A

DICTIONARY

OF THE

HINDEE LANGUAGE

A DICTIONARY OF THE HINDEE LANGUAGE.

COMPILED BY

J. D. BATE

GYAN

Published by

GYAN

Gyan Publishing House
5, Ansari Road
Daryaganj, New Delhi-110002
Phone: 011-47034999, 9811692060
E-mail: books@gyanbooks.com

Distribution Network
gyanbooks.com
India, USA, Canada, UK, Australia, France

ISBN: 978-81-212-7937-6 (PB)
First Published, 1875

2nd Impression 2023

Printed at: Gyan Press, Delhi.

A DICTIONARY OF THE HINDEE LANGUAGE
COMPILER: J. D. BATE

A

DICTIONARY

OF THE

HINDEE LANGUAGE.

COMPILED BY

J. D. BATE, MISSIONARY
(OF THE BAPTIST MISSIONARY SOCIETY, OF LONDON):
MEMBER OF THE UNIVERSITY OF LONDON AND OF THE ASIATIC SOCIETY OF BENGAL.

PRINTED AT THE MEDICAL HALL PRESS, BENARES:

MAY BE HAD OF

E. J. LAZARUS AND CO., BENARES; AND OF TRÜBNER AND CO., LONDON.

1875.

PREFACE.

More than a quarter of a century has passed since the publication of the Hindee Dictionary at present in use, *viz.*, that compiled by the late Rev. J. T. Thompson, Baptist Missionary, of Delhi. Although Forbes, while embodying the whole of 'Thompson' in his more recent Dictionary of the Hindústání language, added many new words, yet experience abundantly proves that the Hindee language is best studied with the help of a Dictionary whose words are arranged in the order of the Devanágarí alphabet. To study Hindee literature by the help of a Hindústání Dictionary would be analogous to studying English with a Dictionary in which the English words should be written in the Arabic character;—the letters have no one point in common, and are arranged, as to their alphabets, on principles exhibiting the utmost diversity; while each alphabet contains some letters and sounds which have no exact equivalents in the other. Every reader of Hindee whose studies have been anything more than elementary, must have many times regretted the inadequacy of Thompson's work. When it is stated that of the fifty thousand words and forms of words contained in the present Dictionary, there are about twenty-five thousand in excess of those given in 'Thompson,' and that these words have been gathered chiefly from the writings of the people's favourite authors, it will be obvious that to facilitate the study of the Hindee literature a new Dictionary was needed.

From the western border of Bengal to the Panjáb, and from the foot of the Himálayas to the borders of the Madras Presidency, this language is the vernacular of the masses both in British India and in the Feudatory States. Within that vast territory, other languages also are spoken, notably the Urdoo of the Muhammadans, especially in the larger cities. Eight dialects of Hindee are generally enumerated, which in their characteristic diversities are sharply marked; nearly all of these peculiarities are, however, more or less clearly traceable to a common parent. There is difference of opinion, even among the best authorities, as to the number of persons to whom this is a mother-tongue,—the figures ranging from fifty to eighty millions: thus much, however, seems to have been ascertained, that no one language in this vast country of Hindústán is spoken by so large a number of the people. With these facts before us, little need be said to shew the importance of the study of Hindee; yet less, probably, has been accomplished by European enterprize for the cultivation of this language, than for almost any other language in the Queen's dominions in the East.

A feeling exists in some quarters that no words are properly entitled to a place in a Hindee Dictionary that are not traceable to Sanskrit: this opinion, however, has to be weighed against the fact that a strong body of accomplished Orientalists are of the contrary opinion; while the literature produced by native writers, whether ancient or modern, poetical or prose, abounds in words which are commonly regarded as Arabic and Persian. The following may be cited as specimens from one work only,—that most popular of Hindee works the *Rámáyaṇ* of Tulsí-Dás; **गरीबनेवाज, सुपेती, बाग, लायक, जीन, जिनिस, सराफ, खबर, दाम, जोर, हर, मसखरी, फराक, खाना, फौज, बख, लगान, बकसीस, जहाज, बाद, दरबार, कागद,** etc. This does not exhaust the list, but the number is sufficient to prove that Hindee, in common with other languages, is composite. Such words are not always given by native authors in their proper form, as the word सुपेती (سفيدي) shews; there is, hence, all the greater reason for giving them a place in a Dictionary of that language. The twenty-five thousand additional words and forms of words contained in this work, are mainly such as the writer has found in Hindee works read by himself.

It would occupy too much space to enumerate the many respects in which the arrangement of the present Dictionary differs from that of its predecessors: the aim has been to prepare a Dictionary that shall meet the wants of students rather than of scholars; and the author will receive with thankfulness any light that may be thrown on the defects of his work.

In the preparation of this Dictionary, the following works have been consulted; *viz.*, Thompson's Hindee Dictionary, the Hindústáni Dictionaries of Shakespear and Forbes, the Bengáli and Sanskrit Dictionary of Sir Graves Haughton, Max Müller's edition of Benfey's Sanskrit Dictionary, and the Sanskrit Dictionary of Prof. Monier Williams. An expression of the author's obligations to his valued and learned friends John Beames, of the Bengal Civil Service, and S. H. Kellogg, of the American Presbyterian Mission, is recorded with very much pleasure; also to Dr. Lazarus, of the Medical Hall Press, for the pains and the patience with which he has conducted the work through the press.

J. D. BATE.

Allahabad, *February*, 1875.

A
DICTIONARY
OF THE
HINDEE LANGUAGE.

अ

अ (a) is the first vowel in the Hindee alphabet, and has the following characteristics and functions:—1, It is said to be short *a*; but if accurately pronounced it has in Hindee the sound of *u* in the English words 'dust,' 'bud,' 'fun,' of *o* in 'come,' or of *a* in 'villa.' 2, It is the letter which is said to be inherent in every consonant, when the consonant is not followed by some other vowel or by *virām* expressed or implied; that is, it serves to indicate the sound which is necessary in order to a consonant becoming pronounceable. Thus म cannot be pronounced unless some vowel-sound be admitted: the vowel-sound which is used for this purpose is that of this letter अ. 3, In a large number of instances (which might, indeed, be increased almost *ad lib.*) contiguous consonants which are to be pronounced without the intervention of this sound are formed into compound letters, thus removing the necessity for the constant recurrence of the *virām*. This is one of the causes of the variety and uncertainty of orthography in Hindee: thus, one writer will use the form समभव (which in the absence of *virām* will inevitably be pronounced wrongly by the uninitiated); while another writes more accurately सम्भव. Though the sound of this letter is in Sanskrit always (and in Bengāli, nearly always) produced at the end of words, it is never, excepting in poetry, pronounced at the end of words in Hindee: words which end in य preceded by some other vowel than अ, form the single exception to this rule; thus इन्द्रिय is pronounced with a slight vowel-sound at the end. It should be added, that in printing Hindee, it is usual to omit the *virām*; so that it is only by long and careful attention of both eye and ear that the learner can know where to drop the sound. 4, It never appears in Hindee excepting at the beginning of a word or of a syllable. 5, Unlike all the other vowels in Hindee this vowel has no medial or final form. 6, In poetry it is *short by nature*, whether used separately or joined to a consonant; before a compound consonant, however, it is, like all the other short vowels, *long by position*. 7, It is sometimes an interjection expressive of pity. 8, It is frequently prefixed to words with the functions of the *alpha privitum* of the Greek, and of the *in* or *un* of many English words of German or Latin origin; for example, in the words 'unfriendly,' 'intact,' 'atheist': thus, अधर्म, अक्षत. When prefixed as a privitive to words beginning with a vowel it is followed by न, presumably to prevent the hiatus; thus, अनन्त. (See also art. अन.) 9, Not unfrequently, however, it is prefixed corruptly and without in any way modifying the sense of a word; thus, अस्थल, more properly स्थल. The explanation of this curious fact seems to be that the natives of India, like the Persians and Arabs, find a difficulty in pronouncing two quiescent consonants at the beginning of a word; with this difference, however, that in Hindee the difficulty does not appear excepting in the pronunciation of a compound consonant whose first element is a sibilant; thus most Hindoos would pronounce the English word 'sprout' as if it were spelt ăsprout or ĭsprout. It has been thought desirable not to expunge from this Dictionary the words which exhibit this phenomenon; for, if the student find, in the course of his reading, the word अस्तुति, he is not to be supposed to be unreasonable if he expect to find it in his Dictionary, albeit it is a corruption: how, indeed, can he know, unless he is told, whether the word he is in search of is an instance of this phenomenon or not? It may, indeed, be fairly presumed that a Dictionary is intended not for those who have acquired the knowledge of a language, but rather for the assistance of those who seek such knowledge. If the student look for अस्तुति and does not find it, he will naturally infer that the word is not in the Dictionary. The cases of such words as अस्पर्शों, in which the अ is both privitive and redundant, seem to leave no room for doubt either as to the duty of the compiler or the interests of the student. In keeping, therefore, with the method adopted by Shakespear, Haughton, Thompson, Forbes and others, such words have, for the most part, been retained in the present work. 10, In such Arabic or Persian words as have found their way into the language and literature of the Hindee speaking people, this letter represents *alif*; also, the *fat'ha* of the Arabs and the *zabar* of the Persians. 11, Printed with a dot under it (अ़) it represents in this Dictionary the Arabic letter *'aīn*: as, however, the proper sound of *'aīn* does not exist in the Hindee or Devanāgarī alphabet, no difference is made in the pronunciation of such words excepting by Muhammadans of education and of taste. Thus, in the very common word अ़र्ज़ or अ़रज़ the अ would be pronounced by a Muhammadan of culture with a *spiritus lenis* which has no corresponding sound in any European language, and can be perceived only by a delicate and cultivated ear: the true sound is observable in the slight catch in the breath with which many persons pronounce the *u* in the word 'tea-urn.' Hindoos, however, together with at least nine tenths of the Muhammadans make no difference between the pronunciation of *'aīn* and of short *a*; and it may even be doubted whether their organs of hearing detect any difference. 12, Sometimes, especially in poetry, in Braj, and in the *patois*, it is inserted like व, and interchangeably with it, to form an extra syllable or to avoid a hiatus; thus सेाअत or सेावत, in the place of the proper form of the present participle of सेाना. 13, This letter is one of the epithets of Vishnu: see ओम. 14, Sometimes it is intensive, like its equivalent in some English words; *e. g.* अधारी, अवश. 15, It is frequently put inaccurately for आ; *e. g.* अघात, more properly आघात. 16, When it is the first letter in the second member of a compound word whose first member ends with a closed syllable, it disappears to the eye though not to the ear; thus, अनवसर = अन + अवसर. 17, It is frequently put inaccurately for य; *e. g.* सवैआ, more properly सवैया. 18, In some instances this letter, when initial, is dropped: *e. g.* धेला, properly अधेला. 19, In Sandhi this letter is liable to certain important changes which will be found specified at length in any good Hindee or Sanskrit Grammar.

अइहै *m. f.* in Braj = आवेगा.

अइहैं *m. f.* in Braj = आवेंगे.

अऊत, *m. f.* a man who dies without leaving issue; an unmarried man; (in Hindoo phraseology) a stupid, blockhead, dunce.

अऋणी, *m.* (*f.* iṇī) a person who is free from debt or from obligation.

अओड़ी, *f.* a kind of basket used in sugarmills.

अओलानिया, *m. pr. n.* a certain tribe of Jāts.

अंक, *m.* a letter of the alphabet; a number, figure, any numerical figure from 1 to 9 (as distinguished from *sun* or *sunna*, a dot or cypher); the stamp on coins, plate, etc.; a mark, spot, the mark on cloth to indicate the price; the flank or part above the hip; the embrace, the bosom; the body; a share, portion. Often inaccurately for अंग, *q. v.*

अंकक, *m.* (*f.* ikā) an accountant, arithmetician.

अंककार, *m.* (*f.* ī) an assayer.

अंकड़ी, *f.* the barb of an arrow; a hook, tenter, catch; a circle; a tendril; a cirrhus; a fishing-hook.

अंकना, 1, *t.* to mark, distinguish a thing by some mark; to page a book; to write numbers: 2, *n.* to be valued, prized, examined, approved.

अंकवार, *f.* an embrace; the bosom. — *bharnā*, to embrace. [mathematics.

अंकविद्या, *f.* the science of numbers, arithmetic,

अंकस, *more prop.* अंकुश, *q. v.*

अंकाना, *t.* to cause to value; to prize, approve of, examine (as cloth).

अंकाव, *m.* valuation, appraisement.

अंकित, *m.* (*f.* ā) marked, spotted, stained, stamped, approved, counted, paged. [seedbud, germ.

अंकुर, *m.* a sprout, shoot, scion, blade, plantlet,

अंकुरना, *a. int.* to sprout.

अंकुरा, *more prop.* अंकुर, *q. v.*

अंकुश, *m.* the iron hook with which elephants are driven; a goad. — *mārnā*, to bring to obedience, reduce to submission.

अंकुशी, *f.* a hook, tenter.

अंकूर }
अंकूरा } *more prop.* अंकुर, *q. v.*

अंक्री, *f.* 1, a kind of vetch (*Vicia sativa*); wet grain: 2, (dim. of अंकुर) a young sprout.

अंखन, *m.* the space between two pillars or beams.

अंखड़ी }
अंखरी } *f.* the eye, the glance of the eye.

अंखाना, *n.* to be angry, displeased, fretful, peevish.

अंखियां, *f.* the eyes; amorous glances.

अंखुआ, *m.* a sprout, shoot, blade, scion, plantlet.

अंग, 1, *m.* the body; a limb, member; a share, portion, division of a country; Bengal proper. As the Veds are divided into six parts, this word, in the ingenious system of reckoning by symbols adopted by the Hindoos in their poetry, is a symbol for 6: 2, *m.* (*f.* ā. *or* ī.) appertaining to the body or to its members.

अंगड़ाई, *f.* a stretching the limbs, yawning.

अंगड़ाना, *a. int.* to yawn, stretch the limbs, oscitate. [concealed in his quilted clothes.

अंगड़िया, *m.* a man who carries money or jewels

अंगढंग = ढंग *q. v.*

अंगद, *m.* a bracelet worn on the upper arm: (in Myth.) the son of Bāli, king of the monkeys.

अंगन }
अंगना } *m.* = अंगनाई, *q. v.*

अंगनाई, *f.* enclosed space adjoining a house, a yard, area, court, compound.

अंगन्यास, *m.* a religious ceremony which consists in touching certain parts of the body according to rules prescribed in the Shāstras.

अंगरखी, *f.* dim. of अंगरखा, *q. v.* [gown, jacket.

अंगरखा, *m.* an upper garment, coat, doublet,

अंगरी, *f.* armour.

अंगलि }
अंगली } *more prop.* अंगुली, *q. v.*

अंगवना, *a. int.* to bear, to endure.

अंगवह्नि, *m. pr. n.*; *lit.* one whose body is of fire.

अंगवारा, *m.* the proprietor of a small portion of a village; mutual aid in tillage.

अंगा, 1. *m.* an upper garment, coat; a long tunic worn by Hindoos and Muhammadans. (The former tie it over the right breast and the latter over the left.) 2, *f.* a maid whose business it is to watch, hold, or amuse a child; a kind of nurse.

अंगार, *m.* charcoal, coal; embers; sparks; a fire, firebrand, bit of fire: wrath. *Angārkā kīrā*, *m.* a salamander. *Angārpar loṭnā* or *angāroṅpar loṭnā*, to be agitated, tormented in mind, highly enraged (*esp.* from jealousy).

अंगारा, 1, a corruption of अंगार, *q. v.*: 2. *m.* (*f.* ī) unprepared, unformed, inexperienced.

अंगारि, *f.* a small portable firepan.

अंगिया, *f.* a bodice, stays. [sages.

अंगिरस, *m. pr. n.* (see ऋषि,) one of the seven

अंगी, *m.* (*f.* inī) bodily, corporeal.

अंगीकार, *m.* agreement, acquiescence; avowal; reception, acceptance; promise; agreeing to, consent, concession, confession. — *k.* to accept, agree to, consent, concede, admit, be willing, receive. [etc.

अंगीकृत, *m.* (*f.* ā) agreed, conceded, promised,

अंगीठी, *f.* a flowerpot.

अंगीठी, *f.* a chafingdish.

अंगुरी, *more prop.* **अंगुली**, *q. v.*

अंगुल, *m.* a thumb; a finger.

अंगुली, *f.* (dim. of **अंगुल**,) a finger; a finger's breadth. *Pairki* —, a toe. *Kalamki* —, the fore-finger. *Bichki* —, the middle finger. *Kanki* —, the the little finger. *Angulikā nok*, the tip of the finger. — *kāṭnā*, to be astonished.

अंगुष्ट, *f.* a finger, toe; a measure of nine inches.

अंगुष्ठ, *m.* the thumb, the great toe; the thumb's breadth as a measure.

अंगुस्त, = **अंगुष्ट**, *q. v.*

अंगू, *adv.* in front, before, preceding.

अंगूठा, *m.* the thumb, great toe. — *chumnā*, to flatter, be subservient to, submit to. — *dikhānā*, to brave, defy, etc. (an attitude resorted to by women in blandishment as a token of prohibition).

अंगूठी, *f.* a finger-ring, a thimble.

अंगूर, *m.* a grape; granulations in a healing sore. — *bannā* or *honā*, to become sound and healthy (said of a sore.)

अंगूरी, *m.* (*f.* inī.) appertaining to the grape.

अंगेट, *f.* appearance, person.

अंगेटी / **अंगेठी** } *f.* a chafingdish, brazier; a flower-pot.

अंगोट, *f.* appearance, person.

अंगोछा, *m.* a towel, handkerchief, a cloth which Hindoos fasten around the waist when bathing, and afterwards wipe themselves with.

अंगोरा, *m.* a midge, gnat.

अंगोंगा, perquisites from the threshing-floor to the Brāhmaṇ, Guru, etc.

अंगोछा, = **अंगोछा**, *q. v.*

अंगोछी, *f.* dim. of **अंगोछा**, *q. v.*

अंगोरिया, *m.* a ploughman; the allowing the use of a plough instead of paying wages in money or in kind.

अंगोखा, *m.* a vest, coat.

अंग्रेज़, 1, *m. pr. n.* England: 2, English.

अंग्रेज़िस्तान, *m. pr. n.* England.

अंग्रेज़ी, 1, *m.* (*f.* inī) an English person: 2, *f.* the English language: *lit.* English.

अंग्लेट, *f.* appearance, person.

अंचड़, stupid, ignorant.

अंचड़पन, *m.* stupidity, ignorance.

अंचर, = **अंचरा**, *q. v.*

अंचरा, *m.* the hem or border of a cloak, veil, or shawl: a kind of sheet used among ascetics.

अंचल, = (1) **अंचरा** (2) **आंचल**, *qq. v.*

अंचला, = **अंचरा**, *q. v.*

अंचवत = **अंचवता** (**अंचवना**): see **न**, 5.

अंचवना, *t.* to cleanse the mouth after eating.

अंचवाना, *t.* to supply a person with water for cleansing the mouth after eating. [on a road.

अंचा, *m.* a post for letters; a stage or station

अंजन, *m.* 1. a collyrium or ointment applied to the eyelashes to darken and improve them (it is a very common article of the Eastern toilet); particular applications, such as antimony, lampblack, and another kind called *rasānjan*: 2. ink; night: 3. the elephant of the west or south-west quarter: 4. a kind of grass much used in the Upper Provinces of India as food for cattle.

अंजनपर्वत, *m. pr. n.* the mountain said to be the residence of the mother of *Hanumān.*

अंजनसार, *m.* collyrium.

अंजनहारी, *f.* a stye on the eyelids.

अंजना, *f.* the mother of *Hanumān*: a lizard.

अंजना, *t.* = **आंजना**, *q. v.*

अंजनिका, *f.* a kind of newt or lizard.

अंजनी, *f.* 1, a woman perfumed with sandal, etc: 2, a small boil on the eyelid, a stye: 3, an epithet of the mother of *Hanumān*: 4, a certain medicinal plant used as a sedative and laxative.

अंजला, *m.* = **अंजलि**, *q. v.*

अंजलि, *m.* (*f.* ?) the cavity formed by putting the hands together and hollowing the palms so as to contain water; this cavity used as a measure, two handfuls: the placing the hands so as to form the shape of a boat; the putting the hands together and then raising them to the forehead in saluting a superior, a goupen; Scottice.

अंजलिगत, *m.* (*f.* ā) received into the hand.

अंजान, *m.* / **अंजाना**, *f.* } *more prop.* **अनजान**, *q. v.*

अंजाम, *m.* 1, accident; vexation: 2, an end; (in comp.) ending, etc.

अंजामको, *adv.* in the end, at last. — *pahunchnā*, to reach fulfilment (prophecy). [grow.

अंजामा, *m.* barren land in which nothing will

अंजिनी = **अंजनी**, *q. v.*

अंजीर, *m.* a fig. [quet.

अंजुमन, *f.* an assembly, meeting, company, ban-

अंजुली, *more prop.* **अंजलि**, *q. v.*

अंट, **अंठ**, **अंड**, **अंत**, **अंद**, **अंध**, **अंब**; for all words beginning with either of these forms, see under the corresponding forms **अयट**, **अयठ**, **अयड**, **अन्त**, **अन्द**, **अन्ध**, **अम्ब**, respectively.

अंवां, *more prop.* **आवा**, 2. *q. v.*

अंश, *m.* a part, division, share, right, possession; a degree of a circle, a degree in latitude or longitude; essence; (in Math.) a fraction, the numerator of a fraction.

अंशधार, *m.* (*f.* ī) = **अंशधारी**, *q. v.*

अंशधारी, *m.* (*f.* inī) a sharer; an incarnation; *lit.* sharing, partaking; (in Theol.) becoming incarnate; successful.

अंशपत्र, *m.* a deed setting forth the shares of property apportioned to the several members of a Hindoo family.

अंशवांसा, *m.* a measure of land twenty of which make a *pilwānsa*.

अंशधारा, *m.* (*f.* ī) a co-heir, joint-sharer, partner.

अंशांश, *m.* a sub-division, a share of a share.

अंशिक, *m.* (*f.* ā) a co-heir, sharer, participator, partner, proprietor : lit. *adj.* sharing, participating.

अंशी, *m.* (*f.* inī) = **अंशिक**, *q. v.*

अंशु, *m.* a ray of light, sunbeam.

अंशुमन्त, *m.* an epithet of the sun ; *lit.* with rays, like rays, possessing rays, radiant.

अंशुमान, = **अंशुमन्त**, *q. v.* [more proper form **अंश**.

अंस, for words beginning thus, see under the

अक, 1, a particle suffixed to substantives to form (1) a class of diminutives : *e. g.* **वृत्तक** (2) a class of adjectives ; *e. g.* **क्षमक** : 2, *m.* pain, affliction ; sin.

अकंटक, free from thorns : *met.* without enemies.

अकड़, *f.* crookedness, pride, strut, airs, conceit.

अकड़ना, *a. int.* to writhe, become distorted, be cramped, stiffen, strut affectedly, give oneself airs.

अकड़तकड़ } = **अकड़मतकड़म**, *q. v.*
अकड़पकड़ }

अकड़बाय, *f.* the cramp.

अकड़बाज़, *m. f.* an affected person, fop, swaggerer.

अकड़बाज़ी, *f.* swaggering, strutting, foppishness, airs. [tiness, pride.

अकड़मतकड़म, *m.* stateliness, affected airs, haugh-

अकड़ाना, *t.* to distress, to impede.

अकडू, *m. f.* = **अकड़ैत**, *q. v.*

अकड़ैत, *m.* (*f.* ā) a swaggerer, fop ; *lit.* swaggering, affected, foppish.

अकथ, *more prop.* **अकथ्य**, *q. v.*

अकथनीय, unsuitable to be spoken, mentioned, or told : incapable of being spoken, mentioned, or told ; unspeakable, unutterable, inexpressible, indescribable ; obscene.

अकथ्य = **अकथनीय**, *q. v.* [en, hear.

अकनना, *a. int.* to listen, give ear, attend, heark-

अकनून, now, at present.

अकबर, *m. pr. n.* a man's name ; *lit.* very great.

अकबराबाद, *m.* the capital of the emperor Akbar, Agra.

अकमा, bold, brave : armed : born blind.

अकम्पन, *m.* firmness, steadiness.

अकम्पित, *m.* (*f.* ā) firm, unshaken.

अकर, exempt from taxes, duty-free.

अकरन = **अकारण**, *q. v.*

अकरा, *f.* a kind of grass, kind of vetch : 2, *m.* (*f.* ī.) dear, costly. [ceiving seed.

अकराया, *f.* ground not properly cleaned for re-

अकर्कस, not hard, soft.

अकर्णी, *m.* (*f.* iṇī) not to be done, unsuitable, inconsistent, indecent. [vice.

कर्म, *m.* a bad or low action, sin, wickedness,

अकर्मक, (in Gram.) intransitive. [profitable.

अकर्मण्य, *m.* (*f.* ā) useless, good-for-nothing, un-

अकर्मी, *m.* (*f.* iṇī) an evil-doer.

अक़्ल, *f.* wisdom, sense, common sense, understanding, opinion. — *kharachnā*, to exercise one's common sense, act wisely. — *thijnā*, to be astonished. — *daumānā*, to consider, think.

अकल, 1, artless, having no limbs : 2, *m.* food, eating. — *o shurb*, meat and drink, eating and drinking.

अकलंक, without stain or rust.

अकल्पित, *m.* (*f.* ā) not wrought, inartificial.

अकल्याण, *m.* (*f.* ā *or* ī) unpropitious, ominous, unlucky ; uncomfortable, disconsolate, unblessed.

अकसर, *more prop.* **अक्सर**, *q. v.*

अक्सर, many, most, nearly all ; often ; much ; for the most part, usually, generally. [sort.

अक़साम, *f.* (pl. of **क़िस्म**) of various kinds, of every

अकसी = **अक्ती** = **अगती**, *q. v.*

अकसीर, *f.* alchemy, chemistry ; the philosopher's stone ; an elixir ; dust, filings.

अकस्मात, *lit.* without a wherefore ; *hence,* without the operation of any known cause, causelessly ; suddenly, abruptly, unexpectedly, unawares, instantaneously, immediately, extempore.

अकस्मातीय, 1, = **अकस्मात**, *q. v.* : 2, *m.* (*f.* ā.) causeless, abrupt. [injury, prejudice.

अकाज, *m.* uselessness ; loss, detriment, hurt,

अकाजना, *t.* to render useless, inflict injury : *a. int.* to die. [diment ; *lit.* useless, detrimental, retarding.

अकाजी, *m.* (*f.* inī.) a useless person, an impe-

अकाबिर, (pl. of **अकबर**) people of rank, nobles, the great, grandees.

अकाम, 1, useless, fruitless, unavailing, unprofitable, unremunerative, vain ; aimless : 2, an epithet of the Supreme ; *lit.* without desire, without lust.

अकार, 1, *m.* the letter **अ** ; 2, = **अकाम**, 1, *q. v.*

अकारत } = **अकाम**, 1, *q. v.*
अकारथ }

अकारण, 1, (sc. **से**,) causelessly, groundlessly, without pretext : 2, *m.* the absence or non-existence of a cause.

अकाल, 1, *m.* famine, scarcity ; unseasonableness, extremity, pinch : 2, unseasonable, untimely, prema-

अकालफल, *m.* fruit produced out of season. [ture.

अकालवृष्टि, *f.* untimely rain.

अकाश, *more prop.* **आकाश**, *q. v.*

अकाशदीवा, *more prop.* **आकाशदीया**, *q. v.*

अकिंचन, *more prop.* **आकिंचन**, *q. v.*

अकोटा, *m.* confidence.

अकीर्त्ति, *f.* disgrace, infamy, ill-repute.

अकुंठ, indestructible, keen, sharp.

अकुल, 1, *m.* a great eater, glutton : 2, without pedigree, relations, or family.

अकुलता, *f.* agitation, distress of mind.

अकुलाना, *a. int.* to tire, weary : to be astonished, be agitated, be distracted, be confused, be disconcerted, be out of order.

अकुली, *m.* (*f.* inī) a low-born person, etc.: *lit.* of low origin or race, of mean extraction, low, base, mean, ignoble, plebeian.

अकुलीन, *m.* (*f.* ā) = **अकुली**, *q. v.*

अकुशल, unlucky, inauspicious.

अकृत, *m.* (*f.* ā) not done or wrought, inartificial; not cultivated; wavering.

अकृति, *more prop.* **आकृति**, *q. v.*

अकृत्रिम, not made or wrought, inartificial.

अकेलपन, = **अकेलापन**, *q. v.*

अकेला, *m.* (*f.* ī) alone, solitary, single; celibate.

अकेलापन, *m.* loneliness, solitude, singularity; celibacy.

अकेलोअकेला, see **अकेलेदुकेले**.

अकेले *adv.* (sc. **में**) solitarily, alone.

अकेलेदुकेले, *adv.* in complete loneliness, entirely alone.

अकैया, *m.* one of the sacks or baskets of a pannier.

अकोर, *f.* a bribe, a coaxing (as a cow that has lost her calf, to make her tractable).

अकोरी, *m.* (*f.* iṇī) one who receives a bribe.

अकोल, *m.* a plant (*Alangium hexapetalum*) the oil of which is used in enchantments.

अक्कलबार, the Indian shot-plant (*Canna Indica*), a beautiful flower.

अक्का, 1, *m.* a father; a dear or intimate friend. 2, *f.* an elder sister.

अक्ती = **अगती**, *q. v.*

अक्रूर, *m.* epithet of the paternal uncle and friend of Krishṇ; *lit.* not cruel, mild, humane, gentle.

अक्रोट = **अख़रोट**, *q. v.*

अक्कन्द, *m.* swallow-wort (*Asclepias gigantea*).

अक्ष, a die (in play; cubic or oblong); the spots on dice.

अक्षत, 1, *m.* whole grain, whole grains of rice used in religious ceremonies; fried grain: 2, *m.* (*f.* ā.) infallible, remaining, abiding, indelible.

अक्षततिलक, *f.* the ceremony of putting a few grains of rice on the forehead of an idol when addressed, or of a Brāhmaṇ when invited to an entertainment.

अक्षपाद, *m. pr. n.* a certain Rishi.

अक्षभाग, *m.* (in Geog.) a degree of latitude.

अक्षय, *m.* (*f.* ā) undecaying, imperishable; permanent, durable.

अक्षयता, *f.* / **अक्षयत्व**, *m.* } imperishableness, durability.

अक्षयलोक, *m.* the world or region of the imperishable, heaven.

अक्षयवट, *m. pr. n.* a certain tree famous in Hindoo legend as being undecaying (the tree in the underground temple in the fort at Allahabad).

अक्षयवर / **अक्षयवृक्ष** } = **अक्षयवट**, *q. v.*

अक्षर, *m.* a letter of an alphabet; a syllable.

अक्षरप्रकाश, *m.* a treatise on an alphabet.

अक्षरी, *m.* (*f.* iṇī) one who writes an elegant hand, a lettered or scientific person.

अक्षरौटी, *f.* orthography; a mode of playing on a stringed instrument so as to express the words of a song.

अक्षविद्यावान, *m.* (*f.* vatī) a soothsayer, necromancer, wizard; *lit.* practising soothsaying.

अक्षांश, *m.* (in Geog.) a degree of latitude or of longitude.

अक्षि, *m.* the eye.

अक्षितारा, *f.* the pupil of the eye.

अक्षिसंकेत, *m.* a sign or wink of the eye.

अक्षेम, *m.* (*f.* ā) a miserable person: *lit.* unfortunate, unhappy.

अक्षोणी / **अक्षोहणी** / **अक्षौणी** } *more prop.* **अक्षौहिणी**, *q. v.*

अक्षौहिणी, *f.* an army (when complete it consists of 109350 foot, 65610 horse, 21870 chariots, and 21870 elephants).

अख, *m.* a brother.

अखंड: for words beginning thus, see under the form **अखण्ड**.

अख़ज़, *f.* objection, cavil, hostility; taking, seizing, intercepting. — *k.* to seize, assume, accept.

अखड़, undisciplined (said of soldiers), barbarous, rude, uncouth, ugly, ill-shapen.

अखण्ड, *m.* (*f.* ā) unbroken, irrefragable, indivisible, indestructible, whole, entire, all.

अखण्डनीय, *m.* (*f.* ā) not to be broken or divided, irrefragable, indestructible, irrefutable, incontestible, undeniable.

अखण्डित, *m.* (*f.* ā) unbroken; unrefuted; continuous.

अखत, *more prop.* **अक्षत**, *q. v.*

अख़तना, *m.* uncircumcision.

अखतीज, the eighteenth day of the month Vaisākh, a Hindoo festival.

अख़नीपुलाव, *m.* a kind of stew.

अख़मीरी, *m.* (*f.* iṇī) unleavened.

अखय, **अखर**: for words beginning with either of these elements, but not given below, see under the more proper form **अक्ष**.

अखर, abundance, plenty.

अख़रोट, *m.* a walnut; the fruit of the *Aleurites triloba*.

अखर्ब, tall, long, large.

अखल = **अखिल**, *q. v.*

अख़लाक़, *m.* (pl. of **ख़ल्क़**) disposition; the good properties of mankind; morals, ethics.

अखाड़ा, *m.* a palaestra, or place for wrestling, arena, scene, circus; a court, any place of assembly; Indra's court.

अखाद्य, *m.* (*f.* ā) forbidden food: *lit.* unsuitable or unlawful for food, uneatable.

अखारा = **अखाड़ा**, *q. v.*

अखिल, the whole, all, entire, every.

अखिलेश्वर, *m.* an epithet of God; also of Rām, Shiv, etc.; *lit.* the Lord of all.

अखोट = **अख़रोट**, *q. v.*

अख्यात, *m.* (*f.* ā) an obscure person: *lit.* unknown to fame, obscure.

अग, *m.* an epithet of any tree or mountain: *lit.* not going or moving, immovable.

अगआ, *m.* (*f.* **अगई**) *more prop.* **अगुआ**, *q. v.*

अगयास = **अग्रयास**, *q. v.*

अगट, *m.* a butcher's stall.

अगटना, *a. int.* to collect, assemble.

अगड़ = **अकड़**, *q. v.*

अगड़बगड़, *m.* trifling employment or talk, trifles, trumpery, trash: *lit.* composed of odds and ends, promiscuous. [numerable.

अगणित, *m.* (*f.* ā) not reckoned or counted, in-

अगति, *m.* one whose funeral ceremonies have not been performed: *lit.* without character, dishonored, disgraced. [demnation, damnation.

अगति, *f.* distress, inconvenience; disgrace; con-

अगती, *f.* the Agati tree (*Alschynomene grandiflora*) the leaves and pods of which are eaten as vegetables.

अगत्तर, *adj.* coming, arriving.

अगना, *more prop.* **अंगना**, *q. v.*

अगनित, *more prop.* **अगणित**, *q. v.*

अगनी, *more prop.* **अग्नि**, *q. v.*

अगम, *more prop.* **आगम** or **अगम्य**, *qq. v.*

अगम्य, *m.* (*f.* ā) impassable, untraversable, inaccessible, inapproachable, impenetrable; unfordable, deep, unfathomable, bottomless; impervious; incomprehensible; unaccomplishable; difficult of acquirement, unattainable.

अगयाना, *t.* to burn metallic vessels for the purpose of cleaning them. [when.

अगर, 1, = **अगुरु**, *q. v.*: 2, if, though, although,

अगरखा, *more prop.* **अंगरखा**, *q. v.*

अगरचि, though, although, even though, notwithstanding, albeit.

अगरबगर, *m.* senseless talk, babble.

अगरवाला, *m.* a race of merchants of the Vais tribe (from Agrohā, a place west of Delhi).

अगरिया = **अगरी**, *q. v.*

अगरी, appertaining to the wood of aloes (see *aguru*): of the colour of the wood of aloes.

अगरु = **अगुरु**, *q. v.*

अगल, *m.* a bar or bolt.

अगलब, 1, superior, stronger: 2, most likely, for for the most part. — *hai*, it is most likely, it generally happens.

अगला, *m.* (*f.* ī) an ancient, ancestor: *lit.* prior, preceding, former; foremost, first, chief, best; other, second, next, forthcoming, future, yet to come.

अगलान्त, *adv.* up to the neck.

अगवा, *more prop.* **अगुआ**, *q. v.*

अगवाई, 1, *more prop.* **अगुआई**, *q. v.*: 2, *f.* a conflagration (of a city, forest, etc.). [of a house.

अगवाड़ा, *m.* the front, forepart, space in front

अगवान, *m.* (*f.* ā) } = **अगुआ**, *q. v.*
अगवानी, *m.* (*f.* inī) }

अगवार, a portion of corn set apart for village servants, like the customary "sharping-corn" in England.

अगवासी, the body of a ploughshare.

अगवाही, *f.* burning, conflagration.

अगसी *more prop.* **अगुई**, *q. v.*

अगस्त, *more prop.* **अगस्त्य**, *q. v.*

अगस्तवार, *m.* a certain small tribe of Rajpoots.

अगस्ति, *m.* a certain tree (*Æschynomena grandiflora*): *pr. n.* (1) of a certain star (*Canopus*); (2) of a certain saint-sage (*rishi*) celebrated in Hindoo legend. He is the son of Mithra and Varan, and is said to have been born in a water-jar. He is represented as of short stature, and is the regent of the star *Canopus*. It is said that he swallowed the ocean when it had given him offence, and that it was at his command that the Vindhya range prostrated itself and [so remains.

अगस्त्य = **अगस्ति**, 2, *q. v.*

अगस्त्यऋषि } = **अगस्ति**, (2) *q. v.*
अगस्त्यमुनि }

अगहन, *m.* the eighth month of the Hindoos (Nov.-Dec.), during which the sun is in Scorpio and the moon is full near the head of Orion.

अगहनी, *m.* the produce of the abovementioned month: *lit.* appertaining to that month.

अगहनीफ़स्ल, *f.* the cold harvest weather.

अगहुड़ = **आग**, *q. v.*

अगाऊ, *m.* an advance of money: a fore-runner, precursor: *lit.* before, in front. — *ānā*, to advance in order to meet a person coming on a visit.

अगाड़ा, *m.* a certain plant (*Achyranthis aspera*) said to cure the bite of venomous reptiles.

अगाड़ी, 1, *f.* the ropes with which a horse's feet are tied; the front, forepart, future; 2, before, in front, onward, forward, further on (whether in space or in time). — *pichhāṛi lagānā*, to confine (*esp.* a horse). — *mārnā*, to attack in front; to defeat a hostile army in a pitched battle. [deep.

अगाध, *m.* (*f.* ā) unfathomable, bottomless, very

अगाधता, *f.* depth, exceeding depth, unfathomableness.

अगार, avarice, covetousness.

अगास, *more prop.* **आकाश**, *q. v.*

अगासी, *f.* a turban; a terrace in front of a room; the cry of the kite. [bird, a sort of lark.

अगिन, 1, *more prop.* **अग्नि**, *q. v.*: 2, *m.* a certain

अगिनबाव, *more prop.* **अग्निबाव**, *q. v.*

अगिनि, *more prop.* **अग्नि**, *q. v.* [told.

अगिनित, *m.* (*f.* ā) countless, incalculable, un-

अगिया, *m.* a bird (*Alauda Aggia*, Buch.).

अगिला, *m.* (*f.* ī) *more prop.* **अगला**, *q. v.*

अगुआ, *m.* (*f.* **अगुई**) a guide, conductor; harbinger; one who negotiates or adjusts a marriage, a matchmaker; *lit.* foremost.

अगुआई, *f.* guidance, leadership.

अगुण, 1, *m.* (*f.* ā) unskilful; without merit; ineffectual; bad; void of qualities (good or bad): an epithet of God: 2, *m.* a defect, fault.

अगुप्त, *m.* (*f.* ā) unconcealed, not hidden.

अगुर, a kind of sweet-smelling gum.

अगुरु, 1, *m.* wood of aloes, a kind of fragrant wood, agallochum (*Aquillaria agallocha*): a certain tree which yields bdellium (*Amyris agallocha*): the sisoo tree (*Dalbergia sisoo*): 2, not heavy, light.

अगुवा, *m.* (*f.* **वी**) *more prop.* **अगुआ**, *q. v.*

अगुवाई, *more prop.* **अगुआई**, *q. v.*

अगूढ़, easy of comprehension, evident, manifest.

अगूढ़भाव, of an open, honest, ingenuous disposition. [thou! Halloa!

अगे, (exclamation addressed to females) O! O

अगेटी, *f.* a chafingdish, brazier; a flowerpot.

अगेही, *m.* (*f.* inī) a homeless person: *lit.* houseless.

अगैया, a certain disease which affects the rice-plant (parching it up).

अगोचर, an epithet of God: *lit.* imperceptible to the senses or the mental faculties.

अगोड़ी, *f.* an advance of money: *lit.* beforehand, in advance.

अगोर = **अगोरिया**, *q. v.*

अगोरना, *t.* to watch, guard.

अगोरबटाई *f.* a division of the crop after reaping.

अगोरिया, *m.* a watchman, guard, one who watches over crops.

अगोरी = **अगोड़ी**, *q. v.*

अगोलना = **अगोरना**, *q. v.*

अगौंट, the top of the sugarcane cut up for seed.

अगौनी, *f.* the going or sending forward to meet and receive a visitant with honor. — *k.* to advance to meet the bridegroom at a wedding or a visitant on the road.

अगौर, *m.* an advance of rent.

अग्नि, *m.* fire; the fire of the stomach, the digestive faculty; appetite; the name of one of the Purāṇs; the south-east; (in Myth.) the god of fire and agent of the south-east quarter. In the ingenious system of reckoning by symbols adopted by Hindoos in their poetry, this word is a symbol for 3.

अग्निक, *m.* an insect of a scarlet colour, the lady-bird. [fire in.

अग्निकुण्ड, *m.* a fire-pit, a hollow for kindling a

अग्निगर्भ = **अग्निमणि**, *q. v.* [is of fire.

अग्नितन, *m. pr. n.* a certain demon whose body

अग्नित्रेता, *f.* the three sacred fires of the Hindoos, taken collectively, *viz.* the southern, the household, and the sacrificial fire.

अग्निदीपक, *m.* a lamp.

अग्निदेवता, *m. pr. n.* the god of fire.

अग्निपरीक्षा, *f.* the fiery ordeal (by a heated iron, or by boiling oil, or by passing through fire).

अग्निपात्र, *m.* any vessel in which fire (and fire only) is kept.

अग्निपुराण, *m. pr. n.* one of the Purāṇs.

अग्निपुरुष, *m. pr. n.* the god of fire.

अग्निपूजक, *m.* (*f.* ikā) a fire-worshipper, guebre.

अग्निप्रस्तर, *m.* firestone, any stone producing fire, flint. [rocket.

अग्निबान, *m.* an arrow of fire, fiery missile,

अग्निबाव, *f.* the farcy in horses; an eruptive disease in men; erysipelas. [eating.

अग्निभोजक, *m.* (*f.* ikā) a fire-eater: lit. *adj.* fire-

अग्निभोजन, *m.* the eating of fire, fire-eating.

अग्निमणि, *m.* the sunstone (a fabulous gem supposed to contain and to impart solar heat).

अग्निशिखा, *f.* a flame of fire.

अग्निसंस्कार, *m.* funeral ceremonies, such as burning a dead body; any ceremony performed with consecrated fire.

अग्निहोत्र, *m.* a ceremony consisting in oblations to consecrated fire; the consecrated fire itself.

अग्निहोत्री, *m.* (*f.* iṇī) one who keeps a perpetual sacrificial fire; a sacrificing priest conversant with the *Rigved.*

अग्निहोम, *m.* sacrifice by fire, burnt sacrifice.

अग्या घास = **अघिन घास**. *q. v.*

अग्याबैताल, *m.* a demon who rules over fire.

अग्यारी, *f.* the kindling the fire at the time of devotion by Hindoos. [prior, first, chief.

अग्र, 1, *m.* the fore part of anything: 2, *m.* (*f.* ā)

अग्रगामी, *m.* (*f.* inī) a forerunner, predecessor: *lit.* preceding.

अग्रगामी सेना, *f.* the advanced guard of an army.

अग्रग्रास, *m.* the first morsel. [birth; firstborn.

अग्रज, *m.* (*f.* ā) an elder brother: *lit.* of prior

अग्रता, *f.* / **अग्रत्व**, *m.* } priority, precedence.

अग्रभाग, *m.* the first, chief, front, or foremost part of anything. [preceding.

अग्रसर, *m.* (*f.* ā *or* ī) a chief, leader, guide: *lit.*

अग्रसोच, *m.* foresight, forethought, providence, precaution. [*lit.* forecasting, provident, cautious.

अग्रसोची, *m.* (*f.* inī) one endued with foresight:

अग्रहायण, *m.* the eight month in the lunar year of the Hindoos (Nov.-Dec.) when the moon is full near the head of Orion.

अग्रा, *f.* = **अग्र**, 2, *q. v.*

अग्रहार, *m.* a village, district or division occupied entirely by Brāhmans. [etc.) to the gods.

अग्रास, *m.* food offered (in oblations, sacrifices,

अग्रासन = **अग्रास**, *q. v.*

अग्राह्य, not to be received, unacceptable.

अग्रिम, *m.* an elder brother: *lit.* first in order or in rank, chief, eldest: *adv.* before, prior.

अघ, *m.* sin, guilt, crime, wickedness; suffering.

अघकारी, *m.* (*f.* iṇī) a sinner, profligate, criminal.

अघटित, unfit, unworthy; the unknown future.

अघन, *more prop.* **अगहन**, *q. v.*

अघनाशक, *m.* (*f.* ikā) a destroyer of sin: *lit.* sin-destroying, freeing from sin, purifying.

अघमय, *m.* (*f.* ī) sinful: *lit.* consisting of or abounding in sin. [of guilt.

अघहरता, *m.* an epithet of God: *lit.* the remover

अघाई, *f.* satiety, surfeit.

अघाट, *m.* land held in perpetuity and not alienable. [of venomous reptiles.

अघाड़ा, *m.* a certain plant said to cure the bite

अघात, *more prop.* आघात, *q. v.* [ed, sound.
अघाती, *m.* (*f.* inī) not wounded, whole, unscath-
अघाना, *t.* to satiate, surfeit; *n.* to be satiated.
अघाना, *m.* (*f.* ī) satiated; affluent, rich.
अघारी, *m.* (*f.* iṇī) a miser; *lit.* affected with avarice.
अघासुर, *m. pr. n.* a certain demon slain by Krishṇ.
अघिन घास, *m.* lemon-grass. [midable, terrible.
अघोर, *m.* an epithet of Shiv: *lit. m.* (*f.* ā.) for-
अघोरपन्थ, *m.* a certain order of religious mendicants among Hindoos. They eat anything and everything, however filthy, even human carcases.
अघोरपन्थी, *m.* (*f.* inī) a member of the abovementioned order; hence, this term is applied in opprobrium to a gross or filthy feeder.
अघोरी, *m.* (*f.* iṇī) 1, = अघोरपन्थी, *q. v.*: 2, a covetous, greedy person. [hard.
अघोष, without noise, without sound: (in Gram.)
अङ्क, अङ्ग for all words beginning with either of these elements, see under the forms अंग अंक, respectively. [fixed, inactive.
अचंचल, *m.* (*f.* ā) unmoved; immovable, firm.
अचकरी, *f.* lasciviousness, wantonness, wickedness.
अचक्षु, 1, *m. f.* eyeless, blind: 2, *f.* spectacles, [eyeglasses.
अचगरी = अचकरी, *q. v.*
अचण्ड, *m.* (*f.* ā) not passionate, gentle.
अचताना, *more prop.* अच्छताना, *q. v.*
अचतुर, *m.* (*f.* ā) stupid, inapt, inactive.
अचना, *t.* to cleanse the mouth after eating.
अचपल, *m.* (*f.* ā) restless, inconstant, unruly, obstinate, playful, wanton, brisk.
अचपलता, *f.* restlessness, inconstancy, wantonness, playfulness, vivacity.
अचपला, 1, *f.* or 2, *m.* (*f.* ī) = अचपल, *q. v.*
अचपलाहट, *f.* = अचपलता, *q. v.*
अचपली, *f.* (1) = अचपला: (2) = अचपलता, *qq. v.*
अचम्भा, 1, *m.* astonishment, amazement, wonderment: — *k.* (with abl.) to make wonder of a thing, be astonished at: 2 *m.* (*f.* ī) a wonderful thing, cause of astonishment: *lit.* wonderful, astonishing, rare.
अचम्भित, *m.* (*f.* ā) astonished, smitten with [wonder.
अचर, *more prop.* अचल, *q. v.*
अचरच, 1, *m.* wonder, astonishment, admiration: 2, *m.* (*f.* ā) astonishing, wonderful.
अचरज, *m.* (*f.* ā) astonishing, wonderful.
अचरजयुत; see आश्चर्य्यित.
अचल, *m.* a mountain; an aged person: *lit. m.* (*f.* ā.) not moving, inanimate; immovable, (whether from strength or weakness). In the ingenious system of reckoning by symbols adopted by Hindoos in their poetry, this word is a symbol for 7.
अचला, *f.* an epithet of the earth (supposed, as the centre of the universe, to be immovable).
अचवें = अचे (अचना).
अचा, corruption of अच्छा, *q. v.*
अचांचक, suddenly, unexpectedly, unawares.

अचानक = अचांचक, *q. v.* [drink.
अचाना, *t.* to rinse the mouth after eating; to
अचार, 1, *more prop.* आचार, *q. v.*: 2, *m.* pickles.
अचार्य्य, *more prop.* आचार्य्य, *q. v.*
अचिक्कन, unpolished, rough.
अचिन्त, *m.* (*f.* ā) a thoughtless person, etc. *lit.* thoughtless, careless, heedless, rash.
अचिन्ता, *f.* absence of (or deficiency in) thought, care, concern or consideration; heedlessness, disregard.
अचीता, *m.* (*f.* ī) unwished-for: not painted (said of paper, etc.). [*lit.* unerring, unfailing, sure.
अचूक, *m.* (*f.* ā) a good marksman, a dead shot:
अचेत, *m.* (*f.* ā) a stupid person: *lit.* out of one's mind, bereft of one's senses, senseless, thoughtless, unmindful, forgetful, stupid. — *honā*, to be thoughtless, be insensible to, be insensible (as in a swoon or dream). [ity, obliviousness.
अचेतता, *f.* senselessness, thoughtlessness, stupid-
अचेतन = अचैतन्य, *q. v.*
अचेतपना, *m.* = अचेतता, *q. v.*
अचैतन = अचैतन्य, *q. v.*
अचैतन्य, *m.* (*f.* ā) not possessing or exhibiting the qualities which distinguish men from brutes, without sensation or consciousness, brutish, irrational, senseless.
अचैन, uneasy, uncomfortable, ill at ease.
अच्छुत *more prop.* अच्युत, *q. v.*
अच्युत, *m.* (*f.* ā) an epithet of Vishnoo or of God: *lit.* fixed, permanent, imperishable, undecaying, immortal, eternal.
अच्युतानन्द, *m.* an epithet of the Supreme Being: *lit.* He whose joy or blessedness is unmoveable or imperishable.
अच्छ: This form is often corruptly interchanged with अछ, अच, अक्ष. For any words, therefore, beginning with this form, but not given below, see under the more proper forms.
अच्छत, *more prop.* अक्षत, *q. v.* [grieve, lament.
अच्छताना पछताना, *a. int.* to repent, be sorry,
अच्छना, *more prop.* आछना, *q. v.*
अच्छा, *m.* (*f.* ī) good, excellent, pleasant; righteous; healthy, sound, well; lucky. — *k.* to cure, heal, cause to recover. — *lagnā.* to beseem, befit; to be agreeable or pleasing. — *honā*, to be in good health, to be well. — *ho jānā*, to recover in health. As an adverb, or as an exclamation, this word is often repeated to intensify the sense; thus, *Achchhā achchhā!* very good! all right! well done!
अच्छोदन, *m.* hunting, the chase.
अछ, This form is often corruptly interchanged with अच्छ, अच, अक्ष. For any words, therefore, beginning with this element, but not given below, see under the more proper forms.
अछत, *more prop.* अक्षत, *q. v.*
अछवानी, *f.* caudle. [children are liable).
अछिर, *m.* the thrush (a complaint to which
अछेद, } in Chand = अक्षय, *q. v.*
अछेह, }

अछूता, *m.* (*f.* ī) not to be touched (said of food dressed for religious persons) : inviolable.

अज, 1, *more prop.* **आज**, *q. v.* : 2, *m.* (*f.* ā) a goat : *lit.* unborn : hence, it is an epithet of God as the Uncreated One : 3, *note*, **ज** is often interchanged corruptly with **य**. For all words, therefore, beginning with **अज**, but not given below, see under the form **अय**.

अजगर, *m.* a kind of large snake; a large serpent, the boa constrictor ; a dragon : *lit.* the goat-eater.

अजगुत, *m.* (*f.* ā) surprizing, wonderful.

अजज़ा, *m.* (pl. of **जुज़**) parts, portions ; sections of the Kurān (of which there are thirty).

अजदहा, *m.* a large snake, dragon.

अजदाद, *m.* (pl. of **जद्द**) ancestors.

अजनबी, foreign, strange, unknown.

अजनास, *f.* (pl. of **जिन्स**) goods and chattels, movables ; kinds, sorts, species.

अजन्त, (in Gram.) ending in a vowel.

अजन्म, *m.* (*f.* ā) unborn ; unbegotten.

अ़जब, wonderful, rare.

अज़बर, by rote, by memory, by heart.

अ़ज़्म, *m.* design, intention, purpose, resolution ; undertaking : a bone.

अजमूद, *m.* parsley (*Apium involucratum*): the common carraway (*Carum carui*) : a kind of lovage (*Ligusticum Ajowān*).

अजमोदा = **अजमूद**, *q. v.*

अजय, 1, not victorious, subdued ; not successful : 2, unvanquished ; invincible : 3, *m.* defeat.

अजयकीर्ति, *f.* the reputation for invincibleness.

अजर, *m.* 1, the reward of good or bad actions, retribution ; fare, hire : 2, an epithet of God ; *lit.* not liable to decay or old age.

अजराम, *m.* (pl. of **जिर्म**,) bodies.

अजरामर, an epithet of God ; *lit.* not liable either to decrepitude or to death.

अजल, *f.* death ; delay ; a stated time ; respite for [the payment of a debt.

अज़ल्लत, *f.* injustice, oppression, injury (suffered without power of redress) ; famine, scarcity, straits.

अजवाइनी, *f.* a kind of caudle.

अजवान, *f.* the seed of a plant of the dill kind (*Ligusticum Ajowān*) ; a kind of aniseed. *Ajwāyani khurāsāni*, henbane.

अजवायन = **अजवान**, *q. v.*

अजवीथी, *f.* the name of a part of the moon's orbit (also, the Milky Way ?).

अजस, *m.* 1, (*f.* ā) a disreputable person ; *lit.* disreputable, infamous : 2, *m.* disrepute, disgrace, dispraise.

अजसाम, *m.* (pl. of **जिस्म**) bodies.

अजहू, (emphatic) to-day even, this very day ; just at the present time, immediately ; hitherto, yet, even now, even yet.

अजहूं = **अजहू**, *q. v.*

अजा, *f.* 1, (*m.* **अज**) a she-goat : 2, the unreality of the universe, illusion (an epithet of *Māyā* considered as God's wife).

अज़ां, therefore, thence.

अ़जाइब, *m.* (pl. of **अ़जीब**) wonders.

अजाड़, *m.* cloth made of hemp, canvas.

अजात, *m.* (*f.* ā) one who has lost his caste, one who has no caste.

अजाती, *m.* (*f.* in *or* inī) = **अजात**, *q. v.*

अजान, *m.* (*f.* ā) a simpleton ; *lit.* unknowing, ignorant, simple, unsophisticated ; indifferent, careless.

अजानी, *f.* innocence, simplicity ; heedlessness.

अ़ज़ाब, *m.* pain, misfortune, torment, punishment, martyrdom.

अजामिल, *m. pr. n.* a certain Brāhmaṇ mentioned in the Rāmāyaṇ (he was a great sinner and a penitent).

अजित, *m.* (*f.* ā) unconquered, unsubdued, unsurpassed ; invincible.

अजिन, *m.* the hide of an antelope, lion, tiger, etc. on which the theological students sit and sleep.

अजिर, *m.* an area or court.

अजी, an interjection used for the purpose of calling attention. In Bengal it is used in addressing one's inferiors, or in cases of great intimacy only : on the other hand, in the western provinces of India it is often used in addressing an equal or a superior to indicate respect.

अ़ज़ीज़, dear, beloved, precious, excellent.——*rakhnā*, to prize, hold dear.

अजीत, *m.* (*f.* ā) unsubdued ; impregnable, in- [vincible.

अजीतवर्ण, *m.* leprosy of a bad kind.

अ़जीब, *m.* a wonder : *lit.* wonderful, surprizing, astonishing, rare.

अज़ीयत, *f.* wanton injury, distress, vexation.

अजीर, *m.* a slave.

अजीर्ण, *m.* indigestion, surfeit, flatulence.

अजीर्ण, *m.* (*f.* ā) undecayed, unimpaired.

अजीव, *m.* 1, deprived of life, lifeless, dead : 2, death ; (according to the Jains,) the inanimate part of the universe.

अजुक्त, *more prop.* **अयुक्त**, *q. v.*

अजुका, *f.* a mother ; (in theatrical language) a [courtesan.

अजूठा, *m.* (*f.* ī) untouched, untasted (as food).

अजूरा, *m.* hire, wages, fare.

अजूरादार, *m.* a hired labourer (whether paid by the day or by the job).

अजे, *more prop.* **अजय**, *q. v.*

अजों, hitherto, as yet, to this day.

अजोड़, *m.* (*f.* ā) without joining : matchless, rare.

अजोत, *m.* (*f.* ā) without splendour, dull.

अजोल, an epithet of the elephant : *lit.* of steady gait or pace.

अज्ञ, 1, *m.* (*f.* ā) an ignorant person, etc. : a stranger : *lit* ; ignorant, unknowing, stupid, idiotic : unknown : 2, unwittingly.

अज्ञता, *f.* ignorance, stupidity, folly.

अज्ञा, 1, *more prop.* **आज्ञा**, *q. v.* : 2, *f.* (*m.* **अज्ञ**) an ignorant or idiotic female.

अज्ञाकारी, *m.* (*f.* iṇī) = आज्ञाकारी, *q. v.*

अज्ञात, *m.* (*f.* ā) unknowing, unsophisticated, simple; unknown. [*m.* ignorance, stupidity, folly.

अज्ञान, 1, ignorant, unwise, simple, witless: 2,

अज्ञानता, *f.*
अज्ञानत्व, *m.* } = **अज्ञानपन**, *q. v.*

अज्ञानपन, *m.* a state of ignorance, stupidity, folly.

अज्ञानी, *m.* (*f.* inī) an ignoramus; *lit.* ignorant, unwise. [see under the form **अंज**.

अञ्ज : For all words beginning with this element,

अटक, *f.* an obstacle, obstruction, prevention, stop, bar: the river Atak.

अटकना, *a. int.* to cease, remain, rest, adhere, stick, get aground: *n.* to be restrained, be prevented, be stopped. [gestures.

अटकमटक, amorous dalliance, fond tricks and

अटकल, 1. *f.* guess, conjecture; judgment; quantity, size: 2, (sc. **से**) by guess, at random. When used as a postposition, as it frequently is, it sometimes takes before it the inflected form of the genitive *masc.*, and sometimes, though less frequently, the genitive *fem.*

अटकलना, to guess, conjecture, suppose.

अटकलपच्चू, *m.* one who guesses at a venture or without grounds for his conjecture. [ing.

अटकलबाज़, *m.* an appraiser: *lit.* adroit at guess-

अटकलमटकल, *m.* the name of a children's game, like our "Guess if you can."

अटका, 1, *m.* a vessel used in performing ablution; the pot in which food is dressed for the public at the door of the temple of Jagannāth: 2, *m.* (*f.* i) stopped, hindered; aground.

अटकाना, *t.* to prevent, hinder, restrain, stop, detain, challenge (as a sentry might).

अटकाव, *m.* prevention, arrest, stop, challenge.

अटकावना = 1, **अटकाना**; 2, **अटकाव**, *qq. v.*

अटकी, *f.*; see **अटका**, 2.

अटखेल, wanton, playful, coquettish.

अटखेली, *f.* wantonness, coquetry; an affected (also, a graceful) mode of walking.

अटट, coarse, strong (said of cloth). [cony.

अटन, *m.* (pl. of **अटा**?) an upper room; a bal-

अटना, *a. int.* to wander about, walk about: to fill up: *n.* to be contained; to be filled up (*e. g.* *kooā aṭ gayā*, the well is filled up).

अटनी, *f.* the notched extremity or horn of a bow.

अटपट = **अटपटी**, *q. v.*

अटपटांग, *m.* (*f.* ā) poor; wicked, disorderly.

अटपटांगी, *f.* poverty; wickedness; absurdity.

अटपटाना, *n.* to be tired, out of sorts, confused.

अटपटी, *m.* (*f.* inī) a thoughtless person: *lit.* thoughtless, inconsiderate; unstudied, irregular.

अटपटीबात, *f.* confused or incoherent talk, pre-

अटपठो = **अटपटी**, *q. v.* [varication.

अटम, *m.* a heap, pile, mass.

अटल, an epithet of God: *lit.* fixed, permanent, immovable, unchangeable, irrefragable, inviolable, incontrovertible; of determined resolution.

अटलता, *f.* unchangeableness, fixedness, incontrovertibleness. [great affliction remains bedridden.

अटवाटखटवाट, *f.* the state of a person who in

अटवाटीखटवाटी, *f.* the being bedridden. — *lenā*, to be confined to bed in some great trouble or affliction.

अटवि
अटवी } *f.* a forest, wood, wilderness, grove.

अटा, *m. f.* an upper room or story.

अटाना, *t.* to fix into, fasten on, fasten on to.

अटामाटी = **आटामाटी**, *q. v.*

अटारी, *f.* a thatched upper room; a roof; a house built of burnt brick.

अटाल, *f.* anything immovable; *hence*, a stack, rick (of grass, etc); a heap (of baggage, etc.).

अटाला, *m.* a heap; goods, furniture.

अटाली, *f.* household furniture. [haustible.

अटूट, *m.* (*f.* ā) not liable to be broken; inex-

अटेक, without a support.

अटेर, *f. pr. n.* a certain town.

अटेरन, *m.* a skein of thread, bundle of thread; reel of thread; the lounge or circle in a manége.

अटेरना, *t.* to reel or make up thread into skeins; to lounge a horse. [interrupted, unquestioned.

अटोक, *m.* (*f.* ā) unrestrained, unhindered, un-

अटोव, *m.* nature, constitution, essence, power.

अटोल, *m.* (*f.* ā) unpolished (stones or jewels); hence (when applied to persons) rude, unmannerly.

अट्टहास, *m.* a horse-laugh.

अट्ठाईस = **अठाईस**, *q. v.*

अट्टाल, *m.* an upper room or pavilion.

अट्टालिका, *f.* a thatched upper chamber.

अट्टी, *f.* a hank or bundle of thread; a cant word

अट्ठा, the eight (at cards). [for a turban.

अट्ठावन = **अठावन**, *q. v.*

अठकेली = **अटखेली**, *q. v.*

अठतालीस, forty-eight, (४८): see **वां, वीं, वे, वें**.

अठतीस, thirty-eight, (३८): see **वां, वीं, वे, वें**.

अठत्तर = **अठहत्तर**, *q. v.*

अठमास, *m.* land constantly ploughed for sugarcane from the month *Asāṛh* to the month *Māgh* inclusive.

अठल, *m.* the bathing of a bride and bridegroom together on the third day after marriage.

अठवाटीखठवाटी = **अटवाटीखटवाटी**, *q. v.* [a week.

अठवारा, *m.* the eight day after any other day;

अठसठ, sixty-eight, (६८): see **वां, वीं, वे, वें**.

अठहत्तर, seventy-eight, (७८): see **वां, वीं, वे, वें**

अठाईस, twenty-eight, (२८): see **वां, वीं, वे, वें**.

अठानवे, ninety-eight, (९८): see **वां, वीं, वे, वें**.

अठारवां = **अठारहवां**, *q. v.*

अठारह, eighteen, (१८): see **वां, वीं, वे, वें**.

अठावन, fifty-eight, (५८): see **वां, वीं, वे, वें**.

अठावीस = **अठाईस**, *q. v.*

अठासी, eighty-eight, (८८): see **वां**, **वीं**, **वे**, **वें**.

अठेआनव / **अठेआनवे** } = **अठानवे**, *q. v.*

अठेआस्सी = **अठासी**, *q. v.*

अठेल, not to be pushed out of its place, immovable; irrefragable, unanswerable.

अठेहत्तर = **अठहत्तर**, *q. v.*

अड़. As **ठ** and **ड़** are often interchanged, some of the words which might have been given above will be found below, and some of those which might have been given below will be found above; *e. g.* if the student find **अड़तीस** in his book, but fail to find it in the Dictionary, he will find it spelt **अठतीस**.

अड़ *f.* contention, contrariety, obstinacy, fault. — *k.* to come to a standstill, be obstinate (as a horse).

अड़ंग, *f.* a manufacturing town; a warehouse where goods are sold wholesale; the place or depôt where goods are manufactured (whether it be a town or not): e. g. *Nilkī* —, an indigo-factory. [obstacle.

अड़ंगा, *m.* a mode of wrestling with the feet; an

अड़क, a surname, title, epithet.

अड़कसब, *m.* a Hindoo who follows a trade different from that of his ancestors. [Madras *fanam*).

अड़का, a small brass coin (the eighth part of a

अड़गसबड़गस, *m.* worthless things, lumber.

अड़चन, light; uneasy.

अड़चनी, *f.* lightness; uneasiness.

अड़िचन = **अड़चन**, *q. v.*

अड़ज़ात, a villain (*lit.* base-born).

अड़ज़ामिनी, a counter-security, a surety for a surety; mutual responsibility.

अड़ठया, *m.* a broker, salesman, agent; a commission agent; a banker who grants and accepts bills on other bankers or correspondents.

अड़ठो = **अड़ठया**, *q. v.*

अड़ड़ाना, *a. int.* to lament aloud, shriek.

अड़तक, erring, astray.

अड़तला, *m.* protection, shelter, defence.

अड़तालीस = **अठतालीस**, *q. v.*

अड़तूक, *m.* a hindrance.

अड़दंग, *m.* rheumatism (in horses).

अड़दगहा, 1, *m.* a stop, impediment, bar, bolt; a yoke (for oxen); 2, *m.* (*f.* ī) athwart, awry.

अड़दावा, mashed grain mixed with a little oil and water and given to horses.

अड़ना, *a. int.* to stop, hesitate, be restive (said of horses). [hard up.

अड़पभड़प, necessity, need. —— *meṅ honā*, to be

अड़बंगा, *m.* (*f.* ī) crooked, uneven.

अड़बड़, *m.* nonsensical talk. —— *baknā*, to speak inconsiderately or without meaning; to rave, talk nonsense, babble.

अड़बड़, *m.* (*f.* ā) rugged, uneven.

अड़बड़ंग, *m.* foolish actions.

अड़बड़ंगी, *m.* (*f.* inī) an inconsiderate person.

अड़बन्द, *m.* a cloth worn by Hindoos passing from the waist between the legs and fastening behind.

अड़बाड़, *f.* a prop; a shelter; an obstacle: *lit.* stopping, impeding. [lative.

अड़बाल, a very distant relative, a pretended re-

अड़मट्टयाल, silly, foolish, indiscreet.

अड़मान, *m.* a deposit, security, pledge.

अड़माप, *m.* measure more than the standard.

अडरउडर, *m.* a ditch and the mound of earth thrown up from it forming the boundary of a field.

अड़यल, *m.* (*f.* ā) an obstinate person: *lit.* perverse, obstinate, sullen, mulish.

अड़सटगी / **अड़सटा** } *f.* sloth, laziness.

अड़सट = **अठसठ**, *q. v.* [sion, brokerage.

अड़हत, *f.* agency, sale by commission, commi-

अड़ा देना, *t.* to give up, abandon.

अड़ाई, *more prop.* **अढ़ाई**, *q. v.*

अड़ाड़, *m.* outhouses for cattle; harvest-floor for the blossoms of the *Māhwa*; the steep bank of a pond or river. [tank.

अड़ाड़ा, *m.* the high steep banks of a river or

अड़ाड़ी, *f.* the measure of a field originally established in a lease or grant to which the occupant appeals in preference to an actual measurement or adjustment. [to another: 2, *m.* a kind of tune.

अड़ाना, 1, *t.* to cause to stop; to fasten one thing

अड़ानी, *f.* a large fan, a parasol.

अड़ू, much given to venery (said of any male animal, such as a stallion, etc., which is kept for procreation). [mulish.

अड़ुआ, *m.* (*f.* **अड़ुई**) obstinate, perverse, restive,

अड़ूसा, *m.* a certain medicinal plant (*Justicia adhenatoda* and *ganderussa*).

अड़ेआना, *t.* to protect, screen, shelter: *a. int.* to become a protection: *n.* to be protected.

अड़ेंच / **अड़ैंच** / **अड़ैंश** } *f.* enmity, malice, hostility.

अडोल, immovable, unshaken, fixed.

अड़ोसपड़ोस, *m.* vicinity, neighbourhood.

अड़ोसीपड़ोसी, *f.* neighbourliness: *m.* a neighbour.

अढ़त, *f.* agency, commission, sale by commission, brokerage. [another, agent, broker.

अढ़तिया, *m.* a man who transacts business for

अढ़वल, *m.* a day-labourer.

अढ़ाई, 1, *f.* a full gallop: 2, two and a half; twice and a half. When used with a noun of number, it means twice and a half of that number; e. g. *arhāi sau*, 250: *arhāi ser*, 5 lbs: *arhāi kos*, two and a half kos.

अढ़ैया, *m.* any weight or measure of two and a

अणावी, *f.*; see **अणु**. [half sers.

अणिया, *m.* = **अणी**, *q. v.*

अणिमन, *m.* the superhuman faculty of making oneself infinitely small; the subtle and invisible state

said to be attainable by austere devotion and the performance of magical rites, or as possessed by a deity; [subtlety.

अणिमा, *m.* = **अणिमन**, *q. v.*

अणी, *f.* the point or the edge of any sharp instrument; the stern of a boat; the pin of an axle.

अणु, *m.* (*f.* **अण्वी**) atomic, minute, small, subtile; hence, *m.* a minute particle, an atom.

अण्टना, *m.* to be contained, be filled up (said of a well, tank, etc,); to be tightened.

अण्टा, *n.* a ball, a marble.

अण्टाघर, *m.* a billiard-room.

अण्टारी, *more prop.* **अटारी**, *q. v.*

अण्ट्टहास, *m.* a horselaugh.

अण्ठई, *f.* a tick, the louse that attacks dogs, etc.

अण्ठना, *more prop.* **अण्टना**, *q. v.*

अण्ठलाना, *a. int.* to twist, writhe, to start, to swagger, walk affectedly, give oneself airs. [into.

अण्ठवाना, *t.* to cause to be contained, to cram

अण्ठाकोड़ी, *f.* a cord with which cattle are tied neck and heels.

अण्ठाचित, *m.* (*f.* ā) one whose fortune is exhausted (a term of abuse): *lit.* unlucky.

अण्ड, *m.* an egg; *semen genitale;* the scrotum, testicles: the castor-oil plant or Palma Christi (*Ricinus vulgaris*).

अण्डकटाह, *m. pr. n.* the egg of Brahm.

अण्डका, *m.* an egg: a pannier, one of the bags forming a pannier. [hernia.

अण्डकोश, *m.* the scrotum, testicles: rupture,

अण्डकोष, } = **अण्डकोश**, *q. v.*
अण्डकोस, }

अण्डज, *m.* (*f.* ā) an epithet of any oviparous animal, as a bird, reptile, or fish; *lit.* egg-born.

अण्डड़ा, *m.* an egg.

अण्डा, *m.* an egg; the egg of Brahm (the egg *par excellence*): a species of firework (so called because the composition is put into an egg-shell). —*denā*, to lay eggs.

अण्डाकृति, egg-shaped.

अण्डाभा, *m.* (*f.* ī) egg-like.

अण्डेल, oviparous; pregnant with egg (said of the females of oviparous animals).

अत = **इतना**, *q. v.* (Frequent in poetry).

अतः, from this cause, therefore; thence.

अतएव, thence, therefore, wherefore.

अतथा, *m.* (*f.* ī) without authority, powerless.

अतन, *m.* an epithet of Kāmdev: *lit.* bodiless.

अतना, *m.* (*f.* i) (*colloquial*) = **इतना**, *q. v.*

अतनु = **अतन**, *q. v.*

अतन्त (*colloquial*) = **अत्यन्त**, *q. v.*

अ़तफ़, *m.* favour, affection, kindness, bounty; a present; a connecting, joining.

अतफ़ाल, *m.* (pl. of **तिफ़्ल**) bairns, children, family.

अ़तर, *m.* scent, perfumery, essence, fragrance.

अ़तरदान, *m.* a perfume-box, scent-bottle.

अतरपाल, *m.* land which is left uncultivated.

अ़तरमाली, *f.* the act of rubbing or applying perfume. [of logical inquiry, uninvestigable.

अतर्क्य, *m.* (*f.* ā) not falling within the province

अतर्पित, *m.* (*f.* ā) unsatisfied; dissatisfied.

अतल, *m.* one of the seven *pātāls*, or divisions of the infernal regions; the portion immediately below the earth: *lit.* bottomless.

अतललोक, *m.* the infernal regions.

अतलस्पर्श, *m.* (*f.* ā) very deep, bottomless.

अतश, *more prop.* **आतश**, *q. v.*

अतसी, *f.* flax (*Linum usitatissimum*).

अता, *more prop.* **आता**, *q. v.*

अताई, *m.* a man who sings and dances gratis.

अताबग, *m.* a master, teacher; a title given to kings or to prime ministers, *lit.* the lord-father.

अतालीक़, *m.* a private tutor. [ship; education.

अतालीक़ी, *f.* private tuition, tutorship, preceptor-

अति. 1, a particle denoting excess, used chiefly in forming compound words: 2, It is also a preposition denoting beyond (whether as to time, place, or degree), over, gone by, passedover, surpassing, exceeding, much, very, very much: 3, *adv.*, exceedingly.

अतिका, much, excessively.

अतिकाय, *m.* (*f.* ā) a giant; a certain *Rākhsas: lit.* having a large body, gigantic.

अतिकाल, *m.* delay, a long time. [nomical yogs.

अतिगण्ड, *m.* the sixth of the twenty-seven astro-

अतिगति, very much, very great. [*thus*).

अतिगन्ध, *m.* lemon-grass (*Andropogon schœnan-*

अतिगर्व्वित, *m.* (*f.* ā) very proud, arrogant.

अतिगुप्त, (*f.* ā) closely hidden or concealed, very secret.

अतिघिन, *f.* intense disgust, abhorrence.

अतिचार, *m.* the rapid motion of a planet from one sign to another. [ful, restless.

अतिजागर, *m.* the black curlew: *lit.* very wake-

अतिजीर्ण, *m.* (*f.* ā) very old, decayed.

अतितीक्ष्ण, *m.* (*f.* ā) very keen, very pungent, sharp, acrid, hot. [to hospitality.

अतिथि, *m.* a guest, a stranger, a person entitled

अतिथिक्रिया, *f.* hospitality (especially contemplated in the light of a religious obligation).

अतिथित्व, *m.* hospitality.

अतिथिपाल, *m.* (*f.* ī) = **अतिथिपालक**, *q. v.*

अतिथिपालक, *m.* (*f.* ikā) a host: lit. *adj.* practising hospitality, hospitable.

अतीथिशला } *more prop.* **अतिथिशाला**, *q. v.*
अतिथिशाल }

अतिथिशाला, *f.* a house or apartment for the reception or entertainment of visitors or of travellers.

अतिथिसेवक, *m.* (*f.* ikā) a host: lit. *adj.* rendering kind offices to guests. [hospitality.

अतिथिसेवा, *f.* the rendering kind offices to guests,

अतिदान, *m.* liberality in giving.

अतिदाह, *m.* great heat, violent inflammation.

अतिदीन, very needy, very distressed, very miser-

अतिदुर्गत, *f.* great difficulty, great distress. [able.

अतिदुष्कर, very difficult. [distance, afar off.

अतिदूर, 1, *m.* a great distance : 2, *adv.* at a great

अतिदोष, *m.* a great fault or crime.

अतिधृति, a certain metre of nineteen syllables; hence, in the ingenious system of reckoning by symbols adopted by Hindoos in their poetry, this word is a symbol for 19.

अतिपराक्रम, 1, *m.* great strength: 2, very strong.

अतिपातक, *m.* a heinous sin, great crime.

अतिपातकी, *m.* (*f.* inī) a criminal : *lit.* guilty of very great or heinous crime, very guilty.

अतिपान, *m.* 1, drunkenness, excessive drinking: 2, a drunkard. [babbler.

अतिवक्ता, *m.* (*f.* trī) a great speaker, great talker,

अतिबल, 1, *m.* great strength : 2, very strong.

अतिबार, frequently, very frequently.

अतिबेल, 1, much, excessive, unlimited : 2, frequently, very often.

अतिभार, *m.* a very great or excessive burden.

अतिभोग, *m.* excess of enjoyment ; *hence,* misuse,

अतियोग्य, very suitable, very worthy. [abuse.

अतिरिक्त, *m.* (*f.* ā) excessive, exceeding.

अतिरोग, *m.* consumption (*Phthisis pulmonaris*).

अतिवास, *m.* a rigid fast observed on certain occasions. [very formidable ; hard, difficult.

अतिविकट, *m.* a fierce elephant : *lit.* very fierce,

अतिविष, *m.* an antidote to poison : *lit.* exceeding or subduing poison.

अतिविषा, *f.* a certain poisonous tree (*Aconitum ferox* or *Betula*) used in medicine; the bark is also used in dying red. It is of three kinds, *viz.* white, red, and black, and is also called *Atis* and *Vishwā*.

अतिविस्तृत, *m.* (*f.* ā) very extended.

अतिव्ययी, *m.* (*f.* inī) a spendthrift : *lit.* extravagant, prodigal, lavish, expensive, spendthrift.

अतिशक्त, *m.* (*f.* ā) very powerful.

अतिशक्ति, *f.* great strength, great power.

अतिशक्तिता, *f.* (*m.* **त्व**) heroic valour, prowess.

अतिशय, very much, exceeding, excessively.

अतिशीत, *m.* (*f.* ā) exceedingly cold.

अतिसंचय, *m.* a great accumulation, a hoard.

अतिसार, *m.* diarrhœa, dysentery. [entery.

अतिसारकी, *m.* (*f.* inī) a person afflicted with dys-

अतिसारी, *m.* (*f.* iṇī) a person afflicted with dysentery : *lit* 1, afflicted with dysentery : 2, purgative.

अतिहर्ष, 1, *m.* great joy: 2, *m.* (*f.* ā) exceedingly delighted.

अतीहास, *m.* violent laughter, a horselaugh.

अती: An occasional corruption of **अति**, *q. v.*

अतीक्ष्ण, *m.* (*f.* ā) not sharp, not keen or shrewd; [dull, obtuse.

अतीक्ष्णता, *f.* bluntness, obtuseness.

अतीत, 1, past, elapsed ; free from, devoid of, destitute of : *hence,* 2, *m.* (*f.* ā) a wanderer, pilgrim, mendicant, ascetic (among the Hindoos).

अतीतकाल, *m.* (in Gram.) the preterite : *lit.* time past and gone.

अतीरिक्त, *more prop.* **अतिरिक्त**, *q. v.*

अतीव, much, very, very much, exceedingly, excessively, indeed.

अतीख, *m.* (*f.* ā) a stupid person, etc : *lit.* not sharp, dull, stupid, uninteresting. [medicine.

अतीस, *m.* (see **अतिविषा**) a certain root used in

अतीसार, *more prop.* **अतिसार**, *q. v.* : See **अती**.

अतुल, *m.* (*f.* ā) not weighed ; not weighable : unequalled, unexampled, unparalleled. [swelled.

अतुलित, *m.* (*f.* ā) not weighed : increased, risen,

अतृप्त, *m.* (*f.* ā) unsatisfied, uneasy, restless.

अतृप्ति, *f.* inability to be satisfied, insatiableness,

अतेक, provincial form = **इतना**. [voraciousness.

अतेजा, *m.* (*f.* ī) dim, dull, dark.

अतोल = **अतुल**, *q. v.* [gist, perfumer.

अत्तार, *m.* a maker or a vendor of scents, drug-

अत्थ in Chand = **अस्त्र**, *q. v.*

अत्यन्त, much, very much, exceedingly, excessively

अत्यन्तता, *f.* } superabundance, excessiveness.
अत्यन्तत्व, *m.* }

अत्यन्तलों, to the utmost, to the very last degree.

अत्यल्प, very little, the least bit, very few.

अत्यल्पतर, (*intensive compar. adj.*) least, meanest.

अत्यष्टि, a certain species of metre of seventeen syllables ; hence, in the ingenious system of reckoning by symbols adopted by Hindoos in their poetry, this word is a symbol for 17.

अत्याचार, *m.* a deviation from prescribed observances, the contemning religious and moral laws.

अत्याचारी, *m.* (*f.* iṇī) a transgressor : lit. *adj.* transgressing religious rules. [ful.

अत्यानन्द, 1, *m.* great joy : 2, *m.* (*f.* ā) very joy-

अत्यानन्दता, *f.* } great gladness.
अत्यानन्दत्व, *m.* } [sary.

अत्यावश्यक, of essential importance, very neces-

अत्युक्त, m. (*f.* ā) a great talker. [tion.

अत्युक्ति, *f.* superfluous talk, garrulity ; exaggera-

अत्युत्तम = **अत्योत्तम**, *q. v.*

अत्योत्तम, (*intensive superl. adj.*) exceedingly good, the very best, most excellent, superexcellent, choice, rare.

अत्र, here, in this place, herein. [used in medicine.

अत्रन, *m.* a climbing plant (*Cynanitum extensum*).

अत्रमुनि, *more prop.* **अत्रिमुनि**, *q. v.*

अत्राफ़, *f.* (pl. of **तरफ़**) sides, environs, confines, skirts, districts : *adv.* all around.

अत्रि, *m. pr. n.* (see **ऋषि**) one of the seven rishis, [the father of Chandra.

अत्रिऋषि } = **अत्रि**, *q. v.*
अत्रिमुनि }

अत्रिप्रिया, *f.* (see **प्रिया**) an epithet of **अनुसूइया**: *lit.* the beloved of Atri.

अत्वार, *m.* (pl. of **तौर**) manners, ways, devoirs, habits, practice, behaviour.

अन्वित, connected with, possessed of, fraught [with.

अथ, 1, *m.* a beginning: 2, It is also used as an inceptive or premising particle for the purpose of introducing a remark, question, theme or affirmation, or to call attention to a logical inference about to be stated; *e. g.* then, thus, so, hence, consequently, therefore, wherefore, further, now, moreover, henceforth, "here beginneth."

अथक, *m.* (*f.* ā) unwearied, insensible of fatigue.

अथवना, sunset, the west.

अथवर्ण, *m.* (see **वेद**) the fourth Ved.

अथल, 1, *m.* (*f.* ā) unsteady, unstable, wavering: 2, *m.* land farmed or rented.

अथवा, or, or even.

अथा = **अथाह**, *q. v.*

अथाई, *f.* any place where people meet for counsel, or to converse and to amuse themselves.

अथाह, *m.* 1. a great depth, an abyss: 2, very deep, unfathomable, bottomless; out of man's depth, unfordable.

अथित, *m.* (*f.* ā) unsteady, unstable, wavering.

अथ्य = **अत्थ**, *q. v.*

अद, half (much used in composition).

अदंद, *more prop.* **अद्वन्द**, *q. v.*

अदकचा, *m.* a cloth for carrying things in; a cover, covering, wrapper.

अदखिला = **अदखीला**, *q. v.*

अदखीला, *m.* (*f.* ī) half open, half blown (said of [flowers).

अदगड़ा, *m.* (*f.* ī) half driven (as a stake).

अदगदरा, *m.* fruit fully formed but unripe.

अदण्ड, 1, *m.* impunity: 2, *m.* (*f.* ā) unpunished.

अदतरी, pendulous, hanging; infirm.

अदत्त, *m.* (*f.* ā) not given. In Hindoo law it is applied to illegal donations, consequently void and resumable.

अदत्ता, *f.* (see **अदत्त**) not given in marriage (said [of females).

अदद, *m.* number.

अदन, 1, *m.* the act of eating; food, nourishment: 2, *f. pr. n.* the garden of Eden.

अदना, *m.* (*f.* ī) inferior, little, low, mean, of no [consequence.

अदन्तर, **अदन्तरी** } = **अदतरी**, *q. v.*

अदब, *m.* the act of preserving the proper boundaries of things; good breeding, politeness, ceremony, urbanity, respectfulness: polite literature.—*k.* to respect; to behave politely.

अदबवाला, *m.* (*f.* ī) a person deserving polite behaviour: a polite or well-bred person.

अदबीच, in the midst of, among.

अदभव, *m.* the act of being born or of springing up (as plants from seed); birth, production.

अदभुत, *more prop.* **अद्भुत**, *q. v.*

अदभ्र, many, much.

अदम, *m.* non-existence, non-entity; privation, nothing; discontinuance, cessation.

अदमड़ा, *m.* (*f.* ī) breathless, dead.

अदमरा, *m.* (*f.* **अदमरी**), **अदमुआ**, *m.* (*f.* **अदमुई**) } half dead.

अदय, *m.* (*f.* ā) merciless, unfeeling, cruel.

अदया, *f.* mercilessness, unfeelingness, cruelty.

अदर = **उदर**, *q. v.*

अदरक, *more prop.* **आर्द्रक**, *q. v.*

अदर्श, *m.* 1, fate, fortune; unseen danger: 2, unseen, unforeseen.

अदर्शण, 1, *m.* (*f.* ā) invisible, unseen: 2, *m.* dis- [appearance, invisibility.

अदर्सा, *m.* a kind of very fine muslin; a kind of fried sweetmeat.

अदल, *m.* a plant (*Eujenia acutangula*): *lit.* with- [out lobes, apetalous.

अदलबदल, *m.* alteration, change, exchange, substitution. *Adl-badlī k.*, *adlā-badlā k.*, *adlī-badlī k.*, *adl-kā badl k.*, to change, exchange; to displace, confuse.

अदलाबदला, *m.*, **अदलीबदली**, *f.* } = **अदलबदल**, *q. v.*

अदवान, *f.* braces for tightening the tape of a bed- [stead.

अदवायन = **अदवान**, *q. v.*

अदवार, *m.* (pl. of **दौर**) revolutions.

अदहन, *m.* water set to boil for the purpose of cook- [ing food.

अदा, *f.* blandishments, coquetry; disharge, payment, performance: voice. —*k.* to pay, liquidate, reimburse.

अदाता, *m.* (*f.* trī) = **अदानी**, *q. v.*

अदानी, *m.* (*f.* inī) a niggard: *lit.* niggardly, illiberal, stingy, avaracious.

अदाबन्दी, *f.* the fixing a period for the performance of a contract, or payment by instalments.

अदालत, *f.* a court of justice; justice, law, equity.

अदावत, *f.* enmity, hatred, strife.

अदिक, *more prop.* **अधिक**, *q. v.*

अदिति, *f. pr. n.* the mother of the gods.

अदितिनन्दन, *m.* an epithet of any male deity; *lit.* a son of Aditi.

अदिन, *m.* an inauspicious or unlucky day.

अदिल्ला, *f.* (pl. of **दलील**) arguments, proofs, indi- [cations.

अदिष्ट, *m.* misfortune, fate.

अदीक = **अधिक**, *q. v.*

अदीब, *m.* 1, a teacher of polite manners: 2, urbanity: 3, courteous, polite.

अदीम, *m.* perfumed goat's leather: the face, surface (of the earth or of the heavens).

अदील, *m.* an administrator of justice: *lit.* alike, equal; equitable, just.

अदृश्य, *m.* (*f.* ā) unseen, invisible.

अदृष्ट, 1, *m.* (*f.* ā) unseen, invisible, unforeseen: hence, 2, *m.* the unseen, fate, fortune, unforeseen danger.

अदेय, *m.* (*f.* ā) not suitable to be given, incap- [able of being given.

अदेवदे, *m.* procrastination.—*k.* to put off, evade, shuffle.

अदीप्त, *m.* (*f.* ā) without splendour.

अदौरी, *f.* a kind of food eaten by Hindoos.

अद्धी, *f.* a half of the coin **दमड़ी** : the half of a piece of cloth.

अद्भुत, 1, *m.* (*f.* ā) surprizing, wonderful ; admirable ; curious, rare : 2, *m.* surprize, astonishment.

अद्भुतकर्म्म, *m.* an astonishing feat, miracle.

अद्भुतवस्तु, *f.* a curiosity ; a phenomenon.

अद्यापि, even to this day, even still, even yet.

अद्यावधि, up to this day, still, yet, even now.

अद्योत, 1, *m.* (*f.* ā) without lustre (see **अ**, 8) : 2, *m.* great light, brilliancy, lustre (see **अ**, 14). [state.

अद्रक, *m.* ginger (*Amomum zinziber*) in the undried

अद्रकी, *f.* a certain kind of sweetmeat.

अद्रि, *m.* a stone ; a hill, mountain. [ness.

अद्रोह, *m.* absence of tyranny, moderation, mild-

अद्रोही, *m.* (*f.* inī) a non-tyrannical person : *lit.* not tyrannical, mild, moderate, innocuous.

अद्वन्द्व, *m.* (*f.* ā) quiet, tranquil, free from strife.

अद्वायन = **अदवायन**, *q. v.*

अद्विती : see (1) **अदिति** (2) **अद्वितीय**.

अद्वितीय, *m.* (*f.* ā) peerless, matchless, unequalled ; only, sole, without a second. In applying this term to the Supreme Being most Hindoos intend to convey the pantheistic idea ; not, the Peerless One, but rather the One who is Himself all things, the universal Soul : there is but One Being, say they ; all existences are but parts of him ; there is no other.

अद्वेष, not malicious, inoffensive, harmless : hence, *m.* (*f.* ā) an inoffensive person.

अद्वेषी, *m.* (*f.* iṇī) = **अद्वेष**, *q. v.*

अद्वैत, *m.* (*f.* ā) peerless : undivided, single.

अद्वैतता, *f.* }
अद्वैतत्व, *m.* } peerlessness : singleness.

अध, 1, as a preposition it is the reverse of **उत**, and denotes down, downward, below (whether as to place, rank, or dgree) : 2, In composition it denotes 'half' : many examples will be found below.

अधंग, *m.* palsy affecting half the body, hemiplegia. [lytic.

अधंगी, *m.* (*f.* inī) a paralytic : *lit.* palsied, para-

अधःपतन, *m.* the falling of anything from a height.

अधक, a half ; a part.

अधकचरा }
अधकचा } *m.* (*f.* ī) half-ripe ; half-cooked.

अधकच्चा, 1, *m.* (*f.* ī) half-ripe ; half-cooked : 2, *m.* a kind of soil in the district of Sahāranpur.

अधकपाली, *f.* a pain affecting half the head ; a nut of Areca shaped like a hemisphere. The nut is so called probably either, first, from the fact of two kernels being contained in one shell ; or secondly, from the fact that to this nut the virtue is ascribed of curing discease of the same name.

अधकर, *m.* half of the tax or duty, (the other half being remitted.)

अधकरी, *f.* an instalment of eight annas in the rupee, or half of the Government impost.

अधकहा, *m.* (*f.* ī) half spoken, half uttered, half

अधखुला, *m.* (*f.* ī) half-open. [pronounced.

अधगदरा, *m.* (*f.* ī) half-ripe, (said of fruit, etc.).

अधगो, *m.* the anus ; a way.

अधतरी = **अदतरी**, *q. v.* [pauper.

अधन, poor, needy, destitute : hence, *m.* (*f.* ā) a

अधनी, *m.* (*f.* inī) = **अधन**, *q. v.*

अधपक्का, *m.* (*f.* ī) half ripe ; half cooked.

अधपत, a corruption of **अधिपति**, *q. v.*

अधपाव, half a quarter. [shares.

अधबटाई, *f.* the division of produce in equal

अधबना, *m.* (*f.* ī) half made, half prepared.

अधबर, half-way, in the middle.

अधबीच, in the midst, in the middle.

अधम, *m.* (*f.* ā) mean, contemptible, vile, unworthy, low, inferior, wretched.

अधमता, *f.* (*m.* **त्व**) contemptibleness, inferiority, unworthiness, wretchedness.

अधमधारण, an epithet of God ; *lit.* affording support to the low, wretched, or unworthy.

अधमरण, *m.* (*f.* ā) }
अधमरा, *m.* (*f.* ī) } half dead.

अधमा, *f.* (*m.* **अधम**) an unworthy female.

अधमाधम, extremely wretched, unworthy or base.

अधमुआ, *m.* (*f.* **मुई**) half dead.

अधर, 1, (sc. **में**) in the middle : 2, *m.* empty space, the space between heaven and earth : the lip, the lower lip : *pudendum muliebre* : 3, *m.* (*f.* ā) inferior, low, insignificant, vile : suspended, separate, at a distance.

अधरबुद्धि, *m. f.* a person whose mind is occupied with sublunary things only : a person of an inferior or superficial understanding. [cloth.

अधरसा, *m.* half of a piece of cloth ; a sort of

अधरामृत, *m.* the moisture of the lips.

अधरेंअधर, aside, separate.

अधर्म्म, 1, *m.* injustice ; sin, crime ; unrighteousness, irreligion, impiousness, immorality : 2, *m.* (*f.* ā) unrighteous, irreligious, impious.

अधर्म्मचारी, *m.* (*f.* iṇī) an impious person ; *lit.* unrighteous, wicked, of irreligious behaviour.

अधर्म्मता, *f.* }
अधर्म्मत्व, *m.* } unrighteousness, irreligion.

अधर्म्मपना, *m.* unrighteousness, injustice, crimi-

अधर्म्ममल, *m.* the filth of irreligion. [nality.

अधर्म्मरत, *m.* (*f.* ā) a person whose inclinations are bent upon irreligion.

अधर्म्मिष्ठ, *m.* (*f.* ā) a very wicked person.

अधर्म्मी, *m.* (*f.* iṇī) an irreligious person ; an outcaste : *lit.* unjust, irreligious, sinful, criminal ; bereft of caste, deprived of caste. [ungodliness, wickedness.

अधर्म्मीपन, *m.* unjustness, sinfulness, impiousness,

अधवन, the half of anything.

अधवाड़, *f.* a half-web ; the half (generally applied to pieces of cloth).

अधान, *m.* oils, unguents. [subsistence.

अधार, *m.* food, aliment, nourishment, support,

अधारी, *m.* (*f.* iṇī) a support, prop.

अधार्मिक, *m.* (*f.* ā) unjust, unrighteous, wicked.

अधासीसी = **आधासीसी**, *q. v.*

अधि : this particle is much used as a preposition in composition denoting over, above, over and above, upon. It implies superiority in point of place, quantity, or quality; and is the reverse of **अप**.

अधिआतम, *more prop.* **अध्यात्म**, *q. v.*

अधिक, more, additional, augmented, abundant, greater, excessive, more than; most: extra, over and above, abounding, superabounding. [than.

अधिकतर, (*intensive comparative*) better than, more

अधिकत्व, *m.* (*f.* tā) excess, addition, superabundance, superiority. [the locative case; an adverb.

अधिकरण, *m.* superiority, title, right: (in Gram.)

अधिकर्म्म, *m.* superintendence, supervision, government. [sor.

अधिकर्म्मकृत, *m.* (*f.* ā) a superintendent, supervi-

अधिकाई, *f.* increase, addition; excess, abundance; supremacy; oppression, violence; aggrandizement.

अधिकाना, *t.* to augment; to aggrandize.

अधिकार, *m.* a kingdom, government, estate; dominion; possession, proprietorship; authority (whether absolute or derived); the bearing the insignia of royalty; inheritance; right, title, privilege.

अधिकारत्व, *m.* (*f.* tā) the possession or the exercise of *adhikār*.

अधिकारी, *m.* (*f.* iṇī) a proprietor, master, ruler, heir, any one who possesses or who is invested with *adhikār*: *lit.* possessing a right, title, or privilege; empowered, entitled or fit to rule, authorized.

अधिकृत, *m.* (*f.* ā) a superintendent, inspector of receipts and disbursements, auditor of public accounts. [prince, commander, chief.

अधिप, *m.* (*f.* ā) an owner, lord, master; a king,

अधिपति, *m.* (*f.* patni) = **अधिप**, *q. v.*

अधिमांस, *m.* a fleshy excrescence on the eye, cancer of the eye.

अधिमास, *m.* an intercalary month formed of the aggregate of the days omitted in reckoning the lunar year. It falls once in three years, when two lunations occur within one solar month.

अधियाना, *t.* to halve; to divide.

अधियार, *m.* a man who passes half his time in one village and half in another.— *k.* to act as an *adhiyār*.

अधियारी, *f.* a half-share.

अधिरथ, *m.* a charioteer. [monarch, potentate.

अधिराज, *m.* a great or supreme king, an emperor,

अधिराज्य, *m.* supreme sway, empire.

अधिवास, *m.* a house, residence, dwelling; perfuming the person, perfumes.

अधिविन्ना, *f.* a superseded wife.

अधिवेदनिक, *m.* dowry or alimony given to a wife who is superseded by a second marriage.

अधिष्ठाता, *m.* (*f.* trī) a ruler, governor, protector, presiding deity: *lit.* governing, protecting, presiding.

अधिष्ठातृ, *m.* (*f.* trī) = **अधिष्ठाता**, *q. v.*

अधीती, firm, good.

अधीन, *m.* (*f.* ā) submissive, obedient, subject to, under the authority of, subservient, obsequious, servile; docile, tractable, humble, dependent. Much used as a suffix in composition; e. g. *āgyādheen*.

अधीनता, *f.* submissiveness, obedience, subjection, obsequiousness, tractableness, humbleness, slavery.

अधीनताई, *f.* } = **अधीनता**, *q. v.*
अधीनत्व, *m.* }

अधीनी, *f.* 1, = **अधीनता**, *q. v.*: 2, a petition.

अधीर, *m.* (*f.* ā) confused, perplexed; irresolute; impatient, unsteady; precipitate, hasty.

अधीरज, 1, *m.* (*f.* ā) = **अधीरजा**, *q. v.*: 2, *m.* perplexity; unsteadiness; distractedness.

अधीरजा, *m.* (*f.* ī) confused, perplexed, distracted; unsteady, impatient, irresolute, feeble.

अधीरता, *f.* perplexity, confusion; impatience, unsteadiness, fickleness; precipitation, haste.

अधीश, *m.* (*f.* ā) a master, lord, chief.

अधीश्वर, *m.* (*f.* ī) a king who is paramount over other kings or princes, an emperor.

अधीस, *more prop.* **अधीश**, *q. v.*

अधूरा, *m.* (*f.* ī) half ready, half dressed, unfinished, immature (said of a fœtus). — jānā, to miscarry (said of females.)

अधेड़, *m.* (*f.* ā) middle-aged, just passed the prime of life (said most generally of women.)

अधेड़पना, *m.* the prime of life, middle age.

अधेला, *m.* a small copper coin amounting in value to twelve and a half *dāms*, or four *damrees*, and equal to a half of the *paisā*, a 'half-pice piece.'

अधेलिया, *m.* the proprietor of a half-share.

अधेली, *f.* a half-rupee piece; half a gold mohur; a kind of measure used for measuring corn.

अधैर्य्य, 1, *m.* = **अधैर्य्या**, *q. v.*: 2, *m.* (*f.* ā) unsteady, irresolute, feeble, impatient, perturbed.

अधैर्य्या, *f.* instability, want of endurance or firmness, perturbation of mind.

अधोतर, *f.* a certain fine kind of cloth.

अधोनाढ, half and half.

अधोबंधन, *m.* an under-girding, martingal.

अधोमुख, *m.* (*f.* ā) turned topsy-turvy, inverted; headlong; drooping the head from shame or grief; having the head downwards (a posture resorted to by Hindoos in performing *tapasyā*). [hide.

अधोड़ी, *f.* the half of a thick strong kind of

अध्यग्नि, property or settlement given to a wife when superseded by a new marriage of the husband: it is given during the marriage ceremony over the nuptial fire.

अध्यन, corruption of **अध्ययन**, *q. v.*

अध्यमता, see **अधमता**.

अध्ययन, *m.* reading, study, application to the study of the sacred books. This is one of the six duties of a Brahman.

अध्यक्ष, *m.* (*f.* ī) a chief, man of rank, lord, ruler, master, governor, superintendent.

अध्यक्षता, *f.* } the status of an **अध्यक्ष**.
अध्यक्षत्व, *m.* }

अध्यात्म, *m.* the supreme soul.

अध्याना, *t.* to halve, to divide.

अध्यापक, *m.* a man who instructs in the sacred books, a teacher, spiritual preceptor, learned man.

अध्यापकता, *f.* the status of an **अध्यापक**. [ing.

अध्यापन, *m.* teaching the sacred books, instruct-

अध्याय, *m.* a section or chapter of a book.

अध्याहृत, (in Gram.) understood, *scire licet.*

अन; 1, a negative or privitive prefix: it is never used excepting in composition, and has the same effect as *in* or *un* in many English words (see art. **अ**, 8). In the case of words in Hindee which are purely Sanskrit, it is prefixed to those only which begin with a vowel; as, **अनुचित**: in the common literature and speech of the Hindee-speaking people, however, it is placed indiscriminately before words beginning with vowels or with consonants. Many examples of these phenomena will be found below. 2, in old Hindee, and in some of the dialects of modern Hindee, this particle is inserted, like **ओं**, between the base and the terminations to indicate plurality; *e. g.* **लोगनका** = **लोगोंका**.

अनअहिवात, *m.* widowhood, bereavedness.

अनइस, ungodly, wicked.

अनओसर, *more prop.* **अनवसर**, *q. v.*

अनंग, *m.* (*f.* ā) an epithet of Kāmdev: *lit.* bodiless, limbless. [versary of Kāmdev.

अनंगआराती, *m.* an epithet of Shiv; *lit.* the ad-

अनंश, *m.* one who has no share, one who is excluded from a share of an inheritance on account of some legal flaw. [lock; a prop, support.

अनकटा, *m.* a dam or embankment of a river; a

अनकट्टा = **अनकटा**, *q. v.*

अनख, anger, envy, enmity, malice, wickedness.

अनखात, *m.* dislike, aversion.

अनखाना, *more com.* **अंखाना**, *q. v.*

अनगढ़, *m.* (*f.* ā) unformed, unwrought, uneducated, unpolished, unfinished, unlicked; unset (as a ring or a jewel); incoherent or ill-arranged (said of talk).

अनगिणत, *m.* (*f.* ā) uncounted; transcending calculation, unnumbered, numberless.

अनगिणात, *m.* (*f.* ā) }
अनगिणाती, *m.* (*f.* inī) } = **अनगिणत**, *q. v.*
अनगिणा, *m.* (*f.* ī) }

अनगिणा महीना, *m.* the eighth month of pregnancy.

अनघ, *m.* (*f.* ā) guiltless, sinless, blameless.

अनचेरी, an unsuitable time.

अनचाहत, *m.* (*f.* ā) not desired.

अनचित, suddenly, unexpectedly, unawares.

अनचेना, *m.* a valuation of standing crops.

अनछोला, *m.* (*f.* ī) awkward, rude, boorish, unlicked, unpared (said of fruit, etc.).

अनजना, 1, *m.* an inferior kind of rice: 2, *m.* (*f.* ī) [unborn.

अनजल, *more prop.* **अञ्जल**, *q. v.*

अनजला, *m.* (*f.* ī) unburnt, unscorched.

अनजस, *more prop.* **अनयश**, *q. v.*

अनजाई, a mongrel or hybrid animal.

अनजान, *m.* (*f.* ā) 1, an ignorant person: *lit.* not knowing, unwitting, ignorant; unintentional: 2, a stranger: *lit.* unknown. —*honā*, to assume the stranger; to feign ignorance.

अनजाना, *m.* (*f.* ī) = **अनजान**, *q. v.* [ligence.

अनजानी, *f.* 1, = **अनजाना**, *q. v.*: 2, ignorance, neg-

अनजाने, unwittingly, ignorantly.

अनजामा, *m.* (*f.* ī) barren (said of land).

अनट, *m.* injustice.

अनडवाई, *f.* a swollen testicle. [upon.

अनडालना, *a. int.* to consider, determine, settle

अनत, elsewhere: another, other.

अनदर्सा = **अदर्सा**, *q. v.*

अनदाई, *m.* (*f.* inī) = **अन्नदाता**, *q. v.*

अनदेखा, *m.* (*f.* ī) unseen, invisible; not yet seen, undiscovered.

अनदोलना, *a. int.* to swing. [dependent.

अनधीन, *m.* (*f.* ā) not subject, not dependent, in-

अनधोया, *m.* (*f.* **धोई**) unwashed, uncleansed.

अनन्त, 1, *m.* (*f.* ā) endless, boundless; infinite, eternal: 2, *m.* (in Myth.) an epithet of the serpent that supports the earth: an epithet of Vishnoo: the name of several plants: the name of a cord with fourteen knots which Hindoos tie on the arm on the fourteenth day of the first half of the moon in the month *Bhādoṅ*: this day is sacred to Vishnoo, and is called *Anantchaudas*. In the ingenious system of reckoning by symbols adopted by Hindoos in their poetry, this word is a symbol for the cypher (0).

अनन्तकाल, *m.* eternity; for ever and ever.

अनन्तचौदस, *m.*; see **अनन्त**.

अनन्तता, *f.* endlessness, eternity without ending.

अनन्तताबाई: see **बाई**.

अनन्तराशि, *f.* (in Arithm.) infinite quantity.

अनन्तरूप, *m.* (*f.* ā) multiform.

अनन्तवात, *m.* rigidity or paralysis of the muscles of the face and neck.

अनन्त्य, 1, *m.* (*f.* ā) endless, unbounded, infinite: 2, *m.* endlessness, infinity, eternity.

अननास, *m.* a pine-apple.

अननासी, *m.* (*f.* inī) formed like a pine-apple, appertaining to the pine-apple.

अनन्य, *m.* (*f.* ā) not other, not different, identical.

अनपढ़ा, *m.* (*f.* ī) unread, unlettered, uneducated, uninformed.

अनपत्य, *m.* (*f.* ā) having no progeny, childless.

अनपराध, 1, *m.* (*f.* ā) = **अनपराधी**, *q. v.*: 2, *m.* guiltlessness, blamelessness, innocence.

अनपराधी, guiltless, faultless, blameless, innocent: hence, *m.* (*f.* inī) an unoffending person.

अनपरिचय, *m.* non-acquaintance.

अनपायिन, *m.* (*f.* ī) indestructible, enduring.
अनपावना, *m.* (*f.* ī) unobtainable.
अनपेक्ष, *adj.* disregarding, neglecting, unheeding: hence, *m.* (*f.* ā) a negligent person.
अनपेक्षा, *f.* disregard, carelessness, indifference.
अनप्रतीती, unfriendly ; unbelieving, faithless.
अनबनाव, *m.* discord, dissension, misunderstanding.
अनबियाहा, *m.* (*f.* ī) unmarried.
अनबेधा, *m.* (*f.* ī) unperforated, unpierced, unbored.
अनबोल, *m.* (*f.* ā) speechless, silent, mute.
अनभई : see (1) **अनभाई** (2) **अभय**.
अनभल, *m.* ill fortune, bad luck.
अनभला, *m.* (*f.* ī) not good, bad.
अनभाई, *f.* a maiden, virgin, spinster.
अनभाया, unmarried : hence, *m.* a bachelor.
अनभिज्ञ, *m.* (*f.* ā) not aware, ignorant.
अनभिज्ञता, *f.* ignorance, stupidity.
अनभिलाष, *m.* absence of desire, indifference.
अनभिलाषी, *m.* (*f.* iṇī) one who is free from desire: *lit.* lacking desire, indifferent.
अनमना, *m.* (*f.* ī) thoughtful, regretful, sad, troubled in mind, agitated, dissatisfied, sickly.
अनमनात, doubt, perplexity.
अनमनाना, *t.* to perplex.
अनमिल, *m.* (*f.* ā) heterogeneous, discordant ; not agreeing to, indisposed towards.
अनमुख, *m.* (*f.* ā *or* ī) having the face turned away or averted.
अनमेल = **अनमिल**, *q. v.*
अनमोल, *m.* (*f.* ā) priceless, invaluable, beyond price.
अनयश, *m.* disrepute, disgrace, infamy.
अनयास, *more prop.* **अनायास**, *q. v.*
अनरस, *m.* absence of flavor, absence of enjoyableness ; nauseousness ; disgust ; coolness, distaste, misunderstanding between friends.
अनरीत, (*colloquial*) = **अनरीति**, *q. v.*
अनरीति, *f.* non-compliance with the rules of good manners or behaviour, unceremoniousness, irregularity.
अनरुद्ध, *more prop.* **अनिरुद्ध**, *q. v.*
अनर्थ, *m.* (*f.* ā) useless, aimless, unmeaning, absurd, nonsensical, improper.
अनर्थक, unmeaning, aimless, not to the purpose.
अनर्थकत्व, *m.* (*f.* tā) unmeaningness, aimlessness, irrelevancy.
अनल, *f.* fire ; flame : a certain plant (*Plumbago zeylanica* and *P. rosea*).
अनलशिख, as hot as fire.
अनलशिखा, *f.* flame of fire.
अनवट, *m.* a ring furnished with little balls and worn on the great toe.
अनवद्य, *m.* (*f.* ā) blameless, faultless ; not to be despised, honorable, distinguished.
अनवधान, 1, *m.* carelessness, inadvertency, inattention, indifference : 2, *m.* (*f.* ā) inattentive, inadvertent, careless.
अनवधानत्व, *m.* (*f.* tā) = **अनवधान**, 1, *q. v.*
अनवसर, *m.* 1, want of opportunity, want of leisure ; inopportuneness : 2, having no leisure, busy ; inopportune.
अनवस्थ, *m.* (*f.* ā) unstable, changeable, incontinent.
अनवस्था, *f.* the absence of a fixed state, instability ; uncertainty, doubt ; incontinence.
अनवस्थित, *m.* (*f.* ā) = **अनवस्थ**, *q. v.*
अनश्वर, not perishing, imperishable, immortal.
अनसमझा, *m.* (*f.* ī) not understanding or knowing ; not understood.
अनसिख, *m.* (*f.* ā) } illiterate, unlearned, untaught.
अनसीखा, *m.* (*f.* ī) }
अनसुना, *m.* (*f.* ī) unheard, not noticed, disregarded.
अनसुनीक°, *a. int.* to pretend not to hear what is said : *t.* to disregard.
अनसुन्धान, *m.* investigation, inquiry.
अनसुयिया, *more prop.* **अनुसुइया**, *q. v.*
अनसूय, *m.* (*f.* ā) a person who is free from a spirit of detraction.
अनहंकार, *m.* absence of pride, humility.
अनहंकारी, *m.* (*f.* iṇī) a humble person : *lit.* not proud.
अनहरना, *t.* to filch, pilfer.
अनहित, *m.* unfriendliness, disaffection, hostility : 2, inimical, disaffected, bad : hence, *m.* (*f.* ā) a foe.
अनहितू, *m. f.* = **अनहित**, 2, *q. v.*
अनहोना, *m.* (*f.* ī) *adj.* not to be ; impossible.
अनाकानी, *f.* the turning a deaf ear, overlooking, conniving at, purposely neglecting.
अनाकार, *m.* (*f.* ā) without form ; shapeless.
अनाक्रान्ता, *f.* a sort of prickly nightshade (*Solanum jacquini*).
अनागत, not come, not yet arrived, future.
अनागम्य, *m.* (*f.* ā) inaccessible ; unapproachable ; unobtainable.
अनाचार, 1, illbehaved, indecorous, indecent : hence, *m.* (*f.* ā *or* ī) an immoral person : 2, *m.* neglect or disregard of religious observances ; improper conduct, indecorum.
अनाचारी, *m.* (*f.* iṇī) = **अनाचार**, 1, *q. v.*
अनाचित, unexpectedly, suddenly, unawares.
अनाचिती } *f.* ignorance, thoughtlessness.
अनाचीती }
अनाज, *m.* grain, corn.
अनाड़, not easily discovered, secret.
अनाड़ी = **अनारी**, *q. v.*
अनातुर, *m.* (*f.* ā) healthy, vigorous, well.
अनात्मा, *adj.* not having subdued one's own mind.
अनाथ, *m. f.* an orphan, a widow : *lit.* without a master, protector, patron, husband, or chief, unprotected, helpless, forlorn.
अनाथक, appertaining to the unprotected.
अनाथबनजर, *f.* land without an owner, unclaimed land.
अनाद, *more prop.* **अनादि**, *q. v.*

अनादअनकर, *f.* land that has been waste from time immemorial.

अनादभुमि, *f.* land transferred by mortgage.

अनादर, *m.* affront, disrespect.

अनादरीय, *m.* (*f.* ā) not to be esteemed or venerated, disreputable.

अनादि, an epithet of the Eternal One: *lit.* without beginning; unborn, uncreated.

अनादित्व, *m.* eternity without beginning.

अनामय, *m.* freedom from disease, healthiness; the name of the salutation proper to be used by a Brāhmaṇ to a Shoodra.

अनामय, *m.* (*f.* ā) healthy, unhurt, uninjured.

अनामा, *m.* the ring-finger.

अनायास, 1, *m.* ease, facility: 2, *m.* (*f.* ā) easy: 3, easily.

अनार, *m.* a pomegranate; a kind of firework.

अनारपन, *m.* ignorance, silliness, awkwardness, clumsiness, inexpertness.

अनारी, *m.* (*f.* iṇī) a simpleton, stupid, novice, bungler: *lit.* unskilful, inexpert, inadept, awkward, clumsy, stupid: 2, appertaining to or resembling the pomegranate.

अनाश्य, *m.* (*f.* ā) indestructible, imperishable.

अनाहार, *m.* abstinence from food, foodlessness, starvation, fasting.

अनाहारी, *m.* (*f.* iṇī) one who fasts: lit. *adj.* fasting.

अनि in Chand = **अन्य**, *q. v.*

अनिच्छा, *f.* absence of desire, disinclination, indifference, unwillingness.

अनित्य, *m.* (*f.* ā) not for ever, temporary, transient, fleeting, perishable, frail.

अनित्यत्व, *m.* (*f.* tā) want of permanency, transitoriness.

अनित्यदत्त, *m.* (*f.* ā) a child adopted for a certain term: *lit.* temporarily bestowed.

अनित्यदत्तक, *m.* (*f.* ikā) = **अनित्यदत्त**, *q. v.*

अनिद्र, *m.* (*f.* ā) sleepless, wakeful; awake.

अनिन्दित, *m.* (*f.* ā) irreproachable.

अनिप, *m.* the commander of an army.

अनिपुण, *m.* (*f.* ā) unskilled, unskilful.

अनिमनि = **अनमनी**, *q. v.*

अनिमा, *more prop.* **अणिमा**, *q. v.*

अनिरुद्ध, *m.* (*f.* ā) unobstructed, unrestrained.

अनिर्णय, *m.* uncertainty.

अनिर्मल, *m.* (*f.* ā) dirty, foul, not pure.

अनिर्वचनीय, *m.* (*f.* ā) not admitting of being expressed in words, indescribable, undefinable.

अनिर्वच्य / **अनिर्वाच्य** } = **अनिर्वचनीय**, *q. v.*

अनिल, *f.* wind, breath, air.

अनिवारित, *m.* (*f.* ā) unchecked, unopposed.

अनिषिद्ध, *m.* (*f.* ā) unforbidden.

अनिष्ट, *m.* (*f.* ā) undesired; evil, ominous, deprecable.

अनिष्ठा, *m. f.* unsteadiness, unsteadfastness.

अनिश्चय, 1, *m.* uncertainty: 2, uncertain.

अनिश्चयवाचक, *m.* (*f.* ikā) speaking undeterminately. — *sarvnām*, (in Gram.) an indefinite pronoun.

अनी, 1, *more prop.* **अणी**: 2, = **अनीक**, *qq. v.*

अनीक, *m.* the face, front; an army, multitude, host.

अनीकिनी, *f.* an army; a certain military force consisting of one tenth of an *akhshauhiṇi*.

अनीत, *more prop.* **अनीति**, *q. v.*

अनीति, *f.* indecorum, rudeness, impropriety, impolicy, injustice.

अनीश्व, *m.* created existence: *lit.* that which is not God.

अनीस, *m.* a companion.

अनीह, *m.* an epithet of Brahm: *lit.* without desire; without authority; without exertion, indolent.

अनु, an inseparable prefix, the reverse of **अभि**, denoting according to, in imitation of, after (whether as to time, place, or status).

अनुकथन, *m.* speaking concurrently.

अनुकम्पा, *f.* tenderness, pity.

अनुकरण, *m.* imitation.

अनुकारी, *m.* (*f.* iṇī) an imitator: *lit.* imitating, following; imitative.

अनुकाल, *m.* an appointed time, due season.

अनुकूल, *m.* (*f.* ā) coïnciding, favorable to, conformable to, acting in concert with; suitable.

अनुकूलत्व, *m.* (*f.* tā) conformity to, concord, favor, proneness.

अनुकूल्य, *m.* assistance, patronage.

अनुक्त, 1, *m.* a trope: 2, *m.* (*f.* ā) not spoken, not mentioned, not told; (in Gram.) not expressed, "understood."

अनुक्रम, *m.* a series, succession, order, method.

अनुख, wickedness, malice, enmity.

अनुखाल, *m.* a creek.

अनुग, *m.* (*f.* ā) = **अनुगामी**, *q. v.*

अनुगत, *m.* (*f.* ā) a follower, successor, servant, dependent, attaché: *lit.* gone after, following, dependent on, attached to.

अनुगमन, *m.* a going after. This term is applied to the ceremony of the burning of a Hindoo widow who has heard of her husband's death when from home.

अनुगामी, *m.* (*f.* inī) a follower, successor, servant, attaché, dependent: *lit.* following, succeeding, obedient, dependent on, attached to.

अनुग्रह, *m.* kindness, favor, indulgence, grace, help, promoting.

अनुग्रहपात्र, *m.* (*f.* ī) a recipient of special favor or kind offices, a protégé, favorite.

अनुग्रही: see **अनुग्राही**.

अनुग्रहीत, *m.* (*f.* ā) a favored object: *lit.* favored, accepted through the exercise of kind indulgence.

अनुग्राहक, *m.* (*f.* ikā) = **अनुग्राही**, *q. v.*

अनुग्राही, *m.* (*f.* iṇī) a supporter, patron: *lit.* favorable to, shewing kindness to, favoring.

अनुचर, *m.* (*f.* ī) a companion, follower, servant, dependent: *lit.* following after.

अनुचित, *m.* (*f.* ā) unfit, improper, unbecoming.

अनुज, *m.* (*f.* ā) a younger brother, a junior: *lit.* born afterwards.

अनुजाई, *adj.* following after, succeeding, according to.

अनुज्ञा, *f.* permission, command, order, dismission.

अनुताप, *m.* regret, repentance, remorse.

अनुतापित, *m.* (*f.* ā) troubled in mind, repentant.

अनुतापी, *m.* (*f.* inī) a penitent : *lit.* penitent, re-

अनुतारा, *m.* a satellite. [morseful contrite.

अनुत्तर, without reply, unable to reply, silent.

अनुदिन, daily, every day, day by day, always.

अनुद्योगी, *m.* (*f.* inī) an idler : *lit.* destitute of vigour or of exertion, indolent.

अनुनासिक, *m.* (in Gram.) nasal : *lit.* through the nose. See notes on the sign °. [parable, excellent.

अनुपम, *m.* (*f.* ā) unexampled, unequalled, incom-

अनुपल, *m.* a second (of time).

अनुपस्थित, *m.* (*f.* ā) not present, not ready.

अनुपातक, *m.* any heinous offence short of a capital crime.

अनुपान, *m.* a vehicle; (in Med.) anything taken to facilitate the swallowing of medicine, whether mixed with the medicine or taken after it.

अनुपाम = अनुपम, *q. v.*

अनुपामी, *m.* (*f.* inī) unexampled, excellent.

अनुबन्ध, *m.* a beginning, uninterrupted succession, consequence, posterity.

अनुबन्धन, *m.* uninterrupted connexion.

अनुबन्धी, *m.* (*f.* inī) connected with, lasting.

अनुवर्त्ती, *m.* (*f.* iṇī) a deputy : *lit.* attached to, observant, following.

अनुबल, *m.* the rear of an army.

अनुभव, *m.* comprehension in the mind, perception; judgment, conjecture, hypothesis; experience; consequence, result.

अनुभाऊ
अनुभाओ } *more prop.* अनुभाव, *q. v.*

अनुभाव, *m.* dignity, authority, power; a sign, indication; opinion, certainty.

अनुभूत, *m.* (*f.* ā) perceived, felt, experienced; guessed; indicated. [sion, sanction; advice.

अनुमति, *f.* a command, order, consent, permis-

अनुमरण, *m.* a following in death (said of the death of a Hindoo widow by *satee*).

अनुमान, *m.* inference, guess, hypothesis, theory, argument, analogy, (in Logic) conclusion. *Mujhe — hotā hai,* it seems to me. — *k.* to suppose, judge, infer.

अनुमानना, *a. int.* to suppose, judge, infer, guess.

अनुमानिक, *m.* (*f.* ā) probable, inferrible, supposable, specious.

अनुमानी, *m.* (*f.* inī) a speculatist, theorizer, guesser : *lit.* inferring, guessing. [sympathy.

अनुमोदन, *m.* praise; the feeling of pleasure from

अनुराग, *m.* affection, love, passion. [with.

अनुरागना, to conceive a passion for, be in love

अनुरागी, 1, *m.* (*f.* inī) a lover : *lit.* impassioned, enamoured, in love : 2, *f.* the making love or friendship, a caressing.

अनुराधा, *f. pr. n.* the 17th *Nakshatra* (designated by a row of oblations); stars in *Libra*.

अनुरूप, 1, *m.* conformity to : 2, *m.* (*f.* ā) conformable, imitating, resembling, similar; suitable, proper, convenient.

अनुरूपी, *m.* (*f.* iṇī) = अनुरूप, 2, *q. v.*

अनुरोध, *m.* the effecting a desired end in the interests of another person, obligingness, a kind office, service, compliance. [in conformity with.

अनुरोधी, (*f.* inī) compliant, kind, partial, acting

अनुरोधू, = (1) अनुरोधी (2) अनुसार (3) रोक, *qq. v.*

अनुवाक, *m.* an invocation; a section in the collection of hymns forming part of each of the Veds.

अनुवाद, *m.* a reply; repetition, tautology; interpretation, translation. [*lit.* replying; opposing.

अनुवादी, *m.* (*f.* inī) a defendant; an opponent :

अनुशासन, *m.* advice, direction, precept, instruction; the giving rules for the acquisition of a science.

अनुसन्धान, *m.* inquiry, investigation, searching; desire. [point and purpose of an inquiry.

अनुसन्धानेच्छा, *f.* the aim of an investigation, the

अनुसरण, *m.* the act of following, succession, imitation; persecution; searching; conformity.

अनुसरना, *a. int.* to follow; to be consequent upon.

अनुसार, 1, *m.* conformity to usage: 2, *postp.* (both separable and inseparable) signifying answering to, following, in conformity to or with, in accordance with. It never occurs before its word; and when written separately it requires the inflected form of the genit. masc. before it. [scrutinizing.

अनुसारी, (*f.* inī) following; according with;

अनुसासन, *more prop.* अनुशासन, *q. v.*

अनुसूया, *f. pr. n.* the wife of अत्रि.

अनुस्वार, *m.* (in Gram.) the nasal sign in printed Devanāgarī: *lit.* after-sound. See notes on °.

अनुहरना, *t.* to imitate, resemble.

अनुहर
अनुहार } *m.* imitation, resemblance.

अनूठा, 1, *m.* a wonder, a curiosity, a rarity: 2, *m.* (*f.* ī) rare, curious, wonderful, uncommon, unexampled.

अनूप, 1, *m.* a watery or moist soil, fen, marsh, swamp, bog; the shore: 2, *m.* (*f.* ā) (1) incomparable, unexampled, rare, best: (2) moist, swampy, watery.

अनूपम, *m.* (*f.* ā) incomparable, unprecedented.

अनूपा, *f.* (*m.* अनूप) a peerless female.

अनूपान, = अनुपान, *q. v.*

अनूवा, *m.* the place where men stand when throwing the *boka* or water-bucket.

अनृणी = अऋणी, *q. v.*

अनृत, *m.* (*f.* ā) untrue, false.

अनेक, many, several, manifold; much, abundant. Liable to be much used in composition.

अनेककाल, *adv.* a long time. [than one *gotra*.

अनेकगोत्रा, *m.* a person who is a member of more

अनेकरूप, *m.* (*f.* ā) multiform; of various kinds or sorts; of fickle, variable mind.

अनेकविध, *m.* (*f.* ā) various, of various kinds;

अनेकाकार, multiform. [in manifold ways.

अनैति = **अनीति**, *q. v.*

अनैस, useless, worthless, bad.

अनैसे = **अनायास**, 3, *q. v.*

अनोखा, *m.* (*f.* ī) rare, uncommon, novel, curious, wonderful. The term is generally applied to men.

अनोना, *m.* (*f.* ī) without salt, not salted.

अनोनासार, *m.* a species of brimstone.

अनौखा = **अनोखा**, *q. v.*

अन्त, 1, *m.* end, completion; boundary, border, limit; death, perdition, destruction; proximity: news, intelligence, an account of: the inward parts, the mind, the heart: 2, ultimate, final: 3, at last, after all: 4, in, within: 5, elsewhere.

अन्तःकरण, *m.* the understanding, the soul, the heart considered as the seat of conscience, will, or emotion.

अन्तःकरणरूपी, *m.* (*f.* iṇī) possessing the manner [or the nature of the heart, cordial.

अन्तःपाती, *m.* (*f.* inī) included, comprised in.

अन्तःपुर, *m.* a king's palace, the inner apartments of a dwelling (*esp.* those occupied by females).

अन्तःशरीर, *m.* the internal and spiritual part of a man, the soul, the conscience.

अन्तःस्थ, *m.* (lit. situated in the interior, in the midst) the letters **य, र, ल, व**. These letters are so called because in the arrangement of the Devanāgaree alphabet they *stand between* the other consonants and the sibilants.

अन्तकाल, *m.* the end, the time of death.

अन्तको, (dat. of **अन्त**) at last, in the end, ultimately.

अन्तगुरु, *m.* (in Pros.) any measure whose last syllable is long or heavy. [*lit.* last-born.

अन्तज, *m.* (*f.* ā) a person of low caste, a *Shoodra*:

अन्तड़ी = **अन्तरी**, *q. v.*

अन्तभाग, *m.* the last part, the latter part, the end. This term is often applied to the New Testament as distinguished from the Old (*ādibhāg*).

अन्तर, 1, *m.* an interval, intermediate space, distance, difference, intermission; midst, the midst, the inside; a hole, rent; a corner, side, quarter of the heavens; a pause, stop; the heart; the supreme soul: 2, in, within; between, amongst: except, without; out of the way, on one side: 3, *m.* (*f.* ā) similar; other: 4, frequent as the former and the latter member of compound nouns, importing the idea of 'interior,' 'between." [sanguinity.

अन्तरंग, *m.* a relative; an intimate friend: con-

अन्तरगति, 1, *f.* emotions of the heart, inward sensations: 2, forgotten.

अन्तरजात, *m.* (*f.* ā) innate, inbred.

अन्तरजामी, = **अन्तरयामी**, *q. v.*

अन्तरजाल, *m.* a stick used in wrestling.

अन्तरज्ञानी, an epithet of God: *lit.* possessing an acquaintance with the inward parts or the heart.

अन्तरदुष्ट, *m.* (*f.* ā) internally bad, wicked.

अन्तरद्वार, *m.* a private door within a house.

अन्तरपट, *m.* a curtain, screen.

अन्तरबेद, *f.* the region of Kanauj lying between the Ganges and Jumna, commonly called The *Do,āb.*

अन्तरभाव, *m.* the internal or inherent nature, disposition.

अन्तरभूत, *m.* (*f.* ā) situated in the midst.

अन्तरमनस / **अन्तरमना** } *m. f.* sad, perplexed.

अन्तरयामी, *m.* (*f.* inī) an epithet of God: *lit.* pervading the inward parts; *hence*, acquainted with the heart, heart-searching.

अन्तरवत्नी, *f.* a pregnant female.

अन्तररहित = **अन्तर्हित**, *q. v.*

अन्तरा, 1, see **अन्तर** 3: 2, *m.* a verse; any verse of a song excepting the first: *lit.* situated in the midst: 3, centrical: 4, amongst, among, in the midst, between, in the interval between morning and evening: near, near at hand; therein: except, without.

अन्तरातप, *f.* an intermittent fever, tertian ague.

अन्तरात्मा, *m.* the inward spirit or self, the soul.

अन्तरापत्य, pregnant (said of the female of any animal). [tral.

अन्तराल, 1, *m.* included space: 2, *m.* (*f.* ā) cen-

अन्तरिक / **अन्तरित** } *m.* (*f.* ā) inward, interior, internal.

अन्तरिक्ष, *more prop.* **अन्तरीक्ष**, *q. v.*

अन्तरिया, 1, *m.* an intermittent fever, tertian ague: 2, *adj.* intermitting.

अन्तरी, *f.* intestine, entrail, gut. *Antarīkā bal kholnā*, to eat one's fill after starving. *Antariyān jalnā*, to be very hungry. *Antariyān hool hooallah parhnā*, to be very hungry (*lit.* the insides repeating, 'There is but one God'). *Antariyonmen āg lagnā*, to be very hungry.

अन्तरीक्ष, 1, *m.* the visible firmament, sky, atmosphere, air: 2, *m.* (*f.* ā) appertaining to the visible heavens, celestial: 3, in the air, out of sight.

अन्तरीक्षग, *m.* (*f.* ā) a bird: *lit.* moving in the air.

अन्तर्धान, 1, *m.* disappearance, concealment, a vanishing away, invisibility: 2, *m.* (*f.* ī) disappeared, concealed, invisible, out of sight, vanished.—*konā*, to vanish, disappear; to be concealed.

अन्तर्ध्यान, *m.* profound meditation.

अन्तर्वेदी = **अन्तरबेद**, *q. v.*

अन्तर्वाला, *m.* (*f.* ī) internal, inward.

अन्तर्हित, secret, concealed.

अन्तलघु, *m.* (in Pros.) any measure whose last syllable is short or light.

अन्तष्करण = **अन्तःकरण**, *q. v.*

अन्तस्थ (*corruption*) = **अन्तःस्थ**, *q. v.*

अन्तावरि, *f.* entrail, intestine, gut.

अन्तिम, last, posterior, final, ultimate.

अन्तेवासी, *m.* (*f.* inī) a pupil who resides with his tutor, a resident student.

अन्त्य, 1, last, lowest: hence, *m.* (*f.* ā) a person of low caste, a *chāṇḍāl*: 2, *m.* (in Math.) the last term of a progression; a hundred billions.

अन्त्यज, *m.* (*f.* ā) a *Shoodra* (*i. e.* one born of the last or fourth caste): *lit.* the last-born, the youngest.

अन्त्यजन्म, *m.* (*f.* nī) a *Shoodra*: *lit.* whose birth was of the last or fourth caste.

अन्त्यवर्णा, *m.* (*f.* ā) a *Shoodra* : *lit.* of the lowest kind or race.

अन्त्र / **अन्त्री** } *f.* the bowels, viscera, guts.

अन्दर, within, inside, inwardly.

अन्दरवार / **अन्दरून** } within, interior, inner apartments.

अन्दरूना, internal, relating to the inside.

अन्दरूनी, internal, intrinsic.

अन्दाख़ता, *m.* (*f.* ī) thrown, cast away.

अन्दाज़, *m.* a valuation, estimate, guess ; measurement, weighing ; mode, manner ; (in Music) time ; (in comp.) a throwing.

अन्दाज़पट्टी, *f.* an estimate of the value of a growing crop.

अन्दाम, *m.* the body, figure, stature.

अन्देशा, *m.* thought, meditation, care, concern ; suspicion.— *k.* to reflect, hesitate, fear, care ; to suspect.

अन्द्रिय, *m. pr. n.* the apostle Andrew.

अन्दोह, *more com.* **अंदोह**, *q. v.*

अन्ध, 1, *m.* darkness ; blindness : 2, *m.* (*f.* ā) dark ; blind of both eyes.

अन्धक, 1, *m.* (*f.* ikā) a blind person : *lit.* blind : 2, a proper name.

अन्धकार, 1, *m.* darkness, obscurity, cloudiness, night : 2, *m.* (*f.* ā) dark, obscure, cloudy.

अन्धकारमय, *m.* (*f.* ī) dark, abounding in darkness.

अन्धकारा, *m.* / **अन्धकारी**, *f.* } = **अन्धकार**, 1, *q. v.*

अन्धकूप, *m.* a well overgrown with weeds or filled with rubbish : *lit.* a blind well.

अन्धतमस, *m.* great darkness, blinding darkness.

अन्धता, *f.* / **अन्धत्व**, *m.* } blindness.

अन्धतामिस्र, *m.* the hell of excessive darkness.

अन्धायन in Braj = **अन्धों** (from **अन्धा**).

अन्धराई, *f.* blindness.

अन्धला, *m.* (*f.* ī) dark, cloudy, obscure, dim ; blind of both eyes.

अन्धलापन, *m.* blindness ; intellectual blindness, acting as if one were blind.

अन्धा, *m.* (*f.* ī) dark ; blind of both eyes.

अन्धाकुआ / **अन्धाकूप** } = **अन्धकूप**, *q. v.*

अन्धाखर्च, *m.* blind expenditure, extravagance, prodigality.

अन्धाधुन्ध, 1, blind : 2, blinding. — *ronā*, to weep excessively. — *lutānā*, to squander, spend extravagantly.

अन्धापन, *m.* darkness, obscurity ; blindness.

अन्धारा, *m.* (*f.* ī) dark, obscure.

अन्धारी, *f.* darkness, obscurity ; a blind over a horse's eyes.

अन्धियारा, 1, *m.* darkness, obscurity ; blindness : 2, *m.* (*f.* ī) dark, obscure ; blind.

अन्धेर, *m.* darkness ; misfortune, calamity ; injustice, tyranny, oppression ; violence, tumult, outrage. — *k.* to act unjustly towards, tyrannize over, oppress.

अन्धेरा, 1, *m.* darkness : 2, *m.* (*f.* ī) dark.

अन्धेरी, *f.* darkness ; a blind for a horse.

अन्धेरी कोठरी, *f.* an epithet of the stomach or of the womb : *lit.* a dark chamber.

अन्न, *m.* food, victuals, grain, corn. The term is applied more particularly to boiled rice.

अन्नकाल, *m.* harvest-time.

अन्नकूट, *m.* a festival celebrated by Hindoos (in commemoration of Krishn's sacrifice) on the day following the *Devālee* by the offering of a large quantity of meats to the gods.

अन्नजल, *m.* victuals, board, subsistence, maintenance ; *lit.* food and drink.

अन्नदाता, *m.* (*f.* trī) a benefactor, supporter : *lit.* food-giver.

अन्नधन, *m.* wealth both in grain and coin.

अन्नपानी = **अन्नजल**, *q. v.*

अन्नपूर्णा, *f.* satiety ; the name of the Ceres of the Hindoo mythology.

अन्नप्राशन, *m.* the ceremony of giving a child for the first time when six months old a food consisting of rice and milk.

अन्नरस, *m.* chyle.

अन्नहीन, *m.* (*f.* ā) destitute of food, needy.

अन्ना, *m.* a nurse's husband ; a kind of male nurse.

अन्नी, *f.* a child's female attendant, a nurse.

अन्मिल / **अन्मेल** } = **अनमिल**, *q. v.*

अन्मोल = **अनमोल**, *q. v.*

अन्य, (*f.* ā) other, different, another.

अन्यगोत्र, appertaining to another race or lineage.

अन्यजन्म, *m.* another birth ; regeneration.

अन्यजातीय, appertaining to another caste.

अन्यत्र, in another place, elsewhere.

अन्यथा, 1, *m.* (*f.* ī) contrary : 2, contrariwise ; in a different manner, otherwise ; inaccurately, untruly.

अन्यदाता, *more prop.* **अन्नदाता**, *q. v.*

अन्यदेशी, *m.* (*f.* inī) a foreigner ; *lit.* foreign, appertaining to another country.

अन्यपुरुष, *m.* (in Gram.) the third person.

अन्यपूर्वा, *f.* a woman who has been previously married.

अन्यभाषिया, *m.* a foreigner : *lit.* foreign, appertaining to another language.

अन्यमनस, *m.* (*f.* ā) absent, fickle, versatile.

अन्याई, 1, *m.* = **अन्याय** : 2, *m.* (*f.* inī) = **अन्यायी**, *qq. v.*

अन्याय, *m.* injustice, oppression, tyranny, outrage, impropriety ; a complaint of injustice.

अन्यायता, *f.* / **अन्यायत्व**, *m.* } injustice, oppression, tyranny.

अन्यायी, *m.* (*f.* inī) an unjust person ; a lawless person ; *lit.* unjust, inequitable, oppression, tyrannical ; lawless.

अन्यास, corruption of **अनायास**, *q. v.*

अन्योन्य, *m.* (*f.* ā) each other, mutual, reciprocal.

अन्वय, *m.* race, lineage ; interpretation, making out the natural order or connection of poetical style.

अन्वय समास, *m.* (in Gram.) connexion, relation.
अन्वयीभाव, *m.* (in Gram.) a compound of which one element is a particle or uninflected word.
अन्वहं, without interval, continuous, consecutive.
अन्वित, *m.* (*f.* ā) connected with, joined; possessed of, fraught with, inherent in.
अन्वेषण, *m.* inquiry, investigation, search, re- [search.
अन्वेषी, *m.* (*f.* inī) an inquirer, investigator: *lit.* inquisitive, searching, investigating.
अन्वाय, *m.* (pl. of नसल) generations, families.
अन्हवाना = नहवाना, *q. v.*
अन्हान = नहान, *q. v.*
अन्हाना = नहाना, *q. v.*
अन्होन्हार, improbable, impossible; unpromising, [hopeless.
अन्होना, *m.* (*f.* ī) impossible; not to be.
अप, an inseparable prefix, the reverse of अधि, importing in Hindee the idea of privation, separation, detraction, contrariety, inferiority, badness. For examples see below.
अपंग, *m.* (*f.* ā) infirm.
अपक, *more prop.* अपक्क, *q. v.*
अपकता, *more prop.* अपक्कता, *q. v.*
अपकर्म्म, *m.* a mean or unworthy action, wicked- [ness.
अपकलंक, *m.* an indelible disgrace.
अपकार, *m.* a hindrance, detriment, injury.
अपकीर्त्ति, *f.* disrepute, dishonor, disgrace.
अपकृष्ट, *m.* (*f.* ā) bad, inferior, deteriorated.
अपकृष्टत्व, *m.* (*f.* tā) badness, inferiority, deterioration; meanness of rank.
अपक्क, *m.* (*f.* ā) unripe, uncooked, immature, im- [perfect.
अपक्कता *f.* / **अपक्कत्व** *m.* } unripeness, immaturity.
अपक्ष, *m.* (*f.* ā) without assistance or protection: *lit.* without wings.
अपगति, *f.* misdemeanour; ill-repute; evil plight, [forlorn condition.
अपच; see अपक्ष.
अपचय, *m.* loss, detriment, waste.
अपछरा = अपछरा, *q. v.*
अपजस = अपयश, *q. v.*
अपजसी, *m.* (*f.* inī) = अपयशी, *q. v.*
अपटक, *m.* (*f.* ā) paralytic, having the hands and [feet useless.
अपटन; see उबटन.
अपटु, sick, diseased: unskilled, incapable, awkward, uncouth; ineloquent.
अपड़ना, *a. int.* to come to hand.
अपडर, *m.* falsehood; fear; fear of oneself.
अपढ़ / **अपढ़े** } *more com.* अनपढ़, *q. v.*
अपत, disreputable, wicked.
अपति, *f.* disrepute, dishonor, disgrace.
अपतिया, *m. f.* treacherous, faithless.
अपतियारा, *m.* (*f.* ī) faithless, treacherous.
अपतिव्रता, unchaste, unfaithful to conjugal allegiance: hence, *f.* an unfaithful wife; a courtesan.
अपत्य, *m.* offspring, race.
अपत्यधर्म्म, *m.* duty to offspring; the duty of offspring to their progenitors.
अपत्यवाचक संज्ञा, *f.* (in Gram.) a patronymic noun.
अपथ, *m.* the want of a road; a wrong path; [error.
अपथ्य, *m.* (*f.* ā) indigestible.
अपन, (*colloquial*) = अपना, *q. v.*
अपनपो, in Braj. = (1) अपने पास (2) अपने पर.
अपना, (gen. of आप) *m.* (*f.* ī) own, appertaining to self. This is the uniform substitute for each and all of the possessive pronouns when they refer to the same person as the agent of the sentence.
अपनाना, *t.* to make a thing one's own, appropriate to one's own use.
अपनायत, *f.* family connexions, kindred, kith [and kin.
अपनिन्दक, *m.* (*f.* ikā) a blasphemer, abuser.
अपनिन्दा, *f.* blasphemy, abuse, reproach.
अपनी गाना, *t.* to sing one's own praises, egotize.
अपनेतईं = अपनेको or आपको (acc. sing. or pl. of [āp, self).
अपनो / **अपनौ** } in Braj. = अपना, *q. v.*
अपनौं, (in Chand) to obtain; to give: *lit.* to appropriate.
अपन्थ, *m.* a wrong road, bad road, devious track; [heresy.
अपन्थी, *m.* (*f.* inī) a wanderer; a heretic: *lit.* having lost one's way, being out of the way; heretical; devious.
अपबस = अपवश, *q. v.*
अपबाद = अपवाद, *q. v.*
अपभ्रंश, *m.* common or vulgar language, a vulgar term, ungrammatical speech.
अपभय, *m.* fear; fear of oneself.
अपभाषा, *f.* low, vulgar, obscene, or abusive lang- [uage.
अपभ्रंस = अपभ्रंश, *q. v.*
अपमान, *m.* disgrace, dishonor, disrespect, affront, contempt. — *k.* (with gen. of the object) to treat disrespectfully.
अपमानित, *m.* (*f.* ā) disrespected, degraded, [disgraced.
अपमानी, *m.* (*f.* inī) a disreputable person: *lit.* disgraced, abased, disreputable, dishonorable.
अपमान्य, *m.* (*f.* ā) dishonorable, disreputable.
अपमृत्यु, *f.* a sudden, untimely or inauspicious death, death from some casualty and not from sickness or decay.
अपस्पा, oneself. It is used in the accusative sense only; *e. g.* — *bachānā*, to guard or protect oneself.
अपयश, *m.* disrepute, disgrace, dishonor, ignominy, infamy.
अपयशी, *m.* (*f.* inī) a disreputable person: *lit.* disreputable, disgraceful, infamous; unfortunate.
अपर, *m.* (*f.* ā) another, other, a second one; following, inferior, posterior, ; opposite, western.
अपरचित; see अपरिचित.
अपरम्पार. (*f.* ā) boundless, infinite.

अपराजय, *m.* victory, non-defeat ; invincibleness.
अपराजित, *m.* (*f.* ā) not defeated ; invincible ; unerring.
अपराजिता, *f.* a twining shrub (*Clitorea ternatea*). The name is applied also to several other plants.
अपराध, *m.* transgression, fault, guilt, crime, injury. — *k.* (with gen. of the object) to sin against.
अपराधक, *m.* (*f.* ikā) appertaining to guilt.
अपराधी, *m.* (*f.* inī) an offender, criminal : *lit.* guilty, faulty, offending, culpable, sinful.
अपराध्नु, *m. f.* = **अपराधी**, *q. v.* [noon; evening.
अपराह्न, *m.* the third watch of the day, after-
अपरिचित, *m.* (*f.* ā) intangible, unappreciable, unrecognizable, unknowable, indefinite.
अपरिच्छा, *more prop.* **अपरीक्षा**, *q. v.*
अपरिपाटी, *f.* deviation from established custom.
अपरिमित, *m.* (*f.* ā) unmeasured ; unlimited.
अपरीक्षा, *f.* want of trial or proof, untriedness ; an inadequate trial of anything.
अपर्स, *m.* 1, a kind of red chalk ; bitumen : a subordinate flavor : leprosy : 2, the state of a Hindoo after bathing (previous to worship or to eating), during which it is unlawful for him to touch any one.
अपलक्षण, *m.* a bad omen, bad sign.
अपलक्षणा, *m.* (*f.* ī) of bad omen, ominous, of suspicious appearance, unlucky.
अपलज्ज, impudent, immodest, shameless : hence, *m.* (*f.* ā) an immodest person. [ness.
अपलज्जा, *f.* impudence, immodesty, shameless-
अपलज्जी, *m.* (*f.* inī) = **अपलज्ज**, *q. v.*
अपलोक, *m.* disrepute, disgrace, dishonor, ignominy, infamy.
अपवर्ग, *m.* completion ; liberation, deliverance, emancipation from the necessity of further transmigration, final beatitude. [trolled.
अपवश, *m.* (*f.* ā) independent, absolute, uncon-
अपवश्य } *more prop.* **अपवश**, *q. v.*
अपवस }
अपवाद, *m.* censure, blame, accusation, reproach, complaint. [ed against, forbidden.
अपवादित, *m.* (*f.* ā) accused, blamed, complain-
अपवादी, *m.* (*f.* inī) a complainer, plaintiff, accuser : *lit.* accusing, blaming, complaining against, rebelling, defaming.
अपवित्र, *m.* (*f.* ā) unholy, defiled, unclean.
अपवित्रता, *f.* } unholiness, uncleanness, filth.
अपवित्रत्व, *m.* }
अपशकुन, *m.* any unlucky omen or portent.
अपशब्द, *m.* a disagreeable sound ; ungrammatical language ; wind expelled backwards.
अपश्लोक, = **अपलोक**, *q. v.* [telligible, inevident.
अपष्ट, *m.* (*f.* ā) hidden, secret ; not clear, unin-
अपसकुन = **अपशकुन**, *q. v.*
अपसर, for words beginning thus see under the more proper form **अपसर**. [2, opposite, contrary.
अपसव्य, 1, *m.* the right side of the body, the right :
अपसोस (*corruption*) = **अफ़सोस**, *q. v.*
अपस्मार, *m.* the falling sickness, epilepsy.
अपस्वार्थ (*contraction*) = **आपस्वार्थ** : see **अ**, 15.
अपस्वार्थी (*contraction*) = **आपस्वार्थी**, *q. v.*
अपहरण, *m.* a taking away, plundering, stealing.
अपहरना, *t.* to take away, plunder, steal, filch.
अपहर्त्ता, *m.* (*f.* trī) a thief, plunderer : *lit.* one who takes away or steals. [taking away, ravishing.
अपहारी, *m.* (*f.* iṇī) a plunderer, destroyer : *lit.*
अपहारे ; see **अपहरना**.
अपह्नव, *m.* denial ; concealment.
अपांग, 1, *m.* the outer corner of the eye ; a sectarial mark on the forehead : 2, maimed, crippled ; hence, *m.* (*f.* ā) a cripple.
अपांगदर्शन, *m.* a side-glance, leer, wink, ogle.
अपाक, 1, *m.* immaturity ; indigestion : 2, raw, unripe, uncooked, immature.
अपात्र, *m.* (*f.* ā) an inferior or worthless person : *lit.* incapable, unfit, unworthy, inferior. [taking away.
अपादान, *m.* (in Gram.) the ablative case : *lit.* a
अपान, *m.* the anus ; the emission of wind backwards.
अपान } in Braj. = **अपना**, *q. v.*
अपाना }
अपाप, *m.* (*f.* ā) sinless, innocent, guiltless, pure.
अपाय, *m.* 1. injury ; destruction : 2. injurious ; destructive.
अपार, *m.* (*f.* ā) boundless, interminable, excessive, impassable, unsurpassed, unrivalled.
अपारतें in Braj. = **अपारसे** (see **तें**, 3).
अपावन, *m.* (*f.* ā) defiling, polluting, impure.
अपाश्रय, 1. *m.* (*f.* ā) without shelter, destitute, helpless : 2, *m.* refuge, support ; an awning spread over a court ; the head.
अपाहज, *m.* (*f.* ā) a cripple, an indolent person, a person who never visits any one : *lit.* crippled, lazy.
अपाहिज = **अपाहज**, *q. v.*
अपि, moreover, also, even, still, though, yet ; as-
अपीड़, *m.* (*f.* ā) without pain. [suredly.
अपीन, *m.* (*f.* ā) light, lean.
अपीनस, *m.* dryness of the nose, want of the pituitary secretion and loss of smell, a cold.
अपेय, *m.* (*f.* ā) unfit to be drunk, forbidden to
अपुच्छ, *m.* (*f.* ā) tailless. [be taken as drink.
अपुच्छा, *f.* a certain tree (*Dalbergia Sisoo*).
अपुण्य, 1. *m.* irreligiousness, unholiness : 2. *m.* (*f.* ā) irreligious, unholy, void of merit, wicked.
अपुत्र, 1, *m.* (*f.* ā) = **अपुत्रक**, *q. v.* : 2, *m.* (*f.* ī) a disreputable, bad, or unfilial child : *lit.* unfilial.
अपुत्रक, *m.* (*f.* kā *or* ikā) a childless person : *lit.* without offspring.
अपुरुष, unmanly, effeminate, impotent.
अपुष्ट, *m.* (*f.* ā) lean ; hidden, secret.
अपुष्पित, *m.* (*f.* ā) without flowers, not bearing flowers, not in flower.

अपूजक, *m.* (*f.* ikā) an irreligious person : *lit.* irreligious, irreverent not deserving respect (if a man) or veneration (if a god). [object of worship.

अपूज्य, *m.* (*f.* ā) unlawful or unsuitable as an

अपूट, unadulterated, pure.

अपूत, *more prop.* **अपुत्र**, *q. v.* [fraction.

अपूर्ण, 1. *m.* (*f.* ā) not full, incomplete : 2. *m.* a

अपूर्णकाल, prematurely, untimely.

अपूर्णता, *f.* } incompleteness.
अपूर्णत्व, *m.* } [tense.

अपूर्णभूतकाल, *m.* (in Gram.) the imperfect past

अपूर्व, *m.* (*f.* ā) unprecedented, unparalleled, unheard-of, uncommon, extraordinary, eminent, wonderful, new.

अपूर्वक, *m.* (*f.* ikā) *adj.* being unprecedented.

अपूर्वी, *m.* (*f.* iṇī) an eminent or uncommon person : *lit.* unprecedented.

अपे = आप, *q. v.* (Frequent in Braj.)

अपेक्षक, *m.*(*f* ikā) an expectant : *lit.* expecting, waiting for, on the look-out for.

अपेक्षा, 1, *f.* expectation, hope.—*k.* (with genit. *f.* of the object) to expect, be in anticipation of, hope for : 2. *postp.* (takes fem. genit.) than.

अपेक्षित, *m.* (*f.* ā) expected, waited for, hoped for.

अपेक्षी, *m.* (*f.* iṇī) an expectant : *lit.* expecting, waiting for, looking to, on the look-out for.

अपेख, *m.* (*f,* ā) unseen, invisible.

अपेय, *m.* (*f.* ā) forbidden liquor : *lit.* undrinkable, unfit for drinking, forbidden to be taken as drink.

अपेल, immovable.

अपेसों अपे in Braj. = **आपसे आप**, *q. v.* [not human.

अपौरुष, *m.* (*f.* ā) unmanly, effeminate, impotent,

अपौरुष्य, *m.* unmanliness ; inhumanity.

अप्यय, *m.* loss, destruction ; final absorption into the Deity.

अप्रकट, *m.* (*f.* ā) unmanifested, not apparent.

अप्रकाश, *m.* (*f.* ā) not displayed, not manifested, secret, private, hidden.

अप्रचण्ड, *m.* (*f.* ā) without dignity, not strong, not violent, not formidable. [vogue, obsolete.

अप्रचलित, not customary, not current, not in

अप्रतच्छ, *more prop.* **अप्रत्यक्ष**, *q. v.*

अप्रताप, *m.* absence of or deficiency in acuteness, power, fortune, or brilliancy ; dulness, bluntness.

अप्रतापी, *m.* (*f* inī) blunt, dull, powerless ; unfor-

अप्रतिपत्ति, *f.* (see **प्रतिपत्ति**) disesteem, etc. [tunate.

अप्रतिबन्धा, *m.* an undisputed inheritance.

अप्रतिष्टा, *f* absence of or deficiency in respectability. [teemed.

अप्रतिष्टित, *m.* (*f.* ā) dishonored, disgraced, dises-

अप्रतिहत, unhindered ; unrepelled ; not alarmed ; not confused.

अप्रतीत, not enjoying the credit or the confidence of one's fellows, unfriended. [trust, unfriendliness.

अप्रतीती, *f.* want of confidence or of credit, mis-

अप्रत्यक्ष, *m.* (*f.* ā) imperceptible, invisible, not evident, not present, absent, secret.

अप्रत्यय, *m.* doubt, distrust, mistrust, unbelief, disbelief, incredulity. [ful, mistrustful, sceptical.

अप्रत्ययी, *m.* (*f.* inī) a sceptic, doubter : *lit.* doubt-

अप्रथा, *f.* deviation from custom ; secrecy.

अप्रधान, not chief, subordinate ; powerless, little, mean. [dulness, darkness.

अप्रभा, *f.* absence of or deficiency in splendour ;

अप्रमाण, *m.* (*f.*ā) without proof, untrue, of doubtful authority. [ity.

अप्रमाणिक, *m.* (*f.*ā) unauthentic ; without author-

अप्रमाण्य, *m.* want of proof or of authority.

अप्रवीण, *m.* (*f.* ā) unskilful, inexperienced.

अप्रवीणता, *f.* } want of skill or of experience.
अप्रवीणत्व, *m.* }

अप्रसन्न, *m.* (*f.* ā) displeased, dissatisfied, unfavorable to, averse, ungracious. [disfavor.

अप्रसन्नत्व, *m.* (*f.* tā) displeasure, dissatisfaction,

अप्रसाद, *m.* disfavor, disapprobation.

अप्रसादी, *m.* (*f.* inī) that which is not presented to the deity. [fame.

अप्रसिद्ध, *m.* (*f.* ā) not celebrated, unknown to

अप्रसिद्धकर्तृक, *m.* (in Gram.) the passive voice.

अप्राचीन, *m.* (*f.* ā) modern, recent.

अप्राप्त, *m.* (*f.* ā) unobtained. [berty.

अप्राप्तयौवन, not having reached the age of pu-

अप्राप्ति, *f.* non-attainment, non-acquisition.

अप्रामाणिक = अप्रमाणिक, *q. v.*

अप्रामाण्य = अप्रमाण्य, *q. v.*

अप्रिय, *m.* (*f.* ā) unlovable, unloving, unfriendly ; unloved, disliked, hated. [sion, indifference to.

अप्रीति, *f.* unfriendliness, enmity, dislike, aver-

अप्रेम, *m.* want of love ; dislike, enmity, hatred.

अप्सरस, *f.* (pl.) female divinities ; (in classical poetry) the courtesans of Indra's heaven. [a courtesan.

अप्सरा, *f.* a female dancer in the court of Indra ;

अप्सरास्वर, *m.* the notes or echoes of the Apsaras.

अफ़ज़ल, more excellent, most excellent.

अफ़ज़ाइश, *f.* the act of increasing or adding.

अफ़ज़ूद, *m.* increase, addition, abundance.

अफ़ज़ून, more, manifold, greater, much, increasing.

अफरना, *a. int.* to swell out (said of the stomach) ; to gormandize, eat to satiety ; to become very rich.

अफराई, *f.* gluttony ; a surfeit.

अफराना, *t.* to feed one till his stomach swells ; to give one money, etc. to the utmost extent of his desire.

अफरिया, *f.* a subdivision of the caste called *aheer.*

अफल, *m.* (*f.* ā) barren, unproductive, unprofitable, ineffectual, useless. [uselessness.

अफलत्व, *m.* (*f.* tā) barrenness, unprofitableness,

अफ़लाक, *m.* (pl. of **फ़लक**) the heavens, the heavenly spheres.

अफ़्लातुन, *m. pr. n.* Plato.
अफलित, *m.* (*f.* ā) not in fruit.
अफलिता, *f.* barrenness, unproductiveness.
अफ़शानी, *f.* scattering over, sprinkling, dispersing.
अफ़सुर्दा, *m. f.* dejected, low-spirited, melancholy.
अफ़सून, *m.* incantation, sorcery, fascination; verses used in spells or enchantments. — *k.* to use spells or enchantments. [sad to relate! ah!
अफ़सोस 1, *m.* sorrow, concern, vexation: 2, alas!
अफ़ीम, *f.* opium.
अफ़ीमन, *f.* / **अफ़ीमी**, *m.* } an opium-eater; a sot.
अफेंडा, *m.* (*f.* ī) obstinate, opinionated, conceited.
अफेन, not frothy, without foam, without vapour.
अफ़्रिका, *m. pr. n.* Africa.
अब, 1, **ब** and **व** are often interchanged, and by many are used indiscriminately: for all words, therefore, beginning with this element, but not given below, see under the form **अव**: 2, an inseparable prefix, the reverse of **आ** denoting from, down, off, away; sometimes also deprivation, disgrace, disjunction, etc.: 3, now, presently, just now, a little while ago.
अबका, (gen. of **अब**) *m.* (*f.* ī) appertaining to the present time. [fruit, barren.
अबकेशी, *m.* (*f.* inī) a barren tree: *lit.* without
अबखान : see **आबख़ाना**.
अबच, *m.* (*f.* ā) that which has not escaped.
अबछरा = **अप्सरा**, *q. v.*
अब्जद, *m.* an alphabet; a mode of reckoning numbers by the letters of the alphabet.
अबड़धबड़, coarse, rough, common.
अबडेर = **अवडेर**, *q. v.*
अबतईं, till now, up to the present time.
अबतक, up to the present time, till now, yet, as yet, still. [death.
अबतब, presently. — *honā*, to be at the point of
अबतरी, *f.* worthlessness.
अबतलक = **अबतक**. *q. v.*
अबतें, from this time, henceforth. (See **तें**, 3.)
अबतोरी = **अबतक**, *q. v.*
अबद, *m.* eternity without end.
अबदतक, to all eternity, for ever and for evermore.
अबध, *m.* (*f.* ā) inviolable, sacred.
अबधा, *f.* a segment of the base of a triangle.
अबधूत, *m.* (*f.* nī) an order of fakeers devoted to God but not attending on ceremonies. Fakeers of this order are Shivites.
अबध्य, *m.* (*f.* ā) not to be slain, not deserving death, sacred, inviolable.
अबनी, *f.* the earth, the world.
अबभाग, *m.* ill-fate, misfortune.
अबभी, yet, still, now too, now even (with the emphasis on the word 'now').

अबर, 1, *m.* a cloud: 2, now, at present.
अबरक, *m.* talc, mica.
अबरस, leprous.
अबरा, *m.* (as distinguished from **अस्तर**, the lining,) the outer fold of a double garment.
अबरू, *f.* (Sk. **भ्रू**) the eyebrow.
अबरेशम, *m.* sewing-silk.
अबर्षणा, *more prop.* **अवर्षणा**, *q. v.* [power, frail.
अबल, *m.* (*f.* ā) an infirm person, etc: *lit.* without
अबलक, piebald, party-colored, black and white.
अबलता, *f.* / **अबलत्व**, *m.* } weakness, frailty.
अबलम्ब, *more prop.* **अविलम्ब**, *q. v.*
अबलम्बी, = **अवलम्बी**, *q. v.*
अबला, *f.* (*m.* **अबल**) a female, a woman.
अबलाई, *f.* weakness, powerlessness, frailty.
अबलापन / **अबलापा** } *m.* = **अबलाई**, *q. v.*
अबलामय, abounding in females.
अबली, 1, *f.* a range, row, continuous line: 2, *m.* (*f.* inī) a powerless person: *lit.* without strength, without power, frail.
अबलोकन, *m.* a seeing; a sight, view.
अबलोकना, *t.* to get a sight of, look at, view.
अबश / **अबस** } *more prop.* **अवश**, *q. v.*
अबसन, *m.* (*f.* ā) not clothed, naked.
अबसि (*Rām.*) = **अवश्य**, *q. v.*
अबसे, from this time, henceforth. — **दूर**, far be it from us! The expression is used by those who after describing some past misfortune deprecate a repetition of it in the future.
अबसेरनी ; see **अवसेरी**.
अबसेषित, *more prop.* **अविशेषित**, *q. v.*
अबसों, *in Braj.* = **अबसे**, *q. v.*
अबस्तु = **अवस्तु**. *q. v.*
अबही, (emphatic) even now, just now, exactly at this point of time; hitherto, yet, just yet.
अबहीं / **अबहूं** } in Braj. = **अबही**, *q. v.*
अबाक, 1, beneath, below, downwards; southwards: 2, *m.* (*f.* ā) speechless; mute, dumb.
अबाधा, *m.* (*f.* ī) true; unobstructed, unopposed, without difficulty; not obstructing, not hindering, not opposing.
अबाबील, *m.* a swallow.
अबार, *m.* the near bank of a river, its hither side.
अबिकार = **अविकार**, *q. v.*
अबिकारी, *m.* (*f.* iṇī) = **अविकारी**, *q. v.*
अबिक्त, *m.* (*f.* ā) any invisible principle: *lit.* hidden, unintelligible. [quantities, algebra.
अबिक्तगणित, *f.* (in Math.) arithmetic of unknown
अबिनीत, *m.* (*f.* ā) an unfaithful spouse: *lit.*

wanton, unfaithful, unchaste, behaving improperly, petulant, pert. [sign.

अबिन्दु, (in Gram.) without point, dot, or nasal

अबिवाहित, *m.* (*f.* ā) an unmarried person : *lit.* un-

अबिला, *m.* a swelling, blister. [married.

अबिवेक, *more prop.* **अभिषेक**, *q. v.*

अबिसन, (*colloquial*) = **अधिसन**, *q. v.*

अबी, corruption of **अबही**, *q. v.*

अबीज, grain that does not germinate.

अबीर, *m.* the red powder used at the *Holee* festival.

अबुद्धि, 1, *f.* want of or deficiency in understanding, ignorance : 2, *m. f.* a stupid, dull person : *lit.* stupid, dull, ignorant, unwise.

अबुद्धिमान, *m.* (*f.* matī) = **अबुद्धि**, 2, *q. v.*

अबुध, *m.* (*f.* ā) void of or deficient in understanding or sense. [Muhammad.

अबुहोरैरा, *m. pr. n.* one of the companions of

अबू, 1, in Braj. = **अबही**. *q. v.* : 2, *m.* father. Frequent as the first member of a man's name in words of Arabic origin. [standing or sense.

अबूझ, *m.* (*f.* ā) void of or deficient in under-

अबूझा, *m.* (*f.* ī) not understood ; incomprehensible. [tary : *lit.* father of excellence.

अबुल्फ़ज़ल, *m. pr. n.* the emperor Akbar's secre-

अबे, (an exclamation expressive of contempt or depreciation) hollon ! you rascal ! you fellow !

अबोध, 1, *m.* want of sense, stupidity, ignorance : 2, *m.* (*f.* ā) wanting in sense, stupid, unintelligent ; perplexed, puzzled.

अबोधगम्य, *m.* (*f.* ā) not falling within the range of intelligence, incomprehensible.

अबोधनीय, *m.* (*f.* ā) not to be understood, not in the nature of things admitting of comprehension, incomprehensible.

अबोल, *m.* (*f.* ā) speechless; silent, mute, dumb.

अबोला, *m.* (*f.* ī) disposed to be silent, accustomed to be silent.

अब्ज, *m.* the lotus : the moon : a conch : a species of tree : the physician of the gods : a million millions.

अब्तर, worthless, spoiled, wanton, dissolute.

अब्द, *m.* a cloud : a year ; an æra.

अब्दाली, (see **दुर्रानी**) appertaining to a devotee.

अब्धि, *m.* the ocean. In the ingenious system of reckoning by symbols adopted by Hindoos in their poetry, this word is a symbol for 4.

अब्धिकफ, *m.* cuttle-fish bone.

अब्ध्यग्नि, *m.* submarine fire.

अब्बा, *m.* father. [broken, entire.

अभंगु, not breakable, imperishable, strong : not

अभक्त, *m.* (*f.* ā) an unbeliever : *lit.* unbelieving, undevout, unattached, indifferent.

अभक्ति, *f.* unbelief, impiety, want of devotion to, want of desire for, indifference, disregard.

अभक्तिमान, *m.* (*f.* matī) an unbeliever : *lit.* unbelieving, not devoted to, indifferent to.

अभक्ष्य, not to be eaten, unlawful (or unsuitable) to be eaten : hence, *m.* forbidden food.

अभय, 1, fearless, undaunted, courageous, bold : hence, *m.* (*f.* ā) a courageous person : 2, *m.* the root of *Andropogon muricatum*, commonly called *Ḳhasḳhas.*

अभयदान, *m.* assurance of safety or of protection, encouragement, amnesty.

अभयपत्र } = **अभयदान**, *q. v.*
अभयवाक }

अभया, *f.* a certain plant (*Terminalia citrina*) and its flower : a courageous female.

अभरण, *more prop.* **आभरण**, *q. v.* : see **अ**, 15.

अभरम, *m.* (*f.* ā) without credit, respect, or character.— *k.* to disgrace.

अभाग, *m.* misfortune, ill-luck, calamity.

अभागा, *m.* (*f.* ī) = **अभागी**, *q. v.*

अभागी, *m.* (*f.* inī) an unfortunate person : *lit.* unfortunate, unlucky, ill-starred, destitute.

अभाग्य, 1, *m.* = **अभाग** : 2, *m.* (*f.* ā) = **अभागी**, *qq. v.*

अभाग्यमान, *m.* (*f.* matī) = **अभागी**, *q. v.*

अभाना, *m.* (*f.* ī) unacceptable, distasteful, unbefitting, improper.

अभाया : see (1) **अभया** (2) **अभाना**.

अभार, *m.* (*f.* ā) light (as to weight).

अभाल, *m.* a cloud.

अभाव, 1, absence, non-existence ; want, deficiency, lack ; annihilation, death : 2, non-existent, brought to naught, annihilated.

अभावता, *f.* } non-existence ; deficiency.
अभावत्व, *m.* }

अभि, an inseparable prefix, the reverse of **अनु**, denoting priority in time or in place ; against ; with [respect to.

अभिअन्तर (*Rām.*) = **अभ्यन्तर**, *q. v.*

अभिक्रम, *m.* an attack ; an undertaking.

अभिगमन, *m.* a coming forward, an approaching, a going towards. [death.

अभिचार, *m.* a charm or spell causing disease or

अभिजात, noble, well-born ; wise, learned ; fit, qualified.

अभिजित, *m. pr. n.* (1) of the 21st *Nakshatra* (2) of the 8th *Muhūrt*.

अभिज्ञ, *m.* (*f.* ā) a patron : *lit.* knowing, conversant with.

अभिधान, *m.* a vocabulary, dictionary ; an appellation : *strictly*, a list of the Sanskrit substantives.

अभिनन्दन, *m.* praise, approbation, consent.

अभिनव, *m.* (*f.* ā) new, quite new, recent.

अभिन्न, 1, *m.* a whole number, integer : 2, not separated, undivided.

अभिप्राय, *m.* sentiment, intention, opinion, design, drift, purpose, sense, scope : *e. g.* the main drift of a book, speech, saw, proverb, etc.

अभिप्रायाज्ञान, *m.* ignorance of any particular purpose or design.

अभिप्रेत, *m.* (*f.* ā) intended, designed.

अभिबाद (*colloquial*) = **अभिवाद**, *q. v.*

अभिबादन (*colloquial*) = **अभिवादन**, *q. v.* [over.

अभिभूत, *m.* (*f.* ā) defeated, subdued, domineered

अभिमत, *m.* (*f.* ā) approved, agreed to, desired, chosen.

अभिमतत्व, *m.* (*f.* tā) approval, desire, love.

अभिमन्यु : see **अभिमान्य**, *q. v.* [weening.

अभिमान, *m.* haughtiness, pride, self-conceit, over-

अभिमानता, *f.*
अभिमानत्व, *m.* } = **अभिमान**, *q. v.*

अभिमानपुत्र, *m.* (*f.* kā *or* ikā) a foster-child.

अभिमानी, *m.* (*f.* inī) a proud person : *lit.* haughty, highminded, proud, overweening, conceited, arrogant.

अभिमान्य, *m.* (*f.* ā) proud, conceited, arrogant.

अभिमुख, 1. *m.* (*f.* ā *or* ī) present, facing, in front of, approaching : 2. *adv.* towards ; in front of, in the presence of.

अभिमुखत्व, *m.* (*f.* tā) proximity, presence.

अभिराम, *m.* (*f.* ā) beautiful, handsome, charming, delightsome.

अभिलषित, *m.* (*f.* ā) wished-for, desired.

अभिलाख (*colloquial*) = **अभिलाष**, *q. v.*

अभिलाष, *m.* longing, wish, desire, inclination.

अभिलाषा, *f.* = **अभिलाष**, *q. v.*

अभिलाषी, *m.* (*f.* iṇī) a wisher : *lit.* wishing, longing for, desirous of. [probrious language.

अभिवाद, *m.* 1, salutation : 2, unfriendly or op-

अभिवादन, *m.* obeisance, a bow or prostration to a person addressed by name, the kissing the feet in adoration. [led, enthroned ; imbued with.

अभिषिक्त, *m.* (*f.* ā) anointed to an office, instal-

अभिषेक, *m.* sprinkling, bathing ; royal unction ; accession to a throne, instalment, inauguration. This word is often used for initiation, royal unction, etc., — ceremonies of which sprinkling with Ganges-water or with water in which certain articles have been immersed, forms an essential part. The term is also used to designate a religious ceremony which includes the presentation of a variety of articles (such as fruits, gems, etc.) along with water or with fluid substances for bathing the idol to which the worship is being offered. [rendezvous ; an attack.

अभिसार, *m.* a lover's appointment, assignation,

अभिसारिका, *f.* a woman who makes or who goes to an assignation, a lewd woman.

अभिसारी, *m.* (*f.* iṇī) a party to an assignation : lit. *adj.* keeping an assignation.

अभी, *more prop.* **अबही**, *q. v.*

अभीच, now, just now. [(*f.* ā) a fearless person.

अभीत, fearless, undaunted, unalarmed : hence, *m.*

अभीतक, till now, heretofore, yet, still.

अभीति, *f.* fearlessness, intrepidity.

अभीप्सित, *m.* (*f.* ā) wished for, desired.

अभीष्ट, *m.* (*f.* ā) beloved, desired, cherished.

अभू
अभूं } in Braj = **अबही**, *q. v.*

अभूत, *m.* (*f.* ā) non-existent : not past.

अभूतरिपु, without enemies.

अभेद, 1, *m.* absence of difference or distinction, similarity, identity : 2, *m.* (*f.* ā) alike : fastened together, united, undivided : impenetrable : known, celebrated, public.

अभेद्य, indivisible, impenetrable, inseparable, [annexed.

अभेव = **अभेद**, *q. v.*

अभोग, unfit for use ; unenjoyed, unpossessed.

अभोगी, *m.* (*f.* inī) a non-participator : *lit.* not partaking in, not enjoying, not possessing.

अभोज, *more prop.* **अभोज्य**, *q. v.*

अभोजन, *m.* an abstaining from food, a fasting.

अभोजी, *m.* (*f.* inī) a faster : *lit.* fasting, not having eaten.

अभोज्य, *m.* (*f.* ā) forbidden food : *lit.* not to be eaten, unsuitable or forbidden to be eaten.

अभ्यन्तर, 1, *m.* an included space, interval of time, inside, the inner part, middle : 2, *m.* (*f.* ā) inward, internal. [ated, accustomed, experienced.

अभ्यस्त, *m.* (*f.* ā) studied, got by heart ; habitu-

अभ्यागत, *m.* (*f.* ā) a guest ; *lit.* arrived.

अभ्यास, *m.* study, meditation, practice, exercise, the frequent repetition of a thing in order to fix it on the mind. [tising, exercising, repeating.

अभ्यासी, *m.* (*f.* inī) a student : *lit.* studious, prac-

अभ्युत्थान, *m.* the act of rising or standing up, rising as a mark of respect ; dignity, elevation, origin.

अभ्र, *m.* the sky, a cloud ; talc, mica.

अभ्रक, *m.* talc, mica.

अभ्रकी, made of or consisting of talc.

अमंगल, 1, *m.* ill luck, an evil omen ; inauspiciousness ; a calamity, disaster : 2, *m.* (*f.* ā) unlucky, inauspicious, disastrous, evil. [little estimation.

अमकाठमका, *m.* trifles ; trifling ; a person of but

अमकाधमका = **अमकाठमका**, *q. v.* [sun.

अमचूर, *m.* the parings of the mango dried in the

अमजी, *f.* compulsory service.

अमत, *m.* disregard, dislike. [unmanly ; inhuman.

अमनुष्य, *m.* a coward ; one who is not a man : *lit.*

अमनुष्यता, *f.*
अमनुष्यत्व, *m.* } unmanliness ; inhumanity.

अमनोनीत, *m.* (*f.* ā) disapproved of, reprobate.

अमनोयोग, *m.* inattention. [inattentive.

अमनोयोगी, *m.* (*f.* inī) an inattentive person : *lit.*

अमनोहर, unattractive, displeasing, disagreeable.

अममत्व, *m.* (*f.* tā) unselfishness, absence of self-interestedness, or of arrogance : want of interest, indifference, stoicism.

अमर, 1, *m. pr. n.* a certain Sanskrit lexicographer : 2, exempt from dying, immortal, everlasting ; longlived. The term is used as an epithet of God.

अमरता, *f.*
अमरत्व, *m.* } immortality, deathlessness.

अमरद, beardless, handsome (youth). [lity.

अमरपद, *m.* the status of an immortal, immorta-

अमरबेल, *m.* a certain parasitical plant similar to the misletoe.

अमरलोक *m.* the region of the immortals, heaven.
अमरा, *m.* the hog-plum *(Spondias mangifera)*.
अमराई *f.* a tope or grove of mangoes.
अमरावती, *f. pr. n.* the capital of Indra and abode of the immortals.
अमरावी, *more prop.* **अमरावती**, *q. v.*
अमरित, a corruption of **अमृत**, *q. v.*
अमरूत, *m.* the guava *(Psydium pyriferum)*.
अमरूद, *m.* a pear.
अमर्य्याद, disrespected, dishonored, affronted.
अमर्य्यादा, *f.* indignity, dishonor, disrespect, slight, affront.
अमर्य्यादिक, not honoring, disrespectful.
अमल, 1, intoxication : 2, *m.* (*f.* ā) clean, pure, bright, clear.
अमलतास, *m.* *Cassia fistula.*
अमलदार, *m.* one who has command ; a collector.
अमलदारी, *f.* government ; a collectorship.
अमलपट्टी, *f.* the hem of cloth, a kind of stitching.
अमला, *m.* (pl. of **आमिल**) agents, officers, subor- [dinates.
अमला, *f.* (*m.* **अमल**) clean, etc.
अमलिन, *m.* (*f.* ā) clean, pure, stainless.
अमवास, *more prop.* **अमावस्या**, *q. v.*
अमात्य, *m.* a minister of state, senator, statesman, councillor, adviser.
अमान, 1, *f.* grace, mercy ; safety, security, protection : 2, *m.* absence of dignity, absence of reverence : 3, unproven, unprovable.
अमानत, 1, *f.* deposit, charge, anything given in trust ; faith, religion : 2, *m.* (*f.* ā) trustworthy, honest, faithful.
अमाननीय, *m.* (*f.* ā) not to be believed, not worthy [of belief, incredible.
अमाना, to go into, to be contained.
अमानी, *m.* (*f.* inī) an incredulous person : *lit.* incredulous, inattentive ; without pride. [inhuman.
अमानुष, *m.* (*f.* ī) not human, other than human,
अमान्य, *m.* (*f.* ā) not to be believed, incredible.
अमाल, *m.* (*f.* ā) not wearing a necklace.
अमावट, *m.* the inspissated juice of the mango.
अमावस } *(colloquial)* = **अमावस्या**, *q. v.*
अमावस्य }
अमावस्या, *f.* the conjunction of the sun and moon, the day of the new moon, the change of the moon.
अमावासी } = **अमावस्या**, *q. v.*
अमावास्या }
अमिट, *m.* (*f.* ā) not effaced ; indelible.
अमित *m.* (*f.* ā) immeasurable ; unmeasured ; undefined.
अमिय, *m.* (*f.* ā) undying, imperishable.
अमी, *f.* the water of life, nectar.
अमीन, *m.* a commissioner, trustee, investigator, arbitrator : *lit.* trustworthy, honest, faithful.
अमीर, *m.* (pl. **उमरा**) a nobleman, grandee. An eastern title nearly answering to the English 'lord.'

अमुआ = **आम** : see **उआ**.
अमुक, (pl. **अमुक**) a certain person, such a one. It corresponds to *fulāna* in Urdoo.
अमुख्य, *m.* (*f* ā) not chief, inferior, ordinary.
अमूर्त्त, *m.* (*f.* ā) formless, shapeless, unembodied.
अमूल, *m.* (*f.* ā) destitute of root, origin, or foundation.
अमृत, immortal : hence, (1) *m.* (*f.* ā) an immortal, a god : (2) *m.* anything sweet, water of life, nectar ; wine ; water ; a guava ; an antidote ; final emancipation, immortality.
अमृतता, *f.* } immortality, deathlessness.
अमृतत्व, *m.* }
अमृतबान, *m.* a certain variety of the plantain.
अमृतरूपी, *m.* (*f.* iṇī) *adj.* possessing immortality.
अमृती, 1, *f.* a small vessel for drinking : a kind of sweetmeat : a kind of cloth : 2, *m* (*f.* inī) nectarious.
अमेठिया, *m.* a certain tribe of Rājpoots.
अमेध्य, *m.* an impure substance, fæces, excrement : *lit.* impure. [lible.
अमोघ, *m.* productive, fruitful ; effectual ; infal-
अमोरा, *m. pr. n.* Gomorrah. [chasable.
अमोल, *m.* (*f.* ā) priceless, invaluable ; unpur-
अम्पड़ना. *a. int.* to come to hand.
अम्ब, 1, in Chand = **आम्बु**, *q. v.* : 2, *m.* a mango, a
अम्बक, *m.* the eye. [mango-tree.
अम्बत, *m.* (*f.* ā) sour, acid, acrid.
अम्बताना, *a. int.* to grow sour, become acidulated.
अम्बर, *m.* a cloud, the sky, atmosphere : clothes, cotton, cloth : a certain perfume *(Ambergris)*.
अम्बराई *f.* a mango-orchard, mango-grove.
अम्बरीष, *m.* a frying-pan ; battle, war : the name of a certain king.
अम्बर्चा, *m.* a kind of ornamental drawing ; a certain mode of decoration : an ornament filled with amber for the neck.
अम्बल, *m.* the after-birth, secundines. [fant.
अम्बलनाल, *m.* the navel-string of a newborn in-
अम्बष्ठ, *m.* a person who is the offspring of a Brāhmaṇ father and a Vaisya mother, by occupation a physician.
अम्बा, *f.* a mother ; a proper name.
अम्बां, *more prop.* **आवां**, *q. v.* [trade.
अम्बाज़, *m.* a companion, associate, partner in
अम्बाड़ा, *m.* the esculent plant hibiscus *(Hibiscus cannabinus)* commonly called the Rozelle.
अम्बाड़ी, *f.* = **अम्बाड़ा**, *q. v.* [barn.
अम्बार, *m.* a heap, stack, pile, magazine, granary,
अम्बारी, *f.* a canopy, a litter used on an elephant or camel. When there is no canopy the litter is called a *houda*.
अम्बाला, *m. pr. n.* a certain city of the Panjāb.
अम्बालिका, *f.* an epithet of Pārvatī.
अम्बासना, *t.* to rinse ; to season a new earthen vessel by letting water remain in it for some time.

अम्बासा, 1, *m.* a handful of corn or of grass cut in reaping: 2, *m.* (*f.* ī) old, stale, seasoned.

अम्बिका, *f.* an epithet of Pārvatī.

अम्बिया, 1, *f.* (dimin. of **अम्ब**) a small mango, a small unripe mango: 2, *m.* (pl. of **नबी**) prophets.

अम्बिल, a kind of pottage.

अम्बोकार, *m.* a sailor, pilot.

अम्बु, *m.* water. [*m.* (*f.* ā) water-born.

अम्बुज, *m.* the lotus (*Nymphœa nelumbo*): lit.

अम्बुधर, *m.* a cloud: *lit.* the water-holder.

अम्बुधि, *m.* the ocean, sea. [waters.

अम्बुपति, *m.* an epithet of Varuṇ; *lit.* lord of the

अम्बोज, (*corruption*) = **अम्भोज**, *q. v.*

अम्बोती, *f.* a species of sorrel (*Oxalis corniculata*).

अम्बोल, *more prop.* **अन्बोल**, *q. v.*

अम्बोह, *m.* a crowd, mob, concourse, great quan-

अम्भोज, *m.* the lotus-flower. [tity, abundance.

अम्मा / **अम्मां** } *more prop.* **अम्बा**, *q. v.*

अम्मास, *more prop.* **अमावस्या**, *q. v.*

अम्र, *m.* the mango-tree (*Mangifera Indica*).

अम्रा, *m.* 1, = **अमरा**, *q. v.*: 2, *m.* (pl. of **अमीर**) nobles, grandees.

अम्रूत, *m.* a guava (*Psydium pyriferum*).

अम्ल, 1, *m.* (*f.* ā) sour, acid: 2, *m.* sourness.

अम्लता, *f.* / **अम्लत्व**, *m.* } sourness, acidity.

अम्लान, 1, *m.* (*f.* ā) clean, pure, clear: 2, *m.* globe amaranth (*Gomphrena globosa*).

अम्व. For all words beginning with this element see under the form **अम्ब**. [a going.

अय, *m.* 1, (= **अयस**) iron: 2, good fortune, luck:

अयं in poetry = (1) **यह** (2) **अयस**, *qq. v.*

अयत्न, *m.* absence of hardship, absence of endeavour: *lit.* without effort, without pains, easy: easily.

अयथार्थ, not accurate, not according to the sense, not true: unrighteous, improper.

अयन, *m.* a place of motion, road, path, line; a place, house, dwelling; the half-year, *i. e.* the sun's course north or south of the equator.

अयनघोष, *m. pr. n.* the husband of Rādhā.

अयना, *more prop.* **आईना**, *q. v.*

अयश, *m.* disrepute, disgrace, dishonor, infamy.

अयस, *m.* iron.

अयाच, unasked, unsolicited.

अयादि, (in Gram.) the designation of a certain modification of vowels.

अयान, not going, not moving.

अयाना, *m.* (*f.* ī) a fool, simpleton; *lit.* unknowing, witless, simple, foolish. [horse's ears.

अयाल, *f.* a horse's mane, the lock between a

अयुक्त, 1, *m.* violence, oppression, compulsion: 2, *m.* (*f.* ā) unfit, incompetent, incompatible.

अयुत, ten thousands, a myriad.

अयुध, *more prop.* **आयुध**, *q. v.*: see **अ**, 15.

अयू, *more properly* **आयु**, *q. v.*: see **अ**, 15.

अयोग्य, *m.* (*f.* ā) unsuitable, unbefitting, improper, unbecoming, unworthy.

अयोग्यत्व, *m.* (*f.* tā) unsuitableness, incongruity, impropriety, unworthiness.

अयोध्य, *m.* (*f.* ā) not to be warred against.

अयोध्या, *f. pr. n.* the country and the capital of Rām, the modern Oude.

अयोध्याकाण्ड, *m. pr. n.* (see **सातोंकाण्ड**) the second section of the Rāmāyaṇ. [weather.

अय्याम, *m.* (pl. of **योम**) days; times; season,

अर, 1, (*contraction*) = **अगर**, if: 2. *m.* a spoke.

अरई, *f.* the root of *Arum colocasia*: a goad at the end of a whip.

अरंड, *more prop.* **अरण्ड**, *q. v.* [ity.

अरकट, *f.* vigilance, activity; cleverness, ingenu-

अरकाट, *m.* the city of Arcot in the Dakkhan.

अरकाटी, *m.* (*f.* inī) a native of Arcot; a pilot: *lit.* appertaining to Arcot. In former times the pilots of Southern India are supposed to have been men of Arcot. [defended.

अरक्षित, *m.* (*f.* ā) unprotected, uncared-for, un-

अरगजा, *m.* a certain yellowish perfume compounded of several scented ingredients.

अरगजी, *m.* (*f.* inī) dyed with **अरगजा**.

अरगा, separate. For this word and its cognates see under the more proper form **अलगा**.

अरघ, = **अर्घ**, *q. v.* [veneration.

अरज़, *m.* price, value; quantity; esteem, honor,

अरज़, *f.* a petition, request; breadth; a military muster; a portion of land; the earth.

अरज़ी, *f.* a petition, request, memorial, representation; letter (from an inferior to a superior).

अरझना, 1, *n.* to be ravelled or entangled (said of thread, hair, or [*met.*] of the heart); to be bound (as in fetters, etc.): 2, *a. int.* to quarrel unreasonably or without cause.

अरणा, *m.* (*f.* ī) a wild buffalo: cowdung found dried in the forest (used as fuel by the native apothecaries in the preparation of medicines).

अरणि, *f.* wood used for kindling fire by attrition.

अरणी. *f.* 1, = **अरणि**, *q. v.*: 2, the female wild buffalo.

अरण्ड, *m.* the tree (*Ricinus vulgaris* or *Palma Christi*) from which castor-oil is made.

अरण्डी, *f.* the fruit of the above-mentioned tree: a sort of firework.

अरण्य, *m.* a forest, desert, wilderness.

अरत / **अरथ** } (*colloquial*) = **अर्थ**, *q. v.*

अरदन (*colloquial*) = **अर्दन**, *q. v.*

अरध (*colloquial*) = **अर्ध**, *q. v.*

अरधंग (*colloquial*) = **अर्द्धांग**, *q. v.*

अरधन : see **अर्दन**.

अरनव *(colloquial)* = **अर्णव**, *q. v.* [tate, stop.

अरना, 1, *more prop.* **अरणा**, *q. v.*: 2, *a. int.* to hesi-

अरनी, *more prop.* **अरणी**, *q. v.*

अरपना, *t.* to present an offering, offer up.

अरब, *m.* 1, *pr. n.* Arabia : 2, an Arab.

अरबराना, to hurry, be confused, be perplexed, be agitated, to hesitate or bungle in speaking.

अरविन्द, *m.* the lotus *(Nymphœa nelumbo)*.

अरबी, Arabian, appertaining to Arabia : hence, (1) *m.* (*f.* inī) an Arabian : (2) *f.* the Arabic language.

अरमज़ाद, desirous : without resource.

अरमीनिया, *pr. n.* the country of Armenia.

अरराना, = **अर्राना**, *q. v.*

अरवन, *m.* the first cuttings of corn (presented to the household gods).

अरवी, *f.* a species of Arum the root of which is used in food *(Arum calocasia)*, called also *ghoyan* or *ghooyan*, and in Bengal *Kuchoo*.

अरस, *m.* (*f.* ā) without juice, useless, insipid; dull, flat, tasteless (said of composition).

अरसट्टा, *m.* guess, conjecture, estimate, valuation, appraisement; a broker; a mediator : a monthly treasury account of receipts and disbursements made up from the daily entries. [counts.

अरसट्टानवीस, *m.* a clerk who keeps monthly ac-

अरसठ, *m.* a monthly account of revenue.

अरसा, *m.* a plain; an area, court : a chess-board : space of time; while, interval, time.

अरसीलेनयन / **अरसीलेनैन** } *m.* (*f.* ā) = **अरसीलेनैना**, *q. v.*

अरसीलेनैना, *m.* (*f.* ī) a person who has weak eyes or eyes as if just awake.

अरसू : see (1) **अरस** (2) **अरसा**.

अरहट, *more properly* **रहट**, *q. v.*

अरहर, *m.* a species of pulse *(Cytisus cajan)*.

अरहु, a poetic imperat. of **अरना**, *q. v.*

अराजक, destitute of a king. [of land.

अराज़ी, *f.* (pl. of **अरज़**) lands, detached portions

अराती, *m.* an enemy.

अराधना, *more prop.* **आराधना**, *q. v.*: see **अ**, 15.

अराबा, *m.* a wheeled carriage, gun-carriage, cart.

अरार, a hut in the jungles used by graziers.

अरारा, *m.* the mark of the nails left after scratching.

अरि, *m.* an enemy : a wheel. In the ingenious system of reckoning by symbols adopted by Hindoos in their poetry, this word is a symbol for 6.

अरित्व, *m.* (*f.* tā) enmity, hostility.

अरिदल, *m.* the host or army of the enemy. [foes.

अरिमर्दन, *m. pr. n.*, *lit.* the destroyer or subduer of

अरिष्ट, *m.* garlic; the neem-tree *(Melia azadirachta)*; a woman's lying-in chamber, a gyneceum; a crow; good fortune; misfortune; a symptom of death : 2, *m.* (*f.* ā) unhurt, not wounded.

अरिष्टनेमी, *m. pr. n.* (occuring in the *Rāmāyaṇ*).

अरी = **अरे**, (properly addressed to females only).

अरीज़, large; wide, broad, expanded.

अरीति, *f.* ill manners, ill breeding, incivility,

अरु, and, more, moreover, again. [impoliteness.

अरुई, corruption of **अरुचि**, *q. v.*

अरुचि, *f.* sickness of stomach arising from pregnancy, nausea, disgust, aversion, disrelish, want of appetite; displeasure : *pr. n.* the wife of king Prithee.

अरुझाना, *t.* to entangle.

अरुण, 1, *m.* the sun, the dawn, the colour of the dawn; blood : 2, *m.* (*f.* ā *or* ī) red, dark red, tawny, of the colour of the dawn.

अरुणचूड़, *m.* a male bird, cock.

अरुणवर्ण, *m.* the colour of the dawn, dark red.

अरुणसिखा, *m.* a male bird, cock.

अरुणाई, *f.* the dawn; the colour of the dawn.

अरुणारा, *m.* (*f.* ī) red, tawny.

अरुणोदय, *m.* the early dawn, daybreak.

अरुणोपल, *m.* a ruby. [shishṭ.

अरुन्धती, *f.* an asterism : *pr. n.* the wife of Va-

अरुस, *m.* a certain medicinal plant *(Justicia adhatoda and gandarussa)*: a wound, sore; a joint, vital part. [country.

अरुज़, *m.* Mecca and Medina with their adjacent

अरुंधती, *more prop.* **अरुन्धती**, *q. v.*

अरूप, 1, *m.* (*f.* ā) without form or shape : 2, *m.* the absence of form or shape.

अरूस, *f.* a bride, spouse.

अरे, *m.* (*f.* **अरी**) (a mode of calling or of address expressive of disrespect or of anger : it is used chiefly in addressing inferiors, and is properly applied to males only) = ho! O! hark ye! look here! look you! holloa there! holloa! sirrah!

अरेअरे = **अरे**, *q. v.*

अरेब, 1, = **अरेबले**, *q. v.*: 2, *m.* guilt.

अरेबले, *f.* stratagem, deception, complication.

अरेरे = **अरे**, *q. v.*

अरोग, 1, *m.* freedom from sickness; soundness, healthiness : 2, free from disease, sound, healthy, well : hence, *m.* (*f.* ā) a healthy person.

अरोगी, *m.* (*f.* inī) = **अरोग**, 2, *q. v.*

अरोग्य, 1, *m.* = **अरोग**, 1, : 2, *m.* (*f.* ā) = **अरोग**, 2, *qq. v.*

अरोग्यकारी, *m.* (*f.* inī) anything producing health, a restorative : *lit.* health-producing, healing, restorative.

अरोग्यता, *f.* / **अरोग्यत्व**, *m.* } healthiness, soundness.

अरोग्यवान, *m.* (*f.* vatī) healing, health-producing,

अरोसीपरोसी = **अड़ोसीपड़ोसी**, *q. v.* [restorative.

अर्क, *m.* a certain plant *(Calatropis gigantea)*: swallow-wort *(Asclepias gigantea)*: the sun; a ray of light : crystal : copper.

अर्कदिन, *m.* a solar day.

अर्कमण्डल, *m.* the disc of the sun.

अर्कवर्ष, *m.* a solar year.

अर्कांश, *m.* a digit or twelfth of the sun's disc.

अर्काटी = **अरकाटी**, *q. v.*

अर्कान, *m.* (pl. of **रुक्न**) pillars; the feet of a verse.

अर्काश्मन, *m.* a crystal lens; a ruby.

अर्कोपल, *m.* the sunstone, a ruby, a crystal lens.

अर्गजा = **अरगजा**, *q. v.*

अर्गजी = **अरगजी**, *q. v.*

अर्गनी, *m.* a rope stretched for drying clothes on or for similar purposes: a wooden rod or a bamboo placed horizontally for this purpose has the same name.

अर्ग़वान, *m.* a plant (*Arbor Judææ*) whose flowers and fruit are of a beautiful red; a red colour.

अर्घ, *m.* a libation in honor of a deity: an oblation of eight ingredients offered in worship to a deity or to a Brāhmaṇ: the act of pouring out water in honor of a deity while performing worship: value, price.

अर्घा, *m.* a certain boat-shaped vessel used by Hindoos for performing libations in their worship.

अर्चक, *m.* (*f.* ikā) a worshipper: *lit.* worshipping, adoring.

अर्चन, *m.* worship, adoration, reverence, respect.

अर्चना, *f.* worship, adoration, homage, ceremoniousness.

अर्चा, *f.* devotion, adoration; an image.

अर्चि, *m.* flame; light, radiance, splendour.

अर्चित, *m.* (*f.* ā) worshipped, adored, revered.

अर्ज़: see **अरज़** and **अ़रज़**. [acquisition, gain.

अर्जन, *m.* the act of gathering or accumulating;

अर्जना, *t.* to gather, accumulate, acquire, gain.

अर्जमन्द, noble; blessed, happy; beloved, dear.

अर्ज़ी, terrestrial, mundane, earthy, earthly.

अर्ज़ीज़, *f.* tin: base or light money.

अर्जुन, *m.* 1, *pr. n.* a certain hero in the Mahābhārat, the third of the Pāṇḍav princes: 2, a certain tree (*Terminalia alata glabra*).

अर्ज़ू, *f.* desire, wish; hope; want, distress.

अर्णव, *m.* the ocean, sea.

अर्तला, *m.* a patron, protector.

अर्थ, *m.* interpretation, definition, meaning, sense, signification, acceptation; intention, purpose, object, design, purport, aim, motive: property, wealth, riches, substance, goods: request, begging. This word is sometimes used in composition; e. g. *Yathārth*, accurate, right, just (*lit.* according to the sense): it is also sometimes used as a suffix in the sense of cause, for the sake of, with a view to; e. g. *Tapasyārth*, for devotional purposes.—*lagānā*, to interpret, translate.

अर्थकारक, *adj.* interpreting: hence, *m.* (*f.* ikā) an interpreter.

अर्थबोधक, *m.* (in Gram.) a significant term, any word which conveys a sense as distinguished from the mere unmeaning root: *lit.* importing a sense, significant.

अर्थलाभ, *m.* the acquisition or attainment of one's purpose; the appreciation of a signification or meaning.

अर्थलोभी, *m. pr. n.* a certain jackal in one of the fables of the *Akhlāḳi Hindī*; lit. *m.* (*f* inī) greedy of gain.

अर्थशास्त्र, *m.* the science which teaches how to obtain things (such as friends, money, or any other object). [purpose.

अर्थसिद्धि, *f.* success, the accomplishment of one's

अर्थात, that is to say, namely.

अर्थान्तर, *m.* another meaning, a variety of signification, difference of interpretation.

अर्थी, 1, (the reverse of **प्रत्यर्थी**) *m.* (*f.* iṇī) a beggar, petitioner, plaintiff, prosecutor: *lit.* suppliant, desirous, craving, having an object to accomplish; self-interested, sinister, designing: 2, *f.* a bier.

अर्थिया, 1, a corruption of **आढ़तिया**, *q. v.*: 2, *m. f.* a follower, client, person recommended, protégé.

अर्दन, *m.* a begging, request; covetousness: wounding, killing.

अर्दावा, *m.* coarsely-ground meal (that has been partially parched previous to the grinding).

अर्दास, *f.* representation; offering to a deity.

अर्द्ध, 1, *m.* a half, a part: 2, *m.* (*f.* ā) halved.

अर्द्धकपारी: see **कपाली**. [half-*kumbh*.

अर्द्धकुम्भ, *m.* (see **कुम्भनी**) the sixth-year fair; *lit.*

अर्द्धचन्द्र, *m.* a half moon, crescent, semicircle.

अर्द्धचौपाई, *f.* (in Pros.) a species of metre.

अर्द्धभाग, *m.* a half.

अर्द्धरात्र, *f.* midnight.

अर्द्धश्लोक, *m.* a hemistich, a line in epic poetry.

अर्द्धांग, *m.* half the body; palsy affecting half the body, hemiplegia. [with hemiplegia: 2, *f.* a wife.

अर्द्धांगी, 1, *m.* (*f.* inī) a paralytic: *lit.* afflicted

अर्ध. **ध** (dh) and **द्ध** (ddh) are constantly interchanged, and by many used indiscriminately: for words, therefore, beginning with this element, see under the form **अर्द्ध**.

अर्धसमवृत्त, *m.* (in Pros.) a species of metre in which the first two lines are similar to each other, but dissimilar from the last two, which are also similar to each other.

अर्नव, *more properly* **अर्णव**, *q. v.*

अर्ना, *more properly* **अरना**, *q. v.*

अर्पण, *m.* the making an offering; delivering, entrusting: an offering —*k.* to present an offering, deliver to, entrust to. Used in comp.; e. g. *Samarpaṇ*.

अर्पणनामा, *m.* a deed of gift (especially to a temple or to an idol). [offering, offer up.

अर्पना, *t.* to deliver over to, present, present an

अर्पि = **अर्पके** (**अर्पना**): see **क**, 7.

अर्पित, *m.* (*f.* ā) appointed, fixed, arranged, placed, deposited, delivered, presented.

अर्ब, one hundred millions.

अर्बखर्ब, innumerable.

अर्बद, one hundred millions. [formerly.

अर्वाक, 1, *m.* (*f.* ā) low, inferior, vile: 2, at first,

अर्बुद, *m.* one hundred millions: the shape of the foetus in the second month after conception: a certain mountain. [pupil.

अर्भक, *m.* the young of any animal, a son, child,

अर्मान, *m.* desire, longing, inclination, wish, hope.

अर्य्य, *m.* (*f.* ā *or* ī) a person belonging to the third or Vaisya caste : *lit.* excellent, good.

अर्रा, *f.* a saw.

अर्राटा, *m.* a loud and prolonged sound as from the discharge of artillery or the fall of a building.

अर्राना, *a. int.* to produce a continued sound (as a mill does); to scream out.

अर्श, *m.* hæmorrhoids, piles.

अर्शपर्श, *m.* partial bathing (as by throwing a very little water on the head with one's hand instead of bathing), sprinkling or aspersion; the act of touching.

अर्शस, 1, *m.* hæmorrhoids : 2, *m.* (*f.* ā) a subject of hæmorrhoids.

अर्सठ = **अरसठ**, *q. v.*

अर्सा, belonging or appertaining to a person.

अर्ह; a suffix (*m.* [*f.* ā]) frequent in comp. in the sense of worthy, entitled to, deserving, fit, suitable, proper : *e. g.* **विश्वासार्ह**, deserving of confidence, trustworthy, etc.

अर्हन्त, *m.* (*f.* **अर्हन्ती**) a venerable person; a *sugat*, or follower of the doctrines of Buddh : *lit.* venerable.

अलंकार, *m.* ornament, any ornament of dress (*hence,* a trinket, jewel); rhetoric, the ornate in prose composition.

अलंकृत, *m.* (*f.* ā) ornamented, ornate, adorned.

अलंकृति, *f.* = **अलंकार**, *q. v.*

अलंस्वार, the treble notes in music.

अलंग, 1, *m.* (*f.* ā) naked : 2, *f.* a side, way, corner, intrenchments. *Is* —, this side, this way (sc. *meṅ* or *par*).

अलक, 1, (*corruption*) = (1) **अलक्ष** (2) **अलग**, *qq. v.* : 2, *f.* a lock of hair, a curl, ringlet.

अलकनन्दा, *f. pr. n.* a certain stream that issues from the Himālaya mountains and falls into the Ganges near Shreenagar.

अलकावलि, *f.* a row of side curls.

अलकिस्सा, in short, in one word.

अलक्ष, unobserved, undistinguishable, invisible, unseen (see *alakh*).

अलक्षण, 1, a bad sign, ill omen, mark of ill fortune : 2, *m.* (*f.* ā) without distinguishing marks : inauspicious. [fortunate, ill-fated.

अलक्षणी, *m.* (*f.* inī) an ill-fated person : *lit.* unfortunate, poor.

अलक्षित, *m.* (*f.* ā) invisible, undistinguishable, unseen.

अलक्ष्मी, 1, *f.* bad luck : 2, not prosperous, unfor- [tunate, poor.

अलख, *m.* (= **अलक्ष**, *q. v.*) an epithet of God : a form of salutation among a certain class of Brāhmaṇs.

अलखगति, *m.* an epithet of the Supreme; lit. *adj.* penetrating the unseen.

अलखनामी, *m.* a mendicant of the Shaiv sect.

अलग, *m.* (*f.* ā) separate, aloof, apart, loose.— *k.* to separate.— *jānā* or *ho jānā*, to separate, get out of the way, break up (as an assembly or crowd might).

अलगअलग, separately, apart. Used with *karnā* it is intensive, distributive, or reciprocal.

अलगटलग = **अलगअलग**, *q. v.*

अलगना, *n.* to be separated, disjoined, set apart.

अलगनी, *f.* any line for hanging clothes on.

अलगा, 1, *m.* a sandal : 2, *m.* (*f.* ī) separate, apart, distinct, free, loose, unconfined. [silent.

अलगाई, *f.* separation, separateness; the being

अलगाना, 1, = **अलगना**, *q. v.* : 2, *t.* to cause to be separate, to put on one side, to separate.

अलगानी = **अलगाई**, *q. v.*

अलग़ोज़ा, *m.* a whistle, pipe, small flageolet.

अलच्छ, *more properly* **अलक्ष**, *q. v.*

अलछि, *more prop.* **अलक्ष्मी**, *q. v.*

अलड़, imperfect; not grown up.

अलड़बलड़, *f.* trifling talk, trifling employment.

अलड़ाना, *a. int.* to scream out, shriek.

अलसनी, *f.* the rope around the neck of an elephant in which the driver puts his feet as in stirrups.

अलता, *m.* cotton strongly impregnated with the dye of lac ready to be used for dyeing, etc. It is used chiefly by Hindoo women for staining their feet red.

अलताफ़, *m.* (pl. of **लुत्फ़**) favors, kindnesses.

अलप (corruption) = **अल्प**, *q. v.*

अलफई, *m. pr. n.* Alphæus. [terms.

अलफ़ाज़, *m.* (pl. of **लफ़्ज़**) articulate sounds, words,

अलबत्ता, certainly, of course, indeed, truly.

अलबेलपन = **अलबेलपना**, *q. v.*

अलबेलपना, *m.* foppishness, spruceness, coquettishness, frivolity, airs and blandishments.

अलबेला, coquettish : hence, *m.* (*f.* ī) a beau, fop, [coquet.

अलभेला, *m.* (*f.* ī) = **अलबेला**, *q. v.*

अलभ्य, not to be attained, unattainable.

अलम, 1, *m.* sticks set up for the support of creeping plants : 2, *m.* (*f.* ā) adequate to, equal to, able, enough, abundant.

अलमायरा, *m.* a moveable cupboard, a wardrobe, a chest of drawers, a bookcase. The word is most probably of European origin.

अलमारी, *f.* = **अलमायरा**, *q. v.*

अलमास, *m.* a diamond. [trict of the Panjāb.

अलमोड़ा, *m. pr. n.* a certain mountain and dis-

अलवः, *m.* a bonfire, blaze, flame.

अलचित = **अलक्षित**, *q. v.* : see **छ** and **क्ष**.

अलस, 1, *m.* (*f.* ā) lazy, slothful, drowsy, weary; slack : 2, *m.* sloth, drowsiness, laziness.

अलसट, *f.* sloth, laziness, indolence, apathy.

अलसटा
अलसटागी } = **अलसट**, *q. v.*
अलसटी

अलसान, drowsy, used-up.

अलसाना, *n.* to doze, be drowsy : to slacken.

अलसी, *f.* linseed (*Linum usitatissimum*).

अलहाल, now, at present; presently, just now.

अला, 1. exaltation, superiority, sublimity : 2. above, high, most high.

अलात, *m.* a firebrand.

अलान, a chain, a chain for binding an elephant to a post.

अलाव, *m.* a bonfire, blaze, flame.

अलि, 1, *f.* = **आली**, 3: 2, *m.* (*f.* ai) = **अलिन**, *qq. v.*

अलिन, *m.* (*f.* i) a bee; a certain large black bee said to be enamoured of the lotus: a scorpion: the Indian cuckoo (*Cuculus Indicus*); a crow: spirituous liquor.

अलिनि, *f.* (*m.* **अलिन**, etc.) a female bee, etc.

अली, *more prop.* (1) **अलि** (2) **आली**, *qq. v.*

अलीक, *m.* (*f.* ā) false; unpleasing: hence, *m.* falsehood, a lie; anything displeasing.

अलीन, *m.* (*f.* ā) not melted, not dissolved, not wiped away, not effaced, not embraced.

अलीम, painful, excruciating.

अलीरंग, *m.* a colour extracted from the *āl* tree.

अलीह, *more properly* **अलीक**, *q. v.*

अलुझना, *more prop.* **उलझना**, *q. v.*

अलेख, that cannot be written, that cannot be taken account of.

अलेमानी, *m.* (*f.* inī) a German: *lit.* German.

अलेयाबलेया, *f.* a sacrifice, victim; lighted wisps with which Hindoos divert themselves at the season of their *Diwālee.*

अलोकन, *m.* invisibility; disappearance.

अलोना, *m.* (*f.* ī) not salted, unseasoned, fresh, insipid.

अलोप, *m.* (*f.* ā) concealed, defaced; run out, destroyed; retired: apparent.—*ho jānā*, to vanish, disappear.

अलोपना, *t.* to hide, conceal: *a. int.* to hide oneself, lie hid, be concealed.

अलोपा, *f.* (*m.* **अलोप**) defaced, etc.

अलोल, 1, *f.* a gambol (generally said of horses): 2, *m.* (*f.* ā) steady.

अलोलकलोल, *f.* wantonness, gambols, playsomeness (of young animals).

अलौकिक, *m.* (*f.* ī) not of this world, supernatural, transcendental, superhuman, not current, not common, rare; unpopular.

अल्क, *more prop.* **अलक**, *q. v.*

अल्प, *m.* (*f.* ā) little, small, of little value, insignificant, few, short, feeble. Much used in composition.

अल्पज्ञ, *m.* (*f.* ā) a person of defective, meagre, or limited knowledge: *lit.* knowing little, ignorant.

अल्पतर, (*adj. compar.*) less, lesser.

अल्पत्व, *m.* (*f.* tā) smallness, insignificance, inferiority, paucity.

अल्पप्रभाव, of little consequence, insignificant.

अल्पप्रमाण, of little authority.

अल्पप्रमाणक, credulous; resting on but little evidence, of small weight, of small significance, of small authority.

अल्पप्राण, *m.* (in Gram.) an unaspirated consonant, *e. g.* **क**, **ग**, etc.: *lit.* lenis or unaspirated.

अल्पबल, *m.* (*f.* ā) of little strength, feeble.

अल्पबुद्धि, *m.* (*f.* in) deficient in understanding, lacking in sense, silly, unwise.

अल्पमात्र, *m.* a little only; a few moments, a short time.

अल्पमूल्य, *m.* (*f.* ā) of little price, of small value.

अल्पयश, 1, *m.* limited notoriety: 2, *adj.* of little note, not known to fame, obscure.

अल्पवय = **अल्पायु**, *q. v.*

अल्पशक्ति, *m.* (*f.* in) of little strength, weak.

अल्पश्वास, *m.* (*f.* ā) a short-winded person: *lit.* short-winded.

अल्पायु, *m. f.* a young person; an ephemeral creature: *lit.* of few years, of little age, of short duration, ephemeral, young.

अल्पाहार, 1, moderate in eating, abstemious: hence, *m.* (*f.* ā) a moderate eater: 2, *m.* moderation in eating, abstemiousness.

अल्पाहारी, *m.* (*f.* inī) = **अल्पाहार**, 1, *q. v.*

अल्पौजस, in Braj = **अल्पयश**, *q. v.*

अल्लाना, *a. int.* to bawl, scream, squeak.

अल्लावा, *m.* a bonfire, flame, blaze.

अल्लाह, *m.* the Supreme Being, God.

अल्लाहतआला, *m.* the Most High God.

अल्हड़, *m.* (*f.* ā) young, unskilful, untaught.

अल्हाना = **आल्हाना**, *q. v.*

अल्हैया, *f.* a certain metre in Hindee versification.

अव, 1, For all words beginning with this element, but not given below, see under the form **अउ**: 2, an inseparable prefix, the reverse of **आ** (much used in composition), denoting negation, deprivation, disjunction; disrespect, disgrace; from, down from, away, off.

अवकलित, certain, ascertained, concluded.

अवकाल = **औकाली**, *q. v.*

अवकाश, *m.* leisure, opportunity, interval of time.

अवकाशबोधक क्रिया, *f.* (in Gram.) a permissive verb, an acquisitive verb.

अवकेशी, *m.* (*f.* inī) having no hair; barren.

अवगत, known, understood.

अवगति, *f.* knowledge.

अवगाह, *m.* bathing, ablution.

अवगाहन, *m.* immersion, ablution.

अवगाहना, *t.* to immerse, bathe.

अवगाहा, *m.* (*f.* ī) immersed, bathed.

अवगीत, 1, *m.* (*f.* ā) reproached, detested, wicked, vile: 2, *m.* reproach, blame.

अवगुण, *m.* blemish, demerit, defect, worthlessness, vice.

अवगुणकथन, *m.* the relating another's demerits.

अवगुणी, *m.* (*f.* inī) a vicious person: *lit.* of a vicious disposition, worthless; ignorant, without virtue or science.

अवघट, uneven, rugged, inaccessible, steep; unfrequented.

अवघड़, awkward, indiscreet, unpleasant.

अवघट = **औघट**, *q. v.*

अवच्छद, *m.* a cover.

अवच्छेद, *m.* boundary, limit, distinction.

अवज्ञा, *f.* disregard, contempt, despite.

अवज्ञाकारी, *m.* (*f.* inī) a contemptuous person: *lit.* contemptuous, derogatory, degrading.

अवढ़ी = **अमोढ़ी**, *q. v.*
अवडेर (*Rām.*) = (1) **कल** (2) **तूफ़ान** (3) **फन्दा**, *qq. v.*
अवडेरना, *t.* to forsake.
अवडेरि (*Rām.*) = **त्याग करके**. (**अवडेरना**.)
अवढर, compassion towards the lowly.
अवतंस, *m.* a crest: an earring; an ornament: a gem, wealth: a halter, rein.
अवतरना, *a. int.* to cross over, pass down, descend (especially as an incarnation of the Deity).
अवतरेउ / **अवतस्यो** } in Braj = **अवतरा**. (**अवतरना**.)
अवतार, *m.* descent, entering into, descent of a deity from heaven, the incarnation of a deity; crossing over, translation, translating: epithet of a *teerth* or sacred place of Hindoo pilgrimage; also, a pious or distinguished person is called, in the language of respect or of flattery, an *avatār* (an incarnation of the Deity). The Hindoos reckon the following ten *avatārs* of Vishṇu:—1, *Matsya*, the fish: 2, *Kachchhap*, the tortoise: 3, *Varāh*, the boar: 4, *Nursingh* the man-lion: 5, *Vāman*, the dwarf: 6, *Parashurām*: 7, *Rām*: 8, *Krishṇ*: 9, *Boodh*: 10, *Kalkee*.
अवतारना, *more prop.* **अवतरना**, *q. v.*
अवतारा, *m.* (*f.* ī) incarnated, incarnate.
अवतीर्ण, (*f.* ā) passed down, descended, incarnated.
अवदीच, *m.* a certain tribe of the Guzerātee Brāhmans.
अवध, 1, *more prop.* **अवधि**, 1, *q. v.*: 2. *f. pr. n.* the province and the city of Oude.
अवधपुरी, *f. pr. n.* the city of Oude.
अवधान, 1, attentive, cautious, careful: 2, *m.* attention, care, caution; staring at.
अवधारण, *m.* a settling, restricting, determining, ascertaining; (in Gram.) emphasis.
अवधारणबोधक क्रिया, *f.* (in Gram.) an intensive verb; e. g. *Mār ḍālnā*, to kill out and out, kill thoroughly, to kill outright, to murder.
अवधि, 1, *m.* an end, limit, term, period; a promise, engagement, stipulation, pledge: the ocean: 2, as far as, up to, till; as long as. Chiefly used as an adverbial suffix; e. g. *Prātukkālāvadhi*, till morning.
अवधूत, *m.* (*f.* ā) large, gigantic; frightful as to form: shaken off, brushed off: 2, *m.* an epithet of a certain kind of fakeer.
अवधेश / **अवधेस** } *m.* the Lord of Oude, *i. e.* Rām.
अवध्य, *m.* (*f.* ā) not fit to be slaughtered.
अवनि / **अवनी** } *f.* the earth, the world.
अवनीप, *m.* an epithet of any king; *lit.* a lord of the earth or of the world.
अवनीश / **अवनीस** } = **अवनीप**, *q. v.*
अवन्तिका, *f. pr. n.* the city of Ujjain (anciently called Ujjayinī).
अवन्ती = **अवन्तिका**, *q. v.*
अवम, *m.* (*f.* ā) low, inglorious, vile, inferior.
अवयव, *m.* a limb, member, part.

अवर, 1, *more prop.* **और**, *q. v.*: 2, low, inferior, hinder: hence, *m.* (*f.* ā) a *Shoodra*.
अवरज; see **आवरज**.
अवराधक, *more prop.* **आराधक**, *q. v.*
अवराधना, *more prop.* **आराधना**, *q. v.*
अवरुद्ध, *m.* (*f.* ā) hindered, restrained, stopped, obstructed, kept in order, besieged, imprisoned, shut up, secluded.
अवरेखना, *a. int.* to write.
अवरेब, badly turned, deformed, ugly.
अवरोध, *m.* (allied to **अवरुद्ध**) the seraglio of a palace, the queen's apartment; a covering, hindrance obstruction.
अवर्गीय, (in Gram.) unclassified.
अवर्त = **आवर्त**, *q. v.* See **अ**, 15.
अवर्षण, *m.* drought.
अवलंब, **अविलंब**. *Note*:—The most confusing variety prevails among Hindee writers and speakers in reference to the orthography of these words and their cognates; even the highest authorities differ among themselves as to the point. In the present work, the spelling adopted by Benfey and Max Müller has, not without some hesitation, been followed. For these words, therefore, and their cognates, see under the form **अविलम्ब**.
अवलक्षण = **अलक्षण**, *q. v.*
अवला, *more prop.* **अबला**, *q. v.*
अवलि, *more prop.* **आवलि**, *q. v.* / **अवली**, *more prop.* **आवली**, *q. v.* } See **अ**, 15.
अवलोकन, *m.* the looking at or the surveying an object, view, sight, inspection.
अवलोकना, *t.* to look at, inspect, see, view.
अवलोकित, 1, *m.* (*f.* ā) looked at, inspected, seen: 2, *m.* a saint of the Jain sect.
अवश, *m.* (*f.* ā) 1, in subjection to another, helpless, powerless, without choice: 2, unsubdued, not under control, disobedient. (See **अ**, 8 and 14.)
अवशिष्ट, *m.* (*f.* ā) left, remaining over and above.
अवशेष, *m.* a residue, remnant, surplus.
अवशेषित, *m.* (*f.* ā) = **अवशिष्ट**, *q. v.*
अवश्य, certainly, inevitably, indispensably, necessarily, actually, of course.
अवश्यक. For this word and its cognates see under the more proper form **आवश्यक**.
अवश्यकार / **अवश्यकरके** } = **अवश्य**, *q. v.*
अवसर, *m.* time, leisure, opportunity, occasion, vacation; a moment.
अवसान, *m.* an end, conclusion, completion, boundary, limit; death, destruction.
अवसि, a corruption of **अवश्य**, *q. v.*
अवसेर, *m.* anxiety, solicitude, care.
अवसेरी, *f.* lateness, delay, slowness; uneasiness, care, regret; longing.
अवस्तु, unreal, unsubstantial, vain, trifling, unessential, not belonging to the true nature of a thing.

अवस्तुत्व, *m.* (*f.* tā) unreality, unsubstantialness, non-essentialness.

अवस्था, *f.* state, condition, any particular state varying with the advance of time (as youth, age, etc.).

अवस्थी, a subdivision of Kanaujiya Brāhmaṇs.

अवही = (1) मैं आता हूं (2) **अबही**, *q. v.*

अवा, *f.* a brick-kiln.

अवाई, *f.* approach, advance, arrival : a saddle-cloth adorned with fringes, etc. : a kind of pickaxe.

अवां ; see (1) **अवा** (2) **आवां**.

अवाक = **अबाक**, *q. v.*

अवागमन, *more prop.* **आवागमन**, *q. v.*

अवाच्य, *m.* (*f.* ā) speechless, dumb.

अवाधी, *f.* unobstructedness.

अवाभक्ति (*corruption*) = **आवभक्ति**, *q. v.*

अवार, *f.* injustice, tyranny : delay.

अवाल, *m.* an enclosed space formed by a cluster of peasants' houses.

अवि, *m.* the sun : a mountain : preservation : a [sheep : the shawl-goat.

अविकार, (see **विकार**) without change, not liable to change.

अविकारी, *m.* (*f.* inī) an unchanging one : *lit.* [not undergoing change ; faithful.

अविगत, diffusive, pervading, spreading or extending widely.

अविचल, *m.* (*f.* ā) motionless, unshaken, unmov-[ed, firm, resolute.

अविचार, *m.* want of consideration or judgment ; injustice.

अविचारित, *m.* (*f.* ā) ill-judged, unconsidered ; [not investigated.

अविचारी, *m.* (*f.* inī) an ill-advised person : *lit.* destitute of or deficient in consideration or reflection ; unjust.

अविच्छिन्न, without interval, close, dense, coarse ; [uninterrupted.

अविज्ञात, *m.* (*f.* ā) not understood ; not known, not celebrated, not famous.

अविदित, *m.* (*f.* ā) not known, not understood.

अविद्या, *f.* absence of or deficiency in learning, illiterateness, ignorance.

अविद्यापंच, the five kinds of trouble which follow [upon illiterateness.

अविद्वान, *m.* (*f.* vatī) an illiterate person : *lit.* illiterate, unlearned, ignorant.

अविनय, *m.* absence of submissiveness, pertness, wantonness.

अविनाश, *m.* exemption from destruction or from [loss, safety.

अविनाशी, *m.* (*f.* inī) anything indestructible : *lit.* exempt from liability to destruction or to loss, imperishable, everlasting ; safe, entire.

अविनीत, *m.* (*f.* ā) behaving improperly, unchaste, unfaithful (conjugally), wanton, petulant, pert.

अविभाज्य, (in Law) indivisible (as property, etc.).

अविरल, uninterrupted, close, dense, coarse.

अविलम्ब ; 1, see note *s. v.* **अवलम्ब** : 2, *m.* a hanging down, depending upon ; asylum, protection : absence of delay, quickness, deligence : 3, without delay, without postponement, quickly.

अविरोध, *m.* absence of contention, quietness, tranquillity, peaceableness.

अविरोधी, *m.* (*f.* inī) a peaceable person : *lit.* non-contentious, non-combative, peaceable, tranquil.

अविलम्बन, *m.* 1, a depending upon ; dependence, support, asylum : 2, non-delay, quickness, diligence.

अविलम्बित, *m.* (*f.* ā) hanging down, dependent on, protected, cherished : 2, expeditious, quick.

अविलम्बी, *m.* (*f.* inī) a dependent, refugee : a procrastinator : *lit.* dependent : delaying.

अविवादी, *m.* (*f.* inī) a peaceable person : *lit.* not contentious, not disputatious, tranquil.

अविवेक, 1, = **अविवेकी**, *q. v.* : 2, *m.* absence of or deficiency in discrimination, insight, or judgment, indiscreetness, indiscretion.

अविवेकता, *f.*
अविवेकत्व, *m.* } = **अविवेक**, 2, *q. v.*

अविवेकी, *m.* (*f.* inī) an undiscriminating person, a stupid : *lit.* undiscriminating, stupid, wanting in judgment, indiscreet.

अविशेष, 1, *m.* absence of distinction or difference : 2, without distinction, not eminent ; without a remainder, entire, whole.

अविशेषित, 1, see **अवशेषित** : 2, *m.* (*f.* ā) not distinguished, not discerned.

अविश्वास, *m.* want of confidence, disbelief, unbelief, distrust ; mistrust, suspicion.

अविश्वासता, *f.*
अविश्वासत्व, *m.* } = **अविश्वास**, *q. v.*

अविश्वासपन, *m.* distrustfulness, unbelievingness, suspiciousness.

अविश्वासी, *m.* (*f.* inī) an unbeliever : *lit.* destitute of or deficient in belief, trust or confidence, unbelieving, mistrustful.

अविष, *m.* (*f.* ā) not venomous ; anti-venomous, [antidotal.

अविषय, 1. *m.* the not being an object of sense ; invisibility : 2. unacquainted with objects of sense.

अविसन, *m.* (*f.* ā) an indifferent person, etc. : *lit.* without application, without desire, indifferent.

अवीर, *m.* (*f.* ā) helpless, weak, impotent.

अवीरा, *f.* (*see above*) a childless widow.

अवेर, *f.* unseasonableness (as to time), lateness, [delay.

अवैया, *m.* (*f.* **अवैई**) *adj.* future, yet to come.

अवैयाजवैया, *m.* (*f.* **अवैईजवैई**) *adj.* coming and going.

अवैये, *m.* ; pl. of **अवैया**, *q. v.*

अवैरो in Braj = **अवेर**, *q. v.*

अव्यक्त, *m.* 1, (*f.* ā) indistinct, non-apparent, invisible, imperceptible : hence, 2, the Supreme Being or Universal Spirit ; soul ; temperament ; nature.

अव्यय, 1, economical, parsimonious : 2, *m.* (in Gram.) an indeclinable word, particle ; an epithet of Vishṇu : *lit.* immutable ; eternal.

अव्ययी, (in Gram.) indeclinable, unchangeable ; relating to an indeclinable word.

अव्ययीभाव, *m.* (in Gram.) an indeclinable com-[pound word.

अव्यवस्था, undecided ; without regulation, irregular.

अव्यवस्थित, *m.* (*f.* ā) not put in order, not re-[gulated, undisciplined.

अव्यवहारित, *m.* (*f.* ā) not customary, not used, obsolete.

अव्यवस्थित, *m.* (*f.* ā) united, joined, not interposed.

अव्याकुल, calm, composed, not preoccupied, firm.

अव्याप्ति, 1, *f.* the not diffusing itself: 2. *m.* (*f.* in *or* inī) *adj.* not diffusing itself, not pervading.

अव्यापक, *m.* (*f.* ikā) *adj.* not pervading, not penetrating, not permeating.

अव्याहत, unrepelled; not alarmed, not disconcerted.

अव्वल, 1, *m.* a beginning: 2, first, chief, principal, best: 3, at first, in the first place.

अशंक, *m.* (*f.* ā) without doubt, undoubting, confident, fearless.

अशक = **अशक्त**, *q. v.*

अशकुन, *m.* a portent, inauspicious omen.

अशकुनी, *m.* (*f.* inī) an evil omen: *lit.* portentous, inauspicious, boding evil luck.

अशक्त, *m.* (*f.* ā) powerless, incompetent, unable.

अशक्ति, *f.* powerlessness, impotence, incapability.

अशक्य, *m.* (*f.* ā) impracticable, impossible.

अशन, *m.* eating, food; the tree (*Terminalia alata tomentosa*) on which the tasar silkworm feeds.

अशनबसन, *m.* food and clothing.

अशनि / **अशनी** } *f.* the thunderbolt of Indra.

अशर, see **असर**.

अशरण, *m.* (*f.* ā) without shelter, unprotected, helpless.

अशरफ़ी, *f.* a certain gold coin (in value £1-11-8 of English money).

अशरीरी, *m.* (*f.* iṇī) incorporeal, unembodied.

अशवारी, *f.* riding, horsemanship; a certain mode of warfare carried on with battleaxes.

अशान्त, *m.* (*f.* ā) anxious, restless, unresigned.

अशान्ति, *f.* anxiety, restlessness in mind.

अशावन्त, 1, (*corruption*) = (1) **आशावन्त** (2) **अशान्त**, *qq. v.*: 2, fearful, timid, unquiet: pitiful.

अशावरी, *f.* a certain metre in Hindee versification: a kind of pigeon: a sort of cotton cloth.

अशास्त्र, *m.* (*f.* ā) contrary to or inconsistent with the rules of science or of law; unlawful, irregular, inconsistent; unscriptural, heterodox, erroneous.

अशास्त्रीय, *m.* (*f.* ā) = **अशास्त्र**, *q. v.*

अशिक्षित, *m.* (*f.* ā) untaught, illiterate.

अशिया, *f.* (pl. of **शै**) things, affairs, effects.

अशिव, *m.* (*f.* ā) inauspicious, not prosperous, unhappy.

अशिष्ट, *m.* (*f.* ā) under the dominion of those habits which are incident to a neglected, defective, or imperfect education; unpolite, ill-behaved, barbarous, boorish, rude, undisciplined, ungoverned.

अशीर्वाद (*contraction*) = **आशीर्वाद**, *q. v.* See **अ**, 15.

अशीष, *more prop.* **आशिस**, *q. v.*

अशुगुण / **अशुगुन** } = **अशकुन**, *q. v.*

अशुगुनी, *m.* (*f.* inī) = **अशकुनी**, *q. v.*

अशुच; see (1) **अशुचि**, 1, (2) **अशौच**, (3) **अशौच**.

अशुचि, 1, *m.* (*f.* in *or* inī) impure, ceremonially unclean: 2, *f.* impurity, ceremonial uncleanness.

अशुद्ध, *m.* (*f.* ā) incorrect, erroneous, impure, inaccurate, corrupt (as language or style).

अशुद्धत्व, *m.* (*f.* tā) uncleanness, impurity, inaccuracy.

अशुद्धिया, *adj.* speaking or writing inaccurately.

अशुभ, 1, *m.* misfortune, calamity, distress, unhappiness, inauspiciousness: 2, *m.* (*f.* ā) unpropitious, unfavorable, unfortunate; unbecoming, inelegant, evil, bad.

अशेख (*colloquial*) = **अशेष**, *q. v.*

अशेष, *m.* (*f.* ā) boundless, endless; without remainder, entire, all.

अशोक, 1, *m.* ease, tranquillity, cheerfulness: quicksilver: a certain 'shrub (*Jonesia asoka*, Roxb.) and its flower: *pr. n.* a certain ancient king: 2, *m.* (*f.* ā) at ease, unmolested, tranquil, cheerful.

अशोच, *m.* absence of care, content, tranquillity.

अशोभा, 1, *f.* want of elegance, ugliness: 2, *m.* (*f.* ī) inelegant, ill-made, shapeless, ugly.

अशौच, *m.* impurity, perfidy; mourning, social or legal uncleanness as from the death of a relation, etc.

अशौचः / **अशौचा** } = **अशौच**, *q. v.*

अश्क, *m.* a tear; tears.

अश्काल, *f.* (pl. of **शकल**) appearances, forms, figures, shapes, resemblances.

अश्नान, *more prop.* **स्नान**, *q. v.* See **अ**, 9.

अश्मरी, *f.* the disease called 'the stone'; strangury.

अश्र, *m.* a tear: blood.

अश्रद्धा, *f.* aversion, loathing, disgust, contempt; disbelief, distrust.

अश्रद्धेय, *m.* (*f.* ā) not to be believed, incredible.

अश्राफ़, *m.* (pl. of **शरीफ़**) men of high extraction, nobles, grandees, gentlefolk.

अश्रु, / **अश्रू**, } *m.* a tear.

अश्लेषा, *m. pr. n.* the 9th *Nakshatra.* It consists of five stars near the southern claw of Cancer.

अश्लोक, *more prop.* **श्लोक**, *q. v.* See **अ**, 9.

अश्व, *m.* (*f.* ā) a horse; the seven-headed horse of Soorya's car; *hence*, in the ingenious system of reckoning by symbols adopted by Hindoos in their poetry, this word is a symbol for 7.

अश्वगन्धा, *f.* a certain plant (*Physalis flexuosa*).

अश्वत्थ, *m.* the holy figtree (*Ficus religiosa*).

अश्वत्थामा, *m. pr. n.* Krishṇ's charioteer. He cut off the heads of the five Pāṇḍav princes, and was himself decapitated by Arjun.

अश्वनी = **अश्विनी**, *q. v.*

अश्वपति, *m.* a horseman, a person of rank attended by horsemen: *lit.* a lord or master of horses. It is used as a title by some of the Hindoo rājās.

अश्वमेध, *m.* the actual or the emblematic sacrificing of a horse. This sacrifice is held to be one of the highest order, and when performed a hundred times it entitles the sacrificer to the dominion of

Paradise. It appears to have been originally typical, — the horse and other animals being simply bound during the performance of certain ceremonies : the actual sacrifice is an introduction of a later period.

अश्वयुज, *f. pr. n.* an epithet of the first *Nakshatra*.

अश्वरक्षक, *m.* (*f.* ikā) a horse-keeper, groom.

अश्ववार, *m.* (*f.* in *or* ī) a horseman.

अश्वशाला, *f.* a stable, horse-repository.

अश्वा, *f.* (*m.* **अश्व**) a mare. [a horseman.

अश्वारूढ़, mounted on horseback: hence, *m.* (*f.* ā)

अश्विन, *m. pr. n.* (a Sanskrit dual form) the twin sons of *Soorya* by the goddess *Ashwinī*: they are (in Myth.) the physicians of the gods. Hence, in the ingenious system of reckoning by symbols adopted by Hindoos in their poetry, this word is a symbol for 2.

अश्विनी, *f. pr. n.* the 1st *Nakshatra* (it consists of three stars in the head of Aries; and is so named from *ashwa*, a horse, because it is represented by a horse's head as its symbol): a certain nymph (this asterism personified).

अश्विनीकुमार, *m. pr. n.* an epithet of the *Ashwin*.

असलोक = **अश्लोक** = **श्लोक**, *q. v.* See **अ**, 9.

असाढ़ } **असाढ़ा** } *more properly* **आषाढ़**, *q. v.*

असाढ़ी, *f.* the day of the full moon in the month *āshāṛh*; also, the harvest of that month.

असुद्ध, *more prop.* **अशुद्ध**, *q. v.*

असुद्धता, *more prop.* **अशुद्धता**, *q. v.*

अष्ट, Sk. (in Hindee **आठ**) eight.

अष्टक, *m.* (*f.* ikā) 1, one eighth : 2, eightfold.

अष्टकोण, *f.* any octagonal figure, an octagon.

अष्टचत्वारिंशत, in Sansk. = **अठतालीस**, *q. v.*

अष्टत्रिंशत, in Sansk. = **अठतीस**, *q. v.*

अष्टधाती, *m.* (*f.* inī) anything consisting of a combination of the eight metals. [eight metals.

अष्टधातीज, *f.* a mixed metal, a compound of the

अष्टधातु, *m.* the eight metals. They are reckoned by the Hindoos as follows:— gold, silver, copper, brass, tin, bell-metal, lead, iron.

अष्टधावी, *f.* a mixed metal of iron and others, a compound of eight metals.

अष्टनवति, in Sansk. = **अठानवे**, *q. v.*

अष्टपंचाशत, in Sansk. = **अठावन**, *q. v.*

अष्टपहर, *lit.* through the eighth watches, *i. e.* all day long and all night long, incessantly.

अष्टप्रहर = **अष्टपहर**, *q. v.*

अष्टभुजी, possessed of eight arms.

अष्टम, 1, *m.* an eighth : 2, *m.* (*f.* ī) *adj.* eighth.

अष्टमंगल, *m.* a horse with the face, tail, breast and hoofs all white; a collection of eight lucky things to be assembled on certain occasions (such as a lion, a bull, an elephant, a water-jar, a fan, a flag, a trumpet, and a lamp: or, a Brāhman, a cow, fire, gold, ghee, the sun, water, and a king).

अष्टमी, *f.* the eighth day of a lunar half-month.

अष्टलोक, *m.* the eight worlds. See **लोक**.

अष्टलोकपाल, *m.* lord of the eight worlds.

अष्टषष्टि, in Sansk. = **अठसठ**, *q. v.*

अष्टसप्तति, in Sansk. = **अठहत्तर**, *q. v.*

अष्टसिद्धि, *m.* the eight *siddhis*; the name of a superior order of beings, a personification of the powers and laws of nature. When those powers are subjected to the will by holiness and austerity, whatever the fancy desires may, it is said, be obtained; even universal sovereignty may be acquired and implicit obedience to any command enforced; the magnitude or weight of the body may be increased or diminished at will, or the body transferred in an instant to any part of the universe.

अष्टांग, 1, *m.* the eight parts of a man, *viz.* the hands, feet, thighs, breast, eyes, head, words, and mind : 2, *m.* (*f.* ī *or* ā) of (with, or consisting of) eight members or parts.

अष्टांगप्रणाम, *m.* a certain method of prostration in adoration or in salutation by which the ground is touched with the eight principal parts of a man.

अष्टादश, in Sansk. = **अठारह**, *q. v.*

अष्टाविंशति, in Sansk. = **अठाईस**, *q. v.*

अष्टाशीति, in Sansk. = **अठासी**, *q. v.*

अष्टि, *f.* a kernel, the stone of a fruit; (in Pros.) a certain metre of sixteen syllables; *hence*, in the ingenious system of reckoning by symbols adopted by Hindoos in their poetry, this word is a symbol for 16.

अखनौं in Chand = to say.

अस = **ऐसा**, *q. v.*

असंक, *more prop.* **अशंक**, *q. v.*

असंख्य, *m.* (*f.* ā) countless. [less.

असंख्यात, not calculated, unnumbered, number-

असंगत, *m.* (*f.* ā) not holding together, incoherent, incongruous, inconsonant, unreasonable, absurd, improper, bad. [intemperateness.

असंयम, *m.* absence of self-restraint, incontinence,

असंयमी, *m.* (*f.* inī) an incontinent person : *lit.* incontinent, unrestrained, intemperate.

असंयोग, *m.* want of opportunity.

असंशय, *m.* 1, absence of doubt : 2, undoubted.

असकत, *f.* drowsiness, laziness, tardiness.

असकती, *m.* (*f.* inī) a lazy person : *lit.* drowsy, lazy, remiss. [used medicinally.

असगन्ध, *m.* a certain plant (*Physalis flexuosa*)

असगुन = **अशकुन**, *q. v.*

असज्जन, *m.* (*f.* ā) unfit, improper, untrue : not respectable, not of good family. [true : non-existent.

असत, *m.* (*f.* ī) unholy, unchaste, ungodly : un-

असती, *f.* an unchaste woman, unfaithful wife.

असत्य, 1, *m.* untruth : 2, *m.* (*f.* ā) untrue.

असत्यवादी, *m.* (*f.* inī) a liar : *lit.* speaking falsely.

असत्यी, *m.* (*f.* inī) a liar : *lit.* untrue.

असन, *more properly* **अशन**, *q. v.*

असनबसन, *more prop.* **अशनबसन**, *q. v.*

असनि, *more properly* **अशनि**, *q. v.*

असन्तान, without offspring, childless.

असन्तुष्ट, *m.* (*f.* ā) dissatisfied, discontented, displeased, hard to please.

असन्तोष, *m.* dissatisfaction, unrest, displeasure.

असन्तोषी, *m.* (*f.* iṇī) unsatisfied, dissatisfied.

असन्मान, *m.* disrespect, irreverence.

असबाब, *m.* (pl. of **सबब**) causes: goods and chattels, furniture; tools, apparatus, baggage.

असभ्य, *m.* (*f.* ā) uncivilized, barbarous, rude, unfit for society, impolite, inurbane.

असभ्यता, *f.* / **असभ्यत्व**, *m.* } impoliteness, barbarity, rudeness.

असम, uneven, not level, dissimilar, unusual.

असमंजस, *m.* doubt, suspense; suspicion; unconformity, disparity, difference.

असमय, 1, *m.* a time of misfortune or distress; an unsuitable time: 2, *m.* (*f.* ā) ill-timed, premature, out of season. *Samay asamay*, in season and out of season.

असमर्थ, *more prop.* **असामर्थ**, *q. v.* See **अ**, 15.

असमसर, *m.* an epithet of Kāmdev.

असमान, uneven, not level, unlike, different, dissimilar, unequal.

असमाप्त, *m.* (*f.* ā) unfinished, incomplete.

असमाप्ति, *f.* incompleteness.

असमें / **असमै** } (*colloquial*) = **असमय**, *q. v.*

असम्पूर्ण, *m.* (*f.* ā) incomplete, imperfect, defective.

असम्बद्ध, *m.* (*f.* ā) not joined, unconnected.

असम्भव, *m.* (*f.* ā) uncommon, inconsistent, incompatible, unlikely, unreasonable, impossible.

असम्भावना, *f.* the being beyond all thought, inconceivableness, unexpectedness; wretchedness.

असम्मत, *m.* (*f.* ā) dissentient, adverse, contrary.

असम्मति, *f.* dis-assent, dissent, dissension, contrariety, dislike.

असम्मान, *m.* disrespect, disgrace.

अस्र, *m.* time; age; the time of prayer before sunset.

असर, *m.* a mark, sign, impress, impression, effect.—*k.* to work upon, operate upon, produce an impression.

असरा, *more prop.* **अप्सरा**, *q. v.*

असरत, *f.* 1, difficulty, distress: 2, pleasure, delight, enjoyment, society.

असरमेल / **असरवेल** } = **इस्पगूल**, *q. v.*

अस्ल, *f.* lineage; foundation, origin, (in Gram.) root; capital, principal sum, stock-in-trade.

असल, having a disjointed, withered, or paralytic hand.

अस़ल, *m.* honey (of bees or of dates).

असवार, *m.* a horseman; cavalry: *lit.* mounted, riding on any thing (as a horse, carriage, ship, etc.).

असहज्ज = **असह्य**, *q. v.*

असहनीय, not to be endured, insufferable.

असहाई, *more prop.* **असहाय**, *q. v.*

असहाय, one who has no assistant, helper, coadjutor, or ally: *lit.* without assistance; absence of help.

असह्य, *m.* (*f.* ā) unbearable, insufferable, intolerable.

असा, *m.* a stick, club, staff, mace, rod.

असांच, *m.* (*f.* ā) untrue, unreal, improper.

असाक्षात, not in the presence of, in the absence of, not manifestly, not openly.

असाखी, *m.* (*f.* iṇī) a false witness, inadmissible witness: *lit.* without credit, without reputation, witnessing falsely, of inadmissible evidence or testimony.

असाख्य, 1, *m.* a want of evidence or testimony: 2, *m.* (*f.* ā) without credit or reputation.

असाक्ष = **असाख्य**, *q. v.* For words beginning with this element see under the form **असाख**.

असाढ़ *more prop.* **आषाढ़**, *q. v.* See **अ**, 15.

असाथ, *m.* (*f.* ā) addicted to bad company.

असाथी, *m.* (*f.* inī) a stranger; an upstart: *lit.* strange, unknown, upstart.

असाद्ध = **असाध**, *q. v.*

असादृश्य, 1, *m.* unsimilarity: 2, non-resembling, unlike.

असाध, (*f.* ā) evil-minded, thievish, without desire or energy, lazy.

असाधपन, *m.* evil-mindness, thievishness, laziness, impurity.

असाधी = **असाध्य**, *q. v.*

असाधु, immoral, unrighteous, wicked.

असाधुता, *f.* / **असाधुत्व**, *m.* } wickedness, unrighteousness.

असाध्य, *m.* (*f.* ā) unable, incapable, weak; impracticable, impossible; incurable.

असामर्थ, *m.* (*f.* ā) powerless, weak, feeble, helpless, unable, unfit, incompetent.

असामान्य, *m.* (*f.* ā) not common, not usual; specific, particular.

असामी, *m.* (pl. of **इस्म**) names.

असार, *m.* (*f.* ā) sapless, pithless; unsubstantial, vain, unprofitable; weak in understanding, silly; hollow (like a reed).

असारत्व, *m.* (*f.* tā) want of solidity, vanity, unreality, unprofitableness, unenduringness, worthlessness.

असार्थ, *m.* (*f.* ā) poor, insignificant.

असार्थता, *f.* / **असार्थत्व**, *m.* } poverty, insignificance.

असालत, *f.* firmness, solidity of judgment, integrity, genuineness.

असावधान, (*f.* ā) careless, inadvertent.

असावधानत्व, *m.* (*f.* tā) carelessness, negligence, inadvertency.

असावधानी, *m.* (*f.* inī) a careless person: *lit.* careless, negligent, inadvertent.

असावन्त, (*f.* vatī) timid, unquiet; pitiful.

असावरी, *f.* a certain kind of metre: a kind of pigeon: a kind of cotton cloth.

असास, *f.* a foundation; a pedestal.

असाहस, *m.* want of bravery, cowardice, fear.

असाहसी, *m.* (*f.* inī) a coward: *lit.* cowardly, tame, chicken-hearted, spiritless.

असि, 1, = **है**: 2, = **ऐसी**: 3, *m.* a sword, scimitar.

असिक्री, *f.* a girl attending upon the inner or female apartments: *pr. n.* a wife of Daksh.

असित, 1, *m.* the colour black: the dark half of the month from full to new moon: 2, *m.* (*f.* ā) black.

असिद्ध, *m.* (*f.* ā) not effected, unaccomplished, imperfect, incomplete, unripe; invalid, false.

असिपत्र, *m.* blade of a sword or scimitar; a scabbard: a hell paved with swords: a sugar-cane.

असिपत्रधारा, *f.* the edge of a sword or scimitar.

असिव, = **अशिव**, *q. v.*

असी, *more properly* **असि**, *q. v.*

असींचा / **असीचा** } *m.* (*f.* ī) not irrigated.

असीम, *m.* (*f.* ā) without limits or boundaries, unbounded.

असीर, *m.* a prisoner, captive.

असीर्बाद, *more prop.* **आशीर्वाद**, *q. v.*

असीस, *more prop.* **आशिस**, *q. v.*

असु, *m.* life, breath; the five vital breaths or airs of the body; reflection, thought (or the heart as the seat of them), affection.

असुख, *m.* uneasiness, restlessness, pain, affliction, sorrow.

असुखी, *m.* (*f.* inī) an afflicted or unhappy person: *lit.* uneasy, restless, in pain, afflicted, unhappy.

असुगन, *more prop.* **अशकुन**, *q. v.*

असुच, *m.* (*f.* ā) impure, foul.

असुची, *f.* impurity, pollution, foulness.

असुद्ध, *more prop.* **अशुद्ध** *q. v.*

असुर, *m.* (*f.* i) a demon. The demons of this order are said to reside at the south pole: they are considered to be demons of the first order and to be in constant hostility with the gods.

असुरतन, *adj.* possessing the body of a demon.

असुरसेन, an epithet of the city of Gayā.

असुरी, *f.* (see **असुर**) black mustard-seed.

असूझ, *m.* (*f.* ā) invisible, incorporeal.

असूया, *f.* malice, detraction, slander.

असूर, *more prop.* **असुर**, *q. v.*

असृज, *m.* (Sk.) blood.

असेवन, *m.* / **असेवा**, *f.* } disobedience, inattention.

असेषा / **असेस** } corruptions of **अशेष**, *q. v.*

असों, this year; the current year.

असोक = **अशोक**, *q. v.*

असोकी, (*f.* inī) a tranquil, cheerful person: *lit.* at ease, free from care.

असोग, *m.* ease, tranquillity: a certain tree (*Uvaria longifolia*) called also *Deva-dāru.*

असोगी, *m.* (*f.* inī) = **असोकी**, *q. v.*

असोच, *m.* (*f.* ā) impossible to be effected by reflection or by study, not contrivable: not to be regretted.

असोची, *m.* (*f.* inī) a careless person: *lit.* careless, unconcerned, indifferent.

असोज, *m.* the sixth solar month.

असोन, *more properly* **असों**, *q. v.*

असोभा, *more properly* **अशोभा**, *q. v.*

असोच *more properly* **अशौच**, *q. v.*

अस्कत, *more properly* **आस्कत**, *q. v.* See **अ**, 15.

अस्कन्ध, *more prop.* **स्कन्ध**, *q. v.* See **अ**, 9.

अस्कर, very heavy: *lit.* heavier, heaviest.

अस्त, *m.* a setting (as of the sun, etc.).— *honā* to set (as the sun and the other heavenly bodies).

अस्तम्भ, *more properly* **स्तम्भ**, *q. v.* See **अ**, 9.

अस्तर, *m.* lining (*see* **अबरा**): a mule.

अस्तव्यस्त, *m.* (*f.* ā) dispersed, scattered, confused, perplexed, helter-skelter.

अस्ताचल, *m. pr. n.* a certain mountain in the west behind which the sun is supposed to set.

अस्ति, (3rd sing. pres. indic. of Sk. vb. **अस**) (he, she, or it) is.

अस्तित्व, *m.* existence.

अस्तुत, 1, *more prop.* **स्तुत**, *q. v.*: see **अ**, 9.: 2, *f.* absence of applause, dispraise.

अस्तुति = **अस्तुत**, 1 and 2, *qq. v.*

अस्त्र, *m.* any weapon, a missile.

अस्त्रधारी, *m.* (*f.* iṇī) an armed person: *lit.* armed, bearing arms.

अस्त्रविद्या, *f.* the science of the use of weapons of defence, the military science.

अस्त्रवेद, *m.* the science of arms and of war.

अस्त्रशस्त्र, *m.* weapons, weapons of war, arms.

अस्त्रहीन, *m.* (*f.* ā) an unarmed person: *lit.* unarmed, defenceless.

अस्त्रहीनता, *f.* / **अस्त्रहीनत्व**, *m.* } unarmedness, defencelessness.

अस्थल, *more prop.* **स्थल**, *q. v.* See **अ**, 9.

अस्थान, *more prop.* **स्थान**, *q. v.* See **अ**, 9.

अस्थावर, not steadfast, unsteady, movable, not fixed, moving.

अस्थि, *m.* a bone: a kernel, seed.

अस्थिपंजर, *m.* a skeleton: *lit.* a cage of bone.

अस्थिबन्धन, *m.* the joining of the bones; sinews.

अस्थिभंग, *m.* fracture of a bone; a certain plant (*Cissus quadrangularis*) of supposed efficacy in fractures.

अस्थिभेद, *m.* the fracture of a bone.

अस्थिमात्र, mere bones, nothing but bones, full of bones.

अस्थिर, *m.* (*f.* ā) unstable, unsteady, uncertain, restless, fickle.

अस्थिरत्व, *m.* (*f.* tā) instability, restlessness, uncertainty, fickleness.

अस्थिवत, osseous, bony, like bone.

अस्थिशोष, *m.* dryness or decay of the bones.

अस्थिसन्धि, *f.* the uniting a broken bone.

अस्थैर्य, *m.* instability, unsteadiness.

अस्नेह, 1, *m.* want of affection, unkindness: 2, *m.* (*f.* ā) wanting in affection, unkind, harsh.

अस्प, *m.* a horse; the knight at chess.

अस्पर्शनीय, *m.* (*f.* ā) not to be touched, literally or ceremonially impure.

अस्पर्शी, 1, *more prop.* **स्पर्शी**, *q. v.*: 2, *m.* (*f.* iṇī) anything intangible: *lit.* intangible, impalpable.

अस्पष्ट, *m.* indistinct, not intelligible.

अस्पृश्य, *m.* (*f.* ā) not to be touched, literally or ceremonially impure.

अस्व = **अश्व**, *q. v.*

अस्वाब = **असबाब**, *q. v.*

अस्मक, *m. pr. n.* a certain ancient Hindoo sage who was born without the sexual intercourse of his parents.

अस्मद, (Sk. pers. pron. 1st pers. sing.) I.

अस्मरण, *m.* oblivion, forgetting, forgetfulness.

अस्मृति, *f.* want of memory, forgetfulness.

अस्र, *m.* a corner : hair : blood : a tear.

असरार, *m.* (pl. of **सिर्र**) secrets, mysteries, confidential concerns.

अखि, *f.* ten millions.

अस्वत्थ, *m.* the sacred figtree (*Ficus religiosa*).

अस्वादित, *m.* (*f.* ā) without taste, without flavor, without relish.

अस्वार्थता, *f.* } unselfishness, disinterestedness.
अस्वार्थत्व, *m.* }

अस्वार्थी, *m.* (*f.* iṇī) a disinterested person : *lit.* unselfish, disinterested.

अस्वीकार, *m.* a withholding or refusal of assent, disassent, denial.

अस्सी, eighty (८०) : see **वां, वीं, वे, वें.**

अह, 1, egoism, self-conceit, pride, self-sufficiency : 2, difficulty, trouble, trial : 3, *m.* a day.

अहई in Braj = **है.** (**अहना.**)

अहउं in Braj = **मैं हूं.** (**अहना.**)

अहं, 1, I ; I am : 2, don't, no, not, nay.

अहंकार, *m.* the conceiving of objects with the notion that they refer to one's own self, egoism, self-conceit, pride, arrogance, haughtiness.

अहंकारता, *f.* } = **अहंकार**, *q. v.*
अहंकारत्व, *m.* }

अहंकारिक, *m.* (*f.* ā *or* ī) = **अहंकारी**, *q. v.*

अहंकारी, *m.* (*f.* iṇī) a self-conceited person : *lit.* egoistical, self-conceited, arrogant, proud, haughty.

अहंकृत, selfish, conceited, proud, arrogant.

अहकाम, *m.* (pl. of **हुकम**) orders, commands, decrees or decisions of a Government or of judges.

अहद, *m.* a compact, treaty, promise, obligation, mandate, will, testament, oath, vow ; conjecture, time, season ; a lifetime ; a reign.

अहदी, 1, a kind of Indian military corps : 2, an idler, indolent person.

अहना, *n.* to be.

अहमक, a blockhead, dunce, fool : *lit.* very foolish, most foolish.

अहमकपन } *m.* stupidity, folly.
अहमकापन }

अहमज्ञ, *adj.* knowing the ego : hence (1) *m.* self-consciousness : (2) *m.* (*f.* ā) one who possesses self-knowledge.

अहमिति = **अहम्मति**, *q. v.*

अहम्मति, *f.* selfism, self-sufficiency, conceit, arrogance, vaunting, pride ; self-love : spiritual ignorance.

अहर, *m.* a reservoir for collecting rain-water to water fields : fuel made of cowdung : a certain tribe of Rājpoots.

अहर: a reservoir, etc. = **अहर**, *q. v.*

अहरी, *more prop.* **आहरी**, *q. v.* See **अ**, 15.

अहर्निश } day and night.
अहर्निशि }

अहर्षित, *m.* (*f.* ā) unhappy, sorrowful.

अहल, *m.* people : a master.

अहलिया, *f.* a wife ; a mistress.

अहल्य, *more prop.* **अहल्या**, *q. v.*

अहल्या, *f. pr. n.* (see **गौतम**) the wife of Gotam and daughter of Brahmā ; one of the Apsarās.

अहवाल, *m.* state, condition ; events, occurrences, circumstances, narration, particulars.

अहसन in Braj = **अहसे** (**अह**). See **सन**, 1.

अहह, alas ! Oh ! O ! (an exclamatory particle implying surprize, pain, pleasure, or calling).

अहहह, a lengthened form of **अहह**, *q. v.*

अहहिं, (3rd pl. pres. indic. of **अहना**) they are.

अहा, (an exclamation denoting sorrow, condolence, or sympathy) alas ! Oh !

अहां, don't, no, nay.

अहार = **आहार**, *q. v.* See **अ**, 15.

अहारना, *t.* to paste, starch.

अहाहाहा, aha ! (an interjection used in praise ; also expressive of pain, surprize, or pleasure).

अहि, *m.* (*f.* nī) a serpent, snake.

अहिंसक, uninjurious, harmless, inoffensive.

अहिंसा, *f.* harmlessness, inoffensiveness ; benevolence.

अहिगिरि, *m.* (= **मलयाचल**, *q. v.*) a mountain where the sandal-tree grows (so called because the snakes are drawn to it by the odour of the sandalwood).

अहित, unfriendly, wanting in affection, prejudicial : hence (1) *m.* (*f.* ā) an enemy : (2) *m.* enmity.

अहितकारी, *m.* (*f.* iṇī) an enemy : *lit.* acting unkindly, operating adversely, inimical.

अहितमना, inimical, hating.

अहिनी, *f.* (*m.* **अहि**) a female serpent or snake.

अहिफेन, *f.* the saliva or the venom of a snake ; the expanded hood of the *Cobra de capello.*

अहिभवन, *m.* an abode of snakes, a snake's hole.

अहिराज, *m.* an epithet of *Shēshnāg*, king of the serpent race.

अहिर्बुध } = **अहिबुध्न**, *q. v.*
अहिर्बुध्य }

अहिल्या = **अहल्या**, *q. v.*

अहिवात, good fortune, auspiciousness ; affection.

अहिविष, *m.* the venom of a snake.

अहिबुध्न, *m. pr. n.* one of the eleven demigods called *Rudra.*

अहिसेज, *m. pr. n.* the bed of Vishṇu in the *Kshīrsamudra* (consisting of the thousand-headed hydra *Sheshnāg*).

अही, *m. f.* (3rd sing. pres. indic. of **अहना**) (he, she, or it) is.

अहोटा, *m.* a person appointed to watch the grain when ripe and to see that the dues are paid ere it be removed.

अहीर, *m.* (*f.* ṇ *or* ṇī) a cowherd, a particular caste of Hindoos whose business it is to attend to cows.

अहीरण, *f.* a cowherd's wife; a female of the above-mentioned caste.

अहीरणी = **अहीरण**, *q. v.*

अहीरिण / **अहीरिणी** } *f.* (*m.* **अहीरी**) = **अहीरण**, *q. v.*

अहीरी, 1, *f.* cowkeeping, the occupation of an *aheer*: 2, *m.* (*f.* iṇ *or* iṇī) an *aheer*: *lit.* following the occupation of an *aheer*, or belonging to that caste.

अहीश, *m.* an epithet of *Sheshnāg*, lord of the serpent race.

अहीस / **अहीसा** } *more properly* **अहीश**, *q. v.*

अहे, (in Gram. a sign of the vocative case) O!

अहेतुक, *m.* (*f.* ā) causeless, groundless; without motive or purpose, careless.

अहेर, *f.* prey, game; the chase, hunting.

अहेरिया, *m.* a sportsman, hunter, fowler.

अहेरी, *m.* (*f.* iṇī) a sportsman, hunter, fowler: lit. *adj.* following the chase (whether as an occupation or as an amusement).

अहेक, *f.* a plant (*Asparagus racemosus*).

अहै, *m. f.* (from **अहना**, to be) we are, they are.

अहो, 1, (in Gram.) one of the signs of the vocative case = O!: 2, an exclamation (holloa! wonderful! alas! etc.) expressive of reproach, compassion, regret, fatigue, surprize, calling, contempt, or praise.

अहोभाग्य, 1, *m.* ill fortune: 2, *m.* (*f.* ā) unfortunate.

अहोरात्र, a day of twenty-four hours, from sunrise to sunrise.

ऐ, *more prop.* **ऐ**: see **ऐ**, 4.

ऐसा, *more prop.* **ऐसा**: see **ऐ**, 4.

ऐहै, (pl. **ऐहैं**) in Braj and in poetry = **आवेगा**.

आ

आ (ā) is the second vowel in the Hindee or Devanāgaree alphabet, and has the following characteristics and functions:—1, In pronunciation it has the broad open sound of *a* in the English words 'far,' 'star.' 2, Its medial and final form is ा, sometimes called *mātra*, sometimes again *ākār*, but most commonly *kānoon*. 3, It is sometimes inaccurately interchanged with **अ**, or with **अव**; thus, **अघात**, more properly **आघात**; **आलि**, more properly **अलि**; **अवराधना**, more properly **आराधना**. 4, It is often inaccurately put for the privitive **अ**; thus, **आधर्म**, more properly **अधर्म**. 5, When it occurs as the first letter in the second member of a compound word, the secondary form only is used; thus **अनाकार** (= **अन** + **आकार**). 6, Standing alone in a sentence it is either (1) the second person singular of the imperative mode of the verb **आना**; or (2) it is the shortest form of the conjunctive participle of that verb; or (3) it is an interjection (Oh! Ah! Alas!) expressive of sudden thought, or of recollecting, or of condolence or participation of sorrowful feeling on any account. 7, It is the sign of the second person singular of the imperative mode of all verbs in which it immediately precedes the **ना** of the infinitive; thus, **जा** (*inf.* **जाना**): **बुझा** (*inf.* **बुझाना**); **करवा** (*inf.* **करवाना**). 8, In the future tense and in the present participle, as also in several of the modes and tenses in which the present participle figures, this letter is the sign of the masculine singular. 9, Inserted between the verbal root and the sign of the infinitive mode, it forms causal verbs; *e. g.* **करना**, **कराना**. 10, In words derived from Arabic or from Persian it represents long *alif*, or *alif* with the sign *madda* written over it. 11, With a dot under it and at the beginning of words or of syllables, it represents *'aīn* followed by *alif*, or long *'aīn*. 12, In some of the words of Arabic origin which appear to have fairly settled themselves down in the language of the Hindee-speaking people, and especially in the larger cities where the Muhammadan influence has long predominated, this letter represents the Arabic letter *'aīn*; e. g. **जमा** (properly *jum'*, pronounced 'jama' with the *a* in each instance like *a* in the English word 'villa'); **बाद** (properly *ba'd*). (See art. **अ**, 11.) In such words the dot is not put unless the full form of the letter is given; *e. g.* **कलआम**. 13, Sometimes this letter is short *a* lengthened according to fixed rules, thus imparting to other words the sense (1) of *origin*; e. g. **सामुद्र**, sea-born (from **समुद्र**): (2) of *ownership, relation*, or *resemblance*; e. g. **आसुर**, appertaining to the *Asurs*, like an *Asur*: (3) of *direction*; e. g. **आश्विन**, directed towards the *Ashwin*: and (4) of *relationship* (patronymic); *e. g.* **आदित्य**, sons of **अदिति**. 14, As the sign of the masculine singular of the present participle (*see* 8) it is, in common with all the other vowels that are used as terminations in the conjugation of the verb, very often omitted in poetry and also by inaccurate speakers; so that it is impossible to know, excepting from the context, either the gender, the number, or the person; e. g. *kahāñ le jāt* or *kahāñ le jāwat*. 15. This letter enjoys no exemption from the remark that in poetry nearly all the vowels are liable to be interchanged; and hence, the ordinary requirements of Grammar as to agreement in the matter of gender are entirely subordinate to the caprice of the poet or to the exigencies of his metre. 16, In composition this letter often appears as a prefix denoting *extent* (as far as), *limitation* (up to, *e. g.* **आगत**), *intensity* (as in **आकम्पन**, **आशंका**), or *direction* (as in **आगमन**): in this class of its functions, therefore, it is the reverse of **अव**. 17, It might be noticed that as a prefix to the words **गमन** and **दान** it has the effect of reversing their meaning. 18, Not only as a prefix, however, but also as a *suffix* it is very common in Hindee; accordingly (1) added to the stems of verbs it forms instrumental nouns; *e. g.* **भुला** (**भुलना**): (2) it is one of the suffixes by means of which masculine adjectives are formed from substantives; *e. g.* **भुखा** (**भुख**): (3) sometimes it forms masculine substantives from adjectives; *e. g.* **अधैर्या** (*adj.* **अधैर्य**): (4) sometimes it forms feminine substantives from adjectives; *e. g.* **अनपेक्षा** (*adj.* **अनपेक्ष**): (5) sometimes it forms masculine substantives from feminine ones; *e. g.* **अकुंगा** (*f.* **अकुंग**): (6) sometimes it forms feminine substantives from masculine ones; *e. g.* **अभिलाषा** (*m.* **अभिलाष**): (7) while it is sometimes *added* (e. g. **दाम**, **दामा**, *m.* **दिश**, **दिशा**, *f.*) and sometimes *rejected* (e. g. **दारा**, **दार**, *f.*) and sometimes *interchanged with* **ई** (*e. g.* **तृषी** **तृषा**)

without affecting the gender at all : (8) it is often used as a Kridanta suffix to form feminine substantives expressive of volition or of reiteration ; *e. g.* जिज्ञासा, पिपासा, प्रशंसा : (9) for many adjectives which in the masculine end with a consonant, this letter suffixed is the sign of the feminine ; *e. g.* प्रिया (*m.* प्रिय) : (10) added to verbal roots ending with a consonant, this letter forms the masculine singular of the Historical Tense (*e. g.* सुना, from सुनना), and of the Past Passive Participle ; *e. g.* देखा (हुआ) (from देखना) : (11) in some few instances it forms diminutives ; *e. g.* कोला (कोल). 19, In compiling a Hindee Dictionary at the present stage of the language, a question arises as to the best method of representing what is called the imperceptible *h* at the end of words obtained from the Urdoo. As an attempt at solving this difficulty, and with the view of indicating the grounds for the method adopted in the present work, the following facts are commended to consideration : (1) The letter is called obscure or imperceptible *h* ; by which is meant simply that the true sound at the end of such words is not that of *h*, — the vowel which happens to precede it having its own proper pronunciation; thus not *nah*, but *na* ; not *kih*, but *ki* ; not *bandah*, but *banda* : (2) In the oblique cases of the singular, and in the nominative plural, of all words at the end of which this inaudible *h* occurs in Urdoo, the inflection which takes place is exactly after the manner of the inflection of the ordinary substantives ending in long *a*, and it is dropped in the oblique cases of the plural ; e. g. *betā*, a son ; *banda*, a slave ; gen. sing. *bete kā*, *bandekā* : nom. pl. *bete*, *bande* ; gen. pl. *betoṅkā*, *bandoṅkā* : (3) The sound of *a* when it precedes this obscure *h* at the end of words is always that of *a* in the English word 'villa'; but if in Hindee there be at the end of a word no vowel-*sign* the genius of the language requires that there be also no vowel-*sound* : (4) The tendency even in Urdoo itself is to drop the imperceptible *h*, and in doing so, to replace it by *alif* : (5) There is in Hindee no other way of representing short *a* (excepting at *the beginning* of words and of syllables) than by आ. For these reasons it seems clear that to represent the inaudible *h*, whether in Hindee by: or ह, or in English by *h*, would be to misrepresent entirely the actual fact as to the sound, to ignore both the facts in relation to inflection and also the usage of natives of all classes, and consequently to countenance an error which to accurate pronunciation must be fatal. It should be observed, therefore, that in dismissing the *h* and representing the sound by आ at the end of such words, the compiler is not arbitrarily attempting to lead the way, but is rather following the way already indicated by the existing phenomena. 20, When it occurs at the end of foreign adjectives as the representative of the inaudible *h* it is not generally exchanged for *i* in the feminine ; *e. g.* ख़फ़ा, *m.* and *f.* 21, When, in Hindee, the long *a* at the end of adjectives represents the nominative form of the Sanskrit substituted for the base, the adjective is the same in form for both genders ; *e. g.* दुष्टचेता (*m.* and *f.*) is the nominative form of the base दुष्टचेतस्. 22, There are several words in regular use in Hindee which end in long *a* to which plural meanings are given : the explanantion is this, that such words are Tatsamas, *i. e.* they are indentical in form with the original Sanskrit words (the said words being in Sanskrit in the plural number) ; excepting, however, that they drop the *visarga* ; *e. g.* दशेन्द्रिया (in Sanskrit, दशेन्द्रियाः). 23. In colloquial usage this letter is sometimes put where we should properly expect य ; *e. g.* संसा, properly संशय : समा, properly समय. 24, In poetry it is, in all situations, *long by nature*. 25, In the formation of many compound words this letter discharges important functions which will be found carefully specified at length in any good Hindee or Sanskrit Grammar. [body.

आअज़ा, *m.* (pl. of उज़्व) the functionaries of the

आइ, life, age, lifetime.

आइन, (in Gram.) a suffix forming the feminine of many titles and family names ; *e. g.* मिश्राइन (मिश्र), पण्डिताइन (पण्डित).

आइना = आईना, *q. v.*

आई, *f.* 1, a maternal grandmother ; a paternal great-grandmother : 2, a coming, arrival : 3, (in Gram.) a suffix forming a large number of abstract substantives feminine ; *e. g.* चतुराई (चतुर). Many of the substantives so formed are each susceptible of four different senses, *viz.* (1) they may signify *a status, art,* or *business* ; *e. g.* लिखाई, writing, *i. e.* the business or status of a writer : (2) they may denote the *act* of discharging the functions which appertain to such business ; *e. g.* निकाई, the act of weeding : (3) they may denote the price paid or the wages received for such work ; e. g. लिखाई, the salary of a writer : (4) they may denote workmanship or the *product* of action ; *e. g.* बिनवाई, weaving. 4, *f.* (*m.* आया) came ; come. [institute, custom, manner.

आईन, *m.* regulation, law, rules, common law ;

आईना, *m.* a mirror, looking-glass ; the kneepan : (frequently, but with doubtful accuracy) eyeglasses, spectacles : (vulg.) a pane of glass.

आउख, *more prop.* सेयुख. *q. v.*

आएती पाएती, low down, low, under, inferior.

आयो in Braj = आया (from vb. आना).

आओं, *m.* fæculent matter, mucus.

आओदी, *m.* a certain tribe of *Jāts*.

आओली, *f.* a certain mode of estimating the produce of land (the produce of one *biswā* is measured, and thence the rest is inferred).

आः = आ 6, (3) *q. v.* See also आ, 22.

आं, (in Gram.) frequently adopted as the sign of the nominative plural of substantives which in the nominative singular end with a short vowel ; *e. g.* लोडआं. It is believed by Trumpp and other Orientalists to be a softened remnant of the sign (आनि) of the neuter plural of nouns in Sanskrit.

आंक is a corrupt form of अंक : for all words, therefore, beginning with this element, but not given below, see under this latter form.

आंक, certain, sure.

आंकदार, *m.* a sharer, partner. [approve of.

आंकना, *t.* to value, prize, estimate, examine,

आंकबन्दी, *f.* an adjustment of rents.

आंकर, conjunctive part. of आकना (= आना) *q. v.*

आंख, *f.* the eye. — *ānā*, to have inflammation of the eyes, to be blear-eyed. — *kisiki dekhnā*, to receive education in anyone's company (*lit.* to look at anyone's eyes). — *kisise roshan karnā*, to meet (*i. e.* to visit) a friend or a person of rank (*lit.* to obtain a look from any one). — *khaṭaknā*, to have pain in the eyes. — *kholnā* = *āṅkh pasārnā*. — *garm k.* to contemplate the beauty of anyone. — *ghuraknā*, to look at with anger. — *chaṛhnā*, to have eyes marked by debauchery. — *chaṛhānā*, to be angry; to be intoxicated. — *chamakānā*, to make the eyes dance, to roll the eyes in anger or as a blandishment. — *chīrke dekhnā* or *chīr chīr dekhnā*, to look with great attention and deep meditation; to look with anger. — *churānā*, not to attend to, to avert one's eyes through shame, dislike, etc., to avoid the sight of any one (*lit.* to steal the eyes). — *chhipānā* (*lit.* to hide or conceal one's eyes), to be ashamed of an improper act; to wink; to connive. — *jornā*, (inelegant) to look steadfastly. — *jhapaknā*, to fear, (*lit.* to move the eyelids quickly, to blink). — *ṭhanḍī k.* to have consolation by meeting friends, to be glad (*lit.* to cool the eyes). — *ḍabḍabānā*, to fill with tears (said of the eyes). — *ḍhaknā*, (obsolete) to have the eyes shut; to be ashamed; to die. — *dābnā*, to shut the eyes, to forbid by signs of the eyes. — *dikhlānā* or *dikhānā*, to frighten, restrain, browbeat (*lit.* to shew the eyes). — *dekhke kuchh k.* to do anything after having consulted the inclination of another. — *na rakhnā*, to have no hope or expectation; to be mentally blind (*lit.* not to have eyes, not to look). — *nam k.* = *āṅkh bharlānā*. — *pattharānā* (*lit.* to become stone), to become dim from long expectation (said of the eyes). — *pasārnā*, or *phailānā*, (obsolete,) to open one's eyes, stare; to be wise and prudent; to discriminate, discern, to be judicious. — *pharaknā*, to feel a pulsation in the eye. (Considered if in the right eye of a man or in the left of a woman, as an omen of some desirable event; if the contrary, it is regarded as unlucky.) — *phuṭnā*, to be blind. — *phuṭī pīr ga,ī*, the eye is lost and the pain is gone (said of a contention which has ceased by the object of it being lost to both parties). — *phernā*, to display aversion after friendship. — *pher lenā*, to turn away the eyes (as through grief, displeasure, etc.). — *phornā*, to make blind; to expect or to watch in vain. — *band kar lenā*, to turn away from one, treat one with neglect: to die. — *bachānā*, to steal away privately and unseen. — *badalnā*, to withdraw one's favor or affection from any one. — *barābar na kar saknā*, not to be able to look steadfastly in another's face, to be ashamed. — *bharke dekhnā*, to look till one's curiosity is fully satisfied. — *bharlānā*, to have the eyes full of tears, to be ready to cry. — *mārnā*, to wink, to stop anyone with a sign of the eyes, to make amorous signs with the eyes. — *minchjānā*, to die, perish. — *milnā*, to look steadfastly. — *milānā*, to contract friendship. — *mūdnā* = *āṅkh band kar lenā* (*lit.* to exchange looks). — *mūndke ek chizkā ikhtiyār k.* to choose or to accept a thing precipitately or without proper consideration (*lit.* having first closed the eyes). — *mūrkh k.* to be angry (*lit.* to make the eyes red). — — *moṛnā*, to shew aversion after friendship. — *rakhnā*, to love, entertain friendship for; to have hopes; to discern (*lit.* to keep the eyes upon). — *lagānā*, to contract friendship or affection for any one, to fall in love with. — *laṛnā*, to encounter the eyes of another; to meet with one's lover unexpectedly. — *laṛānā*, to wink as a hint; to communicate a secret by signs of the eyes. — *seṅknā*, to contemplate the beauty of anyone. — *surkh k.* to be angry.

आंखअंजनी, *f.* a stye on the eyelid.

आंखफोड़ा, *m.* a midge that flies into the eyes at night.

आंखमिचौली, *f.* }
आंखमिचौवल, *m.* } blind-man's buff.
आंखमून्दौरा, *m.* }

आंखसे *girnā*, to become contemptible (*lit.* to fall from the eyes of any one). — *dekhke kuchh k.* to do anything knowingly and with reflection.

आंखाऊ, *m.* a valuation of a growing crop by the eye and without measurement.

आंखि, *more prop.* (1) **आंख** (2) **आंखें**, *qq. v.*

आंखें, *f.* (pl. of **आंख**) the eyes.— *dekhnā*, to study anyone's temper or inclination; to behave respectfully towards anyone. — *nīlipīlī k.* to change the colour of the face from excess of anger.

आंखेंवाला, *m.* (*f.* ī) a spy, an inspector, one of the secret police.

आंखोंका गुलाबी क°, to have redness of the eyes (said of an appearance of intoxication or wantonness).

आंखैं in Braj = **आंखें**, *q. v.*

आंखोंपर बैठना, to sit on a very elevated place; to become dignified; to be beloved.

आंखोंमें *ānā*, to intoxicate (*lit.* to get to the eyes: said especially of wine). — *khāk ḍālnā* (*lit.* to throw dust into the eyes), to commend or to puff wares of an inferior quality; to pilfer, snatch away anything quickly or privately. — *khaṭaknā*, to be seen with envy and dislike. — *ghar k.* to be esteemed or beloved: to persist in one's own erroneous opinions. — *charbī chhānā*, to be wilfully blind, to pretend from pride not to know one's former acquaintances. — *pen lenā*, to be at ease, be secure. — *phirnā*, to be always present in one's eyes, to be ever in one's mind. — *rāt kāṭnā*, or *rāt lejānā*, to pass the night in wakefulness.

आंग, a corrupt form of **अंग**: for all words, therefore, beginning with this element, but not given below, see under this latter form.

आंग, a demand on each head of cattle for pasture, an agistment.

आंगमड़ी, *f.* a yawning, a stretching the body.

आंच, *f.* heat, glare, blaze, flame of a fire (but not of a candle): ashes of cowdung.

आंचर = **अंचरा**, *q. v.*

आंचल, *m.* 1, = **अंचरा**, *q. v.*: 2, the breast of a woman or of any lactescent animal.

आंचला = (1) **अंचरा** (2) **आंचल**, 2, *qq. v.*

आंचू, *m.* the raspberry.

आंजन = **अंजन**, *q. v.*

आंजना, *t.* to tinge the eyes with *añjan*.

आंजनेय, *m. pr. n.* one of the names of Hanoomān.

आंजि, the selvage of a piece of cloth, the hem of a handkerchief.

आंजिनेय, *m.* a certain insect, a kind of newt.

आंसू }
आंभू } *m.* a tear.

आंट, **आंठ**, **आंड**; for words beginning with either of these forms, see under the corresponding forms **आवट**, **आवठ**, **आवड**, respectively.

आंड, *m. f.* a testicle, the scrotum; *semen genitale*.

आंडू = **आंड**, *q. v.*

आंडू, having large testicles.

आंडूबैल, *m.* a bull. It is said to mean, in Dakkhanī, a bull with one testicle.

आंत : a frequent corruption of **अन्त** and of **आन्त** : for all words, therefore, beginning with this element, see under either of these latter forms.

आंध : a frequent corruption of **अन्ध** and of **आन्ध** : for all words, therefore, beginning with this element, see under either of these latter forms.

आंन in Braj = (1) **आज्ञा** (2) **अन्य**, *qq. v.*

आंना in Braj = **आना**, to come.

आंब : a frequent corruption of **अम्ब** and of **आम्ब** : for all words, therefore, beginning with this element, see under either of these latter forms.

आंव, *m.* the glutinous whitish matter voided by people afflicted with tenesmus; a certain affection of the bowels. — *baiṭhnā*, to be afflicted with tenesmus; to be in the act of voiding the above substance.

आंवरा = **आंवला**, *q. v.*

आंवरोग, *m.* the disease in which *ā̃o* is voided.

आंवरोगी, *m.* (*f.* inī) a person afflicted with tenesmus.

आंवलनाल, *f.* the navel-string of a newborn infant.

आंवला, *m.* a certain fruit, a kind of myrobalans (*Phyllanthus emblica*).

आंवलोहू, *m.* dysentery.

आंस, *f.* the fibrous part of anything.

आंसू, *m.* a tear. —*bharnā*, to fill with tears (said of the eyes). — *bhar lenā*, to have the eyes filled with tears.

आक, *m.* 1, a sprout of sugarcane: 2, curled flowered gigantic swallowwort (*Asclepias gigantea*) celebrated among native practitioners for its many medicinal properties.

आकन, grass and weeds collected from a ploughed field.

आकम्पन, *m.* a shaking, trembling.

आकम्पित, *m.* (*f.* ā) *adj.* shaking, trembling.

आकर, 1, conjunctive participle of **आना**, *q. v.*: 2, *f.* the den of a lion or a tiger: 3, *f.* a mine, quarry, source, spring: a multitude: aborigines.

आकर्ष, *m.* attraction, fascination; magnetic attraction; a magnet, loadstone; a spasm.

आकर्षक, drawing, pulling, attractive, magnetic: hence, *m.* anything that attracts, a magnet, loadstone.

आकर्षण, *m.* a drawing, attracting; attraction; absorption.

आकर्षिक = **आकर्षक**, *q. v.*

आकर्षित, *m.* (*f.* ā) attracted, drawn.

आकर्षी, *m.* (*f.* inī) = **आकर्षक**, *q. v.*

आकला, *m.* (*f.* ī) fleet, swift; peevish.

आकली, *f.* agitation, motion (*esp.* of a carriage).

आकश, *more prop.* (1) **आकष** (2) **आकाश**, *qq. v.*

आकष, *m.* a magnet, touchstone.

आकस्मात, *more prop.* **अकस्मात**, *q. v.* See **आ**, 3.

आकस्मिक, *m.* (*f.* ī) sudden, unexpected.

आका, *f.* a hearth, stove, oven, furnace, kiln.

आकांक्षा, *f.* wish, desire, expectation, purpose, intention.

आकांक्षित, *m.* (*f.* ā) desired, wished for, expected.

आकांक्षी, *m.* (*f.* inī) an expectant: *lit.* wishful, desirous, full of hope; asking, inquiring: expectant.

आकार, *m.* 1, the letter **आ**, or any symbol that may represent it: 2. form, appearance, aspect, shape, statue, likeness; a sign, token, hint.

आकारान्त, (in Gram.) ending with **आकार**.

आकाल, *more prop.* (1) **अकाल** (2) **आकार**, *qq. v.*

आकाश, *m.* the fifth element, ether, air, atmosphere, space, the sky, heavens, visible firmament; the subtle and ethereal fluid which is supposed to fill and to pervade the universe, and to be the peculiar vehicle of life and sound. In the ingenious system of reckoning by symbols adopted by Hindoos in their poetry, this word is a symbol for the cypher (0).

आकाशग, moving in or through the air: hence, *m.* (*f.* ā) any bird.

आकाशगंगा, *f. pr. n.* (see **गंगा**) the Ganges of the sky.

आकाशदीया, *m.* a species of lamp which the Hindoos hang aloft on a bamboo in the month Kārtik; any elevated lantern, a beacon.

आकाशनीम, *m.* a certain plant (a kind of Epidendron) which grows on the neem-tree.

आकाशपवन = **आकाशबेल**, *q. v.*

आकाशमण्डल, *m.* the celestial sphere, the firmament.

आकाशमुखी, *m.* epithet of any member of a certain class of devotees of the Shaiv sect. Their devotion consists in holding up the face toward the sun, till at length it becomes difficult to hold it in its proper position.

आकाशवर्ण, *m.* (*f.* ā) cerulean, azure.

आकाशवाणी, *f.* a voice from heaven, a revelation, oracle.

आकाशवृत्ति, *f.* casual subsistence, living from hand to mouth.

आकाशवृत्ती, *m.* (*f.* inī) a cadger, casual, person who has no certain means or source of subsistence, one who lives from hand to mouth.

आकाशबेल, *f.* a certain plant (*Cuscuta reflexa*) which has neither root nor leaves, and which grows on the tops of trees, an air-plant or dodder.

आकाशी, *m.* (*f.* inī) appertaining to space, celestial, aerial, atmospheric.

आकाशीवर्ण, = **आकाशवर्ण**, *q. v.*

आकिंचन, 1, *more prop.* **आकिंचन्य**, *q. v.*: 2, poor, needy, destitute, wretched, miserable.

आकिंचन्य, *m.* poverty; labour, endeavour, exertion.

आक़िल, *m.* a sage: *lit.* wise, sage, sensible.

आक़िबत, *f.* end, conclusion; successful issues: finally.

आकुल, *m.* (*f.* ā) confounded, perplexed, distressed, agitated, crowded, fully occupied. This word is much used as a suffix in compound words; *e. g.* *vyākul*.

आकुलत्व, *m.* (*f.* tī) agitation, disturbance, distress, restlessness.

आकुलित, *m.* (*f.* ā) agitated, disturbed, distracted.

आकूत, *m.* }
आकूति, *f.* } intention.

आकूती, *f.* intention: *pr. n.* the wife of Ruchi.

आकृति, *f.* shape, figure, likeness, image; the body; species.

आकृष्ट, *m.* (*f.* ā) attracted, drawn.

आक्रम, *m.* a beginning; ascending, superiority surmounting, surpassing; invasion; a seizing.

आक्रमण, *m.* an ascending, increase, entering.

आक्रान्ति, *f.* an ascending.

आक्षेप, *m.* a throwing away; convulsion; a putting upon; reproof, irony, sarcasm, abuse, censure, blame.

आखत = **अक्षत**, *q. v.* See **आ**, 3.

आख़ता, *m.* a gelding: *lit.* castrated.

आखन, a frequent Braj pl. of **आंख**, *q. v.*

आखर, 1, *more prop.* (1) **अक्षर** (2) **आख़िर**, *qq. v.*: 2. *f.* the den of a wild beast.

आ खरोट = **अखरोट**, *q. v.* See **आ**, 3.

आखा, *m.* a riddle; a sieve; a pair of bags used as a pannier, a bag of grain (of which two are carried by a beast of burden). [last, in the end.

आख़िर, *m.* the end; the issue; the last: *adv.* at

आख़िरत, *f.* futurity, the future state, the world to come. [late.

आख़िरी, appertaining to the end, last, ultimate,

आख़िरुलअमर, in the end, finally, at last.

आखुपाषाण, *m.* a kind of mineral, a loadstone.

आखेट, *m.* the chase, hunting, pursuing; terror,

आखेटक, (*f.* ikā) = **आखेटिक**, *q. v.* [fright.

आखेटपशु, *m.* a wild animal, beast of chase.

आखेटिक, *adj.* hunting, chasing, pursuing: hence, *m.* (*f.* ā) a hunter; a hound.

आखों, *m.* a preceptor, master, lord.

आखोट = **अखरोट**, *q. v.*

आख्या, *f.* a name, appellation. [by name.

आख्यात, said, spoken; denominated, named: *lit.*

आग, 1, = **आक**, *q. v.*: 2, *f.* fire. — *uṭhānā*, to raise a disturbance; to enrage, provoke. — *k.* to make anything exceedingly warm, to excite anger or envy (used among women). — *jhārnā*, to strike fire (as with a flint). — *denā*, to apply the fire in the burning of a Hindoo corpse. — *parnā*, to be enraged, (e. g. *merī bātoṅse uspar āg partī hai*, he is enraged at my words). — *phāṅknā*, to speak idle words, to boast. — *barnā*, to be enraged, be very angry. — *barasnā*, to rain fire (said of the extreme heat of the sun, or of a hot fire of cannon or musketry in battle). — *bujhānā*, to extinguish fire: to appease a tumult, still resentment, pacify a quarrel. — *lagnā* to be set on fire, be enraged; to be very hungry. — *lagāke pānī le daurnā*, to pretend to appease a quarrel after having oneself purposely excited it; to play tricks, to deceive. — *lagānā*, to set fire to, enflame; to enrage, to raise disturbance. — *lagepar billīkā mūt ḍhūṅḍhnā yā māṅgnā*, to put off, delay, excuse oneself on vain pretences. (The literal translation would be highly expressive, but had better be left to the ingenuity of the inquisitive.) — *leneko ānā*, to come in order to get fire (said of a person who goes to visit his friend and leaves him quickly). — *sulagānā*, to enflame; to excite sedition; to foment a quarrel clandestinely. — *honā*, to be enraged, to flare up. [blighted.

आगड़ा, *m.* an ear of corn or rice that has been

आगत, arrived, come: hence, *m.* (*f.* ā) a guest.

आगति, *f.* arrival: concern.

आगत्व, *m.* concern.

आगम, *m.* futurity: a shāstra containing spells and incantations; a *shāstra* or work on sacred science; (in Law) a voucher, document; a certain Hindoo scripture dictated by Mahādev. — *bāndhnā*, to determine the future, to foretell.

आगमज्ञानी, skilled in the knowledge of the future and in prognosticating: hence, *m.* (*f.* inī) a prognosticator, prophet.

आगमग्यानी, *m.* (*f.* inī) = **आगमज्ञानी**, *q. v.*

आगमन, *m.* a coming, arriving; a proceeding: origin: sexual intercourse.

आगमना, 1, *m.* the advanced guard: the east: 2, *m.* (*f.* ī) venturesome, adventurous; forward, early (as fruit might be).

आगमवक्ता, *m.* (*f.* trī) a prognosticator, one who tells the doctrines of *āgam*; an epithet of Shiv: lit. *adj.* predicting.

आगमबात, *f.* prophecy, prediction.

आगमवाणी, *f.* prophesying, prophecy. [ticating.

आगमविद्या, *f.* the art or the science of prognos-

आगमी, appertaining to the future: hence, *m*, (*f.* inī) a prognosticator, prophet.

आगमें *kisīkī jalnā* or *kisīkī loṭnā* or *ghairkī jalnā*, to bring reproach upon, to accuse; to suffer for another. — *pānī ḍālnā*, to extinguish fire, appease a tumult, pacify a quarrel, still resentment. — *loṭnā*, to be afflicted with grief or melancholy. [clever.

आगर, 1, = **आगार**, *q. v.*: 2, *m.* a saltpit: 3, chief;

आगरा, *m. pr. n.* Agra.

आगरी, 1, *m.* (*f.* iṇī) a manufacturer of salt: 2. *f.* a small room, chamber.

आगरुई, *f.* tinder: *lit.* fire-cotton.

आगरेवाला, *m.* (*f.* ī) a native or a resident of Agra; *lit.* appertaining to Agra.

आगल, before, in front.

आगला, 1, *m.* (*f.* ī) *more prop.* **अगला**, *q. v.*: 2, *f.* (?) an obstructing, hindering, preventing.

आगलान्त, up to the neck.

आगलो, in Braj = **अगला**, *q. v.*

आगवा = (1) **अगुआ** (2) **आगुआ**, *qq. v.*

आगा, *m.* the front part, space in front of a house, fore part of a turban.— *lenā*, to take the lead, [precede.

आग़ा, *m*, a master, lord.

आग़ाज़, *m.* a commencement. — *k.* to make a [beginning.

आगाड़ी = **अगाड़ी**, *q. v.* See **आ**, 3.

आगाध = **अगाध**, *q. v.* See **आ**, 3.

आगापीछा क°, *a. int.* to hesitate, waver, demur, boggle, stand shilly-shally; to prevaricate.

आगामी, *m.* (*f.* inī) anything ensuing: *lit.* coming, ensuing, about to come; future.

आगार, *m.* a dwelling-house.

आगारी, *f.* pay given in advance.

आगाह, 1, informed of, acquainted with, intelligent: 2, an advance of money; usury.

आगि, *more prop.* (1) **आग** (2) **आगे**, *qq. v.*

आग़िल, any device for a sheepcote in a mountain or in open country.

आगिल, future ; possible.

आगू, before, forward ; heretofore.

आगूधा, *m.* a pommel.

आगे, *adv.* and *postp.* (sc. में) before, beyond, more, ago, already, formerly ; in future, forwards, onwards, henceforth, hence : rather, sooner than. —*ānā*, to come forward, to return, revert : to hasten, accelerate. —*kar lenā*, to put forward, put foremost. —*dhar lenā*, to get before, outstrip, surpass; pass (as a horse in a race might). —*lānā*, to bring forward, advance. —*shubh*, fare thee well (used at the end of a letter or written address).

आगेको, (dat. of आगे) further on in time or in space, in future, in the future, ahead, subsequently.

आगौर:, *m.* the first sheaf of the crop presented to the Zamindar.

आगौड़ी, *f.* an advance of money.

आग्नेय, *m.* (*f.* ī) anything appertaining to fire or to the deity of fire, pungent, piquant, stimulating, digestive.

आग्रह, *m.* favor, patronage ; taking, seizing ; surmounting, surpassing : ability, power : pertinacity.

आग्रहायण, = अग्रहायण, *q. v.*

आग्रहायणी, *f.* the day of full moon in the above-mentioned month ; a certain constellation consisting of three stars, the first of which is Orionis (λ) figured by an antelope's head ; *hence*, called also *Mrigsiras*.

आघू, *m.* a species of bird, the thrush.

आघात, *m.* a beating, stroke, blow ; a cast, throw ; a gust ; killing ; a place of execution, slaughterhouse.

आघार, *m.* 1, sacred food which Hindoos place before an idol; ghee, clarified butter : 2, covetousness, avarice.

आघासुर, *more prop.* अघासुर, *q. v.* See आ, 3.

आङ्ग, 1, a corruption of अंग, *q. v.* : 2, *m.* a soft delicate form or body : 3, *m.* (*f.* ī) an inhabitant of Anga.

आचमन, *m.* the rinsing the mouth before religious ceremonies, meals, etc. by sipping water from the hand and spitting it out again ; a ceremony performed before eating.

आचरण, *m.* = आचरणी, *q. v.*

आचरणी, *f.* manner of life, conduct, custom, practice, institute, religious observance.

आचरना, to do, to practice.

आचार, *m.* 1, an established rule of conduct, manner of life, common practice, custom, ordinance, institute, precept, religious observance.

आचारवर्जित, contrary to rule or to established usage, irregular : hence, *m.* (*f.* ā) an outcaste.

आचारी, *m.* (*f.* iṇī) a person who is strict in the observance of religious ceremonies : *lit.* acting in accordance with rules which are admittedly good.

आचार्य्य, *m.* (*f.* ā *or* ānī) a guide or instructor in religious matters, priest, founder or leader of a sect ; a learned paṇḍit, the one who invests the student with the sacrificial thread and instructs him in the mysteries of religion ; a name of Drona the military teacher of the Paṇḍavs.

आचार्य्या, *f.* the wife of an *āchārya* ; a spiritual preceptress, priestess.

आचार्य्यानी = आचार्य्या, *q. v.*

आच्छन्न, *m.* (*f.* ā) covered, concealed, protected.

आच्छादन, *m.* a covering, cloak, garment, cloth.

आच्छादित, *m.* (*f.* ā) covered, concealed, guarded.

आछना, *n.* to be, to remain.

आछा, in Bruj = अच्छा, *q. v.* See आ, 3.

आज, to-day ; now. *Ājke din* or *ājke roz*, to-day. *Āji rāt*, to-night. *Āj dinko*, to-day by day, to-day. *Āj rātko*, to-day at night, to-night.

आजकल, now-a-days, of late ; in a few days.

आज़माइश, *f.* examination, proving, trial, tempting : (in revenue language) the estimating a standing crop by an officer of Government.

आज़माना, *t.* to examine, prove, test, try, tempt ; to touch gold, etc. on the touchstone.

आज़मूदा, examined, tested, tried, proved.

आज़मूदाकार, *m.* one who is experienced in business.

आजरात, (sc. को) to-day at night, to-night.

आजा, *m.* (*f.* ī) a paternal grandfather.

आजागुरु, *m.* one's guru's guru, *i. e.* a grandguru.

आज़ाद, *m.* (*lit.* free, solitary) a kind of fakeer who shaves his beard, eyelashes and eyebrows, and vows chastity, but considers himself exempt from all the ceremonial observances of his religion.—*k.* to manumit ; to set at liberty.

आजाना, *a. int.* to come suddenly, befal, happen ; to come.

आज़ार, *m.* sickness, disorder, disease ; trouble, affliction ; injury, outrage.

आजाव, an imperat. 2nd pers. pl. of आजाना, *q. v.*

आजिज़, weak, impotent, unable, exhausted, helpless, dejected, hopeless.

आज़िर, *m.* an apologist : the scar of a wound.

आजिल, *m.* one who is hastening : *lit.* agile, fleeting, transitory.

आजी, *f.* (*m.* आजा) a paternal grandmother.

आजीव, *m.* means of living, livelihood, profession or calling, maintenance, subsistence.

आजीवका }
आजीविका } *f.* = आजीव, *q. v.*

आजु, to-day, this very day. See उ, 9.

आजुध = आयुध, *q. v.*

आजुर, *f.* unpaid labour.

आज़ुर्दा, afflicted, sad, dispirited, sorrowful, vexed, displeased, weary.

आजूबाजू = आसपास, *q. v.*

आज्ञा, *f.* a command, order, precept, injunction, permission. — *k.* to rule, have the rule, hold sway, command : (with the gen.) to command to. — *denā*, (with the gen.) to give the order.

आज्ञाकार, *m.* (*f.* ī) a servant : lit. *adj.* ministrant.

आज्ञाकारक, *m.* (*f.* ikā) a commander, ruler, chief : lit. *adj.* commanding.

आज्ञाकारी, *m.* (*f.* iṇī) an obedient person : *lit.* acting according to orders, obedient, ministrant, obsequious.

आज्ञाधीन, *m.* (*f.* ā) a manageable person : *lit.* submissive to orders, subservient, dependent, tractable.

आज्ञानुवर्त्त, *m.* (*f.* vati) a subject, obedient person : *lit.* subjected, subdued, brought under control.

आज्ञानुवर्त्ती, *m.* (*f.* iṇī) an observer of orders : *lit.* attentive to orders, obedient.

आज्ञापत्र, *m.* a written order, edict, warrant, [commission.

आज्ञापाल, *m.* (*f.* ī) = **आज्ञापालक**, *q. v.*

आज्ञापालक, law-abiding, obedient : hence, *m.* (*f.* ikā) an obedient person.

आज्ञापालन, *m.* observance of orders, obedience.

आज्ञाभंग, *m.* law-breaking, disobedience, insubordination.

आज्ञाभंगी, law-breaking, disobedient, refractory, insubordinate : hence, *m.* (*f.* inī) a law-breaker.

आज्ञाभंजक, *m.* (*f.* ikā) = **आज्ञाभंगी**, *q. v.*

आज्ञालंघन, *m.* the breaking a command, transgression, disobedience.

आज्ञालंघनकारी, transgressing, disobedient : hence, *m.* (*f.* iṇī) a trangressor.

आट = **आठ**, *q. v.*

आटअठारा, *m.* (*f.* ī) perplexed, distressed.

आटना ; see (1) **अटना** (2) **अटाना**.

आटरूष, *m.* a certain tree (*Justicia adhenatoda*).

आटवां = **आठवां** ; see **आठ**.

आटा; *m.* flour, meal, any ground grain. When sifted, the finer flour (*maidā*) is separated from the coarse meal (*soojee*).

आटामाटी ह°, *n.* to be utterly destroyed or un- [done.

आटि = **अराटि**, *q. v.*

आटो, *more properly* **आठों**, *q. v.*

आठ, eight (८ *or* ⍍) : see **वां**, **वें**, **वे**, **वें**. *Āṭh āṭh ānsoo rōnā*, to shed floods of tears, weep excessively.

आठकोनी, octangular: hence, *m.* (*f.* inī) any thing eight-cornered.

आठखम्भा, *m.* a canopy supported by eight posts.

आठपहर = **आठोंपहर**, *q. v.*

आठमना, *m.* the west (as contrasted with *āgmanā*).

आठवां, *m.* (*f.* wīṅ) eighth. See **आठ**.

आठों, all the eight, the eight of them, the whole eight of them. [constantly.

आठोंपहर, through all the watches, day and night,

आड़, 1, *m.* a prevention, stop, barrier, hindrance, boundary : 2, *f.* a screen, shelter, protection, protector : a line drawn horizontally across the forehead : a kind of ladle used in making sugar.

आड़गीर, *m.* a strip of sward encompassing a field.

आड़ना, *t.* to afford shelter, protect, support, prop.

आड़म्बर, *m.* a charge sounded by musical instruments ; commencement : pride, arrogance ; anger, passion ; pleasure, happiness.

आड़वाड़, 1, *m.* (*f.* ā) stopping, hindering ; protecting : 2, *f.* a stop, barrier, obstacle ; shelter.

आड़ा, 1, *m.* a prop ; shelter : a large saw, hand-saw : a shoemaker's knife : 2, *m.* (*f.* ī) oblique, athwart, transverse ; crooked.

आड़ि = **अराड़ि**, *q. v.*

आड़ी, 1, *m.* (dim. of **आड़ा**) a protector, supporter : 2, *f.* a small saw, small knife : a kind of tone ; tune or mode in music.

आड़ू, 1, = **अड़ू**, *q. v.* (**आ**, 3): 2, *m.* a peach.

आड़े आना, *t.* to protect, screen, shelter : *a. int.* to come under shelter, be protected.

आड्डा, *m.* a stand or station where porters, etc. wait to be hired, a stall, booth, shop, etc.

आड्डादार, *m.* a *pālkī*-bearer, a *ḍāk*-runner.

आढ़, 1, *f.* a kind of fish : 2, alternate (as when there is an interval of a unit between two measures of time or of space ; *e. g. Ek roz āṛh*, every alternate day : *ek kōs āṛh*, every alternate kōs).

आढ़क, *m.* a measure of capacity for dry measure (about seven hundred and fifty of our cubic inches).

आढ़त, *more properly* **अढ़त**, *q. v.*

आढ़तिया, *more prop.* **अढ़तिया**, *q. v.*

आढ्य, *m.* (*f.* ā) wealthy, abounding in riches.

आणि, 1, = **आनि**, *q. v.* : 2, *m.* the edge of a sword ; the pin of the axle of a cart ; a limit, boundary.

आयट, *f.* a knot : envy.

आयटना, *a. int.* to fill (said of a well or tank) : to come into, go into : to reach.

आयटसायट, *f.* partnership ; intrigue.

आयटा, *m.* (*f.* ī) scanty, insufficient ; closely confined : confining closely, restraining, severe.

आयटी, *f.* a handful ; a bundle of grass, etc. ; a small faggot ; a skein of thread, a hank : the stone of fruit : coagulation.

आयठी, *f.* the stone of fruit : coagulation.

आयड, *m. f.* a testicle, the scrotum ; *semen genitale*.

आत, 1, = **आता**, 1, *q. v.* : 2, this is the termination of the ablative case in Sanskrit, and as such frequently occurs in Hindee as a termination of adverbs ; *e. g.* **अकस्मात**.

आतंक = **आतंग**, *q. v.*

आतंग, *m.* fear : pain, sickness, disease, affliction : pomp, shew, dignity, ostentation ; the sound of a drum : an example ? [ers in the Dakkhan.

आतकारी, *m.* (*f.* iṇī) a certain caste of silkweav-

आततार्इ = **आततायी**, *q. v.*

आततायी, felonious, thievish, murderous, incendiary : hence, *m.* (*f.* inī) a felon, etc.

आतप, *m.* sunbeams, sunshine, heat of the sun.

आतम ; for words beginning thus, see under the form **आत्म**.

आतश, *f.* fire, a flame of fire.

आतशगाह, *f.* a furnace, grate, stove ; a temple of the fire-worshippers.

आतशज़दगी, *f.* a conflagration of houses.

आतशपरस्त, *m.* a fire-worshipper, a guebre, of the sect of the magi.

आतशबाज़, *m.* a maker of fireworks.

आतशबाज़ी, *f.* a display of fireworks.

आता, *m.* 1, the custard-apple (*Annona squamosa* or *reticulata*) : 2, a father.

आतातार्इ, *more prop.* **आततायी**, *q. v.*

आतिथेय, 1, *m.* hospitality : 2, *m.* (*f.* ī) a hospitable person, a host : *lit.* attentive to guests : suitable for guests. [a hospitable salutation.

आतिथ्य, 1, = **आतिथेय**, 2, *q.v.*: 2, *m.* hospitality ;

आतिथ्यकारी, *adj.* performing hospitality : hence, *m.* (*f.* iṇī) a hospitable person, a host.

आ़तिर, odoriferous; benevolent, generous, noble.

आतिश = **आतश**, *q.v.*

आतीपाती, *f.* a certain game.

आतुर, 1. *m.* (*f.* ā) sick, diseased; wounded; perplexed, agitated, restless, grieved, afflicted.

आतू / **आतूं** } *f.* a preceptress, governess.

आतूंजी = **आतूं**, *q.v.* See **जी**, 1.

आत्तायी = **आततायी**, *q.v.*

आत्म, *m.* self ; soul, life, breath ; body. (Much used in composition in Hindee, as the following examples will shew.)

आत्मकार्य्य, *m.* one's own private affairs. [cowach.

आत्मगुप्ता, *f.* the plant (*Carpopogon pruriens*)

आत्मघात, *m.* suicide. — *k.* to commit suicide.

आत्मघातक, *m.* (*f.* ikā) = **आत्मघाती**, *q.v.*

आत्मघाती, *adj.* committing suicide, suicidal : hence, *m.* (*f.* inī) a suicide, self-murderer.

आत्मच्छिद, *m.* a cutting or destroying oneself.

आत्मज, *m.* (*f.* ā) a child, one's own offspring : *lit.* born of oneself.

आत्मज्ञ, *m.* (*f.* ā) one who knows the Supreme Being, or spirit, or himself. [ledge.

आत्मज्ञान, *m.* the knowledge of spirit ; self-know-

आत्मज्ञानी, *adj.* knowing spirit or self: hence, *m.* (*f.* inī) a mental philosopher, psychologist.

आत्मत्व, *m.* the peculiar nature of spirit ; sincerity, friendship.

आत्मदेव, *m.* (*f.* ī) = **आत्मदेवता**, *q.v.*

आत्मदेवता, *f.* a tutelar deity.

आत्मनामी, *m.* (*f.* inī) anything self-evident.

आत्मपालक, *adj.* self-cherishing; hence, *m.* (*f.* ikā) a selfish person ; a self-supporting person.

आत्मबन्धु, *m.* one's own kinsman. [spirit.

आत्मबुद्धि, *f.* self-knowledge ; the knowledge of

आत्मबोध, *m.* knowledge of the mind or soul ; self-knowledge, self-consciousness. [ness.

आत्मभिमान, *m.* self-conceit, arrogance, haughti-

आत्मभिमानी, self-conceited, arrogant, haughty, proud, selfish : hence, *m.* (*f.* inī) a coxcomb, etc.

आत्मवादी, *adj.* speaking of self or soul: hence, *m.* (*f.* inī) a mental philosopher, psychologist.

आत्मविक्रयी, *m.* (*f.* inī) a person who sells himself.

आत्मविद्या, *f.* the science of the knowledge of mind or soul, or of self.

आत्मविषयिक, appertaining to self, or to spirit.

आत्मशक्ति, *f.* inherent power. [vanity.

आत्मश्लाघा, *f.* self-applause, egotism, boasting,

आत्मसंयम, *m.* self-restraint.

आत्मसंयमी, *adj.* restraining self: hence, *m.* (*f.* inī) a self-restraining or stoical person.

आत्मसन्देह, *m.* internal doubt.

आत्मसुख, *m.* one's own happiness or pleasure.

आत्महत्या, *f.* self-destruction, suicide.

आत्महन, *m.* (*f.* ī *or* ghnī) / **आत्महन्ता**, *m.* (*f.* trī) } = **आत्मघाती**, *q.v.*

आत्महित, *m.* (*f.* ā) *adj.* benefiting oneself.

आत्मा, (not infl.) *m. f.* (?) the soul, self, the reasoning faculty, the understanding ; the body : Brahm.

आत्माभिमान = **आत्मभिमान**, *q.v.* / **आत्माभिमानी** = **आत्मभिमानी**, *q.v.* } See **आ**, 3.

आत्माराम, *m.* an epithet of animal life, or the all-pervading spirit of Rām.

आत्मिक, mental, appertaining to the spiritual ; own, appertaining to self. [sameness.

आत्मिकत्व, *m.* (*f.* tā) personal identity, identity.

आत्मिय = **आत्मीय**, *q.v.*

आत्मीय, appertaining to one's self, own, special and peculiar ; related, cognate, of kin : hence, *m.* (*f.* ā) a friend, congener.

आथर्व्वण, *m.* (*f.* ī) any Brāhmaṇ versed in the Atharvan Ved ; a collection of prayers, etc. delivered by Atharvan a sage : *lit.* appertaining to the [Atharvan Ved.

आद = **आदि**, *q.v.* See [illegible], 1.

आदअन्त = **आद्यन्त**, *q.v.*

आ़दत, *f.* a habit, custom, usage. — *k.* to accustom, introduce a custom, adopt a habit.

आदम, *m.* Adam, the first man : man in the abstract.

आदमखवार, *m.* a man-eating animal, a cannibal.

आदमखव्वार / **आदमखूर** / **आदमखोर**, } = **आदमखवार**, *q.v.*

आदमज़ाद, *m.* man, mankind, the human race, a descendant of Adam.

आदमी, *m. f.* a descendant of Adam (male or female), a human being, a person, individual ; people.

आदमीयत, *f.* humanity, human nature ; civility, good breeding, complaisance, urbanity. — *k.* to behave politely. — *pakarnā*, to become civilized. — *uṭh jānā*, to become savage, ferocious, or frantic.

आदर, *m.* reverence, respect, politeness, a treating respectfully, or attentively. — *k.* to respect, shew respect, treat respectfully.

आदरणीय, venerable, respectable, estimable : hence, *m.* (*f.* ā) one who is to be revered.

आदरना, *t.* to respect, revere, treat respectfully.

आदरपूर्वक विधि, *m.* (in Gram.) the honorific form of the imperative mode.

आदरभाव, *m.* respect, reverence ; respectability.

आदरमान, *m.* respect, honor, reverence.

आदरयोग्य, worthy of esteem and reverence, venerable, estimable, respectable.

आदरवन्त, devout, respectful, reverential ; respectable, estimable, to be revered : hence, *m.* (*f.* vatī) a devout person, etc.

आदर्श, *m.* a mirror: a commentary; an original manuscript from which a copy is taken, a specimen, a copy; a sign.

आदर्शक, *m.* a mirror.

आदर्शश; see अदर्शन.

आदा, *m.* ginger in the undried state.

आदान, *m.* taking, receiving, acceptance.

आदानप्रदान, *m.* giving and taking.

आदाब, *m.* (pl. of अदब) etiquette, devoirs, ceremony, politeness; respects, compliments, salutations in writing or in speaking.

आदि, 1, *m.* beginning: 2, first, prior; preëminent: 3, It is frequent as a suffix meaning *et cetera* (*lit.* from these or from this as a beginning, onwards, embracing all that comes within the class to which reference has been made); e. g. *Manushyādi jantu*, man and the other animals: *Sooryādi grih*, the sun and the other planets.

आदिअन्त = आद्यन्त, *q. v.*

आदिक, appertaining to the first or to the beginning; appertaining to those implied in the expression *et cetera*.

आदिकवि, *m.* an epithet of Vālmeeki; *lit.* the first or the chief and most eminent poet.

आदिकारण, *m.* a primary cause.

आदिगुरु, *m.* an epithet of Brahmā (the first or the chief *guru*) considered as author of the Veds; (in Pros.) any measure whose first syllable is long.

आदित, 1, = (1) आदिक (2) आदित्य, *qq. v.*: 2, from the beginning; *et cetera*; and the like: first.

आदित्य, *m.* a certain class of deities, sons of Aditi; a deity in general: the sun. The Ādityas are twelve in number, and are forms of the sun, whom they appear to represent as distinct in each of the twelve months.

आदित्यवार, *m.* Sunday.

आदित्व, *m.* priority, precedence.

आदिदेव, *m.* an epithet of Vishṇu or Nārāyaṇ; *lit.* the chief of gods.

आदिपुरुष, *m.* the first male or progenitor, the primeval spirit; usually an epithet of Vishṇu.

आदिभाग, *m.* (see अन्तभाग) the Old Testament.

आदिल, just, upright, sincere.

आदिलघु, *m.* (in Pros.) any measure whose first syllable is short or light.

आदिशिक्षा, *f.* elementary instruction.

आदी, dialectic form = आर्द्रक, *q. v.*

आदेश, *m.* an order, command; a salutation of Jogees: a report, tidings; instruction; prediction: (in Gram.) the substitution of one letter or syllable for another.

आदौ, at first, at the first, in the beginning.

आद्य, *m.* (*f.* ā) first, initial, prior, preëminent.

आद्यन्त, 1, *m.* the first and the last, the beginning and the ending: 2, from first to last, from beginning to end, without cessation or intermission.

आद्रा, *f.* the beginning of the rainy season: *pr. n.* the 6th Nakshatra (*prob.* Orionis).

आध = आधा, *q. v.*

आधकगड़ा, half-cleaned (as rice from the husks).

आधा, 1, *m.* a half, the moiety, a part, the middle: 2, *m.* (*f.* ī) half, mid. — *k.* to halve. In composition it is made to assume a variety of forms; *e. g.* अद, अद्ध, अध, अर्द्ध, अर्ध, आध.

आधान, *m.* pregnancy, conception; a kind of ceremony performed previous to conception as conducive to it: a deposit, surety, pledge.

आधानिक, *m.* a ceremony performed after cohabitation to procure conception or to favor it.

आधार, *m.* one on whom dependence is placed for subsistence, a supporter, patron, prop: comprehension: location: a dike, canal: a basin around the foot of a tree: food, aliment, nourishment.

आधारी, *adj.* obtaining food or nourishment: hence, *m.* (*f.* iṇi) an eater. Much used as a suffix in composition; e. g. *dūdhādhārī*, milk-eating, subsisting on milk.

आधार्म्मिक = अधार्म्मिक, *q. v.* See आ, 3.

आधासीसी, *f.* pain affecting one half of the head, hemicrania.

आधि, *m.* mental agony, anxiety; expectation; calamity: a pawn, pledge, engagement; a site, location, fixing.

आधिक्य, *m.* excess, overplus, abundance.

आधिपत्य, *m.* governorship; lordship, sovereignty.

आधिराज, *m.* a chief king, emperor.

आधिराज्य, *m.* supreme sway, empire, emperorship.

आधीन; for this word and its derivatives see under the more proper form अधीन.

आधीर = अधीर, *q. v.* See आ, 3.

आधीरात, *f.* the middle of the night, midnight.

आधीर्य = अधीरज, *q. v.* See आ, 3.

आधुनिक, *m.* (*f.* ā) belonging to the present time, recent, modern.

आधुनिकत्व, *m.* (*f.* tā) modernness, recentness, novelty.

आधे, in the middle, half-way. — *ādh*, in the middle, midships, midway, in the middle of the road, half the distance.

आधेय, to be held, be maintained, be supported.

आधो आध = आधेआध, *q. v.*

आध्या, the division of produce between two parties in equal shares,—the one having furnished the seed and the other the labour.

आध्यापक = अध्यापक, *q. v.* See आ, 3.

आन, 1, in Braj = (1) अन्य (2) आज्ञा, *qq. v.*: 2, *f.* a graceful attitude, an affected gait; affectation, pride: dignity; honor: modesty, bashfulness: 3, on one's honor, on oath.

आनक, *m.* 1. a kettle-drum; a large drum beaten only at one end; a small drum or tabor: 2. appertaining to another.

आनन, 1, *m.* face, visage, mouth: 2, *f.* a command, order.

आनना, 1, (*corruption*) = आना, 2, *q. v.*: 2, *t.* to bring.

आनन्द, *m.* pleasure, delight; ease, tranquillity, contentment; an epithet of the Supreme Spirit.

आनन्दकन्द, *m.* an epithet of Krishṇ; *lit.* the root or source of enjoyment.

आनन्दत्व, *m.* (*f.* tā) joy, delight, pleasure, happiness.

आनन्दध्वनि, *f.* a shout of joy.

आनन्दबोधक, (in Gram.) said of any interjection or expression indicating joy.

आनन्दमय, *m.* (*f.* ī) an epithet of God considered as the Blessed One; *lit.* made up or consisting of happiness, blessed, blissful.

आनन्दयुक्त, *m.* (*f.* ā) = आनन्दमय, *q. v.*

आनन्दित, *m.* (*f.* ā) delighted, joyful, cheerful.

आनन्दी, joyful, cheerful, delighted, rejoiced hence, *m.* (*f.* inī) a happy or blessed person.

आनपुरना, *a. int.* to happen, come to pass.

आनबाग, *f.* legitimate or proper pride, spirit.

आनमानसे, respectfully; honorably.

आनर्त, *m.* a stage, a theatre: war: *pr. n.* (1) of a certain country in Guzerat (2) of its people (3) of its capital, *viz.* Dwārkā.

आनव } (in Braj) = आनो, *q. v.*
आनवो }

आना, 1, *m.* (in Indian coinage) the sixteenth part of a rupee; a measure of land equal to sixteen roosees. In most Indian dialects the term *ānā*(corruptly 'anna') is conventionally used to denote the fraction $\frac{1}{16}$: thus, a man is said to have a four-*ānā* share in a business, which means that he is entitled to one fourth of the profits. It is similarly used in estimating quality, character, and ability (much as the expression "Sixteen ounces to the pound" is commonly used in England); thus, a man is said to be about twelve annas; *i. e.* that though a decent fellow, he is not quite up to the mark. 2, *a. int.* to come; to be, become. This verb has several important idiomatic usages, among which the following are the chief: 1, It forms some Statistical Verbs; e. g. *Rote ānā*, to come weeping: 2, It forms some Intensives; e. g. *Le ānā*, to bring: 3, In the Conjunctive Participle it sometimes assumes the forms *ān*, *ānke* instead of the regular *ā*, *āke*; e. g. *Itnemeṅ sab-sakhi sahēli ān miliṅ*, in the meantime all the female attendants, having come, met her: 4, When used with nouns it often serves to supply the place of other verbs; e. g. *Mujhe nischay nahiṅ ātā*, I am not certain (*lit.* to me certainty does not come): 5, With *kām* it signifies to come into use, be of use to, be of avail; e. g. *Sarkārke kām āwegā*, it will be of use to the Government. (Obs. that the phrase *kām ānā* is always preceded by the inflected form of the masc. genit.)

आनाकर, *m.* a fee or a levy of one anna per rupee.

आनाकानी, *f.* a turning a deaf ear, purposely neglecting, conniving at.—*denā*, to feign ignorance; to ignore, connive at.

आनाकान्ता, *f.* a sort of prickly nightshade (*Solanum jacquini*).

आनाजाना, *m.* (infl. आनेजाने) a coming and going, thoroughfare, intercourse — *k.* to frequent, be in the habit of coming and going (Historical Tense, *āyājāyā kiyā*).

आनि; in poetry and in Braj this is often the termination of the nominative plural, as it is also of certain substantives in Sanskrit from which it is derived.

आनी; this particle is a distinguishing mark of the feminine of many substantives which designate living creatures, *e. g.* पुरोहितानी.

आनुकूल्य, *m.* help, assistance, patronage: suitability, compliance, favor.

आनुपूर्व्य, *m.* = आनुपूर्व्वी, *q. v.*

आनुपूर्व्वी, *f.* regular succession, order, method; a rank, row.

आनुमानिक = अनुमानिक, *q. v.* See आ, 3.

आनेजाने, the inflected form of आनाजाना, *q. v.*

आनेवाला, *m.* (*f.* i) = आनेहारा, *q. v.*

आनेयार, *m.* the time allotted in the hot season for labor, *viz.* from sunrise till noon.

आनेहारा, *m.* (*f.* ī) one who has yet to come: *lit.* coming, having yet to arrive.

आनो, (imperat. 2nd pers. pl. of आनना) bring.

आन्त, *f.* entrails, viscera, tripe. — *ā,onā*, to be afflicted with the coming down of the rectum. — *girnā*, to void white glutinous stools.

आन्तड़ी = अन्तरी, *q. v.*

आन्तरिक; see (1) आन्त्रिक (2) अन्तरिक.

आन्तरिक्ष, *m.* (*f.* ā) appertaining to the visible firmament, proceeding from the air or sky: *adv.* in the air, out of sight.

आन्तरीक्ष = (1) अन्तरीक्ष (2) आन्तरिक्ष, *qq. v.*

आन्त्रिक, *m.* (*f.* ā) appertaining to the viscera.

आन्दू, *m.* the chain or rope with which the feet of elephants are tied up.

आन्धी, *f.* a storm, hurricane, tempest; a darkening or lowering of the sky. — *chalnā*, to blow keenly or furiously (said of the wind). — *honā*, to engage keenly in a bad action.

आप, I, *m.* water. II, *m. pr. n.* one of the eight demigods called *Vasus*. III, (genit. अपना) self. This is the Reflective Pronoun for all persons, genders, and numbers. With the exception of the genitive case it has in all the cases two sets of forms, the one whose base is आप and the other whose base is अपने. The word is an emphatic one, and as such does not supplant the personal pronoun which may chance to be the subject of the sentence, but rather supplements it: hence, a sentence in which आप *only* is used as the nominative (*i. e.* without the proper personal pronoun) contains nothing to indicate which of the persons it is that is the subject of the sentence; the omission occasions, in fact, inevitable ambiguity: thus, in the sentence *Āp gharmeṅ rahtā* the nominative of *rahtā* may be either *maiṅ*, *tū*, or *wuh*; while in the plural (*Āp gharmeṅ rahte*) there is a *twofold* ambiguity; for, the *āp* may here be not merely the Reflective Pronoun, but even the Honorific one. Apart from the mere difference in declension there is a permanent and unvarying distinction between these two pronouns; for, the latter always has its verb in the plural, and never refers to any other person than the second. The proper function of the word is either to emphasize, or to particularize or single out; thus *Wuh āpse āp girā*, he fell of himself (no one threw him down): *Wuh āphī āp āyā*, he himself came (no one else came for him, but he came *in propriâ personâ*). In the former of these sentences the phrase appears to be used in an instrumental or agentive sense (*āpse āp*, of, or by the agency of one's very self alone, spontaneously), and the latter in a nominative sense (*āphī āp*, oneself, one's very self, oneself alone): in each instance, however, the prevailing idea seems to be aloneness and individuality, personality or identity. It might be added that the second *āp* might be omitted, as it often is, without in any way influencing the sense. This word is sometimes applied to God in the same way as is *ātman* in Sanskrit and 'He' in English, — taking care, however, to begin with a capital letter and to omit the word 'God'; e. g. *Jāke hriday sāṅch hai, tāke hriday āp*, in whose heart there is truth, in his heart there is Himself (*i. e.* God). IV (gen. **आपका**), the Honorific Pronoun. Unlike the last-mentioned word, this word has, in declension, only one set of forms, — the base of these being *āp*; and as it is applied only to the second person it never requires a personal pronoun before it: it differs also from that word by the fact that it invariably requires the plural form of the verb, and this in the third person. It is used when addressing one's superior; or by equals, when in dignified or respectful conversation. Lastly,— the word may be used in addressing either one person or more than one: in the latter circumstance, however, the fact is most generally indicated by adding the word *lōg*; e. g. *Āplōg*, Your Honors, your Worships, You, Sirs: *Āplōg jānte hoeṅge ki*, You, Sirs, may be aware, that, etc.

आपआप, *m.* egotism, selfishness.

आपकाज = **आपकाजी**, *q. v.*

आपकाजी, *m.* (*f.* inī) one who a'tends to his own business, one who is occupied about his own affairs.

आपगति, *more prop.* **अपगति**, *q. v.* See **आ**, 3.

आपत, *f.* a calamity, disaster, accident, misfortune, obstacle, trouble, difficulty, evil, danger, adversity.

आपत्काल, *m.* a season of trouble or distress.

आपत्ति, *f.* = **आपत**, *q. v.*

आपत्य, appertaining to offspring; (in Gram.) appertaining to the formation of patronymic nouns.

आपद, *f.* = **आपत**, *q. v.* [fortunate, unhappy.

आपदग्रस्त, *m.* (*f.* ā) involved in misfortune, un-

आपदा, *f.* = **आपत**, *q. v.* [troublous, risky.

आपदायुक्त, *m.* (*f.* ā) beset with evils, dangerous,

आपन, *more prop.* **अपना**, *q. v.*

आपना, *m.* (*f.* ī) *more prop.* **अपना**, *q. v.*

आपनि in Braj = (1) **अपनी** (2) **आपने**.

आपनिक, *m.* an emerald.

आपनो in Braj = **अपना**, *q. v.*

आपन्न, *m.* (*f.* ā) a refugee: *lit.* coming to another for shelter: gained, acquired: unfortunate, afflicted.

आपरूप, *m.* (*f.* ā) self; an epithet of the Deity: *lit.* own form, self-formed: strange, wonderful, rare.

आपस, 1, *f.* kindred, brotherhood, fellowship: 2, (*recip. pron.*) selves, one another. *Āpasmeṅ rahnā*, adultery (in the speech of women).

आपस्वार्थ / **आपस्वार्थी** } = **स्वार्थ**, *q. v.*

आपा. 1, *f.* an elder sister: 2, self.

आपा आपी = **आपसे आप** *or* **आपही आप**. See **आप**, III.

आपी, *f. pr. n.* the 20th *Nakshatra*.

आपु in Braj = **आप**, *q. v.*

आपुन in Braj = **अपना**, *q. v.*

आपुनि in Braj = (1) **आपने** (2) **अपनी**. [*qq. v.*

आपुस / **आपुसु** } 1, in Braj = **आपस**: 2, *more prop.* **आपूष**,

आपुहि in Braj = **आपको** *or* **आपही**.

आपूष, *m.* tin.

आप्त. *m.* (*f.* ā) authentic, revealed; acquired; trusted, trusty, confidential. [a degree.

आप्ता, *f.* (in Math.) a quotient; an equation of

आप्तोक्त, *m.* an authentic reference. [ablution.

आप्लव, *m.* a pouring upon; a bathing, swimming;

आप्लाव = **आप्लव**, *q. v.*

आप्लुत, 1, *m.* an initiated householder: 2, *m.* (*f.* ā) bathed, sprinkled, washed. overflowed.

आफ़त, *f.* misfortune, calamity, wretchedness.

आफ़तें / **आफ़ात** } *f.* (pl. of **आफ़त**) calamities, evils.

आफ़ियत, *f.* health, safety. [*Papaver somniferum*.

आफ़ीम, *f.* opium, the inspissated juice of the

आफ़ीमन, *f.* / **आफ़ीमी**, *m.* } an opium-eater: *hence*, a sot.

आफ़ू = **आफ़ीम**, *q. v.*

आफ़्ताब, *m.* the sun; sunshine: *fig.* a patron.

आफ़्ताबपरस्त, *m.* a worshipper of the sun.

आफ़्ताबपरस्ती, *f.* the worship of the sun.

आफ़्ताबा, *m.* an ewer, waterpot.

आफ़्रिका, *m. pr. n.* the continent of Africa.

आफ़्रीदगार, *m.* the Creator.

आफ़्रीन, bravo! well done!—*k.* to applaud, praise.

आब, *m.* water: splendour, elegance, dignity, lustre (in gems), temper (of steel), sharpness (of a sword, etc.).

आबकार, *m.* a distiller, wine-merchant; a wine-drinker; a water-carrier, sprinkler.

आबकारी, *f.* the business of a distiller; revenue derived from duty levied on distilleries and on houses of refreshment. [a cellar.

आबख़ाना, *m.* a repository of water, a reservoir;

आबख़ुर्द, *m.* livelihood; victuals; fortune.

आबख़ोरा, *m.* a narrow-mouthed drinking-vessel.

आबगीना, *m.* a looking-glass; a drinking-glass: wine: a diamond. [brush.

आबगीर, *m.* a lake, pond, pool, ditch; a weaver's

आबताब, *f.* lustre, splendour.

आबदार, *m.* the person who takes charge of the drinking-water. [sword, etc.); polish (of gems).

आबदारी, *f.* the office of *ābdār*; sharpness (of a

आबपाशी, *f.* irrigation.

आबनूस, *m.* ebony. [a certain poet.

आबरू, *f.* honour, character, renown, elegance:

आबशार, *m. f.* a cascade, cataract.

आबाद, cultivated, pleasant, peopled, full of buildings and inhabitants: freq. in comp. *e. g.* Allāhābād.

आबादी, *f.* a habitation; a village; a site.

आबाधा, *f.* a segment of the base of a triangle.

आबान, *m.* the eight month among the Persians.

आबिचश्म, *m.* tears (*lit.* water of the eye).

आबिनुक़रा, *m.* quicksilver.
आबिला, *m.* a blister.
आबिस्ता, with young (females); newborn (a child).
आबिहयात, the water of life.
आबोहवा, *f.* climate (*lit.* water and air).
आभरण, *m.* jewels, ornaments, decoration.
आभस, little, few.
आभा, *f.* light, splendour, beauty.
आभाव / **आभास** } *m.* = आभाषकथा, *q.v.*
आभाषकथा, *f.* preface, preämble, exordium.
आभिमुख, 1, *m.* the being face to face with: 2, present, in front of, opposite to, before, fronting.
आभिमुख्य = आभिमुख, *q.v.*
आभीर, *m.* a cowherd (sprung from a Brāhmaṇ by a female of the medical tribe of the *Ambasṭh*).
आभूषण, *m.* ornaments, jewels, finery.
आभोग, *m.* crookedness, roundness; a vault: fulness, plenty, surfeit: the expanded hood of the *cobra*.
आभ्यन्तरीय, interior, internal.
आम, 1, *m.* the mango tree (*Mangifera Indica*) or its fruit: 2, *m.* sickness, disease, sickness in the bowels; the mucous matter voided in diarrhœa: 3, *m.* (*f.* ā) raw, unripe, uncooked.
आमद, *f.* an arrival, coming, approach.
आमदनी, *f.* income; revenue; import; perquisites; the season in which any merchandise generally arrives.
आमदरफ़्त, *m.* intercourse, thoroughfare.
आमदानी, imported, brought in, received.
आमन, *m.* the winter rice-crop. [rice is sown.
आमनिया, *f.* land on which the winter crop of
आमय, *m.* sickness, disease.
आमरस, *m.* the inspissated juice of the mango.
आमर्ष, *m.* peevishness, anger, wrath, rage; envy, impatience of another's success.
आमलक, *m.* = आमला, *q. v.* [*blica*).
आमला, *m.* emblic myrobalan (*Phyllanthus em-*
आमवात, *m.* constipation or torpor of the bowels with flatulence and intumescence, the wind being supposed to be chiefly affected.
आमशूल, *m.* the colic, pain arising from indigestion.
आमा, *f.* (*m.* आम, 3) raw, etc.
आमातिसार, *m.* dysentery.
आमादा, prepared, ready, alert. [visions.
आमान्न, *m.* raw rice, raw grain; uncooked pro-
आमालक, *m.* land near a mountain. [mander.
आमिर, *m.* one who is in command, a ruler, com-
आमिल, *m.* an agent, superintendent of finances, collector of revenue; a ruler, governor.
आमिष, *m.* food, flesh, fleshmeat; enjoyment; an object of enjoyment, pleasing object.
आमीन, the Hindee form of the word 'Amen.'
आमेज़िश, *f.* mirthfulness, sociability, bonhomie.
आमेज़िश, *m.* a mixture, a mixing.
आमेरिका, *m. pr. n.* America. [God).
आमुर्ज़िश, *f.* pardon, grace, forgiveness of sins (by
आमोख़्ता, taught, instructed, trained. [pleasure.
आमोद, *m.* diffusive perfume, odour, fragrance;
आम्हासाम्हा, *m.* an opposing, confronting. —*k.* to oppose, confront.
आम्हेसाम्हे, over against, opposite, facing, fronting,
आम्र, *m.* a mango. [face to face.
आम्बर, *f.* amber.
आम्बात, *m.* a windy tumor, a swelling which comes without pain and goes off as easily and without medicine.
आम्बी, anything which grows spontaneously.
आम्र, *m.* the mango-tree (*Mangifera Indica*).
आम्लिका, *f.* the tamarind tree.
आय, 1, sometimes = आ; see art. आ, 6 (2): 2, *m.* gain, profit, receipt, revenue.
आयत, 1, sunshine, sunbeam: 2, *f.* a sign, mark: a sentence, text, quotation: 3, long, wide, large.
आयतन, *m.* a place, site, groundplot; a seat; an outhouse; an altar.
आयत्त, *m.* (*f.* ā) tractable, docile, dependent.
आयत्तत्व, *m.* (*f.* tā) dependence, tractableness,
आयना = आईना, *q.v.* [docility.
आयसु / **आयसू** } *m.* an order, command.
आया, 1, *m.* (*f.* आई) came; come: 2, *f.* an ayah or female attendant for children: 3, an interrogative particle. It is a mere untranslated sign of interrogation, is invariably found at the beginning of the interrogative clause, and may have either an affirmative or a negative reply. It is much used in localities where Muhammadan influence predominates, and is equivalent to the Hindee क्या, 3. [etc.
आयाजाया, *m.* (= आनाजाना) a coming and going,
आयास, *m.* effort, fatigue, trouble, weariness.
आयीता, ready, prepared. [oppression,
आयु, *f.* age, time of life, duration of life.
आयुध, *m.* a weapon, armour, arms.
आयुपूरी, *f.* fulness of age, full age.
आयुर्दा, *f.* / **आयुर्दाय**, *m.* / **आयुर्बल**, *f.* } age, time of life, lifetime.
आयुष्य, 1, *m.* long life: 2, *m.* (*f.* ā) procuring or granting longevity. [time of life, lifetime, life.
आयुस, 1, *more prop.* आयसु, *q. v.*: 2, *m.* (*f.* ?) age,
आयुसपालक, *m.* (*f.* ikā) = आज्ञापालक, *q. v.*
आयेउं in Braj = आया हूं.
आयो / **आयौ** } in Braj = आया, 1, *q.v.*
आर, 1, *m.* the artificial spur of a game cock: 2, *f.* a goad; a river; a kind of ladle used in sugar-factories.
आर, *f.* bashfulness, modesty; reproach, disgrace, ignominy.

आरक्त, red, blood-red.

आरचा, *f.* adoration, devotion, worship; an image.

आरज = आर्य्य. *q. v.*

आरण्य, 1, *m.* a forest, wilderness: 2, *m.* (*f.* ā) living in forests, growing in forests, wild.

आरण्यककाण्ड, *m. pr. n.* (see सातोंकाण्ड) the third section of the Rāmāyan.

आरण्यषष्ठी, *f.* a certain religious ceremony observed by women. [munity of hermits.

आरण्यसभा, *f.* a forest-court, a court for a com-

आरत = आर्त्त, *q.v.*

आरता, *m.* a certain ceremony in connection with marriage among Hindoos. When the bridegroom first comes to the house of the bride he is received by her relatives, who present to him a platter painted and divided into several compartments, — moving it circularly around his head: in the middle of it there is a lamp made of flour filled with ghee and having several wicks lighted.

आरति = (1) आर्त्ति (2) आरती, *qq. v.*

आरती, *f.* a certain ceremony performed in adoration of the gods by moving circularly around the head of the idol a platter containing a burning lamp with wicks. — *k.* or *lenā*, to perform this ceremony.

आरना, *a. int.* to hesitate, stop.

आरम्भ, *m.* a beginning, prologue. —*k.* to begin.

आरम्भबोधक क्रिया, *f.* (in Gram.) an inchoative verb.

आरव, *m.* sound. [the more proper form आलस.

आरस; for this word and its derivatives see under

आरसी, *f.* a mirror, looking-glass (particularly a mirror used on the thumb, and especially by Hindoo females).

आरस्य, *m.* insipidity, want of flavor, want of spirit.

आरा, 1. = आला, *q. v.*: 2. *m.* a saw; a shoemaker's knife or awl: *pr. n.* a certain district in Shāhābād.

आराजारी }
आराज़ारी } = आनाजाना, *q. v.*

[opponent.

आराति, *m.* (*f.* n *or* nī) an enemy, adversary,

आराती, *m.* (*f.* inī) = आराति, *q. v.*

आराधक, *m.* (*f.* ikā) a worshipper, etc.: *lit.* worshipping, adoring, supplicating; conciliating, gratifying.

आराधन, *m.* worship, adoration, supplication; accomplishment, acquirement; a gratifying.

आराधना, 1, *f.* service, adoration, worship: 2, to worship, adore, serve; to accomplish.

आराध्य, *m.* an epithet of a certain class of Brāhmaṇs; *lit.* venerable, worshipful.

आराम, *m.* 1, pleasure; a garden, pleasure-garden, grove: 2, ease, rest, health, relief, repose. —*k.* to rest, repose, take it easy. —*pānā*, to obtain repose, recover. [person.

आरामी, (*f.* inī) an ease-loving, slothful, or idle

आराइश, *f.* embellishment, adornment, preparation, dressing, equipage; artificial flowers, etc., made of talc and tinsel.

आरास्तगी, *f.* a dressing, preparing, getting into order, regularity, ornament. [regular.

आरास्ता, prepared, dressed, adorned, dressed out,

आरिज़, *m.* the cheek; an accident; a muster-master; the general of an army.

आरिज़ा, *m.* anything necessary to be done: an event, accident: an obstacle: sickness.

आरिफ़, wise, sagacious, ingenious; holy.

आरियत, *f.* the borrowing a thing which is itself (*i. e.* not its equivalent) to be returned, *e. g.* an umbrella, book, etc.

आरी, *f.* (dim. of आरा) a small saw, hand-saw, awl.

आरीया, *m.* a certain plant of the gourd kind.

आरुक, *m.* a certain drug of cooling properties brought from the hills.

आरूढ़, *m.* (*f.* ā) ascended, elevated, mounted (as on a horse, etc). Much used as a suffix in composition.

आरून्धना, *t.* to strangle.

आरे = अरे, *q. v.* See आ, 3.

आरो = आ रव, *q. v.*

आरोग्य; for this word and its kin, see under the more proper form अरोग्य. [ing to, predication.

आरोप, *m.* a transmutation, change: an attribut-

आरोपण, *m.* a causing to ascend; a stringing a bow; a putting on; a planting.

आरोपना, *t.* to plant.

आरोपित, *m.* (*f.* ā) planted, deposited, entrusted; transformed, changed into, feigned.

आर्जव, *m.* rectitude, candour, sincerity.

आर्त्त, *m.* (*f.* ā) pained, injured, hurt, distressed, afflicted, grieved, disturbed, confounded.

आर्त्तवचन, *m.* the complaint or cry of the afflicted.

आर्त्ति, *f.* pain, affliction, distress; intense desire.

आर्द, *m.* flour, meal.

आर्द्र, *m.* (*f.* ā) wet, moist, damp. [dried state.

आर्द्रक, *m.* ginger (*Amomum zinziber*) in the un-

आर्द्रा, 1, = आद्रा, *q. v.*: 2, *f.* (*m.* आर्द्र) wet.

आर्वल, *f.* age, duration of life.

आर्य्य, *m.* (*f.* ā) of a good family, respectable, venerable, honorable.

आर्य्यकुल, *m.* the Āryans (*lit.* the noble race).

आर्य्यवर्त्त, *m.* the land of the noble. It extends from the eastern to the western sea and from the Himālaya to the Vindhya mountains.

आर्य्याभट्ट, *m.* a very learned man.

आर्सी = आरसी, *q. v.*

आल, 1, *m.* yellow orpiment: 2, *f.* a certain tree (*Morinda citrifolia*) from the root of which a red coloring is extracted for staining leather, dyeing silk, etc.: 3, (see औलाद) progeny, race, dynasty, offspring by the mother's side.

आलत, *f.* a tool, instrument, apparatus; the running rigging of a ship; a rope (in the lingo of Indian seamen): *membrum virile; veretrum animalium.*

आलता = अलता, *q. v.* See आ, 3.

आलबाल = आलवाल, *q. v.*

आलम, *m.* the world, the universe: time, condition, mankind.

आलमयां, *m.* mankind, the people of this present world.

आलम्बन, *m.* a supporter; support, maintenance; dependence.

आलय, *m.* a house, dwelling, abode. Much used as a suffix in composition: e. g. *Himālaya.* Frequently shortened or otherwise modified in common speech; e. g. *Shivālā, Divāl.*

आलवाल, *m.* a basin or hole made around the root of a tree to retain water.

आलस = **आलस्य**, *q. v.*

आलसी *m.* (*f.* inī) = **आलस्यी**, *q. v.*

आलसीपना, *m.* laziness, inactivity, weakness.

आलस्य, 1, *m.* laziness, idleness, drowsiness, sloth, inactivity, weakness: 2, lazy, slothful, drowsy, inactive, weak: hence, *m.* (*f.* ā) an idle person, etc.

आलस्यी, *m.* (*f.* inī) = **आलस्य**, 2, *q. v.*

आला, 1. = **आलवाल**, *q. v.*: 2. *m.* a small recess in a pillar or wall (for holding a lamp, etc.): 3. *m.* (*f.* ī) wet; running (as sores); saturated with rain (said of land).

आलाइश, *f.* pollution, filth.

आलात, *f.* (pl. of **आलत**) apparatus, tools, instruments, utensils.

आलातूनी, vague, undetermined.

आलान, *m.* the post to which an elephant may be tied; also, the rope that ties him.

आलाप, 1, *m.* association, intercourse, speaking, conversation, discourse; enumeration of the questions in an arithmetical or algebraic sum: 2. *f.* the prelude to singing.

आलापचारी, *f.* the tuning the voice previous to singing.

आलापना. to sing, tune, tune the voice previous to singing, run over the notes, catch the proper key.

आलापाला, *m.* the leaves of trees.

आलि = (1) **अलि**, 2 (see **आ**, 3): (2) **अराटि**, *qq. v.*

आलिंगन, *m.* the act of embracing, an embrace.

आलिंगी, *adj.* embracing: hence, *m.* (*f.* inī) one who embraces.

आलिम, (pl. **उलमा**) sage, intelligent, learned.

आलिमुलग़ैब, *m.* the world of absence, the world of spirits, the unseen world, the future state.

आलिया, a certain tribe of *banjāras.*

आली, 1. *m.* a scorpion: 2. a land measure equivalent to four *beesees*: 3. *f.* a woman's female friend, a damsel: a line, row, range: 4. appertaining to the *āl* tree.

आलीरंग, *m.* a colour extracted from the *āl* tree.

आलु, 1, = **आलू**, *q. v.*: 2, *f.* a small water-jar, a pitcher: 3, a Kridanta suffix forming many adjectives; *e. g.* **कृपालु**, inclined to compassion, merciful.

आलू, *m.* a certain esculent root (*Arum campanulatum*); a potato, yam.

आलूगाछ, *m.* the potato-tree; the tapioca-shrub.

आलूदा, soiled, stained, smeared, defiled; overwhelmed, loaded with.

आलेप, *m.* liniment, plaster.

आलो, a portion of unripe corn.

आलोक, *m.* sight, looking, appearance; light; panegyric, flattery.

आलोकन, *m.* a looking, a seeing; sight.

आल्ह; for words beginning with this element, see under the more proper form **आह्ल**.

आव, 1, = **आयु**, *q. v.*: 2, (in Gram.) added to the roots of verbs it sometimes forms abstract nouns; *e. g.* **मिलाव (मिलना)**.

आवक़, *m.* insurance or assurance.

आवखल, land reclaimed from waste.

आवृता, *m.* (*f.* ī) covered, concealed, overspread, overshadowed.

आवती, *f.* an approach, advance (as the coming of an army or the approach of a friend): the season in which merchandize is expected: rumour, tidings.

आवन, *m.* a coming, approaching, arrival.

आवनआवन, *f.* the tidings of approach or of arrival.

आवनहार (*colloquial*) = **आनेहारा**, *q. v.*

आवना (*colloquial*) = **आना**, 2, *q. v.*

आवनिहार / **आवनेहार** } (*colloquial*) = **आनेहारा**, *q. v.*

आवनों, in Braj = **आना**, 2, *q. v.*

आवभक्ति, *f.* a civil reception or salutation, welcome, courteousness.

आवभगत / **आवभगति** } = **आवभक्ति**, *q. v.*

आवभाव, *m.* a welcome.

आवरण, *m.* a cover, covering, shield, protection, obstruction, lock.

आवर्दा, 1. = **आयुर्दा**, *q. v.*: 2. that which is brought or carried.

आवर्त्त, *m.* a whirlpool; a curl: *prop.* a turn, a turning.

आवर्त, *m.* a turning; a turn, whirlpool, curl.

आवलि, *f.* a row, range, continuous line; a series, lineage, dynasty.

आवली = (1) **आओली** (2) **आवलि**, *qq. v.*

आवश्यक, 1. *m.* anything necessary; necessity, expediency: 2. *m.* (*f.* ā) necessary, inevitable, indispensable, actual.

आवश्यकत्व, *m.* (*f.* tī) indispensableness, inevitability, necessity.

आवा, 1, (*Rām.*) = **आया (आना)**: 2, *m.* a machine for making pottery, a potter's kiln, a furnace.

आवाई, *f.* rumour, report, mention, tidings.

आवां = **आवा**, 2, *q. v.*

आवागमन, *m.* coming and going; transmigration.

आवागवन = **आवागमन**, *q. v.*

आवाज़, *f.* sound, voice, report, echo, fame, whisper, sentence.—*uṭhānā*, to raise the voice, spread a report.—*k.* to sound, give forth a sound.—*par kān rakhnā*, to hear, listen.—*paṛnā*, to be reported.—*baiṭhnā*, to be suppressed (as the voice, from hoarseness or otherwise).

आवाज़बैठा, *m.* (*f.* ī) hoarse.

आवाज़ा, *m.* report, rumour, fame; conversation, audible talking.

आवाजाई, *f.* coming and going, intercourse, thoroughfare, a dancing attendance upon any one.

आवाती = **आवती**, *q. v.* See **आ**, 3.

आवाभक्ति = **आवभक्ति**, *q. v.* See **आ**, 3.

आवारा, wandering, vagrant, vagabond, out of house and home. [book.

आवारिजा, *m.* a diary, rough note-book, account-

आवास, *m.* a house, habitation.

आवासी, *f.* unripe corn (chiefly barley).

आवाहन, *m.* a summoning, call, summons, respectful invitation.

आविर्भाव, *m.* an unfolding, developing, manifesting; manifestation, presence, a becoming visible.

आविर्भूत, *m.* (*f.* ā) unfolded, developed, manifested, apparent.

आविष्ट, *m.* (*f.* ā) possessed (as by a demon), engrossed (as by a sentiment or feeling).

आवुर्दा, *more prop.* **आवर्दा**, *q. v.*

आवृत, 1, *f.* order, arrangement, manner, ceremony : 2, *m.* (*f.* ā) enclosed, surrounded (as by a ditch, wall, etc.).

आवृत्ति, *f.* order, method ; a returning, a repetition of the same thing ; a resolution.

आवेज़, (in comp.) suspending, adhering. — k. to hang, suspend. [the ears as ornaments.

आवेज़ा, *m.* an earring, drops or pendants worn in

आश ; for all words beginning with this element, but not given below, see under the forms **अश** or **आस**.

आशक्त, *m.* (*f.* ā) fond, attached, enamoured of, devoted to, fascinated, intent upon, zealously active, diligent, addicted to, strongly inclined to : able, powerful : eternal.

आशक्ति, *f.* fondness, attachment : devotedness to, love, zealous application, power, might.

आशक्तिता, *f.* }
आशक्तित्व, *m.* } = **आशक्ति**, *q. v.* [awe; danger.

आशङ्का, *f.* fear, apprehension, doubt, uncertainty ;

आशन = (1) **अशन** (2) **आसन**, *qq. v.*

आशय, *m.* meaning, aim, intention ; an object of desire ; a subject, theme : shelter : the mind, heart : the stomach : a seat : a den : an asylum.

आशा, *f.* a quarter, region ; desire, hope, trust, dependence, reliance. — *k.* or *rakhnā* (each of them taking the genit. *fem.* of the object), to cherish the expectation of, hope for, expect, rely upon.

आशाढ़ = **आषाढ़**, *q. v.*

आशाप्राप्त, *m.* (*f.* ā) a successful person : *lit.* one who has become possessed of the object hoped for.

आशाबन्ध, *m.* confidence, trust, expectation ; a spider's web. [appointed.

आशाभंग, 1. *m.* disappointment; despair : 2. dis-

आशारहित, without hope, without expectation.

आशावत }
आशावन्त } *m.* (*f.* vatī) = **आशावान**, *q. v.*

आशावान, *m.* (*f.* vatī) a candidate, dependent, expectant : *lit.* expecting, desiring, hopeful, dependent.

आशाहीन, *m.* (*f.* ā) hopeless, destitute of hope.

आशिक़, an affectionate person, lover, inamorato.

आशिया, *m. pr. n.* the continent of Asia.

आशिष, *f.* benediction, blessing, the bestowal or the invocation of a blessing upon another ; the return of a compliment from a Hindoo superior : the fang or

आशीति = **अस्सी**, *q. v.* [the venom of a snake.

आशीर्वचन }
आशीर्वाद } *m.* benediction, blessing.

आशीस = **आशिष**, *q. v.*

आशीसमय, *m*, (*f.* ī) blessed, abounding in blessing.

आशु, speedily, forthwith, swiftly, quickly.

आशुतोष, *m.* (*f.* ā) easily pleased, easily satisfied, easily appeased : an epithet of Shiv.

आशोब, *m.* tumult, clamour, storm, tempest ; misfortune ; inflammation of the eyes : an impostor.

आश्चर्य्य, 1. *m.* amazement, astonishment, surprize : 2. *m.* (*f.* ā) astonishing, surprizing, wonderful.

आश्चर्य्यत, *more prop.* **आश्चर्य्यित**, *q. v.* [derfulness.

आश्चर्य्यत्व, *m.* (*f.* tā) wonder, astonishment : won-

आश्चर्य्यबोधक, (in Gram.) said of any interjection or exclamation expressive of surprize.

आश्चर्य्यमान, astonishing, wonderful : hence, *m.* (*f.* matī) a wonderful person.

आश्चर्य्ययुत ; see **आश्चर्य्यित**.

आश्चर्य्यवत }
आश्चर्य्यवन्त } *m.* (*f.* vatī) = **आश्चर्य्यमान**, *q. v.*
आश्चर्य्यवान } [astonishment.

आश्चर्य्यित, *m.* (*f.* ā) astonished, confounded with

आश्रम, *m.* an abode, residence, hermitage ; a school, college : a class or religious order of which the Hindoos reckon four kinds referable to the different periods of a Brāhmaṇ's life : *viz.* 1st, the *Brahmachāree*, who devotes his life to religious exercises, austerity, and celibacy : 2nd, the *Grihee* or *Grihasth*, who lives in the world and rears a family : 3rd, the, *Vānaprasth*, who retires from the world with his family, and passes life in devotion in the forest : 4th the *Bhikshoo*, who subsists on alms.

आश्रमी, *m.* (*f.* inī) belonging to one of the four orders mentioned above.

आश्रय, *m.* a house, residence, abode, asylum, retreat ; vicinity ; a means of defence ; the having recourse to protection or sanctuary ; hope, reliance ; a patron, protector ; cheating, fraud, circumvention.

आश्रा = **आश्रय**, *q. v.* See **आ**, 23.

आश्रित, *m.* (*f.* ā) a refugee, dependent, protégé, etc. : *lit.* relying on the protection of another, hopeful, confiding.

आश्रैत = **आश्रित**, *q. v.* [comfort, completion.

आश्वास, *m.* recreation, rest, repose, cessation,

आश्विन, *m.* (*lit.* directed towards the *Ashwin*) the sixth month of the Hindoos (Sept.-Oct.). It is the first month of the sultry season, commencing when the Sun enters Virgo. During this month the moon is full near the stars at the head of Aries.

आषाढ़, *m.* the third solar month among the Hindoos (June-July), during which the Sun is in Gemini and the moon is near *Ashāṛhā* : it is the first month of the rainy season and, consequently, of cultivation : *pr. n.* the 20th and 21st *Nakshatras*.

आस ; for all words beginning with this element, but not given below, see under the forms **अस** or **आश**.

आसकत; for this word and its kin, see under the form आस्कत, q.v.

आसतर, m. lining; plastering (of a wall): a star.

आसत्ति, f. juxtaposition, connection; (in Gram.) general harmony in a sentence (grammatically or otherwise).

आसन, 1, = अशन, q.v.: 2, m. the inside or under part of the thigh: a seat, stool, a small carpet on which Hindoos sit during prayer; sitting, posture, attitude, particularly the attitude resorted to by Jogees in their devotional exercises of which they enumerate eighty-four: the withers of an elephant, the part where the driver sits: the maintaining a post against an enemy: a market-stall.— *tale ānā*, to come under subjection.—*jornā*, to sit on the hams.—*dolnā* spoken of a holy man who perceiving by supernatural intelligence that some one in distress has invoked him, interposes in his behalf. *Āsanse āsan jornā*, to sit in close contact with another person.— *lagānā*, to sit obstinately in a given posture till one's request be yielded.— *mārnā*, to sit (particularly in an attitude practised by Jogees); to retain one's seat firmly on horseback.

आसनी, f. (dim. of आसन) a small carpet, etc. on which Hindoos sit to worship.

आसन्नभूतकाल, m. (in Gram.) the Perfect Tense.

आसमन्तात, all around, on every side, wholly, altogether.

आसतूं, m. f. one who is dependent on another.

आसरा, *more prop.* आश्रय, q. v. See आ, 3 and 23.

आसरो in Braj = आश्रय, q. v.

आसव, m. rum, an intoxicating liquor distilled from sugar and molasses.

आसा, *more prop.* आशा, q.v.

आसाइश. f. rest, repose, ease, quiet, tranquillity; indulgence, enjoyment.

आसान, easy, convenient, commodious.

आसाभरोसा = आशा, q. v.

आसाम, m. pr. n. the province of Assam.

आसामी, m. (f. inī) 1, an Assamese; *lit.* appertaining to Assam: 2, a defendant in a lawsuit; a culprit, criminal.

आसावसन, naked: without desire.

आसावरी = असावरी, q. v. See आ, 3.

आसिख, 1. = आशिस, q. v.: 2. m. admonition, instruction.

आसिन, *more properly* आश्विन, q. v.

आसिम, virtuous, chaste, protected, safe.

आसिया, f. a mill.

आसियाना, m. a whetstone.

आसियासंग, m. a millstone.

आसिर्बाद, *more prop.* आशीर्वाद, q.v.

आसी, m. f. a rebel, a sinner: *lit.* disobedient, criminal, rebellious.—*k.* to speak depreciatingly of oneself, speak of oneself as unworthy, etc.

आसीन, m. (f. ā) sitting, seated.

आसुर, 1. = असुर, q. v.: 2. m. a form of marriage among Hindoos in which the bridegroom gives to the bride, her father, and her paternal kinsmen, as much as he can afford.

आसुरी, 1, m. (f. inī) appertaining to the *Asurs*, demoniacal: 2, f. a division of medicine, surgery curing by cutting with instruments, applying the cautery, etc.

आसुरीमाया, f. the deception of demons.

आसूदगी, quiet, peaceful, content.

आसूदा, full, glutted, satiated; saturated; quiet, tranquil, contented, at rest, at ease.

आसेब, m. a misfortune, trouble, calamity, damage. It generally refers to such misfortunes as result from the shadow of a demon having fallen upon one.

आसैधः, m. legal arrest.

आस्कत, f. drowsiness, laziness, tardiness.

आस्कताना, n. to be lazy, drowsy, tardy.

आस्कती, m. (f. inī) an idler, etc.: *lit.* drowsy, lazy, remiss.

आस्तर, f. the title of the Book of Esther.

आस्तान, m. a threshold: a fakeer's residence.

आस्तिक, religious, pious, faithful, devout: hence, m. (f. ā) a religious believer.

आस्तीन, f. a sleeve.

आस्ते, *more properly* आहिस्ता. q. v.

आस्था, f. a prop, stay; a place or a means of abiding: effort, pains, care.

आस्पाद, m. a place, situation; a footing, dignity, rank.

आ.स्पास, 1, m. neighbourhood, vicinity; circumference: 2, around, all around, round about, on all sides.

आस्मान, m. the sky, visible heavens, celestial orb.

आसम, for this word and its kin see under the more proper form आश्रम.

आस्वाद, m. savour, flavour, relish.

आस्वास, m. completion, cessation; comfort, consolation, encouragement.

आह, 1, f. a sigh: 2, alas! — *khainchnā*, to draw or heave a sigh. — *bharnā*, to sigh.

आहंग, m. design, purpose: sound, melody; one of the Persian tunes.

आहट, f. sound, noise, clack.

आहन, m. iron.

आहनगर, m. a worker in iron, blacksmith.

आहनगरी, m. the occupation of an ironsmith, smithing.

आहर, a small pond; a salt-pit, a drain; a trough for watering cattle: a certain tribe of Hindoos.

आहरजाहर, f. a coming and going.

आहरी = आहर, q. v. (Its diminutive?)

आहल, m. freshness of soil.

आहला, m. a deluge, inundation, overflow, flood.

आहलो, in Braj = आहला, q. v.

आहा, 1, the distinctive termination of certain epithets; e. g. कजोराहा: 2, *exclam.* aha! alas! woe's me! Bravo! well done!

आहार, m. food, rations, aliment, glue, starch, paste. — *k.* to partake of food. — *band k.* to stop the supplies of food.

आहि, m. f. (अहना) (he, she, it) is, exists.

आहिस्ता, gently, slowly, softly, tenderly.

आहुत, 1, offered, sacrificed; worshipped by offerings: 2, *m.* the offering oblations with fire, burnt-offering.

आहुति, *f.* an oblation, burnt-offering.

आहू, *m.* a deer : vice, defect, fault.

आह्निकी, *m.* the constant or daily ceremonies of religion, daily work : *lit.* daily.

आह्निकी, appertaining to a day, diurnal.

आहा, 1, = **आहला**, *q. v.* : 2, *m. pr. n.* a certain Hindoo soldier and poet from whom a species of poetry takes its name.

आह्लाद, *m.* joy, delight, exultation, mirth, festivity.

आह्लादक, *m.* (*f.* ikī) anything promoting or imparting delight ; *lit.* joy-imparting.

आह्लादित, *m.* (*f.* ā) joyous, mirthful, exultant, merry, pleased, gratified.

आह्लाना, to rejoice, be cheerful, be mirthful.

आह्वान, *m.* a call, summons, respectful invitation.

इ

इ (i) is the third vowel in the Hindee or Devanāgaree alphabet, and has the following characteristics and functions :— 1, In pronunciation it has the sound of short *i* in such English words as 'mill', 'wit'. It is, however, frequently ignored altogether in pronunciation ; *e. g.* **रीति** is oftener pronounced *reet* than *reeti*. This omission of the sound of the letter frequently gives rise to a corrupt spelling of words in which it occurs ; *e. g.* **धूल** is common for **धूलि**. 2, This is its initial form, *i. e.* the form which the letter assumes when it occurs at the beginning of words or of syllables ; in all other situations, however, it assumes the form **ि**, — called its medial and final, or secondary, form. This form, unlike any of the other vowel-forms in Hindee, invariably appears at the left of the letter after which it is sounded, *e. g.* **इति**, (not *iit* but) *iti*. 3, At the beginning of words transliterated from the Arabic it represents *alif* with *kasra* ; and, in like manner, in words from the Persian it represents *alif* with *zer* : with a dot under it, however, it represents *'aīn* with *kasra* or *zer*. 4, This letter is sometimes (especially in poetry) put redundantly with **य** before the vowel terminations in the case of verbs whose root ends in a vowel (according to the caprice or the inadvertence of writers, or the exigencies of metre) ; *e. g.* **उठाइये**, more properly **उठाये** or **उठाय** (**उठाना**). 5, It is sometimes prefixed like **अ** (see **अ**, 9) without in anyway modifying the sense, and seemingly for the same reason ; *e. g.* **इस्पष्टा**, more properly **स्पष्टा**. 6, Words beginning with this letter are often inaccurately spelt with **ई** ; *e. g.* **ईतेकु**, more properly **इतेक**. 7, This letter is often inserted needlessly and corruptly after **ह** ; *e. g.* **कहिना**, more properly **कहना** (vulgarly pronounced as if spelt **कैना**) : and, generally, it is a very common redundancy before the last consonant of the root of a verb ; *e. g.* **जानि**, more properly **जान** or **जानके** (**जानना**). Each of these phenomena is most observable in poetry and in Braj. 8, It is frequently inserted (especially in poetry and in Braj), where we should expect long *i* ; *e. g.* **करयिा**, more properly **करयी**. 9, It is often put in the place of **य** ; *e. g.* **जाइ**, more properly **जाय** (**जाना**). 10, It seems impossible to state a rule in reference to the gender of substantives which end with this letter ; they seem to be as often masculine as feminine. 11, In Braj this letter often appears where we should expect **ए** ; *e. g.* **कामिनिहारो** = **कामेवाला**. 12, In poetry it is *short by nature*, whether used separately or joined to a consonant : before a compound consonant, however, whether that consonant be in the same word with it or in the word that follows, it is, like all the other short vowels, *long by position*. 13, It is sometimes interchanged with **अ** ; *e. g.* **इंग्रेज़ी** = **अंग्रेज़ी**. 14, In the case of those adjectives in Hindee which end with this letter, the form for both genders is the same ; *e. g.* **कुबुद्धि**, *m.* and *f.* Such adjectives are formed by merely prefixing some word or particle to a feminine substantive ending in **इ**. 15, In the formation of some compound words this letter undergoes important changes which will be found carefully specified at length in any good Hindee or Sanskrit Grammar.

इअ ; this element is frequently found at the end of words in the Bhojpurī dialect, especially in the case of dissyllabic words containing two open long syllables, the former of which it shortens ; *e. g.* **करिआ** = **काला**.

इअ़्तिक़ाद, *m.* confidence, faith.

इअ़्तिज़ार, *m.* an excuse, apology.

इअ़्तिबार, *m.* confidence, belief ; esteem, veneration, reliance.

इअ़्तिमाद, *m.* confidence, reliance, hope.

इअ़्तिमादी, *m.* a person in whom confidence is placed, a trustworthy person.

इअ़्तिराज़, *f.* a refusing assent, objection, discussion, criticism, animadversion, displeasure.

इअ़्तिराफ़, *m.* a confession, acknowledgment, avowal.

इअ़्राज, a crippling, making lame.

इअ़्राज़, a flying from, aversion. —*k.* to turn away from anything with abhorrence.

इअ़्राब, *m.* (in Arabic) a vowel, vowel points.

इअ़्लाम, *m.* an announcing, proclaiming, indicating ; a notification, warrant.

इआ ; this element is frequently found as a dialectic increment : its use appears to involve the shortening of the foregoing vowel in the word in which it may occur : it seems sometimes to produce a diminutive effect, but it is most probably merely a jingling termination : *e. g.* **बतिआ** = **बात**.

इंगलण्ड, **इंगलस्थान**, **इंगलिस्थान**, *m. pr. n.* England.

इंगित, *m.* a hint, sign, gesture, motion ; inquiry, search, research.

इंग्रेज़ी = **अंग्रेज़ी**, *q. v.*

इंजोल = **इनजील**, *q. v.*

इक, 1, = **एक**, chiefly in composition : for all words, therefore, beginning with this element but not given below, see under this latter form : 2, Frequent as a suffix forming adjectives or adjectival participles from substantives ; *e. g.* **सांसारिक** (**संसार**).

इकअंग, either of the dishes of a pair of scales.

इकईस, twenty-one (२१); see **वां, वीं, वे, वें.**

इकछत्रराज्य, *m.* universal sway. —*k.* to exercise universal sway.

इकट्ठा } *m.* (*f.* ī) **एकट्ठा**, *q.v.*
इकठा }

इकठान = **इकठौरा**, *q.v.*

इकठौरा, *m.* (*f.* ī) collected together in one place.

इकतक = **एकटक**, *q.v.*

इकपेचा, a head-ornament.

इकरा, a dialectic form = **इसका**.

इकराके, a dialectic form = **इसको**.

इक़रार, *m.* a promise, agreement, assurance, attestation, confession, acknowledgment, confirmation.

इकला, *m.* (*f.* ī) alone, solitary, single, only.

इकलाई, *f.* 1, loneliness, loneness: 2, a certain article of dress consisting of one breadth and generally made of silk.

इकल्ला = **इकला**, *q.v.*

इकहत्तर = **एकहत्तर**, *q.v.*

इका; the characteristic termination of the feminine of certain adjectival participles which in the masculine end in **अक** or **क**; *e.g.* **रक्षक**, *m.* a protector; **रक्षिका**, *f.* a protectress: lit. *adj.* protecting.

इक़ामत, *f.* a resting, staying; abode, dwelling, residence.

इकार, *m.* the letter **इ**. or any symbol that may represent it.

इकारान्त, (in Gram.) ending with **इ**.

इकेला, *m.* (*f.* ī) = **अकेला**, *q.v.*

इक्का, 1, *m.* (*f.* ī) single, incomparable, matchless, superexcellent: 2. *m.* an earring consisting of a single pearl; an ornament worn on the wrist (often hollow) containing perfume: a champion who serves alone without being attached to any corps: a species of carriage used by the natives of Northern India drawn by one horse (whence, as is supposed, its name).

इक्कीस = **इकईस**, *q.v.*

इक्त°; see under the form **एकत°**.

इक्तिसाब, *m.* gain, acquisition.

इक्यावन, fifty-one (५१): see **वां वीं, वे, वें.**

इक्यासी, eighty-one (८१): see **वां, वीं, वे, वें.**

इकराम, *m.* an honoring, complimenting; a treating with attention and ceremony.

इक्षाकु, *more properly* **इक्ष्वाकु**, *q.v.*

इक्षु, *m.* (*f.* ?) sugar-cane (*Saccharum officinarum*).

इक्षुकाण्ड, *m.* a kind of sugar-cane (*Saccharum munja*).

इक्षुमती, *more prop.* **ईक्षुमती**, *q.v.* See **इ**, 6.

इक्षुमेही, diabetic.

इक्षुरस, *m.* the juice of the sugar-cane.

इक्षुसार, *m.* raw or unrefined sugar, molasses.

इक्ष्वाकु, *m. pr. n.* the first king of Oude; a descendant of that king.

इखट्ठा = **इकट्ठा**, *q.v.*

इख़्तिताम, *m.* a completion, finishing, fulfilment.

इख़्तिफ़ा, *m.* the act of hiding, concealing, covering.

इख़्तियार, *m.* authority, power, will, choice, option, election.

इख़्तिरा, *m.* an invention, inventing, discovering, conjecturing.

इख़्तिलात, *m.* friendship, intercourse, conversation; the act of mixing, a mixture, confusion.

इख़्तिलाफ़, *m.* difference of opinion, opposition, discord; misunderstanding between friends, coolness.

इख़्तिलाल, *m.* an interruption, obstacle.

इख़्तिसार, *m.* a reducing, curtailing, contracting, abridgment.

इखत्तर = **एकहत्तर**, *q.v.*

इख़लाक़, *m.* (pl. of **ख़ुल्क़**) disposition, the good qualities of mankind; ethics, morals.

इग़माज़, *m.* dissimulation; superciliousness; ogling, coquetry.

इग़वा, *m.* temptation, seduction.

इङ्गलण्डीय, English, relating to England.

इगारह = **एग्यारह**, *q.v.*

इचकना, to grin, shew the teeth (as a dog might).

इच्छक, *more prop.* **इच्छुक**, *q.v.*

इच्छन, *more properly* **ईक्षण**, *q.v.*

इच्छा, *f.* (not infl.) will, wish, desire. —*k.* or *rakhnā* (with genit. *fem.* of the object), to have a desire for. *Apnī ichchhāko mārnā*, to practice self-denial. *Jis bātkī tumheṅ ichchhā ho*, (*i.e.* with dat. of the agent and the gen. of the object) whatever you may wish for, whatever you may wish.

इच्छाचारी, *m.* (*f.* inī) one who acts according to his own will.

इच्छाबोधकक्रिया, *f.* (in Gram.) a desiderative verb.

इच्छाभोजन, *m.* desired food, choice food, food agreeable and abundant to the utmost desire.

इच्छामय, *m.* (*f.* ī) desirous, willing.

इच्छारूपी, voluntary, according to one's wish.

इच्छित, *m.* (*f.* ā) wished for, desired.

इच्छुक, wishful, desirous.

इछ in Chand = (probably) **इष्ट**, *q.v.*

इछुरस, *more prop.* **इक्षुरस**, *q.v.*

इज्तिनाब, *m.* abstinence, continence.

इज़्तिराब, *m.* agitation, perturbation, restlessness, anguish, trouble, chagrin.

इज़्तिरार, *m.* (*f.* ī) violence, constraint, agitation.

इजतिहाद, *m.* care, effort, diligence; (among Musalmāns) carrying on war against disbelievers in Muhammad.

इज़दहाम, *m.* a concourse, crowd.

इज़्न, *m.* permission; dismission.

इजमाल, *m.* an abstract, abridgment, compendium, synopsis, summary: joint occupancy or possession.

इजरा, *m.* execution, performance. —*k.* to perform, put into practice.

इज़राईल, *more prop.* **इस्राएल**, *q.v.*

इज़हार, *m.* demonstration; revealing, publication, evincing.

इजाज़त, *f.* commands, permission, dispensation, sanction.

इज़ाफ़त, *f.* an addition, adjunct, epithet: name of the sign of the genitive case in Persian.

इज़ाफ़ा, *m.* addition, augmentation, junction; attribute.

इजाज़त, *f.* consent, approbation.

इज़ार, *f.* trowsers, drawers.

इज़ारबन्द, *m.* the string with which drawers are tied.

इजारा, *m.* a farm: a privilege or income of variable amount sold or let for a fixed sum.

इजारादार, *m.* a farmer of land or of revenue; one who has purchased the labor of another; the holder of a monopoly.

इजारादारी, *f.* farming or contracting for rent or revenue.

इजालत, haste, speed: anticipation.

इज़्ज़त, *f.* grandeur, power, honor, respectability, glory.

इटली, *m.* (*f.* inī) an Italian.

इटले, *m. pr. n.* Italy.

इठलाना, *a. int.* to walk affectedly, walk coquettishly; to express tenderness or kindness by gestures.

इया } **इयी** } *see* **इन, इनी**.

इण्डिया, *m. pr. n.* the peninsula of India.

इण्डुआ, *m.* a kind of round cushion placed on the head in carrying burdens.

इण्डुई, *f.* a round ornament worn on the top of the head.

इत, 1, (correl. of उत) here, hither: 2, (in Gram.) as a suffix it forms many adjectives from substantives; *e. g.* आनन्दित (आनन्द), लज्जित (लज्जा), and from, the roots of verbs; *e. g.* विदित (विद).

इतक, so much, thus much, as much as this.

इतना, *m.* (*f.* ī) thus much, as much as this.

इतनीबेर, by this time, all this time.

इतने, *m.* (pl. of **इतना**) so many.

इतनेमें, in the meanwhile, meantime.

इतनौं, in Braj = **इतना**, *q. v.*

इतर, 1, affectation: 2, other, different, low, vile: 3, affected, acting affectedly, giving oneself airs; playful, gay, wanton, coquettish.

इतरदान, *m.* a perfume-box, scent-bottle.

इतरलोग, *m.* people of inferior caste, low people.

इतराना, *a. int.* to give oneself airs, act affectedly, behave in a non-natural or unusual manner.

इतराया, *m.* (*f.* **इतराई**), affected, playful, wanton, coquettish.

इतलाक़, *m.* a setting at liberty; divorcing; disengagedness: (in Law) the office and the records of summonses, also fees thereon.

इतलिया = **इटले**, *q. v.*

इतवार, *m.* Sunday.

इतहि, an emphatic form of **इत**, 1, *q. v.*

इता, now, at present.

इताअत, *f.* subjugation, obsequiousness, reverence, worshipping, obedience, submission.

इताब, *m.* reproach, rebuke, anger, displeasure.

इताल, now, at present.

इति, this much, thus much, so much. A very common use of this word is to place it at the end of books, sections, chapters, treatises, letters, and documents generally; in which case it has the same function as the word *finis* in English books, or "here endeth", "thus endeth" in reading.

इतिहास, *m.* history, annals, tradition, story, fable.

इतिहासकारक, *adj.* history-making: hence, *m.* (*f.* ikā) a historian, narrator.

इतिहासवेत्ता, *m.* (*f.* vettrī) a historian, professor of history: *lit.* learned in history.

इते, in Braj = (1) **इत** (2) **इतने**, *qq. v.*

इतेक, thus much, so much, so many.

इतेकमह } **इतेकमांह** } **इतेकमांहीं** } in Braj = **इतेकमें**, *q. v.*

इतेकमें, in the meanwhile, meantime.

इतो } **इत्ता** } *m.* (*f.* ī) in Braj = **इतना**, *q. v.*

इत्तिक़ा, *m.* the avoiding, shunning or abstaining from (vice); abstinence, piety.

इत्तिफ़ाक़, *m.* equality; friendship, concord, similarity of disposition; chance, fortune, accident, lot, success, incident, opportunity; probability.

इत्तिफ़ाक़न, accidentally, by chance.

इत्तिला, *f.* manifesting, informing, declaring, investigating: information, knowledge. — *k.* to acquaint, inform.

इत्तिसाफ़, *m.* description, qualification, excellence, praise.

इत्तिसाल, *m.* conjunction, adhesion, attachment, union, contiguity, neighbourhood.

इत्तिहाद, *m.* union, concord, intimate friendship.

इत्तिहाम, *m.* suspicion, censure; (in Law) a charge, imputation.

इत्ते = **इतने**, *q. v.*

इत्थं, thus, in this manner.

इत्मीनान, *m.* tranquillity, content, security, repose.

इत्यादि, (**इति** + **आदि**) and so forth, *et cetera*: *lit.* thus beginning, *i. e.* from this as a beginning.

इत्यादिक, appertaining to the rest.

इत्राया = **इतराया**, *q. v.*

इत्रीफल, *m.* an electuary composed of myrobalan with coriander-seed and honey.

इदं } **इदम** } this.

इदमित्थम } **इदमित्थ** } thus far.

इदर, (correl. of **उदर**) this way, hither, here.

इदराज, *m.* the inserting one thing in another.

इदरीस, *m. pr. n.* the prophet Enoch.

इदानीन्तनलोग, *m.* (pl.) the moderns, people of the present day.

इद्राक, *m.* understanding, comprehension.

इधर, (correl. of **उधर**) this way, hither, here.

इधरउधर, here and there, about, around, all about, up and down.

इन, 1, the base of the oblique cases of **वे** (pl. of **यह**): 2, in Braj = **इनने**: 3, as a suffix to substantives designating the occupations of men it gives epithets of the wives of those men or of females who follow those occupations; *e. g.* सोनारिन (सोनार), दुल्हिन (दुल्हा), धोबिन (धोबी): 4, as a termination of adjectival substantives it is in Sanskrit always masculine, but in Hindee sometimes masculine but most frequently feminine.

इनआम, *m.* a gift, present, prize.

इनइकास, *m.* the being turned upside-down; reflexion (from a mirror), repercussion, reverberation.

इनकर } dialectic forms = **इनका**.
इनकरा }

इनकराके, a dialectic form = **इन्हें**.

इनकरासें, a dialectic form = **इनसे**.

इनकरे, a dialectic form = **इनका**.

इनकार, *m.* a denial, disavowal, refusal. — *k.* (with genit. *m.* uninfl. of the object) to disavow, deny.

इनक़िज़ा, elapsed, fulfilled, finished, completed: hence, *m.* the expiration of a term.

इनक़ियाद, *m.* fidelity, obedience, submission, compliance.

इनक़िलाब, *m.* a vicissitude, revolution, alteration, change, inversion, transposition.

इनक़िसाम, *m.* a dividing, division.

इनकिसार, *m.* the being routed; humility, want of courage, despondency.

इनके, a dialectic form = **इन्हें**.

इनजील, *m.* (*f.* ?) the New Testament, the Gospel (Arabic form of the Greek term *Euangelion*).

इननि, in Braj = (1) **इनने** or **इन्होंने**; (2) **इनसे**.

इनफ़िसाल, *m.* a decision, termination of a cause; a settling, separation, division. — *k.* to settle, decide.

इनशा, *f.* writing, literary composition, elegance of style, the *belles lettres*.

इनसें, a dialectic form = **इनसे**.

इनसाफ़, *m.* the decision of a cause, equity, justice. — *k.* to decide a cause, administer justice.

इनायत, *f.* (pl. **इनायात**) a favor, gift, present.

इनी; very frequent in Hindee as a distinctively feminine termination, especially in the case of adjectives and adjectival substantives whose masculine form ends with *in* or with ई; *e. g.* पापिनी (पापी). If, however, this termination be preceded by a cerebral letter (ऋ, ॠ, र, ष) in the same word, the termination assumes the form **इणी**; *e. g.* **मश्क़ारिणी**, a female who writes an elegant hand.

इन्तिक़ाम, *m.* revenge, retaliation. — *lenā*, to take revenge.

इन्तिख़ाब, *m.* selection, picking; a making extracts from books; election, choice.

इन्तिज़ाम, *m.* disposition, arrangement, regularity, order, the dispensations of fate or Providence.

इन्तिज़ार, *m.* expectation. — *k.* to expect, be on the look out for.

इन्तिफ़ा, *m.* profit, advantage.

इन्तिशार, *m.* confusion, want of regularity, dispersion; explanation.

इन्तिहा, 1, *f.* an end, termination; a summit: 2, finished, completed; prohibited.

इन्दस, *m. pr. n.* the river Indus.

इन्दारा, *m.* a large well built of solid masonry.

इन्दिफ़ा, *m.* a warding off, repelling.

इन्दिया, *m. pr. n.* the peninsula of India.

इन्दिरा, *f. pr. n.* (in Myth.) the goddess of wealth.

इन्दिराज, *m.* the becoming extinct (as a family might); a being folded together; insertion.

इन्दु, *m.* the moon. In the ingenious system of reckoning by symbols adopted by Hindoos in their poetry, this word is a symbol for 1 (*one*).

इन्दुरेखा, *f.* a digit of the moon.

इन्दुवार, *m.* the day of the moon, *i. e.* Monday.

इन्दुर, *m.* a rat, a mouse.

इन्दौर, *m. pr. n.* a certain district of Rājputāna.

इन्द्र, *m. pr. n.* (*f.* āṇī) the regent of the visible heavens and king of the gods, the thunderer, the Jove of the Hindoo mythology. He is said to be renewed every fourteen epochs; and hence, in the ingenious system of reckoning by symbols adoped by Hindoos in their poetry, this word is a symbol for 14.

इन्द्रजाल, *m.* deception, magic, illusion, cheating, juggling; stratagem.

इन्द्रजालवत }
इन्द्रजालवन्त } *m.* (*f.* vatī) = **इन्द्रजाली**, *q. v.*
इन्द्रजालवान }

इन्द्रजाली, unreal, deceptive, illusive, magical: hence, *m.* (*f.* inī) a magician, conjuror, juggler, cheat.

इन्द्रजीत, *m.* thunder.

इन्द्रजौ = **इन्द्रयव**, *q. v.*

इन्द्रदमन, *m.* self-mortification, self-restraint.

इन्द्रद्वादशी, *f.* the twelfth day of the month Bhādra, a festival in honor of Indra.

इन्द्रद्युम्न, *m. pr. n.* a certain man with the patronymic *Bhāllaveya*.

इन्द्रनील, *m.* sapphire, emerald.

इन्द्रनीलक, *m.* an emerald.

इन्द्रपुरी, *f. pr. n.* the capital of Indra, and abode of the immortals.

इन्द्रप्रस्थ, *m. pr. n.* an ancient name of Delhi.

इन्द्रप्रोक्षिता, *f.* an epithet of the asterism *Pushya*.

इन्द्रवधू, *f.* the wife of Indra; a certain insect (it is a species of *acarus* of a scarlet colour, and like velvet).

इन्द्रयव, *m.* a certain medicinal seed (sparrow's tongue, *Nerium antidysentericum*) which grows on the plant *kardījā*.

इन्द्रलोक, *m. pr. n.* the abode of Indra, and paradise of the immortals.

इन्द्रसेन, *m. pr. n.* (1) of certain men (2) of a Nāg.

इन्द्राणी, *f.* a certain medicine or plant (*Vitex negundo*): *pr. n.* the wife of Indra.

इन्द्रायण, *f.* colocynth, wild gourd; a certain fruit (*Cucumis colocynthis*) of beautiful appearance but bitter taste: hence, *Indrāyaṇkā phal* is an epithet of any beautifnl but worthless person.

इन्द्रावण = **इन्द्रायण**, *q. v.*

इन्द्रासन, *m.* the throne of Indra.

इन्द्रिय, *m.* (see also **इन्द्री**) power, *semen virile*, any organ of sense.

इन्द्रियज्ञान, *m.* the faculty of perception, sense, consciousness.

इन्द्री, *f.* the senses (internal or external), the organs of action and of perception; *membrum virile; veretrum animalium;* the privities. The Hindoos reckon the organs of action to be the hand, the foot, the voice, the organ of generation and of excretion: those of perception, the mind, the eye, the ear, the tongue, and the skin.

इन्द्रीछिद्र, *m.* the word alludes to a practice of some Hindoo ascetics, *viz.* the piercing (and sometimes the excision) of the male organ. The act is regarded as a work of merit.

इन्द्रीजुलाब *m.* a purgative.

इन्धन, *m.* wood, grass, etc. used for fuel.

इन्स, *m.* mankind, the human race, men.

इन्सान, *m.* mankind, man.

इन्सानियत, *f.* humanity, humaneness, human kindness, affability.

इन्सिराम, *m.* completion, end.

इन्ह = **इन्हों**, *q.v.*

इन्हन, in Braj = **ये** and **इन्हों**, *qq.v.*

इन्हों; an inflective base of the oblique cases of the pl. of **यह**: see **इन**, and **उन्हों**.

इफ़तिख़ार, *m.* glory, honor, elegance, gracefulness.

इफ़तिरा, *f.* calumny, slander, false imputation.

इफ़रीत, *m.* anything frightful or horrifying, as a giant, demon, spectre, ogre.

इफ़लास, *m.* bankruptcy; penury, want.

इफ़शा, *m.* a divulging, publishing. [etc.

इफ़ाक़त, *f.* convalescence, recovery from a swoon,

इफ़ात, *m.* excess, superfluity.

इब; for any words beginning with this element but not given below, see under the form **इव**.

इब्न, *m.* a son, offspring, child.

इबरत, *f.* an example, warning; *met.* fear.

इबलाग़, *m.* a conveying, sending, causing to arrive.

इबलीस, *m. pr. n.* Satan.

इबहाम, 1, *m.* the thumb; suspicion, ambiguity, equivocalness: 2, covered, concealed, unknown.

इबादत, *f.* divine worship, adoration.

इबादतख़ाना, *m.* a place of worship.

इबारत, *f.* style (in writing), speech, dialect, idiom, word, phrase, trope, figure.

इब्तिज़ाल, *m.* vileness, meanness, servitude: carelessness in preserving anything.

इब्तिदा, *f.* beginning, commencement, exordium.

इब्तिसाम, *m.* cheerfulness, a smile.

इब्तिहाज, *m.* gladness, cheerfulness, alacrity.

इभ, *m.* (*f.* **इभ्या**) an elephant.

इभपालक, *m.* (*f.* ikā) the keeper of an elephant.

इम, 1. = **ऐसा**, *q.v.*: 2, it forms many adjectives when subjoined to the past participle passive; *e.g.* **कतिम (कम)**: also some superlatives; *e.g.* **अग्रिम (अग्र)**.

इमकान, *m.* possibility; contingent existence (as opposed to necessity or necessary existence).

इमदाद, *f.* an assisting, aiding, abetting; help; extending.

इमरती, 1. = **अमृती**, *q.v.*: 2. *f.* a kind of sweetmeat; a kind of cloth; a small vessel for drinking out of.

इमरोज़, to-day. [filling up, completing.

इमला, *m.* orthography, a writing correctly; a

इमलादान
उमलानवीस } one who writes correctly.

इमसाक, *m.* parsimony; abstinence; want, scarcity; a medicine taken to prolong pleasure.

इमसाल, this year.

इमान, *more prop.* **ईमान**, *q.v.*

इमाम, *m.* a priest, prelate, chief or leader in religious matters. [the sway of an Ameer.

इमारत, *f.* authority, dominion, a district under

इमि in Braj and in poetry = **ऐसा**.

इमें (*contraction*) = **इसमें**. See **इस**.

इम्तिदाद, *m.* protraction, extension, prorogation.

इम्तिना, *m.* restraint, prohibition.

इम्तियाज़, *m.* discrimination, distinction, separation; preëminence; good breeding. [temptation.

इम्तिहान, *m.* examination, proof, trial, experiment,

इम्मानुएल, *m. pr. n.* Immanuel: *lit.* God (is) with us.

इम्लाक, *m.* (pl. of **मुल्क**) possessions, landed properties. [and its fruit.

इम्लि, *m.* the tamarind-tree (*Tamarindos Indica*)

इम्ली = **इम्लि**, *q.v.*

इय; a suffix (*m.* [*f.* ā]) forming some adjectives from substantives; *e.g.* **समुद्रिय (समुद्र)**.

इया; a suffix forming (1) some masculine nouns of agency from nouns and verbal roots; *e.g.* **अकृतिया (अकृत)**; **जड़िया (जड़ना)**; (2) some diminutives; *e.g.* **अम्बिया (आम्ब)**; (3) some adjectives from substantives; *e.g.* **झांझिया (झांझ)**.

इयां; the uniform termination of the nominative plural of feminine nouns ending in long *i*; *e.g.* **स्त्रियां (स्त्री)**.

इयो; termination of the mild or hortative form of the imperative mode; *e.g.* **देखियो, पाइयो**.

इरफ़ान, *m.* discernment, wisdom, knowledge, [science.

इरसि
इरसी
इरिस } *f.* the axle of a wheel, an axletree.

इर्तिकाब, *m.* perpetration or commission of a crime; commencement or undertaking of an enterprize. [refusing.

इर्तिदाद, *m.* a recantation, apostasy; an opposing,

इर्तिफ़ा, *m.* an elevation, ascent, exaltation, height, grandeur, prosperity.

इर्तिबात, *m.* friendship; connection.

इर्शाद, *m.* a command, order. Frequently used

by an inferior as a respectful interrogation. "What is your pleasure?"

इर्स = इरसी, *q. v.*

इर्साल, *m.* a mission, the act of sending (*esp.* a letter, etc.): (in Rev.) monthly collections of rents, etc. forwarded to head-quarters by the subordinate revenue authorities. [design, intention, plan.

इरादत, *f.* desire, inclination, wish, purpose,

इरादा, *m.* = इरादत, *q. v.*

इल, 1, an Unādi suffix by means of which some nouns are formed from verbal roots; *e. g.* अनिल, from Rt. अन्, to breathe, etc.: 2, as a Taddhita suffix [*m.* (*f.* ā)] it is suffixed to some primitive words to form possessive adjectives; *e. g.* पंकिल, from पंक; शार्करिल, from शर्करा.

इलज़ाम, *m.* blame, reproach, conviction.—*denā*,

इलझना = उलझना, *q. v.* [to blame, reproach.

इलतिज़ाम, *m.* a being necessary or expedient; a being assiduous, the taking upon oneself.

इलतिफ़ात, *f.* friendship, kindness, obligation, courtesy, respect: (in Rhetoric) an apostrophe.

इलतिमास, *m.* a beseeching, supplicating, petitioning; a prayer, request. — *k.* (with abl.) to beseech.

इल्म, *m.* science, knowledge, learning.

इलया = इलीश, *q. v.*

इलहाम, *m.* inspiration, revelation.

इला, *f.* See इल, 2.

इलाइची = इलाची, *q. v.*

इलाक़ा, *m.* relation, connection, interest, sphere of operation, right, pretension; communication, commerce. [thread.

इलाचा, *m.* a kind of cloth woven of silk and

इलाची, *f.* large cardamoms. — *bāṇṭnā*, to distribute cardamoms (a kind of wedding ceremony).

इलाचीडोरा, a capsule of cardamoms.

इलाचीदाने, a kind of sweetmeat.

इलाचीपपड़ू, a kind of wild fruit.

इलाचीबोयडा, *m.* a capsule of cardamoms.

इलायचा = इलाचा, *q. v.*

इलायची }
इलायची } = इलाची, *q. v.*

इलावृत, *m. pr. n.* one of the nine divisions of the world comprehending the highest and most centrical

इलाहाबाद, *m. pr. n.* Allahabad. [part of Asia.

इलिया = एलियाह, *q. v.*

इलिशा, *more prop.* इलीश, *q. v.*

इलीश, *m.* a certain Indian fish (*Clupea alosa*), the hilsa or sable (much esteemed for the table).

इलीशा, *m. pr. n.* the prophet Elisha. [unless.

इल्ला, 1, *m.* a wart: 2, besides, except, otherwise,

इल्लिश = इलीश, *q. v.* [way, almost, scarcely.

इव, thus, like, in like manner as; as; in some

इब्रानी, Hebrew, Jewish: hence (1) *m.* (*f.* inī) a Jew (2) *f.* the Hebrew language.

इब्राहीम, *m. pr. n.* the patriarch Abraham.

इब्री = इब्रानी, *q. v.* [or language.

इब्रीय, Hebrew, appertaining to the Jewish race

इश्क़, *m.* love.

इश्कालना, *t.* to deceive, tempt, delude, wheedle.

इशरत, *f.* society, pleasant and familiar converse; pleasure, delight, enjoyment.

इशा, *f.* the first watch of the night; the prayers said when retiring to rest.

इशारत, *f.* a sign, wink, hint, beck, command.

इशारा, *m.* = इशारत, *q. v.*

इश्तयाक़, *m.* wish, desire, strong inclination.

इश्तिरा, *m.* buying and selling, commerce.

इश्तिहार, *m.* a publishing, divulging; fame, renown, report, rumour: preface, advertisement, notification, notice.

इश्लोक, *more properly* श्लोक, *q. v.* See इ, 5.

इषनौं in Chand = to see.

इष्ट, *m.* (*f.* ā) anything worshipped, a god, a deity; a beloved person, an object of desire: *lit.* desired, wished-for, approved, cherished, beloved; reverenced, worshipped. [loved, most desired.

इष्टतम, (superlative of the above) dearest, best

इष्टतर, (comparative form) dearer, more loved, more desired. [pect, reverence.

इष्टत्व, *m.* (*f.* tā) desirableness, belovedness; res-

इष्टदेव, *m.* (*f.* ī) one's own chosen deity.

इष्टि, *f.* sacrificing; sacrifice; a sacrificial pile.

इस; the base of the oblique cases of the singular of the nearer demonstrative यह.

इसकारण, from this cause, on this account.

इसकेकारण, on account of this, because of this.

इसगन्ध = असगन्ध, *q. v.*

इसघड़ी, this once, for this time.

इसदार, *m.* producing, appearing, issuing.

इसपात, *m.* steel of a tough kind.

इसरार, the act of concealing, keeping secret: also, the divulging a secret, disclosure.

इसहाक़, *m. pr. n.* the patriarch Isaac.

इसाई = ईसाई, *q. v.*

इसारा, *more prop.* इशारा, *q. v.*

इसावल, *m.* a pursuivant.

इसकन्दर, *m. pr. n.* Alexander the Great.

इस्कन्ध, *more prop.* स्कन्ध, *q. v.* See इ, 5.

इस्तबल, *m.* a stablo. [ing, invitation.

इस्तदुआ, *f.* a request, desire, petition, entreat-

इस्तम्प, *m.* (Engl.) a stamp (generally applied to the stamp affixed to legal or Government documents).

इस्तम्पकाग़ज़, *m.* stamped paper (generally applied to paper bearing a legal or Government stamp).

इस्तम्बोल, *m. pr. n.* the city of Constantinople.

इस्तम्भ, *more prop.* स्तम्भ, *q. v.* See इ, 5.

इस्तादा, standing, set up, erected; hence, *m.* a

pole, ensign-staff, etc., a prop for supporting the door of a tent (but not applied to the tent-pole).

इस्तिआरा, *m.* a borrowing, using a word metaphorically; a metaphor. — *k.* to beseech, beg earnestly.

इस्तिख़राज, *m.* expulsion; drawing forth, extracting.

इस्तिख़लास, *m.* a desiring to liberate; liberty.

इस्तिज़हार, *m.* an imploring assistance; a remembering, calling to remembrance.

इस्तिताअत, *f.* power, possibility; dependence, a submitting to.

इस्तिहक़ाक़, *m.* a demanding justice; merit; ability; (in Law) a claim of right preferred by others to the subject of a sale.

इस्तिहकाम, *m.* confirmation, firmness, strength.

इस्तिहज़ार, *m.* a calling, citing to appear, summoning.

इस्तीफ़ा, *m.* a satisfying completely; the paying or receiving the whole of what is due; a relinquishing (as business or a situation).

इस्तीसाल, *m.* a destroying, eradicating.

इस्त्री, 1, *more prop.* **स्त्री**, *q.v.* (see **इ**, 5.) : 2, *m.* a smoothing-iron. — *k.* to iron, smoothe with a heated iron.

इस्त्रीवाला, *m.* (*f.* ī) a person who irons linen.

इस्थ, for words beginning with this element see under the more proper form **स्थ**.

इस्पर, upon this, hereupon.

इस्परमूल, *m.* a certain plant (*Aristolochia Indica*) said to be an antidote to snake-bites.

इस्फ़ंज, *m.* sponge.

इस्पृहा, *more prop.* **स्पृहा**, *q.v.* See **इ**, 5.

इस्पहान, *pr. n.* Ispahan (till recently the capital of Persia).

इस्म, *m.* a name; (in Gram.) a noun or substantive.

इस्मृति, *more properly* **स्मृति**, *q.v.* See **इ**, 5.

इस्राएल, *m. pr. n.* Israel, the patriarch Jacob.

इस्राएली, *m.* (*f.* inī) an Israelite: *lit.* appertaining to Israel, Israelitish, Jewish.

इस्राफ़, *m.* prodigality, dissipation, abuse of wealth, extravagance, ruin.

इस्लाम, *m.* the religion of Muhammad, orthodoxy in the Muhammadan sense.

इस्वी = (1) **ईसाई** (2) **यीश्वी**, *qq.v.*

इससे (abl. sing. of **यह**) from this, on this account, hereupon, wherefore, therefore.

इह, 1, = **यह**, *q.v.*: 2, here, in this place, in this present world.

इहकाल, *m.* this present life, this time state.

इहज़ार, *m.* the act of causing to appear or of calling; a summons.

इहतिमाम, *f.* diligence, solicitude, anxiety, care; inspection, superintendence; a subdivision of a province.

इहतिमाल, *m.* the act of bearing or supporting: doubt, uncertainty, probability. — *honā*, to be probable. — *k.* to doubt, impute.

इहतियात, *f.* caution, circumspection, scrupulousness, foresight.

इहतिराज़, *m.* abstinence, self-restraint, regimen.

इहतिशाम, *m.* having many followers, etc.; pomp, magnificence, retinue.

इहतिसाब, *m.* the making up accounts; the censorship of weights and measures.

इहमाल, *m.* negligence, inadvertence, carelessness, inattention, delay, indolence.

इहलोक, *m.* this present world.

इहवां, a dialectic form of **यहां**, *q.v.*

इहसान, *m.* beneficence, kindness, courtesy. — *k.* to oblige, confer favors, patronize.

इहां, a corruption of **यहां**, *q.v.*

इहाता, *f.* a surrounding; circumference; besieging; a "compound," park.

इहानत, *f.* contempt, disdain, enmity, affront, insult.

इहामुत्र, here and there; in this world and in the next.

इहिं, (*poet.*) = **यहीं**, *q.v.*

इही, (*poet.*) = **यही**, *q.v.*

इहीथान, 1. *m.* this very place: 2. in this very place. (More prop. *yihī sthān: isī sthānmeṅ.*)

इहे, 1, = **इही**, *q.v.*: 2, dialectic form = **ये**, these.

इहें = **इहैं**, *q.v.*

इहै, (pl. **इहैं**); in poetry and in Braj this is the termination of the 2nd and 3rd persons singular of the future tense = *egā*; e. g. **करिहै** = **करेगा**.

इहो, in poetry and in Braj, this is the termination of the 2nd pers. pl. fut.; *e. g.* **पाइहो** = **पाओगे**.

इहौं, in poetry and in Braj, this is the termination of the 1st pers. sing. fut.; *e. g.* **देखिहौं** = **देखुंगा**.

ई

ई (ī) is the fourth vowel in the Hindee or Devanāgaree alphabet, and has the following characteristics and functions: — 1, In pronunciation it has invariably the sound of long *i* in the English word 'police' or of *ee* in 'meek'; *never* that of long *i* in 'kite.' 2, When it occurs as a medial or final letter, *i. e.* when it is in any other situation than at the beginning of a word or syllable, its form is **ी**. Unlike **ि**, this form invariably appears at the right of the letter after which it is to be sounded. 3, In all modes and tenses of verbs, as also in all participles and adjectives, whose masculine form ends in long *a*, this letter, displacing the long *a*, is the sign of the feminine gender: see, however, article **आ**, 14 and 20. 4, It is very common as a particle of emphasis, and so used, it is put at the end of the word it emphasizes; *e. g.* **यही**: if, however, the word it emphasizes be in an oblique case it is generally inserted between the inflective base and the case-sign; *e. g.* **इसीका** (*gen.* of **यही**). 5, It is often (but more especially in poetry), used at the end of the conjunctive participle of verbs whose root ends with a vowel; and where we should therefore expect either **य** or, more properly, nothing excepting the root of the verb (**आ**, 7,); *e. g.* **जाई** often **जाय**, but more properly **जा**. 6, In keeping with the last remark it is proper to observe that **ई** and **य** are often, though inaccurately and needlessly, interchanged; *e. g.* **उपाई**, more properly उपाय. 7, Frequently, in the corrupt speech of the people, and in books not carefully written, and, again, in poetry for the purpose of metre, the feminine form of the past passive participle (ending, of course, with this letter) is used where we might expect the masculine form. 8, It is often used as the sign of the feminine of the past passive participle and of the singular of the feminine of the Historical Tenses of verbs whose root ends in a vowel, this vowel being dropped or represented by short *i*; *e. g.* दई, लई; more generally दिई, लिई: in such case this letter is often inaccurately printed in its secondary form; *e. g.* दी, ली. 9, When this letter stands alone in a sentence it is an interjection of regret, anger, or compassion: it is also used in calling. 10, Added to masculine substantives ending with consonants it frequently yields the corresponding feminine ones; *e. g.* कुकुरी (कुकुर). 11, In the case of some adjectives whose masculine form ends in a consonant, this letter, added, forms the feminine; *e. g.* सुन्दरी (सुन्दर). 12, Displacing आ at the end of substantives, it commonly yields the diminutive form; *e. g.* पोथी (पोथा). 13, It is commonly used for forming abstract substantives feminine from adjectives by being added to the masculine form of them ending in आ; *e. g.* उंचाई (उंचा). 14, It is frequently added to abstract substantives ending in आ; importing, presumably, some such refined distinction as might be supposed to exist between many English words ending in *tion* as distinguished from those ending in *ness*; *e. g.* consideration, considerateness; adaptation, adaptedness; cold, coldness; wonder, wonderfulness; आधीनता, submission, आधीनताई, submissiveness. 15, In the case of nearly all substantives which end with this letter, unless they be adjectival ones, it is the distinguishing mark of their being feminine In the case, however, of adjectival substantives this is the sign of the masculine: the feminine of such ends most commonly in *ini*. 16, It is often used for forming masculine adjectives and masculine adjectival substantives from substantives ending in a consonant; *e. g.* ऊनी (ऊन); रोगी (रोग); कोढ़ी (कोढ़); भागी (भाग). In like manner this letter is suffixed to a very large number of substantives in Hindee, thus forming adjectives which signify 'appertaining to', 'possessed of', 'abounding in'. 'consisting of' the thing indicated by the substantive; like the letter *y* in many adjectives in English; *e. g.* rainy, snowy, lucky, wealthy (धनी). It should be carefully marked, however, that inasmuch as in Hindee it is very seldom indeed that the feminine form of the adjective is used to agree with a feminine substantive, excepting in the case of those adjectives which in the masculine end in long *a*, adjectives ending in long *i* qualify substantives of either gender. The distinctively feminine forms of adjectives are adopted when the adjectives are used substantively: even here, however, it is not at all unusual to make the masculine form do service for the feminine; just as in English the terms 'author'. 'proprietor', are sometimes used where 'authoress' or 'proprietress' would be the more appropriate term. Of all this, one example may suffice; — पापी means sinful', and qualifies *purush* in the phrase पापी पुरुष (a sinful man); but it also qualifies *stri* in the expression पापी स्त्री (a sinful woman): पापिनी स्त्री is not Hindee; but पापिनी (alone) means a female sinner, and पापी, of course, a male sinner, and it may even be used to designate a female sinner too. 17, This letter sometimes serves to distinguish a vocation from those who follow it; *e. g.* ठगी (ठग). 18, Sometimes it imports the idea of money; *e.g.* कतराई (कतरा), खुराकी (खुराक). 19, It is frequently put inaccurately for इ especially at the beginning of words; *e.g.* ईतर, more properly इतर. 20, In the case of those adjectives whose masculine form ends in *āyā*, this letter, supplanting *yā*, yields the feminine form; *e. g.* पराई (*m.* पराया): this same observation applies to past passive participles similarly formed; *e. g.* अनपाई (*m.* अनपाया). 21, In Braj this letter is used in the Historical Tense for either gender; *e. g.* राजा कही (= राजाने कहा). 22, It sometimes forms feminine substantives from masculine ones by displacing आ; *e. g.* घोड़ी (घोड़ा). 23, In words from the Arabic or Persian this letter with a dot under it represents *'aīn* followed by *yā* or *yi* with *kasra* or *zer* written under; *e. g.* ईसा. 24, This letter is often inaccurately put for ए or for य; *e. g.* जाई, more properly जाए (3rd pers. sing. aor. of जाना), also written जाय. 25, As a suffix this letter sometimes forms patronymics; *e. g.* रामानन्दी (रामानन्द). 26, It occasionally forms feminine substantives from masculine ones by taking the place of the short *i* of the masculine: *e. g.* ऋषी (*m.* ऋषि). 27, This letter sometimes distinguishes the workman from his tool; *e. g.* करान्ती (करान्त). 28, Sometimes it distinguishes an instrument from the use to which it is applied; *e. g.* वेधनी (वधन). 29, Occasionally it serves to distinguish between a tree and its produce; *e. g.* कर्पासी (कर्पास). 30, It sometimes, also, distinguishes between an agent and his status, and his business, and his place of business; *e. g.* कोतवाली (कोतवाल). 31, Sometimes it is added or rescinded without affecting the gender; *e g.* मुण्डेरी, लतरी, खटली, etc. 32, n poetry this. like all the other long vowels, is, in all situations, *long by nature*. 33, In the formation of many compound words this letter exercises important functions which will be found carefully specified at length in any good Hindee or Sanskrit [Grammar.

ईंगुर, *m.* red lead, minium, cinnabar.

ईंच = ऐंच, *q. v.*

ईंचना, *t.* to draw, pull, attract.

ईंट; see under the form ईंयट.

ईकार, *m.* the letter ई, or any symbol that may [represent it.

ईकारान्त, (in Gram.) ending with ई.

ईक्षण, *m.* the eye; the power or the act of seeing; sight; care, superintendence.

ईक्षणिक, *m.* (*f.* ई) a fortune-teller.

ईखुमती, *f. pr. n.* a certain river in Bengal, the [Issamutty.

ईख, *f.* sugar-cane. See ऊख.

ईखराज, *m.* the day on which the planting of the sugar-cane commences (generally attended with festive ceremonies).

ईज़ा, *f.* pain, trouble, affliction, vexation, distress.

ईजाद, 1, *m.* an invention: 2, invented. — *k.* to invent.

ईजाब, *m.* a rendering necessary: (in Logic) affirmation as opposed to privation: (in Muhammadan Law) the first proposal made by one of the parties in negotiating or concluding a bargain.

ईट = **ईंट**, *q. v.*

ईठी, *f.* a spear, lance; the "cat" in boys' play.

ईठीदाण्डू, the ball and the crooked stick in the game of *chaugān*.

ईंठ, see (1) **ईंट** (2) **इष्ट**.

ईंट, *f.* a brick.

ईंटकारी } *f.* brick-work.
ईंटगारी }

ईंटवाला, *m.* (*f.* ī) a maker or a vendor of bricks.

ईंटाया, *m.* (*f.* **ईंटाई**) a species of dove.

ईंठ, *more properly* **ईंट**, *q. v.*

ईंडुआ = **इंडुआ**, *q. v.*

ईतर, *more properly* **इतर**, *q. v.*

ईता, *m.* (*f.* ī) in Braj = **इतना**, *q. v.*

ईताल, now, at present.

ईति, the seasons: *see* **ऋतु**.

ईतिलाफ, *m.* familiarity, friendship, society, company, connexion, correspondence.

ईतेकु, *more properly* **इतेक**, *q. v.*

ईदृश, thus, like this, such.

ईधर, *more properly* **इधर**, *q. v.*

ईनू } this; these.
ईना }

ईन्दूर, *more properly* **इन्दूर**, *q. v.*

ईन्धन, *more properly* **इन्धन**, *q. v.*

ईप्सित, *m.* (*f.* ā) longed-for, wished-for.

ईफ़ा, *m.* the performing a promise, paying, satisfying. — *k.* to make good, perform.

ईमन, a kind of metre in Hindee versification.

ईमा, *m.* a sign, nod, wink (indicating departure); an emblem; a symptom.

ईमान, *m.* faith, belief, religion, conscience. —*lānā*, (with *par*) to believe on. — *honā*, to be on oath.

ईमानदार, believing, faithful, trusty, true.

ईमानवाला, *m.* (*f.* ī) a believer, a trusty person.

ईय, *m.* (*f.* **ईया**) a Taddhita suffix with which a large number of adjectives in Hindee are formed. It imports the idea of (1) needing or requiring (2) capable of or suited for (3) worthy of: — the whole of which meanings are expressed in the English phrase 'to be'; *e. g.* **प्रशंसनीय**, to be commended or praised. [*i. e.* praiseworthy.

ईरान, *pr. n.* Persia.

ईरावत, *more prop.* **ऐरावत**, *q. v.*

ईर्खा, a provincial spelling of **ईर्षा**, *q.v.*

ईर्षा, *f.* envy, jealousy, spite, emulation.

ईर्षालु, *m.* or *f.* envious, jealous, spiteful.

ईलम, *m.* an auction or public sale. —*ḍālnā,* to sell by auction.

ईला, (in Gram.) as a suffix to substantives forms some adjectives; *e. g.* **सजीला (सज)**.

ईला, swearing; (in Muhammadan Law) a vow to abstain from carnal knowledge of a wife for four months, the fulfilment of which is equivalent to a divorce.

ईलाम, *more prop.* **ईलम**, *q. v.*

ईलीसा, *more prop.* **इलीशा**, *q. v.*

ईश, *m.* (*f.* ā) a ruler, master, lord, supreme; hence, an epithet (1) of the Supreme Being (2) of Shiv, regent of the north-west quarter (3) of the eleven inferior manifestations of Shiv: hence, in the ingenious system of reckoning by symbols adopted by Hindoos in their poetry, this word is a symbol for 11 (eleven).

ईशन, *m.* (see **न**, 6) a Braj pl. of **ईश**.

ईशा, *f.* 1, (see **ईश**) a governess, mistress, etc.: 2, the beam or pole of a car or of a plough.

ईशान, 1, *m.* (*f.* ī) *adj.* ruling: 2, *m.* light, splendour: 3, *m.* an epithet of the Deity or of Shiv.

ईशानकोण, *m.* an epithet of the North-east quarter.

ईशानी, *f.* (*m.* **ईशान**) an epithet of Durgā.

ईशिता, *f.* = **ईशित्व**, *q. v.*

ईशितृ, *m.* (*f.* trī) a ruler, master, owner, king.

ईशित्व, *m.* superiority, supremacy, lordship, one of the eight attributes of the Deity.

ईश्वर, *m.* (*f.* ā *or* ī) a ruler, lord, owner, king, husband; the Supreme Being; a name of Shiv: a name of Kāmdev.

ईश्वरत्व, *m.* (*f.* tā) supremacy, lordship; divineness of nature, divinity, Godhead, Godship.

ईश्वरभक्त, *m.* (*f.* ā) a worshipper of God, a pious person.

ईश्वरभाव, *m.* the divine nature.

ईश्वरस्मरणस्थान, *m.* any place used for the purpose of the worship of God, a temple, mosque, church.

ईश्वरय; see **ईश्वरीय**.

ईश्वरवाणी, *f.* the voice of God, revelation, inspiration, oracle.

ईश्वरा = **ईश्वरी**, *q. v.*

ईश्वरांश, *m.* a part of God. Applied as an epithet to created objects, *esp.* to animals.

ईश्वरांशी, *m.* (*f.* inī) an epithet of any one possessing special divine endowments.

ईश्वराधीन, *m.* (*f.* ā) subject to or dependent on God.

ईश्वराधीनता, *f.* subjection to God, dependence on God.

ईश्वराराधना, *f.* the worship of God.

ईश्वरावेश, *m.* absorption into the Deity.

ईश्वरी, *f.* (see **ईश्वर**) a mistress, queen, goddess; a name of Durgā, Lakshmee, Saraswatee, or any other of the *Saktis* or female energies of the deities.

ईश्वरीय, appertaining to deity, divine, godlike.

ईषणा, *f.* desire, inclination, choice.

ईषत, a little, somewhat, slightly.

ईस; for all words beginning with this element but not given below, see under the form **ईश**.

ईसा, *m. pr. n.* the most usual form of the word 'Jesus.' **योशु** might probably be a preferable form.

ईसाई, appertaining to the Lord Jesus Christ, or to the Christian religion: hence, *m.* (*f.* in *or* inī) a Christian.

ईसाल, *m.* a winged white ant.

ईस्वी = (1) **ईसाई** (2) **यीश्वी**, *qq.v.*

ईह, *more properly* **यह**, *q.v.*

ईहा, *f.* desire; attempt, exertion, energy.

ईहां, a very com. corruption of **यहां**, *q.v.*

उ

उ (u) is the fifth vowel in the Hindee or Devanāgaree alphabet, and has the following characteristics and functions: — 1, It has in pronunciation the short sound of *u* in the English word 'pull'; *never* that of *u* in 'usage.' 2, Its medial and final form somewhat resembles that of the English comma, and is always written under the letter which it follows in pronunciation: when, however, it follows the letter **र** its form and position are special: all these facts are illustrated in the word **कुमेरु**. When it follows **ह** there is an option; *e. g.* **हु** = **हु** or **हु**. 3, When it occurs at the end of a word the natives of India for the most part make it inaudible or nearly so; thus **कृपालु** is oftener pronounced *kripāl* than *kripālu*: an exception to this remark is seen, of course, in the case of monosyllabic words; *e. g.* **मुंह**. 4, It is very common in Hindee as an *Uṇādi* suffix; *e. g.* **चाकु**. 5, It is used as an interjection implying anger, doubt, calling, command, or respectful address. 6, Words properly beginning with this letter are often inaccurately spelt with **ऊ**, and *vice versâ*. 7, It is frequently interchanged inaccurately with **व**, *e.g.* **तरउ**, more properly **तरु**; **भाउ**, more properly **भाव**; and with **श्र**, *e. g.* **उड़ाड़**, more properly **श्रड़ाड़**. 8, When found in this Dictionary with a dot under it, it represents *'ain* with *zamma* or *pesh*. 9, This letter is sometimes, and especially in Braj, found at the end of a word where we should ordinarily expect **भी**, even, also, both. 10, It is sometimes (especially in Braj) found as a sign of the imperative mode as in Sanskrit; *e. g.* **मानु**, more commonly **मानो** (**मानना**). 11, It is often put by corruption for **श्रो**; *e. g.* **लेउगे**, more properly **लेश्रोगे** (**लेना**): **का करु** = **क्या करो**. 12, In Braj this letter is the termination of the present participle for each person, number, and gender; *e. g.* **चलतु** = **चलता, चलती, चलते**. 13, This letter is one of the epithets of Shiv: see **श्रोम**. 14, In poetry, this is, like the other short vowels, *short by nature*, whether it be used separately or joined to a consonant: when, however, it occurs before a compound consonant whether in the same word with it or in the one that follows, it becomes, like them, *long by position*. 15, In the case of those adjectives in Hindee which end with this letter, the form for both genders is the same; *e. g.* **द्विधातु**, *m.* or *f.* Such adjectives are formed by prefixing some word or particle to a substantive ending in **उ**. In Sanskrit this letter would be lengthened into **ऊ** or exchanged for **वी** in the feminine, but these changes are extremly rare in Hindee. 16, In the formation of some compound words, this letter, like the other vowels, discharges important functions which will be found carefully specified at length in any good Hindee or Sanskrit Grammar.

उश्रना, *a. int.* to rise (said of the sun).

उश्रा; this element is frequently found at the end of words in the Bhojpuri dialect: it is, most probably, merely a jingling termination, and has the effect of shortening a vowel that precedes it in the same word; *e. g.* **श्रमुश्रा** = **श्राम**: also **बेटुश्रा** = **बेटा**; **घरुश्रा** = **घर**; **घसुश्रा** = **घांस**.

उं, an interjection expressive of anger, contempt, or interrogation. [probation, anger, or compassion.

उः, an interjection expressive of surprize, ap-

उऋण = **उरिण**, *q.v.*

उंगन, *m.* = **उंगनी**, *q.v.*

उंगनी, *f.* dozing, drowsiness (from opium, etc.); the greasing a wheel to set it asleep, *i. e.* to prevent it creaking.

उंगल, *more prop.* **श्रंगुल**, *q.v.* } see **उ**, 7.
उंगली, *more prop.* **श्रंगुली**, *q.v.* }

उंच = **उंचा**, *q.v.*

उंचकाना, *more com.* **उचकाना**, *q.v.*

उंचनीच, 1, uneven, high and low; *hence*, 2, inequality, the ups and downs of life, vicissitude: particulars.

उंचा, *m.* (*f.* ī) high, lofty, tall, steep, loud. — *k.* to exalt, elevate, raise. — *bol bolnā*, to speak loudly or proudly. — *sunnā*, to be hard of hearing. *Unche bolkā muṅh nichā*, the proud ones are brought down.

उंचाई, *f.* height, elevation, exaltation, eminence, tallness, steepness.

उंचाउ, *m.* in Braj = **उंचाव** = **उंचाई**, *q.v.*

उंचाकानी, *f.* dullness of hearing, deafness.

उंचान, *m* = **उंचाई**, *q.v.*

उंचाना, *t.* to take up, raise, exalt, elevate.

उंचाव, *m.* in Braj = **उंचाई**, *q.v.*

उंचास, 1, *f.* = **उंचाई**; 2, = **उनचास**, *qq.v.*

उंचाहट, *f.* = **उंचाई**, *q.v.*

उंजिश्राला } *m.* (*f.* ī) = **उजियाला**, *q.v.*
उंजियाला }

उक, (in Gram.) as a suffix, sometimes forms adjectives and adjectival participles from substantives; *e. g.* **इच्छुक** (**इच्छा**); **भिक्षुक** (**भिक्षा**).

उकट, a contrivance, invention. [unearthed.

उकटना, 1, = **उकटाना**, *q.v.*: 2, *n.* to be dug up, be

उकटाना, *t.* to dig up slowly anything buried in the ground, to unearth, to extract a secret gradually and artfully, to pump.

उकडू, *m.* the posture of sitting on the hams with the soles of the feet on the ground.

उकत = (1) **उक्त** (2) **उक्ति**, *qq.v.*

उकताना, *n.* to be melancholy, be dejected, to fret, to be out of humour with, be tired of, to tire.

उकतारना, *t.* to promote, forward, abet.

उकताक, *m.* or *f.* a promoter, abettor, instigator.

उकना = **ऊकना**, *q.v.* [next or future world.

उक़बा, *m.* end, conclusion, accomplishment; the

उकर, a dialectic form = **उसका**.

उकराके, a dialectic form = **उसे**.

उकलना, *a. int.* to boil.

उकलेसर, *m. pr. n.* a certain town in southern India famous for its paper manufacture.

उकलेसरी, *m.* (*f.* iṇī) appertaining to *Uklesar*.

उकसना, to be excited, be moved: to try to move.

उकसाना, *t.* to excite, instigate, arouse, move; to trim (as a lamp).

उक़ाब, *m.* an eagle.

उकार, *m.* the letter उ, or any symbol that may represent it.

उकारान्त, (in Gram.) ending with उ.

उकालना, *t.* to boil water.

उकेलना, *t.* to turn up.

उक्त, *m.* (*f.* ā) spoken, aforesaid, above-mentioned, the said (used in law documents).

उक्ति, *f.* a speaking, speech, voice, language; a contrivance, invention. — *banānā*, to make up a story, fabricate, invent, contrive. — *lenā*, to discover, find out.

उखटना, *a. int.* to trip, stumble.

उखड़ना, *n.* to be rooted up, be plucked up, be raised up: *a. int.* to slip out (as a bone, etc).

उखड़नापुखड़ना, *n.* to be rooted up, be plucked up.

उखड़ाना, *more prop.* **उखाड़ना**, *q.v.*

उखम (*colloquial*) = **उष्म**, *q.v.*

उखमज (*colloquial*) = **उष्मज**, *q.v.*

उखल, *m.* a wooden mortar for pounding rice or other grain.

उखली, *f.* = **उखल**, *q.v.*

उखाड़, *f.* a rooting up, extirpation.

उखाड़ना, *t.* to root up, pluck up, break up, extirpate, eradicate; to dislocate.

उखाड़ू, *m.* or *f.* one who uproots.

उखारना, *more prop.* **उखाड़ना**, *q.v.*

उखाल, *m.* a vomiting; an emetic.

उखालना, *a. int.* to vomit, spue.

उखालपुखाल, *m.* violent vomiting, *cholera morbus*.

उखेड़ना = **उखाड़ना**, *q.v.*

उखेड़वाना, *t.* to cause to root up.

उगटना, to revile, give abusive language.

उगत, a growing, springing up; production.

उगना, *a. int.* to grow, spring (as plants); to rise (as the moon). *Ugtehi jal jānā*, to wither immediately on springing up (said of a hope or expectation which is blasted in the very bud).

उगलना, *t.* to spit out, vomit forth; *met.* to refund property surreptitiously obtained, to disgorge it.

उगसाना, *t.* to snuff a candle, trim a lamp.

उगाना, *t.* to cause to grow, to raise (as plants).

उगाल, *m.* that which is spit out after chewing anything (*esp.* betel leaf). *Apkā ugāl merā adhār*, you, Sir, are my support and benefactor; *lit.* Your Worship's leavings are my nourishment.

उगालदान, *m.* a spittoon, spitting-pot.

उगाहना, *t.* to collect, gather, accumulate.

उगाही, *f.* usury; the trade of lending money on interest of one fourth part, the payment of which is received by instalments.

उगिलना, *more prop.* **उगलना**, *q.v.*

उगुम, *adj.* growing; becoming.

उग्र, 1, *m.* anger, wrath: 2, *m.* (*f.* ā) strong, rigorous, wrathful, cruel, savage, terrible; an epithet of Shiv; the name of a mixed tribe, the offspring of a Kshatriya by a Shoodrā woman. The employment of this tribe is to kill animals that live in holes.

उग्रशर्मा, *m. pr. n.* a certain ancient Hindoo sage.

उग्रसेन, *m. pr. n.* (1) of a certain king (2) of several princes.

उग्रा, *f.* (*m.* **उग्र**) a female of the *Ugra* tribe.

उघड़ना, *n.* to be uncovered, be opened, be pulled off.

उघाड़ना, *t.* to uncover, unveil, unclose, open, pull off, lay bare, disclose.

उघाड़ा, *m.* (*f.* ī) uncovered, disclosed, laid bare.

उघाड़ू, *m.* or *f.* one who discovers or unveils.

उघारना, *more prop.* **उघाड़ना**, *q.v.*

उचकना, *n.* to be raised, be lifted up: *a. int.* to rise, leap, bound, spring up.

उचकाना, *t.* to lift, raise, elevate.

उचक्का, 1, *m.* swindling, theft, pocket-lifting: 2, thievish, swindling, given to pocket-picking: hence, *m.* (*f.* ī) a pocket-lifter, cutpurse, etc.

उचक्कापना, *m.* theft, robbery, swindling.

उचटना, *a. int.* to separate (as plaster might from a wall), slip, slide, rebound (as a sword through striking obliquely on a hard body): *n.* to be separated, be interrupted, be broken (as sleep).

उचपद = **उच्चपद**, *q.v.*

उचरंग, *m.* a moth.

उचरना, 1, *more prop.* (1) **उचलना** (2) **उचारना**, *qq.v.*: 2, *n.* to be uttered, be pronounced, be spoken.

उचलना, *a. int.* to separate (as skin from the flesh, etc.): *n.* to be separated.

उचलाना, *t.* to order or cause a person to separate one thing from another.

उचाट, *m.* (*f.* ā) separate, sorrowful, dejected. — *honā*, to be tired, be disgusted.

उचाटना, *t.* (causat. of **उचटना**) to separate, divide, etc.

उचाटी, *f.* sorrow, vexation, separation.

उचाटू, *m.* or *f.* one who vexes, renders sorrowful, or interrupts.

उचाना, *t.* to raise, hoist up, elevate, lift a burden.

उचापट, *m.* a taking up goods on credit; also the goods so taken up: money borrowed.

उचारना, *t.* or *a. int.* to pronounce, utter, speak out.

उचावा, *m.* a raving or talking incoherently (as in sleep); the nightmare.

उचित, morally right and proper, morally obligatory, becoming, suitable, fit, convenient.

उचितता, *f.* obligatoriness, befittingness, propriety.

उचेलना, *t.* to separate one thing from another.

उच्च, *m.* (*f.* ā) = **ऊंचा**, *q.v.*

उच्चता, *f.* height.

उच्चपद, *m.* high rank, status, office or situation

उच्चपदधारी, *m.* (*f.* iṇī) a person of rank, dignitary, magnate : *lit.* holding high office or position.

उच्चरना, 1. = **उच्चारना**, *q.v.*: 2. = **उचलना**, *q.v.* : 3, *n.* to be pronounced, be uttered, be spoken, be told.

उच्चरित = **उच्चारित**, *q.v.*

उच्चस्वर, *m.* (in Gram.) a long vowel.

उच्चाट = **उचाट**, *q.v.*

उच्चाटन, *m.* a vexing, a rendering sorrowful.

उच्चाटना, *t.* to vex, render sorrowful.

उच्चाटी, *f.* sorrow, vexation ; separation.

उच्चान, *f.* (*m.* ?) height, elevation.

उच्चार = **उच्चारण**, *q.v.*

उच्चारण, *m.* articulation, utterance, pronunciation.

उच्चारना, *t.* to enunciate sounds, pronounce, articulate, utter, speak, tell, express.

उच्चारित, *m.* (*f.* ā) uttered, articulated, pronounced.

उच्चैःश्रवस = **उच्चैःश्रवा**, *q.v.*

उच्चैःश्रवा, *m. pr. n.* (in Myth.) the horse of Indra that was among the things produced at the churning of the ocean : *lit.* high eared, having the ears erect.

उच्चैःश्रवाः = **उच्चैःश्रवा**, *q.v.*

उच्छाह, *m.* joy, gladness.

उच्छाहवाला, *m.* (*f.* ī) a braggart.

उच्छिन्न, ruined, laid waste, destroyed.

उच्छिष्ट, *m.* the remainder of victuals, leavings, fragments.

उच्छ्वास, *m.* breath, a breathing ; expectation, hope ; a division of a book.

उछंग, *more prop.* **उत्संग**, *q.v.*

उछट, retirement, retreat.

उछड़ना = **उखड़ना**, *q.v.*

उछरना, *more com.* **उछलना**, *q.v.*

उछलना, *a. int.* to leap, bound, spout up (as water from a fountain), rebound (as a ball), start up (as in sleep.)

उछल पड़ना, *a. int.* to become deranged.

उछलाना, *t.* to order or cause another to throw up anything.

उछार, *m.* a covering, curtain, screen.

उछालना, *t.* to throw up anything (as a ball, etc.) and catch it in the hand.

उछाह, *m.* a festival, jubilee, public demonstration of joy : impatience, wrath.

उजड़ना, *a. int.* to become desolate.

उजड़वाना, *t.* to cause to be desolated or laid waste (by the hands of a third person).

उजड़ा, *m.* (*f.* ī) desolate, laid waste.

उजड़ापुजड़ा, intensive redupl. of **उजड़ा**, *q.v.*

उजड्ड, inconsiderate, rash, ignorant, clownish.

उज़्ब, *m.* pride, haughtiness.

उज़्र, *m.* an apology, excuse, plea.

उजरत, *f.* reward, wages, hire.

उजरना, *more prop.* **उजड़ना**, *q.v.*

उजरा, *more prop.* **उजड़ा**, *q.v.*

उजड़य्या, *m.* (*f.* °ई) a desolator.

उजलना, *n.* to be bright, become clean, to shine.

उजलाना, *t.* to cause to cleanse ; to brighten.

उजवल, a Prākṛit form of **उज्ज्वल**, *q.v.*

उज़्व, *m.* (pl. **आअ्ज़ा**:) a functionary of the body, member, joint, limb.

उजवाना, *t.* to order or cause a person to pour from one vessel into another.

उजागर, 1, *m.* brightness, splendour : 2, light, bright, splendid, gaudy ; celebrated.

उजागरता, a cause of celebrity.

उजाड़, deserted, abandoned, desolated, demolished, ruined. — *k.* to raze to the ground.

उजाड़ना, *t.* to lay waste, desolate, depopulate, overturn, root up ; to injure, expose to loss. *Maińne terā kyā u ārā*, in what respect have I injured you ?

उजाड़ू, *m.* or *f.* a spoiler, destroyer.

उजान, *m.* the direction or part of a river which is opposite to the course of the stream, — up the river.

उजारना, *t.* to reduce to desolation.

उजालना, *t.* to cleanse, brighten, polish.

उजाला, 1, *m.* = **उजाली**, *q.v.* : 2, *m.* (*f.* ī) clear, bright, shining, luminous.

उजाली, *f.* brightness, splendour, light, illumination, glare. — *k.* to illuminate.

उजालेकी तारा, *f.* the planet Venus.

उजिआरा
उजियारं
उजियारा } *more prop.* **उजियाला**, *q.v.*

उजियाला, 1, *m.* brightness, light, glare : 2, *m.* (*f.* ī) bright, light, brilliant.

उजूबा, *m.* a wonder, wonderful thing.

उज्जयन, *m. pr. n.* a certain Indian province.

उज्जयनी, *more prop.* **उज्जयिनी**, *q.v.*

उज्जयिनी, *f. pr. n.* the capital of the province of *Ujjayan*. It was formerly the residence of Vikramāditya ; it is also one of the seven sacred cities of the Hindoos, and is the point whence their Geographers take their first meridian.

उज्जल ; for this word and its kin, see under the form **उज्ज्वल**.

उज्जैन (*colloquial*) = **उज्जयन**, *q.v.*

उज्जैनी (*colloquial*) = **उज्जयिनी**, *q.v.*

उज्ज्वल *m.* (*f.* ā) clear, bright, splendid, beautiful ; blown, expanded (as a flower).

उज्ज्वलत्व, *m.* (*f.* tā) brightness, brilliancy, splendour, radiance, clearness, beauty.

उज्ज्वलन, *m.* a blazing, shining forth, (fire ?).

उज्ज्वलित, *m.* (*f.* ā) clear, pure, clean, bright.

उज्झड़, (*f.* ā) a clown, etc. : *lit.* ignorant, illiterate, clownish, awkward, clumsy.

उझकना, *t.* to observe, peep, spy.

उझड़ = **उज्झड़**, *q.v.*

उझलना, 1, = **उझालना**, *q.v.* : 2, *a. int.* to flow or be poured from one vessel into another.

उझालना, *t.* to throw or pour quickly from one vessel into another, scatter about. *Ujhāl denā*, to pour.

उटंगन, a certain plant : *pr. n.* a certain river near Goāliyār.

उटक्करलैस, *m.* (*f.* ā) an inconsiderate person : *lit.* precipitate, rash, acting without consideration.

उटज, *m.* a hut made of leaves, a hermitage, residence of anchorites.

उठंगन, *m.* a support, prop.

उठंगना, *a. int.* to lean, rest upon for support.

उठंगल, out of order, without manner, dull, heavy, stupid.

उठना, *a. int.* to rise up, go away, spring. Very frequently used after the past active participle of another verb to express the suddenness or hastiness of the act expressed by that verb : in such cases, *uṭhnā* alone undergoes inflection ; e.g. *Wuh bol uṭhā*, he spoke out on a sudden, spoke up, spoke out hurriedly.

उठबैठ, *f.* restlessness ; name of a kind of exercise. — *lagnā*, to be uneasy in mind.

उठवाना, *t.* to cause to raise, cause to lift, cause to remove : to cause to be raised up, cause to be removed. [lit. *adj.* rising, going away.

उठवैया, *m.* one who rises, one who goes away :

उठाईगीरा, plunderer, pilferer, petty thief.

उठान, 1, *m.* an area, court : 2, *f.* the act of appearing ; a rising, ascension.

उठाना, *t.* to lift, raise up, elevate, hoist, take away, bear away ; to invent, produce, cause ; to get gain, enjoy ; to get rid of, abolish ; to excite, arouse ; to bear, support, carry, remove ; to receive ; to suffer ; to exhibit ; to expend, contract debts, purchase on credit. *Uṭhā denā*, to abolish, do away with : (with the *abl.*) to take away, deprive of, divest of.

उठाबिठाना, *t.* to lead into error, cause to err.

उठाबैठी, *f.* the act of frequently rising up and sitting down, restlessness, inconstancy.

उठाव, *m.* support, expenditure.

उठावत = **उठाता है**. See **त**, 5.

उठावना = **उठाना**, *q.v.* See **व**, 8.

उडगण, *f.* (a pl. of **उडु**) the stars.

उड़चक, *m.* a thief, robber.

उड़चलना, *a. int.* to walk with a stately or affected gait : to walk quickly.

उड़तक, *m.* the housing of a saddle.

उड़द, black grain, a kind of pulse.

उड़दाबेगनी = **उर्दाबेगनी**, *q.v.*

उड़दू = **उर्दू**, *q.v.*

उड़न, *m.* a flying, being on the wing.

उड़ना, 1, = **उढ़ना**, *q.v.* : 2, *a. int.* to fly, soar. *Uṛ jānā*, to fly away, soar away.

उड़नागन, *f.* a flying serpent or dragon.

उड़प, *more prop.* **उडुप**, *q.v.*

उड़फ़ाख़ता, a simpleton, fool.

उड़वाना, *t.* to cause to dissipate, cause to squander, cause to blow up, cause to let fly.

उड़स, *m.* the common bug.

उड़ाऊ, *m.* or *f.* a spendthrift, prodigal, extravagant person.

उड़ाक्कू, *m.* a flying away, disappearing ; a deceitful stratagem, fraud, deceit : an engine.

उड़ाक, capable of flying, fledged.

उड़ाड़ = **अड़ाड़**, *q.v.* See **उ**, 7.

उड़ान, *m.* the act of flying.

उड़ाना, *t.* to cause to fly ; to squander, dissipate, disperse, blow up : to filch : to entice. *Uṛā denā*, to spend extravagantly, squander money. *Uṛā mārnā*, to rob, steal. — *parānā*, to squander.

उडु, *f.* (*m.* ?) a star ; a constellation in the moon's path, lunar mansion.

उडुप, *m.* a raft, float : the moon.

उड्डू, (said of male animals) much given to venery (as a stallion, etc. kept for procreation).

उड़द, *m.* a kind of vetch, black grain.

उडूप, *more prop.* **उडुप**, *q.v.*

उढ़ंगन, *m.* anything placed under a vessel to prevent its upsetting, a support, prop.

उढ़क क°, *a. int.* to seek or cry for an absent person (said only of a child).

उढ़कना, *a. int.* to upset : *n.* to be upset.

उढ़कपर, (**उढ़क+पर**) abroach, atilt, tilted, upset, capsized, bottom upwards.

उढ़गन = **उढ़ंगन**, *q.v.*

उढ़ना, *t.* to put on clothes : *n.* to be clad.

उढ़ाना, *t.* to dress, clothe : to cause to clothe.

उढ़ैया, *m.* a wearer of a dress, putter on of a dress.

उढ़ौना, *m.* clothing.

उतटकटारा, *more prop.* **ऊतटकटारा**, *q.v.*

उतडेलना, *t.* to pour (water).

उत, (correl. of **इत**) there, thither.

उतंग, 1, *more prop.* **उत्तुंग**, *q.v.* : 2, *m. pr. n.* a certain ancient Hindoo sage (*rishi*).

उतकंठा = **उत्कण्ठा**, *q.v*,

उतकल, *m. pr. n.* a name of the province of Orissa.

उतकृति, a certain metre of twenty-six syllables ; *hence*, in the ingenious system of reckoning by symbols adopted by Hindoos in their poetry, this word is a symbol for 26.

उततें, (abl. of **उत**) thence. See **तें**, 3.

उतथ, *m. pr. n.* an elder brother of Parikshit.

उतथ्य, *m. pr. n.* a certain Muni.

उतना, *m.* (*f.* ī) as much as that, that much.

उतनाही, (emphat of **उतना**) exactly as much as that, neither more nor less than that, that much only.

उतने, *m.* (pl. of **उतना**) as many as that, so many.

उतपात = **उत्पात**, *q.v.*

उतरन, *f.* a fragment ; anything taken off from the body, cast-off clothing. *Rinse utran honā*, to be free from debt.

उतरना, *a. int.* to come down from a height, fall in value, diminish in dignity, alight, disembark ; to become insipid, get flat, decay, fade, flag ; to halt ; to bait ; to be freed from debt ; to decrease, subside, pass away, disappear, pass over, go off ; *e.g. Nashā utrā*, (his) intoxication has passed off.

उतरवाना, *t.* (causal of **उतरना**) to cause to be brought down or lowered, etc. [*int.* to boil over.

उतराना, 1, = (1) **उतरवाना** (2) **उतारना**, *qq. v.* : 2, *a.*

उतरि = **उतरके** (**उतरना**). See **कृ**, 7.

उतला, *more prop.* (1) **उतावला** (2) **उथला**, *qq. v.*

उतहि, *an emphatic form of* **उत**, *q. v.*

उतहे, a Braj corrupt. of **उठे** (**उठना**).

उतान, } **उत्तान**, *q. v.*
उताना, }

उतार, *m.* descent, declination, declivity; reduction in price; ebb tide. — *denā*, to bring down; to disgrace, dishonor.

उतारचढ़ाव, *m.* a lowering and raising.

उतारन, *f.* a fragment: descent; disgrace.

उतारना, *t.* to cause to alight, cause to descend, bring down, cause to pass over, to convey over; to degrade; to take off, tear off, strip off, cut off, break off (a portion of anything); to unload, discharge, disembark, dismount; to make a recompense, make a return; to act according to circumstances. *Utāre hooe* (pl. masc. of past passive participle of this verb: *lit.* dismounted) engaged with a desperate resolution in any enterprize (a metaphor taken from the idea of cavalry who dismount in order to fight on foot with a determination to conquer or die). [remedy.

उतारसुतार, *m.* comfort, relief, ease, alleviation,

उतारा, *m.* an answer; a halting-place, stage of a journey; a descent; a crossing over (a river, etc.); ransom; self-devotion; second hand things, cast-off clothing.

उतारिद, *m.* the planet Mercury; quicksilver.

उतावल, *f.* quickness, speed, haste, despatch.

उतावला, *m.* (*f.* ī) swift, quick, speedy, precipitate, rash.

उतावली, *f.* haste, speed; rashness, impatience.

उतीर्ण, *m.* (*f.* ā) worn, cast-off (said of clothing, ornaments, jewels, etc.).

उतृण, *m.* (*f.* ā) free from debt or obligation.

उते = (1) **उत** (2) **उतने**, *qq. v.*

उतेक, a dialectic form = **उतना**.

उत्कट, 1, *m.* intoxication; pride; an elephant in rut: woody cassia or its bark: 2, *m.* (*f.* ā) excessive, abounding in; difficult; intoxicated; furious, mad.

उत्कण्ठ, *m.* (*f.* ā) having the neck erect, eagerly longing for.

उत्कण्ठा, *f.* the longing after anything, the sense of having missed something, uneasiness, care, sorrow, regret.

उत्कण्ठित, *m.* (*f.* ā) one who longs after an absent love: *lit.* the longing after something missed, sorrowful, regretful, uneasy.

उत्कर्ष, *m.* exaltation, distinction; excess.

उत्कल, *m.* thought, care; a fowler; a porter: *pr. n.* a certain ancient king, son of Dhruv.

उत्कृष्ट, *m.* (*f.* ā) good, excellent.

उत्कृष्टभूमि, *f.* a good soil.

उत्कोच, *m.* a bribe; venality.

उत्कोचक, *m.* (*f.* ikā) one who receives bribes.

उत्तंग, *m.* (*f.* ā) *more prop.* **उत्तुंग**, *q. v.*

उत्तड़, the placing one thing over another.

उत्तप्त, *m.* (*f.* ā) anxious, excited.

उत्तम, (adj. superl.) *m.* (*f.* ā) supreme, chief, principal, first, most excellent, best, greatest, great; last. [superiority, greatness, worth.

उत्तमत्व, *m.* (*f.* tā) excellence, super-excellence,

उत्तमपुरुष, *m.* (in Gram.) the first person.

उत्तर, 1, *m.* an answer; superiority; power; defence; arrival; the north: a consequence; (in Arithm.) the difference: 2, *m.* (*f.* ā) farther; surpassing, superior; more powerful; lofty; excellent, best; left (not right); answering; subsequent, posterior, future; northerly.

उत्तरकाण्ड, *m. pr. n.* (see **सातोंकाण्ड**) the seventh and last section of the Rāmāyaṇ. [making answer.

उत्तरकारी, *m.* (*f.* iṇī) one who replies: lit. *adj.*

उत्तरखण्ड, *m. pr. n.* (1) of the last section of the Padm Purāṇ and of the Shiv-Purāṇ (2) of northern India.

उत्तरदाई, (*more prop.* **उत्तरदायी**) *m.* (*f.* inī) one who gives a reply: lit. *adj.* answering.

उत्तरदिशा, *f.* the North, northerly direction.

उत्तरपश्चिम, *m.* the North-west.

उत्तरफलगुनी, *f. pr. n.* (see **फालगुन**) the 12th *Nakshatra.* It contains two stars (one of which is Andromedæ) and is represented by a couch.

उत्तरभाद्रपद, *m. pr. n.* (see **भाद्रपदा**) the 27th *Nakshatra.* It contains two stars (one of which is Andromedae) and is represented by a couch.

उत्तरमीमांसा = **ब्रह्ममीमांसा**, *q. v.* [north.

उत्तरवर्त्ती, *m.* (*f.* inī) northern, existing in the

उत्तरा, *f.* 1, (*m.* **उत्तर**) northern, northerly, to the north: 2, the north wind, Boreas: *pr. n.* the mother of Rājā Parikshit and daughter of Virāṭ.

उत्तराखण्ड, *m. pr. n.* northern India.

उत्तराधिकार, *m.* an inheritance, succession.

उत्तराधिकारी, *m.* (*f.* iṇī) an heir, successor: *lit.* inheriting, succeeding.

उत्तरायण, *m.* a northing, the summer solstice, the six months from *Māgh* when the sun is north of the equator.

उत्तरार्द्ध, *m.* the latter half (of a book, etc.), the last part; the upper part of the body; the northern part; the further end.

उत्तरावन, *m.* a place where fish throng to.

उत्तराषाढ़ा, *f. pr. n.* (see **आषाढ़**) the 21st *Nakshatra.* It contains two stars (one of which is Sagittarius) and is represented by an elephant's tooth or by a bed.

उत्तराहा, *m.* (*f.* ī) northern, appertaining to the north.

उत्तरीय, *m.* an upper and outer garment.

उत्तरोत्तर, 1, *m.* (in Law) a rejoinder to a reply: 2, *adv.* further and further, more and more.

उत्ता, *m.* (*f.* ī) so many as that, so much as that.

उत्तान, *m.* (*f.* ā) lying supinely: shallow, conceited, proud. [of Swayambhūmanu and Satarūpā.

उत्तानपाद, *m. pr. n.* a certain Hindoo sage, son

उत्तीर्ण, arrived: rescued.

उत्तुंग, *m.* (*f.* ā) prominent, tall, high, lofty.

उत्तू, *m.* the plaits of cloth. *Mārkar uttoo banāyā usketain*, he beat him to a mummy (*lit.* he beat him so that his body became marked as with the plaits [of cloth).

उत्तूगर, *m.* a plaiter.

उत्थान, *m.* a rising, awaking from sleep; effort, manly exertion, battle; joy. — *ekādashī* or *devothān*, the eleventh day of the *shuklpaksh* of Kārttik, when Vishnu awakes from sleep. During the four months that he is asleep it is said to be unlawful to marry.

उत्थापन, *m.* the raising anything up; (in Arithm.) the producing an answer or result.

उत्पत्त, *more prop.* **उत्पत्ति**, *q. v.*

उत्पत्ति, *f.* a springing up, origin, rise, birth, production: title of the book of Genesis. — *k.* to create, produce. [origin.

उत्पत्तिसम्बन्धी, *m.* (*f.* inī) anything relating to

उत्पत्तिसूचक, *m.* an epithet of the Supreme as the originator of creation.

उत्पन्न, 1, *m.* proceeds, profits, produce: 2, produced, born; secured; gained. — *k.* to produce. — *honā*, to be produced: *a. int.* to occur.

उत्पल, *m.* a certain blue species of the lotus (*Nymphea cerulea*); a certain plant (*Costus*).

उत्पाटन, *m.* a plucking out, rooting up, extirpating. [jury, injustice.

उत्पात, *m.* a portent, phenomenon: violence, in-

उत्पादक, *m.* (*f.* ikā) an originator, father; a certain fabulous animal with eight legs: *lit.* causing, originating, producing.

उत्पादन, *m.* the producing or creating a thing.

उत्प्रेक्षा, *f.* indifference, carelessness: (in poetry or in Rhetoric) a comparison, illustration.

उत्भाद्रपद, *more prop.* **उत्तरभाद्रपद**, *q. v.*

उत्राई **ह** °, *n.* to be thankful, be grateful.

उत्रिण, *m.* (*f.* ā) free from debt or obligation.

उत्संग, *m.* the lap; the slope of a mountain; a roof.

उत्सर्ग, *m.* an abandoning, resigning, retiring from; a giving, consecrating: any rule or precept.

उत्सव, *m.* a public demonstration of joy, jubilee, festival; impatience, wrath.

उत्साह, *m.* joy, gladness, pleasure; effort, energy, fortitude, perseverance.

उत्साहसों in Braj = **उत्साहसे**. See **सों**, 1 (2).

उत्साही, *m.* (*f.* inī) joyous; active, persevering.

उथलना, *a. int.* to capsize, upset.

उथलना पुथलना, *n.* to be capsized.

उथलपुथल, *m.* (*f.* ā) capsized, topsy-turvy, higgledy-piggledy.

उथला, *m.* (*f.* ī) shallow, shelving. [upset.

उथलाना, *t.* to cause to turn over, cause to be

उथापन, *m.* the raising anything up.

उद = **उत**, *q. v.* [in obsequies; ablution.

उदक, *m.* water; the ceremony of pouring water

उदघाटी, *f.* manifestness; the path of the sun's [rising.

उदधि, *m.* the ocean.

उदभत्र = **उद्भव**, *q. v.*

उदमाद, *m.* lewdness, wantonness.

उदमादी, 1, *f.* a paroxysm of lust: 2, *m.* (*f.* inī) a lewd person: *lit.* lewd, lustful, wanton.

उदय, *m.* a rising (as of the sun, moon, or ocean), dawn, sunrise, ascent; the East as opposed to the West (*ast*); the eastern mountain from behind which the sun is supposed to rise; light, splendour; prosperity, good fortune. — *honā*, to rise (as the sun, etc.). *Uday asttak tumhārā rāj ho*, may your sway extend from the East to the West.

उदयगिरि, *m.* = **उदयाचल**, *q. v.*

उदयाचल, *m. pr. n.* the mountain from behind which the sun is supposed to rise. [sunset.

उदयास्त, from East to West, from sunrise to

उदयी, *m.* (*f.* inī) prosperous, flourishing.

उदर, 1, (correl. of **इदर**) that way, thither: 2, *m.* the interior part, the stomach: war.

उदरपिशाच, *m.* (*f.* ī) a glutton: *lit.* gluttonous, voracious, omnivorous, demon-bellied, one who eats as if he had a demon to feed.

उदररेख, *f.* the line of hair on the abdomen.

उदरवृद्धि, *f.* dropsy.

उदरामय, *m.* diarrhoea, dysentery.

उदरावेष्ट, *m.* the tapeworm.

उदरिन, 1, *m.* = **उदरी**, 1: 2, *f.* = **उदरिणी**, *qq. v.*

उदरिणी, *f.* (*m.* **उदरी**) a corpulent or a pregnant [female.

उदरिल, *m.* (*f.* ā *or* ī) = **उदरी**, 1, *q. v.*

उदरी, 1, appertaining to the abdomen, corpulent, potbellied, pregnant: hence, *m.* (*f.* inī) a corpulent person: 2, *f.* enlargement of the abdomen from [dropsy or from flatulency.

उदवाह, *m.* marriage.

उदवेग = **उद्वेग**, *q. v.*

उदसीन (*contraction*) = **उदासीन**, *q. v.*

उदाई, *f.* brownness, the colour brown.

उदाता = **उदाता**, *q. v.*

उदात्त, 1, *m.* the acute accent, a high sharp tone, an ornament in Rhetoric; a donation, gift; a kind of musical instrument, a large drum: 2, *m.* (*f.* ā) a donor, etc.: *lit.* giving, liberal, generous; great, illustrious, dearly beloved.

उदान, *m.* one of the five vital airs (that which rises up the throat and passes into the head).

उदार, 1, *m.* prodigality, etc.: 2, *m.* (*f.* ā *or* ī) a liberal person, etc.: *lit.* munificent, liberal, bountiful, excellent, distinguished, great: unperplexed; gentle.

उदारत्व, *m.* (*f.* tā) liberality, generosity, munificence.

उदास, 1, *m.* unsettledness, retiredness, loneliness; (in Agriculture) a sickly crop: 2, *m.* (*f.* ā) a dejected person, etc: *lit.* unsettled in mind, retired, lonely, solitary, forlorn, dejected, sad, sorrowful, dull, dead and alive: fearless, without reflection, careless, — *k.* to sadden, dishearten.

उदासा, *m.* a cord worn as a shoulder-belt.

उदासी, 1, *f.* dejection, sorrow, loneliness, solitude: 2, *m.* (*f.* inī) a dejected person, etc.; a certain class of Hindoo fakeers; (in Music) the bass: *lit.* unsettled, solitary, lonely, retired, dejected, forlorn, sad.

उदासीन, *m.* one who is completely detached from

the world, whose family is unknown, and who has neither friend nor foe; a hermit, misanthrope, stoical indifferent person, one who is neither a friend nor an adversary, an umpire: a certain class of mendicants in the Panjāb.

उदासीनता, *f.* indifference, carelessness.

उदासीबाजा, *m.* any bass instrument.

उदाहट, *f.* brownness, the colour brown.

उदाहरण, *m.* a speaking, declaration; (in Rhet.) an example, simile, comparison, illustration; an opposite argument; (in Logic) one of the five modes of reasoning.

उदाहरणी, *f.* उदाहरण, *q.v.*

उदित, *m.* (*f.* ā) risen (as the sun, etc.); distinguished, shining, conspicuous (as valour, etc.).

उदीच्य, *m. pr. n.* (1) of the country north and west of the river *Sarāvatee* (2) of its inhabitants: *lit.* northern.

उदुम्बर, *m.* the glomerous figtree (*Ficus glomerata*) or gūlar-tree.

उदूखल, *m.* a gum resin, bdellium, a mortar.

उदूल, *m.* deviating, declining, refusing, disobeying. — *k.* to disobey.

उदै in Braj = उदय, *q.v.*

उदोत, *more prop.* (1) उदित (2) उद्योत, *qq.v.*

उद्गत, *m.* (*f.* ā) vomited, cast up.

उद्गार, *m.* a spitting, exhalation, throwing out; saliva, vomiting: sound, roar.

उद्घाटन, *m.* the rope and bucket of a well, a leathern bucket for drawing water with; any instrument for opening (as a key, etc.).

उद्घाटित, *m.* (*f.* ā) done with effort; exerted; opened.

उद्दिम, *more prop.* उद्यम, *q.v.*

उद्दीपन, 1. *m.* the blazing or glowing of a luminous body: 2. exciting, inflaming (as passion).

उद्दीप्त, *m.* (*f.* ā) illuminated.

उद्देश, *m.* search, inquiry, scope; an example; a vestige, trace; a place; love, desire, lust.

उद्देश्य, *m.* (*f.* ā) anything noteworthy, etc.; (in Gram.) the subject: *lit.* suitable to be pointed at.

उद्धक, *m.* asthma; a gasping, panting; plethora in the vessels of the head; headache; indigestion.

उद्धत, 1, *m.* a king's wrestler: 2, *m.* (*f.* ā) rude, daring, self-important, arrogant, mischievous, ill-behaved.

उद्धव, *m.* a festival, holiday: *pr. n.* a certain ancient Hindoo devotee.

उद्धार, *m.* a debt (*esp.* one not bearing interest), loan, trust; deduction, discharge, deliverance, a raising up from any place or state, salvation. — *denā*, to lend. — *lenā*, to borrow.

उद्धारक, *m.* (*f.* ikā) a deliverer, etc.: lit. *adj.* delivering, liberating, relieving.

उद्धारना, *t.* to deliver, discharge, liberate.

उद्धारनिक, *m.* (*f.* ā) a deliverer: lit. *adj.* emancipating.

उद्भव, *m.* birth, production, a being born, a springing up (as plants from seed).

उद्भिज, *m.* (*f.* ā) *adj.* sprouting.

उद्यत, 1, *m.* a division of a book, a section, chapter: 2, *m.* (*f.* ā) raised, held up; prepared, ready; active, persevering, laboring diligently and incessantly.

उद्यम, *m.* strenuous and continuous effort, exertion, endeavour, labor, employment, calling, trade.

उद्यमी, *m.* (*f.* inī) active, energetic, persevering, prompt, engaged in trade.

उद्यान, *m.* a royal pleasure-ground: motive, purpose.

उद्यापन, *m.* the accomplishing a thing.

उद्योग, *m.* continued and strenuous endeavour, exertion, perseverance, zeal.

उद्योगी, *m.* (*f.* inī) an energetic person, etc.: *lit.* active, laborious, persevering, zealous.

उद्योत, *m.* light, lustre.

उद्र, *m.* an otter, crab, or any aquatic animal.

उद्विग्न, *m.* (*f.* ā) filled with anxious thought, perplexed, distressed, troubled.

उद्वेग, *m.* perturbation (*esp.* from pain), consternation, anxiety, perplexity, care, exertion, the fruit of the *Areca catechu*, betel-nut.

उद्वेगी, *m.* (*f.* inī) anxious, perplexed, perturbed, agitated.

उद्बोध, *m.* recollection, the recognizing a thing.

उधड़ना = उधेड़ना, *q. v.*

उधर, (correl. of इधर) there, that way, thither, thitherwards, on the other side.

उधरसे, from that side, from the other side, thence.

उधरा, *m.* (*f.* ī) opened, undone, unrolled (as the seam in a garment, or as the thread which was rolled up in a clue). [more proper form उद्धार.

उधार; for this word and its kin, see under the

उधेड़, *m.* an unravelling, unweaving.

उधेड़ना, *t.* to unravel, unfold, undo.

उधेड़बन, *m.* perplexity.

उधेरना, *more properly* उधेड़ना, *q.v.*

उधोरना = उद्धारना, *q. v.*

उन, 1, the inflective base of the oblique cases of the plural (वे) of the remoter demonstrative pronoun: 2, in Hindee numerals this particle is a prefix characteristic of all the nines after nine; *e. g.* nineteen, twenty-nine, etc: eighty-nine and ninety-nine are the only exceptions. But see ऊन.

उनकर / **उनकरा** } dialectic forms = उनका.

उनकराके, a dialectic form = उन्हें.

उनकरासें, a dialectic form = उनसे.

उनकरे, a dialectic form = उनका.

उनके, a dialectic form = उन्हें.

उनचालीस = उनतालीस, *q.v.*

उनचास, forty-nine (४९): see श्रों, वां, वीं, वे, वें.

उनडालना = उपडेलना, *q. v.*

उनतालीस, thirty-nine (३९): see श्रों, वां, वीं, वे, वें.

उनतीस, twenty-nine (२९): see श्रों, वां, वीं, वे, वें.

उनमत्त, *more prop.* उन्मत्त, *q. v.*

उनवाचक संज्ञा, *f.* (in Gram.) a diminutive noun.

उनसठ, fifty-nine (५९): see श्रों, वां, वीं, वे, वें.

उनसठि, *more prop.* उनसठ, *q. v.*

उनसा, like them. See **सा**.

ऊनसो, in Braj = (1) **उनसा** (2) **उनसे**. See **सो**.

उनसों = **उनसो**, *q.v.* [2, = **उनसो**, *q.v.*

उनसौ, 1, ninety-nine (९९): see **ओं, वां, वीं, वे, वें**:

उनसौं = (1) **उनसो** (2) **उनसौ**, *qq.v.*

उनहत्तर, sixty-nine (६९): see **ओं, वां, वीं, वे, वें**.

उनासी, seventy-nine (७९): see **ओं, वां, वीं, वे, वें**.

उनि in Braj = **उनने** (by them, etc.).

उनीदा, *m.* (*f.* ī) unshut (said of the eye), sleepless ; expanded (as a flower might be).

उनीस, nineteen (१९): see **ओं, वां, वीं, वे, वें**.

उनू, *f.* the body.

उने, thither.

उन्नत, high, tall.—*k.* to elevate.

उन्नति, *f.* a rising, increase, loftiness, advancement, prosperity.

उन्मत्त, *m.* (*f.* ā) a lunatic, etc : *lit.* insane, frantic, mad, furious, intoxicated, lustful, extravagant.

उन्मत्तत्व, *m.* (*f.* tā) insanity, madness ; intoxication ; solaciousness ; extravagance.

उन्मद ; for this word and its kin, see under the [more proper form **उन्मत्त**.

उन्माद = **उन्मत्तता**, *q.v.*

उन्मादा = **उन्मत्त**, *q.v.*

उन्मान, *m.* a measure of size or of quantity.

उन्मुख, *m.* (*f.* ā) *adj.* looking upwards.

उन्मेष, *m.* a winking, twinkling of the eyelids.

उन्स, *m.* friendship, love, affection, companionship, society.

उन्सा = **उनसा**, *q.v.*

उन्ह = (1) **उन**, 1 (2) **उन्हों**, *q.v.*

उन्हार, 1, *f.* manner, mode, appearance ; 2, *m.* (*f.* ā) like, resembling, similar.

उन्हें, (a dat. and acc. of **वे**) = them, to them.

उन्है
उन्हैं } in Braj = **उन्हें**, *q.v.*

उन्हों = **उन**, 1, *q.v.* Some hold that the longer form is honorific in its nature ; others affirm that it is redundant, and (so far) corrupt.

उप ; an inseparable prefix much used in composition [denoting vicinity or proximity (*e. g.* **उपताप**), *hence*] to, towards ; near, down, under ; on ; by, by the side of ; with, by means of, or resemblance by inferiority (*e. g.* **उपवेद**). Many examples will be found below.

उपंग, *m.* a kind of musical instrument.

उपकरण, *m.* the insignia of royalty ; means, implements, materials ; a helping, assisting.

उपकार, *m.* favor, kindness, assistance, benefit, beneficence, protection.

उपकारक, *m.* (*f.* ikā) a friend, helper, benefactor.

उपकारार्थ, for the sake of assistance, with a view to assistance.

उपकारी, *m.* (*f.* iṇī) a helper, etc. : *lit.* aiding, beneficent, assisting, helpful, subsidiary, subservient.

उपकार्या, *f.* a king's house.

उपक्रम, *m.* the deliberate commencement of an undertaking, a beginning : a stratagem.

उपगत, *m.* (*f.* ā) promised, agreed : approached, drawn near, attached to.

उपगति, *f.* an approach.

उपगम, *m.* agreement, promise : approximation, [approach.

उपग्रह, *m.* any animal under confinement, a prisoner : encouragement, favor, assistance.

उपङ्ग, *m.* a kind of musical instrument.

उपचार, *m.* service, remedy ; practice, usage, profession ; the practice of medicine ; a present, bribe : enmity.

उपचारी, *m.* (*f.* iṇī) a servant : lit. *adj.* serving.

उपज, 1, *m.* produce, crop ; product : 2, *f.* anything spoken or sung extempore ; the burden of a song, the chorus ; variations in music.

उपजतन, *m.* preparation : exertion.

उपजना, *a. int.* to spring up, originate, grow, shoot forth, be produced, take place, transpire.

उपजाऊ, fertile, productive.

उपजाना, *t.* to cause to grow, cause to spring forth ; to create, produce, cultivate.

उपजायक, *m.* (*f.* ikā) a producer : lit. *adj.* producing.

उपजित, *m.* (*f.* ā) produced, propagated.

उपजीवन, *m.* = **उपजीविका**, *q.v.*

उपजीविका, *f.* means of support, livelihood, subsistence.

उपज्यो, in Braj = (1) **उपजा हुआ** (2) **उपजाया**.

उपजीवी, *m.* (*f.* inī) a dependent ; *lit.* dependent, living by, subsisting on.

उपटन (*corruption*) = **उबटन**, *q. v.*

उपटना (*corruption*) = **उबटना**, *q. v.*

उपठन (*corruption*) = **उबटन**, *q. v.*

उपठना, *n.* to be tired or sick of a business.

उपड़ना, *n.* to be rooted out, be pulled out ; to be skinned.

उपताप *m.* disease, sickness, pain ; misfortune : heat ; hurry.

उपदंश, *m.* flavour, relish, something to promote [drinking : the venereal disease.

उपदर्श, *m.* spectacles.

उपदर्शक, 1, *adj.* doorkeeping ; hence, *m.* (*f.* ikā) a doorkeeper : 2, *m.* spectacles : a wink.

उपदर्शन, *m.* a commentary.

उपदा, *f.* a meeting ; a present or offering made to a king or any great personage on the occasion of an interview : a bribe.

उपदेश, *m.* advice, counsel, admonition, exhortation, sermon, instruction, information. — *k.* to counsel, preach.

उपदेशक, *m.* (*f.* ikā) an adviser, instructor, admonisher, preacher, a guide in moral or spiritual affairs : lit. *adj.* instructing, etc.

उपदेशना, *t.* to counsel, preach, give advice or instruction in spiritual matters.

उपदेशी, *m.* (*f.* in *or* inī) a teacher, preacher.

उपदेष्टा, *m.* (*f.* ṭrī) an adviser, instructor, teacher.

उपद्रव, *m.* any natural phenomenon considered

as a portent; injustice, oppression, tyranny, high-handedness, insult, injury, violence, excess.

उपद्रवी, *m.* (*f.* ini) an overbearing person, etc.: *lit.* portentous; oppressive, high-handed, insulting, [violent.

उपद्रो } (*colloquial*) = **उपद्रव**, *q. v.*
उपद्रौ }

उपधातु, *m.* an inferior mineral; a semimetal (of which seven are specified; *viz.* pyrites, sulphate of copper, talc, antimony, red orpiment, yellow orpiment, calx of brass); secondary secretion (such as the milk, menses, adeps, perspiration, teeth, hair, lymph).

उपधान, *m.* a pillow, bolster, cushion; kindness, affection: poison: religious obligation or observance.

उपनन्द, *m. pr. n.* (1) of a son of Vasudev (2) of a pupil of Sākhya-muni (3) of a king of the Nāgas.

उपनय, (= **उपनयन**) a supplying, an applying.

उपनयन, *m.* a bringing; the initiation of the first three classes of Hindoos; investiture with a peculiar thread or cord worn over the left shoulder and under the right. The sacred thread of the Brāhmaṇ is of cotton, *moonj*, or *kusha*-grass; that of the Kshatriya is of *soon* or flax; that of the Vais is of wool. The investiture is confined to the male sex, — the Brāhmaṇ youths being invested at from eight to sixteen years of age; the Kshatriyas at from eleven to twenty-two; and the Vaishyas at from twelve to twen- [ty-four.

उपनाम, *m.* any title or family name.

उपनामवाची शब्द, *m.* any word indicating a title or family name.

उपनिषद, *f.* a portion of the religious writings of the Hindoos, sacred texts or extracts from the Veds; the theological and argumentative parts of the Veds, whether detached from the principal work or comprized in it. The Upanishads inculcate an abstract and speculative monotheistical worship.

उपनेत्र, *m.* spectacles, eyeglasses.

उपन्यास, *m.* a giving; declaration; law; pretext; prologue; a tale.

उपपति, *m.* an adulterer, paramour, gallant; *lit.* a secret or secondary husband; *hence*, one who keeps a woman to whom he is not married.

उपपातक, *m.* a great but expiable crime (such as killing a cow, selling a daughter, atheism, etc.).

उपपुराण, *m.*; see **पुराण**.

उपबर्हण, *m. pr. n.* a certain celestial minstrel.

उपबाद = **उपवाद**, *q. v.*

उपमय; see (1) **उपमा** (2) **उपमेय**.

उपमा, *f.* a comparison, likeness, illustration, resemblance, simile, metaphor, that to which another thing is likened. — *denā*, (with the abl. of the remoter object) to compare with, liken to.

उपमां } *m.* = **उपमा**, *q. v.*
उपमान }

उपमिति, *f.* a comparison, resemblance, likeness, image; picture; analogy, induction.

उपमेय, to be compared, comparable.

उपयन्ता, *m.* a husband, lord.

उपयुक्त, *m.* (*f.* ā) fit, suitable, worthy, proper, becoming, right; qualified, adapted to, suitable for, appropriate.

उपयुक्तता, *f.* } adaptedness, suitability, fitness.
उपयुक्तत्व, *m.* }

उपयोग, *m.* suitableness; employment, use.

उपयोगी, *m.* (*f.* inī) a useful person, etc.: *lit.* suitable; useful, serviceable.

उपर, (a separable postposition taking the genit. masc. inflected) above, on, over, on the outside, moreover, concerning, on account of.

उपरना, *m.* a covering, scarf.

उपरला, 1, *m.* the surface, the outside (of cloth or a garment as opposed to the lining): 2, *m.* (*f.* ī) superficial.

उपरवाईतरवाई, *f.* surfeit, *mort de chien*, *cholera* [*morbus*.

उपरस, *m.* a subordinate flavour; a secondary mineral (as red chalk, bitumen, etc.). [painting.

उपराग, *m.* a seizing; an eclipse; a calamity;

उपराजना, *t.* to cause to grow, cause to spring forth, to create, produce, cultivate.

उपरान्त, after, afterwards, after which, above and beyond, over and above, besides.

उपरान्ति, *more prop.* **उपरान्त**, *q. v.*

उपराला, *m.* aid, assistance. —*k.* to take anyone's part, protect, stickle for.

उपरि = **उपर**, *q. v.* [tion.

उपरिभाव, *m.* eminence, exaltation, dignity, posi-

उपरिस्थलेख, *m.* an address (at the beginning of a letter or on its cover). [thought or feeling.

उपरीमनसे कहना, to speak other than one's real

उपरोध, *m.* partiality, favour, kindness, support, protection, defence: an obstacle; disturbance; injury.

उपरोधन, *m.* an obstacle.

उपरोधी, *m.* (*f.* inī) an impediment, etc.: *lit.* impeding, disturbing.

उपरोहित, *m.* a chief priest of a Hindoo temple.

उपरौंचा = **उपरौंछा**, *q. v.*

उपरौंछा, 1, *m.* a towel or cloth for wiping the body: 2, *m.* (*f.* ī) superficial.

उपरौठा, *m.* (*f.* ī) above, aloft, upper; e. g. *Uparauthee kothree*, an upstairs room.

उपल, *m.* a rock, stone, precious stone, jewel.

उपलक्षण, *m.* a figure of speech, synecdoche, el-

उपला = **उप्ला**, *q. v.* [liptical expression.

उपलिप्त, *m.* (*f.* ā) smeared, plastered. [cakes.

उपली, *f.* (dim. of **उप्ला**) dried cowdung in small

उपलेप = **उपलेपन**, *q. v.* [(*esp.* with cowdung).

उपलेपन, *m.* an anointing, plastering, smearing

उपवन, *m.* a grove, garden, an artificially planted wood. In the Paurānik literature twenty-four of these are enumerated.

उपवर्णन, *m.* a minute description.

उपवाद, *m.* censure, blame. [a censurer.

उपवादी, *adj.* censuring, blaming: hence, *m.* (*f.* inī)

उपवास, *m.* a fast, fasting, hunger.

उपवासी, *m.* (*f.* inī) one who is fasting: lit. *adj.* fasting, observing a fast.

उपविद्या, *f.* profane science (as opposed to sacred), inferior sort of knowledge.

उपविष, *m.* factitious poison, a narcotic, any deleterious drug (as opium, datura, etc.).

उपवीत, *m.* the Brāhmaṇical thread, the thread worn by the first three classes of the Hindoos over the left shoulder and under the right.

उपवेद, *m.* (*lit.* depending on or deduced from the Veds) a division of Hindoo science deduced immediately from the Veds. Four works are included under this designation which are entitled as follows:—Āyush, Gandharva, Dhanush, Sthāpatya. The first of these is said to have been delivered to mankind by Brahma, Indra, Dhanwantaree, and five other deities, and comprises the theory of disorders and medicines, with the practical methods of curing diseases: the second, or Music, was invented and explained by Bharat: the third was composed by Vishwāmitra, and treats of the construction and use of arms and implements handled in war by the Kshatriyas: the fourth is said to have been revealed by Vishwakarma, and contains various treatises on sixty-four mechanical arts, designed for the improvment of those who exercise them.

उपशम, *m.* tranquillity, calmness, patience.

उपशान्त, *m.* (*f.* ā) calm, clear, pacified.

उपशान्ति, 1, *f.* tranquillity, calmness: 2, *adj.* appeasing, allaying.

उपशान्ती, *m.* (*f.* inī) tranquil, calm, appeased.

उपशास्त्र, *m* sciences connected with the Shāstras or deduced from them.

उपस, *f.* stink; staleness, putrefaction, rottenness.

उपसना, *a. int.* to become musty, grow stinking, rot, putrefy.

उपसर्ग, *m.* a portent, a phenomenon of nature supposed to announce future evil; a disease; possession by an evil spirit: (in Gram.) a particle prefixed to roots, etc., a preposition, prefix.

उपसाना, *t.* to cause to rot.

उपस्त्री *f.* (see **उपपति**) a concubine; *lit.* a secondary woman.

उपस्थ, *n.* the genitals (male or female), the haunches, the anus, the legs, the arms.

उपस्थित, present, at hand, ready, arrived. — *k.* to summon; to present.

उपस्थिति, *f.* a placing, putting, applying, using.

उपहार, *m.* an interview; a complimentary present to a superior; adoration; religious exultation.

उपहास, *m.* a smile, laughter, sneering, ridicule, derision, fun, sport. — *k.* (with gen.) to laugh at.

उपाइ, *more prop.* **उपाय**, *q.v.*

उपाई, *more prop.* (1) **उपाय** (2) **उपायी**, *qq. v.*

उपाउ, *more prop.* **उपाय**, *q.v.*

उपाऊ, in Braj = **उपाय**, *q.v.*

उपांग, *m.* the sectarial mark made with sandal, etc on the forehead.

उपाख्यान, *m.* a legend, tale, story of the olden time.

उपाटना / **उपाड़ना** } *t.* to pluck up by the roots.

उपादान, *m.* seizure, restraining the organs of sense or of perception, abstraction; a cause; a motive.

उपाध, *f.* violence, injury, injustice, tyranny, oppression.

उपाधि, *m.* a virtuous reflection; a discriminative or distinguishing property, modifying circumstance, a condition applied to limit a too general middle term; deception, disguise, a title, a nickname.

उपाधी, *m.* (*f.* inī) a tyrant, etc.: *lit.* violent, unjust, tyrannical, oppressive.

उपाधीतर, (*adj.* compar. deg.) very tyrannical.

उपाध्यानी (*contraction*) = **उपाध्यायानी**, *q. v.*

उपाध्याय, *m.* (*f.* ā, ānī, ī) a preceptor in spiritual things: *lit.* learned.

उपाध्याया / **उपाध्यायानी** / **उपाध्यायी** } *f.* (*m.* **उपाध्याय**) a preceptress.

उपाना, *t.* to create, produce; to earn, get; to devise, contrive, prepare, adopt as an experiment or as a remedy.

उपाय, *m.* a means, expedient, contrivance, device, remedy, redress, preparation. — *k.* to devise, hit upon a contrivance, to remedy, etc.

उपायक, *adj.* contriving, remedy-producing: hence, *m.* (*f.* ikā) a deviser, contriver, helper.

उपाया, *more prop.* **उपाय**, *q. v.*

उपायी, *adj.* contriving, remedying, resorting to expedients, expert in the devising and application of means or of remedies: hence, *m.* (*f.* inī) an expert at devising, etc.

उपारना = **उखाड़ना**, *q. v.*

उपार्जन, *m.* an earning, acquiring, gaining.

उपार्जित, *m.* (*f.* ā) acquired, gotten, earned.

उपालम्भ, *m.* abuse, reviling; a delaying.

उपाव in Braj = **उपाय**, *q.v.*

उपास (*contraction*) = **उपवास**, *q.v.*

उपासक, *m.* (*f.* ikā) a servant, worshipper.

उपासन, *m.* the sitting near and attending upon; religious contemplation, prayer; the sacred fire; archery.

उपासना, 1. *t.* to reverence, worship, serve: 2. *f.* attendance on a superior, service, worship, adoration; prayer, intercession.

उपासा, *m.* (*f.* ī) one who fasts: *lit.* hungry, fasting.

उपासी, *adj.* worshipping, serving: hence, *m.* (*f.* inī) a worshipper, devotee.

उपास्य, *m.* (*f.* ā) an object of reverence, etc.: *lit.* worthy of honor, reverence, worship or service.

उपेक्षा, *f.* indifference, neglect, want of attention, abandonment, one of the minor expedients in war, stratagem, fraud, deceit, trick.

उपेखा, *more prop.* **उपेक्षा**, *q. v.*

उपेन्द्र, *m.* an epithet of Vāman.

उप्पज, *more properly* **उपज**, *q. v.*

उप्राटा, *m.* the West.

उप्रान्त, *more prop.* **उपरान्त**, *q. v.*

उप्राल, above, over.

उप्राला, *more prop.* **उपराला**, *q. v.*

उपावरी, quarrelsome, wrangling: hence, *m.* (*f.* inī)
उप्ल = **उपल**, *q.v.* [a quarrelsome person.
उप्ला, *m.* a cake of dried cowdung.
उफ़ुक़, *m.* the horizon ; any tract or region of the world ; (poetically) the world.
उफ़तादा, fallen, lying horizontally ; poor, wretched, helpless, oppressed.
उफनना, *a. int.* to boil over.
उफालना, *t.* to root up, eradicate.
उबकना, *a. int.* to vomit.
उबकाई, *f.* (see **आई**, 3) the act of vomiting.
उबकाना, *t.* to cause to vomit.
उबटन, *m.* a paste (consisting of perfumes, flour, etc) for scouring the body with before and when bathing, an odour, perfume, cosmetic.
उबटना, 1, *more prop.* **उबटन**, *q.v.*: 2, *t.* to rub on the body the above-mentioned substance.
उबटी, *f.* = **उबटन**, *q.v.*
उबरना, *n.* to remain over, be kept in reserve.
उबराना, *t.* to keep in reserve.
उबलना, *a. int.* to bubble up, boil.
उबलाना, *t.* to cause to boil (by the hands of another). Shakespear, Thompson, and Forbes agree in saying that this verb means, to boil anything so that it becomes fit to eat, to cook, to boil anything with such violence that it is spilled.
उबस; for this word and its kin, see under the
उबसना, *t.* to vomit forth. [form **उपस**.
उबाना, *t.* to sow, plant.
उबार, *m.* release, deliverance. [in reserve.
उबारना, *t.* to liberate, release, deliver : to keep
उबाल, *m.* a boiling, effervescence, fermentation. — *denā*, to cause anything to boil.
उबालना, *t.* to cause anything to boil, to boil.
उभक, *m.* a bear.
उभय, *m. f.* both, the two, the both, both of them.
उभयतः, from both sides, on both sides, to both sides ; in both cases.
उभयथा, in both ways ; in both cases.
उभरना, 1, *a. int.* to swell, rise, overflow: 2, *t.* to unload (a cart or a boat).
उभरा, *m.* (*f.* ī) overflowed: unladen. — *k.* to unload (a cart or a boat). [ing.
उभराना, *t.* to cause to overflow, fill to overflow-
उभाड़ना, *t.* to take away, steal.
उभाना, *t.* to alarm, disturb. [prominence.
उभार, *m.* a swelling, tumefaction, plumpness,
उभारना, *t.* to raise up, excite, persuade, plump up.
उभै in Braj = **उभय**, *q.v.*
उमंग, *f.* excessive joy, exultation, transport ;
उमंगना, *a. int.* to advance with joy. [ambition.
उमंगी, *m.* (*f.* inī) a joyous person, etc : *lit.* sanguine, desirous, ambitious. [more proper form **उमंग**.
उमग; for words beginning thus, see under the

उमघड़ उमघड़ कर रोना, *a. int.* to weep violently.
उमघड़ना, 1, *a. int.* to overflow, abound, swell, increase, fall (as tears) : 2, *n.* to be proud, be conceited ; to be poured out (as a river, clouds, an army, the heart, etc.).
उमड़ा, flooded, overflowing. — *ānā*, to become flooded, to overflow. — *denā*, to cause to overflow, to flood.
उमड़ाना, *t.* to cause to overflow ; to flood.
उ़मर, *f.* age, time of life, lifetime.
उमरा, *m.* (pl. of **अमीर**) nobles, grandees.
उमसना = **उपसना**, *q.v.*
उमा, *f.* an epithet of Pārvatee ; linseed ; light, splendour ; reputation, fame : tranquillity : night : an interjection expressive of astonishment.
उमिर, *more prop.* **उ़मर**, *q.v.* [same belief.
उम्मत, *f.* people ; a religious sect, people of the
उम्मेद, *f.* hope, expectation, trust, dependence ; pregnancy. — *rakhnā*, to hope.
उम्मेदवार, *m.* an expectant, dependent, candidate.
उम्मेदवारी, *f.* hopefulness, expectation.
उम्मेदसे ह°, *n.* to be pregnant.
उम्हर, thither.
उयेउ, (from **उअना**) risen (the sun).
उर, *m.* the bosom, breast, heart. — *lenā*, to take to one's heart, embrace, fondle, caress. As a Kridanta suffix [*m.* (*f.* ā)] this particle is subjoined to some roots to form attributive adjectives ; *e. g.* **विदुर** (Rt. **विद**) : and as a Taddhita suffix it serves to form possessive adjectives from substantives ; *e.g.* **दन्तुर**, from **दन्त**.
उरग, *m.* (*f.* ī) a snake, worm, reptile : *lit.* crawling, creeping, going on its breast.
उरगस्थान, *m.* the infernal regions (supposed to be below the earth). [birds ; *lit.* the worm-eater.
उरगाद, *m.* (in Myth.) an epithet of the regent of
उरगारी = **उरगाद**, *q.v.* : *lit.* the enemy of reptiles.
उरज, *more prop.* **उरुज**, *q.v.* [form **उलझना**.
उरझना; for this word and its kin, see under the
उरतू, *m.* crimping ; plaits (as in clothes).
उरतूगर, *m.* a crimper, plaiter of clothes.
उरपोर, *f.* grief, sorrow, disconsolateness.
उरध = **उर्द**, *q.v.*
उ़रफ़ा, *m.* (pl. of **आरिफ़**) the ingenious, the intelligent, the wise ; the good ; judges, magistrates.
उरबर, *f.* fertile soil.
उरमाँहि in Braj = **उरमें** (**उर**). [Dhātā.
उरराग, *f. pr. n.* one of the four daughters of
उरला, hithermost, belonging to this side.
उरवी, *f.* the earth.
उरस, *m.* the breast, bosom.
उरसिज, *m.* the female breast.
उराड़नो in Braj = **उड़ाना**, *q.v.*
उरिन, freed from an obligation.

उरिहना, *m.* reproach, reproof. [great, ample.
उरु, 1, *more prop.* **ऊरु**, *q.v.*: 2, *m.* (*f.* **उरवी**) large,
उरोज, *m.* the female breast.
उरुज, *more prop.* **ऊरुज**, *q. v.* [aslant, oblique.
उरेब, 1, *f.* complication; deception: 2, crooked,
उर्द, *m.* a kind of vetch (*Dolichos Pilosus*).
उर्दाबेगनी, *f.* an armed female who attends the ladies of a royal harem. [autumn.
उर्दी, *f.* the Persian name of the first month in
उर्दू, *m.* an army, camp, market. The term (Urdoo) is very commonly applied to the Hindustani language as spoken by the Muhammadan population
उर्द्द, *m.* an otter. [of India proper.
उर्द्ध; for all words beginning with this element,
उर्ध = **उर्द**, *q. v.* [see under the form **ऊर्ध्व**.
उर्धंग, *m.* a disease occasioned by the mounting
उर्धंग = **उर्धंग**, *q. v.* [of wind upwards; flatulency.
उर्व्वरा, 1, fertile: 2, *f.* fertile soil, yielding every kind of crop; land in general. [*pr. n.* a certain *Apsarā*.
उर्वशी, *f.* a kind of ornament worn on the breast:
उर्विजा, *f.* one of the epithets of Seetā.
उर्स, *m.* the breast, bosom. [man.
उल, *m.* a kind of wild animal: *pr. n.* a certain
उलंग, *m.* (*f.* ā, ī, inī) a nude person: *lit.* nude.
उलंगना, *t.* to spring over, bound over, overleap.
उलंगनी, *f.* a clothes-line.
उलंघना, *more prop.* **उल्लंघना**, *q. v.*
उलगट, the act of leaping over.
उलगाना, *t.* to cause to leap over.
उलचना, *t.* to throw off the water from anything, to drain, strain. [volvedness.
उलझन, *f.* a being entangled, complication, in-
उलझना, 1, *n.* to be entangled (as thread or hair; *met.* as the heart), to be bound (as in fetters), to be involved in a quarrel or in difficulties: 2, *t.* to quarrel, quarrel causelessly; to debate, dispute.
उलझपुलझ जाना, to become entangled.
उलझा, *m.* (*f.* ī) entangled, involved, intricate.
उलझाना, *t.* to entangle, ravel or entwist (as thread); to involve, embroil; to busy, engage (in difficulties, business, etc.).
उलझाव, *m.* entanglement, complication, involvement, perplexity, intricacy.
उलझेड़ा, *m.* = **उलझन**, *q. v.*
उलट, *m.* the act of upsetting, act of reversing.
उलटकंवल, *m.* a certain plant (*Abroma augustum*).
उलटना, 1, *n.* to be reversed, be turned over, be turned back: 2, *a. int.* to return: 3, *t.* to pervert, subvert, thwart, reverse, overturn; reply.
उलटपुलट, 1, *f.* confusion; interchange; deception, imposition: 2, confused, all in confusion, higgledy-piggledy, topsy-turvy.
उलटा, 1, *m.* a kind of pudding made of meal or of any pulse, pease-pudding: 2, *m.* (*f.* ī) inverted, reversed, turned back; reverse, contrary: opposite — *phirnā*, to return. — *samajhnā*, to misunderstand.
उलटाना, *t.* to reverse, upset, turn topsy-turvy, thwart, pervert; to modify; to interchange; to re-
उलटाना पुलटाना (intensive) = **उलटाना**, *q. v.* [turn.
उलटापलटा, *m.* (*f.* **उलटीपलटी**) }
उलटापुलटा, *m.* (*f.* **उलटीपुलटी**) } = **उलटपुलट**, 2, *q. v.*
उलटाव, *m.* an upsetting, turning upside-down.
उलठना = **उलटना**, *q. v.*
उलठपलठ = **उलटपुलट**, *q. v.*
उलठाना = **उलटाना**, *q. v.*
उलठामार, *m.* a reverse blow, back-stroke.
उलठी समझ, *f.* a misconception, perverse idea,
उलठेपाओं, *adv.* on returning. [absurd idea.
उलथड़ना = **उलेथड़ना**, *q. v.* [ocean by storms).
उलथना, *a. int.* to undulate, be agitated (as the
उलथा, *m.* a translation, rendering, interpretation. — *k.* to translate [ness, familiarity, intimacy.
उलफ़त, *f.* friendship, affection, attachment, kind-
उलमा, *m.* (pl. of **आलिम**) the learned, the wise.
उलरना, *a. int.* to lie down, take rest.
उललना, *n.* to be overset, be laid over to one side.
उलवा = **उलू**, *q. v.*
उलश, *m*, the leavings of a superior.
उलहना, 1, *m.* a complaint, accusation, reproof, chiding, reproach: 2, *a. int.* to grow, vegetate. — *denā*,
उलाग़, *m.* an owl. [to reproach, complain of, abuse.
उलाट जाना, *n.* to be proud, become proud.
उलारना, *t.* to cause to lie down, cause to take rest, cause to sleep.
उलालना, *t.* to overset, lay over to one side.
उलाहना, *m.* a reproach, chiding, complaint.
उलीचना, *t.* to throw off water, to bale.
उलुलभ्रक्रम, endued with constancy.
उलू, *f.* a kind of grass (*Saccharum cylindricum*) used in thatching.
उलूक, *m.* an owl; an epithet of Indra.
उलूखल, *m.* bdellium; a gummy substance; a wooden mortar used for cleaning rice.
उलूवा = **उलू**, *q. v.*
उलेथड़ना, *t.* to pour (water, or any liquid).
उल्का, *f.* a firebrand; fire falling from heaven, meteor, etc.; flame, fire. [or inverted blow).
उल्पट, *m.* a certain stroke in sword-play (a reflex
उल्मुक, *m.* a firebrand, burning wood, charcoal.
उल्लंघक, *adj.* transgressing: hence, *m.* (*f.* ikā) a transgressor. [transgression, infringement.
उल्लंघन, *m.* the transgressing a rule or custom
उल्लंघना, *t.* to disobey, transgress, infringe.
उल्लास, *m.* skipping; alacrity; gladness, joy, happiness: a section, chapter: splendour, light.
उल्लू, *m.* an owl; *met.* a stupid, blockhead, fool.

उल्लूदास, *m.* (*f.* ī) any one who is as stupid as an owl, a simpleton, fool.

उल्लूदासरी = **उल्लूदास**, *q.v.*

उल्लूपन, *m.* owlishness, stupidity.

उवार, the act of ploughing up a standing crop.

उशर, a heifer.

उशीर, *f.* a grass (*Andropogon muricatum*) whose root is sweet-scented and is used for making *tattees.* [Its Persian name is *khas.*

उश्तुर, *m.* a camel.

उषनना = **उसनना**, *q.v.*

उषस, *f.* the dawn, morning, daybreak.

उषा, 1, *m.* = **उषस**, *q.v.*: 2, = **ऊषा**, *q.v.*

उषाकाल, *m.* the early morning.

उष्ट्र, *m.* (*f.* ī) a camel, a buffalo, a bull with a hump: *pr. n.* a certain demon.

उष्ण, 1, *m.* warmth, heat, the hot season: 2, *m.* (*f.* ā) warm, hot, pungent, acrid.

उष्णत्व, *m.* (*f.* tā) warmth, heat.

उष्णीष, *m.* a turban; a diadem.

उष्णोत्पादक, *m.* (*f.* ikā) *adj.* heat-producing.

उष्म, *m.* (*f.* ā) warm, hot.

उष्मकाल, *m.* the hot season, summer.

उष्मज, *m.* (*f.* ā) any animal born of heat, such as gnats, flies, mosquitoes, etc.: *lit.* heatborn (as insects in a dunghill).

उष्मत्व, *m.* (*f.* tā) warmth, heat.

उष्मा, *f.* warmth, heat; wrath.

उस; the inflectional base of the oblique cases of the singular of the remoter demonstrative **वह**.

उसकाना = **उस्काना**, *q.v.*

उसता, *m.* a barber.

उसनना, *a. int.* to simmer, boil.

उसना, *m.* (*f.* ī) boiled.

उसनाना, *t.* to cause to boil.

उसरना, *a. int.* to retreat, shrink from, recede.

उसल, form, figure.

उसलपुसल, *n.* to be agitated, tossed, get into confusion, be disconcerted, be put out, be ill-at-ease.

उसांस, *more com.* **उसास**, *q.v.*

उसानना, *t.* to cause anything to boil, to boil.

उसाना, *t.* to winnow.

उसारना, *t.* to remove, displace.

उसारा, *m.* a porch, portico, peristyle, vestibule.

उसास, *m.* breath, respiration, breathing, sigh.

उसासना, *a. int.* to breathe.

उसिजना, *a. int.* to simmer, boil.

उसीजना }
उसीझना } *t.* to boil anything.

उसीर, *more prop.* **उशीर**, *q.v.*

उसीसा, *m.* a pillow, cushion, head of a bed or of any resting place.

उसुरा; see **ऊसर** and **ऊसारा**.

उसूल, *f.* (pl. of **असल**) causes, roots.

उसे, a dat. and acc. sing of **वह**.

उसेवना, *t.* to throw off the water from boiled rice.

उसै }
उसैं } in Braj = **उसे**, *q.v.*

उस्काना, *t.* to light a fire, light a candle; to excite, stir up, unsettle, incite, instigate.

उस्तरा, *m.* a barber.

उस्तरां, *adv.* free, gratis, for nothing.

उस्ता, *m.* a barber.

उस्ताद, *m.* a teacher, preceptor in religious matters; the chief of a department.

उस्तुख़ान, *m.* a bone: a kernel (of fruit).

उस्तुर्लाब, *f.* an astrolabe.

उस्तुवार, powerful, strong, firm, brave, resolute, solid.

उस्पर, *adv.* upon that, thereupon.

उस्र, *m.* (*f.* ā) a bull: a ray of light.

उस्लूब, *m.* manner, mode, method, order, arrangement.

उस्सा, like him: see **सा**.

उह, a dialectic form = **वह**, *q.v.*

उहरना, *a. int.* to subside (said of a swelling or of an inundation).

उहवां, a dialectic form = **वहां**, *q.v.*

उहां (*corruption*) = **वहां**, *q.v.*

उहार, *m.* a cover, covering of a litter or palki for females.

उहो (*corruption*) = **वहो**, *q.v.*

उहे, a dialectic form = **वे**, those.

ऊ

ऊ (ū) is the sixth vowel of the Hindee or Devanāgaree alphabet and has the following characteristics and functions: —1, In pronunciation it has the long broad sound of *u* as in the English word 'rude'; *never* as in 'mule.' 2, The shape of its medial and final form is nearly that of the foregoing letter (उ) reversed; and it is always placed under the letter after which it is to be pronounced; *e. g.* **सूल**. There is, however, a single exception both as to its form and position where it follows **र**; *e. g.* **रूप**; also when it follows **ह** its form is, generally speaking, peculiar; *e. g.* **हृ** = **हू**. 3, As an Unādi suffix it appears at the end of some substantives which are formed, with or without further modification, from the roots of verbs; *e. g.* **पादू** (**पद**), **उनू** (**उन**), **उड़ाऊ** (**उड़ा**). The substantives so formed are generally feminine. 4, Added to some substantives it forms the corresponding adjectives; *e. g.* **भांडू** (**भांड़**). 5, Words properly beginning with this letter are often inaccurately spelt with **उ**, and *vice versâ*. 6, This letter is often (especially in Braj) used as the sign of the second person plural of the imperative mode, where we should expect **ओ**; *e. g.* **तेजू** = **तेजो** (**तेजना**). 7, In Braj it is an emphatic particle = **भी**; *e. g.* **सोऊ** = **सो भी**; **वेऊ** = **वे भी**. 8, Often, and especially in the Braj dialect, this letter is found where we might expect **व**; *e. g.* **ठांऊ**, more properly **ठांव**. 9, In poetry this, like all the long vowels is in all situations *long* *by nature.* 10, In certain provincial dialects this letter is sometimes found for वह, that. 11, In the case of those adjectives in Hindee which end with this letter, the form for both genders is the same; *e. g.* खाऊ, *m.* or *f.* a glutton. 12, In the formation of many compound words, this letter exercises important functions and undergoes important changes which may be found carefully specified at length in any good Hindee or Sanskrit Grammar.

ऊई, (an exclamation of reproach) Oh fie! Oh!

ऊं, the characteristic termination of the first person singular of the "aorist;" *e.g.* करूं, कराऊं.

ऊः, (an exclamation expressive of sudden pain or distress) Oh!

ऊंगा, *m.* (*f.* ऊंगी) the characteristic termination of the 1st pers. sing. of the future tense; *e. g.* करूंगा.

ऊंघ, *f.* a nodding, sleepiness.

ऊंघना, *a. int.* to doze, droop, nod from sleepiness.

उंघाई = ऊंघास, *q.v.*

ऊंघास, *f.* drowsiness, nodding, sleepiness, dozing, drooping drowsily (*esp.* from the influence of opium).

ऊंच, ऊंट; for all words beginning with either of these elements, see under the more proper forms उंच, उच, ऊपट, respectively.

ऊंजरी, *f.* a small heap of corn set apart by Muhammadans at harvest-time in the name of some saint.

ऊंदी, *more prop.* कुंदी, *q.v.*

ऊंहूं, an interjection denoting refusal or negation.

ऊक, *f.* an error, mistake, slip.

ऊकत = उक्त or उक्ति, *qq.v.*

ऊकना, 1, = ओकना, *q. v.*: 2, *a. int.* to make a mistake, miss, err, slip.

ऊकार, *m.* the letter ऊ or any symbol that may represent it.

ऊकारान्त, (in Gram.) ending with ऊ.

ऊख, *f.* sugarcane (*Saccharum officinarum*). According to the author of the *Araishi Mahfil*, this word is pronounced in the Delhi district as if spelt *ikh*, and *ookh* in that of Oude.

ऊखर, a pot for husking rice.

ऊखरस, *m.* the juice of the sugarcane.

ऊखराज, *m.* the day on which the planting of the sugarcane begins. It is generally attended with some festive ceremonies.

ऊखल, *more prop.* (1) ऊखर (2) उखल, *qq.v.*

ऊखली, *more prop.* उखली, *q.v.*

ऊखा, *more prop.* (1) उखा (2) ऊख (3) ऊषा, *qq.v.*

ऊखाड़ना, *more com.* उखाड़ना, *q.v.*

ऊखाड़ी, *f.* a field of sugarcanes.

ऊखाल, *m.* an emetic.

ऊखालना = उखालना, *q. v.*

ऊछालनी, *f.* the multiplication-table.

ऊजड़ } ऊभड़ } = उजभड़, *q.v.*

ऊटपटंग, 1, *m.* anything without meaning or without foundation, nonsense, absurdity: 2, poor, helpless, destitute; in disorder.

ऊटपटंगी, *m.* (*f.* inī) one who speaks without due consideration or preparation.

ऊटपटांग = ऊटपटंग, *q.v.*

ऊटपटांगी = ऊटपटंगी, *q.v.*

ऊठाईगीरा, *m.* a certain class of robbers who plunder by day, and are commonly followers of an army.

ऊठाना = उठाना, *q.v.*

ऊठाबिठाना, *t.* to excite, stir up, urge on.

ऊड़िया, *m. pr. n.* the province of Orissa.

ऊड़ी मारना, *a. int.* to dive, plunge.

ऊणा, *f.* wool. *Gādar ānī ooṇ koṅ baiṭhī chare kapās*, I bought the sheep for furnishing) wool, and she is eating up the cotton (said of anything done by way of economy, which in the end turns out to be very expensive).

ऊणी, *m.* (*f.* inī) woollen, made of wool.

ऊपट, *m.* (*f.* nī) a camel.

ऊपटकटारा, *m.* a thistle (*Eschinops echinatus*, Roxb.) of which camels are fond.

ऊपटनी, *f.* (*m.* ऊपट) a she-camel.

ऊत 1, *more prop.* उत, *q.v.*: 2, = अऊत, *q.v.*

ऊतना, *m.* (*f.* ī) *more prop.* उतना, *q.v.*

ऊता, *m.* (*f.* ī) = उतना, *q.v.*

ऊतार = उतार, *q.v.*

ऊतारान, *m.* a stripping off; the act of dismounting.

ऊतावलपाना, *m.* haste, urgency.

ऊतिक, that much, as much as that.

ऊत्तम, *more properly* उत्तम, *q.v.*

ऊत्तर, *more properly* उत्तर, *q.v.*

ऊद, *more prop.* उद्, *q.v.*

ऊदबिलाव, *m.* an otter (*lit.* the aquatic cat).

ऊदा, 1, *m.* the colour brown: 2, *m.* (*f.* ī) brown.

ऊदाई } ऊदाहट } *f.* brownness.

ऊदी, *f.* (*m.* ऊदा) brown.

ऊदेस, क°, to search for.

ऊदै, *more prop.* उदय, *q.v.*

ऊधम, *m.* noise, hubbub, uproar, disturbance, rebellion, impudence.

ऊधमी, *m.* (*f.* inī) a noisy person, etc.: *lit.* making a noise; impudent, rebellious.

ऊधर, *more properly* उधर, *q v.*

ऊधार = उद्धार, *q.v.*

ऊधो, *m. pr. n.* a certain friend and companion of Krishṇ's.

ऊन, 1, *more prop.* ऊणा, *q.v.*: 2, *m.* (*f.* ā) less, deficient, minus. Prefixed to Sanskrit numerals it denotes, 'one less': in Hindee it has the same function, but the *u* is generally short; *e g.* उनतीस, *lit.* one less (than) thirty, *i. e.* twenty-nine. Hence, for all numerals beginning with this element, see under the form उन.

ऊनन = उन्नों. Frequent in poetry and in Braj.

ऊनवाचक संज्ञा, *f.* (in Gram.) a diminutive noun.

ऊना, *m.* (*f.* ī) a kind of sword, scimitar, knife, etc., worn down by grinding.

ऊनी, *more properly* ऊर्णी, *q. v.*

ऊनुं
ऊनों } = उन्हों, *q. v.*

ऊपजना, *more prop.* उपजना, *q. v.*

ऊपटना, *a. int.* to exceed.

ऊपर, (*prop.* उपर) 1, *m.* the top, outside, exterior: 2, (a separable postposition taking the inflected form of the genitive masculine) above, on, on the top of, upon, over, outside, up, upwards, passed over.

ऊपरना, *more prop.* उपरना, *q. v.*

ऊपरसे, over, from above, on the outside. *Tūfān ūparse chalā gayā*, the storm passed over.

ऊपरी, upper, external, outside, strange, foreign.

ऊपरीय = ऊपरी, *q. v.* [devious.

ऊबट, *m.* (*f.* ā) impassable, inaccessible, steep,

ऊबलना = उबलना, *q. v.*

ऊबालना = उबालना, *q. v.* [heat.

ऊभ, *m.* oppressive heat, languor occasioned by

ऊभना, *n.* to be agitated, be oppressed with heat; to be angry, be dissatisfied.

ऊमरि, *m.* the glomerous figtree (*Ficus glomerata*).

ऊमी, *f.* an ear of half-ripe corn.

ऊरद, *more prop.* उर्द, *q. v.*

ऊरु, *m.* (*f.* ?) the thigh, upper part of the thigh.

ऊरुज, *m.* (*f.* ā) one of the third or thigh-born caste, *i. e.* a Vaishya: *lit.* born from the thigh.

ऊर्णवस्त्र, *m.* woollen cloth, a woollen garment.

ऊर्द्ध; for all words beginning with this element, see under the form ऊर्ध्व. [superior.

ऊर्ध्व, *m.* (*f.* ā) erect, raised, high, above, on high,

ऊर्ध्वगमन, *m.* an ascending, mounting, ascent; a walking stiffly, walking proudly.— *k.* to ascend, mount aloft.

ऊर्ध्वपुण्ड्र, *m.* a perpendicular line delineated on the forehead by the worshippers of Vishṇu.

ऊर्ध्वबाहु, *m.* a man who holds one or both arms aloft (one of the attitudes of Hindoo ascetics).

ऊर्ध्वमुख, *m.* (*f.* ī) with upturned face (as in supplication).

ऊर्ध्वरेता, *m.* (*lit.* chaste) one who lives in perpetual chastity; epithet of an order of Hindoo mendicants, a *sanyāsee*, a *rishi*.

ऊर्ध्ववस्त्र, *m.* an outer garment, overcoat.

ऊर्ध्ववांह = ऊर्ध्वबाहु, *q. v.*

ऊर्ध्वश्वास, *m.* a deep inspiration, gasp, hard breathing (as in asthma).

ऊर्ध्वसांस = ऊर्ध्वश्वास, *q. v.*

ऊर्मि, *m. f.* a wave, surge.

ऊलू
ऊलूआ } = उलू, *q. v.*

ऊषण, *m.* black pepper.

ऊषर, *m.* saline soil, barren land: lit. *m.* (*f.* ā) impregnated with saline particles.

ऊषा, *f. pr. n.* the wife of Aniruddh, son of Kāmdev.

ऊष्म, *m.* (in Gram.) a sibilant. For words beginning with this element, see under the more proper form उष्म.

ऊष्माण:, an artificial word used by ancient writers on Sanskrit Grammar to denote the sibilants, *viz.*, श, ष, स, ह.

ऊसर, *f.* dry ground, desert soil, sandy land.

ऊसरल्ली, *f.* a chameleon.

ऊसारा, *m.* gamboge.

ऊह, 1, an interjection expressive of pain, distress, disgust, or awe: 2, *m.* connected reasoning, logic, inference: the supplying an ellipsis.

ऊह्य, requiring to be supplied (in reasoning), elliptical; inferrible, to be investigated.

ऋ

ऋ (ṛi) is the seventh vowel in the Hindee or Devanāgaree alphabet, and has the following characteristics and functions:— 1, It has in pronunciation the sound of *ri* in the English word 'rill'. 2, Its medial and final form is merely a hooked figure turned towards the right, and is written under, and attached to, the consonant which it may happen in pronunciation to follow; *e. g.* तृण. 3, As this is one of the cerebral letters, if *n* follows it in the same word, the न becomes ण, provided the न be not final. If the word be a polysyllabic one this change seldom takes place in Hindee unless this letter occur in the syllable immediately preceding the one in which the *n* occurs. 4, This letter is continually liable to be corrupted into रि; *e. g.* रिषि, more properly ऋषि. 5, Through want of exactness it is often (both to the eye and to the ear) separated from its letter in a way that is eminently calculated to mislead; *e. g.* गिरहस्थ, more properly गृहस्थ. 6, In poetry, it is, like the other short vowels, *short by nature*, whether it be used separately or joined to a consonant: when, however, it occurs before a compound consonant, whether in the same word with it or in the one that follows, it becomes, like them, *long by position*. 7. For a full and clear statement of the functions and vicissitudes of this letter in the formation of compound words, see any good Hindee or Sanskrit Grammar.

ऋक, *more properly* ऋग, *q. v.* [represent it.

ऋकार, *m.* the letter ऋ, or any symbol that may

ऋक्ष, *m.* (*f.* ī) a bear: a star; a constellation.

ऋग = ऋग्वेद, *q. v.*

ऋगकेतु, *m. pr. n.* the constellation of the Bear.

ऋग्वेद, *m. pr. n.* (see ऋच) the first and most important of the four Veds (so called because it consists chiefly of hymns in praise of the Hindoo deities).

ऋच, *f.* lustre, splendour; a hymn; stanza; the Rig-Ved (so called because it consists chiefly of hymns to the Hindoo deities); a verse or text from the Rig-Ved, a mystic text from a Ved, magical invocation.

ऋचा, *more com.* ऋच, *q. v.*

ऋचीक, *m. pr. n.* (1) of a certain saint, father of Jamadagni (2) of a certain country.

ऋच्छक, *more prop.* ऋक्ष, *q. v.*

ऋजु, straight; right; sincere, upright.

ऋजुता, *f.* } straightness ; rectitude ; honesty.
ऋजुत्व, *m.* }

ऋण, *m.* an obligation, debt ; (in Algebra) a negative quantity, minus. — *denā*, to lend. — *lenā*, to borrow.

ऋणग्रस्त, *m.* (*f.* ā) involved in debt, indebted to.

ऋणग्राहक, *m.* (*f.* ikā) a borrower, one who contracts debts : lit. *adj.* borrowing.

ऋणदायक, *m.* (*f.* ikā) a lender: lit. *adj.* lending.

ऋणमार, one who does not pay his debts.

ऋणमुक्ति, *f.* = ऋणमोक्ष, *q. v.* [from debt.

ऋणमोक्ष, *m.* the discharging a debt ; freedom

ऋणशोधन, *m.* the clearing off a debt.

ऋणिया, *m.* (*f.* ī) = ऋणी, *q. v.*

ऋणी, indebted, obligated : hence, *m.* (*f.* iṇī) a debtor, one who is under obligation.

ऋणोद्धारक, *adj.* discharging debt : hence, *m.* (*f.* ikā) one who discharges a debt or obligation.

ऋतु, *m.* (*f.* ī) order: the right time ; season of the year ; weather : a month ; the menstrual discharge ; the season approved for sexual intercourse. The Hindoos divide the year into six seasons, each consisting of two months; *viz.* (1) *Vasant* (2) *Greeshm* (3) *Varshā* (4) *Sarad* (5) *Him* (6) *Shishir* : hence, in the ingenious system of reckoning by symbols adopted by Hindoos in their poetry, this word is a symbol for 6.

ऋतुपर्ण, *m. pr. n.* a certain king of Ayodhyā.

ऋतुप्राप्त, productive in due season, fruitful.

ऋतुमती, *f.* a woman in her courses ; a woman in the period approved for sexual intercourse ; a marriageable girl.

ऋतुराजा, *m.* the lord of the seasons, *i. e.* the spring.

ऋतुवर्ण, *m. pr. n.* a certain ancient Hindoo king.

ऋतुसुकत, *m.* an epithet of spring.

ऋतुस्नान, *m.* bathing after menstruation.

ऋद्ध, *m.* (*f.* ā) a prosperous person, etc. : *lit.* prosperous, thriving, rising, etc.

ऋद्धि. 1. *f.* plenty, wealth, property ; prosperity, increase : 2. *f.* a certain medicinal plant ; an epithet of the goddess Pārvatee, the deity of wealth.

ऋन ; for words beginning thus, see under the more proper form ऋण.

ऋभु, *m.* a deity, *esp.* a son of Brahmā.

ऋषभ, *m.* a bull ; a chief : *pr. n.* the first of the 24 principal Jins or Jain saints. As the latter element in compound words it means 'best', 'excellent' ; *e. g.* पुरुषर्षभ, an excellent man ; *lit.* a bull of a man.

ऋषभदेव, *m. pr. n.* (see ऋषभ) a certain sage.

ऋषया (*poet.* and *colloq.*) = ऋषि, *q. v.*

ऋषि, *m.* (*f.* ऋषी) an author of sacred hymns, bard ; a pious person, saint, sage, saint-sage, anchorite : a Ved or sacred composition. The *rishi* of a *mantra*, or mystic prayer of the Veds, is the sage by whom it is supposed to have been remembered, composed, or recited. There are several orders of *rishis*, as the *Devarshi*, the *Maharshi*, the *Rajarshi*, etc. The uncompounded name is applied more particularly to seven ancient sages (*viz.* Vashishtha, Marīchi, Atri, Angiras, Pulastya, Pulah, and Kratu) who hold in the Hindoo mythology an exalted and mysterious rank : they are identified with the seven stars of Ursa Major. In astronomy this term is applied to the seventh asterism of the great Bear. In the ingenious system of reckoning by symbols adopted by Hindoos in their poetry, this word is a symbol for 7.

ऋषिऋण, *m.* an obligation owing to the Rishis, *i. e.* the study of the Veds. [of a *rishi*.

ऋषिकन्या, *f.* an epithet of Sītā ? *lit.* the daughter

ऋषिता, *f.* } the status of a *rishi*, saintship.
ऋषित्व, *m.* }

ऋषीनायक = ऋषीश्वर, *q. v.*

ऋषिनारि }
ऋषिनी } = ऋषी, *q. v.*
ऋषिपत्नि }

ऋषिमुनि = ऋषि or मुनि. This combination is very common in ordinary discourse.

ऋषिराई, *m.* an epithet of the moon ; *lit.* lord of the stars, lord of the bears.

ऋषी, *f.* (*m.* ऋषि) the wife of a *rishi*.

ऋषीश }
ऋषीश्व } = ऋषीश्वर, *q. v.*

ऋषीश्वर, *m.* an epithet of either of the four sons of Brahmā : *lit.* lord or chief of the *Rishis*.

ऋषीसा, *more prop.* ऋषीश, *q. v.*

ऋष्टि, *f.* a spear ; a sword. [spear-bearing.

ऋष्टिमन्त, *m.* (*f.* matī) a spear-bearer : lit. *adj.*

ऋष्य, *m.* the painted or white-footed antelope.

ऋष्यक, *adj.* of the colour of the painted antelope.

ऋष्यमूक, *m. pr. n.* a certain mountain mentioned in the Rāmāyaṇ,

ऋष्यरूपी, *m.* (*f.* iṇī) being of the shape or appearance of an antelope.

ॠ

ॠ (ṛī) is the eighth vowel of the Hindee or Devanāgaree alphabet, and has the following characteristics and functions : — 1, It is the above-mentioned vowel lengthened, and has the sound of *ri* in the English word 'marine.' 2, Its medial and final form is a kind of double hooked figure turned towards the right, and is written under, and attached to, the consonant which in pronunciation it may happen to follow ; *e. g.* पितॄन्. 3, In poetry, this, like all the long vowels, is in all situations *long by nature.* 4, Remark 3, article ऋ applies also to this letter. 5, For a clear statement of the functions and vicissitudes of this letter in the formation of compound words, see any good Hindee or Sanskrit Grammar. 6, *m.* a demon : an epithet of Shiv. 7, *f.* an epithet (1) of the mother of the gods (2) of the mother of the demons.

ॠकार, *m.* the letter ॠ, or any symbol that may represent it.

ऌ

ऌ (lṛi) is the ninth vowel of the Hindee or Devanāgaree alphabet, and has the following characteristics and functions : — 1, In pronunciation it ought to have the power of the combination of the three letters *lṛi*, but it is more usually expressed by the sound of *li* in the English word 'lip'. 2. Its secondary form is the primary form *minus* the horizontal and perpendicular strokes (thus ॢ) and is written under (and attached to) the consonant which it may happen in pronunciation to follow. 3, In poetry, it is, like the other short vowels, *short by nature*, whether used separately or joined to a consonant: when, however, it occurs before a compound consonant, whether in the same word with it or in the one that follows, it becomes, like them, *long by position*. 4, In regard to this letter and the following one it might be observed that there are no words in Hindee commencing with them: when they occur at all, which is very seldom, they occur in the secondary and not in the primary form; and chiefly in a few verbal roots which are usually recorded in Dictionaries of Sanskrit only; *e. g.* क्ळृप. The reason for inserting them in a Hindee Dictionary is to complete the alphabet. 5, For a full and specific statement of the changes to which this letter is liable in the formation of compound words, see any good Sanskrit Grammar.

ऌकार, *m.* the letter ऌ or any symbol that may represent it.

ॡ

ॡ (lṛī) is the tenth vowel of the Hindee or Devanāgaree alphabet, and has the following characteristics and functions: — 1, In pronunciation it ought properly to have the power of the three letters in the combination *lri*: it has, however, the sound of *li* in the English word 'police', and is thus the above-mentioned vowel lengthened. 2, Its secondary form is the primary form *minus* the horizontal and perpendicular strokes (thus ॣ) and is written under (and attached to) the consonant which it may happen in pronunciation to follow. 3, There do not appear to be any words in which this letter occurs; it is never used excepting in technical grammatical phraseology, and its only *raison d'etre* seems to be to contribute to the completeness of the alphabet.

ॡकार, *m.* the letter ॡ or any symbol that may represent it.

ए

ए (ē) is the eleventh vowel of the Hindee or Devanāgaree alphabet, and has the following characteristics and functions: — 1, As this is the only vowel in the Devanāgaree alphabet to represent the *e* sound, its quantity is sometimes short, as in the English word 'grey', and sometimes long, as in the English word 'there', or the French *crême*. This latter pronunciation is by far the more usual one; but, in fact, nothing but long and careful practice can inform the student in what words it should have the one pronunciation, and in what words the other. 2, Its medial and final form is a kind of curve, and is always written above the letter which it follows in pronunciation and is contiguous to it; thus के. 3, As a vocative particle (O!) it implies respect. 4, When preceded by a vowel this letter is frequently interchanged with य, *e. g.* होए = होय; उपाए, more properly उपाय; and occasionally when preceded by the inherent vowel only; *e. g.* बिषे, properly बिषय. 5, It is often interchanged with ये; *e. g.* भए = भये. 6, In provincial brogue, this letter is often put inaccurately for ऐ; *e. g.* हे, more properly है. 7, This letter is the characteristic termination of the second and third persons singular of the "aorist": *e. g.* करे, पाए. 8, in reference to its function as the distinctive termination of the masculine plural of participles, it may be important to remember article आ, 14. 9, This letter is invariably the inflectional substitute of आ; *e. g.* बेटा, बेटेका; होना, होनेका. 10, As the inflection of the infinitive mode this letter is often dropped, especially by the lower classes and by the peasantry; *e. g.* रहन देओ, more properly रहने देओ. 11, This letter forms adverbial ordinals by displacing the आ or the आं of adjectival ordinals; *e. g.* पहिला, first; पहिले in the first place, firstly: दसवां, tenth; दसवे, in the tenth place, tenthly. (See articles वां, वे, वें.) 12, In provincial brogue this letter is often exchanged for इ; more especially in numerals or in words that imply *collectiveness*: e. g. इकावन, more properly एकावन; इकट्ठा, more properly एकट्ठा. 13, Of all inflectible substantives this letter is the sign of the nominative plural; *e. g.* कुत्ते, nominative plural of कुत्ता. 14, In poetry this letter is, in all situations, *long by nature*. 15, In some dialectic pronunciations this letter = यह, this. 16, This letter is one of the names of Vishṇu. 17, For a full and careful statement of the functions and changes of this letter in the formation of compound words, see any good Hindee or Sanskrit Grammar.

एउ; freq. in Braj as the termination of the past part. (*m.* and *f.*); *e. g.* करेउ = किया or किया हुआ.

एऊ = एउ, *q. v.*

एं; 1, This is the characteristic termination of the nominative plural of substantives feminine ending with a consonant (*e. g.* बातें, nominative plural of बात), and of substantives feminine ending in the uninflected आ; *e. g.* आज्ञाएं, nominative plural of आज्ञा. 2, In verbs this is the characteristic termination of the first and third persons plural of the "aorist"; *e. g.* करें, कराएं. 3, This form is often used in Braj where we should expect to find ए; *e. g.* ऐसें, more properly ऐसे.

एंउ; see यहू भी and यों.

एक, *m.* (*f.* ā) one; a, an; the same, similar, alike; alone; any, only; preëminent, chief: somebody. This word is much used in composition, especially in the formation of compound adjectives, just as in Persian; e. g. *Ekdil, ekchit. Ekse din na rahnā* is a phrase that is applied to a change of condition, — most commonly from good to bad, but sometimes the reverse. *Ekkā das sunānā* is a phrase that is applied to a person who replies in many words, especially in giving abuse; *lit.* to reply ten (words) for one. *Ek na ek* (gen. *ek na ekkā, ki, ke*) either, one or other. *Ek* is frequently united to the following word, even when no special reason for the connexion is apparent; e. g. *ekdin*. When used in immediate proximity to another numeral, and *following* it, this word exhibits an important idiom, which is observable, however, in other Indian languages besides Hindee: in such a position it is equivalent to one of the senses of the English word 'about'; e. g. *Ek kos*, one kos; but *kos ek*, about a kos; *das ek kos*, about ten kos; *ādmee das ek*, about ten persons; *sau ek*, about a hundred; (but *ek sau ek* a hundred and one); *sau das ek* or *ek sau das ek* about a hundred and ten. *Ek ek*, each, each severally, each separately, one by one, one at a time, one each. *Ek ek karke*, one by one, singly, in detail, one at a time.

एकई, (emphatic) one and the same, one only.

एकईस, twenty-one (२१): see **चों, वां, वीं, वे, वें**.

एकउ in Braj = **एकई**, *q.v.*

एकक, alone, solitary; the same.

एकक़लम, altogether, entirely, utterly.

एककाल, *m.* one time, the same time: *adv.* once, at one time.

एककालीन, coëval, cotemporary, simultaneous.

एकछत्र, *m.* a supreme monarch, emperor; *hence*, Rāja Rāmchandra. [trunk of a tree.

एकगाछी, *f.* a canoe consisting of the hollowed

एकगुरु, *m.* a pupil of the same preceptor, a spiritual brother.

एकग्रामीय, *m.* (*f.* ā) an occupant of the same village, native of the same village: *lit.* appertaining to the same village.

एकचित्त, *m.* (*f.* ā) collected as to thought, thinking of one thing only, intent upon, absorbed in, being in a state of mental concentration; of one mind, unanimous, concurring, agreeing: collected as to intention, unwavering, determined, resolute.

एकछत्र, *more prop.* **एकच्छत्र**, *q.v.* [sentient.

एकज़बान, of one speech; of the same mind, con-

एकटक, *m.* a looking fixedly at anything without blinking, a fixed look, stare, gaze. – *dekhnā*, to look steadily, fixedly, or carefully at, to eye, gaze at.

एकट्ठा, 1, *m.* a small boat rowed with one oar: 2, *m.* (*f.* ī) collected together, united. — *k.* to bring together, collect, amass. — *honā*, to assemble.

एकट्ठा }
एकठा } *m.* (*f.* ī) = **एकट्ठा**, *q.v.*
एकड़ा }

एकडाल, in one piece, without joining.

एकतनु, *adj.* having but one body, *i.e.* not subject to transmigration.

एकतराज्वर, *m.* a tertian ague or fever.

एकता, *f.* unity, oneness, union, harmony, conjunction, sameness, identity.

एकताई = **एकता**, *q.v.*

एकतान, 1, *m.* musical unison: 2, *adj.* having the mind fixed on one object only, closely attentive.

एकताल, *m.* harmony, unison, the accurate adjustment of song, dance, and instrumental music.

एकतालीस, forty-one (४१): see **चों, वां, वीं, वे, वें**.

एकतीर्थिन, *m.* an associate in religious offices or objects, a spiritual brother.

एकतीस, thirty-one (३१): see **चों, वां, वीं, वे, वें**.

एकतें in Braj = **एकसे**. See **तें**, 3.

एकत्र, 1, = **एकत्रा**, *q.v.*: 2, in one and the same place, together, collectedly.

एकत्रा *m.* a sum-total; interest of one per cent. per month; the numeral 101.

एकत्व, *m.* = **एकता**, *q.v.*

एकथा, *more properly* **एकत्र**, *q.v.*

एकदम, *adv.* in one instant, at once.

एकदस्त, altogether, entirely, utterly.

एकदा, once upon a time, at one time, once; at once, at the same time.

एकदिल, unanimous; determined, resolute.

एकदीगर, one another. [sorrows, sympathizing.

एकदुःखसुख, having (or sharing) the same joys or

एकदृश, one-eyed.

एकपक्ष, *m.* an associate, firm ally, partisan.

एकपत्नी, *f.* a faithful wife, wife devoted to her husband. [on all lands at an equal rate.

एकबाछी, *f.* a distribution of any tax or cess levied

एकबार = **एकदा**, *q.v.*

एकबारगी, all at once, suddenly.

एकबेर = **एकदा**, *q.v.*

एकभक्त, *m.* (*f.* ā) a person who eats but one meal a day: worshipping one deity.

एकभक्ति, 1, *f.* unity of religious belief: 2, of one faith, believing in one deity. [consentient, agreeing.

एकमत, of one way of thinking, of one opinion,

एकमतो in Braj = **एकमत**, *q.v.*

एकमात्रिक, *m.* (in Gram.) a short vowel: *lit.* having [a single *mātra*.

एकमुठ }
एकमूठ } = **एकमत**, *q.v.*

एकर, a dialectic form = **इकला**.

एकरस, 1, *m.* an only flavour, an only pleasure: 2, *m.* (*f.* ā) pleased with one object only; unchanged; not liable to change.

एकराशि, *f.* a heap, crowd.

एकरूप, *m.* (*f.* ā) having the same shape or form or appearance, alike, similar, resembling.

एकरूपी, *m.* (*f.* iṇī) = **एकरूप**, *q.v.* [alone.

एकल, *m.* (*f.* ā) a solitary person: *lit.* solitary,

एकलख़्त, altogether, entirely, utterly.

एकलात, solitarily.

एकले = **एकार**, *q.v.*

एकलोठा }
एकलौता } *m.* (*f.* ī) *more prop.* **एकलोठा**, *q.v.*

एकलोठा, (**एकल + उठा**) *m.* (*f.* ī) an only child (without brother or sister): *lit.* the only one that was picked up (the oriental idea being that the new-born child falls to the ground and is taken up by its father).

एकवचन, *m.* (in Gram.) the singular number.

एकवचनान्त, (in Gram.) ending with a sign of the singular number.

एकवर्ण, 1, *m.* (in Algebra) an unknown quantity: 2, *m.* (*f.* ā) of one color, plain; of one caste, of one race: identical.

एकवर्णी, *f.* beating time, marking musical measure by clapping the hands; an instrument for beating time, a castanet.

एकवार = **एकबार** = **एकदा**, *q.v.*

एकविंश, the twenty-first.

एकविंशति = **एकईस**, *q.v.*

एकशरण, *m.* an epithet of any deity ; *lit.* one only hope and refuge.

एकशरीर, of one body, of one blood.

एकसंग, together, all together, simultaneously.

एकसठ, sixty-one (६१): see **ओं, वां, वीं, वे, वें.**

एकसम = **एकसमान**, *q.v.*

एकसमान, alike, equal, the same, on a level, concordant, harmonizing.

एकसा, *m.* (*f.* ī) alike, having the same qualities, of the same sort, similar, resembling, identical.

एकसाथ, together, all together, simultaneously.

एकसान / **एकसार** } = **एकसा**, *q.v.*

एकसौ, 1, in Braj = **एकसा**, *q.v.*: 2, one hundred.

एकहत्तर, seventy-one (७१): see **ओं, वां, वीं, वे, वें.**

एकहरा, *m.* (*f.* ī) alone, solitary, single.

एकहो, (emphatic) one only; one and the same.

एका, *f.* (*m.* **एक**) alone, single, solitary ; *hence*, a combining together, conspiracy ; a unit ; an ace at cards, etc. — *k.* to act in unison, act together, act simultaneously.

एकाई, *f.* (see **आई**, 3) solitariness ; unanimity, unity.

एकाएक / **एकाएकी** } all at once, suddenly, once.

एकाकार, of the same form, uniform, alike.

एकाकिन, *m.* (*f.* ī) / **एकाकी**, *m.* (*f.* inī) } alone, solitary.

एकाक्ष, 1, *m.* a crow : 2, *m.* (*f.* ī) one-eyed ; blind of one eye : having one axle.

एकाग्र, *m.* (*f.* ā) one whose mind is fixed on one object : *lit.* intent upon : undisturbed, unperplexed.

एकाग्रचित्त, *m.* (*f.* ā) one who has his thoughts or his resolution concentrated on one object : *lit.* attentive ; intent of purpose, resolved upon, resolute.

एकाग्रता, *f.* close attention, intentness ; resolvedness, undisturbedness.

एकाद = **एकाध**, *q.v.*

एकादश, (Sk.) 1, = **ग्यारह**: 2, *m.* (*f.* ī) **ग्यारहवां**, *qq.v.*

एकादशी, *f.* the eleventh day of a lunar fortnight.

एकाध, one half ; some few.

एकाधिपति, *m.* (*f.* **पत्नी**) a sole and absolute monarch.

एकाधिपत्य, *m.* sole and absolute sovereignty.

एकानव, *more prop.* **एकानवे**, *q.v.*

एकानवे, ninety-one (९१): see **ओं, वां, वीं, वे, वें.**

एकान्त, 1, *m.* a solitary place : an extreme : 2, *m.* (*f.* ā) alone, only ; apart, aside, lonely, retired, unfrequented, uninhabited.

एकार, *m.* the letter **ए**, or any symbol that may represent it.

एकारान्त, (in Gram.) ending with **ए**.

एकार्थ, 1, *m.* the same meaning : 2, having one and the same meaning, object, or purpose ; synonymous.

एकार्थक, (in Gram.) synonymous.

एकावन, fifty-one (५१): see **ओं, वां, वीं, वे, वें.**

एकासी, eighty-one (८१) : see **ओं, वां, वीं, वे, वें.**

एकाह्निक, quotidian.

एकौ, *more com.* **एकहो**, *q.v.*

एकीस, *more prop.* **एकईस**, *q.v.*

एकु = **एक भी**, one only : *hence*, with a negative = (not) any, (not) even one.

एके, 1, dialectic form = **इसको** ; 2, = **एकही.**

एकोआनवे = **एकानवे**, *q.v.*

एकोआसी = **एकासी**, *q.v.*

एकोला, *m.* (*f.* ī) = **अकेला**, *q.v.*

एकैक, *m.* (*f.* ā) every one, each successively.

एकैकम, *adv.* one by one, singly.

एको in Braj = **एकभी**. See **ओ**, 5.

एकोत्रा = **एकत्रा**, *q.v.*

एकोह in Braj = **यह कौन.**

एकौ in Braj = **एका** or **एकाई**, *qq.v.*

एक्कीस, *more properly* **एकईस**, *q.v.*

एखड्डा, *more properly* **एकड्डा**, *q.v.*

एग्यारह, eleven (११) : see **ओं, वां, वीं, वे, वें.**

एज़रा, *m. pr. n.* the prophet Ezra, and the Book that bears his name.

एड़, *f.* a striking with the heel, spurring ; a kind of spur for urging on a horse. — *mārnā*, to spur.

एड़क, (*f.* ā) a ram ; a large he-goat trained for fighting : a kind of fireworks.

एड़गज, *m.* a certain medicinal plant (*Cassia Tora*) used for the cure of ringworm.

एड़ी, *f.* the heel. — *dekho*, look at home ; *lit.* look at your heel (a phrase used to neutralize the effect of an evil eye).

एत, so much, so long, so many. (Frequent in composition.)

एतहुंकार = **एत** + **टंकार**, *qq.v.*

एतद्, this. Frequent in composition.

एतदर्थ, for this reason, on this account, therefore, wherefore.

एतद्देश = **एत** + **देश**, *qq.v.*

एतना / **एतनि** } *m.* (*f.* ī) *more prop.* **इतना**, *q.v.*

एतवार, *m.* Sunday.

एतवारी, *m.* (*f.* inī) a person confined for debt who avails himself of the Christian Sabbath for appearing abroad.

एतहि, (1) an emphatic form of **एत** (2) = **इतहि.**

एता, *m.* (*f.* ī) = **इतना**, *q.v.*

एतादृश, like this, similar to this, such.

एताद्वितीय, *adv.* peerless as this.

एताम (Sk.) = **इसको.**

एतावता, on this account, for this reason, by this, hereby.

एतावन्मात्र, thus much only, only this and no more.

एतिक, *more properly* **इतेक**, *q.v.*

एतेहू in Braj = **इतने भी.**

एमन, *m.* a certain musical mode.

एरंड, *m.* = **एरंडी**, *q.v.*

एरंडी, *f.* the castor-oil plant (*Palma Christi* or *Ricinus communis*).

एरफेर }
एराफेर } *m.* = एराफेरी, *q. v.* [ing attendance.

एराफेरी, *f.* exchange, interchange, barter; a danc-

एराख, *m.* the keel of a ship or boat.

एरावत, *more prop.* ऐरावत, *q. v.*

एरावती, *more prop.* ऐरावती, *q. v.*

एरी = (1) एड़ी (2) अरी; see अरे. [persons only.

एल, *f.* a bracelet of gold or silver worn by male

एलची, *m.* an ambassador, agent, envoy, attorney.

एलचीगरी, *f.* = एलचीपना, *q. v.*

एलचीपना, *m.* the office or the dignity of ambassador, etc., ambassadorship, agency. — *k.* to act in the stead of another, discharge the functions of an agent [or ambassador.

एलवा, *m.* aloes (*Aloe perfoliata*).

एलम, *more com.* नीलाम, *q. v.*

एला, 1, *f.* small cardamoms, the seed of *Electeria cardamomum* or *Apinia cardamomum*: 2, as a suffix this particle forms adjectives from substantives; *e. g.* [घरेला (घर).

एलाम = ऐलम, *q. v.*

एलाबालुक, *m.* (see बालु) a kind of drug.

एलियाह, *m. pr. n.* (1) of Elijah (2) of Jerusalem.

एलुआ }
एलुवा } = एलवा, *q. v.* [just, also.

एव, as, like; even so, verily, indeed: only, still,

एवं, thus, so, even so, in this manner; and, moreover. [for, in *lieu* of,

एवज़ी, (takes genit. masc. infl.) in compensation

एवड़, *m.* a flock of goats.

एवम, the composite form of एवं; *see below.*

एवमस्तु, (the Sanskrit imperat. of the verb 'to be') so let it be, Amen. Put at the close of invocations to the Deity.

एवम्भवतु = एवमस्तु, *q. v.* The third person singular of the imperative of the Sanskrit verb 'to become', 'to come to be'.

एशिया, *more prop.* आशिया, *q. v.*

एश्वर्य, *more prop.* ऐश्वर्य, *q. v.*

एसि, 1, in Braj = ऐसे *or* ऐसा, *qq. v.*: 2, an old termin. of the 2nd pers. sing. pres. indic. of verbs; *e. g.* [करेसि = तू करता है.

एसोब, *m.* hyssop.

एसों, a dialectic form = इससे.

एहसान = इहसान, *q. v.*

एहा in Braj = यहां, *q. v.*

एहि in Braj and in poetry = यही, *q. v.*

एहु in Braj = मेंभी; *e.g.* स्वप्नेहु = स्वप्नमें भी.

ऐ

ऐ (ai) is the twelfth vowel of the Hindee or Devanāgaree alphabet, and has the following characteristics and functions:—1, In pronunciation it has the long sound of *ai* in the English word 'aisle'. 2, Its medial and final form is that of the above-mentioned letter doubled, and, like it, is always written above the letter which it follows in pronunciation, and is attached to it; *e. g.* जैसा. 3, In Braj, in poetry, and in the jargon of the peasantry, it is often put inaccurately for ए; *e. g.* करै, more properly करे. 4, This letter is frequently found in Hindee works as a vocative particle: as such, however, it is probably nothing more than a transliteration of the vocative particle of the Urdoo, and is sometimes printed अै,—a form which has properly speaking no existence in Hindee. As a particle of address it implies respect. It is also used in summoning, as are the English expressions, Holloa there! Ho! Heigh! 5, As an interjection or exclamation this letter expresses recollection, after the manner of the English words Ha! Aye! 6, In poetry, this, like all the long vowels, is, in all situations *long by nature.* 7, This letter is frequently put corruptly for ह; *e. g.* बैली, properly बहली; कैना, properly कहना. 8, This letter is one of the epithets of Shiv. 9, The changes and functions of this letter in the formation of compound words will be found carefully specified at length in any good Hindee or Sanskrit Grammar.

ऐं in Braj = एं; *e. g.* बातैं = बातें.

ऐंच, *m.* a drawing, attracting; reserve, security.

ऐंचखेंच, *m.* a quarrelling.

ऐंचना, *t.* to draw, attract, pull.

ऐंचू = ऐंच, *q. v.*

ऐंट; see under the form ऐंठ.

ऐक, by guess, at random, about. As this form is constantly liable to be interchanged with एक, words beginning with the one element will sometimes be found under the other. [represent it.

ऐकार, *m.* the letter ऐ, or any symbol that may

ऐकाहिक, quotidian. [aggregate, product, total.

ऐक्य, *m.* unity, singleness, oneness, harmony;

ऐक्यता, *f.* }
ऐक्यत्व, *m.* } = ऐक्य, *q. v.*

ऐगुण, *m.* stupidity, unskilfulness.

ऐगो in Braj = एगा; *e. g.* करैगो = करेगा.

ऐड़ी = एड़ी, *q. v.* [wheel.

ऐंटन, *m.* the strings or bands of a spinning-

ऐंटनी, *f.* pride, uppishness, peevishness.

ऐंटा, *m.* a snail.

ऐंटू, proud, peevish, stately.

ऐंटूपना, *m.* proudness, stateliness. [a strut.

ऐंठ, *f.* a coil, twist, convolution, tightening;

ऐंठन, *m.* a tightening, twisting, writhing; the cramp.

ऐंठना, 1, *n.* to be pulled, be dragged: 2, *a. int.* to writhe, cramp, twist. be racked with spasms; to strut, stalk, walk affectedly: 3, *t.* to tighten: 4, *m.* the [cramp.

ऐंठाना, *t.* to tighten, twist.

ऐंडना, *a. int.* to stalk about, strut.

ऐतरेय, *m. pr. n.* a certain portion of the Rig-Ved.

ऐनक, *f.* glasses used to assist the sight, spec- [tacles.

ऐनमैन, *adv.* exactly.

ऐने, hither.

ऐनो in Braj = एना; *e. g.* देनो = देना.

ऐन्द्रजालिक, *m.* (*f.* ī) a wizard, magician, juggler: *lit.* magicial, illusory, relating to witchcraft or to legerdemain.

ऐमली, *m.* a certain tribe or caste.

ऐमा, *m.* land given as a reward or favor by the king at a very low rent, a fief; a grant of land, etc. to the people who attend at the tomb of a saint.

ऐयत्य, *m.* quantity; number; value.

ऐम्हर, hither.

ऐयूब, *m. pr. n.* the patriarch Job, and the Book that bears his name.

ऐरावत, *m. pr. n.* Indra's chief elephant, the elephant of the north-east quarter; a particular shape of the rainbow.

ऐरावती, *f.* 1, *pr. n.* (1) of the Ravee river in the Panjāb (2) of the female of Indra's elephant: 2, lightning.

ऐलफैल, *m.* abusive or obscene language.

ऐला; a suffix particle forming adjectives from substantives; *e. g.* **बनेला** (**बन**).

ऐलाड़ }
ऐलार } on this side.

ऐलेवर }
ऐलेवार } on this side.

ऐवान, *m.* a hall, gallery, portico. (Applied generally to a royal palace).

ऐवारः, *m.* a cowshed in a jungle.

ऐश, *m.* pleasure, delight, luxury.

ऐश्वर्य, *m.* control, dominion, sway, supremacy, power, might; grandeur, glory, pomp, wealthiness, greatness, majesty, state: (applied to the attributes of the Deity, thus) superhuman power, omnipotence; the divine faculties of omnipresence, invisibility, etc.

ऐश्वर्यमान, *m.* (*f.* matī) }
ऐश्वर्यवन्त, *m.* (*f.* vatī) } = **ऐश्वर्यीय**, *q. v.*

ऐश्वर्यीय, *m.* (*f.* ā) endowed with superhuman qualities, majestic, glorious, etc.

ऐषीक, made of reeds.

ऐसन, a dialectic form = **ऐसा**, *q. v.*

ऐसा, *m.* (*f.* ī) thus, like this, after this manner. It is sometimes a suffix; *e. g.* **मर्दैसा**, like a man. This word is sometimes inaccurately spelt **अैसा**.

ऐसातैसा, *m.* (*f.* **ऐसीतैसी**) = **ऐसावैसा**, *q. v.*

ऐसावैसा, *m.* (*f.* **ऐसीवैसी**) so so, indifferent: *adv.* indifferently.

ऐसाही = **ऐसेह**, *q. v.*

ऐसे, *m.* this manner: *adv.* in this manner, thus.

ऐसेह, (emphatic) in this very manner, thus and in no other way.

ऐसें in Braj = **ऐसे**, *q. v.*

ऐसेही = **ऐसेह**, *q. v.*

ऐसो in Braj = **ऐसा**, *q. v.*

ऐसोह in Braj = **ऐसेह**, *q. v.*

ऐसों, *adv.* this year.

ऐहलौकिक, relating to this present world.

ऐहहु in Braj = **यही**, *q. v.*

ऐहिक, *m.* (*f.* ī) appertaining to the present state or place, terrestrial, temporal, worldly, local.

ऐहिकदर्शी, *m.* (*f.* inī) a person who is concerned about mundane affairs: *lit.* worldly-minded.

ऐही in Braj = (1) **ऐसाही** (2) **यही**, *qq. v.*

ऐहै, *m. f.* (pl. **ऐहैं**) in Braj = **आवेगा**.

ऐ; this form has, properly speaking, no existence in Hindee; and the only reason for inserting it in a Dictionary is that in Braj it frequently appears as a corruption of **है**.

ओ

ओ (o) is the thirteenth vowel of the Hindee or Devanāgaree alphabet, and has the following characteristics and functions: — 1, In pronunciation it has the long broad sound of *o* in the English word 'go'. 2, Its medial and final form is, in some founts of type, made to approximate too closely to the secondary form of **ई**, — which, indeed, it somewhat resembles: it is always written at the right of the letter which it follows in pronunciation, and is attached to it; *e. g.* **कोना**. 3, It is the invariable termination of the vocative plural of all substantives irrespective of gender or of the manner of their inflection. 4, When used in calling, it indicates respect. 5, It is equivalent to the conjunctions, and, also, too, even, indeed, verily; and when used in these senses it is sometimes attached, like an emphatic suffix particle, to the word it emphasizes; *e. g.* **यको** = **एक भी**. 6, This letter is often interchanged corruptly with **व**; *e. g.* **बवना**, more properly **बोना**; **बिलाओ**, more properly **बिलाव**. 7, This letter is sometimes put corruptly for **आ**, especially in the last syllable; *e. g.* **छोटो**, more properly **छोटा**; **करनो** (but more commonly **करनौं**) is a Braj form of **करना**. 8, This letter is the uniform termination of the second person plural of the "aorist" and of the imperative. 9, In poetry, this, like all the long vowels, is, in all situations, *long by nature*. 10, In certain provincial dialects this letter sometimes = **वह**, that. 11, This is a vocative particle = Oh. 12, It is also an interjection (1) of calling = Ho! Holloa! (2) of reminiscence = Ho! Ah! (3) of compassion = Ah! Oh! 13, This is one of the epithets of Brahma. 14, In the formation of compound words this letter undergoes important changes which will be found carefully specified at length in any good Hindee or Sanskrit Grammar.

ओं, 1, = **ओम**, *q. v.*: 2, This form is invariably inserted between the base and the terminations of all substantives in the oblique cases of the plural; and this, irrespective of their gender or of the manner of their inflection; *e. g.* **बेटोंका**, **जलोंका**, **बातोंका**, **साधुओंका**, **माताओंका**: 3, This is the termination of pronominal numerals in Hindee; *e. g.* **दोनों**, **चारों**, **बीसों**: 4, This is also the termination of aggregate numerals; *e. g.* **सहसों**. In this function this termination imparts various shades of meaning; thus **सहस्रों** = (1) thousands (2) thousands upon thousands, many thousands (3) the whole thousand of them (4) in groups of a thousand, by thousands (5) a thousand times, a thousandfold. It should be observed that we cannot prefix a numeral to any of these aggregate forms; thus, not **तीन सहसों**, but **तीन सहस**; the letter, in fact, is, in aggregate numerals, not merely a mark of pluralization, it is also strongly emphatic, just as when in English we wish to convey a vivid idea of an indefinitely large number, we pluralize the numeral and emphasize strongly in pronunciation; *e. g.* "tons and tons", "hundreds upon hundreds", "thousands". 5, This form is often, in Braj, a sign of the infinitive; *e. g.* पढ़नों = पढ़ना.

ओंकार, *m.* the sacred syllable **ओम**; thanksgiving: grumbling.

ओक, *m.* a house, dwelling; an asylum, place of refuge: sickness at the stomach, nausea, inclination to vomit: a draught of water from the hollow of the hand.

ओकना, *a. int.* to vomit.

ओकरा, a dialectic form = **उसका**.

ओकार, *m.* the letter **ओ**, or any symbol that may represent it.

ओकारान्त, (in Gram.) ending with **ओ**.

ओके, a dialectic form = **उसको**.

ओखली, *f.* a wooden mortar.

ओगर / **ओगरा** } *m.* a kind of pottage or gruel.

ओघ, *m.* a multitude, aggregate, collection; density: a stream.

ओछन, undependable.

ओछा, *m.* (*f.* ī) of little consequence, light, trifling, absurd; lowborn, mean; capricious, silly; fruitless. — *hona*, to want.

ओछाई, *f.* insignificance; absurdity; levity; lowness of extraction; capriciousness.

ओछापन, *m.* = **ओछाई**, *q. v.*

ओज, see (1) **ओजस** (2) **ओझ**.

ओजस, *m.* light, splendour, metallic lustre; gold; manifestation, strength; vitality, vital warmth and action (especially in the foetus).

ओजा, see (1) **ओजस** (2) **ओझा**.

ओझ, *m.* the stomach, entrails.

ओझड़, *f.* a thrust, push.

ओझल, 1, *f.* privacy, retirement; a private apartment; shelter. — *k.* to conceal; to screen, shelter: 2, private, hidden. — *honā*, to be concealed, etc.

ओझा, (see **ओझ**) *m.* (*f.* in) a snake-catcher, charmer: a diviner, wizard, magician. Probably so called, like the Roman *aruspex*, from the practice of the art by examining entrails.

ओझाइन, *f.* (*m.* **ओझा**) a witch, sorceress.

ओट, *f.* a protection, shelter, shade, screen, curtain, partition, covering, concealment. — *k.* to screen, shelter, conceal. — *honā*, to be concealed, be sheltered.

ओटना, *t.* to screen, shelter, defend: to separate the seed from cotton: to thumb: to catch (as a ball).

ओटा, *m.* a partition-wall, screen.

ओठ, *m.* the lip.

ओड़न, *m.* a shield; a target.

ओड़नखाण्डा, *m.* shield and sword.

ओड़ना, *t.* to shield; to ward off a blow in fighting.

ओड़ा, *m.* a basket, pannier.

ओड़िअचि, a screen, protection, shelter.

ओड्र, *m. pr. n.* (1) of Orissa (2) of its inhabitants.

ओढ़ना, 1, *m.* a sheet, cloak, mantle: 2, *t.* to put on (as clothing).

ओढ़नी, *f.* (dim. of **ओढ़ना**) a small sheet; a veil; a woman's cloak.

ओणठ, *m.* the lip.

ओणठखना, a pillow.

ओणडा, *m.* (*f.* ī) deep.

ओत, *f.* overplus, surplus; abatement; recovering from sickness, convalescence.

ओतना / **ओता** } *m.* (*f.* ī) = **उतना**, *q. v.*

ओतिक = **ऊतिक**, *q. v.*

ओत्सुक, *more prop.* **औत्सुक्य**, *q. v.*

ओदन, boiled rice, a kind of pap; food.

ओदनी, *f.* a certain plant (*Sida cordifolia*).

ओदा, *m.* (*f.* ī) wet, damp, moist.

ओधे, 1, *m.* a bunch, cluster: 2, *m.* a proprietor, supreme ruler, one possessing power and authority: *lit.* possessing a right or title.

ओन्ध, *m.* the cord with which rafters or frames for thatching on are pulled into their places and fastened till the roof is finished.

ओन्धना; for this word and its kin, see under the form **औन्धना**.

ओप, *f.* ornament, beauty, elegance, grace, polish, lustre, brightness, brilliancy.

ओपची, *m.* a man armed with weapons or clothed in mail, an armed man.

ओपचीख़ाना, *m.* a guardhouse, post of armed men.

ओपना, polish.

ओम, the mystic name of the Deity. It is said to consist of three letters **अ**, **उ**, **म**, these being names of Vishnu, Shiv, and Brahmā respectively: it hence implies the Divine Triad as recognized by the Hindoos, and is used at the beginning and (like our 'Amen') at the end of prayers and holy recitations: it is also used at the beginning of writings and respectful salutations, and is the subject of many mystical speculations.

ओर, *f.* origin, boundary, limit, side, direction, *ward* as in the English word 'toward'. *Us* —, *adv.* that way, on that side, in that direction, thitherward. — *nibāhnā*, to be constant to, protect for ever.

ओरमा, *m.* the name of a particular kind of sewing, stitching together two breadths.

ओरा = **ओला**, *q. v.*

ओरी, 1, *f.* the eaves of a house; the bank of a pond or rivulet to the water's edge: 2, *m.* (*f.* ini) a sidesman, partisan; a protector, patron: *lit.* partial, belonging to a side.

ओल, *m.* a certain vegetable (*Arum campanulatum*, Roxb.) the root of which is eaten: a hostage or personal security for a debt.

ओलकोबी, *f.* the vegetable commonly called knolcole.

ओलती, *f.* the eaves of a roof.

ओला, *m.* hail: the name of a kind of sweetmeat. — *ho jānā*, to become cold. *Jon sir mundāyā ton ōle parc*, I had no sooner shaved my head than a shower of hail came on (spoken by one who has just engaged in an enterprize when it turns out unfortunate).

ओस, *f.* dew. — *paṛ jānī*, a falling in value, a being deprived of importance, splendour, etc., a becoming less in demand than formerly.

ओषधि = ओषधी, *q. v.*

ओषधी, *f.* a medicinal herb ; an annual plant ; a deciduous herb ; a herb that dies after becoming ripe ; an ingredient of a medicine.

ओष्ठ, *m.* the lip (*esp.* the upper one).

ओष्ठरोग, *m.* any morbid affection of the lips.

ओष्ठी, *f.* a certain creeper (*Bryonia grandis* or *Momordica monodelpha*) bearing a red flower to which the lip is commonly compared.

ओष्ठ्य, (in Gram.) labial.

ओस, *more properly* ओष, *q. v.*

ओसत, *more prop.* औसत, *q. v.*

ओसकर्ग, *m.* a certain medicine.

ओसर, *f.* a heifer.

ओसरा, *m.* a turn ; vicissitude.

ओसराओसरी, by turns, alternately.

ओसार, 1, width, girth : 2, wide.

ओसारा, *m.* a porch, portico, peristyle, vestibule, shed. [place ; a pillow, cushion.

ओसीसा, *m.* the head of a bed or of a resting-

ओसें, a dialectic form = उससे.

ओहो (*corruption*) = वही, *q. v.*

ओहो, (an exclamation of regret) Heigho ! Alas !

औ

औ (au) is the fourteenth vowel of the Hindee or Devanāgaree alphabet, and has the following characteristics and functions. — 1, In pronunciation it has the long broad sound of *ou* in the English word 'round'. 2, The shape of its medial and final form is nearly that of the above-mentioned letter : it is always placed at the right of the letter after which it is to be pronounced, and is attached to it ; *e. g.* गोरिया. 3, As a term of calling or of address, it implies respect. 4, It is also used as an interjection of prohibition and of asseveration. 5, In poetry, in Braj, and in the corrupt jargon called *gaṅwārī* (or the brogue of the peasantry) this letter is frequently put where we might expect (1) आ ; *e. g.* करनौ = करना ; (2) ए ; *e. g.* ऐसौ, = ऐसे ; (3) ओ ; *e. g.* करौ = करो ; (4) अ ; *e. g.* औलगि = अवलग ; (5) भी ; *e. g.* कनकौ = कनक भी ; (6) व ; *e. g.* औतार = अवतार ; (7) और अथा, or औ (and) of which it is, especially among the peasantry, a very common abbreviation and corruption. 6, In poetry, this, like all the other long vowels, is, in all situations, *long by nature*. 7, It is sometimes corrupted into ऊ ; *e. g.* दो सल, properly दो सौ. 8, *m.* sound. 9, *m.* an epithet of the serpent Shesh or Anant. 10, The functions and changes of this letter in the formation of compound words will be found carefully specified at length in any good Hindee or Sanskrit Grammar.

औं, in Braj = (1) अ ; *e. g.* औचौंहियो = अचौंहियो : (2) = आ and ऊं ; *e. g.* करौंगों = करूंगा : (3) = व ; *e. g.* औंतार = अवतार.

औंगो, *f.* silence, dumbness.

औंगो, in Braj = ऊंगा ; *e. g.* करौंगो = करूंगा.

औंला, *m.* a kind of myrobalan (*Phyllanthus emblica*), a species of fruit.

औंलाऔंला, a twin, twins.

औंलासार, *m.* a kind of brimstone.

औकल, restless, uneasy.

औकलबेकल, very restless, very uneasy.

औकात, *m.* (pl. of वक़्त) times, seasons, circumstances, opportunities. [represent it.

औकार, *m.* the letter औ, or any symbol that may

औकारान्त, (in Gram.) ending with औ.

औकाल, a child born before its time : *lit.* untimely, out of season.

औकाली, *m.* (*f.* inī) = औकाल, *q. v.*

औचौंहियो in Braj = अचौंहियो, *q. v.*

औखध, a provincial form of औषध, *q. v.*

औगाह, deep, very deep, unfathomable.

औगी, *f.* a whip like a waggoner's (it is about seven cubits in length and is used in horse-training) : an ornamental edging of superior country-made shoes (peculiar to Delhi).

औगुण ; for words beginning thus, under the more [proper form अवगुण, *q. v.*

औगो = औंगो, *q. v.*

औघट, *more prop.* अवघट, *q. v.*

औघड़, an indiscreet person, etc. : *lit.* awkward, unpleasant, indiscreet.

औचक
औचट } suddenly, unexpectedly.

औचित्य, *m.* fitness, suitableness, aptness, propriety, rightness.

औछ, *m.* a certain root (*Morinda citrifolia*) from which an orange colour is extracted.

औज, *m.* a height, summit, the top ; promotion, preferment, dignity.

औज़ार, *m.* (pl. of वज़र) the rigging and implements of a ship or of a boat ; loads ; weapons ; tools, apparatus : asylums.

औझड़, *f.* a thrust, push.

औटन, *m.* 1, a knife used for cutting tobacco : 2, a boiling, evaporation by boiling.

औटना, 1, *a. int.* to boil (said of milk) ; to evaporate over a fire ; to consume with rage or with vexation : 2, *t.* to burn, parch, dry.

औटाना, *t.* to make hot, cause anything to boil.

औपटा, *m.* (*f.* ī) boiled : parched.

औपडा, *m.* (*f.* ī) deep.

औतरना (*colloquial*) = अवतरना, *q. v.*

औतार (*colloquial*) = अवतार, *q. v.*

औत्सुक्य, *m.* anxiety, perturbation, regret ; eagerness, impatience, desire.

औदात, 1, *m.* the color white : 2, *adj.* white.

औदान, *m.* that which is given over and above beyond what is purchased, gratis, to boot.

औदार्य्य, *m.* munificence, liberality.

औदास्य, *m.* solitude, loneliness.

औदेश, *m.* (अव + देश) a strange or foreign country.

औदेशा, *more prop.* **औदेश**, *q. v.*

औदेशी, *m.* (*f.* inī) a stranger, foreigner: *lit.* appertaining to another country.

औधंगा, *m.* (*f.* ī) improper, out of place.

औधां, *m.* (*f.* īṅ) *more prop.* **औन्धा**, *q. v.*

औनेपौने, *adv.* more or less; partially: on occasion.

औन्धना, *a. int.* to lower (as the sky might).

औन्धा, *m.* (*f.* ī) upside-down, overturned, reversed. — *leṭnā*, to lie on one's face. [turn, spill.

औन्धाना, *t.* to turn upside down, reverse, over-

औन्धाबख़्त, *m.* adverse fortune, misfortune.

औन्धीपेशानी, shortsighted: unfortunate.

औन्धे मुंह गिरना, *a. int.* to fall facewards, fall headlong. [immediate contact.

औपश्लेषिक, *m.* (*f.* ī) appertaining to close or

औबट }
औभट } = ऊबट, *q. v.*

औबाश, *m.* a dissolute fellow, a rake; a mixed crowd of all nations and all sorts of people, especially of the rabble; the mob, the canaille. — *honā*, to become depraved, become dissolute.

और, 1, *conj.* and, also, besides, but: 2, *adj.* more, other, another, different. *Yih aur bāt hai, wuh aur bāt hai*, this is one thing, and that is quite another thing.

औरऔर, others, others besides, other kinds of.

और एक, another, separate, distinct; else.

और क्या, how can it be otherwise? certainly! of course! to be sure! exactly so! [factured for sale.

औरंग, *m.* a throne; places where goods are manu-

औरत, *f.* a woman, a wife.

औरन; frequent in Braj as the inflective base of the oblique cases of the plural of **और**, 2.

और नहीं; a conjunction generally followed by **तो** at the beginning of the next clause: (the "*aur*" is frequently omitted; *e. g. Dekho! [aur] naheeṅ, to tum giroge*); and (if) not, then; and if otherwise, then; or else.

और्व, *m. pr. n.* a certain ancient Hindoo sage.

औरश्रलोम = विरूश्रलोम, *q. v.*

औरस, *m.* (*f.* ī) a legitimate child, *i. e.* a child by a wife of one's own tribe: *lit.* dwelling in one's breast, innate. [length.

औरसचौरस, *m.* vicinity, all around, breadth and

और सब, all other things; the rest, the remainder.

औरहि = (1) **औरको** (2) **औरही**.

औरही, totally different, quite different; extraordinary, otherwise, differently.

औरो }
औरौ } in Braj = **और भी**.

और्णनाभ, *m.* a spider.

और्द्धदेहिक, *m.* obsequies of the deceased: *lit.* serving for the acquisition of merit; belonging to the obsequies of a deceased person; given or performed in remembrance of a wealthy deceased person.

और्व्वानल, *m.* submarine fire.

औल, a virulent plague, cholera, jungle fever.

औलखना }
औलखना } in Braj = **अवलखना** = **अलखना**, *q. v.*

औलगि, till now, hitherto, heretofore.

औला, better, preferable.

औलाद, (see **आल**) *f.* (pl. of **वलद**) descendants, children, sons, progeny, offspring by the father's side.

औलिया, *m.* (pl. of **वली**) friends, companions (particularly of the prophets); apostles, the saints, the holy.

औषध, *m.* (*f.* ?) a medicine, medicament, drug; any herb or mineral used in medicine.

औषधालय, *m.* a dispensary, drugshop.

औषधि }
औषधी } = **औषधि**, *q. v.*

औषधीय, *m.* an ingredient of a medicine, materia medica; *lit.* medicinal, relating to medicine.

औसत, 1, *m.* the middle, interval, medium; mediocrity, moderation: 2, *adj.* middle, intervening.

औसना, *a. int.* to become musty, to putrefy, rot.

औसर, *more properly* **अवसर**, *q. v.*

औसान, *m.* sensation; sense, courage, presence of mind. [endowments.

औसाफ़, *m.* (pl. of **वसफ़**) praises, commendations;

औसुख, *m.* (*f.* ई) without consideration, heedless.

औसेर, *m.* anxiety, solicitude, care.

There are several marks or symbols which are of frequent occurrence in Sanskrit, some of which never occur in Hindee: the following however, will be often found in Hindee:—

ं (ṅg)

This mark (called *Anuswār*, sometimes also *Maste*) is properly of a diamond figure, but in most founts of type used for printing Hindee it is merely a dot. Properly speaking it has in pronunciation the nasal sound of *ṅg* in the English word 'king': many, however, prefer to give it, as often as possible, the sound of the letter which it displaces; thus **संसार** is often pronounced as if spelt **सन्सार**. As the principles which regulate the use of this sign are very fully and carefully specified in all good Hindee or Sanskrit Grammars, it has been deemed needless to occupy space by the repetition of them here: the following observations, however, may be of use to the student in reading Hindee:—1, *Anuswār* is, in Hindee books, frequently inserted where it would not be expected, and dropped where strict accuracy would require that it should be used;—peculiarities which seem to depend sometimes on the caprice or inadvertence of the writer or compositor, and sometimes upon the requirements of metre or of euphony; thus **जों** and **जो** are often used interchangeably; as also **चारों** and **चारो** and the other pronominal numerals. 2, A large number of words in Hindee are spelt sometimes with *Anuswār* and sometimes without it; a great quantity of space has been saved in this Dictionary by the care that has been exercised to avoid the recurrence of such words. In the case of any word in which this variety in spelling may occur, the student will speedily learn for what forms to look; especially if he understand the principles which operate in the use of this sign; *e. g.* if he fail to find in the Dictionary the form भ्रांत he will infer that this is a mis-spelling and will look for भ्रान्त. 3, This sign is often put in Hindee where in Sanskrit and Bengālee we should find *Anunāsika* (ँ) called also *Chandravindu*: it is, in fact, very seldom indeed that this latter sign is found in Hindee books. 4, In poetry, a short vowel followed by *Anuswār* becomes *long by position*. 5, In the transliterations that occur in the present work, this sign is represented by *n* with a dot over it; *e. g.* Kaṅs = कंस. 6, This sign is sometimes interchanged with आ; *e. g.* निरंकाल = निराकार. 7, *Anuswār* written over the final letter of feminine substantives ending in *yā* or *iyā* yields the nom. plural; *e. g.* ठिलियां, water-pots. 8, Lastly, this sign is in some books used as a mark of punctuation inferior in value to the sign । (*chhewā*).

ः (aḥ)

This mark (called *Visarg*, sometimes also *Durbāsee*) consists properly of two small rings written perpendicularly; it is, however, more frequently represented in Hindee by a couple of diamond-shaped figures (:), and most commonly by a couple of dots. For a full statement of the principles which regulate its use the student is referred to the Grammars; the following remarks, however, will be found of importance in reading Hindee: — 1, This sign always occurs after some vowel, which it slightly and almost imperceptibly aspirates; — the aspiration is, in fact, so slight that both to the eye and to the ear the symbol is very commonly dropped; thus दुःख (*duḥkh*) is as often written and pronounced दुख (*dukh*). 2, It is often, both in pronunciation and in writing represented by a sibilant; thus निस्सन्देह, more properly निःसन्देह; अन्तष्करण, more properly अन्तःकरण. 3, Excepting the case of prefixes, there seems to be a tendency in Hindee to drop this sign when it occurs at the end of words, and to substitute ह or आ for it. (See Art. आ, 19.) 4, It is sometimes inflected before the case-signs and sometimes not; *e. g.* श्रेयःको or श्रेयेको (dat. of श्रेयः). 5, In poetry, a short vowel followed by *Visarg* becomes *long by position*. 6, If no vowel-sign intervene between this symbol and the consonant that precedes it, it is usual to transliterate it by *a* (short) or more accurately by *ah*; *e. g.* पुनः, *punah*; also, but less accurately, *puna*. And, conversely *a* and *ah* (final) are properly rendered by *Visarg*; but see 3.

०

This mark (called *Soon*, [prop. *Shūnya*] 'vacant', 'empty') discharges several functions: — 1, It is, in Arithmetic, the cipher (naught). 2, It is a mark of repetition, indicating that the word or sentence which it follows should be repeated. 3, It is used for indicating abbreviation as the dot is in English; *e. g.* क° = करना; उ° = *e. g.* = उदाहरण = *exempli gratiâ*. 4, As a sign of elision or abbreviation it may occur not only at the end of a word but also at the beginning, or even at the beginning and at the end; *e. g.* °लौ° = तिलौदन. Of course, such abbreviations can only be resorted to in cases in which there is no danger of misunderstanding what the elided elements are.

्

This mark (called in Hindee *Virām*, 'rest', 'pause', 'stop') is placed under consonants to indicate the absence of the so-called inherent vowel (अ, 2, 3.). It is sometimes employed by natives like a mark of punctuation at the close of a sentence ending with a quiescent consonant, — all the preceding words being written without separation, because supposed to be pronounced or read without stopping (see the sign ।).

।

This mark is sometimes called छेवा, and in relation to ॥ (*see below*) it is also called a half pause. It is a stop or mark of punctuation, and is usually placed at the end of the first line of a couplet or stanza. In relation to *Virām* (*see above*) it indicates the close of a sentence ending with a vowel, — all the preceding words being written without separation, because supposed to be pronounced or read without stopping.

॥

This mark is sometimes called "double *chhewā*", and in relation to । (*see above*) it is also called a whole or full pause. It has the function of a full stop, — indicating at the close of a couplet, verse, section, paragraph, or chapter, that the subject ends there.

क

क (k) is the first consonant in the Hindee or Devanāgaree alphabet, and has the following characteristics and functions: — 1, It is the first letter of the कवर्ग, or guttural class, and is, in pronunciation, a simple hard consonant, having the sound of *k* in the English word 'king'. 2, With a dot under it, it represents *ḳāf* of the Arabic or Persian alphabet. 3, It is sometimes prefixed with the same effect as कु; *e. g.* कपुत्र. 4, As a suffix it forms diminutives with the effect of expressing (1) simple diminutiveness; *e. g.* पुत्रक: (2) depreciation or contempt; *e. g.* मानवक: (3) endearment; *e. g.* मामक: (4) similarity or resemblance; *e. g.* अश्वक, horse-like. 5, Added to substantives or to the roots of verbs this letter forms certain adjectives, adjectival participles or nouns of agency; *e. g.* स्वादक, रक्षक, प्रवेशक. 6, This letter is sometimes put corruptly for ग; *e. g.* अंक, more properly अंग. 7. This letter is sometimes put corruptly for ब; *e. g.* जोतिक = ज्योतिष; and for श; *e. g.* ढनेक = धनेश. 8, This letter is also a substantive masculine, and as such denotes (1) the highest deities; *e. g.* Brahmā, Vishṇu, etc.: (2) a Brāhmaṇ: (3) air: (4) water: (5) the sun: (6) the soul: (7) the head.

ककइ, *more prop.* कैकेयी, *q. v.*

कइसन, a dialectic form of कैसा, *q. v.*

कई, a few, some; sundry, several.

कईएक, several, sundry; a few.

कईगेर = **किसने**. See **गेर**, 20.

कउचाना, *t.* to steal.

कंक, *m.* (*f.* ā) a heron; one of the eighteen divisions of the continent of India; the back of a sword; a false Brāhmaṇ; an epithet of Yam.

कंकण, *m.* an ornament for the wrist, a bracelet:

कंकणा = **कंकण**, *q. v.* [a kind of weapon.

कंकणी, (*f.* inī) the wearer of a bracelet.

कंकत, *m.}* **कंकती**, *f.*} a comb.

कंकन = **कंकण**, *q. v.*

कंकना, *m.* (*f.* ī) lukewarm.

कंकर, *m.* a nodule of limestone, stone, gravel.

कंकरा, *m.* a stone ball with which boys play, a marble, pebble.

कंकरी, *f.* (dim. of **कंकरा**) a small pebble.

कंकलाट, a sort of stiff sandy loam. [backbone.

कंकाल, *m.* the skeleton; the loins, waist; the

कंकालिन, *f.* a witch, sorceress, hag.

कंकुग्रीव, *more prop.* **कम्बुग्रीव**, *q. v.*

कंकरीला, *m.* (*f.* ī) abounding in gravel. [Roxb.).

कंकोल, *m.* a kind of gourd (*Momordica mixta*,

कंखजूरा, *f.* a centipede (*Scolopendra*).

कंखिया, *f.* a side-glance, ogle. — *dekhnā*, to look with a side-glance, to ogle, leer.

कंखी, *f.* a side-glance, squint, side-look.

कंगन, *m.* an ornament worn as a bracelet by Hindoo females. [wrist.

कंगना, *m.* a thread tied around a bridegroom's

कंगनी, *f.* a cornice: millet (*Panicum Italicum*).

कंगरोड़, *m.* the ridge of the back, the spine: a kind of water-fowl.

कंगलता (*contraction*) = **कंगालता**, *q. v.*

कंगली (*contraction*) = **कंगाली**, *q. v.*

कंगाल, poor, indigent; friendless; miserly.

कंगालटर, vainglorious.

कंगालता, *f.*} **कंगालत्व**, *m.*} penury, destitution, poverty.

कंगालपन, *m.* low estate, poverty, indigence.

कंगालबांका, *m.* (*f.* ī) poor and proud.

कंगालिन = (1) **कंगाली**, 2, (2) **कंकालिन**, *qq. v.*

कंगाली, 1, *f.* indigence: 2, *m.* (*f.* inī) a pauper: *lit.* indigent, poor.

कंघी, *f.* a kind of large jar or vessel in which grain is kept. It is made of split cane or wicker-work plastered with clay.

कंगुरा, *m.* a niched battlement, porthole; a turret, minaret; a parapet-wall; plumes on helmets, ornaments on crowns.

कंगुरादार, spired, having a turret, parapet, etc.

कंगूड़ी, *f.* the lobe of the ear.

कंगूरा = **कंगुरा**, *q. v.*

कंघाई, *f.*} **कंघा**, *m.*} = **कंघी**, *q. v.*

कंघी, *f.* a comb. — *k.* to comb the hair. — *saṅwārnā*, to adjust or tidy the hair after sleeping.

कंघूआ, *m.* a kind of rake or harrow.

कंचन, 1, *m.* gold: 2, *m.* (*f.* ī) a certain tribe somewhat akin to our gypsies, whose females are generally dancers, etc.

कंचनखचित, *m.* (*f.* ā) inlaid with gold.

कंचनपुर, *m.*} **कंचनपुरी**, *f.*} = **कांचनपुर**, *q. v.* [by birth.

कंचनवान, *m.* (*f.* vatī) a real or genuine *kañchan*

कंचनी, *f.* a female of the *kañchan* tribe, dancing-girl, strumpet.

कंचित, *more prop.* **किंचित**, *q. v.*

कंचु, *m.* the skin of a snake.

कंचुक, *m.* the skin of a snake; mail, armour; a bodice, jacket; short trowsers, drawers; clothes.

कंचुकी, *m.* (*f.* inī) an attendant on the women's apartments, confidential attendant; a debauchee: a serpent. [hair: an epithet of Brahmā.

कंज, *m.* the lotus; the food of the immortals:

कंजर, *m.* a class of people of low caste who sell strings, etc.; they also catch and eat snakes.

कंजा, *m.* (*f.* ī) blue-eyed.

कंजाल = **कुजाल**, *q. v.*

कंजिया, *f.* a small stye.

कंजूस, *m.* a miser, niggard.

कंजूसी, *f.* niggardliness, penuriousness.

कंट, कंठ, कंड, कंत, कंथ, कंद, कंध, कंप, कंब; for all words beginning with either of these elements, see under the forms **कण्ट, कण्ठ, कण्ड, कन्त, कन्थ, कन्द, कन्ध, कम्प, कम्ब**, respectively.

कंवल, *m.* the lotus (*Nymphæa nelumbo*): a shade for a candle, made of colored silk or paper, ornamented. [lotuses.

कंवलदह, *m.* very deep water abounding with

कंवलनैन, *adj.* having eyes like the flowers of the

कंवलबाद, the jaundice. [lotus.

कंवार, *m.* a small species of the aloe from which the medical drug is obtained.

कंस, *m. pr. n.* the cousin and implacable foe of Krishṇ who slew him. As the foe of the deity he is considered an *Asur*.

ककड़ी, *f.* a cucumber (*Cucumis utilissimus*, Roxb.).

ककना, *m.*} **ककनी** *f.*} a bracelet, ring worn on the wrist.

ककरी = (1) **ककड़ी** (2) **कखरी**, *qq. v.*

ककरोन्दा, *m.* a certain plant (*Celsia*) and its fruit.

ककहरा, *m.* an alphabet.

कक्का, *m.* (prop. **काका**) a paternal uncle.

ककार, *m.* the letter **क**, or any symbol that may represent it.

ककारवर्ग, *m.* (in Gram.) the guttural consonants collectively.

कखोरना, *t.* to excavate, hollow out, scrape the earth as fowls do.

कख, *m.* the armpit, side, flank.

कछार, *f.* the end of the lower garment, which, after the cloth is carried around the body, is brought up behind and tucked into the waistband; a woman's girdle.

कखरी, *f.* the armpit; soreness of the armpit.

कखिवाली, *f.* a bundle of sheaves of corn given as perquisites to reapers and village servants.

कखौरी, *f.* a painful suppurating tumour in the armpit.

कखौली = **कखौरी**, *q.v.*

कगार, *m.* an edge, border, corner, architrave.

कङ्क, for all words beginning with this element, see under the form **कंक**.

कच, *m.* hairs: water in which rice has been washed: rawness; simplicity: a binding: a dried sore, cicatrix: *pr. n.* (1) of a province in western India (2) of a son of Vrihaspati.

कचक, *f.* the pain of a wound: a limp.

कचकच, *m.* debate, altercation.

कचकचाना, 1, *a. int.* to grind or gnash the teeth: 2, to be very abundant, to swarm: to be gritty.

कचकचाहट, *f.* the act of debating or altercating.

कचकड़ा, *m.* tortoise-shell.

कचकना, *a. int.* to limp; to pain, ache: to strain, sprain, twist.

कचकाना, *t.* to strain, sprain, twist.

कचकेला, *m.* a kind of plantain which is eaten cooked or boiled as a vegetable.

कचकोल, *f.* a cup or bowl (generally a beggar's); a wallet: a miscellany, ollapodrida, common place book.

कच खाना, to suffer grief, suffer vexation.

कचड़ा, *m.* an unripe melon of a very small size.

कचनार = **कचनाल**, *q.v.*

कचनाल, *f.* a tree (*Bauhinia variegata*) the flowers of which are a delicate vegetable.

कचपच, 1, = **कचकच**, *q.v.*: 2, *f.* a crowd: 3, close, thick, stuffed together.

कचपचिया, *m. pr. n.* the Pleiades.

कचपन, *m.* rawness, simplicity, want of experience.

कचबच, *m.* breed, offspring, progeny, brats, children, family.

कचमच, *f.* unintelligible or incorrect language, gibberish, babble, nonsensical talk.

कचरा, *m.* the raw musk-melon: clay; rubbish, dirt, sweepings.

कचरिया, *m.* a fruit (*Cucumis madaraspatanus*).

कचरी = (1) **कचरिया** (2) **कचहरी**, *qq.v.*

कचला, *m.* clay.

कचली, *f.* the skin of a snake.

कचलोन, *m.* a kind of salt said to promote digestion.

कचलोहिया / **कचलोही** } *f.* untempered iron.

कचलोहू, *m.* the bloody ichor discharged along with purulent matter.

कचवांसी, a minute division of surface in land measure.

कचवाट, *f.* vexation, abhorrence, dislike.

कचवाना, *n.* to be grieved, be vexed; to be tired or disgusted with a person.

कचहरी, *f.* a hall of justice, court, town-house, public office for receipt of revenue, etc.

कचा आमदनी, gross import, the payment made by a zamīndār of his rent to Government.

कचाई, *f.* rawness; indigestion; surfeit.

कचाकच, altercation, debate.

कचाकची, *f.* hair against hair, a pulling each other's hairs.

कचा खाना, to become angry.

कचापन, *m.* rawness; unripeness; crudity, inferiority, immaturity.

कचार = **कछार**, *q.v.*

कचालू, *m.* a certain esculent root (*Arum colocasia*).

कचिया, *m.* a reaping-hook, sickle.

कचियाना, *a. int.* to shrink from, draw back, be frightened.

कचियाहट, *f.* abhorrence.

कची = **काछी**, *q.v.*

कचुआर = **कचनार**, *q.v.*

कचुमर, *m.* a kind of pickle. —*kāṭ ḍālnā*, to cut to pieces; *lit.* to make pickles of.

कचू = **कच्चू**, *q.v.*

कचूमर = **कचुमर**, *q.v.*

कचूर, *m.* a certain plant or drug (*Curcuma reclinata* or *zerumbet*, Roxb.).

कचेरा, *m.* name of a certain tribe.

कचेरी = **कचहरी**, *q.v.*

कचेला / **कचैला** } = **कुचेला**, *q.v.*

कचौरी, *f.* a kind of pastry made of wheaten flour and pulse.

कच्चा, *m.* (*f.* ī) unripe, crude, immature; raw, uncooked; silly, simple, unknowing, uninstructed, green, inexperienced; false, unsound, of imperfect make or texture, claybuilt, slight, inferior, incomplete, undeveloped.

कच्चीखुजली, the raw or tumid itch.

कच्चू, *m.* a certain plant (*Arum colocasia*).

कच्छ, *m.* a shore, bank, land contiguous to water: a tortoise.

कच्छप, *m.* (*f.* ī) a tortoise, turtle; *pr. n.* the second of the ten incarnations of Vishṇu (see *Avatār*).

कच्छी, *m.* a horse with a hollow back (from the province of Kachh on the banks of the Sind or Indus).

कच्छू, *f.* a scab, itch.

कछ, *m.* a tortoise: the privities.

कछना, 1, *m.* a kind of breeches which cover very little of the thigh: 2, *n.* to be washed, be rinsed.

कछनी, *f.* (dimin. of **कछना**) a smaller kind of breeches than the preceding.

कछप = **कच्छप**, *q.v.*

कछलम्पट, *m.* a libertine: *lit.* lewd, lecherous, dissolute, incontinent.

कछ्या, low land. [*Kāchhees*.
कछवारा, ground cultivated by gardeners called
कछवाहा, *m.* the designation of a tribe of Rāj-puts who claim descent from Koos the son of Ram-Chandra :— the rājās of Jainagar are of this family.
कछाड़ = कछार, *q.v.* [a river, alluvial formation.
कछार, moist and low land by a river, bank of
कछारना, *t.* to wash, rinse.
कछियाना, 1, *a. int.* to shrink with fear, be fright-ened, draw back : 2, a kitchen-garden.
कछु = कछू, *q.v.*
कछुआ, *more prop.* कछूआ, *q.v.*
कछुक, *more prop.* कछूक, *q.v.*
कछुकी, dimin. of कछूक, *q.v.*
कछुप, *more prop.* कच्छप, *q.v.*
कछू, (gen. काहूको) Braj form of कुछ, *q.v.*
कछूआ, *m.* (*f.* कछूई) a tortoise, turtle.
कछूआदाबर, *adj.* of uneven bottom (said of a river that is deep and shallow alternately).
कछूए, inflected form of कछूआ.
कछूक, the very least, a very small quantity.
कछेरी = कचहरी, *q.v.*
कछोटी, *f.* a cloth worn by the natives between the legs to conceal the privities.
कज, crooked, wry ; *met.* perverse, cross.
कज़क, an iron hook.
कजदुम, *m.* a scorpion, dragon ; *lit.* having a crook-
कजनलोक, *m. pr. n.* one of the *loks.* [ed tail.
कज़ब, *m.* lying ; a lie.
कजमज, athwart and across, distorted.
कजरवा = कजरा, *q.v.*
कजरा, *m.* lampblack (used for painting the eyes).
कजरारा, *m.* (*f.* ī) black (eyes) without painting.
क़ज़लबाशी, *m.* a certain kind of Moghul soldier.
कजल, *m.*, कजला, *m.*, कजली, *f.* } = कज्जल, *q.v.*
कजलौटी, *f.* a kind of pot in which *kajjal* is kept ; an iron instrument like snuffers used to receive smoke or to prepare and keep lampblack.
कज़ाक़, an iron hook.
कजा, where ? whither ? how ?
क़ज़ा, *f.* fate, destiny ; fatality, death : praying at an appointed time : administration of justice ; decree.
कज़ाक = कज़्ज़ाक़, *q.v.*
कज़ाकी, *f.* highway robbery, brigandage.
कजाचित, *more prop.* कदाचित, *q. v.*
क़ज़ात, *f.* vice, disgrace, stain.
कजावा, *m.* a camel's saddle ; a kind of litter in which females travel on camels.
कजिया, *m.* a declaration ; a proposition ; a de-termination ; a narrative ; a syllogism ; a quarrel ; death.
कज्जल, *m.* lampblack, soot, collyrium prepared from soot.
कज्जलगिरि, *m.* any hill from which coal is digged.
कज़्ज़ाक़, *m.* a robber, brigand, ruffian, Cossack.
कज़्ज़ाब, *m.* an enormous liar.
कञ्च ; for all words beginning with this element, see under the form कँच. [2, *f.* the loins, waist.
कट, 1, *m.* black colour for marking chintz with :
कटक, *m.* an army, legion ; a bracelet : the hill of a mountain. [tick-tick.
कटकट, an imitative sound, a clicking, ticking,
कटकटाना, to gnash or grind the teeth.
कटकटी, *f.* grief, trouble, vexation. — *khānā*, to experience grief, trouble, or vexation.
कटकना, 1, *m.* a picture or model on wood, plan, scheme, sketch ; a regulation : 2, *m.* (*f.* ī) shrewd, [cunning.
कटकर = कठघरा, *q. v.*
कटकरंज, (*m.* ?) = कटकलेजी, *q.v.*
कटकरा = कठघरा, *q. v.*
कटकलेजी, *f.* the febrifuge nut (*Guilandina bon-ducella*, Lin. : *Caesalpinia bonducella*, Roxb.).
कटका, a peck or seizure with the beak.—*bhar-nā*, to peck with the beak, bite with the teeth.
कटकाना ; see (1) कटखाना (2) खटकाना.
कटकीना, a sub-lease, under-farm. [tenant.
कटकीनादार, *m.* an under-farmer of revenue, sub-
कटकेहरी, *f.* an epithet of a handsome-waisted female ; *lit.* having a waist as elegant as the lion's.
कटखड़ी, *f.* a species of steatites with which chil-dren learn to write (it is used in polishing stucco).
कटखना, *m.* (*f.* ī) any animal inclined to bite.
कटखाना, *t.* to bite.
कटगर, कटघरा } = कठघरा, *q. v.*
कटना, 1, *n.* to be cut, be clipped, be cut off ; to be interrupted : to be bashful, be abashed : 2, *a. int.* to pass or be spent (as time) ; to die of wounds.
कटनास, *m.* a species of bird (*Coracias*).
कटनी, *f.* harvesting, harvest, harvest-time.
कटफल = कायफल, *q. v.*
कटबन्धन = कठबन्धन, *q. v.*
कटर, 1, = कठोर : 2, *m.* a caitiff.
कटरना, *m.* a species of fish.
कटरहना, *n.* to be cut, be cut off, be intercepted, be divided, be separated, be stopped up (as a road, by being infested with thieves, etc).
कटरा, *m.* a market, the market town belong-ing to a fort ; suburbs.
कटवाना, *t.* to cause to be cut, cause to be bitten.
कटहर, 1, corruption of कटहल, *q. v.* : 2, *m.* a wood-en cage in which wild beasts are kept : 3. *adj.* hard.
कटहरा, *m.* a wooden cage, railing, palisade.
कटहल, *m.* the jack-tree (*Artocarpus integrifolia*, Roxb.), jack-fruit.

कटहा, *m.* (*f.* ī) inclined to bite, snappish.
कटा, *f.* a killing; a cutting. —*k.* to slaughter, murder.
कटाई, *f.* a harvest, crop.
कटाक्ष, *m.* a leer, glance, side-look, ogling. —*k.* to look askance at, to leer.
कटाना, *t.* to cause to cut, cause to bite.
कटार, *m.* a stiletto, dirk, dagger with a broad straight blade (the hilt comes up on either side of the wrist, while it is grasped by a cross-bar in the centre); a polecat.
कटारबन्ध, *m.* (*f.* ā) a murderer, assassin: *lit.* a person who carries a dagger.
कटारा, 1, the aloe plant: 2, *m.* the medicinal plant, Globe thistle (*Echinops echinatus*, Roxb.).
कटारिया, *m.* a kind of silk cloth with stripes in the form of daggers.
कटारी, *f.* (dimin. of **कटार**) a small dagger.
कटाल, *m.* the spring-tide, flood.
कटाव, *m.* 1, in Braj = **कटाई**, *q.v.*: 2, a kind of flowering on cloths.
कटाहा, *m.* (*f.* ī) any animal inclined to bite.
कटाह, *m.* a caldron, frying-vessel, shallow kind of boiler for oil, butter, sugar, etc.
कटि, *f.* loins, waist, buttocks, hip: the cheeks of an elephant.
कटिकेहरी = **कठकेहरी**, *q.v.*
कटित, *m.* vent: sale.
कटिबन्द, **कटिबन्ध** = **कटिबन्धनी**, *q.v.*
कटिबन्धनी, *f.* a girdle for the loins.
कटिया, *f.* a fishing-hook.
कटिसूत्र, *m.* a waistband, girdle, zone.
कटी, *f.* loins, waist, buttocks, hip: the cheeks of an elephant.
कटीरा, *more prop.* **कटीला**, *q.v.*
कटीला, 1, *m.* (*f.* ī) thorny: active, brave (as soldiers): 2, *m.* a species of plant.
कटु, 1, *m.* (*f.* **कटवी**) sharp, pungent, cutting, fierce, hot, impetuous: 2, *m.* pungency (whether in taste, smell, or language): the flower *Michelia campaca.*
कटुक, *m.* (*f.* ā) = **कटु**, *q.v.*
कटुता, *f.* pungency, sharpness; impetuosity, irritability, testiness; wickedness.
कटूसी, *f.* obscenity, smut.
कटेरा, railings, palings, balustrade.
कटेव, *f.* a bad habit.
कटैया, coarse grass growing on fields left fallow.
कटोरा, *m.* a brass bowl, cup, goblet, etc.; a shallow cup.
कटोरी, *f.* (dimin. of **कटोरा**) a small metallic cup.
कटोल, *m.* a man of a degraded tribe, a *Chaṇḍāl*: a kind of plant, perhaps cowage (*Dolichos pruriens*).
कट्टर, *m.* (*f.* ā) any animal inclined to bite or addicted to biting.
कट्टरी, *f.* the horizontal beam to which the bullocks in a sugar-mill are attached: the word also denotes land that has been recovered from large rivers.
कट्ठा, 1, *m.* a large louse: 2, a bundle, bunch, handful, parcel, faggot or bundle of sticks, file of papers: 3, *m.* (*f.* ī) robust, able-bodied, athletic, strong.
कट्ठा, *m.* a certain measure of land, — the twentieth part of a *beeghā*; a corn-measure containing five *sers.*
कठ, a contraction of **काठ**, much used in composition.
कठगुलाब, *m.* a species of rose (*Rosa chinensis*).
कठघरा, *m.* a wooden cage, railing, palisade.
कठड़ा = **कठरा**, *q.v.*
कठन्दर, *m.* dropsy, tympany, hardness of the stomach.
कठपुतरी, **कठपुतली**, *f.* a wooden doll or image.
कठफोड़ा, *m.* a wood-pecker (*Picus*).
कठबन्दन, *more prop.* **कठबन्धन**, *q.v.*
कठबन्धन, *m.* the wooden clog or ring with which an elephant is fastened by a leg.
कठबिकक्की, *f.* a toad.
कठबेल, *m.* the elephant-apple (*Feronia elephantum*) called also the wood-apple.
कठबेला, *m.* the flower *Jasminum multiflorum.*
कठमस्ता, *m.* (*f.* ī) very stout and lusty.
कठर = **कठोर**, *q.v.*
कठरा, *m.* a tub, tray, plate, trough: a young male buffalo.
कठरी, *f.* (dimin. of **कठरा**) a small tray, etc.
कठला, *m.* a wooden ornament or charm put on a child's neck.
कठहंसी, *f.* affected or forced smiles (with internal displeasure).
कठहरा, *m.* a wooden cage, railing, palisade.
कठार; for words beginning thus, see under the more proper form **कटार**.
कठिंजर, *m.* a certain plant (*Ocymum sanctum*, or sacred basil) worshipped by Hindoos and commonly called the *Tulsee.*
कठिन, *m.* (*f.* ā) hard, solid; unkind, severe, cruel; obscure, difficult; painful, troublesome; acute.
कठिनतर, *adj.* (comp. of **कठिन**) very difficult, etc.
कठिनत्व, *m.* (*f.* tā) hardness; severity; difficulty; obscurity.
कठिनहृदय, *m.* (*f.* ā) hardhearted, severe, cruel.
कठिनाई = **कठिनता**, *q.v.*
कठिनान्तःकरण, *m.* (*f.* ā) = **कठिनहृदय**, *q.v.*
कठिनी, *f.* chalk for writing with.
कठिया, *m.* a trencher, platter: a snare, trap, trepan.
कठिल्ल, *m.* a species of balsam-apple (*Momordica charantias*).
कठोर, *m.* (*f.* ā) hard, solid; difficult; severe, cruel, callous, relentless, implacable, hard-hearted, violent, loud; sharp; complete, full-grown; of rough manners.
कठोरता, *f.* hardness; firmness; cruelty, relentlessness, etc.
कठोरताई, *f.*, **कठोरत्व**, *m.*, **कठोरपन**, *m.* = **कठोरता**, *q.v.*
कठोरा, *more prop.* **कटोरा**, *q.v.*

कठोल, *more prop.* **कठोर**, *q. v.*

कठौती, *f.* a tub; a trencher, platter, plate.

कड़, *f.* the seed of the safflower (*Carthamus tinctorius*).

कड़क, *f.* a crash, crack; thunder: agility.— *dauṛnā*, to gallop at full speed.

कड़कड़ा, *m.* (*f.* ī) hard, stiff, strong.

कड़कड़ाना, *a. int.* to give forth such a sound as oil or butter does when boiling.

कड़कना, *a. int.* to crackle, crack; to thunder. *Bijli* —, *a. int.* to crack (said of thunder).

कड़का, *m.* 1, a pæan, song of triumph: 2, the bank of a river, shore, steep bank, precipice.

कड़खा, *m.* commemoration, mention, the encouraging soldiers at the time of battle by pointing out the good effects of steadiness and valour, by extolling the deeds of former heroes, etc.; a warsong for the encouragement of combatants.

कड़खैत, *m.* a kind of bard; an officer in Indian armies whose business it is to encourage the soldiers by the exhortations mentioned under the above word; a kind of Indian Tyrtacus.

कड़ना, *t.* to pierce, perforate.

कड़रखून, *m.* name of a certain plant.

कड़वा, *m.* (*f.* ī) = **कड़ुआ**, *q.v.*

कड़वागी / **कड़वाट** } = **कड़वाहट**, *q. v.*

कड़वातेल, *m.* oil made from sesamum-seed, mustard-oil, bitter oil.

कड़वास = **कड़वाहट**, *q. v.*

कड़वाहट, *f.* bitterness, acidity, pungency, virulence.

कड़वी, *f.* the stubble of a kind of grain.

कड़ही, *f.* a dish consisting of the meal of pulse (*chanā* or *Cicer arietinum*) dressed with sour milk.

कड़ा, 1, *m.* a ring worn on the wrists or on the ankles; a bracelet; a ringlet; the handle of a door or anything in the form of a ring: 2, *m.* (*f.* ī) stiff, hard, obdurate; sharp, harsh, austere; arch, sly, knowing, penetrating.

कड़ाई, *f.* hardness, stiffness; obduracy; severity, rigour.

कड़ाकड़, *m.* successive crashes.

कड़ाका, *m.* the crash of anything breaking: a rigid fast (in which no food or drink has been taken).

कड़ाड़ा, *m.* the perpendicular bank of a river; a precipice, declivity.

कड़ावा, care, charge, trust.

कड़ाह = **कड़ाहा** = **कटाह**, *q. v.*

कड़ाहा, *m.* a cauldron, boiler.

कड़ाही, *f.* (dim. of **कड़ाहा**) a small boiler, frying pan.

कडिरार / **कडिहार** / **कडिहाल** } *m.* a steersman, boatman.

कड़ी, *f.* a rafter, beam; a ring, staple, fetter.

कड़ुआ, 1, *m.* (*f.* **कड़ुई**) bitter, acrid; strong, virulent, coarse, hard-hearted; brave: 2, *m.* myrrh.— *k.* to give or to expend unwillingly.— *honā*, to be enraged. *Karwekasele din*, hard and cruel times.

कड़ुवा, *m.* (*f.* ī) = **कड़ुआ**, *q. v.*

कड़ोड़, *m.* a crore, ten millions, a hundred laks.

कड़ोड़खुख, *m.* a liar.

कड़ोड़पति, *m.* (*f.* **पत्नी**) the owner of a crore of rupees; a millionaire.

कड़ोड़ा, *m.* a taxgather; inspector, overseer.

कड़ोड़ां, (see **ओं**, 4) many crores.

कढ़ना, 1, *n.* to be extracted, be drawn out, be pulled out; to be drawn, be painted, be delineated: 2, *a. int.* to escape, rise, issue forth, slip forth, spring.

कढ़ी = **कड़ही**, *q.v.*

कढ़ुआ, *m.* a loan, debt; a premium on a loan, a deduction from the sum lent.

कण, *m.* corn, grain; a minute particle, grain, eye of corn; a spark or facet of a gem; a drop.

कणकि, *f.* ground rice, the scraps that fly off while pounding rice to separate it from the husk.

कणकी = **कणकि**, *q. v.*

कणरस = **कनरस**, *q. v.*

कणरसिया = **कनरसिया**, *q.v.*

कणसलाई = **कनसलाई**, *q. v.*

कणा, *f.* 1, = **कणिका**, *q.v.*: 2, the dark lunar fortnight of the month Āsin

कणिका, *f.* an atom, particle, grain; a kind of rice; fine sand (particularly grittiness of sand in bread).

कणेर, *m.* a species of tree (*Cascaria ovata*). It grows wild in the beds of rivers and in other moist places in most parts of Asia.

कण्टक, *m.* a thorn; a sharp bone; a stinging pain; an obstacle; a wicked person, mean enemy.

कण्टकारी, *f.* a sort of prickly nightshade (*Solanum jacquini*): the silk-cotton tree (*Bombax heptaphyllum*).

कण्टकी, *m.* (*f.* inī) a vexatious person: *lit.* thorny, vexatious.

कण्टर, miserly, niggardly.

कण्टार, prickly, thorny.

कण्टिया, *f.* a fishing-hook; a vessel for oil.

कण्टीला, *m.* (*f.* ī) thorny.

कण्ठ, 1, *m.* the neck, throat, windpipe, Adam's apple, larynx; the bosom; the voice: proximity.— *phutnā*, to be broken (said of the voice of a boy as he approaches puberty): 2, *adv.* by heart, committed to memory.— *k.* to get a thing by heart.

कण्ठतालव्य, (in Gram.) gutturo-palatal letters; *e. g.* **ए**, **ऐ**.

कण्ठभूषा, *f.* a collar, short necklace.

कण्ठमणि, *m.* a jewel worn on the throat.

कण्ठमाला, *f.* a kind of necklace of gold and jewels; bronchocele or goitre; scrofula.

कण्ठला, *m.* a necklace composed of pieces of gold, silver, etc. put on to children to avert evil.

कण्ठस्थ, by heart, by rote.

कण्ठा, *m.* a necklace or rosary of large beads made of silver, crystal, or the earth of *Karbalā*.

कण्ठाग्र, by rote, by memory.

कण्ठाभरण, *m.* ornaments for the neck.

कण्टाकन्धन, *m.* strangulation.

कण्ठी, *f.* (dim. of **कण्ठा**) a short necklace.

कण्ठौष्ठ्य, *m.* (in Gram.) any gutturo-labial letter; *e. g.* **ओ, औ.**

कण्ठ्य, *m.* (in Gram.) any guttural letter.

कण्डराना, *a. int.* to bristle: *t.* to dislike, abhor.

कण्डरी, *m.* (*f.* ?) a certain vegetable, a kind of mustard-seed.

कण्डा, *m.* dry cowdung picked up in the fields or roads and used for fuel: a reed; a bush.

कण्डारी, *m.* a steersman, boatman.

कण्डाल, *m.* a kind of hautboy.

कण्डु, 1, *m. f.* = **कण्डू**, *q. v.*: 2, *m. pr. n.* a certain *ṛishi.*

कण्डू, *f.* scratching; itching; the itch.

कण्डेरा, *m.* a cleaner of cotton.

कण्व, *m. pr. n.* a certain *Rishi*, author of several of the hymns of the Rig-Ved.

कत, where? whither? why? how? how much? how many?

कतनई, *f.* spinning.

कतना, *n.* to be spun.

कतरन, *f.* parings, clippings.

कतरना, *t.* to clip, cut (as with scissors); to cut out; to pare.

कतरनी, *f.* scissors.

कतरब्योन्त, *m.* a cutting out: *met.* meditation, anxiety, consultation.

कतरभेद, *m.* fraud, guile, deceit.

कतरा, *m.* parings, clippings.

कतराई, 1, *f.* (see **आई**, 3) the price paid for cutting out (clothes, etc.): 2, *adv.* sideways.

कतराना, *t.* to cause to clip; to cut out: *a. int.* to leave the high road, — stealing away by by-paths, go round about, shrink away, slink away, edge off, go sideways. *Katrākar chalnā*, to cut anyone's society, desert one's companions.

कतक, *m.* a cutter.

क़त्ल, *m.* slaughter, murder, homicide. — *k.* to murder, kill, execute.

कतला, 1, *m.* a slice: 2, *m.* (*f.* ī) rank, rancid, musty, flabby.

कतवार; see **कोतवाल**.

कतहुं in Braj = **कत**, *q. v.*

क़ता, *f.* shape, form, cut; segment, portion, section, division. — *k.* to pass or traverse (a road).

कताई, *f.* (see **आई**, 3) spinning: the price paid for spinning. — *k.* to spin.

कताना, *t.* to cause some one to spin anything, cause to be spun, get spun.

क़तार, *f.* a tying or binding together: a string, rope: a rank, order, series, row.

कतारा, *m.* a kind of sugarcane.

कति in Braj = **कितना**, *q. v.*

कतिक = **कितेक**, *q. v.*

कतीरा, *m.* the gum tragacanth from the *Atragalus verus*: a gum resembling tragacanth obtained from the *Sterculia urens.*

कतेक, a dialectic form = **कितना**, *q. v.*

कत्तल, *f.* a lump of stone, brick, or earth.

कत्तान, *m.* a knife, dagger.

कत्थक = **कथक**, *q. v.*

कत्थन, *m.* boasting; a boaster; *lit.* boastful.

कथ, *m.* the astringent vegetable extract which the natives of India eat with betel-leaf: catechu, terra japonica. It is the produce of a species of *mimosa* (*Chadira*).

कथक, *m.* (*f.* ikā) a narrator, teller of stories; a kind of singer; one who reads the Purāṇs in public: lit. *adj.* narrating.

कथन, *m.* a saying, telling, narrating: *pr. n.* a certain ancient Hindoo sage (*muni*).

कथना, *t.* to say, tell, relate, narrate.

कथनीय, admitting of being uttered, lawful to be uttered, fit to be uttered, requiring to be said.

कथा, *f.* (not infl.) a saying, story, tale, narrative, fable; a word.

कथानि, (see **नि**) a Braj pl. of **कथा**.

कथाप्रबन्ध, *m.* literary composition, a literary production.

कथाप्रसंग, *m.* conversation.

कथारूपी, in the form of words, by means of speech, in verbal form.

कथालाभ, *m.* = **कथावार्त्ता**, *q. v.*

कथावार्त्ता, *f.* a conversation, discourse, intercourse, news.

कथासंयुक्त, *m.* literary composition.

कथिक, *more prop.* **कथक**, *q. v.*

कथित, *m.* (*f.* ā) spoken, said, told, uttered.

कथोपकथन, *m.* conversation, intercourse, conference, dialogue, narration.

कद, when? at what time?

कदखुदा, *m.* the head of a family, a married man: a *locum tenens*, viceroy.

कदखुदाई, *f.* marriage; the establishing a family: the office of viceroy. — *k.* to marry.

क़दग़न, care; injunction, prohibition.

कदन, *m.* a killing, destroying: a killer, destroyer.

कदम, 1, = **कदम्ब**, *q. v.*: 2, *m.* a pace, step, footstep; the sole of the foot. — *mārnā*, to walk.

कदमा, a kind of sweetmeat made so as to resemble in form the flowers of the *Nauclea.*

कदम्ब, *m.* a certain tree (*Nauclea cadamba* or *orientalis*): a multitude, crowd; plenty.

कदम्बपुष्पी, *f.* a certain plant (commonly called *mundiri*) whose flowers resemble those of the *Kadamb.*

कदर, *m.* a white sort of *mimosa*: a certain disease: a saw: an iron goad for an elephant.

क़दर, *f.* worth, price; quantity; destiny, fate; the title of the ninety-seventh section of the Kur,ān.

क़दरदान, *m.* a just appreciator, one who appreciates another at his true worth.

कदराई, *f.* idleness.

कदर्य, avaricious, miserly: hence, *m.* (*f.* ā) a niggardly person.

कदल, *m.* (*f.* ?) = **कदलक**, *q. v.*

कदलक, *m.* the plantain-tree (*Musa sapientum*) or its leaf.

कदली, *f.* 1, = **कदलक**, *q. v.*: 2, a kind of deer: a banner.

कदलीपत्र, *m.* the plantain-leaf.

कदहु in Braj = **कभी**, *q. v.*

कदा, when? at what time? once upon a time; perhaps.

कदाकार, ill-shaped, ugly.
कदाचार, following evil practices, abandoned, profligate: hence, *m.* (*f.* ā or ī) a profligate, etc.
कदाचित, ever, at some time or other; sometimes: should, perhaps, perchance, peradventure, possibly.
कदापि = **कदाचित**, *q.v.*
क़दामत, *f.* priority, excellence, precedence.
क़दीम, ancient, old.
क़दीमसे, of old, from time immemorial. [crow.
कदीमा, *m.* a pumpkin (*Cucurbita pepo*): an iron
क़दीर, *m.* the Almighty: *lit.* powerful.
कदूरत, *f.* foulness, impurity (in water, etc.): *met.* perturbation, depression of spirits, affliction; re-
कदेवर, *m.* a gardener. [sentment.
कद्द, 1, *f.* examination, search, inquiry, trouble, labor, endeavour: 2, *m.* stature. [*brum virile.*
कद्दू, *m.* a pumpkin (*Cucurbita lagenaria*): *mem-*
कद्र; see **क़दर**. [the serpent race.
कद्रू, *f. pr. n.* the wife of Kashyap and mother of
कधी, ever, at any time, at some time or other.
कधीं, **कधु**, **कधुं**, **कधू** } in Braj = **कधी**, *q.v.*
कधैआ, *more com.* **कन्धैआ**, *q.v.*
कधैया, *more com.* **कन्धैया**, *q.v.*
कन, 1, = **कण**, *q.v.*: 2, = **कने**, *q.v.*: 3, *m.* appreciating, valuing (a field): a weevil. — *k.* to value, appraise.
कनअंगुली, *f.* the little finger.
कनआन, *m. pr. n.* the land of Canaan, Palestine.
कनआनी, Canaanitish, appertaining to Canaan: hence, *m.* (*f.* inī) a Canaanite.
कनक, *m.* the thorn-apple (*Datura metel*): gold.
कनककशिपु, *m. pr. n.* a certain demon slain by
कनकघट, *m.* a golden pot or jar. [Vishṇu.
कनकटा, *m.* (*f.* ī) a person without ears: *lit.* earcropt, earless.
कनकटी, *f.* a certain disorder in the ears.
कनकमय, *m.* (*f.* ī) consisting of gold, abounding in gold, golden. [eyes: *lit.* the golden-eyed.
कनकलोचन, *m.* (*f.* ā) a person with beautiful
कनकूत, *f.* the estimated valuation of a stand-
कनकौआ, *m.* a species of paper kite. [ing crop.
कनखजूरा, *m.* a centipede (*Scolopendra*).
कनखल, *m. pr. n.* (1) of a certain place of Hindoo pilgrimage (2) of the mountains surrounding it.
कनखी, *f.* a glance of the eye, ogle, leer.
कनड़ो, *f.* a certain mode in versification.
कनपटी, *f.* the upper part of the side of the face between the temples and the ears.
कनफ़, a side; a shore; a wing.
कनफटा, *m.* a Hindoo ascetic with slit ears.
कनफुकवा, *m.* any religious teacher among the Hindoos who whispers his instructions in the ears of his followers. [sic, etc.).
कनरस, *m.* the taking a pleasure in hearing (mu-
कनरसिया, *m.* a lover of music, an amateur in music. [king.
कनल, *m. pr. n.* a certain Shoodra who slew his
कनवई, *f.* a kind of clayey soil.
कनवा, a certain measure (the twentieth part
कनवाई, *f.* the boring the ears. [of a *ser*).
कनवैया, *more prop.* **किनवैया**, *q.v.*
कनशलाई, *f.* a kind of *scolopendra* or *julus* which is said to get into the brain through the ears, and by its bite, to occasion excessive pain and even death.
कनसुई, *f.* a listening, hearing.
कनहर, *m.* a rudder, helm.
कनहरा, *m.* a listening, attention.
कनहरीला, *m.* a helmsman, steersman.
कनहा, *m.* an officer employed by Government to value standing crops.
कनहाई, 1, *m.* in Braj, one of the names of Kṛishṇ: 2, *f.* the appraisement of crops of grain.
कना, *f.* the dark half of the month Āsin.
क़नाअत, *f.* contentment, tranquillity; abstinence.
कनांखी, *f.* a side-glance, sly wink (on the part of a female).
कनाकचू, *m.* a certain vegetable, a species of *Arum.*
कनागत, *f.* a *shrāddh* or religious ceremony performed daily by Hindoos during the dark half of the month *Āsin* in honor of deceased ancestors: that fortnight is hence called *Kanā.*
क़नात, 1, *more prop.* **क़नाअत**, *q.v.*: 2, *f.* the walls of a tent, a screen, canvas enclosure.
कनान, *more prop.* **कनआन**, *q.v.*
कनानी, *m.* (*f.* inī) *more prop.* **कनआनी**, *q.v.*
कनार, *more prop.* **किनारा**, *q.v.*
कनारना = **कराहना**, *q.v.*
कनारा, *more prop.* **किनारा**, *q.v.*
कनिक, *m.* wheaten flour.
कनिका = **कणिका**, *q.v.*
कनिको, a very little, the least bit.
कनिया, *more prop.* **कन्या**, *q.v.*
कनियाना, 1, *t.* to go to one side, avoid any one, shun, dodge: 2, *m.* a contrivance, dodge.
कनियाहट, *f.* shyness, coyness, timidity.
कनिश, *m.* a miser, niggard: an ear of corn.
कनिष्ठ, *m.* (*f.* ā) a younger brother, etc.: *lit.* little, small, least, smallest, youngest.
कनिष्ठा, *f.* the little finger; a younger sister.
कनिष्ठाध्यक्ष, *m.* (*f.* ī) a sub-manager, lieutenant.
कनिष्ठिका, *f.* the little finger. [ful, malevolent.
कनिहा, *m.* (*f.* ī) a malevolent person: *lit.* revenge-
कनी, *f.* a bulbous root: an atom.
कनीज़ = **कनीज़क**, *q.v.*
कनीज़क, *f.* a female servant, handmaid, slavegirl.

कनीज़की / कनीज़ी } *f.* servitude.

कनीरर, *m.* a certain caste of people (generally arrowmakers). [with, in proximity to.

कने, *postp.* (takes genit. *masc.* infl.) near, close by,

कनेटी, *f.* a pulling the ears.

कनेर / कनेल } *more prop.* कणेर, *q.v.*

कनेया, *m.* (*f.* ?) the ceremony of boring the ears.

कनोज, *more prop.* = कनौज, *q.v.*

कनोटी, *f.* the ear of a horse.

कनोठा = कनौठा, *q.v.*

कनौज, *m. pr. n.* an ancient city and kingdom of India where Porus is supposed to have reigned.

कनौजिया, *m.* a native or an inhabitant of Kanauj; also, the designation of various tribes originally from that ancient kingdom.

कनौठा, *m.* any situation in an apartment close to an angle of the wall.

कनौडा / कनौड़ा } *m.* (*f.* ī) = कनौवडा, *q.v.*

कनौवड, *m.* diffidence, bashfulness.

कनौवडा, *m.* (*f.* ī) a diffident person, etc.: *lit.* diffident, standing in awe of a person. — *k.* to gain ascendancy over another, make him stand in awe.

कनौती; see कनोटी.

कन्त, *m.* a husband, sweetheart.

कन्तमन, *m.* a happy mind.

कन्तभाव, *m.* husbandhood, the being a husband; the disposition and sentiments appropriate in an espoused one towards her lover.

कन्था, *f.* (*m.* ?) a patch cloth or garment, rag, quilt of rags, beggar's wallet, coat of shreds worn by a Hindoo ascetic: a wall.

कन्द, *m.* a bulbous or tuberous root; a certain esculent root (*Arum campanulatum*); a cloud; a multitude: garlic: an affection of the female organ: sugar-[candy: strife.

कन्दमूल, *m.* any edible root.

कन्दर, *m.* (*f.* ?) a cave, cavern (natural or artificial), a chasm in a mountain.

कन्दरा, *m.* / कन्दरी, *f.* } = कन्दर, *q.v.*

कन्दर्पकेतु, *m.* a sign or symbol of Kāmdev, the flag over his carriage in pictures or images of him.

कन्दल, *m.* a certain gum (*Sagapenum*): war, battle; strife, dissension, dispute; censure, reproach.

कन्दला, (not infl.) *m.* (*f.* ?) a cave; a precipice: [a kind of silver thread.

कन्दली = कदली, *q.v.*

कन्दसार, *m.* a stag, buck, deer.

कन्दा, 1, *m.* a squill (*Erythonium Indicum*): 2, engraved. — *k.* to engrave (seals, etc.).

कन्दाकार, *m.* an engraver.

कन्दाला, *m.* a priapus, obelisk; the lingam.

क़न्दील, *f.* a candle; a lamp, lantern, chandelier, shade.

कन्दुक, *m.* a ball for playing with: a pillow.

कन्द्रा = (1) कन्दरा (2) कन्दा, 1, *qq.v.*

कन्ध, *m.* the shoulder: a thick branch.

कन्धर, *m.* the neck: a cloud: a certain plant (*Amaranthus oleraceus*).

कन्धरा, *f.* the neck: a cloud. [body.

कन्धा, *m.* the shoulder. — *denā*, to carry a dead

कन्धाई / कन्धाय } *m.* an epithet of Krishṇ.

कन्धियाना, *t.* to place on the shoulder.

कन्धी, *f.* a cloud.

कन्धेली, *f.* a kind of paunch or pack-saddle.

कन्धैआ / कन्धैया } *m.* (not infl.) an epithet of Krishṇ.

कन्ना, *m.* the notches on the two sides of the upper leather of a shoe: that part of a paper kite to which the string is tied.

कन्नादार, *m.* a kind of shoe or slipper.

कन्नी, *f.* a spark of a diamond or of any other gem: bran. — *kāṭnā*, to undermine a person, effect one's ruin by clandestine means. [(*Aloe perfoliata*).

कन्यका, *f.* a girl, maiden: the Socotrine aloe

कन्यस, *m.* (*f.* ī) a younger brother, etc.: *lit.* younger.

कन्या, *f.* an unmarried girl, maiden, virgin, daughter: the sign Virgo: a name of Durgā.

कन्याकुब्ज, the full form of कनौज, *q.v.*

कन्यात्व, *m.* maidenhood, virginity. [a dowry:

कन्यादान, *m.* the bestowing a girl in marriage,

कन्यापुत्र / कन्यासुत } *m.* the son of an unmarried girl.

कन्व, *more prop.* कण्व, *q.v.*

कन्हरीला = कनहरीला, *q.v.*

कन्हाई = कनहाई, *q.v.*

कन्हार, quick of hearing, acute.

कन्हैआ / कन्हैया } *m.* (not infl.) an epithet of Krishṇ.

कपकपी, *f.* a shivering, trembling, quaking, per-[turbation.

कपचा, *m.* a kind of jacket.

कपट, 1, *f. m.* ? fraud, trick, deceit; subterfuge, dissimulation, circumvention, hypocrisy; adulteration: spite: 2, designing; insincere, hypocritical.

कपटत्व, *m.* (*f.* tā) deceitfulness, hypocrisy.

कपटतापस, *m.* (*f.* ī) a feigned ascetic.

कपटभू, *f.* an epithet of the present world.

कपटलेख्य, *m.* a forged document.

कपटवेश, *m.* disguise, hypocrisy.

कपटवेशी, *m.* (*f.* inī) a hypocrite, etc.: *lit.* disguised, hypocritical.

कपटाभिप्राय, *m.* secret or hypocritical design.

कपटिन, 1, *m.* (*f.* ī) = कपटी, *q.v.*: 2, *f.* (= कपटिनी) a female hypocrite, etc.

कपटी, *m.* (*f.* inī) a hypocrite, cheat, etc.: *lit.*

insincere, false, dishonest, hypocritical, designing, fraudulent, deceitful, cheating; adulterated.

कपड़, *m.* cloth.

कपड़कूट, clay made for crucibles, etc.: *lit.* pounded up with rags.

कपड़कोठा, *m.* a tent.

कपड़छन, *adj.* impalpable (powder); deep (consultation); thoroughly sifted (as intelligence, etc.).

कपड़छान क°, *t.* to strain (as through cloth).

कपड़धूल, *m.* a kind of gauze.

कपड़फूल, *m.* a silk cloth wrought with gold and silver flowers worn as a head-dress by females.

कपड़ा, *m.* cloth; clothing. —— *oṛhnā* or *pahinnā*, to dress oneself.

कपड़ावाला, *m.* (*f.* ī) a cloth manufacturer; a cloth vender, draper.

कपड़े, *m.* (pl.) clothes, clothing. —— *rangnā*, to become a fakeer. — *ko jhol denā*, to give an alarm.

कपड़ेवपड़े, *m.* (pl. redupl.) clothes.

कपड़ोंसे होना, *n.* to have the menses.

कपना, 1, *a. int.* to shiver, tremble, quake, quiver: 2, *m.* (*f.* ī) *adj.* trembling, tremulous. [कपड़.

कपर; for words beginning thus, see under the form

कपाट, *m.* a door, shutter, panel of a door, leaf of a door.

कपाटीलगाम, *f.* a snaffle-bridle.

कपार; for words beginning thus, see under the form कपाल.

कपाल, *m.* the forehead; head, skull, cranium; *met.* fate, destiny: either half of a water-jar, a potsherd; either half of an egg: the glene; a kind of leprosy. — *khulnā*, to have a favorable turn of fortune. — *phuṭnā*, to be unfortunate.

कपाली, 1, *m.* (*f.* inī) a shrewd person; *lit.* shrewd, sly: wearing skulls as a necklace; covered with skulls: 2, *f.* a cavesson or noseband for a horse. This is one of the epithets of Shiv, who carries a skull in his hand and wears a chain of skulls around his neck. The feminine form is also an epithet of Durgā. *Arddh* —, *m.* pain of half the head (*hemicrania*): an areca nut having two kernels, or rather, one of those kernels which are convex on the one side and flat on the other side where it was in contact with its fellow. These nuts, from the doctrine of signatures, are said to be a remedy for *hemicrania*.

कपालीआसन, *m.* one of the attitudes of fakeers in worship in which they stand on their heads.

कपालीक्रिया, *f.* a certain ceremony among Hindoos, in which while the body is burning and is nearly reduced to ashes, the nearest relative breaks the skull with the stroke of a bamboo, pours melted butter into the cavity; hence, — *k.* to cudgel one's brains, think intensely.

कपास, *f.* undressed cloth: the cotton-plant (*Gossypium herbaceum*).

कपि, *m.* an ape, monkey; an epithet of Vishṇu: a pulley, block.

कपिकुंजर, *m.* an epithet of अंगद, *q.v.*

कपित्थ, *m.* a certain tree (*Feronia elephantum* or *Crataeva valanga*) and its fruit; also called the elephant-apple, or the wood-apple.

कपिन्द्रा } कपिपति } कपीन्द्र, *q.v.*

कपिल, *m. pr. n.* a certain Hindoo sage, author of the Sānkhya Shāstra: lit. *m.* (*f.* ā) reddish-haired.

कपिला, *f.* a reddish brown cow; *pr. n.* a certain river.

कपिश्रेष्ठ = कपीन्द्र, *q.v.*

कपी, *more properly* कपि, *q.v.*

कपीन्द्र, *m.* an epithet of Vishṇu; *lit.* lord or chief of the monkeys.

कपीस, *more prop.* कपीश = कपीन्द्र, *q.v.*

कपुत्र } कपूत } *m.* a bad or undutiful son. See क, 3.

कपूतन, a Braj pl. of कपूत, *q.v.* See न, 6.

कपूती, *f.* unfilialness (in a son).

कपूर, *m.* camphor: a certain flower.

कपूरकचरी, *f.* a certain medicine.

कपूरी, *m.* a species of betel-leaf.

कपोत, *m.* (*f.* ī) a dove, pigeon, the spotted-necked pigeon.

कपोल, *m.* the cheek.

कपोलगेन्दुआ, *m.* a small pillow of a circular shape to rest the cheek upon.

कफ, *m.* phlegm, spittle, scum, watery froth or foam in general.

कफ़, *f.* the hand, the palm of the hand.

कफ़तान, a robe of honour which Eastern princes present to ambassadors and other persons of distinction.

कफ़दस्त, *f.* the palm of the hand; *met.* a level and desert plain.

कफ़न, *m.* a shroud, coffin. —— *phāṛke bolnā*, expresses the impossibility of remaining silent in the sight of something wonderful.

कफ़नदफ़न, *m.* burial, funeral.

कफ़नाशन, *m.* (*f.* ī) antiphlegmatic.

कफ़नी, *f.* a certain dress worn by fakeers.

कफ़ाफ़, a sufficiency, competency, enough to keep one from begging: a request made with outstretched hand.

कफ़रनाहुम, *m. pr. n.* Capernaum.

कफ़्श, *f.* a shoe, slipper (high-heeled and shod with iron).

क़फ़स, *m.* a cage, lattice, network.

कफ़ाफ़, *m.* pittance, daily bread.

कफ़्फ़ारा, *m.* penitence, penance: expiation, atonement for sin; an epithet of Christ. — *k.* to atone for sin.

कफ़ालत, *m.* a pledge, pawn, security, responsibility.

कफ़ालतनामा, *m.* bail-bond.

कफ़ी, *m.* a (*f.* inī) a person afflicted with a cold: *lit.* phlegmatic, afflicted with rheum.

कफ़ील, *m.* a security, surety, hostage, ransomer, one who stands bail.

कब, 1, (*contraction*) = कवि, *q.v.*: 2, when? The word is declined like a substantive, as the following examples will show.

कबकब, when? at what period? what time?

कबका, *m.* (*f.* ī) of what time? appertaining to what time?

कबको, (dat. of कब) at what period? when?

क़ब्ज़, *f.* contraction; costiveness: a receipt; tribute, tax.

क़ब्ज़ा, *m.* a grasp, grip, clutch; a handle, the gripe of a sword: possession.

कबट, a kind of delicate dish.

कबड्डी, *f.* a certain game among boys who divide themselves into two parties, one of which takes its station on one side of a line or ridge, called *pālā*, made on the ground, and the other on the other side, — one boy, shouting *kabaddee kabaddee*, passes along the line and tries to touch one of those on the opposite side. If he is able to do this and to return to his own party, the boy that was so touched is supposed to be "killed," that is, he has to retire from the game: but if the boy who made the assault be seized and be unable to return, he "dies", or retires in the same manner. The assault is thus made from the two sides alternately, and that party is victorious of which some remain after all their opponents are [slain.

कबतईं } **कबतक** } = **कबतलक**, *q.v.*

कबतलक, up to what time? till when? how long?

कबन्ध, *m.* a headless trunk (still retaining a little life so as to have the power of moving); a belly: cloud, vapour: a certain demon.

क़बर, *f.* a grave, tomb.

कबरकन, *m.* a grave-digger.

कबरगाह, *f.* } **कबरस्थान**, *m.* } a burying-ground, cemetery.

कबरा, 1, *m.* (pl. of **कबीर**) the great, grandees, nobles: 2, *m.* (*f.* ī) grey, dirty white, variegated.

क़ब्ल, 1, *m.* the front, anterior; 2, *adj.* anterior, [foremost, first: 3, *adv.* before.

कबलग } **कबलों** } **कबलौ** } **कबलौं** } = **कबतलक**, *q.v.*

कबस, 1, *m.* the lighting or getting fire from another; a match, or anything for kindling fire with: learning, teaching: 2, *adj.* quick.

कबही, ever, at any time, at some time or other.

कबहीं } **कबहु** } in Braj = **कबही**, *q.v.*

कबा, *f.* a quilted garment; a jacket; a kind of [long gown.

कबाड, 1, *m.* a door, gate: 2, *f.* a bundle of firewood.

कबाब, *m.* a roast; meat cut into slices and then stuck on skewers to be roasted. —*k.* to burn, roast. —*honā*, to burn; *met.* to be enraged; to be desperately [in love.

कबार, *more prop.* (1) **कबाड़** (2) **केवाड़**, *qq.v.*

कबारी, *m.* (*f.* in *or* iṇī) a marine-store dealer.

कबाड, *m. f.* = **कबारी**, *q.v.*

कबाला, *m.* a writing, deed, bond, written agreement, contract; a bill of sale.

कबाहत, *f.* villany, dishonesty, baseness, wrong, evil, ill; deformity; inconvenence.

कबि; for all words beginning thus, see under [the form **कवि**.

कबीं in Braj = **कबहीं**, *q.v.*

कबीर, *m.* (pl. **कबरा**) 1, a nobleman, grandee: *lit.* large, immense, great, full-grown, senior: 2, *m. pr. n.* a famous fakeer, saint, and author who flourished about the close of the fifteenth century.

कबीरपन्थी, *m.* (*f.* inī) } **कबीरहा**, *m.* (*f.* ī *or* in) } a follower of Kabīr.

क़बील, *m.* a species, kind; family, tribe, kindred, [progeny.

क़बीला, *m.* a family, tribe; a wife.

कबीश्वर } **कबीसर** } = **कवीश्वर**, *q.v.*

क़बीह, detestable, vile, shameful, bad; deformed, [ugly.

कबुली, *f.* a kind of white pea.

कबूतर, *m.* (*f.* ī) a pigeon.

कबूतरख़ाना, *m.* a pigeon-house.

कबूतरझाड़, *m.* a certain plant (*Justitia nasuta*).

कबूतरबच्चा, *m.* a young pigeon: an unripe poppy-head wrapped up in pease-meal and fried in butter or [oil.

कबूतरबाज़ } **कबूतरबान** } *m.* a pigeon-fancier.

कबूतरी, *f.* (see **कबूतर**) a female pigeon. The word is frequent as a name of females.

कबूद, *m.* azure, blue: a sort of blue sheepskin: a kind of willow: a heron.

क़बूल, *m.* consent, agreement, concession, approbation, favourable reception. — *k.* to assent, confess, own, admit, agree to, promise.

क़बूलियत, *f.* a written agreement.

कभी } **कभीउं** } **कभीं** } = **कबही**, *q.v.*

कभीकभी, sometimes, at times, now and then.

कभीके, of some time, some time ago.

कभी नकभी, at some time or other.

कभु } **कभू** } **कभूं** } in Braj = **कबही**, *q.v.*

कम, deficient, less, little, minus. —*k.* to diminish; to depreciate. The term is much used as the first member of a compound word, and generally imports the idea of negation or inferiority.

कमका, left, what remains.

कमख़ाब, *m.* brocade, silk wrought with gold and [silver flowers.

कमचोर, *m.* an indolent person who does not turn out a proper amount of work.

कमज़ोर, weak, powerless, infirm.

कमज़ोरी, *f.* weakness, infirmity, powerlessness.

कमठ, *m.* a tortoise, turtle.

कमठा, *m.* a bow made of bamboo.

कमड़ा, *m.* a kind of gourd (*Cucurbita pepo*).

कमण्डल, contracted from **कमण्डलु**, *q.v.*

कमण्डलु, *m.* an earthen or wooden pot used by the ascetic and the theological student; a vessel with a spout: the waved-leaved figtree (*Ficus infectoria*).

कमतर, less, lesser, smaller; least.

कमतरीन, very small, least, smallest.

कमती, *f.* deficiency, lack, abatement, loss.

कमन, *m.* (*f.* ā) a libidinous person: a beautiful person: *lit.* desirous, libidinous: beautiful, desirable.

कमना, *f.* (see **कमन**) a libidinous or a beautiful female.

कमनीय, *m.* (*f.* ā) a desirable person : *lit.* beautiful, pleasing, desirable.

कमनैत, *m.* an archer, bowman.

कमन्द
कमन्ध } *m.* 1, = **कबन्ध**, *q v.* : 2, water.

कमनैती, *f.* archery. [nate (reproachfully).

कमबख़्त, *m.* a rascal, villain, wretch : *lit.* unfortu-

कमबख़्ती, *f.* unfortunateness, adversity.

कमबेश, more or less. [tion of the Kur,ān.

क़मर, *m.* the moon : title of the fifty-fourth sec-

कमर, *f.* (*m.* ?) the loins ; a girdle, belt, zone : an arch : the flank of an army. — *kholnā*, to quit service. —*khol baiṭhnā*. to sit at ease. — *ṭūṭnā*, to be hopeless, be deserted by one's friends ; to become weak in the loins (an incurable disease to which horses in many parts of India are liable). — *tornā*, to take away one's hopes ; to draw over one's adherents to the side of his adversaries. — *pakarnā*, to urge a claim against one. — *bāndhnā*, to get ready, resolve. — *baiṭhnā*, to be helpless. — *mazbut k.* to undertake a work of expense. — *mārnā*, to strike sideways, attack an army in flank. — *sidhi k.* to lie down. — *hilānā*, to endeavour ; to copulate.

कमरकश, *m.* a brave man, hero.

कमरकशाई, *f.* ungirding the loins (a kind of oriental exaction made by officials placed as guards over any one for permission to unfasten the clothes in order to performing the offices of nature).

कमरकोटा, a parapet. [and appearing outside.

कमरकोठा, a part of a beam passing through a wall

कमरख, *m.* a certain fruit (*Averrhoa carambola*).

कमरदार, *m.* a servant, manservant.

कमरदवाल, a leathern belt.

कमरपट्टा, *m.* a kind of ring or zone encircling the waists of women. This kind of girdle is composed of many flat pieces of silver or gold (embossed and ornamented) linked together.

कमरबन्द, 1, *m.* a girdle, zone, long piece of cloth girt about the loins : 2, alert, ready for action, armed.

कमरबन्दी, *f.* preparation for action.

कमरसार = **कमरसाल**, *q. v.* [by women.

कमरसाल, *m.* a kind of ornamental girdle worn

कमरा, *m.* a chamber, room ; a cabin of a ship.

कमरी, 1, = **कमली**, *q. v.* : 2, appertaining to the waist or loins : weak in the loins (said of a horse).

कमरिया = **कमली**, *q. v.* [waistcoat.

कमरी अंगरखा, *m.* a spencer, short jacket or

कमल, *m.* the lotus (*Nilumbrium speciosum*, Willd. ; *Nymphaea nelumbo*, Lin.). [*lit.* lotus-feet.

कमलचरण, *m.* an epithet of the feet of any deity :

कमलनयन, *adj.* having eyes like the lotus-flower : hence, *m.* (*f.* ā) a person with beautiful eyes.

कमलनाल, *m.* the stalk of the water-lily,

कमलपत्र, *m.* the lotus-leaf.

कमलनैन, *m.* (*f.* ā)
कमलनैना, *m.* (*f.* ī) } = **कमलनयन**, *q. v.*

कमलबन, *m.* a forest of lotuses.

कमलबाए
कमलबायु } *m.* jaundice.

कमला, 1, *m.* the name of the caterpillar or larva of a brown moth covered with fine bristles, which, on handling it, adhere to the skin and excite itching (it is destructive to trees), the palmer-worm : 2, *f.* an excellent woman : an epithet of the goddess *Lakshmi*.

कमलापति, *m.* the lord of Lakshmī, *i. e.* Vishṇu.

कमलाक्ष, *m.* (*f.* ī) epithet of a person with beautiful eyes ; *lit.* having eyes like the lotus.

कमलासन, *m.* an epithet of Brahma ; *lit.* seated on the lotus. [bounding in lotuses.

कमलिनी, *f.* a number of lotus-flowers, a place a-

कमली, *f.* (a dim. of **कम्बल**) a small blanket.

कमलीकीड़ा, *m.* a palmer-worm, hairy caterpillar.

कमवाना, *t.* to cause to earn, cause to work : to

कमाइश, *f.* business in general. [use (as a razor).

कमाई, *f.* gain, earnings, gettings, wages ; work, performance. — *k.* to earn ; to work. — *kā beṭā*, a

कमाईपूत, *m.* a grown-up son. [grown-up son.

कमाऊ, *m. f.* a laborer, etc. : *lit.* industrious, laborious, earning a livelihood.

कमातुर, *more prop.* **कामातुर**, *q. v.*

कमान, *f.* a bow : a spring.

कमानअबरू, *f.* epithet of a mistress ; *lit.* having

कमानकश, *m.* an archer. [arched eyebrows.

कमानगर, one who makes holes.

कमानदान, *m.* a bow-case. [bow.

कमानदार, *m.* an archer, a person armed with a

कमाना, *t.* 1, to earn, accumulate, save ; to work ; to perform ; to do (good) ; to perpetrate ; to clean (leather, or a privy) : 2, to diminish, lessen, abate.

कमाल, *m.* perfection, excellence ; completion, conclusion : punctuality.

कमालत ; see (1) **कमाल** (2) **कमालात** (3) **कमालियत**.

कमालात, *m.* (pl. of **कमाल**) perfections, excellences, acquirements, accomplishments.

कमालियत
कमालीयत } *f.* accomplishment, perfection, ex- [cellence.

कमासुत, *m.* (*f.* ā) a servant, earner, workman, journeyman.

कमिया, *m.* an agricultural laborer.

कमी, *f.* deficiency, lack, loss, abatement.

कमींना, *more prop.* **कमीना**, *q. v.*

कमीज़, *m.* a shirt.

कमीन, 1, *f.* an ambush : 2, *m.* a kind of village serf : 3, defective ; mean, abject.

कमीनगाह, *f.* an ambuscade.

कमीना, *m.* or *f.* mean, base, abject, defective.

कमीला = **कमूद**, *q. v.*

क़मीस, *m.* a shirt.

कमूद, *m.* a certain drug used for dyeing. It consists of the dust from the outside of the capsules of *Rottlera tinctoria* : it is said to be also a purgative medicine and aphrodisiac.

कमेरा, *m.* a workman, journeyman, assistant.

कमेरू, 1, *more prop.* कुमेरु; 2, *m.* or *f.* = कमेरा, *qq. v.*

कमोद = कमूद, *q. v.*

कमोदिनी, *f.* a sort of water-lily (*Menyanthes Indica* or *cristata*) said to expand its petals at night and close them by day.

कमोरी, *f.* a small earthen pot.

कम्प, *m.* a trembling, shivering, tremor.

कम्पत्ति, the ocean, sea.

कम्पन, 1, *m.* a trembling, shaking: a certain weapon: *pr. n.* (1) of a man (2) of a country: 2, *m.* (*f.* ā) *adj.* causing to tremble.

कम्पना, 1, *a. int.* to tremble, shake: 2, *f. pr. n.* a certain river.

कम्पमान, *m.* (*f.* matī) tremulous, shaky.

कम्पाना, *t.* to agitate, shake, cause to tremble.

कम्पायमान, *m.* (*f.* matī) tremulous, shaking.

कम्पाहा, *m.* (*f.* ī) tremulous, trembling, timid.

कम्पित, *m.* (*f.* ī) tremulous, shaking, fear-stricken.

कम्बख़्त = कमबख़्त, *q. v.*

कम्बल, *m.* a blanket, woollen garment.

कम्बु, *m.* a shell; a bracelet made of shells.

कम्बुग्रीव, *m.* (*f.* ā) an epithet; *lit.* having a neck marked with three lines like a shell (held to indicate exalted fortune).

कम्बोज, *m. pr. n.* the country of Camboge or Cambay in Northern India.

कम्मल, *m.* 1, = कम्बल, *q. v.*: 2, a kind of ear-ring: a long strip of palm-leaf rolled up and inserted into the aperture bored in the lobe of the ear.

कम्मा, *m.* a document written on a leaf of the palmyra-tree rolled up into a ball; proceedings, intelligence.

कम्मून, *m.* cummin-seed.

कय, see (1) कई (2) काय (3) किया.

कयम, *more prop.* क़ाइम, *q. v.*

कयलास, *more prop.* कैलास, *q. v.*

कयी / **कयो** } in Braj = किया (करना).

कर, 1, *m.* the hand; the trunk of an elephant: a sunbeam, ray of light: a father: hail: royal revenue, toll, tax, fee, custom, duty, tribute: 2, the form of the second person singular of the imperative mode of vb. *karnā*: also, the shortest form of its conjunctive participle: 3, this particle frequently occurs, especially in poetry, as the case-sign of the genitive irrespective of gender or of number; *e. g.* मायाकर = मायाका (की, के): 4, as र is constantly liable to be written as *reph*, words which may begin with कर will sometimes be found under the form क॑; *e. g.* करक = कर्क, and *vice versâ* (see article र): 5, as a suffix [*m.* (*f.* i)] it forms some nouns of agency.

करई, *m.* a granary, storehouse.

करउं in Braj = करूं (करना).

कर उगाहनेहारा, *m.* (*f.* ī) a collector of revenue.

करंज, *m.* a certain plant (*Galedupa arborea*).

करंजा, *m.* a certain tree (*Dalbergia arborea*).

करक, *m.* the drinking-pot of a student or of an ascetic: sickness, pain: hail.

करकच, *m.* a kind of salt, sea-salt made by evaporation.

करकट, *m.* (*f.* ī) a crab; the sign Cancer: the Numidian crane: a certain plant.

करकनाथ, *f.* a species of bird of which even the bones are said to be black.

करकरा, *m.* a bad coin: the Numidian crane.

करकराहट, *f.* a crackling noise, cracking.

करकस, *m.* (*f.* ā) = कर्कश, *q. v.*

करकाना, *t.* to strain, sprain, break.

करके, conjunctive participle of vb. *karnā*. It forms many adverbial phrases; *e. g.* अवश्य करके, most assuredly, of necessity, of course.

करकोटक = कर्कोटक, *q. v.*

करख़्त, austere, rigid, insensible, of no feeling.

करखा, *more prop.* कड़खा, *q. v.*

करग, *m.* a rhinoceros.

करगता, *m.* a string worn around the waist.

करगम, *m.* a vulture: a kind of arrow.

करगहना, *m.* protection.

करग्राहक, *m.* (*f.* ikā) a collector of revenue.

करछी, *f.* a spoon; a skein; a ringlet.

करज, *m.* a finger, a finger-nail.

क़रज़, *m.* a loan, debt, money borrowed at interest. — *denā*, to lend. — *rakhnā*, to owe. — *lenā*, to borrow.

क़रज़दार, *m.* or *f.* a debtor.

क़रज़दारी, *f.* the being in debt.

करजोड़ / **करजोर** } = करजोड़ी, *q. v.*

करजोड़ी, *f.* having the hands placed flat together as in supplication.

करण, *m.* 1, a making, doing; a cause, instrument; an organ of sense; the accomplishing an action; (in Gram.) the instrumental case: 2, an astronomical division of time, of which there are eleven, — seven movable and four fixed, and two of which are equal to a lunar day: 3, the hypothenuse of a triangle; the diagonal of a square, parallelogram, etc.; a secant: 4, the ear: 5, = कारण, *q. v.*: 6, for all words beginning with this element, but not given below, see under the form कर्ण.

करणवाचक संज्ञा, *f.* (in Gram.) an instrumental noun.

करणी, *f.* an action, deed, doing; business: a trowel: (in Arithm.) a surd.

करणीय, lawful to be done, suitable to be done, feasible.

करटक, *m.* a crow: *pr. n.* a certain jackal in the Hitopadesh.

करठक, *more prop.* करटक, *q. v.*

करतब, *m.* action; business; skill.

करतल, *m.* the palm of the hand.

करतव, *more prop.* (1) करतब (2) कर्त्तव्य, *qq. v.*

करतव्य, *more prop.* कर्त्तव्य, *q. v.*

करतार, *m.* an author, doer, creator; The Creator; a proprietor, master, husband: (in Gram.) the nominative case.

करतारा, a poetical form of **करतार**, *q. v.*

करतारी, *more prop.* **करताली**, *q. v.*

करताल, *m.* a kind of small cymbal.

करताली, *f.* the beating time with the hands.

करती, *f.* the skin of a calf stuffed and placed near the cow to make her give milk.

करतूत = **करतूति**, *q. v.*

करतूति, *f.* action, business; manner of life, conduct, practice.

करदा, *m.* exchange, balance made to make up a deficiency in coin, or the difference between the price of new things and old given in exchange.

करदायक, *m.* (*f.* ikā) a tax-payer.

करदिखलाना, *t.* to realize.

करदोरा, a string tied around the waist to which the *laṅgotee* is fastened: a kind of gold or silver chain worn around the waist by men.

करधनी / **करधमरी** } = **कर्धनी**, *q. v.*

करन; for all words beginning thus, but not given below, see under either of the forms **करण** or **कर्ण**.

करन, *m.* lace cut into small pieces and put on a cap.

करनफूल, *m.* a kind of earring.

करनम, *m.* a village accountant.

करनहार, *m.* a doer, maker, originator.

करना, 1, *m.* a kind of citron (*Citrus*): 2, *t.* to do, act, perform, execute, make, effect, to administer; to avail; to set; to thrust; to use; *coire*; to turn or change into; e. g. *Usne use swān kiyā*, he transformed him into a dog. This verb forms what in Grammar are termed Nominals when added to substantives, adjectives, or adverbs; *e. g.* **ध्यान क°**, to meditate: **तंग क°**, to tighten: **शीघ्र क°**, to make haste. With the uninflected form of the masculine of the past participle of any verb this verb forms the corresponding Frequentative; *e. g.* **लिखा क°**, to write frequently, be in the habit of writing.

करनाटक, *pr. n.* the Carnatic country.

करनी, *f.* (prop. **करणी**) an action, deed.

करनेवाला, *m.* (*f.* ī) a doer, maker, agent.

करनीं in Braj = **करना**. See **श्रीं**.

करपान, *m.* an eruptive cutaneous disorder to which children are subject.

करब, vexation, affliction.

करबट = **करवट**, *q. v.*

करबी, *f.* the stalk of the *juwār* or *bājrā* (*Holcus sorgum* and *spicatus*).

करभाजन, *m. pr. n.* (see **नवोयोगेश्वर**) the 9th Yogeshwar.

करम = **कर्म्म**, *q. v.*

करमचारी, *m.* an inferior officer who collects revenue for a certain division of a village; the village accountant.

करमभोग, *m.* the fulfilling of destiny, experiencing the consequences of actions whether good or bad.

करमेवा, *m.* a kind of vegetable.

करयुग, *adj.* with the hands clasped as in earnest entreaty.

कररहित, untaxed, rent-free.

करलगुआ, uxorious.

करलाना, *a. int.* to shriek: *t.* to effect, settle.

करव, a hollow tooth: bitter lettuce, endive.

करवट, *f.* a sleeping on the side, a turning from side to side. — *k.* or *lenā*, to turn over (in bed).

करवरा, calamity, trouble.

करवा, *m.* (*f.* ī) = **कडुआ**, *q. v.*

करवांसी, the twentieth part of a *biswānsee*.

करवाना, *t.* to cause to be made, to cause to make, cause to do.

करवारा, 1, the bucket for raising water from a well: 2, *m.* an oar, paddle; a rudder.

करवाल, *m.* a paddle, oar; a rudder: a sword.

करवीर, *m.* a certain fragrant plant (*Nerium odorum* or *Oleander*) or its flower.

करवैय्या, *m.* a causer, doer; a worker, operative, the person who acts as the instrument in bringing about any result.

करशोथ, *m.* œdematous swelling of the hand.

करषना, *t.* to plough, till: to attract, draw.

करषा, hostility, enmity, anger, envy.

करसी, *f.* the sweepings of a stable (*esp.* of a cowshed) used for fuel.

करस्मा, *more prop.* **किरिश्मा**, *q. v.*

करह, *f.* aversion, detestation, abhorrence, abomination; molestation, trouble.

करहा / **करहाना** } *f.* the loins.

करहु in Braj = **करो** (**करना**).

करा, 1, *m.* (*f.* i) an old form = **क्रिया**, *q. v.*: 2, *m.* (*f.* ī) hard, adulterated, false, bad (as coin).

कराइजा = **कराएजा**, *q. v.*

कराएजा, *m.* the oval-leafed rosebay (*Nerium antidysentericum*); a plant whose seeds are used in medicine as a tonic or febrifuge. See *Indrayav*.

करांजना / **करांग्रना** } = **कराहना**, *q. v.*

कराकुल, *m.* (*f.* ā) a kind of heron or curlew.

कराड़ा = **करारा**, *q. v.*

कराना, *t.* to cause to be done, cause to be made, to actuate, effect.

करान्त, *m.* a saw.

करान्ती, *m.* (*f.* in *or* inī) a sawyer.

करावत, dates which are gathered from the roots of the branches after the clusters are cut off.

करायल, *m.* rosin, resin.

करायहीं in Braj = **कराऊंगा** (**कराना**). See **इहीं**.

करायी, *f.* the pod of a white pea.

करार, 1, *more prop.* **कराल**, *q. v.*: 2, *m.* rest, firmness, ratification: 3, *m.* an attacking violently; a reiterated assault.

करारा, 1, *m.* the shore, coast, bank: 2, *m.* (*f.* ī) hard, rigid, stiff.

कराल, 1, *m.* resin, pitch: 2, *m.* (*f.* ā) great, large, formidable, huge, lofty.

कराला, *f.* an epithet of Durgā.

कराव, a term applied by some inferior tribes to concubinage generally, but more especially to the marriage of a widow with a brother of her deceased husband.

करावल, *m. f.* the advanced guard of an army; a sentinel, picquet: a gamekeeper.

कराहत, *f.* dislike, disgust, aversion.

कराहना, *a. int.* to sigh, groan, moan, utter "ah!" (from pain).

कराहा, *m.* = कड़ाहा, *q. v.*

कराहियत, *f.* disagreeableness; disgust: aversion, abomination, hatred, abhorrance.

कराही, *f.* a flat vessel of iron, brass, or earth in which food is boiled or fried. — *chāṭnā*, to lick the pot (from indigence or extreme avarice); hence, *Usne — chāṭī* is applied as a reproach to a bridegroom if it rain on the occassion of his wedding procession. — *lenā* describes a kind of ordeal in which oil is made boiling hot in the vessel above described, a small piece of gold (as, for example, a ring) is put into it, and the suspected person is to take it out: if he do this without injury to his hand he is pronounced innocent.

करि, 1, *m.* (*f.* ṇī) an elephant: 2, this form is frequently used (especially in poetry and in Braj) for कर in either of its senses.

करिश्र, a dialectic form of काला, *q. v.* See क्रश्र.

करिकर, 1, = करके, *q. v.*: 2, see कर, 3.

करिके, *more prop.* करके, *q. v.*

करिणी, *f.* (*m.* करि) a female elephant.

करिन, *m.* (*f.* ṇī) an elephant.

करिन्थ, *m. pr. n.* the city of Corinth.

करिय, an old form = कीजियेा.

करिल, *m.* a sprout, shoot.

करिवर, *m.* an epithet of Ganesh: *lit.* the beautiful or chief elephant (in allusion to his face).

करिश्मा, *more prop.* किरिश्मा, *q. v.*

करिहांव, *f.* the loins, waist; the buttocks.

करिहै (pl. करिहैं) in Braj = करेगा. See हुवै.

करिहेा in Braj = करोगे. See हुहेा.

करिहेां in Braj = करूंगा. See हुहेां.

करी, 1, *f.* (*m.* करा) an old form = किई, *q. v.*: 2, *m.* (*f.* iṇī) an elephant.

क़रीन, conjoined, contiguous, connected.

क़रीना, *m.* similarity, likeness; symmetry: cause, context, connexion, tenour.

करीपाक, a certain plant the leaves of which are used in cookery.

क़रीब, *postp.* (takes gen. masc. infl.) near, neighbouring, nigh, almost, about, akin.

करीम, bountiful, gracious, benevolent, munificent.

करीर, *m.* a shoot of a bamboo: a thorny leafless plant (*Capparis aphylla*, Roxb.) which grows in deserts and is eaten by camels.

करील }
करीला } *more prop.* करीर, *q. v.*

करीह, detestable, abominable, filthy, dirty.

करुग्रार, an oar.

करुई, *more prop.* कड़ुई (कड़ुश्रा).

करूख, *m. pr. n.* the fourth son of Sudyumn, and progenitor of the Karukh race of Kshatriyas.

करुणा, *f.* compassion, pity, tenderness of feeling, mercy.

करुणाश्रायन, *more prop.* करुणायन, *q. v.*

करुणात्मक, compassionate: hence, *m.* (*f.* ikā) a compassionate person.

करुणानिधान, *m.* an epithet of God; *lit.* the abode of mercy.

करुणानिधि, *m.* an epithet of God; *lit.* the receptacle or treasury of compassion.

करुणापर, *m.* (*f.* ā) a compassionate person; one who is intent upon compassionateness.

करुणामय, *m.* (*f.* ī) a compassionate, tender, merciful person: *lit.* abounding in, or made up of, the quality of pitifulness.

करुणायन, *m.* the abode of compassion; an epithet of God.

करुणासन, *m.* a mercy-seat, throne of grace.

करुन, *more prop.* करुणा, *q. v.*

करुवेा in Braj = कड़ुश्रा, *q. v.*

करुश्रा, *m.* an earthen pipkin, a pot with a spout.

करुश्राचेाथ, *f.* a certain holy-day of the Hindoos which occurs in the month Kārttik.

करुब, *m.* a cherub, a certain superior order of angels.

करेकर, abreast of, even with.

करेजा, *more prop.* कलेजा, *q. v.*

करेरा, *m.* (*f.* ī) hard, stiff, vehement.

करेलनी, *f.* a kind of rake.

करेला, *m.* a certain bitter vegetable (*Momordica charantia*): a kind of firework.

करैगेा in Braj = करेगा. See ऐगेा.

करैत, *m.* a certain snake of a very venomous kind.

करैता = करैत, *q. v.*

करेां in Braj = (1) मैं करूं (2) मैं करूंगा.

करोड़; for this word and its kin, see under the form कड़ेाड़.

करोड़ा, *m.* (*f.* ī *or* in) }
करोड़ेा, *m.* (*f.* in *or* inī } = कड़ेाड़ा, *q. v.*

करेात, *m.* a saw.

करोनी, *f.* the milk that sticks to the bottom of the pot after boiling.

करेान्त, *m.* a saw.

करोर = कड़ेाड़, *q. v.*

करौं in Braj = करूं (करना).

करौन्दा, *m.* the corinda (*Carissa carandus*).

कर्; for all words beginning with this element, but not given below, see under the form कर.

कर्क, *m.* a crab; the sign Cancer: a white horse.

कर्कराशि, *m.* a crab; the sign Cancer.

कर्कश, *m.* (*f.* ā) a violent person: *lit.* violent, harsh, contumelious, obdurate; hard, unfeeling, unkind, cruel, merciless; miserly: intangible: sharp, piercing.

कर्कशा, *f.* a termagant, scold, shrew.

कर्कशास्त्री = कर्कशा, *q. v.*

कर्कसा, *more prop.* कर्कशा, *q. v.*

कर्का, *m.* a pæan, warsong.

कर्कोतर, *m.* a kind of gem.

कर्कोटक, *m.* the bael-tree (*Ægle Marmelos*) and its fruit: a certain plant (*Momordica mixta*): the sugar-cane: *pr. n.* a certain Nāg.

कर्चूर, *m.* a certain plant (*Cucurma reclinata*).

कर्चूरक, *m.* zedoary (*Cucurma zerumbet*).

कर्छनी, *f.* an iron skimmer.

कर्छा, *m.* a ladle, large spoon.

कर्छाल, *f.* a bound, spring, jump.

कर्छी, *f.* (dim. of कर्छा) a spoon; a skein; a ringlet.

कर्छुल, *f.* an iron spoon: a sword made of soft iron.

कर्ज़ = करज़, *q.v.*

कर्ड़ा, *m.* (*f.* ī) hard, stiff; obdurate, harsh.

कर्ण; for all words beginning with this element, but not given below, see under the form करण.

कर्ण, *m.* the ear: the helm of a ship or boat.

कर्णकीटी, *f.* a small centipede (*Julex cornifex*); [*lit.* the ear-worm, ear-insect.

कर्णगूथ, *m.* ear-wax.

कर्णजलूका, *f.* = कर्णकीटी, *q.v.*; *lit.* the ear-leech.

कर्णदर्पण, *m.* an ornament for the ear, earring.

कर्णधार, *m.* a supercargo, pilot, helmsman.

कर्णपाक, *m.* inflammation of the outer ear.

कर्णपाली, *f.* a garland or string of jewels pendent from the ear as an ornament.

कर्णपुर, *m. pr. n.* the ancient Bhāgalpur, capital [of *Rājā Karṇ*.

कर्णप्रतिनाह, *m.* a certain disease of the ear in which there is a suppression of the excretion of wax, which is supposed to have dissolved and passed off by the nose and mouth.

कर्णफल, *m.* the fish *Ophiocephalus Kurrawey*.

कर्णफूल, *m.* a kind of earring.

कर्णमद्गुर, *m.* a kind of sheat-fish (*Silurus unitus*).

कर्णभूषण, *m.* any ornament for the ear.

कर्णमती, *f. pr. n.* a certain female incarnation.

कर्णमल, *m.* ear-wax.

कर्णमुकुट, *m.* an earring.

कर्णमूल, *m.* a swelling near the ear, parotis.

कर्णमोटी, *f.* an epithet of Durgā in one of her [incarnations.

कर्णलतिका, *f.* the lobe of the ear.

कर्णवेधन, *m.* the piercing the ears.

कर्णवेधनी, *f.* an instrument for piercing the ear.

कर्णशूल, *m.* the ear-ache.

कर्णस्राव, *m.* a discharge of ichorous matter [through the ear.

कर्णाट, *m. pr. n.* the Carnatic. Anciently the name was applied to the central districts of the peninsula including Mysore.

कर्णाटक = कर्णाट, *q.v.*

कर्णाटी, *f.* one of the female personifications of [the musical modes.

कर्णालंकार, *m.* an earring.

कर्णिका, *f.* the pericarp of the lotus: an ornament of the ear: *pr. n.* a certain Apsaras.

कर्णिनी, *f.* a disease of the uterus, — *prolapsus* or *polypus uteri*.

कर्णौ, *m. pr. n.* one of the seven principal ranges of mountains which divide the universe.

कर्तब, *m.* action, deed; business; skill.

कर्त्तरी, *f.* a pair of scissors or shears.

कर्त्तव्य, proper to be done, necessary to be done, what ought to be done, proper, fit, necessary, incumbent, obligatory, practicable.

कर्त्तव्यकर्म्म, *m.* a work of necessity, duty, imperative duty.

कर्त्तव्यत्व, *m.* (*f.* tā) propriety, obligatoriness, fitness, necessity, practicability; business.

कर्त्ता, *m.* (uninfl.) author, doer, agent, Maker, Creator; a proprietor, master, chief, husband; (in Gram.) the nominative case. Frequently suffixed to form certain nouns of agency; *e. g.* पालनकर्त्ता.

कर्त्तापन, *m.* agency, Creatorship, proprietorship, etc.

कर्त्तापुरुष, *m.* an epithet of Brahmā, of Vishṇu, [or of Shiv.

कर्त्तार, *m.* author, doer, maker, Creator.

कर्त्ताल, *f.* a certain musical instrument, a kind of cymbal: the beating time with the hands.

कर्त्तृ, *m.* (*f.* trī) a doer, maker, agent.

कर्त्तृता, *f.* (*m.* °त्व) agency, management, government, rule.

कर्त्तृप्रधान क्रिया, *f.* (in Gram.) an active verb (transitive or intransitive).

कर्त्तृवाचक संज्ञा, *f.* (in Gram.) a verbal noun of agency.

कर्त्तृवाच्य क्रिया, *f.* (in Gram.) a transitive verb.

कर्द, *m.* mud, clay, mire.

कर्दन, *m.* the grumbling of the bowels, borborigmi.

कर्दम, *m.* mud, mire, clay; dregs; sin: flesh: a certain plant; *pr. n.* (1) of a certain Nāga (2) of a certain Prajāpati.

कर्द्धनी }
कर्धनी } *f.* a waistband, girdle, zone.

कर्ना, frequently put for करना, *q. v.*

कर्पास, *m.* cotton.

कर्पासी, *f.* the cotton-tree.

कर्पूर, *m.* the camphor-tree (*Laurus camphorifera*); camphor: *pr. n.* (1) of a certain poet (2) of the father of Gajmalla and uncle of Kalyāṇmalla.

कर्पूरक, *m.* zedoary (*Curcuma zerumbet*).

कर्पूरतिलक, *m. pr. n.* (in Myth.) a certain elephant.

कर्पूरतैल, *m.* camphor liniment.

कर्पूरमंजरी, *f.* a certain dramatic work by Rājā [Shekhar.

कर्पूरमणि, *m.* a certain white mineral used medicinally.

कर्बी, *f.* the stalk of *juwār* or *bājrā* (*Holcus sorgum* and *spicatus*).

कर्बुदार, *m.* mountain ebony; blue barleria.

कर्बुरा, *f.* the trumpet-flower (*Bignonia suaveolens*): a sort of basil (*Ocymum gratissimum*).

कर्बूरक = कर्पूरक, *q. v.*

कर्म्म, *m.* an act, deed, proceeding; business, occupation, work; fortune, fate, destiny; Hindoo worship, devotion; (in Gram.) the accusative case: name of a certain bird.

कर्म्मकर्त्ता, *m.* (*f.* trī) an attorney, agent, ambassador, *locum tenens*.

कर्म्मकाण्ड, *m.* (see मीमांसा) the body of religious ceremonies commanded by Hindoo law or established by custom. [a bull.

कर्म्मकार, *m.* a workman, artisan : a blacksmith :

कर्म्मकारक, 1, *m.* (*f.* ikā) = कर्म्मकारी, *q.v.* : 2, *m.* (in Gram.) the accusative case.

कर्म्मकारी, *adj.* performing a business, operative, effectual : hence, *m.* (*f.* iṇī) a worker, workman, agent, operative. [acts.

कर्म्मगुण, *m.* any property resulting from human

कर्म्मच्युत, *m.* a person dismissed from office.

कर्म्मणा, *f.* (see मनसावाचाक°) an act, deed.

कर्म्मत, a name of श्री or of its symbol.

कर्म्मत्व, *m.* (in Gram.) objectivity, the accusative state of any word. [disreputable, immoral.

कर्म्मदुष्ट, *m.* (*f.* ā) a low immoral person : *lit.*

कर्म्मन, (1) = कर्म्म (2) a Braj pl. of कर्म्म, *q.v.*

कर्म्मनाशा, *f. pr. n.* a certain sacred river in Bihār. Its water is said to destroy religious merit.

कर्म्मनिवासक क्रिया, *f.* (in Gram.) a passive verb.

कर्म्मना, *more prop.* कर्म्मणा, *q.v.*

कर्म्ममीमांसा, *f. pr. n.* the prior or practical division of the Mimānsā philosophy (so called because it relates to works, or religious observances undertaken for specific ends).

कर्म्मप्रधान क्रिया, *f.* (in Gram.) a passive verb.

कर्म्मभूमि, *f.* an epithet of आर्य्यावर्त्त, *q.v.* [epoch.

कर्म्मयुग, *m.* (see कलि) an epithet of the present

कर्म्मरेखा, *f.* any mark on the body by which one's fortune is ascertainable ; fate, fortune, destiny.

कर्म्मवाचक संज्ञा, *f.* (in Gram.) a verbal noun indicating the object, the past passive participle.

कर्म्मवाच्य क्रिया, *f.* (in Gram.) a passive verb.

कर्म्मविपाक, *m.* the consequences of actions.

कर्म्मशील, *m.* (*f.* ā) an assiduous person : *lit.* assiduous, persevering, laborious, industrious.

कर्म्मशीलत्व, *m.* (*f.* tā) assiduity, perseverance.

कर्म्मशुद्ध, *m.* approved occupation.

कर्म्मशूर, *m.* assiduous, laborious, hardworking, performing work carefully.

कर्म्मसिद्धि, *f.* success, efficiency : accomplishment.

कर्म्माचल, *m.* = कर्म्मभूमि, *q.v.* (?)

कर्म्माधर्म्मी, *m.* (*f.* iṇī) a devout person, etc. : *lit.* devout, virtuous ; fortunate ; accidental. [tined.

कर्म्माधीन, *m.* (*f.* ā) subject to destiny, fated, des-

कर्म्मारम्भक, *m.* (*f.* ikā) a causer, beginner.

कर्म्मिष्ठ, *m.* (*f.* ā) an assiduous person, etc.: *lit.* active, diligent, assiduous.

कर्म्मी, *m.* (*f.* iṇī) a worker (esp. in the religious sense) etc.: *lit.* relating to any work or to worldly action, doing works : fortunate.

कर्म्मेन्द्रिय, *m.* (see बुद्धीन्द्रिय) an organ of action : five are reckoned, *viz.* the hand, the foot, the larynx (as the organ of voice), the anus and the organ of generation.

कर्रत, *f.* one time : one assault. *Do.* —, twice.

कर्रा, *m.* (*f.* ī) hard, adulterated, false, bad (as

कर्रांद, *m.* a monkey-keeper. [coin).

कर्रांना, *n.* to be hard, be stiff.

कर्रोबी, *m.* a cherub, a certain superior order of angels. [vating the soil.

कर्षक, *m.* (*f.* ikī) a tiller of the soil : *lit.* culti-

कर्षण, *m.* ploughing, tilling ; cultivated land, tillage : bringing, drawing, attracting, bending ; tormenting. [rica).

कर्षफल, *m.* beleric myrobalan (*Terminalia bele-*

कर्षिणी, *f.* a medicinal sort of moon-plant (*Menispermum cordifolium*) : the bit of a bridle.

कर्षी, *m.* (*f.* iṇī) a cultivator of the land, etc. : lit. *adj.* cultivating the soil : attracting, dragging.

कर्षू, *f.* a furrow ; an incision.

कल, 1, *f.* ease, tranquillity, peace, relief, quiet, rest, repose ; a trap, machine, lock, trigger of a gun : 2, scald-headed, bald : 3, *m.* (*f.* ā) a dumb person, etc. ; *lit.* dumb ; beautiful, sweet, low, soft, weak : 4, *m.* to-morrow ; yesterday : — *ratko*, yesternight, to-morrow night : in the Dakkhanee dialect this word is used only in the sense of yesterday : — to-morrow is expressed by *sabāh* or *subāh* : 5, = कलि, *q.v.* : 6, = कली, *q.v.* : 7, a contraction of कोकिल, *q.v.*

क़लई, *f.* tin ; lacker, covering, gilt.

कलंक, *m.* a spot, mark, rust, brand, stigma, reproach, disgrace, calumny, defamation, accusation, reflection, suspicion. [ed, calumniated, defamed.

कलंकित, *m.* (*f.* ā) polluted, stained, contaminat-

कलंगड़ा, a water-melon. [row.

कलंज, *m.* an animal struck with a poisoned ar-

कलंकी, 1, (*corruption*) = कल्की, 1, *q.v.* ; 2, *m.* (*f.* inī) a disreputable person, etc. : *lit.* stained, blemished, disgraced ; liable to reproach.

क़लक़, *m.* disquietude, anxiety, commotion.

कलकण्ठ, *m.* (*f.* ā *or* ī) a person who has a sweet voice : *lit.* having a voice like the *kokil*. [eyes).

कलकम, lamp-black (applied medicinally to the

कलकत्ता = कलिकाता, *q.v.*

कलकल, *m.* a wrangling, quarrel, confused noise, buzz of a crowd : an epithet of Shiv.

कलका, *m.* (*f.* ī.) gen. of कल, 4. Used idiomatically, *e.g.* — *ādmī*, an automaton, puppet ; a very weak person : an upstart, *novus homo.* — *ghora*, a very well-trained and obedient horse. — *din*, yesterday. *Kalkī bāt*, a mere thing of yesterday, recent news. *Kalkī rāt*, last night ; to-morrow night. [*q.v.*

कलकी, 1, *more prop.* कल्की, *q.v.* : 2, *f.*; *m.* कलका,

कलगट, an axe, pickaxe.

कलगा, *m.* a certain flower (*Amaranthus*), the cockscomb, prince's feather.

कलगी, } *f.* an ornament on the turban.
कलग़ी

कलजभवां, *m.* (*f.* °वीं) sallow-complexioned, tawny.

कलजिभा, *m.* (*f.* in *or* ī) one whose curses prevail ; an evil-tongued person : *lit.* malignant, ill-omened.

कलजीबी, *m.* (*f.* in or inī) = कलजिभा, *q.v.*

कलत्र, *f.* a wife. [*Let* (?) man by a *Tīvar woman*).

कलन्दर, *m.* a man of a mixed caste (the son of a

कलप; for all words beginning thus, but not given below, see under the form **कल्प**. [called māndee, *q. v.*

कलप, *m.* a kind of hair-dye; a kind of starch

कलपना, 1, = **कल्पना**, *q.v.*: 2, *n.* to be vexed, be grieved, be in distress, be in pain, be in torture.

कलपाना, *t.* to distress, grieve any one.

कलफ़, *m.* a padlock: attention: a pimple or dot on the face.

क़लब, 1, *m.* the heart, mind, soul, understanding; kernel, marrow: 2, adulterated; inverted. — *k.* to [invert.

कलबल, *more prop.* **कलवल**, *q.v.*

कलबा, *m.* a plough.

क़लबारानी, *f.* driving a plough, ploughing.

कलभ, *m.* a young elephant; a young camel.

क़लम, *f.* a reed, pen: hand-writing.

कलम, *m.* a kind of rice. [traction.

कलमकल, *f.* uneasiness, disquiet, trouble, dis-

कलमख (*colloquial*) = **कल्मष**, *q. v.*

कलमलाना, *a. int.* to writhe, fidget, flutter.

कलमा, *m.* any food stuffed into intestines, *e. g.* sausage, black pudding, haggis. [vegetable.

कलमी, *f. Convolvulus repens* used as an esculent

कलर, a kind of fuller's earth.

कलवल, *f.* misfortune, calamity.

कलवार, *m.* (*f.* in) = **कलार**, *q.v.*

कलविंक, *m.* a sparrow.

कलश, *m.* 1, a dome, cupola, pinnacle; spire, ornament on the top of a dome: 2, an earthen waterpot, pitcher. — *sthāpan k.* to make an offering of a jar of water to any deity, — a twig of each of the following trees, deemed sacred, having been previously placed in it, *viz.* 1, the *ashwattha* (*Ficus religiosa*), 2, the *vata* (*Ficus Indica*), 3, the *udambar* (*Ficus glomerata*), 4, the *shami* (*Mimosa albida*), 5, the *āmra* or mango-tree.

कलशा = **कलश**, *q. v.*

कलशिरा, 1, *m.* a man: 2, blackheaded.

कलशी, 1, *f.* dimin. of **कलश** in both of its senses: 2, *f.* a plant (*Hemionitis cordifolia*, Roxb.): name of a certain holy place. [form **कलश**.

कलस; for words beginning thus, see under the,

कलसिरा, 1, *m.* an enemy: 2, depraved, vicious.

कलह, *m.* quarrel, strife, contention.

कलहंस, *m.* (*f.* ī) a kind of duck or goose.

कलहकार, 1, *m.* (*f.* ī) = **कलहकारी**, *q.v.*: 2, *m.* quarrelsomeness, strifemaking, contention.

कलहकारी, quarrelsome, contentious: hence, *m.* (*f.* iṇī) a strifemaker.

कलहारा, *m.* (*f.* ī) quarrelsome, violent.

कलही, *f.* a termagant, scold, vixen.

कला, *f.* a small part, a part, portion, division; the sixteenth part of the moon's diameter, a digit of the moon: a certain division of time, — about eight seconds, the sixtieth part of a degree: a minute: interest on capital: art, trick, craft. — *na badnā*, to disobey, decline, not to succeed. — *na lagnā*, not to have an advantage, not to avail. In the ingenious system of reckoning by symbols adopted by Hindoos in their poetry, this word is a symbol for 16.

कलाई, *f.* the wrist, the fore-arm: pulse, legumin-

कलां, large, big, elder. [ous seeds in general.

कलांवत, *more prop.* **कलावन्त**, *q. v.*

कलाग़, a crow, rook, raven.

कलान, large, big, elder. [2, *t.* to parch grain.

कलाना, 1, *a. int.* to mix together, get confused:

कलाप, *m.* an assemblage, multitude, bundle, string (of pearls), girdle (of laces, etc.); totality; perfection: a quiver: a peacock's tail.

कलाबत्तुन } **कलाबत्तून** } *m.* gold thread, silver thread.

कलाबाज़ी, *f.* a turning over head and heels, tumbling; juggling. [sation.

कलाम, *m.* word, discourse, speech, talk, conver-

कलामुल्लाह, *m.* (among Muhammadans) an epithet of the Kur,ān; *lit.* the Word of God.

कलाया, a kind of long bean, very nutritious, used as food for horses.

कलार, *m.* (*f.* in) a distiller, man who extracts the juice of the palmyra and date trees.: a seller of spirituous liquors, wine-merchant, tavern-keeper, toddy-drawer.

कलारी, *m.* (*f.* iṇī) a tavern-keeper, vintner.

कलाल, *m.* (*f.* in) = **कलार**, *q. v.*

कलालख़ाना, *m.* a distillery, liquor-shop.

कलालज़मा, *f.* duty on spirituous liquors.

कलाली, *m.* (*f.* inī) = **कलारी**, *q. v.*

कलावन्त, 1, *m* (*f.* vatī) a minstrel: 2, *m.* the moon.

कलाश्क, *m.* a musical instrument.

कलि, 1, *m.* a die; the game of dice personified; *pr. n.* (1) of a certain very wicked king (2) of a certain inferior deity (3) of the fourth or present Age of the world (according to the Hindoos); like the iron age of classic writers, it is supposed to be, as distinguished from its predecessors, the age of vice: see **युग**. The celebrated French astronomer, Bailly, supposes *Kaliyug* to have commenced 3102 years before Christ. The number of its years is 432000; at the expiration of which term the world is to be destroyed: 2, *f.* an unblown flower, blossom, bud: quicklime: 3, *m.* quarrel, strife, contention.

कलिंग, *m.* the febrifuge-nut plant (*Caesalpinia* or *Guilandina bonducella*). This term is applied as a proper name in the Purāṇs to several places, but it is more particularly applied to a district on the Coromandel coast extending from below Cuttack to near Madras.

कलिंगा, *f.* a certain plant (commonly called *teorī*), the bark of which is used as a purgative.

कलिक, 1, *m.* a curlew: 2, appertaining to Kaliyug.

कलिकवि, *m.* an epithet of any poet of Kaliyug.

कलिका, *f.* the sixteenth part of the moon's disc:

कलिकाता, *f. pr n.* the city of Calcutta. [a bud.

कलिकाल, *m.* (see **कलि**) the fourth Age in the Hindoo mythology.

कलिको, in Braj, gen. of **कलि**, *q.v.*

कलित, *m.* (*f.* ā) contrived, beautiful; fabricated.

कलिन्द, *m. pr. n.* the mountain on which the Jumna rises.

कलिप, *m. pr. n.* a certain *avatār*, son of Devhūtī.

कलिमल, *m.* impurity, guilt, sin.

कलिमलसरि, an epithet of the **कर्मनाशा** river.

कलिमा, *m.* a word, saying, speech; an epithet of Christ; the Muhammadan creed or confession of faith.

क़लिया, *m.* (curry ?) the name of a dish of boiled flesh, etc.: a kind of soap-ashes.

कलियान, *m.* a small simple kind of tobacco-pipe [(hukka).

कलिय.ना, *a. int.* to blossom, bloom, bud.

कलियुग, *m.* (see **कलि**) the fourth Age in Hindoo [mythology.

कलियुगी, appertaining to Kaliyug.

कलिल, 1, *m.* confusion; mud: 2, *m.* (*f.* ā) filled; impervious, impenetrable: mixed, blended.

कली, *f.* an unblown flower, blossom, bud: quicklime.

कलीम, *m.* one who speaks with another, a familiar, a speaker.

क़लील, little, small, moderate; a few, rare.

कलीसा / **कलीसिया** } *m.* the Christian Church.

कलुष, 1, *m.* dirt, impurity, sin: 2, *m.* (*f.* ā) turbid, dirty, impure, sinful; choked: unable.

कलूटा, *m.* (*f.* ī) anything tawny or black-complexioned.

कलेऊ, *m.* (= **कलेवा**) a light morning meal.

कलेजा, *m.* the liver: *met.* courage, magnanimity, spirit. — *ulatnā*, to be fatigued with excessive vomiting. — *phatnā*, to be disturbed with grief or with jealousy. — *thandā k.* to obtain one's wish, get ease. — *thandā honā*, to be quiet at ease. — *jalnā kisikā*, to suffer sorrow, to mourn. — *kāmpnā*, to be afraid; to suffer cold. *Kalejepar sāmp phirnā*, to suffer jealousy or envy. *Kalejese lagā rahnā* or *lenā*, to caress, embrace, love exceedingly. *Kalejemeṅ dāl rakhnā*, to love or esteem exceedingly.

कलेला = (1) **करेला** (2) **कलेवा**, *qq.v.*

कलेवर, *m.* the body.

कलेवा, *m.* cold meat, stale victuals, breakfast, [luncheon.

कलेश = **क्लेश**, *q.v.*

कलेसा, a poetical form of **क्लेश**, *q.v.* [3, the moon.

कलेस, 1, = **क्लेश**, *q.v.*: 2, *m.* quarrel, contention:

कलोर, *m.* a heifer.

कलोल, *f.* wantonness, friskiness, play, sport, [frolic, gambol.

कलौंजी, *f.* a certain small blackish pyramid-shaped seed (*Nigella Indica*, Roxb.) of a very pungent smell and used medicinally.

कल्क, 1, *m.* the deposit of oil, ghee, etc., dregs, sediment; dirt, foulness, filth, ordure; sin, fraud: paste: ear-wax: the beleric myrobalan: 2, sinful, wicked.

कल्की, 1, *f.* a kind of instrument for smoking with: 2, *m. pr. n.* (see **अवतार**) the tenth or last incarnation of Vishṇu, — yet to come. This deity is expected to assume the appearance of a Brāhman who will be born in the town of Sambhal and in the family of Vishṇu Sharmā. He will ride on horseback and put to death all the wicked and introduce the reign of righteousness.

कल्प; for all words beginning thus, but not given below, see under the form **कलप**.

कल्प, *m.* a rule, sacred precept, performance, practice prescribed by the Veds for effecting certain results; propriety; manner; alternative; doubt; resolution, purpose; toxicology: the destruction of the world: name of one of the trees of Indra's paradise: a shāstra or sacred book of the Hindoos, one of the six Vedāngas comprehending the description of religious rites: a day and a night of Brahma amounting to a period of 1000 yugs or 4,320,000,000 solar years of mortals (this period, according to the Hindoos, measures the duration of the present world, and a period of equal duration will pass during its annihilation): an epithet of Vishṇu as containing all the sacred precepts.

कल्पक्षय, *m.* the final destruction, the end of the [world.

कल्पतरु = **कल्पवृक्ष**, *q.v.*

कल्पना, 1, *f.* (uninfl.) a scheme, contrivance, fabrication, forgery, imitation; hypothesis: trouble, difficulty: 2, *t.* to form, contrive, fabricate, imitate, commit forgery. [(*see above*).

कल्पनाकारी, *m.* (*f.* iṇī) a contriver, forger, etc.;

कल्पनासे, *adv.* by hypothesis.

कल्पनेहारा, *m.* (*f.* ī) = **कल्पनाकारी**, *q.v.*

कल्पवृक्ष, *m. pr. n.* one of the fabulous trees of Indra's heaven. It is said to yield whatever might be desired.

कल्पान्त, *m.* the end of the world; *lit.* the end of the *kalp* or period of the world's existence.

कल्पान्तर, another *kalp*; from *kalp* to *kalp*; in the midst of a *kalp*.

कल्पित, *m.* (*f.* ā) contrived, fabricated, made, false, made-up, artificially produced, artificially constructed.

कल्मष, *m.* dirt, sediment; a spot; impurity, [guilt, sin.

कल्माख = **कल्माष**, *q.v.*

कल्माष, 1, *m.* (*f.* ī) variegated, spotted; black and white; black: 2, *m.* any variegated colour, black and white; the colour black: a goblin, rakshas: a stain: a kind of fragrant rice: 3, *m. pr. n.* (1) of a certain Nāg (2) of a servant of the sun identified with Yam (3) of Sākhyamuni in a former birth.

कल्माषी, *f. pr. n.* (1) of a certain river (2) of the spotted cow of Jamadagni, the giver of all desires.

कल्य, 1, *m.* dawn, break of day: 2, *m.* (*f.* ā) ready; healthy, recovered from sickness: deaf and dumb: 3, yesterday; to-morrow.

कल्याण, 1, *m.* welfare, prosperity, happiness, good fortune: a virtuous action: an entertainment: the name of one of the musical modes (*rāg*) sung at night: a certain leguminous shrub (*Glycine debilis*): 2, *m.* (*f.* ā or ī) blessed, happy, well, prosperous, lucky: 3, Hail to you! blessing on you!

कल्याणक, *m.* (*f.* ikā) a prosperous person, etc.: *lit.* prosperous; useful; excellent.

कल्याणवचन, *m.* the expression of good wishes.

कल्याणी, *m.* (*f.* inī) a prosperous person, etc.: *lit.* happy, prosperous: auspicious, propitious.

कल्लर, barren, sterile (land): salt (as food).

कल्ला, *m.* a cabbage ; *met.* the head.

कल्लाच = **कल्लाम**, *q.v.*

कल्लाना, *a. int.* to burn, be inflamed (as the skin by rubbing pepper, etc. on it).

कल्लापरवर, *m.* a sort of sweetmeat.

क़ल्लाश, *m.* a drunkard, etc. : *lit.* shrewd ; malicious ; wretched, friendless ; addicted to drinking : cunning.

कल्लोल, *m.* 1, joy, happiness, pleasure : 2, a [billow, surge.

कल्लेदराज़, talkative ; abusive.

कल्लेदराज़ी, *f.* abuse, reviling.

कल्लोलिनी, *f.* a river with large waves.

कल्ह, *m.* yesterday ; to-morrow.

कल्हि, an emphatic form of **कल्ह**, *q.v.*

कवक, 1, = **कवल**, *q.v.* : 2, *m.* a mushroom.

कवच, *m.* armour, a coat of mail : a drum used in battle, a kettle-drum : an amulet, a writing kept about the person as a charm : a certain tree (*Hibiscus populus vides*).

कवचपत्र, *m.* a species of birch-tree (commonly called *Bhojpatr*) pieces of the bark of which, inscribed with mystical verses, serve as amulets, etc.

कवन in Braj = **कौन**, *q.v.*

कवनहीं, **कवनहीं**, **कवनहूं** } emphatic forms of **कवन**, *q.v.*

कवनि = (1) **कवन** (2) **कवनहीं** (3) **कवने**, *qq.v.*

कवने (infl. of **कवन**) = **किसमें**.

कवनेहूं, an emphatic form of **कवने**, *q.v.*

कवन्ध = **कबन्ध**, *q.v.*

कवयी, *f.* a kind of flat-fish (*Coius coboius*) remarkable for going by land from one place to another.

कवर, 1, = **कवल**, *q.v.* : 2, *m.* a braid of hair.

कवर्ग, *m.* (in Gram.) the designation applied to the consonants of the **क**, or guttural, class, viz. **क**, **ख**, **ग**, **घ**, **ङ**.

कवल, *m.* a mouthful, morsel ; an astringent wash for cleansing the mouth, a gargle : a kind of fish.

कवहु in Braj = **कभी**, *q.v.*

कवाकिब, *m.* (pl. of **कौकब**) stars ; constellations.

कवाफ़िर, *m.* (pl. of **काफ़िर**) infidels.

क़वाम, *m.* justice, equity.

कवारना, *t.* to pull up by the roots.

कवि, 1, *m.* (*f.* ī *or* n) a wise man, a poet : 2, *f.* [the bit of a bridle.

कवित = **कवित्त**, *q.v.*

कविता, *f.*, **कविताई**, *f.*, **कवित्व**, *m.* } poetry, the poetic art.

कवित्त, *m.* a certain species of verse in Hindee poetry ; poetry, a poem (applied to certain metrical compositions in Hindee or in Braj).

कविन, *f.* (*m.* **कवि**) a poetess (?).

कविराज, *m.* a prince of poets (applied to any chief or very celebrated poet).

कविरामायण, *m.* the poet of the *Rāmāyaṇ*, i. e. [Vālmīki.

कविराय = **कविराज**, *q.v.*

कवी, *f.* 1, (*m.* **कवि**) a poetess : 2, the bit of a bridle.

कवीर, *more prop.* **कबीर**, *q.v.*

कवीश्वर, *m.* the chief of the wise men ; any first-rate poet, an eminent poet ; *lit.* prince of poets.

कवेलू, *m.* a tile.

कशना, *more com.* **कसना**, *q.v.*

कश्फ़, *m.* an opening, manifestation, revelation, declaration, explanation, solution.

कशाकश, *f.* attraction, allurement : contention, struggle, difficulty, distraction, perplexity, distress, penury, crowding, mutual pulling.

कशूर (*corruption*) = **कसूर**, *q.v.*

कशेरु, *m. pr. n.* one of the nine divisions of Jamboo Dweep : a sort of grass (*Scirpus Kysoor*) ; a certain root (*Cyperus tuberosus*).

कश्मीर, *m. pr. n.* the country or valley of Cashmere in the North-west of India.

कश्मीरी, appertaining to Cashmere : hence (1) *m.* (*f.* in *or* inī) a Cashmerian (2) *f.* the language of Cashmere.

कश्यप, *m. pr. n.* a certain deified sage, son of Marīchi, husband of *Diti* and of *Aditi*, and father of the immortals (both gods and demons) : a kind of deer : a [kind of fish.

कश्यपनन्दन = **काश्यपनन्दन**, *q.v.*

कश्शाफ़, 1, *m.* a discoverer, solver, explainer : 2, very clear, very explicit.

कष, *m.* the touchstone ; assay : the decoction of a colouring substance. [touchstone.

कषण, *m.* the touching or testing gold by the

कषाय, *m.* astringency ; an astringent juice, a decoction ; ointment ; dirt, impurity : stupor : the color red.

कषावट, *f.* an astringent.

कषौटी, *f.* a touchstone, an assay ; proof.

कष्ट, *m.* affliction, pain, distress, hardship, penury, want, difficulty ; vehemence, violence, acuteness of pain, bodily pain or uneasiness ; agony.

कष्टकर, occasioning pain, occasioning trouble.

कष्टसाध्य, accomplishable with difficulty.

कष्टि, *f.* trouble, pain, trial, test.

कष्टित, *m.* (*f.* ā) troubled, tried, tested.

कष्टी, *m.* (*f.* inī) a sufferer, one who suffers pain and tedious labor (esp. a woman) : *lit.* afflicted, suffering, in want.

कस, 1, in Braj and in poetry = **कैसा**, *q.v.* : 2, *m.* strength, power : 3, *more properly* **कष**, *q.v.* : 4, *m.* a man, a person, one, anyone.

कसक, *f.* pain, affliction, the stitch.

कसकना, *n.* to be painful : *a. int.* to suffer pain.

कसकसा, *m.* (*f.* ī) gritty, sandy (said of bread).

कसकुत, *m.* bell-metal.

क़स्द, *m.* desire, wish, inclination ; purpose, intention, project, machination, conspiracy.

कसन, *m.* rack, torture, torment.

कसना, 1, *m.* a bundle, wallet : a kind of poisonous spider : 2. *t.* to tighten, tie, brace : to assay, try, prove, test, examine : to fry in melted butter.

कसन्द, a species of bell-metal.

क़सफ़, m. the wind breaking; a dashing to pieces (a ship); a blowing with a loud noise (the wind); a thundering.

कसब, m. trade, profession, employment; gain, [acquisition (by labor).

क़सबा, m. a small town (esp. one that is inhabited by decent people or by families of some rank); a township (including the town and all the lands attach-[ed to it).

कसबिन = कसबिनी, q. v.

कसबिनी, f. a mistress, strumpet, prostitute.

कसबी, 1, f. = कसबिनी, q. v. 2, m. an artisan, craftsman.

कसबीख़ाना, m. a house of assignation, a stew, [brothel.

कसबीन = कसबिनी, q. v.

कसबीबाज़, m. a whoremonger.

कसबीबाज़ी, f. whoremongery, harlotry.

क़सम, f. an oath. — *khānā*, to take an oath, swear. — *khilānā* or *dilānā*, to administer an oath, put one on his oath.

कसमसाना, a. int. to move, shake, fidget, become [restless.

कसर = कस, q. v.

कसर, m. 1, violence, compulsion, retaliation, revenge: 2, diminution, deficiency, defect; evening twilight (*q. d.* defect of light): an edifice, palace, elegant villa, building. — *k.* to diminish, deduct, keep back anything, speak or act with reservation.

कसरत = कस, q. v.

कसरती, usual, practised, familiar.

कसल, m. laxness, slowness, indolence, cowardice, relaxedness, sickness; *non emittere in coitu.*

कसवाना, t. to cause to be tested: to cause to be tightened.

कसा, m. (f. ī) tight, tense, straightened.

कसाई, 1, m. (f. inī) a butcher: *lit.* cruel, hard-hearted: 2, f. a drawing, tightening.

कसाद, not current, not in use, not in demand; flat sale, bad market: indigence, penury.

कसाना, 1, t. to cause to try, cause to assay, cause to prove: to cause to tighten: 2, n. to be spoiled (as curds, etc.) by standing in a metallic vessel.

कसाफ़त, f. sediment; obscuration, an eclipse: density, fulness, repletion.

कसाया, m. (f. कसाई) ready, tied up.

कसार, m. 1, a kind of sweetmeat: 2, a maker of brass pots and utensils, brazier.

कसावट = कसाहट, q. v. [pain, chagrin.

क़सावत, f. hardness of heart; grief, anguish,

कसावा, a handkerchief tied around the head on going to bed. [astringency, an astringent.

कसाहट, f. a testing, proving: a tightening;

कशिपु, m. a cushion; clothing; food, boiled rice.

कसीदा, m. a poem, a long ode exceeding a hundred couplets. [pleasant.

कसीफ़, impure, thick, dense, opaque; dreary, un-

कसीर, many, much, abundant, fruitful, copious, numerous, excessive.

कसीला, m. (f. ī) strong, vigorous.

कसीस, m. martial (*i. e.* red) vitriol (*Sulphas ferri*).

क़सूर, m. an error, sin, fault, defect, omission, failure, shortcoming; the premium on the exchange of rupees in distinction from *baṭṭā* or discount.

क़सूरवार, m. or f. a guilty person, sinner.

क़सूरी, f. defect, error, failure, shortcoming.

कसेकसाए, tied up, prepared, ready.

कसेरा, m. a brazier, pewterer.

कसेरिन, f. the wife of a brazier.

कसेरू, m. a certain root (*Cyperus tuberosus*, Willd.).

कसेला, m. (f. ī) astringent. [pl. of कसना.

कसो, 1, in Braj = कैसा, q. v.: 2, imperat. 2nd pers.

कसौटी, f. a touchstone, an assay; proof.

कसौन्दी, f. a certain plant (*Cassia sophera*): a kind [of pickle.

कस्क, *more prop.* कसक, q. v.

कस्तूरा, f. an oyster.

कस्तूरी, f. musk, the animal perfume and the substance so called, as brought from Cashmere, Nepāl, Western Assam, and Bhootān (this last is said to be the best): a kind of plant.

कस्यप, *more prop.* कश्यप, q. v.

कस्र, m. (pl. कुसूर) (in Arithm.) a fraction; breach: loss, affliction: a putting an enemy to flight, rout-[ing: the short *i.*

क़स्साब, m. a butcher.

कहई; see (1) कहाई (2) कहीं.

कहई, a poetical form = कहूं or कहूंगो.

कहउं, *more com.* कहऊं, q. v.

कहऊं, a poetical form of कहूं, 1, q. v.

कहं, 1, a contraction of कहां, q. v.: 2, an old poetic [form = को, 1, q. v.

कहंलग = कहांलग, q. v.

कहंलगि = कहंलग = कहांलग, q. v.

कहकशान, m. the milky way, galaxy.

कहकहा, m. loud laughter, a horselaugh. — *k.* or *mārnā*, to laugh aloud or heartily, to giggle.

कहजा, m. the strawberry.

कहत, m. famine, dearth.

कहतरी; see (1) किहतरी (2) खतरी.

कह देना, t. (intensive) to order, bid, tell.

कहन, m. a saying, by-word.

कहना, 1, m. a saying; advice; an order: 2, a. *int.* to speak: *t.* to speak with, converse with (as distinguished from *bolnā*, to speak *to*, to address: and from *baknā*, to talk, prate); to say, tell; to bid, order, call; to affirm, assert; to acquaint; to advise; to compose; to repeat, to read, to quote. It usually takes the abl.; *e. g. Usne usse kahā*; but occasionally also the acc.; *e. g. Usne use kahā*. This verb, though active intransitive in sense, governs as if it were transitive, *i. e.* its agent takes *ne.*

कहनावत, f. a proverb, adage, saying; style.

कहफ़, a large cavern, cave, grotto.

क़हबा, 1, m. a cough: 2, f. an old woman subject to coughing: a whore (notifying her profession by coughing). [judgment, chastisement.

क़हर, m. severity; rage, indignation, vengeance,

कहरना } = कराहना, *q.v.*
कहराना }
[guor, indolence.

कहल, 1, = कहा (कहना); see ल, 3 : 2, sloth, lan-

कहलन = कहा (from कहना, *q.v.*).

कहलना, *n.* to be parched : *a. int.* to wither.

कहलाना, 1, *t.* to cause to say, cause to tell, cause to speak : 2, *n.* to be called, be designated : 3, *t.* to parch : *a. int.* to wither away : 4, *a. int.* to become weak : *n.* to be lazy.

कहला भेजना, *t.* to send to tell, send a message, cause to be announced by word of mouth.

क़हवा, *m.* coffee.

कहवां, a dialectic form = कहां.

क़हवादान, *m.* a coffee-pot. [cause to tell.

कहवाना, *t.* to cause to speak, cause to say,

कहहि (pl. कहहिं) in Braj = कहता है. See हि, 3.

कहा, 1, *m.* (*f.* ī) said, spoken : 2, in Braj (gen. काहेको) what? which? how? why? 3, *m.* an order, command : a saying, word; advice, leave, call, affirmation, confession.

कहां, where? whither? It is declined like a substantive, as some of the following examples will shew.

कहांका, *m.* (*f.* ī) appertaining to what place?

कहांका कहां, to what a degree! *i. e.* extremely, [intensely, immensely.

कहांतक }
कहांतलक } = कहांलग, *q.v.*
कहांलों }

कहांते in Braj = कहांसे, *q.v.*

कहांलग, how far? how long? to what degree?

कहांसे, whence? [versation.

कहाकही, *f.* dialogue, discussion, altercation, con-

कहाना = कहलाना, 1 and 2.

कहानी, *f.* a tale, story, fable.

कहार, *m.* a certain tribe of Shoodras in Bihār who follow the occupation of pālkee-bearers.

कहालत, *f.* inactivity, indolence, sloth.

कहावत, *f.* a proverb, saying, adage.

कहावन, *m.* designation of the aggregate number of 1280 cowries. [designation.

कहावना, *n.* to be called or named by a certain

कहावही (*Rām.*) = कहावते हैं.

कहासुन }
कहासुनी } *f.* = कहाकही, *q.v.*

कहि = कहके (कहना). See इ, 7.

कहिहै (pl. कहिहैं) in Braj = कहेगा. See इहै.

कहिहौं in Braj = कहूंगा (कहना). See इहौं.

कहिए, *more com.* कहिये (कहना).

कही, *f.* 1, (*m.* कहा) said, spoken : 2, a foraging party; forage, supplies.

कहीं, 1, *f.* (pl. of कही, 1) said, spoken : 2, somewhere, anywhere; wherever, whithersoever. *Aur* —, anywhere else. *Jahāṅ* —, wherever, in whatever place, in whatever quarter. *Har* —, everywhere. It is declined like a substantive. — *na kahīṅ*, somewhere or other. — *nahīṅ*, nowhere.

कहीं कहीं, at times, sometimes; at certain places, in some places, here and there, at intervals.

कहींका, *m.* (*f.* ī) relating to somewhere : queer, strange. — *kahīṅ*, here and there.

कहु in Braj = कहीं, 2, *q.v.* [talkative, garrulous.

कहुआ, *m.* (*f.* कहुई) a talker, etc. : *lit.* eloquent,

कहुं, an old poetic form = को, 1, *q.v.*

कहूं, 1, in Braj = कहीं, 2, *q.v.* : 2, = मैं कहूं.

कहेउ (*Rām.*) = कहा है (कहना).

कहेसि in Braj = तू कहता है. See एसि, 2.

कहै in Braj = कहे (कहना). See ए, 3.

कहों in Braj = कहूं or कहूंगा.

कहोंगो in Braj = मैं कहूंगा.

कहौ in Braj = (1) कहा (2) कहूं.

कह्यौ in Braj = कहा (कहना). See य, 14.

का, 1, *m. f.* (gen. काका, *m.* [*f.* ī], Braj काको and काहेको) who? which? what? 2, In Braj this is also the inflective base of the oblique cases of the singular of the interrogative pronoun को (= कौन) gen. काको. It thus corresponds to किस. As such it is sometimes inflected before the case-endings; *e.g.* काहि = किसको (see हि). 3, *m.* (*f.* की) the case-sign of the gen. of the masc. sing. As such, it is also frequently used as an adjectival termination; *e.g* काठका घोड़ा, a wooden horse. 4, Prefixed to Sanskrit words this particle imports some depreciatory idea; *e. g,* कापुरुष, a vile man; a coward. [of the lesser Bear.

क़ाइद, *m.* a leader, general; the star in the tail

क़ाइदा, *m.* base, groundwork; rule, custom, institution; (in Gram.) a rule. [beings, existing creatures.

काइनात, *f.* (pl. of काइनत) the world, universe,

क़ाइम, erect, perpendicular; firm, fixed, durable : attentive, persevering. — *k.* to erect, fix, establish.

क़ाइमा, *m.* a perpendicular line; a right angle : *adj.*

काइर, the Indian thrush. [erect, perpendicular.

क़ाइल, an acquiescing, agreeing, giving up a point : *adj.* subdued, confuted. — *k.* to confute, convince. — *honā*, to acquiesce, give way.

काइला, *more prop.* काहिला, *q. v.*

काई, *f.* the green scum on the surface of stagnant pools, the green mould that sticks to walls and pavements; scum, fur, paste : green, raw, or unripe fruit.

काउ }
काऊ } in Braj = कबहूं = कबही, *q.v.*

काएफल = कायफल, *q. v.*

कां, 1, = कहां, *q.v.* : 2, the sound or cry of the crow.

कांकर, *m.* a nodule of limestone. [the crow.

कांकां क°, *a. int.* to give forth a noise like that of

कांक्षा, *f.* desire, inclination, longing, wish. [ing.

कांक्षित, *m.* (*f.* ā) desired, longed-for : desirous, long-

कांक्षिता, *f.* desire.

कांक्षी, *m.* (*f.* iṇī) an expectant, etc. : *lit.* desiring;

कांख, *f.* the armpit. [expecting.

कांखना, *a. int.* to grunt.

कांखा, *m.* a straining (at stool, etc.).

कांगन, *m.* a certain plant (*Panicum Italicum*) or its seed.

कांगनी, *f.* = **कांगन**, *q. v.*

कांगो, *f.* a chafingdish.

कांच, 1, = **काच**, *q. v.* : 2, = **कच्चा**, *q. v.* : 3, *m.* a disorder (*Prolapsus ani*) in which the *intestinum rectum* is prolapsed. — *nikālnā* = *ani procidentia*.

कांचकूरी, *f.* cowach (*Dolichos pruriens*).

कांचन, 1, *m.* gold ; wealth : 2, *m.* (*f.* ī) golden.

कांचनपुर, *m. pr. n.* a certain Hindoo town.

कांचनमय, *m.* (*f.* ī) consisting of gold, abounding in gold, golden.

कांचना, *f.* a whore (?).

कांचनार = **कचनार**, *q. v.*

कांचा, *m.* (*f.* ī) *more prop.* **कच्चा**, *q.v.*

कांची, *f.* a girdle worn by women and generally adorned with small bells : a kind of marriage ceremony.

कांचो in Braj = (1) **कच्चा** (2) **काच**, *qq. v.*

कांक्ष, **कांछ** ; for words beginning with either of these forms, see under the form **कांक्ष**.

कांजी, *f.* a kind of pickle or vinegar made by steeping rice in water and leaving the liquor to ferment. This liquor is sometimes kept for use twenty years.

कांट, **कांठ**, **कांड**, **कांत**, **कांद**, **कांध**, **कांप**, **कांब** ; for all words beginning with either of these elements, see under the forms **काण्ट**, **काण्ठ**, **काण्ड**, **कान्त**, **कान्द**, **कान्ध**, **काम्प**, **काम्ब**, respectively.

कांड़ना, *t.* to tread, trample.

कांनी, *f.* the little finger.

कान्ह, *m.* a husband : *pr. n.* Kṛishṇ.

कान्हर, *m. pr. n.* a name of Kṛishṇ.

कांवरू, a colloquial form of **कामरूप**, *q.v.* (?)

कांस, 1, = **कांसा**, *q. v.* : 2, *f.* (*m.* ?) a species of grass (*Saccharum spontaneum*).

कांसा, *m.* bell-metal, white copper, brass, queen's metal, any mixture of zinc and copper : a cup, bowl, goblet, glass.

कांसागर, a maker of goblets, etc.

कांसागरी, *f.* the business of cupmaking.

कांस्य, 1, made of brass : 2, *m.* brass : 3, a metallic drinking-vessel.

कांस्यकार, *m.* (*f.* ī) a worker in metals, brazier, pewterer.

कांस्यनील, *m.* blue vitriol (used as collyrium).

काक, *m.* (*f.* ī) a crow.

काकड़ा, *m.* a sort of a leather : a large wick.

काकड़ासिंगी, *f.* a certain medicine.

काकणा, *m.* a kind of leprosy with black and red spots (it is considered incurable).

काकदसिंगी, *f.* the flowers of the ink-nut.

काकन्दि, *m. pr. n.* a certain tribe.

काकन्दी, 1, *f. pr. n.* a certain country : 2, *f.* a certain plant (*Emblic myrobalan*).

काकन्दीय, *m.* any prince of the Kākandis.

काकपक्ष, *m.* a crow's feather, a ringlet, curl, tresses.

काकपीलु, *m.* a kind of ebony.

काकबन्ध्या, *f.* a woman who has borne only one child.

काकभुसुण्ड, *m.* a kind of mountain crow (?).

काकमुंग, *m.* a water-hen, gallinule.

काकमर्द, *m.* the colocynth or bitter apple..

काका, 1, gen. masc. of **का**, 1, *q.v.* : 2, *m.* (not infl.) a paternal uncle : 3, *m.* an elder brother : 4, *m.* (*f.* ī) a slave (belonging to one's father).

काकातुआ, *m.* (*f.* °**तूई**) the cockatoo, a species of large parrot very common in India.

काकासुर, *m. pr. n.* a certain demon slain by Kṛishṇ.

काकिणी, *f.* a certain small coin (a quarter of a *Paṇa*) = twenty cowries ; the cowrie-shell (*Cypræa Moneta*) used as a coin : a cubit.

काकिनी = **काकिणी**, *q. v.*

काकिन्दी ; see **काकन्दी**.

काकी, 1, gen. fem. of **का**, 1, *q. v.* : 2, *f.* (*m.* **काक**) a female crow : 3, *f.* (*m.* **काका**) a paternal aunt : a female slave.

काकु, 1, in Braj = **किसको** and **किसीको** : 2, *m.* a paternal uncle : sarcasm.

काकुल, *f.* a curl, lock, ringlet ; a tuft of hair left on the top of the head.

काकूंजकी, *f.* a ranunculus.

काकबन्ध ; see **काकबन्ध्या**.

काकोल, *m.* a certain poisonous substance of a black colour (possibly the berry of the *Cocculus Indicus*) : name of one of the divisions of the infernal regions : a raven.

काकोली, *f.* a certain sweet and cooling drug used for allaying fever, removing phlegm, etc. It is said to be a root brought from Nepāl or Morung.

काको in Braj, gen. sing. (1) of **का** (2) of **को**, *qq. v.*

काकौं in Braj, dat. and acc. sing. (1) of **का**, (2) of **को**.

काकोरन, *m. pr. n.* a son of king Shishunāg.

काख, *f.* the armpit.

काखमलाई, *f.* a painful suppurating tumour in the armpit.

काखासोती, *f.* the space from the shoulders to the armpit.

काग, (*f.* li) a crow, raven.

काग़ज़, *m.* (*pl.* āt) paper ; a written document, letter ; a charter.

काग़ज़बहा, *m.* office allowance for stationery.

काग़ज़ी, *m.* a stationer, vender of paper ; a paper manufacturer : a paper case.

कागद, a corruption of **काग़ज़**, *q. v.*

कागभुशुण्डि, a kind of mountain crow (?).

कागली, *f.* (*m.* **काग**) a female crow, female raven.

कागा, *m.* a crow, raven.

कागारि, *m.* an epithet of the owl.

कागिज़, *more com.* **काग़ज़**, *q. v.*

काच, *m.* glass ; crystal ; quartz ; ornaments of crystal; alkaline ashes, any salt of potash or of soda in a glassy or crystalline state : a certain disease of the eyes.

काचमणि, *m.* crystal, quartz.

काचमल, *m.* black salt or soda.

काचलवण, *m.* black salt, a medicinal salt prepared by calcining fossil salt and the fruit of the emblic myrobalan together. It consists chiefly of muriate of soda, with a small quantity of iron, lime and sulphur, and is used as a tonic aperient.

काचा, *m.* (*f.* ī) = **कच्चा**, *q.v.*

काची, *f.* milk pottage.

काछ, *m.* the upper part of the thigh: a cloth worn around the hips passing between the legs and tucked in behind.

काछन, *f.* a female gardener.

काछना, 1, *t.* to bind on the *kāchh* or to tie it up; to cover the nakedness: 2, *t.* to skim; to gather.

काछनी, *f.* } = **काछ**, *q.v.*
काछा, *m.* }

काछी, *m.* a gardener who cultivates and sells potherbs.

काज, *m.* work, action, occupation, business, an affair.

काज़, *m.* a duck, goose.

काजन, *m.* 1, (a Braj pl. of **काज**) affairs, works: 2, a cause, account.

काजल, *m.* soot; lampblack with which the eyes are painted. *Kājalkī kothrī*, *f.* a place the going into which (or an affair the being engaged in which) brings disgrace or suspicion on one's character.

काजस, *more com.* **कुयश**, *q.v.*

काजा = **काज**, *q.v.*

काजाने = **क्या जाने**. See **का**, 1.

काज़िब, *m.* a liar: *adj.* false.

काजी, *m.* (*f.* inī) a worker, artisan, industrious person: *lit.* employed, occupied, busy, industrious.

क़ाज़ी, *m.* a Muhammadan judge (civil, criminal, and ecclesiastic).

काजू, *m.* the cashew-nut (*Anacardium occidentale*).

काजे, *postp.* (takes gen. masc. infl.) by reason of, on account of, for the sake of.

काट, *f.* a cut, incision: execution: spur of a cock: scum: virulence.—*k.* to cut, wound.—*khānā*, to bite. —*ḍālnā*, (intensive) to lop off, strike off, chop off, cut off, amputate, to cut down, hew.

काटक, hard, severe, difficult.

काटकूट, *f.* clippings, chips, scraps. — *k.* to clip; to deduct, to cut out.

काटन, *m.* the act of cutting or of clipping.

काटना, *t.* to cut, clip; to bite; to saw; to reap; to waste, spend, pass away the time; to stop, stay; to pass a road; to interrupt, intercept; to shame, make ashamed.

काटा, *m.* (*f.* ī) cut, reaped, spent, etc.

काटि, *f.*; see (1) **काट** (2) **काटना** (3) **काणटा**.

काटिहै (pl. **काटिहैं**) in Braj = **काटेगा**. See **हुहै**.

काटू, *m.* a cutter: *adj.* corrosive.

काठ, *m.* wood, timber; a block, stock, pair of stocks; a scabbard. — *chabānā*, to fare hardly: *lit.* to chew timber. — *honā*, to pine away; to be petrified with astonishment. *Kāthkā ulloo*, *m.* a very great blockhead, an impenetrably stupid person; *lit.* a wooden owl. *Kāthkī bhambo*, *f.* a female blockhead. *Kāthmen panw denā*, to be in the stocks, be imprisoned.

काठक, 1, wooden, appertaining to wood: 2, *m.* a certain Hindoo religious book.

काठकबाड़, wooden articles.

काठकोड़ा, *m.* a bug.

काठड़ा, *m.* a wooden pot.

काठपुतली, *f.* a wooden doll, puppet, toy.

काठमेंढक, *m.* a toad.

काठिन्य, *m.* difficultness, hardness, cruelty, firmness.

काठी, *f.* a body; appearance, shape, person; a sheath, scabbard; a saddle: wood, timber.

काठीकसवय्या, *m.* a saddler.

काढ़ना, *more prop.* **काढ़ना**, *q.v.*

काढ़ा, *m.* a young buffalo: a sick man's beverage, decoction.

काड़ी, *f.* a single straw, blade of grass.

काड़ीकस्पट, clay.

काढ़, *m.* membrum virile.

काढ़ना, *t.* to draw, draw off, draw forth (as a sword), take out, extricate, skin, draw lines or figures, work figures on cloth, draw figures in needlework; to delineate, paint pictures.

काढ़ा, *m.* a sick man's beverage, decoction.

काण; for any words beginning thus, but not given below, see under the form **कान**.

काणा, *m.* (*f.* ī) a one-eyed person; a stupid: fruits, nuts, etc. whose kernel is rotten or which have no kernel: *lit.* one-eyed, blind of one eye; stupid, foolish.

काणाटोरी, *f.* a certain grass.

काणी, *f.* (*m.* **काणा**) a female blind of one eye.

काणीकौड़ी, *f.* a cowrie with a hole in it.

काणटा, *m.* a thorn; spine; a fork; the pricker of a musket; small scales (*e. g.* goldsmith's or apothecary's); a spur; a type; a fishinghook; a fishbone; the tongue of a balance; a kind of firework. *Kāntoṅ par ghasītnā*. to extol or exalt one above his merits; *lit.* to drag upon thorns (the phrase is used by a person who from humility disclaims the praises bestowed upon him).

काणटा मुहर्रिर, *m.* a clerk who notes and registers weighments.

काणटासा निकल जाना, to be freed from distress or injury.

काणटे बोना, *t.* to prepare for oneself distress or misfortune; *lit.* to sow thorns.

काणठा, *m.* (*f.* ī) near, proximate.

काणठे, the bank of a river (?).

काणड, *m.* the part of a plant from one joint to another, a slip, stalk, switch, arrow, section of a book, part, division: a bone: a multitude; sport; exhibition.

काणडना, *t.* to tread, trample.

काणडली, *f.* purslain (*Portulaca*).

काणडी, *f.* a rafter: a sentence of a Ved: the yoke of a vehicle or of a plough.

काणडूर, *m.* a pusillanimous person, coward.

कात, *f.* the spur of a cock.

कातना, *t.* to spin, wrap around.

कातर, 1, *m.* = **कातरत्व**, *q.v.*: 2, *m.* (*f.* ā) a faint-hearted person, etc.; *lit.* timid, timorous, cowardly, fainthearted, irresolute; confused, perplexed, agitated, distressed; gentle: 3, *m.* a large kind of fish (*Cyprinus catla*).

कातरत्व, *m.* (*f.* tā) fear, timidity, agitation, timorousness, cowardice.

कातिक = **कार्तिक**, *q. v.*

कातिब, *m.* an amanuensis, copier, writer, clerk.

क़ातिल, *m.* a murderer, homicide; *lit.* murderous, killing, mortal, deadly.

कात्यायन, (patronymic) *m.* (*f.* ī) a descendant of *Kati* or *Kātya*: in the *fem.* a name of Durgā.

कादर, 1, *m.* = **कातर**, 1; 2, *m.* (*f.* ā) = **कातर**, 2, *qq. v.*

कादराई }
कादरी } *f.* = **कातरत्व**, *q. v.*

कादा, *m.* slime, mud, mire, bog, alluvial deposit, soft clay. [capable of, skilful.

क़ादिर, *m.* the Almighty; *lit.* potent, powerful,

कादो in Braj = **कादा**, *q. v.*

कान; for any words beginning thus, but not given below, see under the form **कानु**.

कान, 1, *m.* the ear: the handle of a vessel: a husband: a make-weight: 2, *f.* modesty, shame: respect: a mine, a quarry: 3, *m* (*f.* ā) a person who is blind of one eye: 4. (for *ki-ān*) since, for that, inasmuch as.—*k.* to shame; *n.* to be ashamed. — *chhornā*, to act immodestly or impudently. — *na mānnā* or *na karnā*, to treat with disrespect. — *kāṭnā*, to get the better of, surpass, overcome, outwit. — *khaṛe honā*, to be alarmed. — *khirolnā*, to scratch the ear. — *kholnā* or *khol denā*, to inform one, caution him, warn him, make him acquainted with; *lit.* to open his ears. — *jhookānā*, to desire to hear. — *dabākar chale jānā*, to run away. — *dabānā* or *lachiyānā*, to throw back the ears (as a horse does when preparing to bite). — *denā* or *dharnā*, to give ear, listen, be attentive. — *bharko sunnā*, to listen attentively. — *bharnā* or *bhar denā*, to give ear, be attentive, listen. — *phooṭnā*, to be deaf. — *phoonknā*, to tell tales, excite quarrels. to tutor — *phoṛnā*, to make a noise. — *pakaṛnā*, to confess one's inferiority. — *meṭnā* and *ameṭnā*, to pull the ears, chastise. — *malnā*, to admonish; to chastise, punish. — *hilānā*, to acquiesce. — *na hilānā*, to be silent. - *honā*, to understand, comprehend: take warning, take example. *Kanoṅ kān kahnā*, to whisper to.

कानकन, *m.* a mine-digger.

कानका परदा, *m.* the tympanum.

कानखजूरा = **कनखजूरा**, *q. v.* See **का**, 3.

कानन, *m.* a wood, grove, forest, desert: a house: the face of Brahmā.

कानपर *jūṇ na chalnā*, to be very negligent. — *rakhnā*, to remember: to abstain.—*hāth dharnā*, to refuse, deny.

कानपुर, *m. pr. n.* (from **कान्ह**, Krishṇ ?) Cawnpore.

कानफल = **कायफल**, *q. v.*

कानमें *anglī de rakhnā*, to stop one's ears, turn a deaf ear to. — *ḍālnā* or *kahnā*, to whisper to, tell. — *tel ḍālnā*, to pretend not to hear. — *tel ḍālke so rahnā* to be inattentive, be negligent. — *paṛnā*, to be heard (any sound). — *bāt mārnā*, to pretend not to hear.

कानमैल, *m.* earwax.

कानमैलवाला, *m.* (*f.* ī) a person whose occupation it is to pick and clean the ears.

कानवाला, *m.* (*f.* ī) having ears, eared.

कानसलाई = **कनसलाई**, *q. v.* [blind of one eye.

काना, 1, = **काला**, *q. v.*: 2, *f.* (*m.* **कान**, 3) a female

कानाकानी, *f.* a whispering into the ear. — *k.*

कानात, *more prop.* **क़नात**, *q. v.* [to whisper to.

कानानी, *m.* (*f.* inī) *more prop.* **कनयानी**, *q. v.*

कानाफूसकी = **कानाफूसी**, *q. v.*

कानाफूसी, *f.* a whispering into the ear. — *k.* to whisper, consult, advise, tell tales.

कानाबाती = **कानाफूसी**, *q. v.*

कानि; see (1) **काणी** (2) **कानी**.

कानी, 1, a corruption of **कहानी**, *q. v.*: 2, *f.* resentment, spite: 3, *f.* the ear: 4, relating to mines, mineral.

क़ानून, *m.* a rule, regulation, statute, canon: a dulcimer, harp: one of the names of the letter **आ**, and more particularly of its secondary form. See **आ**, 2.

क़ानूनगो, *m.* an officer in each district who is acquainted with its customs, the nature of the tenures of land, etc. and who has charge of the public records.

कानो देना, *t.* to give the cold shoulder.

कान्त, *m.* (*f.* ā) a husband, etc.: *lit.* beloved, pleasing, agreeable, beautiful. [dour, light.

कान्ता, *f.* 1, a wife, sweetheart: 2, beauty, splen-

कान्ति, *f.* lustre, splendour, beauty, gloss, decora- [tion.

कान्द. *m.* a wall, embankment.

कान्दा, *m.* an onion.

कान्दू, *m.* a certain tribe whose occupation it is to fry corn, prepare sweetmeats, etc., a sugar-boiler.

कान्दो, *m.* mud, slime, bog, soft clay.

कान्धना, *t.* to protect, assist.

कान्धर, 1, = **कन्धर**, *q. v.*: 2, = **कान्हर** (?) *q. v.*

कान्धा, *m.* the shoulder. — *denā*, to assist; to carry away the dead. — *hilānā*, to shrug the shoulders.

कान्यकुब्ज, *m. pr. n.* the ancient name of the country of Kanauj.

कान्ह, *m.* a husband; *pr. n.* a name of Krishṇ.

कान्हड़ा, *m.* a certain musical mode: a nightingale.

कान्हर, *m. pr. n.* a name of Krishṇ.

कापट्य, *m.* vice, dishonesty, dissimulation, fraud.

कापड़ा, *more com.* **कपड़ा**, *q. v.*

कापथ, *m.* (= **कुपथ**) a wrong road; a bad course.

कापना, *more prop.* **काम्पना**, *q. v.*

कापुरुष, *m.* a mean wretch, contemptible man, [coward.

काफ़ूर, *m.* (*more prop.* **कपूर**) camphor.

कापै in Braj = **किस पर**, *q. v.* See **का** and **पै**.

काफर; see (1) **काफ़ल** (2) **काफ़िर**.

काफल, *m.* a certain bitter seed.

क़ाफ़िया, *m.* rhyme, cadence, metre; the last letter in a verse to which all the other distichs rhyme.

काफ़िर, *m.* an infidel, disbeliever in the Muhammadan faith; one who denies the existence of God: *met.* a sweetheart, a mistress.

क़ाफ़िला, *m.* a body of travellers, caravan.

काफ़ी, sufficient, sufficing, enough.

क़ाब, 1, *m.* a cavern, pit, furrow; a cup: hidden meaning: 2, the case of a watch.

काबर, 1, *more com.* **कबरा**, 2, *q. v.*: 2, a mixed soil of clay and sand suitable for any crop excepting rice.

काबा, *m.* a square building, more particularly the temple of Mecca. [occupant.

क़ाबिज़, *m.* an astringent: a receiver, possessor,

काबिर, great, grand, illustrious.

क़ाबिल, possible: fit, capable, skilful, clever, able, worthy, sufficient, adapted to or for.

क़ाबिला, *f.* a skilful woman, midwife.

काबिश = **काबिस**, *q.v.* [varnished.

काबिस, *f.* an earth with which earthenware is

काबीन, a settlement which a man has to pay his wife if he divorces her on insufficient grounds, a marriage portion.

काबुल, *m. pr. n.* the capital of Afghanistān, formerly a province of the Moghul Empire. [Cabul.

काबुली, *m.* (*f.* in *or* inī) a native or resident of

क़ाबू, *m.* power, command, authority; possession;

काबुक, *f.* a pigeon-house. [opportunity; will.

काबेरी, *more prop.* **कावेरी**, *q.v.*

काम, 1, *m.* the palate: 2, *m.* desire, wish, inclination, inordinate desire; the name of the Cupid of the Hindoo mythology; he is also the lord of the *tithi* or lunar days, and hence, in the ingenious system of reckoning by symbols adopted by Hindoos in their poetry this word is a symbol for 13: 3, *m.* an act, deed, action; business, affair, matter; work, occupation, employment, job, use; a packet, mail, postbag: 4, *m.* (*f.* ā) a loving person, etc.: *lit.* desiring, loving: an object of desire. — *ānā* (sc. *meṅ*) to come into use, be of service, be of avail (*obs.* when the object or the person to whose advantage the action redounds, is stated, it is put in the gen. masc. infl.; *e. g. Yih uske kām āwegā*, this will avail him or be of use to him); to be wanted; to be smitten, be slain in the field. — *chalānā*, to carry on business. — *tamām k.* to accomplish, finish; to make away with, kill. — *tamām honā*, to be finished; to be made away with, be killed. — *parnā* (sc. *meṅ*) to be of use. — *meṅ deh churānā* or *lukānā*, to work in a dilatory manner. — *nikālnā*, to carry into effect, accomplish one's desire. — *meṅ lānā*, to employ, use. — *meṅ lagānā*, to bring into use; to employ. — *rakhnā*, to make a use of. [of Kāmsen.

कामकन्दला, *f. pr. n.* a certain harlot of the court

कामकला, *f.* an epithet of Rati, wife of Kāmdev.

कामका, (gen. of **काम**, 3, very frequent as an adj.) *m.* (*f.* ī) of some use, of any use, of what use?

कामकाज, *m.* work, occupation, business.

कामाजी, *m.* (*f.* inī) a superintendent, worker, etc.: *lit.* laborious, industrious, busy, active: managing, superintending.

कामकार, *m.* freewill: one who effects what he wishes; an absolute monarch; a hunting-bird which infallibly secures its prey.

कामकेल, *m.* sport, amorous dalliance; coition.

कामकेलि, *f. m.* ? = **कामकेल**, *q.v.*

कामकृत, *m.* (*f.* ā) one who has accomplished his object: lit. *adj.* having effected one's desire.

कामग, *m.* (*f.* ā) = **कामगम**, *q.v.*

कामगम, *adj.* coming or going according to one's own desires: hence, *m.* (*f.* ā) a lascivious person, etc.

कामगार = **कामकार**, *q.v.*

कामत, *f.* stature: the shape, form, figure, body.

कामतरु, *m. pr. n.* a fabulous tree of Indra's heaven said to yield whatever may be wished.

कामतौ, a Braj form of **कुमता**, *q.v.*

कामद, *m.* an epithet of Kāmdev: lit. *m.* (*f.* ā) one who yields or fulfils desire.

कामदगाई = **कामधेनु**, *q.v.*

कामदार, *m.* a man of business; a manager, agent,

कामदारी, *f.* stewardship; agency. [steward.

कामदुघ }
कामदुह } *m.* (*f.* ā) *adj.* yielding every wish.

कामदेव, *m. pr. n.* the Cupid of the Hindoo mythology. He was the son of Vishnu by Rukminee, and husband of Rati (or Venus). Having offended Mahādev he was destroyed by the flame from the eyes of the angry deity: he was, however, born again as Pradyumna, son of Krishn, but was immediately seized by Sambara whom it had been foretold he would destroy, and thrown into the ocean where he was swallowed by a fish. This fish, having been caught, was presented to Sambara and happened to be given to Rati to clean: — Rati took out the infant and reared him till he was able to destroy Sambara.

कामधेनु, *m. pr. n.* a certain cow belonging to Indra which is said to have been produced at the churning of the ocean and to yield whatever may be requested of her: any cow that yields much milk may also be so called.

कामना, *f.* desire, wish, inclination, lust.

कामनावश, *m.* (*f.* ā) under the control of inordinate desire, blinded by lust.

कामनावान, *m.* (*f.* vatī) desirous, lustful.

कामप्रिय, *m.* (*f.* ā) *adj.* lust-loving, libidinous.

कामयितृ, *m.* (*f.* trī) libidinous, lustful, desirous.

कामराज, *m.* the sow-thistle (*Sonchus*).

कामरान, a successful person: *lit.* fortunate, suc-

कामरि (*contraction*) = **कामारि**, *q.v.* [cessful.

कामरानी, *f.* fortunateness, successfulness, pros-

कामरी, *f.* a blanket. [perity, felicity.

कामरूप, 1, *m.* (*f.* ā) = **कामरूपिन**, *q.v.*: 2, *m. pr. n.* a district lying to the east of Bengal, — now part of Assam.

कामरूपिन, *m.* (*f.* i) one who is able to change shape or appearance at will: a beautiful person, pleasing object: *lit.* assuming any shape at will: pleasing, beautiful.

कामरूपी, 1, *m.* (*f.* inī) = **कामरूपिन**, *q.v.*: 2, appertaining to the district of Kāmroop: hence, *m.* (*f.* in *or* inī) a native or a resident of Kāmrūp.

कामल, *m. pr. n.* a certain Nāg.

कामलता, *f. pr. n.* (see **लताकाम**) a certain famous woman, a heroine of romance: a certain ornamental climbing-plant (*Ipomœa Quamoclit*).

कामला, *f.* jaundice, the excess or the obstruction of bile. [diced.

कामली, *m.* (*f.* inī) a jaundiced person: *lit.* jaun-

कामवती, *f.* a loving female: *pr. n.* a certain city.

कामवन्त, *m.* (*f.* vatī) a loving person: *lit.* loving.

कामसेन, *m. pr. n.* a certain king of Kāmvatī.

कामसैन in Braj = **कामसेन**, *q.v.*

कामस्वरूप, of the nature of *Kām*.

कामहीन, *m.* (*f.* ā) vacant, unoccupied, unused.

कामा, *f.* 1, see **काम**, 4: 2, *pr. n.* a certain city.

कामाटी, *m.* a mason, builder.

कामातुर, *m.* (*f.* ā) agitated or distracted by lust. — *honā*, to be enamoured of, burn towards.

कामातुरत्व, *m.* (*f.* tā) libidinousness, sensuality.

कामान्ध, *m.* (*f.* ā) blinded by lust, under the influence of conjugal desire.

कामारि, 1, *m.* an epithet of Mahādev; *lit.* the enemy of Kāmdev (see **कामदेव**): 2, *m.* a certain mineral substance used in medicine, — a sort of pyrites.

कामारु = **कामारि**, *q.v.*

कामार्त्त, *m.* (*f.* ā) lovesick, libidinous.

कामार्थी, *m.* (*f.* inī) a person who carries baskets filled with Ganges-water to distant places.

कामासक्त, under the power of lust: occupied, busy: hence, *m.* (*f.* ā) a libidinous person: a person occupied in work.

कामिन, *m.* (*f.* ī) 1, the ruddy goose; a pigeon; a sparrow: a boy dressed in female attire who dances at the season of the Holee: 2, a lascivious person; a beloved object: *lit.* amorous, lascivious; beloved.

कामिनि = **कामिनी**, *q. v.*

कामिया; see **काम्या**.

कामिल, *m.* (*f.* ā) an accomplished person: *lit.* learned, accomplished, perfect, complete, entire.

कामिली, *f.* completeness, entireness, perfectness, accomplishment.

कामी, 1, *f.* a nugget of gold: 2, *m.* (*f.* inī) a lover, etc.: *lit.* libidinous, fond, loving, effectionate; beloved; 3, *m.* (*f.* inī) an industrious person, etc. *lit.* occupied, busy, industrious, workish.

कामुक, desirous, sensual, libidinous: hence, *m.* (*f.* ā *or* ī) a lover, etc.

कामुकत्व, *m.* (*f.* tā) libidinousness, wishfulness.

कामुका / **कामुकी** } *f.* (*m.* **कामुक**) a wanton.

कामून = **कम्मून**, *q. v.*

कामूस, *m.* the ocean.

कामोद, *m.* a certain musical mode sung in the [night.

कामोदक, *m.* an oblation of water to deceased friends exclusive of those for whom it is directed by law.

कामोदा, *m.* a certain musical mode sung at [night.

काम्प, *m.* 1, misfortune, evil luck. — *mārnā*, to happen, befal (said of ill luck): 2, mud thrown up deposited by water-courses or by rivers.

काम्पना, *a. int.* to shiver, tremble, shake.

काम्बोज, 1, *m. pr. n.* a certain country on the western coast of Northern India (Camboge, Cambay, or Kambāch): 2, *m.* (*f.* ā) a native of Camboge, a horse of the Camboge breed: *lit.* appertaining to Camboge.

काम्य, *m.* (*f.* ā) agreeable, desirable, amiable.

काम्यकर्म्म, *m.* any supererogatory work performed at pleasure or through the desire of some advantage.

काम्यदान, *m.* a desirable gift, acceptable gift.

काम्या, *f. pr. n.* (see **काम्य**) a certain Apsarā: desire.

काय, *m.* the body, appearance, person: the root of the little finger: a nuptial form called Prājāpatya.

कायक, *m.* (*f.* ikā *or* ikī) corporeal, bodily, per- [sonal.

कायथ = **कायस्थ**, *q. v.*

कायथी, *f.* a certain modification of the Devānāgarī character used by Hindoo clerks, especially in and about Patna.

कायफल, *m.* a small tree (*Fragaria vesca*) found in the North-west of Hindustān the bark and the seeds of which are used in medicine and as aromatics; the fruit also is eaten. As. Res. vol. 6. p. 380.

कायम, *more prop.* **क़ाइम**, *q.v.*

कायर, *m.* (*f.* ā) timid, timorous, cowardly.

कायल, *more prop.* **क़ाइल**, *q. v.*

कायस्थ, *m.* (*f.* ā) a certain mixed tribe or caste of Hindoos proceeding from a Kshatriya father and a Shoodra mother (they are generally employed as clerks or copyists, and are hence called the writer caste); a writer: a name of the Supreme Being: *lit.* situated in the body, incorporate.

काया, *f.* the body, appearance, person.

कायाधू, *f. pr. n.* the wife of *Hiranyakashyap*.

कायी, *m.* (*f.* inī) bodily, corporeal, personal.

क़ार, *m.* a gulf, abyss; the bottom of a well.

कार, 1, *m.* business, profession, work, action, affair: 2, stubborn, obdurate, strong: 3, *m.* (*f.* ī) very common as a suffix forming nouns of agency; *e. g.* **कारगुज़ार**. 4, It is used for forming the names of the letters of the alphabet in Hindee; *e. g.* **अकार**, **ककार**, etc.

कारक, 1, *m.* action (*esp.* in Gram.): (in Gram.) case: 2, *m.* (*f.* ikā) a doer, agent: *lit.* doing, acting.

कारकरचना, *f.* (in Gram.) the formation of cases, declension. [business it is to keep records; a labourer.

कारकुन, *m.* a director, manager, officer whose

कारख़ाना, *m.* a workshop, manufactory, arsenal, dockyard, any place where public works are carried on; *met.* a great work, the *vulva*.

कारचोब, *m.* embroidery; an embroiderer. [**कार्य्य**.

कारज; for words beginning thus, see under the form

कारण, *m.* cause, motive, principle, purpose, reason, occasion, account; action, agency, means; a father.

कारणकारण, *m.* an epithet of the Great Creator; *prop.* the cause of all things.

कारदाजा, *m.* the cock or mouth of a cistern, barrel, etc.; the mouth of a water-channel.

कारदार, *m.* an agent (esp. of Government).

कारबरदारी, *f.* the undertaking a business.

कारबार, *m.* avocation, business, profession.

कारबारी, *m.* (*f.* inī) a trader, transactor of business,

कारबोस, a species of fish (?). [manager, officer.

काररवाई, *f.* usefulness; occupation, conduct, management, the carrying on a business.

कारसाज़, *m.* an epithet of God; *prop.* the causer of the efficiency of work.

कारा, 1, = **काला**, *q.v.*: 2, a kind of tree (*Webera Tetranda*): 3, *f.* a gaol.

कारागार } *m.* a gaol, prison.
कारागृह }

कारिगर, *more com.* **कारीगर**, *q.v.*

कारिख, 1, see **कारीष**; 2, a water-conductor.

कारिज = **कार्य्य**, *q.v.*

कारिन्दा, *m.* a manager, officer, agent: *lit.* working, laborious.

कारिस्तानी, *f.* workmanship.

कारी, 1, a corruption of **काली**, *q.v.*: 2, effectual, deep, mortal (as a wound): 3, see **कार**, 3: 4, *m.* (*f.* iṇī): a suffix, very frequent in Hindee, denoting agency; *e. g.* **अधिकारी**: 5, *f.* the dish called 'curry.' This word is, perhaps, borrowed from the English name of the dish, just as that name, again, is said to be a corruption of **क़लिया**, a sort of stew differing in some respects from curry. But *query*, a contraction of **तरकारी**?

कारीगर, *m.* a workman, craftsman, good workman.

कारीगरी, *f.* masterly work, workmanship, the product of workmanship.

कारीनून, *m.* black salt, muriate of soda.

कारीष, *m.* a heap of dung, a large quantity of dried cowdung.

कारु, 1, *m.* or *f.* = **कारुकार**, *q.v.*: 2, (*dialectic*) = [**किसीका**.

कारुकार, *m.* (*f.* ī) a worker, agent, maker, artificer, mechanic, artisan: lit. *adj.* working, doing work.

कारुष, *m.* a certain race of Kshatriyas.

कारुणक, *m.* (*f.* ikā) } compassionate, tender, kind.
कारुणिक, *m.* (*f.* ā) }

कारे, 1, infl. form of **कारा** = **काला**; 2, (see **अरे**) = [**अरे काहेके लिये**.

कारेज़, *f.* a canal, aqueduct.

कारेज़ी, *m.* land irrigated from a canal: *lit.* appertaining to a canal.

कारो in Braj = **काला**, *q.v.*

कारोबार, *m.* business, occupation, profession.

कार्त्तवीर्य्य, *m.pr.n.* (1) of a certain king, also called Urjoon (2) of a celebrated hero distinct from the Pandoo prince (3) of one of the Jain Chakravartees or emperors of the world.

कार्त्तिक, *m. pr. n.* the seventh month of the Hindoos (Oct. — Nov.) the full moon of which is near *Krittikā* or the Pleiades.

कार्त्तिकेय, *m.pr.n.* the god of war and son of Shiv.

कार्त्तिकोत्सव, *m.* the day of full moon in the month Kārttik; a certain Hindoo festival.

कार्पण्य, *m.* poverty, indigence.

कार्पास, 1, *m.* cotton, cotton cloth, the cotton plant (*Gossypium hirsutum*): 2, *m.* (*f.* ī) made of cotton, cottony.

कार्पासी, *f.* the cotton-plant (*Gossypium hirsutum*).

कार्म्मिक, 1, *m.* a figured web: 2, *m.* (*f.* ā) worked, embroidered, intermixed with colored thread.

कार्म्मुक, *m.* a bow (in archery).

कार्य्य, *m.* cause, origin, motive, object; work, business, affair, action, possession, occupation.

कार्य्यिक, appertaining to a **कार्य्य**.

कार्य्यकर्त्ता, *m.* (*f.* trī) a manager, agent, negotiator, ambassador, representative.

कार्य्यकारी, *m.* (*f.* iṇī) a workman, operative, agent: *lit.* effectual, efficient, availing, operative.

कार्य्यचिन्ता, *f.* considerateness, prudence, caution.

कार्य्यत्व, *m.* the condition of being an effect.

कार्य्यरहित, unoccupied, unemployed, fallow.

कार्य्यसिद्धि, *f.* the accomplishment of any purpose, the attainment of any object, success.

कार्य्याध्यक्ष, *m.* (*f.* ī) a superintendent of work.

कार्षक, *m.* (*f.* ikā) a husbandman, tiller.

कार्षापन, *m.* a weight of silver equal to sixteen *paṇs* of cowries; a weight of copper equal to eighty rattees; a weight of shells equal to eighty cowries: a husbandman.

कार्षिक, *m.* (*f.* ā) a tiller of the soil, husbandman.

काल, 1, in Braj = **कल**, yesterday; to-morrow: 2, *m.* a certain black poisonous snake (*Coluber nāga*); the black in the eye; a proper name (1) of a person (2) of a mountain: 3, *m.* (*f.* ī) dark, dark blue, black: 4, *m.* time; (in Gram.) tense; time personified; meal-time; season; age; period; fate; calamity; dearth, famine; death, the messenger of death, the regent of the dead, one of the names of Yam or Jam. — *kāṭnā* or *gaṅwānā* or *bitānā*, to spend time, pass the time: to waste time. — *parnā*, the coming on of a famine. — *bas honā*, to be in the hands of death; to be seized by fate.

कालक, 1, *f.* (*m.* ?) blackness; the black in the eye; a spot, mark, freckle: a kind of grain: 2, *m. pr. n.* (1) of a Rakshas (2) of an Asur: 3, *f.* (*m.* ?) one of the expressions of quantity in the science of Beej-ganit or Algebra corresponding to our a, b, x, y, etc: 4, *m.* (*f.* ikā) appertaining to time or to death.

कालंजर = **कालञ्जर**, *q. v.*

कालका, *f. pr. n.* a certain female demon.

कालकोल, *m.* a confused sound, tumult.

कालकूट, *m.* the poison of a snake; a kind of poison destroying even the regent of death.

कालके समाचार, *m. pr. n.* the Books of Chronicles.

कालक्रमिक, according to the process of time.

कालक्षेप, *m.* a spending time; the enduring suffering.

कालख, *m.* a freckle, mark, spot, stain; blackness, lampblack, soot. *Nāmpar — lagānā*, to give a person a bad name, bring a stain on one's reputation. *Kisike muṅhmeṅ — lagānā*, to mortify one, put one to shame give one annoyance.

कालगन्ध, *m.* a kind of Cobra di cappello.

कालचक्र, *m.* a period of time, cycle, epoch.

कालञ्जर, *m. pr. n.* a name of Shiv; a rock in Bundēlkhand, the modern Callinger; also the country adjacent to it: an assemblage of religious mendicants, so called because Callinger is one of their meeting-places, — being enumerated in the Veds among the *tapasyā-sthāns* or localities suitable for the practice of austere devotions.

कालज्ञान, *m.* mundane information, secular knowledge, the knowledge of worldly things as distinguished from things spiritual and eternal.

कालधर्म्म, *m.* death; dying.

कालनिर्य्यास, *m.* a certain fragrant and resinous substance, bdellium.

कालनेमि, *f.* a kind of weapon : *pr.n.* a certain demon.

कालपात्र, *m.* (*f.* ī) a victim of famine.

कालप्रभात, *m.* the sultry season, autumn, the two months following the rainy season.

कालमा, *m.* suspicion, calumny.

कालसूत्र, *m. pr. n.* (in Myth.) one of the hells.

कालमेषिका, *f.* Bengal madder ; black Teoree.

कालमेषी, *f.* a certain plant (*Serratula* or *Conyza anthelmintica*) : Bengal madder (*Rubia manjeth*).

कालयमन, = **कालयवन**, *q. v.*

कालयवन, *m. pr. n.* a certain tyrant prince of the Yavans who after having made great devastations was slain by Nārāyaṇ.

कालरात्रि, *m.* a particular night, one of which occurs on the seventh of the seventh month of the seventy-seventh year. After attaining such a period of life a man is considered exempt from attending to the usual ordinances.

काललवण, *m.* a factitious and purgative salt.

कालवश, *m.* (*f.* ā) liable to death. — *honā*, to be in the hands of death ; to be seized by fate.

कालवा, *m.* a river, watercourse, channel, canal.

कालवाचक, (in Gram.) having reference to time ; as, an adverb of time.

कालसर्प, *m.* the black and most deadly variety of the cobra (*Coluber nāga*).

कालसार, *m.* the black antelope.

कालसूत्र, *m. pr. n.* one of the twenty-one hells.

काला, 1, *f.* (*m.* **काल**) a certain female demon : 2, *m.* a certain snake ; one of the names of Krishn : time : 3, *m.* (*f.* ī) black, dark.

कालांजनी, *f.* a certain small shrub used as a purgative.

काला आंचू, *m.* the hill bramble.

कालागुरु, *m.* a black kind of aloe-wood or agallochum.

कालाचोर, *m.* an unknown person.

कालाजीरा, *m.* seeds of the *Nigella Indica* (Roxb.).

कालादाना, *m.* a certain purgative seed (*Convolvulus nil ?*).

कालानिमक, *m.* a kind of rock salt impregnated with sulphur and bitumen. It leaves a hepatic flavor and is much used medicinally.

कालान्तर, *m.* intervening time, interval ; the process of time ; a suitable time.

कालापत्ती, *f.* the calking a ship or boat. — *k.* to calk.

कालापन, *m.* blackness, the condition of being black.

कालामुँह क॰, *t.* to break off all connexion with a person ; to expel ; to disgrace : to copulate.

कालि, *more prop.* **काली**, *q. v.*

कालिक, 1, *m.* blackness ; lampblack, the soot which collects under pots, etc. : blacking ; ink ; a fault or flaw in gold ; the line of hair extending to the navel ; a small bird commonly called Syām, the curlew ; 2, *m.* (*f.* ā or ī) periodical, temporal, relating to time, (in Gram.) relating to tense.

कालिका, *f. pr. n.* the goddess Kālee.

कालिकावृद्धि, *f.* periodical interest on money.

कालिख, *more prop.* **कालख**, *q. v.*

कालिदास, *m. pr. n.* a celebrated Hindoo poet, — the Shakespeare of India, author of the Shakuntalā, Raghoovans, Naloday, and other poems. He was one of the nine poets or gems of Vikramāditya's court, and is supposed to have flourished in the century preceding the Christian era. The name is, however, applicable to more persons than one, and seems, in some degree, to have been used as a title of honor. The works attributed to this author are among the most elegant compositions in the Sanskrit language.

कालिन्दी, *f.* (contr. of **काली नदी**) the river Jumna : *pr. n.* (1) of a wife of Krishṇ (2) of the wife of Asit and mother of Sagar.

क़ालिब, *m.* a mould, model, form, prototype ; a bust, figure ; the body, lifeless form.

कालिय, *m. pr. n.* (1) of Kaliyug (2) of Kālī-Nāg.

कालिया, 1, *m.* = **काली**, 2, *q. v.* : 2, black-complexioned.

कालीकुण्ड, *more com.* **कालीदह**, *q. v.*

काली, 1, *f. pr. n.* (from **काल**, 2) the Hecate of the Hindoo mythology, and wife of Shiv, to whom human sacrifices are offered : the river Nile : ink : 2, *m. pr. n.* a fabulous serpent (called also Kāliyā) with a hundred and ten hoods, said to have been vanquished and slain by Krishṇ : 3, a corruption of **कल्ह**, *q. v.*

कालीज़ीरी, *f.* blacklead.

कालीतुलसी, *f.* basil (*Ocymum sanctum* or *basilicum*).

कालीदह, *m. pr. n.* a whirlpool in the river Jumna in which the serpent Kālee is said to have lived.

कालीन, timely, seasonable, relating to time.

कालीनाग = **काली**, 2, *q. v.*

कालीभूमि, *f.* a rich black soil, vegetable mould.

कालीमिट्टी, *f.* blacklead.

कालीमिर्च, *f.* black pepper.

कालीखून, *m.* a certain plant.

कालीसर, *m.* a break, stay.

कालुक ; see **कलुष**.

कालुष्य, *m.* foulness ; unfairness ; turbidness ; capacity ; disagreement.

कालेकोस, *m.* a great distance.

कालेबरन, *adj.* of the colour of a snake.

कालेबाल, *m.* the pubes.

कालेश्वर, *m.* a certain drug.

काल्पनिक, *m.* (*f.* ā) factitious, contrived, feigned, hypocritical.

काल्पनिकत्व, *m.* (*f.* tā) hypocrisy, dissimulation.

काल्ह, *more prop.* **कल्ह**, *q. v.*

काल्हि, an emphatic form of **काल्ह**, *q. v.*

कावड़, a stick or bamboo carried on the shoulder to the ends of which are suspended boxes, baskets, etc., called in Urdoo *bahangi*.

कावड़वाला, *m.* (*f* ī) a person who carries baggage, etc. hung to a *Kāwar*.

कावर, *f.* the baskets in which Hindoo pilgrims carry about Ganges-water.

कावल, *m.* surrounding, perambulating, patrolling ; fees paid for protection of property ; black-mail.

कावलगार, *m.* a patrol, sentinel.

कावलपट्टी, *f.* a commitment to jail.

कावली, *f.* = **कावल**, *q. v.*

कावलीगार, *m.* a patrol, sentinel.

कावादेना, *t.* to ring or lounge (a horse, etc.) : to trick ; to shame.

कावित } the wood-apple (see कठबेल).
कावीट }

कावेरी, *f.* turmeric: a harlot: *pr. n.* the river Cavery in the Dakkhan.

काव्य, *m.* a poem; a bard: a patron.

काव्यचोर, *m.* a plagiarist of poetry.

काव्यचौर in Braj = काव्यचोर, *q.v.*

काव्यरस, *m.* taste for poetical composition; the flavour or sweetness of poetry.

काश; for all words beginning thus, but not given below, see under the forms काष or कास.

काश, 1, *m.* cough, catarrh: 2, *f.* a kind of reed or long grass (*Saccharum spontaneum*) of which rope is made: 3, *m.* a cup, goblet, bowl: 4, *m.* a very small copper coin, called by Europeans "cash", current, till late years, in Southern India. Eighty of these coins made one fanam and twelve fanams a rupee.

काशमीर = कश्मीर, *q. v.*

काशरोग } *m.* asthma.
काशस्वास }

काशी, *f. pr. n.* the modern Benares, — the most sacred of all the cities of the Hindoos, and their most important place of pilgrimage.

काशीनरेश, *m. pr. n.* a certain ancient Hindoo king.

काशीपुरी, *f.* the capital of the Kāshees, *i. e.* Benares.

काश्मीर = कश्मीर, *q.v.*

काश्यप, appertaining to Kashyap: *hence* (patronym.) *m.* (*f.* i) a descendant of Kashyap.

काश्यपनन्दन, *m.* (*f.* ā) an epithet of any god: *lit.* offspring of Kashyap.

काष, (*exclam.*) would that! Frequent in Braj; *e. g.* काष चल्यौ होतु, Oh, that I had gone!

काषकी } = काष, *q. v.*
काषके }

काष्ठ, *m.* wood, timber, a piece of wood.

काष्ठक, *m.* aloe-wood or agallochum.

काष्ठकीट, *m.* a certain small insect or worm found in decayed wood.

काष्ठकुट्ट, *m.* the woodpecker.

काष्ठा, *f.* aim; limit, boundary; place, a quarter or point of the compass: a lunar station; a measure of time.

काष्ठी, *m.* (*f.* iṇī) wooden.

कास; for words beginning thus, but not given below, see under the form काश.

कासघ्न, *m.* (*f.* ā) removing or relieving cough, pectoral.

कासघ्नी, *f.* a sort of prickly nightshade (*Solanum jacquini.* [ny plant used as a remedy for cough.

कासनाशिनी, *f.* the cough-destroyer, a certain thorny plant used as a remedy for cough.

कासबी, *m.* (*f.* inī) a weaver.

कासमर्द, *m.* the plant *Cassia* or *Senna esculenta.*

कासा, *m.* a cup, goblet, bowl, plate.

कासालु, *m.* a certain esculent root, a sort of yam.

कासिद, 1, *m.* a courier, express, messenger, postman: 2, deficient, defective, not passing current, not selling, worthless.

कासिब, *m.* an artist, tradesman.

कासिबी, *m.* (*f.* inī) a weaver.

क़ासिम, *m.* a distributor: *lit.* dividing, distributing.

क़ासिर, insufficient, defective, deficient, failing, impotent.

कासी, *more prop.* काशी, *q. v.*

कासीस, *m.* green sulphate of iron, green vitriol, copperas.

कासे (an abl. sing. of को) = किससे.

कासें in Braj, abl. sing. of को, *q. v.*

कास्त, 1, *m.* a certain plant (*Chara*, Bruce MS.): 2, *f.* diminution, loss, damage.

कास्तन, *m.* diminution, loss, damage.

कास्तनी, *f.* a certain plant: diminution, loss, damage.

कास्या, a sickle.

काह, 1, in Braj = क्या, *q.v.*: 2, *f.* grass, straw.

काहकशान, *m. pr. n.* the Milky Way.

काहगिल, plaster for walls made of a mixture of straw and mud.

काहण, *m.* an aggregate number consisting of sixteen *pans*, or 1280 cowries.

काहर, *more com.* (1) काहल (2) कहार, *qq.v.*

काहल, 1, *m.* a cock: a cat: a large drum: sound in general; indistinct speech: 2, *m.* (*f.* ā) mischievous: excessive: withered.

काहलापुष्प, *m.* the thorn-apple (*Datura metel*).

काहि, in Braj, a dat. and acc. of को, 2, *q.v.*

काहिन, *m.* a prophet, priest; a soothsayer, astrologer, conjuror, augur, sorcerer.

काहिल, slow, tardy, indolent, languid, indisposed, sick.

काहिलपना, *m.* indolence, tardiness, sloth, languor, sickness.

काहिला = काहिल, *q. v.*

काहिलागी } *f.* = काहिलपना, *q. v.*
काहिली }

काहिश, *f.* diminution; emaciation: care, anxiety.

काही, *f.* greenness; name of a certain dish: *adj.* appertaining to straw or grass.

काहुक (= काहूको) appertaining to someone or to something.

काहुनसों in Braj = कहांसे.

काहू in Braj, inflective base of कोऊ and of कहू, *qq. v.*

काहूको, the gen. of कोउ and of कहू, *qq. v.*

काहूकों, the dat. and acc. of कोऊ and of कहू, *qq. v.*

काहे, inflective base of क्या, *q.v.*: and in Braj, the inflective base of कहा or of का, *qq. v.*

काहेको, (dat. or acc. of क्या, *q.v.*) why? for why?

काहेकौ, the gen. of कहा or of का, *qq.v.*

काहेकों, the dat. and acc. of कहा or of का, *qq.v.*

काहेलिये, (sc. *ke* = *kaheke liye*?) why? for what purpose? [reason? on what ground? for what occasion?

काहेवास्ते, (sc. *ke* = *kaheke wāste*?) why? for what?

काहेसे, from what cause? wherefore?

कि; this word is used in a variety of ways: — 1, it sometimes = क्या, 3, as the untranslated sign of interrogation: 2, it is occasionally interrogative = why? wherefore? what? 3, sometimes it is used as a relative pronoun = who, which, what, that: 4, sometimes it is a conjunction = that, for, since, inasmuch as, seeing that, whilst, or, whether, when: 5, it is frequent at the beginning of quotations, when it indicates, like the Greek ὅτι, that the *ipsissima verba* follow: in this usage it is, like the Greek word, untranslateable in English; e. g. *Usne kahā ki maiṅ jāuṅgā*, he said, I I will go: 6, It should be added that in pure Hindee this word is of rare occurrence, and that its usage is exceedingly limited: it is, however, of not at all infrequent occurrence in that laxer style both of speaking and of writing which exhibits clear traces of the influence of Urdoo.

किई, *f.* sing. of **किया**, 2, *q.v.*

किईं, fem. pl. of **किया**, 2, *q.v.*

किए (from **किआ** = **किया**) = **किये**, *q.v.*

किंकर, *m.* (*f.* ī) a bondsman, slave, servant: *pr. n.* (1) of a people (2) of a tribe of demons.

किंकिणी, *f.* a kind of girdle with small bells or any tinkling ornaments (worn by women and children).

किंकिणीक, *m.* = **किंकिणी**, *q.v.*

किंकिणीकिन, *m.* (*f.* ī) a person adorned with tinkling things.

किंकिनि / **किंकिनी** } (*Rām.*) = **किंकिणी**, *q.v.*

किंगाढ्य, *f.* parsimony.

किंधी, *f.* a certain musical instrument (something like the *bin*, or *vina* only somewhat smaller) having only two steel strings and three or four pumpkins or calabashes as sounding-boards.

किंचली, *f.* the slough of a snake.

किंचित, a little, a part, somewhat.

किंचितज्ञ, *m.* (*f.* ā) a person of but little or limited knowledge: *lit.* little-knowing.

किंशुक, *m.* a certain tree (*Butea frondosa*) and its blossom which is of a beautiful red.

किकरा, a dialectic form = **किसका**.

किकि, *m.* the blue jay.

किकियाना, *a. int.* to shriek, scream.

किचकिचाना, *a. int.* to gnash the teeth, grind the teeth.

किचड़ा, *m.* the gummy substance that oozes from the eyes.

किचड़ाना, *n.* to be blear-eyed, to have a gummy running at the eyes.

किचपिच, *f.* mud, mire, slush, dirt.

किचरपिचर होना, *n.* to be very wet.

किचरा = **किचड़ा**, *q.v.*

किछु, *more com.* **कुछ**, *q.v.*

किट्ठ, *m.* a kind of sour dish; excrement, dirt.

किड़; for words beginning thus, see under the form **कीड़**.

कित, where? whither? how much? how many?

किण्व, *m.* a certain substance used to produce fermentation in the manufacture of spirits from sugar, ferment, yeast.

कितई (in Braj = **कोतई**, *q.v.*) to, up to, for.

कितक, some, several, a few.

कितना, *m.* (*f.* ī) how much? what quantity? In the pl., how many?

कितने एक, several, some, a few. (*Not much used.*)

किता, *m.* (*f.* ī) *more com.* **कितना**, *q.v.*

किताब, *f.* (pl. **कुतुब**) a book; writing, despatches, an epistle; The Book *par excellence*, *i. e.* the Bible or the Kur,ān.

किताबख़ाना, *m.* a book-repository, library.

किताबवाला, *m.* (*f.* ī) a believer in The Book: a vendor or a maker of books.

किताबिया, *f.* (dimin. of **किताब**) a small book.

किताबी, *m.* (*f.* inī) a believer in The Book, *i. e.* a Jew, a Christian, or a Muhammadan: *lit.* appertaining to a book, of the shape of a book.

क़िताल, massacre, slaughter, fighting, battle.

किते, *more com.* **कितने**, *q.v.*

कितेक, 1, a dialectic form = **कितना**: 2, (a contraction of *kitne ek*) some, several, a few.

किते in Braj = **कितने**, *q.v.*

कित्ता, *m.* (*f.* ī) = **कितना**, *q.v.*

कित्ती in Chand = **कीर्ति**, *q.v.*

कित्ते, *more com.* **कितने**, *q.v.*

क़िदम, *m.* a man who excels in virtue.

क़िदवा, *m.* an example, model, leader.

किदारबसन्त, *m.* a certain musical mode.

किदारा, *m.* a certain musical mode sung in the midnight of summer.

किधर, whither? where? in what direction? — *se*, from what quarter? whence?

किन, 1, in Braj = **क्यों नहीं**: 2, a wound, sore: 3, the inflective base of the oblique cases of the plural of **कौन** and, in Braj, of **को**.

किनकर = (1) **किंकर**, *q.v.* (2) **किनका** (**कौन**). See **कर**, 3.

किनको in Braj, gen. pl. of **को**, *q.v.*

किनकों in Braj, dat. and acc. pl. of **को**, *q.v.*

किनना, *more prop.* **कोनना**, *q.v.*

किनवैया, *more prop.* **कोनवैया**, *q.v.*

किनसों in Braj, abl. pl. of **को**, *q.v.*

क़िनाअ़त = **क़नाअ़त**, *q.v.*

किनान, *more prop.* **कनआन**, *q.v.*

किनाया, *m.* a wink, nod, sign, hint, allusion; a metaphor; an ironical expression.

किनार, *m.* the bosom, embrace; a side, edge, margin, rim. — *khainchnā*, to give up, quit, leave.

किनारा, *m.* a side, margin, edge, brink, rim, hem, border, boundary, limit, shore, bank. — *k.* to refrain, abstain from.

किनारी, *f.* edge, border, gold or silver lace.

किनारीबाफ़, *m.* a lace-maker.

किनारे, *adv.* aside; ashore. — *hojānā*, to withdraw, retire, get out of the way, get aside.

किन्तु, but, however, still, nevertheless; again, moreover.

किन्तुघ्न, *m. pr. n.* one of the eleven *Karaṇs* or astronomical periods.

किन्नर, *m.* (*f.* ī) a class of demigods attached to the service of Kuver the god of riches: a kind of chorister at the court of Indra.

किन्नकर, *m.* (*f.* ī) *more prop.* **किंकर**, *q.v.*

किन्व = **किण्व**, *q.v.*

किन्ह = किन्हों, *q.v.*

किन्हा, *m.* (*f.* i) *more prop.* कीन्हा, *q.v.*

किन्हें, a dat. and acc. pl. of कौन, *q.v.*

किन्हैं in Braj, a dat. and acc. pl. of को, *q.v.*

किन्हों, an inflective base of the oblique cases of the pl. of कौन. See किन and उन्हों.

किफ़ायत, *f.* a sufficiency, enough, abundance, plenty, surplus; economy, thrift. — *k.* to save; to answer, serve, be sufficient, do; to content oneself.

क़िबर, *m.* grandeur, dignity, pride.

किबरीत, *m.* sulphur: fine gold or silver.

क़िबला, *m.* (the direction to which Muhammadans turn the face in prayer; hence) Mecca; worship; an altar, temple: a father: *lit.* anything opposite.

क़िबलेआलम, (an epithet) the *ḳiblā* of the world; His Majesty; Your Majesty.

किबाड़, *more prop.* किवाड़, *q.v.*

किम, 1, a contraction of क्रिमि, *q.v.*: 2, who? which? what?

किमपि = कुछ भी.

क़िमार, *m.* any game of hazard, *e.g.* dice.

किमि = कैसा, *q.v.*

किम्पुरुष, *m.* 1, (*corruption of* कम पुरुष?) a despicable man: 2, a class of horse-faced beings belonging to the suite of Kuver: 3, one of the nine divisions of the world between the Himāchal and Himākoot mountains.

किम्बा, else, moreover, or.

किय; see (1) किया (2) किये.

किया, 1, *m.* an action, deed; doings: 2, *m.* (*f.* किई) base of the historical tenses of vb. *karnā*.

क़ियामत, *f.* the last day, the general resurrection (at the last day); *met.* calamity: excessively great. —*k.* to do anything wonderful, work a wonder; to oppress.

कियारी, *f.* a bed of a garden; a frame.

क़ियास, *m.* a measuring, comparing; judgment, opinion, theory, supposition, guess, thought; a syllogism.

क़ियासत, *f.* ingenuity, cunning, quickness of parts, great vivacity.

किये, *m.* (*f.* किईं) pl. of किया, 2, *q.v.*

कियो in Braj = किया and किये, *qq.v.*

किरकि; see (1) किरकी (2) खिड़की.

किरकिटी, *f.* a mote or particle of dust fallen into the eye.

किरकिरा, *m.* (*f.* ī) gritty, sandy.

किरकिराना, *a. int.* to grate, be gritty.

किरकिराहट, *f.* a cracking, crackling noise.

किरकिरी, *f.* grittiness, sandiness.

किरकी, *f.* a kind of ornament.

किरतन, (see कीर्तन) a dancing.

किरतास, *m.* paper.

किरतिया, *m.* a dancer; a singing-boy.

किरण, *f.* (*m.*?) a ray of light, a sunbeam, a moonbeam.

किरणमय, *m.* (*f.* ī) radiant, refulgent, bright.

किरति, *more prop.* कीर्ति, *q.v.*

किरदार, *m.* deed, act, action, labor, business; conduct, manner.

किरन = किरण, *q.v.*

किरपा, *more prop.* कृपा, *q.v.*

किरमिज, *more prop.* क़िरमिज़, *q.v.*

किरया; see (1) किरिया (2) कीया.

किरयात, *f.* a plant (*Justicia paniculata*) used in medicine, etc. forming the basis of the well-known tincture called the *Drogue amere*.

किरवान, *f.* a sword.

किरसित in Braj = कर्षित, *q.v.*

किरात, *m.* (*f.* ī, in, inī) a savage; a tribe of mountaineers who live by the chase; the Cirrhadae of the ancients.

किरातिन, **किरातिनी**, **किराती**, *f.* a female *kirāt*.

क़िरान, *m.* a conjunction of the planets; propinquity, contiguity; a period of 10, 20, 30, 40, 80, or 120 years. — *k.* to accomplish something wonderful.

किराना, 1, *m.* grocery: 2, *n.* to be hard, be stiff: 3, *t.* to adjust; to sift, separate by turning around in a winnowing-fan (differing from *phaṭaknā*, *q.v.*).

किराया, *m.* hire, fare, rent, freight.

किराव, *m.* a sort of small pea (*Pisum arvense*).

किरिच, *more prop.* किर्च, *q.v.*

किरिम, *more prop.* किरम, *q.v.*

किरिया, *f.* an oath. —— *khānā*, to take one's oath, swear (in the good or in the bad sense).

किरिश्मा, *m.* amorous look or gesture, ogling, wink, glance, blandishment.

किरीट, *m.* a diadem, crest.

किरीटी, *m.* (*f.* inī) a person adorned with a diadem; an epithet of Arjuna: *lit.* adorned with a diadem.

किरूब, *m.* a cherub.

किरूलना, *t.* to scrape.

किरोट; see (1) कड़ोड़ (2) करवट (3) किरीट.

क़िरोड़, *more prop.* करोड़, *q.v.*

किरोलना, *t.* to scrape.

किर्रा, 1, *m.* a hollow tooth: endive: 2, broken, rugged, tattered.

क़िरौना, a worm.

किर्च, *f.* a sword (*esp.* a straight one for thrusting with): a splinter.

किर्म, *m.* (more prop. कृमि) a worm.

किर्मिपीला, *m.* a silkworm.

किर्मी, *f.* the palās tree.

किर्तत, *f.* an action, deed; a doing.

किल, certainly, indeed, verily; probably, possibly.

किलक, *f.* splendour, lustre (of a gem).

किल्क, *f.* a reed, pen.

किलकत, *more prop.* खिलक़त, *q.v.*

किलकार मारना, to make a loud noise.

किलकारी = किल्कारी, *q.v.*

किलकिंचित, *m.* wanton or amorous pastime or gestures.

किलकिल, *m. pr. n.* a name of Shiv.

किलकिलकाँटा, *m.* a certain game among boys. One boy, having drawn several lines upon a stone, hides it; and the others, repeating the words *kilkil kāṅṭā*, run about searching for it. Whoever finds i has a right to strike the boy who hid it three times with his fingers on the back of the hand.

किलकिला, 1, *m.* peevishness, fretfulness, anger : 2, *m.* the kingfisher : 3, *f.* any sound or cry expressive of pleasure, a confused sound of many persons talking together. [2, *n.* to be fretful, be peevish.

किलकिलाना, 1, *a. int.* to snap, snarl, squabble :

किलकिलाहट, *f.* = किलकिला, 1 or 3, *q.v.*

किलना, *a. int.* to groan, lament.

किलनी, *f.* a tick, doglouse.

किलबिख } *more prop.* किल्बिष, *q.v.*
किलबिष }

किलवाई, *f.* a small rake used for gathering grass together into a cocklet.

क़िला, *m.* a fort ; a palace, royal residence.

किलात, *m.* a dwarf : *pr. n.* a certain demon.

क़िलादार, *m.* the commandant of a garrison.

क़िलादारी, *f.* the commandership of a garrison.

किलाना, *t.* to winnow ; to strike with the fist.

किलाह ; see (1) क़िला (2) कुलाह.

किलीद, *f.* a key.

किलोल, *more prop.* कलोल, *q.v.*

किल्कारी, *f.* a chattering, snarling, grinning (as of a monkey) : a shout of joy. — *karnā* or *mārnā*, to shout, express pleasure by any sound or cry.

क़िल्लत, *f.* littleness, paucity, scarcity, penury,

किल्ला ; see (1) कील (2) कीला. [want, indigence.

किल्ली, *f.* a key, bolt. [sin ; injury.

किल्बिष, *m.* fault, offence, transgression, crime,

किवा, (see व) *more prop.* किया, *q.v.* [fuge.

किवांच, *m.* cowach (*Dolichos pruriens*), a vermi-

किवाड़ }
किवाड़ा } *more com.* केवाड़, *q.v.*
किवार }

किशमिश, *f.* raisins, particularly a small kind of stoneless raisin commonly called the Sultana raisin.

किशवर, *m.* a climate, country, region.

किशलय, *more prop.* किसलय, *q v.*

किशोर, *m.* (*f.* ī) a colt ; a child, youth, son, lad under fifteen ; a minor in law, becoming, after attaining his fifteenth year, subject to suits at law.

किशोरा, *m.* (*f.* ī) infantine, young, youthful.

किश्त, 1, *m.* a sown field ; a growing crop : 2, *f.* check (in Chess). [beggar's plate or pot , a tray.

किश्ती, *f.* a ship, sailing-vessel, boat, barque ; a

किश्तीबान, *m.* a pilot ; the master of a vessel.

किश्मश, *more prop.* किशमिश, *q.v.*

किष्किन्ध, for words beginning thus, see under the more proper forms किष्किन्ध or किष्किन्ध्य.

किष्किन्ध, *m. pr. n.* a certain mountain, in or near Orissa. It contains a cave, the residence of Bāli, king of the monkeys. [section of the Rāmāyan.

किष्किन्धकाण्ड, *m. pr. n.* (see वाल्मीकिकाण्ड) the fourth

किष्किन्धा, *f.* = किष्किन्ध, *q. v.*

किष्किन्धाकाण्ड = किष्किन्धकाण्ड, *q. v.*

किष्किन्ध्य, *m.* }
किष्किन्ध्या, *f.* } = किष्किन्ध, *q. v.*

किष्किन्ध्याकाण्ड = किष्किन्धकाण्ड, *q. v.* [monkeys.

किष्किन्ध्याधिप, *m.* an epithet of Bāli, king of the

किष्कु, *m. f.* the forearm ; a span (as a measure), a cubit : *adj.* contemptible, bad.

किस ; the inflective base of the oblique cases of the singular of कौन. This form appears in several compound words of an interrogative character, in which, it will be observed, some case-sign, such as *ke, par, meṅ, se*, etc., has been elided ; thus, *Kis tarah*, in what manner ? how ? *Kis kadr*, how much ? *Kisliye*, why ? from what motive ? *Kiswāste ?* why ? from what cause or occasion ? *Kiskis*, which (of several) ?

किस्सःकहानी, *f.* stories and fables.

किसनई, *f.* agriculture, husbandry.

किसकिन्धाकाण्ड = किष्किन्धकाण्ड, *q.v.* [tribution.

क़िसमत, *f.* fate, fortune, lot, share, division, dis-

किसलय, *m.* a young shoot, sprout.

किसवत, *f.* dress, robe, habit, appearance ; *met.* form, figure, manner.

किसवा, *more prop.* किस्सा, *q. v.* [peasant.

किसान, *m.* a husbandman, farmer, ploughman,

किसारी, *f.* a kind of pulse (*Lathyrus sativus*).

किसी ; the inflective base of the oblique cases of the singular of कोई.

किसु (irregular) in Braj = किसका.

किसू ; the inflective base of the oblique cases of the singular of कुछ.

किसे ; dat. and acc. sing. of कौन, *q.v.*

किसोर, *more prop.* किशोर, *q. v.*

क़िस्त, *f.* (pl. अक़सात) a portion, instalment : tax.

किस्ती, *more prop.* किश्ती, *q. v.*

क़िस्म, *f.* (pl. अक़साम) a sort, kind, species ; a part, division ; (in Law) the equal partition of cohabitation which a husband is required to make his wives when he has more than one. [rel.

क़िस्सा, *m.* a story, tale, narrative : a dispute, quar-

किहतरी, *f.* smallness, diminutiveness, littleness.

किही = (1) किसको (2) किसी (3) किस.

की 1, why ? wherefore ? what ? 2, *f.* (*m.* का) the case-sign of the fem. genitive : 3, it is sometimes put inaccurately for कि, 4, *q. v.* : 4, it is frequently (and especially in poetry and in Braj) put where we should expect किई and even किया.

कीं, (pl. of की, 4) *more prop.* किईं, *q. v.*

कीकड़, *m.* the acacia tree (see बबूल).

कीच, *f.* dirt, mire, slime, mud. [of कीच.

कीचइ, (1) *more prop.* कीचहि (2) an emphat. form

कीचड़, *f.* dirt, mire, mud, slime.

कीचहि (see हि) in Braj = कीचको, etc.

कीजे }
कीजो } in Braj and in poetry = कीजिये.

कीट, *m.* (*f.* ī) a worm, maggot, reptile, insect ; the dregs of oil in a lamp, the dregs collected in a hukka-snake.

कीड़, *m.* (*f.* ī) a worm, maggot, insect : mildew, rot.

कीड़खाया, *m.* (*f.* °खाई) a person marked with small-pox, etc. : *lit.* wormeaten : freckled, pockmarked.

कीड़हा, *m.* (*f.* ī) wormy, wormeaten, weevileaten.

कीड़ा, *m.* (*f.* ī) a worm, insect, reptile, maggot, snake, leech.

कीती, a corruption of कीर्ति, *q.v.*

कीधर, whither? where? which way?

कीन, *m.* malice, rancour, hatred, enmity.

कीनतोज़, *m.* one who foments dissensions and law-suits : *lit.* malevolent.

कीनना, *t.* to purchase, buy.

कीनवैया, *m.* a purchaser.

कीना, 1, (= करना) to make, do, etc. : the verb *karnā* borrows its past participle, and the forms of the tenses into which the past participle enters, from this verb *kīnā* : 2, *m.* (*f.* ī) in poetry and in Braj = किया, *q.v* : 3, *m.* malice, spite, rancour, hatred.

कीनेहु = कीन्हेउ, *q.v.*

कीनै (from कीना) = कीने = कीन्हे, *q. v.*

कीन्ह (*contraction*) = कीन्हा, *q.v.*

कीन्हा, *m.* (*f.* ī) old form = किया. See न्हा.

कीन्हि ; see (1) कीन्ह (2) कीन्ही.

कीन्ही = किई, *q.v.* See कीन्हा.

कीन्हीं = किईं, *q.v.* See कीन्हे.

कीन्हे, *m.* (*f.* °न्हीं) pl. of कीन्हा = किये, *q.v.*

कीन्हेउ, an old form = (1) किया हुआ (2) किया भी.

कीन्हेसि, an old form = तुमने किया.

कीन्हों, }
कीन्हौं, } कीन्हा, *q.v.*

कीप, *f.* a funnel.

क़ीमत, *f.* price, value, worth.

कीमिया, *m.* chemistry, alchemy. —*k.* to do anything very well, to work miracles.

कीमियागर, *m.* a chemist, alchemist.

कीमियागीरी, *f.* chemistry, alchemy.

कीया, *m.* (*f.* ī) *more prop.* किया, *q.v.*

कीर, *m.* a parrot, a parroquet : flesh : *pr.n.* the country of Kāshmīr.

कीरक, *m.* a parrot, a parroquet : a Buddh : a kind of tree.

कीरत, कीरति ; for words beginning with either of these forms, see under the form कीर्ति.

कीरहा, *more prop.* कीड़हा, *q.v.*

कीरा, 1, *more prop.* कीड़ा, *q.v.* : 2, *m.* (see आ, 22) the people of Kāshmīr.

क़ीरात, *m.* a carat, the twenty-fourth part of an ounce, a weight of four grains ; four barley corns.

कीरिल, *f.* virtue.

कीरी = कीड़ी, dimin. of कीड़ा, *q.v.*

कीर्त, *more prop.* कीर्त्ति, *q.v.*

कीर्त्तन, *m.* mention, report ; speech, words ; a shouting for joy, singing aloud, celebrating, praising ; fame, glory.

कीर्त्तनयोग्य, praiseworthy, laudable.

कीर्त्तना, *f.* = कीर्त्तन, *q. v.*

कीर्त्ति, *f.* fame, renown, glory, any news of a kind that reflects credit rather than discredit on its object : *pr. n.* the mother of Radhā.

कीर्त्तिमान, praised, celebrated, renowned, famous, glorious : hence, *m.* (*f.* matī) a famous person, etc.

कीर्त्तिवन्त }
कीर्त्तिवान } *m.* (*f.* vatī) = कीर्त्तिमान, *q. v.*

कील, *f.* a nail, stake, pin, wedge.

कीलकाँटा, *m.* tools, apparatus.

कीलना, *t.* to charm a snake so as to prevent him from biting.

कीला, *f.* a small nail, tack ; a peg.

कीली, *f.* a key ; a peg ; a screw-nail ; an axis.

कीवंजा, the eye.

कीश, *m.* a monkey, ape : the sun : a bird.

कीस, the membrane which envelopes the fœtus in the womb ; the scrotum ; a purse ; a wrinkle, fold.

कीसा, *m.* a purse.

कीसाबुर, *m.* a cutpurse.

कीसी, a corruption of किसी, *q. v.*

कु, 1, *f.* the earth : 2, an inseparable prefix particle the reverse of सु, denoting depreciation and implying sin, guilt, reproach, contempt, inferiority, diminutiveness : 3, as this particle is prefixable almost *ad lib.* to nouns, many words commencing with it will be found in Hindee literature which it has been deemed superfluous to insert in a Dictionary.

कुअभिलाषा, *f.* evil or illicit desire.

कुअर = (1) कूआर (2) कुमार, *qq.v.*

कुअरि, *more prop.* कुमारी, *q. v.*

कुअवसर, *m.* an unseasonable time, unluckytime.

कुआ, *more properly* कूआ, *q.v.*

कुआर ; see (1) कुमार (2) कूआर.

कुआरा, *more prop.* कुमारा, *q.v.*

कुइच्छा, *f.* evil or inordinate desire, lust.

कुए, *more prop.* कूए ; see कूआ.

कुअंक, *m.* a bad or unfortunate mark.

कुंअर = कुमार, *q. v.*

कुंअरि (*contraction*) = कुमारी, *q. v.*

कुंआर = (1) कूआर (2) कुमार, *qq.v.*

कुंआरी = कुमारी, *q. v.*

कुंकुम, *m.* saffron (*Crocus sativas*).

कुंकुमा, *m.* a vessel in which the red mixture (goolāl) is contained with which Hindoos play at the Holee.

कुंगड़ा, *m.* (*f.* ī) an able-bodied person, etc. : *lit.* robust, able-bodied, athletic, stout.

कुंगड़ाई, *f.* robustness, stoutness, strength.

कुंगलता = कंगालता, *q. v.*

कुंचकी, *f.* a bodice, jacket.

कुंचित, *m.* (*f.* ā) crooked, bent, curved, curled ; perverse.

कुंज, *m.* an arbor, bower, grove ; a cavern : an elephant's tusk, ivory : the lower jaw.

कुंअड़, see (1) **कुंअड़ा** (2) **कुंजर** (3) **कुंजल**.

कुंअड़ा, *m.* (*f.* **कुंजड़न**, **कुंअड़ी**) a green-grocer, fruiterer, a certain caste among Hindoos whose business it is to sell fruits, vegetables, etc.

कुंजन, a Braj pl. of **कौंज**, *q.v.* See **न**, 6.

कुंजर, *m.* an elephant, large elephant (as distinguished from *Kumeṅdhyā*); *pr. n.* (1) of a certain Nāga (2) of a certain prince (3) of a certain mountain.

कुंजल, 1, *more prop.* **कुंजर**, *q.v.*: 2, *m.* sour gruel.

कुंजलगिरि, *m.* = **कुंजरगिरि**. See **कुंजर** (3).

कुंजश्क, *f.* a sparrow.

कुंजाद्दश = **गुंजाद्दश**, *q.v.*

कुंजाल, the green scum formed on stagnant water.

कुंजी, *f.* a key.

कुंट, **कुंठ**, **कुंड**, **कुंत**, **कुंद**, **कुंध**, **कुंब**, **कुंभ**, **कुंह**; for all words beginning with either of these elements, see under the forms **कुण्ट**, **कुण्ठ**, **कुण्ड**, **कुन्त**, **कुन्द**, **कुन्ध**, **कुम्ब**, **कुम्भ**, **कुम्ह**, respectively.

कुंड़बोजी, *f.* the name given by husbandmen to the day on which sowing is concluded.

कुंड़मयडला = **कूंड़बोजी**, *q.v.*

कुंवर = **कुमार**, *q.v.*

कुंवरि = **कुमारी**, *q.v.*

कुंवां = **कूआ**, *q.v.*

कुंवार = (1) **कुमार** (2) **कूआर**, *q.v.*

कुंवारपन = **कुमारपन**, *q.v.*

कुंवारा, *m.* (*f.* ī) = (1) **कुमार** (2) **कूआरा**, *q.v.*

कुंवारी = **कुमारी**, *q.v.*

कुक, a voice; the barking of a dog.

कुकड़ = (1) **कुकड़ा** (2) **कुकुर** (3) **कुक्कुट**, *qq.v.*

कुकड़ा, *m.* (*f.* ī) a male bird, cock.

कुकर, *m.* (*f.* ī) = **कुकुर**, *q.v.*

कुकरा = **कुकड़ा**, *q.v.* [sin, fornication.

कुकर्म्म, *m.* misconduct, evil-doing, villainy, vice,

कुकर्म्मकारी, evil-doing, wicked, sinful: hence, *m.* (*f.* iṇī)) a profligate, malefactor, fornicator, etc.

कुकर्म्मा, *m.* (*f.* ī)
कुकर्म्मी, (*m.* iṇī) } = **कुकर्म्मकारी**, *q.v.*

कुकरौन्दा, *m.* a certain plant (*Celsia*) and its fruit.

कुकामना, *f.* evil inclination, concupiscence.

कुकुर, *m.* (*f.* ī) a dog; *met.* a Kshatriya: *pr. n.* (1) of a certain prince (2) of a certain people.

कुकुरखांसी, *f.* a bad cough (as of a dog barking).

कुकुरमुत्ता, *m.* a mushroom, toadstool.

कुकुरी, *f.* a bitch; *met.* a female Kshatriya.

कुकुरौन्धा, *m.* a certain medicinal grass (*Celsia*).

कुकूणक, *m.* weakness of the eyes in infants.

कुक्कट = **कुक्कुट**, *q.v.*

कुक्कटी = **कुक्कुटी**, *q.v.*

कुक्कुट, *m.* (*f.* ī) a male bird, gallinaceous fowl, cock, wild cock (*Phasianus gallus*): a claw.

कुक्कुटव्रत, *m.* a religious observance (worship of Shiv) held by women on the seventh day of the light half of the month *Bhādoṅ* for the sake of obtaining offspring. [*heptaphyllon*).

कुक्कुटी, *f.* a hen: the silk-cotton tree (*Bombax*

कुक्कुर, *m.* (*f.* ī) a dog; *met.* a Kshatriya: *pr. n.* (1) of a certain sage (2) of a certain people.

कुक्रिया, *f.* any bad action, crime, sin, fornication.

कुकुन्दा
कुकौन्दा } = **कुकुरौन्धा**, *q.v.*

कुकौनीर, *m. pr. n.* a certain Nāg.

कुक्षि, *m.* the abdomen, stomach; a cavity, cavern; a bay: *pr. n.* of a man.

कुख्याति, *f.* evil report, infamy, disrepute.

कुगन्ध, *f.* a bad odour, offensive smell, stink.

कुगो, *m.* an infirm bull.

कुच, 1, *more prop.* **कुछ**, *q.v.*: 2, *m. f.* ? the female breast, a teat, nipple, pap.

कुचकचूआ, *m.* (*f.* °**चूई**) an owl.

कुचन, (a Braj pl. of **कुच**) the bubbies, paps.

कुचना, *more com.* **कूंचना**, *q.v.* [saffron, logwood.

कुचन्दन, *m.* red-sanders (*Pterocarpus santalinus*):

कुचर, 1, *m.* a fixed star: 2, *m.* (*f.* ā *or* ī) a calumniator: *prop.* censorious, detracting.

कुचलना, *t.* to bruise, crush. *Kuchal ḍālnā* or *denā*, (intensive) to bruise, crush; to overlay.

कुचला, *m.* the vomic-nut (*Strychnos nux vomica*).

कुचली, *f.* the canine teeth.

कुचा, *more prop.* **कूचा**, *q.v.*

कुचाग्र, *m.* a nipple.

कुचार, *more prop.* **कुचाल**, *q.v.*

कुचाल, *f.* misconduct, misdemeanour, immorality.

कुचाली, *m.* (*f.* inī) an ill-behaved person: *lit.* ill-behaved, of evil manners, of corrupt conduct.

कुचाह, evil tidings.

कुचिया, *m.* the lobe of the ear.

कुचेल, *m.* (*f.* ā) = **कुचेला**, *q.v.*

कुचेला, 1, *m.* coarse cloth, inferior raiment: 2, *m.* (*f.* ī) ill-clad, dressed in old, tattered or dirty garments.

कुचैन, *m.* unrest, uneasiness, restlessness.

कुचैल, *m.* (*f.* ā)
कुचैला, *m.* (*f.* ī) } **कुचेला**, *q.v.*

कुछ, (gen. **किसू का**) any, some, a little, anything, something, somewhat, whatever, partly. Though this indefinite pronoun is generally applied to inanimate objects, as *ko,ī* is generally applied to animate or rational ones, this rule is not without exceptions; *e. g.* *Kuchh log*. It has various shades of meaning and much that is noteworthy in its idiomatic usages, as the following phrases illustrate: — *aur*, something else, something different, something additional. — *aur gānā*, to give a false explanation, tell a different story. — *iswāste*, partly because, partly on this account. — *ek*, some little, some few. *Kuchh kuchh*, a little, somewhat, more or less. — *tumne parā pāyā*, have you found a treasure? *lit.* have you found anything that has been dropped? (an expression applied to one who seems exceedingly pleased without apparent cause). — *tumne khwāb dekhā*, what! have you seen something in a dream? what! have you dreamt this? (an expression used to a person who relates improbabilities.

it is also used to express the astonishment of the speaker at any unexpected act of another's.) — *se* —, from one state to another, from this to that. — *se* — *honā*, to be entirely changed. — *isse* — *usse*, what with this and what with that. — *kā* —, something besides, in a different manner, on the contrary; progression, advancement. — *na* — (gen. *kisā na kiskā*, *ke*, *kī*) some at least, something or other. — *nahīn*, nothing, it is nothing, there is nothing; e. g. *Yih kuchh bāt nahīn*, this is nothing, there is nothing in this, this is neither here nor there, this is of no importance, this is not to the point. — *ho*, come what may, whatever may happen. *Bahut* —, a great deal. *Sab* —, everything, the whole. *Jo* —, whatever. *Jo* — *thoṛā*, whatever little. *Aur* —, something else, something different, something additional. *Har* —, everything, the whole. — *dinse*, for some days. — *thoṛā*, a little. — *bimār*, a trifle poorly, somewhat unwell. — *achchhā*, a trifle better.

कुछु (*very unusual*) = (1) **कुछ**, (2) **कुछ भी**.

कुछेक, some few, some little.

कुज, *m. pr. n.* the planet Mars; Tuesday.

कुजननी, *f.* a bad mother.

कुजना, *a. int.* to wear out, decay: *n.* to be putrescent, be rotten.

कुञ्जलीबन, *m.* a forest frequented by elephants.

कुत्रा, where? whither? how? *Har* —, every where.

कुजात, *m.* (*f.* ā) low-born, of low extraction, of mean origin, of bad caste, one who has lost his caste.

कुजाति, 1, *m.* or *f.* = **कुजात**, *q.v.*: 2, *f.* meanness of origin or birth, low extraction.

कुजाना, *t.* to cause to rot; to waste.

कुजोग, } **कुजोगी**, } = **कुयोगी**, *q. v.*

कुट, *m.* a certain medicine (*Costus arabicus*).

कुटकी, *f.* a gnat: a certain medicine: estrangement from or desertion of friends.

कुटकुट, *m.* a nibbling, itching, scratching.

कुटज, *m.* a certain plant (*Echites antidysenterica*) whose seeds are used as a vermifuge.

कुटना, *m.* (*f.* ī.) a pimp, pander, mischiefmaker.

कुटनाई, *f.* (see **आई**, 3) the wages of a pimp.

कुटनाना, *t.* seduce, entice, inveigle, wheedle, coax.

कुटनापा, *m.* pimping.

कुटनी, *f.* (*m.* **कुटना**) a bawd, procuress, go-between.

कुटबट, *m.* a certain plant (*Bignonia Indica*).

कुटम; for words beginning thus, see under the form **कुटुम्ब**.

कुटमस्ता, *m.* (*f.* ī) an able-bodied person: *lit.* strong-bodied, very powerful, lusty.

कुटाया, *m.* the plant *Solanum jacquini* (Willd.).

कुटार, *m.* an impatient little horse.

कुटासख़्त, *m.* a very dog.

कुटिर, *m.* a small house, cottage, hut, hovel.

कुटिल, *m.* (*f.* ā) a cruel person, etc.: *lit.* crooked, bent, perverse, disingenuous; cruel, ruthless.

कुटिलत्व, *m.* (*f.* tā) crookedness, perversity, dishonesty, disingenuousness, guile, ruthlessness, cruelty.

कुटी, *f.* } **कुटीर**, *m.* } **कुटिर**, *q. v.*

कुटुम, for words beginning thus, see under the form **कुटुम्ब**.

कुटुम्ब, *m.* kith and kin, relatives, kinsfolk, household, family, progeny, race.

कुटुम्बिन, *m.* (*f.* ī) a householder, paterfamilias, kinsman: *lit.* appertaining to the *Kuṭumb*.

कुटुम्बी, *m.* (*f.* inī) = **कुटुम्बिन**, *q. v.*

कुटुर, the sound of hard food (such as grain) being ground between the teeth, a crunching, munching.

कुटेरा; see **कुटिर**.

कुटेव, *f.* a bad habit.

कुट्टनी, *f.* a bawd, procuress, go-between.

कुट्टार, *m.* copulation: oneness: exclusion: a mountain.

कुट्टिनी, *f.* a bawd, procuress, go-between.

कुठर, *m.* the post around which the string of the churningstick winds.

कुठाकु, *m.* the woodpecker.

कुठार, *m.* an axe, a sort of hoe: a tree.

कुठारी, *f.* (dim. of **कुठार**,) a small axe: a crucible, earthen vase for melting gold, silver, etc.

कुठाली = **कुठारी**, *q. v.*

कुठाहर, a low place.

कुठौर, 1, a wrong place; 2, misplaced.

कुड़कना, *a. int.* to speak angrily, grumble, murmur; to cluck (as a laying hen).

कुड़कुड़ाना = **कुड़कना**, *q. v.*

कुड़ता *m.* a coat, jacket.

कुड़ती, *f.* any drinking-vessel for animals.

कुड़ना = **कुढ़ना**, *q. v.*

कुड़मा, *m.* a tribe, caste, family, race.

कुड़ापन, } **कुड़ापा**, } = **कुढ़ापन**, *q. v.*

कुड़ुक, 1, *f.* a clucking: 2, *adj.* clucking.

कुडुमस्बोदी, *f.* incest.

कुडौल, ill-shaped, ugly.

कुढंग, *m.* (*f.* ā) an ill-bred person, etc.: *lit.* ill-bred, unmannerly, rude.

कुढंगी, *f.* ill-breeding, boorishness, rudeness.

कुढ़क } **कुढ़न** } *f.* grief, sorrow, lamentation.

कुढ़ना, *a. int.* to grieve, mourn, lament, pine, repine: *n.* to be afflicted, be angry, be disgusted.

कुढब, ill-shaped, ugly; ill-mannered, rude.

कुढ़ाना, *t.* to vex, afflict, grieve, trouble, anger.

कुढ़ापन, } **कुढ़ापा**, } *m.* vexation, grief, pain, affliction.

कुणबा, *m.* tribe, caste, family, brotherhood.

कुणिठस, *m.* (*f.* ā) ashamed.

कुण्ड, *m.* an abyss; a pit for sacrifice; a hole in the ground for receiving and preserving consecrated fire: a pool, spring, well; a water-jar, water-pot, pitcher, a basin of water especially consecrated to some holy purpose or person: a vessel for holding coals: a son of an adulteress born before the death of the husband: *pr. n.* (1) of Shiv (2) of a certain Naga.

कुण्डल, *m.* a large ring worn in the ears; a circle; a halo around the sun or moon. — *mārnā.* to form a coil.

कुण्डलिया, *m.* a species of stanza in Hindee poetry which is so constructed as to end invariably with the same word or phrase with which it began: it is hence compared to a circle or to the coil of a snake, the opposite ends of which unite.

कुण्डली, circular, spiral, winding, coiling; wearing earrings or bracelets: hence (1) *m.* (*f.* inī) one who wears earrings or bracelets; a snake, serpent; a peacock; the spotted deer: (2) *m.* an epithet of Varun: (3) *f. m* ? a coil, curl, hoop, ring, earring, bracelet. — *banānā*, to curl.

कुण्डा, *f.* an epithet of Durgā.

कुण्डाला, *m.* a large flat vessel in which bottles of drinks are cooled with ice or saltpetre: an earthenware pan in which clothes are washed.

कुण्डिनपुर, *m. pr. n.* the capital of the district of Vidarbh. Identical with the modern Kondavir in Berar.

कुण्डी, 1, *f.* = **कुण्ड**, *q. v.*: 2, *f.* a hasp, staple, chain or any iron catch to fasten a door: 3, *m.* (*f.* inī) one who carries a water-pot; a horse: lit. *adj.* carrying a [water-pot.

कुतक, *more prop.* **कूतक**, *q. v.*

कुतका, *m.* a short stick with which *bhang* is ground.

कुत्न, cotton.

कुतप, *m.* the eighth hour or portion of the day, about noon: a blanket made of the hair of the mountain goat.

कुतब, *m.* the north pole; an axis.

कुतरका, *f.* illogical reasoning.

कुतरन, *m.* that which is gnawed or bitten off by the teeth.

कुतरना, *t.* to gnaw, cut with the teeth.

कुतरू, *m.* a cutter, biter: a puppy: lit. *adj.* cutting, biting.

कुतर्क, *m.* wrong reasoning; a false doctrine: insignificance in judgment or in discernment.

कुतवाल, *more prop.* **कोतवाल**, *q. v.*

कुतापस, *m.* (*f.* ī) a wicked ascetic.

कुतिया, *more prop.* **कुत्तिया**, *q. v.*

कुतुप, *more prop.* **कुतप**, *q. v.*

कुतुब, *f.* (pl. of **किताब**) books.

कुतुबख़ाना, *m.* a repository for books, library.

कुतूणक, *m.* weakness of the eyes in infants.

कुतूहल, *m.* (*f.* ?) eagerness, desire, curiosity; a surprising object, shew, spectacle, entertainment, pastime, festivity, sport.

कुतूहली, *m.* (*f.* inī) an inquisitive person, etc.: *lit.* eager, inquisitive; fond of sport, sportive.

कुत्ता, *m.* (*f.* ī) a dog: the scear of a gunlock, the part which is acted upon by the trigger; a hand-vice.

कुत्तामूता, a toadstool, fungus.

कुत्तिया, *f.* (dim. of **कुत्ती**) a young bitch, small bitch.

कुत्ती, *f.* (*m.* **कुत्ता**) a bitch.

कुत्र, where? whither?

कुत्रापि, wherever, anywhere, somewhere or other.

कुत्सा, *f.* reproach, censure, calumny, contempt.

कुत्सित, *m.* (*f.* ā) a vile person, etc.: *lit.* low, vile, despicable, contemptible; calumniated, reviled, contemned, censured.

कुत्सिताचरण, *m.* bad conduct, low behaviour.

कुत्सितभाषण, *m.* low language; slander.

कुदकना, *a. int.* to frisk, leap, bound, caper, hop, jump, skip.

कुदम, side, direction; *adv.* towards.

कुदमा, *m.* (pl. of **क़दमी**) the ancients.

कुदरत, *f.* authority, power; omnipotence.

कुदरा, a colloquial form of **कुद्दाल**, 2, *q. v.*

कुदराना = **कुदकना**, *q. v.*

कुदवाना, *t.* to cause to dandle, cause to be dandled.

कुदशा, *f.* a bad state, low condition, evil plight.

कुदस, *m.* holiness, sanctity: Jerusalem: the angel Gabriel: *adj.* holy, pure.

कुदाना, *t.* to dandle; to cause to leap: *met.* to provoke.

कुदाया, *m.* a kind of dove.

कुदार, **कुदाल** — colloquial forms of **कुद्दाल**, *q. v.*

कुदारी, dim. of **कुदार**; **कुदाली**, dim. of **कुदाल** — *f.* a dibble.

कुदूम, *m.* an arriving, a coming near.

कुद्दल, *m.* mountain ebony (*Bauhinia variegata*).

कुद्दाल, 1, = **कुद्दल**, *q. v.*: 2, *m.* a pickaxe, mattock, spade, hoe.

कुद्दूस, pure, holy, blessed: *hence*, an epithet of the Supreme Being.

कुद्दूसीयत, *f.* extreme purity or sanctity.

कुदृष्टि, *f.* weak sight, defective vision; the evil eye; a false system; an ill intended look, lascivious glance.

कुधन, side, direction: *adv.* towards.

कुधर, *m.* a mountain.

कुधातु, *m.* iron.

कुधी, *m.* (*f.* inī) a fool.

कुनख, *m.* a disease of the nails.

कुनखी, *m.* (*f.* inī) a person who has diseased nails: lit. *adj.* having diseased nails.

कुनबा, *m.* a tribe, caste, family, brotherhood.

कुनामी, *m.* (*f.* inī) a person of ill repute, etc.: *lit.* disreputable, disgraceful, infamous.

कुनीति, *f.* misconduct: misgovernment: bad policy.

कुनूत, *f.* devotion, obedience to God, perseverence in prayer, supplication.

कुन्त, *m.* a lance, bearded dart, spear: *pr. n.* a certain country.

कुन्तल, *m.* hair: *pr. n.* a certain people.

कुन्ति, *m. pr. n.* (1) of a certain man (2) of a certain people (3) of their king.

कुन्तिभोज, *m. pr. n.* the king of the Kuntis.

कुन्ती, *f.* 1, = **कुन्त**, *q. v.*: 2, *pr. n.* a wife of *Pāṇḍu* and the mother of the five *Pāṇḍava* princes by as many gods.

कुन्द, 1, blunt, obtuse, slow: 2, *m.* a kind of jasmine (*Jasminum grandiflorum* or *multiflorum* or *pubescens*): *pr. n.* (1) of Vishṇu (2) of a certain mountain.

कुन्दड़ा = **कुन्दरा**, *q. v.*

कुन्दन, *m.* 1, very fine gold: 2, a digging, digging up, extirpating; engraving.

कुन्दनकूट, *m.* a certain medicine (*Olibanum*).

कुन्दर, *m.* a kind of sweet-smelling gum (*Gum olibanum* or frankincense).

कुन्दरकूट, *m.* a certain medicine (*Olibanum*).

कुन्दरा, *m.* a stack, rick.

कुन्दन, *m.* the finest gold.

कुन्दला, *m.* a kind of tent.

कुन्दा, *m.* 1, the shoulder: 2, a mark, butt, block; the stock of a gun; a billet of wood.

कुन्दी, *f.* 1, obtuseness, stupidity: 2, the act of calendering (cloth). — *k.* to calender (cloth); to beat,

कुन्दीगर, *m.* a calenderer. [cudgel.

कुन्दुरु, *f.* the resin of the *Boswelia thurifera*, *Gum olibanum* or frankincense.

कुन्ह, 1, *m.* rancour, malice, spite: 2, *f.* substance; essence; quantity; time; mode or reason of a

कुप, *more prop.* कूप, *q. v.* [thing; end, extreme.

कुपथ, *m.* (*lit.* a bad road, the wrong way whether physically or morally, a road or a habit or manner that is bad or that ends badly; *hence*) deviation aberration, immorality; heresy, heterodoxy.

कुपथगामी, *m.* (*f.* inī) a heretic, etc.: *lit.* going in a bad or wrong road; immoral; heterodox.

कुपथ्य, *m.* (*f.* ā) unwholesome diet: *adj.* unfit,

कुपन्थ = कुपथ, *q. v.* [unwholesome, hurtful.

कुपन्थी, *m.* (*f.* inī) a wanderer; an immoral person; a heretic: *lit.* appertaining to a wrong or a bad way.

कुपरामर्श, *m.* bad counsel, ill advice.

कुपात्र, (*f.* ī) an unsuitable person, etc.: *lit.* unworthy, unfit, incapable. [incensed, angry, offended.

कुपित, *m.* (*f.* ā) an offended person, etc.: *lit.*

कुपुत्र, *m.* (*f.* ī) a bad, degenerate, villainous, or unfi-

कुपुरुष, *m.* a vile man, coward, poltroon. [lial son.

कुपूत = कुपुत्र, *q. v.*

कुपेच, badly-turned, deformed, ugly.

कुप्पा, *m.* a large leathern vessel for holding oil, ghee, etc. — *honā*, to become very fat.

कुप्पालुढ़ना, the disease of a king, etc.

कुप्पी, *f.* (dim. of कुप्पा) a leathern bottle, phial.

कुफ़्र, *m.* paganism, infidelity, unbelief, blasphemy, ingratitude. — *baknā*, to talk blasphemy.

कुफ़्ल, *m.* a lock, bolt.

कुब, *m*, a hump on the back.

कुबचन = कुवचन, *q. v.*

कुबज, *m.* (*f.* ā) = कुब्ज, *q. v.*

कुबड़, *m.* a hump on the back.

कुबड़ा, *m.* (*f.* ī) humpbacked, crooked, deformed.

कुबल, 1, difficult, severe: 2, *m.* the jujube-tree (*Ziziphus jujuba*): a water-lily: a pearl.

कुबलय; for words beginning thus, see under the

कुबलया, *more prop.* कुवलय, *q. v.* [form कुवलय.

कुबिचार; for words beginning thus, see under the form कुविचार.

कुबिसन, *m.* bad conduct: *adj.* of bad conduct.

कुबिहग, *m.* a certain bird.

कुबुद्धि, 1, *f.* depravity of mind: 2, depraved.

कुबेर, *more prop.* कुवेर, *q. v.*

कुबेरहु in Braj = कुवेर भी. See हु.

कुबेष, *m.* a term applied to the appearance of ascetics, etc. who mutilate their bodies, or who wear snakes or the skins of brutes, etc.

कुब्ज, *m.* (*f.* ā) humpbacked, crooked, deformed.

कुब्ब, *m.* a hump on the back.

कुब्बा, *m.* (*f.* in *or* ī) = कुब्ज, *q. v.*

कुभाग, *m.* ill-fortune, misfortune, bad luck.

कुभागी, *m.* (*f.* inī) an unfortunate person: *lit.* subject to misfortune, ill-starred, unfortunate.

कुभाड, कुभाण्ड, } *more prop.* कुम्भाण्ड, *q. v.*

कुभार्या, *f.* a bad wife, a wicked wife.

कुभाव, *m.* badness of disposition, ill temper; ill

कुभेष = कुबेष, *q. v.* [treatment.

कुमक, *f.* aid, assistance.

कुमकुम, *m.* saffron.

कुमकुमा, 1, *m.* saffron: 2, *m.* (*f.* ī) lukewarm.

कुमकुमाट, *f.* lukewarmness.

कुमत (*contraction*) = कुमति, *q. v.*

कुमता, *f.* erroneous or dangerous opinions (*esp.* on religious topics), heterodoxy, heresy.

कुमति, 1, *f.* a weak mind; perversity, error, indiscretion, folly, stupidity: 2, weakminded, stupid, foolish, injudicious, indiscreet; wicked, vicious.

कुमद, *more prop.* कुमुद, *q. v.*

कुमदिन, *more prop.* कुमुदिनी, *q. v.*

कुमन्त्रणा, *f.* (*m.*?) evil advice, bad counsel, intrigue.

कुमलाना, कुमह्लाई, } see under the form कुम्ह.

कुमाच, *m.* a kind of unleavened bread, a loaf or roll of unleavened bread.

कुमाचसा मुंह, *m.* a broad face, jolly moonlike countenance. [(the reverse of 'to pet').

कुमाया, *f.* anger. — *k.* to be angry with, rebuff

कुमार, *m.* (*f.* ī) an unmarried youth, son, lad, boy, child, son of a rājā, prince: *pr. n.* (1) of Skand, the god of war (2) of a certain people.

कुमारक, *m.* (*f.* ikī) = कुमार, *q. v.*

कुमारपन, *m.* the time or the condition of youth, youthfulness, youth.

कुमारी, *f.* a girl arrived at marriageable age, maiden, virgin, damsel, lass, maid, daughter, daughter of

कुमारिका = कुमारी, *q. v.* [a rājā, princess.

कुमारीकन्या, *f.* (= कुमारी, *q. v.*) an unmarried damsel.

कुमारीहत्या, *f.* the murder of a virgin.

कुमार्ग = कुपथ, *q. v.* [an ugly face.

कुमुख, *m.* (*f.* ī) an epithet of the hog: *lit.* having

कुमुद, *m.* the white esculent water-lily or lotus (*Nymphæa esculenta*) which expands its petals by night and closes them by day: *pr. n.* (1) of a celestial being (2) of a man (3) of a monkey (4) of a Nāga (5) of a mountain.

कुमुदबन्धु, *m.* an epithet of the moon.

कुमुदिनी, *f.* a group of lotus-flowers; a place abounding in lotuses.

कुमेंढ़ीया, *m.* a small kind of elephant.

कुमेंढ़िया
कुमेंयडया
कुमेंयढया
कुमेंयिढया } = **कुमेंढ़िया**, *q. v.*

कुमेरु, *m.* the southern hemisphere; the south pole (the region of demons and Titans).

कुमोदक, *m.* an epithet of Vishṇu or Kṛishṇ.

कुम्बट, agricultural labour, farming. [form **कुमार**.

कुम्बर; for all words beginning thus, see under the

कुम्बा, *m.* a tribe, caste, family, fraternity.

कुम्बी, *m.* (*f.* inī) a peasant, cultivator of the soil, a tribe of husbandmen.

कुम्भ, *m.* a pot, waterpot; an elephant's head; the paramour of a harlot; a measure of grain equal to twenty *droṇas*: *pr. n.* (1) of a *rākshas* (2) of a *dānav* (3) of the sign Aquarius. *Kumbhkā melā*, the twelfth-year fair of the Hindoo fakeers held at Hardwār and at Allahabad; — so called because the sun is then in Aquarius.

कुम्भक, *m.* a certain religious exercise consisting of the closing the mouth and nostrils so as to suspend breathing.

कुम्भकर्ण, *m.* an epithet of one of the younger brothers of Rāvaṇ; *lit.* having ears like a waterpot.

कुम्भकामला, *f.* a certain bilious affection, sort of

कुम्भकार, *m.* (*f.* ikā *or* in) a potter. [jaundice.

कुम्भज, *m.* (*f.* ā) an epithet of **अगस्त्य**, *q. v.*; *lit.* born in a waterpot.

कुम्भनी, *f.* (dim. of **कुम्भ**) the sixth-year fair; *lit.* the lesser *kumbh*: called also *Arddhkumbh.*

कुम्भला, *f.* a certain plant the flowers of which are compared to those of the *Nauclea cadamba.* [Vāṇ.

कुम्भाण्ड, *m. pr. n.* the minister of the demon-king

कुम्भाण्डा, *m.* (see **भा**, 22) a certain class of demons with testicles shaped like a *kumbh.*

कुम्भिका, *f.* (dimin. of **कुम्भ**) a small pot: a certain disease of the eyes, a stye.

कुम्भिलाना, *a. int.* to wither, fade, pine, droop, take blight, become blasted, dry up: *n.* to be dispirited, be dejected.

कुम्भिलानी, *f.* a fading, withering, taking blight.

कुम्भी, *f.* a small jar or pot; a small vessel for preserving grain in; a measure of grain equal to twenty *droṇas.*

कुम्भीपाक, *m. pr. n.* a hell in which the wicked are supposed to be baked like potter's vessels.

कुम्भीर, *m.* the crocodile of the Ganges, the long-

कुम्भेर; see **कुम्भीर**. [nosed alligator.

कुम्मार; see (1) **कुमार** (2) **कुम्हार**.

कुम्मैत, *m.* the bay colour in horses.

कुम्वर, *more prop.* **कुमार**, *q. v.*

कुम्वारि, *more prop.* **कुमारी**, *q v.*

कुम्वां, *more prop.* **कूआ**, *q. v.* [the form **कुमार**.

कुम्वार; for all words beginning thus, see under

कुम्हल; see (1) **कुम्भला** (2) **कुम्हलाई** (3) **कूम्हल**.

कुम्हलाई, *f.* a fading, withering, taking blight.

कुम्हलाना = **कुम्भिलाना**, *q. v.* [vessels, potter.

कुम्हार, *m.* (*f.* in *or* nī) a manufacturer of earthen

कुम्हारी, *f.* a creature like a wasp which builds

कुम्हिलाना = **कुम्भिलाना**, *q. v.* [its house of clay.

कुम्हीर, *more prop.* **कुम्भीर**, *q. v.*

कुया, *more prop.* **कूआ**, *q. v.*

कुयें, *more prop.* **कूए**, *q. v.* [ture or of injury.

कुयन्त्र, *m.* any instrument for the infliction of tor-

कुयश, *m.* a bad reputation, evil name, disrepute.

कुयोगी, *m.* (*f.* inī) a bad or wicked yogee, false devotee; a magician, juggler.

कुर; some words which may be spelt in this way will be found under the form **कुं**.

कुरआन, *m. pr. n.* the book containing the precepts and the theology of the Muhammadan faith. —*uṭhānā* or — *par hāth dharnā*, to take one's oath.

कुरंग, *m.* (*f.* ī) a species of deer.

कुरकुरी, *f.* belly-fretting, gripes in a horse. [*dum*).

कुरण्ड, *m.* corundum-stone (*Adamantinus corun-*

कुरतनी, *f.* (a dim. of **कुरता**) = **कुरती**, *q. v.* [shirt.

कुरता, *m.* a large tunic, upper garment, coat, frock,

कुरती, *f.* (dim. of **कुरता**) a jacket, short jacket, soldier's jacket, woman's jacket, kind of shirt.

कुरथी, *f.* a kind of vetch (*Dolichos biflorus*).

कुरर, *m.* (*f.* ī) an osprey: *pr. n.* a mountain.

कुरस, 1, *m.* badness of juice, badness of flavor; spirituous or vinous liquors: 2, *m.* (*f.* ā) of bad juice, of bad essence, of bad flavor.

कुरसत, *m.* a kind of coarse sugar.

कुरसी, *f.* a chair, stool, seat, throne: *pr. n.* (1) of the eighth heaven (2 of the throne of God (3) of a place within about fourteen miles of Lucknow the inhabitants of which are said to be foolish or mad.

कुरसीका, *m.* (*f.* ī) an inhabitant of Kursee. —*hai*, he (or she) is mad or foolish. This is precisely what the ancient Greeks used to say in reference to Thracian Abdera and its inhabitants.

कुरसीनशीन, established in office, enthroned.

कुरसीनामा, *m.* a genealogical tree.

कुरह, a circular enclosure.

कुराई, *f.* stocks for imprisoning the feet.

कुरान, *more prop.* **कुरआन**, *q. v.*

कुराह, *f.* = **कुपथ**, *q. v.*

कुरिया, *f.* (not infl.) a lady, proprietress.

कुरियारूपी, in the manner of a lady, lady-like.

कुरी, 1, see (1) **कुर्री** (2) **कूरी** (3) **कोरी**; 2, *f.* a kind of grass or corn.

कुरीति, *f.* misconduct, bad manners.

कुरु, *m. pr. n.* (1) of a people (2) of their progenitor (3) of an ancient sovereign of Delhi and of the surrounding country (4) of the territory governed by him (5) of the most northerly of the four Mahādweeps or principal divisions of the known world, called also *Uttar Kuru*. By other systems it is considered one of the nine divisions (*Varsha*) of the known world: in each case however, it is the country beyond the northernmost range of mountains extending to the frozen ocean.

कुरुक्षेत्र, *m. pr. n.* (1) of the country near Delhi where the great battle was fought between the Kauravas and the Pāṇdavas (2) *pl.* the inhabitants of that country.

कुरुचि, *f.* depraved appetite, low desire; disgust, [dislike.

कुरुक्षेत्र = **कुरुक्षेत्र**, *q.v.*

कुरुज, the moulting of fowls.

कुरुल, *m.* a curl or lock of hair (esp. on the forehead).

कुरुवंश, *m.* the race of *Kuru*.

कुरुवंशी, *m.* (*f.* inī) a person who belongs to the [race of *Kuru*.

कुरुवक, *m.* the crimson amaranth; a purple species of Barleria, also a yellow kind: the flower of these plants.

कुरुविन्द, *m.* a fragrant grass (*Cyperus rotundus*); the name of several plants; a kind of barley: a ruby.

कुरुविल्ल / **कुरुविल्व** } *m.* a ruby.

कुरू = **कुरु** (3), *q.v.*

कुरूप, 1, *m.* (*f.* ā) ugly, deformed, misshapen, unsightly: 2, *m.* malformation, deformity, ugliness.

कुरूपता, *f.* / **कुरूपत्व**, *m.* } = **कुरूप**, 2, *q. v.*

कुरूपा, *f.* an unpresentable female, an ugly woman.

कुरूपी, *m.* (*f.* iṇī) = **कुरूप**, 1, *q.v.*

कुरेलना, *t.* to poke, thrust.

कुरेलनी, see (1) **करेलनी** (2) **कुरेलना**.

कुर् ; some words beginning thus are sometimes [printed **कुर**.

कुर्कुट, *f.* sweepings, rubbish.

कुर्कुरी, *f.* belly-fretting, gripes in a horse.

कुर्छाल, *f.* a bound, leap, jump.

कुर्ता / **कुर्था** } see **कुरता**.

कुर्ब, *m.* proximity; kindred, relationship.

कुर्बान, *m. f.* ? a sacrifice, victim offered in sacrifice, oblation: a quiver. — *k.* to offer up in sacrifice.

कुर्बानी, 1, *f.* = **कुर्बान** : 2, sacrificed.

कुर्ब्बा, 1, *m.* (*f.* ī) a hunchback: *lit.* humpbacked: 2, a kind of sheep that has much wool.

कुर्म, *m. pr. n.* (see **अवतार**) a name of the second incarnation of Vishṇu; *lit.* a tortoise, turtle.

कुर्मपुराण, *m. pr. n.* the Hindoo Purāṇ which contains the history of the second incarnation of Vishṇu.

कुर्मभूमि, *f.* / **कुर्माचल**, *m.* } = **कर्मभूमि**, *q.v.* (?).

कुर्मी, *m.* (also spelt **कुम्बी**) a certain tribe of husbandmen.

कुर्मुक, *m. pr. n.* a certain ancient Hindoo sage (disciple of Bhiṇḍi-Rishi).

कुर्याल, *m.* the state of a bird sitting at ease and in serenity, trimming its wings with its beak; *hence* ease, security, hope, confidence of success. — *meṅ ghulelā lagnā*, to be disappointed, to fall into misfortune at the moment of security or when sure of success.

कुर्री, *f.* cartilage, gristle.

कुर्सल, *m.* a kind of coarse sugar.

कुल, *m.* a herd, flock, multitude; a caste, family, house, pedigree, race, relations; noble lineage: a grange holding as much land as can be tilled by two ploughs each drawn by six bulls.

कुलउजागर, *m.* = **कुलाधीश**, *q.v.*

कुलंग, *m.* any fowl of a large breed, a crane, heron.

कुलंज, *m.* a horse that cuts behind in walking.

कुलंजन, *m.* a certain plant (*Alpinia galanga* or *Galanga major*); a certain seed (*Nigella sativa*).

कुलका, *m.* (*f.* ī) appertaining to a caste or family.

कुलकुला, *m.* a gargling: a kind of hukka.

कुलक्ष = **कुलक्षण**, 1, *q. v.*

कुलक्षण, 1, *m.* an evil omen; ugly visage; bad temper; misconduct: 2, *m.* (*f.* ā) of evil omen; ugly; ill-tempered.

कुलक्षणा, *f.* (**कुलक्षण**, 2,) a female of an evil dis-[position.

कुलगारी, *f.* the abuse of one's own family or tribe.

कुलचा, *m.* capital, principal, stock-in-trade.

कुलच्छण = **कुलक्षण**, *q. v.*

कुलजुम, *m.* a sea; the Red Sea, Arabian Gulf.

कुलटा, *f.* an unchaste woman, prostitute, woman by whom the family honor is injured.

कुलटी, *f.* red arsenic.

कुलतारण, *m.* a youth who is a credit to his family, the saviour of his family or tribe.

कुलत्तन, evil, bad, wicked.

कुलत्था, *f.* a certain blue stone used in medicine (applied as a collyrium to the eyes and as an astringent to sores).

कुलथी, *f.* Madras horse-gram (*Dolichos biflorus*).

कुलदेवता, *m. f.* a principal deity; an epithet of Durgā.

कुलदेवी, *f.* the family goddess, any female deity worshipped in particular by a family through successive generations.

कुलद्रुह = **कुलद्रोही**, *q. v.*

कुलद्रोही, *m.* (*f.* inī) one who brings disgrace or injury on his own family.

कुलधर्म, *m.* observance peculiar to a caste, tribe, or family; the duty of caste or of race.

कुलनाश, *m.* a camel; an outcaste, reprobate.

कुलनायक, *m.* (*f.* ikā) = **कुलपति**, *q. v.*

कुलनायिका, *f.* a girl worshipped at the the celebration of the orgies of the left-hand Shāktas.

कुलपति, *m.* (*f.* patnī) the head or chief of a family or race, a patriarch.

कुलपरिवार, *m.* friends and relatives of the same tribe or caste, kith and kin, family connexions.

कुलपालक, *m.* (*f.* ikā) one who nourishes or provides for a family.

कुलपालि, *f.* a chaste woman.

कुलपूज्य, *m.* the object of worship or reverence in a family, a household god: a family priest.

कुलफुल, *f.* trouble, vexation, distress.

कुलवधू, *f.* a virtuous woman of a noble family.

कुलेरा, *m.* a house, cottage, hut, closet.

कुलबुला, *m.* (*f.* ī) vermicular, peristaltic.

कुलबुलाना, *a. int.* to itch; to fidget, writhe (as a worm or snake); to rumble, grumble (as the bowels).

कुलबुलाहट, *f.* peristaltic or vermicular motion.

कुलबोड़, *m.* (*f.* ā) one who disgraces his family.

कुलबोड़क, *m.* (*f.* ikā) = **कुलबोड़**, *q.v.*

कुलबोड़ना, *t.* to disgrace one's own family.

कुलमा, *m.* a sausage.

कुलला, *m. f.* a cap, hat, bonnet, cowl, tiara, crown.

कुलवत / **कुलवन्त** } *m.* (*f.* vatī) = **कलवान**, *q. v.*

कुलवान, *m.* (*f.* vatī) a person of good family: *lit.* well born, of gentle blood, of noble descent, genteel, pure, chaste.

कुलवन्ती, *f.* (*prop.* **कुलवती**?) a gentlewoman.

कुलह = **कलाह**, *q.v.*

कुलहड़, *m.* a kind of firework.

कुलहड़ा, *m.* a kind of cup or earthen vessel larger [than a *kulhiyā*, *q.v.*

कुलहाड़ी / **कुलहारी** } = **कुल्हाड़ी**, *q. v.*

कुलहिया *f.* a cup, small round vessel. —— *meṅ gooṛ phornā*, to endeavour to do with a few hands a work which requires many; *lit.* to break sugar into a small cup. — *lagānā*, to cup. [*mārnā*, to bound, skip.

कुलांच, *f.* a bound, spring, leap, jump, bounce. ——

कुलाचार, *m.* = **कुलधर्म्म**, *q. v.*

कुलार्णव, *m.* an epithet of any one (*e. g.* Rām; Christ, of the tribe of Judah, etc.) who occasions the [celebrity of his family or tribe.

कुलाल, *m.* a potter.

कुलावन्त *m.* (*f.* vatī) = **कुलवन्त**, *q.v.*

कुलाह, *m. f.* a hat, cap, bonnet, cowl, tiara, crown.

कुलाहल, 1, = **कोलाहल**, *q.v.* : 2, *m.* a certain plant (*Coryza Terebinthina* or *Celsia Coromandelina*) which dogs are fond of smelling before they eject urine.

कुल्लि, 1, all, the whole: 2, *m.* the hand.

कुलिंग, *m.* a kind of mouse; the fork-tailed shrike: *pr. n.* a certain man.

कुलिंज; see (1) **कलंज** (2) **कुलंज** (3) **कुलिंग** (4) **कुलिज**.

कुलिज, *m.* (in Pros.) a species of metre.

कुलिश, *m.* an axe; the thunderbolt of Indra.

कुलिस, *more prop.* **कुलिश**, *q.v.*

कुली, *more com* **कूली**, *q.v.*

कुलीञ्जन, *m.* a certain drug (the root of *Piper betel*).

कुलीन, of noble descent, well-born, of gentle blood: hence, *m.* (*f.* ā) a nobleman.

कुलीनता, *f.* / **कुलीनत्व**, *m.* / **कुलीनाई**, *f.* } nobility of descent, gentility.

कुलीना, 1, *f.* (*m.* **कुलीन**) a gentlewoman: (in Pros.) a species of metre: 2. *m.* a kind of pickle.

कुल्ल, *m.* totality, sum, amount: *adj.* all, the whole, universal.

कुल्ला, (1) *m. f.* = **कुलाह** (2) *m.* = **कुल्ली**, 1, *qq.v.*

कुल्ली, 1, *f.* a gargling, rinsing or washing the mouth: 2, *f.* sum total, the whole: 3, *adj.* universal, total, all, every.

कुल्लूक, *m. pr. n.* a celebrated scholiast on Manu.

कुल्हाड़ा, *m.* an axe, hatchet.

कुल्हाड़ी, *f.* an axe, hatchet; a species of land [tenure.

कुवच, abusive, censorious, detracting.

कुवचन, *m.* abuse, depreciative talk, low language.

कुवर, 1, see **कुबड़** and **कुवेर**: 2, *m.* (*f.* ā) astringent in flavour.

कुवलय, *m.* a water-lily: the terrestrial globe: *pr. n.* [the horse of *Kuvalayāshwa*.

कुवलयपुर, *m. pr. n.* a certain town.

कुवलयादित्य, *m. pr. n.* a certain ancient Hindoo prince.

कुवलयानन्द, *m.* a certain treatise on Rhetoric by [Apyadīkshit.

कुवलयापीड़, *m. pr. n.* 1, = **कुवलयादित्य**, *q.v*: 2, a certain demon who (changed into an elephant) became the vehicle of Kaṅs.

कुवलयावली, *f pr. n.* a certain princess.

कुवलयाश्व, *m. pr. n.* of two ancient Hindoo princes, *viz.* (1) Dhundhumār (2) Pratardan.

कुवलयाश्वक, *m. pr. n.* the prince Dhundhumār.

कुवा / **कुवां** } = **कूआ**, *q. v.*

कुवाक्य, *m.* abuse, evil-speaking, calumny.

कुवाचक, *m.* (*f.* ikā) a person who uses filthy or abusive language, a calumniator.

कुविचार, *m.* a wrong decision, ill-judgment, im- [prudence.

कुवार = **कुमार**, *q. v.*

कुविचारी, *m.* (*f.* inī) an ill-advised person, etc.: *lit.* ill-judging, indiscreet, imprudent.

कुवृत्ति, *f.* a bad character.

कुवेर, *m. pr n.* the Plutus of the Hindoo mythology, — the god of riches.

कुवेरलोक, *m. pr. n.* the place where Kuver reigns or where he keeps his treasures.

कुवेला, *f.* an unsuitable time, unseasonable time. *Velā* --, in season and out of season.

कुव्वत, *f.* power, authority, virtue, faculty, [strength, vigour.

कुश, *m.* the sacred grass of the Hindoos (*Poa cynosuroides*); it is used in many religious observances, and is hence called sacrificial grass: *pr. n.* (1) of one of the dweeps or great divisions of the universe (2) of [one of the sons of Rām.

कुशरात, *f.* = **कुशल**, 1, *q. v.*

कुशल, 1, *m.* (*f.* ?) health, well-being, safety, prosperity, happiness: 2, *m.* (*f.* ā) happy, healthy, well, right, auspicious, prosperous, expert, skilful.

कुशलक्षेम, *m.* health and well-being.

कुशलजनक, *adj.* producing prosperity or well-being.

कुशलता, *f.* / **कुशलताई**, *f.* / **कुशलत्व**, *m.* } = **कुशल**, 1, *q. v.*

कुशलदायक, *adj.* affording happiness or well-being.

कुशलप्रश्न, *m.* enquiry after one's welfare, friendly [salutation.

कुशलमंगल, *m.* happiness and welfare.

कुशला = **कुशल**, 2, *q.v.*

कुशलात, *f.* = **कुशल**, 1, *q. v.*

कुशलानन्द, *m.* welfare, tranquillity, prosperity.

कुशली, *m.* (*f.* inī) = **कुशल**, 2, *q.v.*

कुशा, *adj.* opening, displaying, expanding; solving, loosening; conquering. Much used in composition in words of Persian origin; e. g. *Dilkushā, adj.* heart-conquering.

कुशादा, opened, uncovered, expanded, loosened; wide, ample, extensive, displayed; free, cheerful, frank.

कुशामन्त्र, *m.* a kind of charm.

कुशासन, *m.* a seat or mat made of the *kush*-grass.

कुशिक, *m. pr. n.* (1) of a certain man (2) of his descendants.

कुशी, *m.* (*f.* inī) a person holding the *kush*-grass.

कुशील, *m.* (*f.* ā) an evil-disposed person, etc.: *lit.* evil-disposed, ill-behaved, rude, wicked; ill-tempered.

कुशीलत्व, *m.* (*f.* tā) badness of disposition; ill-temper; misconduct.

कुशीलव, *m.* an actor, mimic, dancer: the two sons [of Rām, viz. *Kush* and *Lav.*

कुश्ती, *f.* wrestling. — *k.* or *larnā* or *khelnā*, to wrestle. — *meṅ paṭak denā*, to throw in wrestling.

कुश्तीगर / **कुश्तीगीर** / **कुश्तीबाज़** } *m.* a wrestler.

कुष्ट, *more prop.* **कुष्ठ**, *q.v.*

कुष्ठ, *m.* a certain plant (*Costus speciosus*): leprosy (of which eighteen varieties are enumerated, — seven great or severe and eleven of minor importance).

कुष्ठनाशन, *m.* white mustard: a sort of yam.

कुष्ठनाशिनी, *f.* the plant *Psoralia corylifolia.*

कुष्ठित, *m.* (*f.* ā) / **कुष्ठी**, *m.* (*f.* inī) } a leper: *lit.* leprous.

कुष्माण्ड, *m.* a kind of imp: a pumpkin, gourd: a drug: a certain religious rite performed as penance or [expiation.

कुष्माण्ड, *m.* / **कुष्माण्डी**, *f.* } certain holy texts.

कुस, *m.* vulva. — *marānā*, to play the strumpet.

कुसंकट, *m.* any very severe misfortune.

कुसंग, *m.* evil intercourse, bad company.

कुसंगत, *m. f.* / **कुसंगति**, *f.* } = **कुसंग**, *q. v.*

कुसकेतु, *m. pr. n.* the brother of Janak.

कुसमउ in Braj = **कुसमय**, *q. v.*

कुसमय, *m.* an inopportune time: *adv.* inopportunely.

कुसमरानी, *f.* a strumpet: harlotry.

कुसमसाना, *more prop.* **कसमसाना**, *q. v.*

कुसरात, *more prop.* **कुशरात**, *q. v.*

कुसल; for words beginning thus see under the [form **कुशल**.

कुसा = **कुश**, *q. v.*

कुसीद, 1, *m* usury, loan with interest; the profession of a usurer: 2. *m.* (*f.* ā) a money-lender.

कुसीदा, 1, *f.* (*m.* **कुसीद**) = **कुसीदिन**, *q. v*: 2, *m.* (*f.* ī *or* in) a money-lender, usurer.

कुसीदायी = **कुसीदिन**, *q. v.*

कुसीदिक, *m* (*f.* ā or ī) a money-lender: *lit.* following the profession of money-lending.

कुसीदिन, *f.* (*m.* **कुसीदा**) the wife of a usurer: a [female money-lender.

कुसीदी = **कुसीदिन**, *q. v.*

कुसुम, *m.* a certain flower (*Carthamus tinctorius*) with which cloth is dyed red, bastard saffron, safflower: the menstrual discharge: ophthalmia: fruit: a theological student's water-pot: gold.

कुसुमांजन, *m.* the calx of brass used as a collyrium.

कुसुमित, *m.* (*f.* ā) blossoming, full-blown, ripe.

कुसुमी, *f.* (see **कुसुम**) a certain dye.

कुसुम्भ = **कुसुम्भा** or **कुसुम**, *qq.v.*

कुसुम्भा, *m.* safflower (*Carthamus tinctorius*); the dye of safflower: *met.* an infusion of *bhang* (*Cannabis sativa*) used for intoxication.

कुसुम्भी, *m.* cloths dyed with safflower.

कुसूफ़, *m.* an eclipse of the sun.

कुसूर, (*pl.* of **कसर**) *m.* (in Arithm.) fractions.

कुसूर, *m.* error, sin, defect, fault, omission, want, failure: premium on the exchange of rupees in distinction from *baṭṭā* (discount).

कुसूरवार, in error, deficient, guilty.

कुस्ती; see **कुश्ती**.

कुस्थली, *f. pr. n.* a certain Apsarā.

कुस्वप्न, *m.* a bad dream; unsound sleep; nightmare.

कुस्वभाव, *m.* an evil disposition.

कुस्वभावी, *m.* (*f.* inī) a person of an evil disposition.

कुहनी, *f.* the elbow.

कुहरा, *m.* fog, vapour, mist.

कुहराम, *m.* weeping, lamentation.

कुहासा, / **कुहिर**, / **कुहिरा**, } *m.* fog, vapour, mist.

कुही, *f.* a species of hawk.

कुहुक, *f.* the notes of the *kokila.*

कुहुकना, *a. int.* to give forth a sound like a *kokila's.*

कुहेसा, *m.* a fog, vapour, mist.

कूआ, *m.* (gen. **कूएका**; nom. pl. **कूए**; gen. **कूओंका**) a well, pit: a slice or division of the jack-fruit: the cocoon of the silkworm: the angle or corner of the eye.

कूआं = **कूआ**, *q. v.*

कूआर; for some words beginning thus, see under [the form **कुमार**.

कूआंर = (1) **कुआर** (2) **कुमार** (3) **कूआर**, *qq.v.*

कूआर, *m.* the sixth month of the Hindoos (Sept.-Oct.), more commonly called *Āsin.*

कूआरा, *m.* (*f.* ī) an unmarried man, bachelor.

कूईरी, *f.* a ring worn as an ornament round the toe.

कूए, infl. sing. and nom. pl. of **कूआ**, *q. v.*

कूएं }
कूंय } more prop. कुए, q. v.
कूंएं }

कूंआं = कूआ, q. v.

कूंआंर = कूआर, q. v.

कूंच, m. the little red and black seeds (*Abrus precatorius*) which goldsmiths use as weights : march-

कूंचक, appertaining to a march. [ing, a march.

कूंचना, t. to thrust, pierce, stab, gore: a. int. to march from a place (as soldiers might do) not to re-

कूंची, f. a brush. [turn.

कूंज, m. a certain bird (perhaps the crane).

कूंया, *more com.* कूआ, q. v.

कूंएं, *more com.* कूए, q. v.

कूक, f. a sobbing, crying. — *mārnā*, to sob, cry.

कूकड़ियाना, t. to cover, overlay.

कूकना, a. to wind up (as a watch, cloth, etc.) : a. int. to sob, cry, scream, vociferate, call (as the *kokil*).

कूकर, m. (f. ā) a dog.

कूकरचल, f. a trot, dogtrot. [wood).

कूकरमुत्ता, m. a toadstool, mushroom (growing on

कूकरा, f. (m. कूकर) a bitch.

कूकरी, f. maize, Indian corn (*Zea mais*): a bundle of thread : the gripes. [dove ; the cooing of a dove.

कूकू, m. the dish called *kūkūpilāū* ; omelet : a

कूच, m. 1, a breast, the female breast (especially that of a young or unmarried woman) : 2, a marching, decamping. — *k.* to decamp, march, depart.

कूचक, small, diminutive, little. [purple.

कूचकी, f. smallness, diminutiveness : the colour

कूचगदा, m. (f. ī) a street-beggar.

कूचगर्द, m. one who perambulates the streets, a vagrant, stroller, street-walker, wanderer, vagabond.

कूचगर्दी, f. a wandering about in the streets.

कूचा, m. a lane, street, narrow passage, row.

कूचिका, f. a small brush, hair pencil.

कूचिया, f. a small tamarind : the lobe of the ear.

कूची, f. a brush.

कूच्छा, m. a tuft, cluster.

कूज़, m. a hump on the back.

कूजना, a int. to speak.

कूज़पुश्त, a hunchback : *lit.* humpbacked.

कूज़पुश्ती, f. humpbackedness.

कूज़ा, m. an earthen water-pot, jug ; a lump of sugar that has been crystallized in an earthen pot : a kind of rose.

कूट, 1, f. mimickry, buffoonery, fraud, trick, falsehood : 2, m. the head, the top, summit of a hill, peak of a mountain : a multitude, heap : an anvil : a hammer : a trap ; an enigma : paper used for making pasteboard.

कूटत्व, m. (f. tā) = कूट, 1, q. v.

कूटना, t. to pound, beat, macerate, cudgel.

कूटस्थ, m. (f. ā) a chief, etc : *lit.* situated at the summit ; unchanging, unalterable.

कूटार्थभाषिता, f. a tale, story, fiction.

कूटी, f. sarcasm.

कूठार, *more prop.* कुठार, q. v.

कूड़, *more properly,* कूढ़, q. v.

कूड़ा, m. sweepings, rubbish, dirt, dung.

कूड़ि, an iron helmet.

कूड़ी, see (1) कूड़ा (2) कूड़ि.

कूढ़, m. a simpleton, sloven, etc. : *lit.* simple, stupid, foolish, slovenly.

कूंडा, m. an earthen vessel for kneading bread in, a platter : the chaff or coarse part of rice. — *kōṛhnā*, to prosper. — *k.* dicitur cum plures viri, unus post alterum, mulierum violant.

कूंडी, f. an instrument or vessel of stone in which *bhang*, snuff, etc. are ground.

कूत, m. the base of a right-angled triangle: a survey, task, guess, appraisement, rough estimate or valuation.

कूतक, m. 1, one of the rules of arithmetic or algebra : 2, a club, pestle, short stick with which bhang is ground. — *mārnā*, to cudgel, thrash with a stick. — *khānā*, to receive a cudgelling.

कूतना, t. to value, appraise, estimate.

कूद, f. a spring, jump, leap, bound.

कूदना, a. int. to spring, jump, leap, bound, hop, hobble : *met.* to rejoice ; to boast. — *phāndnā*, to leap about, jump for joy.

कूदा, m. a spring, jump, leap, bound.

कूदाबीघा, m. a *bīghā* measured by a certain number of leaps or springs of the measurer.

कूनाई, f. a scrap.

कून्स, m. a conjecture, guess.

कून्दला, m. a kind of tent.

कूप, m. a well, hole, hollow, pit.

कूपी, f. (dimin. of कूप) a small well.

कूपैरा, m. (f. ī) unlucky, inauspicious.

कूबड़, m. a hump on the back. [ed.

कूबड़ा, m. (f. ī) humpbacked, hunchbacked, crook-

कूमांक, (f. ī) a kind of bread.

कूमाया, f. estrangement in affection.

कूम्भल, *more prop.* कूम्हल, q.v. [through the wall.

कूम्हल, f. burglary. — *denā*, to break into a house

कूया }
कूयां } *more com.* कूआ, q. v.

कूर, *more properly* क्रूर, q. v.

कूरनी, f. a scoop.

कूर्म = कुर्म, q. v. [pool, pond.

कूल, m. a shore, bank of a river ; a mound, heap, a

कूलटी, f. a wooden poker or stake burnt at one

कूला, the hip, buttock. [end.

कूली, m. a coolie, labourer, porter, carrier.

कूवरा = कूबड़ा, q. v.

कूवा = कूआ, *q.v.*

कूवेर, *more prop.* कुवेर, *q.v.*

कूहरा, *m.*
कूहा, *f.* } a fog, vapour, mist.

कूही, *f.*; see (1) कुही (2) कूहा.

कृच्छ्र, 1, *m.* pain, distress, difficulty, penance: 2, *m.* (*f.* ā) a sufferer, etc.: *lit.* painful, difficult, dangerous, miserable, wicked.

कृत, 1, = कृतयुग (see युग): 2, much used as a suffix [*m.* (*f.* ā)] in compound adjectives: 3, *m.* (*f.* ā) done, made, performed; composed, perfect; proper, fit: 4, *f.* consequence, fruit: 5, *adv.* completely finished, done: 6, anent signification 1, observe that in the ingenious system of reckoning by symbols adopted by Hindoos in their poetry, this word is a symbol for 4.

कृतंघ; see (1) कृतघ्न (2) कृतज्ञ.

कृतकता, *f.*
कृतकत्व, *m.* } adoption, feignedness, falseness.

कृतकर्मा, *m.* or *f.* a clever person, etc.: lit. *adj.* having successfully performed a duty or discharged an undertaking, clever, able, skilful.

कृतकार्य्य, *m.* (*f.* ā) = कृतकर्मा, *q.v.*

कृतकृत्य = कृतार्थ, *q.v.*

कृतघन, *m.* (*f.* ā) *more prop.* कृतघ्न, *q.v.*

कृतघ्न, *m.* (*f.* ā) an ungrateful person, etc.: *lit.* destroying that which has been done (for one), *hence*, ungrateful, neglectful of favours, returning evil for good.

कृतघ्नता, *f.*
कृतघ्नताई, *f.*
कृतघ्नत्व, *m.* } ungratefulness.

कृतघ्नदोष, *m.* the sin of ingratitude.

कृतघ्नी, *m.* (*f.* inī) = कृतघ्न, *q.v.*

कृतज्ञ, *m.* (*f.* ā) a grateful person, etc.: *lit.* taking cognizance of that which has been done (for one), *hence*, mindful of favours, grateful.

कृतज्ञत्व, *m.* (*f.* tā) gratitude, thankfulness.

कृतद्युती, *f. pr. n.* the chief queen of Chitraketu.

कृतमाल, *m.* a certain tree (*Cassia fistula*): a certain animal.

कृतस्थला, *f. pr. n.* a certain Apsarā.

कृतनिन्दक = कृतघ्न, *q.v.*

कृतवर्मा, *m. pr. n.* (1) of several princes (2) of the father of the 13th Arhat of the present Avasarpini.

कृतयुग = सत्ययुग; see युग.

कृतान्त, *m.* an epithet of यम, *q.v.*

कृतार्थ, 1, *m.* the fulfilment of one's wishes, accomplishment or realization of one's purpose, the discharging one's duty, success, satisfaction, the granting supplication: 2, successful, having discharged one's duty, having attained one's purpose or accomplished one's designs.

कृतार्थत्व, *m.* (*f.* tā) = कृतार्थ, 1, *q.v.*

कृतिका, *more prop.* कृत्तिका, *q.v.*

कृती, *m.* (*f.* inī) wise, clever; satisfied.

कृत्तिका, *f. pr. n.* the 3rd *Nakshatra* (consisting of six stars), the Pleiades.

कृत्रिम, *m.* (*f.* ā) an adopted child, etc.: *lit.* the reverse of what is naturally or spontaneously produced: manufactured, made, factitious, fictitious, artificial, feigned, forged, false, adopted (as a child).

कृत्रिमपुत्र, *m.* (*f.* ī) an adopted son; one of the twelve kinds of adoption recognized in law.

कृत्रिममित्र, *m.* (*f.* ā) an acquired friend, — one on whom benefits have been conferred or from whom they have been received.

कृत्य, *m.* a right, duty, need, service, business, motive; *lit.* to be done, be performed; seducible.

कृत्या, *f.* an action; a charm, witchery: pestilence: a goddess to whom sacrifices are offered for magical purposes.

कृदन्त; in Sanskrit a class of suffixes called *krit* is added to verbal roots for the purpose of forming substantives and adjectives: these suffixes are called *Kridanta* suffixes, and the words so formed are described as *Kridanta*.

कृपण, *m.* (*f.* ā) a miser, etc.: *lit.* avaricious, miserly, miserable, lamenting, parsimony.

कृपणत्व, *m.* (*f.* tā) wretchedness, niggardliness,

कृपा, *f.* compassion, pity, tenderness, kindness, favor, mercy, : a common name of females, "Mercy."

कृपाकटाक्ष, *m.* a glance of compassion.

कृपाचार्य, *m. pr. n.* a certain ancient Hindoo sage.

कृपाण, *m.* a sword, scimitar, sacrificial knife.

कृपाणी, *f.* shears, scissors; a dagger.

कृपाते in Braj = कृपासे. See ते, 3.

कृपादृष्टि, *f.* a kind or pitiful look, merciful regard. — *k.* to look in mercy upon, regard pitifully.

कृपानाथ, *m.* an epithet of God.

कृपानि, 1, *more prop.* (1) कृपाण (2) कृपाणी, *qq.v.*: 2, in Braj = कृपाने.

कृपानिधान, *m.* an epithet of God; *lit.* the mansion of compassion.

कृपानिधि, *m.* an epithet of God; *lit.* the treasury or reservoir of compassion.

कृपापात्र, *m.* (*f.* ī) an object of compassion, recipient of special favors, protégé, favorite.

कृपारहित, pitiless, unkind.

कृपामय, *m.* (*f.* ī) abounding in pity, compassionate,

कृपाल, a com. contraction of कृपालु, *q.v.*

कृपाला, a poetical form of कृपाल, *q.v.*

कृपालु, *m. f.* compassionate, pitiful, tender, merciful, propitious, kind, obliging, liberal.

कृपालुत्व, *m.* (*f.* tā) compassionateness, mercifulness, pitifulness, tenderness, kindness.

कृपावान,
कृपावन्त, } *m.* (*f.* vatī) compassionate.

कृपासागर, *m.* an epithet of God; *lit.* the ocean of compassion.

कृपासिन्धु = कृपासागर, *q.v.*

कृपाहीन, *m.* (*f.* ā) unfeeling, pitiless, unkind.

कृपाहीनत्व, *m.* (*f.* tā) unfeelingness, mercilessness.

कृपिण, *more prop.* कृपण, *q.v.*

कृपिनाई = कृपणता, *q.v.*

कृपी, *f. pr. n.* the mother of *Ashvātthāmā*.

कृमरात, *m. pr. n.* one of the divisions of the world.

कृमि, *m.* a worm, an insect in general, the worms (disease): lac, the red dye (which is, in fact, the accumulation of an insect).

कृमिघ्न, 1, *m.* (*f.* ā) the worm-destroyer, vermifuge: lit. *adj.* worm-destroying : 2, *m.* a certain shrub (*Ericybe paniculata*) used in medicine as an anthelmintic, commonly called Bairang.

कृमिज, *m.* agallochum ; *lit.* worm-produced.

कृमिजा, *f.* (*m.* कृमिज) a certain red dye, lac.

कृमिदन्तक, *m.* toothache from decay. [on worms.

कृमिभोजन, *m. pr. n.* one of the hells ; *lit.* feeding

कृमिल, *m.* (*f.* ā) wormy, having worms.

कृमिला, *f.* a fruitful female.

कृमिहर, *m.* vermifuge ; *lit.* the worm-seizer.

कृमी, *m.* (*f.* iṇī) affected with worms, wormy.

कृपावान, *more prop.* क्रियावान, *q. v.*

कृश, *m.* (*f.* ā) a thin animal : *lit.* thin, emaciated, spare, lean ; small, minute.

कृशत्व, *m.* (*f.* tā) emaciatedness, meagreness, spareness, slenderness, leanness, smallness.

कृशांग, *m.* (*f.* ī) a person of a slender shape: *lit.* of meagre slender limbs. [*bago zeylamica*).

कृशानु, *m.* a name of fire : a certain plant (*Plum-*

कृशाश्व, *m. pr. n.* of several persons, but especially of a certain author of directions to players and actors.

कृशित *m.* (*f.* ā) emaciated, spare, lean.

कृष ; see कृश. [husbandman.

कृषक, *m.* (*f.* ikā) a cultivator of the soil: peasant,

कृषाण, *m.* a husbandman, ploughman.

कृषि, *f.* ploughing, agriculture, husbandry.

कृषी, *m.* (*f.* iṇī) = कृषक, *q. v.*

कृष्ण, (the origin of the meaning is doubtful) 1, *m.* (*f.* ā) dark-blue, black : 2, *m.* the color dark-blue or black : black pepper : a certain plant (*Nigella Indica*) : the black antelope : frequently used as an abbreviation for *Krishnpaksh*, *q.v.* : *pr. n.* the eighth and most celebrated of the ten incarnations of Vishṇu, (see *Avatār*). He was the younger brother of the third Rām (Balarām) : his parents were Vasudev and Devakee, but he was brought up in the house of Nand and Yashodā to conceal him from the tyrant Kaṅs, to whom it had been predicted that the eighth-born child of this family would destroy him. In the family of Nand he passed his life among the gopees or cowherds. During his childhood he slew the serpent Kāliya and many giants and monsters. Afterwards he slew Kaṅs, protected Yudhishthir and kindled the war described in the Mahābhārat. He is the Apollo of the Hindoos and is supposed by Capt. Wilford to have lived about 1300 years before Christ. The history of this incarnation is contained in the Bhāgavat Purāṇ or Sukhsāgar. [grimage in Mathurā.

कृष्णकुण्ड, *m. pr. n.* a certain sacred place of pil-

कृष्णखण्ड, *m. pr. n.* a kind of history of Golok, contained in the Brahmavaivart-Purāṇ.

कृष्णचन्द } *m.* an epithet of Kṛishṇ.
कृष्णचन्द्र }

कृष्णचूड़ा, *m.* a plant (*Poinciana pulcherrima*).

कृष्णजटा, *f.* the Indian spikenard.

कृष्णजीरक, *m.* Calonji, a certain plant (*Nigella Indica*) having a small black seed which is used for medicinal and culinary purposes.

कृष्णता, *f.* blackness.

कृष्णताम्र, *m.* a kind of sandal-wood of a dusky

कृष्णत्व, *m.* blackness. [copper hue.

कृष्णद्वैपायन, *m. pr. n.* Vyās considered as the compiler of the Veds and Purāṇs. The epithet alludes to the darkness of his complexion together with the fact that he was brought forth by his mother Satyavatee on an island (*dwip*) in the Ganges.

कृष्णपक्ष, *m.* the dark half of a month, the fifteen days during which the moon is on the wane.

कृष्णपक्षी, (*f.* iṇī) a nickname for the bastard children of a Hindoo by a woman of a different caste.

कृष्णपक्षक = कृष्णपक्ष, *q. v.*

कृष्णफल, *m.* the Corinda fruit. [of Mur.

कृष्णमुरारि, *m.* an epithet of Kṛishṇ as the enemy

कृष्णलवण, *m.* a factitious salt (either that prepared by evaporation from saline soil, or the medicinal kind), a muriate of soda.

कृष्णलोह, *m.* the loadstone.

कृष्णसार } *m.* (*f.* ā or ī) the black antelope.
कृष्णसारंग }

कृष्णा, *f.* (*m.* कृष्ण) long pepper ; an epithet of Durgā ; the name of several plants.

कृष्णानदी, *f. pr. n.* a certain river, — possibly the Kistna in the Dakkhan.

कृष्णार्पण, offered up to Kṛishṇ. [ṇu or Kṛishṇ.

कृष्णावतार, *m.* (see कृष्ण) any incarnation of Vish-

कृष्णावास, *m.* the holy figtree (*Ficus religiosa*).

कृष्णाश्रित, *m.* (*f.* ā) a person depending on

कृष्ट = खोष्ट, *q. v.* [Kṛishṇ or devoted to him.

केस ; for words beginning thus, see under the form कृश or कृष.

के, 1, = कौन, *q. v.*: 2, the inflected form of का (case-sign of the genitive) : 3, sometimes the base of the oblique cases of the singular of का in Braj: 4, sometimes put inaccurately for कि.

केओड़ा, *m.* the flower *Pandanus odoratissimus* [(Roxb.).

केंकड़ा = केकड़ा, *q. v.*

केंचवा, *m.* an earthworm.

केंचुल, *m.* (?) the skin of a snake.

केकई, *more prop.* केकयी, *q. v.*

केकड़ा, *m.* (*f.* ī) a crab ; *pr. n.* the sign Cancer.

केकय, *m. pr. n.* (1) of a certain country (2) of its prince (3) of its people.

केकयदेश, *m. pr. n.* a certain country.

केकयी, *f. pr. n.* a certain princess of the Kekay tribe (wife of Dasharath and mother of Bharat).

केकर, 1, (a dialectic genit. of के, 1,) = किसका, *q. v.* : 2, squint-eyed.

केकरा, 1, *m.* (*f.* ī) = किसका ; 2, = केकड़ा, *qq. v.*

केका, *f.* the cry of the peacock.

केकी, *m.* (*f.* inī) a peacock.

केचुलि, *more com.* केचुली, *q. v.*

केचुली, *f.* the skin of a snake.

केचूक, *m.* the esculent root *Arum colocasia*.

केठां }
केठाई } *interrog.* in what place? where?

केड़ा, *m.* a sapling, tender twig.

केत (*contraction*) = केतु, *q. v.*

केतई = को, case-sign of the dat. and acc.: *e. g.* उसकेतई = उसको = (1) him (2) to or for him.

केतक = (1) कितना (2) केतिक (3) *m.* = केओड़ा, *qq. v.*

केतकी, *f.* = केओड़ा, *q. v.*

केतना, *m.* (*f.* ī) in Braj = कितना, *q. v.*

केता, *m.* (*f.* ī) in Braj = कितना, *q. v.*

केताई, *more prop.* केतई, *q. v.*

केतिक, somewhat, a little, a few, some.

केतु, *m.* a sign by which any object may be recognized, a banner; (in Astronomy) the dragon's tail or descending node; the ninth of the planets; a comet, meteor: (in Myth.) a demon.

केतुतारा, *f.* a comet, falling star.

केतुमाल, *m. pr. n.* one of the nine great divisions of the known world,—the western portion of Jambu- [Dwip.

केतुरत्न, *m.* lapis lazuli.

केते in Braj = कितने; see कितना.

केतें in Braj = (1) केते (2) केतई, *qq. v.*

केतेक in Braj = (1) कई एक (2) कितना (3) केतिक, *qq. v.*

केत्ता, *m.* (*f.* ī) *more prop.* कितना, *q. v.*

केदार, *m.* a field, a cultivated field, a watered field: a mountain: *pr. n.* (1) of a certain place of Hindoo pilgrimage in the Himālaya mountains (2) of a certain race of people in Arabia.

केदारनाथ, *m.* an epithet of Shiv, as the object of worship at Kedār; *lit.* the lord of Kedār.

केदारेश्वर = केदारनाथ, *q. v.*

केनारा = किनारा, *q. v.*

केने, *interrog.* whither?

केन्दु, *m.* a sort of ebony (*Diospyros tomentosa*).

केन्दुक, *m.* a sort of ebony that yields a species of tar (*Diospyros glutinosa*). [the poles.

केन्द्र, *m.* a centre, the centre of a circle; a pole;

केम्हर, *interrog.* whither?

केयूर, *m.* a bracelet worn on the upper arm.

केर, frequently (especially in poetry) the case-sign of the genitive irrespective of gender or of number.

केरा in Braj = (1) किसका (2) केला, *qq. v.*

केरी in Braj = (1) किसकी (2) केलि, *qq. v.*

केरे in Braj = किसके.

केल, *f.* amorous dalliance, coition.

केलन, *f.* a daughter-in-law.

केला, *m.* a plantain, a plantain-tree.

केलि, *m. f.* play, sport, pastime, amusement, amor

केली, *f.* = केलि, *q. v.* [ous dalliance, coition.

केवड़ा = केओड़ा, *q. v.*

केवट, *m.* a fisherman, waterman, boatman.

केवना; see क्यों नहीं. [man.

केवर्त, *m.* a fisherman, waterman, boatman, sea-

केवल, 1, *m.* (*f.* ā) *adj.* only, simple, mere, alone, rare, nothing but, entire, exclusively proper, all, whole: 2, *adv.* merely, only, simply, solely, peculiarly, certainly, absolutely: 3, *m.* a species of knowledge (probably that of the unity of God); the knowledge of the unity of all the universe: 4, *pr. n.* a certain prince.

केवली, 1, *f.* a horoscope, nativity: 2, *m.* (*f.* inī) one who possesses the knowledge of the universal unity: 3, *f. pr. n.* a certain locality.

केवांच, *f.* cowach (*Dolichos pruriens*).

केवाड़, *m.* the shutter of a door, fold of a door, a door, the gate of a city, an entrance. [hatchway.

केवाड़ी, *f.* (dim. of केवाड़) a small door, small gate,

केवार, *more prop.* केवाड़, *q. v.*

केश, 1, *m. f.* hair, hair of the head, a lion's mane, a cock's comb: 2, *f.* faith, religion, manner, quality.

केशर, *m.* a lion's or horse's mane: the filament of a lotus or of any vegetable: the name of several plants and their flowers (1) *Messua ferrea*, called also Nāgesar (2) *Rottleria tinctoria*, used in dyeing (3) [*Mimusops elengi*.

केशरि, *m.* (*f.* ṇī) = केशरी, *q. v.*

केशरिणी, *f.* (*m.* केशरी, etc.) a lioness. [*q. v.*

केशरिन, 1, *f.* = केशरिणी, *q. v.*: 2, *m.* (*f.* ṇī) = केशरी,

केशरी, *m.* (*f.* iṇī) a lion; *pr. n.* the father of Hanumān: *lit.* having a mane.

केशरीवानर, *m. pr. n.* a certain monkey.

केशव, an epithet of Vishṇu: lit. *m.* (*f.* ā) hairy, longhaired, having much or handsome hair.

केशवमूर्ति, *m.* an epithet of Kṛishṇ.

केशवेश, *m.* a tress or fillet of hair.

केशा, a poetical form of केश, *q. v.*

केशाकेशी, *f.* a pulling each other's hair, fighting by a mutual pulling of hair.

केशिन, 1, *m.* (*f.* ī) = केशी, *q. v.*: 2, *m. pr. n.* a certain demon slain by Kṛishṇ.

केशिनी, *f.* a female with much and beautiful hair; a grass (*Andropogon aculeatum*); *pr. n.* a certain courtesan of Indra's paradise.

केशी, 1, hairy, shaggy; having fine hair: hence, (1) *m.* (*f.* inī) a hairy person (2) *m.* an epithet of Kṛishṇ (3) *f.* a lock of hair on the crown of the head (4) *m. pr. n.* a certain demon slain by Kṛishṇ.

केष, *more com.* केश, *q. v.* [the form केश.

केस; for some words beginning thus see under

केसन, 1, (*dialectic*) = कैसा, *q. v.*: 2, a Braj pl. of केश, *q. v.* See न, 6.

केसर, *f.* saffron (*Crocus sativus*); the colour yellow.

केसरिया, saffron-coloured, yellow.

केसरियाबाना, *m.* (*f.* ī) saffron-coloured; dressed in

केसी = (1) कैसा (2) केशी, *qq. v.* [yellow.

केहर, *more prop.* केशर, *q. v.*

केहरी, *m.* (*f.* iṇī) *more prop.* केशरी, *q. v.*

केहि = किसको; see का and हि.

केहिकर }
केहिके } (*Rām.*) = किसके.

केहू, a dialectic form = कोई.

कै, 1, (see कई) several, some, some few, a few: 2,

how many ? 3, when ? 4, or, either : *kai — kai*, either — or, whether — or : 5, in Braj = कि, *q.v.* : 6, *f.* a vomiting, frequent vomiting. —*jullāb*, cholera morbus. — *lānewālā*, an emetic.

कैएक, several, some few, a few.

कैंचली, *f.* the slough of a snake.

कैंची, *f.* scissors, —*k.* to prune trees, cut the hair. — *bāndhnā*, to secure an unskilful rider on his horse.

कैंचुल, *m.* (?) = कैंचली, *q.v.*

कैकय, *more prop.* केकय, *q.v.*

कैकयी, *more prop.* कैकेयी, *q.v.*

कैकेय, (patronym.) *m.* (*f.* ī) a descendant of केकय.

कैकेयी, *f. pr. n.* one of the wives of Dasharath.

कैटभ, *m. pr. n.* a certain demon slain by Vishṇu.

कैटभजित, *m.* the conqueror of Kaitabh } *i.e.* Vishṇu
कैटभहन, *m.* the slayer of Kaitabh }

कैत, *m.* a certain tree (*Feronia elephantum*).

कैतव, *m.* the stake in a game; gambling; deceit, fraud, roguery, treachery : lapis lazuli.

कैतो
कैतौ } in Braj = कैतव, *q.v.*

कैथा, *m.* 1, = कैत, *q.v.*: 2, an intoxicating drink made from the fruit of the *kait*-tree.

कैथी, or कैथी नागरी ; see कायथी.

कैद, *m.* treachery, deceit, fraud; the croaking of a raven ; war : *adj.* vomiting ; menstruous : adjusting.

क़ैद, *f.* a fetter, imprisonment ; an obstacle : an obligation, compact. — *k.* to imprison. — *honā* or *rahnā*, to be imprisoned.

क़ैदख़ाना, *m.* a prison, gaol.

क़ैदी, *m.* (*f.* in *or* inī) a prisoner, captive.

कैन, *f.* a bamboo, twig.

कैफ़, intoxication ; an intoxicating drug.

कैफ़ियत, *f.* (pl. °यात) a story, statement, narrative, account, circumstances; quality, mode, state, condition.

कैर = करीर, *q.v.*

कैरव, *m.* the white esculent water-lily (*Nymphœa lotus*) : a rogue, cheat, enemy.

कैराटक, *m.* one of the fixed kinds of poison.

कैरात, *m.* a prince of the Kirāts ; *lit.* appertaining to the Kirāts.

कैरातक, *m.* (*f.* ī) appertaining to the Kirats.

कैरी, *f.* a small unripe mango. — *ānkh*, *f.* an eye the pupil of which is grey, a wall eye.

कैल, *f.* a sprout, shoot.

कैलाश = कैलास, *q.v.*

कैलास, *m. pr. n.* a certain mountain fabled as the residence of Kuver and the favorite haunt of Shiv : the name is given by the Hindoos to one of the loftiest peaks of the Himālayas lying to the north of the Manus lake.

कैवर्त्त, *m.* a fisherman, boatman, rower; a certain mixed tribe : the son of a Nishād by an Āyogavi woman.

कैवल्य, *m.* eternal emancipation, *i. e.* the release of the soul from further transmigration; complete absorption in the thought of the universal unity, absolute happiness : totality.

कैसन, a dialectic form of कैसा, *q.v.*

कैसर, *m. pr. n.* the emperor Cæsar.

कैसही (*contraction*) = कैसाही, *q.v.*

कैसा, *m.* (*f.* ī) what-like? what sort of? what kind or manner of ? *adv.* in what manner? how ?

कैसाही, (emphatic) howsoever, how much soever.

कैसे, 1, *adj.* (pl.) what-like ? 2, *adv.* how ?

कैसें in Braj = कैसे, *q.v.*

कैसो
कैसी
कैसां } in Braj = कैसा and कैसे, *qq.v.*

कैसोहू — तैसोहू (in Braj, correlatives) however much — still.

कैहों, in Braj, a form = करूं (करना).

को, 1, the case-sign of the dative and accusative : 2, (gen. काको) in Braj = कौन ; and sometimes also = कोई : 3, (*more prop.* कौ) in Braj = का (sign of the genitive)

कोआ, *m.* an angle of the eye.

कोइ, *more prop.* कोई, *q.v.*

कोइल = कोयल ; see कोकिल.

कोई, 1, (gen. किसीका ; nom. pl. कोई, and sometimes कोई कोई) a, an, one, any, anybody, somebody. — *hai*, is there anyone (about, or in attendance, or within hearing) ? — *nahīṅ*, nobody, there is nobody. — *na* —, (gen. *kisī na kisīkā*) some or other, someone or other. Somtimes used as a contraction of *Jo koi*, whoever ; e. g. *Koi ho*, whoever it may be, be it who it may. Sometimes this word is not inflected when it might be expected to be ; e. g. *Koi dammeṅ*, in a few moments, speedily. It corresponds to *bāz* in Urdū (compare अमुक) : 2, *f.* the water-lily (*Nymphœa lotus*) : the pulp of the jackfruit (*Artocarpus integrifolia*).

कोईं = कोई, 2, *q.v.*

कोईका, *m.* (*f.* ī) *more prop.* किसीका.

कोईल = कोयल ; see कोकिल.

कोईला = (1) कोकिला (2) कोयला, *qq.v.*

कोईलां ; a Braj pl. of कोईल, *q.v.*

कोईसा, *m.* (*f.* ī) certain, somebody, something.

कोउ, *more freq.* कोऊ, *q.v.*

कोऊ (gen. काहूको) in Braj = कोई, *q.v.*

कोएड़ी, *m.* a planter, husbandman, gardener : the name of a caste among the Hindoos whose occupation is husbandry. [by toddy-drawers (called also *dāw*).

कोएसा, *m.* a bill-hook, cutting instrument used

कोएला, *m.* charcoal.

कोंई
कोंइ } *more prop.* कोई, 2, *q.v.*

कोंकण, *m. pr. n.* (1) of a country in the south-west of India (2) of the people of that country.

कोंख in Braj = कोख, *q.v.*

कोंचना, *t.* to prick, stab, thrust, pierce, gore.

कोंड, **कोंत**, **कोंप** ; for words beginning with either of these elements, see under the forms कोण्ड, कोन्त, कोम्प, respectively.

कोंचली, *f.* a long tooth; a boar's tusk.

कोंढ़ा, *m.* sweet pumpkin (*Curcurbita pepo*).

कोक, 1, *more com.* **कूक**, *q.v.*: 2, *m.* a wolf: a cuckoo: the ruddy goose (*Anas cascara*): scientia modorum diversorum coeundi; a quodam *Kōk paṇḍit* explicata unde nomen.

कोकशास्त्र, *m. pr. n.* a treatise by *Kōk paṇḍit*.

कोका, *m.* a foster-brother, nurse's son: a small nail, tack: a kind of lotus.

कोकिनी, abbreviated, short.

कोकिल, *m.* (*f.* ā) a kind of mouse: a poisonous insect: the black or Indian cuckoo (*Cuculus*). This bird makes a prominent figure in Hindoo poetry, and is supposed by his musical cry to inspire pleasing and tender emotions.

कोकिलबैनी, kokil-voiced, speaking like the kokil, [eloquent as the kokil.

कोकिला, *f.* the female Indian cuckoo.

कोकिलाक्ष, *m.* the name of certain plants (1) *Capparis spinosa* (2) *Barleria longifolia* (3) *Ruellia longifolia*; *lit.* having eyes resembling those of the *kokil*.

कोख (= **कोष**, *q.v.*) *m. f.*? the womb, abdomen.

कोखबन्द / **कोखबन्ध** } *f.* a barren female.

कोखा, *f. m.* (= **कोष**, *q.v.*) the womb, abdomen.

कोच, 1, *more prop.* **कवच**, *q.v.*: 2, *m.* a shrinking, shrivelling.

कोचक, 1, *more com.* **कूचक**, *q.v.*: 2, appertaining to [**कोच**.

कोचना, *more com.* **कोंचना**, *q.v.*

कोछा, the lap, bosom, embrace.

कोजागर, *m. pr. n.* the day of full moon in the month Āshwin (Sept.-Oct.). It means properly "who is awake?", and is said to have been the call of Lakshmee, who, descending on this night, promised wealth to all who were awake: hence, the night is spent in festivity and games of chance in honor of the goddess.

कोट, *m.* a fort, redoubt, stronghold, castle: *adv.* much, many.

कोटबान्ध बैठना, *a. int.* to sit with the legs crossed as Asiatics do, to sit (as they fancy) at one's ease.

कोटर, *m.* a kind of greens: a cavity; a hollow tree, hollows made in trees by birds.

कोटरा, *f. pr. n.* (= **कोटरी**?) the mother of Vāṇāsur.

कोटरी, *f.* a naked woman; an epithet of Durgā [(the naked goddess).

कोटवार / **कोटवाल** } = **कोतवाल**, *q.v.*

कोटली, *f.* a division in a granary for different [sorts of grain.

कोटापली, *f.* a mallet.

कोटि, *f.* a point; eminence; the edge or point of a sword; a side: a crore, ten millions.

कोटिक, *m.* (*f.* ā) a worm; a kind of frog: *pr. n.* the son of a certain prince.

कोटिन्ह in Braj = **करोड़ों**, *q.v.* See **न्ह**.

कोटी, *f.* an earthen reservoir for grain.

कोठु, see (1) **कोट** (2) **कोठ**.

कोठ, *m.* a species of leprosy with large round spots, [ringworm, impetigo.

कोठमीरका कीरा, *m.* a winged bug.

कोठरी, *f.* a small room, closet, apartment, chamber. *Andherī* —, *f.* the womb.

कोठवार in Braj = **कोतवाल**, *q.v.*

कोठा, *m.* a house built of burnt bricks or of stone; a barn, storehouse; a storey, floor.

कोठी, *f.* (dim. of **कोठा**) a small house built of brick or of stone; a warehouse, storehouse, granary; a mansion, dwelling, barrack, factory, banking-house; a chamber; the chamber of a gun; the inside or well of a shaft; a chest; the womb; the ferrule or mounting at the end of a scabbard.

कोठीवाल, *m.* a warehouse-keeper, wholesale mer- [chant.

कोठौर, out of place, improper, misplaced.

कोड़ = **कोढ़**, *q.v.*

कोड़ना, *t.* to dig out, scoop, bore, hollow, excavate, scrape.

कोड़वाला, *m.* a kind of bird; a kind of flower; [a kind of snake.

कोड़ा, *m.* a whip, horsewhip, lash: the breast, bosom. — *k.* to whip; to reduce to obedience; to put an animal to his speed by whipping. — *mārnā*, to whip, flog, scourge, apply the lash.

कोड़ाना, *t.* to cause to dig out, cause to scrape.

कोड़ी, 1, = **कोढ़ी**, *q.v.*: 2, *f.* a score, twenty: a sloping pavement of stone-work at one end of a tank to let the water off when the tank is too full.

कोढ़, *m.* leprosy, white leprosy which causes a discoloring of the skin.—*meṅ khāj nikalnā*, the breaking out of the itch in leprosy, or in leprosy to catch [the itch.

कोढ़ना, *t.* to vex, grieve, afflict.

कोढ़िन = (1) **कोढ़ी** (2) **कोढ़िनी**, *qq.v.*

कोढ़ी, leprous, afflicted with leprosy: hence, *m.* (*f.* in *or* inī) a leper.

कोण, *m.* a corner, angle: an instrument for [sounding a lute.

कोणदार, *adj.* having corners or angles.

कोणा, *more prop.* **कोण**, *q.v.*

कोणाकुचरा, *m.* a corner of a room, corner of a house, hole and corner, every corner.

कोणादार, *adj.* having corners or angles.

कोणि, *adj.* having a crooked arm.

कोणडना, *t.* to imprison, confine.

कोणडबार, straight, tight, narrow.

कोणढा, *m.* sweet pumpkin (*Cucurbita pepo*).

कोत, *m.* a fort, stronghold.

कोतमीर, *f.* a kind of greens, coriander.

कोतल, *m.* a led horse.

कोतलकश, *m.* a surcingle (particularly for fasten- [ing body-cloths).

कोतवाय / **कोतवार** } (*corruptions*) = **कोतवाल**, *q.v.*

कोतवाल, *m.* the chief officer of the police of a town or city; the superintendent of a market.

कोतवाली, *f.* the status and the business of a kotwāl; a kotwāl's place of business.

कोतवाली चबूतरा, *m.* a place or hall for the office [of a kotwāl.

कोता, small, little, short, mean.

कोथ, *m.* inflammation and ulceration of the angles of the eyelids, gangrene, putrefaction.

कोथमीर, *m.* the coriander plant (the seed is called *dhaniyā*).

कोदण्ड, *m.* a bow (in archery); an eyebrow (from its shape); a creeping-plant: *pr. n.* a country.

कोदण्डा, *more prop.* **कोदण्ड**, *q. v.*

कोदव } **कोदो** } (*contractions*) = **कोद्रव**, *q. v.*

कोद्रव, *m.* a certain small grain (*Paspalum scrobiculatum*, Lin., or *kora*, Willd., or *frumentaceum*, Kœn. MS.). It is sown early in the rainy season, and is eaten by the poorer people.

कोदेा } **कोद्रेा** } in Braj = **कोद्रव**, *q. v.*

कोन, *more prop.* (1) **कोण** (2) **कौन**, *qq. v.*

कोना, *more prop.* **कोण**, *q. v.*

कोनी = **कोहनी**, *q. v.*

कोनेरी, *f.* = **कोण**, *q. v.*

कोनेा, *more prop.* (1) **कोण** (2) **कौन**, *qq. v.*

कोन्त, *f.* a spear.

कोप, *m.* wrath, rage, passion, anger.

कोपज्वलित, *m.* (*f.* ā) burning with wrath, enraged.

कोपदीप्त, *m.* (*f.* ā) inflamed with anger, incensed.

कोपन, 1, *m.* excitement, provocation; *pr. n.* a certain demon: 2, *m.* (*f.* ā) passionate, wrathful.

कोपना, *n.* to be angry, be wrathful, be enraged.

कोपभवन, *m.* any chamber to which a woman retires when angry or affronted.

कोपमय, *m.* (*f.* i) abounding in anger, of an angry nature.

कोपर; see (1) **किसपर** (2) **खोपरा** (3) **खोपरी**.

कोपवान, angry, passionate: hence *m.* (*f.* vatī) a passionate person.

कोपवेग } **कोपवेश** } *m.* violence, impetuosity of passion.

कोपाकुल, *m.* (*f.* ā) an enraged person: *lit.* enraged, furious.

कोपान्वित, *m.* (*f.* ā) a passionate person; *lit.* passionate, rageful, angry, wrathful.

कोपित, *m.* (*f.* ā) an enraged person: *lit.* enraged, wrathful, furious.

कोपि (*contraction*) = **कोपी**, *q. v.*

कोपी, 1, a corruption of **कोई**, *q. v.*: 2, *m.* (*f.* inī) angry, passionate, wrathful.

कोपीन, *m.* (*f.* ?) a cloth worn around the waist and passing between the legs (the *laṅgoṭī*): a privy part.

कोफ़्त, *f.* vexation, grief, anguish; the inlaying gold or silver or any other metal.

कोफ़्तगर, *m.* a gilder.

कोफ़्ता, pounded, beaten (meat); a kind of dish.

कोबा, *m.* a wooden instrument for beating terraces, etc. with.

कोबाकारी, *f.* a beating, thumping.

कोबिद = **कोविद**, *q. v.*

कोबी, *f.* a cabbage, cauliflower.

कोम; see **क़ौम**.

कोमल, *m.* (*f.* ā) bland, soft, sleek, tender, supple, placid, mild, immature, young, unripe.

कोमलता, *f.* blandness, softness, tenderness, mildness, suppleness, agreeableness.

कोमलताई, *f.* } **कोमलत्व**, *m.* } = **कोमलता**, *q. v.*

कोम्पल, *m.* } **कोम्पली**, *f.* } a bud, a young shoot.

कोय, *a corruption of* **कोई**, *q. v.*

कोयण, *m.* a corner, angle.

कोयल, 1, = **कोकिल**, *q. v.*: 2, *f.* a certain flower (*Clitoria tornatea*). See *Aparājitā*.

कोयला, *m.* charcoal.

कोया, the ball of the eye.

कोर, 1, a corruption of **कड़ोड़**, *q. v.*: 2, *m.* a flexible joint (as of the fingers): a bud: 3, *f.* an edge, border, margin, side: a point.

कोरंगी, *f.* small cardamoms.

कोरक, *m.* a bud, blossom, unblown flower.

कोरना, *more prop.* **कोड़ना**, *q. v.*

कोरनिश, *f.* adoration; a certain method of salutation which consists in raising the hand to the forehead and then bending the head and shoulders forward.

कोरा, *m.* (*f.* ī) fresh, unhandled, unused, new; unbleached (applied only to clothes, earthen vessels, and paper; *hence*, it is the mercantile name for plain silk cloth undyed).

कोरा काग़ज़, *m.* white paper, *i. e.* paper not written on.

कोरान (*corruption*) = **क़ुरआन**, *q. v.*

कोरापन, *m.* newness, freshness; *met.* virginity (of a girl).

कोरिन्त, *m. pr. n.* Corinth.

कोरी, 1, = (1) **कड़ोड़** (2) **कोड़ी**, *qq. v.*: 2, *f.* (see **कोरा**) a virgin, maiden: one of the Hindoo castes.

कोरे रहना, *n.* to be disappointed.

कोरो, *m.* a rafter, transverse beam.

कोल, *m.* a hog: a kind of weapon: the fruit of the jujube (*Zizyphus jujuba*): a creek, bay; any long passage way, a lane: an embracing, embrace: *pr. n.* (1) of a tribe of hill-people (the 'Coles' or 'Kols') who occupy the country between Benares and Bundēlkhand (2) of the country (Colinga) on the coast from Cuttack to Madras.

कोलड़ा, *m.* (= **कोड़ा**, *q. v.*) a whip.

कोलसा, *m.* (= **कोयला**, *q. v.*) charcoal.

कोला, *m.* a jackal. *Kolonko daghā denā*, to escape death, rob the gallows; *lit.* to cheat the jackals.

कोलाहल, *m.* an uproar, noise, tumult, screaming, clatter, quarrelling, any great and indistinct noise or confused sound; mirth: *pr. n.* a certain mountain.

कोलिन, *f.* (*m.* **कोल**) a female Cole or Kol.

कोलिया, *m.* (dim. of **कोल**) a lane, narrow street.

कोलियाना, *t.* to embrace, take into one's lap.

कोली, *m.* (*f.* in *or* inī) a weaver.

कोलू, *m.* an oilman, a certain caste whose business it is to sell oil.

कोले, (a loc. form of **कोल** ?) the lap, bosom, embrace.

कोल्हू, *m.* an oilman's press, sugarmill. — *men̤ purwā denā*, to destroy utterly, crush to atoms; *lit.* to macerate in a press.

कोवली, *f.* tiles.

कोविद, knowing, learned, skilful, experienced: hence, *m.* (*f.* ā) a skilful person, a *paṇḍit*.

कोविदार, *m.* a species of ebony (*Bauhinia variegata*): *pr. n.* one of the trees of paradise.

कोवू ; see कोऊ.

कोश, 1, = कोष, *q.v.*: 2, *m.* a piece added to the end of a sleeve, a cuff: 3, *m.* a measure of length equal to about two English miles, but varying in different parts of India. According to some it is 4000 cubits, according to others 8000.

कोशक, *m.* an egg; a testicle.

कोशना, *t.* to curse.

कोशल, *m. pr. n.* (1) of the city of (Oude) Ayodhya (2) of the surrounding district (3) of the country south of Ayodhya (4) of the inhabitants of Ayodhya.

कोशला, *f. pr. n.* = कोशल, 1, *q.v.*

कोशवृद्धि = कोषवृद्धि, *q.v.*

कोशिश, *f.* endeavour, effort, attempt, application, study.— *k.* to attempt, strive, endeavour.

कोष, *m.* a sheath, case, scabbard, shell; a cocoon; the womb; an egg; a testicle; a coop; a bud; a nutmeg; a treasure; a treasury, store-room; an abode; a dictionary, vocabulary, thesaurus, lexicon: judicial trial by oath or by ordeal, attesting a deity and touching or drinking water three times in which some idol has been washed.

कोषवृद्धि, *f.* a swelling of the testicles (from *Hernia humoralis* or from *Hydrocele*, etc.).

कोषाध्यक्ष, *m.* (*f.* ī) a treasurer, keeper or protector of treasure.

कोष्ठ, *m.* an apartment, any place in which grain is kept; any of the viscera (as the heart, lungs, etc.).

कोष्ठाग्नि, *m.* the digestive faculty, gastric juice.

कोस (*corruption*) = कोश and कोष, *qq.v.*

कोसन, 1, a Braj pl. of कोस, *q.v.*: 2, *f.* a curse. (?)

कोसना, *t.* to curse.

कोसल = कोशल, *q.v.*

कोसली, *m.* new leaves just sprouting.

कोसा, *m.* a malediction, curse.

कोसों, *prop.* कोशों. See कोश, 3, and ओं, 4.

कोह, 1, in Braj = (1) कौन (2) कोप, *qq v.*: 2, *m.* a mountain, hill, hillock, mount.

कोहक, the frame of the mouth of a well.

कोहड़ा, *m.* the sweet pumpkin (*Cucurbita pepo*).

कोहनी, *f.* the elbow.

कोहबर, a house in which there is a marriage (?).

कोहर, *m.* a fog, mist: a kind of fruit.

कोहाना, to be displeased, turn away in anger(?).

कोहाब, a being angry or displeased (?).

कोहार, *m.* (*f.* in *or* nī) = कुम्हार, *q. v.*

कोही, 1, = कोपी, *q.v.*: 2, *f.* a species of hawk (*Falco cristatellus*, B.): 3, *m.* (*f.* inī) a mountaineer; mountainous country: *lit.* mountainous; appertaining to mountains.

कौ, 1, = पृथिवीमें; 2, in Braj = कब ; 3, in Braj, the case-sign of the gen.: also frequently that of the dat. and acc.

कौआ, *m.* (*f.* कौई) a crow. See कौवा.

कौइ, a corruption (1) of कोई (2) of कौई, *qq.v.*

कौं, 1, a corruption of कौन, *q. v.*: 2, in Braj, the case-sign of the dat. and acc.: sometimes also that of the genitive.

कौंकि, *more prop.* क्योंकि, *q. v.*

कौंन in Braj, a corruption of कौन, *q. v.*

कौंला in Braj = (1) कौंधा (2) कोमल (3) कौला, *qq. v.*

कौंली हड्डी, *f.* gristle.

कौंहु in Braj, a corruption of कोऊ, *q. v.*

कौकब, *m.* (pl. कवाकिब) a star, constellation.

कौचाना, *t.* to steal.

कौटुम्ब, *m.* affinity, relationship.

कौटुम्बिक, *m.* the father of a family; *lit.* constituting a family.

कौड़ा, *m.* a shell of a large kind.

कौड़ियाला, *m.* (*f.* ī) a wealthy person: a kind of snake: a kingfisher.

कौड़ी, *f.* (dim. of कौड़ा) the cowrie, a small shell (*Cypræa moneta*) used as coin; *hence*, money, fare, hire: a gland; the point of the sternum, ensiform cartilage. *Kānī* or *phūṭī* —, a bit of money of the lowest value. *Kauṛī kauṛī bhar*, the full amount up to the very last cowrie.

कौड़ीबूक, venal.

कौतुक, *m.* joy, pleasure, happiness; a festival, diversion, show, play, pastime, scene, spectacle, trick: eagerness; desire: marriage, the marriage string.

कौतुकिवृन्द, *m.* (a Braj pl. of कौतुकी) mountebanks.

कौतुकी, *m.* (*f.* inī) a mountebank, etc.: *lit.* sportive, contributing to diversion by exhibition, tumbling, tricks, etc.

कौतूहल, *m.* eagerness; curiosity; desire.

कौथा, *m.* (*f.* ī) in Braj = कौनसा, *q. v.*

कौंदना, *more prop.* कौन्धना, *q. v.*

कौंदा, *more prop.* कौन्धा, *q.v.*

कौन, (gen. किसका ; pl. किनका or किन्होंका) who? which? what? In poetry, in Braj, and in the *patois*, this pronoun is but seldom inflected. See the next word.

कौनकौ, in Braj, the gen. of कौन ; sometimes also its dat. and acc.

कौनसा, *m.* (*f.* ī) which? what? what kind of? what manner of?

कौनो, a dialectic form = कुछ, *q. v.*

कौने (an infl. form of कौन) = किसमें.

कौन्ध, *f.* splendour, brightness, flash (of lightning).

कौन्धना, *a. int.* to lighten, flash (as lightning).

कौन्धा, *m.* lightning.

कौबा in Braj = (1) कोबा (2) कौवा, *qq. v.*

कौपीन, *m.* (*f.* ?) the privy parts: a cloth to cover them.

क़ौम, *f.* a tribe, caste, sect, people, nation, family, house or dynasty.

कौमार, 1, *m.* childhood, youth: 2, *m.* (*f.* ī) appertaining to abstinence; appertaining to the god of war

कौमारी, 1, a corruption of कुमारी, *q. v.*: 2, *f.* the energy of the god of war: one of the seven mothers.

कौमुद, *m.* a name of the month Kārttik (Oct.-Nov.).

कौमुदी, *f.* the day of full moon in the month Kārttik; moonlight.

कौमुन्दा, *f. pr. n.* one of Krishṇ's female companions.

कौमोदक ; see (1) कुमोदक (2) कौमोदकी.

कौमोदकी, *f.* the mace or club of Krishṇ.

कौमोदी, *f.* = (1) **कौमुदी** (2) **कौमोदकी**, *q.v.*

कौर = **कौल**. See **कवल**.

कौरवोंका in Braj = **कौरवोंका (कौरव)**.

कौरपाण्डु, *m. pr. n.* the united designation of two ancient families (the Kauravas and the Pāṇḍavas) descended from Kuru by their respective fathers Dhrit-rāshṭr and Pāṇḍu.

कौरव, (patronymic) *m.* (*f.* ī) a descendant from Kuru : *lit.* appertaining to Kuru or to the Kurus.

कौरवन, *m.* (a Braj pl. of **कौरव**) the Kaurav princes.

कौरवान, 1, *m.* (*f.* vatī) = **कौरव**, *q. v.* : 2, *m.* (a Sk. pl. of **कौरव**) the Kaurav princes.

कौरी, *more prop.* **कौड़ी**, *q. v.*

कौल, 1, in Braj = **कवल**, *q.v.* : 2, a wicked, covetous, greedy person (?) : 3, *m.* (*f.* ī) a well-born person: *lit.* appertaining to family or to race, of good family.

कौल, *m.* a word, saying; an agreement, promise, consent, contract : a kind of song.

कौलव, *m. pr. n.* one of the astronomical Karaṇs.

कौला, *m.* a corner (of a room, etc.): a kind of orange: an embrace ; an armful ; a sheaf or armful of corn.

कौलिक, *m.* (*f.* ā *or* ī) 1, a weaver : a heretic : 2, ancestral.

कौलिया, 1, *f.* (dimin. of **कौल**, 1.) a small mouthful : 2, *f.* (dimin. of **कौला**) a bundle of sheaves of corn given as perquisites to reapers and village servants : 3, *m.* a lane, narrow street.

कौलियाना, *t.* to embrace, take into the arms or lap.

कौली, *f.* the embrace, grasp of the arms.

कौलीन, 1, *m.* gossip, rumour : 2, *m.* (*f.* ā) appertaining to high birth.

कौवा, *m.* (*f.* ī) a crow.

कौवाठोंठी, *f.* (see **अपराजिता**) a certain flower (*Clitoria ternatea*).

कौवेका निशास्ता, *m.* a kind of arrowroot; *lit.* crow's starch.

कौवेर, *m.* (*f.* ī) appertaining to Kuver.

कौवेरदिश, *m.* the northern quarter or point of the compass.

कौश, 1, *m. pr. n.* the ancient city of Kanyākubj or Kanauj : 2, *m.* (*f.* ī) made of *kush*-grass : silken.

कौशकी, *more prop.* **कौशिकी**, *q.v.*

कौशल, 1, in Braj = **कुशल**, *q.v.*: 2, *m.* a prosperous event ; skill, cleverness ; a device, stratagem.

कौशलपुरी, *f.* (= **कौशला**) the city of Ayodhya.

कौशली, *f.* a greeting, salutation, friendly inquiry : a respectful present.

कौशलेश, *m.* any king of Ayodhya (but especially Dasharath).

कौशल्य, *m.* good fortune, well-being : ability, capability, cleverness.

कौशल्या, *f. pr. n.* the mother of Rām and wife of Dasharath.

कौशिक, *m.* (*f.* ī) 1, an owl : 2, (patronym.) a descendant of Kushik.

कौशिकगोत्र, *m.* } **कौशिकगोत्री**, *f.* } the race of Kushik.

कौशिकी, *f. pr. n.* a certain river in Bihār.

कौशिल्या = **कौशल्या**, *q.v.*

कौशेय, made of the *kush*-grass : silken.

कौषेय = **कौशेय**, *q.v.*

कौस, see (1) **कोश** (2) **कोष**.

कौसिक, *m. pr. n.* a certain tribe of Rājpoots.

कौसुम्भ, dyed with safflower.

कौसें in Braj = (1) **कैसा** (2) **कैसे** (3) **कोसों**, *qq.v.*

कौस्तुभ, *m. pr. n.* the jewel worn by Krishṇ on his breast.

क्या, 1, *interrog. pron.* (gen. **काहेका**) what ? how ? why ? The form is the same in both numbers ; *e. g. Kyā hai*, what is it ? *Kyā haiṅ*, what are they ? When repeated it has a distributive sense ; *e.g. Kyā kyā*, (what what things?) what things severally or respectively? *Kyā kahe to*, for example, thus. 2, *conj.* or, whether, *e. g. Kyā — kyā*, whether — or. 3, it is the sign of interrogation placed at the beginning of a question, like the Persian *āyā* and the Latin *an* or *num*, and is, like them, untranslated when in such a position : it anticipates agreement with the aim of the speaker ; *e. g. Kyā Ishwar patthar kai ki ātmā*, Is God a stone, or (is He not rather) a spirit ? 4, An exclamation of wonder or surprize ; *e. g. Kyā achchhā*, how fine ! well done ! bravo !

क्यां, of; at the house of, in the neighbourhood of, near, with.

क्यांन ; see **क्यां**.

क्यारी, *f.* a bed of a garden : a frame.

क्याही, (an emphasized exclamation of wonder or surprize); *e. g. — achchhā*, how *very* good ! how *very* fine !

क्यूं, a corruption of **क्यों**, *q.v.*

क्यों, why ? wherefore ? how ? what ? well ? what then ? then; because. — *na ho*, why should it not be ? what for no ? why not ? — *nahiṅ*, why not ? certainly, surely. *Hai — nahiṅ*, what for no ? why not ?

क्योंकर, *interrog.* by *doing* what ? by what means ? on what hypothesis ? how ? *adv.* how : *conj.* because.

क्योंकरके, *more com.* **क्योंकर**, *q.v.*

क्योंकि, because, because that, since.

क्योंके, *more com.* (1) **क्योंकि** (2) **क्योंकर**, *qq.v.*

क्योंक्यों, however much.

क्यौं in Braj = **क्यों**, *q.v.*

क्रता, *more prop.* **कृता**, *f.* ; see **कृत**, 3.

क्रतु, *m.* power : sacrifice : *pr. n.* (1) of one of the seven Rishis (2) of one of the ten Vishwadevs.

क्रन in Chand = **कर्ण**, *q. v.*

क्रन्दन, *m.* a weeping, lamenting. — *k.* to weep.

क्रनों, (in Chand =) to prick up the ears.

क्रम, *m.* a step ; a foot ; a posture for assailing ; a bound ; strength ; order succession, course, method, arrangement; uninterrupted progress ; a way ; a sacred precept ; intention.

क्रमक्रम = **क्रमक्रमसे**, *q.v.*

क्रमक्रमसे, gradually, little by little, by degrees, in due course.

क्रमि, *more prop.* **कृमि**, *q.v.*

क्रमी, *m.* (*f.* inī) *more prop.* **कृमी**, *q. v.*

क्रमेकमे, *more com.* **क्रमक्रमसे**, *q.v.*

क्रम्म in Chand = **कर्म**, *q.v.*

क्रय, *m.* buying ; purchase : purchased objects.

क्रयविक्रय, *m.* buying and selling, trafficking, trade.

क्रानी, *m.* a writer, clerk. The designation is generally applied to native or Eurasian clerks.

क्रान्त=**क्रान्ति**, *q. v.*

क्रान्ति, *f.* an ascending, surmounting (whether literally or figuratively); the declination of any heavenly body; the ecliptic; the sun's course on the ecliptic; the torrid zone: lustre, splendour.

क्रान्तिमंडल, *m.* the space of the heavens included within the tropics, the ecliptic.

क्रिमी, *more prop.* (1) **कृमि** (2) **कर्मी**, *qq. v.*

क्रियन्ह, (see **न्ह**) a Braj plural of **क्रिया**, *q. v.*

क्रिया, *f.* 1, a corruption of **किरिया**, *q. v.*: 2, performance, action, act, deed; business; use; a religious act, duty, act of piety, religious ceremony; obsequies; physical treatment; a literary work; (in Gram.) a verb.

क्रियाकर्म्म, *m.* the performance of obsequies.

क्रियाद्योतक संज्ञा, *f.* (in Gram.) the present participle.

क्रियार्थक संज्ञा, *f.* (in Gram.) a verbal noun.

क्रियावाचक संज्ञा, *f.* (in Gram.) a verbal noun.

क्रियावान, *m.* (*f.* vatī) a person engaged in business, etc.: *lit.* engaged in business; performing religious works.

क्रियाविशेषण, *m.* (in Gram.) an adverb.

क्रियेन्द्रिय = **कर्म्मेन्द्रिय**, *q. v.*

क्रिस्तान = **ख्रीष्टियान**, *q. v.*

क्रीट; see (1) **किरीट** (2) **कीट**.

क्रीटकुण्डल, *m.* the begemmed collar of Kṛishṇ.

क्रीड़पत्र, *m.* an appendix.

क्रीड़ा, *f.* sport, amusement, play, game, pastime, gambol. — *k.* to play, etc.

क्रीड़ारत्न, *m.* copulation.

क्रीड़ावान, *m.* (*f.* vatī) a gamester, etc.: *lit.* sporting, sportive.

क्रीड़ितृ, *m.* (*f.* trī) a gambler.

क्रीत, *m.* (*f.* ā) a child purchased from his parents and adopted as issue (one of the twelve kinds of childhood recognized by the ancient Hindoo law): *lit.* acquired by purchase, bought.

क्रीतक, *m.* (*f.* ikā) = **क्रीत**, *q. v.*

क्रीता, *f.* (*m.* **क्रीत**) an adopted daughter.

क्रीमिज, *m.* the *aguru* or aloe-wood.

क्रुद्ध, *m.* (*f.* ā) angry, wrathful.

क्रुध, *f.* (*m.* ?) anger, wrath, passion.

क्रूर, *m.* (*f.* ā) sore; hot, sharp; hard; cruel, pitiless, hardhearted, harsh, formidable, terrible, severe, savage.

क्रूरकर्मा, *m.* or *f.* fierce, cruel, relentless.

क्रूरकोष्ठ, *m.* torpid or costive bowels unaffected by strong purgatives.

क्रूरत्व, *m.* (*f.* tā) cruelty, fierceness, formidableness.

क्रूरदृश, evil-eyed, mischievous, villainous.

क्रूरदृष्टि, *f.* an evil look, glance of the evil eye.

क्रूश, *m.* across; a crucifix. — *par charhānā*, to crucify.

क्रूशयन्त्र, *m.* the cross as an instrument of punishment.

क्रूशाकार, cruciform.

क्रेत, *f.* a furrow.

क्रेता, **क्रेतृ** } *m.* (*f.* trī) a buyer, purchaser.

क्रोध, *m.* anger, raged, resentment.

क्रोधन, 1, *m.* anger: 2, *m.* (*f.* ā) a choleric person: *lit.* passionate, angry, wrathful, choleric.

क्रोधना, *f.* (*m.* **क्रोधन**, 2,) a vixen, scold.

क्रोधमय, *m.* (*f.* ī) a choleric person, etc.: *lit.* abounding in anger, choleric, passionate, wrathful.

क्रोधवन्त, *m.* (*f.* vatī) = **क्रोधन**, 2, *q. v.*

क्रोधवर्जित, *m.* (*f.* ā) a gentle person: *lit.* free from anger, mild, gentle.

क्रोधवश, *m.* (*f.* ā) a person under the influence or the sway of wrath: *lit.* ruled by wrath.

क्रोधवान, *m.* (*f.* vatī), **क्रोधिन**, (*f.* ī), **क्रोधी**, *m.* (*f.* inī) } = **क्रोधन**, 2, *q. v.*

क्रोश = **कोश**, *q. v.*

क्रौंच, 1, *m. pr. n.* (1) of a certain mountain (2) of a certain demon (3) of one of the dweeps or principal divisions of the world: 2, *m.* (*f.* ī) a kind of heron or curlew.

क्लान्त, wearied, fatigued, exhausted, languid.

क्लान्तमना, *m. f.* low-spirited, melancholy, languid.

क्लान्ति, *f.* languor, weariness, fatigue.

क्लिशित, *m.* (*f.* ā) = **क्लेशित**, *q. v.*

क्लिष्ट, *m.* (*f.* ā) afflicted, weary, distressed.

क्लिष्टत्व, *m.* (*f.* tā) distress, affliction, weariness.

क्लीब, *m.* a eunuch; a coward; an impotent man; (in Gram.) the neuter gender: *lit.* deprived of virility, emasculated, impotent, timorous, cowardly, slothful, idle.

क्लीबत्व, *m.* (*f.* tā) absence of virility.

क्लेद, *m.* humidity, dampness, moisture.

क्लेश, *m.* pain, anguish, affliction, trouble, care.

क्लेशबोधक, *m.* (in Gram.) any word (as an interjection) expressive of distress.

क्लेशित, *m.* (*f.* ā) a care-worn person, etc.: *lit.* pained, distressed, in anguish, afflicted, care-worn, wearied.

क्लैब्य, *m.* absence of virility, impotence, weakness, timidity, cowardliness, unmanliness; (in Gram.) the neuter gender.

क्ष (kṣh) is sometimes treated as a separate consonant in the Hindee alphabet; it is, however, compounded of **क** + **ष**, and has, in Hindee, the sound of *ksh* in the English word 'bookshelf,' or of *cti* in the word 'unction.' It is constantly interchanged with (1) **ख**; *e. g.* **खीन** = **क्षीण**; (2) with **छ**; *e. g.* **छमा** = **क्षमा**; (3) with **च्छ**; *e.g.* **लच्छ** = **लक्ष**; (4) with **ष**; *e.g.* **मोचन** = **मोक्षण**; it is also liable to be corrupted (1) into **झ**; *e. g.* **झिनझुझा**, properly **क्षोयाक्षुझा**; and (2) into **ख**; *e. g.* **लखन** = **लक्ष्मण**. Besides the form given to it in this Dictionary it is sometimes written thus **क्ष**. Lastly, it should be observed that if *n* follow this letter in the same word it is *murdhanya*, unless it be (1) in the sign of the infinitive; *e. g.* **क्षमना**; (2) an element of a compound letter; *e. g.* **क्षान्त**; (3) followed by *virām* written or understood; *e. g.* **क्षेत्रिन्**.

क्षईरोग, *more prop.* **क्षयरोग**, *q.v.*

क्षकार, *m.* the letter **क्ष**, or any symbol that may represent it.

क्षण, *m.* a moment; a measure of time equal to thirty *kalās* or four minutes: vacation from work, leisure; opportunity; a festival; the centre; the time of the new or full moon: *adv.* for a moment.

क्षण क्षण, moment by moment, every moment, continually, without intermission.

क्षणदा, *f.* night: turmeric.

क्षणदाचर, *m.* (*f.* ā *or* ī) any *rākshas* or demon.

क्षणभरमें, in a moment.

क्षणमात्र, momentarily, merely for a moment.

क्षणा; see (1) **दया** (2) **क्षपा**.

क्षणान्तर, *adv.* a moment afterwards, the next moment; moment by moment. [porary, fleeting.

क्षणिक, momentary, transient, transitory, tem-

क्षणी *m.* (*f.* inī) 1, = **क्षणिक**, *q.v.*: 2, *adj.* being at one's leisure. [while: 2, *adv.* in a moment.

क्षणेक, 1, *m.* one moment, an instant, a little

क्षत, *m.* a wound, sore, hurt, scar. [destroying.

क्षति, *f.* hurting, harm, detriment, injury, hurt,

क्षत्तृ, *m.* (*f.* trī) a carver; a doorkeeper; a charioteer; the child of a Shoodra by a Kshatriya woman.

क्षत्रनी (prop. **क्षत्राणी** or **क्षत्रियाणी**) = **क्षत्रिया**, *q.v.*

क्षत्राणी = **क्षत्रिया**, *q.v.*

क्षत्रानी = **क्षत्राणी** = **क्षत्रिया**, *q.v.*

क्षत्रियाणी, *f.* (*m.* **क्षत्री**) = **क्षत्रिया**, *q.v.*

क्षत्रिय, *m.* (*f.* ā) a Hindoo of the second (*i. e.* the military and regal) caste. [of the second caste.

क्षत्रियत्व, *m.* the condition and status of a Hindoo

क्षत्रिया, *f.* (*m.* **क्षत्रिय**) a female Hindoo of the second caste, a Kshatriya's wife.

क्षत्री, 1, *f.*; see *m.* **क्षत्तृ**; 2, *m.* (*f.* iṇī) = **क्षत्रिय**, *q. v.*

क्षद, *more prop.* **क्षुद**, *q.v.* [**क्षण**.

क्षन; for words beginning thus, see under the form

क्षपा, *f.* night: turmeric.

क्षपाचर, *m.* (*f.* ā *or* ī) any *rākshas* or demon.

क्षम, 1, *m.* propriety, fitness: 2, *m.* (*f.* ā) a patient person, etc.: *lit.* patient, enduring, endurable, able, capable, useful, suitable, favorable, benevolent.

क्षमना, *t.* to pardon, forgive.

क्षमस, a corruption of **क्षमस**, *q.v.*

क्षमा, *f.* patience, forbearance, forgiveness, pardon: the earth · night. — *k.* (with acc.) to forgive. — *chāhnā* to ask forgiveness, beg for mercy.

क्षमायुक्त, *m.* (*f.* ā) a patient, enduring, forbearing, forgiving person: *lit.* patient, forgiving.

क्षमायोग्य, pardonable, venial, forgivable.

क्षमारहित, *m.* (*f.* ā) unforgiving, impatient.

क्षमावन्त / **क्षमावान** } *m.* (*f.* vatī) = **क्षमायुक्त**, *q.v.*

क्षमाशील, *m.* (*f.* ā) a person of a patient or forgiving disposition. [forbearance or of forgiveness.

क्षमासागर, *m.* an epithet of God; *lit.* the ocean of

क्षमित, *m.* (*f.* ā) forgiven, pardoned.

क्षमी, *m.* (*f.* inī) = **क्षमायुक्त**, *q.v.*

क्षय, *m.* diminution, decrease in price, loss, waste, a wasting away, destruction, removal, decay, destruction of the universe, any sickness but especially consumption (*Phthisis*); (in Algebra) negative quantity, minus. [versal dissolution.

क्षयकाल, *m.* the end of all things, period of uni-

क्षयकास, *m.* a consumptive or phthisical cough.

क्षयनाशिनी, *f.* a certain plant (*Celtis orientalis*).

क्षयरोग, *m.* consumption (*Phthisis*).

क्षयरोगी, *m.* (*f.* īnī) a person suffering from consumption: *lit.* consumptive, hectic, phthisical.

क्षयवायु, *m.* the wind that is to blow at the end of the world.

क्षयसम्पद, *f.* total loss, destruction, ruin.

क्षया, decaying, perishable, liable to destruction.

क्षयी, *m.* (*f.* iṇī) consumptive, decreasing, decay-

क्षर, *m.* (*f.* ā) anything perishable. [ing.

क्षविका, *f.* a kind of rice.

क्षात्र, 1, *m.* the military caste; royal dignity: 2, *m.* (*f.* ī) appertaining to the military caste.

क्षान्त, *f.* patient, forbearing, endurance.

क्षान्ति, *f.* patience, forbearance, endurance.

क्षाया; see (1) **छाया** (2) **काया**.

क्षार, 1, *m.* (*f.* ā) salty, alkaline: 2, *m.* a burning corrosive substance, either soda or potash, caustic alkali, borax, borate of soda; salt; ashes; one species of cautery; a factitious or medicinal salt commonly called black salt.

क्षारकर्दम, *m.* an epithet of hell.

क्षारकर्म, *m.* the applying caustic alkali (*Lapis infernalis*) to proud flesh, etc. [sulphate of soda.

क्षारमृत्तिका, *f.* saline soil, especially an impure

क्षाररस, *m.* a salt or alkaline flavour. [yields potash.

क्षारवृक्ष, *m.* any tree (*e. g.* the plantain, etc.) which

क्षिति, *f.* a dwelling place; the earth; land: loss, destruction, wane; the period of the destruction of the universe.

क्षितिज, *m.* (*f.* ā) an epithet (1) of any tree (2) of the planet Mars (3) of the horizon: *lit.* sprung

क्षितिधर, *m.* any mountain. [from the earth.

क्षितिपति, *m.* (*f.* °**पत्नी**) a king, prince, sovereign, supreme ruler; *lit.* lord of the earth.

क्षितिपाल, *m.* (*f.* ī) a king, prince, sovereign, supreme ruler; *lit.* keeper or preserver of the earth.

क्षिन, *more prop.* (1) **क्षण** (2) **क्षीण**, *qq. v.*

क्षिपा, 1, *m.* (*f.* ī) *more prop.* **क्षिपा**, *q.v.*: 2, *f.* a sending, casting, throwing: night.

क्षिमा, a corruption of **क्षमा**, *q.v.*

क्षोटा (*corruption*) = **क्षोपटा**, *q.v.*

क्षीण, *m.* (*f.* ā) a decayed person or thing etc.: *lit.* thin, slender, subtle, fine, emaciated, decayed, diminished, wasted away, enfeebled, exhausted, miserable, poor, destroyed, lost.

क्षीणता, *f.* (*m.* °**त्व**) thinness, slenderness, emaciatedness, delicacy, diminution, decay, weakness.

क्षीणमन, of weak or decayed mental powers; of subtle intellect.

क्षीणवन्त } m. (f. vatī) = **क्षीणा**, q.v.
क्षीणवान }

क्षीणशक्ति, m. or f. whose force or power is decayed, impotent, feeble, weak.

क्षीणा, f. (m. **क्षीण**) an emaciated female, etc.

क्षीर, m. milk, thickened milk; the milky juice of plants: water (?).

क्षीरककोलिका, f. a certain medicinal root. It is apparently the root of a species of lily brought from the Himālayas, and is one of the eight principal medicaments of the Hindoos.

क्षीरतोयधि, m. = **क्षीरोद**, q. v. [drinking.

क्षीरप, m. (f. ā ?) a nurse-child: lit. adj. milk-

क्षीरमय, m. (f. ī) onsisting of milk, represented [by milk.

क्षीरनिधि }
क्षीरसमुद्र } m. = **क्षीरोद**, q.v.
क्षीरसागर }

क्षीरस्फटिक, m. a certain precious stone (opal or cat's-eye ?) described as a milky crystal.

क्षीरिणी, f. the name of several plants.

क्षीरी, m. (f. iṇī) anything abounding in or yielding milk; a certain tree (*Mimusops kanki*) and its fruit: lit. milky, yielding milk, having milk.

क्षीरोद, m. pr. n. (in Myth.) the ocean of milk (being one of the seven seas surrounding as many worlds).

क्षुद्र, m. (f. ā) a mean person, etc.: lit. small, mean, insignificant, little, low, contemptible, niggardly, indigent, poor.

क्षुद्रजीव, any lower animal, a brute beast.

क्षुद्रता, f. } smallness, insignificance, meanness.
क्षुद्रत्व, m. }

क्षुद्रबुद्धि, a person of mean intellect; *hence*, simple, ignorant, silly.

क्षुद्ररोग, m. a minor disease, a disease of little importance. [nor disease.

क्षुद्ररोगी, m. (f. iṇī) a person suffering from a mi-

क्षुद्रा, f. (m. **क्षुद्र**) a low female, a dancing-girl, a [harlot.

क्षुध, } f. hunger; appetite.
क्षुधा, }

क्षुधार्त, m. (f. ā) a very hungry person: lit. pain-

क्षुधालु, m. or f. hungry. [ed with hunger, famished.

क्षुधित, m. (f. ā) a hungry person: lit. hungry.

क्षुर, m. a razor: a hoof: name of certain plants (1) *Barleria longifolia* (2) *Tribulus lanuginosus*.

क्षुरपा, a kind of paddle-shaped instrument with a short handle for grubbing up grass for cattle.

क्षुरप, m. (= **क्षुरपा**) a kind of arrow with a horse-shoe head. [barber.

क्षुरी, 1, f. a knife, razor, dagger: 2, m. (f. iṇī) a

क्षेत्र m. landed property; a field; sphere of operation; a wife; any holy place (as Benares, etc.); the body; a place; extent; (in Geom.) plain surface bounded by a figure, a diagram, triangle, etc.

क्षेत्रज्ञ, m. (f. ā) a clever person: the soul: lit. clever, skilful, conversant with the body.

क्षेत्रफल, m. the measurement or superficial contents of a field or of any geometrical figure. [place.

क्षेत्रसीमा, f. the boundaries of a field or of a sacred

क्षेत्रिक, m. (f. ā) } = **क्षेत्री**, q.v.
क्षेत्रिन. m. (f. ṇī) }

क्षेत्री, m. (f. iṇī) the owner or the cultivator of a field, agriculturist; a husband.

क्षेद, m. grief, sorrow, moaning.

क्षेदित, m. (f. ā) a sorrowing, person, etc.: lit. sorrowing, mourning, afflicted, distressed, moaning.

क्षेप, m. a throw, cast; a stroke of an oar; a throw of a casting net: (in Math.) an additive quantity, addendum; abuse; a nosegay.

क्षेपक, m. (in Literature) a spurious or adulterated passage introduced into the text, an interpolation.

क्षेपण, m. a striking; a throwing; a passing the the time; a letting go (the string of a bow); an expelling; a suspension; a sling. [sile weapon.

क्षेपणी, f. an oar; a fishing-net; a sling, any mis-

क्षेम, 1, m. happiness, well-being, safety, prosperity, fortune, wealth: happiness etc. personified: pr. n. (1) of a certain prince (2) of one of the divisions of the continent: the term of civil salutation proper to be used by a Brāhmaṇ to a Vaishya: 2, m. (f. ā) a prosperous person, etc.: lit. safe, dangerless, prosperous, fortunate, happy, well in health.

क्षेमकर, m. (f. ī) one who confers happiness, etc.: lit. propitious, conferring happiness, prosperity, etc.

क्षेमकुशल, m. health and well-being.

क्षेमधर्म, m. the duty of forgiveness.

क्षेमधर्मा, m. pr. n. a son of king Shishunāg.

क्षेमवान, m. (f. vatī) a prosperous person, etc.: lit. safe, happy, prosperous, well-to-do, etc.

क्षेमी, m. (f. iṇī) = **क्षेमवान**, q. v. [several princes.

क्षेम्य, m. (f. ā) salubrious; secure: 2, the name of

क्षोणि, f. the earth.

क्षोणिप, m. a king, monarch; lit. lord of the earth.

क्षोणी, f. the earth.

क्षोभ, m. agitation, excitement, distress, anguish.

क्षौणि, } f. the earth.
क्षौणी, }

क्षौद्र, m. honey; water; a grape: a certain tree (*Michelia champaka*). [made of flax: made of linseed oil.

क्षौम, 1, m. a linen garment: linseed: 2, m. (f. ī)

क्षौर, m. shaving of the head or beard, the office of barber. — *banwānā*, to get oneself shaved.

क्षौरिक. m. (f. ā) a barber.

क्षौरी, f. a razor; shaving.

क्षौहिणी (*contraction*) = **अक्षौहिणी**, q.v. See **अ**, 18.

क्ष्मा, f. the terrestrial globe, the earth.

क्ष्मातल, m. the surface of the earth.

क्ष्मापति, m. (f. °**पत्नी**) a king, sovereign, monarch; lit. lord of the earth.

क्ष्माभृत, m. a king, sovereign, monarch; a mountain; lit. a supporter of the earth.

क्ष्मामण्डल, m. the terrestrial globe.

खेलिका, *f.* play, jest, joke, trick.

ख

ख (kh) is the second consonant in the Hindee alphabet, being the aspirated form of the letter **क**. It is the second letter of the **कवर्ग** or guttural class, and has, in pronunciation, the sound of *kh* in the English word 'blockhead' with the *ead* dropped. This letter is constantly interchanged (1) with the unaspirated form **क** ; *e. g.* **ककरी = कखरी** (2) with **छ** ; *e.g.* **खीन = छीण** (3) with **ष** ; *e. g.* **खट = षट : षट्वांग = खट्वांग**. It is also interchanged with **ह** ; *e. g.* **खरहरा = खरखरा**. In many of the words in common use in Hindee which are of Arabic or Persian origin, this letter has, properly speaking, a guttural sound which does not in reality exist either in Hindee or in English, but which is exactly represented by the sound of *ch* in the Scotch *loch* and in the German *buch* : that this is the required pronunciation in any particular instance will be indicated in this Dictionary by this letter with a dot under it ; *e.g.* **ख़**. Lastly :—this letter is alone a substantive *masculine* signifying the sky, ether ; a cavity, vacuity ; zero ; a cipher ; and hence, in the ingenious system of reckoning by symbols adopted by Hindoos in their poetry, this letter is a symbol for the cipher (0) *naught.*

खं, the sky, the air : the hold of a ship.

खंक, feeble, frail, weak.

खंकली, *f.* a certain plant, polypody, a kind of moss.

खंखल, land that requires to be left fallow for a

खंखड़, dry and crackling. [year or two.

खंखारना, *a. int.* to clear the throat preparatory to expectorating, to hem, hawk.

खंगर, *m.* semi-vitrified bricks.

खंगल, *more prop.* (1) **खंगर** (2) **खंगैल**, *qq.v.*

खंगारना = (1) **खंखारना** (2) **खंगालना**, *qq.v.* [rinse.

खंगाल डालना, *t.* to murder privately : to wash out,

खंगालना, *t*, to wash, wash out, rinse.

खंगैल, *m.* (*f.* ā) tusked. [limping.

खंज, *m.* (*f.* ā) a cripple, etc. : *lit.* lame, crippled,

खंजन, *m.* a species of wagtail (*Motacilla alba*).

खंजर, *m.* a dagger, poignard.

खंजरनी, *f.* (*dialectic*) = **खंजरी** *q.v.*

ख़ंजरी, *f.* a certain mode of printing or staining silk.

खंजरी, *f.* a small tambourine, timbrel.

खंजरीट = **खंजन**, *q. v.*

खंजा, *f.* a species of metre in which there is a stanza of two lines the one containing thirty-two feet and the other thirty.

खंड, खंठ, खंत, खंद, खंध, खंभ ; for all words beginning with either of these elements, see under the forms **खण्ड, खण्ठ, खन्त, खन्द, खन्ध, खम्भ**, respectively.

खंसना ; see (1) **खसना** (2) **खांसना**.

खंड़ाकं, *more prop.* **खड़ाकं**, *q.v.* [represent it.

खकार, *m.* the letter **ख**, or any symbol that may

खकेड़ना, *more prop.* **खखेड़ना**, *q.v.*

खक्खा, *m.* (*f.* ī) old, ancient, long elapsed.

खखेड़ना, *a. int.* (?) to hurry.

खखोरना, *t.* to scrape, scoop.

खग, *m.* (*f.* ā) wind, air ; any bird ; *lit.* sky-going, that which moves in air or the sky.

खगकेतु = **खगेश**, *q. v.*

खगहा, *m.* a rhinoceros.

खगेश, *m.* (*f.* ā) the regent of birds, a species of gigantic crane well known in India as the "adjutant-bird."

खगोल, *m.* the vault or circle of the heavens, the planisphere : the same represented artificially, the

खगोलविद्या, *f.* astronomy. [armillary sphere.

खग्ग / **खग्गो** } old forms of **खड्ग**, *q. v.*

खच, a ball of things fastened together.

खचना, *n.* to be set (as a jewel).

खचर, *adj.* moving or existing in the sky : hence (1) *m.* (*f.* ā *or* ī) any bird (2) *m.* a cloud.

खचा, *m.* (*f.* ī) set (as a jewel) : studded, inlaid,

खचित, *m.* (*f.* ā) = **खचा**, *q. v.* [set with jewels.

खच्चर, *m.* a mule.

खच्चरबान, *m.* a muleteer.

ख़ज़ानची, *m.* (*f.* in) a cashkeeper, treasurer.

ख़ज़ानचीगरी, *f.* treasurership.

ख़ज़ाना, *more prop.* **ख़िज़ाना**, *q. v.*

ख़जिल, modest, bashful, abashed, ashamed.

खजुली = **खुजली**, *q.v.*

खजूर, *m.* a date ; a date-tree (*Phoenix dactylifera*) : the wild date (*Elate silvestris*, Lin. ; *Phoenix silvestris*, Roxb.) : a kind of sweetmeat.

खजूरकड़ी, *f.* a kind of silk cloth stained with waving marks like traces of the old leaves on the trunk of the date-tree. [(as locks of hair).

खजूरा, 1, *m.* the ridge of a thatched roof : 2, plaited

खजूरिया, *m.* (dim. of **खजूर**) a small date-tree, small

खट = (1) **खाट** ; see **आ**, 3 (2) **षट** ; see **ष**, 5. [date.

खटक = **खटका**, *q. v.*

खटकत = **खटकता है** ; see **त**, 5.

खटकना, 1, *m.* doubt, hesitation ; disgust : 2, *a. int.* to doubt, be apprehensive : 3, *t.* to wrangle ; to offend ; to pierce (as a thorn might) ; to rankle : to nibble.

खटका, *m.* apprehension, doubt, scruple, suspicion, suspense, abodement, danger ; the sound of footsteps.

खटकाना, *m.* the rapping at, thumping, or rattling of, a door, etc. [relling ; toil, difficulty, trouble.

खटखट, a noise, voice, sound ; wrangling ; quar-

खटखटाना, *t.* to knock at a door, pat, rap, tap.

खटगोर, *m.* a bug.

खटछप्पर, *m.* a bedstead with curtains.

खटना, *a. int.* to last, continue, hold out.

खटपट, *f.* wrangling, quarrelling, contention, strife, conflict ; a clashing of weapons.

खटपटिया, quarrelsome.

खटपद, *m.* a species of large black bee.

खटपूरा, a kind of rake worked by hoe-men for breaking up the soil into small beds.
खटमल, *m.* a bug; *lit.* the bed-polluter.
खटमीठा, *m.* a mixed taste of sour and sweet, an agreeable taste.
खटमुत्त्वा, *m.* a piss-a-bed.
खटयाल, soiled, filthy, impure.
खटरस = **षटरस**, *q. v.*
खटराग, *m.* wrangling : singing discordantly.
खटरिया, *m.* a species of insect.
खटवा, *f.* a bedstead, couch, cot, hammock.
खटवाई, **खटवाट**, **खटवाटी**, *f.* confinement to bed from sickness.
खटशास्त्र = **षटशास्त्र**, *q. v.*
खटाई, *f.* acidity, sourness ; an acid.
खटाका, *m.* a crash.
खटापटी, *f.* wrangling, quarrelling.
खटापन, **खटापना**, *m.* acidity, sourness, moroseness.
खटाल, *m.* spring-tide.
खटाव, *m.* a pin with which a boat is fastened.
खटास, *m.* a polecat, the zibet or cibet or civet cat (*Vivetra zibetha*).
खटाहि, a remaining still or firm (?).
खटिका, *f.* chalk.
खटिया, *f.* (dim. of **खट** or **खाट**) a small bedstead : a bier. *Khuda kare uskī khatiyā nikale*, God grant that he may die ! *lit.* God grant that his bier may be carried out (a common form of cursing).
खटीक, *m.* a hunter, fowler, one who gets his living by killing and selling game.
खटोलना, a bedstead : a kind of net or snare.
खटोला, *m.* a small bedstead.
खट्टा, *m.* (*f.* ī) acid, sour.
खट्टामिट्ठा, *lit.* sour and sweet. — *khānā*, to take things as they go, take the bitter with the sweet.
खट्टास = **खटास**, *q. v.*
खट्टाहा, *m.* (*f.* ī) sourish : very sour. See **ह**, 2.
खट्टासाग, *m.* the herb sorrel.
खट्टिक = **खटीक**, *q. v.*
खट्टू, 1, *m.* a laborer : 2, ashamed, abashed.
खट्वा, *f.* a bedstead, couch, cot, hammock.
खट्वांग, *m.* one of the attributes of Shiv : one of Shiv's weapons, being a club with a skull at the top : *pr. n.* a certain king in *Tretā-Yug*.
खठोला, *more com.* **खटोला**, *q. v.*
खड़, *f.* grass, straw, grass and trees.
खडंक, dry, dried up, parched : acid.
खड़क, *f.* 1, a cowshed, cowhouse : 2, an imitative sound. — *jānā*, to take warning, be apprised.
खड़कट, chalk for writing with.
खड़कना, *a. int.* to crash, tingle, clang, rattle, rustle.
खड़का, 1, = (1) **खटका** (2) **खड़क**, *qq. v.* : 2, *m.* a toothpick.
खड़खड़ाना, *a. int.* to creak, clatter, rattle, jar ; to snore ; to grind the teeth.
खड़खड़ाहट, *f.* a snoring ; a creaking, clattering, rattling, clashing, jarring (as a door).
खड़ग = **खड्ग**, *q. v.*
खड़तल, 1, spoiled, bad, destroyed : 2, *m.* ruin.
खड़बड़ाहट, = **खड़बड़ी**, *q. v.*
खड़बड़ी, *f.* hurry, bustle, commotion, tumult, uproar, sound, the noise of horses' feet (*esp.* as in galloping) : griping on going to stool.
खड़बिड़, 1, the clang of metals : 2, rough, rugged, uneven.
खड़बीहड़, rough, rugged, uneven.
खड़बेड़, the clang of metals.
खड़मण्डल, *f.* a wrangling.
खड़साम, *m.* a whetstone, grindingstone.
खड़हर, fallen to ruins, laid waste.
खड़ा, *m.* (*f.* ī) erect, standing, standing up, upright, perpendicular, steep, high, aground ; ready ; ripe : *hence*, honest, all right, payable on demand. — *k.* to raise up, stick up, place erect ; to station, locate, pitch ; to procure a fictitious person for some purpose. — *rahnā*, to remain standing, to stay. — *honā*, to stand, rise, stand erect.
खड़ाई, *f.* erectness ; steepness ; uprightness.
खड़ाऊं, *m. f.* a wooden shoe, clogs, pattens.
खड़ाऊंदार, *m.* a kind of shoes fastened to pattens.
खड़ांव = **खड़ाऊं**, *q. v.*
खड़ाका, *m.* a crash, noise made in breaking.
खड़ावां, = **खड़ाऊं**, *q. v.*
खड़िया, *f.* chalk : a mark.
खड़िल, *f.* a mortar.
खड़ी, *f.* chalk.
खड़ीमिट्टी, *f.* chalk.
खड़ुआ, *m.* a bracelet, ornament for the wrist.
खड़ेखड़े, soon, immediately, instantly, presently, quickly.
खड़ेपत्थर, *m.* a slab of stone placed under a pillar or post, the plinth of a column, a flat stone with a hole bored in it in which a pole is set upright.
खड़ेलन्द, *m.* a day-book, journal : an account drawn out on a loose bit of paper.
खड्ग, *m. f.* a sword, scimitar : a rhinoceros. — *mārnā*, to administer a blow with a sword, fight with a sword.
खड्गी, *m.* (*f.* inī) a person armed with a sword ; a rhinoceros.
खड्डा, *m.* the kneepan.
खढ़, *more prop.* **खड़**, *q. v.*
खण, 1, = **क्षण**, *q. v.* : 2, the sky, the air : the hold of a ship.
खणा, an old form = **खण्ड**, *q. v.*
खण्ड, *m.* a side, portion, piece, quarter, section, a subdivision of a literary work, fragment, chapter, apartment, a province, district, region, division of the earth (in this sense much used in the composition of Indian names of places ; *e. g.* Bundēl-Khaṇḍ, popu-

larly Bundlecund): a flaw in a jewel: coarse sugar: the songs of Padmāwat.

खण्डन, *m.* the reducing anything to pieces, a breaking, dividing, rescinding, revoking, removing, averting, refuting, thwarting. — *k.* to divide, cut up, cut to pieces; to refute; to rescind; to revoke; to rescind: to revoke.

खण्डना, *t.* to divide, cut up; to demolish; to interrupt, prevent; to refute; to revoke; to rescind.

खण्डभूमि, *f.* a section of a country, a province, county, shire, zillah, state.

खण्डर, *m.* a broken-down building, ruins (of a [house, town, etc.).

खण्डरिच } **खण्डरीच** } *m.* the wagtail.

खण्डला, *m.* a piece of land, flake, slice (*esp.* of fish).

खण्डहर = **खण्डर**, *q.v.*

खण्डा (*contraction*) = **खाण्डा**, *q.v.*

खण्डित, *m.* (*f.* ā) cut, torn, broken to pieces; controverted; averted; revoked; refuted; destroyed; scattered, dispersed.—*k.* to refute, interrupt, prevent, etc.

खण्डिता, *f.* a woman who, provoked at the infidelities of her husband or lover, becomes somewhat abusive, and speaks her mind freely, but retains no [malice in her breast.

खण्डेर = **खण्डर**, *q.v.*

खण्ठ = **खण्ड**, *q.v.*

खण्ठोर, turbid.

ख़त, *m.* an epistle, letter, note; hand-writing: a [line, stripe: moustache, beard.

ख़तना, *m.* circumcision. — *k.* (with gen. of the [object) to circumcise.

ख़तनावाला, circumcised.

ख़तनाहीन, uncircumcised.

ख़तनाहीनता, *f.* uncircumcision.

ख़तब, *m.* a marrying, betrothing, contracting a marriage: a thing; a cause; a work.

ख़तबा, see (1) **ख़तब** (2) **ख़ुतबा**.

ख़तम, *m.* end, conclusion, seal: *adj.* done, finished. — *k.* to conclude. — *honā*, to be concluded.

ख़तर *m.* coming into the mind, recollection, thought, danger, risk; fortune.

ख़तरा, *m.* danger, fear, risk, venture. — *na k.* to do a thing without compunction, make no bones of. *Khatremeṅ ḍālnā*, to endanger, to risk, to venture.

खतरानी = **छत्राणी** = **छत्रिया**, *q.v.*

खतरी *m.* (*f.* in *or* iṇī) = **छत्री**, *q.v.*

खतवारा, *m.* a dunghill.

ख़ता, *f.* a mistake, error, fault, crime, — *k.* to err, miss; to sin. — *honā*, to be deficient, to fail, to be guilty of a fault.

ख़ताकार, one who fails, one who errs, a sinner.

खत्ता, *m.* a granary, grainpit, cavity in the ground for storing grain in: a kind of liniment for inflamed [eyes.

ख़त्म, *m.* (= **ख़तम**) a conclusion, end, seal.

खत्रानी = **छत्राणी** = **छत्रिया**, *q.v.*

खत्री, *m.* (*f.* in *or* iṇī) = **छत्री**, *q.v.*

खदखदाना } **खदबदाना** } *a.int.* to make a boiling noise, simmer.

ख़दशा, *m.* fear, alarm, apprehension, solicitude, [doubt, question.

खदिर, *m.* a certain tree (*Mimosa catechu*) the resin of which is used in medicine, *kutthā* or catechu.

खदिरोपम, *m.* the bābool (*Acacia Arabica*).

खदी, *f.* a certain grass that grows in ponds.

खदेड़, *f.* pursuit, chase. — *denā*, to drive away.

खदेड़ना, *t.* to pursue, hunt, give chase.

खदेरना, *more com.* **खदेड़ना**, *q.v.*

खद्दा, *m.* a hole dug in the ground.

खद्योत, *m.* (*f.* ā) a firefly: the sun.

खन, 1, = **क्षण**, *q.v.*: 2, *m.* a division of a house; a story, flight of rooms: a mine: a certain day of the fortnight, as the full of the moon, the change of the [moon, etc.

खनकना = **खनखना**, *q.v.*

खनखना, *a. int.* to jingle, ring, clink (as metal [bowls).

खनना, *t.* to scrape, dig.

ख़नब, *m.* an arched building, cupola, portico, porch.

खनी, *f.* a pit or hole in which rice in the husks is [kept.

खन्ती, *f.* a dibble, paddle for digging the ground [with.

खन्द, *more prop.* **खण्ड**, *q. v.*

ख़न्दक़, *m.* a ditch, fosse, moat.

खन्दल, a field, an open plain.

खन्दलाट, *f.* the act of trampling under foot.

ख़न्दान, smiling, laughing, merry.

खन्दाना, *m.* a pit from which earth has been dug out to make bricks or pottery: a notch in a log of wood.

खन्धक; see **ख़न्दक़**, *q.v.*

खन्धा, *more prop.* **कन्धा**, *q.v.*

खपटा, *m.* a broken tile; a slice of a mango.

खपत, 1, *f.* vent; sale: 2, expended.

खपती, *f.* vent; sale; expense: request: a lunatic.

खपना, 1, *m.* a company of travellers: 2, *a. int.* to enter, penetrate, join, mix with; to remain: 3, *n.* to sell, go off; to be dried up, be absorded, be expended, be made away with.

खपर = **खप्पर** = **खर्पर**, *q.v.*

खपरा, *m.* a tile for roofing: an arrow with a broad [point.

खपरिया, a heavier sort of plough for stiff soil.

खपरी, *f.* (dim. of **खपरा**) a small tile: the skull.

खपरेल, *f.* a tile.

खपरेलकी जाली, *f.* a window built of semicircular [tiles.

खपरैल, *f.* a tiled house, a building of tiles, tiling.

खपरैलवाला, *m.* (*f.* ī) tiled.

खपाच, *f.* a piece torn off from a bamboo, splinter: a very lean person.

खपाना, *t.* to dry up, destroy, make away with [despatch, waste, ravage.

खपुर, *m.* the betel-tree (*Areca faufel* or *catechu*).

खप्पर = **खर्पर**, *q.v.*

ख़फ़ा, 1, *m. f.* angry, cross, vexed, enraged; 2, *f.* [a secret; a concealment.

ख़फ़ीफ़, of no consequence, of no weight, of light character, light, undignified; immoral.

खब, a wrinkle, fold, notch, groove.

ख़बर, *f.* news, advices, rumour, report, account, [fame.

ख़बरकाग़ज़, *m.* a newspaper.
ख़बरदार, careful, cautious. — *honā*, (with abl. of the object) to be cautious, have a care.
ख़बरदारी, *f.* carefulness, cautiousness, care. — *k.* (with gen. of the object) to take care, take care of.
ख़ब्स, *m.* malice, malignity, spitefulness, perfidy : [impurity.
खबसा, *m.* slime, mud.
ख़बीस, 1, *m.* (*f.* ī) impure, base, malignant, wicked : 2, *m.* an evil spirit. [female.
ख़बीसी, *f.* impurity, wickedness : a malignant
खब्बा, *m.* (*f.* ī) a lefthanded person.
खभार, *m.* wrangling; trouble, perplexity; encumbrance. [trouble.
खभाड़, *m.* agitation, excitement, anguish, distress,
ख़म, *m.* a jar, a still, an alembic : a fold, ply, coil, curl, that part of a noose which encircles the neck.
खम, *m.* a pillar, post, stake. — *ṭhoṅknā*, to strike the palms of the hands against the arms as wrestlers do preparatory to wrestling; to challenge (as wrestlers do in the above-mentioned manner).
ख़मख़ाना, *m.* a wine-cellar, a tavern.
ख़मची, *f.* a kind of jockey-whip, a lash.
ख़म्र, *m.* a covering, hiding, fermenting, leavening; strong drinks in general and wine in particular.
खमस, the hot weather : *lit.* sultry.
खमसाई. *f.* sultriness, heat.
ख़मदार, twisted, bent, crooked, curled.
खमाच, *f.* one of the musical modes.
ख़मीदा, *m. f.* awry, crooked, bent.
ख़मीदाक़द, bent in form or stature.
ख़मीर, *m.* leaven, anything that is used for fermenting. — *k.* to leaven, ferment.
ख़मीरः }
ख़मीरा } = ख़मीर, *q.v.*
ख़मीरी, *m.* (*f.* iṇī) leavened, fermented.
खमीलन, *m.* lassitude, weariness, sleepiness.
ख़मोश, mute, silent, dumb.
ख़मोशान, the dead ; *lit.* the mute ones.
ख़मोशी, *f.* silence, muteness, dumbness. [porch.
खम्ब, *m.* an arched building, cupola, partico,
खम्बा }
खम्भ } *m.* a pillar, post, stake.
खम्भा }
ख़म्मारी, *m.* (*f.* in *or* iṇī) one who is drunk.
ख़म्सा, five ; an aggregate of five poetical pieces.
खयर; see (1) खैर (2) ख़ैर.
ख़यानत, *f.* perfidy, treachery, embezzlement.
खयाल; see (1) ख्याल (2) ख़्याल.
खर, 1, = खड़, *q.v.* : 2, *m.* a general term for a demon : 3, *m.* (*f.* ī) an ass ; a proper name : 4, solid ; brittle ; pointed, sharp ; hot ; hoarse.
खरंज, *more prop.* खडंज, *q.v.*
खरंजा, *m.* a pavement.

खरक, corruption (1) of खड़क (2) of खड्ग, *qq.v.*
खरका, corruption of खड़का, *q.v.*
खरकाना, *t.* to thump, shake : to frighten away, put [to flight : to sell.
खरखरा, *m.* a currycomb.
खरखरिया, *f.* a chair, litter.
ख़रगोश, *m.* a hare ; a rabbit.
खरगोस, *more prop.* ख़रगोश, *q.v.*
ख़रच, *m.* expenditure, expense, price. — *k.* to draw upon, use, use up, spend. — *lagnā*, to cost (whether money, time, strength, sense, food, or anything else). — *honā*, to be expended, be used up.
खरचक्र, *m.* (in Gram.) a table of vowels.
ख़रचना *t.* to draw upon, use, use up, spend.
ख़रचा, *m.* the costs in lawsuits.
खरछरा, *m.* (*f.* ī) rough.
खरज = खरच, *q.v.* [needle or of an axe.
ख़रत, a hole ; the orifice of the ear ; the eye of a
खरतल, low, vile, wicked, base.
ख़रतूम, *m.* an elephant's trunk. [brothers.
खरदूषण, *m. pr. n.* (खर + दूषण) a couple of demon-
खरपा, *m.* a sandal : the seam of a garment which extends from the armpit down the side.
खरबर, *f.* the sound of horses' feet in galloping ; hurry, bustle, commotion, tumult.
खरबुजा, *more prop.* ख़रबूज़ा, *q.v.* [cumber.
ख़रबूज़ा, *m.* a muskmelon (*Cucumis melo*), a cu-
खरभर, *m.* agitation, excitement, anguish.
खरमस्त, athletic : stupid.
खरल, *m.* a mortar, stone for grinding medicine on.
खरह, *more prop.* खड़, *q.v.*
खरहक, a portion of grain given at the end of
खरहरा = खरखरा, *q.v.* [harvest to village servants.
खरहा, *m.* (*f.* ī) a hare, a rabbit.
खरहारना, *t.* to sweep.
खरही, *f.* a stack, rick : a kind of grass.
खरा, *m.* (*f.* ī) pure, prime, best sort, genuine, honest, sincere, candid.
खराई, *f.* purity, excellence, probity, trustiness, honesty, candour, rectitude, uprightness.
खराऊं }
खरांउ } (Rām.) = खड़ाऊं, *q.v.*
खरांउं }
खराका, *m.* a crashing noise.
ख़राब, bad, wicked, depraved ; gone bad, spoiled, depopulated, deserted, ruined ; miserable, lost ; waste (as land unfit for cultivation). — *k.* to spoil, despoil, etc. — *honā*, to be spoiled. — *ho jānā*, to go bad.
ख़राबी, *f.* badness, wickedness, depravity ; ruin, desolation ; mischief : evil, an evil ; misery ; affliction.
खरारा, *m.* a currycomb. [(who slew them).
खरारी (*Rām*) = खरदूषणका अरि, an epithet of Rām
ख़राश, *m.* excoriation, scraping, scratching.
खराहन्द, *f.* the stalk of burnt grass.

खरिका, *f.* a toothpick. [oilcake.
खरी, 1, *f.* of **खर**, *q.v.*: 2, *f.* of **खरा**, *q.v.*: 3, *f.* chalk:
ख़रीता, *m.* a purse, bag, packet, mail; *met.* a letter.
ख़रीद, *f.* purchase.
ख़रीदा, *m. f.* purchased, bought.
ख़रीदार, *m.* a purchaser, buyer. [demand.
ख़रीदारी, *f.* buying, purchasing; traffic, commerce;
ख़रीफ़, *f.* autumn; the autumnal harvest; the first crop in the year consisting chiefly of rice.
खरी, corruption of **खड़**, *q.v.*
खरोचना, *t.* to scrape, scratch.
खरोञ, *m.* a scraping, a scratching.
खरोटना, *t.* to scrape, scratch.
खरोयट, *f.* a scratch with the nail.
खरोयटना, *t.* to scrape, scratch. [clamour.
ख़रोश, *m.* a crash, loud noise, tumult, shout,
ख॰; for words beginning thus, but not given below, see under the form **खर**; *e.g.* **खर्च** = **खरच**.
खर्घ; see **खड्ग**. [which it is equivalent in sense.
खर्चबर्च, a common jingle on the word **खरच**, to
खर्चराह, *m.* travelling-expenses.
खर्ज, 1, *m.* = **खरच**, *q.v.*: 2, *f.* the bass in music.
खर्जूर, *m.* the date-tree (*Phœnix silvestris*).
खर्जूररस, *m.* the juice or extract of the wild date (*tāṛi*) used (1) to leaven bread (2) as an intoxicating liquor when in a state of spontaneous fermentation.
खर्पर, *m.* the skull, cranium, upper part of the head: the back: a chafingdish: an earthen cup used by yogees: the vessel in which the blood of a victim is offered: a tile: a thief, rogue, cheat: a collyrium for the eyes.
खर्व, **खर्ब्ब**; for words beginning thus, see under the form **खर्व**.
खर्रा, *m.* the rough draft of a letter or of any writing: an iron instrument for rubbing horses with, a curry-comb: an ulcer (with hardness of the skin) on the
खर्राटा, *m.* a snoring. [back of the foot.
खर्व, *m.* a very great number, a billion, ten thousand millions, a quadrillion, 1 followed by 37 naughts.
खर्वट, *m.* a market town, country town.
खर्वनिखर्व, an intensive form = **खर्व** (?).
खर्सम्बल, *m.* a large kind of kidney-bean (*Dolichos lunatus*), the Duffin bean.
खर्ह, *more prop.* **खड़**, *q.v.*
खल, 1, *m.* an oilcake, sediment, deposit of oil: a threshingfloor, granary; stock (of grain): 2, a pit: 3, an entertainment: 4, *m.* (*f.* ā) a bad person, etc.: *lit.* low, vile, base, wicked, mischievous, artful, malignant, cruel: 5, *m.* the plant *Achyranthes lanata* (woolly *Illecrum* or mountain knot-grain: 6, the crash of an earthen vessel breaking to pieces.
खलउ in Braj = **खल**, 4, *q.v.*
खलंगा, *m.* a park.
ख़लक, ethics. [els).
खलखलाना, *a. int.* to rumble, grumble (as the bow-
खलगंजन, *adj.* sin-destroying.

खलड़ा, *m.* the hide, the skin.
खलड़ी, *f.* skin, hide, membrane; the prepuce.
खलता, *f.* malice, wickedness, artfulness, villainy;
खलबल = **खलबली**, *q.v.* [worthlessness; filthiness.
खलबलाना, *a. int.* to bubble, boil; *met.* to be agitated, be in commotion, be tossed up and down.
खलबली, *f.* hurry, bustle, agitation, tumult, hurly-burly, commotion, alarm.
खलयान, *more prop.* **खलियान**, *q.v.*
ख़लल, *m.* interruption, disturbance, confusion; prejudice; damage, detriment, injury, ruin.
ख़लवत, *f.* retirement, solitude, privacy; a private apartment, closet; a conference.
ख़लवतख़ाना, *m.* a place of retirement, private apartment, closet, cabinet.
ख़लवतगाह, *f.* } = **ख़लवतख़ाना**, *q.v.*
ख़लवतस्थान, *m.* }
ख़लवती, *m.* (*f.* in *or* inī) one who is admitted into private apartments, an intimate friend, confidante; a hermit, recluse.
ख़लस, *m.* a true friend, sincere friend.
खला, 1, *f.* of **खल**, *q.v.*: 2, *m.* vacuity, vacancy.
ख़लाइक़, *f.* (pl. of **ख़ल्क़**) the creation, created beings, people, mankind.
खलाड़ी, *f.* the place in which salt is boiled.
खलाफत = **ख़िलाफ़त**, *q.v.*
खलायक = **ख़लाइक़**, *q.v.*
खलार, *m.* a hollow, a bottom.
खलाल, very wet, dripping wet, weltering.
ख़लालत, *f.* sincere friendship: bits of meat sticking between the teeth.
खलाला, *m.* a fountain, a *jet d'eau*.
ख़लास, *m.* freedom, release, discharge, emancipation, redemption. — *k.* to release, — *honā*, to be freed; to emit, calve, be brought to bed.
ख़लासी, 1, *f.* = **ख़लास**, *q.v.*: 2, *m.* a native artillery-man; a native sailor; a tent pitcher (*vulg.* Clashee
खलि, *m.* = **खली**, *q.v.* [or Calashee).
खलियान, *m.* a granary, barn, threshingfloor.
खलियाना, *t.* to flay, skin.
खलिश, *m.* a kind of fish (*Trichopodus colisa*).
खलिहान = **खलियान**, *q.v.*
खली, *f.* the dregs of mustard-seed, etc. after the oil is pressed out; oilcakes.
ख़लीफ़ा, *m.* a sovereign, (popularly) the kaliph; a cook; a tailor: a monitor (at school).
खलील, a sincere and intimate friend.
खलीहान = **खलियान**, *q.v.*
खलु, certainly.
खलेल, *m.* scented oil: a hole made by children for playing at trap-ball or at marbles.
खलेश = **खलिश**, *q.v.*
खलोक्ति, *f.* abuse, low or wicked language.
ख़ल्क़, *f.* (*pl.* **ख़लाइक़**) people, mankind, the creation, created things.

खल्ल, *m.* a mill, a stone or vessel for grinding :
खल्लक ; see (1) **ख़लक़** (2) **ख़ल्क़** (3) **ख़ल्लाक़**. [a bag.
खल्ला, *m.* a shoe : a place where grain is trodden out by oxen, a threshingfloor ; a granary ; a store of grain.
ख़ल्लाक़, *m.* the Creator, the Almighty.
खल्लिट, bald.
खल्ली = **खली**, *q.v.*
खवा, *m.* the shoulder.
ख़वाजा, *m.* man of distinction, rich merchant,
खवाट = **खाट**, *q. v.* [gentleman, governor, master.
ख़वान, *m.* a tray.
खवाना, *t.* (causat. of **खाना**) to cause to eat, *i. e.* to feed ; to administer (or cause to take) an oath ; to cause to suffer ; *e. g. Mār* — , to cause to be beaten.
ख़वानी, *f.* a reading, repeating, recitation.
खवाब, *more prop.* (1) **कबाब** (2) **ख़्वाब**, *qq.v.*
ख़वास, *m.* (pl. of **ख़ास**) domestics ; grandees, ministers of State ; a favorite, a page : properties, qualities. [man on an elephant.
ख़वासी, *m.* the place where one sits behind a great
खवाहिश, *more prop.* **ख़्वाहिश**, *q. v.*
ख़वीद, *m.* a green field ; a sown field; green grass
खवैया, *m.* an eater. [cut for cattle.
खश, *m.* (*f.* ā) a certain caste of Hindoos ; the child of an outcast Kshatriya. [ments are made.
ख़शन, a kind of grass from which coarse gar-
खशरीर, *m.* a celestial, immortal, or ethereal form.
खशरीरी, *m.* (*f.* iṇī) a celestial : *lit.* having an
खशुसन, *more prop.* **ख़ुशूसन**, *q. v.* [ethereal form.
खशतर, *more prop.* **ख़स्तर**, *q.v.*
ख़श्का, *m.* boiled rice.
ख़श्म, *m.* anger, passion, rage, fury.
खस = (1) **खश** (2) **खसखस**, *qq.v.*
खसकन्त, *f.* a separation ; a running away.
खसकाना, *t.* to remove, shove out of the way, slide away, draw back.
खसखस, *f.* the poppy-head ; the scented root of a species of grass (*Andropogon muricatum*) used for making door-screens for use in the hot weather. The screens are sprinkled with water to cool the atmosphere of the rooms.
खसखसरस, *m.* poppy-juice, opium.
खसखसा, *m.* a grinding the teeth.
खसखसाना, *a. int.* to grind the teeth.
खसना, *a. int.* to fall. [tion in value.
ख़सर, *m.* damages, loss, injury, fraud : deprecia-
खसरा, *m.* a day-book, field-book, waste-book ; rough drawings, draught (of an account) : a kind of eruptive disease, a scab.
खसरीर, *more prop.* **खशरीर**, *q. v.*
ख़सलत, *f.* habit, custom, quality, property, disposition, nature ; mode, talent, virtue. [fall in.
खसाना, *t.* to ruin : to open, loosen ; *a. int.* to sink,
ख़सी, *m.* a eunuch; a castrated animal (*esp.* a goat).
खसोटना, *t.* to pull, pluck, pull the hair, scratch, tear, cause the hair to stand on end.
ख़स्तर, noxious insects, reptiles.
ख़स्ता, *m. f.* wounded, sick, infirm.
ख़स्ताहाल, afflicted, grieved.
खस्फटिक, *m.* crystal, the sun-gem, the moon-gem.
ख़स्म, *m.* anger, passion, rage, fury.
ख़ह्हे, *exclam.* well done ! how good ! bravo !
ख़ाइफ़, timid, pusillanimous, afraid.
खाइयां, *f.* (nom. pl. of **खाई**) ditches, trenches.
खाई, 1. *f.* (*m.* **खाया**) eaten : 2, *f.* a ditch, trench, moat, drain (*esp.* a moat as a boundary between two
खाईं, *f.* (pl. of **खाई**, 1) eaten. [estates.)
खाईं } see (1) **खाई** (2) **खाईं**.
खाऊ, voracious, gluttonous : hence, *m.* or *f.* one who eats excessively, a glutton.
खाऊमीत, avaricious, greedy.
खांग. *m.* a tusk.
खांगे, diminution, deficiency.
खांच, *m.* slime, mud.
खांचा, *m.* a tray, basket, pannier ; a cage, aviary, hencoop : muddy or marshy soil, quagmire, a marsh.
खांड़ा = **खांडा**, *q. v.*
खांदान, *more prop.* **ख़ान्दान**, *q.v.*
खांवगा, *more prop.* **खाऊंगा** (**खाना**).
खांसना, 1, *m.* a coughing : 2, *a. int.* to cough.
खांसी, *f.* a cough.
ख़ाक, *f.* dust, earth, ashes. [est caste.
ख़ाकरोब, *m.* a sweeper, menial servant of the low-
ख़ाकसार, *m.* a humble suppliant : *lit.* base, mean,
खाख ; see (1) **काख** (2) **ख़ाक**. [low-born.
खाग, *m.* the horn of a rhinoceros : a pillar or mound marking the boundaries of a village.
ख़ागीना, *m.* fried eggs, a kind of dish made of eggs,
खाज, *f.* (*m.* ?) the itch. [an omelet, pancake, etc.
खाजा, *m.* a certain sweetmeat like pie-crust ; *lit.* hard, firm.
खा जाना, *t.* (intensive) to eat up, eat away, devour. *Merā jān khā gayā*, (*lit.* he has eaten up my life, *i. e.*) he has given me a great deal of trouble or bother, he has worn me out.
खाट, *f.* a bedstead ; a cot on which corpses are conveyed to the pile, a bier.
खाड़ी, 1, see **खड़ी** ; 2, a valley (?).
खाडू, *m.* a decrepit old man : *lit.* very feeble.
खांड, *m.* coarse sugar.
खांडना, *t.* to excavate, to pound.
खांडा, *m.* a straight double-edged sword, a cutlass ; butcher's cleaver ; a flake or slice of fish. *Khāṇḍe-ke dharpar chalnā*, to arbitrate, decide. —*mārnā*, to administer a blow with a *khāṇḍā*.

खात, 1, = **खाट**, *q.v.* : 2, = **खाद**. *q.v.* : 3, *m.* a pit ;
खातगी, *f.* food, eating. [subterraneous granary.
खाता, *m.* 1, the act of eating : 2, a daily account, day-book.
खाताबन्दी, *f.* an abstract of individual accounts.
खाताबाड़ी, *f.* a store-house.
खातावनी, *f.* a ledger.
ख़ातिम, a ring worn on the fingers ; a seal.
ख़ातिमा, *m.* end, conclusion, epilogue, finis.
ख़ातिर, *f.* the heart, soul, inclination, memory, propensity, will, choice ; account, sake.
ख़ातिरजमा, *f.* assurance, encouragement, satisfaction; *lit.* collected, composed, assured, tranquil, at ease.
ख़ातिरदारी, *f.* encouragement, comfort, gratification, satisfaction.
ख़ातिरख़्वाह, agreeable to one's wishes, satisfactory.
खाती, 1, *m.* a carpenter : 2, *f.* a certain caste generally employed as cartwrights.
ख़ातून, *f.* a lady, a matron.
खाद, 1, = **खात**, 2, *q.v.* : 3, *f.* the expense incurred by cultivators in the repairs of their ploughing apparatus : 3, *f.* manure, dung.
खादक, *m.* (*f.* ikā) a borrower, user ; *lit.* an eater.
खादर, low or alluvial lands fit for rice-cultivation.
ख़ादा *m.* a straight branch ; a broomstick; an oar ; a gibbet; a coal-rake.
ख़ादिम, *m.* a servant. [very coarse cotton stuff.
खादी, 1, *m.* (*f.* inī) = **खादक**, *q.v.* : 2, *f.* a kind of
खाद्य, 1, *m.* eatables, victuals : 2, edible, fit to be eaten, lawful to be eaten.
खाद्यवस्तु, *m.* eatables, victuals, food.
ख़ान, *m.* a lord, prince (a title used chiefly by Pathāns : in Hindustān it signifies the lowest order of the Moghal nobility). [abundance.
खान, *f.* a mine: *met.* a nest ; a receptacle ; a heap,
खानक, *m.* (*f.* ikā) a digger, delver, miner. [dry.
खानखर, *m.* a pit, shaft of a mine ; anything very
खानदान, *m.* family, race, house, household.
खानपान, *m.* eating and drinking, feeding.
ख़ानमान, *m.* household furniture, everything belonging to a house, family, household.
ख़ानसामाँ, *m.* a house-steward.
ख़ाना, *m.* a house, place, dwelling: a drawer, partition, compartment, apartment.
खाना, 1, *m.* eating, food, dinner, repast, feast.— *khānā*, to eat : 2, *t.* to eat; to suffer, undergo, experience ; to embezzle ; to get ; *met.* to hold, contain. *Kasam* or *kiriyā* —, to take one's oath, to swear.
ख़ानाजंगी, *f.* domestic strife, civil war, bickering, duel, skirmish. [and drink.
खानापीना, *m.* board, fare, food, victuals; *lit.* food
ख़ानाबदोश, a traveller, pilgrim, gipsy, rover, so-
खानि = **खान**, *q.v.* [journer.
खानिक, 1, *m.* (*f.* ā) *more prop.* **खानक**, *q.v.* : 2, *m.* a breach in a wall : 3, appertaining to a mine.

खानी = **खान**, *q.v.*
खान्दा, a corruption of **कान्धा**, *q.v.* [house.
खान्दान, *m.* retainers, household, family, race,
खान्हारा, *m.* (*f.* ī) an eater, devourer.
खापड़ि ; see **खपरी** or **खोपरी**.
खाब = **ख़्वाब**, *q.v.* [mitory.
खाबगाह, *f.* a sleeping-apartment, bedroom, dor-
खाबड़, uneven.
खाम, *m.* a post, pillar, column, mast of a ship, tent-
खामखाह, *more prop.* **ख़ाहमख़ाह**, *q.v.* [pole.
ख़ामा, *m.* a pen, writing-reed.
ख़ामादान, *m.* a pen-case.
ख़ामी, *f.* rawness, unripeness : loss.
ख़ामोश, *m.* a certain disease in horses.
खाया, *m.* (*f.* **खाई**) eaten. (**खाना**.) [or of soda.
खार, *m.* alkali, potash, impure carbonate of potash
ख़ार, *m.* a thorn, thistle, bramble, spine ; a goad,
खारज, *f.* the bass in music. [spur, cock's-spur.
खारवा, *m.* a sailor (a designation much used on the western coasts of India) : a coarse kind of red
खारवामाटी, *f.* alkaline soil. [cloth of cotton.
खारा, 1, *m.* a net in which straw is tied : 2, *m.* (*f.* ī) salt, saline, brackish, bitter.
ख़ारिज, external, without, beyond, outcast.— *k.* to exclude. — *honā*, to be excluded, be exempted.
ख़ारिश, *f.* the itch, mange, scab.
खारी, *f.* 1, (*m.* **खारा**) saline, etc. : 2, a creek, inlet, backwater : meanness ; ignominy.
खारीशोर, very brackish, very saline.
खारू ; see (1) **खाड़ू** (2) **खारा**, 2.
खारुआ, *m.* a coarse kind of red cloth of cotton.
खाल, *f.* a creek, backwater, bay, inlet of the sea or of a large river ; a canal, rivulet, river : a skin, hide : bellows. — *khainchnā*, to flay. *Bāo bharī* —, of light estimation, of no intrinsic value ; *lit.* a skin full [of wind.
खाला = **खाल**, *q.v.*
ख़ालिक़, *m.* the Creator, the Almighty,
ख़ालिस, *m.* a friend : *lit.* pure, sincere.
ख़ालिसा, *m.* the exchequer or royal office for the collection of revenue, etc. : land held immediately from Government.
ख़ाली, empty, vacant, vacated ; unemployed pure, unmixed, mere, only.— *k.* to empty.
ख़ालीहाथ, empty-handed, penniless, unarmed.
खालीस ; see (1) **ख़ालिस** (2) **खालिसा**.
खाले, 1, a cavity, hole, pit, abyss : 2, low (?).
खाव, *f.* manure.
खावज, a corruption of **ख़्वाब**, *q.v.*
ख़ावर, *m.* the West.
खावहु (*poet.*) = **खाओ** (**खाना**).
ख़ाविन्द, *m.* a lord, master, husband. — *k.* to marry (said of the woman).
खाशकर, *more prop.* **ख़ासकर**, *q.v.*

ख़ास, excellent, noble, pure, unmixed; particular, specific, more especial, private, own, proper, peculiar.

ख़ासकर more particularly, more specifically.

ख़ासकरके = **ख़ासकर**, *q.v.*

ख़ासदान, *m.* a wallet, portmanteau.

ख़ासा, *m.* a dinner, more particularly a king's meal; the king's property; a confidential : a kind of fine cotton cloth : *lit.* excellent, etc.

ख़ासियत, *f.* quality, speciality, particularity, innate property, natural disposition.

खाह, *more prop.* **ख़ाह**, *q.v.*

खाह्श }
खाहिश } *more prop.* **ख़ाहिश**, *q.v.*
खाहिस }

खिंच, *f.* a pull, a pulling, a drawing.

खिंचना, *n.* to be drawn, be tightened, be extracted, be delineated; to be borne, be endured, be suffered.

खिंचवाना, *t.* to cause to be pulled, cause to be drawn, cause to be tightened, cause to be delineated.

खिंचाना, *t.* to pull, draw, tighten, stretch, delineate: to cause to pull, cause to delineate, cause to endure.

खिंचावट }
खिंचाहट } *f.* a drawing, tightening.

खिकसा = **खेकसा**, *q.v.*

खिकोरना, *t.* to scrape, scratch.

खिचड़ा = **खिचड़ी**, *q.v.*

खिचड़ी, *f.* a certain dish made of pulse and rice boiled together : the flower of the ber-tree (*Zizyphus jujuba*) : the earnest to dancing-women when they are engaged for an entertainment : a mixed heap of gold and silver coin : a barbarous mixture of two languages, a *lingua franca*, a jargon.

खिचना = **खिंचना**, *q. v.*

खिचवाना = **खिंचवाना**, *q.v.*

खिचा, *m.* (*f.* ī) tense, tight : slender, fine.

खिचाव, *m.* a drag, pull, draught; tenseness.

ख़िजलत, *f.* shame, modesty, bashfulness.——*uṭhānā* or *khānā*, to blush.

खिजलाना, 1, *t.* to vex, tease, irritate, molest, disturb, trouble, fret : 2, *n.* to get angry.

ख़िज़ान, *f.* autumn; the falling of the leaves.

ख़िज़ाना, *m.* a treasury, granary, magazine, repository; the chamber of a gun : treasure.

खिजाना = **खिजलाना**, *q. v.*

खिजालत = **ख़िजलत**, *q.v.*

खिझ, *f.* teasing; vexation, fretfulness.

खिझना, *n.* to be vexed, be teased, be irritated, be angry, be fretted.

खिझलाना = **खिझाना**, *q.v.*

खिझाना, *t.* to vex, tease, anger, irritate, fret.

खिट, *f.* impurity, filth, dirt, a spot or stain from any dirt.

खिटखिटी, *f.* giggling, the sound of laughter.

खिटजमना, *m.* a collecting or gathering of filth.

खिड़की, *f.* a window, casement, sally-port, shutter; a wicket, back door, gate.

खिड़जाना, *n.* to be dashed out (the brains).

खिथड, a hole, perforation, mine.

खिथडना, *n.* to be scattered.

खिथडाना, *t.* to scatter.

ख़िताब, *m.* a title : a conversation, speech, address.— *k.* to accost, address.

ख़ित्ता, *m.* a boundary, line; region, country, territory.

ख़िदमत, *f.* service, employment, business, appointment, duty, office, use.— *k.* to wait upon, attend; *met.* to satirize; to beat.

ख़िदमतगार, *m.* (*f.* nī) a table-waiter, domestic, servant.

ख़िदमतगारी, *f.* attendance, domestic service.

खिदर देना, *t.* to propel, drive.

खिदरना, *t.* to chase, pursue.

खिनाल; see **छिनाल**.

खिन्दड़ी, *f.* a pallet, beggar's bedding.

खिन्न, distressed, suffering, wearied, exhausted.

खिपला, *m.* a fish-scale; a crust, scab.

ख़िफ़्फ़त, *f.* lightness, levity, want of dignity; disgrace : affront.

ख़िबरत, *f.* wisdom, learning : experiment, trial, proof; experience.

खिमा = **छमा**, *q.v.*

ख़ियात, *f.* a needle.

खियाना, *n.* to be worn, be abraded.

ख़ियार, *m.* choice, election : a cucumber : a second-rate land of two species.

खियारा, *m.* (*f.* ī) artful, sly, deceitful.

खियाल, *more prop.* (1) **ख्याल** (2) **ख़्याल**, *qq. v.*

खिरकिन, *f.* a window.

खिरचा, a toothpick.

ख़िरद, *f.* intellect, sense, wisdom.

ख़िरदमन्द, sagacious, sensible, wise.

खिरन, *f.* a black ring painted on a tambourine.

खिरनी, *f.* a certain tree (*Mimusops kauki*) and its fruit.

खिरसा, *m.* a certain dish made with biestings or the milk of the cow that has just calved.

ख़िराज, *m.* tax, duty, revenue, tribute, rent.

ख़िराम, *f.* pace, gait, stately gait.—— *k.* to pace, march.

ख़िरामख़िराम, walking elegantly. gracefully.

ख़िरामान, walking in a stately manner, moving gracefully.

ख़िर्मन, *m.* harvest : halo round the moon : a barn.

ख़िर्स, *m.* a bear.

ख़िर्सक, leap-frog; blind-man's buff.

खिर्सन, *m.* (a Braj pl. of **ख़िर्स**; see **न**, 6) bears.

ख़िर्सबच्चा, a young bear.

ख़िर्सबाज़ी, *f.* bear's-play, romping, rudeness.

ख़िलअ़त, *m. f.* dress; a robe of honor with which princes confer dignity on subjects.

ख़िलक़त, *f.* the creation, the world, people, mankind, populace.

खिलखिल, tittering, giggling, the sound of laughter.

खिलखिलाना, *a. int.* to laugh loudly, laugh heartily : to giggle, chuckle, titter.

खिलजाना, *a. int.* to blossom, bloom : to laugh, be [delighted.

खिलत ; see (1) ख़िल्त (2) ख़िल्लत.

खिलना, *a. int.* to flower, blow : to laugh, be delighted. [pleasant.

खिलबाड़, humorous, playful, funny, entertaining,

खिलवत = ख़लवत, *q. v.*

खिलवाना, 1, = खेलवाना, *q. v.*: 2, *t.* to cause to be fed ; *lit.* to cause (some one) to feed (some one else).

खिला, *m.* (*f.* ī) blown (as a flower) ; rejoiced.

खिलाई
खिलाईदाई } *f.* a dry-nurse.

खिलाईपिलाई, *f.* charge of maintenance.

खिलाऊ, 1, *m.* a feeder; lit. *adj.* giving to eat, feeding : 2, *adj.* causing to bloom.

खिलाड़ = खिलाड़ी, *q. v.*

खिलाड़ी, *m.* (*f.* inī) a gambler, etc. : *lit.* playsome, funny, facetious, full of tricks, mischievous ; gaming, [gambling.

खिलाना = (1) खवाना (2) खेलाना, *qq. v.*

ख़िलाफ़, *m.* opposition, contrariety, contradiction, falsehood. [tenancy, etc.: imperial dignity, monarchy.

ख़िलाफ़त, *f.* the office of Kaliph, deputyship, lieu-

ख़िलाब, *m.* mire, clay, filth.

खिलार, *more prop.* (1) ख़िलाल (2) खिलाड़, *qq. v.*

ख़िलाल, *m.* a toothpick : middle : defect, detriment, damage, injury, ruin.

ख़िलालत, *f.* sincere friendship; candour, sincerity.

खिलावना, see खिलाना.

खिलोड़ = खिलाड़ी, *q. v.* [gewgaw.

खिलौना, *f.* (*m.*?) any plaything, a toy, bauble,

ख़िल्क़त = ख़िलक़त, *q. v.*

ख़िल्त, *m.* one of the four humours of the body.

ख़िल्लत, *f.* a rich sword-sheath of leather adorned with jewels and gold ; a bow-case.

खिल्ली, *f.* a joke, jest, humour.

खिल्लीबाज़, *m. f.* humorous, playsome, funny.

खिल्लीबाज़ी, *f.* humour, fun, play, jocularity.

खिल्लू, *m. f.* a humorous, jocular, funny or play- [some person.

खिशाना = खिसियाना, 1, *q. v.*

ख़िश्त, *m. f.* a wounded, sick, infirm person.

खिस, *f.* a grinning, shewing the teeth ; a tooth.

खिसक जाना, *a. int.* to slip away, slip away stealthily, to hide.

खिसकना, *a. int.* to stir, slip, slip away, sheer off.

खिसकाना, *t.* to remove, shove out of the way, slide away, draw back. [to become old, decline in years.

खिसना, *a. int.* to fall, sink (as a terrace) ; to drop off ;

खिसयाना, *more com.* खिसियाना, *q. v.*

खिसलना, 1, *a. int.* to slip: 2, *m.* (*f.* ī) slippery.

खिसलहा, *m.* (*f.* ī) slippery.

खिसलाना, *t.* to cause to slip. [periness.

खिसलाव, *m.* a causing to slip ; a slipping ; slip-

खिसलाहट, *f.* a sliding, slipping ; slipperiness.

खिसाना, *n.* to be abashed : *a. int.* to draw back, flinch. [back, flinch.

खिसाय रहना, *n.* to be abashed : *a. int.* to draw

ख़िसारत, *f.* loss, damage, devastation, plunder,

खिसारी, *f.* a kind of pulse. [perfidy, fraud.

खिसियानपत, *f.*
खिसियानपन, *m.*
खिसियानपना, *m.* } = खिसियाहट, *q. v.*

खिसियाना, 1, *a. int.* to grin : 2, *m.* (*f.* ī) fretful, peevish ; bashful, abashed.

खिसियाहट, *f.* vexation, fretfulness, bashfulness.

खींचना = खिंचना, *q. v.*

खींचाखींची, *f.* pulling and hauling.

खीखीर, a fox.

खीच, *m.* reluctance, repugnance.

खीचना = खिंचना, *q. v.*

खीज, *f.* anger, vexation.

खीजना, *n.* to be angry, be vexed.

खीझना ; see (1) खिझना (2) खिझाना (3) खीजना.

खीन = छीण, *q. v.*

ख़ीमा = ख़ैमा, *q. v.*

खीर, *f.* rice-milk, a dish made of rice and milk.

खीरा, 1, *m.* a cucumber (*Cucumis utillissimus*) : 2, *m. f.* dark ; wicked, malignant ; vain.

खीरी, *f.* an udder.

खील, *f.* parched grain inflated or puffed out so as to appear like froth. [gredients.

खीली, *f.* betel-leaf made up with the different in-

खीस, 1, *m.* a kind of cloth, diaper, damask, a sheet or wrapper made of such cloth : 2, *f.* loss : a grin, shrug : biestings. — *nikālnā*, to grin.

खीसना, *a. int.* to shew the teeth, grin.

खीसा, 1, a corruption of कीसा, *q. v.*: 2, *m.* a rubber, hair glove (used in baths).

खीह, *f.* an alkaline earth, fossil alkali.

खुआरा ; see (1) खुवारा (2) खारा.

खुंस, *m.* animosity, spite, rancour, malice, anger.

खुंसाना, *n.* to be angry.

खुंसी, *m.* (*f.* inī) an angry person : *lit.* angry, wrath- [ful.

खुख, poor, miserable.

खुखला, *m.* (*f.* ī) *more com.* खोखला, *q. v.*

खुजराहा, *m.* (*f.* ī) ropy, stringy.

खुजलना, *a. int.* to itch.

खुजला, *m.* a kind of sweetmeat.

खुजलाना, *n.* to itch : *t.* to tickle, scratch.

खुजलापन, *m.*
खुजलाहट, *f.* } an itching, titillation, scratching.

खुजली, *f.* the itch, mange, herpes, scab.

खुजाना, 1, *more prop.* खुज़ाना, *q. v.*: 2, *t.* to scratch, rub gently with the nails, titillate, tickle.

खुभराहा, *m.* (*f.* ī) ropy, stringy.

खुटकना, *more com.* **खटकना**, *q. v.*

खुटका, *more com.* **खटका**, *q.v.*

खुटपचरा, *m.* (*f.* ī) a spiteful malicious person.

खुटाई, *f.* } malice, spite, rancour, perfidy.
खुटापा, *m.* }

खुट्टी, *f.* a treasure, hoard, store : a gnat.

खुड़ला, 1, *m.* a hen-house : 2, *m.* (*f.* ī) rough.

खुड़ाड़ा, an aviary, hen-house, any place in which birds are kept.

खुपठा, *m.* (*f.* ī) *more com.* **खोपटा = खोटा**, *q.v.*

खुपडला, *m.* the hollow of a tree.

खुतन, *m. pr. n.* a country in Turkistan, Tartary, or the north of China, famous for musk.

खुतबा,, *m.* a sermon or oration delivered after divine service on Fridays in which the preacher blesses Muhammad, his successors, and the reigning Sove- [reign.

खुत्ती, *f.* a purse, small bag.

खुद, self (corresponds to **आप**, self ; *q.v.*).

खुदकाश्त, *adj.* cultivating one's own field.

खुदना, *n.* to be dug, be hollowed, be delved, be [engraved.

खुदनी, *more prop.* **खोदनी**, *q.v.*

खुदपरस्त, *m.* self-conceited.

खुदपरस्ती, *f.* self-conceit.

खुदबखुद, of one's own accord, spontaneously.

खुदवाना, *t.* to cause to be dug, cause to be delved, cause to be engraved, cause to be carved.

खुदा, *m.* God, the Almighty.

खुदा तआ़ला, *m.* the Most High God.

खुदाई, 1, *f.* godhead, godship, divinity; providence : the world : 2; *adj.* divine.

खुदाना, *t.* to cause to dig, cause to engrave, cause [to carve.

खुदावन्द, *m.* a possessor, master, husband, lord, Sir ; (in Christian phraseology) Christ, the Lord.

खुड्डे, *f.* the spaces in a necessary between the little brick partitions : the space from which a tooth [has been extracted.

खुद्दा, see **छुद्दा**, *q.v.*

खुद्वाना, *more com.* **खुदवाना**. *q.v.*

खुधवाई, *f.* (see **आई**, 3) the act of digging : the [wages for digging.

खुधा = छुधा, *q.v.*

खुधार्थ, corruption of **छुधार्त्त**, *q.v.*

खुन, *more prop.* **खून**, *q.v.*

खुनया, *m.* melody, singing, minstrelsy.

खुनसाना, *n.* to be angry.

खुनसी, *m.* (*f.* inī) an angry person : *lit.* angry, [wrathful.

खुने, *more prop.* **खूनि**, *q.v.*

खुन्दलना, *t.* to trample, tread, press, beat, or work [with the feet.

खुन्स, *m.* a hermaphrodite : asphodel.

खुपखुपाट, *f.* envy, spite.

खुपखुपाना, *t.* to pierce; to envy : *a. int.* to become [enraged.

खुब, *more prop.* **खूब**, *q.v.*

खुबना, *t.* to affect; to penetrate, stick into; to [adorn.

खुभना = खुबना, *q. v.*

खुम्ब, an earthen vessel for holding wine or water.

खुम्स, the one fifth : (in Law) a double tithe, or 20 per cent. levied on the owners of land in which there are valuable mines of metals.

खुर, *m.* a cloven hoof; a horse's hoof, a hoof.

खुरखुरा, *m.* (*f.* ī) rough.

खुरचन, *f.* pot-scrapings.

खुरचना, *t.* to scrape.

खुरचनी, *f.* a scraper ; a scoop, shovel.

खुरजी, *m.* a wallet, portmanteau, saddle-bag,

खुरंड, *m.* a scab.

खुरद, minute, little, small.

खुरदसाल, *adj.* of tender years.

खुरदिया, *m.* a money-changer.

खुरपा, *m.* an instrument for scraping grass for horses : the kneepan, patella.

खुरपी, *f.* (dimin. of **खुरपा**) a scraper, weeding-knife, a tool with which grass is scraped up for horses ; a shovel for cleaning out a birdcage.

खुरमा, *m.* a kind of sweetmeat.

खुरली, *f.* a stall or manger in a stable.

खुरवाला, *m.* (*f.* ī) hoofed, possessed of hoofs.

खुरशेद, *m.* the sun.

खुरसन्द, contented, satisfied, pleased.

खुराक, *f.* eatables, rations, daily food ; one meal ; one dose of medicine.

खुराकी, *f.* subsistence-money; a daily allowance [of food.

खुरापट, very old.

खुराफ़ात, *f.* a fable, tale, romance, ludicrous say- [ing, smut.

खुरिया, *m.* the kneepan : an instrument like a cup, formed of a cocoanut-shell or other material, with which clothes are marked with stripes.

खुरिश, *f.* eating and drinking, food, fare.

खुरी, *f.* a hoof, horse's hoof, cloven hoof.

खुरेरना, *t.* to run after, persecute, catch, enclose.

खुर्खुरा, *m.* (*f.* ī) rough.

खुर्फ़ा, *m.* that which is plucked from a tree ; autumnal fruit : purslain (*Portulaca oleracea*).

खुर्रम, pleasant, delightful : cheerful, pleased.

खुर्रमदिल, a person of a cheerful disposition.

खुर्रमी, *f.* gladness, pleasedness, cheerfulness.

खुर्रा, *m.* the noise of one being suffocated ; a snore.

खुर्सन्द, contented, satisfied, pleased.

खुलखेलना, *a. int.* to indulge openly in practices which formerly were only practised in secret.

खुलजाना, *intensive of* **खुलना**, *q.v.*

खुल देना, *intensive of* **खोलना**, *q.v.*

खुलना, *n.* to be opened, be revealed, be displeased, be unravelled ; to be laid aside (as restraint) ; to be broken (as meditation) : *a. int.* to clear up (as the sky); to shine ; to expand.

खुलवाना, *t.* to cause to be opened, etc.

खुन्साना, *n.* to be angry, be vexed, be displeased,

खुला, *m.* (*f.* ī) open, wide; naked; loose, unconfined; clear, fair (as the sky).

खुलाना, *t.* to open; to cause to open.

खुलासा, *m.* essence, the prime part of a thing; an abstract, abridgement; the conclusion, inference, moral. [clearish (as the sky, or the weather).

खुलासा, (see **खुला**) somewhat open, etc., fairish,

खुलेबन्दों, 1, unceremonious, free, unconfined, unrestrainted: 2, unceremoniously, unrestrainedly, [openly, freely.

खुलेबन्द = **खुलेबन्दों**, *q.v.*

खुल्क़, *m.* (*pl.* **अख़लाक़**) nature, quality; good disposition; custom, manner.

खुवक, *more prop.* **खूबक** = **खूबसूरत**, *q.v.*

खुवारा, *m.* established order; mode, manner: strengthening food: a frame for turning an arch upon; a scaffold.

खुश, pleased, delighted, cheerful, content, merry; amiable, good, pleasant, delicious, excellent, elegant, healthy. [*adv.* by land.

खुश्की, *f.* dryness; drought, dearth; dry land:

खुशख़बरी, *f.* glad tidings, (in Christian phraseology) the Gospel. — *denā*, to preach the Gospel.

खुशनुद, pleased, contented, delighted.

खुशरंग, of a lively or pleasing colour. [happy.

खुशहाल, in pleasant circumstances, fortunate,

खुशबो, 1, fragrant: 2, *f.* odour, perfume.

खुशामद, *f.* flattery. [— *k.* to rejoice.

खुशी, *f.* delight, pleasure, cheerfulness, gaiety.

खुसूसन, *adv.* particularly, especially.

खुस, **खुष**; for words beginning thus, see under

खुसरफुसर, *m.* a whispering. [the form **खुश**.

खुसूफ़, *m.* an eclipse of the moon.

खुसूस, *m.* an affair, business, thing, particular: a doing anything particular: *adv.* particularly.

खूंच, *m.* (*f.* ?) the *tendo Achillis.* — *mārnā*, to hamstring: to puncture, prick.

खूंचालना, *m.* to puncture, prick.

खूखी, *f.* a little girl, female infant.

खूजिया = **खोजिया**, *q.v.* [etc.

खूझा, *m.* sediment, dregs, mouldiness of vinegar,

खूट, side, direction: *adv.* towards. [tables.

खूटना, *t.* to pluck, pick the leaves, etc. of vege-

खूठी, *f.* a scab.

खूड़, *m.* a furrow. [station; a portion: earwax.

खूपट, *m.* a corner, angle, pivot, central point: a

खूपटला, *m.* a certain drug.

खूपटा, *m.* a wooden stake, post.

खूपटी, *f.* (dim. of **खूपटा**) a peg, small stake.

खूयी, *f.* a scab.

खूद, *f.* refuse.

खूद = **खूद**, *q.v.*

खूदाना, *a. int.* to trot.

खून, *m.* blood; murder. — *k.* to kill, slaughter.

खूनरेज़, *m.* a murderer: lit. *adj.* blood-shedding.

खूनिजिगर पीना or **खाना**, to work oneself to death.

खूनी, *m.* (*f.* inī) a murderer. [when angry.

खून्दना, *t.* to paw or dig up the earth (as a bull does

खूब, good, excellent, well, pleasing, amiable.

खूबक (= **खूबसूरत**, *q.v.*) beautiful-faced.

खूबसूरत, beautiful, well-formed, handsome, elegant, graceful.

खूबसूरती, *f.* handsomeness, elegance, beauty.

खूमना, *n.* to wax old. [of cattle.

खूरापट, old soil, soil trodden down by the hoofs

खूश, *more com.* **खुश**, *q.v.*

खूशनुमा, pleasant to the sight, beautiful, neat, pretty, becoming, seemly.

खूस, *more com.* **खुश**, *q.v.*

खूस्की, *more prop.* **खुश्की**, *q.v.*

खे, (a dialectic form of the substantive verb) is.

खेंचना = **खिंचना**, *q.v.*

खेकटा, hardship, distress, severity.

खेकसा, *m.* a mark, spot, sign.

खेचना, *more prop.* **खिंचना**, *q.v.*

खेचर, *m.* (*f.* ī) a planet; a bird; a *vidyādhar* or kind of demigod; genii; *lit.* moving in the sky, aërial.

ख़ेज़, (in comp.) rising, leaping, bounding, galloping, capering, springing up (as vegetation).

खेटक, *m.* (*f.* ?) 1, sport, hunting, the chase: 2, a shield: 3, a mace, the club of Balarām: a village.

खेटकी, *m.* (*f.* inī) a sportsman, hunter.

खेड़यालू, *m.* a husbandman, villager, rustic.

खेड़ा, *f.* a village, hamlet, the land immediately adjacent to a village.

खेड़ी, *f.* a sort of steel made in India.

खेढ़ी, 1, = **खेड़ी**, *q.v.*: 2, *f.* membranes in which the foetus is developed, secundines.

खेत, *m.* a field, field of battle; ground; a holy place. — *ānā*, to become helpless. — *chhoṛnā*, to flee from the field of battle. — *rahnā*, to remain on the [field to be killed.

खेतखद्दु, mortgage of a field.

खेतचिट्ठा, a rough field-book.

खेतदार, *m.* the owner or the occupant of a field.

खेतबापट, *m.* the allotment of land to villagers.

खेतवार, field by field.

खेति, *more prop.* **खेती**, *q.v.*

खेती, *f.* husbandry, farming; a crop, produce.

खेतीपसारी, *f.* agricultural labour.

खेतीबाड़ी, *f.* husbandry, farming.

खेतीहर, *m.* a husbandman, farmer, peasant.

खेतुआ = **खेत**. See **उआ**.

खेद, *m.* sorrow, grief, affliction, faintness, fatigue, trouble, pain, distress. — *denā*, to grieve, distress, etc. — *mānnā*, to suffer affliction, to grieve.

खेदजनक, *adj.* grief-producing, occasioning trouble.

खेदना, *t.* to persecute, pursue, chase, hunt.

खेदमान, *m.* (*f.* mati) = **खेदित**, *q. v.* [are caught.

खेदा, *m.* the enclosure or trap in which elephants

खेदाई, appertaining to a trap. — *afyāl*, expenses. incurred in entrapping wild elephants; a cess levied for that purpose.

खेदित, *m.* (*f.* ā) a sorrowful person, etc.: *lit.* sorrowful distressed, afflicted, pained, repentant.

खेप, *f.* (compare **क्षेप**) a voyage, trip: cracked coin, a piece of base metal inserted in coin: an apartment: a term in Algebra; something added to a sum. — *karnā*, to sustain a loss.

खेपना, *t.* to pass the time.

खेपा, *m.* (*f.* ī) an idiot, madman, fool: *lit.* ignorant,

खेपिया, *m.* a voyager. [foolish, insane, mad.

खेमकुशल *f.* = **कुशलक्षेम**, *q. v.*

खेमटा, a species of measure in Hindee versification.

खेमा = **ख़ेमा**, *q. v.*

खेयाल; see (1) **ख्याल** (2) **ख़्याल**.

खेरना, to pass away (?).

खेरी, *f.* the after-birth.

खेरे, a city, village (?). [*k.* or *khelnā*, to play.

खेल, *m.* (*f.* ?) play, game, sport, pastime, fun. —

खेलखिलाड़ी, *f.* an unchaste woman, adulteress, strumpet: lit. *adj. f.* playsome, wanton.

खेलत, (in Braj) playful, sportive.

खेलना, *a. int.* to play, frisk, romp, sport.

खेलबाज़ी, *f.* play, sport.

खेलवाड़ = **खिलाड़ी**, *q. v.*

खेलवाना, *t.* (double causat. of **खेलना**) to cause to be played with; *lit.* to cause to cause to play.

खेलवार = **खिलाड़ी**, *q.v.*

खेलहिं (*poet.*) = (1) **खेलको** (2) **खेलते हैं**. See **हिं**.

खेलाड़ी = **खिलाड़ी**, *q.v.*

खेलाना, *t.* (causat. of **खेलना**) to cause to play, to amuse, play with, dandle: to cause to blossom.

खेलिहै (pl. **खेलिहैं**) = **खेलेगा**. See **इहै**.

खेलिहौं = **खेलाइहौं** = **खेलाऊंगा**. See **इहौं**.

खेलौना = **खिलौना**, *q.v.*

खेवक }
खेवट } = **खेवटिया**, *q. v.*

खेवटिया, *m.* a fisherman, boatman, rower.

खेवना, *t.* to row, punt, paddle: to suffer, endure (pain, calamity, etc.). [money, fare: a crossing a river.

खेवा, *m.* the price of passage in a boat, passage-

खेश, *m.* a certain kind of cloth, diaper, damask; a sheet or wrapper made of such cloth.

खेसारत, *more com.* **ख़िसारत**, *q.v.*

खेसड़ा, *m.* a kind of cloth.

खेआल; see **ख्याल** and **ख़्याल**.

खैंच, *f.* a pull, pulling, drawing: scarcity.

खैंचखमेट, struggle, contention.

खैंचना = **खिंचना**, *q. v.*

खैचर, *more prop.* **खेचर**, *q. v.*

खैंचाखैंच }
खैंचाखैंची } *f.* a pulling and hauling.

ख़ैमा, *m.* a tent, pavilion. — *k.* to encamp.

खैयाल; see **ख्याल** and **ख़्याल**.

खैर, *m.* a certain tree (*Mimosa catechu*); an extract made from the interior of it.

ख़ैर, *f.* goodness, health, happiness: *adj.* good, best, well: *adv.* very good, very well.

ख़ैरआफ़ियत, *f.* health, welfare, health and wealth.

ख़ैरख़्वाह, a well-wisher, friend.

खैरयत, *more prop.* **ख़ैरियत**, *q. v.*

खैरा, 1, *m.* a certain tree (*Mimosa catechu*): 2, a sprat (or a fish of a kind very like one): 3, *m.* (*f.* ī) brown.

ख़ैरात, *f.* (pl. of **ख़ैर**) alms, deeds of charity; land given in charity (principally to Musalmāns).

ख़ैरियत, *f.* welfare, happiness, safety.

ख़ैरोआफ़ियत, *f.* health and wealth, health, welfare.

खैला, *m.* a young bullock, steer.

खो, 1, the root of vb. **खोना**; 2, = **खोआ**, 2, *q. v.*: 3, *f.* habit, custom, disposition, nature. — *jānā*, to be lost, be missing. — *denā*, to lose, to squander away.

खोआ, 1, = **खोया**, *q.v.*: 2, *m.* plaster; coarse brick-dust used for making terrace-roofs or floors: milk inspissated by boiling. [to part with.

खोआना, *t.* (causat. of **खोना**) to cause to lose, cause

खोई, 1, *f.* of **खोया**, *q.v.*: 2, *f.* the dry part of sugar-cane after the juice is expressed: clothes folded up and put on the head as a defence against rain.

खोंखना, *a. int.* to cough.

खोंखी, *f.* a cough.

खोंच, *f.* a cut or rent in cloth, etc.

खोंचना, *t.* to thrust; to stuff.

खोंचा, *m.* a thrust, thrusting; a stuffing.

खोंचाखोंची, *f.* a thrusting; a stuffing: a mutual wrangling or quarrelling.

खोंची, *f.* anything stuffed into something else (as grass into thatching): trifling purchases: a part of grain which is to be parched taken as pay by the person who parches it: something paid by those who draw water at a well to the bihishtee who attends there with his bucket, for the use of it.

खोंट, **खोंड**; for words beginning with either of these forms, see under the forms **खोयट**, **खोयड**, respectively.

खोंसना, *t.* to stuff, cram, thrust in. [**खोखा**.

खोखल; see (1) **कोकिल** (2) **कोखा** (3) **खोखला** (4)

खोखला, *m.* (*f.* ī) hollow, excavated (as a tooth, tree, etc.).

खोखा, 1, *m.* (*f.* ī) a boy, little boy, male infant: 2, *m.* a bill of exchange the amount of which has been paid remaining in the hands of him who has paid it, by way of voucher.

खोखी, *f.* a girl, little girl, female infant.

खोज, *m.* (*f.*?) search, inquiry, quest: trace, mark. — *k.* (with gen. of the object) to search for, be in quest of. — *meṅ rahnā*, to try to find fault, endeavour to pick a hole in another's coat.

खोजक, *m.* (*f.* ikā) = **खोजी**, *q. v.*

खोजखाज, *f.* inquiry, investigation : vexation.

खोजना, *t.* to search for, inquire after, seek, explore.

खोजनिहार, *m.* (in Braj) an inquirer, seeker, investigator. [eunuch.

खोजा, 1, *m.* (*f.* ī) sought, searched for : 2, *m.* a

खो जाना, *a. int.* (an intensive of **खोना**); see *s. v.* **खो**.

खोजाना, *t.* to cause to inquire after, cause to seek for. [gator, inquisitive person.

खोजिया, *m.* a searcher, inquirer, seeker, investi-

खोजी, *m.* (*f.* inī) = **खोजिया**, *q. v.* : lit. *adj.* seeking, searching, inquiring, inquisitive.

खोझ, *more prop.* **खोज**, *q. v.* [ception.

खोट, *f.* a blunder, defect, blemish, vice, flaw, de-

खोटा, *m.* (*f.* ī) spiteful, malicious, perfidious, impious, false ; faulty, deficient, defective ; adulterated, base (as coin) ; forged (as a bank-note).

खोटाई, *f.* perfidy, impiousness, faultiness, spitefulness, malice ; forgery.

खोटाएगी = **खोटाई**, *q. v.* [of sandal.

खोड़, 1, = **खोट**, *q. v.* : 2, gold (?) : 3, a largish piece

खोड़का, a dry or withered shrub.

खोडर, *m.* the hollow of a tree.

खोडस = **षोडश**, *q. v.* [the hands.

खोड़ा, *m.* stocks, wooden manacles for securing

खोड़िल, worthy of blame, disgraceful.

खोड़ो, *f.* a cavern, pit.

खोढरा ; see **खोदरा**.

खोयट = **खोट**, *q. v.*

खोयटा, 1, = **खोटा**, *q. v.* : 2, *m.* a pin, peg, nail, tent-pin : protection. *Khonteke bal kūdnā*, to become insolent while relying on some protection (as when one teazes an animal which being fastened by a rope is unable to get at him ; hence, the *khonṭā*, by restraining the adversary becomes indirectly a protection).

खोयडकल, *m.* a hollow.

खोयडर, gleanings or leavings on the threshing-floor after the grain has been removed.

खोयडला, *m.* (*f.* ī) toothless ; hollow.

खोता, *m.* a bird's-nest.

खोद, *m.* a push, thrust : a pass. [to search for.

खोदना, *t.* to dig, delve, engrave, scoop, hollow :

खोदनो, *f.* a searching, investigating : a spade, any instrument for digging or engraving. —*k.* to search for, investigate, find out.

खोदबेवाद, *m.* search, inquiry.

खोदर, *m.* a certain pace of a horse.

खोदरा, *m.* (*f.* ī) a pockmarked person.

खोदा, *more prop.* **खुदा**, *q. v.* [a digging.

खोदाई, 1, *more prop.* **खुदाई**, *q. v.* : 2, *f.* (see **श्राई**, 3)

खोदवाना, *more com.* **खुदवाना**, *q. v.*

खोदिया ; see **खो देना**.

खोदी, *f.* digging, the culture of land.

खो देना, *t.* (an intensive of **खोना**, 1). See *s. v.* **खो**.

खोना, 1, *t.* to lose ; to part with, get rid of, do away with : 2, *m.* a leaf which contains a parcel of [betel or flowers, etc.

खोन्ता, } *m.* a bird's-nest.
खोन्धा, }

खोप, *f.* a rent, fissure ; a cave ; corner.

खोपड़ी = **खोपरी**, *q. v.* [or pulp, kernel ; brain.

खोपरा, *m.* the kernel of a cocoanut, the dried interi-

खोपरी, *f.* a shell, the skull, pate. —*khājānā*, to to spend or lavish another's property.

खोबार, *m.* a hogsty. [on the top of the head.

खोम्पा, *m.* the hair of the head braided or tied up

खोया, *m.* (*f.* **खोई**) refuse, anything or person that is lost, etc. : *lit.* lost, thrown away, destroyed.

खोर, *f.* an alley : a covering : the rage or the curse of a god.

खोरा, 1, a cavity, pit, den : 2, *m.* (*f.* ī) lame (?).

खोराक, *more com.* **खुराक**, *q. v.* [*f.* an alley.

खोरी, 1, = **खोड़**, *q. v.* : 2, wickedness, guilt (?) 3,

खोरिश, *more com.* **खुरिश**, *q. v.* [(of a tree, etc.).

खोल, *m.* (*f.* ?) a case, sheath ; a cavity, hollow

खोलके कहना, *a. int.* to speak plainly, speak without reservation, circumlocution, or evasion.

खोलड़, } *m.* a hollow (as of a tree, etc.).
खोलड़ा, }

खोलना *t.* to open, loosen, unravel, unfold ; to unmoor a ship, set sail : *a. int.* to expand ; to shine.

खोलबन्दी, *f.* the changing or removing horses'

खोलर ; see **खोलड़**. [shoes.

खोलामांजा, a porcupine ; a hedgehog.

खोवैं, in Braj = **खोए** or **खोवें** (**खोना**).

खोश, *more com.* **खुश**, *q. v.* [hairs.

खोसना, *t.* to take away, snatch away ; to pluck out

खोसा, 1, *m.* rind, peel, skin, shell : a certain marauding tribe on the borders of Sind : 2, *m.* (a man) having little or no beard.

खोह, *m.* (*f.* ?) a cavern, abyss, pit.

खौ, a subterraneous vault for storing grain, etc.

ख़ौगीर, *m.* the stuffing of a saddle, a pad, pack-saddle.

खौड़, *f.* the *tilak* or mark which Hindoos make on the forehead with sandal-wood, saffron, etc.

खौता, a corruption of **खोन्धा**, *q. v.*

खौदी = **खोदनी**, *q. v.*

ख़ौफ़, *m.* fear.

ख़ौफ़नाक, terrifying, frightful.

ख़ौफ़रजा, *m.* suspense ; *lit.* fear and hope.

खौभ ; see (1) **ख़ौफ़** (2) **खूब**. [the hairs.

खौरा, *m.* the rot among sheep, the falling off of

खौरी = **खोड़**, *q. v.*

खौरु, the roaring or bellowing of a bull.

खौलना, *a. int.* to boil, be agitated by heat.

ख्यात, *m.* (*f.* ā) a person of reputation, etc. ; *lit.* renowned, famous, celebrated, known, notorious ; styled or designated.

ख्याति, *f.* celebrity, fame, renown, notoriety : title, name or designation. [and renown.

ख्यात्यापन्न, *m.* (*f.* ā) famous, possessed of honor

ख्याल, *m.* play, sport, fun, amusement, pastime : a species of measure in Hindee versification.

ख़्याल, *m.* imagination, fancy, thought, consideration ; a phantom, vision, delusion. — *k.* to think, imagine, fancy, look forwards.

खष्टीय = **ख़ीष्टियान**, *q. v.*

ख़ीष्ट, *m. pr. n.* Christ.

ख़ीष्टियान, *m.* (*f.* ī) a Christian : *lit.* appertaining to Christ or to His religion, Christian.

ख़ाजा, *m.* a man of distinction, rich merchant, gentleman, governor, master.

ख़ान, *m.* a tray.

ख़ानपोश, *m.* a tray-lid, cloth for covering a tray.

ख़ान्दा, a reader, repeater.

ख़ाब, *m. f.* sleep ; a dream : nap (of cloth).

ख़ार, poor, distressed ; deserted, friendless, abandoned ; wretched, contemptible, ruined.

ख़ारा, *m.* stipend, every-day allowance, victuals.

ख़ारी, *f.* baseness ; distress, wretchedness.

ख़ास्त, *f.* desire, wish, request.

ख़ास्तगार, *m.* a candidate, competitor, bidder.

ख़ास्तगारी, *f.* request, petition, candidateship.

ख़ाह, wishful of, desiring : *conj.* either, whether, or. [*volens.*

ख़ाहमख़ाह, whether willing or not willing, *nolens*

ख़ाहिश, *f.* desire, wish, inclination ; request. — *k.* or *rakhnā*, to wish, desire. [own ; self.

ख़ेश, *m.* a kinsman ; a son-in-law : a family ; *lit.*

ग

ग (g) is the third consonant of the Hindee alphabet and the third letter in the **कवर्ग** or guttural class, and has invariably the hard sound of *g* in the English word 'go' ; — in no circumstances has it the soft sound of that letter in the English word 'gem'. This letter is sometimes interchanged inaccurately with **क** ; *e. g.* **अंक**, corruption of **अंग**. It is sometimes found as a suffix [*m.* (*f.* ā)] in compound words derived from Sanskrit, importing in such case the idea of 'motion' ; *e. g.* **खग** : the feminine of such words is formed sometimes by adding **आ** and sometimes by **ई** ; *e. g.* **कामगा**, *f.* a lascivious female : **तुरगी**, *f.* a mare. In works on Prosody this letter is used as an abbreviation of the word **गुरु** to denote a long syllable. In many of the words in common use in Hindee which happen to be of Arabic or Persian origin, this letter has a rough guttural sound which properly speaking has no representative either in Hindee or in English, but which is exactly represented by the sound of *g* in the German *sagen*, and by the sound given to *r* by many of the more uncultivated people about the banks of the Tweed and in some parts of Devonshire, where the word 'round', for example, is often pronounced as if spelt 'ghound'. By the Hindee speaking people, however, the distinction is far from universally observed, so that 'kāghaz' is most frequently corrupted into 'kāgaj'. That this is the required pronunciation of the letter in any given instance will be indicated in this Dictionary by a dot underneath the letter ; *e. g.* **काग़ज़**. This letter is in provincial jargon, sometimes exchanged with a sibilant, *e. g.* **दिग** (= **दिक**) = **दिश** (from Sk. **दृश**).

गइ = **गई**, *q. v.*

गइया क°, to search for.

गई, *f.* (pl. **गईं**) ; see **गया**.

गऊ, *f.* a cow ; any animal of the cow kind.

गऊरूपी, cow-shaped, cow-like.

गए, a *masc.* pl. of **गया**, *q. v.*

गएऊ in Braj = **गया**, *q. v.*

गंग, *m.* = **गंगा**, *q. v.* This form occurs chiefly in composition ; *e. g. Do-gang* (a river) in two streams.

गंगदत्त, *m.* a proper name of males.

गंगबरामद = **गंगबरार**, *q. v.* [pecially from the Ganges.

गंगबरार, alluvial land recovered from a river, es-

गंगय्या, *more prop.* **गौरैया**, *q. v.*

गंगशिकस्त, encroachment of any river by diluvion.

गंगा, *f.* (see **मेरु**) any stream or river, the Ganges (which is, to Hindoos, 'the river' *par excellence*). It is supposed to exist also in the sky and in the lower regions. [either side of the Ganges.

गंगाक्षेत्र, *m.* the land extending about two *kos* on

गंगाजमनी, *f.* a kind of earring : a species of precious

गंगाजल, *m.* river-water, *esp.* Ganges-water. [metal.

गंगाजी = **गंगा**, *q. v.* : See **जी**, 1.

गंगातीर, *m.* the bank of the Ganges.

गंगाद्वार, *m. pr. n.* (= **हरद्वार**) the place where the Ganges issues from the mountains and enters the

गंगाधर, *m.* one of the epithets of Shiv. [plains.

गंगापानी, *m.* river-water, *esp.* Ganges-water.

गंगापार, *m.* the further bank of the Ganges or of any river.

गंगापुत्र, *m.* a Brāhmaṇ who conducts the ceremonies of pilgrimage to the Ganges : a man of low caste employed in removing dead bodies.

गंगायात्रा, *f.* pilgrimage to the Ganges ; the carrying a sick person to the river side to die there. [ges.

गंगाला, lands subjected to inundations of the Gan-

गंगासागर, *m. pr. n.* the place where the Ganges empties itself into the ocean. (of devotion).

गंगास्नान, *m.* bathing in the Ganges (*esp.* as an act

गंगो, *m. pr. n.* a certain *Nāg*.

गंगोतरी = **गंगोत्री**, *q. v.*

गंगोत्री, *f. pr. n.* the source of the Ganges, the place where it springs from the mountains. [river.

गंगोदक, *m.* water of the Ganges or of any sacred

गंगोद्धं, the rising of any river (but especially of the Ganges) in the rains.

गंज, *m.* 1, scaldhead (*Tinea capitis*) : 2, a mine, jewel-mine, jewel-room, place where plate, etc. is preserved ; a treasury ; a granary, mart, market, place of merchandize ; a village, town, or spot where grain is kept stored for sale : a tavern : a case ; disrespect, contempt.

गंजन, *m.* disrespectful treatment, contemptuous language, abuse.

गंजना, *t.* to treat disrespectfully, abuse; to destroy.

गंजनी घास, *f.* a kind of sweet-smelling grass used

गंजमुक्ता, *m.* a pearl. [for a variety of purposes.

गंजा, *m.* (*f.* ī) a scaldhead; *lit.* scaldheaded, bald: destroyed. [their sickle, etc.

गंजिया, *f.* a wallet, bag in which grass-cutters keep

गंजी, *f.* rice gruel, conjee.

गंजीफ़ा, *m.* a pack of cards; a game of cards.

गंजेली = **भंगेला**, *q. v.* [*gānjhā.*

गंझेल, *m.* (*f.*) a person addicted to the use of

गंठ, गंड, गंढ, गंद, गंध, गंभ; for all words beginning with either of these elements, see under either of the forms **गयठ, गयड, गयढ, गन्द, गन्ध, गम्भ**, respectively.

गंव (*contraction*) = **गांव**, *q. v.* See **ग्र**, 15.

गंवरऊ (Rām.) = **गंवारी**, *q. v.*

गंवाई }
गंवाई } corruptions of **गवाही**, *q. v.*

गंवाऊ, *m.* or *f.* a waster, squanderer, prodigal.

गंवाना, *t.* to lose, throw away, get rid of, discharge, spend fruitlessly, waste, squander, pass, trifle.

गंवार, *m.* a villager, peasant, rustic, clown, boor, churl, low-bred person; *hence*, clownish, stupid, boorish.

गंवारी, *f.* rustic or provincial brogue; *lit.* appertaining to villagers or rustics.

गंवाही, a corruption of **गवाही**, *q. v.* [village.

गंवी, *m.* (*f.* inī) a rustic: *lit.* appertaining to a

गंवीगांव, rustic hamlets or villages.

गंहूं, a corruption of **गेहूं**, *q. v.* [represent it.

गकार, *m.* the letter **ग**, or any symbol that may

गगण, *m.* the visible heavens, sky, firmament, atmosphere. — *ki buchchewālī murghi*, *f.* the group of stars called the Pleiades.

गगणधूल, *f.* the dust of the *Pandanus odoratissimus.*

गगणभेड़, *m.* a pelican (*Pelicanus onocrotalus*).

गगर }
गगरी } *f.* a jar, pitcher, waterpot. [from **गंग.**

गङ्ग; for words beginning thus see under the

गच, 1, *m.* mortar, plaster, cement, old mortar knocked off walls, etc.: the floor: 2, thick, close, [dense (as trees).

गचकारी, *adj.* building with **गच.**

गचगोना, *m.* (*f.* ī) a short and stout person.

गचपच, crowded, stuffed together, close, thick.

गची, cemented, plastered. [stick; a yard: a ramrod.

गज़, *m.* any instrument for measuring with, yard-

गज, *m.* (*f.* ī) an elephant: the eight elephants of the eight cardinal points; hence, in the ingenious system of reckoning by symbols adopted by Hindoos in their poetry, this word is a symbol for 8.

गजगमनी, *f.* an epithet of any female of a graceful gait; *lit.* having an elephant's gait.

गजगामिनी = **गजगमनी**, *q. v.*

गजगाह, *m.* a string composed of several tassels made of the hair of a kind of ox. It is suspended as an ornament from an elephant's neck, or fastened to a horse's ears, and extends on both sides to the saddle.

गजगौनी in Braj = **गजगमनी**, *q. v.*

गजदन्त, 1, *m.* elephant's tooth, ivory: 2, an epithet of Gaṇesh; *lit.* having an elephant's tusk.

गजन, a Braj pl. of **गज.** See **न**, 6.

गजनलाल, *m. pr. n.* a common name of males.

गजनाल, *m.* a large gun, cannon.

गजनी, *f.* bole, earth.

गजपति, *m.* the leader in a drove of elephants; any particularly large elephant: a title of any Rājā; *lit.* a lord of elephants. [painted.

गजपाटल, *m.* lampblack with which the eyes are

गजपाल, *m.* the keeper or the driver of an elephant.

ग़ज़ब, *m.* violence, oppression, injustice, compulsion; rage, anger, passion, vengeance. [a post.

गजबन्धन, *m.* a chain for binding an elephant to

गजबन्धनी, *f.* a post to which an elephant is bound.

गजमनिह = **गजमोती**, *q. v.*

गजमुख, *m.* the elephant-faced, *i. e.* Gaṇesh.

गजमुक्ता, *f.* = **गजमोती**, *q. v.*

गजमोती, *m.* an elephant-gem, elephant-pearl. It is a popular idea among Hindoos that the finest gems and pearls are to be found in the heads of elephants and serpents.

गजर, *m.* the chimes rung at the expiration of a watch or *pahar* of the day or of the night: it is, however, sometimes restricted to those at the end of the fourth watch, — the middle chimes being more usually designated by the word *pahar*, *q. v.* [elephant.

गजरथ, *m.* a chief chariot, a chariot drawn by an

गजरभत्त, *m.* a dish of boiled carrots.

गजरा, *m.* the leaf of the carrot: a species of jewels; an ornament for the wrist, a bracelet, armlet: the waving lines on mashroo (a kind of silk cloth).

गजराज, *m.* a specially large elephant; the leader in a drove of elephants (like the "bell-wether" among sheep); *lit.* lord of elephants.

गजरात, *more prop.* **गुजरात**, *q. v.* [of gold

गजराहार, *m.* a wreath or a necklace of flowers or

ग़ज़ल, *f.* an ode, short poem, amatory sonnet.

गजवीथी, *f. pr. n.* the Milky-Way.

गजा, *m.* a part of a cart: a kind of sweetmeat.

गजानन, *m.* the elephant-faced one, *i. e.* Gaṇesh.

गजाना, *a. int.* to work, ferment.

गजाल, *m.* a kind of fish: a pin or peg to hang

गजी, *f.* (*m.* **गज**) a female elephant. [things on.

गज़ी, *f.* a coarse kind of cotton cloth.

गजेन्द्र, *m.* a huge or noble elephant; *lit.* a chief

गज्जर, swampy ground. [among elephants.

गझा, *m.* a gaining, winning.

गझिन, thick, dense (as trees). [form **गंझ.**

गञ्ज; for all words beginning thus see under the

गट, *f.* the bank of a river or tank.

गटगट , the noise made by a liquid poured from a bottle or guglet.

गटड़मल, *m.* a nickname for a monkey.

गटना, *more prop.* **गठना**, *q.v.*

गटपट, higgledy-piggledy, topsy-turvy.

गटरमल, *m.* a nickname for a monkey.

गटवारा, *m.* the designation of a certain tribe of jāts.

गटिया, *f.* (dim. of **गट्ठा**, 1) a small bundle.

गट्टा, *m.* the part of a *hukkā* (a kind of Indian tobacco-pipe) which fixes into the top of the metal part or bottle: the ankle: a row of gems.

गट्टी, *f.* the bank of a river or tank.

गट्ठा, *m.* 1, a bundle, package, pack: root of onion, turmeric. etc.: a clove of garlic: 2, the twentieth part of a jareeb or land-measure.

गठकटा, *m.* (*f.* ī) a cut-purse.

गठकटाई, *f.* (see **आई**, 3) purse-cutting, theft.

गठकटी, *f.* 1, = **गठकटाई**, *q.v.*: 2, a female cutpurse.

गठजोड़ा = **गठबन्धन**, *q.v.*

गठड़ी } *more com.* **गठरी**, *q.v.*
गठड़ि }

गठना, *n.* to be tied together, be knotted together; to be connected, be joined: *a. int.* to unite, to collude.

गठबन्धन, *m.* the Hindoo ceremony of tying the knot. A corner of some article of clothing worn on the occasion of marriage by the bride and by the bridegroom is united by being fastened in a knot: united thus, they form part of a procession to some river or piece of water.

गठर, *m.* a large bundle, bale, package, pack.

गठरी, *f.* (dim. of **गठर**) a bundle, parcel, packet; a sum of money sealed up in a bag: a crew, pack, junto: amount, total. — *k.* to add figures. —*bāndhnā*, to gather, bundle, pack up.

गठवांसी, *f.* the twentieth part of a **गट्ठा**.

गठवाना, *t.* to cause to be joined, cause to adhere.

गठाना, *t.* to attach, connect, join, tie; *lit.* to cause a joining to take place.

गठानी, *f* a kind of tax levied by zamindars on the cultivators of the soil.

गठाव, *m.* a connexion, junction, joining together; a contrivance. — *gānṭhnā*, to contrive well, manage one's cards well.

गठिया, *f.* a bump: pains in the joints: a bag, sack, package, pannier, bundle, small bundle.

गठियाबाई } *f.* gout in the joints, rheumatism.
गठियाबाव }

गठी, *f.* a ball; a small bundle, pack, pad put on the back of a beast of burden.

गठीला, *m.* (*f.* ī) a robust person, etc.: *lit.* knotty, robust.

गठुआ, *m.* the ceremony of **गठबन्धन**, *q.v.*; knots in cloth.

गठे; see (1) **गट्ठा** (2) **गट्ठा** (3) **गठना**.

गठौन्द, a deposit or trust bound up in a bag.

गड, a boundary-mark, landmark.

गडंग } a magazine.
गड़ंग }

गड़क, *m.* a kind of fish, sort of gilt-head.

गड़गड़ाना, *a. int.* to gurgle, rumble, roll, thunder, roar (as a tiger).

गड़गूदर, *m.* old and tattered garments.

गड़च्चा } threatening, snubbing, browbeating.
गड़ड }

गड़ती, a friend, companion.

गड़न, *f.* a swamp, morass.

गड़ना, *n.* to be sunk into the earth, be buried in the earth, be driven into the earth: *a. int.* to penetrate enter, lie.

गड़न्त, *m.* the name of a certain game, tipcat: a certain mode of incantation performed for the destruction of a person (*māraṇ*), — to secure his affection (*mohan*), to subject him to obedience (*bāsīkaraṇ*). — to imprison him or to deprive him of the power of action or of speech (*stambhan*). — to drive him away (*uchchāṭan*), — to call him (*ākarshaṇ*). Certain words are pronounced over an effigy of the person or over his written name, — the document or the effigy being afterwards buried.

गड़बड़, 1, *m.* muddle, confusion: 2, higgledy-piggledy, topsy-turvy.

गडबड = **गड़बड़**, *q.v.*

गड़बड़ा, *m.* bustle, confusion: the motion of the bowels (*Borborygmi*).

गड़बड़ाना, *n.* to be confused, be confounded, be apprehensive.

गड़बड़ाहट, *f.* confusion, flight, alarm, bustle.

गड़बड़ि } = **गड़बड़ाहट**, *q.v.*
गड़बड़ी }

गडरिया } *m.* a shepherd, goatherd, cowherd.
गड़रिया }

गड़लवण, *m.* rock or fossil salt (especially that found in the district of Sāmbhar in the province of Ajmere).

गड़वा, *m.* a kind of waterpot: a flowerpot carried about by musicians and dancing-women at the feast of *Basant-panchamī* as an offering to people of rank, from whom they receive presents in return.

गड़वाट, *f.* a burying; a perforating.

गड़वाना, *t.* to cause to be buried, cause to be driven into the earth, cause to have penetrated, cause to have stuck into.

गड़हा, *m.* (*f.* ई) a cavity, hole, pit, grave, abyss.

गड़ा, *m.* a name given to any large sheaf.

गड़ाना, *t.* to cause to enter, cause to penetrate, to thrust in.

गड़ाबटाई, *f.* division of produce in the sheaf without threshing.

गड़ाव, an instrument for cutting *jawār* stalks.

गड़ासी, *f.* an instrument for cutting sugarcane.

गड़ियार, obstinate, stiffnecked; stouthearted.

गड़ियारी, *f.* obstinacy; stoutheartedness.

गड़ी, 1, = **गढ़ी**, *q.v.*: 2, a friend, companion.

गडुवा = **गड़वा**, *q.v.*

गड़ेरन, the receptacle for the sugarcane before it is cut up.

गड़ेरिया, *m.* a shepherd, goatherd, cowherd.

गड़ेरी, *f.* a joint or piece of the sugarcane, the portion between two knots.

गड़ोना, *t.* to pierce, stick into, perforate.

गड्डा, *m.* a bulbous root.

गड्डी, *f.* a bundle of paper containing ten quires.

गढ़, *m.* a fortress, citadel, castle: a hill.

गढ़ई, *f.* a small pond or tank.

गढ़ट } **गढ़त** } *f.* shape, form, fashion, make.

गढ़ना, 1, = **गड़ना**, *q.v.*: 2, *n.* to be formed, be fashioned, be made: *t.* to make, form, shape, fashion, grave, form by hammering, malleate.

गढ़मुक्तेश्वर, *m. pr. n.* a certain city and celebrated place of Hindoo pilgrimage situated on the Ganges to the east of Merat. A *melā* takes place there in the mouth of *Māgh*.

गढ़वार, coarse, thick, fat.

गढ़हा } **गढ़ा** } = **गड़हा**, *q.v.*

गढ़ाई, *f.* (see **घाई**, 3) the price of malleating or making jewellery: burying.

गढ़ाना, *t.* to cause to make, cause to form by hammering: to bury.

गढ़िया, *f.* 1, a small pond or tank: 2, a pike, javelin, spear.

गढ़ी, *f.* (dim. of **गढ़**) a small fort, castle, village, fortification of mud flanked with towers. Under former Governments there was scarcely a village in India without its gaṛhee; now the word is nearly unknown.

गढ़ीबन्द, a favorable tenure of land in the district of Bundēlkhaṇd to those of the inhabitants who obstinately defended their forts against the Marhattas.

गढ़ेला, *m.* a cavity, hole, pit, abyss.

गढ़ैया, 1, *m.* a burier: 2, *f.* a small tank or pond.

गण, *m.* a troop, flock, multitude, tribe, genus, party, sect, class, etc.; a body of troops consisting of three gulmas, *i. e.* 27 chariots, 27 elephants, 81 horse, and 135 foot; (in Myth.) troops of inferior deities considered as Shiv's attendants and under the especial superintendance of Gaṇesh: (in Arithm.) a number: (in Pros.) a division (1) of time = 30 *kasthas* or about 8 seconds; or (2) of measure = 4, instants or short syllables: (in Gram.) the list of roots (*dhātu*) in the Sanskṛit language: (in Astrol.) a division of the 27 stellar mansions into three parts, each consisting of nine. This word is not unfrequently used to pluralize; *e. g. Tārāgaṇ*, the starry host, stars.

गणाधीश, *more prop.* **गणेश**, *q.v.*

गणक, *m.* (*f.* ī) a calculator, astrologer, arithmetician, one who casts nativities.

गणकी, *f.* (*see above*) the wife of an astrologer, etc.

गणता, *f.* arithmetic.

गणत्व, *m.* (see **गण**) the condition of being an attendant of Shiv.

गणद्रव्य, *m.* public property, common stock.

गणन, *m.* a counting, reckoning, enumeration, calculation.

गणना, 1, *f.* = **गणन**, *q.v.*: 2, *t.* to count, calculate, reckon up.

गणनायक = **गणपति**, *q.v.*

गणनिधान; see (1) **गणपति** (2) **गुणनिधान**.

गणनीय, countable, not innumerable, admitting of or requiring counting.

गणपति. *m.* an epithet of Gaṇesh: *lit.* lord of the inferior deities.

गणराउ } **गणराज** } = **गणपति**, *q.v.*

गणलोग, *m.* (see **गण**) Shiv's attendants.

गणि, *f.* computation, enumeration.

गणिक = **गणक**, *q.v.*

गणिका, *f.* a courtesan, harlot, dancing-girl.

गणित, 1, *m.* calculation, enumeration; arithmetic: 2, *m.* (*f.* ā) counted, reckoned, enumerated.

गणितकर } **गणितकार** } *m.* (*f.* ī) an astrologer, arithmetician.

गणितविद्या, *f.* the science of calculation, mathematics.

गणितस्कन्ध, *m.* = **गणितविद्या**, *q.v.*

गणेश, *m. pr. n.* (1) one of the names of Shiv: but more especially (2) the son of Shiv and Pārvatī, — the Janus of the Hindoo mythology. He is the god of wisdom and the remover of obstacles; hence, he is invoked at the commencement of all undertakings, literary composition, etc. He is represented as a short fat man with an elephant's head, and attended by a rat. The above appellation, with other similar compounds, alludes to his office as chief of the varrious classes of subordinate gods who are regarded as his attendants. Most Hindoo literary compositions begin with the phrase *Sriganeshāya namaḥ*, reverence to the divine Ganesh.

गणेशा, } **गणेस**, } *more prop.* **गणेश**. *q. v.*

गण्टम, *m.* an iron style for writing on palm-leaves.

गण्ठ, *more prop.* **गांठ**, *q.v.*

गण्ठकटा, *m.* (*f.* ī) a cutpurse, thief.

गण्ठजोड़ा, *m.* (see **गठबन्धन**) a knot-joining, splicing, uniting. — *bāndhnā*, to tie together the corners of the skirts of the mantles of a bride and bridegroom. This is a ceremony attending marriage among Hindoos, and is performed by the family-priest (*purohit*).

गण्ठवारा, *m.* the designation of a certain tribe of Jāts.

गण्ठिआ, see (1) **गठिया** (2) **गांठ**.

गण्ड, an old form = **गांड**, *q.v.*

गण्डक, *m.* 1, *pr. n.* = **गण्डकी**, *q.v.*: 2, a rhinoceros; the inhabitants of Videha who reside on the Gaṇḍakī.

गण्डकी, *f. pr. n.* a certain river in northern India.

गण्डमाला, *f.* inflammation of the glands of the neck.

गण्डा, 1. a ring, circle; a kind of horse-collar, a knotted string tied around the neck as a charm: 2. the aggregate number 'four'; *e. g.* a *gaṇḍā* of cowries, *i. e.* four cowries.

गण्डासा, *m.* a sort of axe, pole-axe, a sickle in general.

गण्डासी, *f.* (dim. of **गण्डासा**) a sickle, instrument for cutting sugarcane with.

गण्डिड, *m.* the goitre or bronchocele.

गण्डिया, *m.* (see **गांडू**) a catamite.

गण्डी, *f.* a circle, especially that one which Rām drew around Seetā to protect her from Rāvaṇ: a bank or mound of a tank.

गण्डीला, see **गण्डोला**.

गण्डेरी, *f.* a segment, joint, or portion of the sugarcane.

गण्डोला, *m.* a certain vagrant tribe.

गण्डू, *m.* a certain tribe.

गण्य, not innumerable, admitting of or requiring counting.

गत, 1, = **गति**, *q.v.* : 2, the past, etc. : *lit.* gone ; reached, gained, attained ; understood, known.

गतकाल, *m.* past time, a past opportunity.

गतकुल, unclaimed inheritence (lands etc.) of which the legal owners are extinct.

गतमास, *m.* the month that is gone, last month.

गतार्थ, according to the past, inferred from the past, inferred, understood.

गति, *f.* a going, motion, march, procedure, course ; flight, refuge ; transmigration of souls ; state, condition : course of events, fate ; happiness ; stratagem ; basis ; means of success ; attainment ; custom, habit, way ; gait, pace ; appearance ; funeral rites ; an air or tune. — *k.* to perform funeral rites.

गत्ती, *more prop.* **गति**, *q.v.*

गत्ते, softly, gently, slowly, by degrees.

गथ, price.

गद, *m.* speech, speaking ; a word, spell : disease, sickness : *pr. n.* the younger brother of Krishṇ.

गदका, *m.* a foil for fencing with ; a mace, club.

गदगड़ा, *m.* (*f.* ī) dark, obsure ; muddy, turbid.

गदगद, joyful, rejoicing.

गदगदा, *m.* a certain grain (*Guilandina bonducella*).

गदगरा, a soil abounding in moisture.

गदगा = **गदका**, *q.v.*

गदगोल, *m.* thick and muddy water.

गदबदा, *m.* (*f.* ī) fat, corpulent.

गदर / **गदरा** } = **गद्दर**, *q.v.*

गदल, *m.* a large species of bat, commonly called the flying fox or vampyre.

गदला. *m.* (*f.* ī) turbid, muddy, dull, dirty.

गदलाई, *f.* muddiness, turbidness, dullness.

गदहा, *m.* (*f.* ī) = **गधा**, *q.v.*

गदा, 1, *f.* a club, mace: 2, indigent, poor: hence, *m.* (*f.* in *or* ī) a mendicant, beggar.

गदाई, *f.* poverty, want, mendicity, beggary.

गदाधर, *m.* the mace-bearer, *i. e.* Krishṇ.

गदाया, *m.* = **गदाई**, *q.v.*

गदायुद्ध, *m.* a battle carried on with bludgeons.

गदाला, *m.* an elephant's saddle.

गदावीर, *m.* an epithet of Krishṇ ; *lit.* a warrior skilled in the use of the club.

गदी, *m.* (*f.* inī) a person bearing a mace ; an epithet of Krishṇ : *lit.* armed with a club or mace.

गदीचल, a kind of grass resembling *dūb* but about twice as large ; it is much used as fodder.

गदेल, *m.* a child.

गदेला, *m.* a thick bedding.

गद्द, for words beginning thus, see under the form **गदग**.

गद्दर, half-ripe, unripe (fruit or corn).

गद्दार ; see **गद्दर**.

गद्दी, *f.* a cushion, pad, pack-saddle, bedding or anything stuffed ; a seat, sovereign's throne.

गद्दीगम क°, *t.* to beat thoroughly.

गद्दीनशीन, the occupant of a guddee, *i.e.* a president, principal, prince.

गद्दरी, *f.* the unripe pod of the gram-plant (*Cicer arietinum*).

गद्य, *m.* prose.

गधा, *m.* (*f.* ī) an ass : *met.* a stupid fellow, blockhead. *Gadheká hal,* a donkey's plough. In former times it was not uncommon in the East to yoke donkeys to a plough and drive them over the ruins of a captured town or fort as a mode of insulting a vanquished enemy. *Gadhepar charhānā,* to mount one upon a jackass : — a phrase designating a mode of punishment common in the East, in which the culprit has, first of all, his face blackened and is then seated on a donkey with his face towards its tail ; old shoes, rags, etc. are fastened around his neck, and he is thus paraded through the town.

गधापूरना, *m.* the plant *Boerhavia diffusa.*

गधी, *f.* (*m.* **गधा**) a she-ass.

गन ; for all words beginning thus, but not given below, see under the form **गण**.

गनकटा, (*f.* ī) = **गनकाटा**, *q. v.*

गनकाटा, *m.* (*f.* ī) a person employed in cutting sugarcane into pieces for the mill.

गनती = **गिन्ती**, *q. v.*

गनहिं = (1) **गणको** (2) **गणते हैं**. See **हिं**.

ग़ना, *f.* riches, wealth.

गनि ; see (1) **गणि** (2) **ग़नी** (3) **गनी** (4) **गणना**.

ग़नी, *m.* (*f.* inī) a wealthy person : *lit.* rich, wealthy, opulent ; ind pendent.

गनी, *f.* 1, a kind of coarse stuff of which bags are made : 2, calculation, estimate, judgment.

ग़नीम, *m.* an enemy ; a plunderer.

ग़नीमत, *f.* plunder ; good fortune, affluence.

गनेल, a kind of long grass used in thatching.

गनेस, corruption of **गणेश**, *q.v.*

गनौरी, *f.* a bulrush.

गन्द ; for words beginning thus, but not given below, see under the more proper form **गन्ध**.

गन्दक ; see (1) **गण्डक** (2) **गन्धक**.

गन्दड़वाला, *m.* the receptacle for the sugarcane at the mill before it is cut up.

गन्दना, *f.* a leek (*Allium porum*).

गन्दरवाला, *m.* (*f.* ī) = **गन्दड़वाला**, *q. v.*

गन्दर्कपिन, *f.* a Hindoo dancing-girl.

गन्देरी, *f.* a joint or piece of the sugarcane.

गन्दुम, *m.* wheat.

गन्दुमगून, brown, swarthy ; *lit.* wheat-colour.

गन्दौला, a certain destructive grub.

गन्ध, *f.* smell, odour, stink, scent, perfume ; ordure, filth.

गन्धक *f.* sulphur, brimstone, gunpowder. — *kā tel*, sulphuric acid, oil of vitriol.

गन्धकाष्ट, *m.* any fragrant wood, as sandal-wood, aloe-wood etc.

गन्धबिरोज़ा, frankincense.

गन्धमादन, *m. pr. n.* (1) of Rāvaṇ (2) of a certain monkey (3) of a certain mountain : sulphur.

गन्धरस, *m.* myrrh, frankincense. [smelling flower.
गन्धराज, *m.* sandal (*Gardenia florida*); any sweet-
गन्धर्व *m.* (*f.* ī) an aërial minstrel, kind of celestial musician, a class of demigods who inhabit Indra's heaven and constitute the orchestra at all the banquets of the principal deities: the soul after death and previous to its being born again according to the notions of the Hindoos: a horse; a kind of deer.
गन्धर्वगाना, *m.* the minstrelsy of the celestial choristers. [song.
गन्धर्वगीत, *f.* (*m.*?) the singing of cherubs, a cherub's
गन्धर्वव्याह, *m.* a kind of marriage (like Scotch marriage) by mutual pledge before witnesses or in writing.
गन्धर्वसेन, *m. pr. n.* a certain ancient Hindoo king.
गन्धर्वविनी / **गन्धर्व्विनी** / **गन्धर्व्विनी** } = **गन्धर्वी**, *q. v.*
[court of Indra.
गन्धर्वी, *f.* (*m.* **गन्धर्व**) a female minstrel of the
गन्धवह, 1, *m.* the wind, zephyr: 2, fragrant.
गन्धसार, *m.* sandal-wood.
गन्धा, *m.* (*f.* ī) stinking, foul, nasty, odious.
गन्धार. *m.* a certain musical mode.
गन्धी; *m.* (*f.* inī) a perfumer, one who sells rose-water, essences, and scents; a bug, (*Cimex lectularius*), the green flying bug.
गन्धीला, *m.* (*f.* ī) a scented person, etc.: *lit.* scented, odorous, stinking, fœtid, having a smell (whether good or bad).
गन्धेल, *m.* a certain sweet-smelling grass.
गन्ध्रब in Chand = **गन्धर्व**, *q. v.* [ting).
गन्ना, *m.* the sugarcane (esp. when ready for cut-
गन्नेल, a kind of long grass used in thatching.
गप, *f.* prattle, tattle, chat, gossip, talk.—*chhāntnā*, to indulge in gossip. — *mārnā*, to prattle, tattle.
गपकना, *t.* to swallow, gulp, devour, bolt, gobble.
गपशप, *f.* prattle, tattle, chitchat, gossip.
गपसा, hard soil of a whitish appearance.
गप्पी, *m.* (*f.* inī) a prattler, tattler. gossip: lit.
ग़फ़र, *m.* pardon. *adj.* gossipy.
ग़फ़लत, *f.* carelessness, negligence, inadvertency.
ग़फ़्स, substantial, thick, close (as cloth).
गब; see (1) **गया** (2) **गर्व** (3) **गर्भ** (4) **गव**.
गबरू, *m.* a clown, uninformed youth, lad, young [man, bridgroom.
गबरौटा / **गबरौन्धा** / **गबरौरा** } = **गुबरौता**, *q. v.*
गबा (*corruption*) = **गवा** = **गया**, *q. v.*
ग़बावत, *f.* inadvertency, stupidity.
ग़बी, *m.* (*f.* inī) a weak-minded person, etc.: *lit.* weak-minded, forgetful, negligent, imprudent.
गब्बर, wealthy, rich, prosperous.
जिब्रील, *m. pr. n.* the angel Gabriel.
गभक = **गबरू**, *q. v.*
गभस्ति, *f.* a ray of light, sunbeam, moonbeam.

गभिन, *f.* a pregnant female.
गभीर, more commonly **गम्भीर**, *q. v.*
गभुआरे / **गभुवारे** } *more prop.* **गर्भवाल**, *q. v.*
गम, lost, missing, wanting; distracted.
ग़म, *m.* grief. — *k.* to sorrow, grieve, bemoan.—*khānā*, to suffer grief: to devour one's grief, *i. e.* to have patience. [shake or clash in music; a beat, march.
गमक, *f.* the sound of the kettle-drum; a violent
गमकीला, *m.* (*f.* ī) spicy, fragrant, odoriferous.
गमख्वारक, *m.* (*f.* ikā) a sympathizer, friend.
गमख्वारी, *f.* affliction; condolence, real friendship.
ग़मगीन, sorrowful, disconsolate. [quetry.
ग़मज़ा. *m.* a wink, amorous glance, ogling, co-
गमत, 1, *m.* a road, path: 2, occupation, employment: 3, pleasure, merry-makings, rejoicing.
गमन, *m.* the act of going. — *k.* to go.
गमनपत्र, *m.* a passport.
गमना, *a. int.* to pass, elapse, be spent (as time): *t.* to put off, procrastinate.
गमनागमन, *m.* a coming and going, passing and re-passing, thoroughfare, intercourse.
गमनीय, accessible, passable; practicable; requiring to be traversed, traversable; moveable: relating to carnal approach.
गमला, *m.* a kind of large earthen water-pan.
गमाना, *t.* to pass one's time.
गमानी, *more prop.* **गुमानी**, *q. v.*
गमार, corruption of **गंवार**, *q. v.*
गमिन, *m.* (*f.* i) / **गमी**, *m.* (*f.* inī) } a passenger, traveller.
गमु, a going, proceeding.
गम्वाना = **गंवाना**, *q. v.*
गम्भीर, *m.* (*f.* ā) a sedate person, etc.: *lit.* deep (as soil, or the sea, or a forest, or a secret, or a tone); impervious, thick; grave, sedate, serious, thoughtful.
गम्भीरत्व, *m.* (*f.* tā) depth; profoundness, mysteriousness, seriousness, gravity, dignifiedness.
ग़म्माज़, *m.* a talebearer, informer.
गम्य, *m.* (*f.* ā) approachable, accessible, travers-
गम्वाना = **गंवाना**, *q. v.* [able, attainable.
गम्यत्व, *m.* (*f.* tā) accessibleness, traversability, perceptibility.
गय, 1, = (1) **गये** (2) **गयन्द** (3) **गज**, *qq. v.*: 2, *m. pr. n.* (1) of a Rishi (2) of a mountain (3) of the people living about Gayā (4) of the district they inhabit.
गयन्द, *m.* (*f.* ī) an elephant.
गयल, *f.* (*more prop.* **गैल**) a road, path.
गयहान, *m.* the world; time; fortune.
गया, 1, *m.* (*f.* **गई**) past part. of **जाना** *q. v.*: 2, *f.* a cow: 3, *f. pr. n.* (1) of a certain river (3) of a certain Hindoo city in the province of Bihār: it is a celebrated place of pilgrimage among Hindoos, and is said to have been rendered sacred by the benediction of Vishnu who granted its sanctity to the prayers of its dying chief slain by the deity.

गयारी, *f.* the land of deceased *biswadārs* or tenants lying unclaimed. [or a resident of Gayā.
गयाली, 1, = गयारी, *q.v.*: 2, *m.* (in *or* inī) a native
गयावाल, *m.* (see वाल) designation of a class of Brāhmaṇs who officiate at certain religious ceremonies performed by Hindoo pilgrims at Gayā, a Hindoo priest [of Gayā.
गयी, (pl. गयीं) a corruption गई, *q.v.*
गयऊ in Braj = गया, 1, *q.v.*
ग़यूर, an epithet of God; *lit.* jealous in point of
गये, *m.* pl. of गया, 1, *q.v.* [honor or of love.
गयो, in Braj = गया, 1, *q.v.*
गर, 1, a contraction of अगर, *q.v.*: 2, *m.* (*f.* nī) often a suffix in words of Persian origin, thus exactly corresponding to function 5 of कर in Hindee and Sanskrit: 3, excoriation or scratching of a horse: 4, *m.* sickness, disease: poison: antidote: a fluid: 5, in
ग़रक़ी, *f.* flooded lands: inundation. [Chand = गल, *q.v.*
गरगया / **गरगय्या** = गेरिया, *q.v.*
गरगराना, *a. int.* to gurgle, rumble, roll, thunder, roar (as a tiger). [during the rains.
गरगवा, a kind of grass, which grows in low grounds
गरचि, a contraction of अगरचि, *q.v.*
गरज, *f.* thunder, the rumbling of clouds; a roaring, bellowing, thundering.
गरज़, *m.* a mace, club, bludgeon, battle-axe.
ग़रज़, *f.* design, object, view, wish, intention, purpose, end, meaning; business, occasion, need, use, want; selfishness, hatred: *adv.* in fine.
गरजना, *a. int.* to thunder, bellow, roar.
ग़रज़बावला, one who is a slave to his passions.
ग़रज़मन्द, desirous, wishful for; self-interested.
ग़रज़मन्दी, *f.* desire; self-interestedness.
गरजात, *f.* the noise of thunder.
ग़रज़ामेज़ / **ग़रज़ालूद** selfish, interested, designing.
गरती, *f.* a modest woman, chaste woman.
गरदन, *f.* the back of the neck. — *kāṭnā*, to cut the throat, behead. — *mārnā*, to kill by decapitation.
गरदनकशी, *f.* insolence, rebellion.
गरदा; see गिरदा and गुरदा.
गरदिश, *f.* a turning round, revolution, period, reversion, vicissitude, circulation, roll. [comp.) separation.
गरदी. *f.* misfortune, affliction: (as as a suffix in
गरब, **गरभ**; for words beginning thus, see under forms गर्ब्ब, गर्भ, respectively. [choleric, virulent.
गरम, hot, warm; ardent, zealous, active; fiery,
गरममसाला, *m.* condiments, spices, seasoning.
गरमी, *f.* warmth, heat: the venereal disease. —*k.*
गरमीदार, peevish, diseased. [to affect fondness.
गररा = गर्रा, *q.v.*
गरल, *m.* poison, venom, venom of a snake.
गरली, *m.* (*f.* inī) any venomous animal: *lit.* poisonous, venomous.

गरवा, *m.* (*f.* ī) heavy, important, respectable, demure.
गरवापन, *m.* weightiness, respectability, demure-
गरह; see ग्रह. [ness.
गरहत्या, *f.* murder by poisoning.
गरा, a corruption of गला, *q.v.*
ग़राइब, *m.* (pl. of ग़रीब) strange things, strangers.
गरांवन, a burying: a coarse kind of salt.
गराम, a corruption of ग्राम, *q.v.*
गरारा, *m.* a sack for containing the walls of a tent.
गरारी, *f.* an instrument for twisting thread or string: the block over which a well-rope traverses.
गरावा, light soil, poor soil. [thorn-bushes, etc.
गरासी, *f.* an implement for cutting *jawār* stalks,
गरिमा, *f.* importance, self-importance, vanity; boast. [of his work.
गरियार, *m.* a bullock that lies down in the midst
गरी, 1, *f.* the kernel of a cocoanut: 2, in words of Persian origin this particle is frequently found as a suffix yielding certain abstract nouns feminine.
ग़रीज़ी, innate, natural.
ग़रीब, 1, (pl. ग़राइब) *m.* (*f.* ā) a stranger, foreigner: *lit.* strange, foreign, wonderful: 2, (pl. ग़ुरबा) *m.* (*f.* ā) a pauper, etc.: *lit.* poor, humble, mild.
ग़रीबनी, *f.* (*m.* ग़रीब) a poor female.
ग़रीबनवाज़, hospitable, courteous to strangers, kind to the poor. [nourisher of the poor.
ग़रीबपरवर, epithet of a master or patron; *lit.*
गरीबां, *more prop.* ग़रीबान, *q.v.*
ग़रीबान, *m.* (a Pers. pl. of ग़रीब) the poor, paupers.
ग़रीबिन / **ग़रीबिनी** = ग़रीबनी, *q.v.*
ग़रीबी, *f.* poverty, wretchedness; humility, poorness in spirit: foreignness.
गरीसम, an old form of ग्रीष्म, *q.v.*
गरुआई / **गरुता** = गुरुता, *q.v.*
गरुड, *m.* (in Myth.) the regent of the feathered race and vehicle of Vishṇu: a large kind of heron (*Ardea argula*); a large vulture: the name of a battle-array: *query*, the "adjutant-bird?"
गरुड़, more commonly गरुड, *q.v.*
गरुड़पुराण, *m. pr. n.* one of the Purāṇs.
गरुवा, in Braj = गुरु, adj., *q.v.*
गरेबान; see (1) ग़रीबान (2) गिरेबान.
गरोह, *more prop.* गुरोह, *q.v.*
गर्ग, *m. pr. n.* (1) of one of the ten principal *munis* (2) of a sect of Brāhmaṇs descendants of Garg.
गर्गऋषि / **गर्गपुरोहित** / **गर्गआचार्य** / **गर्गमुनि** see *s.v.* गर्ग.
गर्गज, *m.* a scaffold: a tower, bastion: a cavalier.

गर्गर, *m.* a whirlpool; a churn.
गर्गरी, *f.* a water-vessel, guglet.
गर्गवंशी, a certain class of Rajpoots.
गर्गाचार्य्य, *m.* (= **गर्ग**) an epithet of Garg-muni.
गर्ज, *m.* (*f.* ?) a roaring, bellowing; a rumbling
of the clouds, thunder; war.
गर्जट; see **गर्जन** or **गर्जाट**.
गर्जन, *m.* sound, noise, a roaring noise, bellowing,
roaring, thundering; passion, wrath. [and roaring.
गर्जनतर्जन, *m.* a thundering, storming, bellowing
गर्जना, 1, *f.* = **गर्जन**, *q. v.*: 2, *a. int.* to roar, bellow,
गर्जाट, the noise of thunder. [thunder.
गर्जि, *m.* the sound of distant thunder.
गर्त्त, *m.* a hole, cavity, ditch.
गर्द, *f.* dust: the globe: fortune.
गर्दन, *f.* } = **गरदन**, *q. v.*
गर्दना, *m.* } [reversion, circulation.
गर्दिश, *f.* a turning around, revolution, vicissitude,
गर्दाड़ा, *m.* a small pit.
गर्द्दन, *more prop.* **गरदन**, *q. v.*
गर्द्दभ, 1, *m.* (*f.* ī) an ass: 2, *m.* the white lotus.
गर्द्दभी, *f.* (*see above*) a she ass: a kind of beetle
springing from and living in cowdung. [form **गर्व्व**.
गर्ब, for some words beginning thus see under the
गर्बपहारी, *m.* (*f.* iṇī) *more prop.* **गर्व्वापहारी**, *q. v.*
गर्भ, *m.* the belly, stomach, inside; womb, foetus,
embryo; conception, pregnancy; the interior; a sprout; the bed of the Ganges when the river is fullest, *i. e.* on the fourteenth day of the dark half of the month Bhadr, or in the height of the rains. As high as the river flows at this period, so far extends the '*Garbh*', after which the '*Teer*' or proper bank begins and extends for a hundred and fifty cubits:—this space is holy ground. — *rahnā* or *honā* or — *se honā*, to be
गर्भदा, *f.* a kind of shrub. [pregnant.
गर्भदास, *m.* (*f.* ī) the child of a slave-girl; *lit.* a
womb-slave.
गर्भपात, *m.* miscarriage after the fourth month of
pregnancy. [produce abortion.
गर्भपातक, *m.* a kind of red *Morunga* supposed to
गर्भबाल, *m.* the hair of a new-born child.
गर्भरूप, *m.* (*f.* ā) } a child, infant.
गर्भरूपी, *m.* (*f.* inī) }
गर्भवती } *f.* a pregnant female.
गर्भवन्ती }
गर्भवास, *m.* the womb, the being in the womb.
— *k.* to dwell in the womb (said of an *avatār*).
गर्भस्राव, *m.* miscarriage, abortion.
गर्भाधान, *m.* conception; a certain ceremony sup-
posed to procure conception. [(*Asclepias rosea*).
गर्भिणी, *f.* a pregnant female: a certain plant
गर्भी, with child, pregnant. [**गरम**.
गर्म; for words beginning thus, see under the form
गर्मा, *m.* summer.

गर्रा, *m.* (*f.* ī) bayish (said of the colour in a horse
गर्रिन्दा, abusive, scurrilous. [or in a pigeon).
गर्री, *f.* an instrument for twisting thread or string:
a rick, haystack, rick of thatched grain.
गर्व्व, *m.* pride, arrogance, vanity, conceit. — *k.*
गर्व्वत, *m.* (*f.* ā) = **गर्व्वित**. *q. v.* [to be proud.
गर्व्वता, *f.* pride, arrogance: a proud woman.
गर्व्वमणि, *m. f.* the jewel of pride, *i. e.* very great
गर्व्वर, *m.* (*f.* ā) = **गर्व्वित**, *q. v.* [pride.
गर्व्ववन्त, *m.* (*f.* vatī) = **गर्व्वित**, *q. v.*
गर्व्ववन्ती, *f.* a proud woman.
गर्व्ववास, *m.* proudness, vainness, arrogance.
गर्व्वापहारी, *m.* (*f.* iṇī) *adj.* pride-destroying.
गर्व्वित, *m.* (*f.* ā) an arrogant person: *lit.* proud,
arrogant, haughty, vain, conceited.
गर्व्वी, *m.* (*f.* īṇī) = **गर्व्वित**, *q. v.*
गर्हण, *m.* a censuring, blaming, reproaching.
गर्हा, *f.* censure, blame, reproach, abuse.
गर्ह्य, *m.* (*f.* ā) a mean person: *lit.* contemptible,
mean, vile, low.
गल, *m.* the neck, throat; a noose, snare; a fish-
inghook; the gallows. — *jānā*, to melt away, dissolve, waste away. — *denā*, to throttle, choke, put to death by hanging, hang a criminal. — *bahiyāṅ ḍālnā*, to throw the arms around another's neck.
गलका, *f.* a boil, swelling, tumour.
गलखोर, a horse's halter. [glands of the neck.
गलगण्ड, *m.* inflammation or enlargement of the
गलगन्डा; see **गलगण्ड**.
गलगल, *m.* a citron; a certain bird: a mixture of
of lime and linseed oil forming a kind of mortar impervious to water. [the arm.
गलजन्दड़ा, *m.* a handkerchief used as a sling for
गल जाना, *a. int.* (intens. of **गलना**): see *s. v.* **गल**.
गलगड़ा, *m.* (*f.* ī) a person who has a tremendous-
ly loud voice: *lit.* stentorophonic.
ग़लत, *m.* an error, mistake: *adj.* erroneous.
गलतंस, a person who dies without issue. [neck.
गलतकिया, *m.* a kind of pillow or bolster for the
ग़लतनामा, *m* the table of *Errata* in a book.
गलतनी, *f.* part of the headstalk of a bridle. [yoke.
गलताड़, the name given to the inner pegs of a
ग़लती, *f.* an error, mistake. — *k.* to make a mis-
गल देना; see *s. v.* **गल**. [take.
गलना, *n.* to be dissolved, be melted, be wasted
away: *a. int.* to melt, dissolve, waste away.
गलनी, *f.* wasting, consumption.
गलन्दा, *m.* (*f.* ī) an abusive person: *lit.* abusive,
गलपाल, a pellet-bow. [scurrilous, foulmouthed.
गलफटाकी, *f.* a scolding; a boasting, bragging.
— *k.* to scold; to brag; to utter falsehoods.
गलफड़ा, *m.* the jaws; the angle of the mouth.
गलफूट, *f.* a vaunt; vaunting.

गलफूला, chubby : hence, *m.* (*f.* ī) a chubby person.

गलबही
गलबाह } गलबाह, *q.v.*
गलबाही [of its work.

गलया, *m.* a bullock that lies down in the midst

ग़ल्बा, *m.* superiority, prevalence, conquest, overcoming, assault, strength. — *k.* to overpower, overcome. [throwing the arms around another's neck.

गलबाह *f.* an embrace, embracing, caressing by

गलवाना, *t.* to cause to be dissolved, cause to be melted, cause to be wasted away. [by married women.

गलसरी, *f.* an ornament worn around the neck

गलहड़
गलहर } *m.* the goitre, swelling in the neck.

गलहार, *m.* (*f.* ā) soluble ; corruptible.

गलही, *f.* the prow, forecastle of a boat, etc.

गलहेयडा, abusive, scurrilous . hence, *m.* (*f.* ī) an abusive person.

गलहैया, *m.* the boatswain, forecastle-man.

गला, *m.* the front part of the neck, throat, gullet ; a funnel, tube, syphon ; the voice. — *uṭhānā*, to apply acrid substances, such as pepper, etc., to the *uvula* of a child when it becomes hoarse or when it loses its voice by the relaxation of that part ; *lit.* to lift up the throat. — *kāṭnā*, to cut the throat. — *ghoṇṭnā*, to hold by the throat, throttle, strangle, choke. — *dabānā*, to strangle. — *denā*, to waste. — *paṛnā*, to be hoarse. — *phā̃snā*, to choke, hang by the neck. — *bandhānā*, to ensnare oneself (especially in the bonds of love). — *baiṭhnā*, to be hoarse.

गलाऊ, soluble : septical, melting, dissolving, [weakening.

गलाश्रो, *m.* a solution, fusion.

गलाना, *t.* to melt, dissolve, waste, squander away ; [to soften.

गलानि, *more prop.* ग्लानि, *q.v.*

गलानेवाला, *m.* a menstruum, solvent.

गलाबैठा, *m.* (*f.* ī) hoarse.

गलामाटी, *f.* rich free mould.

गलार, *m.* the *maina*-bird.

गलाव, *more prop.* (1) गलाऊ (2) गलाश्रो, *qq. v.*

गलावट, *f.* solution, the act of dissolving or melt- [ing.

गलि ; see (1) गलना (2) गली.

गलित, *m.* (*f.* ā) melted, dissolved, wasted away : fallen, dropped, sunken.

गलियाना, *t.* to abuse : to force anything (as food or medicine) down the throat, to cram (a horse etc).

गलियारा, *m.*
गलियारी, *f.* } a street, lane, passage, abode.

गली, *f.* a lane ; a narrow pass between mountains.

गलीकूचा, *m.* a narrow lane.

ग़लीज़, dirty, filthy, gross, rude.

गली गली, from lane to lane, from street to street.

गली बगली = गली गली, *q.v.*

गले *paṛnā*, to seek the friendship of one who is averse to it. — *paṛī bajā,e sidh*, we should make a virtue of necessity. — *kā hār honā*, to seek a quarrel or a dispute and to persist in it ; to seek with ardour the friendship or affection of anyone ; to persecute one with attention or with kindness ; to teaze, importune. — *manḍhnā*, to importune. — *lagnā*, to embrace.

गलेगयड, *m.* the adjutant-bird (*Ardea argalla*).

गलेबाज़, a sweet singer.

गलौज = गालीगलौज, *q.v.*

ग़ल्ला, *m.* grain, corn, the produce of the earth.

गल्ला, *m.* a flock, herd.

ग़ल्लादान, *m.* a granary.

गल्लाबान, *m.* a shepherd, pastor : a vessel in which shopkeepers put money for things sold in the course [of the day : a tile.

गल्लाला, *m.* ga garism.

गल्ली, more commonly गली, *q.v.*

गल्ह in Chand = गला, *q.v.* [cow kind.

गव, *f.* (*more prop.* गौ) a cow, any animal of the

गवन, 1, in Braj = गमन, *q. v.* : 2, a Braj pl. of गव.

गवना, *more prop.* गौना, *q. v.*

गवय्या, *more prop.* गवैया, *q. v.*

गवरि
गवरी } in Chand = गौरी, *q. v.*

गवहिं = (1) गांवको (2) गांवसे. See गांव, and हिं.

गवा, a corruption (1) of गवाह (2) of गवाही, *qq. v.*

गवांना, *more prop.* गवाना, *q. v.*

गवांर, *more com.* (1) गंवार (2) गवार, *qq. v.*

गवांरी, *more com.* (1) गंवारी (2) गवारी, *qq. v.*

गवाक्ष, *m.* a skylight, bull's-eye, window, air-hole, loophole, the light that is admitted by a window.

गवाख
गवाच्छ } corruptions of गवाक्ष, *q. v.*

गवाना, *t.* (causat. of गाना) to cause to sing.

गवार, *pr. n.* a certain race of gypsies in India.

गवारी, *f.* a family ; a dwellinghouse, cowhouse.

गवाल (= गयाली, 1) unclaimed land.

गवाशा, *f.* a slaughterhouse. [dence.

गवाह, *m.* (pl. गवाहां) a witness, one who gives evi-

गवाही, *f.* evidence, testimony, witness. — *k.* to bear witness (in writing). — *denā*, to bear witness (by word [of mouth).

गवीश, *m.* (*f.* ā) an owner of kine.

गवेरुक, *m.* red chalk.

गवैया, *m.* a minstrel, singer.

गव्य, *m.* (*f.* ā) appertaining to kine ; produced by a cow ; *hence*, milk, butter, etc.

ग़व्वास, *m.* a diver (*esp.* a diver for pearls). [tion.

गव्वी, *f.* a den of a wild beast ; a pit, hole, excava-

ग़श, *m.* stupor, fainting. — *ānā* or *paṛnā*, to faint.

गस्तान, *f.* a dissolute woman, prostitute.

गस्तानगर, *m.* a clown : *prop.* ignorant, uninformed, foolish. [3, time ; place.

गह, 1, in Chand = ग्रह and ग्रह, *qq. v.* : 2, *f.* a handle :

गहक, *f.* the emotion of intoxication.

गहकना, *a. int.* to be agitated by intoxication.

गहकी, 1, *f.* purchase : 2, *m.* (*f.* inī) a purchaser.

गहगह, from time to time, sometimes.

गहगहाना, *a. int.* to quiver, shake; to undulate.

गहवा = (1) **गहन** (2) **गहवर**, *qq.v.*

गहन, *m.* a thicket, wood, forest; multitude; impenetrability, obscurity: *lit.* adj. *m.* (*f.* ā) deep, impenetrable, impervious, obscure: formidable, great.

गहनता, *f.* } impenetrability, obscurity.
गहनत्व, *m.* }

गहनवन्त, *m.* (*f.* vatī) full of thickets.

गहना, 1, *fem.* of **गहन**, *q.v.*: 2, *m.* jewels, ornaments; mortgage, a pledged or pawned article: 3, *t.* to lay hold of, seize, catch, take, handle: *a. int.* to blush. *Bhaglī*—, false jewels, trinkets.

गहनी, 1, *f.* oakum: the act of caulking: 2, *m.* (*f.* inī) pledged. — *dharnā*, to pledge, pawn.

गहमागहम = **घमाघम**, *q.v.*

गहवर = **गह्वर**, *q.v.*

गहरवार, *pr. n.* a certain tribe of Rajputs.

गहरा, *m.* (*f.* ī) deep, profound.

गहराई, *f.* }
गहराओ, *m.* } deepness, profundity, depth.
गहरापन, *m.* }
गहरावा, *m.* }

गहरारंग, *m.* deep colour.

गहराव, *m.* depth, profundity, deepness.

गहरी, *f.* delay, procrastination, lateness: low swampy ground (fit for rice-cultivation).

गहरू, procrastination, delay, lateness.

गहल, *f.* a bunch or cluster of grapes, etc.

गहलोत, *pr. n.* a certain tribe of Rājputs.

गहवा, *m.* forceps, pincers.

गहवारा, *m.* a swing, cradle.

गहवैया, *m.* one who seizes.

गहाई, *f.* the process of treading sheaves of corn by bullocks for separating the grain from the ears and talks

गहिना, *more prop.* **गहना**, 2. *q.v.*

गहिरा, *m.* (*f.* ī) *more prop.* **गहरा**, *q.v.*

गहिराई, *more prop.* **गहराई**, *q.v.*

गहिराव, *more prop.* **गहराव**, *q.v.*

गहूरी, *f.* demurrage.

गहेसि = **तू गहता है**. See **एसि**.

गह्वर, *m.* a thicket, wood: an enigma: *lit. m.* (*f.* ā *or* ī) impenetrable, dense, obscure, profound.

गा; in Gaṅwārī, an emphatic particle = **हो**, 2.

गाइगोठ, a cowhouse, cowshed.

गाइब, absent, concealed, invisible, vanished.

गाइबबाज़, *m.* a conjuror.

गाई, 1, *f.* of **गाया**, *q.v.*: 2, *f.* (prop. **गो**) a cow.

ग़ाई, *f.* (pl. of **ग़ायत**) ends, extremities.

गाईं, 1, pl. of **गाई**, 1, *q.v.*: 2, *pr. n.* a certain small class of Rājpoots in the district of Kopa-cheet.

गाए, 1, *m.* a pl. of **गाया**, *q.v.*: 2, *f.* (prop. **गो**) a cow.

गाएरों, a calculus or hard substance found in the gall-bladder of oxen and used in medicine.

गाओ, 1, = **गाओं**, *q.v.*: 2, = **गाव**, *q.v.*: 3, the second person plural imperative and conditional of **गाना**, *q.v.*

गाओं, *m.* a village, town, district.

गाओंखरचा, *m.* expenses or charges incurred in the municipal administration of a village.

गाओंटी, appertaining to a village.

गाओंबट, a subdivision of a district into several villages.

गाओली = **गावली**, *q.v.*

गांओं, *m.* a village, town, district.

गांकर, an inferior kind of coarse bread made of arhar.

गांगन, *m.* a certain disorder.

गांजना, *t.* to store, hoard: to stir, agitate, churn.

गांजर, *f.* a kind of grass or verdure.

गांजा, = **गांझा**, *q.v.*

गांजू, *m.* or *f.* an extravagant consumer of *gāñjhā*.

गांझा, *m.* the hemp-plant (*Cannabis sativa*); the leaves or young buds of the hemp-plant. The fructification when nearly ripe is bruised and smoked in order to produce intoxication: the dried leaves of it are ground and mixed with water and drunk for the same purpose; in this latter state it is called *bhang* or *sabzee*.

गांझावाला, *m.* (*f.* ī) a vendor or a consumer of *gāñjhā*.

गांठ, **गांड**; for words beginning thus, see under the forms **गाण्ठ**, **गाण्ड**, respectively.

गांडीव, *more prop.* **गाण्डीव**, *q.v.*

गांड़, *f.* the anus, the privities.

गांम } *m.* a village, town, district.
गांव }

गांवना in Braj = **गाना**, to sing.

गांवबासी, *m.* (*f.* in *or* inī) }
गांववाला, *m.* (*f.* in *or* ī) } a villager, rustic.
गांववासी, *m.* (*f.* in *or* inī) }

गांसना, *t.* to pierce, transfix, spit (a fowl).

गांसी, *f.* the iron point of an arrow.

गांहक, *more prop.* **गाहक**, *q.v.*

गाकर = **गांकर**, *q.v.*

गागर, *f.* (prop. **गगरी**) a water-vessel, guglet.

गागरा, *m.* (*f.* in) a certain low caste of sweepers.

गागरी *f.* (*prop.* **गगरी**) a water-vessel, guglet.

गाच } *m.* a tree.
गाछ }

गाछमिर्च, *f.* cayenne pepper (*Capsicum annuum*).

गाछी, *f.* a pad put over the back of a beast of burden.

गाज, 1, *f.* scum, froth: 2, a thunderbolt: 3, bangles or bracelets made of glass.

गाजन, *m.* a sounding, roaring.

गाजना, *n.* to be pleased, be happy, be cheerful, be delighted: *a. int.* to thunder; to roar as a wild beast.

गाजमारा, *m.* (*f.* ī) an unfortunate person, etc.: *lit.* thunderstruck; afflicted, unfortunate.

गाजर, *f.* a carrot (*Daucus carota*).

गाजल, a seller of glass bangles.

गाजा, a term designating the first or early rice-growing in the districts at the foot of the hills.

गाजाबाजा, *m.* the sound or clangour of various musical instruments, a band of music.

गाजिर = **गाजर,** *q. v.*

ग़ाज़ी, *m.* a conqueror, hero (particularly one who has fought against and slain one or more infidels).

गाज़र, *m.* a washerman, fuller, bleacher.

गाट = (1) **गाटा** (2) **गायठ,** *qq. v.*

गाटा, the yoking of bullocks together for the purpose of treading out grain: a plot or piece of land, a division of a village.

गाटाबन्दी } **गाटेवार** } *f.* the division of a village by gāṭās.

गाठ (*corruption*) = (1) **गाट** (2) **गायठ,** *qq. v.*

गाठि, *more com.* **गायठ,** *q. v.*

गाड (*corruption*) = (1) **गड्हा** (2) **गाड़,** *qq. v.*

गाड़थोप, *f.* burying, burial.

गाड़ना, *t.* to bury, sink, drive down, set in, fix in.

गाडर, 1, *f.* a ewe: 2, a variety of the *khas*-grass.

गाडरू, *m.* a charm or *mantra* against venom or snake-bite.

गाड़ा, *m.* 1, a wagon, cart, carriage: 2, a ditch, pit, hole, cavern; an ambuscade: *Gāre baiṭhnā,* to be concealed, lie in ambush: 3, low land on which water does not lie long: 4, a kind of cloth.

गाड़ी, *f.* a cart, carriage, railway-carriage, railway-train.

गाड़ीबान } **गाड़ीवान** } *m.* a carman, carter, coachman.

गाड्डी, *m.* (*f.* in) a juggler, mountebank, buffoon.

गाढ़, *f.* a difficulty, misfortune.

गाढ़ना, 1, = **गाड़ना** *q. v.*: 2, *t.* to malleate, form by hammering.

गाढ़ा, *m.* (*f.* ī) thick, close, dense; difficult; muddy, turbid; sly, shrewd, knowing, wise; strong (as tea, etc).

गाढ़ापन, *m.* denseness; turbidness; shrewdness.

गायठ, *m.* (*f.* ?) a knot, knob; a joint, articulation; a bundle. — *kā pūrā,* wealthy. — *kā khonā,* to act to one's own prejudice. — *kholnā,* to untie a knot. — *parna,* a phrase applied to designate the fixing enmity towards any one in the breast. *Mankī* — *bāndhnā,* to be prejudiced.

गायठ उखड़ना, *m.* a dislocation.

गायठ खोलना, *m.* prodigality, extravagance, expense: the removal of prejudice; *lit.* the untying a knot.

गायठगठीला, *m.* (*f.* ī) knotty (as a stick); compact (as a man).

गायठजोड़ा, *m.* (see **गठजोड़ा**) a splicing.

गायठदार, knotted.

गायठना, *t.* to tie, knot, join, stitch, cobble, put together, attach, cause to adhre: to reduce to obedience, reduce to subjection.

गायठा, *m.* } **गायिठ** } **गायठी,** *f.* } = **गायठ,** *q. v.*

गायठीदार, an occupant of lands by heritable tenure.

गायड *f.* the anus, the privities.

गायडग़लत, stupid; dead.

गायडमराव, *m.* a sodomite.

गायडर, *f.* a kind of grass (*Andropogon muricatum*) used for thatching. It grows in soil subject to inundation, and its root yields the *khas* or *khaskhas* of which ṭaṭṭees are made.

गायडल = **गायडर,** *q. v.*

गायडा, *m.* sugarcane ready for cutting.

गायिडव } **गायडीव** } *m.* a bow (*esp.* that of Arjun).

गायडीवी, *m.* an epithet of Arjun: lit. *m.* (*f.* inī) armed with a bow.

गायडू, *m.* a catamite; a sodomite (*cinœdus*).

गात, 1, *f.* (from **गात्र**) the body: 2, apparel.

गाता, 1, *m.* pastedoard: 2, *f.* the body.

गाती, *f.* a plaid: a mantle.

गातु, *m.* motion, course (of life); a celestial chorister.

गात्र, *m.* the body; a limb, member.

गाथ, *m.* singing; a song.

गाथक, *m.* (*f.* ikā) a singer, musician, chanter of the Purāṇs: lit. *adj.* singing.

गाथा, *f.* a verse, stanza; a song, chant, verse to be sung or chanted; metre, rhythm.

गाथी, *m.* (*f.* inī) a singer.

गाद, *f.* sediment (of dirty water).

गादना, *t.* to ram down.

गादर, 1, *m.* a heap, stack, rick: 2, half-ripe (fruit or grain).

गादा, *more prop.* **गधा,** *q. v.*

गदी, a corruption (1) of **गद्दी** (2) of **गधी,** *qq. v.*

गादुर, a bat (?).

गाधि, *m. pr. n.* a certain ancient Hindoo king.

गान, *m.* singing; a song. — *k.* to sing.

गानधर्ब, *more prop.* **गान्धर्व,** *q. v.*

गाना, *a. int.* to sing; *t.* to celebrate in song.

गान्थना, *t.* to arrange; to lay bricks in mortar; to unite, thread, stitch, string up.

गान्दिनी = (1) **गान्दी** (2) **गान्धिनी,** *qq. v.*

गान्दी, *f. pr. n.* a certain princess of Kāshī. She was wife of Shwaphalk and mother of Akrūr.

गान्धर्ब, 1, *more prop.* **गन्धर्ब,** *q. v.*: 2, *m.* music and dancing, singing, song; a certain from of marriage which requires only mutual and amorous agreement: 3. *m.* (*f.* ī) musical, appertaining to the Gandharvas.

गान्धार, *m.* one of the seven primary notes of music; *pr. n,* (1) of the country of Candahar between India and Persia (2) of its people (3) of one of its princes.

गान्धारी, *f. pr. n.* (1) of one of the tutelary female deities of the Jains (2) of a princess of the Gāndāria.

गान्धिक, *m.* (*f.* ā *or* ī) a vendor of perfumes: a kind of worm that has a strong foetid smell.

गान्धिनी, *f.* an epithet of the Ganges or of the goddess Gangā.

ग़ाफ़िल, senseless, stupid, apathetic, negligent, careless, thoughtless, imprudent, not on one's guard.

गाब, 1, = गर्भ, *q. v.*: 2, *m.* a certain tree (*Diospyros glutinosa*, Kœn. MS.; *Embryopteris glutinifera*, Roxb. Pl. Cor. 70) the fruit of which contains glutinous astringent juice with which the bottoms of boats are smeared and in which nets are soaked.

गाबा = गाभा, *q. v.*

गाबिन = गर्भिणी, *q. v.*

गाभ = गर्भ, *q. v.*

गाभना, *t.* to snub, chide. [a plantain-tree.

गाभा, *m.* a new leaf springing from the centre of

गाभिन, = गर्भिणी, *q. v.*

गाम, *m.* a village, town, district.

गामिज़, abstruce, difficult, obscure.

गामिन, *m.* (*f.* ī) } = गामुक, *q. v.*
गामी, *m.* (*f.* inī) }

गामुक, *m.* (*f.* ā) *adj.* going, moving, locomotive

गाम्भीर्य्य, *m.* = गम्भीरता, *q. v.* [(used in comp.).

गाय, 1, *f.* (prop. गो) a cow: 2, *m.* a song.

गायक, *adj.* singing: hence, *m.* (*f.* ikā) a singer.

गायकर, 1, an old gen. of गाय, *q. v.*: 2, *m.* (*f.* in, ī, *or* nī) a singer.

ग़ायत, *f.* (pl. ग़ायें) the end; extremity, excess; excrement: a flag, standard: *lit.* very, extremely, chiefly.

गायत्रिन, *m.* (*f.* ī) a singer: a certain tree (*Mimosa catechu*) which yields the resin formerly called *Terra japonica*.

गायत्री, *f.* a certain Vedic metre, — being a stanza of twenty-four syllables, or four lines of six syllables each: a sacred verse from the Rig-Ved to be recited only mentally; this is usually personified and considered as a goddess, — the metaphorical mother of the first three castes of Hindoos regarded in their capacity of twice-born, — the investiture with the distinguishing and sacred thread, etc. being regarded as the new birth. There is but one gāyatree of the Veds; but according to the system of the Tantrikas, there are a number of mystical verses called by the name, — each deity having some one particular gāyatree. The repetition of the gāyatree is considered necessary to salvation. [public singer: 3, *adj.* singing.

गायन, 1, a Braj pl. of गाय, *q. v.*: 2, *m.* a song: a

गायमांस, *m.* cow's flesh, beef.

गाया, *m.* (*f.* गाई) past part. of गाना.

गायिका, *f.* (*m.* गायक) a songstress.

गायें, 1, *f.* (pl. of गाय) cows: 2, = गाएं (गाना).

गायों, see (1) गायें (2) गायो (3) गाऊंगा (गाना). [*qq. v.*

गायो, in Braj a corruption (1) of गया, 1, (2) of गाया,

गार, 1, = गाली, *q. v.*: 2, *m.* hail, frost: 3, frequent as a suffix in words from the Persian denoting agency, corresponding thus to कार in Hindee and Sanskrit.

गारज = गरज, *q. v.*

गारडू, *m.* a snake-charmer.

ग़ारत, *f.* rapine, plunder, devastation. — *k.* to plunder, devastate. — *honā*, to be plundered, be laid waste.

गारना, *t.* to strain, squeeze, milk.

गारला, *m.* (*f.* ī) grey, light blue.

गारा, 1, *m.* mud kneaded or prepared for making pottery: 2, *m.* a certain musical mode: 3, low land on which the water does not lie long.

गारी, *more prop.* (1) गाड़ी (2) गाली, *qq. v.*

गारुड़, 1, appertaining to गरुड़: 2, *m.* an emerald.

गारुड़ी, *adj.* neutralizing the effect of poison (?).

गार्ग्य, *m.* (*f.* ī) a descendant of गर्ग, *q. v.*

गार्हस्थिक, (*more prop.* गार्हस्थ्य) appertaining to the condition of a householder.

गाल, *m.* 1, a sort of tobacco: 2, a cheek: a story; conversation; a tattler. — *bajānā.* to prate, chatter, talk. — *mārnā*, to tell lies.

गालफटाकी, *more com.* गलफटाकी, *q. v.*

गालव, *m. pr. n.* a certain Rishi.

गाला, *m.* a pod of cotton; a ball of carded cotton.

गालागाली = गालीगलूज, *q. v.*

गालि, *f.* (*m.* ?) a curse, imprecation, execration.

ग़ालिब, overcoming, victorious, excelling. — *k.* or *honā*, to overcome, excel, have the predominance.

गालियां, *f.* (pl. of गाली) abusive words; a species of indecent nuptial song. — *denā*, to give abuse; to sing amatory songs. [abuse, revile, call names, scold.

गाली, *f.* abuse, insulting language. — *denā*, to

गालीगलूज, *f.* reciprocal abuse, quarrelling, brawl-

गालीगलौज = गालीगलूज. *q. v.* [ing.

ग़ालीचा, *m.* a small carpet.

गालील, *m. pr. n.* the province of Galilee.

गालीली, appertaining to Galilee: hence, *m.* (*f.* in

गाव, *f.* (*prop.* गो) a cow. [*or* inī) a Galilean.

गावंगर, *m.* a singer, musician.

गावख़ाना, *m.* a house or stall for cattle.

गावघप, deceit, artifice, fraud.

गावघप्पू, deceitful, fraudulent, alluring. [lands.

गावचराई, *f.* grazing: a tax levied on pasture-

गावत in Braj = गाता (गाना).

गावतकिया, *m.* a kind of pillow or bolster; a large bolster for supporting the back when seated.

गावदा, *m.* a simpleton, blockhead.

गावदुम, *f.* a trumpet; a tube; a slope, acclivity, descent: *lit.* thick at one end and thin at the other.

गावना in Braj = गाना, *q. v.*

गावली, *m.* (*f.* inī) a cowherd.

गावगोश्त, *m.* beef.

गावघी, *m.* clarified cow-butter.

गावों, (1) a pl. of गांव (2) a pl. of गाव (3) = गाऊंगा.

गाह, 1, *m.* an alligator; a shark; 2, *f.* time; place. [a receiver, getter, taker, seizer.

गाहक, *m.* (*f.* ikā) a chapman, vendor, dealer:

गाहगाह, again and again, repeatedly.

गाहन, *m.* 1, bathing: 2, a kind of harrow with teeth for eradicating grass from ploughed land.

गाहना, *t.* to caulk; to thrash, tread out corn: to inquire, investigate, search.

गाहब, a fut. form of गहना and of गाहना. See ब, 4.

गाहा = (1) कथा (2) गाथा, *qq. v.*

गाहिगाहि, *adv.* with much inquiry or research.
गाहो, *f.* the aggregate of five, a five.
गाहे, *adv.* at one time, some time.
गिंजाई, *f.* (see **कनखलाई**) a certain insect.
गिंती = **गिन्ती**, *q.v.*
गिचपिचिया, *m. pr. n.* the Pleiades. [nutriment.
ग़िज़ा, *f.* food, victuals, diet, provisions; aliment,
गिजाफ = **गुज़ाफ़**, *q.v.* [young person.
ग़िज़ाल, a young deer, fawn: the sun: a delicate
गिटकारी, *f*, a particular sound of the voice in singing (quavering? warbling?).
गिटकौरी, *f.* a pebble. [humbly.
गिड़गिड़ाना, *t.* to beseech, implore earnestly and
गिड़गिड़ाहट, *f.* imploring, beseeching, entreating.
गिड्डा, *m.* (*f.* ī) of short or small stature.
गिणती = **गिन्ती**, *q.v.*
गिणना, *t.* to count, number, reckon up.
गिण लेना, intensive form of **गिणना**, *q.v.*
गिणवाना, *t.* to cause to be counted, cause to be reckoned up.
गिणाना, *t.* to cause to count, cause to reckon up.
गिण्डुरी, *f.* (see **चूना**) a kind of rope.
गिदड़, *more com.* **गीदड़**, *q.v.*
गिद्ध, *m.* a vulture.
गिनजाई, *f.* (see **कनखलाई**) a kind of insect.
गिनना = **गिणना**, *q.v.*
गिन्ती, *f.* number, reckoning, counting, account; title of the Book of Numbers: the first day of the month: a muster, specimen. [ing grain.
गिन्दर, a certain insect very destructive to grow-
गिन्दुरी, *f.* a circular twist of straw or grass for supporting a vessel with a round bottom.
गियान in Chand = **ज्ञान**, *q.v.*
गिर (*contraction*) = **गिरि**, *q.v.*
ग़ियास, 1, listening to complaints, redressing wrongs; redress, assistance, succours: 2, diving, [studying deeply.
गिरगट, *more prop.* **गिरगिट**, *q.v.*
गिरगिट, *m.* a lizard (*Lacerta striata*); a chameleon; the tree lizard (often called by Europeans, "the blood-
गिरगिटाना, see (1) **गिरगिट** (2) **गिड़गिड़ाना**. [sucker").
गिरगुट = **गिरगिट**, *q.v.*
गिरजा, *m.* (Port.) a place of worship, church. — *k.* to conduct worship in public.
गिर जाना, *a. int.* (intensive) to fall down; to be lost by dropping; *e.g. Merā ek paisā gir gayō*, I've dropped a pice.
गिरते पड़ते, *adv.* with great difficulty, with much toil, with much ado; *lit.* repeatedly failing.
गिरथापन, *m.* economy. [**गरदन**, *q.v.*
गिरदंन, 1, a Braj pl. of **गिरदा**, *q.v.*: 2, *more prop.*
गिरदा, round; hence, *m.* a circle, ring, hoop; the hair cut in a circular form; a round carpet spread under a *hukkā*; a shield; a round pillow; a round flat loaf or cake of bread; a wafer; a barrel (of a drum); [an orb.
गिरधर, *more prop.* **गिरिधर**, *q.v.*
गिरधारी, *more prop.* **गिरिधारी**, *q.v.*
गिरन, a Braj pl. (1) of **गिरि** (2) of **गिरा**, *qq.v.*
गिरना, *a. int.* to fall, drop, sink, tumble: *n.* to be spit. [down.
गिर पड़ना, *a. int.* (intensive) to fall down, tumble
गिरफ्तार, **गिरफतार**, } *more prop.* **गिरिफ़्तार**, *q.v.*
गिरराज, *more prop.* **गिरिराज**, *q.v.*
गिरवर, *more prop.* **गिरिवर**, *q.v.*
गिरवाना, *t.* to cause to overthrow, cause to fell, cause to be thrown down, cause to upset. [ing corn.
गिरवी, *f.* a certain insect mischievous to stand-
गिरह; see (1) **गिरा** (2) **गिरिह** (3) **ग्रह** (4) **ग्रह**.
गिरहस्त; for all words beginning thus see under the
गिरहू, a Braj past part. of **गिरना**, *q.v.* [form **गृहस्थ**.
गिरा, 1, *f.* speech; poetry: an epithet of Saraswatee: 2, *m.* an event, accident: 3, *m.* (*f.* ī) fallen.
गिरां, heavy, important; precious, dear.
गिरांमाया, *m. f.* precious, costly, of great worth, of noble birth. [cast down.
गिरा देना, *t.* (intensive) to throw down, beat down,
गिराना, *t.* to cause to fall; *hence*, to fell, overthrow, overturn, upset, cast down, throw down, break down, abase; to spill, drop, shed: to strike.
गिरानी, 1, *f.* scarcity, dearth, dearness of food, etc.: importance, weight; heaviness of spirit, grief, vexation: 2. *m.* a dull heavy person.
गिरापति, *m.* the lord of Saraswatee *i.e.* Brahmā.
गिरामी, dear, precious; elegant; excellent, great, [revered.
गिरावना, *more com.* **गिराना**, *q.v.*
गिरास, *more prop.* **ग्रास**, *q.v.*
गिरि, *m.* a hill, mountain, elevation, rock.
गिरिजा, *f.* an epithet of Pārvatee considered as daughter of the personified Himālaya mountains; *lit.* the mountain-born.
गिरिजानन्त **गिरिजानन्द** } *m.* epithet of Gaṇesh.
गिरिधर, *m.* (see **गोवर्धन**) an epithet of Krishṇ; *lit.* the mountain-holder.
गिरिधारण, *m.* the upholding or sustaining a mountain. — *k.* to hold up or support a mountain.
गिरिधारी = **गिरिधर**, *q.v.*
गिरिनदी, *f.* a mountain torrent.
गिरिनन्दिनी, *f.* an epithet of any mountain-stream; *lit.* daughter of a mountain.
गिरिनाथ = **गिरिपति**, *q.v.*
गिरिनाथा, *more prop.* **गिरिनाथ**, *q.v.*
गिरिनारी, *f.* the wife of any mountain.
गिरिनिम्नगा, *f.* a mountain-stream.
गिरिन्द्र, an epithet of **मेरु**, *q.v.*
गिरिपति, *m.* the lord or chief of the hills; *hence*, an epithet (1) of mount *Meru* (2) of Mahādev.

गिरिफ़्त, *f.* a taking, seizing, capture; a handle, catch, clutch; an objection, criticism.

गिरिफ़्तार, *m.* a prisoner, captive; *lit.* seized, involved or overwhelmed in trouble, etc.

गिरिफ़्तारी, *f.* captivity, imprisonment, bondage; embarrassment. [on, or by, a mountain.

गिरिभव, *m.* (*f.* ā) mountain-born, produced in,

गिरिर, *m.* a hyena.

गिरिराई = गिरिराज, *q. v.*

गिरिराज, *m. pr. n.* an epithet (1) of Krishṇ (2) of Meru (3) of Govardhan; *lit.* the lord or the chief of hills, the royal hill.

गिरिराजा } = गिरिराज, *q. v.*
गिरिराय }

गिरिवर, *m.* a mountain, hill. [south of India.

गिरिसार, *m. pr. n.* the Malaya mountain in the

गिरिह, *f.* a knot, knob; a knuckle, joint; a division of a *gaz*, three finger-breadths: prejudice, misunderstanding: a purse.

गिरीश, *m.* an epithet of Mahādev and of the Himālaya mountains; *lit.* king of hills.

गिरीस } = गिरीश, *q. v.*
गिरीसा }

गिरेखम, a corruption of ग्रीष्म, *p. v.*

गिरेबान, *m.* a collar; a cap; a pocket; *fig.* the neck. — *meṅ muṅh ḍālnā*, to confess and to be ashamed of one's faults.

गिरेवा, a low hill; an acclivity, ravine, steep pass.

गिरेवान = गिरेबान, *q. v.*

गिरो = (1) गिरा (2) गिराओ (गिराना).

गिर्गिट = गिरगिट, *q. v.*

गिर्दआवर, 1. = गिर्दवार, *q. v.*: 2, = गिर्दओपेश, *q. v.*

गिर्दओपेश, *adv.* around, round about, all around.

गिर्दवार, *m.* a superintendant or inspector of police or of customs: a patrol, watch, guard.

गिर्दावा, *m.* a patrol, watch, guard.

गिर्यान, a weeper: lit. *adj.* weeping.

गिल, *f.* earth, clay, mud, bole.

गिलई, see (1) गिलहरी (2) गिलो (3) गिल्ली.

गिलट *m.* = गिलटी, *q. v.* [knot, tumour.

गिलटी, *f.* a protuberance, hard swelling, gland,

गिलहरी, *f.* a squirrel.

गिला, *m.* complaint, lamentation, reproach, blame.

ग़िलाज़त, *f.* thickness, spissitude, coarseness; hardness, roughness; roughness of manners: filth.

गिलान, *more prop.* ग्लान, *q. v.*

ग़िलाफ़, *m.* a case, cover, sheath; the prepuce.

गिलियर, lazy, indolent.

गिली, earthen, made of clay.

गिलेरी, *f.* a squirrel.

गिलो, *m.* the medicine *Menispermum glabrum.*

गिलोन्दा, *m.* the flower of the *mahooā* (*Bassia latifolia*) after it has fallen off.

गिलोरी, *f.* betel-leaf prepared and folded up.

गिल्ल, see (1) गिल (2) गिल्ला (3) गील.

गिल्ला, *m.* (*f.* ī) moist, damp, wet.

गिल्लावा, *m.* prepared clay; dirt, mud.

गिल्ली, *f.* a span, *i. e.* the measure of circumference indicated by the circle formed by joining the ends of the thumb and forefinger: an ear of Indian corn (*Zea mays*) from which the seeds have been taken out: the short stick in the game of tipcat which is struck by the longer one called *ḍanḍā.* — or *gulli ḍanḍā khelnā*, to play tipcat.

गिह = गेह, *q. v.* [hurrum.

गींज, *f.* a certain dish used in the festival of Mo-

गींजना, *a. int.* to crumple.

गीटम, *m.* a coarse kind of carpet not colored.

गीत, (*m.*?) *f.* (prop. गीति ?) a song, hymn; sing-

गीतबधाई, *f.* a birth-song. [ing. —*gānā*, to sing.

गीता, *f.* a rhapsody or episode (as the *Bhāgavat-Gītā*, an episode of the *Mahābhārat*).

गीती, *f.* the world, universe. [any hymn-book.

गीतों की पुस्तक, *f. pr. n.* title of the Book of Psalms:

गीद, *m.* a kite.

गीदड़, *m.* a jackal (*Canis aureus*).

गीदड़भबकी, *f.* bullying, blustering, bravado.

गीदो, *m.* a blockhead: *lit.* stupid.

गीध, *m.* (prop. गिद्ध) a vulture.

गीर, 1, see (1) गिरि (2) घीर; 2, (in comp.) *adj.* taking, seizing, holding, catching, conquering.

गीरि } corruptions of गिरि, *q. v.*
गीरी }

गील, *f.* (prop. गैल) a road, path.

गीला, 1, *m.* a certain wild creeper (*Mimosa scandens*): 2 *m.* (*f.* ī) moist, damp, wet.

गीलापन, *m.* moistness, dampness, wetness.

गीली, see गीला, 2. [more common form ग्वाल.

गुआल; for words beginning thus, see under the

गुंग, mute, speechless, dumb.

गुंगा, *m.* (*f.* in *or* ī) = गुंग, *q. v.*

गुंगुन, a muttering: speaking softly to oneself.

गुंगुना, 1. *m.* tepidity: 2. *m.* (*f.* ī) tepid, milk-warm;

गुंगुनाट, *f.* a muttering, grumbling. [snuffling.

गुंगुनाना, *m.* to be milkwarm: *a. int.* to mutter, grumble; to sing slowly, sing with a low voice; to [snuffle.

गुंगुनापन, *m.* tepidity.

गुंघी, see गुंगी, घूंगी, and घोंघी.

गुंचा, see कूंच, कूच, कूचा, and गुच्छा.

गुंज, 1. *m.* the shrub *Abrus precatorious* or its seed (which forms the smallest of the jeweller's weights); 2. *f.* an echo, hollow sound, resounding, buzzing.

गुंजत, *adj.* buzzing, humming.

गुंजना, *a. int.* to buzz (said of the bee).

गुंजमाल, *f.* a rosary of *gunj*-seeds.

गुंजरना, *a. int.* to roar, growl.

गुंजहार, *m.* a necklace composed of *gunja*-seed.

गुंजाई, = गुंजाइश, q. v.

गुंजाइश, f. capacity, holding-room ; capability of a village respecting revenue : profit, gain.

गुंजाइशवाला, m. (f. ī) capacious, roomy, profitable.

गुंजान, m. (f. ā) thick, close, dense.

गुंजानी, f. closeness, thickness, denseness (forest).

गुंभा, m. (f. ī) grave, venerable. [bdellium.

गुग्गुल, m. a certain tree (*Amyris agallocha*) or gum,

गुचा, see कूंच, कूच, कूचा, and गुच्छा.

गुची, f. a bundle of a hundred betel-leaves.

गुच्छ, m. = गुच्छा, 1, q. v.

गुच्छा, 1. m. a bunch, cluster of fruit ; an ear of corn ; a tassel : 2. m. (f. ī) dapper, neat, compact.

गुच्छेदार, f. a kind of turban.

गुज़र, f. a ferry, passage, ford ; an elapsing, passing. — k. to cross over. — *jānā*, to pass by, elapse.

गुजरगाह, f. a ferry, ford, passage.

गुज़रना, t. to omit, abstain from, decline : *a. int.* to pass, go, pass by, pass over ; to terminate.

गुजरनी = गूजरनी ; see गूजर.

गुजरात, m. pr. n. Guzrāt in western India.

गुजराती, m. (f. inī) a native of Guzerāt : *lit.* appertaining to Guzrāt. [employment, livelihood.

गुज़रान, f. life, living, course of life ; passing ;

गुजरातु, see (1) गुजरात (2) गुजराती.

गुज़री, f. a market (*esp.* one held in the afternoon by the road-side. [utterance, rash or vain speech.

गुज़ाफ़, f. boasting ; a falsehood, inconsiderate

गुज़ार, m. a ferry, passage ; a passing ; a performing, executing ; a paying.

गुज़ारा, m. a ferry, ferryboat ; a passing, passage.

गुज़ारिश, f. payment ; a representation, explanation ; a petition, request.

गुजिया, f. an earring : a kind of sweetmeat.

गुझन, *adv.* thickly, closely, densely.

गुटकना, t. to swallow : *a. int.* to coo as a dove.

गुटका, m. (?) = गुटिका, q. v. [*quini*, Willd.).

गुटबैंगन, m. a certain prickly plant (*Solanum ja-*

गुटिका, f. a ball prepared by Hindoo devotees by putting which into their months they are supposed to become invisible : a sweetmeat swallowed as a bolus without chewing ; a pill, bolus, any small globe or ball : a pearl : a small book worn as an amulet.

गुठना, *more prop.* गठना, q. v.

गुठला, m. (f. ī) set on edge (the teeth).

गुठली, f. a kernel, seed, stone (of fruit).

गुड, } m. raw sugar ; molasses, treacle.
गुड़, }

गुड़गा, the knee. *Gurge po mundi jhukānā* to pon-

गुड़गी, f. knee-breeches. [der, meditate, reflect.

गुड़गुड़ाना, *a. int.* to rumble (said of the bowels).

गुड़गुड़ी f. a small hukka commonly called the bubble-bubble.

गुड़च, m. the medicine *Menispermum glabrum.*

गुड़पुष्प, m. the plant *Bassia latifolia.* It bears sweet flowers from which a spirituous liquor is distilled, and its nuts yield an oil which is used instead of butter.

गुड़फूल = गुड़पुष्प, q. v. [resembling mango-foule.).

गुड़म्बा, m. mangoes boiled with meal aud sugar

गुड़री, f. (see जूना) a kind of rope.

गुड़सी, f. a cottage, hut, shed.

गुड़ाकू, tobacco prepared for the hukka.

गुड़ाना, t. to dig : to cause to dig, cause to be dug.

गुड़ाम्ब = गुड़म्बा, q. v.

गुड़िया, 1, m. a *gur*-seller : 2, f. a child's puppet, doll.

गुड्डी, f. a child's kite ; a pinion.

गुड़ल, m. the plant *Hibicus Syriacus*, commonly called by Europeans "the shoe-flower."

गुण, m. a string, rope, small tack-rope, lute-string, bow-string : quality, an attribute or property in general but especially of excellence, a good quality, virtue, excellence, merit : mode, method, manner ; gain ; excess : a kindness, a favor : species ; a subordinate element : skill, cleverness, sense, understanding. By the addition of this word to cardinal numbers, proportional numbers are formed ; *e. g. Do-gun*, twofold, double ; *Das-gun*, tenfold. — k. to benefit. — *kā paltā denā* , to repay a benefit. — *chhāndnā*, to pass over a person's good qualities. The term signifies a principle or property incident to humanity of which there are three particularized, *viz.* 1st, *Satwa-gun*, the principle of truth, of benevolence, or of existence ;—supposed to be specially exhibited in Vishnu: 2ndly, *Raja-gun* the love of sensual enjoyment or of pleasure ;—supposed to prevail in Brahm: 3rdly, *Tama-gun*, darkness, ignorance, irascibility, or promptitude to the vindictive passions ;—supposed to prevail in Shiv : hence, in the ingenious system of rekconing by symbols adopted by Hindoos in their poetry, this word is a symbol for 3. (In Gram.) when a word ending in short or long *a* is compounded with a word beginning with a vowel, both of these vowels in blending into one undergo certain modifications according to the laws of combination or Sandhi ; these modifications are termed *gun*-(or quality) changes.

गुणआगार, an epithet of any person of surpassing excellence (like the English phrase 'a paragon of excellence') ; *lit.* a dwelling-place of good qualities.

गुणक, m. (in Arith.) the multiplier.

गुणकारक, m. (f. ikā) } helpful, salutary, fit.
गुणकारी, m. (f. inī) }

गुणखान, an epithet of any very excellent, skilful or learned person ; *lit.* a mine of merit.

गुणगण, pl. of गुण, q. v. See गण.

गुणगाथा, f. the statement of the qualities of a person or thing (whether in praise or in dispraise).

गुणगान, m. panegyric. eulogy, praise. — k. to sing, celebrate in song ; to prattle or crow (as infants).

गुणगाहक, m. (f. ikā) a seeker after knowledge ; an appreciator of another's merits, etc. *lit.* discerning merit, patronizing learning, doing justice to the good qualities of others.

गुणग्राहक, m. (f. ikā) } = गुणगाहक, q. v.
गुणग्राही, (f. inī) }

गुणज्ञ, m. (f. ā) a recognizer of merit, friend of virtue, appreciator of another's worth.

गुणज्ञाता, *m.* (*f.* trī) = गुणज्ञ, *q.v.*

गुणता, *f.* subordination, dependence: excellence, virtue: (in Arithm.) multiplication.

गुणत्व, *m.* the condition of a rope or string: subordination: excellence: the possession of qualities: (in Arithm.) multiplication.

गुणद, *m.* (*f.* ā) = गुणदायक, *q.v.*

गुणदायक. *m.* (*f.* ikā), *adj.* imparting virtue or virtue, profit, beneficial, improving.

गुणधर्म, *m.* the virtue or duty incident to the possession of certain qualities (as clemency is the virtue and duty of royalty, etc.).

गुणना, *t.* to praise: to think upon, consider, judge of. [tralizer, antidote.

गुणनाशक, *m.* (*f.* ikā) a destroyer of qualities, neu-

गुणनिधान, *m.* an epithet of any being of great excellence; *lit.* a treasury of good qualities.

गुणभ्रंश, *m.* the loss of all good qualities.

गुणमय, *m.* (*f.* ī) consisting of virtues, abounding in excellences referable to the three fundamental qualities. [female.

गुणवती, *f.* (*m.* गुणवान) an excellent or virtuous

गुणमान, *m.* (*f.* matī) } गुणवान, *q.v.*
गुणवन्त, *m.* (*f.* vatī) }

गुणवाचक, (in Gram.) any word indicating quality or attribute; *hence*, an adjective.

गुणवाचन; see (1) गुणवाचक (2) गुणवाद.

गुणवाद, *m.* the pointing out or celebrating good qualities or merits. [sessing good qualities.

गुणवान, *m.* (*f.* vatī) an excellent person: *lit.* pos-

गुणवाला, *m.* (*f.* in *or* ī) = गुणवान, *q.v.*

गुणसागर, *m.* an epithet of God or any person of special excellence; *lit.* an ocean of excellences.

गुणस्तुति, *f.* encomium, panegyric, eulogy.

गुणहीन, *m.* (*f.* ā) void of merit, without qualities.

गुणा (infl. *m.* गुणे; *f.* गुणी): by the addition of this element to cardinal numbers, proportional numbers are formed; *e.g. Saugunā*, a hundred-fold.

गुणाकर, *adj.* possessing all excellences: hence (1) *m.* (*f.* ā) one endowed with all virtues (2) *m.* a mine or multitude of merits (3) *m.* an epithet (1) of Buddha Shākya-muni, the founder of Buddhism (2) of Shiv.

गुणाधिप, *m. pr. n.* a certain ancient Hindoo king.

गुणानुवाद, *m.* extolment, glorifying, praising; (chiefly applied to praise offered to the Supreme). — *k.* or *gānā*, to praise, extol, glorify.

गुणायन, *m.* (*f.* ā *or* ī) one who goes on the path of virtue, a virtuous person.

गुणावना, *t.* to cause to praise.

गुणावाद = गुणानुवाद, *q.v.* [of another, a praiser.

गुणावादी, *m.* (*f.* inī) one who rehearses the praises

गुणिता, see गुणता.

गुणित्व, see गुणत्व.

गुणिन, *m.* (*f.* ī) = गुणी, *q.v.*

गुणियन, a Braj. pl. of गुणी, *q.v.*

गुणी, *m.* (*f.* inī) a snake-catcher, snake-charmer, conjuror, sorcerer, etc.: *lit.* possessed of any quality or art, dexterous, skilful, virtuous. [jectival pronoun.

गुणीभूत, (in Gram.) a pronominal adjective or ad-

गुणेश्वर, *m. pr. n.* a certain mountain in Bundēlkhaṇḍ supposed by some to be Chitrcote or Comptah.

गुण्टा, *m.* a tank, pool.

गुण्ड, a furrow.

गुण्डली, *f.* coiling (of a snake).

गुण्डा, *m.* a fop, ridiculous fellow, dissolute fellow.

गुण्डी, *f.* a stud, button, knob. [determine, appoint.

गुतना, *n.* to be occupied, be employed: *a. int.* to

गुताना, *t.* to cause to appoint, etc.; *see above.*

गुत्ता, *m.* rent, lease of land, farm.

गुथना, *n.* to be strung, be threaded (as pearls, etc.); to be plaited; to be arrayed.

गुथवाँ, *m.* (*f.* wīṅ) plaited or strung together.

गुद, 1, *m.* the anus: 2, marrow, kernel; brain.

गुदकीलक, *m.* the piles.

गुदगुदा, *m.* (*f.* ī) soft, plump.

गुदगुदाना, *t.* to tittilate, tickle.

गुदगुदाई }
गुदगुदाहट } *f.* tittilation, prurience, tickling.
गुदगुदी }

गुदग्रह, *m.* constipation, flatulence, etc.

गुदड़िया, *m.* one who hires out quilts: one who is clothed in patched garments or in rags.

गुदड़ियापीर, *m.* a tree near a town or village to which people tie up rags in the manner of votive tablets which they believe to be efficacious for the accomplishment of their wishes.

गुदड़ी, *f.* 1. (corruption of गुज़री ?) a daily market: 2. a pallet, beggar's bedding, quilts, etc.; the garment of a darvesh.

गुदरना, *more com.* गुज़रना, *q.v.*

गुदा, 1, *more prop.* गूदा, *q.v.*: 2, *f.* the anus.

गुदांकुर, *m.* the piles.

गुदाज़, mild, gentle, affable, melting: (in comp.) melting, a melter: *met.* exterminating. [pairing boats.

गुदी, *f.* 1, = गूदा, *q.v.*: 2, a small dock, place for re-

गुदेन्द्रिय, *m.* the anus. [branch.

गुड्डा, *m.* a baby; a doll: a windgall; a bough,

गुद्दी, *f.* the nape of the neck.

गुन; for words beginning thus, but not given below, see under the form गुण.

गुनअयन, *more prop.* गुणायन, *q.v.*

गुनगाथ, *m.* = गुणगाथ = गुणगाथा, *q.v.*

गुनगुना, *more properly* गुंगुना, *q.v.*

गुनगुनाना, *more prop.* गुंगुनाना, *q.v.*

गुनतीस, in Chand = उन्तीस, *q.v.*

गुनन, *m.* (in Braj pl. of गुण; see न, 6) qualities, properties, virtues, merits.

गुनह, *m.* a fault, error, crime, sin, guilt.

गुनहकार, *m.* (*f.* ī) a criminal, sinner.

गुनहकारी *f.* = (1) गुनहकार (2) गुनहगारी, *q. v.*

गुनहगार *m.* (*f.* nī) = गुनहकार, *q. v.*

गुनहगारी, *f.* sinfulness, criminality; a fine for crimes and misdemeanours, revenue derived from judicial fines. [person plural imperative of गुनाना, *q. v.*

गुनहु = 1, गुनह, *q. v.*; 2, an old form of the second

गुना
गुनां } corruptions (1) of गुणा (2) of गुनह, *qq. v.*

गुनाकर, see (1) गुणाकर (2) गुणाकार (3) गुनहकार.

गुनाह; for words beginning thus, see under the [form गुनह.

गुनि, a corruption of गुणी, *q. v.*

गुनिय; an honorific imperative of गुनाना, very frequent in poetry.

गुनीस in Chand = उनीस, *q. v.*

गुनी, *m.* (*f.* in *or* inī) *more prop.* गुणी, *q. v.*

गुन्थवाना, *t.* to cause to string up, etc.

गुन्द, see (1) गुण्ड (2) गुणाद (3) गोन्द (4) गून्द.

गुन्दा, 1, *more prop.* गुण्डा, *q. v.*: 2, coarse, thick, [strong.

गुन्देला, *adj.* producing gum (a tree).

गुन्धना, *n.* to be kneaded; to be plaited.

गुन्धावट, *f.* plaiting, braiding.

गुपाल, *more prop.* गोपाल. *q. v.*

गुन्मा, see (1) गुणामय (2) गुणामें; loc. of गुण.

गुप्त, *m.* frequently the second member of compound proper names of men of the Vaisya caste: 2, *m.* (*f.* ā) preserved, protected; hidden, concealed, invisible: 3, secretly, privately.

गुप्तगति, *m.* a spy, secret emissary.

गुप्तदान, *m.* a certain mode of giving alms secretly to Brāhmaṇs or to a deity.

गुप्तप्रकाशक, *m.* (*f.* ikā) a discoverer.

गुप्ति, *f.* concealment, protection.

गुप्ती, *f.* a hidden sword, sword-stick.

गुफा, *f.* (not infl.) a cave, cavern, den, vault.

गुफ़्तगू, *f.* conversation, talk, discourse, chitchat.

गुफ़्तार, speech, mode of speaking.

गुफ्तोशनीद, *f.* conversation, dialogue; controversy, debate, contention.

गुबरैला, *m.* a certain beetle *Scarabæus stereorarus*, Lin.; *copris*, Geoff.) found in dunghills or in old cowdung.

गुबार, *f.* dust; clouds of dust, vapour; impurity, foulness: *met.* vexation, perplexity, affliction.

गुब्बारा, *m.* a shell, bomb; a mortar.

गुब्बारायन्त्र, *m.* a mortar or any machine for throwing shells.

गुभाना, *t.* to thrust, stick into.

गुभेला, *m.* *scybala*, hard lumps in the intestines produced by costiveness.

गुभेना, *t.* to thrust, stick into.

गुम, lost, missing, wanting; distracted. — *k.* to lose; to be proud. — *ho*, get off! away with you! make yourself scarce!

गुमका, the separation of the corn from the husks.

गुमची, *f.* a kind of wild liquorice (*Abrus precatorius*). Its seed is a small scarlet pea, called ratee, which is used as weights by druggists: women string them together for necklaces and other ornaments.

गुमटा, *m.* a bruise, swelling or tumour resulting from a blow. [vault; a vaulted building.

गुमटी, *f.* a bastion, tower, dome, cupola arch,

गुमड़ा, *m.* a protuberance, swelling, lump.

गुमराह, a wanderer, etc.: *lit.* on the wrong road, wandering, erring; abandoned, depraved.

गुमराही, *f.* wandering, deviation; depravity.

गुमरी, *f.* giddiness, vertigo.

गुमसा, *m.* (*f.* ī) musty, mouldy.

गुमान, *m.* doubt, suspicion, supposition, imagination, fancy, opinion — *k.* or *lānā*, to suppose, imagining, opine, suspect. [jealous, doubtful, suspicious.

गुमानी, *m.* (*f.* inī) a suspicious character: *lit.*

गुमाश्ता, *m.* a factor, agent, envoy with full powers.

गुम्बद
गुम्मज
गुम्मट } *m.* = गुमटी, *q. v.*

गुर (*colloquial*) = गुरु, *q. v.*

गुरखई, *f.* a kind of mortgage.

गुरगी, *f.* knee-breeches; a wench, slave-girl.

गुरज्ञानी, *m.* (*f.* inī) a religious teacher: a receiver of religious instruction.

गुरजना, *a. int.* to snarl.

गुरदच्छिणा, *more prop* गुरुदच्छिणा, *q. v.*

गुरदा, *m.* a sugar-mill: a kidney; *met.* courage: the scrape at a sugar-mill to prevent the sugar from resting at the bottom of the boiler.

गुरनाशक, *m.* (*f.* ikā) one who takes the life of his *guru* or who brings upon him obloquy or disgrace.

गुरब, a certain agricultural process by which the ground is broken and pulverized.

गुरबत, *f.* travelling, being far from one's country and friends; exile; wretchedness.

गुरबा, *m.* a cat.

गुरबा, *m.* (pl. of ग़रीब) poor people, paupers.

गुरभाई, *more prop.* गुरुभाई, *q. v.*

गुरविनी
गुरवी } see गुरु, 1, and गुर्व्वी.

गुरमुख, *more prop.* गुरुमुख, *q. v.*

गुरयं, in Chand = गुरु, *q. v.*

गुरसिंगी = गुरुशृंगी = शृंगी, 2, *q. v.*

गुरहेर, stacks of cowdung.

गुराइब, *more prop.* ग़राइब, *q. v.*

गुराई, *f.* whiteness, fairness; yellowness; pale redness, ruddiness.

गुराब, *m.* a crow, raven, rook, jackdaw.

गुराव, *m.* a stock or collection of sheaves: an instrument for cutting juwār-stalks, etc. for fodder.

गुरिया, *f.* a bead of a rosary, etc.

गुरु, 1, *m.* (*f.* gurvī *or* gurviṇī) large, great; heavy, weighty; important; venerable, honorable, respectable; eminent; excellent, best; dear; violent;

2, m. (f. āin or āini) a spiritual parent, spiritual director from whom a youth receives the initiatory *mantra* or prayer, and who conducts the ceremonies necessary at various periods of infancy and youth up to the time of the investiture with the characteristic sacred thread: this person may be either the natural parent or the religious preceptor; and hence, the term denotes any object of veneration, any venerable male relation, a father, spiritual preceptor or guide, pastor, tutor, teacher, one who explains law and thelogy and instructs his pupils in the Shástras, etc.: an epithet of Vrihaspati.

गुरुआइन } **गुरुआइनी** } f. (see गुरु, 2) the wife of a religious preceptor; a religious preceptress.

गुरुआई, f. (see आई, 3) the office, profession, or condition of a *guru*.

गुरुकार्य्य, m. the office of a *guru*; any weighty affair.

गुरुजन. m. 1, (a pl. of गुरु) great people, eminent persons: 2. m. any venerable person, as one's parents or religious preceptor, an elder.

गुरुतर, m. (f. ā) a venerable person: *lit.* more important, more weighty, highly honorable.

गुरुत्व, m. (f. tā) weightiness, importance, dignity: the status of a religious teacher, guruship, tutorship.

गुरुदक्षिणा, f. a fee given to a spiritual preceptor.

गुरुदेव, m. a respectful epithet of any *guru*.

गुरुदैवत, m. pr. n. the eighth *Nakshatra*. [guide.

गुरुधन्य, m. the pronouncing blessing on a religious

गुरुपाक, difficult of digestion. [religious preceptor.

गुरुपुत्र, m. (f. ī) the natural or the adopted child of a

गुरुभाई, m. a fellow-disciple, fellow-student.

गुरुमुख होना, a. int. to receive from one's *guru* the initiatory *mantra*, to become a pupil.

गुरुमुखी, f. pr. n. the character in which the Pan-

गुरुरत्न, m. a topaz. [jabee language is written.

गुरुर, *more prop.* गुरुड़. q. v.

गुरुलक्षण, m. knowledge which can be acquired from a living instructor only: adj. m. (f. ā) heavy, hard of digestion.

गुरुवाइन, *more prop.* गुरुआइन, q.v.

गुरुवार, m. (= बृहस्पतिवार; see गुरु) Thursday.

गुरू, *more properly* गुरु q.v.

गुरूब, m. setting of the sun; the West. — *honā*, to be set (said of any heavenly body).

गुरूर, m. pride, haughtiness, vainglory, vanity.

गुरूवार, *more prop.* गुरुवार, q.v.

गुरोह, m. f. a band, troop, company, levy of peo-

गुर्ग, m. a wolf. [ple, crew, sect, gang, group.

गुर्गज़ादा, a young wolf, wolf's cub. [knee joint.

गुर्गा, m. a servant-boy; a brat; a vagabond: the

गुर्गाबी, f. a kind of shoe or slipper. [fever.

गुर्गुरी, f. the cold fit of a fever, ague, quotidian

गुर्च, f. the creeping-plant *Menispermum glabrum*.

गुर्ज, a snarling.

गुर्ज़, m. a mace, club, battle-axe.

गुर्ज़मार, m. a Muhammadan fakeer who carries a club armed with spikes with which he wounds himself in order to obtain alms from the people.

गुर्जर, 1, m. pr. n. the country of Guzerat in western India: 2, a native of Guzerat, the people of Guzerat.

गुर्जरी, f. one of the musical modes.

गुर्राज़, m. a hog, boar: a harrow.

गुर्री, f. parched barley.

गुर्व्विणी = गुर्व्वी, q. v.

गुर्व्वी, f. (m. गुरु) a pregnant female: *lit.* heavy.

गुर्सी, f. a cottage, hut, shed.

गुल, 1, = गोल, 1, q. v.: 2, m. a rose; a flower; the snuff of a candle; the albugo; a seton, issue, mark made by burning; balls of charcoal used for burning the tobacco in a hukka: the *caput mortuum* of tobacco left on the tile of a hukka after smoking. — *k.* to extinguish a candle or lamp; to flash in the pan and miss fire (a gun). — *katarnā*, to snuff a candle; to calumniate. — *kāṭnā*, to snuff a candle. — *khānā*, to be cauterized, to cauterize oneself (a practice among lovers, who burn themselves with heated pieces of coin in order to recommend themselves by their fortitude to the notice of their mistresses). — *lagānā*, to brand; mark, — *lenā*, to snuff a candle. — *honā*, to be extinguished, go out (a candle).

गुलकारी, f. a flowering; a painting flowers.

गुलकेश, m. the cock's-comb flower (*Amaranthus*

गुलखयड़ा, m. a bell. [*cruentus*).

गुलगीर, m. snuffers.

गुलगुला, 1, m. (f. ī) soft: 2, m. sweet cakes fried in butter; wheaten flour, sugar, and dahee, with anise and cardamum-seeds, made into dumplings and

गुलगुलाना, t. to soften, mollify. [fried in ghee.

गुलगुलाहट, f. the act of softening; softness.

गुलगुली, f. a kind of dish (swollen rice mixed with molasses and formed into balls).

गुलगूथना, m. (f. ī) plump, chubby, handsome.

गुलघला, m. a musqueteer, rifleman, cannoneer.

गुलज़ार, m. f. a garden (or bed) of roses.

गुलझड़ी, f. conglomeration; a knot. *Dilki* —, mental uneasiness, grief, displeasure.

गुलदुम, a nightingale.

गुलफाम, rose-coloured, rose-like; *met.* a mistress.

गुलफुनना, a certain herb which grows in fields sown with khareef grains.

गुलबकावली, f. pr. n. a certain Hindustani work of fiction by Nihāl Chand Lahorī. [*defolium*.

गुलबेल, m. the creeping-plant *Menispermum cor-*

गुलमख़मल, f. globe amaranth (*Gomphrena globosa*)

गुलमिहिन्दी, f. the flower *Impatiens balsamina*.

गुलमेख़, f. a stud; a tack, nail. [the fair ones.

गुलरुख़ान, (pl. of गुलरुख़) the rosy cheeked ones,

गुलरु, rosy-faced, ruddy: *met.* a mistress, a sweet-

गुलरुख, *more prop.* गुलरुख़, q. v. [heart.

गुलरोख़, *more prop.* गुलरुख़, q. v.

गुलरंग, rose-coloured, red.

गुलशन, cheerful: hence, m. a place of enjoyment, delightful spot, rose-garden.

गुलस्तान, *more prop.* गुलिस्तान, *q. v.*

गुलहसी, *f.* rice-gruel, or rice and water boiled together and seasoned with salt.

गुला, *m.* a ball (from a cannon, musket, etc.); a cotton-reel; a cotton-pod; a ringlet, curl.

गुलाई, *f.* roundness, rotundity.

गुलाब, *m.* a rose; rose-water.

गुलाबजल, *m.* rose-water. [Roxb.).

गुलाबजामन, *f.* the rose-apple (*Eujenia jambos,*

गुलाबनीर
गुलाबपानी } *m.* rose-water. [sprinkled.

गुलाबपाश, *m.* a bottle from which rose-water is

गुलाबपाशी, *f.* a sprinkling of rose-water.

गुलाबी, 1, *f.* a phial, flagon, bottle: a kind of sweetmeat: a pear: 2, rose-coloured, damask. rosy.

गुलाबी जाड़ा, *m.* the spring-season. [a male slave.

गुलाम, *m.* a boy, youth, young man at maturity;

गुलाल, *m.* a certain farinaceous powder dyed red which Hindoos throw on each other's person and clothing during the drunken and indecent frolics of

गुलालचश्म, reddish-eyed. [the Holee festival.

गुलालबाड़ी, *f.* a royal tent, royal pavillion.

गुलाली, *m.* (*f.* inī) a person stained with *gulāl*: *lit.* of the colour of *gulāl.*

गुलिस्तान, *m.* a rose-garden: *pr. n.* a certain well-known work of fiction by *Muslihu-d-din shaikh Sa'di* of Shirāz. [bular substance.

गुली, *f.* a disease: a pill, bolus; any small glo-

गुलू, 1, the pod of the *mahwā*-tree (*Bassia latifolia*) which yields a very useful oil: 2, *m.* the gullet, throat, windpipe.

गुलूगा, *m.* a monkey's pouch.

गुलूगीर, *m.* an accuser: *lit.* that which fastens on the throat (as acrid food, etc.).

गुलूबन्द, *m.* a neck-cloth.

गुलेबकावलि, *more com.* गुलबकावली, *q. v.*

गुलेराना, *m.* a beautiful delicate scented rose.

गुलेरोख, *more prop.* गुलरुख़, *q.v.*

गुलेन्दा = गुलू, 1, *q.v.*

गुलेल
गुलैल } *f.* a pellet-bow. [high ankles.

गुल्फ, 1, *m.* the ankle: 2, *m.* (*f.* ā) a person with

गुल्म, *m.* a shrub: a division of an army consisting of nine platoons, each amounting to nine elephants, nine chariots, twenty-seven horse, and forty-five foot: the spleen, a disease consisting, according to some, in an enlargement of the spleen, according to others it is an induration of the mesenteric glands so as to be perceptible externally.

गुल्ला, *m.* a pellet (shot from a pellet-bow).

गुल्लाल, *more prop.* गुलाल, *q. v.*

गुल्ली, *f.* a kind of pigeon: a species of red coral: a whetstone; a polishing-stone. [*chu*).

गुवाक, *m.* the betel-nut tree (*Areca faufel* or *cate-*

गुवैया, 1, *f.* a woman's female friend, a gossip; 2, eloquent; conversable.

गुष्ट, *m.* an assembly; a cabal.

गुसल, *m.* ablution, bathing.

गुसलख़ाना, *m.* a bath-room, bath, bagnio.

गुसा, *more prop.* गुस्सा. *q. v.*

गुसाई,
गुसाईं, } (*contractions*) = गोसाईं, *q. v.* [irascible.

गुसेला, *m.* (*f.* ī) passionate, furious, choleric,

गुस्ताख़ी, *f.* want of urbanity or politeness, arrogance, sauciness, presumption, rudeness, contempt, of court, freedom, familiarity.

गुस्सा, *m.* strangulation, suffocation: *met.* anxiety, grief: anger, passion, wrath, rage.

गुह, *f.* human excrement, ordure.

गुहत, *m.* (*f.* ā) covered, concealed: plaiting the hair.

गुहनौ, *t.* (Braj) to thread, string: to plait, braid.

गुहराना, *t.* to assist: *a. int.* to call out, bawl.

गुहरी, 1, adorned with gems: high-bred (as horses): 2, a dealer in precious stones: recompense.

गुहा, *f.* a cavern, cave: the heart.

गुहाई, *f.* *meconium* (of infants).

गुहांजनी, *f.* a stye (in the eye). [alarm.

गुहार, 1. = गुहारी, *q.v.*: 2. *f.* a bawling, tumult;

गुहारी, *m.* (*f.* iṇī) a keeper, helper, assistant.

गुहाल, *m.* a cowhouse, cattle-shed.

गुही, *m.* (*f.* inī) defiled with excrement.

गुह्य, 1. *m.* (*f.* ā) requiring concealment, concealable; private, secret: 2. *m.* (*f.* ?) the privities.

गुह्यक, *m.* a certain class of demigods (attendants upon Kuvēr and guardians of his treasures).

गुह्यस्तोत्र, *m.* secret praise or commendation.

गू, *f.* human exerement, ordure.

गूआ, *f.* betel-nut. [more common form ग्वाल.

गूआल; for words beginning thus, see under the

गूइयाँ, *m.* a partner (at a game).

गूँग, mute, speechless, dumb.

गूँगा, *m.* (*f.* ī) = गूँग, *q. v.*

गूँगाई, *f.* speechlessness, dumbness.

गूँज, *f.* an echo, resounding; a hallow sound; a buzz; a roar. [to hum, buzz.

गूँजना, *a. int.* to resound, echo; to roar, growl;

गूँझा, *m.* a kind of sweetmeat.

गूँढ़ा, *m.* a beam of a ship, cross-timbers of a boat.

गूगल, *m.* a certain tree (*Amyris agallocha*, Roxb. cor. pl. vol. iii) or its gum; bdellium.

गूगली, *f.* a cockle-shell.

गूजरना, *more prop.* गुज़रना, *p, v.*

गूजर, 1. *m.* a certain caste among Rājputs formerly notorious for thieving (they were originally from Guzerāt, whence their name): 2. *m.* (*f.* ī *or* nī) appertaining to Guzerāt.

गूजरी, *f.* a certain ornament worn on the wrists and feet: an earthen image representing a milkmaid: [a certain musical mode.

गूजी, *f.* a stick, club.

गुड़िया, *m.* a doll, puppet.

गूढ़, abstruse, difficult, obscure, abstract, mysterious, enigmatical, secret, concealed, hidden.

गूढ़ज, *m.* (*f.* ā) a child whose father is not ascertained: *lit.* mysteriously born.

गूढ़त्व, *m.* (*f.* tā) concealedness, abstruseness, secrecy.

गूढ़पात, *m.* a snake.

गूढ़पुरुष, *m.* a spy, scout, secret embassy, disguised agent.

गूढ़मार्ग, *m.* a secret way, subterraneous passage, bye-road, defile.

गूढ़वक्ता, *m.* (*f.* trī) a pedant, pedagogue: lit. *adj.* saying profound things.

गूढ़ा, *m.* the beam of a boat.

गूढ़ार्थ, of obscure or hidden meaning.

गूढ़ो in Braj = **गूढ़** and **गूढ़ा**, *q.v.*

गूथठना = **गून्थना**, *q.v.*

गूथड़ा, *m.* a beam of a ship, cross-timbers of a boat.

गूथ, *m.* a round ball of cotton, etc.

गूथना = **गून्थना**, *q.v.*

गूद, *more prop.* **गुद**. *q.v.*

गूदड़, *m.* a quilt; a bundle of old cloths, any old tattered clothes; a kind of silk stuff.—*kā lāl* or—*meṅ gandaurā nikalnā*, the proceeding of good from evil. —*sīnā*, to stitch together.

गूदड़खेल, foolish, unmannerly, rude (said of females only).

गूदड़ी, *f.* a bundle; a quilt (especially a fakeer's).

गूदना = **गोदना**, *q.v.*

गूदर, fat, plump.

गूदा, *m.* brain, marrow, kernel, pith; a crumb.

गूदाम, a warehouse (*vulg.* go-down).

गूदिया, desirous, wishful, wishing.

गूदी, 1, *more prop.* **गुदी**; 2, *f.* = **गूदा**, *qq.v.*

गूधड़ी, *more commonly* **गूदड़ी**, *q.v.*

गूधना, *more prop.* **गून्थना**, *q.v.*

गून; for words beginning thus, but not given below, see under the form **गुण**.

गूनगूं, see **गुंगुन**.

गूना, a corruption (1) of **गुणा** (2) of **गुनह**, *qq.v.*

गून्थना, *t.* to thread, string; to plait, stitch; to put on to a spit.

गून्थवाना, *t.* to cause to be threaded, cause to be plaited or stitched, cause to be put on to a spit.

गून्थाना, *t.* to cause to thread, cause to plait or to stitch, cause to put on to a spit.

गून्द, *f.* gum.

गून्दना, *more prop.* **गून्धना**, *q.v.*

गून्दनी, *f.* a certain tree yielding a gummy fruit.

गून्दला, *m.* a ring, circle: lit. *m.* (*f.* ī) circular.

गून्धन, *m.* dough; the act of kneading; plaiting, braid.

गून्धना, *t.* to knead; to plat, plait, braid, weave.

गून्धा, *m.* (*f.* ī) plaited, braided, woven.

गून्धान, *m.* dough.

गूपाल, an iron mace, iron throne.

गूमड़ा, *m.* a swelling, bump.

गूय, *m.* a ball; a globe, sphere; any thing globular.

गूरु, *more prop.* **गुरु**, *q.v.*

गूरुत्व, *more prop.* **गुरुत्व**, *q.v.*

गूल, a channel cut for conveying water to a field; a road, path: a bunch of unripe Indian corn.

गूलर, *f.* a wild fig (*Ficus glomerata*, Roxb.): cotton-pods which have not yet burst.

गूह, *f.* human excrement, ordure.

गूहड़िया, *m.* a dunghill, any place where excrement is thrown.

गूही, *m.* (*f.* inī) defiled with excrement.

गृंजन, *m.* poisoned meat: garlic.

गृध्र, *m.* (*f.* ī) a vulture: *lit.* greedy.

गृध्रकूट, *m. pr. n.* a certain mountain.

गृध्रा / **गृध्नु** } eager, greedy, covetous.

गृध्नुता, *f.* (*m.* °**त्व**) greediness, ravenousness.

गृह, *m.* a house, dwelling; family, wife.

गृहकपोतक, *m.* (*f.* ikā) the domestic pigeon, a tame pigeon.

गृहकाज / **गृहकार्य** } *m.* domestic affairs, household work.

गृहचारी, *m.* (*f.* iṇī) = **गृहस्थ**, *q.v.*

गृहच्छिद्र, 1, *m.* a family quarrel, family fault: burglary: 2, *m.* (*f.* ā) one who tells abroad the secrets of his own family.

गृहतटी, *f.* a terrace in front of a house.

गृहनाशन, *m.* (*f.* ī) a pigeon.

गृहपति, *m.* (*f.* **पत्नी**) a house-holder, head of a family, master of the house.

गृहभूमि, *f.* the site of a house.

गृहवाटिका, *f.* a garden or grove near a house.

गृहसम्बन्धी, *m.* (*f.* inī) any member of a household (including servants).

गृहस्त; for words beginning thus see under the more proper form **गृहस्थ**.

गृहस्थ, *m.* (*f.* ā) a Brāhmaṇ who performs the duties of master of a house; a householder, head of a a family, master of a house; a husbandman: *lit.* adj. being in a house.

गृहस्थाश्रम, *m.* the profession or the condition of a householder or married man.

गृहस्थी, 1, *f.* the duties and functions of a householder; house-keeping, husbandry, house-wifery; household: 2, *m.* (*f.* ini) appertaining to house-keeping or to a householder.

गृहाधि, *more prop.* **गृहव्याधि**. See **व्याधि**.

गृहिन / **गृही** } *m.* (*f.* iṇī) = **गृहस्थ**, *q. v.*

गृहीत, *m.* (*f.* ā) accepted, received, taken, caught, seized, attacked.

गृह्य, *m.* (*f.* ā) a book containing directions for religious rites: a partisan, etc.: *lit.* appertaining to a house, domestic: belonging to a side or party: acceptable, obtainable, to be taken, be received, be seized.

गे, a corruption of **गये**, *q.v.*

गेंडा, *m.* (*f.* ī) a rhinoceros.

गेंडु, *more com.* **गेंडुं**, *q.v.*

गेगटा, *m.* (*f.* ī) a crab.

गेगली, *f.* a trollop, slattern.

गेड़ी, *f.* a certain game (in which one stick is knocked over a line by throwing another stick at it).

गेण्ठ, *f.* a certain kind of fish.

गेण्डक, *m.* a marigold.

गेण्डा, *m.* (*f.* ī) rhinoceros.

गेण्डु } गेण्डू } *m.* a ball (for playing with).

गेती, *f.* the world; the universe.

गेदरा, *m.* (*f.* ī) simple, ignorant, silly.

गेदा, *m.* a young unfledged bird: *met.* an infant.

गेनन, a corruption of गेन्द, *q.v.*

गेन्ती = गैन्ती, *q. v.*

गेन्द, *f.* a ball (for playing with).

गेन्दकपड़ा, *m.* cloth of the colour of the marigold (characteristic of the followers of Kṛishṇ).

गेन्दगहवारा, flowers formed like the scale of a balance tied on to images.

गेन्दतड़ी, *f.* play at ball. — *khelnā*, to play at ball.

गेन्दवा, *m.* a tapeworm, worm in the intestines.

गेन्दा, *m.* a marigold: a ball.

गेन्दी, *f.* (dim. of गेन्द) a little ball.

गेपा, *m.* a nipple.

गेवर, *m.* a certain species of bird.

गेरवा, a kind of quail.

गेरामाटी, *f.* loam of fine clay.

गेरी = गेड़ी, *q. v.*

गेरू, *m.* a kind of red earth or ochre, soil of a red colour.

गेरुआ, *m.* (*f.* गेरुई) of the colour of gēroo, red.

गेरुई, *f.* smut; mildew.

गेला, *m.* (*f.* ī) simple.

गेष्णा = गेष्णु, *q.v.*

गेष्णु, *m.* a professional singer; an actor, mimic; a chanter of the Sām-Ved.

गेसू, *m.* a ringlet, curl, forelock, sidelock, the hair of a woman's head, the whole hair when gathered up twisted and fastened on the top or back of the head.

गेह, *m.* an edifice, house, dwelling, mansion.

गेहुआँ, 1, *m.* (*f.* गेहुई) wheat-coloured: 2, *m.* the colour of wheat; a certain grass.

गेहूँ, *m.* wheat.

गै, 1, *f.* (*prop.* गौ) a cow: 2, an old form of गई, *q.v.*

गैंगला, *m.* (*f.* ī) mad, insane, possessed.

गैण्डा, *m.* (*f.* ī) a rhinoceros.

ग़ैदान, *m.* the tender age of youth.

गैना, 1, a corruption of गहना, *q.v.*: 2, *m.* a bush: a small kind of bullock of Guzerat.

गैनी, *f.* a kind of small chariot drawn by *gaina*-bullocks.

गैन्ता, *f.* a pick-axe.

गैन्ती, *f.* (dim. of गैन्ता) a small pick-axe.

ग़ैब, absent, concealed, invisible, vanished.

गैया, *f.* (prop. गौ) a cow.

गैयाँन, in Braj, a pl. of गाय or of गैया.

ग़ैर, other, different: foreign, alien, extraneous: reverse: *adv.* excepting, besides, unless.

ग़ैरत, *f.* modesty, bashfulness: courage; honor, nice sense of honor: jealousy, emulation; enmity.

ग़ैरतमन्द, jealous; bashful.

गैरा, *m.* a sheaf of corn such as will yield a *ser* and a quarter of grain (given to village servants at harvest-time).

गैरिक, *m.* a kind of red earth or ochre.

गैरू, *more prop.* गेरू, *q. v.*

गैल, *f.* a road, path.

गैहरी, *f.* demurrage.

गैहे, in Braj = (1) गाओगे (2) गाएगा (गाना).

गैहैं, in poetry and in Braj = गाएंगे (गाना).

गैहौं, in Braj = गाऊंगा (गाना).

गो, 1, *m.* a bull: 2, *f.* a cow, any animal of the cow kind: 3, *m. f.* cattle, bulls and cows: 4, *m.* (*pl.*) rays of light: 5, *m. f.* water: 6, *f.* speech: the goddess of speech, *viz.* Sarasvatee: 7, *m. pr. n.* a certain Rishi: 8. *f.* the earth, the world: 9, *m.* heaven or paradise: 10, *m.* the sun: the moon: 11, *m.* the sacrifice of a cow: 12, *m.* a thunderbolt: 13, *m.* a member of the body; the hair of the body: 14, *m.* water: 15, *f.* the eye: 16, *f.* an arrow: 17, *f.* any quarter of the horison, as East, West, etc. 18, *f.* a mother: 19, *adj.* gotten, obtained: 20, In colloquial jargon it is often found at the end of a word implying number without affecting the sense, and is used both in asking questions or in making statements; *e. g.* कईगो = कितने; दोगो or दूगो = दो, two.

गोआ, *m.* (*f.* गोई) concealed.

गोई, *f.* speaking, speech, eloquence: a pair.

गोई, *m.* a pair of plough-oxen.

गोए, *m.* pl. of गोआ, *q. v.*

गोंरा, *m.* a kind of reservoir for water.

गोंचरी, *f.* a tick, insect which annoys cattle.

गोंठ, गोंड, गोंद; for words beginning thus, see under either of the forms गोण्ठ, गोण्ड, गोन्द, respectively.

गोंहु, *more com.* गेहूँ *q. v.*

गोकर्ण, *m.* a kind of deer (the नीलगाय): a cow's ear: a mule: a span: *pr. n.* (1) of a certain place of Hindoo pilgrimage (2) of Shiv.

गोकि, *conj.* although, notwithstanding that.

गोकुल, *m.* 1, *pr. n.* the country around Vrindāvan: 2, a cow-house, cow-station; a herd of kine or of cattle.

गोकुलवासी, *m.* (*f.* inī) an inhabitant of Gokul.

गोखरू, *m.* a certain plant (*Ruellia longifolia* and *Tribulus languinosus*.

गोखरुक, *m.* 1, = गोखरू, *q.v.*: 2, a certain ornament consisting of bells tied around the ankles: a joint: *Baṛā* —, *Pedalium murex*.

गोगा, *m. pr. n.* a certain *pīr* or saint held in much veneration in Delhi and the upper Dōāb.

गोघ्न, *m.* (*f.* ī *or* ā) one who has killed a cow.

गोचना, *t.* to catch, seize.

गोचर, 1, *m.* pasture-ground: 2, *m.* reach, province; the range of the eyes; an object of sense (as sound, shape, etc.); an object of devotion: perception; information acquired by the perception of the senses : 3, m. (f. i) visible, perceived, known.

गोचरी; see **गोचर**, 3.

गोजई, f. wheat and barley sown together in the same field.

गोजर, m. a centipede (*Scolopendra*).

गोजरा, m. barley and *chanā* sown together.

गोजरी, f. wheat and barley sown together in the same field.

गोजांगरिक, m. (f. ā or ī) happy, fortunate, auspicious.

गोजी, f. a walkingstick or staff.

गोझा, m. a species of thorny grass which springs up during the rains.

गोट, f. a border of a garment, hem : a counter, piece, man (at chess, etc.).

गोटबस्ती, f. the chief or first assemblage of houses erected on the settlement of a village (those built subsequently are called *tholā* or *patti*).

गोटा, m. fringe, gold or silver lace or edging (rather narrow).

गोटारा, the rich lands immediately adjacent to a village.

गोटी, f. a pock, small-pox.

गोड़, m. the leg, the foot.

गोड़ना 1, t. to dig, scrape : 2, m. a hoe for digging up sugarcane, etc.

गोडरी, f. (see **जूना**) a kind of rope.

गोड़ी, f. a taking away. — k. to take away, walk off with, steal.

गोड़ैत, m. a village watchman, intelligencer.

गोढ़, a name given to weeds and grasses collected from a ploughed field.

गोढ़ा, fields near a village homestead.

गोढ़िया, a homestead, fields near a village.

गोण, f. a sack, bag made of coarse cloth fastened to the side of a beast of burden to carry grain in.

गोयठ, m. a kind of wide stitch or sewing : lands assigned rent-free for religious purposes ; the endowment of a temple.

गोयठा, m. dried cowdung (used for fuel).

गोपिटया, m. the chief manager of a village.

गोगड, m. the designation of the aboriginal inhabitants of the Sāgar territory.

गोगड़ = **गोगड**, q.v.

गोयडली, f. a certain tree.

गोयडा, m. a certain caste of cowherds : a suburb ; a field near a village.

गोत, m. parentage, lineage, pedigree, family stock, kith and kin ; a caste (collectively) ; a subdivision of a tribe or caste ; genus, species.

गोतम, 1, m. pr. n. a certain saint-sage (*muni*) famous in the Hindoo Mythology. He was the author of the *Nyāy-Shāstra*, and his doctrines in Logic correspond with those of Aristotle. Gotam and his wife Ahalyā resided in a retired forest, where Indra, happening to pass, was struck with Ahalyā's beauty, and, having assumed the appearance of Gotam, he deceived and slept with her. This having been discovered, Gotam cursed them both : — to Indra he said, "May your testicles fall to the ground !" — an event which accordingly took place : but Brahmā advised the sage to restore them to Indra together with those of a ram cut out for that purpose ; hence, Indra is called *Meshāndakosh*, the ram-testicled : the sage then caused his wife Ahalyā to be turned into stone ; in which state she remained till Rām, son of Dasarath, passing that way with his brother Lachhman, relieved her and restored her to her original form : being thus purified by the mercy of Rām, she was again received by her husband : 2, a coarse bag full of stones used in schools by way of practice (in teaching ?).

गोता, m. 1, = **गोत**, q.v. : 2, the mustard-seed.

ग़ोता, m. dipping, diving ; a dip, dive. — *khānā*, to be dipped (contrary to one's own will) ; to be deceived : to wash oneself, dive. — *denā*, to dip, plunge, — *mārnā* or *lagānā*, to be dipped (not in opposition to one's own wish).

गोती, m. (f. inī) a kinsman, relative, family connexion : *lit.* appertaining to the same race, etc.

गोत्र = **गोत**, q.v.

गोत्रज, m. (f. ā) a kinsman, clansman : *lit.* born in the same *gotra*. In law this term is equivalent to 'gentile' in Roman law, and is applied to the kinsmen of the same general family who are connected by offerings of food and water : it is opposed to the *bandhoo*, or cognate kin who do not partake in the offerings to the common ancestors.

गोत्रहत्या, f. a striking or a killing a person of one's own *gotra*.

गोत्रा, 1, = **गोत**, q.v. : 2, f. the earth : a herd of kine.

गोत्री, f. ; see **गोत**.

गोथान, m. the place for assembling the cattle of a village.

गोद, 1, m. the brain : elephantiasis : 2, f. the lap, bosom, embrace, — k. to embrace. — *lenā*, to adopt. — *pasārnā*, to ask, beg.

गोदना, 1, m. mark of tattooing, brand : 2, t. to prick, puncture, tattoo, brand as a criminal.

गोदन्त, m. a cow's tooth ; yellow orpiment : a certain fossil substance of a white color (apparently an earthy salt).

गोदरी, f. a circular twist of grass or twine for supporting a round-bottomed vessel.

गोदहूं in Braj = (1) **गोद** **हों** (2) imperat. of **गोदना**. [See **हूं**.

गोदा, f. ; *more com.* **गोद**, 2, q.v.

गोदान m. the gift of a cow.

गोदारा, a subdivision of the *jāṭ* tribe.

गोदावरी, f. pr. n. the rivery Godavery in the Dakkhan.

गोदी = **गोद**, 2, q.v.

गोदुहन, m. milking a cow.

गोदोहनी, f. a milkpail.

गोधड़, the weeds, etc. collected from a ploughed field by a harrow.

गोधड़ा, m. }
गोधड़ी, f. } a bow, branch.

गोधन, m. property in cattle : a station of cowherds.

गोधा, f. a leathern fence worn by archers on the left arm to protect it from the bowstring ; a kind of lizard.

गोधुम, }
गोधूम, } m. wheat.

गोधूली, f. evening, twilight.

गोधेनु, f. a milch cow.

गोधीरा, m. evening, twilight.

गोन, *more properly* **गोण**, q.v.

गोनस, m. a large serpent, *Boa constrictor*.

गोन्द, 1, f. gum : 2, a kind of sweetmeat : 3, a certain rush which grows in marshy ground (it is much used in making mats and baskets).

गोन्दकश, a certain instrument for spreading gum with in sealing letters.

गोन्ददानी, *f.* a vessel in which gum is kept for sealing letters with.

गोन्दनी, *f.* a certain reed (*Typha*) of the leaves of which coarse mats are made.

गोन्दा, *m.* a thin dough or pap made of the flour of the *Cicer arietinum* for feeding birds with.

गोन्दी, *f.* a certain tree (*Cordia*).

गोप, 1. *m.* (*f.* ī) a cowkeeper, dairy-man, cowherd: a certain caste of Hindoos: 2. *f.* a gold necklace.

गोपग्वाल, *m.* cowkeepers.

गोपद, *m.* the cloven hoof of cattle.

गोपन, *m.* concealment, protection. — *k.* to conceal, hide.

गोपना, *f.* = **गोपन**, *q.v.*

गोपनीय = **गोप्य**, *q.v.*

गोपमहल्ल, *m.* pasture-grounds.

गोपरस, *m.* gum, myrrh.

गोपष्टमी, *f.* the eighth day of the light half of Kārttik.

गोपसुता, *f.* the condition of a cow about to be immolated.

गोपांगा, *f.* (*m.* **गोप**) a cowherd's wife, a milkmaid.

गोपाल, *m.* (*f.* ī) a cowkeeper, cowherd: a king; one of the epithets of Krishṇ: frequent as a proper name of males among Hindoos.

गोपालक, *m.* (*f.* ikā) a cowherd: a king: *lit.* adj. having the charge of kine: having charge of the earth.

गोपालतापनीय, *m. pr. n.* one of the Upanishads.

गोपिकन, a Braj pl. of **गोपिका**, *q.v.*

गोपिका }
गोपिन } = **गोपी**. *q.v.*
गोपिनी }

गोपी, *f.* (*m.* **गोप**) a cowherd's wife, a cowherdess, a milkmaid.

गोपीगंज, *m. pr. n.* of a place.

गोपीग्वाल, (**गोपी** + **ग्वाल**) shepherdess and shepherd.

गोपीचन्दन, *m.* a species of white clay.

गोपीनाथ, *m.* lord of the milkmaids, *i. e.* Krishṇ.

गोपेश्वर, *m.* an epithet (1) of Mahādev (2) of Krishṇ.

गोप्य, *m.* (*f.* ā) anything which it is right, lawful, or possible to conceal, guard, or cherish.

गोफन, *m.* a sling for throwing with, a sling used by persons stationed on the *dāmcha* or platform for watching crops.

गोफना }
गोफनी } *f.* = **गोफन**, *q.v.*
गोफिया }

गोबध, *m.* the killing a bull or a cow.

गोबर, *m.* cowdung dried and used as fuel. — *khānā*, to do penance by eating cowdung.

गोबरगनेश, *m.* a simpleton, fool: *adj.* fat, corpulent, sleek.

गोबरी, *f.* a plaster made with cowdung: the name of a tribe in Rohilkhand.

गोबरौन्दा, *m.* a certain beetle (*Scarabæus*) found in cowdung.

गोबर्द्धन }
गोबर्धन } = **गोवर्द्धन**, *q. v.*

गोबिन्द, *more prop.* **गोविन्द**, *q.v.*

गोभी, *f.* a term at cards: a certain medicinal herb (*Elephantophus scaber*: *Hieracium*, Bruce MSS.).

गोम, *m.* a kind of centipede.

गोमती, *f.* cowdung: *pr. n.* (1) of a certain river in Northern India (2) of a certain Vedic hymn.

गोमतीयं in Chand = **गोमती**, *q.v.*

गोमय, *m.* cowdung.

गोमुख, *m.* a certain musical instrument: a breach in a wall made by thieves.

गोमुखी, *f.* the chasm in the Himālaya mountains through which the Ganges issues (supposed by Hindoos to be of the shape of a cow's mouth): a cloth bag containing a rosary (the hand being thrust in counts the beads).

गोमूत्र, *m.* cow's urine. Certain kinds of penance require that it be imbibed.

गोमेदक, *m.* a kind of gem of a yellowish tawny colour, a topaz, a precious stone brought from the Indus and from the Himālayas (it is described as of four sorts, — white, pale yellow, red, and dark blue: perhaps varieties of agate).

गोमेदसन्निभ, *m.* chalcedony or opal.

गोमेध, *m.* the offering up a cow in sacrifice.

गोया, *adv.* thus, in this manner, as if one should say, it is the same as if, just as if.

गोयाई, *f.* conversation, talk.

गोर, *f.* a tomb, grave: the wild ass.

गोरकन, *m.* a grave-digger.

गोरखधन्धा, life, existence: annoyance, affliction: Chinese puzzle consisting of a number of pins passed through holes in an oblong plate, — the pins having rings at one end through which an oblong ring is passed.

गोरगारी, *f.* a curious method of settling boundary disputes in Chutia Nagpore.

गोरपड, a destroyer of a religious faith.

गोरस, *m.* milk, butter-milk, curdled milk.

गोरसचा, 1, *m.* a sodomite: 2, *m.* (*f.* ī) a child: *lit.* reared on cow's milk.

गोरसी, *f.* a vessel for holding milk, etc., milkpail.

गोरस्तान, *m.* a burying-ground, graveyard.

गोरा, fair-complexioned, fair-skinned: hence (1) *m.* an epithet of Shiv (2) *m.* (*f.* ī) a white man, European.

गोराई, name of a clan of Rājputs in the Agra district.

गोरागुमता, *m.* (*f.* ī) red and white.

गोराक, *m.* a partridge.

गोरिस्तान = **गोरस्तान**, *q.v.*

गोरी, *f.* (*m.* **गोरा**) a fair-complexioned female.

गोरुवारीबेरा, *f.* evening, twilight, time of bringing home the cows.

गोरू, *m.* (*f.* ā) an ox.

गोरूआ, *f.* a cow.

गोरूआकुलान, *m.* }
गोरूआरीबेरा. *f.* } = **गेरुवारीबेरा**, *q.v.*

गोरूचना = **गोरोचना**, *q. v.*

गोरूस, *m.* a measure of distance equal to two *kos*.

गोरेट }
गोरेट } *m.* a watchman, village messenger.

गोरोचन, *m.*; *more com.* **गोरोचना**, *q.v.*

गोरोचना, *f.* a bright yellow pigment prepared from the urine of the cow, or vomited by her in the form of *scibulae.* It is employed in painting and in dyeing, and is considered of especial virtue in marking the *tilak*: it is also used in medicine as a sedative, tonic, and anthelmintic remedy, etc.

गोल, 1, *m.* anything globular, a ball, sphere, circle, water-jar: 2, *m.* (*f.* ?) a party from another village sojourning with their cattle for pasture: 3, an idiot, blockhead: 4, round, globular.

गोलक, *m.* (*f.* ikā) the bastard son of a widow: a ball or globe for playing with; the socket of the eye.

गोलगोल, round.

गोलता, *f.*
गोलत्व, *m.* } = **गोलाई**, *q.v.*

गोलन्दाज़, *m.* a gunner, bombardier, marksman.

गोलन्दाज़ी, *f.* ball-practice, gunnery.

गोलफल, *m.* the testicles.

गोलबात कहना, to give utterance to round, general, indefinite assertions (avoiding particulars as one who lacks faith in himself or in his theme).

गोलमिर्च, *f.* black pepper (*Piper nigrum*).

गोलसा, *m.* (*f.* ī) roundish.

गोला, 1, *m.* a store-room, granary (an Indian granary is often a circular house): a ball; a cannon-ball; the kernel of a cocoanut: a large beam of wood: a kind of pigeon: 2, *f.* a globe, sphere, large water-jar, *mandal.*

गोलाई, *f.* rotundity, globularity, sphericity.

गोलाकार, spherical.

गोलाडण्डा, *m.* the game of tipcat.

गोलादार, *m.* a wholesale grain-merchant.

गोलाध्याय, *m.* the section of the *Surya-siddhānt*, and other astronomical works devoted to the doctrine of spheres: spherics. [globe, sphere.

गोलार, 1, *m.* roundness, globularity: 2, *f.* ? a

गोलारा, *m.* (*f.* ī) round, globular, spherical.

गोलिका, *f.* (*m.* **गोलक**) the bastard daughter of a widow.

गोली, *f.* (dim. of **गोला**) a musket-ball, marble, globule, pellet, pill: a jar: a gunshot (as a measure of distance). — *mārnā*, to shoot at with a bullet.

गोलोक, *m. pr. n.* (see **गो**, 9) the heaven of Vishṇu.

गोवना, *t.* to hide, conceal.

गोवर्द्धन, *m. pr. n.* (*lit.* the nourisher of kine) a celebrated hill in Vrindāvan, fifteen miles to the west of Mathurā. It is the Parnassus of the Hindoos, and is said to have been held up by Krishṇ on one of his fingers as an evidence of his divinity, for the purpose of sheltering the cowherds from a storm excited by Indra; *hence*, one of his epithets, 'Giridhar'.

गोवर्द्धननाथ, *m.* the lord of Govarddhan, *i.e.* Kṛishṇ.

गोवा, cowdung, manure.

गोवारी, a dwellinghouse; a family; a cowhouse, cowshed. [cow-keeping.

गोवाली, *m.* (*f.* inī) a dairyman, cowherd: *lit.* adj.

गोविन्द, *m.* an epithet (1) of Kṛishṇ (2) of a mountain; *lit.* who or what acquires a cow or the earth.

गोविन्दराम, *m. pr. n.* a certain scholiast. The word is rather common as a proper name.

गोश, 1, = **गोश्त**, *q.v.*: 2, *m.* the ear.

गोशत, *more prop.* **गोश्त**, *q.v.*

गोशगुज़ार, 1, heard, reported: 2, a hearer.

गोशपोश, *m.* an ornament worn in the turban; a shawl worn around the head, a kind of turban.

गोशपेच = **गोशपोश**, *q.v.* [way of rebuke.

गोशमाल, a pulling, rubbing or boxing the ears by

गोशमाली, *f.* rebuke, punishment.

गोशवारा, *m.* an earring: an embroidered cloth worn as an ornament over the sides of a turban; the abstract of an account, summary, index: the boring the ears of female children.

गोशा, *m.* a corner; the horn or pointed extremity of a bow; a closet, retirement, privacy; a side.

गोशागीर, *m.* a recluse, hermit. [tirement, seclusion.

गोशागीरी, *f.* withdrawal from worldly affairs, re-

गोशागुज़ीन, *m.* a recluse, hermit.

गोशाल, *m.*
गोशाला, *f.* } a cowhouse, cattleshed.

गोश्त, *m.* flesh, fleshmeat. *Sū,arkā* —, swine's flesh, pork. *Bheṛikā* —, mutton.

गोष्ट, *f.* a plot, cabal, conspiracy.

गोष्ठ, *m.* a station for cattle, cattleshed, cowpen.

गोष्ठी, *f.* an assembly, meeting; conversation, discourse: family connexions (especially the dependent or junior branches).

गोष्पद, *m.* a cow's foot, mark made by a cow's hoof, puddle not larger than a cow's footmark; a certain measure, *viz.* as much as a cow's footprint would hold.

गोसव, *m.* the sacrifice of a cow. This was one of the grand sacrifices of the Hindoos in former times, but it is not permitted in Kaliyug (the present epoch).

गोस्सा, *more prop.* **गुस्सा**, *q.v.*

गोसाइन
गोसाई } *more prop.* **गोसांई**, *q.v.*

गोसांई, *m.* (**गो + स्वामी**) an epithet (1) of the Deity (2) of a monarch (3) of a fakeer, saint, or holy person (4) of the descendants of the disciples of Chaitanya of Nadiyā: *lit.* lord of the earth: lord of the cows.

गोसाला, 1, *more prop.* **गोशाला**, *q.v.*: 2, *m.* a calf: [*met.* a dolt, blockhead.

गोसैंया
गोसैयां } = **गोसांई**, *q.v.*

गोस्तन, *m.* a nosegay, cluster of blossoms.

गोस्तनी, *f.* a grape.

गोस्थान, *m.* a station for cattle, cowpen.

गोस्पन्द, *f.* a sheep; a goat. [Hindoo ascetic.

गोस्वामी, *m.* (see **गोसांई**) an owner of kine: any

गोह, *m.* a lizard, guana; a Gangetic alligator.

गोहत्या, *f.* the killing a cow, cow-murder (among Hindoos a most heinous crime).

गोहर, *m.* a broad pathway for cattle: a pearl, jewel, gem: the lustre of a gem or of a sword: essence; disposition; form, substance: offspring: intellect, wisdom.

गोहरा, 1, *more prop.* **गोहरहा**, *q.v* : 2, *m.* cakes of dried cowdung.

गोहरी, *f.* demurrage.

गोहाई, *f.* the treading out of grain by bullocks.

गोहार, *m.* tumult, uproar.

गोहारी, *f.* rich and highly cultivated land.

गोहाल, *m.* a cowhouse, cattleshed.

गोहूँ, *m.* (*com.* **गेहूँ**) wheat.

गोहुअन / **गोहुनः** / **गोहुना** } *m.* the *Boa constrictor*.

गौ, 1, in Braj = **गा** ; *e. g.* **चलेगौ** = **चलेगा** : 2, *f.* a cow, any animal of the cow kind : 3, *m.* (= **योजन**) a measure of four *kos*.

गौअनका, an old form = **गौओंका**, *q. v.*

गौओंका, gen. pl. of **गौ**, 2, *q. v.*

गौएं, *f.* (pl. of **गौं**, 2) cows.

गौएँ in Braj = **गौएं**, *q. v.*

गौं, *f.* (*m.* ?) opportunity, occasion, advantage.

गौंगीर, *m.* a ruler, controller : *lit.* uncontrolled, invested with authority.

गौंघात, *f.* power, opportunity.

गौंडा, *more prop* (1) **गौं** (2) **गौखा**, *qq. v.*

गौंर, see (1) **गौर** (2) **ग़ौर**.

गौख, *m.* a threshold, portico.

ग़ौग़ा, *m.* noise, disturbance, uproar, clamour, alarm, bawling.

गौंदा ; see (1) **गौन्दा** (2) **गौयडा**.

गौचना, *m.* a field of wheat and *chanā* sown together.

गौकई, *f.* a sprout, shoot.

गौखी / **गौछी** } *f.* a pit, hole.

गौटीका, *m.* the head manager of a village.

गौड़, *m. pr. n.* a certain division of central Bengal : an ancient city (fomerly the capital of Bengal); an inhabitant or inhabitants of Gouṛ.

गौड़कायथ, *m.* one of the twelve divisions of the Kāyath caste.

गौड़ठाकुर, *m.* a certain tribe of Rājputs in the district of Furrakhābad.

गौड़तगा, *m.* a certain important Hindoo tribe (of Brāhmaṇical descent in the North-west of India).

गौड़देश, *m.* the country of the Gauṛ Brāhmaṇs.

गौड़ब्राह्मण, *m.* one of the ten tribes of Brāhmaṇs.

गौड़राजपुत, *m.* a certain class of the Rājputs.

गौड़ा, *m.* one of the musical modes : a certain caste of Hindoos in Orissa who generally serve as palkee-bearers ; they also serve as " bearers" (male domestics who take charge of the wardrobe, bedding, etc.).

गौड़िया, *m.* any inhabitant of Gouṛ ; *hence*, the followers of Chaitanya of Nadiyn are also so called.

गौड़ी, *f.* rum or spirit distilled from *guṛ* ; one of the musical modes (*rāgiṇi*).

गौण, *m.* (*f.* ī) subordinate, secondary, inferior : (in Gram.) metaphorical ; secondary.

ग़ौयटा, village expenses.

गौखिटया, *f.* a small hamlet.

गौतम, 1, a frequent corruption of **गोतम**, *q. v.* : 2, (patronymic) *m.* (*f.* ī) Gotamite, desc·nded from Gotam.

गौतमनारी, *f.* an epithet of **अहल्या**, *q. v.*

गौतमराजपुत, *m*, the designation of a certain numerous tribe of Rājputs about Asimgarh and Gorukpore.

गौतमारन्य, *m. pr. n.* the forest in Central India in which Gotam-rishi did *tapasyā*.

गौतमियान = **गौतमराजपुत**, *q. v.*

गौथन, *m.* a cow's udder.

गौदान, *m.* the presentation of a cow (especially to a Brāhmaṇ) as a work of merit.

गौन, 1, in Braj = **गमन**, *q. v.* : 2, *more prop.* **गौना**, *q. v.*

ग़ौनखी, *f.* a hole in a path (such as that made by the feet of animals).

गौना, *m.* the bringing home a wife.

गौनी, *f.* opportunity, occasion, advantage.

गौनहार, *m.* the company who attend the bride when she is being brought home.

गौमांस, *m.* cow's flesh, beef,

गौमुत्र, *m.* (see **गोमुत्र**) cow's urine.

गौम्भ, *m.* a certain medicinal plant.

गौयें, *more prop.* **गौएं**, *q. v.*

ग़ौर, *m.* reflection, consideration, meditation.

गौर, 1, *m.* (*f.* ī) white, pale, fair-complexioned ; yellow ; red, pale red : 2, a kind of buffalo (*Bos gaurus*) : white mustard : the moon : one of the epithets of Pārvatee : a certain tree (*Grislea tomentosa*) : the filament of a lotus : gold : saffron : 3, *m.* a fire-worshipper, pagan, unbeliever. The term is generally applied by Muhammadans to those who do not believe in Muhammad.

ग़ौरख़ाना, *m.* any apartment for retiring into for the purpose of meditation and reflection ; commonly, the place whither a judge retires before pronouncing sentence.

गौरघर = **ग़ौरख़ाना**, *q. v.*

गौरता, *f.* / **गौरत्व**, *m.* } fairness of complexion.

गौरया, *more prop.* **गौरिया**, *q. v.*

गौरव, *m.* heaviness, importance, dignity, respect ; grandeur, repute, respectability : lit. *m.* (*f.* ā) relating to a *guru*.

गौरवित, *m.* (*f.* ā) a venerable person : *lit.* reputable, important, venerable.

गौरा, *m.* (*f.* **गौरिया** or **गौरैया**) a cock-sparrow : an epithet (1) of the goddess Pārvatee (2) of a certain tribe of Aheers.

गौराहर, the designation of an obscure tribe of Rājputs on the borders of Aligaṛh.

गौरि, *more* ɋ*rop.* **गौरी**, 2, *q. v.*

गौरिया, *f.* (not infl. : *m.* **गौरा**) a hen-sparrow.

गौरी, *f.* 1, a certain musical mode (*rāgiṇī*) : 2, an epithet of the goddess Pārvatee.

गौरीपति, *m.* the husband of Gaurī, *i. e.* Shiv.

गौरीश, *m.* an epithet of Shiv ; *lit.* lord of Pārvatee.

गौरीशंकर, *m.* an epithet of Mahādev.

ग़ौरवा, a certain inferior tribe of Rājputs in Agra and Mathura.

गोरूप } cow-shaped, cow-like.
गोरूपी }

गोरैया, *f.* (not infl.: *m.* गौरा) a hen-sparrow.

गोली, *m.* a grazier, cowherd.

गोवैं in Braj = गोएँ, *q.v.*

गोवोंका, *more prop.* गोओंका, *q.v.*

गोशाल, *m.* } a cowhouse, cattleshed.
गोशाला, *f.* }

गोह, *f.* perseverance, diligence.

गोहत्या, *f.* (see गौहत्या) the crime of cow-killing.

गोहर, *m.* a pearl, gem, jewel; lustre of a gem or of a sword: essence, nature, substance, origin.

गोहरवा, *m.* (*f.* ī) an ally, assistant, succourer.

गोहान, a village made over to any person on a permanent assesement.

गोहानी, *f.* lands situated close around a village; the village itself, fields on which cattle graze.

ग्यान, *m.* in old Hindee = ज्ञान, *q. v.*

ग्यारह, *more prop.* एग्यारह, *q.v.*

ग्रथित, *m.* (*f.* ā) strung together, tied together, composed, formed, built.

ग्रधकूट, *more prop.* गृध्रकूट, *q.v.*

ग्रन्थ, *m.* a literary composition, book, code, particularly the book of the Sikh religion composed by its founder Nānak Shāh.

ग्रन्थकर्त्ता, *m.* (*f.* trī) a book-maker, author, writer, founder of any religious system or sect.

ग्रन्थकार, *m.* (*f.* ī) = ग्रन्थकर्त्ता, *q.v.*

ग्रन्थन, 1, a Braj pl. of ग्रन्थ, *q.v.*: 2, *m.* a tying, stringing together, composing a literary work.

ग्रन्थम, *m.* a character in which Sanskrit is written and printed in Southern India where the Davanāgaree character is unknown.

ग्रन्थालय, *m.* a book-repository, library.

ग्रन्थि, *m.* (*f.* ī) a joint, knot, tie, swelling; the knot in a reed or cane; a joint of the body.

ग्रन्थी, *m.* (*f.* inī) a writer of books; an owner of many books; a reader of many books.

ग्रब्ब in Chand = गर्व्व, *q.v.*

ग्रसद, *m.* a present, offering, gift.

ग्रसहि, (pl. °हिं) (poet.) = ग्रासता (ग्रासना): see हि.

ग्रसि (poet.) = ग्रासके (ग्रासना): see के, 7.

ग्रसित (poet.) = ग्रासित (ग्रासना).

ग्रस्त, inaccurately pronounced, slurred, uttered with the omission of a letter or syllable: frequent as the latter element of compound words, signifying seized, possessed, owned.

ग्रसित्त, seized.

ग्रह, 1, a frequent corruption of गृह, *q.v.*: 2, *m.* an eclipse (*i. e.* a 'seizure' of the sun or moon by Rāhu): any planet: the Hindoo Mythology recognizes nine planets, viz. Mars, Mercury, Jupiter, Venus, Saturn, Rāhu, Ketu, Sun and Moon; and hence, in the ingenious system of reckoning by symbols adopted by Hindoos in their poetry, this word is a symbol for 9.

ग्रहकित, *more prop.* गृहकित, *q.v.*

ग्रहण, *m.* a taking, seizing, receiving, accepting, agreement, assent, buying, putting on, undergoing, protection, pronouncing, perception; study; an eclipse.

ग्रहणस्नान, *m.* bathing for religious purposes at the time of an eclipse.

ग्रहणाई, *f.* the state or condition of ग्रहण, *q.v.*

ग्रहणी, *f.* an organ of the stomach: diarrhoea, dysentery.

ग्रहदशा } *f.* a constellation.
ग्रहदसा }

ग्रहना, *t.* to seize; to assent; to comprehend: to smell.

ग्रहपत्र, *m.* a horoscope.

ग्रहपीड़ा, *f.* the influence of an unpropitious planet.

ग्रहपूजा, *f.* sun-worship, planet-worship.

ग्रहयोग, *m.* the conjunction of the planets.

ग्रहराज, *m.* an epithet of the Sun, the Moon, or Jupiter; *lit.* the chief of planets.

ग्रहस्थापन, *m.* (see ग्रह) the invoking the presence of the nine planets.

ग्रहाधार, *m.* an epithet of the constellation Dhruv, or the polar star (from its remaining fixed amidst the planetary movements).

ग्रहाधीन, *m.* (*f.* ā) subject to planetary influence.

ग्रहामय, *m.* epilepsy, convulsions, demoniacal possession (which, in fact, the complaint is supposed by the Hindoos to be).

ग्रहीता, *m.* (*f.* trī) a receiver, purchaser, debtor: *lit.* adj. receiving, taking, apprehending.

ग्राम, 1, a village, hamlet, an inhabited place in the midst of fields and meadow-land: 2, a scale in music: 3, (as a suffix in comp.) multitude: 4, *m.* (*f.* ṇī) a peasant.

ग्रामणी, 1, *f.* (*m.* ग्राम, 4) a female peasant; a whore: 2, *m.* a chief, the chief of a community; *lit.* best, excellent, chief, eminent: 3, *m.* a barber.

ग्रामनर, *m.* (*f.* °नारी) = ग्रामवास, *q.v.*

ग्रामपुरोहित } *m.* a village-priest.
ग्रामयाजक }

ग्रामवास, *m.* (*f.* ā) an inhabitant of a village.

ग्रामवासी, *m.* (*f.* in *or* inī) = ग्रामवास, *q.v.*

ग्रामसिंह, *m.* (*f.* ī) a dog: *lit.* the village-lion.

ग्रामा; see ग्राम.

ग्रामाधिकारी, *m.* (*f.* iṇī) the headman of a village; *lit.* holding chief authority in a village.

ग्रामाधिपति, *m.* (*f.* पत्नी) *same as the above.*

ग्रामाश्व, *m.* (*f.* ā) a donkey: *lit.* the village-horse.

ग्रामिक, *m.* (*f.* ā *or* ī) a rustic: *lit.* appertaining to a village, rustic, clownish, rude, vulgar.

ग्रामी, *m.* (*f.* iṇī) a rustic, clown, boor: *lit.* appertaining to a village, rustic, vulgar, rude.

ग्रामीण, *m.* (*f.* ā) a rustic: *lit.* inhabiting a village.

ग्रामीणता, *f.* } rusticity, vulgarity, rudeness.
ग्रामीणत्व, *m.* }

ग्राम्य, *m.* (*f.* ā) rustic or homely speech, Prākrit: *lit.* appertaining to a village, village-born, rustic.

ग्राम्यधर्म, *m.* copulation, public sexual intercourse, the customs of tame animals (or of villagers ?).

ग्राम्याश्व, *m.* (*f.* ā) an ass; *lit.* the village-horse.

ग्रास, *m.* a mouthful; fodder for cattle.

ग्रासना, *t.* to eat up, devour.

ग्रासा, 1, *more prop.* **ग्रास**, *q.v.*; 2, *m.* (*f.* ī) eaten.

ग्राह, *m.* (*f.* ī) a shark; according to some, the Gangetic alligator; according to others, the water-elephant (hippopotamus ?): lit. *m.* a taking (whether by acceptance or by seizure); *hence*, a robber; a fit; a disease; an enterprize.

ग्राहक, *m*, (*f.* ikā) a taker, receiver, buyer; a hawk, *lit.* adj. taking, apprehending, accepting, seizing, catching, robbing, holding, choosing, gaining, gathering, charming.

ग्राही, 1, *f.*; *m.* **ग्राह**: 2, *m.* (*f.* iṇī) = **ग्राहक**, *qq. v.*

ग्राह्य, *m.* (*f.* ā) fit to be received, worthy of acceptance, acceptable, requiring to be taken. [form **गृहस्थ**.

ग्रिहस्थ; for words beginning thus, see under the

ग्रीष, 1, *f. pr. n.* the fourth of the six seasons, including from the 15th of Baisāk to the 15th of Ashāṛh: 2, *f.* heat; the hot or summer season.

ग्रीवा, *f.* the neck, the nape of the neck, the tendon of the Trapezium muscle.

ग्रीष्म, *m.* heat, warmth; the hot season.

ग्रीष्मऋतु, *f.* the hot season (comprehending two months about June-July).

ग्रेह in Chand = **गृह**, *q. v.* [lace, collar.

ग्रैव, *m.* a neck-ornament, necklace, close neck-

ग्रैष्म, *m.* (*f.* ī) appertaining to the hot season.

ग्रैष्मी, *f.* double jasmine.

ग्लान, wearied, languid, exhausted, emaciated, feeble. [situde, languor, inertness.

ग्लानि, *f.* fatigue of body, depression in mind, las-

ग्लाल, *more prop.* **गुलाल**, *q.v.*

ग्वाल, *m.* (*f.* in) a cowkeeper, cowherd: a certain caste of Hindoos whose occupation it is to attend to cattle.

ग्वालन, 1, = **ग्वालिन**; 2, a Braj pl. of **ग्वाल**, *qq. v.*

ग्वालबाल, *m.* a child of a cowherd; cowherds'

ग्वाललोग, *m.* cowherds, cowkeepers. [children.

ग्वालबल, *more prop.* **ग्वालबाल**, *q. v.*

ग्वाला, *m.* (*f.* in *or* ī) = **ग्वाल**, *q. v.*

ग्वालावल / **ग्वालावाल** } *more prop.* **ग्वालबाल**, *q. v.*

ग्वालि, *more prop.* **ग्वाली**, *q.v.*

ग्वालिन, *f.* (*m.* **ग्वाल**) any female of the *gwāl* caste, a cowherdess, milkmaid, dairy-woman.

ग्वालिनी, *f.* (*m.* **ग्वाली**) = **ग्वालिन**, *q. v.*

ग्वाली, 1, *m.* (*f.* inī) = **ग्वाल**, *q. v.*: 2, *f.* (*m.* **ग्वाला**) [= **ग्वालिन**, *q. v.*

ग्वैयड, 1, = **गैयड़ा**, *q. v.*: 2, *adv.* near.

ग्वैयड़ा, *m.* suburbs, vicinage; fields near a village; [a homestead.

ग्वैयड़े, *adv.* near.

घ

घ (gh) is the fourth consonant in the Hindee alphabet and the fourth letter in the **कवर्ग** or guttural class: it is the aspirate of **ग**, and has invariably the sound of *gh* in 'loghouse' with the *ouse* dropped. Like all the aspirated consonants, it is constantly interchanged inadvertently with its unaspirated form; *e. g.* **घ्रीष्म**, properly **ग्रीष्म**.

घई, *f.* (see **चुल्ली**) a support, staddles.

घंगोल, the water-lily which produces the celebrated neeloofar-flower.

घंघस, a certain subdivision of the jāts.

घंघेरा, *m.* a petticoat.

घंघेवाला, *m.* (*f.* ī) an artist.

घंघोरना = **घंघोलना**, *q. v.* [ring it about.

घंघोलना, *t.* to rinse; to mix any liquid by stir-

घंच, *m.* the neck. [represent it.

घकार, *m.* the letter **घ**, or any symbol that may

घगरी, *f.* a kind of musical instrument: a hollow metallic ring, having some small shot within it so that it rattles when shaken.

घघरा, *m.* / **घघरी**, *f.* } a petticoat.

घचाघच, thick.

घट, 1, *m.* a large earthen water-jar, waterpot: the body: 2, *f.* the mind, heart, soul, thought: 3, firm, tight, fast, strong, thick, hard, compact.

घटक, *m.* (*f.* ikā) a mediator, go-between, attorney, ambassador, messenger; an agent who ascertains or invents genealogies and negotiates marriages: lit. *adj.* striving. [the Supreme Being.

घटघटव्यापक, *adj.* pervading the inward parts, *i. e.*

घटघटनिवासी, *adj.* dwelling in the inward parts, *i. e.* the Deity. [born in a waterpot.

घटज, *m.* an epithet of **अगस्त्य**, *q. v.*: lit. *m.* (*f.* ā)

घटती, *f.* decrease, diminution, decline, abatement, alleviation; deficiency.

घटदासी, *f.* a bawd, procuress.

घटन, *m.* an occurring, happening: a striving, exertion, endeavour; junction, composition.

घटना, 1, *f.* = **घटन**, *q. v.*: 2, *n.* to be depressed, be deficient, be spent: *a. int.* to abate, decrease, decline, waste, dwindle, subside, fail, fail, become abortive. [requiring abatement, diminution, or decrease.

घटनीय, liable to occur, probable: liable to or

घटन्त, *f.* diminution, decrease.

घटबढ़, more or less, about.

घटव; 1, see **घटाव**; 2, in old Hindee = **घटूंगा**. See **ब**.

घटवाना, *t.* to cause to be diminished, etc.

घटवार / **घटवाल** } *m.* a wharfinger, ghāṭ-keeper.

घटहा, *m.* (*f.* ī) an offender, transgressor.

घटा, *f.* (not infl.) a multitude, crowd; a troop of elephants assembled for martial purposes; a gathering of clouds, clouds, cloudiness.

घटाटोप, *m.* a covering (for a pālkee, carriage, or any article of furniture).

घटाना, *t.* to decrease, diminish, abate, reduce, allay, alleviate: *lit.* to cause to subside, cause to become less.

घटाव, *m.* diminution, deficiency, reduction, depreciation, abbreviation, falling (as a river, or prices).

घटावना, an old form = **घटाना**, *q. v.*

घटि, 1, = (1) **घटिया** (2) **घटी**, *qq. v.* : 2, see **घटना**.

घटिका, 1, *f.* ; *m.* **घटक**, *q. v.* : 2, *f.* the ankle : a jar, bucket : a muhoort or 30th part of a day and night; a *daṇḍ* or period of twenty-four minutes. [plied. (?)

घटित, 1, diminished ; 2, like, resembling : 3, ap-

घटिया, low-priced, cheap, inferior iu quality.

घटिहि, (pl. °**हिं**) in poetry = (1) **करेगा** (2) **होगा**.

घटी, *f.* the gharee or Indian clock, a plate of iron or mixed metal on which the hours are struck : diminution, abatement ; deficiency, lack, disadvantage ; alleviation. — *k.* to diminish ; to alleviate.

घटोत्कच, *m. pr. n.* a certain *rākshas* (son of Bhīmsen by the *rākshasī* Hiḍimbā) slain by Karṇ.

घट्ट, *m.* a landing-place, quay, wharf, steps leading down to the water's edge, bathing-place : (in Chand) a waterpot.

घट्टा, *m.* a corn (of the foot) : a plug, cork.

घट्टी, *f.* (dim. of **घट्ट**) a small, or secondary landing-place, private steps leading down to the water.

घड़ ; see (1) **घट** (2) **घर**.

घड़घड़ाना, *a. int.* to thunder, growl.

घड़ना, 1, *t.* to make, form, fashion, shape; to forge, work (as metals) ; to hammer : 2, *a. int.* to happen (*esp.* a calamity).

घड़याल = (1) **घड़ियाल** (2) **घड़ियाला**, *qq. v.*

घड़ा, *m.* an earthen waterpot, pitcher, jar.

घड़िया, *f.* a crucible : a honey-comb : the womb.

घड़ियाल, *m.* a Gangetic alligator (*Lacerta Gangetica*) : a plate of bell-metal for beating the hours upon ; a watch, clock, gong.

घड़ियाला, *m.* (*f.* ī) = **घड़ियाली**, *q. v.*

घड़ियाली, (*f.* inī) the person who announces the time whether by calling or by striking the hours upon the gharee or ghariyāl.

घड़ी, *f.* a fold, plait : a certain portion of time, *viz.* the space of twenty-four minutes ; it is, however, generally applied to the English hour of sixty minutes : a clock, watch, or any instrument for measuring time : in revenue phraseology the term denotes a subdivision of a village. *Ghaṛīmeṅ tolā ghaṛīmeṅ māshā* describes a person of a variable or uneven disposition ; *lit.* at one time an ounce, at another time a grain. — *chār*, four o'clock.

घड़ीक, appertaining to **घड़ी**, *q. v.*

घड़ोंचा, *m.* }
घड़ोंची, *f.* } a stand for waterpots, etc.

घड़ोला, *m.* a pot, pitcher, jug, mug.

घण्टा, *m.* an hour ; a clock ; a bell, a metallic plate struck as a bell.

घण्टाकर्ण, *m.* one who has bell-like ears, or whose ears are decorated with bells: *pr. n.* (1) of an attendant on Skand (2) of one of Shiv's attendants, who presides over cutaneous complaints, and is worshipped for exemption from them in the month Chaitra (3) of a certain *pishāch* attendant on Kuver.

घण्टाली, *f.* a small bell.

घण्टाशब्द, *m.* bell-metal.

घण्टिका, *f.* the *uvula* or soft palate.

घण्टु, a string of bells tied on to an elephant's chest by way of ornament.

घतर, daybreak, the early morning.

घतिया, *m.* a murderer.

घन, 1, *m.* (*f.* ā) firm, hard, dense, without interstices, compact, impenetrable, solid, gross, impervious, thick (as a liquid or as a forest), close, set, deep, entire : 2, much, very : 3, *m.* a cymbal, bell, metallic plate for striking the hours upon; an anvil; an iron club, sledge-hammer : a cloud, a gathering of clouds ; thunder : extension ; hardness, solidity, a solid mass, substance, heap ; an assemblage, number, quantity ; (in Math.) the cube of any number ; (in Geom.) a solid : a certain fragrant grass (*Cyperus rotundus*).

घनगरज, *m.* the roaring of the clouds, thunder, any loud noise : *lit.* adj. loud-sounding.

घनगेरा, *m.* a petticoat. [*f.* an imitative sound.

घनघन, 1, *m.* (in Math.) the cube of a cube : 2,

घनघनाना, *a. int.* to jingle, ring, tingle, sound like

घनघेरा, *m.* a petticoat. [a wheel going around.

घनघोर, *m.* cloudiness, gathering of the clouds, roaring of the clouds, thunder : *lit.* cloudy : loud-

घनचिड़ी, *f.* the hornbill (*Buceros*). [sounding.

घनज्वाला, *f.* lightning, a flash of lightning.

घनतनवर्ण, *m.* an epithet of Kṛishṇ ; *lit.* whose body is of the colour of the clouds.

घनता, *f.* }
घनत्व, *m.* } compactness, imperviousness, solidity.

घनफल, *m.* (in Geom.) the contents of a solid.

घनमूल, *m.* (in Math.) the cube root.

घनवर्ग, *m.* (in Math.) the square of a cube.

घनश्याम, black as a cloud : *hence* (1) *m.* black clouds : 2, an epithet of Kṛishṇ.

घनसार, *m.* camphor : mercury or some form of it.

घना, 1, *f.* ; see **घन** : 2, *m.* a sporting-preserve, park, chase : 3, *m.* (*f.* ī) thick, close, confused, numerous,

घनाना, *more prop.* **घिनाना**, *q. v.* [many, much.

घनाक्षरी, *adj.* written or printed in very close dense

घनी, *f.* : see **घना**, 3. [type or character.

घनेरा, *m.* (*f.* ī) many, much.

घनेस, *m.* a kind of bird (*Buceros Malabaricus*).

घन्त, a certain subdivision of the jāṭs.

घपची, *f.* embrace, grasp of the both arms.

घबराट, *more prop.* **घबराहट**, *q. v.*

घबराना, *n.* to be confused, be confounded, be disconcerted, be perplexed, be agitated, be embarrassed, etc. [tation, perturbation, alarm, consternation.

घबराहट, *f.* confusion, perplexity, distraction, agi-

घमघमना, *more prop.* **घुमघुमना**, *q. v.*

घमण्ड, *m.* pride, haughtiness, arrogance, conceit, vanity, boastfulness, glorying. [haughty, arrogant, vain.

घमण्डी, *m.* (*f.* inī) a proud person, etc. : *lit.* proud.

घमना, *more prop.* **घुमना**, *q. v.* [gagement,

घमरौल, *f.* a crowd ; confusion in a general en-

घमस, *f.* heat, closeness.

घमसान, *m.* battle, engagement.

घमाघम, thick, crowded, dense (as a population or as a forest).

घमाना, *a. int.* to sun, bask in the sun.

घमासान, *m.* battle, engagement.

घमूई, *f.* a certain plant.

घमोय, *f.* sunbeams, sunshine.

घमोरी, *f.* the prickly-heat.

घम्भीर, affable; patient, enduring.

घर, *m.* a house, dwelling-place, home; a family; apartment, compartment, groove, loop, loophole, button-hole. — *k.* or *banānā*, to fix, settle, establish a family, build up one's house. — *khokar tamāshā dekhnā*, to ruin oneself and spend the time in idle pleasures; *lit.* having done away with one's house, to then turn one's eyes towards amusements. — *ghālnā*, to ruin, utterly destroy. — *chalānā*, to provide the expenses for one's household; *lit.* to set one's house a-going. — *dubonā*, to ruin oneself and family. — *ḍūbnā*, or *baiṭhna*, or *baith-jānā*, or *jānā*, to be ruined. — *honā* expresses affection and unanimity between husband and wife. *Gharkā ḍhelānā rahnā*, to be desolated, be destroyed.

घरऊ, domestic, household.

घरघर, to or in every house, from house to house.

घरड़, the dry moth-plant cut and given as fodder to cattle.

घरत, *f.* form, fashion, make.

घरदार, *m.* housekeeping; household.

घरद्वार, *m.* a dwellingplace, house.

घरद्वारी, *f.* an illegal cess from householders and shopkeepers: a kind of tax, poll-tax, hearth-money.

घरनई, *f.* a raft or a float made of pots.

घरनते in Braj = **घरोंसे**.

घरना, *t.* to make, fashion, form, forge, work, malleate (spoken of metals).

घरनी, *f.* a wife; a female housekeeper.

घरपत्ती, *f.* a kind of house-tax (now abolished).

घरफान्त, an arrangement entered into for paying the government revenue.

घरजन्मी, a slave born in the house.

घरबघर, to or in every house, from house to house.

घरबराव, *m.* household furniture, etc.

घरबसा, *m.* (*f.* ī) one who is at home or who keeps to the house, etc.: *lit.* stay-at-home, inactive, indolent.

घरबार, *m.* family, household concerns, household goods. — *basānā*, to consummate a marriage. — *honā*, to undergo the consummation of a marriage.

घरबारी, 1, *f.* house-wifery, domestic concerns, family affairs: 2. *m.* a householder.

घरभाड़ा, *m.* houserent.

घररा, *m.* the rattling sound in the throats of the dying; pain, agony, pang.

घरराटा, *m.* snoring, snorting.

घरवाला, *m.* (*f.* ī) a housekeeper, householder, master of a house, husband, occupant or inmate of a house.

घरवाली, 1, *fem.* of **घरवाला**, *q.v.*: 2, *f.* housekeeping.

घरसबील, advances of money to peasants to enable them to build cottages for themselves.

घरही, an emphatic form of **घर**, *q.v.*

घरातल, surface.

घराना, *m.* household, family, house (*i. e.* race, generation, dynasty; *e. g.* House of David, House of Brunswick).

घरामी, *m.* a thatcher.

घरारी, *more prop.* **गरारी**, *q.v.*

घरी, 1, = **घड़ी**, *q.v.*: 2, folded up, gathered or tucked up.

घरुआ = **घर**. See **उआ**.

घरूआ, *m.* a small house which children make to play in.

घरेला, *m.* (*f.* ī) domestic, domesticated, tame.

घरौन्दा = **घरूआ**, *q.v.*

घर्घट, *m.* a kind of fish (*Silurus*).

घर्घर, *m.* an inarticulate sound, gurgling, rumbling: *pr. n.* the river Gogra.

घर्म, *m.* heat; sunshine; perspiration; the hot season.

घर्रा, = **घररा**, *q.v.*

घर्राटा, = **घरराटा**, *q.v.*

घर्षण, *m.* a grinding, pounding, rubbing into.

घर्षणी, *f.* turmeric.

घलवा } = **घुलवा**, *q.v.*
घलूआ }

घवरि = **गुच्छा**, *q.v.*

घस, *m. pr. n.* a certain *Rākshas.*

घसटना; see **घसिटना**, *q.v.*

घसन, *f.* (*m.* ?) the act of rubbing.

घसना, 1, *n.* to be rubbed, be abraded, be worn: *a. int.* to fret, wear: *t.* to rub; to beat: 2, *m.* (*f.* ī) apt to be worn by rubbing.

घसिटना, *n.* to be dragged, be trailed along: *a. int.* to trail.

घसियाड़ा = **घसियारा**, *q.v.*

घसियाना, *more com.* **घिसियाना**, *q.v.*

घसियारा, *m.* (*f.* in) a grass-cutter, seller of grass.

घसीटना, *t.* to drag, pull, draw, trail.

घसीठना, *more prop.* **घसीटना**, *q.v.*

घसीला, *m.* (*f.* ī) grassy, yielding grass, abounding in grass.

घसुआ = **घांस**. See **उआ**.

घस्मर, gluttonous, voracious.

घाता, *m.* (*f.* ī) mischievous, hurtful.

घायल, wounded.

घाई, *f.* a cudgeling: stratagem, fraud, decoy: the number five (in reckoning): the interval between the fingers or toes, the junction of the fingers, the space at the root of the fingers where they separate; the angle formed by a branch with the trunk of a tree on the space at the root of a branch: a cut or stroke with the broad-sword or cudgel (the cuts are twelve).

घाईन, *f.* turn, a time.

घाउ, *m.* a hurt, bruise, wound, sore.

घाउघप, a spendthrift, etc.: *lit.* living from hand to mouth, improvident, spendthrift.

घायल, wounded.

घाओ, *m.* a wound, sore, hurt, bruise.

घां; see (1) **घाईन** (2) **घाओ** (3) **घान**.

घांगराघोल, perplexed, bewildered, distracted.

घांघर, *m.* a petticoat.

घांस, *f.* grass, green turf. — *kā chakkā*, a sod of turf, square-cut piece of turf.

घांसी, *f.* a kind of covering.

घागर, the rope tied to the foot of an elephant.

घागरागोल = घांगराघोल, *q.v.*

घागस, *m.* a large kind of fowl.

घाघ, old, aged, experienced ; shrewd, wily, sly.

घाघर ; see (1) घांघर (2) घागर (3) घाघरा.

घाघरा, *m.* a petticoat : *pr. n.* the river Gogra ; a certain plant (*Xanthium Indicum*, Kœn. MS.).

घाघरागोल } = घांगराघोल, *q.v.*
घाघराघोल }

घाघरी, *f.* (dim. of घाघर) a small petticoat, a child's petticoat.

घाट, 1, *m.* mode, manner, shape : abatement, reduction, deficiency, want, detriment, loss : offence : a pitcher, pot : 2, abated, less : 3, *m. f.* the nape or back of the neck, the cervical ligament : 4, *f.* a landingplace, quay, wharf, ferry, ford, bathingplace at a a river-side, steps leading down to the water's edge ; an entrance into a country over mountains or any difficult pass ; a public ferry over any river, a landingplace where tolls or customs are collected. — *mārnā*, to smuggle.

घाट्कपटान, *m.* the master-attendant at a port, harbour-master. [passes.

घाटबारी, *f.* a toll levied on crossingrivers or hill-

घाटबाट, *f.* the way to a घाट, *q.v.*

घाटमांझी, *m.* a ferry-man.

घाटमार, *m.* a smuggler.

घाटमारा, *m.* smuggling : a smuggler.

घाटवाल, *m.* a ferryman ; a person in charge of a landingplace or of a mountain-pass.

घाटवाला, *m.* (*f.* ī *or* in) = घाटवाल, *q.v.*

घाटा, *m.* an ascent, acclivity : deficiency, abate-

घाटानी = घाटबारी, *q. v.* [ment, reduction.

घाटिया, *m.* a Brāhman who takes charge of the clothing of the Hindoos who bathe in a sacred river.

घाटी, *f.* a strait, pass, mountain-pass, ravine, valley, declivity.

घाण्टी, *f.* the windpipe, larynx, Adam's apple : strips of cloth of different colours tied around the ankles by Muharram fakeers.

घात, *f.* aim, design ; the product of a sum in multiplication : ambush, ambuscade, snare : killing, slaughter ; a blow, bruise. — *k.* to waylay, lie in ambush ; to kill. — *taknā*, to watch an opportunity.

घातक, *m.* (*f.* i) an instrument for killing ; a murderer, destroyer, maimer, enemy, hangman, executioner, slaughterman, butcher : *lit.* murderous, destroying savage, ferocious, mischievous, etc. Much used as a suffix in composition.

घातन, *m.* a murderer; killing, slaughter, murder.

घातनी, *f.* a club (as an instrument of slaughter).

घाता, *m.* a kind of plaything.

घातिक, *m.* (*f.* ā *or* ī) a murderer : *lit.* murderous.

घातित, *m.* (*f.* ā) slain, murdered.

घाती, *m.* (*f.* inī) = घातक, *q. v:* Much used as a suffix

घातुक, *m.* (*f.* ī) = घातक, *q.v:* [in composition.

घातू, *m.* a deceiver. [to a mill, mortar, etc.

घान, *f.* as much as is thrown in at one time in-

घाना, *m.* } an oil-mill, sugarcane-press.
घानी, *f.* }

घाब, a provincial form = घाव, *q. v.*

घाबघप, a provincial form = घाऊघप, *q. v.*

घाबरा, *m.* (*f.* ī) confused, confounded.

घाम, *f.* (*m.* ?) heat of the sun ; sunbeams, sunshine.

घामड़, *m.* a blockhead, clown : *lit.* simple, artless.

घायल, *m.* wounded.

घार, a kind of clay soil. — *ho jānā*, to be worn away by running water (said of land).

घारी, *f.* a valley, ravine : cattlesheds.

घाल, *f.* mischief, destruction, ruin.

घालक, *m.* (*f.* ikā) a destroyer, desolator : *lit.* destroying, ruinous, ruining.

घालना, *t.* to desolate, ruin : to thrust in ; to throw ; to mix, jumble. [animal (as a cow, etc.).

घालमल, the drawing milk from any milk-giving

घालमेल, jumbled, topsy-turvy.

घालय, 1, (*corruption*) = घायल ; 2, = घालमेल, *qq. v.*

घाला, calamity, misfortune, evil.

घालि } see (1) घालना (2) घालमेल.
घाली }

घाव, *m.* a wound, sore, hurt, bruise.

घावघप = घाऊघप, *q. v.* [fodder.

घास, *f.* grass (meadow or pasture), hay, straw,

घासकटा = घासकाटा, *q. v.*

घासकाटा, *m.* a man whose occupation it is to cut and supply fresh grass daily for a horse.

घासपात, sweepings, rubbish, fallen and rotting leaves, gardener's refuse.

घासफूंस, } *m.* old dry grass or straw.
घासफूस, }

घिउ, *more com.* घी, *q. v.*

घिंघाना, *n.* to be hoarse.

घिंज़की, a corruption of ज़िन्दगी, *q. v.*

घिघियाना, *n.* to falter, appear very humble, be unable to speak (from shame, fear, joy, etc.) : *a. int.* to coax, wheedle, fawn, beseech, implore.

घिग्घी, *f.* a faltering in speech, — *bandh jānā*, to falter, be unable to speak (from shame, fear, joy etc.).

घिचपिच, thick, muddy, confused, higgledy-piggledy, crowded. — *baknā* or *bolnā*, to speak thickly or confusedly.

घिन, *f.* disgust, hate, hatred, abhorrence, aversion ; reproach, blame, censure ; bashfulness, shame : tenderness, pity, compassion. — *k.* to hate, have an aversion for. — *khānā*, to be disgusted, have the stomach turned : (with abl. of the object) to abhor, hate. — *denā*, to reproach, abash.

घिनघिना, *m.* (*f.* ī) = घिनौना, *q. v.*

घिनाना = (1) घिनियाना (2) घिनौना, *qq.v.*

घिनियाना, *n.* to be disgusted, to nauseate.

घिनौना, *m.* (*f.* ī) disgusting, abominable, nauseous, loathsome, detestable, hateful, obnoxious, ill-favored.

घिनघिनाना, *n.* to be disgusted, to nauseate.

घिनावना = घिनाना = घिनाना, *q.v.*

घिनित, *m.* (*f.* ā) = घिनौना, *q.v.*

घिनोंना
घिनोना } *m.* (*f.* ī) *more com.* घिनौना, *q.v.*
घिनोन्दा

घिच ; see घिया.

घिया, *m.* a pompion (*Cucurbita lagenaria*).

घिया तोरई, *f.* the vegetable *Luffa pentandra*, [(Roxb.).

घिरका, a certain game among children.

घिरना, *n.* to be surrounded, be inclosed ; to be collected around : *a. int.* to gather (as the clouds).

घिरनी, *f.* a pulley ; an instrument for twisting ropes : the tumbler pigeon. — *khānā*, to go round and round.

घिराना, *t.* to surround ; to cause to surround.

घिरान्द, *f.* stink (particularly of urine).

घिसटना = घसिटना, *q.v.*

घिसना = घसना, *q.v.*

घिसनी, *adv.* by rubbing ; *e. g. Gāṅṛ* — *k.* or — *chalnā*, to move along rubbing on the ground as a child on his buttocks before he is able to walk.

घिसाना, *t.* to abrade, wear, cause to rub.

घिसाव, *m.* attrition, rubbing, abrasion, friction.

घिसावट, *f.* = घिसाव, *q.v.*

घिसियाना, to trail, drag.

घी, *m.* butter clarified by boiling and straining. It is boiled gently and then allowed to cool : it is much used in cooking, and is highly esteemed by Hindoos both in food and for religious uses.

घीकरा, a small sort of cucumber much used as a condiment.

घीकुवार, *m.* the medicinal plant *Aloe perfoliata*.

घीच, the neck (both before and behind).

घीया = घिया, *q.v.*

घीला, *m.* a certain very large wild creeper.

घीव, a corruption of घी, *q.v.*

घुंगची, *more prop.* घुंघची, *q.v.*

घुंगरू, *more prop.* घुंघरू, *q. v.*

घुंगौना, *m.* a plaything, child's rattle.

घुंघी, *f.* a cloak or mantle of hairy coarse wollen stuff ; a caterpillar, palmer-worm.

घुंघंची, a corruption of घुंघची, *q.v.*

घुंघची, *f.* a certain small red and black seed (*Abrus precatorius*) used as a weight.

घुंघरू, *m.* a small bell ; an ornament worn (*esp.* by dancing-girls) around the ankles with bells fastened to it, morris-bells.

घुंघुंवारा, *m.* (*f.* ī) *more prop.* घूंघरवाला, *q.v.*

घुंघुरूदार, possessed of, or wearing, a घुंघरू, *q.v.*

घुंघुरू
घुंघुरू } *more prop.* घुंघरू, *q.v.*

घुंस, *more prop.* (1) घुस (2) घूस, *qq.v.*

घुंसी, *m.* (*f.* ini) a receiver of bribes ; a malicious person : *lit.* malicious.

घुघुआ, *m.* (*f.* °ई) a kind of wild bird.

घुघुरवाला, *m.* (*f.* ī) *more prop.* घूंघरवाला, *q.v.*

घुटन, *m.* the knee.

घुटना, 1, *n.* to be rubbed ; to be suffocated, be stifled : *a. int.* to spread (as smoke) : 2, *m.* the knee. *Ghutne teknā*, to kneel. *Ghutnoṅ chalnā*, to crawl about on the knees as a child. [on all fours like a child.

घुटनी, *f.* the knee. — *chalnā* or *dhānā*, to go about

घुटाई, *f.* perfidy, villany.

घुटाना, *t.* to shave clean, polish.

घुटुनी, 1, *more prop.* घुटनी, *q.v.* : 2, *f.* a kind of instrument for mashing and preparing *ḍāl*, a kind of churn.

घुट्टी = घूंटी, *q. v.*

घुड़, *m.* (contraction of घोड़ा) a horse.

घुड़कना, *t.* to frown at, browbeat, reprimand.

घुड़की, *f.* a frowning at, browbeating, rebuking.

घुड़चढ़, *m.* horse-riding, being mounted on horseback. [mounted on horseback.

घुड़चढ़ा, *m.* (*f.* ī) a rider, horseman, trooper : *lit.*

घुड़चढ़ी, 1, fem. of घुड़चढ़ा, *q. v.* : 2, *f.* a riding on [horseback.

घुड़दौड़, *m.* a race-course.

घुड़बहल, *f.* a chariot, four-wheeled carriage for riding in, drawn by horses.

घुड़मुंहा, *m.* (*f.* ī) horse-faced.

घुड़सना, *a. int.* to curl, become curled.

घुड़सार
घुड़साल } *m.* a stable, horse-repository.

घुण, *m.* a certain insect destructive to wood, meal, grain and flower, a wood-worm, weevil : rancour, malice, spite : the pangolin or armadillo.

घुणाक्षर, done by the घुण, *q.v.*

घुणा, *m.* (*f.* ī) infested by the wood-worm, weevil-eaten : rancourous, spiteful, malicious, revengeful ; [designing, secret, cautious.

घुण्डी, *f.* a button.

घुन, a corruption of घुण, *q. v.*

घुनगौना, *m.* a plaything, child's rattle.

घुना, *more prop.* = घुणा, *q.v.*

घुनाक्षर (*corruption*) = घनाक्षर = घनाक्षरी, *q. v.*

घुनिया, designing, malicious, spiteful, revengeful, rancourous.

घुप, dark, hidden, obscure.

घुमघुमा, *m.* a revolving, going round ; evasion, prevarication, subterfuge ; hesitation ; doubt, suspense.

घुमघुमाना, *a. int.* to revolve ; to prevaricate, have recourse to subterfuge.

घूमड़ना = घूमना, *q. v.*

घुमड़ाना = घूमाना, *q. v.*

घुमड़ी = घुमरी, *q. v.*

घुमसड़, *f.* a gathering of the clouds.

घुमना, *more com.* घूमना, *q. v.*

घुमरा, *m.* a certain plant (*Phlomis*); a certain insect.

घुमरी, *f.* a swimming in the head, giddiness, vertigo. [to revolve a thing.

घुमवाना, *t.* (causat. of घुमाना) to cause some one

घुमाना, *t.* (of घूमना) to revolve, whirl, circulate, wheel, roll, brandish, encircle: *t.* to delude, beguile. — *phirānā*, to prevaricate.

घुमाव, *m.* as much land as can be ploughed in a day by a single pair of bullocks.

घुम्मरहिं = घूम रहते हैं = घूमते हैं (घूमना).

घुरकना = घुड़कना, *q. v.*

घुरकी = घुड़की, *q. v.*

घुरघुरा, *m.* the mole-cricket (*Gryllus gryllotalpa*): a phagedenic ulcer (*Herpes exedens*). So named from its digging in the flesh as the mole-cricket does in earth or in sand.

घुरघुराना, *a. int.* to snore, snort, snarl, grumble.

घुरनस, *m.* the *tendo Achillis*.

घुरना, *t.* (= घूरना) to look at.

घुरनाना, *a. int.* to snore, snort, snarl, grumble.

घुरनी, *f.* a swimming in the head, vertigo; a

घुरबाबा, *m.* a groom. [rolling.

घुरुघुराना, *a. int.* to snore, snort, snarl, grumble.

घुलना, *a. int.* to melt, become dissolved; to rot, become mellowed; to waste, become lean. [ness.

घुलमिल, melted, dissolved, mixed; melted in kind-

घुलवा, 1. *m.* a small quantity given above the purchase: 2. *adv.* over and above, to boot.

घुलवाना, *t.* to cause to be melted, cause to melt

घुलाऊ, *adj.* melting. [or to dissolve.

घुलाना, *t.* to melt, dissolve.

घुलावट }
घुलाहट } *f.* a dissolving, melting.

घुवा, *m.* a coarse kind of cotton.

घुस, *m.* (*f.* ई) an entering, penetrating; a creeping.

घुसड़ना, *n.* to be thrust in, be stuffed in.

घुसना, *n.* to be thrust in, be forced in: *a. int.* to enter, penetrate: *t.* to interfere, meddle.

घुसपैठ, *f.* access, entrance. [flower.

घुसरान्द, a kind of creeping grass with a yellow

घुसाना, *t.* to cause to enter, cause to penetrate; *hence*, to thrust in, stuff in, cram in, force in, pene-

घुसायन, a fem. of घोसी ? [trate.

घुसिड़ना, *n.* to be thrust in, be stuffed in.

घुसेड़ना, *t.* to thrust in, stuff in, cram in, force in, run in, pierce, insinuate, foist.

घुस्सा, *m.* a blow of the fist, a thump, buffet.

घूआ, *m.* the carpenter-beetle (an insect which penetrates wood). [rains on high grounds.

घूई, *f.* a certain herb which grows during the

घूंगनी, *f.* a sort of stir-about, or grain of any kind

घूंगर, *m.* a curl. [(pulse, wheat, etc.) boiled whole with sugar.

घूंगरवाले बाल }
घूंगरवाले बाल } *m.* curled hair, curly hair.

घूंगरू = घुंघरू, *q. v.*

घूंगी, *f.* 1, dim. of घोंगा, *q. v.*: 2, cloths folded up and put on the head as a defence against rain: 3, the *gindar* (an insect very destructive to growing grain).

घूंगची, *f.* a certain small red and black seed (*Abrus precatorius*) used as a weight.

घूंघट, *f.* veil: a concealing the face with a veil, etc. — *k.* to veil; to draw back the neck (said of the horse). — *kārhnā*, to draw a veil over the face. — *khānā*, to be broken or defeated (said of an army).

घूंघर, *m.* a curl.

घूंघरवाला, *m.* (*f.* ī) curly, curled.

घूंघरू = घुंघरू, *q. v.*

घूंघी = घूंगी, *q. v.*

घूंघुट, *more prop.* घूंघट, *q. v.*

घूंस = घूस, *q. v.*

घूंसा = घूसा, *q. v.*

घूघर, *more prop.* घूंघर, *q. v.*

घूघरवाला, *m.* (*f.* ī) *more prop.* घूंघरवाला, *q. v.*

घूघू, *m.* the ring-necked dove: an owl.

घूघूआ, *m.* (*f.* घूघूई) an owl: *met.* a blockhead.

घूघुवा, *more prop.* घूघूआ, *q. v.*

घूट, *m.* a gulp, draught, pull.

घूटना, *a. int.* to gulp, drink, guzzle.

घूटनी, *f.* a rubber. [joint.

घूटी, *f.* 1, *more prop.* घुघटी, *q. v.*: 2, the ankle-

घूणा, *more prop.* घुणा, *q. v.*

घूपट, *m.* a gulp, draught, pull.

घूपटना, *t.* to gulp, guzzle, swallow, drink.

घूपटी, *f.* a medicine consisting of aloes, spices and borax (given to newborn infants to clear out the *me*

घून, *m.* (prop. घुण) rancour, malice, spite. [*conium*).

घूना, *more prop.* घुणा, *q. v.* [ligious establishments.

घून्त, rent-free lands assigned as endowments of re-

घून्ची, *f.* 1, = घुघची, *q. v.*: 2, the name of a certain herb which grows in rice-fields after the crop is cut.

घूम, 1, a kind of children's game: 2, *adv.* back, around, about.

घूमघुमाला }
घूमघूमाला } *m.* (*f.* ī) loose, full (as a robe).

घूमघुमेला }
घूमघूमेला } *m.* (*f.* ī) revolving, circling, round.

घूमना, 1, *m.* a whirling, turning, etc.: 2, *a. int.* to revolve, go round and round, turn, roll, wheel, whirl. *Sir* —, to swim (said of the head); *hence*, to be giddy, be dizzy. [day by a pair of bullocks.

घूमाओ, as much land as can be ploughed in a

घूमालाना, *more com.* घुमाना, *q. v.*

घूमिति, a corruption of घूमती (घूमना).

घूमपानयन्त्र, *m.* a pipe, tobacco-pipe.

घूयं }
घूया } *more com.* घोया, *q. v.* [of sandy soil.

घूर, *m.* a staring: a dunghill: the name of a kind

घूरची, *f.* a twist in thread, a tangle, entanglement.

घूरत, cattle-pens. [on, look at angrily.

घूरना, *a. int.* to stare : *t.* to stare at, fix the eyes

घूरबरार, a species of dues or tax.

घूरा, *m.* sweepings ; soil, mauure ; a dunghill.

घूरिया, *m.* a dunghill.

घूलाना, *t.* to deceive, outwit.

घूस, 1, *m.* (for घूशा ?) a bribe. — *denā*, to bribe : 2, a large kind of rat, the bandicote rat (*Mus Malabaricus*, Shaw : *Mus giganteus*, Lin. Trans. vol. vii).

घूसत, *m.* a young owl. [boxing, fisticuffs.

घूसमघूसा, *m.* a thumping and pulling each other,

घूसलेनवाला, *m.* (*f.* ī) a taker of bribes.

घूसा, *m.* 1, = घूस, 2, *q.v.* : 2, a thump, buffet,

घूघा = घिघा, *q.v.* [blow of the fist.

घृत, *m.* (commonly घी, *q.v.*) clarified butter.

घृतकुमारी, **घृतकुवार** } *f.* the aloe-plant (*Aloe perfoliata*).

घेऊं, *m.* (prop. गेहूं) wheat.

घेंगा, a wen, tumour.

घेंचना, *more prop.* खिंचना, *q.v.*

घेगरा, *m.* the unripe pod of gram ; the unripe bole

घेगा = घेघा, *q.v.* [of cotton before it bursts.

घेघरा = घेगरा, *q.v.* [neck.

घेघा, *m.* the bronchocele, goitre, or Derbyshire

घेटना, *t.* to mix, knead together.

घेवट, the neck. [and other pulses.

घेवटा, *m.* (*f.* ī) a pig : the unripe pod of gram

घेसला, *m.* a kind of shoe. [flour and water).

घेपना, *t.* to mix, mingle, unite into a paste (as

घेर, *m.* 1, calumny, reproach, complaint : 2, circuit, circumference, circle, ring, environs : 3. *adj.* surrounding, enclosing ; full, loose (as a robe) ; meandering, winding : 4, *adv.* around. — *lenā*, or *denā*, to encompass, besiege.

घेरघार क°, *t.* to surround, hinder, stop. [sive.

घेरदार, full, loose (as a robe) ; circular ; exten-

घेरदेना ; see *s. v.* घेर.

घेरना, *t.* to surround, encircle, encompass, beset, hem in, blockade, invade, envelope, enclose (as fishes in a net).

घेरमाघारना, *t.* to surround, encompass, besiege.

घेरनी, *f.* a winch, handle for turning a spinning-

घेरलेना ; see *s. v.* घेर. [wheel.

घेरा, *m.* a circle, circumference ; a siege, blockade ; a fence, enclosure, "compound" : vertigo. — *ḍālnā*, to lay siege, besiege, surround. *Gheremeṅ paṛnā*, to be besieged, be encompassed, be surrounded.

घेलौनी, *f.* a gratuity allowed to a purchaser in addition to the article purchased (such as our baker's dozen, *i. e.* thirteen instead of twelve).

घेवर, *f.* a kind of sweetmeat.

घैरा, (prop. गहरा) *m.* (*f.* ī) deep, profound.

घोंगा, 1, *m.* a cockle ; a cockle-shell ; 2, *m.* (*f.* ī) a snail (*Cochlea helix*).

घोंघ, *m.* an intermediate space. [son.

घोंघा, 1, = घोंगा, *q.v.* : 2, *m.* (*f.* ī) a senseless per-

घोंसला, *m.* a bird's nest.

घोखना, *more prop.* घोषना, *q.v.*

घोघा ; see (1) घोंगा (2) घोंघा (3) घोघी.

घोघी, *f.* a pocket, pouch, wallet : a turtle-dove.

घोट, *f.* polish.

घोटक, *m.* (*f.* ī) a horse. [plod.

घोटना, *t.* to polish ; to shave ; to calendar ; to

घोटनी. *f.* a rubber.

घोटा, *m.* a wooden rubber.

घोटी, *f.* land which has been under a rice-crop.

घोट्टू, polished, smooth (said of words).

घोड़चढ़ा, *m.* (*f.* ī) mounted on a horse.

घोड़फोड़, the guana lizard.

घोड़शाला, *f.*, **घोड़सार**, *m.* } = घोड़ाशाला, *q. v.*

घोडा *more com.* घोड़ा, *q.v.*

घोड़ा, *m.* (*f.* ī) a horse ; the cock of a gun ; the knight at chess ; a clothes-horse. — *chaṛhānā*, to cock a gun. *Ghoṛeko sarpaṭ pheṅknā*, to force a horse to his utmost speed.

घोड़शाला, *f.* a horse-repository, a stable.

घोपा, *m.* a sort of hooded cloak or loose garment to cover the head and body in cold or rainy weather.

घोयें, *more com.* घोयां *q. v.*

घोयां, *f.* an esculent root (*Arum colocasia*).

घोर, 1. *m.* a horrible act ; horribleness ; trepidation, horror ; an epithet of Shiv ; dread, awe : the sound of a drum : 2 *m.* (*f.* ā) horrible, frightful, dreadful, awful, violent ; deep (as colour or sleep). — *ghāṇṭnā*, to be inwardly displeased, to conceal one's dislike or indignation.

घोरचढ़ा, *more com.* घुड़चढ़ा *q. v.*

घोरत्व, *m.* (*f.* tā) horribleness, frightfulness.

घोरदर्शन, *m.* (*f.* ā) of horrid or frightful appearance, terrifying. [beverage.

घोरना, 1, see घूरना ; 2, *f.* a kind of refreshing

घोरनाद, *m.* a terrifying sound, thunder.

घोररूप, *m.* (*f.* ā) a hideous appearance, etc. : *lit.* of horrible aspect or form, grim, frightful, hideous,

घोररूपी, *m.* (*f.* iṇī) = घोररूप, *q. v.* [terrifying.

घोराकार, *m.*, **घोराकृति**, *f.* } = घोररूप, *q.v.*

घोल, *m.* buttermilk. [tion.

घोलघुमाव, *m.* evasion, subterfuge, procrastina-

घोलना, *t.* to mix with a liquid, dissolve.

घोलमेल, *m.* a mixture, mixing.

घोला, *m.* an intoxicating potion made of *bhang* or opium ; a solution : the name of a certain fish. *Gholemeṅ ḍālnā*, to involve in difficulty.

घोष, *m.* sound, roar; language: a station of herdsmen; a caste of milkmen; a cowherd: (in Gram.) soft.

घोषक, *m.* = **घोषणा**, *q.v.*

घोषणा, *f.* a speaking aloud, making a great noise, heralding, proclamation. — *k.* to proclaim, preach.

घोषना, to speak aloud, proclaim, reiterate, repeat.

घोषा, *f.* (*m.* **घोष**) a female cowherd.

घोस, see **घोष**.

घोसला, see **घोंसला**.

घोसी, *m.* a Muhammadan milkman or cowherd said to be converted from the Hindoo *aheer* caste.

घोंसुआ, in Braj = **घोंसला**, a bird's nest.

घौद, *f.* a bunch of plantains.

घौद
घौर } = **घौर**, *q.v.*

घ्न, *m.* (*f.* ी *or* ा) a killer, murderer, destroyer: *lit.* striking, killing, destroying, removing. This form never occurs excepting as the last member of a compound word.

घ्यारा, a small sort of cucumber much used as a condiment.

घ्यौं, a Braj corruption of **घोव** = **घो**, *q.v.*

घ्राण, 1, *m.* the nose; smelling; smell: 2, *m.* (*f.* ा) *adj.* smelling.

घ्राणतर्पण, *m.* a fragrance, odour, perfume.

घ्राणा, *f.* the nose. [smell.

घ्राणेन्द्रिय, *f.* the nose, the organ or the sense of

घ्रात, *adj.* smelt, smelled.

घ्रीष्म, a corruption of **ग्रीष्म**, *q.v.*

ङ

ङ (n·) is the fifth consonant in the Hindee alphabet and is generally called '*gnua*'. It is the nasal of the **कवर्ग** or guttural letters, *i. e.* it never occurs in Hindee excepting in connexion with one or the other of these letters, with which it forms compound letters and is always the first element in such combinations: it is hence called the guttural nasal, or nasal of the gutturals. When combined with the letters of its class it generally remains unchanged; thus, **ङ्क**, **ङ्ख**, **ङ्ग**, **ङ्घ**. Followed by **क** or by **ख** it has the sound of *n* in the English word 'blink'; followed by **ग** or by **घ** it has the sound of *n* in the word 'sing'. It is unpronounceble unless there be a vowel before it; and though of very frequent occurrence in the language it never occurs at the beginning of words or of syllables, even though preceded by a vowel-sound. Like all the nasal consonants this letter is liable to be printed interchangeably with *anuswār*; excepting **ञ**, however, this letter is more frequently so represented than either of the other nasals: thus, **अंक** is very frequently put for **अङ्क**; less frequently **कंप** for **कम्प**. It has been usual in Hindee Dictionaries to insert *twice* all words in which *anuswār* and the nasal consonants might be interchanged, together with all their explanations and notes;—a plan which augments needlessly, as it seems, the ultimate bulk of the work. In the present Dictionary it has been thought desirable to avoid all such repetition and to reserve the space for better uses: in pursuance of this plan **ङ** and **ञ** are invariably represented by *anuswār* (— the manner most frequently found in print), and the other nasals (**ण**, **न**, **म**) uniformly in combination with the letters of their respective classes. There are no words in the language beginning with this letter.

च

च (ch) is the sixth consonant in the Hindee alphabet and has the following characteristics and functions:— 1, It is the first letter of the **चवर्ग** or palatal class, and has invariably the sound of *ch* in the English word 'cherry'. 2, As a suffix (1) it is sometimes emphatic like **ही** or **भी** (2) it sometimes forms adjectives derived from prepositional particles; *e.g.* **उच्च** (**उत** + **च**); **नीच** (**नि** + **च**). 3, In Sanskrit (1) it is sometimes an epithet of Shiv, and signifies a tortoise; a thief: seedless: vile, base (2) it is sometimes *adverbial*, signifying mutually, equally (3) it is sometimes disjunctive signifying either — or, otherwise, but (4) it is sometimes prepositional signifying for, on account of (5) it is very common as a copulative particle, signifying and, also, moreover; and is invariably placed *after* its word or clause like the Greek τε and the Latin *que*: like these also, it is frequently repeated, having the signification of both — and, as well — as (6) it is sometimes emphatic, like the English even, and even (7) it is sometimes used as an expletive to fill up the measure of a verse. 4, It is occasionally interchanged (1) with **य**; *e. g.* **लोचन**, properly **लोचन** (2) with **छ**; *e. g.* **चमस**, properly **चमस** (3) with **क**; *e. g.* [**काचा** = **काका**.

चंक; see (1) **चंग** (2) **चंच** (3) **चक**.

चंग, *f.* a claw: the hand expanded: a kind of guitar, a harp: report, fame: a paper kite which they fly at night: the name of a suit at cards.

चंगबाओ
चंगबायु
चंगबाव } *m.* (*f.* ?) a kind of disorder.

चंगर, *m.* a tray, trough.

चंगा, *m.* (*f.* ी) well in health, sound, cured, healed. — *karnā*, to correct, punish, chastise, put to flight. — *k.* to heal, cure. *Bhalā* —, in health; perfect, good.

चंगुल, *m.* a claw, talon, hand, clutch, grasp, hook.

चंगुर, excellent.

चंगेर, *f.* a flowerpot, tray.

चंगेरा, *m.* a large basket; a tray, trough.

चंगेरी, *f.* (dim. of *the above*) a small basket.

चंगेल, a certain herb which grows amidst old buildings, the seed of which, called khabājee, is used in medicine.

चंचनाना, *a. int.* to throb or shoot (as a boil, etc.): to make the noise that butter does in a fryingpan.

चंचनाहट, *f.* a throb, throbbing, shooting pain.

चंचर, land left untilled for one, two, or three years.

चंचरीक = **भ्रमर**, *q.v.*

चंचल, *m.* (*f.* ा) a libertine, fickle person, etc.: *lit.* moving to and fro, unsteady, tremulous; restless, fickle, inconstant, wanton, playful; transient, perishable.

चंचलता, *f.*
चंचलत्व, *m.*
चंचलपन, *m.*
चंचलपना, *m.* } = **चंचलाई**, *q.v.*

चंचलहृदय, *m.* (*f.* ā) false-hearted, of uncertain or uneven disposition, fickle, capricious.

चंचला, *f.* lightning.

चंचलाई, *f.* wantonness, gaiety, unsteadiness, uncertainty, fickleness, capriciousness, restlessness, playfulness; perishableness.

चंचलाना, *n.* to be unsteady, be restless, be wanton, be playful.

चंचलाहट = **चंचलाई**, *q.v.*

चंचु, *f.* the beak of a bird.

चंट, चंड, चंद, चंप, चंब; for all words beginning with either of these elements, see under the forms **चण्ट, चण्ड, चन्द, चम्प, चम्ब**, respectively.

चंवर, *m.* a kind of flapper for driving away flies. It is generally made of peacock's feathers, sometimes also of the tail of a species of ox (*Bos grunniens*), and is waved over the head of any great personage to keep off flies.

चक, *m.* landed property, estate, farm; a portion of land divided off: a shepherd, goatherd.

चकई, *f.* 1, see **चकवा**: 2, a whirligig.

चककार, *more prop.* **चक्र**, *q.v.*

चकचका, *m.* (*f.* ī) resplendent, shining.

चकचकी, *f.* 1, *see above*: 2, a kind of dagger worn on the waist.

चकचूर = **चकनाचूर**, *q.v.*

चकचौन्धी, *f.* the effect on the eyes of a sudden flash of light.

चकछन्दी, *f.* a musk-rat (*Sorex caerulescens*, Shaw; *S. caerulens*, Turton.

चकटुकड़ा, *m.* a plot or parcel of a landed estate.

चकता, *m.* a scraping the skin: a scrape, scar; a slice. — *denā* or *lenā*, to scar.

चकताना, *t.* to sod, turf.

चकती, *f.* the hide of a rhinoceros (of which shields are made); a patch, patch of leather, slice, the round of a cheese, round plate of metal, etc.; a shield; a letter: *lit.* compressed, flattened.

चकत्ता, *m.* a kind of shield (of rhinoceros or buffalo-hide, with brass knobs, used among the Rājpūts); a scar, round blotch on the skin; a compressed substance of a flattened and round form.

चकनाचूर, *m.* atoms, small pieces, filings, scraps. — *k.* to shatter, dash to pieces. — *honā*, to be shattered, dashed to pieces.

चकनामा, *m.* a statement shewing the boundaries of an estate (*chak*); a grant for holding a *chak*.

चकबन्दी, *f.* the defining or making the boundaries of an estate (*chak*).

चकबरार, the collecting the rent of a *chak*.

चकमक, *f.* a flint; the steel for striking fire with from a flint; the lock of a gun. — *jhāṛnā*, to strike a light.

चकमा, *m.* a boot; a stocking: a game at cards.

चकमाक़ = **चक़मक़**, *q.v.*

चकरबा, *m.* revelry. — *machānā*, to revel, riot.

चकरमकर, *m.* evasion, trick, subterfuge.

चकरा, *m.* a kind of dish made of pulse.

चकरानी, *f.* (*m.* **चाकर**) a maid-servant.

चकरिया, *m.* servitude, service.

चकलना, *t.* to squeeze, press upon.

चकला, 1, *m.* (*f.* ī) wide, broad; round: 2, *m.* a brothel: a kind of cloth made of silk and cotton: a district or division of a country containing several parganas: a round plate on which bread is rolled: a log of wood, trunk of a tree; a block or mass.

चकलाई, *f.* width, breadth.

चकलाख़र्च, *m.* the expenses of a *chaklā*.

चकलानवीस, *m.* the accountant of the revenues and charges of a *chaklā*.

चकलाना, *t.* to widen, extend in breadth.

चकलेदार, *m.* the governor of a province or county.

चकलेदारी, *f.* the status or the work of the governor of a province or county.

चकवंड़ = **चकौंड़**, *q.v.*

चकवा, *m.* (*f.* **चकवी** or **चकई**) the ruddy goose or Brāhmaṇī duck (*Anas casarca*): a whirlpool.

चकवाई, a certain small class of Rājputs in the district of Ghāzeepur.

चकवाण्ड, *m.* the egg of the **चकवा**.

चकवापक्षी = **चकवा**, *q.v.*

चकवी, a fem. form of **चकवा**, *q.v.*

चकसा, see (1) **चसका** (2) **चिकसा**.

चकसूनी, *f.* a certain kind of grass.

चका, *more prop.* **चक्का**, *q.v.*

चकाचाक, *f.* the sound of the repeated strokes of a sword, dagger, or mace, a clashing of swords.

चकाचान्ध, *more com.* **चकाचौन्ध**, *q.v.*

चकाचौन्ध, *f.* the state of being dazzled; radiance.

चकाचौन्धी, *more com.* **चकाचौन्ध**, *q.v.*

चकाटे आना, *n.* to be in astonishment, be in perplexity.

चकार, *m.* the letter **च**, or any symbol that may represent it.

चकारी, a corruption of **चाकरी**, *q.v.*

चकाव, *m.* decision: deception, trickery.

चकावर, *m.* a certain disease of horses.

चकावी, *f.* a ringworm.

चकित, *m.* (*f.* ā) astonished; timid, afraid, fearful, perplexed.

चकोदगी, *f.* distillation; a drop.

चकोदा, *m. f.* dropped, distilled.

चकोटा, *m.* (*f.* ī) a goggle-eyed person: *lit.* having large eyes.

चकोंड़ = **चकौंड़**, *q.v.*

चकोट, savoury, delicious.

चकोतरा, *m.* a fruit of the lime kind, citron; pompelmoose, shaddock (*Citrus decumanus*).

चकोत्रा = **चकोतरा**, *q.v.*

चकोर, *m.* (*f.* ī) a partridge, especially the Bartavelle or Greek partridge (*Tetrao rufus*, Lin.: *Perdix rufa*, Lath.) fabulously said to be enamoured of the moon, to subsist upon the moonbeams, and to eat fire at the full moon.

चकोह, *more com.* **चक्र**, *q.v.*

चकौंड़, *m.* a species of cassia (*Cassia obtusifolia* or *C. tora*) esteemed a remedy for ringworm.

चकौटा, *m.* fixed rates of rent, money-rate, settlement.

चकौण्ड, **चकौन्दा** } = **चकौंड़**, *q.v.*

चक्क in Chand = **चक्र**, *q.v.*

चक्कर, *more prop.* **चक्र**, *q. v.*

चक्करवरदेशी, compound interest.

चक्कवे, a poetical form of **चक्रवर्त्ती**, *q. v.*

चक्कस, *m.* a roost, perch for birds (*esp.* falcons).

चक्का, *m.* coagulated milk ; a circle, carriage-wheel, circular lump of earth, round sod of turf : adj. *m.* (*f.* ī) round, circular ; thick. [etc.): dropping, distilling.

चक्कान, *m.* a blot : *lit.* blotted, smeared; thick (*bhang*,

चक्की, *f.* a mill-stone, grinder, mill, grinding-stone, hand-mill ; the timber of a gunlock ; the kneepan ; a thunderbolt.

चक्कीनामा, *m.* a kind of song sung by females at weddings while grinding a perfumed powder.

चक्कीनावरी, the presentation of the above-mentioned powder to the bride and bridegroom.

चक्कू, *m.* a claspknife, penknife.

चक्र, *m.* a wheel, a potter's wheel : an oil-press ; a circle ; an army, multitude, a form of military array, a circular position ; a whirlwind, whirlpool, anything revolving in a circle ; revolution, a circular course, the lounge (in manège); *met.* a misfortune, scrape, perplexity : a sharp discus or iron ring used as a missile principally by Sikhs and thrown by them with great dexterity (it was with this instrument, called *Sudarshan-chakra*, that Nārāyan is fabled to have cut off the head of the Asur Rāhu when, after churning the ocean, the Surs or gods and the Asurs or demons fought for the Amrit or nectar) : (in Gram.) a table or paradigm : a side or quarter, e. g. *Chahoṅ — meṅ*, on the four sides, on all sides ; (in Astron.) the zodiac with its twelve signs ; hence, in the ingenious system of reckoning by symbols adopted by Hindoos in their poetry, this word is a symbol for 12. *Ghoreko — denā*, to lounge a horse. — *denā*, to surround. — *mārnā*, to wheel around, whirl around.

चक्रदारी, *m.* a peacock : an epithet of Vishṇu.

चक्रवत्, *adv.* revolving like a wheel, in rotation.

चक्रवर्त्ती, *m.* (*f.* inī) a sovereign of the world, universal monarch, emperor, the ruler of a *chakra* or country described as extending from sea to sea : twelve princes, beginning with Bharat, are especially considered as Chakravartees ; the title of one of the great families of Brāhmans in Bengal, where the word is commonly corrupted into 'Chuckerbutty'.

चक्रवाक, *m.* (*f.* ī) the ruddy goose (*Anas casarea*).

चक्रवान, *m.* (*f.* vatī) circular, ring-shaped.

चक्रवृद्धि, *f.* interest upon interest, compound interest, interest agreed on the risk of safe carriage.

चक्राकार, circular, ring-shaped.

चक्रायुध, *f.* a fighting with the **चक्र**, *q. v.*

चकित, *m.* (*f.* ā) *more prop.* **चक्रित**, *q. v.*

चक्री, *f.* a round plate on which bread is rolled ; an assembly of singers ; a certain plaything of children, a whirligig.

चक्रोठा, *m.* (*f.* ī) = **चकोठा**, *q. v.*

चक्रोला, *m.* (*f.* ī) round, circular.

चक्षु, *m.* the eye : hence, in the ingenious system of reckoning by symbols adopted by Hindoos in their poetry, this word is a symbol for 2.

चक्षुरोग, *m.* ophthalmia. [= **जैसा**, *q. v.*

चख, 1, *more prop.* (1) **चक्षु** (2) **चख़**, *qq. v.* : 2, (*Rām.*).

चख़, *f.* variance, rupture, quarrel.

L

चख़माक़, = **चकमक**, *q. v.*

चखना, *t.* to taste, relish.

चखाचखी, *f.* discord.

चखाना, *t.* to cause to taste, give a sample of.

चखु, 1, *more prop.* **चक्षु**, *q. v.* : 2, (*Rām.*) = **जैसा**, *q. v.*

चखैबो in Braj = (1) **चखाओ** (2) **चखाया** (**चखाना**).

चगलना, *t.* to eat without appetite.

चगाल, thick, compact, heavy.

चगुली = **चुग़ली** (?) *q. v.*

चगेर, *f.* a flowerpot, tray.

चचर, land which after having lain fallow has been cultivated or ploughed for one year.

चचरा, *m.* a species of tree.

चचहिया, *m.* a whistler.

चचा, *m.* a paternal uncle (father's brother).

चचि, *more prop.* **चची**, *q. v.* [brother's wife.

चची, *f.* a paternal aunt (father's sister, father's

चचोर, *m.* a line, stripe, score.

चचेरा, *m.* (*f.* ī) descended from a paternal uncle, related through a paternal uncle : *e. g. Chacherā-bhāī*, *m.* a cousin, son of a paternal uncle : *Chacherī-bahin*, *f.* a female cousin, daughter of a paternal uncle.

चचोड़ना, = **चचोरना**, *q. v.*

चचोरना, *t.* to suck (a dry substance from which nothing can be obtained).

चच्चल, *m.* large breasts.

चच्चा } **चच्ची** } = **चचा**, etc., *qq. v.*

चट, 1, *f.* an excoriation, sore, scab, cancer : the noise of breaking up, a snap. — *k.* to eat, devour, dissipate. — *honā*, to be dissipated, be consumed. — *de ṭūṭnā*, to snap short, to break : 2, quickly, instantly.

चटक, *m.* (*f.* ā) 1, a sparrow : a crash, crack, smack ; intelligence ; gaudiness, glitter, splendour, prime of life : 2, intelligent, quick.

चटकना, 1, = **चटख़ना**, *q. v.* : 2, *m.* a slap, box, blow, cuff.

चटकवाई, *f.* quickness.

चटकसे, deceiving. — *jānā*, to pay with the fore topsail.

चटका, 1, see **कटक** ; 2, *m.* scarcity. — *lagānā*, to thirst, wish.

चटकाना, *t.* to split ; to crack (a whip) ; to snap the fingers in rejoicing ; to fire off a musket ; to irritate.

चटकारना, *t.* to urge cattle by the clacking noise made by drawing the tongue from the palate.

चटकारी, *f.* urging cattle by the clacking noise made by drawing the tongue from the palate.

चटकीला, *m.* (*f.* ī) splendid, glittering, gaudy.

चटख़ना, *a. int.* to crack, split, crackle (as charcoal or wood when burning).

चटजोरा, *m.* a species of tree.

चटना, *m.* (*f.* ī) a voracious person.

चटनी, *f.* 1, *see above* : 2, a kind of acid sauce or marmalade.

चटपट, hastily, in a hurry, instantly.

चटपटा, *m.* (*f.* ī) active, hasty; stout : meat dressed with little sauce or gravy.

चटपटाना, *a. int.* to flutter, palpitate, wince, become agitated.

चटपटाहट, *f.* agitation, flurry, flutter, palpitation.

चटपटिया, active, quick, alert; hot (with spice); restless, fidgetty.

चटपटी, *f.* haste, hurry, quickness, restlessness.

चटभसम, eating up the whole, licking the platter clean. [licked.

चटवाना, *t.* to cause to lick up, to cause to be

चटरी, *f.* a certain herb used as fodder for cattle.

चटसारी }
चटसाल } *f.* a school, academy.
चटसाला } [lay a mat.

चटाई, *f.* a mat. —— *bichhānā*, to mat, spread or

चटाक, 1, *f.* a crash, explosion: 2, intelligent.

चटाका }
चटाखा } *m.* a crack, explosion, smack, kiss.
चटाख़ा }

चटाचट, *m.* reiterated sound.

चटान, *f.* rocky ground; a rock, block of stone.

चटाना, 1, *m.* the ceremony of feeding a child for the first time: 2, *t.* to cause to lick, cause to lap up.

चटिया, *m.* a learner, pupil.

चटुआ, *m.* a kind of plaything; a sort of hawk.

चटोखा, *m.* a kind of dove.

चटोर }
चटोरा } *m.* an epicure, glutton.

चट्टा, *m.* a school-boy: a jacket, frock-coat.

चट्टान, *f.* rocky ground; a rock, block of stone.

चट्टाबट्टा, *m.* a kind of plaything, rapper or clapper.

चट्टी, *f.* scarcity, want.

चट्टेकार, *m.* a half-caste, a Eurasian.

चड्डा, *m.* a tit-bit, dainties.

चड़, *m.* the sound made by breaking a branch.

चड़का; see **चरका**.

चड़चड़, *m.* an imitative sound.

चड़चड़ाना, *a. int.* to crack, creak.

चड़ड़, *m.* an imitative sound.

चड़पड़ाना, *a. int.* to smart, palpitate, flutter, throb.

चड़बड़, a chattering, prattling. —— *k.* or *bolnā*, to chatter, prattle.

चड़बड़िया, *m.* a prattler, chatterer, idle talker.

चड़र, *m.* an initiative sound.

चड़ाओ, *m.* ascent; flood-tide.

चड़ाना = **चढ़ाना**, *q.v.*

चड़ावा, *m.* an offering to an idol: jewels, etc. presented by a betrothed damsel to her intended.

चड्डा }
चढ्ढा } *m.* the groin; a bubo.

चढ़, increase or augmentation of rent, etc.

चढ़के, *adv.* avowedly, designedly, excellently.

चढ़ता, *m.* an increase of price, the making additional profit, the settlement of revenue at a progressively increasing price. — *honā*, to be excelling, rising, etc. [progressively increasing.

चढ़ता पत्ता, a lease for a term of years, —— the rent

चढ़ती, *f.* advantage, gain, rise.

चढ़ना, *a. int.* to ascend, mount, advance, attack, embark, board, rise, climb, soar, spread, swell, ride; to elapse, pass over (as time): *n.* to be strung (said of a bow); to be braced (a drum); to be offered up (sacrifice); to be fixed (as a bayonet or arrow). — *utarnā*, to hire and dismiss: *congressus.*

चढ़नी, *f.* preparations for battle.

चढ़न्दार, *m.* a passenger, supercargo.

चढ़बनना, to find an opportunity.

चढ़वाँ, *m.* (*f.* wīṅ) rising high.

चढ़वाना, *t.* to cause to be raised, *i. e.* to cause some one to raise, send up, pull on, etc.

चढ़वी, *f.* a raising (rent or prices).

चढ़वैया, *m.* one who ascends, mounts, etc., *hence*, a rider, mounter, climber.

चढ़ाई, *f.* 1, = **चढ़ाओ**, *q.v.*: 2, the price paid for ascending, riding, embarking, etc.

चढ़ाओ, *m.* an ascent, rise, acclivity; rank, dignity: an attack, assault; flood-tide: offerings made to idols; a raising in price or in rent.

चढ़ाना, *t.* to cause to ascend, cause to embark, etc.; to offer up oblations or sacrifice; to string (a bow); to brace (a drum): to pull, draw on, cock, fix (a bayonet or an arrow); to raise, take up, advance, apply, put, spread, bend, dye, run.

चढ़ायता, *m.* a trooper.

चढ़ार्दार, a kind of jacket worn by harlots.

चढ़ाव = **चढ़ाओ**, *q.v.*

चढ़ावा, *m.* anything presented in sacrifice, a religious offering or gift. — *chaṛhānā*, to offer up or present a religious offering.

चढ़ी, *f.* preparations for battle.

चढ़ैत = (1) **चढ़वैया** (2) **चढ़ैता**, *qq. v.*

चढ़ैता, *m.* a trooper who does not ride his own horse; a rider. [wearer.

चढ़ोंवा, *m.* a shoe rising up over the heel of the

चणक, *m.* chick-pea (*Cicer arietinum*), fitches, vetches. This pulse is commonly called 'gram': it is grown in all parts of the East and is used chiefly as food for horses, but it is also frequently eaten by the poor.

चणा = **चणक**, *q. v.*

चणी, *f.* (dim. of **चणा**) a small kind of gram.

चपट, *m.* a miser.

चण्ड, *m.* (*f.* ā *or* ī) a violent person, etc.: *lit.* passionate, violent, furious, fierce; hot, warm, pungent, acrid. [warmth, pungency.

चण्डत्व, *m.* (*f.* tā) passionateness, fierceness,

चण्डल, *more prop.* **चण्डाल**, *q. v.*

चण्डवा, the shaft of a ploughshare.

चण्डवत }
चण्डवान } *m.* (*f.* vatī) = **चण्ड**, *q. v.*

चण्डा, *f.* (see **चण्ड**) *lit.* a passionate or furious woman; hence, applied especially to the goddess Durgā in allusion to her fabled incarnation for the purpose of destroying the demon Mahesh Asur. This exploit forms the theme of a section of the Markaṇdeya Purāṇ, and is particularly celebrated in Bengal at the festival called Durgā-poojā which is held in honor of this goddess in the month Āswin (Sept-Oct).

चण्डार in Braj = **चण्डाल**, *q.v.*

चण्डाल, *m.* (*f.* ā, in, inī, *or* ī) one of the inferior castes among Hindoos: a person of the lowest of the mixed tribes born from a Shoodra father and a Brāhmaṇī mother: *met.* a miser, merciless wretch, outcaste.

चण्डाला, **चण्डालिन**, **चण्डालिनी** } = **चण्डाली**, *q.v.*

चण्डालिया, a certain tribe of the Bhangees.

चण्डाली, *f.* (*m.* **चण्डाल**) a female Chaṇḍāl.

चण्डावल, *m.* the rear guard.

चण्डिका, **चण्डी** } *f.* (see **चण्डा**) names of Durgā.

चण्डीकुसुम, *m.* red oleander.

चण्डोल, *m.* the rear guard: a sort of sedan: a species of lark: a kind of plaything consisting of four little earthen pots joined together.

चतर; for words beginning thus, see under the [form **चतुर**.

चतरमार, *m.* a mushroom, toadstool.

चतरसेन, a corruption of **चित्रसेन**, *q.v.*

चतराव, *more com.* **चतुराई**, *q.v.*

चतरी, *f.* a canopy, parasol, veil; a pavilion, tent.

चतुर, *m.* (*f.* ā *or* ī) a shrewd person, etc.: *lit.* four; *hence.* circumspect, clever, cunning, dexterous, shrewd, ingenious, intelligent, expert, many-sided, sagacious, adroit, sly.

चतुरंग, *m.* the four divisions of an army, *viz.* ele[phants, horses, chariots, and footmen.

चतुरंग, *m.* (*f.* ī), **चतुरंगी**, *m.* (*f.* inī) } consisting of four parts.

चतुरत्व, *m.* (*f.* tā) = **चतुराई**, *q.v.*

चतुरन, a Braj pl. of **चतुर**, *q.v.*

चतुरस्र, *m.* a quadrangle: *lit.* quadrangular.

चतुरा, *f.* (*m.* **चतुर**) a clever female.

चतुराव, *more com.* **चतुराई**, *q.v.*

चतुराई, *f.* alertness, cunning, dexterity, cleverness, skilfulness, ingenuity, wisdom, expertness, subtlety, craftiness, deceit, roguery, fraud, slyness.

चतुरानन, *m.* (*f.* ī) the four-faced one, *i. e.* Brahm.

चतुराय, *more com.* **चतुराई**, *q.v.*

चतुरावत, *f.* a proper name of females.

चतुर्थ, *m.* (*f.* ī) fourth.

चतुर्थांश, 1, *m.* a fourth: 2, entitled to a fourth.

चतुर्थी, *f.* the fourth lunar day.

चतुर्थ्यन्त, (in Gram.) terminating with the suffix or sign of the fourth case (i. e. of the Dative).

चतुर्दश, fourteen.

चतुर्दशी, *f.* the fourteenth day of the moon's age.

चतुर्दिक, the four sides, all around.

चतुर्भद्र = **चतुर्वर्ग**, *q.v.*

चतुर्भुज, *m.* (*f.*) the four-armed one, *i. e.* Vishṇu.

चतुर्भुजी, *f.* the four-armed one, *i. e.* Durgā.

चतुर्मुख, *m.* (*f.* ī) the four-faced one, *i. e.* Brahm.

चतुर्युग, 1, *m.* the aggregate of the four Yugs or epochs of the world: 2, containing the four Yugs.

चतुर्वर्ग, *m.* the aggregate of the four objects of human pursuit, *viz.* Arth, Dharm, Kām, Moksh (*i. e.* virtue, wealth, sensual enjoyment, final beatitude).

चतुर्वर्ण, *m.* the four chief castes among Hindoos, *viz.* Brāhmaṇ, Kshatriya, Vaishya, Shoodra.

चतुर्विंश, *m.* (*f.* ī) the twenty-fourth.

चतुर्विंशति, twenty-four.

चतुर्वेदी, *m.* (*f.* inī) = **चौबे**, *q.v.*

चतुष्कोण, 1, *m.* a quadrangle: 2, quadrangular.

चतुष्पथ, *m.* a place where four roads meet.

चतुष्पद, *m.* (*f.* ā) a quadruped; a metre or stanza consisting of four *pads* or lines: *lit.* four-footed.

चतुष्पदा, **चतुष्पदी** } *f.* = **चतुष्पद**, *q.v.*

चत्र, *m.*, **चत्री**, *f.* } an umbrella.

चद्दर, *f.* a sheet, table-cloth, cloth of more than one breadth. — *bichhānā*, to lay the cloth.

चद्दरअन्दाज़ी, a certain marriage ceremony among Sikhs (when a man marries a widow, a sheet is thrown [over the parties.

चन, *m.* a kind of sugarcane.

चनक, *f.* the bursting of the husk of a seed by exposure to the sun.

चनकना, *a. int.* to burst and fall out (as as a seed [from the husk).

चनगारी, a corruption of **चिंगारी**, *q.v.*

चनवाँ, a cloth wrapper or cover for a book.

चनमिया, a certain tribe of Rājputs.

चनवान, a small species of millet.

चना, *more prop.* **चणा**, *q.v.*

चनांके (*corruption*) = **चुनानचि**, *q.v.*

चनाका, *m.* = **चणक**, *q.v.*

चनाना, *t.* to reflect or cast back (a shadow).

चनी = **चणी**, *q.v.*

चनियादा, **चनेआदा** } land under a crop of **चणा**, *q.v.*

चनेठ, *f.* spices or drugs given to cattle.

चन्द, *m.* the moon: *pr. n.* the earliest of the Hindee poets. He was a native of Lahore, was the bard of the court of the last Hindoo king of Delhi, and the author of the *Prithirāj Rāsau*, and wrote *circa* A. D. 1200.

चन्दन, *m.* the sandal-tree (*Syrium myrtifolium* or *Santalum album*) or its wood: a proper name.

चन्दनदास, *m. pr. n.* a certain merchant.

चन्दना, *m.* light, moonlight.

चन्दमी, *f. pr. n.* a certain river.

चन्दन्हार, an ornament worn on the head by women (it is shaped like a half-moon).

चन्दबदन = **चन्द्रवदन**, *q.v.*

चन्दबदना }
चन्दबदनी } = चन्द्रवदनी, *q. v.*

चन्दमुख = चन्द्रमुख = चन्द्रवदन, *q. v.*

चन्दमुखा }
चन्दमुखी } = चन्द्रमुखी = चन्द्रवदनी, *q. v.*

चन्दरना, *more prop.* चन्दाना, *q. v.*

चन्दरोज़, 1, a few days : 2, how many days ?

चन्दला, 1, *m.* baldness : 2, *m.* (*f.* ī) bald.

चन्दवदन = चन्द्रवदन, *q. v.* [the pomflet-fish.

चन्दवा, *m.* a small canopy, awning : — *mach'hī*,

चन्दा, 1, a corruption of चन्द्र, *q. v.* : 2, *m.* an assessment, contribution, subscription, a "collection". — *uthānā*, to get up a subscription, subscribe, contri-

चन्दालिया, a certain caste of sweepers. [bute.

चन्दिनी, *more prop.* चान्दनी, *q. v.*

चन्दिया, *f.* the crown of the head.

चन्दी, a contraction of चान्दी, *q. v.*

चन्दीन, silvery.

चन्दील, *m.* the designation of a certain tribe of Rājputs who claim descent from the moon.

चन्दीला, (*f.* ī) silvery, white.

चन्दे, a few, some ; sometime.

चन्देरी, *f. pr. n.* a certain place.

चन्देल = (1) चन्दील (2) चन्देरी, *qq. v.*

चन्देला = चन्दील, *q. v.*

चन्देली, *f.* a very fine sort of cotton fabric (manufactured at Chandēl) so costly as to be used in native

चन्दैया, deep places. [courts only.

चन्दोआ }
चन्दोया } = चन्दवा, *q. v.*
[of a certain mountain.

चन्द्र, *m.* the moon ; a moonlike spot : the name

चन्द्रक, *m.* the eye in a peacock's tail : a finger-nail.

चन्द्रकला, *f.* a digit or one sixteenth part of the moon's diameter ; a lunar crescent.

चन्द्रका, *more prop.* चन्द्रिका, *q. v.*

चन्द्रकान्त, *m.* the moon-stone (a fabled gem supposed to be formed of the congealed rays of the moon).

चन्द्रकान्ता, (*f.* ?) (1) = चन्द्रकान्त, *q. v.* : (2) the wife of the moon ; the night. [influence of the moon.

चन्द्रकाल, *m.* (in Astrol.) death occasioned by the

चन्द्रगुप्त, *m.* the fabled registrar of the court of Yam.

चन्द्रगोल, *m.* the disc of the moon.

चन्द्रग्रहण, *m.* a lunar eclipse.

चन्द्रजोत, *f.* moonlight ; blue light.

चन्द्रजोती, *f.* a proper name of females.

चन्द्रदूत, *m.* a messenger from the moon (the planet being regarded in this word as a deity).

चन्द्रदेव, *m.* the moon (regarded as a deity).

चन्द्रभाग, *m. pr. n.* one of the mountains of the Himālaya range in which the river Chenāb is said to have its source.

चन्द्रभागा, *f. pr. n.* a name of the river Chenāb (which is one of the five streams of the Panjāb).

चन्द्रमणि, *m.* = चन्द्रकान्त, *q. v.*

चन्द्रमण्डल, *m.* the moon's disc. [of Atri.

चन्द्रमा, *m. pr. n.* (1) of the moon (2) of the son

चन्द्रमामणि ; see (1) चन्द्रमणि (2) चन्द्रमामुनी.

चन्द्रमामुनी, *m. pr. n.* the son of Atri-Muni.

चन्द्रमुख, *m.* (*f.* ā *or* ī) = चन्द्रवदनी, *q. v.*

चन्द्रमौलि, *m.* the moon-crested one, *i.e.* Shiv.

चन्द्ररेखा, *f.* a digit of the moon.

चन्द्ररेणु, *m.* a poetical thief, plagiarist.

चन्द्रलेखा, *f.* 1, a digit of the moon : 2, a certain plant (*Serratula anthelmintica*) : 3, a species of metre.

चन्द्रलोक, *m. pr. n.* the sphere or heaven of the moon.

चन्द्रवंश, *m.* (the lunar race) a certain race or dynasty of Kshatriyas who claim descent from the moon. [race.

चन्द्रवंशी, *m.* (*f.* inī) appertaining to the lunar

चन्द्रवदन, *m.* (*f.* ā) = चन्द्रवदनी, *q. v.*

चन्द्रवदनी, an epithet of any person with a very beautiful face ; *lit.* moon-faced.

चन्द्रवल्लरी, *f.* the moon-plant (*Asclepias acida*) : rue.

चन्द्रबाला, *f.* large cardamums.

चन्द्रबिन्दु, *m.* the nasal sign ँ. It is very seldom used in Hindee works, *anuswār* being used instead of it.

चन्द्रबिम्ब, *m.* the disc of the moon.

चन्द्रसम्भव, *f.* small cardamums.

चन्द्रसागर, *m.* an epithet of क्षीरसागर as the place whence the moon first came.

चन्द्रहार, *m.* a sort of necklace composed of circular pieces of gold, silver, etc.

चन्द्रहास, *m.* a scimitar.

चन्द्रा, *m.* (*f.* ī) bald ; intelligent, wise.

चन्द्रातप, *m.* moonlight. [to cease to grow.

चन्द्राना, *n.* to be withered or dried up (as a tree) ;

चन्द्रायना, (in Pros.) a species of metre. [panions.

चन्द्रावलि, *f. pr. n.* one of Krishṇ's female com-

चन्द्रिका, *f.* moonlight, moonbeams : a kind of small fish (*Zeus oblongus*) : large cardamums : *pr. n.* (1) of a certain woman (2) of a certain river (3) of a certain metre. [barber : an epithet of Shiv.

चन्द्रिल, *m.* a potherb (*Chenopodium album*) : a

चन्द्रोदय, *m.* moon-rise : a cloth or sheet spread as an awning over the large open courts of Hindoo houses, etc. on the occasions of festivals : a kind of collyrium.

चन्द्रोपल, *m.* (see चन्द्रमणि) the moon-gem.

चन्वा, *m.* light, moonlight.

चन्सुर, *m.* cresses (*Lepidium sativum*).

चपकन, *f.* a tightly-fitting sort of coat, a cassock.

चपकना, *a. int.* to collapse.

चपकन्दार, *m.* a vest like a *chapkan*.

चपक़लिश, *f.* a crowding, want of room.

चपका, *m.* the goat-sucker (*Caprimulgus*).

चपकाना, *t.* to cause to adhere, stick on ; to com-

चपटना, *n.* to be flattened. [press ; to threaten.

चपटबाज़, femina libidini sapphicae indulgens.

चपटबाज़ी, *f.* congressus libidinosus duarum mulierum. [level or even (as ground).

चपटा, *m.* (*f.* ī) flattened, compressed, shallow;

चपटाना, *t.* to flatten.

चपटिहो, *f.* a kind of insect.

चपटी, *f.* congressus mulierum. —*khelnā* or *laṛna*, libidini sapphicae indulgere. [in eating.

चपड़चपड़, *m.* the noise which the mouth makes

चपड़ना, *a. int.* to flee; to desist; to deny.

चपड़ा, *m.* a kind of lac: clear land.

चपड़ाऊ, 1, *m.* slippers: 2, brazen-faced.

चपड़ाना, *t.* to falsify; to brazen.

चपड़ी, *f.* cakes of cowdung.

चपना, *m.* to be abashed, be bashful in company; to be squeezed, be crushed: *a. int.* to blush, submit, stoop.

चपनी, *f.* a lid, cover, top (small); the kneepan. — *chāṭnā*, to be contented with a little; *lit.* to lick the potlid. —*bhar pānīmeṅ* (or *leke*) *dūb marnā*, to be greatly abashed; *lit.* to drown oneself in a saucerful of water.

चपरास, *f.* a buckle, breastplate, clasp, badge.

चपरासी, *m.* a messenger or other servant so called from his wearing a *chaprās*.

चपरि, quickly, instantly, forthwith. [bling *chanā*.

चपरी, *f.* a puddle: a small species of pulse resem-

चपल, *m.* (*f.* ā) an unsteady person, etc.: *lit.* unsteady, shaking, wavering, tremulous, restless, volatile, wanton; expeditious, swift: *adv.* swiftly.

चपलगिड़ी, *f.* a kind of lizard.

चपलता, *f.*
चपलत्व, *m.*
चपलपन, *m.* } = **चपलाई**, *q. v.*

चपला, *f.* (of **चपल**) an epithet of the goddess Lakshmee; a wanton, a whore: lightning.

चपलाई, *f.* fickleness, inconstancy, unsteadiness.

चपलात्मक, *m.* (*f.* ikā) of a fickle, unsteady, inconstant nature. [Oriental shoe lacks the heel piece.

चपात, a shoe or slipper that has a heel-piece. The

चपाता, *m.*
चपाती, *f.* } a thin cake of unleavened bread.

चपाना, *t.* to abash; to pile, place one thing upon another.

चपेट, 1, *m.* the palm of the hand with the fingers extended: 2, *f.* a sudden misfortune, risk: a blow, slap.

चपेटा, 1, *m.* a slap, blow: 2, *m.* (*f.* ī) a bastard,

चपेटी, *f.* an old worn-out turban. [illegitimate.

चपेरास्त, *m.* unsteadiness, want of principle, carelessness; *lit.* left and right.

चप्पन, *m.* a lid or cover of a pot (large).

चप्पल, *f.* a slipper. —*mārnā*, to beat with a

चप्पलसेंढ (= **नागफनी**) the prickly pear. [slipper.

चप्पा, *m.* a hand-breadth, span.

चप्पी, *f.* kneading the limbs, shampooing.

चप्पू, *m.* a paddle, oar. — *mārnā*, to row.

चप्रास = **चपरास**, *q. v.*

चफूत, *m.* a prop: an arbour. [mire.

चफाल, *f.* a place surrounded with marshes and

चबनीहड्डी, *f.* cartilage, gristle.

चबमाक, a corruption of **चकमाक**, *q. v.*

चबलाना, *t.* to chew slowly.

चबवाना, *t.* to cause to chew.

चबाई, *f.* mastication.

चबाभोला, *m.* (*f.* ī) childish, puerile.

चबाना, *t.* to chew, gnaw, champ, masticate, bite. *Chabā-chabāke bāt k.* to speak with study or preparation; to speak without reserve, speak haughtily, speak

चबावला, *m.* (*f.* ī) childish, puerile. [scornfully.

चबूतरा = **चबूत्रा**, *q. v.*

चबूत्रा, *m.* a terrace or mound to sit upon and converse; a custom-house, police-station, guard-house, tribunal or court of justice; a market-place; a boundary mark.

चबेना, *m.* = **चबेनी**, *q. v.*

चबेनी, *f.* parched grain to exercise the teeth with when more substantial food is not at hand.

चब्बा, a corruption of **चौवा**, *q. v.*

चभक, *f.* sting. [flash, glare, gleam.

चमक, *f.* (*m.*?) glitter, splendour, brilliancy, lustre,

चमकटमक, *f.* splendour, refulgence, glitter.

चमकता, *m.* (*f.* ī) bright, glistening, flashing.

चमकना, *a. int.* to glitter, shine, flash, glare, startle, throb; to prosper; to become angry.

चमकवर्णी; see **चम्पकवर्णी**.

चमकवाना = **चमकाना**, *q. v.*

चमका, *m.* (*f.* ī) shining, glistening, flashing, flaring; prosperous; angry. [liancy, much light; flourish.

चमकाई, *f.* glitter, splendour, brightness, bril-

चमकाना, *t.* to cause to glitter, to burnish, brighten, brandish, flourish, wave, display; to cause to start, [startle, provoke.

चमकाव, *m.*
चमकाहट *f.* } = **चमकाई**, *q. v.*

चमकी, *f.* glitter: a spangle.

चमकीला, *m.* (*f.* ī) glittering, splendid.

चमगदल, *m.* the flying fox (*Pteropus edulis*); a bat.

चमगादड़, *m.*
चमगिदरा, *m.*
चमगीदड़, *m.*
चमगुदड़ी, *f.* } = **चमगदल**, *q. v.*

चमच, *more prop.* (1) **चमचा** (2) **चमस**, *qq. v.*

चमचड़क = **चमचड़ख़**, *q. v.*

चमचड़ख़, 1, lean, meagre: 2, *m.* a bat.

चमचमाना, *a. int.* to tingle; to sparkle, glitter,

चमचमाहट, *f.* brightness. [shine; to sleep.

चमचरक, *more prop.* **चमचड़ख़**, *q. v.*

चमचा, *m.* a spoon. —*bhar*, a spoonful.

चमड़ा, *m.* a hide: leather, skin. — *udheṛnā* or *khainchnā* or *churānā* or *nikālnā*, to flay.

चमत्काकर, a corruption of **चमत्कार**, *q.v.*

चमत्कार, 1, *m.* surprize, astonishment, amazement; splendour: 2, *f.* name of a grass: haste.

चमत्कृत, *m.* (*f.* ā) astonished, surprized.

चमत्कारी, *m.* (*f.* iṇī) a sagacious person, etc.: *lit.* astonishing, surprizing, unusual, acute, sagacious.

चमन, *m.* a bed of a garden, a parterre.

चमर, *m.* (*f.* ī) the *Bos gruniens*: the tail of this animal when used to whisk off flies and other insects.

चमरख, *f.* the apparatus of a spinning-wheel: *met.* a lean woman.

चमरनी, 1, *more com.* **चमारनी**, *q.v.*: 2, = **चमरी**, *q.v.*

चमरबगली, *f.* a bittern.

चमरा, an old form of **चमड़ा**, *q.v.*

चमरावट / **चमरावत** the perquisites of a **चमार**, *q.v.*

चमरी, *f.* the female of the Yak (*Bos gruniens*) of whose tail the "chauree" is usually made.

चमरीगो = **चमरी**, *q.v.*

चमला, *m.* / **चमली**, *f.* a mendicant's cup, begging-dish.

चमस, *m.* a kind of ladle or spoon used at sacrifices for drinking the juice of the acid asclepias: a species of plant (*Mollugo pentaphylla*) commonly called [*Khetpaprā*.

चमाई, *m.* (*f.* ini) copper-coloured.

चमाऊ / **चमाऊं** *f.* slippers or shoes fixed to pattens.

चमान, a giving oneself airs, walking haughtily; walking gracefully. [Panipat Bargar.

चमायन, *pr. n.* a small clan of the *gūjar* tribe in

चमार, *m.* (*f.* in, ī, *or* nī) a leather-worker, currier, tanner, shoe-maker. [at hides and leather.

चमारकार, *m.* (*f.* ī) a person of low caste who works

चमारनी / **चमारिन** = **चमारी**, *q.v.*

चमारी, *f.* (*m.* **चमार**) a leather-worker's wife, any female of the caste who work in leather.

चमी, real, true, significant.

चमू, *f.* an army; a squadron, division of an army.

चमूकन, *m.* a kind of tick or louse that infests cattle.

चमेटा, *m.* a box, thump, blow. [oil.

चमेली, *f.* a kind of flower which yields a fragrant

चमोटा, *m.* / **चमोटी**, *f.* a razor-strop.

चम्प, *m.* mountain ebony (*Bauhinia variegata*).

चम्पई = **चम्पकवर्णा**, *q.v.*

चम्पक, *m.* 1, = **चम्पा** 1, *q.v.*: 2, a division of the jack-fruit: 3, *pr. n.* a certain ancient Hindoo king.

चम्पकवर्णी, of the colour of the champā-flower, *i.e.* gold-coloured, orange-coloured. [India ('Chumparun').

चम्पकारण्य, *m. pr. n.* a certain district in northern

चम्पकेश्वर, *m. pr. n.* a certain ancient Hindoo king.

चम्पट *honā* or *ho jānā*, to vanish, disappear, scamper off, run away.

चम्पत = **चम्पट**, *q.v.*

चम्पनों, (Chand) to be hid: to creep.

चम्पा, 1, *m.* a certain tree (*Michelia champaca*) bearing a fragrant yellow flower: 2. *f. pr. n.* a certain [town.

चम्पाई, see (1) **चमाई** (2) **चम्पई** (3) **चम्पा**.

चम्पाकलि / **चम्पाकली** = **चम्पाकाली**, *q.v.*

चम्पाकाली, *f.* a necklace each piece of which resembles the unblown flowers of the *champā*.

चम्पाकेला, *m.* a small kind of plantain.

चम्पाकेली, *f.* = **चम्पाकेला**, *q.v.*

चम्पानगरी / **चम्पापुरी** *f. pr. n.* (= **चम्पा**) a certain town.

चम्पावरनी, *f.* a name or an epithet of females.

चम्पावती, *f. pr. n.* the district of Champā or Bhāgalpore (abounding in ebony-trees).

चम्पि, (Chand) stealthily, secretly; in.

चम्पी, *m.* (*f.* inī) orange-coloured.

चम्पू, *f.* a literary work in which the same subject is continued through alternations in prose and verse.

चम्बल, 1, *m.* a mendicant's cup, begging-dish: 2, *f. pr. n.* a river in Bundēlkhand: 3, a log of wood with grooves fixed on the banks of canals, and used in drawing water for irrigation.

चम्बला, *m.* a mendicant's cup, begging-dish.

चम्बा, *m.* a tribe of beggars who cut or scarify their skin.

चम्बार, *m.* 1, = **चमार**, *q.v.*: 2, an executioner.

चम्बू, *m.* a narrow-necked vessel for holding water, commonly called a 'goglet'.

चम्बेली, *f.* the flower *Jasminum grandiflorum*.

चम्मल, *m.* a mendicant's cup, begging-dish.

चय, *m.* a heap, mass, assemblage, collection, multitude; a rampart consisting of a mound of earth raised from the ditch of a fort; a mound of earth raised to form the foundation of a building.

चयन, a corruption of **चैन**, *q.v.*

चर, 1, *m.* a ford, shoal, sandbank, island in the current of a river: the sound made by tearing cloth, etc.: a wagtail: pasture, forage, food: 2, *m.* (*f.* ī) a spy, secret agent: 3, *m.* (*f.* ā *or* ī) a termination of many adjectival substantives in Hindee importing the idea of 'moveable', 'moving', 'practising'.

चरक, *m.* 1, (*f.* ikā) a spy, secret agent: 2, leprosy: 3, *pr. n.* (1) of a treatise on medicine (2) of its author.

चरकटा, *m.* a person who cuts forage for cattle; an elephant-keeper's mate.

चरका, 1, *m.* a small wound, scratch: 2, *m.* (*f.* ī) white-spotted (as from leprosy).

चरकी, *m.* (*f.* inī) a leper.

चरख़, *m.* a wheel (particularly a potter's); the sky, heavens, celestial sphere; circular motion; fortune, chance: a bow in a very tense state, crossbow: a hyena. — *charnā*, to dress or adorn oneself; to turn (as in a lathe). — *mārnā*, to circulate (as the blood).

चरख़अन्दाज़, an expert archer.

चरख़ज़न, *m.* a spinner.

चरख़ज़नी, *f.* a spinning-wheel; spinning.

चरख़पूजा, *f.* a certain penitential ceremony observed by the lower orders of Hindoos on the day on which the sun enters Aries. They are suspended by an iron hook thrust through the flesh of the back to one end of a lever which is raised on the top of a high pole and whirled around by means of a rope fixed to the other end. The observance is held to be very effectual in the expiation of sin, and, like others of the more self-denying ceremonies of the Hindoos, has often been done by proxy for those who are rich enough to pay accordingly. It is now practised much less frequently than formerly.

चरख़ल, aged and decrepit.

चरख़ा, *m.* a spining-wheel, reel. *Tum apne charkhemeṅ tel lāgṅo*, mind your own business; *lit.* oil your own wheel.

चरखाऊ, *m.* a beast, quadruped.

चरख़ी, *f.* (dim. of **चरख़ा**) a small spinning-wheel; a pulley; the instrument with which the seed is separated from cotton; a globe; catherine-wheels (a kind of fire-work); a dumb waiter; the pulley by which water is raised from a well; a round piece of wood fixed over the top of a tentpole upon which the fly of the tent rests.

चरख़ीदव्वार, *m.* the visible heavens, sky.

चरख़ीफ़ानूस, *f.* a kind of magic lantern which revolves by the smoke of the candle within. It is made of some transparent substance and has pictures all round its sides.

चरच; see (1) **चरचना** (2) **चर्चा**.

चरचना, *t.* to perfume the body of any one by plastering him all over with sandal-wood, etc.

चरचर, *m.* a prating, chattering; an imitative sound.

चरचरा, *m.* (*f.* ī) talkative, chattering.

चरचराना, *a. int.* to crackle (as wood in the fire), to sputter; to chew with a cracking noise; to chide, scold, fret.

चरचा, *more prop.* **चर्चा**, *q.v.*

चरचार, *m.* a crumb.

चरचूँ, *m.* an imitative sound (as of a wheel, carriage, etc.); idle prattle.

चरचेला, *m.* (*f.* ī) a chatterer, prater.

चरचैत, *m.* a reasoner; a mentioner.

चरट, *m.* a wagtail.

चरण, *m.* the foot; a foot in verse; a foot-soldier; shoes; practice, good conduct, fixed observances; a school; a verse.

चरणकमल = **कमलचरण**, *q.v.*

चरणचिह्न, *m.* a footmark, footprint.

चरणन, a Braj pl. of **चरण**. See **न**, 6.

चरणपतन, *m.* falling at one's feet, prostration.

चरणपतित, *m.* (*f.* ā) fallen at one's feet, prostrated.

चरणपीठ, *m.* a wooden shoe; a footstool.

चरणरज, *m. f.* the dust of the feet.

चरणरक्षक, shoes.

चरणसरोज, *m.* the lotus-like foot, *i. e.* of a deity, lover, etc.

चरणसेवक, *m.* (*f.* ikā) a devoted attendant: *lit.* adj. serving the feet (of a person).

चरणसेवा, *f.* service, devotion, obsequious attendance.

चरणा, *more prop.* **चरण**, *q.v.*

चरणाभरण, *m.* an ornament for the feet.

चरणामृत (= **चरणोदक**, *q.v.*); *lit.* ambrosia of the feet.

चरणाम्बुज, *m.* the dust of the feet.

चरणारविन्द, *m.* an epithet of the blessed feet of any deity; *lit.* the lotus-feet.

चरणोदक, *m.* the water in which the feet of an idol (or of a Brāhmaṇ or of a *guru* or of a guest) have been washed. —*lenā*, to sip the water in which their feet have been washed.

चरती, *m.* (*f.* inī) one who does not fast.

चरन; for words beginning thus, but not given below, see under the more proper form **चरण**.

चरना, 1, *a. int.* to graze (as quadrupeds do): 2, *m.* half-trowsers.—*charhānā*, to put on half-trowsers.

चरनी, *f.* a manger, stable.

चरन्द, any animal that grazes, a quadruped, beast.

चरन्नी, *f.* (**चार आने**) a silver coin in value four annas.

चरपटा, a small or slight wound.

चरपर, *more prop.* (1) **चरपरा** (2) **चरफर**, *qq. v.*

चरपरा, *m.* (*f.* ī) acrid; hot (as pepper); smart (in conversation).

चरपराना, *a. int.* to smart.

चरपराहट, *f.* smarting; pungency.

चरपरिया, active; ingenious, smart.

चरपूज़, useless, stupid; miserly, mean; wicked.

चरफ़, active, attentive, vigilant.

चरफर, *m.* activity, quickness, cleverness.

चरफरा, *m.* (*f.* ī) active, quick, clever.

चरफराना = **डोलना**, *q.v.*

चरबना, to overcome, prevail.

चरबरा, *m.* (*f.* ī) active, alert, expert.

चरबराकी, *f.* activity, expertness, dexterity.

चरबराना, *a. int.* to practice plausibility, speak smoothly.

चरबाना, *t.* to brace a drum.

चरबी, *f.* fat, suet, grease, tallow. —*kī jhillī*, caul of fat covering the bowels.

चरबीदार, *adj.* fat, greasy.

चरम, 1, *more prop.* **चर्म**, *q.v.*: 2, *m.* (*f.* ā) last, ultimate, final; western, west.

चरमक्ष्माभृत = **चरमाचल**, *q.v.*

चरमाचल, *m.* the mountain in the west behind which the sun is supposed to set.

चरवाई, *f.* (see **आई**, 3) price or rent paid for pasturage.

चरवाना, *t.* to pasture, graze, feed.

चरवाहा, *m.* (*f.* in) a shepherd, grazier, herdsman.

चरवाही, *f.* the wages of a grazier (paid in grain); the occupation of a grazier.—*k.* to take animals to grass.

चरवैया, *m.* a grazier, shepherd, herdsman.

चरस, *m.* a leathern bucket; an urn: the exudation of the flowers of hemp collected with the dew and prepared for use as an intoxicating drug.

चरसा, *m.* a skin, hide.

चराई, *f.* (see **आई**, 3) pasturage, grazing: the price or rent paid for pasturage.

चरागो, *m.* pasture-ground.

चराक, *m.* any animal that grazes.

चराग़, *more prop.* **चिराग़**, *q.v.*

चरागाह, *f.* a pasture : a meadow, pasture-land.

चराचर, *m.* the heavens, sky, atmosphere ; *lit.* moveable and immoveable, animate and inanimate ; moveable, locomotive, unsteady, shaking, tremulous.

चरान, *m.* lea fallow ; a meadow ; a salt marsh or meadow by the sea-shore.

चराना, *t.* to pasture, graze, feed.

चराव, *m.* pasture-ground.

चरावट, *f.* cattle-feeding, pasturing, grazing.

चरावत ; see (1) **चरावट** (2) **चराता** (**चराना**).

चरिका, see **चरक**.

चरित, *m.* (freq. put for **चरित्र**) a fixed institute, proper or peculiar observance ; disposition of mind : *lit.* gone over, gone through ; done, enacted ; customary.

चरित्र, *m.* ancient usages, custom ; conduct, behaviour, temper, bearing, disposition ; quality, manner ; an account of the deeds of anyone, history, procedure, story, adventures ; humour ; talent.

चरिन्द, *more prop.* **चरन्द**, *q.v.*

चरी, 1, *f.* unripe corn cut for the food of cattle : 2, moveable, locomotive ; unsteady, shaking, tremulous.

चरु, *m.* a cauldron : a kind of oblation to the gods (chiefly of milk and butter).

चरुई, *f.* (dim. of **चरुआ**) a small earthen pot.

चरुप्रसाद, *m.* the distribution of the **चरु** by Brāhmaṇs.

चरू, *more prop.* **चरु**, *q.v.*

चरुआ, *m.* a large earthen pot.

चरों, *more prop.* **चारों**, *q.v.*

चरोत्तर, a life-rent grant.

चर्ख़, *more prop.* **चरख़**, *q.v.*

चर्ख़ा, *more prop.* **चरख़ा**, *q.v.*

चर्ग़ीना, *m. f.* wicked, villainous.

चर्चक, *m.* (*f.* ikā) an arguer, a repeater.

चर्चना, *t.* to consider, reflect, apprehend, conceive.

चर्चर, *m.* a prating, chattering ; an imitative sound.

चर्चराना = **चरचराना**, *q.v.*

चर्चा, 1, *f.* a smearing, plastering, anointing, cleaning the person with sandal-wood and other fragrant substances : 2, *m.* a talking over past events, recapitulation of former occurrences, mention, mentioning ; investigation, inquiry ; argument, discussion, deliberation, reflection, consideration, careful perusal, attention to business ; discourse, report ; engagedness ; prevalence ; practising, applying, cultivating (science, etc.) ; adoration.

चर्ची, *m.* (*f.* inī) = **चर्चक**, *q.v.* : 2, *f.* repetition of words in recitation.

चर्चैला, *m.* (*f.* ā) a chatterer, prater.

चर्चित, *m.* a reasoner ; a mentioner.

चर्च्चा = **चर्चा**, *q.v.*

चर्च्ची = **चर्ची**, *q.v.*

चर्ख ; for words beginning thus see under the form **चरख**.

चर्त, *f.* a nap ; drowsiness, nodding, doziness.

चर्बज़बान, *f.* pleasant or agreeable speech.

चर्बदस्त, active, ingenious : *hence*, a thief.

चर्भुजी = **चतुर्भुजी**, *q.v.*

चर्म, *m.* a skin, hide, leather ; a shield.

चर्मकार, *m.* (*f.* ī) a leather-worker, currier, shoe-maker.

चर्मचटका, **चमचटी** } *f.* a bat.

चर्मण्वती, *f. pr. n.* a river (the modern Chambal) that runs across Bandelkhand into the Ganges.

चर्मतरंग, *m.* a wrinkle, fold of the skin.

चर्मन, *m.* skin, hide, bark ; a shield ; the hide on which a student sits (usually that of an antelope).

चर्मपत्र, *m.*, **चर्मपत्री**, *f.* } a hide-manuscript.

चर्ममय, *m.* (*f.* ī) made of leather, consisting of leather, abounding in leather, leathery, leathern.

चर्मवन्त, *m.* (*f.* vatī) covered with leather, leathern.

चर्मवती, *f.* = (1) **चर्मण्वती** (2) **चर्मवन्त**, *qq.v.*

चर्मार = **चमार**, *q.v.*

चर्मी, *m.* (*f.* inī) 1, = **चर्ममय**, *q.v.* : 2, a person armed with a shield, shield-bearer.

चर्या, *f.* a roaming, going, visiting, practising ; perseverance in religious austerities, the due and regular observance of all rites and customs.

चर्रा, *m.* thunder.

चर्राना, *a. int.* to burst ; to ache ; to smart.

चर्वण, *m.* a chewing, masticating, tasting.

चर्षणी, 1, *m.* (*more prop.* **चर्षणि**) men : 2, *f. pr. n.* the wife of Varuṇ.

चर्स = **चरस**, *q.v.*

चल, 1, *f. m.* a going, dispersion : variation ; departure from truth, deception ; failure in the performance of a promise or in the accomplishment of a prediction : 2, *m.* (*f.* ā) trembling ; loose ; fickle : troubled — *denā*, to march (as an army) : to beguile, to deceive.

चलचलाव, *m.* preparation for journey or for departure.

चलचित्त, 1, *m.* = **चलचित्तता**, *q.v.* : 2, *m.* (*f.* ā) a fickle person, etc. : *lit.* fickle, inconstant, mutable.

चलचित्तत्व, *m.* (*f.* tā) fickleness, inconstancy, mutability.

चलत, *m. f.* = **चलता**, 2. *q.v.*

चलता, 1, *m.* a kind of tree (*Dillenia Indica*) producing an acid fruit : 2, *m.* (*f.* ī) moving, going, saleable, current, passable.

चलती चीज़, *f.* a saleable commodity.

चलदल, *m.* the holy figtree.

चलन, 1, *m.* a trembling, moving, swerving : habit, custom, usage, course, fashion, behaviour, conduct, ceremony ; currency : 2, *m.* (*f.* ā *or* ī) tremulous, unsteady : customary, fashionable, current, — *chalnā*, to behave.

चलनता, *m.* (*f.* ī) saleable.

चलनदरी, *f.* a place where water is supplied gratuitously to travellers as an act of charity or of religious merit.

चलना, *a. int.* to move, go, proceed, walk ; to go off, be discharged (as a gun) ; to be current, be in vogue, pass (as coin) ; to blow ; to flow ; to behave ; to sail ; to work, serve, answer the purpose, succeed ; to last ; to stand. *Chalā* (*m.* ; *f.* ī ; *pl.* e) *chalnā* or *jānā*, to go along, be off, depart

चलनी, *f.* 1, = **चलन**, 2, *q.v.* : 2, a sieve, kind of basket for winnowing grain : 3, a kind of short petticoat worn by women of the humbler classes.

चलफेर, *m.* motion.
चलबिचल, *m.* error, mistake.
चलबिधरा, *m.* (*f.* ī) restive.
चलबिधराहट, *f.* restiveness.
चलवय्या, *more prop.* **चलवैया**, *q.v.*
चलवा, *f.* the anchovy (*Clupea cultrata*).
चलवैया, *m.* one who moves about a great deal : [*lit.* adj. wandering, vagrant.
चला, see **चल**, 2.
चलाई, *fem.* of **चलाया** (**चलाना**).
चलाऊ, *adj.* going ; at the point of death ; frail, [fickle, inconstant,
चलाओ, *m.* habit, custom.
चलाओनी, passing, current (as coin).
चलाचल = **चलाचली**, *q.v.*
चलाचलि, reciprocal motion, motion to and fro.
चलाचली, *f.* the bustle of setting out on a journey or of setting about anything : *lit.* adj. moving to and fro, unsteady, tremulous; moveable and stationary.
चलान, *f.* a clearance, remittance ; an invoice, announcement of despatch ; a passport, pass.
चलानदार, one who has charge of an invoice or despatch.
चलाना, *t.* to cause to move, cause to go, cause to pass ; to set a-going, impel, propel, walk ; to actuate, direct, call into play ; to fire (a gun, etc.), shoot at ; to hasten forward, send, do, act, accustom, advance, utter, throw, thrust.
चलायमान, *m.* (*f.* matī) moveable, unsteady, fickle, [unsettled.
चलाव, *m.* habit, custom.
चलावा, *m.* a going ; motion ; custom.
चलित, *m.* (*f.* ā) moveable or personal property, etc.: *lit.* current, in vogue, usual, customary : shaking, trembling : departed, gone.
चलित्र, *more prop.* **चरित्र**, *q.v.*
चलित्री, *m.* (*f.* inī) (prop. **चरित्री**) an affected person, etc.; *lit.* gay, sportive, affected, inconstant, changeable.
चलु = **चलू**, *q.v.*
चलुक, *m.* the hand hollowed for holding a little water, etc. ; a handful of water ; a small pot, gallipot.
चलू, *m.* the ceremony described under **आचमन**.
चलेन्द्रिय, *m.* (*f.* ā) a sensual person, etc. : *lit.* sensitive, sensual, having the passions unsubdued.
चलो, away ! be off ! come along !
चलौना, *m.* a small stick with which the spinning [wheel is turned.
चल्लू, land under cultivation.
चल्यासा, *m.* a lizard.
चल्यो / **चल्यौ** } (in Braj) = **चला**. See **चलना**.
चवत, a poetical form from **चवना**, *q.v.*
चवँर = **चँवर**, *q.v.*
चवकसाई, *more prop.* **चौकसाई**, *q.v.*
चवना, *more prop.* **चूना**, *q.v.* [four times.
चवर, 1, = **चँवर** and **चौर**, *qq.v.* : 2, land ploughed
चवर्ग, *m.* (in Gram.) the name applied to the consonants of the **च**, or palatal, class, *viz.* **च**, **छ**, **ज**, **झ**, **ञ**.

चवाई, *m.* (*f.* inī) a reporter, backbiter.
चवाला, *m.* (*prop.* **चौपाला**) a chair, sedan.
चवालीस, (see **चौआलीस**) forty-four.
चवाव, *m.* a report, slander. [(*Piper chavya*, Roxb.).
चवि, *f.* the pepper-plant which yields long pepper
चविका / **चव्य** } = **चवि**, *q.v.*
चशम, **चश्म** ; see under the form **चश्म**.
चश्म, *f.m.* the eye : hope; an amulet : a fountain.
चश्मक, *f.* a winking.
चश्मनुमाई, *f.* reproof.
चश्मपोशी, *f.* a turning away the eyes, affecting not to see or hear a petitioner, etc. ; connivance.
चश्मा, *m.* spectacles, eyeglasses : a fountain, spring. [let, bowl, cup : spirituous liquor.
चषक, *m.* any drinking-vessel, a wine-glass, gob-
चषति, *m.* decay, infirmity. [ing pain, stitch.
चसक, *f.* pain, ache, throbbing pain, sharp lacerat-
चसकना, *a. int.* to throb, ache. [tom.
चसका, *m.* love, ardent desire; a relish ; habit, cus-
चसना, *a. int.* to burst, split (as tight clothes).
चस्पान, viscous, slimy, cohesive.
चस्म, *more prop.* **चश्म**, *q. v.*
चस्सी, *f.* a species of itch peculiar to the palms of the hand and the soles of the feet (said to be occasioned by insects).
चह, *m.* a well, pit : a platform, pier-head.
चहं, see **चहना**.
चहकना, *a. int.* to whistle or sing (as birds).
चहका, *m.* a kind of fireworks : the smarting of a wound by the application of medicine. — *lagānā*, to burn the skin slightly by fomenting.
चहकार, *f.* the singing or chirping of birds.
चहकारना, *a. int.* to whistle or sing (as birds).
चहकैंट / **चहकैंठ** } brawny, stout.
चहचहा, 1, *m.* (*f.* ī) deeply-coloured : 2, *m.* the song of a bird (*esp.* the melody of the nightingale).
चहचहाट (*contraction*) = **चहचहाहट**, *q.v.* [birds).
चहचहाना, *a. int.* to sing, whistle, chirp, warble (as
चहचहाहट, *f.* the singing or chirping of birds.
चहचहिया, *m.* a whistler, warbler.
चहना, *more prop.* **चाहना**, *q.v.*
चहराकुनना, to calumniate.
चहल, a certain strong kind of soil ranking between *rosli* and *dānkar*, *qq. v.*
चहलना, *a. int.* to become fatigued, grow tired.
चहलपहल, *f.* jollity, merriment, cheer, mirth.
चहला = **चिहला**, *q. v.*
चहली, *f.* the wheel on which the rope revolves [at the top of a well.
चहार, four.

चहिय / चहिये } *more prop.* चाहिये, *q.v.*

चही, *f.* warbling: a snipe (*Teolopax gallinago*).

चहुं, (= चारों) four: the four, all four.

चहुंओर / चहुंचक्र / चहुंदिश / चहुंदिशा / चहुंदिशि / चहुंदिस / चहुंदिसि / चहुंपास } = चारोंओर, *q.v.*

चहुंयुग = चारोंयुग, *q.v.*

चहूं; for words beginning thus, see under the form [चहुं.

चहूंवोर in Braj = चहुंओर, *q.v.*

चहेल, wet oozy land.

चहै, see चहना.

चहों, 1, = चहुं, *q.v.*: 2, see चहना.

चहोरना, *t.* to transplant.

चहोरा, a fine sort of rice.

चा, 1, *f.* tea: 2, this [*m.* (*f.* ī)] is in Marāṭhī the sign of the genitive case, and as such occurs occasionally in Hindee books.

चाईं, 1, *f.* scaldhead: 2, *m.* the name of a low class of Hindoos: the seed of tamarind.

चाईंचूईं, *f.* scaldhead.

चाउ / चाऊ } in Braj = चाओ, *q.v.*

चाए, *m.* eagerness; pleasure; taste.

चाएचोज = चाओचोज़, *q.v.*

चाओ, *m.* eagerness, desire; pleasure; taste: a measure equal to four fingers: a kind of bamboo.

चाओचोचला, fondling and toying, dalliance, fondness, affection, tenderness, endearments, love.

चाओचोज़ = चाओचोचला, *q.v.*

चांक, *m.* a stamp fixed on a stack or heap of grain, or a piece of cowdung placed on the same to protect [it from the evil eye.

चांका = चांक, *q.v.*

चांकना, *t.* to stamp (see चांक).

चांकी, *more prop.* चक्की, *q.v.*

चांगला, *m.* a colour in horses.

चांचरी, a kind of inferior grain (as *mung* or *jawār*).

चांचल्य, *m.* unsteadiness, fickleness, mutability.

चांट, चांड, चांढ, चांप; for all words beginning with either of these forms, see under the forms चाण्ट, चाण्ड, चान्द, चाम्प, respectively.

चांड़, *f.* a prop, support.

चांणूर, *more prop.* चाणूर, *q.v.*

चांया, a corruption of चौया, *q.v.*

चांवसो, *more prop.* चावसे (चाओ).

चांवर / चांवल } in Braj = चावल, *q.v.*

चाक, *m.* a potter's wheel; a wheel of any kind; rings of earth for forming a well; the pulley over which a well-rope passes; a mill, millstone: a narrow opening intentionally left in clothing, a rent, slit, fissure. — *k.* to slit, split, tear, rend.

चाकट, a kind of bracelet.

चाकड़, 1, *more prop.* चाकर, *q.v.*: 2, wide.

चाकर, *m.* (*f.* चकरानी) a servant, attendant.

चाकरान, *m.* (a pl. of the above) servants. — *zamīn*, *f.* lands exempted from revenue dues and appropriated to the maintenance of public officers and servants.

चाकरी, *f.* service, situation, attendance; service-land, a grant in a village for personal services.

चाका, *more prop.* चक्र, *q.v.*

चाकी = चक्की, *q.v.*

चाकू, *m.* a clasp-knife, penknife.

चाक्षुक / चाक्षुख } *more prop.* चाक्षुष, *q.v.*

चाक्षुष, 1, *m. pr. n.* the sixth Manu: 2, *m.* (*f.* ī) peculiar to the eye; perceptible by the eye: relating to Manu Chākshush.

चाखू, *m.* a certain small black seed used as a medicine for diseases of the eyes.

चाख, a name of the नीलकण्ठ, *q.v.*

चाखना, *t.* to taste, relish, enjoy.

चाचर, *m.* the pole around which Hindoos play at their Holee festival; a fair or assemblage of people collected after the Holee.

चाचा = चचा, *q.v.*

चाची = चची, *q.v.*

चाचोज़, see चाओचोज़.

चाट, 1, *m.* a rogue: 2, *f.* longing, wish, relish, taste; a delicacy, *bonne bouche*; habit, custom. — *lenā*, to lick up, lap.

चाटना, *t.* to lick, lap.

चाटा, the vessel that receives the juice of the sugar-cane as it drops from the mill.

चाटी, *f.* a churn.

चाड़, 1, a corruption of चाव, *q.v.*: 2, *f.* turf: a hurt, knock, wound: a lever.

चाड़ पड़ना, to be necessary.

चाड़ी, slander. — *khānā*, to indulge in calumny.

चाणूर, *m. pr. n.* (1) of a certain ancient Hindoo prince (2) of a certain demon-wrestler in the service of Kaṅs slain by Krishṇ.

चाण्टना, *t.* to press, squeeze.

चाण्टी, cesses levied or "squeezed" from artisans and others.

चाण्ड *f.* a prop, support.

चाण्डाल; for words beginning thus, see under the form चण्डाल.

चाण्डूर, *more prop.* चाणूर, *q.v.* (?)

चातक, *m.* a kind of cuckoo (*Cuculus melanoleucus*) supposed to drink only drops of rain.

चातर, *m.* a seine, large fishing-net: a conspiracy.

चातुर, *more prop.* (1) चातर (2) चतुर, *qq.v.*

चातुरवर्ण्य, *m.* (see चतुर्वर्ण) the aggregate of the four Hindoo castes.

चातुरी, *f.* / चातुर्य्य, *m.* } = चतुराई, *q.v.*

चातुर्वर्ण्य, *more prop.* चतुर्वर्ण्य, *q.v.*

चातुर्वर्ण्यदेश, *m. pr. n.* India; *lit.* the country of the four castes.

चातुर्वेद्य = **चौबे**, *q.v.*

चातक, *m.* a sparrow-hawk (*Falco nisus*).

चात्वाल, *m.* any hole in the ground, especially a hole made in the ground to receive a burnt offering.

चादनी, *more prop.* **चान्दनी**, *q.v.*

चादर, *f.* a sheet, tablecloth, mantle, veil; a cascade. — *bichhānā*, to lay the cloth.

चादान, *m.* a teapot, tea-urn.

चानक, see **चांक**.

चान्ना = **चान्दना**, *q.v.*

चान्द, *m.* the moon; the crown of the head, also many other things that are moonlike, *e.g.* the white spot in the forehead of horses and cattle; a target; an ornament; a lunar month. — *chhipānā*, to change as the moon. — *mārnā*, to shoot at a mark. *Chāndne khet kiyā*, the moon has arisen.

चान्दतारा, *f.* a robe made of flowered muslin, etc.

चान्दना, *m.* light, moonlight.

चान्दनापख, *m.* the light fortnight of the moon.

चान्दनी, *f.* the moonbeams, moonlight; a kind of flower; a white cloth spread over a carpet; anything white and shining. — *kā mārā jānā*, to be effected with a disease supposed to be occasioned by a stroke of the moon (said of a horse).

चान्दनीचान्द, *m.* an epithet of the moon.

चान्दनीचौक *m.* a wide and public street or market (of which there is a celebrated one in Delhi).

चान्दनीकरण, *m.* the practise of Brāhmaṇs and others of wounding themselves in order to extort alms or the payment of a debt.

चान्दनीरात, *f.* a moonlight night.

चान्दम, *pr. n.* a certain clan of Rājpoots.

चान्दरात, *f.* the end of the month; *lit.* the night of the (new) moon.

चान्दा, *m.* (see **चन्दा**) a subscription towards raising a certain sum, assessment, quota, share.

चान्दायण = **चान्द्रायण**, *q.v.*

चान्दिनी, *more prop.* **चान्दनी**, *q.v.*

चान्दी, *f.* (dimin. of **चान्द**) the crown of the head; pure silver, plate.

चान्द्र, 1, *m.* the moon-gem; a lunar month; the half-month during which the moon is on the increase: 2, lunar.

चान्द्रभागा = **चन्द्रभागा**, *q.v.*

चान्द्रमस, 1, *m. pr. n.* the constellation *Mrigshira*; stars in Orion: 2, *m.* (*f.* ī) relating to the moon, lunar.

चान्द्रमास, *m.* a lunar month.

चान्द्रायण, *m.* a religious or expiatory fast regulated by the moon's age (it consists in the diminishing the quantity of one's food by one mouthful every day during the dark half of the moon and increasing it in like manner during the light half.

चाप, *m.* a bow.

चापजरीब, gross measurement of the lands on an estate.

चापड़ा, *m.* a cake of cowdung which when dried is used as fuel.

चापन = **चाम्पना**, *q.v.*

चापना, *more prop.* **चाम्पना**, *q.v.*

चापपट, *m.* a certain tree (*Buchanania latifolia*).

चापल, *m.* unsteadiness; quickness.

चापलूस, *m.* a flatterer, wheedler.

चापा, *more prop.* **चाम्पा**. See **चाम्पना**.

चापाटी, *f.* a thin cake of fine bread.

चापी, *m.* (*f.* inī) an archer.

चाफन्द, *m.* a kind of fishingnet.

चाबना, *t.* to prick, thrust in (a pin, nail, etc.); masticate, chew. *Chāb chāb bāteṅ k.* to mince or chew one's words; to speak little and haughtily.

चाबी, *f.* a key.

चाबुक, *m.* a horsewhip. — *phaṭkārnā*, to crack a whip. — *mārnā*, to whip, lash.

चाबुकसवार, *m.* a jockey, horse-breaker; a good rider; a horse-broker.

चाबुकसवारी, *f.* jockeyship, horsemanship.

चाबुकी, *f.* activity, alertness, celerity, despatch.

चाबू, *m.* a chewer: *lit.* adj. chewing.

चाभट पाड़ना, *t.* to crunch, crush.

चाम, *m.* skin, hide, leather. *Chāmke dām chalānā*, to stretch to the utmost a temporary authority; *lit.* to give currency to coins of leather.

चामचोरी, *f.* adulterous connexion with another man's wife.

चामर = **चमर**, *q.v.*

चामरपुष्प, *m.* the betel-nut tree (*Areca faufel* or *Catechu*).

चामीकर, *m.* gold.

चामुण्डा, *f. pr. n.* Durgā.

चाम्प, the lock of a gun; the stocks (used in punishment).

चाम्पना, *t.* to join: to stuff, cram, squeeze, press, thrust in.

चाय *m.* eagerness, pleasure, taste.

चार, 1, four (४): 2, *m.* (*f.* ī) a spy, secret agent; a slanderer.

चारअंगल, *m.* a palm (four inches).

चारअंगली, *f.* a hand's-breadth.

चारआईना, *m.* iron armour.

चारआंख, **चारआंखें** } *f.* = **चारचश्म**, *q.v.*

चारक, *m.* (*f.* ikā) a spy, secret agent.

चारख़ाना, *m.* a kind of cloth; *lit.* chequered.

चारखूंटा, *m.* (*f.* ī) quadrangular.

चारगुणा, *m.* (*f.* ī) fourfold.

चारचश्म, *f.* the meeting of the eyes of two persons, interview, meeting.

चारज़रब, sensible, intelligent (the term is generally applied to slaves).

चारज़ानू, a mode of sitting, *viz.* as tailors sit at their work.

चारजामा, *m.* a kind of saddle (without a tree).

चारटक, broken into four pieces.

चारण, *m.* a strolling player, dancer, mimic, kind of bard, panegyrist; a spy.

चारतक, ambling (pace of a horse).

चारदीवारी, **चारदीवाली** } *f.* a courtyard, inclosure; area.

चारनज़र } चारनज़रें } *f.* = चारचश्म, *q. v.*

चारन; see (1) चारण (2) चारों (3) चालन.

चारना, a dialectic form of चलना, *q.v.*

चारपथ, *m.* a quadrivium, crossing of two roads.

चारपाई, *f.* a bedstead, bed; a litter for carrying the sick; *lit.* four-footed. — *par paṛnā*, to get sick.

चारपाया, *m.* (*f.* ई) a quadruped.

चारपारा, four-pieced, divided into four.

चारबांग, sensible, quick, intelligent, alert.

चारबालिश, *m.* a throne, couch, sofa.

चारबीसी, *m.* fourscore.

चारमग़ज़, *m.* a walnut; an earthen ball with which children play.

चारयारी, *m.* an epithet of a *Sunnī*, from the fact that the Sunnis venerate equally the four successors of Muhammad.

चारवा, *m.* a quadruped; a pony.

चारवां, (usually चैथा) *m.* (*f.* °वीं) fourth.

चारवाक, *m.* the chief of a tribe of atheists; an atheist, sceptic, sophist.

चारवी = चार्वी, *q.v.*

चारशाना, *m. f.* hardy, tough.

चारसाल, a horse of four years old.

चारसू, a cross-road, where two roads cross.

चारा, *m.* 1, food for cattle, fodder, forage; bait for fish: a young plant. — *ḍālnā*, to bait: 2, a remedy, cure, expedient, help, aid.

चाराना, see चराना.

चारि, a corruption of चार, *q.v.*

चारिअवस्था = चारोंदशा, *q.v.*

चारिउ, (1) a Braj emphatic form of चार (2) = चारों, *qq. v.*

चारिदस, *more com.* चौदह, *q.v.*

चारिपद, *m.* the four feet of religion, *viz.* truth, purity, beneficence, and mercy.

चारी, 1, = चार, *q.v.*: 2, *m.* (*f.* iṇī) a foot-soldier, a walker; much used as the latter element in adjectival substantives, importing the idea of going, moving, roaming, existing, acting, etc.

चारु, *m.* (*f.* चार्वी,) a beautiful person, etc.: *lit.* beautiful, handsome, elegant, agreeable, pleasing.

चारुदन्त, *m.* (*f.* ā *or* ī) *adj.* having beautiful teeth.

चारुदेष्ण, *m. pr. n.* (1) of a son of Gaṇḍush (2) of a son of Krishṇ by Rukmiṇī.

चारू, *more prop.* (1) चारु (2) चारों, *qq.v.*

चारेक, 1, = चार एक (see एक): 2, one of four, a fourth part.

चारों, (see ओं) the four, the four of them, all four.

चारोंअवस्था, = चारोंदशा, *q.v.*

चारोंआश्रम, *m.* (see आश्रम) the four religious orders among Hindoos.

चारोंओर, on all four sides, all around, in all directions, circumjacently.

चारोंतरफ़ = चारोंओर, *q.v.*

चारोंदशा, *f.* the four states of man, but more particularly, of the student of the Vedant philosophy, *viz.* (1) जाग्रत, waking (2) स्वप्न, sleeping (3) सुषुप्ति, unconsciousness (4) तुरीय, absorption into the one universal spirit of Brahm.

चारोंपदार्थ, *m.* the four chief things, viz. अर्थ, धर्म, काम, मोक्ष.

चारोंयुग, *m.* (see युग) the four Yugs or epochs of the world, *viz.*—Satya or Krita, Treta, Dvāpar, Kali.

चारोंवर्ण, (see वर्ण) the four chief castes among Hindoos.

चारोंवेद, *m.* (see वेद) the four Veds.

चारोली, *f.* the kernel of a nut.

चार्य्य, *m.* (*f.* ā) the son of a Vrātya or outcaste Vaishya.

चार्वाक, *m.* any philosopher or sophist who holds materialistic or unorthodox opinions, a sceptic, atheist.

चार्वी, *f.* (*m.* चारु) a beautiful woman, a beauty; splendour, light, moonlight; intellect, understanding.

चाल, 1, *m.* the thatch or roof of a house: 2, *f.* a colour in horses, roan: 3, *f.* movement, motion, gait, pace, procedure, method, way, habit, custom, practise. — *chalnā*, to behave. — *pakaṛnā*, to prevail. — *milnā*, to smell a rat.

चालक, *m.* a laxative: *lit.* laxative.

चालचलन, *f. m.* (?) behaviour, course of conduct, deportment.

चालढाल, *f.* motion, procedure, gait, behaviour, manners, breeding, politeness.

चालति = चालती. See चालना.

चालन, *m.* motion, shaking: a sieve, strainer.

चालनहार, *m.* a sifter, one who sifts.

चालना, *t.* to sift: *n.* to be mischievous.

चालनी, *f.* a sieve, strainer.

चालव्यवहार, *f.* (*m.* ?) = चालचलन, *q.v.*

चालह = चाला, 3, *q.v.*

चाला, 1, = चालाक, *q.v.*: 2, *m.* motion, departure; *met.* a lucky moment: 3, *f.* a kind of sprat (*Clupea cultrata*, Buch.).

चालाक, active, laborious, hardworking, alert, fleet, nimble, ingenious, clever, sharp.

चालाकदस्त, expert of hand, dexterous.

चालाकदस्ती, *f.* expertness, dexterity.

चालाकिया, *more com.* चालाकी, *q.v.*

चालाकी, *f.* activity, alertness, celerity, nimbleness, sharpness, boldness.

चाली, *m.* (*f.* iṇī) a mischievous person, etc.: *lit.* roguish, wicked, mischievous.

चालीस, forty (४०): see ओं, वां, वीं, वे, वें.

चालीसवां, *m.* (*f.* वीं) fortieth; hence, the fortieth day of ceremonial impurity, *i. e.* the fortieth day after the death of a kinsman, after child-birth, etc.; the festival or ceremony held on such day.

चालीससुतून, *m.* a pavilion, palace, etc., having forty (*i. e.* a great many) pillars.

चालीसा, *m.* the fortieth year of any era of a century; an aggregate of forty; a period of forty days; a quarantine; a dimness of sight which is supposed to come on at forty years of age, and often to be removed on approaching the forty-eight or fiftieth year.

चाल्लीस, *more com.* चालीस. *q.v.*

चालीसी, *f.* quarantine, a period of forty days abstinence kept after the death of a kinsman, child-birth, etc.

चावंक, a corruption of चाबुक, *q.v.*

चाव = चाओ, *q.v.*

चावचोचला } चावचोज़ } = चाओचोचला, etc., *qq.v.*

चावड़ी, *f. pr. n.* a place in Delhi; a caravansery.

चावल, *m.* (see **भात**) uncooked rice.

चाशनी, *f.* taste, flavour, relish, mixture of sweet and sour: trial, proof, specimen.

चाशिनी, *more prop,* (1) **चाशनी** (2) **चाषिणी**, *qq. v.*

चाशी, *more prop.* **चाषी**, *q. v.*

चाश्त, *f.* the hour midway between sunrise and the meridian; also what is eaten at that time, breakfast, a collation.

चाष, *m.* the blue jay (*Coracias Indica*).

चाषी, *m.* (*f.* iṇī) a ploughman. [plough.

चास, (prop. °**ष**) *f.* ploughing, cultivation. — *k.* to

चासकू, *more prop.* **चाखू**, *q. v.*

चासना, (prop. °**ष**) *t.* to plough, till, cultivate.

चासनी, *f.* a pan in which the juice of the sugar-cane is boiled. [tiller, husbandman.

चासा, (prop. °**ष**) *m.* (*f.* ī) a cultivator, ploughman,

चासाचासी, *f.* tilling, ploughing, cultivation.

चासी, (prop. °**ष**) 1, *m.* (*f.* inī) = **चासा**, *q. v.*: 2, *f.* = **चासाचासी**, *q. v.*: 3, *f.* (*m.* **चासा**) a ploughman's wife.

चाह, 1, *f.* desire, inclination, volition, will, wish, longing, craving, love, liking, zest, appetite, affection, choice, want: 3, *m.* a pit, well. [fectionate, friendly.

चाहक, *m.* (*f.* ikā) longing, desirous, craving, af-

चाहकन, *m.* a well-digger.

चाहचित, *f.* love, affection, dalliance.

चाहज़नख़, *f.* the dimple of the chin.

चाहट } *more com.* **चाह**, 1, *q. v.*
चाहत }

चाहना, 1, as an infinitival substantive, *f.*: 2, *t.* to love, desire, wish for, will, want, demand, require, need, choose; to pray, ask for, crave, entreat; to approve of; to attempt, try; to see, look to, look for.

चाहा, *m.* = **चाह**, *q. v.*

चाहाचाही, *f.* the love of one's country.

चाहि = **चाहके**; see **चाहना**, 2.

चाहिए, *more com.* **चाहिये**, *q. v.*

चाहिका, see **चाहक**.

चाहियतु in Braj = **चाहिये**, *q. v.*

चाहियत, *more prop.* (1) **अब चाहिये** (2) **मैं चाहूंगा**.

चाहिये, (the respectful imperat. of **चाहना**, commonly used as an impers. verb) it is necessary, it is obligatory, it behoves, it is becoming, proper, or befitting, it is expedient, it is desirable.

चाहिरा } a certain tribe of Rājputs in Hisar.
चाहिल }

चाही, 1, = **चहो**, *q. v.*: 2, = **चाह**; 3, relating to a well.

चाहीत; see **चाहीता**.

चाहीता, *m.* (*f.* ī) a sweetheart, beloved one: *lit.* agreeable, desired, wished, beloved.

चाहींती, *f.* (*see above*) a mistress, etc.

चाहुवान in Chand = **चौहान**, *q. v.*

चाहे — चाहे (*lit.* choose: 2nd pers. sing. condit.) either — or, whether — or.

चाहो — चाहो (pl.) = **चाहे — चाहे**, *q. v.*

चाहोचोज़ = **चाओचोज़**, *q. v.*

चिउंटी }
चिऊपटी } *more prop.* **चीऊपटी**, *q. v.*
चिउटी }

चिउपटा, *more prop.* **चीऊपटा**, *q. v.*

चिंगट, *m.* }
चिंगड़ा, *m.* } a shrimp, prawn.
चिंगड़ी, *f.* }

चिंगनी, *f.* } a chicken.
चिंगा, *m.* }

चिंगारी, *f.* a spark (of fire).

चिंगी, *f.* a spark (of fire): a wicked dwarf. — *chhūṭnā* or *jharnā* or *nikalnā*, to sparkle.

चिंघनी, a corruption of **चिंगनी**, *q. v.*

चिंघाड़, *f.* a scream, screech, clamour. — *chinghāreṅ* or *chinghāṛ mārnā*, to scream.

चिंघाड़ना, *a. int.* to scream, screech (the elephant).

चिंघाड़ा, *m.* = **चिंघाड़**, *q. v.* [children).

चिंचा, *m.* tamarind-stones (used as playthings by

चिंत, **चिंद**; for all words beginning thus see under the forms **चिन्त**, **चिन्द**, respectively.

चिक, *f.* a pain in the loins: a screen or blind made of spilt bamboo.

चिकट, sticky, adhesive, gummy.

चिकटा, *m.* a kind of *tasar* cloth.

चिकटी, *f.* a clayey or sticky soil.

चिकठा, *m.* (*f.* ī) an oil-dealer, etc.: *lit.* greasy, filthy.

चिकण, for words beginning thus, see under one or other of the forms **चिकन** or **चिक्कण**.

चिकन, *m.* a particular mode of working flowers on muslin or other cloth, embroidery.

चिकनकारी, *f.* the executing *chikan*-work.

चिकनगर } *m.* an executor of *chikan*-work.
चिकनदोज़ }

चिकना, 1, *m.* oil, grease: 2, *m.* (*f.* ī) an incontinent person, etc.: *lit.* clean, smooth, sleek, slippery, glossy, polished, beautiful; greasy, oily, fat, slimy, unctuous; bland, mild, soft; incontinent, lewd, wanton.

चिकनाई, *f.* fat of meat, grease; greasiness, unctuousness; smoothness, gloss, polish; incontinence, etc.

चिकनाघड़ा क° = **चिकनाबासन क°**, *q. v.*

चिकनाचान्दा, *m.* (*f.* ī) beautiful.

चिकनाचुपड़ा, *m.* (*f.* ī) funny, humourous, amusing.

चिकनाट = **चिकनाहट**, *q. v.*

चिकनाना, *t.* to clean, smooth, polish.

चिकनाबासन बनना, *n.* to be incontinent, be incorrigible, be deaf to admonition.

चिकनावट } *f.* a clayey, loamy, fat soil.
चिकनावत }

चिकनाहट, *f.* cleanness, smoothness, sleekness, glossiness, beauty; greasiness oiliness, fatness.

चिकनिया, *m.* a beau, a sp rk.
चिकनी, see चिकना, 2.
चिकनीजोरू, *f.* a slippery wife.
चिकनीमिट्टी, *f.* clay, potter's earth. [boiling.
चिकनीसुपारी, *f.* a kind of betel-nut prepared by
चिकनीसूरत, prosperous, flourishing, affluent.
चिकलना, *t.* to masticate, chew (slowly).
चिकसा, *m.* a kind of pulville or perfumed powder
चिकारना, *a. int.* to squeak. [of many ingredients.
चिकारा, 1, *m.* (*f.* ī) useless, worthless, contemptible: 2, *m.* a kind of four-horned antelope found on the banks of the Jumna: a kind of fiddle.
चिकारी, *f.* an insect like a mosquito: smut (ob-
चिकावट, *f.* black clayey soil. [scenity.
चिकित्सक, *m.* a medical practitioner, physician.
चिकित्सा, *f.* the practice of medicine, the healing art, the application of remedies; curing, healing; the attendance of a physician on a patient.
चिकिन, *m.* (*f.* ī) a flat-nosed person.
चिकिल, *m.* mud, mire.
चिकुर, *m.* hair; a lock of hair.
चिकुरा, *m.* (*f.* ī) rashly criminal, inconsiderately guilty, punishing or injuring others without consider-
चिकोरना, *t.* to peck. [ation.
चिकोरा, *m.* (*f.* ī) restless, inconstant.
चिक्क, *m.* a musk-rat.
चिक्कड़, *m.* mud, mire, clay, compost, swamp.
चिक्कट, filthy, covered with grease and dirt.
चिक्कण = चिकना, 2, *q.v.*
चिक्कणी, *f.* the betel-nut.
चिक्कन = चिकना, 2, *q.v.*
चिक्कस, *m.* barley-meal.
चिक्का, *f.* a mouse.
चिक्किणा = चिकना, 2, *q.v.*
चिक्की, 1, *m.* (*f.* inī) a flatnosed person: *lit.* flat-nosed: 2, *f.* a rotten betel-nut.
चिखर, the husk of the चणा, *q. v.*
चिखुरन, *m.* a weed.
चिखुरना, *t.* to weed.
चिखुरवाई, *f.* (see आई, 3) wages for weeding.
चिखूरी, *f.* a squirrel.
चिचड़ा, *f.* a tick or louse (of dogs and sheep).
चिचढ़ी खींचना, *t.* to scrawl; to score.
चिचाना, see चुचाना.
चिचानी, *f.* an aunt (*viz.* a father's brother's wife).
चिचिंडा, *m.* a certain vegetable (*Beta vulgaris*).
चिचियाना, *a. int.* to squeak, shriek, scream, bleat.
चिची, *f.* a woman's bosom; a nipple, teat.
चिचुन्दर, *m.* a musk-rat. [still, be motionless.
चिचोंडा, 1, = चिचिंडा, *q.v.*: 2, — *honā*, to be
चिज, *more prop.* चीज़, *q.v.*

चिट, *f.* a rag, scrap. — *ukharnā*, to splinter, have small pieces knocked off (said of furniture).
चिटका, *m.* a kind of grass or grain: mucus, slime: a place where corpses are burnt.
चिटकाना, see चटकाना.
चिटकारा, *m.* a speck, scar: a cluck with the tongue (occasioned by an acrid taste). — *lagānā*, to brand.
चिटकी, *f.* sunshine.
चिट्ठ, a corruption of चित्त, *q. v.*
चिट्टा, *m.* a silver coin: lit. *m.* (*f.* ī) white, fair. — *ukhāṛnā*, to splinter, knock small pieces off furniture.
चिट्टी, *f.* (see दोगपड़ी चिट्टी) the hen of the little birds called Amaduvades (*Fringilla amandava*).
चिट्ठा, *m.* a memorandum of money paid; the pay of state-servants; a rough note or account; a journal, day-book. [— *ḍhālnā*, to cast lots, vote.
चिट्ठी, *f.* a note, letter, billet; an order, demand.
चिट्ठीतलब, *f.* a summons.
चिट्ठीपत्तर, चिट्ठीपाती } *f.* epistolary correspondence.
चिठी, *more prop.* चिट्ठी, *q. v.* [— *nikālnā*, to banter.
चिड़, *f.* vexation, irritation; aversion, antipathy.
चिड़चिड़हा, see चिड़चिड़ा.
चिड़चिड़ा, 1, *m.* a species of plant (*Achyranthes aspera*): 2, *m.* (*f.* ī) cross, peevish, crabbed, fretful.
चिड़चिड़ाना = चिरचिराना, *q. v.*
चिड़चिड़ाहट, *f.* peevishness, fretfulness. [to fret.
चिड़ना, *n.* to be vexed, be irritated, be provoked:
चिड़न्दोल, *m.* a species of lark.
चिड़पिड़ा, *m.* (*f.* ī) fiery, hot (as pepper); acrid.
चिड़पड़ाहट, *f.* acrimony, crabbedness.
चिड़ा, *m.* (*f.* ī) a sparrow. [jibe, jeer.
चिड़ाना, *t.* to vex, irritate, provoke, offend, mock,
चिड़ालू, peevish, crabbed, fretful. [of sewing.
चिड़िया, *f.* a bird (*esp.* the hen-sparrow): a kind
चिड़ियां, *f.* (pl. of चिड़ी) hen-sparrows.
चिड़ियाख़ाना, *m.* an aviary.
चिड़िवा, *more prop.* चिड़िया, *q. v.*
चिड़िवां, *more prop.* (1) चिड़िया (2) चिड़ियां, *qq. v.*
चिड़ी, *f.* (*m.* चिड़ा) a hen-sparrow.
चिड़ीमार, *m.* birdcatcher, fowler.
चिड़ोया, *more prop.* चिड़िया, *q. v.*
चिढ़, *f.* abhorrence, abomination, dislike, vexa-
चिढ़ाना = चिड़ाना, *q. v.* [tion, provocation.
चिढ़ाव, *m.* a provocation, offending, mocking.
चिढ़ावना = चिड़ाना, *q. v.*
चित, 1, = चितपति, *q. v.*: 2, *f.* (often interchanged with चित्त, *q. v.*) the soul: 3, *f.* a look, glance: 4, supine, lying flat on the back. — *k.* to overcome one's adversary, throw him (in wrestling).
चितइ, चितई, चितईरी; see चितना.
चितकबरा, *m.* (*f.* ī) piebald, spotted, speckled.

चितचाव, that which the heart desires; *prop.* pleasing to the mind, satisfying.
चितचूड़क, *more prop.* **चिताचूड़क**, *q. v.*
चितचेता, attentive, careful, cautious.
चितचोर, *adj.* heart-stealing, heart-alluring: hence, *m.* a heart-ravisher; an epithet of Kṛishṇ.
चितना, 1, *n.* to be painted: 2, *t.* to look, behold, see: 3, *a. int.* to look, appear, seem.
चितपट, a game at wrestling.
चितपित, blotted, stained, defiled, foul. — *k.* to blot paper when writing; to spoil a copy.
चितरना, *t.* to paint.
चितरा, *more prop.* **चित्रा**, *q. v.*
चितराना, *t.* to cause to paint, get painted.
चितलगन, amusing, captivating, pleasant.
चितला, *m.* (*f.* ī) piebald, spotted, speckled.
चितव / **चितवत** } old forms = **चितौता** (**चितौना**).
चितवन, *f.* a sight, look, glance.
चितवना = **चितौना**, *q. v.*
चितवट, *f.* reluctance, repugnance.
चिता, *f.* a funeral pile. It is a heap of dried wood on which the Hindoos burn their dead.
चिताओनी, *f.* a token, warning, admonition.
चितांग, *m.* (*f.* ī) a person lying supine.
चितायता, *f.* a funeral pile.
चिताचूड़क, *m.* a mark where a funeral pile has been; a mausoleum, monument.
चिताना, *t.* to caution, warn, apprize, give an alarm, intimate, remind, suggest, admonish.
चितापिण्ड, *m.* offerings of cakes to the manes at the time of burning a corpse.
चितारना, *t.* to paint.
चितारी, *m.* (*f.* iṇī) a painter.
चितारोहण, *m.* the ascending the funeral pile, the burning with the corpse of a husband.
चितावना an old form = **चिताना**, *q. v.*
चितावनी = **चिताओनी**, *q. v.*
चिति, *f.* a heap; wood raised for burning corpses; an altar: intellect.
चितिका, *f.* a funeral pile.
चितेरा, *m.* (*f.* i) a person who paints flowers, etc. on wood, a painter.
चितैनें in Braj = **चितौना**, *q. v.*
चितौना, *t.* to see, look at, behold.
चितौनी, *f.* a token, warning, admonition.
चितौनें in Braj = **चितौना**, *q. v.*
चित्कार, *m.* a cry, scream, braying of an ass.
चित्त, *m.* the reasoning faculty, mind, understanding, intellect, sense, thought, memory, heart, soul, life. — *k.* to make up one's mind. — *denā* or *lagānā* or *lānā*, to pay attention, apply the mind to.
चित्तड़, the buttocks, hips, thighs.
चित्तड़ान बजाना, to evince pleasure, rejoice.
चित्तचाउ; see **चाओ**.
चित्तपिण्ड, *more prop.* **चितापिण्ड**, *q. v.*
चित्तप्रसन्नत्व, *m.* (*f.* tā) joy, happiness, gaiety.
चित्तरमूल, *m.* a certain plant (*Plumbago zeylanica*).
चित्तल = (1) **चित्रल** (2) **चीतल**, *qq. v.*
चित्तवन; see **चितवन**.
चित्तवान, *m.* (*f.* vatī) kindhearted, amiable.
चित्तविभ्रम, *m.* derangement, madness.
चित्ता, 1, = (1) **चित्तरमूल** (2) **चिन्ता** *qq. v.*: 2, *m.* the application of a blister: 3, *m.* (*f.* ī) lying down, reclining: white.
चित्ताभोग, *m.* consciousness of pleasure or pain, attention of the mind to its own sensations.
चित्ती, 1, = **क्षिति**, *q. v.*: 2, see **चित्ता**, 3: 3, *f.* a scar, spot, freckle:— *lānā*, *t.* to scar: a kind of serpent: a cowrie worn smooth by friction: mildew or rot in cloth. — *khānā*, to become mildewed or rotten (as damp cloth).
चित्तीदार, speckled, freckled, spotted.
चित्य, *m.* any mark of the site of a funeral pile, a monument, tomb.
चित्या, *f.* a funeral pile.
चित्र, 1, *m.* a wonder, surprising appearance; a spot; a painting, picture, delineation, writing, etc.: a circular ornament, sectarial mark on the forehead; 2, *m.* (*f.* ā) variegated, spotted, speckled; various, fluctuating; uncommon, wonderful.
चित्रंगी, *m.* (*f.* inī) a versatile person, etc.: *lit.* versatile, unsteady, deceitful.
चित्रकम्बल, *m.* a variegated carpet; a painted cloth used as an elephant's housing.
चित्रकर, *m.* (*f.* ā) a portrait-painter.
चित्रकरण, 1, *m.* = **चित्रकारी**; 2, *m.* (*f.* ī) = **चित्रकर**.
चित्रकार, *m.* (*f.* ī) a portrait-painter.
चित्रकारी, *f.* the art of portrait-painting.
चित्रकूट, *m. pr. n.* a mountain in Bandelkhaṇḍ, (the modern Compteh), — the first habitation of Rām in his exile.
चित्रकेतु, *m. pr. n.* a certain ancient Hindoo king.
चित्रगर = **चित्रकर**, *q. v.*
चित्रगुप्त, *m. pr. n.* (1) of Yam (2) of Yam's registrar, the recording angel who registers the virtues and the vices of mankind.
चित्रग्रीव, *m. pr. n.* the king of the pigeons; *lit.* the spotted-necked.
चित्रदेव, *m. pr. n.* one of Skand's attendants.
चित्रदेवी, *f.* a certain plant: *pr. n.* a daughter of Indra.
चित्रनेत्रा, *f.* the *mainā*-bird.
चित्रपट, a picture: variegated cloth.
चित्रपदा, *f.* a species of creeper (*Cissus pedata*): a kind of metre.
चित्रपर्णिका, *f.* name of certain plants (1) *Hemionites cordifolia*, Roxb. (2) *Rubia manjeth* or Bengal madder.
चित्रपर्णी = **चित्रपर्णिका**, *q. v.*
चित्रपादा, *f.* the *mainā*-bird.
चित्रबट, *m.* a kind of tree: *pr. n.* a certain king.
चित्रभोजन, *m.* change of diet, the eating unusual food.
चित्रल, *m.* the variegated or spotted colour.
चित्ररथ, *m. pr. n.* a certain king of the Gandharvs. Also, the name of many other mythological personages.

चित्ररेखा = **चित्रलेखा**, *q.v.*

चित्रलेखा, *f.* a picture, portrait: (in Pros.) two species of metres: *pr. n.* (1) of a certain Apsaras born from Brahmā's hand (she was a friend of Ūshā, and was skilful in painting) (2) of a daughter of Kumbhāṇḍ minister of king Vāṇ (she too, was a friend of Ūshā).

चित्रवत, *m.* (*f.* vatī) decorated with paintings.

चित्रवती, *f.* a kind of metre (of four lines of 13 syllables each): *pr. n.* a daughter of Gad or (according to some) of Krishṇ.

चित्रवर्ण, the peacock.

चित्रविचित्र, *m.* (*f.* ā) of various colours, variegated, chequered: an epithet of the chameleon.

चित्रसारी, *f.* a kind of garment: a picture.

चित्रशाला, *f.* a picture-gallery, picture-room, hall adorned with pictures.

चित्रसेन, *m. pr. n.* (1) of a snake-demon (2) of a leader of the Gandharvs and son of Vishwā-vasu (3) of a son of Dhrit-rāshtra (4) of a son of Parikshit (5) of a son of Sambar (6) of a son of Narishyant (7) of a son of the 13th Manu (8) of a son Gad (9) of an adversary of Krishṇ (10) of Jarā-sandh's general, Dimbhak.

चित्रा, 1, **चित्र**, 2: 2, *f. pr. n.* the fourteenth Nakshatra (*Spica Virginis*).

चित्रांग, *m.* (*f.* ī) a kind of snake: a kind of plant (*Plumbago zeylanica*): yellow orpiment: vermilion.

चित्रांगद 1, *m.* (*f.* ā) adorned with splendid or variegated bracelets: 2, *m. pr. n.* one of the sons of king Santanu by Satyavatī.

चित्रांगदा, *f.* a female adorned with splendid bracelets.

चित्रिणी, *f.* (see **पद्मिनी**) the second Hindoo division of women; *lit* surprising, beautiful, ravishing.

चित्रित, *m.* (*f.* ā) painted with a variety of colours, variegated, chequered.

चिथड़ा, *m.* a rag, tatter.

चिथड़िया, ragged, tattered, clothed in rags.

चिथाड़ना, *t.* to tear to pieces; to fill a paper with writing or scribbling; to treat with indignity, revile, abuse.

चिदाकाश, an epithet of the all-pervading spirit.

चिदानन्द, an epithet of God as the seat of blessedness.

चिन, *m.* a kind of sugarcane.

चिनग, *f.* ardor urinae.

चिनगना, *a. int.* to throb, shoot, (as a boil, etc.); to cry, screech.

चिनगारी = **चिंगारी**, *q.v.*

चिनगी = **चिंगी**, *q.v.*

चिनचिनाना, *a. int.* to scream, squeak, squall.

चिनांचे (*corruption*) = **चुनान्चि**, *q.v.*

चिनार, *m.* a poplar-tree, plane-tree.

चिनागारी (*corruption*) = **चिंगारी**, *q.v.*

चिनाल, *m.* a kind of high-heeled slipper.

चिनौनी, *f.* a picking out, selecting.

चिन्त = **चिन्ता**, *q.v.*

चिन्तक, *m.* (*f.* ā *or* ī) used as the latter part of compound words importing the idea of 'thinking about', 'caring for'.

चिन्तति = **चिन्तती**: see **चिन्तना**.

चिन्तन, 1, an old pl. of **चिन्त**, *q.v.*: 2, *m.* thinking, way of thinking, study, reflection.

चिन्तना, 1, *f.* = **चिन्तन**, *q.v.*: 2, *a. int.* to think, reflect, study.

चिन्तनीय, requiring to be thought about, capable or admitting of being thought about.

चिन्ता, *f.* (not infl.) thought, care, anxiety, concern, reflection, consideration, doubt; recollection; risk, danger, peril. — *k.* to be anxious about, etc.

चिन्ताकारी, *m.* (*f.* iṇī) anxious, careful, thoughtful.

चिन्ताकुल, *m.* (*f.* ā) disturbed in thought, distracted by any idea.

चिन्ताना, *t.* to cause to study.

चिन्तापर, *m.* (*f.* ā) an anxious person, etc.: *lit.* anxious, thoughtful.

चिन्तामणि, *m.* a certain fabulous gem (supposed to yield its possessor whatever he might desire).

चिन्तायमान, *m.* (*f.* matī) anxious, concerned, thoughtful, careful, full of care.

चिन्तावत } **चिन्तावान** } *m.* (*f.* vatī) = **चिन्तायमान**, *q.v.*

चिन्तावेश्मन, *m.* a council-room, council-house.

चिन्तित, 1, *m.* thought, care, design: 2, *m.* (*f.* ā) thoughtful, reflective, anxious, solicitous, perplexed.

चिन्तिया, *f.* reflection, consideration, thinking.

चिन्दिया; see **चन्दिया**.

चिन्दी, *f.* a small piece, fragment, tatter, scrap of cloth, rags. *Chindi chindi k.* to break, reduce to small pieces.

चिन, *m.* a kind of grain (*Panicum miliaceum*).

चिन्मय, *m.* (*f.* ī) spiritual; all intelligence: hence (1) *m.* an epithet of the Deity (2) *m.* pure intelligence.

चिन्ह, *m.* a mark; a scar, spot, stain; a token by which anything is known, sign, figure, emblem, symbol, feature, signature. — *charhānā*, to stigmatize.

चिन्हचरण, *m.* a footmark, footprint.

चिन्हवाना, *t.* to cause to be recognized.

चिन्हा, see **चीन्हा**.

चिन्हानी, *f.* a mark, sign, token.

चिन्हार. *m.* (*f.* ī) an acquaintance.

चिन्हारी, 1, *m.* (*f.* iṇī) an acquaintance: 2, *f.* acquaintance.

चिन्हित. *m.* (*f.* ā) marked, known, recognized.

चिन्हितनामा, *m.* any list of descriptions or of names.

चिपकना, *a. int.* to adhere, stick; to spread or sink (as ink on damp paper); to collapse, be compressed.

चिपक जाना, *a. int.* to fall in love at first sight: *n.* to be sold on account of its sweetness.

चिपकाना, *t.* to stick on, cause to adhere.

चिपचिपा, *m.* (*f.* ī) clammy, viscid, glutinous, adhesive.

चिपचिपाना, *a. int.* to adhere, cohere, stick.

चिपचिपाहट, *f.* glutinousness, stickiness.

चिपटना, *a. int.* to adhere, cohere, stick.

चिपटा, *m.* (*f.* ī) clammy, viscous, glutinous, adhesive.

चिपटाना, *t.* to sod, turf, stick, apply patches.

चिपड़ाहा, *m.* (*f.* ī) bleared (as the eyes).

चिपड़ी, *f.* small cakes of dried cowdung.

चिपना, *n.* to be concealed.

चिपरा, *m.* gum (of the eyes). [shallow.
चिप्पक, 1, *f.* (*m.* ?) the goat-sucker (a bird): 2,
चिप्पख, *m.* a sparrow-hawk.
चिबाग्रोला } चिबावला } *m.* (*f.* ī) childish, puerile.
चिबिल = चिबिल्ला, *q.v.*
चिबिल्ला, *m.* (*f.* ī) unpolite, childish, boyish.
चिबिल्लापन, *m.* childishness, boyishness.
चिबुक, *f.* the chin. [pointed instrument.
चिबुकनी, *f.* a wound or puncture from any sharp-
चिमगक्षड़ } चिमगादड़ } = चमगादड़, *q.v.*
चिमचिमा, *m.* oil that has become viscous by age.
चिमट रहना, *a. int.* to cleave, adhere.
चिमटना, *t.* to cling to, adhere, cleave to.
चिमटा, *m.* forceps, tongs, pincers, nippers.
चिमटाना, *t.* to stick, cause to adhere.
चिमटी काटना, *t.* to pinch.
चिमठा, *m.* (*f.* ī) elastic, tough.
चिमड़ना = चिमटना, *q.v.* [tough, hardy, hard.
चिमड़ा, *m.* (*f.* ī) ductile, flexible, irrefrangible,
चिमड़ाई, *f.* ductility, flexibility, toughness, power,
चिमड़ाना, *a.int.* to grow tough, toughen. [vigour.
चिमड़ाहट = चिमड़ाई, *q.v.*
चिमड़ी, see चिमड़ा.
चिमसा, *m.* (*f.* ī) glutinous (as oil by keeping).
चिमि, *m.* a parrot: a plant from the fibres of which coarse cloth and rope are made.
चिम्बुक *more com.* चिबुक, *q.v.*
चिय्यूर, *m.* a kind of grass.
चिर, *m.* delay: lit. *m.* (*f.* ā) olden; long (time).
चिरंजी, *more com.* चिरंजीव, *q.v.*
चिरंजीव, 1, *m.* (*f.* ā) long-lived: 2, (a kind of benediction) long may you live!
चिरंजीवना; see चिरजीवना.
चिरंजीविन, *m.* (*f.* ī) } चिरंजीवी, *m.* (*f.* inī) } = चिरजीवी, *q.v.*
चिरकना, *a. int.* to have a scanty stool.
चिरकारी, *m.* (*f.* iṇī) dilatory, tedious, slow.
चिरकाल, 1, *m.* a long period: 2, *adv.* eternally, always. — *se,* long ago, for a long period.
चिरकुट, *m.* a bit, piece; a rag.
चिरकुटिया, *m.* or *f.* a tatterdemalion: *lit.* ragged.
चिरक्रिया, dilatory, tedious, slow.
चिरचिट्टा, *m.* a species of grass.
चिरचिरा, *m.* a child: a certain medicinal plant (*Achyranthus aspera*) said to be of sovereign virtue to one bitten by a venomous reptile or stung by a scorpion, etc.
चिरचिराना, *a. int.* to crackle (as wood in the fire), sputter: to chew with a crackling noise: to chide.
चिरचिराहट, *f.* peevishness, fretfulness. [long.
चिरजीवना, *a. int.* to get to be of a great age, live
चिरजीवी, *m.* (*f.* inī) a person of great age; an epithet (1) of Vishṇu (2) of Mārkaṇḍeya Rishi (3) of any crow; *lit.* long-lived.
चिरयटी, *f.* a young woman, a woman (married or single) who continues, after maturity, to reside in [her father's house.
चिरयहूल, a species of lark.
चिरतिक्त, *m.* a kind of gentian (*Gentiana cherayta*),
चिरत्न, *more prop.* चिरन्तन, *q.v.* [chiretta.
चिरना, *a.int.* (of चीरना) to be split, be torn; to split.
चिरन्तन, old, ancient, longlasting; hereditary.
चिरम, a corruption of चर्म, *q.v.*
चिरवाना, *t.* to cause to tear, cause to be torn.
चिरवेल, *m.* the chay-root or Indian madder.
चिरवाई, *f.* a causing to tear or rend.
चिरस्थायी, *m.* (*f.* inī) long-enduring, remaining or lasting a long time.
चिरायता, a common form of चिरतिक्त, *q.v.*
चिराश्रो, *m.* a rent, fissure.
चिराग़, *m.* a lamp; a light. — *baṛhānā* or *ṭhaṇḍā k.*, to extinguish a lamp. — *meṅ batti parnā*, an expression denoting that evening sets in, that it grows dark, and that it is time to light the lamp.
चिराग़दान, *m.* a lamp-stand. [cause to tear.
चिराना, 1, = पुराना, *q.v.*: 2, *t.* to cause to split,
चिरान्द, *f.* the smell of burning leather, hair, etc.
चिरायु, *m.* a deity: *lit.* long-lived.
चिरियटी = चिरयटी, *q.v.*
चिरैता = चिरायता = चिरतिक्त, *q.v.* [the tree itself.
चिरोंजी, *f.* the nut of the *Chironjia sapida*; also
चिरौरी, *f.* a beseeching, requesting, begging.
चिर्क, *m.* dirt, filth, ordure; matter.
चिलक, *f.* refulgence, glitter.
चिलकना, *a. int.* to glitter, shine.
चिलचिलाना, *a. int.* to shriek, scream, screech.
चिलड़ाहा, *m.* (*f.* ī) lousy.
चिलता, *m.* the lining of iron armour.
चिलम, *m.* (*f.* ?) the part of a hukka which contains the tobacco and fire.
चिलमची, *f.* a covered metallic wash-hand basin; a ewer: the part of a hukka fixed under the *chilam*.
चिलमन = चिलवन, *q.v.* [Venetian blind, lattice.
चिलवन, *f.* a screen for keeping out the glare,
चिलवाई, *f.* mud, slime.
चिलवान, *m.* a shutter.
चिलहला, *m.* (*f.* ī) splashy, muddy, slimy.
चिलहोरना, *t.* to peck.
चिलिक, *f.* twitch, stitch.
चिल्पासा, *m.* a lizard.
चिल्ल, *m.* the Bengal kite (*Falco ater* or *cheela*).
चिल्लड़ *f.* a louse. — *mārnā*, to louse.

चिल्ला, *m.* 1, a bowstring; gold threads in the borders of a turban: 2, quarantine.—*Khainchna*, to bend a bow, prepare for battle: to keep quarantine.—*chaṛhānā*, to bend a bow.

चिल्लाना, *a. int.* to scream, shriek, cry out, bellow, roar, bawl, shout, exclaim.

चिल्लाहट, *f.* a scream, cry, outcry.

चिल्ली, 1, *f.* a kind of dish made of eggs: a kind of vegetable: 2, *m.* (*f.* inī) a blockhead, one who plays mischievous pranks.

चिल्लू, *more com.* **चुल्लू**, *q.v.*

चिल्हवांस, *m.* the flesh of the kite (the eating of which is said to produce madness): screaming like a kite.

चिल्हार, abounding in kites.

चिवाना, *m.* a place for the cremation of the dead.

चिस्तां, *m.* an enigma.

चिह्न; see (1) **चार** (2) **चिहरा** (3) **ची** (4) **छः** (5) **छी**.

चिहरा, *m.* face, visage, countenance; air; description-roll. — *likhnā*, to write a description-roll. — *likhānā*, to enlist; to take service and horses.

चिहरापट्टी, *f.* a descriptive roll.

चिहलहा, *m.* (*f.* ī) splashy, muddy, slimy.

चिहला, *m.* soft mud, ooze, slime; a splinter of wood. — *nikalnā*, to grow tired, fatigue. — *k.* to split to pieces.

चिहाना, *t.* to embellish, decorate.

चिहिकना, *m.* the warbling of the nightingale; the sound of fireworks.

चिहेल, wet oozy land.

चिहों in Chand = **चारों**, *q.v.*

ची, *f.* 1, see **चा**, 2: 2, pain, ache.

चीऊड़ा, *m.* rice parched in a certain mode and eaten dry.

चीऊंटा, *m.* a large black ant.

चीऊंटी, *f.* (dim. of the above) a small ant.

चीओंटी, *f.* a nip or pinch with the nails of the thumb and finger.

चींट, **चींत**; see under the forms **चीयट**, **चीन्त**.

चीक, *f.* mud, slime; thick milk (?).

चीकट, 1, *f.* a mixture of oil and dust: a sort of clayey soil: 2, greasy or dusty (as cloth).

चीकटी, *f.* a clayey soil.

चीकड़, *f.* mud, slime, land that has been recently irrigated.

चीकर = **चीकड़**, *q.v.*

चीख़, *f.* a scream, screech, shriek. — *mārnā*, to scream, screech, shriek.

चीखना, *t.* to taste: *a. int.* to scream.

चीखाना, *t.* (causat. of **चीखना**) = **चखाना**, *q.v.*

चीखुर, *m.* a squirrel.

चीज़, *f.* a thing, commodity.

चीठी, *more prop.* **चिट्ठी**, *q.v.*

चीयट, *more com.* **छीयट**, *q.v.*

चीयटी, a contraction of **चीऊंटी**, *q.v.*

चीतड़, *m.* hips, buttocks. — *teknā*, to sit down, get rest.

चीतना, *t.* to draw, paint; to wish, think, imagine.

चीतल, 1, *m.* a certain animal of the forest (some think the spotted deer, the leopard, the panther, or some other spotted animal): 2, speckled, variegated, spotted.

चीता, *m* painting: thought, understanding, wisdom; wish, desire: a leopard or panther (*Felis jubata*, Schreb.); a hunting-leopard (*Pennant*): a certain medicinal plant (*Plumbago zeylanica*).

चीथड़ } **चीथड़ा** } *m.* a rag, tatter.

चीथना, *t.* to rend, tear.

चीन, 1, *m. pr. n.* China: 2, *m.* a kind of grass (*Panicum miliaceum*): a sort of cloth: 3, *f.* a fold, plait, wrinkle.

चीनकपूर, *m.* camphor.

चीनपिष्ठ, *m.* minium or red lead. It is brought in cakes or lumps from the hills to the north-west of Bengal.

चीना, 1, *m.* millet (*Panicum Italicum*): 2, to ooze, leak.

चीनी, 1, *f.* sugar (of a common kind; so named, perhaps from *chin*, China, whence, it is supposed, it may have been brought) as distinguished from **मिस्री** (supposed to have been brought from *Misr*, Egypt): the face of a watch: 2, appertaining to China, Chinese; hence (1) *m.* (*f.* inī) a Chinese (2) *f.* the Chinese language.

चीपट, *more com.* **छीपट**, *q.v.*

चीन्तना, *t.* to pull up by the roots.

चीन्थना, *n.* to be bruised by being trodden upon.

चीन्हैं in Braj = **चीन्हना**, *q.v.*

चीन्ह = **चिन्ह**, *q.v.*

चीन्हना, *t.* to known, recognize.

चीन्हा, *m.* an acquaintance.

चीपड़, *f.* rheum of the eyes.

चीभर, land that remains long moist.

चीमटा, *m.* nippers, pincers, forceps, tongs.

चीर, 1, *m.* bark; a vesture of bark; a rag; cloth: a rent, slit, strip; a tearing, rending, splitting, slitting: 2, *f.* cloth, clothes, attire, a sort of covering or dress for women: the pine-tree (*Pinus longifolia*).—*nikālnā*, to break through troops.

चीरना, *t.* to rend, cleave, split, tear, rip, slit, harrow, saw.

चीरहरण, *m.* a stealing, seizing, taking away.

चीरा, 1, *m.* an incision, slit, cut, wound: maidenhood: a turban: — *utārnā*, to deflower: 2, powerful; uncivil, rude.

चीराबन्द } **चीरावली** } *f.* a virgin, maiden.

चीरी, 1, *f.* the ends or hem of a garment: a cricket: 2, *m.* (*f.* iṇī) a person covered with bark or with rags.

चीरेफारे, broken, torn, ragged, rent.

चीरेता, a common form of **चिरतिक्त**, *q.v.*

चील, *f.* a kite (*Falco cheela*, Lath.) — *jhapaṭṭā mārnā*, to snatch.

चीलड़ } **चीलर** } = **चिल्लड़**, *q.v.*

चीला, *m.* a thin cake made of rice-flour and cocoanut milk: a small iron nail.

चील्ह = **चील**, *q.v.*

चील्हड़ } **चील्हर** } **चील्हार** } = **चिल्लड़**, *q.v.*

चील्हैं, *f.* (prop. **चील्हें**; pl. of **चील्ह**) kites.

चीवर, *m.* the tattered dress of any mendicant but especially of a Buddhist.

चीवरिन्, *m.* a Bauddh or Jain mendicant.

चीही / **चीहे** } a subdivision of the gujar tribe.

चीहुटी (*corruption*) = **चीऊपटी**, *q.v.*

चुआ ; see (1) **चूहा** (2) **चोआ**.

चुआन, *f.* a reservoir, cistern. [ing at the bottom.

चुआनखाई, *f.* a very deep ditch with water spring-

चुआना, more commonly **चोआना**, *q.v.*

चुंगना ; see (1) **चुगना** (2) **चूंगना**.

चुंगल, a handful of anything dry (as distinguished from *chullā*, a handful of anything liquid).

चुंगली, *more prop.* **चुग़ली**, *q.v.*

चुंगी, *f.* a tax gathered daily from grain-merchants, being as much grain as a man can take up in his fist : illegal abstraction of handfuls of market produce.

चुंगीपेन्थ, a market held on condition of giving a small portion of each saleable article to the zamīndār.

चुंचुना, *m.* the thread-worm (*Ascarides*).

चुंटी (*corruption*) = **चीऊपटी**, *q.v.*

चुकत, a settlement, contract. [court, etc.

चुकती, *f.* settlement, decree or sentence of a

चुकना, *n.* to have finished or completed ; to be fixed, be agreed upon, be adjusted.

चुक़न्दर, *m.* beet-root (*Beta vulgaris*).

चुकाई, *f.* a task, agreement, adjustment, decision, settlement. — *denā*, to escape one's notice, give one the slip. [fix the price of.

चुकाना, *t.* to finish, complete, settle, adjust ; to

चुकारा, customs-duty. [money-rate.

चुकौता, *m.* 1, = **चुकाई**, *q.v.*: 2, field-rates of rent ;

चुक्कड़, *m.* a small tank, a pit, a shallow hole with

चुक्कार, *m.* the roaring of a lion. [water in it.

चुक्की, *f.* deceit, fraud. — *denā*, to deceive, play tricks. [of vinegar made of fruits.

चुक्र, *m.* sourness ; sorrel ; acid seasoning, a kind

चुक्री, *f.* a fractional division of land.

चुक्रिका, *f.* wood-sorrel (*Oxalis monodelpha*) or *Ru-*

चुग़द, *m.* the small screech-owl. [*max vescicarius.*

चुगन, *f.* a plait or fold in a garment.

चुगना, *t.* to pick up food with the beak, peck. *Chug lenā*, to select, cull, choose.

चुगल, *more prop.* **चुग़ल**, *q.v.*

चुग़ली, *f.* tale-bearing, backbiting, slander. — *khānā*, to tell tales, backbite, slander.

चुगाई, *f.* pasturage. [cause to peck.

चुगाना, *t.* to cause to pick up food with the beak,

चुग़ल, *m.* a tell-tale, slanderer, informer, spy.

चुगुली, *more prop.* **चुग़ली**, *q.v.* [beak.

चुगौ, *m.* (in Braj = **चुगा**) food picked up with the

चुचकारना = **चुमकारना**, *q.v.*

चुचकारी, *f.* blandishment. [drip.

चुचवाना, *t.* to cause to be drenched, cause to

चुचाना, *n.* to drop, be drenched, be dripping wet (with water, perspiration, etc.).

चुचि, *m. f.* ? the female breast or bosom.

चुच्चड़, *m.* large breasts.

चुटकल, a jest.

चुटकी, *f.* a pinch ; a snapping the fingers : the hammer of a gun : a mode of printing cloth or *gulbadan* : a certain ornament worn on the toes. — *denā* or *bharnā* or *lenā*, to pinch, nip ; to throw out provoking insinuations. *Chuṭkiyoṅmeṅ uṛānā*, to put one off with a joke. [mour ; a conundrum.

चुटकुला, *m.* pleasantry, facetiousness, wit, hu-

चुटकुलासा, *m.* (*f.* ī) amusing.

चुटला, *m.* (*f.* ?) a cue or lock of hair worn at [the back of the head.

चुटाना / **चुटालना** } *t.* to wound.

चुटिया, 1, *m.* a spy to thieves, the head of a gang of thieves : 2, *f.* a lock of hair left on the head [when the rest is shaved.

चुटियाना, *t.* to wound.

चुटी ; see (1) **चीऊपटी** (2) **चोटी**.

चुटीला, *m.* (*f.* ī) wounded, bruised, stricken.

चुट्टा, *m.* (see **चोटी**) a lock of hair left on the top

चुड़, *f.* an imitative sound: *vulva.* [of the head, etc.

चुड़ी, *f.* (a fem. of **चिड़ा**) a hen-sparrow.

चुड़वा / **चुड़ुआ** } *m.* a dish prepared from parched rice.

चुड़ैल, *f.* the ghost of a woman who died while pregnant ; a hag, fury ; a dirty woman, slut, slattern.

चुदक्कड़, *m.* a salacious person qui coitu frequenti

चुदना, *n.* feminam subigere. [fruitur.

चुदवाई, *f.* (see **आई**, 3) the wages of prostitution.

चुदवाना = **चुदाना**, *q.v.*

चुदवैया = **चुदक्कड़**, *q.v.*

चुदाई, *f.* copulation.

चुदाना, *t.* viri amplexibus se submittere (mulier).

चुदास, *f.* lust, lasciviousness.

चुदासा, *m.* (*f.* ī) desirous of copulating.

चुनखाऊ, *m.* a bird ; a beggar.

चुनचुना, *m.* (*f.* ī) the thread-worm (*Ascarides*).

चुनत, *f.* plaiting cloths ; plaits, ruffles.

चुनदेना, *t.* (intensive) to pick out, select, choose.

चुनन, *m.* a rumple, crease.

चुनना, 1, *m.* the thread-worm (*Ascarides*) : 2, *t.* to gather, pick, choose, select, cull ; to pick up food (as birds) ; to arrange, place in order ; to plait. *Darwāza* — , to close a door with bricks.

चुनरी, *f.* a certain mode of dyeing cloths in which they are tied in different places previous to dipping them into the dye, so as to prevent the parts tied from receiving the colour ; cloths dyed in this manner.

चुनली मटी / **चुनली मिट्टी** } *f.* potter's-earth.

चुन लेना, *t.* (intensive) to pick out, select, choose.

चुनवाना, *t.* (see **चुनाना**) to cause to be picked, etc.

चुना, *m.* (*more prop.* चूना, *q.v.*) lime.

चुनांकि
चुनांके
चुनांच
चुनांचे
चुनाके
चुनाचे } corruptions of चुनानचि, *q.v.*

चुनानचि, so that, in such manner that, accordingly, consequently.

चुनानचें, *more prop.* चुनानचि, *q.v.*

चुनाना, *t.* to cause to pick, cause to choose, etc.; to arrange, array, put in order, dress oneself, etc.

चुनालेना, *t.* to plait cloth: to kill a person by build- [ing him into a wall.

चुनावट, *f.* a plaiting; a plait.

चुनौटा, *m.* a box for holding the lime used to chew along with betel: the folding the cloth called the *sārī* (worn by Hindoo females).

चुनौटी, *f.* a small box for holding the lime used to chew along with betel; a small spoon used to take out the lime: encouraging troops in the time of battle (for which purpose there is a special officer in Indian armies); the selecting from an army the fittest men for a desperate enterprize: a certain practice which formerly prevailed at Banāras, *viz.* on the 11th day of the Shuklpaksh of Jaith the inhabitants were wont to swim across the river, and, forming themselves into two parties, to fight with swords, clubs, etc.

चुनौती, *f.* envy, spite; reproach, disrespect.

चुन्दरी, *f.* a kind of coloured cloth.

चुन्दी, *f.* a procuress, bawd.

चुन्धला, *m.* (*f.* ī) a blinkard.

चुन्धलाना, *n.* to be purblind, be dim-sighted.

चुन्धा, *m.* (*f.* ī) a blinkard: *lit.* purblind, dim-sighted, dim; bad and crabbed (as hand-writing).

चुवत, *more prop.* चुनत, *q.v.*

चुवन, a Braj pl. (1) of चुवा (2) of चुवो, *qq v.*

चुवा = चुनना, *q. v.*

चुवी, *f.* a small ruby: the thread-worm (*Ascarides*).

चुप, 1, *adj.* silent: 2, *adv.* gratis, for nothing: 3, *interj.* silence! (*rah* or *raho* being understood): 4, *f.* silence.— *lagnā*, to be struck dumb.

चुपका, *m.* (*f.* ī) silent, quiet, mute.

चुपकी, *f.* 1, *see above*: 2, silence. — *lagnā*, to be [struck dumb.

चुपके, *adv.* quickly, silently, with little noise; gratis. — *kahnā*, to speak in a very low voice, speak in a whisper.

चुपकेसे, on the quiet, secretly, clandestinely.

चुपको, *adv.* gratis, for nothing.

चुपचाप, *adj.* silent, perfectly still: *adv.* silently, fur- [tively, stealthily.

चुपचुपाते, *adv.* silently, secretly.

चुपचुपाना, *a. int.* to keep silence, move quietly [or secretly.

चुपड़ना, *t.* to varnish, anoint, besmear; to smoothe; to cover, palliate.

चुपड़ा, *m.* (*f.* ī) greasy, oiled, smooth, plausible [(though false).

चुपड़ीआलू, *m.* the yam.

चुपड़ीबात, *f.* plausible speech, soft words, flattery.

चुपड़ोरोटी, *f.* cakes rich with clarified butter.

चुपरनौं, in Braj = चुपड़ना, *q. v.*

चुपाचुप, *more commonly* चुपचाप, *q. v.*

चुप्पी, *f.* silence.

चुभकी, *f.* a plunge into water, a dip, dive: a [puncture, prick.

चुभना, *n.* to be struck into, be thrust into; to be pierced, be pricked, be stabbed: *a. int.* to prick, pierce, penetrate.

चुभाना, *t.* to stick, into, thrust into, prick, goad, [pierce, stab.

चुभावना
चुभोना } = चुभाना, *q. v.*

चुमकार, *m.* a sound made with the lips for call- [ing dogs and horses.

चुमकारना, *t.* to coax, speak kindly to, fondle, chirp to, soothe or cheer by producing the sound occasioned by drawing the breath with protruded lips.

चुमकारी, *f.* = चुमकार, *q. v.*

चुमटी, *f.* an ant: a pinch or nip.

चुमना, *more com.* चूमना, *q.v.*

चुमली, *f.* = चुम्मल, *q. v.*

चुमा, *m.* (prop. चुम्बा) a kiss.

चुमाक़, *m.* a mace, club, baton with an iron knob [at the end.

चुमाचाटी, *f.* dalliance.

चुमाना, *t.* to cause to kiss.

चुमार, *more prop.* चमार, *q.v.*

चुम्बक, 1, *m.* a magnet, loadstone; an extract from a book, etc.; a quotient; a general scholar, one who knows parts in a variety of books; the upper part or middle of a balance; a rogue, cheat: 2, lit. *m.* (*f.* ikā) a kisser, lecher.

चुम्बकपत्थर, *m.* a loadstone, magnet: *lit.* the kiss- [ing-stone.

चुम्बत = चूमता. See चूमना.

चुम्बन, *m.* kissing; a kiss.

चुम्बा, *m.* a kiss. — *lenā*, to take a kiss.

चुम्मक, *m.* (prop. चुम्बक) a loadstone.

चुम्मल, *m.* a ring made of grass or twigs placed under waterpots to keep them in an upright position.

चुम्मा, *m.* (prop. चुम्बा) a kiss.

चुर, an imitative sound.

चुरकी, *f.* a lock of hair.

चुरकुट, *m.* powder.

चुरगना, *a. int.* to gabble, prattle, chirp.

चुरचुरा, *m.* (*f.* ī) crisp; acid.

चुरचुरी, 1, *see above*: 2, *f.* dregs, sediment.

चुरवा, 1, *more prop.* चूर्वा, *q. v.*: 2, *m.* stealing, thiev- [ing, robbing.

चुरमुरा, an imitative sound.

चुररी, *f.* dregs, refuse.

चुरवाना, *t.* to cause to steal; to cause to be stolen.

चुराना, *t.* to steal, filch, pilfer, rob.

चुरामन; see (1) चूरामणि (2) चूरामन.

चुरी, *f.* (prop. चूड़ी) bangles or rings made of glass, etc. and worn on the wrist; a kind of bracelet: a small well.

चुरीहारा, *m.* (*f.* ī *or* in) a maker or a vendor of bangles.

चुरुक, the chirping of little birds.

चुरगना, *a. int.* to gabble, prattle, chirp.

चुरस, spite, envy, jealousy.

चुर्त, *f.* a nap, drowsiness, nodding.

चुर्मुरा, an imitative sound.

चुर्री, *f.* dregs, refuse.

चुर्रीहारा; see (1) **चुरीहारा** (2) **चुर्री**.

चुर्स, spite, envy, jealousy.

चुर्सी, *m.* (*f.* inī) a spiteful person, etc.: *lit.* spiteful, envious.

चुल, *f.* an itching; a scratching; the itch.

चुलचुल, *m.* wantonness, inconstancy.

चुलचुलाना, *a. int.* to itch, tittilate.

चुलचुली, *f.* wantonness, inconstancy.

चुलना; see **चूरना**.

चुलबुला, *m.* (*f.* ī) restless, fidgetting; airy, gay.

चुलबुलागी, *f.* liveliness, airiness, restlessness, gaiety.

चुलबुलाना, *n.* to be restless, be agog, be fidgetty.

चुलबुलापन, *m.* } = **चुलबुलागी**, *q.v.*
चुलबुलाहट, *f.* }

चुलबुलिया, restless, fidgetting; airy, gay.

चुलाना = **चोआना**, *q.v.*

चुलाव, *m.* a kind of dish consisting of plain boiled rice.

चुली; see (1) **चुल्ली** (2) **चूल्ही** (3) **चोली**.

चुल्ल, *m.* a blear eye.

चुल्ला, *m.* (*f.* ī) blear-eyed.

चुल्ली, 1, *see above*: 2, *f.* a fire-place, chimney: staddles, the support placed beneath a stack of straw, etc.

चुल्लू, *m.* a handful, handful of any liquid, the palm of the hand contracted so as to hold water. *Chullū chullū sādhnā*, to acquire a habit of drinking by gradual increase. *Chullū bhar pānimeṅ dūb marnā*, to be greatly or unreasonably abashed; *lit.* to perish from drowning in a handful of water. *Chullūmeṅ ullū honā*, to be intoxicated by a mouthful.

चुल्लाई, *f.* a lewd libidinous female.

चुल्लारा, *m.* (*f.* ī) lascivious, lewd.

चुवाना = **चोआना**, *q.v.*

चुसकना, *a. int.* to throb, ache.

चुसकी, *f.* a mouthful of drink.

चुसक्कड़, *m.* one who is in the habit of sucking; *met.* a tippler.

चुसनी, *f.* a child's coral, a stick for a child to suck.

चुसाना, *t.* to give or cause to suck.

चुस्त, active, fleet, ingenious: narrow, straight, tight. — *chālāk*, active, fleet, alert.

चुस्ता, *m.* runnet.

चुस्ती, *f.* activity, alertness, fleetness.

चुस्सी, *f.* the juice of fruits.

चुहचुहा, *m.* (*f.* ī) deeply-coloured.

चुहचुहाना, *a. int.* to glow (as a colour); to blush; to dye a deep colour.

चुहल, *f.* mention: cheer, jollity, mirth, festivity. [— *k.* to make merry, carol.

चुहलपुहल, merriment, festivity, good cheer.

चुहला, *m.* a tentpin, large wooden peg.

चुहली, *m.* (*f.* inī) a mirthful person: *lit.* comic, mirthful.

चुहा, *m.* (*f.* ī) *more com.* **चूहा**, *q.v.*

चुहिया, *m.* (dim. of **चूहा**) a small mouse.

चूआ = (1) **चोआ** (2) **चूहा**, *qq.v.*

चूआन = **चुआन**, *q.v.*

चूएदान, *more prop.* **चूहेदान**, *q.v.*

चूं, the sound of breaking wind.

चूंगना, 1, *more prop.* **चुगना**, *q.v.*: 2, *t.* to suck.

चूंगी, *f.* a toll, tax, duty: a small pipe or tube.

चूंचहाट, *f.* the singing of birds.

चूंची = **चूची**, *q.v.*

चूंचूं, the noise of birds.

चूक, 1, *f.* an error, mistake, blunder, inadvertency, fault, miss: 2, *m.* a kind of medicine made of boiled lemon-juice and pomegranates: 3, sour, acid.

चूकना, *a. int.* to blunder, mistake, err, miss, fail, depart from.

चूकसे, *adv.* by mistake.

चूका, *m.* a kind of sorrel (*Rumex vescicarius*): a kind of earthen pot: rice.

चूख, *m.* a kind of medicine, orrice or iris-root, orris-root.

चूची, *f.* breast, pap, dug, nipple, teat, bubby.

चूचुक, *m.* a nipple; the breast.

चूज़ा, *m.* a kite: a young bird, chicken.

चूट, *m.* a crack, noise; a peculiar mode of folding a blanket or sheet.

चूड़, *m.* (= **चूड़ा**, **चूड़ी**) the ceremony of cutting the hair: a crest, top-knot; an amulet, ring; the bracelet put on a bride at her marriage; a gold or silver ornament worn by Hindoo widows.

चूड़ा, 1. *m.* a kind of ornament; the rings fastened to elephants' tusks: a kind of food made of parched rice: 2. *f.* a single lock of hair left at the crown of the head at the ceremony of tonsure; the ceremony of cutting the hair; the hair; a peacock's crest; any crest, plume, diadem; the head, top, summit: a kind of bracelet.

चूड़ाकर्ण, *m.* a shaving, tonsure: *pr. n.* a certain religious mendicant.

चूड़ाभन्दारा, *m.* an allowance for the maintenance of the junior members of a zamindār's family.

चूड़ामणि, *m.* a jewel worn in a crest or diadem: the Gunjā (*Abrus precatorius*).

चूड़ाल, *m.* (*f.* ā) a crested one: *lit.* crested, having a lock of hair on the top of the head.

चूड़ाला, *f.* 1, a kind of grass (*Kyllinga monocephala*): 2, *see above.*

चूड़ावत, *m.* (*f.* ī) = **चूड़ाल**, *q.v.*

चूड़ी, *f.* bangles or rings made of glass, sealing-wax, etc. and worn on the wrist.

चूड़ीदार, drawers or sleeves made too long so as to be crumpled into plaits.

चूड़ीहारा, *m.* (*f.* ī) a maker of bangles.

चूण, *m.* flour, pulse coarsely ground; lime.

चूपटना = **चूपठना**, *q.v.*

चूपटा, *m.* a large ant.

चूपटी, *f.* a small ant.

चूपठना, *t.* to gather (a flower); to claw, pinch.

चूत, 1, *f.* (prop. **च्युति**) *vulva*: 2, *m.* the mango (*Mangofera Indica*).

चूतड़, *m.* the rump, hip, buttock, posterior. —— *bajānā*, to be overjoyed. — *sakornā*, to loiter, hang back. *Chutarse kān gānthnā*, to use far-fetched expressions, speak in parables, equivocate.

चूतमरानी, *f.* a strumpet, harlot.

चूतसलामी, *f.* fees paid by a bridegroom to the kāzee on the morning after his nuptials.

चूतिया, *m.* a blockhead.

चून, *more prop.* **चूर्ण**, *q.v.*

चूनचिरा, wrangling, altercation.

चूना, 1, *m.* lime, chunam: —— *lagānā*, to defame: 2, *a. int.* to leak, drop, distil, ooze, exude; to drop (as ripe fruit from a tree).

चूनांचे, a corruption of **चुनानचि**, *q.v.*

चूनापज़नी, *f.* a dancing-girl.

चूनारी, *m.* (*f.* inī) a lime-burner, worker in lime.

चूनाक, *m.* or *f.* = **चूनारी**, *q.v.*

चूनी, *f.* pulse split or ground very closely; a spark, small ruby or other gem.

चून्नू, *m.* the head-man of a district.

चून्नी = **चुन्नी**, *q.v.*

चून्धला, *m.* (*f.* ī) = **चुन्धला**, *q.v.*

चून्धा, *m.* (*f.* ī) = **चुन्धा**, *q.v.*

चूपड़, *m.* grease. [form **चुपड़ी**.

चुपड़ी; for words beginning thus see under the

चूपान, *m.* a cowherd, shepherd.

चूपानी, *f.* the office of shepherd.

चूभ, *m.* a pricking, prick, puncture.

चूभना = **चुभना**, *q.v.*

चूमकपत्थर, *more prop.* **चुम्बकपत्थर**, *q.v.*

चूमन, *more prop.* **चुम्बन**, *q.v.*

चूमना, *t.* to kiss. [kiss.

चूमा, *m.* (prop. **चुम्बा**) a kiss.—— *lenā*, to take a

चूमाचाटी = **चुमाचाटी**, *q.v.*

चूर, 1, *m.* powder, filings, atoms: 2, bruised.—— *k.* to shatter, break into small pieces. — *rahnā*, to sot. — *honā*, to be enamoured, be in love, dote; to be tired; *lit.* to be broken into small pieces. *Nashemen* — *honā*, to be helplessly intoxicated.

चूरचार, *m.* a crumb, fragment.

चूरचूर, broken to atoms.

चूरण }
चूरन } = **चूर्ण**, *q.v.* [atoms, pulverize.

चूरना, *t.* to reduce to very small pieces, reduce to

चूरा, *m.* filings; sawdust; grain reduced to coarse particles to be chucked into the mouth; a small bit, fragment.

चूरामन = **चूर्णमन**, *q.v.* [clarified butter.

चूरी, *f.* 1, = **चूड़ी**, *q.v.*: 2, a kind of bread rich with

चूर्ण, *m.* any pulverized or minute division of substance, powder, dust, flour; aromatic powder, pounded sandal, etc.; a powder composed of medicines for promoting digestion; fossil alkali, efflorescent salt.

चूर्णकुन्तल, *m.* a lock of hair, curl, curling hair.

चूर्णखण्ड, *m.* pebble, gravel, hardened fragments of earth or brick; limestone nodule (commonly known in India by the name of *kankar*). [tent.

चूर्णमन, contrite, broken-hearted, sorrowful, peni-

चूर्णा = **चूरना**, *q.v.* [crumbled.

चूर्मा, *m.* a kind of sweetmeat made of sugar, and

चूल, *f.* a tenon, a part of a joiner's work which fits into another part (as a dove-tail); a pivot on which a door turns as on a hinge; an axle-arm. *Chūlen ukharnā* or *dhīlī honā*, to be tired, be worn out with labour.

चूलत, *f.* a crest: a certain tribe of Tagās.

चूला, 1, *f.* = **चूलत**, *q.v.*: 2, *m.* a smith's forge,

चूल्या, *m.* }
चूल्हा, *m.* } a fire-place, stove. [trivet, stove, kitchengrate.
चूल्ही, *f.* }

चूल्हिहि, an old dat. and acc. of **चूल्ही**, *q.v.*

चूवना, *a. int.* to drop, leak, ooze, exude.

चूवी, *more prop.* **चूही**, *q.v.*

चूसना, *t.* to suck, absorb, appropriate, kiss.

चूसनी = **चुसनी**, *q. v.*

चूहड़, *m.* the act of hunting by deceiving game with a stalking-horse. [caste of village servants.

चूहड़ा, *m.* (*f.* ī) a Hindoo sweeper, the lowest

चूहना, *t.* to suck.

चूहरी, *f.* a small kind of mouse.

चूहा, *m.* (*f.* ī) a rat. [a small rat; a mouse.

चूही, *f.* 1, (*m.* **चहा**,) a female rat: 2, (dim. of **चूहा**)

चूहेदान, *m.* a mouse-trap, rat-trap.

चूहेमार, *m.* a mouser, sparrow-hawk, cormorant.

चे, the inflected form of **चा**, 2, *q.v.*

चेओली, *f.* a kind of silk cloth.

चेंच, a kind of herb which springs up in uncultivated places during the rains.

चेंचपेंच, *m.* brats, bairns, young ones.

चेंची, *f.* a needlecase. [ble, squeak.

चेंचें, क°, *a. int.* to chatter, chirp, murmur, grum-

चेंड़ा, *m.* (*f.* ī) young, little.

चेचक, *f.* the small-pox.

चेट, *m.* (*f.* ī) a servant, slave. [a deception.

चेटक, 1, *m.* (*f.* ikā) = **चेट**, *q.v.*: 2, *f.* a miracle;

चेटी, *f.* (*m.* **चेट**) a female servant or slave.

चेड़ा, *m.* (*f.* ī) = **चेट**, *q.v.*

चेपटी, *f.* a small ant.

चेत, *m.* memory, remembrance, thought, perception, consciousness, sensation; circumspection.—*k.* to bear in mind.

चेतन, 1, = **चैतन्य**, *q.v.*: 2, *m.* (*f.* ā) a sentient being: *lit.* alive, living, feeling, conscious, sentient, rational.

चेतना, 1, *f.* consciousness; recollection; intellect, understanding, wisdom: 2, *t.* to remember, think of, advise: *a. int.* to reflect, perceive: *n.* to be aware, be aroused, recover the senses.

चेता, 1, = **चित्त**, *q. v.*: 2, *m.* an adviser, admonisher.

चेदि, *m. pr. n.* (1) of a certain country (2) of its people (3) of their king.

चेना, *m.* millet (*Panicum Italicum*).

चेन्द, *m.* a lock of hair left on the top of the head.

चेन्दूल, *m.* a ball to play with.

चेप, stickiness, sliminess.

चेपना, *t.* to stick together.

चेम्प, *m.* the acrid resin of fruits and trees.

चेर, a contraction of **चेरा**, *q. v.*

चेरा, *m.* (*f.* ī) = **चेला**, *q. v.*

चेराई, *f.* slavery, servitude; discipleship.

चेरायता, a common form of **चिरतित्त**, *q. v.*

चेरी, see **चेरा**.

चेरु, the name of a wild tribe in Mirzapore.

चेरुआ, *m.* (*f.* **चेरुई**) a slave.

चेल, *m.* cloth; raiment.

चेलका, *m.* a slave; a pupil, disciple.

चेला, (from **चेट**) *m.* (*f.* ī) a servant, slave brought up in the house; a pupil, disciple.

चेवली, *f.* a kind of silk cloth.

चेष्टा, *f.* bodily action, motion, gesture, exercise, exertion, effort, endeavour, application, search. — *k.* (with the fem. gen. of the object) to strive after.

चेहरा, *m.* a descriptive roll of a servant.

चेंपटा, *m.* a black ant.

चैत, *m. pr. n.* the twelfth month of the Hindoos (March-April) the full moon of which is near *Chitrā*.

चैतन्य, 1, *m.* intellect, reason, understanding, wisdom, intelligence, rationality; consciousness, sensation, perception; animation: caution; the possession of the proper use of the faculties; soul, spirit; the Deity considered as the essence of all being; a sentient being: 2, *adj.* in possession of the senses, perceiving, sensitive, aware, rational, attentive, cautious, awake: 3, *m. pr. n.* the leader of a sect among the Hindoos. This philosopher flourished about the year 1407 of Sālivāhan (about A. D. 1350): he was by birth a Brāhman, and, having become a Sañyasee, he maintained that the doctrines of the Veds had hitherto been misunderstood, and explained them in a manner peculiar to himself. His sect is a branch of the Vaishnav sect (worshippers of Vishṇu), and his followers in various parts of India are said to amount to five millions: they believe Chaitānya to have been an incarnation of the Diety.

चैतन्यचूरण, *m.* snuff; *lit.* quickening-powder.

चैतन्यचोला, *m.* the living human body.

चैतन्यात्मा, *m.* the rational spirit, the living soul.

चैती, *f.* the harvest of the month *Chait*.

चैत्र = **चैत**, *q. v.*

चैत्री, *f.* the day of the full moon in *Chaitra*.

चैन, *m.* ease, relief, repose, quiet, rest, tranquillity; a calm at sea: denying a bet in gaming, imposture: a low caste of Hindoos.

चैनमई = **चैनमय**, at rest, tranquil, reposed, calm.

चैना, *m.* millet (*Panicum Italicum*).

चैल, 1, = **चेल**, *q. v.*: 2, land twice tilled.

चैला, *m.* a billet of wood cut for burning, etc.

चैली, *f.* shavings, chips, saw-dust.

चोआ, *m.* a kind of perfume: the pod or skin of any pulse: a windfall (fruit): a certain plant (*Amaranthus oleaceus*) used as a potherb.

चोआड़, *m.* a mountain robber, outlaw, mountaineer, brigand.

चोआन, *f.* a dripping, dropping.

चोआना, *t.* to cause to drip; to distil, filter, draw off.

चोआर = **चोआड़**, *q. v.*

चोई, *f.* the pip of an orange.

चोईल, land lying low and always moist.

चोंकना, *t.* to prick, pierce, goad.

चोंगला, *m.* a joint of bamboo used for sending letters in.

चोंगा, *m.* a funnel, tub, barrel of a gun: a sort of bread: a young woman.

चोंच, *f.* a point; a beak, bill of a bird.

चोंचला = **चोचला**, *q. v.*

चोकड़ / **चोकर** } *m.* husk of wheat, bran.

चोका, *more com.* **चौका**, *q. v.*

चोख, 1, = **चूख**, *q. v.*: 2, (prop. **चोक्ष**) clean, pure; genuine, unadulterated; neat, good, choice, fine; sharp, pungent, keen; dexterous, clever, skilful; pleasing, delightful, beautiful.

चोखा, 1, *m.* (*f.* ī) = **चोख**, 2: 2 = **चोखा**, *qq. v.*

चोखाई, *f.* sharpness, pungency.

चोखान; see (1) **चोखाई** (2) **चोखा**.

चोखी, *f.* (see **चोखा**) sharp (as tone in music).

चोगा, *m.* food of birds brought up from the crop; food of birds in general. — *badalnā*, to bill, caress (as doves by joining bills).

चोग़ा, *f.* a sort of quilted garment, kind of long gown.

चोच, 1, *more com.* **चोंच**, *q. v.*: 2, *m.* bark, rind; half-eaten fruit: the fruit of the palm; the plantain; the cocoa-nut.

चोचला, *m.* blandishments, endearing arts and expressions, toyishness, coquetry.

चोज, *m.* subtleness; beauty.

चोजी, (*f.* inī) subtle, fine.

चोट, *f.* a hurt, bruise, blow, damage; a fall; spite; assiduity; an effort, attempt, wish, desire, aim, *Choṭ-par choṭ*, one misfortune follows another, misfortunes come not singly. — *khānā*, to be hurt, receive a blow, suffer loss. — *bāndhnā*, to defend; to bind up the edge of a sword, etc.; to restrain by magic, — *mārnā*, to hurt.

चोटा, *m.* discount or premium independent of interest: treacle.

चोटि = **चोटी**, *q. v.*

चोटियाना, *t.* (see **चोटी**) to seize by the hair: to hurt, wound.

चोटी, *f.* the lock of hair left by Hindoos at the top of the head at the time of shaving, the plait or tie of hair at the back of the head, the cue; the crown of the head, summit of a hill, top, pinnacle, summit: a petticoat. *Choṭikā honā*, to excel, be preëminent, be unrivalled.

चोट्टा, *m.* (*f.* ī) a thief.

चोड़, *m.* a boddice, jacket.

चोड़ह; see (1) चोट्टा (2) चोड़.

चोयटी, *f.* (= चोटी, *q.v.*) an ornament worn on the head by women. — *āsmānpar ghisnā*, to be very vain or aspiring. — *katwānā*, to be a slave, be obedient. — *kisi ki hathmeṅ ānā*, to have a power over one, to subdue.

चोथ, *m.* cowdung.

चोदना, to copulate. [cation, whorish.

चोदवांसा, *m.* (*f.* ī) libidinous, addicted to forni-

चोदवा, *m.* (*f.* ī) *more prop.* चोदहवां, *q.v.*

चोदू; see (1) चाऊचप (2) चुदक्कड़.

चोन्धल, darkness, dimness.

चोन्धला, *m.* (*f.* ī) a blinkard.

चोन्धलाना, *n.* to be purblind, see dimly.

चोन्धी, *f.* dulness of sight, dimness.

चोप, *f.* desire, wish, hope.

चोपदार = चोबदार, *q.v.*

चोपना, *t.* to throw water from a *daurī*.

चोब, *f.* wood; a post; a stick, club, drumstick.

चोबक, *f.* a drumstick. [embroidery.

चोबकारी, *f.* a beating with a stick: a kind of

चोबदस्ती, *f.* a staff, mace, stick.

चोबदार, *m.* a mace-bearer, servant whose business it is to announce the arrival of company.

चोबा, *m.* a stake, post.

चोभा, *m.* a nail: a kind of victuals given on great occasions (marriages, etc.): prey: a puncture.

चोम्प, *f.* wish, desire, fondness, avidity, alacrity: a gold ornament worn in the front teeth.

चोया, *m.* husk of grain, fish-scale; a hole (in which water is found) dug in the sandy bed of a river which has dried up; a rivulet.

चोर, 1, *m.* (*f.* in) a thief, robber: 2, sly, hidden, false, treacherous. — *lagnā*, to be injured, be damaged.

चोरख़ाना, *m.* a private room; a secret drawer.

चोरखिड़की, *f.* a bye-door, back-door.

चोरगली, *f.* bye-road, back lane.

चोरचकार, *m.* a thief.

चोरज़मीन, *f.* a quagmire, bog.

चोरजहाज़, *m.* a pirate-ship, privateer.

चोरदरवाज़ा, *m.* a trap-door.

चोरधोर, *m.* plaintiff and defendant; all the parties to a lawsuit; a thief and what he has stolen,

चोरनिमक, *m.* contraband salt (chiefly used in

चोरपहरा, the scouts of an army. [Cuttack).

चोरपुष्पी, *f.* a grass (*Andropogon aciculatum*).

चोरबालू, *f.* quicksand.

चोरमन्दूरा, *m.* a certain child's-game.

चोरमहल्ल, *m.* the apartments of the concubines

चोरमहीचनी, *f.* hide-and-seek. [of great men.

चोररस्ता, *m.*, **चोरराह**, *f.* } a secret path, private road.

चोरसीढ़ी, *f.* back-stairs, secret stairs.

चोरा, see (1) चूड़ा (2) चूरा (3) चोड़ा (4) चौरा.

चोराना, *t.* to steal, filch, pilfer, rob.

चोराया, *m.* (*f.* चोराई) stolen, filched.

चोरावन, *m.* (in Braj) stealing.

चोरिन *f.* (*m.* चोर) a female thief.

चोरी, *f.* theft, robbery, stealth. — *k.* to steal.

चोरीचोरी, *adv.* by stealth, on the sly, clandestinely. [down the thighs.

चोलना, short breeches reaching only half-way

चोला, *m.* a bodice, body of a gown, waistcoat, jacket; a case, mould, form; the body; a garment worn by a bride at her marriage: animal life, being: a small betel-basket: a country (the modern Tanjore); the name is supposed to apply also to a part of Beerbhoom in Bengal. [jacket: a small betel-basket.

चोली, *f.* a bodice, body of a gown, waistcoat,

चोव, *more prop.* चोब, *q.v.* [pulse: a windfall (fruit).

चोवा, *m.* a perfume: the pod or skin of any kind of

चोवे, a corruption of चुभे (चुभना).

चोष्य, *m.* anything (*esp.* fruit) that is capable of being sucked; *hence*, a mango, etc.: *lit.* suckable.

चोहड़नीचला, *m.* the lower jaw.

चोहला, *m.* a large peg or pin.

चोहा, a small well.

चौ, 1, = चार, four (but it is used only in composition as the following examples will shew): 2, *m.* a back tooth; a ploughshare. [*q. v.*

चौअन, 1, an old pl. of चौ, *q.v.*: 2, *more prop.* चौवन,

चौअन्नी, *f.* (चार आना) a small silver coin (in value four annas), a quarter-rupee piece.

चौआलीस, forty-four (४४): see ओं, वां, वीं, वे, वें.

चौंक, *f.* a starting up in a fright, a start. — *uṭhnā*, to start up from or in one's sleep, to start, wince.

चौंकना *a. int.* to start up from or in one's sleep, to start, boggle. — *ānā* or *paṛnā*, to bounce up, start up as from or in sleep.

चौंकाना, *t.* to rouse up from sleep, awaken.

चौंकैल, *m.* an untamed animal, boggler, horse that starts. [money).

चौंगा, *m.* a wheedling. — *k.* to wheedle (out of

चौंगी, *f.* a wheedling, sharp shooting.

चौंगीबाज़, *m. f.* a wheedler.

चौंगीबाज़ी, *f.* wheedling, sharping.

चौंच, a Braj form of चोंच, *q. v.*

चौंचा, the fourth reservoir to which water by the *daurī* for irrigation is raised.

चौंठी, a corruption of चौऊपटी, *q. v.*

चौंडू, *m.* a blockhead.

चौंरा, *m.* an underground apartment for grain.

चौंरी, *f.* a fly-flapper, instrument for driving off flies: a police-station where the *Kotwāl* resides.

चौंलाई, *f.* a kind of plant (*Pertulaca quadrifica*).

चौंसठ, sixty-four (६४): see ओं, वां, वीं, वे, वें.

चौंसर, *m.* 1, = चौसर, *q.v.*: 2, a garland of flowers.

चौक, *m.* (contr. of चौकोण) a square, an open

place in a city where the market is held, and where also the chief of the police-office is stationed, a market (according to Gladwin it denotes "a constant daily market or place of sale in towns, for all articles of wearing-apparel and other second-hand goods, the commodities here sold being for the most part not new; or, if new, coarse of their kind"); a courtyard, quadrangle; a custom at Hindoo and Muhammadan marriages of making a square space of coloured meal in which the bride and bridegroom are seated on chairs, etc.; a square space filled (at marriages and on other festive occasions) with sweetmeats, which, after certain ceremonies, are distributed; the square marked out by Hindoos when they cook or eat their food, within which no one is permitted to enter. — *bharnā* or *pūrnā*, to form a square space of coloured meal in which at marriages the bride and bridegroom are seated on chairs, etc.; to fill a square space with sweetmeats on some occasion of rejoicing; to make chequers or squares.

चौकट, *more prop.* **चौखट**, *q.v.*

चौकड़, good, excellent, fine, well.

चौकड़ा, *m.* a ring of two pearls worn in each ear: a division of a crop (the cultivator giving a fourth part to the zamīndār).

चौकड़ी, *f.* a bound, spring, bounce: a ring of pearls worn in the ear by men.— *bharnā* or *mārnā*, to leap, bound, bounce. — *bhūlnā*, to be fascinated, have one's senses benumbed; *lit.* to forget one's bounds. — *mār baiṭhnā*, to squat.

चौकना, *more com.* **चौंकना**, *q.v.*

चौकनिकास, *m.* a tax on all goods sold in a *chauk*.

चौकन्ना, *m.* (*f.* ī) circumspect, cautious, wary, on one's guard, alert, sly. [the ceremony of *chauk* (*q.v.*).

चौकपट्टा, a seat on which people sit and eat in

चौकमारा, *m.* evading the market-tax, smuggling.

चौकरी, *f.* a certain measure of grain (quarter of a *chauthiyā*).

चौकला, an assemblage of the smaller divisions of a province, the jurisdication of a *faujdār*.

चौकस, 1, *m.* full weight: 2, circumspect, watchful, alert, cautious; diligent, attentive, active, intelligent, accurate, clever, sharp. — *rahnā* (with abl. of the object), to beware of. [tion, alertness, caution.

चौकसाई, *f.* circumspectness, watchfulness, atten-

चौकसी, 1, *f.* circumspection, watching, vigilance, caution, attention, diligence: four persons employed together, or eating from the same dish or plate: 2, *m.* an assayer, examiner.

चौका, *m.* the space in which Hindoos cook or eat their food; a square plate of marble, etc.; a square space of ground; the four front teeth; the cube of a measure called *bāns*.

चौकाबाग, seed sown immediately after a fall of rain.

चौकी, *f.* any stool, sitting-bench, chair, "the chair" *par excellence*: guard, watch; an out-post, police-station, watchhouse; a guard's post; watching; a custom-house; an ornament worn on the breast. — *denā*, to watch, mount guard. — *mārnā*, to smuggle.

चौकीदार, *m.* a watchman: lit. *adj.* keeping watch.

चौकीदारी, *f.* (see **ई**, 17, 18) a keeping watch, the business of a watchman; the wages of a watchman.

चौकुदन / **चौकुधन** } *adv.* on all four sides, all around.

चौकोण / **चौकोणा** / **चौकोना** / **चौकोर** } four-cornered, square.

चौखट, *m. f.?* a door-frame, door, the upper and the lower piece of a door-frame.

चौखा, *m.* a station where four boundaries meet.

चौखी, *more prop.* **चोखी**, *q.v.*

चौखुधन / **चौखूट** } *adv.* on all four sides, all around.

चौखूटा, *m.* (*f.* ī) four-cornered, square.

चौगड़ा, *m.* (*f.* ī) a rabbit, hare. [lages meet.

चौगड्डा, a place where the boundaries of four vil-

चौगाण, **चौगाणः**, **चौगाणा** = **चौगुणा**, *q.v.*

चौगान, *m.* a game (a kind of hockey or shinty) played on horse-back; the bat, crocked stick, or club with which the game is played: a desert, plain, *maidān*. [game is played.

चौगानगाह, *f.* a place where the above-mentioned

चौगानबाज़, *m.* one who plays at *chaugān*.

चौगानबाज़ी, *f.* the playing at *chaugān*.

चौगानी, *f.* a straight *huḳḳā*-pipe or tube for smoking through. [vicinity, environs.

चौगिर्द, on all four sides, all around: hence, *m.*

चौगुणा, *m.* (*f.* ī) quadruple, fourfold.

चौगुना, *more prop.* **चौगुणा**, *q.v.*

चौगोशा, *m.* a kind of oblong tray; a square napkin usually sent with a present of fruit, sweetmeats, etc.

चौगोशिया, four-cornered.

चौगोशी, *f.* an animal with slit ears (particularly a horse: these are generally taught to amble).

चौगोषिया, *m.* a *turkī* horse, horse with slit ears.

चौघड़ा = **चौघरा**, *q.v.*

चौघरा, *m.* a small box with four partitions for holding betel-leaf, nut, chunam and spices which are chewed together, or for perfumes, etc.: a wooden frame for holding four chatties or pots.

चौज, ardour (in old Hindee).

चौटक, four eyes.

चौठाई = **चारों ठांई**, *qq.v.* [quity.

चौजुगी, relating to the **चतुर्युग**, *q.v.*; of vast anti-

चौड़, spoiled, destroyed.

चौड़चौपट, damaged, abandoned, vicious.

चौड़ा, *m.* (*f.* ī) wide, broad. — *k.* to enlarge.

चौड़ाचकला, *m.* (*f.* ī) extensive, spacious.

चौड़ाई, *f.* breadth, width; latitude; extent, extension; boasting.

चौड़ान, *f. m.?* breadth, width.

चौड़ाना, *t.* to increase in breadth, widen, expand.

चौड़ाव, *m.* = **चौड़ाई**, *q.v.*

चौडोल, *m.* a kind of sedan with two poles.

चौपडू, *m.* a blockhead.

चौतग्गी, *f.* a thread of four strands.

चौतनी, *f.* a four-cornered cap.
चौतरका, *m.* a mitre : a kind of tent.
चौतरा, a contraction of चबुत्रा, *q.v.*
चौतह } चौतहा } of four folds. [guitar.
चौतारा, *m.* a four-stringed musical instrument,
चौताल } चौताला } *m.* a certain mode in music.
चौतिया, see (1) चौथिया (2) चौतीया.
चौतीया, *f.* a quartan ague.
चौतीस, more commonly चौन्तीस, *q.v.*
चौत्कीखैआली, *f.* a sum paid to the zamīndār for the privilege of weighing the grain of the cultivators.
चौथ, *f.* the fourth lunar day ; the fourth part ; a species of tribute (consisting of one fourth of the regular Government assessment) demanded by the Marhaṭṭas from the neighbouring princes as the price of forbearing to ravage their country.
चौथपन, *m.* old age.
चौथा, *m.* (*f.* ī) *adj.* fourth.
चौथाई, *f.* a fourth part, quarter ; a fine equal to one fourth of the revenue.
चौथिया, 1, = चौतीया, *q.v.* : 2. *m.* one who receives the *chauth* : a certain grain-measure nearly equal to a *ser.* [the fourth day after marriage.
चौथी, *f.* a fourth day ; a ceremony performed on
चौथे, *adv.* in the fourth place, fourthly.
चौथेपन, *m.* old age.
चौदन्त, *m.* (*f.* ā *or* ī) sturdy, robust, stout : *lit.* crossing the teeth (as elephants do in fighting).
चौदन्ता, *f.* a female elephant (?).
चौदन्ती, *f.* (see चौदन्त) boldness.
चौदवां, a corruption of चौदहवां, *q.v.*
चौदस, *f.* the fourteenth day of the moon.
चौदह, fourteen (१४) : see वां, वीं, वे, वें.
चौदहगुणनिधान, *m.* an epithet of any person possessing all good qualities, a paragon of excellence.
चौदहां, *m.* (*f.* °हीं) (*contraction*) = चौदहवां, *q.v.*
चौदहों, (see ओं, 4) the fourteen of them, the whole fourteen.
चौदहोंभुवन, *m.* the fourteen worlds or states of existence, *i. e.* the seven that are below the earth and the six that are above it, inclusive of the earth.
चौदहोंरत्न, *m.* the fourteen treasures that were produced at the churning of the ocean.
चौदहोंलोक = चौदहोंभुवन, *q.v.*
चौदहोंविद्या, *f.* the fourteen branches of learning taught in the system of the Hindoos.
चौदहीं in Braj = चौदहों, *q.v.*
चौदा = चौदह, *q.v.* [pearls.
चौदानिया, *m.* an ear-ornament formed of four
चौदानी, *f.* = चौदानिया, *q.v.*
चौदिश } चौदिशा } चौदिस } = चहुंदिश = चारोंओर, *q.v.*

चौद्धवा (*corruption*) = चौदहवां, *q.v.*
चौद्री, *more prop.* चौधरी, *q.v.*
चौधमा, *m.* (*f.* ī) *more prop.* चौदहवां, *q.v.*
चौधर, robust, active, vigorous, corpulent.
चौधराई, *f.* (see आई, 3) the status or the business of a *chaudharī*, chaudhareeship.
चौधरायत, a chaudharee's fees of office.
चौधरी, *m.* the headman of a trade, headman of a village ; (in Bengal) a title of landholders (superior [to talluqdār).
चौधिर } चौधीर } चौधेर } on all four sides, all around.
चौन्ताली, *f.* cotton-pods in which the fibre is equal to one fourth of the whole produce.
चौन्तीस, thirty-four (३४) : see, ओं, वां, वीं, वे, वें.
चौन्धियाना, *n.* to be confused, be frightened out of one's senses, be amazed, be dazzled, be astonished.
चौपट, ruined, destroyed, levelled, plain, flat.— *k.* to level, destroy.
चौपड़, 1, a corruption of चौपाड़, *q.v.* : 2, *f.* the name of a game (backgammon ?) played with long dice ; the cloth on which it is played.
चौपत्ती = चौपत्री, *q.v.* [et-book.
चौपत्री, *f.* a small tract, essay, pamphlet ; a pock-
चौपहरा, *adv.*. during four pahars, *i. e.* half the natural day (or twelve hours). — *dend*, to break in a horse by giving him a twelve hours' spell of it.
चौपहल, four sides or four-sided, a square bottle.
चौपहला = चौपाला, *q.v.*
चौपहलू = चौपहरा, *q.v.*
चौपा, a contraction of चौपाया, *q.v.*
चौपाई, *f.* a kind of metre or verse consisting of four short lines. It is used chiefly in Braj compositions.
चौपां = चूपान, *q.v.*
चौपाड़, 1, = चौपाया, *q.v.* : 2, *m.* a kind of small shed, summer-house or pavilion (it is generally built jointly by several persons in a village community as a restingplace common to them all).
चौपान = चूपान, *q.v.*
चौपाय = (1) चौपाई (2) चौपाया, *qq.v.*
चौपाया, *m. f.* any quadruped : any four-footed piece of furniture.
चौपार = (1) चौपाड़ (2) चौपाया, *qq.v.*
चौपारा, made of four pieces.
चौपाल, a corruption of चौपाया, *q.v.*
चौपाला, *m.* a litter, sedan.
चौपास, (= चहुंपास) all around, on all sides.
चौपैआ } चौपैया } = चौपाई, *q.v.* [arms.
चौबग़ला, *m.* a kind of jacket, not open under the
चौबन्दी, *f.* the giving a horse new shoes ; fasten-
चौबर, strong, robust, bold. [ings of baggage.
चौबला, a plebeian form of चौबे, *q.v.*
चौबाइन, *f.* a female of the *chaube* tribe.

चौबाई, *more prop.* चौवाई, *q.v.* [specified things.
चौबाछा, a kind of tax or levy of revenue on four
चौबाईन, *more com.* चौबाइन, *q.v.*
चौबार, *m.* a summer-house, shed; a police-station; a town-hall, assembly, court.
चौबारा, *m.* = चौबार, *q.v.*
चौबीस, twenty-four (२४): see ओं, वां, वीं, वे, वें.
चौबीसा, a track of land containing twenty-four villages occupied by one tribe.
चौबे, *m.* (corrupt. of चतुर्वेदी) a Brāhman who has read (or who professes to have read) the four Veds. The term is now-a-days applied to the supposed descendants of such persons, though they are themselves very far from being learned men.
चौभीर, on all sides, all around.
चौमस्या, *m.* a ploughman hired for a term or season of four months.
चौमहल्ला, of four stories (a house, etc.).
चौमहल = चौमहल्ला, *q.v.*
चौमास, lands tilled during the *chaumāsā.*
चौमासा, *m.* the space of four months (applied particularly to the rainy season (from June to Sept.).
चौमुख, *m.* an epithet of Brahm; a lampstand with four partitions.
चौमुखा, *m.* 1, a kind of पटा, *q.v.*: 2, a lampstand with four partitions: 3, *adj.* having four burners (a lamp).
चौमुखी, *f.* an epithet of the goddess *Devī*; the the seed of a tree (*Scaevola lobelia* or *Eleocarpus ganitrus*) called in Sanskrit *Rudrāksha.*
चौमुहानी, *f.* a place where four roads meet.
चौमेंढा, tying the elbows behind.
चौम्य = चौम्य, *q. v.* [extensive tract of low land.
चौर, *m.* a thief: a large open space in a forest; an
चौरंग, *m.* a practice in sword-exercise, *viz.* the cutting off at one blow the four legs of an animal. — *kaṭnā*, to cut off the four legs of an animal at one blow. — *mārnā*, to lose the use of the limbs by illness; to hamstring a quadruped. [four kinds.
चौरंगा, *m.* (*f.* ī) having four colours, being of
चौरंगी, *m.* (*f.* iṇī) = चौरंगा, *q. v.*
चौरंसा, (in Pros.) a species of metre. [around.
चौरस, level, even: *adv.* on all four sides, all
चौरसाई, *f.* equality of surface, levelness, even-
चौरसाना, *t.* to level, make plain or even. [ness.
चौरसी, *f.* a granary above-ground.
चौरहा, *m.* = चौराहा *q. v.*
चौरा, 1, *more prop.* (1) चबुत्रा (2) चौला, *qq. v.*: 2, *m.* the place where the Hindoo widow (or *sati*) is im- [molated.
चौरानवे } चौरान्वे } = चौरानवे, *q. v.*
चौरानवे, ninety-four (९४): see ओं, वां, वीं, वे, वें.
चौरारा = चौपाड़, 2, *q.v.*
चौरासी, eighty-four (८४): see ओं, वां, वीं, वे, वें.
चौरास्ता = चौराहा, *q.v.*
चौराहा, *m.* a cross-road, the junction of four roads; the meeting of the boundaries of four villages.
चौरिका, *f.* theft; fraud. [house.
चौरी, *f.* 1, *more com.* चोरी, *q. v*: 2, a summer-
चौर्य्य, *m.* theft; stealth; fraud. [tonsure.
चौल, *m.* the ceremony of cutting the hair or of
चौलकर्म, *m.* the ceremony of tonsure,—the cutting off all the hair from the head of a child three years old, excepting one lock on the crown of the head.
चौलड़ा, *m.* } चौलड़ी, *f.* } a necklace of four strings.
चौला, a kind of bean (*Dolichos sinensis*) much cultivated in India. [*mus*).
चौलाई, *f.* a kind of greens (*Amaranthus polyga-*
चौवन, fifty-four (५४): see ओं, वां, वीं, वे, वें.
चौवा, *m.* a quadruped (particularly said of oxen): a hand-breadth.
चौवाई, *f.* a commotion, tempest, hurricane, (*i. e.* the blowing of the wind from all four quarters).
चौवार, *more com.* चौपाड़ or चौबार, *qq. v.*
चौवालीस = चौआलीस, *q. v.*
चौस, *m.* land four times tilled: flour, powder.
चौसठ = चौंसठ, *q. v.*
चौसर, *m.* a certain game played with oblong dice (differing only in the form of the game from *chaupaṛ*); the material on which the game is played.
चौसरी, *f.* 1 an ornament worn by females around the neck: land four times ploughed.
चौसिंघा, a raised mound indicating where the boundaries of four villages meet.
चौहट, a contraction of चौहट्टा, *q. v.*
चौहट्टा, *m.* a market where four roads meet.
चौहड़, the jawbone, the cheekbone.
चौहत्तर, seventy-four (७४): see ओं, वां, वीं, वे, वें.
चौहट्टा, *m.* } चौहट्टी, *f.* } = चौहट्टा, *q. v.*
चौहान, *m.* a certain caste of Rājputs.
च्यमस, 1, = चमस, *q.v.*: 2, *m. pr. n.* (see नवयोगेश्वर) the 8th Yogeshwar.
च्यवन, *m.* motion; loss: *pr. n.* a certain *Rishi.*
च्यार in Chand = चार, *q.v.*
च्युत, fallen, fallen from, fallen off, deviated from, erred, strayed; degraded; dropped, oozed out.
च्युति, *f.* a departing; a flowing out; a fall; a perishing; the not doing one's duty; the vulva; the anus.
च्यूड़ा = चोऊड़ा, *q. v.*
च्यूपटा, = चोऊपटा, *q. v.*
च्यूपटी = चोऊपटी, *q. v.*
च्यौत्न, 1, *m.* (*f.* ī) animating, inspiring, promoting; going, moving; oviparous; abandoned, void of virtue or purity: 2, *m.* concussion, shaking; enterprize, exertion; contrivance, management; strength.

छ

छ (chh) is the seventh consonant in the Hindee

alphabet, and the second letter of the चवर्ग or palatal class. It is the aspirate of the letter च, and has the sound of *chh* in the English word 'watch-house' with the *ouse* dropped. It is constantly used (1) as a contraction of छः (2) as a corruption (α) of क्ष; *e.g.* छुरी (β) of ष; *e.g.* छटाँक (γ) of श (δ) of स; *e.g.* छिर्का (ε) of its unaspirated form.

छई, 1, (क्षत) abolished : 2, (क्षय) *f.* pulmonary consumption : 3, *f.* a thatched roof on a boat : a stuffed pad to prevent bullocks from being hurt when loaded.

छए, *more prop.* छई, *q.v.*

छओ, a corruption of छओं, *q.v.*

छओं, (see ओं, 4) all six, the six of them.

छः, (षष) six (६).

छःओ, *more com.* छओं, *q.v.*

छंकाना, *t.* to concentrate, cause to strain.

छंकाहट, *f.* a concentrating, causing to strain.

छंछनाना, *a. int.* to simmer; to sound, chink : to smart, pain.

छंजन, a certain species of leprosy.

छंडनौं, in Chand = छाड़ना, *q.v.*

छंहाई, *f.* shadiness.

छक, satiated, satisfied, filled, content. — *jānā*, to become satisfied, get to be satiated.

छकड़ा, *m.* a kind of carriage, car, cart.

छकड़ाना, *t.* to slap, cuff.

छकना, *n.* to be content, be satiated, be gratified : to be afflicted, harassed : to be astonished.

छकवाना, *t.* to cause to be satisfied, etc.

छकाई, *f.* satiety, satisfaction.

छकाचक = छकाछक, *q.v.*

छकाछक क°, *t.* to satiate, fill, satisfy, gratify.

छकाना, *t.* to pamper, cloy, satiate : to chastise.

छकार, *m.* the letter छ, or any symbol that may represent it.

छकुर, a division of crops by which one sixth goes to the zemīndār.

छक्कड़, *f.* a slap, blow, cuff.

छक्का, *m.* the sixth (at cards, etc.) : a cage with a net attached to it. — *pakka ronā*, to weep very bitterly. — *panjā k.* to deceive, play tricks.

छग, *m.* a goat.

छगनौं, (*Chand*) to taste, experience, become subject to (?).

छगरी, *f.* a small she-goat.

छगल, 1, = छागल, 2, *q.v.* : 3, *m.* (*f.* ā *or* ī) a goat.

छगला, *f.* 1, *see above*, 2; 2, a certain plant (*Convolvulus pes caprae* or *C. argenteus*).

छगली, 1, see छगल, 2 : 2, = छगला, 2, *qq.v.*

छगुन, sixfold.

छगुनी, *f.* child's coral.

छचकारना, *t.* to reprove, chide.

छछड़ी, *f.* the root of the *phapond*-tree.

छछिआ = (1) छाछ (2) डवा, *qq.v.* See बछिआ.

छछुगडर, a corruption of छुछुन्दर, *q.v.*

छछुआ, *f.* boiled rice.

छज, *m.* a thicket : *lit.* bushy.

छज्जा, *m.* a gallery : the expanded branches of a tree.

छट, (*prop.* षट) six (६)) : see ओं, वाँ, वीं, वे, वें.

छटकना, see छिटकना.

छटकाना, see छुटकाना and छिटकाना.

छटना, 1, *m.* a kind of sieve : 2, *a. int.* to decay; to separate : *n.* to be pruned, be picked out; to be cut to a point and obliquely (as a pen), be cut aslant, be reduced.

छटपटाना, *a. int.* to toss, tumble about, flounder.

छटवाँ, *m.* (*f.* वीं) sixth. See छट.

छटहा, *m.* (*f.* ī) waspish, peevish.

छटा, 1, *m.* (*f.* ī) *more prop.* छठा, *q.v.* : 2, *m.* a lump, mass, assemblage, multitude, number; a glory, splendour, brilliance, lustre, refulgence, a straight or continuous line or mark.

छटाओ, *more prop.* छपटाव, *q.v.*

छटाँक, (prop. ष) *f.* the sixteenth part of a *ser*, or about two ounces avoirdupois.

छटाना, a causat. of छटना, *q.v.*

छटाभा, *f.* lightning.

छटाव, *more prop.* छपटाव, *q.v.*

छटी, 1, see छटा, 1 : 2, *more com.* छठी, *q.v.*

छटे, sixthly, in the sixth place.

छटों, (see ओं, 4) all six, the six of them.

छट्टा, *m.* (*f.* ī) the sixth.

छट्टे = छटे, *q.v.*

छट्ठ, *f.* the sixth day of the moon.

छट्ठा, *m.* (*f.* ī) the sixth.

छट्ठी = (1) छट्ठा (2) छठी, *qq.v.*

छठ = छट्ठ, *q.v.*

छठवाँ, *m.* (*f.* °वीं)
छठा, *m.* (*f.* ī) } *more com.* छटवाँ, *q.v.*
छठाँ, *m.* (*f.* छठीं)

छठी, *f.* (see छठा) a kind of religious ceremony performed among Hindoos on the sixth day after child-birth. *Chhaṭhīkā dūdh yād dilānā*, to administer chastisement.

छठीं, 1, see छठाँ; 2, *more com.* छठी, *q.v.*

छठें, (poet.) = (1) छः (2) छटे, *qq.v.*

छड़, *f.* the pole of a spear : spikenard : straw, stubble, pedule, stalk.

छड़ना, *t.* to beat rice to separate the husk from it.

छड़याछाट, solitary, alone.

छड़ा, 1, *m.* an ear-ornament of pearls : 2, *m.* (*f.* ī) apart, alone, solitary.

छड़ी, *f.* 1, (*m.* छड़ा) a lonely female : 2. a switch, rod, cane, wand : a procession of the followers of Shāh Madār.

छड़ीदार, *m.* a mace-bearer, usher of the rod.

छड़ीला, *f.* a kind of fragrant moss : potter's earth.

छण ; for words beginning thus, see under the form क्षण.

छपटना, *a. int.* to grow thin, diminish : *n.* to be extracted, be separated.

छपटवाना, *t.* to cause to clean rice; to cause to select, cause to prune, cause to lop, cause to clip.

छटाई, *f.* (see **झाई**, 3) cleaning or separating (grain, etc.); the price paid for cleaning grain.

छटाना, transitive of **छटना**, *q.v.*

छटाव, *m.* a beating rice to clean it from the husk: detachment on forage.

छत, 1, a corruption of **क्षत**, *q.v.*: 2, *f.* a roof; a cloth stretched across the roof of a room: a platform. — *pāṭnā* or *banānā* or *lagānā*, to ceil, cover the

छतनार, bunchy; flat. [inner roof of a building.

छत्तर, *m.* (prop. **छत्र**) an umbrella; a house set apart for the charitable entertainment of strangers or guests; a shed, open building, choultry or resting-

छत्ता, *m.* a honey-comb. [place for travellers, etc.

छति = **क्षति**, *q.v.*

छत्तीस, thirty-six (३६): see **ओं, वां, वीं, वे, वें**.

छत्तीसगुणनिधान, *m.* an epithet of any Brāhmaṇ considered as possessing all the virtues possible to one of his order. [food that are lawful to Brāhmaṇs.

छत्तीसव्यंजन, *m.* the thirty-six different kinds of

छत्तीसी, *f.* (prop. an adj. *f.* prudish) a prude, an excessively lewd woman who knows thirty-six postures in copulation, and who yet pretends to modesty.

छतुर, a covering placed on a heap of winnowed

छत्र, *more prop.* **छत्र**, *q.v.* [corn.

छत्रक, an earthquake.

छत्रधारी, *m.* (*f.* iṇī) = **छत्रपति**, *q.v.*

छत्रपति, *m.* (*f.* **पत्नी**) one who is entitled to carry an umbrella, *i. e.* a rājā, prince, etc.

छत्रबन्धु, *m.* (a term of abuse) a mere Kshatriya, a base Kshatriya. [nion, deposition; widowhood.

छत्रभंग, *m.* loss of empire, subversion of domi-

छत्रर in Chand = **छत्र**, *q.v.*

छत्रा, *f.* a kind of fennel (*Anethum sowa*); a pungent seed, coriander; a mushroom; anise.

छत्रियाणी = **क्षत्रियाणी** or **छत्रियाणी**, *qq.v.*

छत्री, 1, *m.* (*f.* iṇī) = (1) **छत्री** (2) **क्षत्री**, *qq.v.*: 2, *f.* a tester or covering of a bed; a small umbrella; a small ornamented pavilion generally built over a place of interment; a frame made of bamboos for pigeons to settle upon: the poop of a ship.

छत्र, *m.* a parasol, umbrella.

छत्रवन्त, *m.* (*f.* vatī) = **छत्री**, *q.v.*

छत्राक, *m.* a mushroom.

छत्री, *m.* (*f.* iṇī) one who has an umbrella.

छत्वर, *m.* a house, dwelling; an arbour, bower.

छद, *m.* a leaf; a cover; a wing; *hence*, in the ingenious system of reckoning by symbols adopted by Hindoos in their poetry, this word is a symbol for 2.

छदना, *more prop.* (1) **छिदना** (2) **छन्दना**, *qq.v.*

छदाम, *m.* a denomination of money equal to six *dām* or two *damṛī* being the fourth part of the *paisā*.

छद्म = **छद्मन**, *q.v.*

छद्मतापस, *m.* (*f.* ī) a hypocrite in religion.

छद्मन, *m.* disguise, hypocrisy, fraud pretext, deceit, trick, masquerade.

छन, *m.* 1, = **क्षण**, *q.v.*: 2, the hissing sound made by the falling of a drop of water upon a warm plate.

छनकाना = **छंकाना**, *q.v.*

छनकाहट = **छंकाहट**, *q.v.*

छनछनाना = **छंछनाना**, *q.v.*

छनना, *n.* to be strained, be percolated.

छनवाना, *t.* to cause to sift, cause to strain.

छनाक, *m.* = **छन**, 2, *q.v.*; *also*, the sound of the breaking of earthenware.

छनाना, *t.* to strain, percolate.

छनिक = **क्षणिक**, *q.v.*

छन्द, *m.* 1, purport, meaning, intention, object, wish, desire, opinion; self-help; power, subjection; a certain measure in music (particularly, the metre of the Veds): 2, *adj.* flattering: solitary; private, secret.

छन्दना, *n.* to be tied. [pocrite.

छन्दपातन, *m.* (*f.* ī) a false ascetic, pretender, hy-

छन्दबन्द, *m.* a trick, cheating, deceiving.

छन्दसम्बन्धीय, versified, in verse.

छन्दा = **छान्दा**, *q.v.*

छन्दी, *m.* (*f.* in *or* inī) deceitful.

छन्दोग / **छन्दोज्ञ** } *m.* a chanter of the Sām-Ved.

छन्दोनिरूपण, *m.* a treatise on Prosody.

छन्न, covered, concealed, hidden.

छन्ना, 1 = **छनना**, *q.v.*: 2. *m.* a sieve, a cloth through which anything is sifted; the cells of a beehive. [splash, squash.

छप, *m.* the sound of anything falling into water,

छपई = **छपय**, *q.v.* [shock; a dent, bruise.

छपक, a dashing against an object, collision,

छपकना, *n.* to be dashed, be thrown, be splashed: to be beaten. [to beat, thrash, flog, whip.

छपकाना, *t.* to dash or throw water, to splash:

छपछप, *m.* the sound occasioned by water being struck with the hand. [printed.

छपना, 1, = **छिपना**, *q.v.*: 2, *n.* to be stamped or

छपय, *m.* a kind of measure in Hindee verse consisting of six hemistichs.

छपर, *more prop.* **छप्पर**, *q.v.*

छपरखट / **छपरखाट** } see **छप्परखाट**.

छपरी, *f.* a puddle.

छपवाना, *t.* to cause to be printed, get printed.

छपा, *m.* (*f.* ī) stamped, printed. [ing; edition.

छपाई, *f.* the act of printing; the price of print-

छपाका, *m.* the sound produced by striking water, splash, squash.

छपाना, 1, = **छिपाना**, *q.v.*: 2, *t.* to cause to print.

छपाय (*corruption*) = (1) **छपय** (2) **छपाई**, *qq.v.*

छप्पड़, *more com.* **छप्पर**, *q.v.*

छप्पन, fifty-six (५६): see **ओं, वां, वीं, वे, वें**.

छप्पर, *m.* a sloping thatch, roof; a tester.

छप्परखट (*contraction*) = **छप्परखाट**, *q.v.* [tains.

छप्परखाट, *m.* a bedstead with a tester and cur-

छप्परबन्द, *m.* a thatcher.
छप्परबन्दी, *f.* thatching; the price of thatching.
छप्यौ, an old form = छपा, *q.v.* [figure.
छब, *f.* beauty, splendour, brilliancy: shape, form,
छबछीन = छबीछीन, *q.v.*
छबड़ा, *m.* a kind of basket.
छबतख़्ती, *f.* handsomeness.
छबि; see छवि.
छबी, *f.* a painting, picture.
छबीछीन, deficient in splendour, destitute of beauty or of form; small, slender.
छबीला, *m.* (*f.* ī) handsome, comely, graceful.
छब्बीस, twenty-six (२६): see ओं, वां, वीं, वे, वें.
छम; for words beginning thus, see under the form छम.
छमछमाना, *a. int.* to shine, glitter; to sound.
छमयड, *m.* a fatherless son, orphan.
छमात्रा, *more prop.* षडमात्र, *q.v.*
छमि = छमा करके (from छमना). [the form छय.
छय, *m. f.*; for words beginning thus, see under
छयकारी, promotive of decay or of destruction.
छयल; see छैल.
छया, 1, = छाया, *q.v.*: 2. *m.* a victim: a boy.
छयालीस, forty-six (४६): see ओं, वां, वीं, वे, वें.
छयासठ, sixty-six (६६): see ओं, वां, वीं, वे, वें.
छयासी, eighty-six (८६): see ओं, वां, वीं, वे, वें.
छर, *f.* spikenard: a shaft, pole, flagstaff, flag,
छरछोबी, *f.* a necessary, jakes. [staff, pike.
छरस, see षटरस. [dened (as a traveller).
छरिन्दा, alone, single, free, not loaded, not bur-
छरी, *more prop.* छुरी, *q.v.*
छर्द, *m.* } छर्दि *f.* } nausea, retching, vomiting.
छर्दिकारिपु, *m.* small cardamoms; *prop.* an anti-
छर्रा, *m.* a small shot. [emetic.
छल, *m.* fraud, artful management, circumvention, deception, knavery, stratagem, trick, artifice, imposture, perfidy, subterfuge, evasion, pretence, pretext, excuse.— *k.* to defraud, etc.
छलंग, *f.* a skip, bound.
छलंगना, *a. int.* to skip, bound.
छलक, 1, *f.* an overflow, running over: 2, *m.* (*f.* ikā) a deceiver: lit. *adj.* deceiving, deceptive, appertaining to *chhal.*
छलकना, *a. int.* to overflow, spill.
छलकाना, *t.* to spill, cause to overflow.
छलछलाना, *a. int.* to murmur.
छलछलाहट, *f.* a murmuring, murmur.
छलछिद्र, *m.* a plot, stratagem.
छलछिद्री, *m.* (*f.* iṇī) deceitful, fraudulent, tricky.
छलज्ञानी, *m.* (*f.* inī) *adj.* understanding tricks, or
छल देना, an intensive form of छलना, *q.v.* [strategy.

छलन, *m.* a deceiving, tricking. [make excuses.
छलना, *t.* to deceive, cheat, impose upon, evade,
छलनी, 1, = छालनी, *q.v.*: 2, battered.—*k.* to batter.
छलबल, *m.* fraud and force, stratagem, artifice,
छलमय, *m.* (*f.* ī) abounding in deception. [trick.
छलांग, *f.* a skipping, jumping; a skip, leap, spring. *Chhalāngeṅ mārnā,* to spring, jump.
छलावा, *m.* ignis fatuus.—*denā,* to lead one a wild goose chase, mislead. — *ho jānā,* to elude one's search or pursuit.
छलिक, 1, = छलक, 2; 2, *m.* a kind of song.
छलिकरूप, *m.* (*f.* a) = छलिकरूपी, *q.v.*
छलिकरूपी, *m.* (*f.* inī) a tricky person, etc.: *lit.* feigning, artful, tricky, false, deceptive.
छलिका, *f.* (see छलक, 2,) a female deceiver.
छलिया = छली, *q.v.*
छली, *m.* (*f.* inī) a cheat, deceiver, trickster, etc.: *lit.* fraudulent, deceitful, false, perfidious, treacherous, traitorous, artful, tricky, swindling.
छलौरी = छिलौरी, *q.v.*
छल्ला, *m.* an ornamented gold or silver ring worn on the fingers or toes: a blister, pock, pustule.
छल्ली, *f.* skin, bark, rind, etc.
छल्लेदार, annular. [brillance, lustre, light.
छवि, *f.* hide, skin: colour; beauty, splendour,
छवो, in Braj = छओं, *q.v.*
छवैया, *m.* a thatcher.
छसट } छसठ } *more com.* छयासठ, *q.v.*
छसात, *m.* a trick, cheating, jugglery.
छह = छः, *q.v.*
छही, *f.* a kind of decoy-bird.
छहूं, a Braj form of छहों.
छहों, (see ओं, 4) all the six, the six of them.
छा; see (1) छह (2) छां (3) चाह.
छाई, *f.* ashes.
छाईं, *f.* discoloration: a ghost, goblin.
छाओं, *f.* (pl. छाएं) shade, shadow, reflection of
छाओंबांह, *f.* auspices. [any object in a mirror.
छाओनी, *f.* cantonments, barracks or huts for soldiers; thatching, the act of thatching.
छां = छाओं, *q.v.* [(छायडना).
छांड़ा, a corruption (1) of छारा (2) of छायडा (see
छांबांह, *f.* auspices.
छाओं } छांव } छांवा } छांह } = छाओं, *q.v.*
छांहक, appertaining to छांह, *q.v.*
छांहबांह, *f.* auspices.
छांहवाला, *m.* (*f.* ī) affording shade, shady.
छांहा = छाओं, *q.v.*

छांहारा, *m.* (*f.* ī) umbrageous, shady.

छाक, *m.* prepared food taken forth by labourers when they go to their daily work, luncheon: a cup, ewer.

छाकना, *t.* to clear the water of a well, etc.

छाके = मत्त, मतवाला.

छाकें ; see (1) छाक (2) छाकना (3) छाके.

छाग, *m.* (*f.* ikā *or* ī) a goat.

छागल, 1. (*f.* ī) a goat: *adj.* produced from a goat: 2. *f.* a leathern bottle with a spout to it, a goatskin.

छागिका / छागी } *f.* (see छाग) a she-goat.

छाछ ; see (1) छाछ (2) छाज.

छाछ, *f.* (*m.* ?) buttermilk.

छाछी = मथठा, *q.v.* [clearing grain.

छाज, *m.* a kind of basket used in winnowing or

छाजन, 1, a Braj pl. of छाज, *q.v.* : 2, see (1) छाजना

छाजना, *t.* to thatch : to befit, become. [(2) छंजन.

छाजा, *m.* (*f.* ī) past part. of छाजना.

छा जाना, to spread, lie, over-shadow. [alluvium.

छाड़, *f.* a river's bank ; land gained from a river,

छाड़कर, see छोड़कर.

छाड़चिट्ठी, *f.* a permit, pass.

छाड़छड़ेला, *m.* a certain medicinal herb.

छाड़ना = छोड़ना, *q.v.*

छाड़ाना = छोड़ाना, *q.v.*

छांटा, *f.* parings, refuse, vomit: selection, fashion of clothes. — *k.* to disgorge, vomit. — *lenā*, to select, [choose.

छांटछटाव, *m.* retrenchment.

छांटन, *f.* a cutting, slip, chip.

छांटना, *t.* to vomit; to husk, separate the husk from grain by pounding it in a mortar; to pare, clip, prune, lop, crop, trim, dress, clean, select.

छांटा ; see (1) छांट (2) छांटना.

छायडना, *t.* to vomit, emit, let go, release, loose, leave, abandon, forsake.

छात, 1, *f.* a roof : 2, thin, feeble, emaciated.

छाता, *m.* a large umbrella ; the breast ; a fungus, mushroom ; mouldiness.

छातिन, a pl. (1) of छाता (2) of छाती, *qq.v.*

छातिया, a familiar form of छाती, *q.v.*

छाती, *f.* a small umbrella, parasol : breast, bosom, dug, bubby. — *bhar*, breast-high. — *bhar ānā*, to weep. — *bhar-jānā*, to be chest-foundered. — *par patthar raknā*, to have patience. — *par mung ḍālnā*, to do anything in the presence of another person by which he is vexed; *lit.* to grind pulse on the breast. — *phaṭnā*, to sympathize ; *lit.* (the heart) to break (with grief or sorrow). — *piṭnā*, to strike the breast in grief, to regret, repent, lament. — *ṭhoknā*, to encourage, reässure, assure. — *ṭhanḍi honā*, to be pleased or overjoyed. — *jalnā*, to lament ; *prop.* to have the heart-burn. — *kā patthar*, nuisance, pest. — *kā jam*, the destroyer of the heart (said of a person or thing the presence of which is unpleasant), a nuisance, pest. — *kholke milnā*, to meet frankly. — *gadranā*, (the breast) to swell (in young women). — *lagānā*, to lament, grieve. — *se lagānā*, to fondle. — *nikalke chalnā*, to stalk, strut.

छात्र, *m.* a pupil, disciple, tyro, novice.

छादन, *m.* the act of covering : raiment ; a screen, [covering.

छादान, *m.* a water-bag.

छादित, *m.* (*f.* ā) covered, concealed.

छान, *f.* a roof, a frame of bamboo for thatching.

छान डालना, *t.* (intensive) to strain out.

छानना, *t.* to strain, percolate ; to sift ; to search, investigate, canvass.

छानबिछान, *f.* investigation, examination, search.

छानबिनान, *m.* = छानबिछान, *q.v.*

छानमारना, *t.* to search, rummage, explore, canvass.

छानलेना, *t.* to select, cull.

छानवे, ninety-six (९६): see चों, वां, वीं, वे, वें.

छानस, *m.* (*f.* ?) chaff.

छाना, *t.* to thatch, shade, cover, roof, spread.

छानी, *f.* a thatch.

छान्द, *f.* a tether, trammel, net.

छान्दना, *t.* to tether, fasten, tie, bind.

छान्दा, *m.* a share, part (among faqeers).

छान्दोग्य, *m. pr n.* the Chāndogya-Upanishad (pertaining to the Sām-Ved) ; the Veds in general.

छाचवे = छानवे, *q.v.*

छाना = छानना, *q.v.*

छान्वे = छानवे, *q.v.*

छाप, *f.* a stamp, print, copy; a seal ; the impression of a stamp or seal ; the Government stamp on coins, papers etc. ; an official stamp in general.

छापती, *f.* a coarse seal of cowdung and mud affixed to a pile of grain on the threshingfloor to pre- [vent its removal.

छापना, *t.* to stamp, print.

छापा, *m.* edition, impression, stamp, print, seal, etc. *Pattharkā* —, lithography : sectarial marks delineated on the body by worshippers of Vishṇu (Vaishnavas) representing a lotus, trident, etc.

छापाना, *more com.* छपाना, *q.v.*

छापाविद्या, *f.* the art of printing.

छापेख़ाना, *m.* a printing-office, printing house.

छापेवाला, *m.* (*f.* ī) a printer.

छाय, a corruption of चय and of छाईं, *qq.v.*

छाया, 1. *f.* shade, shadow, reflected image, reflected light, splendour ; colour ; obscurity, darkness ; 2, (*m.* ?) an apparition, spectre, shade : a mode in music : *met.* somewhat resembling. [shelter.

छायातरु, *m.* a large tree that affords shade and

छायानट, *m.* a certain musical mode (*rāg*).

छायापथ, *m.* æther, the firmament.

छायापाद, an ascertaining the time by observing

छायामित्र, *m.* a parasol. [the shadow of any object.

छायायन्त्र, *m.* a sun-dial ('shadow instrument').

छायावन्त / छायावान } *m.* (*f.* vati) shady, shadowy.

छायावाला, *m.* (*f.* ī) shady, umbrageous.

छार, 1, a corruption of छाड़, *q.v.* : 2, *f.* ashes, dust ; a large clod of earth.

छारकर्दम, *more prop.* चारकर्दम, *q. v.*
छारछबीला, *m.* a kind of fragrant moss.
छारा = छार, 2, *q. v.*
छाल, *m.* the thrush (the disease), a blister.
छाल, *f.* peel, skin, rind, bark. — *utārnā*, to peel, decorticate.
छालनी, *f.* any instrument for flaying.
छाला, *m.* skin; a blister, pustule, pimple.
छालिया, *f.* a kind of betel-nut.
छा लेना, to overspread, overcast, cloud, darken.
छावना = छाना, *q. v.*
छावनी = छाओनी, *q. v.*
छावा, *m.* an elephant aged from ten to twenty [years.
छावों, *more com.* छाओं, *q. v.*
छावो in Braj = छाओं, *q. v.*
छासठ (*contraction*) = छयासठ, *q. v.*
छाह; see (1) छह (2) छां (3) चाह.
छाहीं, *f.* discoloration.
छिंकना, *more com.* छींकना, *q. v.*
छिंकवाना = छिंकाना, *q. v.*
छिंकाई, *f.* sneezing. [strike out, cancel.
छिंकाना, *t.* to cause to stop, cause to seize; to
छिंगुली, *f.* the little finger.
छिंछ, (Chand) a jerk, spirt (?).
छिकाना = छकाना, *q. v.*
छिकुनी, *f.* a wand, stick.
छिक्कन, *m.* sneezing.
छिचड़ा, *m.* sink, slough of a wound, skin, thin skin or pellicle, the cellular membrane that covers the surface of the body, the internal cellular web.
छिचड़ैल, lean, skinny.
छिच्छा = छूछा, *q. v.*
छिछड़ा, *m.* the prepuce.
छिछला, *m.* (*f.* ī) shallow.
छिछलाई, *f.* shallowness.
छिछली, *f.* the play of ducks and drakes.
छिछोड़ा / छिछोरा } *m.* (*f.* ī) trifling, airy, puerile.
छिटकना, *n.* to be scattered, be dissipated, be dispersed: *a. int.* to spread, spirt. — *chāndnikā*, *m.* the diffusion of moonlight.
छिटकनी, *f.* a bolt. [squirt; to desert.
छिटकाना, *t.* to dissipate, disperse, scatter, strew,
छिटकी, *f.* a small spot, speck. — *ḍālnā*, to splash. — *k.* or *denā* or *lagānā*, to flecker, spot, speck, mark with strokes or touches.
छिटुवा, *m.* a sowing broadcast. [stones.
छिटा, the rind or husk of hard seed or of fruit-
छिड़कना, *t.* to sprinkle. *Chhiṛak kar bechnā*, to sprinkle water on stale or faded fruits or vegetables to make them appear fresh; to puff off goods.
छिड़कवाना, 1, = छिड़काना, *q. v.*: 2, *t.* to cause to be sprinked.
छिड़काओ, *m.* the act of sprinkling.
छिड़काना, *t.* to cause to sprinkle.
छिड़काव, *m.* the act of sprinkling.
छिड़ना, *n.* to be vexed, be touched, be excited, be plagued: *a. int.* to take offence, fret. [छया.
छिया; for words beginning thus, see under the form
छियाविधंस, passing away quickly, fading, frail.
छितनी, *f.* a kind of basket without a cover (like a
छितरना, *n.* to be scattered, be spread about. [tray).
छितरवितर, dispersed, scattered.
छितराना, *t.* to scatter, strew, spread.
छिति / छिती } *f.* (prop. चिति) the earth.
छितीछान, covering the earth, prostrate on the ground. — *honā*, to be dispersed, be scattered.
छितोड़ना, *t.* to asperse, sprinkle.
छिदना, *n.* to be pierced, be bored. [pierced.
छिदवाना 1, = छिदाना, *q. v.*: 2, *t.* to cause to be
छिदहा, *m.* (*f.* ī) bored, perforated, pierced.
छिदाना, *t.* to cause to pierce, to perforate.
छिद्र, 1. *m.* a hole, gap, perforation, vacuity, opening, entry, weak point, vulnerable part, defect, fault, flaw: in allusion to the nine inlets of the body, this word, in the ingenious system of reckoning by symbols adopted by Hindoos in their poetry, is a symbol for 9: 2. *m.* (*f.* ā) perforated.
छिद्रत्व, *m.* (*f.* tā) the quality of giving space.
छिद्रा; see छिद्र, 2. [holes or openings.
छिद्रित, *m.* (*f.* ā) perforated, pierced, having
छिन; for words beginning thus, but not given below, see under the form छया.
छिनक, an old form = छिनेक = चयोक, *q. v.*
छिनकना, *t.* to winnow, sift; to blow the nose; *a. int.*
छिनकाना, = छिंकाना, *q. v.* [to go away offended.
छिनला, *m.* a fornicator, whoremonger.
छिनवाना, *t.* to cause to snatch.
छिनविधंस, = छियाविधंस, *q. v.*
छिनाओ, *m.* a seizing, seizure.
छिनाना, *t.* to seize, snatch, pluck.
छिनाल, *f.* (from छिन्न) a harlot.
छिनालपन / छिनालपना } *m.* harlotry.
छिनाला, *m.* fornication. — *k.* to whore, commit fornication, commit adultery.
छिनाव, *m.* a seizing, seizure.
छिनु, a corruption of छया, *q. v.*
छिनेक, a corruption of चयोक, *q. v.*
छिन्न, *m.* (*f.* ā) cut, divided, rent, perforated.
छिन्नभिन्न, cut up, pierced through and through, destroyed, scattered, dispersed, severed, in confusion, all abroad, disheveled. [rum).
छिचकटा, *f.* a certain tree (*Menispermum glab-*

छिचवेष्टिका, *f.* a certain plant (*Cissampelos hexandra*) also called *Uknidhi.*

छिचसंशय, free from doubt, confident.

छिछा, *f.* the tree *Menispermum glabrum* : a harlot.

छिछाल, *f.* (from **छिछ**) a harlot.

छिपकली, *f.* a lizard.

छिपका, *m.* sprinkling.

छिपकिली, *more prop.* **छिपकली**, *q.v.*

छिपकी, *f.* a lizard.

छिप जाना, *a. int.* (intens.) to retire, withdraw.

छिपना, *n.* to be concealed, be hidden, be absent: *a. int.* to disappear, lurk.

छिपवाड़ा (*by inversion*) = **पिछवाड़ा**, *q.v.*

छिपा, *m.* (*f.* ī) concealed, hidden, close. — *rahnā*, to abscond.

छिपाउ / **छिपाऊ** / **छिपाश्रो** } *more com.* **छिपाव**, *q.v.*

छिपाछिपी, *adv.* underhand, secretly.

छिपाना, *t.* to conceal, hide, secrete.

छिपाव, *m.* hiding, concealment, secrecy.

छिपावनी, *f.* clandestine cultivation of land.

छिपेछिपे (*by inversion*) = **पीछेपीछे**, *q.v.*

छिमा; for words beginning thus, see under the form **छमा**.

छिमाजोग = **छमायोग्य**, *q.v.*

छिया; for words beginning thus, but not given below, see under the form **छया**.

छियानव / **छियानवे** / **छियानब्वे** / **छियान्वे** } *more prop.* **छानवे**, *q.v.*

छियूल, a kind of jungle-tree (called also *dhāk*, *q.v.*).

छिरकना, *more prop.* **छिड़कना**, *q.v.*

छिर्का, *m.* (a corruption of **सिर्का**) vinegar.

छिलकना, *a. int.* to glitter, shine.

छिलका, *m.* crust, husk, shell, hull, peel, scale, rind, bark, skin. — *utārnā*, *t.* to blanch, peel, shell, husk, etc.

छिलना, *n.* to be excoriated, be worn away, be rubbed away.

छिलवाना, *t.* (causat. of **छिलना**) to cause to be peeled, etc.

छिलाना, *t.* (causat. of **छीलना**) to cause to peel, etc.

छिलोरी / **छिलौरी** } *f.* a whitlow, blister, felon.

छिल्लड़, *m.* the husk of *chanā*, *q.v.*

छिहत्तर, seventy-six (७६): see **श्रों, वां, वीं, से, सें**.

छिहार्इ, *f.* a crematory.

छी, tush! tut! fie! foh! shameful!

छीऊल = **छियूल**, *q.v.*

छींक, *f.* sneezing, a sneeze. — *lanewālā*, a sternutatory (medicine).

छींकना, *a. int.* to sneeze.

छींका, *m.* a network of strings or cords to hang anything in (as a burthen at either end of a pole the cords of a *bahangi*, an ox-muzzle.

छींचना, *t.* to throw out water.

छीकटूठ, *m.* a wanderer, vagabond.

छीका = **छींका**, *q.v.*

छीछड़ा, *m.* tough and uneatable flesh, the skinny part of meat. — *k.* to flay, tear to pieces.

छीछी, an intensive form of **छी**, *q.v.*

छीजहि, *m. f.* (pl. °**हिं**) old form = **छीजता है**.

छीजना, *a. int.* to decrease, pine away. *Dekhādekhī kīje jog, chhīje kāyā bāṛhe rog*, they who are mere imitators of others in austerity, waste away, and their diseases increase.

छीट, for words beginning thus, see under the form **छीपट**.

छीड़, see (1) **चीर** (2) **छिड़ना** (3) **छीट** (4) **छेड़** (5) **सीर**.

छीया = **चीया**, *q.v.*

छीपट, *f.* spot, splash; spotted cotton cloth, chintz.

छीपटना, *t.* to scatter, sprinkle, irrigate.

छीपटव, a sowing broad cast.

छीपटा, *m.* a spot, splash; a shot; a field in which peas and linseed have been sown broad-cast —*mārnā*, to sprinkle.

छीतर, *m.* a brogue, shoe.

छीदा, *m.* (*f.* ī) thin, not close (said of a person or animal whose legs are much separated: also applied to trees, crops etc. which are scattered or straggling).

छीन, 1, = **चीया**, *q.v.*: 2, the base of **छीनना**; hence, — *lenā*, to snatch up, take possession of, seize, deprive of, pluck, bereave of.

छीनना, *t.* to pull, snatch, pluck, tear, rob.

छीना, 1, = **छूना**, *q.v.*: 2, = **चीया**, *q.v.*: 3, *t.* to bite, sting.

छीनाछानी क°, *t.* to scramble.

छीनू, *adj.* (in comp.) snatching, a snatcher.

छीचा = **छीनना**, *q.v.*

छीप, *f.* discoloration or spot on the skin: a fishing-rod: the act of a buffalo's pushing with his horns.

छीपना, *t.* to print cloths: to push with the horn (as a buffalo): to draw up the rod in fishing.

छीपी, *m.* (f. inī) a cotton-printer or stamper: a flapper or whisk for driving away flies.

छीमी, *f.* a pod, legume, husk.

छीर, a corruption of **चीर** and **सीर**, *qq.v.*

छीलछाल क°, *t.* to pare, peel, etc.

छीलन, *f.* parings, scrapings of rind or peel.

छीलना, *t.* to peel, skin, excoriate, pare, bark, erase, scrape, scratch.

छीलनाछालना, *t.* (intens. of **छीलना**) to pare, peel, etc.

छुश्राना, *more com.* **छूश्राना**, *q. v.*

छुंगलिया, *f.* the little finger.

छुचकारना, *a. int.* to whistle.

छुछकारन, *t.* to drive away contemptuously; to set on or encourage a dog.

छुछली, *f.* the play of a dog or cat with game, etc.

छुछवाना, *t.* to conjure, exercise.

छुछुन्दर, *m.* / **छुछुन्दरी**, *f.* } = **छूछून्दर**, *q. v.*

छछून्दर, *f.* a mole ; a species of musk-rat or shrew (*Sorex caerulescens, Shaw*) : a sort of squib let off from the hand. — *chhornā*, to backbite, calumniate, excite resentment. [a prefix in comp.) little, small.

छुट, (contr. of छोटा) but, excepting, save : (as

छुटक, see (1) छुट (2) छुटका (3) छूट.

छुटकारा, *m.* deliverance.

छुटका, *m.* (*f.* ī) diminutive, small, little, lesser, younger, junior, least in size.

छुटकाना, *t.* to release, set at liberty.

छुटकार, *m.* exemption, liberty, liberation, deliverance, disengagement, release, discharge, emancipation, manumission.

छुटकारा, *m.*
छुटकारी, *f.* } = छुटकार, *q. v.*

छुटखेला, *m.* (*f.* ī) dissolute.

छुटखेली, *f.* dissoluteness.

छुटना, *n.* to be adrift, be discharged, be got rid of, be let go, be let off (a gun), be left, be abandoned, be dismissed, be released, be liberated, be loose, be disheveled (hair) ; to cease ; to slip from, escape, get loose, slip away ; to leave ; to remain.

छुटपन
छुटपना } *m.* childhood, infancy.

छुटभाइया, *m.* middling class of people.

छुटवाना, the causative of छुटना, *q. v.*

छुटाई, *f.* rescue, escape.

छुटान, *f.* leisure, time.

छुटाना, the transitive form of छुटना, *q. v.*

छुटानी, *f.* leisure, time.

छुटापा, *m.* smallness, littleness.

छुटौती, *f.* remission of rent or revenue on the part of Government.

छुट्टी, *f.* discharge, leave of absence, holiday, leisure, time, cessation, disengagement, freedom, dismission, intermission, permission, acquittal.

छुड़वाना, *t.* to cause to let go, cause to set free.

छुड़ाई, *f.* dismissal, discharge.

छुड़ाना, *t.* to free, set free, liberate, extricate, get rid of, discharge, remove, dismiss ; to cause to be freed ; to separate ; to except.

छुड़ाव, *m.* dismissal, discharge.

छुड़ावना, *more prop.* छुड़ाना, *q. v.*

छुड़ावा, *m.* deliverance ; a deliverer.

छुड़ौती, *f.* ransom.

छुतहरा, (*f.* ī) defiled by touching, foul, corrupt, polluted (applied to vessels, dishes, etc).

छुतिहर, ceremonially unclean. [छुद्र.

छुद्र ; for words beginning thus, see under the form

छुद्रम, a corruption of छद्मन, *q. v.* [form छुधा.

छुधा, for words beginning thus, see under the

छुपना = छिपना, *q. v.*

छुपाना = छिपाना, *q. v.*

छुयो, in Braj = छुआ (छुआना). [knife ; a razor.

छुरा, *m.* (prop. क्षुर) a large knife, amputating

छुराछुरी, *f.* (prop. क्षु) snickasnee, fighting with knives, a quarrel : *adj.* at daggers drawn.

छुराना, *more prop.* छुड़ाना, *q. v.*

छुरी, *f.* (prop. क्षुरी) a knife, scalpel. — *tale dam lenā*, to be patient in difficulties.

छुरीकटारी = छुराछुरी, *q. v.*

छुलकना, *a. int.* to make water slowly (as mares

छुलछुलाना, *see above.* [etc. in heat).

छुलाना, *t.* (a causat. of छूना) to cause to touch.

छुलछला
छुलोछला } *m.* (*f.* ī) boyish, puerile, finical.

छुल्लू, boyish, silly.

छुवाव, *m.* resemblance, likeness.

छुहाना, *t.* to whitewash.

छुहारा, *m.* the date (*Phoenix dactylifera*).

छुहावट, *f.* touch.

छुहे = चित्रित, *q. v.* [a prayer of incantation.

छू, the act of blowing or exorcising on uttering

छूआना, *t.* (a causat. of छूना) to cause to touch.

छूआनी, *f.* caudle given to a lying-in woman.

छूई, *f.* chalk.

छूकी, *f.* a gnat.

छूछ = छूछा, 2, *q. v.*

छूछला, *m.* foolish, silly, empty.

छूछा, 1, *m.* conjuration : 2, *m.* (*f.* ī) empty, hollow ; contemptible, despicable, mean.

छूछी, *f.* 1, see छूछा, 2 : 2, a pipe, tube, canula.

छूट, *f.* remission ; leaving ; remission of revenue ; striking off-hand or playing loose in fencing; radiance or splendour of jewels ; reflection of a mirror, etc. ; giving money off-hand or at will to jugglers, etc. at [entertainments.

छूटना = छुटना, *q. v.*

छूटौती = छुटौती, *q. v.*

छूठना, *more com.* छुटना, *q. v.*

छूत, *f.* touch, contamination, defilement. — *lagnā* or *parṇā*, to be infectious (a disease).

छूना, *t.* to touch, meddle with, feel.

छूरिका, *f.* a nostril.

छूरी, a corruption of छुरी, *q. v.*

छे, 1, (a corruption of छः) six : 2, (a dialectic form of the substantive verb) is. [fiscate.

छेंक, *f.* sequestration of goods. — *lenā*, to con-

छेंकना, *t.* to detain, stop, prevent, retain, bar,

छेंकवैया, *m.* a confiscator. [restrain, arrest.

छेंकाव, *m.* = छेक, *q. v.*

छेंचना, *t.* to mince, hack, pound.

छेक, domesticated, tame (as a bird or beast).

छेकना = छेंकना, *q. v.*

छेका, *m.* past part. of छेकना, *q. v.*

छेकोक्ति, *f.* indirect speech, insinuation, double

छेटना ; see छीपटना. [entendre, hint, etc.

छेड़, *f.* an irritating, vexing, etc.

छेड़खानी, *f.* stricture, animadversion; the act of vexing, provoking, exciting, etc.

छेड़छाड़, *see above.*

छेड़ना, *t.* to irritate, vex, excite, fret, trouble, disturb, molest, aggress, abuse, insult, stir up, interrupt, touch, handle, play on a musical instrument.

छेड़ा, *m.* touch, provocation, excitement, etc. [क्षेत्र.

छेत्र; for words beginning thus, see under the form

छेत्री, a corruption (1) of **क्षत्री** (2) of **क्षेत्री**, *qq.v.*

छेद, *m.* a slice, piece, cutting; a cutting off, destruction, dissipation, ceasing; want; limit; a hole, mouth, opening: (in Math.) the denominator of a fraction, divisor. [*lit*: that which penetrates.

छेदक, *m.* anything with which a hole is bored;

छेदन, *m.* a cutting, lopping off, removing: a hole, orifice; a boring, piercing; (in criminal law) mutilation, the cutting off a limb.

छेदना, *t.* to pierce, bore, perforate.

छेदा, *m.* a certain small insect destructive to corn: the disease occasioned by it.

छेना, *m.* curd: a small kind of cymbal.

छेनाल, *more com.* **छिनाल**, *q. v.*

छेनी = **छेवनी**, *q.v.*

छेप, छेम; for words beginning thus, see under the forms **क्षेप, क्षम, क्षेम**, respectively.

छेमंकरी, *f.* a species of kite (*Falco ponticarianus*).

छेमकरी; see (1) **छेमंकरी**, (2) **क्षमकरी**.

छेमघड, *m.* a fatherless son, orphan.

छेरना, *n.* to have a bad digestion.

छेरी, *f.* a she-goat.

छेलछबेला, *m.* (*f.* ī) free, unrestrained.

छेला, *m.* a he-goat. [*mintica*).

छेलु, *m.* a certain medicinal plant (*Conyza anthel-*

छेव, *m.* a mark; a piece of wood cut off. — *mārnā*, to line out, mark. [to extract *tāṛī*.

छेवना, *t.* to mark; to pierce or bleed a *tāṛ*-tree,

छेवनी, *f.* an instrument for piercing with, a chi-

छेवर, *m.* cuticle, skin. [sel, punch.

छेवा, *m.* spaces, comma, etc. See note on the sign ।.

छेवुर, *m.* cuticle, skin.

छेह (from **क्षय**) in Chand = finally, at length.

छै, *f.* for words beginning thus, see under the form

छैया = (1) **छया** (2) **छाया**, *qq.v.* [क्षय.

छैल, *m.* a fop, beau, coxcomb, buck.

छैलचिकनिया, *m.* an exquisite, coxcomb.

छैला, *m.* fop, beau.

छैलापन, *m.* foppishness, spruceness.

छोआ, *m.* treacle.

छोंक, *f.* reasoning, relish.

छोंकन, *m.* spices with which food is seasoned.

छोंचला क°, *t.* to fondle. [for children.

छोंछी, *f.* a bodkin; a needle-case: a small cup

छोकड़ा, *m.* (*f.* ī) *more com.* **छोकरा**, *q.v.*

छोकरा, *m.* a boy: a dancing-man dressed in the

छोकरी, *f.* a girl. [clothes of a female.

छोछो, *f.* a nurse; the bosom. — *k.* to fondle.

छोट, a poet. form of **छोटा**, *q.v.*

छोटा, *m.* (*f.* ī) little, small, less, younger, junior, lesser, subordinate, minor, least, inferior, of but little consequence, insignificant.

छोटाई, *f.* smallness, etc. (*see* **छोटा**).

छोटाचान्द, *m.* a certain climbing plant (*Ophioxylon serpentinum*) the root of which is said to be an excellent remedy for snake-bites. This root, dried and powdered, is applied externally to the bitten part and a decoction of it is given to the patient to drink to the extent of a pint in twenty-four hours.

छोटापन, *m.* smallness, etc. (see **छोटा**).

छोटाबड़ा, *m.* (*f.* ī) great and small, high and low, varied, various.

छोड़, 1, = **छोड़ा**, *q.v.*: 2, *postp.* (takes the acc.) excepting, besides. It is the shortest form of the conjunct.

छोड़कर = **छोड़**, *q.v.* [part. of **छोड़ना**.

छोड़चिट्ठी, *f.* a deed of release, pass, permit; a deed of divorce or abandonment of a betrothed girl.

छोड़छाड़ना, a colloquial combination of **छोड़ना** and

छोड़ जाना, an intensive of **छोड़ना**, *q.v.* [**छाड़ना**.

छोड़ना, *t.* to let go, leave alone, leave, quit, desert, forsake, abandon, abdicate, relinquish, resign, lay aside, abstain, discharge, breathe, spare, emit, emit fire, forgive, pardon, release, loose, omit, except, fire (a gun, etc.).

छोड़ा, *m.* release, deliverance, setting free, relinquishment, sparing, leaving, letting go, omission.

छोड़ाना, *more com.* **छुड़ाना**, *q. v.*

छोड़ाव, **छोड़ावा** } *m.* = **छोड़ा**, *q.v.*

छोड़ावना, *more com.* **छुड़ाना**, *q. v.*

छोड़ेड in Braj = **छोड़ा**, (**छोड़ना**).

छोड़ौती, *f.* ransom.

छोत, *f.* touch, contamination, defilement.

छोनिप, a corruption of **क्षोणिप**, *q. v.*

छोनी, *f.* (prop **क्षोणि**) the earth.

छोप, *m.* a coat of paint, etc. [a wall, etc.

छोपछाप क°, *t.* to shuffle up: to plaster or repair

छोपना, *t.* to fill up, shut; to paint, dye.

छोभ, **छोभा** } corruptions of **क्षोभ**, *q. v.*

छोर, *m.* border, edge, margin, end, tip, point, boundary, limit, shore, summit, brow of a hill: a tow-boat.

छोरण, *m.* an abandoning, leaving.

छोरणा, a corruption of **छोड़ना**, *q.v.*

छोरा, *m.* (contraction of **छोकरा**) a boy.

छोराछोरी, *m.* boys and girls, children.

छोरी, *f.* (contraction of **छोकरी**) a girl. [erase.

छोलना, *t.* to peel, skin, excoriate, pare, scrape,

छोलनी, *f.* an instrument for scraping. [cane.

छोला, *m.* gram: a man who cuts standing sugar-

छोह, *m.* affection : anger.

छोहरा, *m.* (*f.* ī) a child, lad, boy.

छोहरिआं, *f.* (*pl.* of छोहरी) little girls.

छोही, *m.* (*f.* inī) affectionate : angry.

छोहू, an emphat. form of छोह, *q.v.*

छोंक, *f.* seasoning ; relish.

छोंकन, *m.* spices with which food is seasoned.

छोंकना, *t.* to season.

छोकन, *m.* a scrambler.

छोकना, *t.* to scramble.

छोनर, *m.* the young of any animal.

छोनी, *f.* barracks, cantonments.

छौर, 1, *more prop.* (1) चौर (2) चूड़ी, *qq.v.*: 2, a large stack of *jawār* or *bājrā* collected for fodder: the walking a boundary with a raw cowskin on the head under a solemn oath to decide correctly.

छोल, merriment, cheerfulness, joy.

छोलिया, gay, cheerful, happy.

छ्या ; for words beginning thus, see under the form छया.

ज

ज (j) is the eighth consonant in the Hindee alphabet and has the following characteristics and functions :— 1, It is the third letter of the चवर्ग or palatal class, and has in pronunciation the full sound of *j* in the English word 'judge', — never the imperfect sound of *dz* that it often has in Bengālee. 2, It is frequently interchanged with य and even with ज्य ; it is only, however, in certain words that this phenomenon takes place, and these, very common ones ; *e. g.* जात्रा (properly यात्रा), सूरज (properly सूर्य्य), जदि (properly यदि), etc. This change is so widespread that the true pronunciation is the exception ; the attempt, in fact, to keep the two letters ज and य distinctly in their proper places both to the eye and to the ear, seems to many to savour of the pedantic. 3, In the present work such foreign words as contain either of the letters *zāl, ze, zād,* or *zoe* have these letters represented by the present letter with a dot under it, the dot signifying that the true sound is that of *z* in the English word 'zone' ; *e. g.* हाज़िरी, काग़ज़. It should be observed, however, that among the masses of the people, and especially among the lower classes, this foreign sound is very frequently ignored. 4, This letter is sometimes found as a suffix particle (from the root जन) in compound words, especially epithets or descriptive nouns, importing the idea of (1) begotten, born (2) produced (3) caused : the feminine form of such words always ends in long *a* ; *e. g.* अण्डजा, the female of any oviparous animal. In this sense the letter is only used in composition. 5, In Sanskrit treatises on prosody and metre, this letter denotes an amphibrachys. 6, This letter is sometimes put corruptly (1) for छ: *e. g.* जिनहट्टा, properly छीनाहट्टा : (2) for ज्य ; *e.g.* जोत = ज्योति.

जइ, in Chand = जय, *q. v.*

ज़ईफ़, 1, hospitable, convivial: 2, *m.* a stranger, a guest.

जई, *f.* oats ; the small shoots of barley which Hindoos wear in their turbans during the *dasahrā*, the first sprout of germinating rice ; a small species of barley.

जउं, an old form = जौं, *q.v.*

जउंर, a rope.

जंग, *m.* battle, war, combat, fight.

जंगम, 1, *m.* a Hindoo mendicant who has matted hair and rings a bell : 2, *m.* (*f.* ā) wanderer, etc. : *lit.* moveable, removeable, locomotive, in motion, anything which has motion as distinguished from that which is stationary, medicant.

जंगमजंगमा = दंगमदगा, *q. v.*

जंगमत्व, *m.* (*f.* tā) mobility.

जंगमा, *f.* : see जंगम, 2.

जंगर, a dialectic form of जंगल, *q.v.*

जंगल, 1, *m.* a forest, wood, waste, desert ; weeds : —*jānā* or *phirnā*, to ease oneself ; *lit.* to go into the jungle : 2, desert, solitary, waste, wild, etc.

जंगलबुरी, *f.* the act of clearing woodlands.

जंगला, 1, *m.* woody country, forest : 2, *m.* one of the musical modes (rāginī) : 3, *m.* (*f.* ī) wild.

जंगली, *m.* (*f.* inī) a savage, etc. : *lit.* wild, savage ; barbarian, clownish, boorish. — *ām*, *m.* a wild mango. — *kanwār*, hill aloe. — *kawwā*, *m.* a raven. — *kabūd*, the bustard. — *champā*, the red jasmine. — *piyāz*, squills (*Erythonium Indicum*). — *bādām*, wild almond. — *billī*, *f.* a wild cat. — *sarv*, wild cypress, — *singhārā*, *m.* Hermodactyl.

जंगा ; see (1) जंग (2) जंगाह (3) दंगा.

जंगाह, *f.* (जंग + गाह) a battle-field.

जंगी, *m.* (*f.* inī) a warrior, etc. : *lit.* appertaining to war, warlike, martial, military, quarrelsome.

जंघा, *m.* the stalk of autumnal crops.

जंगला, *m.* a coppice or thicket : a kind of flowered cloth : a medley of tunes.

जंघा, *f.* (*m.* ?) the leg, thigh : the shrouds of a ship.

जंघला, name of a rate or clause in a lease.

जंघामथानी, *f.* an adulteress, harlot, strumpet.

जंघारा, name of a large and turbulent tribe of Rājputs.

जंघाल, *m.* a rapid walker.

जंजाल, *m.* trouble, difficulty, perplexity, plague, embarrassment, misfortune: a swivel ; a large musket.

जंजाली, 1, *m.* a gun mounted on a camel or an elephant: 2, *m.* (*f.* inī) one who molests : *lit.* occasioning trouble, etc.

जंजिल, *more prop.* ज़ंजीर, *q. v.*

ज़ंजीर, *f.* a chain, fetters.

ज़ंजीरी, *m.* (*f.* iṇī) a person bound in chains, especially a mad or insane person.

जंजीरें = ज़ंजीरें (pl. of ज़ंजीर).

जंत, जंट, जंप, जंब, ; for words beginning with either of these forms, see under the forms जन्त, जन्ट, जम्प, जम्ब, respectively.

जंह, a corrupted form of जहां, *q. v.*

जक, *m.* (prop. यक्ष) when treasure, etc. is buried, an animal (sometimes a man) is killed and buried with it as a guard : this animal is called *jak*, and receives orders to allow no one to take up the treasure ; hence, *met.* a miser ; called also *Jakkā gumāshta*, Jak's agent.

जकड़ना, *t.* to tighten, draw tight (as a knot); to bind, fasten, tie, pinion.

जकड़बन्द, made fast, tightened, tight.

ज़क़न, *m.* the chin; the beard.

जकरना, *more prop.* ज़िकरना, *q. v.*

ज़करियाह, *m. pr. n.* the prophet Zechariah, and the Book that bears his name.

ज़का, *m.* vivacity, acuteness, penetration.

ज़कात, *f.* alms; a portion of a Muhammadan's property given in charity agreeably to the rules laid down in the Kurān. [represent it.

जकार, *m.* the letter ज, or any symbol that may

ज़कावत, *f.* probity, purity, ingenuousness: acuteness, brightness, ingenuity.

जकावत; see (1) ज़कावत (2) झकावत.

जकी; see (1) ज़की (2) झकी (3) झक्की.

ज़की, 1, *m.* one who regularly pays the *zakāt*; 2, pure, pious, continent: acute, ingenious: fiery.

जच, जछ; for words beginning with either of these forms, see under the form यक्ष. [what time.

जखन (correl. of तखन) when, at whatever time,

जखनि = जखन, *q.v.*

जखनी, a corruption of यक्षिणी, *q.v.* [be wounded.

ज़ख़्म, *m.* a wound, sore, scar, cut. —— *khānā*, to

ज़ख़ामत, *f.* bulkiness, thickness, corpulence.

ज़ख़ीरा, *m.* treasure, provisions, victuals, stores.

जग, a contraction (1) of जगत (2) of जगह (3) of यज्ञ, *qq.v.* Used chiefly as the first element in compound words: for examples see below.

जगआधार, *m.* an epithet of the Supreme; *lit.* the support of the universe.

जगकरतार = जगतकर्त्ता, *q.v.*

जगजगत, *m.* the universe: an entertainment, feast; a sacrifice or religious ceremony at which oblations are presented.

जगयोनि, *m.* an epithet of Brahmā.

जगजगा, *m.* brass tinsel, very thin plates of brass used in decoration.

जगजगाहट, *f.* much light, splendour, glitter.

जगजननी, *f.* an epithet in praise of any chief goddess, *e. g.* Pārvatee, Seetā; etc.: *lit.* mother of the universe.

जगजान, *m. f.* an epithet of any living creature.

जगजीव, *m.* an epithet of any living creature.

जगजीता, *m.* (*f.* ī) victorious over the world.

जगजीवन, *m.* an epithet of the Supreme Being as the giver of life.

जगजोनि, *m.* an epithet of Brahmā.

जगण, (see ज, 5) *m.* (in Pros.) a Scolius or Amphibrach (⏑—⏑) consisting of a foot of two short syllables with one long one between them.

जगत, 1, *m.* the world, universe; the race of men; a buttress: 2, *m.* (*f.* ī) moveable, locomotive, transitory. [enlightening the world.

जगतउजागर, *m.* an epithet of the Supreme; *lit.*

जगतकर्त्ता, *m.* the Creator of the world, *i. e.* Brahmā.

जगतक्षय, *m.* the destruction of the world. [mā.

जगतगुरु, *more prop.* जगद्गुरु, *q.v.* [of the universe.

जगतजनक, *m.* an epithet of the Deity; *lit.* parent

जगततार }
जगतत्राता } = जगत्राता, *q.v.*

जगतदुःखी, *m.* a tyrant.

जगतनिवास = जगन्निवास, *q.v.*

जगतपति = जगपति, *q.v.*

जगतपालक = जगपालक, *q.v.* [world.

जगतपालन, *m.* the sustaining or nourishing of the

जगतप्राण = जगत्प्राण, *q.v.*

जगतमाता = जगन्माता, *q.v.*

जगतबन्ध, see (1) जगद्बन्द्य (2) जगबन्धु.

जगतवंचक = जगवंचक, *q. v.*

जगतवंचित = जगवंचित, *q.v.*

जगतवासी = जगवासी, *q.v.*

जगतविख्यात = जगविख्यात, *q.v.*

जगतसेठ, *m.* an epithet of an exceedingly rich class of men; *lit.* a banker of the world.[preme being.

जगतस्वामी, *m.* Lord of the universe, *i. e.* the Su-

जगता, *m.* (*f.* ī) awake.

जगतारक, *m.* the Saviour of the world, *i. e.* Christ.

जगती, *f.* 1, = जगत, 2, *q.v.*: 2, the earth, world; mankind, people: a kind of metre.

जगतीतल, *m.* the earth, world; sublunary things.

जगत्कर्त्ता, *m.* the Creator of the world, *i. e.* Brahmā.

जगत्तार = जगत्राता, *q. v.*

जगत्तारणी, *f.* the redemption of the world.

जगत्प्राण, *m.* air, wind.

जगत्माता, *more prop.* जगन्माता, *q. v.*

जगत्राता, *m.* the Saviour of the world, *i. e.* Christ.

जगदघमोचक, *m.* an epithet of the Supreme Being: lit. the world's emancipator from sin. [Pārvatī.

जगदम्बा, *f.* the mother of the universe, *i. e.* pa-

जगदम्बिका = जगदम्बा, *q.v.*

जगदात्मा, *m.* the soul of the world, *i. e.* Brahm.

जगदाधार, *m.* 1, = जगआधार, *q.v.*: 2, air, wind.

जगदिन्द्र, *m.* an epithet of Indra.

जगदीश, *m.* an epithet of Vishṇu and of Shiv; *lit.* lord of the universe or of the world.

जगदीस }
जगदीसा } *more prop.* जगदीश, *q.v.*

जगद्गुरु, *m. pr. n.* an epithet (1) of Brahma (2) of Vishṇu (3) of Shiv: *lit.* the teacher of the world.

जगद्बन्द्य, *m.* an epithet of Krishṇ: *lit.* to be praised or adored by the world.

जगद्विनाश, *m.* the expiration of a *Kalp* or period of the world's existence; *lit.* the destruction of the world.

जगधारी *m.* (*f.* inī) an epithet of God, and (in Myth.) of any chief deity; *lit.* the Upholder of the world.

जगन, a Braj pl. of **जग**, *q.v.*

जगनक, *m. pr. n.* a certain ancient Hindoo bard.

जगन्मोहनी, *m.* (*f.* inī) a bewilderer or infatuator of the world.

जगना, *n.* to be awake : *a. int.* to awake, wake up, rouse.

जगनिवास, *m.* the inhabiting the universe, dwelling in the world.

जगनिवासी, *m.* (*f.* inī) = **जगवासी**, *q.v.*

जगनू ; see **जगनूं**.

जगन्नाथ, *m. pr. n.* (see **रथयात्रा**) an epithet of Vishṇu or Krishṇ ; *lit.* lord of the universe. The great place of pilgrimage devoted to this deity is near Cuttack in Orissa, and this name itself is the name under which the place also is recognized by the mass of Hindoos. Pilgrimage to this shrine is believed by Hindoos to be one of the most effectual procuring causes of final emancipation, and it is hence undertaken from all parts of India.

जगन्माता = **जगदम्बा**, *q.v* : also an epithet (1) of Durgā (2) of Lakshmī.

जगम्बंशी, name of a tribe of Brāhman zamindārs in Fatihpur.

जगपति, *m. pr. n.* epithet of Vishṇu and Shiv ; *lit.* lord of the universe.

जगपालक, *m.* an epithet of the Supreme, also of a sovereign ; *lit.* preserver of the world.

जगबन्धु, *m.* an epithet of God; *lit.* Friend of the world.

जगमगा, *m.* (*f.* ī) brilliant, glittering.

जगमगाना, *a. int.* to shine, glitter, glisten.

जगमगाहट, *f.* glitter, glare, much light, splendour, great brilliancy.

जगमाहिं in Braj = **जगमें**, in the world.

जगमूल, *m.* an epithet of God ; *lit.* the root or foundation of the universe.

जगमोहनी, *f.* an epithet of any very charming female.

जगर, *m.* armour, coat of mail.

जगराई, *m.* an epithet of the Supreme ; *lit.* Lord of the universe.

जगराजा, **जगराय**, **जगराया** } = **जगराई**, *q.v.*

जगवंचक, *m.* (*f.* ikā) an epithet of a hypocrite ; *lit.* deceiver of the world.

जगवंचित, *m.* (*f.* ā) = **जगवंचक**, *q.v.*

जगवाना, *t.* (causat. of **जगाना**) to cause to awaken.

जगवासी, *m.* (*f.* inī) an inhabitant of the world.

जगव्यवहार, *m.* the way of the world, custom.

जगविख्याति, *f.* world-wide celebrity.

जगविख्यात, *m.* (*f.* ā) a person of world-wide renown.

जगह, *f.* (*m.* ?) place, station, locality, quarter, room, stead, vacancy. — *chhoṛnā*, to leave a blank.

जगहर, *m.* wakefulness (occasioned by apprehension of disease) ; vigils, vespers ; coughing at night.

जगा, 1, *f.* = **जगह** ; 2, *m.* = **जागा**, *qq.v.*

जगाजोत, **जगाज्योत**, } *more prop.* **जगाज्योति**, *q.v.*

जगाज्योति, *f.* splendour, brilliancy, much light.

जगाना, *t.* to wake, awaken, arouse from sleep.

जगेश्वर, *m. pr. n.* an epithet of Vishṇu and of Shiv ; *lit.* lord of the universe.

जगोपबीत, *more prop.* **यज्ञोपवीत**, *q.v.*

जग्गतर, *m.* the world, universe.

जग्गीसर, **जग्नेश्वर** } **जगेश्वर**, *q.v.*

जघन, *m.* pudenda, mons veneris : the buttocks, hip and loins : the rear-guard of an army.

जघन्य, *m.* (*f.* ā) a Shoodra : *lit.* last, lowest, hindmost, vile, base, low.

जघन्यज, *m.* (*f.* ā) a Shoodra ; a younger or youngest brother : *lit.* last-born, lowest-born.

जचना, *n.* to be guessed, be tried, be assayed, be examined, be proved.

जचा, *f.* a woman in child-bed and for forty days after, a lying-in woman.

जचावट, *f.* test, trial, examination, proof.

जच्चनीं ; see (1) **जचना** (2) **जांचना** (3) **याचना**.

जच्चा = **जचा**, *q.v.*

जक, (*colloquial*) = **यज्ञ**, *q.v.*

जज, 1, in old Hindee = **यज्ञ**, *q.v.* : 2, *m.* (Engl.) a judge (in Law).

जज़्ब, *m.* allurement, attraction, absorption, drawing (as of a plaster). — *k.* to draw, absorb.

जज़्बा, *m.* passion, rage, fury ; violent desire.

जजमान = **यजमान**, *q.v.*

जज़र, *m.* origin, root ; the square root (in Arithm.) : the ebb-tide.

जजर ; see (1) **जज़र** (2) **जर्जर**.

जज़ा, *f.* retaliation, retribution, requital, return, compensation, reward.

जजाति = **ययाति**, *q.v.*

जज़ायल, *m.* a large musket, wall-piece, swivel.

जजिर, a corruption of **ज़ंजीर**, *q.v.*

जजिरेए, **जज़ीरए** } corruption of **ज़ंजीरें**, *q.v.*

जजीर, a corruption of **ज़ंजीर**, *q.v.*

जज़ीरा, *m.* an island, peninsula.

जजीरे, **जजीरेए** } corruption of **ज़ंजीरें**, *q.v.*

जज्ञ ; for all words beginning thus, see under the form **यज्ञ**.

जट = (1) **जटा** (2) **जाट**, *qq.v.*

जटना, *t.* to snatch, seize, pilfer, defraud.

ज़टल, *f.* the talking much and foolishly, prating, chattering, quibbling, tattle, foolish prattle, falsehood. — *mārnā*, to talk nonsense, to chatter, prate. — *hānknā*, to quibble.

जटा, 1, = **जाट**, *q.v.* : 2, *f.* matted hair, especially the hair matted as worn by the god Shiv and by ascetics ; the long hair sometimes clotted together and brought over the head so as to project like a horn from the top of the forehead, and at other times allowed to fall carelessly over the back and shoulders : the root of a tree, a fibrous root : spikenard.

जटाजिनी, *m.* (*f.* inī) a person wearing matted hair and the hide of an antelope.

जटाजूत, *more prop.* **जटाजूट**, *q.v.*

जटाजूट, *f.* the matted and braided hair of Shiv rolled on his head.

जटाधारी, 1, *m.* (*f.* iṇī) one who wears the **जटा** : 2, *f.* the cock's-comb flower (*Celosia cristata*). [*mansi*).

जटामांसी, *f.* Indian spikenard (*Valeriana jata-*

जटामासी = **जटामांसी**, *q.v.*

जटायु, *m.* 1, *pr. n.* (see **रामचन्द्र**), a certain fabulous

जटायुस = **जटायु**, *q.v.* [vulture : 2, bdellium.

जटायू, *more prop.* **जटायु**, *q.v.*

जटाल, *m.* (*f.* ā) }
जटालक, *m.* (*f.* ikā) } = **जटी**, *q.v.*

जटाला, *f.* 1, see **जटाल**; 2, spikenard.

जटि, *f.* the waved-leafed figtree (*Ficus venosa*).

जटित, 1, *m.* (*f.* ā) clotted, matted : set or studded with jewels : 2, *f.* set work of jewels.

जटिन, 1, *m.* = **जटि**, *q.v.* : 2, *m.* (*f.* ī) = **जटी**, *q.v.*

जटिनी, *f.*; see **जटी**. [tangled hair.

जटिल, *m.* (*f.* ā) a lion; a person with matted or

जटिला, *f.* Indian spikenard (*Valeriana jatamansi*); long pepper; orris-root.

जटी, *m.* (*f.* inī) a person with matted or tangled hair : lit *adj.* wearing matted hair.

जटुल, *m.* a freckle, mark.

जठर, 1, *m.* the stomach, womb, interior : 2, *m.* (*f.* ā) hard, firm; old; bound, tied.

जठरनुद, *m.* Cassia fistula.

जठरा, *f.* see **जठर**, 2.

जठराग्नि, *m.* *f.* = **जठरानल**, *q.v.*

जठरानल, *m.* the uneasy sensation arising from hunger; *lit.* the fire of the stomach.

जठराम, *m.* water in the stomach, dropsy.

जठेरा, *m.* (*f.* ī) = **ज्येष्ठ**, *q.v.*

जड़, 1, *f.* (for **जट**) root, origin, foundation, basis : —*pakarnā*, to take root. 2, *m.* an inanimate body, anything that is void of animation : an idiot, dolt, blockhead : *lit.* cold, chilly; rigid; irrational; material; immoveable; unfeeling, apathetic, idiotic, stupid, dumb.

जड़क्रिय, *m.* (*f.* ā) a dilatory person : *lit.* working slowly, etc.

जड़चरचा, *more prop.* (1) **जड़चर्चा** (2) **जड़चर्या**, *qq.v.*

जड़चर्चा, *f.* any enquiry into the nature of inanimate things. [animate substance.

जड़चर्या, *f.* the deportment or manner of any in-

जड़जीव, *m.* (*f.* ā) a brute (applied to beasts and to [senseless ignorant persons).

जड़ता }
जड़ताई } *f.* = **जड़त्व**, *q.v.*

जड़त्व. *m.* coldness, chilliness; immoveableness, torpor, stiffness, rigidity; apathy, insensibility, stu-

जड़न, *f.* the act of setting jewels. [pidity.

जड़ना, *t.* to strike; to shake off : to join, make adhere : to bestud, set with jewels, inlay, enchase.

जड़पदार्थ, *m.* any substance that is devoid of animation. [tirpate.

जड़पेड़, *f.* root and branch. —— *se ukhārnā*, to ex-

जड़बुद्धि, *f.* dullness of intellect, stupidity.

जड़भरत, *m.* (*f.* ī) a dull stupid person, idiot.

जड़मूलसे उखाड़ना, *t.* to completely extirpate, destroy root and branch.

जड़वट, *f.* the trunk of a tree.

जड़वाना, *t.* to cause to be set with jewels.

जड़वी, *f.* the small shoots of the rice-plant when it first springs from the ground.

जड़हन, *m.* a large species of rice cropped at the end of the rainy season.

जड़ा, 1, *m.* cold, frost, winter : sluggishness of mind or body, stupidity, inanition, idiocy, dulness : 2, *f.* cowach (*Carpopogon pruriens*). [setting jewels.

जड़ाई, *f.* the act of setting jewels : the price of

जड़ाऊ, set or studded with jewels.

जड़ाऊं; see (1) **जड़ाऊ**, (2) **जड़ाना**.

जड़ाना, 1, *t.* (causat. of **जड़ना**) to cause to set with jewels : 2, *n.* to be cold, feel cold.

जड़ाव, *m.* }
जड़ावट, *f.* } the act of setting jewels.

जड़ावर }
जड़ावल } *f.* winter dress, warm clothes.

जड़ित, *m.* (*f.* ā) bedecked, studded, set with jewels. [sets jewels, a jeweller : a striker.

जड़िया, *m.* (noun of agency from **जड़ना**) one who

जड़ी, *f.* the root of a medicinal herb.

जड़ोटा, *m.* brushwood, brambles.

जड़ीबूटी, *f.* medicinal herbs, drugs, samples.

जडुल, *m.* a freckle, mark.

जड़ेउ in Braj = **जड़ा** (**जड़ना**).

जढाऊ, *more prop.* **जड़ाऊ**, *q.v.*

जत = (1) **जति** (2) **जाति** (3) **जैसा** (4) **जितना** (5) **यत्न**, *qq.v.*. The form occurs chiefly in Braj and in poetry.

जतन; for words beginning thus, see under the [form **यत्न**.

जतनाईंगी }
जतनाइगी } *f.* carefulness, caution.
जतनागी }

जतर, cultivated land.

जतलाना; see **जताना**.

जताड़ा = **जतारा**, *q.v.*

जताना, *t.* to caution, remind, warn, admonish, inform of, apprize; to declare, proclaim, make known. *Prem* — (with acc.) to make a declaration of love to.

जतारा, *m.* family, race, stock, house, line, lineage, dynasty. [sung at the Holee).

जति, *f.* a kind of musical rhythm (generally

जती, (prop **यती**) *m.* (*f.* inī) one who has brought his passions completely under subjection, a particular order of Hindoo ascetics, a religious person, one who is faithful to the marriage bed.

जतु, *m.* lac, a red dye or animal pigment ana-

जतुक, *m.* lac : assafœtida. [logous to cochineal

जतुका, *f.* a certain fragrant plant commonly called *chakāwat* or *chakwat* : a bat.

जतुपुत्रक, *m.* a piece or man at chess, etc.

जतेक, a dialectic form = जितना, *q. v.*

जतेन्द्रिय, *more prop.* जितेन्द्रिय, *q. v.*

जत्रानी, a certain tribe of *jāts* in Rohilkhaṇḍ.

जत्रु, *m.* the collar-bone, clavicle. [form यथा.

जथा; for words beginning thus, see under the

जद, (correl. of तद) as, while, whilst, when, as soon as, at the time when. — *na tad*, constantly.

जदतक, till, until, yet, whilst, as long as, while.

जदतलक = जदतक, *q. v.*

जदपि = यद्यपि, *q. v.* [so-so.

जदबातदबा, *m.* an ummeaning expression : *adv.*

जदल, *m.* fighting, battle, encounter, altercation.

जदलग
जदलों } = जदतक, *q. v.*

जदवल, *f.* lines drawn in a book as ruling or to separate the margin ; a rivulet ; a table, astronomical

जदवलकश = जदवलपट्टी, *q. v.* [table.

जदवलपट्टी, *f.* a rule consisting of a card of paste-board and threads on which the paper is pressed, and

जदा = यदा, *q. v.* [thus becomes ruled.

जदि = यदि, *q. v.*

जदीद, new, fresh, modern. [यदु.

जदु; for words beginning thus, see under the form

जदोकोब, *m.* assault and battery, beating.

जद्द, *m.* an ancestor, grandfather.

जद्यपि = यद्यपि, *q. v.*

जन, *m.* (*f.* ī) a human creature, person, individual, mankind, man (individually or collectively). The term is sometimes suffixed with the effect of pluralizing ; e. g. *Strijan*, females, women, women-folk : *Shishujan*, children, little folk. [tribe.

जनंगम, *m.* a *chanḍāl* or man of low or degraded

जनक, *m.* a progenitor, producer, father : *pr. n.* a certain king who was sovereign of Mithilā and father of Seetā : *lit.* causing.

जनकपुर, *m. pr. n.* the metropolis of the above-named Rājā in the district of Tirhut. [(of Mithilā).

जनकविदेही, *m.* a certain class of Hindoo princes

जनकसुता, *f.* the daughter of Janak, *i. e.* Seetā.

जनकौरा, *m.* (*f.* ī) an inhabitant of Janakpur.

ज़नख़, *m.* the chin, the pit in the chin.

जनजानवर, *m.* man and beast.

जनत, birth, the being born. [servants, subjects.

जनता, *f.* mankind, a number of men, household

जनन, 1, a Braj plural of जन, *q. v.*: see न, 6 (1) : 2, *m.* birth, child-birth, production, existence ; family, race, lineage : 3, *m.* (*f.* ī) a progenitor : *lit.* causing.

जनना, *n.* to be delivered of a child ; to be born : *t.* to give birth to : to produce young : generate, breed,

जननि, an old form = जनों. See नि, 2 (1). [beget.

जननी, *f.* a mother, the actual mother of a child as distinguished from a step-mother, parent, progenitrix : tenderness, compassion.

जनमस, a certain plant (*Crotalaria juncea*).

जनम; for words beginning thus, see under the

जनमे, *m.* pl. past part. of जन्मना. [form जन्म.

जनमेउ, Braj form of जन्मे ; *see above.*

जनमेजय
जनमेजी
जनमैजय } *more prop.* जन्मेजय, *q. v.*

जनयिता, *m.* (*f.* trī) a father, progenitor, ancestor.

जनरंजन, *m.* an epithet of God ; lit. *adj.* befriending or inspiring one with confidence and joy, conciliating, joy-affording. [noise.

जनरव, *m.* the sound of human voices, clamour,

जनलोक, *m. pr. n.* one of seven Loks or divisions of the universe as recognized by Hindoos. It is a superior sort of Paradise supposed to be situated over the Maharlok, and to be inhabited by pious men after

जनवाद, *m.* report, rumour, news. [death.

जनवाना, *t.* (causal of जनना) to cause to be born, etc.

जनवांसा
जनवास
जनवासत
जनवासा } = जन्वासा, *q. v.*

जनश्रुति, *f.* hearsay, report, tidings, intelligence,

जनहित, salutary, beneficial, beneficent. [news.

जना, *m.* (*f.* ī) a son ; a person, individual : *lit.* born

जनाई, *f.* a midwife. [(past part. of *jannā*).

जनाईसदक़ा, *m.* alms given at the birth of a child.

जनाओ, *m.* a signal.

जनाज़ा, *m.* a bier, hearse ; a funeral.

जनाजात, particularizing or specifying each person, one by one, man by man.

ज़नाना, *m.* female apartments, seraglio.

जनाना, 1, *t.* (= जताना) to inform, remind, tell, warn, point out, shew; to seem (used chiefly in Braj). 2, *t.* to deliver, bring to bed : 3, *m.* midwifery. [males.

ज़नानी, female, effeminate, appertaining to fe-

जनान्तिक, *m.* speaking aside, secret communication, whispering. [excellency : a vestibule, threshold.

जनाब, *f.* side, brink, margin : majesty, highness,

जनाव, *m.* a signal.

जनावना in Braj = जनाना, *q. v.*

जनावर (*by inversion*) = जानवर, *q. v.*

जनाश्रय, *m.* a temporary hall.

जनि, 1, a corruption of जिन 2 and 3, *q. v.*: 2, *f.* a woman : a birthplace.

जनिका, *m.* any expression having more than one meaning, pun, double entendre.

जनित, *m.* (*f.* ā) produced, born. [father.

जनिता, 1, *f. see* जनित्र : 2, *m.* a progenitor, parent,

जनित्री, *f.* a progenitrix, mother.

जनी, *f.* (prop. जनि) a woman in general, mother, maidservant, daughter-in-law (*i. e.* the wife of a son or of a brother's son, etc.) : production, birth : a kind of fainting-fit to which lying-in women are subject.

जनु, 1, in Braj = जानो, *q. v.*: 2, in old Hindee = जैसा, *q. v.* ; 3, *m.* engenderment, production, birth.

जनुक, to wit; though, although.
जनू (*contraction*) = जानू, *q.v.*
जने, *m.* (pl. of जना) persons, individuals.
जनेउ / जनेऊ / जनेओ } (*colloquial*) = जनेव, *q.v.*
[ding or marriage feast.
जनेत, *f.* the company and attendants at a wed-
जनेरा, *m.* a tall species of millet.
जनेला, a window. [in a jewel.
जनेव, *m.* the sacred Brāhmanical thread: a flaw
जनेवा, *f.* the fragrant *dub*-grass (*Agrostislinearis*).
जनेश, *m.* (*f.* ā) an epithet of any king; *lit.* a lord of
जनेषु, (Sk. loc. pl.) = मनुष्योंमें. [men.
जनेस, a corruption of जनेश, *q.v.*
जनो = (1) जनेव (2) जानो, *qq.v.*
जनों, probably, perhaps.
जनोदाहरण, *m.* fame, glory. [form यन्त्र.
जन्तर; for words beginning thus, see under the
जन्ता, *m.* an instrument for drawing wire.
जन्ताना, *n.* to be squeezed, be pressed.
जन्तार, *m.* a charm, amulet. [parturition.
जन्ती, 1, = जनती (जनना): 2, *f.* birth, being born,
जन्तु, *m.* any creature endowed with animal life, an animal, beast, sentient being, man. The term is applied chiefly to animals of the brute creation.
जन्तुघ्न, *m.* a vermifuge.
जन्तुफल, *m.* glomerous figtree (*Ficus glomerata*).
जन्तुमय, *m.* (*f.* ī) *adj.* abounding in animals.
जन्तुला, *f.* a grass (*Saccharum spontaneum*).
जन्त्र: for all words beginning thus see under the
जन्दा; see (1) जन्द्रा (2) जिन्दा. [form यन्त्र.
जन्दोलिया, a certain small class of Rājputs in Banda. [North-west Provinces.
जन्द्रा, *m.* a pitchfork; a kind of rake used in the
जन्न, *m.* suspicion, jealousy, opinion, thought, idea.
जन्नत, *f.* the garden; heaven, paradise.
जन्ना = जनना, *q.v.*
जन्म, *m.* production, birth, existence, life. — *bitānā*, to pass one's life. — *lenā*, to be born.
जन्मकील, *m.* an epithet of Vishṇu; *lit.* the bolt
जन्मजगह, *m.* birthplace. [(or stay) of life.
जन्मकुण्डली, *f.* a horoscope, genealogical table.
जन्मजन्म, in every birth, from birth to birth.
जन्मजन्मान्तर, from birth to birth, one birth after another. [(or spoiled) from its birth.
जन्मजला, *m.* (*f.* ī) originally bad; *lit.* burned
जन्मत in Braj = जन्मता है. See त, 5.
जन्मद, *m.* (*f.* ā) a parent, father.
जन्मदाता, *m.* (*f.* trī) a parent, father: an epithet of
जन्मदिन, *m.* a birth-day. [the Author of existence.

जन्मन, 1, a Braj pl. of जन्म, *q.v.*: 2, *m.* birth, pro-
जन्मना, *n.* to be born. [duction, existence.
जन्मपत्र, *m.* = जन्मपत्री, *q.v.*
जन्मपत्री, *f.* horoscope, nativity, a genealogical table.— *ki bidhi milnā*, to meet one's fate, receive one's [destined award.
जन्मभुम / जन्मभूम } = जन्मभूमि, *q.v.*
जन्मभूमि, *f.* the country or place of one's birth,
जन्ममरण, *m.* eternal death. [fatherland.
जन्मरोगी, *m.* (*f.* inī) a valetudinarian.
जन्मलग्न, *f.* (*m.* ?) the moment of birth, horoscope.
जन्मसि (old form) = तू जन्मता है. [fatherland.
जन्मस्थान, *m.* the place or country of one's birth,
जन्मस्वार्थ, *m.* a fortunate or a well-spent life.
जन्माना, *t.* to beget; to cause to vegetate.
जन्मान्तर, *m.* another birth, another state of existence, regeneration. [ing to another birth.
जन्मान्तरीय, acquired in another birth, appertain-
जन्मान्ध, *m.* (*f.* ā) a person blind from birth.
जन्माष्टमी, *f.* the eighth day of the Krishṇ-paksh of Bhādra, the anniversary of the birthday of Krishṇ.
जन्मिन, *m.* (*f.* ī) / जन्मी, *m.* (*f.* inī) } an animal, living being.
जन्मेजय, *m. pr. n.* the son and successor of Rājā
जन्मेजय, *more prop.* जन्मेजय, *q.v.* [Pareekshit.
जन्मोत्सव, *m. pr. n.* a festival held on the anniversary of Krishṇ's birthday. [war, combat.
जन्य, *m.* the friend of a bridegroom; a father:
जन्या, *f.* a bridesmaid, relation or companion of a bride; a mother's friend.
जन्यो in Braj = जना (जनना).
जन्वाई, *m.* (*f.* inī) a son-in-law.
जन्वासा, *m.* the place at a bride's house where the bridegroom and his train are received.
जन्हाई / जन्हार } = जनाजात, *q.v.*
जन्हु, *m. pr. n.* (see जान्हवी) a certain fabulous king who produced water from his ear and then drank it. This water issuing from him in the natural way became the river Ganges.
जप, *m.* the silent repetition of the name of any deity, the muttering prayers, charms, etc., the repeating inaudibly passages from the Shāstras, the counting silently the beads of a rosary; silent meditation; adoration.[name of any deity, worshipping, repeating.
जपत, *part.* repeating inaudibly or mentally the
जपतप, *m.* adoration, devotion.
जपना, *t.* to count one's beads, repeat the name of any deity inaudibly or internally, mutter prayers inaudibly, recite the bead-roll: to wait for, expect.
जपनों in Braj = जपना, *q.v.*
जपन्ति = जपते हैं (poet.). [tation, a saint-sage.
जपपरायण, *m.* a man devoted to religious medi-

जपमाल, *m.*
जपमाला, *f.* } a rosary.

जपा, 1, *more prop.* जप, *q.v.* : 2, *f.* the flower of the plant *hurhur* (*Cleome viscosa*): the China rose (*Hibiscus rosa Sinensis*).

जपामि = मैं जपता हूं (poet.).

जपी, *m.* (*f.* inī) one who performs जप, *q.v.*

जपीतपी, *m.* an adorer.

जपु, see (1) जप (2) जपी.

जफ़ा, *f.* oppression, violence, injury, injustice.

जब, (correl. of तब) when, at the time when, as soon as. — *na tab*, now and then, perpetually.

जबकभी, whenever, when at any time.

जबकभू
जबकभूं } in Braj = जबकभी, *q.v.*

जबका जब, *m.* (*f.* जबकी जब) = जबका तब, *q.v.*

जबका तब, *m.* (*f.* °की°) at the time when, at the proper moment.

जब कि, at the time when, when; since, inasmuch as.

जब जब, whensoever, at whatever time.

जबड़ा, *m.* the jaw, or the part of the face from the corners of the mouth to the jaws.

जबड़ोबन्द, *m.* lock-jaw.

जबतई
जबतक } as long as, till when, whilst.

जब तब, now and then.

जबतलक
जबतोड़ी } as long as, till when, whilst.

जबदना, *n.* to be filled: to be folded.

जबदी, *f.* a species of rice cultivated in Rohilkhaṇḍ.

जबद्दा, *m.* (*f.* ī) rigid, stiff, awkward.

जबद्धिया, ill-shapen.

जबमें, *adv.* at what time.

जब्र, *m.* oppression, violence, strength, power, force, constraint. [violent, vigorous, strong.

ज़बरदस्त, overbearing, high-handed, oppressive,

ज़बरदस्ती, *f.* high-handedness, oppression, violence. — *k.* to oppress, exercise violence, to force.

जबल, *m.* a mountain, hill.

जबलग, as long as, till when, whilst.

जबलपुर, *m. pr. n.* Jabalpur (in the Central Provinces); *lit.* the hill-city.

जबलें
जबलों } = जबलग, *q.v.*

जबवान, a corruption (1) of ज़बान (2) of जवान, *qq.v.*

जबसे, *adv.* (of time) since.

जबहि, (emphat.) at the very time when.

जबहिं
जबही } = जबहि, *q.v.*

ज़बान, *f.* the tongue; language, speech, dialect.

ज़बानदराज़, abuse.

ज़बानी, traditional, verbal, from the (tongue or) statement of any one, by word, by word of mouth.

जबाहिर, *more prop.* जवाहिर, *q.v.*

ज़बी, *m.* a deer, chevril, gazelle.

जबीन, *f.* the forehead.

ज़बून, a dupe, a capture: *adj.* unlucky, bad, ill, wicked.

ज़बूर, *f. pr. n.* the Book of Psalms.

जबै; see (1) जबहि (2) जब.

जब्बार, *m.* a conqueror; a revenger: a tall palm-tree: *pr. n.* the constellation Orion: *adj.* omnipotent.

ज़ब्ह, *f.* sacrifice, slaughter. — *k.* to sacrifice; to slaughter; to kill (animals for food according to the directions of Muhammadan law).

जब्बूर, *more prop.* ज़बूर, *q.v.*

जब्र = जब्र, *q.v.*

जब्रएल
जब्राएल
जब्रायेल } = गब्रीएल, *q.v.*

जभड़ा
जभा } = जबड़ा, *q.v.*

जभिया, ugly, uncouth.

जभी, *more prop.* जबही, *q.v.*

जम; for words beginning thus, see under the form यम.

जमई, the whole, all; universal.

जमईयत, *f.* a concourse, multitude.

जमक, 1, *more prop.* यमक, *q.v.*: 2, *f.* the state of succeeding or going on well.

जमकना, *n.* to be assembled: *a. int.* to succeed, go on well, fit. *Dūkān jamkī*, buyers and sellers are collected in the shop. *Larāī jamkī*, the fight was joined. *Majlis jāmkī*, the assembly is full. *Muḳaddama jamkā*, the cause is begun to be debated.

जमकाना, *t.* to cause to succeed, adjust, settle, fix: to assemble, crowd together.

जमकूड़ा, *m.* a kind of covering for the head and shoulders. It is made of reeds or palm-leaves plaited, and is worn during the rainy season.

जमघट, *m.* a multitude, crowd.

जमजम, constantly, perpetually, always.

ज़मज़मा, *m.* singing; a concert.

जमद, *m.* congelation; connexion.

जमदग्नि, *m. pr. n.* a certain Rishi, father of Parashurām.

जमदी, a corruption of जलदी, *q.v.*

जमधड़
जमधर } *m.* a dagger.

जमन, *more prop.* यमन or यवन, *qq.v.*

जमना, *n.* to be coagulated, be congealed, be frozen, be collected: *a. int.* to germinate, grow: to clot, consolidate: to stick, adhere, cohere, set: to pace in the manège.

जमनिका = यवनिका, *q.v.*

जमनौटा, *m.* a certain consideration given to one who becomes security for another (generally five per cent. on the amount).

जमनौटिया = जमनौटा, *q.v.*

जमरूद, *more prop.* ज़ुमुर्रुद, *q.v.*

जमस्त, *f.* a kind of blue stone or mineral substance supposed to be a specific against fainting and palpitation of the heart.

ज़मह़रीर, *m.* cold, intense cold.
जमहाई, *f.* gaping, yawning. — *lenā*, to yawn.
जमहाना, *a. int.* to yawn, gape.
जमा, 1, *f.* an accumulation, amount, sum-total; (in Gram.) the plural number: 2, *m.* (*f.* ī) collected, accumulated. — *k.* to accumulate, collect, store, stow.
जमाअत, *f.* a crowd, party, assembly, congregation, meeting, society, senate, troop.
जमाई, *m.* (from **जामाता**) a son-in-law.
जमाओड़ा, *m.* a crowd, assembly, collection; a place of assembly.
जमात, *more prop.* **जमाअत**, *q.v.*
जमादार, *m.* a native officer of an army so called; the head of any body, as of guides, *harkāras*, etc.
जमादारी. *f.* the business or the status of a jamādār.
जमाना, a corruption (1) of **ज़माना** (2) of **जमाना**, *qq. v.*
जमान = (1) **ज़माना** (2) **जवान**, *qq. v.*
ज़माना, *m.* time; an age; the world; fortune; the heavens; (in Gram.) tense.
जमाना, *t.* to collect, sum up, coagulate, congeal, consolidate; to freeze or make ice: to pace in the manège.
जमाबन्दी, *f.* accounts of the revenues, settlement of the revenues.
ज़माम, *f.* a rein, bridle.
जमाल, *m.* beauty, elegance.
जमालगोटा, *m.* a certain purgative nut (*Jatropha cureas*: *Croton triglium*).
जमालपुर, *m. pr. n.* Jamālpur.
जमाव, *m.* a multitude, crowd, accumulation, collection, accretion, coagulation.
जमावट, *f.* coagulation, agglutination, congelation, consolidation.
जमाहना, *more prop.* **जमहाना**, *q. v.*
जमाहिर, a corruption of **जवाहिर**, *q. v.*
जमाही, *more prop.* **जमहाई**, *q. v.*
जमिन, *more prop.* **ज़मीन**, *q. v.*
ज़मिस्तान, *m.* winter: wisdom.
जमी = (1) **जमा**, 2 (2) **यमी** (3) **संयमी**, *qq. v.*
ज़मीन, *f.* the earth, soil, mould, land, ground; a country, region.
ज़मीनकन्द, *m.* a bulbous root.
ज़मीनी, appertaining to the earth.
ज़मीन्दार, *m.* (*f.* nī) a landlord, landholder, revenue farmer.
ज़मीन्दारी, *f.* the estates of a zamīndār; the business of a zamīndār.
ज़मीम, blameable, culpable.
ज़मीमा, *m.* addition, augmentation.
जमील, beautiful, elegant, fair, good.
जमीलः / **जमीला** } *fem.* of **जमील**, *q. v.*
जमुन, 1, *more prop.* **यमुना**, *q. v.*: 2, coagulation, congelation, jelly, curds; rennet or acid employed for curdling milk.
जमुना = **यमुना** *q. v.*
जमुरद,
जमुर्रद / **जमुर्रुद** } *more prop.* **ज़ुमुर्रुद**, *q. v.*
जमुहाई, *more com.* **जमहाई**, *q. v.*
जमूअट = **जमूवट**, *q. v.*
जमूवट, *f.* the foundation of a well; the festive ceremony held on the occasion of laying the foundation of a well.
जमैया, a species of grass in the province of Delhi: Thursday.
जमोआ, indigo planted before the rains and irrigated by artificial means.
जमोग, transfer of liabilities by mutual consent; a conditional mortgage.
जमोगदार, *m.* a person who sends a landed proprietor a sum of money and recovers that money from the cultivators.
जमोगना, *t.* to ascertain.
जम्पती, *more prop.* **दम्पति**, *q. v.*
जम्पना, *more com.* **जपना**, *q. v.*
जम्ब, a side, part, tract of country.
जम्बक, *a corruption of* **जम्बुक**, *q.v.*
जम्बाल, *m.* the aquatic plant *Vallisneria*: mud.
जम्बाला, *m.* a certain fragrant plant (*Pandanus odoratissimus*).
जम्बीर, *more prop.* **जम्भीरी**, *q.v.*
जम्बु, *f.* the rose-apple (*Eugenia Jambu*): *pr. n.* (1) of one of the great Hindoo divisions of the world (2) of a fabulous river.
जम्बुक, 1, = **जम्बु**, *q. v.*: 2, *m.* (*f.* ā *or* ī) a jackal: a low man.
जम्बुकेतु, *m. pr. n.* a certain king of Ceylon.
जम्बुतरु, the rose-apple (*Eugenia Jambu*).
जम्बुद्वीप, *m. pr. n.* one of the seven divisions of the world. According to the Purāṇs this division is the central one, and includes the whole of Hindustan; while according to the Bauddhas, it is confined to India, and is so named from the *Jambu*-plant abounding in it.
जम्बू, for words beginning thus, see under the form **जम्बु**.
ज़म्बूर, *m.* a hornet, bee: a vice, nippers, forceps.
जम्बूल, *m.* a certain fragrant plant (*Pandanus odoratissimus*): the rose-apple.
जम्भीरी, *m.* the common lime or citron (*Citrus acida*): a plant considered by some to be a sort of basil with small leaves.
ज़म्म, *m.* blame, reproach, accusation, detraction.
जम्मश, a species of bird of chase.
जम्मी, *f.* a species of tree or plant.
जय, 1, *m.* (*f.* ?) victory, conquest, triumph; advancement, preferment, promotion: resignation: 2, *exclam.* bravo! hurrah! all hail: 3, *m.* a species of bean (*Phaseolus mungo*): 4, *m. pr. n.* one of the two gatekeepers of the Hindoo paradise.
जयजयकार, *m.* rejoicings, cheers, exultation, triumph. — *k.* to hurrah, shout.
जयजयवन्ती, *f.* a certain musical mode (*rāgiṇī*).
जयजश, *m.* the renown of victory.
जयढक, *m.* a kind of drum.
जयत, *m.* a species of plant (*Œschynomene sesban*): a certain musical mode.
जयति (*poet.*) = **जय होता है**.
जयद्रथ, *m. pr. n.* a certain ancient Hindoo king.

जयध्वज, *m.* a banner or symbol of victory : *pr. n.* the father of Tāljangh.

जयध्वनि, *m.* the shout of victory.

जयनदेव, *m. pr. n.* the founder of the Sarāwagī sect.

जयन्त, *m. pr. n.* a certain hero and demigod, the the son of Indra.

जयन्ती, *f.* a certain tree (*Œschynomene sesban*) : a banner, flag : *pr. n.* (1) of a country (2) of a river.

जयपत्र, *m.* a record of victory or triumph ; (in Law) the written and sealed award of the judge in favour of either party.

जयपाल, *m.* (*f.* ī) a sovereign, king (it is the name of several celebrated Hindoo princes) : a certain plant or tree (*Croton triglium*). [pur in Rājputāna.

जयपुर, *m. pr. n.* the capital and province of Jay-

जयफल, *m.* the reward of triumph.

जयमंगल, *m.* (*f.* ā) the royal elephant.

जयमान, *m.* (*f.* matī) a victor : *lit.* victorious.

जयमाल, *m.* = **जयमाला**, *q. v.*

जयमाला, *f.* a necklace or garland of victory.

जयवन्त } **जयवान** } *m.* (*f.* vatī) = **जयमान**, *q. v.*

जयविजय, *m. pr. n.* (**जय** and **विजय**) the two gate-keepers of the paradise of the Hindoos.

जयशब्द, *m.* the exclamation '*jai jai*,' a shout or song of victory.

जयशाली, victorious, conquering. [Durgā.

जया, 1, in Chand = **जय**, *q. v.* : 2, *f.* an epithet of

जयी, *m.* (*f.* inī) a conquerer, the winning party in a lawsuit : *lit.* victorious, conquering.

जयेउ } **जयेा** } in Braj = (1) **जीता** (2) **बिजय किया**.

जय्या, *m.* (*f.* ī) able to conquer, victorious.

जर, a corruption (1) of **जड़**, 1 (2) of **ज्वर**, *qq. v.*

ज़र, *m.* gold, riches, wealth, money.

ज़रक़, *m.* hypocrisy, fraud, detraction.

ज़रगर, *m.* a goldsmith, jeweller.

ज़रगरी, *f.* the business of a goldsmith.

जरगा, a kind of grass given as fodder to cattle,

जरजर, *more prop.* **जर्जर**, *q. v.* [*esp.* to horses.

जरठ = **जरठा**, 2, *q. v.*

जरठा, *m.* 1, decrepitude : 2. *m.* (*f.* ī) old, decayed, infirm ; hard, solid ; hard-hearted, cruel, harsh.

जरण, 1, old, decayed : 2, *m.* a plant (*Nigella Indica*) yielding a pungent seed, cumin-seed : old age, the becoming old and infirm. [cayed, infirm.

जरत, *m.* (*f.* ī) old, ancient, advanced in years, de-

जरतिका } **जरती** } *f.* an old woman.

ज़र्द, yellow, pale, livid.

ज़रदार, wealthy.

ज़रदुश्त, *m. pr. n.* Zoroaster.

ज़रदोज़ी, *f.* embroidery.

जरन } **जरनि** } *f.* the act of burning.

जरना, *n.* to be on fire, burn.

ज़रब, *f.* a blow, violence ; stamping, coining money.

ज़रबफ़्त } **ज़रबाफ़**, } *m.* bro cade, cloth of gold.

ज़रर, *m.* injury, damage, detriment, loss, ruin,

जररा, see **ज़र्रा**. [affliction, anguish.

जरवाना, *t.* to cause (some one) to ignite a thing, cause (a thing) to be ignited.

जरवाफी, a corruption of **ज़रीबाफ़ी**, *q. v.*

जरा, 1, *more prop.* **ज़र्रा**, *q. v.* : 2, *f.* decrepitude, the general relaxation and debility consequent upon old age : old age : a species of tree (*Mimusops kauki*) : *pr. n.* a certain female demon.

जरांश, *m.* paroxysm of a fever.

जरातुर, *m.* (*f.* ā) an infirm person, etc. : *lit.* infirm, decrepit, debilitated, old.

जराद, *m.* a locust.

जराना, *t.* to ignite, burn, inflame, kindle, light ; to make jealous. [ry ; humour, jocularity, wit.

ज़राफ़त, *f.* beauty ; elegance ; politeness, gallant-

जराभी, *more prop.* **ज़र्रा भी**, *q. v.*

जरामूल ; see **जड़मूल**.

जरायु, *m. f.*? the after-birth ; the uterus.

जरायुज, *m.* (*f.* ā) man and other animals born from

जरावठ, see **जड़ावट**. [the womb : *lit.* viviparous.

जरासन्ध, *m. pr. n.* a certain Kshatriya Rājā, sovereign of Magadha, father-in-law of Kaṅs and foe to Krishṇ. He is said to have been slain in single combat by Bheem. [Bheemsen.

जरासन्धजित, *m.* the conqueror of Jarāsandh, *i. e.*

जरासन्धि } **जरासन्धी** } *f. pr. n.* the wife of **जरासन्ध**, *q. v.*

ज़रासा, *m.* (*f.* ī) a small portion, the least bit,

जराहत, *f.* a wound, sore. [a very little.

जराह, *more prop.* **जर्राह**, *q. v.*

जरि, (poet.) a corruption of **जड़**, *q. v.*

जरिहैां (see **रहैां**) in Braj = **मैं जलूंगा**.

ज़री, *f.* anything woven with gold thread.

जरीदा, *m.* a register, account-book.

जरीदार, *adj.* bordered with gold thread.

ज़रीपतका, *m.* a golden sash granted by the Peshwa as badge of honour to his officers.

ज़रीफ़, ingenuous, polite, gallant ; witty, jocose, elegant in conversation.

जरीब, *f.* a sort of wooden dart with an iron point — *chalānā*, to throw the jareeb.

ज़रीबाफ़ी, *f.* the trade of working gold lace.

जरीमाना, *m.* a penalty, fine, forfeit.

ज़रीह, *f.* a railing or lattice-work surrounding a temple or tomb.

जरुथ, *m.* skinniness, flesh flaccid with old age.

ज़रूर, *f.* necessary, unavoidable, expedient : *adv.*

certainly, of necessity, of course: *met.* a necessary, water-closet. [2, *f.* necessity.

ज़रूरी, 1, necessary, needful, forced, compelled:

ज़रूरत, *f.* necessity, compulsion, constraint: violence, force; indigence, want.

जरे, a corruption of **जले** (**जलाना**). [riegated.

जर्क़बर्क़, shining, glittering, splendid, gaudy, va-

जर्जर, 1, *m.* the banner or emblem of Indra, a certain aquatic plant (*Vallisneria*): 2, old, decayed, thin, infirm, broken, rugged, crushed, torn asunder.

जर्जरीका, ragged, full of holes, decayed, old, per-

जर्णी = **जरण**, *q.v.* [forated.

जर्त्तिल, *m.* sesamum growing wild.

ज़र्द, yellow, pale, livid.

ज़र्दआलु, *m.* an apricot.

ज़र्फ़, *m.* a vase, vessel. [foot of a mountain.

जर्र, *m.* a drawing, dragging; base, foundation,

ज़र्रा, *m.* an atom, particle, little: *adv.* a little,

जर्राह, *m.* a surgeon, anatomist. [the least bit.

जल, 1, *m.* water: 2, (**जड़**?) frigidity (physical or moral): a certain jungle shrub: 3, cold, apathetic, stupid, idiotic: 4, in the ingenious system of reckoning by symbols adopted by Hindoos in their poetry, this word is a symbol for 4. — *bharnā*, to draw water. — *marnā*, to be burnt to death.

जलअलि, *m.* a water-bee: a whirlpool.

जलकणा, *f.* a drop of water. [a crocodile.

जलकण्टक, *m.* an aquatic plant (*Trapa bispinosa*):

जलकपि, *m.* the water-ape or Gangetic porpoise.

जलकर, *m.* revenue assessed on fisheries or on

जलकांक्ष, *m.* an elephant. [water.

जलकाक, *m.* (*f.* ī) the diver or water-crow.

जलकिराट, *m.* a shark: a large alligator.

जलकुकड़ / **जलकुक्कड़** } = **जलकुक्कुट**, *q.v.*

जलकुक्कुट, *m.* (*f.* ī) a kind of water-fowl, diver.

जलकुक्कुटी, *f.* (*see above*) the black-headed gull.

जलकुण्ड, *m.* a spring, a pool of water that never dries up.

जलकुन्तल, *m.* an aquatic plant (*Vallisneria*).

जलकूपी, *f.* a whirlpool; a pond, spring, well.

जलकूर्म, *m.* the Gangetic porpoise.

जलकेलि, *m.* *f.* = **जलक्रीड़ा**, *q.v.*

जलकेश, *m.* an aquatic plant (*Vallisneria*).

जलक्रीड़ा, *f.* bathing for pleasure or amusement, gamboling or sporting in the water.

जलग, a contraction of **जबलग**, *q.v.* [of water, lake.

जलगुल्म, *m.* (*f.* ā) a turtle, tortoise: a whirlpool, piece

जलघुमर, *m.* a whirlpool. [or going in water.

जलचर, *m.* (*f.* ī) any aquatic animal: *lit.* moving

जलछोटा, *m.* a sprinkling or a splashing with water.

जलज, *m.* (*f.* ā) an aquatic animal, etc.; a fish, shell, lotus: *lit.* water-born.

जलजन्तु, *m.* an aquatic or amphibious animal, *e.g.* a fish, porpoise, shark, etc.

जलजन्तुका, *f.* a leech.

जलजल, full of water, wet.

जलजला, *m.* (*f.* ī) indignant: outrageous.

जलजलाना, *n.* to be indignant.

जलजलाहट, *f.* indignation, rage, passion, anger.

जलजा, *f.* (see **जलज**) a species of plant (*Bassia*) growing in or near water.

जलजात / **जलजाता** } = **जलज**, *q.v.*

जलजान, *more prop.* **जलयान**, *q.v.* [abounds.

जलठल, *m.* any place where water settles or

जलडिम्ब, *m.* a bivalve shell.

जलतरंग, *m.* 1, the musical glasses or harmonicon: 2, the sound produced by such instrument: 3, the playing on glasses or china bowls by rubbing the edges: 4, a brass vessel in which water is put and the edges are beaten with two sticks.

जलतरंगी / **जलतरंजो** } *f.* = **जलतररंग**, *q.v.*

जलतापिक, *m.* the hilsa or sable-fish (*Clupea alosa*).

जलताल = **जलतापिक**, *q.v.* [shy ground.

जलथल, *m.* ground half covered with water, mar-

जलद, *m.* (*lit.* the water-giver) a cloud: a species of fragrant grass (*Cyperus rotundus*): *pr. n.* a certain *varsh* or division of the known continent.

जलदबाज़ = **जल्दबाज़**, *q.v.*

जलदाशन, *m.* the *sāl*-tree (*Shorea robusta*).

जलदी, *more prop.* **जल्दी**, *q.v.*

जलधर, *m.* (*lit.* the water-holder) a cloud; the ocean: a species of fragrant grass (*Cyperus rotundus*).

जलधारा, *f.* a current of water.

जलधि, *m.* (contr. of **जलनिधि**?) the ocean. [passion.

जलन, *m.* a burning, inflammation; heat; vexation,

जलनकुल, *m.* (*f.* ī) an otter. [sionate.

जलनशील, *m.* (*f.* ā) ignitable, combustible, pas-

जलना, *n.* to burn, be on fire, be enkindled: *met.* to burn with rage, burn with lust. *Jal uṭhnā*, to break out (as a fire). *Jal paknā*, to rage with passion. *Jal bujhnā*, to brand, burn to ashes. *Jalepar nōn lagānā*, to triumph over, insult; *lit.* to throw salt on a burn.

जलनिधि, *m.* the ocean.

जलनिर्गम, *m.* a drain, watercourse; a pipe along a wall for carrying off water; a waterfall, etc.

जलनीम, *m.* a species of drug (*Herpestes monniera*). It is a bitter herb which grows on the edges of tanks

जलनीली, *f.* an aquatic plant (*Vallisneria*). [etc.

जलन्दर = **जलन्धर**, *q.v.*

जलन्धर, *m.* dropsy, ascites: *lit.* that which retains water; hence, it is applied to flat alluvial land, as the Jalandar Duāb: *pr. n.* a certain Asur or demon.

जलन्धरी, *m.* (*f.* iṇī) a dropsical person.

जलपक्षी, *m.* (*f.* iṇī) any water-fowl.

जलपखी } m. (f. inī) = जलपत्ती, q. v.
जलपच्छी

जलपति, m. lord of the waters. i. e. वरुण, q.v.

जलपाई, f. the olive-tree (*Eleocarpus serrata*) and its fruit.

जलपान, m. drinking (water).—k. to drink, partake of refreshment (in the shape of luncheon or light food between meals).

जलपिप्पली, f. a species of aquatic plant (*Commelina salicifolia*).

जलपीपल, (*same as the above*?) a herb somewhat resembling the pepper-plant.

जलपृष्ठज, m. = जलपृष्ठजा, q. v.

जलपृष्ठजा, f. an aquatic plant (*Pistia stratiotes*).

जलप्रलय, m. the destruction of the world by water.

जलप्रिय, m. (f. ā) any fish : a certain bird (*Cuculus melanoleucos*) commonly called the *chātak*.

जलफ़, m. a miser : *adj.* mean, base.

जलब ; for words beginning thus, but not given below, see under the form जलव.

जलबन्धक, m. a dam, dike, rocks or stones impeding a current.

जलबन्धु, m. any fish.

जलबल, burnt up or consumed by fire.

जलबत्ती, f swimming (striking with the arms and legs in water.

जलबुद्बुद, m. a bubble of water.

जलब्राह्मी, f. a kind of potherb (*Hilancha repens*).

जलभू, m. a cloud ; a certain aquatic plant (*Commelina salicifolia* or *Bengalensis*).

जलभौंरा, m. a water-bee.

जलम, m. (prop. जन्म) birth ; birthright : proprietary right (especially in the soil).

जलमक्षिका, f. any water-fly or water-insect.

जलमण्डल, m. a kind of tarantula or large spider the bite of which is said to be fatal.

जलमय, m. a deluge, inundation; lit. *adj. m.* (f. ī) consisting of water, abounding in water, watery, deluged.

जलमल, m. foam, etc.

जलमानुष, m. a mermaid, the water kelpie, a small species of monkey.

जलमार्ग, m. a drain or issue from a pond.

जलमार्जार, m. (f. ī) an otter.

जलमुर्गा, m- (f. ī) any water-fowl.

जलमूर्त्ति, m. an epithet of Shiv (of whom one form is water, implying his omnipresence).

जलयन्त्र, m. any machine for raising water, waterworks.

जलयन्त्रगृह, m. a house, etc. constructed in the midst of water, or subterraneous apartments constructed on the bank of a river, for retiring to in the hot season, a summer-house, etc.

जलयात्रा, f. a voyage.

जलयान, m. a boat ; *lit.* moving on water.

जलरंक, m. a kind of crane (which feeds chiefly on small fish and haunts swamps, etc.).

जलरंकु, m. a gallinule.

जलरंज, m. the *vak*, a kind of crane.

जलराशि, m. the ocean.

जलराशी, *more prop.* जलराशि, q. v.

जलरुह, m. the lotus.

जलल ; see (1) ज़लल (2) जलाल.

ज़लल, m. meanness, baseness : erring, blundering ; stumbling, falling ; deficiency, loss : an error, crime.

जललता, f. a wave. billow.

जलवा, m. splendour, lustre ; the bridal bed, bridal ornaments.

जलवाना, t. to cause a thing to be burnt.

जलविड़ाल, m. an otter ; *lit.* the water-cat.

जलविन्दु, m. a drop of water : *pr. n.* a certain place of Hindoo pilgrimage.

जलविषुव, m. the autumnal equinox or the moment of the sun's entering Libra near the close of the rainy season.

जलविहंग } m. (f. ā) any water-fowl.
जलविहंगम

जलविहार, m. gamboling or sporting in water.

जलवृश्चिक, m. (*lit.* the water-scorpion) a shrimp, prawn.

जलवैया, m. (noun of agency from जलना) a burner.

जलव्यध, m. (f. ā) a species of pike-fish.

जलशय, m. (*lit.* he who sleeps on the water) an epithet of Vishṇu. The allusion is to the fact that after the destruction of the universe, he alone of all beings remains floating on the water on a leaf of the *bar* (*Ficus Indica*) or on the great snake *Anant*.

जलशयन }
जलशाई }
जलशायी } = जलशय, q. v.
जलसाई }

जलसंस्कार, m. ceremonial purification by means of the external application of water.

जलसा, m. attitude, posture, situation, seat, post, state, bearing ; a sitting, meeting, society.

जलसूचि, f. a sort of pike-fish (*Esox scolopax*) ; the Gangetic porpoise ; a leech ; a certain aquatic plant (*Trapa bispinosa*).

जलसूत, f. the guinea-worm (*Filaria medinensis*).

जलसेनी, f. a fish ; sleeping in water by way of mortification; drowning by sleeping in water as an act of penance. [for religious purposes.

जलस्पर्श, m. touching water (*esp.* Ganges-water)

जलह, m. a summer-house ; a small piece of water, a pond, lake.

जलहास, m. cuttle-fish bone (considered as the indurated foam of the sea).

जला, 1, = जल्ला, q. v.: 2, f. *pr. n.* a certain river.

जलाऊ, m. the act of burning ; a burner.

जलांचल, m. a natural watercourse or channel ; a certain aquatic plant (*Vallisneria*).

जलाकार, m. an appearance of water.

जलाखु, m. an otter or water-cat.

जलाद, *more prop.* जल्लाद, q. v.

जलादत, f. activity, agility, strength.

जलाधार, m. a pond, lake, reservoir.

जलाना, t. to set fire to, burn, kindle, fire, light, enflame ; to excite to rage, jealousy, or lust.

जलापा, *m.* envy, anger, rage, spite.

जलापाखुर, an envious person.

जलाबला } scorched; hot-tempered; fretful.
जलाभुना }

जलामय, *m.* (*f.* ī) consisting of water, abounding in water, full of water, watery, wet.

जलाम्बिका, *f.* a well.

जलाया, *m.* (*f.* **जलाई**) ignited, enflamed.

जलार्णव, *m.* a deluge, great flood, inundation; the rainy season; sea of fresh water.

जलार्द्र, *m.* (*f.* ā) charged with moisture, wet.

जलाल, *m.* dignity, state, majesty, grandeur, splendour, glory, power.

जलालत, *f.* = **जलाल**, *q.v.*

जलाली, glorious, illustrious, majestic.

जलालुका } *f.* a leech.
जलालोका }

जलावन, *f.* firewood.

जलाशय, *m.* 1, any piece of water, a pond, lake, tank, reservoir; the ocean: a certain fragrant grass (*Andropogon muricatum*): 2, apathetic, cold, dull, stupid.

जलासय; see (1) **जलाशय** (2) **जलाशय**.

जलासा, a pool of water, tank.

जलिका, *f.* a leech.

जलिया, *m.* a fisherman.

जलीयप्रलय = **जलप्रलय**, *q.v.*

जलील, great, glorious, illustrious.

ज़लील, submissive, abject, mean, base, contemptible, wretched.

जलीस, *m. f.* a companion, comrade, guest, chum.

जलुका } *f.* a leech.
जलू }

ज़ुलूम, cruel, tyrannical, oppressive.

जलूहुं, an old acc. or emphat. form of **जलू**, *q.v.*

जलेचर, *m.* (*f.* ī) any aquatic animal; *lit.* moving or existing in water.

जलेच्छया, *f.* a plant (*Heliotropium Indicum*).

जलेन्धन, *m.* submarine fire.

जलेपर नोन लगाना, *t.* to triumph over, insult; *lit.* to throw salt on one who is burned.

जलेब, *m.* attendants, equipage, suite.

जलेबी, *f.* a kind of sweetmeat.

जलेश्वर, *m.* the sovereign of the waters: *hence*, an epithet (1) of Varuṇ (2) of the ocean.

जलोका, *f.* a leech.

जलोच्छ्वास = **जलोच्छ्वास**, *q.v.*

जलोच्छ्वास, *m.* a drain or channel (whether natural or artificial) to carry off an excess of water, a conduit.

जलोत्सर्ग, *m.* the ceremony gone through when a pond, bā,oli, or well is married.

जलोदर, 1, *m.* dropsy: 2, *m.* (*f.* ī) a dropsical person: [*lit.* dropsical.

जलोद्गम, *m.* the course of the water.

जलोरगी } *f.* a leech.
जलोर्गी }

जलोर्मी, *f.* a wave: *adj. m.* (*f.* inī) wavy.

जलौकस } *f.* a leech.
जलौका }

जल्क, *m.* a prompt and ready or eloquent tongue.

जल्द, expeditious, quick, brisk, fast, hasty.

जल्दक़दम, fleet of foot.

जल्दबाज़, expeditious, fleet, hasty.

जल्दबाज़ी, *f.* haste, fleetness, expeditiousness.

जल्दमिज़ाज, quick-tempered, passionate.

जल्दरव, swift of motion.

जल्दी, *f.* haste, quickness, rashness, precipitancy. — *k.* to make haste; to act precipitately.

जल्प, *m.* prating, babble, wrangling, dissension.

जल्पक, *adj.* talking much and foolishly: hence, *m.* (*f.* ikā) a prater, babbler, chatterer.

जल्पत in Braj = **जल्पता है**.

जल्पना, to speak; to utter falsehoods.

जल्पसि, (poet.) = **तू बकता है**.

जल्पहि, *m. f.* (pl. **जल्पहिं**) in poet. = **वह बकता है**.

जल्पिका, *f.* (*m.* **जल्पक**) a female chatterer.

जल्पिता, *m.* (*f.* trī) } = **जल्पक**, *q.v.*
जल्पी, *m.* (*f.* inī) }

जल्पाक = **जल्पक**, *q.v.*

जल्ल, great, eminent, glorious.

जल्ला, *m.* a mass of water, lake, reservoir, tank.

जल्लाद, *m.* an executioner: *adj.* hard-hearted.

जल्लादी, *f.* the office of executioner; cruelty.

ज़ल्लाम, a great oppressor, atrocious tyrant.

जल्हो; see (1) **जल** (2) **जल्दी**.

जव, 1, in Braj = **जौ**, *q.v.*: 2, *m.* quickness.

जवं, an old form = **जौं**, *q.v.*

जवखार } = **यवखार**, *q.v.*
जवक्षार }

जवत्री, *f.* mace; nutmeg.

जवन, 1, = (1) **जौं** (2) **जौन** (3) **यवन**, *qq.v.*: 2, *m.* (*f.* ī) a fleet horse, courser, etc.: *lit.* fleet, quick.

जवनिका, *f.* a curtain, screen surrounding a tent.

जवफल = **यवफल**, *q.v.*

जवमध्य = **यवमध्य**, *q.v.*

जवल, *more prop.* **सबल**, *q.v.*

जवा, 1, *m.* = **यव**, *q.v.*: 2, *m.* a clove of garlic: 3, *m.* a kind of stitch in needlework: 4, *f.* the China rose (*Hibiscus rosa Sinensis*).

जवाई = **जमाई**, *q.v.*

जवांकुर = **यवांकुर**, *q.v.*

जवांमर्द, *m.* a fine young fellow, brave fellow, hero: *lit.* brave, manly, generous.

जवांमर्दी, *f.* generosity, manliness, heroism.

जवाखार, a corruption of **यवखार**, *q.v.*

जवाज़, *m.* permission: propriety, lawfulness: a wooden mortar; a sugar-mill, oil-mill.

ज़वाजिर, forbidden things.

जवान, *m.* a youth, lad, one who has 'come of age': *lit.* youthful, young.

जवानी, *f.* adolescence, youthfulness; the season of youth: 'coming of age': a daughter's husband.

जवापुष्प, *m.* = **जवा**, 4, *q.v.*

जवाब, *m.* an answer, anything answering to or matching with another.

जवाबनामा, *m.* a writing fixed to the winding-sheet on the breast of a good Muhammadan deceased which it is intended that Munkir and Nakīr should read in case the poor soul should be too much flurried to answer their questions.

जवाबदार / **जवाबदिह** } *m.* a surety, respondent.

जवामरदी, *more prop.* **जवांमर्दी**, *q.v.*

जवार, = (1) **जुवार** (2) **जोआर**, *qq.v.*

जवारा, *m.* Indian corn: the small shoots of rice which germinate when steeped in water: as much land as can be ploughed by a pair of bullocks: a yoke of bullocks: the barley which is forced into earthen pots by Brāhmaṇs for presentation at the Dasahrā, or by women for presentation to their fathers and brothers on that festival.

ज़वारी, *f.* great millet.

ज़वाल, *m.* decline; wretchedness.

जवाला, *m.* grain mixed with barley as food for cattle.

जवाली, *f.* 1, = **जवाला**, *q.v.*: 2, mixed wheat.

जवास / **जवासा** } *more prop.* **यवास**, *q.v.*

जवाहिर, *m.* (prop. pl. of **जौहर**) a jewel, gem.

जवाहिरात, *m.* (pl. of the above) jewels, gems.

जवेदार, (see **जवा**, 3) sewed in a particular manner.

जश, **जस**; for words beginning thus, but not given below, see under the form **यश**.

जश्न, *m.* a feast, festival (chiefly of royalty).

जस, *more prop.* (1) **जैसा** (2) **यश**, *qq.v.*

जसहुतसहु (*poet.*) = **जैसातैसा**, *q.v.*

जसामत / **जसामी** } *f.* corpulency, bulkiness.

जसारत, *f.* presumption, temerity, boldness, daring, intrepidity.

जसावर, *m. pr. n.* a small tribe of Rājputs in Mathura.

जसु in Braj = **जैसा**, *q.v.*

जसे, *more com.* **जैसे**, *q.v.*

जस्त / **जस्ता** } *m.* pewter, prince's-metal.

जस्ती, made of pewter or tin.

जहँ, a contraction of **जहाँ**, *q.v.*

जहँतहँ (*contraction*) = **जहाँतहाँ**, *q.v.*

जहन्नम, *m.* hell.

ज़हब, gold: the yolk of an egg.

ज़हमत, *f.* disquietude, trouble, pain, injury, sickness, affliction.

ज़हर, *m.* poison, venom.

ज़हरमोहरा, *m.* a bezoar.

ज़हरा, *m.* bile, gall-bladder: spirit, boldness, pluck.

जहल, *m.* ignorance, stupidity, irreligion.

जहवाँ, (Rām.) = **जहाँ**, *q.v.*

जहा, *f.* a species of plant whose flowers resemble those of the *Kadamb.*

जहाँ, (correl. of **तहाँ**) where, in the place which. — *Kahīṅ*, wheresoever. — *kā* (*ki*, *ke*) *tahāṅ*, anywhere and everywhere, everywhere, in the same place as before. — *jahāṅ jahāṅ*, wherever. — *tak* or *talak* or *lag* or *loṅ*, as far as. — *tahāṅ*, here and there, all about, everywhere: *phirnā*, to wander, straggle.

जहाँदीदा, having seen the world, experienced.

जहाँपनाह = **जहानपनाह**, *q.v.*

जहाँसे, whence, from which place.

जहाज़, *m.* a ship; the tree of a camel's saddle; funeral apparatus; *vulva, pudenda mulieris.*

जहाजी, 1, *m.* a sailor: 2, *f.* a kind of scimitar.

जहान, *m.* the world.

जहानक, *m.* the period of the total destruction of the world.

जहानपनाह, *m.* an epithet of Kings and other potentates; *lit.* asylum of the world.

जहापनाह, *more prop.* **जहानपनाह**, *q.v.*

जहानी, a human being: *lit.* worldly, terrestrial.

जहाम, a corruption (1) of **जहान** (2) of **झाम**, *qq.v.*

जहालत, *f.* brutality, barbarism, ignorance, stupidity.

जहालक, a corruption of **जहाँलग**, *q.v.*

जहि, (poet.) = **जिसको**.

जहिया, a poet. form of **जब**, *q.v.*

जही, a corruption (1) of **जहीं** (2) of **यही**, *qq.v.*

जहीं, wherever, in whatsoever place.

ज़हीन, sagacious; ingenious.

ज़हीर, thin, reduced (by sickness); low-spirited, melancholy, sad.

जहेज़, *m.* whatever a wife carries with her to her husband's house, paraphernalia, portion.

जह्नु, *m. pr. n.* a certain king who adopted the river Gangā as his daughter.

जह्नुतनया, *f. pr. n.* an epithet of the river Ganges; *lit.* the daughter of Jahnu. The river is said to have disturbed the devotions of Jahnu, whereupon he drank up its waters: at the intercession of the gods he released them, and is hence considered to have become the parent of the river.

जहुर, a corruption of **ज़हर**, *q.v.*

ज़हूल, *m.* oblivion, forgetting.

जहूल, very ignorant.

जहेर, a corruption of **ज़हर**, *q.v.*

जा, 1, fem. of **ज**; (see **ज**, 4): 2, *f.* a place: 3, (in Braj) the inflected base of **जो** or **जौन**, *q.v.*

ज़ाइ, lost, destroyed, perished, fruitless, abortive. — *k.* to lose, destroy, squander, apply to no purpose, misapply.

जाइ (Rām.) **जाय**, *q.v.*

ज़ाइक़ा, *m.* the sense of tasting, the palate, relish, taste.

जाइय, *more prop.* **जाइयो** (**जाना**).

ज़ाइल, deficient, failing, perishing, vanishing.

जाइयों, a dialectic form of the Honorific Imperat.
जाइहो in Braj = जाओगे (जाना). [of vb. *jānā*.
जाई, *f.* (*m.* जाया) a daughter.
ज़ाइचा, *m.* a horoscope, astronomical table.
जाईये, *more prop.* जाइयो (जाना).
जाईल, twice-ploughed land.
जाउ in Braj = जाव or जाओ (from जाना). [*q.v.*
जाउरि, 1, i.e. जाउ (+ रि for the metre) : 2, = पायस,
जाउब (*poet.*) = जाऊंगा (जाना).
जाऊ in Braj = जाव or जाओ (जाना).
जाएगीर, 1, taking or holding a place; fixed, permanent; efficacious : 2. *f.* pension.
जाएफल, *m.* nutmeg (*Myristica moschata*).
जाएस, a certain tribe of Suraj-vaṅsī Rājputs.
जाएसून = जासून, *q.v.*
जाओ, (imperat. 2nd pl. of जाना) go you.
जां, *more com.* (1) जहां (2) जान, *qq.v.*
जांइ (*poet.*) = (1) जायं (2) जाय, *qq.v.*
जांकड़, *m.* money or other property left as pledge for a thing purchased while it is carried away to be finally approved.
जांगर, *m.* the thigh and leg.
जांगा, *more prop.* जागा, *q.v.*
जांघ, *f.* the thigh.
जांघल, *m.* a kind of heron (*Ardea Indica*).
जांघिया, *m.* a kind of breeches that do not cover the thigh, short breeches.
जांच, *m.* trial, examination, test, assay, proof.—*lenā*, to test, make trial of. [verify, try, prove, assay.
जांचना, *t.* to examine, enquire into, ascertain,
जांफ़िशानी, *f.* zeal, devotedness, extreme diligence. — *k.* to strain every nerve.
जांय, pl. of जाय, 1, *q.v.*
जाकि in Braj = जिसको (जो). [not sell.
जाकड़, 1, *more prop.* जांकड़, *q.v.* : 2, goods that do
जाकर, 1, an old form = जिसका; 2, see जाकड़; 3, a form of the conjunct. part. of verb जाना.
जाकरि = जाकर, 3, *q.v.*
जाका in Braj = जिसका (जो).
ज़ाकिर, one who remembers or praises God: *adj.* re-
जाकी in Braj = जिसकी (जो). [membering, grateful.
जाके, 1, in Braj = जिसके (जो) : 2, the second form of the conjunctive participle of *jānā*.
जाकै = जाके = जिसके.
जाको in Braj = जिसको (जो).
जाकौ in Braj = जिसका (जो).
जाकौं in Braj = जिसको (जो). [of a well.
जाखन, the wooden foundation of the brickwork
जाखर, a subdivision of the *jāt* tribe.
जाग, *m.* 1, = यज्ञ, *q.v.* : 2, vigils.
जागत, a contraction of जागर्ति, *q.v.*

जागतीजोत }
जागतीज्योति } = जाग्रतज्योति, *q.v.*
जागना, *n.* to be awake : *a. int.* to awake.
जागरण, *m.* waking, vigil, wakefulness, keeping watch, sitting up at night at a religious ceremony or at prayers, vespers.
जागर्त्ति, *f.* waking, vigilance, watchfulness.
जागह = जगह, *q.v.* [of the *Bhāt* tribe of Hindoos.
जागा, 1, *more prop.* जगह, *q.v.* : 2, *m.* a designation
जागाबन्दी, *f.* drowsiness, sleepiness.
जागि, an old form = जागके (जागना).
जागी, outward, manifest.
जागीर, *f.* land given by Government as a reward for services or as a fee; a pension in land.
जागीरदार, *m.* the holder of a जागीर.
जागु = जागू, *q.v.* [waking, wakeful, vigilant.
जागू, 1, = जगह, *q.v.* : 2, *m.* one who awakens : *lit.*
जागृवि, *m. f.* watchful.
जाग्रत, awake, vigilant, on the watch. [powers.
जाग्रतज्योति, possessed of or exerting miraculous
जागरी, *f.* coarse sugar, molasses, treacle, refuse of sugar; sugar of the palmyra-tree.
जाङ्गल, *m.* the francoline partridge.
जाङ्गली, 1, = जंगली, *q.v.* : 2, *f.* cowach (*Carpopogon pruriens*): 3, *m.* (*f.* ī) picturesque country : *lit.* rural, picturesque, diversified (with hill, vale, wood and water).
जाङ्गुल, *m.* poison, venom.
जाङ्गुलि, *m.* a snake-catcher; a dealer in antidotes, snake-doctor, one who professes, chiefly by charms, to cure the bites of snakes of other venomous [animals.
जाङ्गुलिक = जाङ्गुलि, *q.v.*
जाङ्गुली, *f.* the knowledge of poisons, the possession of charms or drugs and the employment of them as antidotes : a kind of potherb (*Luffa acutangula*).
जाच; for words beginning thus, see under the
ज़ाज, *m.* copperas, vitriol. [form याच.
ज़ाज़; see (1) ज़ाज (2) जहाज़. [form याज.
जाज; for words beginning thus, see under the
जाजम, *f.* a cloth (thrown over the carpet) to sit on.
जाजल, *m.* a certain school of the Atharva-Ved.
जाजलि, *m. pr. n.* a certain ancient Hindoo sage.
जाजाति, *more prop.* ययाति, *q.v.* [(as a plaster),
जाज़िब, alluring, attractive, absorbent, drawing
जाजुलन, *m.* (Chand) rage, fury.
जाजुलित, (Chand) *m.* (*f.* ā) inflamed with rage.
जाज्य, जाज्ञ; for words beginning thus, see under the forms याज्य, याज्ञ, respectively.
जाज्वल्य *m. pr. n.* a certain ancient Hindoo sage.
जाट, *m.* a certain tribe among Rājputs.
जाटलि, *m.* (*f.* ī) the plant *Bignonia suaveolens*.
जाटली, a certain subdivision of the *gūjar* tribe.
जाटुवा = जाटूआ, *q.v.*
जाटू, a certain Rājput tribe.

जाटूआ, a branch of the *chamār* tribe.

जाठ, *m.* the axis of an oil or sugar-mill which presses the grain or the canes : a post placed by Hindoos in the centre of a tank to indicate that its water has been dedicated to a deity. [gums of the teeth.

जाड़, 1, a corruption of **झड़**, *q.v.* : 2, *f.* (*m.*?) the

जाड़ा, *m.* cold, coldness ; the winter.

जाड़ी, *f.* a row of teeth.

जाड्य, *m.* want of sensation, apathy, coldness, frigidity, senselessness, stupidity, dullness, folly.

जात, 1, *m.* = **ज़ात**, *q.v.* : 2, *m.* (*f.* ā) a child, offspring : *lit.* born, produced, engendered.

ज़ात, *f.* a mistress, possessor ; the soul ; essence, nature, substance ; a person viewed as body and soul : caste.

जातक, *m.* a ceremony on the birth of a child ; astronomical calculation of a nativity : a mendicant.

जातकर्म, *m.* a sacrificial ceremony directed to be performed at the birth of a child.

जातना = **यातना**, *q.v.*

जातपान्त } *f.* = **जातिपान्ति**, *q.v.*
जातपान्ति }

जातभाई, *m.* a person of the same caste as oneself, a brother by caste, a caste-fellow.

जातरूप, 1, *m.* gold : 2, *m.* (*f.* ā) golden.

जाता, *f.* (*m.* **जात**) a daughter.—*rahnā*, to go away entirely, vanish, pass away, be lost, be missing.

जाति, *f.* birth, existence, life, production ; lineage, race, tribe, family ; genus, species, class, kind, sort : according to one principle of calculation the Hindoos are divisible into twenty-two castes ; and hence, in the ingenious system of reckoning by symbols adopted by Hindoos in their poetry, this word is a symbol for 22 : this is sometimes the latter element in compound words ; e. g. *Strijāti*, woman-kind, the female sex, women.

जातित्व, *m.* (*f.* tā) distinction or nature of caste or tribe, special or generic property.

जातिधर्म, *m.* the duties appertaining to any particular tribe or caste. [gree.

जातिपान्ति, *f.* race, lineage, tribe, family, pedi-

जातिभाई = **जातभाई**, *q.v.*

जातिलक्षण, *m.* a mark of tribe or caste, specific or generic characteristic or distinction.

जातिवाचक, *m.* (in Gram.) a generic name.

जातिवाला, *m.* (*f.* ī) a person of high caste, a respectable person. [nature.

जातिस्वभाव, *m.* specific or generic character or

जातिहीन, casteless, without caste, outcaste.

जाती, 1, a corruption of **जाति**, *q.v.* : 2, *f.* the great-flowered jasmine (*Jasminium grandiflorum*) : mace ;

जातीपत्री, *f.* mace. [nutmeg.

जातीफल, *m.* nutmeg.

जातीय, appertaining to caste or to kind.

जातीरस, *m.* gum myrrh.

जातु ; see under the form **यातु**.

जातु, a certain tribe of Rājputs in Karnal of whom many have now become Muhammadans.

जात्य, *m.* (*f.* ā) a person of noble descent ; *lit.* well-born, of noble race, true. [*lit.* born blind.

जात्यन्ध, *m.* (*f.* ā) a person blind from his birth :

जात्याभिमान, *m.* pride of race, family, or pedigree.

जात्युक्त, *m.* (*f.* ā) spoken concerning caste.

जात्र, **जात्य** ; for words beginning thus, see under the forms **यात्र**, **यात्य**, respectively.

ज़ाद, *m.* increase: provisions, food : a child, son.

ज़ादबूम = **जन्मभूमि**, *q.v.*

जादव = **यादव**, *q.v.*

ज़ादा, *m.* (*f.* ī) a child, son : *lit.* born of.

जादाद, *f.* a place, station ; employment, service ;

जादिन (see **जा**, 3) = **जिस दिनमें**. [consignment.

जादू, *m.* enchantment, conjuring, juggling.—*chalānā*, to practice incantations, etc.

जादूगर, *m.* (*f.* nī) an enchanter, juggler, conjuror,

जादूगरी, *f.* necromancy, magic. [sorceror, magician.

जादो, *m.* one of the low castes in a village (employed in menial offices).

जादों, a certain tribe of Rājputs.

जान, 1, *more prop.* (1) **ज्ञानी** (2) **यान**, *qq.v.* : 2, *f.* *m.* life, soul, spirit, understanding, mind, self : a sweetheart. —*rakhnā*, to bear in mind. —*par khelnā*, to run the hazard of one's life, risk one's life. —*se mār ḍālnā*, to slay, murder. [2, cognizant.

जानक, 1, appertaining to life or to the living :

जानकारी, *f.* knowledge ; e. g. *Merī* —— *meṇ*, as far as my knowledge goes, as far as I know.

जानकी, *f. pr. n.* Seetā (daughter of Janak).

जानके ; see (1) **जानना** (2) **जान**.

जानत, *adj.* knowing, understanding.

जानता, *more prop.* **जान्ता**, *q.v.*

जानना, *t.* to know, understand, comprehend ; to suppose, opine, infer, hold, consider, recognize, trust, believe. *Mujhe jān paṛtā hai*, it seems to me, it occurs to me, for aught I know, I suppose. *Jān lenā*, to perceive, recognize, "twig".

जाननिहार in Braj = **जाननेहारा**.

जाननों in Braj = **जानना**, *q.v.* [ledge or of life.

जानपन, *m.* the state of being in possession of know-

जानपना, *m.* } = **जानपन**, *q.v.*
जानपनी, *f.* }

जानपहचान, *m.* (*f.*?) acquaintance, intimate friend.

जानब, 1, = **मैं जानूंगा** ; 2, acquaintance, kith and kin, the things or the persons one knows.

जानबूझकर = **जानबूझके**, *q.v.*

जानबूझके, *adv.* in the exercise of knowledge and of the faculty of intelligence, knowingly, wilfully, purposely.

जानव = **जानब**, *q.v.*

जानवर, *m.* any living creature, an animal. [rosary.

जानवा, a belt ; a Brāhmaṇical thread ; a Hindoo

जानशीन, *m.* a *locum tenens*, deputy, successor,

जानहार, *adj.* going, passing away. [vicegerent.

जाना, *a. int.* to go, pass, reach, continue, be. This

verb has two past participles, the one (जाया) being used only in forming compound verbs, and the other (गया; from Sk. rt. गम्) being the one always used where the past participle of this verb is required. It has certain important idiomatic usages:—1, following the present participle of any verb it yields the Continuative form of that verb; *e. g. Wuh gātī jātī hai*, she continues singing: 2, it yields the Passive form of a verb by following the past participle of that verb; *e. g. Wuh dekhī jaegī*, she will be seen: 3, it yields the Intensive form of many verbs by following their roots; *e. g. Khā jānā*, to eat up, devour.

जानाना; see (1) जनवाना (2) जनाना (3) जाना.

जानामि, divination, soothsaying.

जानि in Braj = जानके (जानना).

जानिब, *f.* a part, side; party. [second.

जानिबदार, *m.* one who takes a side, a supporter,

जानिमर, a corruption of जानवर, *q.v.*

जानिये, (Honorif. Imperat.) understand, suppose, know. *Na—kitne hain*, there is no knowing how many there are.

ज़ानी, *m.* a fornicater, adulterer.

जानी, 1, *more prop.* ज्ञानी, *q.v.*: 2, *f.* a woman: 3, *m.* a lover, friend: *lit.* appertaining to the life or soul; *hence*, cordial, sincere.

जानु, *m.* the knee; the lap.

जानुफलक, *m.* the kneepan or patella.

जानुये, a corruption of जानिये, *q.v.*

जानुसन्धि, *f.* the knee-joint.

ज़ानू, *m.* the knee; the lap.

जाने *denā*, to liberate, let go; to excuse, pass over a fault. *—do*, never mind, let alone, don't. *Kyā jāne*, what does anyone know? how does anyone know? who knows? *Yih sthān na jāne kaisā hai*, as for this place, there's no knowing what sort of a place it is.

जाने अनजाने, wittingly or unwittingly.

जानेहु = (1) जानेमें (2) तुमने जान लिया.

जानो, (2nd pers. pl. condit. of जानना) you would suppose, it seems as if, understand, suppose, to wit, namely, *videlicet*, as if, as, like as if. Preceded by *ki* [expressed or implied.

जानों = (1) जानो (2) मैं जानूं.

जानौ in Braj = (1) जाना (2) जानूं (3) जानो.

जानौं = जानौ, *q.v.*

जान्त, *f.* a wooden trough for raising water.

जान्ता, *f.* a stone mill for grinding corn, a hand-mill of two stones one over the other: bellows: skill, [knowledge.

जान्ताकल, *f.* = जान्त, *q.v.*

जान्ना = जानना, *q.v.*

जान्यौ, an old form = जाना (from जानना).

जान्हवी, *f.* (see जन्हु) an epithet of the Ganges; [*lit.* produced by Janhu.

जाप = जप, *q.v.*

जापक = जपी, *q.v.*

जापन = यापन, *q.v.*

जापर, an old form = जिसपर. See जा, 3.

जापी }
जापु } = जपी, *q.v.*

जापै, an old form = जिसपर. See जा and पै.

ज़ाफ़, *m.* sudden death.

जाफर }
जाफल } जायफल, *q.v.*

जाब, *m.* an ox-muzzle: a fruit-net: a grass.

जाबजा, from place to place, in every place, everywhere; here and there; scatteredly. [other persons.

जाबालि, *m. pr. n.* a certain Rishi; also, several

जाबिध (see जा, 3) in Braj = जिस विधिसे.

जाबी, *f.* (dim. of जाब) a muzzle for small cattle.

जाम, 1, *more prop.* याम, *q.v.*: 2, *m.* the rose-apple (*Eugenia jambu*): a guava (*Psydium pyriferum*): any drinking-vessel, cup, glass, bowl, goblet.

जामघ, *m. pr. n.* a certain ancient Hindoo king, the son of Shishubindu

जामदग्नेय, *m.* (*f.* ī) a descendant of Jamadagni.

जामदग्न्य, *m. pr. n.* a name of Parashurām, son of Jamadagni; *lit.* a descendant of Jamadagni.

जामध in Braj = जिसमें. See जा, 3.

जामन, 1, *m.* sour milk used for coagulating fresh milk, rennet: 2, *f.* the rose-apple tree (*Eugenia jambolana* or *Calyptranthes caryophyllifolia*) and its fruit.

जामना, *n.* to be produced, be born.

जामनी = यावनी, *q. v.* [*Mallaccensis*).

जामफल, *m.* the Malay or star-apple (*Eugenia*

जामव°; for words beginning thus, see under the form जाम्बव°.

जामा, *m.* a garment, robe, vest, shawl.

जामाख़ाना, *m.* a wardrobe.

जामाता }
जामातृ } = यामाता, *q. v.*

जामिक, *more prop.* यामिक, *q.v.*

जामाद, *m.* a son-in-law (daughter's husband).

जामिद, congealed, solid, stiff, astringent; (in Gram.) underived, primitive. [guarantee, sponsor.

ज़ामिन, *m.* a surety, bondsman, security, bail,

जामिन; see (1) ज़ामिन (2) यामिनी.

जामिनि }
जामिनी } see (1) ज़ामिनी (2) यामिनी.

ज़ामिनी, *f.* surety, bail, guarantee. *—kabūl k.* to accept bail. [respectable woman.

जामी, *f.* a sister, female relation, virtuous and

जामीनी; see (1) ज़ामिनी (2) यामिनी.

जामुन = जामन, *q. v.*

जामे, (see जा, 3) in Braj = जिसमें (जो).

जाम्बती, a corruption of जाम्बवती, *q.v.*

जाम्बव, *m.* the rose-apple tree (*Eugenia Jambu*) and its fruit. [at the point of death.

जाम्बलब, at the point of expiring. *—honā*, to be

जाम्बवत, *m. pr n.* the chief of the bears who, with the monkeys, was an ally of Rām and therefore sometimes called a monkey. He was son of Pitāmah.

जाम्बवती, *f. pr. n.* the daughter of Jāmbavat who was a wife of Krishṇ and mother of Sāmb.

जाम्बवन्त
जाम्बवान
जाम्बुवत } = जाम्बवत, *q.v.*

जाम्वती, a corruption of जाम्बवती, *q.v.*

जाय, 1, (from जाना) a form of the third pers. sing. of the dependent mode: 2, in vain, abortive.

ज़ाय:, see (1) ज़ाया (2) ज़ियादः.

ज़ायक़, one who tastes; *adj.* tasting. [taste.

ज़ायक़ा, *m.* the sense of tasting, the palate, relish,

जायगीर (*corruption*) = जागीर, *q.v.*

ज़ायद, redundant, superfluous, more.

जायपत्री, *f.* mace.

जायफल, *m.* nutmeg (*Myristica moschata*).

जाया, 1, see जाना: 2, *m.* (*f.* जाई) a son; *lit.* born; 3, *f.* a spouse, wife, a wife wedded according to the [perfect ritual.

जायापति
जायापती } *m.* husband and wife.

जायी, *adj.* conquering; hence, *m.* (*f.* inī) a con- [queror.

जायें, *more prop.* जाइये (जाना).

जार, *m.* a lover; paramour, gallant, adulterer: virulence, violence.

जारज, *m.* (*f.* ā) the child of a woman by her paramour, an adulterine: *lit.* begotten of a paramour.

जारन, *m.* firewood, fuel.

जारना, *t.* to set alight, set on fire, ignite, en- [kindle, inflame, burn.

जारनौं in Braj = जारना, *q.v.*

जारल, *m.* a kind of wood (*Lagerstræmia flos re-* [*ginae*).

ज़ारा, an assemblage, heap.

जारी, running, flowing, proceeding; current, customary, in force. — *k.* to begin, set on foot, originate, found. — *honā*, to be set agoing, be in vogue, be in force, pass current, proceed.

जारू, *adj.* burning, inflaming.

जारूब, *m.* a broom; a sweeper.

जारूबकश, *m.* a sweeper. [of a sweeper.

जारूबकशी, *f.* the act of sweeping, status or office

जारेहू, an old form = जला दिया.

जारोब, *more prop.* जारूब, *q.v.*

जाल, *m.* a net, sash, eyelet, loophole; a lattice, window; a coat of mail; illusion, supernatural decep- [tion, conjuring, illusion.

जालदार, reticulated.

जालना = जारना, *q.v.*

जालन्धर, *m. pr. n.* a country situated on the North-west of India (perhaps the modern Jallindhar).

जालन्धरी, *m.* (*f.* ī) an inhabitant of Jālandhar.

जालकरी, *f.* valerian. [of mail.

जालवन्त, *m.* (*f.* vatī) a person covered with a coat

जालसिलाही, *f.* a coat of mail.

जाला, *m.* a cobweb, net, pellicle; a jar; a speck [on the eye, cataract.

जालिक, *m.* = जालिका, *q.v.*

जालिका, *f.* a net; a coat of mail.

जालिकी, *m.* one who employs nets for a livelihood: a cheat, juggler, conjuror, rogue; a hunter who uses nets; a fisherman; a spider.

जालिनी, *f.* a painting-room.

ज़ालिम, *m.* tyrant; *met.* a beloved person, mistress: *lit.* tyrannical, oppressive, cruel, barbarous.

जालिया = जालिकी, *q.v.*

जाली, 1, *f.* net-work; the integument in which a foetus is enveloped lattice-work, trellis-work, grating; a coil; a caul; an ox-muzzle: — *parnā* expresses the hardening of a mango-stone: 2, illusory, deceptive.

जालेना, *t.* to overtake, catch up to, outstrip.

जाल्म, *m.* (*f.* ī) a low person, one of a degraded tribe or business, etc.: *lit.* wicked, cruel, harsh, severe; contemptible; acting without thinking, inconsiderate, rash.

जाव, 1, *more prop.* जाओ, *q.v.*: 2, *m.* a going: 3, for words beginning thus, but not given below, see [under the form याव.

जावत्री, *f.* mace.

जावन्त, a corruption of जावत = यावत, *q.v.*

जावहु (*poet.*) = जाओ (जाना).

जावां, *m.* (*f.* °वीं) a twin, twins.

जावान = (1) जवान (2) जवां, *q.v.*

जावित्री, *f.* mace.

जावें, (from जाना) a form of the first and third persons pl. of the dependent mode.

जावैं in Braj = जावें, *q.v.*

जासन = जिससे. See सन, 1.

जासुस, a corruption of जासूस, *q.v.*

जासु = जिससे and जिसके.

जासुन्दो = जासून, *q.v.*

जासू = जासु, *q.v.* [*Syricus* or *Hibiscus Sinensis*).

जासून, the China-rose or shoe-flower (*Hibiscus*

जासूस, *m.* a spy, emissary.

जासूसी, *f.* espionage. — *k.* to act the spy.

जासें = जासों and जहांसे.

जासों in Braj = जिससे (जो).

जाह, *f.* dignity, rank, grandeur.

जाहर, *more prop.* ज़ाहिर, *q.v.*

जाहि, *m. f.* (pl. जाहिं) an old and poetic form = (1) जिसको (2) वह जाता है. See जा, 3. [devout.

ज़ाहिद, *m.* a monk, hermit, recluse: *adj.* religious,

ज़ाहिर, *m.* the external appearance: *adj.* apparent, manifest, plain, clear, obvious, evident.

ज़ाहिरी, outward, external, apparent, visible.

जाहिल, ignorant, illiterate, brutal, barbarous.

जाहिली, *f.* a state of ignorance; paganism.

जाही, 1, = जाहि, *q.v.*: 2, the flower *Jasminum grandiflorum*; a firework resembling that flower.

जाहीतें (poet.) = जिससे.

जाहीं
जाहु } = जाहि, *q.v.* [Braj sometimes = जिसको.

जाहु, 1, (see हु) an old imperat. pl. = जाओ; 2, in

ज़िंगी, a corruption of ज़िन्दगी, *q.v.*

जिंघ, *f.* Bengal madder (*Rubia manjith*).

ज़िंज़िफ़, *f.* fringe, border, edging.
ज़िंदगी, a corruption of ज़िन्दगी, *q.v.*
जिंस, *f.* genus, kind, species, sort, family, race; goods, moveables, merchandize, commodities, produce, grain.
जिक्र; see ज़ौक़.
ज़िक्र, *m.* remembrance, memory, commemoration, mention, recital, narration; praise, fame.
ज़िक्रकरना, *t.* to tell, relate, narrate, mention.
जिकिर, *more prop.* ज़िक्र, *q.v.*
जिगजिगाना, *a. int.* to shine, glitter.
जिगजिगिया, *adj.* fawning, wheedling.
जिगजिगी *f.* an exclamation expressive of surprize and pleasure. — *k.* to wheedle, fawn.
जिगटा, *m.* (*f.* ī) clammy.
जिगटाई, *f.* clamminess.
जिगर, *m.* the life, vitals, heart, mind.
जिगीषा, *f.* wish to overcome or to win or to attain, emulation.
जिजमान = यजमान, *q.v.*
जिज़या, *m.* a tribute, poll-tax (levied by Muhammadans on their subjects of another faith).
जिजिया, *f.* a sister; a dug, breast.
जिजी, *f.* a foster-mother; a wet-nurse; a maid that takes care of children, nursery-maid.
जिजीमां, *f.* a foster-mother.
जिज्जी = जिजी, *q.v.*
जिज्ञासा, *f.* asking, inquiring, examining.
जिज्ञासु, an inquirer: *lit.* desirous of knowing a thing, inquisitive, curious.
जिज्ञास्य, admitting of investigation, deserving investigation, needing or calling for investigation.
जिझोटिया, a low caste of Kanaujiya Brāhmaṇs.
जिठानी, *f.* the wife of a जेठ, *i. e.* of a husband's elder brother.
जित, (correl. of तित) wheresoever.
जितक्रोध, *m.* (*f.* ā) a person whose anger has been brought under control: *lit.* of subdued anger.
जितना, (correl. of तितना) *m.* (*f.* ī) however much, as much (as). *Jitnebhar—utnebhar*, as much as—by so much.
जितनेमें, in as much (time) as.
जितने, pl. (correl. of तितने) *m.* (*f.* ī) as many (as).
जितबर, means of living: housewifery.
जितव, *more prop.* जीतब, *q.v.*
जितवाना, *t.* (causat. of जिताना) to cause to be overcome.
जिता = जित्ता, *q.v.*
जितात्मा, *m.* one who has brought his passions under control: *lit.* self-subdued.
जिताना, *t.* (causat. of जीतना) to cause to win, cause to overcome.
जितेक, (correl. of तितेक) as much as, as many as.
जितेन्द्रिय, *m.* (*f.* ā) one who has completely subdued his senses, an ascetic, chaste person: *lit.* having the senses or passions subdued.
जितेन्द्रियता, *f.* subjugation of the senses or passions, continence, chastity, self-restraint.
जितेन्द्रिया, *f.* (see जितेन्द्रिय) a chaste woman.
जितेन्द्री = जितेन्द्रिय, *q.v.*
जित्ता, *m.* (*f.* ī) = जितना, *q.v.* — *ke*, for all that, notwithstanding.
जित्य, *m* (*f.* ā) capable of being overcome, needing to be overcome, conquerable, vincible.
जित्वर, *m.* (*f.* ī) a victor: *lit.* victorious, triumphant.
जित्वरी, *f.* (victorious) an epithet of the city of Benares.
जिदबर, means of subsistence; furnishing a house; stock in trade and plenishing or fixings.
जिदाल, *m.* altercation, contest.
जिद्द, *m.* trial, endeavour, effort, study.
जिधर, (correl. of तिधर) where, wherever, whither, whithersoever, there. — *tidhar*, withersoever; here, there, and every where, all about, in all directions. *Jidhar niwān udhar pānī ḍhaltā hai*, (*lit.* where there is a declivity, thither flows the water) = "misfortunes never come single": "Evil unites with evil."
जिन, 1, the base of the oblique cases of the plural of जो: 2, (a negative particle) = no, not: 3, a prohibitive particle (like *mat*) = don't: 4, *m. pr. n.* Buddh: 5, *m.* a Buddh, a generic term applied to the chief saints of the Bauddh sect in the same manner as to those of the Jains: 6. *m.* a *Jin*, the generic name of the personage peculiar to the Jain sect who is ranked by them as superior to the gods of the other sects; a saint and teacher: twenty-four Jins are supposed to flourish in an Avasarpini or Jain age, and their writers enumerate those of the ages past, present and future; hence, in the ingenious system of reckoning by symbols adopted by Hindoos in their poetry, this word is a symbol for 24.
जिनका, an old form = जिनका (जिन, 1).
जिनकरहु in Braj = (1) जिनका भी (2) मत करो.
जिनकौ in Braj = जिनका (जो).
जिनकों in Braj = जिनको (जो).
जिनगी, a contraction of ज़िन्दगी, *q.v.*
ज़िनदान, *m.* a prison, goal.
जिननि in Braj = 1, जिनने (जो); 2, but more generally it stands for जिन्हों, *q.v.*; *e.g.* जिननिकौं.
जिनस a very common form of जिंस, *q.v.*
ज़िना, *f.* adultery, fornication.
ज़िनाकार, *m.* an adulterer, whoremonger.
ज़िनाकारी, *f.* adultery, fornication, harlotry.
जिनि in old Hindee = जिन, 1, *q.v.*
जिनिस / जिनिस } very common forms of जिंस, *q.v.*
जिनु in Braj = जिन, 2, 3, *q.v.*
जिनू in old Hindee = जिन, 1, *q.v.*
जिनेत, *more com.* जनेत, *q.v.*
ज़िन्दः, *m. f.* alive, living. — *k.* to make alive, bring back to life.
ज़िन्दगानी, *f.* life, existence; livelihood.
ज़िन्दगी, *f.* life, existence, living.
ज़िन्दा = ज़िन्दः, *q.v.*
जिन्दान, *m.* a gaol, prison.
जिन्न, *m.* (*pl.* āt) a spirit, genius, genie, demon.
जिन्हे = जिनने = जिन्होंने.

जिन्स = जिंस, *q.v.*

जिन्सियत, *f.* kindred nature, similarity of kind, homogeneousness.

जिन्ह = जिन्हों, *q.v.*

जिन्हन in Braj, a form of जिन्हों, *q.v.*

जिन्हें (dat. or acc. pl. of जो) to whom, whom.

जिन्हैं } जिन्हैं } in Braj = जिन्हें, *q.v.*

जिन्हों; an inflective base of the oblique cases of the plural of जो. See उन्हों.

जिबरील = जब्रीयल, *q.v.*

जिबिल्लत, *f.* essence, quality, disposition, temperament, constitution, creation, form.

जिब्बा, *m.* a kind of long vest.

जिभारा, *m.* (*f.* ī) = जीभारा, *q.v.*

जिभ्या, *more prop.* जिह्वा, *q.v.*

जिम (old form; correl. of तिम) = जैसे, *q.v.*

ज़िमन, *m.* anything contained or comprehended, contents suretiship, an obligation, favor, aid.

जिमाना, *t.* to feed, entertain.

जिमि (old form; correl. of तिमि) = जैसे, *q.v.*

जिमीदारी, *more prop.* ज़मीनदारी, *q.v.*

ज़िम्मा, *m.* trust, custody, charge, obligation, duty, service, subjection, fidelity, lineage. — *lenā*, to take custody of, take upon oneself.

जिय, a corruption of जीव, *q.v.*

जियत, a poet. form of जीता (जीना).

जियरा, 1, *m.* life, soul: 2, *m.* (*f.* ī) beloved.

ज़िया, *f.* light, splendour, brilliancy.

ज़ियादः, *m.* augmentation, increase, addition, surplus: *adj.* great, excessive: *adv.* extra, all the more, more, over and above, above and beyond, too much. — *k.* to augment, increase, go beyond, exceed. — *honā*, to increase.

जियादत, *f.* } जियादा, *m.* } = ज़ियादः, *q.v.*

ज़ियान, *m.* loss, damage, deficiency.

जियाना = जिलाना, *q.v.*

ज़ियाफ़त, *f.* a convivial entertainment, banquet, feast; hospitality; invitation.

जियाये = जियाए (जियाना).

ज़ियारत, *f.* pilgrimage, visiting.

जियूड़ा, *m.* annual wages to washermen and others: life, soul; *met.* a beloved object, sweetheart.

जियो; see (1) जिय (2) जीना.

जियौठ in Braj = जीवट, *q.v.*

जिरना, *a. int.* to dry up, wither.

जिरह } जिरा } *f.* iron armour made with rings.

ज़िराअत, *f.* agriculture, husbandry, sown field, cultivation, tillage.

ज़िराब, *m.* a fighting, fencing, conquering: *coiens.*

जिरिया, a species of rice cultivated in Benares.

जिर्म, *m.* the body of anything inanimate: a globe: a flaw, crack.

जिर्यान, *m.* a flowing, running, flux.

जिला, *f.* splendour, lustre, brightness.

ज़िला, *f.* a zillah, district, division of a country.

जिला देना, *t.* to revive or bring to life (the dead).

जिलाना, *t.* (a causat. of जीना) to give life to, cause to live; to bring back to life, recover anything almost dead, vivify, resuscitate; to foster, patronize.

जिलायतन, *m.* emigration, banishment.

जिल्द, *f.* the skin, leather; the binding of a book; a book, volume. — *k.* to bind a book.

ज़िल्ल, *m.* gentleness, ease.

जिव, *more prop.* जीव, *q.v.*

जिवड़ा = जियूड़ा, *q.v.*

जिवनार = जेवनार, *q.v.*

जिवाना = (1) जिमाना (2) जिलाना, *qq.v.*

जिवार, *m.* neighbourhood, propinquity, vicinity, adjacency.

जिव्हा, *more prop.* जिह्वा, *q.v.*

जिश्न; see (1) जश्न (2) जिष्णु.

जिष्णु, victorious, gaining, winning, excelling: hence, an epithet (1) of the sun (2) of Indra (3) of Vishnu (4) of Arjun: *pr. n.* (1) of a Vasu (2) of son of Manu Bhautya (3) of the father of Brahmgupt.

जिस, the inflective base of the oblique cases of the singular of जो. The following are the most common of the idiomatic usages of this inflected form; *Jis-jis*, whichever, each of which. — *jagah* (sc. *meṅ* or *par*) where, wherever. — *tis*, that which, whatever, some or other. — *dam* (sc. *meṅ* or *par*) when, while, whilst. — *tarah* (sc. *par* or *se*) in what manner, according to, as. — *taraf* (sc. *meṅ* or *par*) whatever, — *kadr* (sc. *par* or *se*) to what degree, as, as much as, whatever, whatsoever. *Jis-kisikā, jiskisiko*; see *Jo koi*. *Jiskā khāe uske darānmeṅ denā*, explained by *Namakharāmī k.* to evince ingratitude. — *karke*, by means of which.

जिसतर; see (1) जिसके नीचे (2) जिस तरफ़ (3) जिस तरह.

जिसे = जिसको.

जिसै in Braj = जिसको.

जिसो, an old form = जैसो = जैसा, *q.v.*

जिस्तें = जिस्से. See तें, 3.

जिस्म, *m.* the body of any animated being.

जिहत, *f.* account, cause, reason: side; surface; form, manner, mode.

ज़िह्न, *m.* understanding, memory, genius, ability.

जिहचम, *more prop.* जहचम, *q.v.*

जिहाँ in Chand = जहाँ, *q.v.*

जिहाद, *m.* war (especially that which is waged by Muhammadans against idolaters and disbelievers in Muhammad).

जिहालत, *more prop.* जहालत, *q.v.*

जिहि, 1, in Braj = जिसको (जो): 2, in old Hindee = जो and जिस, *qq.v.*

जिहिं in Braj = जिनको (जो).

जिहिकर (*poet.*) = जिसका.

जिह्वा, *f.* the tongue.

जिह्वामल, *m.* the fur of the tongue.

जिह्वास्वाद, *m.* a licking, lapping.

जी, 1, a term of endearment or of respect = Sir, lord, master, madam : 2, a term of assent or accord = yes : 3, *m.* life, soul, spirit, mind, self. — *uṭhnā*, to come back to life again, rise from the dead. — *uṭhānā*, to withdraw one's friendship or desire. — *ājānā*, to have the mind suddenly fixed (on anything). — *burā k.* to vomit, have a nausea ; *met.* to be displeased. — *baṛhānā*, to be moderately desirous. — *bikharnā*, to faint. — *bhar jānā*, to be at ease and contented. — *ṭūṭnā*, to expire. — *bahlānā*, to dissipate reflection, amuse oneself.— *pānā*, to understand one's temper : to escape from misfortune : to be highly pleased.—*pānī k.* to harass, tease, plague, perplex. — *par kisīke chalnā*, to obey anyone. — *par khelnā*, to risk one's life, run the hazard of one's life. — *pasījnā* or *pighalnā* or *pighal jānā*, to feel affection towards, be compassionate. — *pakṛā jānā*, to be sorry. — *phaṭ jānā*, to be broken-hearted. — *phir jānā*, to be contented, be satiated, be disgusted. — *jalānā*, to befriend : to perplex, plague. — *jalnā*, to be vexed, be troubled in mind. — *chāhnā*, to desire.—*churānā* or *chhipānā*, to neglect, do a work carelessly or lazily. — *chalānā*, to act bravely. — *chalnā*, to desire. — *dān k.* to grant one his life, pardon a capital crime. — *dhaṛaknā*, to have palpitation of the heart. — *ḍūb jānā*, to faint. — *rakhnā*, to be easily pleased ; to please.—*se utar jānā*, to sink in the opinion of another ; to be broken-hearted. — *se mārnā*, to kill. — *k.* or *honā*, to desire, wish for. — *kholke kuchh k.* to do a thing with pleasure, do it cheerfully. — *kī amān māngnā*, to preface a discourse with excuse. — *ke badal jī denā*, to take up the cause of another. — *ghaṭ jānā*, to detest. — *lagnā*, to hanker after, contract an affection for any person or thing. — *lagānā*, to fix or apply the mind ; to excite desire or love. — *lenā*, to penetrate one's thoughts ; to excite one's desire ; to kill. — *mārnā*, to mortify one's desire, practice selfdenial; to displease. — *matlānā*, to be sick at stomach, feel nausea. — *milānā*, to contract friendship. — *meṅ ānā*, to come into the mind, occur to the recollection.— *meṅ jal-jānā*, to be tormented with envy or jealousy. — *meṅ jī ānā*, to be comforted. — *meṅ ghar k.* to be pleasant, agreeable or acceptable to. — *nikalnā*, to die; to desire or love excessively to fear exceedingly. — *hārnā*, to be discouraged, be depressed from fear, be spiritless. — *haṭ jānā*, to detest.

जीउ, *m.* a beloved one, sweetheart. [form ज़िन्द.

जींद ; for words beginning thus, see under the

जींगुराना, *a. int.* to corrugate, wrinkle.

जींजीर, *more prop.* **ज़ंजीर**, *q.v.*

ज़ीक, *m.* anguish, vexation, melancholy, anxiety, doubt, affliction, oppression of spirit.

जीका, a contraction of **जीविका**, *q.v.* [the turban.

जीग़ा, *m.* an ornament of gold and jewels worn in

ज़ीज, *m.* astronomical tables ; a mason's rule.

जीत, *f.* winning, victory, success. — *lenā*, to get the victory, win. [win, conquer, overcome, beat.

जीतना, 1, a corruption of **जितना**, *q.v.*: 2, *t.* to

जीतपत्र, *m.* a favorable decree.

जीतब, *m.* life, existence.

जीतवन्त, *m.* (*f.* vatī) a winner, victor : *lit.* adj. conquering, overcoming, winning. [ner, conqueror.

जीतवैया, *m.* (noun of agency from **जीतना**) a win-

जीता, 1, *m.* mutual assistance in tillage, the allowing the use of a plough and bullocks in lieu of wages in money or in kind : 2, *m.* (*f.* ī) alive: 3, over, more, above. — *honā*, to be over.

जीतापत्र = **जीतपत्र**, *q.v.*

जीतालू, *m.* arrow-root.

जीतिया, *f.* a certain fast observed by Hindoo women who have lost children, with the view of preserving the remainder. In this fast, they sacrifice to Devī and worship her.

जीतू, *m.* a winner, conqueror.

जीतेजी, *m.* the being alive, a living, lifetime.

जीतेरा = **जीता**, 1, *q.v.*

जीद, a long, slender, and beautiful neck.

जीधर, *more prop.* **जिधर**, *q.v.*

जीन, *more prop.* **जीर्ण**, *q.v.*

ज़ीन, *m.* a saddle.— *bāndhnā*, to saddle. [ration.

ज़ीनत, *f.* ornament, beauty, elegant dress, deco-

ज़ीनपोश, *m.* a cloth fastened over a saddle, housing.

ज़ीन्द ; for words beginning thus, see under the form **ज़िन्द**. [patronage.

ज़ीनहार, *m.* care, caution, protection, defence,

जीना, *a. int.* to live, be alive.

ज़ीना, *m.* a ladder, stairs, steps.

जीफ, *more prop* **ज़ीफ़**, *q. v.*

जीब = **जीभ**, *q. v.*

जीबक = **जीवक**, *q. v.*

जीबछिलनी, *f.* a tongue-scraper.

जीबिका = **जीविका**, *q.v.*

जीबी, appertaining to the tongue, lingual.

जीभ, *f.* (a colloquial form of **जिह्वा**) the tongue. — *ulaṭnā*, to express clearly. — *baṛhānā*, to be loquacious and abusive : to pursue pleasures beyond one's reach. — *pakaṛnā*, to silence ; to interrupt one's discourse ; to criticize minutely. — *jhukānā*, to pretend to wealth falsely. — *chāṭnā*, to long after or covet unattainable enjoyment. — *chalānā*, to boast beyond one's ability. — *dābke bāt kahnā*, to speak with reserve. — *kāṭnā*, to forbid by signs : to grant the request of a petitioner : to be struck with terror or amazement. — *nikālnā*, (to put out the tongue ; *hence*) to be extremely fatigued or thirsty.

जीभारा, *m.* (*f.* ī) a loquacious person, etc. : *lit.* plain-spoken, loquacious, long-tongued, abusive, foul-tongued.

जीभी, *f.* an instrument for cleaning the tongue ; [a bit (of a bridle).

जीभीमछली, *f.* a sole-fish.

जीमना, *a. int.* to eat, feed oneself.

जीमार, *m.* (*f.* ī) one who mortifies his desires : *lit.* capital (as a crime) ; mortifying one's desires.

जीर / **जीरक** } *m.* cumin-seed (*Cuminum cyminum*).

जीरन, *more prop* **जीर्ण**, *q.v.*

जीरा, *f.* = **जीर**, *q. v.* [withered, decayed ; digested.

जीर्ण, *m.* (*f.* ā) an old man, etc. : *lit.* old, ancient,

जीर्णता, *f.* (*m.* °त्व) old age, frailty, decay.

जीर्णवस्त्र, *m.* old, worn, or tattered clothing.

जीर्णबध्नक, *m.* a fragrant grass (*Cyperus rotundus*).

जीर्णा, *f.* (see **जीर्ण**) an old woman.

जीर्णि, *f.* old age, infirmity, decay ; digestion.

जील, *f.* a high note or tone in music, the treble.

जीव, 1, = जीओ (imperat. of जीना) : 2, *m.* life, existence, animal being, creature, animal, the sentient individual soul, or emanation of the Deity, which, it is believed, is incorporated in the animal body, giving it life, motion and sensation, and hence called 'Jeevātmau' : it is opposed to that abstract state of the soul ('Paramātman') in which by meditation on its own divine origin and nature, the spirit is supposed eventually to be set at liberty from human feelings and passions : 3, *m.* (*f.* ā) a sweetheart, beloved one : *lit.* living ; causing life : 4, bravo !

जीवंजीव, *m.* a kind of bird, supposed to be a pheasant ; the *chakor* or Greek partridge.

जीवंजीविक = जीवंजीव, *q.v.*

जीवक, *m.* (*f.* ikā) any being endowed with life, any animal : a certain tree (*Pentaptera tomentosa*) ; a medicinal plant considered as one of the eight principal drugs classed together under the name *Ashtvarg*.

जीवका, *more prop.* जीविका, *q.v.*

जीवकोठी, *f.* a house or hospital for vermin, etc. [such as may be seen at Surat.

जीवगर = जीवट, *q.v.*

जीवजीव, *more prop.* जीवंजीव, *q.v.*

जीवट, lively, spirited, courageous, brave, bold, [resolute.

जीवड़ा = जियूड़ा, *q.v.*

जीवत = (1) जीवट (2) जीवन, *qq.v.*

जीवततोका = जीवत्तोका, *q.v.*

जीवतपति = जीवत्पति, *q.v.*

जीवता, *m.* (*f.* ī) alive. —— *rakhnā*, to live on, con-[tinue to live.

जीवतिया = जीतिया, *q.v.*

जीवत्तोका, *f.* a woman whose children are alive.

जिवत्पति, *f.* a woman whose husband is alive.

जीवद, *m.* (*f.* ā) *adj.* life-imparting.

जीवदया, *f.* kindness for animal life.

जीवदान, *m.* a giving life, a rescuing from sickness : a certain manual of medicine composed by Chyavan.

जीवधन, *m.* living property, wealth in flocks and [herds, live stock.

जीवधर्म, *m.* the appropriate functions of animal life.

जीवधारी, *m.* (*f.* iṇī) assuming or possessing life.

जीवन, *m.* life, existence : subsistence ; means of subsistence, livelihood, living, profession ; water ; a son.

जीवनदाई, *m.* (*f.* inī) = जीवनदायक, *q.v.*

जीवनदायक, *m.* (*f.* ikā) a giver of life (an epithet of God) : *lit.* adj. life-giving.

जिवनबिर्त, a stipend allowed to the family of an [old deceased servant.

जीवनमुक्त, *m.* (*f.* ā) *adj.* having in this life obtained deliverance from transmigration.

जीवनमुक्ति, *f.* (in the Vedānta system) a secondary sort of liberation of the soul which conducts it after death to live with Brahm, not, however, divested of a subtle corporeal frame.

जीवनवत, *m.* (*f.* vatī) possessed of, or appertain-[ing to, life.

जीवनवती, *f.* a pregnant female.

जीवनवन्त } **जीवनवान** } *m.* (*f.* vatī) = जीवनवत, *q.v.*

जीवना, *a. int.* to live, be alive.

जीवनी, *f.* jasmine.

जीवनोपाय, *m.* means of subsistence.

जीवनौषध, *m.* a drug to revive the dead.

जीवन्त, *m.* (*f.* vatī) a living creature : *lit.* alive.

जीवन्तिक, *m.* a fowler, bird-catcher.

जीवन्तिका, *f.* a certain parasite plant (*Epidendron tapeloides*, etc.) ; a plant (*Menispermum Glabrum*).

जीवन्ती, *f.* the name of several plants and trees, (1) *Celtis orientalis* ; (2) *Menispermum glabrum* ; (3) the Sam or Sāen tree (*Mimosa albida*); (4) yellow myrobalan (*Terminalia chebula*).

जीवपुत्रक, *m.* a certain plant bearing seeds which [are used in rosaries.

जीवमन्दिर, *m.* the body ; *lit.* the temple of life.

जीवमार = जीमार, *q.v.*

जीवसू, *f.* a mother of living children.

जीवस्थान, *m.* an articulation, joint.

जीवहिंसा, *f.* the injury or the destruction of life.

जिवातु, *m.* a drug for reänimating the dead ; life, existence.

जीवात्मा, *m.* (see जीव) the individual soul, the vital principle or spirit, that spiritual essence which renders bodies susceptible of motion or sensation.

जीवाधार, *m.* the earth ; *lit.* the receptacle of life.

जीवान्तक, *m.* (*f.* ā) a fowler, bird-catcher.

जीविका, *f.* life ; means of subsistence, occupation or profession by which a subsistence is obtained, livelihood, pension, allowance, pittance.

जीवित, 1, *m.* life, existence ; 2, *m.* (*f.* ā) alive, existent, living.

जीवितकाल, *m.* a lifetime, period of life.

जीवितेश, *m.* (*f.* ā) one who rules the life of another : *hence*, a lord or master of one's existence, a lover, husband ; a drug to revive the dead ; *pr. n.* Yam (the regent of death): *lit.* adj. ruling life (applicable to objects either of reverence or affection).

जीवी, *m.* (*f.* inī) a living being : *lit.* alive, ani-[mate, living.

जीस ; see (1) जिस (2) जैसा.

जीस्त, *f.* life, existence, living.

जीह, *more prop.* (1) जिह्वा (2) जीव, *qq.v.*

जीहारना, *n.* to be discouraged, be depressed from [fear, be spiritless.

जीहुन, *f. pr. n.* a certain river.

जु in Braj = जो, 2, *q.v.*

जुआ ; for words beginning thus, but not given below, see under the more proper form जूआ.

जुआर = जुवार and जोआर, *qq.v.*

जुआरि, *more prop.* जूआरी, *q.v.*

जुआरी = जुवारी and जूआरी, *qq.v.*

जुंग, 1, *m.* (*f.* ?) a potherb (*Convolvulus argentius*) : 2, *f.* emotion, impulse : a volume containing several books.

जुंगित, *m.* (*f.* ā) outcast, deserted, abandoned, [injured.

जुकति = युक्ति, *q.v.*

जुकाम, *m.* rheum, defluxion ; a cold.

जुकूरा, *m.* the male sex.

जुक्ति = युक्ति, *q.v.* [low, see under the form जुग.

जुग; for words beginning thus, but not given be-

जुगत, *f.* manner, mode, skill, cleverness, dexterity, address, contrivance, counsel, wit, art, pun, double meaning. — *bolnā*, to pun.

जुगतबाज़, *m.* a punster, one who is fond of uttering language with double meaning.

जुगतबाज़ी, *f.* quibble, pun, witticism; economy.

जुगती, *m.* (*f.* inī) a punster, etc. : *lit.* artful, cunning, clever, facetious, humorous, funny, punning.

जुगना = जुगनू, *q.v.*

जुगनी, *f.* a firefly, glowworm : an ornament worn around the neck : a small grain from which oil is ex-

जुगनू, *m.* the firefly (*Lampyris*). [tracted.

जुगनूं, a jewel worn about the neck.

जुगम, *more prop.* युग्म, *q.v.*

जुगाना, *t.* to be careful of, keep with care : to lend labour, *i. e.* to assist another in his work in expectation of similar assistance being returned hereafter.

जुगाल, *more prop.* युगल, *q v.*

जुगालना, *t.* to chew the cud.

जुगाली, *f.* the cud. — *k.* to chew the cud.

जुगिनिपुर, *m. pr. n.* a certain ancient Hindoo city.

जुगुत in Braj = युक्ति, *q.v.*

जुगुनू = जुगनू, *q.v.*

जुगुप्सन, *m.*
जुगुप्सा, *f.* } censure, reproach, abuse, aversion.

जुगुप्सित, *m.* (*f.* ā) censured, reproached, abused.

जुज़, *m.* a part, portion; an ingredient.

जुजमान = यजमान, *q.v.* [whole.

जुज़ोकुल, totally, entirely, great and small, the

जुझ, *m.* an engagement, battle.

जुझनौं in Chand = to make war, fight.

जुझाऊ बाजना, *a. int.* to sound or strike up (as warlike instruments in battle).

जुझार
जुझारा } *m.* a fighter, warrior.

जुटक, *m. f.*? the matted hair of Shiv or of ascetics; any knot or fillet of hair.

जुटना, *t.* to close with, engage in close fight : *a. int.* to unite, close, join (as the edges of a wound);

जुटाना, *t.* to conglutinate. [to stay, wait.

जुट्टा, *m.* a span; the space from the tip of the thumb to the tip of the forefinger when stretched.

जुड़ना, *n.* to be joined, to unite.

जुड़वाई, *f.* the state of being joined, adhesion.

जुड़वां, see (1) जोड़वान (2) जोड़ुआं.

जुड़वाट = जुड़वाई, *q.v.*

जुड़ला, *m.* twins.

जुड़हि, *m. f.* (pl. °हिं) = जुड़ता है (जुड़ना).

जुड़ाई, *f.* the price of joining or of mending.

जुड़ाट, *f.* joining, annexation.

जुड़ाना, *t.* to cause to couple, cause to join, to get (a thing) mended : to tear the hair in token of

जुढ़ा = जुड़ला, *q.v.* [grief and vexation.

जुत, *more prop.* (1) ज्योति (2) युत, *qq.v.*

जुतवाना, *t.* to cause to be joined, cause to be yoked.

जुता, *m.* the rope which connects the irrigating basket with its handle.

जुताई, *f.* tillage : *adj.* arable.

जुताना, *t.* to conglutinate; to yoke : *n.* to be joined; to be tilled [ed an act of great degradation).

जुतियाना, *t.* to beat with a shoe or slipper (deem-

जुदा, separate, away, absent, different. *Judā judā*, various; one by one, severally. *Judā judā kahnā*, to particularize.

जुदाई, *f.* separation, absence, difference.

जुद्ध, जुध; for words beginning thus, see under the

जुन, *m.* time. [forms युद्ध, युध, respectively.

जुना, *t.* to yoke together.

जुनून, *m.* madness, insanity, frenzy : a demoniac.

जुन्द, a certain medicinal substance found in the

जुन्हरी, *f.* a kind of grain. [castor beaver.

जुन्हाई, *f.* the moonlight.

जुन्हार, *m.* a kind of grain (comprising many species of which Indian corn is one).

जुन्हैया, *f.* the moonlight.

जुफ़्त, *m.* evenness, parity; a pair, couple, match.

जुब°; for words beginning thus, but not given below, see under the form युव°.

जुबदा, *m.* cream, butter (the best of anything).

जुब्बा; see (1) जभा (2) युवा.

जुबान, *more prop.* (1) ज़बान (2) जवान, *qq.v.*

जुबानी; see (1) ज़बानी (2) जवानी (3) यवानी.

जुबानू = जवानपुरुष.

जुमा, *m.* Friday (on which day Muhammadans assemble to pray at the great mosque).

जुमारात, *f.* Thursday.

जुमाहिर, *more prop.* जवाहिर, *q.v.*

जुमुर्रद, *m.* an emerald.

जुमेरात, *f.* Thursday.

जुम्बिश, *f.* agitation, motion, gesture.

जुम्मा; see (1) जमा (2) जिम्मा (3) जुमा.

जुयारी, *m.* (*f.* iṇī) *more prop.* जुआरि, *q.v.*

जुरना, *n.* to be procured, be obtained, come to hand; to be joined, to unite.

जुरनो
जुरनौं } in Braj = जुरना, *q.v.*

जुरवाना = जुराना, *q.v.*

जुरा, *m.* one draught; a drop. [boldness, temerity.

जुरात, *f.* courage, bravery, valour, audacity,

जुरा देना, *t.* (intensive) to procure.

जुराना, *n.* to be comforted, be pacified : to procure :

जुराव, *m.* procurement. [to cause to unite.

जुरावन, procurable.

जुरुवा, *f.* a woman, female.
जुरेला, *m.* a species of rice grown in Rohilkhaṇḍ.
जुर्म, *m.* a crime, fault, sin.
जुल, *m.* deceit, cheating, a trick.
जुलना, *a. int.* to meet, be united.
जुलबाज़, *m.* a knave, cheat.
जुलबाज़ी, *f.* knavery.
जुलम, *more com.* ज़ुल्म, *q.v.*
जुलाहनी, *f.* a weaver's wife, female weaver.
जुलाई, *m.* (*f.* inī) a weaver.
जुलाईवाड़ी, *f.* a ward inhabited by weavers.
जुलाब, *more prop.* जुल्लाब, *q.v.* [head, fool.
जुलाह, *m.* a Muhammadan weaver : *met.* a block-
जुलाहा = जुलाह, *q.v.*
जुलुफ, *more prop.* ज़ुल्फ़, *q.v.*
ज़ुल्फ़, *m.* a curling lock, ringlet, whisker.
जुलूस, *m.* accession (to a throne); the reign or era of a monarch.
ज़ुल्म, *m.* oppression, tyranny, injustice, extortion; a heavier assessment than people can bear.
ज़ुल्मत, *f.* darkness, obscurity.
ज़ुल्मात, *f.* darkness, regions of darkness; a dark place where the water of immortality is said to be.
जुल्ल, *f.* a housing or covering for an elephant, bullock, etc.
जुल्ला, *m.* anything shady, a covering, a cloud.
जुल्लाब, *m.* a purge, purgative.
जुव; for words beginning thus, but not given
जुवान; see जवान. [below, see under the form युव.
जुवार, 1, = जोआर, *q.v.* : 2, *m.* large maize.
जुवारा = (1) जुवार (2) जुवारी, *qq.v.*
जुवारी, 1, *m.* a thread stretched over the bridge of a musical instrument, beneath the cords, whereby the sound is said to be improved : 2, *m.* (*f.* in *or* iṇī) a gambler.
जुवाहिर, *more prop.* जवाहिर, *q.v.* [porridge, etc.
जुष्कक, *m.* the water of boiled pulse, pease soup,
जुष्ट, *m.* the crumbs, remnants, or leavings of a meal. [tified by service.
जुष्टा, *m.* (*f.* ī) served, obliged, worshipped, gra-
जुस; 1, see (1) यश (2) युष; 2, a pair (?).
जुस्त, seeking, searching, search, enquiry.
जुस्त, strong, sharp, pungent, harsh, violent, passionate; clear.
जुहद, *m.* continence, abstinence, devotion.
जुहर, *m.* midday, or a little time after the sun has passed the meridian, when it is most sultry.
जुहल, *m. pr. n.* the planet Saturn.
जुहला, pl. of जाहिल, *q.v.*
जुहा, *m.* breakfast-time, the brightest part of the day, *viz.* that about half-way between sunrise and meridian.
जुहार, *f.* Hindoo salutation, obeisance.

जुहारना, to speak with reverence, to do obeisance,
जुहूर, *m.* appearing, rising, apparency. [salute.
जुहूल; see (1) जुहूर (2) जहूल (3) ज़हूल.
जू, 1, (in Braj) Sir, lord, master : 2, *f.* a river, brook, rivulet, stream : 3, this is sometimes the base of the oblique cases of the singular of जो in Braj; *e.g.*
जूआर; see (1) जवार (2) ज़ोर. [जूके = जिसके.
जूआ, *m.* (gen. जूएका) a yoke, yoke of a carriage or plough : a die, dice; a game, gambling. — *khelnā*, to play at dice; to gamble.
जूआचोर, *m.* a cheat, sharper.
जूआचोरी, *f.* cheating at gambling.
जूआठ, *m.* a yoke.
जूआरी, *m.* (*f.* iṇī) a gambler. See जुवारी.
जूई, *f.* an insect destructive to certain crops.
जूएख़ाना, *m.* a gambling-room, gambling-house.
जूएबाज़, *m.* a gambler.
जूएबाज़ी, *f.* gambling.
जूं, *f.* a louse.
जूंमुंहा, *m.* (*f.* ī) smooth-faced, hypocritical.
जूका, 1, = यूका, *q.v.*: 2, *m.* (*f.* ī) in Braj = जिसका.
जूको in Braj = जिसको. See जू, 3.
जूगत; for words beginning thus, see under the more proper form जुगत. [*marnā*, to die fighting.
जूझना, *a. int.* to fight, be killed in battle. *Jūjh*
जूझा, *m.* battle, combat, fighting.
जूट, *m.* the matted hair of Shiv; the clotted hair of an ascetic. [men near the Sewalik hills.
जूटियाल, a certain class of hereditary watch-
जूठ; for words beginning thus, see under the more proper form झूठ.
जूड़, *m.* the cold, coldness : *adj.* cold.
जूड़ा, *m.* the cold : the hair done up in a knot behind; the hinder part of a turban.
जूड़ी, *f.* ague : a small bundle of sugarcane.
जूड़ीमारी, *f.* land in actual possession.
जूगठी; see झूगठी.
जूतखोरा, one who has been beaten with a slipper; *hence*, degraded, infamous, abject, mean.
जूतन, *m.* (a Braj pl. of जूता) shoes, slippers.
जूतनखोरा = जूतखोरा, *q.v.*
जूता, 1, = जुता, *q.v.*: 2, *m.* a shoe, slipper.
जूतियां, 1, *f.* (pl. of जूती) shoes, slippers : 2, land bearing two crops in the course of one year.
जूतियाल = जूटियाल, *q.v.*
जूती, *f.* a slipper, shoe.
जूतीकारी, *f.* the act of beating with a slipper.
जूतीखोर = जूतखोरा, *q.v.*
जूतीपैज़ार, *f.* a scuffle.
जूतीमार = जूतीकारी, *q.v.* [form यूथ.
जूथ; for words beginning thus, see under the

जूथवार, corporate, joint, possessed in common.
जूथाली }
जूथेली } *f.* land which bears two harvests a year.
जूद, *m.* a present; munificence, beneficence.
जून, *m.* time: *adj.* old. [*Andropogon sorghum*).
जूनरी, *f.* a species of grain (*Holcus sorgum* or
जूना, *m.* a rope of grass; a ring of twisted grass put under a round-bottomed jar to prevent its upsetting.
जूप, *more prop.* यूप, *q.v.* [the god).
जूपिटर, (Lat.) *m. pr. n.* Jupiter (the planet and
जूय, *f.* a rivulet, brook.
जूया, *more prop.* (1) जूआ (2) युवा, *qq.v.*
जूरत, the forepart of a bird's crop where the
जूरना, see जोड़ना. [water lodges.
जूरी (poet.) = (1) समूह (2) जोड़ करके.
जूल, *m.* fraud, guile, deceit.
जूलम, *more prop.* ज़ुल्म, *q.v.*
जूला, a land-measure of sixteen *bīsīs*.
जूवा, *more prop.* (1) जूआ (2) युवा, *qq.v.*
जूष }
जूस } *more prop.* यूष, *q.v.*
जूह, 1, = यूथ, *q.v.*; 2, *m.* a yoke.
जूहड़, *m.* pits filled with water at the bottom of mountains; a lake or large pond.
जूहा (poet.) = यूथ, *q.v.*
जूही, *f.* jasmine (*Jasminum auriculatum*); a kind of fireworks. [opening (as of a flower).
जृम्भ, *m.* (*f.* ā) kind of animal: a gaping, yawning,
जृम्भक, *m. pr. n.* (1) of certain demons (2) of a spell that produces drowsiness.
जृम्भा, *f.* (see जृम्भ) a yawning, etc.
जृम्भिका, *f.* a yawning, gaping.
जृम्भिनी, *f.* a kind of mimosa (*Mimosa octandra*).
जे, 1, in Braj, pl. of जो: 2, often found (but especially in Braj) in the place of the proper termination of the Honorific form of the Imperative mode; *e. g.* कीजे, *more prop.* कीजिये.
जेइ, old form = जो and जिसको.
जेईं (poet.) = भोजन किया (जेवना).
जेउ }
जेऊ } emphatic forms = जे, 1, *q.v.* [servants.
जेओड़ा, *m.* a cord, string: perquisites of village
जेओड़ी, *f.* a cord, string; a worm.
जेओनार = जेवनार, *q.v.*
जेंवना, *more com.* जेवना, *q.v.* [*q.v.*
जेंवनारा, 1, = जेवनार, *q.v.*: 2, *m.* (*f.* in *or* ī) जेवनहरी,
जेट, *f.* a heap, accumulation.
जेठ = ज्येष्ठ, *q.v.* [brother.
जेठरा, *m.* (*f.* ī) first-born, eldest: a husband's elder
जेठराईयत, *m.* the head villager who conducts the ordinary business of a village.

जेठा, 1, = ज्येष्ठा, *q.v.*: 2, *m.* the first and strongest tint obtained from *kusum* (*Carthamus tinctorius*).
जेठानी, *f.* the wife of a husband's elder brother.
जेठी; see (1) जेठानी (2) ज्येष्ठा.
जेठीमधू, *m.* liquorice (*Glycirrhiza glabra*).
जेठुघडा, the right or share of an eldest son.
जेठौत, *m.* the son of a husband's elder brother.
जेत = जयत, *q.v.*
जेतना, *m.* (*f.* ī) *more com.* जितना, *q.v.*
जेता, (correl of तेता) *m.* (*f.* ī) = जितना. *Jetā ki*, though, although.
जेतिक (correl. of तेतिक) = जितेक, *q.v.*
जेतु in Braj = जेता, *q.v.*
जेते, (correl. of तेते) old form = जितने.
जेतो in Braj = जितना, *q.v.*
जेने, whithersoever.
जेब, *f.* a pocket.
जेबकत्र }
जेबकतू्र } *m.* a cutpurse, pickpocket.
जेबी, appertaining to the pocket.
जेम्हर, whithersoever.
जेया, conquerable, *i. e.* needing, liable, or fit to be conquered. [veloped. after-birth, secundines.
जेर, *m.* the membrane in which the foetus is de-
ज़ेरबन्द, *m.* a martingal, belly-band.
जेरी, in poet. = जो or जिसे (+ री for the metre).
जेल, *m.* a line or string of captives chained together; a string of buckets passed over the Persian wheel.
जेलख़ाना, *m.* a jail, prison.
जेली, *f.* a kind of pitchfork or rake for collecting and adjusting the ears of corn on a threshing-ground.
जेवड़ा }
जेवड़ी } = जेओड़ा, *q.v.*
जेवन; see (1) जीवन (2) जेवना (3) ज्यों.
जेवनहरी, *m.* (*f.* iṇī) a guest.
जेवना, *t.* to eat.
जेवनार, *f.* a treat, feast, entertainment, banquet.
ज़ेवर, *m.* (pl. āt) a jewel, ornament (of gold, silver,
जेवरी, *f.* a string, cord; a measure of land. [etc.).
जेवाना, *t.* to cause to eat.
जेवार, a certain clan of Rājputs.
जेष्ट, जेष्ठ; for words beginning thus, see under
जेह, a string. [the form ज्येष्ठ.
जेहखानि; an old form = जिस तरह.
जेहड़, *f.* a pile of pots filled with water and placed one upon the other in order to be carried on the head; a certain ceremony preparatory to marriage in which pots filled with water are piled one on the other,—the whole being crowned with a bowl of sherbet, and watched by during the night by friends.
जेहर, *m. f.* ? a kind of ornament for females.
जेहि in Braj = जिसे.

जोहिये in Braj = जिसको.
जोहते in Braj = जिस्से.
जे, 1, *more prop.* जय, *q.v.*: 2, often found (but especially in Braj) in the place of the proper form of the Honorific Imperative; *e. g.* दंजे, *more prop.* दीजिये: 3, an old form = जितना, *q. v.*: 4, in Braj = जो
जैसा, *m.* (*f.* ī) *more prop.* जैसा, *q.v.* [and जो, *qq. v.*
जैची = जैती, *q v.*
जैजैकार, *more prop.* जयजयकार, *q.v.*
जैजैवन्ती, *more prop.* जयजयवन्ती, *q.v.*
जैढक, *m.* a kind of drum.
जैत = जयत, *q.v.*
जैती, *f.* a sort of weed which grows up with the spring crops and yields a kind of oil.
ज़ैतून, *m.* an olive-tree. [triumphant, successful.
जैत्र, *m.* (*f.* ī) a conqueror, victor: lit. victorious,
जैत्ररथ, *adj.* possessing a triumphal car: hence (1) *m.* a triumphal car (2) *m.* (*f.* ā) a conqueror, hero.
जैत्रा = जैत्र, *q.v.*
जैत्री, *f.* (see जैत्र) a heroine.
ज़ैद, *m.* increasing, augmenting, adding, overflowing: a fictitious name employed like John Nokes and Thomas Stiles in English.
जैन, *m.* the designation applied to any follower of the principles of a *Jin*, or teacher of heterodox notions. The Jains are worshippers of a number of *Jins*, whom they regard as divine teachers and incarnations of God: they hold these spiritual pontiffs to be superior to the gods of the Hindoos; they also deny the divine authority of the Veds, and disregard the distinctions of caste. [*m.* (*f* iṇī) a *Jain*.
जैनधर्मी, appertaining to the *Jain* religion: hence,
जैनी, appertaining to the *Jain* sect.
ज़ैनुलमलूक, *m. pr. n.* a certain Persian king: *lit.* the [honourer of kings.
जैपाल = जयपाल, *q.v.*
ज़ैफ़, *m.* a guest, stranger: *adj.* convivial, hospitable. [a garment.
जैब, *f.* the breast, heart; the breast or collar of
जैबेर, an old form (= जितने बेर) as many times as,
जैमान, *more prop.* जयमान, *q.v.* [as often as.
जैमाल, *m.* = जयमाला, *q.v.*
जैमिनि, *m. pr. n.* a celebrated saint and philosopher, founder of the *Pūrv-Mīmāṅsā* school.
जैये, an old form = जाइये (जाना).
ज़ैयादा, a corruption of ज़ियादा, *q.v.*
ज़ैल, *m.* the skirt of a garment, train of a robe; the last, hinder, or supplemental part of anything, sequel.
जैवार, the head inhabitants of a village.
जैवो, a Braj form for जाना, *q.v.*
जैश, *m.* an army, troops: enjoyment, pleasure.
जैसन, a dialectic form = जैसा, *q.v.*
जैसवार, a name of certain low-caste tribes.
जैसवारा = जैसवार, *q. v.*
जैसही (*contraction*) = जैसेही, *q.v.*
जैसा, *m* (*f.* ī) what-like, as, such as: *adv.* as, according as, in the manner which. — *chāhiye*, as it ought, as occasion may require, sufficiently. — *taisā*, as well as, so-so. — *ki*, as though, as if. [which, just as.
जैसाही, (emphat.) in exactly the same manner in
जैसीही, the fem. form of जैसाही, *q.v.*
जैसे, in the same manner in which, just as, like.
जैसें *more com.* जैसे, *q. v.*
जैसेकातैसा, *m.* (*f.* जैसेकीतैसी) = ज्योंकात्यों, *q. v.*
जैसेही, the inflected form of the masc. of जैसाही, *q.v.*
जैसो / जैसौ } in Braj = जैसा, *q.v.*
जैहसि, an old form = तू जाएगा.
जैहै, (pl. जैहैं) a Braj and poet. form of जाएगा.
जैहों, *more prop.* जैहौं, *q. v.*
जैहो, a Braj and poet. form of जाओगे.
जैहौं, a Braj and poet. form of जाऊंगा.
जो, 1, (gen. जिसका [के, की], in Braj जाको or जाकौ [के, की]) who, what, which, that. *Jo koī*, (gen. *jis kisikā*) whoever (the verb may be either sing. or pl.). *Jo kuchh* (gen. *jis kisīkā*) whatever, whatsoever. *Jo chīz*, whatever, what thing soever. *Jo jo*, whoever, whosoever. *Jo ki*, though, although, whichever: 2, *conj.* if, that, as, when, in that, inasmuch as: 3, *f.* a river, brook, rivulet.
जोअर; see (1) जुवार (2) जोआर (3) ज़ोर.
जोआर, 1, *f.* Indian corn (*Holcus sorgum* or *Sorgum vulgaris*): 2, *m.* flood tide.
जोआरभाटा, *m.* the flood-tide and ebb-tide.
जोई, 1, *f.* (*m.* जोया, *q.v.*) saw, beheld: 2, an emphatic form of जो. See ई, 4.
जोऊ, 1, a seeing, beholding, looking at: 2, the Braj emphatic form of जो. See ऊ, 7.
जोए, *f.* a rivulet, brook.
जों, as, when. — *toṅ*, as before, *in statu quo*, in some way. — *toṅ karke*, in any way, by some means, by any means, somehow or other, as it could be done. — *kā toṅ*, as originally, in the same way as it was, *in statu quo*, as it was, the same as ever, as in reality, unaltered, precisely the same, unchanged.
जोंक, *f.* a leech. — *lagānā*, to apply leeches.
जोंकर, as, in any way, by any means.
जोंका; see (1) जों (2) जोंक.
जोंका तों, *m.* (pl. जोंके तों; fem. जोंकी तों); see *s. v.* जों.
जोंग / जोंगक } *m.* aloe-wood or agallochum.
जोंघ; see जोंग.
जोंजों, a redupl. form; see (1) जों (2) जैसा.
जोंतों; see *s. v.* जों.
जोंही / जोंहीं } see (1) जोही (2) ज्योंही.
जोक, *more com.* जोंक, *q. v.*
जोकमा = जोखमा, *q. v.*
जोख, *f.* weight.

जोखना, *t.* to weigh.

जोखाई, *f.* (see **आई**, 3), a weighman's perquisite.

जोखिम, *f.* risk, danger, peril, venture, enterprize, achievement. — *uṭhānā*, to venture, run the hazard.

जोखिमी, *m.* (*f.* in *or* inī) one who risks.

जोखों, *f.* risk, venture, danger; harm, damage.

जोग, 1, = (1) **योग** (2) **योग्य**, *qq. v.*; for words, therefore, beginning thus, see under either of these latter forms: 2, the name of the person on whom a draft or bill of exchange is drawn.

जोगनपुर, *m.* an ancient name of Delhi.

जोगनी, *more prop.* **योगिनी**, *q. v.*

जोगवत = **जुगाता है**.

जोगवना = **जुगाना**, *q.v.*

जोगा, *more prop.* **योग्य**, *q.v.*

जोगिनीय in Chand = **योगिनी**, *q. v.*

जोगिया, 1, *m.* a certain colour: 2, *f.* one of the musical modes (*rāgiṇī*); a kind of pigeon.

जोगू; see **जोग**.

जोगेश / **जोगेसर** } *more prop.* **योगेश्वर**, *q. v.*

ज़ोज, *m.* a couple, pair; a husband, spouse.

जोजन = **योजन**, *q. v.*

जोजा, *f.* a wife.

जोट, 1, *m.* a fellow, peer, one of a pair, mate, match: 2, equal, even, not odd. — *bāndhanā*, to pair.

जोटा = **जोट** and **जोड़ा**, *qq. v.*

जोड़, *m.* junction, connexion; joints, joining, a seam, patch, tie, bond, union, society; addition, sum-total. — *denā*, to add up a sum, cast it up.

जोड़गड़ती, *f.* a companion, consort, wife.

जोड़जाड़, *m.* savings; a collecting by small quantities, scraping together.

जोड़ती, *f.* calculation, reckoning.

जोड़तोड़, *m.* contrivance, mechanism, joining.

जोड़न, *m.* solder: rennet. [adds, one who joins.

जोड़नहारा, *m.* (*f.* in *or* ī) one who collects, one who

जोड़ना, *t.* to collect; to add up; to join.

जोड़वान, *f.* a companion, helpmate, consort, wife.

जोड़ा, *m.* joining, connexion; a pair, couple; a pair of shoes; a suit (of clothes): alchemy: a rope of twisted grass made to support a round-bottomed jar.

जोड़ाई, *f.* (see **आई**, 3) the act or the profession of joining; the price of joining.

जोड़ि = **जोड़के** (**जोड़ना**).

जोड़ी, *f.* a pair, couple; an assessor; a peer or fellow (to some one): a small pond.

जोड़ु, 1, *more prop.* **जोरू**, *q. v.*: 2, an old 2nd pers. imperat. of **जोड़ना**.

जोत, 1, *more prop.* **ज्योति**, *q. v.*: 2, *f.* cultivation, tillage, cultivated land; the tenure of a cultivator, rent paid by a cultivator.

जोतदार, *m.* a husbandman, one who has a tenure.

जोतन, *m.* ploughing: a ploughman.

जोतना, *t.* to yoke: to plough, till.

जोतमान, *more prop.* **ज्योतिमान**, *q. v.*

जोता, *m.* a ploughman, husbandman, agriculturist, cultivator of the soil, one who tills his own land.

जोतार = **जोता**, *q. v.*

जोति; for words beginning thus, but not given below, see under the form **ज्योति**.

जोतिक, *more prop.* **ज्योतिष**, *q. v.*

जोतिग in Chand = **ज्योतिष**, *q. v.*

जोतिया = **जोता**, *q. v.*

जोतिब (an old future of **जोतना**) = **जोतूंगा**.

जोती, 1, a corruption of **ज्योति**, *q. v.*: 2, *f.* the string which suspends the scale of a balance; the string which goes around the neck of a bullock to fasten the yoke.

जोद्धा, **जोध**; for words beginning with either of these elements, see under the forms **योद्धा**, **योध**, respectively.

जोधान, *m.* (a Braj pl. of **योद्धा**) warriors, heroes.

जोन, *more com.* (1) **जौं** (2) **योनि**, *qq. v.* [form **योनि**.

जोनि; for words beginning thus, see under the

जोनी, (poet.) = (1) **ज्ञाति** (2) **योनि**, *qq. v.*

जोप; see **यूप**.

जोपै, an old form = **जिसपर**. [the strength of youth.

जोबनज़ोर, 1, youthful strength; 2, strong with

जोबन; for words beginning thus, see under the

जोबना; see (1) **जोवना** (2) **यौवन**. [form **यौवन**.

जोय, 1, = **जोई**, 2, *q. v.*: 2, *f.* a wife.

जोयसी, a Braj corruption of **ज्योतिषी**, *q. v.*

जोये (*poet.*) = **ये जो हैं**.

ज़ोर, *m.* force, strength, power, vigour, violence, effort, weight. — *pakaṛnā*, to gain strength. — *k.* to exercise force, compel; to exercise. — *denā*, to assist.

जोरना, *more prop.* **जोड़ना**, *q. v.*

जोरबार, *more com.* **ज़ोरावर**, *q. v.*

ज़ोरावर, strong, mighty, robust.

ज़ोरावरी, *f.* strength, vigorousness.

जोरि; see (1) **जोड़ि** (2) **जोरी**.

ज़ोरी, *f.* strength, force, power.

जोरी; see (1) **जोड़ी** (2) **जोली** (3) **ज़ोरी**.

जोरू, *f.* (pl. **जोरुआं**) a wife.

जोला, *m.* guile, fraud, deceit: — *denā*, to deceive: a tract of land containing sixteen *bisās*.

जोली, a companion, fellow.

जोलीदा, scattered, confused.

जोवत, part. (Braj; from **जोवनौं**) sees, etc.

जोवना, *t.* to look, see, look at, regard, observe.

जोवनो / **जोवनौं** } in Braj = **जोवना**, *q. v.*

जोवा, *m.* (*f.* **जोई**) past. part of **जोवना**. [lust.

जोश, *m.* heat; ebullition, effervescence; passion;

जोष; for words beginning thus, see under the form योष.

जोषी, m. an astrologer; a low caste of Brāhmaṇs [employed in casting nativities.

जोसी, m. a certain tribe of Hindoos.

जोहड़ = जूहड़, q. v.

जोहना, t. to look, see, look at, regard, observe. *Bāt* —, (with gen. *f.*) to be on the look out for.

जोहर, m. a large pond or lake; inundated land.

जोहा, past part. from जोहना, q. v.

जोहारना, t. to salute, do obeisance to.

जोहिया, a certain tribe of Rājputs.

जोहो = जोहके (जोहना).

जोहीं, (correl. of योहीं) = जैसेही, q. v.

जौ, 1, in Braj = जब and जो, qq. v.: 2, m. barley (*Hordeum hexastichon*); the measure of a barley-corn, equal to six mustard-seeds: the mark between the joints of the fingers. *Jau jau hisāb lenā*, to take a [strict account.

जौआ = जवा, q. v.

जौं, 1, in Braj = जोन, q. v.: 2, = जौ, q. v.

जौंक, *more com.* जोंक, q. v.

जौकना, t. to scold, rail.

जौंची, f. a kind of disease in barley or wheat,— the ears producing no grain.

जौड़ा, m. payment of village servants in kind.

जौतरी, f. mace (the spice so called).

जौंप, (in Braj) = supposing, although.

जौंपैं (जौं + पै) in Braj = यद्यपि, q. v. [privacy.

जौराभौरा, m. a retired room, vault, retirement,

जौंलगि in Braj = जबलग, q. v.

जौंहरी, *more prop.* जौहरी, q. v.

जौंहीं in Braj = (1) जोहीं (2) ज्योंही, qq. v.

जौक, *more com.* जोंक, q. v.

जौचनी, f. a mixed crop of barley and *chanā*.

जौघडरी }
जौघडी } = जूनरी, q. v.

जौतुक = यौतक, q. v.

जौथा in Braj = जिसका or जैसा.

जौदत, f. ingenuity, intelligence, quickness of apprehension; benignity.

जौन, 1, = जो, 1, q. v.: 2, = यौन, q. v.: 3, m. time.

जौनार, f. a feast, entertainment: land ready for the seed. [ed for spring and autumn crops alternately.

जौनाल, land in constant cultivation, or cultivat-

जौनी = यौनी, q. v.

जौबन = यौवन, q. v.

जौमध्य = यवमध्य, q. v.

जौर, *more prop.* ज़ौर, q. v.

जौलग }
जौलों } in Braj = जबलग, q. v.
जौलौं }

जौवन; for words beginning thus, see under the [form यौवन.

जौशन, m. a cuirass, armour, coat of mail.

जौहर, m. (*pl.* āt) a gem, jewel, pearl.

जौहरि, *more prop.* जौहरी, q. v. [2, *adj.* essential.

जौहरी, 1, m. (*f.* in *or* inī) a jeweller, lapidary:

ज्वारी, a corruption of जूआरी, q. v.

ज्ञ (gy): this letter is compounded of ज + ञ: its true pronunciation is said to be represented by the combination *jña*; but in Hindee it is invariably pronounced *gya*, as if it were compounded of g + y. It frequently occurs in Hindee as the latter element in compound words, importing the idea of wise, intelligent, knowing, learned, acquainted with; and when so used it has a feminine form in *ā*; *e. g.* धर्मज्ञा, *f.* (*m.* धर्मज्ञ) a woman acquainted with law, etc.

ज्ञपित, taught, expounded, made known.

ज्ञप्ति, f. comprehension, knowing, understanding, the exercise of the intellectual faculty.

ज्ञात, known, comprehended, understood.

ज्ञातसिद्धान्त, m. a man completely versed in any science or shāstra.

ज्ञाता, m. (*f.* trī) one who knows, etc.: *lit.* knowing, intelligent, wise, acquainted with anything.

ज्ञातान्वय, m. *pr. n.* a name of Varddhamān (the last Jin or Jain Pontiff).

ज्ञाति, m. a father: a distant kinsman who does not participate in the oblations of food and water offered to deceased ancestors.

ज्ञातृ, m. (*f.* ज्ञात्री) = ज्ञाता, q. v.

ज्ञातेय, m. relationship, affinity.

ज्ञान, m. knowledge (in general); intellect, understanding, intelligence; knowledge of a specific and religious kind, which is such as to exempt the soul from further transmigration and to secure for it reünion with the universal spirit. This sort of knowledge is said to be derived from meditation and the study of philosophy, which teaches man the divine nature and origin of his immaterial part, together with the unreality of corporeal enjoyments or worldly forms, and which separates him during this life from terrestrial objects and secures for him after death final emancipation from separate existence. — *daurānā*, to meditate deeply. — *sikhnā*, to acquire know- [ledge.

ज्ञानउपदेश, *more prop.* ज्ञानोपदेश, q. v.

ज्ञानकाण्ड, m. *pr. n.* (see मीमांसा) the philosophical portion of each Ved, or that which treats of knowledge as distinguished from ceremonies.

ज्ञानक, appertaining to ज्ञान.

ज्ञानचक्षु, m. the intellect, eyes of the mind.

ज्ञानचर्चा, f. the pursuit or practice of wisdom.

ज्ञानदर्पण, m. *pr. n.* one of the Jain saints (Manjunī).

ज्ञानदशा, f. a state of intelligence or knowledge.

ज्ञानदृष्टि, f. clear vision or perception (untainted either by ignorance or by sin).

ज्ञानमान, m. (*f.* matī) }
ज्ञानवान, m. (*f.* vatī) } = ज्ञानी, q. v.

ज्ञानविज्ञान, m. sacred and miscellaneous knowledge; the Veds with the supplementary branches of knowledge, medicine, arms, etc.

ज्ञानविषय, m. the thing called ज्ञान, q. v. [telligence.

ज्ञानाधिक्य, m. superiority or preëminence in in-

ज्ञानिन्, *m.* (*f.* ī) = ज्ञानी, *q.v.*

ज्ञानी, *m.* (*f.* inī) one who understands fully, one possessing *gyān* or religious wisdom, one who knows future events, prognosticator, sage, fortune-teller, astrologer : *lit.* wise, knowing, intelligent, learned, sage, judicious.

ज्ञानेच्छु, desirous of wisdom.

ज्ञानेन्द्रिय, *m.* an organ of perception or of consciousness ; *e. g.* the skin, tongue, eye, ear, mental powers, intellect.

ज्ञानोपदेश, *m.* wise instruction.

ज्ञापक, *m.* (*f.* ikā) a teacher, one who heralds or makes known : *lit.* adj. making known, giving information, proclaiming.

ज्ञापन, *m.* a notifying, apprizing, informing, making known, communicating.

ज्ञापनार्थ, *adv.* for the purpose of apprizing.

ज्ञापिका, *f.* (*m.* ज्ञापक) a preceptress, etc.

ज्ञापित, *m.* (*f.* ā) notified, revealed, discovered.

ज्यफत, a corruption of ज़ियाफ़त, *q.v.*

ज्या, *f.* a bowstring ; (in Math.) the chord of an arc : a mother ; the earth.

ज्यादा = ज़ियादः, *q. v.*

ज्याना, *more prop.* जियाना, *q. v.*

ज्यानो / **ज्यानौं** } in Braj = जियाना, *q. v.*

ज्याफत, *more prop.* ज़ियाफ़त, *q.v.*

ज्याये = ज्याए (जियाना).

ज्यारी, a corruption of जुआरी, *q. v.*

ज्यूं = ज्यों, *q. v.*

ज्येष्ठ, 1, *m. pr. n.* the second month of the Hindoos (May-June): 2, *m.* (*f.* ā) an older brother : *lit.* eldest-born, oldest, very old : best, most excellent, preëminent.

ज्येष्ठता, *f.* / **ज्येष्ठत्व**, *m.* } primogeniture : superiority.

ज्येष्ठतात, *m.* a father's elder brother.

ज्येष्ठवर्ण, *m.* (*f.* ā) a Brāhmaṇ (considered as the elder or best-born).

ज्येष्ठा, *f.* (*m.* ज्येष्ठ) an elder sister : *pr. n.* the eighteenth *Nakshatra* (it is figured by a ring or ear-ring, and comprizes three stars of which one is Scorpionis) : the middle finger : misfortune.

ज्येष्ठांश, *m.* that share of a father's property which belongs to his eldest son.

ज्येष्ठाधिकार, *m.* a birthright, a right of primogeniture.

ज्यो ; see (1) जीउ (2) जीव (3) ज्यों.

ज्यों, *adv.* how much, the more so, when, as, as if.

ज्योंज्यों, (correl. of त्योंत्यों) as, as by degrees.

ज्योंकात्यों, *m.* (*pl.* ज्योंकेत्यों ; *f.* ज्योंकीत्यों) = जोंका तों ; see *s. v.* जों.

ज्योंही, (emph. of ज्यों) just at the very time when, as soon as, the moment when; just exactly as if.

ज्योति, *f.* light, splendour, lustre, brilliancy ; sunbeams ; the flame of a lamp or candle ; a vision ; intelligence.

ज्योतिमय = ज्योतिर्मय, *q. v.*

ज्योतिमान, *m.* (*f.* matī) luminous, bright.

ज्योतिर्गण, *m.* the celestial bodies collectively.

ज्योतिर्मय, *m.* (*f.* ī) consisting of light, brilliant ; abounding in stars, starry.

ज्योतिष, *m.* astrology, astronomy ; a kind of spell.

ज्योतिषपुर, *m. pr. n.* a certain ancient Hindoo city.

ज्योतिषविद्या, *f.* the science of astrology or of astronomy.

ज्योतिषिक, *m.* an astrologer ; an astronomer.

ज्योतिषी, 1, *m.* (*f.* iṇī) an astrologer, astronomer : *lit.* appertaining to astrology or to astronomy : 2, *f.* a star, planet, asterism.

ज्योतिषीय, *m.* (*f.* ā) = ज्योतिषी, *q.v.*

ज्योतिष्क, *m.* any heavenly body ; the generic term for the sun, the moon, a planet, an asterism, a star.

ज्योतिष्का, *m.* pl. of the above (see आ, 22) signifying the sun, the moon, a planet, an asterism, a star.

ज्योतिष्मान, *m.* (*f.* matī) luminous, splendid, radiant, resplendent, glorious.

ज्योतिस्वरूप, *m.* an epithet of God ; *lit.* resplendence itself.

ज्योती (*poet.*) = ज्योति, *q. v.*

ज्योतीरथ, *m. pr. n.* the pole-star.

ज्योत्स्ना, *f.* moonlight.

ज्योत्स्नाप्रिय, *m.* (*f.* ā) the *chakor* or Greek partridge.

ज्योत्स्नावृक्ष, *m.* the tripod or tree of a lampstand, a candlestick.

ज्योत्स्नी, *f.* a moonlight night, a night in which the moon is full.

ज्योनार = जेओनार, *q. v.*

ज्यौं (in Braj, correl. of त्यौं) = ज्यों, *q. v.*

ज्यौंका तौं, *more prop.* ज्यौंकात्यौं, *q. v.*

ज्यौंकात्यौं, *m.* (*f.* ज्यौंकीत्यौं) in Braj = ज्योंकात्यों, *q. v.*

ज्वर, *m.* fever.

ज्वरनाशक, *adj.* febrifuge, anti-febrile.

ज्वराग्नि, *m.* the hot paroxysm of fever, feverish heat.

ज्वरापहा, *f.* a plant (*Medicago esculenta*).

ज्वरी, *m.* (*f.* iṇī) feverish, affected with fever, febrile.

ज्वरोत्पत्ति, *f.* the origin of fever.

ज्वरौषध, *m. f.* any fever-medicine.

ज्वल, *m.* flame, blaze, light.

ज्वलका, *f.* flame.

ज्वलन, *m.* fire, Agni : caustic potash : *adj.* shining, blazing, burning.

ज्वलित, *m.* (*f.* ā) burnt, consumed by fire ; ignited, blazing, enflamed, flaming.

ज्वार = जोआर, *q. v.*

ज्वारभाटा = जोआरभाटा, *q. v.*

ज्वारी in Braj = जुआरी, *q. v.*

ज्वाल, *m.* / **ज्वाला**, *f.* } flame, blaze, light.

ज्वालाजिह्वा, an epithet of Agni ; *lit.* the flame-tongued.

ज्वालामुख = ज्वालामुखी, *q. v.*

ज्वालामुखी, *f.* a volcano or any place where subterraneous fire breaks forth from the soil. Such spots are objects of veneration to Hindoos. A *jwālāmukhee* famous among the Hindoos exists near Balkh in Chinese Tartary, to which pilgrimages are made from Hindustān : the soil abounds in hydrogenous gas, so that fire can always be produced by slightly rubbing the earth.—the gas taking fire when it comes into contact with the external air. Vents are sometimes made, and, a light being applied to the orifice, the flame is kindled and is fed by the stream of gas that [escapes.

झवेर, a corruption of ज़ेवर, *q. v.*

झ

झ (jh) is the ninth consonant in the Hindee alphabet, and the fourth letter of the चवर्ग or palatal class. It is the aspirate of ज, and is pronounced like *dgeh* in the word 'bridgehouse' with the *ouse* dropped. Besides the form given it in this work it has sometimes three other forms, *viz* भ, म, and झ. Like the other aspirated letters, it is occasionally interchanged corruptly with its unaspirated form. It is also occasionally found where we might expect to find च; *e. g.* झौन = चौना.

झं, *m.* the sound of platters or of vessels of metal striking against each other, clash of arms (as of swords, [etc.).

झंई, *f.* a swoon, stupefaction.

झंकाड़, a tree without leaves.

झंकार, *f.* a clinking, tinkling, clanking, jingling, ringing, rattling, humming, buzzing.

झंकारना, *t.* to cause to give forth a clinking sound, [to ring.

झंकोरना, *more com.* झकोरना, *q. v.*

झंखड़ा, *m.* an elk : a tree without leaves.

झंखना, *n.* to be horror-struck, have the hair standing on end : *a. int.* to shudder, rave, chatter, lament.

झंखनो } in Braj = झंखना, *q. v.*
झंखनों }

झंखाड़ा, *m.* an elk : a tree without leaves.

झंखिल, *m.* (*f.* ā) horror-struck, having the hair standing on end ; terrified, raving, lamenting.

झंगा, *m.* an upper garment, vest, coat, gown.

झंगिया, *f.* (dim. of झंगा) a child's vest.

झंझिया, a species of *sēr* in the lower Doāb.

झंझ, *more com.* झांझ, *q. v.*

झंझकार, *f.* a clinking, tingling, ringing.

झंझट, *m.* wrangling, perplexity, incumbrance.

झंझटी, perplexing.

झंझन, *m.* an indistinct noise like the clanging of metal ornaments, a ringing, rattling.

झंझना, *m.* (*f.* ī) peevish, fretful.

झंझनाना, *a. int.* to tinkle, clank, tingle, jingle, [ring, rattle.

झंझनाहट, *f.* clinking, ringing ; peevishness.

झंझर, a kind of largeish water-jar.

झंझरी, *f.* a lattice, window.

झंझलना, 1, *a. int.* to become angry : 2, *t.* to swing, vibrate (as dyers do cloth in order to dry it).

झंझा, *f.* wind, wind and rain, a hurricane, gale : raining in large drops : a sharp clanging sound, rattling, jangling.

झंझानिल, *m.* wind with rain, a high wind in the rainy season, a typhoon or the kind of tempest frequent in the south-west monsoon.

झंझावात, *m.* wind with rain, a storm, squall.

झंझाहट, *f.* trouble, difficulty, perplexity, vexation, dilemma.

झंझिया, *f.* (dim. of झांझ) small cymbals.

झंड, झंप ; for words beginning thus, see under [the forms झयड, झय्य.

झंय = झई, *q. v.*

झंवाना, *a. int.* to tan (in the sun) : *t.* to wash the feet by rubbing *jhāṅwāṅ*.

झक, *f.* passion, emotion ; rant, nonsense. — *mārnā*, to act fruitlessly or absurdly, to talk nonsense.

झकझकना, *a. int.* to talk nonsense.

झकझोर = झकझोरी, *q. v.*

झकझोरी, *f.* scrambling and wrangling, snatching.

झकड़ी, *more com.* झकरी, *q. v.*

झकना, *a. int.* to rave, chatter, reflect, lament.

झकमर्गी, *f.* the acting fruitlessly or absurdly, talking nonsense, prating, prattling.

झकरी, *f.* a milkpail, milk-vessel.

झकाझक, *adj.* shining, glittering with gold and silver, etc. (brocade).

झकार, *m.* the letter झ, or any symbol that may [represent it.

झकावन्त, *m.* (*f.* vatī) wrathful, passionate.

झकी, (*f.* inī) passionate, wrathful.

झकोर, *f.* loss, misfortune.

झकोरना, *t.* to drive or beat (as wind and rain in a squall) ; to shake.

झकोरा, *m.* raining, a shower, squall, breeze, gust, [blast of wind.

झकोरनौ } in Braj = झकोरना, *q. v.*
झकोरनौं }

झकोल, *f.* the act of shaking in the water.

झकोलना, *t.* to shake.

झक्कड़, *m.* a squall, storm, tempest, 'Nor-wester'.

झक्की, *m.* (*f.* inī) one who talks to himself, chatterer, prater, useless or idle talker.

झखन, a weeping, lamenting, deploring, regret-[ting.

झखना, *a. int.* to chatter, rave : to weep.

झगटा, *more com.* झगड़ा, *q. v.*

झगड़, *m.* a kind of hawk.

झगड़ना, *t.* to wrangle, quarrel, cavil, squabble.

झगड़ा, *m.* wrangling, quarrelling, strife, squabble, contention, dispute. — *k.* to quarrel. — *pakaṛnā*, to engage in another's quarrel.

झगड़ाना, *t.* to cause to quarrel, set a-quarrelling.

झगड़ारगड़ा, *m.* squabbling and wrangling, brawl.

झगड़ालिन, *f.* = झगड़ालू, *q. v.*

झगड़ालू, *m.* a brawler, disputer : *lit.* contentious, quarrelsome, disputatious, wrangling.

झगा = झंगा, *q. v.*

झगुला } *m.* a child's frock or shirt.
झगुलिया }

झझ ; for words beginning thus, see under the [form झंझ.

झझर, *m.* a goblet.

झझ, *m.* a long beard.

झझकाना = झिझकना, *q.v.*

झझकारना, *t.* to browbeat, speak snappishly to.

झझरका = झझलका, *q.v.*

झझरी = झंझरी, *q.v.*

झझलका, *m.* early dawn (before it is easy to distinguish objects).

झझला, *m.* a kind of sweetmeat.

झझा, a violent wind with rain.

झट, quickness: quick: quickly, instantly.

झटक, *f.* a twitch, wrench, twist, stitch, toss, throw, pull, jerk, knock, shake. — *lenā*, to snatch.

झटकना, *a. int.* to shake; to become lean: *t.* to touse, twitch, pull, jerk.

झटका, 1, *m.* = झटक, *q.v.*: 2, *m.* (*f.* ī) any animal which has been beheaded, broken asunder, or torn by a sudden jerk, torn to pieces.

झटकाना, *t.* to shake, pull.

झटति, *more prop.* झटिति, *q.v.*

झटना, *a. int.* to become thin, diminish: to argue, dispute.

झटपट / **झटसे** } quickly, speedily, instantly.

झटास, *m.* rain blown with a strong wind, clap, flap.

झटि, *m.* a small tree, shrub, bush.

झटिति, instantly, in a moment, on a sudden, quickly, speedily.

झटियाना, a certain small clan of Rājputs in the upper Doāb.

झड़, *m.* a kind of lock: *f.* heavy rain: the heat from a fire.

झड़कना, *t.* to browbeat, speak snappishly to, scold; to threaten; to jerk.

झड़काझड़की, *f.* a mutual wrangling.

झड़की, *f.* rebuff, snappishness, frowning, jerk, repercussion.

झड़झड़ाट, *f.* a flapping, shaking.

झड़झड़ाना, *t.* to flap, shake, jerk.

झड़त = झड़न, *q. v.*

झड़ती लेना, *t.* to take an account; to search, rummage, examine.

झड़न, *f.* the act of falling off (as fruit from a tree): snuff.

झड़ना, *a. int.* to fall off (as fruit, leaves, etc. from a tree), to drop, fall, shake, strain: *t.* to emit, pour: *n.* to be sounded (as the *naubat*), to be discharged (as a volley).

झड़प, *f.* heat, fieriness (as of pepper), acrimony, sparring, contention.

झड़पना, *t.* to spar, contend, fight (as cocks).

झड़पाझड़पी, *f.* fighting (particularly of birds), sparring, contention.

झड़पाना, *t.* to fight (*i.e.* to set a-fighting, as cocks or other birds), to cause to spar, cause to contend.

झड़बरना, *a. int.* to burn, be all in flames.

झड़बराना; see (1) झड़बरना (2) लड़बड़ाना.

झड़बेर, *m.* the wild *ber*-tree, *jujube* (*Zizyphus jujuba*).

झड़बेरी / **झड़बेल** } *f.* = झड़बेर, *q. v.*

झड़वाना, *t.* to cause (some one else) to sweep, cause to be swept.

झड़ाक / **झड़ाका** } *m.* speed, haste, hurry.

झड़ाखा, *m.* a skylight.

झड़ाझड़, hastily, rapidly, in a hurry.

झड़ाता, *m.* the close of the fruit season.

झड़ाना, *t.* to cause to be swept, get swept: to cause to be exorcised.

झड़ो = झड़ी, *q.v.*

झड़ी, *f.* continued rain, showers, wet weather, storm: perquisites: a procession in honor of a saint, etc.

झड़ोटा = झड़ोता, *q.v.*

झड़ोता, *m.* the end of the season (of fruits, etc.): *adj.* going out of season.

झणक, *f.* a ringing, tinkling, clinking, tingling, clank, jingle.

झणकना, *a. int.* to clink, tinkle, jingle, tingle, ring.

झणड = झणक, *q. v.*

झणडा, *m.* a banner, flag, standard, ensign, streamer; flagstaff.

झणडी, *f.* = झणडा, *q. v.*

झणडू, petals, foliage of a tree; a lock of hair.

झणडूला, *m.* (*f.* ī) with a fine head of hair (a child); with thick handsome foliage.

झन; for words beginning thus, see under either of the forms झं, झण.

झनकबाई, *f.* acute rheumatism.

झनवां, *m.* a kind of rice.

झप, *adj.* quick; *adv.* quickly, in a trice. —*khānā*, to overset (as a paper kite while flying).

झपक, *f.* the act of fanning, or of winking, etc.

झपकना, *t.* to fan, move to and fro (a fan); to snatch: *a. int.* to wink; to spring (as a tiger).

झपका, *m.* a snatch, spring, puff or gust of wind.

झपकाना, *a. int.* to wink, twinkle.

झपकी, *f.* a snatch, spring (as of a tiger); drowsiness, wink, twinkle.

झपझप, very quickly, with great haste.

झपट, *f.* a snatch, spring (as of a tiger), a rush, snap, onslaught, assault. —*lenā*, to snatch, seize, snap up.

झपटना, *t.* to snatch, spring, attack suddenly, spring upon, pounce upon, fly at, snap at.

झपट्टा, *m.* an assault, sudden attack, snatch, the spring of a tiger. — *mārnā*, to snatch.

झपना, *more prop.* झम्पना, *q. v.*

झपलाना, *t.* to wash, rinse.

झपसे, quickly, in a trice.

झपाझपी, *f.* haste, hurry.

झपाट / **झपात** } *f.* haste, quickness.

झपाना, *t.* to take a snap.

झपास, *f.* a shower.

झपासिया, deceitful, fraudulent.

झपेट = झपट, *q. v.*

झपेटना = झपटना, *q. v.*

झप्पान, a kind of sedan chair for travelling.

झबकाना, *t.* to astonish.

झबरा, covered with long hair (said of the ears of animals).
झबिया, *m.* a kind of ornament.
झबूआ, *m.* (*f.* झबूई) = झब्बूआ, *q. v.*
झब्बा, *m.* a tassel.
झब्बी, *f.* trappings.
झब्बूआ, *m.* (*f.* झब्बूई) long-haired, shaggy (as cattle or dogs): bent, curved, bending (as the bough of a tree).
झमक, *f.* glitter, splendour.
झमकड़ा, *m.* splendour, beauty.
झमकना, *a. int.* to glitter; to dance.
झमका, *m.* splendour, refulgence; the clash or clatter of metallic substances.
झमकाना, *t.* to cause to shine, cause to glitter; to cause to dance.
झमकी, *f.* glare, glitter, lustre, brilliancy.
झमझम, *adv.* raining heavily and continuously, raining the whole day.
झमझमाना, *a. int.* to shine, glitter, sparkle.
झमना, *more prop.* झूमना, *q. v.*
झमरझमर, *adv.* drop by drop (as small rain).
झमाका, *m.* a heavy shower; quickness, haste.
झमाझम = झमझम, *q. v.*
झमेला, a disturbance, row, tumult, squabble.
झम्प, *m.* a jump, spring, plunge, sally.
झम्पना; see (1) झपटना (2) झाम्पना.
झम्मर, a flight of birds, swarm of flies, etc.
झर, *f.* heavy rain: the heat from a fire. — *barnā*, to burn furiously, be all in flames.
झरझर, *m.* a goglet.
झरना, *m.* a skimmer: a spring, cascade: *a. int.* to spring, flow; to fall off (as fruit, etc. from a tree).
झरपत्ति, *m. f.* (pl. °त्तिं) an old form = झड़पता है.
झरपना } *more prop.* झड़पना, *q. v.*
झरफना }
झरबरना, see झड़बरना.
झरबेरी = झड़बेरी, *q. v.*
झरी, *f.* waterfall.
झरुवा, *m.* a nutritious kind of grass resembling *panik.*
झरुआ = झरुवा, *q. v.*
झरोखा, *m.* a lattice, window.
झर्झर, *m.* a goglet.
झर्ना = झरना, *q. v.*
झर्रा, *m.* a spring, fountain, *jet d'eau.*
झल, *f.* passion, anger, jealousy; the heat from a fire.
झलक, *f.* brightness, glitter, glare, refulgence; reflection of light.
झलकना, *a. int.* to shine, glare.
झलका } *m.* a blister.
झलकाट }
झलकाना, *t.* to cause to shine, to brighten, burnish.
झलकार, *m.* brightness, splendour, light.
झलकी, *f.* a glance.
झलझल, *m.* glare, glitter.
झलझलाट, a contraction of झलझलाहट, *q. v.*
झलझलाना, *a. int.* to glitter, glare; to throb, ache, smart; to be in a passion.
झलझलाहट, *f.* glitter, glare, splendour; smart.
झलना, *t.* to fan, move to and fro (as a fan), to flap: *n.* to be soldered, be repaired by soldering: to be sifted.
झलनी, *f.* a sieve.
झलवाना, *t.* to cause a thing to be repaired by soldering.
झलहायी, *m.* (*f.* ī) jealous, suspicious.
झलाझल, *f.* splendour, glitter: *adj.* luminous, resplendent, embroidered.
झलाना, *t.* to repair by soldering.
झलाबोर, *f.* splendour: *adj.* splendid, shining, glittering with jewels.
झलार, *m.* a thicket, underwood, copse.
झवर क°, to quarrel.
झष, *m.* a fish; the sign Pisces.
झषकेतु, *m.* the sign Pisces: Kamdev.
झहरना, *a. int.* to blink with pain (as the eyes by by too much light).
झाईं, *f.* a shadow: a freckle or black mark on the face (not a mole).
झांई, *more com.* झाईं, *q. v.*
झाऊ, *m.* the tamarisk-tree (*Tamarix Indica* or *Dioica*): it is called in Arab. *asl*, and in Pers. *shoragaz*, from its growing in marshy ground. Its tender branches are worked into baskets, and its dry wood is used as fuel.
झांक, *m.* a herd of deer, flock of birds, etc.: *f.* a peep.
झांकड़, *m.* bushes, brambles, underwood.
झांकना, *t.* to peep, spy, peer.
झांकाझोंकी, *f.* a peeping, bo-peep.
झांख, *m.* a kind of deer.
झांगी, a kind of bramble and brushwood.
झांझ, *f.* cymbals: anger, rage, passion, pet: stillness, dreariness; impatience (in a horse expecting his food).
झांझट, *f.* wrangling, squabbling, quarrelling.
झांझर; see (1) झाझर, (2) छिद्रित.
झांझा, *m.* a kind of insect, caterpillar, cabbage-worm.
झांझिया, passionate, furious.
झांझी, *f.* a kind of play (in which children, in the month Āsin, go about at night dancing, begging and carrying on their heads earthen pots, perforated on all sides, within which lamps are kept burning.
झांट, झांप; for words beginning thus, see under the forms झाट, झाम्प, respectively.
झांवरा, *m.* (*f.* ī) black, dusky.
झांवली, *f.* a wink, coquetry: hot wind. — *lenā*, to ogle.
झांवलीबाज़, *m.* a coquetter.
झांवा } *m.* = झामा, *q. v.*
झांवां }
झांसना, *t.* to debauch, seduce; to wheedle, coax: to covet: *n.* to be inclined, be intent or set (on), be agog.
झांसा, *m.* love, desire, eagerness, lust: an assessment formed by a general estimate without regular data.

झांसू, *m.* a wheedler, flatterer, seducer.

झाकड़ी, *f.* a kind of milkpail.

झाकना = झांकना, *q.v.*

झाकरी, *f.* a kind of milkpail.

झाग, *m.* foam, froth (of the ocean), scum.

झाझर, *m.* cymbals or bells for the aukles.

झाझा, *m.* an intoxicating mixture made with *bhang* or hemp.

झाड, *m.* an arbor, bower, place overgrown with creepers, thicket, wood.

झाटा, *f.* jasmine (*Jasminium Amiculatum*).

झाटिका / झाटीका } *f.* a plant (*Flacourtia catafracta*).

झाड़, *m.* bushes, brambles; bush, shrub, underwood, brake: a kind of fireworks: a lustre or chandelier: a purge: continued rain. — *bāṅdhnā*, to rain without ceasing. In southern India this is the general term for 'tree.' *Jhāṛkā nimak*, potass, impure carbonate of potass.

झाड, a tree (in general).

झाड़खण्ड, *m. pr. n.* the forest of *Baijnāth*; *prop.* full of brambles, bushy.

झाड़झंकार, *more com.* झाड़झंखार, *q.v.*

झाड़झंखार, *m.* brambles, large dry bushes; a purge.

झाड़झटक, *f.* a sweeping.

झाड़झनखार, *more com.* झाड़झंखार, *q.v.*

झाड़झूड़, *f.* sweepings: perquisites: a thicket.

झाड़न, *f.* sweepings; a coarse cloth for wiping furniture, a duster, dishclout. — *k.* to dust, wipe; sweep.

झाड़ना, *t.* to sweep, brush; to clean, strain, shift, knock off, dash, strike, flap: to strike fire (as with a flint); to beat (bushes, etc.). *Jhāṛ ḍālnā*, to sweep out, sweep away. *Jhāṛ denā*, to brush, brush off, clear away. *Jhāṛ pachhorkar deknā*, to test, try, examine. *Jhāṛnā phūṅknā*, to exorcise, repeat spells or charms.

झाड़न्त, entirely.

झाड़पहाड़, digression.

झाड़फूंक, *f.* juggling, conjuring, hocus-pocus (particularly for the purpose of curing a disease or a snake bite).

झाड़बहारना, *t.* to sweep up, clean.

झाड़ा, *m.* a stool, purge. — *jhapṭe jānā*, to go to the necessary. — *jhapṭā lenā*, to search. — *phirnā* or — *jhuṭkā phirnā*, to walk among bushes, *i. e.* to go to the necessary. — *denā*, to submit to search.

झाड़ी, *f.* forest, wood, underwood, brushwood, shrub, bush, copse, brake.

झाड़ू, *m. f.* a broom, besom, whisk; a sweeper by caste and occupation; a comet.

झाडूकश, *m.* a sweeper; the caste of Halālkhor.

झाडूबरदार = झाडूकश, *q.v.*

झाटट, *f.* the hair of the private parts, *pubes*: *adv.* far.

झाब, land on which jungly bushes grow.

झाप, *more prop.* झाम्प, *q.v.*

झापा, *m.* a narrow-mouthed basket.

झाबर, *f.* marshy land (on which water lies, and which produces rice), fen.

झाबा, *m.* a leathern pot for measuring oil, ghee, etc.

झाम, a large hoe-shaped instrument used for excavating earth in well-sinking.

झामक, *m.* burnt or vitrified brick.

झामर, *m.* a small whetstone (used chiefly by housewives for sharpening their spindles, needles, etc.).

झाम्प, *m.* a matted shutter: a large wicker-work cage or enclosure for fowls, etc.

झाम्पना, *t.* to cover, shut.

झामा, *m.* pumice-stone, brick burnt to cinder, vitrified brick, slag.

झारखंड, in Chand = झाड़खण्ड, *q.v.*

झारि, see झारी.

झारी, *f.* 1, = झाड़ी, *q.v.*: 2, a pitcher with a long neck and a spout to it, a ewer, kettle.

झाल, *m.* sharpness, heat, fieriness (as of pepper); acrimony: a large basket: joining or soldering of metals.

झालना, *t.* to season (pickles); to polish, clean (plate); to solder.

झालर, *f.* fringe.

झालरदार, fringed, having a fringe, mounted with a fringe.

झालरा, *m.* a water-spring.

झालरी, *f.* cymbals.

झावर = झाबर. *q.v.*

झावु = झाऊ, *q.v.*

झाषा (poet.) = झंखा (झखना).

झिंगलिया, *f.* a child's jacket or tunic.

झिंगुर, *more prop.* झींगुर, *q.v.*

झिंगूर, *m.* a cockroach.

झिंजर, a subdivision of the *gujar* tribe.

झिंझुर / झिंझूर } morning twilight, dawn of day.

झिंझोती, a certain musical mode.

झिजकना; see झिझकना.

झिझक, *f.* a start.

झिझकना, *a. int.* to start, feel the sensation of the limbs being asleep or as if pins and needles were sticking into them.

झिझकाना, see झिझकना.

झिझकारना = झझकारना, *q.v.*

झिझना; see (1) झिझरना (2) झंझना.

झिझरना, to be angry, be peevish, be fretful.

झिड़क, *f.* a jerk, a threat, an augury.

झिड़कना = झड़कना, *q.v.*

झिड़काझिड़की = झड़काझड़की, *q.v.*

झिड़काना = झड़कना, *q.v.*

झिड़की = झड़की, *q.v.*

झिड़झिड़ाट, *f.* a chiding, scolding.

झिड़झिड़ाना, *a. int.* to rage, storm, rail.

झियाहड्डा, (*more prop* छीयाहड्डा) raw-boned.

झियांटी, *f.* a kind of shrub (*Barleria cristata*).

झिनजोड़ना = झिनझोड़ना, *q.v.*

झिनझिनी, *f.* the tingling sensation felt when a limb is asleep.

झिनझोड़ना, *t.* to break with the teeth (as a dog does a bone); to gnaw, tear, rend with the teeth.

झिरझिर, *adj.* running in a slender stream (as water, etc.).

झिरझिरा, *m.* (*f.* ी) very thin.

झिरझिराना, *a. int.* to trickle, rill, flow in a small stream.

झिरी, *f.* (= झिल्ली, *q.v.*): withered wheat, blight.

झिलंगा, 1, = झिलगा, *q.v.*: 2, *m.* a kind of soldier.

झिलख़ाना, *m.* a jail.

झिलगा, *m.* the netted bottom of a bed or couch when worn out and separated: *adj.* (a couch or bed is said to be *jhilgā* when the bottom is) worn out or broken. [helmet. — *kā top*, an iron helmet.

झिलम, *f.* armour, a coat of mail, the visor of a

झिलमिल, *m.* a kind of gauze; a shutter, Venetian blind, hanging shutter.

झिलमिला, *m.* (*f.* ī) thin, sparkling.

झिलमिलाना, *a. int.* to undulate (as the flame of a candle or as water); to scintillate, twinkle.

झिलमिली, *f.* 1, see झिलमिला: 2, a kind of cloth.

झिलली }
झिल्लि } *f.* a cricket.
झिल्लिका }

झिल्ली, *f.* a cricket: a thin skin, pellicle: the membrane in which the foetus is enveloped (*secundines*); the caul (omentum).

झिल्लीक, *m.* a cricket.

झींकना, *a. int.* to grieve, lament, be vexed, think of anything with sorrow: *t.* to recommend anything

झींगट, *m.* a steersman. [seriously.

झींगर, *more prop.* झींगुर, *q. v.*

झींगा, 1, *m.* the plant *Cercumis acutangulus*, Lin.; *Luffa acutangula*, Roxb.: 2, *f.* a shrimp, prawn.

झींगुर }
झींगुल } *m.* a kind of insect, cricket.

झीकना }
झीखना } = झींकना, *q. v.*

झीका, a corruption of झोका, *q. v.*

झीन, *m.* (*f.* ā) a corruption of छीना, *q. v.*

झील, *f.* a shallow lake or morass.

झीसी, *m.* a shower.

झुंकना, *more com.* झकना, *q. v.*

झुंझनी, *more prop.* झुनझुनी, *q. v.*

झुंझलाट = झुंझलाहट, *q. v.*

झुंझलाना, *n.* to be peevish, be fretful, be petulant, be irritable: *a. int.* to rage, storm.

झुंझलाहट, *f.* peevishness; rage, fury.

झुकना, *a. int.* to nod, bow, stoop: *n.* to be tilted, be bent (especially downwards, as the bough of a tree): to be angry, be perplexed.

झुकताझूमता, *m.* (*f.* ī) *adj.* crouching and dodging to escape observation.

झुकनी, *f.* affliction, suffering.

झुकाओ = झुकाव, *q. v.* [tilt, nod, cause to nod.

झुकाना, *t.* to cause to stoop, to bend downwards,

झुकाया, *m.* (*f.* झुकाई) caused to bend. [bend, stoop.

झुकाव, *m.* the state of being bent downwards,

झुकावट, *f.* a bending downwards, stooping, nod-

झुझकना = झिझकना, *q. v.* [ding.

झुझलाना }
झुझुलाना } *more com.* झुंझलाना, *q. v.*

झुट, *more prop.* झूठ, *q. v.*

झुटलाना }
झुटालना } *more com.* झुठालना, *q. v.*
झुठलाना }

झुठालना, *t.* to prove to be false, prove to be in the wrong; to falsify, belie; to assert falsely, pretend: to pollute victuals by touching them, etc. *Muṅh* —, to eat something.

झुड़, *m.* a bush, bramble.

झुड़के झुड़, *more prop.* झुण्डके झुण्ड, *q. v.*

झुड़मुताना, *a. int.* to wither, fade.

झुड्डुप, brushwood, underwood, bushes.

झुण्ट, *m.* a shrub, bush.

झुण्टिया, *f.* a lock of hair left at the back of the head when the rest is shaven.

झुण्ड, *m.* a crowd, swarm, flock, troop; the buzzing noise of a crowd; a clump of trees, shrubbery. — *charhānā*, to feed flocks, take them to grass. [crowds.

झुण्डके झुण्ड, (used intensively) crowds, dense

झुण्डनि; 1, an old pl. of झुण्ड; 2, an old inflected base of झुण्ड; 3, an old agentive = झुण्डने.

झुण्डा = झण्डा, *q. v.*

झुण्डी, *f.* a bush, tuft of grass, thicket, jungle.

झुन, *f.* a slight resemblance.

झुनझुना, *m.* a child's rattle.

झुनझुनी, *f.* little bells worn on the feet.

झुमका, *m.* the bell-shaped pendant of an ear-ring: the wain, *Ursa Major*: a bunch of flowers or fruit: a kind of flower (*Gloriosa superba*). [a blow, etc.

झुमझुमाना, *a. int.* to smart or feel pain (as after

झुमटि, *f.* a certain Hindoo festival.

झुमरि }
झुमेरि } *f.* a certain musical tone (*rāgiṇī*).

झुरना, *a. int.* to wither, fade, pine (from grief).

झुरमट, *m.* a multitude, crowd, assembly, ball: a conflict, battle: a shawl twisted around the head.

झुरमुटाना, *a. int.* to fade, decay.

झुरा, *m.* (*f.* ī) withered, faded away. [house, etc.).

झुरियाना, *t.* to weed: to wipe, clean, plaster (a

झुरी, *f.* a wrinkle (of the body), a blemish.

झुलक, *more prop.* झुलुक, *q. v.* [of a plucked fowl.

झुलकाना, *t.* to scorch, singe (as the small feathers

झुलडी }
झुलड़ी } *f.* a fold, wrinkle.

झुलना, *a. int.* to swing, dandle.

झुलमट = झूरमट, *q. v.*

झुलस जाना, *a. int.* to become scorched or singed.

झुलस देना, *t.* to scorch, singe, sear.

झुलसना, *n.* to be singed, be scorched, be seared.
झुलसाना, *t.* to singe, scorch, sear.
झुलाना, *t.* to swing, push a swing in which others are, rock (a cradle); to make another (as a dun) dance after one; to dangle, hang.
झुलुक, drowsiness, slumber.
झुल्ला, *m.* a shirt or vest that covers the body from the shoulders downwards.
झुल्ली, *f.* a fold, wrinkle, plaits in cloth.
झुल्वां, *m.* a wreath or garland of flowers.
झूंझ, *m.* a bird's-nest.
झूंझल, *f.* petulance, peevishness, irritableness, rage.
झूंझा, *m.* (*f.* ī) dissatisfied, discontented.
झूंट, झूंठ, झूंड, झूंव; for words beginning with either of these forms, see under the forms झूयट, झूयठ, झूयड, झून्व, respectively.
झूझलाना, *more com.* झुंझलाना, *q. v.*
झूट = झूठ, *q. v.*
झूटसच, misrepresentation. — *lagānā*, to misrepresent, calumniate.
झूटा = झठा, *q. v.*
झूटाझाटा, *m.* leavings of food, offals, refuse.
झूटालना = झुठालना, *q. v.*
झूठ, *m.* a lie: *adj.* false, feigned, counterfeit.— *bolnā*, to utter falsehood.
झूठन, a Braj pl. (1) of झूठ (2) of झूठा, *qq. v.*
झूठमूठ, *adj.* untrue: *adv.* falsely.
झूठलाना = झुठालना, *q. v.*
झूठा, 1, *m.* leavings of food, offal, refuse; (among Hindoos) that which has touched food and is thereby defiled:— *chāṭnā*, to eat leavings; to be very wretched; *Jhūṭhi na pūchhnā*, to refuse even common civility: 2, *m.* (*f.* ī) a liar: *lit.* untrue, false:— *banānā*, (with acc.) to make one out a liar.
झूठाई, *f.* untrueness; untruthfulness.
झूठान, land yielding a double crop.
झूठि, *f.* lying, untruth.
झूठिईल, land yielding a double crop.
झूठी, *f.* 1, = झूठा, 1,: 2, (*m.* झूठा, 2) an untruthful female.
झूठे, uselessly, in vain, needlessly.
झूड़, *m.* a bush, bramble; shrubbery.
झूड़झाड़, *m.* a thicket.
झूढ़, *more prop.* झूठ, *q. v.*
झूयटर, *f.* ground that produces two crops a year.
झूयठनझायठन, *f.* leavings, offals, refuse.
झूयठ, *more prop.* झूठ, *q. v.*
झूना, *m.* a ripe cocoanut: a kind of muslin.
झून्व, *m.* a heap; a crowd; an association.
झून्वी, *f.* a lot or parcel of land in a coparcenary village.
झूयठर = झूयटर, *q. v.*
झूपा, *m.* a pile of mangoes or other fruit.
झूम, *m.* abundance of foliage: waving, undulating.
झूयठी = झूठी, *q. v.*
झूयड़ी, *f.* a bush, a clump of grass: the amount due from each sharer in a *bhaiyāchārā* estate.
झूमक, *f.* an assembly, ball: *met.* a battle, engagement. [(a beautiful flower growing wild in India).
झूमका, *m.* (= झुमका, *q. v.*) the *Gloriosa superba*
झूमकी, *f.* a kind of ear-ring.
झूमझूम, *m.* a gathering of the clouds.
झूमना, *a. int.* to wave, move the head up and down (said of elephants), slumber, move loose, gather (said of clouds).
झूम्झल, anger, fury, a storming.
झूमा, *m.* (*f.* ī) = झूमेला, *q. v.*
झूमाझूम, *m.* mutual or repeated attack.
झूमेला, *m.* (*f.* ī) *adj.* moving the head up and down (as quadrupeds in walking).
झूरना, *t.* to pound, grind: to shake fruit from a tree: *n.* to pine.
झूरा, *m.* (*f.* ī) withered.
झूल, *f.* body-clothes of cattle, loose trapping, housings; a bag, wallet, knapsack; a swing.
झूलनयात्रा, *f.* a certain festival of the Hindoos kept about new moon in August in honor of Krishn and his mistress Rādhā. Idols representing these personages are placed in a chair suspended from the roof of the temple or house and swung to and fro, while offerings of fruits, etc. are presented. The Brāhmaṇs are feasted, and love-songs of the most indecent description are chanted all night. This festival is usually celebrated for five days and nights.
झूलना, 1, *m.* a kind of poem: 2, *a. int.* to swing (for exercise); to dangle, hang, oscillate, swing.
झूला, *m.* a swing, a swinging-rope.
झूली, *f.* a cloth or sheet made into a fan for winnowing grain when there is no wind; a hammock or swinging cot.
झूसा, *m.* mizzling rain.
झूसी, *f. pr. n.* a certain town near Allahabad.
झूहा, a large stack of *bājra* (or *Holcus sorghum*) amounting to from ten to twenty loads.
झेलना, *t.* to brush off, waft away, fan; to swing gently.
झेल लेना, *t.* to grasp, fold in the arms.
झोंक, *f.* a shove or push in swinging; the impulse of a squall or sudden blast of wind.— *khānā*, *a. int.* to roll. — *denā*, to set fire to (particularly straw, etc.); to throw dust, etc.; to throw away (the lives of men uselessly).
झोंप°; see under the form झोम्प°.
झोंकना, *t.* to cast, push, throw, toss, cast (fuel into an oven).
झोंकिया, *m.* the man who keeps up the fire when sugar is boiling.
झोंरा, *m.* a bunch, cluster (of fruit).
झोक, *f.* a jolt, push, collision, shove; a puff, gust of wind; a bunch, cluster (of grapes, etc.).
झोकना, *t.* to cast, throw.
झोकन्व, the spot on which the *jhoṅkiyā* stands.
झोका, *m.* a blow, contact, collision; a blast, breeze, gust, current (of wind).
झोकाबाझोका, a current of wind.
झोझ, *m.* a nest: the stomach, a pendulous belly: a quarrel. — *k.* to quarrel.

झोझा, *m.* the stomach: an inferior class of Musalmāns in the Doāb, etc., chiefly converts from Hindooism.

झोझुक, a kind of grass on which camels and horned beasts feed.

झोटा, *m.* the hair on the back part of the head: the motion of a swing. — *denā*, to shake one's head with violence.

झोटटी, *f.* = झोटटा, *q.v.*

झोनैया, a division of the Kurmi tribe.

झोम्पड़ा, *m.* = झोम्पड़ी, *q.v.*

झोम्पड़ी, *f.* a small hovel, cottage, but (chiefly made of straw or bamboo), a thatched roof or shed.

झोम्पा, *m.* a bunch of fruit: a cloth with eyelets which covers the whole body: a spike.

झोरा, the stalk of a leguminous plant (such as *moth*) used as fodder.

झोल, *m.* a puckering or wrinkling (as of illmade clothes): a litter, brood, farrow, batch, birth.

झोला, *m.* a stroke of the sun: palsy: a knapsack, wallet: a bleak cold wind which dries up the ears of wheat.

झोली, *f.* a wallet, sack, pouch.

झोंरा, *m.* (*f.* ī) tawny.

झोंसा, *m.* (*f.* ī) greatly burnt or scorched.

झोड़, *f.* a squabbling; a sounding all the strings of a musical instrument at once.

झोड़ा, a disturbance, row, tumult, squabble.

झोवा, *m.* a certain tree (*Tamarix Indica*) whose branches when tender are used for making baskets, and the wood of which, when dry, is used as fuel: a large basket (without a cover) made from the twigs of this tree. The tree grows in marshes.

ञ

ञ (ṅ) is the tenth consonant in the Hindee alphabet, and is commonly called 'ṅia' or 'ṅa'. It is the nasal of the चवर्ग or palatal letters, *i. e.* it never occurs in Hindee excepting in connexion with one or the other of these letters, with which it forms compound letters, and is always the first element in such combinations: it is hence called the palatal nasal or nasal of the palatals. When combined with the letters of its class, it generally loses its horizontal and perpendicular strokes; thus, ञ्च, ञ्छ, ञ्ज, ञ्झ. Its sound is that of *n* in the English words 'flinch', 'cringe'. Much of what has been said in the article on the guttural nasal ङ applies equally to the present letter. There are no words in the language beginning with this letter.

ट

ट (ṭ) is the eleventh consonant of the Hindee alphabet, and the first letter of the टवर्ग or cerebral class. In transliteration into the Roman character this letter is most commonly represented by *t* with a dot under it (ṭ); all attempts, however, to describe its exact sound must be unavailing and misleading, —it can only be learnt by the ear. Though it is generally pronounced like *t* in the English word 'top,' yet its true pronunciation requires that the tip of the tongue be brought further back than in pronouncing that letter, and kept more firmly up against the roof of the mouth. In books this letter is constantly interchanged inadvertently with its aspirate ठ (*e. g.* कटघरा), and with ड (*e. g.* कडाह), and with त (*e.g.* टसर).

टंक, *m.* a weight equal to four *māshas*: a sword, scimitar, sacrificial knife; a hatchet, stone-cutter's chisel; a spade, hoe: borax: slope: a kind of elephant-apple or wood-apple: a weight of silver put for a coin.

टंकना, *n.* to be stitched.

टंकपति, *m.* the master of a mint.

टंकशाला, *f.* a mint.

टंका, *m.* a jingle (of plates, dishes, etc.).

टंकानक, *m.* the mulberry (*Morus Indica*).

टंकार, *m.* (*f.*?) the twang of a bow-string; sound, howling; surprize, wonder; fame, notoriety.

टंकोरना, *a. int.* to twang (as a bow).

टंग, *m.* the leg: borax.

टंगजाना = टंगना, *q.v.*

टंगड़ी, *f.* the leg, thigh.

टंगना, *n.* to hang, *i.e.* to be hung, be suspended.

टंगरी, = टंगड़ी, *q.v.*

टंगा, a large reedy kind of grass (*Saccharum procrum*) which grows on high ground.

टंगारी, *f.* (dim. of टांगी) a small axe.

टंगिनी, *f.* a certain plant (*Cissampelos hexandra*).

टंच, miserly, hard, untractable.

टंटा = टपटा, *q.v.*

टक, *f.* temper, disposition: nature: a look, stare.— *bāṇdhnā*, to stare at, gaze.—*lagānā*, to long for, expect.

टकटकी, *f.* a fixed look, gaze, staring.—*bāndhnā*, or *lagānā*, to fix one's gaze on an object.

टकटका, *m.* = टकटकी, *q.v.*

टकना, 1, = ताकना, *q.v.*: 2, *n.* to be stitched, be studded with gems or embroidery.

टकराना, *t.* to knock together the heads of two persons, to dash together, dash against, dash the head on something, to butt: *a. int.* to grope in a dark place or passage.

टकसार = टकसाल, *q.v.*

टकसाल, *f.* a mint.—*chaṛhnā*, to be educated.— *bāhar*, uneducated, unpolished, rude, unclassical.—*kā khoṭā*, spoiled in education.

टकसालिया = टकसाली, *q.v.*

टकसाली, *m.* (*f.* inī) an officer or master of a mint.

टका, *m.* a copper coin of northern India equal to two pice; money in general.

टकाई, *f.* a tax, duty, collection, imposition; a cheap trull.

टकार, *m.* the letter ट, or any symbol that may represent it.

टकी, *f.* a fixed look, stare; aim.

टकुए, *more prop.* तकुए. See तकुआ.

टकुरानी, *more prop.* ठाकुरानी, *q.v.*

टकूआ, *m.* a spindle.

टकैटा, *m.* (*f.* ī) a moneyed person: *lit.* possessed of ready money, rich.

टकैत / टकैत } *m.* (*f.* ā) = टकैटा, *q.v.*

टकोर, *f.* fillip, tap; the sound of a drum.

टकोरना, *t.* to foment. [mango.
टकोरा, *m.* 1, = **टकोरा**, *q.v.* : 2, a very small unripe
टकौना = **ढका**, *q.v.*
टक्कड़, resemblance, comparison.
टक्कवेशी, *m.* a kind of potherb (*Chenopodium album*).
टक्कर, *f.* (*m.* ?) a shoving, pushing, shouldering, knocking against, butting, striking a blow, collision, push, the knocking of head to head : equality.— *Khānā*, to stumble, be dashed against anything, to meet with misfortune or loss.— *pahārse lenā*, to enter the lists against an antagonist of greatly superior force. — *mārnā*, to knock against ; hence, *met.* to pray, to curse (from the suppliant striking his head on the ground).
टखना, *m.* the ankle-joint.
टगण, a combination of six short syllables.
टगर, *m.* borax : wanton play or sport : a wandering of the mind, confusion, perplexity.
टगरना, *a. int.* to roll.
टगरा, *m.* (*f.* ī) squint-eyed.
टगराना, *t.* to roll.
टघरना = **टगरना**, *q.v.*
टघराना = **टगराना**, *q.v.*
टघलना = (1) **टगरना** (2) **टिघलना**, *qq.v.*
टघलाना = (1) **टगराना** (2) **टिघलाना**, *qq.v.*
टङ्क, **टङ्ग**, **टञ्च** ; for words beginning thus, see under the forms **टंक**, **टंग**, **टंच**, respectively.
टटकना, *more com.* **ठिठकना**, *q.v.*
टटका, *m.* (*f.* ī) fresh, new, recent.
टटड़ी, *f.* the crown of the head : a hedge, fence.
टटपूंजिया = **दुटपूंजिया**, *q.v.*
टटवानी, *f.* a pony-mare.
टटाना, *n.* to be dried. (A low term.)
टटिया, *f.* a screen, matted shutter.
टटिरी, *f.* the sand-piper (*Tringa goensis*).
टटोना, *more prop.* **टटोलना**, *q.v.*
टटोलना, *t.* to feel for, search for by feeling with the hand, grope, touch, handle, finger.
टटोहरा, *m.* (*f.* ī) the sand-piper (*Tringa goensis*): a kind of rattle. *Ṭaṭoharese āsmān thāmā jāegā*, will the sky be supported by the sand-piper ? This bird is said to sleep with its legs extended upwards, as if to sustain the firmament ; hence, the phrase is applied to a person who undertakes an enterprize far above [his capacities.
टट्टर, *m.* a matted shutter.
टट्टरी, *f.* a falsehood : a kettle-drum.
टट्टा, *m.* a screen.
टट्टी, *f.* a screen, matted shutter ; a necessary office ; a frame for illumination. — *bāndnā*, to draw up (men in a close rank). *Shikārkī — kī oṭ baiṭhnā*, to do secretly ; to form an ambuscade.
टट्टू, *m.* (*f.* **टटवानी**) a pony.
टठिया, *f.* a flat dish used by Hindoos.
टण्टा, *m.* wrangling, altercation, quarrel, squabble, [strife.
टण्टाल = **टण्टा**, *q.v.*
टण्टालमार, *m.* (*f.* ī) quarrelsome.
टण्डेढ़ा, a corruption of **तिरेन्दा**, *q.v.*
टन, *m.* twang : pride, conceit, vanity.
टनक, *f.* a harsh sound.
टनका = **टंका**, *q.v.*
टनटन, *m.* an imitative sound (like the English 'ding-dong').
टनमन, strong at the period of feebleness (*viz.* [in infancy or in advanced age).
टना, *m.* pudendum muliebre, clitoris.
टनाना, *t.* to extend, stretch, pull.
टन्टा, a corruption of **टण्टा**, *q.v.*
टप, *m.* a spring, leap, bound : a drop : a sound. — *jānā*, to jump over, leap over.— *parnā*, to thrust oneself into other people's concerns, intermeddle, interfere.
टपक, *f.* pain, throbbing ; a dripping, the sound [made by dropping.—*paṛnā*, to drip.
टपकनवीस, *m.* one who reports erroneously what he pretends to have overheard.
टपकना, *a. int.* to drop when ripe (as fruit, etc.) ; to drip, drop, dribble, distil ; to throb, palpitate.
टपका, *m.* a drop of rain ; a windfall, fruit which falls through ripeness (particularly mangoes).
टपकाना, *t.* to cause to drip, to distil.
टपकाव, *m.* distillation, dripping.
टपकी, *f.* dim. of **टपका**, *q.v.* — *paṛnī aurat kī*, to be wanton (said of a woman).
टपना, *t.* to jump over, overleap.
टपा, an island in a river.
टपाटोआ, (part.). *m.* (*f.* °ई) groping.
टपाना, *t.* to cause to overleap, cause to bound.
टप्पा, *m.* a post-office : a jump, bound, the bound of a ball, etc. : a sort of hook : a certain mode in music : a relay of palanquin-bearers : a raft, catamaran. — *khānā*, to bound or ricochet (as a shot). — *mārnā*, to sew or stitch with intervals ; to read in a desultory manner.
टप्पाल, *m.* the post for letters ; a mail or packet ; post-office ; relays of runners or carriers for the conveyance of letters or other things.
टप्पालवाला, *m.* (*f.* in *or* ī) = **टप्पाली**, *q.v.*
टप्पाली, *m.* (*f.* in *or* inī) a postman, post-runner, [letter-carrier.
टब्बर, *m.* (prop. **तब्बार**) family.
टमकी, *f.* a small drum ; a gong. — *pīṭnā*, to issue a proclamation.
टमटम, a small drum ; the sound of such a drum.
टर, intoxicated ; inattentive, listless (like a person intoxicated).
टरख़ल, *m.* a contemptuous epithet for a woman, [a low-priced trull.
टरटर, *f.* a chattering.
टरटराना, *a. int.* to chatter.
टरटरी, *f.* a chattering.
टरना, *more prop.* **टलना**, *q.v.*
टर्रा, *m.* (*f.* ī) stout ; wicked, vicious (said particularly of horses).
टर्राना, *a. int.* to chatter.
टल जाना, an intensive form of **टलना**, *q.v.*

टलना, *a. int.* to get out of the way, disappear, vanish, pass away, retire, shrink from, flinch.

टलप, *f.* a fragment, morsel, bit, piece.

टलमलाना, *a. int.* to totter : *t.* to tantalize.

टलवाना, *t.* to cause to be given away, cause to disappear. [cause to flinch.

टलाना, *t.* to cause to give way, cause to disappear.

टलूआ, *m.* (*f.* ई) a person who watches over a stack

टल्ला, *m.* impetus sive successus in coitu. [(*ṭāl*).

टल्ले, *m.* congressus, sonitus collisionis in coitu. —*navisi*, *f.* unprofitable employment, wasting of time.

टवर्ग, *m.* (in Gram.) the designation applied to the consonants of the ट, or cerebral, class, *viz.* ट, ठ, ड, ढ, [ण.

टसक, *f.* shooting pain, stitch, throb.

टसकना, *a. int.* to move, shake; to decline in quality; to have pain. [pain.

टसकाना, *t.* to shake, move : *a. int.* to shoot with

टसना, *a. int.* to burst, split, crack (as tight clothes or a pillow stuffed too full).

टसर, *more prop.* तसर, *q.v.*

टसवे, *m.* tears.

टहक, *f.* pain in the joints.

टहकना, *a. int.* to pain, hurt, smart.

टहटह, *m.* beauty, freshness, splendour, conspic-

टहटहा, *m.* = टहटह, *q.v.* [uousness at a distance.

टहना, *m.* a branch or large bough.

टहनी, *f.* a branch.

टहनै; see (1) टहना (2) टेवना.

टहरना, *more com.* टहलना, *q.v.*

टहल, *f.* house-keeping, house-wifery, duty, task, service, business, use, work, job, drudgery. — *k.* to serve, drudge. — *lagānā*, to dance attendance.

टहलटकोर (a jingling term) = टहल, *q.v.*

टहलना, *a. int.* to walk backwards and forwards, take the air, promenade, rove, ramble.

टहलनी, *f.* a house-wife.

टहलाना, *t.* to cause to walk backwards and forwards (as a horse or a child), lead about, cause to dance attendance.

टहलू, 1, a poetical form of टहल, *q.v.*: 2, an old imperat. 2nd pers. of टहलना, *q.v.*: 3, = टहलूआ, *q.v.*

टहलूआ, *m.* (*f.* टहलूई) a manager of household concerns, a servant, drudge, laborer.

टहों, *m.* the voice of a new-born child.

टहोका, *m.* a blow, thump.

टांक, 1, *m.* a weight equal to four *māshas* : 2, *f.* an iron pin : a stitch : solder for uniting metals.

टांकना, *t.* to stitch, cobble.

टांकर, *m.* a blackguard, lecher, libertine.

टांका, *m.* a stitch : solder : a tub made of stones.

टांकी, *f.* a venereal chancre : a square piece cut out of a melon to examine its quality : a chisel.

टांके लगाना, *t.* to stitch : to solder.

टांख, an underground reservoir for water, a tank.

टांग, *f.* the leg. — *uṭhānā*, to copulate. — *denā*, to hang up, hang : to be a catamite.

टांगड़ी, *f.* the leg, foot.

टांगन, 1, a Braj pl. of टांग, *q.v.* : 2, = टांघन, *q.v.*

टांगना, *t.* to hang up, dangle, hang up by a string,

टांगी, *f.* a hatchet. [etc. (*i. e.* not on a peg).

टांघन, *m.* a kind of horse, highland pony.

टांच = टांचड़ा, *q. v.*

टांघनतुमा, *m.* (*f.* ī) *adj.* like a *tāṅghan*.

टांचड़ा, *m.* (*f.* ī) perverse, audacious, troublesome.

टांछा मारना, *t.* to hamstring (a horse, etc.).

टाकन = टांघन, *q.v.*

टाकना; see (1) टांकना (2) ताकना.

टाकी, *f.* a venereal chancre : a natural basin or fountain in a rock.

टाट, *m.* canvas, sackcloth; hemp, tow.

टाटक, 1, a charm, juggling : 2, fresh, new, recent.

टाटबाफ़, *m.* a weaver of canvas.

टाटबाफ़ी, *f.* embroidery.

टाटी, *f.* a screen, matted shutter.

टाड़ी, *f.* a small axe or hatchet.

टाघट, *f.* the crown of the head.

टाघठा, *m.* (*f.* ī) powerful, strong, firm, solid.

टाघठाई, *f.* solidity.

टाघड, *f.* a stage, raised seat, platform.

टाघडा, *m.* any station where the wandering grain-sellers called Brinjārās or Labanas deposit their stores; a venture (of goods); a caravan or large company of travelling merchants; the name of a place in Oude : the goods of a *banjārā*. [arm.

टाघडी, *f.* a kind of bracelet worn on the upper

टानना, *t.* to stretch, extend, pull.

टाप, *f.* a tap, sound of beating; a stroke with the fore foot of a horse, the sound of a horse's hoof in travelling : a bamboo fishing-frame.

टापना, *t.* to tap, beat down, flatten; to paw with the fore foot (as a horse); to whore (low phrase).

टापर, a sheet, wrapper, etc.

टापरा, *m.* a sort of boat or raft.

टापा, *m.* a hen-coop : a sort of boat or raft.

टापाटोई क°, to trifle; to grope, rummage.

टापाठोइया, **टापाटोया** } see टापाटोई क°.

टापू, *m.* (*f.* ?) an island.

टाबर, *f.* a small lake.

टाबरा, *m.* a waterpot.

टामस, *pr. n.* a certain river.

टाम्बरा, *m.* a waterpot.

टार, (prop. टाल) evasion, etc.

टारना = टालना, *q.v.*

टारी, *f.* distance, remoteness.

टाल, *f.* a stack, rick, heap (of grain, etc.) : baldness from age : a turn or trick in wrestling : evasion, shuffling, rejecting a request, putting aside, putting off, putting out of the way. — *k.* to heap: to put off. — *denā*, to evade, defer, postpone.— *mārnā*, to heap: to turn the scale fraudulently in weighing.

टालटोल, *m.* (a jingle of **टाल**) evasion, shuffling, prevarication, putting off.

टालना, *t.* to drive out of the way, put aside, turn aside, remove, move, move out of the way; to ward off, fend, obviate, avoid, prevent, avert; to evade, prevaricate, postpone, defer.

टालमटोल, *m.* = **टालटोल**, *q.v.*

टाला, *m.* evasion: a rick, stack, heap: a quagmire, piece of stagnant water: decayed vegetable matter.

टालाटोली, *f.* = **टालटोल**, *q.v.* [to deceive.

टालाबाला बताना, *t.* to put off; to drive away;

टाली, *f.* a kind of musical instrument.

टिंगटिंगाना, *t.* to twang or sound a single string of a musical instrument.

टिकट, *m.* (Engl. 'ticket', now fairly established in the vernacular, and applied to) a postage-stamp, a railway-ticket, a label, a badge, a visiting-card.

टिकटिकाना, *t.* to wag (as the tail or the head).

टिकटिकि; see **टिकटिकी**.

टिकटिकी, *f.* 1, = **टकटकी**, *q.v.*: 2, a lizard.

टिकठी, *f.* a three-footed stool, 'teapoy'.

टिकड़ी, 1, = **टिकली**, *q.v.*: 2, *f.* the spreading hog-weed (*Boerhavia diffusa*).

टिकना, *a. int.* to stop, remain in any place, lodge, tarry, stay: *n.* to be detained. [moisture.

टिकरी, *f.* a kind of soil which is irretentive of

टिकली, *f.* a wafer, small round cake; an ornament worn on the forehead, spangle.

टिकाऊ, durable, stationary, lasting, firm.

टिकाना, *t.* to detain, fix in any place, stop, lodge, station, billet, let lodgings.

टिकाव, *m.* stability, permanence, residence.

टिकाश्रय, *m.* a haltingplace, restingplace, caravansery.

टिकिया, *f.* a small cake of bread, small cake of charcoal for the hukkā; a wafer, bolus; a small loaf.

टिकी = **टिक्की**, *q.v.*

टिकोर, *m.* a cataplasm, poultice.

टिक्कड़, *f.* a thick cake of bread.

टिक्कली=**टिकली**, *q.v.*

टिक्की, *f.* a small cake or loaf of bread.—*lagānā*, *t.* to form a connexion, make interest: to earn a scanty

टिघलना, *a. int.* to rarefy, be melted. [livelihood.

टिघलाना, *t.* to rarefy, melt, dissolve.

टिटकारना, *t.* to urge an animal by making the noise described below.

टिटकारी, *f.* the noise made by drawing the tongue from the roof of the mouth to make horses, [etc. proceed.

टिटिहरी } = **टिटीहरी**, *q.v.*
टिटिहिरी }

टिटीह, a contraction of **टटीहरा**, *q.v.*

टिटीहर, *m.* (*f.* ī) = **टटीहरा**, *q.v.*

टिटोर = **टटीहरा**, *q.v.* [goensis).

टिट्टिभ, *m.* (*f.* ī) a kind of bird (*Parra jacuna* or

टिटिभ, *more prop.* **टिट्टिभ**, *q.v.*

टिड्डा, *m.* a grasshopper.

टिड्डी, *f.* a locust.

टिपका, *m.* a stain of any colour applied by the finger: the focus of a burning-lens. [press.

टिपड़ी, *f.* stocks (for the legs); a book-binder's

टिप्पन, *f.* annotation, comment.

टिप्पनी, *f.* a gloss, comment.

टिप्पस, *f.* pride, arrogance.

टिब्बा, *m.* a rising ground, a height; a sand bank or shoal in the sea.

टिभाना, *t.* to give one a small daily allowance such as merely to save him from starving.

टिभाव, *m.* a small daily allowance.

टिमटिम, *m.* a sound.

टिमटिमाना, *a. int.* to glimmer, give a faint light.

टिरेन्दा = **तिरेन्दा**, *q.v.*

टिलिया, *f.* a young hen.

टिलूआ, *m.* (*f.* **टिलूई**) a flatterer.

टिहरा, *f.* (*m.* ?) a small village.

टींट = **टीपट**, *q.v.*

टीक, *f.* an ornament for the head and neck.

टीकर = **टेकर**, *q.v.*

टीकरी, *f.* a small field of inferior land.

टीका, 1, *f.* a gloss or commentary; 2, *m.* inoculation: the nuptial gifts: a badge of sovereignty: an ornament worn on the forehead: a mark or marks made on the forehead and between the eyebrows among Hindoos (the mark is made with coloured earths or unguents, and is intended either for ornament or for sectarial distinction). — *bhejnā*, to send the nuptial gifts (they are presented by the relations of the bride to the bridegroom). —*lenā*, to receive or accept the nuptial gifts.

टीकाकर्त्ता, *m.* (*f.* trī) a commentator, annotator, paraphrast. [of sovereignty.

टीकैत, *m.* (*f.* ā) invested with the *ṭikā* or badge

टीखना, *a. int.* to cry (as a partridge).

टीटली, *f.* a kind of medicine.

टीटा, *f.* lingula vulvæ mulierum.

टीडी } *more prop.* **टिड्डी**, *q.v.*
टीड़ी }

टीपट, *m.* the ripe fruit of *karēl*: a speck on the eye.

टीप, *f.* a note of hand, cheque: the drawing a card: the raising the voice in singing: the noting anything; the act of pressing, compressing.—*lenā*, to draw a card. [compressing.

टीपटाप, *f.* ornament: the act of pressing or of

टीपड़ी, *f.* wooden stocks or thumbscrews used for torture; an instrument in which the prepuce of a boy is fixed when he is to undergo the operation of circumcision.

टीपना, *t.* to press, squeeze, compress; to grope, feel.

टीमटाम, *m.* dressing.

टीर, *f.* a transverse piece in cloths, or a breadth cut diagonally.

टील, *f.* a young hen; a woman (term of contempt).

टीलड़ा = टीला, *q.v.*

टीला, *m.* a rising ground, small hill, hillock, mount, ridge. [*nā*, to throb, shoot (as pain).

टीस, *f.* a shooting pain, throbbing, throb. — *mār-*

टीसना, *a. int.* to throb, palpitate.

टुँइया, *m.* (*f.* ī) tiny.

टुँइयाटोटा, *m.* (*f.* ī) a kind of parrot.

टुँईया, *m.* (*f.* ī) tiny.

टुँगा, *m.* scut, a short tail.

टुँगार, *f.* a pecking, nibbling (fruit, etc., more for amusement than from appetite).

टुक, a little. — *ek*, a little way. [etc.

टुकड़गदा, *m.* (*f.* ī) one who begs for bits of bread,

टुकड़ा, *m.* a piece, portion, fragment, part, division, particle, morsel, bit. *Chār—ho jānā*, to go all to pieces. *Ṭukṛe ṭukṛe kar ḍālnā*, to pound, hew to pieces, reduce to atoms, make mincemeat of.

टुकड़ापुरज़ा, *m.* scraps, clippings, shavings. — *māngnā*, to beg for the bits.

टुकड़ी, *f.* dimin. of **टुकड़ा**, *q.v.*

टुकमुक देखना, to stare, fix one's look.

टुकर; for words beginning thus, see under the

टुकसा, *m.* (*f.* ī) a very little. [form **टकर**.

टुच्चा, *m.* a rake, blackguard.

टुटका = टोटका, *q.v.*

टुटपूँजिया, *m.* a merchant of broken fortunes, man in reduced circumstances, a bankrupt.

टुणटुनाना, *t.* to tune slowly.

टुण्ड, *m.* a hand or branch that has been cut off.

टुण्डा, 1, *m.* the knob in the back part of a turban; 2, *m.* (*f.* ī) a person born without hands or whose hands have been cut off: *lit.* handless.

टुण्डियां *kasnā* or *chaṛhānā* or *bāndhnā*, to tie the hands behind the back.

टुण्डी, *f.* 1, see **टुण्डा**, 2 : 2, the navel. [der part.

टुण्डेदार, *m.* a turban that has a knob in the hin-

टुपाना, *t.* to cause to cover, cause to be buried.

टुभक, *f.* the sound of water dropping, sound of

टुमना, *t.* to vex, irritate. [guggling or gurgling.

टुरना, *more prop.* **टरना = टलना**, *q. v.*

टुर्मटुर्म, the noise made by frogs.

टुसकना }
टुहुकना } *a. int.* to weep, cry: to squeak.

टूँ, *m.* ventris crepitus. — *k.* crepitum ventris edere.

टूँग, *f.* = **टुँगार**, *q.v.* [for amusement.

टूँगना, *t.* to pick, peck, nibble, chew straws, etc.

टूँगाटाँगी, *f.* a pecking and nibbling.

टूँड़ी, *more prop.* **टूण्डी**, *q.v.* [of a drum.

टूक, *m.* a piece, bit, particle, atom: a single beat

टूकड़ा, *more com.* **टुकड़ा**, *q.v.*

टूकन, a Braj plural of **टूक**. See **न**, 6 (1).

टूका, *m.* = **टूक**, *q.v.*

टूट, *f.* a breaking, fracture; a misunderstanding or coolness between friends; harm, deficiency, loss; a passage omitted in the writing of a book which is afterwards inserted in the margin. — *jānā*, to be broken; to become ill, pine. — *parnā*, to break in upon, rush in, be collected in crowds. — *rahnā*, to be distressed, be weary, be separated, be reduced to poverty, pine away.

टूटना, *a. int.* to break, become fractured, burst, fail: *t.* to break forth upon, rush upon, assault, attack, charge, invade. [broken, decayed.

टूटा, 1, *m.* loss, deficiency, failure: 2, *m.* (*f.* ī)

टूटाफूटा, *m.* fragments: *adj.* broken to pieces.

टूटि = टूटके (टूटना).

टूटी, *f.* damage, injury, loss, failure, discomfiture.

टूण्डी, *f.* the navel; a small branch or stump of a tree broken at the end and leafless.

टूम, *m.* trifles: an ornament: a frame for pigeons to perch on. — *denā*, to push gently.

टूमटाम, *m.* a few trifles: an ornament.

टूमना, *t.* to push gently, jog gently, strike softly

टूल; see **टोल**. [(so as to draw a person's notice).

टूलगी, *f.* fun, jesting, joking.

टूसी, *f.* a bud, young flower.

टेआ, *m.* (*f.* **टेई**) sharpened.

टेओ, *f.* habit, custom.

टेओरी = तेवरी, *q.v.*

टेँक, *f.* shelter, support: a recognizing.

टेँगरा, *m.* (*f.* ī) a kind of fish (*Silurus*).

टेँगी, *f.* a teasing.

टेँरना, *more prop.* **टेरना**, *q.v.*

टेँरि = टेँरके (टेँरना). See **इ**, 7.

टेक, *f.* a prop, support, pillar; reliance; a promise, vow. — *k.* to fix, prop, establish. — *dharnā*, to be resolved on, be bent upon. — *rahnā*, to lean upon.

टेकन, *m.* a prop, support.

टेकना, *t.* to support, prop.

टेकनी, *f.* a prop, support. [indifferent quality.

टेकर, *m.* a height, rising ground; high lands of

टेकरा, *m.* = **टेकर**, *q.v.*

टेका, *m.* trust, reliance, confidence, support.

टेकान, *m.* a height, elevation.

टेकी (*Rām.*) = (1) **हठके** (2) **निश्चययुत** (3) **थापी**.

टेकेवाला, (see **ठीका**) *m.* (*f.* ī) a leaseholder, farmer

टेगरा = टेकरा, *q.v.* [of revenue.

टेघरना, *t.* to rarefy, melt, dissolve.

टेटवा, *m.* the head of a snake.

टेड़ा, *m.* the trunk of a tree: an instrument for twisting coarse thread or twine. — *hilānā*, to be afflicted with the venereal disease. [to bend, distort, crook.

टेढ़ा, *m.* (*f.* ī) crooked, bent, distorted, awry. — *k.*

टेढ़ाई, *f.* crookedness, distortion.

टेढ़ाबेढ़ा, *m.* (*f.* टेढ़ीबेढ़ी) } distorted, athwart.
टेढ़ामेढ़ा, *m.* (*f.* टेढ़ीमेढ़ी) }

टेढ़ी, *f.* 1, (*m.* टेढ़ा) crooked, etc. : 2, pride, vanity,
टेपट = टीपट, *q.v.* [haughtiness, perverseness.
टेपटर, *m.* a kind of fruit. [ing inconsiderately.
टेपटा, *m.* a large ripe fruit of *karīl*; a fizgig: speak-
टेपटी, *f.* a kind of fruit: speaking inconsiderately.
टेपटूआ, *m.* the windpipe, throat.
टेपटें, *m.* an imitative sound, inarticulate sound.
टेना, *m.* (*f.* ī) a fowl of the breed called *ṭenī* : *lit.*
टेनी, *m.* a particular breed of fowls. [tiny, small.
टेपी, *f.* a cork,
टेम, *f.* the snuff of a candle; the flame of a candle
टेमटाम, *m.* dressing. [or lamp.
टेर, *f.* tune ; voice, call.
टेरन, 1, a Braj pl. of टर, *q.v.*: 2, a calling, shouting, hallooing. [halloo : to tune.
टेरना, *a. int.* to bawl, roar, call loudly, shout,
टेरा, 1, *m.* a curtain : 2, *m.* (*f.* ī) squint-eyed,
टेलना, *t.* to remove. [cock-eyed.
टेला, *more com.* ठेला, *q.v.*
टेलूआ, *m.* a beam.
टेव, *f.* habit, custom.
टेवकी, *f.* a prop, pillar.
टैवना, *t.* to sharpen.
टेवा, *m.* calculation of nativity : habit, custom.
टेसवा, *m.* a tear. [blossoms : a kind of play.
टेसू, *m.* the *palās*-tree (*Bhutea frondosa*) and its
टेहर ; see (1) टेहरा (2) तेहर.
टैहरा, *m.* a village.
टेहला, *m.* the customs of marriage.
टोआ, *f.* the act of feeling or groping.
टोआटोई, *f.* a searching, feeling for, feeling (with
टोंक ; see (1) टोंग (2) टोक (3) ठोंग. [the hand).
टोंग, end, completion, limit, extreme.
टोक, *f.* hindrance, prevention : the influence of an evil eye.—*kar bolnā*, to speak from experience.
टोकटाक, *f.* hindrance, prevention.
टोकना, *t.* to accost, challenge, interrogate, prevent : to envy ; to look at with an evil eye.
टोकनी, *f.* a cauldron.
टोकरा, *m.* a large basket (without a lid) : a broad shallow basket ; a wicker boat covered with leather (for crossing a river, etc.). — *denā*, to beat a person at a game.
टोकरी, *f.* a small basket (without a lid).
टोकाटोकी, *f.* hindrance, prevention.
टोकापट्टा, *m.* a permanent lease.
टोटक, *m.* (in Pros.) a kind of metre consisting of four lines of twelve syllables each. [tious remedy.
टोटका, *m.* a charm, amulet, philter, supersti-
टोटक, *m.* a kind of turtle-dove. [a candle's end.
टोटा, *m.* loss, deficiency, detriment: a cartridge,
टोटी, *more com.* टोपटी, *q. v.*
टोड़ा, *more prop.* टोटा, *q. v.*
टोड़ी, *f.* a certain musical mode (*rāgiṇī*).
टोपटा, 1, *m.* a cracker, serpent (in fireworks): a joint of a bamboo, etc. ; a cartridge: 2, *m.* (*f.* ī) handless.
टोपटी, *f.* a spout.—*wālā loṭā*, an ewer.
टोनवा, *m.* a kind of hawk: enchantment.
टोनहा, *m.* (*f.* in) *more com.* टोन्हा, *q. v.*
टोना, 1, *m.* enchantment, charm, magic, witchcraft, fascination : a wedding song : 2, *t.* to grope for, feel, handle.

टोनाटानी, *f.* } juggling, hocus-pocus.
टोनाटामन, *m.* }

टोन्हा, *m.* (*f.* in) a juggler, conjurer, wizard.
टोन्हाई, *f.* a female conjurer, witch.
टोप, *m.* a hat, cap, helmet, head, cover, thimble: a bait : a stitch. [earth.
टोपना, *t.* to hang, suspend: to bury, cover with
टोपा, *m.* a hat, helmet, cap.
टोपी, *f.* a hat, cap.
टोपीवाला, *m.* (*f.* ī) one who wears a hat, an animal with a comb, crest, etc. The term was once a designation of the Persian or Moghul troops, but is now generally applied to Europeans.
टोबना, *t.* to hang, suspend.
टोरा, *m.* a ledge extending out from a wall (to keep off the weather) without pillars, eaves.
टोल, *m.* a company, assemblage, society ; a hamlet. — *mārnā*, to dash one top against another while in motion.
टोला, *m.* 1, a quarter, section, or particular part of a town : 2, a set of anything (as of chessmen, etc.); a complete assortment.
टोली, *f.* 1, = टोला, 2, *q. v.*: 2, a company, society,
टोह, *f.* watching secretly, espionage. [crowd.
टोहना ; see (1) टोना (2) टोन्हा.
टौन्हा in Braj = टोन्हा, *q. v.*

ठ

ठ (ṭh) is the twelfth consonant in the Hindee alphabet, and the second letter of the टवर्ग or cerebral class.

It is the aspirate of ट, and its pronunciation, like the pronunciation of that letter, can only be learnt by the ear. Its nearest representative in English is the sound of *th* in such English expressions as 'fathen', 'penthouse', 'sweetheart'. In transliterating into the Roman character, this letter is generally represented by *th* with a dot under the *t* (*ṭh*). Like the other aspirated letters, it is constantly interchanged inadvertently with its unaspirated form. In a very large number of the instances in which this letter occurs in Hindee, it is a Prākṛitized modification of some Sanskrit combination such as स्थ (*e. g.* ठान; Sk. स्थान), or ष्ट (*e. g.* काठ ; Sk. काष्ट).

ठई, *f.* (*m.* ठया) determined on, fixed.

ठकठक, *m.* *f.*? hard work, harassing labour, difficulties: a sound, tapping or rapping sound as of a hammer, etc.

ठकठकाना, *t.* to rat, tap, pat, sound.

ठकठकिया, *m.* a stickler, wrangler.

ठकठेला, *m.* (*f.* ī) stuffed together in a crowd, [crowded.

ठकठौवा, *f.* a kind of small boat, shallop, skiff.

ठकार, *m.* the letter **ठ**, or any symbol that may [represent it.

ठकुर = **ठक्कुर**, *q.v.*

ठकुरसुहाती, *f.* flattery?

ठकुराई, *f.* the rank or status of *ṭhākur*; nobility, lordliness; godship, divinity.

ठकुरानी } **ठकुरायन** } = **ठाकुरानी**, etc., *qq.v.*

ठक्कुर, *m.* an idol, deity, object of reverence or of worship; an honorary title = Mr. (mister).

ठख़ठख़, clack, jangling, chatter.

ठख़ठख़ी, *m.* (*f.* in *or* inī) a chatterer.

ठग, *m.* (*f.* nī, in, *or* inī) a robber, assassin, garrotter, cutthroat, knave, cheat, impostor. The term is applied as the designation of a sneaking sort of highwaymen chiefly in Central India who first strangle the unwary traveller and then rob him: hence, they are also called *phansigar*. — *lānā*, to rob, cheat. [— *lenā*, to cheat.

ठगई = **ठगाई**, *q.v.*

ठगण, a combination of five short syllables.

ठगना, *t.* to cheat, deceive; to rob. [cheat.

ठगनी, *f.* the wife of a *ṭhag*, a female robber or

ठगबाज़ी, *f.* = **ठगविद्या**, *q.v.*

ठगविद्या, *f.* the art of the assassin, robber, or impostor; cunning, fraudulent dexterity. [theft.

ठगाई, *f.* ṭhuggery, robbing, knavery, cheating,

ठगाना, 1, = **ठगना**, *q.v.*: 2, to be cheated.

ठगिन } **ठगिनी** } = **ठगनी**, *q.v.*

ठगिया, *m.* a robber, cheater.

ठगी = **ठगाई**, *q.v.*

ठगौरी, *f.* cheating, robbing, trick.

ठचरा, *m.* wrangling, quarrelling.

ठट, *m.* bank, shore, margin.

ठट्ठ } **ठट्टा** } **ठट्ठ** } = **समूह** and **ठठोल**, *qq.v.*

ठट्ठनौं, in Chand = to stand amazed, to be in a state of wonderment. [the shell of a house.

ठट्टर, *m.* the frame made of bamboo for thatching,

ठट्ठा, *m.* fun, sport, jest, joking: the name of a place. — *k.* or *mārnā* (with abl. of the object) to jest, crack a joke; to deride, ridicule.

ठट्ठामिज़ाज = **ठट्ठेबाज़**, *q.v.*

ठट्ठाय; see (1) **ठट्ठा** (2) **ठठाना**.

ठट्ठेबाज़, *m.* a humorous person, joker, jester, etc.: *lit.* jocular, facetious, funny, comical, arch, waggish.

ठट्ठेबाज़ी, *f.* waggishness, jocularity, jesting, sport, fun.

ठठ, *m.* a throng, crowd.

ठठकना = **ठिठकना**, *q.v.*

ठठना, *t.* to arrange, set in order, adorn.

ठठरा, *m.* a fence.

ठठरी, *f.* the frame of a matted screen, bamboo frame of a thatched roof, shell of a house; a very thin person; a bier.

ठठाना, *t.* to strike, beat, beat one's own head, etc. (in token of vexation), to harass oneself.

ठठुकि, *more prop.* **ठठके** (**ठठकना**).

ठठेरा, *m.* (*f.* ī) a brazier, tinker, smith: the stalk of the *joār* (*Holcus sorghum*). *Ṭhaṭhere ṭhaṭhereki badlai*, a bargain between two persons equally knowing or acute, "diamond cut diamond".

ठठेरी, *f.* a female brazier, brazier's wife.

ठठोर = **ठठोल**, *q.v.*

ठठोल, *m.* a banterer, wag, jester, etc.: *lit.* facetious, waggish, jocular, humourous.

ठठोली, *f.* humour, joking, sport, fun, jesting, waggishness, comicalness, scoffing, derision.

ठठौना in Braj = **ठठाना**, *q.v.*

ठड्ढा, *m.* (*f.* ī) standing, erect.

ठड्ढा, *m.* the beak of a paper kite.

ठणठनाना, *a. int.* to jingle, rattle.

ठण्ड, *f.* coldness, cold; a cold. [sensation.

ठण्डक, *f.* coldness, coolness; *met.* a refreshing

ठण्डा, *m.* (*f.* ī) cold, cool: free from weeds (said of a soil). — *k.* to make cold, cool, refresh, comfort, pacify, appease, assuage, extinguish. *Kalejā ṭhanḍā honā*, to have one's revenge gratified, to be pleased, be happy (by seeing a friend, son, etc. after a period of separation). — *parnā*, to abate (said of anger, virility, or wantonness). — *honā*, to cool, become cold; to be extinguished; to be pacified, be comforted; to rest; to lose virility.

ठण्डकाल, *m.* cold weather, the cold season, winter.

ठण्डाई, *f.* coldness, coolness; a refrigerant; the intoxicating drug made of *bhang*.

ठण्डी, *adj. f.* (*m.* **ठण्डा**) cold. — *sāns bharnī*, the heaving a cold sigh, sighing.

ठण्ढ; for any words beginning thus, see under the more proper form **ठण्ड**.

ठनकना, *a. int.* to throb, shoot (as pain); to jingle,

ठनठनाना = **ठणठनाना**, *q.v.* [tinkle, clink, tingle.

ठनना, *n.* to be fixed, be ascertained.

ठनाक, *m.* a clinking noise, jingle.

ठनी, *f.* a branch.

ठपना, *t.* to strike, beat.

ठप्पा, *m.* an instrument for stamping leather with, stamp, die, printing-type; printing.

ठमकना, *a. int.* to strut.

ठय; see **ठनना**.

ठयऊ } **ठयेउ** } (*Braj*) settled, resolved upon.

ठरक, *m.* snoring, a snore. — *pārnā*, to snore.

ठरर = **ठरक**, *q.v.* [of shoe worn by villagers.

ठरा, *f.* a kind of wine or spirituous liquor : a kind

ठराव, *more prop.* **ठहराव**, *q. v.*

ठरिया, *m.* a kind of earthen hukkā.

ठर्रा } **ठर्री** } = **ठरा**, *q. v.*

ठवनि (in poet.) = (1) **चाल** (2) **उठनेकी रीति**.

ठस, an imitative sound (as of a musket ill-discharg-

ठसक, *f.* state, dignity. [ed or flashing in the pan).

ठसकना, *t.* to break a piece off from any vessel of earthenware (by knocking two vessels together) without completely destroying it, to chip.

ठसनी, *f.* a rammer.

ठसाठस, filled, crowded.

ठस्सा, *m.* a mould or form into which plates of metal, etc. are beaten to take the form of pastes of ornaments, etc. ; a type (in printing), stamp or impression on coins, etc.: vanity, pride.

ठह, an iconoclast (?).

ठहर, a place, station, settlement?

ठहरना, *n.* to be stopped, be fixed, be fixed upon, be concluded, be settled, be determined, be proved: *a. int.* to stop, stay, remain, abide, reside, rest, stand, last.

ठहराना, *t.* to come to a decision, fix, stop, determine, settle, ascertain, appoint, constitute, authorize, fix on, demonstrate, prove, conclude, ascribe.

ठहराव, *m.* settlement, agreement, fixture, permanency, stability ; appropriation ; proof.

ठहल; see (1) **ठहर** (2) **टहल**.

ठहाका, *m.* a peal, explosion, succession of sounds. *Ṭhahākeki mulākāt*, meeting with great demonstrations of friendship. [against another.

ठा, *m.* a sound made by striking one thing

ठाई } **ठाईं** } *f.* a place, residence, station.

ठाउ, a Braj form of **ठाव**, *q. v.*

ठाओं, *m. f.* a residence, place, station.

ठां, *m. f.* a place, station, residence.

ठांई } **ठांईं** } *f.* a place, station, residence.

ठांउ } **ठांऊ** } Braj forms of **ठांव**, *q. v.*

ठांव, *m. f.* a residence, place, station.

ठांस, coughing, a cough.

ठांसना, *t.* to stuff, cram, ram.

ठांसा, *m.* stuffing, wadding (of a gun, etc.).

ठाकुर, *m.* the divinity, an idol ; a lord, master, chief (mong Rājputs) : a landholder : a barber.

ठाकुरद्वारा, *m.* an idol-temple.

ठाकुरबाप, *m.* a grandfather.

ठाकुरबारी, *f.* an idol-temple.

ठाकुरमा, *f.* a grandmother.

ठाकुरसेवा, *f.* (*lit.* the service of an idol ; hence,) a grant of revenue for the support of an idol temple.

ठाकुराइन, *f.* a goddess ; a lady, Madam ; the wife or daughter of a *ṭhākur*.

ठाकुराई, *f.* the rank or office of *ṭhākur*.

ठाकुरानी } **ठाकुरायन** } = **ठाकुराइन**, *q. v.*

ठाट, *m.* the frame of a thatched roof on which the straw is laid : arrangement, adjustment.

ठाठ, *m.* state, dignity, pomp, equipage ; conveniency ; plenty, abundance.

ठाड़, a contraction of **ठाड़ा**, *q. v.*

ठाड़ा, *m.* (*f.* ī) *more prop.* **ठाढ़ा**, *q. v.*

ठाढ़, steep, lofty.

ठाढ़ना, *n.* to be fixed, be erect, to stand.

ठाढ़ा, *m.* (*f.* ī) erect, straight, standing.

ठाढ़ो in Braj = **ठाढ़ा**, *q. v.*

ठान, a place for tying up an animal.

ठानठू, 1, *m.* the report of a musket: 2, worthy of belief, trusty (vulgar).

ठानना, *t.* to resolve, determine on, be intent upon, set one's heart upon, settle ; to perform.

ठाना, *m.* a place, station.

ठानादार, *m.* a station-keeper, station-master.

ठानि ; see **ठानना**, and **इ**, 7.

ठाम, *m. f.* a place, station, residence.

ठामो, *f.* a place, station, residence.

ठामू, a poet. form of **ठाम**, *q. v.* [sidence.

ठार, *m.* determination : snow, frost : place, re-

ठाल, *m.* a branch (of a tree, etc.).

ठाला, *m.* (*f.* ī) unoccupied, disengaged, at leisure.

ठाला, *m.* } **ठाली**, *f.* } = **ठाल**, *q. v.*

ठाव, *m. f.* place, station, residence.

ठासना, *t.* to stuff, cram, ram.

ठाहर } **ठाहरू** } = **ठहर**, *q. v.*

ठिंगना, *m.* (*f.* ī) dwarfish, short.

ठिंगनाई, *f.* lowness of stature, dwarfishness.

ठिकरा, *m.* a fragment of an earthen vessel, shard, potsherd ; a vessel (such as mendicants use) for carrying fire.

ठिकाना, *m.* residence, abode, dwelling, whereabouts, station, place, site ; a boundary, limit ; fixing. — *k.* to account for, search or trace an affair to its commencement. — *ḍhūnḍhnā*, to seek a residence or employment. — *lagānā*, to establish, settle, prove ; to find out one's residence. — *Ṭhikāne lagnā*, to be killed, be put an end to, be terminated, to die. *Ṭhikāne lagānā*, to put to death, kill, assassinate, make away with one ; to waylay ; to establish, settle, prove ; to find out one's residence.

ठिकांना, *more com.* (1) **टिकाना** (2) **ठिकाना**, *qq. v.*

ठिग; see (1) **ठीक** (2) **ठिग**. [or *rahnā*, to stop short.

ठिठक, *f.* the state of standing amazed. — *jānā*

ठिठकना, *a. int.* to stop, stand amazed, stop short, draw back in surprize, shrink, boggle, stagnate.

ठिठर = ठिठराहट, *q.v.*
ठिठरना, *n.* to be chill, be numbed.
ठिठरा, *m.* (*f.* ī) numbed, benumbed, torpid.
ठिठराहट, *f.* numbedness, numbness, chilliness, torpidness, torpor.
ठिठिर = ठिठराहट, *q.v.*
ठिठिरना = ठिठरना, *q.v.*
ठिठुर = ठिठराहट, *q.v.*
ठिठुरना = ठिठरना, *q.v.*
ठिठुरा, *m.* (*f.* ī) = ठिठरा, *q.v.*
ठिठुराना, *t.* to benumb, numb, chill.
ठिठोली; see ठठोली.
ठिनक, *f.* a sob.
ठिनकना, *a. int.* to sob.
ठिर, *f.* frost, coldness.
ठिरना, *a. int.* to freeze, become chilled.
ठिराना, *t.* to cause to freeze, cause to congeal.
ठिलिया, *f.* a waterpot.
ठिवना = ठेवना, *q.v.*
ठिस = ठस, *q.v.*
ठिहुनी, *f.* the knee.
ठीक, 1, *m.* sum, addition: 2, exact, even, accurate, complete, just, fit, meet, proper, true, reasonable, regular, right; *met.* parsimonious: 3, *adv.* exactly. — *ānā*, to suit, fit, answer, correspond, apply. — *k.* to put to rights, correct, adjust, adapt, fit; to beat.
ठीकठाक, exact, fit, proper, accurate, quite right, right and tight: *adv.* properly, fitly, accurately, adequately. — *k.* to put to rights, correct, adjust, fit.
ठीकमठीक, *adv.* exactly, truly, rightly, quite right.
ठीकमठीका, *m.* abuse.
ठीकरा, *m.* a broken piece of earthenware.
ठीकरी, *f.* a broken piece of earthenware, potsherd: mons veneris: the upper or moveable jaw of the cock of a musket. — *chunnā*, to evince madness, be mad.
ठीका, 1, = ठीक, 2, *q.v.*: 3, *m.* hire, fare, fixed price; work done by contract, a task.
ठीप, *f.* a kind of lamp.
ठुकड़ा, *more prop.* टुकड़ा, *q.v.*
ठुकराना, *t.* to kick, strike with the toes.
ठुड्डी, *f.* the chin: parched grain. — *pakaṛnā*, to flatter, curry favour.
ठुनकाना, *t.* to cause to knock, cause to hammer.
ठुनुक, *f.* a sob.
ठुनुकना, *a. int.* to sob.
ठुमक, *f.* the act of waving or of walking with a graceful easy air.
ठुमकचाल, *f.* a dignified pace, stately gait, graceful carriage.
ठुमकना, *a. int.* to strut, walk with grace, stateliness, and dignity.
ठुमका, *m.* (*f.* ī) short, of low stature.
ठुमकी, 1, *f.* the act of playing a paper kite to keep it up when the wind is light: 2, *f. see above*: 3, *m.* (*f.* inī) a lazy person: *lit.* lazy.
ठुमरी, *f.* (in Pros.) a species of metre.
ठुस = ठस, *q.v.*
ठुसकना, *a. int.* to weep (but not aloud): peditum ciere, suppedere.
ठुसकी, *f.* ventris crepitus surdus.
ठुसना, *n.* to be crammed, be stuffed.
ठुसाना, *t.* to cause to stuff, cause to be stuffed.
ठूण्टिया, *m.* a eunuch: *lit.* mutilated.
ठूण्ठ, *m.* a stump, branch of a tree broken off at the end and leafless; an amputated hand.
ठूण्ठा, *m.* (*f.* ī) having the hand amputated; having the branches lopped and leafless (a tree).
ठूण्ठिया, see ठूण्टिया and ठूण्ठा.
ठूण्ठी, *f.* 1, see ठूण्ठा: 2, stubble.
ठेउना = ठेवना, *q.v.*
ठेंगना, *m.* (*f.* ī) short, dwarfish.
ठेंगा, *m.* a stick, small club; a tool (*penis*). — *bājnā*, to spoil, destroy.
ठेंठ, pure, genuine: contentious.
ठेक, *f.* 1, *more com.* टेक, *q.v.*: 2, a large sack filled with grain, a portable granary.
ठेकहदार, *m.* a farmer, leaseholder.
ठेका, *m.* a plug, stopper.
ठेकी, *f.* the act of resting on the way (as a porter with a load). — *denā* or *lagānā*, to rest (as a porter with a load).
ठेगा, (in Gram.) an enclitic word.
ठेठ / ठेण्ठ } pure, genuine: contentious.
ठेप, *f.* a lamp.
ठेपी, *f.* a cork, plug, stopper. — *muṅhmen denā*, to be silent.
ठेलना, 1, *m.* acting the buffoon: 2, *t.* to shove, push, move forward by pushing.
ठेलमठेल, *f.* a shoving and shouldering, pushing, jostling.
ठेला, *m.* a shove, push.
ठेलाठेली = ठेलमठेला, *q.v.*
ठेवना, *m.* the knee; the pastern (of a horse).
ठेस, *f.* (*m.* ?) a knock, blow, tripping (against a stone, etc.); a shove, push, thrust.
ठेसना, *t.* to knock against; to pierce; to stuff, cram, ram; to eat ravenously.
ठेसरा, *m.* a sneer, oblique reflection or inuendo.
ठैरना (*colloquial*) = ठहरना, *q.v.*
ठोंकना, *t.* to knock, hammer; to drive (as a stake); to thrust with the finger, fillip, drive, beat, tap, thump. *Thoṅk denā*, to hammer, knock, drive down. *Piṭh* —, to pat on the back.
ठोंग, *f.* the act of striking with a finger or a beak, pecking.
ठोंगना, see ठोंगाना, *q.v.*
ठोंगा, *m.* a striking with the beak, pecking at.
ठोंगाना, *t.* to peck, strike with the beak.
ठोंठ, a beak (of a bird).
ठोंडी / ठोंड़ी } *more com.* ठोढ़ी, *q.v.*
ठोंसना = ठोसना, *q.v.*

ठोकन, *m.* the act of beating, striking, or driving in.

ठोकना, *t.* to beat, strike, drive (as a stake).

ठोकर, *f.* a blow, stroke, thump; a tripping or striking the foot against anything, stumble, kick; a stumbling-block, cause of stumbling. — *khānā*, to trip, stumble; to meet with misfortune or loss, encounter obstacles or difficulties. — *khilānā*, to cause a person to stumble, trip him. — *lagnā*, the striking of the foot against a stumbling-block or obstacle.

ठोकरा, 1, *m.* a fillip: 2, *m.* (*f.* ī) hard (as bad bread).

ठोकवा, a cake, pancake.

ठोका, *m.* reproof, chiding, scolding.

ठोढ़ी, *f.* the chin.

ठोयठ, a beak (of a bird).

ठोर, *f.* a bird's beak, bill.

ठोला, *m.* a cup for the food and drink of a bird in a cage: the knuckles. — *mārnā*, to strike with the knuckles.

ठोस, *m.* solid, compact, firm.

ठोसना, *t.* to stuff, cram in; to stab.

ठोसा, *m.* the presenting the thumb in token of denial (a manner peculiar to women).

ठोसाई, *f.* solidity, firmness.

ठौर, *f.* place, locality, spot, room, residence: *adv.* on the spot. — *rahnā*, to be murdered, be knocked down lifeless on the spot. — *Ṭhaur thaur*, *adv.* in many places, in various places, in certain parts.

ड

ड (ḍ) is the thirteenth consonant in the Hindee alphabet, and the third letter of the **टवर्ग** or cerebral class. Though it is said generally to be pronounced like the English letter *d*, yet it should be borne in mind that this letter, like the other letters of its class, has, strictly speaking, no exact representative in any European language nor even in Arabic;—its true sound can only be perceived by the ear. Instead of being pronounced by the upper surface of the tip of the tongue striking against the foremost part of the palate, as is the case with the English *d*, it requires that the tongue be drawn further back and that the tip of its *under* surface be kept well up against the palate. Its true sound is much more perceptibly explosive than that of the English *d*. In Hindee, this letter is frequently (excepting at the beginning of words and syllables) printed with a dot under it (**ड़**); it then loses its characteristic sound, and is pronounced nearly like the letter *r* in the more outlandish parts of the northern and western counties of England, or as in the French 'eternel'. In this its secondary form it is frequently interchanged corruptly with **ढ़**, **र**, and even with **ल**, while in its first form it is similarly interchanged with **ठ** and **ढ**. It is generally represented in Roman character by *d* with a dot under it (ḍ), and **ड़** by *r* with a dot under it (ṛ).

डंक, *m.* the sting of a reptile, wasp, or other insect, but particularly of a scorpion. — *mārnā*, to sting.

डंका, *m.* a double drum, kettle-drum; the sound of the kettle-drum.

डंकाई, *f.* the wages of a beater of the kettle-drum.

डंकारना = **डकारना**, *q.v.*

डंकिनी, *more prop.* **डाकिनी**, *q.v.*

डंकियाना, *t.* to sting (as a reptile).

डंकी, *m.* (*f.* inī) = **डंकीला**, *q.v.*

डंकीला, *m.* (*f.* ī) any animal that has a sting: *lit.* armed with a sting.

डंगवार: / **डंगवारा** } *m.* reciprocal assistance in tillage.

डंड = **डण्ड**, *q.v.*

डंवांडोली, *more com.* **डांवांडोली**, *q.v.*

डंसना = **डसना**, *q.v.*

डक = **डंक**, *q.v.*

डकडकाना = **डगडगाना**, *q.v.*

डकराना, *a. int.* to cry bitterly.

डकार, 1, *m.* the letter **ड**, or any symbol that may represent it: 2, *f.* an eructation, belch; a bellowing. —*jānā* or *baiṭhnā*, to embezzle. — *lenā*, to belch.

डकारना, *a. int.* to belch; to bellow, low.

डकैत, *m.* a robber, highwayman, pirate.

डकैती, *f.* robbing, robbery, piracy.

डकोरी, *f.* a wasp, hornet.

डकौत, *m.* a certain caste of Hindoos descended from a Brāhman on the father's side and a Gwālin on the mother's. They subsist on alms on Saturdays and are considered by all decent people as troublesome vagabonds: they are also said to be skilled in astrology.

डकौतिया = **डकौत**, *q.v.*

डग, *f.* a pace, step (in walking).

डगडगाना, *a. int.* to shake; to burn bright and clear (as charcoal). *Ḍagdagākar pānī pinā*, to drink greedily, take a large quantity at a draught.

डगण, a combination of four short syllables.

डगमग, 1, *f.* the act of shivering or of tottering: 2, unsteady, tottering.

डगमगाना, *a. int.* to shiver, totter, stagger, quake.

डगर, *f.* a road, path, highway.

डगरना, *a. int.* to walk (on the road), travel, roll.

डगराना, *t.* to roll, propel.

डगी, a shaking, moving, tottering?

डगा, *m.* a lean long-legged horse, garran, Rosinante.

डघा, a kind of vessel.

डटना, *a. int.* to stop, stand still.

डटाना, *t.* to stop, restrain.

डट्टा, *m.* a plug, stopple, spigot, cork; a fence.

डठा, *m.* a stalk.

डढोरा, *more prop.* **डण्ढोरा**, *q.v.*

डढ़मुण्डा, *adj.* having the beard cropped, deprived of beard, shaved.

डढ़ियल, having a long beard.

डण्ड, *m.* the part of the arm above the elbow; a kind of exercise (the placing the hands on the ground, and then bending down so as almost to touch the earth with the breast); (in Chand) depth.

डण्डपेल, *m.* one who exercises himself at the *ḍanḍ*.

डण्डवत, *f.* a Hindoo salutation, bow, obeisance, prostration. — *k.* to do obeisance.

डण्डवारा, a south wind.

डण्डा, *m.* a staff, ensign-staff; the beam of a pair of scales: a collector of market dues.

डण्डाज़नी, a certain mode of torture.

डण्डावत = **डण्डवत**, *q.v.* [lector of market dues.

डण्डिया, *m.* a kind of garment for women: a col-

डण्डी, 1, *m.* any one who carries a staff, a weighman, a mendicant who carries a staff: 2, *f.* a handle; the beam of a pair of scales: the tube of the corolla of the *Nyctanthes arbortristis*, which is used for dyeing.

डण्डीर, *f.* a line, stripe, score, lineament.

डण्डौत in Braj = **डण्डवत**, *q.v.*

डपटटा, *more prop.* **दुपट्टा**, *q.v.*

डपटना, *a. int.* to call out, shout, bawl; to gallop: *t.* to shout at, rebuke.

डपरा, a kind of musical instrument. [nothing.

डपोलसंख, *adj.* promising much and performing

डफ, *m.* a kind of musical instrument, tambourine,

डफ़र, a kind of sail (of a ship). [small drum.

डफारना, *a. int.* to cry bitterly, blubber, roar.

डफाली, *m.* a kind of Muhammadan mendicant who plays on the musical instrument called the *ḍaph*; *met.* a chatterer.

डब्ब, *m.* strength, power, authority: a kind of pocket: the leather with which oil-pots are made.

डबकना, *a. int.* to glitter.

डबका, 1, *m.* fresh water drawn from a well: 2, *m.*

डबगर, *m.* a currier. [(*f.* ī) corpulent, fat.

डबडबाना, *a. int.* to fill with water or tears (the eye). *Ānkeṅ or āṅsū*—, to be on the point of shedding tears.

डबडा = **डबरा**, *q.v.*

डबरा, *m.* marshy land, a puddle, small pond.

डबराडहरा, *m.* a hole or pit of water, puddle.

डबरिया, left-handed.

डबरी, *f.* a division of profits among a village community according to their respective shares.

डबवाना, *more prop.* **डुबवाना**, *q.v.*

डबस, *m.* sea-stock, provisions, stores.

डबोना = **डुबोना**, *q.v.*

डब्बा, *m.* a leathern vessel for holding oil.

डब्बू, *m.* an iron spoon. [of a river (?).

डभडेभा, uneven ground, *esp.* the uneven bottom

डमरिन } 1, see **डमरु**; 2, a prostitute. (?)
डमरी }

डमरु, *m.* a tabor or small drum shaped like an hour-glass (held in one hand and beaten with the fingers: it is one of the ten attributes of Shiv).

डमरुआ, pain in the knee-joints.

डमरू, *more prop.* **डमरु**, *q.v.* [dwelling.

डमाडोल, *adj.* having no certain restingplace or

डयन, *m.* a car or litter carried on men's shoulders, a doolie, palkee: a flying, flight (of a bird).

डर, *m. f.* ? fear, dread, awe.

डरक्का, *m.* terror, fright.

डरना, to fear, dread, be frightened, be daunted.

डरप, afraid.

डरपना, **डरना**, *q.v.*

डरपोकना } **डरवैया**, *q.v.*
डरवाला }

डरवैया, *m.* a shy or timid person, a coward: *lit.*

डराऊ, terrific, terrible. [timid, shy, cowardly.

डराक, timorous, fearful.

डराना, 1, *t.* to cause to fear, frighten, alarm, terrify, daunt, deter: 2, *m.* (*f.* ī) frightful, terrible, terrifying, tremendous, formidable, dreadful, fearful.

डराबू, *more com.* **डरालू**, *q.v.*

डरालू, a coward: *lit.* timid, fearing.

डरावना } *m.* (*f.* ī) = **डराना**, *q.v.*
डरौना }

डलक, 1, a corruption of **ढलक**, *q.v.*: 2, *m.* a sling, basket, *ḍālī* (carried on men's shoulders by means of a stick and ropes like the beam and strings of a balance. Presents of fruit, sweetmeats, etc. are usually sent in [this manner).

डलमलाना = **डगमगाना**, *q.v.*

डलवा, *m.* a large basket (without a lid).

डलवाना, *t.* causat. of **डालना**, *q.v.*

डला, *m.* a large lump, clod: a large basket.

डलिया, *m.* a basket (without a lid, like a tray): a lump of meat, etc.

डलियाझाड़, the conclusion of the sowing-season; *lit.* the brushing out of the basket.

डली, *f.* a lump (of sugar, meat, etc.).

डवड़ी, see (1) **डिब्बी** (2) **डेवढ़ी**.

डवा, *m.* a large wooden spoon.

डस, *m.* the string by which scales are suspended or held in the hand; the threads of the warp at the end of a piece of cloth which are left unwoven; the end of a piece of cloth.

डसना, *t.* to bite or sting (as a venomous animal).

डसाना, *t.* to make a bed.

डसि, (poet.) = **डसके** (**डसना**).

डसौना, *m.* bedding.

डहक, *m.* (*f.* ?) a cavern, abyss, pitfall.

डहकना, see **डहकाना**.

डहकाना, *t.* to deceive, disappoint, baulk, tantalize; to spoil, throw away uselessly.

डहकि = (poet.) **डहके** (**डहकना**). [fresh, pleasing.

डहडहा, *m.* (*f.* ī) flourishing, blooming, green,

डहडहाना, *a. int.* to flourish, blossom.

डहर, a road, path; low lands flooded with water.

डहरा, *m.* a pond, pool.

डाइन } = **डायन**, *q.v.*
डाई }

डांक, 1, = **डंक**, *q.v.*: 2, *m.* foil (under precious

डांकना; see (1) **डाकना** (2) **ढांकना**. [stones).

डांका = **डाका**, *q.v.*

डांकी = **डाकी**, *q.v.*

डांकू = **डाकू**, *q.v.*

डांग, *f.* a stick, club: the greatest height or summit of a mountain.
डांगर, 1, *m.* flowering stems of radishes or mustard : 2, a lean beast, starveling : *lit.* thin, spare, lean.
डांगरा, 1, *m.* a bull : a wooden trough or manger sufficient for the feeding of one horse, ox, etc. : 2, tall, lean, spare.
डांट, डांठ, डांड; for words beginning thus, see under the forms **डायट, डायठ, डायड**, respectively.
डांड़, *m.* 1, = **डायड**, *q.v.*: 2, an oar.
डांड़ा; see (1) **डांड़** (2) **डायड** (3) **डांड़ी** (4) **डायडा**.
डांड़ी, *f.* the beam of a pair of scales.
डांर, the waist.
डांवरू, *m.* a tiger's cub or whelp.
डांवां, *m.* the left hand ; *lit.* left. [tute, ruined.
डांवांडोल, wandering without house or home, desti-
डांवांडोलगी = **डांवाडोली**, *q.v.*
डांवाडोल = **डांवांडोल**, *q.v.* [state of destitution.
डांवाडोली, *f.* the wandering without house or home,
डांवाराडोल; see **डांवांडोल**.
डावाडोल; see **डांवांडोल**. [gadfly.
डांस, *m.* the sting of a reptile; a large mosquito,
डांसना; see (1) **डसना** (2) **डासना**.
डाक, 1, *m.* the husband of a **डाकिनी** : 2, *f.* a post (for the conveyance of letters; also, relay of horses or of pālkee-bearers); a post-office : perpetual vomiting. — *lagnī*, the being seized with constant vomiting.
डाकगाड़ी, *f.* the mail train, the post-carriage of
डाकघर, *m.* a post-office. [a mail train.
डाकचौकी, *f.* a stage in a journey where a relay of
डाकटर, *m.* (Engl.) a physician. [horses is posted.
डाकटरी, *f.* the profession of a physician.
डाकना, *a. int.* to vomit.
डाका, *m.* an attack by a gang of armed robbers. — *ḍālnā* or *denā* or *paṛnā*, to commit robbery.
डाकिन, *f.* 1, (*m.* **डाकिया**) a female robber; the wife of a robber or of a postman : 2, = **डाकिनी**, *q.v.*
डाकिनी, *f.* a kind of female demon, female imp, a witch whose evil eye causes children to pine and die (she is said to consume their liver); *met.* a termagant.
डाकिया, *m.* a robber : a postman.
डाकी, *m.* (*f.* inī) a glutton: *lit.* gluttonous, vo-
डाकू, *m.* a robber, pirate. [racious.
डाकैत, *m.* a member of a gang of robbers.
डाकैती, *f.* robbery by gangs. [checking.
डाट, *f.* threatening, snubbing, browbeating,
डाटना = **डायटना**, *q.v.*
डाढ़, *f.* a jaw-tooth or grinder.—or *ḍāṛheṅ mārnā*, to grind or gnash the teeth (from rage, despair, grief, etc.).
डाढा, fire.
डाढ़ी, *f.* the beard.
डाढे, burnt.
डाढ़ें, *f.* (pl. of **डाढ़**) the jaw-teeth.

डायटडपट, *f.* a gallop; swiftness. [threaten, menace.
डायटना, *t.* to chide, rebuke, check, snub, browbeat.
डायठ, the refuse of harvest-floors.
डायठल, *m.* pedicle, petiole, footstalk.
डायठी, *f.* a straw, stubble, pedicle, stalk.
डायड, *m.* retaliation, punishment, revenge, fine, amercement, forfeit; a stick; the backbone; an oar; a line. — *bharnā*, to pay a fine, undergo a penalty. — *lenā*, to fine, amerce.
डायडना; see (1) **डयडना** (2) **डायड लेना**.
डायडा, *m.* landmarks : a road.
डायडामेयडा, *m.* the frontier boundary between the lands of two proprietors.
डायडी, *m.* (*f.* inī) a rower, boatman.
डायड़ी, *f.* the beam of a pair of scales.
डाब, 1, *m.* a sword-belt : an unripe cocoa-nut : 2, *f.* the *kush*-grass (*Poa cynosuroides*).
डाबक, *m.* fresh water drawn from a well.
डाबर, *m.* a vessel for washing hands in; a small round tank; low ground where water settles, a pit.
डाबरनैनी, *f.* a laudatory epithet applied to females; *lit.* having large eyes.
डाभ, *m.* 1, a forest : 2, = **डाब**, 2, *q.v.* [surprize.
डामर, *m.* pitch, resin; a torch : an object causing
डायन / **डायिन** } *f.* a witch.
डार, *f.* a branch, bough : a line, rank, row. *Ḍārkī ḍār*, a succession of ranks, a band, troop.
डारना, *more prop.* **डालना**, *q.v.*
डारावना, *m.* (*f.* ī) *more com.* **डराना**, *q.v.*
डारि in Braj = (1) **डार** (2) **डालके** (**डालना**).
डारिम, *more prop.* **दाड़िम**, *q.v.*
डाल, *f.* a branch, bough; a kind of basket for raising water. [to cause, occasion.
डाल देना, *t.* (intensive) to throw away, cast away;
डालना, *t.* to throw down, fling, cast, throw away; to put, drop, shed, pour, inject, lay, push, thrust, set, shake, submit, throw, hurl, destroy; to cause, pro- [duce, occasion, excite.
डाललेना = **डाल देना**, *q.v.*
डाला, *m.* a large branch; a litter.
डालिम, *more prop.* **दाड़िम**, *q.v.*
डाली, *f.* (dim. of **डाला**) a small branch, bough; a tray (or rather a couple of trays) fastened by strings for carrying presents (the tray being generally made of twigs); *hence*, a basket of fruit, etc., especially such a basket sent as a present. — *lāgānā*, to graft.
डावर = **डाबर**, *q.v.* [form **डांवां**.
डावां, for words beginning thus, see under the
डासन, *m.* bedding.
डासना, *t.* to make a bed.
डासी (poet.) = **डासके** (**डासना**). [burning.
डाह, *f.* malice, rancour, spite, envy, jealousy,
डाहना, *a. int.* to be under the influence of the above-mentioned emotions; to become heated or fused (said of metals).

डाहल, *m. pr. n.* the country of Tripura.

डाही, malicious, rancorous, jealous, spiteful : hence, *m.* (*f.* inī) a malicious person, etc.

डाहुक, *m.* a gallinule.

डिउदाड़, a corruption of **डेवढ़ीदार**, *q.v.*

डिंगर, *m.* (*f.* ī) a rogue, cheat ; a low depraved person ; a servant, slave ; a fat person.

डिंगल, low, irregular, inaccurate (= **डिंगर**) ?

डिंगी, *more prop.* **डींगी**, *q.v.*

डिक्की, *f.* an attack, onslaught, butting with the horns (as by an animal).

डिगना, *a. int.* to shrink, go back, relapse, slide from the right path : to shake, vibrate, tremble, quaver, move, slip, stumble.

डिगर जाना, *a. int.* to go away. [cause to shake, etc.

डिगाना, *t.* (causat. of **डिगना**) to cause to relapse; to

डिटना } **डिठना** } = **डीठना**, *q.v.*

डिठियारा, *m.* (*f.* ī) possessed of the power of seeing.

डिंडिम, *m.* a kind of musical instrument (sort of small drum or tabor) : a kind of plant (*Carissa carandas*) bearing a small fruit.

डिंडिमी, *f.* = **डिंडिम**, *q.v*

डिंडिर, *m.* cuttle-fish bone (considered to be congealed foam of the sea).

डिपडी, *more prop.* **डपडी**, *q.v.*

डिबरिया = **डबरिया**, *q.v.*

डिबिया, *f.* a very small box (for medicines, etc.).

डिबियां ; see (1) **डिबिया** (2) **डिबियाएं**.

डिबियाएं, pl. of **डिबिया**, *q.v.*

डिब्बा, *m.* a small box ; a soldier's cartridge-box.

डिब्बी, *f.* a small box of any kind, cartouche-box.

डिम, *m.* a dramatic entertainment, dramatic exhibition of battle or tumult.

डिमडिमी, *more prop.* **डमरू**, *q.v.*

डिम्ब, *m.* an egg, ball ; a chrysalis ; the uterus ; any young animal ; the bladder; the spleen : an affray, conflict ; a battle carried on after the king has been

डिम्बिका, *f.* a libidinous woman. [slain.

डिम्भ, 1, *m.* pride, vanity ; 2, *m.* (*f.* ā) any young animal, infant, child ; a blockhead, idiot, fool.

डिकड़ी }
डिहड़ी }
डिहुड़ी } corruptions of **डेवढ़ी**, *q.v.*
डिहूड़ी }
डिहोड़ी }

डींग, *m.* pride, vaunting, boasting, gasconading. — *mārnā*, to make boast of, boast.

डींगमार, *m.* (*f.* ī) a boaster : *lit.* boastful.

डींगी, *f.* a boat, ferry-boat.

डींगीवाला, *m.* (*f.* ī) a rower, boatman, ferry-man.

डीठना, *t.* to see, look at, behold, to take aim.

डीठ, *f.* a look, glance, view, sight, vision.

डीठबन्द, *m.* a juggler : *prop.* adj. enchanting the sight, preventing (by conjuration) one's seeing.

डीठबन्दी, *f.* conjuring, the enchanting the sight, the preventing (by conjuration) one's seeing.

डीड़ाई, see **ढूढ़ाई**.

डील, *m.f.* stature, size, body, bulk, figure, shape, likeness : ploughed land. [site of a deserted village.

डीह, *m.* a haunt, place, dwelling, village ; the

डीहा, *m.* a small bank or mound.

डुक, *m.* a blow with the fist.

डुकरिया, *f.* an old woman.

डुगडुगाना, *a. int.* to sound (as a kettle-drum) ; to twinkle. [by jugglers.

डुगडुगी, *f.* the drum used by snake-catchers and

डुघना, a corruption of **डुबना**, *q.v.*

डुडका, a kind of disease in the rice-plant.

डुण्डु = **डुण्डुभ**, *q.v.*

डुण्डुभ, *m*, (*f.* ā) a kind of lizard (*Amphisbœna*).

डुपट्टा, *more prop.* **दुपट्टा**, *q.v.* [submerge.

डुबकी, *f.* a dip, dive, plunge. — *denā*, to immerse,

डुबना, *a. int.* to sink, become immersed. [etc.

डुबवाना, *t.* (see **डुबाना**) to cause to be submerged,

डुबसी, inundated land, land liable to be flooded.

डुबाना, *t.* to immerse, submerge, sink, dip, drown, flood ; to exhaust, ruin, demolish, destroy ; *lit.* to cause (a thing) to sink. [in, out of a man's depth.

डुबाव, *m.* a drowning : *adj.* deep enough to drown

डुबुना, *more prop.* **डुबना**, *q.v.*

डुबोदेना } **डुबोना** } = **डुबाना**, *q.v.*

डुब्बी, *f.* a dive. — *mārnewālā*, *m.* (*f.* ī) a diver.

डुभा, a small kind of waterpot.

डुरियाना, *t.* to lead about (as a horse), to lead in hand.

डुरिया लेना, an intensive form of **डुरियाना**, *q.v.*

डुलना; 1, = **डोलना**, *q.v.* : 2, *a. int.* to walk with a peculiar twisting of the body (a gait much affected by women).

डुलाडुलाना, an intensive form of **डुलाना**, *q.v.*

डुलाना, *t.* to move, shake, swing, agitate.

डुलि, *f.* a small turtle : female turtle.

डुलिका, *f.* a kind of small bird resembling a wag-

डूंगा, *m.* (*f.* ī) deep. [tail.

डूण्डा, *m.* a bullock with only one horn.

डूब, *m.* a dip, plunge, dive ; immersion. — *marnā*, to be drowned, die by drowning. — *lenā*, to receive or experience immersion, be immersed. — *denā*, to immerse.

डूबना, *a. int.* to dive, sink, become immersed, become drowned ; to set (as the sun, etc.) ; to get to be destroyed or ruined ; to become absorbed (as in business, study, etc.).

डूबाई, *f.* an unconditional bribe.

डूबाचर, *m.* an island or bank left in the channel of a river ; any low ground that is liable to be flooded.

डूबाना = डुबाना, *q. v.*

डूबारा = डूबाघर, *q. v.*

डूबोना = डुबाना, *q. v.*

डूलाना, *more prop.* डुलाना, *q. v.*

डूही, *f.* alluvial formations; a mark of village boundaries.

डेओढ़ी = डेवढ़ी, *q. v.*

डेओला = डेवला, *q. v.*

डेग, *m.* step, pace.

डेढ़, *more prop.* (1) डाढ़ (2) डेढ़, *qq. v.*

डेढ़, one and a half. The term is much used, and signifies one and a half of the thing denoted by the term which follows it; *e.g.* *Ḍeṛh ser*, a sēr and a half: *Ḍeṛh rupiyā*, a rupee and a half: *Ḍeṛh sau*, a hundred and fifty. *Ḍeṛh inṭki musjid judi banānā*, (*lit.* to make a separate temple of a brick and a half; *i. e.*) to withdraw (through pride) from the society of others. *Ḍeṛh bakāyan miyāṅ baghmeṅ*, *lit.* the gentleman is in his garden consisting of a tree and a half; the saying is applied to a person who assumes consequence without reason,— the bakāyan (*Melia sempervirens*) being a tree of no estimation or use. *Ḍeṛh pāw*, three eighths. *Ḍeṛh pauwā*, a weight, three eighths of a sēr.

डेढ़गत, *f.* a kind of dance.

डेना, *m.* a log tied to the neck of a vicious ox.

डेरः, *m.* a tent, marquee, pavilion, dwelling.— *khaṛā k.* to pitch a tent, encamp.

डेरा, 1, = डेरः, *q. v.*: 2, *m.* (*f.* ī) squint-eyed.

डेराना } डेरावना } *m.* (*f.* ī) = डराना, *q. v.*

डेल } डेला } *m.* a lump of earth.

डेवड़ी, *more prop.* डेवढ़ी, *q. v.*

डेवढ़, a contraction of डेवढ़ा, *q. v.*

डेवढ़ा, *m.* half as much again; a mode of reckoning used to denote interest in kind or in grain at the rate of fifty per cent.

डेवढ़ाना, *t.* to take once and a half more; to receive back the sum lent with fifty per cent. interest.

डेवढ़ी, *f.* a door, threshold, antechamber, porch.

डेवढ़ीदार } डेवढ़ीवान } *m.* a door-keeper, porter.

डेवलः } डेवला } *m.* mounds, high ground.

डेहुड़, *f.* a volley (as when several muskets are discharged at once).

डेहुड़ी = डेवढ़ी, *q. v.*

डैन, *m.* wings of birds.

डैना, *m.* a branch, bough.

डैसे, a corruption of जैसे, *q. v.*

डोई, *f.* a wooden spoon, ladle, oar, paddle.

डोंगर, *m.* a mountain, hill.

डोंगरी, *f.* a hillock, mount.

डोंगा, *m.* a spoon; a trough; a canoe.

डोंगी, *f.* (dim. of डोंगा) a small boat.

डोंची, *f.* a branch of a tree.

डौंर } डौंरा } = डुगडुगी, *q. v.*

डोक, *f.* vomiting.

डोकना, *a. int.* to vomit.

डोकरा, *m.* (*f.* ī) an old person: *lit.* old, ancient.

डोकी, *f.* the act of vomiting.

डोगर = डोंगर, *q. v.*

डोड़, a certain race of Rājputs said to be now extinct.

डोड़ा, *m.* a stone, a fragment of stone or brick, a brickbat.

डोडी } डोड़ी } *more com.* डोयढ़ी, *q. v.*

डोयढ़ी, *f.* proclamation by beat of drum.

डोनी, *f.* a boat, canoe, ship, coasting-vessel.

डोब, *m.* a plunge, dive, dip (in dye or colouring-matter). — *denā*, to dip into dye.

डोबा, *m.* a reservoir: fainting.

डोम, *m.* (*f.* nī) a certain low caste of Hindoos: a certain caste of Muhammadans the males of which are musicians while the females sing and dance in the company of females only.

डोमड़ा, *m.* (*f.* ī), = डोम, *q. v.*

डोमनपना, *m.* the art or practice of a male or female of the *dom* caste.

डोमनी, *f.* (pl. डोमनियाँ; see डोम) a female of the *dom* caste.

डोम्ब, *m.* a man of low caste who earns his living by singing and dancing.

डोर, 1, *m.* = डोरक, *q. v.*: 2, *f.* = डोरी, *q. v.*

डोरक, *m.* a fillet of thread or cord tied around the arm or waist; the string of a parcel or packet.

डोरा, *m.* thread, line, string, cord; the edge of a sword, etc.; a ladle; a capsule (of a poppy, etc.). *Āṅkhkā* —, a bloodshot eye, vessels distended with blood on the *tunica conjunctiva* of the eye (from intoxication or other cause). *Gardankā* —, a graceful motion of the neck in dancing. *Ḍore ḍālnā*, to stitch a quilt; to utter a long-continued sound like the amaduvade (*Fringilla amandava*). *Kis chitīne ḍore ḍāle, tukṛe ho ho lāl laṛā hai*; what female amaduvade uttered this prolonged strain (at hearing which), the male has fought so desperately!

डोरियः, *m.* lace.

डोरिया, *m.* striped muslin; lace: a dog-keeper.

डोरी, *f.* a string, cord, thread, rope.

डोरीवाला, *m.* (*f.* ī) a rope-maker.

डोरीहार, a pedlar (of thread, etc.).

डोल, *m.* a leathern bucket for drawing water: a rich black soil.

डोलः, *m.* manner: coition.

डोलचः } डोलचा } *m.* = डोलची, *q. v.*

डोलची, *f.* a small bucket for drawing water.

डोलडोल, *m.* a roving, perambulating.

डोलना, *a. int.* to move, shake; to swing; to roam, rove, wander, ramble; to waver.

डोला, 1, *m.* manner: coition: a kind of sedan; a swing: a bier on which a corpse is carried: 2, *f.* a wife from an inferior family, married by a person of rank who gives a present to her parents (she ranks below wives of equal family, but above concubines). —*denā*, to give a daughter to a superior by way of [tribute.

डोलाना = **डुलाना**, *q.v.*

डोली, *f.* a kind of sedan or litter (for females). It is an inferior sort of palanquin commonly called [a 'doolie.'

डोंज = **डोंजा** (?) *q.v.*

डोंजा, *m.* a scaffold.

डोढ़ी, *f.* 1, *more prop.* **डेवढ़ी**, *q.v.*: 2, *adj.* one and a half, half as much again (as any given quantity), raised one half higher (as a tone in music).

डोढ़ीवान, *more prop.* **डेवढ़ीवान**, *q.v.*

डोयहो in Braj = **डोयहो**, *q.v.*

डोल, *m.* manner, mode, method; shape, form, figure, image, appearance, fashion: estimate of assets for the purpose of assessment.

डोलपट्टा, *m.* the rent-roll of a farm.

डोला, *m.* a limit, boundary.

ड्योढ़ा, *more prop.* **डेवढ़ा**, *q.v.*

ड्योढ़ी, *more prop.* **डेवढ़ी**, *q.v.*

ढ

ढ (ḍh) is the fourteenth consonant in the Hindee alphabet and the fourth letter of the **टवर्ग** or cerebral class. All that is said in the article on **ड** as to the question of pronunciation applies equally to this letter, excepting that this is the aspirated form of **ड** and requires to be pronounced nearly like *dh* in the English word 'land*h*older'. In Hindee this letter is frequently (excepting at the beginning of words and of syllables) printed with a dot under it (**ढ़**): it then loses its characteristic sound and is pronounced as *r* in the French 'eternel' would be if it were aspirated. **ढ़** is constantly interchanged corruptly with **ड़**, **र**, and **ल**; and **ढ** with **ड**, **द** and **ध**; while in some founts of type this letter is printed in the Bengālee form; thus **ঢ** for **ढ**, and **ঢ়** for **ढ़**. It is generally represented in the Roman character by *dh* with a dot under the *d* (ḍh); and **ढ़** by *rh* with a dot under the *r* (ṛh).

ढई देना, *t.* to force an invitation (by fixing oneself in a house till dinner is put on the table).

ढंकनी = **ढकनी**, *q.v.* [ness; method, mode.

ढंग, *m.* manners, behaviour, breeding, graceful-

ढंगिआ, a dialectic form of **ढंग**, *q.v.*

ढंढ; see under the form **ढण्ढ**.

ढंढना, *more prop.* **ढूंढ़ना**, *q.v.*

ढंढ़ोरा, *more com.* **ढण्ढोरा**, *q.v.*

ढक, *m.* a weight. [conceal.

ढकना, 1, *m.* a cover, lid, potlid: 2, *t.* to cover,

ढकनी, *f.* (dim. of **ढकना**) a lid, cover, potlid, small cover. [quash a suit.

ढकल देना, *t.* to dismiss a complaint, reject a claim,

ढकार, 1, *m.* the letter **ढ**, or any syllable that may represent it: 2, = **डकार**, 2, *q.v.*

ढकेल, *m.* a shove, push, thrust.—*denā*, to give a push, to precipitate.

ढकेलना, *t.* to shove, thrust, push, jostle.

ढकेलू, *m.* one who pushes, etc.

ढक्का, *m. pr. n.* the city or the district of **Dacca** (*prop.* Ḍhakka); a disappearance, covering.

ढक्कन, *m.* a cover, covering. [drum.

ढक्का, 1, = **धक्का**, *q.v.*: 2, *f.* a large drum, double

ढगण, a combination of three short syllables.

ढङ्ग = **ढंग**, *q.v.*

ढटिया } **ढठिया**, *q.v.*
ढट्ठी }

ढट्ठा, *m.* a plug, cork, bung.

ढठिया, *f.* a cord used instead of a bridle.

ढडकोवा, *m.* (*f.* ī) a raven.

ढड़वा, *m.* (*f.* ī) a kind of *mainā*-bird.

ढड्ढा } a term applied to low ground.
ढड्ढी }

ढढोरना, *t.* to seek, investigate.

ढणोरिया, *more com.* **ढण्ढोरिया**, *q.v.*

ढण्डोरा = **ढण्ढोरा**, *q.v.* [subterfuge, trick (?).

ढण्ढकाढण्ढ, 1, see **ढूण्ढकाढण्ढ**; 2, deception, hypocrisy,

ढण्ढोर्ई, *f.* the scum of the sugarcane when boiling.

ढण्ढोर; see (1) **ढण्ढोरा** (2) **ढण्ढोरिया**.

ढण्ढोरा, *m.* a proclamation by beat of drum.—*piṭānā*, to proclaim by beat of drum.

ढण्ढोरिया, *m.* a public crier, one who proclaims by beat of drum. [set, spill.

ढनमनाना, *a. int.* to roll, be tossed about, be up-

ढनमनो, upset, spilt.

ढना, *n.* to be demolished, be razed, be destroyed.

ढनेक, a corruption of **धनेश**, *q.v.*

ढपढपाना, *t.* to thump a drum (as children do).

ढपना, 1, *m.* a cover, covering: 2, *n.* to be covered, be hidden, be concealed; to be submerged, to sink.

ढब, *m.* shape, form, fashion, mode, method, way, knack, style; manners, breeding, behaviour, address, art, dexterity; knowledge; position; idiom.

ढबरा, *m.* (*f.* ī) turbid.

ढबीला, *m.* (*f.* ī) well-formed, graceful.

ढबूआ, *m.* a certain copper coin equal in value to [a *paisā*.

ढबूस, corpulent, fat.

ढमलाना, *a. int.* to roll.

ढम्प, a tambourine.

ढम्पना = **ढपना**, *q.v.*

ढरकना, *a. int.* to fall.

ढरकाना = **ढलकाना**, *q.v.*

ढरखा, *m.* a scarecrow. [flow down.

ढरना, *a. int.* to draw near, come, come down,

ढरला, *m.* a scarecrow.

ढलक, *f.* a rolling, tilting.

ढलकना, *a. int.* to roll, be spilt.

ढलका, *m.* (*f.* ī) blear-eyed; spilling.

ढलकाना, *t.* to overturn, tilt, spill, pour, roll.

ढलना, *a. int.* to flow, spill, roll, be poured out, be cast (as metal); to incline, decline (as the day towards evening). *Din* —, *a. int.* to decline (as day). *Ḍhalti phirti chhāṅw, lit.* rolling and turning shade: the phrase is applied (1) to the changeable character and state of worldly concerns, (2) *met.* to a person of capricious or unsteady temper or disposition.

ढलमलाना, *a. int.* to totter, move from side to side.

ढलाऊ, *adj.* sloping. [cause to cast (as metal).

ढलाना, *t.* (causat. of **ढालना**) to cause to pour,

ढलैत, *m.* a person in the equipage of great men armed with sword and buckler, constable, targeteer, shield-beam. [ing to a *ḍhalait*.

ढलैती, *f.* the status of *ḍhalait*: *adj.* appertain-

ढल्ला, *m.* a piece of clay, clod.

ढवाना, *t.* (causat. of **ढाना**) to cause to be razed, cause to be demolished.

ढहना, *a. int.* to fall, tumble down (as a house): *n.* to be destroyed, be demolished.

ढहपड़ना / **ढहेपड़ना** } intensives of **ढहना**, *q. v.*

ढाई, (= **अढ़ाई**, 2: see **अ**, 18) two and a half.

ढांकना, *t.* to cover, shut.

ढांग, *f.* a precipice, cliff.

ढांचा, *m.* a frame; a plan.

ढांपना, *t.* to cover, conceal, hide.

ढांस, a cough, cold.

ढांसना, *t.* to blame, accuse.

ढांसा, *m.* calumny, defamation, undeserved abuse.

ढाक, *m.* a certain tree (*Butea frondosa*).

ढाका, *m. pr. n.* the district or the city of Dacca (*prop.* Ḍhākkā): *lit.* a thick wood of *ḍhāk*-trees.

ढाख, *more com.* **ढाक**, *q.v.*

ढाखा; see (1) **ढाक** (2) **ढाका**.

ढाटा, *m.* a handkerchief tied over the head and over the ears. [fastened on a horse's nose.

ढाठो, *f.* rack, torment, torture; a noose or gin

ढाड़स, *f. m.*? firmness of mind, confidence, animation, encouragement, comfort.— *denā*, to animate, encourage, to take heart.— *bandhānā*, to encourage, comfort, keep one in spirits.

ढाड़ी, *m.* (*f.* in) a kind of musician, singer.

ढाढ़स = **ढाड़स**, *q. v.*

ढाढ़िन, *f.* / **ढाढ़ी**, *m.* } = **ढाड़ी**, *q. v.*

ढान, *m.* an inclosure, hedge.

ढाना, *t.* to break, batter, knock down, demolish, raze (a building. etc.).

ढापना, *t.* to cover, conceal, hide.

ढाबर, filth, dirt.

ढाबा, *m.* a net: the eaves of a house (extending three or four feet beyond the wall, so that persons might sit under them).

ढाम्पना, *t.* to cover, conceal, hide. [target.

ढार, *m.* a declivity; a heap of corn; a shield; a

ढारना, *more prop.* **ढालना**, *q. v.*

ढारी, *f.* a certain Hindoo caste. [target.

ढाल, 1, *m.* a declivity, slope: 2, *f.* a shield; a

ढालना, *t.* to cast (metal in fusion); to pour out, spill, tilt: *met.* to do mischief, mar, spoil.

ढालमोल, complete transfer by sale. [metal).

ढालवां, *m.* (*f.* **वीं**) sloping, declivitous: cast (as

ढाला, *m.* a branch, bough.

ढाली, 1, *f.* = **डाली**, *q.v.*: 2, *m.* (*f.* inī) a shield-bearer, warrior armed with a shield.

ढालू, *adj.* slant, sloping: spoiling, doing mischief: casting (metals). — *bhār k.* to shift goods, etc. occasionally over shallows, etc.

ढाहना = **ढाना**, *q. v.*

ढाहा, *m.* the precipitous or high bank of a river.

ढिग, *m.* (*f.* ?) side, quarter: *postp.* near, close to.

ढिगार, *m.* a store, heap. [ram, etc.)

ढिच्चा, *m.* a blow of the head (from a fighting-

ढिठाई, *f.* forwardness, impudence, audacity, presumption, pertness, temerity, petulance.

ढिठाय, *more com.* **ढिठाई**, *q.v.*

ढिढोर, 1, see (1) **ढपढोरा** (2) **ढपढोरिया**; 2, a certain caste of Hindoos.

ढिढोरा, *more com.* **ढपढोरा**, *q. v.*

ढिबका, *m.* protuberance.

ढिमढिमी, *f.* a tambourine.

ढिलवांस; see **ढेलवांस**.

ढिल्लड़, lazy, indolent.

ढिल्लाई, *f.* laziness, indolence.

ढींखर, a kind of harrow consisting of a bundle of thorns tied together and drawn by bullocks.

ढींग, a heap, store.

ढीठ, *m.* (*f.* ā) an impudent person, etc.: *lit.* forward, bold, impudent, familiar, daring, confident, pert, presumptuous, troublesome, rebellious, overweening, more free than welcome: seen.

ढीठाई = **ढिठाई**, *q. v.*

ढीढ़, *m.* a large belly: pregnancy.

ढीढा, the back.

ढील, *f.* looseness, remissness, relaxedness, laziness, inattention, delay, caution, foresight.

ढीला, *m.* (*f.* ī) not tight, loose, remiss, lazy, inattentive, dilatory.

ढीलाई, *f.* = **ढील**, *q. v.*

ढीहा, *m.* a rising ground; mounds. [form **ढुपढ**.

ढुपढ; for words beginning thus, see under the

ढुंढेरा, *more prop.* **ढपढोरा**, *q.v.*

ढुकना, *a. int.* to enter, penetrate: *t.* to look, take aim, have regard or inclination to, sympathize.

ढुकली, *f.* a machine for raising water.

ढुक्की लगाना, *t.* to take aim.

ढुलना, *a. int.* to be poured out, roll, be spilt.

ढुलवाना, see **ढलाना**.

ढुलाई, *f.* the act of carrying or removing: the price paid for carrying, etc.

ढुलाना, *t.* to cause to be carried: to spill (as water etc.). [dary.

ढुस्रा, *m.* a mound, bank of earth raised as a boun-

ढूंढ, ढूंठ, ढूंढू; for words beginning thus, see under [the form ढूंढ.

ढूड़ना } more prop. ढूपढना, *q.v.*
ढूढ़ना }

ढूकना, *t.* to shut, close; to steal upon, approach, draw nigh; to go into, enter.

ढूका, *m.* a tapping or shoving a person by way of calling his attention: a hidingplace, lair.

ढूपढठांढ़ = ढूपढठापढ, *q.v.*

ढूपढ, *m. f.* (?) a seeking, search. [inquiry.

ढूपढठापढ, *m.* a strict search, investigation, quest,

ढूपढन, *m.* a seeking, search.

ढूपढना, *t.* to seek, search for. [tion.

ढूपढनाठापढना, *t.* to carry on a strict investiga-

ढूपढ़ना = ढूपढना, *q.v.*

ढूपढनेहार, one by whom an inquiry is carried on.

ढूपढलाना, *t.* to seek, search for.

ढूपढवाना, *t.* to cause to seek.

ढूपढाढ़ = ढपढठापढ, *q.v.*

ढूपिठया, *m.* a mendicant of the *Jain* sect.

ढूरवा, *m.* a pea.

ढूलो = ढोली, *q.v.*

ढूसर, *m.* a certain caste of Hindoos.

ढूह = ढोह, *q.v.*

ढूहा, *m.* a scarecrow: a mound.

ढे, a certain subdivision of the *Jāṭ* tribe.

ढेऊ, *m.* a wave, surge: a whim.

ढेंकर; see ढींखर.

ढेंकली, *f.* a certain mode of joining breadths of cloth or of cutting out cloth: a kind of machine for drawing water (being a lever supported on a long post, and having a bucket suspended at one end and a weight of earth or stone at the other).

ढेंका, *m.* } a pounding-machine.
ढेंकी, *f.* }

ढेंगा, a walking-stick.

ढेंड़स, *m.* a kind of gourd.

ढेंढ़ी, *f.* the poppy-head, capsule of the poppy or of the cotton-tree: an ear-ornament.

ढेक, *m.* the Indian crane (*Ardea Sibirica*).

ढेड़, *more prop.* ढेढ़, *q.v.*

ढेड़ी, *f.* (prop. ढेरी) a heap.

ढेढ़, *m.* name of a tribe of workers in leather; a a certain low caste of Hindoos: a crow.

ढेढ़ी, *f.* an ear-ornament.

ढेपढा, *m.* a large belly; pregnancy.

ढेन, *f.* a milch cow.

ढेपा, 1, a large lump or clod of earth; arable land: 2, *m.* (*f.* ई) corpulent, bulky. [dia as 'pice'.

ढेबुआ, the unstamped lump of copper used in In-

ढेर, *m.* a heap, mound, accumulation; a parcel: *adj.* much, abundant, enough.

ढेरा, *m.* (*f.* ई) squint-eyed, squinting. [property.

ढेरी, 1, *f.* a heap: 2, *m.* (*f.* इनी) a sharer in landed

ढेलवांस, *m.* a sling. [sling.

ढेलवांसी, *m.* (*f.* इनी) a person who throws with a

ढेला, *m.* a clod, lump of earth, lump of chalk, pellet of clay for shooting at birds.

ढेलाचौथ, *f.* the fourth day of the light half of *Bhādoṅ*,—a festival on which Hindoos pelt each other with lumps of earth or with stones, and even throw them into each other's houses; and if they are abused, they consider the abuse an honour.

ढेलो डारी देना, to act remissly.

ढेव, *m.* a wave, surge: a whim.

ढेहा, *m.* a kind of Hindoo fakeer; a tribe of Jāṭs.

ढैया, *m.* a measure of two and a half sérs.

ढैयाटेकर, desolated. [on festival days.

ढैःआ, *m.* fruit and flowers presented by inferiors

ढोंग, fraud, trickery, deceit.

ढोंगिया, fraudulent, deceitful.

ढोंचा = ढौंचा, *q.v.*

ढोंढ } = ढोपढ, *q.v.*
ढोंढ़ }

ढोंस (from डसना); see ढूल.

ढोक, *f.* salutation, obeisance.

ढोकना, *t.* to drink, tope.

ढोकर, a certain Hindoo metre (?).

ढोका, *m.* a piece of stone, small stones of an inferior quality extracted from the Chanār quarries.

ढोटा, *m.* (*f.* ई) a child, son (*esp.* a very fine, fat,

ढोढ़ा = ढोरा, *q.v.* [robust one).

ढोपढ, *f.* a capsule or seed-vessel (especially of the

ढोना, *t.* to take up, carry, bear away. [poppy.)

ढोर, *m.* cattle.

ढोरा, *m.* the representation of a tomb carried about on the Muharram: a kind of insect very de-

ढोरी, *f.* eagerness, ardour. [structive to *chanā*, etc.

ढोल, *m.* a large drum, kettle-drum.

ढोलक, *f.* a small drum.

ढोलकिया, *m.* a person who plays on the *ḍholak*.

ढोलकी, *f.* a small drum.

ढोलन, *m.* a friend, sweetheart.

ढोलना, *m.* a little amulet in the shape of a drum.

ढोला, *m.* a boy: *pr. n.* a famous lover in Hin-

ढोलिया, *m.* a drummer. [dustan.

ढोली, 1, *m.* a drummer: 2, *f.* a bundle of one hun-

ढोस (from डसना); see ढूल. [dred betel leaves.

ढोह, elevated grounds in the midst of ravines.

ढौ, deep water, a deep pool in a river; an eddy.

ढौंचा, four and a half.

ण

ण (ṇ) is the fifteenth consonant in the Hindee alphabet, and the fifth letter of the टवर्ग or cerebral class. It is called ṇa, and is sometimes said to be equivalent in sound to n in the English word 'can': it has, however, no exact representative in any English sound, so that it is impossible to describe accurately its true sound, — the ear only can guide. When it is properly pronounced there seems to the ear to be an attempt at a compromise between न and ड़, so that मणि, for example, might seem to the unaccustomed ear to be pronounced *muṛi*, with, however, an infusion of the n-sound distinctly traceable in the sound of these ṛs. This letter is represented in the present work by ṇ with a dot under it; *e. g.* Brāhmaṇ = ब्राह्मण. It is doubled by two faint oblique strokes joining each of the outer strokes to the middle one; *e. g.* ण्ण. It is the nasal of the टवर्ग letters, and stands in the same relation to them that ङ and ञ stand in to the letters of their respective classes. Combined with the cerebrals, it loses only its last stroke to the right; thus ण्ट, ण्ठ, ण्ड, ण्ढ. Like the other nasals, this letter is constantly liable to be represented in print by *anuswār*; *e. g.* खंड: it has, accordingly, been usual to insert nearly all such words twice. In the present work it has been thought important to avoid this needless prodigality of space, and to insert such words only once, — the more correct form being the one fixed upon for insertion; *e. g.* खण्ड: the pronunciation of this form is nearly *khaṇd*, while that of the form खंड should be nearly *khangd*, — a corrupt sound. To the eye it is usual to distinguish this letter (in transliterating into Roman characters) from the dental n (न) by putting a dot under it; thus *bhaṇḍār*. It might be observed that in the Hindee literature this letter is constantly interchanged inaccurately with न, and this, even to the extent of forming what are, theoretically, impossible combinations; *e. g.* टन्टा: this combination might be said to be impossible; for when the n-sound precedes any letter of the टवर्ग in the same word, and without the intervention of a vowel, it must always be represented by this letter ण; — this, indeed, is what is meant when it is said that ण is the nasal of the टवर्ग. If, again, the n-sound be preceded in the same word by either of the letters ऋ, ॠ, र or ष, it should always be written ण, and this, even though any letter of the guttural or labial class, any vowel, the semivowels य or व and the letter ह, or *visarg* or *anuswār* intervene. If the n-sound be *final* in a word (*i. e.* if no vowel-sound follow it, — not even the inherent vowel-sound) it is always written न, whatever letters may precede it in the same word: immediately, however, any vowel-sound is added in the same word, the न gives place to ण if the foregoing letters be such as to call for the change; thus अचरिन्, *m.*: अचरिणी, *f.* When न occurs under such circumstances, it is always (in theory if not to the eye) followed by *virām*. As has been already observed (Art. अ), the genius of the Hindee language requires (contrary to the rule which is uniform in the case of Sanscrit) that the inherent vowel be not pronounced at the end of all words and syllables: accordingly, although ण terminate a word (thus indicating that in Sanscrit that word must be pronounced with the inherent vowel at the end), yet in Hindee the inherent vowel is, generally speaking, not pronounced in such case, excepting in poetry where the metre may require that it be retained. The retention of ण serves to shew the true mode of spelling the word, and indicates what the pronunciation of the word would be in Sanscrit and in metrical composition; thus रामायण would be pronounced in Hindee 'Rāmāyaṇ' but in Sanscrit 'Rāmāyaṇa'. If the n-sound be followed in the same word by a letter which is not of the टवर्ग, and without the intervention of a vowel-sound, it should be written न (never ण); and this, even though, in the absence of that letter, the ण would, properly speaking, be required; *e. g.* गिण; but गिन्ती (not गिणती). Lastly, in Hindee the rule for the change of न into ण never operates in the case of the ना of the infinitive mode, even though the verbal substantive end in ण; *e. g.* पढ़ना (never पढ़णा, although पढ़ण).

Inasmuch as this letter always requires a vowel-sound before it in the same word, there are no words in Hindee that begin with it: in the older Prākrit dialects, however, it is very frequently found at the beginning of words; *e.g.* णारियलो, *i.e* नारियल; in fact, inasmuch as the letter न does not occur in those dialects, this letter is uniformly substituted for it.

णकार, *m.* the letter ण, or any symbol that may represent it.

णगण, a combination of two short syllables.

त

त (t) is the sixteenth consonant in the Hindee alphabet, and the first letter of the तवर्ग or dental class. 1, It is almost as difficult to quote exact equivalents in English of the Devanāgaree dental letters as of the cerebrals, — the ear only can safely guide. It may be observed that though the sound of this letter resembles that of the English t, yet instead of the front edge of the tongue being placed against the front part of the roof of the mouth near the roots of the teeth, the exact pronunciation of त requires rather that the upper surface of the tip of the tongue be pressed gently against the upper front teeth: the sound, indeed, should be very perceptibly softer than the ordinary sound of the English t, as in the Irish pronunciation of t in the word 'water.' 2, As a Kridanta suffix this letter forms the masculine of past passive participles, — the feminine being formed by the addition of आ; *e. g.* कृत, *m.* (*f.* कृता). 3, Standing alone this letter has a variety of unconnected meanings, *viz.* an outcaste, barbarian: a wicked man: a thief: nectar: a tail: the flank: crossing: a tree. 4. When followed by त or by र without the intervention of any vowel-sound, this letter assumes the form of a single horizontal stroke; *e. g.* त्त = tt; त्र (freq. त्र) = tr; त्त्र = ttr. 5, In Braj, in the *patois*, and in poetry, this letter is often the only sign of the present participle, — the gender and the number of the nominative being a matter of inference; *e. g.* वह चलत (= चलता or चलती) है: also वे कहत (= कहते or कहतीं) हैं. 6, In works on prosody this letter is used for the metrical foot called Hypo-bacchic(— — ⏑) consisting of two long syllables followed by one short one.

तअ़रीफ़, *more com.* **तारीफ़**, *q.v.*

तअ़ल्लुक़, *more com.* **ताल्लुक़**, *q.v.*

तआ़क़ुब, *m.* a pursuit; a persecuting; a following; alternate succession.

तआ़ब, *m.f.* labour, toil, trouble, lassitude, weariness.

तआ़बीर, *f.* explanation, interpretation.

तआ़वुन, *m.* assistance; a conspiring.

तआ़रुफ़, *m.* mutual acquaintance; rule, fashion, custom; handing a thing to a person.

तआ़ला, *adj.* the Most High.

तई, 1, *more prop.* **तईं**, *q.v.*: 2, in Braj = **वहीं**, *q.v.*

तईं = **तक**, 2, *q.v.* This postposition always imparts the accusative sense to the word to which it may be subjoined, and always requires that that word be in the inflected form of the genit. masc.; *e.g. Maiṅ shahr-ke taiṅ gayā.*

तइ } **तइं** } *more prop.* **तईं**, *q.v.*

तइयार, *more prop.* **तैय्यार**, *q.v.*

तईयार, *more prop.* **तैय्यार**, *q.v.*

तउ } **तऊ** } in Braj = (1) **तो** (2) **तौ** (3) **तोभी**, *qq.v.*

तउला, a kind of large earthen vessel.

तंग, 1, strait, narrow; tight; wanting, scarce, barren: 2, *m.* a girth: a sack: a bell: half a load. — *ānā*, to be distressed, be exhausted, be dejected.

तंगा, *m.* a copper coin equal in value to two *paisā.*

तंगी, *f.* want: a sack, bag. — *k.* to act the miser, act parsimoniously.

तंकी; see **तंग**.

तंज़, *f.* mirth, joking, pleasantry, jest; a ridiculing, sneering, taunting.

तंजीम, *f.* astrology; the predicting anything from the appearance of stars.

तक, 1, *f.* a scale, balance: aim. — *bāndhnā* or *lagānā*, to fix one's gaze, stare at: 2, *postp.* up to, to, near to, towards, at, till, while, as long as, as far as.

तकतक, *m.* the sound of feet.

तकतकी, *f.* a carpenter's level.

तक़दीर, *f.* fate, predestination, Divine decree, ordination of the Supreme.

तकना, *n.* to be looked at, be stared at: *t.* to look at, observe, watch, aim at.

तकफुंस, wrapping (herself) up in her garments (said of an old woman).

तकरार, *f.* repetition, tautology; altercation, dispute, contention. — *k.* to carry on an altercation.

तकला, *m.* a spindle.

तकली, *f.* a weaver's reel.

तकलीफ़, *f.* (*pll.* āt *or* eṅ) ceremony, imposition of a burden; trouble, distress, difficulty, inconvenience, annoyance, molestation, affliction, ailment. — *k.* to take the trouble. — *denā*, to annoy, etc.

तकलुफ; see (1) **तकल्लुफ़** (2) **तकलीफ़**.

तकवाही, *f.* a watching, overseeing, superintending, looking sharp after (as after a silversmith).

तक़सीर, *f.* (*pll.* āt *or* eṅ) deficiency, fault, error, crime.

तक़सीरवार, faulty, blameable, transgressing, criminal.

तकल्लुफ़, (*pl.* āt) undertaking, attempting; undergoing, enduring; taking pains, striving; pains, attention, industry, perseverance; inconvenience, trouble: ceremony, dissimulation, insincerity.

तकान, *m.* motion, agitation, gesture.

तकाना, *t.* to aim, take aim.

तकार, *m.* the letter **त**, or any symbol that may represent it.

तकिआ, *more com.* (1) **तक** (2) **तकिया**, *qq.v.*

तकिया, *m.* a pillow; a fakeer's stand; the reserve of an army. — *kisipar k.* to depend upon some one. — *k.* to support, encourage. — *denā*, to receive respectfully. — *lagānā*, to lean upon.

तकियादार } **तकियानिशीन** } *m.* a fakeer, dervise.

तकीनी, *m.* a small pillow.

तकूआ, *m.* a spindle.

तकोरे, a small kettle-drum.

तक्का, *more prop.* **तकता** (**तकना**).

तक्र, *m.* buttermilk with a fourth part water.

तक्राट, *m.* a churning-stick.

तक्षक, *m.* one of the principal serpents (*nāg*) of the lower regions; a snake of a middle size and of a red colour: a cutter, wood-cutter.

तक्षण, *m.* a planing.

तक्षणी, *f.* a carpenter's adze.

तक्षन्, *m.* a carpenter.

तक्षशिला, *f. pr. n.* a certain city in the Panjāb, (the Taxila of Ptolemy).

तख़्त, *m.* a throne. — *se utarnā*, to dethrone.

तख़्तगाह, *f.* the royal residence, seat of government, metropolis.

तखतनर्द = **तख़्तानर्द**, *q.v.*

तख़्तनिशीन, *m.* a king, monarch, prince.

तख़्तनिशीनी, *f.* accession to a throne, reign.

तख़्तपोश, *f.* a stage, platform, covered stage.

तख़्ता, *m.* a plank, board; a stool; a bier; a sheet of paper.

तख़्तानर्द, *m.* backgammon or the game of *chausar.*

तख़्ती, *f.* a small plank, a little board like a slate which children write on; a signet of stone; a kind of amulet; a small sign-board, notice-board, the breast.

तख्तेनर्द } **तखतेनर्द** } = **तख़्तानर्द**, *q.v.*

तखन; see **तक्षण** and **तक्षन्**.

तखन, (correl. of **जखन**, *q.v.*) then.

तखतनशीन, *more prop.* **तख़्तनिशीन**, *q. v.*

तख़ना, *m.* the ankle, ankle-joint.

तखनि = **तखन**, *q. v.*

तख़फ़ीफ़, making light, lifting up; despising; abbreviating; alleviation, remission, diminution, decay.

तख़मा, *m.* indigestion.

तख़मीनन्, *adv.* by guess, hypothetically, by appraisement, nearly, about.

तख़मीना, *m.* guess, conjecture, appraisement, valuation.

तख़मीर, *f.* fermentation, leavening.

तख़य्युल, *f.* fancying, imagining, supposing, suspicion.
तख़री, *f.* scales (of a balance). [waste (a country).
तख़रीब, *f.* devastation, destruction, razing, laying
तख़ल्लुल, *m.* disturbance, discord, dissension, inter-
तख़वीफ़, *f.* a terrifying, threatening. [ruption.
तख़सीस, *f.* particularity, peculiarity, preserving for oneself, appropriating.
तखान, *m.* (prop. तक्षन्) a carpenter.
तख़ालुफ़, *m.* opposition, enmity.
तग, *more prop.* तक, 2, *q.v.*
तगईर = तग़ैयुर, *q.v.*
तग़ज़िया, *m.* food, nourishment.
तगट, gold or silver tinsel or leaf.
तगड़, any thin flat piece of metal, a plate of metal, a device on a shield, a medal.
तगण, (see त, 6) *m.* (in Pros.) the measure called Hypo-bacchic or Anti-bacchic.
तगना, *t.* to stitch together, quilt. [ductions.
तग़मा, *m.* a mark which artists put on their pro-
तगय्युर = तग़ैयर, *q.v.*
तगर, *m.* a certain ornamental plant (*Tabernaemontana coronaria*) and an aromatic powder made from it. [sition, forgery, embezzlement.
तग़ल्लुब, *m.* a taking advantage, cheating, impo-
तगा, *m.* the manna of bamboos. [quilting.
तगाई, *f.* price paid for quilting, etc.; the act of
तगाना, *t.* to cause to be quilted, to get a thing stitched together. [sorbed, as in sleep, etc.
तग़ाफ़ुल, *m.* negligence, inadvertency, a being ab-
तगापू, *f.* bustle, labour, toil.
तग़ायुर, *m.* a differing from each other, discrepancy.
तग़ार, *m.* a tub, bucket, trough, platter.
तग़ीर, 1, *f.* alteration, change: 2, changed, discharged, dismissed. — *k.* to remove from office, dis-
तगेड़ना, *t.* to pursue closely, chase. [miss; to alter.
तग़ैयुर, *m.* change, alteration, removal.
तग़ैर; see (1) तग़ीर (2) तग़ैयुर.
तग्गा, *f.* a strand or thread of a twist, thread for sewing with. [fishing-line not used with a rod.
तग्गी, *f.* a strand or thread of a twist; a kind of
तग्याना, *t.* to cause to run or gallop.
तघड़ी, *f.* a girdle, zone.
तचना, *a. int.* to become heated, to parch.
तचाना, *t.* to scorch, to parch.
तज, 1, (as a verbal root) abandoning, forsaking: 2, *f.* the bay-tree (*Laurus cassia*) or its bark, woody cassia.
तज़ईन, *f.* a dressing oneself, decoration, orna-
तज़ईफ़, a doubling, duplication. [ment, jewel, honor.
तज़किरा, *m.* memory, remembrance; a memoir; a schedule; obligation. [mentioning; admonishing.
तज़कीर, *f.* a bringing to memory, commemoration,
तजज़ी, *f.* a separating into small pieces, analysis.
तजत, (old form) = तजता (तजना). See त, 5.
तजदीद, *f.* renovation, renewal.
तजना, *t.* to abandon, desert, quit, leave.
तजनीस, *f.* resemblance, analogy; equivocation; punning (to the eye instead of the ear).
तजम्मुल, *m.* (*pl.* āt) dignity, retinue, pomp, parade, furniture, conveniences. [assay, experience.
तजरिबा, *m.* experiment, trial, proof, probation,
तजरीद, *f.* solitude, separation, celibacy.
तजरुबा, *more prop.* तजरिबा, *q.v.*
तजर्रुद, *m.* solitude, living in solitude, celibacy.
तज़लील, *f.* abasement, debasement, depression.
तजल्ली, *f.* splendour, brilliancy, clearness.
तजवीज़, *f.* approbation; enquiring into, examining, considering; contrivance; judgment, sentence; trial; plan; permission.
तजवीफ़, *f.* a hollowing, making concave.
तज़वीर, *f.* imposture, fraud, deceit, deception, lie, stratagem. [inquiry, curiosity, inquisitiveness.
तजस्सुस, *m.* a spying, espionage, exploring, search,
तज़हीक, *f.* mocking, derision, ridicule.
तज़ाद, *m.* contradiction, contrariety, absurdity,
तज़ायुद, *m.* increase, augmentation. [inconsistency.
तजावुज़, *m.* diversity, departing, deviating, transgressing, offending. — *k.* (with abl.) to deviate, stray, err.
तजि = तजके (तजना). See इ, 7.
तजु in Braj = तजो. See उ, 10.
तजै = तजे (तजना). See ए, 3.
तज्ज्ञ, (*f.* ā) a connoisseur, one who is versed in a thing: *lit.* adj. knowing that.
तज्ञ, (Rām). = तज्ज्ञ or तत्वज्ञ, *qq.v.*
तट, *m.* a field: bank of a river, shore, coast: fortifications of a city; outskirts of a town; slope; horizon.
तटतटाना, *t.* to pain or vex greatly.
तटवा = तट्टू, *q.v.*
तटवानी, *f.* a female or mare pony.
तटस्थ, *m.* (*f.* ā) an indifferent person, one who is neither a friend nor a foe: *lit.* indifferent.
तटोलना, *t.* to touch, grope, feel (with the hand).
तट्टा, *more com.* टट्टा, *q.v.*
तट्टी, *more com.* टट्टी, *q.v.*
तट्टू, *m.* a pony, a sorry horse of a small kind.
तट्टुआ, a colloquial form of तट्टू, *q.v.*
तठ, the crash made by the breaking of wood.
तड़, *m.* party, faction, division; an imitative sound.
तड़क, a cleft, fissure, crevice, split, crack.
तड़कना, *n.* to be cracked, be split: *a. int.* to burst,
तड़का, *m.* the dawn of day. [split, crack.
तड़काना, *t.* to crack, split; *lit.* to cause to be cracked.
तड़के, *adv.* at dawn, at the beginning of dawn, just before morning, in the very early morning, early.
तड़ख़ = तड़क, *q.v.*
तड़जन, see तर्जन.

तड़तड़ाना, *a. int.* to trickle, drop, patter, bluster, welter; to warp or crack with a noise (as a plank exposed to the sun).

तड़तड़ाहट, *f.* the act of dropping.

तड़ना, a crack of thunder, report of fire-arms.

तड़प, *f.* haste, hurry; outrageousness, explosion, fury; leap, jump.

तड़पड़ा, *m.* the noise of falling water.

तड़पड़ी, *f.* flutter, agitation, palpitation.

तड़पना, *a. int.* to flutter, palpitate, be agitated, flounce, writhe, jump, spring, bound, wriggle, toss, be very desirous about anything.

तड़पाना, *t.* to put into a state of great agitation, cause to flutter, cause to stumble, etc.

तड़पीला, *m.* (*f.* ī) hasty, hurrying.

तड़फ, *f.* agitation, palpitation, timidity, perplexity, tossing about.

तड़फड़ाना, *a. int.* to flutter, palpitate.

तड़फड़ाहट, *f.* the act of fluttering, palpitation.

तड़फना = **तड़पना**, *q.v.*

तड़फाना = **तड़पाना**, *q.v.*

तड़वड़, *m.* a shrub (*Cassia auriculata*) the bark of which is used in tanning, and whose seeds and leaves are used medicinally by native doctors.

तड़स, *m.* a hyena.

तड़ा, *m.* an island.

तड़ाक, *more com.* (1) **तड़ाका** (2) **तड़ाग**, *qq.v.*

तड़ाकड़ी, *f.* the beam of a balance.

तड़ाका, 1, *m.* the sound of striking: 2, *m.* (*f.* ī) pretty, showy, splendid, gaudy.

तड़ाग, *m.* a pond, pool, tank deep enough for the growth of the lotus and other aquatic plants; a trap for catching deer.

तड़ाड़ना, *a. int.* to rear (as a horse).

तड़ाड़ा, *m.* a throwing water.

तड़ाया, *m.* the wearing smart clothes, gaudiness in dress, foppery.

तड़ायादार, *m.* one who is particular in having fine and well-made clothes, one who dresses well.

तड़ावा, *m.* show, ostentation, vanity.

तड़ित, *f.* lightning.

तण्डुल, *m.* rice (cleared from the husk), any grain after threshing and winnowing: a vermifuge plant.

तपटा, *more prop.* **टपटा**, *q.v.*

तपटाल, *more prop.* **टपटाल**, *q.v.*

तपटालमारी = **टपटालमारी**, *q.v.* [a vermifuge.

तण्डुल, *f.* a plant the seeds of which are used as

तत, 1, *more prop.* **तत्त्व**, *q.v.*: 2, (*pron.*) that: (used in comp.; e. g. *Tat-kāl*) 3, *m.* a father.

ततकाल, *more prop.* **तत्काल**, *q.v.*

ततछण, *more prop.* **तत्क्षण**, *q.v.*

ततत्व; see (1) **तत्त्व** (2) **तत्काल** (3) **तत्क्षण**.

ततप्रयुक्त = (1) **उसका कहा हुआ** (2) **तत्त्वप्रयुक्त**, *q.v.*

ततबोक, *f.* a likening, comparing; confronting (as hostile armies).

ततरी, 1, *more prop.* **तातारी**, *q.v.*: 2, *f.* a playful or wanton girl. [ing, prorogation.

ततवोल, *f.* an extending, stretching out, prolong-

ततहरा, *m.* a vessel for warming water in, a kettle.

ततहरी *f.* = **ततहरा**, *q. v.* [rence, cohesion.

तताबुक, *m.* similarity, congruity, analogy; cohe-

ततार, 1, *more prop.* **तातार**, *q. v.* 2, *f.* embrocation, a pouring water on a diseased part.

ततारना, *t.* to embrocate.

ताबुल, *m.* usurpation, oppression, tyranny, conquest, rudeness, insolence.

ततिम्मा, *m.* an appendix, supplement, continuation, remainder, balance.

ततैव, even so, just so, so also, in like manner.

तत्काल, 1, *m.* the time being, the present, the time when a thing occurs: 2, *adv.* at that time, then, forthwith. [is wise or intelligent for the time being.

तत्कालधी, *m.* one who has presence of mind, who

तत्त, *more prop.* **तत्त्व**, *q.v.*

तत्क्षण, 1, *m.* time present, time being: 2, *adv.* at that time, immediately, instantly, forthwith.

तत्तजाति, that caste. [caste.

तत्तजात्युचित, whatever rightly appertains to that

तत्ततकर्म, that kind of deed or business.

ततत्स्थान, that kind of place.

तत्तदवतार, that kind of incarnation.

तत्तद्व्यवहार, that kind of behaviour or custom.

तत्तद्देश, that kind of country.

तत्तद्धर्म, that kind of religion.

तत्तद्रूप, that same manner.

तत्तल्लोक, that kind of people.

तत्ता, *m.* (*f.* ī) hot, warm, fiery, furious, outrageous, wrathful, passionate, zealous.

तत्पर, *m.* (*f.* ā) an adept, etc.: *lit.* intent only on that, completely devoted to, attending to a thing closely and anxiously, engaged in, attentive to, addicted to, adept. [compound word.

तत्पुरुषसमास, *m.* (in Gram.) a particular kind of

तत्र, (in Sk. loc. of **तद**) in that, in that case, therein, on account of that, there.

तत्रजात, *m.* (in Gram.) an adjective of origin.

तत्रभवन्त, *m.* (*f.* vatī) an estimable person, etc.: *lit.* estimable, respectable, venerable, reverend. The term is used in respectful allusion to absent persons.

तत्व; for words beginning thus, see under the more proper form **तत्त्व**.

तत्त्व, (**तद** + **त्व**, Thou art *that*: hence, an epithet of the Supreme) *m.* the very essence, an element, a principle, essential nature, the essential reality or substance of a thing as opposed to what is illusory or fallacious, truth; an element or elementary property (differently enumerated in different systems of philosophy; from the three which are the same with the three *guṇs*, to twenty-seven which include the elements, organs, faculties, matter, spirit, life and God; hence, in the ingenious system of reckoning by symbols adopted by Hindoos in their poetry, this word is a symbol for 25); essential nature, the real nature of the human soul (considered in the Hindoo system as one and the same with the Divine spirit which pervades and animates the universe); a first principle, axiom; mind, intellect: a musical instrument; slow time in music.

तत्वज्ञ, *m.* (*f.* ā) a profoundly skilful person, etc.: *lit.* adj. knowing the exact facts of anything.

तत्वज्ञान, 1, *m.* knowledge of the Divine: 2, *m.* (*f.* ā) an inspired person, etc.: *lit.* one who knows divine things.

तत्वप्रयुक्त = **यथार्थ कहा हुआ**.

तत्वमसि, *m.* (*f.* ī) ink; the stalk of the *Nyctanthes tristis.*

तत्वसम्बन्धी, *adj.* connected with **तत्व**, *q. v.*

तथ, true, right, perfect.

तथा, 1, (correl. of **यथा**) so, thus; in that manner, thence, and, ditto: 2, *f.* power, might, ability.

तथागत, *m.* a divine teacher, a Jain or Buddh.

तथापि, *adv.* then even, still, notwithstanding, yet, nevertheless.

तथास्तु, (Sk. imperat.) be it so, yes.

तथैव, *adv.* even thus, in the same manner, just so.

तद, (correl. of **जद**) then, at that time; afterwards; therefore; in that case; so soon. — *to*, then, in that case. *Jad na tad*, constantly.

तदनन्तर, afterwards, thereafter, after that, thereupon, after which, then.

तदन्तर, in the midst of it; besides this, without this, besides.

तदन्तर्गत, situated in the midst of that.

तदपि, still, nevertheless.

तदभी, still, nevertheless, however, notwithstanding.

तदय्युन = **तदैयुन**, *q. v.*

तदरीज, *f.* gradation, scale.

तदरीस, *f.* giving lectures, lecturing.

तदबीर, *f.* deliberation, counsel, opinion, advice; government, regulation, order, plan, arrangement, contrivance.

तदसे. thence, thenceforward, since that time.

तदही, at that very time; in that case only.

तदहु
तदहू } (old forms) = **तिसपर भी**.

तदा, then, at that time.

तदारुक, *m.* chastisement, reparation, retaliation; provision, remedy, precaution. preparation (*esp.* to obtain justice); the means used to procure justice (as lawyers, witnesses, writing, etc.). — *k.* to provide against, prepare for; to oppose; to chastise.

तदुक्तं = **उसका** (or **उन्होंका**) **कहा हुआ**.

तदैयुन, *m.* religiousness, sanctity.

तद्धत = **उसका मारा हुआ**.

तद्धन, *m.* (*f.* ā) a miser, etc.: *lit.* miserly, niggardly.

तद्धित, *m.* (in Gram.) the class of secondary derivations, *i. e.* those words which have no immediate reference to any root, but to other parts of speech which are themselves already derived from roots.

तद्यपि, still, nevertheless.

तधी=**तदही**, *q.v.*

तन, (*prop.* **तनु**) *m. f.*? the body, the person. — *denā*, to pay attention. *Tan-o-man mārnā*, to restrain one's desires and be silent.

तनआसानी, *f.* bodily ease.

तनक, *more prop.* **तनुक**, *q.v.*

तनकाऊ = **थोड़ा भी** (see **ऊ**, 7). In Braj and in poetry.

तनख़ाह, *f.* salary, wages, an assignment (on the revenues), a money-order, draft.

तनक्षीन, *more prop.* **तनक्षीणा**, *q. v.*

तनक्षीणा, *m.* (*f.* ā) a slender-bodied person.

तनज़ीम, *f.* an ordering, arranging; composing verses; threading pearls.

तनज़ीर, *f.* a resembling; a beholding.

तनज़्ज़ुल, *m.* descent, declining slowly, diminution; a condescending.

तनतनहा=**तनितनहा**, *q.v.*

तनदिह, a person of application.

तनदिही, *f.* application, exertion, attention, diligence.

तनदुरुस्त, sound in bodily health, vigorous.

तनदुरुस्ती, *f.* healthiness, vigour.

तनना, *t.* to stretch, pull tight: *a. int.* to sit upright.

तनपरवर, careful of the body, over-attentive to the body.

तनपरवरी, *f.* self-indulgence.

तनफ़्फ़ुर, *m.* aversion, disgust.

तनफ़्फ़ुस, *m.* respiration, breathing.

तनब्बी, *f.* a beam, rafter.

तनमन, *m.* body and soul, one's whole self.

तनय, *m.* a son; a male descendant.

तनया, *f.* a daughter; a female descendant.

तनवीर, *f.* enlightening, illumination.

तनसीफ़, *f.* a dividing in the middle or into two equal parts.

तनस्सुल, *m.* pedigree, genealogy.

तनहा, alone, solitary, apart, private; single, only; singular, unique: *adv.* only.

तनहाई, *f.* solitariness, loneliness, solitude, privacy.

तनाख़ोरी, *f.* solitary living or enjoyment.

तनाज़ुल, *m.* descent, decline, falling off (in price, rank, etc.); the leaping from a horse for the purpose of fighting.

तनाब, *f.* a tent-rope; a measure for measuring land (formerly made of rope).

तनावर, corpulent, stout.

तनावुल, *m.* eating. — *k.* to eat.

तनासुब, *m.* a resembling, relation, proportion.

तनाही, *f.* a finishing, completing, arriving at the end or place of destination.

तनिक, *more prop.* **तनुक**, *q. v.*

तनिको
तनिकौ } (Braj and poet.) = **तनिक**, *q. v.*

तनितनहा, alone, solitary.

तनिया, *m.* a kind of covering for the waist.

तनी, *f.* a string with which garments are tied: a daughter.

तनु = (1) *f.* **तन** (2) **तनुक** (3) **विस्तार**, *qq. v.*

तनुक, *adj.* small, slight: *adv.* a little, slightly, somewhat, the very least.

तनुकूप, *m.* a pore of the skin.

तनुज, *m.* (*f.* ā) an offspring, child.

तनू, *more prop.* **तनु**, *q.v.*

तनूर, *m.* an oven, stove.

तने (*corruption*)=**तरहसे**. See **तरह**.

तनै; see (1) **तनना** (2) **तनय** (3) **तने**.

तनोतु=**विस्तार करे; फैलावे** (from **तानना**, with the termin. of the 3rd sing. imperat. of the Sansk.).

तन्नना, *m.* sound, rumour, fame; pomp, dignity, state.

तन्ननाना, *a. int.* to twang, tingle.

तन्ननाहट, *f.* a sharp pricking pain from inflammation.

तन्ना, *more prop.* **टपटा**, *q.v.*

तन्ताल, *more prop.* **टपटाल**, *q.v.*

तन्तालमारी= **टपटालमारी**, *q.v.*

तन्ति, *m.* a weaver.

तन्तु, *m.* a thread, cobweb, filament; propagation of a family, offspring, race, issue, descendants.

तन्तुकीट, *m.* a silkworm.

तन्त्र, *m.* demonstration, clear and right conclusion: raiment, vesture: a medicament, drug, a chief medicament or perhaps a charm considered as producing medicinal effects, an enchantment, charm. The term is specially applied as the designation of one of the sacred books of the Hindoos, a theological treatise teaching peculiar and mystical rites and formulae for the worship of the Gods or for the attainment of superhuman power. It is mostly in the form of a dialogue between Shiv and Durgā, who are the peculiar deities of the Tantrikas. There are a number of these works, and their authority seems, in many parts of India, to have, in great measure, superseded that of the Veds. According to one account, a *tantra* comprizes five subjects, viz. (1) the creation and the destruction of the world; (2) the worship of the gods; (3) the attainment of all objects; (4) magical rites for the acquirement of six superhuman faculties; and (5) four modes of union with spirit by meditation. A variety of subjects are, however, introduced into many of them, while some, again, are limited to a single topic, such as the mode of breathing in certain rites, the language of birds, beasts, etc. The term is also applied to that branch of the Veds which teaches spells, charms, *mantras*, or mystical and magical formulae.

तन्त्री, *m.* (*f.* iṇī) a musician.

तन्द, see **तुन्द**.

तन्दुल, a corruption of **तण्डुल**, *q.v.*

तन्दूर, *m.* an oven.

तन्द्रा = **तन्द्री**, *q.v.*

तन्द्रालु, slothful, sluggish, overcome with fatigue or sleepiness.

तन्द्री, *f.* sleepiness, drowsiness; exhaustion, want of energy, fatigue, lassitude, fainting.

तन्वनि, in Chand = **तन्विनी**, *q.v.*

तन्ना = **तनना**, *q.v.*

तन्नाज़, facetious, playful, mirthful.

तन्नाना, *a. int.* to twang: to have a sharp pricking pain from inflammation.

तन्निर्मित = **उसका बनाया हुआ**.

तन्नीर = **उसका पानी**.

तन्मात्र, that merely.

तन्विनी, *f.* (= **तन्वी**) a graceful female.

तन्विन, *m. pr. n.* a son of Manu by Tāmas.

तन्वी, *f.* a delicate and slender female: a certain plant: (in Pros.) a kind of stanza of 4 lines with 24 syllables in each: *pr. n.* one of the wives of Krishṇ.

तन्विन्द्रिय, *m.* (*f.* ā) having slender limbs, delicately-formed, graceful, slender.

तन्हाख़ोरी, *f.* solitary living or enjoyment.

तप, 1, *m.* the hot season, summer: prayer, adoration, devotion, penance; the term is applied in particular to that form of penance in which the devotee sits so many hours a day (6 ?) in the open air in the hot season surrounded by several (5 ?) fires, during twelve years. — *k.* to do penance: 2, *f.* heat, warmth; fever. — *utarnā*, to go off (as a fever). — *charhnā*, to come on (as a fever).

तपआधार, *m.* the depending on the merit of penance.

तपआधारी, *m.* (*f.* iṇī) a person who depends for his salvation on the merit of his deeds of penance.

तपः, *m.* a division of land smaller than a *pargana*.

तपक, a sledge-hammer.

तपड़तपड़ (*by inversion*) = **तड़पतड़प**. See **तड़पना**.

तपकना, *a. int.* to throb, palpitate. — *phorekā*, the throbbing of a phlegmon or boil when coming to suppuration.

तपत, *more prop.* (1) **तप्त** (2) **तप्ति**, *qq. v.*

तपतिल्ली, *f.* a disorder of the spleen.

तपन, 1. *f.* (*m.* ?) heat, warmth, burning, fervour, glow: 2, *m.* the sun; the hot season; name of one of the divisions of hell; mental distress, grieving, pining.

तपना, *n.* to be glorified; to be heated, to burn with pain or grief: *a. int.* to glow; to frisk about.

तपनि in Braj = (1) pl. of **तप**; (2) **तपने**.

तपनी, *f. pr. n.* the Godāvaree river.

तपबल = **तपोबल**, *q.v.*

तपरिहाऊ, land cultivated in small patches among the uncultivated portions of an estate.

तपरी, *f.* a mound, small height, acclivity.

तपलोक = **तपोलोक**, *q. v.*

तपश्री, *more prop.* **तपसी**, *q.v.*

तपश्या, *more prop.* **तपस्या**, *q.v.*

तपस, *m.* religious austerity, penance, self-mortification, the practice of self-denial; name of the region or world inhabited by saints or devotees after death; virtue, merit, duty, the observance of certain special practices; thus, the *tapas* of a Brāhman is sacred learning; that of a Kshatree, the protection of subjects; that of a Vaisya, almsgiving to Brāhmans; that of a Sudra, the service of the same sect; and that of a Rishi (or saint-sage) the feeding on herbs and roots.

तपसी, *more prop.* **तपस्वी**, *q.v.*

तपसीमछली = **तपस्वी मछली**, *q.v.*

तपस्य, 1, *m.* = **तपस्या**, *q.v.*: 2, *m. pr. n.* the month Phālgun (Feb. — March).

तपस्या, *f.* religious penance, devout austerity, devotion.

तपस्विन, *m.* (*f.* ī) = **तपस्वी**, *q.v.*

तपस्वी, *m.* (*f.* inī) a religious devotee or ascetic, yogee, etc.: *lit.* engaged in the practice of rigorous and devout penance, devout.

तपस्सी, *more prop.* **तपस्वी**, *q.v.* [*disea*).

तपस्सी मछली, *f.* the mango-fish (*Polynemus para-*

तपा = **तपस्वी**, *q.v.*

तपाक, *m.* affection, esteem, regard, love; ardour, zeal; consternation; affliction.

तपाना, *t.* to pour out a libation: to make one warm himself by the fire or in the sunshine, cause to glow, to heat, warm.

तपावन, *m.* a libation, the pouring out a libation.

तपास, *f.* sunshine, sunbeams; labour, toil.

तपिश, *f.* heat, warmth; affliction.

तपी = **तपस्वी**, *q.v.*

तपीदन, *m.* agitation, palpitation.

तपोधन, *m.* (*f.* ā) an ascetic, devotee, one who performs religious penance: *prop.* one who treasures up the merit of *tapas*. [land.

तपोवट, *m. pr. n.* a part of central India or holy

तपोवन, *m.* a sacred grove, forest frequented by ascetics or in which religious austerities are practised.

तपोबल, *m.* the power or strength acquired by the performance of religious austerities. [worlds.

तपोलोक, *m. pr. n.* (in Myth.) one of the seven

तपोव्रत, *m.* penance and religious fasting.

तप्त, *m.* (*f.* ā) hot, heated, fervent, inflamed, burnt or burning with heat, pain or sorrow.

तप्तकृच्छ्र, *m.* a kind of penance consisting in drinking hot water, milk or ghee for three days.

तप्ति, *f.* heat.

तप्ती, *more prop.* **तप्ति**, *q.v.*

तप्प in Chand = **तप**, *q.v.*

तप्पा, *m.* a division, district, parish.

तफ, *m.* vapour, steam, mist.

तफ़सीर, *f.* an explanation, comment, commentary, paraphrase, interpretation.

तफ़ावुत, 1, *m.* distance; difference, distinction, disparity: 2, distant, separate, far away, remote. absent. — *bolnā*, to prevaricate.

तब, (correl. of **जब**) then, at that time; afterwards.

तबईयत, *more prop.* **तबीअ़त**, *q.v.*

तबंचा, *m.* a pistol. — *mārnā*, to fire a pistol, shoot with a pistol.

तबका, *m.* (*f.* ī) appertaining to that time.

तबक्कुर, being profoundly learned; abounding in wealth: remaining in the city or village (whilst one's family continue in the field): being open, wide and spacious.

तबख़्तुर, walking stately, strutting vainly.

तबज्ज्व, a corruption of **तबज्जुब**, *q.v.*

तबतईं / **तबतक** } = **तबतलक**, *q.v.* [those very times.

तबतब, (correl. of **जबजब**) at that very time, at

तबतलक, up to that time, till then, so long.

तबते (see **ते**, 3) in Braj = **उस समयसे**.

तबतोड़ी = **तबतलक**, *q.v.* [transposition, difference.

तबदील, *f.* a change, alteration, substitution,

तबन्नी, *f.* adoption (of a child).

तबभी, even then, then even, then too (with the emphasis on the word 'then').

तबर, *m.* a hatchet, axe.

तबरीद, *f.* the act of cooling, refreshing.

तबर्रुक, *m.* benediction, congratulation; sacred relics, a portion of presents (or what is left of the food that has been presented to great men, etc.) given to their dependents.

तबलग / **तबलों** } = **तबतलक**, *q.v.*

तबलों in Braj = **तबलें** = **तबतलक**, *q.v.*

तबस्सुम, *m.* a smile. [consideration.

तबस्सुर, *m.* sight, distinct perception, attentive

तबह, *more com.* **तबाह**, *q.v.*

तबहि / **तबहिं** } = **तबही**, *q.v.*

तबही, (emph. of **तब**) at that very time, exactly then, even then. — *to*, then indeed. — *se*, from that [very time forward.

तबहीं / **तबहूं** } = **तबही**, *q.v.*

तबा = **तबाह**, *q.v.*

तबायुन, difference, contradiction, inconsistency; (in Arithm.) incommensurability.

तबार, *m.* people, nation, tribe, family.

तबाह, bad, wicked, depraved, abject, spoiled, wretched, ruined. [ruin. — *khānā*, to be afflicted.

तबाही, *f.* wickedness, depravity, wreck, perdition,

तबीअ़त, *f.* disposition, temperament, constitution, essence, property: following, dependence.

तबीच = **तबही**, *q.v.*

तबीब, *m.* a physician.

तबीयत, *more prop.* **तबीअ़त**, *q.v.*

तबीह; see (1) **तबही** (2) **सबीह**.

तबुबास, *see* **तम्बबास**.

तबैं / **तभी** } = **तबही**, *q.v.*

तम, 1, a contraction of **तमस**, *q.v.*: 2, a termin. of the Sk. superl.; *e.g.* **प्रियतम**.

तमः = **तमस**, *q.v.*

तमंचा, *m.* a pistol.

तमक, 1, *m.* a kind of asthma: 2, *f.* a growing red in the face: vanity, arrogance, pride.

तमकनत, *f.* dignity, authority.

तमकना, *a. int.* to grow red in the face, be enraged without adequate cause, or to break out in violence at a temperate and reasonable speech.

तमका, *m.* a stroke of the sun.

तमकि = **तमके** (**तमकना**). See **क**, 7.

तमकीन, *f.* majesty, authority, power.

तमग़ा, *m.* a stamp, mark, brand; a species of tax; royal charter, seal.

तमत्र, *adj.* longing after, hankering after, desirous, cupidinous. [sparkle, twinkle, flash.

तमतमाना, *a. int.* to grow red in the face; to glow,

तमतमाहट, *f.* the state of growing red in the face, [glow.

तमचा } *f.* a request, prayer, petition.
तमचो }

तमर, *m.* a date.

तमरिहिन्द = तमरिहिन्दी, *q.v.*

तमरिहिन्दी, *f.* a tamarind; *lit.* the date of India.

तमर्रुद, *m.* refractoriness, stubbornness, disobedience, insolence, rebellion.

तमर्रुदी, *f.* = तमर्रुद, *q.v.*

तमल्लुक, *m.* a cajoling, adulation, ceremony.

तमस, *m.* (see तमोगुण) darkness (physical or moral), gloom, the quality of darkness incident to humanity; illusion of mind, headstrong passion, anger, irascibility, promptitude to the vindictive passions; sorrow, grief; the gloom of hell: *m. pr. n.* (1) of one of the hells (2) of Rāhu, or the personified ascending node.

तमसा, *f. pr. n.* a certain river (the Tamasā or Tonse falling into the Ganges below Pratishthān).

तमसील, *f.* (*pl.* āt) a comparison, similitude, example, parable, allegory; prologue. — *lānā*, to speak in parables, allegorize. [ceipt.

तमस्सुक, *m.* a note of hand, bond, obligation, re-

तमस्सुल, *m.* an imitating, resembling; the apply-

तमस्विनी, *f.* night: *lit.* adj. dark. [ing allegories.

तमहीद, *f.* arrangement, disposition, settlement, management, confirmation; preliminary, preämble, preparation, introduction, preface.

तमांचा, *m.* a pistol: a slap, blow, cuff, box, thump.

तमाकू } = तम्बाकू, *q.v.*
तमाखू }

तमाचा, *more prop.* तमांचा, *q.v.*

तमादी, *f.* perseverance: a long time: (in Law) a limitation as to time which bars a civil prosecution.

तमान, *more prop.* तम्बान, *q.v.*

तमानियत, *f.* rest, repose, tranquillity.

तमाम, entire, all, whole, complete, perfect. — *k.* to complete. — *honā*, to be finished, to die.

तमारि, *m. pr. n.* an epithet of the sun; *lit.* the enemy of darkness. [clusion.

तमामियत, *f.* complement, consummation, con-

तमामी, 1, *f.* completion, perfection, conclusion, totality: brocade, cloth of gold, tissue: 2, *adj.* entire, the whole.

तमाल, *m.* a kind of tree (*Xanthocymus pictorius*, Roxb.) noted for the dark hue of its blossoms: the sectarial mark of the Hindoos (made with sandal, etc.): a tobacco-pipe?

तमालक, *m.* a species of potherb (*Marsilea dentata*).

तमालिका, *f. pr. n.* a district in Bengal, — the modern Tamluk.

तमाली, *f.* a certain medicinal plant (used as an emollient in affections of the mouth and fauces).

तमाशबीन, *m.* a sight-seer; an epicure; a rake, whore-master.

तमाशबीनी, *f.* sight-seeing, luxury, libertinism.

तमाशा, *m.* a sight, spectacle, show, entertainment — *k.* to see; to take a walk; to jeer, jest.

तमाशाई, 1, a spectator, on-looker; a rake, epicure: 2, fit for a spectacle. [more proper form तमाशा.

तमास; for words beginning thus, see under the

तमिस्र, *m.* darkness; a dark night; the dark half of the month (from the full to the change).

तमिस्रा, *f.* a dark night, a night without moon or star, a night during the wane of the moon.

तमी, *f.* night.

तमीज़, *f.* sense, discretion, discernment, judgment.

तमो = तमस, *q. v.*

तमोगुण, *m.* (see तमस and गुण) the third of the qualities incident to creation or the state of humanity, *viz.* the property of darkness, whence proceed folly, ignorance, stupidity, mental blindness, worldly delusion, etc.

तमोगुणी, *m.* (*f.* inī) = तामस, *q. v.* [lusion, etc.

तमोघ्न, *m. pr. n.* an epithet of the legislator of Buddh: *lit.* the destroyer of darkness; *hence*, the sun moon, fire. [*lit.* the night-walker.

तमोचर, *m.* (*f.* ī *or* ā) an epithet of any *rākshas*;

तमोरूह, *m.* the hair of the body. [Bengal.

तमोलिप्ती, *f. pr. n.* the district of Tamluk in

तमोवृत, overcome by any of the effects of the property of darkness (*Tamogun*), such as rage, fear, etc.

तम्बाकू, *m.* tobacco. Though this word is of foreign origin, it is now quite naturalized in the language.

तम्बान, *m.* trowsers, drawers.

तम्बालू, *m.* a brass vessel in which Hindoos dress their food; a small round brass pot for water.

तम्बिया, *m.* a pot.

तम्बीह, *f.* admonition, correction, punishment, flogging. — *k.* or *denā*, to administer chastisement.

तम्बुरा, *more prop.* तम्बूरा, *q. v.*

तम्बूमछी, *f.* a species of lamprey.

तम्बू, *m.* a tent: an eel. — *tānnā*, to pitch tents.

तम्बूबास, *m.* a dwelling in tents, encamping.

तम्बूर } *m.* a drum; a kind of Turkish guitar.
तम्बूरा }

तम्बोल, *m.* the betel-leaf. — *ānā*, to bleed from the bridle (a horse's mouth). [betel-leaf: a kind of tree.

तम्बोलिन, *f.* a woman whose business it is to sell

तम्बोली, *m.* (*f.* in *or* inī) a caste whose business it is to sell betel-leaf.

तम्माकू = तम्बाकू, *q. v.*

तय, an old form = तू, thou.

तयक्कुन, *m.* certainty, knowing for certain, prying into, ascertaining.

तयसहि (*poet.*) = तैसाही.

तयम्मुम, *m.* purifying the person before prayer with sand or dust when water cannot be had.

तयार } *more prop.* तैय्यार, *q. v.*
तय्यार }

तर, 1, *more prop.* **तले**, *q.v.*: 2, wet, fresh, juicy, green, young: 3, a termin. of the Sansk. comparat.; *e.g.* उत्तर (north) = उत + तर.

तरई, *f.* (pl. **तराइन**) a star.

तरंग, *f.* a wave; an emotion, whim, fancy, caprice, conceit; becoming state and dignity.

तरंगिणी, *f.* a river; a braggart female.

तरंगित, *m.* (*f.* ā) wavy: overflowing.

तरंगिनि, *more prop.* **तरंगिणी**, *q. v.*

तरंगी, *m.* (*f.* iṇī) a braggart, etc.: *lit.* wavy, unsteady, braggart, fanciful, whimsical, fantastical.

तरक, 1 = **तर्क**, *q. v.*: 2, *f.* a beam, rafter.

तरक़्क़ुब, *m.* a contemplating, expecting, hoping.

तरकना = (1) **कूदना** (2) **बिचारना**, *qq. v.*

तरकश, 1, *more prop.* **तरकस**, *q. v.*: 2, *m.* a quiver.

तरकस, 1, *more prop.* **तरकश**, *q.v.*: 2, bent, crooked, cornerwise.

तरकारी = **तर्कारी**, *q. v.*

तरकी = **तर्की**, *q. v.*

तरकुल = **तर्कुल**, *q. v.*

तरके, *more prop.* **तड़के**, *q. v.*

तरकुशाया = **तर्कुशाया**, *q. v.*

तरकेउ in Braj = **तरका**. See **तरकना**.

तरक़्क़ी, *f.* advancement, promotion, preferment; increase; a making progress in learning, proficiency.

तरख़ना, *a. int.* to warp, crack, split.

तरखा = **तर्खा**, *q. v.*

तरग़ीब, *f.* temptation, stimulation, exciting desire.—*denā*, to set agog, tempt, excite, induce.

तरछट, *f.* dregs, sediment, lees.

तरजत = **तर्जता है**. See **त**, 5.

तरजना = **तर्जना**, *q. v.*

तरजा = **तर्जा**, past. part. of **तर्जना**.

तरण, *m.* a passing over, crossing; escape, deliverance, a being saved: a name of paradise (Swarg): one who is saved or delivered.

तरणतारण, *m.* the saved and the saviour.

तरणि, *m.* (*f.* ī) one who overcomes: lit. *adj.* overcoming: *hence*, the sun; a ray of light; a boat, raft, float.

तरणी, *f.* a ship, boat, float; the Socotrine aloe (*A. perfoliata*); a certain plant (*Hibiscus mutabilis*).

तरण्ड, *m.* a raft or float (made of bamboos, etc. tied together, and sometimes floated on jars or hollow gourds inverted); the float of a fishingline.

तरण्डी, *f.* a boat, ship, float.

तरत = **तरता है**. See **त**, 5.

तरतरा, *m.* a kind of dish.

तरदद / **तरद्दुत** } *more prop.* **तरद्दुद**, *q. v.*

तरद्दुद, *m.* (*pl.* āt) irresolution; contrivance; debating, hesitation, fluctuation, suspension of judgment.

तरन; for words beginning thus, but not given below, see under the form **तरण**.

तरना, *a. int*, to cross over, pass over; to be ferried, be saved.

तरनिजा, a species of Hindee versification in which the first few syllables are short and the remainder all long.

तरन्त, *m.* a fog; a heavy shower, torrent of rain; the ocean.

तरन्ती, *f.* a boat.

तरप, see **तड़प**.

तरपन, *more prop.* **तर्पण**, *q.v.*

तरपाहैं (poet.) = **तड़पते हैं**.

तरफ़, *f.* direction, quarter; side, margin, corner, extremity: *postp.* (with genit. *f.*) towards.

तरफ़दार, *m.* a partisan, sectary, follower; an assistant, subordinate officer of revenue and police.

तरफ़दारी, *f.* partisanship, sectarianism, partiality, following. — *k.* to shew partiality, take a side.

तरफना = **तड़फना**, *q. v.*

तरफराना; see **तड़फड़ाना**.

तरफ़ैन, (dual of **तरफ़**) both sides, both parties.

तरब, a corruption (1) of **तरफ़** ((2) of **तरव**, *q. v.*

तरबर = **तरवर**, *q. v.*

तरबूज़, *m.* the water-melon (*Cucurbita citrullus*).

तरल, *m* (*f.* ā) a wanton person, etc.: *lit* trembling, tremulous, unsteady, inconstant, changeable, fickle, volatile, ticklish, wanton, libidinous, lecherous; sparkling, resplendent, radiant.

तरला, 1, *m.* a kind of bamboo: a bottom, depth, lower or under part: 2, *m.* (*f.* ī) nethermost, lower: 3 *f.* spirituous liquor; a wanton, etc.; see **तरल**.

तरव, *m.* (prop. **तरु**) a tree.

तरवर, *m.* (prop. **तरुवर**) any large tree; a shrub, small species of cassia.

तरवरिया = **तर्वरिया**, *q. v.*

तरवारि, *m. f.* a sword, scimitar.

तरवार, *f.* a sword, scimitar.

तरस, *more com.* **तर्स**, *q.v.*

तरसना = **तर्सना**, *q. v.*

तरसनाक, terrified, timid, cowardly.

तरसान, timid, fearful, afraid.

तरस्ता, *m.* (*f.* ī) = **तरसता** = **तर्सता** (**तर्सना**).

तरस्सुद, *m.* expectation, hope.

तरहबतरह = **तरहतरह**, *q. v.*

तरह, *f.* manner, mode; kind, sort.

तरहतरह, in different ways, of diffent kinds, various kinds of.

तरा, *m.* the bottom of anything.

तराइन, *f.* (*pl.* of **तरई**) stars.

तराई, *f.* a marsh, low ground flooded with water on which rice is generally cultivated, marshy ground; a vale, valley, meadow, mead.

तराईखेवा, a waterfowl, water-spaniel, etc.: *lit.* living in or near water.

तराक, the noise of any thing splitting, a cracking, snapping, breaking.

तराकड़ी, *f.* the beam of a balance.

तराज़ू, *f.* a scale, balance.—*ho jānā*, to hit right through (as an arrow).

तरान, *m.* revenue, income.

तराना, *t.* to cause to pass over, cause to swim, cause (instrumentally) the salvation of another, to save.

तराना, *m.* modulation, harmony, melody, symphony; voice, trill, quaver; a kind of song.

तरार, quick, rapid.

तरारा, *m.* quickness, expedition.

तराव, *m.* a swimming.

तरावट, *more prop.* तरावत, *q.v.*

तरावत, *f.* freshness, verdure; moisture, humidity, dampness.

तराश, *f.* a cutting, paring, trimming; shape, form. — *ḍālnā*, to pare off, pare away.

तराशना, *t.* to cut, clip, pare, shave, shape, cut out. *Apnetain* —, to value or esteem oneself above others.

तरि, *f.* a boat.

तरिक, *m.* a ferryman.

तरित्र, *m.* a boat.

तरी, *f.* a boat: moisture, water, wet land: sugar.

तरीक़, *f.* way, road, path; manner, mode, custom, fashion; rite; profession, persuasion, sect, religion.

तरीक़त, *f.* } = तरीक़, *q.v.*
तरीक़ा, *m.* }

तरीत्र, *m.* a boat.

तरु, *m.* a tree.

तरुजीवन, *m.* the root of a tree.

तरुण, 1, *m.* a kind of plant (*Achyranthes aspera?*); the castor-oil tree (*Ricinus communis*): cartilage: 2, *m.* (*f.* ī) a young person of the virile age: *lit.* young, juvenile, fresh, new, novel, beginning; adult.

तरुणता, *f.* }
तरुणत्व, *m.* } तरुणापन, *q.v.*
तरुणाई, *f.* }

तरुणापन, *m.* adolescence, youth, puberty.

तरुणी, *f.* (see तरुण, 2) a young woman (from 16 to 30 years of age; generally, however, one about the former age), a young wife.

तरुणय, *m.* = तरुणापन, *q.v.*

तरुतर = तरु तले, *qq.v.*

तरुन; for words beginning thus, see under the form तरुण.

तरुनि in Braj = (1) pl. of तरु (2) तरुने (3) तरुणी, *qq.v.*

तरुनिन, a poetical pl. of तरुणी, *q.v.*

तरुराज, *m.* an epithet of any large or mythologically important tree, *e.g.* the peepal, the Kalpvṛiksh, etc.

तरुवर, *m.* any large tree.

तरे, 1, *more prop.* तले, *q.v.*: 2, like.

तरेड़ा, *m.* the falling of water from a spout or from any height.

तरेल, *m.* a buoy.

तरेरना, *a. int.* to stare: *t.* to stare at.

तरै in Braj = तले, *q.v.*

तरैया, *f.* a star.

तरैस, a corruption of तरस, *q.v.*

तरौवर, *more prop.* (1) तरुवर (2) तलाव, *qq. v.*

तर्क, *m.* supposition, doubt, disputation, discussion, consideration, reasoning; the science of reasoning, *viz.* Logic; a proposition (in Logic). In the ingenious system of reckoning by symbols adopted by Hindoos in their poetry, this word is a symbol for 6.

तर्कताज़ी = तुर्कताज़ी, *q.v.*

तर्कना, 1, *t.* to consider, investigate, reason: 2, *f.* reasoning, consideration, investigation.

तर्कविद्या, *f.* the science of reasoning or disputation, Logic.

तर्कश } = तरकश, etc. *qq.v.*
तर्कस }

तर्कसवार = तुर्कसवार, *q.v.*

तर्का, *f.* logical reasoning.

तर्कारी, *f.* esculent vegetables.

तर्कित, (*f.* ā) a disputatious person: *lit.* doubtful, disputatious.

तर्किन, *m.* (*f.* तर्किणी) a follower of the *Tark-shāstra*, one skilled in speculative reasoning, logician, disputant.

तर्किल, *m.* the plant *Cassia tora.*

तर्की, 1, *m.* (*f.* iṇī) = तर्किन, *q. v.*: 2, *f.* a kind of ear-ornament made of the leaves of the *tāṛ*-tree.

तर्क़ीक़, *f.* a softening, thinning, dilution, rarefaction.

तर्कीब, *f.* (*pl.* āt) composition, mixture, cement; make, form, mechanism. — *k.* to organize.

तर्क़ीम, *f.* a writing, noting, marking.

तर्कु, *f.* (*m.*?) a spindle, distaff, an iron pin upon which the cotton is first drawn out (it also serves as the distaff,—the cotton being next transferred from it to the wheel).

तर्कुट, *m.* spinning, the drawing out the cotton upon the distaff or upon the wheel.

तर्कुटी, *f.* a spindle or a distaff.

तर्कुपिंड, *m.*; see तर्कुपेठी.

तर्कुपेठी, *f.* a ball of clay, etc. on the lower end of the spindle to assist in giving it a rotatory motion.

तर्कुल, *m.* the fruit of the *tāṛ*-tree.

तर्कुलासक, *m.* a concave shell or saucer in which the lower end of a spindle is placed and whirled round.

तर्कुशाण, *m.* a small whetstone for sharpening spindles, etc.

तर्खा, *m.* (*f.* ī) rapid (as a stream).

तर्ख़ीम, *f.* abbreviation, contraction, apocope.

तर्जन, *m.* a menacing, blaming, reprehending, terrifying; wrath, anger.

तर्जना, *t.* to censure; to threaten; to terrify.

तर्जनी, *f.* the fore-finger; *i. e.* the finger of menace, etc.

तर्जमा = तर्जुमा, *q. v.*

तर्जीह, *f.* the gaining a superiority, excelling, preference, preëminence. — *rahnā*, to surpass, excel.

तर्जुमा, *m.* a translation, interpretation, rendering.

तर्जुमानवीस, *m.* a translator.

तर्तराता, *m.* (*f.* ī) very greasy, dripping with moisture.

तर्तराना, *a. int.* to bluster, boast.

तर्तराहट, *f.* bluster, boasting.

तर्तीब, *f.* arrangement, disposition, order, method. — *denā*, to put in order.

तर्दस्ती, *f.* handiness, adroitness, activity.

तर्दीद, *f.* an opposing.

तर्पण, *m.* satisfaction (given or received), the act of pleasing, the state of being pleased, gratification, satiety, fulness; an oblation to the deities or a libation of water to the *manes* of deceased ancestors.

तर्प्पण = **तर्पण**, *q. v.*

तर्ब, *f.* a kind of musical tone.

तर्बियत, *f.* education, instruction, tuition, breeding, correction. — *k.* to instruct, educate.

तर्राना, *a. int.* to grudge, grumble, murmur.

तर्रार, *m.* a cutpurse, pickpocket.

तर्रारा, *m.* rapidity, flow. — *bharnā*, to gallop, rush on at full speed.

तर्वरिया, *m.* a swordsman, sword-player, fencer: [*f.* a sword.

तर्वार, *f.* a sword, scimitar.

तर्षना, *more com.* **तरसना**, *q. v.*

तर्ष, *m.* thirst, desire, wish.

तर्षण, *m.* a thirsting, thirst (literal or metaphorical).

तर्षित, *more prop.* **तृषित**, *q. v.*

तर्स, *m.* compassion, mercy. — *khānā*, to feel pity, to compassionate.

तर्सना, *a. int.* to long, desire eagerly, be agog: [to pity, compassionate.

तर्साना, *t.* to cause to long, set agog, tantalize, tease, vex.

तर्सील, *f.* a sending, transmitting.

तर्सों, the third day past or yet to come (not including the present, *i. e.* with two days intervening).

तल, *m.* surface, bottom, depth, lowness, inferiority of position, the place under, underneath part, the sole of the foot, the palm of the hand, the ground, floor, deck, back: sometimes for *tale*, underneath.

तलऊपर, upside down, topsy-turvy, confused.

तलवकी, *more prop.* **तलवेकी** (**तलवा**).

तलक = **तक**, 2, *q. v.*

तलक़, *m.* divorce, repudiation: talc.

तलक़ीन, *f.* an instructing, informing, initiating; religious instruction, funeral service. — *k.* to instruct, to initiate.

तलख़, bitter, rancid; acrimonious, malicious; sorrowful.

तलग = **तक**, 2, *q. v.*

तलछम, a light soil above clay.

तलछट, *f.* dregs, sediment, scum, lees, offal, refuse, leavings.

तलतलाना, *a. int.* to shake.

तलताला, *m.* the slapping the hands together.

तलन, *m.* a frying; fried meat.

तलना, *n.* to be fried: *t.* to fry.

तलपट, ruined, destroyed (as crops by the trampling of cattle).

तलपना = **तलफना**, *q. v.*

तलफ़, *m.* ruin, destruction, loss; prodigality, consumption, expense. — *k.* to waste, consume. — *honā*, to be unfortunate, meet with loss.

तलफना, *a. int.* to flutter, palpitate, flounce, be agitated, be restless.

तलफें in Braj = **तलफे** (**तलफना**).

तलब, *f.* pay, wages, salary; desire, request, demand, sending for, application, inquiry, searching.

तलबचिट्ठी, *f.* a summons, citation.

तलबाना, *m.* daily pay of constables and others paid by those they guard, etc.

तलबी, *f.* a call, summons; demand, request, application; wish, desire

तलबीस, *f.* cheating, fraud, imposture; fallacy; mixture, confusion; misrepresentation.

तलमलाना, *a. int.* to grieve, be agitated, be tantalized.

तलमीज़, *m.* a student, pupil, disciple.

तलव, *more prop.* **तलब**, *q. v.*

तलवरिया = **तर्वरिया**, *q. v.*

तलवा, *m.* the sole of the foot, heel. — *chātnā* or *talwe tale hāth dharnā*, *t.* to flatter. *Talwe sahlānā*, (*lit.* to stroke the soles of the feet; *i. e.*) to flatter excessively. *Talwonse āg lagni*, *lit.* a burning in the soles of the feet; the phrase implies excessive anger.

तलवाना, *n.* to have feet that are blistered from the heat of the sun.

तलवार = **तर्वार**, *q. v.*

तलवासना, *a. int.* to wear out (said of the feet of an animal which are worn by treading on hard ground).

तलव्वुन, *m.* changing colours like a chameleon; fidgeting, restlessness, capriciousness.

तला, 1, *f.* the leathern fence worn by archers on the left arm: 2, *m.* (?) the bottom of anything, the sole of a shoe; the stand or support of anything (that which is under or below it): protection.

तलाई, *f.* 1, (dim. of **तलाव**) a small tank: 2, see **तलाना**.

तलाओं, low grounds.

तलाक़, *f.* divorce, repudiation.

तलाटा, *m.* the East.

तलाटे, downwards.

तलातल, *m. pr. n.* one of the seven divisions of the infernal regions.

तलातुम, *m.* a buffeting, dashing.

तलाना, *t.* (causat. of **तलना**) to cause to fry.

तलाफ़ी, *f.* compensation, recompense.

तलार, (= **तले**) underneath, below.

तलाव, *m.* a reservoir of water, a pond, large tank.

तलावत, *f.* religious meditation or reading: grace, beauty, elegance.

तलावा = **तलाव**, *q. v.*

तलाश, *f.* search, inquiry, study.

तलाशना, *t.* to rub the palms of the hands or the soles of the feet.

तलाशी, *m.* (*f.* inī) one who searches goods.

तलिस्म = **तिलस्म**, *q. v.*

तलिहडू, one who acts at the command of another: *lit.* inferior, next, below.

तली, *f.* the bottom of anything, the neath or under part; the sole of a shoe; impalpable.

तलीनो, *f.* a kind of beetle the wings of which are used for blistering as a substitute for cantharides. This insect makes its appearance chiefly during the rainy season.

तलीपु (*by inversion*) = **पुतली**, *q. v.*

तलुआ = **तलवा**, *q. v.*

तले, *postp.* (takes genit. *m.* infl.) at the foot of, below, beneath, under: *adv.* down. *Tale tale dekhnā*, *t.* to see clandestinely. *Taleki zamin ūpar honī* is a phrase that is used to express great disturbance and confusion. The sign of the genitive is often dropped before this postposition; *e.g. Talwe tale* = *talweke tale*: *Vriksh e* = *vrikshke tale*.

तले ऊपर = तलोपरि, *q. v.*

तलैया, *f.* (dim. of तलाव) a small pond.

तलेहा, *m.* a turtle-dove.

तलोपरि, upside-down, topsy-turvy, confused.

तल्ल, a hillock, hill, heap.

तल्लास, तल्लाश, corruptions of तलाश, *q. v.*

तल्लिका, *f.* a key.

तव, (Sk.; freq. in poet.) = तेरा, *q.v.*

तवकुश्र = तवक्क़ा, *q. v.*

तवक्क़ा, *f.* request, desire, wish, hope, expectation, trust, reliance.

तवताई, *more prop.* तबतई, *q. v.*

तवज्जुह, *f.* (*pl.* āt) turning towards, regarding, attending to; kindness, favour, oblig'ngness.

तवर्ग, *m.* (in Gram.) the designation applied to the consonants of the त, or dental, class; *viz.* त, थ, द, ध, न.

तवा, *m.* the iron plate on which bread is baked; an iron mirror, the part of a hukkā to which tobacco is fixed, or the tobacco itself.

तवारीख़, *f.* (pl. of तारीख़.) dates; chronicles, annals, histories; *pr. n.* the Books of Chronicles.

तवे, *more prop.* तबही, *q. v.*

तश्रीफ़, *f.* honoring, exalting; investing with a splendid robe.

तश्तड़ी } *f.* a salver, small plate, saucer.
तश्तरी }

तस, a corruption of तैसा (poet.).

तस्दियत, *f.* a clapping the hands; doing a favour.

तसदु, a coming up in front of, opposing, confronting.

तसद्दुक़, *m.* alms; giving alms; sacrificing, devoting. — *honā*, to become devoted heart and soul to a beloved object, to become a sacrifice.

तसबीर, *more prop.* तसवीर, *q. v.*

तसर, *m.* a shuttle: a kind of coarse silk, the produce of a certain worm (*Bombyx paphia*) that feeds on the *ashan*-tree.

तसला, *m.* a kind of vessel in which Hindoos dress their food.

तसलीम, *f.* (*pl.* āt) delivery, consignment; a certain respectful mode of doing obeisance. — *k.* to resign, cede, surrender, give up with resignation; to do homage.

तसल्ली, *f.* consolation, solace, comfort. — *denā*, to assure, secure, animate, exhilarate.

तसल्लुत, *m.* command, absolute rule, sway.

तसवीर, *f.* a picture, likeness, image. — *khainchnā* or *banānā*, to draw, paint.

तसावी, *f.* similarity, equality, neutrality.

तसाहुल, *m.* conniving at, condoning, pardoning; carelessness.

तसु (old form) = तिसका.

तस्कर, *m.* (*f.* ī) a stealer, thief, robber: a kind of potherb (*Medicago esculenta*); a certain tree (*Vangueria spinosa*).

तस्करता, *f.* (*m.* °त्व) thieving; thievishness.

तस्करी, *f.* theft; a female thief, a passionate woman.

तस्म, *m.* a razor-strop.

तस्मा, *m.* a thong, strap of leather. — *khainchnā*, *t.* to strangle.

तस्मात्, (Sk. abl. sing. of तद्, that) from that, *i. e.* therefore, on that account.

तस्सू, *m.* a measure of nearly one inch.

तह, *f.* a fold, plait; a layer, stratum; bottom, beneath.

तहउं in Braj = तैसौं, *q.v.*

तहं, a contraction of तहां, *q.u.*

तहंवा } (*Rām.*) = तहां, *q.v.*
तहंवां }

तहक़ीक़, *f.* (*pl.* āt) investigation, enquiry, trial, verification, proving, ascertaining; exactness, precision; truth, certainty: *adv.* for certain.

तहक़ीर, *f.* a despising, neglect, disdain.

तहक़्क़ुक़, *m.* ascertainment, certain knowledge, verification.

तहक्कुम, *m.* a commanding, ruling, dominion, power, authority; the usurping authority; condemning, passing sentence.

तहख़ाना, *m.* an apartment underground, lower story, vault, cellar, cave, grotto.

तहत, *m.* below, the inferior part: possession.

तहते in Braj = उससे. See ते, 3.

तहत्तुक, *m.* disgrace, dishonor.

तहदीद, *f.* a terrifying, menacing.

तहफा, *more prop.* तुहफा, *q.v.*

तहबन्द, *m.* a cloth worn around the waist and passing between the legs.

तहमत, *more prop.* तुहमत, *q. v.*

तहमील, *f.* an emburdening, imposing a load upon; asking more than one's claim, importuning.

तहम्मुल, *m.* patience, endurance, longsuffering, forbearance, resignation, truce, meekness, humility, peace.

तहरीर, *f.* writing correctly: manumission.

तहर्रुक, *m.* movement, move.

तहलील, *f.* the acknowledging God and Muhammad by repeating the Arabic formula.

तहवा } (Rām.) = तहां, *q. v.*
तहवां }

तहवील, *f.* trusts, charges; cash; return; renovation, change, transfer; the passing of the sun, moon or planets from one sign to another.

तहवीलदार, *m.* a cash-keeper, treasurer.

तहसनहस, ruined, destroyed; dispersed.

तहसीन, *f.* approbation, applause, acclamation; (in Gram.) euphony. — *k.* to applaud.

तहसील, *f.* (*pl.* āt) collecting (esp. of revenues); the district allotted to a collector of revenue; acquisition.

तहसीलदार, *m.* a collector of revenue.

तहसीलदारी, *f.* the status or the work of a collector of revenue.

तहसीलना, *t.* to gather taxes; *hence*, to oppress, afflict.

तहस्सुर, *m.* grieving, regretting; condolence.

तहा, *more prop.* तहां, *q.v.*

तहाइफ़, *m.* (pl. of तुहफ़ा) curiosities, rarities, choice articles, presents.

तहां, (correl. of जहां) at that juncture, there, thither, then.

तहांतहां, (correl. of जहांजहां, wherever) there, in each place.

तहाना, *t.* to fold, ply, wrap.

तहायफ, *more prop.* तहाइफ़, *q.v.*

तहारत, *f.* purity; cleanliness; sanctity; ceremonial purification, ablution.

तहिया, see तहिश्रा and तहीया.

तहिश्रा (poet.: correl. of जहिश्रा) then.

तही, a corruption of तेहि, *q.v.*

तहीया, *m.* a preparing, putting in order.

तहीं, (emphatic form of तहां) there, in that same place, exactly there, in that very direction, thither.

तहोबाला क°, *t.* to subvert, overthrow.

ता; this particle performs various functions in Hindee; 1, It is one of the inflective bases of the singular of वह or वुह in Braj or old Hindee; *e.g.* Nom. वह; Gen. ताको or वाको. 2, This is the masculine form of the termination of the present participle in Hindee,—the feminine form being ती; *e.g.* करता, *m.* (*f.* करती). 3, This is the feminine form of the termination of a large class of past passive participles of Sanskrit whose masculine form ends in त: in Hindee they are used as adjectives; *e.g.* तृषित, *m.* (*f.* तृषिता). 4, Many masculine nouns of agency in Hindee end with this termination, — the feminine ending in त्री. This is the form of the nominative case of such words in Sanskrit, — the Dictionary form being *m.* तृ (*f.* त्री); *e.g.* दाता, *m.* (*f.* दात्री) =Sk. दातृ, *m.* (*f.* दात्री). 5, As a Taddhita suffix it forms abstract substantives feminine from substantives and adjectives; *e.g.* मित्रता; कुशलता. Such words are always susceptible of a corresponding masculine form by adding त्व instead of ता: in Hindee, however, the form in ता is by far the more usual of the two. 6, This is one of the forms of the remoter demonstrative pronoun in Braj or old Hindee (he, she, it): it is both masculine and feminine, and is inflected thus, ते. 7, It is frequently a corruption of था, was.

ताइत, *m.* an amulet, charm.

ताइफ़ा, *m.* people, nation, tribe, suit, equipage; a troop, band (*esp.* of musicians and dancing-women).

ताइब, *m.* a penitent: *lit.* adj. penitent, repenting.

ताइरख़ाना, *m.* (*lit.* a bird-house) an aviary.

ताई, *f.* (of ताऊ) an aunt, *i. e.* a paternal uncle's wife, a father's elder brother's wife: an earthen frying-pot.

ताईयार, *more prop.* तैय्यार, *q.v.*

ताईं, see तईं, तई, and ताईं.

ताउ, *more com.* (1) ताऊ (2) ताव, *qq.v*

ताऊ, *m.* (*f.* ताई) a paternal uncle, a father's elder brother.

ताएरा, *m.* (*f.* ī) born of a father's elder brother.

ताएराभाई, *m.* }
ताएरीबहिन, *f.* } a cousin.

तां, a contraction of तहां, *q.v.*

तांई; see (1) तई (2) तई (3) ताईं.

तांऊ, *more prop.* ताऊ, *q.v.*

तांगल, *m.* a small tank or pond.

तांगा, *m.* a small two-wheeled car (without a covering, in which only one person can sit): the rostrum or fore-part of a Hindoo car (to which the bullocks are yoked).

तांगासवार, *m.* a person who rides on a *tāngā*, *q.v.*

तांडव = ताण्डव, *q.v.*

तांवर; see ताम्बर.

ताक, *f.* a vine, creeper; grasses: a look, fixed gaze; a glance, view, peep; the act of aiming, aim, pointing (of a dog). — *bāndhnā*, to covet, point (as a dog). — *rahnā*, to aspire.

ताक़त, *f.* strength, power, ability, force, patience. — *se tāk honā*, to be powerless, be feeble.

ताकना, *t.* to stare at, behold, look, see, view, watch, spy, peep; to look for; to aim; to attend.

ताकबाक़, *f.* the nick of time.

ताकह, *m.* a single garment, a piece of woollen cloth.

ताका = तिसका. (Braj or old Hindee.)

ताकाताकी, *f.* a mutual staring, bo-peep.

ताकि, so that, to the end that, in order that; until, so long.

ताकी = तिसकी. (Braj or old Hindee.) See ता, 1.

ताकीद, *f.* confirmation; superintendence; ascertaining; injunction; (in Gram.) emphasis. — *k.* to urge, press, enjoin strictly.

ताके, 1, in poetry = तिसके; 2, *more prop.* ताकि.

ताको, *more com.* (1) ताका (2) ताकों, *qq. v.*

ताको = तिसका }
ताकों = तिसको } (Braj or old Hindee.) See ता, 1.

ताख़, *m.* a veil; darkness: firewood.

ताख़्त, *f.* assault, attack, incursion, invasion. — *k.* to assault, invade.

ताख़्ततराज, *m.* assault and plunder, depredation, devastation. — *k.* to depopulate, devastate, ruin.

ताख़ीर, *f.* procrastination; impediment. — *k.* to postpone, delay.

ताग, *m.* thread.

तागतोड़, *m.* lace.

तागना, *t.* to thread.

तागा, *m.* thread.

तागी, *m.* an insurgent, leader of rebels: *lit.* violent, refractory, rebellious.

ताचन्द, how long? how many? by how much?

ताज, *m.* a crown, diadem; a crest, comb of a bird, cap.

ताज़गी, *f.* freshness, greenness, plumpness, fatness, tenderness; pleasure.

ताजजुब = ताअज्जुब, *q. v.*

ताजवरी, *f.* royalty, sovereignty.

ताज़ा, fresh, young, green, raw; fat; happy, pleased. — *k.* to renew, refresh.—*honā*, to be in good case, increase, flourish.

ताज़ादम, *m.* hilarity, cheerfulness, good spirits.

ताजिम (*corruption*) = ताअज़ीम, *q.v.*

ताज़िया, *m.* condolence, a comforting: a model of

the tomb of Hasan and Husain, which is thrown into a river or buried in the earth at the Muhammadan festival of the Muharram.

ताज़ियाना, *m.* a whip, scourge. —*jaṛnā* or *lagānā* or *mārnā*, to apply the lash.

ताज़िर, *f.* discretionary punishment (not specified by the law) correction, reproof, censure, reprimand.

ताज़ीम, *f.* reverence, respect, honour; treating with ceremony or respect, honouring; politeness, gentility.

ताज़ी, *m.* (*f.* inī) an Arabian horse.

ताजुब, a colloquial form of **ताज्जुब**, *q.v.*

ताजुलमलूक, *m. pr. n.* a certain Persian king: *lit.* the crown of kings.

ताज्जुब, *m.* wonderment, amaze, surprize, astonishment, admiration. —*k.* to be astonished.

ताट, *m.* hemp, tow, flax; sackcloth, a very coarse kind of cloth made of hemp, commonly called 'gunny.'

ताटंक, *m.* a kind of ear-ornament.

ताड़, 1, *m.* the palmyra-tree (*Borassus flabelliformis*), called also the fan-palm or toddy-tree: 2, *f.* understanding. —*jānā*, to understand, comprehend, conceive, guess. —*lenā*, to examine the accuracy of a pair of scales.

ताड़ंक, *m.* a kind of ear-ornament.

ताड़क, *m.* (*f.* ikā) a reprover, chastiser.

ताड़न, *m.* beating, whipping, chastisement, punishment, penalty, rebuke, admonition, reproof. —*k.* to reprove, chastise.

ताड़ना, 1, *f. m.*? = **ताड़न**, *q.v.*: 2, = **ताकना**, *q.v.*: 3, *t.* to understand, comprehend, apprehend, conceive, guess.

ताड़नी, *f.* a whip.

ताड़नीय, needing admonition, reproof or punishment, reproveable, punishable.

ताड़पत्र, *m.* the palm-leaf prepared for writing on; a document so written.

ताड़फल, *m.* the gelatinous pulp of the palmyra-tree.

ताड़वन, *m.* a grove of palmyra-trees.

ताड़बाज़, quick of apprehension, intelligent.

ताड़बाज़ी, *f.* quickness of apprehension.

ताड़सा, *m.* (*f.* ī) resembling the toddy-tree.

ताड़िका; see **ताड़क**.

ताड़ी, *f.* the juice of the palmyra-tree, 'toddy': the hilt of a dagger.

ताड़ीवाला, *m.* a man who climbs palmyra-trees and extracts the juice from them.

ताण्डव, *m.* dancing, frantic dancing, dancing with violent gesticulation. The term is applied in particular to the frantic dance of Shiv and his votaries.

तात, 1, = **ताता**, *q.v.*: 2, *m.* father. It is a term of affection or caressment addressed exclusively to males; *e.g.* (1) by parents to their children (2) by teachers to their pupils (3) by children to their fathers (4) by friends and brothers to each other.

तातः, venerable, respect-worthy, reverend.

तातनी, *f.* (Braj) of her, of that, of it.

तातनो, *m.* (Braj) of him, of that, of it.

तातपर्य, *more prop.* **तात्पर्य**, *q.v.*

तातप्यमान, *m.* (*f.* mati) a very afflicted person.

तातमात / **तातमातु** } *m.* father and mother, parents.

तातल, hot, warm; heating.

ताता, *m.* (*f.* ī) hot, warm; heating.

तातार, *m.* a Tartar; the Tartars: *pr. n.* Tartary.

तातारी, 1, *m.* (*f.* in *or* inī) appertaining to Tartary, Scythian, Tartaric: an agreeable friend: 2. *f.* a kind of slashed doublet open at the sides usually worn by the Tartars: fine musk.

ताति (poetic form) = **ताता**, *q. v.*

तातो; see **ताता**.

ताते in Braj and old Hindee = **तिससे**, from him, her, it, or that; *hence*, therefore, from which cause, whence, whereby, thereby, hence.

तातें = **ताते**, *q. v.*

तातौ, a Braj corruption (1) of **तता** (2) of **ताते**, *qq.v.*

तात्कालिक, *m.* (*f.* ā) appertaining to that time or period; lasting for a time of equal length (to that); instantly appearing.

तादिन (see **ता**, 1) = **उस दिन में**.

तात्पर्ज, *more prop.* **तात्पर्य**, *q. v.*

तात्पर्य, *m.* purport, object, aim, design, purpose, meaning, intent, drift, explanation, the apprehension of an implied wish or thought: need.

तात्पर्ययुत, *m.* (*f.* ā) having an object, pregnant with meaning.

तादात्म्य, *m.* identity; similarity, likeness.

तादीब, *f.* correction, chastisement, amendment, erudition; (in Law) a notice, summons. —*k.* to correct, instruct.

तादृश, such-like, that-like, like him, her, or it.

ताधराम, poor.

तान, 1, *m.* a species of vervain: 2, *f.* a kind of plant (*Verbena nodiflora*): 3, *m. f* ? a stretching, tension; knitting the eyebrows; thread; a musical tone, note in music, a tune, the seven octaves of seven notes each; hence, in the ingenious system of reckoning by symbols adopted by Hindoos in their poetry, this word is a symbol for 49.— *tornā*, to crack a joke; to strike up a tune; to drop a word that might induce conversation or excite a quarrel; to animadvert.

तानडव, a corruption of **ताण्डव**, *q.v.*

तानना, *t.* to extend, stretch, tighten, expand, pull; to knit the eyebrows. *Tambū* —, to pitch tents.

ताना, 1, a corruption of **तावना**, *q. v.*: 2, *m.* the threads that are extended lengthwise on a loom, the warp. *Tāne tānnā*, to wander hither and thither without profit: 3, *m.* taunting, sarcasm, reproach, ignominy, disgrace, aspersion. — *mārnā*, to taunt.

तानाबाना क', to fidget, dance attendance.

तानी, *f.* (see **ताना**, 2) the warp; the price paid for weaving.

तानीताना, the warp and the woof.

ताने in Braj = **उसने**. See **ता**, 1.

तानेतानना, *a. int.* to wander hither and thither without profit.

तान्त, 1, *m.* a weaving apparatus, loom: thread, fibre, etc.: 2, *f.* catgut, sinew, a string of a musical instrument. — *bāndhnā*, *t.* to put to silence an idle talker. — *bāt aur rāg bujhā*, he understood from the first word.

तान्ता, *m.* a series, range, row, train, string (of camels, horses, etc.).

तान्ती, *m.* (*f.* inī) a weaver.

तान्त्र, *m.* instrumental music.

तान्त्रिक, *m.* (*f.* ī) a person completely versed in any science or system, a scholar, a follower of the doctrines of the Tantras : *lit.* appertaining to the Tantras.

ताचा = तानना, *q. v.*

ताचो, *f.* procrastination, delay.

ताप, 1, *f.* = तप, 2, *q. v.* : 2, *m.* warmth, heat, burning (physical or metaphorical : *hence*) affliction in mind, pain, sorrow, distress, passion. *Trivid* —, the three kinds of suffering, *viz.* (1) *Deh tāp*, that which is occasioned by the body (2) *Daivik tāp*, that which comes from Providence, *e. g.* calamity, etc. (3) *Bhautik tāp*, that which arises from existence, or contact with the world. [ikā) burning, inflaming, heating.

तापक, 1, *m.* fever, morbid heat : 2, *adj. m.* (*f.*

तापठगड, *m.* ague ; *lit.* fever and shivering.

तापतिल्ली = ताबतिल्ली, *q. v.*

तापन, 1, *m.* heating, inflaming ; the sun ; name of a hell : 2, *adj. m.* (*f.* ī) tormenting.

तापना, *t.* to heat, warm, warm oneself: *a. int.* to bask in the sun or at a fire.

तापर = तिस पर. Braj or old Hindee.

तापस, *m.* (*f.* ī) a practiser of religious austerities, ascetic, devotee : *lit.* practising penance.

तापसप्रिय, *f.* an epithet of Ahalyā, the wife of Gautam ; *lit.* the wife of the ascetic.

तापहारी, *m.* (*f.* iṇī) a remover of trouble ; (epithet of a deity). [ship, affection, friendship.

तापाक, *m.* the anguish of love, solicitude of friend-

तापित, *m.* (*f.* ā) inflamed ; pained, distressed.

तापी, 1, *f. pr. n.* (1) of the Surāt river, Tāptee (2) of the Jumnā river : 2, *m.* (*f.* ī) anything heated or glowing : *prop.* heated, glowing, oppressed by heat (physical or metaphorical) : 3, *f.* a bricklayer's trowel.

तापे in Braj = उसपर.

ताप्य, *m.* a mineral substance (a sulphuret of iron) said to be procured from the Tāpee river.

ताब, *f.* power ; heat ; endurance, brooking ; twisting, contortion ; rage, fury ; light, splendour.

ताबजोस्त, while life remains.

ताबड़तोड़, successively, repeatedly.

ताबतिल्ली, *f.* an induration of the spleen attended with fever or preceded by it ; ague-cake, *splenitis.*

ताबानी, *f.* brilliancy, splendour, light.

ताबिअ, *adj.* dependent, subject. — *k.* to subject, control. — *rahnā*, to remain in subjection.

ताबिअदार, *more com.* ताबिदार, *q. v.*

ताबिच (old form) = उसके बीचमें.

ताबिदार, *m.* a dependent, follower. [fidelity.

ताबिदारी, *f.* dependence, allegiance, obedience,

ताबिनु (old form) = उसके बिना.

ताबिन्ददार (*corruption*) = ताबिदार, *q. v.*

ताबिया, *m.* an arranging (furniture) ; exercising,

ताबिस्तान, *m.* hot weather, summer. [training.

ताबीज, *m.* a small box in which charms are kept.

ताबूत, *m.* a coffin ; a bier ; the ark of the covenant presented by God to Adam (which, according to the Muhammadans, contained the portraits of all the prophets) ; the representation of a coffin carried about at the time of the Muharram.

ताबे = ताबिअ, *q. v.*

ताम, 1, see (1) ताम्ब (2) ताम्र ; 2, *m.* an object of terror ; fault, defect, vice ; anxiety, distress, desire.

तामचीनी, *f.* enamelled copper.

तामटगर = ताम्बटगर, *q. v.*

तामड़ा, *m.* a copper-coloured gem of inferior value.

तामरस, *m.* a lotus (*Nymphæa nelumbo*) ; copper ; [gold.

तामरसी, *f.* a pond full of lotus-flowers.

तामलकी, *f.* a species of plant (*Flacourtia cataphracta*). [ern Bengal.

तामलिप्त, *f. pr. n.* the district of Tamluk in south-

तामस, *m.* (*f.* ī) a person under the influence of *tamogun* ; hence, a mischievous and malignant person, incendiary, villain, etc. : *lit.* affected by or appertaining to the third *gun*, *viz.* that of darkness or vice, partaking of or influenced by the principle of vindictiveness, ignorance, mental darkness, etc. ; *hence*, inert, stupid, ignorant, vindictive, irascible, dark.

तामसी, *f.* (see तामस) a vindictive woman, etc.

तामा, *m.* (prop. ताम्र) copper.

तामात, inconsistent talk, words barbarously pronounced.

तामाम, *more prop.* तमाम, *q. v.*

तामाशा, *more prop.* तमाशा, *q. v.*

तामुस, feigning ignorance or negligence ; leaving anyone in doubt or uncertainty.

तामिस्र, *m.* wrath : *pr. n.* (1) of the dark half of the month from full moon to new moon (2) of one of the hells.

तामेश्वर, *m.* calx or scoriae of copper.

ताम्ब = ताम्बा, *q. v.*

ताम्बट, *m.* copper.

ताम्बटगर, *m.* a plumber. [resembling a ruby.

ताम्बड़ा, *m.* a copper colour in pigeons ; a false stone

ताम्बर, ताम्बा } *m.* (prop. ताम्र) copper.

ताम्बून, *m.* betel (*Piper betel*, Lin.) ; betel-leaf ; the areca-nut.

ताम्बूनराग, *m.* a species of pulse (*Ervum lens*).

ताम्बूलवल्ली, *f.* a small plant (*Piper betel*) bearing a pungent leaf, which, with the areca-nut, caustic lime or chunām, catechu, etc. form the *pān* or betel of the Asiatics.

ताम्बूली, 1, *f.* betel (*Piper betel*) or its pungent leaf : 2, *m.* (*f.* inī) the *pān*-bearer of a magnate, a servant whose business it is to prepare and present the *pān*.

ताम्बेन, a tortoise, turtle.

ताम्ब्रा = ताम्बड़ा, *q. v.*

ताम्म, perfect, entire, complete, full.

ताम्मुल, *m.* meditation, reflection, consideration, hesitation ; purpose. — *k.* to consider, reflect, collect oneself.

ताम्र, 1, *m.* copper ; a dark or coppery red ; a kind of sandal-wood said to be of a dark red colour and to smell like the lotus : 2, *m.* (*f.* ā) of a coppery-red colour : 3, *m.* (*f.* ī) consisting of copper.

ताम्रकर्णी, *f. pr. n.* the female elephant of the western quarter.

ताम्रकार, *m.* (*f.* ī) a coppersmith, plumber.

ताम्रकेतु, *m. pr. n.* a brother of Balarām.

ताम्रगर्भ, *m.* sulphate of copper or blue vitriol.

ताम्रपट्ट, *m.* a copper plate such as Hindoo grants of land, etc. are frequently engraved on.

ताम्रपर्णी, *f. pr. n.* of a river in the Dakkhan and of a district in its vicinity.

ताम्रपुष्प, *m.* a kind of ebony (*Bauhinia variegata*); a certain plant (*Kempferia rotunda*).

ताम्रपुष्पा, *f.* the trumpet-flower (*Bignonia suaveolens*).

ताम्रपुष्पी, *f. Lythrum fruticosum.*

ताम्रफल, *m. Alangium hexapetalum.*

ताम्रवर्णी, *f.* the blossom of sesamum.

ताम्रवल्ली, *f.* Bengal madder (*Rubia mangith*).

ताम्रबीज, *m.* a kind of vetch.

ताम्रवृक्ष, *m.* a kind of sandal-wood. [*santolinum*).

ताम्रसार, *m.* a red kind of sandal (*Pterospermum*

ताम्राकु, *m. pr. n.* one of the eighteen divisions of the known continent.

तामा; see **ताम्र**, 2.

ताम्रिक, *m.* (*f.* ā) a coppersmith, brazier: *lit.* coppery, consisting of or made of copper.

ताम्रिका, *f.* 1, a coppersmith's wife: 2, see **ताम्री**.

ताम्री, 1, see **ताम्र**, 3: 2, *f.* a kind of vessel for marking time, consisting of a copper or metallic cup of prescribed capacity and perforated by a small hole at the bottom, answering the purpose of an hour-glass. It is put into a vessel of water, and the sinking of the cup by its becoming gradually filled with water, indicates the time that has elapsed.

तायत, *more prop.* **ताइत**, *q.v.*

तायफा, *more prop.* **ताइफ़ा**, *q.v.*

ताया, *m.* an uncle (father's eldest brother).

तायेरा; see (1) **ताएरा** (2) **तेरा**.

तार, *m.* a shrill, loud sound, high note or tone in music; a thread; a wire, chord, string of a musical instrument. — *ṭuṭnā*, to be disjointed, be separated. — *bāndhnā*, to continue or to repeat an action without interruption. — *denā*, to pass over, free, absolve, save.

तारक, *m.* (*f.* ikā) a deliverer, protector, saviour, preserver: a star: the pupil of the eye: *pr. n.* a certain *daitya*.

तारकश, *m.* a wire-drawer.

तारकशी, *f.* wire-drawing. — *k.* to draw wires.

तारका, *f.* a star; the pupil of the eye.

तारकुन, a name of the secondary form of **उ**, *viz.* **ु**

तारख़, the root of the tongue, the palate.

तारख़ाना = **तारघर**, *q.v.*

तारघर, *m.* a telegraph-office; a wire-manufactory.

तारण, 1, *m.* a passing over, crossing over; a raft, float; the act of delivering, saving, freeing: 2, *m.* (*f.* ī) a saviour, one who delivers: *lit.* adj. saving.

तारणकर्ता, *m.* (*f.* trī) a deliverer, saviour.

तारणकारक, *adj.* delivering, effecting deliverance, saving; *hence*, *m.* (*f.* ika) a deliverer, saviour.

तारणतरण, *m.* (*f.* ī) the saviour and the saved.

तारणहार, *adj.* delivering, saving: hence; *m.* (*f.* ī) a deliverer, saviour.

तारणहारक, *m.* (*f.* ikā) = **तारणहार**, *q.v.*

तारणा, *more prop.* **तारना**, *q.v.*

तारणी, *f.* (see **तारण**, 2) a female deliverer.

तारतम्य, *m.* distinction, discrimination, proportion: *lit.* the state or condition of more or less, more-or-lessness.

तारतार बोलना, *a. int.* to speak in detail or circumstantially.

तारतोड़, *m.* a kind of sewing or needlework, open work, pulling out some threads, etc.

तारना, *t.* to exempt from further transmigration, free, rid, absolve from sin, save.

तारपतार, dispersed, scattered.

तारपीन, *m.* (Engl.) turpentine.

तारबिजुली, *f.* a lightning-conductor; the electric spark.

तारयन्त्र, *m.* a telegraph-machine.

तारा, *m. f.* a star; the pupil of the eye: a proper name among Hindoo females. *Tāre ginnā*, to count the stars, *i. e.* to get no sleep.

तारागण, *m.* (see **गण**) the stars, the starry host.

ताराग्रह, *m.* (star-planet) one of the five lesser planets, exclusive of the sun and moon.

ताराज, *m.* plunder, devastation. — *k.* to devastate, lay waste, spoil.

तारापथ, *m.* the starry region; *hence*, the firmament, sky, visible heavens.

तारामण्डल, *m.* the starry sphere; *hence*, the firmament, sky, visible heavens.

तारि = **तारके** (**तारना**). See **इ**, 7.

तारिक, *m.* a deserter: toll for passage.

तारिका, 1, *more prop.* **तारका**, *q.v.*: 2, *f.* (see **तारक**) a female deliverer.

तारिख़, *more prop.* **तारीख़**, *q.v.*

तारिणी, *f. pr. n.* (1) of a goddess peculiar to the Jains (2) of Durgā; *lit.* a female deliverer; (see below).

तारी, 1, *m.* (*f.* iṇī) a saviour, deliverer: 2, *f.* the clapping of hands: a key: absorption in devotion or in thought, abstraction, absence of mind: obscurity, darkness.

तारीक, obscure, dark, benighted.

तारीख़, *f.* a (historical) date; era; annals.

तारीफ़, *f.* a praising; an asserting; an explaining, description; a table of rates of export and import duties, 'tariff'.

तारुण्य, *m.* youth; youthfulness.

तालु, *m.* the palate.

तारे तोड़ना, to act deceitfully.

तारौ, in Braj = **तारो** (**तारना**).

तार्किक, *m.* (*f.* ā *or* ī) a dialectician, philosopher, sophist, follower of either of the six schools of Hindoo philosophy: *lit.* appertaining to the science of reasoning.

तार्किकः = **तार्किक**, *q.v.*

तार्क्ष, *m.* 1, *more prop.* **तार्क्ष्य**, *q.v.*: 2, a kind of bird; a species of plant: a name of Kashyap.

तार्क्ष्य = **गरुड़**, *q.v.*

तार्ना, *more prop.* **तारना**, *q.v.*

ताल, *m.* a pond: the slapping or clapping the hands together whether with the view of beating time in music or previous to wrestling or fighting;

beating time in music, musical measure, chime ; a sort of cymbal (of bell-metal or brass) played with a stick : the palmyra-tree or fan-palm (*Borassus flabelliformis*), also (1) its fruit, and (2) its leaf used as a banner. —*denā*, to chime; to slap the hands together or against the arms before fighting. *Tālbetāl*, out of tune.—*thoknā* or *mārnā*, to strike the hands against the arms preparatory to wrestling or fighting.

तालक, *m.* a kind of lock, bolt, latch.

तालजंघ, *m.* (*f.* ā) *adj.* having legs as long as a palm-tree : *pr. n.* (1) of a prince of the Tāljanghās (2) of their ancestor (3) of a son of Jaydhvaj (4) of a Rākshas (5) of a Daitya.

तालपत्र, *m.* a hollow cylinder of gold (with or without a ring attached to it) thrust through the lobe of the ear, and worn as an ornament.

तालपर्णी, *f.* a sort of anise (*Anethum panmorium*).

तालपुष्पक, *m.* a medicinal application to the eyes.

तालमखाना, *m.* a species of medicinal herb (*Barleria longifolia*).

तालमूली, *f.* a certain plant (*Curculigo orchioides*).

तालवृन्त, *m.* a fan.

तालव्य, (in Gram.) palatal.

तालव्यवर्ण, *m.* (in Gram.) a palatal.

ताला, *m.* a lock, door-lock ; the lid of a vessel. —*denā* or *de denā*, to lock. —*diyā gaya*, locked. —*kholnā*, to unlock.

तालाख्य, *f.* a perfume.

तालाब, = **तालाव**, *q. v.*

तालाव, *m.* an artificial pond, tank, reservoir for water.

तालाबि, *more com.* **तालाव**, *q. v.*

तालाश, *more prop.* **तलाश**, *q. v.*

तालिक, *m.* the clapping the hands together.

तालिका, *f.* the palm of the hand.

तालिब, *adj.* asking, demanding, interrogating : hence, *m.* a requirer, demander, inquirer.

तालिशपत्री, *f.* a certain restringent plant and fragrant stomachic (*Flacourtia cataphracta*).

ताली, 1, *m.* (*f.* inī) a person provided with cymbals : 2, *f.* a sort of key or pin : a clapping the hands together : a species of mountain palm (*Corypha taliera*, Roxb.) ; a certain plant (*Flacourtia cataphracta*). —*ek hāthse bajnā*, (*lit.* to produce a clapping with one hand, *i. e.*) to attempt an impossibility. —*bajānā*, to clap the hands (not in token of approbation but of ridicule or censure) ; to hoot a person. —*mārnā*, to hoot, damn (in the theatrical sense) ; also, to applaud.

तालीका, *m.* a list, catalogue, inventory.

तालीफ़, *f.* composition, compiling ; connecting, reconciling, joining in friendship.

तालीम, *f.* (*pl.* āt) teaching, instruction, tuition. [—*denā*, to instruct.

तालीयक, *m.* a cymbal.

तालु, *m.* the palate, the ridge or slit in the roof of the mouth : a disorder in horses, the lampreys.

तालू, a corruption of 1, **ताल** ; 2, **तालाव**; 3, **तालु**.

तालूषक, *m.* the palate.

तालों, a poetical form of **तबलों**, *q. v.*

ताल्लुक़, *m.* (*pl.* āt) relationship, connexion, dependence; consideration, reflection ; commerce, correspondence, property, appurtenance, possession; a manor, lordship, lease in perpetuity, subdivision of a county (or *zillah*, which consists of several *ta'alluks*).

ताव, *m.* a sheet of paper : proof, assay, trial: speed ; heat ; passion, rage ; strength, power ; splendour, dignity: twist, contortion, coil.—*khānā* or—*pech khānā*, to be heated; to be angry. —*denā*, to twist; to stroke the whiskers ; to heat (as iron).

तावत, (correl. of **यावत**) so much, so many, so far, so long, unto, until.

तावत्पर्यन्त, (Sansk.) = **तबतलक**, *q. v.*

तावना, *t.* to heat, raise heat by blowing with bellows, anneal ; to assay, prove: to twist.

तावान, *m.* retaliation, recompense ; debt, loan ; fine, mulct. — *bāndhnā* or *lagānā* or *lenā*, to amerce.

तावील, *f.* explanation, elucidation, interpretation, paraphrase.

ताश, *f.* gold foil, tinsel, cloth of gold, brocade.

तास, 1, *more prop*, **ताश**, *q. v.*: 2, *m.* playing-cards; the game of cards.

तासन (old form) = **तिस्से**.

तासनास = **सत्यानाश**, *q. v.*

तासीर, *f.* (*pl.* āt)) penetration, passing through; an effect, impression.

तासु = **तिसके**. An old form frequent in Braj and in poetry (esp. in the Rāmāyaṇ).

तासुको, *m.* (*f.* °की) = **तिसका**. A redundant or double genitive (Braj).

तासे = **तासु** or **तासों**, *qq. v.*

तासों (Braj or old Hindee) = **तिस्से**.

ताह, *f.* a plait, fold, ply; multiplicity, perplexity.

ताहा ; see (1) **ताह** (2) **तहां** (3) **वह**.

ताहां, in Chand = **तहां**, *q. v.*

ताहाल, hitherto, till now, yet.

ताहि = **तिसको**. (Braj or old Hindee).

ताहिं = **तिसको** and **तिसको भी**. (Braj or old Hindee.)

ताहिको (in Braj) = **तिसका**. (A double genitive.)

ताहिकों (in Braj) = **तिसको**. (A double dative and accusative.)

ताहिरी, *f.* a kind of dish, *viz.* rice boiled with *barī* which consists of pulse (*Phaseolus radiatus*) ground in a wet state and mixed with ginger, pepper, etc. and then dried in small lumps.

ताहिसों (in Braj) = **तिस्से**.

ताही, *more prop.* **ताहि**, *q. v.*

ताहू, in old Hindee = **वहां**, and **वह भी**.

ति ; 1, in Braj this particle sometimes means 'three' : *in composition* this is sometimes its meaning in regular Hindee ; *e. g.* **तिबारा**: 2, In Braj or old Hindee this is the inflective base of the singular of one of the forms of the personal pronoun of the third person ; *e. g.* **तिहि**: 3, This is a Kridanta suffix by means of which a large number of substantives, feminine, expressive of the result of an act, or of the act itself generally, are derived from verbal roots; *e.g.* **गति** (from root **गम्**) ; **शक्ति** (from root **शक्**) : 4, In Braj and in poetry, this is frequently the termination, for all genders and numbers, of the present participle ; *e. g.* **करति** = **करता, करती, करते**. 5, In poetry and in Braj this most frequently stands for **ती** of the present participle feminine ; thus **देति** = **देती**.

तिआग, *more com.* **त्याग**, *q. v.*

तिउरी ; see **तेवरी**.

तित, तिंद ; see तिन्त, तिन्द.
तिकट, = टिकट, q.v.
तिकतिक, f. a sound used in driving a cart.
तिकार, three ploughings.
तिकोनिया, a triangular figure : *lit.* three-cornered.
तिक्का, m. a small piece of flesh, a steak, slice, chop, collop.
तिक्काबोटी क°, t. to tear (a prey) to small pieces.
तिक्त, m. (f. ikā) a bitter taste, bitterness ; fragrance, perfume : *adj.* bitter ; fragrant.
तिक्तक, m. anything of a bitter taste; the name of several plants, *e.g.* a kind of gourd (*Trichosanthes diœca*, Roxb.) ; a sort of gentian (*G. cherayta*): *lit.* bitter.
तिक्तकगन्धा, f. a species of plant (*Lycopodium imbricatum*.
तिक्ततुम्बी, f. a bitter gourd.
तिक्तदुग्धा, f. a medicinal kind of moon-plant.
तिक्तपत्र, m. a kind of cucurbitaceous plant (*Momordica mixta*). [a species of plant (*Menispermum glabrum*).
तिक्तपर्व्वन, f. a kind of potherb (*Hilancha repens*);
तिक्तभद्रक, m. a kind of cucumber (*Trichosanthes diœca*).
तिक्तरोहिणिका, f. a certain medicinal plant.
तिक्तवल्ली, f. the plant *Aletris hyacinthoides*.
तिक्तसाक, m. the plant *Capparis trifoliata*.
तिक्तसार, m. a species of Mimos (*Mimosa catechu*).
तिक्तिका, f. (of. तिक्तक) a bitter gourd.
तिच्छा ; for all words beginning thus, see under the more proper form तीच्छा.
तिखरा क°, to trifallow, plough three times.
तिखाना = तिखारना, q.v.
तिखारना, 1, = तिखरा क°, q.v.: 2, t. to enquire earnestly, establish by argument, prove, confirm.
तिगुण, m. a tone in music (treble ?) : *lit.* adj. threefold, triple, treble.
तिगुणा }
तिगुना } threefold, triple, treble.
तिग्म, 1, m. (f. ā) hot, sharp, pungent, acrid ; sharp (as a weapon) : 2, m. heat, the heat of spices, pungency.
तिग्मग, m. (f. ā) flying swiftly.
तिच्छन, m. (f. ā) a corruption of तीच्छण, q.v.
तिजरी, f. a tertian fever or ague.
तिजाउज़, m. diversity, deviating, transgressing, offending. —*k.* to deviate, stray, err, offend, transgress.
तिजारत, f. trade, commerce.—*k.* to carry on trade.
तिजारी = तिजरी, q.v. [apathy, indifference.
तिजाहुल, m. pretending ignorance, connivance,
तिटकारना, t. to urge on a horse by giving utterance to any sound.
तिठना, a. int. to stay, remain.
तिड़ीबिड़ी, f. medley, mishmash.
तिड्डा, m. a grasshopper, locust.
तिड्डी, 1, m. ? a troop or body of men: 2, f. a locust.
तियठी, f. the *teorī*-plant.
तित, that way, thither, there.
तितउ, m. a sieve.
तितग्गी, f. a thread of three strands.
तितना, (correl. of जितना) m. (f. ī) so much, that much. *Titnemeṅ*, in so much time.
तितने, *pl.* (correl. of जितने) m. (f. ī) so many.
तितरबितर, dispersed, scattered.
तितलिया, a butterfly (?).
तितली, f. a butterfly.
तितहूं, (correl. of जितहूं) = तिधर, q.v.
तितिक्षा, f. suffering, patience, sufferance, endurance, resignation.
तितिक्षित, m. (f. ā) patient, enduring, resigned.
तितिक्षु = तितिक्षित, q.v.
तितिम्बा, m. an obstacle, impediment, stratagem.
तितिल, m. *pr. n.* one of the seven *karaṇs* or astronomical periods : a species of sweetmeat made of sesamum ground and baked with sugar.
तितेक, (correl. of जितेक) so much, so many.
तित्तरबित्तर, dispersed, scattered.
तित्तार ; see (1) तित्ताल (2) तीतर. [ing, knavish.
तित्ताल, m. a cheat, knave : *lit.* deceitful, cheat-
तित्ताली, f. deceitfulness, cheating, knavery.
तित्तिर, m. = तित्तिरि, q. v.
तित्तिरि, m. the Francoline partridge (*Perdrix Francolinus*) : *pr. n.* (1) of the black Yajur Ved (2) of a certain *Muni*, one of its early teachers (the Ved being thus named after him).
तिथ, *more prop.* तिथि, q.v.
तिथयग्म, *more com.* तिथिग्राम, q.v.
तिथि, m. f. a lunar day, the thirtieth part of an entire lunation : the 15th is a semi-lunation ; hence, in the ingenious system of reckoning by symbols adopted by Hindoos in their poetry, this word is a symbol for 15.
तिथिक्षय, m. the day of new moon ; the day or space in which a *tithi* begins or ends without one sunrising ; the difference between the solar and lunar days in a *yug*.
तिथी, f. = तिथि, q. v.
तिथिग्रन्थ, m. any book containing an account of the *tithis*.
तिथिग्राम, m. the aggregate of the *tithis*.
तिदरी, *adj.* three-doored. [thither.
तिधर, (correl. of जिधर) there, in that direction,
तिधारा, m. a certain plant (*Euphorbia antiquorum*) : the meeting of three streams.
तिधारी, f. ? the meeting of three streams.
तिन, 1, *more prop.* तीन, q.v.: 2, (correl. of जिन) the inflective base of the oblique cases of the plural of सो (or तीन).
तिनकना, a. int. to flutter, palpitate, throb.
तिनकर = तिनका, 1 : see कर, 3.
तिनका, 1, m. (f. ī) gen. of तिन, q.v.: 2, m. a straw, bit of the stalk of grass. *Tinke chunnā*, to be intoxicated ; *lit.* to pick straws. *Tinkā dañtoṅmeṅ lenā*, to make submission, confess inferiority, ask for quarter.
तिनको in Braj = उसका. See तिन, 2.

तिनहूं, old form = (1) तिनको (2) उनको भी (3) तीनों.

तिनि in Chand = तिन, 2, *q.v.*

तिनिश, *m.* the tree *Dalbergia ougeinensis.*

तिनु, *more com.* (1) तिन (2) तीनों, *qq.v.*

तिनुका, *more com.* तिनका, *q.v.*

तिनै in Chand = तिन, 2, *q.v.*

तिनो (*corruption*) = तीनों, *q.v.*

तिन्तिड़ी, *m.* the tamarind-tree.

तिन्दु, *m.* a species of ebony (*Diospyros glutinosa*) from the fruit of which a kind of resin is obtained that is used in India as pitch for caulking vessels.

तिन्दुकी, *f.* the resinous fruit of the above-mentioned kind of ebony.

तिन्नी, *f.* a kind of rice.

तिन्ह = तिन, *q.v.*

तिन्हन (corrupt) = तिन्हों, *q.v.*

तिन्हपर = तिनपर (तिन).

तिन्हे, *more prop.* तिन्हें, *q.v.*

तिन्हें = तिनको (तिन).

तिन्है, *more prop.* तिन्हें, *q.v.*

तिन्हैं, in Braj = तिनको (तिन).

तिन्हों = तिन. See also उन्हों.

तिपत = तृप्त, *q.v.*

तिपाई, *f.* a three-legged table (*vulg.* 'teapoy').

तिपारी, *f.* a kind of Indian fruit commonly called Cape gooseberry or Brazil cherry.

तिफ़्ल, *m.* an infant, child.

तिबारा, *m.* a hall or room with three doors: *lit.* thrice, three times.

तिम, (correl. of जिम) old form = तैसे, *q.v.*

तिमाना, *t.* to moisten, wet (?)

तिमि, 1, (correl. of जिमि) = तैसे: (old form, frequent in poetry and in Braj:) 2, *m. pr. n.* (1) of a certain fabulous fish of an enormous size said to be one hundred Yojans in length (2) of a certain king son of Dūrv father of Bribadrath.

तिमिंगिल, *m. pr. n.* (1) of a fabulous colossal fish, father of the sea serpent (2) of a people (3) of their prince.

तिमिंगिलगिल, *m. pr. n.* a fabulous fish (said to be larger than the one above-mentioned).

तिमित, *m.* (*f.* ā) wet, moist, damp, moistened: fixed, steady, unmoved, unshaken.

तिमितिमिंगिल = तिमिंगिलगिल, *q.v.*

तिमिर, 1, *m.* darkness, obscurity; total blindness from an affection of the optic nerve: a certain plant: *pr. n.* a certain town: 2, *m.* (*f.* ā) dark.

तिमिष, *m.* a kind of pumpkin, gourd, water-melon.

तिमिहानी, *more prop.* (1) तिमि हानि (2) त्रिमुहानी.

तिमी, *f.* a fish: *pr. n.* a daughter of Daksh (she was wife of Kashyap and mother of the sea monsters).

तिमुहानी = त्रिमुहानी, *q.v.*

तिय = तिया, *q.v.*

तियन, a Braj pl. of तिय. See न, 6.

तिया, *f.* (from स्त्री) a woman, wife.

तियाने, a certain small charge on revenue.

तिरकस, bent, crooked, cornerwise.

तिरकुटा, *m.* a certain kind of mixture (of dry ginger, long pepper, and black pepper).

तिरखा = तृषा, *q.v.*

तिरखावन्त, *m.* (*f.* vati) तृषावन्त, *q.v.*

तिरखित, *m.* (*f.* ā) = तृषित, *q.v.*

तिरखुंटी / **तिरखूंटी** } *f.* a trivet.

तिरछा, *m.* (*f.* ī) crooked, bent, crosswise, oblique, awry, askant, squint, goggle; perverse, affected, foolish. — *dekhnā*, to look askant, squint. — *lagnā*, to strike obliquely, glance. *Tirchhī ānkh k.*, to look angrily at, cast unkind looks.

तिरछाना, *n.* to be perverse; to be affected: *t.* to crook, slant, place in a transverse position.

तिरछियाना, *a. int.* to edge, go obliquely.

तिरछीनज़र, *f.* an ogle, leer, squint.

तिरता, threefold, triple, treble.

तिरतालीस = तैंतालीस, *q.v.*

तिरतिराना, *a. int.* to drop, trickle.

तिरतीय = तृतीय, *q.v.*

तिरना, *a. int.* to swim, float.

तिरपत = तृप्त, *q.v.*

तिरपद = त्रिपद, *q.v.*

तिरपन = तिर्पन, *q.v.*

तिरपित = तृप्त, *q.v.*

तिरपौलिया = त्रिपौलिया, *q.v.*

तिरफला = त्रिफला, *q.v.*

तिरबेणी = त्रिवेणी, *q.v.*

तिरभंगा = त्रिभंगा, *q.v.*

तिरभंगी = त्रिभंगी, *q.v.*

तिरमिराता, *m.* (*f.* ī) dazzling.

तिरमिराना = तिर्मिराना, *q.v.*

तिरस, *adv.* crookedly, awry, indirectly, underhandedly, covertly, secretly (a particle of depreciation or abuse).

तिरसठ = तिर्सठ, *q.v.*

तिरस्करी, *m.* (*f.* iṇī) a curtain, hiding-veil.

तिरस्कार, *m.* abuse, disrespect, reproach, contempt.

तिरस्क्रिया, *f.* = तिरस्कार, *q.v.*

तिरस्कृत, *m.* (*f.* ā) reviled, abused, reproached, censured.

तिरहुत = तिर्हुत, *q.v.*

तिरहुति = तिर्हुत, *q.v.*

तिरहुतिया = तिर्हुतिया, *q.v.*

तिरा, *m.* (*f.* ī) a corruption of तेरा, *q.v.*

तिराज़, *m.* lace, fringe, embroidery, any ornament on the border of a garment.

तिरानवे, ninety-three (९३): see ओं, वां, वीं, वे, वें.

तिरानव्वे = तिरानवे, *q.v.*

तिराना = तराना, *q.v.*

तिरान्वे = तिरानवे, *q.v.*

तिराव = तराव, *q.v.*

तिरास = त्रास, 1; *q.v.*

तिरासी, eighty-three (८३): see ओं, वां, वीं, वे, वें.

तिरिश्रा, तिरिया ; for words beginning thus, see under the form त्रिया.

तिरी, a corruption (1) of तेरी (2) of त्रय, *qq. v.*

तिरीबिरी, dispersed, scattered.

तिरेन्द, *m.* the float of a fishing-line, a float or buoy.

तिरेन्दा, *m.* = तिरेन्द, *q. v.*

तिरोहित, *m.* (*f.* ā) removed or withdrawn from sight, concealed, hidden, covered.

तिरोन्दा, *m.* a float, buoy, beacon.

तिर्तिराना, *a. int.* to trickle, drop.

तिर्पन, fifty-three (५३) : see श्रों, वां, वीं, वे, वें.

तिर्पौलिया = त्रिपौलिया, *q. v.*

तिर्मिरा, *m.* a spot of oil, etc. swimming on water; an ocular spectrum or spark appearing before the eye from the internal affection of that organ.

तिर्मिराना, *a. int.* to vibrate, dazzle, thrill, shake; to glisten as grease or oil swimming on water.

तिर्मिराहट, *f.* vibration, shaking.

तिर्मिरी, *f.* vertigo, darkness (perhaps, amaurosis or blindness from disease).

तिर्यक्ता, *f.* the nature of brute animals.

तिर्यग, *m.* (*f.* ā) any animal that moves crookedly [or horizontally.

तिर्यग, *m.* (*f.* ā) a quadruped.

तिर्यग्ज, *m.* (*f.* ā) brought forth by animals, brute-born.

तिर्यंच, *m.* (*f.* ī) a wild animal, brute, beast ; amphibious animal.

तिर्यग्योन, *m.* (*f.* i ?) a brute animal.

तिर्यग्योनि, *f.* the womb of a brute animal.

तिर्हुत, *f. pr. n.* the district of Tirhut (Tirhoot) [on the river Gandak.

तिर्हुति = तिर्हुत, *q. v.*

तिर्हुतिया, a native of Tirhut : *lit.* appertaining to Tirhut, grown in Tirhut.

तिल, *m.* the sesame-plant (*Sesamum orientale* or *Indicum*, Lin) and its seed (the plant bears an oily seed. and both the seed and the oil are much used in oriental cooking); a mole or spot (compared to a seed of sesamum); a very small piece ; an instant, moment. *Tiloṅmeṅ tel nahīṅ kahnā*, to say that there is no oil in the seeds of sesamum, *i. e.* to deny the most evident truth, to swear that white is black.

तिलंगा, 1, *m.* = तिलंगी, *q. v.* : 2, *m.* (*f.* ī) तैलंगा, *q. v.*

तिलंगान, *m.* (*f.* ī) = तैलंगा, *q. v.*

तिलंगी, *f.* a kind of paper kite.

तिलक, 1, *m.* the mark or marks made by Hindoos, with coloured earths or unguents, on the forehead and between the eyebrows, either as a sectarial distinction or as an ornament ; a freckle, mole, natural mark on the person ; a title (especially in composition) implying preëminence : a commentary ; name of a tree : 2, *f.* a gown, sleeveless robe.

तिलकट, *m.* the farina of sesamum.

तिलकधारी, *m.* (*f.* iṇi) a person who wears the *tilăk*.

तिलका, *f.* a kind of necklace : *adj.* a person having moles or spots, etc. : *lit.* spotted, freckled : chief, principal. [body : a man so marked.

तिलकालक, *m.* a mole or natural spot on the

तिलकुट, *m.* a kind of sweetmeat composed of pounded sesamum and sugar.

तिलचट्टा, *m.* a cockroach (*Blatta*).

तिलचावली, *f.* a mixture composed of rice and sesamum seeds ; a mixture of black and grey hairs [on the head.

तिलचूरी, *f.* a kind of sweetmeat.

तिलड़ा, *m.* a necklace or any ornament of three [strings.

तिलड़ी, *f.* = तिलड़ा, *q. v.*

तिलतैल, *m.* sesamum-oil.

तिलधेनु, *f.* sesamum made up in the shape of a cow for the purpose of being presented to Brāhmans.

तिलना ; see (1) तिरना (2) तिल (3) तोलना.

तिलपर्णी, *f.* red sanders (*Pterocarpus santolinus*).

तिलपिंज = तिलपेज, *q. v.* [of ground sesamum.

तिलपिच्चट, *m.* a kind of sweetmeat made chiefly

तिलपेज, *m.* barren sesamum (which bears no blossom, or whose seed yields no oil).

तिलबर, *m.* a species of bird.

तिलमय, made of sesamum, consisting of sesamum, abounding in sesamum.

तिलमयूर, *m.* a kind of pea-fowl (marked with spots resembling the seed of sesamum.

तिलवट, a kind of sweetmeat.

तिलवा = तिलुश्रा, *q. v.* [same and sugar.)

तिलशकरी, *f.* a kind of sweetmeat (made of se-

तिलस्म, *m.* (*pl.* āt) a talisman, spell ; anything that [occasions astonishment.

तिलहा, *m.* (*f.* ī) oily.

तिलहाई, *f.* oiliness. [ment, embrocation.

तिला, *m.* gold ; gold fringe : an ointment, lini-

तिलाई, *f.* a small frying-pan.

तिलांजुलि, *m. f.* (?) the ceremony of feeding the dead with sesamum-seeds and water.

तिलाक, long drawers : the clitoris.

तिलावडी, *f. pr. n.* a certain plain in the vicinity of Sirhind abounding in robbers ; the term is hence applied to any situation of danger.

तिलावा, *m.* night-watch, rounds, picket.

तिलिंगा, *more prop.* तैलंगा, *q. v.*

तिलुश्रा, *m.* a kind of sweetmeat (eaten particularly by Hindoos when the sun enters Capricorn).

तिलिहा, *m.* a turtle-dove. [may reach the wick.

तिलोंहा, (said of a lamp) sloped so that the oil

तिलोत्तमा, *f. pr. n.* a certain *Apsarā*.

तिलोदन, *m.* a kind of dish (consisting of milk, rice, and sesamum).

तिल्ला, *m.* the golden border of a turban.

तिल्ली, *f.* the spleen or milt.

तिवई in old Hindee = तिया, *q. v.*

तिवराइन, *f.* (*m.* तिवारी) the wife of a *tivārī*.

तिवारा = तिबारा, *q. v.* [three Veds ?

तिवारी, *m.* (see त्रयी, 3) a man who has read the

तिवासी, 1, state, three days old : 2, *f.* a kind of small embroidered carpet or tapestry.

तिश्न, *more prop.* तृष्णा, *q.v.*
तिष, *more prop.* तृष, *q.v.*
तिष्टति (Sk.) in Chand = he (she, or it) stands.
तिष्ठे = तिठळे (तिठळना).
तिष्णा, *more prop.* तृष्णा, *q.v.*
तिष्य, 1, *m. pr. n.* (1) of the eighth *Nakshatra*, (an asterism figured by an arrow and containing three stars of which one is (δ) Caneri (2) of Kaliyug): 2, *m.* (*f.* ā) auspicious, fortunate, lucky.
तिष्यपुष्य, *m.* } = तिष्या, *q.v.*
तिष्यफला, *f.* }
तिष्या, *f.* emblic myrobalan (*Phyllanthus emblica*); *lit.* auspicious flower.
तिस, 1, a corruption of तृष, *q.v.*: 2, the inflective base of the oblique cases of the singular of सो or तौन. —*uparānt* or *par* or *pe*, over and above that, moreover, besides, yet; where upon, then, after that, thereon, whereat; nevertheless —*par bhī* (emphatic form of the foregoing) notwithstanding, nevertheless, yet, still. —*pichhe*, after that, thereupon.
तिसरा, *m.* (*f.* ī) *more prop.* तीसरा, *q.v.*
तिसरायत, *m.* a third person, arbitrator, umpire; a court of inquiry or arbitration, three or four persons who act as arbitrators in a cause.
तिसूत, *m.* a kind of medicine.
तिस्तें = तिस्से. See तें, 1.
तिस्वांसी, *f.* the 20th part of a बिस्वांसी, *q.v.*
तिहत्तर, seventy-three (७३): see श्रों, वां, वीं, वे, वें.
तिहरा, *m.* (*f.* ī) threefold, triple.
तिहराना, *t.* to do anything for the third time, [tertiate, triple.
तिहरावट, *f.* triplication.
तिहरे, 1, = तिहारे, *q.v.*: 2, *m.* pl. of तिहरा, *q.v.*
तिहाई, *f.* a third part; the third part of a piece of cloth for making trowsers.
तिहाएत } = तिसरायत, *q.v.*
तिहायत }
तिहार, a contraction of तिहारो, *q.v.*
तिहारी, fem. of तिहारो, *q.v.*
तिहारे, inflected form of तिहारो, *q.v.*
तिहारो, Braj or old Hindee = तुम्हारा, *q.v.*
तिहाली, *f.* a species of cotton pod.
तिहि in Braj = उसको, उसको भी.
तिहिं in Braj = उसको भी.
तिहु, *more prop.* तिहुं, *q.v.*
तिहुपन, *m.* the three states or stages of temporal existence, *viz. Larkāpan, Juvāpan*, and *Vriddhāpan.*
तिहुं in Braj = (1) उसको भी (2) तीनों.
तिहू } = तिहुं, *q.v.*
तिहूं }
तिहूंपुर, *m.* three forts?
तिहूंलोक = तीनों लोक. See त्रिलोक.
ती, *f.*; see ता, 2.
तीश्रन, vegetables.
तीश्राने = तियाने, *q.v.*
तीकठ, *m.* the posteriors.
तीकूर, *f.* a starchy substance obtained from the root of the *Cucurma angustifolia.*
तीच्ण, *more prop.* तीक्ष्ण, *q.v.*
तीक्ष्ण, *m.* (*f.* ā) hot, warm, pungent, ardent, zealous, active; keen, subtle, intelligent, shrewd, penetrating, sharp (as an instrument, or an intellect, or tone in music); angry, passionate, harsh.
तीक्ष्णकराटक, *m.* thorn-apple (*Datura metel*).
तीक्ष्णकन्द, *m.* the onion.
तीक्ष्णकर्म्मन, *m.* (*f.* ṇī) active, zealous.
तीक्ष्णगन्ध, *m.* the plant *Morunga hyperanthera*; the gum-olibanum tree; small cardamoms.
तीक्ष्णगन्धा, *f.* several plants (1) mustard-seed (2) orris-root (3) *Pandanus odoratissimus.*
तीक्ष्णता, *f.* sharpness, pungency, subtlety, acuteness, shrewdness, harshness.
तीक्ष्णतैल, *m.* resin; the milky juice of the *Euphorbia*; spirituous or vinous liquors.
तीक्ष्णत्व, *m.* = तीक्ष्णता, *q.v.*
तीक्ष्णपत्र, *m.* coriander.
तीक्ष्णपुष्प, *m.* cloves.
तीक्ष्णफल, *m.* coriander.
तीक्ष्णबुद्धि, 1, *f.* acuteness of intellect, sagacity: 2, acute, sagacious, shrewd, witty.
तीक्ष्णरस, *m.* saltpetre.
तीक्ष्णशूक, *m.* barley.
तीक्ष्णा, *f.* (see तीक्ष्ण) a shrewd woman, etc.
तीखा, *m.* (*f.* ī) = तीक्ष्ण, *q.v.*
तीखुर = तीकूर, *q.v.*
तीछन, a corruption of तीक्ष्ण, *q.v.*
तीछी, a corruption of तीक्ष्णा, *q.v.*
तीछे, a corruption of तीक्ष्ण, *q.v.*
तीज, *f.* the third day of a lunar fortnight.
तीजा, 1, *m.* (*f.* ī) third, a third one: hence, 2, *m.* the third day after the death of a relation (on which oblations are offered), also the oblations so offered. The term is used among Muhammadans.
तीत, *m.* (*f.* ā) bitter, pungent, hot, acrid.
तीतर, *m.* (*f.* ī) a partridge (*Perdrix Francolinus*). —*ke munh Lacchmī* is a saying that is used when a person of mean understanding is chosen to decide in matters of which he is not competent to judge; *lit.* good fortune proceeds from the mouth of the partridge (which is a small bird of little estimation).
तीतरी, *f.* a kind of a medicine: a butterfly: a female [partridge.
तीतिर, *more prop.* तीतर, *q.v.*
तीता, *f.*; see तीत, *q.v.*
तीन, three (३). —*rakmī ḳānūn*, (in Arithm.) the rule of three. *Tin-tin*, three each, three at a time, [by threes, in threes.
तीनकाल = त्रिकाल, *q.v.*
तीनगुण = तीनोंगुण, *q.v.* [temperament, genius.
तीनत, *f.* a piece of clay: nature, disposition,
तीनतेरह, dispersed, scattered, broken, distracted, ruined.

तीनथान, *m.* the private parts of a male animal; also the *penis* only.
तीर्नान in Braj = तीनों, *q. v.*
तीनहु, *more com.* तीनों, *q. v.*
तीनि; see (1) तीन (2) तीनों.
तीनिउ (*Rām.*)=तीनों, *q. v.*
तीनों, (see श्रों, 4) all three, the three of them.
तीनोंअवस्था, *f.* the three periods into which human life divides itself, *viz.* Childhood, Manhood, and Senility.
तीनोंऋण, *m.* (see देवऋण, पितृऋण, ऋषिऋण) the [three kinds of human obligations.
तीनोंकाल = त्रिकाल, *q, v.*
तीनोंगुण, *m.* (see गुण) *i. e.* सतोगुण, रजोगुण, तमोगुण.
तीनोंथान = तीनथान, *q. v.*
तीनोंदशा = तीनोंअवस्था, *q. v.*
तीनोंदुख, *m.* the three kinds of trouble, *viz.* Daihik, Bautik, and Daivik.
तीनोंदेवता, the three persons of the Hindoo triad, *viz.* Brahmā, Vishṇu, and Shiv.
तीनोंभवन = त्रिलोक, *q. v.*
तीनोंलोक = त्रिलोक, *q. v.*
तीब, *m.* perfume, odour; essence.
तीमार, *m.* care, attention, regimen of the sick; sickness, indisposition, infirmity, affliction.
तीय = तिया, *q. v.*
तीयल, *f.* a suit of female's clothes.
तीर, *m.* a shore, bank: an arrow: *pr. n.* the planet Mercury: *adv.* near, close at hand.— *mārnā*, to shoot arrows, shoot by means of an arrow.
तीरगी, *f.* darkness, obscurity.
तीरज, *m.* an abstract of a long list of accounts, etc.: a tree grown on a shore.
तीरथ, *more prop.* तीर्थ, *q. v.*
तीरना, *more prop.* तैरना, *q. v.*
तीरन्दाज, *m.* an archer.
तीर्वा, (in Pros.) a species of metre.
तीरभुक्ति, *m. pr. n.* Tirhut (Tirhoot). A province of India lying to the north of Bihār: it is bounded on the west and east by the Gandak and Kausik rivers, on the south by the Ganges, and on the north by the skirts of the Himālaya mountains.
तीरसा, dart-like. *Unko* — *lag gayā*, they were [pierced as by a dart.
तीरह, dark, obscure.
तीरा, *m.* ? an arrow.
तीर्ण, crossed, passed over: spread, expanded.
तीर्णपदी, *f.* a kind of plant (*Curculigo orchioides.*
तीर्थ, *m.* the Hindoo term for pilgrimage. — *k.* to go on pilgrimage. The term is applied to any place held to be sacred and which is on that account an object of pilgrimage: these places lie generally along the course of sacred rivers, such as the Ganges, etc., or in the vicinity of some piece of water or sacred springs. Allahabad, Benāres, Gyā, Jagannāth and Mathurā are among the chief teerths of the [Hindoos.
तीर्थकार, *m.* (*f.* ī) a holy personage.
तीर्थपति = तीर्थराज, *q.v.*
तीर्थयात्रा, *f.* pilgrimage to holy places, a holy [journey.
तीर्थराऊ = तीर्थराज, *q.v.*
तीर्थराज, *m.* an epithet of Pryāg (the modern Allahabad); *lit.* the chief place of the teerths. It is the chief place of pilgrimage, though inferior in point of sanctity to Benares: to this latter place the Hindoo goes rather to die than merely to bathe.
तीर्थराजी, *f.* an epithet of the city of Kāshī the modern Benares); *lit.* the chief of the teerths.
तीर्थस्नान, *m.* bathing at a holy place.
तीर्थवासी, *m.* (*f.* inī) one who much frequents (or who dwells at) some place of Hindoo pilgrimage.
तीली, *f.* a bar; the leg, calf of the leg.
तीवर, *m.* (*f.* ī) a hunter, any one who lives by killing and selling game; a fisherman, any one who lives by catching and selling fish.
तीवरी, *f.* a hunter's wife; a fisherman's wife.
तीव्र, *m.* (*f.* ā) sharp, flashing, violent, pungent, warm, hot: much, excessive, endless, boundless: *adv.* excessively, much, boundlessly.
तीव्रता, *f.* } heat, pungency, sharpness.
तीव्रत्व, *m.* }
तीव्रवेदना, *f.* excessive pain, agony, the torments of damnation.
तीव्रा, *f.* (see तीव्र) a violent female, etc.: *pr. n.* [a river in eastern Bengal.
तीस, 1, thirty (३०): see श्रों, वां, वीं, वे, वें; 2, *more prop.* तिस, *q.v.*
तीसरा, *m.* (*f.* ī) third; a third party, *i. e.* an um- [pire, arbitrator.
तीसरे, in the third place, thirdly.
तीसी, *f.* flax (*Linum usitatissimum*).
तु (= ता, ती, or ते) one of the terminations of the present participle in Braj and in the *patois.*
तुश्र = तेरा, (old poetical form: Sk. तव ?).
तुंग, *m.* (*f.* ā) prominent, elevated, high, tall; hot, passionate: *hence*, height, top, vertex, a mount tain, culmination; a kind of tree (*Rottleria tinctoria*).
तुंगबल, *m. pr. n.* a certain warrior.
तुंगभद्र, *m.* a restive elephant, an elephant in rut.
तुंगभद्रा, *f. pr. n.* a river in Mysore.
तुंगा, *f.* (see तुंग) a passionate woman, etc.
तुंगी, 1, *f.* a kind of basil (*Ocymum gratissimum*): 2, *m.* (*f.* inī) lofty.
तुंत, तुंद, तुंब; for words beginning with either of these elements, see under the forms तुन्त, तुन्द, तुम्ब, [respectively.
तुंह, a dialectic form of तू, thou.
तुंही, an emphat. form of तुंह, *q.v.*
तुक, *f.* one line of a poem, a rhyme: a moment.
तुकड़ी, *f.* a flight or swarm (of birds or insects).
तुकला, *m.* } = तुक्कल, *q.v.*
तुकली, *f.* }
तुकाचरी, *more prop.* तुगाक्षीरी, *q.v.*
तुक्कल, *f.* a kind of paper kite.
तुक्का, *m.* a sort of arrow blunt at the end: a small hill or mountain; an eminence.
तुखता, *more prop.* तुषित, *q.v.*

तुख़्म, *m.* seed, sperm, an egg; a testicle.
तुख़्मरेज़ी, *f.* a scattering seed, sowing.
तुखार, *m. pr. n.* a certain people mentioned in the Rāmāyan).
तुखित, *more prop.* तुषित, *q.v.* [solence.
तुग़यान, *m.* rebellion, sedition, perverseness, in-
तुग़यानी, *f.* excess, a flood, an overflowing.
तुगा, *f.* the manna of bamboos.
तुगाक्षीरी = तुगा, *q.v.*
तुच्छ, void, empty, vain, worthless, despicable, contemptible, absurd. — *jānnā*, to esteem at a low figure, to despise. [picableness.
तुच्छता, *f.* (*m.* °त्व) emptiness, worthlessness, des-
तुच्छद्रु, *m.* an epithet of the castor-oil tree (considered as having no sap).
तुच्छनीय, *m.* (*f.* ā) contemptible, insignificant, base.
तुज, *more prop.* तुझ, *q.v.* [institutes.
तुज़ुक, *m.* routine, pomp, regulation, ordinance,
तुज्जार, *m.* a merchant.
तुझका, *m.* (*f.* ī) *more com.* तेरा, *q.v.*
तुझतक, as far as to thee.
तुझको (dat. and acc. of तू) = तुझे, *q.v.*
तुझसा, *m.* (*f.* ī) like thee. See सा.
तुझसे, 1, abl. of तू: 2, = तुझसा, *q.v.*
तुझे (dat. and acc. of तू) thee, to thee.
तुझै } in Braj = तुझे, *q.v.*
तुझै }
तुटना, *more prop.* टूटना, *q.v.*
तुटापा, *m.* helplessness, inability.
तुठ, the crash made by the breaking of wood.
तुड़वाट, *f.*? a breach, fracture, breakage.
तुड़वाना = तुड़ाना, *q.v.*
तुड़ाना, *t.* to cause some one to break a thing, cause to be broken or changed (money), cause to be devoured. [large piece of wood.
तुण्ड, *m.* a beak, snout; *pr. n.* of a Rakshas: a
तुण्डका, a large piece of wood.
तुतई, *f.* a vessel with a spout.
तुतक, the deck of a ship.
तुतराना, *more com.* तुतलाना, *q.v.*
तुतलाई, *f.* lisping. [a child).
तुतलाना, *a. int.* to lisp, speak imperfectly (as a
तुता, *m.* (*f.* ī) *more com.* तोता, *q.v.*
तुत्थ, *m.* a collyrium extracted from the *Amomum Xanthorhiza*, blue vitriol, sulphate of copper applied to the eyes medicinally (as an *anjan*).
तुत्थांजन, *m.* blue vitriol considered as an *anjan*, or medicinal application to the eyes. [muslin).
तुनकी, *f.* a fine kind of bread or wafers (thin as
तुनुक, a thin cake or fritter: *lit.* slight, thin, de-
तुने, *more prop.* तूने, *q.v.* [licate, effeminate.
तुन्तुनाना, *a. int.* to sound.

तुन्द, 1, *m.* the belly, abdomen: 2, *f.* the navel; 3, hot, fierce sharp, severe, acrid, spirited, active, strong.
तुन्दकूप, *m.* } the navel.
तुन्दकूपी, *f.* }
तुन्दख़ोई, *f.* passionateness, peevishness, aptitude to unseasonable and excessive anger.
तुन्दपरिमार्ज, *m.* an epithet of a lazy sluggish person; *lit.* stroking or wiping the belly.
तुन्दपरिमृज = तुन्दपरिमार्ज, *q.v.*
तुन्दिक }
तुन्दिभ } = तुन्दी, *q.v.*
तुन्दिल }
तुन्दी, *m.* (*f.* inī) a person having a large, prominent or elevated stomach or navel.
तुन्न, 1, *m.* a kind of tree (*Cedrela toona*) the timber of which bears some resemblance to mahogany and is much used for making furniture, etc.: 2, *f.* the flower of that tree (used for dyeing a yellow colour): 3, tormented, vexed, injured, cut, cut down,
तुन्नवाय, *m.* a tailor. [broken.
तुप, *more prop.* तोप, *q.v.*
तुपक, *f.* a musket.
तुपाना, *more prop.* तोपाना, *q.v.*
तुफ़, *m.* saliva, spittle; a curse.
तुफ़ूलियत, *f.* infancy, childhood.
तुभ्यं (Sk. dat.) = तुमको. (Rāmāyaṇ.)
तुम, *m. f.* (the personal pronoun of the second person plural) you. — *āp*, you yourself.
तुमड़ी, *f.* 1, = (1) तोमड़ी (2) तुम्बी, *qq.v.*: 2, a kind
तुमैं in Chand = तुम, *q.v.* [of rocket.
तुम्तनौ, *m.* (*f.* ī) in Braj = तुम्हारा, *q.v.*
तुमतुराक़, *m.* magnificence, grandeur.
तुमन, *m.* brotherhood, connexion, caste; a bevy, crowd, troop, squadron. — *bāndhnā*, to collect a body
तुमना = तुमको (an old form). [of troops.
तुमनि, in Braj, one of the inflective bases of the dat. acc. and abl. of तुम.
तुमनिकौं, in Braj = तुमको.
तुमनिसौं in Braj = तुमसे.
तुमपाहीं in Braj = तुम्हारे पास.
तुमरा, *m.* (*f.* ī) *more prop.* तुम्हारा, *q.v.*
तुमरो, a corruption of तुम्हारा, *q.v.*
तुमसन = तुमसे (तुम). See सन.
तुमसा, like you. See सा.
तुमहि in old Hindee = तुमको.
तुमाई, *f.* the price of carding.
तुमाना, *t.* to cause to be carded.
तुमार = (1) तुम्हारा (2) तुषार, *qq.v.*
तुमारा, *m.* (*f.* ī) *more prop.* तुम्हारा, *q.v.*
तुमुल, 1, *m.* mingled or tumultuous combat, *mêlée*, tumult, tumultuous noise, uproar, clangour: a kind of plant (*Beleric myrobalan*): 2, *m.* (*f.* ā) a noisy person, etc.: *lit.* excited, tumultuous, noisy.

तुमे, तुमें } 1, nom. forms of तुम, you: 2, = तुम्हें, *q.v.*

तुमै, *more prop.* तुम्हें, *q.v.*

तुम्बा, *m.* a hollowed gourd; the rind of a gourd in which mendicants carry water, etc.

तुम्बिया, *m.* a pot.

तुम्बी, *f.* a long gourd (*Lagenaria vulgaris* or *Cucurbita lagenaria*); a small hollow gourd; the rind of a gourd in which medicants carry water, etc; a kind of pipe (chiefly used by those who exhibit snakes).

तुम्बुरु, *m. pr. n.* (1) of the attendant of the fifth Arhat of the present Avasarpiṇī (2) of a certain pupil of Kalāpin (3) of a certain Gandharv.

तुम्ह, an inflective base of the oblique cases of तुम.

तुम्हरो in Braj = तुम्हारा, *q.v.*

तुम्हहिं, (an old form) = तुमको.

तुम्हार, a contraction of तुम्हारा, *q.v.*

तुम्हारा, (gen. of तुम) *m.* (*f.* ī) your, yours.

तुम्ही, emphatic form of तुम, you.

तुम्हें, (a dat. and acc. of तुम) you, to you.

तुम्है, तुम्हैं } in Braj = तुम्हें, *q.v.*

तुम्हों = तुम्ह, *q.v.*: see also उन्हों.

तुरई, 1, a corruption of तरही, *q.v.*: 2, *f.* a species of cucumber (*Cercumis acutangulis*, Roxb.).

तुरंग, *adj.* moving quickly: hence, *m.* (*f.* ī) a horse.

तुरंगनी, *f.* a dragon-fly.

तुरंगम, *m.* (*f.* ī) a horse.

तुरंगी = तुरगी, *q.v.*

तुरंत, *more prop.* तुरन्त, *q.v.*

तुरक, *more com.* तुर्क, *q.v.*

तुरकानी, *more prop.* तुर्काना, *q.v.*

तुरकी, *m.* (*f.* in *or* iṇī) appertaining to the Turks or to their country, Turkish.

तुरग, *m.* (*f.* ī) a horse.

तुरगब्रह्मचार्य्यक, *m.* enforced celibacy, continence arising merely from the absence of women.

तुरगी, 1, *f.* (see तुरग) a mare: 2, *f.* a species of plant (*Physalis flexuosa*): 3, *m.* (*f.* iṇī) a horse-man, cavalier, equestrian: *lit.* mounted, riding or carried on a horse.

तुरत, तुर्रत } *more prop.* तुरन्त, *q.v.*

तुरन, *more prop.* (1) तूर्ण (2) तोर्ण, *qq.v.*

तुरन्त, quickly, instantly, directly, forthwith, immediately, in haste.

तुरपन, *f.* a kind of stitch.

तुरपना, *t.* to sew (in a particular manner), to stitch.

तुरपाना, *t.* to stitch, darn, hem.

तुरफ़ा, new, strange, rare, wonderful, surprizing, rare, agreeable.

तुरबसु, *more prop.* तुर्वसु, *q.v.*

तुरमती, *f.* a kind of hawk (*Falco cyanellus*, *B.*: *Falco fasciatus*, *B.*: *Tinnunculus dubius*).

तुरम्नी, *f.* a kind of instrument for rasping cocoa-nuts.

तुरवसु, *more prop.* तुर्वसु, *q.v.*

तुरवाई, *more com.* तोड़वाई, *q.v.*

तुरही, *f.* a trumpet, clarion, flageolet. — *phūṅknā*, to blow a trumpet. — *bajānā*, to sound or play a trumpet.

तुराइ = (1) तोड़ करके (2) तोड़कर (3) बेगसे (4) तुराई.

तुराई, 1, = (1) तम्हारी (2) उत्तम, *qq.v.*: 2, *f.* a species of cucumber.

तुराना, rice boiled and kept overnight in the cold weather.

तुराब, *m.* earth, ground, dust.

तुरावती (poet.) = त्वरावती, *q.v.*

तुरी, 1, a corruption of तरही, *q.v.*: 2, *f.* a brush or fibrous stick used by weavers to clean and separate the threads of the woof, also a painter's brush.

तुरीय, *m.* the fourth state of the student of the Vedanta philosophy; hence, the Divine Being or universal Spirit: *lit. m.* (*f.* ā) the fourth; a fourth part.

तुरुक, *m.* (see तुरुष्क) Turkey: a Turk.

तुरुत = तुरन्त, *q.v.*

तुरुष्क, *m. pr. n.* a certain country (perhaps Tūrān, now called Turkistan, the original country of the Turks): incense.

तुरुष्का, *m.* (pl.: see आ, 22) the inhabitants or the people of Turushk.

तुर्क, *m.* a Turk; a soldier; a Muhammadan; a barbarian; a plunderer; a vagabond: a beautiful-faced person.

तुर्कताज़, *m.* an inroad, depredation, attack; feigned anger (of a lover); a walking affectedly or with a tossing about of the body.

तुर्कताज़ी *f.* = तुर्कताज़, *q. v.*

तुर्कमिज़ाज, of a savage disposition; wicked, depraved; sly.

तुर्कसवार, *m.* a cavalier, equestrian.

तुर्कान, (pl. of तुर्क) Turks: *fig.* beautiful women.

तुर्काना, like a Turk, Turk-like, Turkish.

तुर्कानिय = तुर्काना, *q. v.*

तुर्कानी, *f.* a kind of spacious upper garment worn by the females of Turkistān.

तुर्त, *more com.* तुरन्त, *q. v.*

तुर्तफुर्त (a redupl. of तुर्त) = तुरन्त, *q. v.*

तुर्ताव = तुरन्त, *q. v.*

तुर्तोफुर्तो = तुर्तफुर्त = तुरन्त, *q.v.*

तुर्तुरा, *m.* (*f.* ī) nimble, active; flippant.

तुर्तुरी, *f.* a kind of horn or trumpet of great length (generally used at festivals, and commonly called the Coleroon horn).

तुर्बत, *f.* a tomb, sepulchre.

तुर्बतर, completely wet, dripping, soaking, saturated. — *honā*, to drip with wet, (but generally) to be covered with blood.

तुर्वसु, *m. pa. n.* a son of king *Yayāti*.

तुर्श, sour, harsh, crabbed, ill-tempered.

तुल, 1, (prop. तुल्य) alike, like: — *baiṭhnā*, to be weighed against valuable things which are to be given in alms; to sit straight and compact (as in a boat which might capsize by sitting in it unevenly or carelessly) — *rahnā*, to stand front to front or opposed: 2, *m.* the breadth of a field.

तुलतुलाना, *a. int.* to become soft (from moisture, as a mud wall in the rains, as a sore or boil when suppurating, or as a fruit getting ripe).

तुलना, *n.* to be weighed in a balance: to be drawn up in array (as one army against another).

तुलबुल = **तोतला**, *q.v.*

तुलवाना = **तुलाना**, *q.v.*

तुलसी, *f.* a certain shrub, holy basil (*Ocymum sanctum*) held in great veneration by Hindoos, among whom it is also an object of worship. Tulsee is said to have been a nymph beloved by Krishṇ, and by him, metamorphosed into this plant. — *kā kirā*, beads made of the wood of the tulsee-plant.

तुलसीदल, *m.* the leaf of the *tulsī*-plant. — *chaṛhānā*, to place or sprinkle *tulsī*-leaves on the head of an idol or of a Brāhmaṇ.

तुलसीदान, *m.* a gold ornament.

तुलसीदास, *m. pr. n.* a *gosāīṅ* and celebrated Hindoo poet, who died A. D. 1623. He is the author of the Bhāshā translation of the Rāmāyaṇ of Vālmeeki, commonly called 'Tulseekrit Rāmāyaṇ,' — the most popular (among those of the Hindoos who speak Hindee) of all the works in their literature.

तुला, *f.* equality; a balance, weight, beam of a balance; especially a fine balance, goldsmith's or assay-scales; *pr. n.* the seventh sign of the Zodiac, Libra; the being weighed against gold or any kind of valuable substance, which is afterwards given to priests. [hundred millions.

तुलाकोटि, *f.* an ornament of the feet or toes: a

तुलाकोश, *m.* = **तुलापरीक्षा**, *q.v.*

तुलादान, *m.* (see **तुला**) a gift of gold to Brāhmaṇs equal in weight to the person of the donor.

तुलाना, *t.* to cause a person to weigh a thing, cause a thing to be weighed.

तुलापरीक्षा, *f.* an ordeal by balance. The accused is accurately weighed; then, removed, and certain prayers, etc. are said: he is then weighed again, and if lighter than before, it is deemed an infallible sign of innocence; if equal or heavier, he is deemed guilty.

तुलाबीज, *m.* the berry of the *Abrus precatorius*, from which the goldsmith's or jeweller's weight in India is taken. The berry weighs about $1\frac{5}{16}$ grs. Troy, the factitious weight about $2\frac{3}{16}$.

तुलालग्न, *f.* the entrance of the sun into Libra.

तुलावा, *m.* the part of a Hindustānee carriage which rests on the arm of the axletree and supports the body of the carriage: an advanced guard, patrol or reconnoitering party, forlorn hope. [the wagtail).

तुलिका, *f.* a species of small bird (said to resemble

तुलिफला, *f.* the silk-cotton tree.

तुली, *f.* a steel-yard; a weaver's fibrous stick or brush used for cleansing the threads of the woof; a pencil, painter's brush, a stick with a fibrous extremity used as a brush; a rod, etc. dipped into crucibles to try whether their contents are in fusion.

तुले, *more com.* **तुल्य**, *q.v.* [to amble.

तुलुंग, a kind of ambling pace in a horse.—*jāna*,

तुल्य, 1, *m.* (*f.* ā) equal, like, resembling, analogous to, of the same class, indifferent: 2, *postp.* (takes gen. *m.* infl.) like, equal to. [equality.

तुल्यता, *f.* (*m.* °**त्व**) resemblance, analogousness,

तुल्यपान, *m.* a drinking together.

तुल्यबल, *m.* (*f.* ā) of equal strength.

तुव, *more com.* **तव**, *q.v.*

तुअर. *m. pr. n.* a certain tribe among the Rājputs.

तुवरी, *f.* a kind of lentil (*Cytisus cajan*).

तुवावा, *m.* a species of bird.

तुष, *m.* the husk or chaff of grain, especially of rice: *Beleric myrobalan.*

तुषानल, *m.* a conflagration of chaff; a form of capital punishment in which dry straw is twisted around the limbs of a criminal and then ignited.

तुषार, *m.* frost, cold, ice, snow; thin rain, mist, dew: *lit.* adj. *m.* (*f.* ā) cold, frosty.

तुषारगिरि, *m.* an epithet of the Himālaya mountains; *lit.* the snowy mountain.

तुषारा, *f.*; see **तुषार.**

तुषारु = **तुषार**, *q.v.*

तुषित, *m.* (*pl.* ā; see **आ** 22,) a class of subordinate deities: one of a class of thirty-six subordinate deities: an epithet of Vishṇu. [ed, rejoiced.

तुष्ट, *m.* (*f.* ā) contented, satisfied, gratified, pleas-

तुष्टता, *f.* } = **तुष्टि**, *q.v.*
तुष्टत्व, *m.* } [delight, pleasedness.

तुष्टि, *f.* contentment, satisfaction, gratification,

तुस; for words beginning thus, see under the form [**तुष**.

तुहनी, a dialectic form for **तुम**, *q.v.*

तुहनोका, a dialectic form = **तुम्हारा**, *q.v.*

तुहनोके, a dialectic form = **तुम्हें**, *q.v.*

तुहनोसों, a dialectic form = **तुमसे**.

तुहफ़ा, *m.* a curiosity, rarity; a present.

तुहमत, *f.* suspicion of guilt; a charging one with a crime, accusation. — *k.* or *denā* or *lagānā*, to accuse one falsely, belie, etc.

तुहर, a dialectic form = **तेरा** *q.v.*

तुहरा, *m.* (*f.* ī) a dialectic form = **तेरा**, *q.v.*

तुहराके, a dialectic form = **तुझे** and **तुम्हें**, *qq.v.*

तुहरासों, a dialectic form = **तुझसे** and **तुमसे**.

तहरे, a dialectic form = **तेरा**, *q.v.*

तुहार, a dialectic form = **तुम्हारा** *q.v.*

तुहि, 1, an old dat. and acc. of **तू**, *q.v.*: 2, an emphatic form of **तू**. [moonshine.

तुहिन, *m.* frost, snow, ice,; mist, dew: moonlight,

तुहिनगिरि = **तुषारगिरि**, *q.v.*

तुही = **तुहि**, *q.v.*

तुहे, (pl. **तुहें**) *more com.* **तुझे**, *q.v.*

तू, *m. f.* (personal pronoun of the second person singular) thou Its use implies depreciation, contempt; familiarity, endearment; and, when applied to the Supreme Being, extreme reverence.

तूअर, *f.* a kind of lentil (*Cytisus cajan*).

तूं, a corruption of **तू**, thou.

तूंअर, a Prākrit form of **तोमर**, *q.v.*

तूंगा, *m.* a reed, flag, rush.

तूंतां, **क**°, *t.* to dispute, wrangle, abuse.

तूंबा, *more com.* **तुम्बा**, *q.v.*

तूकारना, *t.* to 'thou' a person, to 'thee' and 'thou' [(French, *tutoyer*).

तूख, *more prop.* तुख, *q.v.*

तूटना, *more prop.* टूटना, *q.v.*

तूटापा, *m.* helplessness. [(*Chand.*)

तूठनो, (Sk. तुष्ट) *n.* to be satisfied, be pleased.

तूण, 1, a corruption of तुच्छ, *q.v.*: 2, *m.* a quiver.

तूणि, *m.* a quiver.

तूणी, 1, *f.* a quiver: a certain disease of the nerves: 2. *m.* (*f.* inī) a person provided with quivers.

तूणीर, *f.* a quiver.

तूत, *m.* the mulberry-tree, a mulberry.

तूतई, *f.* a vessel with a spout.

तूतक, *m.* = तूतिया, 1, *q.v.*

तूतन, *m.* chips, clippings, fragments, filings.

तूता, *m.* = (1) तूतिया, 1 (2) तोता, *q.v.*

तूतिया, *m.* 1, sulphate of copper, blue vitriol, tutty: 2, report, tale, slander.

तूती, *more prop.* तोती, *q.v.*

तूतू, the sound of calling a dog.

तूदा, *m.* the butt or mark at which arrows are shot: [a mound, heap, stack.

तून = तूण, 1, 2; *q.v.*

तूनीर, *more prop.* तूणीर, *q.v.*

तूने, (agentive case of तू) by thee.

तूपक, *f.* a musket.

तूफ़ान, *m.* an inundation, deluge; a storm of wind and rain, hurricane: *met.* a quarrelsome person. — *lenā*, to calumniate, defame.

तूम, *more prop.* तुम, *q.v.*

तूमना, *t.* to card or arrange wool or cotton with the fingers preparatory to combing.

तूमरी, *f.* the snout of a crocodile, alligator, etc.

तूमार, *m.* a book, volume, roll, account-book; a story.

तूमियाँ, *m.* the thread made of carded cotton in distinction from that made of cotton which has only [been beaten.

तूम्बा = तूमना, *q.v.*

तूम्बरी = तुमड़ी, *q.v.* (Rāmāyaṇ).

तूम्बा = तुम्बा, *q.v.*

तूम्बी, *f.* 1, dim. of तूम्बा, *q.v.*: 2, the snout of a crocodile, alligator, etc.: 3, a kind of musical pipe (chiefly used by those who exhibit snakes).

तूरना, a corruption of तोड़ना, *q.v.*

तूरही, *more com.* तुरही, *q.v.*

तूरी, 1, (*Rām.*) = तुल्य, *q.v.*: 2, *more com.* तुरही, *q.v.*

तूर्ण, *adj.* quick, expeditious: *adv.* quickly, swift- [ly, expeditiously.

तूर्त, *more prop.* तुरन्त, *q.v.*

तूल, 1, a corruption of तुल्य, *q.v.*: 2, *m.* length: 3, tall, extensive, long, lasting long: 4, *f.* cotton.

तूलनाली, *f.* a thick roll of cotton from which the cotton is drawn out in spinning.

तूला, a corruption of तुल्य, *q.v.*

तूली, *more prop.* तुली, *q.v.*

तूवर, 1, *more prop.* तुवर, *q.v.*: 2, *m.* a bull without horns though of an age to have them; a beardless man; a eunuch.

तूसना, *a. int.* to fade, wither (a flower).

तूसा, *m.* (*f.* ī) = तेरे समान. See सा.

तूसे, *more prop.* तूमा, *q.v.*

तूहिन, *more prop.* तुहिन, *q.v.*

तूही, (emphatic form of तू) thou thyself, thou [even.

तृजग = त्रिजग; see त्रिलोक.

तृण, *m.* grass, a grass-blade, any gramineous [plant.

तृणजम्भ, *m.* (*f.* ā) an epithet of any animal whose food is grass: *lit.* graminivorous.

तृणजाति, *m.* the vegetable kingdom.

तृणता, *f.* the state or the abstract property of [grass.

तृणपल्लव, *m.* a blade of grass.

तृणपीड, *m.* a mode of close fighting.

तृणमय, *m.* (*f.* ī) made of grass, abounding in grass, grassy.

तृणराज, *m.* an epithet of the palmyra-tree; *lit.* [lord of the grasses.

तृणवत, *m.* (*f.* vatī) abounding in grass; grass-like, like a straw; *hence,* insignificant, worthless.

तृणवन्त, तृणवान, } *m.* (*f.* vatī) = तृणवत, *q.v.*

तृणविन्दु, *m.pr.n.* a certain ancient sage and prince.

तृणस, grassy, made, etc. with grass.

तृणांकु, *m. pr. n.* a certain *rishi.*

तृणाग्नि, *m.* = तृणानल, *q.v.*

तृणावर्त, *m. pr. n.* a certain *Rākshas.*

तृणाविन्द, (*corruption*) = तृणविन्दु, *q.v.*

तृतीय, *m.* (*f.* ā) the third: a third.

तृतीयप्रकृति, *f.* (*lit.* the third nature, *i. e.*) a eunuch's nature; *hence,* a eunuch; (in Gram.) the neuter [gender.

तृतीया, *f.*; see तृतीय.

तृतीयांश, *m.* a third part.

तृतीयी, *m.* (*f.* inī) a person of the third rank; [person entitled to a third part.

तृतीत; see तृतीय.

तृन, *more prop.* तृण, *q.v.*

तृप्त, *m.* (*f.* ā) contented, satisfied, pleased.

तृप्तात्मा, satisfied, content, tranquil.

तृप्ति, *f.* content, satisfaction, pleasure.

तृप्तिकारी, *m.* (*f.* iṇī) *adj.* affording satisfaction, [etc.

तृफला = त्रिफला, *q.v.*

तृमूर्ति, 1, *f.* an epithet of the Hindoo Triad or three principal Hindoo deities, *viz.* Brahma, Vishnu and Shiv: *lit.* having three forms; *hence,* a trinity: [2, *m.* a Jain saint.

तृष, *f.* thirst, wish, desire.

तृषा, *f.* thirst, wish, desire: a species of plant [(*Commelina salicifolia*).

तृषावत, तृषावन्त, तृषावान } *m.* (*f.* vatī) = तृषित, *q.v.*

तृषित, *m.* (*f.* ā) athirst, thirsty, thirsting, desirous [of, longing for, cupidinous.

तृष्णज, *m.* (*f.* ā) = तृषित, *q.v.*

तृष्णा, *f.* thirst, wish, desire, ambition, avarice.

तृष्णाक्षय, *m.* contentment, resignation, patience.

तृषा, *more prop.* **तृष्णा**, *q v.*

ते, 1, the inflective base of the singular of **ता**; *e. g.* **तेहि = तिसको**: 2, the plural of **ता**, 6: 3, this is an old Hindee form of the ablative sign **से** *q.v.*: 4, — **तेरा**: 5, in comp. it sometimes = 3; *e. g.* **तेसरी**.

तेइ, see (1) **तेऊ** (2) **तेहि** (3) **तेही**.

तेईस, twenty-three (२३). See **ओं, वां, वीं, वे, वें**.

तेउ = तेऊ, *q. v.* [and in Braj.

तेऊ, an emphatic form of **ते**, 2. Frequent in poetry

तेऊर, land ploughed three times.

तेओं, *more prop.* **त्यों**, *q. v.*

तेओंधा, *more prop.* **त्योन्धा**, *q. v.* [of **तू**, thou.

तैं = 1, **ते**, 3: 2, **तई**; 3, **से**, *qq. v.*: 4, a dialectic form

तेंईस *more prop.* **तेईस**, *q. v.*

तेंत, तेंद; for words beginning with either of these forms, see under the forms **तेन्त, तेन्द**, respectively.

तेग़, *f.* a scimitar, sword, cutlass, dagger.

तेग़ा, *m.* a short broad scimitar. —*numā*, a sword like a scimitar. — *bāz*, a sword-player, a hero.

तेज, *m.* ardour, splendour, glory, refulgence, strength, energy, sharpness, pungency, essence of a thing.

तेजनक, *m.* a kind of reed (*Saccharum sara*).

तेजना, *more com.* **तजना**, *q. v.*

तेजनी, *f.* a certain plant (*Aletris hyacinthoides*).

तेजपात, *m.* cassia, the leaf of the *Laurus cassia*.

तेजबल, *m.* the power of ardour or of refulgence.

तेजमती, *f.* (*m.* **तेजमान**) an energetic female.

तेजमान, *m.* (*f.* mati) an illustrious or energetic person, etc.: lit. glorious, refulgent, splendid, luminous, awful, brilliant, pungent, strong, energetic, famous, celebrated.

तेजयत, *m.* (*f.* vatī); see **तेजमान**.

तेजवती, 1, = **तेजमती**, *q. v.*: 2, *f.* a species of aromatic plant (*Pothos officinalis*).

तेजवन्त / **तेजवान** } *m.* (*f.* vatī) = **तेजमान**, *q. v.*

तेजस, *m.* splendour, flame, light, lustre; glory, beauty; dignity, consequence; strength, power; violence; semen virile.

तेजसी, *more prop.* **तेजस्वी**, *q. v.*

तेजसों in Braj = **तेजसे** (**तेज**). See **सों**.

तेजस्कर, *m.* (*f.* ī) irradiating, illuminating; conferring strength, power, or glory; restorative, invigorating, provocative, tonic.

तेजस्वी, *m.* (*f.* inī) = **तेजमान**, *q. v.*

तेजोमन्थ, *m.* a species of tree (*Premna spinosa*).

तेजोमय, *m.* (*f.* ī) consisting of light, brilliant, illustrious.

तेजोरूप, *m.* (*f.* ā) whose form is light, consisting only of splendour: hence (1) *m.* the nature of light (2) an epithet of Brahm, the supreme spirit.

तेजोवती, *f.* a certain plant which bears a fruit resembling pepper.

तेढ़ा, *m.* (*f.* ī) crooked, bent, uneven, awry.

तेता, (correl. of **जेता**) *m.* (*f.* ī) so much, that much: *pl.* so many, that many.

तेतालीस = तेन्तालीस, *q. v.*

तेति = ते; **अति. बहुत** (Rāmāyaṇ).

तेतिक, (correl. of **जेतिक**) = **तितेक**, *q. v.*

तेतीस = तेन्तीस, *q. v.*

तेते, (correl. of **जेते**) old form = **तितने**, *q. v.*

तेने, thither.

तेन्तालीस, forty-three (४३). See **ओं, वां, वीं, वे, वें**.

तेन्तीस, thirty-three (३३). See **ओं, वां, वीं, वे, वें**.

तेन्दवा, *m.* (*f.* ī) = **तेन्दुआ**, *q. v.*

तेन्दुआ, *m.* (*f.* **तेन्दुई**) a leopard (*Felis lepardus*).

तेन्दू, *m.* a species of fruit (*Diospyros ebenum* or [*D. glutinosa*).

तेपची, *f.* a kind of stitch.

तेपि; see (1) **वे भी** (2) **तोभी**.

तेम, freshness, verdure.

तेमन, *m.* a wetting, moistening; moisture, damp, wetness: a sauce or condiment.

तेमनी, *f.* a chimney, fireplace.

तेमहे, a corruption of **तुम्हें**, *q. v.*

तेम्हर, thither.

तेरस, *f.* the thirteenth day of the moon.

तेरह, thirteen (१३). See **ओं, वां, वीं, वे, वें**.

तेरहतेज़ी, the first thirteen days of the Muhammadan month Safar (which are held to be unlucky).

तेरहां = तेरहवां, (see **तेरह**).

तेरा, (gen. of **तू**) *m.* (*f* ī) thy, thine.

तेरुस, *m.* the third year past or to come, *i. e.* the year before last or the year after next.

तेरो, a Braj form of **तेरा**, *q. v.* [**तैल**.

तेल; for words beginning thus, see under the form

तेलिया, *m.* the colour dark bay.

तेलियासुरंग, *m.* (*f.* ā) light bay-coloured.

तेवड़ी = तेवरी, *q. v.*

तेवन, *m.* a garden, pleasure-garden, pleasure-ground: play, sport, pastime. [ance, physiognomy.

तेवर, *m.* giddiness in the head, vertigo: counten-

तेवरस = तेरुस, *q. v.*

तेवरहो / **तेवरहीं** } = **तेवरी**, *q. v.*

तेवराना, *n.* to have a swimming in the head, be faint: *a. int.* to stagger, fall down senseless from a blow.

तेवरी, *f.* a frown. — *chaṛhnī*, the coming on of a frown. — *chaṛhānā*, to frown.

तेवहार, *m.* a holiday, festival.

तेवां = त्यों, *q. v.*

तेवोन्धा = त्योन्धा, *q. v.*

तेशा, *f.* (*m.*?) a hatchet, axe, adze; a mattock, pickaxe; a halbert, battle-axe.

तेसरी, *f.*? thrice-ploughed land.

तेह, wrath, rage, vehemence of anger.

तेहर, *f.* a kind of ornament worn around the ankles by females.
तेहरा = तेहारा, *q.v.*
तेहा, *m.* steadfastness, firmness, speaking with warmth, vehemence of manner, peremptoriness, perseverance.
तेहारा, *m.* (*f.* ī) treble.
तेहारो (old and poet.) = **तेरा,** *q.v.*
तेहि = तिसको. See **ता,** 6 ; and **हि.**
तेहिमहं (in poetry) = **तिस्में.**
तेहिसों (in poetry) = **तिस्से.**
तेहिके = तिसके.
तेही, 1, *more prop.* **तेहि,** *q.v.* : 2, emphatic form (sc. **बेर** or **समय**), exactly then, immediately, instantly. (Braj or old Hindee.)
तै, 1, in Braj and old Hindee = (1) **तितने** (2) **तू,** *qq.v.* 2, a rolling up, folding. — *k.* to roll up, fold : to constrain ; to abridge : to travel, traverse, pass over.
तैग्रार (*corruption*) = **तैय्यार,** *q.v.*
तैग्रारि (*corruption*) = **तैय्यारी,** *q.v.*
तैं, in Braj or old Hindee = **तू,** *q.v.*
तैंतोस in Braj = **तैंतोस,** *q.v.*
तैंने (an Agentive case of **तैं**) = **तूने,** *q.v.*
तैतिल, *m. pr. n.* one of the astronomical periods called *Karan* : Deity.
तैत्तिर, *m.* a flock of partridges ; a francoline partridge : *prop.* produced from partridges.
तैत्तिरीय, *m.* (*f.* ā) appertaining to the Tittiri portion of the Yajur Ved ; as, a student, a teacher, a section, a text, etc. The texts of this Ved were disgorged by Yajnyavalkya in a tangible form, and picked up by the rest of Vaisampayana's disciples, who for this purpose assumed the form of partridges.
तैत्तिरीयक, *m.* a follower of the Tittiri branch of the Yajur-Ved.
तैने (an Agentive case of **तै**) = **तूने,** *q.v.*
तैब ; compare (1) **तू** **है** (2) **तैयिब.**
तैबेर, (Braj) so often, so many times.
तैयार, *more prop.* **तैय्यार,** *q.v.*
तैयिब, good, sweet, agreeable.
तैय्यार, ready, prepared, finished, complete ; alert, prompt, accomplished, ripe, mature, duly qualified.
तैय्यारी, *f.* readiness, completeness, promptitude, preparedness, preparation. — *k.* (with *f.* gen. of object) to prepare.
तैर, *m.* (*pl.* ān) a bird.
तैरख़ाना, *m.* an aviary.
तैरना, *t.* to swim, float, cross over.
तैल, *m.* oil, expressed oil (prepared from sesamum, mustard, etc.): storax, gum benzoin, incense. — *malnā,* to oil, rub on oil, anoint. — *charhānā,* to anoint the head, shoulders, hands and feet of the bride and bridegroom with oil mixed with turmeric during the marriage ceremony.
तैलंग, *m. pr. n.* the modern Carnatic.
तैलंगा, *m.* (*f.* ī) an inhabitant or a native of Tailang : a sepoy or native foot-soldier dressed in European costume. [after expression).
तैलकिट्ट, *m.* the oil-cake (made of the oily seed
तैलचोरिका, *f.* an epithet of the cockroach ; *lit.* the oil-stealer.
तैलपक, *m.* a cockroach, any oil-drinking beetle ; *lit.* the oil-drinker.
तैलपर्णिक, *m.* a kind of sandal.
तैलपायिका, *f.* a kind of beetle, cockroach.
तैलपायी, *m.* (*f.* inī) a cockroach.
तैलमाली, *f.* wick, the cotton of a lamp.
तैलस्फटिक, *m.* amber.
तैलिक, *m.* (*f.* ā *or* ī) an oil-grinder.
तैलिन, *f.* an oilman's wife, a female who prepares oil.
तैलिनी, *f.* the wife of an oilman, a female who prepares oil ; the wick or cotton of a lamp.
तैलिसाला, *f.* an oil-mill.
तैली, *m.* (*f.* in *or* inī) a caste whose business it is to make or to sell oil, an oilman, oil-grinder, oil-preparer : *lit.* oily, appertaining to oil.
तैल्वक, prepared from the Tilvak-tree.
तैश, *f.* levity, folly ; anger, passion, indignation, choler.
तैस, 1, (*contraction*) = **तैसा,** *q.v.* : 2, *m.* a he-goat (*esp.* one that is old and rank) : a stag.
तैसन, dialectic form = **तैसा,** *q.v.*
तैसा, (correl. of **जैसा**), *m.* (*f.* ī) such, such as that, like that : *adv.* in that manner, in like manner, so ; at the same moment.
तैसे, *adv.* in that manner, in like manner, so.
तो, 1, often used inaccurately for **तौ,** *q.v.* : 2, in Braj, the inflective base of the dative, accusative, and ablative of **तू** ; *e.g.* **तोहि = तुझको** : 3, Used immediately after **नहीं,** it yields the sense of 'otherwise', 'else', 'if not' ; *e.g.* **खाओ, नहीं तो तू मरेगा** : 4, It is a conjunction introducing the second clause of a conditional proposition ; *e.g. Jo tu āwegā, to pawega,* if thou shalt come, *then* wilt thou receive : 5, It is also a kind of expletive particle used chiefly for emphasis ; *e.g. Main to āti thi, par usne āne na diyā,* I was, *in point of fact,* coming, but he prevented me.
तोउ, a Braj form for **तौभी,** *q.v.*
तों = तौं, *q.v.*
तोंतों, *more com.* **त्योंत्यों,** *q.v.*
तोंसा, *more com.* **तौंसा,** *q.v.*
तोंहीं, (emphatic) exactly then, at that very instant, then even ; in that very manner.
तोकों = तुझको (Braj or old Hindee). [form **तोख.**
तोख ; for words beginning thus, see under the
तोग़दार, *m.* the bustard.
तोटका, *m.* a charm, amulet, philter.
तोटा, *m.* loss, deficiency : a cartridge.
तोड़, 1, *f.* a net thrown over a woman's pālkee ; 2, *m.* the breach made by a gun, etc. : the strength of a current : whey. — *k.* to make a breach (as a ball). — *dālnā,* to break and destroy, pull down. — *denā,* to break to pieces, spoil. — *lenā,* to gather or pluck fruit.
तोड़कम, (in Arithm.) fractions.
तोड़जोड़, *m.* a cutting out (as cloth by a tailor) ; an arranging a speech, etc.
तोड़टा, *m.* a dried pod of toree (mustard-seed) kept for seed.
तोड़ता = तोड़टा, *q.v.*
तोड़ताड़, *m.* a breaking and destroying ; plain speaking.

तोड़ना, *t.* to break, tear, rend, burst, split, demolish; to grind (grain); to change (money); to pluck or gather (fruit, flowers, etc.); to reduce (in Arithm.). *Dam* —, to be at the point of death. *Roṭī* —, to eat the bread of idleness. — *jornā* is a phrase which expresses absolute power over everything; *lit.* to break and to join. [*denā* or *lagānā*, to tighten; to distress.

तोड़नी, *f.* a claim (for debt, etc.), a dunning.——

तोड़फोड़, *m.* breaking; plain speaking.

तोड़ल, *m.* a large thick ring worn on the wrist.

तोड़लमल, *m. pr. n.* a certain statesman of the reign of Akbar. [coin, discount.

तोड़वाई, *f.* price paid for breaking or changing

तोड़वाना, *t.* to cause to be broken, cause to be changed (as coin).

तोड़ा, *m.* scarcity, want: a purse, bag containing one thousand rupees: the match of a gun: an island, bank, bar: a ploughshare: a piece of rope: an ornament like a chain. [coin).

तोड़ाना, *t.* to cause to break, cause to change (as

तोड़ी, *f.* mustard-seed: a certain musical mode

तोड़ेदार, a matchlock. [(*rāgiṇī*): *adv.* till, up to.

तोतना, *t.* to weave tape or ribbon.

तोतनी; see (1) तोतना (2) तोती.

तोतर = तोतला, *q.v.*

तोतरवचन, *m.* lisping.

तोतरि = तोतला, *q.v.*

तोतला, *m.* (*f.* ī) a stutterer, stammerer, etc.: *lit.* articulating imperfectly as a child, stuttering, stammering, lisping. [child, to lisp, stutter, stammer.

तोतलाना, *a. int.* to articulate imperfectly as a

तोता, *m.* (*f.* ī) a parrot: the cock of a matchlock.

तोती, *f.* a parrot, parroquet. — *kese honth mal dālnā* (*lit.* to rub or twist one's parrot-like lips) is used by way of an affectionate or friendly admonition.

तोन्द, *f.* a large belly, pot-belly.

तोन्दार, **तोन्दाला** } = तोन्दैला, *q.v.*

तोन्दी, *f.* the navel.

तोन्दैल, pot-bellied, gor-bellied, corpulent.

तोन्दैला, *m.* (*f.* ī) = तोन्दैल, *q.v.*

तोप, 1, *m.* ? a wood, grove, garden, orchard, tuft of trees, orchard of palmettoes: 2, *f.* a cannon, gun. — *chalānā* or *chhornā* or *dāghnā* or *mārnā* or *lagānā*, to fire a cannon, to cannonade.

तोपक, *f.* (dim. of तोप) a musket.

तोपख़ाना, *m.* a naval or military arsenal, place where cannon and artillery stores are kept, a park of artillery. [of ordnance, bombardier.

तोपची, *m.* a conductor of artillery, commissary

तोपड़ा, *m.* (*f.* ī) a kind of pigeon: a fly.

तोपना, *t.* to cover, bury.

तोपाना, *t.* to cause some one to cover or bury a thing, cause a thing to be covered or buried.

तोपी, *f.* a hat (especially of the kind that Anglo-Indians wear).

तोपीवाला, *m.* (*f.* ī) one who wears a topee, an Anglo-Indian.

तोपै in Braj and in poetry = (1) तिसपर (2) तेरे पास

तोप्यो (old form) = तोपा (तोपना). [(3) तुझपर.

तोबः, *more prop.* तोबा, *q.v.*

तोबड़ः, *more com.* तोबड़ा, *q.v.*

तोबड़ा, *m.* a bag in which horses eat their corn.

तोबन्द, a kind of petticoat.

तोबरः = तोबड़ा, *q.v.*

तोभी, *more prop.* तौभी, *q.v.*

तोमड़ा, *m.* = तोमड़ी, *q.v.*

तोमड़ी, *f.* a hollow gourd (*Cucurbita lagenaria*).

तोमर, 1, *more prop.* तोमरा, *q.v.*: 2, *m. pr. n.* a certain king of the Tomarās: 3, *m.* a javelin; an

तोय, *m.* water. [iron crow: a species of metre.

तोमरा, *m.* (see ग्रा, 22) a certain class of Rājpoots.

तोयकाम, *m.* a species of cane (*Calamus fasciculatus*) which grows in or near water.

तोयकृच्छ्र, *m.* a kind of penance in which nothing but water is taken for a fixed period.

तोयद, *m.* a certain fragrant grass (*Cyperus rotundus*): a cloud; *lit.* the water-giver.

तोयधर, *m.* a species of potherb (*Marsilia dentata*).

तोयधि, *m.* a sea, ocean, reservoir.

तोयपिप्पली, *f.* a species of plant (*Jussicua repens*).

तोयपुष्पी, *f.* trumpet-flower.

तोयप्रसादन, *m.* the clearing-nut plant (*Strychnos potatorum*). This nut being rubbed upon the inner surface of a water-jar occasions the precipitation of the impurities of the water poured into it. [in water.

तोयमय, *m.* (*f.* ī) consisting of water, abounding

तोयमुच, *m.* a cloud. [*tia*).

तोयवल्ली, *f.* a kind of gourd (*Mormordica charan-*

तोर, 1, an old form = तेरा: 2, *f.* a kind of pulse: a net thrown over a female's pālkee, etc.

तोरण, *m.* an arch, gateway, the ornamented arch of a door or gateway, the decorations of a gate-post, a bundle of flowers enclosed in a cloth-of-gold tissue and hung at a door or gateway, strings of flowers suspended across gateways on public festivals.

तोरना, *more prop.* तोड़ना, *q.v.*

तोरह, *m.* a dish of various meats presented to others by great men, a number of trays containing such dishes: a nobleman, minister of state: pride.

तोरहपोश, *m.* a covering for dishes, etc.

तोरहबन्दी, *f.* the arrangement or the sending out of trays of food as presents.

तोरही, *more prop.* तुरही, *q.v.*

तोरा, *m.* (*f.* ī) = तेरा, *q.v.*

तोरावलि, *more prop.* त्वरावली, *q.v.*

तोरि, a proposition.

तोरी = (1) तुरई (2) तेरी, *qq.v.*

तोल, *m.* weight; weighing.

तोलः = तोला, *q.v.*

तोलना = तौलना, *q.v.*

तोला, *m.* a designation of a weight (especially of gold or silver), the weight of the Indian Rupee. The *tolā* consists of a number of *māshas*,-the number varying in different parts of India. The standard *tolā*, or sicca weight of Calcutta, is 12½ *māshas*, agreeably to the following table:—

			grains troy.
4	*panks*	=1 *dhān* or grain,	·44916
4	*dhān*	=1 *ratti*,	1 ·79666
8	*ratti*	=1 *māsha*,	14 ·37333
12½	*māshas*	=1 *tolā*,	179 ·66666

तोलादार, *m.* a weighman, one who weighs coins [or goods in a market.

तोशक, *f.* a quilt, mattress.

तोशकख़ाना, *m.* a wardrobe, a place where furniture is kept, a store-room.

तोशल = **तोसल**, *q.v.*

तोशा, *m.* provisions (especially those of a traveller, or those which are carried with the funeral of a deceased person to support him during his journey to the other world); viaticum.

तोशाख़ाना = **तोशकख़ाना**, *q.v.*

तोष, *m.* content, satisfaction, pleasure, joy, happiness: contentment personified as a son of Bhagavat and one of the twelve Tushilas.

तोषक, *m.* (*f.* ikā) one who causes pleasure, etc.: *lit.* gratifying, affording satisfaction or happiness.

तोषता, *f.* }
तोषत्व, *m.* } = **तोष**, *q.v.*

तोषदान, *m.* a cartridge-box, pouch.

तोषण, 1, *m.* the pleasing or gratifying any one: 2, *m.* (*f.* ī) *adj.* gratifying, appeasing pleasing, affording [satisfaction.

तोषना, *t.* to gratify, please, delight.

तोषये (a Sansk. dat.) = **प्रसन्नताके लिये**. (Rāmāyaṇ.)

तोषी, *m.* (*f.* iṇī) a contented person, etc.: *lit.* contented; liking: gladdening.

तोसक, *more prop.* **तोशक**, *q.v.*

तोसदान, *m.* a cartridge-box, pouch.

तोसल, *m. pr. n.* a certain demon slain by Kṛishṇ.

तोसा in Braj = **तूसा**, *q.v.*

तोसों in Braj = (1) **तुझसे** (2) **तूसा**, *qq.v.*

तोहको in Braj = **तुझे**, *q.v.*

तोहमत, *more prop.* **तुहमत**, *q.v.*

तोहनी, dialectic form = **तुम**, *q.v.*

तोहरो, *m.* (*f.* ī) in Braj = **तेरा**, *q.v.*

तोहसो }
तोहसों } = (1) **तुझसा** (2) **तुझसे**. See **सा**.

तोहि = **तुझको** (Braj or old Hindee).

तोही }
तोहीं } in Braj (emphat.) = **तुझीको**.

तौ, 1, frequently in Braj = **तो**: 2, then, in that case, at that time, moreover, that, also, for, yes, well. 3, one of the terminations of the present participle (*m.* sing.) in Braj; *e. g.* **कहतौ** = **कहता**.

तौअम, *m.* (*pl.* ān) a twin.

तौउ, a Braj form = **तौभी**, *q.v.* [then.

तौं, 1, in Braj = **तौन**, *q.v.*: 2, so, in that manner;

तौंदा, *m.* (*f.* ī) pot-bellied, gorbellied, corpulent.

तौंसना, *m.* to be heated in the sunshine, be affected or overcome by heat.

तौंसा, *m.* sunstroke.

तौंहु }
तौंहुं }
तौंहू }
तौंहूं } Braj = (1) **तौभी** (2) **तिसपर भी**.

तौक़दार, 1, lunar: collared: pilloried: 2, *m.* a prisoner: a youth whose beard begins to appear.

तौज़ीह, *f.* a calling one's attention, an explaining, accounting for; an adjustment of accounts; assessment; a description-roll.

तौड़नों in Braj = **तौड़ना**, *q.v.* [that, that same.

तौन, infl. **तिस** (correl. of **जौन**) *m. f.* he, she, it,

तौफ़, *m.* pilgrimage, the procession around the temple of Mecca; *lit.* a surrounding, perambulating.

तौफ़ीर, *f.* increase, perfecting, augmenting of revenue.

तौबा, *f.* (*m.* ?) the promising to sin no more, repentance, penitence, conversion.—*k.* to repent.

तौबाधाड़, *f.* the sound of punishing, etc.

तौभी, even then, admitting even that much, still, nevertheless, notwithstanding that; in that case only; even then.

तौर, *m.* mode, manner; condition, state.

तौरत, *more prop.* **तौरेत**, *q.v.*

तौरात }
तौरीत } = **तौरेत**, *q.v.*

तौरेत, *f. pr. n.* the Old Testament, but more commonly (and more properly) the Pentateuch.

तौल, *m.* weight, weighing.

तौलग }
तौलगि } in Braj = **तबलगि**, *q.v.*

तौलताल, *m.* a weighing and measuring.

तौलना, *t.* to weigh, balance; to confront (as two armies). — *nazaroṅmeṅ ānā*, to estimate the worth of [a person.

तौलवाई, *f.* the cost of weighing.

तौला, a kind of intoxicating liquor made from the flowers of the *Mahwa*-tree.

तौलाई, *f.* the cost of weighing.

तौलाना, causat. of **तौलना**, *q.v.*

तौलिया, *m.* 1, = **तौलो**, *q.v.*: 2, (Engl.) a towel.

तौलो, *f.* a vessel used by Hindoos.

तौलों }
तौलौं } in Braj = **तबलों**, *q.v.*

तौसन, *m.* a horse; a young unbroken horse, colt: a high-blooded noble steed, war-horse, plump horse, unmanageable horse, horse with a hard mouth.

तौसीफ़, *f.* description, commendation.

तौहो in Braj = **तबहो** and **तौभी**, *q.v.* [Deity.

तौहीद, *f.* unity; the believing in the unity of the

तौहू in Braj = **तबहो** and **तौभी**, *qq.v.*

त्यक्त, *m.* (*f.* ā) an abandoned person, etc.: *lit.* left, abandoned, forsaken, deserted, resigned, rejected, thrown away as useless or as reprobate.

त्यजना = त्यागना, *q. v.*

त्याग, *m.* abdication, renouncing, leaving, abandoning, forsaking, parting from, separation, divorce, abstinence, deserting, disowning, relinquishing, resigning. — *k.* or *denā*, to renounce, forsake, abandon, etc.

त्यागन, *m.*; see त्याग.

त्यागना, *t.* to leave, abandon, desert, forsake, quit, relinquish, resign, abdicate.

त्यागपत्र, *m.* a writ of divorce.

त्यागित, *m.* (*f.* ā) a forsaken one: *lit.* abandoned, forsaken, quitted, relinquished.

त्यागिन, *m.* (*f.* ī) = त्यागी, *q. v.*

त्यागी, *m.* (*f.* inī) an abandoner, deserter: applied chiefly to the religious ascetic or to any one who abandons terrestrial objects, thoughts, passions, etc.: lit. *adj.* leaving, forsaking, abandoning, resigning, relinquishing, deserting, disowning

त्याज्य, to be abandoned, *i. e.* capable of being abandoned, requiring to be abandoned, suitable to be [abandoned.

त्यूं, *more prop.* त्यों, *q. v.*

त्यों, (correl. of ज्यों) so, as, like, in like manner: at the same time, then, forthwith.

त्योंत्यों, correl. of ज्योंज्यों, *q. v.*

त्योंही / **त्योंहीं** } in Braj, emphat. of त्यों, *q. v.*

त्योन्धा, *m.* (*f.* ī) dim-sighted, purblind.

त्यौं in Braj = त्यों, *q. v.*

त्यौंहीं in Braj, emphat. of त्यों, *q. v.*

त्यौन्धा in Braj = त्योन्धा, *q. v.*

त्यौर in Braj = तेवर, *q. v.*

त्यौरस in Braj = तेवरस, *q. v.*

त्यौराना in Braj = तेवराना, *q. v.*

त्यौरी in Braj = तेवरी, *q. v.*

त्यौहार in Braj = तेवहार, *q. v.*

त्रंग, *m. f. pr. n.* the city of Harischandra (supposed to be suspended in the air).

त्रपा, *f.* shame: an unchaste woman.

त्रपारण्डा, *f.* a harlot. [three.

त्रय, 1, *m.* triad: 2, *m* (*f.* ī) threefold: 3, (in comp.)

त्रयताप; see ताप, 2.

त्रयरेखा, *f.* (Rām.) = (1) त्रिवली (2) तीन पंक्ति.

त्रयी, 1, *f.* see त्रय, 2: 2, *f.* a species of plant (*Conyza serratula*): 3, *f.* triad: the three Veds (Rig, Yajush, and Sām) regarded collectively (the Atharva is omitted as being very generally considered rather as an appendix to the other three than as a fourth work of equal authority with them, inasmuch as it is not a text-book for the customary religious rites of the Hindoos). [prescribed in the three Veds.

त्रयीधर्म, *m.* duties, rites, modes of sacrifice, etc.

त्रयोदश, *m.* = त्रयोदशी, *q. v.* [night.

त्रयोदशी, *f.* the thirteenth day of the lunar fort-

त्र्यारुण, *m. pr. n.* (1) of a certain prince, son of Tridhanvan (2) of a son of Urukshay (3 of the Vyās [in the 15th Dwāpar.

त्रसित, *m.* (*f.* ā) = त्रस्त, *q. v.*

त्रस्त, *m.* (*f.* ā) a trembler, etc.: *lit.* trembling, timid, fearful.

त्राण, *m* shelter, protection, safety, preservation, deliverance, salvation; a coat of mail. — *k.* to free, [protect, save.

त्राणक, *m.* (*f.* ikā) / **त्राणकर्त्ता**, *m.* (*f.* trī) / **त्राणकारी**, *m.* (*f.* iṇī) } = त्राणी, *q. v.*

त्राणार्थी, *m.* (*f.* iṇī) a person full of desire for deliverance or salvation.

त्राणिका, *f.* (see त्राणक) a female deliverer.

त्राणी, *m.* (*f.* iṇī) a deliverer, protector, saviour: *lit.* delivering, protecting, preserving, saving; appertaining to deliverance, etc.

त्राता / **त्रातृ** } *m.* (*f.* trī) = त्राणी, *q. v.*

त्रानक, *more prop.* त्राणक, *q. v.*

त्रायमाण, *m.* (*f.* ā *or* matī ?) = त्राणी, *q. v.*

त्रास, 1, *f.* thirst: — *ānā* or *lagānā*, to be thirsty: 2, *m.* alarm, fear, dread, terror.

त्रासक, *m.* (*f.* ikā) = त्रासी, *q. v.*

त्रासदायी, *m.* (*f.* inī) a terrifier, etc.; *lit.* adj. occasioning dread, alarm or terror.

त्रासन, 1, *m.* a fright, frightening: 2, *m.* (*f.* ī) one who causes alarm: *lit.* adj. frightening.

त्रासा, timid, fearful, alarmed.

त्रासिका, *f.* (*m.* त्रासक) a timid female, etc.

त्रासित, *m.* (*f.* ā) = त्रासी, *q. v.*

त्रासी, *m.* (*f.* inī) a timid person, etc.: *lit.* timid, fearful, alarmed, affrighted.

त्राह, (*contraction*) = त्राहि, *q. v.*

त्राहि, (*exclam.*) pardon! mercy! save! *Trāhi trāhi k.*, to cry out for deliverance or for mercy, repent of sin. [mercy.

त्राहिकार, *m.* a calling out for deliverance or for

त्रि, (*only in comp.*) three.

त्रिंश, *m.* (*f.* ī) thirtieth.

त्रिंशत, thirty. [(*f.* ā) forming a triad.

त्रिक, *m.* a triad; the chine-bone, the hip: *lit. m.*

त्रिकट, *m.* a species of plant (*Ruellia longifolia*).

त्रिकटु, *m.* a mixture consisting of dry ginger, long pepper and black pepper. [*Silurus*).

त्रिकण्टक, *m.* 1, = त्रिकट, *q. v.*: 2, a kind of fish

त्रिका, *f.* (see त्रिक) a triangular frame or bar, across the mouth of a well, over which passes the rope of a bucket or to which one end of it is tied to guard against its slipping; a frame at the bottom of a well, on which the masonry rests.

त्रिकाल, *m.* past, present, and future time; the past, the present, and the future: morning, noon, and evening.

त्रिकालज्ञ, *m.* (*f.* ā) *adj.* knowing the past, the present and the future; hence, an epithet (1) of the Omniscient One (2) of Buddh.

त्रिकालदर्शी, *m. pr. n.* an epithet of Buddh; also of any *rishi* or saint-sage: *prop. m.* (*f.* iṇī) the Omniscient One: *lit.* the all-seeing One.

त्रिकूट, *m. pr. n.* of several mountains in India: any three-peaked mountain: sea salt prepared by evaporation.

त्रिकोण, triangular: hence, *m.* a triangular figure; [the vulva.
त्रिगण = त्रिवर्ग, *q. v.*

त्रिगर्त्त, *m. pr. n.* (1) of a country in the north-western division of India, apparently part of Lahore (2) of its inhabitants. [ous woman, a wanton.

त्रिगर्त्ता, 1, *m. pl.* = त्रिगर्त्त, 2, *q. v.*: 2, *f.* a lascivi-

त्रिगुण, 1, *m.* (see गुण) the aggregate of the three principal qualities of human nature: 2, *m.* (*f.* ā) any creature possessing those three qualities: *lit.* possessing the three qualities: consisting of three strings: three times as many, triple, thrice.

त्रिगुणात्मक, *m.* (see गुण) an epithet of man: *lit.* the one who possesses the three qualities.

त्रिजग }
त्रिजगत } = त्रिलोक, *q. v.*

त्रिण; for words beginning thus, see under the

त्रिणयन = त्रिलोचन, *q. v.* [form तृण.

त्रिणाचिकेत, *m. pr. n.* a certain portion of the Yājur-Ved; *hence,* one who practises a certain vow prescribed in that portion.

त्रितय, *m.* }
त्रिता, *f.* } = त्रित्व, *q. v.*

त्रिताप; see ताप, 2.

त्रित्व, *m.* an assemblage of three, a triad, trinity.

त्रिदण्डी, *m.* (*f.* inī) one who has attained command over the three seats of action (mind, body, and speech): a kind of wandering Hindoo ascetic who carries three long bamboos in his right hand.

त्रिदला, *f.* the creeping-plant *Cissus pedata.*

त्रिदश, *m.* a name of the thirty-three gods; a god, deity, immortal: heaven. [of the immortals.

त्रिदशाहार, *m. amrit* or ambrosia; *prop.* the food

त्रिदेव, *m. pr. n.* the Hindoo Triad (*viz.* Brahmā, Vishṇu, and Shiv).

त्रिदोष, *m.* disorder of the three humours of the body, defect in the functions of bile, phlegm, and wind. [of three sorts, in a threefold manner.

त्रिधा, threefold, in three places, in three parts,

त्रिपताक, *m.* the forehead (marked naturally with three horizontal lines).

त्रिपथ, *m.* any place where three roads meet.

त्रिपद, *m.* a tripod: (in Math.) trinomial.

त्रिपदी, *f.* a species of creeper (*Cissus pedata*): the girth of an elephant.

त्रिपाद, *m.* an epithet of fever. The demon of fever is described in the Purāṇs as having three feet and three heads, in allusion, probably, to its three stages of cold, hot, and sweating.

त्रिपुंड (*Rām.*) = त्रिपुण्ड्र, *q. v.*

त्रिपुण्ड्र, *m.* the three-curved horizontal lines worn on the forehead by the followers of Shiv and Shakti (they are delineated with the ashes of cowdung, and are indispensable in the worship of Shiv).

त्रिपुर, *m. pr. n.* a certain demon.

त्रिपुरा, *f. pr. n.* the modern Tipperah.

त्रिपुरारि, *m.* an epithet of Shiv; *lit.* the destroyer of Tripur. [or arches.

त्रिपोलिया, *m.* a building which has three doors

त्रिफला, *m.* a certain medicine composed of the three kinds of myrobalan. [form त्रिव.

त्रिब; for words beginning thus, see under the

त्रिभंग, *m.* (*f.* ā) a person who stands awry: *lit.* having three bends (with legs, loins, and neck bent) as have many images of Krishn.

त्रिभंगी, 1, *m.* an epithet of Krishṇ; *lit. tribhang* (see above): 2, *f.* a species of poetical measure.

त्रिभुन, a contraction of त्रिभुवन, *q. v.*

त्रिभुवन = त्रिलोक, *q. v.*

त्रिभुवनउजागर, the splendour of the three worlds.

त्रिभुवननाथ }
त्रिभुवनपति } = त्रिलोकीनाथ, *q. v.*

त्रिभुवनसुन्दरी, *f.* an epithet of a lady; *lit.* the beauty of the three worlds (Durgā ?).

त्रिमधु, *m. pr. n.* a portion of the Rig-Ved beginning with *madhu*; *hence,* one who knows or who recites the three verses beginning with *madhu.*

त्रिमात्रिक, *m.* a प्लुत, *q. v.*: *lit.* appertaining to a *plut.*

त्रिमार्गी }
त्रिमार्गी } *f.* = त्रिपथ, *q. v.*

त्रिमुकुट, *m.* any mountain with three peaks.

त्रिमुख, *m.* the junction of three rivers; lit. *m.* (*f.* i) having three mouths or faces.

त्रिमुहानी = त्रिमुख, *q v.*

त्रिमूर्त्ति = तृमूर्ति, *q. v.*

त्रिय (Rām.) = त्रिया, *q. v.* [*pentaphylla*).

त्रियष्टि, *m.* a certain medicinal plant (*Mollugo*

त्रिया, *f.* a woman, maid, female, wife.

त्रियाचरित्र, *m.* female wiles.

त्रियामक, *m.* an epithet of sin (as the impeder of the three objects of life).

त्रियामा, *f.* 1, an epithet of night; *lit.* consisting of three watches: 2, an epithet of the Jamunā river.

त्रियाराज्य, *m.* amazon-country, petticoat-government. [females.

त्रियावेद, *f.* the science of the knowledge of

त्रिरात्र, *m.* three nights collectively or consecutively, or the duration of three nights.

त्रिरात्रि }
त्रिरात्री } *f.* = त्रिरात्र, *q. v.*

त्रिलोक, *m.* the universe, the three worlds, *viz.* heaven, sky and earth; or, heaven, earth, and the lower regions: the inhabitants of the three worlds.

त्रिलोकी, *f.* the three worlds considered as an aggregate.

त्रिलोकीनाथ, *m.* an epithet (1) of Shiv (2) of Vishṇu (3) of Krishṇ: *lit.* lord of the three worlds, *i. e.* of the entire universe.

त्रिलोचन, *m.* the three-eyed one, *i. e.* Shiv.

त्रिवर्ग, *m.* the three human pursuits, *viz.* love, duty, wealth: the three conditions of a state, *viz.* prosperity, evenness, decay; or, gain, equality, loss: the three qualities of nature, *viz.* purity, blindness, depravity.

त्रिवर्णक, *m.* a certain plant (*Ruella longifolia*).

त्रिवली, *f.* three folds of skin on the abdomen; (applied chiefly to the wrinkles in the skin of females between the ensiform cartilage and the navel).

त्रिविक्रम, *m.* an epithet of Vishṇu as the sun; *lit.* three steps; *i. e.* the one who crosses over the three worlds in three steps.

त्रिविध; see ताप, 2.

त्रिवृतपर्णी, *f.* a species of potherb (*Hilancha repens*).

त्रिवेणी, *f. pr. n.* (1) of the junction of the three rivers, Ganges, Jamunā and (as the mythology teaches) Saraswatee at Pryāg (Allahabad); and hence (2) of Pryāg itself: *lit.* three streams or three braids of hair?

त्रिवेद, *m. pr. n.* (see त्रयी, 3) the three Veds.

त्रिवेदी, *m.* (*f.* inī) a person acquainted with the three Veds.

त्रिशंकु, *m. pr. n.* a certain ancient Hindoo king.

त्रिशरण, *m.* a sanctified teacher of the *Jain* sect; *lit.* the refuge or asylum of the three worlds.

त्रिशिरा, *m. pr. n.* (1) of a certain Asur (2) of a certain Rākshas; *lit.* three-headed.

त्रिशुक; see त्रिशंकु.

त्रिशूल, *m.* a trident or three-pronged lance (especially the one borne by Shiv).

त्रिशूली, *m.* the trident-bearer, *i. e.* Shiv.

त्रिशृंग, *m.* a hill with three peaks: a triangle.

त्रिशृंगी, *m.* (*f.* iṇī) a species of fish (*Cyprinus denticulatus*).

त्रिष्टुभ, *f.* a sort of metre in which the stanza consists of three lines of various lengths.

त्रिसन्ध्य, *m.* = त्रिसन्ध्या, *q.v.*

त्रिसन्ध्या, *f.* the three periods of the day, *viz.* morning, noon, and eve.

त्रिसुपर्ण, *m. pr. n.* a certain portion of the Rig-Ved and Yajur-Ved; hence, a person acquainted with those portions.

त्रिसूल, *more prop.* त्रिशूल, *q. v.*

त्रुटि, *f.* a moment (as a measure of time); small cardamoms.

त्रुटी, *f.* loss, destruction.

त्रेता, *f. pr. n.* (see युग) the second or silver age of the Hindoo mythology (said to consist of 1296000 years).

त्रेताग्नि, *m. pr. n.* = अग्नित्रेता, *q. v.*

त्रैएकत्व, *m.* the union of three in one, trinity in unity.

त्रैकत्व = त्रैएकत्व, *q. v.*

त्रैपुर, *m.* (pl.) the inhabitants of त्रिपुरा, *q. v.*

त्रैलोक्य, *m. pr. n.* = त्रिलोक, *q. v.*

त्रैविद्य, *m.* the three Veds: an assemblage of Brāhmans skilled in the three Veds, a person who possesses the knowledge of the three Veds or of three sciences.

त्रैलोक, *m.* the ruler of the three worlds, *i. e.* Indra.

त्रोटक, *m.* a kind of drama: (in Pros.) a species of metre.

त्रोटकी, *f.* one of the female personifications of music (*rāgiṇī*).

त्रोटी, *f.* the beak of a bird: a kind of pike (*Esox scolopax*).

त्रोण, a quiver.

त्व, (see ता, 5) a Taddhita suffix by means of which abstract substantives masculine, expressive of state or condition, are derived from adjectives or concrete nouns; *e. g.* प्रियत्व (प्रिय); कवित्व (कवि).

त्वक, *f.* the bark of the bamboo, bark in general; skin.

त्वक्कणडुर, *m.* a sore or wound.

त्वक्क्षीरा, *f.* the manna of the bamboo.

त्वकछेद, *m.* circumcision (*lit.* a rent of the skin).

त्वच, 1, *m.* cinnamon: 2, *f.* skin, hide, bark.

त्वचा, *f.* skin, hide, bark, rind: woody cassia.

त्वदन्घि, (Sk. त्वद = अंघ्रि) thy feet (Rām.).

त्वदीय, thine (Sk. poss. pron.). Rāmāyaṇ.

त्वरा, *f.* haste, speed.

त्वरावन्त, *m.* (*f.* vatī) quick, swift, expeditious.

त्वरित, 1. *m.* dispatch, haste: 2, *m.* (*f.* ā) hastening, swift, expeditious: 3, *adv.* quickly, swiftly.

त्वष्टि, *f.* the profession of a carpenter.

त्वष्टा, *m.* (*f.* ṭrī) a carpenter: *pr. n.* a certain deity, the artist of the gods.

थ

थ (th) is the seventeenth consonant in the Hindee alphabet, and the second letter of the तवर्ग or dental class. It is the aspirate of त; and it is as difficult to convey the true idea as to the pronunciation of this letter as of that one. There are several words which in Hindee begin with this letter which in Sanskrit would begin with स्त or स्थ; *e. g.* थन (Sk. स्तन); थिति (Sk. स्थिति).

थई, *f.* a heap (of clothes, etc.).

थंड, थंप, थंब, थंभ; for words beginning with either of these forms, see under the forms थण्ड, थम्प, थम्ब, थम्भ, respectively.

थक, *m.* a clot, lump (congealed). — *jānā,* to grow weary, to tire, fag.

थकथक, very wet, drenched.

थकना, *n.* to be wearied, be fatigued.

थका, *m.* (*f.* ī) weary, tired, fatigued.

थकाई, *f.* weariness, fatigue, exhaustion.

थकाना, *t.* to cause to be tired; *hence,* to tire a person, weary, harass, fatigue, fag, jade.

थकापिक्का, *m.* (*f.* ī-ī) distracted, troubled, perplexed, confounded.

थकाफक्का, थकाबक्का } *m.* (*f.* ī—ī) = थकापिक्का, *q. v.*

थकार, *m.* the letter थ, or any symbol that may represent it.

थकाव, *m.*, थकावट, *f.*, थकाहट, *f.* } = थकाई, *q. v.*

थकि = थकके (थकना). See क्, 7.

थकित, *m.* (*f.* ā) wearied, tired, exhausted; motionless, stopped, astonished.

थकैनी, *f.* weariness, fatigue, exhaustion.

थक्का, *m.* a clot, lump (congealed). *Thakke thakke,* congealed, conglomerated, thick.

थगित, stood, remained.

थज जाना, *a. int.* to become fixed (said of the eyes).

थटकना, *a. int.* to stop, stagnate.

थटा, *more com.* ठट्ठा, *q. v.*

थड़; see **थर.**

थपड; for words beginning thus see under the more common form **ठपड.**

थद्दई, *m. pr. n.* the apostle Thaddeus.

थन, *m*, (prop. **स्तन**) an udder, nipple.

थनदार, an animal with a large udder, or having an udder.

थनी, *f.* a certain blemish in horses.

थनेला, *m.* an inflamed breast (of a woman): name of an animal.

थनेश्वर, *m. pr. n.* a famous Hindoo shrine in Kurukshetra near Karnāl.

थनेश्वरी / **थनेसरी** } *m.* a Brāhmaṇ of Thaneshwar.

थपक, *m.* a pat, tap.

थपकना, *t.* to pat, tap.

थपड़ा, *m.* a slap, box, cuff, blow.

थपड़ी, *f.* a clapping of hands.— *bajānā*, to clap the hands.— *mārnā*, to damn (in the theatrical sense); to hoot at.

थपत = थपता है. See **त**, 5.

थपना, *t.* to establish, fix, settle, place.

थपेड़ = थप्पड़, *q.v.*

थपेड़ा, *m.* 1, = **थप्पड़**, *q.v.*: 2, the scalp.

थप्पड़, *m.* a slap, box, cuff, clout, claw, blow.

थम, **थम्ब**; for words beginning with either of these elements, see under the form **थम्भ.**

थमड़ा, *m.* (*f.* ī) thick, corpulent.

थम्बा = थम्भ, *q.v.*

थम्भ, *m.* (from **स्तम्भ**) a pillar, post, column, support, prop; an obstruction, obstacle, anything that restrains.

थम्भना, *a. int.* to stand still, stop, cease, give over: *n.* to be restrained: to be supported.

थम्भाना, *t.* (a causat. of **थम्भना**) to stop, restrain, quiet.

थम्ह; for words beginning thus, see under the form **थम्भ.**

थर, *m.* (from **स्थल**) a lion's or tiger's den: a layer, bed of anything.

थरथर, *adj.* trembling.— *kāmpnā*, to tremble.

थरथरना, *a. int.* to tremble, shake, quiver, shiver, vibrate.

थरथराना, 1, = **थरथरना**, *q.v.*: 2, *t.* (causat. of that verb) to make tremble, etc.

थरथराहट, *f.* = **थरथरी**, *q.v.*

थरथरी, *f.* tremor, shaking, shivering, quivering, trembling, vibration.

थरहर; for words beginning thus, see under the form **थरथर.**

थरथरैव, an old form = **थरथरा** (**थरथराना**).

थर्राना = थरथराना, *q.v.*

थरिआ, (see **दुआ**) a dialectic form = **थाली**, *q.v.*

थरीआ, a dialectic form = **थाली**, *q.v.*

थल, *m.* (from **स्थल**) a place; firm or dry ground, terra firma: a lion's or tiger's den.

थलकना, *a. int.* to palpitate, tremble, flutter.

थलचर, *m.* (*f.* ī) any land-animal; *lit.* moving on the land.

थलचारी, *m.* (*f.* iṇī) = **थलचर**, *q.v.*

थलथल क°, *a. int.* to undulate, fluctuate (as a thick or glutinous fluid), shake (as the flabby flesh of a corpulent person).

थलथलाना = थलथल क°, *q v.*

थलबेड़ा, *m.* a place of abode, and means of attaining one's desires.

थलिया, *f.* a salver, platter, flat dish (generally of brass) for eating from.

थवई, *m.* a house-mason, bricklayer, builder, architect.

थहराना, *more com.* **थरथराना**, *q.v.*

था, *m.* (*f.* ī) he (or it) was.

थां. *more prop.* **थान**, *q.v.*

थांग, *m.* a den of thieves.

थांगी, *m.* (*f.* inī) a receiver of stolen goods.

थांगीदार = थांगी, *q.v.*

थांगीदारी, *f.* the receiving stolen goods.

थांन, *more prop.* **थान**, *q.v.*

थांवला, *m.* the mound or earthen basin constructed around the base of a tree for retaining water.

थाकना, 1, *more prop.* **थकना**, *q.v.*: 2, *t.* (a causat. of **थकना**) = **थकाना**, *q.v.*

थाट, state, dignity: abundance.

थाती, *f.* a trust, charge, anything given in charge.

थाथी = थाती, *q.v.*

थान, *m.* a place, a stall for cattle, manger: a piece of cloth; a piece of coin (as *ek — ashrafi*, one gold mohur). *Tinoṅ* —, the private parts of a male.

थानः = थाना, *q.v.*

थानःजात / **थानःहात** } pll. of **थाना**, *q.v.*

थाना, *m.* a station, guard-house, police-station: the inside of the lines of an army: a heap of bamboos.

थानादार, *m.* an officer in charge of a *thānā*.

थानादारी, 1, *f.* the occupation or the status of a *thānādār*: 2, appertaining to the office of *thānādār*.

थानी, 1, *m.* the owner of a *thān*; a householder, master of a house; a permanent cultivator: 2, *f.* a den of thieves: 3, *adj.* resident, stationary.

थानेदार = थानादार *q.v.*

थाप, *f.* a tap, pat, slap, flap, paw; the sound of a small drum.

थापना, 1, *t.* to patch (as a wall with cowdung); to pat, slap: 2, *f.* a certain religious ceremony performed at a certain season at Agra and its vicinity.

थापा, *m.* a mark of a paw: gleanings (of corn, etc. left on the field after harvest).

थापी, *f.* the noise of tapping; the instrument with which potters beat their earth, or with which terraces are beaten.

थाम, (from **स्तम्भ**) = **थम्भ**, *q v.*

थामज़ान, *m.* a kind of sedan chair (commonly called in India, "tomjon"). (From **थाम्भ + जांघ ?**)

थामना = थाम्भना, *q. v.*

थाम्भ, (from **स्तम्भ**) = **थम्भ**, *q v.*

थाम्भना, *t.* (a causat. of **थम्भना**) to prop, support, assist; to keep, retain, maintain; to shield, protect, shelter; to prevent, restrain, withhold, stop, pull up (a horse); to calm; to resist; to bear.

थाम्यौ = थाम्भा (**थाम्भना**): Braj or old Hindee.

थम्हना, *more prop.* **थाम्हना**, *q.v.*
थार, a corruption (1) of **ठार** (2) of **थाल**, *qq.v.*
थारी, *more prop.* **थाली**, *q.v.*
थाल, *m.* a large flat dish, tray.
थाला, *m.* a large flat dish; the excavation in which a tree is to be planted: the mound or earthen basin constructed around the base of a tree for retaining water.
थाली, *f.* a salver, platter, tray, flat dish: the mound, etc. (see **थाला**).
थाह, *f.* a bottom, ford. — *lenā*, to sound.
थाहौ, *f.* fordableness.
थिगला, *m.* a binding; a patch.
थिजना, *a. int.* to become senseless and motionless: *n.* to be congealed; to be astonished.
थिजाना, *t.* to congeal; to astonish.
थिति = (1) **स्थिति** (2) **ठहराव** (3) **पालन**, *qq.v.*
थिर, (from **स्थिर**) fixed, stable, settled; tranquil, calm, smooth.
थिरकना, *a. int.* to set oneself off well in dancing, dance with expressive action and gesture. [quillity.
थिरता, *f.* rest, settlement, steadfastness, tran-
थिराना, *a. int.* to settle (as liquor).
थी, *f.* (*m.* **था**) she was. [abl. ending, **से**.
थीं, 1, *f.* (*m.* **थे**) pl. of **थी**: 2, a dialectic form of the
थीकर, *m.* the duty of keeping the village watch (taken by the villagers in turn).
थीकरा, *m.* = **थीकर**, *q.v.* [**स्थिर**.
थीर; for words beginning thus, see under the form
थुकथुकाना, *a. int.* to spit (on the mention of any disease, as a preservative against it); to spit (as a precaution against the influence of an evil eye).
थुकहाई, *m.* (*f.* inī) a contemptible person, etc: *lit.* base, contemptible, fit to be spit upon.
थुकाई (*contraction*) = **थुकहाई**, *q.v.*
थुकाना, *t.* (causat. of **थूकना**) to cause to spit; to cause to reproach.
थुड़दिला, (**थोड़ा** + **दिल**) *m.* (*f.* ī) miserly, small-souled.
थुतकारना, *t.* to drive away scornfully.
थुथनी, *more prop.* **थूथनी**, *q.v.*
थुथाना, *a. int.* to frown, scowl; to pout. *Muṅh*—,
थुनी, *more prop.* **थूनी**, *q.v.* [to make a wry face.
थुपाना, *t.* (causat. of **थोपना**) to cause to prop, etc.; to cause to be propped, etc. [a small height).
थुलथुल, gently falling or dropping (as water from
थूक, *m.* spittle, saliva: the gossamer. — *chāṭnā*, to break one's promise. — *denā*, to leave, give up. — *lagākar chhoṛnā*, to treat with sovereign contempt. — *lagānā*, to apply spittle (a term of abuse, and of most indecent import).
थूकना, *a. int.* to spit: *t.* to spit at.
थूणी, *f.* } = **थूनी**, *q.v.*
थूणय, *m.* }
थूतड़ा, *more prop.* **थूथड़ा**, *q.v.*
थूथड़ा, *m.* the mouth.

थूथना, *m.* the mouth of a horse, camel, etc.
थूथनी, *f.* = **थूथन**, *q.v.* [post over the mouth of a well.
थूनी, *f.* a post, prop, pillar, column; the upright
थूम्बा, a lump of earth put on the end of a lever
थूली, *f.* a kind of sweet dish. [as a balance.
थूहर = **थोहर**, *q.v.*
थे, (pl. of **था**) *m.* (*f.* **थीं**) they were.
थेईथेई, *f.* merry-making. — *k.* to make merry.
थेगा, *m.* a club, stick.
थेगली, *f.* a patch (on a garment).
थेयोथेयो = **थेईथेई**, *q.v.*
थेर, a corruption of **फेर**, *q.v.*
थेवा, *m.* a stone set in a ring. [a bag; the scrotum.
थैला, *m.* a purse, a purse tied around the waist;
थैलिया } *f.* = **थैला**, *q.v.*
थैली }
[tion.
थोक, *m.* heap, amount, ready money; share, por-
थोकदार, *m.* a wholesale dealer. [from the stem.
थोड़, *m.* the spathe of a plantain-tree before it shoots
थोड़ा, *m.* (*f.* ī) a little, some, a few; scanty, scarce; less; seldom. *Thoṛā-thoṛā*, a very little: *adv.* little by little, by degrees, by littles. *Thoṛā-thoṛā honā*, to be ashamed, shrink with shame. *Thoṛa* (*f.* ī) *bahut*, more or less. *Thoṛese thoṛā*, very little. [very few.
थोड़ासा, *m.* (*f.* **थोड़ासी**) a very little: pl. *thoṛese*,
थोतरा, *m.* (*f.* ī) toothless; bruised and spoiled as the head of a mallet).
थोतला, *m.* (*f.* ī) blunt, not sharp, dull.
थोथ, *m.* the mouth.
थोथना, *m.* (*f.* ī) blunt, not sharp, dull.
थोथा, 1, *m.* a certain medicine: an arrow without a point: 2, *m.* (*f.* ī) toothless; hollow, empty. *Thothī bāt*, words without meaning, nonsense.
थोप, *m.* head, topping, an ornament or mounting at the end of the pole of a pālkee, etc.
थोपड़ा, *m.* the jaw. [pile.
थोपना, *t.* to prop, support: to plaster: to heap,
थोपियाना, *a. int.* to trickle.
थोपी, *f.* a thump, box, clout.
थोमा, *m. pr. n.* the apostle Thomas.
थोर = (1) **थोड़** (2) **थोड़ा**, *qq.v.*
थोरा, *m.* (*f.* ī) *more com.* **थोड़ा**, *q.v.*
थोरेऊ, in Braj = **थोड़े भी**. See **ऊ**, 7.
थोरिक = **थोड़ा एक**. See **एक**.
थोहर, *m.* the plant *Euphorbia neriifolia*, Roxb.

द

द (d) is the eighteenth consonant in the Hindee alphabet, and the third letter of the **तवर्ग** or dental class. In power it corresponds to the English letter *d*, though as to its exact pronunciation see Art. **त**, 1. This letter is frequently found as a suffix in compounds, thus importing the idea of 'giving': such words are masculine, — the feminine being invariably formed by adding *ā*; *e. g.* जन्मद, *m.* (*f.* जन्मदा) father; *lit.* the birth-giver. It is occasionally liable to be interchanged with त्त; *e. g.* उन्मद = उन्मत्त.

दअ़वत, *f.* invitation, convocation; an entertainment, feast: the pressing persons to become Muhammadans: pretention, exorcism, invocation of the powers of darkness.

दअ़वी, *f.* a claim, pretention, plaint, suit at law.

दइहै, (pl. दइहैं) (old form) = देगा (देना).

दई, 1, *more prop.* दिई, *q.v.*: 2, *f.* (prop. दया) a gift: 3, *f.* the godhead: 4, *m. f.* destiny, the Deity. — *lagni*, the being unfortunate. [the Deity.

दईमारा, *m.* (*f.* ī) an accursed one: *lit.* struck by

दंग, astonished; foolish, careless.

दं-इत, *more prop.* दंगैत. See दंगई.

दंगई, *m.* (*f.* inī) mutineer, rebel: *lit.* turbulent, mutinous, seditious, rebellious.

दंगईत, *more prop.* दंगैत = दगई, *q. v.*

दंगत. *more com.* दंगा, *q. v.*

दंगमदंगा, an alliteration of दंगा, *q. v.*

दंगया, *m.* (*f.* दंगई) = दंगल, *q. v.*

दंगल, 1, *more com.* दंगा, *q. v.*: 2, *m.* a kind of chair. 3, *m. f.* a crowd, assembly; the sitting face to face in an assembly.

दंगस्त, *m.* a certain class of Rājputs in Ghazeepur.

दंगा, *m.* wrangling, discord, confusion, hubbub, sedition, rebellion, mutiny. — *k.* to occasion a hubbub, rebellion, or insurrection.

दंगेबाज़, turbulent, mutinous.

दंगैड़त, *m.* (*f.* in *or* ī) = दंगई, *q. v.* [दंगई, *q. v.*

दंगैत, 1, *more com.* दंगा, *q. v.*: 2, *m.* (*f.* in or ī) =

दंड, दंत, दंथ, दंद, दंप; for all words beginning with either of these elements, see under the forms दण्ड, दन्त, दन्थ, दन्द, दम्प, respectively.

दंश, *m.* a biting, a bite; a tooth; a gadfly; the sting of a snake; a coat of mail.

दंशन, *m.* a biting, a stinging.

दंशमूल, *m.* a plant (*Hyperanthera morunga*).

दंशित, *m.* (*f.* ā) bitten, stung: protected by mail.

दंशी, *f.* (dim. of दंश) a small gadfly.

दंशेर, cruel, mischievous, noxious.

ंस, *more prop.* दंश, *q. v.*

दकर; see डकार, 2.

दकार, *m.* the letter द, or any symbol that may represent it. [difficult.

दक़ीक़, *m.* flour, meal: *adj.* fine, minute, abstruse,

दक़ीक़ा, *m.* anything small, a subtle question, a trifling business, a moment of time, a minute.

दक़्क़, subtle, minute, thin.

दक्खिन = दखिन, *q. v.*

दक्ष, *m.* (*f.* ā) an able, clever, dexterous person, scholar, pandit: *lit.* able, clever, dexterous; suitable: *m. pr. n.* (1) of one of the Prajāpatis, sons of Brahmā (he is said to have been born from the thumb of the right hand of Brahmā for the purpose of peopling the world: Daksh is said to have had sixty daughters, of whom twenty-seven are represented as the nymphs who form the lunar asterisms and wives of the moon: one of his daughters was Satī or Durgā, the wife of Shiv; while seventeen were married to Kashyap and became the mothers of all created being: Daksh was on one occasion decapitated by Shiv: he is sometimes regarded as an *avatār* of Brahmā himself): (2) of a certain *muni* and legislator who flourished in the beginning of the Tretā Yug. [(called also Pārvatī, Satī, Devī, etc.).

दक्षकन्या, *f.* the daughter of Daksh, *i. e.* Durgā

दक्षजा = दक्षकन्या, *q. v.*

दक्षत्व, *m.* (*f.* tā) cleverness, dexterity.

दक्षप्रजापति, *m. pr. n.* (see प्रजापति) = दक्ष (1), *q. v.*

दक्षसुत, *m.* (= प्रचेतस, *q. v.*) *lit.* a son of Daksh.

दक्षसुता = दक्षकन्या, *q. v.*

दक्षाध्वरध्वंसकृत, *m.* an epithet of Shiv (from his having on one occasion disturbed a sacrifice prepared by Daksh. It seems that he invited on this occasion all the deities excepting his own daughter Satī and her husband Shiv: they, however, went unbidden, and being received impolitely, Satī threw herself into the fire and was burnt: a furious quarrel ensued between Shiv and Daksh, in which Shiv decapitated his father-in-law.

दक्षिण, 1, *m.* (*f.* ā) a dexterous person, etc.: *lit.* right (not left); southern: clever; honest, upright: 2, *m.* the south; *lit.* the right side. According to the Hindoos, the earth (of which Hindustān is supposed to be the navel) has its head to the west, its feet to the east, its right side to the south, and its left to the north. The allusion may, however, be to the position of Orientals (turning the face eastward) in their adoration of the rising sun. In the Arabian method, and (according to Livy) in that of the Roman augurs, as also in the Gaelic dialects, the south and the north correspond, in like manner, with the right and the left respectively.

दक्षिणदिशा, *m. pr. n.* the Southern quarter.

दक्षिणपश्चिम, *m. pr n.* the South-west quarter.

दक्षिणपूर्व्वा, *f. pr. n.* the South-east quarter.

दक्षिणा, *f.* a present to Brāhmans on occasions of sacrifice, a reward, donation or fee to Brāhmans: a figure of Durgā in which the right side is said to be advanced: personified as a goddess, and said to have been born from Krishn's right side.

दक्षिणाग्नि, *m.* one kind of sacred fire (that which being taken from the domestic or consecrated fire, is placed to the south).

दक्षिणाचल, *m pr. n.* the Malay mountain. [estly.

दक्षिणाचार, *m.* (*f.* ā) one who conducts himself hon-

दक्षिणामुख, *m.* (*f.* ī) one who turns towards the south: *lit.* adj. having the face turned southwards.

दक्षिणायन, *m.* a southing, the half of the year when the sun moves to the south of the equator.

दक्षिणायनासूर्य्य, *m.* the sun's southing, the period of the sun's being in the southern hemisphere, the southern declination, winter solstice.

दक्षिणावर्त्त, *m.* (*f.* ā) turning towards the right, turning to the south: hence (1) *m. pr. n.* the south country, the Dakkhan (2) *m.* a conch-shell with the valve opening to the right.

दक्षिणीय, *m.* (*f.* ā) worthy to be honoured with presents, deserving of reward.

दक्षिणेन, (Sk. instr., to the right hand; hence) south-
दक्षिण्य = दक्षिणीय, *q.v.* [ward, southerly.
दक्षी, *m.* (*f.* iṇī) able, capable, well-qualified. [दखिन.
दखन; for words beginning thus, see under the form
दख़ल, *m.* entrance, access, an entering; possibility or practicability; produce, income, receipt; intrusion, interference, molestation. — *k.* to meddle, interrupt, take possession. — *pānā*, to have access.
दखिन, *m. pr. n.* the southern part of Hindustān (commonly called the Deccan); *lit.* adj. *m.* south.
दखिना, *f.* a southerly wind; *lit.* adj. *f.* south.
दखिनायन, *more prop.* **दक्षिणायन**, *q.v.*
दखिनी, southern, appertaining to the Deccan or southern India (generally applied to things or persons
दखिनीपूदीना, *m.* horse-mint. [from the south).
दख़ील, *m.* a friend, confidant, protegé, one who claims protection or mercy; (in Law) the party in possession, occupant: *lit.* familiar, intimate, allowed
दगड़, *m.* a kettle-drum. [entrance.
दगड़ना, *t.* to disbelieve a true testimony.
दगड़ा, *m.* a highway.
दगड़ाना, *t.* to propel, roll.
दगदगा, *m.* (*f.* ī) shining, bright.
दगदगाट, a contraction of **दगदगाहट**.
दगदगाना, *a. int.* to glow, gleam, twinkle.
दगदगाहट, *f.* splendour, sparkling, twinkling (as
दगध, *more prop.* **दग्ध**, *q.v.* [of a star).
दगधना, *t.* to burn; to tease, vex; to chide, pester, upraid, revile, threaten.
दगमगाना, *a. int.* to tremble.
दग़ल, *m.* vice, corruption, depravity, treachery; a villain, pickpocket; luxuriant and entangled herbage: *adj.* false, deceitful; base (as coin).
दग़लफ़सल, treachery, deceit, depravity.
दगला, *m.* a kind of quilted vest worn as armour or under armour.
दग़ा, *f.* deceit, imposture, treachery, deceptiveness, sharp practice. — *khānā*, to be imposed upon.
दग़ादार = दग़ाबाज़, *q. v.*
दग़ादारी = दग़ाबाज़ी, *q.v.*
दग़ाबाज़, *m.* a deceiver, cheat, impostor, traitor.
दग़ाबाज़ी, *f.* imposition, sharp practice.
दग्ध, *m.* (*f.* ā) burnt, scorched, consumed by fire; cauterizing; cunning. [crow).
दग्धकाक, *m.* (*f.* ī) a raven (or, perhaps, the carrion-
दग्धाचार = धधक्कर, *q.v.*
दच, a homestead (East Oude).
दच्छ, दछ; for words beginning with either of these forms, see under the form **दच**.
दच्छिन, *m.* (*f.* ā) = (1) **दच्छिणा** (2) **दखिन**, *qq. v.*
दज्जल, *m.* a liar, impostor, antichrist.
दटना, 1, *more prop.* **दतना**, *q.v.*? 2, *a. int.* to stop:
दटाना = दबकाना, *q.v.* [*n.* to be confronted?
दट्टा, *m.* a cork, stopper, plug.

दड़कना, *a. int.* to split, crack, become torn or
दड़्हूकना, *a. int.* to bellow (said of the ox). [rent.
दड़ेड़ा, *m.* impetuosity; a violent attack; hard and impetuous rain. — *k.* to assault.
दड़ेला, *m.* a rush of water, waterfall.
दढ़मुण्डा, *m.* (*f.* ī) beard-shaven, beardless.
दढ़ियल, *adj.* having a long beard.
दढूकना, *a. int.* to bellow (said of the ox).
दण्ड, *m.* a staff, stick, stem, handle; violence; punishment (whether corporal or by amercement; hence) fine, penalty; a long measure (pole of four cubits); a measure of time (twenty-four minutes).
दण्डक, *m.* the staff of a banner: a species of metre the stanza of which exceeds twenty-seven syllables and may extend to two hundred: *pr. n.* (1) of a great forest in the Dakkhan (2, *m. pl.*) of its inhabitants (3) of a certain king.
दण्डकवन, *m. pr. n.* = **दण्डकारण्य**, *q. v.*
दण्डका, *f. pr. n.* a country on the North-east coast of Hindustān containing the celebrated forest *Daṇḍakāraṇya*.
दण्डकारक, *m.* (*f.* ikā) an administrator of punishment, avenger: *lit.* adj. awarding punishment.
दण्डकारण्य, *m. pr. n.* a certain forest (on the north-east coast of Hindustān) in which for some time
दण्डढक्का, *f.* a kind of drum. [Rām resided.
दण्डतामी, *f.* a kind of time-measurer (consisting of a perforated copper vessel of given capacity placed in a vessel full of water: after gradually filling, it sinks, marking a certain portion of time). [investigate?
दण्डना, *t.* to inflict a penalty, punish, fine: to
दण्डनीति, *f.* the system of ethics taught by Chānyaka. [ment.
दण्डनीय, *m.* (*f.* ā) punishable, deserving punish-
दण्डपारुष्य, *m.* assault and battery. [*biger*?).
दण्डपाल, *m.* a small kind of fish (*Cyprinus bar-*
दण्डयोग्य, *m.* (*f.* ā) worthy of punishment, guilty.
दण्डवत, *f.* a mode of salutation among Hindoos, obeisance, bow, prostration. — *k.* to do obeisance.
दण्डा, *m.* a post, stake; the pole of a carriage.
दण्डादण्डी, *f.* single-stick; a cudgeling, fighting with sticks or staves.
दण्डायमान, *m.* (*f.* matī) *adj.* standing erect.
दण्डित, *m.* (*f.* ā) punished, chastised, sentenced,
दण्डिन, *m.* (*f.* ī) a mace-bearer. [fined.
दण्डिया = डण्डिया, *q. v.*
दण्डी, 1, *m. pr. n.* an epithet of Yam; lit. *m.* (*f.* inī) the staff-bearer; *hence*, a mendicant who carries a staff in his hand: the handle or haft of an instrument; the penis: 2, *f.* a pole, staff, post; the yard of a sail; the beam of a pair of scales.
दण्डोचना = दण्डना, *q. v.*
दण्डोत in Chand = **दण्डवत**, *q. v.*
दण्य = दण्डनीय, *q. v.*
दतकारना, *t.* to reproach, abuse.
दतना, *t.* to oppose, confute, fight.

दतरा, *m.* a large rake used for gathering high grass together into a cocklet. [a twig).

दतवन, *m.* (Sk. **दन्तधावन**) a toothbrush (generally

दतुवन, *more com.* **दतवन**, *q.v.*

दतून = **दतवन**, *q.v.* [the grain called *bājrā* or *juār*.

दताई, *f.* land which has been lately cropped with

दतौन in Braj = **दतवन**, *q.v.*

दत्त, 1, *m.* (*f.* ā) given, presented, made over to, assigned: 2, *m. pr. n.* a certain king: a title or surname of any man of the Vaisya caste, also of some Kāyasths.

दत्तकपुत्र, *m.* a son given away by his natural parents to persons engaging to adopt him. This is one of the twelve kinds of heirs acknowledged by the old Hindoo [law.

दत्तप्रदानिक, *m.* the resumption of a gift.

दत्ता, *f.* (*m.* **दत्त**) a damsel that is given in marriage.

दत्तात्मन, *m.* a youth or orphan who gives himself to persons disposed to take the place of parents.

दत्तात्रेय, *m. pr. n.* a certain ancient Hindoo sage, son of Atri and Anasūiyā.

दत्तानपकर्म्मन, *m.* non-resumption of gifts.

दत्ति, *f.* an offering, donation, gift.

दत्ती, *f.* a match.

ददकना, *more com.* **धधकना**, *q.v.*

ददकर, evil omen, misfortune.

ददलाना, *t.* to chide, snub. [grandfather's family.

ददियाल, *m.* descent, pedigree; ancestors, paternal

ददोड़ा, *m.* a bump (occasioned by the bite of an

ददौ, *f.* unripe corn (chiefly barley). [insect).

दद्रु, *m.* cutaneous and herpetic eruptions.

दद्रुरोगिन, *m.* (*f.* ṇī) = **दद्रुरोगी**, *q.v.*

दद्रुरोगी, *m.* (*f.* iṇi) a person diseased by herpes. [lit. *adj.* herpetic.

दद्रू, *f.* = **दद्रु**, *q.v.*

दधकना, *more com.* **धधकना**, *q.v.*

दधच्कर = **धधक्कर**, *q.v.*

दधि, *m.* milk curdled or coagulated by heat or by the addition of buttermilk. It is of general use among Hindoos, who esteem it highly as an article of food and as a remedy or a preventative of most disorders.

दधिकरण, *m. pr. n.* (1) of a certain Nāg (2) of a certain cat in the Panch-tantra.

दधिकादो, *m.* coagulated milk and clay thrown by persons at each other in sport on the festival of Krishṇ's [birthday.

दधिकादौं } = **दधिकादो**, *q.v.*
दधिकान्दो }

दधिदान, *m.* an offering or a presentation of milk.

दधिपुष्पिका, *f.* a certain flower (*Clitorea terncata*).

दधिफल, *m.* the elephant or wood-apple. [butter.

दधिमन्थन, *m.* the churning curds for making

दधिवक्र, *m. pr. n.* (in Myth.) a certain monkey.

दधीच, *m. pr. n.* a certain saint-sage (famous for having devoted himself to death that the gods might be armed with his bones in lieu of thunderbolts, — they being the only effective weapons against the demon [Tārak).

दधीचि } = **दधीच**, *q.v.*
दध्यंच }

दध्यानी, *f.* a certain medicinal plant.

दनु, *f. pr. n.* a daughter of Daksh. She was wife of Kashyap and mother of the Dānavas.

दनुज, *m.* (*f.* a) a Dānav or demon.

दन्त, *m.* a tooth; an elephant's tusk. This word is frequent in Hindee as the latter element in compound adjectives and in epithets, in which case its feminine form is sometimes *ā* and sometimes *ī*. In allusion to the fact that the human teeth number thirty-two, this word, in the ingenious system of reckoning by symbols adopted by Hindoos in their poetry, is a symbol for 32.

दन्तकथा, *f.* proof (or attempted proof) by mere word of mouth (as distinguished from literary quotation), tradition.

दन्तधावन, *m.* a certain tree (*Mimosa catechu*) yielding an astringent resin: a certain plant (*Mimosops elengi*): a toothbrush or a fibrous stick used for cleaning the teeth.

दन्तपत्रक, *m.* a species of jasmine (*Jasminum pubescens*) the petals of which resemble teeth in [colour and in shape.

दन्तपीर, *f.* toothache.

दन्तपुष्प, *m.* a species of plant (*Strychnos potatorum*) the flower of which is compared to a tooth.

दन्तमल, *m.* the tartar of the teeth.

दन्तमांस, *m.* the gums.

दन्तमान, *m. pr. n.* a brother of Balarām.

दन्तयं, in Chand = **दन्त** or **दान्त**, *qq. v.* [Karūshas.

दन्तवक्र, *m. pr. n.* a certain demon, prince of the

दन्तवक्र } *more prop.* **दन्तवक्र**, *q.v.*
दन्तवल्क }

दन्तशठ, *m.* the name of several plants (1) the elephant or wood-apple (2) the common lime (*Citrus acida*) (3) a species of plant (*Averrhoa carambola*) which bears an acid fruit.

दन्तशठा, *f.* wood-sorrel (*Oxalis monodelpha*).

दन्तशाण, *m.* a dentifrice (composed chiefly of the powdered fruit of the *Chebulic myrobalan* and green [sulphate of iron.

दन्तशूल, *m.* toothache.

दन्तशोधनी, *f.* a toothpick. [the gums, gum-boil.

दन्तार्बुद, *m.* a disease of the teeth, ulceration of

दन्तावली, *f.* a harrow or rake.

दन्ती, *m.* (*f.* inī) an elephant; *lit.* toothed, tusked.

दन्तीबीज, *m.* a strong purgative nut (the fruit of the croton).

दन्तुर, *m.* (*f.* ā) an elephant, boar, or any other animal that has large or prominent tusks: *lit.* tusked.

दन्तैल }
दन्तैला } = **दन्तुर**, *q.v.*
दन्तौल }

दन्त्य, dental, appertaining to the teeth (as the

दन्त्योष्ठ्य, (in Gram.) dento-labial. [dental letters).

दन्थल, the bare stalks of *bājrā*, *joār*, and Indian [corn.

दन्थला = **दन्थल**, *q.v.*

दन्द, enmity, hatred.

दन्दनाना, *a. int.* to enjoy oneself, live at one's ease, be content or independent.

दन्द:, 1, *m.* the middle of a mountain : a rib : 2,
दन्दारू, *m.* a blister, pimple. [lost.
दन्दी, *m.* (*f.* inī) an enemy, adversary.
दचा, *m.* membrum virile: *adj.* large, great, ample.
दपट, *f.* a course, gallop.
दपटना, *a. int.* to gallop, rush ; *t.* to rebuke, repri-
दपटाना, *t.* to put to the gallop. [mand.
दपदप क° / **दपदपाना** } *a. int.* to shine.
दपदपाहट, *f.* a shining, splendour.
दपू, *f.* the anus (vulgar term).
दफ़, *m.* a small tambourine.
दफ़अ़तन, *adv.* often ; all at once. [bout.
दफ़:, *f.* time, a moment ; one time, one turn, a-
दफ़तर, *m.* a book, journal, record, register, book of accounts ; an office, counting-house ; archives.
दफ़तरख़र्च, *m.* office-charges.
दफ़तरख़ाना, *m.* an office, counting-house ; archives.
दफ़तरदार, *m.* a registrar, recorder.
दफ़तरदारी, *f.* the office of registrar.
दफ़तरनवीस, *m.* a registrar, recorder.
दफ़्तरबन्द, *m.* a man employed in preparing articles of stationery and in ruling and binding office-books.
दफ़तरी, *m.* (*f.* in or iṇī) = **दफ़्तरबन्द**, *q.v.*
दफ़ती, *f.* the boards of the binding of a book, pasteboard.
दफ़्न, *m.* burial, hiding, concealing. —*k.* to bury,
दफ़नाना, *t.* to bury. [hide, conceal.
दफा:, *more prop.* **दफ:**, *q.v.*
दफोना, *m.* buried or concealed treasure, hoard.
दफे, inflected. sing. and nom. pl. of **दफ:**, *q.v.*
दबआना, *a. int.* to advance.
दबंग, *m.* (*f.* ā) a dolt, lout, clown: *lit.* ill-bred, brutish, barbarous, foolish.
दबकना, *a. int.* to crouch, cower, skulk, lie in ambush, lurk : to twinkle : *n.* to be awed : *t.* to set (a dog). *Dabak ānā* or *jānā* or *rahnā*, to sneak, skulk, etc. *Dabak baiṭhnā*, to crouch.
दबकनी = **दबकी**, *q.v.*
दबक्कर, *f.* a trap, snare.
दबकाना, *t.* to snub, check, chide, threaten, awe, daunt : to conceal, hide. [in ambush (a tiger etc.).
दबकी, *f.* ambush, crouching. —*mārnā*, to lie
दबकोला, *m.* (*f.* ī) = **दबकेल**, *q v.*
दबकेल, *m.* a skulker : lit. *adj.* skulking.
दबज़, thick, coarse (as cloth).
दबना, *n.* to be snubbed ; to be pressed down, to be mowed down ; to be awed ; to be concealed : *a. int.* to crouch, shrink, give way. *Dab chalnā* or *dab nikalnā*, to be overawed, be overpowered. *Dab jānā*, to to retire, withdraw, be mortified, be suppressed. *Dab marnā*, to be crushed to death. *Dab ānā*, to advance.
दबरा, a marsh, puddle; a small field.

दबल, 1, a colloquial form of **दबा**, 1, *q.v.* : 2, (Engl.) twofold, double : a pice (coin).
दबलाना = **दबाना**, *q.v.* [bed, etc.
दबवाना, *t.* (causat. of **दबना**) to cause to be snub-
दबा, 1, *m.* (*f.* ī) snubbed, etc.: crouched, etc.: 2, *m.* ambush.— *mārnā*, to lie in wait : to overcome, get the better of, crush to death.—*lenā*, to encroach upon.
दबाऊ, *m.* or *f.* (from **दबाना**) an oppressor, etc.
दबाए डालना, *t.* to keep concealed, to hide (generally furtively).
दबादबाया, *m.* (*f.* **दबीदबाई**) covered, concealed, restrained, pent-up, repressed, curbed.
दबाना, *t.* to press down, keep under, repress, restrain, depress, suppress, bow down, curb, check, chide, snub.
दबाव, *m.* pressure, crush, suppression, depression; strength, power authority ; resignation, submissiveness. — *mānnā*, to stand in awe.
दबिंग, *m.* (*f.* ā) = **दबंग**, *q.v.* [corn, etc.).
दबिया, *m.* a measure of about ten handfuls (of
दबिस्तान, *m.* a school.
दबीर, *m.* a writer, secretary, notary.
दबोला, *m.* a species of medicine : a paddle.
दबेपांव, *adv.* with silent steps, silently, softly.
दबेल, *m.* a person under dominion, a subject.
दबेहरा, *m.* a large ploughshare.
दबेहरी, *f.* a kind of light plough. [to strangle.
दबोचना, *t.* to conceal, hide (generally furtively) :
दबोस, *m.* a flint.
दबोसना, *t.* to tope, tipple.
दब्बा, *m.* a leathern oil-vessel.
दम, *m.* a taming, subduing ; self-restraint, self-command, suppressing the appetites, passions, etc. ; the endurance of the most painful austerities : breath, life; boasting: spring ; ambition; cheerfulness : a moment : the stewing over a slow fire. — *ulaṭnā*, to breathe one's last ; to relinquish one's usual habits. — *bharnā*, to boast. — *phūnknā*, to breathe, inhale, inspire. — *ṭuṭnā*, to die.—*chhoṛnā*, to breathe, expire.—*khainchnā*, to be silent. — *lenā*, to take breath, to rest. — *mārnā*, to speak ; to boast. — *nikalnā*, to die.
दमई, *f.* amount of assessment.
दमंमा, *more prop.* **दमामा**, *q. v.*
दमक, 1, *m.* (*f.* ikā) a tamer, subduer of passions : lit. *adj.* subduing : 2, *f.* ardour ; glitter, brilliancy.
दमकना, *a. int.* to shine, glitter, glisten, glow, flare. [(for raising weights).
दमकला, *m.* a squirt; a fire-engine; a jack or crane
दमका, a hillock, eminence.
दमघोख, *more prop.* **दमघोष**, *q.v.*
दमघोष, *m. pr. n.* a certain king of the lunar race, king of Chedi and father of Shishupāl.
दमड़ा, *m.* gold, silver ; riches.
दमड़ी, *f.* the eighth part of a *paisā*, or very nearly three *dāms*. In the emperor Akbar's time, the *damṛi* was rated one eighth of a *dām*, or one three-hundred-and-twentieth of a rupee. — *ke tīn tīn honā*, to be ruined, be abolished.

दमदमा, *m.* a cavalier: (in Fortific.) a mound, raised battery. [coaxing.

दमदिलासा, encouragement, comfort, soothing,

दमन, 1, *m.* (*f.* ī) a hero: lit. *adj.* taming, subduing: 2, *m.* a kind of flower (*Artemisia Indica*).

दमनक, 1, *m.* = **दमन**, 2, *q.v.*: 2, *m. pr. n.* (1) of a certain man (2) of a certain jackal: 3, *m.* the name of two kinds of metre. [ticity, to spring.

दमना, *a. int.* to glitter, flash; to bend with elas-

दमनी, *f.* (*m.* **दमन**) a heroine, etc.

दमनीय, *m.* (*f.* ā) tameable, subdueable, restrainable, requiring to be subdued.

दमनू, *m. f.* a destroyer.

दमबदम, *adv.* perpetually, continually.

दमबाज़, *m.* a wheedler, deceiver, cheat.

दमबाज़ी, *f.* wheedling, imposture. [Mahābhārat.

दमयन्ती, *f. pr. n.* the heroine of a tale in the

दमरफ़्तन, an expiring, dying.

दमरी, *more prop.* **दमड़ी**, *q.v.* [Benares district.

दमवस्त, *m.* a certain low tribe of Rājputs in the

दमां, powerful, terrible, fierce. [organ of smell.

दमाग़, *m.* the brain; haughtiness, pride: the

दमाद, *more prop.* **दामाद**, *q.v.* See **अ**, 15.

दमाना, *a. int.* to bend (with elasticity).

दमामा, *m.* a kettledrum.

दमिका, *f.* (*m.* **दमक**) a heroine, etc.

दमिश्क़, *m. pr. n.* Damascus in Syria.

दमीदा, blown, expanded, vegetated; broken forth (as the dawn of day).

दमेसर्द, *m.* a cold sigh; a sigh of despair.

दम्पति, 1, *more prop.* **दम्पती**, *q.v.*: 2, *m.* (*f.* °**पत्नी**) the master of a house. [and mistress, the couple.

दम्पती, *m.* (Sk. dual) husband and wife, master

दम्मा, *m.* (*f.* ī) fat, thick, corpulent.

दम्भ, *m.* arrogance, pride, boast, self-inflation, ostentation; hypocrisy, feigning, deceit, fraud; wickedness. [guage.

दम्भवक्की, *m.* (*f.* inī) one who uses boastful lan-

दम्भी, *m.* (*f.* inī) a hypocrite, impostor, etc.: *lit.* adj. feigning: arrogant. [subjected.

दम्य, *m.* (*f.* ā) a young bullock, steer: *lit.* tamed,

दय = (1) **दई** (2) **दाई** (3) **दाय** (4) **दिया** (5) **देके**, *qq.v.*

दयऊ in Braj = **दया** or **दिया**, *qq.v.*

दया, *f.* compassion, sympathy, pity, tenderness, clemency, mercy, favour, kindness, affection: a gift.

दयाकर, *m.* (*f.* ī) exercising compassion, merciful, pitiful, sympathetic, benevolent, beneficent, generous, liberal, affectionate, kind, etc.

दयाकार, *m.* (*f.* ī) }
दयाकृत, *m.* (*f.* ā) } = **दयाकर**, *q.v.*

दयाजुत, *more prop.* **दयायुत**, *q.v.*

दयान, a corruption of **दीवान**, *q.v.*

दयानिधि, *m.* an epithet of God or of any one of special compassionateness; *lit.* the treasury of compassion. [passion.

दयापूर्व्वक, *adv.* pitifully, kindly.

दयामती, *f.* (*m.* **दयामान**) a compassionate female.

दयामान, *m.* (*f.* matī) compassionate, kind, etc.

दयामय, *m.* (*f.* ī) abounding in or consisting of [compassion.

दयामुर्त्ति = **दयामय**, *q.v.*

दयायुक्त }
दयायुत } *m.* (*f.* ā) = **दयासंयुक्त**, *q.v.*

दयाराम, *m.* any pitiful or sympathetic person: the name of several men.

दयारूप, *m.* (*f.* ā) of the nature, appearance, or form of compassion; *hence*, compassionate, pitiful, merciful, beneficent, generous, affectionate, kind, etc.

दयारूपी, *m.* (*f.* inī) = **दयारूप**, *q.v.*

दयाल }
दयालु } **दयामान**, *q.v.*

दयालुता, *f.* (*m.* °**त्व**) compassionateness, tenderness, pitifulness, charity, mercifulness, beneficence, kindness, graciousness.

दयावत, *m.* (*f.* vatī) }
दयावन, *m.* (*f.* vā) }
दयावन्त, *m.* (*f.* vatī) }
दयावान, *m.* (*f.* vatī) } **दयामान**, *q.v.*

दयावीर, *m.* a hero of compassion (an epithet of any very merciful person).

दयाशील, *m.* (*f.* ā) of a compassionate disposition, pitiful, merciful, kind, etc.

दयासंयुक्त, *m.* (*f.* ā) connected with (possessed of, or endowed with) compassion, mercy, etc.

दयासागर, *m.* an epithet of God or of any being of special compassionateness; *lit.* the ocean of compassion, etc. [passion, etc.

दयासिन्धु = **दयासागर**, *q.v.*

दयासील, *more prop.* **दयाशील**, *q.v.*

दयित, *m.* (*f.* ā) beloved, dear, desired.

दयिता, *f.* (*see above*) a wife, sweetheart, spouse.

दयिताधीन, *m.* epithet of a hen-pecked husband; lit. *adj.* in subjection to a wife.

दयी = **दिई** (part.): freq. in poetry.

दयो = **दिया** (part.): freq. in poetry.

दयौ in Braj = **दिया** (part.), *q.v.*

दर, 1, a corruption of **डर**, *q.v.*: 2, *m.* price, rate, a number or quantity fixed as a standard: a door, hatchway, gate: a cave, cavity, shell. *Note*:— For all words beginning thus, but not given below, see under the form **दर्**; *e.g.* not **दरप**, but **दर्प**.

दरक, *m.* a crack, fissure, breach.

दरकना, *a. int.* to split, rend, crack, be torn.

दरकार = **दर्कार**, *q.v.*

दरकि = **दरकके** (**दरकना**); see **इ**, 7.

दरख़्त, *m.* a tree.

दरख़्वास्त, *more prop.* **दर्ख़्वास्त**, *q.v.*

दरगुज़र = **दर्गुज़र**, *q.v.*

दरजा, 1, = **दर्जा**, *q.v.*: 2, *more prop.* **दर्वाज़ा**, *q.v.*

दरदालान, *m.* an outer hall.

दरन्द = दरिन्दा, *q.v.* [to pass.
दरपेश, in front. — *honā*, to await one ; to come
दरपै, following, in pursuit of, intent upon.— *k.* or *honā*, to follow, pursue, prosecute, persecute.
दरबारि, *more prop.* दर्बारी, *q.v.*
दरबेश, *more prop.* दर्वेश, *q.v.*
दरया = दर्या, *q.v.*
दरयाई, appertaining to the sea or to a river, marine. — *ādmi*, a merman. — *totā* (*lit.* the sea-parrot) the flamingo (also called *rāj-hāṅs*).
दरयाफ़त = दर्याफ़त, *q.v.*
दरवेश = दर्वेश, *q.v.*
दरस, *more prop.* दर्श, *q.v.*
दरसन = दर्शन, *q.v.*
दरसाया, *more prop.* दर्शाया, *q.v.*
दरसी, *more prop.* दर्शी, *q.v.*
दरहम, angry ; highledy-piggledy ; confounded. — *barham*, confounded.
दरा, 1, = दरी, 1 : 2, = दर्रा : 3, = दिरा, *qq.v.*
दराई, *f.* a bell : contradiction : a blacksmith's [hammer.
दराए, *f.* a bell.
दराज़, long, tall, extended.
दराज़गोश, long-eared (as an ass or a hare).
दराज़दस्त, long-handed ; *met.* oppressive.
दराज़दस्ती, *f.* oppressiveness, oppression, tyranny.
दराज़ी, *f.* extension, length.
दरान्ती, *f.* a sickle.
दराय, *more prop.* दराई, *q.v.* [ture, breach,
दरार, *m.* a crack, fissure, rift, rent, opening, aper-
दरिद्र, 1, *m.* (*f.* ā) poor, indigent, needy, distressed, wretched : 2, *m.* poverty, indigence.
दरिद्रता, *f.* (*m.*° त्व) poverty, wretchedness.
दरिद्रनी = दरिद्रा or दारिद्रयाणी, *qq.v.*
दरिद्रा, *m.* (*f.* दरिद्र) a poor woman.
दरिद्री, *m.* (*f.* iṇī) a contraction of दारिद्री, *q.v.*
दरिन्दा, tearing, rapacious, fierce, ravenous.
दरिया, *more prop.* दर्या, *q.v.*
दरियाफ़्त = दर्याफ़्त, *q.v.*
दरी, *f.* 1, a natural or artificial excavation in a mountain, a cave, cavern, grotto ; a valley : 2, a small [carpet.
दरीआव, *more prop.* दर्या, *q.v.*
दरीचा, *m.* a window.
दरीबा = दरेबा, *q.v.*
दरु, a well of the largest size. [within,
दरून, *m.* the interior ; the heart, bowels : *lit.* in,
दरेग़, *m.* a sigh ; sorrow ; repugnance, disinclination. — *k.* to withhold.
दरेबा, *m.* a stall (in a market) where betel is sold.
दरेस, a road ; a margin ; any very straight line.
दरोग़, *m.* a falsehood : *adj.* false.
दरोगा, *more prop.* दारोग़ा, *q.v.*
दरोग़ी, *m.* (*f.* in *or* inī) a liar : *adj.* false, lying.
दरोबस्त, the whole of an estate as opposed to a *kismat* or share of it : *lit.* all, entire.
दरोश, *m.* an awl ; a lancet.
दरौनी, *more prop.* डरौनी, *q.v.*
दर्क, *m.* an understanding, comprehending, knowledge ; (in Law) a contingency, possible event.
दर्का, *m.* a crack, crevice, cranny. [or split.
दर्काना, *t.* to split ; *lit.* to cause a thing to crack
दर्कार, necessary, needed, wanting.
दर्खत, *more prop.* दरख़्त, *q.v.*
दर्खाल, a cattle-enclosure.
दर्ख़ास्त, *f.* an application, request, entreaty, petition ; (in Law) an appeal, petition of appeal.
दर्गाह, *f.* a place ; a court ; a mosque, shrine ; a threshold, door. [cuse, overlook, pass by.
दर्गुज़र, an excusing or passing over. — *k.* to ex-
दर्ज़, *m.* sewing : a rag, narrow shred, slip of cloth ; a rent in a garment.
दर्ज़न, *f.* a needle : a door-knocker.
दर्जा, *m.* a step, stair, gradation, degree, rank, dignity, station ; an act (of a play) ; a degree of a circle.
दर्ज़ी, *m.* (*f.* in *or* inī) a tailor.
दर्द, *m.* pain, affliction ; sympathy. — *ānā*, to be affected with pity, — *khānā*, to feel pity ; to suffer
दर्दनाक = दर्दमन्द, *q.v.* [the pangs of childbirth.
दर्दमन्द, afflicted, sad ; sympathizing, compassion-
दर्दर, *m.* cinnabar. [ate.
दर्दरा, *m.* (*f.* ī) half-pounded, coarsely-ground.
दर्दा, 1, *m. pr. n.* a certain tribe of barbarians : 2, *f. pr. n.* a country bordering on Cashmere (the mountains about Cashmere and above Peshawar).
दर्दालान, *m.* an outer hall.
दर्दुर, *m.* a frog : a flute : a certain mountain.
दर्दू, *more prop.* दद्रू, *q.v.*
दर्दूरोगी = दद्रुरोगी, *q.v.*
दर्प, *m.* pride, conceit, arrogance, boastfulness.
दर्पई, *more prop.* दरपै, *q.v.*
दर्पण, *m.* a mirror, looking-glass.
दर्पा, *more prop.* दर्प, *q.v.*
दर्पी, *m.* (*f.* iṇī) insolent, proud, boastful.
दर्ब, *more prop.* द्रव्य, *q.v.*
दर्बड़, war, contest, battle.
दर्बन्द, a door-bolt.
दर्बन्दी, *f.* a statement of the different rates of a village : the assessing the prices of produce.
दर्बहरा, *m.* an intoxicating spirit drawn from rice.
दर्बान = दर्वान, *q.v.*
दर्बानी = दर्वानी, *q.v.*
दर्बार, *m.* a house, dwelling, court (of kings and other magnates), hall of audience. — *bāndhna*, to fix or secure the court ; to give a bribe.
दर्बारी, *m.* (*f.* in *or* iṇī) a courtier ; the language of the court : *lit.* appertaining to the court.

दभ, *m.* the *kush* or sacrificial grass (*Poa cynosuroides*): a kind of reed (*Saccharum spontaneum* [or *S. cylindricum*).

दर्मा, *m.* a kind of mat.

दर्मान, *m.* medicine, cure.

दर्मान्दा, helpless, without remedy, destitute.

दर्माहा, *m.* (*f.* ī) monthly salary.

दर्मियान, *m.* interval, middle: *postp.* during, in the course of, among, in the midst, between, before, in view. — *denā*, to employ as a mediator.

दर्मियानी, *m.* a mediator; (in theological language) [an epithet of Christ.

दर्मुस, *more prop.* **दुर्मुस**, *q.v.*

दर्या, *m.* the waters, the sea, any large river.

दर्याफ़्त, *f.* conceiving, understanding, comprehension; investigation, search, discovery.— *k.* to search out, investigate, perceive, understand.

दर्रा, *m.* a valley or glen with a stream winding through it; a depth; a pass.

दर्राना, 1, *m.* (*f.* ī) straight forwards: 2, *a. int.* to go straight and quickly, go on fearlessly and boldly.

दर्व, *more prop.* **द्रव्य**, *q.v.*

दर्वाज़ा, *m.* a door. — *ṭhoknā*, to knock at a door.

दर्वी, *f.* a ladle, spoon.

दर्वेश, *m.* a religious medicant, dervesh, beggar.

दर्श, *m.* a seeing, a sight; the day of new moon, the conjunction of sun and moon.

दर्शक, *m.* (*f.* ikā) a spectator; a searcher; an exhibiter, one who points out or shews anything: lit. *adj.* seeing; searching; shewing, displaying, explaining, making to be perceived.

दर्शन, 1, *m.* a seeing, looking, sight; a vision, dream: appearance, aspect; interview, the visiting any sacred shrine, worshipping in the presence of any image; intellect, understanding, opinion; a shastra, one of the six religious or philosophical systems of the Hindoos. — *k.* to visit, pay an interview (*esp.* at a shrine).— *denā*, to afford or vouchsafe an interview. — *pānā*, to be admitted to an interview.

दर्शनधारी, *m.* (*f.* iṇī) beautiful, handsome.

दर्शनप्रताप, *m.* the blessing (or result) arising out of a visit to a shrine or out of an interview.

दर्शनप्रतिभू, *m.* a surety for appearance, sponsor, [bail.

दर्शनी, 1, *f.* a present at a meeting; an offering, present: a bill of exchange payable at sight: an epithet of Durgā: 2, handsome, sightly. —*juvān*, a beautiful youth. —*hundi*, *f.* a bill of exchange or money-order payable at sight. [visible, to be seen.

दर्शनीय, *m.* (*f.* ī) agreeable, handsome, beautiful:

दर्शनीयमानी, *m.* (*f.* inī) vain, conceited, arrogant, thinking oneself handsome.

दर्शनेन्द्रिय, *m.* the eye; the sense of sight.

दर्शप, *m.* (*f.* ā) *adj.* drinking the new moon [oblation.

दर्शप्रताप = **दर्शनप्रताप**, *q.v.*

दर्शाना, *t.* to shew, cause to be seen.

दर्शाया, *m.* (*f.* **दर्शाई**) shewn, seen.

दर्शित, *m.* (*f.* ā) visible, apparent, seen, exposed to view, displayed, shewn, explained.

दर्शी, *m.* (*f.* inī) freq. as a suffix in comp. in the adjectival sense of looking, seeing, knowing, shewing, teaching.

दर्सी, *f.* a species of carp-fish (*Cyprinus*).

दल, *m.* a leaf of a tree: wild rice: destruction: a large army; a heap, quantity; a party, sect, body of people united together for a common object; *hence*, sometimes used as a sign of the plural; *e g.* **कर्षीदल**, [farmers.

दलक, *f.* glitter, splendour.

दलकना, *a. int.* to glitter, shine.

दलकपाट, *m* a folded petal or leaf.

दलकि, 1, = **दलकके**; 2 = **दरकि**. See **क**, 7.

दलकोष, *m.* a species of jasmine (*Jasminum pubescens*).

दलगंजना, *m.* a species of rice.

दलदल, *f.* a quagmire, slough, bog, swamp.

दलदला, *m.* (*f.* ī) miry, boggy, swampy.

दलदलाना, *a. int.* to shake, undulate.

दलदलाहट, *f.* a tremour, shaking.

दलदली, *f.*; see **दलदला**.

दलदहृदय, *m.* (*f.* ā) broken-hearted, cut to the [heart.

दलदार, fleshy, thick.

दलन, 1, *m.* a breaking to pieces, tearing asunder, rending, dividing, crushing: 2, *m.* (*f.* ī) a tearer: lit. *adj.* tearing.

दलना, *t.* to grind coarsely, split pulse.

दलनाश, *m. f.* (?) the destruction of an army or of a body of people.

दलनिर्मोक, *m.* the *Bhojpatra-tree* (the bark of which is used for wrapping woollens in, and for *hukkā*-snakes, etc).

दलपुष्पी, *f.* a certain fragrant plant (*Pandanus* [*odoratissimus*).

दलबादल, *m.* a mass of clouds; a large army; a [large tent.

दलमलना (*intensive*) = **दलना**, *q.v.*

दलमसल क°, *t.* to thrash; to crumple.

दलव, *m.* a bucket, urn; the hopper of a mill; *pr. n.* [Aquarius.

दलवाना, *t.* to cause to be coarsely ground.

दलवाल, *m.* the commander of an army.

दलवैया, *m.* a corn-grinder.

दलसूत्र, *f.* the fibre or vein of a leaf.

दलहारन, *f.* a female grain-dealer, a grain-dealer's [wife.

दलहारा, *m.* (*f.* ī) a grain-dealer.

दलहारी, *f.* = **दलहारन**, *q.v.*

दलाढक, *m.* the name of several plants, (1) Sesamum growing wild or spontaneously; (2) a certain aquatic plant (*Pistia Stratioites*); (3) a certain plant (*Mesua ferrea*) commonly called *Nagesar*; (4) a species of tree (*Mimosa sirisha*); (5) a sort of jasmine (*Jasminum pubescens*).

दलाना, *t.* to grind coarsely, cause to be coarsely [ground.

दलामल, *m.* a kind of tree (*Vangueria spinosa*).

दलाल, *m.* a certain tribe of jāts: a looking haughtily or angrily through half-shut eyes (as lovers etc.); [*cinædus libidine infamis.*

दलालत = **दिलालत**, *q.v.*

दलि = **दलके** (**दलना**). See **क**, 7.

दलित, *m.* (*f.* ā) rent, torn, broken.

दलिद्र; for words beginning thus, see under the [form **दरिद्र**.

दलिया, *m.* half-ground or coarsely-pounded grain; split pulse (ground more finely than *dāl.*)

दलिहन, *f.* any sort of pulse which may be split (as *dāl*).

दली, *f.* a clod of clay or mould.

दलीप, *more prop.* **दिलीप**, *q.v.*

दलीमः, *m. pr. n.* a certain class of ṭagās in Murādābād.

दलील, *f.* argument, demonstration, proof; a guide, director.

दलेउ in Braj = **दला**(**दलना**).

दलेगन्नी, *m.* a certain plant (*Echites scholaris*).

दलेन्ती, *f.* a hand-mill.

दलेपंजा, a sign of weakness in a horse.

दल्क, *more prop.* **दिल्क**, *q.v.*

दल्ला, *m.* a lump, piece.

दल्लाल, *m.* a broker, salesman.

दल्लालः, *f.* a female guide, a bawd, procuress.

दल्लाली, *f.* brokerage; the business of a broker.

दव, *m.* a forest conflagration.

दवश्री ; see **दबाऊ** and **दबाव**.

दवा, *f.* medicine, a remedy.

दवाई ; see **दवा** and **दोहाई**.

दवां, walking fast, running.

दवाख़ाना, *m.* a dispensary.

दवाग्नि, *m.* a forest conflagration.

दवात, *f.* an inkstand; ink.

दवादौ, *f.* labour and fatigue.

दवानल, *m.* a forest conflagration.

दवाम, *m.* perpetuity : *adv.* always.

दवार / **दवारि** } *m.* a forest conflagration.

दवाव, see **दबाऊ** and **दबाव**.

दश, ten (१०). See **ओं, वां, वीं, वे, वें**.

दशकण्ठ / **दशकन्ध** / **दशकन्धर** } *m.* the ten-necked, *i.e.* Rāvaṇ.

दशकण्ठजित, the conqueror of Dashkaṇṭh, *i.e.* Rām.

दशकण्ठारि, the enemy of Dashkaṇṭh, *i. e.* Rām.

दशकामजव्यसन, *m.* the aggregate of ten vices proceeding from *Kām* (the quality of desire), *viz.* hunting, gambling, sleeping by day, abusiveness, lechery, drunkenness, dancing, singing, playing, hypocrisy.

दशगुण, *m.* (*f.* ā) tenfold, ten-times, ten times over.

दशगुणा, *m.* (*f.* ī) = **दशगुण**, *q.v.*

दशग्राम, *m.* a district or a collection of ten villages.

दशत, *f.* an aggregate of ten; a decade.

दशति, *f.* a hundred.

दशत्रा, ten per cent. : a tenth.

दशन, *m.* a tooth. When it is the latter member of epithets the fem. ends in *ā*.

दशना, *m.* a poignard.

दशपुर, *m. pr. n.* a certain district (part of Malwa in Bandēlkhand) : the fragrant grass *Cyperus rotundus*.

दशम, 1, *m.* a tenth part : 2, *m.* (*f.* ī) *adj.* tenth.

दशमन, *more prop.* **दुशमन**, *q.v.*

दशमाल, *m.* a collection of ten garlands.

दशमी, 1, *f.* the tenth day of a lunar fortnight: the tenth or last stage of human life : the last ten years of a century : 2, *m.* (*f.* inī) a very aged person : *adj.* very old, very aged.

दशमुख / **दशमुह** / **दशमुण्ड** } *m.* the ten-faced one, *i. e.* Rāvaṇ.

दशमूल, *m.* a certain tonic prepared from the roots of ten plants.

दशरथ, *m. pr. n.* an ancient sovereign of Ayodhyā (Oude) and father of Rām; *lit.* having ten chariots.

दशलक्षण, *m.* an aggregate of ten marks or attributes.

दशवां, *m.* (*f.* wīṅ) the tenth. See **दश**.

दशशीस, *m.* the ten-headed one, *i.e.* Rāvaṇ.

दशसत, *m.* a thousand; *lit.* ten hundreds.

दशसहस्र, *m.* a myriad; *lit.* ten thousands.

दशहरा, *m.* (*lit.* the seizer of ten) an epithet of two days (or of the festivals held on them) in the Hindoo year : — (1) the tenth day of *Jaith shukl-paksh*, which is reckoned the birthday of Gangā : whoever bathes in the Ganges on this day is said to be purified from the ten sorts of sins : (2) the tenth day of *Asin shukl-paksh*, on which after the worship and religious ceremonies performed during nine nights (*Navarātri*) they throw the images of Devī into the river. It is said that on this day Rām marched against Rāvaṇ, on which account it is called 'Vijaidasamee'. This day is celebrated with great pomp by Hindoo princes; the weapons and instruments of war are hallowed, and, if war be intended, the campaign is then opened.

दशा, *f.* state, condition, circumstances; period or time of life (as youth, manhood, old age, etc.).

दशांगुल, *m.* a melon, musk-melon : *adj.* ten fingers long.

दशांश, *m.* a tenth part, tithe.

दशानन, *m.* the ten-faced one, *i. e.* Rāvaṇ.

दशानिक, *m.* the plant *Croton polyandrum*.

दशाफल, *m.* a result of circumstances or of condition in life.

दशार्ण, *m. pr. n.* a country in Central India (south-east of the Vindhya range).

दशार्णा, *f. pr. n.* a river rising in the Vindhya mountains, — the Dosarene of the ancients.

दशार्ह, *m. pr. n.* (1) of the kingdom of Yadu, in the south of India (2) of its people.

दशावतार, *m.* (see **अवतार**) an epithet of Vishṇu (of whom the Hindoos believe that there were ten incarnations for the protection or the punishment of mankind) : *lit.* he of the ten incarnations.

दशाविशेष, *m.* special or peculiar circumstances or condition.

दशी, 1, *m.* (*f.* inī) a lord of ten towns : 2, *f.* thread : the unwoven threads at the end of a piece of cloth.

दशीला, *adj.* in good circumstances.

दशेन्द्रिय = **दशेन्द्रिया**, *q.v.*

दशेन्द्रिया, *m.* (pl. : see **आ**, 22) the aggregate of the ten organs of sense and action, *viz.* the skin, the eye, the tongue, the nose, the ear, the organ of speech, the hand, the foot, the anus, the pudendum.

दशेश, *m.* a lord of ten towns.

दशों, (see **औं**, 4) the ten of them, the whole ten.

दशोंइन्द्री, *more prop.* **दशेन्द्रिया**, *q.v.*

दशोंदिग = **दशोंदिशा**, *q.v*

दशोंदिशा, *f.* the ten regions or quarters of the world.

दशोंद्वार, *m.* the ten passages for the action of the faculties, *viz.* the eyes, the ears, the nostrils, the mouth, the crown of the head, the anus, the penis.

दश्त, *m.* a desert; a forest; a plain.

दस; for all words beginning thus, but not given below, see under the form **दश**.

दसईं (Rām.) = **दशवीं**. See **दशवां**.

दसना in Braj = **दिसना**, *q.v.*

दसरान, a kind of trick in wrestling.

दसवां, *m.* (*f.* wīṅ) = **दशवां**, *q. v.*

दसवाना, *m.* a tenth part (added to the revenue, etc.).

दसहत (by inversion) = **दहशत**, *q.v.*

दसहूं, in Braj = **दशों**, *q. v.*

दसोखा, *m.* the moulting of birds.—*jhāṛnā*, to moult.

दसोतरा, *m.* ten per cent.; a tenth.

दसौना, *more prop.* **डसौना**, *q.v.*

दसौन्धा } **दसौन्धी** } *m.* a panegyrist, bard.

दस्त, *m.* the hand; a cubit: stool, evacuation: a shoulder of mutton, an animal's fore-quarter.

दस्तअन्दाज़, *m.* one who commences a business; an oppressor, plunderer.

दस्तक, *f.* a clapping of the hands; rapping at a door; a pass, passport; a summons: commission.

दस्तकार, *m.* a craftsman: *lit.* dexterous.

दस्तकारी, *f.* handicraft; dexterity.

दस्तख़त, *m.* a signature; chirography.

दस्तनिगार, needy, in want, wanting.

दस्तपनाह, *m.* tongs.

दस्तबस्ता, with joined hands (in token of respect).

दस्तबुकचा, *m.* cloth in which a small bundle is wrapped up.

दस्तबुर्द, *m.* superiority, advantage, victory.

दस्तरखान } **दस्तरख़ान** } *more prop.* **दस्तारख़ान**, *q.v.*

दस्ता, *m.* zinc, tutenag; *lapis calaminaris*: a handful; a handle; a pestle; a quire of paper; a skein of thread; a division of an army, brigade; a bundle of arrows (consisting of twenty-four).

दस्ताना, *m.* a glove, gauntlet.

दस्तान्दाज = **दस्तअन्दाज़**, *q.v.*

दस्तार, *m.* a turban.

दस्तारबन्द, *m.* a servant whose business it is to make up the turban.

दस्तारख़ान, *m.* a kind of tablecloth.

दस्तावेज़, *f.* signature, note of hand, bond, title-deed.

दस्तूर, *m.* custom, manner, fashion, habit, regulation.

दस्तूरी, *f.* perquisites paid to a servant by one who sells to his master (it is a gratuity varying in amount in different places from one to three per cent.).

दस्यु, *m.* an enemy, ruffian, thief, oppressor, violator, committer of injustice: name of one of the mixed classes.

दस्युवृत्ति, *f.* theft, dishonest mode of subsistence.

दह, 1, in Chand = **दश**, *q.v.*: 2, *m.* very deep water; a pool or eddy in a river, a whirlpool; an abyss.

दहक, *f.* ardour; conflagration.

दहकना, *n.* to burn, be burnt, be ruined, be lost, be destroyed: to regret.

दहकाना, *t.* to burn, kindle; to ruin, destroy; to lose; to cause to regret; to heat (iron, etc.).

दहगी, *f.* heat, warmth.

दहज, *more prop.* **दिहेज़**, *q. v.*

दहड़दहड़ = **धड़धड़**, *q. v.*

दहत, scorching, burning.

दहदल, *m.* *f.*? a swamp, bog.

दहन, 1, *m.* fire; Agni; burning, combustion: the marking-nut plant; lead-wort (*Plumbago zeylanica*, etc.); a gold coin (in value six rupees): 2. *f.* conflagration; sultriness.

दहना, 1, *more prop.* **दहिना**, *q.v.*: 2, *a. int.* to burn; *n.* to be burnt.

दहनीय, *m.* (*f.* ā) anything combustible: *lit.* combustible, requiring to be burnt, fit to be burnt.

दहनोपल, *m.* the sun-gem, a crystal lens.

दहनैं in Braj = **दहना**, 2, *q. v.*

दहबाशी, *m.* a commander of ten men: a person holding a place of trust; a valet.

दहयो in Braj = **दहा** (past part. of *dahnā*).

दहर, *m.* time, an age; custom, habit, mode, manner; solicitude: the world: atheism: fortune, chance.

दहरिया, *m.* an atheist.

दहरी, stiff clay soil (in low ground).

दहल, a quagmire, quicksand.

दहलना, *a. int.* to shake, tremble, fear.

दहलान, a certain tribe of Jagas in the upper Doāb.

दहलाना, *t.* to shake, agitate.

दहश, stupefied with amazement, stricken with astonishment or consternation.

दहशत, *f.* fear, dread.

दहसनी, a book of accounts, registers, etc. kept for the space of ten years; *lit.* appertaining to ten years.

दहसेरा, *m.* (*f.* ī) a weight of ten *sērs*.

दहा, *m.* the ten days of the Muharram.

दहाई, *f.* the figure ten; the tenth part; (in Arithm.) the decimal place of figures.

दहाड़ना, *a. int.* to roar (as a tiger).

दहान, an orifice, the mouth.

दहाना, *t.* to set fire to, burn.

दहित, *m.* (*f.* ā) burnt, scorched.

दहिना, (from **दक्षिण**) *m.* (*f.* ī) right (not left),

दहिनावर्त्त = **दक्षिणावर्त्त**, *q. v.*

दहिने, *adv.* (sc. *hāthko* or *hāthpar*) to the right, on the right, at the right.

दही, *m.* thick sour milk, coagulated milk.

दहीवाला, *m.* (*f.* ī) a seller of *dahī*.

दहेंगर, *m.* a vessel for carrying sour milk in (particularly at festivals).

दहेंड़ी, *more prop.* **दहेयड़ी**, *q. v.*

दहेज = **दिहेज़**, *q. v.*

दहेड़, *m.* a certain bird (*Coracias*).

दहेयड़ी, *f.* a vessel in which sour milk (*dahī*) is [kept.

दहेल, *m.* a certain bird (*Coracias*).

दहेयड़ी in Braj = **दहेयड़ी**, *q. v.*

दहोवा, *m.* a tenth part, tithe.

दा, 1, *f.* (*m.* **द**) see art. **द**: 2, a Taddhita suffix by means of which adverbs of time are derived from pronouns and pronominal adjectives; *e. g.* **यदा**: 3, a sickle, bill-hook, iron cleaver.

दाइक, *more prop.* **दायक**, *q. v.*

दाइज } = **दाएजा**, *q. v.*
दाइजा }

दाइनी, *f.* of **दाई**, *q. v.*

दाइमां, everlastingly, perpetually, permanently.

दाइमी, 1, *f.* = **दाइमीयत**, *q. v.* : 2, perpetual, continual, lasting, durable, standing.

दाइमीयत, *f.* perpetuity, eternity.

दाइयां, nom. pl. of **दाई**, 2, *q. v.*

दाइर, going round, revolving, encircling; in process, agitated (as a suit at Law); capable of being agitated; cognizable. [tambourine; a monastery.

दाइरा, *m.* a circle, ring, circumference, orbit; a

दाई, 1, *m.* (*f.* **दाइनी**) a giver: lit. *adj*: giving (freq. as a suffix in comp.; e. g. *Duhkhdāi*): 2, *f.* a wet-nurse, milk-nurse; a midwife. — *ko sompnā*, (*lit.* to deliver to a wet-nurse, *i. e.*) to put out to nurse.

दाईखिलाई, *f.* a dry-nurse.

दाईगरी, *f.* midwifery.

दाईजनाई, *f.* a midwife.

दाईपिलाई, *f.* a wet-nurse.

दाऊ, *m.* an appellation of a father or of an elder brother: 2, *m. pr. n.* used by contraction for Baladev, the foster-brother of Krishṇ: 3, deception, fraud, cheating.

दाऊद, *m. pr. n.* the Psalmist David.

दाऊदी, 1, *f.* a certain shrub (*Chrysanthemum Indicum*) which bears a flower like chamomile; a kind of firework resembling that shrub: a kind of armour, coat of mail (so named from its being supposed to have been originally made by Dā,ūd, as we employ the terms 'Ferrara' and 'Joe Manton'): 2, *adj. m.* (*f.* inī) Davidic, appertaining to David.

दाएं, the tying a number of bullocks together for the purpose of treading out the grain from the ear.

दाएंबाएं, *adv.* on the right and left.

दाएजा, *m.* a nuptial present, dowry, portion.

दाओ = **दाव**, *q. v.*

दाओघाओ, feint or stratagem in war.

दां, a corruption (1) of **दांव** (2) of **दाम्न**, *qq. v.*

दांग, a hill, precipice, mountain-summit. [idiot.

दांगर, a superannuated horned beast; *met.* a fool,

दांगी, a name given to the *bũndela rājputs*.

दांड, दांत, दांभ; for words beginning with either of these forms, see under the forms **दायड, दान्त, दाम्भ**, [respectively.

दांयेबांये, unsteadiness.

दांव, 1, = **दाव**, *q. v.*: 2, *m.* ambuscade, ambush, snare: power, opportunity; time, turn, vicissitude; the twisting one another in wrestling. — *chalnā*, to have the advantage. — *chalānā*, to take advantage of. — *tāknā*, to watch an opportunity. — *pakaṛnā*, to wrestle. — *baiṭhnā*, to lie in ambush, lurk.

दांवपेच, watching one's opportunity. [threshing.

दांवरी, *f.* a rope that binds bullocks together when

दांवान, *m.* burning stubble; a forest conflagration.

दांहा, *m.* the right hand.

दाक, 1, = **दाख**, *q. v.*: 2, *m.* a donor, one who makes presents (*esp.* to Brāhmaṇs); a sacrificer, one who pays the expenses of the ceremony and employs the officiating priests.

दाकगाड़ी, *f.* a mail train; a locomotive post-office.

दाक्ष, appertaining to **दक्ष**, *q. v.*

दाक्षायिणी, *f. pr. n.* (1) of the twenty-seven lunar mansions (considered mythologically as the daughters of Daksh and wives of the moon) (2) of the nymph and asterism Rohiṇī: a certain plant (*Croton polyandrum*). [country of Vahlīk or Balkh).

दाक्षिकन्था, *f. pr. n.* a place north of India (in the

दाक्षिकन्थीय, *m.* (*f.* ā) native of Dākshikanthā.

दाक्ष्य, *m.* ability, skill.

दाख, *f.* a raisin, grape.

दाखरस, *m. f.* grape-juice, wine.

दाखलता, *f.* a vine.

दाख़िल, 1, entering, penetrating, arriving; taking possession: 2, an entry in a book: 3, entered; produced. — *k.* to cause to enter, cause to arrive; to place in, fix in, insert, include; to produce. — *honā*, to enter, arrive, penetrate: to appertain: *n.* to be inserted.

दाख़िलख़ारिज, erasure of an entry.

दाख़िलदफ़्तर, entered upon the record.

दाख़िलदार, *m.* an occupant. [conveyance.

दाख़िलनामा, *m.* a warrant or deed of possession; a

दाख़िला, *m.* a receipt for money; a list, entry, muster-roll; a concern or business; a connexion.

दाग़, *m.* a spot, stain, mark, scar, cicatrix, blemish, freckle, speck; a brand, cautery, stigma. — *khānā*, to receive a mark or brand. — *charhānā* or *lagānā* or *lānā*, to vilify, defame. — *denā*, to brand, cauterize; to blemish. — *lagnā*, to be damaged, get a bad name. — *honā*, to be scarred, be cauterized.

दाग़दार, spotted, marked, scarred, branded, cauterized. [gun, etc.).

दाग़ना, *t.* to mark, brand, cauterize; to fire (a

दाग़ी, stained, blemished, spotted. — *k.* to stain.

दाज, *m.* darkness, a dark night.

दाढ़क, *m.* a tooth, tusk. [*tum*) or its fruit.

दाड़िम, *m.* the pomegranate-tree (*Punica grana-*

दाड़िमपुष्पक, *m.* a certain medicinal plant (*An-dersonia rohitaka*). [fond of the pomegranate).

दाड़िमप्रिय, *m.* an epithet of the parrot (as being

दाड़िम्ब, *more prop.* **दाड़िम**, *q.v.*

दाड़ी = **दाढ़ी**, *q.v.*

दाढ़, *f.* a jaw-tooth, grinder. — *mārnā*, to gnash or grind the teeth in wrath, anguish, etc. [titude.

दाढ़ा, *m. f.*? a large tooth, tusk: a number, mul-

दाढ़ि } = **दाढ़ी**, *q.v.*
दाढिका }

दाढ़ी, *f.* a beard: a tendril. — *banānā* or *muṇḍnā*,

दाढ़ू; see (1) **दाढ़ी** (2) **ढूढ़ता**. [to shave.

दाण्ड, *m.* (**दण्ड**) oppression, injury, injustice; punishment; fine. [the lands of two proprietors.

दाण्डामेण्डा, *m.* the frontier or boundary between

दाण्डिक, *m.* (*f.* ī) *adj.* chastising, punishing.

दाण्डी, 1, *f.* (**दण्डी**) a balance: 2, *m.* a rower, waterman.

दाण्डू, a ball for playing with; a bat for striking

दाण्डोरगी, *f.* mischief, wickedness. [such a ball.

दात, 1, a corruption of **दान्त**, *q.v.*: 2, *m.* bounti-

दातन = **दान्तन**, *q.v.* [fulness, liberality.

दातपन = **दातापन**, *q.v.* [with a tooth-brush.

दातवन, 1, = **दतवन**, *q.v.*: 2, the cleaning the teeth

दातव्य, *m.* (*f.* ā) anything that may be (or that ought to be) given: *lit.* adj. to be given.

दाता, *m.* (*f.* trī) a donor, benefactor: *lit.* adj. giving, liberal, generous.

दातान, a corrupt. pl. of **दाता**, *q.v.*

दातापन, *m.* beneficence, benevolence, liberality.

दातार (from **दातृ**) = **दाता**, *q.v.*

दातृ, *m.* (*f.* trī) = **दाता**, *q.v.* [berality.

दातृता, *f.* (*m.* °**त्व**) beneficence, bountifulness, li-

दात्र, *m.* a kind of sickle, large knife.

दाद, *m.* the ringworm, herpes: oblation.

दादनी, *f.* advances, money advanced for providing goods or merchandize of any kind.

दादमर्दन, *m.* a certain plant (*Cassia alata*) used for

दादबेदाद क°, to demand justice. [curing ringworm.

दादरा, *m.* a kind of song.

दादा, *m.* a paternal grandfather: an elder brother.

दादी, 1, *f.* a paternal grandmother: 2, *m.* a plaintiff, complainant.

दादीफर्यादी, *m.* a complainant, one suing for justice.

दादुर } *m.* a frog.
दादुरवा }

दादू, *m. pr. n.* a famous fakeer (born in the state of Jaipur, and founder of the Dādoopanthee sect).

दादुपन्थी, *m.* a follower of Dādoo.

दाधना, *a. int.* to burn.

दान, *m.* the act of giving; a donation, gift, present, bestowment; alms, charity; liberality; anything demanded by law or by custom (as toll, etc.); the fluid that flows from the temples of an elephant in rut; a certain religious rite in which the Brāhmans pronounce a charm or incantation over anything, in the wish of a happy futurity, and give it (*dān*) as a present to another person. — *k.* or *denā*, to bestow, bestow upon, endow with.

दानता, *f.* giving, bountifulness, liberality.

दानदक्षिणा, *f.* a religious gift to a mendicant or to a Brāhmaṇ priest. [making donations.

दानधर्म्म, *m.* almsgiving, charity: the rules for

दानपति, *m.* (*f.* patnī) a liberal or munificent

दानपत्तर, *more prop.* **दानपत्र**, *q.v.* [person.

दानपत्र, *m.* a deed of conveyance, deed of gift by which land is conveyed to Brāhmaṇs, a will.

दानपत्रदार, *m.* a Brāhmaṇ to whom lands have been assigned by deed.

दानपन, *m.* bountifulness, beneficence.

दानपुण्य, *m.* almsgiving, charity.

दानपुन, *more prop.* **दानपुण्य**, *q. v.*

दानयोग्य, *m.* (*f.* ā) fit for or meriting a donation.

दानव, 1, *m.* a demon, giant, Titan: 2, *m.* (*f.* ī) appertaining to Dānavs.

दानवीर, *m.* (*f.* ā) an epithet of any very beneficent person: *lit.* a hero of beneficence.

दानशील, *m.* (*f.* ā) liberal, munificent, bountiful.

दानशीलता, *f.* (*m.* °**त्व**) beneficence of disposition.

दाना, *m.* grain, seed, berry, corn; a pimple, speck: *adj.* wise, sensible, learned.

दानाई, *f.* wisdom, knowledge, cleverness.

दानाकेश, *m.* a kind of embroidered neckcloth (worn in the cold weather over the cloak).

दानाध्यक्ष, *m.* (*f.* ā *or* ī) an almoner.

दानापानी, *m.* food, victuals.

दानियल, *m. pr. n.* the prophet Daniel.

दानिनी, *f.* (*m.* **दानी**) a benefactress.

दानिस्त, *f.* knowledge; opinion.

दानिस्तगी, *f.* knowledge, science, learning.

दानी, *m.* (*f.* inī) beneficent, liberal, bountiful, charitable, giving.

दानीय, *m.* (*f.* ā) worthy of having anything given: fit to be given, requiring to be given.

दानेज़ाद, an avaricious person, miser.

दान्त, 1, *m.* a tooth; a tusk (of an elephant or of a boar). — *ungli kāṭnā*, (to bite the finger) a phrase expressive of surprize or of perplexity. — *kachkachānā*, to grin, shew the teeth. — *kaṭkaṭānā*, to gnash the teeth. — *kāṭī roṭī khānā* to be united in intimate friendship. — *kā dard*, toothache. — *khaṭṭe k.*, to dishearten; to displease. — *tale ungli kāṭnā* or *dabānā*, to stand in amaze, be amazed, wonder. — *nikālnā*, to laugh, grin; to express or confess inability or helplessness: to teeth. — *par charhānā*, to detract from the praises or virtues of another. — *pisnā*, to grin, gnash or grind the teeth as in anger or pain. — *bajnā* or *bājnā*, the chattering of the teeth, squabbling, wrangling, sparring. — *rakhnā* or — *honā kisī-par*, to desire anything exceedingly: to hate. — *lagnā*, trismus or locked-jaw. — *lānā*, to teeth, to grow (said of the teeth). *Dānton* (sc. *ko* ?) *mārnā*, to gnash the teeth (with anger). *Dānton* (sc. *se* ?) *zamin pakarnā* (*lit.* to bite the ground; *hence*) to be reduced to extremities; to suffer great pain: 2, *adj.* ivory: 3, *m.* (*f.* ā) tamed, subdued.

दान्ततिंका, the taking a piece of straw or grass in the teeth to deprecate wrath or as a sign of complete submission.

दान्तन, *m.* 1, (a Braj pl. of **दान्त**) teeth; tusks: 2, a toothbrush (consisting of a piece of twig).

दान्तना, to get teeth (said of kine, horses, etc.).

दान्तपीसना; see *s.v.* **दान्त**.

दान्ताकिलकिल, *f.* quarrel.

दान्तिक, *adj. m.* (*f.* ā *or* ī) ivory.

दान्ती, *f.* the tooth of a saw or other instrument; the cog of a wheel; a rake; a harrow; a kind of sickle. — *denā*, to insist upon. — *parnā*, to be knotched or indented (as the edge of any instrument). — *lagnā*, to have a locked jaw.

दाप, *m.* arrogance, boastfulness, self-importance, strength, potency; a stamping forcibly.

दाब, *m.* fear, dread, awe, reverence: magnificence, pomp, ostentation: custom; institution, manner; situation, condition; vehement or forcible propulsion. See *dābnā*.

दाबत, an imprecation, curse.

दाबना, *t.* to press down; to suppress, snub; to squeeze, hug. *Dāb rakhnā*, to conceal, to steal and conceal; to press (*esp.* with the thighs); to retain by pressure; to grip (as money). *Dāb lenā*, to outgrow.

दाबाग्नि } **दाबानल** } *m.* a forest conflagration.

दाबी, *f.* a measure of about ten handfuls (of autumn crop, etc.). [ruled.

दाम्य, *m.* (*f.* ā) capable of being governed or

दाम, 1, *m.* (*f.* ?) any kind of string, thread, cord, rope: 2, *m.* a net, snare: 3, *m.* a quadruped: 4, *m.* price, cost; the name of a copper coin. In the *āyini akbarī*, (and consequently in most revenue accounts,) the *dām* is considered to be the fortieth part of a rupee: the *dām* was divided into eight parts, called *damṛī*. Two damrees make one *pāolā*, and two pāolās one *adhelā* or half a *dām*. Since the time of Akbar, however, the *dām* has greatly fallen off in value; so that at present, in upper India, it is only one twenty-fifth of a *paisā*, or one sixteen-hundredth of a rupee.

दामचः, *m.* the erection on which a person is posted for the protection of crops.

दामन, *m.* 1, a rope, string: 2, a skirt of a garment; a sail-sheet: the foot or the declivity of a mountain.

दामनी, 1, *f.* a string (*esp.* rope for tying cattle): 2, *adj.* appertaining to the artemisia flower.

दामलिप्त, *m. pr. n.* the district of Tamluk.

दामा, *m.* a rope, string, cord: a garland.

दामाद, *m.* a son-in-law (daughter's husband); a bridegroom.

दामादी, *f.* the relationship of son-in-law.

दामान = **दामन**, 2, *q.v.*

दामासाह, *m. pr. n.* a certain merchant who died insolvent, and whose effects were divided among his creditors in proportion to their claims.

दामासाही, *f.* a proportioning, equal assessment, dividend of a bankrupt's property; composition of a debt.

दामिनि, *f.* lightning. [huntress: 2, lightning.

दामिनी, *f.* 1, (*m.* **दामी**) a sportsman's wife; a

दामी, 1, *m.* (*f.* inī) a setter of snares, sportsman, hunter, fowler: 2, *f.* (*m.* ?) an assessment. — *lagānā*, to assess.

दामीवासिलात, gross assets of a village.

दामोदर, *m.* an epithet of Krishṇ (the allusion being to the fact that his foster-mother Yashodā in vain passed the folds of a rope around his body when he was a child, to keep him in confinement).

दाम्भिक, *m.* (*f.* ā) a hypocrite, cheat: *lit.* hypocritical: a kind of crane (*Ardea nivea*).

दाय, 1, in Chand = **दया**, *q.v.*: 2, *m.* a gift; a nuptial present, separate property of a wife, paternal property; inheritance.

दायक, *m.* (*f.* ikā) a giver: *lit.* adj. giving. Freq. in Hindee as the latter element in many substantival adjectives; *e.g.* **भिक्षादायक**, *m.* (*f.* **भिक्षादायिका**) an almsgiver. [marriage-gift.

दायजा, *m.* a dowry, portion, nuptial present,

दायभाग = **दायविभाग**, *q.v.*

दायर, *more prop.* **दाइर**, *q.v.* [different heirs.

दायविभाग, *m.* a division of property among

दाया, 1, a corruption of **दया**, *q.v.*: 2, *m.* (*f.* **दाई**) the husband of a *dāī*, a male nurse: 3, = **दाय**, *q.v.*: 4. *m.* a demand, claim, plaint.

दायाद, *m.* (*f.* ī) an heir, claimant; a son or other kinsman who is entitled to partake of an inheritance.

दायादव, *m.* an heir, kinsman.

दायादी, *f.* (*m.* **दायाद**) an heiress, daughter.

दायापवर्त्तन, *m.* privation, forfeiture of property.

दायिका, *f.* (*m.* **दायक**) a benefactress.

दायित, *m.* (*f.* a) condemned, sentenced; adjudged,

दायिनी, *f.* (*m.* **दायी**) a benefactress. [awarded.

दायिम, *more prop.* **दाइम**, *q.v.*

दायिरा, *m.* a ring, circumference, circle, orbit; a tambourine; a monastery.

दायी, *m.* (*f.* inī) frequent as the latter element in substantival adjectives, importing the idea of 'giving'; 'causing'.

दार, 1, *f.* a wife: 2, a corruption of **दाल**, *q.v.*: 3, *m.* a gallows, impaling-stake: 4, *m.* a mansion.

दारक, *m.* (*f.* ikā) a young animal, child, son.

दारचीनी, *f.* cinnamon (*Laurus cinnamomum*): *lit.* China-wood. [*tatorum*).

दारण, *m.* the clearing-nut plant (*Strychnos po-*

दारद, *m.* a sort of poison brought from the country

दारना, *t.* to rend, split, break. [called Darad.

दारमदार, *m.* an agreement, stipulation, adjustment of a dispute, settlement of a quarrel.

दारय = **दारो** (**दारना**). See **य**.

दारा, 1, *f.* a wife: 2, *m. pr. n.* king Darius.

दाराधीन, *m.* a henpecked husband: lit. *adj.* dependent on or subject to a wife.

दारिका, *f.* (*m.* **दारक**) a daughter, a girl.

दारिकादान, *m.* the giving a daughter in marriage.

दारिद, *more prop.* **दारिद्र**, *q. v.*

दारिद्र, *m.* poverty, indigence, wretchedness. — *khednā* (*lit.* to drive away poverty) alludes to a ceremony of the Hindoos in which they take a sieve or winnowing-basket, and beating it in every corner of the house, exclaim:—'*Ishwar paiṭho, dāridr niklo!*' Enter, O God! depart, O poverty!

दारिद्री, *m.* (*f.* iṇī) poor, indigent, needy, wretch-

दारिद्र्य = **दारिद्र**, *q. v.* [ed, unfortunate.

दारी, *f.* a female slave taken in war.

दारु, *m.* wood, timber; a species of pine (*Pinus devadaru* or *P. deodora*, Roxb.).

दारुक, *m.* 1, (*f.* ā) a doll, puppet: 2, *m. pr. n.* (1) of Krishṇ's charioteer (2) of a certain incarnation of Shiv.

दारुज, *m.* (*f.* ā) made of wood, wooden.

दारुण, 1, *m.* severity; horribleness: lead-wort (*Plumbago zeylanica*): 2, *m.* (*f.* ā) hard, harsh, severe, austere, horrible, terrifying, fearful, dreadful, shocking.

दारुणारि, *m.* an enemy of cruelty (epithet of God or of any merciful being).

दारुणारी, *more prop.* (1) **दारुणारि** (2) **दारुनारि**, *qq. v.*

दारुनारि, *f.* (*lit.* a female doll, or a doll's wife) a

दारुन, *more prop.* **दारुण**, *q. v.* [wooden doll, puppet.

दारुनिशा, *f.* the plant *Cucurma xanthorrhiza.*

दारुपुत्रिका
दारुपुत्री } = **दारुनारि**, *q. v.*

दारुमय, *m.* (*f.* ā) abounding in wood, consisting of

दारुस्त्री = **दारुनारि**, *q. v.* [wood, woody, wooden.

दारुहरिद्रा, *f.* the plant *Cucurma xanthorrhiza.*

दारू, 1, *more prop.* **दारु**, *q. v.*: 2, *f.* spirituous liquor, gunpowder.

दारूड़ा, *m.*
दारूड़ी, *f.* } wine, spirituous liquor.

दारूसीसा, military stores, ammunition; *lit.* powder and lead.

दारोग़, *more prop.* (1) **दारोग़ा** (2) **दरोग़**, *qq. v.*

दारोग़गी, *f.* the office of darghā.

दारोग़ा, *m.* the head man of an office; an overseer, manager; the superintendent of police, etc., the prefect of a town or village.

दारोग़ाना, the pay of a daroghā.

दारोमदार, *m.* agreement, adjustment, settlement (of a dispute or quarrel), reconciliation, stipulation.

दार्ढ्य, *m.* hardness, strength, stability, fixedness.

दार्विका, *f.* a sort of collyrium made from an infusion of the *Cucurma xanthorrhiza*: a sort of potherb.

दार्वी, *f.* the plant *Cucurma xanthorrhiza.*

दाल, 1, *more prop.* **डाल**, *q. v.*: 2, *f.* pulse, vetches; a kind of split pea much used for food: 3, *f. m.* ? a species of grain (*Paspalum fumentaceum*). — *galnā kisikī*, to have an advantage, to avail. *Kuchh — meṅ kālā hai* (there is something black in the pea soup, *i. e.*) there is something wrong. 'there is a flaw in the indenture,' 'there is a screw loose.'

दालचीनी = **दारचीनी**, *q. v.*

दालवाला, *m.* (*f.* in *or* ī) a dealer in **दाल**, *q. v.*

दाला, 1, *f.* colocynth: 2, peculiar kind of tenure in

दालान, *m.* a hall. [the Doāb.

दालिद्र, for words beginning thus, see under the

दालिम, a corruption of **दाड़िम**, *q. v.* [form **दारिद्र**.

दालिल, a corruption of **दारिद्र**, *q. v.*

दालून, *more com.* (1) **दालवाला** (2) **दालान**, *qq. v.*

दाव, *m.* a bill or kind of hatchet with a hooked point: vicissitude, turn, opportunity: a stake, wager, stroke at a game, throw of the dice, etc.: a forest; a forest conflagration.—*badnā* or *bāndhnā*, to wager, bet.

दावन, *m.* destruction. [treading out corn.

दावना, 1, *t.* to thresh, tread: 2, *m.* the act of

दावा = **दाया**, 2, *q. v.*

दावारा (*corruption*) = **दुबारा**, *q. v.*

दावाग्नि
दावानल } *m.* a forest conflagration.

दावों, *more prop.* **दाँव**, *q. v.* [fisherman, boatman.

दाश, 1, a corruption of **दास**, *q. v.*: 2, *m.* (*f.* ī) a

दाशपुर, *m.* the fragrant grass *Cyperus rotundus.*

दाशरथ, *m.* (patronym.) a descendant of Dasharath: *adj.* appertaining to Dasharath.

दाशी, 1, *more prop.* **दासी**, *q. v.*: 2, *f.* a fish-woman, the wife or daughter of a fisherman.

दाशेय, *m.* (*f.* ī) a fish-woman's child.

दाशेरक, *m. pr. n.* the province of Mālwā.

दाश्त, *f.* a bringing up, breeding, taking care of, patronage; service.

दास, 1, *m.* (*f.* ī) a servant, slave: a Shoodra; a suffix to names of Shoodras: 2, *m.* a sickle, scythe.

दासक, 1, *m.* (*f.* ikā) a servant, slave; 2, appertaining

दासतान, *more prop.* **दास्तान**, *q. v.* [to servants.

दासत्व, *m.* (*f.* tā) servitude, service, slavery.

दासदासी, *f.* a slave's female slave: male and female slaves, servants and handmaidens.

दासन, *m.* (a Braj pl. of **दास**; see **न**, 6) slaves, etc.

दासपुर
दासपूर } = **दाशपुर**, *q. v.*

दासरथ, *more prop.* **दाशरथ**, *q. v.*

दासा, *m.* a piece of wood projecting from a wall to support the thatch (*chhappar*): a reaping-hook.

दासानुदास, *m.* a servant of servants (an epithet expressive of unworthiness and lowliness).

दासिका, *f.* (*m.* **दासक**) = **दासी**, *q. v.*

दासी, *f.* a female slave, maid-servant, handmaid.

दासीपुत्र, *m.* (*f.* ī) the child of a slave-girl.

दासेय, *m.* (*f.* ī) a fish-woman's child.

दास्तान, *f.* a story, fable, tale.

दास्य, *m.* servitude, service, slavery.

दाह, *m.* a burning, combustion, conflagration; ardour; inflammation, morbid heat, feverish heat; cauterizing. — *denā*, to light the funeral pile. — *rakhnā*, to grudge.

दाहक, 1, *m.* (*f.* ikā) an incendiary, etc.: *lit.* adj.

setting on fire; burning, inflammatory, caustic, cauterizing: 2, *m.* a species of plant (*Plumbago zeylanica*).

दाहकरण }
दाहकर्म } *m.* = दाहक्रिया, *q.v.*

दाहक्रिया, *f.* the act or the ceremony of burning

दाहज्वर, *m.* an inflammatory fever. [a corpse.

दाहन, *m.* setting fire to, burning, cauterizing.

दाहना, 1, *m.* (*f.* ī) *more prop.* दहिना, *q. v.*: 2, *t.* (of दहना) to burn, scorch.

दाहसर, *m.* a place where corpses are burnt.

दाहहरण, *m.* the root of the fragrant grass *Andropogon muricatum.* This root is woven into a kind of screen (called the 'tattie') which is kept wet for the purpose of diminishing the temperature of the hot winds.

दाहा, *more prop.* दहा, *q.v.*

दाहिका, *f.* (*m.* दाहक) a female incendiary.

दाहिजा, *more com.* दाएजा, *q.v.*

दाहिना, *m.* (*f.* ī) *more prop.* दहिना, *q.v.*

दाही, *m.* (*f.* inī) *adj.* setting on fire; burning;

दाहु; see (1) दाह (2) दाही (3) दाऊ. [paining.

दिआ, *more com.* दिया, *q.v.*

दिआले, a lamp; a light.

दिई, (pl. दिईं), *f.* of दिया, *q.v.*

दिक (*prop.* दिश). See दिग.

दिकपति, *m. pr. n.* (*lit.* lord of the ten regions) the designation applied to the guardian deities of the different quarters of the world: of these there are two divisions (1) *astronomical, viz.* the Sun, of the east; Saturn, of the west; Mercury, of the north; Mars, of the south; Venus, of the south-east: Rahoo of the south-west; the Moon, of the north-west; Jupiter, of the north-east: (2) *mythological, viz.* Brahmā, for upwards; Ananta, for downwards; Indra, of the east; Varuṇ, of the west; Kuver, of the north; Yam, of the south; Agni, of the south-east; Nairrit, of the south west; Marut or Vāyu, of the north-west; Íshan or Shiv, of the north-east.

दिकपाल, *m. pr. n.* = दिकपति, *q.v.*

दिकशूल, *m.* any inauspicious planetary conjunction (as, for the Sun and Venus to be in the west, etc.).

दिक़ाक़, *m.* a shred; a chip: *adj.* minute; intelligent.

दिकोड़ी, *f.* a wasp, hornet. [plague, bother.

दिक़्क़, *m.* teazing, trouble, etc. — *k.* to perplex,

दिक़्क़त, *f.* abstrusity, difficulty, trouble, uneasiness; close application, diligence, industry; accuracy.

दिखना = देखना, *q.v.*

दिखराना, *more prop.* दिखलाना, *q.v.*

दिखरावना, *more prop.* दिखलाना, *q.v.* See व.

दिखराशूल, *m.* flatulency (?). [to denote.

दिखलाना, *t.* to shew, exhibit, display; to direct;

दिखलाई = दिखाई, *q.v.*

दिखलावना = दिखलाना. See व.

दिखलावा, *m.* show, pageantry. [viewer, observer.

दिखवैया, *m.* an on-looker, spectator, beholder,

दिखाई, *f.* a shewing, show, appearance, display, exhibition. — *denā* or *parnā*, to appear, be apparent, [come in sight, seem.

दिखाउना = देखाना, *q. v.*

दिखाऊ, fit to be shewn, presentable, comely.

दिखाओ = दिखाव, *q.v.*

दिखाना = देखाना, *q.v.*

दिखाव, *m.* }
दिखावट, *f.* } show, display, exhibition.

दिखावटी, forged.

दिखावत = दिखावट, *q.v.*

दिखित, a certain tribe of Rājputs.

दिग, *m.* (दिश) quarter, region, direction, tract, side, way; point (of the compass): (in *comp.*) = wards; e. g. *Uttar-dig*, northwards.

दिगदिगाना, *a. int.* to chatter (as the teeth).

दिगन्त, *m.* the horizon.

दिगन्तर, *m.* aerial space, atmosphere.

दिगपति }
दिगपाल } = दिकपति, *q.v.*

दिगपालन, *m.* the functions of the guardian deity of any region. [more proper form दिग्व.

दिगब; for words beginning thus, see under the

दिगम्बर, (*lit.* clad by the regions of space, *i. e.* naked) *m.* (*f.* ā) a naked person: *prop.* unclad; hence (1) any Hindoo ascetic who goes unclad: (2) an epithat of Shiv (from his being naked) and of certain of his devotees (who also go naked): (3) an order of ascetics of the *Jain* sect who either go naked or are clad in cloth dyed with red chalk.

दिगर, (*pl.* ān) other, another: again.

दिगवान }
दिगवार } *m.* a watchman, guard.

दिगविजय = दिग्विजय, *q.v.*

दिगशूल, *m.* the direction in which it is deemed unlucky to travel on particular days.

दिग्गज, *m.* an epithet of either of the eight elephants which are supposed to support the world at the different quarters of the compass.

दिग्गी = दिघी, *q.v.*

दिग्विजय, *m.* the subjugation of an extensive country (whether in arms or in controversy).

दिग्विजयक्रम, *m.* invasion, going forth to conquer the world. [tract of country or of the world.

दिग्विजयी, *m.* (*f.* inī) a subjugator of an extensive

दिग्विभाग, *m.* a point or quarter of the compass.

दिग्व्यापी, *m.* (*f.* inī) spreading through all space.

दिघी, *f.* any large tank or reservoir in the form of an oblong quadrangle.

दिच्छाय in Chand = दिया, *q. v.*

दिठवन, *more prop.* देवठान, *q. v.*

दिठौना, *m.* a patch, an artificial mole on the face.

दिड्डी, *f.* a wicket, small door.

दिढ़, दित; for words beginning with either of these forms, see under the forms दृढ़, दिति, respectively.

दिति, *f. pr. n.* one of the two wives of Kashyap and mother of the Daityas.

दितिज, *m.* (*f.* ā) any Daitya (or demon) : *prop.* an offspring of Diti.

दितिनन्दन, *m.* (*f.* ā) = **दितिज**, *q. v.*

दितिया, *f.* the second lunar day.

दितिसुत, *m.* (*f.* ā) = **दितिज**, *q.v.*

दिती, *more prop.* **दिति**, *q. v.*

दित्य, *more prop.* **दैत्य**, *q.v.*

दिदार, *more prop.* **दीदार**, *q. v.*

दिद्धिय } in Chand = **दिया**, *q. v.*
दिद्धौ }

दिधा, *more prop.* **द्विधा**, *q. v.*

दिधि, *f.* firmness, stability, fixedness.

दिन, *m.* day, a day. — *kāṭnā*, to pass the time with difficulty. — *ko* — , *rāt ko rāt na jānnā*, (not to perceive that day is day and that night is night, *i. e.*) to be totally absorbed in thought or in business. — *khulnā* or *phirnā*, to begin to prosper after adversity. — *gaṅwānā*, to spend time carelessly or to trifle it away. — *charhnā*, the day being far advanced; the period of menstruation being protracted. — *charhā-nā*, to commence any business late in the day; to eat the bread of idleness, or earn one's wages without labour. — *dhalnā*, to grow late, to decline (the sun). — *parnā*, to be unfortunate. — *phūlnā*, to dawn. — *bharnā*, to occupy the whole day about a thing. — *mundnā*, to grow late, to close (the day). *Din-ba* (or *par*)-*din*, day after day, day by day. *Baṛā*—, broad day, late in the morning.

दिनकर, *m.* the day-maker, *i. e.* the sun.

दिनकरस्कर, 1, a poet. genit. of **दिनकर**, *q.v.*: 2, *m.* a ray of the sun.

दिनज्योतिष, *m.* sunshine, daylight.

दिनदानी, *m.* (*f.* inī) a very beneficent person: lit. *adj.* giving daily.

दिनदिन, every day, daily, always.

दिनदिया, *m.* daylight.

दिनदिवाले } *adv.* in daylight.
दिनधोले }

दिनन, a Braj pl. of **दिन**. See **न**, 6 (1).

दिनपति, *m.* the lord of day, *i. e.* the sun.

दिनप्रति = **प्रत्येक दिन**, every day, daily.

दिनभर, *adv.* all day, the whole day.

दिनमणि, *m.* the gem of day, *i. e.* the sun.

दिनमान, *m.* the length of day.

दिनरात }
दिनराता } = **दिवारात्र**, *q.v.*
दिनराति }
दिनरैन }

दिना, a poet. form for **दिन**, *q.v.*

दिनाई, *f.* a tetter, ringworm.

दिनाती, *f.* the daily work of labourers; the time of a plough's working in the course of a single day.

दिनान्त, *m.* close of day, sunset, evening.

दिनान्ध, *m.* (*f.* ā) day-blind, *i. e.* the owl.

दिनारम्भ, *m.* beginning of day, morning.

दिनावसान, *m.* close of day, evening.

दिनिका, *f.* a day's wages, payment for one day's labour.

दिनिया } aged (gen. applied to animals).
दिनो }

दिनेश = **दिनपति**, *q.v.*

दिनेस } *more prop.* **दिनेश**, *q.v.*
दिनेसा }

दिनों, (a Braj pl. of **दिन**) days.

दिनोन्धा, *m.* day-blindness, dysopia.

दिन्न } in Chand = **दिया**, 1, *q. v.*
दिन्नौ }

दिपत, *m.* (*f.* ā) *more prop.* **दीप्त**, *q.v.*

दिब ; for words beginning thus, see under the form **दिव**.

दिब्य, *more prop.* **दिव्य**, *q.v.*

दिमात्रा, *more prop.* **द्विमात्रा**, *q. v.*

दिमस क°, *t.* to lay down turf, place the sods and pound them with a rammer.

दियत, *f.* the law of retaliation, the price of blood, the fine paid for murder or for maiming.

दियन (*colloquial*) = **दिया**, *q. v.*

दिया, 1, *m.* (*f.* **दिई**) base of the historical tenses of the verb *denā*: 2, *m.* a gift : 3, *m.* a lamp, lantern. — *bārnā*, to strike a light.

दियाड़ा, an island formed in the bed of a river, alluvion.

दियानत, *f.* conscience, honesty, justice, piety, virtue.

दियानतदार, honest, etc.; see **दियानत**.

दियानतदारी, *f.* honesty, etc.; see **दियानत**.

दियार, *m.* countries, regions, provinces, districts : houses, mansions.

दियासलाई, *f.* any match (for kindling a lamp), lucifer-match.

दियेा } in Braj = **दिया**, *q. v.*
दियेा }

दिरंगी, *f.* lateness, delay : tardiness.

दिरख़्त, *m.* a tree.

दिरसटी in Chand = **दृष्टि**, *q.v.*

दिरहम, *m.* money; the name (1) of a certain silver coin (2) of a certain weight.

दिरा, *f.* a bell.

दिरेस, dressed, adjusted, put into exact line. — *k.* to dress; to put into exact line.

दिरो, *m.* a reaping, cutting corn at harvest. — *k.* to reap, harvest.

दिल, 1, (*colloquial*) = **दिया**, *q.v.*: 2, *m.* heart, mind, soul; valour.

दिलख़स्ता, broken-hearted, sorely grieved.

दिलजमा, collected in mind, at ease.

दिलदार, *m.* a lover, sweetheart, one to whom the heart has been given : lit. *adj.* heart-holding.

दिलदारी, *f.* demonstrations of love : comfort, consolation.

दिलदिही, *f.* heartiness, earnestness, cheerfulness, alacrity.

दिलबर, *adj.* heart-ravishing : *hence*, a beloved object, sweetheart, mistress.

दिलबरी, *f.* comfort, pacification.

दिलरी, *more prop.* **दिलेरी**, *q. v.*

दिलरुबाई, *f.* the ravishment of the heart. [tion.

दिलरोआई, *f.* (*lit.* heart-weeping) bitter lamenta-

दिलरोवाई, *more prop.* (1) दिलरुबाई (2) दिलरोआई, *qq.v.* [given.

दिलवाना, 1, = दिलाना, *q.v.*: 2, *t.* to cause to be

दिलवाली, *m.* an inhabitant of Delhi. [given.

दिलवैया, *m.* one who causes another to give or to

दिलहींदिल = मनही मन, *q.v.* [pay.

दिलाना, *t.* (causat. of देना) to cause to give, cause to give up, cause to yield, cause to pay; to occasion; to consign; to assign.

दिलाराम, *m.* (*lit.* heart-easing) a sweetheart.

दिलालत, *f.* direction, indication, sign, token; argument, demonstration; brokerage.

दिलावर, intrepid, brave. [couragement.

दिलासा, *m.* comfort, soothing, consolation, en-

दिलो, *f. pr. n.* (see दिल्ली) the city of Delhi.

दिलीप, *m. pr. n.* a certain king of Hastināpur (the ancient Delhi) and an ancestor of Rām.

दिलेरी, *f.* intrepidity, boldness, presumption, daring, impudence.

दिलोजान, *adv.* heart and soul; tooth and nail. — *se*, with heart and soul, heartily, in right earnest.

दिल्क, *m.* a medicant's habit (made of patches and shreds. [*dilk*: *prop.* ragged, clothed in rags.

दिल्कपोश, *m.* a mendicant or one who wears the

दिल्ली, *f. pr. n.* (see दिल्ली) the city of Delhi.

दिल्लीवाल, *m.* (*f.* in or ī) = दिल्लीवाला, *q.v.* [Delhi.

दिल्लीवाला, *m.* (*f.* ī) a native or an inhabitant of

दिव, *more prop.* दिव्य, *q.v.* [tials, paradise.

दिवग्रह, *m.* the divine abode, abode of the celes-

दिवद, 1, *m.* heaven: 2, *adj.* heaven-imparting.

दिवधाम, *m.* = दिवग्रह, *q.v.*

दिवधामी, *m.* (*f.* inī) a celestial.

दिवराणी } दिवरानी } *more prop.* देवराणी, *q.v.*

दिवस, *m.* day, a day.

दिवस्पति, *m.* the lord of day, *i. e.* the Sun.

दिवा, 1, *more prop.* दिया, *q.v.*: 2, (prop. Sk. instr. of दिव; hence) *adv.* by day: 3, *m.* day, daylight.

दिवाकर, *m.* the day-maker, *i. e.* the Sun.

दिवातन, *m.* (*f.* ī) daily, diurnal.

दिवान, *more prop.* दीवान, *q.v.*

दिवाना = (1) दिलाना (2) दीवाना, *qq.v.*

दिवानिश = दिवारात्र, *q.v.* [blind by day.

दिवान्ध, *m.* (*f.* ā) an epithet of the owl; *lit.*

दिवामध्य, *m.* midday, noon.

दिवार, *more prop.* दीवार, *q.v.*

दिवारात्र, *m.* a day and a night, day or night, day and night; *hence*, incessantly, uninterruptedly, without intermission, constantly.

दिवारात्रि, *f.* = दिवारात्र, *q.v.*

दिवाल, *more prop.* दीवार, *q.v.*

दिवाला, *m.* insolvency, bankruptcy.

दिवाली, *f. pr. n.* (prop. दीपाली, a row or range of lamps) a certain festival of the Hindoos celebrated on the day of the new moon of Kārttik in honor of Kārttikeya, the god of war. At this festival, the Hindoos after bathing in some river, put on their best attire, and perform a *shrāddh*; and at night worship Lakshmee and indulge in excessive gambling. On this night the houses and streets are illuminated, and the night is spent in gaming.

दिवेसलाई = दियासलाई, *q.v.*

दिवैया, *m.* a giver, bestower.

दिवोदास, *m. pr. n.* a certain king of Benares, founder of the Indian school of medicine.

दिव्य, 1, *m.* an ordeal; an oath: 2, *m.* (*f.* ā) divine, celestial; magical; brilliant, beautiful, agreeable, charming.

दिव्यकवच, *m.* the armour of the gods.

दिव्यज्ञान, *m.* supernatural knowledge.

दिव्यतनु, *m.* an epithet of the Apsaras; *lit.* celestial-bodied.

दिव्यदृष्टि, *f.* supernatural knowledge.

दिव्यधर्मा, *m.* (*f.* inī) virtuous, agreeable.

दिव्यपंचामृत, *m.* a mixture consisting of the five ingredients ghee, curds, milk, butter, sugar.

दिव्यरत्न, *m. pr. n.* = चिन्तामणि, *q.v.*

दिव्यरस, *m.* quicksilver.

दिव्यवस्त्र, clothed in celestial raiment.

दिव्यवाक्य, *m.* a celestial voice, oracle, divine revelation. [celestial-limbed.

दिव्यांगा, *f.* (*m.* दिव्यांग) a beautiful female; *lit.*

दिव्यास्त्र, *m.* celestial weapons. [celestial, divine.

दिव्योपपादुक, *m.* (*f.* ā) of heavenly birth or being,

दिश, *f.* region, direction, quarter, side, space, point of the compass. There are variously reckoned four, eight, and ten quarters or cardinal points; and hence, in the ingenious system of reckoning by symbols adopted by Hindoos in their poetry, this word is

दिशा, *f.* = दिश, *q.v.* [a symbol for 10.

दिशाशूल, *m.* a sign in the heavens that is consulted on commencing a journey; the quarter towards which it is deemed unlucky to travel on par-

दिशि (in poet.) = दिश, *q.v.* [ticular days.

दिष्ट, *more prop.* दृष्ट, *q.v.*

दिष्टि in Chand = दृष्टि, *q.v.*

दिष्टिबन्धक, *m.* the pledge of real property (such as land, houses, etc.).

दिस, *more prop.* दिश, *q.v.*

दिसना, *a. int.* to appear, come into view; to seem: *n.* to be visible, be in sight: *t.* to see: to shew, exhibit.

दिसा, *f.* = दिशा, *q.v.* — *k.* to travel. — *jānā* or *phirnā*, to go into the fields (*i. e.* for a privy).

दिसावर, 1, *more prop.* देशावर, *q.v.*: 2, *m.* climate.

दिसावरी, *m.* (*f.* inī) *more prop.* देशावरी, *q.v.*

दिसि (in poet.) = दिश, *q.v.*

दिसिप = दिसिराज, *q.v.* See प.

दिसिराज = दिक्पति, *q.v.*

दिह, *m.* (*pl.* āt) a village.
दिहन्दा, *m.* a giver: *lit.* beneficent.
दिहरा, *m.* an idol-temple.
दिहली, *f.* a threshold.
दिहात, *m.* (pl. of दिह) villages; "the country" as distinguished from town.
दिहाय = दिहात, *q.v.*
दिहाती, *m.* (*f.* inī) a villager.
दिहिश, charity, bounty, liberality.
दिहुड़ी, *f.* a threshold, door.
दिहुड़ीदार, *m.* a doorkeeper.
दिहुरा, *m.* an idol-temple.
दिहुला, *m.* a species of rice grown in the Benares district. [takes with her to her husband.
दिहेज़, *m.* a dowry, portion, everything a wife
दिह्ली, *f. pr. n.* the city of Delhi. The word is supposed to be derived from दहल,—the city being said to have been built on soil so loose that even tent-pegs could not be fastened into it. Several rival theories are current among both natives and Europeans as to the true spelling and derivation of the name of this city: some spell it Dilī (from दिली); others, Dillī (from दिल्ली); others Dihlī (from दिहली); others, again, spell it Dilhi, or more commonly Delhi. Each of these theories is defended by some rather interesting speculations.
दी, a corruption of दिई, *q.v.*
दीअट, *f.* a lampstand.
दीआ (*poet.*) = दिया, *q.v.*
दीऊनल = देवनल, *q.v.*
दीं, *more prop.* दिईं, *q.v.*
दीक्षा, *f.* consecration, undergoing religious observances, receiving the initiatory *mantra*, engaging in a course of austerities, devotion; offering sacrifices; devotion.
दीक्षित, *m.* (*f.* ā) one who has undergone the above-mentioned ceremony: *lit.* initiated; ready; performed (as the *dikshā* ceremony).
दीक्षिता, 1, *f.* = दीक्षित, *q.v.*: 2, *m.* (*f.* trī) = दीक्षितृ, *q.v.*
दीक्षितृ, *m.* the communicator of the initiatory *mantra*, initiator, spiritual father.
दीखना = दिखना, *q.v.*
दीखित, *m. pr. n.* a certain tribe of Rājputs.
दीगम्बर, *more prop.* दिगम्बर, *q. v.*
दीगर, other, another: again.
दीक्षा = दीचा, *q.v.* [tribe of Kanaujiyā Brāhmaṇs.
दीछित, 1, = दीक्षित, *q.v.*: 2. *m. pr. n.* a certain
दीजे
दीजै } in Braj = दीजिये (देना).
दीजो in Braj = दीजियो (देना).
दीठ, *f.* a sight, view, glance, look, vision.
दीठि
दीठी } *f.* = दीठ, *q.v.*
दीद, *m. f.* sight, seeing, show, spectacle.
दीदः = दीदा, *q.v.*
दीदबाज़ी, *f.* a looking about; amorous ogling; recreation, taking air; reconnoitring.
दीदा, *m.* the eye; a sight, thing seen; a wanton or impudent eye: *met.* impudence.
दीदार, *m.* a sight, look; an interview: an over-
दीदारन; see दीदार. [seer, inspector.
दीदारू, well-looking, personable, presentable.
दीदेदिल, *m.* the eye of the mind.
दीधित (*contraction*) = दीधिति, *q. v.*
दीधिति, *f.* a ray of light, a sunbeam, moonbeam; light (in general). [*more prop.* द्विधा, *q. v.*
दीधा, 1, *m.* (*f.* ī) in Chand = दिया, 1, *q.v.*: 2,
दीन, 1, an old form = दिया, *q.v.* 2, poor, indigent, needy, distressed; lowly, humble: 3, *m.* faith, religion, following, sect. [distressed, dejected.
दीनचेतन, *m.* (*f.* ā) a distressed person, etc.: *lit.*
दीनताई, *f.* = दीनत्व, *q.v.*
दीनत्व, *m.* (*f.* tā) poverty, indigence, want, distress; humility. [for the lowly.
दीनदयाकर, *m.* (*f.* ī) an exerciser of compassion
दीनदयानिधि, *m.* an epithet of God; *lit.* the Treasury of compassion for the lowly. [the lowly.
दीनदयाल, *m.* an epithet of God; *lit.* merciful to
दीनदाता, *m.* (*f.* trī) one who is beneficent to the
दीनदार, virtuous, religious. [poor.
दीनदारी, *f.* religiousness, the state of belonging to a faith. [tector of the poor.
दीननाथ, *m.* an epithet of God; *lit.* Lord or Pro-
दीनबन्धु, *m.* an epithet of God; *lit.* Friend of the poor. [minded.
दीनमन, troubled or afflicted in mind, lowly-
दीनमुख, *m.* (*f.* ī) a person with a down-cast look: *lit.* of melancholy aspect, of rueful countenance, down-cast.
दीनहीन, *m.* (*f.* ā) poor, poverty-stricken. [plication.
दीनवचन, *m.* utterance of distress, humble sup-
दीना (old form) = (1) देना (2, *m.* [*f.* ī]) दिया, *qq. v.*
दीनाचार्य, *m.* an epithet of God; *lit.* the spiritual teacher of the humble.
दीनादयाल, *more prop.* दीनदयाल, *q. v.*
दीनानाथ, *more prop.* दीननाथ, *q.v.*
दीनार, *m.* a kind of coin: a certain weight of gold:
दीनी = दिई. See दीना, 2. [a gold ornament,
दीनो in Braj = (1) दिया (2) देना, *qq. v.*
दीनों = दीनो, *q. v.*
दीन्हा, *m.* (*f.* ī) = दिया. See न्हा.
दीन्हे, *m.* (*f.* °न्हीं) pl. of दीन्हा, *q. v.*
दीन्हों
दीन्हौं } = दीन्हा, *q. v.*
दीप, 1, a corruption of द्वीप, *q. v.*: 2, *m.* a lamp.
दीपक, *lit.* adj. inflaming, making luminous, kindling; hence, *m.* a lamp, light, candle; a kind of fireworks; a musical mode (*rāg*) sung at noon in the hot weather; a certain aromatic seed (*Ligustum ajaen*).

दीपकिट्ट, *m.* lampblack, the condensed smoke or soot of a lamp, snuff of a candle.

दीपकूपी } *f.* the wick of a lamp.
दीपखोरी }

दीपदान, *m.* land assigned to Brāhmans on the banks of rivers to deprecate river encroachment; name of a ceremony observed for ten days after a relative's decease (it consists in the suspending a lamp on the peepal or some other tree for the purpose of lighting the departed spirit on the road to Yampuri); the offering a lamp to an idol.

दीपध्वज, *m.* = दीपकिट्ट, *q.v.*

दीपन, *m.* (*f.* ī) inflaming, light-exciting, heat-exciting; exciting, stimulating, tonic.

दीपपुष्प, *m.* the champac (*Michelia champaca*).

दीपमाला, *f.* a row of lamps, an illumination.

दीपमालिका, *f.* = दीपमाला, *q.v.* [stick.

दीपवृक्ष, *m.* the stand or stem of a lamp, candle-

दीपशिखा, *f.* lamp-flame, candle-flame.

दीपाली, corrupted into **दिवाली**, *q.v.*

दीपिका, *f.* a lamp.

दीप्त, *m.* (*f.* ā) blazing, luminous, radiant.

दीप्तमान, *more prop.* **दीप्तिमान**, *q.v.*

दीप्ति, *f.* light, splendour, lustre. [splendid.

दीप्तिमन्त, *m.* (*f.*matī) radiant, lustrous, shining,

दीप्तिमान, *m.* (*f.* matī) = दीप्तिमन्त, *q.v.*

दीबाचा, *m.* preface, introduction, preamble.

दीबाना, *more prop.* **दीवाना**, *q.v.*

दीमक, *f.* the white ant.

दीयत, *more prop.* **दियत**, *q.v.*

दीया, *more prop.* **दिया**, 3, *q.v.*

दीर, 1, old, antique: 2, late, after: a while ago, a long while: slowly, tardily.

दीरोज़, yesterday.

दीर्घ, *m.* the *sāl*-tree; (in Gram.) a long vowel: lit. *m.*(*f.* ā) long (applied to space or to time).

दीर्घआयु, *more com.* **दीर्घायु**, *q.v.*

दीर्घकण्टक } *m.*(*f.* ā) a sort of crane (*Ardea nivea*).
दीर्घकन्धर }

दीर्घकाल, *m.* a long period of time.

दीर्घकील, *m.* the tree *Alangium hexapetalum*.

दीर्घकेश, *m.* (*f.* ā *or* ī) long-haired.

दीर्घजंगल, *m.* a kind of fish.

दीर्घजंघ, *m.* (*f.* ā) an epithet of the camel and of the crane; *lit.* long-legged, spindle-shanked.

दीर्घजिभा = **दीर्घजिह्व**, *q.v.* [the long-tongued.

दीर्घजिह्व, *m.* (*f.* ā) an epithet of the snake; *lit.*

दीर्घजीव, *m.* long life.

दीर्घजीवी, *m.* (*f.* inī) any long-lived creature: *lit.* living or existing a long time. [bodied, tall.

दीर्घतनु, *m.* (*f.* tanvī) any tall animal; *lit.* long-

दीर्घदर्शी, *m.* (*f.* inī) a wise or learned person, seer, prophet: *lit.* far-seeing, provident, wise.

दीर्घदृष्टि, 1, = **दीर्घदर्शी**, *q.v.*: 2, *f.* long sight.

दीर्घनिद्रा, *f.* death (the long sleep).

दीर्घनिश्वास, *m.* a deep-drawn sigh.

दीर्घपक्ष, *m.* the fork-tailed shrike.

दीर्घपत्र, *m.* garlic; *lit.* long-leaved.

दीर्घपत्रक, *m.* garlic; a species of thorny plant; a kind of Bassia that grows in marshy places.

दीर्घपत्रा, *f.* a sort of Eugenia.

दीर्घपर्ण, long-leaved, longifolium.

दीर्घपल्लव, *m.* the sun-plant (*Crotolaria juncea*); *lit.* having long shoots or tendrils. [the long-footed.

दीर्घपाद, *m.*(*f.* ā *or* ī) an epithet of the heron; *lit.*

दीर्घफल, *m.* a certain plant (*Cassia fistula*).

दीर्घमूल, *m.* a kind of *bilwā*-tree; a sort of sensitive-plant: *lit.* having a long root.

दीर्घमूला, *f.* a creeper (*Echites frutescens*).

दीर्घमूली, *f.* a kind of plant (*Hedysarum alhagi* or *H. Gangeticum*). [winded talker; a proper name.

दीर्घरव, *m.* (*f.* ā) any loud-voiced creature, a long-

दीर्घरात्र, *m.* a long night, long period.

दीर्घरोगी, *m.*(*f.* inī) a person who has been long ill.

दीर्घवंश, *m.* (*f.* ī) a person of an ancient family.

दीर्घवर्ण, *m.* (in Gram.) a long vowel.

दीर्घवृन्त, *m.* a species of plant (*Bignonia Indica*).

दीर्घवृन्तिका, *f.* a species of plant (*Mimosa octandra*).

दीर्घशाख, *m.* the *sāl*-tree (*Shorea robusta*).

दीर्घसूत्र = **दीर्घसूत्री**, *q.v.* [slowness.

दीर्घसूत्रता, *f.* (*m.* °त्व) dilatoriness, tediousness,

दीर्घसूत्री, *m.* (*f.* inī) a dilatory person: *lit.* dilatory, slow, tedious. [a long note.

दीर्घस्वर, *m.* (in Gram.) a long vowel: (in Music)

दीर्घा, *f.*; see **दीर्घ**.

दीर्घायु, 1, *m.* longevity: 2, long-lived, long-living.

दीर्घायुस, *m.* the silk-cotton tree (*Bombax heptaphyllum*): *lit.* long-lived.

दीर्घिका, *f.* an oblong pond.

दील; for words beginning thus, see under the more proper form **दिल**.

दीवक, *f.* the white ant: a weevil, moth.

दीवट, *f.* a lampstand.

दीवली, *f.* a small lamp.

दीवा, *m.* a lamp.

दीवान, *m.* a tribunal: a steward; the collector-general of a province; a court-minister.

दीवाना, *m.*(*f.* ī) mad, insane, possessed, inspired.

दीवानी, *f.* the office of the king's *dīvān*, and superintendence of the administration of civil justice.

दीवार, *f.* a wall: the bridge of the nose.

दीवारगीरी, *f.* tapestry, wall-hangings.

दीवारा, *more prop.* **दीवार**, *q.v.*

दीवारी; see (1) **दीवार** (2) **दीवाली** (3) **दिवाली**.

दीवाल, *more prop.* **दीवार**, *q.v.*

दीवाली, *f.* a leathern strap, belt.

दौंचि, *m.* the blue jay.
दौंसना = दिसना, *q.v.*
दौसे, *adj.* like : *adv.* likely.
दौह, 1, in Chand = देह, *q.v.*: 2, *m.* (*pl.* āt) a village, town.
दौहात, *m.* villages ; 'the country' as distinguished from 'town'.
दौहाती, *m.* (*f.* inī) a villager : *lit.* appertaining to villages or to the country.
दौही, *m.* (*f.* inī) = दौहाती, *q.v.*
दौहीन, a corrupt form = दिया, 1, *q.v.*
दौहुई, *more prop.* दिई हुई (pl. दिये हुये).
दु ; frequent as a prefix in comp. in the sense of two, twofold, double, divided ; *e. g.* दुचित्त.
दुआ, *f.* benediction, salutation, congratulation, invocation, imprecation. — *k.* or *māṅgnā*, to pray. — *denā*, to bless ; to pray for.
दुआब, *m. pr. n.* (*lit.* the two waters, *i.e.*) the country lying between the Ganges and the Jamunā.
दुआर, *more prop.* द्वार, *q.v.*
दुइ (poet.) = दो, two.
दुंका, *m.* a crumb, scrap.
दुंयी, *f.* a coarse kind of cloth.
दुंड, दुंद ; for words beginning thus, see under the forms दुण्ड, दुन्द, respectively.
दुःकंत, *more prop.* दुष्यन्त, *q.v.*
दुःख, 1, *m.* pain, ache ; difficulty, trouble, annoyance, bother, distress, grief, affliction, sorrow, unhappiness ; fatigue, labour. — *kā mārā*, afflicted. — *uṭhānā* or *pānā*, to be afflicted. — *denā*, to occasion trouble, to bother. — *bharnā*, to labour, toil, suffer distress or trouble : 2, *m.* (*f.* ā) painful, unpleasant, troublous.
दुःखकर, *m.* (*f.* ī) one who occasions pain, etc. : *lit.* adj. causing or occasioning pain, sorrow, or trouble.
दुःखकर्त्ता, *m.* (*f.* trī), दुःखकारक, *m.* (*f.* ikā), दुःखकारी, *m.* (*f.* iṇī) = दुःखकर, *q.v.*
दुःखखण्डन, *m.* (*f.* ā *or* ī) one who destroys the trouble, etc. of another : *lit.* adj. pain-destroying.
दुःखग्राहक, *m.* (*f.* ikā) one who takes away the grief, etc. of another : *lit.* adj. grief-removing.
दुःखक्लिष्ट, *m.* (*f.* ā) pained, afflicted, distressed.
दुःखजीवी, *m.* (*f.* inī) one who passes life in pain or distress.
दुःखड़ा, *m.* misfortunes, calamities.
दुःखद, pain-imparting, afflictive, troublesome, vexatious, troublous, painful : hence, *m.* (*f.* ā) one who gives or occasions pain, a tormentor, a persecutor.
दुःखदग्ध, *m* (*f.* ā) consumed by affliction, pained, distressed.
दुःखदाई, *m.* (*f.* inī), दुःखदानी, *m.* (*f.* inī), दुःखदायक, *m.* (*f.* ikā), दुःखदायी, *m.* (*f.* inī) = दुःखद, *q.v.*
दुःखदाहक, *m.* (*f.* ikā) one who burns up the miseries, etc. of another : *lit.* adj. burning up affliction.
दुःखदीन, (a poet. form) = दुःख दिया.

दुःखना, *a. int.* to ache, pain, smart.
दुःखनिकन्द, 1, *m.* the uprooting of grief or trouble : 2, *m.* a destroyer of trouble.
दुःखनिवारण, 1, *m.* the prevention of trouble : 2, *adj.* preventing or warding off affliction.
दुःखप्रद, *m* (*f.* ā) a giver or a causer of pain, etc. : lit. *adj.* pain-imparting.
दुःखबहुल, *m.* (*f.* ā) painful, distressful, abounding with trouble, etc.
दुःखभंजन, *m.* a breaking or destroying of grief or affliction : an epithet of the Supreme Being (considered as the destroyer of affliction).
दुःखभोग, *m.* suffering, affliction.
दुःखभोगिन, *m.* (*f.* ī) one whose portion is pain, etc. : *lit.* suffering or sharing pain, sorrow, or trouble.
दुःखभोगी, *m.* (*f.* inī) = दुःखभोगिन, *q.v.*
दुःखमय, *m.* (*f.* ī) *adj.* abounding in or consisting of pain, etc.
दुःखलभ्य, *m.* (*f.* ā) *adj.* to be obtained or effected with pain or trouble.
दुःखसागर, *m.* an epithet of the world ; *lit.* the ocean of trouble, deep distress.
दुःखहन, *m.* (*f.* ī) a pain-destroyer : *lit.* destroying or removing pain, trouble, or sorrow.
दुःखहरण, *m.* (*f.* ā *or* ī), दुःखहर्त्ता, *m.* (*f.* trī) = दुःखहारी, *q.v.*
दुखहारी, *m.* (*f.* iṇī) a remover of pain, etc. : *lit.* adj. taking away pain or grief ; *hence*, an anodyne.
दुःखा, *f.* ; see दुःख, 2.
दुःखाना, *t.* to hurt, torment, inflict pain, grieve.
दुःखारी, *m.* (*f.* iṇī), दुःखित, *m.* (*f.* ā), दुःखिन, *m.* (*f.* ī) = दुःखिया, *q.v.*
दुःखिया, in distress or pain, afflicted, poor, indigent, unfortunate, wretched, sorrowful, sad, grieved, troubled, sick.
दुःखियारा, *m.* (*f.* ī), दुःखी, *m.* (*f.* inī) = दुःखिया, *q.v.*
दुःशासन, unmanageable, intractable, ill-managed : *pr. n.* one of the 100 sons of Dritrāshtra.
दुःशील, of a wicked disposition, ill-behaved, abandoned, reprobate : hence, *m.* (*f.* ā) a reprobate, etc.
दुःसम, unseasonable, improper.
दुःसमय, *m.* a time of affliction, distress, or trouble.
दुःसह, *m.* (*f.* ā) intolerable, difficult to be borne.
दुःसाध्य, not easily accomplished, difficult, arduous.
दुःसासन, *more prop.* दुःशासन, *q.v.*
दुःसाहसी, *m.* (*f.* inī) rash, irreverent, presumptuous, bold.
दुःस्पर्श, *m.* a certain plant (*Hedysarum alhagi*) : lit. *m.* (*f.* ā) difficult or unfit to be touched, disagreeable to the touch.
दुःस्पर्शा, *f.* a prickly sort of nightshade.
दुकड़ा, *m.* the fourth part of a *paisā*.
दुकड़ी, *f.* a snaffle.
दुकान, *f.* (see दूकान) a shop.
दुकानझाड़ा, *m.* sweeping of a (druggist's) shop ; compound medicine.

दुकाल, *m.* famine, scarcity. [garment.
दुकूल, *m.* a species of plant; very fine cloth; a
दुकेले; see अकेलेदुकेले. [form दुःख.
दुख; for words beginning thus, see under the
दुख़त / दुख़तर } *f.* a daughter, girl, virgin.
दुखहू = दुःखभी. See हू.
दुख़ान, *m.* smoke, tobacco-fumes.
दुखारा, *m.* (*f.* ī) = दुःखिया, *q.v.*
दुखिआरा, *m.* (*f.* ī) = दुःखियारा, *q.v.*
दुगण, 1, = दुगुणा, *q.v.*: 2, *m.* a second degree or
दुगणा = दुगुणा, *q.v.* [tone in music.
दुगदुगी, *f.* the cavity at the bottom of the throat.
दुगन = दुगण, *q.v.*
दुगनी, *more prop.* दुगुणा, *q.v.*
दुगाड़ा = दोगाड़ा, *q.v.*
दुगाड़ी = दोगाड़ी, *q.v.*
दुगुणा, *m.* (*f.* ī) twofold, double, twice.
दुग्ध, *m.* milk.
दुग्धता, *f.* the nature of milk, milkiness.
दुग्धतालीय, *m.* milk and mangoes, mango-foule.
दुग्धफेन, *m.* the froth or skim of milk, cream, sylla-
दुग्धफेनी, *f.* a certain small medicinal shrub. [bub.
दुग्धवती, *f.* any milch animal.
दुग्धा, *m.* a certain tribe of inferior Brāhmaṇs on
the borders of Allahabad.
दुग्धिका, *f.* a certain plant (*Asclepias rosea*).
दुग्धिन, *m.* (*f.* ī) milky, having milk. [*ranthes aspera*).
दुग्धिनिका, *f.* a red sort of the *apang* plant (*Achy-*
दुग्धी, *m.* (*f.* inī) milky, having milk.
दुचल्लः, *m.* a roof sloping two ways. [form दुचित्त.
दुचित; for words beginning thus, see under the
दुचित्त, *m.* (*f.* ā) a waverer: *lit.* of two minds, di-
vided in thought or sentiment, puzzled, distracted, vacillating, irresolute, wavering, fluctuating.
दुचिताई, *f.* the being of two minds, vacillation,
दुज in Chand = द्विज, *q.v.* [indecision.
दुजन, *m.* (in Chand, a pl. of दुज) Brāhmaṇs.
दुजा, *m.* (*f.* ī) = दूजा, *q.v.*
दुत, 1, = दुति, *q.v.*: 2, avaunt! begone!
दुतकार, *m.* (*f.* ī) reproof, reprimand.
दुत कारना, *t.* to reprove, reprimand.
दुतदक्क, *m.* reproof, reprimand.
दुतर्फा, *adj. m.* (*f.* ī) having to do with the two
different sides of a question, trying to agree or to side
दुता = दोता, *q.v.* [with both parts, deceitful.
दुताना, *t.* to press down, keep under, chide, snub.
दुतारा = दोतारा, *q.v.*
दुति, *f.* light, splendour, beauty: spite, malice.
दुती, *more prop.* दूति, *q.v.*

दुत्ता देना, *t.* to drive away scornfully: to deceive,
दुद्धि = दुद्धी, *q.v.* [baulk, cheat.
दुद्धी, *f.* the medicinal herb (*Euphorbia hirta*
दुधार, *more prop.* दूधार, *q.v.* [and *thymifolia*).
दुधारा, *m.* (*f.* ī) two-edged (a sword).
दुधैल, *more prop.* दूधैल, *q.v.*
दुना, *m.* (*f.* ī) *more prop.* दूना, *q.v.*
दूनिअवी = दुनियवी, *q.v.*
दुनियवी, worldly, of the world, appertaining to
the present state of existence, secularly, earthly.
दुनिया, *f.* (not infl.) the world: *met.* people.
दुनियां (*corruption*) = दुनिया, *q.v.*: 2, a pl. of दुनिया.
दुनियादार, worldly, worldly-minded.
दुनियादारी, *f.* worldliness; economy. [दूनी, *q.v.*
दुनी, 1, a poet. contr. of दुनिया, *q.v.*: 2, *more prop.*
दुनीआ / दुनीया / दुनीयां } *more prop.* दुन्या, *q.v.*
दुन्द, *m.* = दुन्दुभी, *q.v.*
दुन्दका, *m.* a sugar-mill.
दुन्दम / दुन्दु } *m.* = दुन्दुभी, *q.v.*
दुन्दुभि, *m.* 1, = दुन्दुभी, *q.v.*: 2, an epithet (1) of
Krishṇ (2) of a certain Daitya.
दुन्दुभी, *f.* a large kettle-drum: a pair.
दुन्दुमार, *m.* a sort of red worm.
दुन्या, *f.* (not infl.) the world: *met.* people.
दुन्यावी = दुनियवी, *q.v.*
दुपटी, *more prop.* दुपट्टी, *q.v.*
दुपट्टा, *m.* a kind of veil, or a piece of linen in
which there are two breadths. — *tānke sonā* (to draw the sheet [over one's head] and sleep) is a phrase used to express a state of security or carelessness: it also denotes the resigning oneself to death. — *phirānā* or *hilānā*, the holding out a flag of truce, the
दुपट्टी, *f.* = दुपट्टा, *q.v.* [offering to surrender (a fort).
दुपसता, pregnant.
दुपहर = दोपहर, *q.v.* [*Phœnicea*): *lit.* adj. meridian.
दुपहरिया, *m.* (*f.* ?) a species of flower (*Pentapetes*
दुपहरी = दोपहरी, *q.v.* [dilemma.
दुबधा, *f.* doubt, suspense, uncertainty, perplexity,
दुबला, *m.* (*f.* ī) lean, meagre, thin, poor, barren,
weak. [ciatedness.
दुबलाई, *f.* leanness, meagreness, thinness, ema-
दुबलाना, *a. int.* to become emaciated or thin.
दुबलापन / दुबलापना / दुबलापा } *m.* = दुबलाई, *q.v.*
दुबसी, *f.* the percentage allowed to Government
farmers on the revenue paid to Government (viz. two in twenty, or ten per cent.). [a *dubē*.
दुबाइन, *f.* any female of the *dubē* caste, wife of
दुबारा, a second time, over again.

दुबासी = दुभाषिया, *q.v.*
दुबे, *m.* an epithet of any Brāhmaṇ who is learn-
दुभाखी = दुभाषिया, *q.v.* [ed in two of the four Veds.
दुभाग्यता, *more prop.* दुर्भाग्यता, *q.v.*
दुभाषिया, *m.* one who speaks two languages; *hence*, an interpreter; also an agent in general, like the continental 'commissaire,' manager, factotum.
दुभाषी, *m.* (*f.* iṇī) = दुभाषिया, *q.v.*
दुभुक, *m.* a famine, scarcity.
दुम, *f.* tail; end, extremity. — *ka tārā*, a comet. —*dabānā*, to put the tail between the legs, *i.e.* to run away. [a man's back.
दुमबाल, *m.* a tail; the stern of a ship, a rudder;
दुमीढ़ (*corruption*) = दुमीढ़, *q.v.*
दुमुंहा, *m.* (*f.* ī) a kind of serpent with two mouths (*Amphisbæna*); *lit.* two-mouthed; two-faced, deceitful.
दुर, (Sk. दुस) an inseparable prefix, the reverse of सु. It corresponds in general to the English prefixes 'in,' 'un,' etc.; *e.g.* infamous, unbearable, etc.; and imports the idea of (1) bad (2) wicked (3) wrong (4) contemptible (5) inauspicious (6) difficult (7) painful (8) troublous (9) inferiority (10) prohibition. In Hindee it is for the most part written दु॰. See art. द.
दुरतिक्रम, hard to be overcome, unconquerable; difficult of accomplishment. [*a. int.* to disappear, lurk.
दुरना, *n.* to be hidden, be concealed, be absent:
दुरन्त, *m.* (*f.* ā) having a bad ending, ending ill;
दुरस्त, *more prop.* दुरुस्त, *q.v.* [miserable.
दुराऊ in Braj = दुराव, *q.v.*
दुराचार, *m.* (*f.* ā) = दुराचारी, *q.v.*
दुराचारी, *m.* (*f.* iṇī) a profligate, etc.: *lit.* following evil practices, disregarding or deviating from established practices, wicked, depraved, vicious, irreligious, profligate, reprobate. [ed, bad, vile.
दुरात्मा, *m.* a rascal, scoundrel, villain: *adj.* wick-
दुराधर्ष, *m.* white mustard: lit. *m.* (*f.* ā) difficult to be attacked, dangerous. [to remove, send away.
दुराना, *t.* to hide, conceal; to cause to disappear;
दुरायनु (Rām.) = दुराया (दराना).
दुराराध्य, *m.* (*f.* ā) one who is worthy of devotion even at the cost of pain or trouble to oneself.
दुरारोह, *m.* (*f.* ā) of difficult ascent; *hence*, an epithet of (1) the palm-tree (2) the date-tree (3) the silk-cotton tree.
दुरालभ, *m.* (*f.* ā) difficult of attainment.
दुरालभा, *f.* an epithet of a certain prickly plant, — the Jawāsā (*Hedysarum alhagi*).
दुरालाप, *m.* scurrilous language, abuse.
दुराव, *m.* concealment; hypocrisy. — *k.* to attempt to deceive, to keep one away from the point, to trick.
दुरावना = दुराना, *q.v.* See व.
दुराशा, *f.* hopelessness, poverty of hope.
दुराहा, *m.* a road that branches off in two different directions. [*m.* sin.
दुरित, 1, *m.* (*f.* ā) sinful, wicked; concealed: 2,
दुरिष्ठ, 1, *m.* great crime, extreme wickedness: 2, *lit. m.* (*f.* ā) a very wicked person: *adj.* most wicked, very bad.
दुरी, *f.* the two on dice, the deuce.
दुरुखा, *m.* (*f.* ī) that which is the same on both sides, not having a wrong side, double-faced.
दुरुत्तर, unanswerable. [oppressive, morose.
दुरुश्त, rough, hard, stiff, rigid; stern, fierce,
दुरुश्ती, *f.* severity, fierceness.
दुरुस्त, right, fit, proper, just, true, accurate, correct, straight, well, safe, sound, entire. — *k.* to arrange, adjust, rectify. — *rakhnā*, to admit; to follow.
दुरुस्ती, *f.* rectitude, soundness, propriety, exactness, fitness, justness, reformation, amendment.
दुरूद, *f. m.* congratulation, benediction, salutation, thanksgiving. — *bhejnā*, to bless.
दुरुस्त, *more prop.* दुरुस्त, *q.v.*
दुर्कर्मन, 1, *m.* a bad action: 2, *m.* (*f.* ī) an evil-doer,
दुर्कर्मनि, *more prop.* दुर्कर्मनी, *q.v.* [wicked person.
दुर्काम, *m.* a bad action.
दुर्कामी, *m.* (*f.* inī) evil-doing, wicked, iniquitous, bad, lustful. [destructive to young indigo.
दुर्खी, *f.* a certain insect whose ravages are very
दुर्ग, 1, a stronghold, fort, hill-fort; a pass, defile, difficult or narrow passage over a stream or over a mountain or through a wood, etc.: 2, lit. *m.* (*f.* ā) difficult of access or of attainment, inaccessible, impenetrable, impervious, unattainable: 3, *m. pr. n.* (1) of a certain Asur (supposed to have been slain by Durgā who, according to some, received her name from him) (2) of a certain Hindoo grammarian.
दुर्गकर्म्म, *m.* a difficult undertaking.
दुर्गत, *m.* (*f.* ā) poor, indigent, distressed, undergoing pain or affliction. [meanness; hell.
दुर्गति, *f.* distress, poverty, indigence, abjectness,
दुर्गन्ध, 1, *f.* (*m.* ?) a bad smell, stink, stench, any ill-smelling substance. —*ānā*, to stink: 2, *m.* (*f.* ā) a stinkard, etc.: *prop.* ill-smelling, fetid, ill-scented, stinking.
दुर्गन्धी, *m.* (*f.* inī) = दुर्गन्ध, 2, *q.v.*
दुर्गम, *m.* (*f.* ā) anything difficult or profound, etc.: *lit.* difficult to be reached, attained, crossed or passed (as a mountain, a bad or muddy road, a science, etc.), inaccessible, hard to be traversed; profound, deep.
दुर्गमता, *f.* (*m.* °त्व) inaccessibleness, difficultness, profundity, depth.
दुर्गवंशी, *m.* (*f.* inī) appertaining to the race of Durg.
दुर्गा, *f.* (see दुर्ग, 2) an epithet of the wife of Shiv, in allusion to the fact that she is represented to be a goddess of terrific form and of irascible temper (she is variously called Durgā, Umā, Bhawānī, and Pārvatī; and is the mother of Kārttikeya (the god of war) and Ganesh (the god of wisdom): the chief annual festival of the Bengālees (the Durgā-pūjā) held in the month Āswin (Sept.-Oct.) is held in her honour): a Hindoo book containing the narration of this goddess: *met.* a word.
दुर्गादेवी, *f. pr. n.* the goddess Durgā. [fort.
दुर्गाधिकारी, *m.* (*f.* iṇī) the governor or chief of a
दुर्गाध्यक्ष, *m.* (*f.* ī) = दुर्गाधिकारी, *q.v.*
दुर्गानवमी, *f.* the ninth of the light half of Kārttik (sacred to Durgā as Jagddhātri).
दुर्गापूजा, *f.* the chief annual festival of the Bengālees

held in honour of Durgā in the month Āswin (Sept. — Oct.).

दुर्गाश्रयण, *m.* the taking refuge in a fortress.

दुर्गोत्सव, *m.* = **दुर्गापूजा**, *q.v.*

दुर्घट, *m.* (*f.* ā *or* ī) difficult of accomplishment, arduous.

दुर्चार = **दुराचार**, *q.v.*

दुर्जन, *m.* (*f.* ī) a bad person : *lit.* low-bred, vile, bad, wicked, malicious, mischief-making.

दुर्जनता, *f.*
दुर्जनताई, *f.*
दुर्जनत्व, *m.* } low-breeding, wickedness, villainy.

दुर्जय, *m.* (*f.* ā) difficult to be subdued or overcome, invincible.

दुर्जर, difficult to be digested, hard, indigestible.

दुर्जात, 1, *m.* misfortune, calamity; disparity; uniformity; impropriety: 2, *m.* (*f.* ā) inauspiciously born or produced; improper; miserable; wicked.

दुर्जाति, vile, low, outcast, wicked.

दुर्ज्ञेय, difficult to be discerned or ascertained.

दुर्णीत, 1, *m.* misconduct; impolicy: 2, *m.* (*f.* ā) ill-behaved; ill-governed; impolitic.

दुर्णीति, *f.* misconduct, impolicy.

दुर्दन्त, *m.* (*f.* ā *or* ī) a creature with formidable teeth.

दुर्दभी, *more prop.* **दुन्दुभी**, *q.v.*

दुर्दम, difficult to be subdued.

दुर्दर्श, difficult to be seen, difficult to be met with.

दुर्दर्शनयन्त्र, *m.* a telescope, spy-glass.

दुर्दशा, *f.* evil plight, adversity, misfortune, calamity, misery. — *k.* to ill-use.

दुर्दशाग्रस्त, *m.* (*f.* ā) in straitened, difficult, or unpleasant circumstances, in evil plight, badly off, distressed.

दुर्दिन, *m.* a dark, cloudy, or rainy day; bad weather.

दुर्दुभी, *more prop.* **दुन्दुभी**, *q.v.*

दुर्दुराना, *t.* to order off, drive away.

दुर्देव
दुर्दैव } *m.* bad luck, misfortune.

दुर्दृष्ट, ill-seen, not well examined, imperfectly investigated, not well ascertained; looked at with an evil eye.

दुर्नाम, *m.* a bad name, obloquy, slander, discredit, infamy.

दुर्नामा, *m.* piles or hæmorrhoids.

दुर्नामी, *m.* (*f.* inī) a slandered person, infamous person.

दुर्नाम्नी, *f.* a cockle.

दुर्निवार, difficult to be stopped, hindered, contradicted, etc.; invincible.

दुर्ब; for words beginning thus, see under the form **दुर्व**.

दुर्बल, *m.* (*f.* ā) impotent, infirm, weak, nerveless, powerless, feeble, faint, thin, emaciated, poor.

दुर्बलता, *f.* (*m.* °**त्व**) impotence, etc. (see **दुर्बल**).

दुर्बहरा, *m.* a certain intoxicating spirit drawn from rice.

दुर्बास, 1, *more prop.* **दुर्वासस**, *q.v.*; 2, *f.* a bad odour.

दुर्बासा = **दुर्वासस**, *q.v.*

दुर्बासी, 1, *more prop.* **दुर्वासी**, *q.v.*; 2, *m.* (*f.* in *or* inī) ill-odoured, stinking : 3, *f.* a colloquial name for Visarg.

दुर्बुद्धि, 1, *f.* obstinacy, stupidity, dulness, evil-mindedness : 2, perverse, foolish, silly, ignorant, narrow minded, evil-disposed.

दुर्भक्ष, difficult to be eaten.

दुर्भगा, *f.* a wife not liked by her husband; a bad or ill-tempered woman.

दुर्भाग, *m.* ill luck, misfortune.

दुर्भागी, *m.* (*f.* inī) an unfortunate person : *lit.* ill-fated, unfortunate.

दुर्भाग्य, *m.* (*f.* ā) = **दुर्भागी**, *q.v.*

दुर्भाव, *m.* bad disposition, ill-temper, ill-manners, bad behaviour.

दुर्भाग्यत्व, *m.* (*f.* tī) ill luck, a misfortune.

दुर्भिक्ष, *m.* famine, dearth, scarcity.

दुर्भिपत्र, *m.* a certain tree (*Achyranthes aspera*).

दुर्भिग्रहा, *f.* cowach.

दुर्मतकचे, a name of **ओंकार**, or of its symbol.

दुर्मति, 1, *f.* foolishness, folly : 2, a blockhead : *prop.* foolish, silly, simple, ignorant.

दुर्मती = **दुर्मति**, *q.v.*

दुर्मना, *m. f.* sad, distressed, meditating or thinking sorrowfully.

दुर्मलिक्ष, *m. pr. n.* a certain Rākshas.

दुर्मिल, *m. pr. n.* (see **नवयोगेश्वर**) the 7th Yogeshwar.

दुर्मिला, *f.* the name of two species of metre, *viz.* (1) of one consisting of 4 × 32 syllabic instants (2) the other consisting of 4 × 8 anapests.

दुर्मिलिका, *f.* = **दुर्मिला** (1), *q.v.*

दुर्मुख, *m.* (*f.* ī) a foulmouthed person : an ugly person : *lit.* foulmouthed, scurrilous : ugly, hideous.

दुर्मुट = **दुर्मुस**, *q.v.*

दुर्मुस, *m.* a pounder, rammer, implement for pounding pavements.

दुर्मुहूर्त, *m.* an inauspicious moment.

दुर्मूल्य, 1, *m.* costliness: 2, *m.* (*f.* ā) dear, costly, precious, of exorbitant price.

दुर्मेध, *m.* (*f.* ā) of little or contemptible understanding, uninformed, ignorant, stupid, dull.

दुर्योधन, *m. pr. n.* the eldest of the Kuru princes. He is one of the heroes of the Mahābhārat, and the leader of the war against his cousins, the Pāndavas and Krishṇ.

दुर्र, *m.* a pearl.

दुर्रानी, *m.* a certain tribe of Paṭhāns who inhabit the country about Kandhār. They are said to have got this name from their wearing pearls in their ears. They are also called Abdālees.

दुर्लक्षण, *m.* an evil mark, unlucky sign, evil omen.

दुर्लभ, 1, *m.* a species of *Hedysarum* (plant): 2, *m.* (*f.* ā) difficult of attainment or of acquirement, hard to be got, scarce, rare, excellent, eminent, beloved, dear.

दुर्लभा, *f.* a sort of prickly nightshade.

दुर्वचन, *m.* censure, reproach, abuse, obloquy, slander, any unlucky or ill-omened utterance.

दुर्वन, *m.* a dense, impenetrable forest.

दुर्वाच
दुर्वाच्य
दुर्वाद } = **दुर्वचन**, *q.v.*

दुर्वासस, *m. pr. n.* a certain Hindoo *rishi* : *lit.* poorly clad.

दुर्विधि, 1, *m.* ill fate : 2, = दुर्भाव, *q.v.*
दुर्वृत्त, *m.* (*f.* ā) a cheat, rogue, blackguard, juggler, etc. : lit. *adj.* leading a low or infamous life, following disreputable habits or occupation, wicked, vile.
दुर्वृत्ति, *f.* the leading a disreputable life, following a degrading occupation ; juggling, fraud.
दुर्हृदय, *m.* (*f.* ā) bad-hearted, evil-minded.
दुलकी, *f.* a trot ; a dog-trot. — *chalnā* or *jānā*, to trot.
दुलड़ा, 1, *m.* a necklace of two rows or strings : 2, *m.* (*f.* ī) two-fold, of two rows or strings.
दुलड़ी, *f.* a necklace of two strings.
दुलत्ती, *f.* a kick of the two hind legs of a quadruped. — *mārnā*, to wince, kick with the two hind legs.
दुलबन्द, *m.* a turban, the fine cloth of which a turban is made.
दुलमियान, *m.* a small purse.
दुलयिन, *f.* a bride.
दुलह, *more com.* दुल्हा, *q.v.*
दुलहन, दुलहिन, दुलहिनि } *f.* a bride.
दुलाई, *f.* a kind of veil or covering made of two breadths and used by females.
दुलाना, *t.* to agitate, shake, toss.
दुलार, *m.* love, affection. — *k.* to love.
दुलारा, *m.* (*f.* ī) darling, beloved, dear.
दुलाव, *m.* an agitating, shaking.
दुलिचा, दुलीचा } a carpet.
दुलोह = दुलोही, *q.v.*
दुलोही, *f.* a scimetar made of two plates of steel joined together.
दुल्लह, *m.* a bridegroom.
दुल्ले, a name of ऐकार or of its symbol.
दुल्हः, *m.* a bridegroom.
दुल्हन, *f.* a bride.
दुल्हा, *m.* a bridegroom.
दुल्हिन, दुल्हैया } *f.* a bride.
दुवाब, दुवाबा } = दुआब, *q.v.*
दुशाला, *m.* (see दोशाला) a pair of shawls.
दुश्चर, *m.* (*f.* ā) *adj.* acting ill, behaving wickedly: difficult to be passed ; difficult to be performed.
दुश्चरत्व, *m.* (*f.* tā) difficulty of practising.
दुश्चरित, 1, *m.* misconduct, evil purpose, error ; 2, *m.* (*f.* ā) doing ill, misbehaving, designing ill.
दुश्नाम, *m.* abuse, scurrility.
दुश्मन, *m.* an enemy.
दुश्मनी, *f.* enmity, hatred, detestation. — *rakhnā*, (with abl. of object) to entertain dislike towards.
दुश्वारी, *f.* difficultness, arduousness.
दुश्शासन = दुःशासन, *q.v.*
दुष्कर, difficult to be performed.
दुष्कर्म, *m.* vice, wickedness, sin.
दुष्कर्मी, *m.* (*f.* iṇī) a malefactor, criminal, sinner.
दुष्कुन्त, *more prop.* दुष्यन्त, *q.v.*
दुष्कुल, *m.* a low family or race.
दुष्कुलीन, *m.* (*f.* ā) of low or degraded family or race.
दुष्कृत, *m.* evil-doing, crime, sin.
दुष्कर्ता, *m.* (*f.* inī) an evil-doer, criminal, sinner.
दुष्ख, *m.* (दुःख) pain (in general).
दुष्ट, *m.* (*f.* ā) a wicked person, enemy, etc. : *lit.* bad, wicked, depraved, faulty, low.
दुष्टचारी, *m.* (*f.* iṇī) a wicked person.
दुष्टचेता, *m.* or *f.* malevolent : stupid.
दुष्टजन्तु, *m.* evil creatures, *i.e.* snakes, etc.
दुष्टतर, (*Sk. comparat.*) very wicked.
दुष्टता, *f.* (*m.* °त्व) wickedness, badness, depravity. — *k.* to be up to wickedness.
दुष्टताई, *f.* = दुष्टता, *q.v.*
दुष्टदलन, *m.* (*f.* ī) a destroyer, breaker, or crusher of the wicked : an epithet of Krishṇ.
दुष्टन ; a poet. pl. form of दुष्ट, *q.v.*
दुष्टनि in Braj = 1, दष्टन (see न, 6); 2, दष्टने (see नि).
दुष्टभाव, innately bad, depraved.
दुष्टभावता, *f.* (*m.* °त्व) innate depravity, wickedness.
दुष्टमति, depraved, wicked.
दुष्टर, unconquerable.
दुष्टवचन, *m.* (= दुर्वचन) abuse, etc.
दुष्टा, *f.* (*m.* दुष्ट) a harlot, wanton, adulteress.
दुष्टाचार, 1, *m.* bad conduct : 2, *m.* (*f.* ā) a wicked person : *lit.* adj. following evil practices.
दुष्टाचारी, *m.* (*f.* iṇī) = दुष्टाचार, 2.
दुष्टात्मा, *m. f.* a very wicked person.
दुष्नाम, *m.* abuse, scurrility.
दुष्पर्श, *m.* a plant (*Hedysarum alhagi*) ; *lit.* unfit (unpleasant, forbidden, or difficult) to be touched.
दुष्पर्शा, *f.* = दुष्पर्श, *q.v.*
दुष्प्रकृति, *adj.* of a bad nature or disposition.
दुष्प्राप, दुष्प्राप्त } = दुष्प्राप्य, *q. v.*
दुष्प्राप्य, difficult of attainment, difficult to be got at or reached.
दुष्मन्त, *m. pr. n.* a certain prince, husband of Sakuntalā.
दुष्यन्त, दुष्वन्त } = दुष्मन्त, *q. v.*
दुसमन, *more prop.* दुश्मन, *q. v.*
दुसह, *more prop.* दुस्सह, *q. v.*
दुसाद = दोसाद, *q.v.*
दुसेरा, *m.* (or *f.* ī) a weight of two *sērs.*
दुस्कुन्त, *more prop.* दुष्यन्त, *q. v.*
दुस्तर, difficult of passage, almost impassable.
दुस्त्यज, difficult to be relinquished or parted with.
दुस्सर, *m.* double stakes at dice, etc., playing double or quits.

दुस्सह, difficult to be borne, painful to be endured.
दुह, *m.* (*f.* ā) found only as the latter element in compound words, when it signifies 'yielder': lit. *adj.* imparting, yielding.
दुहन, *m.* milking, the act of milking.
दुहना, *n.* to be milked : *t.* to milk.
दुहरना, *n.* to be folded or doubled up.
दुहरा, *m.* (*f.* ī) double, twofold.
दुहराना, *t.* to fold, double, reduplicate ; to repeat.
दुहराव, *m.* repetition ; disputation.
दुहरिट, double, twofold.
दुहल, *m.* a kind of drum, a tabor.
दुहल्ल ; see (1) दुहल (2) दुल्लह.
दुहाई = दोहाई, *q.v.*
दुहाना, *t.* to cause to milk.
दुहार, *m.* (*f.* in *or* ī) a milker.
दुहि, desire, inclination, lust.
दुहिता, *f.* a daughter.
दुहितृपति, *m.* a daughter's husband.
दुहितृ, *f.* a daughter.
दुहु / दुहुं } in Braj = दोनों, *q.v.*
दुहुनि in Braj = (1) दोनों (2) दोनोंने.
दुहुल, *m.* a kind of drum, a tabor.
दुहू / दुहूं } in Braj = दोनों, *q.v.*
दुहूंते in Braj = दोनोंसे. See ते, 3.
दुहेला, *m.* (*f.* ī) difficult, arduous, weighty.
दुह्य, *m.* = दुह्या, *q.v.*
दुह्या, *f.* a milch animal : lit. *adj.* that may be milked, milkable, requiring to be milked.
दू ; frequent in composition as a prefix in the sense of two, twofold, double, divided.
दूआ, *m.* the two or deuce at cards, etc.
दूइ (poet.) = दो, two.
दूई, *f.* duality (as opposed to unity), the being two or twofold, disunion, separation, dispersion.
दूंगड़ा, a heavy shower.
दूकान, *f.* a shop ; a workshop.
दूकानदार, *m.* a shopkeeper, tradesman.
दूकानदारी, *f.* shopkeeping, trade, commerce.
दूकानी, 1, *m.* (*f.* inī) a shopkeeper : 2, *f.* shop-
दूख ; see (1) दुःख (2) दोष. [keeping.
दूखे in Braj = दुःखे or दुःखेगा (दुखना).
दूगलः, = दूगला, *q.v.*
दूगला, *m.* a sling-basket of a large size (round and deep) used in irrigating land.
दूगुणा, *m.* (*f.* ī) twofold, double.
दूज, *f.* the second day of a lunar fortnight.
दूजवर, *m.* a bigamist. [another.
दूजा, *m.* (*f.* ī) second, the other, a second one,

दूजे, *adv.* in the second place, secondly.
दूजै in Braj = दूजे, *q.v.*
दूजो, a poet. form of दूजा, *q.v.*
दूजौ in Braj = दूजा, *q.v.*
दूत, *m.* (*f.* i *or* ī) a messenger, envoy, news-carrier, ambassador, angel which passes between God and man, a go-between.
दूतक, *m.* (*f.* ikā) a messenger, envoy. [envoy.
दूतता, *f.* (*m.* °त्व) the status of a messenger or
दूति, *f.* (*m.* दूत) a female messenger or angel, confidante, procuress, go-between, bawd.
दूतिका, *f.* (*m.* दूतक) = दूति, *q.v.*
दूतिया, second, the second.
दूती = दूति, *q.v.* See also दूत.
दूद, 1, *more prop.* दूध, *q.v.* : 2, *m.* smoke, vapour.
दूदमान, *m.* race, generation.
दूदा, *m.* family, race : lamp-black, soot.
दूध, *m.* milk ; the juice ('milk') of certain bushes. *Dūdhkā dūdh aur pānikā pānī karnā*, to exercise unerring and flawless justice (said of God). — *duhnā*, to milk. — *pilānā*, to suckle. — *baṛhnā*, to be weaned. [milk : *adj.* living on milk.
दूधआधारी, *m.* (*f.* iṇī) one whose sustenance is
दूधपिलाई, *f.* a wet-nurse.
दूधबहन / दूधबहिन } *f.* a foster-sister.
दूधभाई, *m.* a foster-brother.
दूधभाती, *f.* a certain ceremony performed on the fourth day after marriage (wherein the bride and bridegroom eat together a mixture consisting of milk, boiled rice, and sugar).
दूधमुख, *m.* (*f.* ā) the young of any animal.
दूधल = दूधार, *q.v.*
दूधवाला, *m.* (*f.* ī) a milk-vendor, milk-yielder.
दूधहंडी, *f.* a vessel for holding milk.
दूधा, *m.* lamp-black : a kind of rice.
दूधाभाती = दूधभाती, *q.v.* [much milk.
दूधार, *f.* a milch cow, etc. : *lit.* milch, giving
दूधारी, two-edged (as a sword).
दूधिया, *m.* the name of several plants with milky juice : *lit.* milky.
दूधियापत्थर, *m.* a kind of white stone of which plaster is made, and utensils formed ; the opal.
दूधी, *f.* starch : the name of several kinds of plants with milky juice, such as various species of *Asclepias*, *Echites*, *Euphorbia*, *Asclepias rosea*, etc. : *lit.* milky, containing milky juice.
दूधैल = दूधार, *q.v.* [poor, vile.
दून, 1, a valley : 2, base, mean, ignoble, inferior,
दूना, *m.* (*f.* ī) double, twofold, doubled. — *k.* to
दूनिया, *more prop.* दुन्या, *q.v.* [double.
दूनों, a Braj form (1) of दोनों (2) of दूना, *qq.v.*
दूपसा, pregnant.
दूब, *f.* (*m.*?) a species of grass (*Agrostis linearis*, Koen. : *Cynodon dactylon*, Royle).

दूबड़घसड़ू, unknown, insignificant, helpless, hiding through weakness.

दूबर, (prop. **दुर्बल**) weak, lean : difficult.

दूबरा = (1) **दुबला** (2) **दोबरा**, *qq.v.*

दूबिया, *f.* a kind of green colour, grass-green.

दूबे, *more commonly* **दुबे**, *q.v.*

दूभक, *f.* a scarcity, famine.

दूमः, *m.* the leathern case (containing about six pounds) in which tea is imported from Thibet into [Garhwāl and Kamā,on.

दूमा = **दूमः**, *q.v.*

दूर, 1, *f.* distance : 2, *adj.* distant, far, remote : 3, *adv.* far, afar, far off, beyond. — *k.* to remove, dispel, reject, avert, repel, keep at a distance. — *durānā*, to send away to a distance. — *bhāgnā*, to abstain from, avoid, shun, abominate, abhor. — *rahnā*, (with abl. of object) to abstain from, shun. — *honā*, to be removed, be dispelled ; to be remote. — *ho*, begone ! avaunt ! be off !

दूरअन्देश, *adj.* far-seeing, fore-seeing, provident, sagacious, prudent, wise, of deep reflection.

दूरअन्देशी, *f.* far-sightedness, foresight, forecast, providentness, sagaciousness, prudence.

दूरगामी, *m.* (*f.* inī) one who goes to a distance ; *lit.* adj. going far, far-reaching.

दूरत्व, *m.* (*f.* tā) remoteness, distance.

दूरदर्शक, *m.* (*f.* ikā) far-seeing, far-sighted.

दूरदर्शकयन्त्र, *m.* a telescope, spyglass.

दूरदर्शन, *m.* longsightedness ; foresight.

दूरदर्शी, *m.* (*f.* iṇī) a seer, prophet ; a vulture ; a learned man, teacher : *lit.* long-sighted, far-seeing (whether literally or metaphorically).

दूरदृश = **दूरदर्शी**, *q.v.*

दूरदृष्टि, *f.* longsightedness; foresight.

दूरबीन, *m.* a spyglass, telescope : *lit.* having the quality of seeing or of shewing a distant object ; hence, *met.* far-seeing, provident, prudent, sagacious.

दूरबीनी, *f.* = **दूरअन्देशी**, *q. v.*

दूरवर्त्ती, *m.* (*f.* iṇī) one who is at a distance : *lit.* situated at a distance, remote, residing at a distance.

दूरवासी, *m.* (*f.* inī) one who resides at a distance or in a foreign country, an outlandish person : *lit.* adj. residing at a distance.

दूरस्थ, *m.* (*f.* ā) situated at a distance, remote, far off.

दूरान्देश, *more prop.* **दूरअन्देश**, *q.v.*

दूरि } **दूरी** } *f.* (see **दूर**) distance ; separation.

दूरीकृत, *m.* (*f.* ī) removed to a distance, placed afar off. [afar off.

दूरीभूत, *m.* (*f.* ā) situated at a distance, remote,

दूर्दर्शनयन्त्र, *m.* a telescope, spyglass.

दूर्वा, *f.* a kind of millet-grass, the Dūb (*Panicum dactylon*).

दूलत्ती = **दुलत्ती**, *q.v.*

दूलम, *m.* non-entity, non-existence.

दूलह = **दूल्हा**, *q.v.*

दूली, *more commonly* **डोली**, *q.v.*

दूल्हा, *m.* a bridegroom, husband.

दूल्हिन, *f.* a bride.

दूषक, *m.* (*f.* ikā) = **दोषक**, *q.v.*

दूषण, 1, = **दोषण**, *q.v.* : 2, *m.* a defiling, hurting, reducing, calumniating : 3, *m.* (*f.* ī) *adj.* defiling, hurting, disgracing : 4, *m. pr. n.* a certain Rākshas.

दूषणा, *f. pr. n.* a certain goddess.

दूषन, *more prop.* **दूषण**, *q.v.*

दूषिका, *f.* (*m.* **दषक**) concretion on the eyes: a kind [of rice.

दूषिणी = **दोषिणी**, *q.v.*

दूषित = **दोषित**, *q.v.*

दूषिता = **दोषिता**, *q.v.*

दूषिन, *m.* (*f.* ṇī) = **दोषिन**, *q.v.* [of the eye.

दूषी, 1, = **दोषी**, *q.v.* : 2, *f.* the secretion or rheum

दूषीका, *f.* = **दूषी**, 2, *q.v.* [bad.

दूष्य, *m.* (*f.* ā) reprehensible ; contemptible, vile,

दूसना, *more prop.* **दोषना**, *q.v.*

दूसर, *n.* the second. [another, a second one.

दूसरा, *m.* (*f.* ī) an equal, a match : *lit.* second, other,

दूसरे, *adv.* in the second place, secondly.

दूसाद = **दोसाद**, *q.v.*

दूहा, *more prop.* **दोहा**, *q.v.*

दूहाई = **दोहाई**, *q.v.*

दूहिया, *m.* a kind of fireplace.

दूहो in Chand = **दोहा**, *q. v.*

दृक, *m. f.* ? the eye ; sight ; wisdom.

दृक्कर्ण, *m.* (*f.* ā *or* ī) a species of snake which has no visible ear ; *lit.* the eye-eared, — the Hindoos being of opinion that his eyes are also his ears.

दृग = **दृक**, *q.v.*

दृगंचल, *m.* the eyelid, eyelash.

दृगन, (a poet. pl. of **दृग**) eyes.

दृग्गोल, *m.* a small circle on the axis of the earth within the great circle of the armillary sphere, and accompanying each planetary orbit.

दृङमण्डल = **दृग्गोल**, *q.v.*

दृढ़, *m.* (*f.* ā) firm, hard, solid, strong, able, powerful, massive, bulky ; confirmed ; (in Math.) reduced to the least term. — *k.* to confirm, establish.

दृढ़काण्ड, *m.* a bamboo. [ing.

दृढ़कारी, *m.* (*f.* iṇī) resolute, determined, persever-

दृढ़चित्त, 1, *m.* resoluteness : 2, *m.* (*f.* ā) a resolute person, etc : *lit.* firm or resolute of mind.

दृढ़ता, 1, *f.* (*m.* °**त्व**) strength, hardness, solidity, firmness, fixedness, steadiness, corroboration, confirmation. [doubted.

दृढ़निश्चय, certain, confirmed, corroborated, un-

दृढ़फल, *m.* the cocoanut. [cens.

दृढ़बन्धिनी, *f.* a species of creeper (*Echites frutes-*

दृढ़भक्ति, faithful, devoted. [serly.

दृढ़मुष्टि, tight-fisted, close-fisted, niggardly, mi-

दृढ़लोम, 1, *m.* coarse hair, bristles : 2, *m.* (*f.* ā) a wild hog : *lit.* having coarse hair.

दृढ़सूत्रिका, *f.* a plant from the fibres of which bow-strings are made. [(*f.* ā) a firm friend.
दृढ़सौहृद, firm in friendship, constant: hence, *m.*
दृढ़स्कन्ध, *m.* a species of *Mimusops*.
दृढ़हास्य, *m. pr. n.* (1) of a son of Dhundhumār (2) [of a son of Kāshya.
दृढ़ाई = दृढ़ता, *q.v.*
दृढ़ांग, *m.* (*f.* ī *or* ā) firm-bodied, strong, hard; *hence*, a diamond. [ascetic.
दृढ़ाचारी, *m.* (*f.* iṇī) an ascetic, etc.: *lit.* orthodox,
दृढ़ाना, *t.* to strengthen, confirm; to prove.
दृढ़ाभक्ति, *f.* a faithful wife or mistress.
दृढ़ायुध, *m.* (*f.* ā) a hero; *lit.* firm in battle.
दृगा } *f.* the eye.
दृगी, }
दृशोपम, *m.* the white lotus (*Nelumbium speciosum*).
दृश्य, 1, *m.* (*f.* ā) visible, to be seen; beautiful, pleasing: 2, *m.* (in Arithm.) a given number or quantity.
दृश्यता, *f.* (*m.* °त्व) visibility; vision, sight.
दृश्यमान, *m.* (*f.* matī) under the view, under survey.
दृषद्वती, *f. pr. n.* a certain river.
दृष्ट, *m.* (*f.* ā) seen, apparent, visible.
दृष्टआकार, *m.* a visible form or appearance.
दृष्टकूट, *m.* a riddle, enigma. [seen.
दृष्टवत, *m.* (*f.* vatī) *adj.* seeing, beholding; having
दृष्टवन्त } *m.* (*f.* vatī) = दृष्टवत, *q.v.*
दृष्टवान }
दृष्टान्त, *m.* an example, illustration, parable, simile, trope. — *k.* to liken, give an example.
दृष्टि, *f.* a looking at, seeing, sight, view, vision; the eye, pupil of the eye. —*k.* to look, look at, take a view of, cast the eyes upon.
दृष्टिकूट, *more commonly* दृष्टकूट, *q.v.*
दृष्टिकृत, *m.* a species of flower (*Hibiscus mutabilis*).
दृष्टिगोचर, perceptible, visible, in view.
दृष्टिधक, *m. pr. n.* a son of Ikshwāku.
दृष्टिनिपात } *m.* a look, glance at.
दृष्टिपात }
दृष्टिविषयक, *m.* any visible object.
दे, 1, imperat. 2nd pers. sing. of देना; 2, (*pl.* दें) the third pers. sing. of the dependent mode of देना.
देआड़ा, *m.* a white ants' hill.
देइ (a Braj form) = दिया, *q.v.*
देइहौं (see इहौं) in Braj = मैं देऊंगा.
देई in Braj = (1) दिया (2) दीजिये, *qq.v.*
देउ = देव, *q.v.*
देउब (*poet.*) = मैं देऊंगा. [pers. pl. imperat. of देना.
देओ, 1, = देव, *q.v.*: 2, *m.* a demon, sprite: 3, 2nd
देओट, *more com.* दीवट, *q.v.*
देओनल = देवनल, *q.v.*
देओटी, *more com.* देवटी, *q.v.*
देंउ in Braj = देऊं or देऊंगा.
देंगी, *f.* bounty, liberality.

देंगे, *m. pl.* (*f.* देंगी) *fut. of* देना.
देंलें, *m.* pecuniary transactions on interest, debts and credits, gambling, commercial transaction, traffic, [barter.
देंहिं in Braj = देंगे, *q.v.*
देखना, *a. int.* to see, look: *t.* to look at, behold, see, view, observe, perceive, inspect, mark; to experience.—*bhālnā*, to look at, see. *Dekh lenā*, to take and see; e. g. *Dekh to lo*, take and see! look and see!
देखत्यों, a poetical form of देखता हूं.
देखनिहार in Braj = देखनेहारा. See नि.
देखपेख, redupl. of the bases of देखना and पेखना.
देखलाना = दिखलाना, *q.v.*
देखलेना; see *s.v.* देखना. [tator, observer.
देखवैया, *m.* an on-looker, beholder, viewer, spec-
देखा, 1, *m.* (*f.* ī) seen, perceived: 2, *m.* a seeing,
देखाई = दिखाई, *q.v.* [sight. —*k.* to see, look at.
देखादेखी, *f.* the looking at each other, competition, emulation, the being within sight (of objects).
देखाना, *t.* to shew, exhibit, display, expose; *lit.* to
देखेये (corruption) = देखाये. [cause to see.
देखो, *exclam.* see! lo! behold!
देख्यो in Braj = (1) देखा (2) देखियो.
देग, *f.* a cooking-pot, cauldron, crock, kettle.
देगचा, *m.* } dimin. of देग, *q.v.*
देगची, *f.* }
देगम्बर, *more prop.* दिगम्बर, *q.v.*
देजा, *m.* a dowry, portion which the wife brings to the husband in marriage; presents made by the bride's family to the bridegroom with the view of securing a husband of higher rank.
देजू, *m.* part of a portion or dowry.
देढ़पेला, *m.* a swelled testicle.
देढ़, *more prop.* डेढ़, *q.v.*
देत = देता (देना). See त, 5.
देदी = दे दिई (दे देना).
देदीप्यमान, *m.* (*f.* matī) very radiant or lustrous.
देन, *m.* a giving (in comp.; *e. g.* लेनदेन).
देनदार, *m.* a debtor.
देनदारी, *f.* debt.
देनलेन = देंलें, *q.v.*
देनवारा, *m.* (*f.* ī) *more prop.* देनेवाला (देना).
देनहार } *m.* (*f.* in *or* ī) a giver. See हार.
देनहारा }
देना, *t.* to give, grant, yield, resign, allow, let, permit, afford, emit, cause, occasion, produce, lay eggs.
देनापाना, *m.* profit and loss; a settling one's affairs.
देनालेना = देंलें, *q.v.*
देनौं in Braj = देना, *q.v.*
देवदार, *m.* the mast-tree (*Uvaria longifolia*).
देवरा, *m.* (*f.* ī) left (not right).
देबाचा, *m.* preface, introduction.
देबी, *more prop.* देवी, *q.v.*
देमारना, *t.* to dash to the ground, throw, stamp.

देय, fit to be given, proper to be given, due.
देयगी, a Braj form = **देगा** (**देना**).
देर, *f.* slowness, tardiness, delay, lateness.
देरा, *m.* a tent, dwelling.
देरी, *f.* lateness, delay, slowness. — *k.* to delay, be late. — *lagnā*, to be late, be slow.
देरीना, old, ancient, wise, cunning.
देलही } **देह्ली** } *more prop.* **दिल्ली**, *q.v.*
देव, 1, a corruption of **देओ**, 3, *q.v.*: 2, *m.* (*f.* ī) a deity, god; a king; a husband's brother; the term is applicable as a surname to Brāhmaṇs and to Kāyaths: also, to either of the thirty-three crores of the gods of the Hindoos; and hence, in the ingenious system of reckoning by symbols adopted by Hindoos in their poetry, this word is a symbol for 33.
देवऋण = **देवर्ण** = **देवकर्म्म**, *q.v.*
देवक, *m.* (*f.* ikā) the inhabitants of one of the Varshas or divisions of the world: *lit.* like a deity, celestial, divine.
देवकन्या, *f.* a celestial nymph, divine maiden.
देवकर्द्दम, *m.* a certain fragrant paste (of sandal, agallochum, camphor, and saffron-flower).
देवकर्म, *more prop.* **देवकर्म्म**, *q.v.*
देवकायहर, *m.* water-cresses.
देवकाष्ट, *m.* a species of pine (*Pinus devadāru*).
देवकिरी, *f.* one of the female personifications (*rāgiṇi*) of the musical modes. [dev, and mother of Krishṇ.
देवकी, *f. pr. n.* the daughter of Devak, wife of Vasu-
देवकीनन्दन, *m.* the son of Devakī, *i. e.* Kṛishṇ.
देवकीय, appertaining to any deity.
देवकुण्ड, *m.* a natural spring.
देवकुसुम, *m.* cloves. [(*rāgiṇī*) of the musical modes.
देवगान्धारी, *f.* one of the female personifications
देवगायन, *m.* (*f.* ā *or* ī) a celestial chorister.
देवगिरी, *f. pr. n.* (1) of one of the female personifications (*rāgiṇi*) of the musical modes (2) of a
देवगीरी = **देवगिरी**, *q.v.* [certain mountain.
देवगृह, *m.* a dwelling of the gods, a celestial or planetary sphere, a temple.
देवगे, *m.* (*f.* ī) *more com.* **देओगे** (**देना**).
देवजानी, *more prop.* **देवयानी**, *q.v.*
देवट, *more com.* **दीवट**, *q.v.*
देवटी, *f.* a torch, lamp.
देवट्टी, *f.* a kind of gull (*Larus ridibundus*).
देवठान, *f. pr. n.* the second day of the moon of Kārttik *shukl-paksh* (on which Vishṇu awakes from his sleep of four months).
देवढ़ी } **देवढ़ी** } *more prop.* **ड्योढ़ी**, *q.v.*
देवतरु, *m.* the holy fig-tree; a tree of paradise, the tree of plenty; any venerable or ancient tree; the place of assembling in a village.
देवतस्थान = **देवथान**, *q.v.*
देवता, (not infl.) 1, *f.* the state or the nature of a deity, the attribute of divinity: 2, *m. f.* any Hindoo deity: the term is applied (in respectful address) to a religious superior, "Your Holiness".
देवताड़, *m.* a grass (*Andropogon serratus*).
देवतान्तार, 1, another god: 2, in the midst of
देवतिन, *f.* a goddess. [the gods.
देवतीर्थ, *m.* the part of the hand that is sacred to the gods, viz. the tips of the fingers.
देवते, often used as a nom. pl. of **देवता**.
देवत्व *m.* = **देवता**, *q.v.* [the rain.
देवथान, *f. m.* (?) a place of idols, an idol-temple: *met.*
देवदत्त, *m.* (*f.* ā) an epithet of anything god-given: *lit.* given by (or to) the gods. [Hāteeghosh).
देवदानी, *f.* a species of creeper (commonly called
देवदारु, *m.* an epithet applied to (1) a species of pine (*Pinus devadāru*) (2, in Bengal) a certain medicinal tree (*Uvaria longifolia*) (3, in the peninsula) another tree (*Erythoxylon sideroxyloidex*).
देवदूत, *m.* (*f.* ī) = **देवदूतक**, *q.v.*
देवदूतक, *m.* (*f.* ikā) a messenger of the gods, a divine envoy, an angel.
देवदृष्टी, *f.* divine vision, divine intelligence.
देवद्विज, *m. pr. n.* (1) of one of the divisions of Shākdweep (2) of Vrihaspati.
देवधान्य, *m.* a kind of grain (*Andropogon saccharatus*) cultivated in many parts of Hindustan.
देवधुनि, *f. pr. n.* the Ganges. [used in incense.
देवधूप, *m.* a certain fragrant resin (*Bdellium*)
देवन, a Braj pl. of **देव**. See **न**, 6.
देवनल, *m.* a kind of reed (*Arundo Bengalensis*) the stem of which is used in writing.
देवनागर, *m.* = **देवनागरी**, *q.v.*
देवनागरी, *f. pr. n.* the Sanskrit character (used by the Hindoos in their sacred writings).
देवनामरवा, *m.* a kind of shrub (*Ocymum*).
देवनिन्दक, *m.* (*f.* ikā) a reviler of the gods, heretic, unbeliever. [the gods, blasphemy, heresy, atheism.
देवनिन्दा, *f.* contemptuous speech in reference to
देवनिर्मित, *m.* (*f.* ā) any natural or created object: *lit.* god-formed.
देवपति, *m.* lord of the deities, *i. e.* Indra.
देवपथ, *m.* the celestial path or way, the firmament, heaven. [the gods, an idolater, pagan.
देवपूजक, *m.* (*f.* ikā) a worshipper of idols or of
देवपूजा, *f.* the worship of idols or of the gods, idolatry, paganism.
देवपूजिका, *f.* (*m.* **देवपूजक**) an idolatress.
देवबल्लभ, *m.* a species of tree (*Rottleria tinctoria*) used in dyeing. [of paradise (3) of any temple.
देवभवन, *m.* an epithet (1) of the holy figtree (2)
देवभाषितमिति, (**देव भाषितम इति**) thus spake the god. [*pr. n.* a minister of King Shālva.
देवमान, *m.* the residence or dwelling of the gods:
देवमास, *m.* the eighth month of pregnancy.
देवयान, *m.* the car or vehicle of a god.
देवयानी, *f. pr. n.* a daughter of Ushanas or wife of Yayāti and mother of Yadu and Turvasu.

देवर, *m.* a husband's brother (*esp.* his younger [brother).
देवराज, *m.* an epithet of Indra.
देवराणी, *f.* a husband's younger brother's wife.
देवरात, *m.* (*f.* ā) god-given: a sort of crane: *pr. n.* (1) of a certain king, son of Suketu and descendant of Nimi (2) of a certain king, son of Karambhi: an epithet (1) of Rājā Pareekshit (2) of Shunah-sheph after he was received into the family of Vishwāmitra.
देवरिषि, *more prop.* **देवर्षि**, *q.v.*
देवरूप, *m.* (*f.* ā) = **देवरूपी**, *q.v.*
देवरूपी, *m.* (*f.* iṇī) of divine form, godlike.
देवर्धा = **देवकर्म्म**, *q.v.*
देवर्षि, *more prop.* **देवर्षि**, *q v.*
देवर्षि, *m.* a sage of the class of demigods, a divine sage: an epithet of Nārad.
देवल, 1, = **देवालय**, *q.v.*: 2, *m.* an attendant upon an idol: 3, *m. pr. n.* a certain *rishi.*
देवलता, *f.* double jasmine.
देवली, *f.* a fish-scale; scab, scar, cicatrix: a small [lamp.
देवलोक, *m. pr. n.* heaven, paradise, the particular sphere or heaven of any deity, any one of the seven superior worlds from earth to the highest (*Satyalok*) as distinguished from those below the earth.
देववर, *m.* any divine boon or blessing.
देववान, *m. pr. n.* a son of Devak.
देववाणी, 1, *more prop.* **देववाणी**, *q.v.*: 2, *f. pr. n.* an epithet of the Sanskrit language; *lit.* the language of the gods.
देववृक्ष, *m.* an epithet of certain trees (1) of a tree of paradise (2) of *Echites scholaris* (3) of *Bdellium.*
देवव्रत, *m.* a vow or obligation to any deity.
देवशर्मन, *m. pr. n.* a certain Brāhmaṇ.
देवसभा, *f.* an assembly of the gods.
देवसर, *m. pr. n.* a certain place (*lit.* the pool of the [gods).
देवस्थान, *m.* = **देवथान**, *q.v.*
देवस्व, *m.* religious endowments, property applicable to the purposes of religion.
देवहरा, *m.* a temple where idols are worshipped.
देवहिं (poet.) = **देवको**. See **हिं**.
देवहू, a designation of the left ear: prop. *adj.* in[voking the gods.
देवहूति, *f.* invocation of a deity; a certain invocation presented to the gods: *pr. n.* a daughter of Swayambhū-Manu, and wife of Kardam.
देवहूती, *f.* a kind of spell; *pr. n.* a daughter of Swayambhū-Manu and Satrūpa.
देवा, 1, *m.* a god, a deity: 2, *m.* a giver: 3, *f.* a certain flower (*Hibiscus mutabilis*); a certain plant (*Marsilea* [*quadrifolia*).
देवागत, *more prop.* **दैवागत**, *q. v.*
देवान, *more prop.* **दीवान**, *q.v.*
देवाना = (1) **दिलाना** (2) **दीवाना**, *qq.v.*
देवापि, *m. pr. n.* a certain Hindoo sage.
देवार्पी, *m. pr. n.* a certain *rishi*, son of Ṛishṭisheṇ.
देवाल, 1, = **देवालय**, *q.v.*: 2, *m.* a giver.
देवालई, *more prop.* (1) **देवालय** (2) **देवालेई**, *qq.v.*
देवालबन्द, *m.* a soldier.
देवालय, *m.* a residence of the gods, a division of heaven, any idol-temple, a pagoda.
देवाला, 1, *more prop.* **देवालय**, *q.v.*: 2, *m.* bankruptcy.
देवालिया, *m.* a bankrupt.
देवाली = **दिवाली**, *q.v.*
देवालेई, *f.* (= **देलें**) traffic, barter.
देवाले, *more prop.* **देवालय**, *q. v.*
देवावृद्ध, *m. pr. n.* (1) of a certain mountain (2) of a certain prince, father of Babhru.
देवाहुति, *f.* an oblation to the gods.
देवाहूत, *adj.* invoking the gods.
देवि, *more prop.* **देवी**, *q.v.*
देविका, *f. pr. n.* (see **देवक**) a certain river.
देवी, *f.* (*m.* **देव**) a goddess; the wife of any deity, but especially Durgā (wife of Shiv); a queen: a certain plant (*Trigonella corniculata*).
देवीकोट्ट, *m. pr. n.* the city of Vān, probably Davicotta, on the Coromandel coast.
देवीपति, *m.* an epithet of the husband of any goddess, but especially of Shiv.
देवेन्द्र, *m.* the chief of the gods (an epithet (1) [of Indra (2) of Shiv.
देवैं in Braj = **देवें** = **दें**, *q.v.*
देवैया, *m.* a giver, bestower.
देवैश्वर्य, *m.* the dominion of the gods.
देवोत्तर, *m.* land held free in the name of Hindoo deities (ostensibly for the provision of all the necessaries of divine worship).
देवोत्थान, *m. pr. n.* the awaking and rising of Vishṇu on the eleventh of the bright half of Kārttik.
देवोद्यान, *m.* a sacred grove.
देव्यागम, *more prop.* **दैव्यागम**, *q.v.*
देश, *m.* a place, part, side, direction, country, region, territory. *Desh-desh*, from country to country.
देशकार, *m.* a certain musical mode (*rāg*?) sung in the morning.
देशकारी, *f.* a certain musical mode (*rāgiṇī*).
देशत्याग, *m.* the abandoning one's country, emigration, voluntary exile.
देशत्यागी, *m.* (*f.* inī) an emigrant, exile.
देशधर्म्म, *m.* the law or usage of a country.
देशनिकाला, *m.* banishment, exile.
देशबहन / **देशबहिन** } *f.* a fellow-countrywoman.
देशबेवहार, *more prop.* **देशव्यवहार**, *q.v.*
देशभाई, *m.* a fellow-countryman.
देशभाषा, *f.* vernacular language, local dialect.
देशरीति, *f.* the customs of a country, local usage.
देशवाला, *m.* (*f.* ī) a native of a country.
देशव्यवस्था, *f.* the laws of a country.
देशव्यवहार, *m.* customs of a country, local usage.
देशव्यहार (*corruption*) = **देशव्यवहार**, *q.v.*
देशाख, *m.* a certain musical mode (*rāg*?) sung at noon in the spring.
देशाचार, *m.* the usage of a country, local usage.

देशाटन, *m.* the wandering through a country or countries, peregrination.

देशाधिकारी. *m.* (*f.* iṇī) = **देशाधिपति**.

देशाधिपति, *m.* (*f.* patnī) the ruler of a country, a governor, monarch.

देशान्त, *m.* the frontier of a country.

देशान्तर, *m.* a foreign country.

देशान्तरी, *m.* (*f.* iṇī) a foreigner.

देशावर, *m.* a foreign country.

देशावरी, *m.* (*f.* iṇī) a foreigner; a kind of dove; a kind of betel-leaf: *lit.* foreign.

देशिनी, *f.* the index or fore-finger.

देशी, 1, *m.* (*f.* iṇī) a native of a country: *lit.* appertaining to a country, indigenous, local: 2, *f.* appearance. [locality, native.

देशीय, *m.* (*f.* ā) appertaining to a country or

देशैश्वर्य, *m.* the magnificence of a country.

देश्य, *m.* (*f.* ā) 1, a witness: 2, a native of a country, (one) belonging to a country.

देषना = **देखना**, *q.v.*

देष्ण, *m.* giving, a gift. [देश.

देस, for words beginning thus, see under the form

देसवाल, *more prop.* **देशवाला**, *q.v.*

देसारना; see **दशार्णा**.

देसू in Braj = **देश**, *q. v.*

देह, *f.* (*m.*?) the body. — *durānā*, to conceal or cover one's nakedness. — *sambhālnā*, to keep one's spirits up, be firm, recover oneself.

देहक, *m.* (*f.* ikā) appertaining to the body.

देहक्षय, *m.* sickness, disease.

देहच्युत, *m.* (*f.* ā) separated or detached from the body (as excrement, or the spirit).

देहत्याग, *m.* death, voluntary death. [incarnate.

देहधारी, *m.* (*f.* iṇī) possessing a body, embodied,

देहयात्रा, *f.* dying, death. [Jains; a Hindu temple.

देहरा, *m.* a temple where idols are worshipped by

देहरी / **देहलि** } *f.* = **देहली**, *q.v.*

देहली, *f.* the threshold of a door, the lower part of the wooden frame of a door, the raised terrace in front of a door.

देहवत / **देहवन्त** } *m.* (*f.* vatī) = **देहवान**, *q. v.*

देहवान, *m.* (*f.* vatī) any embodied creature: *lit.* embodied, corporeal, appertaining to the body.

देहा, a poetical form of **देह**, *q. v.*

देहात्मवादी, *m.* (*f.* inī) a materialist, charvak: *lit.* attributing spiritual nature to the body.

देहान्त, *m.* the end of the body, *i. e.* death.

देहान्तर, *m.* another body, another embodied state (in the doctrine of Metempsychosis).

देहि, 1, **देह**, *q.v.*: 2, (pl. **देहिं**) = **देता है**.

देहिका, *f.*; see **देहक**.

देहिन, *m.* (*f.* ī) = **देहवान**, *q.v.*

देही, 1, *m.* (*f.* inī) = **देहवान**, *q. v.*: 2, = **देहीको** (an emphat. poet. form of the acc. of **देह**: see **ई**, 4): 3, *f.* = [**देह**, *q. v.*

देहु in Braj = **देओ**, give ye (**देना**).

देहौं in Braj = **मैं देऊंगा**.

दै in Braj = **दे**, give thou (**देना**).

दैअहिं (poet.) = **दैवको**. See **हिं**.

दैखना in Braj = **देखना**, *q. v.*

दैजा = **देजा**, *q. v.* [binder of the Daityas.

दैतनबन्धेव, *m.* an epithet of Vishṇu; *lit.* the

दैतेय, *m.* (*f.* ī) a Daitya, an offspring of Diti; *lit.* appertaining to the Daityas, sprung from Diti.

दैत्य, *m.* (*f.* ā) a being hostile to the gods, demon, evil spirit, Titan or giant of the Hindoo mythology; *lit.* a descendant of Diti.

दैत्ययुग, *m.* an age of the demons (consisting of 12000 divine years, or the sum of the four yugs or cycles of men.

दैत्ययोनि, *m.* *f.* the place or source of demons.

दैदीप्यमान, *m.* (*f.* matī) = **देदीप्यमान**, *q. v.*

दैन, 1, *m.* poverty, wretchedness: 2, *adj.* daily.

दैना in Braj = **देना**, *q. v.*

दैनिक, *m.* (*f.* ī) diurnal, daily.

दैनिकी, *f.* a day's hire or wages.

दैनौ in Braj = **देना**, *q. v.*

दैन्य, *m.* affliction, humbleness, miserable state, poverty, meanness, covetousness.

दैबी, *more prop.* **दैवी**, *q. v.*

दैमारयौ in Braj = **देमारा**.

दैमारा, *more prop.* **देमारा**. See **देसारना**.

दैतय, a corruption of **दैत्य**, *q. v.*

दैया, *f.* a mother; the stand that children run to in playing at hide-and-seek.

दैयौ in Braj = **दिया**, 1, *q. v.*

दैव, 1, *m.* one of the forms of marriage (the gift of a daughter at a sacrifice to the officiating priest); the part of the hand sacred to the gods (the tips of the fingers); an oblation to the gods; divine power; destiny, fate, fortune: 2, *m.* (*f.* ī) a celestial being: *lit.* appertaining to divinity or to a deity.

दैवः, *more prop.* **दैव**, 2, *q. v.*

दैवक, *m.* (*f.* ikā) an astrologer, almanac-maker.

दैवकर्म, *m* a religious rite, sacrificing, any observance due to a deity from a worshipper.

दैवगति, *f.* the run of fate, an event for which the gods rather than men are answerable, misfortune, accident.

दैवघटना, *f.* = **दैवगति**, *q. v.*

दैवचिन्तक, *m.* (*f.* ikā) a fatalist.

दैवचिन्ता, *f.* reliance on fate, fatalism.

दैवज्ञ, *m.* (*f.* ā) an astrologer, fortune-teller, prophet: *lit.* acquainted with fate.

दैवज्ञान, *m.* supernatural knowledge.

दैवत, 1. appertaining to a god or to the gods, divine: 2, *m.* a deity, an idol, the deities.

दैवतपति, *m.* lord of the deities, i.e. Indra.

दैवयुग, *m.* an age or cycle of the immortals.

दैवयोग, *m.* the occurrence of any unforeseen event, the intervention of destiny, chance, fortune.
दैवयोग्य, worthy of chance or fortune.
दैवलक्षक, *m.* (*f.* ikā) an astrologer, fortune-teller.
दैववाणी, *f.* a voice from heaven, oracle, divine revelation.
दैवसंयोग, connected with a deity or with fate.
दैवागत, *f.*; see **दैवागति**.
दैवागति, *f.* sudden misfortune, unforeseen disaster, accident, providential dispensation.
दैवात, (Sk. abl. of **दैव**) by the interposition of fate, by chance, accidentally, providentially, fatally: at length.
दैविका, *f.* (*m.* **दैवज्ञ**) a female astrologer, an astrologer's wife.
दैवी = (1) **दैवागति** (2) **दैवात**, *qq.v.*
दैवीगति = **दैवागति**, *q.v.*
दैवीय, *m.* (*f.* ā) appertaining to the gods or to fate.
दैवे, (*pl.* **दैवें**) in Braj = **दे**, 2, *q.v.*
दैव्य, *m.* fate, fortune, chance.
दैव्यागम = **दैवागति**, *q.v.*
दैहे (pl. **दैहैं**) } in Braj = **देंगा** (**देना**).
दैहै (pl. **दैहैं**) }
दैहौ, in Braj = **देओगे** (**देना**).
दैहौं, in Braj = **देऊंगा** (**देना**).
दो, two (२). *Do jīse honā*, to be pregnant (female). This word is frequent in composition as an inseparable prefix; and so used, it is often qualified into **दु** and **दू**, *qq.v.* It is very commonly repeated, and is then reduplicative or descriptive; *e. g.* **दो**₂ two each, two at a time, in twos, by twos. When used to double past participles it is placed between the root and the termination (e. g. **जा**₂ **कर**, i.e. **जा जाकर**), but when it is used to double *present* participles it is placed after the sign; e. g. **जाते**₂, i.e. **जाते जाते**.
दोआ; see (1) **दुआ** (2) **दूआ** (3) **दोहा**.
दोइ in Braj, emphatic for **दो**, *q. v.*
दोउ in Braj = **दोइ** and **दोनों**, *qq.v.*
दोउअन in Braj = **दोनों**, *q.v.*
दोऊ (Rām). = **दोइ** and **दोनों**, *qq.v.*
दोऊन in Braj = **दोनों**, *q.v.*
दों in Braj = **दूं** or **दूंगा** (**देना**).
दोंकना, *a. int.* to growl.
दोंकी, *f.* bellows.
दोंर, *m.* a species of snake.
दोक, *m.* a two-year old foal.
दोकला, *m.* a double padlock; iron chains for the feet of criminals.
दोकसी, two-personed, fit for two persons.
दोकाल, *m.* both worlds.
दोकोहा, *m.* a two-hunched camel (*Camelus Bactrianus*).
दोख, *provincial for* **दोष**, *q. v.*
दोख़्त, *f.* sewing, a stitch.
दोख़्तर, *more prop.* **दुख़्तर**, *q. v.*
दोखी, 1, *m.* (*f.* in or inī) *provincial for* **दोषी**, *q.v.*: 2, *f.* a mound raised to indicate the junction between two boundaries.
दोगंग, in two streams (a river).
दोगण्डीचिट्टी, a fomenter of quarrels; a go-between, one who flatters both parties in a dispute. The allusion is to a certain children's game, in which they rub a tamarind-seed on one side till a mark is produced on it, and then throw it like a die: the thrower wins if the mark turn up. The seed thus prepared is called *chiṭṭi*, and if by fraud it be marked on both sides (so as always to win) it is called *dogandi*.
दोगर, *m.* a certain marauding tribe in north-western India.
दोगाड़ा, *m.* a musket that carries two balls: *lit.* *m.* (*f.* ī) twice, double.
दोगाना, *m.* two genuflexions in prayer: *lit.* double, two-fold.
दोचः, *m.* the second reservoir to which water is raised for the purpose of irrigation.
दोचल्ला, *m.* a roof sloping two ways.
दोचार, *f.* an interview.
दोचिताई, *f.* suspense, absence of mind, abstraction.
दोचित्ता = **दुचित्ता**, *q.v.*
दोचोबा, two-poled (a tent).
दोज़ख़, *m.* hell; *met.* the stomach.
दोज़ख़वाला, *m.* (*f.* ī) = **दोज़ख़ी**, *q.v.*
दोज़ख़ी, the people of hell (i.e. the damned); *met.* a glutton: *lit.* hellish, hell-deserving.
दोज़र्बी, double-barrelled (a gun).
दोज़ानू बैठना, *a. int.* to sit in the Persian fashion, *i. e.* to kneel and sit back on the heels.
दोजिया, *f.* a pregnant female.
दोजीरा, *m.* a kind of rice.
दोजीवा, *f.* a pregnant female.
दोभा, married to a second wife.
दोटूक, two-pieced: clear, plain, clean.—*honā*, to be adjusted, be completed.
दोड़, *more prop.* **दौड़**, *q.v.*
दोता, a kind of cloth; a bending the body: *lit.* twice, double, doubled, bent.
दोतारा, *m.* a kind of shawl; a guitar with two strings: [*lit.* double-threaded.
दोताव } **दोता**, *q.v.*
दोताह }
दोताही, *f.* cloths that are lined: *lit.* two-plied, double.
दोदाना, *t.* to deny.
दोदामी, *f.* flowered muslin, the flowers worked with a needle.
दोदिला, wavering, doubtful, in suspense, absent in mind.
दोधारा, *m.* (*f.* ī) two-edged (a sword).
दोनली, double-barrelled (a gun).
दोना, *m.* a kind of flower (species of *Artemisia*); southern-wood: leaves folded up in the shape of a cup (for holding betel, flowers, boiled rice, sweetmeats, etc.); a basket or bucket made of large leaves.
दोनाली, double-barrelled (a gun).
दोनों, (see **ओं**) both, the both, the both of them.—*wakt milnā* (the two times [*i. e.* day and night] meeting) expresses the evening twilight. *Donoṅke donoṅ*, a strengthened form for *donoṅ*.

दोनौ / दोनौं } in Braj = **दोनों**, *q.v.*

दोपट्टा = **दुपट्टा**, *q.v.*

दोपयाज़ा, *m.* a kind of stew (meat dressed with onions).

दोपर = **दोके ऊपर**.

दोपरता, double, of two folds.

दोपलका, *m.* a kind of pigeon; a kind of stone for a ring: *lit.* adj. *m.* (*f.* ī) having two eyelids.

दोपस्ता, pregnant.

दोपहर, *f.* the end of the second watch, mid-day, noon.—*rātko*, midnight.

दोपहरिया = **दुपहरिया**, *q.v.*

दोपहरी, adj. *m.* (*f.* iṇī) meridian.

दोपैकर, *pr. n.* the sign Gemini.

दोबर, double, twofold.

दोबारा, twice.

दोबासी = **दुभाषिया**, *q.v.*

दोबिसवी, *f.* an allowance of ten per cent., *i. e.* of two biswas out of twenty.

दोबे = **दुबे**, *q.v.*

दोबेर, twice.

दोभयान, two-fisted, ambidextrous, strong.

दोभाषिया = **दुभाषिया**, *q.v.*

दोमट, *m.* a mixture of two soils, clay and sand.

दोमटिकार, a certain subdivision of the Brāhmaṇ tribe.

दोमुंहा, (*f.* ī) = **दुमुंहा**, *q.v.*

दोय, a Braj emph. form of **दो**, *q.v.*

दोयम, the second.

दोर, twice-ploughed land.

दोरंग, *m.* (*f.* ā) a double-dealer, hypocrite; a piebald animal, mongrel: *lit.* of two colours, piebald; mongrel: *met.* whimsical, capricious, double-dealing.

दोरंगी, 1, *m.* (*f.* inī) = **दोरंग**, *q.v.*: 2, *f.* the having two colours: *met.* double-dealing, duplicity, deceit, hypocrisy, capriciousness.

दोरगा; see (1) **दुर्गा** (2) **दोरग्गा**.

दोरग्गा, *m.* (*f.* ī) a mongrel; a person of double breed having good qualities on one side and bad on the other: *adj.* capricious, whimsical.

दोरस, *m.* a mixture of two soils.

दोराहा, *m.* a road that branches off into two different directions.

दोरी, *f.* a chain or line with which land is measured.

दोरुखा, *m.* (*f.* ī) = **दुरुख़ा**, *q.v.*

दोरोया, two-faced, double.

दोल, *m.* a swinging; a swing, litter, doolie, swinging cot; a certain festival on the fourteenth of Phāgun, (the swinging of the juvenile Kṛishṇ).

दोलड़, double, having two rows.

दोलड़ा, *m.* (*f.* ī) a double-dealer, etc.; a double-stringed necklace: lit. *adj.* acting a double part, going from one party to another.

दोलत्ती = **दुलत्ती**, *q.v.*

दोलमाल क°, to swing, wave, undulate; to hesitate.

दोलयात्रा (*contraction*) = **दोलायात्रा**, *q.v.*

दोला, *f.* a swing, swinging hammock, small litter suspended on a bamboo and carried by men; fluctuation, incertitude.

दोलायमान, *m.* (*f.* matī) *adj.* swinging, being swung; vacillating, doubting, perplexed.

दोलायात्रा, *f.* the swing-festival (a certain festival in honour of Krishṇ when figures of him and of Rādhā are carried about in a litter or swung in an ornamental swing).

दोलावः, *m.* any well that has two buckets and ropes.

दोलिका, *f.* a swing.

दोलोही = **दुलोही**, *q.v.*

दोवचन, *m.* (in Gram.) the dual number.

दोवापी, *more prop.* **देवापी**, *q.v.*

दोविधि = **द्विविध**, *q.v.*

दोश, the shoulder: a kind of lac.

दोशमाल, *m.* a towel used by butchers.

दोशाला, a kind of plaid made of two shawls sewed together. A single breadth of a shawl is never worn by Indians.

दोशीज़गी, *f.* virginity.

दोशीज़ा, *f.* a virgin.

दोष, *m.* defect, blemish, fault, damage, vice, crime, sin, offence, blame, reproach, calumny; disorder of the humours of the body, defect in the functions of bile, circulation, phlegm, or wind.—*lagānā*, to blame, calumniate, accuse.—*honā*, to be sick after childbirth (from neglect of regimen).

दोषक, *m.* (*f.* ikā) ill, low, infamous, contemptible.

दोषकर, *m.* (*f.* ī) hurtful, doing injury to, deteriorating.

दोषकल्पन, *m.* a reprehending, condemning.

दोषगायक, *m.* (*f.* ikā) a calumniator, etc.: lit. *adj.* singing the defects (of others); *hence*, censorious, slanderous, etc.

दोषग्रस्त, *m.* (*f.* ā) a sinner: *prop.* seized by or sunk in crime, guilty.

दोषग्राहक, *m.* (*f.* ikā) = **दोषग्राही**, *q.v.*

दोषग्राही, *m.* (*f.* iṇī) *adj.* laying hold of defects; *hence*, censorious, malicious, malignant.

दोषता, *m.* fault, defect, blame, objection.

दोषदायक, *m.* (*f.* ikā) a fault-finder, accuser, calumniator: lit. *adj.* attributing blame, etc.

दोषना, *t.* to find fault, blame, accuse.

दोषपत्र, *m.* an indictment, bill of accusation.

दोषवत / **दोषवन्त** / **दोषवान** } *m.* (*f.* vatī) = **दोषी**, *q.v.*

दोषाच्छादन, *m.* a covering sin or fault.

दोषापत्ति, *f.* the misfortune or calamity of guilt.

दोषिक, *m.* (*f.* ā *or* ī) = **दोषी**, *q.v.*

दोषित, *m.* (*f.* ā) blamed, censured, calumniated, falsely accused (*esp.* of adultery); violated, contaminated, corrupted, spoiled.

दोषिता, *f.* a girl who has been violated or deflowered.

दोषिन, *m.* (*f.* ṇī) = **दोषी**, *q.v.*

दोषी, *m.* (*f.* iṇī) a criminal, etc.: *lit.* faulty, blameworthy, defective, bad, wicked, guilty, criminal.

दोस; for words beginning thus, but not given below, see under the form **दोष** or **दोश**.

दोसर, *a corruption of* **दूसरा**, *q.v.*

दोसरी, *f.* ? the ploughing land twice; twice-ploughed land.

दोसाई = **दोसाही**, *q. v.*

दोसाद, *m.* a certain low caste of Hindoos residing in and about Patna whose occupation it is to remove carcases and act as executioners; hog-keepers.

दोसाही, *adj.* (lands) yielding two crops a-year.

दोसी, *m.* thick sour milk: a Muhammadan milkman.

दोसूता, *m.* a kind of cloth the threads of which are double.

दोसेरा, *m.* (or *f.* ī) a weight of two sérs.

दोस्त, *m.* a friend, sweetheart.

दोस्तदार, *m.* a friend, sweetheart.

दोस्तदारी, *f.* = **दोस्ती**, *q.v.*

दोस्ती, *f.* friendship, friendliness, love, affection.

दोहड़िका, *f.* the Prākrit metre called *Dohā* (a species of stanza of four lines, containing thirteen and eleven syllabic instants alternately).

दोहता, *m.* a grandson (daughter's son).

दोहती, *f.* a granddaughter (daughter's daughter).

दोहत्तड़, *f.* (*m.* ?) a blow, slap or pat with both hands.

दोहद, *m.* wish, desire, morbid desire, the longing of pregnant females, the desired object of a pregnant female, pregnancy.

दोहदलक्षण, *m.* the fœtus, embryo.

दोहदवती, *f.* a pregnant female longing for anything.

दोहदान्विता, *f.* = **दोहदवती**, *q. v.*

दोहन, 1, *m.* a milk-vessel, milk-pail; milking: 2, *m.* (*f.* ā) anything that yields milk or other desirable objects.

दोहना, 1, see **दोहन**, 2: 2, *t.* to milk.

दोहनी, *f.* a milk-vessel, milk-pail.

दोहर, *m.* double sheet: a sheath: the old bed of a river: land that yields two crops in a year.

दोहरा, *m.* a distich: *adj. m.* (*f.* ī) twofold.

दोहराना, *t.* to double, repeat.

दोहराव, *m.* the act of doubling, reduplication, repetition.

दोहलवती, *more prop.* **दोहदवती**, *q. v.*

दोहली, *f.* ? service-lands; lands given to Brāhmaṇs.

दोहा, *m.* (see **दोहड़िका**) a couplet, distich.

दोहाई, *f.* a crying out for justice (*lit.* a crying twice, 'alas!'), complaint, plaint, exclamation; an oath. — *tihāī k.* to make reïterated complaints. — *dená*, (with gen. *fem.* of object) to make an appeal to.

दोहान, *m.* (*f.* ī) a young bullock, steer.

दोहाय, *more com.* **दोहाई**, *q. v.*

दोहाव, *m.* the zamīndār's perquisite of milk from the cultivator's cows.

दोहिन, *m.* (*f.* ī) = **दोही**, *q. v.*

दोहिनी, *f.* a milkmaid (see **दोही**).

दोही, *m.* (*f.* inī) (anything) yielding desirable objects: a milkman.

दोहुर, a sandy sub-soil.

दौ in Braj = **दौ**, *q. v.*

दौं, *f.* a fire, flame.

दौंगड़ा, *f. m.* a heavy shower.

दौंजा, *m.* a scaffold.

दौड़, *f.* a run, incursion, attack, onset, assault, endeavour, struggle, effort, race, running, gallop, course, career, military expedition.

दौड़धूप, *f.* labour and fatigue, toil, bustle. — *k.* to use great labor and exertion, to toil, bustle.

दौड़ना, *a. int.* to run, gallop, drive, rush, assault, invade; to toil.

दौड़नाधूपना, *a. int.* to run violently, use great exertion, toil.

दौड़ा, *m.* a large basket (without a lid): a highwayman (who robs on horseback).

दौड़ाक, *m.* a racer, runner.

दौड़ादौड़ी, *f.* running, contest in running, race, hurry.

दौड़ाना, *t.* to run, drive, impel, actuate, expedite, speed, despatch; *lit.* to cause to run or gallop.

दौड़ापा, *m.* a village runner or messenger.

दौड़ाहा, *m.* a runner, messenger, courier, guide.

दौड़ी, *f.* a drawn game at *chaupaṛ*.

दौतल, a corruption of **दौलत**, *q. v.*

दौना = **दोना**, *q. v.*

दौर, *m.* 1, a revolution; a windlass; reasoning in a circle; vicissitude; circuit; age: 2, the slings attached to an irrigating-basket.

दौरहा, *m.* a forest conflagration.

दौरा, *m.* a large basket (without a lid).

दौरात्म्य, *m.* wickedness, depravity.

दौरान, *m.* time, age; fortune, vicissitude; a revolution, period, cycle.

दौरी, *f.* a basket (without a lid): a rope with which a string of cattle are bound together (as in the case of a number of bullocks when threshing or when treading out the corn): a kind of sling basket used in irrigation.

दौर्गन्धि, *f.* fœtor, bad smell.

दौर्जन्य, *m.* wickedness, vileness, depravity.

दौर्भाग्य, *m.* ill-luck, misfortune.

दौर्बल्य, *m.* weakness, debility.

दौर्हा, *m.* a forest conflagration.

दौलत, *f.* happiness, riches, wealth, fortune, prosperity, state, empire, kingdom.

दौलतख़ाना, *m.* (house of fortune) a palace, a house (your house).

दौलतमन्द, wealthy, fortunate.

दौवल, a corruption of **दुर्बल**, *q. v.*

दौवान, a corruption of **दीवान**, *q. v.*

दौस, trampling, treading, thrashing, drubbing; polishing (a sword): baseness, meanness.

दौहित्र, *m.* a grandson (daughter's son).

दौहित्री, *f.* a granddaughter (daughter's daughter).

द्युत / **द्युति** } *f.* light, radiance, splendour.

द्युतिमान, *m.* (*f.* matī) a dignified person, etc.: *lit.* radiant, brilliant.

द्युतिला, *f.* a plant (*Hemionites cordifolia*).

द्यूत, *m.* gaming, playing with dice, etc.

द्यूतकार, *m.* (*f.* ī) the keeper of a gaming-house; a gambler.

द्यूतपूर्णिमा, *f.* the day of full moon in Kārttik (the night of which is spent at games of chance in honour of Lakshmee, goddess of fortune.

द्यूतसभा, *f.* a gaming-house, gaming-assembly.

द्यूताधिकारी, *m.* (*f.* iṇī) the keeper of a gaming house.

द्योतक, *adj.* shewing, explaining, making clear or manifest, illustrating; (in Gram.) *m.* an insepara-[ble particle.

द्योरानी / **द्यौरानी** } = **देवरानी**, *q.v.*

द्रविड़, *more prop.* (1) **द्रविड** (2) **द्राविड़**, *qq.v.*

द्रवना, *a.int.* to rarify, melt, dissolve; to flow: *met.* to exercise mercy, to melt in compassion towards.

द्रवहु, a poet. imperat. 2nd pers. pl. of **द्रवना**.

द्रवि in Chand = **द्रव्य**, *q.v.*

द्रविड़, *m.* (*f.* ī) a person of an out-caste tribe descended from a degraded Kshatriya.

द्रविड़ी, *f. pr. n.* of one of the female personifications (*rāgiṇī*) of music.

द्रविणनाशन, *m.* the plant *Hyperanthera morunga.*

द्रवौ / **द्रवो** } (poet.) = **द्रवहु**, *q.v.*

द्रव्य, *m.* an object, thing, substance, matter; an elementary substance (of which nine kinds are reckoned in the Hindoo philosophy, viz. earth, water, fire, air, æther, time, space, soul, intellect); wealth, property; a drug, medicament.

द्रव्यप्रिय, *m.* (*f.* ā) *adj.* loving material wealth.

द्रव्यवत / **द्रव्यवन्त** } *m.* (*f.* vatī) = **द्रव्यवान**, *q.v.*

द्रव्यवान, *m.* (*f.* vatī) *adj.* having material wealth, [rich.

द्रव्यसंचय, *m.* accumulation of wealth.

द्रव्यार्जन, *m.* the acquisition of property.

द्राक्षा, *f.* a vine; a grape.

द्राक्षाफल, *m.* a grape, g.apes.

द्राक्षारस, *m.* grape-juice, wine.

द्राघिमा, *m.* length.

द्रावक, diuretic, solvent, discutient.

द्रावकर, *m.* a kind of borax.

द्रावण, *m.* the clearing-nut; a fusing.

द्राविका, *f.* saliva.

द्राविड, 1, *m. pr. n.* (1) of the country which terminates the peninsula of Hindustān on the south; the coast of Coromandel, or the country in which Tamil is spoken (its northern limits appear to lie between the twelfth and thirteenth degrees of north latitude): (2) in a more general sense the term applies to four other countries, *viz.* Karnāṭ, Gujjarāt, Mahārāshtra, and Tilinga: 2, *m.* (*f.* i) a native of Drāvid, a Drāvidian Brāhmaṇ. [salt.

द्राविड़क, *m.* zedoary (*Curcuma zerumbet*); black

द्राविड़ी, a Dravidian female: cardamom.

द्रुकिलिम, *m.* a species of pine (*Pinus devadāru*).

द्रुत, quick, swift; run-away, escaped, flown.

द्रुतपद, *m.* a quick pa e: *adv.* quickly.

द्रुपद, *m.pr.n.* a certain ancient Hindoo king, father

द्रुम, *m.* any tree; a tree of paradise. [of Draupadī.

द्रुमन, *m.* (a Braj. pl. of **द्रुम**) trees.

द्रुमनख, *m.* a tree-claw, *i. e.* a thorn.

द्रुमल्लिक (*corruption*) = **द्रुर्मलिक**, *q.v.*

द्रुमव्याधि, *m.* lac, the animal dye or disease of trees.

द्रुमामय = **द्रुमव्याधि**, *q.v.*

द्रुमीढ़, *m. pr. n.* a certain ancient Hindoo king who on becoming a Brāhmaṇ (from a Kshatriya) abdicated his kingdom. [chief or sovereign of trees.

द्रुमेश्वर, *m.* an epithet of the palm-tree; *lit.* the

द्रुसल्लक, *m.* a certain tree (*Chironjia sapida*).

द्रुह्यु, *m. pr. n.* a certain ancient Hindoo king, son of Yayāti and Sarmishṭā.

द्रेक्काण, *m.* the regent of one third of a planetary sign (the Decanus of European astrology).

द्रोण, 1, *m.* the name (1) of a measure of capacity the same as an *ādhak* (2) of a measure of four *ādhaks* (3) of the sixteenth part of a *khari*, or forty-eight gallons (4) of a weight of thirty-six sērs, or about sixty-four pounds avoirdupois (5) of the military preceptor of the Pāṇḍus and Kurus: 2, *m.* a raven, carrion-crow: a wooden tub.

द्रोणकाक, *m.* (*f.* ī) a raven.

द्रोणपारय, *m. pr. n.* = **द्रोणाचार्य**, *q.v.*

द्रोणमुख, *m.* the capital of a district; the principal of four hundred villages. [Sinhahanu.

द्रोणा, *f.* a kind of shrub: *pr. n.* a daughter of

द्रोणाचार्य, *m. pr. n.* the military preceptor of the Pāṇḍus and Kurus.

द्रोणी, *f.* a canoe, raft, small boat made from the sheath of a plaintain-tree; a wooden tub, bucket; a [valley.

द्रोणीमुख = **द्रोणमुख**, *q.v.*

द्रोह, *m.* injury, insidious wounding, perfidy, mischief, malice, hatred, spite, trespass, offence, wrong, rebellion.

द्रोहचिन्तक, *m.* (*f.* ikā) malicious, designing.

द्रोहचिन्तन, *m.* injurious design, malice prepense, the wish, thought, or attempt to injure.

द्रोहाट, *m.* (see **दोहड़िका**) a species of metre, viz. the *Dohā* or stanza of Hindee poetry.

द्रोहिया, *m.* or *f.* = **द्रोही**, *q.v.*

द्रोही, *m.* (*f.* inī) *adj.* injuring, harming, hurting, endeavouring to hurt, mischievous, spiteful, malicious, malignant.

द्रौणिक, *m.* a field which many be sown with a *droṇ* of grain: *lit.* adj. *m.* (*f.* i) containing a *droṇ*.

द्रौणिकी, *f.* any ve.sel holding a *droṇ*.

द्रौपद, *m.* (*f.* ī) *patronym.* of **द्रुपद**, *q. v.*

द्रौपदी, *f. pr. n.* (patronym.) the daughter of Drupad and wife in common of the five Pāṇḍu princes.

द्वन्द = **द्वन्द्व**, *q. v.*

द्वन्द्व, *m.* a pair, brace, couple (especially, male and female); union of the sexes, coupling; a pair of opposite things (as heat and cold).

द्वन्द्वचारी, *m.* (*f.* iṇī) the ruddy goose, flying in cou-

द्वयाग्नि, *m.* a plant (*Plumbago zeylanica*). [ples.

द्वादश, *m.* (*f.* ī) the twelfth.

द्वादशी, *f.* the twelfth day of the half month.

द्वापर, (see **युग**) *m.pr.n.* (in Myth.) the third of the four great cycles (*yug*) comprizing 864000 years: uncertainty, doubt; the die which is marked with two points.

द्वार, *m. f.* a door, gate, gateway, passage, entrance, opening: *met.* opportunity, means, vehicle, expedient, medium by which anything is effected.

द्वारका, *f. pr. n.* a sacred place of the Hindoos on the bank of the western sea near the mouth of the gulf of Katch. It was at one time the capital of Krishṇ and is supposed to have been submerged by the sea.

द्वारकानाथ, *m.* the lord of Dwārkā, *i. e.* Krishṇ.

द्वारकापुरि / **द्वारकापुरी** } *f* = द्वारका, *q. v.*

द्वारकावासी, *m.* (*f.* inī) an inhabitant of Dwārkā (said especially of Krishṇ). [porter, warder.

द्वारपाल, *m.* (*f.* ī *or* in) a door-keeper, gate-keeper,

द्वारपालक, *m.* (*f.* ikā) / **द्वारपाली**, *m.* (*f.* inī) } = द्वारपाल, *q. v.*

द्वारबलिभुज, *m.* an epithet of the *Vak* (a sort of crane, viz. *Ardea nivea*).

द्वारा, *postp.* by means of, through. It takes the gen. m. infl., and does not itself suffer infl., e.g. *kiskedwārāse.*

द्वाराबती / **द्वारावती** } *f.* = द्वारका, *q. v.*

द्वारिक, *m.* (*f.* ā *or* ī) a doorkeeper, warder, chamberlain at the court of a Hindoo prince.

द्वारिका, 1, *more prop.* द्वारका, *q. v.*: 2, *f.* = द्वारिक, *q. v.*

द्वारिन् / **द्वारी** } *m.* (*f.* inī = द्वारिक, *q. v.*

द्वावश, a corruption of द्वादश, *q. v.*

द्वि, two. (Used in Hindee only in comp.)

द्विकर्म्मक, *adj.* having two functions or objects; (in Gram.) *m.* a causative verb.

द्विखण्ड, *m.* (*f.* ā) divided into two parts, cloven, split. [first member is a numeral.

द्विगु, *n.* (scil. समास) a compound word whose

द्विगुण, twice, doubled, towfold.

द्विगुणगित, *more prop.* द्विगुणित, *q. v.*

द्विगुणता, *f.* (*m.* °त्व) duplication.

द्विगुणाकृत, twice-ploughed (as a field).

द्विगुणित, doubled, multiplied by two, folded, invested, enveloped.

द्विगुणीकृत / **द्विगुणीभूत** } *m.* (*f.* ā) doubled, augmented.

द्विगुणोत्तर, *m.* an ambiguous reply.

द्विगुसमास = द्विगु, *q. v.*

द्विज, *m.* (*f.* ā) twice-born; *hence*, a man of either of the first three castes of the Hindoos, but particularly a Brāhmaṇ whose investiture with the sacred thread (when he arrives at the proper age) is considered a second birth.

द्विजकुत्सित, *m.* a certain tree (*Cordia myxa*).

द्विजदास, *m.* (*f.* ī) a person of the servile caste, i.e. a Shoodra (*lit.* a servant of the *dvij*). [born.

द्विजन्मा, *m.* an epithet of any Brāhmaṇ; *lit.* a twice

द्विजपत्नी, *f.* an epithet of any Brāhmaṇ's wife; *lit.* the wife of a twice-born.

द्विजप्रिया, *f.* the moon-plant (*Asclepias acida*).

द्विजराज, *m.* an epithet (1) of the moon, as lord of the twice-born (2) of Garuṛ, as king of the birds (3) of Anant, as king of the serpents.

द्विजराजा / **द्विजराजू** } *more com.* द्विजराज, *q. v.*

द्विजसेवक, *m.* (*f.* ikā) = द्विजदास, *q. v.*

द्विजा, *f.* a species of plant (*Siphonanthus Indicus*); gum olibanum. [three first castes.

द्विजाति, *m.* a Brāhmaṇ, or a man of either of the

द्विजायनी, *f.* the sacred thread worn by the three first castes of Hindoos. [speech.

द्विजिह्व, *m.* (*f.* ā) double-tongued, deceitful in

द्वितीय, *m.* (*f.* ā) second, the second.

द्वितीया, *f.* (*prop.* a second self) a wife legally wedded according to Vedic rites; the second day of a lunar fortnight. [*thorrhiza*).

द्वितीयाभा, *f.* a scitamineous plant (*Cucurma xan-*

द्वित्व, *m.* twofoldness, repetition, corroboration. — *k.* to corroborate; to repeat. [in a twofold manner.

द्विधा, of two kinds; in two ways; in two directions;

द्विधातु, *adj.* having two natures.

द्विप, 1, *m.* a species of plant (*Messua ferrea*): 2, *m.* (*f.* ā) the elephant; *lit.* twice-drinking.

द्विपथ, *m.* a place where two roads meet.

द्विपद, *m.* (*f.* ā *or* ī) any biped (including four genera viz. gods, demons, men, birds): *lit.* twofooted.

द्विमात्र, *m.* (*f.* ā) = द्विमात्रिक, *q. v.*

द्विमात्रिक, *m.* (in Gram.) a long vowel; *lit.* appertaining to a double *mātra*; containing two syllabic consonants.

द्विमुख, *m.* (*f.* ī) the serpent *Amphisboena*: a leech.

द्विमुखाहि, *m.* a species of serpent (*Amphisboena*).

द्विमूर्द्धो, *f. pr. n.* (in Myth.) a certain demon.

द्विरुक्त, *m.* (*f.* ā) said or told in two ways, said

द्विरुक्ति, *f.* repetition, tautology. [twice, repeated.

द्विरूप, *m.* (*f.* ā) *adj.* having two forms.

द्विरूपी, *m.* (*f.* iṇī) = द्विरूप, *q. v.*

द्विवचन, *m.* (in Gram.) the dual number.

द्विविद, *m. pr. n.* a certain monkey slain by Balarām.

द्विविध, of two kinds; in two ways.

द्विवेदी, *m.* (*f.* inī) = दुबे, *q. v.*

द्विशफ, any cloven-footed animal.

द्विसप्ताह, *m.* a fortnight.

द्विहृदया, *f.* a pregnant female.

द्वीतीय, *more prop.* द्वितीय, *q. v.*

द्वीप, *m.* an island, any land surrounded by water: a large portion of the earth, a clime, region: shelter. According to the Hindoo philosophy, the terrestrial globe is divided into four, seven, or thirteen grand divisions, each of which is separated from its neighbours by a circumambient ocean; these divisions are called 'dweeps.' The seven dweeps, reckoning from the central one, are (1) Jambu (2) Kus (3) Plaksh (4) Shālmali (5) Krauñch (6) Sāk (7) Pushkar. The central *dwip* (or the known continent) is again portioned into ten divisions likewise termed 'dweeps,' viz. (1) Kuru (2) Chandra (3) Varun (4) Saumya (5) Nāg (6) Kumārikā (7) Gabbastimān (8) Tāmrapūrn (9) Kaseru (10) Indra. According to another division there are said to be eighteen minor dweeps.

द्वीपी, *m.* (*f.* inī) an islander; a tiger.

द्वेष, *m.* hatred, abhorrence, aversion, enmity, spite, malignity.

द्वेषी, *m.* (*f.* iṇī) *adj.* disliking, having an aversion to, adverse, inimical, hostile, obnoxious. [ful.

द्वेष्य, *m.* (*f.* ā) detestable, deserving hatred, hate-

द्वेष्यता, *f.* (*m.* °त्व) odiousness, detestableness;

द्वै, two. [dislike, aversion.

द्वैत, *m.* duality, doubling, being doubled, duplication; (in Philos.) the assertion of two principles (as, the distinctness of life and soul, spirit and matter, God and the universe); doubt; separation.

द्वैतवादी, *m.* (*f.* inī) a philosopher who asserts two principles.

द्वैध, *m.* duality; difference; contradiction; a contest, conflict; duplicity; division into two parts; doubt: *adj.* twofold; of two sorts. [parating.

द्वैधीकरण, *m.* a making into two, disuniting, se-

द्वैधीभाव, *m.* duality; duplicity; doubt, uncertainty; division of an army. [midnight.

द्वैपहर, *m.* the end of the second watch, noon,

द्वैपायन, *m. pr. n.* a name of Vyāsa.

द्वैप्य, *m.* (*f.* ī) appertaining to an island.

द्वैव, appertaining to heaven or to divine things, divine, heavenly, supernatural.

द्वैविध्य, *m.* duality, twofold character; duplicity.

द्वौ, two.

द्वौउ (*Rām.*) = **दोनों**, *q.v.*

द्व्यर्थ, *m.* a twofold meaning, double entendre: *lit.* having two senses or meanings, meaning two different things, having two different objects.

ध

ध (dh) is the nineteenth consonant in the Hindee alphabet and the fourth letter of the **तवर्ग** or dental class. It is the aspirate of **द**, and (given the proper dental sound) is pronounced like *dh* in the English word 'madhouse' with the *ouse* dropped. It is often interchanged inadvertently with its unaspirated form; also with **द्ध**; *e. g.* **जोध**, more properly **योद्ध**.

धई, a corruption of **दही**, *q.v.*

धंगर, *m.* a cowherd, shepherd.

धंढ, धंध; for words beginning thus, see under the forms **धगढ, धन्ध**, respectively.

धंस, *more prop.* **ध्वंस**, *q.v.*

धंसना, *n.* to be pierced, be penetrated; to be thrust into, be stuck into: *a. int.* to sink, enter, run into.

धकधक, *m.* palpitation, perturbation, apprehen-

धकधकाना, *a. int.* to palpitate; to glitter. [sion.

धकधकी, *f.* = **धकधक**, *q.v.*

धकरहजाना, to be confounded at a sudden disaster.

धकहोजाना = **धकरहजाना**, *q.v.*

धकाना, *more com.* **धक्का देना**, *q.v.* [represent it.

धकार, *m.* the letter **ध**, or any symbol that may

धकेल, *m.* a shove, push, thrust.—*denā*, to push;

धकेलना, *t.* to shove, push, jostle. [to precipitate.

धकेला, *m.* (*f.* ī) = **धकेलू**, *q.v.* [ing, jostling.

धकेलू, *m.* one who pushes: *lit.* adj. shoving, push-

धक्कमधक्का, *m.* a pushing and shoving, jostling.

धक्कमधुक्का = **धक्कमधक्का**, *q.v.*

धक्का, *m.* a shove, push, jolt, jog. — *khānā*, to be shoved.—*denā*, to shove, push, jolt.

धक्काधक्की, *f.* = **धक्कमधक्का**, *q. v.*

धगड़बाज़, *f.* an adulteress.

धगड़ा, *m.* a paramour.

धगधगाना, *a. int.* to shine, glitter.

धगाड़, *m.* a paramour.

धगोलना, *a. int.* to roll, wallow.

धगड़, *m.* a paramour. *Kāzī* (or *bakshī*) *kā* —, (an expression of pride and independence, meaning) a fig for parson and squire, independent of judge or general.

धगड़बाज़, *f.* an adulteress.

धचकचाना, *t.* to frighten, terrify.

धचकना, to give way, sink (as a bog, slough, etc.).

धज, *m. f.*? shape, form, figure, appearance, person; posture, attitude. — *palaṭnā*, to change one's attitude in fencing.

धजभंग, *m.* impotency.

धजभंगी, *m.* (*f.* inī) an impotent person.

धजा, 1, *m.* attitude, posture: 2, *f.* a slip of cloth, ship's pendant, flag, banner, standard; the pole to which the strip of cloth is attached.

धजीर, *f.* = **धज्जी**, *q.v.*

धजीला, well-looking, personable.

धज्जियां, *f.* (pl. of **धज्जी**) shreds. — *k.* to tear to pieces. — *uṛānā*, to disgrace, expose to infamy.

धज्जी, *f.* a slip of cloth or paper, a shred.

धटीनगर, ignoble; spurious.

धड़, *m.* the body, carcase, trunk. — *jīvko laṛānā*,

धड़ंग, naked, bare. [to consider, reflect.

धड़क, *f.* palpitation, fear.

धड़कना, *a. int.* to palpitate; to blaze.

धड़का, *m.* palpitation; suspense, doubt, fear;

धड़काना, *t.* to frighten, alarm. [thunder.

धड़क्का, *m.* the sound of hammering, etc.; alarming, frightening; bullying; bravado; a crowd.

धड़खा, *m.* a scarecrow.

धड़गुत्ती, *f.* peace of mind, comfort.

धड़धड़जलना, *a. int.* to burn furiously.

धड़धड़रहना, *a. int.* to flutter, palpitate.

धड़धड़ाना, *a. int.* to flutter, palpitate.

धड़ल्ला = **धड़क्का**, *q.v.*

धड़वा, *m.* (*f.* ī) a species of *mainā*-bird.

धड़वाई, *m.* (*f.* inī) the paṭwāree who weighs grain

(so named from *dhari*, a measure of five sérs, this being generally considered his perquisite at the harvest).

धड़ा, *m.* a party : a weight. — *bāndhnā*, to make up a standard to weigh by (with bricks or anything else; as, by having one weight (of a pound, for instance) it is doubled, quadrupled, and so on, till the weight requisite is obtained).

धड़ाका, *m.* a crash, report of a gun, explosion.

धड़ी, *f.* a line (particularly the black lines made on the lips with *missī*): a weight of five sérs; the quantity weighed at a time.

धड़ूआ, *m.* (*f.* धड़ूई) a species of *mainā*-bird.

धपडलाट, *f.* a going and returning without effecting one's purpose, wandering about uselessly.

धपडोरा } = ठपठोरा, *q. v.*
धपठोरा }

धपठोलना = टटोलना, *q. v.*

धत, *f.* a word used to encourage elephants.

धतकारना, *t.* to reprove.

धतीनगर, ignoble, spurious. [powerful narcotic.

धतूरा, *m.* the thorn-apple (*Datura fatuosa*). It is a

धतूरिया, *m.* a cheat, impostor.

धदकार, *m.* an igniting, setting fire to.

धधकता, *m.* (*f.* ī) *adj.* blazing, flaring.

धधकना, *a. int.* to blaze, flare.

धधक्कर, *m.* (prop. दग्धाक्षर, burnt letters) certain words or letters which are considered by Hindee poets to be unlucky; thus, the Devanāgaree letters झ, ग, न, at the beginning of a verse; र, ज, स, in the middle; and क, ट, ज, at the end, are of this description.

धधा, *m.* (*f.* ī) enflamed, blazing, ignited.

धन, 1, a corruption of धन्य, *q. v.* : 2, *m.* property (of any description), chattles, substance, wealth, cattle, gold, money, riches; thanks. — *mānnā*, (with object in gen. *m.* uninfl.) to thank.

धनंजय, *m.* an epithet of Agni and of Arjun (*lit.* conqueror of wealth ?); fire; a species of tree (*Pentaptera arjuna*).

धनंजया, *more prop.* धनंजय, *q. v.*

धनक, *f.* embroidery, lace.

धनकटी, *f.* the rice-cutting season: a kind of cloth.

धनकर, *m.* a kind of stiff soil (producing *dhān*) which is such that it can be ploughed and sown only in the event of sufficient rain falling : a field that has been cropped with rice during the previous season.

धनगर्व्वित, *m.* (*f.* ā) proud of (one's) wealth, purse-proud.

धनचिड़ी, *f.* the hornbill (*Buceros*).

धनता ; *see* धन्यता.

धनतृष्णा, *f.* thirst for wealth, greed.

धनत्तर, 1, *m. pr. n.* a certain physician in the court of Indra : 2, opulent; powerful.

धनचिया, a field on which rice has been cut.

धनद, 1, *m.* an epithet of Kuver : 2, *m.* (*f.* ā) *adj.* giving away wealth, beneficent, liberal.

धनदण्ड, *m.* amercement, fine.

धनदर्प, *m.* pride of wealth. [woman.

धनदा, 1, *more prop.* धन्धा, *q. v.* : 2, *f.* a beneficent

धनदायक, *m.* (*f.* ikā) } = धनद, 2, *q. v.*
धनदायी, *m.* (*f.* inī) }

धनन्तर } = धनत्तर = धन्वन्तरि, *q. v.*
धनन्तरी }

धनपति, *m.* an epithet of Kuver; *lit.* the lord of riches : hence, *m.* (*f.* patnī) a wealthy person.

धनपत्र, *m.* an inventory of property.

धनपात्र, *m.* (*f.* ī) = धनवान, *q. v.*

धनप्रिय, *m.* (*f.* ā) fond of wealth, avaricious.

धनप्रिया, *f.* an avaricious woman : a species of vegetable (*Ardisia solanacea*).

धनमद, *m.* (*f.* ā) intoxicated with wealth, inflated with the pride of wealth, purse-proud.

धनमान, *m.* (*f.* matī) = धनवान, *q. v.* [bravo !

धनमानी, 1, *adj.* thankful : 2, *interj.* well done !

धनलोभ, *m.* desire for wealth, avarice, greed, covetousness.

धनवत, *m.* (*f.* vatī) = धनवान, *q. v.*

धनवती, *f.* (*m.* धनवान, etc.) a wealthy female.

धनवत्त ; *see* (1) धनवत (2) धनवत्ता.

धनवत्ता, *f.* wealth.

धनवन्त, *m.* (*f.* vatī) = धनवान, *q. v.*

धनवा, *more prop.* धन्वा, *q. v.*

धनवान, wealthy, opulent, affluent, rich: hence, *m.* (*f.* vatī) a wealthy person.

धनव्यय, *m.* expenditure, extravagance.

धनषमान, *more prop.* धनुष्मान, *q. v.*

धनसम्पत्ति, *f.* accumulation of wealth.

धनसू, *m.* the fork-tailed shrike.

धनहरी, *f.* a sort of perfume (commonly called *chor*).

धनहा, *m.* a cultivator of rice: *adj.* (a country) in which rice is cultivated.

धनहारी, *m.* (*f.* iṇī) a thief, pilferer.

धनहीन, *m.* (*f.* ā) deprived of wealth, reduced to poverty, poor.

धनहु (poet. and Braj) = धनभी.

धनागार, *m.* any very rich man; *lit.* a dwelling or treasury of wealth.

धनाठ्य, *m.* (*f.* ā) infrequent = धनाढ्य, *q. v.*

धनाढ्य, *m.* (*f.* ā) *more prop.* धनाढ्य, *q. v.*

धनाढ्य, *m.* (*f.* ā) abounding in riches, wealthy.

धनाढ्यत्व, *f.* (*m.* °त्व) opulence, wealthiness.

धनाधिकार, *m.* a title or right to property.

धनाधिकारी, *m.* (*f.* iṇī) an heir.

धनाध्यक्ष, *m.* (*f.* ī) a treasurer; *hence*, an epithet of Kuver.

धनान्ध, *m.* (*f.* ā) blinded by wealth, purse-proud.

धनार्ज्जन, *m.* acquisition of property.

धनार्थी, *m.* (*f.* iṇī) a beggar, avaricious person, etc. : lit. *adj.* seeking for wealth, having wealth as an object, covetous, greedy, miserly.

धनाशा, *f.* thirst for wealth, longing for riches.

धनाश्री, *f.* one of the female personifications (*rāgiṇī*) of the musical modes.

धनि, *more prop.* (1) धनी (2) धन्य, *q. v.*

धनिक, 1, = **धनी**, 1, *q.v.*: 2 *m.*(*f.* ā *or* ī) a creditor: a pious person.

धनिया, *m.* coriander-seed (*Coriandrum sativum*). *Dhaniyeki khopṛimen pānī pilōnā*, to harass, disturb, tantalize.

धनियानी, *f.* a lady, mistress; one who has control.

धनिष्टा, *f.pr.n.* the 24th *Nakshatra* (*i. e.* the dolphin). It comprizes four stars, and is figured by a drum or tabor.

धनी, 1, *m.* (*f.* inī) an owner, proprietor; an epithet of God: *lit.* rich, wealthy, fortunate: 2, *f.* a beam.

धनीपात्र, *m.* (*f.* ī) = **धनपात्र**, *q.v.*

धनु, 1, *m. pr. n.* Sagittarius; *lit.* a bow: 2, *m.* a measure of length.

धनुः, *more com.* **धनुष**, *q. v.*

धनुःपट, *m.* a species of tree (*Buchanania latifolia*).

धनुःशाखा, *f.* a certain plant (*Sansevieria zeylanica*) from the leaves of which a tough thread is extracted of which bow-strings were formerly made.

धनुक, *f.* a bow; hence, *m.* (*f.* ā) an archer.

धनुकधर, *m.* an epithet of Krishṇ; *lit.* carrying a bow; hence, *m.* (*f.* ā) an archer.

धनुकधरा, *f.* a certain ceremony in honour of Shiv: a female archer.

धनुकधारी, *m.* (*f.* iṇī) an archer, bowyer, bowman.

धनुकबाई } **धनुकबाय** } *f.* (in Medicine) Tetanus.

धनुपाणि, *adj.* armed with a bow.

धनुपानी, *more prop.* **धनुपाणि**, *q v.*

धनुर्धरी, *m.* (*f.* iṇī) an archer, bowyer, bowman.

धनुर्म्मला, *f.* a certain plant (from the leaves of which bowstrings are made).

धनुर्लता, *f.* the moon-plant.

धनुष, *m.* a bow; the rainbow. — *ṭūṭnā*, to go off (said of a bow). — *torṇā*, to fire off a bow.

धनुषधर, *m.* (*f.* ā) = **धनुकधर**, *q.v.*

धनुषधरा = **धनुकधरा**, *q. v.*

धनुषधार, *m.* (*f.* ā) = **धनुकधर**, *q. v.*

धनुषधारा = **धनुकधरा**, *qq.v.*

धनुषधारी, *m.* (*f.* iṇī) an archer, bowman.

धनुषयज्ञ, *m.* any religious ceremony in which the bow figures as an emblem.

धनुषबाण, *m.* bow and arrow.

धनुषवान, *m.* (*f.* vati) an archer.

धनुषविद्या, *f.* the science of archery.

धनुष्कोटि, *f.* the points or ends of a bow.

धनुष्टंकार, *m.* the twang of a bow: a severe spasmodic affection.

धनुष्मत } **धनुष्मान** } *m.* (*f.* matī) an archer, bowman.

धनेश, 1, = **धनेश्वर**, *q.v.*: 2, *m.* (*f.* ā) the hornbill (*Buceros*).

धनेश्वर, *m.* the god of wealth, *i.e.* Kuver.

धनेस } **धनेसा** } = **धनेश्वर**, *q. v.*

धन्धक = **धन्धा**, *q. v.*

धन्धका, *m.* a kind of drum.

धन्धकी, *f.* a small drum.

धन्धला, *m.* trick, deception.

धन्धलाना, *t.* to trick.

धन्धा, *m.* business, employment, occupation, avocation, calling, trade, profession, work.

धन्धार, solitary, lonely.

धन्धारी, *f.* loneliness, solitude.

धन्धाला, *f.* a procuress, bawd.

धन्धो } **धन्धौ** } in Braj = **धन्धा**, *q. v.*

धन्नासेठ, successful: true-speaking.

धन्नोटा, *m.* crossbeams that sustain the supports of thatch.

धन्य, 1, *m.* (*f.* ā) bringing wealth, auspicious, fortunate, lucky, wellfated; virtuous, good, worthy of greatness or glory, blessed: 2, *interj.* (an exclamation of praise or of congratulation) well done! what happiness! how fortunate! — *mānna* (with object in gen. *m.* uninfl.) to express devout and adoring thanks. — *kahnā*, to bless, pronounce blessed, pronounce blessings on. — *mere bhōgya*, blessed is my lot! blessed man am I! what a fortunate thing for me!

धन्यता, *f.* (*m.* °**त्व**) fortunate condition.

धन्यभाग्य, *m.* good fortune, happy lot.

धन्यवाद, *m.* the verbal expression of gratitude, thanksgiving: praise, applause; congratulation.

धन्यवादी, *m.* (*f.* inī) one who gives utterance to thanks: one who praises or congratulates.

धन्या, *f. pr. n.* a certain river.

धन्याक, *m.* a certain plant (*Coriandrum sativum*) bearing a small seed used by Hindoos as a condiment.

धन्यानी, *f.* a lady, mistress; one who has control.

धन्वन्तर = **धन्वन्तरि**, *q. v.*

धन्वन्तरि, *m. pr. n.* (1) of the physician of the gods, said to have been produced at the churning of the ocean (2) of a celebrated physician who appears to have been the founder of the Hindoo medical school.

धन्वयवास, *m.* a certain plant (*Hedysarum alhagi*).

धन्वा, *m.* a country scantily supplied with water, a desert, waste; a firm spot, land, ground: a bow.

धन्वी, 1, *m.* an epithet (1) of Sagittarius (2) of Shiv (3) of Arjun: 2, *m.* a kind of tree (*Pentaptera arjuna*): 3, *m.* (*f.* inī) an archer, bowman; a sharp or shrewd man, wit, wag.

धप, 1, *more prop.* **धप्पा**, *q.v.*: 2, *m.* a voice, sound, noise, crack.

धपाड़, *m.* a running, race.

धपिया, *m.* a fourth part of a *kos* (supposed to be so named from *dhāv*, a running, being such a distance as a man may run in a single race without stopping to take breath).

धप्पा, *m.* a stain on cloth: a slap, box, thump, blow: deception.

धब्बा, *m.* a stain on cloth.

धमक, 1, *f.* noise of footsteps over-head, thumping, etc.: threat, threatening; awe: 2, *m.* (*f.* ikā) a blacksmith.

धमकना, *a. int.* to throb, shoot (as pain); to palpitate, thump; to flash, glimmer.

धमका, *m.* great heat: a threatening, chiding: a thump, noise produced by the fall of any heavy body.

धमकाना, *t.* to threaten, menace, chide, reprimand, [snub, cow, daunt.
धमकाहट, *f.* = **धमकी**, *q.v.*
धमकी, *f.* a threat, threatening, menace, reprimand, snubbing. — *denā*, to reprimand, etc.
धमकीला, *m.* a bright colour.
धमधमाना, *a. int.* to make a noise (with the feet by running about overhead).
धमधमाहट, *f.* a stumping overhead.
धमधूसर, *m.* (*f.* ā) a fat person: *lit.* corpulent.
धमना, *n.* to be grieved, be amazed.
धमनि } **धमनी** } *f.* a vein, artery.
धमस = **धम्मस**, *q.v.*
धमाका, *m.* a kind of cannon (carried on an [elephant).
धमाचौकरी, *f.* noise, tumult, bustle.
धमाधम, *m.* the sound of stamping, thumping.
धमार = **धमाल**, *q.v.*
धमाल, *m.* a chime or time in music; a kind of song that is sung at the Holee festival: running through fire on various occasions (among Muhammadan fakeers).
धमिका, *f.* (*m.* **धमक**) a blacksmith's wife.
धमोका, *m.* a kind of tambourine.
धम्मस, a kind of mallet.—*k.* to lay down turf and pound it with a mallet.
धम्माल, *m.* the running through fire on various occasions (among Muhammadan mendicants).
धयल = **धरा** (**धरना**). See **ल**.
धर, 1, a corruption of **धड़**, *q.v.*: 2, *m.* (*f.* ā) frequent as the latter element in compound words in the sense of bearing, holding, sustaining, possessed of: 3, *m.* side, direction: a rope, line: the earth.
धरकना, *more prop.* **धड़कना**, *q.v.*
धरण, 1, *m.* a holding, having, possessing; a measure or weight; a female breast: 2. *f.* a beam: accent, tone: the navel (or rather, the umbilical vein, perhaps the aorta or cœliac artery, as it is said to pulsate) which is supposed by Hindoo physicians to be occasionally removed from its place, and thus to give rise to various morbid symptoms. This is called *dharan digni* or *nāf talnā* or *ukharnā*, and the cure is attempted by friction of the stomach.
धरणि } **धरणी** } *f.* the earth, the globe.
धरणीकन्द, *m.* any esculent root.
धरणीधर, *m.* an epithet (1) of Sheshnāg, the serpent which is said to uphold the earth (2) of Vishṇu in the form of a tortoise and of a boar (3) any mountain; *lit.* the earth-supporter.
धरणीसुता, *f.* an epithet of Seetā; *lit.* the earth-born (she having been turned up from the earth by a plough as Janak was ploughing a spot to prepare it for sacrifice).
धरतः, *m.* discount and commission.
धरता = (1) **धरतः** (2) **धर्त्ता**, *qq.v.*
धरती, *f.* the earth, the land, ground, soil, mould. — *kā phūl*, *m.* a mushroom, fungus, toadstool.
धरदी = **धर दिई**. See **दी**.

धरधमकना, *a. int.* to proceed with tumultuous rapidity, move violently, rush.
धरन, *f.* (prop. **धरण**) a beam.
धरना, *t.* to place, put down, lay, put on, apply; to assume; to give in charge; to seize, lay hold of, catch, keep. — *denā* or *baithnā* describes a certain mode of extorting payment of a debt or compliance with a demand.
धरनि, *more prop.* **धरणि**, *q. v.*
धरनी = (1) **धरणी** (2) **धरनेत**, *qq.v.*
धरनेत } **धरनैत** } *m.* a dun.
धरम; for words beginning thus, see under the [form **धर्म्म**.
धरयाना = **धुरियाना**, *q.v.*
धरवाना, *t.* to cause to be placed, etc.
धरषना, *t.* to repress, restrain, curb, chide.
धरषि = **धरषके** (**धरषना**). See **इ**, 7.
धरा, *f.* (*m.* **धर**) the earth.
धराई, *f.* a placing, putting down; a laying hold [of, seizing.
धराना, *t.* to owe.
धराव, *m.* = **धराई**, *q. v.*
धरावट, *f.* land ascertained and apportioned by estimate (not by measurement).
धरावत = **धराता** (**धराना**). See **त**, 5.
धरावना, *f.* a woman married a second time.
धरासुर, *m.* (*f.* ī) an epithet of any Brāhmaṇ.
धरि = **धरके** (**धरना**). See **इ**, 7.
धरिंगा, a kind of rice.
धरियाना = **धुरियाना**, *q.v.*
धरित्री, *f.* a supporter; the earth.
धरिहौं (see **इहौं**) in Braj = **धरूंगा** (**धरना**).
धरीचा, *m.* the second husband of a Hindoo widow among the lower classes. This connexion, being contrary to the spirit of the Hindoo institutions, is formed without any particular ceremony, excepting the marking the bride's head with minium.
धरुत, a pledge, pawn, trust, deposit, substitute.
धरेव in Braj = **धरा** (**धरना**).
धरोहर, *f.* anything given in charge, a trust, charge, [deposit.
धरौक्षी, *f.* ascertainment by guess.
धर्ती = **धरती**, *q.v.*
धर्त्ता, *m.* (*f.* trī) a debtor: a bearer, supporter, [preserver.
धर्म्म, *m.* virtue, merit, righteousness, justice (or, these attributes personified); right, law; practice, usage, the customary observances of caste, etc.; duty (especially that enjoined by the Veds); business, profession; propriety, fitness; innocence; any peculiar or prescribed practice or duty (thus, giving alms, etc. is the *dharm* of a householder; administering justice is the *dharm* of a king; loyalty is the *dharm* of a subject; piety, that of a Brāhmaṇ; courage that of a Kshatree, etc.).
धर्म्मउपदेश, *more prop.* **धर्म्मोपदेश**, *q. v.*
धर्म्मकर्म्म, *m.* a religious act, work of merit, religious duty, religious exercise, any indispensable act of religion, righteous conduct, acting according to law.

धर्म्मकार्य्य, *m.* } = **धर्म्मकर्म्म**, *q.v.*
धर्म्मक्रिया, *f.* }

धर्म्मक्षेत्र, *m. pr. n.* a certain plain near Delhi, the scene of the great battle between the Kurus and the Pāṇḍus.

धर्म्मगुरु, *m.* (*f.* āīn *or* āīnī) a teacher of religion.

धर्म्मगौर, *m.* any Brāhmaṇ of Gauṛ.

धर्म्मग्रन्थ, *m.* the book that is the repository of the teaching and precepts of any religion, *e. g.* the Bible, the Veds, the Kurān, etc.

धर्म्मग्रहण, *m.* the observance of moral or religious institutes, the accepting or following the law.

धर्म्मचारी, *m.* (*f.* iṇī) one who cherishes the observance of religion or of duty, an honest spouse: *lit.* virtuous, moral, dutiful.

धर्म्मचिन्तन, *m.* (*f.* **धर्म्मचिन्ता**) virtuous reflection.

धर्म्मज्ञ, *m.* (*f.* ā) *adj.* knowing (one's) duty, conversant with virtue, etc.

धर्म्मज्ञान, *m.* the knowledge of duty (moral, legal, or religious).

धर्म्मढीहा, *m.* an accumulation of **धर्म्म**, *q. v.*

धर्म्मण, *m.* a sort of tree: a kind of large snake (not poisonous).

धर्म्मता, *f.* = **धर्म्मत्व**, *q. v.*

धर्म्मतुला, *f.* the scales of religion; *hence*, a weighing (or consideration of) religion for the purpose of enquiry.

धर्म्मत्याग, *m.* the abandonment of religion, virtue, or duty, apostasy.

धर्म्मत्यागी, *m.* (*f.* inī) a renegade, apostate.

धर्म्मत्व, *m.* rectitude, morality, piety; inherent nature, peculiar property, etc.

धर्म्मदिवाकर, *m.* an epithet of the chief light of a religion, *e. g.* Christ, Rām, Muhammad, etc.

धर्म्मदूत, *m.* (*f.* i *or* ī) a messenger in the cause of religion.

धर्म्मद्रोह, *m.* injustice, oppression.

धर्म्मद्रोही, *m.* (*f.* inī) a wicked, unjust, inequitable person: *lit.* adj. injuring the right.

धर्म्मधारी, *m.* (*f.* iṇī) a maintainer of justice.

धर्म्मध्वज, *m.* (*f.* ā) = **धर्म्मध्वजी**, *q. v.*

धर्म्मध्वजी, *m.* (*f.* inī) a hypocrite, one who makes a livelihood by assumed devotion: lit. *adj.* displaying the flag of virtue.

धर्म्मनिबन्ध, *m.* piety, virtue.

धर्म्मनिबन्धी, *m.* (*f.* inī) engaged in or conducive to virtue, pious, holy.

धर्म्मनिष्ट, *m.* the ordinances of religion.

धर्म्मनिष्टा, *f.* firmness in religion, steadfastness in virtue.

धर्म्मनिष्पत्ति, *f.* duty, moral or religious observance, discharge or fulfilment of duty.

धर्म्मपति, *m.* a man who in the name of religion exercises care for a defenceless widow: a lawfully married man, a man who has a first and only wife.

धर्म्मपत्नी, (or °**पत्नि**) *f.* a lawful wife, *i. e.* a man's first wife and of the same caste.

धर्म्मपत्र, *m.* glomerous figtree (*Ficus glomerata*).

धर्म्मपालक, *m.* (*f.* ikā) *adj.* cherishing the observance of the law, law-abiding, dutiful.

धर्म्मपुत्र, *m.* an epithet of the Pāṇḍu prince Yudhisthir: *lit.* a son of piety or duty.

धर्म्मपुस्तक, *m.* (*f.*?) the Bible.

धर्म्मप्रधान, *m.* (*f.* ā) a person eminent in piety.

धर्म्मप्रवर्त्तक, *m.* (*f.* ikā) an advocate of religion.

धर्म्मप्रवृत्यर्थ, 1, *m.* (*f.* ā) a seeker after **धर्म्म**, *q. v.*: 2, *adv.* for the sake of establishing religion.

धर्म्मबाप, *m.* an adopted father, a god-father.

धर्म्मबेटा, *m.* (*f.* ī) an adopted child, a god-child.

धर्म्मभागिनी, *f.* a virtuous and amiable wife.

धर्म्मभागी, *m.* (*f.* inī) a virtuous person.

धर्म्मभेष, *m.* a profession of religion.

धर्म्मभेषी, *m.* (*f.* iṇī) a professor of a religion.

धर्म्ममय, *m.* (*f.* ī) made up of (or replete with) virtue, righteous.

धर्म्ममूर्त्ति, *m.* an epithet of respect; *lit.* the very image of righteousness.

धर्म्ममूल, *m.* an epithet of the Veds; *lit.* the foundation of (Hindoo) law and religion.

धर्म्मयुद्ध, *f.* a religious war, crusade.

धर्म्मरक्षक, *m.* (*f.* ikā) a patron or guardian of religion or of justice.

धर्म्मरक्षा, *f.* zeal for religion (whether ceremonial or otherwise).

धर्म्मराज, 1, *m.* an epithet (1) of Yam, regent of the dead (2) of Yudhisthir (3) of Arjun: 2, *m.* a king (in general); any kingdom where justice is administered. — *k.* to govern justly.

धर्म्मरूप, *m.* (*f.* ā) = **धर्म्मरूपी**, *q. v.*

धर्म्मरूपी, *m.* (*f.* iṇī) having the form of virtue, consisting of (or replete with) virtue, righteous.

धर्म्मरोधी, *m.* (*f.* inī) a law-breaker, etc.: lit. *adj.* obstructing the law, immoral, illegal.

धर्म्मवत } *m.* (*f.* vatī) = **धर्म्मवान**, *q. v.*
धर्म्मवन्त }

धर्म्मवादी, *m.* (*f.* inī) *adj.* contending or talking about religion.

धर्म्मवान, *m.* (*f.* vatī) virtuous, pious, upright, just.

धर्म्मविवाद, *m.* contention about religion.

धर्म्मविवाह, *m.* legal marriage (it is of five sorts, *viz.* (1) Brāhma (2) Daiva (3) Ārsha (4) Gandharb (5) Prājapatya).

धर्म्मविवेचन, *m.* judicial investigation.

धर्म्मवेत्ता, *m.* (*f.* trī) one who is acquainted with religion.

धर्म्मशाला, *f.* an edifice erected for pious purposes, alms-house, hospital, court of justice.

धर्म्मशास्त्र, *m.* any body or code of law civil and ecclesiastical, especially that of the Hindoos.

धर्म्मशास्त्रीय, *m.* (*f.* ā) lawful, appertaining to the civil or ecclesiastical code of the Hindoos.

धर्म्मशील, *m.* (*f.* ā) of a pious disposition, virtuous, just.

धर्म्मशीलत्व, *m.* (*f.* tā) piety of disposition, virtuousness.

धर्म्मसंहिता, *f.* any code of laws (especially the work of some saint or divine person, as Manu, etc.).

धर्म्मसभा, *f.* a court of justice, assembly of pious persons.

धर्म्मसम्बन्धी, *m.* (*f.* inī) anything inherent in or appertaining to religion.

धर्म्मसाला, *more prop.* **धर्म्मशाला**, *q. v.*

धर्म्मसूय, *m.* sacrifice, religious oblation.

धर्म्मसेतु, *m.* barrier of justice; an epithet of Shiv: *pr. n.* a son of Āryak. [*lit.* a pillar of righteousness.
धर्म्मस्तम्भ, *m.* an epithet of a very religious man;
धर्म्मस्थल, *m. pr. n.* a certain town: *lit.* a place of justice, a religious locality.
धर्म्महीन, *m.* (*f.* ā) unrighteous, faithless, worthless.
धर्म्माचार, 1, *m.* (*f.* ā) = **धर्म्माचारी**. *q. v.*: 2, *m.* the observance of religion (whether ceremonial or otherwise); religiousness of behaviour.
धर्म्मचारी, *m.* (*f.* iṇī) one who practises either the ceremonies or the principles of religion.
धर्म्मात, *a contraction of* **धर्म्मात्मा**, *q. v.*
धर्म्मातर, a charitable grant.
धर्म्मात्मा, 1, *m. f.* a pious or virtuous person, saint; *pr. n.* the Holy Spirit: lit. *adj.* pious: 2, *f.* justice.
धर्म्माधर्म्म, *m.* religion and irreligion.
धर्म्माधर्म्मपरीक्षा, *f.* an ordeal by drawing lots or slips of white and black paper.
धर्म्माधिकार, *m.* the administration of justice, the right to administer law.
धर्म्माधिकारी, *m.* (*f.* iṇī) an authoritative administrator of law, a magistrate, judge.
धर्म्माध्यक्ष, *m.* (*f.* ī) = **धर्म्माधिकारी**, *q. v.*
धर्म्मानुराग, *m.* passion for religion, zeal.
धर्म्मानुरागी, *m.* (*f.* inī) a religious zealot, etc.: lit. *adj.* having a passion for religion, zealous, enthusiastic in religious matters. [or practice of duty.
धर्म्मानुसार, *m.* conformity to law or virtue, course
धर्म्मारन्य, *m. pr. n.* a certain forest.
धर्म्मार्थ, *adv.* for the sake of justice or religion.
धर्म्मार्थी, *m.* (*f.* inī) one who is jealous for justice or religion. [man; *lit.* an incarnation of justice, etc.
धर्म्मावतार, *m.* an epithet of respect for an upright
धर्म्मावहीन, *m.* (*f.* ā) *more com.* **धर्म्महीन**, *q. v.*
धर्म्मासन, *m.* a judge's seat, 'the bench.'
धर्म्मिष्ठ, *m.* (*f.* ā) a very pious person: lit. *adj.* (superl.) most or very pious or virtuous.
धर्म्मी, *m.* (*f.* inī) a virtuous person, etc.: *lit.* virtuous, pious, righteous, upright, just, godly.
धर्म्मोपदेश, *m.* instruction in morals or religion.
धर्म्मोपदेशक, *m.* (*f.* ikā) an instructor in religious matters, preacher.
धर्षे, an irregular imperat. 2nd pl. of **धरना**, *q. v.*
धर्ष, *m.* (**धरषना**) a repressing, curbing, overcoming.
धलाइत, an armed attendant or peon.
धव, *m.* a man, husband, lord; a species of shrub
धवनि, (*see* **ध्वनि**) bellows. [*Grislea tomentosa*).
धवरी, *see* **धवली** and **धौरी**.
धवल, 1, *m.* the colour white; a species of shrub (*Grislea tomentosa*); an inferior mode in music: 2, *m.* (*f.* ā *or* ī) dazzling white; handsome, beautiful.
धवलगिरि, *m. pr. n.* a certain mountain.
धवलपक्ष, *m.* the fortnight of the moon's increase.
धवलमृत्तिका, *f.* chalk.
धवला, *f.*: see **धवल**, 2.

धवलित, *m.* (*f.* ā) made dazzling white, whitened.
धवली, *f.* (*m.* **धवल**, 2,) a white cow.
धवलीकृत, *m.* (*f.* ā) = **धवलित**, *q. v.*
धवलीभूत, *m.* (*f.* ā) become white.
धवलु, a poet. form of **धवल**, 2, *q. v.*
धवा, *m.* a certain caste of palkee-bearers who are
धविया in Braj = **धोबी**, *q. v.* [Musalmāns.
धस, a sloping elevation of ground; *hence*, the glacis of a fort; sterile sandy eminences; a kind of soil in the Lower Doāb. [or slough).
धसकना, *a. int.* to give way, sink (as quagmire
धसन, *f.* a quagmire: the state of being thrust into.
धसना = **धंसना**, *q. v.*
धसम, *m.* a quagmire, swamp, slough, bog.
धसान, *m.*: see (1) **धसम** (2) **धसाना**.
धसाना, *t.* to sink; *lit.* to cause to be thrust into.
धसाव, *m.* = **धसम**, *q. v.*
धाई, *f.* a wetnurse, foster-mother, midwife.
धाय, *f.* a wetnurse. — *mārnā*, to cry, groan. — *mār ronā*, to cry, groan, weep bitterly.
धांगर, *m.* a certain caste whose business it is to dig the earth. [form **धान्य**.
धांध; for words beginning thus, see under the
धांयधांय, *f.* the report of cannon heard at a distance; the sound made by anything being burned.
धांविया, *m.* a thresher or a seller of rice.
धांसना, *a. int.* to cough (a horse).
धांसी, *f.* a cough (of a horse).
धाक, *f.* pomp, glory, fame, renown: fear, terror: a species of tree (*Butea frondosa*): a post.
धाकर, *m.* a mongrel. [district of Agra.
धाकरः, *m.* a certain small tribe of Rājputs in the
धाकरा = **धाकरः**, *q. v.*
धाख, see (1) **धाक** (2) **धाखा**. [swing.
धाखा, *m.* a species of tree (*Butea frondosa*): a
धागा, *m.* a thread. — *ḍālnā*, to quilt.
धाचक, dread, aversion. [ing an enemy.
धाटी, *f.* advancing towards an enemy, confront-
धाड़, *f.* a crowd, multitude: water falling from
धाड़स, *more prop.* **ढाड़स**, *q. v.* [above: a robbery.
धाड़ा, *m.* = **धाड़**, *q. v.* [metal: 3, *f.* semen virile.
धात, 1, *more prop.* **धातु**, *q. v.*: 2, *m.* mineral, ore,
धातकी, *f.* a species of tree (*Grislea tomentosa*).
धाता, *m.* (*f.* trī) a supporter, preserver, sustainer, nourisher, parent; *pr. n.* (1) of Brahmā (2) of one of the Ādityas. [of the deities.
धाताविधाता, *m. pr. n.* (1) of Brahmā (2) of two
धातु, *m.* a primary or elementary substance (*viz.* earth, fire, water, air, atmosphere); a principle or humour of the body (as phlegm, wind, bile); any constituent part of the body (as blood, flesh, etc.); any property of a primary element (as odour, flavour, colour, touch, sound); semen, the matter which oozes

in a gleet; a metal, mineral, fossil; (in Gram.) a root, crude form, radical, verbal root.

धातुकाशीश, *m.* red sulphate of iron.

धातुप, *m.* alimentary juice or chyle.

धातुपदार्थ, a tautological form = **धातु**, *q.v.*

धातुभृत, *adj.* promoting the animal secretions.

धातुमाक्षिक, *m.* a sulphuret of iron.

धातुमारिणी, *f.* borax.

धातुराजक, *m* semen virile.

धातुवल्लभ, *m.* borax.

धातुवस्तु, a tautological form = **धातु**, *q. v.*

धातुवादी, *m.* (*f.* inī) an assayer, mineralogist, miner.

धातुवैरी, *m.* sulphur.

धातुशेखर, *m.* green vitriol.

धातूपल, *m.* chalk.

धातृपुष्पिका, *f.* a species of tree (*Grislea tomentosa*).

धातृ, *f.* (*m.* **धातृ**, i.e. **धाता**) an epithet of Saraswatee.

धात्रिका, *f.* emblic myrobalan.

धात्री, *f.* a mother; a nurse, waiting-woman, foster-mother; the earth; emblic myrobalan. [from the husk.

धान, *m.* the rice-plant, rice before it is separated

धानः, *m.* the *gond* portion of a village (which is always separated from the rest of it).

धानाकाटी, *f.* the rice-cutting season.

धाना, 1, *f.* = **धान**, *q. v.*; 2, *m.* = **धानः**, *q. v.*; 3, *a. int.* to run, make haste; to toil, labour, drudge; to worship.

धानी, *f.* a kind of rice in husk: a good soil (fit for grain): the colour light green.

धानुक, *m.* an archer, bowman; a watchman armed with a bow; a certain caste of hill people who use bows and arrows (they are employed as archers, fowlers, house-guards, and in several menial occupations both of the house and of the field, wherever they may reside; while their females are in special request as midwives).

धानुष्क, *m.* an archer, bowman.

धानुष्का, *f.* a certain tree (*Achyranthus aspera*).

धान्धना, *t.* to gormandize. [jugglery, chicanery.

धान्धल, *f.* wrangling, subterfuge, trick, cheating,

धान्धलपना, *m.* chicanery, jugglery, cheating, subterfuge. [some.

धान्धलो, *m.* (*f.* inī) a wrangler: lit. *adj.* quarrel-

धान्य, *m.* corn (*esp.* rice, *Oriza sativa*); coriander: a measure equal to four sesamum-seeds.

धान्यराज, *m.* barley.

धान्यवत, *adj.* abounding in corn.

धाप, *f.* a foot (measure of length): as far as a man can run without taking breath, one quarter of a *kos* or nearly half a mile; a *ghāṭ* or passage; a large expanse of low ground.

धाबरी, *f.* a pigeon-house, dove-cot.

धाबा, an upper story; a terraced roof.

धाभाई, *m.* a foster-brother.

धाम, 1, *m.* a dwelling, house, place; paradise, heaven; 2, *m. pr. n.* (pl.) a certain class of super-human beings.

धामद, *m.* (*f.* ā) any person or means by which paradise is obtained: lit. *adj.* heaven-giving.

धामन, 1, *m.* an abode; state, dignity; host; splendour, light: 2, a certain species of grass of a good quality found in the Bhatti territory.

धामनी, *f.* any tubular vessel of the body, a vein.

धामवत, *m.* (*f.* vati) splendid, luminous, eminent, exalted, illustrious.

धामवन्त / **धामवान** } *m.* (*f.* vatī) = **धामवत**, *q v.*

धामा, *m.* a large cane basket.

धामिन, *m.* (*f.* ī) a kind of harmless serpent (which is said to suck cows); a kind of wood; a kind of bamboo.

धामियां, (*f.* ?) *pr. n.* (pl. of **धामी**) a certain sect. They are followers of Prānāth, a Hindoo reformer who flourished in the 17th century in Bandēlkhaṇḍ.

धामी = (1) **धामा** (2) **धामिन**, *qq. v.*

धाय; see **धाई** and **धाए**.

धार, 1, *m.* debt: slight sprinkling rain: end, bound, limit: 2. *m.* ? a hollow tree inserted in the mouth of wells to prevent their falling in: 3. *f.* a line; lineament; a stream; current; edge of a sword, etc.; sharpness. — *mārnā* or *par mārnā*, to despise.

धारक, *m.* (*f.* ikā) a debtor.

धारण, *m.* a holding, upholding, maintaining, sustaining, having, keeping, bearing, an assuming. — *k.* to draw, absorb, seize, retain.

धारणा, *f.* continuance in rectitude, keeping in the right way, steadiness, fortitude, firmness, resolution: mental retention, memory. [the body.

धारणी, *f.* a straight line; any tubular vessel of

धारता, *m.* (*f.* trī) *more com.* **धर्ता**, *q.v.*

धारधरना, *t.* to winnow.

धारधूरा, the boundary formed by a stream.

धारन, *more prop.* **धारण**, *q. v.*

धारना, *t.* to hold, bear, have, keep, uphold, support, sustain; to pour (water). [ges, rates, etc.

धारबाछ, an equal or general distribution of char-

धारस, tranquillity, consolation.

धारा, *f.* a torrent, river, stream, current; a shower; a drop; a multitude: the sharp edge of any cutting instrument; the circumference of a wheel.

धारासार, *m.* a heavy shower; a large drop of rain.

धारि, (*prop.* **धारी**) an army, host.

धारिणी, *f.*; *see* **धारी**, 2.

धारित, *m.* (*f.* ā) upheld, sustained; assumed.

धारिय (poet.) = **धरिये** or **धारिये**.

धारिष्ट, *m.* a certain subordinate Hindoo caste.

धारी, 1, *f.* a line; lineament: a small buttress: an army, host: a margin, extremity, edge: a certain plant used in dyeing (*Lythrum fructicosum*, Lin.: *Grislea tomentosa*, Roxb.): 2, *m.* (*f.* iṇī) very frequent as a termination of substantival adjectives, when it imports the sense of bearing, holding, having, wearing.

धारीदार, streaked, lined, striped. [devout.

धार्म्मिक, *m.* (*f.* ī) just, virtuous, pious, faithful,

धार्म्मिकत्व, *m.* (*f.* tā) justice, virtuousness.

धालः, *m.* a stream, current: a kind of cess (about an *ānā* in the rupee) levied on villagers.

धाला = धालः, *q.v.*

धाव, *m.* a certain plant (*Grislea tomentosa*) used [in dyeing.

धावक, *m.* (*f.* ikā) *adj.* running, going, expeditious, swift; cleaning, cleansing.

धावत, *adj.* running, going quickly.

धावन, *m.* motion, going: a runner, messenger: a cleansing, purifying.

धावना, *a. int.* to run; to range, roam, rove; to trudge; to worship: *t.* to run at, attack.

धावनिका, *f.* a prickly nightshade.

धावनी, *f.* a species of creeping-plant (*Hedysarum lagopodioides*).

धावमान, *m.* (*f.* matī) *adj.* going, running; swift, [expeditious.

धावा, *m.* a running; an overrunning an enemy's country, assaulting, attack; a crowding together; a store, stock; a kind of tree.—*mārnā, a. int.* to go expeditiously from a distant place, to run on, run about.

धावित, *m.* (*f.* ā) purified, cleaned, cleansed; gone, run away, gone away; run to, advanced towards or against.

धाह, *f* a cry, noise.—— *mārnā*, to cry, groan.

धि; used only as the latter member of compound words (*m.*) and signifying the receptable for retaining that which the preceding part denotes.

धिंगाधांगी, *more com.* धींगाधांगी, *q.v.*

धिंगाना, *m.* clamour, oppression.

धिक, an *interj.* expressing blame, reproach, disapprobation, aversion, contempt, menace, or regret; *e.g.* fie! shame! out upon! what a pity!

धिकार; see (1) अधिकार (2) धिक्कार.

धिक्कार, *m.* reproach, censure, disrespect, contempt, anathema, curse.—*k.* or *denā*, to swear, lay one's oath, [utter a curse.

धिक्कारना, *t.* to reproach; to curse.

धिक्कारी, 1, *f.* a curse, damnation: 2, *m.* (*f.* iṇī) [cursed, damned.

धिग, *more prop.* धिक, *q.v.*

धिगधिग, a repetition (for emphasis) of धिक, *q. v.*

धिगयाचना, *f.* an invocation of धिक, *q. v.*

धिमचा, *m.* a kind of tamarind.

धिया, *f.* a daughter.

धिरकार, *more prop.* धिक्कार, *q.v.*

धिराज, a contraction of अधिराज, *q.v.* See अ, 18.

धिराना, *t.* to threaten; to bully.

धिर्कार, *more prop.* धिक्कार, *q. v.*

धिर्कारना, *more prop.* धिक्कारना, *q. v.*

धिर्काल, *m.* a certain caste of bamboo-workers.

धी, *f.* knowledge, intellect, mind, understanding, intelligence, sense: a daughter.

धींग, धींगड़ा } *m.* a paramour.

धींगाधांगी, *f.* a teasing: defiance.

धींवर, *more prop.* धीवर, *q.v.*

धींट, धींठ } *more prop.* ढीठ, *q.v.*

धीड़, *more prop.* ढीड़, *q.v.*

धीदा, *f.* a virgin, maid.

धीन, *m.* slowness, gentleness.

धीन्द्रिय, *m.* any organ of intellectual perception, as the mind, the eye, the ear, the nose, the tongue, the skin.

धीम, *m.* slowness, gentleness.

धीमत, धीमन्त } *m.* (*f.* matī) = धीमान, *q. v.*

धीमर, 1, *m.* (*f.* ī) a fisherman: 2, *m.* a certain fisherman caste.

धीमा, *m.* (*f.* ī) slow, lazy, gentle, mild, temper- [ate, abated, allayed.

धीमाई, *f.* slowness, tardiness, gentleness, mildness.

धीमान, *m.* (*f.* matī) sagacious, shrewd, sensible, wise, intelligent, learned.

धीमेधीमे, slowly, gently, softly.

धीया, *f.* a daughter.

धीर, 1, *m.* (*f.* ā) lasting, firm, resolute, courageous, steady, patient, deliberate, sedate, solemn, grave: 2, *m.* firmness, resoluteness, patience, endurance, bravery, deliberateness, fortitude, sedateness.

धीरज, *m.* = धीर, 2, *q. v.*—— *dharnā* or *rakhnā*, to exercise patience, have patience, be firm.

धीरजता, *f.*, धीरजत्व, *m.* } = धीर, 2, *q. v.*

धीरजमान, *m.* (*f.* matī) patient, endowed with endurance, resolute, deliberate, sedate.

धीरजवत, धीरजवन्त, धीरजवान } *m.* (*f.* vatī) = धीरजमान, *q. v.*

धीरता, *f.* (*m.* °त्व) = धीर, 2, *q. v.*

धीरह = धीरेधीरे, *q. v.*

धीरा, *f.* (*m.* धीर) a patient woman, etc.

धीरिया, *f.* a daughter.

धीरी, *f.* the pupil of the eye.

धीरेधीरे, slowly, gently, deliberately, patiently.

धीर्य, *m.* gravity; firmness; constancy; courage.

धीर्यमान, *m.* (*f.* matī) = धीरजमान, *q. v.*

धीवर, 1, *m.* (*f.* ī) a fisherman: 2, *m.* a certain fisherman caste.

धीवरी, *f.* a fishwoman, fisherman's wife: a sort of [harpoon for catching fish with.

धीवान, *m.* (*f.* vatī) = धीमान, *q. v.*

धीशक्ति, *f.* any intellectual faculty or power of the understanding (as, attention, comprehension, etc.).

धुअ in Chand = धुआ, *q. v.*

धुआ, *m.* smoke, vapour.

धुआं, *m* dying; a corpse: smoke, vapour.

धुंआ, *m.* smoke, vapour.

धुंएकी नौका, *f.* a steamboat.

धुंगार, *m.* seasoning with which anything is fried.

धुंगारना, *t.* to season with spices.

धुंध; for words beginning thus, see under the form [धुन्ध.

धुंवा, *m.* smoke, vapour.

धुकड़पुकड़, *f.* agitation, palpitation.
धुकड़ी, *f.* a purse.
धुकधुकी, *f.* consideration, reflection; perturbation, anxiety, apprehension: an ornament worn on [the breast.
धुगा, *more prop.* धुनि, *q.v.*
धुत्ता, *m.* trick, deception. — *denā*, to deceive.
धुधु, a driving away.
धुन, 1, *more prop.* धुनि, *q.v.*: 2, *f.* inclination, propensity; application, diligence, assiduity, perseverance; ambitation, ardour: pains in the bones.
धुनकना, *t.* to card or comb (cotton).
धुनध, *more prop.* धुन्ध, *q.v.*
धुनना, *t.* to comb, card (cotton); to beat (the head). *Sir* —, to beat one's head with vexation, etc.
धुनकी, *f.* the bow with which cotton is carded.
धुनि, 1, = धुनके (धुनना); see क, 7: 2, *f.* sound, musical sound: a frog: a river.
धुनिया, *m.* a carder, cotton-comber.
धुनिस्राव, *m.* pains in the bones. [river.
धुनी, 1, *more prop.* (1) धुनि (2) धूनी, *qq.v.*: 2, *f.* a
धुनीस्राव, *m.* pains in the bones.
धुनेहा, *m.* a carder, cotton-comber.
धुन्द, 1, *m.* a design, intention, attempt; an idea, thought: 2, *adj.* drunk. — *k.* to stupefy.
धुन्ध, 1, *more prop.* धुन्धु, *q.v.*: 2, *m.* dimsightedness, haziness, mistiness.
धुन्धक, *m. pr. n.* a certain demon (*rākshas*).
धुन्धकार, *m.* darkness, obscurity, mistiness.
धुन्धकारी, *m. pr. n.* a son of Átmdev and Dhundli.
धुन्धकिया, *adj.* producing haziness, mistifying.
धुन्धराना, *n.* to be dull, be misty.
धुन्धला, *m.* (*f.* ī) foggy, misty, dull, dim (as the eyes of the aged). [ness (as of the eyesight).
धुन्धलाई, *f.* mistiness, cloudiness, dulness, dim-
धुन्धलेपन, *m.* = धुन्धलाई, *q.v.*
धुन्धु, *m. pr. n.* a certain demon.
धुन्धुमार, *m.* a species of insect (*Coccinella*): an epithet of Kuvalyāshwa, the slayer of Dhundu.
धुन्धेला, *m.* (*f.* ī) knavish.
धुवा = धुनना, *q.v.*
धुन्वी, *f.* the bow with which cotton is carded.
धुबला, *m.* a petticoat or any loose garment for
धुबिया, *more com.* धोबी, *q.v.* [covering the legs.
धुमधड़क्का, *m.* pomp, pageantry.
धुमरा, *m.* (*f.* ī) *more prop.* धुमला, *q.v.*
धुमला, *m.* (*f.* ī) dimsighted, blind.
धुमलाई, *f.* gloominess, dimness.
धुर, *m.* 1, beginning; limit, end, extremity. *Dhurse dhurtak*, from beginning to end: 2, a yoke; a load; the fore part of a pole where the yoke is fixed; the head (as the place of honour).
धुरधर, *more com.* धुरन्धर, *q.v.*
धुरना, *more prop.* धरना, *q.v.*

धुरन्धर, *m.* (*f.* ā) a beast of burden; a chief: *pr. n.* (1) of a Rakshas (2) of a people: lit. *adj.* bearing a burden; helping. [the burden of a song.
धुरपद, *m.* a kind of song in the Hindee or Braj;
धुरसांझ, *f.* dusk, twilight, evening.
धुरियाना, *t.* to throw dust; to sift, winnow, separate
धुरी, *f.* an axletree, pole. [good grain from bad.
धुरीण, *m.* a chief: a beast of burden.
धुलना, *a. int.* to swing: to roll: *n.* to be washed (?).
धुलवाना, *t.* to cause a thing to be washed, *i. e.* to get it washed.
धुलाई, *f.* washing; remuneration for washing.
धुलाना, *t.* to cause to wash.
धुलियाना = धुरियाना, *q.v.*
धुलेण्डी, *f. pr. n.* (1) of the second day of the Holee festival (on which it is the practice of Hindoos to scatter a fine red powder) (2) of the first day of the month *Chait* (on which they scatter ashes).
धुलेड़ी = धुलेण्डी, *q.v.*
धुवका, *f.* the introductory stanza of a song (repeated afterwards as the burden of each verse).
धुवा, *m.* smoke, vapour.
धुस्तूर, *f.* thorn-apple (*Datura fatuosa*). [flannel.
धुस्सा, *m.* a kind of coarse stuff made of shawl-wool,
धूआ, धूआं } *m.* smoke, vapour.
धूआंरा, a chimney, any hole for letting out smoke.
धूआंधार, 1, much smoke: 2, smoky: beautiful, [adorned.
धूई = धोई, *q.v.*
धूंआ, धूंआं } *m.* smoke, vapour.
धूंका, the chimney of a sugarcane-mill.
धूंधली, a corruption (1) of धुन्धली (2) of धुन्धलाई, *qq.v.*
धूंरा = धूंका, *q.v.*
धूंवर, *adj.* of a blue or dark grey or smoke colour.
धूंवा, धूंवां } *m.* smoke, vapour.
धूंवाधार = धूआंधार, *q.v.* [smoke.
धूंवारा, *m.* a chimney, any hole for letting out
धूंवाराना, *t.* to smoke. [*ta*).
धूणक, *m.* rosin, resin (*esp.* that of the *Shorea robus-*
धूणचि, *f.* an incense-pot, censer.
धूयठधायठ, *more prop.* कूयककायठ, *q.v.*
धूयडना, धूयठना } *more prop.* कूयकना, *q.v.*
धूत, 1, *m.* (*f.* ā) shaken, agitated, shaken off, removed; fanned, rinsed, cleansed; deserted, abandoned; reproached, reviled; judged, discriminated: 2,
धूतना, *t.* to cheat, trick, defraud. [*m.* good behaviour.
धूता, *f.* a wife.
धूति = धुतके (धुतना). See क, 7.
धून, *m.* an explosion, loud report.

धूनक }
धूना } = धूयाक, *q. v.*

धूनि, *more com.* **धूनी**, 2, *q.v.*

धूनी, 1, *m.* (*f.* inī) *adj.* preserving: 2, *f.* smoke; fumigation by way of exorcising one possessed, or, as a medical application: a fire lighted by a Hindoo ascetic, who sits over it inhaling the smoke by way of penance. It is often practised by them in the manner of *dharnā*, to extort compliance with their demands; hence, — *denā*, to dun, importune; to smoke. — *lagānā*, to lay on the smoking process, *i. e.* to insist obstinately in a demand, persevere in it; to fumigate by way of exorcising one possessed, or, as a medical application. — *lenā*, to inhale smoke, undergo fumigation (*esp.* as a penance).

धूप, 1, *m.* incense; the aromatic vapour that proceeds from burning incense; the perfume burnt by Hindoos at the time of worshipping: 2, *f.* sunshine, sunlight, heat of the sun.

धूपकाल, *m.* the sunny season, the hot weather.

धूपकाला, *m.* = **धूपकाल**, *q. v.*

धूपदानी, *f.* an incense-pot, censer, box for keeping increase.

धूपदीप, *m.* an offering of incense to an idol.

धूपना, *t.* to perfume; to besmear with pith.

धूपपात्र, *m.* = **धूपदानी**, *q.v.*

धूपवृक्ष, *m.* a species of pine (*Pinus longifolia*).

धूपांग, *m.* turpentine.

धूपेलियां, *f.* the prickly-heat.

धूबिया, *more prop.* **धोबी**, *q. v.*

धूम, 1, *m.* smoke, vapour: 2, *f.* tumult, noise, bustle; fame, report, rumour; pomp: 3, *m. pr. n* a certain ancient Hindoo sage.

धूमउ in Braj = **धूमभी**. *See* **उ**, 9.

धूमकेतु, *m.* fire; a comet; a falling star: lit. *adj.* having a flag or standard of smoke.

धूमधाम, *f.* tumult, noise, bustle, uproar; pomp, parade.

धूमप्रभा, *f. pr. n.* one of the divisions of hell, *viz.* the hell of smoke.

धूमरा, 1, *m.* tumult, bustle, uproar, confusion: 2, *m.* (*f.* ī) smoke-coloured, purple-coloured.

धूमला = **धूमरा**, *q.v.*

धूमा, *m.* a colour (like that of smoke) compounded of black and red.

धूमिला, *m.* (*f.* ī) smoke-coloured, purple-coloured.

धूम्र, 1, *m.* the colour purple: 2, *m.* (*f.* ā) smoke-coloured, obscure, grey, purple: 3, *m. pr. n.* (1) of one of Skand's attendants (2) of a certain demon (3) of a certain sage (4) of a certain monkey or bear (5) of the 28th astronomical *Yog*: 4, *m.* an epithet (1) of Shiv (2) of Parāshar.

धूम्रकान्त, *m.* jacinth.

धूम्रकेतु = **धूमकेतु**, *q. v.*

धूम्रकेश, *m. pr. n.* (1) of a son of Prithu and Archis (2) of a son of Krishāshwa (3) of a son of Danu.

धूर, 1, *f.* (*prop.* **धूल**) dust: 2, the twentieth part of a *biswā*: 3, a kind of coarse grass.

धूरकट, an advance of rent paid by villagers to the zamindār in the months of *Jeth* and *Asāṛh*.

धूरकी, *f.* the twentieth part of a **धूर**, *q.v.*

धूरधानी, 1, *m.* a tall stout fellow: 2, *f.* a firelock (without a chamber).

धूरसंझा, *m.* evening.

धूरा देना, *t.* to deceive, wheedle, take in.

धूरि, *f.* (*prop.* **धूलि**) dust.

धूरियाबेला, *m.* a species of jasmine.

धूरियामल्लार, *m.* a certain musical mode (sung particularly at the beginning of the rains).

धूरी, *f.* an axletree: a strand of a rope.

धूर्त्त, *m.* (*f.* ā) a gamester, rogue, cheat: *lit.* fraudulent, crafty, cunning, knavish, sly, dishonest, mischievous, injurious.

धूर्त्तता, *f.* (*m.* °**त्व**) fraudulence, knavery.

धूल, *f.* (*prop.* **धूलि**) dust.

धूलक, *m.* poison.

धूलधानी, dispersed, troubled, perplexed, trampled under foot, ruined.

धूलि, *f.* dust.

धूलिगुच्छक, *m.* the red vegetable powder thrown about at the Holee festival.

धूलीधोया, *m.* a washer of refuse or dust.

धूसना, *t.* to ram, stuff; to butt (as horned cattle).

धूसर, 1, *m.* the colour grey: 2, *m.* (*f.* ā) dust-colour, grey.

धूसाधासी, *f.* cramming and stuffing.

धूहा, *m.* a scarecrow.

धग = **धिक्क**, *q. v.*

धगधग, *more com.* **धिगधिग**, *q.v.*

धृत, *m.* (*f.* ā) carried, held, possessed, sustained, contained, kept, maintained.

धृतराष्ट्र, *m. pr. n.* a certain king, father of Durodhana and uncle of the five Pāndu princes.

धृताची, *f. pr. n.* a certain courtesan of Indra's paradise.

धृतात्मा, *m.* or *f.* calm, collected, firm, steady.

धृति, *f.* holding: steadiness, firmness; satisfaction, content: a species of metre in which the stanza is of four lines of eighteen syllables each; hence, in the ingenious system of reckoning by symbols adopted by Hindoos in their poetry, this word is a symbol for 18.

धृतिमत }
धृतिमन्त } *m.* (*f.* mati) steady, firm, calm.
धृतिमान }

धृष्ट, *m.* (*f.* ā) bold, confident, forward, impudent.

धृष्टकेतु, *m. pr. n.* (1) of a king of Chedi (2) of a king of Videhā or Mithilā (3) of a son of Satyadhriti (4) of a son of Sukumār (5) of the father of Sukumār (6) of a son of Dhrishtadyumn (7) of a king of the Kaikayas (8) of a son of Manu.

धृष्टता, *f.* (*m.* °**त्व**) boldness, impudence.

धृष्टद्युम्न, *m. pr. n.* one of the sons of King Drupad.

धेंगामुष्टी, *f.* fistcuffs.

धेड़ीकौवा, *m.* a large black crow, raven.

धेन, *more prop.* **धेनु**, *q.v.* See **उ**, 3.

धेनु, *f.* a milch cow, a cow that has lately calved; the earth; a gift, present.

धेनुक, *m. pr. n.* a certain demon slain by Balarām.

धेनुका, *f.* a milch cow; a present.

धेनुमति, *f. pr. n.* the Gomtee river.

धेनू, *more prop.* **धेनु**, *q.v.*

धेरा, *m.* (*f.* ī) squint-eyed.

धेला, *a contraction of* **अधेला**, *q.v.* See **अ**, 18.

धैरज, *more prop.* **धैर्य**, *q.v.*

धैर्य, *m.* gravity, steadiness, firmness, constancy, courage.

धैर्यकलित, *m.* (*f.* ā) steady, calm, assuming composure or firmness.

धैर्यमत / **धैर्यमन्त** } *m.* (*f.* matī) = **धैर्यमान**, *q.v.*

धैर्यमान, *m.* (*f*, matī) firm, steady, constant, patient, forbearing.

धैर्यवत / **धैर्यवन्त** / **धैर्यवान** } *m.* (*f.* vatī) = **धैर्यमान**, *q.v.*

धैवत, *m.* the sixth note of the gamut.

धोअन / **धोंअन** } = **धोवन**, *q.v.*

धोआ, 1, *m.* (*f.* **धोई**) washed: 2, *m.* a present of fruit.

धोई, *f.* pulse that has been soaked previous to boiling, a mash.

धोएन्धी डकार, *f.* a sour belch.

धोंचा, (in Surveying) four and a half.

धोंवाला, *m.* a chimney, any hole for letting out smoke.

धोक, *f.* bowing down to idols, salutation.

धोकः, *m.* a measure of about ten handfuls of *kharif* produce.

धोकड़, robust, athletic.

धोका = (1) **धोकः** (2) **धोखा**, *qq. v.*

धोखा, *m.* deceit, deception, delusion, blunder; disappointment; hesitation, doubt; a scarecrow; alarm, panic; anything imaginary, not real, as a vapour resembling water at a distance (Fr. *mirage*). — *khānā*, to be deceived. — *denā*, to deceive.

धोड़, *m.* a kind of water-snake.

धोगड़ा, *m*, a grass that grows in rice-fields and sometimes chokes the plant.

धोगड़ी, *f*, 1. = **धोगड़ा**, *q. v.*: 2, the ordinary kettle-drum of India.

धोता, *m.* (*f.* ī) false, treacherous, perfidious.

धोती, 1, *m.* a kind of falcon (the female of which is called *besarā* : 2, *f.* a cloth worn around the waist (it is passed between the legs and fastened behind).

धोधाकर, *adj.* having thoroughly washed and cleansed.

धोना, *t.* to wash, cleanse.

धोन्धा, *m.* a small mound of earth; *met.* a pot-belly, large belly.

धोनाधाना, an alliterative form of **धोना**, *q. v.*

धोप, *f.* a kind of sword; a race, running; exertion.

धोब, *m.* washing.

धोबिन, *f.* a washerwoman, washerman's wife.

धोबिनी = **धोबिन**, *q. v.*

धोबी, *m.* (*f.* in *or* inī) a washerman.

धोय; *see* (1) **धोई** (2) **धोना**.

धोया, 1, *m.* a cleansing: 2, *m.* (*f.* **धोई**) cleansed.

धोयाधाया, washed, ready washed.

धोयेयड़ीडकार / **धोयेयढ़ीडकार** } *f.* a sour belch.

धौरखि, *f.* tradition.

धौरा, 1, *m.* a kind of medicine: 2, *m.* (*f.* ī) white.

धौरी, 1, a contraction of **अधौरी**, *q. v*: 2, *m.* a bullock.

धौरो in Braj = **धौरा**, *q. v.*

धौलवाना, *more com.* **धुलवाना**, *q. v.*

धौलाना; *see* **धुलाना** and **धौलाना**.

धौवन, *m.* (*f.*?) water in which anything (*e.g.* clothes, dishes, rice, etc.) has been washed.

धौवा = **धोआ**, 1, *q. v.*

धौसा, *m.* a coarse kind of shawl.

धौ, *f.* a species of wood (*Lythrum fruticosum*, Lin: *Grislea tomentosa*, Roxb.).

धौं, 1, *conj.* whether: 2, *m.* a weight of twenty sérs.

धौंक, *f.* a breathing, panting; asthma.

धौंकना, *t.* to blow with bellows.

धौंकनी, *f.* bellows.

धौंज, *f.* consideration, reflection, thought.

धौंस, *m.* an assault; a threatening.

धौसधड़ल्ला, *m.* a blustering, tumult, bullying, the impetuous assault of a crowd or of a body of men.

धौंसा, *m.* a large kettledrum.

धौंसिया, *m.* the leader of a hue and cry, *posse comitatus.*

धौजन, botheration, worry.

धौत, *m.* (*f.* ā) washed, cleansed, purified.

धौतशिल, *m.* crystal.

धौना = **धोना**, *q. v.*

धौन्ताल, wealthy; stout, strong; bold; vicious, mischievous.

धौन्ताली, *f.* riches; strength; courage; viciousness, mischievousness.

धौर, *m.* a large kind of dove.

धौरा, *more prop.* (1) **धौला** (2) **धौरा**, *qq. v.*

धौरी, *f.* (*corrupt. of* **अधौड़ी**?) a bull's hide cut into two pieces.

धौर्त्तिक, knavish, fraudulent, dishonest; *lit.* appertaining to a cheat.

धौल, *f.* a thump, rap, slap; a kind of sugarcane. — *jarnā* or *mārnā* or *lagānā*, to thump. — *lagnā*, to suffer loss.

धौलधप्पा, *m.* a thumping and slapping.

धौला, (from **धवल**) *m.* (*f.* ī) white.

धौलाई, *f.* whiteness.

धौलागिर, *m. pr. n.* a certain mountain.

धौलाना, *t.* to thump, box, slap, cuff.

धौलियाना = **धौलाना**, *q. v.*

ध्यजा, a corruption of **ध्वजा**, *q. v.*

ध्यान, *m.* pious meditation, religious contemplation, reflection, thought, consideration, imagination (especially that profound and abstract consideration which brings objects fully and undisturbedly before the mind). mental representation of the personal attributes of the divinity to whom worship may happen to be addressed; intuition. — *dharnā* or *lagānā*, to apply the mind to contemplation.

ध्यानपर, *m.* (*f.* ā) a person engaged in meditation, one whose highest object is meditation.

ध्यानयोग, *m.* the performance of religious abstraction

ध्याना, *t.* to meditate on, think on, adore; to know.

ध्यानी, *m.* (*f.* inī) one who applies himself to religious meditation: *lit.* contemplative, meditative, religious, thoughtful, considerate.

ध्यानीय, *m.* (*f.* ā) any object suitable for or requiring contemplation: *lit. adj.* to be meditated upon.

ध्यानौं in Braj = **ध्याना**, *q. v.*

ध्यावा = **ध्याना**, *q. v.*

ध्याम, *m.* a certain fragrant grass.

ध्यावत = **ध्याता** (**ध्याना**). See **त**, 5.

ध्यावना = **ध्याना**, *q. v.* See **व**.

ध्यावनौं in Braj = **ध्याना**, *q. v.*

ध्रम in Chand = **धर्म**, *q. v.*

ध्रुपद = **ध्रुवपद**, *q. v.*

ध्रुव, 1, *m.* (*f.* ā) firm, stable, permanent, fixed, certain, true, right: 2, *m.* permanence; *pr. n.* (1) of the polar star (2) of the north pole (3) of one of the twenty-seven astronomical yōgs (4) of Vishṇu (5) of others.

ध्रुवतारा, *m. pr. n.* the polar star.

ध्रुवपद, *m.* a kind of Hindoo song.

ध्रुवलोक, *m. pr. n.* (in Myth.) one of the divisions of paradise.

ध्रुवा, *f.* (*m.* **ध्रुव**) a virtuous woman; a species of plant (*Hedysarum Gangeticum*); a small tree from the fibres of which bowstrings are made; the introductory stanza of a song (it is distinct from the verses of the song, after each of which it is repeated as the burden or chorus).

ध्रू, *m. pr. n.* (1) of the polar star (2) of the north pole (3) of a son of Uttānpād.

ध्वंस, *m.* destruction, loss.

ध्वंसन, 1, *m.* destruction, loss: 2, *adj.* destroying, destructive.

ध्वंसित, *m.* (*f.* ā) destroyed, lost.

ध्वंसी, 1, *m.* (*f.* inī) destructive, destroying; perishing: 2, *f.* a mote in a sunbeam.

ध्वज, *m.* a flag or banner, standard, ship's pendant, flagstaff; a mark, sign, symbol; the penis.

ध्वजा, *m. f.* **ध्वज**, *q.v.*

ध्वजी, *m.* (*f.* inī) a standard-bearer: *lit.* furnished with or bearing a flag.

ध्वन, *more prop.* **ध्वनि**, *q. v.* See **इ**, 1.

ध्वनमोदी, *m.* the umble-bee.

ध्वनि, *m.* sound; the sound of a drum.

ध्वनित, *m.* (*f.* ā) sounded, giving forth a noise (as a drum).

ध्वनिनाला, *f.* the *vīnā* or lute; a fife, pipe; a kind of trumpet.

ध्वांक्ष, *m.* any aquatic bird (feeding on fish), as a crane, gull, etc.; a crow.

न

न (n) is the twentieth consonant of the Hindee alphabet, and has the following characteristics and functions:—1, Its pronunciation is nearly that of the English letter *n*. 2, It is the fifth letter of the **तवर्ग** or dental class, of which it is called 'the nasal'. By calling it 'the nasal of the dentals' is meant that if a compound letter is formed in which the *n*-sound precedes a dental without the intervention of a vowel-sound, the *n*-sound must be represented by this letter (*i. e.* never by **ण**); *e. g.* **गिन्ती**; never **गिणती**. Accordingly, if a simple nexus be formed, the first element of which is the *n*-sound and the second a letter of the **टवर्ग**, or cerebral class, this sound is to be represented by **ण** even though it were originally **न**; *e. g.* **पणडुब्बो**, a diver, from **पन** (the composite form of **पानी**) and the verb, **डूबना**. 3, In conformity with the principles mentioned in Art. **ण**, it is sometimes necessary that these two letters displace each other; frequently, however, they are interchanged inaccurately; *e. g.* **गुन**, more properly **गुण**. 4, This letter is frequently a sign of simple negation (= no, not, nay, neither, nor); frequently also, it is prohibitive, and, as such, it is much less strong than **मत**; *e. g. Aisā nā kaho*, pray don't say so. 5, When this letter precedes a labial without the intervention of a vowel-sound, it loses its natural sound and is most frequently represented by either ˙(*Anuswār*) between the letter that precedes and the letter that follows it, or by **म**; *e. g.* **संपत्ति** or **सम्पत्ति**, etc.: when, however, it is so followed by a dental (*i. e.* by a letter of its own class) it is more properly represented by its secondary form (**न्**) than by *Anuswār*; *e.g.* **दान्त** (rather than **दांत**): when, again, it is so followed by any letter of the **कवर्ग**, **चवर्ग**, or **टवर्ग**, its sound is represented either by *anuswār* or by the secondary forms of the letters **ङ**, **ञ**, **ण** (see the notes on these letters): Lastly, it should be observed that this letter is sometimes interchanged inaccurately with *Anuswār*; *e. g.* **सन्सार**, properly **संसार**. See the art. on *Anuswār* (˙) 6. The provincial usages of this letter, especially its usages in Braj and in poetry, it will be important to notice: (1) It is frequently added to the nominative singular to form the nominative plural; *e. g.* **जनन**, persons; **फलन**, fruits: (2) It is not unfrequently carried into the oblique cases of the plural; *e. g.* **मनुष्यनको** = **मनुष्योंको**: (3) It is sometimes displaced by **व**; *e.g.* **चलवो** = **चलना**; **टिकवेके** = **टिकनेके**. In the case of some words this letter added distinguishes the feminine form from the masculine; *e. g.* **दुल्हन**, **साहन**, **सेठन**, etc. It is also the frequent termination of the infinitival substantive; *e g.* **मरन** = modern **मरण** or **मरना**. 7, As a Kridanta suffix, this letter is frequently added to verbal roots, thus forming substantives masculine expressive of the act denoted by the verb to whose root it is subjoined; *e.g.* **यत्न** (root **यत्**, striving). 8, As a Taddhita suffix, this letter, added to substantives, forms some adjectives masculine: the feminine form of these is sometimes obtained by adding *ā*, sometimes by adding *i*, and in some instances by adding either of these vowels. 9, This letter is sometimes interchanged colloquially with **ल** [see **ल**, 4, (2)]; *e.g.* **लूरी**, properly **नूरी**. 10, In Sanskrit prosody, this letter is the abbreviated term for the foot called 'tribrachys' (⏑⏑⏑) consisting of three short syllables.

नइ, *more prop.* (1) **नई** (2 **नहीं**, *qq. v.*

नईं, *more prop.* (1) **नई** (2) **नवै** (3) **नहीं**, *qq. v.*

नइते (poet.) = **न** + **इते**, *qq. v.*

नई, *f.* (*m.* **नया**) new: a river.

नए, 1, infl. sing. and nom. pl. of **नया**, *q.v.*: 2, a contraction of **नाए**, 2, *q. v.*

नएसिरसे, (see **नया**) anew, afresh, *de novo*.

नंका, *m.* (*f.* ī) *more prop.* **ननका**, *q.v.*

नंग, 1, *m.* (*f.* ā) naked : shameless : 2, *f.* honour, reputation, esteem : (*contra*) disgrace, infamy.

नंगखूल, (*not freq.*) completely naked.

नंगटा, *m.* (*f.* ī) naked.

नंगधड़ंग, stark naked.

नंगधड़ंगी, *f.* nakedness.

नंगा, 1, *f.* (*m.* **नंग**) a naked female : 2, *m.* (*f.* ī) naked : shameless. — *k.* to bare, uncover. — *mādar zād*, stark naked as from the womb. — *pairoṅ* or *pāoṅ*, barefooted. — *pāoṅ hond*, to be prepared for a fight. *Nangī talwār* or *shamsher*, a naked or drawn sword : *met.* a person who speaks his mind freely and without [reserve.

नंगाई, *f.* nakedness.

नंगाझूरी, *f.* a searching, examining (as people on leaving a workshop, to prevent them pilfering).

नंगामुंगा, *m* (*f.* **नंगीमुंगी**) } stark naked.
नंगामुनंगा, *m.* (*f.* **नंगीमुनंगी**) }

नंगाशिर, *m.* (*f.* ā) bareheaded, with uncovered [head.

नंगिया लेना, *t.* to take and strip.

नंचहि, (pl. **हिं**) a poetical form = **नाचता है**.

नंद, **नंध** ; for words beginning thus, see under the forms **नन्द**, **नन्ध**, respectively.

नंघनौं, *t.* (Chand) to pass (as urine), to emit, to let fall : *a. int.* to pass, fall, drop, pass away.

नक, 1, *m.* a corruption of **नख**, *q.v.* : 2, *f.* (a contraction of **नाक**, the nose) used chiefly in composition, as illustrated by the words which follow.

नकघिसनी, *f.* the rubbing the nose on the ground in humble prostration, or as a punishment.

नकचढ़ा, *m.* (*f.* ī) petulant, fretful, ill-tempered, fastidious, passionate, angry.

नकछिकनी, *f.* the sternutatory plant *Artemisia sternutatoria.* [2, the comb-duck.

नकटा, *m.* (*f.* ī) 1, a rogue; *lit.* nose-clipt, noseless:

नकड़ा, *m.* inflammation in the nose, polypus.

नकतोड़ा, *m.* (*f.* ī) droll, waggish, roguish.

नक़द, *m.* ready money, cash. — *o jins*, money and commodities.

नकपूड़ो, *f.* } the nose, nostrils.
नकपोड़ा, *m.* }

नकर (*imperat.*) = **न + कर (करना)**.

नकल, *more prop.* **नक़ल**, *q.v.*

नकवासा, *m.* a certain disease of the nose.

नकश = **नक़शा**, *q.v.*

नकशना } *more com.* **निकसना**, *q.v.*
नकसना }

नक़शा, *m.* a delineation, portrait, model, pattern, plan, chart, map.

नकसा, *more prop.* **नकशा**, *q.v.*

नकसान, *more prop.* **नुक़सान**, *q.v.*

नकसीर, *f.* the veins of the nose. — *phūṭnā*, the [bleeding at the nose.

नकसूर, *m.* the nostrils.

नकार, *m.* the letter **न**, or any symbol that may represent it : refusal, denial.

नकारना, *t.* to withhold consent, refuse, deny.

नकारा, *m.* (*f.* ī) worthless, useless, invalid.

नक़ारा, *m.* a kettledrum (or, rather, a pair of kettledrums of brass or iron).

नकाला, *m.* an eruption on the skin.

नकियाना, *more prop*, **निखयाना**, *q.v.*

नकुछ, (**न + कुछ**) not anything, nothing.

नकुट, *m.* the nose.

नकुल, 1, *m. pr. n.* the fourth of the five Pāṇḍu princes : 2, *m.* (*f.* ī) the Bengal mungoose (*Viverra ichneumon*).

नकुलेष्टका. *f.* a certain plant (*Croton polyandrum*) said to be used by the mungoose as an antidote for snakebites.

नकुलेष्टा, *f.* = **नकुलेष्टका**, *q. v.* [ease of the nose.

नकूआ, *m.* the nose ; the point of the nose ; a dis-

नकेल, *f.* the wooden or iron instrument fixed to a camel's nose and to which the string by which he is led is fastened ; a cavesson or cavezon.

नक्का, *m.* the ace at cards or on dice.

नक्कादूआ, *m.* a kind of game at dice.

नक्कारा = **नक़ारा**, *q.v.* [ary, embroidery.

नक्काशी, *f.* drawing, painting, sculpture, statu-

नक्को, *f.* a speaking through the nose, nasal sound.

नक्कोमूपठ, *f.* a certain game.

नक्खू, wicked, vile, infamous.

नक्तमाल, *m.* a species of tree (*Galedupa arborea* or *Pongamia glabra*, Vent.).

नक्र, *m.* a crocodile, alligator : the nose.

नक्रराज, *m.* the royal alligator, shark.

नक़्ल, *f.* a history, narrative, tale, story; copying, mimicking, acting ; transcribing ; a copy.

नक्वारा, *more prop.* **नक़ारा**, *q.v.*

नक्षत्र, *m.* a star : a lunar mansion or asterism in the moon's path. Besides the common division of the zodiac into twelve signs, the Hindoos divide it into twenty-seven Nakshatras, each of which has a name of its own, and two and a quarter of which are included in each sign. This is the Paurāṇik and popular enumeration of those constellations ; twenty eight, however, distinct in name, figure, and number of stars, are enumerated, *Abhijit*, the twenty-first, being considered as formed of portions of the two contiguous asterisms, and not as being distinct from them. Mythologically, these Nakshatras are regarded as wives of the moon and daughters of Daksh. In the ingenious system of reckoning by symbols adopted by Hindoos in their poetry, this word is a symbol for 27.

नक्षत्रचक्र, *m.* a diagram for astrological purposes.

नक्षत्रमाला, *f.* a necklace of twenty-seven pearls ; the table of lunar asterisms.

नक्षत्रिन, *m.* an epithet of Vishṇu.

नक्षत्री, *m.* (*f.* inī) a person born under a lucky planet, a fortunate person.

नख, 1, *m.* the string of a paper kite : 2, *m.* a finger-nail, toe-nail.— *sikh* or — *se sikhtalak* (*lit.* from the (toe) nails to the hair on the crown of the head ; *hence*) from top to toe, entirely, throughout. In allusion to the number of nails on the fingers and toes, this word, in the ingenious system of reckoning by symbols adopted by Hindoos in their poetry, is a symbol for 20.

नखखादी, *m.* (*f.* inī) any creature that eats with its claws.

नखत / **नखत्र** } *more prop.* नक्षत्र, *q.v.*

नखत्री, *m.* (*f.* iṇī) *more prop.* नक्षत्री.

नखपद, *m.* the scratch of a claw, a scratch.

नखर, *m.* a finger-nail, claw; a knife.

नखरेख / **नखरेखा** / **नखलेखा** } *f.* = नखांक, *q.v.*

नखलौ (*corruption*) = लखनौं, *q.v.*

नखसिख, (from toe-nail to topknot, *i.e.*) from head to foot.

नखांक, *m.* a mark left by the claws, a scratch.

नखानखि, *f.* a mutual clawing, a scratching and tearing one another.

नखियाना, *t.* to scratch, claw.

नखी, 1, *m.* (*f.* inī) a beast with talons: lit. *adj.* having nails or talons: 2, *f.* a certain dried substance (of a brown colour and of the shape of a nail, apparently a dried shell-fish) used as a perfume; a certain vegetable perfume.

नग, *m.* (*f.* ā) anything immoveable; *hence*, a mountain, a tree; the stone of a ring, a stone on which a name, etc. is cut, a gem, precious stone, jewel. In the ingenious system of reckoning by symbols adopted by Hindoos in their poetry, this word is a symbol for 7.

नगचाई, *f.* an approach, arriving.

नगचाना, *a. int.* to approach.

नगचाहट, *f.* an approach, arriving.

नगज, *m.* (*f.* ā) a mountaineer: *lit.* mountain-born.

नगण, *m.* (in Pros.) a tribrach. See न, 10.

नगणा, *f.* heart-pea (*Cardiospermum halicacabum*).

नगद = नक़द. *q.v.*

नगदजिनिस = नक़द ओ जिंस, *q.v.*

नगदौना, *more prop.* नागदौना, *q.v.*

नगन; for words beginning thus, see under the form नग्न.

नगनि, *f.* a nude female.

नगपति, *m.* an epithet of the Himālaya range; *lit.* the lord or chief of mountains.

नगभिद, *m.* the plant *Plectranthrus scutellaroides.*

नगभू, *m.* a mountaineer: *lit.* adj. of the moumtain, mountain.

नगर, *m.* a city, town.

नगरकोट, *m. pr. n.* the town of Kāngrā in the Panjāb.

नगरजन, *m.* (*f.* ī) town's-folk, citizens.

नगरनरनारी / **नगरनारिनर** } = नगरजन, *q.v.*

नगरनारी, *f.* a woman of the town, courtesan.

नगरनिवासी, *m.* (*f.* inī) one who resides in a city.

नगरवर्त्ती, *m.* (*f.* inī) one who dwells in a city.

नगरस्वरूपिणी, *f.* (in Pros.) a species of metre.

नगराध्यक्ष, *m.* (*f.* ī) the chief civil officer of a city.

नगरी, 1, *f.* a city, town; a village: 2, *m.* (*f.* iṇī) a townsman: *lit.* appertaining to a city, town, or village.

नगरोपान्त, *m.* suburbs.

नगारा, 1, (*Rām.*) = निशान, *q.v.*: 2, = नक़ारा, *q.v.*

नगाश्रय, *m.* (*f.* ā) any creature that resides in or frequents mountains.

नगीच, a corruption of नज़दीक, *q.v.*

नगीना, *m.* a ring (*esp.* the signet-ring of a prince); the stone or bezel of a ring.

नग्न, *m.* (*f.* ā) a naked person: *lit.* naked.

नग्नक, *m.* (*f.* ikā) a naked mendicant.

नग्नजित, *m. pr. n.* (1) of a certain prince of the Gandhārs, father of one of Krishṇ's wives (2) of the author of a certain work on architecture (3) of a certain poet.

नग्नता, *f.* (*m.* °त्व) nudity.

नग्नहू, *m.* a drug used for throwing into fermentation the mixture for spirituous liquors, ferment.

नग्ना, *f.* (*m.* नग्न) a naked female; a girl before menstruation.

नग्नाट, *m.* a naked man; *hence*, a kind of religious mendicant who goes about naked, a Jain, Bauddh.

नग्निका, *f.* (*m.* नग्नक) = नग्ना, *q.v.*

नग्निजित, *more prop.* नग्नजित, *q.v.*

नग्नीकरण, *m.* an undressing, stripping.

नग्नीकृत, *m.* (*f.* ā) made naked, undressed, stripped.

नङ्क, for words beginning thus, see under the form नंक.

नचनिया = नर्त्तक, *q.v.*

नचमचाना, *t.* lead a dance: to teaze.

नचवाना, *t.* to cause to be danced.

नचवैया, *m.* a dancer.

नचाना, *t.* to cause to dance, to set a-dancing, to spin a top.

नछत्तर, *more prop.* नक्षत्र, *q.v.*

नछत्तरी / **नछत्री** } *m.* (*f.* iṇī) *more prop.* नक्षत्री, *q.v.*

नज़दीक, *postp.* (takes gen. *m.* infl.) near, hard by, close to, neighbouring, contiguous, almost, about.

नज़दीकी, *f.* propinquity, vicinity.

नज़्म, *m.* a star, planet; fortune; a horoscope, calculation of nativity.

नज़र, *f.* the sight, vision; a look, glance: a vow; a present, offering, gift; an interview. — *ānā*, to appear, come in sight.

नजात, *f.* freedom, deliverance, liberation, absolution, salvation.

नजिक / **नजीक** } corruptions of नज़दीक, *q.v.*

नजूम, *more prop.* नुजूम, *q.v.*

नट, *m.* (*f.* ī; also, but less correctly, n, nī, in, inī) a mime, actor, dancer, tumbler, rope-dancer; a certain tribe who are generally jugglers: the son of a degraded Kshatriya by a woman of the second caste: a subordinate mode in music: a certain tree (*Calorauthes Indica* or *Jonesia asoca*); a sort of reed (*Arundo tibialis* or *Arundo karka*).

नटखट, *m.* a cheat, rogue, etc.: *lit.* trickish, roguish, artful, shrewd, waggish; naughty or fretful (as a child).

नटखटी, *f.* artfulness, trickery, roguishness, wickedness; naughtiness (in children).

नटत (*Rām.*) = **नाचता.** See **त**, 5.
नटता, *f.* actorship.
नटन, 1, *f.* (*m.* **नट**) = **नटनी**, *q.v.*: 2, *m.* the art or or the act of dancing: 3. *f.* denial, negation.
नटना, 1, *t.* to deny: 2, *a. int.* to dance.
नटनारायण, *m.* a certain musical mode (*rāg*). According to some, the sixth; according to others, a subdivision of Deepak or of Megh.
नटनी, *f.* (*m.* **नट**) an actress, female rope-dancer, female tumbler, *nāch*-girl.
नटपत्रिका, *f.* the egg-plant (*Solanum melongena*).
नटबर, *m.* an actor, rope-dancer, mimic, juggler, etc.; a chief dancer or actor.
नटमण्डन, *m.* yellow orpiment.
नटवा, *m.* = **नटबर**, *q.v.*
नटा, *f.* a certain shrub (*Cæsalpinia bonducella*).
नटिन } **नटिनी** } *f.* (*m.* **नट**) = **नटनी**, *q.v.*
नटी, *f.* an actress, dancing-girl, whore: red arsenic: a certain medicinal plant.
नटुआ } **नटुवा** } **नटूआ** } *m.* = **नटबर**, *q.v.*
नट्ठ } **नठ** } (Sk. **नष्ट**) destroyed. (*Chand.*)
नड़, *m.* a species of reed (*Arundo tibialis* or *Arundo karka*): a certain tribe whose special employment is the making a sort of glass bracelets.
नड़कीय, (a field, etc.) abounding in reeds.
नड़डा, *m.* } **नड़डी**, *f.* } the throat, windpipe.
नड़मीन, *m.* a kind of sprat which inhabits reedy places.
नड़ला, *m.* the throat, windpipe.
नड़ी, *f.* a kind of fireworks.
नड्वल, *m.* a reed-bed.
नड्वान, *m.* (*f.* vati) abounding in reeds, reedy.
नत, *m.* the zenith distance of a planet.
नतगुल्ला, *m.* a small shell-fish, cockle, muscle.
नतनी = (1) **नतिनी** (2) **नथनी**, *qq.v.*
नतसंवत, *m.* the beginning of a holy text.
नतमुख, *m.* (*f.* ī) a person who looks down: *lit.* downfaced, looking downwards.
नतरु (*Rām.*) = **नहीं तो**, *q.v.*
नतांग, *m.* (*f.* ī) bent, bowed, stooping, curved.
नतांगी, *f.* (*m.* **नतांग**) a woman.
नतांश, *m.* (in Astron.) zenith distance.
नतान्त; see **नितान्त**.
नति, *f.* a bending, bowing, stooping; curvature, crookedness; a bow, curtsey; modest behaviour.
नतिनी, *f.* a granddaughter (daughter's daughter).
नतु; see **नहीं तो**.
नतैत, *m.* a relative, kinsman.
नत्थ, *more com.* **नथ**, *q.v.*
नथ, *m. f.?* a large ornamental ring worn on the left nostril; a rope passed through the nose of a draught ox.
नथन, a Braj pl. of **नथ**, *q.v.*
नथना, 1, *n.* to have the nose pierced (said of a bullock): 2, *m.* a nostril; a nose-ring. *Nathne charhānā*, to be angry or displeased. *Merā prān nathnoṅtak ā gayā*, my soul has come as far as to my nostrils, *i.e.* I am ready to drop, to faint, or to die (said in a fit of physical exhaustion).
नथनी, *f.* a small nose-ring; a ring inserted in the hilt of a sword; a cord tied around a bullock's nose by which to guide him.
नथी, *f.* a file or bundle of official papers (especially those belonging to a lawsuit) tied up together.
नथुन, *more com.* **नथ**, *q.v.*
नद, 1, in Chand = **नाद**, *q.v.*: 2. *m.* a river. The term is applied only to a river of which the personification is *male*, as the Brahmaputtra, the Indus, etc.
नदनन्द } **नदनन्दन** } corruptions of **नन्दनन्दन**, *q.v.*
नदान, a contraction of **नादान**, *q.v.*
नदाना, a poet. form of **नादान**, *q.v.*
नदिया, *m.* a river; a small stream.
नदियां, *f.* (pl. of **नदी**) rivers.
नदी, *f.* a river (in the more general sense,—the common personification of rivers being female).
नदीकान्त, *m.* (1) a certain tree (*Barringtonia acutangula*): (2) a certain small tree (*Vitex negundo*).
नदीकान्ता, *f.* (1) the rose-apple (*Eugenia jambu*) (2) a kind of shrub (*Leea hirta*).
नदीकूल, *m.* a river's bank.
नदीकूलप्रिय, *m.* a sort of reed (*Calamus rotang*).
नदीज, *m.* (*f.* ā) any creature born in river-water; a certain tree (*Pentaptera arjuna*); the marshy datetree: *lit.* river-produced, aquatic.
नदीतीर, *m.* a river's bank.
नदीबैल, *more prop.* **नन्दीबैल**, *q.v.*
नदीश, *m.* the ocean (*lit.* lord of the rivers).
नदीसर्ज, *m.* a certain tree (*Pentaptera arjuna*).
नदेयी, *f.* a certain plant (*Premna herbacea*).
नदोला, *m.* a large earthen pan.
नद्द in Chand = **नाद**, *q.v.*
ननका, *m.* (*f.* ī) a little child, son (or daughter). (An expression of endearment.)
ननद = (1) **ननदी** (2) **नन्द**, *qq.v.*
ननदिनी } **ननदिया** } = **ननदी**, *q.v.*
ननदी, *f.* a woman's sister-in-law, *i.e.* her husband's sister.
ननन्दा = **ननदी**, *q.v.*
ननान्दा = **ननदी**, *q.v.*
ननिहाल, *f.* a maternal grandfather's family.
नन्द, 1, = **ननदी**, *q.v.*: 2, *m. pr. n.* (1) of Vishṇu (2) of the foster-father of Krishṇ and Durgā (3) of a certain mountain (4) of one of Yudhisthir's drums.
नन्दक, 1, *m.* (*f.* ikā) joyous: causing joy: 2, *m. pr. n.* Krishṇ's sword.

नन्दकन्द (*contraction*) = आनन्दकन्द, *q.v.* See आ, 18.

नन्दकिशोर / नन्दकुमार } *m.* the son of Nand, *i.e.* Kṛishṇ.

नन्दगोप, *m.* an epithet of the cowherd Nand.

नन्दतात, *m.* an epithet of Nand, the foster-father of Kṛishṇ.

नन्दन, 1, *m.* (*f.* ई) a son: lit. *adj.* gladdening: 2, *m. pr. n.* (1) of Vishṇu (2) Shiv (3) of a certain mountain (4) of the pleasure-ground of Indra (5) of the paradise of the Hindoos.

नन्दननन्दन, *m.* the foster-son of Nand, *i.e.* Kṛishṇ.

नन्दननन्दनी, *f.* the daughter of Nand, *i.e.* Durgā.

नन्दनबाग़ / नन्दनवन } *m.pr.n.* the pleasure-grove of the gods.

नन्दनवाटिका, *f.*; see नन्दन, 4, 5.

नन्दना, *f.* (*m.* नन्दन) a daughter.

नन्दप, *m. pr. n.* a son of Swarg.

नन्दमहर, *m.* an epithet of Nand (Kṛishṇ's foster-father).

नन्दरानी, *f.* an epithet of Yashodā (wife of Nand).

नन्दराय, *m.* an epithet of Nand (Kṛishṇ's foster-father).

नन्दलाल, *m.* the beloved of Nand, *i.e.* Kṛishṇ.

नन्दश्याम, *m.* an epithet of Kṛishṇ.

नन्दसुत, *m.* the son of Nand, *i.e.* Kṛishṇ.

नन्दा, *f.* prosperity, happiness, joy: a husband's sister: *pr. n.* (1) of Durgā (2) of a certain river.

नन्दिक, *m.* the toon-tree (*Cedrella toona*, Roxb.) the wood of which resembles mahogany and is much used for making furniture.

नन्दिका, *f.* (*m.* नन्दक) a joyous female: a female who causes happiness.

नन्दिनि (Rām.) = नन्दिनी, *q.v.*

नन्दिनी, *f.* a daughter; a husband's sister; a wife's sister; *pr. n.* a certain fabulous cow.

नन्दिवृक्ष / नन्दिवृक्षक } *m.* = नन्दिक, *q.v.*

नन्दी, 1, *f.* = नन्दक, *q.v.*: 2, = ननदी, *q.v.*: 3, *m. pr. n.* (1) of the bull of Shiv (2) of one of Shiv's chief attendants: 3, *f* a benedictive verse eulogizing a king or a deity.

नन्दीगण, *m.* (pl. of नन्दी) Shiv's attendants.

नन्दीबैल, *m. pr. n.* (see नन्दी) the bull of Shiv.

नन्दीमुख, *m.* 1, = नान्दीमुख, *q.v.*: 2, a kind of water-fowl: a kind of rice: an epithet of Shiv.

नन्दीवृक्ष, *m.* = नन्दिक, *q.v.*

नन्दोई = नन्दोसी, *q.v.*

नन्दोला, *m.* a large earthen vessel, trough for animals to feed from.

नन्दोसी, *m.* a husband's sister's husband.

नन्धना, *t.* to begin.

ननहा, *m.* (*f.* ī) = ननहां, *q.v.*

ननहां, *m.* (*f.* ननहीं) small, diminutive, neat, natty, tidy; insignificant, unimportant.

नन्हा, *m.* (*f.* ī) = ननहां, *q.v.*

नपात, *m.* (*f.* नप्ती) a grandchild (son's child).

नपुआ, *m.* a vessel for measuring with.

नपुंसक, *adj. m.* destitute of virility, of neither sex; *hence*, a eunuch, hermaphrodite; an impotent man; (in Gram.) the neuter gender: *also*, imbecile, unmanly, cowardly.

नपुंसकता, *f.* (*m.* °त्व) the condition of one who is of neither sex; impotence; unmanliness.

नपुंसकलिंग, *m.* (in Gram.) the neuter gender.

नप्ता, *m.* (*f.* नप्त्री) = नपात, *q.v.*

नप्ती, *f.* (*m.* नपात) a granddaughter.

नप्तृ, *m.* (*f.* नप्त्री) = नपात, *q.v.*

नफ़स, *m.* soul, spirit, essence, substance.

नफ़रत, *f.* abomination, aversion: terror, flight: concupiscence; desire: sperm: the penis: gravity: pride: envy: vice.

नफ़ा, *m.* profit, interest, advantage, gain. — *k.* to benefit. — *honā*, to be benefited.

नफ़ीरी, *f.* a kind of brazen trumpet.

नबल, *more com.* नवल, *q.v.*

नबवां, *m.* (*f.* नबवीं) *more prop.* नववां, *q.v.*

नबी, *m.* a divinely-commissioned prophet.

नबीन, *more prop.* नवीन, *q.v.*

नबीरा / नबीसा } *m.* (*f.* ī) a grandchild (son's child).

नबूवत, *f.* prophecy; divining: *pr. n.* the prophetical books of Scripture. — *k.* to prophecy, divine.

नब्बे = नव्वे, *q.v.*

नभ = नभः, *q.v.*

नभः, *m.* the sky, atmosphere, firmament, space, æther (as one of the five elements).

नभग, *adj.* moving in the atmosphere, aerial: hence (1) *m.* (*f.* ā) a bird; (2) *m.* a cloud, air, wind.

नभगनाथ = नभगेश, *q.v.*

नभगिरा, *f.* a voice from the skies, a revelation, an oracle.

नभगेश, *m.* lord of the birds, *i.e.* Garuṛ.

नभगेस, *more prop.* नभगेश, *q.v.*

नभचर *m.* (*f.* ī) = नभग, *q.v.*

नभय, *m.* (*f.* ā) fearless, undaunted, courageous, bold.

नभश्चर *m.* (*f.* ī) = नभचर. See नभग.

नभस = (1) नभः (2) नभस्य, *qq.v.*

नभस्य, *m. pr. n.* one of the months of the rainy season, *viz.* July-August.

नभस्थित, *m. pr. n.* one of the divisions of hell; lit. *m.* (*f.* ā) situated in the sky.

नम, 1, no, not: 2, moistness, humidity: 3, damp, moist, wet.

नमः, *m.* bowing, salutation, obeisance, reverence; a gift, present.

नमक = निमक, *q.v.*

नमकहराम, *m.* a traitor, etc.: *adj.* disloyal, perfidious, treacherous, ungrateful, disobedient.

नमकहरामी, *f.* disloyalty, etc.; (*see above*).

नमकीन, 1, *f.* pickled onions: 2, salted, salt, brackish; witty, poignant, sarcastic; handsome, beautiful. — *pānī*, *m.* pickle, brine.

नमकीनी, *f.* saltness; agreeableness.

नमगीरा, *m.* an awning, canopy.

नमत = (1) नमन, 2 (2) नमस्कार करता है.

नमति = नमत, *q.v.*
नमन, 1, *m.* bowing, obeisance : 2, *m.* (*f.* ā) bowed, bending, stooping : 3, like, resembling : 4, *adv.* like that, in that way.
नमना, *a. int.* to bow in obeisance.
नमनासिब, *more prop.* नमुनासिब, *q.v.*
नमश, *m.* a kind of food made of milk, whipt cream.
नमसित, *m.* (*f.* ā) reverenced, respected, worshipped.
नमस्कार, *m.* respectful or revential address or salutation, adoration. — *k.* (with the acc. rather than the abl. of the object) to salute, do obeisance to.
नमस्कारी, *f.* a kind of sensitive-plant.
नमस्य, *m.* (*f.* ā) venerable, adorable, estimable, entitled to salutation or civility.
नमस्यित, *m.* (*f.* ā) reverenced, worshipped, respected.
नमाज़, *f.* prayer. Specially applied to the prayers prescribed by the Muhammadan law, which are to be offered five times a day.
नमाज़गाह, *f.* the place in a mosque where prayers are read.
नमामहे (*Rām.*) = हम लोग प्रणाम करते हैं.
नमामि / नमामी } (*Rām.*) = मैं प्रणाम करता हूं.
नमालूम, it is not known, there's no knowing, it is not possible to conjecture.
नमित, *m.* (*f.* ā) caused to stop, bent.
नमुचि, *m. pr. n.* (1) of a certain demon who was subdued by Indra (2) of Kāmdev.
नमुचिसूदन, *m.* an epithet of Indra ; *lit.* the destroyer of Namuchi.
नमुची ; see नमुचि.
नमुनासिब, not to the purpose, improper, unbefitting, incongruous.
नमूद, 1, apparent, shewn, exhibited, public, prominent, famous : 2, *f.* index, guide, appearance.
नमूना, *m.* a model, type, specimen, pattern, example (whether in the good or in the bad sense, — for imitation or for avoidance, for admiration or the reverse).
नमेगुरु, *m.* (*f.* āīn *or* āīnī) a spiritual teacher.
नमेरु / नमेरू } *m.* the seed of the eleocarpus.
नम्र, *m.* (*f.* ā) bent, bending, bowed, crooked ; *met.* courteous, mild, meek, soft.
नम्रचित्त, *m.* (*f.* ā) a lowly-minded person : *lit.* of a humble gracious mind or disposition.
नम्रता, *f.* (*m.* °त्व) a bowing ; respectfulness; humbleness, meekness, mildness, tenderness.
नम्रमुख, *m.* (*f.* ī) *adj.* having the head bent, having the face turned downwards, shamefaced, bashful, modest.
नय, *m.* leading ; conduct, way of life ; prudence, policy ; design ; guidance ; justice, fitness, right.
नयऊ (*Rām.*) = झुकाया, *q.v.* (From नाना)
नयन, *m.* leading, bringing, ruling ; the eye ; *hence,* in the ingenious system of reckoning by symbols adopted by Hindoos in their poetry, this word is a symbol for 2.
नयनन, (a Braj pl. of नयन : see न, 6) the eyes.
नयनपट, *m.* the eyelid.
नयनहु (poet. form) = नयन भी.
नयना, *f.* the pupil of the eye.
नयनोत्सव, 1, *m.* a lamp : 2, *m.* (*f.* ā) any loved or desired object.
नयनोपान्त, *m.* the outer angle or canthus of the eye.
नयनौषध, *m.* green sulphate of iron.
नयर in Chand = नगर, *q.v.*
नया, *m.* (*f.* नई) new, modern. *Nayesirse,* anew, afresh, *de novo.*
नयाजन्म, *m.* new birth, (in Theol.) regeneration.
नयो (*Rām.*) = झुकाया, *q.v.* (नाना).
नर, 1, in Chand = नगर, *q.v.* : 2, *m.* a man, a male : 3, *m.* (pl.) mankind, man, men : 4, *m*, the Eternal (*i. e.* the divine imperishable spirit pervading the universe) : 5, certain fabulous beings : 6, masculine, male.
नरः, *m.* a male : *adj.* rough, rude, ugly.
नरक, *m. pr. n.* (1) of the infernal regions, hell (2) of a certain demon (3) of a certain country.
नरककुण्ड, *m.* a well or pit in Tartarus (eight-six such are enumerated).
नरकट = नरकल, *q.v.*
नरकयन्त्रना, *f.* the torments of hell.
नरकवास, *m.* dwelling in hell, being in hell.
नरकल, *m.* a species of reed (*Arundo tibialis,* Roxb.) of which mats are made.
नरकवासी, *m.* (*f.* inī) inhabitant of the infernal regions : *lit.* adj. dwelling in hell.
नरकस, *m.* the windpipe.
नरकस्था, *f. pr. n.* the river of hell.
नरकासुर, *m.* an epithet of Bhaumāsur.
नरकी, appertaining to the infernal regions, hellish.
नरकेशर / नरकेशरी } = नरसिंह, *q.v.*
नरखड़ा, *m.* (or *f.* ī) the throat, throttle.
नरगा, *m.* a kind of long drum : surrounding. — *k.* to surround.
नरगिस, *f.* a narcissus : *met.* the eye of a mistress.
नरजः / नरजा } *m.* small scales.
नरतकी, *more prop.* नर्त्तकी, *q.v.*
नरतन / नरतनु } = मनुष्यतन, *q.v.*
नरत्व, *m.* (*f.* tā) the human state, humanity.
नरदेवा, *more prop.* नृदेव, *q.v.*
नरदेह, *m.* (*f.* ?) = मनुष्यतन, *q.v.*
नरन, (a Braj pl. of नर : see न, 6) men.
नरनारायण, *m. pr. n.* (1) of Kṛishṇ (2) of the author of Krishṇkhaṇḍ.
नरनारि, men and women, males and females.
नरनि, [a Braj pl. of नर : see नि, 2 (2)] men.
नरनाह, *m.* an epithet of any king: *lit.* a lord of men.
नरन्हि, in Braj (1) an emphatic nom. pl. of नर (2) an accus. pl. of नर.
नरपति, *m.* (*f.* patni *or* patnī) a king, monarch, prince ; *lit.* a lord of men.
नरपुर, *m.* the abode of men, *i. e.* the earth.
नरप्रिय, *m.* (*f.* ā) a philanthropist ; lit. *adj.* loving mankind.

नरबलि, *m.* the sacrifice of a human creature.

नरभू. *f.* an epithet of *Bhārat-varsh* (India); *lit.* the land or the birthplace of men.

नरभूप, *m.* an epithet = either (1) lord of the abode of mortals, or (2) lord of men and of the earth.

नरभेप, *m.* an epithet = either (1) the lord of men and of brightness and of wealth, or more probably (2) the lord of the glory and wealth of men.

नरमदा, *more prop.* **नर्मदा**, *q.v.*

नरमाना, *t.* to soften, appease, subdue.

नरमेध, *m.* the sacrifice of a human creature.

नरमोहिनी, *f.* a fascinating woman.

नरमोही, *m.* (*f.* inī) a fascinator of men.

नररूप, 1, *m.* the human form: 2, *m.* (*f.* ā) any creature having the human form.

नररूपी, *m.* (*f.* iṇī) = **नररूप**, 2, *q.v.*

नरलोक, *m.* the state or locality of mortals, *i.e.* the earth.

नरवर, *m.* an excellent man, a chief.

नरश्रेणि, *m. f.* a multitude of men or people.

नरसल, a reed, pen?

नरसिंगा, *m.* a (musical) horn, a wind-instrument. — *phūnknā*, to blow a wind-instrument.

नरसिंगिया, *m.* one who plays the horn.

नरसिंघ (Chand) = **नरसिंह**, *q. v.*

नरसिंह, *m.* 1, *pr. n.* the lion-man or fourth *Avatār* of Vishnu, which appeared in Satya-yug under the following circumstances. Hiranya-kashyap, a certain impious prince, was enraged at his son Prahlād for worshipping the Almighty, and tried various means of destroying him (as, by throwing him into the fire or into the ocean, by poison, etc.); yet Prahlād lived. 'If,' said Hiranya-kashyap, 'your God is present everywhere, let Him come from an alabaster pillar': whereupon, it is said, Narsingh appeared with the lower part of a man and the upper part of a lion; and, destroying the father, he set the son upon the throne: 2, a chief, hero, lion-like man, great, man.

नरसों, the fourth day past or to come (with three days intervening); several days ago or hence.

नरसेनी, *f.* = **नरश्रेणि**, *q. v.*

नरहड़, *m.* a shank, leg.

नरहरि = (1) **नरसिंह** (2) **नरहरिदास**, *qq. v.*

नरहरिदास, *m. pr. n.* Tulsee Dās's *guru*.

नरहिंसक, *m.* (*f.* ikā) homicidal, murderous.

नरहिंसा, *f.* homicide, murder.

नरा, *m.* (poet.) = **नर**, a man.

नराधम, *m.* (*f.* ā) the lowest of mortals, a very low or vile person, a wretch.

नरायण, *more com.* **नारायण**, *q.v.*

नरिंद in Chand = **नरेन्द्र** = **नरपति**, *q. v.*

नरिया, *f.* a tile.

नरी, *f.* a kind of leather, skin, goatskin or sheepskin leather coloured or dyed: a weaver's shuttle.

नरुख, masculine, male.

नरेट, **नरेटा** } *m.* = **नरेटी**, *q. v.*

नरेटी, *f.* the throat, windpipe. —*dalānā*, to throttle.

नरेन्द्र, **नरेश**, **नरेश्वर** } *m.* = **नरपति**, *q. v.*

नर्क; for words beginning thus, see under the form **नरक**.

नर्त्तक, *m.* (*f.* ī) a dancer, actor, mimic, juggler, player; a dancing-master. [*m.* (*f.* ā *or* ī) a dancer.

नर्त्तन, 1, *m.* dancing, gesticulation, acting: 2,

नर्त्तयिता, **नर्त्तयितृ** } *m.* (*f.* °त्री) a dancing-master.

नर्द, *f.* a counter, chessman, etc.; any game (as draughts, etc.) played with counters, backgammon.

नर्दुटक, *m.* a species of stanza of four parts of seventeen syllables each.

नर्बल; see (1) **निर्बल** (2) **नरबलि**.

नर्म, soft; easy, gentle, silly; defective (as coin).

नर्मदा, *f. pr. n.* the Nerbudda river, which, rising in the mountain Amrkūṭ or Amrkantak in the Vindhya range in the province of Gondwana, runs nearly due west about 750 miles, when it falls into the sea in the gulf of Cambay below Baroach.

नर्माई, **नर्माहट** } = **नर्मी**, *q. v.*

नर्मी, *f.* softness, tenderness, delicacy, sweetness; simplicity, silliness.

नर्मीयत, *f.* = **नर्मी**, *q. v.*

नरः, *m.* a male; the male organ; the trunk of a tree; a wave, billow; the ward of a key; a beggar; a hermaphrodite: *lit.* adj. male; rough, rude, abominable, ugly.

नल, *m.* 1, *pr. n.* a certain king who is the hero of several poetical works famous among Hindoos, but especially of the episode of Nala and Damayantee: 2, a kind of reed (*Amphidonax karka*, Lindl., or *Arundo karka* or *Arundo tibialis*); a tube, spout, joint of bamboo or other hollow wood, the bamboo which fowlers use for entangling game by applying birdlime to the top of it; a measuring-rod; a measure of four hundred cubits. — *chalānā* (setting the bamboo in motion) refers to a magical practice resorted to for the discovery of theft; *viz.* two pieces of split bamboo of equal lengths are applied to one another side by side, and held by two men, one at each end (any persons, taken at random, may, it is said, be employed for this purpose): the magician then pronounces certain incantations the efficacy of which is pretended to be such that the bamboos spontaneously move towards the place where the thief or the stolen goods are, — dragging the men along with them. *Nal dar nal*, one tube within another.

नलकूवर, *m. pr. n.* one of the two sons of Kuver.

नलका, **नलड़ा** } *m.* (or *f.* ī) the throat, windpipe.

नलद, *m.* (or *f.* ā) Indian spikenard (*Nardostachys jatamansi*); the root of *Andropogan muricatus*.

नला, *m.* the ureters, urinary ducts: the arm, the arm-bone. *Āhanī nalā*— or *bhūīn nalā*, a sort of fire-works (Roman candle, made of iron, buffalo-horn, or bamboo, placed on the ground). *Dam*—, a variety of the above-mentioned, but with occasional globes of bright light bursting up. *Hath* —, a small species of the above, and held in the hand.

नलायक, *more prop.* **नालायक**, *q.v.*

नलि ; see **नली**.

नलिका, *f.* a kind of perfume.

नलिन, *m.* a lotus-flower : the Indian crane.

नलिनी, *f.* a lotus (*Nelumbium speciosum* or *Nymphœa nelumbo*); an assemblage of lotuses ; a place where the lotus grows or may grow; a branch of the heavenly Ganges ; a mystical name of one of the nostrils.

नलिया, *m.* a certain caste whose occupation it is to catch birds with lined tubes (*nal*).

नली, *f.* a tube, reed, pipe, spout, windpipe, ureter, etc. ; a gun-barrel ; *morbus plerumque a manustupratione ortus in quo membrum virile exile fit nec erigi potest* ; the bone of the leg, the *tibia* ; a weaver's shuttle, the little tube within the shuttle on which the woof is wound. [letters are conveyed ; straw.

नलूआ, *m.* a tube ; a joint of bamboo in which

नल्ली, tight. [hundred (?) cubits.

नल्व, *m.* a furlong, a distance measured by four

नव, 1, *m.* (*f.* ā) new, young, fresh, raw, recent : nine : 2, this form is constantly interchanged with **नौ** ; for all words, therefore, beginning with it, but not given below, see under this latter form.

नवकन्या, *f.* a female who has never known a male.

नवकालिका, *f.* a young woman (either one recently married, or one in whom menstruation has lately com- [menced).

नवखण्ड = **नौखण्ड**, *q.v.*

नवग्रह = **नवग्रहा**, *q.v.*

नवग्रहा, *m.* (pl.: See **आ**, 22) the nine planets, *i.e.* the seven planets, and the ascending and descending nodes.

नवची ; see **नौची**.

नवछात्र, *m.* a student, novice.

नवछावर, *f.* a propitiatory offering, sacrifice, victim.

नवजल, *m.* the rain of the rainy season.

नवजोवना } *more prop.* **नवयौवना**, *q.v.*
नवजौवना }

नवता, *f.* (*m.* °त्व) novelty, freshness, newness.

नवदुल्हः, *m.* a recently-married man, bridegroom.

नवद्वार, *m.* an epithet applied to the body in allusion to its nine outlets, *viz.* the nostrils, the eyes, the ears, the mouth, the generative organ, and the anus ; lit. *adj.* having nine doors.

नवधा, nine-fold, nine times ; nine kinds of.

नवधाभक्ति = **नवभक्ति**, *q.v.*

नवन, 1, see **नौन** : 2, nine : 3, *m.* a praising.

नवना ; see **नौना**.

नवनागरी, *f.* a female who has never known a male.

नवनिधि, *m.* (*f.* ?) the treasure of Kuver (which consists of nine fabulous gems).

नवनी, *f.* } fresh butter.
नवनीत, *m.* }

नवनीता, *more prop.* **नवनीत**, *q.v.*

नवफलिका = **नवकालिका**, *q.v.*

नवबधू, *f.* a newly-married woman.

नवबाला, *f.* a girl just grown up to puberty.

नवभक्ति, *f.* the nine kinds of devotion recognized by Hindoos.

नवम, *m.* (*f.* ī) ninth.

नवमालिका, *f.* double jasmine (*Jasminum zambac*).

नवमी, *f.* (*m.* **नवम**) the ninth day of a lunar half [month.

नवमीं = **नवमी**, *q.v.*

नवम्बर, *m. pr. n.* (Engl.) November.

नवयौवना, *f.* a girl just grown up to puberty, a young woman.

नवरत्न, 1, *m.* the nine precious gems, *viz.* pearl, ruby, topaz, diamond, emerald, *lapis lazuli*, coral, sapphire, and *gomed* : 2, *m. pr. n.* the nine men of letters at the court of Vikramāditya, *viz.* Danvantaree, Kshapanak, Amarsingh, Shanku, Vetalabhatt, Ghatakarpar, Kālidās, Varāhamihir, and Vararuchi : 3, *m.* (*f.* ?) a kind of ornament worn on the arm and wrist consisting of nine different gems.

नवरस, 1, *m.* (*f.* ā) young, fresh, tender, recent, newly arrived or come forth : 2, *m.* the aggregate of the nine kinds of pleasure recognized by the Hindoo system.

नवरात्र, *m.* the term applied to the first nine nights of the light half of Aswin, which are devoted to Durgā.

नवरात्रि, *f.* } = **नवरात्र**, *q.v.*
नवरात्रिक, *m.* }

नवल, 1, *m.* a sapling: 2, *m.* (*f.* ā) a youth : *lit.*

नवला, *f.* a young woman. [beautiful, rare, young.

नववरिका, *f.* a newly-married woman.

नववस्त्र, *m.* new clothing.

नववां, *m.* (*f.* wīṅ) = **नवां**, *q.v.*

नवशायक, *m.* the designation applied to either of the nine inferior classes, *viz.* cowherds, gardeners, oilmen, weavers, confectioners, water-carriers, potters, blacksmiths, and barbers.

नवश्राद्ध, *m.* the first of the series of sacrifices to the manes of a deceased relative, *viz.* on the first, third, fifth, seventh, ninth, and eleventh days after the death.

नवसप्त, (*i. e.* 16: see **शृंगार**) the aggregate of the sixteen kinds of Shringār. [new pupil, beginner.

नवसिख्खा, *m.* (*f.* ī or in) one who has begun to learn, a

नवसूतिका, *f.* a woman recently delivered.

नवसै, (**नव** + **सौ**) nine hundred.

नवा, *f.* 1, = **नव**, *q.v.*: 2, voice, sound, modulation,

नवाई, *f.*; see **नवाया**. [song; opulence; subsistence.

नवां, *m.* (*f.* īṅ) ninth.

नवांश, *m.* a ninth, ninth part.

नवाछात्र ; see **नवछात्र**.

नवाज़ना, *t.* to cherish, caress, favour.

नवाज़िश, *f.* (*pl.* āt) caressing, blandishment, kindness, politeness.

नवाड़ा, *m.* a large boat, a barge.

नवाना, *t.* to cause to stoop, cause to submit to, to bend downwards, bow ; to fold, double.

नवान्न, *m.* new grain or rice ; a certain ceremony observed on first eating the rice, etc. of a preceding [harvest.

नवाब, *more prop.* **नव्वाब**, *q.v.*

नवाम्बर, *m.* new unbleached cloth.

नवाया, *m.* (*f.* **नवाई**) bent, bowed: folded.

नवारना, *a. int.* to travel, walk, wander, stray; *t.* to surround: to exclude.

नवारा, *m.* a large boat, a barge.

नवारी, *f.* a sort of jasmine.

नवासा, *m.* (*f.* ī) a grandchild (daughter's child).

नवासी, eighty-nine (८६). See श्रों, वां, वीं, वे, वें.

नवाह, *m.* (pl. of नाहियः) environs.

नवी, *f.* the string with which a cow's feet are tied

नवीं, *f.* (*m.* नवां) ninth. [during milking, a tether.

नवीकृत, *m.* (*f.* ā) renewed, revived.

नवीन, new, novel, fresh, recent, youthful: hence, *m.* (*f.* ā) a novice, etc. [freshness, youthfulness.

नवीनता, *f.* (*m.* °त्व) newness, recentness, novelty,

नवीभाव, *m.* renovation.

नवीभूत, *m.* (*f.* ā) renewed, revived.

नवें, masc. inflection of नवां, *q.v.* [ninth place.

नवे, 1, = (1) नवी (2) नव्वे, *qq.v.*: 2, ninthly, in the

नवों, (see श्रों, 4) the nine, all nine of them.

नवोंयेागीश्वर, *m.* the nine sons of Bharat, *viz.* (1) Kashyap (2) Hari (3) Antariksh (4) Prabuddh (5) Pippalāyan (6) Upavirhotra (7) Durmil (8) Chyamas (9) Karbhājan.

नवोंनिधि, *m. pr. n.* (see निधि) the nine treasures of

नव्य, *m.* (*f.* ā) = नवीन, *q.v.* [Kuver.

नव्यता, *f.* (*m.* °त्व) = नवीनता, *q.v.*

नव्वां, *m.* (*f.* wīṅ) = नवां, *q.v.*

नव्वाब, *m.* (pl. of नाइब) vicegerents, deputies, lieutenants, governors; *vulg.* 'nabob.'

नव्वासी, *more prop.* नवासी, *q.v.*

नव्वे, ninety (६०). See श्रों, वां, वीं, वे, वें.

नश; see (1) नस (2) नाश (3) नशा.

नशा, *m.* intoxication; intoxicating liquor; headache or crop-sickness from over-drinking.

नशाक, *m.* a species of crow.

नशाखेार, *m.* a drunkard.

नशाना, *more com.* नसाना, *q.v.*

नशीला / नशेला } inebrient, intoxicating.

नश्यत, *adj. m.* (*f.* ā) perishing, decaying, wasting, being destroyed. [chievous, destructive.

नश्वर, *m.* (*f.* ā *or* ī) perishable, evanescent; mis-

नश्वरता *f.* (*m.* °त्व,) perishableness; mischievous-

नश्वरा / नश्वरी } *f.*; see नश्वर. [ness.

नष्ट, *m.* (*f.* ā) destroyed, spoilt, lost, removed, ruined, annihilated. [either half of Bhadra.

नष्टचन्द्र, *m.* the moon on the fourth lunation of

नष्टचेतन, *m.* (*f.* ā) faint, insensible.

नष्टता, *f.* (*m.* °त्व) ruin, annihilation.

नष्टा, *f.* (*m.* नष्ट) an adultress, harlot.

नष्टि, *f.* destruction, ruin.

नस, *f.* a vein; fibre; sinew; nerve.

नसल, *f.* race, pedigree, genealogy, descent, breed, origin, caste, family.

नसहा, *m.* (*f.* ī) veined, veiny.

नसा, 1, *more prop.* नशा, *q.v.*: 2, *f.* a nose.

नसाना, *t.* (नाश) to spoil, squander, destroy, annihilate: *n.* to be destroyed, be annihilated.

नसावन, destructive, destroying.

नसावना, *more prop.* नसाना, *q.v.*

नसावा, *more prop.* नसाया (नसाना).

नसी, *f.* a coulter, ploughshare: a certain plant.

नसीठ, *m.* (*f.* ā) ill-omened. [fate, destiny.

नसीब, *m.* fortune, lot, luck, chance, portion, part,

नसीम, *f.* a gentle zephyr, fragrant air, breeze.

नसीला, *m.* (*f.* ī) veined; of good breed.

नसीहत, *f.* counsel, admonition, advice. — *k.* or *denā*, to admonish; to reprove, reprimand, chastise.

नसीहा, a light plough for tender soils.

नसेनी (*Rām.*) = निःश्रेणी, *q.v.*

नस्त, *m.* a sternutatory, snuff: the nose.

नस्तक, *m.* a hole bored through the bridge of the nose of draught-cattle.

नस्तरन, *m.* the white rose of India (*Rosa glandulifera*, Roxb.): a kind of cloth.

नस्ता, *f.* a hole bored in the septum of the nose.

नस्य, 1, *m.* a sternutatory, snuff: 2, *m.* (*f.* ā) appertaining to the nose, nasal.

नस्या, *f.* a nose-bridle. [the septum of the nose:

नस्योत, *m.* (*f.* ā) an animal led by a string through

नस्वर, *more prop.* नश्वर, *q.v.*

नह, 1, in Chand = नहि, *q.v.*: 2, *m.* a nail, claw, talon. — *lenā*, to trip, stumble.

नहक, meagre, lean.

नहट्टा, *m.* a scratch (of a claw).

नहन, *more com.* नाखून, *q.v.*

नहना, *a. int.* to flow, streem.

नहनियो = नहाइयो (नहाना).

नहनी, *f.* an instrument for cutting the nails; a kind of chisel used in turning and polishing brass, etc.

नहमियाह, *m. pr. n.* of the prophet Nehemiah and of the Book which bears his name.

नहर, *f.* a stream, rivulet, canal.

नहरनी, *f.* an instrument for paring the nails with; a shoemaker's awl.

नहरुआ, *m.* a kind of disease of the skin. [washed.

नहलवाना, *t.* to cause to be bathed, cause to be

नहलाना, *t.* to cause to bathe.

नहलानाधुलाना (a jingling combination of नहाना and धुलाना) = नहलाना, *q.v.*

नहवाना, *t.* to cause to bathe.

नहस, *m.* an evil omen; bad luck: *adj.* inauspicious, unlucky, bad.

नहान, *m.* ablution, bathing.

नहाना, to bathe, wash, perform ablutions.

नहानाधोना (see **नहलानाधुलाना**) = **नहाना**, *q.v.*

नहानी, *f.* menstruation, menses.

नहायत, *more prop.* **निहायत**, *q.v.* [bathing.

नहाया, 1, *m.* (*f.* **नहाई**) bathed ; bathing : 2, *m.*

नहारमुंह, *adj.* without eating, fasting.

नहारू, *m.* a piece of leather: a tiger. [*ensis.*

नहारूआ, *m.* (*f.* °**ई**) the guinea-worm (*Filaria medin-*

नहि } nay, no, not.
नहिं }

नहियर } *more com.* **नैहर**, *q.v.*
नहिहर }

नही } nay, no, not.
नहीं }

नहीं तेा; see **श्रेार नहीं**, and **तेा**, 3.

नहुष, *m. pr. n.* (1) of a certain ancient Hindoo king (2) of a certain Nāg. [Book that bears his name.

नहूम, *m. pr. n.* of the prophet Nahum and of the

नहेर; see (1) **नहर** (2) **नैहर**. [it happen that.

नहेा कि, else, otherwise, lest it be so that, lest

ना, 1, nay, no, not : 2, this is a sign of the feminine of many adjectives of Sanskrit origin ; see **न**, 8 : 3, *m.* (*f.* ī) this is the invariable sign of the infinitive of the Hindee verb : it should be observed, however, that, as such, it is, in Braj, constantly liable to be displaced by the forms **नि**, **नेा**, **नेां**, **वेा**.

नाइ (*Rām.*) = **नवाके** (from **नाना**, 3).

नाइन, *f.* (*m.* **नाई**) a female barber, a barber's wife.

नाइब, *m.* a deputy, vicegerent, lieutenant, substitute, subordinate.

नाइरत = **नाइरा**, *q.v.* [enmity, hatred.

नाइरा, *m.* fire, flame, heat, inflammation : *met.*

नाई, 1, *m.* (*f.* **नाइन**) a barber : 2, = **नाए**, *q.v.* : 3, *more prop.* **नाईं**, *q.v.* : 4, *f.* a kind of herb or plant.

नाईं, *postp.* (takes gen. *fem.*) like, resembling, in the

नाउमेद, hopeless, despairing. [same manner as.

नाऊ in Braj = **नाई**, *q.v.*

नाऊं, 1, (*Rām.*) = **नाम**, *q.v.* : 2, 1st. pers. sing. of the dependent mode of the verb **नाना**.

नाऊदान, *more prop.* **नावदान**, *q.v.*

नाए, 1, a reed, pipe, flageolet, flute, fife : 2, *m.* pl. aor. of **नाना**, 3, *q.v.*

नाश्रेां, *m.* (*prop.* **नाम**) a name, a noun.

नां, no, not, nay.

नांई (Rām.) = **नाईं**, *q.v.*

नांई } *more com.* **नाईं**, *q.v.*
नांईं }

नांश्रेां, *m.* (*prop.* **नाम**) a name, a noun.

नांक, *f.* (*more com.* **नाक**) the nose. [cross, pass.

नांघना, *t.* to step across, leap over, jump over,

नांचना, *more prop.* **नाचना**, *q.v.*

नांड़िया, *m. pr. n.* the bull and vehicle of Shiv.

नांदीमुख = **नान्दीमुख**, *q.v.*

नांव = (1) **नांश्रेां** (2) **नाव**, *qq.v.*

नांवठांव (= **नाम** + **ठाम**) name and place.

नांह }
नांहि } nay, no, not.
नांहीं }

नाक, 1, *m.* heaven, paradise ; the heavens, atmosphere, æther ; sky : 2, *f.* the nose. — *katānā* or *katī honā*, to lose one's honour. — *charhānā* or *sakoṛnā* to turn up one's nose (whether in displeasure or in anger). — *rakhnā*, to preserve one's honour.

नाकड़ा, *m.* an inflammation in the nose, polypus.

नाकनटी, *f.* (= **अप्सरा**) a female dancer of the court of Indra.

नाका, *m.* an alligator, crocodile : the extremity of a road : the eye of a needle : an alley, avenue, passage, lane.

नाकानाकि, *adv.* nose to nose.

नाकारा, *m.* (*f.* ī) useless, worthless, bad.

नाकिस, imperfect, unfinished, deficient, defective, mutilated, inexpert. — *honā*, to want.

नाकी, *m.* (*f.* inī) appertaining to the nose.

नाकुल, *m.* (*f.* ī) ichneumon-like, appertaining to the ichneumon.

नाकुली, *f.* the ichneumon-plant (*Ophioxylon serpentinum*) supposed to furnish the mungoose with an antidote to snake-bite.

नाकेदार, *m.* a receiver of customs or transit-duties.

नाकेबन्दी, *f.* the collecting customs or transit-dues : the shutting up a road.

नाक्षत्र, *m.* a month as computed by the moon's passage through her twenty-seven asterisms (*Nakshatra*) ; *i. e.* a month of thirty days of six gharees each.

नाक्षत्रिक, *m.* (*f.* ā *or* ī) appertaining to the lunar asterisms (*Nakshatra*).

नाक्षत्रिकी, *f.* stellar influence.

नाखुन, *m.* a nail, a talon, a claw. — *lenā*, to pare the nails : to trip or stumble (said of a horse).

नाखुना, *m.* a plectrum, instrument for striking the strings of a guitar with : a haw or web in the eye.

नाखुश, displeased, angry. [stantive verb =) is not.

नाखे, (a dialectic form of the negative of the sub-

नाग, 1, *m.* (*f.* ī) a snake, serpent ; the hooded snake (*Coluber naga*) commonly called *Cobra di capello*, considered by the Hindoos to be a sacred reptile : an elephant : the name of certain trees, *viz.* (1) *Messua ferrea* or *Messua Roxburghii Wight.* (2) *Rottleria tinctoria*, — used in dyeing (3) a species of grass (*Cyperus pertenuis*) : lead : poison : *pr. n.* (1) of one of the five vital airs (2) of a certain country (3) of a certain mountain (4) of one of the 'invariable' astronomical periods called *Karaṇ* : 2, *m.* (*f.* ī) consisting of serpents : produced from an elephant. This term has a special application as the designation of a certain class of demigods, *viz.* the fabulous serpents with a human face, the tail of a serpent and the expanded neck of the *Coluber naga* : they are said to have sprung from Kadru the wife of Kashyap for the purpose of peopling the regions below the earth (*pātāl*). In allusion to the eight species of serpents, this word, in the ingenious system of reckoning by symbols adopted by Hindoos in their poetry, is a symbol for 8.

नागकन्या, *f.* a certain race of very beautiful females, said to be of serpentine extraction and to inhabit the regions (*pātāl*) below the earth.

नागकेशर, *m.* a species of small tree (*Messua ferrea*).

नागजिह्वा, *f.* a kind of plant (*Asclepias pseudosarsa*).

नागजिह्विका, *f.* red arsenic.

नागजीवन, *m.* tin.

नागदन्त, *m.* elephant's tooth, *i.e.* ivory.

नागदन्ती, *f.* a species of sunflower (*Heliotropium Indicum*).

नागदौन, *m.* a kind of wood by touching which it is said that fetters spontaneously fall off: the plant asparagus.

नागदौना, *m.* wormwood (*Artemisia vulgaris*).

नागन, 1, *f.* (*m.* **नाग**) = **नागी**, *q.v.*: 2, *m.* (a Braj. pl. of **नाग**) serpents, etc. See **न**, 6.

नागपंचमी, *f.* a certain Hindoo holiday, *viz.* the fifth day of the shuklpaksh of Shrāvan, on which they worship a snake to procure blessings on their children.

नागपत्नी, *f.* (= **नागकन्या**) a female of the serpent race.

नागपाश, *m.* a noose, a sort of noose used for seizing an enemy in battle, resembling the arms of the Retiarii among the Roman gladiators.

नागपास = (1) **नागपाश** (2) = **नागौर**, *qq. v.*

नागपुष्प, *m.* (1) a certain tree used in dyeing (*Rottleria tinctoria*): (2) a certain small tree (*Messua ferrea*): (3) a kind of flower (*Michelia champaca*).

नागफनी, *f.* the prickly pear (*Cactus ficus Indica*).

नागफांस } **नागफास** } *f.* = **नागपाश**, *q. v.*

नागबन्धु, *m.* the holy figtree (*Ficus religiosa*).

नागबला, *f.* a certain creeping-plant (*Hedysarum lagopodioides*).

नागबेल, *m.* the betel-plant (*Piper betel*).

नागभाषा, *f.* a certain Prākrit language said to be used by the serpentine race who inhabit *Pātāl*.

नागभिद, *m.* a sort of snake (*Amphisbæna*).

नागमातृ, *f.* an epithet of Surasā, mother of the serpent-race: red arsenic.

नागर, 1 = **देवनागरी**, *q.v.*: 2, *m.* (*f.* ī) a citizen, person whose breeding and habits are of the city; *hence*, a clever, sharp, knowing person, wag, buck: *lit.* appertaining to town: 3, *m.* a kind of grass (*Cyperus pertenuis*).

नागरंग, *m.* the orange, especially the Silhet orange (*Citrus aurantium*).

नागरमुस्ता, *f.* a certain grass (*Cyperus*).

नागरमोथा, *m.* a certain sweet-smelling grass (*Cyperus pertenuis* or *C. juncifolius* or rush-leaved *Cyperus*).

नागरिक, *m.* (*f.* ā or ī) a citizen; a polite person; a superintendent of police: *lit.* appertaining to town.

नागरिपु, *m.* an epithet of the lion.

नागरी, *f.* 1, = **देवनागरी**, *q.v.*: 2, (*m.* **नागर**) a clever or intriguing woman: 3, city dialect as compared with the dialect of the village: 4, a kind of Euphorbia.

नागल, *m.* a plough.

नागलोक, *m. pr. n.* the regions under the earth (*Pātāl*) the abode of serpents and hydras. Not being accessible to the sun, it is supposed to be illuminated by very resplendent jewels.

नागहा, *more com.* **नागाह**, *q. v.*

नागहानी, 1, suddenly: 2, sudden, unexpected, accidental.

नागा, 1, vacant, void, unemployed: 2, *m.* adjournment, respite; nought. — *k.* to adjourn, discontinue, intermit.

नागा, *m.* (**नग्न**) a certain caste of Hindoo mendicants (so called from their going naked). Sometimes they are armed, and serve as mercenaries to native princes.

नागांग, *m. pr. n.* Hastināpur (ancient Delhi).

नागांचला, *f.* a boring-rod, a stick or pole driven into a square piece of earth in the centre of a newly dug pond.

नागाख्या } **नागाभा** } = **नागांग**, *q. v.*

नागाह, in no time, suddenly, unexpectedly, unawares.

नागिन } **नागिनी** } **नागीनी** } *f.* = **नागी**, *q. v.*

नागी, *f.* (*m.* **नाग**) a female serpent; a female elephant.

नागूरी, *more com.* **नागौरी**, *q. v.*

नागेश्वर, *f.* a kind of flower (*Messua ferrea*); Indian rose-chesnut.

नागेश्वरी, *m.* (*f.* iṇī) *adj.* yellow; *lit.* of the colour of the *Nāgeshar*.

नागोद, *m.* armour for the front or for the belly, a breastplate, cuirass.

नागोदर, *m.* = **नागोद**, *q. v.*

नागौर, *m. pr. n.* a certain country near *Mārwār*.

नागौरा, *m.* a certain fine breed of bullocks: *lit.* appertaining to *Nāgaur*.

नागौरी, *m.* (*f.* iṇī) a native of Nāgaur: *lit.* appertaining to Nāgaur.

नाग्नजित, *m.* (*f.* ī) a descendant of Nagujit.

नाग्नता, *more prop.* **नग्नता**, *q. v.*

नाच, *m.* a dance, ball, entertainment. — *k.* or *nāchnā*, to dance. — *nachānā*, to cause to dance; to tease.

नाचना, *a. int.* to dance.

नाचनी, *f.* a female dancer, dancing-girl.

नाचरंग, *m.* an entertainment by dancing.

नाचार, *more prop.* **लाचार**, *q. v.* See **न**, 9.

नाचीज़, of no importance, insignificant, trifling.

नाज़, *m.* blandishments, fondling, coquetry, playfulness; gracefulness, elegance; soothing; softness; consequential airs, pride.

नाज, a contraction of **अनाज**, *q.v.* See **अ**, 18.

नाज़िर, *m.* a spectator, supervisor, keeper, superintendent, inspector, guard, a sheriff, a certain officer employed in judicial courts superior to all peons, bailiffs, etc.

नाज़िरी, *f.* the status and the functions of a *nāzir*.

नाज़नीन, 1, delicate, beautiful, lovely, charming: 2, *f.* a lovely female, belle, mistress.

नाजु (*Rām.*) = **अनाज** or **अन्न**, *qq.v.* See **अ**, 18.

नाज़ुक, thin, light, subtile, delicate, nice, tender, brittle, fragile, elegant; genteel, gracious, facetious.

नाट, *m.* a pillar, obelisk: a dance; a pantomime: *pr. n.* the Carnatic country.

नाटक, *m.* (*f.* ikā or ī) an actor: acting, dancing, etc.; a play, drama, comedy; the first of the ten species of Sanskrit dramatic compositions of the first order.

नाटकशाला, *f.* a room or hall for dramatic representations, a theatre, ball-room, dancing-saloon.

नाटकसाल, *m.* an actor, player, mimic.

नाटकसाला, *more prop.* **नाटकशाला**, *q.v.*

नाटकी, *f.* (*m.* **नाटक**) a dancing-girl: a kind of drama-

नाटकीय, dramatic, comic. [tic writing.

नाटम्गार, *m.* a great merchant.

नाटमन्दिर, *m.* = **नाटकशाला**, *q.v.*

नाटा, *m.* (*f.* ī) a dwarf: *lit.* dwarfish, short, dapper.

नाटापन, *m.* lowness of stature, dwarfishness.

नाटिका, *f.* (*m.* **नाटक**) an actress: a short or light comedy, the first of the dramas of the second order.

नाटोर, *more com.* (1) **नटबर** (2) **नाठोर**, *q v.*

नाट्य, *m.* the science or the art of acting or of dancing; the union of song, dance, and instrumental music.

नाट्यशाला, *f* = **नाटकशाला**, *q.v.*

नाठ, *m.* non-existence.

नाठो (*Rām.*) = **नष्ट भई** or **नाश किई.**

नाठोर, *adj.* (**ना + ठोर**) = **जिसका स्थान नहीं है.**

नाड़, *more prop.* **नाड़ो**, *q.v.*

नाड़ा, *m.* tape.

नाड़ि, *more prop.* **नाड़ो**, *q.v.*

नाड़िका, *f.* an Indian hour (being twenty-four minutes or one-sixtieth of a sideral day): a certain measure of length, *viz.* half a *ḍaṇḍa*: an Indian clock.

नाड़िपत्र, *m.* the esculent root *Arum colocasia.*

नाड़िमण्डल, *m.* the celestial equator.

नाड़ो, *f.* the stalk or culm of any plant; any tubular organ of the body (as an artery, vein, intestine); a fistula, sinus; the pulse: an hour of twenty-four minutes. —*dekhnā*, to beat, strike.

नाड़ोच, *m.* a certain esculent root (*Arum colocasia*).

नाड़ोनक्षत्र, *m.* the planet of a person's nativity.

नाड़ोव्रण, *m.* an ulcer.

नाणिडया, *m. pr. n.* the bull and vehicle of Shiv.

नात = (1) **नाता** (2) **नाथ**, *qq. v.*

नातर (= **नहीं तो**) if not—then; else, otherwise.

नाता, *m.* kinsmanship, alliance, relationship, kin.

नातारिस्ता, *m.* kinsmanship, family-alliance.

नातिन, *f.* (*m.* **नाती**, 2) a granddaughter (daughter's

नातिनो = **नातिन**, *q. v.* [daughter).

नाती, 1, *more com.* **नातिन**, *q.v.*: 2, *m.* (*f.* in *or* inī) a grandchild (daughter's child).

नातेदार, *m.* a kinsman, relation.

नातेदारी, *f.* kinsmanship, family-alliance.

नाते; see (1) **नाती** (2) **नाता.**

नातो in Braj = **नहीं तो**, *q.v.*

नाथ, 1, *m.* (*f.* ā) a protector, master, lord, husband: often used as the latter element in compound designations of Hindoo ascetics; *e. g.* Gorakhnāth: 2, *f.* a rope passed through the nose of a draft-ox; a seton.

नाथता, *f.* (*m.* **°त्व**) the status of a protector.

नाथना, *t.* to bore a bullock's nose for the purpose of putting into it a string to guide him by, to insert the string.

नाथवत / **नाथवन्त** / **नाथवान** } *m.* (*f.* vatī) = **नाथी**, *q.v.*

नाथा, 1, *more prop.* **नाता**, *q.v.*: 2, *f.* (*m.* **नाथ**) a protectress.

नाथि, 1, *more prop.* **नाथो**, *q.v.*: 2, = **नाथके** (**नाथना**).

नाथित, *adj.* having the nose pierced (said of a draft-bullock). [dependent, subject to.

नाथी, *m* (*f.* inī) having a protector or husband,

नाद, 1, *m.* sound in general, roaring, noise, cry; a song: a semicircle used especially (in the mystical works of the Hindoos) as an abbreviation or as a hieroglyphic or to represent the nasal sound. — *k.* to

नादना, *t.* to begin. [sing; to roar (as a tiger).

नादन (*contraction*) = **नादान**, *q.v.*

नादली, *f.* a kind of charm or talisman (being a stone inscribed with words from the Kur,ān and hung, as a preserving amulet, around children's necks).

नादान, *m.* a fool, simpleton: *lit.* unlearned, ignorant, stupid, simple.

नादानी, *f.* ignorance, simpleness, stupidity, folly.

नादारी, *f.* poverty, insolvency.

नादाहा, *m.* a spout, canal. [choice.

नादिर, *m.* (*pl.* āt) a wonder: *lit.* wonderful, rare,

नादी, *m.* (*f.* inī) *adj.* sounding, sounding aloud.

नादुरस्त, crooked, untrue, inaccurate, unjust, improper. [river, river-produced, fluviatic, aquatic.

नादेय, *m.* (*f.* ī) an aquatic: *lit.* coming from a

नादेयी, *f.* a kind of water-reed (*Calamus fasciculatus*); a certain plant (*Pranna herbacea*); the China

नाधना, *t.* to yoke. [rose.

नानक, *m. pr. n.* a certain religious mendicant, founder of the sect of Sikhs.

नानकपन्थ, *m.* the religion of Nānak, Sikhism.

नानकपन्थी, *m.* (*f.* inī) a follower of Nānak, a Sikh.

नानकमता / **नानकशाही** } = **नानकपन्थी**, *q.v.*

नाना, 1, *m.* (*f.* ī) a maternal grandfather: 2, different, various, several, sundry, divers: 3, *t.* to bend bow, bow the head.

नानाकार, 1, (**नाना + आकार**) = **नानाविध**, *q. v.*: 2, = **नाना कार्य्य जिसका.**

नानाता, *f.* (*m.* **°त्व**) difference, manifoldness.

नानाप्रकार / **नानाभान्ति** } = **नानाविध**, *q.v.*

नानारूप, *m.* (*f.* ā) many-shaped, multiform, various.

नानारूपी, *m.* (*f.* inī) = **नानारूप**, *q.v.*

नानावर्ण, *m.* (*f.* ā) many-coloured, variegated.

नानाविध, *adj.* of various sorts, kinds, modes or methods, multiform: *adv.* in various ways.

नानी, *f.* (*m.* **नाना**) a maternal grandmother.

नानें in Chand = **नाना**, 3, *q.v.*

नान्द, *f.* a kind of large earthen pan.

नान्दना, 1, a corruption of **नान्धना**, *q.v.*: 2, *a. int.* to live; to become domesticated: *t.* to associate with.

नान्दिया, *m. pr. n.* the bull and vehicle of Shiv.

नान्दी, *f.* joy; prosperity, increase, growth; a eulogy or benedictory address pronounced at the commencement of a dramatic representation or of a sacrifice.

नान्दीमुख, *m.* a certain kind of funeral obsequies (*shrāddh*) performed on festive occasions (such as initiation, marriage, etc.) to the manes of deceased ancestors. In this ceremony a ball of meat is offered to each of the following, *viz.* to the deceased father, paternal grandfather, and paternal great-grandfather; to the deceased mother, paternal grandmother, and paternal great-grandmother; to the maternal grandfather, maternal great-grandfather, and maternal [great great-grandfather.

नान्धना, *t.* to begin.

नान्हक, *more com.* **नानक**, *q.v.*

नान्हा, *m.* (*f.* ī) *more com.* **नन्हा**, *q.v.*

नान्हियाल, *f.* a maternal grandfather's family.

नान्हो in Braj = **नन्हा**, *q.v.*

नाप, *f.* measure. —— *k.* or *lenā*, to measure.

नापजोख, *f.* measuring and weighing.

नापना, *t.* to measure; to weigh.

नापसन्द, unchosen, unacceptable, disapproved of, disagreeable. [filthy.

नापाक, unclean, impure, polluted, defiled, dirty,

नापाकी, *f.* uncleanness, impurity, defilement.

नापित, *m.* (*f.* ī) a barber, shaver, surgeon.

नापितशाला, *f.* a hair-cutting saloon, barber's shop.

नापिती, *f.* (*m.* **नापित**) a barber's wife.

नाब, *m.* a groove, fluting, channel.

नाबदार, grooved, fluted, indented.

नाबार, *m.* one who denies.

नाबीनाई, *f.* weaksightedness, blindness.

नाबीना } **नाबीनी** } weaksighted, blind. [of spell.

नाभ, *m. pr. n.* (1) of Vishṇu (2) of Shiv: a kind

नाभक, *m.* a myrobalan (*Terminalia chebula*).

नाभा, *m. pr. n.* a celebrated Hindoo, author of the *Bhaktmāl.* [torical personages of the Hindoos.

नाभाग, *m. pr. n.* the name of several of the his-

नाभागि, *m.* (patronym.) a descendant of Nābhāg.

नाभाजी = **नाभा**, *q.v.* See **जी**, 1.

नाभि, *f. m.* the navel; a centre, the nave of a wheel; a chief; musk, the musk animal: *pr. n.* the eldest son of king Agnīdhra.

नाभिगोलक, *m.* a prominent or a ruptured navel.

नाभिछेदन, *m.* the dividing the umbilical cord.

नाभिनाड़ी } **नाभिनाला** } *f.* the umbilical cord.

नाभी, *f.* = **नाभि**, *q.v.* [ceeding from the navel.

नाभ्य, *m.* an epithet of Shiv; *lit.* adj. *m.* (*f.* ā) pro-

नाम, *m.* name, appellation; character, fame, repute, honour. — *dharnā*, to name, fix a name upon (*esp.* a bad name), to nickname, miscall. — *dharwānā*, *t.* to name a child: *n.* to be defamed. — *k.* to establish a name for oneself, *i. e.* to become famous. — *denā*, to give a name to, make conspicuous. — *dabonā*, to lose one's character. — *rakhnā* or *lagānā*, to give a name to. — *nikālnā*, to become celebrated; to investigate who the perpetrator of a crime is. — *lenā*, to praise anyone; to repeat the name of a deity. — *lekar māṅg khānā*, to beg alms in the name of another. — *honā*, to be conspicuous, famous, or renowned. — *leke pukārnā*, to call a person by name. (*Pl.*) — *leleke pukārnā*, to call them by their respective names.

नामः, *m.* a letter, book, writing: frequently used as the latter element in compound words, in the sense of history, account, treatise.

नामक, *m.* (*f.* ikā): used as the latter member of compounds, in the sense of having or bearing a name.

नामकरण, *m.* the naming a child first after birth; an acquiring or taking a name (*esp.* of honour).

नामजतन = **नामयत्न**, *q.v.*

नामठाम, 1, probably a tautological play on the word **नाम**, *q.v.*: 2, it may also refer to the *place* (**ठाम**) (in a document, etc.) where the signature or name should be put.

नामदार, famous, celebrated: hence, *m.* a celebrity.

नामदारी, *f.* celebrity, renown.

नामधराई, *f.* ill-repute, disrepute, degradation.

नामना, *t.* to name; to panegyrize.

नामम, white clay, pipe-clay: the mark made on the forehead by Hindoos.

नामयत्न, *m.* effort after reputation, ambition or exertion for the sake of notoriety.

नामयुत, possessing a name; hence (1) famed, noted, renowned (2) signed with one's name, not anonymous.

नामवर, renowned, celebrated, famous.

नामवाचकसंज्ञा, *f.* (in Gram.) a proper name; *lit.* an appellation expressive of a name.

नामवाला, *m.* (*f.* ī) = **नामी**, *q. v.*

नामशेष, *m.* (*f.* ā) one of whom only the name is left, *i. e.* a dead person. [the name of a deity.

नामस्मरण, *m.* the remembrance or repetition of

नामा, *m.* = **नामः**, *q. v.*

नामानि, (*Rām.*) a Sk. pl. of the word **नाम**, *q.v.*

नामी, *m.* (*f.* inī) a person of a repute, a celebrity, etc: *lit.* reputable, celebrated, famous, illustrious, notorious; nominal.

नामुनासिब, not to the purpose, improper, wrong.

नामूस, *f.* reputation, fame, renown: disgrace: the female part of a family.

नामे, *adv.* by name, named, called. [**नाम**, *q. v.*

नामें, 1, see (1) **नामे** (2) **नामना**; 2, a false pl. of

नामों, *f.* = **नामे**, *q.v.*

नाय, 1, *more prop.* **नाय**, *q.v.*: 2, = **नाकरके** (**नाना**, 3).

नायउ, 1, an old imperat. of the verb **नाना**, *q.v.*: 2, an old form = **नाया**, *q. v.*

नायक, *m.* (*f.* ikā) a guide, conductor, chief, principal, preëminent person, husband, lover; a native military officer of the lowest rank (corresponding to the English 'corporal'); a person well conversant in dancing, singing, etc.: the central gem of a necklace.

नायकवार, *adj.* under the authority of *nāyak*.

नायका, *more prop.* **नायिका**, *q.v.*

नायड़, *m. pr. n.* a certain tribe of Telingas or Gentoos (Hindoos of Southern India) who claim the second degree of blood and family antiquity in that nation.

नायन, *more prop.* **नाइन**, *q.v.*

नायब, *more prop.* **नाइब**, *q.v.*

नायर = **नायड़**, *q.v.*

नायरत, *more prop.* **नाइरत**, *q.v.*

नायव; see (1) **नाइब** (2) **नायउ** (3) **नाऊंगा** (**नाना**).

नाया, *m.* (*f.* **नाई**) past part. of vb. **नाना**, *q.v.*

नायिका, *f.* (*m.* **नायक**) a mistress (whether of a house or of a brothel); a damsel, lass; a noble lady; the heroine of a drama; an inferior form (or Shakti) —of Durgā of which there are eight *viz.*(1)Ugra-chaṇḍā (2) Prachaṇḍā (3) Chaṇḍogrā (4) Chaṇḍnāyikā (5) Atichaṇḍā (6) Chāmuṇḍā (7) Chaṇḍā (8) Chaṇḍāvatī.

नायो; see (1) **नयो** (2) **नाया**.

नार, 1, a corruption (1) of **नारी** (2) of **नाल**, *qq.v.*: 2, *m.* water: a calf; a herd, drove: advice, counsel: *lit.* appertaining to a man.

नारंग, *m.* 1, = **नारंगी**, *q.v.*: 2, the juice of the pepper-plant: a libertine, a catamite: any animal: a twin, one of twins: a carrot.

नारंगी, *f.* the orange-tree (*Citrus aurantium*) and [its fruit.

नारंज, *m.* an orange.

नारक, 1, *more prop.* **नरक**, *q.v.*: 2, *m.* (*f.* ī) an inhabitant of the infernal regions: *lit* appertaining to hell, hellish, infernal, hell-deserving.

नारकी, *m.* (*f.* inī) } = **नारक**, 2, *q.v.*
नारकीय, *m.* (*f.* ā) }

नारद, *m.* 1, *pr. n.* a certain celestial *rishi* (Devarshi): he is one of the four sons of Brahmā and one of the ten principal and original munis or rishis, the friend of Krishṇ, a celebrated legislator, and the inventor of the lute (*Vīṇā*); he is also said to have occasioned frequent quarrels among the gods by carrying tales: *hence*, 2, *met.* one who is fond of altercation, a disputant.

नारदपुराण, *m. pr. n.* one of the Purāṇs.

नारबिवार, *m.* the membrane in which the foetus is developed, *secundines.*

नारा, *m.* red thread; fibres of the cocoanut or palm (commonly called 'coir') of which ropes, etc. are made.

नाराच, *m.* a kind of iron arrow: a species of [Sanskrit metre.

नाराचस्त्र, *m.* a kind of iron arrow.

नाराज़, dissatisfied, displeased, unwilling.

नारात, 1, *more prop.* **नारद**, *q.v.*: 2, *m.* (*f.* ā) any animal that subsists on water: lit. *adj.* water-feeding.

नारायण, *m.* an epithet of the Supreme. The origin of the term is unsettled; either (1) from **नर**, man, and **अयन**, an abode (referring to Vishṇu as the first of living beings and the dwellingplace of mortals); or (2) from **नार**, water, and **अयन**, an abode (referring to Vishṇu as the beingwho existed before all worlds and moved on the waters of creation; *lit.* whose dwellingplace is the water): or (3) = whose dwellingplace is man (in the pantheistic sense).

नारायणक्षेत्र, *m.* the term applied to four cubits of the soil on either side of the stream of the Ganges.

नारायणतैल, *m.* a certain oil expressed from a variety of plants, and of great reputed efficacy in many complaints.

नारायणी, *f.* 1, an epithet of Lakshmee, the goddess of prosperity and wife of Nārāyaṇ or Vishṇu; *lit.* appertaining to Nārāyaṇ: 2, a certain plant (*Asparagus racemosa*).

नारास्त, wrong, unfair, unjust, dishonest.

नारि, *more prop.* **नारी**, *q.v.*

नारिंगी = **नारंगी**, *q.v.*

नारिकेर } *m.* the cocoanut.
नारिकेल }

नारिया } Braj and poet. pll of **नारी**, 2, *q.v.*
नारिन }

नारिनरा, (prop. **नारीनर**) = **नरनारी**, *q.v.*

नारिमय, *more prop.* **नारीमय**, *q.v.*

नारियर = **नारियल**, *q.v.*

नारियल, *m.* the cocoanut-tree (*Cocos nucifera*) or its fruit; a hukkā made of a cocoanut. — *kī rūī*, *f.* a certain soft downy substance of a light brown colour found on the exterior of the lower part of the leaves or branches of the cocoanut-tree: it is used as a styptic and for tinder.

नारियली, *f.* a hukkā made of a cocoanut; a cup made of a cocoanut-shell; a sap or liquor extracted from the cocoanut-tree, called by Europeans 'toddy'.

नारिया, *m.* a person who feels the pulse.

नारिवृन्द, *m.* any crowd of females.

नारी, *f.* 1, *a corruption of* **नाड़ी**, *q.v.*: 2, a woman, female; *lit.* appertaining to a man: 3, a species of Sanskrit poetry. Added to a man's name, this term often yields an epithet of a wife, *e.g.* **गौतमनारी**.

नारीच = **नाड़ीच**, *q.v.*

नारीचतुर, *m.* (*f.* ā) one who is a skilful judge of [females.

नारीदूषण, *m.* a vice or breach of duty in a woman. Six of these are reckoned, *viz.* (1) drinking spirits (2) keeping bad company (3) quitting a husband (4) rambling abroad (5 and 6) sleeping or dwelling in a strange house.

नारीधर्म्म, *m.* the duties specially incumbent on [women: the menstrual flux.

नारीन, 1, a Braj and poet. pl. of **नारी**, 2, *q.v.*: 2, *m.* an epithet of the moon: *lit.* the lord of females.

नारीपरायण, passionately fond of women.

नारीप्रसंग, *m.* coition, libertinism, lechery.

नारीप्रिय, a lover of women: one loved by women: lit. *adj.* loving women: dear to women.

नारीमय, *adj.* *m.* (*f.* ī) consisting of women, [abounding in women.

नारू, *m.* the guinea-worm.

नाल, 1, *m.* a hollow tubular stalk (*esp.* that of the lotus); any tubular vessel of the body, the navel-string, a tube, a gun-barrel: *lit.* consisting of reed: 2, along with, accompanying, near. *Soch bhaī bharī kharī sakhī lakhī nālkī*, her accompanying friends, seeing this, were filled with anxiety and fear.

नालकी, *f.* a sort of sedan or litter generally used by persons of rank.

नालना, *a. int.* to weep, lament.

नाला, *f.* a ravine, 'nullah', rivulet, brook, canal, gutter, furrow : a weeping, lamentation.

नालाइक़, unfit, unworthy, unbecoming, improper.

नालिका, *f.* the esculent root *Arum colocasia.*

नालिकेर / **नालिकेल** } *m.* the cocoanut.

नालिता, *f.* a kind of potherb (*Hibiscus cannabinus*).

नालिनी, *f.* a mystic name of one of the nostrils.

नालिश, *f.* complaint, lamentation, exclamation, a groan : (in Law) a plaint. — *k.* to lodge a complaint, to sue (*esp.* in the legal sense).

नालिशी, *adj.* complaining : hence, *m.* (*f.* in *or* inī) a complainant, plaintiff.

नाली, *f.* any tubular vessel of the body ; the pulse; a tubulated tile ; a straw ; a stalk ; a drain ; a sinuous ulcer or fistula.

नालीव्रण, *m.* a fistulous or sinuous sore.

नाव, *f.* anything long and hollow within, a sailing-vessel, boat, ship, a trough.

नावक, *f.* a tube, canal, the tube through which an arrow is projected ; an arrow ; a bee's sting.

नावकी ; see (1) नाविकी (2) नौका.

नावदान, *m.* a dock, aqueduct, gutter.

नावना, *more prop.* (1) नवाना (2) नाना, 3, *qq. v.*

नावरि (*Rām.*) = नाव घुमाना.

नाविक, appertaining to a sailing-vessel : hence, *m.* (*f.* ī) a helmsman, steersman, pilot ; a sailor ; a ship's passenger.

नाविका ; see (1) नाविकी (2) नौका.

नाविकी, *f.* ; see नाविक.

नाश, *m.* loss, disappearance, destruction, devastation, non-existence, annihilation, death.

नाशक, *m.* (*f.* ikā) a destroyer, antidote: *lit.* destructive, destroying.

नाशकर्त्ता, *m.* (*f.* trī) a destroyer.

नाशन, 1, *m.* (*f.* ī) a destroyer : 2, *m.* destruction, a destroying ; a perishing.

नाशपाती, *f.* the pear (*Pyrus communis*).

नाशमान, destructible, perishable.

नाशिक, *more prop.* नासिक, *q. v.*

नाशिका, *f.* (*m.* नाशक) a female destroyer.

नाशित, *m.* (*f.* ā) destroyed, lost.

नाशी, *m.* (*f.* inī) a destroyer, etc. : *lit.* destructive, destroying, removing ; perishable.

नास, 1, *more prop.* नाश, *q.v.*: 2, *f.* snuff. —— *kichuṭkī*, a pinch of snuff.

नासक, *more prop.* नाशक, *q. v.*

नासदान, *m.* a snuff-box.

नासन, *more prop.* नाशन, *q. v.*

नासना, *a. int.* to run away, flee: *t.* to destroy, exterminate, ruin.

नासपाल, *m.* the rind of an unripe pomegranate (used in dyeing).

नासपाली, *adj.* appertaining to *nāspāl*. —— *rang*, *m.* the colour extracted from *nāspāl.*

नासमझ, unintelligent, not understanding, ignorant.

नासमझी, *f.* unintelligence, ignorance.

नासरत, *m. pr. n.* the city of Nazareth.

नासा, 1, *more prop.* नाश, *q. v.*: 2, *f.* the nose : 3, *m.* inflammation of the nose, the polypus.

नासादक्षिणावर्त्त, *m.* the wearing the nose-ring on the right nostril (by women who have money and children).

नासावंश, *m.* the bridge of the nose.

नासावामावर्त्त, *m.* the wearing the nose-ring on the left nostril (by women, as a mark of sorrow or distress).

नासाशोष, *m.* drying of the nostrils.

नासिक, devoted to God.

नासिका, *f.* (uninfl.) a nostril; the nose; the trunk of an elephant.

नासिकामल, *m.* mucus of the nose.

नास्त, *more prop.* नास्ति, *q. v.*

नास्ति, (Sk. ना अस्ति, it is not: *hence*) 1, no, not so: 2, *f.* non-existence, non-entity, annihilation.

नास्तिक, *m.* (*f.* ā *or* ī) *lit.* one who says 'Nāsti', *i. e.* a denier ; *hence*, an atheist, unbeliever, one who denies a future state. The epithet is applied by the orthodox among the Hindoos to any one who denies the divine authority of the Veds, or expresses doubts as to the authenticity of the Purāṇs.

नास्तिकत्व, *m.* (*f.* ta) heterodoxy (esp. in reference to the accepted authorities and orthodoxy of the Hindoos), unbelief, infidelity, atheism.

नास्तिकमत, *m.* an atheistical opinion, a tenet of atheism.

नास्तिका / **नास्तिकी** } *f.* (*m.* नास्तिक) a female heretic.

नास्तिक्य, *m.* = नास्तिकत्व, *q. v.*

नास्तित्व, *m.* (*f.* tā) non-existence.

नास्य, *m.* the rein of an ox (passed through the septum of the nostrils).

नाह, *m.* 1, (*Rām.*) = नाथ, *q. v.* : 2, obstruction: 3, no, nay, not.

नाहक़, 1, *adj.* unjust, wrong, illegal, undeserved, useless, vain : untrue : 2. *adv.* unjustly, undeservedly, improperly : 3, *m.* injustice, injury, wrong.

नाहनुह, *m.* the withholding one's consent, refusal.

नाहर, *m.* a tiger.

नाहा, an old form of नाथ, *q. v.*

नाहि, nay, no, not.

नाहिं / **नाहिन** } = नाहीं, *q. v.*

नाहिनहों (poet.) = मैं नहीं हूं.

नाहिया, *m.* territory, country, district, tract ; coast, shore.

नाहिर, *m.* (*prop.* नाहर) a tiger.

नाही = नाहीं, *q. v.*

नाहीं, no, not, nay, no indeed, certainly not. —— *nāhīṅ*, not at all.

नाहीनुही, *f.* = नाहनुह, *q. v.*

नाहु, an emphatic form of नाह, *q. v.*

नाहुष, *m.* (patronym.) a descendant of king Nahush : *pr. n.* a certain serpent-demon.

नाहू, an emphatic form of नाह, *q. v.*

नि ; 1, an inseparable prefix (1) the reverse of निर. As such, it is positive and intensive; and denotes in, within, into, on, upon. (2) The reverse of उत, and a corruption or a contraction of निः. As such it is negative; and denotes down, downward, under, below, backward, failure, hindrance, negation, deprivation, without: 2, it is important to observe the functions of this particle in Braj: (1) in the oblique cases of the plural it commonly takes the place of श्रों; *e.g.* पुत्रनिकों = पुत्रोंको (2) it is occasionally the sign of the nominative plural, *e. g.* फलनि, fruits (3) it occasionally stands for नो of the infinitive, and (4) it is very commonly the inflective termination of the oblique cases of the infinitive; *e. g.* करनिकौ = करनेका; देखनिहार = देखनेहार (5) this is almost invariably (= ने) the sign of the agent case; *e. g.* कुत्तेनि [(= कुत्तेने).

निश्रर, *more prop.* **नियर**, *q.v.*

निश्रमत, *f.* favour, graciousness, benefit; delight, joy; affluence, wealth, ease.

निश्रराना, *more prop.* **नियराना**, *q. v.*

निश्रारा, *more prop.* **नियारा**, *q.v.*

निऋति / **निऋती** } *more prop.* **निर्ऋति**, *q. v.*

निंदरि (*Rām.*) = निरादर करके.

निंदा, *more prop.* **निद्रा** or **निन्दा**, *qq. v.*

निः, an inseparable prefix = **निर**, *q. v.*

निःकपट, *more com.* **निष्कपट**, *q. v.*

निःकाम, *more com.* **निष्काम**, *q. v.*

निःकारण, *more com.* **निष्कारण**, *q. v.*

निःक्षिप्त, etc., *more com.* **निक्षिप्त**, etc., *qq. v.*

निःखेद, without sorrow or pain.

निःपश्चाताप, *m.* impenitence.[impenitent person.

निःपश्चातापी, impenitent: hence, *m.* (*f.* inī) an

निःपाप / **निःपापी** } *more com.* **निष्पाप**, *q.v.*

निःफल, *m.* (*f.* ā *or* i) *more com.* **निष्फल**, *q. v.*

निःशंक / **निःशंका** } *more com.* **निशंक**, *q. v.*

निःशंसय, *more prop.* **निःसंशय**, *q. v.* [lent, quiet, still.

निःशब्द, without sound, noiseless, voiceless, si-

निःशब्दता, *f.* / **निःशब्दत्व**, *m.* } stillness, etc. (*see above*).

निःशेष, *m.* (*f.* ā) without leaving a residue, without sparing anybody or anything, completely destroyed, without remainder, complete, entire, whole, all.

निःशेषता, *f.* (*m.* °त्व) complete destruction.

निःश्रेणि / **निःश्रेणी** } *f.* a ladder, wooden ladder.

निःश्रेयस, *m.* final beatitude (according to the Hindoos) *viz.* the release of the soul from the necessity for further transmigration, and its reünion with the primary and universal Spirit.

निःश्वास, *m.* a breathing out, expiration, breath,

निःसंक, *more prop.* **निशंक**, *q. v.* [sigh.

निःसंकोच, wanting in reserve or diffidence, shameless, forward, bold.

निःसंग, unconnected, separated, unimpeded, free from desire, indifferent, disinterested.

निःसंशय, doubtless, undoubted.

निःसत्य, untrue; insincere. [rity, lying disposition.

निःसत्यता, *f.* (*m.* °त्व) untrueness, falseness, insince-

निःसन्तान, without offspring or posterity.

निःसन्देह, *more com.* **निस्सन्देह**, *q. v.*

निःसरण, *m.* a going forth or out; death, dying; final beatitude: a means against, an expedient.

निःसह, *m.* (*f.* ā) powerless, unable to bear; intolerable; irresistible.

निःसहता, *f.* (*m.* °त्व) inability to support or bear, unendurance, impatience; insufferableness.

निःसार, 1, *m.* (*f.* ā) sapless, pithless, powerless, insipid, vain, unsubstantial, perishable, worthless: 2, *m.* a species of plant (*Trophis aspera*).

निःसीम, boundless, unbounded.

निःसुख, unhappy, sad; disagreeable, distressing.

निःस्नेहा, *f.* linseed (*Linum utilitissimum*).

निःस्पृह, *m.* (*f.* ā) free from desire or wish, indifferent to, disregarding. [indigent.

निःस्व, *m.* (*f.* ā) deprived of one's property, poor,

निःस्वादु, un-sweet, tasteless, insipid.

निःसहाय, without helpers, associates, or allies; [without assistance.

निक, *more prop.* **नीक**, *q. v.*

निकंमा, *more prop.* **निकम्मा**, *q.v.*

निकट, 1, *m.* (*f.* ā) near, proximate: 2, *postp.* (takes gen. masc. infl.) near, with, about: 3, *m.* proximity. *Mere* —, in my opinion, according to my calculation, in my esteem, in my judgment.

निकटता, *f.* (*m.* °त्व) proximity, nearness.

निकटपना, *m.* the state of being in proximity.

निकटवर्ती, *m.* (*f.* inī) a bystander, neighbour: *lit.* near, proximate, neighbouring.

निकटी, 1, *f.* = निकटता, *q. v.*: 2, *m.* (*f.* in *or* inī) = निकटवर्ती, *q. v.*

निकण्टक, *m.* (*f.* ikā) free from thorns, (*i.e.* obstacles) without enmity or opposition, happy; plain, easy.

निकती, *f.* a balance, small scales (such as gold-

निकन्द, rooted up, extirpated. [smiths use).

निकन्दन, 1, *m.* destruction: 2, *m.* (*f.* inī) destructive.

निकपट = **निष्कपट**, *q. v.* [fitable, worthless, base.

निकम्मा, *m.* (*f.* i) good-for-nothing, useless, unpro-

निकर, *m.* a flock, multitude; a heap; a bundle; [pith, sap, essence.

निकरना = **निकलना**, *q. v.*

निकल; this base forms several compound verbs of an intensive nature (1) — *chalnā*, to escape; *met.* to speak much or display one's talent (said in reference to any person who formerly, from the modesty of a stranger, had been silent); to surpass another, to be advanced or promoted (2) — *jānā*, to escape, get away, be off (3) — *parnā*, to come out, be drawn forth (4) — *bhāgnā*, to flee, run away, get away off, be off.

निकलना, *a. int.* to issue, go forth, go out, come out, get out, secede, depart, proceed, exceed, appear, turn out, result, prove, begin, escape, arise, slip, spring; to be extracted, drawn, pulled or taken out, be performed or accomplished; to be uttered; to be taken off; to be produced, be invented.

निकलवाना, *t.* to cause to go out, to drive out, to cause to be sent out. *Nikalwā denā*, to expel, to banish.

निकलाना; see (1) **निकलवाना** (2) **निकालना**.

निकष, *m.* the touchstone; the test appearing on [the touchstone.

निकषण, *m.* a touchstone.

निकषा, *f. pr. n.* the mother of the goblins.

निकसना = **निकलना**, *q.v.*

निकाई, *f.* weeding; the act of weeding; the price paid for weeding: goodness, beauty, prosperity.

निकाना, *t.* to weed.

निकाम, 1, voluntarily, willingly, at one's own discretion (implying certainty): 2, very, exceedingly.

निकामा, *m.* (*f.* ī) = **निकम्मा**, *q.v.*

निकाय, *m.* a collection, assembly, multitude, flock: [a house, habitation.

निकायी; see **निकाई**, *q.v.*

निकारना; see **निकालना**, *q.v.*

निकाल, *m.* contrivance, outlet, vent, issue, discharge, projection, expulsion. —*dālnā*, to deduct, strike out.—*denā*, to expel, turn out, drive out, eject, exclude, discard, cashier. — *lānā*, to bring off. — *lenā*, to extract, take out, dig up.

निकालना, *t.* (of **निकलना**) to cause to issue, to take out, turn out, expel, exclude, extract, deduce, undo, protrude, extricate, exhibit, display, illustrate, make manifest, bring out, produce, put forth, hatch, pull, pick, accomplish, invent, take off, discover, utter, cause to exceed.

निकास, *m.* outer boundary of land attached to a town, etc., skirts, suburbs; issue, discharge, outlet, vent, egress, source, spring, origin; adjustment of accounts: accomplishment.—*nawis*, an officer in the *Zamindāri Kachahri* who receives and examines the accounts of the collections of revenue in the mufassil.

निकासना = **निकालना**, *q.v.*

निकासपत्र, *m.* a statement of adjusted accounts.

निकासी, *f.* taxes collected on goods passing out of town, export duties, etc.—*ki chitthi*, a passport, permit.

निकास्त; see (1) **निकास** (2) **निकासना** (3) **निकास्ता**.

निकास्ता, *m.* a prop, pillar.

निकाह, *m.* matrimony, marriage, nuptials. It denotes the most honourable kind of marriage. in Bengal, however, the term is applied also to left-handed marriage.

निकिष्ट; see **निकृष्ट**. [arbour, bower, thicket.

निकुंज, *m.* a place overgrown with creepers, an

निकुम्भ, *m.* a species of plant (*Croton polyandrum*): *pr. n.* a certain demon, son of Kumbhakaraṇ and brother of Rāvaṇ. [countersign.

निकेत, *m.* a mansion, dwelling, habitation: a mark,

निकेतन, *m.* a mansion; a temple.

निकेतु, *more prop.* **निकेत**, *q.v.*

निकेवल.(= **निष्केवल**) merely, only, solely.

निकोचक, *m.* the tree *Alangium hexapetalum.*

निकोसना, *a. int.* to grin. [low, base.

निकृत, *m.* (*f.* ā) dishonest, wicked, perverse, vile,

निकृति, *f.* wickedness, dishonesty; abuse.

निकृष्ट, *m.* (*f.* ā) outcast, castaway, reprobate, uncultivated, neglected, low, vile, despised.

निकृष्टत्व, *m.* (*f.* tā) the state of being an outcast vileness, badness, contemptibleness. [caste.

निक्षत्र, 1, see **नक्षत्र**: 2, *adj.* without the military

निक्षिप्त, *m.* (*f.* ā) thrown away, rejected, abandoned, given away, sent away, spent, passed; foregone; pledged, deposited.

निक्षेप, *m.* an abandoning, throwing, sending, or putting away; a spending, passing (time); wiping away (tears), what is left, a pledge, deposit.

निक्षेपक, *m.* (*f.* ikā) a depositor: *lit.* adj. making a deposit, giving a thing as a pledge.

निक्षेप्ता / **निक्षेप्तृ** } *m.* (*f.* °**प्त्री**) a depositor.

निक्षेपण, *m.* a putting down: a place for keeping something. [quietness.

निक्षोभ, *m.* undisturbedness, repose, tranquillity,

निखंग, *f.* a quiver.

निखटर, spiteful, implacable.

निखटरपना, *m.* spitefulness, implacability.

निखट्टू, idle; thriftless: merciless.

निखण्ड, *adj.* half, mid, midway.

निखद, ominous, pernicious.

निखदा, *m.* ominousness, perniciousness.

निखमा, *m.* (*f.* ī) *more prop.* **निकम्मा**, *q.v.*

निखरना, *n.* to be peeled, be skinned, be cleaned, be cleared, be settled. [to be cleaned, etc.

निखरवाना, *t.* (double causat. of **निखारना**) to cause

निखराना, *t.* (causat. of **निखारना**) to cause to clean, etc.

निखर्व, 1, *m.* (*f.* ā) a dwarf: *lit.* dwarfish: 2, *m.* a very high number concerning the limits of which there is the following diversity of statement (1) a thousand millions (2) a hundred thousand millions (3) a million of millions (4) ten millions (5) ten *Kharb.*

निखारना, *t.* (of **निखरना**) to peel, clean, clear, [bleach, settle.

निखिल, complete, entire, all.

निखेदित, 1, *more prop.* **निषेधित**, *q.v.*: 2, *m.* (*f.* ā) whose affliction has been removed. [plain-dealing.

निखोट, free from defect or blemish, faultless,

निखोड़ना = **निखोरना**, *q.v.*

निखोड़ा, *m.* (*f.* ī) inhuman, pitiless.

निखोड़ागी, *f.* pitilessness.

निखोरना, *t.* to peel, decorticate, clean.

निखोसना, *a. int.* to grin. [elephant), fetters, stocks.

निगड़, *m.* an iron chain for the feet (*esp.* of an

निगड़घट, impudent, bold.

निगत, naked. [tition of a prayer.

निगद, *m.* conversation, speech; the audible repe-

निगन्दना, *t.* to quilt.

निगन्दा, *m.* / **निगन्दाई**, *f.* } quilting.

निगम, *m.* Holy Writ, Scripture, the Veds; a passage of the Veds; a precept: a road, way; access, entrance: a city, town, market, fair; traffic; a trader: assurance, certainty.

निगमन, *m.* the fifth or last member of a com-

plete syllogism according to the Nyāya system, logical conclusion. [dwelling in the Veds.
निगमनिवासी, *m.* an epithet of Brahmā; lit. *adj.*
निगमागम, *m.* (निगम = आगम) Veds and Shāstras.
निगमी, *m.* (*f.* inī) a person versed in Holy Writ or the Veds. [ing, gulping, eating.
निगर, 1, *more prop.* निगार, *q.v.*: 2, *m.* a swallow-
निगरण, *m.* a swallowing: the throat.
निगलना, *t.* to swallow, gulp down, swallow up.
निगलिहै, (pl. °हैं) in old Hindee = निगलेगा. See हुई.
निगह, *more com.* निगाह, *q.v.* [observer.
निगहबान, *m.* a watchman, keeper, guardian; an
निगहबानी, *f.* watching, taking care of; observing.
निगार, *m.* a picture, painting, portrait, effigy, idol: a beautiful woman, mistress, belle.
निगारख़ाना } **निगारिस्तान** } *m.* a picture-gallery.
निगारी, *f.* = निगार, *q.v.*
निगाल, *m.* the throat or neck of a horse.
निगालवान, *m.* (*f.* vatī) a horse: lit. *adj.* having the neck of a horse. [of a *hukkā*-snake.
निगाली, *f.* a small *hukkā*-snake; the wooden pipe
निगाह, *f.* a look, glance; aspect; observation, watching; custody, care. — *k.* or *dālnā* or *rakhnā* to look at, etc.
निगुण, *m.* (*f.* ā) without a string; without qualities; without virtue, evil, worthless.
निगुनी, *m.* (*f.* in *or* inī) = निगुण, *q.v.* [guage.
निगुरी, *m.* (among females) abuse, insulting lan-
निगूढ़, *m.* (*f.* ā) secret, mysterious, hidden, profound, obscure, abstruse, difficult to be understood.
निगूढ़ार्थ, *adj.* having a mysterious meaning or hidden significance.
निगोड़ा, *m.* (*f.* ī) an ill-natured person, wretch, wight: *lit.* without feet: *adj.* ill-tempered, cross-
निग्गर, solid. [grained.
निग्यानी, *m.* (*f.* inī) weak in mind, silly, ignorant.
निग्रह, *m.* a seizing, confining, subduing, restraining, chastising; aversion, disfavour, discouragement.
निग्रहण, *m.* suppression; punishment.
निग्रहस्थान, *m.* the predicament of rebuke for failure in argument.
निग्रहार्थ, (see अर्थ) with a view to निग्रह, *q.v.*
निघटना, (*Rām.*) intensive of घटना, *q.v.*
निघण्टु, *m.* a collection of words or names, a vo-
निघर्षण, *m.* friction; crushing. [cabulary.
निघाति, *f.* an iron club or mace.
निघाती, *m.* (*f.* inī) *adj.* killing, destroying.
निघ्न, *m.* (*f.* ā) subservient, docile, dependent,
निचंत, *m.* (*f.* ā) = निश्चिन्त, *q.v.* [domestic.
निचंताई = निश्चिन्ताई, *q.v.*
निचय, 1, = निश्चय, *q.v.*: 2, *m.* a heaping; a collection, heap, assemblage, multitude.
निचला, *m.* (*f.* ī) lower, underneath.
निचाई, *more prop.* नीचाई, *q.v.*
निचान = (1) विशेष (2) नीचपन, *qq.v.*
निचिन्त, *m.* (*f.* ā) = निश्चिन्त, *q.v.*
निचिन्ताई, *f.* freedom from care or anxiety, thoughtlessness, unconcern, fearlessness, leisure.
निचीत, *m.* (*f.* ā) = निश्चिन्त, *q.v.*
निचू = (1) नीच (2) नीचे, *qq.v.* [(Gaertn).
निचुल, *m.* the tree *Barringtonia acutangula*,
निचैताई, *more prop.* निचिन्ताई, *q.v.*
निचेष्ट, *m.* (*f.* ā) = निश्चेष्ट, *q.v.*
निचोड़, *m.* the termination of any affair: the burthen, or that on which anything depends.
निचोड़ना, *t.* to wring, squeeze, strain, press, ex-
निचोड़वा = निचोड़ू, *q.v.* [tort, exact.
निचोड़वाना, *t.* (double caus. of निचोड़ना) to cause to be squeezed, etc. [squeeze, etc.
निचोड़ाना, *t.* (causat. of निचोड़ना) to cause to
निचोड़ी, *m.* (*f.* inī) = निचोड़ू, *q.v.*
निचोड़ू, *m.* an extortioner: *lit.* extortionate, rapacious, exacting, niggardly. [form निचोड़.
निचोर; for words beginning thus, see under the
निचोल, *m.* a cover, wrapper, mantle, outer gar-
निचोलक, *m.* } **निचोली**, *f.* } = निचोल, *q.v.* [ment, veil.
निच्छिवि, *m.* a certain mixed class among Hindoos; the son of a Vrātya Kshatriya. [nocent, genuine, pure.
निछक्का, *m.* (*f.* ī) free from defect, untainted, in-
निछल, clean, clear, pure.
निछावर } **निछावरि** } = नेवछावर, *q.v.*
निज, *m.* (*f.* ā) own, special, peculiar, personal, individual, particular: good, excellent: eternal, perpetual. — *k.* to particularize. — *karke, adv.* more particularly, to take a particular instance, to give the point a personal application or exemplification, to apply the case personally, for instance, for example.
निजका, (gen. of निज) *m.* (*f.* ī) appertaining to self,
निजगति (*Rām.*) = अपनी गति. [own, peculiar.
निजतन्त्र (*Rām.*) = स्वतन्त्र, *q.v.*
निजतिजसे, *adv.* as it ought to be, as is requisite,
निजधर्म (*Rām.*) = मुख्यधर्म, *q.v.* [properly.
निजसन्धि (*Rām.*) = (1) अपना हित (2) अवसर.
निजसुख (*Rām.*) = आत्मसुख, *q.v.*
निजस्थान = अपना स्थान.
निजस्सी, of evil omen, unlucky.
निजहि = (1) अपना ही (2) अपनेको.
निजा, *f.* (*m.* निज) a faithful wife, one who follows her husband on the funeral pile.
निजात, *more prop.* नजात, *q.v.*
निजानन्द, (*Rām.*) = स्वरूपानन्द, *q.v.*
निजुत, *more prop.* नियुत, *q.v.*
निज्जोत, lands cultivated by the proprietors or revenue-payers for their own benefit.

निभ्रतिभ्र, *f.* propriety, correctness.
निभ्राना, *t.* to spy, pry into, observe.
निभ्रोटना, *t.* to twitch.
निभोल, an epithet of the elephant; *lit.* steady-going, easy-paced, walking or running smoothly and without agitation.
निट; see (1) **निज** (2) **नित** (3) **नीट**.
निटर, poor, worn-out (applied to land that has been over-cultivated.
निटारा, *more prop.* **निबटेरा**, *q. v.*
निठल्ला, 1, *m.* idleness: 2, *m.* (*f.* ī) idle.
निठुर; for words beginning thus, see under the form **निष्ठुर**.
निठुरताई, **निठु**.**राई** = **निष्ठुरता**, *q.v.*
निडर, *adj.* fearless, dauntless: *adv.* fearlessly.
निडरता, *f.*, **निडरताई**, *f.*, **निडरत्व**, *m.*, **निडरपन**, *m.*, **निडरपना**, *m.*, **निडरी**, *f.* fearlessness.
निढाल, **निढोल** motionless, still.
नित, 1, = **नित्य**, *q.v.*: 2, a contraction of **निमित्त**, *q.v.*: 3, the base of an obtuse angled triangle.
नितई (*Rām.*) = **नित्य**, *q. v.*
नितउठ, **नितउठके** constantly.
नितनव, ever new, ever fresh.
नितनित, **नितप्रति** = **नित्य**, 2, *q. v.*
नितम्ब, *m.* buttocks, rump; the slope or the prominences of a mountain: a bank; gibbosity.
नितम्बी, *m.* (*f.* inī) a person with large and beautiful buttocks.
नितराम, *adv.* always, constantly, perpetually, eternally.
नितल, *m. pr.n.* one of the seven divisions of hell.
नितान्त, 1, much, excessive: 2, exceedingly.
नित्ता, *more prop.* **नित्यता**, *q. v.*
नित्ती, *more prop.* **निकृती**, *q.v.*
नित्य, 1, *m.* (*f.* ā) constant, perpetual, eternal, regular, essential, fixed, invariable: 2, *adv.* continually, always, at all times, constantly, unceasingly, perpetually, for ever, for ever and ever.
नित्यकर्म्म, *m.* an indispensable act or ceremony (such as the observance of the five greater sacrifices, or any necessary or daily rite).
नित्यक्रिया, *f.* = **नित्यकर्म्म**, *q. v.*
नित्यता, *f.* (*m.* °**त्व**) perpetuity, permanency, lastingness, continuity, eternity; perseverance; necessity.
नित्यताबोधक क्रिया, *f.* (in Gram.) the continuative form of any verb; *e. g.* *Āyā-karnā*, to be in the habit of coming.
नित्यदा, *adv.* always, constantly, perpetually, eternally, for ever and ever.
नित्यदान, *m.* daily alms.
नित्यनित्य, (intens. of **नित्य**, 2) = **नित्यदा**, *q.v.*
नित्यप्रलय, *m.* the constant loss of living beings.
नित्यमय, *m.* (*f.* ī) durable, eternal.
नित्ययुक्त, *m.* (*f.* ā) always engaged or busy, much occupied.
नित्ययौवन, 1, *m.* perpetual youth: 2, *m.* (*f.* ā) ever young.
नित्यबोधक, *adj.* (in Gram.) implying continuity.
नित्यसाधन, *m.* a preserving.
नित्यस्थायी, of eternal duration, ineradicable.
नित्या, *f.*; see **नित्य**.
नित्यानध्याय, *m.* any period when the perusal of the Veds is invariably prohibited; *e g.* on the day of full moon or new moon, on the eighth and fourteenth days of the half month.
नित्यानन्द, 1, *m.* perpetual happiness: 2, *m.* (*f.* ā) a person who is always joyous.
नित्यानित्य, 1, *m.* (*f.* ā) eternal and non-eternal, everlasting and perishable, permanent and temporary.
नियरा, clear (said of water the impurity of which has subsided).
नियारना, *t.* to pour; to purify water or other liquid by letting the feculent matter subside and pouring off the clear water: to milk a cow.
निदर, *more prop.* **निडर**, *q. v.*
निदरना (*Rām.*) = **अनादर करना**.
निदर्शन, 1, (*f.* ī) a teacher: *lit.* adj. shewing, announcing, teaching: 2, *m.* sight, seeing; example, illustration; injunction, precept, authority, text; evidence, foreboding, prognostic, symptom.
निदाघ, *m.* the hot season just previous to the rains (May-June); *lit.* heat, warmth; perspiration.
निदाघकाल, *m.* = **निदाघ**, *q.v.*
निदान, 1, *m.* (*f.* ?) a first cause; the causes of disease; ascertainment of the causes of disease by observation of its symptoms, diagnosis: 2, *adv.* at last, at length, last of all, in the end, finally, after all; altogether, in brief, at the least.
निदिग्धिका, *f.* a sort of prickly nightshade (*Solanum jacquini*, Willd.).
निदिष्ट, *m.* (*f.* ā) ordered, directed, enjoined, explained.
निदेश, *m.* an order, command, word of command, direction, instruction: neighbourhood, proximity.
निदेशी, *m.* (*f.* inī) *adj.* showing, directing, pointing out.
निद्रा, *f.* sleep; sleepiness; sloth.
निद्राकर, *m.* a narcotic: lit. *adj.* sleep-producing, soporific, narcotic.
निद्राकर्षण, *m.* drowsiness, sleepiness, slothfulness.
निद्रागत होना, to be asleep.
निद्रायमान, *m.* (*f.* matī) asleep, sleeping.
निद्रालु, 1, sleepy, drowsy, slothful, lethargic, indolent: 2, *f.* a kind of perfume.
निद्रालुता, *f.* (*m.* °**त्व**) sleepiness, slothfulness.
निद्रित, *m.* (*f.* ā) asleep.
निधड़क, without fear, fearlessly, without reflection, abruptly. — *honā*, to be at one's ease, make oneself at home.
निधन, 1, *m.* (*f.* ā) = **निर्धन**, *q. v.*: 2, *m.* conclusion, death, destruction, extinction, annihilation; decrease,

detriment, loss: the head of a family, race, family, lineage: the seventh lunar asterism reckoning from that under which a person is born.

निधनता, *f.* (*m.* °**त्व**) poverty, indigence.

निधना, *f.*; see **निधन**, 1.

निधनी, *m.* (*f.* in *or* inī) = **निर्धन**, *q. v.*

निधान, *m.* a putting aside; *hence*, a receptacle or vessel in which anything is collected or deposited; a place of cessation or of rest, house, mansion, abode; the subject in which any quality inheres; the term is also applied to the nine treasures of Kuver; see *Nidhi*.

निधि, *m.* a receptacle, treasury; a place of asylum or of accumulation (as a granary, nest, etc.); any sum or quantity of wealth or valuables, a treasure; the ocean. This term is the special designation of the nine treasures of Kuver, *viz.* Kachchap, Kharb, Naud, Nil, Padm, Mahāpadm, Makar, Mukund, Sankh. The nature of these treasures is not exactly defined, though some of them appear to be precious gems. According to the Tantrik system, they are personified and worshipped as demigods attendant either upon Kuver, or upon Lakshmee (the goddess of prosperity).

निधिप, *m.* the guardian of a treasure.

निधुवन, *m.* agitation; enjoyment; coïtion.

निनद, *m.* sound in general; cry; buzzing.

निनयन, *m.* performance of a ceremony.

निनांवा / **निनांवां** } *m.* the thrush, *aphthœ.*

निनाद, *m.* = **निनद**, *q. v.*

निनादी, *m.* (*f.* inī) *adj.* sounding, playing; accom[panied by the sound of.

निनानवे / **निनान्वे** / **निनानव्वे** } = **निन्नानवे**, *q. v.*

निनाया, *m.* a bug.

निनिवी, *pr. n.* the city of Nineveh.

निन्दक, *m.* (*f.* ikā) a calumniator, scorner, blasphemer: lit. *adj.* blaming, reproaching, defaming, abusive, scurrilous, censorious, querulous.

निन्दकाई, *f.* censoriousness, querulousness.

निन्दकी = **निन्दक**, *q. v.*

निन्दन, 1, *m.* (*f.* ā *or* ī) = **निन्दक**, *q. v.*: 2, *m.* blame, [censure, reproach.

निन्दना, *t.* to blame, reproach, defame, revile, blaspheme.

निन्दनीय, *m.* (*f.* ā) deserving censure, reproach, [or contempt, contemptible.

निन्दनीयता, *f.* (*m.* °**त्व**) contemptibleness, censur[ableness.

निन्दरि (*Rām*) = **निरादर करके**.

निन्दा, *f.* blame, reproof, reproach, censure, abuse, reviling, defamation, slander, blasphemy, scorn, contempt, insult. — *k.* (with gen. *fem.* of the object) to slander, abuse, vilify, blaspheme, insult.

निन्दास, *f.* desire for sleep, drowsiness.

निन्दासंयुक्त, *m.* (*f.* ā) abusive, blasphemous.

निन्दासा, *m.* (*f.* ī) drowsy, sleepy.

निन्दास्तुति, *f.* ironical praise.

निन्दित, *m.* (*f.* ā) calumniated, blamed, reproved, reviled, abused; worthy of being reviled, despicable, contemptible, low.

निन्द्रा, *more prop.* (1) **निद्रा** (2) **निन्दा**, *qq. v.*

निन्द्य, *m.* (*f.* ā) = **निन्दनीय**, *q. v.*

निन्द्यता, *f.* (*m.* °**त्व**) contemptibleness, infamy.

निन्नानवे, ninety-nine (९९). See **श्रों**, **वां**, **वीं**, **वे**, **वें**. — *ke phermen parnā*, to be entirely absorbed in the acquisition of wealth; to be involved in difficulties.

निन्नान्वे / **निन्यानवे** } = **निन्नानवे**, *q. v.*

निप, *m.* a water-jar: the kadamb-tree (*Nauclea* [*cadamba*).

निपट, very, exceedingly, excessively.

निपटना, *a. int.* to terminate: *n.* to be settled, be [finished.

निपटाना, *t.* to conclude, decide, settle.

निपटारा, *m.* a termination, finishing.

निपटाऊ, *m.* one who terminates or finishes.

निपठ, see (1) **निपट** (2) **निपाट**.

निपत, *m.* an overthrow, destruction, ruin, death.

निपतन, *m.* a falling: a flying.

निपतित, *m.* (*f.* ā) fallen, overthrown.

निपाट, *m.* reading, study of the sacred books, public perusal of popular poems, lecturing.

निपाटना = **निपटाना**, *q. v.*

निपात, *m.* a falling, coming down, alighting; a casting; death, dying; the opposite extremity: (in Gram.) an irregularity, exception; an indeclinable word, particle.

निपातन, *m.* the causing a downfall, an overthrow, knocking down, beating, killing; a flying down, hurrying down, falling down: (in Gram.) an irregularity, an exception.

निपातना, *t.* to overthrow; to destroy.

निपाता, *m.* (*f.* ī) overthrown, destroyed.

निपाती, *m.* (*f.* inī) *adj.* falling down, alighting: an overthrower, destroyer.

निपान, *m.* drinking; a pool, reservoir of water, a trough or ditch near a well for watering cattle.

निपुण, *m.* (*f.* ā) perfect, clever, expert, skilful, conversant, distinguished, eminent.

निपुणता, *f.* / **निपुणत्व**, *m.* / **निपुणाई**, *f.* } cleverness; eminence.

निपूता, *m.* (*f.* ī) having no child, sonless.

निबटेरा, *m.* determination, final settlement, decree.

निबड़ना, *n.* to be settled, be accomplished, be ended, be decided, be spent.

निबन्ध, *m.* fastening, binding, confinement, fetter, suppression of the urine, constipation, fixed property; root; a literary work.

निबन्धन, *m.* a binding, ligation, bond, fetter; ratification; firmness; a receptacle: cause, motive: (in [Gram.) syntax.

निबन्धनी, *f.* a fetter.

निबन्धित, *m.* (*f.* ā) tied, bound, fixed.

निबन्धी, *m.* (*f.* inī) *adj.* binding; joined, bound.

निबल, *m.* (*f.* ā) = **निर्बल**, *q. v.*

निबलाई = **निर्बलाई**, *q. v.*

निबहना, *more com.* (1) **निभना** (2) **निबाहना**, *qq. v.*

निबहि (*Rām.*) = **निभके** (**निभना**).

निबहे; see **निबहना**.

निबाश्रो, *more prop.* निबाहू, *q. v.* [separation.
निबाड़न, *m.* an accomplishing, ending, cessation,
निबाड़ना, *t.* to keep one's engagements ; to accomplish, end ; to manage ; to spend ; to separate.
निबाड़ा, *m.* a passing, transit, passage. [form निवार.
निबार; for words beginning thus, see under the
निबाव, *more prop.* निबाहू, *q. v.* [form निवास.
निबास ; for words beginning thus, see under the
निबाह, *m.* accomplishment, keeping an engagement, maintenance, keeping, guarding, supply, sufficiency.
निबाहना, *t.* to accomplish, achieve, perfect, carry on to completion; to take care of, protect, guard; to keep one's faith ; to behave ; to afford ; to conduct ; to wear, last for a long time.
निबाहू, lasting, permanent, sufficient for one's
निबिड़ (*Rām.*) = निविड़, *q.v.* [purpose.
निबुकना (*Rām.*) = छुड़ाना or निकलना, *qq.v.*
निबुकि (*Rām.*) = निबुकके (निबुकना). [to, spend.
निबेड़ना, *t.* to complete, perfect, finish, put an end
निबेड़ा, *m.* a finishing, decision, settlement, end.
निबेड़ू, *adj.* performing, finishing.
निबेदन = निवेदन, *q.v.*
निबेरी (*Rām.*) = (1) चकाई (2) युवती, *qq.v.*
निबेही (*Rām.*) = (1) निबहि (2) निरन्तर, *qq.v.*
निभ, (found as the latter element in compounds) *m.* (*f.* ā) similar, resembling, like.
निभना, *a. int.* serve, succeed, pass, live, last : *n.* to be accomplished, be perfected : *t.* to take care of, preserve, afford, conduct, perform.
निभाश्रो, *m.* permanence, durability, lasting quali-
निभागा, (*f.* ī) ill-fated, unfortunate. [ty.
निभाड़ना, *more prop.* निबाड़ना, *q.v.*
निभाना, *more prop.* निबाहना, *q.v.*
निभ्रमा, *m.* (*f.* ī) without respect, worthless.
निमक, *m.* salt ; *met.* subsistence, bread ; animation, spirit. *Katepar-lagānā*, to apply salt to a wound; *i. e.* to aggravate a trouble, add one grief or vexation to another.
निमकचखी, *f.* the first feeding of a child at about six months old, which is attended by certain ceremonies.
निमकदान, *m.* a saltcellar.
निमकमहाल्ल, *m.* revenue derived from salt.
निमकसार, 1, *m.* a saltpit : 2, saline.
निमकहराम, ungrateful, perfidious, disloyal, disobedient, wicked, evil. [disobedience, wickedness.
निमकहरामी, *f.* ingratitude, perfidy, disloyalty,
निमकहलाल, loyal, submissive, faithful, grateful.
निमकी, *f.* pickled lemons.
निमकीन, salted, salt, brackish; *met.* witty, poignant, sarcastic; handsome, beautiful.
निमकौड़ी = निम्बकौड़ी, *q. v.*
निमखी, *f.* any grove of *neem*-trees.
निमछावर, *more com.* नेवछावर, *q. v.*
निमन, stout, strong, tight, good.
निमनाई, *f.* stoutness, strength, tightness.
निमनाना, *t.* to strengthen, ameliorate.
निमन्त्र, *m.* a call, summons, invitation.—*k.* to call, summon, invite.
निमन्त्रक, *m.* (*f.* ikā) *adj.* calling, summoning,
निमन्त्रण, *m.* = निमन्त्र, *q v.* [inviting.
निमन्त्रणपत्र, *m.* a summons or invitation.
निमन्त्रित, *m.* (*f.* ā) called, summoned, invited.
निमाना, *m.* (*f.* ī) simple, without guile ; unlike all others, singular, sheepish.
निमि, *m. pr. n.* a certain ancient Hindoo king.
निमिख = निमिष, *q.v.* See ख, (3).
निमित्त, 1, *m.* aim, mark, sign, omen ; cause, motive, instrumental cause : *met.* fortune : 2, *postp.* (takes gen. *m.* infl.) by reason of, for the benefit of, for the sake of, with a view to, for, on account of ; *e. g. Anantkāl nimitt*, for ever. *Us nimitt*, instead of that, for him. *Uske nimitt*, for his sake, in his interests. Let us ask (*ujālenimitt*) for a light. My thanks are due to you (*is udhār nimitt*) for this deliverance. *Is nimitt*, on this account. *Iske nimitt*, for the sake of this. *Isi nimitt*, on this very account. *Isike nimitt*, on account of this very thing.
निमित्तकारण, *m.* an efficient cause.
निमित्तता, *f.* (*m.* °त्व) causality, instrumentality.
निमित्तमान, *m.* (*f.* matī) prosperous, fortunate.
निमित्तार्त्त, *m.* (in Gram.) the infinitive mode.
निमित्ती, *m.* (*f.* inī) = निमित्तमान, *q. v.*
निमिष, *m.* the twinkling of the eye ; *hence*, a measure of time, a twinkling, moment, instant.
निमीलन, *m.* a closing the eyelids, twinkling, winking ; death, dying.
निमीलिका, *f.* a twinkling of the eye.
निमीली, *m.* (*f.* inī) one who has the eyes shut.
निमेष, *m.* = निमिष, *q.v.*
निमोची, *f. pr. n.* (in Myth.) a certain demon.
निम्न, 1, *m.* (*f.* ā) deep, low, profound, depressed, sunken, stooping : 2, *m.* low ground, declivity, slope.
निम्नग, *m.* (*f.* ā) *adj.* going deep, going downwards,
निम्नगा, *f.* (*m.* निम्नग) a river. [descending.
निम्नता, *f.* (*m.* °त्व) deepness, profundity.
निम्बा, *f.* ; see निम्ब. [*Azadirachta Indica*, Juss.).
निम्ब, *m.* the neem-tree (*Melia azad-dirachta* or
निम्बकौड़ी, *f.* the fruit or berry of the *neem*-tree.
निम्बतरु, *m.* the coral-tree (*Erythrina fulgens*). It is considered to be one of the trees of Paradise.
निम्बू, *m.* the common lime-tree (*Citrus acida*) or its fruit.
निम्बोली, appertaining to the *neem*-tree.
निम्लोच, *m.* the setting of the sun.
निम्लोचा, *f. pr. n.* a daughter of Vishwāmitra.
निय, an old form = निज, *q. v.*
नियत, *m.* (*f.* ā) self-governed, subdued, restrained : established, confirmed, prescribed, constituted.
नियतात्मा = नियत, *q.v.* [stemious.
नियताहार, *m.* (*f.* ī) self-controlled as to food, ab-

नियति, *f.* destiny, good or bad fortune; a regulation, injunction; a religious duty. [ed passions.
नियतेन्द्रिय, *m.* (*f.* ā) *adj.* of restrained or subdu-
नियन्ता, *m.* (*f.* trī) a restrainer, ruler, governor, master, charioteer, coachman.
नियन्तृ, *m.* (*f.* trī) = नियन्ता, *q.v.*
नियन्तृता, *f.* (*m.* °त्व) the faculty of restraining.
नियम, *m.* a restraining, preventing. restriction, rule, precept, usage, practice, any religious observance voluntarily practised (as fasting, watching, pilgrimage, praying, etc.), religious observance or observation in general; certainty; a contract, agreement, bond, engagement, regulation, arrangement, vow, promise, assent.
नियमन, *m.* a subduing, restraining, binding,
नियमरहित, (in Gram.) irregular. [checking.
नियमित, *m.* (*f.* ā) agreed upon, appointed, stipulated, covenanted, regulated, prescribed, established.
नियमी, *m.* (*f.* inī) conscientious, abstemious, con-
नियर, near, beside, close by. [tinent, chaste.
नियराई, *f.* nearness, proximity, contiguity.
नियराना, *a. int.* to draw nigh, approach.
नियरे = नियर, *q.v.* [gence: an offering.
नियाज़, *f.* supplication, petition, prayer: indi-
नियामक, *m.* (*f.* ikā) a controller, superintendent, helmsman, pilot, sailor, boatman, charioteer, coachman: lit. *adj.* controlling, regulating.
नियामकत्व, *m.* (*f.* tā) a superintending, controlling, regulating; exact determination, explanation.
नियाय; for words beginning thus, see under the form न्याय.
नियार, *m.* forage, fodder, food for cattle.
नियारा, *m.* the *scoriæ* left after refining gold, silver, or other metals, from which a minute portion of those metals is obtainable: adj. *m.* (*f.* ī) apart; aloof, separate, distinct, different, extraordinary, uncommon.
नियारिया, *m.* one who extracts metals from their *scoriæ*: *adj.* prudent, cautious, not easily imposed upon.
नियारे, *adv.* apart.
नियुक्त, *m.* (*f.* ā) appointed, fixed upon, ordained, authorized, called, engaged in, applying or attached to.
नियुत, *m.* a great number, *e.g.* a million; also, a hundred thousands.
नियुद्ध, *m.* close fight, personal struggle.
नियोक्ता / नियोक्तृ } *m.* (*f.* trī) a ruler, governor.
नियोग, *m.* a fastening, appointment, authority, commission, order, command; (in Gram.) the impera- [tive mode.
नियोगा (*Rām.*) = नियोग, *q.v.*
नियोगी, *m.* (*f.* inī) an authorized functionary, deputy, agent, minister: *lit.* appointed, entrusted with authority, authorized, engaged in any pursuit, engrossed in or attached to anything.
नियोजन, *m.* an order; an ordering, commanding, directing. [authorized.
नियोजित, *m.* (*f.* ā) entrusted with, appointed to,
निर्, an inseparable prefix, the reverse of नि. Its pervading and permanent import is *negation*, out, forth, without, deprived of, on the outside, destitute of, separation from, removal. This particle is liable to be variously spelt निः, निश्, निष्, निस्, in harmony with principles which will be found carefully explained in any good Hindee or Sanskrit Grammar.
निरउपाधि, *more prop.* निरुपाधि, *q.v.*
निरंकार / निरंकाल } *more prop.* निराकार, *q.v.*
निरंकुश, uncontrolled, unchecked, independent, free, unruly, disorderly, self-willed.
निरंजन, 1, *m.* an epithet of the Supreme: 2, *m.* (*f.* ā) unblackened, unstained, void of passion or emotion, artless.
निरंजना, *f.* (*m.* निरंजन) an artless female; the day
निरंश = निरंशी, *q.v.* [of full moon.
निरंशी, *m.* (*f.* inī) without a share, not having a share.
निरकेवल = निष्केवल, *q.v.*
निरक्कास in Chand = a taking out, extraction.
निरक्ष, *m.* (in Astron.) the terrestrial equator: lit. *adj.* having no latitude. [dian, as Lankā (Ceylon).
निरक्षदेश, *m.* the equatorial region, a first meri-
निरख, *more prop.* निर्ख, *q.v.*
निरखना, *t.* to look at, view, see.
निरखि (*Rām.*) = निरखके (निरखना).
निरत, 1, *more prop.* निर्त, *q.v.*: 2, pleased, delighted: ceased, desisted, reposed.
निरतक, *more prop.* निर्तक, *q.v.*
निरतना, *more prop.* निर्तना, *q.v.*
निरधार, *more com.* निर्धार, *q.v.* [or authority.
निरधिकारी, *m.* (*f.* inī) one who acts without right
निरनाई, *more prop.* निर्णय, *q.v.*
निरनुगृहीत, *m.* (*f.* ā) unfavoured, unhonoured, un-
निरनुनासिक, (in Gram.) non-nasal. [pitied.
निरन्तर, *m.* (*f.* ā) without any interstice, completely filled, without interval, continuous, uninterrupted, continual, faithful: *adv.* incessantly, constantly.
निरन्तराभ्यास, *m.* diligent and unintermitting pursuit of study; private study, reading to oneself the sacred books; exercise, practice.
निरपक्ष; for words beginning thus, see under the
निरपति, *more prop.* नृपति, *q.v.* [form निर्पेक्ष.
निरपराध, 1, = निरपराधी, *q.v.*: 2, *m.* guiltlessness, unoffendingness, innocence, sinlessness.
निरपराधता, *f.* / निरपराधत्व, *m.* } = निरपराध, 2, *q.v.*
निरपराधवान / निरपराधवन्त } *m.* (*f.* vatī) = निरपराधी, *q.v.*
निरपराधी, *m.* (*f.* inī) unoffending, guiltless, innocent.
निरपेक्ष, *m.* (*f.* ā) without purpose or expectation, without desire, indifferent, careless, unconnected with, unconcerned with, independent of.
निरपेक्षता, *f.* (*m.* °त्व) independence.
निरफल, *more com.* निष्फल, *q.v.*
निरबहई (*Rām.*) = निबहै, *q.v.*
निरबहा (*Rām.*) = निबहा, *q.v.*

निरवान, *more prop.* निर्वाण, *q.v.*
निरबाह (*Rām.*) = निबाहके (निबाहना).
निरबुद्धि = निर्बुद्धि, *q. v.*
निरबैना, *m.* (*f.* ī) speechless, silent, mute, dumb.
निरभिलाष, *m.* (*f.* ā) without desire, indifferent to.
निरभिप्राय, meaningless, purposeless, aimless.
निरभै, *more prop.* निर्भय, *q.v.*
निरमय (*Rām.*) = निर्माण करना.
निरमल, *m.* (*f.* ā) *more com.* निर्मल, *q. v.*
निरमाना, *more prop.* निर्माना, *q.v.*
निरमाल ; see (1) निर्मल (2) निर्माल्य.
निरमित्र, 1, *m.* (*f.* ā) free from foes : 2, *m. pr. n.* (1) of a son of Nakul (2) of a king of Trigart (3) of several others.
निरम्बु, destitute of water ; abstaining from water.
निरमोक, *more com.* निर्मोक, *q. v.*
निरमोही, *m.* (*f.* inī) *more com.* निर्मोही, *q.v.*
निरयुक्तिक, *more com.* निर्युक्तिक, *q. v.* [ing, useless.
निरर्थ, *m.* nonsense : *lit.* purposeless, poor, unmean-
निरर्थक, *m.* (*f.* ā *or* ikā) to no purpose, useless, vain, fruitless, unprofitable, meaningless, absurd, insignificant, trivial, obsolete.
निरर्थी, *m.* (*f.* iṇī) = निरर्थक, *q. v.*
निरलेप, free from spots.
निरखि = निरखके. See ख (3), and ब, 7.
निरस, 1, *m.* saplessness, insipidity, want of juice or flavor, want of passion, dryness : 2. *m.* (*f.* ā) sapless, dry, insipid, charmless, merciless. [ed, deserted, left.
निरस्त, thrown out, discharged, expelled, abandon-
निरस्त्र, destitute of arms, unarmed.
निरस्य = निरस, 1, *q. v.* [humble.
निरहंकार, free from selfishness, free from pride,
निरा, *m.* (*f.* ī) mere, pure, only, unalloyed, simple, single. [ing anything, content.
निराकांक्षी, *m.* (*f.* inī) free from desire, not covet-
निराकार, *m.* an epithet of the Supreme ; *lit.* deprived of one's natural form, devoid of form, incorporeal, disguised.
निरादर, *m.* (*f.* ā) without respect, unrespected, disrespected ; disrespectful, unceremonious, impolite. —*k.* to behave rudely, to insult, to scorn.
निरादरबोधक, (in Gram.) expressive of disrespect.
निराधार, without support or prop.
निराधीन, not subject or dependent, free.
निराना, *t.* to reap a harvest.
निरापद, 1, *f.* absence of misfortune : 2, free from misfortune, fortunate, prosperous.
निरामय, *m.* a wild goat ; a hog, boar : *lit.* free from sickness, healthy, pure.
निरामालु, *m.* the wood-apple. [without meat or prey.
निरामिष, *m.* (*f.* ā *or* ī) 1, = निरामिषी, *q.v* : 2, fleshless,
निरामिषी, *m.* (*f.* iṇī) *adj.* living without eating flesh ; free from sensual desires. [ready, easy.
निरायास, not giving trouble, easily attainable,
निरायुध, *m.* (*f.* ā) disarmed, unarmed, defenceless.

निरालस्य, 1, *m.* absence of indolence, zeal : 2, not slothful, active, zealous.
निराला, *m.* (*f.* ī) apart, retired, aloof, lonely, private, odd, extraordinary, strange ; pure, unmixed, simple, mere, unalloyed. [vately.
निराले, *adv.* (sc. में) aside, apart, in private, pri-
निराश, *m.* (*f.* ā) hopeless, disappointed, de-
निराशता, *f.* (*m.* °त्व) = निराशा, 2, *q. v.* [spairing.
निराशा, *f.* 1, (see निराश) a forlorn female : 2, hopelessness, despondency, despair.
निराशिस, *adj.* without a blessing, unblessed.
निराशी, *f.* = निराशा, 2, *q. v.* [refuge, destitute.
निराश्रय, *m.* (*f.* ā) *adj.* having no support, without
निरास, for words beginning thus, see under the form निराश.
निरासन, *m.* a throwing out, a casting away, rejection, refutation, contradiction ; destruction, slaughter.
निराहार, *m.* (*f.* ī) a faster (whether from choice or from necessity) : *lit.* without food.
निरिन्द्रिय, *m.* (*f.* ā) not having the use of the limbs, mutilated, maimed. [expecting, hoping.
निरीक्षण, *m* a look, a looking at, regarding, seeing,
निरीक्षमन्त, *m.* (*f.* matī)
निरीक्षमान, *m.* (*f.* matī)
निरीक्षवान, *m.* (*f.* vatī)
} = निरीक्षी, *q. v.*
निरीक्षा, *f.* a looking at, regarding, seeing ; expecting, hoping ; hope, expectation. [hoped.
निरीक्षित, *m.* (*f.* ā) looked at, beheld ; expected,
निरीक्षी, *m.* (*f.* inī) looking, looking at, regarding, expecting, hoping. [to spy ; to expect.
निरीखना, to look at, behold, see ; to look out ;
निरीछा
निरींछा
} *more prop.* निरीक्षा, *q. v.*
निरीश, 1, = निरीष, *q. v.* : 2, without a proprietor, without a master, or ruler.
निरीष, *m.* the body of a plough.
निरीस, *more prop.* निरीश, 2, *q. v.*
निरीहता, *f.*
निरीहत्व, *m.*
} indifference.
निरुआरना (*Rām.*) = सुर्झाना, *q. v.*
निरुक्त, *m, pr. n.* one of the Vedāngas (by Yāska), being an explanation of obsolete and obscure words occurring in the Veds : lit. *m.* (*f.* ā) not spoken, not said, not declared, obscure, obsolete.
निरुक्ति, *f.* 1, = निरुक्त, *q.v.* : 2, interpretation, etymological explanation.
निरुत्तर, *m.* (*f.* ā) unable to answer, without an answer, without excuse, nonplussed, silenced. —*k.* (with acc. of the object) to silence (in argument).
निरुत्साहता, *f.*
निरुत्साहत्व, *m.*
} cowardice, cowardliness.
निरूपण, *m.* an ascertaining, determining, settling, arranging ; the laying down a rule or precept, doubt, discussion, investigation.
निरुपद्रव, 1, *m.* (*f.* ā) secure from attacks, free

from danger or calamity, unharmed: 2, *m.* security, tranquillity, ease. [bold, fearless; safe, secure.

निरुपधि, 1, (*Rām.*) = **निरुपाधि**, *q.v.*: 2, guileless;

निरुपन, *more prop.* **निरूपण**, *q.v.*

निरुपम, *m.* (*f.* ā) unexampled, unequalled, peerless.

निरुपाधि, causelessly, needlessly. [helpless.

निरुपाय, without help or expedient, remediless,

निरुवारना (*Rām.*) = **खोलना**, *q.v.*

निरूप, *m.* an epithet of the Supreme: *lit. m.* (*f.* ā) a person who is without form: *adj.* without form incorporal. [ing; shape: *adj.* determining.

निरूपण, *m.* sight; a seeking, ascertaining, determin-

निरूपधि, *more prop.* **निरुपधि**, *q.v.*

निरूपाधि, *more prop.* **निरुपाधि**, *q.v.*

निरूपित, *m.* (*f.* ā) fixed upon, settled, determined, arranged, ascertained, appointed, directed to do a thing. [fined or ascertained.

निरूप्य, *m.* (*f.* ā) admitting of being seen or de-

निरूप्यता, *f.* (*m.* °त्व) ascertainableness, define-

निरेखना = **निरीखना**, *q.v.* [ableness, visibility.

निरोग, 1, *m.* healthiness: 2, *m.* (*f.* ā) free from sickness, healthy, in good spirits.

निरोगित, *m.* (*f.* ā) } = **निरोग**, 2, *q.v.*
निरोगी, *m.* (*f.* inī) }

निरोध, *m.* confinement, imprisonment, coërcion, obstruction, disappointment, destruction.

निरोधन, *m.* a confining, obstructing, imprisonment, coërcion, disappointment.

निरौषध, without a medicine, incurable.

निर्भ्राश; see (1) **निराश** (2) **निर्भाजन**.

निर्ऋति, *f. pr. n.* a certain female demigod, patroness of the south-west: *lit.* imprecation; calamity; [gentleness.

निर्क, a corruption of **नरक**, *q.v.*

निर्केवल = **निष्केवल**, *q.v.*

निर्ख़, *m.* price (as fixed by the officers of police), market-price, price current, tariff, assize.

निर्ख़दरोग़ा, *m.* a clerk of the market.

निर्ख़नामा, *m.* an account or bill of current or settled market-prices. [corded, price-list.

निर्ख़बन्दी, *f.* a document in which prices are re-

निर्ख़ी, *m.* the person who fixes the prices current, an appraiser, assizer. [departed, expended, extinct.

निर्गत, *m.* (*f.* ā) gone out, gone forth, gone through,

निर्गन्ध, *m.* (*f.* ā) inodorous, void of fragrance.

निर्गन्धता, *f.* (*m.* °त्व) inodorousness.

निर्गन्धपुष्पी, *f.* the silk-cotton tree.

निर्गम, *m.* a going forth, setting out, issue, exit, vanishing, export, an outlet, a door.

निर्गुण, *m.* (*f.* ā) void of all properties (the term is hence applied to the Supreme, as being without passions or qualities); destitute of good or estimable qualities, unskilful, worthless, bad.

निर्गुणता, *f.* (*m.* °त्व) (an attribute of the Supreme especially) the state of being destitute of all properties; want of good qualities, worthlessness, wickedness.

निर्गुणिया, *m.* one who believes God to be void of all qualities. [root of the lotus.

निर्गुण्ठी, *f.* a certain shrub (*Vitex negundo*): the

निर्घण्ट, *m.* a vocabulary; an index.

निर्घण्टक, *m.* a thorough investigation; a table of contents, summary, list, vocabulary; *strictly*, the singling out the words of a verse or sentence and setting them up in their absolute form, — neglecting the rules of Sandhi or euphonical connexion.

निर्घिन, not odious, not detestable: abominable; shameless: cruel.

निर्घृणता, *f.* (*m.* °त्व) unmercifulness.

निर्चा, *m.* a kind of greens (*Corchorus capsularis*).

निर्छल, guileless, simple. [unfrequented, lonely.

निर्जन, unpeopled, without inhabitants, deserted,

निर्जय, *m.* conquest, victory.

निर्जर, *m.* ambrosia, the food of the gods; *lit.* undecaying, imperishable, immortal.

निर्जल, *m.* a desert, waste; *lit.* without water, dry, desert. [unconquered.

निर्जित, *m.* (*f.* ā) overcome, subdued, conquered:

निर्जेता }
निर्जेतृ } *m.* (*f.* °त्री) a vanquisher.

निर्जीव, 1, *m.* death: 2, *m.* (*f.* ā) devoid of life, inanimate, dead.

निर्जोव (*Rām.*) = **निश्चय**, *q.v.* [mate, dead.

निर्झर, *m.* a waterfall, cascade, torrent, spring.

निर्णय, *m.* removal; investigation, demonstration, certainty, accuracy; (in Logic) complete ascertainment, deduction, conclusion; (in Law) decision, sentence. [sentenced.

निर्णीत, *m.* (*f.* ā) ascertained, determined; decreed,

निर्णेता }
निर्णेतृ } *m.* (*f.* °त्री) one who demonstrates.

निर्त, *m.* (a dialectic form of **नृत्य**) dance.

निर्तक, *m.* (*f.* ikā *or* ī) a dancer, mime.

निर्तना, *a. int.* to jump about playfully, to dance.

निर्ताना, *t.* to cause to dance: to clean.

निर्दई }
निर्दय } *m.* (*f.* inī) = **निर्दयी**, *q.v.*

निर्दयता, *f.* }
निर्दयत्व, *m.* } = **निर्दया**, *q.v.*

निर्दया, *f.* mercilessness, hardheartedness, severity, cruelty, pitilessness. [ed, unkind, severe, cruel.

निर्दयी, *m.* (*f.* inī) merciless, unfeeling, hardheart-

निर्दयीपन, *m.* = **निर्दया**, *q.v.*

निर्दर, *m.* a cave, cavern.

निर्दहन, *m.* marking-nut.

निर्दहनी, *f.* a species of creeper (*Sanseveria zeylanica*) from the fibres of which bowstrings are made.

निर्दिष्ट, *m.* (*f.* ā) pointed out, depicted, described, shewn, ascertained, determined.

निर्देश, *m.* a command, order; detail; description, depicting, pointing out, exhibiting.

निर्दोष = निर्दोषी, *q.v.*
निर्दोषता, *f.* (*m.* °त्व) faultlessness, innocence.
निर्दोषी, *m.* (*f.* iṇī) faultless, unblemished, innocent.
निर्दई / **निर्दयी** } *m.* (*f.* inī) = निर्दयी, *q.v.*
निर्द्वन्द्व, indifferent in regard to the opposite pairs (as pleasure and pain, etc.), free from either of two principles or alternatives, independent, free from jealousy, neither glad nor sorry, not double, uncontested.
निर्धन, *m.* (*f.* ā) without wealth, indigent, poor.
निर्धनता, *f.* / **निर्धनत्व**, *m.* } indigence.
निर्धर्म, 1, *m.* injustice, irreligion, impiety: 2, *m.* (*f.* ā *or* ī) destitute of law or religion, unrighteous, immoral, impious. [2, free from debt.
निर्धार, 1, *m.* ascertainment, certainty, accuracy:
निर्धारण, *m.* the settling or fixing with accuracy, ascertainment, agreement, arrangement.
निर्धारित, *m.* (*f.* ā) ascertained, determined, fixed [upon, settled.
निर्नय, *more prop.* निर्णय, *q.v.*
रिर्नमस्कार, *m.* (*f.* ī) without respect, *i.e.* respecting nobody; respected by nobody. [superior.
निर्नाथ, *m.* (*f.* ā) without protector, master, or
निर्नाथता, *f.* (*m.* °त्व) the being without protection, the being without a master, widowhood.
निर्नाथा, *f.* (*m.* निर्नाथ) an unprotected female.
निर्पक्ष = निर्पक्षी, *q.v.*
निर्पक्षता, *f.* (*m.* °त्व) want of protection.
निर्पक्षी, *m.* (*f.* iṇī) without wings; without preoccupation, not prejudiced, impartial, of no party, [friendless, helpless.
निर्पख, *more prop.* निर्पक्ष, *q.v.*
निर्पेक्ष, *m.* (*f.* ā) without regard, indifferent, without desire, careless, independent of.
निर्पेक्षता, *f.* / **निर्पेक्षत्व**, *m.* } = निर्पेक्षा, *q.v.* [independence.
निर्पेक्षा, *f.* indifference, heedlessness, carelessness,
निर्फल, *more com.* निष्फल, *q.v.* [form निर्वेश.
निर्बेश; for words beginning thus see under the
निर्बन्ध, *m.* an insisting upon, pertinacity, persistence, accusing; seizure; bondage, captivity: *adj.* freed,
निर्बन्धत्व, *m.* (*f.* tā) freedom, emancipation. [free.
निर्बन्धी, *m.* (*f.* inī) intent, tenacious in any pursuit, insisting on anything; persistently devoted to spiritual things; loosed from an obligation, unfettered, free.
निर्बन्धु, without kin, without friends.
लिर्बल, *m.* (*f.* ā) without strength, powerless, weak, [feeble.
निर्बलता, *f.* / **निर्बलत्व**, *m.* } = निर्बलाई, *q.v.*
निर्बला, *f.* (*m.* निर्बल) a weak woman.
निर्बलाई, *f.* powerlessness, impotence, prostration of strength, weakness.
निर्बश, *more prop.* निर्वंश, *q.v.*
निर्बहा (*Rām.*) = बीत गया.

निर्बाद = निर्वाद, *q.v.*
निर्बान, *more prop.* निर्वाण, *q.v.*
निर्बाह = निर्वाह, *q.v.*
निर्बिकल्प (*Rām.*) = भेदरहित.
निर्बिकारता, *f.* (*m.* °त्व) absence of fickleness or mutability, unchangingness, uniformity.
निर्बिखी, *more prop.* निर्बिषी, *q.v.*
निर्बीज, *more prop.* निर्वीज, *q.v.*
निर्बुद्धि, destitute of reason or understanding, senseless, irrational, ignorant.
निर्बुद्धिता, *f.* (*m.* °त्व) senselessness.
निर्बूझ, not to be understood, incomprehensible.
निर्बैर, *more prop.* निर्वैर, *q.v.*
निर्भय, *m.* (*f.* ā) fearless, undaunted, brave, rash.
निर्भयता, *f.* (*m.* °त्व) fearlessness.
निर्भोजन, destitute of food.
निर्भया, *f.* (*m.* निर्भय) a fearless woman.
निर्भर, 1, *m.* anything to depend upon, a prop, fulcrum; reliance, dependence: 2, much, excessive, exceedingly.
निर्मद, *m.* (*f.* ā) an elephant after the frontal juice has ceased to exude, one out of rut: *lit.* free from arrogance, sober, quiet, unintoxicated.
निर्मनुष, *more com.* निर्मनुष्य, *q.v.* [desolate.
निर्मनुष्य, without a man, deserted, uninhabited,
निर्मम, *m.* (*f.* ā) claiming or wishing for nothing, disinterested, indifferent.
निर्ममता, *f.* (*m.* °त्व) disregard of worldly possessions or interests, disinterestedness, indifference.
निर्ममा, *f.* (*m.* निर्मम) a disinterested woman.
निर्मय (*Rām.*) = निर्माण करना.
निर्मयउ (*Rām.*) = निर्माण किया.
निर्मल, *f.* (*m.* ā) spotless, free from dirt or impurities, clean, pellucid, transparent, limpid, pure, clear, cloudless.
निर्मलता, *f.* unspottedness, clearness, cleanness, pellucidness, limpidness, transparency, cloudlessness.
निर्मलत्व, *m.* = निर्मलता, *q.v.*
निर्मला, *f.* (*m.* निर्मल) a spotless female.
निर्मली, *f.* a certain seed (*Strychnos potatorum*) with which water is cleared; clearing-nut.
निर्माण, *m.* measure; a part; forming, creating, making, production, contriving, constructing, work; pith, marrow, essence.
निर्माणकर्त्ता, *m.* (*f.* trī) / **निर्माणकारक**, *m.* (*f.* ikā) } = निर्माता, *q.v.*
निर्माता, *m.* (*f.* trī) a maker, builder, creator, former, [producer.
निर्माना, *t.* to form, make, create.
निर्माल्य, 1, *m.* cleanness, purity, clearness: the remains of an offering made to a deity: 2, *m.* (*f.* ā) clean, pure, clear.
निर्मित, *m.* (*f.* ā) formed, fabricated, artificial.
निर्मेउ = निर्माया हुआ (निर्माना).
निर्मोक, *m. pr. n.* (1) of a son of the 8th Manu (2) of one of the Saptarshis under the 13th Manu.

निर्मूल, *m.* (*f.* ā) without root, eradicated, baseless, unfounded. [fascinated, without affection, unkind.

निर्मोही, *m.* (*f.* inī) free from attachment, not

निर्यास, *m.* exudations of trees and plants (as gum, milk, extract, etc.); extract, decoction, infusion.

निर्युक्ति, *f.* disunion; inappropriateness; (in Gram.) want of connexion or government.

निर्युक्तिक, *m.* (*f.* ā) detached; un connected, un meaning, illogical; inappropriate, improper.

निर्लज्ज, *m.* (*f.* ā) shameless, immodest, impudent.

निर्लज्जता, *f.* (*m.* °त्व) shamelessness.

निर्लज्जा, *f.* (*m.* **निर्लज्ज**) an immodest female: shamelessness, immodesty, obscenity.

निर्लिप्त, *m.* an epithet of Krishṇ; lit. *m.* (*f.* ā) unconnected with, unsmeared, uncontaminated, unpolluted, unanointed.

निर्लेप, free from spots.

निर्लोभ, *m.* absence of greed, unselfishness, contentment: 2, *m.* (*f.* ā) void of avarice or greed, uncovetous, contented.

निर्लोभी, *m.* (*f.* inī) = **निर्लोभ**, 2, *q.v.*

निर्वंश, *m.* (*f.* ā) without family or lineage, without offspring, childless; extinct (race or family).

निर्वंशता, *f.* the being without family or lineage,

निर्वंशत्व, *m.* = **निर्वंशता**, *q.v.* [childlessness.

निर्वचन, *m.* a proverb; etymological explanation: 2, *m.* (*f.* ā) speechless, silent, blameless.

निर्वन, *m.* (*f.* ā) one who has left a forest; a bare open country: *lit.* without jungle.

निर्वपण, *m.* an offering (*esp.* to *manes*); a gift. [tion.

निर्वर्त्तन, *m.* accomplishment, completion, execu-

निर्वाण, 1, *m.* (*f.* ā) extinguished, liberated from existence, deceased: 2, *m.* a becoming extinguished; *hence*, final emancipation from matter and from the necessity for further transmigration, and reünion with the universal Spirit; complete satisfaction, eternal happiness.

निर्वात, 1, *m.* absence of wind, a calm: 2, not windy, calm, still; sheltered from the wind.

निर्वाद, *m.* censure: rumour: the decision of a controversy: absence of dispute.

निर्वाह, *m.* accomplishing, completion, an end; a carrying on, supporting, maintaining; a providing means; sufficiency, adequacy; livelihood. — *k.* to give success, to support.

निर्विकार, unchanged, unaltered, uniform.

निर्विघ्न, 1, *m.* absence of obstruction or impediment: 2, unobstructed, unimpeded: 3, unobstructedly, freely. [nity from encounters, safety.

निर्विघ्नता, *f.* (*m.* °त्व) unobstructedness, immu-

निर्विन्ध्या, *f. pr. n.* a certain river that rises in the Vindhya mountains. [less, foolish.

निर्विवेक, undiscriminating, inconsiderate, thought-

निर्विवेकता, *f.* (*m.* °त्व) inconsiderateness.

निर्विष, *m.* (*f.* ā) without poison, deprived of poison.

निर्विषा, *f.* = (1) **निर्विष** (2) **निर्विषी**, *q.v.*

निर्विषी, *f.* zedoary (*Amomum zedoaria*, Willd.; *Cucurma zedoaria*, Roxb.; *Kylingia monocephala*), a spicy plant somewhat like ginger in its leaves, but of a sweet scent. [less; extinct (a race or family).

निर्वीज, *m.* (*f.* ā) without seed, impotent, child-

निर्वीर्य, powerless, impotent, feeble, spiritless, tame.

निर्वृत, *m.* (*f.* ā) accomplished, ended, emancipated free from occupation or interest, contented, happy.

निर्वृति, *f.* completion, accomplishment, conclusion, ceasing or abstaining from, repose, tranquillity, final emancipation from existence, rest, death; happiness.

निर्वेद, 1, *m.* disgust; loathsomeness; self-disparagement, humility; indifference: desperation: 2, not having the Veds; unscriptural, infidel.

निर्वैर, 1, *m.* peaceableness: 2, without enmity, peaceable, friendly.

निर्हँस, averse to laughter, grave, dull.

निलज्ज, *m.* (*f.* ā) *more com.* **निर्लज्ज**, *q.v.*

निलाहट, *f.* blueness.

निवछावर = **नेवछावर**, *q.v.*

निवटेरा; see **निबटेरा**.

निवड़ना, *a. int.* to bend, stoop, incline.

निवड़ाना, *t.* to cause to bend or stoop, to bend,

निवरा, *f.* an unmarried girl, maiden. [turn, direct.

निवसना, *more com.* **निवासना**, *q.v.*

निवहना, *more prop.* **निभना**, *q.v.* [on.

निवाज़ना, *t.* to entice, decoy, wheedle: to have mercy

निवाड़ = **निवार**, 2, *q.v.*

निवाड़ा, *m.* a large kind of boat.

निवान, low (as ground), level.

निवाना, *t.* to cause to bend, cause to stoop, cause to submit to, to bend downwards; to fold, double.

निवार, 1, *m.* a hindering; opposition, impediment: 2, *f.* a coarse kind of tape.

निवारक, *m.* (*f.* ikā) *adj.* preventative, hindering, prohibitive, impeding, keeping off.

निवारण, *m.* a keeping off, preventing, stopping, hindering, prohibiting, opposing, impediment.

निवारना, *t.* to keep off, prevent, hinder, oppose, prohibit, impede, stop.

निवारबाफ़, *m.* a tape-weaver.

निवारिका, *f.* (*m.* **निवारक**) a female opposer.

निवारित, *m.* (*f.* ā) hindered, checked, opposed,

निवारी, *f.* a species of jasmine. [prohibited.

निवाला, *m.* a morsel, mouthful: the wadding of a gun. *Sonekā* —, an expensive banquet, delicious morsel.

निवावना = **निवाना**, *q.v.*

निवास, *m.* a dwelling, passing the night, an abode, residence, house; night-quarters.

निवासना, *a. int.* to dwell.

निवासस्थान, *m.* a dwellingplace.

निवाहना = **निबाहना**, *q.v.*

निविड, 1, *m. pr. n.* a certain mountain; 2, *m.* (*f.* ā) a crooked-nosed person, etc.: *lit.* without interstices, dense, impervious, thick, firm, coarse, gross, large.

निवासी, *m.* (*f.* inī) an inhabitant, a native: *lit.* *adj.* inhabiting, abiding in, dwelling.

निवृत, ceased, desisted, discontinued, stopped, hindered, quenched. — *k*, to put a stop to.

निवृति, *f.* return, disappearance, cessation, relaxation, abstinence, inactivity, repose, final emancipation.

निवृतिमार्ग, *m.* the path of emancipation, way of salvation. [of emancipation.

निवृतिमार्गी, *m.* (*f.* inī) one who pursues the path

निवृत्यर्थ, (see अर्थ) for the sake of निवृत, *q.v.*

निवेड़ा = निबेड़ा, *q.v.*

निवेदन, *m.* a making known, announcement; a representation to a superior, a petition, address. — *k.* to plead, make an application. [presented.

निवेदित, made known, announced, reported, re-

निश, 1, = निर, *q.v.*: 2, *f.* night.

निशंक, 1, *m.* (*f.* ā) free from doubt, suspicion, or fear:

निशश्वास = निश्श्वास, *q.v.* [2, fearlessly.

निशा, *f.* night: a dream: turmeric.

निशाकर, *m.* the moon (*lit.* the night-maker).

निशाकार, 1, see (1) निशाकर (2) निशाकाल: 2, *m.* the form or aspect of night: *adj.* nightlike.

निशाकाल, *m.* the time of night.

निशाचर, *m.* (*f.* ī) any animal that feeds and watches by night, nocturnal animal, night-prowler, burglar, fiend, demon, goblin, *rākshas*: lit. *adj.* going about or moving by night, nightwalking.

निशाचरी, *f.* (*m.* निशाचर) a female fiend (*Rākshas*), she-devil; a woman who keeps an assignation, a harlot: a kind of perfume. [nished.

निशात, *m.* (*f.* ā) sharpened, sharp; polished, var-

निशान, *m.* a mark, sign, signal, ensign, flag, standard, colours, armorial bearings, family arms; a butt, a scar.

निशानपट्टी, *f.* a descriptive-roll (of fugitive slaves,

निशाना, *m.* a mark; a butt. [deserters, etc.).

निशानाथ, *m.* the ruler of the night, *i.e.* the moon.

निशानी, *f.* a mark, sign, token, keepsake.

निशान्त, 1, *m.* (*f.* ā) quiet, patient, tranquil: 2, *m.* a house, dwelling: 3, *m.* the dawn: *lit.* the end of night.

निशान्तनारी, *f.* a housewife. [*lit.* night-blind.

निशान्ध, *m.* (*f.* ā) a person who is blind at night:

निशापुष्प, *m.* the white water-lily.

निशि, *f.* (prop. निशा) night.

निशिचर *m.* (*f.* ī) = निशाचर, *q.v.*

निशित, *m.* iron: *lit.* whetted, sharpened, ground.

निशिदिन = निशिबासर, *q.v.*

निशिनाथ, *m.* lord of the night, *i. e.* the moon.

निशिनाश, *m.* the destruction of night, *i.e.* the moon.

निशिपुष्पा, *f.* a species of flower (*Nyctanthes tristis*).

निशिबासर, day and night, without intemission,

निशीथ, *m.* midnight; night. [continually.

निशुम्भ, *m. pr. n.* a certain demon (brother of Shumbh) slain by Durgā.

निशेला, inebriant, intoxicating.

निशेश, *m.* an epithet of the moon; *lit.* lord of night.

निशेत, *m.* a crane (*Ardea nivea*).

निश्चय, 1, *m.* ascertainment, certainty, decision, positive conclusion; trust, belief, faith: 2, ascertained, certain, indubitable, sure, actual, real: 3, for a certainty, indubitably, really, actually. [pronoun.

निश्चयवाचक सर्वनाम, *m.* (in Gram.) the definite

निश्चर, (see निशाचर) *m.* (*f.* ī) a night-prowler.

निश्चराई, *f.* night-walking. — *k.* to prowl about at night.

निश्चरी, *f.* (*m.* निश्चर) a female night-walker.

निश्चल, *m.* (*f.* ā) immoveable, still, fixed.

निश्चला, *f.* the earth.

निश्चलांग, *m.* (*f.* ī *or* ā) a kind of crane (*Ardea nivea*): a mountain: rock.

निश्चा, *more prop.* निश्चय, *q.v.*

निश्चित, 1, *m.* (*f.* ā) ascertained, determined, certain, concluded: 2, *m.* certainty, conclusion.

निश्छिद्र, *m.* (*f.* ā) *more prop.* निश्छिद्र, *q.v.*

निश्चिन्त, *m.* (*f.* ā) inconsiderate, thoughtless, heedless, void of reflection, unconcerned, careless, at leisure, free from anxiety or care. — *honā*, to be free from care or worry, be at leisure, to have finished.

निश्चिन्ती = निश्चिन्तताई = निश्चिन्ताई, *q.v.*

निश्चुक्कण, *m.* a kind of tooth-powder prepared from sulphate of iron, etc. It destroys the tartar, but blackens the teeth. [of effort, powerless, helpless.

निश्चेष्ट, *m.* (*f.* ā) deprived of motion, incapable

निश्चै, *more prop.* निश्चय, *q.v.*

निश्छिद्र, *m.* (*f.* ā) without holes, rents, flaws, or defects; without vent. [piration.

निश्श्वास *m.* expired breath; a breathing out, ex-

निष, an inseparable prefix = निर, *q. v.*

निषंग, *m.* a quiver: union, meeting, association.

निषंगी, *m.* (*f.* inī) an archer, bowman: *lit.* armed with a quiver.

निषध, *m. pr. n.* (1) of a country in the south-east division of India (2) of the king of that country (3) of the inhabitants of that country (4) of a mountain or mountainous range which forms one of the chief ranges of the world, and is said to lie immediately south of Ilāvrat and north of the Himālaya range.

निषधक, *m.* a kind of potherb (*Marsilea dentata*).

निषप्रयोजन, *more com.* निष्प्रयोजन, *q.v.*

निषाद, *m.* the first of the seven musical notes: the designation of certain aboriginal tribes of India described as fishermen, hunters and robbers; and who, as being the offspring of a Brāhman by a Shoodra woman, are held to be outcastes.

निषिद्ध, forbidden, prohibited, denied.

निषिद्धता, *f.* (*m.* °त्व) prohibitedness.

निषेक, *m.* the ceremony performed on the occasion of conception, sprinkling, distilling, impregnation.

निषेध, *m.* a keeping off, forbiddance, prohibition, negation, prevention, restriction. [ing.

निषेधकारी, *m.* (*f.* iṇī) prohibitive, forbidding, deny-

निषेधता, *f.*
निषेधत्व, *m.* } = निषेध, *q. v.*

निषेधित, *m.* (*f.* ā) forbidden, prohibited, denied.

निष्कण्टक, *m.* (*f.* ikā) free from thorns, *i. e.* from trouble, danger, or harm.

निष्कपठ, *m.* a certain plant (*Capparis trifoliata*).

निष्कपट, without fraud or deceit, artless, honest,

निष्कर्ष, *m.* ascertainment, certainty. [open, sincere

निष्कलंक, spotless, immaculate, unstained, pure.

निष्कलंकित, *m.* (*f.* ā) } = **निष्कलंक**, *q. v.*
निष्कलंकी, *m.* (*f.* inī) }

निष्काम, 1, *m.* (*f.* ā) free from wish or desire, disinterested : 2, unwillingly.

निष्कारण, causeless, groundless.

निष्कास, *m.* (= **निकास**) issue. [pletely.

निष्केवल, only, exclusively, merely, solely, com-

निष्क्रमण, *m.* a going out or forth ; the taking a child out of the house for the first time. This is done in the fourth month, is considered an essential ceremony, and is accompanied by sacrifice.

निष्खोट, unblemished, without defect, blameless, faultless, sound.

निष्ठा, *f.* basis, certain knowledge, confirmation, belief, faith, accomplishment, end, catastrophe, death.

निष्ठान, *m.* sauce, condiment.

निष्ठावत, *m.* (*f.* vatī) a person possessed of complete knowledge, one who fulfils all religious duties.

निष्ठावन्त } *m.* (*f.* vatī) = **निष्ठावत**, *q. v.*
निष्ठावान }

निष्ठुर, *m.* (*f.* ā) harsh, contumelious, coarse, hard, solid. [ness, reviling, abuse, severity.

निष्ठुरता, *f.* (*m.* °**त्व**) harshness of speech, coarse-

निष्ठुरा, *f.* (*m.* **निष्ठुर**) a harsh female.

निष्पक्ष, *m.* (*f.* ā *or* iṇī) = **निर्पक्ष**, *q. v.*

निष्पत्ति, *f.* the condition of being brought about, completion, consummation, termination.

निष्पन्द, *m.* (*f.* ā) motionless.

निष्पन्न, *m.* (*f.* ā) done, finished, completed.

निष्पराक्रम, destitute of power, weak.

निष्पादन, *m.* a doing, effecting, accomplishing, concluding, causing, engendering, producing.

निष्पादित, *m.* (*f.* ā) done, effected, produced.

निष्पाप, *m.* (*f.* ā *or* ī) free from sin, guiltless, innocent.

निष्पापी, *m.* (*f.* inī) = **निष्पाप**, *q. v.*

निष्पाव, *m.* a species of pulse (*Dolichos sinensis*, Lin.); pulse in general.

निष्पुत्र, *m.* (*f.* ā) a sonless person : *lit.* sonless.

निष्पुरुष, *m.* an impotent man, a eunuch ; a coward : *lit.* without male issue, devoid of men, devoid of manliness. [ing.

निष्पेष, *m.* a striking, the sound produced by strik-

निष्प्रभ, *m.* (*f.* ā) deprived of light or radiance, gloomy, obscure, dark.

निष्प्रभावता, *f.* (*m.* °**त्व**) powerlessness. [authority.

निष्प्रमाण, unproven, unauthorized, wanting in

निष्प्रमाणिक, *m.* (*f.* ā *or* ī) wanting in authority.

निष्प्रयोजन, not induced by motives, causeless, groundless ; absolute.

निष्पृह = **निस्पृह**, *q. v.*

निष्फल, *m.* (*f.* ā) without fruit, unproductive, unprofitable, inefficacious, impotent, seedless.

निष्फलता, *f.* (*m.* °**त्व**) fruitlessness, barrenness, unproductiveness, inefficacy, uselessness.

निष्फला, *f.* (*m.* **निष्फल**) a woman past child-bearing, female in whom menstruation has ceased.

निष्फली = **निष्फला**, *q. v.*

निस, 1, = **निर**, *q. v.* : 2, *more prop.* **निश**, 2, *q. v.*

निसंक, *more prop.* **निशंक**, *q. v.* [with ease.

निसंकट, *m.* (*f.* ā) without difficulty or trouble,

निसंकोच, *adj.* without contracting, without shame

निसंदेह, *more com.* **निस्सन्देह**, *q. v.* [or reserve.

निसचर ; for words beginning thus, see under the form **निश्चर**.

निसन्धाई, *f.* compactness, solidity.

निसन्धि, compact, solid, tight, not leaky.

निसन्धे (*corruption*) = **निस्सन्देह**, *q. v.*

निसपति, *m.* lord of night, *i.e.* the moon.

निसबत, *f.* relation, affinity, reference, attribute ; relationship, alliance.— *k.* to refer, to attribute.

निसबासर, *more prop.* **निशिबासर**, *q. v.* [issue.

निसरना, *a. int.* to move out, come out, go forth,

निसा ; for words beginning thus, see under the

निसांसा ; see (1) **निसास** (2) **निश्श्वास**. [form **निशा**.

निसागम (*Rām.*) = **रात आये**. [expel, exclude.

निसारना, *t.* to cause to issue forth, to turn out,

निसास, *m.* respiration, breath. [**निशि**.

निसि, for words beginning thus, see under the form

निसिन्धु } *m.* the shrub *Vitex negundo.*
निसिन्धा }

निसेनि } (*Rām.*) = **निःश्रेणी**, *q. v.*
निसेनी }

निसेस, *more prop.* **निशेश**, *q. v.*

निसैनी, *more prop.* **निःश्रेणी**, *q. v.*

निसोत (*Rām.*) = **निराला**, *q. v.*

निस्कपट = **निष्कपट**, *q. v.*

निस्तार, *m.* crossing, passing over, acquittal, release, salvation, final beatitude ; payment.

निस्तारक, *m.* (*f.* ikā) one who effects delivery or salvation, a rescuer, deliverer, preserver, saviour : lit. *adj.* releasing, delivering, saving.

निस्तारकर्त्ता } *m.* (*f.* trī) = **निस्तारक**, *q. v.*
निस्तारकर्तृ }

निस्तारना, *t.* to release, acquit, save, exempt from further transmigration, beatify. [in any deity.

निस्तारबीज, *m.* the cause of final liberation, faith

निस्तारा, *m.* definitive settlement, adjustment, decision, decree : blessing.

निस्तारिका, *f.* (*m.* **निस्तारक**) a female deliverer.

निस्तारिहौं (*poet.*) = **मैं निस्तारूंगा**. See **इहौं**.

निस्तुक, *more prop.* **निस्तुष**, *q. v.*

निस्तुष, *m.* (*f.* ā) freed from chaff or husk; *met.* purified, cleansed, simplified. [potent.

निस्तेज, obscure, dull, spiritless, powerless, im-

निस्तेजस = **निस्तेज**, *q. v.* [decision, decree.

निस्तोक, *m.* definitive settlement, adjustment,

निस्पन्द, 1. *m.* motion: 2, motionless, still, steady; immovable. [content, not envious, indifferent.

निस्पृह, *m.* (*f.* ā) exempt from desire or wish,

निस्पृहा, *f.* (*m.* **निस्पृह**) a contented female: a certain plant (*Gloriosa superba*).

निस्पृही, *m.* (*f.* in *or* inī) = **निस्पृह**, *q. v.*

निस्प्रोह, *more prop.* **निस्पृह**, *q. v.*

निस्सन्देह, 1, free from doubt, undoubted: 2, without hesitation, undoubtedly, certainly, freely.

निस्वास, *more prop.* **निश्श्वास**, *q. v.*

निह, an inseparable prefix = **निर**, *q. v.*

निहंग, *m.* (*f.* ī *or* ā) naked, free from care.

निहंगलाड़ला, *m.* (*f.* ī) a careless child or person.

निहचय / **निहचे** / **निहचै** / **निहचैं** } in old Hindee = **निश्चय**, *q. v.*

निहत्था, unarmed.

निहल, alluvial land recovered from water-courses.

निहलवाना, *more prop.* **नहलवाना**, *q. v.*

निहाई, *f.* an anvil.

निहाका, *f.* an iguana or the Gangetic alligator.

निहानी, 1, *f.* the menses: 2, *f.* concealment: 3, secretly, privately.

निहायत, 1, *f.* extremity, boundary; excess: 2, very much, extreme, excessive: 3, extremely, to the utmost.

निहार, *m.* cold, frost: fog, vapour. [spy, see.

निहारना, *t.* to look at, regard, watch, look after,

निहारनौं in Braj = **निहारना**, *q. v.* [*medinensis*).

निहारुआ, *m.* (*f.* °**रुई**) the guinea-worm (*Filaria*

निहाल, exalted, pleased, happy.

निहाली, *f.* an anvil.

निहुड़ना = **निहुरना**, *q. v.* [bow, lean, condescend.

निहुरना, *a. int.* to bend downwards, incline, stoop,

निहुराना, *t.* to cause to bend, *i. e.* to bend, bow, [crook.

निहूड़ना / **निहूरना** } = **निहुरना**, *q. v.*

निहूरा / **निहोर** } *more prop.* **निहोरा**, *q. v.*

निहोरा, *m.* favour, kindness, kind offices; obligation, connexion, necessity; a requesting humbly, begging, coaxing. *Maiṅ tumhārā baṛā — māntā huṅ* I acknowledge my great indebtedness to you.

नी, 1, *f.*; see **ना**, 3: 2, this, in the Bhojpurī dialect, is sometimes a suffixed emphatic particle: 3, this particle is not unfrequently found in the sense of **नि** (2), *q. v.*; *e. g.* **नीरस**: 4, as a termination, this particle is the distinguishing mark of the feminine of many substantives which designate living creatures; *e. g.* **पिशाचनी**.

नीओ, *more com.* **नेव**, *q. v.*

नीं, (= **नी**, 2) this, in the Bhojpurī dialect, is sometimes a suffixed emphatic particle.

नींद, **नींब**; for words beginning thus, see under the forms **नीन्द**, **निम्ब**, respectively.

नीक, *more prop.* **नीका**, *q. v.* [rightly, easily.

नीका, *m.* (*f.* ī) good, beautiful, elegant: *adv.* well,

नीकाश, *m.* (*f.* ā); used as the latter part of some compounds in the sense of like, resembling.

नीकू / **नीके** / **नीको** / **नीकौ** } archaic and poet. forms of **नीका**, *q. v.*

नीच. *m.* (*f.* ā) low, *i. e.* (1) dwarfish, short, small (2) vile, base, inferior, mean, vulgar (3) deep (down).

नीचऊंच, *f.* inequality, unevenness, the ups and

नीचकमाई, *f.* ill-gotten gain. [downs of life.

नीचग, *m.* (*f.* ā) *adj.* going downwards, moving downwards; *hence*, low, base, vile.

नीचगा, *f.* (*m.* **नीचग**) a river.

नीचगामी (= **नीचग**) *m.* (*f.* inī) water.

नीचग्रह, *m.* (in Astrol.) the house or station of the heavens in which a planet stands at its lowest point.

नीचता, *f.* / **नीचत्व**, *m.* } = **नीचपन**, *q. v.*

नीचनी, *f.* a feminine form of **नीच**, *q. v.*

नीचपन, *m.* lowness, humbleness, inferiority, vileness, baseness, meanness, abjectness. [of low caste.

नीचसोनार, *m.* (*f.* in *or* nī) a jeweller or goldsmith

नीचन्हावो, *m.* an inferior sort of barber.

नीचा, 1, *f.*; see **नीच**: 2, *m.* (*f.* ī) = **नीच**, *q. v.*: 3, *adv.* below, down, low. *Nīche suroṅse bolnā*, to sing with a low voice, hum a tune (jocosè autem, crepitus ventris hācce voce subintelligitur). *Kalāṅwatnī, tere gānese dikk huṅ*; *bahut nīche suroṅse boltī hai*, Songstress, I am tired of your lays, you sing too low (the latter clause having a double meaning).

नीचाई, *f.* = **नीचपन**, *q. v.*

नीचाऊंचा, *m.* (*f.* **नीचीऊंची**) up and down, uneven, not level or equal, abrupt.

नीचान, *m.* low lands, a valley.

नीचू in Braj = **नीचे**, *q. v.*

नीचे, (sc. **में**) below, down, beneath, under: also a *postp.* taking the gen. *m.* infl. *Nīche k.* to abase. — *jānā*, to descend. submit, succumb, subside. — *girānā*, to throw down, knock down.

नीचेऊपर, *adv.* upside-down, topsy-turvy.

नीट, straight, upright.

नीठ; see (1) **नीट** (2) **निष्ठा**. [of a chariot.

नीड़, *m.* a bird's-nest; a den; the seat or inner room

नीड़ज, *m.* (*f.* ā) a bird: *lit.* nest-born.

नीडल, water.

नीड़े = **नेरे**, *q. v.*

नीडोद्भव, *m.* (*f.* ā) = **नीड़ज**, *q.v.*

नीत, *more prop.* **नीति**, *q.v.*

नीतक, appertaining to **नीत**, *q.v.*

नीति, *f.* guidance, moral behaviour, prudent behaviour, the correct thing, good policy, prudence, prudent counsel, policy, polity, political science (treating specially of the administration of government including the practice of morality in private life, both by a sovereign and by his subjects).

नीतिकथा, *f.* any treatise on polity or good government, a discourse on ethics, moral tale.

नीतिज्ञ, *m.* (*f.* ā) a politician, statesman, moralist: *lit.* acquainted with polity or with morals.

नीतिमत / **नीतिमन्त** } *m.* (*f.* matī) = **नीतिमान**, *q.v.*

नीतिमान, *m.* (*f.* matī) a moral person, one who knows the rules of prudent behaviour.

नीतियुक्ति, *f.* = **नीतिका उपाय**, *qq.v.*

नीतिविद्या, *f.* the science of ethics and of politics.

नीतिशास्त्र, *m.* any treatise on the science of ethics or of politics: the science of ethics and of politics.

नीती, *more prop.* **नीति**, *q.v.*

नीद, *more com.* **नीन्द**, *q.v.*

नीदना, *a. int.* (*more com.* **नीन्दना**) to sleep.

नीदनि = **मीदने**. See **नि**, 2 (4).

नीनवः, *m. pr. n.* the city of Nineveh.

नीन्द, *f.* (*prop.* **निद्रा**) sleep. —*uchāṭ honā*, to have one's rest broken, be unable to sleep.

नीन्दना, *a. int.* to sleep: *t.* to censure, blame: to deny.

नीन्दभर, *adj.* having had abundance of sleep. —*sonā*, to sleep soundly; to be at ease.

नीन्दा in Chand = **नीन्द**, *q. v.*

नीन्दी, *m.* (*f.* inī) drowsy, sleepy, sleeping.

नीन्दु = **नीन्दी**, *q.v.*

नीप, *m.* the name of certain trees (1) *Nauclea orientalis*, Carey; or *N. Kadamba*, Wilson (2) *Ixora bandhuca* (3) *Nil Asoka*.

नीपूर, *m.* the penis, membrum virile.

नीबू, *more prop.* **नींम्बू**, *q.v.*

नीवेंदन, *more prop.* **निवेंदन**, *q.v.*

नीम, *more prop.* **निम्ब**, *q. v.*

नीमन, strong; well-finished; solid; good.

नीमषार = **नैंमिष**, *q.v.*

नीमानन्द, *m. pr.n.* a certain Hindoo saint, founder of the Neemāvat sect.

नीमावत, *f. pr. n.* the system held by the followers [of the above-named saint.

नीमिषार = **नैंमिष**, *q.v.*

नीम्ब, *more prop.* **निम्ब**, *q.v.*

नीम्बू, *more prop.* **निम्बू**, *q. v.*

नीयत, *f.* wish, intention, design, purpose, aim.

नीर, *m.* water; sap, juice, liquor.

नीरज, *m.* (*f.* ā) any aquatic creature, otter; any kind of lotus; a sort of costus (*Costus speciosus*): *lit.* water-producer, water-born.

नीरजस, *f.* a female who has ceased to menstruate: *lit.* free from dust, pollen, menses, or passion.

नीरजस्क = **नीरजस**, *q.v.*

नीरथ, a contraction of **निरर्थ**, *q.v.*

नीरद, *m.* a cloud (*lit.* the water-giver).

नीरधर, *m.* a cloud (*lit.* the water-holder).

नीरन्ध्र, faultless.

नीरस = **निरस**, *q.v.*

नीरसता, *f.* / **नीरसत्व**, *m.* } = **निरस**, 1, *q.v.*

नीरा, *more prop.* **नीर**, *q.v.*

नीराजन, *m.* lustration of arms (a certain military and religious ceremony held on the nineteenth day of the month Ashwini, and by kings and generals before taking the field; it is still observed in some Hindoo states under the name of *Dasahara*).

नीराजना, *f.* = **नीराजन**, *q.v.*

नीरे = **नेरे**, *q.v.*

नीरेफ, (in Gram.) without *reph*. See **रेफ**.

नीरोग, 1, *m.* freedom from disease or sickness, healthiness, soundness: 2, *m.* (*f.* ā) free from sickness or disease, healthy, sound.

नीरोगता, *f.* / **नीरोगत्व**, *m.* } = **नीरोग**, 1, *q.v.*

नीरोगा, *f.* (*m.* **नीरोग**, 2) a healthy female.

नीरोगी, *m.* (*f.* iṇī) = **नीरोग**, 2, *q.v.*

नीरोग्यता, *f.* / **नीरोग्यत्व**, *m.* } = **नीरोग**, 1, *q.v.*

नील, 1, *m.* (*f.* ā *or* ī) blue, dark blue, black: 2, *m.* the color blue; indigo (1) the plant *Indigofera tinctoria* (2) the dye, blue; blue vitriol; the sapphire; the blue *mainā*-bird: *pr. n.* (1) of one of the divine treasures of Kuver (see **निधि**) (2) of one of the principal ranges of mountains (dividing the world into nine portions) which lies immediately north of Ilāvrat or the central division (3) of the blue mountain (4) of the river Nile. —*kā māṭh bigaṛnā* (*lit.* the spoiling of a vat of indigo) is a saying employed (1) to express the persecutions of fortune (2) on hearing something very wonderful or incredible. Its application in this latter sense is said to have originated in a notion entertained by dyers, that when their dye has, by any accident, been spoiled, it may be restored by telling some miraculous story.

नीलक, 1, stained or dyed blue: 2, *m.* (in Algeb.) the third unknown quantity in an equation, with its products, etc.

नीलकण्ठ, *m.* (*lit. m.* [*f.* ī] blue-necked) the name of several birds (1) the blue jay (*Coracias Bengalensis*) (2) a peacock (3) a wagtail (4) a gallinule (5) a sparrow: a certain plant (*Hyperanthera morunga*): *pr. n.* (1) of a certain celebrated commentator on the Mahābhārat (2) of Shiv or Mahādev. This epithet is applied to Shiv in allusion to the fact that his throat was stained blue by his swallowing the poison produced by overchurning the ocean with the mountain Mandar by the Surs and Asurs, which he did to procure the *Amrit*.

नीलकण्ठाक्ष, *m.* the *elæocarpus*-seed.

नीलकमल, *m.* the blue lotus.

नीलकान्त, *m.* the blue-coloured gem. *i. e.* the sap- [phire.

नीलकार, *m.* (*f.* ī) an indigo-maker.
नीलकुरुण्टक, *m.* blue Barleria.
नीलकोठी, *f.* an indigo-factory.
नीलक्रौंच, *m.* (*f.* ī) a sort of curlew or heron.
नीलगन्दन, a bruise.
नीलगर, *m.* (*f.* nī) an indigo-maker.
नीलगाव, *f.* the white-footed antelope of Pennant and *Antelope picta* of Pallas.
नीलगुण, *m.* (*f.* ā) of a dark blue colour, cerulean.
नीलगूदाम, an indigo-factory.
नीलचर, *m. pr. n.* the blue mountain near Balasore.
नीलज, *m.* blue steel.
नीलजा, *f. pr. n.* the river Vitasta.
नीलझिंझटी, *f.* the flowering plant *Barleria cristata.*
नीलता, *f.* (*m.* °त्व) dark-blue colour.
नीलपद्म, *m.* the blue lotus (*Nymphaea cerulea*).
नीलपाचन, *m.* the steeping or maceration of indigo.
नीलपाचनभाण्ड, *m.* an indigo-vat.
नीलपिच्छ, *m.* (*f.* ā) a falcon.
नीलपुष्पिका, *f.* the indigo-plant (*Indigofera tinctoria*).
नीलपृष्ठ, *m.* the *roki*-fish (*Cyprinus denticulatus*).
नीलबड़ी, *f.* a lump of indigo.
नीलम, a contraction of नीलमणि, *q. v.*
नीलमणि, *m.* the blue-coloured gem, *i. e.* the sapphire.
नीलमन; see नीलमणि and नीलिमन.
नीलमृत्तिका, *f.* iron pyrites ; black mould.
नीलम्बर, *m.* black or dark blue raiment.
नीललोह, *m.* blue steel.
नीललोहित, 1, *m.* a mixture of red and blue, purple: 2, *m.* (*f.* ā) of a purple colour.
नीलवर्ण, *m.* (*f.* ā) of a blue colour.
नीलवारा, *more prop.* नीलवाला, *q. v.*
नीलवाला, *m.* (*f.* ī) a maker or a vendor of indigo ; a dyer.
नीला, 1, *f.* see नील : 2, *m.* (*f.* ī) = नील, 1, *q. v.* : 3, *f.* a blue fly.
नीलाई, *f.* blueness, dark blue colour.
नीलांग, *m.* (*f.* ī or ā) the Indian crane; the blue jay.
नीलांजन, *m.* blue vitriol.
नीलातोता = नीलाथोथा, *q. v.*
नीलाथोथा, *m.* blue vitriol, blue-stone, sulphate of copper.
नीलापीला, black and blue. — *k.* to render (the eyes) blue and yellow, *i. e.* to be greatly enraged.
नीलाकत्तर, *m.* sapphire.
नीलाब, *m. pr. n.* the river Attock or Indus.
नीलाम, *m.* an auction, public sale.
नीलामची, *m.* an auctioneer.
नीलामदार, *m.* one who holds an estate purchased at a public sale.
नीलामी, to be sold by auction, saleable by auction, auctionable.
नीलाम्बर, 1, = नीलम्बर, *q. v.* : 2, *m.* (*f.* ā) a person dressed in dark blue clothing.
नीलाश्मन, *m.* a blue stone, sapphire.
नीलाहट, *f.* blueness.
नीलिका, *f.* a certain plant (*Nyctanthus arbor tristis*) with blue flowers ; the indigo-plant (*Indigofera tinctoria*) : a malady attended with blue marks on the body.
नीलिनी, *f.* the indigo-plant (*Indigofera tinctoria*).
नीलिमन, *m.* a blackness.
नीली, *f.* the indigo-plant (*Indigofera tinctoria*).
नीलोपल, *m.* blue-stone (*Lapis lazuli*).
नीलोफल, *m.* the lotus.
नीव, *more prop.* नेव, 2, *q. v.*
नीवा, *m.* stillness, calmness, a calm.
नीवार, *m.* rice growing wild.
नीवारा, *f. pr. n.* a certain river.
नीवि, नीवी } *f.* cloth worn around a woman's waist.
नीवेदन, *more prop.* निवेदन, *q. v.*
नीसरना = निसरना, *q. v.*
नीसरनौं in Braj = निसरना, *q. v.*
नीसान, a kettle-drum.
नीस्ती, *f.* non-existence, nullity, annihilation.
नीहार, *m.* frost, hoar-frost ; heavy dew.
नीहारकर, *m.* the moon (*lit.* the dew-maker).
नुक़सान, *m.* loss, defect, deficiency, detriment, injury, prejudice, mischief.
नुकीला, pointed, sharp at the top.
नुचना, *more prop.* नोचना, *q. v.*
नुचवाना, *t.* (causat. of नोचना) to cause to pinch, cause to pluck out, etc.
नुजूम, *m.* (pl. of नजूम) stars, planets.
नुजूमी, 1, *m.* (*f.* in *or* inī) an astrologer, astronomer, a fortune-teller : 2, *f.* the science or the art of astrology or of astronomy.
नुत, *m.* (*f.* ā) commended, applauded, eulogized.
नुपूर, *more com.* नूपुर, *q. v.*
नुह = (1) नख (2) नूह, *qq. v.*
नुहट्टा, *m.* a scratch with the talon.
नूं, a dialectic enclitic imparting to its sentence a certain accent of conviction or energy.
नूतन, *m.* (*f.* ā) new, fresh, recent, young, strange, — *k.* to renew.
नूतनता, *f.* (*m.* °त्व) newness, novelty.
नूत्न, *m.* (*f.* ā) = नूतन, *q. v.*
नूद, *m.* the mulberry-tree (*Morus Indica*).
नूधा, *m.* a species of tobacco.
नून, *m.* salt.
नूनिया = नोनिया, *q. v.*
नूनी, *m.* penis puerilis.
नूपुर, *m.* a kind of ornament for the ankles and toes. It consists of a hollowed ring, about a finger and a half in breadth, containing bits of copper or iron of the size of a vetch, which cause it to sound.
नूपुरवान, *m.* (*f.* vatī) a person adorned with the above-mentioned ornament.

नूरी, *f.* a certain bird (*Psittacus*) of the parrot kind, commonly called *lūri*.

नूह, *m. pr. n.* the patriarch Noah.

नृ, *m.* a man: (pl.) mankind.

नृग, *m. pr. n.* (1) of a certain ancient king (2) of a grandson of Oghavat (3) of a son of Uśīnar by Nṛigā (4) of a son of Manu (5) of the father of Sumati.

नृगा, *f. pr. n.* the wife of Uśīnar and mother of Nṛig.

नृति, *f.* = **नृत्य**, 1, *q.v.*

नृतू, *m.* a dancer, actor, mimic.

नृत्य, 1, *m.* dancing, the science or the practice of dancing, a jumping, skipping, motion: 2, *m.* (*f.* ā) a dancer, actor.

नृत्यक, *m.* (*f.* ikā or ī) a dancer, actor, mimic, juggler.

नृत्यकारी, *m.* (*f.* iṇī) = **नृत्यक**, *q.v.*

नृत्यकी, *f.* (*m.* **नृत्यक**) a dancing-girl, actress.

नृत्या, *f.* (*m.* **नृत्य**) } = **नृत्यकी**, *q.v.*
नृत्यिका, *f.* (*m.* **नृत्यक**) }

नृदेव, *m.* (*f.* ī) a sovereign, monarch, king.

नृधर्म्म, *m.* a manly property or duty.

नृप, *m.* a prince, king, sovereign. In the ingenious system of reckoning by symbols adopted by the Hindoos in their poetry, this word is a symbol for 16.

नृपतनय, *m.* (*f.* ā) the offspring of a prince or sovereign.

नृपता, *f.* (*m.* °**त्व**) kingship, sovereignty.

नृपति, *m.* a prince, king, sovereign.

नृपद्रुम, *m.* a certain tree (*Cassia fistula*).

नृपनन्दन, *m.* (*f.* ā) = **नृपतनय**, *q.v.*

नृपनीति, *f.* regal polity, rules of conduct and government for a king.

नृपप्रिय, *m.* a certain thorny species of bamboo (*Bambusa spinosa*).

नृपबाल, *m.* (*f.* ā) the child of a sovereign.

नृपराज, *m.* a prince, king, sovereign.

नृपवाला, *m.* (*f.* ī) appertaining to a sovereign.

नृपसुत, *m.* (*f.* ā) = **नृपतनय**, *q.v.*

नृपसों in Braj = **नृपसे**. See **सों**.

नृपांश, *m.* the royal portion or revenue (*e. g.* of grain, a sixth, eighth, or twelfth; of fruits, etc., a sixth; of merchandise, a fiftieth).

नृपात्मज, *m.* (*f.* ā) = **नृपतनय**, *q.v.*

नृपात्वा, a corruption of **नृपत्व**, *q.v.*

नृपाभीर, *m.* music played at royal meals.

नृपामय, *m.* consumption (the disease).

नृपाल, *m.* (*f.* ī) a sovereign, monarch; *lit.* a guardian or protector of men.

नृपावर्त्त, *m.* a kind of gem.

नृपासन, *m.* a sovereign's throne.

नृपोचित, suited to a sovereign, princely, kingly.

नृवराह, *m. pr. n.* (see **अवतार**) an epithet of the third incarnation of Vishṇu; *lit.* the man-boar.

नृसिंह = **नरसिंह**, *q.v.*

ने, (Sk. **ना**) the sign of the agent case in the sing. and pl. in Hindee.

नेई, *f.*, *more com.* **नेव**, *q.v.*

नेउता, *more prop.* **नेवता**, *q.v*

नेउर (*Rām.*) = **नेवल**, 2, *q.v.*

नेऊन, *m.* butter.

नें, 1, (*prop.* **ने**) by, through: 2, an old sign of the dative case.

नेंमा, *more prop.* **नियम**, *q.v.*

नेक, 1, a contraction of **अनेक**, *q.v.*: 2, little, a little: 3, good, pious; lucky.

नेकनाम, 1, *m.* good name, celebrity,: 2, renowned, of good character.

नेकनामी, *f.* good name, good character, renown, celebrity, praise.

नेकबख़्ती, *f.* virtue; good fortune.

नेकसाअ़त, *f.* a fortunate moment, happy juncture, auspicious occasion.

नेका, *m.* (*f.* ī) = **नीका**, *q.v.*

नेकी, *f.* goodness, virtue, piety, probity, beauty.

नेकु in Braj = **नेक**, *q.v.*

नेकुन; see (1) **नेकु** (2) **नेकु न** (3) **नाखुन**.

नेकुसो in Braj = **थोड़ासा**, *q.v.*

नेको = **नीका**, *q.v.*

नेकोकर, *more com.* **नेकोकार**, *q.v.*

नेकोकार, *m.* (*f.* ī) *adj.* of good actions, beneficent.

नेकोकारी, *f.* 1, a benefactress; 2, good actions, virtuous living, beneficence.

नेख़्वा, *m.* a well-wisher.

नेख़्वेपना, *m.* good-will, benevolence.

नेग, *f.* presents made, at marriages and on other festive occasions, to relatives and particular servants (*e. g.* the *purohit*), and considered by them as perquisites to which they are entitled.

नेगी, *m.* a village servant; any public servant who claims a fee or present on certain occasions.

नेगीजोगी, those to whom it is customary to give the *neg*, viz. tenants and dependents.

नेछावर = **नेवछावर**, *q.v.*

नेज़ा, *m.* a spear, lance, javelin, dart, pike: a piece of reed from which pens are made.

नेटा, *m.* mucus of the nose.

नेड़ना, *t.* to take care for, look after.

नेड़े, in the shelter of, beside, near.

नेता, *m.* (*f.* **नेत्री**) a leader, conductor, guide; an owner, master.

नेति (*Rām.*) = (1) **न** + **इति** = **नहीं ऐसा** (2) **नित्य**, *qq.v.*

नेती, *f.* any cord used for whirling the churning-staff.

नेतृ, *m.* (*f.* trī) = **नेता**, *q.v.*

नेत्र, *m.* the eye: the string of a churning-rope: the root of a tree. In the ingenious system of reckoning by symbols adopted by Hindoos in their poetry, this word is a symbol for 2.

नेत्रजल, *m.* tears, a tear.

नेत्रपिण्ड, *m.* the ball of the eye.

नेत्ररंजन, *m.* collyrium.

नेत्ररोग, *m.* any disease of the eye.

नेत्ररोगी, *m.* (*f.* iṇī) a person afflicted with a disease of the eyes.

नेत्रलोस, *m.* a prisoner.

नेत्रवान, *m.* (*f.* vatī) possessing eyes, clear-sighted.

नेत्रहीन, *m.* (*f.* ā) eyeless.

नेत्राम्बु, *m.* a tear. [prietress.

नेत्री, *f.* (*m.* नेता and नेतृ) a female guide; a pro-

नेत्रोत्सव, *m.* (*f.* ā) any pleasing or beautiful object.

नेत्रौषध, *m.* green sulphate of iron considered as a collyrium; collyrium in general.

नेत्रौषधी, *f.* a kind of drug.

नेदिष्ट, *m.* a certain tree (*Alangium hexapetalum*).

नेपथ्य, *m.* ornament, attire; the attire of an actor; the tiring-room of a stage, the part behind the scenes.

नेपाल, *m. pr. n.* a country in the north of India.

नेपालिका, *f.* arsenic.

नेपाली, *m.* (*f.* in *or* inī) a native of Nepāl.

नेपुर, *m. f.* ? = नूपुर, *q.v.*

नेम, a contraction of नियम, *q.v.*

नेमछावर = नेवछावर, *q.v.*

नेमधर्म्म, *m.* abstinence, good conduct.

नेमि, *f.* a circumference, edge; the frame-work for the rope of a well.

नेमिचक्र, *m. pr. n.* a certain prince descended from Pareekshit. On the occasion of the inundation of Hastināpur, he is said to have removed the capital of India from that place to Kausāmbi.

नेमी, 1, *m.* (*f.* inī) *more prop.* नियमी, *q.v.*: 2, *f.* a species of tree (*Dalbergia Oujeinensis*).

नेमीचक्र = नेमिचक्र, *q.v.*

नेर in Chand = नगर, *q.v.*

नेरूआ, *m.* straw.

नेरे, *postp.* (takes gen. *m.* infl.) near, close by, beside.

नेरो, a poetical form of नेरे, *q.v.*

नेरौ in Braj = नेरे, *q.v.*

नेव, 1, (*Rām.*) = (1) नेग (2) नेह, *qq.v.*: 2, *f.* foundation. — *ḍālnā*, *f.* to lay a foundation.

नेवँ; see नेऊन.

नेवंजी, *f.* a certain flower.

नेवछावर, (*i. e.* नियम + क्षय + वर) *f.* a propitiatory offering, sacrifice, victim.

नेवत (*contraction*) = नेवता, *q.v.*

नेवतना = नेवताना, *q.v.*

नेवतहरी, *m.* (*f.* iṇī) a person who has received an invitation to a feast, a formally invited guest.

नेवतहारी, *m.* (*f.* iṇī) = नेवतहरी, *q.v.*

नेवता, *m.* an invitation; the presents sent to the person invited, and accompanying the invitation; the present made by a guest.— *k.* to invite. — *denā*, to give an invitation.

नेवताना, *t.* to invite (*esp.* to an entertainment).

नेवतेवाला, *m.* (*f.* ī) one who receives an invitation, a guest.

नेवना, *a. int.* to stoop, bow, bend.

नेवर, *f.* a kind of sore in a horse's foot.

नेवल, 1, *more prop.* नेवर, *q.v.*: 2, *m.* (*f.* ī) a weasel, ferret, mungoose, ichneumon (*Viverra mungo* or *V. ichneumon*).

नेवला, *more prop.* नेवल, 2, *q.v.*

नेवाजू, *m.* a nourisher, cherisher, protector.

नेवाना, *t.* to cause to bend, *i. e.* to bow down, bend.

नेवार, *f.* = (1) निवार (2) नेवर, *qq.v.*

नेवारना, *t.* to shut out, exclude.

नेवारी, 1, *m.* (*f.* iṇī) a certain high caste of Brāhmans; 2, *f.* a certain tree.

नेस्त, *f.* (*lit.* it is not) nought. — *k.* to abolish, ruin, destroy, annihilate.

नेस्ती, *f.* non-existence, nullity, annihilation.

नेह, a dialectic form of स्नेह, *q.v.* See स, 9.

नेहक, (prop. स्नेहक,) appertaining to love or affection.

नेहा = नेह, *q.v.*

नेहाइत / नेहायत } *more prop.* निहायत, *q.v.*

नेही, *m.* (*f.* inī) *more prop.* स्नेही, *q.v.*

नेहू, (*poet.*) = नेह = स्नेह, *q.v.*

नैऋत, *more prop.* नैर्ऋत, *q.v.*

नैं, no, nay, not.

नैक, (= नेक) many, various: little, a little.

नैकट्य, *m.* nearness, proximity.

नैकधा, *adv.* in many parts; to many directions.

नैकभेद, various, multiform, manifold.

नैकरूप, *m.* (*f.* ā) multiform.

नैगम, *m.* (*lit.* appertaining to the Veds) an Upanishad: a means: a trader.

नैचै, a dialectic form of निश्चय, *q.v.*

नैज, *more prop.* निज, *q.v.*

नैजाना, *a. int.* to bow down, stoop.

नैन, 1, a corruption of नयन, *q.v.*: 2, = नैना, 2, *q.v.*

नैनन a Braj pl. of नैन. See न, 6 (1).

नैननि in Braj = (1) नैनन (2) नैनने.

नैनसुख, *m.* a species of flower: a kind of cloth: an epithet of a blind person.

नैना, 1, (corruption) = नयना, *q.v.*: 2, *m.* a rope fastened around the neck or foot of a bullock, etc., a tether.

नैनान, (a contraction of the Sk. pl. नयनानि) eyes.

नैनोत्सव, *more prop.* नयनोत्सव, *q.v.*

नैनोपान्त, *more prop.* नयनोपान्त, *q.v.*

नैनौषध, *more prop.* नयनौषध, *q.v.*

नैपाल, *m.* (*f.* ī) appertaining to Nepāl, produced there or brought thence.

नैपालिक, *m.* (*f.* ā *or* ī) = नैपाल, *q.v.*

नैपाली, *f.* double jasmine; red arsenic; sephalica (*Nycanthes tristis*).

नैपुण = नैपुण्य, *q.v.*

नैपुण्य, *m.* cleverness, dexterity, skill, artfulness, experience, exactness, strictness, completion.

नैबेद, *more prop.* नैवेद्य, *q. v.*

नैमिष, *m. pr. n.* a certain forest celebrated as the residence of the Rishis and where Sauti recited to them the Mahābhārat.

नैमिषारण्य = नैमिष, *q. v.* [mentioned forest.

नैमिषीय, *m.* (*f.* ā) appertaining to the above-

नैमिषेय, *m.* (*f.* ī) a person residing in the Naimish forest.

नैयन, a corruption of नयन, *q. v.*

नैयमिक, *m.* (*f.* ā *or* ī) appertaining to a religious precept, regular, enjoined.
नैया, *m.* a boatman, ferryman.
नैयायिक, *m.* (*f.* ā *or* ī) appertaining to the Nyāya system of philosophy; *hence*, a logician, sophist, arguer.
नैर in Chand = **नगर**, *q.v.*
नैरंग, *m.* (or *f.* ī) deceit, trick, pretence, evasion, incantation, magic, sorcery : a miracle.
नैराश = **नैराश्य**, *q.v.* [appointment.
नैराश्य, hopelessness, despair, despondency, dis-
नैरास्य, *more prop.* **नैराश्य**, *q.v.*
नैरित, a corruption of **नैर्ऋत**, *q.v.*
नैरुक्त, *m.* (*f.* ā) one who is conversant with etymological interpretation : *adj.* belonging to the glossary of the Veds ; obsolete, uncommon.
नैर्ऋत, *m.* (*f* ī) south-western : appertaining to the Rakshases : a son of Nirriti. *i.e.* a demon, goblin : *pr. n.* the ruler of the south-west quarter.
नैर्ऋती, *f. pr. n.* (1) of the south-west quarter (2)
नैर्गुण्य = **नैर्गुण्य**, 1, *q.v.* [of Durgā.
नैर्गुण्य, 1, *m.* the absence of qualities : lack of good qualities : 2, adj. *m.* (*f.* ā) not having any relation to qualities.
नैर्मल्य, *m.* cleanness, purity. [oblation.
नैवेद्य, *m.* food consecrated to a deity, an offering,
नैषध, (see **निषध**) *lit.* appertaining to Nishadh ; hence, *m. pr. n.* (1) of the people of that country (2) of Nala, their prince (3) of the story of Nala.
नैषाद = **नैषध**, 1, *q.v.*
नैषादि, *m.* a prince of the Nishadas.
नैहर, *f.* a wife's mother's family, wife's family, her own house (*i. e.* her relations).
नो, 1, = **में**, *q.v.* : 2, *more prop.* **नौ**, *q.v.*
नोइ } **नोइनि** } (*Rām.*) = **नवी**, *q.v.*
नोंचा, *more prop.* **नोञ्चा**, *q.v.*
नोंचे, *more prop.* **नोञ्चे**, *q.v.*
नोक, *f.* a beak, bill ; an angle, end, point, point
नोकझोंक, *f.* a pulling and hauling. [of a weapon.
नोकदार, pointed.
नोकसान, a corruption of **नुकसान**, *q.v.*
नोकीला, *m.* (*f.* ī) sharp-pointed.
नोच, *m.* a grip, pinch, scratch.
नोचना, *t.* to grip, pinch, scratch.
नोचानाची, *f.* a pinching and scratching each other.
नोछावर = **नेवछावर**, *q.v.*
नोट, *m.* (Engl.) a bank-note, cheque, draft.
नोतना = **नेवतना**, *q. v.*
नोता, *more prop.* **नेवता**, *q.v.*
नोन, *m.* (prop. **लवण**) salt.
नोनखार, *m.* brine.
नोना, 1, *t.* to tie the feet of a cow when she is to be milked : 2, *m.* a kind of custard-apple (*Annona reticulata*): 3, *m.* (*f.* ī) salt, saline, brackish.
नोनापानी, *m.* salt water, sea-water, brine.
नोनामट्टी, *f.* earth abounding in salt.
नोनिया, *m.* purslain (*Portulaca oleracea*) : a maker or a vendor of salt ; a manufacturer of saltpetre.
नोनी, *f.* efflorescence of salt on a wall.
नोनेर, saline (said of soil).
नोन्चा, land abounding in saline matter.
नोन्चे, a kind of factitious salt.
नोरस, *more prop.* **नवरस**, *q.v.* [decanter or flask.
नोल, *f.* a bird's beak, the neck or spout of a
नौ, 1, this form is constantly interchanged with **नव** ; for all words, therefore, beginning with it, but not given below, see under this latter form : 2, this is the most common sign of the infinitive mode in the Braj dialect : 3, *f.* a ship, boat : 4, nine.
नौआ, 1, = **नवा** *q.v.* : 2, *m.* (*f.* **नौई**) a barber.
नौआं, *m.* (*f.* **नौई**) *more prop.* **नवां**, *q.v.*
नौं in Braj = **नौ**, 2 and 4, *qq.v.*
नौंतना = **नेवताना**, *q.v.*
नौकर, *m.* (*f.* ānī or nī) a servant.
नौकरचाकर, *m.* domestics. [woman.
नौकरनी, *f.* (*m.* **नौकर**) a female servant, waiting-
नौकरानी = **नौकरनी**, *q.v.* [attendance.
नौकरी, *f.* the situation of a servant, service,
नौका, *f.* a small sailing-vessel, boat : (in Chess) a rook. *Dhuchkī* —, a steamboat. [marine traffic.
नौकागमनागमन, *m.* thoroughfare of boats or ships,
नौखण्ड, (*i. e.* **पृथिवीके**) *m. pr. n.* (see **द्वीप** and **वर्ष**) the nine sections, divisions, or climes of the earth which constitute *Jambu-dwip*, the central portion of the world or the known world.
नौगरी, *f.* a kind of wrist-ornament worn by
नौचना = **नोचना**, *q.v.* [females.
नौचन्दी, appertaining to new moon.
नौची, *f.* a young girl kept by a bawd.
नौछावर = **नेवछावर**, *q.v.*
नौजवान 1, fresh and young, in the bloom of youth, in the prime of life : *hence*, 2, *m.* a lad, youth, young man. [life.
नौजवानी, *f.* bloom or flower of youth, prime of
नौजोबना } **नौजोबना** } *more prop.* **नवयौवना**, *q.v.*
नौढ़ना, *a. int.* to incline downwards, bend, stoop,
नौढ़ाना, *t.* to bow, bend, subdue. [be obedient.
नौतना = **नेवतना**, *q.v.*
नौता, 1, = (1) **नवता** (2) = **नेवता**, *qq.v.* : 2, *m.* a portico : 3, adj. *m.* (*f.* ī) bending downwards, stooping.
नौध, *m.* a young plant, a fresh shoot or branch
नौन, *m.* (prop. **लवण**) salt. [of a plant.
नौना, *a. int.* to bend downwards, stoop, bend, sub-
नौन्तना = **नेवताना**, *q.v.* [mit, become obedient.
नौबत, *f.* a kettle-drum or other instruments played at certain times as the gate of a great personage.

नौबती, *m.* (*f.* inī) one who plays a *naubat*.

नौबन्धन, *m.pr.n.* one of the peaks of the Himālaya range.

नौमतौम, dull, sing-song (as speech).

नौमहीन, *m.* the period of nine months.

नौमासा, *m.* a feast given in the ninth month of pregnancy.

नौमि (*Rām.*) = मैं स्तुति करता हूँ.

नौमी } नौमीं } *more prop.* नवमी, *q.v.*

नौरत्न = नवरत्न, *q.v.*

नौल, 1, नवल, *q.v.*: 2, *m.* freight, fare, hire.

नौला, *more prop.* नवला, *q.v.*

नौलासो, soft, tender, delicate.

नौलेवा, alluvial deposit by an inundation.

नौवत, *more prop.* नौबत, *q.v.*

नौवबत, *more prop.* नौबत, *q.v.*

नौवां, *m.* (*f.* win) *more prop.* नवां, *q.v.*

नौवाला, *m.* (*f.* ī) a boatman, ferryman.

नौशिख, *m.* one in his noviciate, a novice, freshman, young student.

नौशादर, *m.* sal-ammoniac.

नौसात, (*lit.* nine and seven) a certain division of a crop by which the zamīndār gets nine parts out of sixteen, and the cultivator seven.

नौसादर, *m.* sal-ammoniac.

नौसिख, *more prop.* नौशिख, *q. v.*

नौसिखिया = नौशिख, *q.v.*

नौसिर, new, recent. — *tālāo*, a newly excavated tank.

नौसीक } नौसीख } *more prop.* नौशिख, *q.v.*

न्यक्कार, *m* humiliation, disregard, contempt.

न्यग्रोध, *m.* the Indian figtree (*Ficus Indica*).

न्यग्रोधी, *f.* a kind of plant (*Salvinia cucullata*).

न्यर्बुद, *m.* a hundred millions.

न्यवकार, a contraction of न्यवछावर, *q.v.*

न्यवछावर = नेवछावर, *q. v.*

न्यस्त, deposited, consigned, delivered, pledged, accumulated, hoarded.

न्याई, 1, *m.* (*f.* inī) = न्यायी *q.v.*: 2, = न्याय, *q. v.*

न्याए, *more prop.* न्याय, *q. v.*

न्याति, caste, kind, sort.

न्यामड़, a tree which has sprung up of itself in a cultivated field and which the cultivator may legally cut down.

न्यामत, *more prop.* निअमत, *q.v.*

न्याय, *m.* rule; method, manner; suitable manner, propriety, fitness, equity, justice, truth; reason, argument, disputation, logic, proof; a syllogism; policy, good government: *pr. n.* (1) of the Nyāya doctrine, which consists principally in Logic (2) of a certain school of Hindoo philosophy.— *k.* (with gen. masc. of the object) to administer justice, decide, judge. — *chāhnā*, to desire or demand justice, to seek redress.

न्यायक, *m.* (*f.* ikā) = न्यायी, *q.v.*

न्यायकर्ता, *m.* (*f.* trī) a person who acts with equity or justice.

न्यायता, *f.* (*m.* °त्व) fitness, propriety.

न्यायपत्र, *m.* the decree of a judge.

न्यायवान, *m.* (*f.* vatī) a person who behaves with propriety.

न्यायशास्त्र, *m.* the philosophical system of the Nyāya school; a treatise on the Nyāya system; the science of Logic.

न्यायसंयुक्त, suitably, justly, logically, etc.

न्यायसभा, *f.* a court of justice.

न्यायसूत्र, *m.* the aphorisms of the Nyāya philosophy by Gautam.

न्यायस्थान, *m.* a court of law.

न्यायाचार, *m.* (*f.* ā) a virtuous person.

न्यायाधार, *m.* an example of virtue or propriety.

न्यायान्याय, *m.* (न्याय + अन्याय) justice and injustice.

न्यायिक, *m.* (*f.* ā or ī) a reasoner, logician, arguer, sophist.

न्यायिका, *f.*; see न्यायक and न्यायिक.

न्यायिन, *m.* (*f.* ī) = न्यायी, *q.v.*

न्यायी, *m.* (*f.* inī) a rational person, equitable person, just reasoner, logician, administrator of justice, judge: *lit.* right, rational, proper, fit, just, equitable.

न्याय्य, right, equitable, just, fit, proper; lawfully claimable, litigable.

न्यार, न्याव; for words beginning thus, see under the forms नियार, न्याय, respectively.

न्यास, *m.* a depositing, placing, entrusting; a pledge, deposit; the keeping a thing in mind.

न्यून, *m.* (*f.* ā) defective, deficient, lacking, less, low, inferior, vile, despicable, blameable, wicked.

न्यूनत्व, *m.* (*f.* tā) deficiency, paucity, inferiority.

न्यूनांग, *m.* (*f.* ī or ā) of defective limbs, deficient as to limbs, maimed, mutilated, imperfect.

न्यूनाधिक, less or more, unequal.

न्यूनाधिक्य, *m.* more-or-lessness, *i.e.* deficiency or excess, inequality.

न्यूनेन्द्रिय, *m.* (*f.* ā) deficient in some organ, imperfect (*e.g.* blind, deaf, etc.).

न्यौछावर = नेवछावर, *q. v.*

न्योंता (*colloquial*) = नेवता, *q.v.*

न्योड़ना, *a. int.* to bend, bow, stoop.

न्योड़ाना, *t.* to bend, bow.

न्योढ़ना, *a. int.* to bend, bow, stoop.

न्योढ़ाना, *t.* to bend, bow.

न्योत; for words beginning thus, see under the form नेवत.

न्योला, *more com.* नेवला, *q.v.*

न्योर, *more com.* (1) नेवर (2) नेवल, *qq.v.*

न्ह = न in functions 6 (1) and (2).

न्हवा, *m.* (*f.* ī) small, little, young.

न्हन्वाद, *m. f.* a child.

न्हा; a termination (very common in poetry and especially in the Rāmāyaṇ) of the Historical past tense of verbs; *e.g.* कीन्हा = किया. It is inflected; thus °न्हा, *m.* (*f.* °न्ही): pl. °न्हे, *m.* (*f.* °न्हीं).

न्हाटना, *a. int.* to run away, flee.

न्हाटान्हाटी } न्हाटाभागी } *f.* a fleeing, mutual flight.

न्हाटू, a runaway, fugitive, deserter, renegade.

न्हाय़टना, *a. int.* to run away, flee.

न्हाना, *more prop.* **नहाना**, *q.v.*

न्हाय, a conjunctive participle of **न्हाना**, *q.v.*

न्हि = **न** in functions 6 (1) and (2).

न्हो, न्हीं, न्हे; see *s. v.* **न्हा**.

प

प (p) is the twenty-first consonant of the Hindee alphabet, and has the following characteristics and functions: — 1, It is the first letter of the **पवर्ग** or labial class, and has exactly the pronunciation of the English letter *p*. 2, It is occasionally interchanged inaccurately with **ब**; *e. g.* **उपटन**, *more prop.* **उबटन**. It is also liable to be interchanged corruptly with its aspirate. 3, This letter is of somewhat frequent occurrence as the latter member in compound adjectival substantives; *viz.* (1) from the root **पा**, drinking; *e. g.* **द्विप**, the elephant; *lit.* twice-drinking (*i. e.* he first draws the water with his trunk and then conveys it to his mouth): when so used its feminine is **पा** (2) from the root **पा**, guarding; *e. g.* **भूप**, a king; *lit.* earth-protecting. 4, As a substantive masculine this letter denotes (1) the wind (2) the god of the wind, *viz.* Œolus. 5, This letter is occasionally found in composition as a contraction of **पांच**; *e. g.* **पसेरी**.

पइना; see (1) **पईना** (2) **पैना**.

पइये in Braj = **पाए**, 1, *q.v.*

पई, *m.* a reservoir of water; a rill.

पईना, a walking-stick or staff.

पउना, *t.* to eat.

पः, *m.* a contraction of **पर**, used chiefly in verse.

पंक, *m.* mud, mire, clay.

पंककीर, *m.* a lapwing.

पंकगड़क, *m.* the small fish *Macrognathus pancalus.*

पंकग्राह, *m.* (*f.* ī) a certain marine monster (the *makar*).

पंकज, *m.* any species of the lotus.

पंकजी, *f.* an epithet of Durgā.

पंकट, muddy, miry, clayey.

पंकड़ी, *more com.* **पंखडी**, *q.v.*

पंकधूम, *m. pr. n.* one of the divisions of hell.

पंकप्रभा, *f. pr. n.* one of the hells, *i. e.* the hell of mud or mire.

पंकरुह, *m.* (*f.* ā) the Indian crane.

पंकवास, *m.* (*f.* ā) the dweller in mud, *i. e.* the crab.

पंकशुक्ति, *f.* a cockle.

पंकार, *m.* a certain aquatic plant (*Vallisneria: Trapa bispinosa*): a mound, embankment.

पंकचर, *m.* (*f.* ī *or* ā) an osprey.

पंकेरुह, *m.* a water-lily.

पंक्ति, *f.* a row, line, range, series; a company, flock, multitude; (prefixed in comp.) the number (10) ten; a species of Sanskrit metre in which the stanza consists of four lines and each line of ten syllables; the number (5) five.

पंक्तिरथ, *m.* an epithet of king Dasharath; *lit.* having ten chariots.

पंक्ती, *f.* = **पंक्ति**, *q. v.*

पंख, *m.* (from **पक्ष**) a wing, feather, fin.

पंखड़ी, *f.* (from **पक्ष**) a petal, flower-leaf.

पंखन, a Braj pl. of **पंख**, *q.v.* See **न**, 6.

पंखरी = **पंखड़ी**, *q. v.*

पंखवाला, *m.* (*f.* ī) winged, feathered, finned.

पंखा, *m.* (see **पंख**) a fan.

पंखिया, 1, *f.* (a dim. of **पंखा**) a small fan: 2, *m.* a kind of mendicant who fans everybody: a wicked man.

पंखी, 1, *f.* (a dim. of **पंखा**) a small fan: 2, *m.* (*f.* inī) a bird: 3, *f.* a kind of woollen cloth which comes from the hilly countries.

पंखेरू = **मचला**, *q. v.*

पंगत, **पंगति** } *f.* (*prop.* **पंक्ति**) a row, line.

पंगला, *m.* (*f.* ī) = **पंगु**, *q. v.*

पंगवी, *f.* (*m.* **पंगु**) a crippled female.

पंगास, *m.* a kind of fish (*Silurus sagittatus*, Buch.).

पंगु, *m.* (*f.* **पंगवी** *or* **पंगू**) a cripple, bandy-begged person, who has lost his legs: *prop.* adj. lame, halt, crippled.

पंगुता, *f.*, **पंगुत्व**, *m.* } bandy-leggedness, lameness.

पंगुल, 1, = (1) **पंगु** (2) **पंगुता**, *qq. v.*: 2, *m.* a horse of a glossy or silvery white colour.

पंगू, *f.* (*m.* **पंगु**) a crippled female.

पंघूरा, **पंघूला** } = **पिंगूरा**, *q. v.*

पंच, 1, five: 2, *m.* a council, assembly, meeting; arbitators, umpires. —*mānnā*, to regard a person as an arbitrator, constitute him an umpire.

पंचक, 1, appertaining to five, consisting (or made up) of five, bought with five: 2, *m.* the number five: a collection or aggregate of five, a five.

पंचकन्या, *f.* (in Myth.) the five virgins, *viz.* Tārā, Kuntī, Ahalyā, Mandodarī, Sītā, Anusuiyā, Drupadī.

पंचकर्म्म, *m.* the five actions of the body, *viz.* (1) vomiting (2) evacuation by bleeding (3) evacuation by stool (4) discased excretion by fæces or purging (5) the blowing the nose.

पंचकवलि = **पंचग्रास**, *q. v.*

पंचकोण, *m.* a pentagon.

पंचकोल, *m.* the aggregate of the following five spices or pungent plants, *viz.* 1, long pepper (*Piper longum*); 2, its root; 3, *chai* (*Piper chavya*); 4, leadwort (*Plumbago ceylonica*); 5, dry ginger.

पंचकोश, *m.* (pl.: see **आ**, 22) the five sheathes supposed to invest the soul, *viz.* 1, the *Annamay Kosh*, the gross form; *lit.* the form supported by food: 2, the *Prānamay Kosh*, the organs of action: 3, the *Manamay Kosh*, the organs of perception, including the mind (*man*): 4, the *Vijnānamay Kosh*, the intellect: 5, the *Anandamay Kosh*, consisting of the elements of identity and of divine wisdom.

पंचकोशी, *f.* the aggregate of five kos: *pr. n.* the pilgrimage-road around the city of Benares.

पंचक्की, *f.* a water-mill.

पंचखन, consisting of five floors, stories, or apartments (said of buildings).

पंचखना = **पंचखन**, *q. v.*

पंचगव्य, *m.* the five articles yielded by the cow, *viz.* milk, curds, clarified butter, dung, urine.

पंचगुण, five-fold, five times. [by the hand.

पंचग्रास, *m.* five morsels of food taken to the mouth

पंचजन, *m.* the five higher classes of beings, *viz.* gods, men, Gandharvas with the Apsaras, serpents, and manes.

पंचजनी, *f.* an assemblage or aggregate of five persons: *pr.n.* a daughter of Vishwarūp and wife of Bharat.

पंचजन्य; see (1) पंचजन (2) पांचजन्य.

पंचतत्त्व, *m.* the five elements (according to the Hindoos) *viz.* fire, earth, air, water, aether or space: the five essentials of certain rites, *viz.* wine, meat, fish, sexual intercourse, and mystic gesticulations.

पंचतपा, *m.* a kind of Hindoo ascetic who in the hot weather sits amidst four fires, and has the sun for a fifth.

पंचता, *f.* death, dying (*i.e.* the dissolution of the five elements of whose aggregate the body consists).

पंचतीर्थी, *f.* any five chief places of pilgrimage, *esp.* Visrānti, Saukar, Naimish, Pryāg, and Pushkar: bathing on the day of the Equinox,

पंचत्र, *m.* a fee or duty of five *per cent.* levied on a successful litigant.

पंचत्व, *m.* = पंचता, *q. v.*

पंचदश (*Rām.*) = पन्द्रह, *q. v.*

पंचधा, in five ways, in five parts, five-fold.

पंचन, 1, five: 2, (see न, 6 [1]) *m.* (pl. of पंच, 2) associates, friends.

पंचनख, *m.* (*f.* ī) any creature with five claws, *e. g.* the elephant, tiger, tortoise, etc. The term is used as the designation of such animals as are proper for food.

पंचनद, *m.* an epithet of the Panjāb; *lit.* having five rivers, *viz.* the Yamunā, the Satadru, the Vepāsā, the Chandnabhāgā, and the Vitasthā.

पंचपंचनख, *m.* the five kinds of animals allowed to be killed and eaten, *viz.* the hare, the porcupine, the alligator, the rhinosceros, and the tortoise.

पंचपर्णी, *f.* (*m.* ?) a certain small shrub.

पंचपल्लव, *m.* a medical preparation from the sprouts of five trees, *viz.* the spondias (*Spondias mangifera*), the rose-apple (*Eugenia Jambos*), the bēl (*Ægle Marmelos*), the citron (*Citrus acida*), and the wood-apple (*Feronia elephantum*).

पंचपात्र, *m.* five plates collectively; a kind of *shrāddh* in which offerings are made in five vessels.

पंचपिरिया, *m.* any person (Hindoo or other) who worships the five saints (pīr) of the Muhammadans.

पंचप्राण, *m.* the five vital airs of the body.

पंचबन्ध, *m.* a fine equivalent to the fifth part of anything lost or stolen.

पंचभद्र, *m.* (*f.* ā) a horse with five auspicious marks, *i. e.* spotted on the chest, back, face, and flanks: a condiment of five vegetables.

पंचभूत, *m.* the five elements (according to the Hindoos), *viz.* fire, air, earth, water, and aether or space.

पंचभूतात्मा, an epithet of any individual human being; *lit.* consisting of the five primary elements.

पंचम, *m.* (*f.* ī) fifth: one of the musical modes (*rāg*); one of the seven musical notes, originally the fifth, afterwards the seventh; — said to have been so designated from its being said to be performed by air drawn from five places, *viz.* the navel, the breast, the heart, the throat, and the forehead.

पंचमकार, *m.* the five essentials of the left hand, *viz.* wine, man's flesh, fish, copulation, and gesticulation.

पंचमहल्ल, of five stories (a building).

पंचमहायज्ञ, *m.* the five great sacraments of the Hindoos, *viz.* 1, the worship of spirits (by offerings of perfumes and flowers); 2, the worship of progenitors (by obsequial rites); 3, the worship of gods (by oblations with fire); 4, the worship of the Veds (by studying them); 5, the worship of mankind (by hospitality).

पंचमांश, *m.* a fifth part.

पंचमानना; see *s. v.* पंच.

पंचमास्य, *m.* (*f.* ā) the Indian cuckoo (*koil*).

पंचमी, *f.* the fifth day of a lunation: *pr. n.* a certain river.

पंचर्मी, *more prop.* पंचमी, *q.v.*

पंचमूल, *m.* an aggregate of the following five roots, *viz.* *Bēl*, *Premna longifolia*, *Cassia*, *Gmelina arborea*, and the trumpet-flower.

पंचमूली, *f.* an aggregate of the following five roots, *viz.* *Hedysarum Gangeticum*, *Hedysarum lagopodioides* *Solanum melongena*, *Solanum jacquini*, and *Tribulus*, *lanuginosus*.

पंचरत्न, *m.* a collection of five precious objects, *viz.* gold, a diamond, a pearl, a ruby, an amethyst.

पंचरात्र, 1, *adj.* lasting five nights or days: 2, *m.* a period of five nights; a certain sacrifice which lasts five days: a general term for the sacred books of various Vaishnav sects.

पंचरी, *f.* (in Pros.) a species of metre.

पंचलक्षण, *m.* an epithet of a Purāṇ or mythological poem, the allusion being to the fact that a Purāṇ should embrace the following five topics, *viz.* 1, the creation of worlds; 2, their destruction and renovation; 3, the genealogy of gods and heroes; 4, the reigns of the Manus; and 5, the actions of their descendants.

पंचलड़ा, *m.* } **पंचलड़ी**, *f.* } a necklace of five rows.

पंचलोह, *m.* a compound containing the following five metals, *viz.* copper, brass, tin, lead, and iron.

पंचवटी, *f. pr. n.* a certain locality near the river Godāvaree.

पंचवय, *more prop.* पनसोई, *q. v.*

पंचविंशति, five and twenty.

पंचविंशतितम, the twenty-fifth.

पंचशब्द, *m.* five kinds of sounds, five kinds of musical instruments.

पंचशाख, *m.* (or *f.* ā) the hand; *lit.* having five branches.

पंचसबद = पंचशब्द, *q. v.*

पंचसुगन्धक, *m.* the aggregate of five aromatic vegetable substances, *viz.* cloves, nutmeg, camphor, aloe-wood, and kakkolā.

पंचसूना, *m.* (pl.: see आ, 22) the five things in a house by which animal life may be accidentally destroyed, *viz.* the fireplace, the curry-stone, the broom, the pestle and mortar, and the waterpot.

पंचाइत, *more prop.* पंचायत, *q. v.*

पंचांग, *m.* 1, five modes of devotion, *viz.* (1) silent prayer (2) burnt offering (3) libations (4) bathing idols, and (5) feeding Brāhmaṇs: 2, an almanac describing (1) solar days (2) lunar days (3) the periods of asterisms (4) Yogs, and (5) Karaṇs: 3, reverence as expressed (1) by the extending the hands (2) by bending the knees (3) by bowing the head (4) in speech and (5) in look.

पंचागनि, *more prop.* **पंचाग्नि**, *q.v.*

पंचाग्नि, *m.* a collection of five fires amidst which certain Hindoo devotees perform penance during the hot season, *viz.* one fire placed respectively to the east, west, north, and south of them, — the sun being overhead: five mystic fires supposed to be present in the body.

पंचाध्याई, *f.* the aggregate of five chapters of the Bhāgavat Purān detailing the sports of Krishn with the Gopees.

पंचाध्याय, *m.* five readings, sections, or chapters.

पंचाध्यायी, *more com.* **पंचाध्याई**, *q.v.*

पंचानन, *m.* an epithet of Shiv; also, used at the end of the names of scholars; *lit.* the five-faced.

पंचाननी, *f.* spouse of Panchānan, *i. e.* Durgā.

पंचानवे = **पचान्वे**, *q.v.*

पंचामृत, *m.* a mixture consisting of milk, curds, sugar, ghee, and honey: the aggregate of any five drugs of supposed efficacy.

पंचाम्ल, *m.* the aggregate of five acid plants, *viz.* the jujube, the pomegranate, sorrel, spondias, and citron.

पंचायत, *f.* a meeting of any particular society (generally, as a court of inquiry); a deliberative assembly; an Indian jury, inquest (originally consisting of five members).

पंचायतनामा, *m.* the written award of a court of arbitration.

पंचायती, *f.* 1, = **पंचायत**, *q.v.*: 2, relationship, affinity: 3, the award of a panchāyat court. [rels, etc.

पंचायतीखांगी, *f.* domestic settlement of family quar-

पंचायतीभाती, *f.* an arbitration carried on by persons who are of the same caste as the litigant parties.

पंचायतीसर्कार, *m.* a court held by public authority.

पंचायित = **पंचायत**, *q.v.*

पंचाल, *m. pr. n.* (1) of a country in the north of India (2) of its people (3) of a prince of theirs (4) of a metre in Sanskrit poetry: *adj.* deceitful, cunning.

पंचावन, (*more com.* **पचपन**) fifty-five.

पंचेन्द्रिय, *m.* 1, the five organs of sense, *viz.* the eye, the ear, the nose, the tongue, the skin; or 2, the five organs of action, *viz.* the hand, the foot, the wind-pipe, the anus, and the organ of generation.

पंचें = (1) **पांचें** (2) = **पैंचन**, 2, *qq.v.*

पंचोतर, *m.* a transit duty of five per cent.; a deduction from rent, etc. of five per cent.: a toll-house,

पंचोरा, *more prop.* **पनचोरा**, *q.v.* [custom-house.

पंचौ in Braj = **पंचन**, *q.v.*

पंचौंसे, a Braj abl. pl. of **पंच**, *q.v.*

पंछाला, *m.* the tail of a paper kite.

पंछियन, a corrupt pl. of **पंछी**, *q.v.*

पंछी, *more prop.* **पछी**, *q.v.*

पंज, 1, five: fifth: in fives: 2, the five senses.

पंजन, a Braj pl. of **पंजा**, *q.v.*

पंजर, *m.* a cage, aviary; a skeleton; the ribs, the

पंजरी, *f.* a rib. [side; a rib.

पंजशम्बा, *m.* Thursday.

पंजा, *m.* a claw; the bunch of fives; a sort of link or torch resembling the five fingers. — *k.* to play at a kind of wrestling in which the antagonists lock their fingers together.

पंजाब, *m. pr. n.* (see **पंचनद** and **आब**) the Panjāb, the country of the Sikhs, in northern India.

पंजाबी, appertaining to the Panjāb: hence (1) *f.* the language of the Sikhs: 2, *m.* (*f.* inī) a Panjābi or

पंजारा, *m.* a cotton-carder. [Sikh.

पंजिका, *f.* an almanac, calendar, the register or journal of Yam, the record of human actions.

पंजिकाकार, *m.* (*f.* ī) an almanac-maker; an astronomer.

पंजीरी, *f.* a kind of medicine composed of sugar, ghee, flour, etc. given to puerperal women: caudle.

पंजुम, the fifth.

पंठ, पंथ, पंद, पंप; for words beginning thus, see under the forms **पयठ, पन्थ, पन्द, पम्प**, respectively.

पंवाड़ा, *m.* a story, fable, tale.

पंवाड़िया, *m.* a story-teller, bard.

पंवाड़ी, *f.* a betel-garden.

पंवार, *m.* a certain plant (*Cassia tora* or *C. obtusifolia*): *pr. n.* a certain tribe of Rājputs.

पंवार; for words beginning thus, see under the

पंश्चिलू, *m.* the penis. [form **पंवाड़**.

पंसारी, *more prop.* **पनसारी**, *q.v.*

पंसारीता, *f.* the dealing in spices.

पंसेरी, *f.* a weight or measure of five sérs.

पकड़, *f.* the act of seizing; seizure, capture, catch, hold, grip; objection, difficulty.

पकड़ना, *t.* to lay hold of, seize, capture, catch, grip, take, apprehend, handle; to object.

पकड़बन्दी, *f.* a seizing, capture; evidence, proof.

पकड़वाना, *t.* to cause to be seized, cause to be captured, cause to be apprehended, to deliver over, give in custody, to hand over. [tured.

पकड़ाई, *f.* seizing, capture. — *denā*, to be cap-

पकड़ाना, *t.* to cause to seize or capture.

पकदपड़ी = **पगदपड़ी**, *q.v.*

पकना, *n.* to be cooked: *a. int.* to ripen; to suppurate; to turn grey (hair).

पकपन, *m.* ripeness; expertness, cleverness, cunning. [moisture.

पकला, *m.* a sore between the toes produced by

पकवाई, *f.* (see **आई**, 3) price paid for cooking.

पकवान, *more prop.* **पक्वान्न**, *q.v.*

पकवाना, *t.* to cause to be dressed or cooked, cause

पका, *m.* (*f.* ī) *more prop.* **पक्का**, *q.v.* [to ripen.

पकाई, *f.* ripeness: dressing.

पकाऊ, suppurative.

पकाना, *t.* to cook, bake; to ripen.

पकापकाया, ready cooked. [present it.

पकार, *m.* the letter **प**, or any symbol that may re-

पकाव, *m.* suppuration.

पकोड़ा, *m.* a kind of dish made of pease-meal.

पकोड़ी } **पकौड़ी** } *f.* = **पकौड़ा**, *q. v.*

पक्क, *more prop.* **पक्व**, *q. v.*

पक्का, *m.* (*f.* ī) = **पक्व**, *q. v.* — *k.* to establish a claim or an agreement or a proposition, so that no doubt or subject for dispute can remain; to build with bricks.

पक्काघर, *m.* a house built of baked bricks or of stone.

पक्काचिट्ठा, *m.* an authenticated, revised, or accredited account.

पक्कासेर, *m.* a sér of full and standard weight.

पक्तिशूल, *m.* inflammation of the bowels, cholic.

पक्व, *m.* (*f.* ā) cooked, baked, ripe, mature, matured (whether by nature or by art), accomplished, come to perfection, experienced, knowing, cunning, shrewd, instructed, able, firm, dependable, strong; grey (as hair); on the eve of decay; digested.

पक्वकृत, *m.* an epithet of the *neem*-tree, the leaves of which are applied to phlegmonoid swellings to induce suppuration.

पक्वान्न, *m.* dressed food, victuals fried in butter or oil, sweetmeats.

पक्वाशय, *m.* the stomach, abdomen.

पक्ष, *m.* a wing; the feathers of an arrow, a feather, a fin; a side, flank; a half; the half of a lunar month, comprizing fifteen days; party, class; alternative: a partisan, friend; confirmation, protection, defence; a host, troop, army; a position, opinion, thesis, side of an argument; partiality, assistance, protection; a rejoinder; a plaint in law; two. In the ingenious system of reckoning by symbols adopted by Hindoos in their poetry, this word is a symbol for 2. — *k.* to be partial or one-sided in argument; to take a side, espouse the cause of a party by identifying oneself with it; to patronize, protect.

पक्षगम, *m.* (*f.* ā) any bird: *lit.* adj. moving by means of wings, flying.

पक्षता, *f.* the taking up a side or argument, alliance.

पक्षति, *f.* = **पक्षती**, *q. v.*

पक्षती, *f.* the first day of the waxing or waning of the moon: the root or insertion of a wing.

पक्षद्वेष, *m.* the enmity of partisanship.

पक्षधर, *m.* (*f.* ā) a partisan: lit. *adj.* taking a side.

पक्षपात, 1, = **पक्षपाती**, *q. v.*: 2, *m.* the adopting a side or argument, partisanship, partiality, respect of persons, collusion, chicane.

पक्षपातिता, *f.* (*m.* °**त्व**) adherence, fellowship.

पक्षपाती, *m.* (*f.* inī) a partisan, adherent, friend: *lit.* attached to party, associated with.

पक्षभेद, *m.* distinction between the two sides of an argument; the difference between the two halves of a lunar month.

पक्षवन्त, *m.* (*f.* vatī) winged, feathered, fledged.

पक्षवान, *m.* (*f.* vatī) = **पक्षवन्त**, *q. v.*

पक्षहीन, *m.* (*f.* ā) wingless.

पक्षाघात, *m.* hemiplegia, palsy.

पक्षि, *more prop.* **पक्षी**, *q. v.*

पक्षिणी, *f.* (*m.* **पक्षी**) a hen-bird; a female partisan; a night with the days preceding and following it.

पक्षिमृगता, *f.* the form of a bird or beast.

पक्षिराज, *m.* an epithet of Garuḍa; *lit.* king of the birds; hence, also, the peacock.

पक्षिशाल, *m.* } **पक्षिशाला**, *f.* } a nest; an aviary.

पक्षी, *m.* (*f.* iṇī) a bird; an arrow; a partisan, ally, assistant, favorer, advocate, patron: *lit.* winged, siding with.

पख, *more prop.* **पक्ष**, *q. v.*

पखड़ी, *f.* a petal, flower-leaf.

पखरौटा, *m.* a bit of gold or silver leaf covering a *bīṛā* or mouthful of betel.

पखवा = **पखुआ**, *q. v.*

पखाउज (*Rām.*) = **पखावज**, *q. v.*

पखाटा, *m.* the horn or corner of a bow.

पखान } **पखाना** } *m.* (prop. **पाषाण**) stone.

पखारना, *t.* to wash.

पखाल, *f.* a large leathern bag for carrying water (it is generally double, and is thrown over the back of a bullock); a leathern bag for raising water from a well.

पखालना, *t.* to wash.

पखाला, *m.* = **पखाल**, *q. v.*

पखाली, *m.* (*f.* inī) a water-carrier.

पखावज, *f.* a kind of drum, timbrel.

पखावजी, *m.* (*f.* in *or* inī) a drummer.

पखुरी, *f.* the shoulder-blade.

पखुआ, *m.* a side, wing, flank, gable end of a building.

पखेरु } **पखेरू** } *m.* a bird.

पखेव, *m.* a mark, stamp.

पखौटा, *m.* a wing; fin of a fish; a side or flank.

पखौड़ा, *m.* the shoulder-blade.

पग, *m.* the foot. — *uṭhānā*, to give over running. — *dhārnā*, to travel, depart, leave, go. *Pag pag par*, at every step. — *paṭ tār bajnā*, to beat time with the foot.

पगडंडी, *f.* a by-path, by-way, footpath, track. — *lena*, to track, trace.

पगड़ी, *f.* a turban: a species of poll-tax (see *pāg*) — *aṭaknā*, to persevere, persist, be obstinate. — *chhapaṭnā*, to act treacherously, practise deceit.

पगदंडी = **पगडंडी**, *q. v.*

पगन, *m.* (a Braj pl. of **पग**) feet. See **न**, 6.

पगना, *n.* to be dipped in (or covered with) syrup; *met.* to be in love.

पगला, *m.* (*f.* ī) foolish, demented.

पगहा = **पगा**, *q. v.*

पगा, 1, *m.* (*f.* ī) enamoured: 2, *m.* a rope fastened around the neck or foot of a bullock, a tether, the rope which passes under the tail of a bullock and is connected with the harness on the back.

पगार, *m.* mud kneaded or prepared for building or plastering: wages: an enclosure around a field, a trench, mound, bank.

पगाह, *f.* dawn, twilight, morning.

पगिया, *f.* a turban.

पगी, *f.* (*m.* **पगा**) an enamoured female.

पगु, (*Rām.*) = (1) **पांव** (2) **लगन**, *qq. v.*

पगुराना, *a. int.* to ruminate, chew the cud.

पघा = पगा, *q.v.*

पघाया = पघैया, *q.v.*

पघाल, *m.* a kind of hard iron or steel.

पघिलाना, *more com.* टिघलाना, *q.v.*

पघैया, *m.* a dealer in cloth, metals, etc.

पच, 1, prefixed in comp. it = पच, 1, *q.v.*: 2, suffixed in comp. it = *adj.* cooking, baking, roasting.

पचक, *m.* (*f.* ikī) a cook: lit. *adj.* cooking.

पचखन } पचखना } *more prop.* पंचखन, *q.v.*

पचखा, *m.* (pl.?) six days (from Shravaṇ to Revatī) on which several kinds of work are unlawful.

पचत; for words beginning thus, see under the form पछत.

पचतोलिया, *m.* a kind of cloth.

पचन, *m.* cooking, the act of cooking; a becoming entirely cooked, ripening; putrefying; anything that cooks or matures, a fryingpan.

पचना, *n.* to be digested, be consumed: *a. int.* to dissolve, rot: to take pains, to labour.

पचनीय, *m.* (*f.* ā) fit to be cooked, etc.

पचपच, 1, *m.* the noise made by walking in damp places: 2, soft or plashy (as soil or rotten vegetable matter and mud).

पचपचाना, *n.* to be damp, be wet: *a. int.* to perspire, sweat.

पचपन, fifty-five (५५): see ओं, वां, वीं, वे, वें.

पचमहल्ला, consisting of five stories, apartments or rooms (said of buildings).

पचमेल, *m.* (*f.* ā) mixed, confused.

पचम्पचा, *f.* a species of cucurma (*Curcuma xanthorrhiza*.

पचरा, *m.* a kind of wedge, a spike or large nail.

पचलड़ा, *m.* } पचलड़ी, *f.* } = पंचलड़ा, *q.v.*

पचलोना, *m.* a certain medicine composed of five kinds of salt.

पचहत्तर, *more com.* पछत्तर, *q.v.*

पचा, *f.* the act of cooking, cooking. — *ḍālnā*, to digest, to rot.

पचानवे } पचानव्वे } = पचान्वे, *q.v.*

पचाना, *t.* to cause to rot, to digest, ferment, rot.

पचान्वे, ninety-five (९५): see ओं, वां, वीं, वे, वें.

पचाव, *m.* digestion.

पचास, fifty (५०): see ओं, वां, वीं, वे, वें.

पचासी, eighty-five (८५): see ओं, वां, वीं, वे, वें.

पचि (*Rām.*) = पच्ची and कामसे.

पचिका, *f*, (*m.* पचक) a female cook.

पचीस, twenty-five (२५): see ओं, वां, वीं, वे, वें.

पचीसी, *f.* a certain game which is played with cowries instead of dice, and is so named from the highest throw, which is twenty-five.

पचूका, *m.* a squirt, syringe.

पचोतरा, *m.* a duty of five *per cent.* on merchandise.

पचोत्तर, *m.* (see above) five *per cent.*

पचौनी, *f.* the stomach.

पच्चर, *f.* a wedge. — *mārnā*, *t.* to teaze, harass, distress.

पच्ची, adherent, sticking, joined: *met.* (in Music) in unison. — *honā*, to be stuck together as with glue; to be in unison; to be strongly attached by love.

पच्चीकारी, *f.* mosaic; patching or darning damaged cloth.

पच्चीस, *more com.* पचीस, *q.v.*

पच्छ, *more prop.* पक्ष, *q.v.*

पच्छम } पच्छिम } *more prop.* पश्चिम, *q.v.*

पच्छी, *m.* (*f.* inī) = पक्षी, *q.v.*

पच्छीकारी, *more prop.* पच्चीकारी, *q.v.*

पछ, *more prop.* पक्ष, *q.v.*

पछड़जाना, *n.* to be overcome.

पछड़ना, *a. int.* to fall, tumble, stumble.

पछताना, *a. int.* to regret, rue, feel sorry or vexed, grieve, repent.

पछताव = पछतावा, *q.v.*

पछतावा, *m.* regret, compunction, remorse, contrition, grief, sorrow, concern, repentance, penitence. — *k.* to repent.

पछत्तर, seventy-five (७५): see ओं, वां, वीं, वे, वें.

पछना, *m.* the act of scarifying, tattooing; an instrument for scarifying, a lancet: inoculation.

पछनी, *f.* scarifying, tattooing.

पछवा, *f.* westerly wind.

पछाँ, *m.* the west, the setting of the sun.

पछाँह, *more com.* पछाँ, *q v.*

पछाड़, *f.* a fall, a throwing down; the act of winnowing.—*khānā*, to fall down, suffer pain.

पछाड़ना, *t.* to throw down, upset, abase, conquer.

पछान, *more prop.* (1) पछाँ (2) पहचान, *qq.v.*

पछानत, *f.* knowledge, acquaintance, discovery.

पछार = पछाड़, *q.v.*

पछारना = पछाड़ना, *q.v.*

पछित; for words beginning thus, see under the form पछत.

पछिम } पछीम } *more prop.* पश्चिम, *q.v.*

पछिया } पछियाव } *f.* a westerly wind.

पछेरू, *m. f.* winged.

पछोड़ना, *t.* to winnow with a winnowing-basket.

पछोड़ी, *f.* = पिछौरी, *q.v.*

पज़मुर्दा, withered, pallid, fading, decayed, blighted.

पजर, an oozing, dripping, distillation; a fountain, jet d'eau.

पजरना, *a. int.* to drip, drop, leak, ooze, distil.

पजावा, *m.* a brick-kiln.

पज़ीरा, acceptable, agreeable.

पजेब, *f.* a kind of ornament for the feet.

पजोड़ा } पजौड़ा } *m.* (*f.* ī) low, mean, shabby.

पझिम, a corruption of पश्चिम, *q.v.*

पञ्च, पञ्ज; for words beginning thus, see under the forms **पंच, पंज**, respectively.

पट, 1, *m.* woven cloth, cloth, a piece of cloth, a garment, coarse cloth or canvas, a checkered cloth on which chess, etc. may be played: a table, a plate (for painting and writing): sound, the sound resulting from anything falling or being beaten: a shutter, the valve of a folding-door: 2, overturned, upside-down.

पटंबर, a contraction of **पाटम्बर**, *q.v.* [encampment.

पटक, 1, a dash: 2, *m.* cotton cloth: a camp,

पटकन, *f.* a fall, slip of the foot, stumble; a knock. —*khānā*, to fall down, get a knock.—*mārnā*, to knock down. [(as burning wood), crack, sputter; to fret.

पटकना, 1, = **पटकाना**, *q.v.*: 2, *a. int.* to crackle

पटकनिया = **पटकनी**, *q.v.*

पटकनी, *f.* a dash, throw, fling to the ground.—*khānā*, to be dashed to the ground.—*denā*, to dash to the ground, throw against anything with violence.

पटका = **पटूका**, *q.v.* *Zarī* —, the golden girdle, being an ensign conferred by the Peshwā on generals who are invested with authority immediately by him.

पटकाना, *t.* to dash against anything, throw to the ground with violence, to knock.

पटकारना = **पटकाना**, *q.v.*

पटकी देना = **पटकनी द°**, *q.v.*

पटड़ा = **पटरा**, *q.v.*

पटड़ी = **पटरी**, *q.v.*

पटतर (*Rām.*) = (1) **उपमा** (2) **बरोबर**, *qq.v.*

पटन, *m.* roofing.

पटना, 1, = **पाटलिपुत्र**, *q.v.*: 2, *n.* to be paid, be procured; to be watered; to be covered, be roofed, be piled: *a. int.* to fill.

पटनी, 1, *m.* a ferryman: 2, *f.* a city.

पटपट, *f.* the sound of beating. [course.

पटपड़, a level and desert plain or field, a race-

पटपर = **पटपड़**, *q.v.*

पटम्बर, a contraction of **पाटम्बर**, *q.v.*

पटरा, *m.* a plank, a plank for sitting on, a plank on which a washerman beats clothes: unripe grain (*Cicer arietinum*).—*kar denā*, to deprive one of his power; to convict an adversary and leave him with-

पटरानी, a contraction of **पाटरानी**, *q.v.* [out reply.

पटरी, *f.* (dim. of **पटरा**) a board for writing on; the vanes of a Venetian window; a narrow slip or plank of wood, iron, etc.; a firm seat on horseback; a tile.

पटल, *m.* a coverture, veil, roof, thatch; a film on the eye: a heap, collection, multitude; retinue, train: a book, division of a book; a formulary of ritual worship: a basket: a sandal-wood mark on the forehead.

पटली, 1, (*Rām.*) = **पंक्ति**, *q.v.*: 2, *more com.* **पटरी**, *q.v.*

पटलीपुत्र, *more prop.* **पाटलिपुत्र**, *q.v.*

पटवस्त्र, the kind of cloth called **पट**, *q.v.*

पटवा, 1, *m.* (*f.* ī) = **पटूआ**, *q.v.*: 2, *m.* irrigation.

पटवाज़मीन, *f.* land artificially watered.

पटवाना, *t.* to provide money: to water.

पटवार, *m.* = **पटवारी**, *q.v.*

पटवारी, *m.* a person who keeps accounts of lands, land-steward. His business is to keep the accounts of the rents realized in his village or department, and to account for them to his superior. He is also employed by the cultivator to keep his accounts. No village is without its paṭwāree.

पटवी, *f.*: see (1) **पटवा** (2) **पटु**.

पटवीगर, *m.* (*f.* nī) = **पटूआ**, *q.v.*

पटसन, *m.* a species of plant (*Crotolaria juncea*).

पटसाल, *more prop.* **पाठशाला**, *q.v.*

पटह, *m.*, **पटहा**, *f.* } a drum, kettle-drum.

पटा, *m.* a foil, wooden scimetar for cudgelling with, a straight long broad sword with two edges; a board on which Hindoos sit whilst eating their meals or whilst performing religious ceremonies: a streak, stripe, broad line: the half of the beard or one side of the face: a leaf of the American aloe or of any similar plant; the head-stall of a bridle: a code of regulations for the guidance of rent-collectors: a long narrow strip of coarse cloth, matting, etc. —*kāṭnā*, to discharge from service.

पटाक, *m.* a sound, crash, explosion, report of artil-

पटाका, *f.* a flag, banner. [lery: a kind of bird.

पटाख़ा, *m.* a cracker, squib, fireworks.

पटाना, *t.* to water, irrigate: to prepare a *chaukā* with cowdung dissolved in water: to place the beams on the roof of a house: to pay money.

पटापट, *m.* the sound of beating or of the falling of

पटापर, *m.* a kind of fruit. [drops of rain.

पटालन, **पटालम** } *more com.* **पलटन**, *q.v.*

पटाव, *m.* irrigating, flooding a field: roofing a house with tiles, etc.

पटिया, *f.* a slate, slab of stone, tablet; any slip of board used as a slate for writing on.

पटी, *f.* the curtain of a stage.

पटीना, *m.* (*f.* ī) a species of bird, the green flycatcher (*Merops viridis*). [printing.

पटीमा, *m.* the planks on which cloth is spread for

पटीलना, *t.* to exact; to subdue; to beat.

पटु, *m.* (*f.* **पटु** *or* **पटत्री**,) hot, sharp, cruel, diligent, clear, smart, clever, dexterous, skilful, cunning.

पटुआ, *m.* (*f.* **पटुई**) a draughtsman, designer, painter.

पटुका = **पटूका**, *q.v.*

पटुता, *f.* (*m.* **°त्व**) keenness, cleverness, dexterity, adroitness, expertness, skill, vigilance, activity, vigour, virility; eloquence.

पटुया = **पटुआ**, *q.v.*

पटुवा; see (1) **पटुआ** (2) **पटूआ** (3) **पटूका**.

पटूआ, *m.* (*f.* **पटूई**) a man who strings pearls; a maker of fringe and tape, a braider: a tow made from the *Hibiscus cannabinus*.

पटूका, *m.* a cloth worn around the waist, a girdle, belt, sash.—or *paṭkā bāndhnā*, to determine on or to prepare for any act.—or *paṭkā pakaṛnā*, to hinder or obstruct.

पटूत, *m.*, **पटूता**, *f.*, **पटूत्व**, *m.* } = **पटुता**, *q.v.*

पटेबाज़, *m.* a fencer, cudgeller, man who fights with sword and shield, warrior : *met.* a coquette, wanton, strumpet.

पटेर ; see (1) **पटीना** (2) **पटेरा.**

पटेरा, *m.* papyrus : a kind of long grass eaten by elephants and used by the poor for making hoods to protect them from rain.

पटेल, *m.* cudgelling: sovereignty ; a chief among the Kuñbee tribe; a title of Marhattas, the head man of a village. — *ḍālnā*, to interrupt, throw obstacles in the way of business ; to beat.

पटेला = पटैला, *q.v.*

पटेली, *f.* (dim. of **पटेला**) a small flat-bottomed boat.

पटैत, *m.* a cudgeller, cudgel-player.

पटैना = पटेना, *q.v.*

पटैला, *m.* a kind of large flat-bottomed boat used for conveying merchandise on the Ganges : a log or beam used to roll or harrow ground.

पटोतन, *m.* roofing with planks and boards, transom.

पटोर
पटोरा } (*Rām.*) = **पाटम्बर,** *q.v.*

पटोल, *m.* a kind of cucumber (*Trichosanthes dioicea*).

पटोलिका, *f.* = **पटोल,** *q.v.*

पटोहिया, *m.* an owl.

पटौनी, *m.* a ferryman.

पट्ट, *m.* a table, plate (for painting); a patent, document ; a seat, chair, throne ; a strip ; a frontlet, diadem, turban ; woven silk ; a city, town, village ; a royal grant or order written on copper, stone, etc. ; cloth ; an upper or outer garment ; a bandage, ligament, etc. ; a certain plant (*Corchorus olitorius*) from the fibres of the bark of which (called Jute) a coarse sackcloth and cordage are prepared.

पट्टक, *m.* a document; a bandage; a frontlet.

पट्टज, *m.* a kind of cloth.

पट्टदार = पट्टादार, *q. v.*

पट्टदेवी, *f.* a principal queen, queen-consort.

पट्टन, *m.* a city: the act of ordering goods from a manufacturer.

पट्टनी, *f.* a city : commissioned goods, goods made to order.

पट्टरंग, *m.* a certain plant (*Cœsalpinia sappan*) used in dyeing.

पट्टरानी, *more com.* **पाटरानी,** *q.v.*

पट्टशाक, *m.* the potherb *Corchorus capsularis.*

पट्टा, 1, *m.* a lock of hair, ringlet, curl ; a dog-collar ; harness : a deed (*esp.* a title-deed to land), deed of lease ; a grant or lease specifying the quantity of land possessed by each tenant and the amount of rent with which it is charged : 2, *f.* an ornament for the forehead. — *turānā*, to run away, flee.

पट्टाजनाजात, leases granted to tenants individually.

पट्टाठोका, *f.* a deed assigning land for farming on certain conditions.

पट्टाताल्लुक, *m.* a dependent lease.

पट्टादहसाला, a ten years' lease.

पट्टादार, *m.* one who holds his lands by a written engagement, a leaseholder.

पट्टिका, *f.* a ribbon ; turban-cloth.

पट्टिल, *m.* the plant *Caesalpinia bonducella.*

पट्टिलोध, *m.* the red species of the *lodh*-tree (*Symplocos racemosa*) the bark of which is used in dyeing and as an astringent.

पट्टिश, *m.* a spear with a sharp edge.

पट्टिशी, *m.* (*f.* inī) a person armed with the above-mentioned weapon.

पट्टी, *f.* a bandage, fillet, brace ; plaster ; tape ; a head-band or narrow plate of silver or brass worn by sipāhis and their native officers across the turban : a rafter, the whole series of rafters that cover one side of a house : a quarter of a place : the side-pieces of the frame of a bedstead : a row, line : a kind of sweetmeat : the division of the hair which is combed towards the two sides and divided by a line in the middle : a certain custom observed in the Dakkhan on the third day after a woman has been delivered ; also, a ceremony sometimes practised before marriage; the side-locks of hair over each temple : a written order, charter, patent ; a list, statement, invoice ; documents of any kind : laths of split bamboo : spokes of a wheel : a small plank : a tablet : pasteboard : a rule to draw lines with : assessment : a cataplasm : a bolt : a door-knocker : a ledge : a morsel of betel leaf (with betel-nut, lime, etc) : a wooden fencing-sword, a straight long broad sword with two edges : monthly pay : (in Surgery) splints : a public subscription-paper. —*pakarke hilte rahnā* expresses excessive weakness and laziness. — *tornā*, to be bedridden. *Pattise patti milānā* expresses the most intimate proximity.

पट्टीदार, *m.* a patentee; a person who holds a tenure by *patti* ; one who has a share in a coparcenary village or estate.

पट्टीदारी, *f.* a coparcenary tenure.

पट्टीवार, according to shares or assessments.

पट्टू, *m.* a kind of woollen cloth, a cloth to protect from rain, etc.

पट्ठा, *m.* a young full-grown animal, a youth ; a wrestler : a sinew, tendon ; the buttock, the hip, the breech : a kind of plant with long leaves.

पठ, 1, = **पट्ठा** *q.v.*: 2, (*Rām.*) = **पठन,** *q. v.*

पठई, an old conjunct. part. of **पठाना.**

पठओं in Braj = **मैं पठाऊंगा.**

पठंगो = either (1) **मैं पठूंगा,** or (2) **पठाऊंगा.** (?)

पठक, *m.* (*f.* ikā) a reader, reciter.

पठड़ा, *more com.* **पटरा,** *q.v.*

पठन, *m.* reading, reciting, mentioning: a reader, student.

पठनपठन, an intensive redupl. of **पठन,** *q.v.*

पठना, to read, recite; study.

पठबहु = either (1) **तुम पठोगे** or (2) **तुम पठाओगे.** (?)

पठयो, a Braj form of **पठाया (पठाना).**

पठान, *m. pr. n.* (1) of a race or dynasty that once reigned in Dehli (2) of an *Afghān* race settled in Rohilkhand.

पठाना, *t.* to send, despatch.

पठिंगा, *m.* shelter, refuge.

पठिका, *f.* (*m.* **पठक,**) a female reader, female student.

पठित, *m.* (*f.* ā) read, studied, recited.

पठिया, *f.* a young full-grown animal (generally applied to kids, fowls, etc.).

पठेया, sent, despatched.

पठौनो in Braj = **पठाना**, *q.v.*

पड़छटी, *f.* a small thatch thrown over mud walls.

पड़ जाना; see *s.v.* **पड़ना**.

पड़तन (poet.) = **नहीं पड़ता है**.

पड़ती, *f.* fallow land.

पड़ना, *a. int.* to fall, drop; to lie down, repose; to befal, happen, occur: to encamp; to be confined to bed by sickness. *Parjānā*, to lie down, repose, abate, cease (as wind). *Par rahnā* (or *pare rahnā*) to remain helpless, poor, or destitute, to be utterly helpless, be in a regular fix, be in a desperate state. *Jhagra*—, to break out (said of a quarrel).

पड़नेवाला, *m.* (*f.* ī) *more prop.* **पढ़नेवाला**, *q.v.*

पड़पड़ रहना, *a. int.* to chat, prattle.

पड़पड़ाना, *a. int.* to prattle, chatter; to throb with pain (as the tongue from an acid substance).

पड़म, *m.* a coarse kind of cotton cloth (used for tents, etc).

पड़मर्गी, *f.* shamelessness, immodesty.

पड़ रहना; see *s.v.* **पड़ना**.

पड़वा, *m.* a large boat, ferry-boat.

पड़वाना, *t.* (causat. of **पड़ाना**) to cause to lie down, etc.

पड़वी, *f.* a sort of sugarcane sown in autumn.

पड़ा, *m.* the boundary of a field.

पड़ाइन, *f.*; see **पांड़े**.

पड़ाना, 1, *more prop.* **पढ़ाना**, *q.v.*: 2, *t.* to lay down; to cause to repose, put to sleep; to cull, gather, pluck.

पड़ापड़, *adv.* with reïterated strokes.

पड़ापाना, *t.* to find or get easily.

पड़ाव, *m.* a halting, resting, sleeping; a halting-place, encampment, camp; an army, crowd, assembly.

पड़ि = **पड़के** (**पड़ना**). See **इ**, 7.

पड़िया, *f.* a female buffalo-calf.

पड़ियान, a Braj pl. of **पड़िया**, *q.v.* See **न**, 6.

पड़िवा, *more prop.* (1) **पड़िया** (2) **परिवा**, *qq.v.*

पड़ी, *f.* a certain measure for dry or liquid goods.

पड़े रहना; see *s.v.* **पड़ना**.

पड़ेव, an old poet. form = **पड़ा** (**पड़ना**).

पड़ोस, *m.* neighbourhood, vicinity.

पड़ोसन / **पड़ोसिन** } *more prop.* **पड़ोसिनी**, *q.v.*

पड़ोसिनी, *f.* (*m.* **पड़ोसी**) a female neighbour.

पड़ोसी, *m.* (*f.* inī) a neighbour.

पढ़न, *f.* the act of reading, reading.

पढ़ना, *t.* to read, repeat, say, recite, quote, decipher, speak.

पढ़नी, *f.* the act of reading, reading.

पढ़नेवाला / **पढ़नेहारा** } *m.* (*f.* ī) a reader, reciter, student.

पढ़न्त, *f.* a reading, spell, charm.

पढ़यल, *f.* sweepings.

पढ़वाना, *t.* to cause (a person) to be taught reading.

पढ़ा, *m.* (*f.* ī) read, well read, of extensive reading, learned, lettered.

पढ़ागुणा, a learned experienced man.

पढ़ाना, *t.* to cause to read, to teach, to teach birds to sing.

पढ़िन, *f.* a mullet.

पढ़िना; see (1) **पढ़िन** (2) **पढ़ना**.

पण, *m.* play, gaming; a wager, bet, stake; a throw (at play); wages, hire, reward, price, purchase-money, marriage-portion or fee; wealth, property, money; an agreement, stipulation, contract, promise, vow, a clause in an agreement: an aggregate number consisting of twenty *gandā*, i. e. eighty cowries; also, a weight of copper of similar value.

पणव, *m.* a kind of small drum: (in Pros.) a species of metre.

पणवा, *f.* a kind of small drum.

पणी, *m.* (*f.* inī) under a vow or promise, resolute.

पणढ, 1, = **पणढक**, *q.v.*: 2, (in Chand) = **पन्द्रह**, *q.v.*

पणढक, *m.* a eunuch, catamite.

पण्डा, 1, *f.* wisdom, understanding, learning, science: 2, *m.* a minister or priest who presides at the temple of an idol.

पण्डित, *m.* (*f.* ā) a learned man, scholar, teacher: *lit.* learned, wise, skilled, shrewd. The term is applied as a title of respect to Hindoos who are learned in the Brāhmanical theology.

पण्डितख़ाना, a corruption of **बन्दीख़ाना**, *q.v.*

पण्डितता, *f.* / **पण्डितत्व**, *m.* } = **पण्डिताई**, *q.v.*

पण्डितमानी, *m.* (*f.* inī) an ignorant pedant, one who esteems himself a scholar.

पण्डिता, *f.* (*m.* **पण्डित**) a learned woman.

पण्डिताइन, *more com.* **पण्डिताईन** / **पण्डिताइनि**, *more com.* **पण्डितानी** } *qq. v.*

पण्डिताई, *f.* (see **आई**, 3) learning, scholarship, knowledge, wisdom, the learning and status of a paṇḍit.

पण्डिताईन / **पण्डितानी** } *f.* (*m.* **पण्डित**) the wife of a paṇḍit.

पण्डियायन, *f.* the wife of a paṇḍā. See **पण्डा**, 2.

पण्डु, *more prop.* **पाण्डु**, *q.v.*

पण्डुक, *m.* a turtle-dove.

पण्डुनि, either (1) a plural or agentive form of **पाण्डु**, or (2) a Hindee form of **पाण्डवी**, *q.v.*

पण्डुबी, *f.* a water-fowl, the coot, the diver.

पण्डू, fruit, ripe fruit; a berry.

पण्डूरी, *f.* a kind of bird (*Falco*).

पण्डे, a corruption of **पण्डा**, 2, *q.v.*

पण्य, *m.* any saleable article: *lit.* saleable, vendible.

पण्यसाला, *f.* a market-place.

पत, 1, a contraction of **पति**, *q.v.*: 2, *f.* good name, honour, character: temperance in diet.

पतंग, 1, *m.* (*f.* ī) a bird, grasshopper, moth; a paper kite; the sun; sappan-wood; a kind of playing-ball: 2, *m. pr. n.* (1) of Krishṇ (2) of a certain caste in Plakshadwip (3) of a certain mountain (4) of a certain village.

पतंगा, *m.* a spark: a moth. — *honā*, to go rapidly about a business.

पतंगिका, *f.* a small bird; a sort of bee.

पतंगिया, *f.* (pl. of **पतंगी**) moths.

पतंगी, *f.* (*m.* **पतंग**) a hen, etc.: *pr. n.* one of the wives of Tārksh and mother of the flying animals (*patag*).

पतंजलि, *m. pr. n.* an ancient Hindoo philosopher, founder of the Yog doctrine and author of the Mahābhāshya.

पतंति (*Rām.*) = **गिरते हैं**.

पतका, *m.* a girdle, sash.

पतकी, *f.* a small kind of earthen vessel.

पतग, *m.* (*f.* ā) any winged creature, a bird.

पतगी, *more prop.* **पतंगी**, *q. v.*

पतझड़, *f.* the fall of the leaf, *i. e.* autumn: *lit.* bereft of leaves. — *honā*, to lose its leaves (said of a tree in autumn); *met.* to decay (said of an aged person).

पतझड़ी, *f.* the fall of the leaf, *i. e.* autumn.

पतता, *more prop.* **पत्ता**, *q. v.*

पतत्री, *m.* (*f.* iṇī) a bird; an arrow: *lit.* winged.

पतथर, *more prop.* **पत्थर**, *q. v.*

पतदिन, a contraction of **प्रतिदिन**, *q. v.*

पतन, *m.* falling, a fall; falling from dignity, virtue, etc.; hanging down, becoming slack; death; ruin: *pr. n.* a certain Rākshas.

पतनि } **पतनी** } *f.* (*m.* **पति**) a wife. See **पत्नी**.

पतपड़, land susceptible of alluvial deposits.

पतपड़ी, *f.* the surface of soft land caked by sunshine after rain.

पतपिती, *f.* a small kind of bird, the grass-warbler.

पतमई, *f.* the sowing fresh sugarcane after cutting the old.

पतयाना, *more com.* **पतियाना**, *q. v.*

पतरिंगा, *m.* a species of bird, *viz.* the fly-catcher (*Merops viridis*).

पतरिया, *f.* a prostitute.

पतरियाबाज़, *m.* a whoremonger.

पतला, *m.* (*f.* ī) thin, fine, subtle, minute; meagre, slender, lean, delicate, weak. — *k.* to thin.

पतलाई, *f.* thinness, fineness, attenuation, minuteness, meagreness, weakness, subtleness, delicateness.

पतलो, *m.* the dead leaves fallen from a tree; the leaves cut off from the culm of a certain reed (*Saccharum spontaneum*) and used for thatching.

पतवन्ती, *more prop.* **पतिवन्ती**, *q. v.*

पतवार } **पतवाल** } *f.* a rudder, helm.

पता, *m.* a sign, mark, signal, symptom, token, hint, direction, address (or place to which one is directed), labél: a book of instructions and regulations for rent-collectors. — *raknā* or *lagānā*, to seek for, endeavour to find out.

पताका, *f.* a sign, symbol, mark, emblem, standard, banner; flag, flagstaff; a certain great number; an episode in a drama.

पताकी, *m.* (*f.* inī) a standard-bearer, ensign; one who gives a signal.

पताल, a contraction of **पाताल**, *q. v.*

पति, *m.* (*f.* **पत्नि** *or* **पत्नी**) a master, lord, owner, proprietor, governor, husband.

पतिंगा, *m.* a moth.

पतिश्राला; see (1) **पतियारा** (2) **पतियाला**.

पतिग्रह, *more prop.* **प्रतिग्रह**, *q. v.*

पतिघ्नी, *f.* the murderess of her husband: a line on the hand indicating that a woman will be faithless or treacherous to her husband.

पतित, *m.* (*f.* ā) fallen, abject, abandoned, degraded, outcast, guilty, wicked; fallow (land).

पतितन, a Braj pl. of **पतित**. See **न**, 6 (1).

पतितपावन, *m.* an epithet of the Supreme; *lit.* adj. purifying the guilty.

पतिता, *f.* 1, = **पतित्व**, *q. v.*: 2, (*m.* **पतित**) an abandoned female.

पतित्व, *m.* proprietorship, mastership, lordship; the marital or conjugal state, matrimony.

पतिदिन, a contraction of **प्रतिदिन**, *q. v.*

पतिदेवता (*Rām.*) = **पतिव्रता**, *q. v.*

पतिनिहि (*Rām.*) = **पत्नीको**.

पतिपद, *m.* the status of **पति**, *q. v.*

पतिप्राणा, *f.* an epithet of a faithful or virtuous wife, or one who burns with her husband's corpse; *strictly*, valuing her husband as her own life.

पतिभाव, *m.* the disposition and sentiments appropriate in an espoused one towards her lover.

पतिम्बरा, *f.* a bride who chooses her husband: a certain pungent seed (*Nigella Indica*).

पतिया, *f.* a written opinion given by paṇḍits on a point of Hindoo law; a small note, letter.

पतियाना, *t.* to confide in, depend on, trust, believe.

पतियारा, *m.* trust, dependence, confidence, belief.

पतियार, *f.* a rudder, helm.

पतियाला, *m. pr. n.* a certain town N.W. of Delhi.

पतिलोक (*Rām.*) = **हिमाचल**, *q. v.*

पतिवती } **पतिवन्ती** } = **पतिवत्नी**, *q. v*

पतिवत्नी, *f.* a married woman whose husband is still living.

पतिवियोग, *m.* separation from a husband.

पतिव्रत, *m.* fidelity to a husband.

पतिव्रता, *f.* a faithful, virtuous, and devoted wife.

पतिसेवा, *f.* the devotion of a wife to her husband.

पतीत, *m.* uncultivated waste land.

पतीतकमी, *f.* a decrease occasioned by lands being left uncultivated.

पतीरी, *f.* a kind of mat.

पतील, 1, = **पतला**, *q. v*: 3, *m.* a match for a lamp, a linstock, candle-wick.

पतीला, *m.* 1, = **पतील**, 2, *q. v.*: 2, *m.* a pan, pot.

पतुकी, *f.* a small pot, pan.

पतुरिया } **पतूरिया** } *f.* a prostitute.

पत्ती, straw or grass thrown over a field to protect the fresh-planted roots from the sun.

पतोह } **पतोहू** } *f.* a daughter-in-law (son's wife).

पतोवा, *m.* a leaf.

पत्तन, *m.* a city, town, settlement, colony (chiefly used in comp. *e. g.* Srīrangpattan, *i.e.* Seringapatam): the act of ordering goods from a manufacturer.

पत्तनी, commissioned, manufactured by order.

पत्तर, *more prop.* (1) **पत्थर** (2) **पत्र**, *qq.v.*

पत्तल, *f.* a plate or trencher formed of leaves.

पत्ता, *m.* a leaf; a trinket. — *honā*, to run away, flee.

पत्तान, *more prop.* (1) **पत्तल** (2) **पाताल**, *qq.v.*

पत्ति, *m.* a pedestrian, foot-soldier; a company, platoon (consisting of one chariot, one elephant, three horse and five foot).

पत्तिपंक्ति, *f.* a line of infantry.

पत्तिसंहति, *f.* a body of troops.

पत्ती, 1, a corruption (1) of **पति** (2) of **पत्ति**, *qq. v.*: 2, *f.* a leaf; hemp (of which an intoxicating liquor is made): the hem of cloth.

पत्थर, *m.* stone, a stone. — *chhātīpar rakhnā*, to be patient by compulsion or from being without remedy. — *kā chhāpā*, lithography. — *pasijnā*, to be softened or melted (a stony heart). — *pānī ho jānā*, the melting of a stony heart; the facilitating of a difficult task. — *sā phenk mārnā*, to reply rashly and without understanding the meaning of the question. — *se sir phornā* or *mārnā*, to teach or instruct a fool. — *honā*, to be heavy; to stand still, be stable; to be unmerciful.

पत्थरकला, *m.* a firelock.

पत्थरचटा, 1, *m.* (*f.* ī) one who is attached to his own house and who remains there even in distress; a skinflint; a kind of serpent; a sort of fish: 2, *m.* a sort of greens. [*maticus*. Roxb.).

पत्थरचूर, *m.* a species of plant (*Plectranthus aro-*

पत्थरफोड़, *m.* the woodpecker (*Picus*).

पत्थरबाज़, *m.* one who plays at stone-throwing.

पत्थरबाज़ी, *f.* stone-throwing, playing with stones.

पत्थरवाह, *m* stoning (as a punishment). — *k.* to [stone.

पत्थरा, *m.* a kind of stone weight.

पत्थराओ / **पत्थराव** } *m.* stoning, the act of stoning.

पत्थरी, *f.* gravel, grit; the flint of a musket; stone in the bladder, calculus; a gizzard.

पत्थरैल / **पत्थरैला** } stony, rocky.

पत्थल, a common corruption of **पत्थर**, *q.v.*

पत्नि / **पत्नी** } *f.* (*m.* **पति**) a wife.

पत्नीभाग, *m.* the division of property among a [man's widows.

पत्यालय, *m.* a husband's house.

पत्र, *m.* the wing of a bird, the feather of an arrow; any vehicle, *e. g.* a horse, camel, car, etc.: a leaf, the leaf of the *Laurus cassia*, a leaf prepared for writing on, paper, a letter, epistle, document, deed, leaf of a book, gold leaf, etc., a thin piece of metal; lines and signs painted on the face by means of musk and other fragrant substances.

पत्रंग, *m.* red sanders (*Pterocarpus santalinus*).

पत्रक, *m.* (*f.* ikī) a substitute for **पत्र** when the latter element of a compound adjective.

पत्रगुप्त, *m.* a species of Euphorbia.

पत्रनाड़िका, *f.* the fibre or vein of a leaf. [*sum*).

पत्रपुष्प, *m.* a red sort of basil-plant (*Ocymum pilo-*

पत्रपुष्पक, *m.* a kind of birch from the bark of which hukkā-snakes, etc. are made. [gilding, etc.

पत्ररंजन, *m.* the embellishing a page, illuminating,

पत्रशिरा, *f.* the vein or fibre of a leaf.

पत्रा, *m.* an almanac, ephemeral, calendar.

पत्रांक, *m.* the figure or number of the page of a book, paging.

पत्रांग, *m.* red sanders (*Pterocarpus santalinus*); red or sappan-wood (*Caesalpinia sappan*); the *bhojpatra*-tree; a kind of birch. [letter.

पत्रिका, *f.* a leaf, written leaf, page, document,

पत्री, 1, *f.* (dim. of **पत्र**) a note, epistle, letter: 2, *m.* (*f.* inī) a bird, an arrow: a person riding on any vehicle; a mountain: *lit.* winged, feathered.

पत्रोत्तर, *m.* a reply to an epistle.

पत्रोपस्कर, *m.* a certain tree (*Cassia esculenta*).

पत्रोर्णा, *m.* a certain plant (*Bignonia Indica*).

पत्वन्ती, a contraction of **पतिवन्ती**, *q.v.*

पथ, *m.* a way, path, road, highway.

पथख़र्च, *m.* travelling-expenses; provisions for a journey. [conductor: *lit.* adj. shewing the way.

पथदर्शक, *m.* (*f.* ikā) a guide, director, leader,

पथन, (1) = **पथ**, *q.v.*: 2, a Braj pl. of **पथ**. See **न**, 6.

पथपथ, an intensive redupl. of **पथ**, *q.v.*

पथर; for words beginning thus, see under the more proper form **पत्थर**. [(as a boil).

पथराना, *a. int.* to petrify, indurate, become hard

पथरीला / **पथरैला** } *more prop.* **पत्थरैल**, *q.v.*

पथरोधक, *m.* (*f.* ikā) one who guards a way.

पथिक, *m.* (*f.* ā *or* ī) a traveller, wayfarer, passenger, sojourner: a guide, one who knows the way.

पथिकगृह = **पथिकाश्रय**, *q.v.*

पथिकनि, a Braj pl. of **पथिक**. See **नि**, 2 (2).

पथिकहीन, deserted, unfrequented (as a road or [caravansary).

पथिका = **पथिकी**, *q.v.*

पथिकाश्रय, *m.* a refuge for travellers, haltingplace. caravansary, inn, waitingplace.

पथिकी, *f.* (*m.* **पथिक**) a female traveller.

पथिगृह = **पथिकाश्रय**, *q. v.*

पथिद्रुम, *m.* a sort of khyar (*Mimosa alba*). [hell.

पथिन, *m.* a road, way; *pr. n.* one of the divisions of

पथ्य, *m.* (*f.* ā) belonging to a road; furthering, helpful, agreeing with, proper, fit, suitable. Applied chiefly medically, with reference to regimen, diet, etc.

पथ्या, *f.* yellow myrobalan (*Terminalia chebula*); a species of metre in Sanskrit poetry.

पद, *m.* a foot; a step, footstep, footprint, trace, mark, sign; an abode, home; rank, status, station, place, dignity, character, office; a word, (in Gram.) an inflected word (whether with or without its termination); a foot, verse, or line of a stanza; (in Law) a head, title, or topic of legal or judicial proceedings.

पदक, *m.* a step; an office: an ornament of the neck; a badge; a flat plate of gold or other metal.

पदकमल, *m.* an epithet of the feet of any venerated personage or deity.

पदक्रम, *m.* step, pace.

पदचर, *m.* (*f.* ā) one who goes on foot.

पदचारी, (*f.* iṇī) = **पदचर**, *q.v.*

पदचिह्न, *m.* a footprint.

पदच्युत, *m.* (*f.* ā) fallen from station or dignity, disgraced.—*k.* to remove from office, degrade.

पदज, *m.* (*f.* ā) foot-born, *i.e.* a Shoodra.

पदतल, *m.* the sole of the foot.

पदत्रान, *m.* a shoe or slipper.

पदना, *m.* (*f.* ī) = **पदोड़ा**, *q.v.*

पदपंकज, 1, *m.* a lotus-like foot: 2, *adj.* possessing a lotus-like foot.

पदपीठा, *m.* a footstool.

पदबि / **पदबी** } *more prop.* **पदवी**, *q.v.*

पदभंजन, *m.* explanation of obscure or obsolete words, etymology.

पदम, *more prop.* **पद्म**, *q.v.*

पदमन / **पदमनी** / **पदमिन** / **पदमोनि** } *more prop.* **पद्मिनी**, *q.v.*

पदर, bottom, beneath.

पदवी, *f.* a road, way, path; station, rank, status, dignity, character, title, degree, titular name, surname, patronymic; situation, site, place.

पदवीवाचक, *adj.* (in Gram.) indicating status or title, patronymic.

पदांक, *m.* a footprint, vestige.

पदाजि / **पदात** / **पदाति** } = **पदातिक**, *q.v.*

पदातिक, *m.* (*f.* ā *or* ī) a foot-soldier, pedestrian, footman, peon; (in Chess) a pawn.

पदाती, *m.* (*f.* inī) a foot-soldier.

पदादपि (*Rām.*) = **पदसे भी**.

पदाना, *t.* to cause to break wind; *met.* to frighten, put to flight.

पदाभिलाषी, *m.* (*f.* iṇī) an aspirant, candidate: *lit.* wishful of office.

पदाभिषिक्त, *m.* (*f.* ā) one who is anointed or installed in rank or office, especially in the regal dignity.

पदारथ, *more prop.* **पदार्थ**, *q.v.*

पदार्घ, *more prop.* **पदार्घ्य**, *q.v.*

पदार्घ्य, *m.* an offering of curds, honey, etc. to a guest or to a Brāhmaṇ.

पदार्थ, *m.* the meaning of a word or sentence: a thing, substance, substantial or material form of being; a good, rarity, blessing, a delicacy, exquisite food; a category or predicament in logic, of which, according to the Sāṅkhya system, there are six, *viz.* substance, quality, action, community or identity, particularity or variety, and aggregation or intimate relation; some add a seventh, *viz.* annihilation or nonentity: another enumeration gives sixteen.

पदार्पण, *m.* appointment to office.

पदास, *f.* the inclination to break wind, flatulency.

पदासन, *m.* a footstool.

पदासना; see (1) **पदासन** (2) **प्रार्थना**.

पदासा, *m.* (*f.* ī) flatulent.

पदिक, *adj.* going on foot, pedestrian; (in Pros.) one *pad* long; containing only one division: *hence* (1) *m.* (*f.* ā) a footman, footsoldier (2) *m.* the point of the foot.

पदिकहारा, *m.* (*f.* ī) a footman, pedestrian.

पदी, *f.* the tonnage or measurement of boats or ships.

पदीद, open, public, clear, evident, manifest, conspicuous, visible.

पदीम, *more prop.* **प्रदीप**, *q.v.*

पदुम; for words beginning thus, see under the form **पद्म**.

पदोड़ा, *m.* (*f.* ī) having the quality of breaking wind; *met.* a coward.

पदोदक, *m.* water in which a Brāhmaṇ's feet have been washed, and which is drunk by Hindoo devotees as an act of religious merit.

पद्धी, *f.* a way, path, alley.

पद्दू = **पदोड़ा**, *q.v.*

पद्धति, *f.* = **पद्धती**, *q.v.*

पद्धती, *f.* a road, way, path; a line, row, range; a guide, the designation of a class of literary compositions, a ritual, manual, treatise on any particular science, a work on any act or ceremony detailing the mode of its performance and collecting the texts connected with it; a title, surname, family name; manner, custom.

पद्धरी, *f.* (in Pros.) a species of metre.

पद्म, *m.* the lotus (*Nelumbium speciosum* or *Prunus cerasus*), it is often confounded with the water-lily (*Nymphaea*); an ornament; marks or moles on the body, a spot, coloured marks on the face and trunk of an elephant; a lotus-like form of array; a certain sitting-posture when absorbed in meditation: *pr. n.* (1) of one of Kuver's treasures (see *Nidhi*) (2) of a *Nāg*: a certain fragrant plant; a certain large number, either 1, (according to the Shāstras) ten billions; or 2, (according to the *Dastūr-ul-'amal* or royal ordinances of Akbar) one thousand billions; or 3, (Colebr. Alg. p. 4) one thousand millions.

पद्मक, *m.* an army arrayed in the form of a lotus-flower; a certain tree (*Costus speciosus* or *Arabicus*) and its wood: a kind of leprosy.

पद्मकाष्ठ, *m.* a certain fragrant wood used in medicine, and described as cooling and tonic.

पद्मकी, *m.* the *bhojpatra* or birch-tree. The bark is used for writing on, wrapping up shawls, etc.

पद्मकेल, *f.* play with lotuses.

पद्मगंध, *m.* (poet.) the pollen of the feet.

पद्मगर्भ, *m.* an epithet of Brahmā; *lit.* the lotus-born.

पद्मचारिणी, *f.* the small tree *Hibiscus mutabilis*.

पद्मदर्शन, *m.* resin of the *Pinus longifolia*.

पद्मनी, *more prop.* **पद्मिनी**, *q.v.*

पद्मपत्र, *m.* a sort of costus (*C. speciosus*).

पद्मपुराण, *m. pr. n.* (see **पुराण**) one of the Purāṇs of the Hindoos.

पद्ममुखी, *f.* a short of prickly nightshade.

पद्मराग, *m.* a ruby; *lit.* lotus-coloured.

पद्मवर्णक, *m.* a sort of costus (*C. speciosus*)

पद्मा, *f.* 1, the name of two plants (1) *Hibiscus mutabilis* (2) *Clerodendrum siphonanthus*: 2, an epithet (1) of Lakshmee (2) of Shree.

पद्माकर, *m.* a large deep pond in which the lotus grows (or may grow).

पद्माट, *m.* a sort of cassia (*C. tora*).

पद्मालया, *f.* an epithet of Lakshmee; *lit.* whose dwelling is in the lotus-flower.

पद्मावत = **पद्मावती**, *q.v.*

पद्मावती, *f. pr. n.* (1) of a celebrated princess whose adventures are related in a romance entitled Padmāvatī (2) of Lakshmee (3) of the wife of the sage Jaratkāru (4) of the main stream of the Ganges between the Kāsimbāzār river and the sea: *lit.* adj. abounding in lotus-flowers.

पद्मासन, *m.* a seat consisting of a lotus-flower, a seat made in the shape of a lotus (*esp.* one on which idols are placed); a certain posture of Hindoo ascetics when absorbed in religious meditation, in which they sit with the thighs crossed, one hand resting on the left thigh and the other held up with the thumb upon the heart,—the eyes being concentrated on the tip of the nose.

पद्मिनी, *f.* a lotus (*Nelumbium speciosum*), a multitude of lotuses, a lake abounding in lotuses; a sort of witchcraft; a woman of the first or most excellent of the four classes into which womankind is divided according to the Hindoos. The four classes are these, *viz.* Padminī, Chitriṇī, Sankhinī, and Hastinī.

पद्मोत्तर, *m.* safflower.

पद्य, *m.* metre, verse, poetry.

पधारना, *a. int.* to take leave, set out, depart, go away, proceed; to arrive.

पन; 1, a termination forming substantives masculine by being added to substantives and adjectives. The words so formed denote the abstract quality of the words to which this particle is added, and express either (1) condition, state (2) time of life, or (3) occupation: they thus correspond to the English words which end in 'hood,' 'ship,' 'ness'; *e. g.* manhood, chancellorship, boyishness. It is sometimes displaced by its modifications **पना** and **पा**; but these, though by no means infrequent, are less frequent than **पन**, and do not affect the gender. It should be observed that a feminine form, **पनी**, is also (but very rarely) used; *e.g.* **लुच्चपनी**: 2, this form (as may be observed in several of the words below, which begin with it) is, when found as the first element in a compound word, a contraction (1) of **पान**, betel (2) of **पानीय**, appertaining to water (3) a modification of the Sanskrit root **पण**, buying, trading: 3, this form is a corruption of the word **पण**, a bet; a vow, etc.

पनकपड़ा, *m.* soft cloth wetted for application to a wound or sore.

पनकुकरी, *f.* }
पनकुकड़ी, *f.* } a water-fowl.
पनकौआ, *m.* }

पनग, *more prop.* **पन्नग**, *q. v.*

पनगाधा, *m.* a field covered and saturated with water.

पनगोटी, *f.* chicken-pox.

पनघट, *m.* a passage to a river, river-stairs, a quay for drawing water.

पनघटा }
पनघाट } *more prop.* **पनघट**, *q. v.*

पनच, *f.* a bowstring.

पनचक्की, *f.* a water-mill.

पनचोरा, *m.* an earthen vessel with a narrow neck and a hole in the bottom. It is used by followers of Aristotle to illustrate the *horror vacui.* When it is filled with water, and the mouth is stopped, no water flows from the hole below till the hand, or whatever stopped the mouth, be removed.

पनछी = **पंछी** = **पच्छी**, *q. v.*

पनडुब्बी, *f.* a water-fowl, the coot, the diver.

पनतव्वा = **पन्तवा**, *q.v.*

पनपना, *a. int.* to commence increasing in bulk (as a man, a tree, etc.); to prosper, flourish, thrive, shoot, grow, be refreshed or restored.

पनपनाहट, *f.* the whizzing of an arrow or shot.

पनपाना, *t.* to cause to flourish, to promote another's prosperity, to refresh (little used).

पनबट्टा }
पनभट्टा } *m.* a betel-box.

पनभत्ता, *m.* a mixture of water and boiled rice for drinking.

पनमल्ला, *m.* a betel-garden.

पनमार, a soil submerged so as to be incapable of cultivation.

पनव (*Rām.*) = **ढोल**, *q.v.*

पनवाड़ी }
पनवारी } *f.* a betel-garden.

पनवारा, *m.* a plate or dish made of leaves (to eat from).

पनस, *m.* the bread-fruit or Jak-tree (*Artocarpus integrifolia*): a kind of snake.

पनसल्ला, *f. m.* (?) a stand where water is provided for passengers, wateringplace.

पनसा, 1, *m.* (*f.* ī) insipid; *lit.* water-like: 2, *f.* a pustule, malady, pustular and phlegmonoid inflammation of the skin or external organs.

पनसारहट्टा, *m.* a locality where there are many druggists' shops.

पनसारी, *m.* (*f.* iṇī) a vendor of drugs, herbs, species, groceries, etc., a spicer, druggist, apothecary.

पनसाल, *m.* }
पनसाला, *f.* } = **पनसल्ला**, *q. v.*

पनसोइ }
पनसोई } *f.* a kind of small boat.

पनहरा, *m.* (*f.* in *or* ī) a man carrying waterpots on the head.

पनहरिन, *f.* a woman carrying waterpots on the head.

पनहाना, *t.* to cause the milk to come into the udder of animals.

पनहारन }
पनहारनी } *f.* (*m.* **पनहारा**) = **पनहरिन**, *q. v.*

पनहारा, *m.* (*f.* in, ī, n, *or* nī) = **पनहरा**, *q. v.*

पनहारिणी, *f.* (*m.* **पनहारी**) }
पनहारिन, *f.* (*m.* **पनहारा**) } = **पनहरिन**, *q. v.*

पनहारी, 1, *m.* (*f.* iṇī) = **पनहरा**, *q. v.*: 2, *f.* (*m.* **पनहारा**) = **पनहरिन**, *q.v.*

पनहियाई, *m.* (*f.* inī) a person afflicted with the fluor albus.

पनही }
पनहीं } *f.* a slipper.

पना, (*m.*) a modification of **पन**, *q.v.* [of animals.
पनाना, *t.* to cause the milk to come into the udder

पनारा, *m.* / **पनारी**, *f.* / **पनाला**, *m.* } = **पनाली**, *q.v.*

पनाली, *f.* (prop. **प्रणाली**) a drain or pipe by which water runs off from the roof of a house, a conduit, gutter, spout. — *paṛnā*, to become very fat (said of horses).
पनाह, *f.* shade, shelter, protection, asylum, refuge. — *kisise māṅgnā*, to seek protection; to avoid. — *denā*, to afford protection.
पनाही, *f.* = **पनाह**, *q.v.*
पनिघट = **पनघट**, *q.v.* [water-snake.
पनिया, *m.* water: anything that lives in water, a
पनियाना, *t.* to irrigate, water: to yield water.
पनियारा, *m.* (*f.* ī) inundated.
पनियाला, *m.* a kind of fruit (*Flacourtia catafracta*).
पनिहारा, *m.* (*f.* in, ī, n, *or* nī) = **पनहरा**, *q.v.*
पनी, (*f.*) a modification of **पन**, *q.v.*
पनीर, *m.* cheese.
पनीरक, *f.* a young flower-tree.
पनीरमाया, *f.* rennet. [cheesy.
पनीरी, 1, *f.* a young flower-tree: 2, made of cheese,
पनीहा, *m.* (*f.* ī) anything that lives in water, an aquatic, a water-snake.
पनेरी, *f.* a young flowering shrub.
पनोला, land watered after ploughing.
पन्तवा, *m.* a kind of sweetmeat.
पन्तीकोस्त = **पेंपिटकोष्ट**, *q.v.*
पन्थ, *m.* a road, path, way; a religious order, sect.
पन्थकथा, *f.* the special and peculiar teachings of
पन्था, *m.* = **पन्थ**, *q.v.* [any religious sect.
पन्थान, *m. pr. n.* one of the divisions of the infernal regions.
पन्थी, *m.* (*f.* inī) a traveller; the observer of any particular custom or class of opinions, an adherent of any sect or party in religious matters.
पन्द, *m.* advice, admonition, counsel, moral maxim.

पन्दर / **पन्दरह** } *more prop.* **पन्द्रह**, *q.v.*

पन्द्रवारा, *m.* (**पन्द्रह + वार**) a fortnight.
पन्द्रह, fifteen (१५): see **श्रों, वां, वीं, वे, वें**.
पन्द्रहवीं, *f.* the fifteenth day of a half month, *i. e.* the full or the new moon.
पन्धलाना, *t.* to coax, wheedle. [snake-shaped demon.
पन्नग, *m.* (*f.* ā) any reptile, a snake, serpent; a
पन्ना, *m.* a beverage; the upper part of a shoe: an emerald: a leaf. [tinfoil.
पन्नी, 1, *m. pr. n.* a certain tribe of Paṭhāns: 2, *f.*

पपड़ / **पपड़ा** } *m.* a crust, a scale.

पपड़ियाकथ, *f.* a kind of white-coloured *kath* (being the extract of *Mimosa catechu*).
पपड़ी, *f.* a scab, scale, scurf; scales formed by the drying up of moist earth: thin cakes of bread.
पपड़ोला, *m.* (*f.* in *or* ī) scabby, scurfy.
पपनी, *f.* the eyelash.
पपरमास, *m.* the shaddock (*Citrus decumanus*) called also pumpelmose, pumpelmās, pumpelmauz, or pummelo.

पपिहा / **पपीहा** } *m.* the sparrow-hawk (*Falco nisus*).

पपैया, *m.* a kind of child's whistle: the papaw-tree (*Carica papaya*) and its fruit.
पपोटा, *f.* the eyelid.
पबारना, *t.* (*Rām.*) to throw.
पबि, *more prop.* **पवि**, *q.v.*
पम्पा, *f. pr.n.* a certain river in southern India.
पम्पाना = **पन्पाना**, *q.v.*
पम्पापुर, *m. pr. n.* the locality in southern India where the army of the monkeys dwelt during the war between Rām and Rāvaṇ.
पय = **पै**, *q.v.*
पयजेब, *more prop.* **पाएज़ेब**, *q. v.*
पयद, *m.* the female breast or nipple; a cloud: lit. *adj.* yielding milk or water.
पयनिधि, *m.* the ocean; (in Myth.) the ocean of
पयस, *m.* juice, water, milk. [milk.
पयस्या, *f.* a kind of shrub (*Asclepias rosea*); a medicinal kind of moon-plant.
पयस्वल, *m.* (*f.* ā) abounding in milk.
पयस्विनी, *f.* a cow with abundance of milk.
पयादे (*Rām.*) = **पैदल**, *q.v.*
पयान, a contraction (1) of **प्रयाण** (2) of **पायान**, *qq.v.*
पयानक, appertaining to departure or setting out.
पयाना (*Rām.*) = **प्रयाण**, *q.v.*
पयापय = **पैआपै**, *q.v.*
पयाम, *m.* a message, advice, intelligence, news.
पयाम्बर, *m.* a message-bearer, prophet.
पयार, *m.* a species of grass: metre, a measure of verse consisting of two lines.
पयाल, *f.* (*prop.* **पलाल**) straw.
पयोद, *m.* a cloud: *pr. n.* a son of Yadu. [Skand.
पयोदा, *f. pr. n.* one of the Mātṛis attendant on
पयोधर, *m.* a cloud; a woman's breast, an udder: a sort of rush (*Scirpus Kysoor*); a certain fragrant grass (*Cyperus rotundus*).

पयोधस / **पयोधि** } *m.* = **पयोनिधि**, *q.v.*

पयोधिक, *m.* cuttle-fish bone.
पयोनिधि, *m.* the ocean, a cloud, a pond, lake.
पयोमुच, *m.* a cloud.
पयोर, *m.* the *khayar*-tree (*Mimosa catechu*).
पयोव्रत, *m.* the vow of living only on milk for a month, which, with prayer and residence in a cow-house, is an expiation for having received an unsuitable present: the offering milk to Vishṇu and subsist

ing on it for twelve days as act of merit; also for one day or for three days. [Vindhya mountains.

पयोष्णी, *f. pr. n.* a certain river that rises in the

पर; this form is the representative in Hindee of several different originals, and it is to this fact that the great diversity of its meanings is to be attributed. It is constantly liable to be used as the first element in compound words, imparting to them one or other of its many different senses:—1, (Sk. **पर**) *m.* (*f.* ā) an enemy, etc.: *lit.* distant, removed, remote, far, ulterior, being beyond, exceeding, opposite, left or remaining, longest, ancient, other, another, different, strange, alien, foreign, inimical, principal, chief, preëminent, higher, superior, highest, distinguished, greatest, best, subsequent, successive, succeeding, next: 2, *adv.* over, above, through, after, according to, in, at, by, for, of, after the manner of, accordingly: 3, *conj.* but, still, yet, notwithstanding, however, nevertheless: 4, *postp.* (Sk. **उपरि**, Gr. υπερ) on, upon, at: 5, As a suffix in composition it imports the idea of engaged in, occupied with, intent upon, absorbed in, devoted to, filled with, affected with.

परई, (pl. **परईं**) (*Rām.*) = **पड़ेगा**.

परउपकार; for words beginning thus, see under the more proper form **परोपकार**.

परंतु, *more prop.* **परन्तु**, *q.v.*

परंद, *more prop.* **परन्द**, *q.v.*

परंपराय = **परम्पराई**, *q.v.*

परकट, *more* **पर्कट**, *q.v.*

परकना, 1, *more prop.* **परखना**, *q.v.*: 2, *a. int.* to acquire a habit, become habituated.

परकाज, *more prop.* **परकार्य्य**, *q.v.*

परकाजी, *m.* (*f.* ini) a beneficent person, a busybody: *lit.* attentive to the business, concerns, or interests of others.

परकान, *m.* a trunnion.

परकाना, *t.* to habituate, accustom.

परकार्य्य, *m.* the business, concerns, affairs, or interests of another. — *meṅ hāth dālnā*, to intermeddle in the affairs of another.

परकाल = **पर्काल**, *q.v.*

परकाला, *more com.* **पर्काला**, *q.v.*

परकास, *more prop.* **प्रकाश**, *q.v.* [other, hostile.

परकीय, *m.* (*f.* ā) another's, appertaining to an-

परकीया, *f.* another's wife or mistress; a wife who entertains a paramour, an adulteress.

परकोटा, walls of a city.

परक्रिय, *more prop.* **परकीय**, *q.v.* [other's wife.

परक्षेत्र, *m.* another's field, another's body, an-

परख = **परीक्षा**, *q.v.*

परखना, *t.* to test, prove, try, examine, inspect.

परखवाना, *t.* to cause to be tested, etc.

परखाई, *f.* the act of testing, trying, proving, examining, or inspecting; *also*, the price paid for so doing.

परखाना, *t.* (causat. of **परखना**) to cause to test, etc.

परखावनी, *f.* examination, assaying of coin, etc.

परखी, *m.* a banker who examines and approves money, an assayer, tester, inspector, examiner, prover.

परखेरा }
परखैया } = **परखी**, *q.v.*

परग, *m.* a step, footstep, stride.

परगट, *more prop.* **प्रगट**, *q.v.*

परगना, *m.* (*pl.* āt) a lesser division of a country, nearly equal to a barony, the largest division of land in a zamindārī. [lord of a barony.

परगनादार, *m.* the superior officer of a pargana,

परगनावार, according to district (settlement, etc.).

परगाछ, *m.* epidendron.

परगास = **प्रकाश**, *q.v.*

परगासना = **प्रकाशना**, *q.v.*

परगासा = **प्रकाश**, *q.v.*

परगृहवास, *m.* the dwelling in the house of another.

परघट, *more prop.* **प्रगट**, *q.v.*

परघटी = (1) **प्रघटी** (2) **प्रगटता**, *qq.v.*

परचना, *n.* to be tried, etc.; to be introduced, be made acquainted.

परचर in Chand = **प्रचुर**, *q.v.*

परचा, 1, = **परीक्षा**, *q.v.*: 2, *m.* demonstration, proof.

परचाना = **पर्चाना**, *q.v.*

परचार, *more prop.* **प्रचार**, *q.v.*

परचारी, *more prop.* **प्रचारी**, *q.v.*

परचूनिया = **पर्चूनिया**, *q.v.*

परचूनी = **पर्चूनी**, *q.v.*

परचै, a dialectic form = **परिचय**, *q.v.*

परछांहीं (*Rām.*) = **पर्छाईं**, *q.v.*

परछती = **पर्छत्ती**, *q.v.*

परछना, *t.* to move a lamp or candle over the heads of a bride and bridegroom, drive away evil spirits, propitiate good spirits; to kindle a fire.

परछाई }
परछाईं }
परछां }
परछांई } = **पर्छाईं**, *q.v.*
परछांवां }
परछाहीं }

[in another.

परछिद्र, *m.* 1, = **छन्दोछिद्र**, *q.v.*: 2, a fault or defect

परज, *m.* (*f.* ā) a stranger; an adopted child: *lit.* born of another; fostered by a stranger.

परजंक, *more prop.* **पर्य्यंक**, *q.v.*

परजंत = **पर्यन्त**, *q.v.*

परजटन }
परजतन } *more prop.* **पर्य्यटन**, *q.v.*

परजन्त = **पर्यन्त**, *q.v.*

परजवट, *m.* quit-rent, tax.

परजा, 1, *more prop.* **प्रजा**; 2, *f.* (*m.* **परज**) a female stranger; an adopted female.

परजात, *m.* (*f.* ā) = **परज**, *q.v.*

परजाति, *f.* another genus or caste.

परजित, *m.* (*f.* ā) conquered, vanquished, subdued.

परठनें (in Chand) = to offer, present, consecrate.

परत, *m.* a fold, plait, ply, layer, crust, incrustation, stratum.

परतछ, a corruption of **प्रत्यच्छ**, *q.v.*

परतन्त्र, *m.* (*f.* ī) subject to another, dependent.

परतन्त्रत्व, *m* (*f.* tā) dependence, subjection.

परतम, *m.* (*f.* ā) greatest, supreme.

परतमालन, *more prop.* **प्रतिपालन**, *q.v.*

परतमा, *more prop.* **प्रतिमा**, *q.v.*

परतल, *m. f.* ? the baggage of a horseman carried all on one bullock or pony (*ṭaṭṭū*). — *kā ṭaṭṭū*, a pack-horse, bat-horse.

परतला, *m.* a sword-belt, shoulder-belt.

परता, *m.* a reel (for winding thread).

परताप, *more prop.* **प्रताप**, *q.v.*

परताल, remeasurement of a field.

परतालजरीब = **परताल**, *q.v.*

परतिछ, a corruption of **प्रत्यच्छ**, *q.v.*

परतित in Chand = (1) **प्रतीत** (2) **प्रतीति**, *qq.v.*

परतियगामी, *m.* an adulterer ; lit. *adj.* having recourse to the wife of another.

परतिरिया = **परस्त्री**, *q.v.*

परती, *f.* waste or uncultivated land.

परतीत, *more prop.* (1) **प्रतीत** (2) **प्रतीति**, *qq.v.*

परतीति / **परतीती** } *more prop.* **प्रतीति**, *q.v.*

परत्र, elsewhere ; in another world.

परत्रिया = **परस्त्री**, *q.v.*

परदच्छिन, *more prop.* **प्रदक्षिण**, *q.v.*

परदा, a colloquial form = **पर्दा**, *q.v.*

परदाद, a contraction of **परदादा** = **पर्दादा**, *q.v.*

परदादा, *m.* (*f.* ī) = **पर्दादा**, *q.v.*

परदार, *f.* another's wife.

परदारगमन, *m.* adulterous intercourse.

परदारगामी, *m.* an adulterer ; lit. *adj.* having recourse to the wife of another.

परदुःख, *m.* the trouble of another.

परदुःखनिवारण, *m.* (*f.* ā *or* ī) one who wards off trouble from another.

परदुमन, *more prop.* **प्रद्युम्न**, *q.v.*

परदूषन, *m.* the guilt or crime of another.

परदेश, *m.* a foreign country : *adj.* in a foreign land, abroad, in another country.

परदेशी, *m.*(*f.* inī) a foreigner ; one residing abroad: *lit.* appertaining to another country, foreign, exotic.

परदोष, *m.* another's fault or crime.

परदोषकीर्त्तन, *m.* obloquy, calumny, slander.

परद्रव्य, *m.* another's property.

परद्रोहिता, *more com.* **परद्रोही**, *q.v.*

परद्रोही, *m.* (*f.* inī) tyrannizing over others, hurting or injuring others, oppressive, tyrannical.

परद्वेष, *m.* hostility towards another.

परद्वेषी, *m.* (*f.* iṇī) inimical, hostile, adverse.

परधन, *m.* another's wealth or property.

परधनास्वाधनसुख, *m.* a feeding luxuriously at another's expense.

परधर्म्म, *m.* another's duty or business, the occupation of another caste.

परधर्म्मग्रहण, *m.* the adopting another religion, changing one's religion.

परधर्म्मग्राही, *m.* (*f.* iṇī) *adj.* adopting another religion.

परधर्म्मसहिष्णुता, *f.* (°त्व) religious toleration.

परधान / **परधाना** } *more prop.* **प्रधान**, *q.v.*

परधामा, *m.* an epithet of the Supreme (who occupies the chief or highest dwelling).

परन, 1, *more prop.* **प्रण**, *q.v.* : 2, *f.* a very quick time in music.

परना, 1, (*Rām.*) = **पर्ण**, *q.v.* : 2, see (1) **पड़ना** (2) **पढ़ना**.

परनाना, *m.* (*f.* ī) a great-grandparent (by the mother's side).

परनानीं, *t.* to marry (said of the man). (*Chand.*)

परनाम (*Rām.*) = **प्रणाम**, *q.v.*

परनामा, a poet. form of **प्रणाम**, *q.v.*

परनारी, *f.* another woman, another's wife.

परनाला, *m.* / **परनाली**, *f.* } = **प्रणाल**, *q.v.*

परनि = **परनी**, *q.v.*

परनिन्दा, *f.* abuse or ridicule of others, slander, calumny.

परनिये, (**परनानीं**) having married. (*Chand.*)

परनी, *f.* (**परनानीं**) a bride ; a maiden. (*Chand.*)

परनीये = **परनिये**, *q.v.*

परन्तु, but, yet, on the other hand, still, notwithstanding, however ; afterwards, also.

परन्त्र, subservient, dependent, obedient.

परन्द, *m.* a bird : *lit.* winged, flying, fleet. — *ho jānā*, to move with great rapidity.

परपंच ; for words beginning thus, see under the form **प्रपंच**.

परपट, *more prop.* **पर्पट**, *q.v.*

परपद, *m.* 1, = **परमपद**, *q.v.* : 2, high rank or status, eminence.

परपराना, *a. int.* to smart.

परपराहट, *f* smart ; acrimony.

परपरिग्रह, *m.* the family or dependents of another.

परपाता, *m.* (*f.* trī) an excellent protector : a benefactor.

परपुरुष, *m.* a gallant, paramour, stranger ; *lit.* another man (than her own husband), or another's man.

परपुष्ट, (see **परभृत**) *m.* (*f.* ā) an epithet of the Indian cuckoo ; *lit.* nourished by another.

परपुष्टा, *f.* (*m.* **परपुष्ट**) a harlot ; the female kokil ; a parasitical plant.

परपूरण, *m.* (*f.* ī) brimful. [*lit.* another's formerly.

परपूर्व्वा, *f.* a woman who has been married again.

परपैठ, *m.* a duplicate of a bill of exchange.

परपोता / **परपोत्रा** } *m.* (*f.* ī) *more prop.* **प्रपौत्र**, *q.v.*

परब, *more prop.* **पर्व**, *q.v.*

परबल, *more prop.* **प्रबल**, *q.v.*

परबस ; for words beginning thus, see under the form **परवश**.

परब्रह्म, *m.* the Supreme Being.

परभाग, *m.* excellence, supremacy, superior merit ; good fortune, prosperity ; the last, residue, remainder.

परभात (*Rām.*) = **प्रभात**, *q.v.*

परभूमि, *f.* a foreign land, enemy's country.

परभूषण, *m.* an excellent ornament : another's ornament.

परभृत, *m.* (*f.* ā) the Indian cuckoo (which is supposed to leave its eggs in the nest of the crow to be hatched) ; the crow : *lit.* adj. nourishing another ; cherished by another, fostered, adopted.

परम, (Sk. superl. of **पर**) *m.* (*f.* ā) most excellent, highest, chief, extreme, supreme, principal, best.

परमगत = **परमगति**, *q.v.*

परमगति, *f.* the highest attainment or condition, *i. e.* emancipation and absorption, final happiness, heavenly bliss : a chief object or refuge (as, a protector, a god).

परमज्ञान, *m.* the highest wisdom : the knowledge of the Highest, *i. e.* God.

परमत, *m.* a different opinion or doctrine.

परमधन्य, *m.* an epithet of the ever-blessed God ; *lit.* blessed in the highest sense.

परमधाम, *m.* the heavenly paradise.

परमनागरी, *f.* an epithet of Rādhā : *lit.* the chief of courtesans.

परमनाश, *m.* complete destruction, utter ruin ; the ruin of one's highest interests.

परमपद = **परम्पद**, *q.v.*

परमपदार्थ, *m.* the chief thing, *i. e.* salvation (the attainment of emancipation from the necessity of further transmigration).

परमपावन, *m.* an epithet of God or of any river or deity by whom spiritual purification is effected.

परमपुरुष, *m.* the Supreme Spirit.

परमपुरुषार्थ = **परमपदार्थ**, *q.v.*

परमप्रताप, *m.* the highest degree of splendour of effulgence.

परमप्रतापी, *m.* (*f.* inī) *adj.* possessing the highest splendour or glory.

परमभक्त, *m.* (*f.* ā) a very pious person, a fervent devotee, a chief devotee.

परमराज, *m.* any supreme monarch, emperor.

परमर्षि, *m.* any distinguished saint-sage, a saint-sage of the first rank.

परमल, *more prop.* **परिमल**, *q. v.*

परमलोचा, *f. pr. n.* a certain Apsarā.

परमसुख, *m.* the highest happiness, salvation.

परमसुखदायक, *m.* (*f.* ikā) one who bestows the highest happiness or salvation.

परमहंस, *m.* an ascetic of the highest order, who has subdued all his senses by abstract meditation.

परमा, 1, *f.* ; see **परम** : 2, = **परमेव**, *q.v.*

परमागति, *f.* the proceeding to heaven and final beatitude ; *lit.* the supreme pathway.

परमाणु, *m.* an atom, the invisible base of all aggregate bodies (thirty of them are supposed to form a mote in a sunbeam) ; the lowest measure of weight ; a certain measure of time, the sun's passage past an atom of matter.

परमाणुता, *f.* the condition of an atom : an infinitely short space of time.

परमात्मा, *m.* the Supreme Spirit (*esp.* considered as the all-embracing, all-pervading, all-quickening soul of the universe).

परमात्मापुरुष = **परमात्मा**, *q. v.*

परमाद्वैत, *m.* pure Unitarianism.

परमान (*Rām.*) = **प्रमाण**, *q. v.*

परमानन, *m.* an epithet of the sun ; *lit.* having a large face.

परमानन्द, *m.* great pleasure, high delight, crowning joy.

परमाना (*Rām.*) = **प्रमाण**, *q. v.*

परमान्न, *m.* a kind of oblation to progenitors or to deities, consisting of rice boiled with milk and sugar.

परमाभूषण, *m.* an excellent ornament, splendid attire.

परमायुः, *m f.* the longest period of life either in men or in brutes.

परमार्थ, *m.* the most sublime truth, the whole truth, the first pursuit, the best end, the best sense, any excellent or important aim or object, spiritual knowledge, virtue, merit : an epithet of the Supreme Being.

परमार्थवादी, *m.* (*f.* inī) one who teaches **परमार्थ**, *q. v.*

परमार्थी, in pursuit of the highest purpose ; hence, *m.* (*f.* inī) a religious or virtuous person.

परमित, *more prop.* **परिमिति**, *q. v.*

परमितव्यय = **परिमितव्यय**, *q. v.*

परमिति, *more prop.* **परिमिति**, *q. v.*

परमिलू, *f.* a kind of dance.

परमेश्री } *more prop.* **प्रमेह**, *q. v.*
परमेव }

परमेश = **परमेश्वर**, *q. v.*

परमेशा = **परमेश्वरी**, *q. v.*

परमेश्वर, *m. pr. n.* (*f.* ī) the Supreme Lord, the Almighty ; also (sometimes) Shiv.

परमेश्वराय, (*poet.*) the Sk. dat. of **परमेश्वर**, *q.v.*

परमेश्वरी, *f.* an epithet applied to Durgā or Devī by her worshippers ; *lit.* the supreme goddess, or the consort of the supreme lord, *i. e.* of Shiv.

परमेश्वरीय, appertaining to **परमेश्वर**, *q. v.*

परमेष्ठी, *m.* an epithet of the Supreme Being ; *lit.* situated in the highest.

परम्पद, *m.* high rank or status, eminence ; final happiness, eternal felicity, heaven.

परम्पर, *m.* (*f.* ā) a great great-grandchild ; *lit.* one after another, successive, continuous, traditionary, hereditary, propagated from one to another or from father to son.

परम्परा, *f.* (*m.* **परम्पर**) a great great-granddaughter : an uninterrupted succession, regular series, continuous arrangement, chain, method, order, lineage, race, tradition.

परम्पराई, *f.* tradition, that which comes down from ancient times.

परम्परीण, come by inheritance or by descent, hereditary, traditional.

परव, *m.* a kind of potherb (*Eclipta prostrata*).

परलय, *more prop.* **प्रलय**, *q.v.*

परला, *m.* (*f.* ī) appertaining to the other side, [beyond.

परले, *more prop.* **प्रलय**, *q.v.*

परलोक, *m. pr. n.* the other world, the future state, hereafter; the heavenly paradise.

परलोकगम, *m.* a going to the other state, *i. e.* dying, death.

परलोकगमन = परलोकगम, *q.v.*

परलोकगामी, *m.*(*f.* inī) *adj.* going to the other state, [dying.

परव = पर्व, *q.v.*

परवत, *more prop.* **पर्वत**, *q.v.*

परवर, a dialectic form of **पलवल**, *q.v.*

परवर्दिगार, *m.* a cherisher (an epithet of the [Deity).

परवरिश, *f.* breeding, fostering, rearing, patronizing, protection, education.

परवल, *m.* the plant *Trichosanthes dioica*, Roxb.

परवश, *m.* (*f.* ā) dependent on another, under authority, dependent, subservient, precarious.

परवशी, *m.* (*f.* inī) = **परवश**, *q.v.*

परवश्यता, *f.* } dependence on another.
परवश्यत्व, *m.* }

परवस, *more prop.* **परवश**, *q.v.*

परवा, *f.* care, concern, anxiety, vexation; desire, affection, inclination, concupiscence; rest, quiet. *Kuchh—nahīn* (vulg. *kuchh parwānī*) no matter, it is of no consequence.

परवान, *m.* the yard of a sail. — *chaṛhnā*, to grow up (a phrase peculiar to females).

परवानगी, *f.* order, command, permission, leave.

परवाना, *m.* a grant or letter under a great seal from any man of power to a dependent; an order, pass, licence, leave, command, warrant, precept; a butterfly, moth. — *kisikā honā*, to be desperately in love with anyone (the allusion being to the moth and the candle).

परवानी, 1, *more prop.* **परवानगी**, *q.v.*: 2, see **परवा**.

परवार; see **परिवार**.

परवाह; see **परवा** and **प्रवाह**.

परवेश
परवेशा } *more prop.* **प्रवेश**, *q.v.*
परवेस

परश, *m.* a kind of gem: touch.

परशाद, *more prop.* **प्रसाद**, *q.v.*

परशु, *m.* an axe, hatchet, battle-axe.

परशुराम, *m. pr. n.* (see **अवतार; राम**) a certain hero and demigod, the first of the three renowned Rāms and the sixth *avatār* of Vishṇu. He is said to have been the son of the sage Jamadagni and contemporary of the principal Rām, the son of Dasharath: he is also sometimes called Jāmadagni, after his father. Parashurām, or Rām of the battle-axe, is said to have appeared in the world for the purpose of repressing the tyranny of the Kshatriyas and punishing their violence. Reṇukā, the mother of Parashurām, was interrupted while bringing water from the river, by Kārtaveerjārjun, a prince of the Kshatriyas, who was sporting in the water with his thousand wives, for which Jamadagni, her husband, cursed him. The Kshatriya prince killed Jamadagni, whereupon Parashurām vowed that he would not leave a Kshatriya on the face of the earth. He is reported to have extirpated them twenty-one times,—the women with child producing each time a new race. It is said that there have been no real Kshatriyas since that time,—those so called being Varnasankars (of spurious or mixed breed). Parashurām and his feats appear to typify the race of Brāhmaṇs and their contests with the Kshatriyas.

परश्वस, the day after tomorrow.

परस, 1, *m.* (prop. **स्पर्श**) touch: 2, = **पारसपत्थर**, *q.v.*

परसना, *t.* to touch: to distribute (?).

परसम्बन्ध, *m.* relation to or connexion with another.

परसम्बन्धी, *m* (*f.* inī) appertaining to another, belonging to another.

परसराम (*colloquial*) = **परशुराम**, *q.v.*

परसि (*Rām.*) = **परसके** (**परसना**).

परसिया, *m.* a reaping-hook, sickle.

परसु, *more prop.* **परशु**, *q.v.*

परसुधर (*Rām.*) = **परशुराम**, *q.v.*

परसुराम, *more prop.* **परशुराम**, *q.v.*

परसूत, *more prop.* **प्रसूत**, 1, *q.v.*

परसों, the day before yesterday, the day after tomorrow.

परस्त, (in comp.) an adorer, worshipper: *lit.* devoted to, worshipping, adoring.

परस्ता, *m.* any object of worship.

परस्तार, obedient, submission: *hence*, an adorer, worshipper, servant, slave.

परस्तिश, *f.* the act of worshipping, worship, devotion.

परस्ती, *f.* (only in comp.) worship, adoration.

परस्त्री, *f.* another's wife.

परस्त्रीगमन, *m.* unlawful intercourse with the wife of another, adultery.

परस्त्रीगामी, *adj.* having recourse to the wife of another: hence, *m.* an adulterer.

परस्त्रीपक्ष्या }
परस्त्रीप्रसंग } = **परस्त्रीगमन**, *q.v.*

परस्पर, *m.* (*f.* ā) each other, mutual, reciprocal, interchanging: *adv.* mutually, reciprocally.

परस्परयुद्ध, *m.* civil war, feud.

परस्परानुमति, *f.* mutual concurrence.

परस्परोपकार, *m.* mutual assistance, offensive and defensive alliance.

परस्परोपकारी, *m.* (*f.* iṇī) an ally, associate, helper.

परस्मैपद, *m.* (in Sk. Gram.) the transitive form of a verb, the active voice; *lit.* word directed to another.

परस्वार्थ, *m.* the welfare of another; beneficence, benevolence.

परस्वार्थी, benevolent: hence, *m.* (*f.* inī) a benevolent person.

परहिंसा, *f.* inquiry of others.

परहित, profitable to another, contributing to another's wellbeing, friendly, benevolent.

परहेज़, *m.* continence, control of the passions, abstinence, forbearance. — *k.* to control the passions, abstain, observe a regimen.

परहेज़गार, *m.* one who controls himself.

परहेज़गारी, *f.* self-control, abstinence.

परा, 1, *f.* see **पर**: 2, an inseparable preposition signifying away, over, on, inverted, reaction, wrong, back, sideward, backward, return, reverse, retreat, defeat, superiority: 3, *m.* a company, body of troops, rank, file, row.

पराइ, *more prop.* **पराई**, *q. v.*

पराई, *f.* (*m.* **पराया**) another's.

पराए, the masc. infl. form of **पराया**, *q.v.*

परांठा, *m.* (see **पराग**) cake; a kind of paste.

परांमुख, *m.* (*f.* ī) having the face turned away, averse to, disinclined.

परांमुखत्व, *m.* (*f.* tā) the conditionof having one's face averted, aversion, disinclination.

पराक, *m.* a sacrificial sword or scimetar; a kind of penance practised with a view to expiation, consisting in the observance of a fast for twelve days and nights, keeping the mind attentive and the organs subdued.

पराक्काल, *more prop.* **प्राक्काल**, *q.v.*

पराक्रम, *m.* prowess, exertion, strength, power, ability, valour. [courage.

पराक्रमवन्त, *m.* (*f.* vatī) endowed with power or

पराक्रमी, *m.* (*f.* inī) powerful, strong, valiant, bold.

पराग, *m.* the pollen or farina of a flower, any scented powder, dust, a fragrant powder used after bathing: an eclipse: *pr. n.* a certain mountain.

परागन्वगी, *f.* dispersion, defeat.

परागा (*Rām.*) = **पराग**, *q.v.*

पराचित, *m.* (from **प्रायश्चित्त**) a fine or penance imposed on religious occasions as the price of absolution; expiation, atonement.

पराचीन, 1, a corruption of **प्राचीन**, *q.v.*: 2, turned away, averting the face, not minding: being beyond.

पराजय, *m.* a being deprived of, loss, discomfiture, defeat, overthrow, victory; being cast on a trial.

पराजयकर्त्ता, *m.* (*f.* trī) } a victor.
पराजयकारक, *m.* (*f.* ikā) }

पराजयमान, *m.* (*f.* matī) one who has been defeated (especially in a law-suit): *lit.* overcome.

पराजयी, *m.* (*f.* inī) = **पराजयमान**, *q.v.*

पराजित, *m.* (*f.* ā) *adj.* suffering defeat, losing a suit, overcome, defeated.

पराजै, *more prop.* **पराजय**, *q. v.*

पराठा, *m.* a kind of bread made with butter (or ghee) and of several layers, like piecrust.

पराणिक; see **प्राणिक**.

परायठा, *m.* (see **पराठा**) a kind of cake; paste.

परात, 1, *more prop.* **प्रात**, *q.v.*: 2, *f.* a kind of large

पराती = **परात**, 2, *q.v.* [brass plate.

परात्रिय, *m.* a kind of reed (*Saccharum spontaneum*).

परात्म, another person, one's neighbour.

परावन, *m.* a horse of the Persian breed.

पराधिकार, *m.* another's office or post.

पराधिकारचर्चा, *f.* interference with another's affairs, officiousness. [other, subject, humble.

पराधीन, *m.* (*f.* ā) subject to or dependent on an-

पराधीनता, *f.* } dependence, subjection.
पराधीनत्व, *m.* }

पराधीना, *f.* (*m.* **पराधीन**) a dependent female.

परान, a corruption of **प्राण**, *q. v.*

परानसा, *f.* the practice of medicine, administer-

पराना, *a. int.* to run, flee. [ing remedies.

परान्न, 1, *m.* food supplied by another: 2, *adj.* living at another's expense.

परान्नभोजी, *m.* (*f.* inī) one who lives on food provided at the expense of another.

परापत, *more prop.* **प्राप्त**, *q. v.*

परापरत्व, *m.* (*f.* tā) priority and posteriority; the condition of being both a genus and a species.

परापवाद, 1, *m.* slander, calumny, laying blame on another: 2, *adj.* accusing another, slanderous.

परापवादक, *m.* (*f.* ikā) } = **परापवाद**, 2, *q. v.*
परापवादी, *m.* (*f.* inī) }

पराभव, *m.* disappearance; defeat, discomfiting, overcoming, mortification, humiliation, disregard.

पराभूत, *m.* (*f.* ā) defeated, discomfited, overcome, vanquished.

परामर्श, *m.* consideration, reflection, advice, discrimination, judgment. [counsellor.

परामर्शक, *m.* (*f.* ikā) a discriminator, adviser,

परामर्शी, *m.* (*f.* inī) }
परामर्षक, *m.* (*f.* ikā) } = **परामर्शक**, *q.v.*
परामर्षी, *m.* (*f.* iṇī) }

परामोधना, *m.* wheedling.

परायण, 1, *m.* attachment, devotedness to a thing, adherence to: as the latter member of compounds, it signifies 2, *m.* (*f.* ā) wholly occupied with, intent on, devoted to, adhering to, connected with, affected by, depending on.

परायत्त, *m.* (*f.* ā) subject to or dependent on others.

परायन; see **परायण** and **पलायन**.

पराया, *m.* (*f.* **पराई**) 1, appertaining to another, another's, alien, other, strange, foreign: 2, taken flight, run away.

पराऊ, *m.* a kind of gourd (*Momordica charantia*).

परार्थ, 1, *m.* great importance; the interests of another; sexual intercourse: 2, *adj.* having another object or sense; designed or purposed by another; having the advantage of another person for one's object: 3, *adv.* in the interests of another person.

परार्थप्रार्थना, *f.* intercession, intercessory prayer.

परार्थवादी, meddlesome, officious: hence, *m.* (*f.* inī) a busybody, etc. [person.

परार्थी, *m.* (*f.* inī) 1, = **परमार्थी**, *q.v.*: 2, a benevolent

परार्ध, *m.* the other part, the ulterior part, half of the term of Brahm's life, as many days of mortals as are equal to fifty of Brahm's years, a lac of lacs of crores, or a hundred thousand billions: *hence*, adj. immense, infinite.

परार्ध्य, 1, *m.* an infinite number, a maximum: 2, *m.* (*f.* ā) most excellent, beautiful, best.

पराल, *f.* straw.

परावर, *m.* ancestors and descendants, the universe, totality; *lit.* far and near.

परावर्त्त, *m.* reversal of a sentence.

परावर्त्तव्यवहार, *m.* (in Law) appeal.

परावृत, reversed (as a judgment).

पराशर, *m. pr. n.* a certain Hindoo sage, father of the ancient poet Vyās.

पराशरी = **पाराशरी**, *q.v.*

पराश्चित, *more prop.* **प्रायश्चित**, *q.v.*

पराश्रय, 1, *m.* dependence: 2, *m.* (*f.* ā) dependent (or relying) upon another.

पराश्रया, *f.* (*m.* **पराश्रय**) a female dependent; a parasitical plant.

पराश्रित, *m.* (*f.* ā) = **पराश्रय**, 2, *q.v.*

परास, *more prop.* **पलाश**, *q.v.*

परासर; see **पराशर**.

परासु, dying, expired, dead.

परासुत्व, *m.* (*f.* tā) death, extinction; drowsiness, sleepiness, apathy.

परास्त, *m.* (*f.* ā) defeated, overthrown, vanquished.

पराह, 1, = **पलाय**, *q.v.*: 2, *m.* the next day.

पराह्न, *m.* afternoon, the latter part of the day.

परि, (Gr. περί) an inseparable prefix implying completeness, intensity, about, around, all around, round about, entirely, thoroughly, full, excessively, quite. It should be observed, however, that in many instances the influence of this prefix on the sense of the word is scarcely appreciable. The **रि** of this prefix is sometimes inaccurately lengthened.

परीवार, *more prop.* **परिवार**, *q.v.*

परिकथा, *f.* the history or adventures of any fabulous person, a work of fiction, tale, story.

परिकर, *m.* a girth, zone; a train of dependents, retinue; a bed: lit. *adj.* surrounding, embracing.

परिकल्पित, *m.* (*f.* ā) invented, made, contrived, devised, found out, forged.

परिकीर्त्तन, *m.* telling, talking of, boasting.

परिक्रमा, *f.* the going around a person or an idol to the right as an indication of reverence, circumambulating, a going round about; (in Astron.) a revolution, revolving. — *lena* or *k.* to walk around a person or an idol in worship.

परिक्रय, *m.* purchasing back, redemption; the giving up part of a treasure to preserve the rest.

परिक्लेश, *m.* trouble, vexation.

परिक्लिष्ट, *m.* (*f.* ā) annoyed, vexed, troubled.

परिक्षित = **परीक्षित**, *q.v.*

परिखत; see (1) **परखना** (2) **परीक्षित**.

परिखा, *f.* a moat, ditch surrounding a fortified place.

परिख्यात, *m.* (*f.* ā) celebrated, famous.

परिख्याति, *f.* celebrity, fame, repute.

परिग्रह, *m.* an embracing, putting on, seizing, taking, selecting, accepting, undertaking, possession, property; admission; marrying, marriage, a wife, a husband, family, dependents, retinue; honouring; grace; dominion; number: abode: root, origin.

परिघ, *m.* an iron bar for shutting a gate, an iron club, iron-mounted bludgeon: a line of clouds covering partially the rising or setting sun: the gate of a palace: *pr. n.* the nineteenth stellar mansion.

परिचय, *m.* acquaintance, intimacy.

परिचरजा, *more prop.* **परिचर्य्या**, *q.v.*

परिचर्य्या, *f.* service, dependence, veneration, worship.

परिचारक, *m.* (*f.* ikā) } a servant, attendant.
परिचारी, *m.* (*f.* iṇī) }

परिचित, *m.* (*f.* ā) known, made known, acquainted with.

परिचेय, *m.* (*f.* ā) fit to become acquainted with, sociable.

परिच्छद, *m.* a cover, covering, clothing; domestic implements, implements in general; necessaries for travelling; retinue, train, attendants, followers.

परिच्छन्न, *m.* (*f.* ī) surrounded, encompassed, attended, covered, clothed.

परिच्छा, *more prop.* **परीक्षा**, *q.v.*

परिच्छित, *more prop.* **परीक्षित**, *q.v.*

परिच्छिन्न, cut off, detached, singled out, defined; polished, clean, clear; excellent, good.

परिच्छेद, *m.* separation, exact discrimination, determination, decision, a segment, division, a section or chapter of a book.

परिछन; see **परिच्छन्न** and **परीक्षण**.

परिछांही (*Rām.*) = **प्रतिछाया**, *q.v.*

परिछेद = **परिच्छेद**, *q.v.*

परिजन, *m.* surrounding company, attendants, dependents, followers, servants, family, relations kith and kin.

परिजाद, *more prop.* **परीज़ाद**, *q.v.*

परिज्ञान, *m.* thorough knowledge, learning.

परिणय } *m.* marriage.
परिणयन }

परिणाम, *m.* transformation, change, digestion, termination, last stage, ripeness, fulness, maturity.

परिणामदर्शी, *m.* (*f.* inī) *adj.* looking forward to the end, provident, forecasting.

परिणाह, *m.* circumference, breadth.

परितः, *adv.* in every direction, all around.

परिताप, *m.* heat, warmth, pain, sorrow, anguish: *pr. n.* one of the division of hell.

परितापी, *m.* (*f.* inī) very hot; causing much pain or sorrow.

परितुष्ट, *m.* (*f.* ā) contented, satisfied, pleased.

परितोष, *m.* contentedness, gratification, satiety, satisfaction, pleasure, delight.

परितोषक, *m.* (*f.* ikā) *adj.* satisfying, pleasure-giving, gratifying.

परितोषण, 1, *m.* satisfying: 2, *m.* (*f.* ā) *adj.* satisfying.

परितोषना, *t.* to afford satisfaction or pleasure.

परितोषयिता } *m.* (*f.* trī) a satisfier.
परितोषयितृ }

परितोषवत }
परितोषवन्त } *m.* (*f.* vatī) = **परितोषी**, *q.v.*
परितोषवान }

परितोषिक; see (1) **परितोषक** (2) **पारितोषिक**.

परितोषिका, *f.*; see **परितोषक**.

परितोषी, *m.* (*f.* iṇī) contented, satisfied.

परित्यक्त, *m.* (*f.* ā) void, of, deprived of, quitted, abandoned, left.

परित्याग, *m.* abandonment, desertion, neglect, loss.

परित्यागन, *m.* an abandoning, deserting, repudiating, resigning.

परित्यागी, *m.* (*f* inī) *adj.* abandoning, repudiating, deserting, relinquishing, resigning.

परित्राण, *m.* protection, shelter, preserving, defence, deliverance, salvation.

परित्राता } **परित्रातृ** } *m.* (*f.* trī) a protector, saviour.

परिदा, f. the giving oneself up to the favour or protection of another; surrender; devotion.

परिदाह, *m.* burning, combustion; mental anguish, pain, sorrow.

परिधन; see (1) **परधन** (2) **परिधान**.

परिधान, *m.* putting around, wrapping around, putting on, dressing, clothing; a lower garment, clothes.

परिधारण, *m.* a suffering, indulging.

परिधि, *m.* that by which something is bordered, a halo, horizon, circumference, the disc of the sun or moon; pieces of fresh wood surrounding the sacrificial fire. [able to be worn, wearable.

परिधेय, *m.* an under-garment: *lit.* proper or suit-

परिनाम (Rām.) = **परिणाम**, *q.v.*

परिन्द, *more prop.* **परन्द**, *q.v.*

परिपक्व, *m.* (*f.* ā) fully cooked, quite ripe, mature, decaying, digested; shrewd, knowing.

परिपक्वत्व, *m.* (*f.* tā) ripeness, maturity, perfection, digestion; knowingness; fluency.

परिपन्थक, *m.* (*f.* ikā) } **परिपन्थिक**, *m.* (*f.* ā *or* ī) } = **परिपन्थी**, *q.v.*

परिपन्थी, *m.* (*f.* inī) an opposer, antagonist, enemy, highwayman, bandit, robber.

परिपाक, *m.* the becoming fully cooked, ripening, digesting; maturity, perfection, experience, cleverness, shrewdness.

परिपाका (*Rām.*) = **परिपाक**, *q.v.* [*thum*).

परिपाकिनी, *f.* a kind of drug (*Convolvulus turpe-*

परिपाटि, *f.* = **परिपाटी**, *q.v.* [metic.

परिपाटी, *f.* arrangement, order, method: arith-

परिपालक, *m.* (*f.* ikā) a nourisher, guardian, protector, maintainer. [keeping, protection.

परिपालन, *m.* nurture, cherishing, maintaining,

परिपालित, *m.* (*f.* ā) cherished, protected.

परिपुष्करा, *f.* a sort of cucumber (*Cucumis Madras-*

परिपूजन, *m.* a worshipping, adoring. [*patanus.*

परिपूजित, *m.* (*f.* ā) worshipped, adored, served.

परिपूरित, *m.* (*f.* ā) fulfilled, completed, satisfied: brimful. [complete, satisfied, content.

परिपूर्ण, 1, *m.* a filling: 2, *m.* (*f.* ā) quite full, full,

परिपूर्णत्व, *m.* (*f.* tā) fulness, completeness, entireness, satiety, satisfaction. [*tundus*).

परिपेल, *m.* a certain fragrant grass (*Cyperus ro-*

परिप्लव, 1, *m.* a bathing, immersing; an inundation a ship, boat: 2, undulating, tremulous, shaking.

परिप्लुत, *m.* (*f.* ā) immersed, bathed, inundated.

परिभव, *m.* disrespect, humiliation, disregard, contempt, contumely, disgrace.

परिभवन } **परिभाव** } = **परिभव**, *q.v.*

परिभावी, *m.* (*f.* inī) a slighter, despiser.

परिभाषा, *f.* speech, conversation, discourse; an agreement, promise; a general maxim; abuse, ridicule; preface; a summary description of difficult terms; any conventional term in a science, technical terms; (in Gram.) a maxim given by the ancient grammarians as a summary interpretation of the rules of Pāṇini; (in Med.) prognosis.

परिभाषी, *m.* (*f.* iṇī) *adj.* speaking, discoursing.

परिभोग, *m.* enjoyment, sexual intercourse, the illegal enjoyment or use of another person's property, possession. [tray, mistake, error.

परिभ्रम, *m.* a going about, wandering, going as-

परिभ्रष्ट, *m.* (*f.* ā) corrupted, degraded, fallen, deprived of.

परिमण्डल, 1, *m.* an orbit, circle, globe, ball, circumference; a poisonous kind of gnat: 2, *m.* (*f.* ā) round, circular, globular.

परिमण्डलता, *f.* } **परिमण्डलत्व**, *m.* } globularity.

परिमल, *m.* fragrance, a fragrant substance, an exquisite scent (esp. such as arises from the trituration of fragrant substances); the trituration of perfumes: sexual intercourse.

परिमाण, *m.* measure, weight, length of time, capacity of a vessel, circumference; the act of measuring.

परिमाणदण्ड, *m.* a measuring-rod.

परिमाणवाचक, (in Gram.) having reference to degree or quantity (as an 'adverb of degree', etc.).

परिमाणज्ञ, *m.* (*f.* ā) a geometrician.

परिमाता } **परिमातृ** } *m.* (*f.* trī) a measurer.

परिमार्गण, *m.* a tracing, searching, pursuing.

परिमार्गी, *m.* (*f.* inī) a pursuer, searcher.

परिमित, *m.* (*f.* ā) meted, defined, regulated.

परिमितत्व, *m.* (*f.* tā) measuredness, definiteness.

परिमितव्यय, *m* economy, parsimony. [frugal.

परिमितव्ययी, *m.* (*f.* inī) economical, parsimonious,

परिमितभुज, *m.* (*f.* ā) = **परिमिताहार**, *q.v.*

परिमिताहार, *m.* (*f.* ī) *adj.* eating moderately, abstemious, temperate.

परिमिति, *f.* quantity, measure.

परिमोहन, *m.* a fascinating, beguiling, infatuation.

परिमोही, *m.* (*f.* inī) *adj.* bewitching, fascinating, infatuating. [ished, impaired.

परिम्लान, soiled, stained, waned, withered, dimin-

परियां, *f.* (pl. of **परी**) fairies.

परिवर्त्त, *m.* a turning, turning back, going back, turning around, retreat, flight, revolving. end of the period of four ages, the destruction of the world, revolution, palingenesia, transmigration, return, requital, exchange, barter, recompense; reciprocity.

परिवर्त्तन, *m.* requital, recompense, exchange, barter.
परिवर्त्तित, *m.* (*f.* ā) turned around, revolved; returned, retreated; taken or put on in a wrong direction; exchanged.
परिवर्त्ती, *m.* (*f.* inī) *adj.* turning, revolving, recompensing, exchanging.
परिवा, *f.* the first day of the moon's increase or wane.
परिवाद, *m.* detraction, censure, reproach, abuse, slander, calumny, stigma, accusation, charge.
परिवादक, *m.* (*f.* ikā) an accuser, calumniator, reprover, plaintiff, prosecutor: lit. *adj.* calumniating, reproaching, charging, abusing, slandering.
परिवादी, *m.* (*f.* inī) = **परिवादक**, *q.*.
परिवार, *m.* attendants, retinue, dependents, family, household, friends and relatives.
परिवारत्व, *m.* (*f.* tā) dependence, subjection.
परिवारवन्त, *m.* (*f.* vatī) one who has a great retinue: lit. *adj.* abounding in dependents, etc.
परिवारवान, *m.* (*f.* vatī) = **परिवारवन्त**, *q.v.*
परिवाक *more prop.* **परिवार**, *q.v.*
परिवास, *m.* abiding, sojourn; an abode.
परिवाह, *m.* an overflowing, inundation, water-course, drain.
परिविष्ट, *m.* (*f.* ā) surrounded, enclosed.
परिवृत्त, *m.* (*f.* ā) surrounded, attended; gone around, revolved; exchanged.
परिवेदन, *m.* anguish, pain, misery; marriage, marrying, the marrying of a younger brother before the elder: complete knowledge.
परिवेदना, *f.* anguish: foresight, caution.
परिवेषण, *m.* a surrounding, enclosing, circumference, halo: serving up dinner, distributing food to guests.
परिवेष्टन, *m.* a surrounding, encompassing, circumference.
परिवेष्टा / **परिवेष्टृ** } *m.* (*f.* trī) a carver, waiter.
परिवेष्टित, *m.* (*f.* ā) surrounded, enclosed, compassed; covered, veiled.
परिव्याध, *m.* a kind of tree (*Pterospermum acerifolia*); a certain water-reed (*Calamus faciculatus*).
परिव्रज्या, *f.* a strolling, religious wandering, mendicancy, abandonment of the world.
परिव्राजक, *m.* (*f.* ikā *or* kā) a strolling religious mendicant.
परिशंकनीय, *m.* (*f.* ā) to be doubted, be feared, be apprehended.
परिशंख्या, *more prop* **परिसंख्या**, *q.v.*
परिशाप, *m.* a cursing, reviling.
परिशिष्ट, *m.* a supplement, appendix: *lit.* left, remaining, finished.
परिशुद्ध, cleansed, purified; paid, discharged [(as a debt).
परिशेष, *m.* remainder; completion.
परिशोध, *m.* cleansing, purifying, correcting; requital, retaliation; discharge of a debt.
परिशोधन, *m.* a cleansing, purging, purifying; the liquidating a debt.
परिशोष, *m.* an evaporation, drying.

परिश्रम, *m.* *f.* fatigue, exertion, labour, effort, endeavour, toil, pains, trouble, industry, distress.
परिश्रमी, *m.* (*f.* inī) active, laborious, painstaking, energetic, industrious.
परिश्रान्त, *m.* (*f.* ā) overcome with fatigue or distress, exhausted, wearied.
परिश्रान्ति, *f* fatigue, exhaustion, labour, distress, toil, trouble.
परिषद, *f.* an assembly, audience, congregation.
परिष्कार, *m.* cleanness, purification by essential rites, initiation, embellishment, decoration, the repairing a building.
परिष्कृत, *m.* (*f.* ā) cleansed, scoured, purified, embellished, adorned, decorated.
परिष्कृतभूमि, *f.* an altar or ground prepared for sacrificing.
परिसंख्या, *f.* a total or complete enumeration (leaving nothing unsaid), recapitulation, reckoning.
परिसंख्यात, *m.* (*f.* ā) counted, enumerated.
परिसमापन, *m.* an entire completion.
परिसमाप्त, *m.* (*f.* ā) completely finished.
परिसमाप्ति, *f.* an entire completion.
परिहविशे (*poet.*) = **तू जनेगी (जनना)**.
परिसर, *m.* border, proximity, standingplace; ground contiguous to a town, river, mountain, etc.; width, extent, dimension: *lit.* near at hand, contiguous, encompassing.
परिसाधन, *m.* an accomplishing, effecting, ascertaining, determining.
परिसीमन, *m.* a boundary, border, extreme term or limit; the upshot of a business.
परिसीमा, *f.* = **परिसीमन**, *q.v.*
परिहरण, *m.* a seizing, taking; leaving, abandoning; a confuting, the repelling a charge; disrespectful treatment.
परिहरना, *t.* to take away, clear off, leave, forsake, abandon, desert.
परिहार, *m.* the repelling a charge: disrespect, disregard.
परिहास, *m.* mirth, amusement, pleasantry, laughter, sport, jest, derision, mockery.
परिहासक, *m.* (*f.* ikā) a jester, wag, wit: lit. *adj.* laughing at, ridiculing, joking.
परिहासवेदी / **परिहासी** } *m.* (*f.* inī) = **परिहासक**, *q.v.*
परिहीण, *m.* (*f.* ā) waned, faded, wasted, deserted, deprived of.
परी, 1, = **परि**, *q.v.*: 2, *f.* a fairy: a kind of net or contrivance for catching fish.
परीक्षक, *m.* (*f.* ikā) an examiner, experimenter, assayer, investigator, prover, judge: *lit.* possessing the function of testing, investigating acutely, bringing to the test, trying.
परीक्षण, *m.* / **परीक्षणा**, *f.* } = **परीक्षा**, *q.v.*
परीक्षा, *f.* investigation, trial, experiment, test, investigation, discrimination, trial by ordeal of various kinds.—*k*, to examine, test, etc.
परीक्षायुक्त, *m.* (*f.* ā) connected with proof, etc.
परीक्षायुक्ति, *f.* an arrangement for proof, etc.
परीक्षिका, (*m.* **परीक्षक**) a female experimenter, etc.
परीक्षिणी, *f.* (*m.* **परीक्षी**) = **परीक्षिका**.
परीक्षित, 1, *m.* (*f.* ā) tried, tested, examined, prov-

ed, investigated: 2, *m. pr. n.* a certain king, son of Abhimanyu and grandson of Arjun. It is to this king that the Bhāgavat Purāṇ was related.

परीक्षी, *m.* (*f.* iṇī) = **परीक्षक**, *q.v.*

परीच्छा / **परीछा** } *more prop.* **परीक्षा**, *q.v.*

परीछक, *more prop.* **परीक्षक**, *q v.* [a beauty.

परीज़ाद, fairy-born, *i.e.* beautiful: *hence*, a fairy,

परीठा; see (1) **परिठा** (2) **पर्दा**.

परीधावी, *m.* the forty-first year of the Indian [cycle.

परीयाँ *more prop.* **परियाँ**, *q.v.*

परीव; for words beginning thus, see under the [form **परिव**.

परीवा, *f.* the first day of the moon.

परीहास, *more prop.* **परिहास**, *q.v.*

परु = **परुस**, *q.v.*

परुंच, a corruption of **पहुँच**, *q.v.*

परुख (*Rām.*) = **परुष**, *q.v.*

परुष, *m.* 1, (*f.* ā) rough, rugged, harsh, severe, coarse, unkind, contumelious, abusive (as speech): 2, *m.* unkind harsh contumelious speech, abuse: a certain plant (*Barleria Prionitis*); a species of tree (*Xylocarpus granatum*).

परुषवचन, *m.* harsh unkind contumelious speech, abuse, scurrility, reproach.

परुषवाच / **परुषोक्ति** } *f.* = **परुषवचन**, *q.v.*

परुषोक्तिक, *m.* (*f.* ā *or* ī) *adj.* uttering harsh language, abusive, scurrilous.

परुस, *m.* a knot or joint in a reed, cane, or plant.

परे, (Sk. loc. of **पर**) beyond, yonder, at a distance, after, afterwards, hereafter, in another world.—*rahnā*, to remain at a distance, keep aloof, abstain from.

परेंर, a beam.

परेखन = **परीक्षण**, *q.v.* [contrition, concern.

परेखा, 1, *f.* = **परीक्षा**, *q.v.*: 2, *m.* regret, repentance,

परेत, *more prop.* **प्रेत**, *q.v.*

परेतना, *t.* to reel (thread or yarn).

परेता, *m.* a reel (for winding yarn).

परेव in Braj = **पड़ा** (**पड़ना**).

परेवा, *m.* a pigeon.

परेश (Rām.) = **परमेश्वर**, *q.v.*

परेशान, dispersed, dishevelled, preplexed, distressed, wretched, ruined. — *k.* to scatter, discomfit, outdo. — *kahnā*, to talk foolishly. [struction.

परेशानी, *f.* dispersion, perplexity, distress, de-

परेशावशान, a kind of medicinal herb which springs up on brick walls during the rains.

परेस = (1) **परेश** (2) **परदेश**, *qq.v.*

परेह = **परेहा** and **पलेव**, *qq.v.*

परेहा, *m.* land that has been watered after ploughing, or flooded before the final ploughing and levelling

परैखा in Braj = **परीक्षा**, *q.v.* [of the ground.

परोक्ष, 1, *m.* an ascetic, hermit: invisibility, absence, secrecy: (in Gram.) past time, past tense: 2, *m.* (*f.* ā) beyond sight, invisible, imperceptible.

परोक्षभूत, *m.* (in Gram.) the perfect tense.

परोक्षविधि, *m.* (in Gram.) the mild or hortative form of the imperative mode.

परोजन, *more prop.* **प्रयोजन**, *q.v.*

परोना, *more prop.* **पिरोना** *q.v.*

परोपकार, *m.* the assisting others, doing good, beneficence, benevolence, charity.

परोपकारक, *m.* (*f.* ikā) = **परोपकारी**, *q.v.*

परोपकारित्व, (*f.* tā) readiness to assist or do good to others, humanity, kindness.

परोपकारी, *m.* (*f.* iṇī) *adj.* acting in the interests of others and with a view to their wellbeing, charitable, beneficent, hospitable.

परोपदेश, *m.* a giving advice, counselling, admon- [ishing.

परोश, *m.* (*prop.* **पड़ोस**) vicinity.

परोष्टी / **परोष्णी** } *f.* a cockroach.

परोस, *m.* (*prop.* **पड़ोस**) vicinity.

परोसना, *t.* to act the neighbour, serve up dinner, distribute food to guests.

परोसा, *m.* a dish of food which is sent to a friend.

परोसिन, *f.* (= **परोसिनी**) a female neighbour.

परोसी, *m.* (*f.* inī) a neighbour.

परोसैया, *m.* a distributer of food to guests, one who serves up dinner, a waiter.

परोसैया, in Braj = **परोसैया**, *q.v.* [transportation.

परोहन, *m.* a carriage, vehicle; instruments of

परोहा, *m.* a leathern water-bucket.

परौती, *f.* land which is kept out of cultivation for a short time in order that the soil may recover [its strength.

पर्कट, *m* a heron.

पर्कटि, *f.* / **पर्कटिन**, *m.* / **पर्कटी**, *f.* } = **पर्क्कटी**, *q.v.*

पर्काल; see (1) **परकाल** (2) **पर्काला** (3) **प्रकार**.

पर्काला, *m.* a spark: a pane of glass: fine calico, dimity. [*tiosa*).

पर्क्कटी, *f.* the waved-leaved figtree (*Ficus infec-*

पर्खाश, *m.* war, conflict, battle, commotion, tumult, violence, injury, oppression, severe inquisition.

पर्ग, *m.* a step, footstep, stride.

पर्गना = **परगना**, *q.v.*

पर्गास, *more prop.* **प्रकाश**, *q.v.*

पर्चत, *f.* mark, trace, effect, impression.

पर्चा = **परचा**, 1 and 2, *qq.v.* [conversation.

पर्चाना, *t.* to introduce to a person, engage in

पर्चूनिया, *m.* a meal-merchant, flour-seller.

पर्चूनी, *f.* the act of selling meal, etc.

पर्चौ in Braj = **पर्चा**, *q.v.*

पर्छटी / **पर्छती** } *more prop.* **पर्छती**, *q.v.*

पर्छती, *f.* a small thatch thrown over mud walls.

पर्छा, 1, *m.* self-sown paddy (rice): a spindle for winding thread on: 2, cleared up (as the sky after rain).

पर्छाई, *f.* reflection, image, shadow, shade.—*apnī-se bhāgnā*, to be frightened at one's own shadow.

पर्छां }
पर्छांई } **पर्छाई**, *q.v.*
पर्छांव }
पर्छांवां }

पर्ज, *f*, a certain musical mode (*rāgiṇī*); the

पर्जंक, *m.* a bed, bedstead. [handle of a shield.

पर्जंत = **पर्यन्त**, *q.v.*

पर्जदार, black-hilted (a scimetar). [*rhiza*).

पर्जनी, *f.* a species of curcuma (*Curcuma xanthor-*

पर्जन्त = **पर्यन्त**, *q.v.* [the deity of rain.

पर्जन्य, *m.* a rain-threatening cloud; rain: *pr. n.*

पर्जा, *more prop.* **प्रजा**, *q.v.*

पर्जाय, *f.* custom, manner: room, place.

पर्ण, *m.* a wing, feather, leaf; the *pān* or betel-leaf; the *palās*-tree (*Butea frondosa*, Roxb.).

पर्णनर, *m.* a mass of leaves, *i.e.* an effigy stuffed with leaves and intended to represent a person deceased whose body cannot be found and for whom obsequial rites are performed with this representative.

पर्णमाचाल, *m.* a certain acid fruit (*Averrhoa carambola*) called also *kumrāngā*.

पर्णलता, *f.* the betel-plant.

पर्णवल्ली, *f.* the *palās*-tree (*Butea frondosa*, Roxb.).

पर्णशाला, *f.* a hermitage (*prop.* a hut of leaves).

पर्णासि, *m.* a sort of basil (*Ocymum sanctum*) with small leaves.

पर्णी, 1, *m.* = **पर्णवल्ली**, *q.v.*: 2, *f.* a certain aquatic plant (*Pistia stratiotes*): the leaf of the assafœtida?

पर्णोटज = **उटज**, *q.v.*

पर्ताब, *more prop.* **प्रताप**, *q.v.*

पर्दा, *m.* a curtain, screen, partition in a room; a blind, veil; sail of a ship: *met.* modesty.—*k.* to screen, [hide, conceal.

पर्दाख़्त, *f.* a patronizing.

पर्दाज़, *adj.* performing, finishing.

पर्दादा, *m.* (*f.* ī) a great-grandparent by the father's side. [modest.

पर्दानिशीन, *adj.* remaining behind the screen,

पर्द्दन, *m.* the emitting wind backwards; wind

पर्नाला = **प्रणाल**, *q.v.* [emitted backwards.

पर्प, *m.* a wheel-chair, or a chair on which a cripple can move about.

पर्पट, *m.* a certain small medicinal plant with bitter leaves (apparently the *Oldenlandia biflora* or the *Gardenia latifolia* and other species).

पर्पटद्रुम, *m.* bdellium.

पर्पटी, *f.* a thin crisp cake made of any pulse: a kind of red aluminous earth brought from Surāt.

पर्ब्ब, *more prop.* **पर्व**, *q.v.*

पर्यंक, *m.* a bed, bedstead. [nation, travelling.

पर्यटन, *m.* a wandering about, roaming, peregri-

पर्यन्त, *m.* limit, term, boundary, skirt, border, end *adv.* up to, as far as, to the extent of, until, unto.

पर्यवसान, *m.* conclusion, termination.

पर्याय, *m.* expiration of time, change, regular and methodical disposal or succession, order, arrangement, return, repetition, succession, turn, manner, kind, opportunity, occasion; a synonyme, list of synonymes, the text of a vocabulary or the order of the synonymes for any term.

पर्ला, *m.* (*f.* ī) = **परला**, *q.v.*

पर्व, *m.* a knot, knuckle, joint; division of a book, section, chapter; a designation of certain days in a lunar month (as the full and the change of the moon, and the sixth, eighth, and tenth of each half-month); particular periods of the year (as the equinox, solstice, etc.); the moment of the sun's entering a new sign; a festival, holiday, anniversary festival, feast or sacred day; an opportunity, occasion; an instant, moment: a gem, flat diamond.

पर्वकारी, *m.* (*f.* iṇī) a Brāhmaṇ who performs ceremonies for hire out of season.

पर्वगामी, *m.* a man who associates with his wife on festival or other holy-days.

पर्वणिका, *f.* specks (attended with pain) on the edge of the cornea of the eye.

पर्वत, 1, = **पर्वित**, *q.v.*: 2, *m.* a mountain, hill. In the ingenious system of reckoning by symbols adopted by Hindoos in their poetry, this word is a symbol for 7.

पर्वतकाक, *m.* (*f.* ī) the raven.

पर्वतवासी, *m.* (*f.* inī) a mountaineer: lit. *adj.* residing in mountains.

पर्वतश्रेणी, *f.* a range or chain of mountains.

पर्वताश्रय, *m.* (*f.* ā) a mountaineer: *lit.* whose abode is in the mountains.

पर्वतिया, *m.* a kind of pumpkin.

पर्वती, 1, *f.* = **पर्वतिया**, *q.v.*: 2, *m.* (*f.* inī) = **पर्वतीय**, *q.v.*

पर्वतीय, *m.* (*f.* ā) a mountaineer, hill-man: *lit.* appertaining to mountains, mountainous.

पर्वताग्निमान, burning (as a volcanic mountain).

पर्वयोग, *m.* a conjunction of **पर्व**, *q.v.* [Roxb.

पर्वर, *m.* a kind of gourd (*Trichosanthes dioica*,

पर्वरिश, *f.* breeding, fostering, rearing, patronizing, protection, education. — *k.* to patronize, etc.

पर्वर्दिगार, *m.* an epithet of t e Supreme; *lit.* the cherisher. [brought up.

पर्वर्दा, *m.* a protegé, slave; *lit.* bred, reared,

पर्वसन्धि, *m.* the junction of the fifteenth and the first of a lunar fortnight, *i. e.* the precise moment of the full and change of the moon: *prop.* a knuckle, joint.

पर्वस्ती, *f.* cherishing, patronage, protection, care, favor. The term is applied especially to the cherishing of old servants who are past work.

पर्वा = **परवा**, *q.v.*

पर्वाज़, flying, flight. — *k.* to fly.

पर्वानगी, *f.* command; permission.

पर्वाना = **परवाना**, *q.v.*

पर्वाल, *m.* a certain disease of the eyelids in which the eyelashes fall off, a stye.

पर्विणी, *f.* a festival.

पर्वित, *m.* a kind of fish (*Silurus pubda*).

पर्वेस, *more prop.* **प्रवेश**, *q.v.* [form **परशु**.

पर्शु, for words beginning thus, see under the

पर्षद, *more prop.* **परिषद**, *q.v.*

पर्सन, *more prop.* **प्रसन्न**, *q.v.* [morrow.

पर्सों, the day before yesterday, the day after to-

पल, *m.* a weight of gold or silver equal to four *karshas*: one sixtieth part of a *daṇḍ* or a period of twenty-four seconds, a moment: flesh: straw after threshing. — *mārte*, instantly, immediately, in the twinkling of an eye. — *mārnā*, to make a movement of the eyelid. — *ot* for an instant.

पलई, *f.* a young branch or spray of a tree.

पलंग, *m.* a bed without curtains, bedstead: a tiger, panther, leopard. — *tin chor*, the constellation, called 'Charles's Wain'; *lit.* the bed and three thieves.

पलंगपोश, *m.* a coverlet, counterpane, (*corruptly*)

पलंगड़ी, *f.* a small bedstead. ['palampore'.

पलंगी, *f.* ferocity of the leopard, etc.: *adj.* appertaining to the tiger, etc.: *hence*, ferocious.

पलक, *f.* (*m.* ?) the eyelid, the twinkling of the eye, a wink, a moment, a twinkling. — *maṭkānā* or *mārnā*, to wink, twinkle.

पलकदरिया, *m.* clouds. [*lenā* = *palṭā lenā*, *q.v.*

पलट = **पलटा**, *q.v.* *Palaṭ denā*, to repel. *Palaṭ-*

पलटन, *f.* (Fr. *peloton*) a battalion, regiment.

पलटना, *a. int.* to return, turn back, retreat; to overturn; to rebound; to undergo a change, alter.

पलटा, *m.* turn, stead, exchange, return, recompense, revenge, retaliation, retribution. — *khānā*, to turn over head and heels; to overturn, be tilted; to rebound. — *lenā*, (with gen. *m.* uninfl. of object) to take back, take in return, take revenge, exact retribution. [vert, repel.

पलटाना, *t.* to cause to turn, to turn, return, con-

पलटाव, *m.* contradiction, reäction, rebound.

पलटे, *postp.* (sc. **में**) instead of, in revenge for.

पलठा, *m.* = **पलथी**, *q.v.*

पलड़ा, *m.* one of the dishes of a pair of scales.

पलड़ी, *f.* forced meat.

पलथा = **पलथी**, *q.v.*

पलथी, *f.* a mode of sitting on the ground resting on the buttocks. — *bāndhnā* or *mārnā*, to sit in that position. [*a. int.* to thrive.

पलना, *n.* to be reared, be nourished, be fattened:

पलरा, *m.* one of the dishes of a pair of scales.

पलल, *m.* mud, mire; pounded sesamum.

पलवल, *m.* the plant *Trichosanthes dioica*, Roxb.

पलवललती, *f.* the plant of *palwal*.

पलवाना, *t.* to cause to be reared or nourished.

पलवार, *m.* a kind of boat for carrying goods. The designation is applied chiefly to the slow heavy craft of from fifteen to twenty tons burthen which ply in Sundarbans. [belonging to a *palwār*.

पलवारी, *m.* (*f.* in *or* inī) a boatman or person

पलवैया, *m.* a nourisher, cherisher, rearer.

पलस्त = **पिलिस्त**, *q.v.*

पला, *m.* an oil-ladle, spoon.

पलाऊ, *m.* one who laments: *lit.* adj. lamenting.

पलाओ = **पलाव**, 1 and 2, *qq.v.*

पलांग, *m.* (*f.* ī *or* ā) the Gangetic porpoise.

पलाग्नि, *m.* bilious humour, bile.

पलाण्डु, *m.* an onion (*Allium Cepa*).

पलाद, *m. f.* a Rākshas (male or female).

पलान, 1, *more prop.* **पालान**, *q.v.*: 2, a space of ground between two occupied lots left for future disposal.

पलानना, *t.* to saddle a horse or bullock.

पलाना, 1, *more prop.* **पालान**, *q.v.*: 2, *a. int.* to run

पलानी, *f.* thatching. [away, flee, escape.

पलायक, taking to flight, fleeing, flying; hence, *m.* (*f.* ikā, iki, *or* ā) a fugitive, runaway, deserter.

पलायन, *m.* flight, escape, retreat, elopement.

पलायनपरायण, *adj.* fugitive.

पलायमान, *m.* (*f.* matī) running away, fugitive.

पलाल, *m.* the stalk of sorghum, straw, driedgrass.

पलाव, *m.* = **पलानी** and **पिलाव**, *qq.v.*

पलावनों in Braj = **पलाना**, 2, *q.v.*

पलाश, *m.* a leaf, foliage; a certain tree (*Butea frondosa*) bearing red blossoms and fed on by the lac insect; a sort of curcuma (*Curcuma reclinata*): *pr. n.* ancient Bihār or Magadhā.

पलाशक, *m.* (see **पलाश**) *Butea frondosa*; *Curcuma reclinata*. [used in medicine.

पलाशपपड़ा, *m.* the seeds of the *Butea frondosa*

पलाशाख्य, *m.* assafœtida.

पलाशिनी, *f. pr. n.* a certain river.

पलाशी, 1, *f.* lac: 2, *m.* a sort of mimusops (*Mimusops Kanki*); a tree in general and the *Butea frondosa* in particular: *pr. n.* a certain town: 3, *m.* (*f.* inī) a goblin: *lit.* leafy.

पलिक्नी, *f.* an old woman; a cow with calf.

पलित, 1, *m.* greyness of the hair: 2, *m.* (*f.* ā) greyhaired, hoary, aged.

पलिता, *f.* an old woman.

पलिबोथरा, *m. pr. n.* an ancient name of Patna.

पलिहपडा, *m.* } = **पल्लिहपडा**, *q.v.*
पलिहपडी, *f.* }

पली, *f.* (dim. of **पला**) an oil-ladle.

पलीत, *m.* a ghost, spirit of the dead.

पलीता, *m.* a match (of a gun); a candle. — *chāṭ jānā*, to flash in the pan.

पलीदी, *f.* uncleanness; excrement.

पलुआ, *m.* a certain plant (*Hibiscus cannabinus*).

पलेऊ, *m.* land watered after ploughing.

पलेथन, *m.* dry flour laid under and over bread when it is rolled. — *pakānā*, to contrive the ruin of anyone. — *nikālnā*, to beat severely.

पलेव, *m.* 1, = **पलेऊ**, *q.v.*: 2, soup; flour or pounded rice put into soup to thicken it.

पलोक, a corruption of **परलोक**, *q.v.*

पलोटना, *a. int.* to tread gently.

पलोठा, *m.* (*f.* ī) a contraction of **पहिलोठा**, *q.v.*

पल्लव, *m.* a sprout, shoot, twig, blade, blossom, the extremity of a branch bearing new leaves, branch with the leaves attached: the red dye of lac.

पल्लवक, *m.* a kind of fish (*Cyprinus denticulatus*).

पल्लवग्राही, *m.* (*f.* inī) *adj.* picking up straws, *i.e.* laying hold of trifles, fastidious.

पल्लवित, 1, *adj.* having young shoots, having many sprouts: possessing the red dye of lac: 2, *m.* the red dye of the lac insect.

पल्लवी, *adj.* having young shoots, sprouting: [hence, *m.* a tree.

पल्लह = **पल्ला**, *q.v.*

पल्ला, *m.* space, distance: margin, border; a border of cloths: a sheet (generally applied to chintz or shawl): a bag: labium vulvæ: one shutter of a door, etc.: assistance: one dish of a pair of scales.

पल्लि, *f.* a hamlet, small village.

पल्लिग्राम, *m.* a country, district, village.

पल्लिग्रामी, *m.* (*f.* inī) a countryman, villager.

पल्ली, *f.* 1, = **पल्लि**, *q.v.*: 2, a house-lizard.

पल्लू, *m.* the hem or the border of a garment.

पल्लूदार, *m.* a garment with a gold or silver border.

पल्लो; see (1) **पल्लव** (2) **पल्ला** (3) **पल्लू**.

पल्लोठा, *m.* (*f.* ī) a contraction of **पहिलोठा**, *q.v.*

पल्हियड़ा, *m.* a shelf on which waterpots are placed, a place where water is kept.

पल्हियड़ी, *f.* = **पल्हियड़ा**, *q.v.*

पवन, *m.* (*f.* ?) wind, air: *pr. n.* the Regent of the winds and of the north-west quarter: the sacred fire: a cleansing or purifying; winnowing grain.—*kā pūt*, the son of Ravan, *i.e.* the ape Hanumān.

पवनकुमार = **पवनका पूत**. See **पवन**.

पवनचक्की, *f.* a windmill.

पवनपानी, *m.* climate (*lit.* wind and water).

पवनरेखा, *f. pr. n.* the queen of king Ugrasēn.

पवनबाण, *m.* an arrow projected by means of air; an arrow which when projected raises the wind.

पवनव्याधि, *m.* wind (as affected morbidly) or rheumatism, etc.

पवनसुत = **पवनका पूत**. See **पवन**.

पवनाल, *m.* the grain *Andropogon saccharatus*.

पवनाहत, rheumatic.

पवमान, *m.* air, wind: an epithet (1) of Agni, the deity of fire (2) of the moon.

पवर्ग, *m.* (in Gram.) the designation applied to the consonants of the **प**, or labial, class; *viz.* **प, फ, ब, भ, म, व**.

पवाई, *f.* a chain fastened to the legs of horses to prevent their being stolen, chains with which the legs of criminals are fastened, fetters: the leg of a boot or of a stocking.

पवाड़ा, *m.* a narration or an explanation of a story, a story or the circumstances of a story.

पवि, *m.* the iron band of a wheel: *pr. n.* the thunderbolt of Indra.

पवित, a corruption of **पवित्र**, *q.v.*

पवित्र, 1, *m.* a means of purifying; *hence*, sacrificial grass (*Poa cynosuroides*): prayer: the Brāhmanical cord: 2, *m. pr. n.* a certain class of deities: 3, *m.* (*f.* ā) morally or physically pure, holy, free from sin or from sensual propensities, undefiled, clean, nice.

पवित्रआत्मा, *m. pr. n.* the Holy Spirit.

पवित्रता / **पवित्रताई** } *f.* = **पवित्रत्व**, *q.v.*

पवित्रत्व, *m.* moral or physical purity, holiness, sanctity, cleanness.

पवित्रा, 1, *f.* (*m.* **पवित्र**, 3) a holy female: holy basil (*Ocymum sanctum*): the twelfth day of the light fortnight of the month Shrāvan, a festival in honour of Vishnu: *pr. n.* the Pabar river, a little to the north-west of Hardwār: 2, *m.* a means of purifying; *hence*, a knotted piece of *kush*-grass used by the Hindoos in purification; the Brāhmanical thread; a string of silken beads.

पवित्री, *f.* a ring of *kush*-grass (*Poa cynosuroides*), or of gold, silver, or copper, worn on the ring-finger and fore-finger by Hindoos during religious worship.

पवी, *f.* a dike cut to let water either in or out.

पवेरा, the act of sowing seed with the hand.

पश; for words beginning thus, but not given below, see under the more proper form **पशु**.

पशली, *more prop.* (1) **पसली** (2) **पुशली**, *qq. v.*

पशम, *f.* wool, fur, down, hair, the hair of the privities.

पशमीना, woollen, hairy, downy.

पशर, *f.* the feeding of cattle at night.

पशाना, *a. int.* to stink.

पशीना, *more prop.* **पसीना**, *q.v.*

पशु, *m.* a beast, cattle (viz. neat-cattle, horses, goats, sheep, asses, and dogs); an animal to be immolated: an inferior deity attendant on Shiv: the soul (according to the tenets of Pashupatas).

पशुका, *f.* any small animal.

पशुक्रिया, *f.* copulation, coïtion.

पशुगायत्री, *f.* a parody of the holy verse of the Ved whispered into the ear of an animal about to be sacrificed.

पशुत्व, *m.* (*f.* tā) the condition or the nature of beasts, the condition of an animal about to be immolated.

पशुधर्म, *m.* action or function of animals, promiscuous cohabitation; the marrying of widows.

पशुपति, *m.* lord of the Pashus, *i.e.* Shiv.

पशुपतिनाथ, *m.* an epithet of Pashupati.

पशुपल्वल, *m.* the fragrant grass *Cyperus rotundus*.

पशुपाल, *m.* (*f.* ī) a herdsman, cattle-rearer.

पशुपालक, *m.* (*f.* ikā) = **पशुपाल**, *q.v.*

पशुपालन, *m.* cattle-rearing, tending cattle.

पशुरज्जु, *m. f.* a string or tie for fastening cattle.

पशुराज, *m.* the king of beasts, *i.e.* the lion.

पशुरोमन, *m.* the hair of a beast.

पशुली; see **पसली**.

पशुवंगामी, *more prop.* **पशुवद्गामी**, *q.v.*

पशुवत, *m.* (*f.* ī) animal-like, brutish, irrational.

पशुवद्गामी, *m.* (*f.* inī) walking like a brute.
पशुहरीतकी, *f.* the hog-plum. [grief, penitent.
पशेमान, sorry, ashamed, disgraced, filled with
पशेमानी, *f.* shame, regret, repentance penitence.
पश्चमीय, *more prop.* पश्चिमीय, *q.v.*
पश्चात, *adv.* behind, from behind, after, afterwards, backwards, westward.
पश्चातगामी = पश्चादगामी, *q.v.*
पश्चात्ताप, *m.* regret, remorse, repentance.
पश्चात्तापी, *m.* (*f.* inī) regretful, remorseful, repentant. [ing, following.
पश्चादगामी, *m.* (*f.* inī) *adj.* going after, succeed-
पश्चिम (see दक्षिण) *m.* (*f.* ā) hinder, hindermost, last, behind, after; west, western: *hence*, the west, sunset.
पश्चिमसमुद्र, *m.* the ocean to the west of India.
पश्चिमा, *f.* (*m.* पश्चिम) the west.
पश्चिमी, appertaining to the west, occidental: hence, *m.* (*f.* inī) one whose residence is in the west.
पश्चिमीय, *m.* (*f.* ā) westerly.
पश्ताना, *more prop.* पछताना, *q.v.*
पश्तावा, *more prop.* पछतावा, *q.v.*
पश्तू }
पश्ता } = पुश्तू, *q.v.*
पश्यन्ति (*Rām.*) = देखते हैं.
पश्यामि (*Rām.*) = मैं देखता हूं.
पश्शा, *m.* a gnat, mosquito, fly.
पषंड, *more prop.* पाखण्ड, *q.v.*
पषवारा (*Rām.*) = पक्ष or पन्द्रहदिन, *qq. v.*
पषाउज (*Rām.*) = पखावज, *q.v.*
पषान, *m.* (prop. पाषाण) stone.
पषारना, (*Rām.*) *t.* to wash.
पस, 1, after, behind; at length, then, then surely, assuredly, consequently, therefore, wherefore, finally: 2, a buffalo-heifer.
पसन्द, *f.* choice, approbation, liking. — *k.* to choose, approve of, like. — *honā* (with gen. *f.* or dat. of the person pleased) to be pleasing to.
पसर, *f.* grazing cattle at night.
पसरना, *n.* to be spread out, be stretched out, be expanded, be distended. [equipage.
पसरौ, *f.* a follower, train, retinue, dependents,
पसला, *m.* a shower.
पसली, *f.* a rib; the præcordia. — *pharaknī* is applied to describe the perception of the condition of an absent person; *lit.* a thrilling over the ribs.
पसलीखण्ड, *m.* side: a tract of country. [ponds.
पसही, *f.* a kind of wild rice that grows in shallow
पसा, *m.* (= अंजलि) as much as can be contained in both hands open, two handfuls.
पसाई, *f.* a kind of rice.
पसाउ }
पसाऊ } (*Rām.*) = पसाव, *q.v.*
पसाना, *t.* to skim; to pour off superfluous water (from boiled rice); to stroke.
पसारना, *t.* to spread, stretch out, open, expand, extend, reach, distend, display.
पसारा, *m.* the act of spreading or stretching out, expansion. — *k.* to procrastinate, raise obstacles in an easy matter.
पसारी, 1, *more prop.* पनसारी, *q.v.*: 2, = पसेरी, *q.v.*
पसाव (Chand) = प्रसाद, *q.v.*
पसीजना, *a. int.* to perspire; to melt; to compassionate. [sudorific.
पसीना, *m.* perspiration. — *nikālnewālā*, (in Med.)
पसु; for words beginning thus, see under the
पसुरी, *more com.* पसेरी, *q.v.* [form पशु.
पसूजना, *t.* to stitch.
पसेरी, *f.* (i. e. पांच + सेर + ी) a measure of five *sêrs*.
पसेव, *m.* perspiration.
पसेवड़ा, *m.* perspiration.
पसोपेश, *m.* evasion, prevarication; *lit.* behind and before. — *k.* to evade, prevaricate.
पस्त, below, low, lowly.
पस्ताना = पछताना, *q. v.*
पस्तावा = पछतावा, *q.v.* [swamp, marsh.
पस्ती, *f.* lowness, baseness, inferiority, humility; a
पस्ता, (in Pros.) a species of metre.
पह, 1, = पै, 4, *q.v.*: 2, *f.* dawn. — *phaṭnā*, to dawn, [grow luminous.
पहं = पै, 4, *q. v.*
पहचान, *f.* acquaintance, knowledge, recognition.
पहचानना, *t.* to know, be acquainted with, recognize, discriminate, distinguish, perceive.
पहन, *m.* width, breadth, ampleness.
पहनना = पहिनना, *q.v.*
पहना, *m.* (*f.* ī) broad, wide,-extensive.
पहनाई, *f.* width, breadth, ampleness, extensiveness, spaciousness.
पहनाना, *t.* to cause to be dressed, to clothe.
पहनावा, *m.* dress, clothing, raiment, garments.
पहर, *m.* (prop. प्रहर: see गजर) a division of time consisting of eight gharees, being an eighth part of a day, *i. e.* three hours. *Aṭh'oṅ* —, all day long and all night long, night and day, continually. — *ek din*, at the end of the first watch of the day. Strictly speaking the *pahar* is the fourth part of the natural day or night, and consequently varies in length from six to nine gharees according to the latitude and the season of the year; *e g.* in the province of Kashmeer in the north of India, the *pahar* of the day at midsummer will be nearly nine gharees, and that of the night about six; while at Cape Comorin, in the extreme south, there is very little variation during the whole year.
पहरदिन, *m.* a watch of the day, a day's watch.
पहरना = पहिरना, *q. v.*
पहररात, *m.* a watch of the night, a night's watch.
पहरा, *m.* a sentinel, watch, patrol; a tour of watch; a corporal and six. — *denā*, to watch. *Pahremeṅ ḍālnā*, to give in charge to a watch or guard. *Pahremeṅ paṛnā*, to be given in custody, be confined in a guard.

पहरा ा = पहिराना, *q.v.*
पहरावन = पहिरावन, *q.v.*
पहरावनी = पहिरावनी, *q.v.*
पहरावा = पहिरावा, *q.v.*
पहरिया, *m.* or *f.* } = पहरू, *q.v.*
पहरी, *m.*(*f.* inī) }
पहरुआ, *m.* (*f.* पहरुइन or पहरुई) = पहरू, *q.v.*
पहरुए. *more prop.* पहरुए (pl. of पहरुआ) guards.
पहरुया = पहरू, *q.v.*
पहरू, *m. f.* a watchman, sentinel, guard.
पहरेवाला, *m.* (*f.* in *or* ī) = पहरू, *q.v.*
पहल, *m.* a flock of cotton: beginning, aggression: the side of a rectangular figure.
पहलवान, *m.* a hero, champion, brave warrior, strong athletic man, stout fellow, wrestler, boxer.
पहलवी = पह्लवी, *q.v.*
पहला, *m.* (*f.* ī) *more com.* पहिला, *q.v.*
पहलू, *m.* the side; the flank of an army: utility, profit, advantage. — *tihī k.* to retire, withdraw, retreat, decline, evade.
पहले } *more com.* पहिले, *q.v.*
पहलें }
पहलेपहल = पहिलेपहिले, *q.v.*
पहलौठा, *m.* (*f.* ī) *more prop.* पहिलौठा, *q.v*
पहाड़, *m.* a mountain. — *sī rātēn* (mountain-like nights) long and tedious nights (especially of sorrow).
पहाड़ा, *m.* (in Arithm.) the multiplication-table: [a fable, story.
पहाड़िया = पहाड़ी, 2, *q.v.*
पहाड़ी, 1, *f* (dim. of पहाड़) a small mountain, hill: 2, *m.* (*f.* inī) a mountaineer: *lit.* appertaining to hills or mountains, mountainous.
पहाड़ीभंग, henbane.
पहारा; see (1) पहरा (2) पहाड़ा.
पहिचान = पहचान, *q.v.* [See पहचानेगा.
पहिचानिहै (pl. पहिचानिहैं) in Braj = पहचानेगा.
पहिनना, 1, *m.* clothing, dress: 2, *t.* to put on clothes, clothe oneself, dress; to wear.
पहिनाना, *t.* to cause to be dressed, to clothe.
पहिनाव; see पहनावा.
पहि[illegible], *m.* a wheel, carriage-wheel.
पहिरना = पहिनना, 2, *q.v.*
पहिरा; see (1) पहरा (2) पहिरना.
पहिराना = पहिनाना, 2, *q.v.* [ment.
पहिरावन, *f.* (*m.* ?) dress, clothing, garments, raiment.
पहिरावनी, *f.* 1, = पहिरावन, *q.v.*: 2, a woman who dresses the guests at a wedding, a tire-woman.
पहिरावा *m.* ? = पहिरावन, *q.v.*
पहिलना, *more prop.* पहिनना, *q.v.*
पहिला, *m.* (*f.* ī) first, the first: *adv.* before, previously, soon, rather.
पहिले, (sc. में or समयमें) at first, in the first place firstly, first, chiefly, sooner, before, rather.—*par*, on the other side.—*se*, at first, at the first, in the first place, first of all, at the outset, from the first, from the very commencement.
पहिलेपहल = पहिलेपहिले, *q.v.*
पहिलेपहिले, at first, when the things narrated took place: first of all, in the first instance, at the very commencement. The repetition refers probably either (1) to the *time*, contemplated as consisting of parts, or (2) to the facts or circumstances of the things narrated, contemplated in their separateness.
पहिलौटा, *m.* (*f.* ī) *more prop.* पहिलौठा, *q.v.*
पहिलौठा, (पहिला + उठा) *m.* (*f.* ī) firstborn.
पहिलौठपन, *m.* primogeniture.
पहुंच, *f.* arrival; reach; access, admittance; penetration, sagacity; a receipt.
पहुंचना, *a. int.* to arrive, reach, come, extend, amount, belong, befal, happen to, overtake (as a calamity). [conveyed, etc.
पहुंचवाना, *t.* to cause to be carried, cause to be conveyed, etc.
पहुंचा, *m.* the wrist.
पहुंचाना, *t.* to cause to arrive, to lead to, cause to reach or attain unto, to send, carry, convey, transmit, bring, conduct, to cause, occasion, bring about.
पहुंचावनों, in Braj = पहुंचाना, *q.v.* [of bracelet.
पहुंची, *f.* an ornament worn on the wrist, kind of bracelet.
पहुकर in Chand = पोखर, *q.v.*
पहुचना, *more prop.* पहुंचना, *q.v.*
पहुड़ना, *a. int.* to lie down, repose, rest, sleep.
पहुनई, *f.* hospitality, entertainment.— *k.* with gen. *fem.* of object) to entertain, receive, act the host.
पहुना, *m.* (*f.* ī) *more com.* पाहुना, *q.v.*
पहुनाई, *more prop.* पहुनई, *q.v.*
पहुप, *m.* (*prop.* पुष्प) a flower.
पहुमि (*in Chand*) = पृथवी, *q.v.*
पहूंचना, *more prop.* पहुंचना, *q.v.*
पहूंचब, a dialectic form = पहुंचूंगा. See ब, 4.
पहूंकना, *more prop.* पहुंचना, *q.v.*
पहूचना, a corruption of पहुंचना, *q.v.*
पहेचानना, *more prop.* पहचानना, *q.v.*
पहेनना, *more prop.* पहिनना, *q.v.*
पहेनाना, *more prop.* पहिनाना, *q.v.*
पहेर; see (1) पहर (2) पहिर.
पहेल; see (1) पहिले (2) पहेली.
पहेली, *f.* a riddle, enigma. — *pūchhnā*, to ask anyone a riddle, propound an enigma.
पहेलें, *more prop.* पहिले, *q.v.*
पहोंचना, *more prop.* पहुंचना, *q.v.*
पह्लव, *m.* one of the degraded Kshatriya races sentenced by Sagar to wear beards (perhaps a Parthian).
पन्हिका, *f.* a certain plant (*Pistia stratioites*).
पह्नव, *m.* one of the barbarous tribes enumerated by Manu, the Persians: a city; a hero, wrestler; a saint.
पह्लवी, 1, *f.* the language of Persia in its transition from the Zand to that now spoken: 2, *m.* (*f.* in *or* inī) a citizen, a saintly person; an ancient Persian and what appertains to him; heroic: *lit.* appertaining to Pahlav.
पा, 1, *m.* = पन, *q.v.*: 2, *m.* the leg, the foot: 3, the

shortest form of the conjuntive participle of *ch. pānā*: 4, the feminine form of the adjectival termination ए; see ए, 3 (1).

पाइ, 1, in Braj = पा, 3, *q.v.*: 2, *more prop.* पाए, 3, *q. v.*: 3, *more prop.* पाई, 1, *q.v.*

पाइक (Rām.) = (1) पियादा (2) मल्ल, *qq. v.*

पाइये in Braj = 1, पाए, 1, *q.v.*: 2, पाओगे (पाना).

पाइहै *m.* and *f.* (pl पाइहैं) in Braj = पावेगा.

पाइहौ, *m.* and *f.* in Braj = पाओगे } (पाना).
पाइहौं, *m.* and *f.* in Braj = पाऊंगा. }

पाई, 1, *f.* see पाया: 2, *m.* (*f.* in *or* inī) = पाजी, *q.v.*: 3, *f.* a copper coin, being the fourth part of the ānā a 'pice'. The term is, however, chiefly applied to the smallest copper coin of India: these are twelve 'pies' in an 'anna', and eight in the penny: a 'pie' is, accordingly, equivalent to a half a farthing or mite.

पाईं, *f.* 1, = पाई, 3, *q.v.*: 2, pl. of पाई, 1, *q.v.*: 3, pins used by weavers to wind off the warp from.

पाईकाश्त, *more prop.* पायकाश्त, *q.v.*

पाईन्ती, *f.* the foot of a bed, the side towards [the feet.

पाउक, *more prop.* पावक, *q.v.*

पाउना, in old Hindee = पाना, *q. v.*

पाउब, in old Hindee = मैं पाऊंगा. See ब, 4.

पाऊती, *f.* a kind of lamp.

पाए, *m.* 1, pl. of पाया, 1: 2, a peasant who resides in one village and cultivates land belonging to another village: 3, a foot, leg, the foot or stand of a table, chair, etc.—*dharnā*, to intermeddle.

पाएकार, *m.* (*f.* ī) a person who purchases goods from the manufacturer to sell to the merchant: a non-resident labourer hired to cultivate land.

पाएकाश्त, lands let out to non-resident tenants. —*zamīn*, *f.* land cultivated by tenants not residing on the spot.

पाएख़ाना, *m.* a water-closet, necessary, place of [convenience.

पाएज़हर, *m.* the bezoar stone.

पाएजामा, *m.* drawers, trowsers, long loose drawers. [females.

पाएज़ेब, *f.* a kind of ankle-ornament worn by

पाएतख़्त, *m.* a residence of the royal family.

पाएदार, firm, steady, durable, permanent.

पाएबन्द, tied by the leg, fettered, captivated: *met.* encumbered with a family.

पाएबन्दी, *f.* the condition of being fettered, captivated, or encumbered.

पाओ, *more com.* पाव, *q.v.*

पाओं, *m.* (pl. of पा) feet.—*par teshā mār-lenā, to* hit one's own feet with the adze, *i. e.* to occasion one's own failure.

पाओज़हर, *m.* the bezoar stone.

पाओंपाओं, *more prop.* पांवोंपांवों, *q.v.*

पाओंभूल, *f.* calamity, misfortune.

पाओती, *f.* a kind of lamp.

पांओं, *more prop.* पांवों, *q. v.*

पांक, *m.* bog, mire, mud, slough, quagmire.

पांख, linear, in (or by) line or row.

पांखा; see (1) पंखी (2) चूर्ण (3) शलभ.

पांग, *m.* mud left by inundation, alluvial soil.

पांगा, *m.* culinary salt obtained from sea-sand (as by the process used on the sea coast of Bengal.

पांच, five (५).

पांचकर्म्म, *more com.* पंचकर्म्म, *q.v.*

पांचकटांक, a toll of five *chhaṭānk* in a rupee's worth of rice or paddy. The toll is levied in large cities to defray the expenses of inspectors of weighmen stationed in the bāzārs to prevent fraud in the weight and measure of commodities sold therein.

पांचजन्य, *m. pr. n.* (1) of a certain part of Jambu-dweep (2) of Krishn's conch.

पांचज्ञान, *more com.* पंचज्ञान, *q. v.*

पांचतत्त्व, *more com.* पंचतत्त्व, *q.v.*

पांचवां, *m.* (*f.* °वीं) the fifth. See पांच and वां.

पांचवीं, *f.* the fifth day of the moon, or of the half month.

पांचवे, (see वे, 2) fifthly, in the fifth place.

पांचवें, (see वें, 1) infl. of पांचवां, *q.v.*

पांचसात, *f.* perplexity.

पांचाल, *m.* 1, the company or association of five trades, viz. carpenter, weaver, barber, washerman, and shoemaker: 2, the sovereign of Panchāl: 3, appertaining to the country of Panchāl.

पांची, *f.* a kind of weed which grows in tanks [and pools.

पांचेक, (पांच + एक) about five, a few. See एक.

पांचों, the five, all five of them. See ओं, 3.

पांचोंतत्त्व, *more com.* पंचतत्त्व, *q. v.*

पांचोंभाई, *m.* the five Pāṇḍav princes, *viz.* Yudhishthir, Bheemsen, Arjun, Nakul and Sahdev.

पांचोंभूतात्मा, *more com.* पंचभूत, *q.v.*

पांत; see पंक्ति.

पांजर, *m.* the ribs, the side: a side or quarter.

पांड, पांत, पांप; for words beginning with either of these elements, see under the forms पाण्ड, पान्त, पाम्प, respectively.

पांड़े, *m.* a schoolmaster (a title of Brāhmaṇs).

पांय; see पाए, 3.

पांयती = पाईन्ती, *q.v.*

पांव, *m.* leg, foot.— *uṭhānā* or *chalānā*, to go quickly. — *urānā*, to interfere unprofitably in anyone's affairs. —*utarnā*, to be dislocated (the foot.) — *kā anguṭhā*, *m.* the great toe. — *kampnā* or *tharthar-ānā*, to fear to attempt a thing. — *kāim k.* to occupy a fixed habitation, to adopt a new resolution. — *kisikā ukhārnā*, to move anyone from his place or from his purpose. — *kisika galemeṅ ḍālnā*, to convict one by his own arguments. — *kī ungli*, *f.* a toe. — *chal jānā*, to totter, become unstable. — *jamānā*, to stand firmly. — *zamīnpar na ṭhaharnā* is used to indicate expressive joy. — *Ḍālnā* or *denā*, to prepare for and commence an undertaking. —*dignā*, to slip. — *tale malnā*, to give one pain, to annoy. — *tornā*, to desist from visiting a person; to visit a person very often; to be tired. *Dabe — ānā*, to come gently and unperceived (as a spy). — *dharnā*, to interfere, meddle with. — *dho dho pina* (*lit.* to drink the water with which one's feet are washed) denotes perfect confidence in one. — *nikālnā*, to exceed one's proper limits; to withdraw from an undertaking:

to be a ringleader in a criminal action. — *pakarnā*, to beseech submissively : to prevent one from going. — *parnā*, to entreat submissively. — *par* — *rakhnā*, to walk in the footsteps of another, *i. e.* to imitate his conduct; to sit cross-legged, sit at ease. —*piṭnā*, to stamp the foot with impatience.— *pūjnā*, to honour a person ; to avoid a person. — *phūk phūk rakhnā*, to do a thing carefully. —*phailākar sonā* (*lit.* to sleep with the legs extended) is applied to signify perfect content and security. — *phailānā*, to be obstinate, to insist. — *baṛhānā*, to take the lead among one's equals; to desist from one's former courses. — *bharjānā*, to sleep or become numb (said of the feet). —*ragaṛnā*, to go about foolishly and unprofitably; to be in the agonies of death. — *lagnā*, to make obeisance.— *sābit rakhnā*, to persevere firmly in a resolution. — *se* — *bāndhnā*, to watch one closely. — *se* — *bhirānā*, to be near. — *sonā*, to sleep or become numbed (said of the feet). —*gāṛnā*, to plant one's foot, *i. e.* to stand immoveable.

पांवड़ा, *m.* a cloth or carpet spread for great per-
पांवपांव, *adv.* a-foot, on foot. [sonages to walk on.

पांवर (*Rām.*) = **पामर**, *q.v.*

पांवरी, *f.* a shoe, slipper, sandal.

पांवरोटी, *more prop.* **पावरोटी**, *q.v.*

पांवला, *more prop.* **पावला**, *q.v.*

पांवों, *m.* (pl. of **पांव**) the feet.

पांवोंतक, reaching to the feet.

पांवोंपांवों, *adv.* a-foot, on foot, walking.

पांशज, *m.* rock or fossil salt.

पांशु, *m.* manure: dust, a particle of dust. [simus.
पांशुका, *f.* the fragrant plant *Pandanus odoratis-*
पांशुकासीस, *m.* sulphuret of iron. [sil salt.
पांशुज, *m.* salt extracted from soil, rock or fos-

पांशुपुत्र, *m.* the potherb *Chenopdium album.*

पांशुल, 1, *m.* a certain tree (*Cæsalpinia bonducellu*) : 2, *m.* (*f.* ā) dusty, covered with dust; disgraced.

पांस, *m.* manure ; a dunghill. —*ho jānā*, to rot; to become mellow (said of land).

पांसना, *t.* to manure.

पांसा, *m.* a die : *lit.* a throw.

पांसी, *f.* a net for carrying grass or straw in.

पांसु, 1, *f.* a rib, the rib bones: 2, *m.* dust, a particle of dust.

पांसे }
पांसेा } (*colloquial*) = **पांच सेा**.

पांहो, 1, (*Rām.*) = **पास**, *q.v.*: 2, *more prop.* **पाहो**, *q. v.*

पाक, *m.* 1, an electuary medicine, a confection: 2, clean, pure, holy, upright: 3, *pr. n.* a certain *Asur.*

पाकज़ादा, *m.* (*f.* ī) a washerman.

पाकड़, *m.* the citron-leaved Indian figtree (*Ficus*
पाकड़िया = **पाकड़**, *q. v.* [*venosa*).

पाकना, *t.* to boil in syrup.

पाकफल, *m.* the caronda (*Carissa carondus*).

पाकबाज़, undefiled, pure (generally applied to
पाकरद्वीप = **प्लक्षद्वीप**, *q. v.* [the mind).
पाकरंजन, *m.* the leaf of the *Laurus cassia.* [of *Pāk.*
पाकरिपु, *m.* an epithet of Indra ; *lit.* the enemy

पाकल, *m.* a species of costus (*Costus speciosus*): *lit.* suppurative, producing maturity.

पाकलि, *m.* a certain plant (*Bauhinia candida*).

पाकली, *f.* a species of cucumber (*Cucumis utilatis-*
पाकवान = **पकवान**, *q. v.* [*simus.*

पाकशाला, *f.* a cookhouse, kitchen.

पाकसंड़सी, *f.* a table-vice, bench-vice.

पाकस्थान, *m.* a cooking-place, kitchen.

पाकी, *f.* cleansing, purity, sanctity, cleanliness. — *lenā*, to shave (or pluck hairs from) parts concealed.

पाकीज़गी, *f.* cleanliness, neatness, purity, sancti-
पाकीज़ा, clean, neat, pure, holy. [ty, holiness.

पाक्य, *m.* a medicinal salt (*biṭlaban*) impregnated with iron; nitre, saltpetre.

पाक्ष्य, appertaining to a side or party.

पाख (*Rām.*) = (1) **पक्ष** (2) **पान्द्रह दिन**.

पाखण्ड, for all words beginning thus, see under the form **पाषण्ड**.

पाखदिन, *m.* the period of fifteen days, a fortnight.

पाखर, *f.* iron armour for the defence of a horse or of an elephant.

पाखा, *m.* a shed, any small building leaning against the wall of a yard or area.

पाखान, *more prop.* **पाषाण**, *q.v.*

पाख़ाना = **पायख़ाना**, *q. v.*

पाग, *f.* a turban : syrup : a poll-tax formerly levied on all males over twelve years of age.

पागना, *a. int.* to come to a head, ripen.

पागर ; see (1) **पगरी** (2) **पागल**.

पागराना, *more prop.* **पागुराना**, *q.v.*

पागल, *m.* (*f.* ā) demented, deranged, mad, insane, crazy, cracked, idiotic, foolish.

पागलख़ाना, *m.* a mad-house.

पागलपन, *m.* madness, insanity, idiotcy, craziness.

पागला, 1, *m.* (*f.* ī) = **पागल**, *q. v.*: 2, *f.* (*m.* **पागल**) =
पागलामी, *f.* = **पागलपन**, *q. v.* [**पागली**, *q.v.*

पागली, *f.* (*m.* **पागला**) a mad woman.

पागा, 1, *m.* (among Marhaṭṭas) a troop of horse, a stud: 2, *m.* (*f.* ī) come to a head, ripened, ripe.

पागुर, *m.* the chewing the cud, rumination.

पागुराना, *t.* to chew the cud, ruminate.

पागे, *m.* (*f.* **पागीं**) pl. of **पागा**, 2, *q. v.*

पाच, a kind of gem, emerald.

पाचक, 1, *m.* (*f.* ikā) a cook : *lit.* adj. cooking, concocting, aiding or effecting digestion, causing to ripen, tonic ; *hence*, the bile which assists in digestion, a digestive, stomachic, solvent : 2, *m.* cowdung dried for fuel.

पाचन, *m.* a medicinal preparation, an infusion of various drugs (chiefly carminatives or gentle stimuli given to bring the vitiated humours in fever, etc. to maturity, a decoction, sort of diet-drink : expiation, penance : fire : *lit.* adj. ripening, maturing, digestive, suppurative.

पाचनक, *m.* borax ; a sort of diet-drink.

पाचनशक्ति, *f.* the digestive power.

पाचना ; see (1) **पचना** (2) **पाचन** (3) **पाछना**.

पाचनी, *f.* a sort of myrobalan (*Terminalia chebula*).

पाचल, *adj.* aiding or promoting digestion.

पाचिका, *f.* (*m.* **पाचक**) a female cook.

पाचों in Braj = **पांचों**, *q.v.*

पाछ, *m.* the act of inoculating, inoculation.

पाछना, *t.* to inoculate : to rend.

पाछला, *m.* (*f.* ī) in Braj = **पिछला**, *q.v.*

पाछलि in Braj = **पिछली**, *q.v.*

पाछा, *m.* a sheep's foot, a foot.

पाछिल, *more com.* **पिछला**, *q.v.*

पाछिला, *m.* (*f.* ī) *more prop.* **पिछला**, *q.v.*

पाछे, afterwards, after, behind, in the absence of.

पाछें, *more com.* **पाछे**, *q.v.*

पाछेहो, an emphatic form of **पाछे**, *q.v.*

पाछै }
पाछैं } in Braj = **पाछे**, *q.v.*

पाञ्च ; for words beginning thus, see under the form **पांच**.

पाज, a corrupted form of **पास**, *q.v.*

पाजामा = **पाएजामा**, *q.v.*

पाजी, mean, base.

पाजीपन }
पाजीपना } *m.* mean-spiritedness, meanness.
पाजीपा }

पाजीमिज़ाज, of a mean disposition, mean-spirited, base-souled.

पाजेब, *more prop.* **पाएज़ेब**, *q.v.*

पाट, *m.* extension, expansion, width, breadth : an intersection in a triangle formed by a perpendicular drawn from one of the angles : tow : silk, a cocoon of silk : a millstone : a throne, seat, stool ; a board, shutter, slab, plank, plank on which washermen beat clothes, the leaf of a door : a bed or plot in a garden or field : a terrace : a sack or load of corn : an earthen hoop or brace to prevent a well from falling in : a folding clothes or laying them in order : a certain plant (*Corchorus olitorius*). This term also signifies a note or obligation to pay a sum of money for one's own account on an appointed day : it is often usual to accept these pāṭs from creditable persons in payment of the arrears of the zamīndārs.

पाटंबर = **पाटम्बर**, *q.v.*

पाटकृम, *m.* a silkworm.

पाटन, 1, a pl. of **पाट** (see **न**, 6) : 2, *f.* a roof : 3, *m.* a city, mart ; *pr. n.* Patna.

पाटना, *t.* to roof, cover, shut ; to fill, fill up, overstock, heap, pile, accumulate; to irrigate, water: to pay.

पाटमहिषी (Rām.) = **पाटरानी**, *q.v.*

पाटम्बर, *m.* silk cloth, silk clothing.

पाटरानी, *f.* a queen who is installed or consecrated with the king, the principal wife of a rājā, a queen-consort.

पाटल, *m.* pale red, rose-colour ; a kind of rice that ripens in the rains ; the tree of trumpet-flower : lit. *m.* (*f.* ā) of a pale red colour, pallid, pink.

पाटला }
पाटलि } = **पाटली**, *q.v.*

पाटलिपुत्र, *m. pr. n.* the modern Pātna (supposed to be the ancient Palibothra).

पाटली, *f.* the trumpet-flower (*Bignonia swaveolens*) and its tree.

पाटलोपल, *m.* a ruby.

पाटव, *m.* sharpness, energy, cleverness, talent, dexterity, skill, quickness, precipitation : *lit.* dexterous, able, talented, clever.

पाटविक, *m.* (*f.* ā *or* ī) dexterous, clever, cunning, crafty, fraudulent.

पाटच्चिका, *f.* a kind of small shrub (*Abrus precatorius*).

पाटा, *m.* a bench, board, plank (such as that on which washermen beat clothes).

पाटिन, *m.* a sort of fish described as having many teeth.

पाटी, 1, *m.* = **पाटिन**, *q.v.* : 2, *f.* the side-pieces of a bedstead : a kind of mat : a kind of board on which children learn to write : the divisions of the hair when it is combed towards the two sides and parted by a line in the middle : a kind of sweetmeat : arithmetic.

पाटीर, *m.* sandal : a certain pungent root, sort of radish.

पाटूनी, *m.* a ferryman.

पाटोपल, *more com.* **पाटलोपल**, *q.v.*

पाटौनी, *m.* a ferryman.

पाठ, *m.* reading, perusal, study, recital (*esp.* sacred study, *viz.* perusal of the Veds considered as one of the five great sacraments of the Hindoos) ; a text or reading ; a lesson.— *denā*, to give a lecture.— *k.* or *paṛhnā*, to read.

पाठक, *m.* (*f.* ikā) a reader, lecturer, preceptor, teacher, professor ; a spiritual preceptor ; a man who reads in public the Purāṇs or other sacred works of the Hindoos, a paṇḍit who declares what is the law or custom according to the sacred writings : a title of Brāhmaṇs : *lit.* adj. reading, perusing.

पाठगुरु, *m.* a reading-master, professor of elocution, preceptor, schoolmaster.

पाठन, *m.* reading, lecturing, teaching.

पाठभू, *f.* a place where the Veds are read or studied.

पाठमंजरी, *f.* a certain small bird (*Gracula religiosa*).

पाठमार, *m.* a courier or messenger sent from place to place.

पाठवन्त }
पाठवान } *m.* (*f.* matī) a learned person.

पाठशाला, *f.* a reading-room, lecture-hall, school-house, college.

पाठशालिनी, *f.* a certain small bird (*Gracula religiosa*).

पाठा, *m.* (*f.* ī) a young full-grown animal (generally a goat or an elephant), a youth, young wrestler.

पाठान, *m.* bdellium.

पाठिका, *f.* (*m.* **पाठक**) a female student, female lecturer.

पाठित, *m.* (*f.* ā) instructed, taught, lectured.

पाठी, 1, *m.* (*f.* inī) a Brāhmaṇ who has finished his studies, one who gives lessons, a teacher, professor : a kind of plant (*Plumago zeylanica*) : a kind of fish : 2, *f.* a young (female ?) goat.

पाठीन, 1, = **पाठक**, *q.v.* : 2, *m.* the sheat-fish (*Silurus boalis* or *S. pelorius*, Buch.).

पाठ्य, fit (or requiring) to be perused or studied, worth reading, legible, admitting of being read.

पाड़, *f.* a beam laid on pillars to support other beams, a scaffold. —*parnā*, to sustain an injury, receive a blow.

पाड़ना, *t.* to cause to fall, to let fall, throw down; to accomplish, finish, kill: to collect lampblack.

पाड़वा, *f.* the end of the month or the day of the moon.

पाड़ा, *m.* a quarter of a town, ward, canton, neighbourhood.

पाढ़ा, *m.* a hog-deer (*Cervus porcinus*).

पाढ़ी, *f.* crossing a river (when travelling on it): a young buffalo, buffalo-calf.

पाणि, *m.f.* the hand. *Jori*—, with the hands put flat together as in suplication.

पाणिगृहीता, *f.* a bride wedded according to the ritual; *lit.* taken by the hand.

पाणिग्रह = **पाणिग्रहण**, *q.v.*

पाणिग्रहण, *m.* marriage; *lit.* a laying hold of the hand (the junction of the hands of the bride and bridegroom forming part of the ceremony).

पाणिग्रहणिक, *m.* a nuptial present: *lit.* nuptial, matrimonial.

पाणिघ, *m.* a tabor-player, drummer: *lit.* adj. striking or beating with the hands.

पाणिघात = **पाणिघ**, *q.v.*

पाणिनि, *m. pr. n.* Pāṇini, the celebrated Hindoo *muni* and inspired Sanskrit grammarian.

पाणिनीय, connected with or derived from Pāṇini (as a rule, a scholar, etc.).

पाणिभुज, *m.* the glomerous figtree (*Ficus glomerata*).

पाणी, *more com.* (1) **पाणि** (2) **पानी**, *qq.v.*

पाण्डर, *m.* many-flowered jasmine (*Jasminum elongatum*): the colour pale or yellowish-white; *pr. n.* (1) of a certain *Nāg* (2) of a certain mountain: *lit. m.* (*f.* ā) pale, yellowish white.

पाण्डरपुष्पिका, *f.* a certain plant commonly called *sitalā* (perhaps *Phrygnium dichotomum*).

पाण्डरा, *m.* a species of sugarcane.

पाण्डव, 1, *m.* (patronym.) a descendant of Pāṇdu (*esp.* Yudhisthir and his four brothers): 2, *m.*(*f.* i) a partisan of the five Pāṇḍav princes: *lit.* appertaining to the five Pāṇḍavs.

पाण्डवान, *m.* (a Sk. pl. of **पाण्डव**) the five Pāṇḍav princes.

पाण्डिती, *f.* scholarship, learning, wisdom, prudence.

पाण्डित्य, *m.* = **पाण्डिती**, *q.v.*

पाण्डु, 1, pale, white, yellowish white: 2, *m.* the colour pale or yellowish white: 3, *m. pr. n.* a sovereign of Hastināpur (ancient Delhi), and nominal father of Yudhisthir and the other four Pāṇḍav princes who are distinguished in the great wars related in the Mahābhārat: 4, *f.* a certain plant (*Glycine debilis*) commonly called *Mashani*.

पाण्डुकम्बल, *m.* a kind of stone (limestone or marble?).

पाण्डुकम्बली, *f.* a carriage covered with a sort of blanket: the housings of a royal elephant.

पाण्डुक्ष्मा, *f.* an epithet of Hastināpur: *lit.* the the land of the Pāṇḍavs.

पाण्डुनाग, *m.* a species of plant (*Rottleria tinctoria*).

पाण्डुपुत्र, *m.* an epithet of either of the Pāṇḍav princes; *lit.* a son of Pāṇḍu.

पाण्डुभूम, *m. f.* a country with a light-coloured soil.

पाण्डुभूमि, *f.* = see (1) **पाण्डुक्ष्मा** (2) **पाण्डुभूम**.

पाण्डुमृत्तिका, *f.* the opal; a pale soil.

पाण्डुर, *m.* the colour pale or yellowish-white; white leprosy, vitiligo: lit. *m.* (*f.* ā) of a yellowish-white colour.

पाण्डुरद्रुम, *m.* the plant *Echites antidysenterica*.

पाण्डुरोग, *m.* a kind of disease.

पाण्डुलोमा, *f.* a certain plant (*Glycine debilis*).

पाण्डुवर्ण, *m.* whiteness: *adj. m.* (*f.* ā) white.

पाण्डुवा, *m.* a light-coloured soil, a mixed soil of clay and sand.

पाण्डुशर्करा, *f.* light-coloured gravel (disease).

पाण्डुसुतन, (a Braj pl of **पाण्डुसुत**) *m.* the Pāṇḍav princes. See **पाण्डु** and **न**, 6.

पाण्डे, *m.* a schoolmaster (a title of Brāhmaṇs).

पाण्य, *m.* (*f.* ā) praiseworthy, excellent.

पात, *m.* flying, manner of flying, a throwing oneself, falling, a fall, sin, wickedness; a leaf, leaf of a book; an ornament worn in the upper part of the ear; a draft or cheque on a banker. *Pāton ā-lagnā*, applied to trees, indicates the fall of their leaves in autumn: *met.* the phrase signifies the exhaustion of one's power or ability; and thus, this expression is often applied to express the exhaustion of patience by the scorn of a beloved person, or to a condition of destitution from adverse fortune.

पातंजल, appertaining to Patanjali, or to the system of which he was founder.

पातक, *m.* that which causes to fall or to sink; *hence*, sin, crime, guilt.

पातकवा, *m.* a messenger.

पातकिरम = **पातकृम** = **पातकृमि**, *q.v.*

पातकी, fallen, sinful, guilty, criminal: hence, *m.* (*f.* ini) a criminal, sinner.

पातकृम, *more prop.* **पातकृमि**, *q. v.*

पातकृमि, *m.* the leaf-worm, *i. e.* caterpillar.

पातबन्दी, *f.* a statement of the assets and liabilities of an estate.

पातर, 1, = **पातुर**, *q.v.*: 2, *m.* (*f.* nī) a moth, butterfly.

पातरनी, *f.* (*m.* **पातर**, 2) a female butterfly.

पाता, 1, *m.* (*f.* tri) = **पातृ**, *q.v.*: 2, preserved, protected: 3, *m.* a leaf.

पाताल, 1, *m. pr. n.* (1) of hell, the infernal regions, which, according to the Hindoo system, is situated under the earth, or towards the south pole and is the abode of the serpent race (2) of one of the seven hells: 2, *m.* a hole, chasm; a submarine fire; a sort of apparatus for calcining and subliming metals, formed of two earthen pots, the upper one inverted over the lower, and the two joined together by their necks with cement and placed in a hole containing fire.

पातालगंगा, *f. pr. n.* (see **गंगा**) the Ganges of the infernal regions.

पाति, *more com.* (1) **पत्ति**, (2) **पान्ति** *q.v.*

पातिक, *m.* the Gangetic porpoise.

पातित, *m.*(*f.* ā) lowered, depressed, humbled, downcast, overthrown.

पातिला = **पातीला**, *q.v.*

पातिली, *f.* a kind of small earthen pot used by religious mendicants.

पातिव्रत; see (1) **पतिव्रत** (2) **पातिव्रत्य**.

पातिव्रत्य, *m*, the devotedness and attachment of a wife to her husband.

पाती, 1, *f*. a letter, note, epistle, leaf: 2, adj. *m*. (*f*. inī) flying, falling, causing to fall.

पातीला, *m*. a kind of wide-mouthed saucepan used by confectioners.

पातुक, *m*. an aquatic animal of a large size; *figuratively*, the water-elephant; a precipice, declivity: *lit*. apt to fall. [lean.

पातुर, 1, *f*. a prostitute, dancing-girl: 2, weak,

पातुरबाज़, *m*. a whoremonger.

पातुरिया, 1, *f*. a prostitute: 2, *m*. a whoremonger.

पातृ, *m*. (*f*. trī) *adj*. drinking: nourishing or protecting.

पातृता, *m*. a certain plant (*Ocymum pilosum*).

पातें; see *s. v*. **पात**. [viour.

पात्र, *m*. a preservative from sin, a preserver, sa-

पात्रत्व, *m*. (*f*. tā) the quality of preserving from sin, the power or function of a preserver.

पात्र, 1, *m*. a vessel in general, a plate, cup, jar, receptacle; a leaf; the bed of a river; a king's counsellor or minister; what holds or supports: 2, *m* (*f*. ī) used in compounds in the sense of capable of, worthy of, eligible, fit, deserving, accomplished.

पात्रत्व, *m*. (*f*. tā) the condition of being a receptacle or a receiver, capacity, fitness, propriety, worthiness, dignity. [of Durgā.

पात्री, *f*. (*m*. **पात्र**) a vessel, a plate, etc.: a name

पाथ (*Rām*.) = **जल**, *q. v*.

पाथना, *t*. to make up cowdung into cakes for fuel.

पाथर, *more prop*. **पत्थर**, *q.v*.

पाथस, *m*. water.

पाथेय, *m*. provisions for a journey.

पाथोज, *m*. a lotus.

पाथोद, *m*. a cloud.

पाथोधि }
पाथोनिधि } *m*. the ocean, the sea.

पाद, *m*. a foot, leg; the root of a tree; the foot of a mountain; a hill at the foot of a mountain; the bottom of a bag; a ray, beam; a quarter, one fourth, (in Pros.) the fourth part of a shlok, stanza, or verse, a line of poetry: wind expelled from behind.

पादकटक, *m*. an ornament for the feet or toes. [feet.

पादगण्डिर, *m*. morbid enlargement of the legs and

पादग्रहण, *m*. a mode of respectful obeisance, *viz*. the touching the feet of a Brāhman, or superior.

पादग्राही, *m*. (*f*. inī) a humble, or servile person: *lit*. adj. seizing the feet.

पादघाबरा, *m*. (*f*. ī) frightened out of one's wits.

पादचत्वर, *m*. the religious figtree (*Ficus religiosa*).

पादचापल्य, *m*. a beating or shuffling with the feet.

पादचार, *adv*. a-foot, on foot, walking.

पादचारी, *m*. (*f*. inī) a walker, footman, foot-soldier.

पादज, *m*. (*f*. ā) Shoodra, man of the lowest caste: *lit*. born from the foot (of Brahmā).

पादतल, *m*. the sole or the lower part of the foot: *adv*. as low as the feet, under the feet.

पाददारी, *f*. a chap in the foot, chilblain.

पादधावन, *m*. washing the feet.

पादना, *a. int*. to break wind. [feet.

पादप, *m*. a tree: a footstool or a cushion for the

पादपरुहा, *f*. a creeping-plant, parasitical plant.

पादपा, *f*. a shoe, slipper.

पादप्रक्षालन, *m*. washing the feet. [to the feet.

पादप्रणाम, *m*. prostration in salutation, bowing

पादप्रहार, *m*. a kick.

पादमूल, *m*. the heel.

पादरी, *m*. (Portug.) a Christian minister or missionary of any denomination, a Christian priest.

पादरोहण, *m*. the Indian figtree.

पादवल्मीक, *m*. morbid enlargement of the legs and feet, elephantiasis.

पादवन्त }
पादवान } *m*. (*f*. vatī) = **पादी**, 1, *q.v*.

पादविक, *m*. (*f*. ī, in, ā) a traveller, wayfarer.

पादशब्द, *m*. the sound of feet, the footfall.

पादशाखा, *f*. a toe.

पादशोथ, *m*. swelling of the feet, gout.

पादसेवन, *m*. = **पादसेवा**, *q.v*. [mark of respect.

पादसेवा, *f*. the touching a person's feet as a

पादस्फोट, *m*. a sore or ulcer on the foot, a chilblain, kibe. [with the feet.

पादहत, *m*. (*f*. ā) trodden on, kicked, touched

पादहर्ष, *m*. the tingling of the feet after pressure upon the crural nerves. [anything with his feet.

पादहारक, *m*. (*f*. ikā) one who seizes or steals

पादांगुलि, *m*. }
पादांगुली, *f*. } a toe.

पादांगुष्ठ, *m*. the great toe. [great toes.

पादांगुष्ठिका, *f*. an ornament or ring worn on the

पादाकुलक, *m*. a sort of metre in Sanskrit prosody.

पादाघात, *m*. a kick, a trampling.

पादानोन, *m*. black salt. It is prepared by melting common salt with a small proportion of myrobalans, and contains sulphur.

पादार्घ्य, *m*. a donation to Brāhmaṇs or venerable persons (*lit*. offering to the feet).

पादार्थ, *more prop*. **पदार्थ**, *q.v*.

पादार्द्ध }
पादार्ध } *m*. half a line of a stanza.

पादाश, *m*. revenge, retaliation, retribution, re-

पादासन, *m*. a footstool. [compense, reward.

पादाहत *m*. (*f*. ā) = **पादहत**, *q.v*.

पादी, *m*. (*f*. inī) 1, a footed creature: *lit*. having feet, footed: 2, a footed aquatic animal, an amphibious animal: 3, entitled to a fourth part or share.

पादुक, *m*. (*f*. ā) any creature that goes on feet: [*lit*. footed.

पादुका, *f*. a shoe, slipper; sandal.

पादु, *f.* a shoe, slipper.

पादोदक, *m.* water for the feet (*esp.* water in which a Brāhmaṇ has washed or dipped his feet).

पाद्य, *m.* water, etc. for washing the feet.

पाद्यपात्र, *m.* a metallic vessel for washing the feet.

पाद्माकीड़ा, *m.* the ant-lion, an insect which constructs a hole in the ground as a trap for ants on which [it feeds.

पाढ़ी, *more prop.* **पाढ़री**, *q.v.*

पाधा, *m.* a school-master.

पान, 1, *more prop.* **पाणि**, *q. v.*; 2, *m.* the act of drinking; drink, beverage: a hand: any leaf; betel-leaf or leaves of *Piper betel.*—*k.* to drink.—*uṭhānā* or *lenā*, to accept or take the betel-leaf, *i. e.* to consent, agree. [tus is kept.

पानदान, *m.* a box in which betel or its appara-

पानपात्र, *m.* any vessel for drinking from, a glass.

पाना, 1, *t.* to get, acquire, find, realize, experience, enjoy, undergo, sustain, suffer, overtake, reach, attain, obtain, accept: 2, *m.* a plant growing in stagnant water: a solution: sherbet.

पानि, *more prop.* (1) **पाणि** (2) **पानी**, *qq. v.*

पानी, 1, *more prop.* **पाणि**, *q.v.*: 2. *m.* water; sperm; lustre; character, honor.—*k.* to abash; to facilitate; to void water.—*kā bulbulā* (a water-bubble) indicates instability.—*chalnā*, to be afflicted with *fluor albus.* —*jānā*, to be afflicted with *fluor albus*; to be disgraced; to shed tears.—*denā*, to offer a libation of water to satisfy the manes of a deceased person after the corpse has been burnt.—*na māngnā*, to be slain with a single stroke of a sword, etc. and die instantly.—*paṛnā*, to rain.—*pī pī kosnā*, to curse till the throat, being dry, must be moistened by drinking, *i. e.* to curse excessively.—*pīnā*, to drink water.—*bharnā*, to confess inferiority.—*marnā*, to dry up, become evaporated; to exhibit signs confirmatory of a suspicion.—*meṅ āg lagānā*, to revive a contention which had subsided.—*se patlā k.* to abash, put to shame.—*toṛnā* or *mārnā*, to draw (in nautical phraseology); e. g. *Yih jahāz kitnā pāni mārtā* (or *toṛtā*) *hai*, how much water does this ship draw? *i. e.* what is the draught of this ship?

पानीपत, *m. pr. n.* the the country of Pānīpat.

पानीय, to be drunk, *i. e.* fit, proper, or necessary to be drunk, drinkable.

पानीयनकुल, *m.* (*f.* ī) an otter.

पानीयपृष्ठज, *m.* the aquatic plant *Pistia stratioites.*

पानीयमूलक, *m.* the plant *Serratula anthelmintica.*

पानीयामलक, *m.* the fruit *Flacourtia cataphracta.*

पान्त, a contraction of **पान्ति**, *q.v.*

पान्तर, *m.* a desert field. [soldiers.

पान्ति *f.* a row, line (in writing), a note, a row of

पान्तिपान्ति, *adv.* in rows, in lines.

पान्ती, a lengthening of **पान्ति**, *q. v.*

पान्तुपान्तु, *adv.* in rows, in lines.

पान्थ, *m.* (*f.* ā) a traveller, passenger.

पान्य; see **पाथय**.

पान्हर, *m.* a kind of reed.

पाप, 1, *m.* wickedness, evil, crime, sin, guilt, depravity, fault, vice: 2, *m.* (*f.* ā or ī) sinful, wicked, depred, criminal, guilty.—*mānnā*, to confess sin or fault.

पापक, 1, *m.* (*f.* ikā *or* ī) = **पाप**, 2; *q.v.*: 2, appertaining to or consisting of sin.

पापकर, *m.* (*f.* ī) a criminal, sinner: *lit.* adj. doing bad actions, committing crime, criminal, sinful.

पापकर्त्ता, *m.* (*f.* trī)
पापकर्तृ, *m.* (*f.* trī)
पापकारक, *m.* (*f.* ikā)
पापकारी, *m.* (*f.* iṇī)
} = **पापकर**, *q. v.*

पापकृत, 1, *m.* (*f.* ā) = **पापकर**, *q. v.*: 2, *m.* an evil action, misdeed, crime.

पापग्रह, *m.* 1, an inauspicious planet, any ill-omened aspect of the heavenly bodies, such as the conjunction of the sun or *Budh* with the moon in its last quarter: *hence*, an epithet of Rāhu, Saturn, and Mars: 2, calamity, misfortune, fatal destiny.

पापघ्न, *m.* (*f.* ī *or* ā) *adj.* destroying (*i.e.* removing or expiating) sin. [commonly called *aknidhi.*

पापचेली, *f.* a certain plant (*Cissampelos hexandra*)

पापड़, *m.* a thin crisp cake made of any grain of the pea kind.—*belnā*, to undergo great labour or pain.

पापड़खार = **पापड़ाखार**, *q.v.*

पापड़ा, *m.* a certain plant (*Gardenia latifolia*).

पापड़ाखार, *m.* ashes of the plaintain-tree (*Musa paradisiaca*) used instead of salt for seasoning the cakes called *pāpaṛ*.

पापदर्शी, *m.* (*f.* inī) a malevolent person: *lit.* adj. looking at faults. [sequent on sinning.

पापदुःख, *m.* the misery or the punishment con-

पापदृश्वन, *m.* (*f.* ā) a person who is conscious of or conversant with sin: *lit.* conscious of sin, knowing an act to be wicked.

पापन, *m.* (a Braj pl. of **पाप**; see **न**, 6) sins.

पापनाशिन, *m.* (*f.* ī)
पापनाशिक, *m.* (*f.* ā)
} = **पापनाशी**, *q. v.*

पापनाशी, *m.* (*f.* inī) *adj.* sin-destroying, purifying.

पापनी, a contraction of **पापिनी**, *q. v.*

पापपति, *m.* (*f* °**पत्नि**) a paramour, gallant.

पापपुरुष, *m.* a personification of all sin.

पापफल, *m.* (*f.* ā) having evil consequences, inauspicious.

पापबुद्धि, evil-minded, of a corrupt intellect, sinful, ungodly, wicked, depraved, graceless.

पापमति = **पापबुद्धि**, *q.v.*

पापमती, *f.* (*m.* **पापमान**) a sinful woman.

पापमय, *m.* (*f.* ī) abounding in sin, totally depraved.

पापमान, *m.* (*f.* matī) sinful, bad, wicked.

पापमुक्त, *m.* (*f.* ā) a person who has been freed from sin or crime: *lit.* liberated from guilt. [tion.

पापमोक्षण, *m.* liberation from sin, pardon, salva-

पापमोचन
पापमोच्छन
पापमोछन
} = **पापमोक्षण**, *q. v.*

पापयुक्त, *m.* (*f.* ā) connected with sin, sinful.

पापर, *m.* 1, *more prop.* **पापड़**, *q.v.*: 2, a fertile soil.

पापरोग, *m.* a disease (*e. g.* leprosy, small-pox) considered as the punishment of sin committed in a for-

पापसम्मित, equally sinful. [mer, birth.

पापहर, *m.* (*f.* ā) *adj.* removing evil, sin-destroying.

पापहारक, *m.* (*f.* ikā) = **पापहर**, *q.v.*

पापा, 1, *f.* (*m.* **पाप**, 2) a female criminal: 2, *m.* an insect bred in rice, weevil: 2, *m. pr. n.* the Pope.

पापाचरण, *m.* the pursuit of sin. —— *k.* to live a life of sin.

पापाचार, *m.* (*f.* ā) a wicked person: *lit.* adj. following an evil course of life, wicked, vicious.

पापात्मा, a sinner, reprobate, wretch: *lit.* of a wicked or vicious disposition, sinful, criminal.

पापाधीन, *m.* (*f.* ā) in subjection to sin.

पापिन, 1, = **पापी**, 2, *q.v.*: 2, a common contraction

पापिनी, *f.* (*m.* **पापी**) a wicked woman. [of **पापिनी**.

पापिया, 1, *m.* the castor-oil tree: 2, wicked, sinful, malicious. [very sinful.

पापिष्ठ, *m.* (*f.* ā) *adj.* (superl.) most wicked,

पापी, 1, *f.* (*m.* **पाप**, 2) a female criminal: 2. *m.* (*f.* inī) a sinner, criminal: *lit.* wicked, sinful, bad.

पापोश, *f.* a slipper.

पाम, *m.* = **पामा**, *q.v.*

पामन, 1, *m.* = **पामा**, *q.v.*: 2, *m.* (*f.* ā *or* ī) afflicted with herpes or any cutaneous disease.

पामर, *m.* (*f.* ī) a sinner; a low person; an idiot: *lit.* wicked, vile, low, mean, base, stupid, idiotic, foolish.

पामरी, *f.* 1, (*m.* **पामर**) the wife of a man of inferior caste: 2, silk clothing.

पामर्दी, *f.* strength, valour, resolution.

पामा, *f.* cutaneous eruption, herpes, scab, the itch.

पामारि, *m.* sulphur.

पामारी; see (1) **पामरी** (2) **पामारि**.

पामाल, trodden under foot, devastated, ruined.

पाम्य, 1, *more prop.* **पाप**, 1, *q.v.*: 2, *m.* agony, anguish,

पाम्यी, *more prop.* **पापी**, *q.v.* [torture.

पाय, 1, *m.* (prop. **पाइ**) the foot, leg: 2, = **पा**, 3

पायंती = **पायन्ती**, *q.v.* [(see **प**).

पायक, *adj.* drinking: hence, *m.* (*f.* ikā) a drinker.

पायगी, *f.* degree, rank: a troop

पायजमा, a contraction of **पाएजामा**, *q.v.*

पायजामा } *more prop.* **पाएजामा**, *q.v.*
पायजामी }

पायठ, *m.* a scaffold.

पायतख़्त, *more prop.* **पाएतख़्त**, *q.v.*

पायदार, *more prop.* **पाएदार**, *q.v.*

पायन, a Braj pl. of **पाय**, *q.v.*: see **न**, 6 (1).

पायन्ती *f.* the foot of a bed, the side towards the feet.

पायबन्द, *more prop.* **पाएबन्द**, *q.v.*

पायरा, *m.* (*f.* ī) a pigeon.

पायल, 1, *f.* an ornament for the foot or ankle: a bamboo ladder: 2, sure-footed, easy-paced (as the elephant).

पायस, *m.* an oblation of milk, rice, and sugar: turpentine: *lit.* made of or from milk or water.

पाया, 1, *m.* (*f.* **पाई**) base of the Historical Tenses of the verb *pānā*: 2. *m.* the leg or foot of any piece of furniture: the foundations of a building: a step, degree, rank, dignity.

पायान, *m.* } extremity, end, completion.
पायानी, *f.* }

पायाब, 1, *m.* a ford: 2, within a man's depth, fordable. [messenger, harbinger.

पायिक, *m.* (*f.* ā *or* ī) a footman, foot-soldier,

पायिन्ती, *f.* = **पायन्ती**, *q.v.*

पायिल = **पायल**, *q.v.*

पायी, *m.* (*f.* inī) a drinker: lit. *adj.* drinking. This form occurs only as the latter element in compound words.

पायु, *m.* the anus.

पाये, *more prop.* **पाए**, 1, *q.v.* [an agent, broker.

पायो, 1, (in poet.) = **पाया**, 1, *q.v.*; 2, (in Mārwāṛī)

पायें, 1, *more com.* **पांवें**, *q.v.*: 2, **मैं पाऊंगा**.

पायौ in Braj = **पाया**, 1, *q.v.*

पार, 1, *m.* the further or opposite bank or shore of a river or sea: end, extremity, limit: quick-silver: a crossing or passing over: 2, adj. *m.* (*f.* ā) last, past: 3, *adv.* over, across, on the opposite side or shore, through, beyond.—*k.* to ferry over; to cross; to finish, accomplish, carry through; to perforate, transfix; to relieve; to carry off. — *ho jānā*, to go away, be off, escape, attain refuge. — *honā*, to penetrate, permeate, imbue; to survive, succeed in, get through.— *utarnā*, to get across (especially, the ocean of existence), *i. e.* to attain salvation.

पारक, *m.* (*f.* ikā) purifying, protecting, cherishing, pleasing: enabling anyone to cross a river or to get through the world; getting through; accomplishing, able, expert, clever, active. [ability, activity.

पारकत्व, *m.* (*f.* tā) accomplishment, cleverness,

पारक्य, *m.* (*f.* ā) appertaining to another, hostile.

पारख, *m.* (*f.* in *or* nī) = **पारखी**, *q.v.*

पारखी, *m.* (*f.* inī) an examiner, discriminator.

पारग, *m.* (*f.* ā) *adj.* crossing over, *e.g.* a river, or the ocean of existence; *hence*, getting through a task.

पारगत, *m.* (*f.* ā) a Jin or Jain, deified teacher: lit. *adj.* having crossed over; *hence*, pure, holy.

पारगत्व, *m.* (*f.* tā) perseverance in a pursuit,

पारगा, *f.*; see **पारग**. [steadiness of purpose.

पारगामी, *m.* (*f.* inī) = **पारग**, *q.v.*

पारग्रामिक, hostile: hence, *m.* (*f.* ī) an enemy.

पारजातक, *m. pr. n.* one of the five trees of Indra's

पारजायिक, *m.* an adulterer. [Paradise.

पारण, 1, *m.* a fulfilling; the accomplishing a thing; reading, studying: a cloud: the first meal after a fast, breakfast: 2, *m.* (*f.* ā) a person who eats after a fast.

पारणा, *f.* 1, = **पारण**, 1, *q.v.*: 2, (*m.* **पारण**, 2) a female who eats after a fast.

पारतन्त्र्य, *m.* the being subject to another, subordinateness, dependence, subservience.

पारतौकिक, *more prop.* **पारलौकिक** *q.v.*

पारथिव } (Rām.) = **पार्थिव**, *q.v.*
पारथी }

पारद, *m.* quicksilver : *pr. n.* a certain barbarous nation mentioned by Manu. [Orissa).

पारदयहक, *m. pr. n.* a certain country (part of

पारदर्शी, *m.* (*f* inī) a far-seeing person, etc. : *lit.* adj. seeing the opposite shore, far-seeing, long sighted, wise, profound. skilful.

पारदारिक, an adulterer : *lit.* adj. having unlawful intercourse with the wife of another.

पारदारिकत्व, *m.* (*f.* tā) = **पारदार्य्य**, *q.v.*

पारदार्य्य, *m.* unlawful intercourse with the wife

पारदृश्वन = **पारदर्शी**, *q.v.* [of another, adultery.

पारदेशिक, *m.* (*f.* ā *or* ī) } = **पारदेश्य**, *q.v.*
पारदेशी, *m.* (*f.* inī) }

पारदेश्य, *m.* (*f.* ā) a foreigner, traveller : *lit.* appertaining to another or foreign country, foreign.

पारन, *more prop.* **पारण**, *q.v.*

पारना, 1, *more prop.* **पारणा**, *q.v.* : 2, *t.* to finish, accomplish, perform : 3, *n.* to be able.

पारबती, *more prop.* **पार्वती**, *q.v.*

पारमार्थिक, appertaining to a high or spiritual object, of the highest importance, preferable, most desirable, best, excellent, superior, real.

पारमेश्वर, *m.* (*f.* ī) appertaining to or coming from the supreme, *i. e.* Shiv.

पारम्पर्य्य, *m.* a passing on from one to another, continuous order or succession, traditional knowledge, hereditary property.

पारम्पर्य्योपदेश, *m.* traditional instruction.

पारल, *m.* a certain plant (*Bignonia chelonoides* or *suareolens*). [world.

पारलौकिक, *m.* (*f.* ā *or* ī) appertaining to the next

पारवती, *more prop.* **पार्वती**, *q.v.* [through.

पारवार, on both sides (of a river), quite through,

पारशव, 1, *m.* iron ; an iron weapon : 2, *m.* (*f.* ī) consisting of iron : 3, *m.* (*f.* ī) a certain mixed class among the Hindoos, *i. e.* the offspring of a Shoodrā (*i. e.* woman) by a Brāhmaṇ; *hence*, a child by the wife of another, bastard.

पारशीक, *more prop.* **पारसीक**, *q.v.* [Persic, Persian.

पारस, 1, = **पारसपत्थर**, *q.v.* : 2, *m. pr. n.* Persia : 3,

पारसपत्थर, *m.* the philosopher's stone (which, according to Hindoo legend, immediately converted into gold any metal it might touch).

पारसपत्थल, *more prop.* **पारसपत्थर**, *q. v.*

पारसपीपल, *m.* the tree *Hibiscus populnioides.*

पारसाल, (the year before, *i. e.*) last year.

पारसिक, *more com.* **पारसीक**, *q. v.*

पारसी, Persic, Persian : hence, 1, *f.* the Persian language : 2, *m.* (*f.* inī) a Persian.

पारसीक, *m.* a Persian ; the Persian language ; a Persian horse: lit. *adj.* Persian. [language.

पारसीय, appertaining to Persia or to the Persian

पारह = **पारा**, 4, *q.v.*

पारहि (pl. **पारहिं**) = **सकता है** (**पारना**).

पारा, 1, *m.* quicksilver : 2, *f. pr. n.* a certain river said to flow from the Pāriyātra mountain : 3, *m.* sentinel ; a watchman : 4, *m.* a strap, slip, piece, bit.

पारापार, *m.* the two opposite banks of a river.

पारायण, *m.* a crossing over : totality, completeness, entirety : study : the act of reading a Purāṇ continually (or of causing it to be read) without expressing its meaning.

पारायणिक, *m.* a lecturer ; a reader of the Purāṇs.

पारावत, *m.* a sort of ebony (*Diospyros glutinosa* or *D. embryopteris*) : a kind of snake : a pigeon, dove.

पारावती, *f.* the fruit of the *Annona reticulata* : a form of song peculiar to cowherds : *pr. n.* a certain Indian river.

पारावार, *m.* the ocean, sea, limit (of sea): the opposite banks of a river: *adv.* through and through, entirely, on both sides.

पाराशर, *m.* (*lit.* the son of Parāshar) the poet Vyās : the rules of Vyās for the conduct of the mendicant orders.

पाराशरी, *m.* the religious mendicant or Brāhmaṇ who, having passed through the three stages of student, householder, and ascetic, leads a vagrant life and subsists on alms.

पारिका, *f.* (*m.* **पारक**) a protectress, etc.

पारिकांक्षी, *m.* (*f.* inī) an ascetic, contemplative saint, one who gives himself to devout contemplation.

पारिजात, *m.* the coral-tree (*Erythrina fulgens* or *E. Indica*, Lam.): *pr. n.* a certain tree in the Hindoo paradise produced at the churning of the ocean.

पारिजातक = **पारिजात**, *q.v.*

पारिजायिक ; see **पारजायिक**.

पारिणाय्य, *m.* property received by a woman at the time of her marriage : *lit.* appertaining to marriage : obtained on the occasion of marriage.

पारितथ्या, *f.* a kind of trinket worn on the forehead where the hair is parted.

पारितोषिक, *m.* a reward, compensation, remuneration, gratuity : *lit.* adj. delighting, gratifying, satisfying, pleasing.

पारिपन्थिक, *m.* a robber, highwayman, thief.

पारियात्र, *m. pr. n.* a certain mountain (apparently the central or western portion of the Vindhya range were it skirts the province of Mālwa).

पारियात्रक = **पारियात्र**, *q.v.*

पारिभद्र, *m.* the name of several trees (1) the coral-tree (*Erythrina fulgens* and *E. ovalifolia*) (2) the *nimb*-tree (3) two species of pine (*Pinus devadaru* and *P. longifolia* (4, the *surul.*

पारिभद्रक = **पारिभद्र**, *q.v.* [*tus speciosus*).

पारिभाव्य, *m.* a certain drug, a sort of costus (*Cos-*

पारियात्र = **पारिपात्र**, *q.v.*

पारिलौकिक, *more prop.* **पारलौकिक**, *q. v.*

पारिषद, *m.* a king's companion; the retinue of a god ; an attendant ; a spectator, person present at an assembly : *lit.* appertaining to an assembly.

पारिस, *m. pr. n.* Persia.

पारी, *f.* a time, tour, turn : a cup. — *bāndhnā*, to arrange to take by turns.

पारीक्षित, (patronym.) *m.* (*f.* ā) a descendant of Parīkshit: *lit.* appertaining to Rājā Parīkshit.

पारीन्द्र, *m.* a lion: a large snake (*Boa*).

पारीपारी, *adv.* by turns, in rotation.

पारुष्य, *m.* roughness, violence, abuse, contumelious speech, misdemeanour: aloe-wood or agallochum.

पार्चा, *m.* a fragment, piece, scrap; cloth, web, a piece of cloth.

पार्थ, *m.* (patronym. of **पृथा**) an epithet of Yudhishthir, Bhīmsen, and Arjun.

पार्थक्य, *m.* severalty, separateness, singleness, individuality difference.

पार्थिव, 1, *m.* a king, prince: an epithet of Shiv: an earthen vessel: 2, *m.* (*f.* ī) an inhabitant of the earth: *lit.* (1) made of earth (2) ruling or possessing the earth (3) terrestrial.

पार्थो (*Rām.*) = **पार्थिव**, *q.v.*

पार्वण, *lit.* relating to the *parv*; *then* to the changes of the moon, to the full and new moon; hence, *m.* a particular *shrāddh* or funeral ceremony to all the manes at the *parv* or junction of the sun and moon, at which double oblations are offered, *viz.* three cakes to the father, paternal grandfather and great-grandfather; and three to the maternal grandfather, great-grandfather and great great-grandfather; and the crumbs of each set to the remoter ancestors in each line.

पार्वणश्राद्ध; see **पार्वण**.

पार्वत, *m.* a certain tree (*Melia sempervirens*) called the large *nimb*: *lit.* belonging to (or produced in) the mountains.

पार्वती, *f. pr. n.* an epithet of Durgā (wife of Shiv) in her capacity of daughter of Himālaya, sovereign the snowy mountains: the olibanum-tree (*Boswellia thurifera*); also another tree (*Celtis orientalis*).

पार्वतीय, (*f.* ā) a mountaineer: *pr. n.* a certain mountain prince: *lit.* appertaining to the mountains, mountainous.

पार्श्व, *m.* a side, the part of the body below the armpit, the ribs collectively, *i. e.* the side; the side of any square figure: *adv.* by the side of, near, proximate.

पार्श्वग, *m.* (*f.* ā) an attendant.

पार्श्वगत, *adj.* close to, beside.

पार्श्वभाग, *m.* the side, the flank.

पार्श्ववर्ती, *adj.* standing by the side, situated at the side, adjacent: hence, *m.* (*f.* inī) an attendant.

पार्श्वशूल, *m.* spasm of the chest, stitch.

पार्श्वस्थ, *m.* (*f.* ā) one who stays at or near the side of another.

पार्श्विक, *m.* (*f.* ā or ī) a partisan, sidesman, associate or companion: *lit.* appertaining to the side, lateral.

पार्षद = **पारिषद**, *q.v.*

पार्स, *m. pr. n.* (see **पारस**) Persia.

पार्सा, *m.* a holy man, devotee, hermit: *lit.* abstemious, chaste, watchful.

पार्साई, *f.* abstinence, chastity, purity, holiness.

पार्साल = **पारसाल**, *q.v.*

पाल, 1, *m.* (*f.* ?) shelter; a sail; a small tent; layers of straw, leaves, etc. between which unripe mangoes are put to ripen; a dyke or dam; crown lands kept in the hands of Government.—*charhānā*, to hoist sail.—*rakhnā*, to keep, maintain, nourish, cherish.—2, *m.* (*f.* ī): this word sometimes occurs as the latter element in compound words, in which position it means protector, nourisher, cherisher, guardian, preserver.

पालंक, *m.* the olibanum-tree (*Boswellia thurifera*) a kind of beet-root (*Beta Bengalensis*): a hawk.

पालंकी, *f.* the resin of the olibanum, gum olibanum, incense.

पालंक्या, *f.* = **पालंकी**, *q.v.*

पालक, *adj.* cherishing, nourishing, preserving, supporting, protecting; hence, *m.* (*f.* ikā) a cherisher, protector, guardian, preserver, keeper, groom; a sort of spinach; a bedstead.

पालकजूही, *f.* two medicinal trees, *viz. Justicia nasuta* and *Ixora undulata*.

पालकड़ा, *m.* (*f.* ī) an adopted child.

पालकपुत्र, *m.* (*f.* kā *or* ikā) an adopted child.

पालकरी, *f.* blocks of wood placed under the feet of a bed to raise it. It is the custom to have two such blocks ready to raise the head of a bed to give it a sloping position.

पालकसाग, *m.* spinach.

पालकी, *f.* a palanquin, litter, sedan.

पालकीनिशीन, entitled to be carried in a pālkee (a privilege granted in former times by a king or a Viceroy).

पालकीसवार, *m.* (*f.* ī *or* nī) one who rides in a pālkee.

पालन, 1, *m.* (*f.* ī) = **पालक**, *q.v.*: 2, *m.* (*f.* ?) the act of preserving, cherishing, protecting, or keeping a thing, breeding, nourishing, rearing, fostering, bringing up.

पालनकर्ता, *m.* (*f.* trī), **पालनहार**, *m.* (*f.* ī) = **पालक**, *q.v.*

पालना, 1, *m.* a cradle: 2, *t.* to nourish, cherish, breed, foster, keep, maintain, rear, bring up, preserve, guard, protect, educate, patronize.

पालनी, *f.* (*m.* **पालन**) a protectress, etc.

पालव (*Rām.*) = **पल्लव**, *q.v.*

पाला, *m.* the maintenance of a person, charge, trust: frost, hoar-frost, snow, ice: a rick of corn: a spell: secundine of an animal: coagulation: a twig: a time or turn in rotation: a heap of earth made by children to separate the two parties in the game called *kabaddee*: leaves of a species of *zizyphus*-tree called *jharberee*.—*parnā*, to snow. *Pāle parnā*, to fall within the power of another.

पालागन, obeisance by embracing the feet, respect, reverence, veneration.

पालान, *m.* packsaddles, dorsers: an udder.

पालापोसा, *m.* (*f.* **पालीपोसी**) nourished and cherished.

पालाश, *m.* (*f.* ī) made of the wood of the *palāsh*-tree, appertaining to the *palāsh*-tree; *hence* (1) of a green colour (2) the colour green.

पालाशखण्ड, *m. pr. n.* the western part of the province of Bihār.

पालि, *f.* = **पाली**, 3, *q.v.*

पालिक, *m.* (*f.* ā *or* ī) = **पालक**, *q.v.*

पालिका, *f.* (*m.* **पालक**) a protectress; the wife of a cowherd.

पालित, *m.* (*f.* ā) cherished, nourished, reared, supported, protected, kept (as a promise).

पालिन्द, *m.* a sort of jasmine (*Jasminum pubescens*).

पालिन्धी, *f.* the black kind of the *teorī*-plant (*Convolvulus turpethum*).

पालिबोथरा, *m. pr. n.* one of the ancient names of Patna.

पाली, 1, *f.*; see **पाल**, 2: 2, *m.* (*f.* inī) a cowherd, etc.: *lit.* adj. nourishing, protecting: 3, *f.* the tip of the ear: the point or edge of a cutting instrument: a line, row, range: a raised bank, dike: a boundary, margin: a mark, stain: a louse: a woman with a beard: the hollow upon the thigh: a measure of five sérs : a bridge, causeway : praise, eulogium : a battle between birds; a place where birds fight, cockpit : a covering of a pot.

पाले (Rām.) = **आधीन**, *q. v.*

पालेज़, *f.* a melon-field. [part, a quarter.

पाव, 1, inaccurately for **पांव**, *q. v.* : 2, *m.* a fourth

पावक, 1, *m.* (*f.* ikā) purificatory, purifying; appertaining to Agni; pure: *hence*, 2, *m.* fire; Agni the deified personification of fire; a saint or person purified by religious abstraction: 3, *m.* the designation of several plants, *viz.* (1) a certain tree (*Premna spinosa*) the wood of which is used to procure fire by attrition (2) leadwort (*Plumbago zeylanica*) (3) the marking-nut plant (*Semicarpus anacardium*).

पावटकी = **पायतकी**, *q. v.*

पावड़ा = **साड़ी**, *q. v.*

पावत = **पावता** = **पाता** (**पावना**). See **त**, 5.

पावतकी, *f.* the present fee of a *kānūngo* allowed by Government at the rate of four annas per hundred rupees on the net revenue of each district, to defray the expenses of the establishment.

पावती, *f.* what one gets, income, gain.

पावन, purificatory, expurgatory, purifying; purified, pure: *hence*, 1, *m.* (*f.* ī) a purifier: 2, *m.* a purifying, cleansing fire; water; cowdung; incense; austere devotion, penance; expiation: the seed of Eleocarpus; kind of grass (*Costus*).

पावनता, *f.* }
पावनत्व, *m.* } purification, cleanness.

पावनध्वनि, *m.* a conch-shell.

पावना, *more prop.* **पाना**, 1, 2, *q. v.*

पावनी, *f. pr. n.* (*m.* **पावन**, 1) a certain river.

पावनी }
पावनीं } in Braj = **पाना**, 1, *q. v.*

पावमान, *m.* (*f.* matī) purificatory, purifying.

पावमानी, *f.* the name of hymns referring to the preparation of the *som*.

पावरोटी, *f.* bread made in the form of loaves each weighing a quarter (*pāo*) of a sér.

पावल, *m. pr. n.* the apostle Paul.

पावला, *m.* a quarter of any coin (as of a rupee, etc.).

पावस, *m.* the rainy-season; rain.

पावा (Rām.) = **पाया**, *q. v.*

पाविका, *f.*; see **पावक**.

पावित, *m.* (*f.* ā) purified.

पावी, *m.* (*f.* inī) a purifier: *lit.* purificatory, pu-

पावीं = **पाओं**, *q. v.* [rifying.

पाश, *m.* a tie, string, chain, fetter; a string for fastening tamed animals, a net or noose for catching birds, deer, etc.; a noose as a weapon of combat, a noose as principal attribute of Varuṇ: dice. As the latter element in compound words it signifies (1) quantity (2) beauty (3) depreciation.

पाशक, *m.* a die (particularly the long sort used in playing *chaupaṛ*).

पाशक्रीड़क, *adj.* playing with dice, gambling: *hence*, *m.* (*f.* ikā) a gambler.

पाशक्रीड़ा, *f.* playing with dice, gambling.

पाशद्युम्न, *m. pr. n.* a certain ancient Hindoo prince.

पाशपाश, broken to shivers.

पाशबद्ध, noosed, bound, snared, caught.

पाशबन्ध, *m.* a noose, halter, snare, net.

पाशा, *m.* a die; a throw of dice: an ear-ornament: a rope tied to the foot to assist a person in climbing a tree.

पाशिकस्ता, infirm, reduced; *lit.* broken-footed.

पाशित, *m.* (*f.* ā) tied, bound, fettered.

पाशी, *m.* (*f.* inī) one armed with a net or noose; *hence*, a fowler, deer-catcher; an epithet of Varuṇ and of Yam.

पाशुपत, *m.* (*f.* ī) a follower or a worshipper of Shiv in one of his forms as the supreme deity of the Hindoo triad: *lit.* appertaining to Pashupati (Shiv).

पाश्चात्य, *adj.* behind, being behind, hinder; *hence*, the hinder part, western, subsequent.

पाष (Rām.) = **पक्ष** (*i. e.* **पन्द्रहदिन**), *q. v.*

पाषंडी, *m.* (*f.* inī) = **पाषण्डी**, *q. v.*

पाषक, *m.* an ornament for the feet.

पाषण्ड, 1, *m.* (*f.* ā) = **पाषण्डी**, *q. v.* : 2, *m.* heresy, heterodoxy, false doctrine, hypocrisy, deceit in religious matters, wickedness, blasphemy.

पाषण्डता, *f.* }
पाषण्डत्व, *m.* }
पाषण्डमत, *m.* } = **पाषण्ड**, 2, *q. v.*
पाषण्डित्व, *m.* }

पाषण्डी, *m.* (*f.* inī) a heretic, heterodox Hindoo, hypocrite, religious impostor, sectarian, Jain, Bauddh, one who adopts the external marks or characteristics of a tribe or sect, but does not conform to the orthodox tenets of the Hindoo faith nor respect the ordinances of the Veds.

पाषाण, *m.* stone; a stone.

पाषाणचतुर्दशी, *f.* a certain Hindoo festival held on the fourteenth day of the first half of the month Mārgshir.

पाषाणभेदी, *m.* a certain plant (*Plectranthus aromaticus*, Carey; *P. scutellaroides*, Wilson).

पाषाणमय, *m.* (*f.* ī) consisting of or abounding in stone, stony.

पाषाणरूप, *m.* (*f.* ā) of the nature of stone, stony.

पाषाणरूपी, *m.* (*f.* iṇī) = **पाषाणरूप**, *q. v.*

पाषाणी, *f.* (dim. of **पाषाण**) a small stone used as a weight: a stonecutter's chisel, mason's hammer, [pickaxe.

पाषाणीय, *m.* (*f.* ā) = **पाषाणमय**, *q. v.*

पास, 1, *more prop.* **पाश**, *q. v.* : 2, (in Māṛwāṛī) = **फांसी**, *q. v.* : 3, *m.* a watch, guard, defence, preservation, observation; a space of about three hours (= *pahar*, *q. v.*): 4, *postp.* (takes gen. *m.* infl.) near, about at, beside, in the neighbourhood of, in the possession of.

पासंग, *m.* a weight, make-weight, equipoise, balance.

पासबान, *m.* a watchman, sentinel, guard, protector, shepherd.

पासबानी, *f.* watch, guard, protection, keeping.

पासा, *m.* a die, the long die with which *chaupaṛ* is played; a throw of dice.

पासाग = **पाषाण**. *q. v.*

पासी, 1, *f.* a net ; a rope with which the legs of a horse are bound : 2, *m.* (*f.* inī) a fowler ; one whose occupation it is to make or sell *tāṛī* (so called from the rope around his leg when he climbs the *tāṛ*-tree) : 3, *m.* a watchman.

पासू, a poetical form of **पास**, *q. v.*

पासे, *m.* (pl. of **पासा**) dice.

पाहण } **पाहन** } in Braj = **पाषाण**, *q. v.*

पाहरू, *more prop.* **पहरू**, *q. v.*

पाहल, the ceremony of initiation into the Sikh religion and community.

पाहाण, *more prop* **पाषाण**, *q. v.*

पाहात, *m.* the mulberry-tree (*Morus Indica*).

पाहि (*Rām.*) = (1) **रक्षा करो** (2) **पास**, *qq. v.*

पाही, *m.* (*f.* inī) a non-resident cultivator.

पाहीअसामी, *m.* a non-resident cultivator.

पाहीं (*Rām.*) = **पास**, *q. v.*

पाहीकाश्त, cultivation carried on by non-resident [cultivators.

पाहुन, *m.* (*f.* ī) a guest. — *k.* to be a guest.

पाहुना, *m.* (*f.* ī) a guest : a son-in-law.

पाहुनी, *f.* (*m.* **पाहुन**) a female guest.

पाहू, *m.* a person, individual.

पाहूंचना, *more prop.* **पहुंचना**, *q. v.*

पाहूणा = **पाहुना**, *q. v.*

पिअत in Braj = **पीता (पीना)** See **अ**, 12, and **त**, 5.

पिआ, *partic. m.* (*f.* **पिई**) = **पिया**, *q. v.*

पिआज, *more prop.* **पियाज़**, *q. v.*

पिआना, *more com.* **पिलाना**, *q. v.*

पिआर, *more com.* **प्यार**, *q. v.*

पिआस, *more com.* **प्यास**, *q. v.*

पिई, *partic. f.* (*m.* **पिया**) drunk.

पिउ, *more prop.* **पिऊ**, *q. v.* [*lit.* beloved, dear.

पिऊ, *m.* (from **प्रिय**) a lover, sweetheart, husband :

पिंग, 1, *m.* (*f.* ā) of a tawny colour, yellowish, brown : 2, *m.* the colour tawny.

पिंगकपिशा, *f.* a cockroach.

पिंगचक्षु, *m.* an epithet of the crab.

पिंगल, 1, *m.* (*f.* ā) of a tawny colour, brown, bay, yellowish, red-eyed : 2, *m.* the colour tawny, a dull brown or yellow ; *hence*, a tiger ; the sun : *pr. n.* (1) of the 51st year of the Hindoo cycle (2) of an ancient Hindoo grammarian, author of a treatise on the prosody of the Veds (3) of a fabulous being in the form of a *Nāg* (a serpent of the lower regions) to whom a treatise on prosody is ascribed, and who is hence considered as an inspired and divine personage (*Muni*); *hence*, the art of prosody.

पिंगला, *f.* a certain vessel of the body, *viz.* the left of the three canals which run from the *Os cocoygis* to the head, which, in the anatomical system of the Yog school of philosophy, are the chief passages of breath and air : *pr. n.* (1) of the female elephant of the south-west quarter (2) of a certain courtesan who become remarkable for her piety.

पिंगलिका, *f.* a species of crane; a kind of bee ; a variety of the owl.

पिंगलित, *m.* (*f.* ā) of a tawny colour.

पिंगा, *f.* ; see **पिंग**.

पिंगाक्ष, *m.* (*f.* ī) any brown-eyed creature; *hence*, a monkey ; an epithet of Shiv : *lit.* brown-eyed.

पिंगाक्षी, *f. pr. n.* a certain goddess.

पिंगाश, *m.* a sort of fish (*Silurus sagittatus*, Buch. or *Pimelodius pangasius*): the chief of a community of wild tribes, the headman or proprietor of a village : [virgin gold.

पिंगुरा } **पिंगूरा** } **पिंगूला** } *m.* a cradle.

पिंछ, *m.* slaughter : power, strength : the moon.

पिंजट, *m.* the concrete rheum of the eyes.

पिंजड़ा = **पिंजरा**, *q. v.*

पिंजन, *m.* a bow used for cleaning cotton.

पिंजर, 1, *m.* (*f.* ā) yellow or tawny, reddish yellow : hence, *m.* a colour consisting of a mixture of red and yellow, tawny brown, reddish yellow ; yellow orpiment ; gold ; a horse (probably a bay or chesnut horse) : 2, a birdcage ; the ribs, the cavity formed by the ribs, the thorax.

पिंजरा, 1, *f.*; see **पिंजर** : 2, *m.* a birdcage ; a trap. — *honā*, to be or to become lean or thin.

पिंजली, *f.* two blades of *kush*-grass used as a vessel to take up articles with at sacrifices.

पिंजिका, *f.* a roll of cotton from which threads are spun. [or to separate cotton.

पिंजियारा, *m.* (*f.* ī) one whose business it is to beat

पिंजूल, *m.* the wick of a lamp.

पिंजूष, *m.* earwax.

पिंजेट, *m.* the concrete rheum of the eyes.

पिंड, **पिंद** ; for words beginning thus, see under the forms **पिण्ड**, **पिन्द**, respectively.

पिंड़ी = **पिण्डड़ी**, *q. v.*

पिक, 1 *m.* (*f.* ī) the Indian cuckoo (*Cuculus Indicus*) : 2, *f.* spittle coloured red by chewing betel.

पिकदान, *m.* } **पिकदानी**, *f.* } a spitoon.

पिकबन्धु, *m.* the mango-tree.

पिकबयनी, *f.* an epithet of females; *lit.* possessing [a voice like the kokil's.

पिकबैनी = **पिकबयनी**, *q. v.*

पिका ; see (1) **पिकी** (2) **पिक्क** (3) **फीका**.

पिकांग, *m.* (*f.* ī *or* ā) a certain small bird, called also the *chātakiya*.

पिकाख्य, *m.* a certain vegetable and perfume, called [also *rochanī*.

पिकानन्द, *m.* an epithet of spring.

पिकी, *f.* (*m.* **पिक**) the female of the Indian cuckoo.

पिक्क, *m.* a young elephant.

पिक्का, *more com.* **फीका**, *q. v.*

पिघलना, *a. int.* to melt, fuse, flow (as molten metal).

पिघलवाना, *t.* (causat. of **पिघलना**) to cause to be melted.

पिघलाना, *t.* to melt, fuse ; *met.* to soften, assuage, [mollify (as an angry person).

पिघलाओ } m. fusion, flux.
पिघलाव }

पिंघलना, *more com.* **पिघलना**, *q. v.*

पिचकना, *n.* to be squeezed, be shrivelled.

पिचकाना, *t.* to press together, squeeze, shrivel, wrinkle, burst.

पिचकारी, *f.* a syringe, squirt. *Pichkāriyāṅ marnā*, to squirt water through a syringe.

पिचण्ड = **पिचिण्ड**, *q.v.*

पिचण्डिका, *f.* the instep.

पिचण्डिल, *m.* (*f.* ā) corpulent, bigbellied, pot-[bellied.

पिचपिचा, *m.* (*f.* ī) flabby, watery, clammy, soft, flaccid, moist.

पिचिण्ड, *m.* the abdomen, stomach : the back of [an animal.

पिचिण्डिल, *m.* (*f.* ā) = **पिचण्डिल**, *q. v.*

पिचु, *m.* a sort of leprosy : cotton : *pr. n.* a certain [demon (*Asur*).

पिचुक, *m.* a certain plant (*Vangueria spinosa*).

पिचुक्का, *m.* a syringe, squirt.

पिचुमन्द, *m.* the *nimb*-tree (*Azadirachta Indica* or *Melia azadirachta*).

पिचुमर्द, *more prop.* **पिचुमन्द**, *q. v.*

पिचुल, *m.* the tamarisk-tree (*Tamarix Indica*); a certain plant (*Barringtonia acutangula*): the diver or water-crow : cotton.

पिचोर, *m.* garden-ground, etc. in the rear of a tank.

पिच्चट, *m.* inflammation of the eyes, ophthalmia.

पिच्छ, *m.* a tail (*esp.* of a peacock); a tail feather; a crest.

पिच्छलदला, *f.* the jujube (*Zizyphus jujuba*).

पिच्छवान्, *m* (*f.* vatī) tailed, having a tail.

पिच्छिका, *f.* a bundle of feathers of a peacock's tail.

पिच्छितिका, *f.* the *sisu*-tree (*Dalbergia sisu*).

पिच्छिला, *f.* sauce, gravy : the silk-cotton tree (*Bombax heptaphyllum*) : a certain potherb (*Basella rubra* and *lucida*); the *sisu*-tree (*Dalbergia sisu*); a certain esculent root (*Arum Indicum*).

पिछपांव होना, *a. int.* to fall back, withdraw, [retreat.

पिछलग, *m,* (*f.* ā) } a follower.
पिछलगा, *m.* (*f.* ī) }

पिछलन, 1, *m.* a sliding, slipping : 2, next, second, [again.

पिछलना, *a. int.* to slide, slip.

पिछलपाई, *f.* an ugly or frightful woman, one who is a satire upon the sex, a ghost of a woman, an ogress.

पिछला, *m.* (*f.* ī) hind, hinder, hindmost, last, latter, late, recent, modern.—*varsh*, last year. *Pichhli rāt*, last night, the past night (said early in the morning).—*din*, the past day (not of necessity yesterday, but rather said in the evening of the day referred to).

पछिलेपांव हटना, *a. int.* to withdraw from one's [agreement.

पिछवाड़ा, *m.* (*f.* ī) hinder, hindmost, in the rear, abaft; *hence*, the after part, the rear.

पिछा, *f.* the scum of boiled rice and of other grain; the gum of the silk-cotton tree; the venomous saliva of a snake; a multitude, heap; the calf of the leg : a sheath, cover, cort; the areca-nut, betel-nut; a line, row range; a diseased affection of horses' feet; armour, a sort of cuirass or jacket : the *sisu*-tree; a plantain.

पिछाड़ी, 1 *f.* the rear; the stern; the ropes by which the hind legs of a horse are tied : 2, in the rear, behind.—*mārnā*, to attack in the rear.

पिछाना, *more prop.* **पहचानना**, *q. v.*

पिछिला; see **पिच्छिला** and **पिछला**.

पिछूत, *m.* the back of a house : *lit.* behind, back-[ward.

पिछे, *more com.* **पीछे**, *q. v.*

पिछेत, *m.* the back of a house; a yard or enclosure (compound) behind a house.

पिछोड़ा = **पिछौरा**, *q. v.*

पिछोड़ी = **पिछौरी**, *q. v.*

पिछौरा, *m.* a cloth or sheet worn around the waist or thrown carelessly over the head; a table cloth.

पिछौरी, *f.*; dim. of **पिछौरा**, *q. v.*

पिटंकाकी, *f.* colocynth.

पिटंकाश, *m.* a species of pike (*Esox scolopax*).

पिटना, *n.* to be beaten.

पिटपिटिया, one who combs or cards wool, cotton, etc.

पिटवाना, *t.* (causat of **पिटना**) to cause to be beaten.

पिटाना, *t.* (causat. of **पीटना**) to cause to beat.

पिटारा, *m.* a large basket, portmanteau, box, a kind of square box much used in travelling.

पिटारी, *f.* (dim. of **पिटारा**) a small basket, portmanteau, hamper, pannier, : a kind of insect bred in rice, etc., weevil.

पिटाक, *m.* (= **अघोरपन्थी**) a certain order of Hin-[doo mendicants.

पिठाना, *more prop.* **पठाना**, *q. v.*

पिट्टक, *m.* the tartar of the teeth.

पिड़वाना, *t.* to cause to press, squeeze, or pound.

पिण्ड, *m.* a lump, heap, ball, globe, cluster, quantity, mouthful, roundish lump of food; livelihood; alms; a little button; the body : an oblation offered by Hindoos to their deceased ancestors (as a ball or lump of meat, or rice mixed up with milk, curds, flowers, etc., and offered to the manes at the several *shrāddhs* by the nearest surviving male relations); a funeral cake.

पिण्डक, *m.* a lump, a lump of food : the frontal [globes of an elephant in rut : incense.

पिण्डकी, *more prop.* **पिण्डुकी**, *q. v.*

पिण्डखर्जूर, *m.* the wild date-tree.

पिण्डगोस, *m.* gum myrrh.

पिण्डज, *m.* (*f.* ā) any creature born of or with a body.

पिण्डली, *f.* the leg, shin, calf.

पिण्डतैलक, *m.* olibanum, incense.

पिण्डद, *m.* (*f.* ā) the relation who presents the funeral cake to the manes of a deceased ancestor.

पिण्डदाता } *m.* (*f.* trī) = **पिण्डद**, *q. v.*
पिण्डदातृ }

पिण्डदान, *m.* the presentation of the obsequial cake.

पिण्डपुष्प, *m.* the flower of the *asoca*-tree (*Jonesia asoka*); another flower (*Tabernaemontana coronaria*); the China rose; a lotus.

पिण्डपुष्पक, *m.* a certain potherb (*Chenopodium album*).

पिण्डफला, *f.* a bitter gourd.

पिण्डभाक = पिण्डभागी, *q.v.*

पिण्डभागी, *m.* (*f.* inī) one who partakes of (or who is entitled to a share of) the funeral cake.

पिण्डमुस्ता, *f.* a species of grass (*Cyperus pertenuis*).

पिण्डमूल / **पिण्डमूलक** } *m.* the carrot (*Daucus carota*).

पिण्डरोग, *m.* a certain dreadful disease.

पिण्डरोगी, *m.* (*f.* inī) a person afflicted with the above-mentioned disease.

पिण्डली, *f.* the calf of the leg.

पिण्डवीज, *m.* a certain flowering shrub (*Oleander odorum*).

पिण्डा, *m.* (see **पिण्ड**) the body, person; a lump of clay; a bundle or ball of string, clue; balls of flour or rice.

पिण्डाधिकारी, *m.* the superintendent of a funeral (usually the nearest male relation) to whom belongs the right of presenting the funeral cake.

पिण्डार, *m.* a certain tree (*Trewia nudiflora*).

पिण्डारक, *m. pr. n.* (1) of a certain Nāg (2) of a son of Vrishṇi (3) of a son of Vasudev by Rohiṇī (4) of a certain sacred river (5) of a certain place of Hindoo pilgrimage in Guzerat.

पिण्डारकक्षेत्र, *m. pr. n.* = पिण्डारक (5), *q. v.* See **क्षेत्र**.

पिण्डारा, *m.* (*f.* ī) a plunderer, pillager (among Marhaṭṭās).

पिण्डालु, *m.* a certain fruit (*Trewia nudiflora*, Lin.: *Rottlera Indica*, Willd.); a certain esculent root (described as sweet, cooling, and diuretic); yam.

पिण्डिका, *f.* a fleshy part of the body (as the calf); the nave of a wheel.

पिण्डिखर्जूर, *m.* the wild date-tree.

पिण्डिला, *f.* a sort of cucumber (*Cucumis madraspatanus*).

पिण्डी, *f.* (= **पिण्ड**) the nave of a wheel; a long gourd (*Cucurbita lagenaria*); a species of palm (*Phœnix dactylifera*); a certain flowering shrub (*Tabernæmontana coronaria, flor. plen.*); the upper part of a *Shiv-ling*; a lump of anything that may be contained in the fist; a small clue or ball of string: a small altar of sand a cubit square on which oblations to the manes are offered.

पिण्डीतक, *m.* the name of two trees (1) *Vangueria spinosa* (2) *Tabernæmontana coronaria.*

पिण्डीतगर, *m.* a species of the *Tabernæmontana.*

पिण्डीर, *m.* cuttle-fish bone.

पिण्डुक, *m.* (*f.* ī) a turtle-dove.

पिण्डोल, *f.* a kind of white earth used by Hindoos to cover or wash the walls of their houses with.

पिण्डोलि, *f.* orts, leavings of a meal, or fragments dropped from the mouth.

पिण्या, *f.* heart-pea (*Cardiospermum Halicacabum*).

पिण्याक, *m.* assafœtida.

पित, 1, *more prop.* **पित्त**, *q.v.*: 2, in Chand = **पिता**.

पितपापड़ा, *m.* a certain medicinal plant (*Oldenlandia biflora*).

पितर, 1, *more prop.* **पितरः**, *q.v.*: 2, *m. pr. n.* the apostle Peter.

पितरः, *m.* (pl.) paternal ancestors, forefathers, the fathers.

पितरकर्म्म = **पितृकर्म्म** = **पितृक्रिया**, *q.v.*

पितरपक्ष, *more prop.* **पितृपक्ष**, *q.v.*

पितराई, 1, *m.* a kinsman, a paternal relation from three generations: 2, *f.* verdigris.

पितरौ, *m.* (Sk. dual) parents, *i. e.* mother and father.

पितलाना, *more prop.* **पित्तलाना**, *q. v.*

पिता, *m.* (uninfl.) a father. Applied *par excellence* to the First Person in the Christian Triad.

पितापुत्र, *m.* father and son.

पितामह, *m.* a paternal grandfather; an epithet of Brahmā, the great father of all.

पितामही, *f.* a paternal grandmother.

पिताम्बर, *more prop.* **पीताम्बर**, *q. v.*

पितिया, *m.* an uncle (father's brother).

पितियानी, *f.* an aunt (father's sister).

पितु, 1, *m.* drink: 2, a poet. form of **पिता**, *q. v.*

पितृ, *m.* a father: (*pl.*) paternal ancestors; the manes or the deceased and deified progenitors of mankind, inhabiting a peculiar region of heaven, or, according to some, the orbit of the moon.

पितृऋण, *m.* 1, = **पितृक्रिया**, *q.v.*: 2, the obligation of an ancestor to posterity (*i. e.* procreation).

पितृक, appertaining to parents or progenitors, parental, paternal, ancestral, obsequial.

पितृकर्म्म / **पितृकार्य्य** } *m.* = **पितृक्रिया**, *q. v.*

पितृक्रिया, *f.* solemn obsequial rites in honour of deceased ancestors.

पितृगण, *m.* a certain class of progenitors the sons of Rishis or Prajāpatis.

पितृगृह, *m.* 1, a burial-ground, cemetery; *lit.* the ancestral home: 2, paternal relations.

पितृघात, *m.* parricide.

पितृघातक, *m.* (*f.* ī) a child who is hostile to his father, a paricide.

पितृतर्पण, *m.* oblation to the manes of deceased ancestors distributed at the *shrāddhs* (funeral ceremonies); the act of throwing water out of the hand at seasons of ablution by way of offering to the manes of deceased ancestors; the part of the hand between the middle finger and the thumb, sacred to the manes.

पितृता, *f.* = **पितृत्व**, *q. v.*

पितृतिथि, *m.* the day of new moon (on which she rises invisible).

पितृतीर्थ, *m.* an epithet of the city of Gayā, where the performance of funeral sacrifices is thought to be peculiarly efficacious and meritorious: the part between the forefinger and the thumb, sacred to the manes.

पितृत्व, *m.* fatherhood, paternity, the state or condition of a deified progenitor (*pitṛi*).

पितृदान, *m.* a gift presented in honour of deceased ancestors.

पितृधन, *m.* wealth inherited from a father, ancestral property.

पितृपक्ष, *m.* the dark fortnight of the month Bhādra: paternal relationship: *adj.* of the father's side.

पितृपिता / **पितृपितृ** } *m.* a grandfather (father's father).

पितृपैतामह, 1, *m.* (pl.) fathers and ancestors: 2, *m.* (*f.* ī) inherited by the father from the grandfather: *lit.* appertaining to the father and grandfather.

पितृप्रसू, *f.* a grandmother (father's mother): twilight (the time when the manes of deceased ancestors are abroad).

पितृप्राप्त, *m.* (*f.* ā) received from a father, inherited patrimonially.

पितृबन्धु, *m.* a remote or cognate kinsman by the father's side (as the son of the paternal grandfather's sister, or of the paternal grandmother's sister, or of the father's maternal uncle).

पितृभक्त, (*f.* ā) a child fondly attached to his father.

पितृभक्ति, *f.* filial attachment to a father.

पितृभोजन, *m.* food offered to the manes of deceased ancestors.

पितृमन्दिर, *m.* the paternal mansion, a cemetery.

पितृयज्ञ, *m.* = पितृक्रिया, *q. v.*

पितृलोक, *m.* a father's house, paternal mansion; the world or sphere of the manes of the deceased. It is variously situated, but principally in the Bhuvar region or mid-heaven.

पितृलोग, *m.* paternal ancestors, forefathers, the [fathers.

पितृवन, *m.* }
पितृवसति, *f.* } a cemetery.

पितृव्य, *m.* a paternal uncle; any elderly male re- [lation.

पितृश्राद्ध, *m.* = पितृक्रिया, *q. v.*

पितृस्थान, *m.* the abode of the manes: a protector, [guardian.

पितृस्वसा, *f.* a paternal aunt.

पितृस्वस्रीय, *m.* (*f.* ā) a cousin (child of a paternal [aunt).

पितृहत्या, *f.* parricide.

पितृहन, *m.* (*f.* ī) a parricide.

पित्त, *m.* bilious humour, bile, gall; anger.

पित्तघ्न, *m.* (*f.* ī) antibilious.

पित्तघ्नी, *f.* a certain antibilious plant (*Menispermum* [*glabrum*).

पित्तज्वर, *m.* bilious fever.

पित्तल, 1, *m.* (*f.* ā) appertaining to the bilious humour, bilious: 2, *m.* the *bhojpatra* or birch tree, the bark of which is used for writing upon: 3, *m.* brass.

पित्तला, *f.* a certain plant (*Jussicua repens*).

पित्तलाना, *n.* to be contaminated with verdigris (as food [*esp.* of an acid quality] kept in copper vessels).

पित्तली, made of brass, brasen.

पित्ता, *m.* bile, the gall-bladder: *met.* anger, emotion of mind. — *nikālnā*, to chastise. — *marnā*, to subside, cool (as anger or emotion).

पित्थापड़ा = पितपापड़ा, *q. v.*

पित्र, *more com.* पितर = पितरः = पितृ, *q. v.*

पित्रनुमति, *f.* the commands or ordinances of the [fathers.

पिदड़ी, *f.* a tomtit.

पिदर, *m.* a father.

पिदरमिज़ाजी, *m.* a representative father, or one [who has adopted a child.

पिद्दा, *m.* a species of small bird.

पिधान, *m.* a covering, shutting; a cover, lid, sheath, wrapper, cloak; concealment.

पिन, *m.* a sound, noise.

पिनकी, *f.* = पीनक, *q. v.*

पिनजियारा, *m.* (*f.* ī) a person whose occupation it is to beat and separate cotton.

पिनड़ी, *more prop.* पिपड़ी, *q. v.*

पिनपिनहाँ, *m.* (*f.* °हीं) hateful, odious, detestable, [bad.

पिनपिनाना, *a. int.* to twang, whiz.

पिनपिनाहट, *f.* the whizzing of an arrow or shot.

पिनहना, *more com.* पहिनना, *q. v.*

पिनहाना, *more com.* पहिनाना, *q. v.*

पिना, *more prop.* पीना, *q. v.*

पिनाक, *m.* a stuff, club, trident; particularly the bow and trident or club of Shiv.

पिनाकनयन, *m.* (*f.* ā *or* ī) a person with unfeeling- [looking eyes.

पिनाकि, a contraction of पिनाकी, *q. v.*

पिनाकी, 1, *m.* an epithet of Shiv; lit. *adj.* trident-bearing: 2, *f.* a kind of musical instrument (a sort of [viol).

पिनाना, *more prop.* पहिनाना, *q. v.*

पिन्दार, *m.* thought, imagination self-opinion, pride.

पिन्ना, *m.* a cake of mustard-seed remaining after the expression of the oil. It is given to cows, etc. for food.

पिन्नी, *f.* a kind of sweetmeat.

पिपासन, *m.* (*f.* ā *or* ī) = पिपासी, *q. v.*

पिपासा, *f.* thirst; desire in general.

पिपासावन्त }
पिपासावान } *m.* (*f.* vatī) = पिपासी, *q. v.*

पिपासित, *m.* (*f.* ā) = पिपासी, *q. v.*

पिपासी, *m.* (*f.* inī) thirsty, thirsting, athirst, [eagerly desirous.

पिपासु = पिपासी, *q. v.*

पिपीतकी, *f.* the twelfth day of the month Vaisākh when giving away water is an act of merit.

पिपीलक, *m.* (*f.* ikī) a large black ant.

पिपीलिका, *f.* (dim.) the common small red ant.

पिपोहा; see पपीहा.

पिप्पटा, *f.* a kind of sweetmeat.

पिप्पल, *m.* the holy figtree (*Ficus religiosa*) and its fruit: sensual enjoyment.

पिप्पलक, *m.* a nipple.

पिप्पलाद, *m. pr. n.* a certain ancient Hindoo sage.

पिप्पलायन, *m. pr. n.* (see नवयोगेश्वर) the 5th Yogesh- [war.

पिप्पलि }
पिप्पली } *f.* long pepper (*Piper longum*).

पिप्पलीमूल, *m.* the root of long pepper.

पिप्पी, *f.* the dregs, lees, or refuse of anything when poured out or strained.

पिप्पलाध, *m. pr. n.* a certain ancient Hindoo sage.

पिय, *more prop.* पिऊ, *q. v.*

पिया, 1, = पिऊ, *q. v.*: 2, partic. *m.* (*f.* पिई) drunk.

पियाज़, *f.* an onion.

पियादा, *m.* a footman, foot-soldier, a species of foot-soldiers employed as servants or attendants, one who goes on errands, a messenger, peon; (at Chess) the pawn.

पियाना, *t.* (a causat. of पीना) to cause to drink, give to drink, to water, irrigate.

पियार; for words beginning thus, see under the form प्यार.

पियाल, *m.* a certain tree (*Buchanania latifolia*, Roxb.: or *Chironjia sapida*) and its fruit.

पियाला = **प्याला**, *q.v.*

पियास, *more com.* **प्यास**, *q.v.*

पियासा, *m.* (*f.* ī) *more com.* **प्यासा**, *q.v.*

पियूड़ी = **पेवड़ी**, *q.v.*

पियूष (Rām.) = **पीयूष**, *q.v.*

पिरथमी
पिरथी } corruptions of **पृथिवी**, *q.v.*

पिराना, to pain, ache, be painful, to have pain.

पिरिच a saucer.

पिरीती, a corruption of **प्रीति**, *q.v.*

पिरीते (*Rām.*) = (1) **प्रीति** (2) **प्रीतम** (3) **प्रीतियुक्त**, *qq.v.*

पिरोज, a saucer.

पिरोजा (Rām.) = **आंगली रंगका मणि.**

पिरोना, *t.* to thread (as a needle), to string (as pearls), to fix on a spit or skewer.

पिर्तम, *more prop.* (1) **प्रथम** (2) **पृथिवी**, *qq.v.*

पिर्थी = **पृथिवी**, *q.v.*

पिर्मन, *m.* the yard of a sail.

पिलई, *f.* the spleen: the disease so called (arising from enlargement or inflammation of the spleen).

पिलचना, *a. int.* to adhere.

पिलड़ी, *f.* forced meat.

पिलना, *t.* to attack, assault: *n.* to be bruised, be thrashed, be trodden, be pressed, be ground.

पिलपिल, *m.* pepper.

पिलपिला, *m.* (*f.* ī) soft, flabby, flaccid.

पिलपिलाना, *t.* to soften.

पिलपिलाहट, *f.* a softening; softness.

पिलवाना, *t.* to cause drink to be given.

पिलहि, 1, *more com.* **पिलई**, *q.v.*: 2, (pl. °**हि**) = **पिलता**.

पिलाई, 1, *f.* (*m.* **पिलाया**) past part. of **पिलाना**, *q.v.*: 2, *more com.* (1) **पिलई** (2) **पिल्ली** (3) **पीलाई**, *qq.v.*

पिलाना, *t.* (a causat. of **पीना**) to cause to drink, give to drink, to water, irrigate.

पिलानेवाला, *m.* (*f.* ī) a cup-bearer.

पिलाव, *m.* a kind of Indian dish made of rice, spices, and flesh or fowl.

पिलिश्त, *f.* a strumpet, adulteress: *lit.* unclean, impure, polluted.

पिलुआ
पिलूआ } = **पिल्लू**, *q.v.*

पिल्ला, *m.* (*f.* ī) a puppy, whelp, cub.

पिल्लू, *m.* a worm.

पिल्हा = **प्लीहा**, *q.v.*

पिवत
पिवेन } *adj.* drinking.

पिशंग, 1, *m.* (*f.* ī *or* ā) tawny, brownish, yellowish: 2, *m.* the colour tawny.

पिशंगत्व, *m.* (*f.* tā) tawniness, yellowishness.

पिशंगा
पिशंगी } *f.*; see **पिशंग**.

पिशाच, *m.* (*f.* ī) a certain species of evil spirit described as a malignant demigod, something between an infernal imp and a ghost, but always held to be malevolent, and fierce, a vampire, goblin, spirit, demon, spectre, fiend. It is said to haunt the places where dead bodies are burnt or buried.

पिशाचक, *m.* (*f.* ikā) a fiend.

पिशाचग्रस्त, *m.* (*f.* ā) possessed of a demon, demoniac.

पिशाचद्रु, *m.* a certain tree (*Trophis aspera*) believed to be a favourite haunt of goblins.

पिशाचनी, (a *fem.* form of **पिशाच**) a female fiend.

पिशाचपति, *m.* an arch-fiend, demon-chief.

पिशाचिका, *f.* (*m.* **पिशाचक**) a female fiend.

पिशाची, *f.* (*m.* **पिशाच**) a female fiend.

पिशाब = **पेशाब**, *q.v.*

पिशित, *m.* flesh.

पिशिता, *f.* spikenard.

पिशितेप्सु, desirous of flesh, longing after a meal of flesh.

पिशुन, 1, *m.* (*f.* ā) a backbiter, spy, informer, talebearer, one who excites hopes and disappoints them, a stupid person, fool: *lit.* malignant, cruel, mischievous, betraying, backbiting, unkind, wicked, vile, low, contemptible, stupid, foolish: 2, *m.* sycophancy: a crow: cotton: an epithet of Nārad.

पिशुनत्व, *m.* (*f.* tā) backbiting, cruelty, sycophancy, wickedness, meanness, stupidity, folly.

पिशुनवचन, *m.* malicious speech, backbiting, evil report, slander, detraction.

पिशुनवाक्य = **पिशुनवचन**, *q.v.*

पिशुना, *f.* (*m.* **पिशुन**) a malignant woman, etc.: a certain gramineous plant (*Trigonella corniculata*).

पिष्टक, *m.* a certain disease of the eyes, *viz.* opacity of the cornea.

पिष्टप, *m.* a world, a division of the universe.

पिसना, *n.* to be bruised or broken to powder, be ground, be reduced to meal: *met.* to be distressed or ruined; to be desperately in love.

पिसर, *m.* a boy, son, child.

पिसलाना, *t.* (causat. of **पिसाना**) to cause to grind or to reduce to powder.

पिसवाना, *t.* (causat. of **पिसना**) to cause to be ground or reduced to powder.

पिसाई, *f.* (see **आई**, 3) a grinding; the occupation of grinder; the price paid for grinding.

पिसाच; for words beginning thus, see under the form **पिशाच**.

पिसान, *m.* meal, flour.

पिसाना, *t.* to reduce to powder, grind.

पिसाब = **पेशाब**, *q.v.*

पिसुन (*Rām.*) = **पिशुन**, *q.v.*

पिसू, *m.* a flea.

पिस्ता, *m.* a pistachio-nut.

पिस्तान, *m.* the breasts, bubbies.

पिस्सू, *m.* a flea.

पिहर, *more com.* **पीहर**, *q.v.*

पिहुआ, a certain bird (probably so called in imitation of the sound of its note).

पिह्नना, *more prop.* **पहिनना** *q.v.*

पी, 1, *more prop.* **पिऊ**, *q.v.*: 2, the 2nd pers. sing. imperat. of the verb **पीना**.

पीश्राज, *more prop.* **पियाज़**.

पीओ, 1, *more prop.* **पिऊ**, *q.v.*: 2, the 2nd pers. pl. aor. and imperat. of the verb **पीना**.

पींजना, *t.* to clean cotton from the seeds.

पींड, *m.* a roller.

पीक, 1, = **पिक**, 2, *q.v.*: 2, *m.* a certain bird (*Cuculus Indicus*).

पीकदान, *m.* } **पीकदानी**, *f.* } a spittoon.

पीकना, *a. int.* to ripen, grow, be produced.

पीच = **पीछ**, *q.v.*

पीचना, *t.* to tread under foot.

पीचू, *m.* the fruit of the Capparis.

पीचे, *more prop.* **पीछे**, *q.v.*

पीछ, *f.* water in which rice has been boiled, rice-water, rice-gruel, slip-slop, water-gruel, pap, pottage, food, victual, sustenance: strength.

पीछन, a provincial form of **पीछा**, *q.v.*

पीछवा, *m.* the hinder part (particularly of a saddle).

पीछवाना, to run after.

पीछा, *m.* the hinder part, the rear; a following, pursuit, persecution; absence.—*k.* to follow, pursue, chase; to recoil (as firearms).—*phernā*, to withdraw, leave.—*lenā*, to pursue, importune, obstinately persevere.

पीछू, a provincial form of **पीछा**, *q.v.*

पीछूत, afterwards, rearwards.

पीछें, *adv.* (sc. **में**) in the rear, behind, after, astern, in the absence; afterwards, ago. —*dālnā*, to leave behind, outstrip. —*parnā*, to run after or behind, dance attendance; to importune, dun; to persecute, torment, to be outstripped. —*lagnā*, to pursue, set after, follow. —*ho lenā*, to follow.

पीछें, *more prop.* **पीछे**, *q.v.*

पीछेसे, *adv.* (abl. of **पीछा**) afterwards, from behind.

पीजाना, *t.* to drink, absorb, drink up, drink to the point of intoxication; to stifle one's passions; to refrain from answering.

पीटना, *t.* to beat, thrash, strike, knock, dash, comminute, pound. *Chhātī*—, to beat the breast, *i.e.* to lament, repent. *Muṅh*—, to wrinkle the mouth in anger.

पीठ, 1, *m.* a stool, seat, chair, bench; a pedestal, base; the seat of a deity, an altar; a kind of ornament; the complement of a segment in any geometrical figure: 2, *f.* the back. —*k.* to turn the back upon. —*kā bāṅs*, *m.* the spine. —*ke pichhe dāl lenā*, to afford an asylum, shelter, protect, defend.—*ke bal* (*par*) adj. back downwards, *i.e.* supine. —*ke pichhe parnā*, to seek shelter of any one, take refuge or shelter.—*thoknā* to encourage. —*denā*, to turn tail, run away, flee; to turn, shrink from, veer; to turn away in displeasure. —*par hāth phernā*, to pat on the back, encourage. —*phernā*, to turn one's back, withdraw, leave, depart, flee. —*lagnā*, to have a sore on the back (said of horses); to mount or to back a horse. —*lagānā*, to throw down in wrestling.

पीठसर्पी, *m.* (*f.* iṇī) a cripple.

पीठस्थान, *m.* a place consecrated to the worship of Pārvatee.

पीठा, *m.* a kind of food made of rice and flour.

पीठियाठोंक, closely.

पीठी, *f.* a stool, bench, seat, pedestal.

पीठौता, *m.* a page of a book.

पीड़, *f.* pain, labour (in childbirth); compassion.

पीड़क, *adj.* occasioning pain, squeezing, oppressing, vexing, annoying: hence *m.* (*f.* ikā) an oppressor, persecutor.

पीड़ना, *a. int.* to be pained.

पीड़ा, *f.* pain, suffering, anguish, torture, distress, affliction, persecution.

पीड़ाकर, *m.* (*f.* ī) = **पीड़क**, *q.v.*

पीड़ाना, *t.* to occasion pain, cause to smart.

पीड़ाबोधक, (in Gram.) expressive of pain (as, an interjection or exclamation).

पीड़ित, *m.* (*f.* ā) pained, tortured, afflicted, ill, oppressed.

पीढ़ा, *m.* a seat, stool, chair.

पीढ़ाबन्ध, *m.* preface, introduction, preliminary discourse (to a book).

पीढ़ी, *f.* (dim. of **पीढ़ा**) a small stool or chair: a race or series of generations, progenitors, or descendants.

पीढ़ीपीढ़ी, *adv.* from generation to generation, for successive generations, from age to age.

पीणड, *m.* a roller.

पीत, 1, a corruption of **प्रीति**, *q.v.*: 2, *m.* (*f.* ā) yellow: 3, *m.* the colour yellow. *Pitki pit rahe aur mitkā mit hāth lage*, let friendship continue, and the sweets of it will be obtained.

पीतक, 1, *m.* (*f.* ikā) of a yellow colour: 2, *m.* yellow orpiment.

पीतकदली, *f.* a sort of plantain.

पीतकन्द, *m.* the carrot.

पीतकाष्ठ, *m.* yellow sanders.

पीतघोषा, *f.* a sort of creeper with yellow flowers.

पीतचन्दन, *m.* a yellow fragrant species of sandalwood.

पीतता, *f.* yellowness; the colour yellow.

पीततुण्ड, *m.* the tailor-bird (*Silvia sutoria*, Carey: *Motacilla sutoria*, Carey).

पीतदारु, *m.* two kinds of pine, *viz.* *Pinus devadaru* and *P. longifolia*

पीतन, *m.* the hog-plum (*Spondias mangifera*); a certain tree (*Pentaptera tomentosa*); the waved leafed figtree; saffron.

पीतपट = **पीताम्बर**, 1, *q. v.*

पीतपर्णी, *f.* a kind of nettle (*Tragia involucrata*); a certain plant commonly called *bichhati*.

पीतपादा, *f.* the *mainā*-bird (*Turdus salica*).

पीतपुष्प, *m.* a certain plant (*Barleria prionitis*); a sort of *Tabernæmontana*; a species of *karnikārā*.

पीतपुष्पी, *f.* yellow *Barleria*.

पीतफल, *m.* a certain plant (*Trophis aspera*).

पीतम, a contraction of **प्रियतम**, *q. v.*

पीतमणि, *m.* a yellow gem, topaz.

पीतमस्तक, *m.* the small bird *Loxia philippensis*.

पीतमुण्ड, *m.* a gallinule.

पीतम्बर, *more prop.* **पीताम्बर**, *q.v.*

पीतयूथी, *f.* yellow jasmine (*Jasminum chrysanthemum*).

पीतरक्त, *m.* a yellow gem, topaz.

पीतरस, *m.* turmeric (*Curcuma*).

पीतल, 1, *m.* (*f.* ā) yellow: 2, *m.* the colour yellow: 3, *m.* brass.

पीतला, 1, *f.*; see **पीतल**: 2, *m.* (*f.* ī) of brass, brazen.

पीतलोह, *m.* yellow brass, queen's metal, or a mixed metal.

पीतवर्ण, 1, *m.* the yellow colour: 2, *adj.* yellow.

पीतशाल, *m.* a certain tree (*Pentaptera tomentosa*).

पीतसार, *m.* sandal: a yellow gem, topaz; a certain tree (*Alangium hexpetalum*).

पीतस्फटिक, *m.* a precious yellow gem, topaz.

पीता, 1, *more prop.* पिता, *q.v.*: 2, *f.* (*m.* पीत) turmeric.

पीताम्बर, 1, *m.* silk cloth of a yellow colour, *vulg.* a silk cloth: 2, *m.* (*f.* ā) a mime, dancer; a religious mendicant wearing yellow clothes; an epithet of of Krishn.: *lit.* clad in yellow.

पीति, *more prop.* प्रीति, *q.v.*

पीतिका, *f.* (*m.* पीतक) saffron.

पीती, *m.* (*f.* inī) a horse.

पीतडी, *f.* a tomtit.

पीन, *m.* (*f.* ā) fat, corpulent, bulky, full, round, heavy, large.

पीनक, *f.* intoxication from opium, drowsiness, [nodding, stupefaction.

पीनस, 1, *m.* a cold, catarrh, inflammation of the schneiderian membrane: 2, *f.* a chair, litter: a barge, [pinnace.

पीनसी, *m.* (*f.* inī) affected with a cold.

पीना, 1. *f.* (*m.* पीन) a corpulent female: 2, *t.* to drink; to smoke tobacco: 3, *m.* drinking: dregs or refuse (of linseed, etc.), the oil-cake.

पीप, *more prop.* पीब, *q.v.*

पीपर; see पीपल.

पीपल, a corruption of (1) *m.* पिप्पल (2) *f.* पिप्पली.

पीपला, *m.* the point of a sword.

पीपलामूर, *more prop.* पीपलामूल, *q.v.*

पीपलामूल, *m.* the root of the long-pepper tree.

पीपा, *m.* a pipe, barrel, cask.

पीब *f.* purulent running, pus, matter.

पीबियाना, *t.* to suppurate.

पीबियाहट, *f.* suppuration.

पीय }
पीयू } = पिऊ, *q. v.*

पीयूष, *m.* the food or beverage of the gods, ambrosia, nectar; the milk of the cow during the first seven days after calving; biestings.

पीयूस, *more prop.* पीयूष, *q. v.*

पीर, 1, *f.* (prop. पीड़ा) pain, ache, sickness; feeling, pity, compassion, mercy: 2, *m.* (*pl.* ān) an old man, a saint, a founder of a religious sect, a spiritual guide, a canonized saint: Monday.

पीरपत्तरी, *f.* an agate.

पीरपरस्ती, *f.* saint-worship (among Muhammadans)

पीरपाल = पीरान, 2, *q.v.*

पीरहन, *m.* a shirt, a shift, a tunic.

पीरा, 1, = पीर, 1, *q.v.*: 2, *m.* (*f.* ī) = पीला, *q.v.*

पीराई, *m.* (*f.* inī) a certain tribe or caste who beat a kind of drum called *ḍhol.*

पीराकर; see (1) पिराना (2) पीड़ाकर.

पीरान, *m.* 1, (pl. of पीर, 2) old men, sages, saints: 2, charity-lands bestowed on the poor in honour of a saint; land granted for the erection of a tomb over the remains of a Muhammadan saint (*pīr*).

पीराना, like an old man, elderly; appertaining to a saint, worthy of a saint, saintly.

पीरामन }
पीरामून } = पैरामून, *q. v.*

पीराया, *m.* ornament, decoration.

पीरी, *f.* (*m.* पीरा) = पीली, *q.v.*

पीर्त, *more prop.* प्रीति, *q.v.*

पील, *m.* an elephant: (at Chess) the bishop: a [young bird.

पीलक, *m.* the large black ant (*Formica compressa*? Carey): a certain pretty little bird called the oriole [or mango-bird.

पीलपर्णी; see पीलुपर्णी.

पीलपा, afflicted with elephantiasis.

पीलपाया, *m.* a pillar, prop.

पीलबन्द, *m.* (in Chess) the mutual support of a bishop and two pawns.

पीलसाट; see पीताम्बर.

पीला, *m.* (*f.* ī) yellow.

पीलाई, *f.* yellowness.

पीलाफूल, *m.* lattice-work (?).

पीलाम, *m.* satin.

पीली, *f.* (see पीला) a gold mohur.

पीलीभीत, *f. pr. n.* a certain town in Rohilkhaṇḍ.

पीलु, *m.* an elephant: an arrow: a flower: an insect: the blossom of the *Saccharum sara.* This term is very commonly applied to all exotic and unknown trees, and, in particular, to the *Careya arborea*, Roxb. and to the *Salvadora persica.*

पीलुपर्णी, *f.* a certain plant (*Bryonia grandis* or *Aletris hyacinthoides* or *Dracona nervosa*); a kind of [drug.

पीलू, *more prop.* पीलु, *q.v.*

पील्हा = प्लीहा, *q.v.*

पीव, *more prop.* (1) पिऊ (2) पीयो (3) पीब, *qq. v.*

पीवक्कड़, *m.* a drinker, tippler.

पीवन in Braj = पीना, *q. v.*

पीवनि in Braj = पीनेको. See नि, 2.

पीवनो in Braj = पीना, *q. v.*

पीवन्त, *adj.* drinking.

पीवर, *m.* (*f.* ā *or* ī) fat, corpulent, large, dense.

पीवरत्व, *m.* (*f.* tā) corpulence, largeness, heaviness.

पीवरस्तनी, *f.* an epithet of a cow with large udders.

पीवरा, *f.* (*m.* पीवर) a corpulent female.

पीवरी, *f.* 1, = पीवरा, *q.v.*: 2, a certain plant (*Asparagus racemosus*).

पीवरे (*poet.*) = पिऊ, *q. v.* See रे.

पीवा, *f.* water, drink.

पीवे, (pl. पीवें) in Braj = पीवे (पीना).

पीसना, 1, *t.* to grind, bruise, triturate, reduce to powder; to gnash the teeth: 2. *m.* corn or grain for [grinding.

पीसपास क॰, *t.* to grind down, triturate.

पीसाच, *more prop.* पिशाच, *q.v.*

पीह, *f.* grease, tallow.

पीहर, *m.* maternal kinsfolk, mother's family.

पीसू, *m.* a flea.

पुआल, *f.* straw.

पुंग (*Rām.*) = सुपारी, *q.v.*

पुंगव (*Rām.*) = श्रेष्ठ, *q.v.*

पुंगीफल = सुपारी, *q.v.*

पुंज, *m.* a quantity, collection, heap.

पुंजकुस्थली, *f. pr. n.* a certain Apsarā of the court of Indra.

पुंजी, *f.* a heap, store, quantity, collection; capital (in trade), wealth.

पुंजीवाला, *m.* (*f.* ī) opulent, rich.

पुंलिंग, *m.* the male organ; manhood: (in Gram.) the masculine gender.

पुंवार = पंवार, *q. v.*

पुंश्चली, *f.* an unchaste woman, harlot: *lit.* one who goes after males.

पुंश्चिह्न, *m.* the male organ.

पुंस, *m.* a male, man; the soul: a servant.

पुंसवन, *m.* a ceremony performed as soon as a mother perceives the first signs of a living fœtus, a religious and domestic festival held on such an occasion, the first of the essential ceremonies of Hindoo initiation.

पुंस्त्व, *m.* (*f.* पुंस्ता) manhood, virility, semen.

पुकार, *f.* a calling out loud, a bawl, shout, cry, call. — *denā*, to call, to proclaim aloud.

पुकारना, *a.int.* to call aloud, cry out, bawl, shout, cry, call, call upon or call to, exclaim: *t.* to call, to summon.

पुकारा, *m.* = पुकार, *q.v.*

पुखराज, *m.* a topaz: *pr. n.* the 8th *Nakshatra.*

पुख्तघाट, *f.* a *pakkā* wharf or landingplace.

पुख़्ता, dressed (as food); ripe: *met.* experienced in the ways of the world, wise, knowing, shrewd, sly.

पुगनों in Chand = पहुंचना, *q.v.*

पुगानों in Chand = पहुंचाना, *q.v.*

पुच; see पुच्छ.

पुचकारना = पुच्कारना, *q.v.*

पुचकारा = पुचारा, *q.v.*

पुचरस, *m.* a composition of iron and other metals, kind of bronze.

पुचारा, *m.* a thin coat of clay for laying on a wall: the sponge of a gun. — *denā*, to lay a thin coat of clay on the walls of a house, to whitewash a wall. — *phernā*, to sponge a gun.

पुच्छ, *m.* (*f.* ?) a tail; the hinder part.

पुछना, *more com.* पूछना, *q.v.*

पुछवैया, *m.* an interrogator, enquirer.

पुछार, *m.* an investigation, enquiring, asking.

पुजना, 1, *more prop.* पूजना, *q.v.*: 2, *n.* to be filled, be completed.

पुजवाना, *t.* to cause to fill, cause to complete: to cause to worship.

पुजा; for words beginning thus, see under the form पूजा.

पुजाना, 1, = पूजाना, *q.v.*: 2, *t.* to fill, complete.

पुट, *m.* the contracting or folding anything, a concavity, a cup made of a folded leaf; a cover, covering, a cloth worn on the privities; a horse's hoof: a menstruum, solvent, flux.

पुटरी, *more com.* पोटली, *q.v.*

पुटी (Rām.) = पुट and दोना, *qq.v.*

पुट्ठी, *f.* a basket for catching fish.

पुट्ठा, *m.* the buttock, hip.

पुड़ा, *m.* a large parcel (of physic, etc.).

पुड़िया, *f.* 1, = पुड़ा: 2, a dose of medicine in powder.

पुड़ी, *f.* a skin with which a drum is made.

पुण, *more com.* पुण्य, *q.v.*

पुण्डरीक, *m.* the white lotus (*Nelumbium speciosum*), any lotus: a kind of sacrifice: a kind of rice: a kind of leprosy: a sort of snake (*Amphisbœna*): a leopard: *pr. n.* the elephant of the south-east quarter.

पुण्डरीकाक्ष, *m.* lotus-eyed (an epithet of Vishṇu).

पुण्डरीयक, *m.* a certain flower (*Hibiscus mutabilis*): a certain drug commonly called *punderiyā*: *pr.n.* a certain divine being.

पुण्य, 1, *m.* (*f.* ā) beautiful, fragrant, pure, virtuous, holy, righteous; propitious: 2, *m.* a good or meritorious act, moral or religious merit, virtue; happiness.

पुण्यकर्मा, a person whose acts are holy or meritorious: *adj.* virtuous, pious in act.

पुण्यकर्म्म, *m.* any virtuous or meritorious act.

पुण्यकाज = पुण्यकर्म्म, *q.v.*

पुण्यगन्ध, *m.* an epithet of the *champak*-flower (*Michelia champaca*): *lit.* of a pure or pleasing scent.

पुण्यतीर्थ, *m.* a holy shrine considered as a place of pilgrimage.

पुण्यतृण, *m.* an epithet of the white *kush* grass.

पुण्यदर्शन, *m.* (*f.* ā) an epithet of the blue jay; *lit.* of beautiful aspect.

पुण्यदर्शी, *m.* (*f.* inī) *adj.* inspecting or taking note of religious merit.

पुण्यदायक, *m.* (*f.* ikī) *adj.* imparting religious merit.

पुण्यप्रताप, *m.* the might and efficacy of virtue or of the merit acquired by a course of virtuous acts.

पुण्यफल, *m.* the reward of piety or the consequence of good actions.

पुण्यभू, *f.* = पुण्यभूमि, *q.v.*

पुण्यभूमि, *f. pr. n.* the holy land of the Hindoos (bounded on the north by the Himālaya, on the south by the Vindhya, and on the east and west by the sea: the mother of a male child.

पुण्यलोक, *m.* the abode of the holy and blessed, the paradise of heaven.

पुण्यवन्त } पुण्यवान } *m.* (*f.* vatī) = पुण्य, 1, *q.v.*

पुण्यशील, *m.* (*f.* ā) of a virtuous, pious, or righteous disposition.

पुण्यस्थान, *m.* holy ground, a sacred place.

पुण्या, *f.* (*m.* पुण्य) a beautiful or holy female. This word is used by landholders to designate the first day of the collections of the Government officer in the new year. The head officer of Government in this department sits in state at the office (*Kachahrī*) and adjusts the amount of the revenue to be collected in the ensuing year.

पुण्याई, *f.* a virtuous action performed (according to the theory of metempsychosis) in one state of existence, the reward of which is received in a subsequent birth: the merit of an ancestor rewarded in the person of his decendants.

पुण्यात्मा, holy, pious, virtuous, religious, righteous, continent.

पुण्यार्थ लगाना, *t.* to leave as legacy.

पुण्याह, *m.* a good or happy day, a holyday: the the day on which tenants make the first payment of annual rents to their landlords.

पुण्योदय, *m.* good fortune considered as the result of virtuous acts in a former life.

पुत, 1, in Chand = **पुत्र**, *q.v.* : 2, *m.* (*f.*?) *pr. n.* a certain division of the infernal regions which is the abode of the manes of those who die childless.

पुतरी, *more com.* **पुतली**, *q.v.*

पुतला, *m.* an idol, image.

पुतलिका = **पुत्तलिका**, *q.v.*

पुतली, *f.* a small image, puppet, doll, idol; the image in the eye, the pupil of the eye; the frog of a horse's hoof. — *kā tārā k.* to honour one as the apple of the eye.

पुताई, *f.* (see **थाई**, 3) the act of plastering; the occupation of a plasterer; the price paid for plastering.

पुतोह, *f.* a daughter-in-law (son's wife).

पुत्तलिका, *f.* a small image, doll, puppet, idol.

पुत्तिका, *f.* a small bee: the white ant.

पुत्र, *m.* (*f.* ī) a son, child (*lit.* who rescues his progenitors from hell). This term is also applied to the Second Person in the Christian Triad, The Son.

पुत्रक, *m.* (*f.* ā *or* ikā) a son.

पुत्रकाम्या, *f.* desire for progeny, love for offspring.

पुत्रजीव, *m.* a certain tree (*Nagelia putranjiva*, Roxb.) from whose fruit necklaces of supposed prolific efficacy are made.

पुत्रत्व, *m.* (*f.* tā) the circumstance or the condition of being a son, the filial relation, sonship.

पुत्रपौत्री, *m.* (*f.* iṇī) one who has children and grandchildren.

पुत्रपौत्रीण, descended from son to son.

पुत्रभाव, *m.* the being a son, the state or condition of a son, sonship.

पुत्रवत, like a son, resembling a son, filial.

पुत्रवधू, *f.* a daughter-in-law (son's wife).

पुत्रवन्त / **पुत्रवान** } *m.* (*f.* vatī) = **पुत्री**, 2, *q.v.*

पुत्रश्रेणी, *f.* a certain plant (*Salvinia cucullata*).

पुत्रह in Chand = **पुत्र**, *q.v.*

पुत्रार्थी, *m.* (*f.* inī) one who wishes for a son: *lit.* desirous of a son.

पुत्रिका, *f.* (*m.* **पुत्रक**) a daughter; especially one who is appointed to marry in order that her son may perform the solemn obsequies to her own father and not to her husband: a doll, puppet.

पुत्रिकापुत्र, *m.* (see **पुत्रिका**) the son of a daughter who was appointed to raise issue for her father; one of the twelve kinds of heirs acknowledged by the old Hindoo law; a grandson (daughter's son).

पुत्रिकासुत = **पत्रिकापुत्र**, *q.v.*

पुत्रिय, *m.* (*f.* ā) = **पुत्रीय**, *q.v.*

पुत्री, 1, *f.* (*m.* **पुत्र**) a daughter: 2, *m.* (*f.* iṇī) a person who has a son: *lit.* adj. having a son or sons or children: 3, *f.* a species of plant (*Siphonanthus Indica*).

पुत्रीय, *m.* (*f.* ā) appertaining to a son or child, procuring a son.

पुत्रेष्टि, *f.* a sacrifice performed for the sake of obtaining children.

पुन, a corruption of **पुण्य** and of **पुनः**, *qq. v.*

पुनः, back, in an opposite way, on the contrary, again, but, however, nevertheless; also, afterwards.

पुनःकथन, *m.* tautology, repetition.

पुनःपुनः, again and again, over and over again, repeatedly, day by day.

पुनःपुनर = **पुनःपुनः**, *q.v.*

पुनःपुना, *f. pr. n.* the Pumpun river in the province of Bihār.

पुनना, *t.* to abuse, revile, reproach.

पुनम, a dialectic form of **पुण्य**, *q.v.*

पुनर = **पुनः**, *q.v.*

पुनरजन्मा, *m.* palingenesia by transmigration of the soul: *adj.* re-born, born again.

पुनराय = **पुनः**, *q.v.*

पुनरारम्भ, *m.* a fresh beginning, renewal.

पुनरावर्त्तित, repeated.

पुनरुक्त, *m.* repetition, tautology: *lit.* repeated, said over again.

पुनरुक्ति, *f.* repetition, tautology.

पुनरुत्थान, *m.* resurrection.

पुनर्जन्म, *m.* palingenesia by transmigration of the soul; the birth of new principles within leading to a change of life and character, regeneration; *lit.* second birth.

पुनर्जन्मा = **पुनरजन्मा**, *q.v.*

पुनर्नवा, *f.* hogweed (*Boerhavia diffusa alata*).

पुनर्भू, *f.* a virgin-widow remarried.

पुनर्वसु, *m. pr. n.* (1) of the seventh *Nakshatra* (2) an epithet of Vishṇu and of Shiv.

पुनवाना, *t.* to cause to be abused or reproched by another.

पुनाना, *t.* to cause to abuse, cause to reproach.

पुनि (*Rām.*) = **पुनः**, *q.v.*

पुनिपुनि, *more prop.* **पुनःपुनः**, *q.v.*

पुनी; see (1) **पुनि** (2) **पुनित** (3) **पूनी**.

पुनीत, *m.* (*f.* ā) pure, clean.

पुनीम, *m.* the full moon.

पुन्नक्षत्र, *m.* an asterism under which males are procreated.

पुन्ना = **पुनना**, *q.v.*

पुन्नाग, *m.* a preëminent man: a certain tree (*Rottleria tinctoria*) from the flowers of which a yellowish dye is prepared: a white elephant: a white lotus: nutmeg.

पुफ in old Hindee = **पुष्प**, *q.v.*

पुब्ब in Chand = **पूर्ब**, *q.v.*

पुम / **पुमन** / **पुमस** / **पुमांस** / **पुमान** } = **पुंस**, *q.v.*

पुर, *m.* (*f.*?) a fortified town, a town, city; an abode, house; the body: a kind of *Cyperus*: a sort of resin, bdellium: *pr. n.* a certain demon. Properly, this term designates a place containing large buildings surrounded by a ditch, and extending not less than one *kos*, in length; if it extend not less than half a *kos*, it is called a *khet*, or town; if less than half a *kos*, it is called a *karvaṭ*, or market town; while any smaller cluster of houses is called a *grām*, or village.

पुरइनि (*Rām.*) = **कमलपत्र**, *q.v.*

पुरःसर, *m.* (*f.* ā *or* ī) a leader, preceder : *lit.* adj. going in advance, preceeding, leading.

पुरंजन, *m.* the soul personified as a king.

पुरंजनी, *f.* the intellect personified as the queen of Purañjan.

पुरंजय, *m. pr. n.* a name of several ancient Hindoo personages.

पुरंजर, *m.* the armpit.

पुरख, *more prop.* **पुरुष**, *q.v.*

पुरखा = **पुर्खा**, *q.v.*

पुरगोई, *f.* loquacity, volubility.

पुरजित, *m. pr. n.* a certain ancient Hindoo king.

पुरट, *m.* gold.

पुरणिया } = **पुरैनिया**, *q.v.*
पुरणीया }

पुरता, fully, completely.

पुरदर्द, full of pain, painful.

पुरदेवता, *f.* the tutelary deity of a town.

पुरद्वार, *m.* the gate of a town or city.

पुरनिया, *m.* an old man, an elder; a patron : *lit.* old, ancient.

पुरनियां; see (1) **पुरणिया** (2) **पुरनिया**.

पुरनी, *f.* a ferrule, tube, thimble, the ramrod-pipes of a musket, a bugle or oblong bead.

पुरन्दर, *m.* a species of pepper (*Piper chavya*): an epithet of Indra ; *lit.* the destroyer of castles.

पुरब, *more prop.* **पूर्व**, *q.v.*

पुरभूप, *m.* (*f.* ā) the magistrate or protector of a town or city.

पुररुख, in the direction of the city.

पुरलोग, *m.* citizens, townsmen, inhabitants.

पुरवट, *m.* a large leathern water-bag.

पुरवना, *t.* to cause to be filled, *i. e.* to fill.

पुरवाना, *t.* to cause to be filled (by some one).

पुरवास, *m.* (*f.* ā) = **पुरवासी**, *q. v.*

पुरवासी, *adj.* inhabiting a city or town : hence, *m.* (*f.* inī) a citizen, townsman, inhabitant.

पुरवैआ } *more prop.* **पुर्वैया**, *q.v.*
पुरवैया }

पुरश्चरण, *m.* a repetition of the name of a deity, attended with burnt offerings, etc.

पुरश्छद, *m.* a species of grass (*Saccharum cylindricum*).

पुरसा, *more prop.* **पुर्सा**, *q. v.*

पुरसान, asking, enquiring.

पुरस्कर्त्ता } *m.* (*f.* trī) = **पुरस्कारी**, *q. v.*
पुरस्कर्त्तृ }

पुरस्कार, *m.* the placing a thing in front, preference, distinction, promotion, advancement, honour, deference, respect, worshipping ; an honorary gift.

पुरस्कारी, *m.* (*f.* iṇī) *adj.* placing a thing in front, advancing or promoting.

पुरस्थ, *m.* (*f.* ā) situated in a city or town.

पुरा, *m.* a large village, assemblage of habitations, a town : (in comp.) an apartment.

पुराकृत (*Rām.*) = **पहिले किया गया**.

पुराण, *m.* (*f.* ā *or* ī) primeval, ancient, old, aged, worn-out ; *hence*, a tale of bygone ages, old history, legends. This term is applied especially as the designation of an extensive class of sacred compositions : they were originally written in Sanskrit, and are supposed to have been composed or compiled by the poet Vyās, and to comprize the entire body of the Hindoo theology. The Hindoos acknowledge eighteen Purāṇs, *viz.* (1) the Brahm (2) the Padm (3) the Brāhmāṇd (4) the Agni (5) the Vishṇav (6) the Garur (7) the Brahm-vaivartt (8) the Shiv (9) the Ling (10) the Nārad (11) the Skand (12) the Markandey (13) the Bhavishyat (14) the Matsya (15) the Vārāh (16) the Kūrm (17) the Vāman (18) the Bhāgavat. This last mentioned Purāṇ is by some considered to be a spurious and modern work ; the Brahm-vaivartt (7) is also of very modern origin. The Purāṇs are reckoned to contain four hundred thousand stanzas : each of them should treat especially of five topics, *viz.* (1) the creation (2) the destruction and renovation of worlds (3) the genealogy of deities and heroes (4) the reigns of the Manus, and (5) the transactions of their descendants ; great variety, however, prevails in this respect, and but few of them contain historical or genealogical matter. There are also eighteen Upapurāṇs : which are similar poems, but of inferior sanctity and have different appellations. The whole constitute the popular or poetical creed of the Hindoos, and some of them or particular parts of them are very generally read and studied.

पुराणा, 1, *f.*; see **पुराण** : 2, *m.* (*f.* ī) primeval, ancient, old, aged, worn-out.

पुराणी, *f.*; see **पुराणा**.

पुरातन, 1, *m.* (*f.* ī) old, ancient : 2, *m.* an old tale.

पुरातम, *m.* (*f.* ā) very old, ancient.

पुरातिम; see **पुरातम**.

पुराना, 1, *m.* (*f.* ī) *more prop.* **पुराणा**, *q.v.* : 2, *t.* to make full, to fill : to pierce, bore, string pearls.

पुराराति } *m.* epithets (1) of Shiv (2) of Vishṇu.
पुरारि }

पुरारी, a poetical form of **पुरारि**, *q.v.*

पुरावनो in Braj = **पुराना**, 2, *q.v.*

पुरि, *f.* (*m.* **पुर**) *more com.* **पुरी**, *q.v.*

पुरी, *f.* a city, town, abode, habitation, palace, the body ; *pr. n.* the city of Puree (the head quarters of the worship of Jagannāth) in Orissa.

पुरीमोह, *m.* the thorn-apple (*Datura*).

पुरीष, *m.* fœces, excrement, ordure : the remains of food (left in a pot).

पुरीषी, *f.* a certain religious ceremony.

पुरीषोत्सर्ग, *m.* the voiding of excrement.

पुरु, 1, *m.* the farina of a flower : *pr. n.* (1) of an old king, the sixth monarch of the solar (lunar ?) line (2) *f.* of a river said to run a little to the north-west of the Saraswatee.

पुरुख = **पुरुष**, *q. v.*

पुरुखा = **पुर्खा**, *q. v.*

पुरुखे = **पुर्खे**, *q. v.*

पुरुजित, *m. pr. n.* (1) of a certain hero (brother of Kuntibhoj) on the side of the Paṇḍus (2) of a certain prince, son of Ruchak (3) of a son of Ānak.

पुरुरवा, *more prop.* **पुरूरवा**, *q.v.*

पुरुष, *m.* (*f.* ī) a male, a man, man, mankind: soul, an epithet of the Supreme, the universal soul: (in Gram.) person.

पुरुषकार, *m.* human exertion or activity (as opposed to fate), any act of man, a manly act, manhood, virility, effort, exertion, care.

पुरुषकेशर = **नरसिंह**, *q. v.*

पुरुषगमन, *m.* sodomy.

पुरुषगामी, *m.* a sodomite.

पुरुषत्व, *m.* (*f.* tā) manly nature or property, manhood, manliness, virility, valour, prowess.

पुरुषद्वेषी, *m.* (*f.* iṇī) a misanthrope: lit. *adj.* man-hating, inimical to man; *hence*, ill-tempered, factious.

पुरुषन in Braj = (1) pl. of **पुरुष** (2) **पुरुषा**, *qq. v.*

पुरुषभाव, *m.* the especial disposition of males.

पुरुषमय, *m.* (*f.* ī) abounding in males.

पुरुषमात्र, *m.* (*f.* ā *or* ī) of the height or measure of a man.

पुरुषमुख, *m.* (*f.* ī) having a man's face.

पुरुषवंशी, *m.* (*f.* inī) appertaining to the race of men.

पुरुषवर्जित, destitute of human beings, desolate.

पुरुषवाचक, *adj.* (in Gram.) indicating or appertaining to the masculine gender.

पुरुषवाची सर्वनाम, *m.* (in Gram.) a personal pronoun.

पुरुषबोधक, (in Gram.) masculine.

पुरुषसिंह, *m.* (= **नरसिंह**?) a man-lion, a lion of a man, a brave man, hero, an eminent man.

पुरुषसूक्त, *m. pr. n.* a certain celebrated hymn (the 90th hymn of the 10th Maṇḍal of the Rig-Ved).

पुरुषा; see (1) **पुरुषाः** (2) **पुरखा**.

पुरुषाः, *m.* (pl. of **पुरुष**; see **आ**, 22) people of old, the ancients, ancestors, predecessors, the fathers.

पुरुषातन in Chand = **पुरुषात्म्य**, *q. v.*

पुरुषात्म्य, *m.* manhood, manliness, virility.

पुरुषाधम, *m.* (*f.* ā) the vilest of men, a low or base person, outcaste.

पुरुषाधिकार, *m.* the proper function or sphere of a man.

पुरुषानुक्रम, *m.* lineal succession.

पुरुषान्तर, *m.* a succeeding generation: a treaty by which it is stipulated that the affairs of the one party shall be settled by warriors selected from both parties.

पुरुषायु, *m. f.* the life of man, human existence.

पुरुषालोग = **पुरुषाः**, *q.v.*

पुरुषार्थ, *m.* the end of man, *i. e.* the object of his creation and existence; *hence*, either of the four objects of human pursuit, *viz.* (1) *Kām*, the gratification of desire (2) *Arth*, the acquisition of wealth (3) *Dharm*, the discharge of duty (4) *Moksh*, final emancipation of the soul from contact with matter.

पुरुषाशी, *m.* (*f.* inī) a man-eater, cannibal, rakhshas.

पुरुषी, *f.* (*m.* **पुरुष**) a female.

पुरुषे = **पुरखे**, *q. v.*

पुरुषोत्तम, *m.* an epithet of Vishṇu; *lit.* the most excellent of men, a superior man.

पुरू, *more prop.* **पुरु**, *q. v.*

पुरूरवा, *more prop.* **पुरुरवा**, *q. v.*

पुरुरवा = **पुरुरवस**, *q. v.*

पुरुरवस, *m. pr. n.* the second king of the lunar dynasty, and son of Buddh.

पुरैन, *f.* the placenta; the plant of the lotus.

पुरैनिया, *m. pr. n.* the district and the town of 'Purneah' in Bengal.

पुरोजन्मता, *f.* (*m.* °त्व) priority of birth, primogeniture.

पुरोडस, *more prop.* **पुरोडाश**, *q. v.*

पुरोडाश, *m.* an oblation to the gods, consisting of cakes of ground meal that have been steeped in ghee: a sort of flat ladle used for placing the cake in the sacrificial fire.

पुरोध, **पुरोधस**, **पुरोधा**, **पुरोधाः** } *more com.* **पुरोहित**, *q. v.*

पुरोधिका, *f.* a favorite wife.

पुरोना, *more prop.* **पिरोना**, *q. v.*

पुरोहित, *m.* the family-priest of a prince, who conducts all the religious ceremonies and sacrifices of the family, any family-priest.

पुरोहिताई, *f.* the status or the functions of a family priest, purohitship.

पुरोहितानी, *f.* the wife of a *purohit*.

पुरोहिती = **पुरोहिताई**, *q. v.*

पुर्कार, thick, coarse, fat: well-executed, well-manufactured; efficient, skilful, artful.

पुर्ज़ीना, malicious, spiteful.

पुर्खा, 1, = **पुर्खे**, *q. v.* (see **आ**, 23): 2, *m.* (from **पुरुष**) an old man, elder, ancestor.

पुर्खे, *m.* (pl. of **पुर्खा**) ancestors, forefathers, ancestry, the ancients, the patriarchs, the fathers.

पुर्चक, *f.* deceit, trick, coaxing.

पुर्मीढ़, *m. pr. n.* one of the sons of Hastī. Their names were Ajmīṛh, Drumīṛh, and Purmīṛh.

पुर्व, *more prop.* **पूर्व**, *q. v.*

पुर्वा, *f.* (**पूर्व**) an easterly wind.

पुर्वाना = **पुरवाना**, *q. v.*

पुर्वैया, *f.* easterly wind.

पुर्षा, *more com.* **पुर्खा**, *q. v.*

पुर्षे, *more com.* **पुर्खे**, *q. v.*

पुर्सा, *m.* the extent of a man's reach in height when extending the arms and fingers; a fathom: *adj.* of man's height.

पुल, *m.* the erection of the hairs of the body considered as a proof of exquisite delight: a bridge, embankment, dam, dike.—*bāndhnā*, to make a bridge; *hence*, to limit; to abound.

पुलक, *m.* joy, pleasure; the erection of the hairs of the body considered as occasioned by pleasure: a flaw or defect in a gem: a ball of bread and sweetmeats with which elephants are fed: yellow orpiment: a wineglass, goblet: any insect that infects animals: a kind of esculent plant: a sort of stone.

पुलकाना, *t.* to cause the hair to stand erect.

पुलकित, *m.* (*f.* ā) *adj.*. having the hair standing erect with delight, rejoiced, overjoyed.

पुलकी, *f.* a species of kadamb (*Naucleacadamla*).

पुलपुला, *m.* (*f.* ī) soft, flabby, flaccid.

पुलपुलाना, *a. int.* to fear, dread: *t.* to take a morsel into the mouth, and, being unable to chew from want of teeth, to turn it about in the mouth.

पुलपुलाहट, *f.* fear: the turning about a morsel in the mouth from want of teeth to chew it.

पुलबन्दी, *f.* an embankment, dikes or mounds raised to prevent inundations; the keeping a bridge, etc. in repair; also, a tax levied for such repairs: sodomy.—*k.* to commit sodomy, to violate, ravish.

पुलसरात, *more prop.* पुलसिरात, *q.v.*

पुलसिरात, *m. pr. n.* a certain bridge over which, according to the Muhammadan faith, the righteous will pass to paradise in the day of judgment, and from which the wicked will be precipitated into hell.

पुलस्ति (*Rām.*) = पुलस्त्य, *q.v.*

पुलस्त्य, *m. pr.n.* (see ऋषि) one of the seven ṛishis and mental sons of Brahm.

पुलह, *m. pr. n.* (see ऋषि) one of the seven ṛishis and mental sons of Brahm.

पुलहाना, *t.* to persuade.

पुलहाश्रम, *m. pr. n.* one of the places of Hindoo pilgrimage.

पुला, *m.* a small bundle of plants or sticks; a sheaf.

पुलाव = पिलाव, *q.v.*

पुलिंग, *more prop.* पुंलिंग, *q.v.*

पुलिज, land which is cultivated for every harvest, — being never allowed to lie fallow.

पुलिन, *m.* an alluvial formation, a small island or bank left in the middle of a river when the waters have subsided, a sandbank, any island.

पुलिन्द, *m.* one who speaks an unintelligible dialect, one who inhabits mountains and forests, an outcast, a barbarian, a boatman: *pr. n.* (1) of a certain barbarian tribe (2) of their prince.

पुलिन्दा, *m.* a bundle, parcel.

पुलिसिरात = पुलसिरात, *q.v.*

पुलोम, *m. pr. n.* a certain demon, father-in-law of Indra, by whom he was slain.

पुलोमजा, *f.* an epithet of Shachī, wife of Indra: [*lit.* born of Pulom.

पुलोमन = पुलोम, *q. v.*

पुलोमा, *f. pr. n.* the mother of Pulom.

पुल्लिंग, *more prop.* पुंलिंग, *q.v.*

पुवाल, *f.* straw.

पुंश्चली, *more prop.* पुंश्चली, *q.v.*

पुश्त, *f.* ancestry, a generation of progenitors; the back; a second, assistant.

पुश्ता, *m.* a buttress, prop; a quay, bank; a hill, eminence: a heap, load, bundle.

पुश्तारा, *m.* a truss, pack, load (borne on the back).

पुश्ती, *m.* a backing, alliance, support, aid, prop; the cover of a book. — *k.* to back, second, assist, support.

पुश्तीबानी, *f.* support, alliance, aid.

पुश्तू, *f. pr. n.* the language of the Afghans.

पुष, *m.* the sun.

पुषा, *f.* a certain plant.

पुषित, *m.* (*f.* ā) nourished, nurtured, fed.

पुष्कर, *m.* water; the sky, firmament, heaven, atmosphere; the tip of an elephant's trunk; the skin of a drum; a drum, a kettledrum; the blade of a sword, the sheath of a sword: an arrow: the art or the science of dancing; war, battle; intoxication; a cage; a part; a pond or lake; the Indian crane; a species of snake; union: a kind of drug (*Costus speciosus*): the blue lotus-flower (*Nelumbium speciosum* or *Nymphœa nelumbo*): *pr. n.* (1) of a celebrated place of Hindoo pilgrimage (*Pokar*) in the province of Ajmeer (2) of one of the seven great divisions (*dwip*) of the world (3) of a mountain in that dweep (4) of one of the principal clouds (that which occasions dearth).

पुष्करद्वीप, *m. pr. n.*; see पुष्कर, (2).

पुष्करमूलक, *m.* the root of the *Costus speciosus*.

पुष्करिणी, *f.* a piece of water, large pond, lake, tank: *lit.* a pool where the lotus grows or may grow.

पुष्करी, 1, *m.* (*f.* iṇī) an elephant; 2, *adj.* abounding in lotus-flowers.

पुष्कल, *m.* a certain kind of drum; a certain measure; alms to the extent of four mouthfuls of food: *pr. n.* (1) of the mountain Meru (2) of the holy place Pushkar: lit. *m.* (*f.*ā) excellent, eminent, chief, best, good, salutary, complete, much, many.

पुष्कारना, *t.* to put a horse to speed.

पुष्ट, *m.* (*f.* ā) well-fed, fat, nourished, maintained; eminent; loud; restorative, provocative.—*k.* to fatten.

पुष्टई, *f.* nourishment, nutrition: a restorative, cordial: *adj.* restorative, provocative.

पुष्टत्व, *m.* (*f.* tā) the being well fed, a prosperous and thriving condition, fatness; restorative power, invigoration.

पुष्टा, *f.* (*m.* पुष्ट) a fat female, etc.

पुष्टांग, *m.* (*f.* ī *or* ā) fat-limbed.

पुष्टि, *f.* thriving, increase; the supplying with food, maintenance, nourishment; a cherishing; an abutment to preserve any place from decay, a bank, prop.

पुष्टिकर, *m.* any food or medicine of a nutritive or provocative quality: *adj.* causing growth or prosperity.

पुष्टिका, *f.* an oyster.

पुष्टिद, *m.* (*f.* ā) a certain class of Manes: *lit.* adj. yielding prosperity, nourishing, cherishing.

पुष्टिदा, *f.* a certain plant (*Physalis flexuosa*).

पुष्प, *m.* expansion: a flower; the menses; a disease of the eye (*Albugo*); a topaz: *pr.n.* the car of Kuver.

पुष्पक, *m.* a flower; a kind of snake; the calx of brass, green vitriol or copperas; a disease of the eye (*Albugo*); a bracelet of diamonds or jewels: *pr. n.* the chariot of Kuver.

पुष्पकरण्डक, *m.pr.n.* Avantee or Ujjain or the grove in its vicinity sacred to Mahādev.

पुष्पकासीश, *m.* green sulphate of iron in a state of partial decomposition: the inflorescence of salts.

पुष्पकीट, *m.* (*f.* ī) an insect that affects flowers.

पुष्पकेतु, *m.* calx of brass.

पुष्पचामर, *m.* a certain plant (*Artemisia*); a certain fragrant plant (*Pandanus odoratissimus*) having a large bushy flower. [quarter.

पुष्पदन्त, *m. pr. n.* the elephant of the north-east

पुष्पदामन = फुल्लदामन, *q.v.*

पुष्पध, *m.* one of the degraded tribes, the offspring of an outcast Brāhmaṇ.

पुष्पपथ, *m.* the vulva. [bothra (Patna).
पुष्पपुर, *m. pr. n.* the city of Pātāliputra or Pali-
पुष्पफल, *m.* the wood-apple (*Feronia elephantum*).
पुष्पभूषित, *m.* (*f.* ā) adorned with flowers: 2, *m.* a kind
पुष्पमास, *m.* the spring season. [of Prakaraṇ.
पुष्परक्त, *m.* a certain shrub (*Hibiscus phoeniceus*).
पुष्परस, *m.* flower-juice, nectar.
पुष्परेणु, *m.* the pollen of a flower.
पुष्परोचन, *m.* a certain plant (*Messua ferrea*).
पुष्पवत, *m.* (*f.* vatī) having flowers, flowery; like a flower or flowers, flower-like.
पुष्पवती, *f.* a menstruous woman.
पुष्पवाटी, *f.* a flower-garden.
पुष्पवन्त / **पुष्पवान** } *m.* (*f.* vatī) = **पुष्पवत**, *q. v.*
पुष्पशून्य, *m.* (*f.* ā) destitute of flowers.
पुष्पसमय, *m.* the springtime (*lit.* time of flowers).
पुष्पसार, *m.* the nectar or honey of flowers.
पुष्पहीन, *m.* (*f.* ā) flowerless, not flowering.
पुष्पहीना, *f.* a female in whom menstruation has ceased, a barren female; the glomerous figtree.
पुष्पा, *f. pr. n.* the capital of Karṇ.
पुष्पांजन, *m.* the calx of brass.
पुष्पांजलि = **पुष्पांजली**, *q. v.*
पुष्पांजली, *f.* the presenting a nosegay held in both hands open and hollowed.
पुष्पिका, *f.* a division of a book, chapter: the tartar of the teeth; mucus of the glans penis or urethra.
पुष्पित, *m.* (*f.* ā) flowered, in flower, momentarily
पुष्पिता, *f.* a menstruous female. [pleasing.
पुष्पिताग्रा, *f.* a species of Sanskrit metre, in which the line consists of four or six short syllables, a pyrrhic, or a dactyl, two trochees, and a spondee.
पुष्पी, *m.* (*f.* iṇī) flowering, bearing flowers, blossoming.
पुष्य, *m. pr. n.* (1) of the 8th *Nakshatra*, comprizing three stars of which one is Cancer (2) of the Hindoo month *Paus* (3) of Kaliyug: *adj.* requiring to be cherished.
पुष्यपुत्र, *m.* (*f.* ī) an adopted child.—*k.* to adopt [a child.
पुष्या, *f.* = **पुष्य** (1), *q. v.*
पुसपूत, *more prop.* **पुष्यपुत्र**, *q. v.*
पुसा; see (1) **पूषा** (2) **पौष**.
पुस्त, *m.* smearing, anointing, plastering, painting; working in clay, modelling: a book, manuscript.
पुस्तक, *m. f.* a book, volume, manuscript.
पुस्तकागार / **पुस्तकालय** } *m.* a library, book-depôt.
पुस्तकी, *f.* a book, volume, manuscript.
पुस्तकें, *f.* (pl. of **पुस्तक**) books, manuscripts.
पुस्तारा, *more prop.* **पुश्तारा**, *q. v.*
पुस्ती, *more prop.* **पुश्ती**, *q. v.*

पुस्य, *more prop.* **पुष्य**, *q. v.*
पुहप, an old form = **पुष्प**, *q. v.*
पुहुकर in Chand = **पोखर**, *q. v.*
पुहुप, an old form = **पुष्प**, *q. v.*
पुहुमि / **पुहुमी** } (*Rām.*) = **पृथवी**, *q. v.*
पूआ, *m.* pancake.
पूँ, *m.* the sound of the emission of wind backwards. [by jugglers.
पूँगी, *f.* a flute, pipe, a kind of pipe played upon
पूँया, *m.* (*f.* ī) a male child, a boy.
पूँछ, *f.* a tail.
पूँछना, *t.* to wipe.
पूँछपाछ, *more prop.* **पूछपाछ**, *q. v.*
पूँछल', *m.* a tail.
पूँछार, tailed, having a tail.
पूँछि, *more prop.* **पूँछ**, *q. v.* [fund.
पूँजी, *f.* (in trade) capital, stock, principal sum,
पूकार, *more prop.* **पुकार**, *q. v.*
पूग, *m.* a heap, quantity, multitude, assembly: nature, disposition, property: the betel-nut tree (*Areca faufel* or *A. catechu*) and its fruit; the *jak*-tree (*Artocarpus intigrifolius*).
पूगफल, *m.* the *areca*-nut. [*paludosa*).
पूगरोट, *m.* the marshy date-tree (*Phœnix* or *Elate*
पूगवो, in Māṛwāṛī = to send; to meet.
पूच, of no moment, insignificant, absurd, nonsensical, injudicious, inordinate, obscene.
पूछ, 1, *more prop.* **पुच्छ**, *q. v.*: 2, *f.* an asking, inquiry, investigation.
पूछना, *t.* to ask, enquire, interrogate.
पूछपछ, *more com.* **पूछपाछ**, *q. v.* [quiry.
पूछपाछ, *f.* interrogation, investigation by in-
पूछविचार, investigation, discovery.
पूछापाछी, *m. more com.* **पूछपाछ**, *q. v.*
पूछिनों / **पूछिहनो** } old forms = **पूछना**, *q. v.*
पूछी, *f.* the tail of a fish: an insect.
पूजक, *adj.* honouring, venerating, adoring, worshipping: hence, *m.* (*f.* ikā) an idolator, etc.
पूजत, *adj.* reverencing, worshipping.
पूजन, *m.* (*f.* ?) the act of adoring, respect, reverence, worship; the shewing attentions to a visitor.
पूजना, 1, *t.* to reverence, venerate, adore, worship; to idolatrize: 2, *a. int.* to elapse (as time): 3, *n.* to be filled, be fulfilled, be accomplished, be perfected.
पूजनीय, *m.* (*f.* ā) = **पूजमान**, *q. v.*
पूजमान, *m.* (*f.* matī) entitled to or deserving respect, veneration, or homage, venerable, adorable, worshipful.
पूजयिता / **पूजयितृ** } *m.* (*f.* trī) a worshipper.
पूजवाना, *t.* (prop. **पुजवाना**) to cause to worship: to cause to be worshipped.

पूजा, 1, *m.* (*f.* ī) filled, etc. (from **पूजना**): 2, *f.* worship, honour, homage, respect, reverence, adoration, idol-worship.
पूजाना, *t.* to cause to worship.
पूजा.पा, *m.* the apparatus of worshipping.
पूजा.पाठ, *f.* (**पूजा + पाठ**) the attending for religious purposes on study and idol worship.
पूजारी, *m.* (*f.* in *or* ini) a worshipper, adorer, venerator, priest.
पूजावना, *t.* to cause to worship.
पूजास्थान, *m.* any place of idol-worship.
पूजिका, *f.* (*m.* **पूजक**) a female idolator.
पूजित, *m.* (*f.* ā) venerated, adored, worshipped; hospitably received.
पूजिहि, *m. f.* (pl. **पूजिहिं**) = (1) **पूजता है** (2) **पूर्ण होगा**.
पूजी, *f.* (*m.* **पूजा**, 1) filled, etc. (from **पूजना**).
पूजेरी } = **पुजारी**, *q. v.*
पूजेरु }
पूज्य, 1, *m.* (*f.* ā) = **पूजनीय**, *q. v.*: 2, *m.* a father-in-law.
पूज्यत्व, *m.* (*f.* tā) the being entitled to honour or to worship, worshipfulness, adorableness.
पूज्यमान, *m.* (*f.* matī) = **पूजमान**, *q. v.*
पूट, *m.* a certain bone that lies over the tail of a cow: a flux for metals; a menstruum.
पूटकी, *f.* (a term of abuse) the anus.
पूठ, *m.* the buttock, hip.
पूठा, *m.* the cover of a book (whether paper or pasteboard).
पूड़ा, *m.* a kind of cake made of peasemeal.
पूण, *more com.* **पुण्य**, *q. v.*
पूणी, *f.* rolls of cotton prepared for spinning.
पूत, 1, *m.* a son; the young of any animal: 2, *m.* (*f.* ā) cleansed, purified; sincere, true: foul-smelling.
पूतज़म्बूरा, *m.* a young monkey.
पूतत्व, *m.* (*f.* tī) cleanness, purity, sanctity, honesty, sincerity, truth: a stinking.
पूतना, *f.* yellow myrobalan (*Terminalia chebula*): *pr. n.* a certain female demon killed by Krishn; *hence*, a certain disease (atrophy and wasting in a child) ascribed to the malignant operations of that fiend.
पूतफल, *m.* the jack-fruit.
पूतरी, *more prop.* **पुतली**, *q. v.*
पूतला, *more prop.* **पुतला**, *q. v.*
पूतली, *more prop.* **पुतली**, *q. v.*
पूतात्मा, a pure or purified person, a saint, ascetic; a cleanly person, one purified by ablution; *lit.* pure, virtuous, sincere, veracious.
पूति, *f.* purification, purity, sanctity: pus, matter: the civet-cat: a stench: *adj.* stinking, putrid.
पूतिक, *m.* grey bonduc (*Cæsalpinia bonducella*).
पूतिकरंज } = **पूतिक**, *q. v.*
पूतिकरज }
पूतिकर्णक, *m.* fetid ulceration of the ear.
पूतिका, *f.* a species of potherb (*Basella lucida*): a civet cat (*Viverra zibethina*).
पूतिकामुख, *m.* a bivalve shell.
पूतिकाष्ठ, *m.* a species of pine (*Pinus devadaru*).
पूतिफला, *f.* a certain plant (*Psoralea corilifolia*).
पूतिफली, *f.* a certain medicinal plant (*Serratula anthelmintica*).
पूतिवृक्ष, *m.* a certain plant (*Bignonia Indica*).
पूतिशारिजा *f.* the pole-cat (*Viverra zibethina*).
पूतीक = **पूतिक**, *q. v.*
पूत्यण्ड, *m.* the musk-deer: an insect with a fetid smell, the flying bug.
पूथी, *more prop.* **पोथी**, *q. v.*
पूदीना, *m.* garden mint (*Mentha sativa*).
पून, *m.* a ferrule or cap of metal, the mounting of a sword-hilt, walking-cane.
पूनसलाई, *f.* a thin roller on which cotton is prepared for spinning.
पूनियो = **पुन्यो**, *q. v.*
पूनी, *f.* rolls of cotton prepared for spinning.
पूनें, *f.* the day of full moon.
पूनो } in Braj = **पूनें**, *q. v.*
पूनों }
पून्या, *f.* the day of full moon.
पून्यो } in Braj = **पून्यो**, *q. v.*
पून्यों }
पूप, *m.* a cake, loaf, bread.
पूपकर } *m.* (*f.* ī) a baker.
पूपकार }
पूपला, *m.* a sort of sweet cake fried with oil or ghee.
पूपालिक, *m.* } a cake.
पूपालिका, *f.* }
पूपाली, *f.* a sort of cake or biscuit made of meal or barley, half baked or fried.
पूपाष्टिका, *f.* a certain Hindoo festival on the eighth day of the second half of the month Mārgshir, at which cakes of rice are offered to the manes.
पूय, *m.* 1, (*Rām.*) = **प्रिय**, *q. v.*: 2, discharge from any sore, matter, pus.
पूयन = **पूय**, *q. v.*
पूयारस, *m.* suppuration at the joints, white swelling.
पूर, *m.* a filling; a large quantity of water; a kind of cake fried in oil or butter; the healing or cleansing of ulcers; the drawing in breath through the nose as religious exercise; a reply; an ear-ornament —*purnā*, to be able to perform an engagement, to discharge an obligation, to be successful.
पूरक, 1, *m.* a certain religious ceremony consisting in the drawing in the breath by the left nostril, while one is kept closed: a citron (*Citrus medica*): the final obsequial cake: 2, *m.* (*f.* ikā) that which fills or completes: *lit.* adj. filling, completing; full, filled, complete, accomplished, perfect, entire, all, total; exact; ripe; strong, powerful, able.
पूरण, 1, *m.* the act of filling, completing, satisfying; a dike; the ocean; (in Arithm.) multiplication: a certain fragrant grass (*Cyperus rotundus.*)
पूरणार्थसंख्यावाचक, *m.* ordinal numbers.
पूरणी, *f.* the cross-threads in weaving a piece of cloth: the silk-cotton tree.
पूरदर्द, *more prop.* **पुरदर्द**, *q. v.*

पूरन, *more prop.* **पूरण**, *q.v.*
पूरना, *t.* to fill, fulfil, complete.
पूरब, *more prop.* **पूर्व**, *q.v.*
पूरयिता / **पूरयितृ** } *m.* (*f.* trī) one who satisfies.
पूरवा, *m.* (from **पुर**) a small village.
पूरहि, *m.* or *f.* (pl. °**हिं**) = **पूरता है**. See **पूरता** and **हि**.
पूरा, *m.* the act of filling or completing: adj. *m.* (*f.* ī) full, complete, entire, perfect, copious, sufficient; total, ripe, powerful, accomplished. — *k.* to fill, fulfil, complete, accomplish; to reïmburse.
पूराई, *f.* fulness, completeness, entireness, completion, accomplishment.
पूरातन, *m.* (*f.* ī) *more prop.* **पुरातन**, *q.v.*
पूरान, *more prop.* **पुराण**, *q.v.*
पूरिक, *m.* / **पूरिका**, *f.* } a kind of cake.
पूरित, *m.* (*f.* ā) full, filled, complete, accomplished.
पूरिया, *f.* a certain musical mode (*rāgiṇī*).
पूरी, *f.* a kind of fresh unleavened cake fried in oil [or ghee.
पूरुष, *more prop.* **पुरुष**, *q.v.*
पूर्ण = **पूरण**, *q.v.*
पूर्णक, *m.* (*f.* ikā) the blue jay: a certain tree.
पूर्णकाम, *m.* (*f.* ā.) *adj.* having the desires fulfilled, satisfied, satiated.
पूर्णकुम्भ, *m.* a vessel filled with holy water used at the consecration of a king, a water-vessel.
पूर्णचन्द्र, 1, *m. f.* the full moon: 2, *m. pr. n.* (1) of a Bodhisattva (2) of a certain author.
पूर्णतावोधक क्रिया, *f.* (in Gram.) the completive form of any verb; *e. g. Kah-chuknā.*
पूर्णत्व, *m.* (*f.* tā) fulness, completeness.
पूर्णपात्र, *m.* a full cup or vessel, a vessel filled with clothes or ornaments which are scrambled for at a festival by the relations and guests; a vessel full of rice presented as a sacrifice to the superintending and officiating priests. It is properly a measure of two hundred and fifty-six handfuls of rice, but it may also consist of as much as would satisfy one great [eater.
पूर्णपोली, *f.* a kind of bread.
पूर्णप्रतापी, *m.* (*f.* inī) one whose glory is complete.
पूर्णवैनाशी, *m.* (*f.* inī) an epithet applied by orthodox Hindoos to Buddhists; *prop.* adj. arguing total perishableness.
पूर्णब्रह्म, *m.* an epithet of the Supreme Being.
पूर्णभूत, *m.* (in Gram.) the pluperfect tense; *lit.* the complete past.
पूर्णमा, a contraction of **पूर्णमासी**, *q.v.*
पूर्णमास, *m.* a monthly sacrifice performed on the day of full moon. [moon.
पूर्णमासी, *f.* the night or day of full moon, full
पूर्णवासी = **पूर्णमासी** *q. v.*
पूर्णा, *more prop.* **पूरना**, *q. v.*
पूर्णाई, *f.* (= **पूर्त्ति**) fulness, completeness.
पूर्णाहुत, *more prop.* **पूर्णाहुति**, *q. v.*
पूर्णाहुति, *f.* a final oblation, *viz.* that presented at the conclusion of a religious sacrifice, the burnt-offering which completes any ceremony.
पूर्णिका, *f.* (*m.* **पूर्णक**) a certain bird.
पूर्णिमा, a contraction of **पूर्णमासी**, *q. v.*
पूर्त्ति, *f.* fulness, completeness; the accomplishment of any thing. completion.
पूर्त्ती, *m.* (*f.* inī) *adj.* filling, completing.
पूर्ब or **पूर्ब्ब**; for words beginning thus, see under the form **पूर्व**.
पूर्व, 1, *m.* (see **दक्षिण**) the East: 2, *m.* (*f.* ā) fore, former, prior, anterior, preceding, previous, antecedent, initial, first; east, eastward, easterly, eastern: 3, before, prior to, beforehand: at first, formerly, aforetime; immemorially; in front of.
पूर्वअवस्था, *f.* antecedents (*lit.* former condition).
पूर्वक, *m.* (*f.* ikā) an ancestor: *lit.* prior, before, preceding, first. As the latter part of compound words it has an adverbial function, and imports the idea of associated with, accompanied by; *e. g.* **विश्वासपूर्वक**, (*lit.* accompanied by faith, *i.e.*) believingly.
पूर्वकाल, *m.* former time; (in Gram.) past time.
पूर्वकालिक, (in Gram.) appertaining to former or past time; also, to future time. [ancient.
पूर्वकालीन, *m.* (*f.* ā) belonging to former times,
पूर्वकृत, done formerly or in a previous state of
पूर्वग, *m.* (*f.* ā) = **पूर्वगामी**, *q. v.* [existence.
पूर्वगंगा, *f. pr. n.* the Narmada river (formerly called the 'Ganges'). [ceder: *lit.* adj. preceding.
पूर्वगामी, *m.* (*f.* inī) a forerunner, predecessor, pre-
पूर्वचित्ति, *f. pr. n.* a certain Apsaras; *lit.* the first thought, foreboding, presentiment.
पूर्वज, *m.* (*f.* ā) an elder, elder brother; an oriental: *lit.* (1) born or produced before, elder (2) born in the East, oriental.
पूर्वजन्म, *m.* a former birth or state of existence.
पूर्वजा, *f.* (*m.* **पूर्वज**) an elder sister; an ancestress; an oriental female.
पूर्वजाः, *m.* (a Sk. pl. of **पूर्वज**; see **आ** 22) ancestors, progenitors, the deified progenitors of mankind.
पूर्वदिक, *more prop.* **पूर्वदिश**, *q. v.*
पूर्वदिश / **पूर्वदिशा** } *f.* the eastern region.
पूर्वदिसा, *more prop.* **पूर्वदिशा**, *q. v.*
पूर्वदेश, *m. pr. n.* the eastern part of India; *lit.* the east country. [the east.
पूर्वदेशी, *m.* (*f.* inī) an inhabitant or a native of
पूर्वदेह, *m.* a former existence; *lit.* a former body.
पूर्वदेहिक, appertaining to a previous state of
पूर्वनिरूपण, *m.* predestination. [existence.
पूर्वनिवासी, *m.* (*f.* inī) an ancestor: an oriental.
पूर्वनी, *more prop.* **पूर्विणी**; see **पूर्वी**, 3.
पूर्वपक्ष, *m.* the first side or part of an argument, a proposition, a *primâ facie* argument or assertion: the former half of a lunar month.
पूर्वपर्वत, *m. pr. n.* the mountain in the east from behind which the sun is supposed to rise.

पूर्वपुरुष, *m.* (pl. आः) an ancestor, forefather.

पूर्वफल्गुनी, *f. pr. n.* (see फाल्गुन) the eleventh Nakshatra (figured by a conch-shell, and containing two stars, one of which is Leonis).

पूर्वभाद्रपदा, *f. pr. n.* (see भाद्रपदा) the twenty-sixth Nakshatra (containing two stars).

पूर्वमीमांसा = कर्म्ममीमांसा. *q. v.* [yesternight.

पूर्वरात्र, *m.* the earlier or first part of the night;

पूर्वलक्षण, *m.* an indication of something about to occur (as sickness, etc.).

पूर्ववत्, as before, as heretofore, as formerly, in accordance with what has preceded. The term is applied in the Nyāya syst m of philosophy to a kind of syllogism, *e. g.* when from the appearance of a dark cloud, the inference is drawn that rain will fall.

पूर्ववर्त्तिता, *f.* } priority, precedence.
पूर्ववर्त्तित्व, *m.* }

पूर्ववर्त्ती, *m.* (*f.* inī) one who is in the presence of another, etc.: *lit.* situated before (one); preceding, prior, previous.

पूर्ववादी, *adj.* speaking first or in the first instance: hence, *m.* (*f.* inī) a plaintiff.

पूर्वशैल = पूर्वपर्वत, *q. v.*

पूर्वसन्ध्या, *f.* the early dawn.

पूर्वसमुद्र, *m.* the eastern sea.

पूर्वसूचक, *m.* (*f.* ikā) one who relates a forgotten circumstance, a reminder.

पूर्वहि, a poetic form (emphatic and accusative) of पूर्व, 3. *q. v.*

पूर्वा, 1, = पूरवा, *q. v.*: 2, *f.* (*m.* पूर्व) the East; an ancestress; an oriental female. [ancestors.

पूर्वाः, *m.* (Sk. pl. of पूर्व; see आ, 22) forefathers,

पूर्वाधिकारी, *m.* (*f.* iṇī) a prior owner or proprietor.

पूर्वाफाल्गुनी, *more com.* पूर्वफल्गुनी, *q. v.*

पूर्वाभाद्रपद, *more prop.* पूर्वभाद्रपदा, *q. v.*

पूर्वाभिमुख, *m.* (*f.* ā *or* ī) *adj.* facing or fronting the east. looking eastward.

पूर्वाभ्यास, *m.* former practice or experience.

पूर्वार्द्ध, *m.* the first or eastern half of anything, the former half, part the first.

पूर्वाषाढ़ा, *f. pr. n.* (see आषाढ़) the 20th Nakshatra (containing two stars, one of which is Sagittari).

पूर्वाह्ण, *m.* the morning, the forenoon. [female.

पूर्विका, *f.* (*m.* पूर्वक) an ancestress; an oriental

पूर्वी, 1, *f.* a certain *rāgiṇī* sung before evening: 2, *m.* a kind of rice from the east (or Bengal): 3, *m.* (*f.* iṇī) an oriental; an ancestor: *lit.* appertaining to ancestors or to the east, ancestral, eastern.

पूर्वीममांसा (*corruption*) = पूर्वमीमांसा, *q. v.*

पूर्वीय, eastern, easterly.

पूर्वोक्त, said before, before-mentioned.

पूर्वोत्तर, *m. pr. n.* the North-east.

पूला, *m.* a bundle of grass or straw. *Pūle tale guzrān k.* to pass one's days under a bundle of straw, *i. e.* to live in a very destitute plight.

पूलिया, *m.* a certain class of persons in southern India who profess a species of Muhammadanism extremely corrupted by the Indian superstitions. The Muhammadan Arabs in India propagated their religion by buying slaves, to whom, after they had been circumcised and instructed in their doctrines, they gave freedom. In course of time these latter became a distinct people inhabiting the coast of India from Goa around the cape to Madras. In Malabar they are called 'pooliyās', while on the Coromandel they are called 'coolies'.

पूली, *f.* (dim. of पूला) a small bundle of any grass or straw; a small quantity of corn given at harvest to village officers and servants.

पूलीचो, *m.* a certain degraded race of men who inhabit the forests of Malabar, where they are not permitted to build huts, but are obliged to live in a kind of nest which they make on the trees. When oppressed with hunger they howl. to excite the compassion of passers-by: the charitable deposit some rice or other food at the foot of a tree and retire with all possible haste, to give the famished wretch an opportunity of taking it without meeting with his benefactor.

पूष, 1, a corruption of पुष्य, *q. v.*: 2, *m.* the mulberry (*Morus Indica*) or the *Hibiscus populneoides.*

पूषन्, 1, (Rām.) = पूर्णमासी, *q. v.*: 2, *m. pr. n.* (1) of a certain Vedic deity (2) of one of the Ādityas (3) of the sun.

पूषा, *m.* the sun.

पूस, a corruption of पौष, *q. v.*

पूहप, an old form = पुष्प, *q. v.* [*corniculata*).

पृक्का, *f.* a certain gramineous plant (*Trigonella*

पृक्ति, *f.* contact, contiguity, touch.

पृथन्धर, *m. pr. n.* a certain ancient Hindoo king.

पृच्छक, *adj.* inquiring: hence, *m.* (*f.* ikā) an inquirer, inquisitive person, investigator.

पृच्छण, *m.* an asking, inquiring, questioning, investigating.

पृच्छा, *f.* an asking, inquiring; a question, inquiry.

पृतना, *f.* an army; a division of an army consisting of 243 elephants, 243 chariots, 729 horses, and 1215 foot.

पृतनानी, *m.* the commander of an army.

पृथक्, separate, apart: *adv.* separately, severally, distinctly, apart: *conj.* without, except.

पृथकत्व, *m.* (*f.* tā) individuality, separateness, severality, separation.

पृथक्करण, *m.* a separating, distinguishing.

पृथक्कृत, *m.* (*f.* ā) made distinct, separated, sundered.

पृथकत्वचा, *f.* a certain plant (*Sanseviera zeylanica*) commonly called 'moorva'.

पृथक्पर्णी, *f.* a certain plant (*Hemionites cordifolia*).

पृथगात्मा, *m.* individualized spirit, or the spirit of an individual considered as detached from the universal spirit.

पृथग्गुण, *adj.* having distinct properties.

पृथग्विध, diversified, multiform, various.

पृथमी, a corruption of पृथिवी, *q. v.*

पृथवी = पृथिवी and पृथ्वी, *qq. v.*

पृथवीतल, *m.* the surface of the ground.

पृथा, *f.* a name of कुन्ती, *q. v.*

पृथिवी, *f.* (from **पृथु**) the earth; the earth personified; earth, soil. In the ingenious system of reckoning by symbols adopted by Hindoos in their poetry, this word is a symbol for 1 (*one*).

पृथिवीक्षित, *m.* (*f.* ā) an epithet of any monarch; *lit.* adj. ruling the earth.

पृथिवीतल, *m.* the surface of the ground.

पृथिवीनाथ, *m.* (*f.* ā) an epithet of any monarch; *lit.* protector of the earth.

पृथिवीपति, *m.* (*f.* patnī) an epithet of any monarch; *lit.* proprietor of the earth.

पृथिवीपाल, *m.* (*f.* ī) an epithet of any monarch; *lit.* guardian or nourisher of the earth.

पृथिवीपालक, *m.* (*f.* ikā) = **पृथिवीपाल**, *q.v.*

पृथिवीभुज, *m.* (*f.* ā) an epithet of any monarch; *lit.* adj. governing the earth.

पृथिवीमण्डल, *m.* the circuit or whole surface of the world.

पृथी; for words beginning thus, see under the form **पृथिवी**.

पृथीराज, *m. pr. n.* an ancient king of the Chahuvan race who resided at Delhi.

पृथु, 1, *m. pr. n.* (1) of the fifth monarch of the solar dynasty (in the second age) (2) of an ancient *rājā*, the son of Ven, Rājā of Bettūr (he was married to a form of the goddess Lakshmee, and taught men to cultivate the earth, etc.): 2, *f.* a certain pungent seed (*Nigella Indica*); a certain medicinal substance commonly called Hingupatrī (perhaps the leaf of the assafœtida plant): 3, *lit. m.* (*f.* **पृथु** or **पृथ्वी**) large, great, wide.

पृथुत्व, *m.* (*f.* tā) largeness, width, greatness.

पृथुराज, *m. pr. n.* = **पृथु**, (1), *q.v.*

पृथूदर, *m.* (*f.* ī) a ram; a stout person: *lit.* large-bellied, corpulent.

पृथ्वी, *f.* 1, = **पृथिवी** and **पृथु**, 2 and 3, *qq.v.*: 2, a kind of metre in Sanskrit prosody.

पृथ्वीनाथ = **पृथिवीनाथ**, *q.v.*

पृथ्वीभर, *m.* a species of the *atyasti* metre.

पृश्निका, *f.* the aquatic plant *Pistia stratiotes*.

पृश्निपर्णी, *f.* a certain plant (*Hemionites cordifolia* or *Hedisarum lagopodioides*).

पृष्ट, *m.* (*f.* ā) asked, interrogated, inquired.

पृष्ठ, *m.* the back, the hinder or upper part of anything, the rear, the surface, the last.

पृष्ठदृष्टि, *m.* an epithet of the bear (from his looking behind him).

पृश्नि, *f. pr. n.* the wife of the sun.

पे = **पै**, 4, *q.v.*

पेई, *f.* a small basket; a portmanteau.

पें, *m.* an imitative sound.

पेंग, 1, *m.* a certain bird (*Gracula chattareah*, Buch.): 2, *f.* the exertion made by persons in a swing when two persons keep it in motion without assistance from bystanders.

पेंच, *more prop.* **पेच**, *q.v.*

पेंजनी, *f.* little bells fastened around the feet of pigeons and of children, foot-bells, ankle-bells.

पेंठ, पेंड, पेंत, पेंद; for words beginning thus, see under the forms **पेयठ, पेयड, पेन्त, पेन्द**, respectively.

पेखना, 1, *t.* to see, behold: 2, *m.* a play, farce, sham, comedy.

पेखनिया, *m.* a player, actor.

पेगाम, *more prop.* **पैग़ाम**, *q.v.*

पेच, *m.* twist, fold, coil, revolution; a screw; complication, deceit, perplexity, difficulty.

पेचक, *m.* (*f.* ikā) an owl: a louse: the root of an elephant's tail: a cloud: a bed.

पेचताब, *m.* twisting and twining, contortion; folds, twists, knots; restlessness, alarm, suspense, perplexity; words, angry discourse. silence through anger.—*khānā*, to twist, twine; to suffer distress or anxiety.

पेचदार, twisted, coiled.

पेचा, *m.* (*f.* ī?) an owl.

पेचिका, *f.* (*m.* **पेचक**) a female owl.

पेचिश, *f.* inflection, contortion, writhing, pain in the bowels, gripes, tenesmus; perplexity, trouble; circumvention, contention.

पेचु, *m.* a certain esculent root (*Arum colocasia*).

पेचोताब = **पेचताब**, *q.v.*

पेट, *m.* (*lit.* a basket, bag) the stomach; the womb; pregnancy; the bore of a gun, etc.; a cavity, capacity: *met.* a livelihood, a living. — *ānā*, to be purged. — *kāṭnā*, to pinch one's stomach, starve oneself; to be griped. — *kā duhkh denā*, to starve. — *kā parda*, *m.* the omentum. — *kā pānī na hilnā* is applied to the steady motion of a horse, etc. which does not agitate the rider. — *kī āg*, *f.* motherly affection: hunger. — *kī āg bujhānā*, to pacify hunger by eating. — *kī bāteṅ*, *f.* bosom secrets. — *ke pāṅw bāhar nikālnā*, to shew the cloven foot, to practise baseness or viciousness. — *gargaṛānā*, to have borborgmi. — *girnā*, *m.* miscarriage, abortion; to miscarry (a female). — *girānā*, to cause an abortion. — *chalnā* or *chhūṭnā*, to be purged, have a diarrhœa or flux. — *jalnā*, to be very hungry. — *jārī honā*, to be purged, be fluxed. — *ḍālnā*, to procure abortion. — *dikhānā*, to complain of poverty and hunger. — *paknā*, to burst with laughter. — *pānī honā*, to be violently purged, have watery stools. — *pālnā*, to be able to live decently; to be selfish. — *piṭh ek honā*, to be greatly emaciated. — *piṭh batānā*, to evince extreme weakness, act submissively. — *phūlnā*, to burst with laughter. — *baṛhānā*, to eat voraciously; to encroach on the share or rights of another. — *bāndhnā*, to eat less than one's appetite demands. — *bharnā*, to fill one's stomach, eat to satisfaction. — *mārnā*, to stab oneself, commit suicide by stabbing. — *meṅ paṛnā*, to be begotten or conceived. — *meṅ paiṭhnā*, to worm oneself into the secrets of another, become intimate. — *meṅ lenā*, to endure, put up with, have patience: to conceive, become pregnant. — *rakhnā*, to get with child. — *rahnā*, to be pregnant. — *lag jānā*, to be starving, be famished. — *lag rahnā*, to be very hungry. — *haṛbaṛānā*, to have a griping or inclination to go to stool.

पेटक, *m.* a covered wicker-basket for holding clothes, books, etc.: a multitude.

पेटगिरना; see *s.v.* **पेट**.

पेटचिसनी, in Māṛwāṛī = a thief.

पेटपोठ; see *s. v.* **पेट**.

पेटपोंछन, **पेटपोंछन**, **पेटपोछन**, *m.* (*f.* ī) a woman's last child.

पेटपोसू = **पेटपोसूआ**, *q.v.*

पेटपोसुआ, (*f.* ई) a glutton: *lit.* gluttonous.

पेटभर, a bellyful. See *s.v.* पेट

पेटवाली, *f.* a pregnant female.

पेटसे, pregnant (as a female).—*honā*, to be pregnant.

पेटा, *f.* a basket, large basket.

पेटारा, *m.* a large basket, travelling clothes-basket, portmanteau.

पेटारी, *f.* a certain plant (*Sida Asiatica*): a small clothes-basket.

पेटार्थ, for the sake of the stomach.

पेटार्थी, *m.* (*f.* inī) a glutton, epicure: *lit.* desirous for the stomach, gluttonous, epicurean.

पेटार्थु = पेटार्थी, *q.v.*

पेटिका, *f.* a box.

पेटिया, *m.* pension, daily food, board.

पेटी, *f.* a basket, box, chest, case, tumbril, portmanteau; a martingale, belly-band, girth; the thorax, chest.—*larnā* or *mārnā*, to copulate.

पेटुक = पेटू, *q.v.*

पेटुनी, *f.* pregnant female.

पेटू, *m. f.* a glutton: *lit.* gluttonous, voracious, ravenous.

पेटोखा, *m.* looseness, purging, flux.

पेठ, a village or small town (used in comp. like *pur, paṭṭan, ābād*).

पेठा, *m.* a kind of gourd.

पेड़, *f. m.* a tree, plant; a trunk or stem of a tree. —*lagānā*, to plant trees.

पेड़ना, *t.* to press (as oil by means of a mill), squeeze, rack.

पेड़ा, *m.* a kind of sweetmeat made with curds; a globular mass of leaven prepared for baking.

पेड़ी, *f.* a kind of sweetmeat made with curds: a kind of betel-leaf: the indigo-plant after being once cut: the trunk of a tree.

पेडू, 1, a corruption of पेट, *q.v.*: 2, *m.* the belly below the navel, the pubes.

पेंपिटकोष्ट, *m. pr.n.* Pentecost (the second of the great festivals of the Hebrews).

पेयठ, 1, a corruption of पैठ, *q.v.*: 2, *f.* a market, mart.

पेयड, *f.* a pace, step: rising ground, eminence.

पेनी, *more prop.* पैनी, *q.v.*

पेन्ताना, *m.* the foot of a bed, the side towards the feet.

पेन्तिकोष्ट = पेंपिटकोष्ट, *q.v.*

पेन्दा, *m.* the bottom (of a vessel, box, pot, etc.); the breach of a cannon.

पेन्दी, *f.* the fundament.

पेन्हा, *more prop.* पहिनना, *q.v.*

पेन्हाई, *f.* tenderness, fondness, affection.

पेम, a contraction of प्रेम, *q.v.*

पेमी, *m.* (*f.* inī) a contraction of प्रेमी, *q.v.*

पेय, *m.* any drink, water, milk: *lit.* suitable to be taken as drink, drinkable.

पेयाला, *more prop.* प्याला, *q.v.*

पेयी, *f.* a small basket, a portmanteau.

पेयूष } **पेयूस** } = पीयूष, *q.v.*

पेरना, *t.* to till, plant, sow: to oppress.

पेरवा, *m.* a large earthen vessel.

पेरा, *f.* a certain musical instrument.

पेरु, *m.* the ocean: the sun: fire.

पेरू, *m.* (Portug.) a turkey.

पेरोज़, *m.* the turquoise.

पेल, *m.* 1, = पेला, *q.v.*: 2, a shove, push, thrust.

पेलड़ } **पेलड़ा** } *m.* a testicle: a cowrie.

पेलना, *t.* to shove, push, stuff, cram; to squeeze out, express.

पेलपाल, shoving and pushing.

पेला, *m.* a testicle: fault; oppression: a prop, support.

पेलिहहि, (pl. °हिं) old form = पेलेगा (पेलना).

पेलू, *m.* a wrestler, athlete, pusher, shover.

पेल्हड़ } **पेल्हड़ा** } *m.* a testicle.

पेवक्कड़, *m.* a drunkard, tippler.

पेवड़ी, *f.* a kind of yellow colour (said to be obtained from the urine of a cow fed, according to some, on the flowers of *Butea frondosa*, and according to others, on the leaves of the mango-tree).

पेवसी, *f.* more prop. पीयूष, *q.v.*

पेश, 1, *adj.* promoted, advanced, respected, confided in, possessing influence: 2, *m.* front, before: 3, *adv.* before, in front of.—*k.* to produce, bring forward, put forward.

पेशकश, *m.* a present, tribute, fine, quit-rent (paid to Government as an acknowledgement for any tenure).

पेशकार, *m.* a deputy, agent, manager, assistant, minister.

पेशगी, *f.* an advance, earnest-money given on confirming an agreement, etc.

पेशतर, before, formerly, heretofore, prior.

पेशदस्ती, *f.* an excelling, surpassing, preëminence preëxcellence.

पेशबन्द, *m.* the belt that passes over a horse's breast to prevent the saddle from slipping back.

पेशबन्दी, *f.* timely preparation, precaution, foresight.

पेशरो, *m.* a precursor, leader, advanced guard.

पेशवा, *m.* a title of the Marhaṭṭa minister; *lit.* a leader, guide.

पेशवाई, *f.* the office and the functions of a *peshwā*; the honorable meeting and reception of a visitor.

पेशवाज़, *f.* a gown, female dress: going out to meet a person of distinction.

पेशा, *m.* trade, profession; habit, custom, practice.

पेशानी, *f.* the forehead, brow, front.

पेशाब, *m.* urine. —*kā aṭkāo*, *m.* a suppression or stoppage of urine.—*lānewālā*, *m.* (in Med.) a diuretic.

पेशाबबन्द, *m.* strangury.

पेशी, *f.* an egg: a blown bud: spikenard (*Valeriana jatamansi*): a ball of flesh or meat: a scabbard: an advance; precedency, superior rank.

पेशीन, former, prior, anterior, ancient.

पेशीनगोई, *f.* foretelling, prediction, prophecy.

पेषण, 1, (Rām.) = **प्रेक्षण**, *q.v.* : 2, *m.* a grinding, pulverizing ; any apparatus for pounding, a handmill, a stone and muller ; a threshingfloor : a certain plant (a sort of *Euphorbia* with three lobes, commonly called *tekāntā-sij*).

पेषणी, *f.* a stone slab for grinding condiments, etc. with a muller, a grindstone, millstone.

पेखिय (Rām.) = **प्रेक्ष्य**, *q.v.*

पेस, *m.* leprosy : *adj.* white ; vile, ignoble.

पेसवाज, *more prop.* **पेशवाज़**, *q.v.*

पेसानी, *more prop.* **पेशानी**, *q.v.*

पै, 1, *m.* (from **पयस**) anything to drink, juice, water, milk : 2, *m.* the foot, the heel ; a nerve, tendon, sinew : — *ānā*, to have a splint (a horse) : — *k.* to pursue, to seize ; to be importunate : 3, *f.* a fault, blemish, vice : 4, *postp.* (from **उपरि**) on, upon, over, at, to : 5, *conj.* (from **पर**) nevertheless, yet, still, but.

पैआपै, step by step, successively.

पैएं, *f.* (pl. of **पै**, 3) faults, blemishes, vices.

पैं, 1, = **पै**, *q.v.* : 2, = **पई**, *q.v.* : 3, see **ओंपैं**.

पैंआं, *m.* (pl. of **पै**, 2) the feet, etc.

पैंछना, *t.* to winnow.

पैंचा, *m.* return, retribution ; a loan, repayment of a loan.

पैंजनी (pl: **पैंजनियां** or **पैंजनिआं**) = **पैजनी**, *q.v.*

पैंड, पैंठ, पैंत ; for words beginning thus, see under the forms **पैयड, पैयठ, पैन्त**, respectively.

पैंड़ा in Braj = **पैयडा**, *q.v.*

पैंसठ, sixty-five (६५) : see **ओं, वां, वीं, वे, वें**.

पैक, *m.* a messenger, runner ; a watchman employed as a guard at night ; a footman or runner employed on the business of the lands.

पैकड़ा, *m.* iron chains for the legs of culprits, fetters; ornamental rings worn on the ankles.

पैकड़ी, *f.*
पैकढ़ा, *m.* } = **पैकड़ा**, *q.v.*

पैकर, *m. f.* face, visage, countenance, appearance, form ; a portrait, likeness : (in comp.) similitude.

पैकार, *m.* a dealer, agent, broker, hawker, pedlar : war, battle, contest.

पैकी, *m.* a man who carries about a hukkā for hire at a fair or in a market or camp.

पैग़म्बर, *m.* a messenger, apostle, prophet, envoy, legate.

पैग़म्बरी, *f.* the calling, office, or functions of a messenger or prophet, mission, envoyship ; prophecy, message.

पैगश्ती, *m.* a collector of market-dues ; a policeman who patrols at night ; a guard who goes about from station to station.

पैग़ाम, *m.* a message, report, advice, embassy, mission.

पैग़ाम्बर, *more com.* **पैग़म्बर**, *q.v.*

पैग़ाम्बरी, *more com.* **पैग़म्बरी**, *q.v.*

पैग़ार, *m.* a ditch, furrow.

पैगू, *m.* a sort of green-coloured stone imported from Pegu.

पैचताब, *more prop.* **पेचताब**, *q.v.*

पैज, 1, (Rām.) = (1) **पैठ** (2) **पैरवी**, *qq.v.* : 2, *m.* a promise, vow. — *k.* to make a vow.

पैज़ना ; see (1) **पैठना** (2) **पैज करना**, *qq.v.*

पैज़ार, *f.* a slipper, shoe. — *khānā*, to undergo a beating with a slipper.

पैठ, *m.* a duplicate of a bill of exchange : entrance, ingress, admission, access.

पैठना, *a. int.* to rush in, run in, enter, penetrate, pierce, run through, pervade.

पैठारना, *more com.* **पैठालना**, *q.v.*

पैठालना, *t.* to cause to penetrate or to pervade, to force in, run in, introduce, insinuate.

पैठाव, *m.* entering, access, admission.

पैड़, the noise of a blow or knock.

पैड़ी, *f.* a ladder, staircase, flight of steps, stairs ; the inclined plane leading down to a reservoir of water, on which oxen travel for the purpose of drinking or drawing water for irrigation.

पैयठ, *m.* a duplicate of a bill of exchange.

पैयड = **पैयड**, *q.v.*

पैयड़ा in Braj = **पैयडा**, *q.v.*

पैयडा, *m.* a road, highway, path. — *mārnā*, to stop a road ; to commit highway-robbery.

पैयठा = **पैयडा**, *q.v.*

पैतरा, *m.* a flourishing about a weapon before cudgelling, etc. ; the science of sword-exercise.

पैतला, *m.* (*f.* ī) shallow.

पैताना, *m.* (see **सिरहाना**) the foot-part of anything (as of a tomb or of a bedstead).

पैतृक, *m.* (*f.* ī) appertaining to ancestors, progenitors, or the manes ; paternal, ancestral, hereditary.

पैतृकभूमि, *f.* a paternal estate, the country of one's ancestors, fatherland.

पैत्त, *m.* (*f.* ī) appertaining to the bilious humour, proceeding from bile, bilious, biliary.

पैत्तिक, *m.* (*f.* ī) of a bilious temperament, bilious.

पैत्रिक, *m.* (*f.* ī) = **पैतृक**, *q.v.*

पैत्रिकभूमि = **पैतृकभूमि**, *q.v.*

पैदल, 1, *adv.* a-foot, on foot, walking : 2, *m.* infantry.

पैदा, begotten, born, produced, created, given rise to, invented, discovered, exhibited, manifest, evident. — *k.* to produce, etc.

पैदाइश, *f.* birth, origin, rise, existence, production, earnings, profit : *pr. n.* one of the titles of the Book of Genesis.

पैदाईश
पैदायश } *more prop.* **पैदाइश**, *q.v.*

पैदावार, *m.* produce, profit, fruit.

पैदावारी, *f.* a statement of the produce of land.

पैन, *m.* a reservoir of water ; a rill.

पैना, *m.* a goad : lit. *m.* (*f.* ī) sharp.

पैनाना, *t.* to sharpen.

पैनाम, a division of a province (like the 'Ridings' of Yorkshire).

पैनाला, *m.* a gutter, spout.

पैनी, *f.* (*m.* **पैना**) sharp.

पैन्ताना, *m.* (see **पैताना**) the foot of a bed, the side towards the feet.

पैन्तालीस, forty-five (४५): see **ओं, वां, वीं, वे, वें.**

पैन्तीस, thirty-five (३५): see **ओं, वां, वीं, वे, वें.**

पैमाइश, *f.* measuring, the measure or survey of a country, measurement and allotment of lands.

पैमान, *m.* a promise, agreement, compact, treaty, confirmation, oath, asseveration, convention.

पैमाना, *m.* a certain measure for dry or liquid

पैया, *m.* a wheel. [goods; a goblet.

पैयान, *m.* departure.

पैयाल, *f.* straw, dried grass. [tread, step.

पैर, *m.* the foot; a step.—*dharnā* or *rakhnā*, to

पैरना, *a. int.* to float, swim.

पैरव, *m.* a follower: lit. *partic.* following.

पैरवी, *f.* a following, pursuit, hunting after, prosecution, imitation. —*k.* to pursue, hunt, imitate.

पैरवो in Māṛwīṛī = **पहरना**, *q.v.*

पैराई, *f.* a place for swimming in, distance over which it is necessary to swim; the art of swimming; wages for teaching swimming.

पैराक, *m.* (*f.* ī) a swimmer.

पैराकी, *f.* the act or the art of swimming.

पैराना, *t.* to cause to float or swim.

पैरामून, *m.* circuit, circumference; adjacent places, environs; the skirt or flap of a garment.

पैराव, *m.* the place beyond a man's depth, where it becomes necessary to swim.

पैरावा, *m.* tillage, cultivation. [shirt, a shift.

पैराहन, *m.* a long robe, a kind of loose vest, a

पैरी, *f.* 1, *more prop.* **पैड़ी** *q.v.*: 2, a kind of ornament

पैरो, *more prop.* **पैरव**, *q.v.* [worn on the legs.

पैरौ in Braj = **पैरव**, *q.v.* [of the Rig-Ved.

पैल, *m. pr. n.* a certain sage, the promulgator

पैलन, *m.* a firstborn: *lit.* first, foremost, in the

पैलवार, yonder, on that side. [first place.

पैला, *m.* a kind of vessel for measuring grain.

पैलार, removed in time by a whole unit; *e. g. Pailārkā buras*, the year before last, or the year after next.

पैले, a contraction of **पहिले**, *q.v.*

पैलेवार, yonder, on that side.

पैवन्द, *m.* junction, conjunction, connexion; a relative or kindred; a patch; a graft or bud.

पैवन्दकारी, *f.* grafting, patching, cobbling.

पैवन्दी, engrafted.

पैवन्दीगुदड़ी, *f.* patched garments.

पैवन्दीबेर, *m.* an engrafted bēr (*Zizyphus jujuba*).

पैवन्दीमूछें, *f.* the mustachios joining the beard.

पैवस्त, *f.* junction, connexion, friendship.

पैवस्ता, *m.* the year before last: *adv.* continually, always: *lit.* joined, continuous, successive.

पैशाच, *m.* (*f.* ī) a Pishāch: a certain mode of marriage (in which the damsel is forced away and ravished by her lover): *lit.* appertaining to the Pisāchas, demonlike, demoniacal.

पैशाची, *f.* (see **पैशाच**) a sort of gibberish put into the lips of demons by the dramatic poets.

पैशुन, *m.* talebearing, backbiting; slanderousness, malignity. [pravity.

पैशुन्य, *m.* espionage, backbiting, wickedness, de-

पैसठ, *more prop.* **पैंसठ**, *q.v.*

पैसना, *a. int.* to enter, plunge in.

पैसन्दाज़ी, *m.* (*f.* in *or* inī) wealthy, rich.

पैसा, *m.* a copper coin of India equal in size and nearly equal in value to the English 'halfpenny'; it is the sixty-fourth part of a rupee, and is commonly called the 'pice.' In common parlance the word is used as a general term for money, cash, or small change. —*uṛānā*, to spend money extravagantly; to obtain the money of another by theft or by fraud. —*khānā*, to spend money extravagantly, waste money; to subsist by wages or the produce of labour; to take bribes; to embezzle. —*dubnā*, to be sunk (said of money). —*dubonā*, to sink money, lay out money without return. —*pherphār k.* to turn the penny. —*lagānā*, to lay out or apply money. —*soṅ darbār bandhna*, to give bribes, to bribe.

पैसार, *m.* access, admission, ability. [dibs.

पैसे, *m.* (pl. of **पैसा**) small change, coppers, browns,

पैसेवाला, *m.* (*f.* ī) moneyed, wealthy; worth one pice (as to value or price).

पैहम, close together, thickly.

पैहहि, (pl. **हिं**) in Braj = **पाएगा (पाना)**.

पैहै, pl. (**पैहैं**) in Braj = **पाएगा (पाना)**.

पैहौ in Braj = **पाओगे (पाना)**.

पै (= **पर**) on, upon, at.

पोआ, *m.* (*f.* **पोई**) a nursling of any animal; a very young serpent; a plant.

पोआड़ा = **पवाड़ा**, *q.v.* [the steam of water.

पोआना, *t.* to bask, to warm by the sun or by

पोआर } *f.* straw.
पोआल }

पोईस, look you! see! have a care! ho! holloa! holloa you! holloa there! (used in calling to people in the road to get out of the way).

पोंकना, *n.* to be fluxed.

पोंका, *m.* the ship-worm (*Teredo navalis*).

पोंगा, *m.* (*f.* ī) a blockhead; a sort of drum; a thin joint of bamboo: *lit.* empty.

पोंचा, (in Surveying) five and a half.

पोंछन, *m.* a wiping: a rag, etc. with which anything is wiped: anything thrown away after wiping.

पोंछना, *t.* to wipe, to clean.

पोंटा = **पोपटा**, *q.v.*

पोंटी = **पोपटी**, *q.v.*

पोक्की, *m.* a blackguard, low fellow.

पोक्कीलोग, *m.* blackguards, low people, riff-raff.

पोख; see **पोष.**

पोखन, *more prop.* **पोषण**, *q.v.*

पोखर } *m.* a pond, lake, tank.
पोखरा }

पोगण्ड, *m.* a boy from five to fifteen years of age.

पोछ (*Rām.*) = **पूछ**, *q. v.*

पोछना, *t.* to wipe, to clean.

पोख़िश, *f.* excuse, palliation, apology, pretence, pretext.

पोट, *f.* a bundle, bale, pa·kage: a spout.

पोटगल, *m.* a species of reed (*Arundo tibialis*, Roxb.); a sort of grass (*Saccharum spontaneum*).

पोटला, *m.* a large bundle.

पोटलिका = **पोटली**, *q. v.*

पोटली, *f.* (dim. of **पोटला**) a small bundle, a parcel, packet.

पोटा, 1, *m.* (*f.* ī) an unfledged bird: 2, *m.* the eyelid: the crop or craw of birds; the stomach, maw: the mucus of the nose: 3, *f.* a woman with a beard: a hermaphrodite: a female servant.

पोठा, *m.* the stomach, maw, crop or craw of a bird.

पोठी; see (1) **पोटी** (2) **पोठा** (3) **पोथी**.

पोढ़ी, *f.* a stiff strong species of soil.

पोढ़ = **पोढ़ा**, *q. v.*

पोढा, *m.* (*f.* ī) strong, firm: wide, broad.

पोढ़ाई, *f.* strength, firmness: breath.

पोपटा, *m.* the mucus of the nose.

पोपटी, *f.* a certain small fish (*Cyprinus chrysoparius*.

पोत, 1, *m.* (*f.* ī) the young of any animal; an elephant of ten years old: 2, *m.* nature, quality, disposition: an assessment on cultivated fields: glass beads: a young shoot of a plant, a young tree: the site or foundation of a house: cloth: a species of stone: 3, *m. f.* ? a vessel, ship, boat.

पोतक, 1, *m.* (*f.* ikā) the young of any animal: 2, *m.* the young of any plant; a young mango: the foundation of a house.

पोतकी, *f.* a kind of potherb (*Basella lucida*): a certain bird (*Turdus macrourus*).

पोतज, *m.* (*f.* ā) an animal that produces young at once, without the intervention of any medium (elephants and some other animals being supposed, in the physiology of the Hindoos, to carry their young without the aid of an ovarium or uterus).

पोतड़ा, *m.* baby-cloths, clouts.

पोतड़ी, *f.* the after-birth.

पोतना, *t.* to plaster, besmear.

पोतरा, *m.* baby-clothes, clouts.

पोता, 1, *m.* (*f.* ī) a grandchild (son's child): 2, *m.* the scrotum, testicles.

पोतादार, *m.* (see **पोत**, 2) a treasurer.

पोतादारी, *f.* the office of treasurer, treasurership.

पोतिका, *f.* 1, (*m.* **पोतक**) a young female of any animal: 2, a certain potherb (*Basella lucida*).

पोतिया, *m.* a cloth worn at the time of bathing: a kind of plaything.

पोती, *f.* 1, (*m.* **पोत**) a young female of any animal: 2, (*m.* **पोता**) a granddaughter (son's daughter).

पोतो in Māṛwāṛī = an opium-bag.

पोत्र, *m.* the snout of a hog: a ploughshare.

पोत्री, *m.* (*f.* iṇī) a hog.

पोथ, *m.* a small glass bead, beads.

पोथकी, *f.* red pimples on the eyelids.

पोथला, *m.* a porter's load (*esp.* of grain).

पोथा, *m.* a book, a large book, especially a manuscript-book written on long separate leaves of paper or palmyra connected by a string through the centre.

पोथी, *f.* (dim. of **पोथा**) a little book. The word is, however, used for a book irrespective of the question of size.

पोदना, *m.* (*f.* ī) a certain bird (*Sylvia olivacea*).

पोदीन }
पोदीना } *more prop.* **पुदीना**, *q. v.*

पोना, 1 *more prop.* **पौना**, *q. v.*: 2, *t.* to make bread: to string (as pearls), to thread (as a needle).

पोपनी, *f.* any wind instrument of music, but especially a kind made by children of the seeds of mango and the leaves of the *Borassus*.

पोपला, *m.* (*f.* ī) a toothless person.

पोफटना = **पौ फटना**, *q. v.*

पोफटी, *f.* break of day, dawn.

पोय, *f.* a kind of vegetable (*Basella alba* or *B. rubra*).

पोया, *m.* = **पोय**, *q. v.*

पोर, *f.* the space or interval between two joints (of the body, or of a bamboo, sugarcane, etc.).

पोरपोर, every joint, joint after joint.

पोरवाल, *m.* a certain mercantile caste of Hindoos in Mālwā.

पोरा, *m.* a complete set or assortment of anything.

पोरी, *f.* a joint of bamboo, sugarcane, etc.: a stiff strong kind of soil.

पोरुआ, *m.* a joint or phalanx of the fingers, a joint of a tamarind.

पोल, *m.* a courtyard; a gate; a ward or quarter of a town having its own gateway: offspring, family, a litter, brood.

पोलक, *m.* straw bands at the end of a staff used with a *charkhī* to frighten and restrain a furious elephant.

पोलच, land constantly under cultivation.

पोला, *m.* (*f.* ī) soft, hollow (used as a term of abuse = simpleton).

पोलाद, *m.* steel, but especially the finest Damascus steel, which, with that of Kum, is esteemed the best in the East.

पोलिच = **पोलच**, *q. v.*

पोलिया, *m.* a gatekeeper, janitor, doorkeeper, porter.

पोवना, a colloquial form for **पोना**, 2, *q. v.*

पोवनो }
पोवनौं } in Braj = **पोना**, 2, *q. v.*

पोशाक, *f.* vestments, dress, habits, clothing, garments, accoutrements.

पोशीदा, covered, concealed.

पोष, *m.* a thriving; prosperity; nourishing, cherishing.

पोषक, *m.* (*f.* ikā) a nourisher, cherisher, supporter, breeder, keeper: *lit.* adj. cherishing.

पोषण, *m.* a nourishing, cherishing, breeding, rearing.

पोषणभरण क° = **पोषना**, *q. v.*

पोषत (*Rām.*) = **पोसता**, etc. (see **स**, 5).

पोषना, *t.* to nourish, cherish, foster, breed, rear, tame.

पोषिका, *f.* (*m.* पोषक) a female cherisher or keeper.

पोषी, *m.* (*f.* iṇī) = पोषक, *q. v.*

पोष्य, *m.* (*f.* ā) fit or requiring to be nourished, cherished, or taken care of.

पोष्यपुत्र, *m.* (*f.* ī) an adopted child.

पोष्यवर्ग, *m.* a class of persons or objects which it is a duty to cherish, *e.g.* household, parents, children, guests, the sacred fire.

पोसना, *more prop.* पोषना, *q. v.*

पोसो (*Rām.*) = पोसा (पोसना).

पोस्त, *m.* crust, skin, rind; the poppy-plant; an infusion of the poppy formerly much used as a slow poison. [quay.

पोस्ता, *m.* a bulwark, prop, buttress, embankment,

पोस्ताबन्दि = पोस्ता, *q.v.*

पोस्ती, *m.* (*f.* inī) a lazy indolent person: *prop.* one who intoxicates himself with infusion of poppy-heads.

पोस्तीन, leathern (garment): a fault, blemish.

पोह, *f.* the dawn of day. —*phaṭnā*, to dawn, break forth (as the daylight).

पोहदा, *more prop.* पौधा, *q. v.*

पोहना, *t.* to make bread. [on waste land.

पोहा, *m.* the cattle of a village permitted to graze

पौ, *f.* the one or ace on dice: a stand where water is provided for passengers: an overflooding of low lands in the rainy season; the entrance of brightness, the dawn of day. —*phaṭnā*, to dawn (said of the morning).

पौंगी, *f.* a flute, pipe, a kind of pipe played upon by jugglers. [form पहुंच.

पौंच, पौंछ; for words beginning thus, see under the

पौंकना, *more prop.* (1) पहुंचना (2) पौंछना, *qq.v.*

पौंड; for words beginning thus, see under the form [पौण्ड.

पौंश्चल्य, *m.* female incontinence.

पौंसरा; see पौसरा.

पौंसवन = पुंसवन, *q.v.*

पौंहचना, *more prop.* पहुंचना, *q.v.*

पौचना } see (1) पहुंचना (2) पोछना.
पौछना }

पौड़ी, *f.* a stiff strong species of soil.

पौढ़ना, *a. int.* to lie down, rest, repose, sleep.

पौढ़ा, *m.* (*f.* ī) strong, firm: broad.

पौढ़ाई, *f.* strength, firmness, breadth.

पौढ़ाना, *t.* cause to lie down, put to sleep.

पौण्ड, *more prop.* पौण्ड्र, *q.v.*

पौण्डा, *m.* a kind of sugarcane.

पौण्ड्र = पौण्ड्रक, *q.v.*

पौण्ड्रक, *m.* the designation of one of the degraded races of Kshatriyas (from the Vaishya and female of the distiller caste) whose occupation is sugar-boiling; the pale straw coloured species of sugarcane.

पौण्ड्रकवर्द्धन, *m.* an epithet of the province of Bihār.

पौतलना = पौढ़ना, *q. v.*

पौत्तलिक, *m.* (*f.* ā *or* ī) an image-worshipper, idolater.

पौत्र, *m.* (*f.* ī) a grandchild (either a daughter's child or a son's, but more properly a son's).

पौत्रिक, appertaining to a son or to a grandson.

पौत्री, *f* (*m.* पौत्र) a granddaughter.

पौदा } = पौधा, *q. v.*
पौध }

पौधा, *m.* a young tree or plant for transplanting, a sapling. [future transplantation.

पौधेला, ground on which plants are sown for

पौन, 1, *more prop.* पवन, *q. v.*: 2, = पौने, *q. v.*

पौनक्त } *m.* repetition, tautology.
पौनरुक्त्य }

पौनर्भव, *m.* son of a twice-married woman. This is one of the twelve kinds of heirs recognized by the old Hindoo law.

पौनह = पौना, *q. v.* [for skimming with, etc.

पौना, *m.* a spoon with holes in it like a colander

पौनी, a collective name for certain lower castes, such as barbers, shoemakers, etc.

पौने, one quarter less (either of one or of any given number, *hence*), three quarters. It is always prefixed to the number which is required to be reduced by one quarter, *e. g. Paune-tīn*, three, less one quarter, *i. e.* two and three quarters. *Paune-do*, one and three quarters. *Paune-sau*, seventy-five. *Paune do sau*, one hundred and seventy-five.

पौफटना; see *s. v.* पौ.

पौर, 1, *f. more prop.* पौली, *q. v.*: 2, *m.* a certain fragrant grass: 3, *m.* (*f.* ī) a citizen: *lit.* appertaining to town, town-bred, town-made.

पौरणमासी, *f.* a day or a night of full moon.

पौरणिक, *more prop.* पौराणिक, *q.v.*

पौरव, (patronym.) *m.* (*f.* ī) descended from Puru.

पौरवी, *f. pr. n.* a wife of Yudishṭhir.

पौरवेय, *more prop.* पौरुषेय, *q.v.*

पौरसख्य, *m.* fellow-citizenship, *prop.* connexion or equality by having inhabited the same city for ten years.

पौराणिक, *m.* (*f.* ī) one who is conversant with the events of former times: *lit.* appertaining to the former ages, old, appertaining to the Purāṇs.

पौरिया, *m.* a doorkeeper, gatekeeper, porter, janitor.

पौरी, *f.* (*m.* पौर, 3) a female citizen: a gate, door.

पौरुष, 1, *m.* (*f.* ī) one who has the measure of a man with both arms elevated and the fingers extended: *lit.* manly, human: 2, *m.* the measure of a man equal to the height to which he reaches with both arms elevated and the fingers extended: the load which a man may bear: 3, *m.* the property of manhood, virility, manliness, bravery, manly strength or spirit, vigour, power, effort, exertion, endeavours, man's work, action of man; *membrum virile, semen.*

पौरुषता, *f.* } = पौरुष, 3, *q. v.*
पौरुषत्व, *m.* }

पौरुषी, *f.* = पौरुष, 1 and 2, *qq. v.*

पौरुषीय, masculine, manly, male.

पौरुषेय, appertaining to man or to the soul; human, spiritual.

पौरोहित्य, *m.* the office, character, or functions of a family priest.

पौर्णमासी, *f.* the day or t' e night of full moon.

पौर्णिमा, *more prop.* **पौर्णमासी**, *q.v.*

पौर्वदेहिक, appertaining to a former body or state of existence. [primary, former, previous, old.

पौर्विक, *m.* (*f.* ī) appertaining to former times, prior,

पौलन (*provincial*) = **पाया**, *q.v.*

पौला, rice-straw ?

पौलिया, *m.* a doorkeeper, gatekeeper, porter, janitor.

पौली, *f.* a gate, door.

पौलुस, *m. pr. n.* the apostle Paul.

पौलोम, appertaining to Pulomā: (1) hence, *m.* (*f.* ī) a descendant of Puloman (2) *m. pr. n.* a certain class of demons.

पौलोमा, *more prop.* **पौलोमी**, *q.v.*

पौलोमी, *f. pr. n.* the wife of Indra.

पौवा, *m.* a quarter; a weight or measure of a quarter of a sēr.

पौवानौ } **पौवानौं** } in Braj = **पोवाना**, *q.v.*

पौशाक, *more prop.* **पोशाक**, *q.v.*

पौष, *m. pr. n.* the ninth solar month of the Hindoos (Dec.-Jan.) the full moon of which is near Pushya (three stars in Cancer).

पौषी, *f.* the day or the night of full moon in the above-mentioned month.

पौष्करिणी, *f.* a large pond, reservoir.

पौष्टिक, *m.* (*f.* ī) relating to or furthering increase, furthering, fattening, preservative, nutritive.

पौष्ण, *m. pr. n.* the twenty-eighth *Nakshatra*.

पौष्प, *m.* (*f.* ī) appertaining to flowers, made of flowers, flowery, floral. [collyrium.

पौष्पक, *m.* the oxide of brass considered as a

पौष्पी, *m. pr. n.* Pātaliputra or Palibothra.

पौसरा, *m.* (see **पौ**) a stand where water is pro-

पौसला, *m.* = **पौसरा**, *q.v.* [vided for travellers.

पौहे, a herd of oxen.

प्याज, *f.* (prop. **पियाज**) an onion.

प्यादा, *more prop.* **पियादा**, *q.v.*

प्याना = **पियाना**, *q.v.*

प्यार, 1, a corruption of **पियाल**, *q.v.*: 2, *m. f.* ? love, affection, fondness, friendship. — *k.* (with abl. or [more commonly] acc. of the object) to love, fondle.

प्यारा, *m.* (*f.* ī) an object of affection, a sweetheart: *lit.* beloved, pleasant. — *jānā*, to cherish an affection for. [grass.

प्याल, *f.* 1, *more prop.* **पियाल**, *q.v.*: 2, straw, dried

प्याला, *m.* a cup, glass; a fire-pan, priming-pan of a musket, etc. — *bharnā*, to be proud or conceited. — *honā*, (in the talk of fakeers) to die. [drink.

प्यालानिवाला, (in the slang of debauchees) food and

प्याली, *f.* (dim. of **प्याला**) a small cup or goblet.

प्यावना, *more prop.* **पियाना**, *q.v.*

प्यावनौ } **प्यावनौं** } in Braj = **पियाना**, *q.v.*

प्यास, *f.* thirst. — *bujhānā*, to quench thirst. — *marnā* describes the vanishing of thirst without drinking. — *mārnā*, to suffer thirst. — *lagnā*, to be thirsty.

प्यासा, *m.* (*f.* ī) thirsty, athirst. — *marnā*, to be very thirsty, be dying of thirst.

प्र; an inseparable prefix (= Gr. πρὸ; Lat. pro, præ; Engl. pre-, for-, fore-) importing the idea of advance in time, place, or degree, fore, before, forth, forward, away, off, abroad, preëminent, excessive, much, very, beginning. The **र** influences a following **न** according to rule; *e. g.* **प्रणाम**. The influence of this particle on the sense of the words to which it is prefixed, is frequently unappreciable.

प्रकट, *m.* (*f.* ā) unfolded, manifest, displayed, apparent, clear.

प्रकटता, *f.* } **प्रकटत्व**, *m.* } = **प्रगटत्व**, *q.v.*

प्रकटना = **प्रगटना**, *q.v.* [apparent, evident.

प्रकटित, *m.* (*f.* ā) opened, expanded, displayed,

प्रकटीकृत, *m.* (*f.* ā) made visible or manifest.

प्रकटे, pl. of **प्रकटा** (**प्रकटना**).

प्रकम्प, *m.* a shaking, trembling, violent motion.

प्रकम्पन, *m.* violent motion, great trembling, shaking: wind: *pr. n.* a hell: *lit.* adj. causing to tremble.

प्रकम्पमान, *m.* (*f.* matī) trembling violently, shaking.

प्रकम्पी, *m.* (*f.* inī) = **प्रकम्पमान**, *q. v.*

प्रकर, *m.* a heap, multitude, quantity, plenty: aid: custom, use: aloe-wood (*Agallochum*).

प्रकरण, *m.* a treating, expounding; subject, topic; context; prelude, prologue, introduction; a paragraph, section, chapter; a book; a place of pausing or of stopping: a dramatic poem the story of which is wholly imaginary: an event, circumstance, occurrence, affair: opportunity, occasion: relation.

प्रकरणी, *f.* a kind of drama. [drama.

प्रकरी, *f.* a kind of song; a short interlude in a

प्रकर्ष, *m.* excellence, distinction, superiority, length, intensity; (in Gram.) the effect of **प्र** on roots.

प्रकाण्ड, *m.* the stem of a tree, the part between the root and the branches, a branch, shoot: excellence, happiness: *lit.* excellent, strong, stout, robust, very large, enormous.

प्रकार, *m.* sort, kind, species; speciality, specific peculiarity; way, mode, manner, method, fashion.

प्रकारवाचक, (in Gram.) expressive of kind, quality, or manner.

प्रकाश, *m.* (*f.* ā) clear, bright, open, manifest, visible, expanded, blown, displayed, generally known, notorious, famous, celebrated, public: *hence*, this word is applied equally to physical or to abstract subjects, as the blowing of a flower, the diffusion of celebrity, the publicity of an event, the manifestation of a truth, etc.; lustre, splendour, light, sunshine, expansion, diffusion, manifestation, display, notoriety, publicity: *adv.* openly, publicly, manifestly, aloud. — *k.* to illumine, make manifest, display. — *pānā*, to come to light, transpire, come into notoriety.

प्रकाशक, *m.* (*f.* ikā) an illuminator, illustrator, expounder, discoverer, publisher; *hence*, the sun: *lit.* adj. making apparent or manifest, displaying, etc.

प्रकाशकत्व, *m.* (*f.* tā) the property of displaying or manifesting. [brity, fame, renown.

प्रकाशत्व, *m.* (*f.* tā) brightness, shining; cele-

प्रकाशन, *m.* a making clear or manifest, an imparting light to, illuminating, shewing.

प्रकाशना, *t.* to illumine, make manifest, display.

प्रकाशमन्त, *more com.* प्रकाशमान, *q.v.*

प्रकाशमान, *m.* (*f.* matī) *adj.* becoming manifest, appearing, splendid, radiant, brilliant.

प्रकाशहीन, *m.* (*f.* ā) destitute of प्रकाश, *q.v.*

प्रकाशा, *f.*; see प्रकाश.

प्रकाशिक, *m.* (*f* ā) = प्रकाशक, *q.v.*

प्रकाशिका, *f.* (*m.* प्रकाशक) a female discoverer, etc.

प्रकाशित, *m.* (*f.* ā) displayed, unfolded, discovered, apparent, manifest, visible, published, promulgated.

प्रकाशिता, *f.* } clearness, light.
प्रकाशित्व, *m.* }

प्रकाशी, *m.* (*f.* inī) = प्रकाशक, *q.v.*

प्रकाश्य, 1, a contraction of प्राकाश्य, *q.v.*: 2, fit or requiring to be illuminated or manifested. [प्रकाश.

प्रकास; for words beginning thus, see under the form

प्रकीर्ण, 1, = प्रकीर्णक, *q.v.*: 2, *m.* a chapter, section: *lit.* spread out, spread abroad, scattered, diffused, displ yed, expanded, open, promulgated, published.

प्रकीर्णक, *m.* the tail of the Tartarian ox (*Bos grunniens*) used as a fan or whisp, and as an ornament of horses: a section, chapter; (in Law) a decision, decree.

प्रकीर्त्ति, *f.* declaration; celebrity, fame, praise.

प्रकीर्त्तित, *m.* (*f.* ā) declared, explained, revealed, said, stated, mentioned; renowned, celebrated.

प्रकृत, *m.* (*f.* ā) made, completed, accomplished; genuine, real, true, just, right, accurate, proper.

प्रकृतत्व, *m.* (*f.* tā) genuineness, realness, truth, accuracy, propriety.

प्रकृति, *f.* the original or natural state or disposition of anything, nature; a radical form or predicament of being, as illusion, intelligence, etc.; the eight elements from which all is produced; temper, temperament, disposition, habit, custom, manner; the original source, cause; the requisites of royal administration, the chief objects of royal consideration; a king's minister; inhabitants, subjects, people; affairs, business; (in Gram.) the crude form of a word: (in Pros.) a sort of metre consisting of a stanza of four lines, each line containing twenty-one syllables; (in Math.) a coëfficient, multiplier; (in Anat.) the predominence of one of the humours at the time of generation; (in Philos.) the passive or material cause of the world as opposed to the active or spiritual; (in Myth.) a goddess, the personified will of the Supreme in the creation (identified with *Māyā*, or illusion, and in an especial manner the prototype of the female sex). In some Hindoo systems, Prakriti is considered the same with the Supreme Being.

प्रकृतिज्ञान, *m.* the knowledge of प्रकृति, *q.v.*

प्रकृतितरल, *m.* (*f.* ā) volatile, fickle.

प्रकृतिस्थ, stripped of everything, bare, natural, genuine, in its natural state, unadulterated, unmixed, inherent, innate.

प्रकृष्ट, *m.* (*f.* ā) exalted, prominent, eminent, superior, principal, chief, distinguished. [cellence.

प्रकृष्टत्व, *m.* (*f.* tā) eminence, superiority, ex-

प्रकोप, *m.* effervescence, emotion, provocation, irritation, wrath.

प्रकोपन, *m.* an irritating, provoking.

प्रकोपित, *m.* (*f.* ā) irritated, provoked, angry.

प्रक्रम, *m.* a coming forth, proceeding, beginning: opportunity, leisure: proportion.

प्रक्रिया, *f.* manner, way, rite, observance. elevation, dignity; insignia; the bearing royal insignia.

प्रक्षालन, *m.* a cleansing, bathing, washing away; the expiation of a crime.

प्रक्षालित, *m.* (*f.* ā) cleansed; expiated. [hurled.

प्रक्षिप्त, *m.* (*f.* ā) thrown, projected, cast forth,

प्रक्षीण, *m.* (*f.* ā) decayed, wasting away.

प्रक्षेप, *m.* a casting forth or forward, a projecting,

प्रक्षेपण, *m.* a throwing or hurling. [hurling.

प्रक्षोभण, *m.* an agitating. [keen, eminent.

प्रखर, very hot, acrid, pungent, sharp, smart, acute,

प्रख्यात, *m.* (*f.* ā) celebrated, renowned, famous.

प्रख्याति, *f.* celebrity, notoriety, fame, eulogium,

प्रख्यान, *m.* = प्रख्याति, *q.v.* [praise; a making known.

प्रगट, obvious, notorious, manifest, public, issued out, apparent, visible; (in the Drama) audibly, openly, aloud (as distinguished from, 'aside,' to himself).—*k.* to divulge, make public.

प्रगटत्व, *m.* (*f.* tā) visibility, apparency, manifestation, clearness, publicity. [appear.

प्रगटना, *a. int.* to become manifest, issue forth,

प्रगटेउ (*Rām.*) = प्रगट हुआ.

प्रगटेसि = तू प्रगट करता है. See असि.

प्रगमन, *m.* advance, progress, proceeding.

प्रगल्भ, *m.* (*f.* ā) bold, confident, prompt, courageous, resolute, energetic, strong, active, intrepid, audacious, shameless.

प्रगल्भत्व, *m.* (*f.* tā) boldness, confidence, energy, power, resolution, impudence, prevalence, eminence.

प्रगाढ़, *m.* (*f.* ā) much, excessive, difficult, hard, firm, steady, serious; *hence*, pain, privation, penance.

प्रगाढ़त्व, *m.* (*f* tā) excessiveness, abundance, difficulty, hardness, firmness, steadiness, seriousness.

प्रगाता } *m.* (*f.* trī) a singer.
प्रगातृ }

प्रगामी, *m.* (*f.* inī) one who is about to depart.

प्रगायी, *m.* (*f.* inī) a singer.

प्रगीति, *f.* a sort of metre in Sanskrit prosody.

प्रगोपण, *m.* protection, preservation, salvation.

प्रग्रहण, *m.* a seizing, taking, assuming.

प्रघट = प्रगट, *q.v.*

प्रघटी, 1, (*corruption*) = प्रगटत्व, *q.v.*: 2, *f.* a mould in which silver or gold is cast previous to working it.

प्रघण = प्रघन, 1, *q.v.*

प्रघन, *m.* 1, a covered terrace before the door of

a house, a porch, portico : a copper pot: an iron club: 2. a species of bean (*Phascolus mungo*).

प्रघाण }
प्रघान } = प्रघन, 1, *q.v.*

प्रचण्ड, *m.* (*f.* ā) a violent person ; *pr. n.* a certain Dānav ; a sort of *Nerium* with white flowers : *lit.* excessively hot or violent, burning, wrathful, passionate, violent, furious, mighty, insupportable, bold, confident, daring.

प्रचण्डत्व, *m.* (*f.* tā) wrathfulness ; boldness.

प्रचण्डमूर्त्ति, *m.* a certain tree (*Tapia cratæva*).

प्रचय, *m.* (in Math.) the common increase or decrease in the terms of a progression.

प्रचरित, pursued, practised (as an art).

प्रचलत = प्रचलित, *q.v.*

प्रचलन, *m.* a moving about, a circulating, being customary or current ; activity.

प्रचलित, circulating, prevailing, current, in vogue, customary, common, recognized, received (as authority or law, etc.).

प्रचार, *m.* a going, proceeding ; conduct, custom, usage, currency, appearance, manifestation, divulging, promulgation, publicity, notoriety : attendance on cattle while grazing ; pasture-ground.

प्रचारक, *m.* (*f.* ikā) a proclaimer, herald, etc. : lit. *adj.* making public, divulging : attending, grazing cattle.

प्रचारकर्त्ता, *m.* (*f.* trī) a promulgator, herald.

प्रचारना, *t.* to vent, let out, divulge.

प्रचारित, made known, proclaimed, heralded, divulged: grazed: betrayed, deceived, cheated; penetrating.

प्रचारी (*Rām.*) = प्रचारि = प्रचार करके (प्रचारना).

प्रचित, *m.* a species of Sanskrit metre.

प्रचुर, *m.* (*f.* ā) much, many, abundant, enough; frequent ; abounding in. [plenty.

प्रचुरत्व, *m.* (*f.* tā) an abounding ; abundance,

प्रचेता }
प्रचेताः } = प्रचेतस, *q.v.*

प्रचेतस, *m. pr. n.* (1) of a certain ancient saint and lawgiver (2) of a certain king (3) an epithet of Varuṇ : *lit.* wise, intelligent, delighted, happy.

प्रचेल, *m.* yellow sandal-wood.

प्रचोदन, *m.* a saying, inciting, enjoining, prescribing, directing, sending : a rule, order, law.

प्रचोदित, prescribed, directed, sent. [*quini*).

प्रचोदिनी, *f.* a prickly nightshade (*Solanum jac-*

प्रच्छना, *f.* an asking, addressing, inviting.

प्रच्छद, *m.* a wrapper, cover, blanket.

प्रच्छन्न, *m.* (*f.* ā) a person in disguise ; a private door, private entrance, loophole, lattice : *lit.* covered, clothed, concealed, secret, private, disguised, incognito, unavowed.

प्रच्युत, fallen from, deviated from.

प्रजन्त (Rām.) = पर्यन्त, *q.v.*

प्रजा, *f.* offspring, progeny, descendants ; a subject, dependent, tenant, renter ; people, subjects.

प्रजागर, *m.* (*f.* ā) one who wakes, a watcher, guardian ; the act of waking, watching, or guarding.

प्रजाघ्न, *m.* (*f.* ā or ī) = प्रजाहन, *q.v.*

प्रजाता, *f.* a woman who has borne a child.

प्रजाधर्म्म, *m.* the duties appropriate and peculiar to children and to subjects.

प्रजापति, *m.* (*f.* patnī) *lit.* lord of creatures; *hence,* an epithet (1) of the Deity, Brahmā (2) of a monarch, sovereign, or prince (3) of a husband (4) of a father (5) of a daughter's husband (6) of the sun (7) of fire ; also, a potter. This epithet is also applied to the eleven divine personages first created by Brahmā, *viz.* (1) Marichi (2) Atri (3) Angiras (4) Pulastya (5) Pulah (6) Kratu (7) Prachetas (8) Daksha (9) Vasishtha (10) Bhrigu (11) Nārad. Some authorities make their number twenty-one ; others, ten ; others, seven , others, three.

प्रजापत्य, *more prop.* प्राजापत्य, *q.v.*

प्रजापालक, *m.* (*f.* ikā) an epithet of any monarch: lit. *adj.* guarding or protecting his subjects.

प्रजापालन, *m.* the protection or nurturing of subjects or dependents by a master or monarch.

प्रजापोषण, *m.* the cherishing of subjects.

प्रजायिनी, *f.* a mother.

प्रजारना (Rām.) = जलाना, *q.v.*

प्रजालोग, *m.* subjects, people, peasantry, ryots ; dependents. [ing progeny, pregnant.

प्रजावती, *f.* a mother ; a brother's wife : *lit.* hav-

प्रजाशन, 1, *m.* the food of subjects : 2, *adj.* eating up his subjects : hence, *m.* (*f.* ā) one whose food is his subjects, *i. e.* a cruel and oppressive ruler.

प्रजाहन, *m.* (*f.* ī) *adj.* destroying offspring ; slaying (one's) subjects.

प्रजाहित, *m.* (*f.* ā) one who is kind to his dependents, etc. : *lit.* favorable or good for children or subjects, kind to them, useful to them.

प्रजीवन, *m.* subsistence, livelihood.

प्रजेश, *m.* (lord of created beings) an epithet of the god presiding over the procreation of offspring ; (lord of subjects) a prince, sovereign, king.

प्रज्ञ, *m.* (*f.* ā) a clever person : *lit.* intelligent, learned, wise, sensible, clever.

प्रज्ञा, *f.* 1, (*m.* प्रज्ञ) a clever female : 2, intelligence, understanding, wisdom, knowledge.

प्रज्ञात, *m.* (*f.* ā) known, understood, notorious, famous. [ledge : a mark.

प्रज्ञान, 1, *m.* (*f.* ā) = प्रज्ञ, *q.v.* : 2, *m.* wisdom, know-

प्रज्ञावन्त }
प्रज्ञावान } *m.* (*f.* vatī) = प्रज्ञ, *q.v.*

प्रज्वलन, *m.* a taking fire, blazing, burning.

प्रज्वलित, ignited, blazing, radiant. [Gandharv.

प्रज्वार, *m.* the heat of fever : *pr. n.* a certain

प्रटग by inversion = प्रगट, *q.v.*

प्रण, *m.* (prop. पण) a promise, agreement, stipulation, contract, vow, resolution. — *k.* or *bāndhnā*, to make a promise, take a vow, to resolve.

प्रणाऊं (*Rām.*) = मैं प्रणाम करता हूं (प्रणाना).

प्रणत, *m.* (*f.* ā) bowed, obeisant, courteous, reverential. [sant.

प्रणतपाल, *adj.* nourishing or cherishing the obei-

प्रणति, *f.* an inclination, bending, bowing, obeisance, salutation, courtesy, reverence.

प्रणदाई, *m.* (*f.* inī) one who gives his pledge.

प्रणमना, *t.* to do obeisance to, salute reverentially.

प्रणय, *m.* friendly or fond regard, affection, love; trust, confidence reverence, obeisance; acquaintance; affectionate solicitation, request, asking, begging; final emancipation or beatitude.

प्रणयवन्त / **प्रणयवान्** } *m.* (*f.* vatī) = **प्रणयी**, *q.v.*

प्रणयी, *m.* (*f.* inī) an affectionate friend, favorite, husband, lover: *lit.* affectionate, attached, beloved, affable, kind, confident, familiar.

प्रणव, *m.* the holy and mystic monosyllable *Om*.

प्रणवक = **प्रणव**, *q.v.*

प्रणवना, *t.* to do obeisance to, salute reverentially.

प्रणवौं = मैं प्रणाम करता हूं (प्रणवना).

प्रणाद, *m.* a loud noise, roar, shout, neighing, an exclamation of delight or approbation; a buzzing or tingling in the ear from thickening of the membranes, etc.

प्रणाम, *m.* an inclination, bowing; a bow, salutation, prostration (esp. the reverential salutation addressed to a Brāhmaṇ or to a deity). —*k.* (with acc. of object) to salute.

प्रणामी, *m.* (*f.* inī) a worhipper, etc.: lit. *adj.* bowing or prostrating oneself in salutation or worship.

प्रणाल, *m.* = **प्रणाली**, *q.v.* [of the body.

प्रणालिका, *f.* 1, = **प्रणाली**, *q.v.*: 2, a tubular vessel

प्रणाली, *f.* a channel from a pond, a watercourse, drain, gutter, conduit. [perdition, death.

प्रणाश, *m.* disappearance, loss, decay, destruction,

प्रणाशी, *m.* (*f.* inī) *adj.* destroying, removing.

प्रणिधान, *m.* great effort, energy, exertion, stress; profound religious meditation; attention, regard; prayer; entrance, access. [age.

प्रणिपतन, *m.* prostration in salutation or in hom-

प्रणिपात, *m.* prostration, a bow, obeisance, rever-

प्रणी, *more prop.* **पणी**, *q.v.* [ence, salutation.

प्रणीत, produced, made, prepared, constructed, done, cooked; sent, thrown; approached, entered; proper, fit.

प्रतःकाल (*contraction*) = **प्रातःकाल**, *q.v.* See **प**, 15.

प्रतक्ष, *more prop.* **प्रत्यक्ष**, *q.v.*

प्रतल, *m.* tho palm of the hand: *pr. n.* one of the seven principal divisions of the lower regions.

प्रतान, *m.* a tendril, a plant that has tendrils, a climber: fainting, epilepsy.

प्रताप, *m.* heat, splendour, brilliancy; ardour, energy, spirit, highspiritedness; the possession of power and rank, and the high spirit arising from such possessions, majesty, dignity, glory, famousness, prosperousness. [pain, distressing.

प्रतापन, *m. pr. n.* a certain hell: lit. *adj.* inflicting

प्रतापमय, *m.* (*f.* ī) / **प्रतापवन्त**, *m.* (*f.* vatī) / **प्रतापवान्**, *m.* (*f.* vatī) } = **प्रतापी**, *q.v.*

प्रतापस, *m.* a species of the *Asclepias gigantea* with white flowers.

प्रतापी, *m.* (*f.* inī) burning, shining, splendid, glorious, majestic, dignified, potent, powerful, illustrious, noted, famous, replete with splendour or dignity.

प्रतारक, *m.* (*f.* ikā) a cheat, impostor, deceiver: *lit.* adj. cheating, fraudulent, perfidious.

प्रतारकत्व, *m.* (*f.* tā) perfidiousness, deceitfulness, roguery, cheating. [ing, fraud, deceit.

प्रतारण, *m.* a crossing over, over-reaching, cheat-

प्रतारणा, *f.* = **प्रतारण**, *q.v.*

प्रतारिका, *f.* (*m.* **प्रतारक**) a female imposter.

प्रतारित, *m.* (*f.* ā) deceived, tricked, cheated.

प्रति; an inseparable prefix importing the idea of reïteration, repetition, reäction, retaliation, opposition, retribution, back, again, returning, back again, against, for, in exchange for, instead of, each, every. It should be observed that this prefix is not unfrequently corrupted into **प्रती**.

प्रतिउत्तर, *more prop.* **प्रत्युत्तर**, *q.v.*

प्रतिउपकार (*Rām.*) = **प्रत्युपकार**, *q.v.*

प्रतिकर्म, *m.* (= **प्रतिकर्मा**) personal embellishment or decoration, dress. [an opposing.

प्रतिकर्मा, *m.* retaliation, requital, remedy, redress;

प्रतिकामिनी, *f.* a female rival.

प्रतिकार, *m.* an obviating, remedying, counteracting, return, requital, retaliation, revenge.

प्रतिकारक, *m.* (*f.* ikā) a retaliator; an amanuensis, etc.: lit. *adj.* administering retribution, retaliation, or revenge.

प्रतिकूल, *m.* (*f.* ā) contrary, adverse, cross-grained, reverse, inverted, preverse, cross, refractory.

प्रतिकूलत्व, *m.* (*f.* tā) cross-grainedness, contrariety, refractoriness, hostility, opposition.

प्रतिकूला, *f.* (*m.* **प्रतिकूल**) a refractory female.

प्रतिक्रिया, *f.* = **प्रतिकार**, *q.v.* [mentarily, constantly.

प्रतिक्षण, moment by moment, every moment, mo-

प्रतिगर्जन, *m.* an echoing, a reverberating, an an-

प्रतिगर्जना, *f.* = **प्रतिगर्जन**, *q.v.* [swering roar.

प्रतिग्रह, *m.* acceptance, the receiving a donation; whatever is suitable as a present to Brāhmaṇs on certain occasions, a present; a receiver; a spittingpot; the reserve of an army; the sun near the moon's node.

प्रतिघात, *m.* a return blow, repulse; the warding off a blow; a preventing, prohibiting, resistance, combat.

प्रतिघातक, *m.* (*f.* ikā) = **प्रतिघाती**, *q.v.*

प्रतिघातन, *m.* slaughter, killing.

प्रतिघाती, *m.* (*f.* inī) a foe, etc: lit, *adj.* repelling, repulsing, injuring, hostile, opposed to.

प्रतिचिन्तन, *m.* a thinking repeatedly, considering, meditating upon.

प्रतिछांहीं (*Rām.*) = **प्रतिछाया**, *q.v.*

प्रतिछाया, *f.* a reflected image, shadow, picture, image, statue, bas-relief.

प्रतिछाहीं (*Rām.*) = **प्रतिछाया**, *q v.*

प्रतिजिह्वा, *f.* the uvula or soft palate.

प्रतिजीवन, *m.* resuscitation.

प्रतिज्ञा, *f.* promise, assent, agreement, engagement, assertion, acknowledgement, admission; (in Law) a plaint; (in Logic) the proposition; the first of the five members of a complete syllogism (according to the Nyāya system).

प्रतिज्ञात, promised, agreed, acknowledged, admitted, asserted, propounded, alleged, deposed to.

प्रतिज्ञापत्र = **प्रतिज्ञापत्रक**, *q. v.*

प्रतिज्ञापत्रक, *m.* a written contract, bond, promissory note.

प्रतिज्ञाबोधक, *adj.* making known the **प्रतिज्ञा**, *q. v.*

प्रतिताल, *m.* a kind of air or melody.

प्रतिदत्त, *m.* (*f.* ā) given back; given in exchange.

प्रतिदान, *m.* the return or re-delivery of a deposit; a giving back or in return for; exchange, barter.

प्रतिदिन, from day to day, day by day, every day, daily; always, continually.

प्रतिदिशा, everywhere, in all directions.

प्रतिध्वनि, *f.* reïterated sound, echo, resonance, an echo.

प्रतिध्यान } **प्रतिनाद** } *m.* = **प्रतिध्वनि**, *q. v.*

प्रतिनिधि, *m.* a resemblance of a real form; *hence*, an image, picture, statue, a substitute, surety, proxy, deputy, lieutenant, ambassador, attorney, representative. — *k.* to take security.

प्रतिनिधिकर्म, *m.* the work of a representative, etc., embassy.

प्रतिनिधित्व, *m.* (*f.* tā) the status or the condition of a representative, etc., lieutenancy, ambassadorship.

प्रतिनिशा, night by night, every night.

प्रतिपक्षी, *m.* (*f.* iṇī) a rival, opponent, adversary.

प्रतिपक्षी, *m.* (*f.* in *or* inī) = **प्रतिपक्षी**, *q. v.*

प्रतिपत, *f.* = **प्रतिपद**, *q. v.*

प्रतिपत्ति, an obtaining, acquirement, perception, knowledge, ascertainment, determination; respectful behaviour, honouring, reputation, fame.

प्रतिपद, 1, *f.* the first day of a lunar fortnight, but especially that of the moon's increase: understanding, rank, consequence: 2, at each step, step by step; every moment, continually.

प्रतिपन्न, reached, approached, come up to, effected, ascertained, understood, known, agreed to.

प्रतिपन्नत्व, *m.* (*f.* tā) the being acquired or accomplished; demonstration.

प्रतिपादन, *m.* an accomplishing, effecting, ascertainment, demonstration; donation, gift.

प्रतिपादित, accomplished, effected, established, demonstrated, ascertained, signified, treated of.

प्रतिपाद्य, *m.* (*f.* ā) *adj.* to be treated of or discussed, to be explained or expounded.

प्रतिपाल, 1, *m.* (*f.* ī) = **प्रतीपालक**, *q. v.*: 2, *m.* = **प्रतिपालन**.

प्रतिपालक, *m.* (*f.* ikā) a protector, benefactor, guardian, nourisher, cherisher, patron, king: lit. *adj.* cherishing, protecting, preserving, defending.

प्रतिपालन, *m.* the cherishing or protecting a person, the providing for anyone, fostering, breeding, rearing, patronizing, defending.

प्रतिपालना, *t.* to cherish, maintain, foster, rear, protect, feed.

प्रतिपालिका, *f.* (*m.* °**पालक**) a benefactress.

प्रतिपालित, *m.* (*f.* ā) cherished, provided for, protected.

प्रतिपुरुष, man by man, every man.

प्रतिपूजक, *m.* (*f.* ikā) one who does homage, a reverer, venerator, adorer, worshipper.

प्रतिपूजन, *m.* exchange of civilities, mutual obeisance or reverence; the offering homage or respect.

प्रतिप्रसव, *m.* a license, precept for an act which under other circumstances is forbidden.

प्रतिफल, *m.* reward, return, recompense, requital, retribution, retaliation.

प्रतिफलदाता, *m.* (*f.* trī) an avenger, rewarder. An epithet of God as The Avenger *par excellence.*

प्रतिबन्ध, *m.* an obstacle, blocking up, impediment; connexion.

प्रतिबन्धक, *m.* an impediment; an obstructing; a branch; an opposer; *lit.* adj. impeding, obstructing.

प्रतिबर्ष = **प्रतिवर्ष**, *q: v.*

प्रतिबोधक, *m.* (*f.* ikā) awakening; admonishing, instructing.

प्रतिबासी, *m* (*f.* inī) *more prop.* **प्रतिवासी**, *q. v.*

प्रतिबिम्ब } **प्रतिबिम्भ** } *more prop.* **प्रतिबिम्ब**, *q. v.*

प्रतिभट, *m.* (*f.* ā) *adj.* vying with, rivalling, emulating.

प्रतिभटता, *f.* (*m.* °**त्व**) emulousness, emulating, rivalry.

प्रतिभय, 1, *m.* fear: 2, *m.* (*f.* ā) formidable, terrifying, frightful.

प्रतिभा, *f.* light, a reflected light, splendour; manifestation; brilliancy of conception, sharpness of understanding, intellect (especially contemplated as opening or expanding); wit; dignity: boldness.

प्रतिभाव, *m.* corresponding character or disposition.

प्रतिभाषा, *f.* a reply, rejoinder, defence.

प्रतिभास, *m.* appearance, look, similitude; appearing or occurring to the mind; illusion.

प्रतिभासन, *m.* appearing, appearance, look, semblance.

प्रतिभिन्न, *m.* (*f.* ā) pierced through; separated, divided.

प्रतिभू, *m.* bail, security, surety, bondman, sponsor, pledge. — *honā*, to stand security.

प्रतिभेदन, *m.* piercing, cutting, penetrating, separating, dividing.

प्रतिमा, *f.* a resemblance, likeness, figure, image, picture, statue, idol; the part of an elephant's head between the tusks: (in Pros.) a species of metre consisting twelve syllables.

प्रतिमान, *m.* = **प्रतिमा**, *q. v.*

प्रतिमास, from month to month, month by month, every month, monthly.

प्रतिमासिक, appertaining to every month, monthly.

प्रतिमूरति, *f.* a resemblance, likeness, image, picture.

प्रतिमूषिका, *f.* a species of rat.

प्रतियोग, *m.* enmity, opposition, contradiction, resistance, repulsion, controversy; association, coöperation.

प्रतियोगित्व, *m.* (*f.* tā) coöperation, coädjutorship, equality in power.

प्रतियोगी, *m.* (*f.* inī) an opponent; a coadjutor, associate, partner; a match; *lit.* adj. counteracting; coöperating with; answering to; equal in power.

प्रतियोधा, *m.* (*f.* dhrī) an antagonist, opponent, adversary.

प्रतिरक्षण, *m.* a preserving.

प्रतिरात्र, from night to night, night by night, every night, nightly. [image, picture.

प्रतिरूप, *m.* the counterpart of any real form, an

प्रतिरोध, *m.* obstruction, opposition, hindrance, impediment, stoppage, seige.

प्रतिरोधक, *m.* (*f.* ikā) a thief, robber, opponent, lit. *adj.* obstructing, stopping, besieging.

प्रतिरोधी, *m.* (*f.* inī) = **प्रतिरोधक**, *q. v.*

प्रतिलम्भ, *m.* an obtaining: censure, reviling, abuse.

प्रतिलोम, *m.* (*f.* ā) a base-born person, etc.: *lit.* inverted, reverse; left (not right); contrary to the natural order, low, vile, base, depraved.

प्रतिलोमज, *m.* (*f.* ā) a person born from the adverse mixture of different castes; *i. e.* from a marriage in which the wife is of a higher caste than the husband.

प्रतिवचन, *m.* a reply, rejoinder; an echo.

प्रतिवर्ष, every year, year by year, yearly.

प्रतिवाक्य, *m.* } = **प्रतिवचन**, *q.v.*
प्रतिवाच, *f.* }
प्रतिवाणि, *f.* }

प्रतिवादिता, *f.* (in Law) the situation of respondent or defendant.

प्रतिवादी, *m.* (*f.* inī) (in Law) a respondent or defendant, etc.: *lit.* adj. answering, rejoining, contending against, calumniating, slandering.

प्रतिबाधी, *m.* (*f.* inī) an opponent adversary, defendant: *lit.* adj. opposing.

प्रतिवासी, *m.* (*f.* inī) a neighbour: *lit.* adj. dwelling near, neighbouring.

प्रतिबिम्ब, *m.* a resemblance or counterpart of real forms, an image, shadow, reflection, picture, likeness.

प्रतिबिम्बित, *m.* (*f.* ā) reflected (as an image).

प्रतिविषा, *f.* a certain plant (*Betula*).

प्रतिशंका, *f.* constant fear or doubt.

प्रतिशब्द, *m.* a reverberating sound, echo.

प्रतिश्या, *f.* } catarrh.
प्रतिश्याय, *m.* }

प्रतिश्रुत, *f.* an echo; a promise, assent: *lit.* agreed to, granted, accepted, promised.

प्रतिश्रोता, *m.* (*f.* trī) a promiser, assentor.

प्रतिषिद्ध, prohibited, refused, denied.

प्रतिषेध, *m.* a prohibition, contradiction, denial, rejection, exception.

प्रतिष्ठ, *m.* (*f.* ā) renowned, famous.

प्रतिष्ठा, *f.* (*lit.* place; firm standing, staying; accomplishment, completion; *hence*) fame, reputation, celebrity, notoriety, honour, glory, dignity, renown; consecration of a temple or monument erected in honour of a deity or of the image of a deity; the endowment of a temple; the portioning or marriage of a daughter; the completion of a vow; (in Pros.) a metre consisting of a stanza of four lines of four syllables each; a variety of the *gāyatrī* metre consisting of three lines of eight, seven, and six syllables respectively.

प्रतिष्ठान, *m.* a firm standing, base, site, situation: *pr. n.* (1) of the capital of the early kings of the lunar dynasty, opposite Allahabad (2) of the capital of Sālivāhan in the Dakkhan.

प्रतिष्ठावस्त्र, *m.* a robe of honour.

प्रतिष्ठित, *m.* (*f.* ā) placed, situated, established, fixed: renowned, celebrated, famous; consecrated; portioned, endowed.

प्रतिसर, *m.* a servant, dependent; the rear of an army; a garland, bracelet, ornament, a string worn around the hand at nuptials; a form of magic or incantation; cicatrizing or healing as a sore: *lit.* following, dependent, subject to, servile.

प्रतिसर्ग, *m.* secondary creation, *i. e.* the creation of the world by the agency of Brahmā and other divine beings as the agents of the one Supreme Being; *hence*, that portion of a Purān which treats of the destruction and renovation of the world.

प्रतिस्पर्द्धा, *f.* the wish or the effort to excel or overcome, emulation, rivalry.

प्रतिस्पर्द्धी, *m.* (*f.* iṇī) a rival, etc.: *lit.* emulous, envious; refractory, rebellious.

प्रतिस्याय = **प्रतिश्याय**, *q.v.*

प्रतिहत, *m.* (*f.* ā) obstructed, opposed, repulsed, overthrown, fallen, disappointed.

प्रतिहति, *f.* repulse, rebound; disappointment.

प्रतिहार, 1, *m.* a door: trick, disguise: 2, *m.* (*f.* ī) a doorkeeper, porter, warder, chamberlain: a juggler.

प्रतिहारत्व, *m.* (*f.* tā) the office of doorkeeper or chamberlain.

प्रतिहास, *m.* a certain shrub (*Nerium odorum*)

प्रतिहिंसा, *f.* retaliation, revenge.

प्रतिहिंसित, *m.* (*f.* ā) injured by way of requital [or revenge.

प्रती; see **प्रति**.

प्रतीक, 1, *m.* a limb, member, part, portion: 2, *m.* (*f.* ā) against the natural order or state, reversed, inverted, contrary, adverse.

प्रतीक्षक, *m.* (*f.* ikā) = **प्रतीक्षी**, *q. v.*

प्रतीक्षण, *m.* the looking out for or awaiting a thing, a looking to or at, referring to, regard to, considering, respecting, expecting, expectation, hope.

प्रतीक्षा, *f.* = **प्रतीक्षण**, *q.v.* [awaiting, expecting.

प्रतीक्षी, *m.* (*f.* iṇī) *adj.* looking at, looking for,

प्रतीची, *f. pr. n.* the west quarter, the west.

प्रतीचीन } western, west.
प्रतीच्य }

प्रतीत, 1, *m.* (*f.* ā) gone by, passed, come up to; known, heard of, acquainted with, believed: renowned, celebrated, famous, venerated, respected; delighted, glad: 2, *f.* faith, confidence, trust. — *k.* to examine; to believe, trust.

प्रतीति, *f.* knowledge, understanding, conviction; experience, belief, faith; fame, notoriety.

प्रतीतार्थ, *m.* (*f.* ā) having a recognized or acknowledged meaning.

प्रतीप, *m.* (*f.* ā) backward, retrograde, against the grain, turned away, averted, contradictory, opposite, refractory, disobedient. [ted, learnt.

प्रतीयमान, *m.* (*f.* matī) believed, trusted, admit-

प्रतीर, *m.* a bank, shore.

प्रतीवाप, *m.* the calcining or fluxing metals; the throwing one substance into another to alter its form or state; the adding anything to a medicine during or after decoction; a public danger or calamity (as a plague, etc.).

प्रतीहार = प्रतिहार, *q. v.* [the bowels.

प्रतूणी, *f.* pain shooting from the rectum along

प्रत्यंग, *m.* an organ of perception, a limb of the body; a minor member (as the chin, nose, etc.): *adv.* on the limbs severally, limb by limb.

प्रत्यंच, *m.* (*f.* प्रतीची) proceeding to; following in time or place, behind, subsequent, following; west,

प्रत्यक = प्रत्यंच, *q. v.* [western.

प्रत्यकपर्णी / **प्रत्यकपुष्पी** } *f.* the plant *Achyranthes aspera.*

प्रत्यकश्रेणी, *f.* a certain plant (commonly called *Danti*); another plant (*Salvinia cucullata*).

प्रत्यक्ष, *m.* (*f.* ā) *lit.* before the eyes; *hence*, cognizable by the eyes or by any of the organs of sense, present, visible, perceptible, tangible, apparent, evident, axiomatic, plain, clear.—*k.* to make manifest.

प्रत्यक्षकारक, *m.* (*f.* ikā) *adj.* rendering manifest.

प्रत्यक्षदर्शन, *m.* (*f.* ā *or* ī) an eye-witness.

प्रत्यक्षप्रमाण, *m.* (in the Nyāy system) the evidence of the senses, ocular demonstration, visible or tangible proof; an organ or faculty of perception.

प्रत्यक्षा, *f.*, see प्रत्यक्ष.

प्रत्यक्षी, 1, *f.* consciousness of what is perceptible: 2, *m.* (*f.* iṇī) one who has the exercise of his senses: *lit.* adj. perceiving, seeing. [ifested, displayed.

प्रत्यक्षीकृत, *m.* (*f.* ā) made present or visible, man-

प्रत्यच, *more prop.* प्रत्यंच, *q. v.* [in succession.

प्रत्यनन्तर, *m.* (*f.* ā) the next heir: *lit.* next, next

प्रत्यन्त, *m. pr. n.* the country of the Mlechchhas, or savage and barbarous tribes: *lit.* bordering, skirting, contiguous.

प्रत्यभियोग, *m.* a counteraccusation, charge brought against the plaintiff, a recrimination.

प्रत्यय, *m.* (*lit.* the approach or coming against a thing; *hence*) apprehension, ascertainment, knowledge, certainty, proof; truth; belief, confidence, reliance, faith; decisive sentence: oath; ordeal; instrument, means of agency, helpmate; celebrity; (in Gram.) an affix to roots and words forming derivatives and inflections; (in the tenets of the Bauddhas) a concurrent occasion of an event as distinguished from its proximate cause. [confidential.

प्रत्ययित, *m.* (*f.* ā) confided in, relied on, trusted,

प्रत्ययी, *m.* (*f.* inī) a trustworthy person; a believer: *lit.* trustworthy; relying on, believing, trusting.

प्रत्यर्थी, (see अर्थी) *m.* (*f.* inī) an opponent, adversary; (in Law) a defendant: *lit* opposed to, inimical.

प्रत्यवाय, *m.* decrease; disappearance; non-production; disappointment; the contrary course, reverse, contrariety; sin. [loss; suffering.

प्रत्यवायी, *m.* (*f.* inī) detrimental; attended with

प्रत्यश्मन, *m.* red chalk.

प्रत्यह / **प्रत्यहः** } = प्रत्यहम, *q. v.*

प्रत्यहम, day by day, from day to day, every day, daily. [ed; arrived at.

प्रत्यागत, *m.* (*f.* ā) come back, come again, return-

प्रत्यागमन, *m.* a coming back, return.

प्रत्यादिष्ट, *m.* (*f.* ā) set aside, removed; informed, apprised; warned, cautioned; declared (as from heaven).

प्रत्यादेश, *m.* rejection, repudiation, disallowance, refusal, prevention; abstemiousness; eclipsing, informing, apprizing, caution, warning, annunciation or declaration from heaven.

प्रत्यावृत्ति, *f.* a coming back, return. [tion, desire.

प्रत्याशा, *f.* reliance, confidence, trust; hope, expecta-

प्रत्याशी, *m.* (*f.* inī) an expectant: lit. *adj.* hoping, expecting, trusting, relying on.

प्रत्यासत्ति, *f.* immediate proximity (in space, time, etc.), close contact, juxtaposition; analogy.

प्रत्याहार, *m.* a taking back, recovering, restraining the organs of sense: abstraction, abridgement; (in Gram.) the artificial arrangement of certain letters of the alphabet for the purpose of forming a class of letters for the concise expression of grammatical

प्रत्युक्त, answered, replied, rejoinded. [rules.

प्रत्युक्ति, *f.* answer, reply, rejoinder. [a retort.

प्रत्युत्तर, *m.* a reply to an answer, a rejoinder, a

प्रत्युत्थान, *m.* the rising (as a mark of respect) to welcome a visitor, respectful reception.

प्रत्युत्पन्न, *m.* (*f.* ā) reproduced, regenerated; produced by multiplication; ready, prompt; (in Math.) multiplied: multiplication; the product of a sum in multiplication. [meet anyone.

प्रत्युद्गमन, *m.* (= प्रत्युत्थान) the going forth or out to

प्रत्युपकार, *m.* a grateful return, requital of aid or assistance, mutual assistance, gratitude.

प्रत्युपकारक, *m.* (*f.* ikā) = प्रत्युपकारी, *q. v.*

प्रत्युपकारी, *m.* (*f.* iṇī) a grateful person: lit. *adj.* making a return for a kindness.

प्रत्युष, *m.* the early morning, daybreak, dawn.

प्रत्युषस / **प्रत्यूष** / **प्रत्यूषस** } = प्रत्युष, *q. v.*

प्रत्यूह, *m.* an obstacle, impediment, hindrance.

प्रत्येक, one by one, singly, each, every.

प्रत्येकत्व, *m.* (*f.* tā) respectiveness.

प्रथम, (in Hindee = प्रथमतः, *q. v.*) *m.* (*f.* ā) first, the first, prior, before, initial, chief, principal, excellent: (in Arithm.) a first product.

प्रथमकारक, *m.* (in Gram.) the nominative case.

प्रथमगति (Rām.) = दान, *q. v.*

प्रथमतः, in the first place, firstly, previously.

प्रथमपुरुष, *m.* the first (= in European grammars the third) person of the verb; a termination of the first (or, according to European grammars, the third) person.

प्रथमसाहस, *m.* the first or lowest degree of fine or punishment: a capital crime. [breadth.

प्रथमा, 1, *f.*; see प्रथम: 2, *m.* greatness, width,

प्रथमी, a corruption of पृथिवी, *q. v.* [custom.

प्रथा, *f.* fame, notoriety, celebrity: immemorial

प्रथित, *m.* (*f.* ā) renowned, famous, celebrated, notorious, made known, declared.

प्रथिति, *f* celebrity, renown.

प्रथिवी, *more prop.* **पृथिवी**, *q.v.*

प्रथुक, *m.* (*f.* ā) the young of any animal.

प्रथुराय = **पृथुराज** = **पृथु**, *q.v.*

प्रद, *m.* (*f.* ā) a giver : lit. *adj.* giving.

प्रदक्षिण, 1, *m.* (*f.* ā) one who is at the right hand of another : 2, *m.* a method of reverential salutation in which the person saluting circumambulates the person or the object saluted, with his right side towards it (it is also called *Parikramā*).

प्रदक्षिणा, *f.* = **प्रदक्षिण**, 1 and 2, *q.v.*

प्रदक्खिन, *more prop.* **प्रदक्षिण**, *q.v.*

प्रदर, *m.* the flooding of females (*Menorrhagia*): *lit.* a splitting, fracture, a cleft : an arrow.

प्रदर्शक, *m.* (*f.* ikā) a person who sees or views, or exhibits and shews ; *hence*, a teacher, expounder, prophet : *lit.* adj. viewing ; exhibiting.

प्रदर्शन, *m.* a seeing, viewing; a pointing out, exhibiting ; a prophecying.

प्रदर्शनी, *f.* an offering, a present of ceremony, a fee.

प्रदर्शित, shewn, exhibited, pointed out, declared, mentioned ; prophesied.

प्रदल = **प्रदर**, *q.v.*

प्रदा, *f.* 1, (*m.* **प्रद**) a female giver: 2, a gift.

प्रदाता }
प्रदातृ } *m.* (*f.* trī) a giver, bestower.

प्रदान, *m.* a giving, surrendering, bestowing in marriage ; a gift, donation ; marriage.

प्रदिक, *more prop.* **प्रदिश**, *q.v.*

प्रदिश, *f.* an intermediate point of the compass, or half-quarter (as, south-west, etc.).

प्रदीप, *m.* a lamp, lantern, light, splendour.

प्रदीपन, *m.* a kindling, inflaming; a kind of mineral poison of a red colour and caustic.

प्रदेश, *m.* a place in general; a country, foreign country, abroad , a district, province : a short span, measure from the tip of the thumb to the tip of the fore-finger.

प्रदेशन, *m.* a present, gift, offering, bribe.

प्रदेशनी, *f.* the fore-finger, the index-finger.

प्रदेशिन, see (1) **प्रदेशन** (2) **प्रदेशिनी** (3) **प्रदेशी**.

प्रदेशिनी, *f.* (*m.* **प्रदेशी**) a female foreigner, etc. : the fore-finger, the index-finger, the corresponding toe.

प्रदेशी, appertaining to *pradesh*: hence *m.* (*f.* inī) a foreigner, etc.

प्रदेह, *m.* unguent; unction.

प्रदोष, *m.* fault, defect, offence, transgression, sin, guilt : the first part of the night, evening-twilight.

प्रद्युम्न, *m.* an epithet of Kāmdev ; *lit.* the preëminently powerful one.

प्रधा, *f. pr. n.* one of the daughters of Daksh.

प्रधान, 1, *m.* nature, the cause of the material world, the natural state of anything; matter : intellect, understanding : 2, *m.* (*f.* ā) a chief, principal, commander, noble, the chief companion of a king, his minister, eunuch, or confidant ; a chief minister or counsellor of state, courtier, leader, chieftain, president ; *hence*, an epithet of the Supreme God : *lit.* chief, principal.

प्रधानता, *f.* (*m.* °**त्व**) preëminence, principalship, chiefship, presidentship, superiority, excellence.

प्रधानधातु, *m.* the chief element or ingredient of the body, *i. e. semen virile.*

प्रधानमन्त्री, *m.* (*f.* iṇī) a prime minister.

प्रधानयाजक, *m.* (*f.* ikā) a high priest.

प्रधाना, *f.* (*m.* **प्रधान**, 2) a female chief.

प्रधानोत्तम, *m.* (*f.* ā) illustrious, emminent.

प्रध्वंस, *m.* destruction, loss.

प्रध्वंसी, *m.* (*f.* inī) a destroyer : lit. *adj.* destroying, annihilating.

प्रन; for word beginning thus, see under the form [**प्रण**.

प्रपंच, *m.* extent, diffusion, copiousness, prolixity, development, analysis ; inversion, opposition ; error, illusion, unreal or ideal existence ; treachery, imposition, artifice, trick, fraud, delusion, deceit.

प्रपंचित, *m.* (*f.* ā) extended, expanded, expatiated upon, related at length, fully explained ; mistaken, erring ; deceived, beguiled, tricked.

प्रपंची, *m.* (*f.* inī) a cheat, etc. : *lit.* insidious, artful, fraudulent, deceitful, tricky.

प्रपलायन, *m.* a running away, flight.

प्रपलायित, *m.* (*f.* ā) put to flight: routed.

प्रपलायी, *m.* (*f.* inī) a fugitive, one who deserts his cause.

प्रपितामह, *m.* (*f.* ī) a great-grandparent by the father's side.

प्रपुनाट, *m.* a certain tree (*Cassia tora*) ; the ring-worm-shrub (*Cassia alata*).

प्रपुनाड }
प्रपुन्नड }
प्रपुन्नाट } = **प्रपुनाट**, *q.v.*
प्रपुन्नाड }
प्रपुन्नाल }

प्रपुषा, *f.* a certain grass (*Hedysarum alhagi*).

प्रपूर्ण, *m.* the act of filling a vessel or of completing a thing : the drawing a bowstring.

प्रपूरिका, *f.* a prickly nightshade (*Solanum jacquini*).

प्रपौण्डरीक, *m.* a certain small herbaceous plant used in medicine and as a perfume, commonly called *punḍeryā*. In medicine it forms the basis of applications to ulcers and bad eyes.

प्रपौत्र, *m.* (*f.* ī) a great-grandchild (the child of a son's son).

प्रफुल्ल, *m.* (*f.* ā) blown (as a flower), expanded, opened (as the eye); smiling, pleased, glad, cheerful, gay, shining.

प्रफुल्लत्व, *m.* (*f.* tā) cheerfulness, gayness.

प्रफुल्लनयन, *m.* (*f.* ā) an epithet of a joyous person ; lit. *adj.* having the eyes expanded and sparkling with joy.

प्रफुल्लनेत्र, *m.* (*f.* ā *or* ī) = **प्रफुल्लनयन**, *q.v.*

प्रफुल्लमुख, *m.* (*f.* ī) = **प्रफुल्लवदन**, *q.v.*

प्रफुल्लवदन, *m.* (*f.* ā) an epithet of a cheerful-looking person; *lit.* adj. having the countenance expanded with cheerfulness, happy-looking.

प्रफुल्लित, *m.* (*f.* ā) = **प्रफुल्ल**, *q.v.*

प्रबत in Chand = **पर्वत**, *q.v.*

प्रबन्ध, *m.* uninterrupted connexion, arrangement, continuous application, a connected narrative, discourse or discussion, a literary production, composition, style ; continuance, uninterruptedness ; a kind of song.

प्रबन्धकल्पना, *f.* a feigned story (whether founded in fact or not), a work of the imagination.

प्रबन्धित, connected, arranged, agreed on.

प्रबर्षण, *m.* raining, a causing to rain, the first rain: *pr. n.* (1) of a certain treatise (2) of a certain mountain.

प्रबल, *m.* (*f.* ā) prevailing, predominant, powerful, mighty, violent.

प्रबलत्व, *m.* (*f.* tā) predominance, powerfulness, mightiness, violence. [obstinate female.

प्रबला, *f.* (*m.* **प्रबल**) a powerful female, a self-willed

प्रबाल, *m.* coral: a young shoot, sprout, new leaf: the bridge of a lute through which the strings are drawn.

प्रबास, प्रबाह, प्रबीण; for words beginning thus, see under the forms **प्रवास, प्रवाह, प्रवीण**, respectively.

प्रबुद्ध, 1, *m.* (*f.* ā) awake, wakened; expanded; wise, learned: 2, *m. pr. n.* (see **नवयोगेश्वर**) the 4th Yogeshwar. [the form **प्रवेश**.

प्रबेश, प्रबेस; for words beginning thus, see under

प्रबोध, *m.* waking, an awaking either from sleep or from ignorance; a vigilant active state of being, wakefulness, watchfulness, vigilance; knowledge, understanding, wisdom, consciousness, sense; persuasion, consolation, demonstration.

प्रबोधक, *m.* (*f.* ikā) *adj.* arousing, awakening, making aware of, convincing.

प्रबोधन, *m.* an awakening; a recalling to life, resuscitating, reviving, exciting; an instructing, producing conviction, persuading, persuation. [of, convinced.

प्रबोधित, *m.* (*f.* ā) awakened, excited, made aware

प्रबोधिता, *f.* a species of the *Atijagatī* metre.

प्रभंजन, *m.* air, wind: *lit.* adj. breaking down.

प्रभव, *m.* generative cause, the root of existence, origin, production, birth; *hence*, a father, mother, birthplace: family, lineage; strength, superiority; authority: *adj.* produced, born.

प्रभवी, *f.* (*m.* **प्रभु**) a mistress, proprietress.

प्रभा, *f.* light, radiance, splendour, lustre: shadow.

प्रभाउ, **प्रभाऊ** } (Rām.) = **प्रभाव**, *q.v.*

प्रभांजन, *m.* a certain tree (*Hyperanthera morunga*).

प्रभाकर, *m.* an epithet of the sun, the moon, or fire; *lit.* causing light, illuminating, luminous.

प्रभाकीट, *m.* (*f.* ī) the firefly. [sub-fraction.

प्रभाग, *m.* (in Math.) a fraction of a fraction, a

प्रभागजाति, *f.* (in Math.) the reduction of subfractions to a common denominator.

प्रभात, *m.* daybreak, dawn, morning.

प्रभाती, *adj.* sung in a tune (*rāgiṇī*) peculiar to

प्रभान, *m.* a shining, radiance, light. [morning.

प्रभाव, *m.* power, celestial power, might, influence; majesty, dignity, magnanimity, high spirit.

प्रभावती, *f.* a species of Sanskrit metre.

प्रभावन्त, *m.* (*f.* vatī) luminous, shining, splendid,

प्रभावान, *m.* (*f.* vatī) = **प्रभावन्त**, *q.v.* [majestic.

प्रभाष = **प्रभास**, *q. v.*

प्रभास, *m. pr. n.* a certain place of pilgrimage in

प्रभासक्षेत्र, (see **क्षेत्र**) = **प्रभास**, *q.v.* [the west of India.

प्रभु, *m.* (*f.* **प्रभवी** or **प्रभु**) a master, lord, owner, proprietor, commander, superior, principal: *lit.* strong, able; eternal. [superiority, influence, legislation.

प्रभुत, *m.* ability, government, liberty, option,

प्रभुता, *f.*, **प्रभुताई**, *f.*, **प्रभुत्व**, *m.* } = **प्रभुपना**, *q. v.*

प्रभुपना, *m.* the status of a proprietor, etc., mastership, lordship, sovereignty, ascendancy, supremacy, superiority, sway, power, influence, greatness, dignity.

प्रभुभक्त, *m.* (*f.* ā) faithful, loyal, attached, devoted, dutiful.

प्रभुभक्ति, *f.* dutifulness, loyalty, devotedness.

प्रभू, *more prop.* **प्रभु**, *q. v.*

प्रभूतता, *f.*, **प्रभूतत्व**, *m.* } plenty, abundance.

प्रभूभक्त, *m.* (*f.* ā) *more prop.* **प्रभुभक्त**, *q. v.*

प्रभृति, *f.* manner, kind, sort. It is used chiefly as the last member in *Bahuvrīhi* compounds, signifying *etcetera*, the others, the rest, the remainder (of the sort or class just mentioned); *e. g.* **बृहस्पतिप्रभृति**, Jupiter, etc.; *i. e.* Jupiter and the other planets.

प्रभेद, *m.* a cutting through; division, difference, disparity; a sort, kind; a nickname.

प्रभेदक, *m.* (*f.* ikā) *adj.* severing; discriminating.

प्रमग्न, *m.* (*f.* ā) immersed, drowned.

प्रमत्त, *m.* (*f.* ā) intoxicated with delight, enraptured, inadvertent, inattentive.

प्रमथ, *m.* (*f.* ā) a horse: an attendant on Shiv.

प्रमथन, 1, *m.* a paining; a killing, slaughter: 2, *m.* (*f.* ī) a killer, etc.: *lit.* adj. paining, killing.

प्रमथा, *f.* yellow myrobalan (*Terminalia chebula*).

प्रमथाधिप, *m.* an epithet of Shiv; *lit.* lord of Pramath. [of pain.

प्रमथालय, *m.* an epithet of hell; *lit.* the abode

प्रमद, 1, *m.* joy, pleasure, delight, rapture: 2, *m.* (*f.* ā) mad, impassioned, intoxicated (whether physically, with liquor, or figuratively, with passion).

प्रमदा, *f.* (*m.* **प्रमद**) a handsome or impassioned female: a certain Sanskrit metre.

प्रमा, *f.* true perception, true knowledge, exemption from all error; consciousness; authority; example.

प्रमाण, *m.* measure; a scale; analogy; quantity; power; decision; proof; evidence, authority, testimony; cause, motive; attestation, verification; instance, example; detail; a work of sacred authority, a scripture; *adj.* authentic, actual, substantial, real, approved of, admissible, agreeable, acceptable. — *k.* or *denā*, to give evidence, to witness. — *chaṛhnā*, to rise to a high rank.

प्रमाणकथा, *f.* proof (or attempted proof) by appeal to records or to books (as distinguished from hearsay or tradition).

प्रमाणपत्र, *m.* a warrant, affidavit, voucher.

प्रमाणपुरुष, *m.* (*f.* ī) an umpire, arbitrator, judge.

प्रमाणसिद्ध, proven, proved.

प्रमाणाभाव, *m.* absence of (or deficiency in) proof or authority.

प्रमाणिक, *more prop.* **प्रामाणिक**, *q.v.*

प्रमाणिका, *f.* a species of the *Anushṭubh* metre.

प्रमाणी, *f.* a certain Sanskrit metre.

प्रमाणीकरण, *m.* an establishing or admitting as authority or proof.

प्रमाणय, *more prop.* **प्रामाणय**, *q.v.*

प्रमाता, *m.* (*f.* trī) one who knows well, an authority: *lit.* adj. measuring evidence or proof.

प्रमातामह, *m.* (*f.* ī) a great-grandparent by the mother's side.

प्रमाद, *m.* intoxication, insanity, distraction, confusion, distress, stupidity, inadvertence, inaccuracy, error.

प्रमादी, *m.* (*f.* inī) a careless person, etc.: *lit.* intoxicated, insane, confused, inadvertent, etc.

प्रमादु, 1, in poet. = **प्रमाद**, *q.v.*: 2, *m.* or *f.* = **प्रमादी**, *q.v.*

प्रमानन्द, *more prop.* **परमानन्द**, *q.v.*

प्रमित, measured, demonstrated, established by argument, known, authentic.

प्रमिताक्षरा, *f.* a species of the *Jagatī* metre.

प्रमिति, *f.* measure; true knowledge, knowledge established by proof.

प्रमुख, *m.* (*f.* ī) a distinguished person, chief, leader, sage; a certain tree (*Rottleria tinctoria*) used for dyeing: *lit.* first, chief, principal, most excellent, best. [leadership.

प्रमुखत्व, *m.* (*f.* tā) predominance, superiority,

प्रमुखी, *f.* (*m.* **प्रमुख**) a distinguished female.

प्रमुद = **प्रमुदित**, *q.v.* [glad, contented.

प्रमुदित, *m.* (*f.* ā) overjoyed, delighted, very pleased,

प्रमेह, *m.* a urinary affection (as change in the colour, quantity, or consistence of the urine). Twenty-one varieties are enumerated, including diabetes, gleet, gonorrhœa, venereal clap, pox, etc.

प्रमोचक, *m.* (*f.* ikā) a liberator: lit. *adj.* setting free, liberating.

प्रमोचन, *m.* a setting free, releasing.

प्रमोचनी, *f.* a species of cucumber.

प्रमोद, *m.* exceeding joy, delight, hilarity, happiness, pleasure.

प्रमोदक, *m.* (*f.* ikā) one who occasions delight: *lit.* adj. causing delight or happiness.

प्रमोदित, *m.* (*f.* ā) delighted, glad, happy.

प्रमोदी, *m.* (*f.* inī) a happy person; one who makes others happy: *lit.* delighted, happy; delighting, making happy. [pefaction, stupor, confusion.

प्रमोह, *m.* fascination; fainting, insensibility, stu-

प्रयत्न, *m.* persevering exertion, effort, action, act; great care, caution; difficulty; articulation of sound; (in Logic) active effort of three kinds, *viz.* (1) the engaging in any act (2) the prosecuting it (3) the completing it. [terprizing, active, zealous.

प्रयत्नवान, *m.* (*f.* vatī) assiduous, persevering, en-

प्रयश्चित (*contraction*) = **प्रायश्चित**, *q.v.*

प्रयाति (*Rām.*) = **प्राप्त होते हैं**.

प्रयाग, *m. pr. n.* (lit. sacrifice: *qy.* chief sacrifice?) the modern Allahabad situated at the confluence of the Ganges and the Jamunā, with the supposed subterraneous addition of the Saraswatī, whence its other name *Triveṇī* (the three streams). It is a celebrated *tīrth* of the Hindoos and is visited annually in the month of Māgh by a large concourse of pilgrims from all parts of Hindoostān. In composition, this term is applied also to several other places of reputed sanctity which are situated at the junction of two rivers, *e.g.* Devprayāg, Rudrprayāg, Karṇprayāg, and Nandprayāg, in the Himālayas, which, with Prayāg (Allahabad) constitute the five principal places so termed, and where worship is deemed peculiarly efficacious. The name seems to contain an allusion to the legend that it was at Allahabad that Brahmā consummated ten Aswamedhs (sacrifices of the horse) in commemoration of his recovery of the four Veds from Sankhāsur.

प्रयागराज, *m.* (see **तीर्थराज**) an epithet of **प्रयाग**.

प्रयागवाल, *m.* (see **पयागवाल**) a Hindoo priest of Prayāg.

प्रयाण, *m.* a going forth, going to a distance, departure, death; the march of a hostile force, invasion, attack.

प्रयाणकाल, *m.* time of departure, time of death.

प्रयाश्चित (*corruption*) = **प्रायश्चित**, *q.v.*

प्रयास, *m.* labour, fatigue, effort, endeavour, trouble; desire for (or pursuit of) any object.

प्रयासी, *m.* (*f.* inī) diligent, industrious, laborious, persevering.

प्रयुक्त, closely united, compact, connected with, associated, possessing as an attribute, endowed with. Used in comp. in the sense of produced by, caused by, arising from, owing to, in consequence of.

प्रयुत, *m.* a million.

प्रयोग, *m.* action, effort, exertion; direction; occasion, cause, motive, object, consequence, result; contrivance, device; comparison, example; dramatic representation; an authority, a text; a capital bearing interest; usage, application (of a word).

प्रयोगी, *m.* (*f.* inī) one who strives for any object; *lit.* adj. striving for any purpose, calculated for any object, causing, stimulating.

प्रयोज; see **प्रयोज्य**.

प्रयोजक, *m.* (*f.* ikā) the author or instigator of any act, founder or institutor of any ceremony, a director, lawgiver, legislator; a creditor: *lit.* adj. causing, inducing, stimulating, arousing, exciting; deputing, appointing.

प्रयोजन, *m.* cause, motive, purpose, intention, design, occasion, origin; use, need, profit, interest; exigence.

प्रयोजनवान, *m.* (*f.* vatī) *adj.* designing, purposing.

प्रयोजनिक, requisite, necessary.

प्रयोजनी, necessary, requisite.

प्रयोजनीय = **प्रयोज्य**, *q.v.*

प्रयोज्य, proper to be put forth or to be represented, fit, suitable, proper, necessary.

प्ररकार, a corruption of **प्रकार**, *q.v.*

प्रलम्ब, *m.* 1, *pr. n.* a certain demon killed by Balarām; *lit.* pendulous; dilatory; *hence* 2, procrastination, delay; the new shoot or bud of a creeping-plant; a garland of flowers worn around the neck.

प्रलय, *m.* (*f.* ?) dissolution, destruction, end, death, dying, annihilation; loss; the loss of sense or consciousness, fainting, syncope: *met.* vexation, fatigue, oppression, languor, disgust. The term is applied to the destruction of the world at the end of a *Kalp*; also, to the Flood (of the Bible).

प्रलव, *m.* a part cut off, a chip, fragment (as of a reed, etc.); the sheath of a leaf.

प्रलाप, *m.* discourse, conversation; talk (*esp.* incoherent, unmeaning, useless, or delirious talk); lamentation.

प्रलापी, (*f.* inī) a prattler, etc.: *lit.* adj. talking incoherently, unmeaningly, uselessly, or deliriously.

प्रलेप, *m.* an ointment, plaster, salve.

प्रलेपक, *m.* (*f.* ikā) *adj.* amointing, smearing.

प्रलेपन, *m.* the smearing or anointing the body with unguents.

प्रलै in Chand = **प्रलय**, *q.v.*

प्रलोठन, *m.* a rolling on the ground; a heaving, tossing (as of the ocean).

प्रलोठित, *adj.* rolling, heaving, tossing.

प्रलोभ, *m.* allurement; desire, cupidity, greediness.

प्रलोभन, *m.* an alluring, inducing, reducing, attracting.

प्रलोभी, *m.* (*f.* inī) *adj.* alluring, inducing, seducing, attracting, desirous, avaricious, greedy.

प्रल्हाद, *more prop.* **प्रह्लाद**, *q.v.*

प्रवंचक, *m.* (*f.* ikā) an impost r, cheat, etc: *lit.* deceitful, treacherous, imposing, fraudulent.

प्रवंचना, *f.* imposture, deceit, treachery, imposition.

प्रवंचित, *m.* (*f.* ā) imposed upon, deceived, cheated.

प्रवक्ता, *m.* (*f.* inī) an eloquent speaker, a teacher, expounder, propounder.

प्रवर, *m.* (*f.* ā) a chief, etc.; a Muni who contributes to the credit of a particular family (*gotra*); one of the forty-nine gotras, as opposed to the eight principal ones; family, offspring, descendants, kindred, race, lineage: *lit.* chief, excellent, eminent, best.

प्रवरललित, *m.* a species of the *Ashtī* metre.

प्रवर्त्त, *m.* a commencement, engagement, excitement, instigation, stimulus: *adj.* appointed, ready, determined, engaged in, undertaking.

प्रवर्त्तक, *m.* (*f.* ikā) an instigator, causer, author, founder, principal actor, arbiter, judge; the entrance of the first person of the drama at the close of the introduction: lit. *adj.* setting in motion, inciting, inducing, stimulating.

प्रवसन, *m.* a going abroad, sojourning in a foreign country.

प्रवह, *m.* wind: hence (1) *pr. n.* one of the seven Vayus or winds (2) an epithet of Indra.

प्रवहण, *m.* the act of flowing; a covered car, a litter or carriage for females.

प्रवाचक, explanatory, significant, technical (as a term).

प्रवाद, *m.* rumour, report; a proverb; speaking, discourse; litigious language.

प्रवापी, *m.* (*f.* inī) one who sows seed.

प्रवारण, *m.* prohibition, opposition, objection: a desirable gift.

प्रवास, *m.* living abroad or away from home; a temporary or foreign residence.

प्रवासत, *adj.* dwelling or being absent or abroad.

प्रवासन, *m.* a dwelling abroad, sojourning, lodging; banishment, exile; a killing.

प्रवासी, *m.* (*f.* inī) a traveller, sojourner, one who lives away from his home: *lit.* adj. sojourning abroad.

प्रवाह, *m.* anything moving forwards like a stream, *hence*, a stream, current, torrent, continuous passage, a drove of cattle; a pond; a swift horse; usage, custom, activity, life, occupation.

प्रवाहक, *m.* (*f.* ikā) one who carries well; a demon; *lit.* adj. carrying off; flowing off.

प्रवाहिका, *f.* diarrhœa.

प्रविख्याति, *f.* celebrity, renown, fame.

प्रविभक्त, partitioned, divided, separated, shared.

प्रविभाग, *m.* a division, share, part.

प्रविर, *m.* a certain yellow fragrant wood.

प्रविष्ट, *m.* (*f.* ā) gone in, gone into, entered upon (as an affair), engaged in.

प्रवीण, *m.* (*f.* ā) an able person, etc.: *lit.* skilful, clever, able, accomplished, knowing, wise, acute, sagacious, shrewd, conversant with.

प्रवीणत्व, *m.* (*f.* tā) skill, cleverness, accomplishment, sagaciousness, acuteness, shrewdness, ability.

प्रवीणा, *f.* (*m.* **प्रवीण**) a clever female.

प्रवीर, *m* (*f.* ā) a person of distinction or of rank, a hero, chief, king, prince, warrior: *lit.* best, most excellent, bravest.

प्रवृत्त, fixed, settled, determined, done; engaged in; undertaking; occupied.

प्रवृत्ति, *f.* the being engaged or occupied, active life (as opposed to a life of contemplation), activity; prosecution; perseverance; instigation; inclination; addiction to, predilection for; tidings, intelligence; continuous flow, stream, current; a beginning, origin; the applicableness of any precept or rule; the juice that exudes from an elephant's temples when in rut; an epithet of Ujjain or any holy place; (in Gram.) the crude form; (in Arithm.) the multiplier.

प्रवेक्षण, *m.* a foreseeing.

प्रवेक्षित, foreseen, anticipated.

प्रवेक्ष्यत, *adj.* foreseeing, anticipating.

प्रवेट, *m.* barley.

प्रवेणि, *f.* unormented and twisted hair (as worn by women in the absence of their husbands).

प्रवेणी, *f.* = **प्रवेणि**, *q.v.*

प्रवेल, *m.* the yellow variety of kidney-bean.

प्रवेश, *m.* an entering; entrance, admittance, access, penetration; engagedness in a pursuit, intentness on an object. — *k.* to penetrate, etc.

प्रवेशक, 1, *m.* an entry; an interlude: 2, *m.* (*f.* ikā) *adj.* going into, entering, penetrating.

प्रवेशन, *m.* the entering into a place; an entrance to a house, etc.

प्रवेशी, *m.* (*f.* inī) *adj.* going into, entering, penetrating.

प्रशंस; for words beginning thus, see under the form **प्रशंस**.

प्रशंसक, *m.* (*f.* ikā) a flatterer, encomiast, etc.: *lit.* adj. praising, eulogizing, laudatory, flattering.

प्रशंसन, *m.* a praising, eulogizing.

प्रशंसना, *t.* to praise, eulogize, applaud.

प्रशंसनीय, *m.* (*f.* ā) deserving praise, praiseworthy, laudable.

प्रशंसहि (pl. °हिं) in Braj = **प्रशंसता है**. See **हिं**.

प्रशंसा, *f.* praise, eulogy, applause, panegyric, commendation, flattery. — *k.* to laud, extol, panegyrize, express approval of. [encomiast.

प्रशंसाकारी, *adj.* eulogizing : hence, *m.* (*f.* iṇī) an

प्रशंसायोग्य, *m.* (*f.* ā) = **प्रशंसनीय**, *q.v.*

प्रशंसार्थी, *m.* (*f.* inī) a seeker of approval or of notoriety : *lit.* desirous of approval.

प्रशंसित, *m.* (*f.* ā) praised, lauded, eulogized.

प्रशंसी, *m.* (*f.* inī) = **प्रशंसक**, *q.v.*

प्रशब, *more prop.* **प्रसव**, *q.v.*

प्रशमन, *m.* disbursement of wealth ; tranquillizing, pacifying; securing; killing, slaughter, destruction.

प्रशस्त, *m.* (*f.* ā) eulogized ; good, excellent, best ; happy, well, right.

प्रशस्तत्व, *m.* (*f.* tā) excellence, goodness.

प्रशस्ति, *f.* eulogy, praise ; excellence, eminence.

प्रशाखा / **प्रशाखिका** } *f.* a small branch or twig.

प्रशान्त, *m.* (*f.* ā) calmed, composed, tranquillized, calm, peaceful. [serene.

प्रशान्तात्मा, peaceful, calm, composed, tranquil,

प्रशान्ति, *f.* calm (physical or moral), tranquillity, quiet, calm.

प्रशासन, *m.* governing, dominion, ruling.

प्रशास्ता, *m.* (*f.* trī) a ruler, governor.

प्रश्न, *m.* an inquiry, question, demand, a problem for calculation. — *k.* to make an inquiry, ask.

प्रश्नकर्त्ता, *m.* (*f.* trī) an inquirer, asker.

प्रश्नदूती, *f.* an intricate or enigmatical inquiry, an enigma, riddle, conundrum.

प्रश्नलिपी, *f.* (in Law) interrogatories.

प्रश्नवाचक सर्वनाम, *m.* (in Gram.) an interrogative pronoun.

प्रश्नी, *f.* the aquatic plant *Pistia stratioites.*

प्रश्नोत्तर, *m.* question and answer ; a catechism ; discussion, controversy.

प्रष्टा, *m.* (*f.* tri) an interrogator, querist, inquirer : *lit.* enquiring. interrogating.

प्रष्ठ, *m.* (*f.* ī) a chief, leader, conductor : *lit.* adj. going first or before : preceding, prior, chief, best.

प्रष्ठी, *f.* (*m.* **प्रष्ठ**) a female chief.

प्रसंग, *m.* association, union, attachment, introduction, insertion, connexion, coïtion (*esp.* illicit); connected reasoning ; conjuncture, occasion, time ; a topic, treatise, section of a book.

प्रसंगसंगति, *f.* conversation, intercourse.

प्रसंगित, *m.* (*f.* ā) = **प्रसंग हुआ जिसका.**

प्रसंस, प्रसंश; for words beginning thus, see under the form **प्रशंस.**

प्रसक्त, 1, *m.* (*f.* ā) in contact with, attached to, devoted to, engaged in ; attained, obtained, gained ; continual, constant, everlasting, eternal: 2, incessantly, continually, eternally. [ness, engagedness.

प्रसक्ति, *f.* adherence or attachment to, devoted-

प्रसन्द, a corruption of **पसन्द**, *q.v.*

प्रसन्न, *m.* (*f.* ā) pleased, rejoiced, delighted, favourable, complacent. satisfied with, favourable to, kind ; bright, pellucid, pure, clear. — *k.* to gratify. — *honā*, to be pleased.

प्रसन्नत्व, *m.* (*f.* tā) a being pleased with, complacency, favour, kindness, goodwill ; cheerfulness, pleasedness, happiness ; brightness, clearness.

प्रसन्नमुख, *m.* (*f.* ī) a complacent person, etc. : *lit.* agreeable-looking, looking cheerful or pleased, smiling.

प्रसन्ना, *f.* (*m.* **प्रसन्न**) a cheerful female.

प्रसम्बन्धन, a strengthened form of **सम्बन्धन**, *q.v.*

प्रसव, *m.* a bringing forth, being in labour, parturition ; production, birth; offspring, posterity ; fruit, a flower. [commonly called *piyā.*

प्रसवक, *m.* a certain tree (*Buchanania latifolia*)

प्रसवगृह, *m.* a lying-in hospital, a lying-in chamber. [puerperal.

प्रसवत, *m.* (*f.* vatī) a parent : lit. *adj.* bearing,

प्रसवती / **प्रसवन्ती** } *f.* a female in labour.

प्रसवबन्धन, *m.* the footstalk of a leaf or flower, petiole, peduncle.

प्रसविता / **प्रसवितृ** } *m.* (*f.* trī) a parent ; an ancestor.

प्रसवी, *m.* (*f.* inī) = **प्रसवत**, *q.v.*

प्रसाद, *m.* clearness, perspicuity, calmness of mind, favour, kind behaviour, propitiousness ; well-being, blessing, boon, present, gift. The term is specially applied to food that has been offered to the deities or to an idol ; also, to the leavings of food that has been partaken of by a great personage or by a spiritual guide.

प्रसादभोगी, *m.* (*f.* inī) a pensioner, etc. : *lit.* adj. enjoying or subsisting on favours.

प्रसादी, *m.* (*f.* inī) *adj.* shewing favours, treating with kindness ; offered to idols.

प्रसाधक, *m.* (*f.* ikā) *adj.* accomplishing, perfecting.

प्रसाधन, *m.* a dressing, decking, adorning, decoration, ornament; accomplishing, effecting ; embellishment, dress : a comb. [a comb.

प्रसाधनी, *f.* a certain drug commonly called *siddhi:*

प्रसाधित, accomplished, done ; decorated, ornamented. [a going to forage.

प्रसार, *m.* a going about, spreading, extending ;

प्रसारण, *m.* a spreading, expanding, extending.

प्रसारणी, *f.* a spreading ; the surrounding an enemy ; the dispersing of an army by detachments for the purpose of collecting forage.

प्रसारित, spread, expanded, extended.

प्रसारी, *m.* (*f.* iṇī) *adj.* breaking forth, going along, gliding, creeping, expanding, spreading.

प्रसिद्ध, *m.* (*f.* ā) ornamented, adorned ; aforesaid; well-known, celebrated. [brity, notoriety.

प्रसिद्धि, *f.* accomplishment, ornament, fame, cele-

प्रसीद (Rām.) = **प्रसन्न हो.** [the plaintain.

प्रसू, *f.* a mother ; a mare ; the spreading creeper ;

प्रसूत, *m.* the whites, fluor albus : lit. *m.* (*f.* ā) born: delivered, bringing forth.

प्रसूता, *f.* (*m.* **प्रसूत**) a female who has borne a child or who has been recently delivered, a lying-in woman.

प्रसूति, *f.* a bringing forth, birth, progeneration; offspring, progeny, children of either sex.

प्रसूतिका, *f.* a female who has had a child, or who has been recently delivered.

प्रसूती (Rām.) = **प्रसूति**, *q.v.*

प्रसून, *m.* a flower, blossom, bud; fruit: *lit.* produced, born.

प्रसेन, *m. pr. n.* (1) of a son of Nighu (2) of a king of Ujjayinī.

प्रसोती in Braj = **प्रसवती**, *q.v.*

प्रस्कन्दन, *m.* purging, diarrhœa.

प्रस्कन्दिका, *f.* = **प्रस्कन्दन**, *q.v.*

प्रस्तर, *m.* a handful or bundle of *kush*-grass used at sacrifices; a bunch of flowers: a plain, level: a stone, rock, a precious stone, gem.

प्रस्तार, *m.* the spreading a thing out; a bed; a thicket or wood overgrown with grass: (in Math.) an enumeration of all the possible combinations of given numbers.

प्रस्ताव, *m.* an introductory eulogium, a beginning; an occasion, opportunity, turn, season.

प्रस्तावना, *f.* a causing to be praised; a commencement, introduction, prologue, eulogium.

प्रस्ताविक, suited to the occasion, appropriate, seasonable.

प्रस्तुत, *m.* (*f.* ā) eulogized, panegyrized; mentioned, said, declared; accomplished, prepared, ready.

प्रस्तुतत्व, *m.* (*f.* tā) preparedness.

प्रस्थ, *m.* (*f.* ā) *adj.* going forth, expanding, spreading; solid; *hence*, table-land on the top of a mountain; a certain measure of quantity (equal to four *kudav*) or forty-eight double handfuls.

प्रस्थपुष्प, *m.* a sort of *tulsī*-plant (or *Basil*) with small leaves.

प्रस्था, *f.*; see **प्रस्थ**.

प्रस्थान, *m.* a departing, going forth, setting out, proceeding; the march of an army, march of an assailant. — *k.* to depart, to march.

प्रस्थापन, *m.* the causing a person to depart, a sending away, despatching; appointment on an embassy.

प्रस्थापना, *t.* to appoint, establish.

प्रस्थापित, *m.* (*f.* ā) made to depart, despatched, sent.

प्रस्थित, departed, set out, gone.

प्रस्थिति (Rām.) = **कीर्ति**, *q.v.*

प्रस्फुट, *m.* (*f.* ā) cleft open, blown, expanded, spread abroad, divulged, published; manifest, clear, plain, apparent, evident.

प्रस्फुटित, *m.* (*f.* ā) = **प्रस्फुट**, *q. v.*

प्रस्फोटन, *m.* an expanding, opening; a striking; a winnowing corn: winnowing-basket.

प्रस्फोटित, *m.* (*f.* ā) = **पस्फट**, *q. v.*

प्रस्मृति, *f.* a forgetting; forgetfulness.

प्रस्राव, *m.* a flowing, dropping; urine.

प्रहर, *m.* a watch, a certain division of time consisting of eight gharees or an eighth part of a day, *i. e.* about three hours.

प्रहरण, *m.* a striking, pecking, biting; a weapon; battle; a small covered car, litter.

प्रहरणकलिका, *f.* a species of the *sarkarī* metre.

प्रहरिता, *f.* vigilance; the office of a watchman or sentry.

प्रहरिय = **प्रहरी**, *q.v.*

प्रहरी, *m.* (*f.* iṇī) a watchman, sentry, sentinel, bellman, patrol.

प्रहर्ष, *m.* a joy, gladness, hilarity, mirth, merriness.

प्रहर्षिणी, *f.* a species of the *atijagatī* metre.

प्रहर्षित, *m.* (*f.* ā) very happy, delighted, merry.

प्रहलाद, *more prop.* **प्रह्लाद**, *q.v.*

प्रहसत, *adj.* laughing violently or heartily.

प्रहसन, *m.* violent or hearty laughter, merriment, mirth; sarcasm, satire, mockery, ridicule, irony, reproof.

प्रहसन्ती, *f.* Arabian jasmine.

प्रहार, *m.* a striking, pecking, wounding, killing; a blow, stroke, shot, kick.

प्रहारक, *m.* (*f.* ikā) a striker, smiter, warrior, hero, destroyer, murderer, debaser, humbler: lit. *adj.* beating, smiting, killing.

प्रहारण, *m.* a striking: a desirable gift.

प्रहारना, *t.* to strike.

प्रहारित, discharged (as a missile).

प्रहारी, *m.* (*f.* iṇī) = **प्रहारक**, *q.v.*

प्रहास, *m.* loud laughter; an actor; an epithet of Shiv.

प्रहासी, *m.* (*f.* inī) *adj.* laughing aloud: diverting, causing laughter.

प्रहेलिका, *f.* a puzzling question, enigma, riddle.

प्रहृष्ट, *m.* (*f.* ā) = **प्रह्लादित**, *q.v.*

प्रह्लाद, *m.* joy, pleasure, happiness: *pr. n.* Hiraṇyāksha's pious son, who is a Daitya and regent of one of the divisions of Pātāl.

प्रह्लादन, *m.* (*f.* ī) one who causes joy: *lit.* adj. rejoicing, refreshing.

प्रह्लादित, *m.* (*f.* ā) joyous, happy, delighted, pleased.

प्रांगण, *m.* (=**पागन**) a sort of drum.

प्रांगन, *m.* a court, courtyard.

प्रांच, *m.* (*f.* **पाची**) = **प्राक**, *q. v.*

प्रांजलि, *f.* the putting the hands together to the forehead as a mark of respect.

प्राक, preceding in time or in place, former, prior, before, in front; at early morning; east, eastern, eastward.

प्राक्काल, *m.* former time or age.

प्राक्फल्गुणी, *f. pr. n.* the eleventh *Nakshastra.*

प्राकरमी, a corruption of **पराक्रमी**, *q.v.*

प्राकार, *m.* a surrounding wall, enclosure, rampart, fence.

प्राकाश्य, *m.* clearness, brightness; celebrity.

प्राकृत, *m.* (*f.* ī) natural, material, illusory; low, uncultivated, unrefined, provincial, plebeian, vulgar: *lit.* appertaining to *Prakriti.* This term is used to designate a peculiarly broken dialectic form of the Sanskrit language which is used particularly in dramatic compositions by the females and inferior personages; it is also applied to any of the simplified provincial dialects derived from Sanskrit.

प्राकृतकवि (*Rām.*) = **सूरदास आदि**.

प्राकृतज्वर, *m.* common or usual fever (occurring from affections of the wind, bile, and phlegm severally, in as many seasons, *viz.* in the rains, the autumn, and the spring.

प्राकृतप्रलय, *m.* the total dissolution of the world.

प्राकृतभाषा, *f.* = **प्राकृत**, *q.v.*

प्राकृतमित्र, *m.* (*f.* ā) a natural friend or ally.

प्राक्काल, *m.* a former age, former time ; a crisis.

प्राक्कालीन, *m.* (*f.* ā) appertaining to an ancient or previous time, former, previous.

प्राक्तन, *m.* (*f.* ī) ancient, old, former, preceding, anterior, prior ; appertaining to a former state of existence, resulting from the acts of a former birth; *hence*, fate, destiny.

प्राक्तनकर्म्म, *m.* any act formerly done, fate, destiny.

प्राग (*contraction*) = **प्रयाग**, *q.v.*

प्राग्ज्योतिष, *m.* an epithet of the country of *Kāmrūp*, in Assam, being the scene of Brahmā's penance.

प्रागभाव, *m.* antecedent privation, or the non-existence of any effect previous to production ; (in Law) the non-possession of property that may yet be possessed.

प्रागल्भ्य, *m.* confidence, boldness, arrogance, effrontery, determination ; pomp ; rank ; proficiency.

प्रागवाल = **प्रयागवाल**, *q.v.*

प्राग्गामी, *adj.* going before: hence, *m.* (*f.* inī) a precursor.

प्राग्भाव, *m.* prior existence ; superiority, excellence.

प्राग्य, *m.* (*f.* ā) a chief: *lit.* principal, chief.

प्राग्रहर, *m.* (*f.* ā *or* ī) a chief, principal : *lit.* adj. going before.

प्राच, *m.* (*f.* ī) *more prop.* **प्रांच**, *q.v.*

प्राचार, deviating from ordinary institutions and observances, contrary to rectitude.

प्राचार्य्य, *m.* (*f.* ā) a scholar, pupil.

प्राची, *f.* (*m.* **प्रांच**) east, eastern : the East.

प्राचीन, 1, *m.* (*f.* ā) an ancient : *lit.* belonging to the front or former part, prior, former, ancient ; east, eastern : 2, *f.* a bound, hedge, fence, a wall.

प्राचीनत्व, *m.* (*f.* tā) oldness, antiquity.

प्राचीनपनस, *m.* the bael-tree (*Ægle marmelos*).

प्राचीनबर्हिष, *m. pr. n.* the eldest son of Horadhān.

प्राचीना, *f.* (*m.* **प्राचीन**) a certain plant (*Cissampelos hexandra.*)

प्राचीनामलक, *m.* a certain fruit (*Flacourtia cataphracta*).

प्राचीनावीत, *m.* the sacrificial thread (worn over the right arm and passing under the left).

प्राचीर, *m.* a bound hedge, fence, inclosure, rampart, wall.

प्राच्य, *m. pr. n.* the eastern country, *i.e.* the country south or east of the river Saraswatee (which flows from the north-east to the south-west) ; *lit.* eastern, easterly.

प्राजापति, *more prop.* **प्रजापति**, *q.v.*

प्राजापत्य, *m. lit.* appertaining to Prajāpati (Brahmā) or to the Prajāpatis; *hence* (1) an appellation of Prayāg (Allahabad) (2) a form of marriage in which the damsel is presented respectfully to the bridegroom by her father (3) a certain festival on the eighth day of the second half of the month *Paush* (4) a certain sacrifice performed before appointing a daughter to raise issue in default of male heirs (5) the asterism *Rohinī* (6) a kind of penance which consists in eating but once a day for three days in the morning ; then, once in the night for three nights ; then, subsisting for three days on food given as alms ; and then fasting three days more.

प्राजापत्या, *f.* the giving away the whole of one's property before entering on the life of an ascetic or mendicant.

प्राङ्मुख, facing the east.

प्राज्ञ, *m.* (*f.* ā *or* ī) a learned person, etc. : *lit.* patient in investigation, wise, clever, sensible, learned.

प्राज्ञत्व, *m.* (*f.* tā) learning, wisdom, skill, cleverness.

प्राज्ञमान, *m.* respect for the learned.

प्राज्ञमानी, *m* (*f.* inī) one who respects the learned; *lit.* adj. respecting the learned.

प्राज्ञा, *f.* (*m.* **प्राज्ञ**) a clever female ; a paṇḍit's wife.

प्राज्ञी = **प्राज्ञा**, *q.v.*

प्राज्वार, *more prop.* **प्रज्वार**, *q.v.* See **ज्व**, 15.

प्राट (*Rām.*) = **वर्षा**, *q.v.*

प्राड्विवाक, *m.* a judge, chief magistrate.

प्राण, *m.* breath, respiration, vital action generally, air inhaled, wind, inspiration ; one of the five vital airs ; a vital organ, the senses and organs : poetical talent or inspiration : *met. m.* (*f.* ā) a sweetheart, mistress : (in Gram.) aspiration in the articulation of letters : an appellation of Brahm, the Supreme Soul. — *tajnā*, to die. — *denā*, to make a sacrifice of one's life. In allusion to the five modes of inspiration, this word, in the ingenious system of reckoning by symbols adopted by Hindoos in their poetry, is a symbol for 5.

प्राणक, *m.* any animal or sentient being: a certain plant (*Celtis orientalis*).

प्राणग्राहक, *adj.* seizing life, destroying : hence, *m.* (*f.* ikā) a destroyer.

प्राणग्राही, *m.* (*f.* iṇī) = **प्राणग्राहक**, *q.v.*

प्राणघात, *m.* the destroying life, killing, murder.

प्राणघातक, *m.* (*f.* ikā) *adj.* destroying life, killing.

प्राणतुल्य, *m.* (*f.* ā) = **प्राणसम**, *q.v.*

प्राणतुल्या, *f.* = **प्राणसमा**, *q.v.*

प्राणत्याग, *m.* relinquishment of life, dying; suicide. — *k.* to give up the ghost.

प्राणदण्ड, *m.* the punishment of death, capital punishment. *Kisike* — *kā bichār k.* to try someone for a capital offence. — *khānā*, to suffer capital punishment. — *denā*, to pronounce or to execute the sentence of death.

प्राणदाता, *m.* (*f.* tri) a life-giver ; one who saves another's life.

प्राणदान, *m.* the gift of life ; saving anyone's life ; the resigning or laying down life.

प्राणधारण, *m.* supporting life ; sustenance.

प्राणन, *m.* the throat ; respiratiou, breathing ; living, life ; producing life, calling into life : *adj.* life-producing.

प्राणनाथ, *m.* an epithet of a husband, also of the Supreme ; *lit.* the lord or sovereign of life (an expression of endearment).

प्राणनाश, *m.* destruction or cessation of breath ; destruction of the life.

प्राणनाशक, *m.* (*f.* ikā) *adj.* stopping the breath ; life-destroying.

प्राणान्त, *m.* a sort of collyrium.

प्राणान्ती, *f.* hiccough ; sneezing.

प्राणपति = **प्राणनाथ**, *q.v.*

प्राणप्यारा, dear as life, dear to one's soul, beloved, dear : hence, *m.* (*f.* ī) a sweetheart, spouse, darling.

प्राणप्रतिष्ठा, *f.* the ceremony of consecrating (*lit.* imparting life to) an idol.

प्राणप्रदा, *f.* a certain medicinal plant commonly called *Riddhi*.

प्राणप्रिय, *m.* (*f.* ā) = **प्राणप्यारा**, *q.v.*

प्राणबाध, *m.* fear of life, extreme peril or distress.

प्राणमय, *m.* (*f.* ī) any living being: *lit.* consisting in (or endowed with) breath or life.

प्राणमयकोष, *m.* the vital or organic case (one of the cases or investitures of the soul).

प्राणमयी, *f.* (*m.* **प्राणमय**) a living female.

प्राणयात्रा, *f.* support of life, subsistence.

प्राणवान, *m.* (*f.* vatī) endowed with life.

प्राणव्यय, *m.* an epithet of death; *lit.* expenditure of life.

प्राणसंयम, *m.* a certain religious exercise consisting in the suspending the breath.

प्राणसम, *m.* (*f.* ā) one who is as dear as life itself: *lit.* similar or equal to life.

प्राणसमा, *f.* (*m.* **प्राणसम**) a wife (considered as one's life, or as equal to life).

प्राणसमान, *m.* (*f.* a *or* ī) = **प्राणसम**, *q.v.*

प्राणसमाना / **प्राणसमानी** } = **प्राणसमा**, *q.v.*

प्राणहर, *m.* (*f.* ī) taking away life, murderous, mortal, deadly.

प्राणहारक, *m.* (*f.* ikā) / **प्राणहारी**, *m.* (*f.* iṇī) } = **प्राणहर**, *q.v.*

प्राणा, *f.* (*m.* **प्राण**) a mistress, etc.

प्राणाधिक, an epithet of one who is dearer than life; *lit.* more than life.

प्राणाधिनाथ = **प्राणनाथ**, *q.v.*

प्राणान्त, *m.* the end of life, *i.e.* death.

प्राणान्तिक, *m.* murder, assassination: *adj.* destructive of life, fatal, capital (as punishment).

प्राणापहारी, taking away life, fatal, deadly.

प्राणायाम, *m.* a restraining the breath. The term is particularly applied to describe a peculiar method of breathing through the nostrils during the time of the mental recitation of the names or attributes of some deity. It is differently performed, *e. g.* the Vaidyas first close the right nostril with the thumb, and inhale breath through the left; then, they close both nostrils, and, finally, open the right for exhalation: the followers of the Tantras, again, close the left nostril first, and ultimately exhale also through it.

प्राणिक, *adj.* appertaining to life, animal.

प्राणी, *m.* (*f.* inī) any animated being, an animal: lit. *adj.* possessing life, living, breathing.

प्राणीपीड़ा, *f.* cruelty to animals.

प्राणीमाता, *f.* a mother.

प्राणीवाचक शब्द, *m.* (in Gram.) a word indicating an animate object (as distinguished from an inanimate one).

प्राणीहिंसा, *f.* injury to life.

प्राणोचित, salutary to life.

प्राणेश = **प्राणनाथ**, *q.v.*

प्राणेशा, *f.* an epithet of a wife; *lit.* queen of life (an expression of endearment).

प्राणेश्वर = **प्राणनाथ**, *q.v.*

प्रायठा; see **पराठा** and **परायठा**.

प्रात, *more prop.* **प्रातः**, *q.v.*

प्रातः, in the morning, early, at dawn.

प्रातःकर्म, *m.* a matutine ceremony, a religious duty to be performed in the morning.

प्रातःकाल, *m.* early morning, the dawn of day, the early part of the day: *adv.* at early morning.

प्रातःक्रिया, *f.* / **प्रातःकृत्य**, *m.* } = **प्रातःकर्म**, *q.v.*

प्रातःसमय = **प्रातःकाल**, *q.v.*

प्रातःस्नान, *m.* morning ablution (*esp.* as a religious exercise).

प्रातकाल, *more prop.* **प्रातःकाल**, *q.v.*

प्रातकृत (*Rām.*) = **प्रातःकृत्य**, *q.v.*

प्रातक्रिया (*Rām.*) = **प्रातःक्रिया**, *q.v.*

प्रातर = **प्रातः**, *q.v.*

प्रातराश / **प्रातर्भोजन** } *m.* a morning meal, breakfast.

प्रातष्काल = **प्रातःकाल**, *q.v.*

प्रातसमय, *more prop.* **प्रातःसमय**, *q.v.*

प्राताप (*corruption*) = **प्रताप**, *q.v.*

प्रातिपदिक, *m.* (in Gram.) a crude noun, a noun in its uninflected state.

प्रातिभाव्य, *m.* the becoming bail or surety for anyone, surety, suretyship.

प्रात्ययिक, *m.* (*f.* ā *or* ī) a surety, etc.: *lit.* attended with confidence, having faith in, confidential, trusty.

प्राथमिक, appertaining to the first, prior, first, previous, initial, initiative.

प्राथमिकता, *f.* / **प्राथमिकत्व**, *m.* } = **प्राथम्य**, *q.v.*

प्राथम्य, *m.* firstness, priority, precedence.

प्रादक्षिण्य, *m.* circumambulation.

प्रादुर्भाव, *m.* the being evident, appearance, manifestation; greatness, ascendancy.

प्रादेश, *m.* the span of the thumb and forefinger: place, country.

प्रान; for words beginning thus, see under the form **प्राण**.

प्रान्त, *m.* edge, margin, border, end, extremity.

प्रापक, *m.* (*f.* ikā): used in comp. in the sense of obtainer, procurer; *lit.* adj. obtaining, procuring, causing to obtain.

प्रापण, *m.* an obtaining, acquiring, attaining, procuring.

प्रापना, to obtain, get, require, attain.

प्रापित, obtained, procured.

प्रापे in Braj = **प्राप्त करनेसे** (**प्रापना**).

प्राप्त, *m.* (*f.* ā) obtained, gained, acquired, received, procured; fixed, placed; proper, right. — *k.* to obtain, receive.

प्राप्तकाल, 1, *m.* a fitting time, proper season: 2, *m.* (*f.* ā) one whose fated time has come; fated, destined: 3, opportune, in season.

प्राप्तबुद्धि, instructed, intelligent, enlightened: recovering, becoming conscious (after fainting).

प्राप्तार्थ, successful, having attained one's object.

प्राप्तावसर, opportune, seasonable; taking or finding occasion.

प्राप्ति, *f.* an obtaining, getting, acquisition; profit, gain, income, produce, advantage, benefit; success; improvement; ascent; rise: *pr. n.* a sister of Asti, daughter of Jarāsandh and wife of Sham.

प्राप्य, obtainable, procurable, acquirable, attainable.

प्राबल्य, *m.* predominance, ascendancy, vigour, power.

प्राभव, *m.* superiority, preëminence.

प्राभवत्व, *m.* superiority in power, authority, ascendancy.

प्रामर्श, *more prop.* **परामर्श**, *q. v.*

प्रामाणिक, *m.* (*f.* ā *or* ī) one who supports his arguments by reference to written authorities, a learned man; a president, the chief or head of a trade, etc.: *lit.* established by proof, supported by authority, authentic, credible: possessing or exercising authority, authoritative.

प्रामाण्य, *m.* susceptibility of proof; the being established by proof or supported by authority, credibility, authenticity, genuineness, authority, proof.

प्रामाद्य, *m.* madness, frenzy, fury, intoxication; a certain tree (*Justicia adhenotoda*).

प्राय, *m.* (= **प्रायः**) a going away, departure, death (particularly a fasting to death by way of penance, and especially after the abandonment of all worldly goods and desires): age: sin: quantity, plenty, abundance; a banquet, feast. Used as a suffix in comp. in the sense of almost, like, resembling; *e. g.* **अमृतप्राय**, nectarlike. It is also used (like **प्रायः**) as a separable prefix.

प्रायः, generally, commonly, for the most part, in nearly all cases, nearly, about, nearly all, probably.

प्रायण, *m.* death, voluntary death.

प्रायश्चित्त, *m.* penance, expiation, atonement, punishment.

प्रायश्चित्तकर्त्ता, *m.* (*f.* trī) one who effects expiation.

प्रायश्चित्तमुक्तावली, *f.* any work prescribing the rules of expiation.

प्रायश्चित्तवाला, *m.* (*f.* ī) one who effects expiation.

प्रायश्चित्तविधि, *f.* rules for penance or for expiation.

प्रारब्ध (= **प्रारब्धि**, *q. v.*) begun, commenced; caused by fate.

प्रारब्धहीन, *m.* (*f.* ā) luckless, ill-fated, unfortunate.

प्रारब्धि, *f.* beginning; predestination, destiny, fortune, fate, lot, venture, chance: a rope for binding an elephant.

प्रारम्भ, *m.* beginning; undertaking.

प्रार्थक, *m.* (*f.* ikā) one who sues or woos, a petitioner, suitor, candidate, asker: *lit.* adj. asking, sueing, begging, soliciting.

प्रार्थना, *f.* an asking, petitioning, begging; supplication, suit, desire, request, petition, prayer.—*k.* (with gen. or acc. of object) to sue, petition, beseech, pray.

प्रार्थनापत्र, *m.* a written petition.

प्रार्थनीय, *m.* an epithet of the third or Dwāpar age: *lit.* adj. to be asked or begged.

प्रार्थित, solicited, begged, wished for, entreated.

प्रालब्ध, *m.* predestination, destiny, fate, fortune, lot, venture, chance.

प्रालम्ब, *m.* a necklace, garland hanging down from the neck to the breast.

प्रालम्बिका, *f.* = **प्रालम्ब**, *q. v.*

प्रावट, *m.* barley.

प्रावन्य, *more com.* **प्राबल्य**, *q. v.*

प्राविट (*Rām.*) = **प्रावृट**, *q. v.*

प्रावीण्य, *m.* cleverness, skilfulness; accurate knowledge.

प्रावृट = **प्रावृष**, *q. v.*

प्रावृत, *m.* a mantle, cloak, wrapper, veil.

प्रावृता, *f.* = **प्रावृत**, *q. v.*

प्रावृत्ति, *f.* an inclosure, fence, hedge.

प्रावृष, *m.* the rainy season, the two months Shrāvaṇ and Bhādra (July and August).

प्रावृषा, *f.* = **प्रावृष**, *q. v.*

प्रावृषायणी, *f.* cowach (*Carpopogon pruriens*).

प्रावृषेण्य, *m.* the *kadamb*-tree (*Nauclea cadamba*).

प्राशन, *m.* (esp. = **अन्नप्राशन**) a causing to eat; the act of eating.

प्रास, *m.* a bearded dart.

प्रासंगिक, inseparably connected, contiguous, pertaining to, inherent, innate.

प्रासक, *m.* a die, dice.

प्रासाद, *m.* a building consecrated to a deity or inhabited by a prince, a temple, a palace.

प्रिय, *m.* (*f.* ā) a beloved object, a husband, a lover; a sort of drug commonly called *Riddhi*; a sort of drug: *lit.* beloved, dear, agreeable, desired. — *lagnā*, (with acc. of agent) to like, to esteem dear; *e. g. Majhe priyā lagtī hai*, I love her, *i. e.* she is dear to me.

प्रियंगु, *m.* a certain medicinal plant and perfume (described as a fragrant seed) sometimes called *phalī*; panic-seed (*Panicum Italicum*); black mustard-seed; long pepper.

प्रियक, *m.* the plants *Nauclea cadamba* and *Pentaptera tomentosa*; a kind of deer; a certain bird; a bee.

प्रियकर / **प्रियंकार** } *m.* (*f.* ī) = **प्रियकारी**, *q. v*

प्रियकारी, *m.* (*f.* iṇī) a benefactor, friend, etc.: *lit.* adj. doing that which is agreeable and pleasing, doing good or treating kindly, beneficent, affectionate, kind, friendly.

प्रियकृत, *m.* (*f.* ā) = **प्रियकारी**, *q v.*

प्रियतम, *m.* (*f.* ā) a favorite friend, lover, sweetheart, husband, beloved: *lit.* (superl.) most beloved, dearest.

प्रियतर, (compar.) dearer, more beloved.

प्रियत्व, *m.* (*f.* tā) the being dear or beloved; affection, love.

प्रियदर्शन, *m.* (*f.* ā) a lovely-looking person; a certain tree (*Mimusops kauki*): *lit.* lovely-looking, beautiful, handsome.

प्रियभाषण, *m.* a speaking kindly.

प्रियभाषी, *m.* (*f.* iṇī) = **प्रियवादी**, *q. v.*

प्रियमान, *m.* (*f.* matī) a beloved person; an affectionate person: *lit.* beloved; affectionate.

प्रियम्भावुक, become dear to or beloved by.

प्रियम्भावुकत्व, *m.* (*f.* tā) the state or condition of amiability or of becoming beloved.

प्रियवचन, *m.* a word of love.

प्रियवर्णी, *f.* the creeping-plant *Echites frutescens*.

प्रियवादी, *m.* (*f.* inī) a pleasant-spoken person; a flatterer: *lit.* sweet or pleasant-spoken, flattering.

प्रियव्रत, *m. pr. n.* a certain Hindoo sage, son of Swaymbhū-Manu and Satrūpā.

प्रियसख, *m.* a certain tree (*Mimosa catechu*).

प्रियसखी, *f.* a female friend or companion, a confidante.

प्रियसन्देश, *m.* a certain tree (*Michælia champaca*) that bears a fragrant flower.

प्रिया, *f.* (*m.* प्रिय) a beloved female, a mistress, sweetheart, wife. This word is sometimes added to the name of a man for the purpose of forming an epithet of his wife; *e.g.* रामप्रिया, Rām's beloved, *i.e.* Seetā.

प्रियाख्य, *adj.* announcing good tidings.

प्रियाल, *m.* a certain tree (*Buchanania latifolia*) commonly called *piyal.*

प्रियावत, *m.* (*f.* vatī) = प्रियावान, *q.v.* [heart.

प्रियावती, *f.* (*m.* प्रियावान) a female spouse, sweet-

प्रियावर्त्त; see (1) प्रियव्रत (2) प्रियावत.

प्रियावान, *m.* (*f.* vatī) having a mistress, enamoured, being in love with.

प्रीत, 1, a contraction of प्रीति, *q.v.*: 2, *m.* (*f.* ā) beloved, pleased, delighted, satisfied, kind, affectionate.

प्रीतम = प्रियतम, *q.v.*

प्रीता, *f.* (*m.* प्रीत) a female friend, etc.

प्रीति, *f.* joy, enjoyment, gratification; love, affection, amiableness, friendliness, regard, good fellowship; *pr. n.* (1) of the second Nakshatra (2) of the wife of Kāmdev. [love or regard.

प्रीतिकर, *m.* (*f.* ī) kind, affectionate; inspiring

प्रीतिकारक, *m.* (*f.* ikā) } = प्रीतिकर, *q.v.*
प्रीतिकारी, *m.* (*f.* iṇī) }

प्रीतिदान, *m.* a friendly present, a gift of love, token of affection or of regard.

प्रीतिदाय, *m.* = प्रीतिदान, *q.v.*

प्रीतिपूर्वक, through favor or kind regard.

प्रीतिभाव, *m.* courteousness. [friendly, charitable.

प्रीतिमान, *m.* (*f.* matī) affectionate, loving, kind,

प्रीतियुक्त, *m.* (*f.* ā) प्रीतिमान, *q.v.*

प्रीतियुत, *more prop.* प्रीतियुक्त, *q.v.*

प्रीतिवती } = प्रीतिमती, *q.v.*
प्रीतिवन्ती }

प्रीतिवान, *m.* (*f.* vatī) = प्रीतिमान, *q v.*

प्रीती, *more prop.* प्रीति, *q.v.*

प्रीबीन (*corruption*) = प्रवीन, *q.v.*

प्रेक्षण, *m.* a seeing, looking, viewing; the eye; any shew or spectacle, a sight.

प्रेक्षा, *f.* a seeing, beholding, observing; the intellect; consideration; dancing; any public spectacle.

प्रेक्षित, seen, viewed, beheld. [be seen.

प्रेक्ष्य, admitting of being seen, fit or requiring to

प्रेत, *m.* (*lit.* departed; deceased, dead; *hence*) a spirit of the dead, a ghost, goblin, sprite, evil spirit, fiend. [ed ancestors.

प्रेतकर्म्म, *m.* solemn obsequies in honour of deceas-

प्रेतकार्य्य, *m.* } = प्रेतकर्म्म, *q.v.*
प्रेतक्रिया, *f.* }

प्रेतगृह, *m.* a burial-ground, cemetery.

प्रेतजोनी, *more prop.* प्रेतयोनि, *q.v.*

प्रेतनदी, *f. pr. n.* the river of hell.

प्रेतनिवास = प्रेतगृह or मसान, *qq. v.*

प्रेतनी, *f.* (*m.* प्रेत) a female ghost. See नी, 4.

प्रेतपक्ष, *m.* the dark half of the month.

प्रेतयोनि = प्रेतलोक, *q.v.*

प्रेतलोक, *m. pr. n.* the region or habitation of disembodied spirits, in which they remain for one year (or, according to some, for a thousand years), or until the obsequial rites are completed.

प्रेम, *m.* love, affection, tender regard, kindliness, friendship. — *k.* (with acc. or [more commonly] abl. of the object) to love.

प्रेमपर, *m.* (*f.* ā) one who is constant in love: *lit.*

प्रेमबस = प्रेमवश, *q.v.* [constant, loving, affectionate.

प्रेमभक्त, *f. m.* (*f.* ā) devoted to the exercise of love.

प्रेमरंगराता, *lit.* colored with the dye of love, *i.e.* strongly attached, enamoured of.

प्रेमरस, *m.* the quality or the essence of love.

प्रेमलता, *f.* a creeping-plant, parasitic plant.

प्रेमवती, *f.* (*m.* प्रेमवान) a mistress, spouse.

प्रेमवश, *m.* (*f.* ā) under the power of love, steeped in it, over head and ears in it, enamoured.

प्रेमवान, *m.* (*f.* vatī) full of love, affectionate.

प्रेमवाला, *m.* (*f.* ī) *adj.* possessing affection, loving.

प्रेमसंयुक्त, *m.* (*f.* ā) connected with love, having relation to love.

प्रेमसागर, *m. pr. n.* (1) of the tenth section of the Bhāgavat Purāṇ, in which the love-sports of Krishn are related (2) an epithet of God; *lit.* the ocean of love.

प्रेमी, *m.* (*f.* inī) an affectionate person, a lover: *lit.* affectionate, loving, friendly. [ing, ordering.

प्रेरक, *m.* (*f.* ikā) *adj.* sending, despatching, direct-

प्रेरण, *m.* a sending, directing, ordering; command; sensual excitement, passion; (in Gram.) a causal verb.

प्रेरणा, *f.* instigation, injunction, directing, sending, ordering; command.

प्रेरणायुक्त, *m.* (*f.* ā) connected with a प्रेरणा, *q. v.*

प्रेरणार्थक, *adj.* having the sense of inciting or of the causal verb; hence, — *kriyā*, (in Gram.) the causal verb. [tor, commander.

प्रेरयिता, *m.* (*f.* trī) an instigator, sender, direc-

प्रेरित, *m.* (*f.* ā) an envoy, messenger, apostle, missionary: *lit.* sent, directed, despatched. [an apostle.

प्रेरितसंगी, *m.* (*f.* inī) a companion of an envoy or of

प्रेरिताई } *f.* = प्रेरितत्व, *q.v.*
प्रेरितता }

प्रेरितत्व, *m.* the occupation or the status of a messenger, etc., envoyship, mission, apostleship.

प्रेरे, (*Rām.*) sent, despatched.

प्रेषित, sent, directed, ordered, despatched.

प्रेष्ठ, (superl.) *m.* (*f.* ā) very dear, most beloved,

प्रेष्ठा, *f.* (*m.* प्रेष्ठ) a wife, sweetheart. [dearest.

प्रेस, *m.* (Engl.) a printing-press; a printing-office.

प्रोक्त, *m.* (*f.* ā) uttered, said, declared.

प्रोक्षण, *m.* sprinkling with water (*esp.* for purification); immolation of animals in sacrifice; killing; a text to be repeated when animals are offered up.

प्रोक्षित, sprinkled, purified by sprinkling; slaughtered; offered up in sacrifice, immolated.

प्रोत्साह, *m.* great zeal, exertion, effort, incitement, stimulus.

प्रोत्साहक, *m.* (*f.* ikā) the instigator of any act, or (in Law) of any crime.

प्रोत्साहन, *m.* instigating, inciting, stimulating.

प्रोत्साहिका, *f.* (*m.* **प्रोत्साहक**) a female instigator.

प्रोत्साहित, *m.* (*f.* ā) instigated, incited, stimulated, encouraged.

प्रोष्ठ, *m.* a sort of carp (*Cyprinus pransius*, or *C. chrysoparius*, Buch.).

प्रोष्ठपद, *m.* the month *Bhādra* (Aug.-Sept.).

प्रोष्ठपदा, *f. pr. n.* (= **भाद्रपदा**) the 26th and 27th *Nakshatras* (containing stars in the wing of Pegasus).

प्रोष्ठपदी; see **प्रौष्ठपदी**.

प्रोहित, *more prop.* **पुरोहित**, *q.v.*

प्रौढ़, *m.* (*f.* ā) full-grown, adult, married; confident, audacious, bold, able, clever.

प्रौढ़त्व, *m.* (*f.* tā) strength, firmness; breadth.

प्रौढ़ा, *f.* (*m.* **प्रौढ़**) a woman between thirty and fifty-five years of age; a violent or impetuous female.

प्रौढ़ि, *f.* confident or audacious exertion, enterprize, zeal, exertion; discussion, investigation.

प्रौष्ठपद, *m.* the month *Bhādra* (Aug.-Sept.).

प्रौष्ठपदी, *f.* full moon in *Bhādra*.

प्लक्ष, *m.* the waved-leaf figtree (*Ficus infectoria*): the holy fig-tree (*Ficus religiosa*); another tree (*Hibiscus popuincoides*) a side door; *m. pr. n.* one of the seven dweeps.

प्लक्षद्वीप, *m.pr.n.* (see **द्वीप**) one of the seven dweeps.

प्लव, *m.* a leaping, jumping, swimming, floating; a raft, float; a frog; a monkey; a species of water-bird, (*Pelicanus fusicollis*, Buch.); a sort of grass (*Cyperus rotundus*); waved-leaf figtree (*Ficus infectoria*); fragrant grass in general: lit. *adj.* jumping, leaping, floating.

प्लवंग / **प्लवंगम** } *m.* (*f.* ā) = **प्लवग**, *q.v.*

प्लवग, *m.* (*f.* ā) an ape, monkey; a frog; a deer; a bird: *lit.* adj. going leaping.

प्लवन, *m.* 1, *more prop.* **प्लावन**, *q.v.*: 2, a plunging, jumping, leaping, or bounding.

प्लाक्ष, *m.* the fruit of the several trees called *Plaksh*.

प्लाव, *m.* submersion.

प्लावन, *m.* an inundation, deluge, flood.

प्लिनीयूस, *m. pr. n.* Pliny.

प्लिहन, *m.* / **प्लिहा**, *f.* } = **प्लीहा**, *q.v.*

प्लीहघ्न, *m.* a certain medicinal plant (*Andersonia rohitaka*, Roxb.) commonly called *Roherā* or *Rohini*.

प्लीहन = **प्लीहा**, *q.v.*

प्लीहशत्रु = **प्लीहघ्न**, *q.v.*

प्लीहा, *f.* the spleen; the disease called the spleen (in this latter sense, however, the word is equally applied to the enlargement of the mesenteric glands).

प्लीहारि, *f.* an epithet of the holy figtree (*Ficus religiosa*) which is deemed an enemy to the spleen.

प्लुत, *m.* the third sound given to vowels, *i.e.* the protracted or continuous sound, being three times the length of a short vowel, and occupying three moments in its utterance.

प्लेटफ़ार्म, *m.* (Engl.) a railway platform.

फ

फ (ph) is the twenty-second consonant in the Hindee alphabet, and the second letter of the **पवर्ग** or labial class. It is the aspirate of **प**, and its legitimate sound is nearly that of *ph* in the English word 'loophole' with the *ole* dropped; in words, however, of Persian or Arabic parentage, it is sometimes pronounced like *f* (*e.g.* **दर्याफ़्त**), and occasionally like *v* (*e.g.* **लफ़्ज़**): that either of these latter is the true pronunciation in any case is indicated in the present work by a dot under the letter. Like all the aspirated letters, it is occasionally interchanged inadvertently or provincially with its simple or unaspirated form; *e.g.* **फत्तर = पत्तर**.

फंकना = **फिंकना**, *q.v.*

फंका, *m.* a handful (or rather, a mouthful) of anything eaten by being chucked into the mouth.—*mārnā*, to eat by chucking into the mouth, to chuck food into the mouth.

फंकी, *f.* = **फंका**, *q.v.*

फंगा, *m.* a grasshopper.

फंजिका, *f.* a certain plant (*Siphonanthus Indicus*): a species of Hedysarum (*H. alhagi*).

फंजिपुत्रिका, *f.* a certain plant (*Salvinia cucullata*).

फंद, **फंफ**; for words beginning thus, see under the forms **फन्द**, **फम्फ**, respectively.

फंसड़ी (Rām.) = **फांसी**, *q.v.*

फंसना, *n.* to be entangled, be ensnared, be noosed, be entrapped, be caught, be involved in calamity; to stick.

फंसली; see **पसली** and **फसली**.

फंसवाना, *t.* (causat. of **फसना**) to cause to be ensnared, etc.

फंसाना, *t.* to entrap, ensnare, catch.

फंसाव, *m.* entanglement.

फंसियारा, *m.* a footpad who strangles travellers (applied esp. to the *Thag*).

फंसीगार = **फंसियारा**, *q.v.*

फक, a sound, voice, noise.

फ़क़त, only, merely, simply, solely, no more.

फकड़ी, *f.* the act of treating with rudeness.

फकार, *m.* the letter **फ**, or any symbol that may represent it.

फकिया, *f.* a slice, a piece of fruit.

फकिर, *more prop.* **फ़क़ीर**, *q.v.*

फ़क़ीर, indigent, poor; *hence*, *m.* (*f.* ā, in, *or* nī) a beggar, dervesh, mendicant. This term is sometimes used to describe a person in whom are combined great apparent sanctity and an unusual degree of voluntary self-denial; but its usual and more restricted application is to a class of persons who assume a life of professedly religious poverty. Both Hindooism and Muhammadanism have their fakeers, whose relations to their respective religions are much the same as those of the monks to the Church of Rome. They are divided up into almost unnumbered sects which are more or less hostile to each other: their characters are said to be of the worst, and their poverty unreal.

फ़क़ीरी, *f.* fakeerism, poverty, humility.

फक़ीह, *m.* a man who is conversant with religion and law, a theologian, lawyer. [decent talker.

फकोड़िया, *m.* a fop, an absurd prattler, an in-

फकोड़ियात, *f.* absurdity, foppery. [raillery.

फक्कड़, *m.* mutual abuse, wrangling, brawling,

फक्कड़बाज़, *m.* an abuser, an indecent chatterer.

फक्कड़बाज़ी, *f.* abuse, indecent talk.

फक्का, *m.* (see **फंका**) a small quantity of parched grain to be chucked into the mouth.

फक्रिया, *f.* a sophism, a trick, illusion, fraud.

फक्त, *more prop.* **फ़क़त**, *q.v.*

फ़ख़र, *m.* glory, ornament, grace, nobility; boasting, egotism, pride, ostentation. — *k.* to boast, glory.

फगत in Mārwārī = **फ़क़त**, *q.v.*

फगली, *f.* = **फाग**, *q.v.* [ing the Holee holidays.

फगुआ, *m.* 1. = **होली**, *q.v.*: 2, presents made dur-

फ़जर, *f.* morning, dawn of day, early.

फ़ज़ल, *m.* excellence, virtue; increase, gain; favour,

फजिर, *more prop.* **फ़जर**, *q.v.* [gift, reward.

फजीत, in Mārwārī = **फ़ज़ीहत**, *q.v.* [ledge, learning.

फ़ज़ीलत, *f.* excellence, virtue, perfection; know-

फ़ज़ीहत, *f.* disgrace, ignominy, infamy.

फट पड़ना, to be produced plentifully; to become fat suddenly; to be confounded with too much business. *Āsmān phaṭ parnā*, to rain heavily.

फटक, *m.* (*prop.* **स्फटिक**) crystal.

फटकना, 1, *t.* to winnow; to dust, to shake or knock off any light thing which slightly adheres (as crumbs or dust): 2, *m.* to be separated; 3, *m.* the tape in a pellet-bow which strikes the ball.

फटकरी, *m.* (*f.*?) alum.

फटकार, ; see **फिटकार**.

फटकारना; see **फिटकारना**.

फटकी, *f.* a fowler's net; a large cage; a rope tied to a tree to frighten birds with its sound.

फटकी, *m.* (*f.*?) alum.

फटना, *n.* to be torn, be split, be rent, be broken, be cracked: *a. int.* to tear, split, crack, break, burst.

फटफटाना, *t.* to shake, flap, or clap the wings as birds just about fly; to give a sound as the shoes of a person walking.

फटा, 1, *m.* (*f.* ī) torn, split, rent, broken, cracked: 2, *m.* a crack, rent. *Phaṭemeṅ pāoṅ denā*, to interfere in any matter.

फटाना, *t.* to split, rend, tear, crack, break.

फटिक, *m.* (*prop.* **स्फटिक**) crystal.

फटी, *f.* = **फटा**, 1, *q.v.*

फटीआंखी, blear-eyed.

फठिक, *more prop.* **फटिक**, *q.v.*

फड़, *f.* a public house, open house, gambling-house, a gaming house where they play at dice: a place where goods are exposed for sale: the shaft or pole of a carriage. [brating, a flutter; a flap.

फड़क, *f.* a fluttering, palpitating, throbbing, vi-

फड़कना, *a. int.* to vibrate with convulsive, involuntary motion (as the muscles or eyelids), to twitch, to flutter, throb, palpitate, writhe (as the shoulders, etc.).

फड़काना, *t.* to cause to flutter, cause convulsive motion in the muscles, etc.: *met.* to shew.

फड़की, *f.* a coarse screen, a partition.

फड़फड़ाट = **फड़फड़ाहट**, *q.v.*

फड़फड़ाना, *a. int.* to flutter, wave, twinkle, move with convulsive emotion.

फड़फड़ाहट, *f.* agitation, flutter, disquietude.

फड़फड़िया, *m.* a flutterer: *adj.* quick, swift.

फड़बाज़, *m.* a dice-player, gambler: a talkative fellow, prater.

फड़बाज़ी, *f.* dice-playing, gambling: prating.

फड़वाना = **फड़ाना**, *q.v.* [split, or cleaved.

फड़ाना, *t.* (causat. of **फाड़ना**) to cause to be torn,

फड़ाफड़ी, *f.* quarrel, squabble, fight, battle, war.

फड़िंगा, *f.* a cricket. [inghouse or dice-table.

फड़िया, *m.* a pedlar, retailer: the keeper of a gam-

फड़ो, finally, at last, hence.

फण, *m.* the expanded hood or neck of a snake, but especially of the Cobra di capello (*Coluber naga*). — *uṭhānā*, to spread the hood (said of snakes).

फणाकर, *m.* (*f.* ī) a snake, especially the Cobra di capello (*Coluber naga*).

फणधर, *m.* (*f.* ā) = **फणाकर**, *q.v.* [of a snake.

फणमणि, *m.* the jewel supposed to be in the head

फणवन्त / **फणवान** } *m.* (*f.* vatī) = **फणाकर**, *q.v.*

फणा, *f.* = **फण**, *q.v.*

फणिक, *m.* (*f.* ā *or* ī) a snake, serpent.

फणिकेशर, *m.* a certain plant (*Messua ferrea*).

फणिखेल, *m.* a quail.

फणिज्झक, *m.* a certain plant, also called *marua*: a species of basil and of citron.

फणिज्झका, *f.* a certain plant (apparently a sort of basil with small leaves) commonly called *Rāmdūti*.

फणिन, *m.* (*f.* ī) = **फणाकर**, *q.v.* [Patañjali.

फणिनाथ, *m.* an epithet (1) of Sheshnāg (2) of

फणी, *m.* (*f.* inī) = **फणाकर**, *q.v.*

फणीपति / **फणीन्द्र** / **फणीश्वर** } = **फणिनाथ**, *q.v.*

फ़तवा, *m.* a judicial decree, judgment, sentence.

फ़ता, *m.* a youth: *adj.* young (animals).

फतिंगा, a moth, grasshopper, locust.

फ़तीला, *m.* a match, torch, wick: a wick composed of paper inscribed with mystic words, by inhaling the smoke of which demons are expelled from those possessed: a cord of twisted thread sewn between the two folds of the hem of a garment to strengthen it.

फतूर, *more prop.* **फ़ुतूर**, *q.v.* [rackmoss.

फत्तर, *m.* stone, a stone. — *kā phūl*, *m.* lichen,

फत्तरबन्दी, *f.* stone-work, masonry, paving.

फत्तरी, *f.* a small stone, a whetstone, hone, a flint,

फ़त्तान, *m.* an assayer of gold: *adj.* seditious, mischievous, malicious.

फत्री, *f.* = **फत्तरी**, *q.v.*

फदफदाना, *a. int.* to ferment (as sour milk, curds, etc.): *n.* to be inflamed with lust.

फन; for words beginning thus, but not given below, see under the form **फण**.

फनगा, *more com.* **फंगा**, *q.v.*

फनफना, the hiss of a snake.

फनफनाना, *a. int.* to hiss (as a snake); to spring up suddenly (as a fast-growing plant); to move about briskly (as a playful child).

फनस, *more com.* **पनस**, *q.v.*

फ़ना, *f.* mortality, frailty, death.

फना, *f.* (prop. **फणा**) a snake's hood: the forecastle of a ship.

फनि (Rām.) = **फणी**, *q.v.*

फनिक, (Rām.) *m.* (*f.* a *or* ī) = **फणिक**, *q.v.*

फनिगा; see **फनगा**.

फनिनाथ, *more prop.* **फणिनाथ**, *q.v.*

फनी, *m.* (prop. **फणी**) a serpent: a wedge.

फन्द (*contraction*) = **फन्दा**, *q.v.*

फन्दना, *n.* to be imprisoned, be ensnared.

फन्दलाना, *t.* to ensnare, entrap.

फन्दा, *m.* a noose, net, snare, trap, plot: *met.* difficulty, perplexity.

फन्दाना, *t.* to cause to jump over, cause to leap over.

फनूस, a corruption of **फ़ानूस**, *q.v.*

फपोला = **फफोला**, *q.v.*

फफसा, *m.* (*f.* ī) swollen: insipid.

फफुन्दी }
फफून्दी } *f.* mouldiness, mildew.

फफूला, *more prop.* **फफोला**, *q.v.*

फफोला, *m.* a blister, a bubble. — *phūṭnā*, to be blistered: *met.* to be afflicted in mind. *Phaphole dilke phornā*, to satisfy a revenge that has long been rankling in one's breast.

फब, *f.* embellishment, ornament, dress.

फबकना, *a. int.* to shoot forth (said of plants).

फबता, *m.* (*f.* ī) pertinent, fit, becoming, proper.

फबती, *f.* ornament; conjecturing what a person is by his dress.— *kahnā*, to say or conjecture by one's dress what sort of person (or of what caste) he is.

फबन, *f.* embellishment, ornament.

फबना, *a. int.* to become, befit, fit, be pertinent.

फबा }
फबीला } *m.* (*f.* ī) = **फबता**, *q.v.*

फ़म, *m.* the mouth.

फम्फ, land that requires to be left fallow for some time.

फ़यज़ान, *m.* abundance, overflow, redundance.

फयदा, *more prop.* **फ़ाइदा**, *q.v.*

फ़यार, employ, work, business, art.

फ़य्याज़, liberal, generous, profuse, copious, munificent, benevolent.

फर, 1, in Braj = **फिर**, *q.v.*: 2, *m.* a shield: a kind of fruit.

फरऊन, *more com.* **फिरऊन**, *q.v.*

फरंगी, *adj.* European: hence, *m.* (*f.* in *or* inī) a Frank, a European in general.

फरक, 1, *more prop.* **फड़क** or **फ़र्क़**, *qq.v.*: 2, *m.* a shield.

फरकना = **फड़कना**, *q.v.*

फरकाना = **फड़काना**, *q. v.*

फरचा, *m.* a clearing away or dispersion (as of clouds, or a multitude of people), fair weather: decision, definitive sentence (of a judge).

फरचाना, *t.* to decide, give a final sentence or decree.

फरका, 1, = **फरचा**, *q.v.*: 2, *m.* (*f.* ī) pure, honest, candid, fair, clear (not cloudy). — *k.* to clean, settle, sweep. — *honā*, to clear up (as the weather).

फरकाई, *f.* pureness, honesty, fairness, clearness of the sky, settledness of the weather.

फरकाना, *t.* to clean, wipe, settle: *a. int.* to clear away (said of clouds).

फ़रज, 1, = **फ़र्ज़**, *q.v.*: 2, *f.* cheerfulness, delight, pleasure, joy: the private parts.

फ़रजाम, *m.* end, conclusion, issue; happiness, prosperity; utility.

फ़रतूत, old and decrepit.

फरफन्द, *m.* deceit, trick, wickedness.

फरफन्दिया, deceitful, treacherous, wicked.

फरफराना; see **फुरफुराना**.

फरमबरदार = **फ़र्मान्बर्दार**, *q.v.*

फ़रमाइश, *f.* an order (particularly for goods, etc.), a commission; will, pleasure, commands.

फ़रमान, *m.* a mandate, command, order, decree, a royal patent, a royal commission.

फ़रमाना, *t.* to order, command; to give one's orders, speak by way of command; (when put into the mouths of kings or superiors it may signify) to say, to do, to accomplish.

फरमाबरदार = **फ़र्मान्बर्दार**, *q.v.*

फ़रयाद, *more prop.* **फ़र्याद**, *q.v.*

फरसा, *m.* (**परशु**) an axe, hatchet.

फ़रहंग, *f.* wisdom, understanding: a glossary, vocabulary, dictionary.

फरहरा, 1, *m.* a vane, pennant: 2, (*m. f.* ī) half dried.

फरहरी, *f.* = **फरहरा**, 1 and 2, *qq. v.*

फ़रहाद, *m.* a stone-cutter, digger of mines. So named from a celebrated Persian statuary who is said to have dug through an immense mountain to please his mistress Shirin.

फ़रा, back, behind, again, on, over, above, towards.

फराक़; see (1) **फ़राख़** (2) **फ़िराक़**.

फ़राख़, a joke, jest, pleasantry: *lit.* ample, abundant, large, wide, plentiful, cheap.

फ़राग़, *m.* cessation from labour, repose, rest, leisure, happiness; competency.

फ़राग़त, *f.* leisure, repose, ease, happiness, competency, abundance.

फ़राज़, *m.* an ascent, acclivity.

फ़रामोशी, *f.* forgetfulness, oblivion.

फरिंगी, *m.* (*f.* in *or* inī) *more prop.* **फ़रंगी**, *q.v.*

फरिया, *f.* a kind of bordered vestment worn by Hindoos: a contractor for reaping.

फरियाद, *more prop.* फ़र्याद, *q.v.*

फरी, *f.* a shield, buckler, target: one of several [fishes.

फ़रीक़, *m.* a troop, squadron, corps.

फरीशी } *m.* (in the New Test.) a pharisee.
फरीसी }

फरुवक, *m.* a betel-box.

फरुस्त, *more prop.* (1) फ़ुर्सत (2) फुरूसत, *qq.v.*

फरुहा, *m.* a kind of instrument for raking together.

फ़रेफ़्ता, deceived; enamoured.

फ़रेब, *m.* (*f.* ?) deceit, trick, deception, fraud, duplicity, treachery, imposture, fallacy.

फ़रोख़्त *f.* sale.—*k.* to sell.

फ़रोतनी, *f.* humility, submissiveness.

फ़रोद, *m.* a descending, alighting, stopping.

फ़रोमान्दा, dejected, tired, depressed, fatigued, weak, helpless.

फ़रोमाया, worthless, low, sordid, mean, ignoble.

फ़र्क़, *m.* difference, distinction, division, distance, dispersion; head, top, summit.

फर्काई = फरकाई, *q.v.* [mount duty, an obligation.

फ़र्ज़, *m.* a divine command, an absolute and para-

फ़र्ज़द, *m.* a great-grandfather.

फ़र्ज़न, hypothetically, for instance.

फ़र्ज़न्द, *m.* offspring, a child, son, daughter.

फ़र्ज़ाना, wise, intelligent, excellent, distinguished.

फ़र्त, excess, superfluity, abundance: a small hill, a hill-top; a road-mark.

फ़र्द, *f.* a sheet of paper; a statement; a list; a roll; a verse, a piece: an individual, one, single, odd.

फ़र्दा, to-morrow; *met.* the day of resurrection (to express the rapidity and the certainty of its approach).

फ़र्दी, *f.* a roll, catalogue.

फर्करीक, *m.* the palm of the hand with the fingers extended: sweetness: a shoot.

फ़र्मान्बर्दार, subject to orders, obedient.

फ़र्मान्बर्दारी, *f.* obedience, subjection.

फ़र्माना = फ़रमाना, *q.v.*

फ़र्याद, *f.* complaint, exclamation, lamentation, cry for help, petition. [plaintiff.

फ़र्यादी, one who sues for justice, a complainant,

फर्राटा, *m.* a piece of of bamboo: the sound made by the flying of a flag or by the breathing of a horse.

फर्राना, *a. int.* to fly, flutter (as a flag).

फ़र्राश, *m.* a servant whose business it is to spread carpets, etc., a sweeper, job-man.

फर्रास, *m.* a certain tree whose leaves resemble those of the cypress or of the tamarisk, and make a whistling noise in the wind (whence the name).

फ़र्रुख़, happy, fortunate.

फ़रोग़, *m.* illumination, light, splendour.

फ़रोश, *m.* a seller, vendor: selling, sale.

फ़र्श, *m.* a spreading; carpeting, bedding; a cushion, mat, carpet. [amusement.

फ़र्हत, *f.* delight, pleasure, cheerfulness, joy,

फल, *m.* fruit: *met.* result, consequence, effect, produce, advantage, acquisition, profit, gain, recompense, reward; offspring, progeny; the fulfilment of an omen; a fragrant sort of berry and drug commonly called *kakoli*; a nutmeg; a ploughshare, the blade of a sword or knife, the head of an arrow, spear; etc.; (in Arithm.) the quotient of a sum; a shield.—*denā*, to yield fruit.—*pānā*, to reap the reward of good or bad actions.—*phalnā* or *lānā*, to bring forth fruit.

फलई = फल्लकी, *q.v.*

फलंग, *f.* a stride, leap, bound, spring, jump.

फलंगना, *a int.* to frisk, bound, spring, leap, jump.

फलक, *m.* a board, a bench; a layer, a base; surface; a leaf for writing on; a shield; the bone of the forehead (*Os frontis*); a certain plant (*Mesua ferrea*).

फ़लक, *m.* the heavens, sky, firmament: fortune, fate.

फलकर, *m.* a branch of revenue arising from the rent of orchards; profits arising from the fruit-trees on an estate. [quence or result.

फलकामना, *f.* desire in reference to any conse-

फलकी, 1, = फल्लकी, *q.v.*: 2, *m.* (*f.* inī) one who is armed with a shield or who carries a shield.

फलकच्या, *m.* a certain small fruit (*Carissa carandas*) of a black colour.

फलकेशर, *m.* the cocoanut-tree.

फलकोषक, *m.* the scrotum or testicles.

फलखण्डन, *m.* a disappointing.

फलग्रहि, fruitful, bearing fruit in due season.

फलचमस, *m.* the bark of the Indian fig ground and eaten with curds, by way of penance. [prolific.

फलजनक, *m.* (*f.* ikā) fruitful, fruit-producing,

फलड़ा } *m.* blade (of a sword, knife, etc.).
फलड़ा }

फलत, fruitful, profitable, advantageous.

फलताड़, *m.* the fruit-bearing *tāṛ* (the female palm).

फलत्रय, *m.* three sorts of fruit collectively (*viz.* the fruit of the vine with those of the *Grewia Asiatica* or *Xylocarpus Granatum* and *Gmelina arborea*); the three myrobalans.

फलत्रिक = फलत्रय, *q.v.*

फलद, 1, *m.* a tree (*prop.* a fruit-tree): 2, *m.* (*f.* ā) one who rewards, a benefactor: lit. *adj.* yielding or bearing fruit, results, etc.; fertile, profitable, advantageous, efficacious, useful, yielding gain, rewarding.

फलदाई, *m.* (*f.* inī) }
फलदाता, *m.* (*f.* trī) }
फलदातृ, *m.* (*f.* trī) } = फलद, 2, *q.v.*
फलदायक, *m.* (*f.* ikā) }
फलदायी, *m.* (*f.* inī) }

फलदार, fruitful, fruit-bearing, profitable.

फलन, *m.* (see न, 6) a fructifying, bearing fruit, producing consequences.

फलनवा } (*Ayodhyā*) = फुलाना, *q.v.*
फलनवां }

फलना, *a. int.* to bear fruit, be in fruit, to produce; to result, be produced; to be fortunate.

फलनि, a Braj pl. of फल. See नि, 2 (2).

फलनिर्वृत्ति, *f.* cessation of consequences.

फलनिर्वृत्ति, *f.* final consequence or result.

फलनिष्पत्ति, *f.* a bearing fruit, a yielding profit or desired results.

फलन्ता, fruitful, bearing fruit.

फलपाक, *m.* the ripening of fruit; the fulness of consequence; the Coronda.

फलपाकान्ता, *f.* a certain annual plant which dies after bearing fruit.

फलपूर, *m.* common citron (*Citrus medica*).

फलप्राप्त, *adj.* obtaining the consequences of actions, rewarded, recompensed, punished.

फलप्राप्ति, *f.* the obtaining the desired fruit or result.

फलफलारी / **धलफलालो** } *f.* fruits of various kinds.

फलबुझौवल, *m.* a certain game, called also *Mankelā*; thus, "Think of a number, double it, add ten to it, take five from it, etc.; how many remain?" "Twenty-one." "The number was eight."

फलभोग, *m.* the receipt or enjoyment of consequences, the possession of rent or profit, usufruct.

फलभोगी, *m.* (*f.* inī) one who reaps consequences, profits, etc.: *lit.* adj. experiencing fruits.

फलवत / **फलवन्त** } *m.* (*f.* vatī) = **फलवान**, *q.v.*

फलवान, *m.* (*f.* vatī) fruitful, bearing fruit, yielding results or consequences.

फलश्रेष्ठ, *m.* the mango.

फनस, *m.* the *jak* or bread-fruit tree.

फलसई = **फल्लकी**, *q.v.*

फलसम्पत / **फलसम्पद** } *f.* prosperity, success.

फलसिद्धि, *f.* the reaping the fruit of any act, realizing consequences.

फलहानि, *f.* loss of fruit or profit.

फलहीन, *m.* (*f.* ā) without fruit, fruitless, barren, ineffectual, useless.

फला, *m.* a compound letter: the head of a dart or arrow: the head or bowl of a spoon: *adj.* abounding with fruit.

फलांग = **फलंग**, *q.v.*

फ़लाकत, *f.* an evil, a disgrace, a misfortune, adversity.

फलाकांक्षी, *f.* expectation of favorable consequences.

फ़लाख़ुन, *f.* a sling for throwing stones.

फ़लातून, *m. pr. n.* Plato.

फ़लान, *f.* pudendum muliebre.

फ़लाना, *m.* penis virilis.

फलाना, 1, *more prop.* **फुलाना**, *q.v.*: 2, *t.* (causat. of **फलना**) to cause to bear or produce, to make fruitful, to fructify.

फ़लानो, *f.* pudendum muliebre.

फलापेक्षा, *f.* regard to or expectation of consequences.

फलालेन, (Engl.) flannel.

फलाशी, *m.* (*f.* inī) any creature that subsists on fruits: *lit.* adj. fruit-eating.

फलास, 1, = **फलंग**, *q.v.*: 2, *m.* a step, stride.

फ़लाह, *f.* prosperity, happiness, safety, refuge.

फलित, *m.* (*f.* ā) fruitful, successful, fruit-bearing, yielding results.

फलितार्थ, *m.* a meaning implied or involved though not expressed: *adv.* on the whole, in fine, in effect.

फलिनी, *f.* (*m.* **फली**) 1, = **प्रियंगु**, *q.v.*: 2, a certain potherb (*Echites dichotoma*); a certain flower (*Celosia cristata*).

फलिया, *f.* a cod, a pod (or the seed) of any leguminous plant, but particularly of peas: a loop.

फलियाकश, *m.* a hook for drawing the strings through the holes by which the walls of a tent are laced to the top.

फलियाना, to bear fruit.

फली, 1, *m.* (*f.* inī) = **फलवान**, *q.v.*: 2, *f.* = **फलिया**, *q.v.*: 3, *m.* = **फल्लकी**, *q.v.*: 4, *f.* = **प्रियंगु**, *q.v.*: 5, *f.* a shield.

फलीता (*by inversion*) = **फ़तीला**, *q.v.*

फलुआ, *m.* a knotted fringe.

फलेरुहा, *f.* trumpet-flower (*Bignonia suaveolens*).

फलेल, *more prop.* **फुलेल**, *q.v.*

फलोत्तमा, *f.* the highest recompense, *viz.* that arising from sacred study.

फलोदय, *m.* profit, advantage, gain, result, happiness, heaven.

फलोद्देश, *m.* regard to results.

फल्गु, *f.* the opposite-leaved figtree (*Ficus oppositifolia*): a certain red powder, usually of the root of wild ginger, coloured with sappan-wood, and thrown over one another by Hindoos at the Holee festival: the spring season: falsehood: *pr. n.* a certain river which is said to flow underneath Gayā: *lit.* pithless, sapless, worthless, vain, weak.

फल्गुन; for words beginning thus, see under the form **फाल्गुन**.

फल्य, *m.* a bud, flower.

फल्लकी, *m.* a certain fish (*Mystus capirat*) caught in ponds, commonly called *Phabāī* or *Phalsaī*.

फ़व्वारा, *m.* a fountain, spring, jet, drain.

फसकट, *m.* the squatting in the oriental fashion as tailors sit at their work.

फसकड़, *m.* the sitting on the ground with legs extended.

फसकना, *a. int.* to split, burst, break.

फसकाना, *t.* to split, burst, break; to loosen, slacken.

फसना, *n.* to stick (as in mud or in a narrow passage), to be noosed, be caught, be ensnared, be imprisoned, be entangled, be involved in calamity, etc., be impeded.

फसफसा, *m.* (*f.* ī) flabby, loose, not rigid.

फसरी = **फांसी**, *q.v.*

फ़सल, *f.* a section, article, chapter: time, season, harvest, crop.

फसली, *more prop.* **पसली**, *q.v.*

फसाकू, bad tobacco (inelegant).

फ़साद, *m.* depravity, iniquity, wickedness, violence, horror, war, mutiny, sedition, rebellion.

फसाना, *t.* (of **फसना**) to cause to stick (as in mud etc.); to cause to be imprisoned, to mire, entangle catch, embroil, squash.

फसारना ; see पसारना.

फसालेना ; an intensive form of फसाना, *q.v.*

फसाव, *m.* a sticking, entanglement, ensnaring.

फसावट, *f.* = फसाव, *q.v.* [of style.

फ़साहत, *f.* eloquence, pure language, elegance

फसियारा, *m.* (= ठग) a strangler. [writings.

फ़सीह, eloquent, sweet or pure in language or

फ़स्साद, m. a surgeon, phlebotomist.

फ़ह, an oar, paddle. [sion.

फ़ह्म, *m.* understanding, intellect, comprehen-

फ़हमीद, *f.* understanding.

फ़हमीदा, understood : intelligent.

फहरना, *a. int.* to fly, wave, stream, flutter in the breeze (as a banner, etc.).

फ़हरसत, *f.* making an index or catalogue.

फहराई (Rām.) = कूदते हैं or फहराते हैं.

फहराना, *t.* to cause a flag to fly. [meaning.

फ़हवा, *m.* style, contents, signification, sense,

फ़हहाश, salacious, obscene, talking indecently.

फ़हीम, intelligent, learned.

फ़ाइक़, superior, excelling, preferable, paramount. [olument.

फ़ाइदा, *m.* profit, gain, advantage, utility, em-

फ़ाइदामन्द, profitable, advantageous; gratified,

फाएदा, *more prop.* फ़ाइदा, *q. v.* [edified.

फांक, *f.* a slice, piece of fruit.

फांकड़ / फांकड़ा } *m.* a fop, vain fellow.

फांकना, *t.* to chuck (grain, meal, etc.) into the mouth from the palm of the hand : to squander: to elapse (as time): to disappear (as clouds, etc.).

फांकी, *f.* 1, = फांक, *q. v.*: 2, (in Logic) an objection.

फांद = फान्द, *q.v.*

फांदना, *t.* to chop, score.

फांद, फांप, फांफ ; for words beginning thus, see under the forms फान्द, फाम्प, फाम्फ, respectively.

फांस, *m.* a splinter of bamboo : a noose ; an impediment : a die for playing with.

फांसना, 1, *t.* to noose, ensnare, entrap, throttle, strangle, choke: 2, *a. int.* to stick (as in mud): 3, *n.* to be impeded, be perplexed.

फांसा, *m.* a noose ; an impediment.

फांसी, *f.* a slipknot, noose, loop, halter ; *met.* strangulation, the punishment of hanging by the neck. — *denā*, to hang by the neck, strangle. — *parnā*, or *pānā*, to be hanged by the neck. — *lagānā*, to hang oneself.

फांसीकाठ, *m.* a gallows, gibbet.

फांसीगर / फांसीगार } *m.* (= ठग) a strangler.

फाक = फाग, *q. v.*

फ़ाक़:, *m.* poverty, necessity, want ; a fast (from want, not as a religious act). — *khainchnā*, to starve.

फाकड़ा = फाग, *q. v.*

फाका = फ़ाक़:, *q. v.*

फ़ाख़ता, *f.* a dove, ring-dove : dove-colour.

फ़ाख़िर, *m.* a boaster, an egotist : *lit.* excellent, precious, honorable.

फाग, *m.* a red powder which Hindoos throw over each other at the time of the Holee ; the act of throwing the coloured powders at the time of the Holee ; the gambols of the Holee.

फागन = फाल्गुन, *q. v.*

फागली, *f.* = फाग, *q.v.*

फागुन = फल्गुन, *q. v.* [triumphal arch.

फ़ाटक़, an awning supported by two poles, a

फाजिर, 1, disobedient, rebellious ; false (an oath): rich; 2, *m.* a sinner, a liar, a corrupter ; an adulterer, fornicator : a magician, enchanter.

फाज़िल, excellent, learned, virtuous ; abundant ; an overplus, remainder. [sharers in joint tenantry.

फाट, division of revenue, assessment among the

फाटक, *m.* a gate; a large shutter; an obstruction, check, impediment; the bar of a court of justice where the plaintiff and defendant take their stand : a watchman in charge of a gate.

फाटकबन्दी, *f.* imprisonment, safe custody, the being under lock and key.

फाटना = (1) फटना (2) फटाना, *qq. v.*

फाड़, *m.* a fissure, split, rent, crack. — *khānā*, to worry. — *lenā*, to be torn.

फाड़खाऊ, a ravenous beast: *lit.* ravenous.

फाड़खाना, *t.* to worry : to bite, gnaw ; to tear, rend (as a wild beast might).

फाड़खाव, a ravenous beast : *lit.* ravenous.

फाड़ना, *t.* (of फटना) to tear, rend, split, break, cleave, burst open, rip. [bursted, ripped.

फाड़ा, *m.* (*f.* i) torn, rent, broken, split, cleft,

फाणि, *f.* flour or meal mixed with curds.

फाणट, *m.* diluted decoction : the first particles of butter prepared by churning.

फाणटा, *m.* a branch of a tree ; a neck of land.

फ़ातिमा, *f. pr. n.* the daughter of Muhammad and wife of 'Ali.

फ़ातिहा, *f.* commencement, exordium.

फ़ानी, frail, transitory, inconstant, perishable.

फ़ानूस, *f.* a shade (to keep the wind from a candle), a lantern.

फान्त, *m.* a village register. [difficulty.

फान्द, *m.* a noose, snare, net : *met.* perplexity,

फान्दना, *t.* to leap, jump, or spring over : to imprison, entrap, ensnare ; to tie.

फान्दा, *m.* = फान्द, *q.v.*

फान्दी, *f.* a bundle of fifty or a hundred sugar-canes.

फाबी (Rām.) = फबी, *q. v.*

फ़ाम, 1, form, appearance : 2, resembling, like.

फाम्पना, *a. int.* to swell.

फाम्फड़, *m.* a hole, orifice.

फाय:, *m.* a plaster, blister.

फायदा, *more prop.* **फ़ाइदा**, *q. v.*

फाया, *m.* a plaster, blister.

फार, *m.* a ploughshare.

फारतोड़ना, a jingle on **फाड़ना** and **तोड़ना**, *qq. v.*

फारना, *more prop.* **फाड़ना**, *q. v.*

फ़ारयाब, ground watered by irrigation: *pr. n.* a certain country and city in Turkistān.

फ़ारिग़ख़त्ती, *f.* a deed of release or discharge, written acquittance.

फ़ार्स, *m. pr. n.* one of the southern provinces of Persia, ancient Parthia; Persia.

फ़ार्सी, *f.* the Persian language: *lit.* Persic, Persian; *hence*, a Persian.

फाल, 1, *m.* the share of a plough: 2, *m.* an epithet of Shiv and of Balarām: 2, *f.* a lump of betel-nut (*Areca*): a step, footstep.

फालगुण / **फालगुन** } *more prop.* **फाल्गुन**, *q. v.*

फालज; see **फालिज**.

फालतू, spare, surplus, remainder.

फालना, *a. int.* to spring, leap, jump.

फालसा, *m.* a certain fruit (*Grewia Asiatica*) from the juice of which a refreshing beverage is made.

फाला, *m.* a ploughshare.

फ़ालिज, *m.* palsy (esp. *hemiplegia*).

फालिसा, a shrike.

फाली, *f.* a kind of small pillow, a child's napkin.

फालूदा, a kind of flummery or sweetmeat: *lit.* smooth, clear.

फाल्गुन, *m.* 1, *pr. n.* (1) of the eleventh month of the Hindoos (Feb.-Mar.) the full moon of which is near *Pūrvaphōlguni* (2) of Arjun: 2, a certain tree (*Pentaptera arjuna*).

फाल्गुनी, *f.* the day of full moon in *Phālgun*, on which is celebrated the great spring festival of the Hindoos (*Holi*): *pr. n.* of the 11th and 12th *Nakshatras* which are distinguished by the epithets *uttar* (latter) and *pūrv* (former).

फाव, *m.* a small quantity given over and above the quantity purchased: *adv.* to boot.

फावड़ा, *m.* a mattock, spade, hoe.

फावड़ी, *f.* a crutch on which a *yogī* leans; a piece of wood or staff with a support at each end, which is held in both hands and laid horizontally in performing the exercise of *dand*; an instrument like a small rake or hoe for removing the dung of a horse.

फावदा, *more prop.* **फ़ाइदा**, *q. v.*

फावना = **फबना**, *q. v.*

फ़ाश, apparent, manifest, known, divulged.

फासदा; see **फ़ासिद**.

फ़ासिक़, *m.* (*f.* ā) an evil-doer, fornicator, adulterer, unchaste person, worthless person, one who is unworthy of credit as a witness in a court of law.

फ़ासिद, *m.* (*f.* ā) vicious, perverse, depraved, corrupt, noxious, pernicious, bad.

फ़ासिला, *m.* separation, intermediate space, interstice, interval, break.

फासी, *more prop.* **फ़ांसी**, *q. v.*

फाहा, *m.* a flock of cotton wet with *'atr*, or scented water: a plaster, pledget.

फ़ाहिश, *m.* (*f.* ā) obscene, indecent, impudent, shameful: gross, enormous.

फिंकना, *n.* to be thrown.

फिंगक, *m.* the fork-tailed shrike.

फिकर, *more prop.* **फ़िक्र**, *q.v.*

फ़िक़रा, *m.* a line, sentence, paragraph.

फिकवाना, *t.* (causat of **फिंकना**) to cause to be thrown.

फिका, *m.* (*f.* ī) *more prop.* **फीका**, *q.v.*

फिकाना, *t.* to cause or teach to throw.

फिकारना, *t.* to bare or uncover the head, to unplait the hair of the head.

फिकैत, *m.* a thrower (of missiles).

फिकिर, *more prop.* **फ़िक्र**, *q.v.*

फिक्का, *m.* (*f.* ī) = **फीका**, *q.v.*

फ़िक्र, *f. m.* thought, reflection, consideration, concern, solicitude, council, advice.

फ़िक्रमन्द, thoughtful, pensive, anxious, sorrowful.

फिख़फिख़, the imitative sound uttered by birds.

फिग़ान, *m.* lamentation, complaint, clamour: *interj.* alas!

फिगार, lame, crippled, wounded, afflicted, confused, distracted.

फिट, *m.* curse, malediction: *adv.* fie!

फिटकरी, *m.* (*f.*?) alum.

फिटकार, *f.* curse, malediction: the removing a thing to a distance.

फिटकारना, *t.* to curse; to reject.

फिटकिरी, *m.* (*f.*?) alum.

फिटना, *n.* to be paid off, liquidated, discharged (as a debt).

फिटफिट, fie upon it! curse it!

फिटाना, *t.* to beat up and mix, work up into a froth.

फिटिक, a snare, net, cage.

फ़ितना, *m.* calamity, sedition, perfidy, sin, temptation, seduction.

फ़ितर:, *m.* wisdom, sagacity; deceit, trick: nature, creation, form.

फ़ितरत, *f.* = **फ़ितर:**, *q.v.*

फितूर, *more prop.* **फ़ुतूर**, *q.v.*

फ़िदवी, *m.* (*f.* **फ़िदविया**) a devoted servant, subject or vassal: *lit.* devoted.

फ़िदा, *f.* sacrifice, the devoting oneself to save another, consecration, exchange, ransom, redemption.

फ़िन्दुक़, *f.* a filbert-nut; a ball or bullet; the tips of the fingers or toes stained so as to resemble the filbert.

फिर, again, moreover, on the other hand, afterwards, then, any more. — *kahnā*, to say again, say in reply, to retort. — *jānā*, to return, to revolt, to warp, to become distorted. — *parnā*, to be dissatisfied, be displeased, be indisposed.

फिरऊन, *m. pr. n.* Pharaoh king of Egypt.

फिरंगी, *m.* (*f.* inī) *more prop.* **फ़रंगी**, *q. v.*

फ़िरक़ा, *m.* a religious or philosophic sect, party, side, society, company, tribe, troop.

फिरकी, *f.* anything that turns as on an axis, a whirligig, a reel for thread.

फिरजाना ; see फिर. [woman to her paramour.

फिरत, *m.* rejected things ; money paid by a lewd

फिरता, *m.* (*f.* ī) *adj.* turning, returning, walking about.—*rahnā*, to walk about, wander, perambulate.

फिरताबारा, *m.* a whirlwind.

फिरताभाड़ा, *m.* half or return hire.

फिरती, *f.* 1, *m.* फिरता, *q. v* : 2, a returning, return, homeward-bound.— *kā bhārā*, *m.* the hire of a boat, carriage, etc.

फिरतीकिश्ती, *f.* a return boat.

फिरदौस, *m.* a garden: *pr. n.* Paradise.

फिरना, *a. int.* to turn, return, to walk about, ramble, travel, wander about, to whirl, circulate, roll, wheel ; to change ; to revolt ; to go about, *e. g. Munādi karte phirte hain*, they go about preaching. Following another verb (that verb being in the present participial form) it signifies 'about' in reference to the action expressed by that verb ; *e. g. Uṛte phirte hain*, they fly about.

फ़िरनी, *f.* a dish (resembling hasty pudding) made

फिरपड़ना ; see फिर. [of ground rice and milk.

फिरवाना, *t.* to cause to be turned.

फिराई, *f.* (see आई, 3) the act of returning.

फ़िराक़, *m.* distance, separation, distinction, absence.

फिराना, *t.* to cause a thing to turn, cause to go about, to whirl, wheel, return, change, roll, shift.

फिराव, *m.* a turning, rotation, return, restitution.

फिरावना, *more com.* फिराना, *q. v.* [opulent.

फिरावान, much, abundant, copious, sufficient,

फिरासत, *f.* physiognomy: penetration, sagacity, understanding, acuteness.

फिरि, *more com.* (1) फिर (2) फिरके (फिरना).

फिरिना, *more com.* फिरना, *q. v.*

फिरिफिरि, a redupl. of फिर or of फिरना, *qq. v.*

फिरिश्ता, *m.* (*lit.* sent : *hence*) a messenger, ambassador, legate, angel, apostle, prophet, missionary.

फिरुशि } फिरुशी } *more com.* फरोशी, *q. v.*

फिरोज, *more prop.* फ़ीरोज़, *q. v.*

फिरोना ; see (1) पिरोना (2) फिराना. [ligig.

फिर्नी, *f.* anything that turns as on an axis, a whir-

फिल, *more prop.* फील, *q. v.*

फ़िलफ़ौर, in haste, quickly, instantly, immediately.

फिलसना (*by inversion*) = फिसलना, *q. v.*

फ़िलिज़्ज़, *m.* ore, metal, dross, scoria.

फिल्ली, *f.* the leg.

फिश, pish ! pshaw ! tush !

फिसकना, the hiss of a snake.

फिसफिसाना, *n.* to be terrified. [error.

फिसलन, *m.* the act of slipping or sliding ; *met.*

फिसलना, 1, *a. int.* to slip, slide ; *met.* to err : 2, *m.* (*f.* ī) slippery.

फिसलबन्दा, *m.* sliding down a smooth bank (a favorite sport among children).

फिसलहा, *m.* (*f.* ī) slippery. [cause to err.

फिसलाना, *t.* to cause to slip, cause to slide : to

फिसलाहट, *f.* slipping, slipperiness.

फ़िस्क़, *m.* adultery, obscenity, impudence, iniquity, sin, falsehood. [contents, schedule.

फ़िहरिस्त, *f.* an inventory, list, index, table of

फींकना ; see (1) फिंकना (2) फेंकना.

फींका *m.* (*f.* ī) = फीका, *q.v.*

फींचडालना, an intensive form = पींचना, *q. v.*

फींचना, *t.* to wash cloth, to rinse, squeeze.

फीक, *f.* the point of a scourge.

फीका, *m.* (*f.* ī) weak, vapid, tasteless, insipid ; pale, dim, sallow, light (in colour).

फीपस, flabby, flaccid.

फीपसा, *m.* the lights or lungs.

फीर ; see (1) फिर (2) फ़ीर.

फ़ीर, laughter; a laughingstock : vexation.

फीरनी = फ़िरनी, *q. v.*

फ़ीरोज़, victorious, happy, fortunate.

फ़ीरोज़ा, *m.* a turquoise-stone (used as a talisman to bring good luck to the wearer).

फ़ीरोज़ी, *f.* victory, triumph, success. [bishop.

फ़ील, *m.* (*pl.* ān) an elephant : (in Chess) the

फ़ीलपा, 1, *adj.* having a swelling in one's leg, having elephantiasis : 2, elephantiasis.

फ़ीलपाया, *m.* a pillar, prop ; the upright post over the mouth of a well.

फीलफौर, *more prop.* फ़िलफ़ौर, *q.v.*

फ़ीस, (Engl.) fees. The term is more particularly applied to the money paid by native children to their school-master for their education.

फुंकार, *f.* the hiss of a snake. — *mārnā*, to hiss,

फुंकारना, *a. int.* to hiss (as a snake). [(as a snake).

फुंकारी, *f.* the hissing of a snake.— *mārnā*, to hiss

फुंगनी, *f.* a pimple or pustule. [(as a snake).

फुंगी, *f.* a sprout, bud; the point of an ear of corn.

फुंदना, *m.* a tassel.

फुंहार, *f.* small drops of rain.

फुंहारा, *m.* a fountain, jet d'eau.

फुकना, 1, *n.* (of फूंकना) to be inflated, be blown, be blown up, be blown up into a flame: 2, *m.* a bladder, bag, purse.

फुकनी, *f.* a blowpipe ; a firelock, pistol.

फुक़रा, *m* (pl. of फ़क़ीर) derveshes, religious men-

फुगना, to swell, enlarge, puff out. [dicants.

फुट = (1) फुटकर (2) *m.* फुटा, *qq.v.*

फुटकर, odd, unmatched, unpaired, separate, dispersed (as a horseman) : arrogant, overbearing.

फुटकी, *f.* a blot, spot, stain : *adj.* odd, unpaired.

फुटना, *a. int.* to increase ; to obtain advance-

फुटा, *f.* the expanded hood of a snake. [ment.

फुटाना, *t.* to increase ; to promote.

फुठफुठ रोना, *a. int.* to burst out a-crying; to burst with crying.

फुड़वाना, *t.* (causat. of **फोड़ना**) to cause to break.

फुड़िया, *f.* a sore, pimple, boil. [contempt.

फुत, an interjection expressive of disregard or

फुतकार, *m.* (*f.* ī) arrogant, contemptuous, dis-

फुतुव्वत, *f.* liberality, generosity. [dainful.

फुतूर, *m.* weakness, infirmity: insubordination; mutiny, rebellion, quarrelling.

फुदकना, *a. int.* to jump, leap, hop (said of small birds), to dance about in token of delight.

फुदका, *m.* (*f.* ī) a certain bird (*Certhia tula*).

फुनंग, *f.* the top, summit.

फुनगी, *f.* a sprout, bud, the point of an ear of corn.

फुनसी, *f.* a pimple.

फुनि in Chand = **पुनि** = **पुनः**, *q. v.*

फुनिया, *f.* a tassel, knot; penis puerilis.

फुन्दना, *m.* a tassel.

फुचा, *m.* the silk lash of a whip.

फुची / **फुचेा** } *f.* = **फुनिया**, *q. v.*

फुप, *m.* (*prop.* **पुष्प**) a flower. [any liquid.

फुपकार, *f.* a bubbling, a blowing or breathing into

फुपा, *more prop.* **फुप्फा**, *q. v.*

फुपी, *more prop.* **फुप्फी**, *q. v.*

फुपू, *more prop.* **फूफू**, *q. v.*

फुप्पा, *more prop.* **फुप्फा**, *q. v.*

फुप्पी, *more prop.* **फुप्फी**, *q. v.*

फुप्फा, *m* an uncle (the husband of a paternal aunt).

फुप्फी, *f.* an aunt (a father's sister).

फुफकार, *f.* the hissing of a snake.

फुफकारना, *a. int.* to hiss (said of the snake).

फुफा, *more prop.* **फुप्फा**, *q. v.* [sister.

फुफियाससुर, *m.* the husband of a father-in-law's

फुफियासास, *f.* a father-in-law's sister.

फुफियासुसुर = **फुफियाससुर**, *q. v.*

फुफी, *more prop.* **फुप्फी**, *q. v.*

फुफू, *more prop.* **फूफू**, *q. v.*

फुफेरा, *m* (*f.* ī) a cousin: *prop.* descended from, or related through, a paternal aunt.

फुफेरा भाई, *m.* / **फुफेरी बहिन**, *f.* } (see **फुफेरा**) a cousin.

फुर, 1, *more prop.* **फुर्र**, *q. v.*: 2, true, right.

फुरकत, *f.* distance, separation, distinction, absence, bereavement. [form **फुर्ती**.

फुरती; for words beginning thus, see under the

फुरफुराना, *a. int.* to tremble, to wave (as hair in the wind). [pitation.

फुरफुरी, *f.* a trembling, quivering, tremour, pal-

फुरसूत / **फुरसत** } *more prop.* **फुर्सत**, *q. v.*

फुरहारी, *f.* horripilation.

फुरात, *m. pr. n.* the river Euphrates.

फुरि, true, right, just.

फुरूश, *m.* (pl. of **फ़र्श**) carpets.

फुरूसत, *f.* skill in whatever relates to horses, the art of horsemanship, manège: sharpness of intellect.

फुरूसियत = **फुरूसत**, *q. v.*

फुर्त = **फुर्ती**, *q. v.*

फुर्ती, *f.* activity, quickness, alertness, agility.

फुर्तीला, *m.* (*f.* ī) quick, active, nimble, brisk, smart, expert, fleeting, alert.

फुर्र, *m.* the noise as of a bird suddenly taking wing, or of a small quantity of gunpowder exploding.

फुर्सत, *f.* leisure, opportunity, convenience, freedom, ease, relief, rest.

फुलका, *m.* a blister; a kind of cake or small loaf: an area or arena for wrestlers: *lit.* inflated, puffed up: light. [a snake's hood).

फुलकारना, *a. int.* to inflate, expand, swell out (as

फुलकारी, *f.* flowered or embroidered cloth.

फुलकी, *f.* a cake, raised bread, fritters.

फुलझड़ी, *f.* a kind of fireworks like a fountain.

फुलना, *more com.* **फूलना**, *q. v.*

फुलवाई (*Rām.*) = **फुलवाड़ी**, *q. v.*

फुलवाड़ी / **फुलवारी** } *f.* a flower-garden.

फुलहथा, *m.* a cudgelling, beating.

फुलाना, *t.* (of **फूलना**) to cause to swell, to inflate, distend, fatten: *met.* to make proud, puff up with flattery. [so and so.

फुलाना, (= **अमुक**) *m.* (*f.* ī) a certain one, such a one,

फुलासरा, *m.* flattery.

फुलूस, *m.* small coins, pice; money.

फुलेरी, *f.* romping, playing.

फुलेल, (*i. e.* **फुल + तेल**) *m.* oil impregnated with the essence of flowers by steeping them in it; essence (as a perfume). [and fried in ghee or oil.

फुलौरी, *f.* bread or cake made of fruit and pulse

फुल्ल, blown, opened, expanded (as a flower).

फुल्लदामन, *m.* a species of the *Atidhriti* metre.

फुल्लनयन, *m.* (*f.* ā) a happy-looking person, etc.: *lit.* full-eyed, large-eyed; smiling, looking pleased or happy.

फुल्ललोचन, 1, *m.* (*f.* ā) = **फुल्लनयन**, *q. v.*: 2, *m.* a large full eye: 3, *m.* (*f.* ā) species of the antelope.

फुल्लवत / **फुलवन्त** / **फुल्लवान** } *m.* (*f.* vatī) *adj.* blooming, flowering.

फुल्ला, *m.* cataract (the disease of the eye).

फुल्लित, *m.* (*f.* ā) swollen, blown, inflated.

फुल्ली, *f.* the *albugo* (a disorder of the eye): a kind of ear-ornament: the tumbler nail of the cock of a musket.

फुल्लीहून, the star pagoda, a gold coin worth three and a half rupees, or seven shillings sterling.

फुल्लोत्पल, *m.* a full-blown flower.

फुल्लोरी; see **फुलौरी**.

फुस, a voice, sound, noise.

फुसफुसर, *m.* a whispering, buzzing in the ear.

फुसफुसाना, *a. int.* to whisper in the ear.

फुसफुसावट, *f.* a whispering, buzzing in the ear.

फुसला; see (1) **फुसलाना** (2) **फूसरा**.

फुसलाऊ, a coaxer, wheedler, seducer, flatterer: *lit.* adj. coaxing, seductive, etc.

फुसलाश्रो = फुसलाव, *q.v.*

फुसलाट, a contraction of **फुसलाहट**, *q.v.*

फुसलाना, *t.* to coax, wheedle, cajole, entice, seduce, flatter, instigate.

फुसलाहट, *f.* = **फुसलाव**, *q.v.*

फुसलाव, *m.* wheedling, coaxing, cajolling, flattery, seduction, blandishment.

फुसलौनिया, *m.* a coaxer, wheedler, seducer, flatterer.

फुसायढा, *m.* (*f.* ī) = **फुसाहिन्दा**, *q.v.*

फुसायढी, *f.* mouldiness; scum.

फुसाहिन्दा, *m.* (*f.* ī) stinking, fetid, disgusting.

फुस्का, *m.* (*f.* ī) without strength, weak, slack (as a knot).

फुहार, *f.* small drizzling rain.

फूश्रा, *f.* an aunt (father's sister): a lizard.

फूई, *f.* small drizzling rain.

फूं, *m.* an affected fellow, fop, rake, swaggerer.

फूंक, *f.* the act of blowing, a puff, blast, the blowing up a fire.—*denā*, to set on fire. *Phūṅkphūṅkkar pāṅw dharnā*, to act (or walk) carefully and cautiously.

फूंकना, *t.* to blow with the breath, to blow a horn, blow up a fire, to inflame. set on fire, kindle.

फूंकार, *f.* a hissing (as of snakes); snorting.

फूंकारना, *a. int.* to hiss (as a snake); to snort.

फूंश्रार, **फूंही** } *f.* small drizzling rain.

फूक, *more prop* **फूंक**, *q.v.*

फूकना, 1, *t.* to blow, puff: 2, *m.* the bladder.

फूकर, *m.* any fine sensible young fellow.

फूट, *f.* a kind of melon (*Cucumis momordica*, Roxb.); a ripe cucumber that bursts elastically (as the *Cucumis utilissimus*, Roxb. and *Momordica mixta*, Roxb.); difference of opinion, discord, dissension, separation; a flaw, breach: *adj.* odd, unpaired.—*parnā*, to arise (dissension), to have disaggreement. *Phūtphūt* (or *phūtkar*) *ronā*, to weep excessively.—*rahnā*, to be broken; to be dispersed; to be unpaired.—*honā*, to be divided in opinion.

फूटन, *f.* wrangling, disagreement, misunderstanding.

फूटना, *n.* to be broken; to be broken into, be broken down; to be dispersed, be separated; to be unpaired: *a. int.* to separate, to burst, split; to arise or burst forth (as a smell); to burst forth (as sobs); to transpire; to be made public: to get promotion or advancement.

फूटबिखेरा, *m.* (*f.* ī) scattered, dispersed.

फूटला, *m.* (*f.* i) bad or false (as coin).

फूटा, *m.* (*f.* ī) broken.

फूटी, *f.* disparity, disagreement.

फूनंग, *more prop.* **फुनंग**, *q.v.*

फूनियारा, *m.* a jet d'eau.

फून्दना, *m.* a tassel.

फूप; see (1) **फुप** (2) **फूफा**.

फूफा, *m.* an uncle (a father's sister's husband).

फूफी, *f.* an aunt (a father's sister).

फूफीरी, *f.* extravagance; prodigality.

फूफू, *m. f.* an uncle or aunt (a father's sister, or her husband).

फूफेरा, *m.* (*f.* ī) = **फुफेरा**, *q.v.*

फूयां, *f.* small drizzling rain.

फूरोरी, *f.* extravagance, prodigality.

फूरुश, *m.* (pl. of **फ़र्श**) carpets.

फूल, *m.* a flower, blossom; a boss, stud, bunch of ribands, cockade; menses (of which children are the fruit); a swelling; the bones of a corpse after the fleshy parts are burned; lights or fire seen at night; a certain ceremony performed among Muhammadans in honour of a deceased person on the third day after his death (on which occasion a portion of the Kur,ān is recited, and flowers are placed on trays in the midst of the assembly).—*uṭhnā*, to be performed (said of the funeral ceremony above mentioned); to complete the forty days of mourning.—*jānā*, to swell, become fat, be delighted, be pleased.—*jharnā*, to speak eloquently: to fall from a lamp (said of drops of burning oil).—*parnā*, to break out (as a fire)—*baiṭhnā*, to be glad.

फूलकोबी, *f.* a cauliflower.

फूलचड़ी, **फूलभड़ी**, **फूलभाड़** } = **फुलभड़ी**, *q.v.*

फूलडोल, *m.* a kind of Hindoo sport or show.

फूलना, *a. int.* to blossom, blow, flower; to bloom, *hence*, to be in health and spirits, to be pleased; to swell, be inflated, be puffed up (as with pride).

फूलपट्टा, *f.* a knot of ribands, cockade.

फूलवारी, *more prop.* **फुलवाड़ी**, *q.v.*

फूलवाला, *m.* (*f.* ī) flowering, in flower.

फूला, *m.* (*f.* ī) swollen; blossomed, flowered, having flowers, puffed up or out.—*na sāmānā*, to be not able to contain oneself from delight, to be overjoyed, be exultant.

फूलाद, *f.* steel.

फूलादी, *f.* a pikestaff: *adj.* of steel.

फूलाफला, *m.* (*f.* ī) flourishing.

फूलाव, *m.* a swelling.

फूली, *f.* (see *m.* **फूला**) the *albugo* (a disorder of the eye).

फूलेल = फुलेल, *q.v.*

फूस, *m.* old dry grass or straw. — *meṅ chingārī dālnā*, to excite contention or strife.

फूसड़ा, **फूसरा** } *m.* a rag, bundle of rags.

फूसी, *f.* chaff, rubbish.

फूहड़, *f.* a bad housewife, slattern, slut: *lit.* undisciplined, uneducated, stupid, rude, foolish, obscene. The term is applied to females.

फूहड़पन, *m.* stupidity, obscenity, rudeness, foolishness, affectation.

फूहड़पना = **फूहड़पन**, *q.v.*

फूहड़ा, *m.* (*f.* ī) *adj.* talking obscenely.

फूहर; see **फूहड़**.

फूहा, *m.* an artificial pap or nipple made of cotton or other such substance, by means of which milk is given to young animals and infants when they are unable to suck their mothers.

फूहार / **फूही** } *f.* small drizzling rain.

फेंक, *f.* a throw, cast. — *denā*, to throw away; to fly a hawk after prey; to rush off on horseback at full speed.

फेंकना, *t.* to throw, fling, dart; to let fly (a hawk etc. after prey); to set off a horse at full speed, to gallop.

फेंकवाना, *more com.* **फिकवाना**, *q.v.*

फेंकाऊ / **फेंकाव** } requiring to be thrown.

फेंगड़ा, *m.* (*f.* ī) club-footed, lame.

फेंट, for words beginning thus, see under the form **फेयट**.

फेकना, *more prop.* **पेंकना**, *q.v.*

फेट, *f.* the waist when bound with a belt.

फेटना = **फेयटना**, *q.v.*

फेटा, *m.* a small turban; a waistband without a fringe.

फेड़ना, *t.* to accomplish, perform; to liquidate a debt.

फेयट, *f.* a waistband, belt, fob. — *bāndhnā*, to get ready, to resolve.

फेयटना, *t.* to mix by trituration, to beat up eggs etc., to mix, to triturate.

फेयटा, *f.* a small turban; a waistband; a fob.

फेयटी, *f.* a skein (of thread, etc.).

फेन, *m.* (*f.* ई) foam, froth; moisture, vapour; cuttle-fish bone (supposed by the Hindoos to be indurated foam of the sea). — *bahanā*, to foam, emit foam.

फेनक, *m.* cuttle-fish bone.

फेनका, *f.* the soapberry.

फेनता, *f.* frothiness; vapour.

फेनल, frothy, foamy, foaming, bubbling, frothing.

फेनवत / **फेनवन्त** / **फेनवान** } *m.* (*f.* vati) = **फेनल**, *q.v.*

फेना, *m.* = **फेन**, *q.v.*

फेनाना, *a. int.* to foam, froth.

फेनायमान, *m.* (*f.* matī) = **फेनल**, *q.v.*

फेनिल, *m.* (= **फेनल**) the soap-plant (*Sapindus detergens*, Roxb.); the fruit of the jujube; the fruit of the *Vangueria spinosa.*

फेनी, 1, *m.* (*f.* inī) = **फेनल**, *q.v.* 2: *f.* a kind of sweetmeat.

फेनुस, *m.* biesting, the milk of a cow, etc. for some days after calving.

फेफड़ा, *m.* the lights or lungs.

फेफड़ी, *f.* inability to move: *adv.* again, afterwards.

फेफरा, *more com.* **फेफड़ा**, *q.v.*

फेर, 1, *m.* a turning, turn, return, change, meander, maze, curvature, coil, twisting, fold; circumference; equivocation, ambiguity; difficulty; distance: 2, *adv.* again, back. — *khānā*, to go round about; to wind, meander (a river); to meet with difficulties. — *denā*, to restore, return, refund. — *parnā*, to differ. — *meṅ dālnā*, to throw obstacles into another's way.

फेरना, *t.* (of **फिरना**) to turn, turn back, invert, reverse, avert, turn away, to make to walk backwards and forwards, to bring back, carry back; to shift; to repeat; to plaster; to stroke. — *hāth*, to caress, fondle. *Sirpar hāth* —, to deceive by coaxing.

फेरफार, alternate. — *k.* to alternate.

फेरबोटी, *f.* the paunch and abdomen.

फेरव, *m.* (*f.* ī) a rogue, cheat; a jackal; Rākshas; *lit.* fraudulent, crafty, malicious, injurious, noxious.

फेरवाना, *more com.* **फिरवाना**, *q.v.*

फेरवी; see **फेरव** and **फेरु**.

फेरा, *m.* a turning, circuit, perambulation; a roll: a kind of wooden frame with which lime, sand, etc. are measured: a set or assortment (as a set of chessmen, a dinner-service, etc.).

फेराना, *more com.* **फिराना**, *q.v.*

फेराफेरि, *more com.* **फेराफेरी**, *q.v.*

फेराफेरी, *f.* walking backwards and forwards, going and coming, returning, alternating, alternation.

फेरि, *more prop.* **फेर**, *q.v.*

फेरी, *f.* (see **परिक्रमा**) the going round to the right of an object by way of adoration, circumambulation: the knuckles: a set or assortment: (in Mārwārī) the profession of a wandering beggar.

फेरीदार, *m.* a vagrant, vagabond.

फेरीवाला, *m.* (*f.* ī) a pedlar.

फेरु, *m.* (*f.* **फेरवी**) a jackal.

फेल, *m.* orts, leavings of a meal, or droppings from the mouth: *lit.* thrown away, cast off.

फेला / **फेलि** / **फेलिका** / **फेली** } *f.* = **फेल**, *q.v.*

फैंकले in Braj = **फेंकना**, *q.v.*

फैंट, for words begining thus, see under the form **फेयट**.

फ़ैज़, *m.* abundance, plenty, bounty, favour, grace.

फैजान, *more prop.* **फ़यज़ान**, *q.v.*

फैयट, **फैदा**, for words beginning thus, see under the forms **फेयट**, **फ़ाइदा**, respectively.

फैन in Braj = **फेन**, *q.v.*

फैनानौं in Braj = **फेनाना**, *q.v.*

फैम in Mārwārī = **फ़हम**, *q.v.*

फैलजाना, an intensive form of **फैलना**, *q.v.*

फैलना, *n.* to be spread, be expanded, be dilated, be diffused, be scattered, be dispersed: *a. int.* to spread abroad, disperse, become public, spread (as news).

फ़ैलसूफ़, intelligent, knowing, shrewd, cunning, artful: *hence*, a philosopher.

फैलाओ = **फैलाव**, *q.v.*

फैलाना, *t.* to spread, expand, scatter, diffuse,

widen, extend, stretch out, stretch forth, distend, dilate, branch out; to proclaim, publish. *Pāṅw* —, to insist, be obstinate. *Hāth*—, to solicit, supplicate, beg.

फैलाव, *m.* spread, expansion, extension, diffusion, publication, display, extent, profusion, plenty.

फैलावा, *m.* (= **फैलाव**) prolixity.

फ़ैसल, *m.* decision, decree, determination; division, separation.

फ़ैसला, *m.* a decree, settlement.

फोंक, 1, *f.* the notch of an arrow: 2, hollow, not solid (said particularly of jewels).

फोंकार, *more prop.* **फुंकार**, *q.v.*

फोंफी, *f.* anything perforated or hollow, a pipe, tube.

फोंहार, *f.* small drizzling rain.

फोक, 1, = **फोंक**, 2, *q.v.*: 3, *m.* dregs, sediment: grains.

फोकट, *m.* an indigent person.

फोकड़, *m.* dross, refuse, trash; grains.

फोकल, empty, void.

फोड़ना, *t.* to break, pierce, burst, split, disclose, divulge, betray a secret.

फोंड़नी, *f.* (= **तौज़ीह**) an explaining.

फोड़ा, *m.* a boil, sore, abscess, imposthume, ulcer.

फ़ोता, *m.* a bag, purse; the testicle: tax, revenue: a cloth wrapped around the middle when bathing.

फोना, *t.* to unfasten, untie, undo.

फोर, for words beginning thus, see under the form **फोड़**.

फोरन, *more prop.* **फ़ौरन**, *q.v.*

फोला, *m.* (see **फोड़ा**) a blister.

फोलाद, *more prop.* **फ़ूलाद**, *q.v.*

फोली, *f.* (in Mārwāṛī) a title addressed to a woman of rank.

फौरन, *more prop.* **फ़ौरन**, *q.v.*

फ़ौक़, *m.* altitude, loftiness, superiority, excellence.

फ़ौज, *f.* a body of men, multitude, troop, company, army, squadron, regiment.

फ़ौजदार, *m.* an officer of police, a chief magistrate of a chaklah; a military officer.

फ़ौजदारी, *f.* the office or the status of a *faujdār*, magistracy; military officership.

फौड़ा, *m.* a mattock, spade, hoe.

फ़ौत, *f.* death.—*honā*, to die; to be interred.

फ़ौती, (in Law) property which escheats to the sovereign by the owner dying intestate and without legal heirs: *lit.* dead.

फ़ौर, *m.* celerity, haste, speed.

फ़ौरन, quickly, instantly, suddenly, directly, forthwith.

फ़्रांस, *m. pr. n.* the country of France.

फ़्रांसनिवासी, *m.* (*f.* inī) a resident of France.

फ़्रांसीस = **फ़्रांसीसी**, *q.v.*

फ़्रांसीसी, appertaining to France, French: *hence* (1) *f.* the French language (2) *m.* (*f.* inī) a French person.

ब

ब (b) is the twenty-third consonant in the Hindee alphabet, and has the following characteristics and functions:— 1, It is the third letter of the **पवर्ग** or labial class, and has in pronunciation the sound of the English letter *b*: one of the most common phænomena, however, of the Hindee language is the interchange of this letter with **व**. This is particularly so in the case of Sanskrit words commencing with **व**; and to such an extent has the process been carried that every such word occurring in Hindee is liable to be spelt with **ब**, and the careful observance of the distinction between these two letters is usually condemned as pedantic. It has been usual to record twice, with all their meanings, those words in which either of these letters occurs, especially if they occur at the beginning of words: an attempt has been made in the present work to economize the space that might thus be absorbed, by giving the meanings under the original form of the word only. By so doing, however, it is not by any means the author's intention to administer a sweeping condemnation to a practice which is, in fact, almost universal, but rather to compass the twofold purpose of economizing valuable space, and of indicating (for the benefit of any student who may wish it) the true or original form of the word. It may be added that careful native writers and speakers usually prefer the uncorrupted Sanskrit form of Tatsama words. 2. Standing alone, this letter may denote (1) the Sun (2) the ocean (3) water in general, and (4) the god of the waters, *viz.* Varuṇ. 3, This letter is sometimes interchanged with **म**; *e.g.* **नरबदा**, more properly **नर्मदा**; **ताजिम**, properly **ताज्जुब**; and sometimes even with **ह**; thus, **बिलम्हना**, more properly, **विलम्बना**. 4, In one of the dialectic forms of the future tense, very much used in poetry and in the villages, this letter with *virām* under it is the sign of the first person singular and plural (*e.g.* **जानब्**, I [or we] shall know); and without *virām* it is the sign of the second person singular and plural (*e.g.* **जानब**, thou shalt know, or you shall know). Of course, in pronunciation the distinction is indicated by the expression of the inherent vowel in the latter case (thus, *jānaba*) and the omission of it in the former (thus, *jānab*). 5. In a few foreign compounds that have become current in Hindee speech and books this letter is prefixed *pleonastically* (as in **बग़ैर**) and in some instances *intensively* (as in **बग़ैर**).

बअद = **बाद**, 3, *q.v.* See **आ**, 12.

बइयर; see (1) **बेर** (2) **वैर**.

बईद, far, remote, distant, absent.

बंक, 1, = **वंक**, *q.v.*: 2, *m.* (English) a Bank.

बंकघर, *m.* (Engl. 'bank' + **घर**) a banking-house.

बंकटा, the crop on the field irrecoverably spoiled.

बंकटैया, *m.* a certain useless prickly plant resembling the thistle.

बंका, for words beginning thus, see under the form **वंका**.

बंग, 1 = **वंग**, *q. v.*: 2, *f.* hemp (*Cannabis sativa*): a kind of intoxicating potion made from the leaves of hemp.

बंगकटिया = **बंकटैया**, *q.v.*

बंगका, *m.* a certain aquatic beetle that eats the rice-plant.

बंगकी, *f.* a certain kind of rice cultivated in the Benares district.

बंगड़ी, *f.* a kind of ornament (*prop.* of glass) worn on the wrist; a bangle or bracelet made of glass or lac.

बंगला, *m.* a kind of thatched house, 'bungalow', summer-house, lodge, cottage: a sort of betel-leaf.

बंगलिया, *f.* a certain species of rice.

बंगा, *m.* a joint of bamboo-root: a kind of soil: well-water slightly brackish.

बंगाल, *more com.* **बंगाला**, *q.v.*

बंगाला, *m. pr. n.* the province of Bengal.

बंगालिन, *f.* (*m.* **बगाली**) a female Bengālee.

बंगालिनी = **बगालिन**, *q.v.*

बंगाली, appertaining to Bengal, Bengālee: hence (1) *f.* the Bengālee language (2) *m.* (*f.* in *or* inī) a native of Bengal.

बंगी, 1, *f.* a humming-top: 2, *m.* (*f.* in *or* inī) one who intoxicates himself with *bang*.

बंच, for words beginning thus, but not given below, see under the form **वंच**.

बंचन; see (1) **वंचन** (2) **बचन**.

बंचना, *n.* to be read, be perused.

बंचाना, 1, *more prop.* **बचाना**, *q.v*: 2, *t.* to cause to be read, cause anyone to read, to hear one read.

बंचाव, *more prop.* **बचाव**, *q.v.*

बंज; for words beginning thus, see under the form **बनज**.

बंझोटी, *f.* a kind of medicine taken to produce barrenness.

बंट, बंठ, बंड, बंद, बंध, बंब; for words beginning with either of these elements, see under the forms **बण्ट, बण्ठ, बण्ड, बन्द, बन्ध, बम्ब**, respectively.

बंयरै, an occasional contraction of **बोरबानी**, *q.v.*

बंवंड़, **बंवड़**, **बंवर** } *m. f.* a creeper, tendril, vine.

बंश, बंस; for words beginning with either of these elements, but not given below, see under the form **वंश**.

बंशाउरी, **बंशावरी** } *more prop.* **वंशावली**, *q.v.*

बंसा, *m.* a species of grass which grows in rice-fields. (It is used as fodder for cattle.)

बक; for words beginning thus, but not given below, see under the form **वक**.

बक, *f.* prattle, foolish, talk, chat, garrulity.

बकची, *f.* a certain plant (*Conyza* or *Serratula anthelmintica*) the seed of which is used for curing the itch.

बकझक, *f.* chat, prattle, foolish talk, clack, babble, gabble, garrulity. — *k.* to prattle, chatter, gabble, babble, talk nonsense.

बकत, 1, (*by inversion*) = **बतक**, *q.v.*: 2, *more prop.* **वक्त**, *q.v.*

बकता, *m.* (*f.* trī) = **वक्ता**, *q.v.*

बकना, *a. int.* to prate, chatter, talk, chat, jabber, babble, cackle, talk nonsense.

बकबक, (redupl. of **बक**) = **बकझक**, *q.v.*

बकबकाना, *a. int.* to talk nonsensically, jabber, gabble, babble, cackle, prattle, clack, chatter.

बकबाद = **बकवाद**, *q.v.*

बकरा, *m.* a he-goat; (erroneously) a ram, a sheep.

बकरी, *f.* a she-goat; a goat generally; (erroneously) a ewe, a sheep.

बकल; see (1) **बकुल** (2) **बक्कल** (3) **बक़**.

बकलगनी, *f.* talkativeness, garrulity.

बकला, *m.* bark, skin, rind, husk, shell (of fruit).

बकवाद, *m. f.* foolish or empty talk, prattle, nonsense.

बकवादी, *m.* (*f.* inī) one who talks foolishly or nonsensically, an idle talker, mere talker, a babbler, cackler, chatterbox, prater.

बकवास, 1, *f.* talkativeness: 2, *n.* an incessant talker.

बकवाहा, *m.* (*f.* ī) a chatterer, idle talker.

बकशवाला, *m.* (*f.* in *or* ī) = **बकसवाला**, *q.v.*

बकशीश, *more prop.* **बख़शिश**, *q.v.*

बकसवाला, (Engl. 'box' + **वाला**) *m.* (*f.* in *or* ī) a kind of pedlar who carries a box from house to house and offers miscellaneous goods (*esp.* haberdashery, stationery, etc., etc.) for sale: *lit.* box-man.

बकसा, *m.* (*f.* ī) astringent.

बकसाहट, *f.* astringency.

बकसुआ, *m.* the tongue of a buckle.

बकसैला, *m.* (*f.* ī) astringent.

बकायन, *f.* a certain tree (*Melia sempervirens*).

बकार, 1, *m.* the letter **ब**, or any symbol that may represent it: 2, the amount or value of a crop fixed by an appraiser by word of mouth.

बकारवो, *t.* (in Māṛwāṛī) to excite, stir up.

बकारा, 1, *m.* (*f.* in *or* ī) a forerunner, harbinger; a traveller: 2, intelligence forwarded by word of mouth.

बकावल, *m.* (*f.* nī) a cupbearer, a steward; a superintendent of the kitchen, head cook.

बकावली, 1, appertaining to a *bakāwal*: 2, *f.* cooking-materials.

बकासुर = **वकासुर**, *q.v.*

बकिया, *f.* a clasp-knife, a penknife.

बक़ीयां, *m.* remainder, balance.

बकुल = **वकुल**, *q.v.*

बकुला; see (1) **बकला** (2) **बगुला**.

बकेल, twine made from the root of the *ḍhāk*-tree.

बकेलू, *m.* the root of a certain grass (*munj*?) of which rope is made.

बकोटना, *t.* to lacerate with the nails, to claw, scratch.

बकोला, *m.* a covering for the head (as a piece of a blanket, etc.) used by fakeers.

बकोली, *f.* a kind of green caterpiller destructive of rice-crops.

बक़ौल, by the word or saying, according to the word of, according to.

बक्कम, *m. f.*? sappan-wood (*Cæsalpinia sappan*).

बक्कल, *m.* bark, skin, rind, husk, shell (of fruit).

बक़्क़ाल, *m.* a vendor of provisions, green-grocer.

बक्कासुर, *more prop.* **वकासुर**, *q.v.*

बक्की, talkative: hence, *m.* (*f.* inī) a prater, jabberer, chatterer.

बक्तर, *m.* iron armour, coat of mail, cuirass.

बक्ता, *m.* (*f.* trī) = **वक्ता**, *q.v.*

बख; for words beginning thus, see under the form **वख**.

बक, speaking foolishly: mixture, confusion: booty, spoil, prey, plunder.

बख, *m.* the world, the universe.

बखतर, *m.* armour, mail.

बखर, a kind of plough or bullock-hoe: a house, an enclosure, a cattle-shed.

बखरा, *m.* share, portion, lot, allowance, part.

बखरिया, *m.* a householder.

बखरी, *f.* a cottage, a house, a round granary (made of grass, reeds, and mud) raised on piles.

बखलाफ़, *more prop.* **बरख़िलाफ़**, *q v.*

बख़्श, *m.* gift, donation; pay; pardon, forgiveness; share, portion, lot. — *denā*, to bestow, vouchsafe. *Gunāhoṅko — denā*, to vouchsafe forgiveness of sins.

बख़्शना, *t.* to give, present, confer, vouchsafe, grant, bestow; to spare, to pardon, to forgive.

बख़्शा, *m.* a giver; a portion.

बख़्शिश, *f.* a gift, donation, present, gratuity, reward; generosity; beneficence; forgiveness.

बख़्शी, *m.* (*f.* in *or* inī) a giver; a pay-master: *hence*, a general, a commander-in-chief.

बख़्शीश = **बख़्शिश**, *q. v.*

बखान, *m.* explanation, description, account, definition, praise. — *k.* to explain, define, relate; to commend, praise.

बखानना = **बखान क°**, *q. v.*

बखानी; see **बखान** and **बखानना**.

बखार, 1, *m.* = **बखारी**, *q. v.*: 2, *more prop.* **बुख़ार**, *q. v.*

बखारी, *f.* a storehouse, granary, barn.

बख़िया, *m.* a kind of stitching, strong quilting; a stitched cloth, a clout.

बखियाना, *t.* to stitch, quilt.

बखी, *f.* the side under the armpit.

बख़ुद, one's very self.

बखुबि, a corruption of **बख़ूबी**, *q. v.*

बख़ुशी, with pleasure, without hesitation, readily.

बख़ूबी, *adv.* in perfection, through and through, out and out, thoroughly, in a good manner, well.

बख़ूर, *m.* perfume, odour, frankincense.

बखेड़ा, *m.* a wrangling, broil, contention, quarrel, dispute, uproar, tumult, row.

बखेड़ित; see (1) **बखेड़ा** (2) **बखेड़िया** (3) **बखेरना**.

बखेड़िया, *m.* a quarrelsome person, a wrangler, brawler: *lit.* contentious, quarrelsome.

बखेरना, *t.* (a transit. of **बिखरना**?) to despise, scatter, sow.

बग = **बक**, *q. v.*

बगचाल = **बकचाल**, *q. v.*

बगछन्दा लगाना, *n.* to be stupefied or petrified with fear at the sight of a tiger.

बगछूट, *f.* a galloping. — *daurnā*, to gallop.

बगड़, *m.* a kind of rice.

बगड़ा, *m.* trouble: deceit, cheating. — *k.* to evade the payment of one's debts or the performance of a promise.

बगड़िया, a deceitful person, cheat.

बगदना, *n.* to be spoiled: *a. int.* to return.

बग़दाद, *m. pr. n.* the city of Bagdad.

बगदाना, *t.* to cause to return, to put to the rout.

बगपाती, *f.* the side under the armpit.

बगपान्ती = **बकपान्ती**, *q. v.*

बगमेल (*Rām.*) = **बागमिलाके** or **हल्ला करके**.

बग़र, a sudden and excessive fall of rain; a kind of disease incident to camels from excessive thirst; bad water that is injurious to the cattle that drink it.

बगरना, *n.* to be spread, be expanded.

बगराना, *t.* to cause to expand, to spread out.

बगराय = **बकराजा**, *q. v.*

बगरी, *f.* a kind of rice cultivated chiefly in the province of Benares.

बगरेण्डी, *f.* a certain plant (*Jatropha curcas*, Linn.).

बग़ल, 1, *f.* the armpit; the embrace: 2, *postp.* (takes *fem.* genit.) near, close by. — *jānā* or *hojānā*, to get aside, get out of the way.

बगला, *more com.* **बगुला**, *q. v.*

बगलभगत, *m.* (*f.* in *or* ī) a hypocrite.

बगसना, *a. int.* to blow, expand (said of flowers).

बगसरिया, *m. pr. n.* (1) of a certain small class of Rājpūts in the Murādabād district (2) of a certain branch of Kanauj Brāhmaṇs.

बगहंस, *m.* (*f.* ī) the grey goose.

बगार, *m.* pasture-ground: forced labour, compulsory service (without pay or reward).

बगारना, *t.* to throw away: to spread over.

बगाह, *adv.* in time, opportunely, seasonably, timely.

बग़िया, *m. f.* (a dim. of **बाग़**) a small garden, a flower-garden, a small orchard, a private garden.

बग़ी, 1, *f.* infraction of the laws; insurrection, rebellion; tyranny, oppression: 2, rebellious, refractory: hence, *m.* (*f.* in *or* inī) a rebel, rebel, mutineer.

बगीचा = **बग़िया**, *q. v.*

बगुला, *m.* a heron (*Ardea torra* or *A. putea*, Buch.).

बगूला, *m.* a whirlwind.

बगेरी, *f.* an ortolan.

बग़ैर, save and except, without, apart from, independently of, besides.

बग़ैरह, *more prop.* **वग़ैरः**, *q. v.*

बगोकड़ा, *m.* a slap with the fist: a kind of short dagger.

बगोला; see (1) **बगुला** (2) **बगूला**.

बग़ोना, to float.

बग़ौर, with reflection, thoughtfully.

बग्गी, *f.* a kind of light chaise or two-wheeled carriage drawn by one horse.

बघनखा, *m.* a certain medicinal herb with a fragrant root.

बघना, *m.* the teeth and nails of a tiger which are hung around the neck of a child as a charm.

बघवा, a provincial form of **बाघ**, *q. v.*

बघार, *m.* the spices that are mixed with food to give it relish, condiments, seasoning.

बघारना, *t.* to season with condiments, to spice.

बघी, *f.* a horsefly.

बघेल, *m. pr. n.* a certain tribe of Rājpūts (*lit.* tiger's whelps.

बघेला, *m.* (*f.* in *or* ī) a tiger's whelp, a Rājpūt of the above-mentioned tribe.

बच, 1, = **वच**, *q.v.*: 2, a contraction of **वचन**, *q.v.*: 3, *m. pr. n.* a certain inferior tribe of Rājpūts in the district of Jaunpur. — *rahnā*, to avoid, take precautions.

बचकच, *more com.* **कचबच**, *q.v.*

बचकाना, 1, *m.* (*f.* ī) small (generally applied to clothes and shoes): 2, *m.* a dancing-boy.

बचकानी, *f.* a girl adopted by an old prostitute.

बचगूती, *f. pr. n.* a certain tribe of Rājpūts.

बचती, *f.* remainder, residue, surplus; end, conclusion.

बचन; for words beginning thus, see under the form **वचन**.

बचनन, *m.* (a Braj pl. of **बचन**) words. See **न**, 6.

बचनहारा, *m.* (*f.* in *or* ī) a promiser, vower.

बचना, *a. int.* to be saved, be spared, remain unexpended; to escape, survive, recover, to avoid, get out of the way when there is danger.

बचनाग = **बच्छनाग**, *q.v.*

बचपन, *m.* infancy, childhood.

बचा, *more com.* (1) **बच्चा** (2) **बाचा**, *qq.v.*

बचांसि (*Rām.*) = **बातें**, words.

बचाना, 1, a corruption of **बजाना**, *q.v.*: 2. *t.* to save, spare, secure, preserve, protect, defend, guard, to extricate, to reserve, to leave, to avoid, to conceal.

बचानेवाला, **बचानेहार**, **बचानेहारा** } *m.* (*f.* in *or* ī) = **बचान्हार**, *q.v.*

बचान्हार, *m.* (*f.* in) a protector, preserver, deliverer, saviour.

बचापा, *m.* deliverance, escape, safety.

बचाव, *m.* protection, defence, preservation, safety, security, escape, salvation.

बच्चा, *m.* (*f.* ī) the young of any animal (a child, calf, etc.). *Buchchewālī mūrghī*, *f.* an epithet of the Pleiades (*lit.* the hen with her chickens).

बच्चादान, *m.* an epithet of the womb.

बच्छ = (1) **बछा** (2) **वत्स**, *qq.v.*

बच्छनाग, *m.* certain vegetable poison (*Aconitum ferox* ?) said to be brought from China.

बच्छल = **वत्सल**, *q.v.*

बच्छा, *m.* (*f.* ī) = **बछा**, *q.v.*

बछ = (1) **बछा** (2) **वत्स**, *qq. v.*

बछड़ा, *m.* (*f.* ī) a calf, a colt.

बछड़ू, *m.* or *f.* a calf, a colt.

बछरा, *m.* (*f.* ī) a calf, a colt.

बछरू, *m.* or *f.* a calf, a colt.

बछल = **वत्सल**, *q.v.*

बछवा, *m.* (*f.* ī) a calf.

बछा, (Sk. **वत्स**) *m.* (*f.* ī) the young of any animal, a calf, a child.

बछिआबछिआ, a play upon the word **बछिया**, *q.v.*

बछिया, *f.* (dim. of **बछी**) a little female calf.

बछी, *f.* (*m.* **बछा**) a female calf; a little girl; a young female of any animal.

बछेड़ा, *m.* (*f.* ī) a colt.

बछेड़ी, *f.* a foal, filly.

बछेरा, *m.* (*f.* ī) a colt.

बछेरी, *f.* a foal, filly.

बछोरबटा, *m.* the distribution of an aggregate sum among several individuals.

बज:, 1, = **बजा**, *q.v.*: 2, joy, gladness: greatness of rank.

बजत्तर; see **बजन्त्री**.

बजत्तरी, *more prop.* **बजन्त्री**, *q.v.*

बजना, 1, *m.* a rupee (used among brokers): 2, *n.* to be struck, to be sounded, to be famous: *a. int.* to sound (as a bell, gong, etc.). *Das baje*, ten have sounded, *i. e.* it has struck the hour of ten.

बजनिया, *m.* one who plays on an instrument of music, a minstrel.

बजनी, *f.* a quarrel, uproar, row, fight.

बजनूकर्धनी; see **कर्धनी**.

बजन्तर; see **बजन्त्री**.

बजन्त्री, 1, *m.* (*f.* in *or* iṇī) one who plays on musical instruments: 2, *f.* a tax on musicians and female dancers.

बजन्त्रीमहल्ला, *m.* the quarter or locality inhabited by musicians; a brothel.

बजबजाना, *a. int.* to effervesce with noise in putrefying; to boil.

बजम, being quiet, lying still through fear or fatigue; delaying; being contracted, contracting oneself.

बजर, 1, = **वज्र**, *q.v.*: 2, having some distemper affecting the navel, having a projection of the belly, hanging down.

बजरबट्टू, *m.* a kind of fruit; a large kind of seed of which necklaces are made.

बजरा, *m.* a travelling-boat, large kind of pleasure-boat (*vulg.* 'budgerow').

बज़ल = **बज़्ल**, *q.v.*

बज़ला, *m.* a jest, pleasantry, *bon mot*.

बजवाना, *t.* to cause a person to sound an instrument, cause one to play on an instrument.

बजाह, 1, = **बजा**, *q.v.*: 2, joy, gladness; greatness of rank.

बजा, in place, fit, opportune, right, proper, true, accurate, just so: properly, fitly.

बजाक, *m.* a kind of serpent.

बजान, with all one's soul, heartily, in (or to) the soul: after that, afterwards, after.

बजाना, *t.* to cause an instrument to give forth a sound, to play on an instrument of music, to perform or execute music, to beat a drum.

बजानेवाला, *m.* (*f.* in *or* ī) a player on any instrument of music.

बजार, *more prop.* **बाज़ार**, *q.v.*

बजालाना, *t.* to perform, accomplish, execute, effect: to observe, obey, keep (as a law).

बज़ाहिर, on the outside, in appearance, externally.

बजिद, diligent, serious, attentive, urgent, pressing, earnest, quick. — *honā*, to be in earnest, be importunate: *a. int.* to insist upon a thing: *t.* to tempt, to urge.

बजिन्स, in kind, in detail, particularly, in some sort, by kind.

बजीदार, *m.* (see **मिसहदार**) an agricultural servant who takes corn as a recompense for his labour.

बजोर, 1, = (1) **बज़ोर** (2) **बज़्ोर**, *qq. v.*: 2, very plentiful, extremely numerous. [uiator, accuser.
बज़्ोर, unable to keep a secret: *hence*, a calum-
बजुज़, with the exception, without, besides, except.
बजोड़ना, *t.* to strike, smite.
बज्ज, cutting open (a boil); piercing (with a spear); swelling almost to bursting (as cattle from over-eating).
बज्ज़ाज़, *m.* a cloth-dealer, linen-draper, mercer; a general mercer, trader, shopkeeper, inn-keeper.
बज्ज; for words beginning thus, see under the
बज़्ल, *m.* expense; gift; munificence. [form **वज्ज**.
बझना, *n.* to be ensnared or caught (as game or
बझवट, stalk without ear. [fish): *a. int.* to stick.
बझा, *m.* marshy soil.
बझाओना = **बझाना**, *q. v.*
बझाना, *t.* to entangle, ensnare, entrap.
बझावना = **बझाना**, *q. v.*
बट, 1, = (1) **बटखरा** (2) **बटाई** (3) **वट**, *qq. v.*: 2, a contraction of **बाट** (found chiefly in composition): 3, *m.* a twist, fold, plait; a wrinkle or fold of the abdomen; tripe.
बटई, *f.* the art of making gold thread.
बटखरा, *m.* a kind of weight (for weighing with) made of metal or hard stone.
बटना, 1, *t.* to twist, form by convolution (as ropes): to divide, share: to make profit, to gain: *n.* to be twisted, be plaited, be woven together (as a rope): to be divided: 2, *m.* an instrument with which ropes are twisted. [vision), a shareholder.
बटनिया, *m.* the proprietor of a *baṭ* (share, di-
बटपाड़, *m.* a highwayman, footpad, villain, assassin, cut-throat. [the status of an assassin.
बटपाड़ी, *f.* highway robbery, the occupation or
बटपार; for words beginning thus, see under the
बटमार = **बटपाड़**, *q. v.* [form **बटपाड़**.
बटमारी = **बटपाड़ी**, *q. v.*
बटमोगरा, *m.* double jasmine (*Jasminum zambac*).
बटया, 1, = **बटिया**, *q. v.*: 2, *f.* a silken cord adorned with three fringes which females use for tying their hair behind.
बटरी, *f.* a small cup. [doos dress their food.
बटलोही, *f.* a kind of brass vessel in which Hin-
बटवा = **बटूआ**, *q. v.*
बटवाना, *t.* (causat. of **बटना**) to cause to be divided, etc.: to divide, etc.: to cause to twist.
बटवार, *m.* a tax-gatherer who collects a tax levied in kind; a revenue-officer stationed on a road to collect transit-duties.
बटवारा, *m.* a share; the partition or division of lands; the division of a crop in shares.
बटवाल = **बटवार**, *q. v.*
बटाई, *f.* a division, partition; a certain share of a crop given to a landlord for rent: wages paid for twisting ropes, etc. [the zamindar.
बटाईदार, *m.* a cultivator who shares his crop with
बटाऊ, *m.* a traveller: a highway robber.
बटाना, 1, *more com.* **बटवाना**, *q. v.*: 2, *m.* a pea.
बटार, a certain branch of the *gūjar*-tribe.
बटावना; see (1) **बटवाना** (2) **बटाना**.
बटाही; see **बटाई**.
बटिया, *f.* a narrow passage, alley, lane: a small weight-measure made of a small stone.
बटु = **वटु**, *q. v.*
बटुआ = **बटूआ**, *q. v.*
बटुर; see (1) **बटुरना** (2) **बटोर**. [be convened.
बटुरना, *m.* to be together, be collected together,
बटुवा = **बटूआ**, *q. v.*
बटूआ, *m.* a purse, a small bag (generally used for holding betel, etc.); a kind of brass vessel in which Hindoos cook their food.
बटे, 1, = **बाटे** = **हैं** (**बाटना**): 2, see **बटना**.
बटेन्य = **बटनिया**, *q. v.*
बटेर, *f.* a kind of quail (*Perdix olivacea*, Buch.).
बटेह, *m.* a pathway, passage.
बटोर, *m.* a crowd, gathering; a resort.
बटोरन, *m.* a gathering or heaping grain in one place at the time of harvest.
बटोरना, *t.* to gather up, collect, accumulate, purse.
बटोह; for words beginning thus, see under the
बटोही, *m.* (*f.* inī) a traveller, wayfarer. [form **बटोर**.
बट्टख = **बतक**, *q. v.*
बट्टा, *m.* deficiency, loss; exchange or discount, difference of exchange, anything extra, extra allowance paid to the military when on field-duty: defect, blemish, injury, offence: a bale of wood or stone: a box in which gems are kept, a casket.
बट्टाढार } level, even.
बट्टाढाल }
बट्टासट्टा, *more com.* **सट्टामट्टा**, *q. v.* [tilling spirits.
बट्टी, 1, *more prop.* **बत्ती**, *q. v.*: 2, *f.* a still for dis-
बट्टेबाज़, *m.* a juggler, trickster.
बट्टेबाज़ी, *f.* the occupation or the performance of a juggler, sleight of hand, juggling, jugglery.
बठई = **बटई**, *q. v.*
बठना, 1, = **बटना**, *q. v.*: 2, *a. int.* to enter.
बठान, pasture-ground.
बठिया; see (1) **बटया** (2) **बिटिया**.
बठो; see (1) **बठई** (2) **बठना**. [village.
बठोठ, (in Mārwāṛī) the name of Dungar-Singh's
बठुवा } *m.* a kind of herb.
बठूआ }
बड़, 1, *m.* the large Indian figtree (*Ficus Indica*): 2, this form often occurs in composition (especially at the beginning of words) as a contraction of **बड़ा**, *q. v.*
बड़ई; see (1) **बड़ाई** (2) **बढ़ई**.
बड़कबड़क, *f.* the sound of the motion of water.
बड़का, *m.* (*f.* ī) large, great, senior: *hence*, an elder brother, elder son.
बड़कूयान, *m.* a well without a cylinder of masonry.

बड़गट, *m.* the Bengal figtree. [Rājpūts.

बड़गूजर, *m.* one of the thirty-six royal castes of

बड़त ; see **बड़ना**.

बड़ती, 1, *more prop.* **बढ़ती**, *q.v.* : 2, see **बड़ना**.

बड़ना, *a. int.* (prop. **बठना**?) to enter.

बड़पन / **बड़पना** / **बड़पा** } = **बड़ापन**, *q.v.*

बड़पेटा, *m.* (*f.* in *or* ī) big-bellied : *hence*, a great eater, a greedy or an avaricious person.

बड़प्पन = **बड़पन** = **बड़ापन**, *q.v.*

बड़बड़, *f.* the light-headed talk of a person in delirium, muttering. — *k.* to gurgle.

बड़बड़ाई / **बड़बड़ाट** } = **बड़बड़ाहट**, *q.v.*

बड़बड़ाना, *a. int.* to mutter, grumble; to chatter nonsense, talk light-headedly, rave.

बड़बड़ाहट, *f.* muttering, grumbling; muttering in one's sleep as in delirium, talking light-headedly, raving ; gibberish. — *k.* to talk gibberish, to blabber, to rave. [nonsensical talker.

बड़बड़िया, *m.* a mutterer, grumbler, chatterer,

बड़बोला, *m.* (*f.* ī) a noisy talkative person.

बड़भकूआ, *m.* (*f.* **बड़भकूई**) a blockhead.

बड़यींमें in Braj = **बड़ोंमें**, *q.v.*

बड़वा ; see **बड़ा**.

बड़वाग्नि = **बड़वानल**, *q. v.*

बड़वानल, *m.* submarine fire; (in Myth.) a being (with the head of a mare) consisting of flame, who sprang from the thighs of *Urwā* and was received by the ocean.

बड़वामुख, *m.* submarine fire ; the infernal regions.

बड़हर / **बड़हल** } = **बढ़ल**, *q.v.*

बड़हेला, *n.* (*f.* in *or* ī) a wild hog.

बड़ा, *m.* (*f.* ī) great, large, big; elder, senior, major ; old ; eldest ; chief, principal. Often used adverbially in the sense of very, exceedingly. — *k.* to enlarge, exalt, promote : to extinguish a lamp, etc. (to use the direct phrase is deemed unlucky). —*din*, late (*prop.* the day has become great) : the expression is applied also to any great feast-day (as Sunday, Christmas-day, etc.). —*miyāñ*, a form of address to an elderly person = Venerable or honoured Sir. *Baṛe peṭwālā* (*f. baṛe peṭwālī*) *honā*, to be patient. *Baṛā rāstā pakaṛnā*, to enter on the long journey, *i. e.* to die. *Baṛī rātri*, late at night.

बड़ाई, *f.* greatness, bigness, largeness, bulk, bulkiness ; excellence ; boasting ; magnifying, extolling ; exalting, laudation. — *k.* or *mārnā*, to extol, magnify ; to boast, vaunt. — *denā*, to honour.

बड़ाओ, *more prop.* **बढ़ाव**, *q.v.*

बड़ाना, *a. int.* to speak in a dream or delirium, to talk incoherently in one's sleep.

बड़ापन, *m.* greatness, grandeur, magnificence, superiority, dignity, elevation, exaltation, adult state, seniority.

बड़ापा, *m.* = **बड़ापन**, *q. v.* See **पा**.

बड़ाभाव, *m.* a kind of appraisement ; money borrowed at a very high interest.

बड़ाही, 1, (*provincial*) = **बढ़ई**, *q.v.*: 2, (*emphatic*) =

बड़ियाभूम, *f.* rich and fertile soil. [**बड़ा**, *q. v.*

बड़ी, *f.* (see **बड़ा**) a kind of dish made of pulse: the charcoal fireball of the *hukkā*.

बड़ूखा, *m.* a kind of sugarcane with long thin joints

बड़ेमीयां ; see *s. v.* **बड़ा**.

बड़ेरा, *m.* (in Māṛwāṛī) a venerable old man, a sage.

बड़ोंमें, among seniors, among the great. — *milnā*, to be grown-up (*lit.* to associate with one's seniors).

बड़ोती, *more com.* **बढ़ती**, *q.v.*

बढ़इन, *f.* (*m.* **बढ़ई**) a carpenter's wife.

बढ़ई, *m.* (from **वर्द्धकि**) a carpenter, cartwright.

बढ़का, *m.* (*f.* ī) *more com.* **बड़का**, *q.v.*

बढ़ता, 1, *m.* (*f.* ī) see **बढ़ना** ; 2, *m.* = **बढ़ती**, *q.v.*

बढ़ती, *f.* augmentation, increase, enlargement, enhancement, overplus, more, promotion, advancement, elevation, vantage-ground, advantage, aggrandizement.

बढ़न, *f.* (*m.* **बढ़ई**) a carpenter's wife.

बढ़ना, *a. int.* to increase, enlarge, go on, proceed, advance, grow, rise, swell, amount, lengthen, get beyond, be promoted.

बढ़नी, *f.* a broom : advance made for cultivation, or for manufacture, or for a contract.

बढ़न्त, *f. more com.* **बढ़ती**, *q. v.*

बढ़ल, *m.* a certain small round fruit (*Artocarpus lacucha* ?) sweet and acid, and of a yellowish-red colour.

बढ़वार, *m.* / **बढ़वारी**, *f.* } see **बढ़ाई**.

बढ़ाई, *f.* prolongation, increase, enlargement, augmentation, advancement, promotion.

बढ़ाना, *t.* to increase, augment, enlarge, lengthen, forward, make advance, raise, exalt, elevate, promote push forward, aggrandize, extend, stretch out, amplify, dilate ; to rear up ; to shut up shop, leave work (at the end of the day); to extinguish ; to remove a tablecloth.

बढ़ालाना, *t.* to bring forward, lead on an army.

बढ़ाव, *m.* = **बढ़ाई**, *q. v.*

बढ़ावड़, a poet. emphat. form of **बढ़ाव**, *q.v.*

बढ़ावन, a round cake of cowdung placed on the top of a heap of corn as a charm against the effect of the evil eye.

बढ़ावा, *m.* population : excitement : flattery.

बढ़िया, 1, *m.* = **बढ़ेआ**, *q.v.* : 2, highly-priced, costly : 2, a certain small class of Rājpūts.

बढ़िया, *m.* a certain disease affecting sugarcane, Indian corn, etc., which prevents the head from shooting.

बढ़ियाल ; see (1) **बढ़ाई** (2) **बढ़िया** (3) **बढ़ेला**.

बढ़ी, 1, *m.* = **बढ़ई**, *q. v.* : 2, *f.* = **बढ़ोतरी**, *q. v.*

बढ़ेआ, *m.* a kind of sugarmill-stone extracted from the quarries of Chunār. [tribe.

बढ़ेरिया, one of the subdivisions of the *chamār*

बढ़ेला, *m.* (*f.* in *or* ī) a wild hog.

बढ़ैया, *m.* a certain species of pulse; a kind of grain-measure (in some places it is one *sér*, in other places a *sér* and a half).

बढ़ोतर, *m.* = **बढ़ोतरी**, *q.v.*

बढ़ोतरी, *f.* increase, profit, advantage, interest.

बढ़ोलिया, *m.* a certain branch of Rājpūts near Benares.

बणिक, 1, *m.* a merchant, trader: 2, *f.* trade, traffic, merchandise, commerce.

बणिकपथ, *m.* = **बणिक**, 2, *q.v.*

बणिकपुत्र, *m.* (*f.* ī) the child of a merchant or trader; a young merchant or trader.

बणिग्भाव, *m.* = **बणिक**, 2, *q.v.*

बणिज, *m.* 1, = **बणिक**, 1 and 2, *qq.v.*: 2. *pr. n.* the sixth of the astronomical periods called *karaṇ*, corresponding to the half of a lunar day.

बणिज्य, *m.* = **बणिक**, 2, *q.v.*

बणिया, *m.* a shopkeeper, merchant, trader, *usually* a corn-dealer; a Hindoo money-changer. In Calcutta, this term is also applied to the Hindoo partner or cashkeeper in a European firm.

बण्टना, *n.* to be parted, be shared, be divided, be distributed.

बण्टवाना, *t.* (causat. of **बण्टना**) to cause to be shared, etc.

बण्टवैया, *m.* a sharer, distributer, divider.

बण्टाना, *t.* to share, distribute, divide, participate.

बण्टैत, *m.* (*f.* in *or* ī) = **बण्टवैया**, *q.v.*

बण्टोई; see (1) **बण्टवैया** (2) **बण्टैत**.

बण्ठना, *n.* to be plaited, be braided, be woven, be twisted, be twined.

बण्डा, *m.* misletoe (*Epidendrum tasselatum*): a kind of ear-ornament: stone, a great stone, a rock, cliff.

बण्डी, *f.* a short robe, a short full *jāma*: a kind of bullock-carriage, *vulg.* a 'bandy.'

बण्डेरी, *f.* a ridge-pole, the ridge of a house.

बण्डोरा, *m.* a whirlwind: a devil.

बत, 1, *m.* a certain worm (*Teredo*) destructive to ships: 2, the form is frequently used in composition (especially at the beginning of words) as a contraction for **बात**, as the following examples will shew.

बतक, *f.* a duck, a duckling: a vessel formed in imitation of a duck.

बतकहा, *m.* (*f.* in *or* ī) loqacious, garrulous, talkative, conversible.

बतकहाव, *m.* loquaciousness, garrulity, conversibleness; dialogue, discourse.

बतकही, *f.* = (1) **बतकहा** (2) **बतकहाव**, *qq. v.*

बतबकड़, *m.* (*f.* in *or* ī) = **बतकहा**, *q.v.* *Bātkā*—*k.* to multiply words, talk much on little.

बतन; see (1) **बत्न** (2) **वतन**.

बतबढ़ाव, *m.* prolixity, talkativeness, wrangling, chicanery.

बतबना, *m.* (*f.* ī) a great talker, orator, sophist.

बतबाहरी, external, extraneous, foreign.

बतर, land in a state fit for the plough.

बतराना, *a. int.* to talk, speak, converse.

बतरीक़, by way of; by means of; in the manner of; on account of.

बतलाना; see (1) **बतराना** (2) **बताना**.

बतवोन, the preparation of land for the reception of seed.

बतसोंहा करना, *t.* to ventilate.

बता, *m.* a thin slip of bamboo, bomboo lath; an oblong stone on which powders are levigated.

बताई, *f.* a pointing out, shewing, indicating, informing, explaining.

बतान, a place of assemblage of cattle at night in an open field.

बताना, 1, *t.* to point out, shew, indicate, denote, signify, express, teach, tell, inform, explain, adduce, account for: *a. int.* to appear: 2, *m.* an under turban: a small bracelet of metal.

बताव; see (1) **बताई** (2) **बताना**.

बतावना = **बताना**, *q.v.* See **व**.

बतावीनीम्बू, *m.* the shaddock.

बताशा, *m.* a kind of sugarcake of a spongy texture (or filled with air, as the word implies); an air-bubble.

बतास, *f.* wind, air.

बतासफेनी, *f.* a kind of spongy sugarcake.

बतासा = (1) **बताशा** (2) **बतास**, *qq.v.*

बतिआ, 1, a dialectic form of **बात**, *q.v.*: 2, = **बतिया**.

बतिया, *f.* a certain small kind of fruit.

बतियाना, *a. int.* to speak, talk, converse, discourse, say.

बती, *more prop.* (1) **बत्ती** (2) **बात**, *qq.v.*

बतीस, *more prop.* **बत्तीस**, *q.v.*

बतूनी, talkative: *hence*, an idle talker, tattler.

बतूरी, *f.* (in the Benares district) = **चपो**, *q.v.*

बतौं, a cold refreshing wind which blows down from the snows of the Himālayas at night, commencing soon after sunset. The term is chiefly used by the hill-people: in the plains this wind is called **डाढू**.

बतोरन } **बतोलन** } *more prop.* **बटोरन**, *q.v.*

बतोली, *f.* buffoonery.

बतौरी, *f.* a flatulent or œdematous swelling.

बत्त in old Hindee = **बात**, *q.v.*

बत्ती, *f.* a candle; a wick; a match; a stick of sealing-wax: a tent or bougie. — *lekar chandhir dhūṇḍhnā*, to search, rummage.

बत्तीस, thirty-two (३२). See **औं**, **वाँ**, **वीं**, **वे**, **वें**.

बत्तीसा, *m.* a certain medicine composed of thirty-two ingredients (usually given to mares after foaling).

बत्तीसी, *f.* any aggregate of thirty-two parts; (*hence*) a set of teeth. — *dikhānā*, to shew the thirty-two (teeth), *i. e.* to make faces at anyone, to laugh, to scoff.

बत्न, *m.* the inside, stomach, womb.

बत्नी, appertaining to the belly; born of.

बत्स, for words beginning thus, see under the form **वत्स**.

बत्सा, 1, = **वत्सा**, *q. v.*: 2, *m.* a kind of rice.

बथान, a hut in the jungles (used by graziers).

बथिया, *f.* a heap of dried cowdung.

बथुआ, *m.* a kind of potherb or greens (*Chenopo-*

dium album): a kind of weed which grows with the spring crops in the vicinity of water.

बद, *f.* a bubo, a syphilitic or pestilential swelling of any of the glands: 2, (in comp.) bad, evil.

बदक, *more prop.* **बतक**, *q. v.*

बदकना, *n.* to be moved: *a. int.* to move, stir, get along, get out of the way, budge.

बदकार, *adj.* evil-doing: *hence*, an evil-doer, a sinner.

बदकारी, *f.* wickedness, wrong-doing, sin. (That is, *first*, the state of mind which originates evil action: *secondly*, the action itself: and *lastly*, the product of the action, *i. e.* sin. *Note*: — All words similarly constructed admit of these three distinct stages in sense.)

बदख़, *more prop.* **बतक**, *q. v.*

बदगमन, *m.* a bad gait; *morally*, an evil course.

बदगोई, *f.* evil-speaking, calumny, slander.

बदज़ात, of bad breed, low-born, base, vicious, of evil disposition, unprincipled, wicked.

बदज़ाती, *f.* ill-breeding, baseness, viciousness, villainy, wickedness.

बदति, (pl. **बदन्ति**) in Sk. = **वे कहते हैं**. See **बदना**.

बदन, 1, = **वदन**, *q.v.*: 2, *m.* the body. —— *phal jānā*, to have the body covered with an eruption of pustules.

बदनज़री, *f.* badness or wickedness of look.

बदना, 1, *more prop.* **बधना**, 2, *q. v.*: 2. *t.* to wager, bet, stake; to predestinate, to settle; to take or invoke as a witness; to acknowledge, to agree, to obey, not to refuse: to speak; to empannel a jury.

बदनाम, calumniated; infamous. —— *k.* to slander depreciate, abuse, speak evil of a person (generally, in his absence and with malicious intent).

बदनामी, *f.* calumny, scandal, abuse, disrepute, ignominy.

बदनी, *f.* a species of contract by which a borrower gives a bond at high interest, and (as a further security to the lender) assigns his crops valued far below the market-price: a pipkin of a small size.

बदपरहेज़ी, *f.* excess, intemperance.

बदबाचा, *m.* a false or fraudulent division (*bāchh*).

बदबू, 1, fetid, stinking: 2, *f.* a disagreeable smell, a stink.

बदबो = **बदबू**, *q. v.*

बदमआश, of a bad profession, of infamous trade, immoral: *hence*, a lowlived person, lowbred person, blackguard.

बदमआशी, *f.* immorality, dissoluteness, profligacy.

बदर, *m.* the seed of the cotton-pod, the pod of the cotton: the jujube (*Zizyphus jujubus* or *Z. scandens*).

बदरा, *m.* a cloud; cloudiness: cotton: the plant *Mimosa octandra*: a certain medicinal drug.

बदरिका, *f.* the jujube (*Zizyphus jujubus*).

बदरिकाश्रम = **बदरीशैल**, *q. v.*

बदरी, 1, = **बदरीशैल**, *q. v.*: 2, *f.* cotton.

बदरीकेदार = **बदरीशैल**, *q. v.*

बदरीछदा, *f.* a kind of perfume (apparently, a dried shell-fish): a species of the *Zizyphus* tree.

बदरीनाथ = **बदरीशैल**, *q. v.*

बदरीपत्रक, *m.* a certain leaf used as a perfume.

बदरीफला, *f.* a certain plant (blue *Sephalika* or *Nyctanthes*).

बदरीशैल, *m. pr. n.* (1) of a certain place of Hindoo pilgrimage situated in the Himālaya range (2) of a certain town and temple on the west bank of the Alaknandā river in the province of Shreenagar.

बदल, 1, a contraction of **बादल**, *q. v.*: 2, *m.* exchange, substitution, retaliation: 3, in exchange for, on account of.— *lenā*, to exchange, take in exchange.

बदलना, *t.* to alter, change, exchange.

बदलवाना, *t.* to cause to be exchanged, cause to be altered.

बदला, *m.* exchange, lieu, stead; a substitute; recompence, requital, revenge.— *lenā*, to alter: (with abl.) to take the change out of (one), take vengeance, be revenged on.

बदलाई, *f.* the price of exchange.

बदलाना, *t.* to cause to alter, to put one thing for another, to change.

बदलाम, *more prop.* **बदनाम**, *q. v.* See **न**, 9.

बदली, *f.* exchange; a relief of watches; a substitute, a person or thing taken, representation or exchange of some other person or thing: cloudiness: a small piece of cloud.

बदले, *postp.* (takes gen. *m.* infl.) in exchange, in substitution for, in return for, instead of.

बदवी, appertaining to the country or desert: hence, *m.* (*f.* in *or* ini) a countryman, Arab of the desert, Bedouin.

बदशग्यत, *more prop.* **बदसाअ़त**, *q. v.*

बदसरंजामी, *f.* badness of end or conclusion.

बदसला, *m.* a hogsty.

बदसाअ़त, *f.* an unlucky moment, unsuitable time, inauspicious occasion: *adj.* ill-timed, unlucky.

बदसुलूकी, *f*, misbehaviour, maltreatment, abuse.

बदस्त, *adv.* in hand, into hand.

बदस्तूर, according to custom, as usual, in the usual manner.

बदा, 1, *m.* (*f.* ī) said, predestinated, fated: 2, *m.* fate, destiny, predestination, the divine decree.

बदाबदी, *adv.* contentiously, with emulation or rivalry.

बदाम, a contraction of **बादाम**, *q. v.*

बदामी, *f.* a certain kind of rice.

बदि, 1, (*Rām.*) = **कहके** (**बदना**): 2. *f.* the dark half of the lunar month from full moon to new moon, the wane of the moon.

बदी, 1, = (1) **बदि** (2) **बद्धी**, *qq. v.*: 2, *f.* badness, wickedness.

बदीहा, *m.* anything done without premeditation; an extempore, an impromptu, an unexpected event; an axiom.

बदौलत, *postp.* (takes *fem.* genit.) by the fortune of, by the bounty of, by means of, through.

बद्दई; see (1) **बदी** (2) **बद्धी**.

बद्दल, *m.* (from **बादल**) a cloud.

बद्दी; see (1) **बदी** (2) **बद्धी**.

बद्ध, bound, tied, suppressed, checked, withheld, obstructed, fixed, firmly rooted.

बद्धक, one who is bound, a captive, prisoner.

बद्धकोप, *m.* (*f.* ā) one who governs or suppresses wrath.

बद्धमूल, firmly rooted, fast.

बद्धशिख, *m.* (*f.* ā) pupil; a child whose hair has has not been shaven: *adj.* young.

बद्धशिखा, *f.* a certain pungent root (said, by some, to be a kind of garlic). [saluting respectfully.

बद्धांजुलि, *f.* putting the hands to the forehead,

बद्धी, *f.* a kind of ornament worn around the neck and hanging down to the waist and crossing behind and before, a belt, or sash, a pair of braces.

बद्री; for words beginning thus, see under the form बदरी.

बध, *m.* killing, slaying, slaughter, murder.

बधक, *m.* (*f.* ikā) = **बधिक**, *q.v.* [of dying.

बधकांक्षी, *m.* (*f.* iṇī) wishful for death, desirous

बधकाम्या, *f.* desire or intent to kill or hurt.

बधदण्ड, *m.* punishment of death, capital punishment. [ing, murdering.

बधन, *m.* a smiting, wounding, killing, slaughter-

बधना, 1, *t.* to smite, to kill: *n.* to be wounded: *a. int.* to increase, grow: 2, *m.* a kind of drinking-pot with a spout to it.

बधनी, *f.* (dim. of **बधना**, 2) a kind of small drinking-pot with a spout to it. [slaughtered.

बधयोग्य, *m.* (*f.* ā) deserving to be killed, fit to be

बधवंश, *m.* the slaughter of a whole race.

बधस्थल, *m.* a place of slaughter or of execution.

बधस्थली, *f.*
बधस्थान, *m.* } = **बधस्थल**, *q.v.*

बधा, *m.* (*f.* ī) smitten, wounded, killed; grown.

बधाई, *f.* a song in congratulation; presents, etc. carried to the house of a woman on the sixth or the fortieth day after childbirth.

बधाना = (1) **बढ़ाना** (2) **बजाना**, *qq.v.*

बधावा, *m.* = (1) **बधाई** (2) **बधाया** (**बधाना**).

बधिक, murderous, destructive, injurious: hence, *m.* (*f.* ā) a killer, slayer, slaughterer, murderer, executioner; a sportsman, huntsman, fowler.

बधिका, *f.* (*m.* **बधक** and **बधिक**) a murderess, sportsman's wife, etc.

बधिया, any castrated animal, a bullock, a gelding.

बधिर, *m.* (*f.* ā) deaf.

बधिरता, *f.* (*m.* °**त्व**) deafness.

बधी, *m.* (*f.* inī) = **बधिक**, *q.v.* [form **बधू**.

बधू; for words beginning thus, see under the

बधेउ
बधेव } (*Rām.*) = **बधा हुआ** (**बधना**).

बधोपाय, *m.* any instrument or means of putting to death.

बध्य, *m.* (*f.* ā) requiring to be killed, fit to be slaughtered, deserving or doomed to die.

बध्यता, *f.* (*m.* °**त्व**) fitness to be killed.

बध्यभूमि, *f.*
बध्यस्थान, *m.* } = **बधस्थल**, *q. v.*

बन; for all words beginning thus, but not given below, see under the form **वन**.

बन, 1, *m. f.* ? a forest, wood, grove: 2, *m.* cotton; a crop of cotton: 3, (= **बनी**?) wages for harvesting, *viz.* one bundle for oneself for having reaped so many. — *jhāṛnā* or *majhāṛnā* or *mārnā*, or to beat the forests. — *jānā*, to get to be, to become. — *parnā*, to succeed, answer, suit, come to pass, come to a conclusion.

बनआना, *a. int.* to succeed in life, to prosper.

बनक, 1, *more prop.* **वणिक**, *q.v.*: 2. *f.* a sort of fruit: a kind of satin: a pimple: drops of sweat on the face.

बनकटी, *f.* a fee paid for cutting timber: the right obtained by clearing a jungle and bringing it under cultivation.

बनकट्टी = **बनकटी**, *q. v.* [ed and used as fuel.

बनकण्डा, cowdung found in the jungle and dri-

बनकर, *m.* spontaneous produce of jungle or forest-land (such as gums, honey, etc.); revenue from woods and forests.

बनकस, grass used in making ropes.

बनखण्ड, *m.* a wood, forest.

बनखण्डी, *m. pr. n.* a certain Indian forest.

बनखरा, land on which cotton has grown during the past season.

बनगोयटा
बनगोयटा } = **बनकण्डा**, *q. v.*

बनचर, *m.* (*f.* ī) = **वनचर**, *q. v.*

बनचरी, (*f.* a kind of high jungle-grass of which elephants are very fond. [chandise, commerce.

बनज, 1, = **वनज**, *q. v.*: 2, *m.* trade, traffic, mer-

बनजर, *f.* waste land, land that has not been cultivated for five years and upwards. [some years.

बनजरकदीम, land that has been left fallow for

बनजरकमी, *f.* abatement of rent for fallow land.

बनजरजदीद, land brought under cultivation after lying for some time fallow.

बनजात्रा = **वनयात्रा**, *q. v.*

बनजाना, an intensive form of **बनना**, *q. v.*

बनजारा, *m.* (*f.* in *or* ī) a grain-merchant; a grain-carrier. This term (as also the term *birinjārā*) is likewise applied as the designation of a certain distinct class of vagrants: they are Hindoos, but do not belong to any particular part of the country or to any caste, but travel about like gypsies and live in tents.

बनजारी, *f.* the wife of a *banjārā*: a kind of tent used by *banjārās*: half-boiled grain.

बनजिन, lands close to a village: a certain weed about three feet high which springs up among harvest-crops.

बनठन, dressed out (as a bridegroom, etc.).

बनत, *f.* lace, gold or silver lace, a ribbon studded with spangles. [' wild *tarāī*.'

बनतराई, *f.* a certain plant (*Luffa*), called also

बनतरिया, *m.* a certain class of people who formerly acted as wood-rangers in Gorakhpur.

बनना, *n.* to be made, be prepared; to be adjusted, be mended: *a. int.* to chime, agree, fall in with; to answer (the purpose), do, serve, avail succeed: to be, become, counterfeit.— *ṭhannā*, to be fully adorned, be decked out.

बनपड़ना, an intensive form of **बनना**, *q. v.*

बनपशु, *m.* or *f.* any wild animal.

बनप्रस्थ = **वनप्रस्थ**, *q. v.* [aquatic plant.
बनफ़शा, *f.* a violet; violet colour: a certain
बनबास; see under the form **वनवास**.
बनबिडाल } **बनबिलाव** } **बनबिल्लि** } = **वनविड़ाल**, *q. v.*
बनबिहार; see under the form **वनविहार**. [*ena*).
बनभाटा, *m.* the wild egg-plant (*Solanum melong-*
बनमाखी, *f.* the jungle-bee, the wild-honey bee.
बनमानुष, *m.* a man of the woods, a wild man, an *oran-ūtang*.
बनमाल, *f.* a garland of various kinds of flowers (usually of the *tulsī*, the *kund*, the *mandār*, the *pārijāt*, and the lotus) reaching down to the feet.
बनमाला = **बनमाल**, *q. v.* [or wearing a *banmāl*.
बनमाली, *m.* an epithet of Kṛishṇ: *lit.* having
बनया, 1, *more prop.* **बणिया**, *q. v.*: 2, victuals which people carry into the country; a picnic.
बनयुवति, *f.* a female residing in a jungle.
बनरा, *m.* a bridegroom.
बनरी, *f.* a bride. [anything.
बनवाई, *f.* (see **आई**) the price paid for making
बनवाना, *t.* (causat. of **बनना**) to cause to be made, cause to be formed, cause to be prepared.
बनवारी = **बनमाली**, *q. v.*
बनवास; see under the form **वनवास**. [facturer.
बनवैया, *m.* a maker, fabricator, former, manu-
बनस; for words beginning thus, but not given below, see under the form **वंश**. [blackish ears.
बनसी, *f.* a fishing-hook: a kind of wheat with
बनस्पति, 1, = **वनस्पति**, *q. v.*: 2, see **बनास्पत्ति**.
बना, 1, a colloquial form of **बिना**, *q. v.*: 2, *m.* (*f.* ī) made, prepared; having made, etc.: *hence*, a bridegroom; land dressed and ready for the seed. — *thannā*, to be fully adorned, be decked out. — *rahnā*, to remain waiting. — *lānā*, to make and bring.
बनांतर = **वनान्तर**, *q. v.* [ranged.
बनाचुना, *m.* (*f.* **बनीचुनी**) dressed, decked out, ar-
बनात, *f.* woollen cloth, broadcloth.
बनाती, appertaining to *banāt*, woollen.
बनातुनश, *f. pr. n.* the constellation of the Bear (as having the stars scattered, in opposition to the Pleiades in which they cluster).
बनाना, *t.* to make, fabricate, manufacture, do, fashion, form, prepare, compose, invent, build, perform, transform, change into, to make agree, to adjust, to adorn, to reconcile, to pluck a fowl, to dress victuals, to mend, repair, to rectify, to feign, mock.
बनान्तर = **वनान्तर**, *q. v.*
बनाबनाया, *m.* (*f.* **बनीबनाई**) ready-made, finished, complete, perfect, entire.
बनाय (in poet.) = **बनाके** (**बनाना**). [be in hand.
बनायाजाना, to be in process of being made, to
बनारस, a modern form of **वाराणसी**, *q. v.*
बनालाना; see *s. v.* **बना**.

बनाव, *m.* a dressing, preparing, decking oneself; preparation, formation, composition, fabric, fashion, decoration: concord, understanding, reconciliation, making up.—*k.* to adorn, bedeck, decorate.
बनावट, *f.* make, formation, composition, fiction, fabrication, contrivance, invention, affectation, sham.
बनावना = **बनाना**, *q. v.* See **व**.
बनावरी, *f.* a getting ready, preparing, prepara-
बनावाना; see (1) **बनवाना** (2) **बनाना**. [tion.
बनावो; see **बनाव** and **बनाना**.
बनास्पत्ति } **बनास्पत्ती** } **बनास्पत्थी** } *f.* forest-leaves.
बनि; for words beginning thus, but not given below, see under the form **बणि**.
बनि, *more prop.* (1) **बन** (2) **बनी** (3) **बणी**, *qq. v.*
बनिता = **वनिता**, *q. v.*
बनियाइन, *f.* (*m.* **बणिया**) the wife of a baṇiyā, a female baṇiyā, any female of the baṇiyā class.
बनियां, *more prop.* **बणिया**, *q. v.*
बनियायन, *more prop.* **बनियाइन**, *q. v.*
बनिस्बत, *postp.* (takes gen. *f.* or *m.* infl.) with relation to, with respect to, with regard to, concerning.
बनिहार, *m.* (*f.* in, ī, *or* nī) a ploughman or labourer whose services are paid in kind (*bannī*), a reaper, harvestman, farm-labourer.
बनी, *f.* 1, (dim. of **बन**) a small forest, a wood: 2, a corruption of **बणी**, *q. v.*: 3, (*m.* **बना**) a bride.
बनीक, *more prop.* **बणिक**, *q. v.*
बनीचुनी, *f.*; see **बनाचुना**.
बनीज, *more prop.* **बणिज**, *q. v.*
बनीबनाई, *f.*; see **बनाबनाया**.
बनीवाल, a certain subdivision of the *bhangī*-caste.
बनुफशा } **बनूफशा** } *more prop.* **बुनफ़शा** = **बनफ़शा**, *q. v.*
बनेटी, *more com.* **बनैटी**, *q. v.*
बनेला, *m.* (*f.* ī) = **वनेला**, *q. v.*
बनैटी, *f.* a kind of torch lighted at both ends and whirled around so as to form a double circle of fire.
बनैनी, *f.* (= **बनियाइन**) the wife of a *baṇiyā*.
बनैयाकण्डा, *m.* cowdung dried for fuel (not made
बनैला, *m.* (*f.* ī) = **वनेला**, *q. v.* [up).
बनोत्सर्ग, *m.* a certain ceremony (much resembling a marriage-ceremony) performed in honour of a newly-planted orchard, and without which it is not proper to partake of its fruit.
बनोला, *more prop.* **बिनोला**, *q. v.* [cotton-plant.
बनौरी, *f.* hail (of a small kind); the seeds of the
बन्ध, *m.* a fastening, bandage, knot; a binding; a tie, cord; fetters; imprisonment, captivity, arrest, bondage; an agreement, pledge, contract, promise, regulation; a mound, dike, dam, embankment; a belt; a roll; a string; a joint, knuckle. — *k.* to make fast, shut or bar a door; to stop, prevent; to confine, imprison, captivate. — *bāndhnā*, to restrain an inundation with dikes.

बन्दश्रोबस्त = **बन्दोबस्त**, *q.v.*

बन्दःनवाज़, an epithet of a patron: *lit.* cherisher of servants or dependents.

बन्दख़ाना, *m.* a prison-house, gaol.

बन्दगी, *f.* slavery; service, devotion; compliment (a term used in salutation).

बन्दटाल, damming up a watercourse for the purpose of irrigation.

बन्दताल = **बन्दटाल**, *q.v.*

बन्दन; for words beginning thus, but not given below, see under the form **वन्दन**.

बन्दनवार = **बन्दन्वार**, *q.v.*

बन्दना, 1, = (1) **बन्धना** (2) **वन्दना**, *qq.v.*: 2, *t.* to worship, adore, praise.

बन्दनिवार = **बन्दन्वार**, *q.v.*

बन्दन्वार, *f.* a wreath or garland of wreaths and flowers suspended across gateways on the occasion of marriages or public festivals.

बन्दफान्ता, an account of the shares of the liabilities of a village.

बन्दबटाई, *f.* an account of each share of assessment in grain.

बन्दबेहरी, *f.* a statement of the amount of each money-instalment or share of a village.

बन्दर, 1, *m.* (*f.* ī) a monkey: 2, *m.* a city, emporium, trading-town to which numbers of foreign merchants resort; a harbour, port; a market, mart.

बन्दरा, *m.* misletoe (*Epidendron tasselloides*).

बन्दराखत, *m.* a sore that does not heal, a running sore, an issue.

बन्दरिया, *f.* a female monkey.

बन्दरी, *f.* (*m.* **बन्दर**) a female monkey; a sort of chintz from *Machhli-bandar*; a sword from *Rāj-bandari*; a certain grass used as fodder for cattle.

बन्दलो, *f.* a species of Rohilkhaṇḍ rice.

बन्दा, 1, *m.* misletoe (*Epidendron tasselloides*): a grain-magazine above-ground: 2, *m.* (*f.* ī) a slave, a servant.

बन्दाना, *more prop.* **बन्धाना**, *q.v.*

बन्दारा, *m.* a shore, coast.

बन्दि; see (1) **बन्दना** (2) **बन्दी**.

बन्दित, *m.* (*f.* ā) = **वन्दित**, *q.v.*

बन्दिन, *f.* (*m.* **बन्दी**, 3) a female captive or prisoner.

बन्दिय; see (1) **बन्दना** (2) **बन्दी** (3) **वन्दनीय**.

बन्दी, 1, *f.* (*m.* **बन्दा**, 2) a female servant or slave, a handmaid: 2, *m* a certain tribe called *bhāṭ* (they are generally bards or panegyrists; *hence*) a bard: 3, *m.* (*f.* in *or* inī) a prisoner, captive: 4, *f.* a kind of ornament worn on the forehead: a dress shorter than the *jāma*; (in the language of Law and Revenue) arrangement, agreement; distribution, allowance, reduction or charge: a certain dry-measure: imprisonment, captivity.

बन्दीख़ाना, *m.* a house for captives, a place of confinement, a prison-house, gaol.

बन्दीगृह / **बन्दीघर** } = **बन्दीख़ाना**, *q.v.*

बन्दीजन, *m.* a kind of ornament: a person of the *bhāṭ*-tribe; (*hence*) a bard.

बन्दीवान, *m.* (*f.* vati) a prisoner, captive.

बन्दीशाल, *m.* / **बन्दीशाला**, *f.* } = **बन्दीख़ाना**, *q.v.*

बन्दीसार, *m.* the substance of a *bhāṭ's* teaching.

बन्दूआ, *m.* (*f.* **बन्दूई**) a prisoner, captive.

बन्दूक़, *f.* a musket, firelock.

बन्दूहा, *m.* a whirlwind.

बन्दोड़, *f.* a female slave.

बन्दोबस्त, *m.* (*lit.* binding and fastening: *hence*) settlement, regulation, disposition, agreement, management, government, economy.

बन्दोल, *m.* (*f.* in *or* ī) the child of a slave.

बन्दौं (*poet.*) = **मैं बन्दता हूं** (**बन्दना**).

बन्ध, *m. f.*? a binding, tying, holding in fetters; a bandage, tie, knot, fastening, fetter; bondage, imprisonment; a deposit, pledge; agreement, union; an embankment, dike, mound for confining water; a village-boundary. —*meṅ ānā* or *parnā*, to become a captive.

बन्धक, *m.* binding; confinement; barter; pledge, deposit, pawn, mortgage, deposit, hostage, wages.

बन्धकी, *f.* an unchaste female, harlot, wanton; a a barren female: a she-elephant.

बन्धतन्त्र, *m.* a complete army (*i.e.* an army with its four divisions of elephants, chariots, horse, and foot).

बन्धन, *m.* binding, tying, confining, fastening; the instrument with which tying is effected, a rope, thread, chain, snare, rope for tying cattle, bandage; a bond; bondage, imprisonment; a prison; an obstacle, hindrance.

बन्धनग्रन्थि, *m.* the knot of a ligature.

बन्धनरज्जु, *f.* any rope or string used for tying.

बन्धना, 1. = **बन्धनी**, *q.v.*: 2, *n.* to be tied, be fastened, be bound, be kept, be enclosed, be laid, be formed or composed, be continuous or uninterrupted.

बन्धनालय = **बन्दीख़ाना**, *q.v.*

बन्धनी, *f.* any instrument for tying or holding together, a tie, string, rope, thread, chain, snare.

बन्धव = **बन्धु**, *q.v.*

बन्धवाना, *t.* (causat. of **बन्धना**) to cause to be bound, cause to be constructed: to accuse.

बन्धवास, *f.* land embanked all around in such a manner as to retain water.

बन्धा; see **बन्धना**.

बन्धाई, *f.* a bond, binding, fastening.

बन्धान, *m.* a fixed allowance made to anyone, stipend, wages, salary, pension: raised embankments of earth for flooding lands: purchase of grain in advance of harvest.

बन्धाना, *t.* (of **बन्धना**) to bind, fasten, shut, etc.; to enjoin upon.

बन्धानी, *m.* (*f.* in *or* inī) one whose occupation it is to carry stone, timber, etc. slung over his shoulder; a pensioner; an artilleryman, gunner.

बन्धायमान, *m.* (*f.* mati) fastened, bound.

बन्धिया, *f.* a raised earthen embankment for flooding lands.

बन्धी, fastened, fettered: hence, *m.* (*f.* inī) a prisoner, captive, felon.

बन्धीमूठी, *f.* an undisclosed intention.

बन्धु, *m.* (*lit.* one who is bound: *hence*) a kinsman, relation; a friend; a brother; a prisoner, captive; a certain flower (*Pentapetes phœnicea*). The term is specially applied to a distant or cognate kinsman subsequent in right or inheritance to the gentile (*sagotra*). The *bandhu* is of three kinds (1) the kinsman of the person himself (2) his kinsman through his father (3) his kinsman through his mother.

बन्धुआ, *m.* (*f.* **बन्धुई**) one who is bound, a bondsman, captive, prisoner; a kinsman, relative, friend.

बन्धुआई, *m.* (*f.* see **आई**, 3) relationship, kinship, friendship; captivity.

बन्धुजन, *m.* a kinsman, relation, friend.

बन्धुजीव, *m.* the flower *Pentapetes phœnicea.*

बन्धुता, *f.* (*m.* °**त्व**) relationship, friendship, intimacy; a multitude of relations or friends.

बन्धुदत्त, *m.* one kind of female property, *viz.* that given to a girl at her marriage by her own relations: *lit. m.* (*f.* ā) given by a kinsman or friend.

बन्धुर, 1, uneven, undulating, bent; pleasing, handsome: injurious: deaf: 2. *m.* (*f.* ā) a crane: a goose: 3, *m.* a certain flower (*Pentapetes phœnicea*): two kinds of drugs, *viz.* (1) *Virang* (2) *Rishabh*: a diadem: the dregs of oil. [a harlot.

बन्धुरा, *f.* (*m.* **बन्धुर**) a handsome or pleasing female,

बन्धुवा, *m.* (*f.* in *or* ī) = **बन्धुआ**, *q.v.*

बन्धुवाई = **बन्धुआई**, *q.v.* [less.

बन्धुहीन, *m.* (*f.* ā) without kin, relationless, friend-

बन्धु, for words beginning thus, but not given below, see under form **बन्धु**.

बन्धुक, *m.* a certain red-flowering shrub (*Pentapetes phœnicea*): a certain tree (*Pentaptera tomentosa*): the *Ixora bandhuli.*

बन्धूकपुष्प, *m.* the tree *Pentaptera tomentosa.*

बन्धूर, *m.* purchase of grain in advance of harvest.

बन्धवाना, *more prop.* **बन्धवाना**, *q.v.* [simony.

बन्धेज, *m.* stability, steadiness, persistence: par-

बन्ध्य, *m.* (*f.* ā) bound, confined, detained, under arrest; not bearing fruit in due season, unfruitful, barren.

बन्ध्या, *f.* (*m.* **बन्ध्य**) a barren female (woman, cow, etc.), a childless woman: a certain perfume commonly called *bālā.* [a mason, builder.

बना, 1, = **बनना**, *q.v.*: 2, *m.* (*f.* ī) a bridegroom:

बनाफिर, *m.* a certain tribe of Rājpūts.

बनी, *f.* a portion of grain given to a labourer as a remuneration for his services: the touchstone: a bride.

बन्य; for words beginning thus, see under the form **बन्य**.

बन्या, 1, *more prop.* **बनिया**, *q.v.*: 2, = **वन्या**, *q.v.*

बन्हा, *m.* a conjuror, magician, wizard.

बन्हाई, *f.* a female conjuror, enchantress.

बन्हियान, *m* a bridegroom.

बपंश, *m.* (**बाप** + **अंश**) father's share, paternal estate; patrimony, heritage.

बपत, secret, hidden, concealed.

बपतिसमा, *more prop.* **बप्तिस्मा**, *q.v.*

बपसी in Bhojpurī = **बाप**, *q.v.*

बपा, *adv.* on the feet. — *honā*, to be raised, be established, be pitched.

बपु, a poetical form of **वपुष**, *q.v.*

बपुख = **बपुष**, *q.v.* See **ब** (3).

बपुरा, *m.* (*f.* ī) helpless, distressed, poor.

बपुष = **वपुष**, *q.v.* See **ब**, 1.

बपौती }
बपोती } *f.* = **बपंश**, *q.v.*
बपौती }

बप्त, secret, hidden, concealed, See. **बपत**.

बप्तिस्मा, *m.* (Greek) the Christian rite of baptism. The term has been introduced into the Indian dialects by some of the propagators of Christianity.

बप्पारे, *more com.* **बापरे**, *q.v.*

बफपै, *m.* (a corruption of **बृहस्पति**) Thursday.

बफा, *more prop.* **वफ़ा**, *q.v.*

बफारा, *m.* vapour; a vapour-bath.

बब, *more prop.* **बर्बर**, *q.v.* [a tiger, a lion.

बबर, *m.* a man who crops the manes of horses:

बबरची }
बबरजी } = **बावरची**, *q.v.*

बबराखेरी, *f.* dissension, contention, quarrelling.

बबरी, *f.* the act of cropping hair (*esp.* the manes of horses); cropped hair; tresses.

बबडता, *m.* a clumsy awkward young man, a clown, lout, bumpkin.

बबल; see (1) **बबूल** (2) **बब्बर**.

बबुआ, *m.* (*f.* **बबुई**) = **बबुवा**, *q.v.*

बबुरी, *f.* a certain tree of the *Mimosa* kind; the acacia-tree. There are several species, but the commonest is the *Arabica* (Roxb.). The *babūl* yields a valuable gum; and its bark, being a powerful astringent, is used by *chamārs* in tanning.

बबुल, *more com.* **बबूल**, *q.v.*

बबुवा, *m.* (*f.* ī) a child, a boy. (A term of fondness.)

बबूर }
बबूरी }
बबूल } *f.* = **बबुरी**, *q.v.*
बबूला }

बबोसिया, *m.* a catamite: *adj.* talking nonsense.

बबेसी, *f.* the piles.

बबै, *m.* the seed of a certain sweet-scented herb (*Ocymum pilosum*, Roxb.): a certain bird.

बब्बी, *f.* a kiss.

बभनी, *f.* a stye on the eyelids: a lizard.

बभूव, (Sk.) = **भया**, *q.v.*

बभूवुः, *more prop.* **बभूव**, *q.v.*

बभ्रु, *m.* a large ichneumon: a tawny or brown colour; any creature or object of that colour: *hence*, an epithet (1) of Vishṇu (2) of Shiv (3) of fire: *pr. n.* a certain sage: *lit.* large, great, baldheaded through disease. [hodaya.

बभ्रुवाहन, *m. pr. n.* a son of Arjun, king of Ma-

बम, *f.* a spring (of water): a measuring-rod of 3½ cubits: a fathom: (in Music) the bass; a bass or lowest string; a drum that has the deepest tone; deep sound (as that of a drum, or of the large pipes of an organ). The term is much used by Hindoo pilgrims to the temple of Vaidyanath (*vulg* Byjnath) as an interjection addressed to Shiv; thus, they shout in chorus, 'Bam Mahādev!'

बमकना, *a. int.* to swell.

बमड़ी, *interj.* alas! *Bamṛī mārnā*, to bewail the dead in the Hindoo fashion, *viz.* by uttering loud cries or wails, and slapping the mouth with the hand at the same time.

बमतेले, *m.* a certain tribe of Rājpūts (of low repute) in the Doab.

बमन; for words beginning thus, but not given below, see under the form **वमन**.

बमन, a dialectic form of **ब्राह्मण**, *q.v.*

बमना, *a. int.* to vomit: *t.* to vomit forth.

बमनी, a dialectic form of **ब्राह्मणी**, *q.v.*

बमनेटा = **ब्राह्मणेटा**, *q. v.*

बमला, a hole from which water springs up.

बमहनिया, a certain subdivision of the *kāchhi*-tribe.

बमहनी, *f.* light red soil.

बमोठा, *m.* a term applied in Upper India to anthills and to snakes' holes.

बमोल, *m.* a certain grass.

बमूजिब / **बमूजिम** / **बमोझिम** / **बमोजिब** / **बमोजीब** / **बमौजिब** } *more prop.* **बमूजिब** = **बिमूजिब**, *q. v.*

बम्म, *m.* a revenue-defaulter, one who owes a balance to the State.

बम्बई, *f. pr. n.* the city or presidency of Bombay.

बम्बा, *m.* a well; a *jet d'eau*; the spout of a fountain: a pump: a boss or nave, a large nave.

बम्बी, *f.* the navel.

बम्बू, *m.* the bamboo (*Bambusa arundinacea*). The word is said to be derived from Tamil or Telugu: it occurs, however, in Chand, *Prithirāj* I, 21.

बम्बूड़, a kind of disease in elephants (a kind of ulceration above the nails of their feet or in the lower parts of their extremities.

बम्भं; see (1) **बभ्रु** (2) **ब्राह्मण**.

बम्हन, for words beginning thus, see under the form **ब्राह्मण**.

बम्हनगौर, *m.* a certain class of the Gaur Rājpūts.

बय; for words beginning thus, but not given below, see under the form **वय**.

बय, *f.* (**वयस**) age, time of life.

बयऊ (*Rām.*) = **बोया**. See **बोना**.

बयन, *m. f.* (**वचन**) a word, saying, speech.

बयर, for words beginning thus, see under the form **वैर**.

बयल; for words beginning thus, see under the forms **बैल** and **वैल**.

बयस, *more prop.* (1) **वयस** (2) **वयस्य**, *qq. v.*

बया, *m.* an assizer: a certain small bird (*Lexia* or *Loxia Indica* or *Fringilla euplectes*) that learns to fetch and carry, and which Hindoos teach to snatch the ornamental patch or wafer from the forehead of their mistresses.

बयां; see (1) **बया** (2) **बायां**.

बयाज = **व्याज**, *q. v.*

बयान, *m. f.* explanation, relation, disclosure, unfolding. — *k.* to explain, unfold, relate, tell.

बयाना, 1, *more prop.* **बैयाना**, *q. v.*: 2, *m.* an assurance, guarantee, earnest.

बयापिक; see **व्यापक**.

बयाबान, *m.* a wilderness, desert.

बयार, *f.* wind, air.

बयारी, *f.* 1, = **बयार**, *q. v.*: 2, supper.

बयाला, *m.* (*f.* ī) flatulent: heavy or indigestible (said of esculents).

बयालीस, forty-two (४२). See **श्रों, वां, वीं, वे, वें**.

बयासी, eighty-two (८२). See **श्रों, वां, वीं, वे, वें**.

बये; see **बया**.

बर, 1, = **वर**, *q. v.*: 2, a contraction of **बरं**, *q. v.*: 3, *m.* a breadth of cloth: 4, *f.* the breast, bosom: fruit.

बरश्राना, *a. int.* to succeed, follow, remain at a distance, keep aloof, abstain, withdraw.

बरश्रामद, *f.* (*lit.* coming up: *hence*) issue; expenditure; informing (*esp.* of bribery), accusation.— *honā*, to ascend, to appear, to come forth.

बरश्राव, *m.* abstinence.

बरश्रावुर्द, *f.* a calculating, casting up, estimating, considering beforehand what may be necessary for a feast; an estimate.— *k.* to calculate, estimate, carry to account: to strike out of a muster-roll.

बरई, *m.* (*f.* **बरइन**) a seller of betel-leaf, a cultivator of betel.

बरं, (Sk. **वरम**) moreover, but, still, even, rather, better, in preference, on the contrary, on the other hand, over and above, and even, but even.

बरंग, 1, an allowance of provisions: a bell: a key: a bolt, bar: 2, *adv.* in kind; in the mode or manner of.

बरकत, *f.* (*pl.* āt) blessing; abundance, prosperity; auspiciousness; an inherent prosperity which produces success or abundance. — *denā* or *bakhshnā*, to vouchsafe a blessing, to bless, prosper. — *chāhnā* or *māngnā*, to bless, *i e.* to invoke a blessing upon.

बरकन्दाज़ = **बर्क़न्दाज़**, *q. v.*

बरक़रार, fixed, firm, established.

बरक्ष; see **वृक्ष**.

बरख = **वर्ष**, *q. v.*

बरखना, *a. int.* (from **वर्ष**) to rain.

बरखा = **वर्षा**, *q. v.*

बरख़ास्त, *f.* a recalling or removing from office, a breaking up of a court of justice, a going away.

बरख़िलाफ़, *postp.* (takes gen. *m.* infl.) on the contrary, in opposition to, against: *adj.* contrary, adverse, opposite.

बरख़िलाफ़ी, *f.* contrariety, adverseness, opposition.

बरगत, *m.* the Indian figtree (*Ficus Indica*).

बरगद = **बरगत**, *q. v.*

बरगन, a partition, division, share.

बरगा, *m.* a rafter.

बरगेल, *m.* an ortolan (*Alauda*).

बरघोष, *m.* an excellent cowherd.

बरका, *m.* } **बर्क्का**, *q.v.*
बरक्की, *f.* }

बरज = व्रज, *q.v.*

बरजतिया, *m.* a harmless kind of snake.

बरजना, *t.* to prohibit, forbid.

बरज़ोरी, *adv.* by force, violently, oppressively.

बरण = (1) **बरं** (2) **वरण** (3) **वर्ण**, *qq.v.*

बरणाऊं (*Rām.*) = **मैं वर्णता हूं** (**वर्णना**).

बरणन = वर्णन, *q.v.*

बरणनकर्त्ता, *m.* (*f.* trī) = **वर्णनकर्त्ता**, *q.v.*

बरणव (*Rām.*) = **मैं वर्णता हूं** (**वर्णना**).

बरणा = वरणा, *q.v.*

बरणी, *f.* an eyelash.

बरणौं (*Rām.*) = **मैं वर्णता हूं** (**वर्णना**).

बरडा, *m.* any kind of light sandy or stony soil.

बरडी, *f.* = **बरडा**, *q.v.*

बरत, 1, = **व्रत**, *q.v.* : 2, *f.* a thong, leathern girth, rope, cable, the rope attached to the bucket of a well: 3, *m.* use, practice : 4, a certain disease which affects [rice-crops.

बरतन = बर्त्तन, *q.v.*

बरतना, *a. int.* to consider, reflect.

बरतनी = बरत्नी, *q.v.*

बरतमान, *more prop.* **वर्त्तमान**, *q.v.*

बरता, *m.* (*f.* ī) that which has been used.

बरताना = बर्त्ताना, *q.v.*

बरताव ; see **बर्त्ताना**.

बरतुआ, land sown with sugarcane after a rice-crop.

बरत्नी, *f.* orthography.

बरथ, land situated in the midst of jungles.

बरद, 1, *m.* (*f.* ā) = **वरद**, *q.v.*: 2, *m.* (contracted from **बलीवर्द**) a bull, a bullock.

बरदमान, *more prop.* **वर्द्धमान**, *q.v.*

बरदाई, *adv.* blessing-giving : hence, *m.* (*f.* inī) the giver of a choice, vouchsafer of a blessing.

बरदान = वरदान, *q.v.*

बरदानी, *m.* (*f.* inī) } = **बरदाई**, *q.v.*
बरदायक, *m.* (*f.* ikā) }

बरदार, wide, broad (said of cloth).

बरदी, *f.* a drove of loaded cattle.

बरदैत, *m.* a panegyrist, bard.

बरदैही, *f.* compensation for pasture-ground.

बरध = बरद, *q.v.*

बरधना, *t.* to cover or bull a cow. [cow to the bull.

बरधाना, *t.* to cause a cow to be bulled, put the

बरन = (1) **बरं** (2) **वरण** (3) **वर्ण**, *qq.v.*

बरनन = वर्णन, *q.v.*

बरनना = वर्णना, *q.v.*.

बरना, 1, = **वरणा**, *q.v.*: 2, *m.* a certain fruit-tree (*Cratæva tapia*) : 3, *t.* to marry : 4, *a. int.* to burn : 5, *m.* a youth.

बरनि, 1, in Braj = **वर्णने** (**वर्णना**): 2, in Chand (a pl. of **वर**) heroes.

बरनी, 1, see **बरना** and **बरनि** ; 2, *f.* an eyelash : an advance made for cultivation or manufacture.

बरनो }
बरनों } in Braj = **बरना**, *q.v.*
बरनौ }

बरनौं in Braj = (1) **बरना** (2) **मैं वर्णता हूं**.

बरपा, on foot, raised, erected, established. — *k.* to set on foot, pitch, establish, raise, cause, produce, occasion, introduce. — *rahnā*, to continue firm or standing. — *honā*, to be raised, be set on foot, be pitched, be established, be occasioned, be introduced.

बरफ, *more prop.* **बर्फ़**, *q.v.*

बरबन, a north wind.

बरबरना, *m.* (*f.* ī) of the best colour, of an excellent colour, fair, white. [Barbary).

बरबरी, *f.* a certain large kind of goat (from

बरबस, *m.* strength, vigour, force, violence, prowess, [bravery.

बरबस्ती, *f.* = (1) **ज्यादती** (2) **बरबस**, *qq.v.*

बरबाद, given to the wind, thrown away, destroyed, laid waste, ruined. — *k.* or *denā*, to cast away, misapply, lavish, squander. — *honā*, to be squandered, be desolated, be laid waste, be ruined.

बरभसिया = बुरभसिया, *q.v.*

बरमला, *m.* (*f.* ī) public, conspicuous.

बरमा = बर्मा, *q.v.*

बरयार = बरयारा, *q.v.*

बरयारा, *m.* (*f.* ī) strong, violent : rich or fertile (said of soil) : a certain medicinal herb.

बरयोग, (= **वरयोग्य**) marriageable (said of girls).

बरराना, *a. int.* to talk in one's sleep or in delirium.

बररुचि, *more prop.* **वररुचि**, *q.v.*

बरवट, *m.* a tumour in the stomach.

बरवत, *f.* a kind of snake.

बरवह, *m.* a certain bird that feeds on fish.

बरवा, *f.* a certain musical mode (*ragiṇī*) by which deer and serpents are said to be tamed.

बरवायक, *m.* a certain class of hereditary watchmen near the Siwālik hills.

बरवार, *m.* a certain class of people whose occupation it is to cleanse and sell rice.

बरवै, *f.* a kind of measure or cadence in language.

बरष, बरस ; for words beginning thus, but not given below, see under the form **वर्ष**.

बरस, *m.* a certain intoxicating drug made of opium : a year : rain.

बरसगांठ, *f.* (*lit.* the year-knot : *hence*) the ceremony of tying a knot on the anniversary of the birthday of a child : (*hence*) a birthday, an anniversary.

बरसना, *a. int.* (from **वर्ष**) to rain.

बरसदिन }
बरसभर } = **वर्षदिन**, *q.v.*
बरसरोज़ }

बरसवां, *m.* (*f.* °वीं) = **वर्षवां**, *q.v.*

बरसवान = **वर्षवां**, *q.v.*

बरसात = **बर्सात**, *q.v.*

बरसाती = **बर्साती**, *q.v.*

बरसान, *m. pr. n.* a certain village near Mathurā.

बरसाना = **बर्साना**, *q.v.*

बरसालिया, *m.* a servant engaged in cultivation who contracts for one year's service, a servant engaged by the year.

बरसावना = **बर्साना**, *q.v.* See **ब**.

बरसी = **बर्सी**, *q.v.*

बरसोड़ी, *f.* an annual tax or rent.

बरसोदिया / **बरसोलिया** } = **बरसालिया**, *q.v.*

बरसोड़ी, *f.* an annual tax or rent.

बरस्सा, *m.* rain.

बरहक़, in truth, indeed, forsooth; for a certainty; by right, rightful; incumbent, inevitable.

बरहना, *m.* (*f.* ī) naked, bare.

बरहम, confused, entangled, spoiled; angry, vexed, sullen.

बरहमन; for words beginning thus, see under the form **ब्राह्मण**.

बरहा, *m.* a field where cows feed: a rope, string, thong: a channel for the passage of water from a well to a field or from one field to another: the land of a township which is farthest from the homestead.

बरहाई, *m.* (*f.* in *or* inī) *more prop.* **बढ़ई**, *q.v.*

बरही (*Rām.*) = **बर्ही**, *q.v.*

बरहेला, *m.* (*f.* in *or* ī) a wild hog.

बरा, 1, *m.* (*f.* ī) = **बड़ा**, *q.v.*: 2, *m.* cakes made of pulse-meal and fried in butter or ghee.

बराइ; see (1) **बराई** (2) **बराय** (3) **बराना**.

बराई, *f.* a certain kind of grain.

बराएं (*Rām.*) = **बचा करके**.

बराका, (**वराक** ?) a sinner.

बराठा, *m.* (*f.* in *or* ī) a washerman.

बरात, *f.* (**व्रात**) a marriage-possession: a commission, warrant, assignment, letter, draft.

बराती, *m.* (**व्राती**) the company and attendants at a marriage.

बराना = **बरआना**, *q.v.*

बराबर, abreast, even, level, plain, in continuity, smooth, uniform, like, alike, on a par, equal, up to, opposite to, over against, adequate, correspondent, suitable, exact, accurate, straight.

बराबरवाला, *m.* (*f.* ī) an equal.

बराबरी, *f.* equality, correspondence, exactness, emulation, rivalry, competition. — *k.* to vie with, compete with.

बरामद = **बरआमद**, *q.v.*

बराय; see (1) **बराए** (2) **बराना**.

बरार, *m.* a species of taxation; division of property.

बरारा, *f.* a thong, rope (*esp.* of a swing).

बरारी, *m.* (*f.* in *or* iṇī) a shareholder paying his portion of the *barār*-taxation.

बराव = **बरआव**, *q.v.*

बरावप; see **बड़ापन**.

बराह = **वराह**, *q v.*

बराही, *f.* a small species of sugarcane.

बरि (*Rām.*) = **बट करके** (**बरना**). See **इ**, 7.

बरिआ; see **बरिआं**.

बरिआं (*Rām.*) = (1) **बाग** (2) **बिरियां**, *qq.v.*

बरिआर = **बरयारा**, *q.v.*

बरिआइ; see **बरिआं**.

बरिंज; see **बिरिंज**.

बरिया; see **बरिआं**.

बरियाई, *f.* boastfulness, exultation.

बरियार = **बरयारा**, *q.v.*

बरियारा, *m.* (*f.* ī) = **बरयारा**, *q.v.*

बरिवंड (*Rām.*) = **बलवन्त**, *q.v.*

बरिवंडा, a poet. lengthening of **बरिवंड**, *q.v.*

बरिस (*Rām.*) = **वर्ष**, *q.v*

बरिसना, *more com.* **बरसना**, *q.v.*

बरी, 1, *more prop.* (1) **बड़ी** (2) **बली**, *qq.v.*: 2. *f.* quicklime: a kind of dish made of pulse: a wedding-garment (together with some jewels and eatables) sent in a procession from the bridegroom's house to the bride previous to a marriage; the marriage-ceremony; the wedding-day.

बरीस, *m.* (from **वर्ष**) a year.

बरीसा, a poetical form of **बरीस**, *q.v.*

बरु / **बरुक** } in Braj = **बरं**, *q.v.*

बरुण, 1, = **वरुण**, *q.v.*: 2, *m.* a certain tree (*Cratæva tapia or Capparis trifoliata*).

बरुथ, 1, *more prop.* **वरुथ**, *q.v.*: 2, a heap, multitude.

बरुथा; see (1) **बरुथ** (2) **वरुथ**.

बरू, the reed *Arundo karka* (used for writing with); a tube, pipe, conduit, canal.

बरुआ, *m.* a soil consisting of sand and clay.

बरूं; see **बरू**.

बरूत, *f.* whiskers, moustaches.

बरूथ; see (1) **बरुथ** (2) **वरुथ**.

बरे, in Ayodhyā = **लिये**, *q.v.*

बरेज, *m.* a garden for the cultivation of the *betel*-plant.

बरेजः / **बरेजा** } = **बरेज**, *q.v.*

बरेठन, *f.* a washerman's wife, a washerwoman.

बरेठा, *m.* (*f.* **बरेठन**) a washerman.

बरेरा, *f.* (*m.* ?) a wasp.

बरेषी, *f.* the negotiating of a marriage.

बरेसिरी, a certain tribe of inferior Rājpūts.

बरेहटा, 1, *more com.* **बरेठा**, *q.v.*: 2, a certain village.

बरै, *more prop.* (1) **बरई** (2) **बढ़ई**, *qq.v.*

बरैन, *more prop.* (1) **बरइन** (2) **बढ़इन**, *qq.v.*

बरो, a certain high jungle-grass.

बरोंखा = **बढ़ूंखा**, *q.v.*

बरोठा, 1, = **बरेठा**, *q.v.*: 2, *m.* a vestibule.

बरोथी, a certain tribe of cowherds (*ahīr*) in the Mynpore district.

बरोध, *m.* the branch of the baniyan-tree.

बरोबर = **बराबर**. *q.v*

बरोरु = **वरोरु**, *q.v.*

बरोसी, *f.* any vessel in which fire is kept.

बरोठा, 1, = **बरेठा**, *q.v.* : 2, *m.* a vestibule.

बरोन्धा, *m.* cotton-land.

बर्क़, *f.* lightning.

बर्क़न्दाज़, *m.* (*lit.* lightning-throwing: *hence*) a musketeer, matchlockman; a watchman, guard, escort.

बर्ग्ग, बर्ग; for words beginning thus, see under the forms **वर्षा, वर्ग**, respectively.

बर्गद = **बरगद**, *q.v.*

बर्गश्ता, turned, inverted, changed, turned back, turned away, apostatized, rebelled.

बर्गी, *m.* (from **वर्गीय**) an epithet of the Marhaṭṭas.

बर्छा, *m.* a long slender spear, a dart, javelin.—*mārnā*, to spear, kill with a spear or dart.

बर्छाबर्दार = **बर्छैत**, *q.v.*

बर्छी, *f.* = **बर्छा**, *q.v.*

बर्छीबर्दार
बर्छबर्दार } = **बर्छैत**, *q.v.*

बर्छैत, *m*, a man who uses a javelin or dart, a spearsman.

बर्जन = **वर्ज्जन**, *q.v.*

बर्जना, *t.* to prohibit, forbid.

बर्जित, *m.* (*f.* ā) = **वर्ज्जित**, *q.v.*

बर्जोरी = **बरजोरी**, *q.v.*

बर्ण; for words beginning thus, see under the form **वर्ण**.

बर्णारमट्टी, *f.* coloured soil of two kinds (the one tinged with yellow, and the other with yellow and white).

बर्त = **बरत**, *q.v.*

बर्तन, *m.* a dish, plate, basin, vessel, utensil.

बर्तना, *t.* to use.

बर्तनी, *f.* orthography.

बर्ताना, 1, *t.* to cause to use, make to use: 2, *t.* to distribute: 3, *m.* old clothes.

बर्तमान = **वर्त्तमान**, *q.v.*

बर्त्तिका = **वर्त्तिका**, *q.v.*

बर्थलमई, *m. pr. n.* the apostle Bartholomew.

बर्द, *m.* cold, frigidity; frosty weather.

बर्दान, *more prop.* **बरदान**, *q.v.*

बर्दाश्त, *f.* endurance, patience: stores, supplies.—*k.* to bear, endure.

बर्द्धमान = **वर्द्धमान**, *q.v.*

बर्फ़, *m. f.* ice, frost, snow.

बर्ब; for words beginning thus, see under the form **वर्व**.

बर्म, *m.* armour, mail.

बर्मा, *m.* a kind of gimlet or borer worked with a string (used for drilling holes by Indian carpenters): a certain plant (*Trichosanthes incisa*).

बर्माना, *t.* to drill holes, bore.

बर्म्हा, *m. pr. n.* (1) of the country of Burmah (2) of the people of Ava, the Burmese.

बर्य = **वर्य**, *q.v.*

बर्र, 1 *m.* land: 2, *f.* a wasp.

बर्रतीतर, *m.* the Indian grouse (commonly called 'Rock-partridge').

बर्रा, *m.* a kind of rope used in a village game on the 14th of the light half of *Kā,ār*.

बर्राक़ी, *f.* brilliancy, splendour, flash.

बर्राहट, *f.* chattering, prate, rant.

बर्राह, *pr. n.* the uplands on the right bank of the Yamunā.

बर्ष; for words beginning thus, but not given below, see under the form **वर्ष**.

बर्षगाँठ = **बरसगाँठ**, *q.v.*

बर्षवान = **वर्षवां**, *q.v.*

बर्षा; for words beginning thus, see under the form **वर्षा**.

बर्षात; see under the form **बर्सात**.

बर्षौड़ी, *f.* an annual tax or rent.

बर्स; for words beginning thus, but not given below, see under the forms **बरस** and **वर्ष**.

बर्सना, *a., int.* to rain.

बर्सात, *f.* (from **वर्षर्तु**) the rainy season, the rains: rain: the leathern cover or apron that protects the occupants of a carriage from rain.

बर्साती, *f.* a certain eruptive disease to which horses and kine are liable in the rains: *adj.* appertaining to rain, rainy.

बर्साना, *t.* to cause to rain, to rain down, shower down: to winnow grain.

बर्सालिया = **बरसोलिया**, *q.v.*

बर्सी, *m.* annual ceremony in commemoration of deceased relations.

बर्सौदिया
बर्सौलिया } = **बरसालिया**, *q.v.*

बर्हम; see (1) **बरहम** (2) **ब्रह्म**.

बर्हा = **बरहा**, *q.v.*

बर्हिष = **वर्हिस**, *q.v.*

बर्हिषद, *m.* a certain class of the original progenitors (*pitṛī*) of mankind.

बर्हिस = **वर्हिस**, *q.v.*

बर्ही, *m.* (*f.* in *or* inī) a peacock.

बल, 1, a corruption of **भल**, 2, *q.v.*: 2, *m.* a coil, twist, convolution, crook: strength, power, force, violence, vigour: a crow: an army: bulkiness: the body: a sacrifice, offering: 3, *m. pr. n.* (1) of Balarām or Balrām, the elder brother of Krishṇ (2) of the king of Pātāl (*more properly*, Bali).—*k.* to put forth one's strength: to sacrifice.—*khānā*, to be twisted.—*jānā*, to be sacrificed.—*denā*, to twist: to sacrifice.

बलकट, rent taken in advance; the cutting ears of corn without going through the usual process of reaping: a kind of ship or boat.

बलकटी, *f.* a certain tax formerly exacted at the commencement of reaping.

बलकन, a corruption of **बल्कि**, *q.v.*

बलकना, *a. int.* to speak indistinctly from excessive joy or intoxication: *t.* to open.

बलकल; see (1) **वल्कल** (2) **बिल्कुल**.

बलकावा, affected or distorted language.

बलकि }
बलके } *more prop.* **बल्कि**, *q.v.*

बलगना, *m.* a sobbing; a sob.

बलगा = बल्गा, *q.v.*

बलताड़, *m.* the toddy-tree (*Borassus flabelliformis*): *lit.* the strong or male palm.

बलतोड़, *m.* a pimple or sore, a small boil (supposed, as the word strictly implies, to be occasioned by the breaking or pulling out of a hair).

बलतोर, *more prop.* **बलतोड़**, *q.v.*

बलत्कार; see under the form **बलात्कार**.

बलद, *m.* horned cattle, bullocks; a burden-bearing bullock: a city, town: a country.

बलदाऊ = (1) **बलदिया** (2) **बलदेव**, *qq.v.*

बलदाना, *m.* a tax on laden oxen.

बलदार, 1, crooked, twisted, coiled, convoluted: 2, strong, powerful: 3, *m.* a kind of wheaten cake.

बलदिया, *m.* one who loads bullocks, a bullock-driver, cowherd, drover: a grain-merchant.

बलदी, *m.* (*f.* in *or* inī) = **बलदिया**, *q.v.*

बलदेव, 1, *more com.* **बलदिया**, *q.v.*: *m.* air, wind; 3, *m.* an epithet of Balarām. [called *Trāyumān*).

बलदेवा, *f.* a certain medicinal plant (commonly

बलधारी, *m.* (*f.* iṇī) a powerful person.

बलना, *a. int.* to burn, be burnt.

बलनिग्रह, *m.* a weakening, reducing strength or

बलन्द, *more prop.* **बुलन्द**, *q.v.* [power.

बलबकरा, *m.* a person who dies (in a battle, etc.) without doing anything.

बलबक्रा, *more com.* **बलबकरा**, *q.v.*

बलबलाना, *a. int.* to ferment; to be inflamed with lust; to make a noise from feelings of lust (said of the camel).

बलबीर = बलवीर, *q.v.*

बलबे, *exclam.* bravo! hurrah! well done!

बलभद्र, *m.* (*f.* ā) strong, powerful, robust: *hence*, an epithet (1) of Balarām (2) of Anant.

बलभाना, *t.* to allure.

बलभिद, *m.* (the slayer of Bali, *i.e.*) Indra.

बलभोग, *m.* the taking forcible possession of anoth-

बलम, *m.* (from **वल्लभ**) a lover, husband. [er's right.

बलमा = बलम, *q.v.*

बलरख, *m.* a person put in charge of property under distraint for arrears of revenue. [while very young.

बलरांड, *f.* a widow who has lost her husband

बलराम, *m. pr. n.* (see **राम**) the third Rām, and elder half-brother of Krishṇ. He was son of Rohiṇī, and was born at the end of the third epoch (*Dwāpar*). By some, he is identified with the eighth incarnation of Vishṇu.

बलवत, *m.* (*f.* vatī) = **बलवान**, *q.v.*

बलवती, *f.* (*m.* **बलवन्त**, etc.) an able-bodied and powerful female.

बलवत्ता, *f.* stoutness, firmness, strength, power.

बलवन्त, *m.* (*f.* vatī) strong, powerful, able-bodied, stout, lusty, robust, athletic, firm, valid.

बलवन्द, a dialectic form of **बलवन्त**, *q.v.*

बलवर्द्धन, *adj.* strengthening, ennobling.

बलवल, *more prop.* (1) **बल्वल** (2) **बुलबुल**, *qq.v.*

बलवा, *m.* disturbance, tumult, riot, alarm, sedition, rising, rebellion, disobedience, concourse, mutiny.

बलवान, *m.* (*f.* vatī) }
बलवाला, *m.* (*f.* ī) } = **बलवन्त**, *q.v.*

बलवीर, *m.* (the mighty hero, *i.e.*) Balarām.

बलसुन्दर, *m.* a kind of soil in Azīmgaṛh; clay much mixed with sand.

बलहन, *m.* phlegmatic humour, phlegm.

बलहना, *more prop.* **उलहना**, *q.v.*

बलही, *f.* a faggot. [weak, infirm.

बलहीन, *m.* (*f.* ā) powerless, without strength,

बलहीनता, *f.* (*m* °**त्व**) prostration of strength, infirmity, weakness, powerlessness, exhaustion.

बला, *f. m.* ? a certain aquatic and medicinal plant (*Sida rhombifolia* or *Sida rhomboides* or *S. Cordifolia*).

बलाई लेना }
बलायं लेना } = **बलैया लेना**, *q.v.*

बलांचिता, *f.* a sort of lute (*vīṇā*), called also Rām's lute. [form **बलाक**.

बलाक; for words beginning thus, see under the

बलागत, *f.* eloquence: maturity.

बलाट, *m.* a sort of bean.

बलात्कार, *m.* the doing anything by violence; any act of violence (such as robbery, rape, etc.); oppression, exaction: (in Law) the detention of the person of a debtor by his creditor, and the violent measures (flogging, etc.) taken by the latter to recover his debt.

बलात्कारक, *adj.* doing anything by force or violence: hence, *m.* (*f.* ikā) an oppressor, robber, etc.

बलात्कारिक, *m.* (*f.* ā) }
बलात्कारी, *m.* (*f.* iṇī) } = **बलात्कारक**, *q.v.*

बलात्मिका, *f.* the plant *Tiaridium Indicum*: a species of sunflower (*Heliotropium Indicum*).

बलान्वित, *m.* (*f.* ā) possessed of power, powerful, strong; leading an army.

बलाबल, *m.* strength and weakness; relative importance and unimportance: 2, *m.* (*f.* ā) strong and weak; strong at one time and weak at another.

बलाय, *m.* disease, sickness: a certain plant (*Capparis trifoliata*).

बलालक, *m.* the caronda (*Carissa carandus*).

बलाश, very cheaply purchased, bought at a rate far short of the real value, dog-cheap, dirt-cheap.

बलास, *m.* phlegmatic humour, phlegm.

बलाहक = वलाहक, *q.v.*

बलाहर, *m.* (*f.* nī) a low-caste servant; a village guide or messenger. [leather.

बलाही, *m.* (*f.* in *or* inī) a worker in hides and

बलि, 1, *m.* a religious offering, oblation, sacrifice; an animal that is fit for sacrifice; presentation of food to all created beings (one of the five great sacrifices of the Hindoo religion, consisting in throwing a small parcel of the offering into the air at the back of the house); fragments of food left at an oblation or at a meal: **tax**, royal revenue: the handle of a fly-flapper: 2, *f.* a wrinkle, the fold of the skin in stout persons (*esp.* females) on the upper part of the belly, or between the ensiform cartilage and the navel; skin shrivelled by old age: 3, *m. pr. n.* (1) of a certain king and *daitya* (2) of Mahābali, the virtuous sovereign of Mahābalipur who was tricked out of the dominion he had over earth and heaven by Vishṇu in the Dwarf-*Avatār* (*Vāman*), and was left (in consideration of his merits) the sovereignty of the infernal regions (*Pātāl*). — *k.* to sacrifice, make a sacrifice.— *charhānā*, to offer up sacrifice.— *denā*, to present a sacrifice.

बलित, *m.* (*f.* ā) surrounded, enveloped.

बलिदान, *m.* the offering up victims, etc. in sacrifice to a deity, the act of sacrificing a victim: the presentation of grain, etc. to all creatures.

बलिदानव, *m.* the *daitya* Bali. See **बलि**, 3.

बलिन, *m.* a bull: a camel: a hog: a sort of jasmine: a kind of pulse (*Phaseolus radiatus*): *adj.* strong: shrivelled, wrinkled: flabby, flaccid.

बलिनी, *f.* (*m.* **बली**, 2) a powerful female: a certain plant (*Sida cordifolia*).

बलिमुख, *m.* (*f.* ī) the wrinkled-faced, *i.e.* the monkey.

बलिष्ठ, *m.* (*f.* ā) strongest, most powerful, very

बलिस्थान, *m.* a place of sacrifice, an altar. [strong.

बलिहार, *m.* the slaying of oblation, sacrifice.

बलिहारी, *f.* sacrifice.— *jānā*, to be sacrificed.

बली; for words beginning thus, see under the form **बलि**.

बली, 1, *more prop.* **बलि**, *q.v.*: 2, *m.* (*f.* inī) = **बलवन्त**, *q.v.*: 3, *f.* = **बलि**, 2, *q.v.*: 4, *f.* anything offered in sacrifice to an idol (as, flowers, rice, goats, etc.).

बलु
बलुक } in Braj = **बरं**, *q.v.*

बलुवा, *m.* (*f.* **बलुवी**)
बलूआ, *m.* (*f.* **बलूई**) } (from **बालू**) sandy.

बलूत; see **बल्लूत**.

बलूरना, *t.* to tear with the nails, scratch.

बलूला, *m.* a water-bubble.

बले, yes, true, even so, well, right.

बलेंडा, *m.* a ridge-pole of a cottage: a whirlwind.

बलेंडी, *f.* a ridge-pole of a cottage.

बलेसर, a certain subdivision of the *Gūjar*-tribe.

बलेश्रा, *m.* kind of disease: *pr. n.* a certain forest in Faizābād.

बलैया लेना, *t.* to draw one's hands over the head of another in token of taking all his misfortunes on oneself. (Generally practised by women.)

बल्कल = **वल्कल**, *q.v.*

बल्कि, the Urdoo equivalent of **बरं**, *q.v.*

बल्के, *more prop.* **बल्कि**, *q.v.*

बल्य, connected with strength, strong, vigorous; [hence, *m.* semen virile.

बल्लभ = **वल्लभ**, *q.v.*

बल्लम, *m.* a spear, pike, javelin, lance.

बल्लमबर्दार, *m.* (*f.* inī) a spearman.

बल्ला, *m.* a pole or boat-hook.

बल्लाई, *m.* (*f.* inī) a kind of village servant who cuts wood and preserves the village boundaries.

बल्ली, *f.* a prop, pole, long pole or bamboo to move or steer boats with: a climbing-plant, vine. — *mārnā*, to push or steer a boat.

बल्लूत, *m.* an acorn; an oak; a chesnut-tree.

बल्वल, *m. pr. n.* a certain Daitya, the son of Ilval.

बवंडर, *m.* a whirlwind: a devil, demon.

बवंर, *f.* a creeping-plant, a vine.

बवघडर, *m.* a whirlwind: a devil, demon.

बवना = **बोना**, *q.v.* See **श्रो**, 6.

बवर, *f.* a creeping-plant, a vine. [foot.

बवाई, *f.* a kibe, chilblain, blister or chap on the

बवादा, *m.* a kind of herb somewhat like turmeric.

बवासीर, hœmorrhoids, piles.

बवाहा, *m.* (*f.* ī) affected with *Luco venerea*, pocky.

बवेःर, *m.* sowing, seed-time.

बवेसिया, *adj.* talking nonsense; *hence*, a babbler; a catamite, a sodomite.

बभ्रुवाहन, *more prop.* **बभ्रुवाहन**, *q.v.*

बश; for words beginning thus, but not given below, see under the form **वश**.

बशमा, *m.* undressed leather: a certain black grain used in anointing the eyes. [tals.

बशर, *m.* a human being, a man; mankind, mor-

बशा = (1) **वशा** (2) **बसा**, *qq.v.*

बशाई, *more prop.* **बसाई**, *q.v.*

बशात, ill-flavoured, stinking, unwholesome, bitter, disagreeable, sour, morose.

बशारत, *f.* glad tidings, good news.

बशिष्ठ = **वशिष्ठ**, *q.v.*

बशीठ = (1) **बसीठ** (2) **वशिष्ठ**, *qq.v.*

बशीठी = **बसीठी**, *q.v.*

बशीभूत, *m.* (*f.* ā) = **वशीभूत**, *q.v.*

बशीष्ठ = **वशिष्ठ**, *q.v.*

बश्य = **वश्य**, *q.v.*

बषत; see (1) **बसत** (2) **वक्त** (3) **वसति**. [form **बखान**.

बषान; for words beginning thus, see under the

बस; for words beginning thus, but not given below, see under the form **वश**.

बस, no more, enough, sufficient, plenty, abundance, very much, too much. — *k.* to stop, seize; to put an end to; to have done, finish.

बसगत = **बसगित**, *q.v.* [residence.

बसगित, *f.* residence, homestead, site of a village

बसत, inhabited, cultivated (said of land).

बसतक, *m.* a servant, minister, attendant.

बसति
बसती } = **वसति**, *q.v.*

बसन = (1) **वसन** (2) **बस**, *qq.v.* [resident, settler.

बसनहार, *m.* (*f.* nī *or* ī) an inhabitant, dweller,

बसना, 1, = **बसा**, *q.v.*: 2, *a. int.* to dwell, reside, abide, settle, inhabit: *n.* to be peopled, be built (as a city, town, etc.).

बसनी, *f*, a purse. [form बसन्त.

बसन्त; for words beginning thus, see under the

बसबास = बसवास, *q v.*

बसर, at an end, to an end. — *ānā*, to come to an end, be accomplished; to get away from: to succeed, — *k.* to bring to an end, finish, accomplish, execute: to spend, pass (time). — *jānā*, to pass away, to be finished. — *lejānā*, to bring to an end, finish, accomplish, execute; to acquit oneself; to outstrip. — *honā*, to be ended, be finished; to be spent, be passed (said of time).

बसल, *f.* an onion: millet: the heel: an iron

बसवर्त्ती, *m.* (*f.* inī) = वशवर्त्ती, *q.v.* [helmet.

बसवा = वेश्या, *q.v.*

बससि (*poet.*) = तू बसता है (बसना).

बसह, *m.* an ox, a bull.

बसा; see under the form वसा.

बसाई, *f.* (*m.* बसाया): See बसाना.

बसाना, *a. int.* to stink: *t.* to cause to dwell; to people, colonize, settle a country, bring a country under cultivation.

बसारत = बशारत, *q.v.*

बसावरी, *f.* ground-rent, rent paid by villagers who do not occupy any of the village lands.

बसिष्ठ = वशिष्ठ, *q.v.*

बसीकत, inhabited, peopled.

बसोट = वसोठ, *q.v.*

बसोठी = (1) बसोठ (2) बसोठी, *qq.v.*

बसीत, 1, *m.* the headman of a village: 2, simple, elementary, uncompounded. [dence.

बसीरत, *f.* sight, perception, circumspection, pru-

बसु; for words beginning thus, see under the form वसु. [proper forms बसु and वसू.

बसू; for words beginning thus, see under the more

बसूला, *m.* a kind of axe used by carpenters, an adze. [ting bricks.

बसूली, *f.* a small adze; an instrument for cut-

बसेरक, *m.* a certain edible root found in ponds and

बसेन्धा, *m.* (*f.* ī) fetid, stinking. [lakes: a sweeper.

बसेरा, *m.* the time before evening when birds return to their nest; a bird's nest, bird's roost; a bird's remaining on its roost; a night's lodging. — *k.* to roost.

बसेसि (*poet.*) = तू बसता है (बसना). See एसि.

बसोबास, *m.* residence, dwellingplace, home, coun-

बसोर, *m.* (from बांस) a bamboo-garden. [try.

बस्त; for words beginning thus, but not given below, see under the form वस्तु. [form वस्त.

बस्तर; for words beginning thus, see under the

बस्तरा, *m.* the plant *Callicarpa Americana.*

बस्ता, *m.* cloth in which anything is tied up, a bundle, parcel.

बस्ती, **बस्तु**; for words beginning thus, see under the forms वसति, वस्तु, respectively.

बस्तुन, *f.* (a Braj pl. of वस्तु) things.

बस्तैं, *f.* (pl. of the form बस्त = वस्तु) things.

बस्त्र; for words beginning thus, see under the

बस्त्रा = बस्तरा, *q.v.* [form वस्त्र.

बस्ना, *m.* a cloth, wrapper, pack-cloth.

बस्य; see under the form वश्य.

बस्वारी, *f.* (from बांस) a bamboo garden.

बह; the base of बहना, *q.v.* — *jānā*, to flow, pass, flow away, go with the stream; to be destroyed, be

बहइ; see वहई. [ruined.

बहंगी, *f.* a stick (generally a bamboo) with ropes hanging from each end for slinging baggage to. This stick (*vulg.* banghy) is carried on the shoulder.

बहंगीबर्दार, *m.* (*f.* in, ī, nī) = बहंगीवाला, *q.v.*

बहंगीवाला, *m.* (*f.* in or ī) one who carries a *bahangī*,

बहंत = वहन्त, *q.v.* [a 'banghywallah'.

बहकना, *a. int.* to stray: *n.* to be baulked, be disappointed, be deceived, be taken in; to be intoxicated.

बहकाना, *t.* to send astray, to baulk, disappoint, deceive, take in, foil, beguile, inveigle, mislead, humbug, tempt.

बहजाना, intensive form of बहना. See बह.

बहतर, 1, *more prop.* (1) बहत्तर (2) बिहतर, *qq.v.*: 2, a lie.

बहता, *m.* (*f.* ī) running, flowing, afloat, gliding away. *Bahte pānīmeṅ hāth dhonā*, to pay attention to one's friends, to attend to one's own duty or affairs while the opportunity is favourable, to make hay while the sun shines.

बहत्तर, seventy-two (७२). See वों, वां, वीं, वे, वें.

बहधा, *f.* pain, distress; obstruction, hindrance, prevention.

बहन, 1, *more com.* बहिन, *q.v.*: 2, = वहन, *q.v.*

बहना, 1, a dialectic form of बहिन, *q.v.*: 2, *a. int.* to flow, run, glide, pass away, drive, blow; to float.

बहनि in Braj = बहिन, *q.v.*: 2, see बहना, 2.

बहनेऊ, *m.* a brother-in-law (sister's husband).

बहनेली, *f.* an adopted sister.

बहनोई = बहनेऊ, *q.v.*

बहन्त = वहन्त, *q.v.* [ous, public; bold, brave.

बहबहा, *m.* (*f.* ī) flowing, gliding along; notori-

बहम, *adv.* one with another, one against another, together. — *ānā* or *pahunchnā*, to be procured, be acquired. — *pahunchānā*, to get, acquire, procure.

बहमन; for words beginning thus, see under the form ब्राह्मण. [fleet.

बहर, 1, = बहिर, *q.v.*: 2, *m.* a sea, a bay: 3, *f.* a

बहरमुख, *m.* (*f.* ī) = बहिर्मुख, *q.v.*

बहरखाल = बहिरका खाल. See बहर, 1.

बहरा, 1, *m.* (*f.* ī) = बहिरा, *q.v.*: 2, *m.* property, fortune; share, portion, quota; advantage, profit, gain.

बहराम, *m. pr. n.* (1) of the plant Mars (2) of several of the kings of Persia.

बहराऊ, *m.* an outsider, stranger, upstart, foreigner.

बहरावा, *m.* a feigning deafness.

बहरिया = **बाहरिया**, *q. v.*

बहरी, *f.* (*m.* **बहरा**) a deaf female: a falcon, a female hawk (*Falco calidus*, Lath.).

बहरीबचा, *m.* the male of the *bahrī*.

बहल, *f.* a two-wheeled car (for riding in, not for baggage); a coach, carriage.

बहलना, *n.* to be diverted, be amused: *a. int.* to pass agreeably, glide happily (said of time or leisure).

बहलाना, *t.* to amuse, divert, recreate.

बहलिया, *m.* a kind of retainer armed with bows and arrows; a huntsman.

बहली, *f.* = **बहल**, *q. v.* (Vulg. 'bylee'.)

बहलीम, a certain small tribe of Muhammadans near Merat and Dasna.

बहस, thirst.

बहसना, *a. int.* to argue, debate, dispute, talk.

बहहि, (pl. **बहहिं**) a poet. form = **बहता है**.

बहा, 1, *m.* (*f.* ī) flowed, floated, glided away: 2, *m.* price, value. — *denā*, to set afloat; to demolish, destroy, ruin; to deprive of fortune or felicity, to impoverish. — *phirnā*, to wander; to be in a distressed condition; to be intoxicated.

बहादुर, brave, valiant, courageous, bold, invincible: *hence*, a hero, champion, knight (a title bestowed on military officers): *contemptuously*, a martinet, a proud and haughty mortal dressed in a little brief authority.

बहान, *more com.* **बहाना**, 2, *q. v.*

बहाना, 1, *t.* to cause to flow, set afloat, launch, set adrift; to give currency to: 2, *m.* pretence, evasion, contrivance, excuse, pretext.

बहाबहा फिरना = **बहा फिरना**, *q. v.*

बहार, *f.* spring; beauty, elegance; delight.

बहाल, prosperous, flourishing, happy: reinstated, restored.

बहाव, *m.* a flooding; a flow, flood, flux, afflux; effusion; fluidity.

बहिः = **वहिः**, *q. v.*

बहिआना, *more com.* **बहजाना**, *q. v.*

बहिन }
बहिनि } *f.* (from **भगिनी**) a sister.

बहिया = **बहा** (**बहना**).

बहियार, lands at a distance from a village.

बहिर, out, without, on the outside. — *ānā*, to issue forth, come out.

बहिरमुख, *m.* (*f.* ī) = **बहिर्मुख**, *q. v.*

बहिरा, *m.* (*f.* ī) dull of hearing, deaf.

बहिराना, *t.* to amuse, divert, recreate.

बहिर्देश, *m.* a foreign or remote country.

बहिर्मुख, 1, *m.* the neglect or violation of any moral or religious duty: 2, impious: hence, *m.* (*f.* ī) an impious person.

बहिला, *f.* barren (generally applied to cattle).

बही, *f.* a book (not stitched at the sides, but at the end); a book of accounts, ledger; a register.

बहीखसरा }
बहीखता } *f.* a merchant's day-book.
बहीखाता }

बहीड़, *f.* the baggage accompanying an army: the lines near a camp where the soldiers' families live: a camp-follower of any kind.

बहीपटवारी, *f.* a village-accountant's register.

बहीमहाजन, *f.* a merchant's or banker's book.

बहीर, *more prop.* (1) **बहिर** (2) **बहीड़**, *qq. v.*

बहीरोबुना, the baggage of an army.

बहु, much, many: large, great.

बहुक, *m.* a certain plant (*Asclepias gigantea*).

बहुकण्टक, *m.* the marshy date-tree; the prickly plant *Hedysarum alhagi* (and several others).

बहुकाल, *m.* a long while, a length of time.

बहुकालीन, *m.* (*f.* ā) of long standing, old, antiquated, ancient.

बहुगन्ध, *m.* olibanum (the resin of *Boswellia thurifera*): cinnamon.

बहुगन्धा, *f.* a bud of *Michelia champaka*: certain plants (1) *Jasminum auriculatum* (2) *Nigella Indica* (3 Arabian jasmine.

बहुगुण, *m.* (*f.* ā) many-threaded, composed of many threads: manifold, many times over, multifarious, much: having many good qualities, possessed of many virtues, variously excellent.

बहुत, much, many, more, over-much, most, very, abundant, numerous. — *yār honā*, to become more intimate than formerly.

बहुतकुछ, a great deal, plenty.

बहुतय = **बहुताई** = **बहुता**, *q. v.*

बहुतसा, *m.* (*f.* ī) a great deal, very much, rather too much, somewhat beyond or exceeding.

बहुता, *f.* muchness, abundance, plentitude, excess, plenty, multitude, majority: (in Gram.) plurality.

बहुतात }
बहुताई }
बहुतास } = **बहुता**, *q. v.*
बहुतायत }

बहुति; see (1) **बहुत** (2) **बहुता** (3) **बहति** (4) **बहती**.

बहुतेरा, *m.* (*f.* ī) many, very many, much, very much, abundant, most.

बहुत्र, in many ways or manners, in many places.

बहुत्व, *m.* = **बहुता**, *q. v.*

बहुत्वक्क, *m.* a species of birch-tree (*Bhoj*).

बहुदर्शक, *m.* (*f.* ikā) }
बहुदर्शी, *m.* (*f.* inī) } = **बहुदृष्ट**, *q. v.*

बहुदुग्धिका, *f.* any plant (as, the various species of *Euphorbia*) yielding a caustic milky juice.

बहुदृष्ट, *m.* (*f.* ā) seeing much; paying attention to many things, far-seeing, much-seeing, taking a broad and comprehensive view, circumspect, cautious, forecasting, prudent, experienced.

बहुदोष, *m.* (*f.* ā) full of faults or defects, very wicked, very bad.

बहुधन, *m.* (*f.* ā) having much wealth, very rich.

बहुधा, manifoldly, in many ways or manners, in many instances, many times, often, usually, generally, mostly, in most cases, nearly always.

बहुधागत, scattered, dispersed.

बहुपटु, *m.* (*f.* **बहुपटवी**) a very clever person.

बहुपत्र, *m.* talc.

बहुपत्री, *f.* the drug *Trigonella fœnum grœcum.*

बहुपुत्र, 1, *m.* (*f.* ā) *adj.* having many children: 2, *m.* a certain tree (*Echites scholaris*).

बहुपुत्री, *f.* the plant *Asparagus racemosus.*

बहुप्रवाह, *adj.* flowing in many streams.

बहुफल, *m.* the *kadamb*-tree (*Nauclea cadamba*): adj. *m.* (*f.* ā) very fruitful, fertile.

बहुफली, *f.* the opposite-leaved figtree.

बहुब्रचन = **बहुवचन**, *q. v.*

बहुबार, many times, repeatedly, often.

बहुबाहु, *m.* (the many-armed, *i.e.*) Rāvaṇ.

बहुभाग्य, *m.* (*f.* ā) very fortunate.

बहुभान्ति, in a variety of ways.

बहुमान, *m.* great respect, reverence.

बहुमित्र, *m.* (*f.* ā) *adj.* having many friends; *pr. n.* a certain man. [form.

बहुमूर्त्ति, many-formed, variously-shaped, multi-

बहुमूल, *m.* (*f.* ā) many-rooted: a sort of reed or grass (*Hyperanthera moringa*).

बहुमूला, *f.* the plant *Asparagus racemosus.*

बहुमूली, *f.* the plant *Emblica officinalis.*

बहुमूल्य, 1, *m.* (*f.* ā) high-priced, of a high price, costly, precious, expensive: 2, *m.* a great price, a large sum of money. [valuableness, preciousness.

बहुमूल्यता, *f.* (*m.* °त्व) expensiveness, costliness,

बहुमोल = **बहुमूल्य**, *q. v.*

बहुर, again, a second time.

बहुरंगी, *m.* (*f.* inī) variable in colour, various, changeable, fickle, unsteady.

बहुरना, *a int.* to come back, return.

बहुरहि, (pl. °हिं) in poet. = **बहुरता है**.

बहुराना, *t.* to cause to return, to bring back.

बहुरि, again, a second time.

बहुरिय, *more com.* (1) **बहुरि** (2) **बहुरिया**, *qq. v.*

बहुरिया, *f.* a daughter-in-law (son's wife).

बहुरूप, many-formed, variously-shaped, multiform; many-hued, variegated, checkered; of varied aspect, varied, manifold: hence (1) *m.* (*f.* ā) the chameleon: (2) *m.* mimicry; the resin of *Shorea robusta*; the sun; hair: (3) *m.* an epithet (1) of Brahm (2) of Vishṇu (3) of Shiv (4) of the god of love (5) of a Rudra (6) of a Buddh (7) of a son of Medhātithi and of a Varsh named after him.

बहुरूपा, *f.* one of the seven tongues of fire.

बहुरूपिन, *f.* (*m.* **बहुरूपिया**) a female mimic.

बहुरूपिया, of various shapes or forms: hence, *m.* (*f.* °पिन) a person who assumes various characters and disguises, an actor, mimic.

बहुरूपी, *m.* (*f.* iṇī) = (1) **बहुरूप** (2) **बहुरूपिया**, *qq. v.*

बहुरूप्य, *m.* mimicry.

बहुरे; see (1) **बहुरना** (2) **बहुरि**.

बहुरेखा, *m.* (pl.: see **आ**, 22) many lines, wrinkles, furrows, marks of care or pain or trouble.

बहुरों }
बहुरैं } in Braj = **बहुरि**, *q. v.*

बहुल, *m.* (*f.* ā) thick, dense, compact, solid; broad, wide, widespread, spacious; capacious, ample, large; abundant, exceeding, numerous, manifold, many, much; abounding in, rich, full of; accompanied with, attended by; variously applicable, comprehensive (as a rule); born under the Pleiades; black: hence, *m.* the dark half of the month; fire or the god of fire (Agni); the sky, air; white pepper; a certain high number: *pr. n.* (1) of a certain Prajāpati (2) of a king of the Tāljanghas: *adv.* often, frequently.

बहुलता, *f.* (*m.* °त्व) abundance; multiplicity; comprehensiveness.

बहुला, 1, *m.* (pl.: see **आ**, 22) the Pleiades: a certain people: 2, *f.* a cow: cardamoms: the indigo-plant: the dark fortnight of a lunar month: 3, *f. pr. n.* (1) of the 12th *kalā* of the moon (2) of a certain goddess (3) of one of the Mātṛis attending on Skand (4) of the wife of Uttam who was son of Uttānpād (5) of a certain mythical cow (6) of a certain river.

बहुलाश्व, *m. pr. n.* a certain ancient Hindoo king.

बहुवचन, *m.* (in Gram.) the plural number.

बहुवचनान्त, (in Gram.) ending with a sign of the plural number. [*Cordia myxa*).

बहुवार, *m.* a certain fruit (*Cordia latifolia* or

बहुविध, of several descriptions, of many sorts or

बहुविधि = **बहुविध**, *q. v.* [kinds, manifold, various.

बहुबीज, containing much seed, many-seeded: hence, *m.* the custard-apple (*Annona squamosa*).

बहुवीर्य, containing much seed, many-seeded: hence, *m.* the name of several plants (1) *Terminalia bellerica* (2) *Amaranthus polygonoides* (3) *Bombax heptaphyllum* (4) *Vangueria spinosa.*

बहुव्रीहि, *m.* (in Gram.) a relative or adjective compound, a class of compounds in which the last member being a substantive loses its independence as well as its original grammatical character and together with the first member serves only to qualify or define another word. The words so formed are usually called epithets; *e. g.* **चतुर्भुज**, an epithet of Vishṇu; *lit.* the four-armed. The only title of the word *Bahuvrihi* (possessing much rice) to be the designation of such words is that it is itself an example of the rule.

बहुशत्रु, *adj.* having many enemies. [tions.

बहुशाख, *adj.* having many branches or ramifica-

बहुसुता, *f.* the plant *Asparagus racemosus.*

बहुसू, *f.* a female who has given birth to many children.

बहू, 1, *f.* (pll. **बहूएं** and **बहूओं**) a daughter-in-law (son's wife); a wife: 2, *more prop.* **बहु**, *q. v.*

बहूआर = **बहुवार**, *q. v.*

बहूत, *more prop.* **बहुत**, *q. v.*

बहूबेटी, *f.* a daughter-in-law (son's wife).

बहूमोल्य, *more prop.* **बहुमुल्य**, *q. v.*

बहूस्यों (poet.) = **मैं बहुत हो जाऊं**

बहेड़ा, *m.* beleric myrobalan (*Terminalia bellerica*).

बहेतू, *m.* a vagrant, vagabond, wanderer.

बहेन, *more prop.* **बहिन**, *q. v.*

बहेरा, 1, *m.* (*f.* ī) = बहिरा, *q.v.*: 2, = बहेड़ा, *q.v.*

बहैया, a certain class of Rājpūts in Jaunpur and Chunār.

बहेलिया, *m.* a fowler, sportsman, gamekeeper:

बहोयडा = बहोपड़ा, *q.v.* [a certain tribe of Hindoos.

बहोत, a corruption of बहुत, *q.v.*

बहोरना; see (1) बहुरना (2) बहुराना.

बहोरा, *m.* (*f.* in *or* ī) a shopkeeper or monied man in a village who advances money to (or on account of) the cultivators.

बहोरि, again, a second time.

बहोरी (*Rām.*) = (1) बनाव (2) बहोरि, *qq.v.*

बहोरो, a kind of sloping pathway for bullocks engaged in drawing water from a well.

बहोपडा, land given rent-free to the watchman (*chaukīdār*) of a village.

बह्नन; for words beginning thus, see under the

बा, *more prop.* वा, *q.v.* [form आह्नया.

बाइ = बाई, 2, *q.v.*

बाइज्जत, *more com.* बेइज़्ज़त, *q.v.*

बाइबल, *f.* (Engl.) the Bible.

बाइयां, a provincial form of बायां, *q.v.*

बाइस, 1, *more prop.* बाईस, *q.v.*: 2, *m.* cause, occasion, motive, reason, account, subject, author.

बाई, *f.* a mistress, lady (among Marhaṭṭas); a dancing-girl; a harlot; a woman: wind, air; flatulency; rheumatism.—*pachnā*, to be mortified, to be depressed, to die away.—*meṅ bharaknā*, to talk foolishly, to prate.—*sarnā*, to be discharged backward (said of wind).

बाईं, *f.* 1, (*m.* बायां) left (not right): 2, (= बावली) [a large well.

बाईका
बाईकू
बाईको } *f.* a woman, a wife.

बाईगोला = बायगोला, *q.v.*

बाईजी, *f.* (see बाई, 1, and जी, 1) the mother-bawd, the old abbess, '*la bonne.*'

बाईनी, *f.* a kind of basket in which snakes are carried about for show.

बाईस, twenty-two (२२). See ओं, वां, वीं, वे, वें.

बाईसी, *f.* the royal army (so called because composed of the troops of twenty-two provinces then constituting the Mughal empire); a command of twenty-two thousand men.—*ṭūṭnā*, to attack with one's whole force.

बाईहा, *m.* rheumatism. [the forms बायु, बाव.

बाउ, बाऊ; for words beginning thus, see under

बाउन्ह, *f.* (from बांह?) the hand.

बाए, *f.* wind, air; flatulency; rheumatism.

बाएं, *adv.* (infl. of बायां) to the left, on the left, at the left hand.

बाएगोला = बायगोला, *q.v.* [*ribes*?).

बाएबिडंग, *m.* a certain medicinal seed (*Embelia*

बाओ; for words beginning thus, see under the more common form बाव.

बां; see (1) बांह (2) बाया (3) बाम.

बांई, 1, *f.* (*m.* बांया) *more com.* बाईं, *q.v.*: 2, *more com.* बाई, *q.v.* [*com.* बाई, *q.v.*

बांईं, 1, *f.* (*m.* बांयां) *more com.* बाईं, *q.v.*: 2, *more*

बांए, (from. बांया) *more com.* बाएं, *q.v.*

बांएं, the inflected form of बांयां, *q.v.*

बांओं; for words beginning thus, see under the more common form बाव.

बांक, 1, *m.* a bending, curvature, crook: a reach or turning of a river: fault, offence, wickedness: 2, *f.* a kind of semicircular ornament worn on the arms; a kind of dagger having a curved blade; an exercise with the dagger; a settee. [ger and cutlass.

बांकपट्टा, *m.* a kind of fencing with wooden dag-

बांकपन, *m.* foppishness; debauchery; disorderly conduct.

बांका, 1, *m.* (*f.* ī) crooked; foppish, coxcombish, coquettish: *hence*, a fop, beau, coxcomb, buck, bravo, bully: 2, *m.* a knife or hook to cut bamboo with; a bent trumpet (of brass): 3, *f. pr. n.* a certain river.

बांकाचूर, *m.* a fop, beau, coxcomb, buck, bravo, bully. [a belle, etc.

बांकी, 1, *more prop.* बाक़ी, *q.v.*: 2, *f.* (*m.* बांका)

बांग, *f.* sound, voice, cry; the call of Muhammadans to worship; the crowing of a cock.—*denā* or *mārnā*, to cry out, call, crow.

बांगर, *m.* high ground, uplands.

बांगा, *m.* a kind of cotton produced exclusively in the Dacca district. Though not otherwise of superior quality, it is indispensably necessary to form the stripes of some of the finest kinds of muslin.

बांचना, 1, *more prop.* बचना, *q.v.*: 2, *t.* to read.

बांचहुगे (poet.) = बचोगे (बचना). [form बांछ.

बांछ; for words beginning thus, see under the

बांज, *more prop.* बांझ, *q.v.*

बांजर, lying waste or fallow (said of land).

बांझ, barren (said of females); sterile (said of land).

बांट, बांठ, बांड, बांद, बांध, बांब; for words beginning with either of these elements, see under the forms बायट, बायठ, बायड, बान्द, बान्ध, बाम्ब, respectively.

बांन, a corruption of बान, *q.v.*

बांनर, *m.* (*f.* ī) *more prop.* वानर, *q.v.*

बांबां क°, *a. int.* to prate idly, talk foolishly.

बांय, *more prop.* (1) बाएं (2) बायां (3) बाय, *qq.v.*

बांया, 1, *m.* (*f.* बांई) *more com.* बायां, *q.v.*: 2, *more com.* बांयां, *q.v.*

बांयां, 1, *m.* (*f.* बांईं) *more com.* बायां, *q.v.*: 2, *m.* (infl. बांयें or बांएं) the left hand, the left side.

बांये (infl. of बांया) *more com.* बाएं, *q.v.*

बांयें (infl. of बांयां) = (1) बाएं (2) बांएं, *qq.v.*

बांवां, *m.* (infl. बांवें) the left hand, the left side.

बांस, *m.* a bamboo: a certain measure (it consists of about ten feet, and is used for measuring excavations, such as tanks, ditches, etc. a cube of one *bāṅs* is called a *chaukā*).—*par charhnā*, to be branded with

बांसनी; see (1) बसनी (2) बांस (3) बांसली. [infamy.

बांसफोड़, *m.* a certain caste of Hindoos who work on (or trade in) bamboos.

बांसरी, *f.* a flute, fife, pipe: a kind of noxious weed found in parts of the Doāb, near the Yamunā.

बांसली, *f.* a flute, fife, pipe: a purse. — *bajānā*, to play on a flute or pipe.

बांसा, *m.* the bridge of the nose: the channel (in a drilling-machine) through which the seeds descend.

बांसी, 1, *f.* a flute, fife, pipe: 2, appertaining to

बांसुरी = **बांसरी**, *q.v.* [bamboo, made of bamboo.

बांसुली, *more com.* **बांसली**, *q.v.*

बांह, *f.* the arm (from the shoulder to the elbow); a sleeve: guarantee, security, protector (as when a person trusts himself in the power of an enemy, a third person who engages to return him to his house or fort in security, is his *bāṅh*). — *gahnā* or *pakaṛnā*, (to seize the arm, *i. e.*) to rescue, protect. — *chaṛhānā*, to get ready, prepare. — *ṭutnā*, to be destitute of friends or protectors. — *denā*, to assist.

बांहबल, *m.* strength of arm. [the arm.

बांहबली, *m.* (*f.* inī) a person who is strong in

बांहियां, *m.* a patron, protector.

बांहुक; see **बाहुक**. [get ready, prepare.

बांहें, *f.* (pl. of **बांह**) the arms. — *charhānā*, to

बाक, 1, *more prop.* **वाक**, *q.v.*: 2, *m.* (in Revenue) a verbal estimate of the produce of a field (without measuring the field): apprehension, fear.

बाकन्द, a certain proportion of a crop (about two fifths) paid as rent by the cultivators to the zamīndārs. [pregnancy: a young buffalo.

बाकरी, *f.* a cow advanced about five months in

बाकला, *m.* a bean, pea, potherb.

बाकस, *m.* a certain shrub (*Justicia adhatoda* or *J. gandarussa*) of which charcoal is made for the manufacture of gunpowder: (Engl.) a box.

बाक़ियात, *f.* remainders, balances, arrears.

बाकिरा, *f.* an unblemished virgin.

बाक़िला, *m.* a bean, a pea, a potherb.

बाक़ी, 1, *f.* a remnant, remainder, balance, arrears; 2, (*lit.*) remaining, left in arrear, permanent, enduring, eternal: 3, but, *i. e.* albeit, it remains to be said over and above. — *rahnā*, to remain, be left, be saved.

बाक़ीदार, *m.* (*f.* nī, ī, in) a revenue-defaulter, one who owes a balance. [form **बाख**.

बाख; for words beginning thus, see under the

बाखर, *m.* an area, courtyard; a house; several houses contained within one enclosure; an enclosure; cattlesheds: a certain drug used as a ferment: a kind of bullock-hoe.

बाखल; see (1) **बाखर** (2) **बाख़िल**.

बाख़िल, covetous.

बाग, 1, = (1) **बाघ** (2) **वाघ** (3) **वागी**, *qq.v.*: 2, *f.* a rein, bridle. — *moṛnā*, to turn the reins (this phrase is applied also to the drying up of the small-pox: thus, when the pustules begin to blacken and dry up, the people say '*Sitlāne* [or *Mātāne*] *bāg moṛī*). — *lenā*, to take the rein, *i. e.* to curb or pull up a horse. — *hāthse chāṭnā*, to slip from the hands (said of reins), *hence*, = the loss of choice, or power, or control.

बाग़, *m.* a garden, grove, orchard.

बाग़चा, *m. f.* (a dim. of **बाग़**) a small garden, a private garden, a flower-garden.

बागडोर, *f.* a long rein with which horses are led.

बागन, *m.* (a Braj pl. of **बाग़**) gardens. See **न**, 6.

बागनि, *m.* (a Braj pl. of **बाग़**) gardens. See **नि**, 2.

बाग़बान, *m.* a gardener, horticulturist.

बागम, *m.* any cultivated spot.

बागर, *m.* a hedge of thorns or twigs: *pr. n.* a certain large tract of country in Mālwa belonging to Rājpūts. [a native of Bāgar.

बागरी, appertaining to Bāgar: hence, *m.* (*f.* inī)

बाग़वान, *m.* a gardener, horticulturist.

बागवो, in Māṛwāṛī = to be called.

बागा, *m.* an honorary dress; a vestment.

बागी, *m.* (*f.* inī) a horseman, rider.

बाग़ी, *m.* (*f.* inī) a mutineer, rebel, traitor.

बाग़ीआ
बाग़ीचा
बाग़ीया } (diminutives of **बाग़**) = **बाग़चा**, *q.v.*

बागीसा, a poetical lengthening of **वागीश**, *q.v.*

बागुर; see **वागुर** and **वागुरा**.

बाघ, *m.* (*f.* n, nī, in, inī) a tiger. [**बाघ**) tigers.

बाघन, 1, *f.* = **बाघिनी**, *q.v.*: 2, *m.* (a Braj pl. of

बाघनी = **बाघिनी**, *q.v.*

बाघबकरी, *f.* 'tiger and goat.' (It is a children's-game, like our 'Fox and geese.')

बाघम्बर, *m.* a tiger's skin.

बाघा, a lengthened poet. form of **बाघ**, *q.v.*

बाघिन = **बाघिनी**, *q.v.*

बाघिनी, *f.* (*m.* **बाघ**) a tigress.

बाघी, *f.* a bubo. [form **बाच**.

बाच; for words beginning thus, see under the

बाचना, *t.* (*more com.* **बांचना**) to read.

बाछ, 1, useless: 2, *f.* selection: the corner of the lip: (in Revenue) the proportionate rate or division either of lands, or of liabilities to them.

बाछना, *t.* to choose, select.

बाछबरार, *m.* adjustment of liabilities, etc.

बाछल, a certain tribe of Rājpūts about Aligaṛh.

बाछा, *m.* (*f.* ī) *more com.* **बछा**, *q.v.*

बाछो in Māṛwāṛī = **बादशाह**, *q.v.*

बाज, 1, *more prop.* **वाज़**, *q.v.*: 2, *m.* a tax, duty, toll, import, tribute (*originally*, the tribute taken by one king from another): 3, without, in the absence of.

बाज़, 1, = **बाज़ा**, *q.v.*: 2, *m.* a hawk: a female falcon: 3, again, once more, back: 4, (in comp.) a player or practiser; e.g. *Shatranjbāz*, a chess-player: *Randibāz*, a whoremonger. — *ānā*, to leave off, decline, refuse, reject, resist. — *rakhnā*, to hold back, prevent, forbid. — *rahnā*, to decline, refuse, reject, leave off, desist, cease from, refrain from.

बाज़गश्त, returned, retreated.

बाजगाज, *m.* the sound or clangour of various musical instruments, a band of music.

बाजगाह, *f.* toll-gate, custom-house, revenue-office.

बाजगीर, *m.* (*f.* in, ī, nī) a collector of tribute or revenue, a tax-gatherer.

बाजत in poet. = **बाजता है**. See त, 5.

बाजदार = (1) **बाज़दार** (2) **बाजगीर**, *qq.v.*

बाज़दार, *m.* (*f.* nī, ī, in) a falconer. [hawks.

बाज़दारी, *f.* falcon-keeping, the care or charge of

बाजन, *m.* (a Braj pl. of **बाज** and of **बाजा**) taxes, tolls: instruments of music.

बाजनबाजा, *m.* (pl.) instruments of music.

बाजना, *a. int.* to sound (as a musical instrument), to strike (as a clock); to resound, be published: *t.* to play, strike up, perform on a musical instrument.

बाजन्तरी, *f.* a kind of tax formerly exacted from musicians and dancing-girls. [tion or examination.

बाज़फुर्स, *f.* reïterated inquiry, minute investiga-

बाजपेय = **वाजपेय**, *q.v.*

बाज़बहरी, *f.* a kind of hawk (*Falco calidus*, Lath.).

बाजबी, a corruption of **वाजिबी**, *q.v.*

बाज़रगान, *m.* a merchant, trader.

बाज़रगानी, *f.* trading, traffic, merchandise.

बाजरा, *m.* a certain grain (*Holcus spicatus* or *Panicum spicatum*, Roxb.), a kind of millet, Indian corn.

बाजरी, *f.* (dim.) a smaller kind of *bājrā*.

बाजवाना, *more prop.* **बजवाना**, *q.v.*

बाजा, *m.* music, any instrument of music. — *bajānā*, to play on an instrument of music.

बाज़ा, (= **कोई**) *m.* (*f.* ī) some, certain, sundry.

बाजाबजत्तर
बाजाबजन्तर
बाजागाजा } = **बाजगाज**, *q.v.*

बाज़ार, *m.* a market-place; a market, a constant and established market as distinguished from an occasional or periodical one.

बाज़ारी, *m.* appertaining to a market: hence, *m.* (*f.* in *or* inī) market-people, common people.

बाज़ारीबात, *f.* low language, vulgar language or dialect, Billingsgate, patois.

बाज़ारू = **बाज़ारी**, *q.v.*

बाजि; see (1) **बाजना** (2) **बाजी** (3) **बाज़ी**.

बाजिमेध = **वाजीमेध**, *q.v.*

बाजी, 1, *more prop.* (1) **बाज़ी** (2) **वाजी**, *qq.v.*: 2, (in Mārwāṛī) a title of respect: 3, *f.* nitre.

बाज़ी, 1, *f.* (*m.* **बाज़ा**) some, etc.: 2, *f.* play, sport; a game; a stake.

बाज़ीगर, *m.* (*f.* n, in, nī, ī) a tumbler, actor, one who exhibits feats of agility.

बाजीद, *m. pr. n.* a certain Panjābī poet.

बाजुगान, *more prop.* **बाज़रगान**, *q.v.*

बाज़ू, *m.* the arm; an ornament worn on the arm, armlet, bracelet; the fold a door; the side of a bedstead. [armlet, bracelet.

बाज़ूबन्द, *m.* an ornament worn on the arm, an

बाजे, 1, *more prop.* **बाज़े**, *q.v.*: 2, *m.* (pl. of **बाजा**) instruments of music.

बाज़े, *m.* (pl. of **बाज़ा**) some, certain ones.

बाजेगाजे, infl. form of **बाजागाजा**, *q.v.*

बाजेवाला, *m.* (*f.* ī) a maker or a vendor of musical instruments, a player on any instrument of music, a musician. [to be, to be.

बाझना, *n.* to be considered, be called, be held

बाञ्छ; for words beginning thus, see under the form **वांछ**.

बाट, *more com.* (1) **बायट** (2) **वाट**, *qq.v.*

बाटछाप, *f.* the stamp on weights and measures to guarantee their being genuine. [ing weights.

बाटछापी, *f.* weight-stamping: the fee for stamp-

बाटदेना, an intensive form of **बाटना**, *q.v.* [twist.

बाटना, 1, *more com.* **बायटना**, *q.v.*: 2, *t.* to spin,

बाटसाक = **वाटसाक**, *q.v.* [twisted.

बाटा, *m.* (*f.* ī) 1, *more com.* **बायटा**, *q.v.*: 2, spun,

बाटिका = **वाटिका**, *q.v.*

बाटी = (1) **बाटा** (2) **वाटी**, *qq.v.*

बाटेघाटे, somewhere or other.

बाठना, *more com.* **बाटना**, *q.v.*

बाड़, 1, = **वाड़**, *q.v.*: 2, *f.* edge (of an instrument): verge, margin, edge; fence, hedge; a line (of soldiers): *pr. n.* a certain place between Patna and Mungēr: 3, (in comp.) an enclosure, a garden. — *uṛānā* or *jhāṛnā*, to fire a volley.— *chirnā* or *chirwānā* or *rakhnā*, to sharpen, put an edge on. — *dilwānā* or *denā*, to give an edge to, to sharpen, grind; to instigate, animate, excite. — *pakāṛanā*, to urge on, encourage, teach, instruct. — *bāndhnā*, to enclose a field with thorns.

बाड़व, *m.* any Brāhmaṇ: a submarine fire: a stud or collection of mares.

बाड़वानल, *m.* a submarine fire. [charity.

बाड़ा, 1, = **वाड़ा**, *q.v.*: 2, *m.* an enclosure: alms,

बाड़िया, *m.* a whetter of cutting-instruments.

बाड़ी, *f.* an enclosed piece of ground, a garden, a kitchen-garden, an orchard; a house, dwelling, abode, home (*esp.* a house together with the garden, orchard, etc. attached to it): cotton.

बाढ़, *f.* promotion; increase: a flood.

बाढ, *f.* stubble.

बाढ़ना, *a.int.* to increase, go on, advance, enlarge, proceed, grow, swell, rise, amount, lengthen, be promoted.

बाढ़नो
बाढ़नों } in Braj = **बाढ़ना**, *q.v.*

बाढ़ही, *f.* usurious profit or interest taken on grain; interest in kind paid on seed-grain.

बाढ़ा, *m.* (*f.* ī) increased, grown, risen, amounted.

बाढ़ी = (1) **बाढ़ही** (2) **बाढ़ा**, *q.v.*

बाण; for words beginning thus, but not given below, see under the forms **वाण** and **बान**.

बाण, 1, *more prop.* (1) **वाण** (2) **बान**, *qq.v.*: 2, *f.* temper, quality, manners, disposition, method, way, custom: 3, a kind of rope made of *munj* used to form the bottom of beds and for other purposes.

बाणप्रस्थ, *more prop.* **बानप्रस्थ**, *q.v.*

बाणासज्या, *more prop.* **बाणशय्या**, *q.v.*

बाणिज्य, *m.* trade, commerce, merchandise, traffic.

बाणी = **वाणी**, *q.v.*

बाँट, *m.* share, distribution: food given to a cow while she is being milked: a weight (*i.e.* a standard whether of metal or of stone) by which things are weighed.— *denā*, to share, divide up, distribute. —*lenā*, to go shares, participate.

बाँटचोँट, *m.* share, distrbution.

बाँटना, *t.* to share, distribute, divide, portion out, divide up, dispose of, to participate, go shares.

बाँटा, 1, *m.* (*f.* ī) shared, portioned out, divided up, distributed: 2, *m.* a share, portion, allotment.

बाँठना, *more com.* **बाँटना**, *q.v.*

बाँडा, *m.* (*f.* ī) tailless, docked; *hence*, a serpent or a bird that has lost its tail. [calamity.

बाँडी, *f.* a cudgel: a kind of dress: misfortune,

बात, 1, *more prop.* **वात**, *q.v.*: 2, *f.* (Sk. **वार्त्ता**) speech, language; a word, saying; a report; a discourse; a subject, question, topic, theme; a cause, account, affair, business, fact, matter, circumstance, particular, article.—*k.* to speak, say; to converse, talk; to address.—*kāṭnā*, to interrupt anyone in speaking (whether rudely or for the purpose of inquiry). — *kā jān*, in short. — *kānko lenā*, to accept, agree to. — *kā batakkaṛ k.* to multiply words, talk much on little. *Bātki*—*f.* mere talk, verba et proeterea nil, unmeaning orders, commands not intended to be obeyed. *Bātki*—*meṅ*, in an instant.—*kursi nishin honā*, to be acceptable be approved of (said of a word, speech, affair, or proposal).—*ko pinā*, to have patience. — *gaṛhnā*, to speak to the purpose, speak so that one's words have effect or make an impression.—*ghaṭ k.* to determine, settle.—*chalānā*, to start a subject, strike up a conversation.— *ṭālnā*, to put off, excuse oneself. — *ḍālnā*, to throw away one's words, to ask in vain. — *ḍharānā*, to persist in making excuses, to put off, evade. —*pānā*, to accomplish one's wishes, to effect one's purpose.— *pinā*, to have patience. —*pheṅknā*, to jeer at, mock, speak at (but not *to*).— *phernā*, to equivocate. — *baṛhānā*, to prolong a contest. — *banānā*, to make up a story, make excuses. — *bāndhnā*, to speak with sophistication, to prevaricate. — *bigārnā*, to mar a plot, spoil an affair. — *mārnā*, to turn off, evade, divert a discourse. — *meṅ kuchh k.* to perform an affair in a word (*i. e.* in a short time), to lose no time in doing a thing. — *meṅ girānā*, to floor an opponent in an argument. — *rakhnā*, to assist; to agree, comply. — *rahnā*, to make good one's words; to be fulfilled or accomplished (said of declarations); to succeed, overcome, get the better in argument; to be accepted; to preserve perfect. — *lagānā*, to calumniate, insinuate something maliciously.

बातकहाव, *m.* = **बातचीत**, *q.v.* [confabulation.

बातचीत, *f.* conversation, discourse, talk, chitchat,

बातन, *f.* (a Braj pl. of **बात**) words, etc. See **न**, 6.

बातदबीर, *adv.* with deliberation, with good council, prudently, advisedly.

बातराग, *m.* fondness for words.

बाता; see (1) **बात** (2) **वात** (3) **वार्त्ता**.

बातांखानी, talkative.

बातापि }
बातापी } = **वातापि**, *q.v.*

बाति = (1) **बत्ती** (2) **वर्त्तिका**, *qq.v.*

बातिन, *pr. n.* a certain tract of land in Etāwah.

बातिल, false, vain, absurd, fertile; ignorant; abolished. [bougie put into a wound to keep it open.

बाती, *f.* a candle; the wick of a lamp: a tent or

बातुल = **वातुल**, *q.v.* [ing.

बातूनिया, talkative, chatty, conversible, entertain-

बातूनी, *m.* (*f.* in *or* inī) = **बातूनिया**, *q.v.*

बातेँ, *f.* (pl. of **बात**) words. *Peṭkī* —, bosom secrets. — *sunnā*, to receive abuse or harsh reproof. — *sunānā*, to abuse, speak harshly.

बातैं in Braj = **बातें**, *q.v.*

बातों, the inflective base of the oblique cases of the plural of **बात**, *q.v.* *Bātoṅ bātmeṅ* or *Bātoṅ bātoṅmeṅ* or *Bātoṅhi bātoṅmeṅ*, in the course of conversation.

बात्स्यायन = **वात्स्यायन**, *q.v.*

बाद, 1, = **वाद**, *q.v.*: 2, *f.* wind, air, breeze, gale: 3, *postp.* (takes gen. *m.* infl.) after, behind; afterwards; subsequently.

बादः, *m.* wine, spirits.

बादना = **वादना**, *q.v.*

बादप्रतिबाद = **वादप्रतिवाद**, *q.v.*

बादबान, *m.* a sail: a kind of vessel in which a lamp is placed to protect it from the wind.

बादविबाद = **वादविवाद**, *q.v.*

बादर, 1, = **बादल**, *q.v.*: 2, *m.* the cotton-plant: *adj.* made of cotton. [weather, continous rain.

बादल, *m.* a cloud, rain-cloud; a rainy day, rainy

बादलः = **बादला**, *q.v.* [stuff variegated.

बादला, *m.* gold or silver wire; brocade of silken

बादली, *f.* silver cloth: cloudiness.

बादले; see (1) **बादल** (2) **बादला** (3) **बदले**.

बादशाह, *m.* a king, sovereign, monarch, emperor.

बादशाहज़ादा, *m.* (*f.* ī) a king's child.

बादशाहत, *f.* royalty, sovereignty, kingship, empire, reign, sway, government, rule.

बादशाही, 1, *f.* = **बादशाहत**, *q.v.*: 2, appertaining to a monarch, kingly, royal, imperial.

बादह, *m.* wine, spirits.

बादहवाई, *f.* useless, fruitlessness, waste.

बादा, 1, *m.* wine, spirits: 2, *m.* (*f.* ī); see **बादना**.

बादानुबाद = **वादानुवाद**, *q.v.*

बादान्य = **वादान्य**, *q.v.*

बादाम, *m.* an almond; the fruit of the *Terminalia catappa* (which resembles the almond).

बादामी, 1, appertaining to almonds, almond-shaped: 2, *m.* a kind of dish of which almonds form a main ingredient: any eunuch.

बादार, a large house, a granary raised on piles.

बादि; see (1) **बादना** (2) **प्रयोजन** (3) **वृथा**.

बादिनि, *more prop.* **वादिनी**, *q.v.* [see **बादना**.

बादी, 1, *m.* (*f.* inī) = **वादी**, *q.v.*: 2, *f.* (*m.* **बादा**);

बादीचोर, *m.* (*f.* in) an inveterate thief.

बादुर, *m.* a flying fox, a bat.

बाध, *m.* prohibition, hindrance, opposing; annoyance ; damage; danger : a string, chord : a lesser division of an estate : a plain, desert.

बाधक, obstructive,annoying,painful,damaging : hence, *m.* (*f.* ika) an obstructor, opponent, foe.

बाधन, *m.* an opposing, obstruction, impeding ; refutation ; pain. [thwart, check, frustrate.

बाधना, *t.* to oppose, hinder, obstruct, resist,

बाधा, *f.* obstruction,impediment,hindrance,prevention, interruption, disturbance, annoyance : refutation : pain, affliction, distress, anguish.

बाधाकारक, *m.* (*f.* ikā) } **बाधक**, *q.v.*
बाधाकारी, *m.* (*f.* iṇī)

बाधिका, *f.* (*m.* **बाधक**) a female opponent.

बाधित, *m.* (*f.* ā) obstructed, impeded ; pained, tormented.

बाधी, *m.* (*f.* inī) *more com.* **बाधक**, *q. v.*

बाध्य, *m.* (*f.* ā) *adj.* requiring to be stopped.

बान = (1) **बाण** (2) **वाण** (3) **वान** (4) **वाना** (5) **रंग**, *qq.v.*

बानगी, *f.* a sample, specimen, pattern, example, muster.

बानदार, *m.* (*f.* in *or* nī) a rocket-thrower.

बानप्रस्थ = **वानप्रस्थ**, *q.v.*

बानर, *m.* (*f.* ī) = **वानर**, *q.v.*

बानवे, ninety-two (९२). See **ओं, वां, वीं, वे, वें**.

बानव्वे = **बानवे**, *q.v.*

बाना, 1, *t.* to open, spread out, stretch out : to cast : 2, *m.* habit : profession : fashion in dress (peculiar to individuals or to bodies of persons regarded collectively ; thus, a regimental uniform might be called '*bānā.*') ; uniformity : a kind of weapon ; a veil : the woof (in weaving) : (in the Dakkhanī dialect) a vat, earthen jar or pot having a round bottom and no feet : a kind of hemispherical bucket made of iron plates closely riveted together, used in raising water for irrigation.—*bāndhnā*, to be ready, to be determined.

बानात, *f.* broadcloth. [broadcloth, woollen.

बानाती, appertaining to broadcloth, made of

बानाना, *more prop.* **बनाना**, *q.v.*

बानारस = **वाराणसी**, *q.v.*

बानावाला, *m.* (*f.* ī) an archer, bowman.

बानासुर = **वाणासुर**, *q.v.*

बानि ; see (1) **बानी** (2) **वाणि** (3) **वाणी**.

बानिया in Braj = **बणिया**, *q.v.*

बानी, 1, *more prop.* **वाणी**, *q.v.* : 2, *f.* the price paid for any work : a fabric or manufacture : a certain yellow earth with which potters ornament vessels : the thread with which cloth is woven : a certain weight = 80 rupees : ashes.

बानीकार, *m.* (*f.* nī) an architect ; a composer, author, beginner ; an investigator.

बानीकारी, *f.* architecture ; composing, composition ; investigation ; commencing a business.

बानीबानी, *f.* the price of weaving.

बानु in Māṛwāṛī = dress.

बानू, *f.* a woman of rank, lady, gentlewoman.

बानूआ, *m.* (*f.* **बानूई**) a certain water-bird.

बानूसा, *m.* } a kind of cloth.
बानूसी, *f.*

बानैत, *m.* an archer, bowyer, bowman.

बान्वना, *more prop.* **बान्धना**, *q.v.*

बान्दर, *m.* (*f.* ī *or* nī) an ape, monkey, marmoset.

बान्दरा, *m.* (*f.* ī) = **बान्दर**, *q. v.*

बान्दा, 1, *m.* a kind of parasitical plant (*Epidendrum*, esp. *Tassellatum*, Roxb.) : 2, *m. pr. n.* a certain district of Būndēlkhaṇḍ.

बान्दी, a lengthened form of **बन्दी**, *q.v.* [sonment.

बान्ध, *m.* an embankment, confinement, impri-

बान्धना, *t.* to bind, tie, fasten, shut ; to stop water, to embank ; to stop ; to pack ; to invent, contrive, devise, compose, fabricate, form, build ; to aim ; to put ; to settle.

बान्धनू, *m.* a certain mode of dyeing (in which the cloth is tied in different places to prevent the parts tied from receiving the dye) : a kind of silk cloth : a kind of parrot : slander : plot, plan. [Būndēlkhaṇḍ.

बान्धलगोती, a certain tribe who inhabit part of

बान्धव, *m.* (*f.* ī) a kinsman, relative, friend.

बान्धा, *m.* (*f.* ī) fastened, etc. (see **बान्धना**).

बान्धी, *more prop.* **बन्धी**, *q. v.*

बान्वे, *more prop.* **बानवे**, *q. v.*

बाप, *m.* father.—*k.* to regard anyone as father. *Bāp merā* or *Bāp re* or *Bāp re bāp* are exclamations expressive of surprize, grief, etc. = O father! *Bāp jī*, (my) honoured or beloved father!

बापजी = **बाप जी**. See *s.v.* **बाप**.

बापड़ा, (= **बपुरा**) *m.* (*f.* ī) helpless, poor, destitute.

बापतिस्म } *more com.* **बप्तिस्मा**, *q.v.*
बापतिस्मा

बापदादा, *m.* forefathers (*lit.* father and grand-

बापरा, *m.* (*f.* ī) *more com.* **बापड़ा**, *q. v.* [father).

बापरे = **बाप रे**. See *s.v.* **बाप**.

बापरो in Braj = **बापड़ा**, *q. v.*

बापिका = **बावली**, *q. v.*

बापी = **वापी**, *q. v.*

बापुरा, *m.* (*f.* ī)
बापुरो (*Rām.*) } = **बापड़ा**, *q. v.*
बापो in Braj

बाफ, *f.* (Sk. **बाष्प**) steam, vapour, exhalation.

बाब, *m.* a door,gate : a chapter,section,division of a book; a subject,head, topic, affair, business,point, matter, reason, manner, method, mode, sort,species.

बाबजद
बाबजुद } *more prop.* **बावुजूद**, *q. v.*
बाबजूद

बाबत, *postp.* (takes *fem.* genit.) on account of, concerning, for.

बाबन = **बामन**, *q. v.*

बाबनी, *f.* a snake's hole. [a filbert: a ball, bullet.

बाबर, *m.* a kind of sweetmeat : a species of grass :

बाबरियां, a man's head of hair (long and uncut).

बाबर्ची, *more prop.* **बावर्ची**, *q. v.*

बाबल in Māṛwāṛī = **बाबा**, *q.v.*

बाबा, *m.* father, dad; sire, sir; (endearingly) child: a *sannyāsī*. [dear; dear child.

बाबाजान, (expressive of endearment) father

बाबुल, *m. pr. n.* the city of Babylon, Babel.

बाबुली, appertaining to Babylon, Babylonish: hence, *m.* (*f.* inī) a Babylonian.

बाबू, *m.* a child: a prince: master, gentleman (commonly used, especially among Bengālees, as a term of respectful address = Mr., Sir, Esq.).

बाबूली; see (1) **बाबुली** (2) **बबुरी**. [of, for.

बाबें, by reason of, on account of, for the sake

बाभन, *m.* a certain caste of bastard Brāhmaṇs concerning whose origin many curious legends are told.

बाम, 1, a contraction (1) of **बामन** (2) of **बामा**, *qq.v.*: 2, = **वाम**, *q.v.*: 3, *f.* an eel (*Ophidium Simack*, Buch.); a snake: 4, *m.* an upper story, the terrace or roof of a house: morning, dawn: a fathom (a measure of six feet, or three and a half cubits, or the space embraced by the extended arms).

बामशृंग = **वामशृंग**, *q.v.* [morning.

बामदाद, *f.* morning, dawn; aurora: *adv.* in the

बामदेव = **वामदेव**, *q.v.* [of the forms **ब्राह्मण**, **वामन**.

बामन; for words beginning thus, see under either

बामनहट्टी, *f.* the plant *Ovieda verticillata*, Roxb.

बामननी, a colloquial form of **ब्राह्मणी**, *q.v.*

बामनी / **बामनो** } = **बामननी**, *q.v.*

बामन्ह, 1, a Braj pl. of **बामे**, *q.v.* (see **न्ह**): 2, a colloquial form of **ब्राह्मण**, *q.v.*

बाम्ब, *f. m.?* an eel, snake. — *andhūā*, an eel.

बाम्बी / **बाम्बई** / **बाम्बनी** / **बाम्भी** } *f.* a snake's hole: an anthill.

बाम्हन; for words beginning thus, see under the

बाम्हनहट्टी = **बामनहट्टी**, *q.v.* [form **ब्राह्मण**.

बाम्हनी, 1, = **ब्राह्मणी**, *q.v.*: 2, *f.* a stye on the eyelid: a lizard: a certain medicinal herb, the moonplant.

बाय, 1, = **पसारके** (**बाना**, 1): 2, for words beginning thus, but not given below, see under the form **वाय**.

बायल, 1, = **वायल**, *q.v.*: 2, apart, separate, distinct, strange, other, different. *Yih bāt — hai*, this is another matter.

बाया, 1, = **बया**, *q.v.*: 2, *m.* (*f.* **बाई**) opened, spread out; cast: 3, *m.* a weighman.

बायाँ, 1, *m.* (*f.* **बाईं**) left (not right): 2, *m.* (in Music) the bass; the bass sound (*esp.* of the *tabla*, *dholak*, and *pakhāwaj*, which are played with the left hand).— *pāṅw pūjnā*, to acknowledge the cunning of an artful person.

बायु; for words beginning thus, see under the

बाये; see **बाया**. [form **वायु**.

बायें, *more prop.* **बाएं**, *q.v.*

बार, 1, *more prop.* (1) **बाड़** (2) **बाल** (3) **बाला** (4) **वार**, *qq.v.*: 2, *m.* prohibition; obstacle; a load, burden; pregnancy: a court, tribunal, sitting of a sovereign to give audience: repetition: fruit: leave, permission; admission: the perquisite of the cow-herd in milk (generally, the milk of every eighth day): 3, this word (in the sense of 'time', 'once') is put at the end of numerals to form ordinals; e. g. *Ekbār*, once: 4, in Māṛwāṛī = assistance: a door. — *lagānā*, to delay, hesitate. — *denā*, to load, impose, cucumber, give charge; to afford trouble; to give leave; to give admission.

बारंबार = **बारम्बार**, *q.v.*

बारख़ाना, *m.* a warehouse.

बारगाह, *f.* a court, palace, place of audience.

बारचाप, a kind of cloth.

बारजुन, *m.* a name of (ू) the secondary form of **ऊ**.

बारण = **वारण**, *q.v.*

बारणा = (1) **बारना** (2) **वारना**, *qq.v.*

बारत = **बारता है** (**बारना**). See **त**, 5.

बारदेना; see *s. v.* **बार**.

बारन, 1, a Braj pl. of **बार**, *q.v.*: 2, = **वारण**, *q. v.*

बारना, *a. int.* to leave off; to separate: *t.* to quit: to prohibit, forbid: to light, kindle.

बारनी; see (1) **बारना** (2) **वारुणी**.

बारबटाई, *f.* division of crops by sheaves or shocks before the corn is trodden out.

बारबार = **बारम्बार**, *q.v.*

बारबारी, *f.* delay, procrastination.

बारबिलास, *m.* whoremongery.

बारबिलासिनी, *f.* a harlot.

बारबिलासी, *m.* a whoremonger.

बारम्बः, *m.* revenue derived from the lease of mangoe-groves (*lit.* fruit of mangoes).

बारम्बार, time after time, times and again, again and again, over and over again, often and often, repeatedly, often, frequently, continuously, concurrently, alternately.

बारय, an old poet. imperat. of **बारना**, *q.v.*

बारह, 1, twelve (१२): 2, land near to (or surrounding) a village (generally enriched by manure).

बारहदरी, *f.* a summer-house (*lit.* having twelve doors).

बारहपुली, *f.* an aggregate of twelve bridges, or, perhaps, a bridge with twelve arches.

बारहबाट, divided into twelve, *i. e.* ruined, destroyed. — *honā*, to be a vagabond, be ruined, be harassed.

बारहवाँ, *m.* (*f.* °**वीं**) twelfth, the twelfth. See **वाँ**, **वीं**.

बारहवे, *adv.* twelfthly, in the twelfth place. See **वे**, 2.

बारहवें, the inflected form of **बारहवाँ**, *q. v.* See **वें**, 1.

बारहसिंगा, *m.* a certain large kind of stag (*Cervus elaphus*) with horns of twelve branches.

बारहा, (Pers. collective pl. of **बार**, time) again and again, repeatedly, often, times and again.

बारहाँ, 1, *m.* (*f.* °**हीं**) *more com.* **बारहवाँ**, *q. v.*: 2, *more com.* **बारहों**, *q.v.*: 3, dozens (see **हाँ**, 2).

बारहि, 1, (pl. **बारहिं**) a poetical form = **बारता है** (**बारना**): 2, (*Rām.*) = **बालकपन** (**बार** = **बाल**).

बारहिंबार } poet. forms of बारम्बार, *q.v.*
बारहिबार }

बारही; see (1) बारहि (2) बाराही.

बारहों, (see ओं, 4) the whole twelve, the twelve,

बारहोंबाट = बारहबाट, *q.v.* [the twelve of tnem.

बारहोंमास = बारहोंमहीना, *q.v.*

बारहोंमहीना, 1, *m.* a twelvemonth: 2, *adv.* for the period of a twelvemonth, the whole year round, all the year through, at all times, continually.

बारा, 1, = बारह, 2, *q.v.* : 2, a colloquial form of बारह, 1, *q. v.* : 3, a corruption of बाल and of बाला, *qq.v.* : 4, *m.* the cowherd's perquisite (generally the milk of every eighth day) : wind, air, atmosphere.

बाराखरी, *f.* (in Gram.) the aggregate of the vowel-symbols in combination with consonants.

बारादरी, *f.* } = बारहदरी, *q.v.*
बाराद्वार, *m.* }

बारान, *m.* rain : the rainy season, the rains.

बारानसी, *more prop.* बाराणसी, *q.v.*

बाराबार; see (1) बराबर (2) बारबार.

बारासिंगा, *more prop.* बारहसिंगा, *q.v.*

बाराह, *more prop.* (1) बारह (2) वाराह, *qq.v.*

बाराही, (1) *more prop.* वाराही, *q.v.*: 2, *f.* land. [वारि.

बारि, for words beginning thus, see under the form

बारिन, *f.* (*m.* बारी, 3) a female of a certain Hin-

बारिश, *f.* rain: a shower of rain. [doo caste.

बारिस, *more prop.* (1) बारिश (2) वारीश, *qq.v.*

बारी, 1, *more prop.* (1) बाड़ी (2) वारी, *qq.v.* : 2, *f. m.*? a window : a kind of ornament worn in the ear and nose : 3, *m.* (*f.* in) a certain caste of Hindoos whose occupation it is to sell torches, and leaves which are used as platters (the same caste occasionally act as barbers): 4, *f.* a garden, orchard ; a house : a girl not exceeding sixteen : time, tour, turn ; spell, rotation. *Bārikī tap*, an intermittent fever.

बारीक, fine, slender, minute, subtle.

बारीचर; see वारिचर.

बारीतआला, *m.* the Most High God.

बारीदार, *m.* (*f.* in *or* nī) an attendant who waits

बारुणी = वारुणी, *q.v.* [in turn with others.

बारू, 1, (provincial) = बालू, *q.v.* : 2, *m.* (बाल?) a child : 3, *f.* gunpowder ; saltpetre.

बारूत } *f.* gunpowder ; saltpetre.
बारूद }

बारे, 1, (*Rām.*) = (1) बालक (2) बारके (बारना), *qq.v.*: 2, once, one time or turn ; all at once ; at last, at

बारेक, (= एकबार) once (not twice). [length, finally.

बारेहि, an emphatic or an acc. form of बारे, *q.v.*

बारोंबाट = बारहबाट, *q.v.*

बार्गीर, *m.* a cavalryman who does not find his own horse : a beast of burden. [form बार्त्ता.

बार्त्ता, for words beginning thus, see under the

बार्बरदार, *m.* (*f.* in *or* nī) a burden-bearer, porter.

बार्बरदारी, *f.* the business of a porter, expenses of travelling, coolie-hire, carriage-hire : means of con-

बार्बार = बारबार = बारम्बार, *q.v.* [veyance.

बाल, 1, a contraction of बाला, *q.v.* : 2, = वाल, *q.v.*: 3, young, ignorant, uninstructed, unwise, infantine, childish : hence, *m.* (*f.* ā) a child under sixteen years of age (though generally applied rather to an infant or child under five years of age) ; a colt ; a five-year-old elephant : 4, *m.* hair ; a tail ; an elephant's or a horse's tail : the thread on which sugar is crystallized : a kind of perfume (*Andropogon schœnanthus*) : a wing : heart, mind : state : the whole arm : power : 5, *f.* an ear or spike of corn : a crack in a cup or glass. — *bāndhī kauri mārnā*, (to shoot at without missing; *hence*) to act with great care, not to fail or mistake. — *bīkā na howe*, (let not a hair be disordered; *i. e.*) take every care that not the least harm be done (the phrase is used to express the idea of the smallest harm or inconvenience). *Uskā bāl bingā na kar sakā*, he could not do it the least harm.

बालअवस्था, *f.* the state and condition of infancy or of childhood.

बालक, *m.* (*f.* ikā) a young child, infant; a boy: a foot : the tail of a horse or of an elephant : a finger-ring ; a kind of perfume.

बालकता, *f.* (*m.* °त्व) childhood, infancy; boyhood; childishness, boyishness, puerility.

बालकन, (see न, 6) } Braj pll. of बालक, *q.v.*
बालकन्ह, (see न्ह) }

बालकपन }
बालकपना } *m.* = बालअवस्था, *q.v.*
बालकपा }

बालकवि, *m.* (see बाल, 3) a minor poet.

बालका, *m.* a young follower or disciple of a yogī, sannyāsi, judge, etc.

बालकाण्ड, *m. pr. n.* (see सातोंकाण्ड) the first section of the Rāmāyaṇ. [infantine, childish.

बालकीय, appertaining to a child or to childhood,

बालखिल्य, *m.* a kind of divine personage of the size of the thumb (sixty thousand of whom are produced from the hair of Brahmā's body, and surround the chariot of the sun).

बालगोपाल, *m.* offspring, family.

बालघात, *f.* infanticide, child-murder.

बालघातक, *m.* (*f.* ī) a murderer of children.

बालचरित्र, *m. f.*? the tricks, games, and general conduct peculiar to children, childish frolics.

बालछड़, *f.* a certain medicine or perfume, spike-nard, hyacinth.

बालज़िबूल, *m. pr. n.* (in Scripture) Beelzebub.

बालति } = बाल्ति, *q.v.*
बालती }

बालतोड़, *m.* a pimple, sore. [etc.): 2, winged.

बालदार, 1, *m.* a cracked vessel (of china, glass,

बालना, *t.* to light, kindle, ignite.

बालन्द, a certain tribe inhabiting the southern

बालपन, *m.* = बालअवस्था, *q. v.* [parts of Mirzapur.

बालप्पन in Chand = बालअवस्था, *q. v.*

बालबंचे, *more com.* बालबच्चे, *q.v.* [offspring.

बालबच्चे, *m.* little folks (of either sex), children,

बालबाल, hair by hair, every hair.

बालबीका; see *s. v.* **बाल**.

बालबोध, *m.* a very small book: *pr. n.* a certain Hindoo astrologer. [early morning.

बालभोग, *m.* an offering to Krishṇ presented at

बालम, *m.* a kind of cloth: a beloved person, lover, husband.

बालमखीरा, *m.* a species of cucumber (a variety of *Cucumis sativus*) in season in the rains.

बालमीक / **बालमीकि** } *more prop.* **वाल्मीकि**, *q. v.*

बालयती, *m.* (*f.* trī) any ascetic whose passions have been subdued from childhood.

बालराज, *m.* lapis lazuli.

बालरांड, *f.* a very young widow, or a widow who lost her husband when she was very young.

बालरूप, 1, *m.* (*f.* ā) childish, youthful: 2, *m.* a certain Hindoo literary work.

बाललीला, *f.* = **बालचरित्र**, *q.v.*

बालवायज, *m.* lapis lazuli.

बालशिकस्ता, distressed, wretched.

बालसा, a fever when it attacks a child.

बालसूर्य, *m.* lapis lazuli.

बालहत्या, *f.* child-murder, infanticide.

बालहत्यारा, *m.* (*f.* ī) a murderer of children.

बाला, 1, *f.* (*m.* **बाल**, 2,) a female child, a girl not arrived at the age of sixteen; a woman: small cardamoms: a certain medicinal and fragrant plant (*Andropogon muricatum* or *Hibiscus tortuosus*, Roxb.) from the roots of which tatties are made; 'cus-cus': 2, *m.* a male child, boy: an earring: a kind of grub which eats the young plants of wheat or barley when they are about six inches high: 3, above, aloft, up; high: *hence*, 4, *m.* top; stature.

बालाख़ाना, *m.* an upper story, upper room, balcony.

बालाचान्द, *m.* the new moon.

बालातप, *m.* the rays of the rising sun.

बालापन, *m.* = **बालअवस्था**, *q. v.*

बालाबन्द, *m.* part of the native dress, a kind of turban, a coat of a particular kind.

बालाबर, *m.* the part of the *angarkhā* that laps over the thigh, foreskirt.

बालाभोला, *m.* (*f.* **बालीभोली**) artless (as a child), guileless, innocent, childlike.

बालावस्था = **बालअवस्था**, *q. v.*

बालि, 1, *m. pr. n.* (in Myth.) the monkey-chief (son of Indra and brother of Sugrīv: he was slain by *Rām-Chandra*): 2, *m.* the leaf of a folding-door; the leaf of a palm-tree with its sheath.

बालिका, 1, *f.* (*m.* **बालक**) a (female child); a woman: 2, a corruption of **बालुका**, *q. v.*

बालिकी, *f.* (*m.* **बालक**,) a female child; a woman.

बालिग़, *m.* (*f.* ā) a youth just arrived at the age of maturity: *lit.* of age; marriageable.

बालिन = **बालि**, 1, *q. v.*

बालिनी, *f. pr. n.* the constellation Ashwinī.

बालिश, 1, *m.* a pillow, cushion: 2, young, ignorant, foolish, careless.

बालिश्त, *f.* a span: a pillow, cushion.

बाली, 1, *more prop.* **बालि**, *q. v.*: 2, *f.* (*m.* **बाला**, 2) a female child: 3. *f.* a kind of earring which passes through the centre of the ear: an ear of corn.

बालीका; see (1) **बालिका** 2 **बालि**.

बालीदा, extended, grown. — *honā*, to vegetate.

बालीवान्दर = **बालि**, 1, *q. v.* [water.

बालीश, *m.* pain (from gravel, etc.) in making

बालु = **बालुक**, *q. v.* [ly called *Elābāluk*).

बालुक, *m.* a certain drug and perfume (common-

बालुका, *f.* sand, gravel; powder: camphor.

बालुकागड़, *m.* a kind of fish (*Cheilodiptens culins Cheilodipterus butis*). [or gravel, sandy, gravelly.

बालुकामय, consisting of (or abounding in) sand

बालू, *f.* sand, gravel.

बालूक, *m.* a kind of poison.

बालूचर, *m. pr. n.* a certain city near Murshidābād.

बालूचरी, *f.* a kind of silk cloth manufactured in Balūchar.

बालूबुर्द, land covered with a deposit of sand after an inundation; *also*, a remission of revenue on that account.

बालेपन = **बालापन** = **बालअवस्था**, *q. v.*

बालेय, 1, = **बालेयशाक**, *q. v.*: 2, fit for a child, soft, gentle, mild: 3, *m.* an ass: a demon.

बालेयशाक, *m.* the plant *Siphonanthus Indica*.

बालेश्वर, *m. pr. n.* Balasore (in Orissa).

बालेहीपन, an emphatic form of **बालेपन**, *q. v.*

बालोपवीत, *m.* the sacrificial thread (or any substitute for it) as worn by children: a cloth for covering the privities. [tub.

बाल्ति, *f.* a wooden water-vessel, a bucket, pail,

बाल्मीक, *more prop.* **वाल्मीकि**, *q. v.*

बाल्य, *m.* infancy, childhood, youth; foolishness.

बाल्यावस्था = **बालअवस्था**, *q. v.*

बाव, *f.* wind, air: the venereal decease: a bubo. — *khānā*, to live in pleasure and enjoyment; to court anyone's inspirations; to lead a protracted and miserable existence. — *kā rukh batānā*, to cheat, deceive, impose upon. — *bāndhnā*, to prevail over an adversary by flattery or invective (without argument). — *bharī khāl*, of light estimation, of no intrinsic value (*lit.* a skinful of wind). — *sārnā*, to be discharged backwards (said of wind).

बावग, *m.* seed-time; sowing. — *k.* to sow.

बावगोला, *m.* the colic, flatulency, flatulency with impaired function of the bowels, flatulency from indigestion in which the wind seems to move about like a ball (*golā*) in the bowels. [prater

बावभक, *m.* a talker of trifles, babbler, prattler,

बावटा, *m.* a flag or banner; a sail: a sort of armlet worn by females.

बावड़ा, *m.* a well of the largest size.

बावड़ी, *f.* a well, a large well, a pit.

बावता = बावटा, *q.v.* [2, = बामन, *q.v.*
बावन, 1, fifty-two (५२): see ओं, वां, वीं, वे, वें:
बावना, *m.* (*f.* ī) dwarfish. (From बामन.)
बावनी, *f.* seed-time; sowing.
बावबतास, *f.* calamity, misfortune (*esp.* such as is believed to result from the evil influence of a demon).
बावबन्दी, *f.* wind.
बावभक = बावभक्क, *q.v.*
बावर, *m.* belief, faith, confidence, credit, truth: *adv.* credible, true.—*k.* (with acc.) to credit, believe.
बावरा, *m.* (*f.* ī) crazy, insane, mad.
बावरी, 1, = (1) बावरा (2) बावड़ी, *qq.v.*: 2, *f.* a certain tribe of vagrants to the west of Delhi. [wife.
बावर्चिन, *f.* (*m.* बावर्ची) a female cook; a bāwarchī's
बावर्चिनी = बावर्चिन, *q.v.* [person.
बावर्ची, *m.* (*f.* in *or* inī) a cook; *met.* a confidential
बावर्चीख़ाना, *m.* a cook-house, kitchen.
बावर्चीगरी, *f.* the culinary art.
बावला, *m.* (*f.* ī) crazy, insane, mad.
बावली, 1, *f.* (*m.* बावला) an insane female: 2, *f.* a large well into which persons descend to get water; the drag (whether a thing or an animal) with which hawks, dogs, etc. are taught to hunt; a trick.—*denā*, to initiate.
बावलेना, *m.* a kind of defect in horses.
बावशूल / **बावसूल** } *m.* the colic.
बावा, *more com.* बाबा, *q.v.*
बावां, *m.* (= बायां) the left hand or side.
बावाजान = बाबाजान, *q.v.* [notwithstanding,
बावुजूद, *postp.* (takes gen. *m.* infl.) nevertheless.
बावो, in Māṛwāṛī = बहाना, *q.v.*
बाशा, *m.* (*f.* īn) a kind of falcon, a hawk.
बाशिन्दा, *m.* (*f.* ī) an inhabitant, dweller.
बाशीन, *f.* (*m.* बाशा) a female falcon. [weeds.
बाषगिया, crops being choked and destroyed by
बास, 1, *m.* = बासा, *q.v.*: 2, *f.* odour, scent, smell.
बासक, *m.* a certain shrub (*Justicia ganderussa*).
बासका, *f.* = बासक, *q.v.*
बासठ, sixty-two (६२). See ओं, वां, वीं, वे, वें.
बासदेव = वासुदेव, *q.v.*
बासन, 1, (*Rām.*) = (1) निवास (2) सुगन्ध, *qq.v.*: 2, *m.* a basin, dish, goblet, pot, plate.
बासना, 1, = वासना, *q.v.*: 2, *t.* to scent, perfume.
बासबन्या, *m.* (*f.* °न्याइन) a vendor of perfumes.
बासर = वासर, *q.v.*
बासव = वासव, *q.v.*
बासा, *m.* a dwellingplace, habitation, house, abode, lodging, temporary residence.—*k.* to lodge, stay with, dwell.
बासियान, a certain tribe of cowherds. [seeing.
बासिरा, *m.* the sense of sight, the faculty of vision,

बासी, 1, a colloquial form of बाक़ी, *q.v.*: 2, *m.* (*f.* inī) = वासी, *q.v.*: 2, perfumed; odoriferous, fusty, stale.—*k.* to make stale: to vomit.
बासु, for words beginning thus, see under the form वासु.
बासुक / **बासुकी** } *more prop.* वासुकि, *q.v.* [form वास्त.
बास्त, for words beginning thus, see under the
बाह, 1, *f.* = बांह, *q.v.*: 2, *m.* a horse: 3, *f.* manhood, virility; coïtus.
बाहत्तर, *more com.* बहत्तर, *q.v.*
बाहन, 1, = वाहन, *q.v.*: 2, *m.* fallow land.
बाहना, *t.* to discharge a weapon, to shoot: to comb the hair, to plough, till.
बाहम, together, mutually, inter se.
बाहर = बाहिर, *q.v.* [from the stomach.
बाहरन, a kind of medicine for removing wind
बाहरवाला, *m.* (*f.* ī) = बाहरिया, *q.v.*
बाहरा, *m.* (*f.* in *or* ī) the person who stands at the well to upset the (*charas*) leathern bucket.
बाहरि, *more com.* (1) बाहरी (2) बाहिरी, *qq.v.*
बाहरिया, *m.* (see भीतरिया) an outsider, stranger, foreigner, upstart.
बाहरी, 1, *m.* (*f.* iṇī) = बाहिरी, *q.v.*: 2, *f.* = बाहरा.
बाहा, 1, *f.* the arm: 2, a watercourse, channel.
बाहिज (*Rām.*) = बाह्य, *q.v.*
बाहिनी = वाहिनी, *q.v.*
बाहिर, (Sk. बहिर) outside, out, without, away, foreign, abroad.—*ānā*, to issue forth, come out.
बाहिरका, (gen. of बाहिर) *m.* (*f.* ī) = बाहिरी, *q.v.*
बाहिरह = बाहिरा, *q.v.* [exercise, etc.
बाहिरा, *m.* the off-side, the left side (in sword-
बाहिरे, in Braj = (1) बाहिरा (2) बाहिरी, *qq.v.*
बाहिरी, appertaining to without, outer, outside, outward, extraneous, strange, foreign: hence, *m.* (*f.* iṇī) an outsider, stranger, foreigner, upstart.
बाहु, *m. f.?* the arm (from the elbow to the shoulder): *hence*, in the ingenious system of reckoning by symbols adopted by Hindoos in their poetry, this word is a symbol for 2.
बाहुक, 1, subject to others, dependent, servile: 2, *m.* a servant, slave: a monkey: the name of Nala after his change of form.
बाहुज, 1, arm-born: hence, *m.* (*f.* ā) a Kshatriya: 2, *m.* sesamum growing wild or spontaneously.
बाहुदण्ड, *m.* an arm as hard as a staff.
बाहुदा, *f. pr. n.* a certain river said to rise in the Himālayas (probably the modern Behut, the Hydaspes of classical writers). [arm, an armlet.
बाहुभूषा, *f.* an ornament worn around the upper
बाहुमूल, *m.* the shoulder-blade; the armpit.
बाहुयुद्ध, *m.* hand-to-hand fight, close fight, personal struggle; wrestling; boxing.
बाहुल, *m.* mail or armour for the arm: fire: (in Gram.) the optional applicability of different rules: an epithet (1) of Kārttik (2) of Agni.

बाहुल्य, *m.* variety, multiplicity, manifoldness; plenty, abundance, excess, quantity.
बाहुल्यता, *f.* (*m.* °त्व) = **बाहुल्य**, *q.v.*
बाहु, *f.* 1, = **बाहु**, *q.v.* : 2, a walking-stick, club, shepherd's staff.
बाहेर, *more prop.* **बाहिर**, *q.v.* [form **ब्राह्मण**.
ब्राह्मन; for words beginning thus, see under the
ब्राह्मनहट्टी, *f.* a certain plant (*Ovieda verticellata*).
ब्राह्मनीचील, *f.* the sacred or Brāhmanī kite.
ब्राह्मनीबदक़, *f.* the **चकवा**, *q.v.*
बि; for all words beginning thus, but not given below, see under the form **वि**.
बिआई, *f.* any pregnant female.
बिआरि / **बिआरी** } *f.* supper.
बिआसी, *more com.* **बयासी**, *q.v.*
बिंगा, *m.* (*f.* ī) crooked, distorted, awry, askew, oblique, aslant, curved, bent.
बिंजन = **व्यंजन**, *q.v.*
बिंड, **बिंत**, **बिंद**, **बिंध**, **बिंब**; for words beginning with either of these elements, see under the corresponding forms **बिण्ड**, **बिन्त**, **बिन्द**, **बिन्ध**, **बिम्ब**, respectively.
बिंसना, *a. int.* to go bad, to spoil.
बिक, *m.* (from **वृक**) a wolf. — *jānā*, to be sold, be sold off: *met.* to be dependent on, to be obliged.
बिकट = **विकट**, *q.v.*
बिकत, wife and family. This word is used in a general sense; thus, a man will say, 'I have five bikats; meaning that his family consists of five persons. When the wife only is referred to, she is called *bikatī*.
बिकना, *n.* to be sold: *a. int.* to sell, *se vendre*.
बिकर, **बिकल**; for words beginning thus, see under the forms **विकर**, **विकल**, respectively.
बिकरार = **विकराल**, *q.v.*
बिकवान, *m.* a certain subdivision of the Gauṛtagas.
बिकवाना, *t.* (causat. of **बिकना**) to cause to be sold.
बिकस; for words beginning thus, see under the form **विकस**.
बिका, *m.* (*f.* ī) sold, disposed of by sale.
बिकाऊ, to be sold, saleable, for sale. [sell.
बिकाना, *t.* (of **बिकना**) to cause a thing to sell; to
बिकार = **विकार**, *q.v.*
बिकाल = **विकाल**, *q.v.*
बिकाव, *m.* sale, selling, vending, demand; vent.
बिकास, 1, = **विकाश**, *q.v.* : 2, pleased, delighted,
बिक्की, *m.* a partner (at play, etc.). [happy.
बिक्रम, **बिक्रय**; for words beginning thus, see under the forms **विक्रम**, **विक्रय**, respectively.
बिक्रमजीत / **बिक्रमाजीत** } *more prop.* **विक्रमादित्य**, *q.v.*
बिक्री, *f.* sale, selling, vending, demand; vent.
बिक्रीत, *m.* (*f.* ā) sold, disposed of by sale.
बिक्ष; for words beginning thus, see under the form **विक्ष**.
बिखोद, *more prop.* **बिछोह**, *q.v.* [form **विख**.
बिख; for words beginning thus, see under the
बिखरना, *n.* to be scattered, be dispersed, be dishevelled: to be confounded, be amazed: *a. int.* to become angry.
बिखेरना, *t.* to scatter, disperse. [form **विख्य**.
बिख्य; for words beginning thus, see under the
बिगड़ जाना, (intensive of **बिगड़ना**) to deteriorate, go bad, go to the bad.
बिगड़ना, *n.* to be spoiled, be damaged, be marred: to be at variance, be enraged: *a. int.* to miscarry; deteriorate, degenerate, go to the bad; to fail of success; to disagree, quarrel.
बिगड़ाना, 1, *more com.* **बिगाड़ना**, *q.v.* : 2, *t.* to scatter, spread about, sprinkle, strew.
बिगड़ाव, *more com.* **बिगाड़**, *q.v.*
बिगड़ी, *f.* spoil; damage; misunderstanding between friends; war, battle.
बिगत; for words beginning thus, see under the
बिगन्ध = **विगन्ध**, *q.v.* [form **विगत**.
बिगरना, *more prop.* **बिगड़ना**, *q.v.*
बिगसना = **विकसना**, *q.v.*
बिगहटी, *f.* rent of land at per *bighā*.
बिगहा / **बिगा** } *more prop.* **बीघा**, *q.v.*
बिगाड़, *m.* injury, damage; violation; discord, difference, misunderstanding, quarrelling. — *k.* to quarrel; to forfeit friendship. — *paṛ ānā*, to be ready for a quarrel.
बिगाड़ना, *t.* to spoil, mar, damage, injure, ruin, make a bungle; to cause misunderstanding between friends. [lator, destroyer, bungler.
बिगाड़ू, *m.* a spoiler, injurer, mischief-maker, vio-
बिगाना, *m.* (*f.* ī) *more com.* **बेगाना**, *q.v.*
बिगारना, *more prop.* **बिगाड़ना**, *q.v.*
बिगोना, *t.* to destroy.
बिगोया, *m.* (*f.* **बिगोई**) destroyed.
बिग्रह = **विग्रह**, *q.v.*
बिघटन = **विघटन**, *q.v.* [the form **विघ्न**.
बिघन, **बिघ्न**; for words beginning thus, see under
बिच; for words beginning thus, but not given below, see under the forms **बीच** and **विच**.
बिचक, fear, fight, alarm; disappointment.
बिचकना, *n.* to be disappointed, be baulked: *a. int.* to run away, retreat; to withdraw a consent that has been given: start with fear: *t.* to sprain.
बिचकवा, *m.* an ornament worn in the anterior lobe of the ear.
बिचकाना, *t.* to baulk, disappoint, back out of an agreement, break one's promise; to threaten, terrify, frighten.
बिचत्र, *more prop.* **विचित्र**, *q.v.*

बिचमना, *t.* to vex anyone with questions.
बिचरना = **फिरना**, *q.v.*
बिचरहि, (pl. °हिं) in poet. = **बिचरता है**. [middle.
बिचला, *m.* (*f.* ī) situated in the midst, intervening,
बिचवई, *m.* (*f.* in *or* inī)
बिचवाई, *m.* (*f.* inī *or* in)
बिचवानी, *m.* (*f.* in *or* inī)
बिचवैत, *m.* (*f.* in, nī, inī) } = **बिचौलिया**, *q. v.*
बिचार; for words beginning thus, see under the form **विचार**.
बिचारा, *m.* (*f.* ī) *more com.* **बेचारा**, *q.v.*
बिचाली, *f.* straw.
बिचित्र; see under the form **विचित्र**.
बिचूआ, *m.* the plant *Crotalaria juneca ?*
बिचौलिया, *m.* one who interposes, a middleman, mediator, arbitrator, umpire, agent, ambassador, broker.
बिच्छाना; see **बिछाना**. [the sign Scorpio.
बिच्छू, *m.* a scorpion: a kind of firework: *pr. n.*
बिच्छूआ, *more com.* (1) **बिच्छू** (2) **बिछूआ**, *qq. v.*
बिच्छौना, *more prop.* **बिछौना**, *q. v.*
बिछ, *more prop.* **बिच्छू**, *q.v.*
बिछड़ना, *n.* to be separated, be set apart: *a. int.* to separate, turn away, slide, slip, turn away the face.
बिछड़ा, 1, *m* = **बिछड़ाहट**, *q.v.*: 2, *m.* (*f.* ī) set apart, separated; slipped, turned away.
बिछड़ाट (*contraction*) = **बिछड़ाहट**, *q.v.*
बिछड़ाना, *t.* to cause to be separated, to separate, divide, part, sunder.
बिछड़ाव, *m.* = **बिछड़ाहट**, *q.v.*
बिछड़ाहट, *f.* a separating, parting, parting asunder, separation, turning away.
बिछड़ी, *f.* = **बिछड़ा**, 2, *q.v.*
बिछना, *n.* to be spread: *a. int.* to spread.
बिछर, **बिछल**; for words beginning thus, see under the form **बिछड़**.
बिछलहा, *m.* (*f.* ī) slippery.
बिछवय्या, *m.* a person who sweeps, a sweeper.
बिछवाना, *t.* to cause to be spread, *i.e.* to spread (as, a bed): to cause to spread.
बिछा, *m.* (*f.* ī) spread out, extended. —*denā*, to spread out: *met.* to floor, prevail over, knock down, drub.
बिछाता, *m.* a stinging-nettle (*Urtica interrupta*).
बिछाना, 1, = **बिछावन**, *q.v.*: 2, *t.* (of **बिछना**) to spread, extend.
बिछानां
बिछावन } *m.* a bed, bedding, carpet.
बिछावना, *more com.* (1) **बिछाना** (2) **बिछौना**, *qq.v.*
बिछुड़, **बिछुर**, **बिछुल**; for words beginning with either of these elements, see under the form **बिछड़**.
बिछूआ, *m.* a sort of dagger; a small stiletto with a carved or serpentine blade; a kind of ornament worn on the toes; a scorpion: *pr. n.* the sign Scorpio.

बिछूई, *f.* a ring or ornament formed like the scorpion's sting and worn by females on the great toe.
बिछोड़ना = **बिछड़ाना**, *q.v.*
बिछोना, *more com.* **बिछौना**, *q.v.*
बिछोह
बिछोहा } *m.* separation; absence.
बिछौना, *m.* a bed; bedding, bedclothes; carpeting, a carpet. *Bichhaunepar*, in bed.
बिज, *more com.* **बीज**, *q.v.*
बिजन = **विजन**, *q.v.*
बिजना, *m.* a fan, punkah. [form **विजय**.
बिजय; for words beginning thus, see under the
बिजली, *f.* lightning; a thunderbolt. —*karaknā*, to crack (said of thunder).
बिजा, *m.* a stallion. [mission.
बिज़ाअत, *f.* stock-in-trade, capital: agency, com-
बिजाई, *f.* a portion of seed-corn which the poorer classes are allowed to take from the field.
बिजायठ, *m.* a kind of ornament worn on the arm, an armlet, bracelet.
बिजार, *m.* a stallion; a bull.
बिजाला, *m.* (*f.* ī) appertaining to seed, abounding in seed, seedy, gone to seed.
बिजिया = **विजया**, *q.v.*
बिजुली, *more com.* **बिजली**, *q.v.*
बिजू, *more com.* **बेजू**, *q. v.*
बिजूखाभेरारा = **बेजू**, *q. v.*
बिजै, **बिजोग**, **बिज्ञ**; for words beginning with either of these elements, see under the forms **विजय**, **वियोग**, **विज्ञ**, respectively.
बिज्जुी, *more prop.* **बिजली**, *q. v.*
बिज्ञाप्य = **विज्ञाप**, *q.v.* [startled, be scared.
बिझकना, *n.* to be frightened, be alarmed, be
बिझकाना, *t.* to frighten, alarm, startle, scare.
बिझगाह, *m.* a scarecrow.
बिझोनिया, a certain tribe of Rājpūts in Jaunpur.
बिटप = **विटप**, *q. v.* [*kalāya* species.
बिटमास, *m.* a certain coarse kind of pulse of the
बिटलाना = (1) **बिटवाना** (2) **बिठलाना**, *qq.v.*
बिटवा, *m.* (dim. of **बेटा**) a little son.
बिटवाना, *t.* to cause to scatter, cause to sprinkle.
बिटाना, *t.* to scatter, sprinkle.
बिटाअना, *m.* (*f.* ī) = **बिटौना**, *q. v.*: 2, = **बिटाना**, *q.v.*
बिटिया, *f.* (dim. of **बेटी**) a little daughter.
बिटौना, *m.* (*f.* ī) a little child. [(used for fuel).
बिटौरा, *m.* a heap of cakes of dried cowdung
बिटौरी, *f.* a tax on shopkeepers, etc. in a village.
बिठक, *m.* an anthill: (pl.) anthills.
बिठना, *more prop.* **बैठना**, *q.v.*
बिठलाना
बिठाना
बिठालना } *t.* (causals of **बैठना**) = **बैठाना**, *q. v.*

बिड़की, *f.* a drove of bullocks (laden with grain, betel, cotton, etc.).

बिड़ता, *m.* ability, power; purpose, object. *Kis birtepar tattā pānī*, Why do you call for hot water? (a proverbial expression applied to a man who has not done his matrimonial duty over-night).

बिड़ती, *f.* = बिड़ता, *q.v.* [form विडम्ब.

बिडम्ब; for words beginning thus, see under the

बिडारना, *t.* to drive away, to turn away: to

बिहरना, *t.* to scatter, strew, spread. [efface.

बिड़ाड़, *f.* = बिड़की, *q.v.*

बिढ़ई, an old conjunct. partic. of बिढवना, *q.v.*

बिढवना, *t.* to diminish, lessen, abate. [a faggot.

बिपड़ा, *m.* a bundle of firewood (sticks or straw),

बित; for words beginning thus, but not given below, see under the more proper forms वित्त, वित, वित्त.

बितना, 1, = बीतना, *q.v.*: 2, *m.* (*f.* ī) = उतना, *q.v.*

बितनो; see बितना.

बितरना, *t.* to grant, vouchsafe, bestow.

बितान = (1) चन्दवा (2) मण्डप (3) वितान, *qq.v.*

बिताना, *t.* (of बीतना) to pass (one's life), to spend

बितार = विस्तार, *q.v.* [or pass (the time).

बितीत = व्यतीत, *q.v.*

बितौरा = बिटौरा, *q.v.*

बित्त; for words beginning thus, but not given below, see under the form वित्त.

बित्तमबित्तम, little by little, bit by bit, piece by piece, in detail, piecemeal, gradually.

बित्ता, *m.* a span.

बित्तिया, *m.* a dwarf (*prop.* a span high).

बित्राबन्दी = बिलबन्दी, *q.v.*

बिथकना, *n.* to be astonished, be terrified.

बिथकाहि (pl. °हिं) = बिथकता है.

बिथरना, *n.* to be scattered, be sprinkled, be spread.

बिथरवाना, *t.* to cause to be scattered, etc.

बिथराना, *t.* to scatter, sprinkle, spread.

बिथा, *f.* (व्यथा) pain, affliction, distress.

बिथारना, *t.* to cause to scatter, cause to sprinkle, cause to spread.

बिथारी, *f.* cleansing the warp. [form विथुर.

बिथुर; for words beginning thus, see under the

बिद; for words beginning thus, but not given below, see under the form विद.

बिद, *f.* a little pit into which children in play endeavour to throw balls or marbles.

बिदअ़त, *f.* the introduction of novelty or change in religion, innovation, schism, heresy, blasphemy, violence, oppression, wrong.

बिदअ़ती, *m.* (*f.* in *or* inī) a schismatic, blasphemer; an oppressor, tyrant. [form विदर.

बिदर; for words beginning thus, see under the

बिदरी, *f.* a certain mixture of metals; a kind of tutenag inlaid with silver. It is used for making *hukkā*-bottoms, cups, etc., and is named from Bidra.

बिदरेउ = विदरा हुआ = torn, rent. [form विदा.

बिदा; for words beginning thus, see under the

बिदारहि (pl. °हिं) = विदारता है.

बिदाहना, *t.* to turn the plough over a field after the seed is come up; to plough immediately after sowing for the purpose of covering the seed; to harrow. [form विदि.

बिदि; for words beginning thus, see under the

बिदिसा } *more prop.* विदिशा, *q.v.*
बिदिसि }

बिदोर्यो *m.* (*f.* ā) = बिदीर्यो, *q.v.*

बिदुर, *m.* (*f.* ā) = विदुर, *q.v.*

बिदुष, बिदूर, बिदूष, बिदेश; for words beginning thus, see under the forms विदुष, विदूर, विदूष, विदेश, respectively.

बिदेस, बिदेह; for words beginning thus, see under the forms विदेश, विदेह, respectively.

बिदोकना, *t.* to mock, laugh at, ridicule.

बिदोरना, 1, = बिदोकना, *q.v.*: 2, *t.* to screw.

बिद्य; for words beginning thus, see under the

बिद्रुम = विद्रुम, *q.v.* [form विद्य.

बिद्व; for words beginning thus, see under the form विद्व. [below, see under the form विध.

बिध; for words beginning thus, but not given

बिधवा, 1, = विधवा, *q.v.*: 2, *m.* (from विधाता?) an epithet of the Supreme Being. [form विधा.

बिधा; for words beginning thus, see under the

बिधावट, *f.* (from बेधना) perforation. [form विधि.

बिधि; for words beginning thus, see under the

बिधिअण्ड (*Rām.*) = ब्रह्माण्ड, *q.v.*

बिधिबिबहार = विधिव्यवहार, *q.v.* [form विधु.

बिधु; for words beginning thus, see under the

बिधेआ, an old form = विद्या, *q.v.*

बिध्वंस = विध्वंस, *q.v.*

बिन; for word beginning thus, but not given below, see under the form विन.

बिन, freq. as a contraction of बिना, *q.v.* *Bin jāne*, without knowing, unwittingly. — *dāne pānī*, without eating or drinking. — *māre* (or *tegh*) *shahīd honā*, (said in love affairs) to be slain without a blow (or without a sword). — *māre tauba k.* to be afraid without cause.

बिनऊं (*poet.*) = मैं बिनौता हूं (बिनौना).

बिनत = (1) विनत (2) विनति, *qq.v.*

बिनता; see (1) बिनना (2) विनता.

बिनति = विनति, *q.v.*

बिनती, 1, = विनति, *q.v.*: 2, see बिनना. [form विन्ध्य.

बिनध्य; for words beginning thus, see under the

बिनध्यान, without meditation, without reflection, unthinkingly, inconsiderately.

बिनना, *n.* to be picked: *t.* to knit, weave.

बिनफ़शा = बनफ़शा, *q.v.*

बिनय; for words beginning thus, see under the form **बिनय**.

बिनवऊं (*poet.*) = **मैं बिनौता हूं**.

बिनवना = **बिनौना**, *q.v.*

बिनवा, *m.* (*f.* **बिनवी**) = **बिनौया**, *q.v.*

बिनवाई, *f.* (see **आई**) the price paid for weaving.

बिनवाना, *t.* to cause to be picked: to cause to weave.

बिनवौं (*poet.*) = **मैं बिनौता हूं**.

बिनश, बिनस; for words beginning thus, see under the form **बिनश**.

बिनसार, morning.

बिनस्वार्थ, uselessly, fruitlessly.

बिनस्सनो, in Chand = **बिनशना**, *q.v.*

बिनहर, *m.* (*f.* ī *or* nī) a gatherer of cotton.

बिनहि (pl.° **हिं**) = **बिनता है** (**बिनना**).

बिना; for words beginning thus, but not given below, see under the form **बिना**.

बिनाई, *f.* (see **आई**, 3) weaving.

बिनाबर, on account of, by reason of, owing to.

बिनायक, *m.* (*f.* ikā) = **विनायक**, *q.v.*

बिनावट, *f.* weaving.

बिनाश, बिनास; for words beginning thus, see under the form **बिनाश**.

बिनिंद, बिनीत; for words beginning thus, see under the forms **विनिन्द, विनीत**, respectively.

बिनु (freq. in poetry) = **बिना**, *q.v.*

बिनैं (in poet.) = **मैं बिनौऊं** (**बिनौना**).

बिनोद = **विनोद**, *q.v.*

बिनोला = **बिनौला**, *q.v.*

बिनौ (in poet.) = **मैं बिनौऊं** (**बिनौना**).

बिनौना, *t.* to adore, venerate, revere, laud.

बिनौया, *m.* (*f.* **बिनौई**) venerated, lauded.

बिनौरिया, *m.* a certain herb which is used as fodder for cattle.

बिनौला, *m.* the seed of the cotton-tree (said to be very fattening for cattle). — *chābnā*, to say unpleasant things.

बिनौली, *f.* hail (of a small kind).

बिन्ति / **बिन्ती** } = **बिनति**, *q.v.*

बिन्द, *more prop.* (1) **विन्द** (2) **विन्दु**, *qq.v.*

बिन्दक = **विन्दक**, *q.v.*

बिन्दसर = **विन्दुसर**, *q.v.*

बिन्दसेन = **विन्दुसेन**, *q.v.*

बिन्दा, *m.* a bundle, sheaf, faggot.

बिन्दाक्ष, *m. pr. n.* a certain demon (*rākshas*).

बिन्दाल, *f.* a certain medicinal herb.

बिन्दी, *f.* = **विन्दु**, *q.v.*

बिन्दु; for words beginning thus, see under the form **विन्दु**.

बिन्द्राबन (*corruption*) = **वृन्दावन**, *q.v.*

बिन्धन, *m.* (*f.* ā) without wealth, indigent, poor.

बिन्धना, *t.* to sting, to bite: *n.* to be pierced, be bored.

बिन्धा, बिन्ध्य; for words beginning with either of these elements, see under the form **विन्ध्य**.

बिन्हा = **बिनना**, *q.v.*

बिन्याचल (*corruption*) = **विन्ध्याचल**, *q.v.*

बिन्सार, morning.

बिपत, बिपत्त, बिपर; for words beginning thus, see under the forms **विपत, विपत्त, विपर**, respectively.

बिपरना, *t.* to attack, assault: *n.* to be initiated: *a. int.* to break out into a passion.

बिपल, बिपिन; for words beginning thus, see under the forms **विपल, विपिन**, respectively.

बिपिनि, *more prop.* **विपिन**, *q.v.*

बिपिरीत, *more prop.* **विपरीत**, *q.v.*

बिपुल, बिप्त, बिप्र; for words beginning thus, see under the forms **विपुल, विपत, विप्र**, respectively.

बिप्रन, (see **न**, 6) / **बिप्रन्ह**, (see **न्ह**) / **बिप्रन्हि**, (see **न्हि**) } Braj pll. of **विप्र**, *q.v.*

बिप्रहि, an old dat. and acc. of **विप्र**, *q.v.* See **हि**, 2 (3).

बिफपै, *m.* (from **बृहस्पति**) Thursday.

बिफरना, *n.* to be perverse, be disobedient, be refractory, be cross, be obstinate, be pert.

बिफै, *m.* (from **बृहस्पति**) Thursday.

बिबर, बिबश, बिबस; for words beginning thus, see under the forms **विवर, विवश, विवस**, respectively.

बिबाइन, a plural of **बिवाई**, 2, *q.v.*

बिबाकी, *f.*; see (1) **नाश** (2) **बिवाक**.

बिबाद, बिबाह; for words beginning thus, see under the forms **विवाद, विवाह**, respectively.

बिबित्त, *m.* (*f.* ā) = **विवित्त**, *q.v.*

बिबिध / **बिबिधबिध** / **बिबिधि** } = **विविध**, *q.v.*

बिबुद्ध; for words beginning thus, see under the form **विबुद्ध** or **विबुध**.

बिबुधबैद (*Rām.*) = **बिबुधबैद्य**, *q.v.*

बिबेक, बिबेच; for words beginning thus, see under the forms **विवेक, विवेच**, respectively.

बिध्वंस, a corruption of **विध्वंस**, *q.v.*

बिभंजन, बिभक्त; for words beginning thus, see under the forms **विभंजन, विभक्त**, respectively.

बिभचार, *more prop.* **व्यभिचार**, *q.v.*

बिभति, *more prop.* **विभक्ति**, *q.v.*

बिभलता, *more prop.* **विह्वलता**, *q.v.*

बिभव, बिभाग, बिभात, बिभिचार, बिभिच, बिभीष, बिभु, बिभू, बिभेद, बिभेा; for words beginning with either of these elements, but not given below, see under the corresponding forms **विभव, विभाग, विभात, व्यभिचार, विभिच, विभीष, विभु, विभू, विभेद, विभव**.

बिभागा, *more prop.* **विभाग**, *q.v.*

बिभाती, *more prop.* **विभाति**, *q.v.*

बिभुन्ह, an old plural of विभु, q.v. See न्ह.

बिभूती = विभूति, q.v.

बिभौ in Braj = विभव, q.v.

बिभचार, *more prop.* व्यभिचार, q.v.

बिमरिहा, *m.* (*f.* ī) sickly, diseased, ill.

बिम; for words beginning thus, but not given below, see under the form विम.

बिमात्र, *more prop.* विमातृ, q.v.

बिमार, *more prop.* बीमार, q.v.

बिमूजिब, *postp.* (takes gen. *m.* infl.) on account of, in conformity with, by reason of, according to.

बिमोचना, *more prop.* विमोचयिता, q.v.

बिमोह, बिम्ब, बिय; for words beginning thus, but not given below, see under the forms विमोह, विम्ब, विय, respectively.

बिया, *m.* (from वीर्य) seed.

बियाज = व्याज, q.v.

बियाबान, *m.* a desert, wilderness.

बियार, *more com.* (1) बयार (2) बियारि, q.v.

बियारि, *f.*
बियारी, *f.* } supper.
बियालू, *m.*

बियास, land cultivated and prepared for being sown in the following year.

बियाह, *m. f.* (from विवाह) marriage. — *k.* (with abl. of the object) to contract marriage with anyone, to marry (said of either sex).—*denā*, (with acc. of the object) to give in marriage (said of some third party). —*rachānā*, to celebrate a marriage. — *lenā* or *le-ānā* or *le-jānā* (said of the man) to marry, to take in marriage, to bring home a wife.

बियाहता, *f.* (= विवाहिता) a married female.

बियाहन, *m.* marrying, marriage. — *k.* to wed.

बियाहनयोग, marriageable.

बियाहना, 1, = ब्याना, q.v.: 2, *t.* to marry, wed (*i. e.* to give or to take in marriage).

बियाहवाला, *m.* (*f.* ī) married.

बियाहा, *m.* (*f.* ī) married. —*jānā*, to get married.

बियोग, बिरंग, बिरंच, बिरक्त, बिरच, बिरज; for words beginning thus, but not given below, see under the forms वियोग, विरंग, विरंच, विरक्त, विरच, विरज, respectively.

बिरकत, *more prop.* विरक्त, q.v.

बिरचत = विरचता है (विरचना). See त, 5.

बिरचन, 1, = विरचन, q.v.: 2, *m.* a kind of flour made of the fruit of the *bēr*-tree (*Rhamnus jujuba*).

बिरचना = विरचना, q.v.

बिरच्यो in Braj = विरचा हुआ.

बिरछिक = वृश्चिक, q.v.

बिरजिया, *m.* one of the subdivisions of the cow-herd-tribe (*ahīr*).

बिरत = (1) बिर्त (2) विरत, qq.v.

बिरति = विरति, q.v.

बिरतिया, *m.* a tenant who holds his land on a fixed unalterable annual assessment.

बिरती, 1, *more prop.* विरति, q.v.: 2, *m. f.* a certain plant (a species of *Panicum*).

बिरथ = विरथ, q.v.

बिरद, *m.* fame, reputation, panegyric.

बिरदैत, *m.* an archer, bowyer, bowman.

बिरनी, *f.* a wasp: a small seed or grain.

बिरमना = विलम्बना, q.v.

बिरमां, *m.* the plant *Trichosanthes incisa.*

बिरमाऊ, 1, = बिरमाया, q.v.: 2, *adj.* taming.

बिरमाना, 1, = विलम्बाना, q.v.: 2, *t.* to allure, to tantalize; to reduce to obedience, to tame.

बिरमाया, *m.* (*f.* बिरमाई) tamed, allured.

बिरयानी, *f.* a kind of dish made of flesh and rice.

बिरल; for words beginning thus, see under the form विरल.

बिरव (*Rām.*) = (1) पौधा (2) बिरवा, 1, qq.v.

बिरवा, 1, *m.* a plant, a tree: 2, *m.* (*f.* in *or* ī) the labourer employed at the basket used in raising water for the purpose of irrigation.

बिरवाही, *f.* an orchard. — *k.* to enclose with a hedge; to make an orchard.

बिरसना = (1) विलम्बना (2) बिलसना, q.v.

बिरह, बिराग, बिराज, बिराट; for words beginning thus, but not given below, see under the forms विरह, विराग, विराज, विराट, respectively.

बिरहन, an old form = विरहिणी, q.v.

बिरहनी, 1, = विरहिणी, q.v.: 2, *f.* (in love) sickness resulting from separation, lovesickness.

बिरहमन; for words beginning thus, see under the form ब्राह्मण.

बिरहा, 1, = विरहा, q.v.: 2, *m.* a kind of song peculiar to washermen.

बिरहागि (*Rām.*) = विरहाग्नि, q.v.

बिरहाना, *m.* land in which culinary herbs are produced.

बिरागा, *more prop.* विराग, q.v.

बिराज = विराज, q.v.

बिरादर, *m.* a brother.

बिरादरख़ावन्दगी, *f.* profession of fraternal affection.

बिरादरपरवर, kind to friends and relations.

बिरादरी, *f.* brotherhood, fraternity, kin, relationship, company.

बिरानवे = बानवे, q.v.

बिराना, 1, *t.* to mock, jibe, jeer, taunt, vex, make faces at: 2, *m.* (*f.* ī) appertaining to another, strange, foreign, alien.

बिराम 1, = विराम, q.v.: 2, *more prop.* बीमार, q.v.

बिरावनो in Braj = बिराना, q.v.

बिरासी, *more com.* बयासी, q.v.

बिराहमन, बिराह्मन; for words beginning thus, see under the form ब्राह्मण.

बिरिंजारा = बनजारा, q.v.

बिरिंचि; see (1) विरंचि (2) विरिंचि.

बिरिया, 1, = बिरियां, q.v.: 2, *f.* women's ear-ornaments.

बिरियां, *f.* time; space of time. *Ek.*— once, one time, at one time, once upon a time.

बिरियानी, *f.* (in Māṛwāṛī) the wife of a baniyā.

बिरौजा, *m.* galbanum.

बिरुज, बिरुद्ध, बिरूप; for words beginning thus, but not given below, see under the forms **विरुज, विरुद्ध, विरूप**, respectively.

बिरुदैत, *m.* an archer, bowman, bowyer.

बिरुद्धता, *more prop.* **विरुद्धता**, *q.v.*

बिरुल, *m.* (*f.* ā) *more prop.* **विरल**, *q.v.*

बियोग, बिरोध; for words beginning thus, see under the forms **वियोग, विरोध**, respectively.

बियोगन; see (1) **वियोगन** (2) **वियोगिनी**.

बिर्ज = (1) **बिरज** (2) **ब्रज**, *qq.v.*

बिर्त, a custom, right, privilege; a religious endowment.

बिर्तांत, *more prop.* **वृत्तान्त**, *q.v.*

बिर्मभाट, a certain subdivision of the *bhāṭ*-tribe.

बिर्रः = **बिर्रां**, *q.v.*

बिर्रां, *m.* gram and barley sown together in the same field.

बिर्रांबरार, *m.* (in Revenue) collection in kind.

बिल; for words beginning thus, but not given below, see under the form **विल**.

बिलंगना, *t.* to climb, ascend, mount.

बिलंब, बिलंभ; for words beginning thus, see under the form **विलम्ब**.

बिलकना, *a. int.* to sob, cry violently (as a child): to long, desire eagerly: *t.* to take fast hold of, to catch, grasp.

बिलकुल, *more prop.* **बिलकुल्ल**, *q.v.*

बिलकुल्ल, totally, altogether, entirely, wholly, completely, universally.

बिलकैल, *more prop.* **बिलकुल्ल**, *q.v.*

बिलखना, *a. int.* to sob, cry violently (as a child): *t.* to look at, behold, see, perceive: *n.* to be displeased.

बिलखरिया, a certain tribe of Rājpūts (so called from *Bilkhar* in Oudh).

बिलखाना, *t.* causative of **बिलखना**, *q.v.*

बिलग, *m.* separation, disunion, difference: *adj.* separate, detached.—*mānnā*, to be displeased, be angry, be offended.

बिलगना, *a. int.* to separate: to curdle, turn (as milk).

बिलगाई, *f.* separating, parting, separation.

बिलगाना, *t.* to separate, detach, disjoin.

बिलगाव, *m.* separating, parting, separation.

बिलचना, *t.* to extract, select, pick, cull (as passages from books).

बिलटना, *a. int.* to become bad.

बिलन, *m.* (pl. of **बिल**) holes, crevices. See **न**, 6.

बिलनी, *f.* a stye in the eyelid.

बिलपाना (by inversion) = **बिलापना**, *q.v.*

बिलफ़र्ज़, granted that, on the supposition or condition that.

बिलफ़ेल, in fact, actually; now, for the present moment; in short; in the mean-time.

बिलबिलाना, *a. int.* to be restless, be tormented with pain: to complain from pain or grief, to lament, whine, whimper, blubber.

बिलम, बिलम्ब, बिलम्भ, बिलम्ह; for words beginning with either of these elements, see under the form **बिलम्ब**.

बिलमा; see (1) **बिरमा** (2) **बिलमना** (3) **बिलमें**.

बिलमाना = (1) **बिरमाना** (2) **बिलम्बाना**, *qq.v.*

बिलरा, *m.* a male cat: a kind of cloth.

बिललाना, *a. int.* to lament, whine, whimper.

बिलल्ला, *m.* (*f.* ī) simple, silly, foolish, stupid, ninny, gawky.

बिलव = **विल्व**, *q.v.* See **व**.

बिलवना, *more com.* **बिलखना**, *q.v.*

बिलवाना, *more com.* **बिलखाना**, *q.v.*

बिलसना, *a. int.* to be pleased, be satisfied, be delighted.

बिलस्त, *f.* a span (*i.e.* the space from the tip of the thumb to that of the little finger when stretched).

बिलहबन्द, *m.* settlement, regulation.

बिलहबन्दी, *f.* an account of the settlement of a district (specifying the name of each *mahall*, the farmer of it, and the amount at which it is let).

बिलहरा, *m.* a kind of long narrrow basket generally used for holding betel-leaf (*pān*).

बिलहरी, *f.* 1, (dim. of **बिलहरा**) a small basket for holding betel-leaf: 2, an oil-ladle.

बिलहार; see **बिलहरा**.

बिलहारी; see **बिलहरी**.

बिला, *m.* (from **बिल**) a hole, burrow.

बिलाई, *f.* 1, (*m.* **बिलाया**) a strumpet: 2, a she-cat: a kind of grater for scraping pumpkins, etc.

बिलाईकन्द, *m.* a certain medicine.

बिलाना, *a. int.* to vanish, retire, be lost: *t.* to cause to vanish, to dispose of, distribute, dissipate.

बिलान्द, *f.* a span. See **बिलस्त**.

बिलाप; for words beginning thus, see under the form **विलाप**.

बिलाया, *m.* (*f.* **बिलाई**) corrupt, degenerate, bad: *hence*, an impudent person.

बिलार, *m.* (*f.* ī) a cat.

बिलाला, *m.* (*f.* ī) = **बिलल्ला**, *q.v.*

बिलाव / **बिलावड़** } *m.* a male cat.

बिलावल, *f.* one of the minor musical modes (*rāgiṇī*).

बिलास; for words beginning thus, see under the form **विलास**.

बिलाहि (pl. °**हिं**) an old form = **बिलाता है**.

बिलिश / **बिलिश्त** } = **बिलस्त**, *q.v.*

बिलूखा, a rent, fissure, crack, crevice.

बिलोक, बिलोच; for words beginning thus, see under the forms **विलोक, विलोच**, respectively.

बिलोकि / **बिलोक्य** } (*Rām.*) = **बिलोकके** (**बिलोकना**).

बिलोना, *t.* to churn.

बिलोवनी in Braj = **बिलोना**, *q.v.*

बिलैंगी, *f.* a certain species of grass.

बिलोटा, *m.* (*f.* ī) = (1) **बिलहरा**, *q.v.*: (2) a cat.

बिलोना, *t.* to churn.

बिलौर = **बिल्लौर**, *q.v.*

बिलोवनो in Braj = **बिलोना**, *q.v.*

बिल्ब = **बिल्व**, *q.v.*

बिल्ला, 1, *m.* (*f.* ī) a cat: 2, *m.* a breastplate or badge as worn by peons, policemen, etc.: any tablet or flat piece of metal: a string confining the hilt of a sword or dagger to the sheath.

बिल्लाना, *a. int.* to weep or complain from grief or pain; to whine, whimper.

बिल्लार, *m.* (*f.* ī) a cat.

बिल्ली, *f.* 1, (*m.* **बिल्ला**) a she-cat: 2, the bolt of a door, a bar.

बिल्लीलोटन, *m.* valerian.

बिल्लोर = **बिल्लौर**, *q.v.*

बिल्लौर, *m.* a kind of stone, crystal; glass of the finest quality, cut glass; beryl (*Aqua marina*).

बिल्व = **विल्व**, *q.v.*

बिल्वन्त, *m.* (*f.* vatī) *more prop.* **बलवन्त**, *q.v.*

बिवस्वान = **विवस्वान**, *q.v.*

बिवहार, **बिवहारा** } *more prop.* **व्यवहार**, *q.v.*

बिवाई, 1, = **विवाही**, *q.v.*: 2, *f.* a blister or chap on the foot or the hand, a kibe, a chilblain.

बिवाद, बिवास, बिवाह; for words beginning thus, but not given below, see under the forms **विवाद, विवास, विवाह**, respectively.

बिवाहि, *more prop.* **विवाही**, *q.v.*

बिश; for words beginning thus, but not given below, see under the forms **विश** or **विष**.

बिशद, *more prop.* (1) **विशद** (2) **बिष्ट**, *qq.v.*

बिशन; for words beginning thus, see under the forms **बिसन** and **विष्णु**.

बिशिख; see (1) **विशिख** (2) **विशेष**.

बिशुक = **विशुष्क**, *q.v.*

बिशेख, बिशेष, बिशेश; for words beginning with either of these elements, see under the form **विशेष**.

बिशेय, a corruption of **विषय**, *q.v.*

बिशोक = **विशोक**, *q.v.*

बिश्न, बिश्व, बिश्वस, बिष; for words beginning thus, but not given below, see under the forms **विष्णु, विश्व, विश्वस, विष**, respectively.

बिश्नोत्तर, *more prop.* **विष्णूत्तर**, *q.v.*

बिशुआ, *more prop.* **विष्णु**, *q.v.*

बिषे, **बिषै** } = (1) **बीचमें** (2) **विषय**, 1 and 2, *qq.v.*

बिष्ट, बिष्ठ; for words beginning thus, see under the forms **विष्ट, विष्ठ**, respectively.

बिष्ट, *m.* a provincial term in Kamāōn for a *ta'allukdār* whose office is in the gift of Government.

बिष्टी, *more prop.* (1) **बिहिश्ती** (2) **वृष्टि**, *qq.v.*

बिष्णु, बिष्म; for words beginning with either of these elements, see under the form **विष्णु**.

बिष्णोत्तर, *more prop.* **विष्णूत्तर**, *q.v.*

बिस; for words beginning thus, but not given below, see under the forms **विश, विष, विस**.

बिसकर्मा, *more prop.* **विश्वकर्म्मा**, *q.v.*

बिसन, 1, *more prop.* **विष्णु**, *q.v.*: 2, *m.* evil, fault; desire, lust.

बिसनपट, *m.* a habit of indulging desire.

बिसनपद = **विष्णुपद**, *q.v.*

बिसनपन, *m.* a habit of indulging desire.

बिसनी, delicate, nice, showy in dress; hence, *m.* a rake, lecher, debauchee.

बिसबास, *more prop.* **विश्वास**, *q.v.*

बिसबिसाना, *a. int.* to yield a sound (as in the fermentation of putrefying vegetables or of vinous liquors).

बिसमय, *more prop.* (1) **विषमय** (2) **विस्मय**, *qq.v.*

बिसमार, *m.* a certain kind of bush.

बिसमित, *m.* (*f.* ā) *more prop.* **विस्मित**, *q.v.*

बिसमिल, sacrificed. — *k.* to sacrifice an animal.

बिसमिल्लाह, *more prop.* **बिस्मिल्लाह**, *q.v.*

बिसयारी, *f.* superfluity, abundance.

बिसर, *m.f.* forgetfulness, obliviousness, oblivion.

बिसरना, to forget: to be forgotten.

बिसरा, *m.* (*f.* ī) forgetful, oblivious.

बिसराट, a contraction of **बिसराहट**, *q.v.*

बिसराना, *t.* to forget; to cause to forget; to mislead.

बिसराहट, *f.* = **बिसर**, *q.v.*

बिसर्ग = **विसर्ग**, *q.v.*

बिसर्जन = **विसर्ज्जन**, *q.v.*

बिसल, *m.* a proper name of males.

बिसवाबरार = **बिस्वाबरार**, *q.v.*

बिसवांसः, *more prop.* **बिस्वांसः**, *q.v.*

बिसवांसी, *more prop.* **बिस्वांसी**, *q.v.*

बिसवास, *more prop.* **विश्वास**, *q.v.*

बिसहरी, 1, *f.* (*m.* **बिसहक**) a female purchaser: 2, *f.* a phlegmon or boil on the hand.

बिसहक, *m.* (*f.* °**सहरी**), **बिसहकआ**, *m.* (*f.* °**कई**) } a purchaser.

बिसाएन्ध, *f.* evil odour, fetidness, stink.

बिसाखा = **विशाखा**, *q.v.*

बिसात, *f.* means, power, ability; capital, estate, stock-in-trade: what is spread out; *hence*, carpeting, bedding; a chessboard; expanse, expansion, surface.

बिसाती, appertaining to *bisāt*: hence, *m.* (*f.* inī) one who sells all kinds of things, a dealer, pedlar, haberdasher.

बिसान, *f.* an offensive smell (as of fish, onions, etc.).

बिसाना = (1) **बिसराना** (2) **बिसाहना**, *qq.v.*

बिसान्ध, **बिसायन्ध** } = **बिसाहिन्द**, *q.v.*

बिसार, 1, *more prop.* (1) **विशाल** (2) **बिसरा**, *qq.v.*:

2, a load of seed given on the stipulation of an ample refund after the harvest.

बिसारद = **विशारद**, *q.v.*

बिसाल = (1) **बिसार** (2) **विशाल**, *qq.v.*

बिसाह, *f.* buying, purchasing, purchase.

बिसाहन, 1, *m.* = **बिसाह**, *q.v.*: 2, *f.* = **बिसाहिन्द**, *q.v.*

बिसाहना, *t.* to purchase, buy.

बिसाहिन्द, *f.* evil odour, fetidness, stink.

बिसाहिन्दा, *m.* (*f.* ī) fetid, stinking.

बिसिख = **विशिख**, *q.v.*

बिसी, *more prop.* **बीसी**, *q.v.*

बिसुरना, *a. int.* to cry slowly, to sob.

बिसेख; for words beginning thus, see under the [form **विशेष**.

बिसेखो in Braj = **विशेष**, *q.v.*

बिसेन, a certain powerful tribe of Rājpūts.

बिसेला, *m.* (*f.* ī) = **विषेला**, *q.v.* [form **विशेष**.

बिसेष; for words beginning thus, see under the

बिशोक = **विशोक**, *q.v.*

बिसोका, a poet. form of **विशोक**, *q.v.* [form **बिस्त**.

बिस्त; for words beginning thus, see under the

बिस्तर, *m.* bedding, carpeting; a bed.

बिस्तरा, *m.* a bed, etc. peculiar to a faqeer; the abode of a faqeer.

बिस्तुइया, **बिस्तुई**, **बिस्तूइया**, **बिस्तूई** } *f.* (from **बिष**) a lizard.

बिस्प, **बिस्फ**, **बिस्म**, **बिस्र**; for words beginning thus, see under the forms **बिस्प**, **बिस्फ**, **बिस्म**, **बिसर**, respectively.

बिस्मिल्लाह (*lit.* in the name of God) is a phrase used by Muhammadans at the beginning of all actions, literary works, etc.: it has passed, however, into a common phrase, and, as such, is frequent even in the lips of Hindoos: hence, *Bismillāh k.* to make a beginning, to commence. *Bismillāh hū,ā* is said of a a child who has just commenced learning to read.

बिस्व; for words beginning thus, but not given below, see under the forms **बिश्व**, **बिस्व**. [*bīghā*.

बिस्वा, *m.* (from **बीस**) the 20th part (*esp.* of a

बिस्वांसः, *m.*, **बिस्वांसी**, *f.* } a fraction of a *biswā*.

बिस्वादार, *m.* (*f.* nī *or* in) the holder of a share or shares in a coparcenary.

बिस्वादारी, *f.* the tenure of independent village communities holding under a superior *ta'allukdār*.

बिस्वाबरार, *m.* collecting or assessment by the *biswā*. [curry-stuff, curry-powder.

बिस्वार, a mixture of spices, etc. for making curry,

बिस्वास = **विश्वास**, *q.v.* See **बिस्व**.

बिह; for words beginning thus, but not given below, see under the form **बिह**.

बिहंसना, *a. int.* to smile, laugh.

बिहड़, land cut up by a torrent.

बिहतर, preferable, better, good, well, very good, [excellent.

बिहन, *m.* seed.

बिहनौर, *f.* a seedplot, nursery for plants.

बिहफै, *m.* (from **बृहस्पति**) Thursday.

बिहबल = **विह्वल**, *q.v.*

बिहबूदि, *f.* health, vigour, goodness, welfare.

बिहरन = **विहरण**, *q.v.* See **बिह**.

बिहरी, *f.* a subscription towards raising a certain sum, a contribution, share, rate, quota, assessment.

बिहर, a bursting, splitting, rending, tearing.

बिहसना, *a. int.* to smile, laugh.

बिहाइ = (1) **बिहाई** (2) **बिहाय**, *qq.v.*

बिहाई, *f.* a kind of spirit supposed to teaze infants by whispering alternately in their ears things pleasing and things sad (which is believed to be the occasion of their laughing and crying when asleep or awake).

बिहाग, *m.* a certain musical mode (*rāg*).

बिहागड़ा = **बिहाग**, *q.v.* [(yesterday or to-morrow).

बिहान, *m.* the morning, dawn; the next day

बिहाना, *t.* to spend or pass the time.

बिहाने, *adv.* (sc. **पर** or **में**) at dawn, in the morning, early, soon.

बिहाय; see (1) **बिहाना** (2) **बिहायना**.

बिहायना, *t.* to leave, let go, forsake.

बिहार; for words beginning thus, see under the [form **विहार**.

बिहाल, *more com.* **बेहाल**, *q.v.*

बिहित, *m.* (*f.* ā) = **विहित**, *q.v.*

बिहिन, *m.* seed.

बिहिश्त, *f. pr. n.* paradise, heaven.

बिहिश्तवाला, paradisiacal: hence, *m.* (*f.* ī) an inhabitant of paradise, a celestial being.

बिहिश्ती, appertaining to Bihisht, celestial, paradisiacal: hence, *m.* (*f.* in *or* ini) an inhabitant of paradise, a celestial being: a water-carrier. [cure.

बिही, *f.* a guava: a quince: goodness: recovery,

बिहीन, *m.* (*f.* ā) = **विहीन**, *q.v.*

बी, 1, (*contraction*) = **बीबी**, *q.v.*: 2, (*corruption*) = **भी**, *q.v.*: 3, a vocative particle used in addressing females.

बीअड़, *f.* a seedbed, seedplot: evening.

बीअर, *m.* a hole (of a snake, rat, etc.).

बीआर; see (1) **बीअड़** (2) **बीअर** (3) **बयार**.

बीआस, land cultivated to be sown in the follow- [ing year.

बींच, a colloquial form of **बीच**, *q.v.*

बींज, a colloquial form of **बीज**, *q.v.*

बींड, **बींत**, **बींद**, **बींध**; for words beginning thus, see under the forms **बीण्ड**, **बीन्त**, **बीन्द**, **बीन्ध**, respectively.

बीक, *m.* (from **वृक**) a wolf. [damaged.

बीका, (see **बाल**) *m.* (*f.* ī) crooked, awry; injured,

बीको in Braj = **बीका**, *q.v.*

बीगा, *more prop.* (1) **बीका** (2) **बीघा**, *qq.v.*

बीघा, *m.* a certain measure of land. The *bīghā* varies much in different parts of India: thus in Bengal it consists of 20 *katthā* or 120 feet square, *i. e.* 1600 square yards or nearly a third of an English acre; while in the upper Provinces it is usually 3025 square yards, or nearly five eighths of an acre.

बीघादफ़्तरी, *f.* a record of the measurement of lands in a district.

बीघादाम, *m.* settlement of revenue at so much per bighā; rate levied at per bighā.

बीच, 1, in, into, in the midst of, among, between, during, meanwhile: 2, *m.* middle, midst, centre; difference; hostility; quarrel. — *ki angli*, the middle finger. — *parnā*, to differ; to raise a quarrel between. — *meṅ parnā*, to mediate, interpose.

बीचबिचाव, *m.* mediation, interposition, arbitration. — *k.* to mediate, interpose, arbitrate.

बीचबोली, *f.* the middle language or dialect (*i.e.* the Urdoo and Hindee mixture).

बीचरा, *m.* a bed for growing plants that are to be [transplanted.

बीचवाई } **बीचवानी** } *m.* (*f.* inī) = **बिचौलिया**, *q.v.*

बीचवाला, *m.* (*f.* ī) situated between or in the midst.

बीचाबीच, 1, *m.* the very middle: 2, *adv.* in the very middle: 3, *adj.* middlemost, central.

बीचि = **वीचि**, *q.v.*

बीचोंबीच = **बीचाबीच**, *q.v.*

बीचा = **बीचरा**, *q.v.*

बीछा } **बीछू** } *more com.* **बिच्छू**, *q. v.*

बीज; for words beginning thus, but not given below, see under the form **वीज.**

बीज, (in Chand) the 2nd day of the light half [of the month.

बीजक, *m.* a ticket tied to goods, or on bags of grain, etc. to mark their contents, price, etc.; a list, catalogue, inventory, invoice.

बीजना, *m.* a kind of fan.

बीजर, a description of soil in which the cereal grains are generally sown.

बीजवार, a perquisite of the lower classes consisting of a portion of seed-corn brought away each day from the field.

बीजाई, *f.* a perquisite of a certain allowance of [seed-grain.

बीजार, seedy, abounding in seed.

बीजावरखण्ड, *m.* a forest.

बीजी, 1, *m.* (*f.* inī) = **बीजी**, *q.v.*: 2, *f.* a weasel, mungoose (*Viverra ichneumon*).

बीजोसर, *m.* a certain tree (called in Urdoo *'shāl'*).

बीझना, *t.* to tear up the earth with horns or hoofs (as a bull): to push, shove, shoulder.

बीझेरया or **बीझेर्या**, a certain class of Rājpūts in the district of Gorakhpur.

बीझोनिया, a certain tribe of Rājpūts in Jaunpur.

बीट, *f.* 1, = **बीठ**, *q.v.*: 2, a factitious salt containing sulphur: a kind of agistment (an allowance per head of cattle, paid to the cowherd). — *k.* to evacuate.

बीटना, *t.* to pour out, spill, scatter.

बीठ, *f.* (from **विष्ठा**) the dung of birds.

बीठा, *m.* an annular cushion put on the head for carrying pots of water on.

बीढा, *m.* a mound, a cluster of mounds.

बीड़ा, *m.* a betel-leaf made up with a preparation of the areca-nut, spices, and chunam: a thong tied to the hilt of a sword by which the sword is retained in the scabbard, a sword-knot. — *uṭhānā*, to undertake a business, accept a challenge, take up the gauntlet. — *dālnā*, to propose a premium for the performance of a task, to make challenge, throw down the gauntlet. These expressions originated in a custom that once prevailed, of throwing a *birā* of betel into the midst of an assembly in token of proposal to any person to undertake some difficult affair then requiring to be performed: the person who took up the betel bound himself by that act to perform the business in question.

बीड़िया, *f.* a certain class of harlots.

बीड़ी, *f*, (dim. of **बीड़ा**) a small parcel of betel-leaf: the colour that adheres to the lips from shewing betel: a certain composition which being rubbed on the teeth stains their interstices of a red colour.

बीण = **वीण** = **वीणा**, *q. v.*

बीणा = **वीणा**, *q.v.*

बीण्डा, *m.* a roll of paper: a kind of rope made of grass or of the fibres of the *arhar*-plant.

बीण्डी, *f.* the hair twisted or plaited behind; a [tail.

बीतखेत, *m.* land cultivated by forced labour.

बीतना, *a. int.* to pass, elapse, expire (as time): to occur, to come to pass, happen, befal, arrive.

बीतनेहारा, *m.* (*f.* ī) passing, transient, temporary.

बीता, a span (from the tip of the little finger to [that of the thumb).

बीति = **वीति**, *q.v.*

बीथि } **बीथी** } = **वीथी**, *q. v.*

बीद, *f.* a street, lane.

बीदर, a kind of rake or harrow worked by oxen: *pr. n.* a certain province and city.

बीधा, settlement, arrangement, determination of the amount to be paid as revenue.

बीन = **वीण** = **वीणा**, *q. v.*

बीनडी, *more prop.* **बीण्डी**, *q. v.*

बीनना, *t.* (of **बिनना**) to select, peck, pick up (as fowls do), glean (as corn).

बीना, 1, = **बीणा**, *q.v.*: 2, having sight, seeing, clearsighted, discerning. — *k.* to impart the faculty of vision or of discernment.

बीनाकरन, *more prop.* **वीणाकरण**, *q. v.*

बीनिश, *f*, sight; seeing; discernment.

बीनी, *f.* the nose: the guard of a sword.

बीन्तना, *t.* to cut out clothes.

बीन्द, *m.* a reed, rush. [fibres of the *arhar*-plant.

बीन्दा, *m.* a kind of rope made of grass or of the

बीन्धना, *t.* to bore, perforate. [a wife.

बीबी, *f.* a lady, dame, madam; (*euphemistically*)

बीभीषण, *more prop.* **विभीषण**, *q.v.*

बीम, *m*, fear, terror, dread; danger.

बीमा, *m.* insurance, the rate of insurance, money [paid for the insurance of goods.

बीमां = **बीमा**, *q.v.*

बीमार, sick, ill, indisposed, invalid.

बीमारख़ाना, *m.* a sick-ward, a hospital.

बीमारदार, *m.* (*f.* nī *or* in) an attendant on sick persons, a nurse.

बीमारदारी, *f.* attendance on the sick, nursing.

बीमारी, *f.* illness, sickness, disorder, disease, distemper.

बीर; for words beginning thus, but not given below, see under the form **वीर**.

बीर, 1, *m.* a brother: a jewel worn in the ear: 2, *f.* a sister: a tusk: 3, *m. f.* pasture-land.

बीरण, a kind of tough grass spreading over uncultivated lands.

बीरन, 1, = **बीरण**, *q.v.*: 2, *m.* (a Braj pl. of **बीर**) brothers, etc.: 3, *m.* a brother: 4, *m.* (a Braj pl. of **वीर**) heroes.

बीरबहोटी / **बीरबहुटी** } = **बीरबहुट्टी**, *q.v.*

बीरबहुट्टी, *f.* (**वीर + वधूटी**) a certain small insect (*Bucella carniola?*) with a back of a bright red colour. It is commonly called 'the red velvet-insect,' 'the scarlet fly,' 'the lady-cow' or 'the lady-fly,' also 'the rain-insect,' from its making its appearance when the first rains have fallen: it is covered with a bright scarlet down.

बीरबधूटी = **बीरबहुट्टी**, *q.v.*

बीरबानी, *f.* a man's own wife. The term is used [by the Jāṭs of the North-west.

बीरा = **बीड़ा**, *q.v.*

बीराम; see (1) **बीमार** (2) **बेआराम** (3) **विराम**.

बीरामी; see (1) **बीमारी** (2) **बेआरामी**.

बीरी = **बीड़ी**, *q.v.*

बीरूआ, a colloquial form of **बीर**, a hero, etc.

बीरो, a small tree, a sapling.

बीर्य = **वीर्य**, *q.v.* See **बीर**.

बील; see **बेल** and **बिल**.

बीलार, *m.* (*f.* in *or* ī) a cat.

बीवत, the fit of a suit of clothes, etc.

बीस, twenty (२०).

बीसबाहु, *m.* (the twenty-armed, *i.e.*) Rāvaṇ.

बीसर, gleanings left in the fields for the lower orders to gather.

बीसल, *m.* a proper name of males.

बीसवां, *m.* (*f.* °**वीं**) twentieth. [ethly.

बीसवे, (see **वे**, 2) in the twentieth place, twenti-

बीसवें, the inflected form of **बीसवां**. See **वें**, 1.

बीसा, 1, *m.* a score: 2, *m.* (*f.* ī) a dog that has twenty nails.

बीसी, *f.* a score: a certain measure of grain: a land-measure equivalent to twenty *nalis*.

बीसों, 1, scores; 2, *adv.* in twenties. See **ओं**, 4.

बीहड़, land that is sterile, rugged, and craggy, [waste land, land full of ravines.

बीहन, *m.* seed.

बीहार, **बुंद**; for words beginning thus, see under the forms **विहार**, **बुन्द**, respectively.

बुंबास, *more prop.* **बूबाश**, *q.v.*

बुकट / **बुकटा** } *m.* = **बुक्कट**, *q.v.*

बुकनी, *f.* a kind of digestive-powder.

बुकलाना, *a. int.* to talk incoherently to oneself; to act or talk foolishly.

बुकात, *f.* a kind of sweetmeat. [nails.

बुकोटना, *t.* to scratch, claw, lacerate with the

बुक्कट, *m.* a claw: a handful.

बुक्का, *m.* a handful.

बुक्की, *f.* a cloth worn over the shoulders, under the armpits, and tied behind: a handful. — *mārnā*, to pass a cloth under the armpit and tie it behind.

बुख़्ल, *m.* parsimony, stinginess, avarice, sparingness.

बुख़ार, *m.* steam, mist, fog, exalation; glowing heat (such as is felt in fever or such as arises from the ground). — *nikalnā*, to break out (as an eruption on the skin).

बुग़्ज़, *m.* malice, spite, revenge, hatred.

बुगमार, *m.* a musketoon or blunderbuss.

बुग्गा, a fountain, spring, *jet d'eau*.

बुजना, 1, *more prop.* **बुझना**, *q.v.*: 2, *m.* a cloth used by menstruous women; a pessary.

बुजबुरा, *m.* a vessel for warm water.

बुजाना, *more prop.* **बुझाना**, *q.v.*

बुज़ुर्ग, great; venerable: hence, *m.* a great man, grandee, celebrity; a saint; an elder; an ancestor.

बुज़ुर्गी, *f.* grandeur, greatness, exaltation, respectability, aggrandizement.

बुझना, *n.* to be extinguished, be put out (said of fire or a lamp), to be quenched (said of thirst), to be damped or dejected (said of the spirits).

बुझबुझवल, *m.* a conundrum, riddle, enigma.

बुझाई, *f.* an explaining, instructing.

बुझाउनो in Braj = **बुझाना**, *q.v.*

बुझाना, 1, *t.* (of **बुझना**) to extinguish, quench, put out, to damp, deject, depress (the spirits): 2, *t.* (causat. of **बूझना**) to cause to comprehend or understand, to instruct, to assure, to push (as, with argument), to demonstrate, to persuade, to cause to believe, to signify.

बुझारत, *f.* adjustment of accounts.

बुझावनौं, in Braj = **बुझाना**, *q.v.*

बुझेल, laden: *hence*, a beast, etc. of burden.

बुझोन्ता, an abstract account of a village proprietary.

बुझौवल; see (1) **फलबुझौवल** (2) **बुझबुझवल** (3) **बुझेल**.

बुझ्झनौं in Chand = **बूझना**, *q.v.*

बुड़, *f.* pudenda fœminæ, vulva.

बुड़क = **बुडुक**, *q.v.* [scoundrel.

बुड़चोद, *m.* (a term of abuse) blackguard, rascal,

बुडढा, *m.* (*f.* ī) *more prop.* **बुड्ढा**, *q.v.*

बुड़ना, *more prop.* **बूड़ना**, *q.v.*

बुड़पन
बुड़पना } *more prop.* **बुड्ढापन**, *q.v.*
बुड़पा

बुड़बुड़ा, *m.* a bubble.

बुड़म, the sound of water.

बुड़ा, *m.* (*f.* ī) *more com.* **बुड्ढा**, *q.v.*

बुड़ाना, *t.* (a causat. of **बूड़ना**) to cause to sink, to immerse, dip, drown.

बुड़ी, *f.* (*m.* **बुड़ा**) *more com.* **बुड्ढी**, *q.v.*

बुडुक, the sound of anything falling into (or sinking in) water.

बुड़ूक, *m.* a basket-maker, a mat-maker.

बुड्डा, *m.* (*f.* ī) *more prop.* **बुड्ढा**, *q.v.*

बुड्डापन
बुड्डापना } *more prop.* **बुड्ढापन**, *q.v.*
बुड्डापा

बुड्डी, *f.* (*m.* **बुड्डा**) *more prop.* **बुड्ढी**, *q.v.*

बुड्ढा, *m.* (*f.* ī) advanced in years, old, aged.

बुड्ढापन
बुड्ढापना } *m.* old age, senility. See **पन**.
बुड्ढापा

बुड्ढी, *f.* (*m.* **बुड्ढा**) an aged female.

बुढगंगा, *f.* the old bed of the Ganges where it has shifted its stream. [airs of youth.

बुढभस, *adj.* affecting in old age the manners and

बुढ़रा, *m.* (*f.* ī) in Braj = **बुड्ढा**, *q.v.*

बुढ़वता, *m.*
बुढ़वती, *f.* } old age, senility.

बुढ़वा, *m.* (*f.* ī) *more com.* **बुड्ढा**, *q.v.*

बुढ़ा, *m.* (*f.* ī) *more prop.* **बुड्ढा**, *q. v.*

बुढ़ाई, *f.* (see **ई**, 13) old age, senility.

बुढ़ाप, a contraction of **बुढ़ापा**, *q.v.*

बुढ़ापन
बुढ़ापना } *more prop.* **बुड्ढापन**, etc., *q.v.*
बुढ़ापा

बुढिया, *more com.* **बुढ़िया**, *q.v.*

बुढ़िया, *f.* an aged female.

बुढ़ियाँ, *more com.* **बुढ़िया**, *q.v.*

बुढ़ी, *f.* (*m.* **बुढ़ा**) *more prop.* **बुड्ढी**, *q.v.*

बुढ़ौती, *f.* old age, senility.

बुण्डा, *m.* a kind of ear-ornament.

बुत, *m.* a hazard-table: a blow with the fist: an idol, image, statue; *met.* a beloved object, a darling, a mistress.

बुतक, *f.* (dim. of **बुत**) a little idol. See **क**, 4.

बुतकदा
बुतख़ाना } *m.* an idol-temple, pagoda.

बुततराश, *m.* an idol-maker, carver of images,

बुतना, *more com.* **बुझना**, *q.v.* [graver, sculptor.

बुतपरस्त, *m.* (*f.* nī *or* in) a worshipper of images,

बुतपरस्ती, *f.* image-worship, idolatry. [idolater.

बुताना, *more com.* **बुझाना**, *q.v.*

बुतायी, *f.* an explaining, instructing.

बुतारत, the name given to an extra cess upon

बुतावनौं, in Braj = **बुताना**, *q.v.* [the cultivator.

बुत्ता, *m.* over-reaching, fraud, trick, take-in.

बुत्ती, *f.* provision for travelling. — *lekar chaudhīr dhūṅḍhnā*, to go in search of anything. [oil or grease.

बुदला, *m.* a leathern bottle or vessel for holding

बुदली, *f.* (dim. of **बुदला**) a small leathern bottle.

बुदबुद, *more prop.* **बुद्बुद**, *q. v.*

बुद्ध, 1, known, perceived, apprehended, discerned, understood: 2, *adj.* knowing: *hence*, 3, *m.* a wise or learned man, a sage: 4, *m. pr. n.* (1) of the 9th incarnation (*Avatar*) of Vishṇu, and the supposed founder of the Bauddh religion: *hence*, a generic name for a deified teacher of that religion, a Bauddh (2) of the planet Mercury (3) of Wednesday.

बुद्धि, *f.* understanding, intellect, sense, mind, thought, opinion, reflection, knowledge, wisdom, discretion.

बुद्धिबल, *m.* strength of intellect, mental power.

बुद्धिभत, *m.* (*f.* ā) wise, intelligent.

बुद्धिभ्रम, *m.* aberration of the mind or intellect.

बुद्धिभ्रष्ट, 1, *m.* the deterioration or destruction of intellect: 2, *m.* (*f.* ā) *adj.* of a deteriorated intellect.

बुद्धिमत, *m.* (*f.* matī) = **बुद्धिमान**, *q.v.*

बुद्धिमती, *f.* (*m.* **बुद्धिमान**) a woman of understanding, a sensible or a learned female.

बुद्धिमन्त, *m.* (*f.* matī) = **बुद्धिमान**, *q.v.*

बुद्धिमान, *m.* (*f.* matī) endowed with understanding, intelligent, sagacious, sensible, wise, intellectual, learned; ingenious, skilful: known, famed, celebrated.

बुद्धिराशि, *m.* an epithet of Gaṇesh (as the god of wisdom).

बुद्धिरूप, 1, *m.* the form or embodiment of intelligence: 2, *m.* (*f.* ā) of the manner or nature of intelligence.

बुद्धिरूपी, *m.* (*f.* iṇī) = **बुद्धिरूप**, 2, *q. v.*

बुद्धिवत, *m.* (*f.* vatī) = **बुद्धिमान**, *q. v.*

बुद्धिवती, *f.* (*m.* **बुद्धिवान**, etc.) = **बुद्धिमती**, *q.v.*

बुद्धिवन्त, *m.* (*f.* vatī) = **बुद्धिमान**, *q.v.*

बुद्धिवन्ती, *more com.* **बुद्धिवती**, *q.v.*

बुद्धिवान, *m.* (*f.* vatī) = **बुद्धिमान**, *q.v.*

बुद्धिशक्ति, *f.* an intellectual faculty.

बुद्धिसागर, *m.* (an epithet and a proper name: *lit.*) an ocean of intelligence. [ignorant.

बुद्धिहीन, *m.* (*f.* ā) senseless, silly, simple, foolish,

बुद्धिहीनता, *f.* (*m.* °त्व) senselessness, foolishness, silliness, ignorance. [female.

बुद्धिहीना, *f.* (*m.* **बुद्धिहीन**) a senseless or ignorant

बुद्धीन्द्रिय, *m.* (see **कर्मेन्द्रिय**) an organ of the intellect as distinguished from an organ of action. Six are enumerated, *viz.* mind, eye, ear, nose, tongue, skin.

बुद्बुद, *m.* a bubble; a vesicle: *adv.* little by little, by littles.

बुदबुदाना, *a. int.* to mutter, grumble.

बुध, 1, wise, intelligent, learned: *hence*, a wise and learned man, a sage: 2, *m. pr. n.* (1) of the son of the moon, and regent of the planet Mercury with whom he is identified (2) of Wednesday.

बुधजन, *m.* a wise and learned person.

बुधवार / **बुधबार** } *m.* (see **बुध**) Wednesday.

बुधि, a corruption of **बुद्धि**, *q.v.*

बुधित, *m.* (*f.* ā) known, perceived, understood.

बुन, 1, *m.* unground coffee: an allowance of grain given to a day-labourer: 2, *f.* root, stem: basis, foundation.

बुनना, *t.* to weave, intertwine, knit.

बुनफशा = **बनफ़शा**, *q.v.*

बुनियाद, *more prop.* **बुन्याद**, *q.v.*

बुन्द, *more com.* **बून्द**, *q.v.*

बुन्दा, *m. f.* a drop; a point, dot.

बुन्दिया, *f*, a kind of sweetmeat (like drops).

बुन्देला = **बून्देला**, *q.v.*

बुना = **बुनना**, *q.v.*

बुन्याद, *f.* groundwork, base, foundation, origin. — *ḍālnā*, to lay a foundation, to found (a house, city, dynasty, etc.).

बुबास, *more prop.* **बूबाश**, *q.v.*

बुभुक्षा, *f.* desire for food, hunger.

बुभुक्षित, *m.* (*f.* ā) desirous of food, hungry.

बुम्बी, *f.* the navel.

बुर, *f.* pudenda fœminæ, vulva.

बुरखोला, *m.* (*f.* ī) foul-tongued, abusive, scurrilous.

बुरभसिया, a person who affects in old age the manners and airs of youth.

बुरला, *m.* a wasp.

बुरा, *m.* (*f.* ī) bad, wicked; ugly; naught; worse. —*mānnā*, to take amiss, take ill (as, an affront); to be displeased, be affronted, feel oneself insulted.—*lagnā*, to be unpleasant.

बुराई, *f.* (the reverse of **भलाई**) badness, wickedness, sinfulness, vice, villainy, evil, mischief, dissension. *Burāīpar uṭhnā* or *Burāīpar kamar bāndhnā*, to resolve on mischief.

बुरांस, *m.* the rhododendron.

बुरास, *f.* badness, evil; anger, displeasure; vexation, regret: *adj.* displeased, angry, vexed.

बुरिंज; see **बिरिंज**.

बुरी, *f.* (*m.* **बुरा**) bad, etc.

बुरीचुड़ी, *f.* the small screech-owl.

बुकल, *f.* whiskers, moustaches.

बुरो / **बुरौ** } in Braj = **बुरा**, *q.v.*

बुर्ज, *m.* a large track-rope, a cable: a bastion, tower, bulwark: a constellation: a sign of the zodiac.

बुर्जेरी, *f.* (a term of abuse applied to females, such as) brimstone, strumpet, etc.

बुर्द, *f.* a bearing, carrying off: *met.* an opportunity of making some acquisition. The term is used at Chess when the king only, on one side, remains on the board: it is a species of victory, but not so creditable as checkmate.

बुर्बुरा, *m.* a bubble.

बुर्खोला, *m.* (*f.* ī) = **बुरखोला**, *q.v.*

बुर्रा, 1, *m.* the interior cavity of anything; the belly of a drum: 2, *f.* a dry and hollow pumpkin or cocoanut.

बुर्री, *f.* sowing by dropping seed from the hand into the furrow instead of sowing broadcast or with the drill.

बुर्हा, *m.* (*f.* ī) *more com.* (1) **बुरा** (2) **बुड्ढा**, *qq.v.*

बुल, *f.* pudenda fœminæ, vulva.

बुलन्द, high, tall, elevated, exalted, sublime.

बुलबुल, *f.* a nightingale: (in India) a shrike (*Lanius boulboul*, Lath.).

बुलबुला, *m.* a bubble.

बुलवाना, *t.* to cause to call, cause to send for or summon: to cause to be called, cause to be sent for or summoned.

बुलवालेना, an intensive form of **बुलवाना**, *q. v.*

बुला, *particip.* summoning. —*denā*, to summon, call. — *bhejnā*, to send for, summon. — *lānā*, to send and bring, to summon.

बुलाक, *m.* a kind of ornament worn on the nose and generally set with some gem.

बुलाना, *t.* (of **बोलना**) to summon, call, invite, bid.

बुलावन, *m.* = **बुलावा**, *q.v.*

बुलावनौं in Braj = **बुलाना**, *q.v.*

बुलावा, *m.* the act of calling or summoning.

बुलाहट, *f.* a calling, call, summons, invitation, bidding.

बुलि, *f.* pudendum fœminæ, vulva.

बुलुक, a large prominent eye.

बुल्लनौं in Chand = **बोलना**, *q. v.*

बुल्ला, *m.* a bubble.

बुल्लानौं in Chand = **बुलाना**, *q. v.*

बुवाई; see (1) **बिवाई** (2) **बोआई**.

बुहनी, *f.* (also **बोहनी**) the first ready-money sale in the morning, handsel; earnest-money.

बुहरी, *f.* fried or parched barley.

बुहारन, *f.* sweepings.

बुहारना, *t.* to sweep, to gather.

बुहारनी, *f.* an instrument for sweeping, a broom, besom.

बुहारी, 1, *f.* = **बुहारनी**, *q. v.*: 2, *m.* (*f.* iṇī) = **बुहारू**, *q.v.*

बुहारू, *m.* a sweeper, one who sweeps.

बू, *f.* a sister: hobgoblin: scent, odour, smell.

बूआ, *f.* a sister: an aunt (by the father's side).

बूई, *f.* (a word used for frightening children; like our) bogie, goblin.

बूंगा, a stack of straw, a heap of chaff.

बूंज, mouldiness, mustiness, mould.

बूंजभरा, *m.* (*f.* ī) mouldy, musty.

बूंट, **बूंद**; for words beginning thus, see under the forms **बूयट**, **बून्द**, respectively.

बूक, land recovered by the receding of a river.

बूकना, *t.* to reduce to powder, to pulverize, grind, powder.

बूक़लमून, various, wonderful : *hence*, anything of various hues, as a chameleon, etc.

बूका, *m.* powder : small pearls.

बूकारा, (see **बूक**) land that has been recovered by the receding of a river, but is rendered useless by a deposit of sand.

बूचना, *a.int.* to sit in a confined posture, to crouch.

बूचा, *m.* (*f.* ī) ear-cropt, without ears.

बूची, *f.* a hobgoblin.

बूज़ा, *m.* a kind of beer.

बूज़ागर, *m.* (*f.* in *or* nī) a brewer ; a beer-seller.

बूज़ागरी, *f.* brewing ; beer-selling.

बूज़ेख़ाना, *m.* a beer-shop, 'boozing-ken.'

बूझ, *f.* understanding, comprehension, thought. —*parnā*, (with dat. of the person) to seem. —*lenā*, (at Cards) to settle the amount of gain and loss.

बूझकर=**बूझके**, *q.v.*

बूझके, understandingly, wittingly, knowingly.

बूझनहार, thoughtful, intelligent, reflective.

बूझना, to understand, comprehend, make out, conceive : to think.

बूझबिचार, *m.* understanding and discretion.

बूझाई, *f.* teaching, explaining, instruction.

बूझाबूझी, *f.* a certain game among children in which one of them is blindfolded and must guess which of the others touched him.

बूट, *m.* chick-pea (*Cicer arietinum*) and its plant.

बूटा, *m.* a flower (*esp.* one worked on cloth, or painted on paper, etc.) : a bush, shrub.

बूटाकद is applied to describe the small stature and exquisite proportions of a beloved person.

बूटी, *f.* (see **बूटा**) flowers or sprigs on muslin ; sprigs of a plant : drugs.

बूटेदार, flowered (said of cloth).

बूड़ना, *n.* to be immersed, be submerged : *a. int.* to dive, dip, drown, to set (as the sun or any planet).

बूड़पन / **बूड़पना** / **बूड़पा** } *more prop.* **बुढ़ापन**, *q. v.*

बूड़मरना, *a. int.* to die of drowning, to drown.

बूड़ा, *m.* (*f.* ī) *more prop.* (1) **बुड्ढा** (2) **बुरा**, *qq.v.*

बूड़िया, 1, *more prop.* **बुढ़िया**, *q.v.* : 2, *m.* (from **बूड़ना**) a diver.

बूड़ी, 1, *more prop.* **बुड्ढी**, *q.v.* : 2, *f.* the point of a spear ; a spike at the end of a staff.

बूढ़गंगा, *more prop.* **बुढ़गंगा**, *q.v.*

बूढ़ा, *m.* (*f.* ī) *more prop.* **बुड्ढा**, *q.v.*

बूढ़ाआरहा, *m.* (*f.* **बूढ़ीआरही**) of mature years, aged : *hence*, an old person, an oldest person.

बूढ़ापन / **बूढ़ापना** / **बूढ़ापा** } *more prop.* **बुड्ढापन**, *q.v.*

बूढ़ी, *f.* (*m.* **बूढ़ा**) *more prop.* **बुड्ढी**, *q.v.*

बूणट, 1, = **बूट**, *q.v.* : 2, *m.* a stalk : green unripe gram.

बूणटपुलाव, *m.* a kind of *pulāo* made of *būnṭ*.

बूत ; see (1) **बूता** (2) **बहूत**.

बूता, *m.* strength, power, ability.

बूतात, *m.* an account of household expense, marketing-charges.

बूद, 1, *m.* (prop. **बुध**) Wednesday : 2, *f.* existence, being : a dwellingplace.

बूनियाद, *more prop.* **बुन्याद**, *q.v.*

बून्द, *f.* a drop : *adj.* good, excellent, well : high-soaring (said of kites). *Būndkī būnd*, very strong drink (*prop.* double-distilled, rectified).

बून्दकी, *f.* a spot, speck.

बून्दकीदार, spotted.

बून्दबून्द, *adv.* drop by drop, by drops, in driblets.

बून्दा, *m.* a large drop.

बून्दाबान्दी, *f.* a small and interrupted dropping of rain ; distillation, filtration.

बून्दी, 1, *f.* (dim. of **बून्दा**) a small drop ; small rain, rain-drops, droppings ; a kind of sweetmeat like drops : 2, *f. pr. n.* a certain place.

बून्देलखण्ड, *m. pr. n.* a certain province in North-western India.

बून्देला, *m.* a certain spurious tribe of Rājpūts who gave name to the province of Būndēlkhaṇḍ.

बूबक, *m.* an old simpleton.

बूबाश, ancient, perpetual, everlasting.

बूबू, *f.* (in western India = **बीबी**) a sister : a favourite concubine, or one of superior rank.

बूर, 1, barren (said of land) : 2, *f.* husk, chaff. *Būrkā laḍḍū*, a kind of sweetmeat made with the husk of grain : *met.* any person or thing that is fair without and foul within ; or, that promises well but turns out badly : *hence*, a well-looking but stupid fellow. The makers or vendors of the above-mentioned sweetmeat themselves own the imposition, and cry out to passers-by, 'You'll repent if you eat it, or regret not tasting it.' Hence, great folk are sometimes called '*Būrkā laḍḍū*' when they make a practice of encouraging their dependents to hope, but do nothing for them at last ; so that, dancing attendance on them, or neglecting them, are each likely to end in regret.

बूरना, *t.* to scatter abroad, strew, shed, besprinkle.

बूरा, 1, *m.* (*f.* ī) *more prop.* **बुरा**, *q.v.* : 2, *m.* a coarse kind of sugar ; sawdust ; filings ; powder : redeemable mortgage.

बूस ; see (1) **बोस** (2) **भूस**.

बृंह, बृक, बृच, बृज, बृत, बृत्त, बृथ, बृद्ध, बृन्द, बृश, बृष, बृह ; for words beginning with either of these elements, see under the forms **वृंह, वृक, वृच, वृज, वृत, वृत्त, वृथ, वृद्ध, वृन्द, वृश, वृष, वृह**, respectively.

बृख ; for words beginning thus, see under the forms **वृक्ष** and **वृष**.

बृक्ष. बृक्ष ; for words beginning thus, see under the form **वृक्ष**.

बृज, 1, = **वृज**, *q.v.* : 2, *more prop.* **ब्रज**, *q.v.*

बृति, *more prop.* (1) **वृति** (2) **वृत्ति**, *qq.v.*

बृद्धवस्था, *more prop.* **वृद्धावस्था**, *q.v.*

बे, 1, a vocative particle used to express contempt; like, 'You fellow!' 'You rascal!' 'Sirrah! 'O you!' 2, (from Sk. वि) without, out of; void of, minus. In this latter sense it is found as a prefix in some compound words from the Persian which are very commonly found in the Hindee speech and literature.

बेअदबी, *f.* ill-manners, rudeness, presumptuousness, impudence.

बेअर्थ, *more com.* व्यर्थ, *q.v.*

बेआकूफ, *more prop.* बेवकूफ़, *q.v.*

बेआदर, *more com.* निरादर, *q.v.*

बेआरामी, *f.* restlessness, uneasiness, disquiet, disease.

बेआलीस, *more com.* बयालीस, *q.v.*

बेआसी, *more com.* बयासी, *q.v.*

बेइज़्ज़त, *f.* ingloriousness, disesteem.

बेइख़्तियार, without choice, in spite of oneself.

बेईमान, without faith, unbelieving, irreligious; untrustworthy, treacherous.

बेईमानी, *f.* infidelity, irreligiousness, untrustworthiness, dishonesty, treacherousness.

बेऊ in Braj = वे भी. See ऊ, 7.

बेओपटना, *more com.* ब्योन्तना, *q.v.*

बेंग, *m.* (from व्यंग) a frog, paddock, toad.

बेंगत, *m.* seed given to a needy peasant at the time of sowing, to be repaid, with interest, at harvest.

बेंच, *more prop.* बेच, *q.v.*

बेंजन, *more prop.* व्यंजन, *q.v.*

बेंजनी = बैंगनी, *q.v.*

बेंट, बेंढ, बेंद, बेंध; for words beginning thus, see under the forms बेयट, बेयढ, बेन्द, बेन्ध, respectively.

बेकट्ठर, ruffianly, brutal, cruel.

बेकदर, of no value, of no importance, worthless.

बेकरार, restless, unsettled, variable, fickle, inconstant.

बेकरारी, *f.* restlessness, variableness, fickleness, instability.

बेकल, out of order, restless, uneasy, disturbed, agitated in mind.

बेकली, *f.* restlessness, perturbation, agitation of mind, uneasiness, disturbance.

बेकसूर, *more prop.* बेकुसूर, *q.v.*

बेकाज, बेकाम, बेकार } unemployed; idle; useless.

बेकारण, causelessly, aimlessly, uselessly.

बेकारी, *f.* unoccupiedness, unemployedness; idleness; uselessness.

बेकुपाई in Māṛwāṛī = बेवुकूफ़ी, *q.v.*

बेकुसूर, unoffending, innocent, faultless; without fail; entirely, completely.

बेख, *more prop.* (1) बेख़ (2) वेष, *qq.v.*

बेख़, *f.* root, origin, foundation.

बेखटके, *adv.* (sc. से) without apprehension or doubt.

बेखा, a poetical form of वेष, *q.v.*

बेख़ार, without thorns, without anxiety, without fear or solicitude.

बेखुद, beside oneself, enraptured.

बेखुदी, *f.* ecstasy, rapture.

बेग, 1, = वेग, *q.v.*: 2, a Mughal title corresponding to the English title 'lord.'

बेगड़, *m.* gold-tinsel; tinfoil: varnish.

बेगनी, *f.* the wife of a Beg. See बेग, 2.

बेगम, *f.* (*pl.* āt *or* ān) a lady, a woman of rank, a queen.

बेगव; for words beginning thus, see under the form बेग.

बेगा, *more prop.* (1) वेग (2) बेगाह, *qq.v.*

बेगाना, not domestic, strange, foreign, unknown: hence, *m.* (*f.* ī) a stranger, foreigner.

बेगार, a person forced to work whether with or without pay. — *pakaṛnā*, to press one into service with or without pay.

बेगारी, *f.* the act of pressing or forcing one to work. — *lenā*, to take forcibly or press into work with or without pay.

बेगारीपकड़ेला, *m.* (*f.* in *or* ī) a pressed man, one compelled to work with or without pay.

बेगाह, *adv.* out of season, untimely, unseasonably.

बेगि; see वेग and वेगि.

बेगिन, *m.* (*f.* ī) } = वेगी, *q.v.*
बेगी, *m.* (*f.* inī) }

बेगुनाह, sinless, faultless, innocent.

बेगैर; see (1) बग़ैर (2) बेग़ौर.

बेग़ौर, without premeditation, without reflection, without consideration, thoughtlessly.

बेचना, *t.* to sell, dispose of by sale. *Bech-ḍālnā*, (intensive) to sell off.

बेचाबाची, *f.* buying and selling, trade, commerce.

बेचारा, without choice, without remedy, helpless, wretched, poor: hence, *m.* (*f.* ī) a helpless creature, poor wretch, unlucky wight.

बेचैन, uneasy, restless.

बेचैनी, *f.* restlessness, uneasiness.

बेछना, *more com.* बेचना, *q. v.*

बेजना, *more prop.* भेजना, *q.v.*

बेज़र, without money, without the means of getting money, helpless.

बेजा, ill-placed, ill-timed, inaccurate.

बेज्जू, *m.* a certain animal that feeds on carcases (*Ursus Indicus*, Shaw; *Indian badger*, Penn.).

बेजून, out of occasion, untimely, unseasonable.

बेजोत, untilled: *hence*, a farm that has been abandoned by the cultivators.

बेझड़ा, *m.* a mixed crop (generally, grain and barley).

बेझा, *m.* a butt or mark for archers.

बेटा, *m.* (*f.* ī) a child, boy, son. — *kar lenā*, to adopt a child.

बेटी, *f.* a girl, damsel, daughter.

बेटुआ = बेटा, *q.v.* See उआ.

बेठ, sandy unproductive soil.

बेठन, *m.* the envelope in which cloth purchased is folded up to which the purchaser is entitled: pack-cloth, a wrapper.

बेठिकाना, *m.* (*f.* ī) uncertain, groundless.

बेठौर, out of place, groundless, inconsistent: *adv.*

groundlessly, inconsistently, improperly. — *thikāne*, improperly, inconsistently.

बेड़, *m*. an enclosure around a dwelling, a 'compound'. [enclose a field.

बेड़बन्दी, *f*. the making an enclosure. — *k*. to

बेडर, *adj*. fearless, dauntless: *adv*. fearlessly.

बेड़ा, *m*. a raft, float; the raft which is floated by Muhammadans in honour of Khwāja-khizr. Besides the anniversary *berā* offered to propitiate this saint, hundreds of smaller ones with lamps may be seen on Thursdays of the month Bhādoṅ in particular, which are offered to him by the Muhammadans. — *pār k*. or *lagānā*, (*lit*. to ferry over a raft; *hence*) to help one through a business, relieve from distress, remove difficulties. — *kiskā pār honā*, to be propitious, to succeed. — *pār honā*, to obtain deliverance from misfortune or distress, to succeed. — *bāndhnā*, to collect a crowd. [or tribe of Hindoos.

बेड़िया, *m*. 1, dim. of **बेड़ा**, *q.v.*: 2, a certain caste

बेड़ी, *f*. a ring worn around the ankle, iron fastenings for the legs of criminals or quadrupeds, fetters: a kind of basket used to irrigate fields with.

बेडौल, shapeless, misshapen, ugly, clumsy, ill-fashioned, ill-mannered, ill-bred, uneducated.

बेढ़ना, *t*. to enclose with a fence; to surround; to beseige; to pound (cattle, etc.); to drive away cattle (as in a foray).

बेढब, ill-shapen, ugly, deformed.

बेढ़ा, 1, *m*. (*f*. ī) = **बेपढ़ा**, *q.v.*: 2, *m*. a paling, railing, enclosure, hedge. [form **बेण**.

बेण; for words beginning thus, see under the

बेणु, a contraction of **वेणु**, *q.v*. See उ, 3.

बेण्ठ, *m*. a handle (of a knife, axe, etc.).

बेपढ़ा, *m*. (*f*. ī) crooked, bent, athwart, awry: *met*. not straightforward; absurd.

बेपठना, *t*. to plait, fold, braid.

बेत, 1, *m*. the sky, heaven: 2, *f*. a cane, reed, ratan (*Calamus rotang*); a blow or stroke with a cane.

बेतक़सीर, innocent, blameless, not guilty, acquitted.

बेतन = **वेतन**, *q.v.*

बेतर, *m*. a cane or willow.

बेतरफ़दार, of no party, impartial, unsectarian.

बेतरफ़दारी, *f*. non-partisanship, impartiality, unsectarianism.

बेताक़त, beyond the power of endurance.

बेताब, impotent, feeble, faint; impatient, restless.

बेताल = **वेताल**, *q.v.*

बेतौबः, *m*. impenitence.

बेतौर, mannerless, ill-omened.

बेत्र, *m*. a cane or willow. [in packing goods.

बेत्रबन्दी, *f*. an allowance for mats or wicker-work

बेद; for words beginning thus, but not given below, see under the form **वेद**.

बेदतत्त्व, *more prop*. **वेदतत्त्व**, *q.v.*

बेदर्द, painless; pitiless, unfeeling, merciless.

बेदलत, *more prop*. **बेदौलत**, *q.v.*

बेदवा, *m*. a reader of the Veds.

बेदार, awake. [tion.

बेदिली, *f*. heartlessness: want of courage, dejec-

बेदौलत, poverty-stricken, destitute, unfortunate.

बेध; for words beginning thus, see under the form **वेध**.

बेधड़क, without fear or doubt, fearless, dauntless; unsuspecting: *adv*. confidently; on a sudden.

बेधड़का, *m*. (*f*. ī) = **बेधड़क**, *q.v.*

बेन, *more prop*. (1) **वेणु** (2) **बैन**, *qq.v.*

बेनज़ीर, incomparable, peerless, matchless.

बेना, *m*. a fan: a certain kind of grass (*Andropogon muricatum*) commonly called *khas*.

बेनाप, unmeasured, unsurveyed. — *kā paṭṭā*, *m*. a lease guaranteeing that the average rates of land remain as before. [without rule.

बेनियम, without restraint, without restriction,

बेनी, *more prop*. **वेणी**, *q.v.*

बेनीव = **वेणीव** (*i. e*. **वेणी** + **इव**) = **वेणीके सदृश**.

बेनु; for words beginning thus, see under the form **वेणु**.

बेनीधा, *pr. n*. the country between Allahabad and Sarwar. [small river in Faizābād.

बेन्त, 1, *more prop*. **बेत**, *q.v.*: 2, *pr. n*. a certain

बेन्दी, *more prop*. **बिन्दी**, *q.v.*

बेन्धना, *t*. to plait, braid, fold.

बेपरवा, without reflection, careless, fearless.

बेपरवाई, *f*. freedom from danger or apprehension, indifference, tranquillity, security.

बेपरवाह, *more prop*. **बेपरवा**, *q.v.*

बेपार, a colloquial form of **व्यापार**, *q.v.*

बेप्रमाण, *more com*. **निष्प्रमाण**, *q.v.*

बेफ़ाइदा, profitless, useless, vain: *adv*. in vain.

बेफ़िक्र, thoughtless; contented; tranquil.

बेब, *f*. a certain grass used for making a sort of

बेबस = **बेवश**, *q.v.* [twine and for thatching.

बेबस्त्र = **बेवस्त्र**, *q.v.* [ly, completely, fully.

बेबाक, fearless: without remainder: *adv*. entire-

बेमात, *f*. (from **विमाता**) a step-mother.

बेमातभाई, *m*. a brother born of a different mother by the same father, a half-brother by the father's side.

बेमेल, without unison, unharmonious, unreconciled.

बेर, 1. *m*. the jujube-tree (*Zizyphus jujuba*) and its fruit: 2, *f*. time, tour, turn, vicissitude, delay, while: the lotus of the ancients.

बेरंग, colourless. The term is generally believed to be the English word 'bearing,' and in the jargon of the Post-offices is equivalent to the technical expression 'unstamped,' i.e. not pre-paid.

बेरबेर, again and again, repeatedly, over and over again, often, frequently.

बेरहम, merciless, cruel, barbarous.

बेरा, 1, *more com*. **बेर**, 2, *q.v.*: 2, *m*. a boat.

बेरां, in Chand = **बेर**, 2, *q.v.*

बेराना, 1, *m.* (*f.* ī) *more com.* बिराना, *q.v.*: 2, *m.*

बेरामी = बेआरामी, *q.v.* [a grove of *bér*-trees.

बेरार, *m.* a village accountant or registrar.

बेरि, *more prop.* (1) बेरी (2) बेरि, *qq.v.*

बेरी, *f.* a betel-leaf made up with spices, etc.: the colour which adheres to the lips from chewing betel: the tree of *Zizyphus jujuba*: the lees (or sediment) of oil or of clarified butter.

बेरून, *adv.* on the outside, without, out.

बेरे; see (1) बेरा (2) बेड़ा.

बेल, 1, *m.* a spade, shovel, pickaxe, hoe, mattock: a pole for directing a boat: a spot in which the receiving-pans are placed when sugar is being manufactured: a line marked out on a road or in a garden with an axe to point out the direction of any proposed work: a creeper, tendril: a well: a certain fruit (*Cratæva* or *Ægle marmelos*): a certain flower (*Jasminum zambac*) 2, *f.* any climbing-plant, a creeper, climber, tendril: offspring, descendants.

बेलकी, *m.* (*f.* in *or* inī) a cattle-breeder, grazier.

बेलदार, *m.* (*f.* in *or* nī) one who uses a spade, a digger, pioneer: a certain class of Hindoo employed in excavating.

बेलन, 1, *m.* a rolling-pin: 2, a Braj pl. of बेल, *q.v.*

बेलना, 1, *t.* to spread out, laminate: 2, *m.* a rolling-pin. [2, *m.* a branch.

बेलनी, 1, *f.* (dim. of बेलन) a small rolling-pin:

बेलपात, *m.* the leaf of the *bél*-tree.

बेलफल, *m.* the fruit of the *bél*-tree.

बेलबचला, a certain plant (*Basella alba*). [cloth.

बेलबूटा, *m.* a shrub, bush: a creeper: flowers on

बेला, 1, = वेला, *q.v.*: 2, *m.* a bag of money carried in the hand by a person of rank for distribution among the poor: 3, *f.* a certain shrub (*Jasminum zambac*) or its flower: a cup: an instrument of music resembling a fiddle.

बेलावना, *t.* to collect cattle.

बेलि, *f.* a creeper, tendril of a vine.

बेलिबिरह, afflicted, desolate, disconsolate.

बेली, *f.* a creeper, tendril of a vine.

बेलू, *m.* the act of rolling.

बेलोकन, *more com.* विलोकन, *q.v.*

बेलौ, dispirited, disheartened, heartless.

बेवकूफ़, *more prop.* बेवुकूफ, *q.v.*

बेवपार = ब्योपार, *q.v.*

बेवपारी, *m.* (*f.* iṇī) = ब्योपारी, *q.v.*

बेवरा, *m.* difference, distinction: explanation, account, history, detail of circumstances, account of particulars, detailed account in book-keeping.

बेवरेवार, explicitly, distinctly, in detail.

बेवश, *m.* (*f.* ā) without power or authority, helpless: not under subjection or control, independent.

बेवस्त्र, destitute of clothes, naked.

बेवह, *more com.* बेवा, *q.v.*

बेवहर, *m.* (from व्यवहार) a loan. [ditor, trader.

बेवहरा, *m.* (*f.* in, ī, inī, nī) a money-lender, cre-

बेवहरिया = बेवहरा, *q.v.*

बेवहार = व्यवहार, *q.v.*

बेवा, *f.* a widow.

बेवाई, *f.* the state or situation of widowhood, widowhood. [of any Hindoo deity; a Hindoo bier.

बेवान, *m.* (from विमान) vehicle or self-moving car

बेवापन } *m.* = बेवाई, *q.v.*
बेवापा }

बेवार = बेवरा, *q.v.*

बेवुकूफ़, ignorant, foolish, stupid, inexpert: *hence*, a blockhead. [norance, stupidity, foolishness.

बेवुकूफ़ी, *f.* want of understanding or sense, ig-

बेश, more, greater, superior, preferable, excellent, good, proper, well, elegant, delightful.

बेशक, *more prop.* बेशक्क, *q.v.*

बेशकम, more or less.

बेशक़ीमत, of great value, costly, precious.

बेशक्क, *adj.* free from apprehension, fearless, indubitable, certain: *adv.* without doubt, certainly.

बेशा, *m.* a forest, desert, jungle.

बेशी, *f.* excess, surplus, increase.

बेशुभ = बेशक्क, *q.v.*

बेशुमार, numberless, unnumbered, innumerable, much. [usually, exceeding, better, rather.

बेश्तर, more, most, mostly, for the most part,

बेश्या, बेश्वा; for words beginning with either of these elements, see under the form वेश्या. [form वेष.

बेष; for words beginning thus, see under the

बेस; see (1) बेश (2) वेश (3) वेष.

बेसन, *m.* the flour or meal of pulse (*esp.* of *chaṇā*). It is also used as a substitute for soap.

बेसनी, made of (or mixed with) *besan*.

बेसनौटी, *f.* a cake made of pease-meal.

बेसबा, *more prop.* वेश्या, *q.v.* [the nose.

बेसर, 1, = वेसर, *q.v.*: 2, *f.* the small ring worn on

बेसरा, *f.* a kind of falcon (*Falco nisus*) being the female or hen-bird of the species called *dhotī*.

बेसवा, *more prop.* वेश्या, *q.v.*

बेसा, *more prop.* (1) वेश्या (2) वेष, *q.v.*

बेसुध, beside oneself, senseless, in a faint or swoon, [entranced, enraptured.

बेसुरा, *m.* (*f.* ī) out of tune.

बेस्मा, बेस्य, बेस्या, बेस्वा; for words beginning with either of these elements, see under the form वेश्या.

बेह, *m.* (from वेध) a perforation, hole.

बेहड } (see बीहड़) uneven, rugged, abrupt.
बेहड़ }

बेहतर, *more prop.* बिहतर, *q.v.*

बेहद्द, without boundary, unlimited, boundless.

बेहन, a nursery for rice-plants.

बेहर: } *m.* grass kept for pasturage.
बेहरा }

बेहरी, *f.* a subscription, instalment, or assessment on a share; the distribution of an aggregate sum.

बेहरीदार, *m.* (*f.* in *or* nī) the holder of a *behrī*.

बेहरीबन्दी, *f.* an allowance for repairs (of roads, etc.).

बेहरीबरार, *m.* collection on shares of revenue in [kind.

बेहान, *more com.* **बिहान**, *q.v.*

बेहाल, out of condition, ill-circumstanced, in- [disposed.

बेहिया, *m.* a comber, carder (of cotton).

बेहुरमत, disgraced, debased.

बेहू, poet. or emphat. form of **बेह**, *q.v.*

बेहूदा, *m.* (*f.* ī) foolish, silly, stupid.

बेहोश, not in one's senses, intoxicated, delirious, stupefied, senseless, silly, foolish, insane.

बैआना, *m.* earnest-money.

बैओरा, *more com.* **बेवरा**, *q.v.*

बैंगन, *m.* the egg-plant (*Solanum melongena*).

बैंगनी, of the colour of the *Solanum melongena*, [i. e. purple.

बैंजनी = **बैंगनी**, *q.v.*

बैंट, बैंद; for words beginning with either of these elements, see under the forms **बैपट, बैन्द**.

बैंना, *more prop.* **बैणा**, *q.v.*

बैंसी, a certain subdivision of the Gūjar-tribe.

बैकारिक = **वैकारिक**, *q.v.*

बैकाल, *m.* (from **विकाल**) afternoon.

बैकुण्ठ; for words beginning thus, see under the [form **वैकुण्ठ**.

बैखट, a sale, a selling.

बैगन, *more com.* **बैंगन**, *q.v.*

बैगन्ती, *f.* a kind of wood.

बैगार, *m.* the Khaiwār tribe.

बैजनाथ = **वैद्यनाथ**, *q.v.*

बैजनी = **बैंगनी**, *q.v.*

बैजन्ती / **बैजयंती** } = **वैजयन्ती**, *q.v.*

बैज़वी, appertaining to eggs, made of eggs, egg- [shaped.

बैज़ः, *m.* an egg-shell: a testicle.

बैज़ा, *m.* the sun: adj. *m.* (*f.* ī) white.

बैजला, *m.* a species of black pulse.

बैट; see **बेठ** and **बैठ**.

बैटा, 1, *m.* (*f.* ī) = **बेटा**, *q.v.*: 2, = **बैठा**, *q.v.*

बैठ, the value of Government share of produce; the amount settled on land.—*jānā*, to sit down.—*rahnā*, to continue sitting, to sit.

बैठक, *f.* a seat, bench; a place where people (e.g. in a village) meet to sit and converse: a deliberative assembly: a sitting, the act or the condition of sitting.

बैठकख़ाना, *m.* a chamber (or hall or house) where meetings are held, an assembly-room, house of relaxation, clubhouse.

बैठका, *m.* = **बैठक**, *q.v.*

बैठना, *a. int.* to seat oneself, to sit: *hence*, to be unemployed, be out of work, be idle: to ride (on a horse): to sit in *dharna*, or as a dun: to perch (said of birds): to subside, abate, settle; to settle down (as in a home or at an occupation): to visit a person in grief for the purpose of condolence.

बैठलाना = **बैठाना**, *q.v.*

बैठवां, *m.* (*f.* **बैठवीं**) flat.

बैठवान = **बैठवां**, *q.v.*

बैठा, 1, *m.* (*f.* ī) seated, settled down: 2, *m.* a paddle for rowing a boat.

बैठाई, *f.* a seating, settling, allaying.

बैठाओ, 1, imperat. 2nd pers. of **बैठाना**, *q.v.*: 2, *more com.* **बैठाव**, *q.v.*

बैठाना, *t.* (causat. of **बैठना**) to cause to sit, make one sit, to seat, set, place, settle, station, plant, apply, calm, becalm, allay, assuage.

बैठारना = **बैठालना** = **बैठाना**, *q.v.*

बैठारिनि (*Rām.*) = **बैठाया** (**बैठाना**).

बैठालदेना, an intensive form of **बैठाना**, *q.v.*

बैठालना = **बैठाना**, *q.v.*

बैठाव, *m.* allocation, situation, position.

बैठिका = **बैठक**, *q.v.*

बैठू, *m.* or *f.* a sitter, one who sits.

बैण; for words beginning thus, see under the [form **वेण**.

बैण, 1, *m.* (from **वाणी**) a word, speech: 2, *f.* (from **वेणु**) a flute, fife, pipe.

बैणटा, *m.* a handle (of an axe, hoe, hatchet, etc.).

बैणड़ी, *f.* the throwing up water with a basket from a pond or reservoir for the purpose of irrigation.

बैत, *f.* a couplet (in poetry): an edifice, house, [temple.

बैतबन्दी, *f.* verse-making, prosody.

बैतरणी = **वैतरणी**, *q.v.*

बैतरा, *f.* dry ginger.

बैतलहम, *m. pr. n.* the city of Bethlehem.

बैताल = **वेताल**, *q.v.*

बैतालपचीसी, *f.* a certain Hindoo work (so called because it contains 25 tales related by a *Baitāl*).

बैतुलमाल, *m.* the treasure-house, the public treasury or exchequer: an escheat, property that falls in failure of heirs: *met.* an unfortunate person.

बैद, *m.* (*f.* in *or* nī) a physician.

बैदक, *m.* the science or the practice of medicine: (at Chess) a pawn.

बैदाई, *f.* (from **वैदिकी**) the practice of medicine.

बैदिक, बैदेश, बैदेह, बैद्य, बैध, बैन; for words beginning thus, see under the forms **वैदिक, वैदेश, वैदेह, वैद्य, वैध, वैण**, respectively.

बैन = (1) **बयन** (2) **बहिन** (3) **बैण**, *qq.v.*

बैनतेय = **वैनतेय**, *q.v.*

बैना, 1, (*Rām.*) = **बैणा**, *q.v.*: 2, (in Mārwāṛī) = **बयाना**, *q.v.*: 3, *m.* a kind of ornament worn on the forehead: sweetmeats, cakes, etc. distributed at marriages and at other ceremonies.

बैन्दा, *m.* a mark placed on the forehead (among Hindoos) as a preparative to devotion.

बैन्दी, *f.* an ornamental circlet made (with a coloured earth or unguent) on the forehead and between the eyebrows; a kind of ornament worn by Hindoo females on the forehead.

बैपार = **व्यापार**, *q.v.*

बैपारिन = **व्यापारिणी**, *q.v.*

बैपारी, *m.* (*f.* in *or* iṇi) = **व्यापारी**, *q.v.*

बैल, at a distance, afar off.

बैबल, *f.* (Engl.) the Bible.

बैभव = **वैभव**, *q.v.*

बैमात्र = **वैमात्र**, *q.v.*

बैमान, *more prop.* **बेईमान**, *q.v.*

बैमानी = (1) **वैमानी** (2) **बेईमानी**, *qq.v.*

बैया = **बया**, *q.v.* [or a weigher of grain.

बैयाई, *f.* the perquisite or the fee of a measurer

बैयाक, **बैयाप**, **बैयाम**, **बैयाल**, **बैयास**; for words beginning thus, see under the forms **व्याक**, **व्याप**, **व्याम**, **व्याल**, **व्यास**, respectively.

बैयान, *more com.* (1) **बयान** (2) **व्यान** (3) **व्याम**, *qq.v.*

बैयाला = **बयाला**, *q.v.*

बैर; for words beginning thus, but not given below, see under the form **वैर**.

बैरक, **बैरख** } *m.* a banner, ensign, colours.

बैरण, **बैरन** } *f.* (*m.* **बैर**) a female enemy.

बैरखान, in Gaṛhwālī = **बीरखामी**, *q.v.*

बैरयुत = **वैरयुक्त**, *q.v.*

बैराखेरी, *f.* quarrelling, wrangling, dissension.

बैरागन, 1, = **वैरागिणी**, *q v.*: 2, a Braj pl. of **बैरागा**.

बैरागा, *m.* a small crooked stick or piece of iron which a *vairāgi* places under his armpit to lean upon as he sits.

बैरामी = **बेआरामी**, *q.v.* [its fruit.

बैरि, *f.* the jujube-tree (*Zizyphus jujuba*) and

बैरी, *m.* (*f.* iṇī) = **वैरी**, *q.v.*

बैरोचन = **वैरोचन**, *q.v.* [beef-suet; tallow.

बैल, *m.* a bull, ox: *met.* a blockhead.— *kī charbī*,

बैला, *m.* a kind of bird.

बैलोचन = **वैरोचन**, *q.v.*

बैवर्त्त = **वैवर्त्त**, *q.v.*

बैवाहिक, *m.* (*f.* ā *or* ī) = **वैवाहिक**, *q.v.*

बैश, *more prop.* **वैश्य**, *q.v.*

बैशाख = **वैशाख**, *q.v.* [of a certain town.

बैशाली, *f. pr. n.* (1) of the wife of Vasudev (2)

बैश्नव, *more prop.* **वैष्णव**, *q.v.*

बैश्रवसन = **वैश्रवसन**, *q.v.*

बैषानस = **वैखानस**, *q.v.*

बैष्णव, **बैष्णी**; for words beginning with either of these elements, see under the form **वैष्णव**.

बैस = (1) **वयस** (2) **वैश्य**, *qq.v.* See **बैसवाड़ा**.

बैसक, 1, = **बैठक**, *q.v.*: 2, a spot in a jungle to which cattle are sent to graze; an old worn-out animal.

बैसना, *more com.* (1) **बैठना** (2) **पैठना**, *qq.v.* [caste.

बैसनी, *f.* [*m.* **बैस** (2)] a female of the Vaishya

बैसन्दर = **वैश्वानर**, *q.v.*

बैसम्पायन = **वैशम्पायन**, *q.v.*

बैसलाना, *more com.* **बैठलाना**, *q.v.*

बैसवाड़ा, *m.* the residence of Bais; the nativity of Bais. The province of Baiswāṛā is situated in Oudh, and is so named from a certain tribe of Rājpūts named *Bais* who formerly resided there. A prince of that tribe formerly reigned at *Dunḍia-khera*. His dominions, which extended over a great part of the province of Oudh, on the north bank of the Ganges, are still called Baiswāṛā.

बैसा, *m.* (*f.* ī) seated, settled down.

बैसाख = **वैशाख**, *q.v.*

बैसाखा, *m.* a crutch; a club armed with iron; a club consecrated to the month Vaiśākh.

बैसाखी = **वैशाखी**, *q.v.*

बैसाखू, *m.* or *f.* sedentary, idle, lazy.

बैसानी; see **बैसनी**.

बैसाख = **वैशाख**, *q.v.*

बैसे, 1, (corruption) = **वैसे**, *q.v.*: 2, pl. of **बैसा**, *q.v.*

बैसाख, a colloquial form of **वैसाख**, *q.v.*

बो, 1, *f.* smell, odour, scent: 2, sowing, cultivation.

बोआई, *f.* (see **आई**, 3) the act of sowing; sowing, cultivation; seed-time.

बोआना, 1, *a.int.* (from **बो**) to emit a bad smell, to stink: 2, *t.* (of **बोना**) to cause to sow.

बोआरा, *m.* seed-time; sowing, cultivation.

बोइया, *m.* a small basket.

बोई, *f.* 1, (*m.* **बोया**) sown: 2, sowing, cultivation.

बोईबाढ़, assessment to be realized on cultivation.

बोउ, 1, *more com.* **बू**, *q.v.*: 2, the 2nd and 3rd persons sing. of the dependent mode of the verb **बोना**.

बोंगा, a stack of straw, heap of chaff.

बोंट. **बोंड**; for words beginning thus, see under the forms **बोवट**, **बोवड**, respectively.

बोक, *m.* a he-goat, ram, tup.

बोकड़, *m.* a he-goat (big-bearded); a bell-wether.

बोकरा, *m.* a he-goat, a ram.

बोकरी, *f.* a she-goat.

बोकला, *more com.* **बकला**, *q.v.*

बोका, *m.* a basket, pail, or leathern bag used for throwing water to a higher elevation.

बोच, *m.* an alligator.

बोचरा, clipt or notched on the edge.

बोचा, *m.* a kind of sedan, a chair-palkee.

बोज़ना, *m.* a monkey, ape. [*deundata*, *Buch.*).

बोज़ा, 1, = **बूज़ा**, *q.v.*: *m.* 2, a kind of bird (*Ibis*

बोजोत, *f.* sowing, cultivation.

बोझ, *m.* a load, burden, weight; ballast (of a boat or ship): freight; (in Agric.) about five dhokas of corn; pregnancy, importance. — *pakaṛnā*, to affect a new delicacy or consequence, to give oneself airs (generally said in raillery).— *lādnā*, to emburden, lade, load. — *sirpar honā* is applied to a task the performance of which is become indispensable.

बोझना, *t.* to lade, load, emburden: to scald or parch rice. [corn by stacks or bundles.
बोझबटाई, *f.* a certain mode of division of mowed
बोझल, loaded, laden, burdened: heavy.
बोझा, *m.* = **बोझ**, *q.v.*
बोझाई, *f.* cargo, load, burden, lading.
बोझेल, loaded, laden, burdened: heavy. [inch.
बोट, *m.* a finger; a finger's-breadth, a digit, an
बोटी, *f.* a morsel (slice or lump) of meat; tripe.
बोड़ना, *t.* (causat. of **बूड़ना**) to cause to dive or dip; to immerse, sink, drown.
बोड़ा, 1, *m.* (*f.* ī) dull of hearing, deaf: 2, *m.* a species of bean (*Dolichos catsang*).
बोढैया, *f.* old age, senility.
बोणट, *m.* 1, = **बोट**, *q.v.*: 2, a stalk.
बोण्डा, *m.* a capsule, pod, seed-vessel (applied to cardamoms, cotton, the poppy, etc.). [shed.
बोण्डी, *f.* the germ of a plant after the flower is
बोत in Māṛwāṛī = **बहुत**, *q.v.*
बोतल, *f.* (Engl.) a bottle. [is kept, a pantry.
बोतलख़ाना, *m.* any apartment in which crockery
बोतू, *m.* a he-goat. [water from a well).
बोदर, a place to stand on (for those who raise
बोदलो, *f.* a simple woman; a trollop; a woman who lives with a *benawā* faqeer and dresses like a man. [hearted, low-spirited.
बोदा, 1, *m.* a buffalo: 2, *m.* (*f.* ī) weak, faint-
बोदाकाग़ज़, *m.* blotting-paper.
बोदी in Māṛwāṛī = **बहुत**, *q.v.*
बोद्ध = **बोध**, *q.v.*
बोद्धा, *m.* (*f.* ī) intelligent, sensible, ingenious.
बोध, *m.* intellect, understanding, capacity, wisdom; knowledge, intelligence; security.
बोधक, *adj.* causing to know: hence, *m.* (*f.* ikā) a teacher, informer, spy.
बोधन, 1, *m.* perception by the understanding, comprehension; knowledge; teaching, informing; arousing, awakening: 2, incense-burning: 3, *pr. n.* (1) of a certain Hindoo festival on the 9th of the month Bhādra (2) of the planet Mercury.
बोधना, *t.* to wheedle, cajole, coax, flatter.
बोधनी, *f.* = **बोधन**, 1, *q.v.*
बोधि, *m.* intellect, understanding: sacred study: the holy figtree (*Ficus religiosa*).
बोधिका, *f.* (*m.* **बोधक**) a female teacher, informer, or spy. [apprized.
बोधित, *m.* (*f.* ā) made known, taught, expressed,
बोना, 1, *t*, to sow, plant: 2, *m.* sowing; seed-time.
बोनी, *f.* the season of sowing, seed-time.
बोब, grain-sowing by the drill.
बोबा, *m.* goods and chattels, property: a bundle.
बोम = **बोमड़ो**, *q.v.*
बोमड़ो, *f.* howling, yelling, wailing aloud, lamentation, weeping: *interj.* alas!

बोयर, land that is never allowed to lie fallow.
बोया, *m.* (*f.* **बोई**) *past part.* sown, planted.
बोर, *m.* studs of gold or silver; little bells for the *pājeb*: a hole, opening, aperture: *adj.* deep.
बोरना; see (1) **बोड़ना** (2) **बोलना**.
बोरबच्चा, *m.* (*f.* ī) a leopard. [taining fire.
बोरसी, *f.* a kind of large earthen pan for con-
बोरहा, *m.* (*f.* ī) *more com.* **बोरहा**, *q.v.*
बोरा, *m.* a sack, canvas bag (particularly for containing two maunds of rice): a kind of bean like French beans (*Dolichos catsang*): redeemable mortgage.
बोराहट, *more com.* **बोराहट**, *q.v.*
बोरी; see (1) **बोड़ा** (2) **बोरहा** (3) **बोरा**.
बोरो, *m.* a rainbow: a kind of rice which is cut in March; marsh-rice.
बोल, *m.* myrrh: speech, word, conversation, talk; the words of a song. — *uthnā*, to speak out, exclaim, speak up, speak on a sudden. — *chālnā*, to converse, speak together. — *bhejnā*, to send for, to summon.
बोलंस, *m.* the making over one's share to another.
बोलंसी, *m.* (*f.* inī) the holder of another's share or inheritance; an adopted heir. [lation.
बोलचाल, *f.* diction, talk; conversation, confabu-
बोलता, 1, *m.* (*f.* ī) *pres. part.* saying: 2, *m.* the faculty of speech: soul, life.
बोलतियां, nom. pl. of **बोलती** (**बोलता**).
बोलना, *a. int.* to emit sound, to sound, to articulate, speak, talk, say, tell, address with the living voice. *Bole so* —, to speak repeatedly. This verb has, most frequently, the dative of the person spoken to; thus differing from *kahnā*, which generally has the ablative.
बोलबाला, *m.* a kind of benediction (*lit.* high speech or diction). — *honā*, to prosper.
बोला, 1, in Māṛwāṛī = **बहुत**, *q.v.*: 2, *m.* (*f.* ī) *partic.* spoke, spoken: 3, *m.* a verbal agreement between two parties.
बोलाचाली, *more com.* **बोलचाल**, *q.v.*
बोलाना, *more com.* **बुलाना**, *q.v.*
बोलि, see (1) **बोल** (2) **बोलना** (3) **बोला** (4) **बोली**.
बोलियां, *f.* (pl. of **बोली**) languages, dialects.
बोली, *f.* speech, dialect, brogue, language, saying, talk, conversation. — *k.* to jeer, jest.
बोलीठोली, *f.* jeering, speaking at (but not *to*) a person; altercation; conversation, chitchat. — *mārnā* or *sunānā*, to reproach, blame.
बोलेहु, an old form = (1) **बोलो**, 2nd pers. pl. imperat. of **बोलना** (2) **बोले**, aor. 2nd pers. pl. of **बोलना**.
बोवनों in Braj = **बोना**, *q.v.*
बोवे, (pl. **बावें**) in Braj = **बोय**, 2, *q.v.*
बोवैया, *m.* a sower of seed.
बोस, *m.* a kiss, buss; kissing, saluting.
बोसा, *m.* a kiss. — *denā* or *lenā*, to kiss.
बोसाबाज़ी, *f.* kissing and toying.
बोसीदा, stale, rotten, fœtid.
बोस्तान, *m. pr. n.* a certain celebrated book by

the Persian poet and moralist Sa'dī (*lit.* a place of odour, a flower-garden).

बोहनी, *f.* the money realized by hucksters, etc. for the first sale in the morning (no credit is allowed, nothing but ready money being accepted on such occasions). [bankers.

बोहरा, *m.* a certain class of money-lenders or

बोहाना, *t.* to set afloat, to send away, to separate.

बोहित = (1) बोहित (2) बोहित्य, *qq. v.*

बोहोदिया, *m.* a man who has no plough of his own and who works with a borrowed one.

बौर, the fee or perquisite of a zamīndār whenever a daughter of a cultivator in his village is married.

बौंड ; for words beginning thus, see under the form बौंयड. [drift.

बौछाड़, *f.* wind and driving rain, wind and rain,

बौछार = बौछाड़, *q. v.*

बौझका, *m.* (*f.* ī) foolish, insane, mad.

बौंड़. *m.* a creeping-plant, a vine.

बौड़हा, *m.* (*f.* ī) insane, rabid, mad.

बौड़हापन, *m.* = बौराई, *q. v.*

बौड़ा, *m.* (*f.* ī) insane, rabid, mad.

बौढ़िया, *f.* old age, senility.

बौंयड, *m.* a creeping-plant, a vine.

बौंयडना, *t.* to entwine (creepers or vines).

बौयडर ; see बवयडर.

बौयडा ; see बौयडा.

बौंयडियाना, *a. int.* to twine, run irregularly in a crooked direction with turns and windings.

बौतोज़मीन, *f.* land held by the owner of a village in his own possession to give out to the peasants for cultivation. [Bauddh or Buddhist.

बौद्ध, *m.* a follower of the religion of Buddh, a

बौद्धमत, *m.* the Buddhist class of opinions, the Buddhist sect, Buddhism.

बौद्धमतावलम्बी, attached to the Buddhist opinions: hence, *m.* (*f.* inī) a Buddhist.

बौध, 1, speechless : 2, *m. pr. n.* a certain king.

बौधनी ; see बोधनी.

बौना, dwarfish : hence (1) *m.* (*f.* ī) a dwarf (2) *m. pr. n.* the 5th incarnation of Vishṇu. See *Avatar.*

बौनी, *f.* (*m.* बौना) a female dwarf. [starveling.

बौभुख, *m.* (*f.* ī) one who is always hungry, a

बौंर ; see (1) बौड़ (2) बोर (3) बौरहा.

बौरहा, *m.* (*f.* ī) insane, rabid, mad.

बौरा, *m.* (*f.* ī) insane, rabid, mad.

बौराई, *f.* the state or condition of dementedness; insanity, rabidness, madness.

बौराना, *n.* to be mad: *a. int.* to go mad, to madden.

बौरापन } *m.* = बौराई, *q. v.*
बौरापा }

बौराया, 1, *m.* (*f.* बौराई) = बौड़ा, *q. v.* : 2, see बौराना.

बौराह ; see बौरहा.

बौराहट, *f.* = बौराई, *q. v.*

बौराहा, *m.* (*f.* ī) insane, rabid, mad.

बौरी, *f.* (*m.* बौरा) a mad female.

बौल, *m.* urine.

बौलगाह, *f.* the urethra.

बौलदान, *m.* a chamber-pot.

बौला, *m.* (*f.* ī) toothless.

बौलाना, *more prop.* बौराना, *q. v.*

बौली, *f.* 1, (*m.* बौला) a toothless female: 2, a kind of assessment, settlement with the peasant direct.

बौहा, *m.* (*f.* ī) affected with the venereal disease,

बौहाई, 1, = बौही, *q. v.* : 2, *f.* pockiness. [pocky.

बौहित, *m.* a sailing-vessel, ship, boat.

बौही, *f.* (*m.* बौहा) a female who is affected with the venereal disease.

ब्यजा, a corruption of ख्वाजा, *q. v.*

ब्य ; for words beginning thus, but not given below, see under the form व्य.

ब्यपार, a contraction of ब्यापार, *q. v.*

ब्याथा ; see (1) बियाहा (2) व्यथा.

ब्यान, *m.* birth ; the act of parturition. *Chār byān gā,e,* a cow that has calved four times. *Ek byān jāmak,* having produced two calves at a birth.

ब्याना, *a. int.* (applied to the lower animals only) to be delivered of young ; *hence,* to calve, foal, farrow, litter, pup, yean.

ब्यान्त = ब्यान, *q. v.*

ब्यार ; see बयार.

ब्यारी = बियारी, *q. v.*

ब्यार्थ, a colloquial form of व्यर्थ, *q. v.*

ब्यालु } *m.* supper.
ब्यालू }

ब्याह ; for words beginning thus, see under the form बियाह.

ब्यिंजन, a corruption of व्यंजन, *q. v.*

ब्यिारी, a corruption of बियारी, *q. v.*

ब्योंगा, *m.* the instrument with which leather is scraped and cleaned. — *phirā nahīṇ,* the *byongā* has not yet passed over (his hide), *i. e.* his hide has not yet been curried (said of a spoiled child, etc.).

ब्योंगी, *f.* ; dimin. of ब्योंगा, *q. v.* [or gate.

ब्योंड़ा, a kind of wooden bar for fastening a door

ब्योटना = ब्योन्तना, *q. v.* [clothes.

ब्योन्त, *m.* shape, fashion : the act of cutting out

ब्योन्तना, *t.* to cut or shape clothes.

ब्योपार, *m.* trade, commerce, business, traffic, labour, merchandise. [man of business, merchant.

ब्योपारी, *m.* (*f.* iṇī) a tradesman, commercial man,

ब्योम ; see under the form व्योम.

ब्योरा = बेवरा, *q. v.* [form बेवहार.

ब्योहर ; for words beginning thus, see under the

ब्योहार ; for words beginning thus, see under the form व्यवहार.

ब्योन्ता, *more com.* ब्योन्त, *q. v.*

ब्यौपार = ब्योपार, *q. v.*

ब्यौपारी, *m.* (*f.* iṇī) = ब्योपारी, *q. v.*

ब्यौरा = **बेवरा**, *q.v.*

ब्यौहार ; for words beginning thus, see under the form **व्यवहार**.

ब्रंच in Chand = **वर्णन**, *q.v.*

ब्रकत, a corruption of **बरकत**, *q.v.*

ब्रज ; for words beginning thus, see under the form **व्रज**.

ब्रजति (pl. **ब्रजन्ति**) = (1) **जाता है** (2) **प्राप्त होता है**. (It is a Sanskṛit form, and occurs in Tulsī's *Rāmāyaṇ*.)

ब्रण = **व्रण**, *q.v.*

ब्रत, 1, = **व्रत**, *q.v.* : 2, *m.* use : 3, *f.* a leathern girth, thong : a rope : 4, *adj.* blazing, flaming.

ब्रतमान ; see (1) **वर्त्तमान** (2) **व्रतमान**.

ब्रती, *m.* (*f.* inī) = **व्रती**, *q.v.*

ब्रथा, *more prop.* **वृथा**, *q.v.*

ब्रन, 1, = **व्रण**, *q.v.* : 2, in Chand = **वर्ण**, *q.v.*

ब्रनना, in Chand = **वर्णन**, *q.v.*

ब्रषभ, *more prop.* **वृषभ**, *q.v.*

ब्रह्म, *m.* God, the divine source and essence of the universe, or the Deity considered in the abstract, and divested of action, quality, and attribute (when in action, He is *masc.* and is termed Brahmā) ; from Him all things are believed (according to the Hindoo system) to proceed, and to Him they return : spirit, the very soul : Scripture (*i.e.* the Veds) : religious knowledge : the practice of religious austerity.

ब्रह्मक्यं, *more prop.* **ब्रह्मैक्य**, *q.v.*

ब्रह्मकुण्ड, *m. pr. n.* a certain sacred pool.

ब्रह्मगिरा, *f.* the voice of Brahm.

ब्रह्मघात, *f.* the murder of a Brāhmaṇ.

ब्रह्मघातक, *adj.* Brāhmaṇ-killing : hence, *m.* (*f.* ikā) the slayer of a Brahmaṇ.

ब्रह्मघोष, *m.* (the word of Brahm, *i.e.*) the Veds.

ब्रह्मघ्न, *m.* (*f.* ī) = **ब्रह्मघातक**, *q.v.*

ब्रह्मचर्य्य, *m.* (see **ब्रह्मचारी**) the condition, profession, or way of life of a Hindoo religious student, the order of a religious student, studentship, pious austerity, charity.

ब्रह्मचारिणी, *f.* (*m.* **ब्रह्मचारी**) a female who leads a life of continence.

ब्रह्मचारी, *m.* (*f.* iṇī) *adj.* performing religious austerities, abstaining from sexual intercourse ; *hence*, this term is applied (1) to a Hindoo religious student (2) to a Brāhmaṇ from the time of his investiture with the sacred thread till he becomes a *Grihasth*, or householder (3) to a person who continues with his spiritual teacher (*Guru*) studying the Veds (4) to a paṇdit learned in the Veds (5) to an ascetic. By the Tantras the term is assigned to persons whose chief virtue is the observance of continence : it is also assumed by many religious vagabonds.

ब्रह्मजन्म, *m.* Brāhmaṇical investiture (regarded as a second or spiritual birth).

ब्रह्मज्ञ, possessed of spiritual wisdom and of knowledge of God : hence, *m.* (*f.* ā) a religious sage.

ब्रह्मज्ञान, *m.* knowledge of the Supreme, spiritual wisdom.

ब्रह्मज्ञानवाला, *m.* (*f.* ī) }
ब्रह्मज्ञानी, *m.* (*f.* inī) } = **ब्रह्मज्ञ**, *q.v.*

ब्रह्मण, *m.* (*f.* ī) a contraction of **ब्राह्मण**, *q.v.*

ब्रह्मणभोजना, *f.* the distributing food to Brāhmaṇs.

ब्रह्मणी, a contraction of **ब्राह्मणी**, *q.v.*

ब्रह्मण्य, appertaining to Brahmā or to a Brāhmaṇ ; devoted to the worship of the Deity : hence *m.* (*f.* ā) a pious person.

ब्रह्मतत्त्व, *m.* the true knowledge of supreme spirit.

ब्रह्मतेज, *m.* Brāhmaṇical virtue.

ब्रह्मता, *f.* (*m.* °**त्व**) identification with Brahm ; the state or the nature of Brahm, God.

ब्रह्मद, *adj.* imparting knowledge of the Divine ; hence, *m.* (*f.* ā) a spiritual teacher.

ब्रह्मदण्ड, *m.* an anathema ; a curse.

ब्रह्मदर्भा, *f.* the plant *Ligusticum ajwaen*, Roxb.

ब्रह्मदाता }
ब्रह्मदातृ } *m.* (*f.* trī) = **ब्रह्मद**, *q.v.*

ब्रह्मदारु, *m.* the mulberry-tree (*Morus Indica*).

ब्रह्मदैत्य, *m.* an apparition, ghost, Satan.

ब्रह्मधाम = **ब्रह्मलोक**, *q.v.*

ब्रह्मन = (1) **ब्रह्म** (2) **ब्रह्मा** (3) **ब्राह्मण**, *qq.v.*

ब्रह्मनाल, *m. pr. n.* a certain sacred bathingplace in Benares.

ब्रह्मनिर्व्वाण, *m.* absorption into (or identification with) the supreme spirit of the universe.

ब्रह्मनेटा (*contraction*) = **ब्राह्मणेटा**, *q.v.*

ब्रह्मपुत्र, *m. pr. n.* (1) of the Brahmaputtra river in northern India (2) of a certain place of Hindoo pilgrimage (probably the source of the river) : a kind of poison.

ब्रह्मपुत्री, *f.* an epithet of the river Saraswatī.

ब्रह्मपुर, *m. pr. n.* the city of 'Berhampore.'

ब्रह्मपुरी, 1, *f. pr. n.* (1) of the city of Brahm in heaven (2) of the capital of Brahm on mount Kailas (3) of a certain peak in the Himālaya range : 2, *f.* an epithet (1) of the city of Benares (2) of any city the inhabitants of which are mostly Brāhmaṇs.

ब्रह्मबाण = **ब्रह्मवाण** = **ब्रह्मास्त्र**, *q.v.*

ब्रह्मभवन = **ब्रह्मलोक**, *q.v.*

ब्रह्मभोज, *m.* the act of feeding Brāhmaṇs.

ब्रह्ममय, pervaded by Brahm, consisting of Brahm, possessed of Brahm.

ब्रह्ममीमांसा, *f. pr. n.* the second or theoretical division of the Mīmāṅsā philosophy (so called because it has for its object the investigation of theological proof deducible from the Veds).

ब्रह्मरन्ध्र, *m.* the suture on the top of the head.

ब्रह्मराक्षस, *m.* a certain kind of demon (*viz.* one of the Brāhmaṇical class).

ब्रह्मरात्री, *f.* a night of Brahmā (embracing 1000 ages of the gods, or 216000000 of those of mortals).

ब्रह्मर्षि, *m.* (1) a saint-sage (*ṛishī*) of the Brāhmaṇ caste, as Vashishṭh (2) an epithet of a certain class of countries.

ब्रह्मर्षीय, appertaining to a Brahmarshi.

ब्रह्मलोक, *m. pr. n.* one of the divisions of the universe (*viz.* the eternal residence of Brahmā and of the spirits of the pious).

ब्रह्मवाण = **ब्रह्मास्त्र**, *q.v.*

ब्रह्मवाणी, *f.* the voice of God, a voice from heaven, an oracle.

ब्रह्मवादी, *m.* (*f.* inī) an expounder or a defender

of the Veds; a follower of the Vedantic system of philosophy who maintains that all things are spirit.

ब्रह्मवैवर्त्त, *m. pr. n.* (see **पुराण**) one of the Hindoo Purāṇs. [Brāhmaṇs.

ब्रह्मशासन, *m.* an edict, grant, etc. addressed to

ब्रह्मशेष, *m.* the leavings of Brāhmaṇs.

ब्रह्मसुख, *more com.* **ब्रह्मानन्द**, *q.v.*

ब्रह्मस्त्र, a contraction of **ब्रह्मास्त्र**, *q. v.*

ब्रह्मस्वरूप, of the same essence as the godhead, of the nature of spirit.

ब्रह्महत्य, *m.* = **ब्रह्महत्या**, *q.v.*

ब्रह्महत्या, *f.* the administering a blow to a Brāhman, Brāhman-beating, the murder of a Brāhmaṇ.

ब्रह्महत्यारा, *m.* (*f.* ī) the murderer of a Brāhmaṇ.

ब्रह्महन / **ब्रह्महा** } *m.* (*f.* **ब्रह्मघ्नी**) = **ब्रह्मघातक**, *q.v.*

ब्रह्महृदय, *m.pr.n.* a certain star. [offered to Brahm.

ब्रह्महोत्र, *m.* a ceremony consisting in oblations

ब्रह्मा, 1, *m. pr. n.* (1) of the First Person in the Hindoo Triad, being Brahm in action, or in the character of Creator viewed as the plastic Cause of the universe, but not considered as having a distinct personality (2) of one of the astronomical *yogs*: 2, *m.* a Brāhman; an officiating priest.

ब्रह्माणी, *f.* a female energy of Brahmā.

ब्रह्माण्ड, *m.* (*lit.* the egg of Brahm; *i.e.*) the world, a world: the top of the head. [doo Purāṇs.

ब्रह्माण्डपुराण, *m.pr. n.* (see **पुराण**) one of the Hin-

ब्रह्माण्डभाण्डोदर, *m.* the interior of the vessel-like egg of Brahmā. [a Brāhmaṇ.

ब्रह्मादय, *m.* any grant or perquisite bestowed on

ब्रह्मानन्द, *m.* the rapture of absorption into the supreme spirit, final beatitude, eternal bliss.

ब्रह्मानी, *more prop.* **ब्रह्माणी**, *q. v.*

ब्रह्मारण्य, *m.* 1, *pr. n.* a certain forest: 2, any grove in which the Veds are read and explained.

ब्रह्मावर्त्त, *m.pr.n.* the country to the North-west of Delhi (lying between the rivers Saraswatī and Drishadwatī).

ब्रह्मासन, *m.* a certain posture suited to devout religious meditation. [ing among Brāhmaṇs.)

ब्रह्मास्मि (Sk.) = **मैं ब्रह्म हूं**. (It is common as a say-

ब्रह्मास्त्र, *m.* 1, *pr. n.* a certain fabled weapon which, consecrated by a formula addressed to Brahmā, deals infallible destruction: 2, the sacred Brāhmanical thread: the imprecation of a Brāhman (the term applied to a certain kind of incantation).

ब्रह्मास्य, *m.* the mouth of Brahm or of a Brāhmaṇ.

ब्रह्मैक्य, *m.* the oneness of Brahm, the unity of

ब्राज, a corruption of **व्रज**, *q. v.* [the Godhead.

ब्रात = **व्रात**, *q.v.*

ब्रादर, *more prop.* **बिरादर**, *q.v.*

ब्राह, a corruption of **वराह**, *q. v.*

ब्राह्मण, *m.* (*f.* ī) a Hindoo of the first caste, a Brāhmaṇ: an assemblage of Brāhmaṇs: the theological portion of the Veds. [the wife of a Brāhmaṇ.

ब्राह्मणी, *f.* a female of the Brāhmaṇical caste,

ब्राह्मणेटा, *m.* (*f.* ī) a young Brāhmaṇ.

ब्राह्मण्य, *m.* the state, quality, business, or dignity of a Brāhmaṇ, Brāhmaṇhood; priestly character: *pr. n.* the planet Saturn.

ब्राह्मन, *m.* (*f.* ī) in Braj = **ब्राह्मण**, *q.v.*

ब्राह्म, *m.* one of the five sacraments (*viz.* the worship or veneration of Brāhmaṇs): astonishment.

ब्रिछ (*rare*) = **वृच्छ**, *q. v.*

ब्रिता, *m.* a grant (generally of land) to a religious person or to a tenant on certain stipulations.

ब्रिस्पति, *more prop.* **बृहस्पति**, *q.v.*

ब्रीड़ा = **व्रीड़ा**, *q. v.*

ब्रुज, *m.* a large track-rope, a cable.

भ

भ (bh) is the twenty-fourth consonant in the Hindee or Devanāgarī alphabet, and has the following characteristics and functions:—1, It is the fourth letter of the **पवर्ग** or labial class, and is described as the aspirate of **ब**; that is, it is pronounced as *b* would be pronounced if followed by *h* without the intervention of either a vowel-sound or a hiatus; as in 'cabhorse', 'clubhouse' with the *orse* or *ouse* dropped. 2, This letter, like the other aspirated letters, is constantly liable to be interchanged inaccurately with its unaspirated form: it is also sometimes interchanged with **ह**; thus **सम्हालना**, more properly **सम्भालना**. 3, In poetry, and more particularly in Sanskrit, this letter is sometimes used alone as a substantive masculine in the following senses (1) a dactyl (2) a bee (3) semblance, mere semblance, delusion, error (4) a star (5) a planet (6) an asterism (7) an epithet of the planet Venus (8) a sign of the Zodiac (9) a lunar mansion (*Nakshatra*); and hence, in the ingenious system of reckoning by symbols adopted by Hindoos in their poetry, this letter is a symbol for 27.

भइ is constantly found in poetry for **भई**, *q. v.*

भइन (an old form of **भगिनी**) = **बहिन**, *q.v.*

भइय in Chand = **भई**, *q, v.*

भइहि, an old form = **भई**, *q. v.*

भइहू (*Rām.*) = **तू भई**, etc. (**भया**).

भई, *f.* (*m.* **भया**) been, taken place, etc.

भईं, pl. of **भई**, and fem. of **भए**, *qq.v.*

भईरी, *f.* a species of falcon (?).

भए, *m.* (*f.* **भईं**) plural of **भया**, *q.v.*

भएउ in Braj = **भए**, *q. v.*

भंग, 1, *more prop.* (1) **भग** (2) **भग्न**, *qq. v.*: 2, *m.* a breaking, splitting, breach, chasm, fissure: defeat, destruction, discomfiture, disappointment; interruption; breach of faith, fraud; a wave, breaker: the palsy: 3, *f.* hemp (*Cannabis sativa*); a kind of intoxicating potion made from hemp-leaves.

भंगड़ा, *m.* a certain small creeping-herb (*Eclipta* or *Verbesina prostrata*).

भंगन, 1, = **भंगिनी**, *q.v.*: 2, a Braj pl. of **भंग**, *q. v.*

भंगना, *f.* a certain kind of fish.

भंगराज, *more prop.* **भृंगराज**, *q. v.*

भंगा, 1, *m* = **भृंगराज**, *q.v*: 2, *f.* = **भंग**, 3, *q.v.*

भंगान, *m.* a certain fish (*Cyprinus banggana*).

भंगिश्रा = **भांग**, *q.v* See **इश्रा**.

भंगिनी, *f.* (*m.* **भंगी**) the wife of a *bhangī*; any female of the *bhangī* caste: a female who drinks *bhang*.

भंगी, 1, *f.* fracture, division, separation; fraud, deception, trick, disguise: a kind of small insect: 2, *m.* (*f.* inī) a certain caste of Hindoo sweepers (or *halāl-khors*) descended from a Shoodra by a Brāhmaṇ's widow: a drinker of *bhang*.

भंगेरन, *f.* a female who sells *bhang*, the wife of a *bhang*-seller.

भंगेरा, *m.* (*f.* **भंगेरन**) a *bhang*-seller.

भंगेला, *m.* coarse hempen cloth; a sack or pannier made from the fibres of the *bhang*-plant.

भंगोरिया, *m.* a certain tribe of *tagas*.

भंजक, *adj.* breaking, severing, dividing, afflicting, destroying: hence, *m.* (*f* ikā) a severer, a destroyer.

भंजत, *adj.* breaking, severing, destroying.

भंजन, 1, *m.* (*f.* ā) = **भंजक**, *q v.*: 2, *m.* breaking, separating, dividing, demolishing, destroying, afflicting.

भंजना, *t.* to break: *a. int.* to break.

भंजाना, *t.* to change money (*lit.* to break).

भंजिका, *f.* (*m.* **भंजक**) a female destroyer.

भंजेउ (*Rām.*) = he (or she) has broken.

भंट, भंड, भंब, भंभ; for words beginning thus, see under the forms **भंवट, भण्ड, भम्ब, भम्भ**, respectively.

भंवग, *m.* a certain small class of Rājpūts.

भंवर, *m.* (*f.* ī) a large black bee: a beetle: an eddy, vortex, whirlpool: a climbing-plant, creeper.

भंवरकली, *f.* a kind of halter (for dogs, horses, goats, etc.): a swivel.

भंवरगीत, *m. f.* the songs which the cowherdesses of Mathurā addressed to the bees.

भंवरा, *m.* (*f.* ī) = **भंवर**, *q.v.*

भंवेरी, see (1) **भईरी** (2) **भंवरी**.

भंसना, *a. int.* to float, swim.

भंसरा, *m.* a certain subdivision of the cowherd-tribe.

भकसी, *f.* a dungeon, a dark room in which defaulters in native States are confined.

भकार, *m.* the letter **भ**, or any symbol that may represent it.

भकूश्रा, *m.* (*f.* **भकूई**,) stupid, foolish.

भकूश्राना, *a. int.* to become stupefied or foolish.

भकोसना, *t.* to devour, stuff, eat.

भक्त, cooked, dressed: attached, devoted, believing, attentive, engrossed by, desirous, pious: hence (1) *m.* (*f.* ā) one who has devoted himself to a religious life, an adorer, devotee, follower, votary, zealot, a Hindoo who performs for entertainment, a dancer, player (2) *m.* food, a meal, boiled rice.

भक्तश्राधीन, in subjection to his worshippers.

भक्तजन, 1, = **भक्त** (1), *q. v.*: 2, a pl. of **भक्त**. See **जन**.

भक्तता, *f.* (*m.* °**त्व**) devotedness, implied faith in, attachment to, religiousness, piety.

भक्तन, a Braj pl. of **भक्त**, *q.v.* See **न**, 6.

भक्तबछल, *more prop.* **भक्तवत्सल**, *q.v.*

भक्तमाल, *m. pr. n.* a certain book written in Sanskrit by Nābhā (containing a brief biography of the principal Hindoo religious leaders, reformers, and wonder-workers).

भक्तराज, *m.* (the lord of the devout; *i. e.*) the Supreme Being.

भक्तवत्सल, kind to worshippers, suppliants, or faithful attendants: hence, *m.* (*f.* ā) a gracious being.

भक्तहितकारक, *m.* (*f.* ikā) }
भक्तहितकारी, *m.* (iṇī) } = **भक्तवत्सल**, *q. v.*

भक्ता, 1, *f.* (*m.* **भक्त**) a religious female: 2, *m.* (see **श्रा**, 22) an epithet (1) of a certain Vaishṇav sect (2) of a certain Shaiv sect: *lit.* the devoted, the faithful.

भक्ताई, *f.* = **भक्तता**, *q. v.*

भक्ति, *f.* worship, adoration, devotion, attachment; desire; devotedness, service; religion; faith, belief: breaking, fracture.

भक्तिभक्त, *m.* (*f.* ā) one who performs **भक्ति**, *q.v.*

भक्तिभव, *m.* the origin or source of **भक्ति**, *q.v.*

भक्तिमत, *m.* (*f.* matī) = **भक्तिमान**, *q.v.*

भक्तिमती, *f.* (*m.* **भक्तिमान**, etc.) a pious female.

भक्तिमन्त, *m.* (*f.* matī) = **भक्तिमान**, *q.v.*

भक्तिमान, *m.* (*f.* matī) endowed with *bhakti*, attached, devoted, devout, religious, pious, faithful.

भक्तिवत, *m.* (*f.* vatī) = **भक्तिमान**, *q.v.*

भक्तवती, *f.* (*m.* **भक्तिवान**, etc.) a pious female.

भक्तिवन्त }
भक्तिवान } *m.* (*f.* vatī) = **भक्तिमान**, *q.v.*

भक्तिहीन, destitute of *bhakti*: hence, *m.* (*f.* ā); an impious person, a disobedient person.

भक्ष, 1, *m.* eating: 2, *m.* (*f.* ā); found as the latter element in compound adjectives in the sense of 'devouring.'

भक्षक, *adj.* feeding upon, eating, devouring, voracious, gluttonous: hence, *m.* (*f.* ikā) an eater, feeder, devourer, glutton.

भक्षण, *m.* eating, feeding, devouring, gormandizing: a meal. — *k.* to eat, feed, devour, gormandize.

भक्षणीय, *m.* eatable, suitable or lawful to be eaten, proper for food, edible.

भक्षना, to eat, feed, devour, gormandize.

भक्षहो = (1) **भक्षण करो** (2) **भक्षण करते हो**. (The form is Braj, and occurs in the Rāmāyaṇ.)

भक्षा, *f.* 1, eating: 2; see **भक्ष**, 2.

भक्षिका, *f.* (*m.* **भक्षक**) a female eater; a voracious female: a meal.

भक्षित, *m.* (*f.* ā) eaten.

भक्षी, *m.* (*f.* iṇī) = **भक्षक**, *q.v.*

भक्ष्य, *m.* (*f.* ā) = **भक्षणीय**, *q. v.*

भखना, to take food, eat, feed, devour, gormandize.

भग, *m.* divine power, omnipotence; excellence, virtue, glory, fame, greatness, strength; splendour, beauty; prosperity, fortune: wish; effort, exertion: religious tranquillity or absence of passion: *pudendum muliebre*: *pr. n.* (1) of Shiv (2) of the sun (3) of the moon (4) of one of the *ādiṭya*.

भगदत्त, *m. pr. n.* (1) of a prince of Prāg-jyotish (2) of a king of Kāmrūp.

भगीता (*corruption*) = **भगवद्गीता**, *q.v.*

भगण, *m.* the zodiac; an assemblage of stars; the heavenly tribe; (in Pros.) a dactyl.

भगत, provincial form = **भक्त** (1), *q.v.*— *khelnā*, to act a play, to imitate, mimic. —*honā*, to be initiated as a devotee, to be affiliated to a religious order. The ceremony alluded to is peculiar to the low tribes, and consists in putting a necklace of beads around the neck of the person to be initiated and marking a circle on his forehead; after which he is bound to refrain from the use of spirituous liquors, flesh, etc.

भगतन, *f.* the wife of a *bhagat*; (*ironically*) a lewd woman, a prostitute.

भगता, *m.* a certain tribe of cowherds (*ahīr*).

भगताई, *f.* (*colloquial*) = **भक्तता**, *q.v.*

भगति (*colloquial*) = **भक्ति**, *q.v.* [cing-girl.

भगतिया, *m.* a dancing-boy dressed up like a dan-

भगना (*contraction*) = **भागना**. See **श्र**, 15.

भगन्दर, *m.* a fistula *in ano*.

भगल, *m.* affectation, hypocrisy, deception, trick. —*nikālnā*, to affect, to play a trick, to pretend poverty.

भगलिया, *m.* an impostor, trickster, cheat: imposture, cheating, trick. [false jewels, trinkets.

भगली, affected, deceptive, false. — *gahnā*, *m.*

भगवद्गीता, *f.pr. n.* a certain philosophic poem (an episode of the Mahābhārat)held in high esteem by the Vaishnavas.

भगवत, *m.* (*f.* vatī) = **भगवान**, *q.v.*

भगवती, *f.* (*m.* **भगवान**, etc.) an estimable female an epithet (1) of Gaurī (2) of Bhawānī.

भगवन्त, *m.* (*f.* vatī) = **भगवान**, *q.v.*

भगवां, *m.* cloth dyed with **गेरू**, *q.v.*

भगवान, *m.* (*f.* vatī) an epithet (1) of the Supreme Being (2) of Vishṇu (3) of Kṛishṇ (4) of any respectable or estimable person: *lit.* possessing fortune, fortunate, prosperous, happy; glorious, illustrious, adorable, divine, worshipful, respectable, estimable. [to drive away.

भगवाना, *t.* to cause to be driven away; to cause

भगान; see (1)**भगवान** (2) **भगाना**.

भगाना, *t.* (of **भागना**) to cause to flee, cause to run away, cause to escape; to drive away.

भगाल, *m.* the human skull. [man skulls.

भगालिन, *m.* an epithet of Shiv; *prop.* having hu-

भगिना, *m.* a brother.

भगिनी, *f.* a sister; a woman, female.

भगीरथ, *m. pr. n.* a certain ancient king (son of *Dilip*) who by his austere devotion caused the descent of the Ganges from heaven; he is hence, called, the father of the Ganges. [fugitive, deserter, renegade.

भगेल, 1, *f.* overthrow, defeat: 2, *m.* a runaway,

भगोंहा, *m.* the reddish colour extracted from **गेरू**.

भगोड़ा, *m.* (*f.* in *or* ī) = **भगेल**, *q.v.*

भग्गू = **भगेल**, 2, *q.v.*

भग्न, *m.* (*f.* **ā**) broken, torn, defeated, vanquished, afflicted, wretched, despised, disregarded.

भग्ना, 1, a provincial form = **भागना**, *q.v.*: 2, *more prop.* **भगिना**, *q. v.*: 3, *f.* (*m.* **भग्न**) a wretched female.

भग्नाश, *m.* (*f.* ā) a disappointed person: *lit.* of broken hopes, disappointed, discouraged.

भग्नी, a contraction of **भगिनी**, *q.v.*

भचक, alarmed, starting, aghast. — *rahnā*, to be amazed or astonished at a sudden or unexpected event.

भचकना, *n.* to be astonished or amazed.

भचकाना, *t.* to alarm, astonish, amaze.

भच्छना = **भखना**, *q v.*

भछ, *more prop.* **भक्ष**, *q.v.*

भछक, *m.* (*f.* ikī) *more prop.* **भक्षक**, *q.v.*

भछना = **भखना**, *q.v.*

भछी, *m.* (*f.* in *or* inī) *more prop.* **भक्षी**, *q.v.*

भजई (Rām.) = **सुमिरै** or **सेवै**, *qq. v.* (**भजना**, 2.)

भजत, *adj.* serving, waiting upon: enjoying carnally.

भजन, *m.* service, waiting upon, attendance, adoration, worship: a hymn: sharing, possession, possessing or enjoying carnally.

भजनग्रालय, *more prop.* **भजनालय**, *q.v.*

भजनगृह } = **भजनालय**, *q. v.*
भजनघर }

भजनपुस्तक, *m. f.* a book for guidance in worship, a liturgy. [to the needs of others, kind offices.

भजनभाव, *m.* reverence of disposition; attention

भजना, 1, *f.* = **भजन**, *q.v.*: 2, *t.* to adore, worship, to count one's beads: *a. int.* to run away, take flight.

भजनालय, *m*, a house for worship, a temple.

भजनीक, *m.* a singer; an adorer, worshipper.

भजमान, *m.* (*f.* ā) *adj.* apportioning, dividing, sharing; possessing, enjoying; loving, honouring, courting; waiting on. serving; fitting, meet, appropriate, proper, fit, right: the proper name of several princes. [away, put to flight.

भजाना, *t.* (of **भजना**, 2) to cause to flee, to drive

भजामहे (*Rām.*) = **हम भजते हैं**.

भजामि (*Rām.*) = **मैं भजता हूं**.

भजि = **भजके** (**भजना**, 2) fleeing, taking to one's heels. —*jānā*, to take flight, run away.

भजे (*Rām.*) = **मैं भजता हूं**.

भट, 1, *m.* a warrior, soldier, combatant, hero: a kind of grass: an outcaste of a particular tribe a barbarian: a goblin, ghost: 2, *f.* an oven, furnace, kiln: misfortune, curse. — *parnā*, (*lit.* to fall into the furnace; *hence*) to be unfortunate, be cursed, be lost.

भटई, *f.* the encomiums of a **भाट**, panegyric, praise.

भटकटाई, *f.* a certain prickly plant (*Solanum jacquini*, Willd.) used in medicine.

भटकटैया = **भटकटाई**, *q.v.*

भटकना, *a. int.* to go astray, miss the right path, lose the way, wander, stray.

भटकरिया, *m.* a certain class of inferior Rājpūts.

भटकवाना = **भटकाना**, *q. v.*

भटका, *m.* (*f.* ī) astray, wandering.

भटकाना, *t.* to cause to miss the way, cause to wander, to mislead, deceive, bewilder, scare.

भटगौर, *m.* a certain subdivision of the Gau Rājpūts.

भटनागर, *m.* a certain tribe of Kāyasths.

भटभेरे (*Rām.*) = **धक्का खाते फिरते हैं**.

भटयुग = **कलियुग**, *q.v.*

भटयोगा in Garhwālī = पुकाड़ना, q. v. [apple).
भटा, f. coloquintida or colocynth (i. e. the bitter
भटिया, m. land of the poorest kind in Sāgar and Bundēlkhand. [form भठियार.
भटियार, for words beginning thus, see under the
भटुला, m. a kind of bread made from the flour of the arhar, chanā, and mūng.
भटू, interj. O sister! [form भठियार.
भटेआर; for words beginning thus, see under the
भटेआरन / भटेआरनी } f. (m. भटेआर) = भठियारिन, q.v.
भटेआरा, m. (f. n, nī, ī, or in) = भठियारा, q.v.
भटोत्तर, m. lands alloted to bards (bhāṭ); lands allotted to Brāhmaṇs.
भट्ट, m. a learned man, scholar, philosopher (esp. one who is conversant with the philosophical systems): an enemy: an authority: adj. chief, eminent, best. The term is applied as a title to Mahārātta Brāhmaṇs.
भट्टा, 1, more com. भंटा, q.v.: 2, m. a ploughman's wages in kind: a pair of bellows.
भट्टाचार्य, m. the most learned of the learned, a scholar, philosopher, doctor, teacher. The term is applied as a title to the Kanaujiya Brāhmaṇs, also to anyone who teaches any branch of Sanskrit literature.
भट्टियाना, m. pr. n. the country of the bhaṭṭi Rājpūts. [of Rājpūts.
भट्टी, f. 1, = भट्ठी, 1, q.v.: 2, pr. n. a certain tribe
भट्ठा, m. a furnace, kiln, oven, still, brick-kiln.
भट्ठी, f. 1, (dim. of भट्ठा, q.v.) a small fireplace, a kind of furnace: 2, a distillery, a liquor-shop. [liquors.
भट्ठीदार, m. one who makes and sells spirituous
भठियाख़ाना = भठियारख़ाना, q.v. [of the tide).
भठियाना, a. int. to go down the river, to ebb (said
भठियारख़ाना, m. an inn, eating-house, travellers' lodgingplace, caravanserai. [thiyārā.
भठियारपन, m. the business or the status of a bha-
भठियारा, m. (f. ī) one who prepares food for travellers in a sarāī, a sutler, inn-keeper, baker, cook.
भठियारिन, f. the wife of a bhaṭhiyārā, a female who carries on the business of an inn-keeper.
भठियारी, f. (m. भठियारा) = भठियारिन, q.v.
भठियाल, m. a kind of elegiac verse (marsiya) sung in praise of Hasan and Husain: adj. with the current, i. e. down the river and not with the flood-tide.
भठी, f. a furnace, kiln; a small fire-place.
भड़, m. a large boat, a lighter, a transport-boat:
भड़ंक, more prop. भड़क, q.v. [a wasp, hornet (?).
भड़ंग, simple, undesigning; artless, silly, having the quality of telling secrets without reserve.
भड़क, f. splendour, blaze, flash, glare, show, pomp: perturbation, agitation, alarm, starting, shyness.
भड़कना, a. int. to start, shrink: n. to be scared, be alarmed; to be blown up into a flame.
भड़कन, a large gate or door.
भड़काना, t. to blow up into a flame, to kindle (a fire): to frighten, scare.

भड़कीला, m. (f. ī) splendid, glittering, flashy, gaudy.
भड़कैल, wild, untamed, skittish, coy, shy.
भड़ड़ा, m. the beleric myrobalan.
भड़भड़ाना, a. int. to flutter.
भड़भड़िया, an artless person: lit. without guile, candid, simple, artless.
भड़भूंजन, f. a female who parches grain.
भड़भूंजा, m. a man who parches grain.
भड़रिया, m. a conjuror. [tribe.
भडरिया, m. a certain subdivision of the ḍakaut
भड़वा, m. (f. ī or in) more prop. भड़ूआ, q. v.
भडा, m. a kind of grass which grows in poor soils (it attains a height of a little more than a foot, and is used for fodder).
भड़ा, more com. भडा, q. v.
भडिल, m. an attendant: a hero.
भडिहाई, f pilfering, theft.
भडुआ, more prop. भड़ूआ, q. v.
भड़ूआ, m. (f. भड़ुई) one who lives on the earnings of a prostitute, a pimp, pander, blackguard. [tution.
भड़ुआई, f. panderism, pimping: the wages of prosti-
भड़ुई, f. (m. भड़ुआ) a bawd, procuress.
भड़ैत, m. (f. in or ī) a tenant, lessee.
भणक, f. a low sound, a distant sound, a hum, buzz of insects; rumour, report.
भणित, m. (f. ā) sounded, uttered, spoken, said.
भणिति, f. speech, talking, talk, discourse.
भणिता / भणितृ } m. (f. trī) an author, composer.
भण्टवास, m. a certain grain, the fruit of the water lily (koṇ). [ploughman's wages in kind.
भण्टा, m. the egg-plant (Solanum melongena): a
भण्ड, m. a mimic, jester, buffoon, dissembler: deceit, imposition; confusion, spoiling.
भण्डक, m. a wagtail.
भण्डन, m. deception, mischief, evil, wickedness: armour, mail; war, battle.
भण्डसार, more prop. भण्डसाल, q. v.
भण्डसाल, f. the provision which is previously reserved for years. [for years.
भण्डसाली, m. (f. inī) one who reserves provisions
भण्डा, m. a kind of large earthen pot. —phūṭnā, to be disclosed (said of a secret).
भण्डार, a contraction of भाण्डागार, q. v.
भण्डारपन = भाण्डारोपन, q. v.
भण्डारा, m. a feast of Jogees, Sunnyāsees, etc.
भण्डारोपन = भाण्डारोपन, q. v.
भण्डारी m. (f. in or inī) = भाण्डारी, q. v. [Roxb.).
भण्डि, f. a wave: Bengal madder (Rubia manjith,
भण्डिल, 1, m. a messenger: 2, happy, fortunate, auspicious: a certain tree (Mimosa sirisha).
भण्डी = भण्डि, q. v.
भण्डीर = भण्डिल, q. v.

भणडौरी = **भणिड**, *q. v.*

भणडौल = **भणिडल**, *q. v.*

भणडेरिया, *m.* an actor.

भणडेलन, *f.* an actress.

भणडेला, *m.* an actor.

भणडोली, *f.* two or more jars carried one over the other.

भणडोवा, *m.* satire, ribaldry.

भतार, *m.* (from **भर्त्ता**) a husband.

भतीजन, a Braj pl. of **भतीजा**, *q.v.*

भतीजा, *m.* (*f.* ī) a nephew (a brother's son, or a wife's brother's son).

भतीजान, a corruption (1) of **भतीजा** (2) of (**भतीजे**) the pl. of **भतीजा**.

भतीजी, *f.* a niece (a brother's daughter, or a wife's brother's daughter).

भत्तः, *m.* an extra allowance for troops on service or on the march, 'batta'.

भत्ता, *m.* 1, = **भत्तः**, *q.v.*: 2, a pair of bellows.

भद, *f.* a slap ; a crash. — *se gir paṛā*, it fell down with a crash.

भदई, *f.* the produce of the month Bhādoṅ.

भदन्त, *m.* a Bauddh mendicant.

भदभद, *m.* the sound made by the falling of fruit or by the walking of a person.

भदभदाना, 1, *t.* to make a sound by striking two bodies together ; to strike repeatedly : to shake fruit from a tree : 2, *m.* the cutting grain when only half ripe : the shaking fruit from a tree.

भदभदाहट, *f.* the sound made by the falling of fruit from a tree.

भदवरिया, a certain tribe of Rājpūts.

भदवार, *m.* land prepared for sugarcane.

भदाक, *m.* the noise made by anything falling, a crash.— *se gir paṛā*, it fell down with a crash.

भदाका, *m.* a sound or noise.

भदाहर, grain cut when only half ripe.

भदेस = **भदेसल**, *q. v.*

भदेसल, ill-shapen, ugly, awkward, clumsy, ridiculous.

भदेसला = **भदेसल**, *q. v.*

भदेसा, *m.* (*f.* ī) *more com.* **भदेसल**, *q. v.*

भद्दव in Chand = **भाद्र**, *q. v.*

भद्दा, *m.* (*f.* ī) stupid, senseless, dull.

भद्र, 1, *m.* (*f.* ā) an excellent person ; a fortune-teller, an impostor ; a wagtail, etc.: *lit.* excellent, best, worthy, dear, good, virtuous, pious, pure ; auspicious, propitious, happy, lucky, prosperous : 2, *m.* auspiciousness, prosperity, happiness, welfare : a certain fragrant grass (*Cyperus*) : gold : iron or steel : a heap : a bull ; an epithet of Shiv : one of the astronomical periods called *karan*. — *honā*, to be clean or purified by shaving the head and beard after mourning or in a holy place.

भद्रक, 1, *m.* (*f.* ikā) an estimable person, etc.: *lit.* beautiful, pleasing, agreeable, good, respectable, worthy, estimable, fortunate, lucky : 2, *m.* a certain grass (*Cyperus pertenuis*); a species of pine (*Pinus devadaru*) : 3, *f.* advantage, produce, beauty, pleasantness, goodness ; nature, genius, reason.

भद्रकाली, *f.* the fragrant grass *Cyperus pertenuis* or *C. rotundus* : an epithet of the goddess Durgā.

भद्रगन्धिका, *f.* a certain creeping-plant (*Asclepias pseudosarsa*, the arrow-leaved variety).

भद्रचूड़, *m.* a species of euphorbia (*E. tirucalli*).

भद्रजौ in Braj = **भद्रयव**, *q. v.*

भद्रदारु, *m.* a species of pine (*Pinus devadaru*).

भद्रदेश, *m.* an epithet of Pryāg (?).

भद्रनामा, *m.* the woodpecker ; the water-wagtail.

भद्रपदा, *f. pr. n.* the twenty-sixth and twenty-seventh lunar asterisms (*Nakshatra*) which are distinguished from each other by the terms **पूर्व** and **उत्तर** being prefixed to this designation.

भद्रपर्णा, *f.* a certain shrub (*Pœderia fœtida*).

भद्रपर्णी, *f.* 1, = **भद्रपर्णा**, *q.v.*: 2, a certain tree (*Gmelina arborea*).

भद्रमुस्तक, *m.* the fragrant grass *Cyperus pertenuis*.

भद्रयव, *m.* the seed of the *Echites* or *Wrightea antidysenterica*.

भद्रवल्ली, *f.* Arabian jasmine (*Jasminum zambac*) ; the large Bengal creeper (*Gœrtnera racemosa*).

भद्रा, 1, *f.* (*m.* **भद्र**) an excellent female, etc. : an unlucky moment ; bad luck : an epithet (1) of the second, seventh, and twelfth days of a lunar fortnight (2) of the Ganges of heaven (see **गंगा**).

भद्राकरण, *m.* shaving.

भद्रारक, *m. pr. n.* one of the eighteen minor divisions of the world (*dwip*).

भद्राश्व, *m. pr. n.* (1 of one of the four larger divisions (*mahādwip*) into which the known world is divided (2) according to another system of philosophy, it is one of the nine smaller divisions (*khaṇḍ*) of the continent ; — in either case it is the eastern division.

भद्रासन, *m.* a throne : a certain peculiar posture of a Hindoo devotee while meditating, *viz.* the legs are bent and crossed underneath, and turned so as to bring the ankles into contact with the perineum, while the soles of the feet are held close to the sides.

भद्रिका, *f.* (*m.* **भद्रक**) an estimable female, etc.

भद्री, *m.* (*f.* iṇī) an astrologer, palmister.

भद्रोदनी, *f.* a certain plant (*Sida cordifolia*).

भनई
भनंता } (*Rām.*) = **कहते हैं** (**भनना**).

भनक, *a corruption of* **भणक**, *q. v.*

भनगा, *a corruption of* **भंगा**, *q. v.*

भनत = **भनता** (**भनना**) : see **त**, 5.

भनना, *a. int.* (Sk. root **भण**) to speak.

भनाना, *t.* to cause to speak.

भनित, *more prop.* **भणित**, *q. v.*

भनो (*Rām.*) = **कह करके** (**भनना**).

भनु (*Rām.*) = (1) **कहते हो** (2) **कहो** (**भनना**).

भने (*Rām.*) = **कहे** (**भनना**).

भनै in Braj = **भने** = **कहे** (**भनना**).

भना ; see (1) **भनना** (2) **भुनना**.

भपकना, a dialectic form of **भभकना**, *q. v.*

भपकारा, **भपारा** = **भफारा**, *q.v.*

भपोला, *m.* a blister.

भफारा, *m.* steam, vapour, mist, exhalation, fumigation.

भबकना, *n.* to be enraged : *a. int.* to rush on with rage, to run with great rapidity (said of the horse), to catch fire; to bubble (as boiling water); to roar; to grumble.

भबका, *m.* a kind of drinking-vessel with a large mouth, an alembic, a still.

भबकाना, *t.* to kindle, to light; to provoke, enrage, exasperate; to spur on a horse.

भबकी, *f.* a threat.

भबभर, *more prop.* (1) **भबभल** (2) **भभर**, *qq.v.*

भबभल, fat, corpulent.

भबूत, **भबूती**, **भबूल** *f.* = **भभूत**, *q. v.*

भभक, *f.* a sudden bursting forth of flame; a forcible expulsion of water from a fountain or pipe; smell arising suddenly.

भभकना, *a. int.* to emit steam, to fume, simmer, bubble, boil.

भभर, *m.* solicitude, alarm. —*paṛnā*, to be alarmed, be frightened.

भभरना, *n.* to be solicitous, be alarmed, be frightened.

भभरा (*Rām.*) = **घबराया** (**भभरना**).

भभराना, *a. int.* to swell (said particularly of the face); to entertain doubt.

भभरि (*Rām.*) = **घबराके** (**भभरना**).

भभूका, 1, *m.* (*f.* ī) red (said of burning coal; also, of the splendour of a beloved person's countenance); splendid, beautiful : 2, *m.* blaze, flame : explosion.

भभूत, *f.* ashes of cowdung (which Hindoo fakeers and ascetics rub over their bodies).

भमना, *a. int.* to revolve.

भमभेरी, *more prop.* **भम्भेरी**, *q. v.*

भमी, *f.* a going around, revolution, whirling; a wandering.

भम्खेरी, *more prop.* **भम्भेरी**, *q. v.*

भम्खेा; see *s. v.* **काठ**.

भम्भनाना, *a. int.* to buzz, hum (as insects).

भम्भूखा, *m.* an ascetic or fakeer who is pressed by hunger to rob.

भम्भेरी, *f.* a butterfly.

भम्भोड़ना, *t.* to bite and mumble (as a dog); to worry.

भम्भोरना = **भम्भोड़ना**, *q. v.*

भय, *m.* (*f.* ?) fear, alarm, flight, dread, terror, peril, danger : the flower of the *Trapa bispinosa.*—*k.* to fear.—*khānā*, to be frightened, be afraid.—*denā*, or *dikhānā*, to terrify, alarm, frighten.—*mānnā*, to regard with fear.—*rakhnā*, to entertain apprehension.

भयउ in Braj = (1) **भय** (2) **भया**, *qq.v.*

भयंकर, *m.* (*f.* ī) terrifying, frightful, fearful, horrible, terrific, formidable.

भयकम्पित, *m.* (*f.* ā) shaken with fear, terrified.

भयकारक, *m.* (*f.* ikā) = **भयंकर**, *q. v.*

भयचक, alarmed, aghast, starting. —*rahnā*, to be amazed or astonished at a sudden or unexpected event.

भयथरी; see **भरथरी**.

भयद, *m.* (*f.* ī) imparting or occasioning fear, alarming, fearful, frightful, terrifying, formidable.

भयदर्शक, *m.* (*f.* ikā), **भयदर्शी**, *m.* (*f.* inī) = **भयद**, *q.v.*

भयभंजन, *m.* the breaking or dispersion of fear: *adj.* fear-destroying, fear-dispelling.

भयभीत, *m.* (*f.* ā) = **भयमान**, *q.v.*

भयमान, *m.* (*f.* matī) frightened, alarmed, terrified, afraid, timid.

भययुक्त, *m.* (*f.* ā) = (1) **भयंकर** (2) **भयमान**, *qq. v.*

भयल (*dialectic*) = **भया**, *q.v.*

भयसों in Braj = **भयसे**. See **सों**.

भयस्थान, *m.* seat or part exposed to peril or hurt.

भयहू, *f.* a sister-in-law (a younger brother's wife).

भयहूं, 1, *more prop.* **भयहू**, *q. v.* : 2, see **भय** and **भया**.

भया, *m.* (*f.* **भई**) the base of the historical tenses of the verb substantive (from Sk. root **भू**) = came to be, became, took place, occurred.

भयातुर, *m.* (*f.* ā) distressed or distracted with fear, terrified.

भयानक, *m.* the sentiment of terror excited by poetical composition; a tiger; Rāhu : *lit.* terrific, fearful, terrible, frightful, dreadful, alarming, formidable, dismal.

भयानकत्व, *m.* (*f.* tā) awfulness, dreadfulness, terribleness, formidableness.

भयापत, **भयापा** *more prop.* **भैयापत**, *q. v.*

भयार्त्त, *m.* (*f.* ā) distressed with fear, frightened, terrified.

भयावना, *m.* (*f.* ī) frightful, terrible, alarming, dreadful, formidable.

भयावह, *m.* (*f.* ā) = **भयावना**, *q.v.*

भयाविष्ट, *m.* (*f.* ā) possessed by fear, terrified.

भयी, *f.* (*m.* **भया**) *more prop.* **भई**, *q. v.*

भयीं, *f.* (*m.* **भय**) *more prop.* **भईं**, *q. v.*

भये, **भयें** *more prop.* **भए**, *q.v.*

भयो, a colloquial form of **भया**, *q. v.*

भयौ in Braj = **भया**, *q. v.*

भर, 1, *m.* a load, burden; plenty; size, bulk; a measure of value of two thousand *pal* : 2, *adj.* much, excessive, full: 3, whole, all, every, each : *adv.* 4, as much as, as far as, up to, to the extent of, fully : 5, *pr. n.* one of the aboriginal races of India: 6, *m.* (*f.* ā) used in forming some compound epithets, in the sense of carrying, bearing, supporting, sustaining : 7, In reference to the senses given under 2, 3, 4, observe (1) that the word is used idiomatically, and is often united to the word it modifies; *e. g.* *'Umr* —, all (one's) lifetime : *Din*—, all day, the whole day: *Maḳdūr* —, to the extent of (one's) power, to the utmost of (one's) ability, with all (one's) might : *Pahar*—, fully three hours : *Main baras bhar bhar ṭikātā hun*, I let lodgings by the year (2) that it is sometimes put before its word and sometimes after it; most commonly, however, after it : when placed *before* it, it has the sense of full, fully; *e.g.* *Bhar kos*, a full kos: *Bhar ser*, a full sér : when placed *after* it, its meaning seems equivalent to 'a'; *e. g.* *Kos* —, a kos; *Ser* —, a sér :

Bāṅs —, (the height or length of) a bamboo. —*jānā*, to be filled; to be lined (said of a bitch); to be broken-winded (said of a horse from severe exercise). — *denā*, to fill, fill up; to reïmburse, pay: to darn. — *pānā*, to receive the amount; *hence*, to be paid: it is used when a person is disappointed; *e.g. Mainne bhar pāyā*, I am paid, I am paid with a witness.

भरई, *f.* a kind of cess or tax.

भरक, *m.* a fruit-garden, orchard.

भरका, *m.* slaked lime.

भरकाना, *t.* to slake lime.

भरजाना; see *s.v.* **भर**.

भरट, *m.* a potter.

भरण, *m.* the act of carrying, bearing, supporting, sustaining, nourishing, maintaining: the act of filling or satisfying; paying in full; wages, hire.

भरणपोषण, *m.* the supplying a person with food and raiment, maintenance.

भरणी, *f. pr. n.* the second *Nakshatra* (containing three stars in *Musca*, and figured by the *pudendum muliebre*).

भरडावड = **भड़डावड**, *q.v.*

भरत, 1, *more prop.* **भर्त**, *q.v.*: 2, *m. pr. n.* (1) of a a younger brother of Rām, and son of Dasharath by Kaikeyī (2) of several princes (3) of a certain sage, the inventor of dramatic composition: 3, *m.* an actor, mimic; a weaver.

भरतकूल, *m.* a certain tribe of Brāhmaṇs.

भरतखण्ड, *m. pr. n.* one of the nine divisions of the world between Lankā and Sumeru (*i.e.* India from Ceylon to Tartary).

भरतण्ड; see (1) **भरतखण्ड** (2) **भरदावड** (3) **भरतण्ड**.

भरतपुर, *m. pr. n.* a certain city and district in [Northern India.

भरतरी; see **भरथरी**.

भरतवंश *m.* the offspring of Bharat.

भरतवंशी, *m.* (*f.* inī) a descendant of Bharat.

भरतवर्ष = **भारतवर्ष**, *q.v.*

भरती, *more prop.* **भर्ती**, *q.v.*

भरथरी; see **भर्तृहरि**.

भरदावड, *m.* galloping at full speed. — *denā* or *pheṅknā*, to cause to gallop, to set agoing at full speed.

भरदेना; see *s.v.* **भर**.

भरदाँक़, (see **भर**, 7) to the extent of (one's) power, to the utmost of (one's) ability, with all (one's) might.

भरद्वाज, 1, *m. pr. n.* a certain ancient *muni*: 2, *m.* a skylark (*Alauda arvensis*). [to, as far as, till.

भरन, 1, *more prop.* **भरण**, *q.v.*: 2, (= **तक**) to, up

भरना, 1, *t.* to fill, to load, to satisfy, to perform, to charge, to daub, to pay, repay, reïmburse, liquidate or discharge a debt, fine, etc.; to give evidence; to undergo, suffer: *n.* to be filled, be sated; to be performed, be completed: *a. int.* to heal; to abound: 2, *m.* the act of filling, completing, etc.: the vessel that receives the expressed juice of the sugarcane.

भरनी, *f.* 1, *more prop.* **भरणी**, *q.v.*: 2, weft, woof.

भरपतवा, *m.* a certain subdivision of the *bhar*

भरपाई, *f.* a receipt in full. [tribe.

भरपाना; see *s.v.* **भर**.

भरपूर, full, brimful, quite full, chokeful, replete, overflowing; high (said of the tide); full (the moon).

भरपूरण = **भरपूर**, *q.v.* [abundance, fulness.

भरपूरी, *f.* the state of being full or overflowing,

भरपेट, a bellyful.

भरपेटी, *m.* (*f.* in *or* inī) pot-bellied.

भरभण्डा; see (1) **भरभावड** (2) **भड़भावड**.

भरभराना, *a. int.* to swell and be glossy (said esp. of the face in fever).

भरभरी, *f.* a swelling, a sore. [*Mexicana*).

भरभावड, *m.* a certain prickly poppy (*Argemone*

भरम, 1, = **भ्रम**, *q.v.*: 2, *m.* character, credit, reputation. — *gaṅwānā*, to lose credit or character.

भरमना, *a. int.* to roam, wander, stray, err.

भरमाना, *t.* to deceive, mislead: to excite by throwing out temptation: to perplex, to alarm.

भरमित, colloquial = **भ्रमित**, *q.v.*

भरमी, a colloquial form of **भ्रमी**, *q.v.*

भरमीला, *m.* (*f.* ī) ambiguous, doubtful; confounded: scrupulous.

भरया, *a dialectic form of* **भरा**, *q.v.*

भरवाना, *t.* (causat. of **भरना**) to cause to be filled, etc.: to cause to fill, etc.

भरशक, to the extent of one's ability, with all one's might, as far as may be, as far as possible.

भरशक्य, *more com.* **भरशक**, *q.v.* See **भर**, 7.

भरसक = **भरशक**, *q.v.*

भरसांई }
भरसारी } *f.* a furnace, oven, kiln.

भरा, 1, *m.* (*f.* ī) filled, full, replete, brimful, overflowing: 2, *m.* the filling a thing, fulness; a load, cargo; the charge of a gun.

भराई, *f.* a filling, stuffing.

भराइवेको in Braj = **भरानेको** (**भराना**).

भराना, *t.* to cause to fill; to fill; to cover (or to cause to cover) a mare.

भरावट, *f.* the act of filling, stuffing: anything in in which a substance is filled.

भरि, 1, (*colloquial*) = **भर**, *q.v.*: 2, see **भरना**.

भरित, *m.* (*f.* ā) filled, full.

भरिभरि, a distributive form of **भरि**, *q.v.*

भरिया, *m.* land watered by irrigation.

भरी, *f.* 1, (*m.* **भरा**) full, etc.: 2, the weight of one sicca rupee (*i.e.* one *tolā*, or twelve *māshā*).

भरु, *m.* an epithet (1) of Shiv (2) of Vishṇu: 2, [gold: a lord.

भरुज, *m.* a small species of jackal.

भरुटक, *m.* fried meat.

भरे, 1, *m.* inflect. of **भरा**, *q.v.*: 2, a certain grass which grows in the jungles to the height of about nine feet, and is used for ṭaṭṭies, thatching, etc.

भरेत }
भरेती } *more prop.* **भड़ैत**, *q.v.*

भरोटा, *m.* a load (of grass, hay, etc.).

भरोस, a contraction of **भरोसा**, *q.v.*

भरोसा, *m.* hope, dependence, trust, reliance, assurance, confidence, faith. — *k.* to hope; (with gen. of object) to hope in, rely on.

भरोसो in Braj = **भरोसा**, *q.v.*

भरौती, *f.* a release in full.

भरौना, *m.* a load of wood. [or baking.

भर्जन, *m.* the act of scorching, parching, frying,

भर्त, *m.* a certain mixed metal (composed of copper and lead): a certain bird (a species of lark), a skylark: the full amount of rent or revenue paid by an individual or by a party.

भर्तपुर, *more prop*, **भरतपुर**, *q.v.*

भर्ता, 1, *more com.* **भर्त्ता**, *q.v.*: 2, = **भुर्ता**, *q.v.*

भर्तार in Braj = **भर्त्ता**, *q.v.* [called *bhart.*

भर्तिया, *m.* a brazier; *lit.* a worker in the metal

भर्ती, *f.* filling, completion; loading, lading, burden, cargo; recruiting (soldiers); *vulg.* promotion. — *k.* to load, to recruit.

भर्त्ता, *m.* (*f.* trī) a cherisher, nourisher, supporter, protector, holder; a lord, master, commander, husband.

भर्त्तार in Braj = **भर्त्ता**, *q v.*

भर्तृहरि, *m. pr. n.* a well-known Hindoo author. He wrote in Sanskrit three hundred moral, political, and religious maxims or apothegms comprised in three Shatakas (called Shringār-S., Nīti-S., and Vairāgya-S.), also some Grammatical Kārikās, and the Vākya-padīya; also (according to some) the Bhatti-kāvya. He is often designated by the one name Hari, and, though little is really asertained about his history, is said to have been the brother of Vikramāditya, who lived in the 1st century B. C. According to a legend, he wrote his apothegms when leading the life of an ascetic, after a licentious youth.

भर्त्सना, *f.* an upbraiding, reviling, cursing; reproach, abuse; threat, menace. [seized with panic.

भर्रा, *m.* a panic. *Faujmeṅ* —— *parā*, the army was

भल, 1, a contraction of **भला**, *q.v.*: 2, *m.* side, direction. *Sirke bhal* (sc. *par*) head-foremost, headlong. *Muṅhke* —, face downwards, prone, prostrate.

भलक; see **भल्लक**.

भलका, *m.* a gold patch fixed on the nose-ring: a kind of bamboo: dawn of day.

भलघोड़िया, *m.* a cavalier: *lit.* adj. having a good horse, well-mounted.

भलता, *f.* a certain shrub (*Pœderia fœtida*).

भलपन, *m.* = **भलाई**, *q.v.*

भलपुच्छी, *f.* the plant *Hedysarum logopodioides.*

भलभलउजाला, *m.* broad daylight.

भलमनसाई, *f.* good nature, benevolence, humanity, benignity, civility, decorum.

भलमनसाहगी, **भलमनसागी**, **भलमनसात**, **भलमनसायत**, **भलमनसी** = **भलमनसाई**, *q.v.*

भलमानुस, (**भला** + **मनुष्य**) courteous, polite, urbane, respectable, humane.

भला, 1, *m.* = **भलाई**, *q.v.*: 2, *m.* (*f.* ī) good, excellent, virtuous, righteous, benevolent, kind; healthy, well, sound; strange, wonderful, admirable, comical, droll: 3, *adv.* well, very good. — *ādmī* or — *mānush*, a person of respectability, a gentleman: (*ironically*) a silly fellow. — *k.* to do good to, to prosper. — *mānnā*, to take well (*i. e.* not to take amiss).

भलाई, *f.* (antithesis of **बुराई**) good, goodness, excellency, virtue: good health; welfare. — *k.* (with abl. of the object) to do good to.

भलाचंगा, *m.* (*f.* **भलीचंगी**) in good order, in sound health, hale, well; good, perfect.

भली, *f.* (*m.* **भला**, 2) good, etc.

भलेउ, **भलो**, **भलौ** in Braj = **भला**, *q. v.*

भल्ल, *m.* 1, = **भल्लात**, *q.v.*: 2, a bear: a kind of arrow.

भल्लक, *m.* a bear. [*dioides*).

भल्लपुच्छी, *f.* a certain plant (*Hedysarum lagopo-*

भल्लात, *m.* the marking-nut plant (*Semicarpus anacardium*), marking-nut.

भल्लातक, *m.*, **भल्लिका**, *f.* = **भल्लात**, *q. v.*

भल्ली, *f.* 1 = **भल्लात**, *q.v.*: 2, a kind of arrow with a crescent-shaped head.

भल्लुक, **भल्लूक** *m.* a bear (*Ursus labiosus*).

भव, *m.* being, existing; existence, birth, origin; the place or the means of being, the world; acquisition, gain, prosperity, welfare; excellence: a god: an epithet of Shiv and of Rudra.

भवंर, *more prop.* **भंवर**, *q. v.*

भवचक्र, *m.* the wheel or course of nature, the established arrangements of created things.

भवचाप, *m.* the bow of Shiv. [ary cares.

भवजाल, *m.* the concerns of the world, sublun-

भवती, *f.* (*m.* **भवन्त**) an honorific term of address to females = "my lady."

भवदन्घि (*Rām.*) = **आपका चरण**.

भवन, *m.* being, production, birth, nature; a place of abiding or of being, a dwelling, habitation, abode, house, mansion, temple; a site, spot; a field: the various celestial paradises.

भवनाशिनी, *f.* an epithet of the Sarju river (which flows from the Himālayas into the Goggra, with which it then becomes confounded).

भवन्त, *m.* (*f.* vatī) an honorific pronoun used in the *Rāmāyan* (1) in respectful address instead of 'thou' or 'you' (2) in respectful reference to third persons or persons not present.

भवन्ती, *f.* a house surrounded by a dead wall.

भवभंजनी, *f.* an epithet of Kālī (*lit.* the destroyer [of existence).

भवभामा, *f.* women.

भवरजनी, *f.* moral blindness (*lit.* the night or darkness of existence).

भवरा; see (1) **भंवरा** (2) **भौरा** (3) **भैरा**.

भवरें, *more com.* **भंवरे** (pl. of **भंवरा**).

भवसमुद्र }
भवसागर } = भवाम्बु, *q.v.*
भवसिन्धु }

भवानी, *f.* (see **भव**) an epithet of the wife of Shiv (Pārvati or Durgā) in her mild and pacific form.

भवाम्बु, *m.* the ocean of existence, the world of being, this present life, the state of mortals.

भवाम्बुनाथ }
भवाम्बुराशि } *m.* the ocean of existence.

भवार्णव, *m.* the ocean of existence.

भवितव्य, likely or necessary to be or to occur, ordained by Heaven, fated, decreed, destined, unavoidable.

भवितव्यता, *f.* necessity of coming into existence or of taking place, fate, destiny.

भविय्यत, *more prop.* **भविष्यत**, *q.v.*

भविष्य, *m.* (*f.* ā) future; *hence*, subst. *m.* what has yet to be, the future.

भविष्यकाल, *more com.* **भविष्यत्काल**, *q.v.*

भविष्यकालिक, *more com.* **भविष्यत्कालिक**, *q.v.*

भविष्यत, *m.* what has yet to be, what will be, the future. [Gram.) the future tense.

भविष्यत्काल, *m.* the time to come, futurity; (in

भविष्यत्कालिक, (in Gram.) appertaining to future time or to a future tense.

भविष्यत्वक्ता }
भविष्यद्वक्ता } *m.* (*f.* trī) = **भवष्यद्वादी**, *q.v.*

भविष्यद्वाक्य, *m.* }
भविष्यद्वाणी, *f.* } prophecy, prediction.

भविष्यद्वादी, *m.* (*f.* inī) a predicter, prophet: *lit.* adj. speaking of the future, prophesying, predicting.

भविष्यमान, *m.* (*f.* matī) appertaining to the future.

भविष्यवाणी, *f.* a voice of the future, prophecy, [prediction.

भवीष्यत, *more prop.* **भविष्यत**, *q.v.*

भवें; see (1) **भव** (2) **भएं**.

भवैया, *m.* a dancer: a story-teller.

भव्य, likely or necessary to be or to occur; *hence*, 1, *m.* existence, being; a result, consequence, fruit: 2, proper, fit, right, true, well-bred, prosperous, happy.

भव्यत्व, *m.* (*f.* tā) politeness, civility, courtesy.

भशिरा, *f.* a sort of beet (*Beta Bengalensis*).

भस, *m.* a colloquial form of **भस्म**, *q.v.*

भसकना, *a. int.* to fall, drop down.

भसतिक्का, *m.* a steak, chop, collop.

भसद, *f.* pudendum muliebre, mons veneris: the [sun: a mouth.

भसना, *a. int.* to float.

भसभसा, *m.* (*f.* ī) weak, soft, loose, flabby (as meat).

भसम, a colloquial form of **भस्म**, *q.v.*

भसरा, *a corruption of* **भुसरा**, *q.v.*

भसवाना, *t.* to cause to be floated, cause some one to make a thing float.

भसाना, *t.* to cause to float, to launch, set afloat.

भसावन, *m.* a tax on boats freighted with grain.

भसेरा, *a corruption of* **भुसेरा**, *q.v.*

भस्म, *m. f.* (?) ashes, cinders.

भस्मंत, *more prop.* **भस्मन्त**, *q.v.*

भस्मक, *m.* a certain disease of the eyes (thickening of the membranes and indistinctness of vision): morbid appetite (constant craving for food) with general decay. [variety of it.

भस्मगर्भा, *f.* the *sisu*-tree (*Dalbergia sisu*) or a

भस्मनं }
भस्मन्त } *m.* ashes, cinders.

भस्मस्नान, *m.* the act of smearing the body with the ashes of cowdung.

भस्मासुर, *m. pr. n.* a certain demon who had the power to reduce to ashes anyone on whose head he might place his hand.

भस्मीकरण, *m.* the act of calcining.

भस्मीकृत, reduced to ashes, calcined.

भस्वाना, *more prop.* **भसवाना**, *q.v.*

भहराना, *a. int.* to shiver, tremble, totter, stagger.

भहो, *f.* a sister-in-law (younger brother's wife).

भा, 1, (*dialectic*) = **भया**, *q.v.*: 2, *m.* the sun: 3, *f.* light, radiance, lustre, splendour, beauty; the shadow of any object.

भाइया, (voc. sing. of **भाई**) O brother!

भाइयनका in Braj = **भाइयोंका**. See **न**, 6 (2).

भाई, 1, *fem.* of **भाया**, *q.v.*: 2, *m.* (from **भ्राता**) a brother; a friend or comrade. *Baṛā* —, an elder brother. *Chhoṭā* or *lauharā* —, a younger brother.

भाईअंश, *m.* the share or portion of a brother.

भाईचारा, *m.* the quality or property of the brother-relationship, the relationship of brothers, brotherhood, fraternity, intimacy, a community of brothers or of people from one common stock.

भाईचारी, *f.* = **भाईचारा**, *q.v.*

भाईन, terrible, awful.

भाईपंसी, *f.* the share or portion of a brother.

भाईपन }
भाईपना } = **भाईचारा**, *q.v.*
भाईपा }

भाईबत, *more prop.* **भाईवत्**, *q.v.*

भाईबन्द, *m.* brotherhood, relations, kin, friends, [comrades; fraternity.

भाईबन्दी, *f.* = **भाईबन्द**, *q.v.*

भाईबाएट, *m.* (a term applied to a village owned by descendants [brothers] from one common stock) a fraternal community. [fraternal.

भाईवत, like (or becoming to) a brother, brotherly,

भाईहिस्सा, *m.* the share or portion of a brother.

भाउ (*Rām.*) = (1) **जन्म** (2) **प्रेम** (3) **भावना** (4) **सत्ता**.

भाओं, with respect to, concerning.

भाऊ in Braj = **भाव**, *q.v.*

भाऊज = **भावज**, 2, *q.v.*

भाएं, 1, *more prop.* **भावें**, *q.v.*: 2, *f.* pl. of **भा**, 3, *q.v.*

भांकड़ा, *m.* a fop: a parasite.

भांग, *f.* hemp (*Cannabis sativa*) of which an intoxicating liquor is made: the drink itself. [use of *bhāng*.

भांगरा, *m.* (*f.* i.) a person who is addicted to the

भांगी, *m.* (*f.* inī) = **भांगरा**, *q. v.*
भांगेरा, *m.* (*f.* ī.) a vendor of *bhāng*.
भांज, *m.* a twisting, twist.
भांजना, *t.* to put into circular motion, to turn on a lathe; to wave, brandish; to twist, break, destroy.
भांजा, *m.* a nephew (a sister's son).
भांजी, *f.* a niece (a sister's daughter): interruption, hindrance: tale-bearing. — *khanā*, to give a malicious piece of intelligence.—*denā* or *mārnā*, to interrupt, break in upon, put a stop to.
भांजीख़ोर, *m.* an interrupter; a tale-bearer.
भांट, भांड, भांत; for words beginning thus, see un- under the forms **भायट, भायड, भान्त**, respectively.
भांड़म; see **भायड़ा**.
भांड़ीर = **भायड़ीर**, *q.v.*
भांड़े, a pl. form of **भांड़ा** = **भायड़ा**, *q.v.* [*folia?*).
भांनकरी, *f.* a certain jungle shrub (*Ruelia longi-*
भांनि; see **भान**.
भांवर, *f.* revolution, circulation.—*paṛnā* or *phirnā*, to circumambulate, to circle: *n.* to be sacrificed.
भांवरि; see (1) **भांवरना** (2) **भांवरी**.
भांवरना = **भांवर फिरना**, *q. v.*
भांवरी, *f.* = **भांवर**, *q. v.*
भांस, a provincial form = **बांस**, *q. v.*
भांसी, a provincial form = **बांसी**, *q. v.*
भाकसी, *f.* a furnace, kiln.
भाक्त, *m.* (*f.* ā) a follower, dependent, retainer, one who is regularly fed by another.
भाक्तिक, *m.* (*f.* ā *or* ī) = **भाक्त**, *q. v.*
भाखना = **भाषना**, *q. v.*
भाखा = **भाषा**, *q. v.*
भाग, *m.* a portion, part, allowance, participation, share, division, lot, fate, destiny, fortune, luck; side, direction; department; tax, duty; a fraction, the numerator of a fraction; a degree (the 360th part of the circumference of a circle); a division of time (the 30th part of a zodiacal sign). —*jāgnā*, to be fortunate. —*jānā*, to run away, take flight, abscond, be off.
भागड़, *f.* flight, a general emigration, escape from
भागदार, *m.* a sharer. [immediate danger.
भागनर, the rich alluvial lands under the banks of the Yamunā. [self scarce, abscond, be off.
भागना, *a. int.* to run away, take flight, make one-
भागबटाई, *f.* the apportionment of the shares of
भागभरोसा, *m.* consolation. [a crop.
भागमती, *f.* (*m.* **भागमान**) a fortunate female.
भागमान, *m.* (*f.* matī) favoured of the fates, fortunate, rich, prosperous.
भागमानी, *f.* fortunateness, prosperity, good for-
भागल, trick, affectation. [tune, felicity.
भागलपुर, *m. pr. n.* a certain city and district of Bengal. [Bhāgalpur from silk and cotton.
भागलपूरी, *m.* a kind of cloth manufactured at
भागलिया, *f.* imitation, imposture, hypocrisy.
भागली, *adj.* false, mock, imitation.

भागवत, *m. pr. n.* (see **पुराण**) one of the most celebrated of the eighteen Purāṇs.
भागवतरूपी, after the manner of the Bhāgvat.
भागवान, *m.* (*f.* vatī) = (1) **भगवान** (2) **भागमान**, *qq. v.*
भागवानी = **भाग्यवानी**, *q. v.*
भागवार, held upon a joint tenure or share (said
भागसी, *f.* a jail. [of land).
भागहार, *m.* (in Arithm.) division.
भागाभाग, *m.* running away, scampering off, flight.
भागिनी, *f.* (*m.* **भागी**) an heiress.
भागिनेय, *m.* a nephew (a sister's son).
भागिनेयी, *f.* a niece (sister's daughter).
भागी, *m.* (*f.* inī) a partner, sharer, participator; an heir; a fortunate person: *lit.* adj. participating: fortunate.
भागीदार, *m.* a sharer, participator, partner.
भागीरथ, *more prop.* **भगीरथ**, *q. v.*
भागीरथी, *f. pr. n.* (patronym.) an epithet (1) of the Ganges (2) of one of the rivers that flow into it; *lit.* daughter of Bhagīrath.
भागुरि, *m. pr. n.* a certain ancient Hindoo sage.
भागू, *m. f.* a fugitive, runaway, deserter, coward.
भागेल, 1, = **भागू**, *q.v.*: 2, flight, desertion.
भागोड़ा, *m.* (*f.* ī) = **भागू**, *q.v.*
भाग्य, *m.* merit and demerit acquired in former existences, fate, fortune, luck, chance, destiny (good or ill, but especially good).
भाग्यमान, *m.* (*f.* matī) = **भागमान**, *q. v.*
भाग्यमानी = **भागमानी**, *q. v.*
भाग्यवन्त } **भाग्यवान** } *m.* (*f.* vatī) = **भागमान**, *q. v.*
भाग्यवानी, *f.* luckiness, fortunateness, prosperity, felicity. [fortunate, wretched, poor.
भाग्यहीन, *m.* (*f.* ā) not favoured by fortune, un-
भाग्यहीनत्व, *m.* (*f.* tā) unfortunateness, wretchedness, poverty. [nate female.
भाग्यहीना, *f.* (*m.* **भाग्यहीन**) a wretched unfortu-
भाचर, a kind of large earthen jar.
भाज; see (1) **भांज** (2) **भाजना**.
भाजड़, *f.* a running off, flight.
भाजन, *m.* any vessel (as a pot, plate, cup, etc.): (in Arithm.) division. [abscond: *t.* to fry.
भाजना, *a. int.* to run away, scamper off, flee,
भाजर, *f.* a running off, flight.
भाजी, *f.* a portion or share of food: greens. *Māṭ-ki* —, *f.* the edible amaranth (*Amaranthus oleaceus*).
भाज्य, fit or requiring to be divided or distributed, divisible; hence, *m.* a portion, share, inheritance; (in Arithm.) the dividend.
भाट, *m.* (**भट** or **भट्ट**?) a certain tribe of bards; a bard, minstrel, panegyrist, a genealogist or family bard. [*bhāṭ*, a female minstrel.
भाटन, *f.* a female of the *bhāṭ*-tribe, the wife of
भाटा, a provincial form of **भाठा**, *q. v.* [Bhaṭṭa.
भाट्ट, *m.* (patronym.) a follower of Kumārila

भाठ ; see भाट्ठ.

भाठा, *m.* a current, stream ; the ebb-tide.

भाठियाल, down, below, down the river, with the stream. [bellows.

भाठी, *f.* the way of the current, down the river ;

भाड़, *m.* the wages of fornication : a furnace, kiln (particularly for parching grain). — *khānā*, to subsist on the wages of prostitution (said not of the woman herself, but of those dependent on her gains). [pense.

भाड़ा, *m.* settled fare, hire, rent ; price ; recom-

भाणट, *m.* a certain medicinal plant (*Clerodendrum infortunatum*, Linn. : *Volkameria infortunata*, Roxb.).

भाणटा, *m.* the egg-plant (*Solanum melongena*).

भाण्ड, *m.* any vessel (as a plate, cup, pot, vat, etc.), a small earthen pot ; any implement or utensil ; a case, a razor-case; capital, principal, stock, goods, wares ; any ornament ; any musical instrument ; the bed of a river : buffoonery, mimicry ; a mimic, actor, buffoon, jester.

भाण्डना, t. to abuse, reproach, calumniate.

भाण्डा, *m.* a large earthen pot ; estate ; equipage. — *phūṭnā*, to lose one's character.

भाण्डागार, *m.* (भाण्ड + आगार) a place where household goods or merchandize are kept, a store-house, 'godam,' magazine, treasury.

भाण्डार } contractions of भाण्डागार, *q.v.*
भाण्डारा }

भाण्डारख़ाना = भाण्डागार, *q.v.*

भाण्डारी, *m.* (*f.* inī) one who has charge of a store-house or magazine, a house-steward, butler, store-keeper, purveyor, caterer, keeper, guard, treasurer, superintendent.

भाण्डारीपन, *m.* the status of store-keeper, stewardship, purveyorship, treasurership. [an actress.

भाण्डिन, *f.* (*m.* भाण्ड) a female mimic or jester,

भाण्डीर, *m.* the Indian figtree (*Ficus Indica*).

भाण्डू, *m.* a mimic, actor, buffoon, jester.

भाण्डैत, *m.* (*f.* ī) a mimic, buffoon, jester, actor.

भाण्डैती, *f.* (*m.* भाण्डैत) a female mimic or jester, an actress : mimicry, buffoonery, jesting, acting.

भाणो in the hill dialect = पकाना, *q.v.*

भात, *m.* dawn, the early morning : boiled rice, cooked food : advances made to ploughmen without interest : (in Māṛwāṛī) the second day's feast at a marriage.

भाता, *m.* an extra allowance to troops on service

भाथा, *f.* a quiver. [or on the march, 'batta.'

भादवा } = भाद्र, *q.v.*
भादों }

भादोंवी, *m.* the autumnal crop : *lit.* appertaining

भादों in Braj = भाद्र, *q.v.* [to the month *Bhādoṅ*.

भाद्र, *m.* the fifth month of the Hindoos (Aug.-Sept.) when the moon is full near the wing of Pegasus.

भाद्रपद = भाद्र, *q.v.*

भाद्रपदा, *more prop.* भद्रपदा, *q.v.*

भान, 1, *m.* a contraction of भानु, 2, *q.v.* : 2, *f.* a provincial form of बहिन, *q.v.* : 3, *m.* appearance; perception, consciousness, recollection : the trumping up of a story.

भानचारा, *m.* (see भान, 2, and भाईचारा) the quality or property of sister, the relationship of sister, sisterhood, sisterly affection.

भानज ; for words beginning thus, see under the more proper form भांज.

भानना, *more prop.* भांजना, *q.v.*

भानमती, *f.* a female juggler, actress.

भाना, *n.* to be approved of, be acceptable : *a. int.* to please, suit, fit, seem good or befitting to.

भानु, 1, *f.* = भानुमती, *q.v.* : 2, *m.* a ray of light ; light ; the sun, a planet, any luminary : a master, a sovereign. [female.

भानुमती, *f.* (*m.* भानुमान) a beautiful or handsome

भानुमान, *m.* (*f.* matī) a handsome person ; the sun : *lit.* luminous, splendid, radiant, beautiful, handsome.

भानुवार, *m* (see भानु) Sunday.

भानू, a corruption of भानु, *q.v.*

भानेज ; see under the form भांज.

भानोली, *f.* a certain kind of bread.

भान्त, *more prop.* भान्ति, *q.v.*

भान्तभान्त, *more prop.* भान्तिभान्ति, *q.v.*

भान्ति, *f.* manner, mode, method, kind, sort, style.

भान्तिक, appertaining to manner or to sort.

भान्तिभान्ति, various, of various kinds, of different sorts or styles.

भाना, *more prop.* भांजना, *q.v.*

भाप } *more comm.* बाफ, *q.v.*
भाफ }

भाफना, *t.* to conceive, to guess, to comprehend.

भाबर, *pr. n.* a certain large forest at the foot of

भाबी, *more prop.* भावी, *q.v.* [the Sevālik hills.

भाभी, *f.* a brother's wife.

भाम, *m.* anger, passion, wrath : light, radiance; the sun : a brother-in-law (sister's husband).

भामा, *f.* a passionate female.

भामिन, *m.* (*f.* ī) = भामी, *q.v.*

भामिनि (*Rām.*) = भामिनी, *q.v.*

भामिनी, *f.* (*m.* भामी) a passionate female (often used as a term of endearment).

भामी, passionate, wrathful, indignant : hence, *m.* (*f.* inī) a passionate person, etc.

भाय, 1, a corruption of भाई, *q.v.* : 2, see भावना.

भायप (*Rām.*) = भाईपन, *q.v.* [ing, acceptable.

भाया, *m.* (*f.* भाई) agreeable, fitting, suitable, pleas-

भाये (*Rām.*) = (1) भाव (2) pl. of भाया, *qq.v.*

भार, 1, a corruption of बाहिर, *q.v.* : 2, *m.* weight, burden, load, a great weight, a certain weight of gold (= 2000 *pal*) : a yoke for carrying burdens ; a faggot ; weight, gravity ; a charge, trust, responsibility.

भारग्रस्त, *m.* (*f.* ā) an oppressed person, etc.: *lit.* weight, loaded, burdened, oppressed.

भारत,(patronym.) *m.*(*f.* ī) a descendant of Bharat: an actor, mimic: *pr. n.* (1) of India Proper; so called, because it was the patrimony of Bharat, the son of Dushyant, who is said to have been the first monarch of all India (2) of the great epic of the Hindoos, usually called the Mahābhārat (3) an epithet of fire.

भारतखण्ड = **भरतखण्ड**, *q. v.*

भारतवर्ष, *m. pr. n.* = **भारत** (1), *q.v.*

भारती, *f.* speech, eloquence; the goddess of speech (*Saraswati*); dramatic recitation; a quail (*Perdix chinensis*).

भारद्वाज, *m.* a skylark: wild cotton: a bone: *pr.n.* an epithet (1) of Droṇ (2) of one of the seven ṛishis (3) of Agastya (3) of the son of Vrihaspati.

भारवाह, *m.* a bearer of burdens, porter, carrier.

भारवाहक }
भारवाहिक } = **भारवाह**, *q.v.*

भारवृक्ष, *m.* a certain fragrant substance (commonly called *kākshi*) considered variously as a vegetable and a mineral product.

भारा, *m.* a load, burden: the throwing any charge or responsibility on a person: scaffolding.

भारी, *m.* (*f.* iṇi) a carrier of burdens, porter, etc.: *lit.* loaden, laden, laden, burden-bearing; heavy, weighty, big, great, large, fat, thick, strong, loud: *met.* of importance, momentous, important; valuable; grave, steady, patient; burdensome, troublesome. —*putthar chūmkar chhorṇā*, to withdraw from a difficult or impracticable undertaking. —*lagnā*, to become heavy.

भारीपन, *m.* weightiness, heaviness, weight.

भारीभरकम, grave, sedate; patient.

भारो, a poetical form = **भार** or **भारा**, *qq. v.*

भार्ग, *m.* any king of the Bhargas: *pr. n.* (1) of a king called also Bharg (2) of a son of Pratardan.

भार्गभूमि, *m. pr. n.* a certain king.

भार्य, requiring to be borne, be supported, be cherished, be nourished; dependent for a livelihood on another: hence, *m.* (*f.* ā) a servant, dependent, mercenary.

भार्या, *f.* she who is maintained by her husband, a wife (espoused according to the ritual of the Veds), a married female: a musical mode, the wife of a deity (*rāg*) presiding over a musical mode.

भार्याटिक, *m.* one who is over-ruled by his wife, a henpecked husband. [a female.

भार्यात्व, *m.* the state or condition of a wife or of

भाल, 1, *m.* a bear: the forehead: fortune: light, lustre: a certain tribe of Rājpūts: 2, *f.* the point or head of an arrow.

भालना, *t.* to see, perceive, look, contemplate.

भालदार, *m.* a spearman, pikeman.

भाला, *m.* a kind of spear (about seven cubits long); a kind of lance with a narrow head.

भालांक, *m.* a kind of fish (*Cyprinus rohita*) commonly called the *rohi*: a sort of potherb.

भालु, *m.* the sun.

भालुक, *m.* a bear (*Ursus labiosus*).

भालू, *m.* a bear: an old jackal.

भालूकोला, *m.* a hyena, or (as some say) a hybrid between a wolf and a jackal.

भालैत, *m.* a spearman, pikeman.

भाल्लुक }
भाल्लूक } *m.* a bear (*Ursus labiosus*).

भाव, *m.* existence, being; birth; state or condition of being, natural state, nature, property, disposition, intention, design, purpose, signification, meaning; mind, heart, soul; emotion, sentiment, passion, affection, choice, liking, will; a sudden idea or emotion of the mind, notion, idea; corporeal expression of amorous sentiment, the expressing meaning by signs, blandishment, gesticulation, acting, pantomime; a being, substance, thing, object; the world; superhuman power; the Supreme Being; a learned or clever person: friendship: price, value. —*batānā*, to gesticulate.

भावई, 1, *more prop.* **भावी**, *q. v.*: 2, (pl. °**ईं**) = **भावता है** (**भावना**, 1).

भावक, 1, *m.* (*f.* ikā) a friend, lover: 2, *m.* the external expression of amatory sentiments.

भावज, 1, *m.* love: 2, *f.* a brother's wife, the wife of a wife's brother.

भावता, *m.* (*f.* ī) amiable, dear, beloved.

भावन, 1, = **भाओं**, *q.v.*: 2, *m.* = **भावना**, 2, *q.v.*: 3, *m.* a creator, producer; efficient cause; a founder.

भावना, 1, a provincial form of **भाना**, *q.v.*: 2, *f.* mental perception, the present consciousness of past ideas or perceptions, recollection, imagination, contemplation, thought, meditation (religious and abstract); looking about, observing, investigating; consideration, anxiety, apprehension, doubt, concern; (in Math.) the accomplishing a thing by combination.

भावनायुक्त, *m.* (*f.* ā) anxious, concerned, thoughtful.

भावप्रधान, (in Gram.) impersonal (said of the verb).

भावली, *f.* rent paid in kind to a zamīndār; the distribution of a crop between a zamīndār and the cultivator. [vation.

भावलीलील, land recently brought under culti-

भावलीपा, land that has long been cultivated.

भाववाचक संज्ञा, *f.* (in Gram.) an abstract substantive. [tion.

भाववान, *m.* (*f.* vati) *adj.* being in a state or condi-

भावह, *f.* a sister-in-law (younger brother's wife).

भावा, *m.* (*f.* ī) *more com.* **भाया**, *q.v.*

भावार्थ, *m.* the simple or inherent meaning, the obvious purport, drift, scope, sense, subject-matter.

भाविउ, 1, an old poetical form of **भावी**, *q.v.*: an old imperat. 2nd pers. of **भावना** (**भाना**).

भाविक, natural, innate, appertaining to feeling, sentimental: (in Math.) an equation involving products of unknown quantities.

भाविका, *f.* (*m.* **भावक**) a female friend.

भावित, *m.* (*f.* ā) animated, inspired: thoughtful, anxious, apprehensive, alarmed.

भाविनी, *f.* (*m.* **भावी**) a distinguished woman, a beloved woman, a wanton woman.

भावी, 1, *m.* (*f.* inī) future, yet to be, proximately future, about to be; predestined: 2, *f.* (*m.* **भावा**) beautiful.

भावीकाल, *m.* future time, the future.

भावीवश, subject to the future.

भावे, *postp.m.* in the manner of, after the fashion of, like, as; with a view to, for the purpose that, in order that, in the sentiment, perception, mind, notion or idea; in one's eyes, in sight, near, before.

भावैं } **भावै** } **भावे**, *q.v.*

भाव्य, future, about to be or to occur, what must be, what will be or ought to be, possible, probable.

भावय, *more prop.* **भाव्य**, *q.v.*

भाषण, *m.* a speaking, talking; speech.

भाषना, *a. int.* to speak, say, tell: *t.* to call.

भाषा, *f.* speech, language; the vernacular of any country; dialect; a word; a plaint at law; an epithet of Saraswatī (the goddess of speech): one of the musical modes (*rāgiṇī*).

भाषातमक, *more prop.* **भाषात्मक**, *q.v.*

भाषात्मक } **भाषाबन्ध** } written in a vernacular (*bhāshā*).

भाषित, *m.* (*f.* ā) spoken, uttered, said.

भाष्य, *m.* speaking, talking; any literary work in vernacular speech; any commentary.

भासना, *n.* to be known, to appear.

भासा; see (1) **भासना** (2) **भाषा**.

भासुर, 1, *adj.* shining: 2, *m.* crystal: a hero: a brother-in-law (husband's elder brother): a species of costus (*Costus speciosus*).

भास्कर, *lit.* light-making, resplendant, shining; *hence*, *m.* the sun; fire; gold; a hero: *pr. n.* a celebrated ancient Hindoo astronomer (author of the *Siddhānt Shiromaṇi*, and other works).

भास्वर, *lit.* luminous, shining, radiant, splendid; hence, *m.* the sun, daylight; a day: a species of costus (*Costus speciosus*).

भिंगाना, *more prop.* **भिगाना**, *q.v.*

भिंट, **भिंड**; for words beginning thus, see under the corresponding forms **भिण्ट**, **भिण्ड**.

भिकारी, *m.* (*f.* iṇī) = **भिक्षाहारी**, *q.v.*

भिक्षा, *f.* begging, asking alms: the thing obtained by begging, alms, begged food: hire; service. — *māngnā*, to ask for alms.

भिक्षापात्र, *m.* a begger's bowl or wallet, any vessel in which alms are collected.

भिक्षाहारी, *m.* (*f.* iṇī) a beggar, mendicant.

भिक्षु, *m.* one who subsists only on alms, a mendicant, religious mendicant: the fourth Hindoo *āshram*.

भिक्षुक, *m.* (*f.* ī) a beggar, mendicant.

भिखमंगा, *m.* (*f.* ī) a beggar, mendicant.

भिखरी, *f.* an unfilled grain, a shrivelled grain.

भिखारी, *m.* (*f.* iṇī) = **भिक्षाहारी**, *q.v.* [etc.

भिगवाना, *t.* (causat. of **भिगाना**) to cause to drench,

भिगाना, *t.* (of **भिगना**) to wet, moisten, bedew, steep, drench.

भिगोना = **भिगाना**, *q.v.* [drenched.

भिगोया, *m.* (*f.* **भिगोई**) moistened, wet, steeped,

भिच्छुक } **भिछुक** } *m.* (*f.* ī) colloquial = **भिक्षुक**, *q.v.*

भिजवाना, *t.* (causat. of **भेजना**) to cause to be sent; to cause to send.

भिजाना, *t.* 1, (causat. of **भीजना**) to cause to be wet, to wet, moisten, steep, drench: 2, (causat. of **भेजना**) to cause to send.

भिटनी, *f.* a nipple.

भिड़, 1, = **भिर**, *q.v.*: 2, an enclosing or surrounding, an enclosure, fence; a crowd.

भिड़ना, *n.* to be placed together (touching each other), be continuous, be joined: *a. int.* to close (as two armies), to join battle, come together, join, shoulder, approach.

भिड़ाई, *f.* the closing of two armies in battle.

भिड़ाना, *t.* to place close to, to join, to close: to cause to fight.

भिड़ो; see (1) **भिड़ना** (2) **भिण्डो**.

भिढ़ा, *m.* (*f.* ī) a wolf.

भिण्डवास, *m.* a certain species of pulse.

भिण्ड, *m.* } **भिण्डा**, *f.* } a kind of shrub.

भिण्डी, 1, *f.* a certain vegetable (*Hibiscus esculentus*): 2, *m. pr. n.* a certain Hindoo sage.

भिण्डेखाना, *m.* the room appropriated to the apparatus of the *hukkā*.

भिण्डो in the hill dialect = much.

भित्ति, *f.* a breaking; a thing broken or divided; a figure, a fragment, a defect: a place, spot: an opportunity, occasion: an asylum: a wall of earth or masonry.

भित्तिका, *f.* a wall: a small house-lizard.

भिदनौं, *t.* (in Chand) to penetrate, sever, separate.

भिनक; see (1) **भिक्षुक** (2) **भयानक** (3) **भिनकना**.

भिनकना, *a. int.* to buzz (said of the fly): *n.* to be covered with flies, to swarm.

भिनभिनाना, *a. int.* to buzz, hum (as insects).

भिनभिनाहट, *f.* a buzzing, buzz, hum.

भिनुसार, *more prop.* **भिनसार**, *q.v.*

भिन्दपाल, *m.* a short arrow thrown from the hand or shot through a tube, a sling.

भिन्दिपाल, *more prop.* **भिन्दपाल**, *q.v.*

भिन्न, *m.* (*f.* ā) broken, split, divided, disunited, detached, distinguished, other, different, separate, apart, distinct, diverse; opened, unfolded, expanded, blown; hence, *m.* (in Math.) a fraction.

भिन्नक, *m.* a heterodox sectary, separatist, seceder; a Bauddh; a certain musical mode.

भिन्नगुणन, *m.* (in Math.) multiplication of fractions.

भिन्नगोत्र, one not belonging to the same family or tribe, one of a different lineage.

भिन्नघन, *m.* (in Math.) the cube of a fraction.

भिन्नता, *f.* (*m.* °त्व) distinction, difference, separateness, separation.

भिन्नभागहर, *m.* (in Math.) division of fractions.

भिन्नभिन्न, *adj.* various, diverse, separate, different; *adv.* severally, one by one.

भिन्नवत्, disjoined, divided, scattered.

भिन्नवर्ग, *m.* (in Math.) the square of a fraction.

भिन्नवर्णी, *m.* (*f.* ई) a person of a different caste, etc.: *lit.* of different colour: of a different tribe or caste.

भिन्नव्यवकलित, *m.* (in Math.) subtraction of fractions.

भिन्नसंकलित, *m.* (in Math.) addition of fractions.

भिन्नसार, *m.* an epithet of the dawn, morning.

भिन्ना, *f.*; see **भिन्न**.

भिन्नाना, *n.* to have a singing in the ears, to be giddy: *a. int.* to sound (as brass pots, etc.).

भिन्नाभिन्न, distinct and not distinct, separate and not separate.

भिन्नोदर, *m.* a half-brother (a brother not by the same mother).

भिन्नोदरी, *f.* a half-sister (a sister not by the same mother).

भिन्सार, *m.* dawn, break of day.

भिया, *f.* fear.

भियाव, *m.* espousals, marriage.

भिर, *m.* (Sk. **भृंग**?) a species of insect, a wasp, bee.

भिरना, *n.* to be open or ajar (a door).

भिराना in Bhojpurī = **फिराना**, *q.v.*

भिलावन }
भिलावां } *m.* = **भल्लात**, *q.v.*

भिलांजी, *f.* the seed of the marking-nut.

भिल्ल, *m.* (see **भील**) a barbarian of a certain tribe (perhaps the modern Bhills of the province of Mālwā).

भिल्लिन, *f.* a female of the above-mentioned race.

भिषज, *m.* a physician.

भिष्टल, *f.* a foolish or stupid female.

भिस, the edible root of the lotus.

भिसलना, *n.* to be dazzled (said of the sight).

भी, also, too, even, forsooth, and, moreover, both; in fact, at all events, at any rate. With a negative particle before the verb, it = neither—nor. *Dūdhbhi hai aur pānībhi hai*, there is both milk and water.

भींगना = **भीगना**, *q. v.*

भीक, a provincial form = **भीख**, *q. v.*

भीकारी, *m.* (*f.* iṇī) = **भिखाहारी**, *q. v.*

भीख, *f.* begging, mendicity; charity, alms. —*denā*, to give alms. —*māngnā*, to ask alms, beg.

भीखमंगा, *m.* (*f.* in *or* ī) a beggar, pauper.

भीगना, *n.* to be wet. *Rāt bhīgnī* is applied to the night passing in mirth and musical entertainment.

भीगनां; see (1) **भीगना** (2) **फेंकना**.

भीगा, *m.* (*f.* ī) wet, saturated, moist.

भीचना, *t.* to squeeze, compress, crush.

भीजना, *n.* to be wet: to be affected with grief.

भीजा, *m.* (*f.* ī) wet, moistened.

भीट, an elevation of earth made near a tank for the purpose of planting *pān*; the mound of a tank or artificial pond; the vestige of an old house.

भीटा, *m.* an old house, a former residence (provided some vestige remain).

भीटी = **भीट**, *q.v.*

भीड़, *f.* a multitude, crowd, assemblage, mob, throng, concourse; a press of work; trouble, difficulty.

भीड़बंगा, *m.* the rabble of camp-followers, the *impedimenta* of an army on the march.

भीड़भाड़, a multitude, crowd.

भीड़ा, *m.* (*f.* ī) crowded, thronged.

भीत, 1, *m.* a contraction of **भीति**, *q.v.*: 2, *f.* a wall or breadth of a wall: 3, a corruption of **भीट**, *q v.*: 3, *m.* (*f.* ā) frightened, fearful, timid, afraid. *Ochhekī prīt jon bālūkī bhīt*, the friendship of the mean is like a wall of sand (*i. e.* it is unstable).

भीतर, 1, *m.* the interior, the space or part within: 2, *adv.* within, inside: 3, *postp.* (takes gen. *m.* infl.) on the inside of, in the interior part of.

भीतरवाला, *m.* (*f.* ī) an inmate.

भीतरिया, the people who live in a house or family, not strangers or outsiders, inmates, domestics; those among the guests at a wedding feast who eat in company with the relations of the bride (those who partake of the feast *without*, are called *Bāhariya*); the men who are attached to a Hindoo temple, *viz.* the *Bhāṇḍārī*, the *Pūjārī*, and the *Rasoīyā*.

भीतरी, *m.* or *f.* the inward parts, the heart, etc.: *lit.* appertaining to the inside, inward, internal, essential, inner, interior, inside.

भीति, *f.* alarm, apprehension, fear, trembling.

भीती (*Rām.*) = (1) **भीति** (2) **भित्ति**, *q. v.*

भीतैरी, *f.* ground-rent paid for the site of a house by a stranger.

भीत्ति, a corruption of **भित्ति**, *q.v.*

भीनसार, *m.* dawn, break of day, morning.

भीना, 1, *m.* a brother-in-law (sister's husband): 2, *m.* (*f.* ī) wet.

भीनौ, *m.* (*f.* ī) 1, in Chand = **भरा** (?), *q. v.*: 2, in Braj = **भीना**, *q. v.*

भीन्त, *f.* (from **भित्ति**) a wall.

भीम, 1, *m. pr. n.* (1) of the second of the five Pāṇḍu princes, the second brother of Yudhiṣṭir (2) an epithet of Shiv: 2, *m.* horror, terror; danger: *lit. m.* (*f.* ā) fearful, terrible, terrific, horrible, dreadful, frightful, tremendous.

भीमरथ, *m. pr. n.* a certain Asur.

भीमरथी, *f.* the seventh night of the seventh month in the seventy-seventh year of a man's life (supposed to be the ordinary period of human life); extreme old age; dotage: *pr. n.* a certain river.

भीमसेन = **भीम** (1), *q. v.*

भीमसेनी, *f.* a kind of camphor.

भीमा, *f.* (*m.* **भीम**) an epithet of Durgā, the wife of Shiv: a whip.

भीर, 1, *a corruption of* **वीर**, *q. v.*: 2, see **भीड़**.

भीरा (*Rām.*) = (1) **बोझा** (2) **भीड़** (3) **डर**.

भीरी, a species of falcon.

भीरु, *m.* (*f.* **भीरु** or **भीरू**) a shy or timid person; a jackal, a tiger, a goat, a centipede; a sort of prickly nightshade; a certain plant (*Asparagus racemosus*); *lit.* timid, shy, cowardly, pusillanimous.

भीरुक, 1, *m.* a coward ; an owl : *lit.* timid, afraid, shy, pusillanimous : 2, formidable.

भील, *m.* (*f.* nī) a certain race of wild mountaineers who dwell especially along the course of the Nerbudda (*Narmada*) and subsist chiefly by plunder.

भीलनी, *f.* (*m.* भील) a female of the above-mentioned race.

भीलु } timid, fearful.
भीलुक }

भीषण, *m.* the sentiment of horror; the property that excites fear ; horror, terror; an object of horror : the olibanum-tree (*Boswellia thurifera*) : *lit. m.* (*f.* ā) horrible, terrific, formidable, awful.

भीषा, *f.* fear, terror, fright ; intimidation, terrifying.

भीष्म, *m.* horror, the sentiment of horror ; a goblin, imp: *pr. n.* the grand-uncle of the Pāṇḍus, and son of the Ganges: an epithet of Shiv : *lit.* fearful, frightful, horrible, terrific.

भीष्मक, *m.* the contemptible Bhīshm.

भीष्मजननी, *f.* the mother of Bhīshm, *i.e.* the Ganges.

भीष्मपितामह, *m. pr. n.* a certain ancient Hindoo sage and warrior, the son of Santanu and Gangā.

भीस, the edible root of the lotus.

भीहर, *m.pr.n.* a certain tribe (supposed to be the aborigines of Rohilkhaṇḍ).

भुअंग, *m.* (*f.* i *or* ini) a snake.

भुआल } *Rām.*) = भूप, *q.v.*
भुआला }

भुइंफोर, *m.* a toadstool, a mushroom.

भुइंडोल }
भुईंडोल } (colloquialisms) = भूमिडोल, *q.v.*
भुइँडोल }

भुंजना (*Rām.*) = भोगना, *q.v.*

भुंडली = भुयड़ली, *q.v.*

भुंडा in Mārwāṛī = बुरा, *q.v.*

भुकसा, *m.* a certain forest tribe of Rājpūts.

भुक्त, *m.* (*f.* ā) an eater : food, eating : *lit.* eaten : eating, having eaten : comprized in.

भुक्ति, *f.* eating; food, a meal ; fruition, possession, enjoyment.

भुगतना, *t.* to receive the reward of virtue or the punishment of crime, to undergo, experience, suffer, enjoy, get requital.

भुगतमान, *m.* (*f.* matī) one who deserves punishment: *lit.* fit to undergo (*i.e.* fit to suffer or to enjoy), deserving punishment.

भुगताना, *t.* to cause to experience or to enjoy, to requite, to distribute.

भुगति ; see (1) भुक्ति (2) भुगतना (3) भोग.

भुगन्दर, *m.* a fistula *in ano.*

भुग्गा, *m.* (*f.* ī) simple, foolish.

भुच्च, barbarous, uncivilized, ignorant.

भुचंग = भुजंगा, *q.v.*

भुचम्पा, *more prop* भूंचम्पा, *q.v.*

भुज, *m.* a bending, curve ; the arm above the elbow, the hand, the proboscis of an elephant : (in Geom.) the side of a plane figure ; one of the shorter sides of a right angled triangle (*i.e.* either the perpendicular or the base) : (in Astron.) the distance of the sun from the equator, or of the moon from the nearest node: (in the hill dialect) birch-bark. —*bharnā*, to clasp in the arms, embrace.

भुजंग, *m.* (*f* ī) a snake or serpent.

भुजंगप्रयात, *m.* (in Pros.) a species of metre.

भुजंगम, *m.* (*f.* ā) a snake or serpent.

भुजंगा, *m.* a kind of shrike (*Lanius cœrulescens*) commonly called the 'king crow.' *Bhujange urānā*, to be in great poverty and distress : to spread false reports.

भुजंगिनी, *f.* a female snake or serpent.

भुजंगी, *f.* (in Pros.) a species of metre.

भुजग, *m.* (*f.* ī) a snake or serpent.

भुजदण्डा, *m.* an arm as hard as a staff.

भुजना, *m.* parched or scorched grain.

भुजबन्ध, *m.* an ornament worn on the arm, an armlet.

भुजभर, *m.* an armful, an embrace.

भुजमूल, *m.* the upper part of the arm near the shoulder.

भुजा, *f.* the arm above the elbow, the proboscis of an elephant.

भूजाभूषण, *m.* an ornament for the arm, an armlet.

भुजिआ, *f.* greens.

भुजिष्य, 1, *m.* an independent man : a kind of string worn around the waist : 2, *m.* (*f.* ā) a servant, slave.

भुजिष्या, *f.* (*m.* भुजिष्य) a female servant or slave ; a harlot.

भुट्टा, 1, *m.* Indian corn (*Zea mays*); the head or ear of corn ripened ; any large bunch : 2, *m.* (*f.* ī) small.

भुट्टासा, *m.* (*f.* भुट्टौसी) smallish, very small.

भुड़, *f.* a hole through which water runs out.

भुयड़ली, *f.* a kind of worm covered with hair, the palmer-worm.

भुत ; see भूत.

भुतना, (dim. of भूत) *m.* (*f.* ī) a small devil, imp, demon, ghost, or goblin.

भुतहा, *m.* (*f.* ī) devilish, demoniacal, peevish, fierce.

भुताहा, *m.* (*f.* ī) = भुतहा, *q.v.*

भुतियाना, *n.* to be like a demon.

भुत्ता, *more com.* भुट्टा *q.v.*

भुनना, *n.* (see भूनना) to be parched, be grilled, be broiled, be fried : to be changed (said of money).

भुना ; see भुनना and भूना.

भुनाना, *t.* (and causat. of भुनना) to cause to parch or to grill, etc. : to change (money).

भुपाल, *more prop.* भूपाल, *q.v.*

भुभुक्षित, *m.* (*f.* ā) *more prop.* बुभुक्षित, *q.v.*

भुमयां, *more prop.* भूमियां, *q.v.*

भुमुण्डी, *f.* a large kind of basket.

भुरभुरा, *m.* (*f.* ī) dry and in a state of powder.

भुरभुराना, *t.* to throw or sprinkle salt or sugar on meat.

भुरकी, *f.* a yogee's spell performed by casting a handful of ashes on the head of anyone and uttering a *mantra.*

भुरा in Mārwārī = बुरा, *q.v.*

भुराना, *t.* to wheedle.

भुर्ता, *m.* vegetables boiled or fried and then broken or pressed in the hand.

भुलसना, *n.* to be singed, be scorched.

भुलाऊ, *m. f.* a misleader, inveigler, deceiver : *lit.* [*adj.* misleading.

भुलाट (contraction) भुलावट, *q.v.*

भुलाना, *t.* (causat. of भूलना) to cause to be forgotten, cause to forget, to bewilder, mislead, inveigle, deceive, fascinate, wheedle, coax, allure, amuse.

भुलानी, a poetical form of भुलाना.

भुलाव = (1) भुलाऊ (2) भुलावा, *qq.v.*

भुलावट, *f.* forgetfulness, obliviousness.

भुलावना = भुलाना, *q.v.*

भुलावा, *m.* a leading into error, misleading, deception, fraud, cheating; deceit, feint. — *denā*, to play a trick on one, to deceive, mislead.

भुल्लड़, forgetful, blundering, stupid.

भुव, contracted from भुवः, *q.v.*

भुवः, *m.* heaven, ether, sky, atmosphere. This expression forms part of the mystical triverbial phrase भूर भुवः स्वर.

भुवंग, *m.* (*f.* ī) a snake or serpent.

भुवंगिनि, *f.* a female snake or serpent.

भुवन, *m.* a being, creature, mankind, man; a world; water; heaven; one of the three mundane regions (earth, sky, the intervening space).

भुवनमोहनी, *f.* an epithet of *Māyā*, and of any charming female : *lit.* the enchantress of mankind.

भुवर्लोक, *m. pr. n.* one of the mundane regions, *viz.* the ethereal, or the space between the earth and the sun.

भुवस = भुवः, *q.v.*

भुवाल (*Rām.*) = भुआल = भूपाल, *q.v.*

भुवि (*Rām.*) = (1) पृथिवी (2) पृथिवीमें.

भुशुण्डी, *f.* a weapon (apparently a kind of fire-arms), a small gun.

भुस, *m.* bran, husk, chaff. — *par barāt*, an assignment on chaff, *i.e.* an assignment from which nothing can be obtained.

भुसकारना, *a. int.* to hiss (said of snakes).

भुसकारा, *m.* the breathing or hissing of a snake.

भुसरा, *m.* an inferior kind of wheat.

भुसुण्डि }
भुसुण्डी } *more prop.* भुशुण्डी, *q.v.*

भुसुल }
भुसेरा } = भुसेला, *q.v.*

भुसेला, *m.* a place where corn or chaff is kept.

भुसेहरा, *m.* the place in a dwelling-house where straw is kept. [chaff into.

भुसौण्डा, *m.* a place, hole or cavity for putting

भुसौरी, *f.* }
भुसौला, *m.* } = भसौण्डा, *q.v.*

भू, *f.* the earth, the world; land, ground, soil; a site, a place : sacrificial fire : (in Geom.) the base of a plane figure : in the ingenious method of reckoning by symbols adopted by Hindoos in their poetry, this word is a symbol for 1 (*one*).

भूआ, *f.* an aunt (father's sister) : a worm, a cater-[pillar.

भूई, *m. more com.* भोई, *q.v.*

भूई, *f.* 1, a colloquial form of भूमि, *q.v.*: 2, a kind of caterpillar covered with hair, and destructive to plants, flowers, and trees (esp. the *bēr*-tree).

भूईआंवला, a certain plant (*Phyllanthus niruri*).

भूईचम्पा, 1, *more prop.* भुंचम्पा, *q.v.*: 2, *m.* a kind of fireworks like a flower-pot (resembling that commonly called *anār*).

भूईडोल, *a colloquial form of* भूमिदोल, *q.v.*

भूईदगधा, gifts at marriages and funerals.

भूईमाली, a certain low caste of Hindoos engaged in the vilest offices. [rakhpur, etc.

भूईहार, a certain tribe of Hindoos settled in Go-

भूईहारी, *f.* land let at a low rent to military re-[tainers.

भूं *f. a colloquial form of* भूमि, *q.v.*

भूंई = भूई, *q.v.*

भूंईकम्प, *colloquial form of* भूमिकम्प, *q.v.*

भूंईचाल, *a colloquial form of* भूमिचाल, *q.v.*

भूंईडोल, *a colloquial form of* भूमिदोल *q.v.*

भूंईहार, *m.* country-people : a certain caste of bastard Brāhmans concerning whose origin many curious legends are told.

भूंकना; see भोंकना and भौंकना.

भूंगई }
भूंगाई } *f.* a kind of tax on forest-produce.

भूंचम्पा, *m.* a certain plant (*Kœmpferia rotunda*); a kind of firework like the flower of that plant.

भूंड; see under the form भूनड.

भूंभाई = भूम्भाई, *q.v.*

भूंयारा, *m.* a cellar; a cavern.

भूंस = भूस, *q.v.*

भूंसना, *a. int.* to bark (said of the dog).

भूंसा = भूसा, *q.v.*

भूंसाजिंस, all kinds of grain in husk.

भूंसी = भूसी, *q.v.*

भूंहार, *m.* a certain tribe of Hindoos.

भूंहारा, *m.* a kind of subterraneous dwelling.

भूक, 1, *a dialectic form of* भूख, *q.v.*: 2, *m.* darkness : a hole : the head of a fountain : time.

भूकड़, *a dialectic form of* भूखा, *q.v.*

भूकदम्ब, *m.* a certain plant (*Ligustum ajwaen*).

भूकम्प, *m.* an earthquake.

भूकल, *m.* (*f.* ā) a restive horse.

भूख, *f.* appetite, desire, hunger, craving for food. — *marnā*, to be dying of hunger, be famished, be starving. — *lagnā* (with the subject in the dat.) to be hungry.

भूका, *m.* (*f.* ī) *a dialectic form of* भूखा, *q.v.*

भूखित, *m.* (*f.* ā) a hog.

भूखन, *a colloquial form of* भूषण, *q.v.*

भूखा, m. (f. ī) hungry, desirous, craving, starv-
भूगल, m. ashes, embers of fire. [ing, destitute.
भूगोल, m. the terrestrial globe, the earth.
भूगोलविद्या, f. the science of Geography.
भूचर, m. (f. ī) any land-animal : *lit.* moving on land or on the ground.
भूचक्र, m. the equinoctial line. [quake.
भूचाल, f. the motion or course of the earth; earth-
भूजना ; see भुजना and भजना.
भूजन्तु, m. an earthworm. [*courtia sapida*).
भूजम्बू, f. wheat : the fruit of the Vaikunta (*Fla-*
भूजेल, m. a certain kind of bird.
भूट, land irretentive of water.
भूड़, f. very sandy soil. [process of treading.
भूड़री, f. corn still remaining in the ear after the
भूडल, m. talc, mica.
भूपडपैरा, m. (f. ī) ill-omened, unlucky.
भूपडरी, f. a small patch of cultivation allotted rent-free to village servants.
भूपिडया, m. one who cultivates with a borrowed plough or hand-instrument.
भूत, 1, m. (f. ā) been, former, past, gone; become, being, existing : proper, right, true ; *hence.* any created being ; a child ; (in Myth.) a certain kind of demigod ; a kind of malignant spirit (believed, by the Hindoos, to haunt graveyards, lurk in trees, animate carcases, and delude or devour human beings), a demon, goblin, fiend, evil spirit, sprite, ghost, apparition : an epithet of Shiv : (in Gram.) the preterite tense : (in Philos.) an element (of which the Hindoos reckon five, *viz.* earth, air, fire, water, and ether) : (in Law) the real state of the case, the matter of fact. — *lagnā* (with the dat. of the person) to be possessed of an evil spirit. — *honā*, to be distracted with rage.
भूतकाल, m. (in Gram.) past time, past tense.
भूतकालिक, (in Gram.) appertaining to past time or to a past tense.
भूतगण, m. a class of sprites or goblins.
भूतगन्धा, f. a sort of perfume (*Mūra*).
भूतग्रस्त, m. (f. ā) a maniac, etc. : *lit.* possessed by an evil spirit.
भूतघ्न, 1, m. garlic : 2, m. (f. ā) a camel.
भूतघ्ना, f. holy basil.
भूतजटा, f. Indian spikenard (*Valeriana jatamansi*).
भूतनाथ, m. an epithet of Shiv.
भूतनाशन, m. the marking-nut plant (*Semicarpus anacardium*); the *Eleocarpus*-seed. [demon's wife.
भूतनी, f. (m. भूत) a female demon or goblin, a
भूतप्रेत, m. ghosts and goblins. [*uosum*).
भूतराज, m. a certain plant (*Ophioglossum flex-*
भूतल, m. the earth, the ground, the face of the
भूतवार्त्ता, f. conversation about the past. [earth.
भूतवास, m. beleric myrobalan (*Terminalia belerica*).
भूतविक्रिया, f. possession by evil spirits, epilepsy.
भूतवीर, m. a certain ancient race of people.
भूतवेशी, f. a species of nebari (*Nyctanthes tristis*).
भूतवृक्ष, m. the name of two kinds of trees (1) *Trophis aspera* (2) *Bignonia Indica*.
भूतसंचार, m. possession by evil spirits. [ing things.
भूतसृष्टि, f. the creation or origination of exist-
भूता, f. (m. भूत) any female creature, etc.
भूतात्मा, m. (*lit.* composed of the five elements) an epithet of the body : the elementary or vital principle, or the proximate cause of life and action : an epithet of Brahmā and of Shiv.
भूताद, excess, abundance ; much, many.
भूतारि, m. a safœtida. [refuge of created beings.
भूतालय, m. an epithet of the Divine Being : *lit.* the
भूताविष्ट, m. (f. ā) a maniac : *lit.* occupied or possessed by an evil spirit. [spirit.
भूतावेश, m. the being possessed by a malignant
भूति, f. state of being, existence, production, birth ; pure and undisturbed existence aloof from matter and passion : power, dignity ; prosperity, wealth ; superhuman power as attainable by the practice of austere and magical rites : ashes : fried meat : plunder, booty : the rut of elephants.
भूतिनी = भूतनी, *q.v.*
भूतेश्वर, m. one of the epithets of Shiv : *pr. n.* a certain town and temple situated between Agra and Etawah on the banks of the Yamunā, being one of the sacred places of the Hindoos.
भूदान, m. a grant of land, or of the revenue
भूदानपत्र, m. a deed of a grant of land. [thereof.
भूदार, m. (f. ā) a hog : *lit.* the tearer of the earth.
भूदेव, m. (f. ī) an epithet of any Brāhmaṇ.
भूधर, m. any mountain : a kind of chemical or medical apparatus (a kind of sand-bath in which a covered crucible is placed, the fire being lighted above as well as below). [inflame.
भूनना, t. to parch, grill, broil, roast, toast, fry,
भूना, m. (f. ī) parched, broiled, roasted, grilled.
भूनाग, m. an earth-worm.
भूनामास, m. roasted meat.
भूनिम्ब, m. a certain plant (*Gentiana (cherayta)*.
भूनी, f. (m. भूना) roasted, etc.
भून्दरी, f. land given rent-free to village servants.
भूना = भूनना, *q.v.*
भूप, m. an epithet of any king, sovereign, prince, *rājā*, or landlord ; *lit.* a guardian, protector, nourisher or cherisher of the world or of the land.
भूपविमान, m. the carriage of a monarch.
भूपति, m. (f. patnī) } = भूप, *q.v.*
भूपाल, m. (f. ī) } = भूप, *q.v.*
भूपालक, m. (f. ikā) } = भूप, *q.v.*
भूपाली, f. a certain musical mode (*rāgiṇī*).
भूपावमान, m. disrespect of a monarch.
भूपृष्ठ, m. the back (*i.e.* the surface) of the earth.
भूभंग, *more prop.* भ्रूभंग, *q.v.*
भूभल, m. hot ashes, embers.

भूभार, *m.* the burden of the world (as sustained by Vishṇu through incarnation).

भूम, *a contraction of* **भूमि**, *q.v.*

भूमण्डल, *m.* the terrestrial globe, the earth.

भूमध्यस्थ, situated in the middle of the earth or in the centre of the world.

भूमध्यस्थसागर, *m. pr. n.* the Mediterranean Sea.

भूमय, *m.* (*f.* ī) made of earth, abounding in earth, terrene.

भूमयाल, *m.* one's native country, native place, home: a native of a place, an inhabitant.

भूमयी, *f. pr. n.* an epithet of *Chhāyā* (or shadow personified) the wife of the sun.

भूमि, *f.* the earth, the world; land, soil, earth, mould, ground; place, site; estate, domain; (in Geom.) the base of any plane figure: in the ingenious system of reckoning by symbols adopted by Hindoos in their poetry, this word is a symbol for 1 (*one*).

भूमिकम्प, *m.* an earthquake.

भूमिचम्पक = **भूंचम्पा**, *q.v.*

भूमिचाल, *f.* the motion or course of the earth; [earthquake.

भूमिज, *m. pr. n.* (1) of the planet Mars (2) of hell; a certain low caste of Hindoos: *lit. m.* (*f.* ā) earthborn, *i. e.* born of the earth, sprung from the ground, born on the earth.

भूमिजम्बु, *m.* (and *f.* kā) a certain tree (*Premna herbacea*).

भूमिजा, *f.* an epithet of Sītā.

भूमिदान, *m.* a donation of landed property.

भूमिदोल, *m.* a trembling or shaking of the earth, [earthquake.

भूमिनाग (*Rām.*) = **पृथिवीपरके सांप**.

भूमिप, *m.* an epithet of any king, sovereign, or prince; *lit.* a guardian or cherisher of the earth.

भूमिपति, *m.* (*f.* patnī) }
भूमिपाल, *m.* (*f.* ī) } = **भूमिप**, *q.v.*
भूमिपालक, *m.* (*f.* ikā) }

भूमियां, *m.* a land-holder, landlord, zamīndār.

भूमियापति, *m.* (*f.* patnī) = **भूमियां**, *q.v.*

भूमियाल, accomplished, proficient.

भूमियावत, *f.* a general plundering.

भूमियावती, *m.* an insurgent chief.

भूमी, *more prop.* **भूमि**, *q.v.*

भूमीदार, *m.* a landholder, headman or chief.

भूमीदाहा, being burnt or reduced to earth (said [of corpses).

भूमें (see **भू**) = **पृथ्वीमें**.

भूम्भाई, *m.* a man invested by a proprietor with a portion of land which he must not dispose of to others.

भूयः, further, more; again, repeatedly; afterwards.

भूयन, *m.* a chief holding by military service; the headman of a village.

भूयात्रा, *f.* the tour of the world; a wandering about [without any definite purpose.

भूयी = **भूयन**, *q.v.*

भूयोभूयः, again and again, repeatedly.

भूर, 1, a contraction of **भूरि**, *q.v.*: 2, the earth: the word forms part of the mystical triverbial expression **भूर भवः स्वर**: 3, *f.* alms, charity: a fountain, spring. — *bānṭnā*, to give alms to a numerous assembly of the poor.

भूरज; see **भुरज**.

भूरवन्ती, *f.* a proper name of females.

भूरश्रेण, *m. pr. n.* a certain ancient Hindoo king.

भूरा, 1, *m.* (*f.* ī) fair, auburn, or brownish (said of hair): 2, a certain ceremony performed on the third day after marriage: land belonging to a village furthest from the inhabitants.

भूरि, 1, *adj.* much, many: 2, *adv.* much, exceedingly, frequently, repeatedly: 3, *m.* a day: gold: 4, *m.* an epithet (1) of Brahmā (2) of Vishṇu (3) of Shiv.

भूरिधामन, splendid, bright, illustrious.

भूरिलाभ, *m.* great gain: *lit.* very profitable or beneficial.

भूरिश्रवा, *m. pr. n.* a son of Somdatt.

भूरी, *f.* light sandy soil.

भूरुण्डी, *f.* a species of sun-flower (*Heliotropum Indicum*).

भूर्ज, *m.* a kind of birch-tree (*Betula bhūrja*), commonly called *bhoj* or *bhojpath*, which grows in the snowy mountains.

भूर्जतरु (*Rām.*) = **भूर्ज**, *q.v.*

भूर्जपत्र, *m.* (see **भूर्ज**) the leaf and the bark of the *bhūrj*-tree (which are used for writing on, and also in the manufacture of *hukkā*-snakes).

भूर्भि, *f.* }
भूर्लोक, *m.* } = **भूलोक**, *q.v.*

भूल, *f.* forgetfulness; mistake, error, miss, blunder.

भूलता, *f.* a worm, earth-worm.

भूलना, *n.* to be forgotten: to be misled, be deceived: *a. int.* to forget, err, stray, mistake, blunder: *t.* to miss, to omit, to forget (with acc. of the object).

भूलाना, *more prop.* **भुलाना**, *q.v.*

भूलाबिसरा, *m.* (*f.* ī) a person who calls on another in consequence of some accident, etc. and not for the express purpose of paying a visit: *adj.* missing the road, astray, wandering.

भूलाभटका, *m.* (*f.* ī) = **भूलाबिसरा**, *q.v.*

भूलावनों in Braj = **भुलाना**, *q.v.*

भूलि = **भूल गया** (**भूलना**): see **कृ**, 7.

भूलोक, *m.* the earth, the habitation of mortals.

भूवृत्त, *m.* the equator.

भूषण, *m.* an adorning or decorating; ornament, jewel, dress, decoration, embellishment.

भूषित, *m.* (*f.* ā) adorned, decorated, bejewelled, bedecked, dressed.

भूस, *m.* 1, = **भूसा**, *q.v.*: 2, mouldiness, mould.

भूसना; see **भूंसना**.

भूसरा, a certain inferior kind of wheat.

भूसावन, *m.* a tax on boats freighted with grain.

भूसा, *m.* stalks chopped up and given as food to animals, straw, chaff.

भूसी, *f.* husk of grain, chaff, bran.

भूसुर, *m.* (*f.* ā *or* ī) an epithet of any Brāhmaṇ.

भूसेहरा, *more com.* **भुसेहरा**, *q.v.*

भूसौरी, *f.* }
भूसौला, *m.* } = भुसौरा, *q.v.*

भूस्तृण, *m.* a certain fragrant grass (*Andropogon schœnanthus*).

भूस्वर्ग, *m.* an epithet of the mountain Sumeru.

भूस्वामी, *m.* (*f.* inī) a proprietor of land.

भृंग, 1, *m.* (*f.* ī) a large black bee: the fork-tailed shrike (*Lanius cœrulescens* or *Corvus balicassius*): 2, *m.* a golden vase: a libertine: woody cassia: a certain plant (*Verbesina prostrata*).

भृंगक, *m.* a species of shrike (*Lanius Malabaricus*).

भृंगरजाः, *m.* 1, = भृंगक, *q. v.*: 2, a certain medicinal herb or spreading shrub (*Eclipta prostrata* or *Verbesina prostrata* or *Verbesina scandens* or *Verbesina calendulacca*).

भृंगराज }
भृंगराजा } = भृंगरजाः, *q. v.*

भृंगार, *m.* a kind of golden vase used at royal ceremonials: gold: cloves: a certain plant (*Verbesina calendulacca*).

भृंगारी, *f.* a cricket.

भृंगी, *f.* (*m.* भृंग) a large black bee; a kind of wasp (*Vespa solitaria*).

भृंगीफल, *m.* the hog-plum.

भृकुंश }
भृकुंस } = भूकुंस, *q. v.*

भृकुटि }
भृकुटी } = भ्रकुटी, *q. v.*

भृगु, 1, *m.* a cliff, mountain, precipice, table-land: 2, *m. pr. n.* (1) of one of the ten Mahārshis, or primeval sages (2) of Jamadagni (3) of Shiv (4) of Shukra (5) of the descendants of Bhṛigu.

भृगुटी, a corruption of भ्रंकुटी, *q. v.*

भृगुनाथ, *m.* an epithet of Parashurām.

भृगुलता, *f. pr. n.* the mark made by Kṛishṇ on on his own breast to shew the place where Bhṛigu kicked him.

भृगुवंशी, *m.* a certain tribe of Rājpūts: *lit.* descended from Bhṛigu.

भृत, *m.* (*f.* ā) = भृत्य, *q.v.*: used as the latter element in compound epithets, in the sense of bearing, supporting, carrying, nourishing.

भृति, *f.* nourishment, maintenance; wages, hire; service; capital, principal.

भृत्य, *m.* (*f.* ā) a hired labourer, servant, slave, dependent.

भृत्यत्व, *m.* (*f.* tā) service, servitude, slavery, dependence.

भृत्या, *f.* maintenance, support; hire, wages.

भृष्ट, *m.* (*f.* ā) baked, fried, parched.

भे, (*Rām.*) = भए, *q. v.*

भेई, *f.* (*m.* भेया) wet, moist.

भेउ }
भेऊ } *in Braj* = (1) भेघ (2) भेद (3) भया, *qq. v.*

भें, 1, *a dialectic form of* भूमि, *q. v.*: 2, the bleating of sheep. *Bheṅ bheṅ k.* to bleat (as sheep).

भेंगा, *m.* (*f* ī) squint-eyed.

भेंट, भेंड़; for words beginning thus, see under the corresponding forms भेयट, भेयड.

भेंस, *f.* (*m.* भेंसा) *more prop.* भैंस, *q. v.*

भेक, 1, *m.* a cloud: 2, *m.* (*f.* ī) a frog, toad.

भेकी, *f.* 1, (*m.* भेक) a female frog or toad: 2, (dim. of भेक) a small frog or toad: 3, a kind of creeping plant (*Hydrocotyle Asiatica*).

भेख, a colloquial form of भेष, *q. v.*

भेज, rent, an instalment.

भेजना, *t.* to send, to transmit: to utter, ejaculate.

भेजबरार, *m.* a kind of complex tenure.

भेजवाना, *more com.* भिजवाना, *q. v.*

भेजा, 1, *m.* the brain: 2, *m.* (*f.* ī) sent.

भेट, *f.* an interview, meeting, visit; a present to a superior on the occasion of a visit. — *k.* (with abl. of the object) to hold an interview with, pay a visit to.

भेटन, *m.* the act of meeting, the having an interview.

भेटना, *t.* to meet, visit, have an interview, join company; to make a present to a superior.

भेटपत्र, *m.* a deed of gift on the occasion of the *bheṭ-bakrā*.

भेटबकरा, *m.* a present made to a newly-appointed governor by the villagers.

भेटा, 1, the brinjal: 2, *m.* (*f.* ī) met (भेटना).

भेटी, *f.* a present made to a superior on the occasion of an interview: a stalk, stem.

भेटू, *m.* a stalk, stem.

भेड़, *m.* (*f.* ī) a ram, sheep. —*kā gosht*, *m.* mutton.

भेड़क, *m.* (*f.* ā, ikā, ī) a ram, sheep.

भेड़ना, *t.* to shut, to close.

भेड़शाला, *f.* a sheepfold, pen.

भेड़ा, 1, *more prop.* भड़िया, *q. v.*: 2, *m.* (*f.* i) a ram, sheep.

भेड़िया = (1) भेड़िया (2) भेड़. See बूआ.

भेड़िया, *m.* a wolf.

भेड़ियाधसान, *m.* a multitude crowded together like sheep in a pen; the act of following the example of another.

भेड़ी, *f.* (*m.* भेड़) a sheep, ewe.

भेयट, *more prop.* भेट, *q. v.*

भेयटना, *more prop.* भेटना, *q. v.*

भेयटमुलाक़ात, *f.* a meeting, interview.

भेयटा, *more prop.* भेट, *q. v.*

भेयड, *m.* a kind of reed or aquatic plant (*Æschynomene paludosa*) whose stem resembles pith and is exceedingly light. A variety of articles are made of this substance, and, being a non-conductor, it is admirably adapted for making hats, covers for wine-bottles which have been cooled with ice, etc. This substance, when cut in very thin plates, is commonly called "Rice-paper." The plant is also called *sholā*.

भेयडक; see (1) भेड़क (2) भेयडक.

भेयडी, *f.* a certain nutritious culinary vegetable (*Hibiscus esculentus*).

भेता, *m.* (*f.* trī) one who causes a division or sows dissension, a seditious or factious person, a traitor: *lit.* adj. dividing, breaking, severing.

भेतृ, *m.* (*f.* trī) = भेता, *q. v.*

भेद, *m.* a breaking, separation, disunion, difference, disagreement; betrayal ; a chasm, cleft, fissure; kind, sort, species: secrecy, mystery, a secret. — *lenā*, to spy, pry into, worm oneself into another's confidence, to sound. *Jaṛkā* —, *m.* the nature, quality, or essence of a thing.

भेदक, *m.* (*f.* ikā) *adj.* breaking, breaking up or open, dividing, causing disunion.

भेदकर. *m.* (*f.* ī) = **भेदक**, *q.v.*

भेदकिया, *m.* a scout, spy, secret-keeper, confidant.

भेदिका, *f.* (*m.* **भेदक**) a female mischief-maker, etc.

भेदित, *m.* (*f.* ā) divided, separated, severed.

भेदिया, *m.* a scout, spy, secret-keeper, confidant.

भेदी, 1, *m.* (*f.* inī) = **भेदक**, *q.v.*: 2, *m.* (*f.* in *or* inī) = **भेदिया**, *q.v.*: 3, *m.* (*f.* inī) intelligent, knowing: 4, *m.* the ratan.

भेदू, *m. f.* one who is acquainted with the secrets of others, a secret-keeper, confidant.

भेद्य, requiring to be separated or distinguished, separable: requiring to be kept secret, worthy of secrecy.

भेना, *f.* a sister.

भेया, (from **भेवना**) *m.* (*f.* **भेई**) wet, moist.

भेर, *f.* a contraction of **भेरि**, *q.v.*

भेरि, *f.* a kind of musical instrument, a kind of pipe, a kettle-drum.

भेरी, 1, *f.* = **भेरि**, *q.v.* : 2, *m.* (*f.* iṇī) a piper.

भेल (*dialectic*) = **भया**, *q.v.*

भेलसेल, *m.* alloy of metal (in coinage, etc.).

भेला, *m.* the marking-nut plant (*Semicarpus anacardium*).

भेली, *f.* a large lump of coarse sugar (*guṛ*) generally consisting of five or six sérs.

भेव, *m.* 1, (*Rām.*) = **भेद**, *q.v.*: 2, (**भाव**) state or condition of being, innate property, nature, disposition.

भेवना (*Rām.*) = **भिगोना**, *q.v.*

भेवा, 1, (*poet.*) = **भेव** = **भेद**, *q.v.*: 2, *m.* (*f.* ī) wet, moist.

भेष, *m.* disguise, feigned appearance, assumed likeness, counterfeit dress, guise, garb.

भेषज, *m.* a medicament, drug, remedy ; a species of fennel (*Nigella Indica*).

भेषधारी, *m.* (*f.* iṇī) a disguised or hypocritical person : lit. *adj.* putting on a disguise, assuming an appearance.

भेस (*colloquial*) = (1) **भेष** (2) **भैंस**, *qq.v.*

भै, *more prop.* (1) **भई** (2) **भय** (3) **भव** (4) **भाई**, *qq.v.*

भैअंकर, a corrupt spelling of **भयंकर**, *q.v.*

भैअंश, a corrupt spelling of **भाईअंश**, *q.v.*

भैआ, *more prop.* (1) **भया** (2) **भैया**, *qq.v.*

भैआतुर, a corrupt spelling of **भयातुर**, *q.v.*

भैआनक, a corrupt spelling of **भयानक**, *q.v.*

भैऊ; see (1) **भय** (2) **भया** (3) **भाई** (4) **भेव** (5) **भयहू**.

भैंस, *f.* (pl. **भैंसें**) a female buffalo.

भैंसा, *m.* (pl. **भैंसे**) a male buffalo.

भैंसादाद, *m.* a kind of ringworm.

भैंसिया, a dialectic form of **भैंस**, *q.v.*

भैंसियादाद, *m.* a kind of ringworm.

भैंसी (a mistaken fem. of **भैंसा**) = **भैंस**, *q.v.*

भैंसोन्धा, *m.* a tax or cess for the privilege of grazing buffaloes.

भैक्ष, 1, *m.* (*f.* ī) living by alms, subsisting by charity: 2, *m.* asking alms; begging, mendicity: 3, *m.* anything obtained by begging, begged food, charity, alms.

भैचक. a corrupt spelling of **भयचक**, *q.v.*

भैजनीं in Braj = **भेजना**, *q.v.*

भैपंसी, a corrupt spelling of **भाईपंसी**, *q.v.*

भैबट, paying and receiving on the footing of a member of some fraternity.

भैमान, a corrupt spelling of **भयमान**, *q.v.*

भैमी, *f.* (patronym.) Damayantī, daughter of Bhīm: the eleventh day of the bright half of the month Māgh ; a festival on that day.

भैयल (*dialectic*) = **भया**, *q.v.*

भैया (*very com.*) = (1) **भाइया** (2) **भाई**, *qq.v.*

भैयाचारा = **भाईचारा**, *q.v.*

भैयापत }
भैयापा } *m.* brotherhood, friendship.

भैयाबापट, *m.* = **भाईबापट**, *q.v.*

भैरव, 1, *m.* (*f.* ī) formidable, horrid, terrific, horrible, miserable : 2, *m.* horror, terror, formidableness, horribleness, dreadfulness ; abhorrence, hatred : 3, *m. pr. n.* (1) an epithet of Shiv; but more especially an inferior manifestation of that deity : of these, eight are reckoned, *viz.* Asitang, Ruru, Chand, Krodh, Unmatt, Kupati, Bishān, and Sanghār, all of which allude to terrific properties of mind or body (2) of a certain river (3) of a certain musical mode (*rāg*) which is calculated to excite emotions of terror : it is sung at early dawn in autumn, and is represented in pictures by Mahādev with the Ganges flowing from the hair of his head and this musical deity (*rāg*) issuing from his mouth.

भैरवता, *f.* }
भैरवत्व, *m.* } = **भैरव**, 2, *q.v.*

भैरवी, *f.* (*m.* **भैरव**) an epithet of Durgā ; a certain musical mode (*rāgiṇi*) the wife of *Bhairoṅ rāg*.

भैरारी, *f.* a certain musical mode (*rāgiṇī*).

भैरी, a certain species of falcon.

भैरो }
भैरों } corrupt spellings of **भैरव**, *q.v.*

भैल, 1, (*dialectic*) = **भया**, *q.v.*: 2, *more prop.* **बैल**, *q.v.*

भैवाद, paying and receiving on the footing of one of some brotherhood or fraternity.

भैहिस्सा, *f.* the shares of a brotherhood (especially in the lands of a township).

भैहू }
भैहूं } = **भयहू**, *q.v.*

भो, a Sanskrit interjection or vocative particle generally translatable by 'O!' 'Ho there!' 'Hallo!' 'Ah!' 'Alas!'

भोइनी, *f.* (*m.* **भोई**) a female bearer, the wife of a chair-porter, etc.

भोइल (*dialectic*) = **भया**, *q.v.*

भोई, *m.* (*f.* inī) a chair-porter, palkee-bearer, a bearer, "boy": a white cat : the head of a Gond village.

भोएं, *more prop.* **भौंएं**, *q.v.*

भों, 1, = **भौं**, 2, *q.v.*: 2, the sound of a trumpet or clarion.

भोंय / **भोंयं** } *more prop.* **भोंएं**, *q.v.*

भोंक, *m.* a stab, thrust.

भोंकड़ा, *m.* (*f.* ī) very fat.

भोंकना, *t.* to thrust, drive (as a nail).

भोंकस, *m.* a kind of wizard who preys upon persons till he brings them to the grave, a sorcerer, magician.

भोंकाभोंकी, *f.* thrusting and stabbing.

भोंघरा, *m.* an underground vault, cavern, or cellar.

भोंचाल, a colloquial form of **भुमिचाल**, *q.v.*

भोंड, भोंथ, भोंद, भोंप; for all words beginning with either of these elements, see under the corresponding forms **भोण्ड, भोन्थ, भोन्द, भोम्प**.

भोंह (pl. **भोंहें**) = **भों**, 2, *q.v.*

भोकना; see (1) **भोंकना** (2) **भूकना** (3) **भोखना**.

भोकस = **भोंकस**, *q.v.*

भोक्ता, *m.* (*f.* **भोक्त्री**) the enjoyer, or agent in fruition; an eater; one who consumes, enjoys, or suffers; *hence*, a husband, a possessor, the soul.

भोखना = **भोंखना**, *q.v.*

भोग, *m.* an affection generally; (in particular) possession, enjoyment, pleasure, satisfaction; (also) suffering, passion: dressed food offered to an idol: eating, feasting, food; nourishing, cherishing: a snake, a snake's body, a snake's expanded hood: an army in column: abuse; rudeness: wealth: hire, the hire of dancing-girls: (in Arithm.) the numerator of a fraction. — *k.* to experience, undergo, to enjoy, to suffer; to hold sensual intercourse with (abl.).

भोगत = **भोगता है**, etc. (**भोगना**): see **त**, 5.

भोगकर, *m.* (*f.* ī) one who affords enjoyment.

भोगदार, a person who is in the possession or enjoyment of any property.

भोगन, 1, a Braj pl. of **भोग**, *q.v.*: 2, see **भोगना**.

भोगबन्धक, *m.* a bond granting the use of a pledged article; mortgage.

भोगना, *a. int.* to experience, undergo, enjoy, suffer; to live stoically, take in with indifference pleasure and pain as they may chance to come.

भोगवती, *f.* (*m.* **भोगवन्त**) a female who yields enjoyment: *pr. n.* (1) of the capital of the serpent-race (2) of the Ganges of the lower regions.

भोगवन्त, *m.* (*f.* vatī) 1, = **भोगी**, *q.v.*: 2, one who yields enjoyment: a snake: *lit.* yielding enjoyment, delightsome.

भोगविलास, *m.* luxurious living, sensual pleasure, amorous enjoyment. [luxuriousness or pleasure.

भोगविलासी, *m.* (*f.* inī) one who is abandoned to

भोगा, *m.* deception, imposition, fraud, trick, deceit, illusion, treachery, roguery, cheating.

भोगाधिकार, *m.* the possession of the usufruct of mortgaged or pledged property.

भोगाधिकारी, *m.* (*f.* iṇī) the possessor of the usufruct of mortgaged or pledged property.

भोगावति / **भोगावती** } (*Rām.*) = **भोगवती**, *q.v.*

भोगिनी, *f.* (*m.* **भोगी**) a royal concubine; a female enjoyer: *pr. n.* the capital of the serpents.

भोगी, *m.* (*f.* inī) the person who enjoys or possesses anything, one who makes mere pleasure a pursuit: a snake: a king: the head-man of a village: a barber: *lit.* subject to affections generally, partaking in, possessing, suffering, enjoying, jovial, jolly.

भोगोत्र, *m.* a grant of revenue for the use or enjoyment of an individual, especially of a Brāhmaṇ or religious person.

भोग्य, *m.* (*f.* ā) any object of fruition; wealth: *lit.* adj. to be possessed, to be participated in, to be experienced, to be endured, to be enjoyed. [his seed.

भोघिया, *f.* a small basket in which a sower carries

भोज, *m.* eating; a feast, meal, banquet: a cowherd: *pr. n.* (1) of the country of Patna and Bhāgalpur (2) of a sovereign of Ujjain, who is celebrated in the *Singhāsan-batīsī*: he is supposed to have flourished about the end of the 10th century, and is celebrated as a patron of philosophers and learned men: the nine gems or poets (**नवरत्न**) are often, but erroneously, ascribed to his era.

भोजकट, *m. pr. n.* = **भोजपुर**, *q.v.*

भोजन, *m.* enjoying; eating; food, victuals, a meal.

भोजनख़र्च, *m.* table-expenses. [—*k.* to eat food.

भोजनख़ानो / **भोजनशाला** } *f.* a dining-hall.

भोजनचतुर, *m.* (*f.* ā) one who is a skilful judge of

भोजनीय, *m.* (*f.* ā) = **भोज्य**, *q.v.* [food.

भोजपत्र, a colloquial form of **भूर्जपत्र**, *q.v.*

भोजपुर, *m. pr n.* the country of Bhoj (the vicinity of Patna, Bhāgalpur, and Chhaprā).

भोजपुरी, appertaining to Bhojpur: hence (1) *f.* the dialect of Hindee spoken in Bhojpur (2) *m.* (*f.* iṇī) an inhabitant of Bhojpur.

भोजवंश, *m.* a certain branch of the lunar race.

भोजवंशी, *m.* (*f.* inī) a member of the Bhojvaṅsh.

भोजाइ, *more com.* **भोजाई**, *q.v.*

भोज्य, *m.* (*f.* ā) anything eatable or enjoyable; food: *lit.* suitable or proper to be eaten, edible.

भोज्यवस्तु, *m.* anything eatable, food.

भोट, *m.* 1, *pr. n.* a certain country (believed to be Bhootān): 2, cloth or clothing from Bhoṭ.

भोटांग, *m. pr. n.* the country of Bhootān.

भोटिया, *m.* a native of Bhoṭ.

भोडल, *m* talc, mica.

भोण्डा, *m.* (*f.* ī) ill-shaped, misshapen, uncouth, ugly; useless; unlucky, bad: austere, morose, dismal.

भोता, *m.* (*f.* ī) blunt, dull, obtuse.

भोती, *f.* labour, toil, work.

भोतीहार, *m.* (*f.* ī) a labourer.

भोन्थरा / **भोन्था** } *m.* (*f.* ī) = **भोता**, *q.v.*

भोन्दना, *t.* to deceive, impose upon, take in.

भोन्दू, *m.* or *f.* a simpleton, etc.: *lit.* silly, quiet, mild, artless, simple: artful, deceitful.

भोपा, *m.* a kind of fakeer, a magician.

भोमीरा, *f.* coral.

भोम्प / भोम्पू } a wind instrument, a horn.

भोर, 1, in Chand = भुरा, *q.v.*: 2, *f.* dawn of day, the early morning. — *honā*, to be finished, be terminated.

भोरको, *adj.* at early morning, at dawn.

भोरना, a poet. form of भूलना, *q.v.*

भोरवौं ; see (1) भोरना (2) भोरको (3) भूलना.

भोरा, 1, a poet. form of भूला (भूलना): 2, *m.* (*f.* ī) a corruption of भोला, *q.v.*

भोरी, *f.* (*m.* भोरा) *more prop.* भोली, *q.v.*

भोरे (*Rām.*) = भूलके भी (भोरना).

भोला, *m.* (*f.* ī) simple, artless, undesigning, innocent, harmless, meek: an epithet of Shiv.

भोलानाथ, *m.* an epithet of Mahādev.

भोलापन, *m.* artlessness, undesigningness, simplicity, innocence, harmlessness, meekness.

भोली, *f.* (*m.* भोला) an artless female.

भोलीबातें, *f.* innocent artless prattle.

भोसड़ा, *m.* / भोसड़ी, *f.* / भोसा, *m.* } vulva valde magna.

भौ, 1, a provincial form of बहु, *q.v.*: 2, in Braj = (1) भय (2) भया (3) भव, *qq.v.*: 3, = भौं, 2, *q.v.*

भौएं (pl. of भौ, 3) = भौंहें, *q.v.*

भौं, *f.* 1, a colloquialism for भूमि, *q.v.*: 2, (from भ्रू) the eyebrow. — *ṭeṛhī k.*, to crook the eyebrows, scowl, frown, to browbeat, to look angrily at (raising the eyebrows). — *tānnā*, to knit the eyebrows.

भौंएं, *f.* (pl. of भौं) the eyebrows.

भौंकना, *a. int.* to bark: *met.* to talk foolishly.

भौंकमान, *f.* an arched eyebrow.

भौंचाल, a colloquial form of भूमिचाल, *q.v.*

भौंयें, *f.* (pl. of भौं, 2) the eyebrows.

भौंर, *m.* a whirlpool, eddy, vortex.

भौंरकली = भंवरकली, *q.v.*

भौंरा, *m.* (*f.* ī) a large black bee (enamoured of the lotus): a whirlpool, gulf, eddy, vortex: *met.* dilemma.

भौंरियाना, *t.* to whirl, turn.

भौंरी, *f.* (*m.* भौंरा) a large black female bee: feathered hair: a kind of defect in horses.

भौंवरकली = भंवरकली, *q.v.*

भौंसना, *a. int.* to bark (said of dogs, etc.).

भौंह (pl. भौंहें) = भौं, 2, *q.v.*

भौंहैं, *f.* (Braj pl. of भौंह) the eyebrows.

भौचक (inelegant) = भचक, *q.v.*

भौजाई, *f.* (from भ्रातृजाया) a sister-in-law (brother's wife).

भौजी = भौजाई, *q.v.*

भौतिक, *m.* an epithet of Shiv: *lit.* (1) appertaining to the corporeal elements, elemental (2) appertaining to the goblins or evil spirits (3) existing.

भौतिकमठ, *m.* a college of monks, a monastery, convent.

भौतिकविद्या, *f.* (spirit-science, *i.e.*) witchcraft, sorcery.

भौतिकसृष्टि, *f.* the creation of beings, corporeal creation.

भौन ; see (1) भौं (2) भौं (3) भवन (4) भौम.

भौना, *a. int.* to revolve.

भौनाई, *m.* a brother-in-law (sister's husband).

भौनास, *m.* a large and strong post driven into the ground for chaining elephants to.

भौम, *m.* 1, *pr. n.* (1) of the planet Mars (2) of hell: 2, ambergris: *lit.* appertaining to the earth or to the ground, terrestrial: appertaining to the planet Mars.

भौमवार, *m.* Tuesday; *lit.* Mars' day.

भौमासुर, *m. pr. n.* a certain demon slain by Krishṇ.

भौमी, *f.* (*m.* भौम) earthly, etc.: an epithet of Sītā.

भौमीं / भौयों } see *s.v.* भौ.

भौर (*colloquial*) = भंवर, *q.v.*

भौरा ; see भूरा and भौंरा.

भौला, *m.* (*f.* ī) *more com.* भोला, *q.v.*

भौसागर (*colloquial*) = भवसागर, *q.v.*

भ्यासना, *more prop.* अभ्यासना, *q.v.*

भ्रंश, *m.* a falling off, falling from, falling off, declining from a height or from propriety, fall from virtue, abandoning, dropping, desertion, overthrow, destruction, ruin.

भ्रकुंश / भ्रकुंस } = भ्रूकुंस, *q.v.*

भ्रकुटी, *f.* the eyebrow; a contraction of the eyebrows, an angry look, a frown, a scowl.

भ्रम, *m.* a moving about, whirling, erring, straying, roaming, wandering, error, misapprehension; blunder, mistake, slip, doubt, suspicion, apprehension, perplexity; a whirlwind, whirlpool, lathe, potter's wheel.

भ्रमण, *m.* a roaming or wandering about, whirling, turn around, perambulation; giddiness; the falling into error or mistake.

भ्रमणकारी, *m.* (*f.* iṇī) a wanderer.

भ्रमणी, *f.* a sort of game performed by women for the amusement of a husband or lover.

भ्रमत, *adj.* whirling about, going around, revolving; wandering, roaming, erring.

भ्रमना, *a. int.* to roam, wander, stray, err.

भ्रमर, *m.* (*f.* ī) a large black bee: a lover, gallant: giddiness, vertigo, epilepsy.

भ्रमरी, *f.* a bee: two plants (1) *Jatuka* (2) *Putra-dātrī*.

भ्रमवाला, *m.* (*f.* ī) mixed with error.

भ्रमाना, *t.* to cause to stray, cause to err, to mislead, misguide, deceive.

भ्रमि, *f.* a going around, whirling about; *hence*, a lathe, whirlwind, whirlpool, vertigo, stupor, error, blunder, mistake, forgetfulness, a sceptic.

भ्रमित, *m.* (*f.* ā) / भ्रमी, *m.* (*f.* iṇī) } = भ्रमत, *q.v.*

भ्रष्ट, *m.* (*f.* ā) a fallen one, etc.: *lit.* fallen, fallen from virtue, depraved, debased, vicious, polluted, defiled, abominable, dissolute.

भ्रष्टत्व, *m.* (*f.* tā) a fallen condition, degradation, depravity, corruptness, dissoluteness.

भ्रष्टपन / **भ्रष्टपना** / **भ्रष्टपा** } = भ्रष्टत्व, *q. v.*

भ्रष्टराज्य, deprived of empire, deposed.

भ्रष्टा, *f.* (*m.* भ्रष्ट) a fallen female, unchaste woman, adulteress, harlot.

भ्रष्टाचरण, *m.* depraved behaviour.

भ्राजना (*Rām.*) = (1) शोभना (2) विराजना, *qq. v.*

भ्राजी, *m.* (*f.* ī) shining, splendid.

भ्रात (*contraction*) = भ्राता, *q. v.*

भ्राता / **भ्रातृ** } *m.* a uterine brother.

भ्रातृक, appertaining to a brother, paternal.

भ्रातृवृद्धि, *f.* the wealth or prosperity of a brother.

भ्रात्रीय, *m.* (*f.* ā) a brother's child: *lit.* appertaining to a brother, fraternal.

भ्रान्त, *m.* (*f.* ā) whirled, revolved; gone astray, wandering, erring, fallen into error, mistaken.

भ्रान्ति, *f.* a whirling around; wandering, going about, error, mistake, blunder, ignorance.

भ्रान्तिमान, *m.* (*f.* matī) = भ्रान्त, *q. v.*

भ्रान्ती, a corruption of भ्रान्ति, *q.v.*

भ्रामक, *m.* (*f.* ikā) a deceiver, inveigler, cheat, swindler, rogue; a jackal; the load-stone; the sunflower (*Helianthus annuus*): *lit.* adj. causing to whirl, causing to err or mistake, misleading.

भ्रामर, *m.* a whirling around; a sort of load-stone; a kind of dance; epilepsy: honey: a village.

भ्रामरी, 1, *m.* (*f.* iṇī) an epileptic: *lit.* whirling; epileptic: made of honey: 2, *f.* an epithet of Durgā or Pārvatī; a female attendant on Durgā.

भ्रामिका, *f.* (*m.* भ्रामक) a female swindler, etc.

भ्रुकुंश / **भ्रुकुंस** } = भ्रूकुंस, *q. v.*

भ्रुकुटि / **भ्रुकुटी** } = भ्रकुटी, *q. v.*

भ्रू, *f.* an eye-brow. When required as the latter member of compound epithets, it takes the form भ्रुव.

भ्रूकुंस, *m.* an actor or dancer attired in the dress of a female.

भ्रूकुटि / **भ्रूकुटी** } = भ्रकुटी, *q.v.*

भ्रूण, *m.* the embryo or fœtus; an unborn child; pregnancy.

भ्रूणघ्न, *m.* (*f.* ī) one who occasions or procures abortion: *lit.* adj. fœtus-killing.

भ्रूणहत्या, *f.* murder of the fœtus, the causing or procuring abortion.

भ्रूणहन / **भ्रूणहा** } *m.* (*f.* भ्रूणघ्नी) = भ्रूणघ्न, *q. v.*

भ्रूभंग, *m.* a contraction of the eyebrows, an angry look, a frown.

भ्रूलता, *f.* the eyebrow compared to the gentle bends of a climbing-plant.

म

म (m) is the twenty-fifth consonant in the Hindee alphabet, and the fifth letter of the पवर्ग or labial class, of which it is the nasal. Its sound is identical with that of the English letter *m.* It is occasionally interchanged inaccurately (1) with व; *e. g.* मिन्ती, more properly विनति (2) with ब; *e.g.* नरबदा, more properly नर्मदा. In Prosody it signifies a molossus, or metrical foot of three long syllables. This letter is one of the epithets of Brahmā: see *s.v.* ओम. It is also an Unadi suffix by means of which a number of substantives and adjectives are derived from verbal roots; *e. g.* होम, from the Sanskrit root हु, offering. It occurs also as a Taddhita suffix, and is used to derive adjectives from a limited number of other words; *e. g.* मध्यम, from मध्य. Lastly, it is sometimes found as equivalent to में the sign of the locative case.

मअलूम, *more com.* मालूम, *q. v.*

मइके (Rām.) = नैहर, *q. v.*

मई, *f.* a harrow: a ladder.

मऊआ, *m.* an uncle (mother's brother).

मऊओ, *f.* an aunt (mother's sister).

मंका, *m.* a rosary, a bead of gold, silver, etc. (beads of glass are called *pot*): the vertebræ of the neck.— *dhalakna*, (*lit.* the bending of the neck) to be at the point of death.

मंग, *m.* the head of a boat.

मंगट, the wrist.

मंगटबन्ध, *m.* a wristband, wrist-ornament.

मंगटीका; see (1) मंगटबन्ध (2) मांगटीका.

मंगत / **मंगता** } *m.* a beggar; a borrower.

मंगती, *f.* an asking; a request.—*lagānā*, to perform the duty of a *sazāwal.*

मंगन, 1, *m.* an asking, dunning: 2, *f.* debt.

मंगना (contraction) = मांगना, *q. v.*

मंगनी, *f.* an asking in marriage, espousing, betrothal; a loan.—*denā*, to lend.

मंगरा, *m.* the ridge of a house.

मंगल, 1, *m.* (*f.* ā) lucky, auspicious, propitious, conferring happiness; beautiful, pleasing, agreeable, brave: 2, *m.* luckiness, auspiciousness, prosperity, welfare, happiness, bliss; rejoicing; a festival; burnt offering on various occasions of rejoicing; blessing: *pr. n.* (1) of the planet Mars, or its deified personification (2) of Tuesday. In the ingenious system of reckoning by symbols adopted by Hindoos in their poetry, this word is a symbol for 8.

मंगलकलस, *m.* a kind of vessel in which a light is placed when a wedding is about to take place. This vessel is held on the head by women (whose husbands are alive) who stand at the door of the bride to shew the light as a good omen.

मंगलकारक, *m.* (*f.* ikā) = मंगलकारी, *q. v.*

मंगलकारी, *m.* (*f.* inī) a beneficent person, etc: *lit.* causing or producing welfare, propitious, beneficial, beneficent, benevolent.

मंगलकोट, *m. pr. n.* a certain place.

मंगलकोटी, *f.* a kind of carpet made at Mangalkoṭ.

मंगलग्रह, *m.* an auspicious planet, a lucky star.

मंगलचार, *m.* an auspicious observance, pious custom or usage; festive decoration; festivity, rejoicing, congratulation: a song of congratulation, a marriage-song, epithalamium; worship or salutation to Ganesh at the commencement of an undertaking or of a treatise, *hence*, a preface, introduction.

मंगलजनक, *m.* (*f.* ikā) = मंगलकारी, *q. v.*

मंगलदायक, *m.* (*f.* ikā) a beneficent person, etc.: lit. *adj.* contributing to well-being, beneficial, beneficent, benevolent.

मंगलदायी, *m.* (*f.* inī) = मंगलदायक, *q. v.*

मंगलद्रव्य, *m.* the various subtances (such as flowers, fruits, etc.) which are offered as good omens.

मंगलरासी, *m. f.* good fortune, well-being, weal.

मंगलवादी, *m.* (*f.* inī) a proclaimer of good news, preacher of the Gospel: lit. *adj.* speaking to the profit of others or concerning their welfare, felicitating.

मंगलवार, *m.* Tuesday.

मंगलसमाचार, *m. pr. n.* the Gospel; *lit.* tidings of wellbeing, auspicious news.

मंगलसमाचारक, *m.* (*f.* ikā) = मंगलवादी, *q. v.*

मंगलसूत्र, *m.* the string used in the marriage ceremony among the Hindoos: *lit.* the lucky thread.

मंगला, *f.* (*m.* मंगल) an agreeable female, etc.: a. sort of bent grass (*Panicum dactylon*): an epithet of Uma the wife of Shiv.

मंगलाचरण, मंगलाचार } = मंगलचार, *q. v.*

मंगलामुख, *m.* (*f.* ī.) a musician, minstrel.

मंगलायतन, *m.* the abode of wellbeing. Often used as an epithet.

मंगली, triumphant, rejoicing. — *log*, persons employed on occasions of rejoicing.

मंगलोपकार, *m.* beneficence, benevolence.

मंगलोपकारक, *m.* (*f.* ikā) a benevolent person: *lit.* beneficent, benevolent; beneficial.

मंगलोपदेश, *m.* salutary instruction, the Gospel.

मंगलोपदेशक, *m.* (*f.* ikā) an imparter of salutary instruction, preacher of the Gospel.

मंगवाना, *t.* to cause to ask for, to send for, to procure.

मंगसिर, *m.* (from मार्गशिर) the eighth solar month of the Hindoos (Nov.-Dec.). According to some systems it is the first month.

मंगा, *part.* sending for, asking for. — *bhejnā*, to send for, ask for, call for, procure. — *lenā*, to ask for and bring, to procure.

मंगाना, *t.* to send for, ask for, call for, procure.

मंगाभेजना; see *s.v.* मंगा.

मंगाया, *m.* (*f.* °ई), मंगावा, *m.* (*f.* ī) } sent for, asked for, procured.

मंगूला, *m.* a small tassel.

मंगूस, *m.* (*more com.* नेवल) a mungoose.

मंगेतर, *m. f.* the party (male or female) to whom a man or a woman is betrothed.

मंच, *m.* a bedstead, bed; a scaffold, platform, chair, a sort of throne or chair of state, or the platform on which it is raised, the dais, a high place, alcove, altar, stage, an elevated shed raised on bamboos in a field where a watchman is stationed to protect the crops.

मंचा, *m.* a platform, stage, scaffold.

मंचूवा; see (1) मंच (2) मंचा (3) मचवा.

मंझ in Mārwāṛī (= मध्य) central.

मंजन, *m.* tooth-powder, dentifrice: the cleaning the person by wiping, bathing, or rubbing it with oil or fragrant unguents.

मंजना, *t.* to be scoured, be smoothed, be cleaned, be polished.

मंजर, *m.*, मंजरि, *f.* } = मंजरी, *q. v.*

मंजरी, *f.* a stalk, flower-spike, ear of corn; a sprout, shoot; a creeper; a cluster of flowers; blossom: a pearl: a certain musical mode (*rāgiṇī*).

मंजलता, *more prop.* मंजुलता, *q. v.*

मंजा, 1, *m.* a bedstead; a sort of throne or chair of state: a kind of religious ceremony (anointing the body with turmeric on certain festive occasions): any high place where one may escape from an inundation: a certain large species of grass (*Saccharum munja*): 2, *f.* any creeping-plant.

मंजाड़, मंजार } *m.* (*f.* ī) a cat.

मंजिर (*Rām.*) = मंजीर, *q. v.*

मंज़िल, *f.* a day's journey; a stage, caravansery, abode, habitation: rank, dignity: boundary; goal: a story or floor: deck of a ship.

मंजीठ, *more prop.* मजीठ, *q. v.*

मंजीर, *m.* any ornament for the feet or toes: a. a stick around which passes the string that works the stick of a churn.

मंजीरा, *m.* a kind of cymbal consisting of two small cups tied together with a string and played by striking the one against the other.

मंजु, *m. f.* beautiful, pleasant, agreeable, pleasing, good.

मंजुल, 1, *m.* (*f.* ā) beautiful, pleasing, agreeable: 2, *m.* a gallinule: a bower: a watercourse.

मंजुलता, *f.* (*m.* °त्व) beautifulness, agreeableness.

मंजून, *more prop.* मंजुल, *q. v.*

मंजूषा, *f.* a large basket; a receptacle.

मंजेखाना, *m.* the room in which a young person about to be married is seated for a certain number of days.

मंझ, मंझं } in Chand = मध्य, *q. v.*

मंझला, मंझारा } *m.* (*f.* ī) = मझला, *q. v.*

मंझारे, मंझिले } = मझिले, *q. v.*

मंझोला, *m.* (*f.* ī) = मझोला, *q. v.*

मंझोली = मझोली, *q. v.*

मंठ, मंड, मंढ, मंत, मंथ, मंद; for words beginning with either of these forms, see under the corresponding forms मण्ठ, मण्ड, मण्ढ, मन्त, मन्थ, मन्द.

मंडुआ = **मगडुआ**, *q. v.*

मंडुई = **मगडुई**, *q. v.*

मंढ़ी ; see **मगढी**.

मंसूवा, *more prop.* **मनसूबा**, *q.v.*

मंह, a corruption (1) of **महं** (2) of **मुहं**, *qq. v.*

मंहगा, *m.* (*f.* ī) *more prop.* **महंगा**, *q.v.*

मक (Rām.) = **बरु**, *q. v.*

मकई, *f.* Indian corn (*Zea mays*).

मकड़, *m.* (*f.* ī) a spider.

मकड़ा, 1, *m.* a kind of grain: 2, *m.* (*f.* ī) a spider.

मकड़ाना, *a. int.* to move by winding about, move crookedly ; to fidget : *met.* to waver, to counteract, to be averse, act contrary.

मकड़ी, *f.* (*m.* **मकड़ा**) a female spider. — *kā jālā*, *m* a spider's web; hence, *met.* anything very fine and slender. [fate, predestination.

मक़दूर, *m.* power, ability, capability ; possibility;

मक़बूल, agreeable, acceptable ; taking in good part, agreed on : *hence*, the elect, one of the faithful ; a mistress.

मकर, *m.* a certain marine monster usually confounded with the crocodile and shark, but properly a fabulous animal (as a fish it might be conjectured to be the horned shark, or the unicorn-fish ; but it is often drawn, as in the pictured signs of the Zodiac, with the head and fore-legs of an antelope and the body and tail of a fish : it is the emblem of the god of love) : the tenth sign of the Zodiac (Capricorn) represented by a water-animal with the body and tail of a fish and the neck and head of an antelope : a certain form of marching an army : one of Kuver's treasures.

मकरन्द, *m.* the nectar of any flower : a kind of jasmine (*Jasminum pubescens*) : the filament of the lotus : a fragrant kind of mango : the Indian cuckoo (*Kokilā*). [*veolens*).

मकरन्दवती, *f.* the trumpet-flower (*Bignonia sua-*

मकरमहीना, *m.* the Hindoo month of *Māgh*.

मकरसाई, *f.* a deceitful or cunning woman.

मकराकृत, *m.* (*f.* ā) shaped like the *makar*.

मकरी, 1, *f.* the wife of the fabulous monster called *makar* : 2, fraudulent, deceitful.

मकरोना, *t.* to wet (slightly).

मक़सद, *m.* desire, wish, purpose, design, meaning, intention, object, scope.

मकसिद (corruption) = **मक़सद**, *q. v.*

मकाई, *f.* Indian corn (*Zea mays*).

मकान, *m.* a place, station, situation, site, dwelling, room, abode, home.

मकाना ; see (1) **मकान** (2) **मखन** (3) **मखाना**.

मकानात, *m.* (pl. of **मकान**) places ; dignities, posts of honour. [tings or assemblies.

मक़ामात, *m.* sittings, conversations held at sit-

मकार, *m.* the letter **म**, or any symbol that may represent it.

मकोजारी, *f.* Indian corn (*Zea mays*).

मकु (Rām.) = **बरु**, *q. v.*

मकुट, *more com.* **मुकुट**, *q. v.*

मकुर, *more com.* **मुकुर**, *q. v.*

मकुल, *more com.* **मुकुल**, *q.v* [*nigrum ?*).

मको, *m.* a certain species of solanum (*Solanum*

मकोए, *m.* 1, = **मको**, *q. v.* : 2, sarsaparilla.

मकोड़ा / **मकौड़ा** } *m.* (*f.* ī) a large ant.

मक्खन, *m.* a butter.

मक्खी, *f.* a fly; the sight of a gun. — *uṛānā*, to flatter, to perform servile offices for anyone : to have ulcers on the body (so as to be constantly employed in driving away the flies from them) : to be a good marksman (so as to be able to hit a fly with a ball or arrow). — *jhalnā*, to have venereal ulcers. — *mārnā*, (*lit.* to kill flies; *hence*) to be unemployed, be idle, to trifle, to fool.

मक्खीचूस, *m.* a miser, niggard, skinflint.

मक्खीर in the hill dialect = honey.

मक्कार, *m.* (*f.* ā) a cheat, knave, impostor, feigner.

मक्कारी, *f.* fraud, imposture, cheating, roguery.

मक्र, *m.* hypocrisy : wrath : multitude.

मक्षिका / **मक्षीका** } *f.* a fly ; a bee.

मख, *m.* sacrifice, oblation : a warrior.

मखगुरु, *m.* the priest or preceptor who gives directions in the offering of sacrifices or oblations.

मखन, *m.* butter.

मखनचोर / **मखनलाल** } *m.* epithets of Krishṇ.

मखना, *m.* a kind of elephant which has no tusk ; a cock without spurs. [butter, a butterman.

मखनिया, *m.* a man who makes (or who sells)

मख़मल, *m.* velvet.

मख़मली, appertaining to velvet, made of velvet.

मख़रज, *m.* pronunciation.

मख़लूक़, (*pl.* āt) a created thing, creature : *lit.* created, formed, produced.

मखा, a poetical lengthening of **मख**, *q. v.*

मखान ; see (1) **मकान** (2) **मखन** (3) **मखाना**.

मखाना, *m.* a certain plant (*Euryalis ferox* or *Annesleia spinosa*).

मखारविन्द (corruption) = **मुखारविन्द**, *q. v.*

मख़ारिज, *m* (pl. of **मुख़रज**) disbursements, expens- [es, outlay.

मखी, *f.* a fly.

मखून, *m.* a bug, a flea.

मखूरा / **मखौड़ा** } *m.* any large ant.

मग, 1, *m.* (contr. of **मार्ग**) a road, path, way : 2, (contraction) = **मगध**, *q.v.* — *dekhnā*, to be on the look-out for, to expect, wait for. [gance, pride.

मग़ज़, *m.* brain, marrow ; kernel, pith : *met.* arro-

मग़ज़रोशन, *m.* ('brain-clearer,' *i. e.*) snuff.

मग़ज़ी, *f.* edging, border.

मगण, *m.* (in Pros.) a Molussus : see **म**.

मगध, *m. pr. n.* the country of south Bihār, including Patnā, Gayā, etc.: an inhabitant of that country: a bard whose peculiar province it is to sing the praises of a chief's ancestry in his presence; a family bard or minstrel.

मगधपति = **मगधेश्वर**, *q. v.*

मगधभाषा, *f. pr. n.* a certain Prākṛit dialect much used in Siam and Burmah, where it is called Pālik (Pālī ?).

मगधेश्वर, *m.* king of the Magadhas: an epithet (1) of Parantap (2) of Jarāsandh.

मगन, *m.* (*f.* ā) (colloquial) = **मग्न**, *q. v.*

मगनता, *f.* (*m.* °**त्व**) (colloquial) = **मग्नता**, *q. v.*

मगनी, *more prop.* **मंगनी**, *q. v.*

मगर, 1, (from **मकर**) *m.* (*f.* ī) an alligator, crocodile: 2, unless, perhaps, except, only, if it is not, moreover, but.

मगरचे, a corruption of **अगरचि**, *q. v.*

मगरमच्छ = **मगर**, 1, *q. v.*

मगरा, *m.* (*f.* ī) proud, haughty, presuming, arrogant, insolent; fastidious, cross, refractory, stubborn, obstinate, sulky, sullen, impatient.

मगराई, *f.* pride, haughtiness, arrogance, insolence, presumption, stubbornness, obstinacy, refractoriness.

मगरापन, *m.* / **मगराही**, *f.* } = **मगराई**, *q. v.*

मगरी, *f.* 1, (*m.* **मगर**) a female alligator: 2, (*m.* **मगरा**) a haughty or refractory female: 3, the flat roof of a house.

मग़रूर, proud, arrogant, haughty; fastidious: deceived, taken in; (in Law) a man who marries a woman under a misconception.

मग़रूरी, *f.* pride, arrogance.

मगरेला, *m.* a small blackish triangular pyramid-shaped seed (*Nigella Indica*) of a very pungent smell.

मगसरोशन, *more prop.* **मग़ज़रोशन**, *q. v.*

मगसिर = **मंगसिर**, *q. v.*

मगह, 1, see **मगध** and **मघ**; 2, in Chand = **मार्ग**, *q. v.*

मगही, *more prop.* **मघी**, *q. v.*

मगहिया, *more prop.* **मघया**, *q. v.*

मगाना, *more com.* **मंगाना**, *q. v.*

मगाही, *m.* a certain tribe of agriculturists in [Bihār.

मगु, emphat. of **मग**, *q. v.*: see **उ**, 9.

मगुरी, *f.* a certain fish (*Silurus pelorius* or *Macropteronatus magur*, Ham.).

मग्ग in Chand = **मार्ग**, *q. v.*

मग्न, *m.* (*f.* ā) plunged, immersed, dipped, sunk, drowned; immersed in joy, pleased, glad, happy, delighted, jovial, jolly; immersed in love, enamoured.

मग्नत्व, *m.* (*f.* tā) transport, delight, rapture, cheerfulness, vivacity, amusement, mirth, pleasure.

मग्सरोशन, *more prop.* **मग़ज़रोशन**, *q. v.*

मघ, *m. pr. n.* (1) of one of the divisions (*dwīp*) of the universe (2) of the country of the people called Mugs, *i. e.* the modern Arracan: a certain flower; a certain drug: power, wealth, pleasure.

मघन, fragrant, odoriferous. [caste of Brāhmaṇs.

मघया, *m.* an inhabitant of Magadh: *pr. n.* a certain

मघवन्, *m.* (*f.* vatī) a wealthy person: a sacrificer: one of the epithets of Indra.

मघवन्त / **मघवा** / **मघवान** } *m.* (*f.* vatī) = **मघवन्**, *q. v.*

मघा, *f. pr. n.* the tenth *Nakshatra* containing five stars (α [*Regulus*], γ, ζ, η, and ν [*Leonis*]) figured by a house: a species of grain.

मघी, 1, *m.* (*f.* inī) appertaining to Magadh: 2, *f.* [a species of grain.

मच, *f.* drowsiness, inattention, negligence, apathy: a standard for judging of the purity of gold.

मचक, *f.* pain in the joints.

मचकना, *n.* to have pain in the joints: *a. int.* to creak (said of a bedstead).

मचकाना, *a. int.* to wink.

मचना, *n.* to be perpetrated, be made, be committed, be stired up, be occasioned, be produced.

मचमच, an imitative sound.

मचमचाना, *a. int.* to creak (as a bedstead or any- [thing else heavily laden).

मचल = **मचला**, *q. v.*

मचलना, *n.* to be perverse, be refractory, be cross, [be disobedient.

मचलपन, *m.* = **मचलाई**, *q. v.*

मचला, *m.* (*f.* ī) perverse, refractory, disobedient, cross, restive, pert, obstinate, [crossness, pertness.

मचलाई, *f.* perverseness, obstinacy, disobedience,

मचलाना, *n.* to feel nausea, to be sick at the stomach: *a. int.* to feign ignorance.

मचलापन, *m.* / **मचलाहट**, *f.* } = **मचलाई**, *q. v.*

मचलाहा, *m.* (*f.* ī) squeamish, stubborn, cross.

मचली, 1, *more prop.* **मछली**, *q. v.*: 2, *f.* (*m.* **मचला**) [a refractory female.

मचवा, *m.* a boat.

मचवाना, *t.* to cause someone to make, cause to [be made.

मचा, *more com.* **मचान**, *q. v.*

मचान, *m.* a platform, scaffold, stage, raised seat, frame, bench.

मचाना, *t.* (of **मचना**) to make, occasion, cause, stir up, excite, produce, perpetrate, commit.

मचामच, filled up, stuffed full, chokeful.

मचाला (dialectic) = **मचान**, *q. v.*

मचावना = **मचाना**, *q. v.*

मचिया, *m.* a stool, a chair.

मचियाव, *m.* honey.

मचोड़ना, *t.* to twist; to break by twisting.

मच्वा, *m.* (see **मचवा**) a boat.

मच्वाना, *more prop.* **मचवाना**, *q. v.*

मच्छ, (from **मत्स्य**, *q. v.*) *m.* (*f.* ī) a fish.

मच्छड़, *more com.* **मच्छर**, *q. v.*

मच्छर, *m.* a mosquito, gnat, midge. — *kī jhūlkā chor*, a mean, petty, pilferer, one who would steal the minutest thing.

मच्छरी, *f.* (from **मत्सी**) a fish.

मच्छवा, *more com.* **मछुवा**, *q. v.*

मच्छी, *f.* (*m.* मच्छ) a fish : a kiss. *Machchhiyāṅ lenā*, to kiss.

मछ, 1, = मच्च, *q.v.*: 2, *m.* (*f.* ī) a fish : see मत्स्य.

मछड़, *more com.* मच्छर, *q.v.*

मछन्दर, *m.* 1 *pr. n.* a certain *Yogī* : 2, a rat : *met.* [stupid.

मछरंगा, *m.* a species of kingfisher.

मछरी }
मछली } *f.* (from मत्स्यी) a fish.

मछलीबन्दर, *m. pr. n.* the port of Masulipatam.

मछवा, *more com.* मछुवा, *q.v.*

मछिली, *f.* (more com. मछली) a fish.

मछी, *f.* (*m.* मछ) a fish.

मछुवा, *m.* (*f.* in *or* ī) a fisherman.

मज, ripe, mellow.

मज़कूर, remembered, related, afore-said, above-mentioned, the said; (in Gram.) expressed: hence, *m.* mention, discourse.

मज़दूर, *m.* (*f.* in) a labourer, carrier, porter; hireling, a day-labourer. [wages : labour ; labouring.

मज़दूरी, *f.* the price of labour, pay, hire, fare,

मज़बूत, strong, firm, compact. [ability.

मज़बूती, *f.* strength, firmness, compactness, dur-

मजबूर, constrained, forced, restricted.

मज़बूर, written, afore-said, above-mentioned.

मजमा, *m.* an assembly, meeting, convention, collection. — *honā*, to be convened, be assembled, be congregated.

मजमूदार, *m.* a record-keeper, document-holder. The term is applied as a title to the servants of a *Kānūngo*. [sense, purport, signification.

मजमून, *m.* (*f.* ?) contents (of a book or document);

मज़रा, *m.* a field sown or prepared for sowing, a

मजरूह, wounded, lacerated. [corn-field.

मजलिस, *f.* an assembly, meeting, company, congregation, convention. [submissive.

मज़लूम, injured, oppressed: mild, gentle, modest,

मज़हब, *m.* mode, religion, sect.

मजहब, *more prop.* मज़हब, *q. v.* See ज, 3.

मज़ा, *m.* (*f.* ?) flavour, taste, savour ; anything agreeable to the taste. [or of a document.

मज़ामीन, *m.* (pl. of मज़मून) the contents of a book

मजाल, *f.* power, strength, ability.

मजालिस, *f.* (pl. of मजलिस) conferences, convivial conversations, sederunts, assemblies.

मंजिल, *more prop.* मंज़िल, *q.v.*

मजिस्ट्रेट, *m.* (Engl.) a magistrate.

मजीठ, *f.* a certain drug (*Rubia manjith*, Roxb.) the root of which is used for dyeing red.

मजील, cheap, sold at an under-price ; bought at

मजीरा, *m.* small symbals. [second-hand.

मजूत, a corruption of मज़बूत, *q. v.*

मजूर }
मजूरा } corruptions of मज़दूर, *q. v.*

मजूरी, a corruption of मज़दूरी, *q. v.*

मजे, the inflected form of मज़ा, *q.v.*

मज्जन, *m.* bathing, immersion, drowning.

मज्जनौं, *t.* (old) to bathe, immerse, submerge.

मज्जा, *f.* (from मध्य) the marrow of the bones and flesh, fat, grease; the pith or sap of trees and plants.

मझ }
मझं } in Chand = मध्य, *q. v.*
मझमं }

मझला, *m.* (*f.* ī) = मझोला, *q. v.*

मझार, 1, *m.* the middle, centre : 2, in the midst of, in the middle : 3, in.

मझारा, *m.* (*f.* ī) = मझला = मझोला, *q. v.*

मझारि }
मझारो } = मझिले, *q. v.*

मझि, the older form of में, *q. v.*

मझिला, *m.* (*f.* ī) = मझला = मझोला, *q. v.*

मझिले, (= मझि) in the middle, in the midst.

मझेला, *m.* (*f.* ī) = मझोला, *q. v.*

मझेली = मझोली, *q. v.*

मझोला, *m.* (*f.* ī) middle, second of three, middlemost, intermediate, middling.

मझोली, *f.* a smallish sort of car or carriage on two wheels drawn by bullocks.

मटक }
मटकन } *f.* coquetry, ogling.

मटकना, 1, *a. int.* to wink, ogle, coquet : 2, *m.* a small vessel for taking water out of a larger one, a small earthen vessel.

मटका, *m.* a large earthen jar or pot.

मटकाना, *t.* (causat. of मटकना) to cause to twinkle or to wink.

मटकी, *f.* a child's coral, or plaything which infants suck : a small earthen pot or jar : a vessel in which milk is churned : a wink, twinkle, closing of the eyes.

मटकुला, *m.* a kind of sweet dumpling made of

मटकोठा, *m.* a house of earth. [wheaten flour.

मटर, *m.* a pea (*Pisum sativum*).

मटरा, *m.* a kind of pea : a kind of silk cloth.

मटरी, *f.* a kind of pea.

मटरीला, *m.* (*f.* ī) mixed with peas.

मटाकाना = मटकाना, *q. v.*

मटियाना, *t.* to wink at, connive at, to suffer, tolerate.

मटियारा, *m.* arable land, rich soil.

मटियाव, *m.* connivance, toleration, sufferance.

मटुक = (1) मटक (2 मटका (3) मुकुट, *qq. v.*

मटुका, *more prop.* मटका, *q.v.*

मटुकी, *more com.* मटकी, *q. v.*

मट्ठा, *m.* a club or bat : a bough of the *tāṛ*-tree or of the cocoanut-tree. [excavated.

मट्ठिया, a well without a frame, *i. e.* a well merely

मट्टी, *f.* earth, ground, land, soil, mould, clay. —

k. to destroy, ruin. — *khānā*, to eat flesh. — *ḍālnā*, to conceal the fault or crime of another. — *denā*, to bury, inter. — *pakaṛnā*, to bite the ground, to be overturned or overcome; to be obstinate, be perverse; to resist. — *par laṛnā*, to have a dispute about land. *meṅ milnā*, to be ruined or disgraced. — *meṅ milānā*, to disgrace, to ruin. — *honā*, to become weak or faint; to be ruined. — *kā tel*, petroleum, a kind of bitumen supposed to possess marvellous salutary qualities. [sour milk.

मट्ठा, 1, *m.* (*f.* ī.) = **मठा**, 1, *q.v.* : 2, *m.* buttermilk,

मठ, *m.* a residence for young Brāhmaṇs prosecuting sacred studies, a school, college, convent, cloister, monastery, pagoda, pagan temple, a building inhabited by Brāhmaṇ ascetics.

मठड़ी, *f.* a kind of sweetmeat.

मठा, 1, *more com.* **मट्ठा**, 2, *q. v.* : 2, *m.* (*f.* ī) slow, indolent, lazy, preverse, obstinate.

मठी, 1, *more prop.* **मट्ठी**, *q.v.*: 2, *f.* (*m.* **मठा**) a perverse or indolent female: 3, *f.* a cell, cloister.

मठोर, *m. f.* ? a jar.

मठोली, *f.* (from **मुष्टि**) onanism.

मठौट, a poll-tax, an impost.

मठौरी, *f.* a jar.

मड़या, a contraction of **माड़या**, *q.v.*

मडव, *m. pr. n.* a certain district in Kashmir.

मड़वा, *m.* a kind of fish.

मड़ार, the pit of an old well that has gone to ruins.

मढ़ियाना, *t.* to paste.

मँड़ी, *f.* (in Agriculture) a border, bank, division: a section of a rice-field; a bed, plat, parterre.

मड़ोड़; for words beginning thus, see under the form **मरोड़**.

मड्डी, *f.* dregs, sediment, grounds, lees, feculency.

मढ़न, *f.* lining; the heading of a drum, etc.

मढ़ना, *t.* to cover (as a book with leather or a drum with parchment), to case; to gild.

मढ़ा, 1, *m.* (*f.* ī) lined, covered, headed, topped (as a drum with parchment), bound (as a book): 2, *m.* a temporary shed or building erected for a marriage ceremony, etc.

मढ़ी, *f.* a cottage: a temple.

मढ़ैया, *f.* a cottage, hut.

मण, a contraction of **मणि**, *q.v.* See **म**, 1.

मणि, *m. f.* a precious stone, gem, pearl, jewel; fleshy processes hanging from the neck of a goat: the wrist: a waterpot.

मणिआकार, of the form of a *maṇi*, gem-like.

मणिक्य (*contraction*) = **माणिक्य**, *q.v.*

मणिग्रीव, *m. pr. n.* a son of Kuver.

मणिजड़ित, set with gems, bedecked with jewels.

मणिजला, *pr. n.* a certain river.

मणिजाला, *f.* a net interwoven with gems.

मणिदीप, *m.* a lamp having jewels.

मणिद्वीप, *m. pr. n.* (1) of a certain mythical island in the ocean of nectar (2) of the hood of the great serpent Anant.

मणिनायक, *m.* (the chief of jewels, i.e.) Kaustubh.

मणिमय, *m.* (*f.* ī) made of (consisting of, or set with) precious gems or jewels.

मणिमाला, *f.* a necklace, zone, or fillet of precious gems or jewels.

मणियारा, *m.* (*f.* ī); see (1) **मणियुत** (2) **मणिहार**.

मणियुत, *m.* (*f.* ā) appertaining to gems, bedecked with jewels, inlaid with gems.

मणिवैगनी, *f.* a purple gem.

मणिशैल, *m. pr. n.* a certain mountain.

मणिहार, *m.* (*f.* ī) a person who makes or sells the glass bracelets (*chūṛī*) which females wear on their wrists.

मणिहारी, *f.* the jewel-trade.

मणी, *f.* = **मणि**, *q.v.* [tinct.

मण्ठा, *m.* (*f.* ī) desolate, ruined, non-existent, ex-

मण्ड, *m.* ornament: the castor-oil tree (*Palma Christi*): scum, skimmings, froth, foam, barm; pith, essence: the head: rice-water, gruel, starch, paste.

मण्डन, *m.* the act of ornamenting: ornament, decoration, jewels, trinkets, etc. [adorn.

मण्डना, 1, see **माण्डना** and **मुण्डना**; 2, *t.* to array,

मण्डप, *m.* a temporary building, an open shed or hall adorned with flowers and erected on festive occasions (such as marriages, etc.); an open temple or building consecrated to a deity, a family temple; a bower.

मण्डल, *m.* the disc of the sun or moon, a circle, halo, circumference, orb, sphere, the globe; a round tent; an officer employed in villages, an exciseman; a province, region, district (extending according to some authorities twenty, and according to others, forty Yojans in every direction); the country or empire over which the twelve princes termed *Chakravarti* are supposed to have ruled (perhaps the peninsula of India); the visible horizon; a sort of leprosy with circular spots; a form of military array (an army drawn up in a circle); a nest; a globe, ball; a wheel.

मण्डलाकार, round, circular.

मण्डलाना, *a. int.* to make a circuit, to hover (as birds): *n.* to be enveloped.

मण्डलिक, *m.* (*f.* ā *or* ī) = **मण्डलेश्वर**, *q.v.*

मण्डलिया, *m.* a tumbler-pigeon.

मण्डली, 1, *f.* the disc of the sun or moon; a circle; bent grass; a nest: a society, assembly, congregation, flock, church, sect, corporation: 2, *m.* (*f.* inī) a snake; a cat.

मण्डलेश्वर, (*f.* ī) a monarch, sovereign, the lord of any district or region.

मण्डवा = **मण्डूआ**, *q.v.*

मण्डवी, *f.* 1, = **मण्डूआ**, *q.v.* : 2, a kind of food.

मण्डा, *m.* a sort of sweetmeat made in small nuts.

मण्डित, *m.* (*f.* ā) ornamented, adorned, overlaid (with gold, etc.), covered (with dust, etc.). [the hair.

मण्डियाना, *t.* to starch, to apply starch or dye to

मण्डी, *f.* a market, a market for any one particular thing; a shop or warehouse for the sale of goods on commission or by auction; a shop for the sale of grain having a storehouse attached.

मण्डुआ, *m.* a certain grain (*Cynosurus coracanus* or *Eleusine coracana*).

मण्डुई, *f.* = **मण्डुआ**, *q.v.*

मण्डूआ, *m.* an alcove, arbour, bower, a temporary gallery or shade.

मण्डूक, *m.* (*f.* ī) a frog: a certain flower (*Bignonia Indica*).

मण्डूकी, *f.* 1, (*m.* **मण्डूक**) a female frog: 2, (dim. of **मण्डूक**) a small frog: a certain plant (*Siphonanthus Indica* or *Hydrocotyle Asiatica*).

मण्ढना = **मढ़ना**, *q. v.*

मण्ढप, *m.* (= **मण्डप**) a small round temple or cell.

मण्ढवाना, *t.* to cause to cover (as a book, a drum, etc).

मण्ढा, *m.* a temporary building, an open shed or hall adorned with flowers for the bride and bridegroom on a wedding occasion.

मण्ढाया, *m.* (*f.* **मण्ढाई**) starched.

मण्ढियाना = **मढ़ियाना**, *q. v.*

मण्ढी, *f.* a cottage, a yogee's hut, a temple.

मत, 1, *m.* a purpose, intention, disposition of the mind, wish; knowledge, doctrine, belief, tenet, opinion: 2, *f.* wisdom, understanding, intellect; manner, method, way, mode, system, sect: 3, a prohibitive particle (= don't) used with the imperative only: 4, a Taddhita suffix which serves to form adjectives which in Hindee are masculine though in Sanskrit they are neuter: the feminine form of such adjectives ends in **मती**.

मतंग, 1, *m.* (*f.* ī) an elephant: 2, *m.* a cloud.

मतखण्डन, *m.* destruction of religious belief, heresy, heterodoxy, infidelity.

मतन, *m.* the text of a book, the middle.

मतना, 1, *m.* a kind of sugarcane: 2, *more prop.* **मथना**, *q. v.*: 3, *a. int.* to consult together.

मतपरीक्षा, *f.* an investigation of religious belief.

मतपरीक्षाख्य, (see **आख्य**) *Matparīkshā* by name.

मतप्रवर्त्तक, *m.* (*f.* ikā) the originator or founder of any religious or philosophical sect.

मतप्रवर्त्तकत्व, *m.* (*f.* tā) the originating or establishing new opinions or theories.

मतबल (corruption by inversion) = **मतलब**, *q. v.*

मतराना, *t.* to persnade.

मतलक, *more prop.* **मुतलक़**, *q. v.*

मतलब, *m.* a question, petition, desire, wish, intention, object, purpose, meaning, drift, purport.

मतला; for words beginning thus, see under the form **मत्ला**.

मतली = **मत्ली**, *q. v.*

मतल्लिका, *f.* excellence, happiness; a sort of metre in Sanskrit prosody.

मतवत, *m.* (*f.* vatī) like one intoxicated, in the manner of a drunkard; drunken, inebriated.

मतवाद, *m.* contention concerning opinion.

मतवारा, *m.* (*f.* ī) *more com.* **मतवाला**, *q. v.*

मतवालपन, *m.* a state of intoxication, inebriation, drunkenness.

मतवाला, *m.* (*f.* ī) intoxicated, drunk. [(**मत**).

मतस्य, 1, *more prop.* **मत्स्य**, *q v.*: 2, (Sk.) = **मतका**

मतहीन, *m.* (*f.* ā) destitute of understanding, stupid, senseless, ignorant.

मतहु; **मत** and **मतना**.

मता, *m.* counsel, advice, consultation; opinion. — *k.* to advise. — *ṭhānnā*, to agree in a consultation, to resolve.

मताचार, *m.* the observance of any method or opinion, following a sect.

मतानुसार, conformably to an opinion or sect.

मतान्तर, *m.* a different opinion or tenet, another method, a different sect or party.

मतान्तराचार, *m.* the observance of another method, the following another sect.

मतारा, wealth, substance, merchandize.

मतारी, *f.* a mother.

मतावलम्बी, *m.* (*f.* inī) an adherent to any specified class of religious opinions: lit. *adj.* embracing or holding the tenets of any particular religious sect.

मति, 1, a corruption of **मत**, 3, *q. v.*: 2, *f.* mind, understanding, intellect, intelligence, thought, resolution: perception; opinion, belief; wish, desire, inclination; advice; recollection; respect.

मतिधीर, *m.* (*f.* ā) grave, sedate, collected, resolved.

मतिभ्रम, *m.* misapprehension in judgment, error, mistake.

मतिभ्रान्ति, *f.* = **मतिभ्रम**, *q. v.*

मतिमन्द = **मन्दमति**, *q. v.*

मतिमान, *m.* (*f.* matī) sensible, intelligent, wise, clever.

मतिरंक, *m.* (*f.* ā) poor of understanding, of a barren or unfurnished mind.

मतिहीन, *m.* (*f.* ā) = **मतहीन**, *q. v.*

मती, *more prop.* **मति**, *q. v.*

मतो }
मतौ } 1, in Braj = **मता** or **मति**, *qq. v.*: 2, see **मतना**.

मतौना, *m.* the grain called *kodo* (when it has an inebriating quality).

मत्त, *m.* (*f.* ā) a drunken person; an elephant in rut: *lit.* intoxicated (with liquor or with passion or with pride); maddened; pleased.

मत्तत्व, *m.* (*f.* tā) intoxication, excitement of the passions, infatuation, madness.

मत्तवत, like a drunkard, drunk-like, as if drunk.

मत्ता, *f.* (*m.* **मत्त**) a drunken female; a female elephant; intoxicating or vinous liquor.

मत्ती, *m. pr. n.* the evangelist Matthew and the Book that bears his name.

मत्राना, *t.* to persuade.

मत्लाई, *f.* sickness at stomach, nausea.

मत्लाना (**जी का**), to be sick at the stomach, to feel nausea.

मत्लाहट, *f.* sickness at stomach, nausea.

मत्ली, *f.* sickness at stomach, nausea.

मत्सर, 1, *m.* (*f.* ā) a niggard, etc.: *lit.* envious, jealous, covetous, niggardly; hostile: 2, *m.* envy, jealousy, anger, passion.

मत्सरा, 1, *f.* (*m.* **मत्सर**) a greedy female, etc.: 2, *f.* impatience of another's success or prosperity, jealousy, envy, passion, anger.

मत्सरी, *m.* (*f.* iṇī) a niggard, etc.: *lit.* envious, niggardly; wicked, depraved, bad.

मत्स्य, *m.* (*f.* ī) a fish in general: *pr. n.* (1) of the first incarnation (see *Avatār*) of Vishṇu who is fabled to have appeared, in the shape of the small fish

Saphari, to Satyavrata or Hayagrīv to warn him of the general deluge and to desire him to place the four Veds in the boat which he (Vishṇu) would preserve: the fish was first taken up by Hayagrīv in his hands when bathing, it being then of the size of a *Saphari* or *Pūthi*; but it grew too large to be contained in a tank or a river, and was carried to the sea, where it subsequently supported the ark with its horn: Satyavrata lived about B. C. 3000 (2) of one of the Hindoo Purāṇs (3) of a country (Dinājpur and Rangpur) enumerated among the midland divisions of India.

मत्स्यराज, *m.* the *rohi*-fish (*Cyprinus rohita*): *pr. n.* the country called Matsya. See **मत्स्य** (3).

मत्स्यी, *f.* (*m.* **मत्स्य**) a female fish.

मत्स्यावतार, *m. pr. n.* = **मत्स्य** (1), *q. v.*

मथन, *m.* churning, stirring; a certain tree (*Premna longifolia*) the wood of which is used to produce fire by attrition.

मथनसिन्धु by inversion = **सिन्धुमथन**, *q. v.*

मथना, 1, *t.* to churn; to knead, work, squeeze: 2, *m.* a churning-staff.

मथनिया, *f.* a churning-vessel.

मथनी, *f.* a churning-staff.

मथा, 1, (*contraction*) = **माथा**, *q. v.*: 2, see **मथना**.

मथानी, *f.* a churning-vessel.

मथित, *m.* butter-milk without any watery admixture: *lit.* stirred, agitated, churned.

मथिन, *m.* a churning-staff; the *penis*.

मथुरा, *m. pr. n.* a district and city ("Muttra") in the province of Agra celebrated as the birth-place and early residence of Krishṇ (still important as a favorite resort of Hindoo pilgrims).

मथुरापुरी, *f. pr. n.* the city of Mathurā.

मथुरावाला, *m* (*f.* inorī) } **मथुरावासी**, *m.* (*f.* inī) } an inhabitant of Mathura.

मथुरिश्रा = **मथुरिया**, *q. v.* [thurā.

मथुरिया, *m.* a certain caste of Brāhmaṇs of Ma-

मथुरैनी, *f.* a female of the Mathuriyā caste; the wife of a Mathuriyā. [scription.

मथोट, *m.* capitation, poll-tax, contribution, sub-

मथौरा, *m.* a parasol, parapluie, umbrella.

मथ्थ in Chand = **माथा**, *q. v.*

मद, 1, *m.* spirituous liquor, wine, spirits: intoxication, sensual enjoyment, passion, love, joy; pride, arrogance, haughtiness, conceit; insanity; the juice that flows from an elephant's temples when in rut, the rut of an elephant, *semen virile*; musk: 2, *adj.* having a bad smell.

मदक, *m.* a pellet of opium or other drug for smoking, an opiate. [revenue.

मदख़ल, place of entrance, entrance; income,

मदख़ोर, *m.* (*f.* nī, ī, in) a drunkard.

मदद, *f.* help, succour, assistance.

मददगार, *m.* a helper, protector, ally.

मदन, *m.* the act of gladdening or exhilarating; an epithet of Kāmdev; love, lust; bee's-wax; a bee; the season of spring; the name of certain plants or trees (1) *Datura metel* (2) *Vangueria spinosa*, Roxb. (3) *Gardenia dumetorum*, Kœn. (4) *Mimosa catechu*.

मदनपूजक, *m.* (*f.* ikā) worshipper of Kāmdev, a vo-

मदनबान, *m.* a certain flower. [tary of lust.

मदनबुद्धि, *f.* a nature or disposition like that of

मदनभान } **मदनमस्त** } = **मदनबान**, *q. v.* [Kāmdev.

मदनमोहन, *m.* (the infatuator of the god of love, *i. e.*) Krishṇ. [subdued by love.

मदनवश, *m.* (*f.* ā) under the ifluence of love,

मदपीना, *m.* imbibing intoxicating liquor, tippling.

मदमता, *m.* (*f.* ī) contraction = **मदमाता**, *q. v.*

मदमाता, *m.* (*f.* ī) intoxicated, drunk.

मदमान्ता, *m.* (*f.* ī) = **मदमाता**, *q. v.*

मदरास, *m. pr. n.* the city of Madras.

मदार, 1, a contraction of **मन्दार**, *q. v.*: 2, *m.* an elephant: a hog: a rogue: an orbit, circle, circumference; a place of turning or returning, a place where one stops or stands, a centre, station, seat: *pr. n.* a celebrated Muhammadan saint and mendicant.

मदारिज, ways, roads, paths, steps, ascents, degrees.

मदारिया, *m.* a follower of Madār. [to Madār.

मदारी, 1, *m.* (*f.* iṇī) a juggler: 2, appertaining

मदिक, *m.* (*f.* ā *or* ī) a proud person: *lit.* intoxicated with wealth, purse-proud.

मदिर, *m.* a red species of Khayar (*Mimosa catechu*).

मदिरा, *f.* spirituous liquor, wine, spirits; nectar: the wagtail: a species of metre in Sanskrit prosody.

मदेरा = **मदिरा**, *q. v.*

मदोत्कट, *m.* (*f.* ā) an elephant in rut; a furious creature: *lit.* furious, arrogant. [*teronatus magur*).

मद्गुर, *m.* sheat-fish (*Silurus pelorius* or *Macrop-*

मद्गुरसी, *f.* = **मद्गुर**, *q. v.*

मद्ध, 1, *more prop.* **मध्य**, *q. v.*: 2, *m.* temperament.

मद्धस्त, *more prop.* **मध्यस्थ**, *q. v.*

मद्धम, *more prop.* **मध्यम**, *q. v.*

मद्धि in Chand = **मध्य**, *q. v.*

मद्र, *m. pr. n.* (1) of a country enumerated among the countries of the Nort-west of Hindustan (2) of a king of that country.

मद्रजा, a corruption of **मद्रसा**, *q. v.*

मद्रसा, *m.* a college, university, (more especially) a school for the diffusion of Muhammadan learning.

मद्रा, *f. pr. n.* a certain river.

मद्य, *m.* spirituous liquor, wine. [cating liquors.

मद्यप, *m.* (*f.* ā) *adj.* drinking spirituous or intoxi-

मद्यपान, *m.* drinking wine or spirituous liquors.

मद्यपीत, drunk, intoxicated: hence, *m.* (*f.* ā) a drunkard.

मद्यपीना, *m.* imbibing intoxicating liquor, tippling.

मध = (1) **मद** (2) **मधु** (3) **मध्य**, *qq. v.*

मधमाता, *m.* (*f.* ī) intoxicated, drunk.

मधस्त, a corruption of **मध्यस्थ**, *q. v.*

मधि in Chand = **मध्य**, 2, *q. v.*

मधु, (*lit.* sweet; hence) *m.* the nectar of flowers, honey, sugar, liquorice, spirituous liquor from the blossoms of the *Bassia latifolia*, wine, water; the season of spring: the month Chaitra (Mar.—April); a certain Daitya slain by Vishṇu; a certain tree (*Bassia latifolia*); a sort of metre in Sanskrit prosody.

मधुकर, *m.* (*f.* ī) a bee; a lover; the round sweet lime; a certain plant (*Achyranthus aspera*); a name of Uddhav, a relation of Krishṇ's.

मधुकरी, 1, = **मधूकरी**, *q.v.*: 2, see **मधुकर**.

मधुकैटभ, *m. pr. n.* a certain demon slain by Vishṇu.

मधुकोष, *m.* a honey-comb; a bee-hive: the testicles of a goat.

मधुच्छन्दसा, *m.* (see **श्वा**, 22) all the 101 sons of [Vishwāmitra.

मधुच्छन्दा, *m. pr. n.* the middlemost (*i. e.* the 51st) of Vishwāmitra's 101 sons.

मधुतृण, *m.* sugarcane (*lit.* sweet grass, honey-grass).

मधुप, *m.* a bee (*lit.* the honey-drinker).

मधुपरस, *m.* ripe juicy fruit.

मधुपर्क, *m.* a dish of honey and milk to be offered to a respectable guest on his arrival.

मधुपुर, *m.* } **मधुपुरी**, *f.* } epithets of Mathurā.

मधुमय, *m.* (*f.* ī) consisting of or abounding in honey, sweet, luscious.

मधुमल, *m.* bee's-wax.

मधुमाखी, *f.* a honey-bee.

मधुमात, *m.* a certain musical mode (*rāgiṇī*).

मधुमाता, *m.* (*f.* ī) intoxicated, drunk.

मधुमास, *m.* the month Chaitra (March-April).

मधुर, *m.* (*f.* ā) sweet, agreeable, pleasing, liked; tender: hence, *m.* sweetness, treacle, syrup; poison; tin.

मधुरत्व, *m.* (*f.* tā) sweetness, agreeableness, tenderness, suavity.

मधुरवाक्य, 1, *m.* pleasant speech, honied words, eloquent language: **2**, *m.* (*f.* ā) one who speaks pleasantly or agreeably or eloquently: lit. *adj.* sweet-speaking, fair of speech.

मधुरवाचक, *m.* (*f.* ikā) = **मधुरवाक्य**, 2, *q.v.*

मधुरस, *m.* sweetness (in flavour or in speech).

मधुरा, *f.* (*m.* **मधुर**) an agreeable female: marrow: a certain town: anise-seed (*Anethum sowa*), and some other plants.

मधुराम्ल, *m.* (*f.* ā) sweet and sour, sub-acid.

मधुरी, *f.* (*more prop.* **मधुरा**?) sweet.

मधुल, *m.* spirituous liquor.

मधुवन, *m.* an epithet of Mathurā.

मधुसूदन, *m.* (see **मधु**) an epithet of Krishṇ; *lit.* the [slayer of Madhu.

मधुहन = **मधुहा**, *q.v.*

मधुहा, *m.* a destroyer of honey; a collector of honey; a soothsayer; a certain bird of prey; an epithet of Krishṇ (the slayer of the *daitya* Madhu).

मधूकरी, *f.* a kind of bread baked on live coals (used among Hindoo ascetics); food given as alms to pilgrims.

मधूलक, *m.* sweetness; a sort of *Bassia latifolia* which grows in watery or mountainous places.

मध्य, 1, *m.* (*f.* ā) a middle-sized person: *lit.* middle, middle-sized, of middling sort, amongst, intermediate, central; right, proper; low: hence, *m.* the middle, the centre, the waist, a horse's flank; cessation, interval: the west: a very high number, ten thousand billions: (in Music) mean or common time: (in Arithm.) the middle term or the mean of a progression: **2**, *adv.* in the middle, in the midst, among, amongst, amid, between.

मध्यगति (Rām.) = **उदासीन**, *q.v.*

मध्यगुरु, *m.* (in Pros.) any measure whose middle syllable is long or heavy.

मध्यदिवस, *m.* mid-day, noon.

मध्यदेश, *m.* the central or middle part of anything; the waist; intervening country. The term is specially applied to the middle region of India, *viz.* that bounded by Kurukshetra on the north, Allahabad on the south, the Himālaya mountains on the east, and the Vindhya mountains on the west;—comprising, therefore, the modern provinces of Allahabad, Agra, Delhi, Oude, etc. The northern limit is, by some, defined to be the place where the Saraswatee disappears.

मध्यप, *m.* (*f.* ā) *more prop.* **मद्यप**, *q.v.*

मध्यपीत, *m.* (*f.* ā) *more prop.* **मद्यपीत**, *q.v.*

मध्यभाग, *m.* the central portion.

मध्यम, *m.* (*f.* ā) middle, midmost, intervening, intermediate, middling, moderate, temperate, of middle sort, of moderate strength, middle-born (neither the oldest nor the youngest), mediocre, so so, indifferently good or bad: hence, *m.* the middle part of anything, the waist; the middle country (= *Madhyadesh*); the fifth note of the Hindoo gamut.

मध्यमता, *f.* the state of being midmost or moderate, middlingness, mediocrity.

मध्यममति, *f.* an intellect of but moderate calibre, [mediocrity.

मध्यमपुरुष, *m.* (in Gram.) the second person.

मध्यमलोक = **मध्यलोक**, *q.v.*

मध्यमा, *f.* (*m.* **मध्यम**) a girl arrived at puberty; the middle finger; a central blossom.

मध्यलघु, *m.* (in Pros.) any measure whose middle syllable is short or light.

मध्यलोक, *m.* the earth, the abode of mortals (considered as the intermediate state between heaven and hell).

मध्यवर्त्ती, *m.* (*f.* inī) a mediator, an associate, etc.: *lit.* abiding in the midst, dwelling amongst, indwelling, central, internal.

मध्यस्थ, *m.* (*f.* ā) a middle-man, mediator, arbitrator, umpire, go-between: *lit.* standing between, situated in the midst, intermediate, central, internal.

मध्यस्थत्व, *m.* (*f.* tā) intermediate situation or state, mediatorship, umpireship, arbitratorship, arbitration.

मध्यस्थल } **मध्यस्थान** } *m.* the centre; the waist.

मध्या, *f.* (*m.* **मध्य**) a young woman, a girl arrived at puberty; the middle finger.

मध्यावस्था, *f.* an epithet of the period of youth as the middlemost of the three conditions of mankind, viz. *Bālāvasthā*, *Yuvāvasthā*, and *Vriddhāvasthā*.

मध्याह्न, *m.* mid-day, noon.

मध्ये, (not freq. in Hindee) = **मध्य**, 2, *q.v.*

मन, *m.* 1, *a corruption of* **मणि**, *q.v.*: 2, a certain weight (consisting of forty sérs or about seventy eight pounds) incorrectly called a "maund": 3, the mind (considered as the seat of perception and of passion), the heart; the intellect; power of mind; purpose, inclination; character, disposition; soul, spirit. Often used idiomatically like the English 'self'; e. g. *Usne manmeṅ kahā*, he said to himself.—*bhānā*, to be agreeable to the mind.—*bhānā mundiyā hilānā*, to pretend to refuse that which one secretly desires.—*mār-rahnā*, to suffer pain or grief with patience.—*lānā* or *lagānā*, to apply the mind to, be attentive.—*mārnā*, to resist one's own inclination; to be grieved or troubled in mind.

मनः = **मनस**, *q.v.*

मनका, *more prop.* **मंका**, *q.v.*

मनकामना, *f.* desire, inclination, wish, purpose.

मनकेला; see **फलबुझौवल**.

मनक्रमबचन } **मनक्रमबानी** } (*Rām.*) = **मनसावाचाकर्म्मणा**, *q.v.*

मनगढ़ा, *m.* (*f.* ī) powerful, strong.

मनगसिर = **मंगसिर**, *q.v.*

मनघटा, *m.* the raised masonry around the mouth [of a well.

मनचला, *m.* (*f.* ī) assiduous, intent, eager, zealous, active, bold.

मनचली, *f.* eagerness of mind, assiduity, intentness, zeal.

मनची = **मनकी** (**मन**). See **ची**, 1.

मनचोर, *m.* (*f.* nī, ī, in) heart-stealer.

मनजन, 1, *more prop.* **मंजन**, *q.v.*: 2, = **मनुष्य**, *q.v.*

मनजात (Rām.) = **कामदेव**, *q.v.*

मनज़िल = **मंज़िल**, *q.v.*

मनत, *f.* acknowledgment, assent.

मनतर (colloquial) = **मन्त्र**, *q.v.*

मनतलब (corruption) = **मतलब**, *q.v* (or story).

मनदरावर्दी, fanciful, invented (said of a speech

मनबचक्रम (*Rām.*) = **मनसावाचाकर्म्मणा**, *q.v.*

मनन, *m.* the act of thinking, a minding: understanding, reflection, thought; (in the Vedanta system) intuitive knowledge, or science without need of study.

मनना, *n.* to be soothed, be propitiated, be conciliated, be tranquilized.

मनपूरण, *m.* satisfaction of mind, confidence.

मनभाना, *m.* (*f.* **मनभानी**) } **मनभाया**, *m.* (*f.* **मनभाई**) } = **मनभावन**, *q.v.*

मनभायौ in Braj = **मनभाया**, *q.v.*

मनभावन, agreeable to the mind or soul, acceptable, pleasing, charming, amusing: *hence*, a sweetheart, mistress, spouse.

मनभावना, *m.* (*f.* ī) = **मनभावन**, *q.v.*

मनमता, *m.* (*f.* ī) mere opinion, surmise, conjecture.

मनमथ, *more prop.* **मन्मथ**, *q.v.*

मनमलीन, *m.* (*f.* ā *or* ī) sad, melancholy, troubled, vexed, distressed, downcast.

मनमांह in Braj = **मनमें** (**मन**).

मनमान, *m.* the heart's desire, choice.

मनमाना, *m.* (*f.* ī) = **मनमान्ता**, *q.v.*

मनमानी, *f.*; see (1) **मनमान** (2) **मनमाना**.

मनमाने, *adv.* as the mind may desire.

मनमान्ता, conformable to one's wishes or inclination, pleasing to the mind, agreeable, soothing, charming: hence, *m.* (*f.* ī) a sweetheart, spouse.

मनमार; see *s.v.* **मन**.

मनमारा, *m* (*f.* ī) = **उदास**, *q.v.* See *s. v.* **मन**.

मनमारना; see *s. v.* **मन**.

मनमोहन, *m.* (*f.* ī) a heart-ravisher, a sweetheart, a mistress; an epithet of Krishṇ: *lit.* heart-ravishing, fascinating, charming, captivating.

मनमोहनप्यारा, *m.* (*f.* ī) = **मनमोहन**, *q.v.*

मनमौज, *m.* self-conceit.

मनमौजी, *m.* (*f.* in *or* inī) self-conceited.

मनरंजक, *m.* (*f.* ikā) agreeable, pleasing to the mind, gratifying.

मनरंजन, *m.* pleasingness, agreeableness, loveliness, pleasantness; captivation of the mind.

मनलगन, *m.* heart-attachment, heart-engaging.

मनवन्तर, *more prop.* **मन्वन्तर**, *q. v.*

मनष in Chand = **मनुष्य**, *q v.*

मनस, *m.* the heart or mind considered as the seat of perception and of passion, and reckoned by the followers of the Sānkhya and Nyāya schools as an organ of both sense and action; the intellect, the understanding.

मनसर्वा, *m.* a male, a man.

मनसल = **मैनसिल**, *q.v.*

मनसहिं (Rām.) = **मनमें**.

मनसा, *f.* 1, desire, inclination, wish, intention, purport, design, purpose: 2, *pr. n.* the goddess of the serpent-race, and the particular protectress of their venom.

मनसादेवी = **मनसा**, 2, *q.v.*

मनसावाचाकर्म्मणा, *f.* thought, word, and deed.

मनसिज, *m.* an epithet of Kāmdev: *lit.* born in the soul, mental, intellectual.

मनसील, *more com.* **मनसल** = **मैनसिल**, *q.v.*

मनसूख़, cancelled, abrogated, obliterated, abolished, broken, superseded.

मनसूब, *m.* *f.* ā) related to, addicted to, belonging to, depending on.—*k.* to connect with, attribute to.

मनसेरू, *m.* (from **मानुष**) a man, a male.

मनस्क, mental, intellectual.

मनस्कार, *m.* the cognizance which the mind takes of its own sensations, self-consciousness.

मनस्ताप, *m.* mental agony or distress.

मनहरण, *m.* heart-ravishment, fascination, captivation.

मनहरणप्यारा, *m.* (*f.* ī) an epithet of any heart-ravisher; *e. g.* of Krishṇ.

मनहाई, *f.* prohibition, forbidding.

मनहारक, *m.* (*f.* ikā) a heart-stealer: *lit.* captivating the mind or heart, fascinating, charming, delighting, enchanting.

मनहारी, *m.* (*f.* iṇī) = **मनहारक**, *q.v.*

मनहिं मन, in the heart of hearts, with a sincere heart.

मनहीं में, in the very soul, in one's heart of hearts.

मनहु } मनहू } मनहूं } in Braj = (1) मनको (2) मनभी (3) मानेा, *q.v.*

मना, 1, *m.* prohibition, forbidding, refusal, denial, hindrance : — *k.* to prohibit : 2, the nominative form of the Sanskrit base मनस, used as the termination of a class of adjectives the same in both genders ; *e.g.* दुर्मना, *m. f.*

मनाक, a little, somewhat ; slow, dull, tardy.

मनागपि = मनाक + अपि.

मनाका, *f.* a female elephant.

मनादी, *f.* heralding, proclamation, publication, [preaching.

मनाना, *t.* (causat. of मानना) to cause someone to agree to a thing, to persuade, conciliate, propitiate, appease, soothe, coax, assuage ; to put in mind: to do, act, perform, make : to invoke (whether for good or evil). — *danānā*, to conciliate, appease.

मनायी, *f. pr. n.* the wife of Manu.

मनार्थ, *m.* intention, desire, aim, purpose.

मनावनों in Braj = मनाना, *q.v.*

मनावी, *f. pr. n.* the wife of Manu.

मनासिब, *more prop.* मुनासिब, *q.v.* [from मणि.

मनि ; for words beginning thus, see see under the

मनी, 1, *a corruption of* मणि, *q.v.* : 2, *f.* death, fate: presumption, boasting, egotism : *sperma genitale (viri aut mulieris).*

मनीचनी, *m.* a certain blemish in horses.

मनु, 1, *a corruption of* मानेा, 1, *q.v.* : 2, *m.* a man (in general) : 3, *m. pr. n.* Manu, the legislator and saint, the son of Brahmā, or a personification of Brahmā himself, the creator of the world and the progenitor of mankind. The name is, however, a generic term ; and in every *kalp*, or interval from one creation to another, there are fourteen successive Manus presiding over the universe, each of them for the period of a Manwantar. In the present creation there have been the six following Manus (1) Manu, called Swāyambhava, the supposed revealer of the code of law possessed by the Hindoos (2) Swārochish (3) Uttam (4) Tāmas (5) Raivat (6) Chākshush. The seventh, or the present Manu, is Vaivaswat, or Raivat the Second. In the ingenious system of reckoning by symbols adopted by Hindoos in their poetry, this word (in allusion to the number of Manus in a *Kalp*) is a symbol for 14.

मनुआ (corruption) = (1) मनुष्य (2) मनूआ, 3, *qq.v.*

मनुआं = मनुआ, *q. v.*

मनुख = मनुष, *q.v.*

मनुग, a corruption of मनुज, *q.v.*

मनुज, *m.* (*f.* ā) a human being: *lit.* born of Manu, sprung from Manu.

मनुजाद, *m.* (*f.* ā *or* ī) any Rākshas: lit. *adj.* devouring human beings, man-eating.

मनुष (*contraction*) = मनुष्य, *q. v.*

मनुषी, *more accurately* मनुष्यी, *q. v.*

मनुष्य, *m.* (*f.* ī) an offspring of Manu, a human creature, man, mankind, being, person, individual.

मनुष्यघात, *m.* homicide, manslaughter, murder.

मनुष्यघातक, *m.* (*f.* ikā) one who slays a human creature, murderer, homicide : lit. *adj.* manslaying, homicidal.

मनुष्यघाती, *m.* (*f.* inī) = मनुष्यघातक, *q.v.*

मनुष्यचोला, *m.* the human form, human existence.

मनुष्यतन, *m.* the human body, the human form, mortal flesh. — *pānā* or *dharnā*, to get or assume the human form, to become incarnate.

मनुष्यत्व, *m.* (*f.* tā) the state or condition of man, manhood, humanity ; manliness.

मनुष्यविक्री, *f.* trade in human beings.

मनुष्यरचित, *m.* (*f.* ā) formed by man.

मनुष्यलोग, *m.* mankind, the human race, people.

मनुष्यी, *f.* (*m.* मनुष्य) a human female, a woman, the wife or female of the man.

मनुसाई (Rām.) = पुरुषार्थ, *q. v.* [by Manu.

मनुस्मृति, *f. pr. n.* the code of laws promulgated

मनुहार, *m.* (*f.* ī) = मनहारक, *q.v.*

मनू (*corruption*) = (1) मनु (2) मानेा, 1, *qq.v.*

मनूआ, 1, *m.* (*f.* मनूई) a cat, puss : 2, *f.* a kind of cotton : 3, *m.* mind, soul, life.

मने, a corruption of मना, 1, *q.v.*

मनेा, *a contraction of* मानेा, 1, *q.v.*

मनों, 1, a pl. form of मन, 2 (= maunds): see ओं, 4 : 2, a corruption of मानेा, 1, *q.v.*

मनोकामना, *f.* inclination or bias of the mind, heart's desire, wish, purpose, design.

मनोगत, 1, gone to the heart, affecting the soul, seated in the mind : 2, *m.* thought : wish.

मनोगुप्त, thought on or pondered over in secret.

मनोज } मनोजात } (Rām.) = कामदेव, *q.v.*

मनोज्ञ, *m.* (*f.* ā) heart-winning, beautiful, pleasing, agreeable, lovely, handsome. [acceptable, approved.

मनोनीत, *m.* (*f.* ā) made choice of, wished for,

मनोभव } मनोभूत } *m.* epithets of Kāmdev.

मनोमय, *m.* (*f.* ī) mental. The term is applied to the second of the three subtle sheaths in which (according to the Vedantic system) the soul is encased.

मनोमल, *m.* the defilement of the mind, sin, im-

मनोरंजन = मनरंजन, *q.v.* [purity.

मनोरथ, *m.* wish, desire, design, intention, good pleasure, purpose, aim.

मनोरम, *m.* (*f.* ā) a lovely person, etc.: *lit.* pleasing, lovely, agreeable, beautiful.

मनोरमा, *f.* a species of metre in Sanskrit prosody.

मनोर्थ, *more prop.* मनोरथ, *q.v.*

मनोलौल्य, *m.* caprice, whim, fancy. [mind).

मनोवृत, full, complete, developed (said of the

मनोवृत्ति, *f.* operation or activity of the mind, fancy, volition, desire, wish.

मनोहर, *m.* (*f.* ī) a charming person, etc. : *lit.* captivating the heart or mind, fascinating, charming, beautiful, pleasing, agreeable, lovely.

मनोहरता } f. = मनोहरत्व, q.v.
मनोहरताई }

मनोहरत्व, *m.* (*f.* tā) captivatingness, charmingness, pleasantness fascination, beauty.

मनोहरी, *f.* (*m.* मनोहर) a fascinating beautiful [female.

मनोहारी, *m.* (*f.* iṇī) = मनोहर, *q.v.*

मनौती, *f.* bail, security, surety, assurance, acknowledgment: a person referred to for payment of the debt of another. [another.

मनौतीदार, *m.* a person who becomes surety for

मन्त, *m.* (*f.* matī); the plural termination of the Sanskrit Taddhita suffix मत्. Frequent in Hindee as a distinctive termination of adjectives.

मन्तर (*colloquial*) = मन्त्र, *q.v.*

मन्त्र, *m.* that part of each Ved which comprizes the hymns (as distinguished from the theological part, or the Brāhmaṇas); a mystic verse or incantation, a charm, spell; any formula sacred to any particular deity; a holy text: secret consultation, private advice.

मन्त्रगुप्ति, *f.* secret counsel, private consultation.

मन्त्रजन्त्र = मन्त्रयन्त्र, *q.v.*

मन्त्रज्ञ, *m.* (*f.* ā) a priest; a spy.

मन्त्रणा, *f.* consultation, deliberation, advising, persuasion, counsel.

मन्त्रधारी, *adj.* possessing good counsel: hence, *m.* (*f.* iṇī) an adviser, counsellor.

मन्त्रयन्त्र, *m.* incantation, exorcism. [formula.

मन्त्रराज, *m.* (king of spells) a certain magical

मन्त्रसिद्धि, *f.* the accomplishment or operation of a spell; the effecting or carrying out of a deliberation or advice. [recital of sacred texts.

मन्त्रित, *m.* (*f.* ā) initiated or consecrated by the

मन्त्रित्व, *m.* (*f.* tā) the condition, office, or functions of a councillor, ministership.

मन्त्री, *m.* (*f.* iṇī) a councillor, adviser, king's minister; an enchanter.

मन्त्रोपदेश, *m.* (among Hindoos) the instruction or formulæ imparted by a religious reacher.

मन्थ, *m.* a churning-stick; a dish made of barley-meal with ghee and water; a sort of gruel or porridge; a disease of the eyes (cataract or opacity); excretion of the eyes, rheum: the sun: stirring, churning: killing. [slaughter, murder.

मन्थन, *m.* churning, agitating, stirring: injury,

मन्थनी, *f.* a churning-vessel.

मन्थर, *m.* (= मन्दर) treasure: fruit: an obstacle: a churning-stick: safflower: *adj.* slow, torpid; large; crooked; stupid; low.

मन्थित, *m.* (*f.* ā) *more prop.* मथित, *q.v.*

मन्द, 1, *m.* (*f.* ā) a stupid person, etc.: *lit.* slow, stupid, tedious, dull, foolish, abated, allayed, tardy, gentle, mild, affable, cheap, bad, ill, vile, wicked, coarse, low, trifling, little, small, fertile: 2, an epithet (1) of Saturn (2) of Saturday (3) of Yam.

मन्दगति, *f.* slow motion, slow progress: *adj.* moving with a slow pace.

मन्दगामी, *m.* (*f.* inī) one who moves or marches slowly, etc.: *lit.* slow-moving; given to evil courses.

मन्दत, *m.* (*f.* antī) *adj.* rejoicing, delighting.

मन्दतर, (Sk. compar. of मन्द, *q.v.*) *m.* (*f.* ā) very stupid, very bad, very tardy, etc.

मन्दत्व, *m.* (*f.* tā) slowness, dulness, littleness, feebleness, tardiness, folly, wickedness.

मन्दबुद्धि, *m.* *f.* slow of apprehension, wanting in energy, dull, stupid, senseless, foolish, indifferent, bad.

मन्दभागी, *m.* (*f.* inī) an unfortunate person, etc.: *lit.* ill-fated, wretched, unhappy.

मन्दभाग्य, 1, *m.* = मन्दभाग्यत्व: 2, *m.* (*f.* ā) = मन्दभागी.

मन्दभाग्यत्व, *m.* (*f.* tā) adverse fortune, bad luck, [misfortune, ill-fatedness.

मन्दमति = मन्दबुद्धि, *q.v.*

मन्दमन्द, gently, softly, slowly, tardily, sluggishly, badly.

मन्दयमान, *m.* (*f.* matī) tardy, slow, delaying.

मन्दर, 1, slow, tardy, lazy, dull, large, bulky: 2, *m. pr. n.* (1) of the mountain with which the ocean is said to have been churned by the Surs and Asurs after the deluge, in order to recover the things lost in it during that catastrophe (2) of one of the trees of paradise (3) of paradise (*Swarg*).

मन्दरगिरि, *m. pr. n.* = मन्दर, 2 (1), *q.v.*

मन्दरा, *m.* (*f.* ī) squat, dapper.

मन्दराकिनी, a corruption of मन्दाकिनी, *q.v.*

मन्दराचल = मन्दर, 2 (1), *q.v.* [goddess Kāli.

मन्दरालसा, *f.* (see मन्दालसा) an epithet of the

मन्दल, 1, *m.* (corruption) = (1) मन्दिर (2) मण्डल (3) मन्दर, 2, *qq.v.*: 2, *f.* a kind of wooden drum beaten with the fingers: a fountain, jet d'eau.

मन्दलिपति, *more prop.* मण्डलिपति, *q.v.*

मन्दविष, 1, *m.* (*f.* ā) containing but little poison, having but little venom: 2, *m. pr. n.* a certain snake.

मन्दहास्य, *m.* a gentle laugh, a smile, simper.

मन्दा, *f.* (*m.* मन्द) a dull female, etc.

मन्दाकिनी, *f.* (see गंगा) the Ganges of heaven: (in Pros.) a species of metre: (in Astron.) a certain conjunction.

मन्दात्मा, *m.* *f.* slow of apprehension.

मन्दादर, *m.* (*f.* ā) a disrespectful person, etc.: lit. neglecting, disregarding, disrespecting.

मन्दायमान, *m.* (*f.* matī) = मन्दयमान, *q.v.*

मन्दार, *m.* one of the five trees in Indra's paradise; the coral-tree (*Erythrina fulgens*); swallow-wort (*Asclepias gigantea*). [thet of Kāli.

मन्दालसा, *f. pr. n.* the wife of king Alark: an epi-

मन्दिकुकुर, *f.* a sort of fish.

मन्दिर, *m.* a house, dwelling, palace, temple; a town: the sea: the back of the knee.

मन्दिरसेवक, *m.* (*f.* ikā) a temple-servant.

मन्दिरा, *f.* a house, dwelling, palace, temple; a town: a stable: a bed; a mat used as a couch.

मन्दिल, *more prop.* (1) मन्दिर (2) मन्दल, *qq.v.*

मन्दोदरी, *f. pr. n.* the favourite wife of Rāvaṇ, [and mother of Indra-jit.

मन्न, *m.* manna.

मन्नत, *f.* acknowledgment, assent, promise, vow; desire, intention. — *mānnā* to take a vow.

मथा, 1, = **मनना**, *q.v.* : 2, *more prop.* **मच**, *q.v.*

मन्मथ, *m.* an epithet of Kāmdev: amorous passion or desire, love, lust ; the elephant or wood-apple.

मन्मथी, *m.* (*f.* inī) amorous, impassioned, in love.

मन्वन्तर, *m.* the period of the reign of a Manu. The Manwantar is equivalent to seventy-one ages of the gods, or 306720000 years of mortals; or, with its *sandhi* or interval of universal deluge, 308448000 years. Fourteen Manwantars constitute a *kalp*, the grand period of creation and destruction, *i. e.* 4320000000 years. Each manwantar is governed by its distinct Manu, and is provided with its own Indra and minor deities. According to the Hindoo cosmogony there have been innumerable Manwantars since the first creation of the world.

मन्वान, *m.* (*f.* vatī) *adj.* thinking, conceiving, minding, regarding. [of the English term.)

मन्स्क्रप, *f.* manuscript. (The Indian printer's form

मपतखपत, *f.* measure.

मपना, *n.* to be measured.

मपवाना, *t.* to cause to be measured, to have a thing measured, to cause to measure.

मपान, *m.* measuring; measure.

मपाना, *t.* (causat. of **मापना**) to cause to measure.

मफ़तून, tried (as gold by fire); insane, fascinated, mad with love.

मफ़र, *m.* a place of refuge, asylum.

मबादी, *f.* beginnings, origins.

मबालिग़, *m.* sums of money, money.

मम, (a gen. of the Sk. **अस्मत**) of me, my, mine.

ममकिन, *more prop.* **मुमकिन**, *q.v.*

ममता, *f.* the interest or affection entertained for objects from the considering them as belonging to or connected with one's self, appropriation; selfsufficiency, pride, arrogance, selfism ; avarice, covetousness, selfishness; affection.

ममतायुक्त, *m.* (*f.* ā) a selfish person, niggard, miser:

ममत्व, *m.* = **ममता**, *q.v.* [*lit.* selfinterested, selfish.

ममधाम (*poet.*) = **मेरा धाम** = my dwellingplace.

ममलुकत, *f.* dominion, empire, kingdom, state ; grandeur. [purchased slave, a captive.

ममलूक, in one's power, possessed: hence, *m.* a

ममालिक, *f.* kingdoms, provinces, states, coun-

ममशीश (*poet.*) = **मेरा सिर** = my head. [tries.

ममियाना, *a. int.* to bleat (said of sheep). [uncle.

ममियाससुर, *m.* a husband's or wife's maternal

ममियासास, *f.* a husband's or wife's maternal

ममिहौं (*poet.*) = **मैं हूं**. [aunt.

ममेरा, *m.* (*f.* ī) appertaining to a maternal uncle.

ममेरा भाई, *m.* a cousin (a mother's brother's son).

ममेरी बहिन, *f.* a cousin (a mother's brother's daughter). [ly in the bowels).

ममोड़ा, *m.* twist, wreath ; ache, pain (particular-

मय, 1, *m.* (*f.* ī) a Taddhita suffix very extensively subjoined to substantives to form adjectives attributive of that of which a thing consists, or is chiefly made, or in which it abounds ; *e. g.* **मट्टीमय** means either (1) consisting of (or composed of) earth (2) abounding in (or replete with) earth, or (3) mixed with earth ; and thus = earthen, earthy : **2**, *m.* a camel : a mule : *3*, *m. pr. n.* a certain demon, the carpenter and architect of the Daityas : **4**, more properly **मै**, 2, *q. v.* As a suffix, this form is often printed **मई** ; *e. g.* **चैनमई** (see **य**, 2).

मयंक (Rām.) = **चन्द्रमा**, *q.v.*

मयत्री (Rām.) = **मैत्री**, *q.v.*

मयदानव, *m. pr. n.* = **मय**, 3, *q.v.*

मयन (Rām.) = **कामदेव**, *q.v.*

मयना, *f.* a kind of jay-bird (*Gracula religiosa* or *Coracias Indica*) commonly called the 'myna' or 'maina'.

मया ; for words beginning thus, see under the

मयारी ; see **मभक्की**. [more proper form **माया**.

मयी, 1, *more prop.* **मई**, *q.v.* : 2, *f.* : see **मय**, 1.

मयूख, *m.* a ray of light; light, splendour, lustre, beauty ; flame : the pin or gnomon of a sun-dial.

मयूड़, *m.* (*f.* ī) *more prop.* **मयूर**, *q.v.*

मयूर, *m.* (*f.* ī) a peacock ; the coxcomb-flower (*Celosia cristata*); a certain plant (*Achyranthes aspera*).

मयूरचूड़ा / **मयूरचूरा** } *f.* coxcomb (*Celosia cristata*).

मयूरारि, *m.* an epithet of the chameleon and of the lizard ; *lit.* the enemy of the *mayūr*.

मयूरारी, *more prop.* **मयूरारि**, *q. v.*

मयूरी, *f.* (*m.* **मयूर**) the peahen.

मयूष (corruption) = **मयूख**, *q.v.*

मर, (root of **मरना**) dying.—*jānā*, to die, die away, die off.—*pachnā*, to labour excessively, to suffer pain or sorrow.—*rahnā*, to be dead : to be deeply in love.

मरक, *m.* epidemic or pestilential disease.

मरकचा, *m.* the ridge of a house.

मरकट, *more prop.* **मर्कट**, *q. v.*

मरकटी, *more prop.* **मर्कटी**, *q. v.*

मरकत, *m.* an emerald. [difficulty.

मरकर, *lit.* having died; hence, *adv.* with great

मरक्त, *m.* an emerald.

मरकहा / **मरखना** } *m.* (*f.* ī) = **मरखाहा**, *q. v.*

मरखपना, *a. int.* to die.

मरखाहा, *m.* (*f.* ī) addicted to beating, striking, or butting (said of men or of brutes).

मरगल, fried (said of fish). [burn their dead.

मरघट, *m.* a crematory, or place where Hindoos

मरजाद, *more prop.* **मर्य्यादा**, *q.v.*

मरजाना ; see *s.v.* **मर**. [ceptable; taking favorably.

मरज़ी, *f.* will, pleasure, assent : *lit.* agreeable, ac-

मरजीया, *m.* a diver (for pearls).

मरण, *m.* dying ; death.

मरणकाल / **मरणसमय** } *m.* the dying moments, time of death.

मरतक (by inversion) = **मरकत**, *q. v.*

मरतबा, 1, *m.* step, degree, dignity office, employment, charge, rank of honour; class, order: 2, *f.* time, turn, occasion; *e. g. Tin martabe*, thrice: *Ek*—, once, one time, once upon a time, on one occasion.

मरतार (corruption) = **भरतार** = **भर्त्ता**, *q. v.*

मरतिब, *more prop.* (1) **मरतबा** (2) **मरातिब**, *qq. v.*

मरतूल } **मरतोल** } = **मारतोल**, *q. v.*

मरतेकाल, *m.* the dying moments, time of death.

मरत्तबा, *more prop.* **मरतबा**, *q. v.*

मरद, *more prop.* **मर्द**, *q. v.*

मरदनियां, *more prop* **मर्दनियां**, *q. v.*

मरदाना, *m.* (*f.* ी) appertaining to males, male, manly, brave; propria quæ maribus (as male apartments, etc.).

मरदानी, *f.* a masculine woman.

मरदी, *f.* manhood, virility, manliness.

मरदूद, rejected, excluded, reprobated, repulsed, confuted: hence, *m.* an apostate.

मरद्द in Chand = **मर्द**, *q. v.*

मरनहार, *m.* (*f.* ī) **मरनेहारा**, *q. v.*

मरना, 1, = **मरण**, *q. v.*: 2, *a. int.* to expire, die, cease: *met.* to desire vehemently, to set one's heart on a thing.

मरनेहारा, *m.* (*f.* ī) a mortal: *lit.* destined to die, dying, mortal.

मरपच, rotten, fermented, macerated.

मरपचना; see *s. v.* **मर**.

मरब्बत, *f.* rule, dominion.

मरभूक्खा, *more com.* **मरभूखा**, *q. v.*

मरभूखा, *m.* (*f.* ī) starved to death, voracious, ravenous, greedy.

मरम (*colloquial*) = **मर्म्म**, *q. v.*

मरमर, 1, *more prop.* **मर्म्मर**, *q. v.*: 2, *m.* marble.

मरमराना, *a. int.* to creak (as new shoes).

मररहना; see *s. v.* **मर**.

मरवाना, *t.* (causat. of **मरना**) to cause to be killed, cause to be beaten. *Marwā ḍālnā*, to dismiss a charge or complaint.

मरवाही, *m.* (*f.* inī) = **मरोही**, *q. v.*

मरवैया, *m.* one who is dying, one who is at the point of death; a corpse.

मरषा, *m.* (Sk. **मारिष**) a certain potherb (*Amaranthus oleraceus*).

मरसा, *more prop.* **मरषा**, *q. v.*

मरहटा } **मरहट्टा** } *m.* (prop. **महाराष्ट्र**) a Marhaṭṭā.

मरहम, *m.* a plaster, ointment, salve.

मरा, *m.* a corpse, carcase; base metal: *lit. m.* (*f.* ī) dead.

मरातिब, degrees, gradations of rank, dignities; affairs, matters: times.

मराना, *t.* (causat. of **मारना**) to cause to strike, cause to kill.

मराल, *m.* a sort of goose with red legs and bill; a duck; a horse; a rogue, scoundrel; a cloud; a grove of pomegranate-trees; lampblack used as a collyrium: *lit.* soft, mild, bland.

मराव, *m.* (*f.* nī ?) mortal, deadly, fatal.

मरिच, *m.* (*f.* ?) black pepper, and its plant (*Piper nigrum*).

मरियल, emaciated, lean, much reduced by sickness.

मरिष्या, *f. pr. n.* the daughter of a certain *rishi* and wife of Sūrsen.

मरिषा, *m.* mustard-seed (*Sinapis dichotoma*).

मरिहि (pl. °हिं; see **इहि**) } **मरिहै** (pl. °हैं; see **इहै**) } = **मरेगा** (**मरना**).

मरी, *f.* plague, pestilence, cholera morbus.

मरीच, *more prop.* (1) **मरिच** (2) **मरीचि**, *qq. v.*

मरीचा, *more prop.* **मरिच**, *q. v.*

मरीचि, 1, *m. f.* a ray of light, a sunbeam: 2, *m.* a niggard, miser: 3, *m. pr. n.* (1) of one of the ten Mahārishis or primeval sages and procreators of mankind, a Prajāpati and son of Brahmā (2) of one of the seven ṛishis represented by the seven stars in Ursa Major.

मरीचिका, *f.* the mirage.

मरीची, *more com.* **मरीचि**, *q. v.*

मरीज़, sick, diseased.

मरु, *m.* 1, dry ground, soil destitute of water, desert, sands: a mountain: 2, *pr. n.* (1) of a certain ancient Hindoo king (2) of the province of Māṛwāṛ, and of its people.

मरुआ, *m.* a certain strong-scented plant (*Artemisia vulgaris*); the plant *Ocymum pilosum*, Roxb.

मरुत, *m.* wind, air: *pr. n.* the deities of wind and of the North-west quarter.

मरुतकोण, *m. pr. n.* the North-west quarter.

मरुत्त, *m. pr. n.* a certain fabulous king.

मरुदेश, *m.* } **मरुभू**, *f.* (*m.* ?) } **मरुभूमि**, *f.* } = **मरुस्थल**, *q. v.*

मरुस्थल, *m.* (= **मरु**, 1, 2) a dry and desert tract of country, barren land.

मरू; for words beginning thus, see under the more proper form **मरु**.

मरुव्वत; see **मुरुव्वत**.

मरेठा, *m.* twisted, bound around, wound up.

मरोड़, *f.* twist, flexion, turn, writhe, convolution, contortion.— *ḍālnā*, to tear by twisting.

मरोड़ना, to twist, writhe, contort, distort, gripe, yearn.

मरोड़फली, *f.* a certain plant (*Helicteres isora*) the fruit of which is used in medicine.

मरोड़ा, *m.* a twisting of the bowels, pain in the bowels, gripes, flux.

मरोड़ी, *f.* twisting, contortion, writhing; a screw.

मरोर, *more prop.* **मरोड़**, *q. v.*

मरोल, *more prop.* (1) **मरोलि** (2) **मरोड़**, *qq. v.*

मरोलि } **मरोली** } *m.* (= **मकर**) the *makar*.

मरोह, *f.* affection, kindness, humanity, compassion, pity, mercy.

मरोही, *m.* (*f.* inī) affectionate, humane, compassionate, merciful.

मर्क, *m.* a body; the vital breath which pervades the body: a monkey: an imp: *pr. n.* a son of Shukrāchārya.

मर्कट, *m.* (*f.* ī) a monkey, ape: a spider: a large crane (*Ardea argala*): a kind of venom.

मर्कटी, *f.* 1, (*m.* **मर्कट**) a female monkey: 2, (dim. of **मर्कट**) a small monkey.

मर्कटेन्दु, *m.* a sort of ebony (*Diospyros melanoxylon*).

मर्करा, *f.* a chasm, hole; a vessel; a barren female.

मर्गाबियां, a corruption of **मुर्ग़ाबियां**, *q.v.*

मर्ज़ी = **मरज़ी**, *q. v.*

मर्तबा = **मरतबा**, *q. v.*

मर्त्तलोक, *more prop.* **मर्त्त्यलोक**, *q. v.* [mortal.

मर्त्तव्य, *m.* (*f.* ā) liable to death, doomed to die,

मर्त्य, *m.* (*f.* ā) a mortal, a human creature; the body; the earth: *lit.* liable to death, doomed to die, mortal.

मर्त्यपुर = **मर्त्यलोक**, *q. v.*

मर्त्यलोक, *m.* the habitation of mortals, *i. e.* the earth, the present world: *lit.* that state which is such that those who exist in it are all liable to death.

मर्द, *m.* a male, a man, a brave man, hero (*vir*): *lit.* male, brave, bold.

मर्दन = **मर्द्दन**, *q. v.* [break, subdue, destroy.

मर्दना, *t.* to rub, touch, anoint; to grind, pound,

मर्दनिया, *m.* one who anoints.

मर्दनियां, *m.* (pl. of **मर्दनी**) anointers, attendants whose business it is to rub oil, perfumed paste, etc. over the body.

मर्दनी, *m.* (*f.* inī) one who anoints.

मर्दि (Rām.) = **मर्दके** (**मर्दना**): see **कृ**, 7.

मर्दित, *m.* (*f.* ā) = **मर्द्दित**, *q. v.*

मर्दी, *m.* (*f.* inī) *adj.* grinding, breaking.

मर्दुआ, *m.* (see **उआ**) a man, male.

मर्द्दन, 1, *m.* rubbing, friction, grinding, pounding, bruising, trampling, treading down, anointing, touching: 2, *m.* (*f.* ā) *adj.* grinding, pounding, breaking, subduing, destroying.

मर्द्दित, *m.* (*f.* ā) rubbed, touched, anointed, ground, pounded, broken, bruised, subdued, destroyed.

मर्म्मी, *m.* (*f.* inī) = **मर्म्मज्ञ**, *q. v.*

मर्म्म, *m.* a vital member or organ, a joint, the core, the quick; anything hidden or recondite, secret meaning or purpose, the secret recesses of the heart, a secret, design, truth.

मर्म्मज्ञ, *m.* (*f.* ā) a learned man; a Brāhmaṇ; a spy: *lit.* acquainted with secret things, learned, intelligent, acute. [leaves or of the wind).

मर्म्मर, *m.* a rustling sound (as of cloth or of dry

मर्म्मरी, *f.* a species of pine-tree (*Pinus devadaru*).

मर्म्मभेदी / **मर्म्मी** } *m.* (*f.* inī) = **मर्म्मज्ञ**, *q. v.*

मर्याद, *more prop.* **मर्य्यादा**, *q. v.*

मर्य्यादवान, *m.* (*f.* vatī) a respectable person, etc.: *lit.* observing propriety of conduct, respectable, estimable, aristocratic, honorable, dignified.

मर्य्यादा, *f.* a landmark, boundary, limit; the keeping within proper limits, propriety of conduct, steadiness, uprightness, straightforwardness, rectitude, dignity, respect, reputation, station, rank, honour.

मर्य्यादिक, *m.* (*f.* ā *or* ī) = **मर्य्यादवान**, *q. v.*

मर्री, *f.* plague, pestilence, cholera morbus.

मर्वा / **मर्सा** } more prop. **मरवा**, *q. v.*

मल, *m.* dirt, filth, sediment, dregs, filthy refuse, excretion of the body (as serum, semen, blood, marrow, earwax, nails, phlegm, tears, rheum, sweat, urine, fœces); rust: a spot; defilement; sin: camphor: cuttle-fish bone. [ty, excommunicated.

मलऊन, execrated, accursed, driven out of socie-

मलंग, *m.* a kind of Muhammadan ascetic who lets his hair grow loose and uncombed: a kind of bird.

मलंगी, *m.* (*f.* inī) a salt-maker.

मलक, doubt, suspicion, apprehension.

मलकना, *a. int.* to walk trotting and raising the shoulders (like a chair-carrier, etc.). [sion.

मलखाट, bile, excess of bile: doubt, apprehen-

मलस, *m.* (from **मलना**) a worn rupee (or other coin).

मलदल, *m.* a rubbing, grinding.

मलन, *m.* a rubbing, grinding, threshing; a path.

मलना, *t.* to rub; to tread or trample on; to thresh by treading; to anoint.

मलनादलना, a play on the word **मलना**, *q. v.*

मलवा, *m.* rubbish, refuse, sweepings, dirt.

मलवाख़र्च, *m.* village-expenses, etc.

मलम, more prop. **मरहम**, *q. v.*

मलमल, *f.* muslin.

मलमला, *m.* (*f.* ī) brackish. [vities.

मलमल्लक, *m.* a piece of cloth worn over the pri-

मलमास, *m.* an intercalary month.

मलमेट, ruined: decided (said of a dispute). —*k.* to raze, destroy. — *honā*, to be destroyed.

मलय, *m. pr. n.* (1) of a mountain or mountainous range (from which the best sandal-wood is brought) answering to the western ghāṭs in the peninsula of India (2) of the country (Malayālim or Malabār) which lies along that range (3) of one of the minor dweeps or divisions of the world (4) of the garden of Indra.

मलयज, *m.* sandal-wood.

मलयध्वज, *m. pr. n.* (1) of a certain king of the Pāṇdyas (2) of a son of Meru-dhvaj. [Malayālim.

मलयघाट, *m. pr. n.* the country of Malabar or

मलया, 1, *f.* a plant (*convolvulus turpethum*) commonly called *teori*: 2, (in Pros.) a species of metre.

मलयागर / **मलयागिरि** / **मलयागीर** } = **मलयाचल**, *q. v.*

मलयागीरी, *m.* the colour of sandal-wood.

मलयाचल, *m. pr. n.* (see **मलया**, 1) a mountain (or mountainous range) from which the best sandal-wood is brought, answering to the western ghāṭs in the peninsula of India.

मलवाई, *f.* (see **वाई**, 3) the price for scouring, etc.

मलवाना, *t.* to cause to be rubbed, cause to be scoured, cause to be ground.

मलवैया, *m.* one who rubs or scours, a scrubber.

मलहती, *more prop.* मूलहट्टी, *q.v.*
मलहम, *more prop.* मरहम, *q.v.*
मलहानी, *f.* the removal or destruction of filth.
मलहारक, *m.* (*f.* ikā)
मलहारी, *m.* (*f.* iṇī) } *adj.* filth-destroying.
मलाई, *f.* cream; a kind of dish made of milk.
मलाका, *f.* a lewd female; a female messenger: a female elephant.
मलाकात, *more prop.* मुलाक़ात, *q.v.*
मलाकी, *m. pr. n.* the prophet Malachi and the Book that bears his name.
मलागिर
मलागिरि } = मलयाचल, *q.v.*
मलागोरि; see मलागोरी and मलागिरि.
मलागोरी, *m.* the colour of sandal-wood.
मलान (Rām.) = म्लान, *q.v.* [to grind.
मलाना, *t.* to cause to rub, cause to scour, cause
मलाम, *m.* reproach, reprehension, rebuke, blame,
मलामत, *f.* = मलाम, *q.v.* [accusation, reviling.
मलार, *a contraction of* मल्लारी, *q.v.*
मलाह, 1, *more prop.* मल्लाह, *q.v.*: 2, a bulrush.
मलिछ (*colloquial*) = म्लेच्छ, *q.v.*
मलाहत, *f.* being salt, savoury, well (or highly) flavoured; elegancy; beauty, excellence.
मलिदलि (see मलनादलना) = मलदल, *q.v.*
मलिन, *m.* (*f.* ā *or* ī) dirty, filthy, soiled, unclean, polluted, foul, vile, bad, sinful, depraved, vicious; black; obscured; sad, indisposed, troubled, disturbed, vexed, melancholy. [ness; sediment.
मलिनता, *f.* (*m.* °त्व) filth, impurity, vileness; black-
मलिनमति, a person of a polluted or troubled mind.
मलिनमुख, *m.* (*f.* ī) a cruel person; a goblin; the black-faced monkey; an epithet of Agni: *lit.* black-faced; *hence,* savage, fierce, cruel, vile, wicked.
मलिना, *f.* (*m.* मलिन) a foul female; a female during
मलिनी, *f.* (*m.* मली) = मलिना, *q.v.* [menstruation.
मलिया, *m.* a small vessel (of wood or of the shell of a cocoanut) for holding the oil used in unction.
मलिष्ठ, *m.* (*f.* ā) an exceedingly vile person: *lit.* (superl.) very foul, very polluted, very wicked.
मलिष्ठा, *f.* (*m.* मलिष्ठ) an exceedingly vile female; a female during menstruation.
मली, *m.* (*f.* inī)
मलीन, *m.* (*f.* ā or ī) } *more com.* मलिन, *q.v.*
मलुक; see (1) मलूक (2) मुलुक.
मलूक, *m.* a kind of worm: *pr. n.* a certain an-
मलूम, blamed, reproached. [cient Hindoo faqeer.
मलेआल
मलेआली } = मलयवाट, *q.v.*
मलेछ (*colloquial*) = म्लेच्छ, *q.v.*
मलेपंज, aged above ten years (said of horses, because their age is no longer evident from their teeth).
मलेवार
मलेवारी } = मलयवाट, *q.v.*

मलेया, *more prop.* मलय, *q.v.*
मल्खम, the upright post in a sugar-mill.
मल्ल, *m.* (*f.* ā) the offspring of an outcaste Kshatriya: a boxer, wrestler (by birth): a cup; the hemimnium: the residue of an oblation: *lit.* strong, robust, stout, athletic; best, chief, eminent, excellent.
मल्लभू, *f.* a place for athletic contests, the site of any conflict, a palæstrum, arena, gymnasium, battlefield.
मल्लयात्रा, *f.* a match of wrestling or boxing.
मल्लयुद्ध, *m.* wrestling, boxing, fisticuffs, fighting. — *k.* to wrestle. [athletic female: Arabian jasmine.
मल्ला, *f.* (*m.* मल्ल) a female of the *mall* caste; an
मल्लार, *more prop.* मल्लारी, *q.v.* [during the rains.
मल्लारी, *f.* one of the musical modes (*rāgiṇī*) sung
मल्लाह, *m.* a waterman, boatman, sailor, seaman;
मल्लि = मल्ली, *q.v.* [a manufacturer of salt.
मल्लिका, *f.* Arabian jasmine (*Jasminum zambac*): a species of metre in Sanskrit prosody.
मल्लिगन्धि
मल्लिगन्धी } *m.* aloe-wood.
मल्ली, *f.* Arabian jasmine (*Jasminum zambac*), a
मल्लु, *m.* a bear. [beautiful flowering shrub.
मल्लू, 1, *more prop.* मल्लु, *q.v.*: 2, a monkey.
मल्हार, *more prop.* मल्लारी, *q.v.*
मल्हारराव, *m.* the sound of the *mallārī*.
मवा in Gaṛhwāl = honey.
मवाठी, *more prop.* मवादी, *q.v.*
मवाफरोश, *more prop.* मेवाफ़रोश, *q.v.*
मवाशी, quadrupeds, cattle (esp. domestic beasts, as cows, buffaloes, sheep, and goats).
मवास, *m.* protection, refuge, asylum, retreat: a
मवासी; see मवाशी and मवास. [collection of trees.
मश, *m.* a mosquito, gnat.
मशक, *m.* 1, a gnat, mosquito: a kind of cutaneous eruption, the formation of small pustules or warts: 2. *f.* a leathern water-bag. This term *Mashak* is applied chiefly to the entire goat's hide which is commonly used by the native water-carriers; it is also applied to the inflated buffalo-hide which in some parts of the country is used as a boat.
मशहक, *more prop.* मशक, *q.v.*
मश्क, 1, *m.* musk: 2, *f. more prop.* मशक, 2, *q.v.*
मशक्कत, *f.* trouble, labour, pains, toil, assiduity.
मशगूल, employed, occupied, busy, diligent, anxious.
मशन, striking gently (with a sword or scourge), scratching, excoriating, grazing the skin: lying with: rubbing with the hand in order to make smooth: giving.
मशर, one who goes with a graceful sprightly air.
मशल, *more prop.* मसल, *q.v.* [practiser, a proficient.
मश्शाक़, well-versed, well-practised: hence, *m.* a
मश्शाक़गी, *f.* the art of attiring a bride.
मश्शाता, *f.* a comber, waiting-maid, bride-dresser, tire-woman; a woman who makes or concerts marriages, a go-between.

मशहरी, *f.* mosquito-curtains.
मशहूर, celebrated, famous, notorious, published, [divulged, conspicuous.
मशा, a gnat, mosquito.
मशाता, *more prop.* **मश्शाता**, *q.v.*
मशान (contraction) = **श्मशान**, *q.v.* See **मसान**.
मशाल, *f.* a torch, flambeau, lantern.
मशालची, *m.* (*f.* in, inī, nī) a torch-bearer.
मशाबिह, *more prop.* **मुशाबिह**, *q.v.*
मशाला, *m.* a torch, flambeau, lantern.
मशालाढार, *m.* a torch-bearer.
मषरंगी, *f.* a kind of pulse fried.
मषी, *f.* ink: the stalk of the *Nyctanthes tristis.*
मष्ट, *f.* silence. — *mārnā,* to remain silent.
मसक, 1, *more prop.* **मशक**, *q.v.* : 2, see **मसकाना**.
मसकना, *n.* to be torn, be split, be rent, be burst.
मसकरी, *more prop.* **मस्करी**, *q.v.*
मसकाना, *t.* to tear, rend, split, burst.
मसख़री, *f.* jest, drollery, buffoonery.
मसगुल, *more prop.* **मशग़ूल**, *q.v.*
मसजिद, *f.* a Muhammadan temple, mosque.
मसन, *m.* a certain medicinal fruit (*Serratula anthelmintica*).
मसनंद, *more prop.* **मसनद**, *q.v.*
मसनद, *f.* a throne, a large cushion, a chair, a prop.
मसबिर्द, *m.* a fleshy excrescence or swelling, a wart.
मसमसाना, to suppress one's sentiments from fear, to be mealy-mouthed.
मसरंगी, *f.* a kind of pulse fried.
मसल, *f.* a fable, allegory, simile, metaphor, example; an adage, proverb; department, post.
मसलन, for example, for instance.
मसलना, *t.* to break with the hand, crush, bruise.
मसलहत, *f.* an action, occupation: expediency, the best thing to be done; counsel, advice. — *k.* to consult, combine.
मसशातः, *more prop.* **मश्शाता**, *q.v.*
मसहर; see (1) **मशहरी** (2) **मशहूर** (3) **मुशहर**.
मसहरी, *more prop.* **मशहरी**, *q.v.*
मसहलत (*by inversion*) = **मसलहत**, *q.v.*
मसहूर, *more prop.* **मशहूर**, *q.v.*
मसा, *m.* a fleshy excrescence, a wart: the sight of a gun: a mosquito, gnat.
मसान, *m.* (from **श्मशान**) a place where Hindoos burn their dead, a crematory; a cemetery: a demon.
मसार, *m.* a sapphire, an emerald.
मसाला, *m.* condiments, drugs, spices, seasoning.
मसाहिब, *more prop.* **मुसाहिब**, *q.v.*
मसि, *f.* ink.
मसिधान, *m.* } an inkstand.
मसिधानी, *f.* } an inkstand.
मसिहरी (*corruption*) = **मशहरी**, *q.v.*
मसी, *f.* ink.
मसीत in Māṛwāṛī = **मसजिद**, *q.v.*
मसीन, *m.* a vetch, pulse; linseed (*Linum usitatissimum*), flax.
मसीना, *f.* = **मसीन**, *q.v.*
मसीपात्र, *m.* an ink-bottle, an inkstand.
मसीह, *m. pr. n.* the Messiah, Christ. The word properly means 'anointed' (*i.e.* to office, whether ecclesiastical or regal).
मसीहा, 1, *more com.* **मसीह**, *q.v.*: 2, = **मसीही**, 2, *q.v.*
मसीहाई, *m.* (*f.* inī) *more com.* **मसीही**, *q.v.*
मसीही, 1, *f.* the office or the works of the Messiah: 2, *m.* (inī) a follower of the Messiah, a Christian: *lit.* appertaining to the Messiah, Christlike, Christian.
मसुर = **मसूर**, *q.v.*
मसुरा = **मसूरा**, *q.v.*
मसूड़ा, *m.* the gums (of the teeth).
मसूर, *m.* a certain small flat yellow bean or lentil (*Urvum hirsutum* or *Cicer lens*).
मसूरा, *f.* 1, = **मसूर**, *q.v.* 2, a harlot.
मसूरिका, *f.* procuress: the small-pox.
मसूरिया, *f.* (from **मसूरिका**) a kind of small-pox.
मसूरी = **मसूरिया**, *q.v.*
मसें, *f.* (pl.) the hair or down on the upper lip which appears in early youth.
मसोसना, *t.* to twist, squeeze, wring: *a. int.* to grieve, regret.
मसोसा, 1, *m.* (*f.* ī) twisted; grieved, afflicted: 2, *m.* remorse, regret, affliction.
मस्करिन } *m.* a religious mendicant: the moon.
मस्करी } *m.* a religious mendicant: the moon.
मस्कोदा, *more com.* **मशक**, 2, *q.v.*
मस्त, intoxicated; wanton, lustful; proud.
मस्तक, *m.* (*f.* ?) the forehead, the head, the skull; the top, the summit; the chief.
मस्तकी, appertaining to the head.
मस्ती, *f.* intoxication, wantonness, lust.
मस्तूल, *m.* the mast of a ship. — *girānā,* to strike sail.
मस्याधार, *m.* (**मसि** + **आधार**) an inkstand.
मस्स, *m.* touch. — *k.* to touch, feel.
मस्सा, *m.* a fleshy excrescence, a wart; the sight of a gun.
मह, 1, (*contraction*) = **माह**, *q.v.*: 2, in Braj = **में**, 2.
महं in Braj and in poetry = **में**, 2, *q.v.*
महंग (contraction) = **महंगा**, *q.v.*
महंगमोल, *m.* high price.
महंगा, *m.* (*f.* ī) high-priced, expensive, costly, dear.
महंगी, *f.* expensiveness; dearth, scarcity, famine.
महक, *f.* perfume, fragrance, odour, scent, smell.
महकना, *a. int.* to smell pleasant, to exhale agreeable odours, to perfume.
महकाज = **महाकर्म्म**, *q.v.*
महकाना, *t.* to exhale, to perfume.
महकीला, *m.* (*f.* ī) odoriferous, fragrant, spicy, aromatic.
महक्क, *m.* diffusive fragrance.
महज़, pure, unmixed, mere: *adv.* purely, merely, entirely, wholly.
महजाला (dialectic) = **महाजाल**, *q.v.*

महज़ुय, a corruption of **महज़ूज़**, *q.v.* [pleased.

महज़ूज़, glad, cheerful, contented, delighted,

महटिआना; see **मटियाना**.

महत, *m.* (*f.* ī) = **महन्त**, *q.v.*

महतत्व, *more prop.* **महत्तत्व**, *q.v.*

महता, 1, = **महतो**, *q.v.*: 2, *more prop.* **महत्ता**, *q.v.*

महताज, *more prop.* **मुहताज**, *q.v.* [village constable.

महतादी, *m.* a head village peon; a village bailiff,

महताब, *m.* the moon; moonlight; a kind of fire-

महतारी, *f.* a mother. [works (blue-lights).

महति (Rām.) = **महती**, *q.v.*

महती, *f.* (*m.* **महन्त**, etc.) an eminent female, an abbess, a 'lady-superior'; the lute of Nārad containing seven or one hundred strings; the egg-plant (*Solanum melongena*); (in Arīthm.) a great surd or the sum of two original irrational numbers.

महतो, *m.* a land-bailiff, or person employed by a land-holder to collect the rent from a village, an agent, scribe, clerk. [tellect.

महत्तत्व, *m.* the *mahat* or great principle, *i. e.* In-

महत्ता, *f.* = **महत्त्व**, *q.v.* [ance, grandeur, dignity.

महत्त्व, *m.* greatness, magnitude, bulk; import-

महत्व, *more prop.* **महत्त्व**, *q.v.*

महदाश्रय, *m.* (*f.* ā) one who is dependent on the great: *lit.* whose asylum is the great.

महदोज, very powerful, very strong.

महदौषध = **महौषध**, *q.v.*

महनरकी, *m.* (*f.* inī) a dweller in Mahānarak.

महना, *t.* to churn.

महन्त, 1, *m.* (*f.* **महती**) an eminent personage; a religious superior, prior, abbot, a chief of fakeers, a monk: *lit.* large, bulky, great, eminent, chief, excellent, illustrious, glorious, greatest, best, preëminent: 2, *m.* greatness, magnitude, importance, grandeur, dignity; infinity; kingdom: the intellectual principle.

महन्ताई, *f.* the status, office, or functions of a *mahant*, mahantship.

महन्ती, *f.* 1, *more prop.* **महती**, *q.v.*: 2, = **महन्ताई**, *q.v.*

महफ़िल, *f.* a time or place of meeting; assembly, congregation, congress. [ted to memory.

महफ़ूज़, guarded, protected, preserved, commit-

महब्बत, *f.* friendship, charity, affection, love, attachment.

महबूबी, *f.* exceeding loveliness, great beauty.

महमूदा, *f.* scammony.

महम्मद, *more prop.* **मुहम्मद**, *q.v.*

महर, 1, *m.* = **महर्लोक**, *q.v.*: 2, *m.* a chief: 3, *f.* a female, woman, wife: 4, *m.* a marriage portion.

महरबान, *more prop.* **मिहरबान**, *q.v.*

महरम, a spouse, an intimate friend; anyone who is admitted into the women's apartments: the boddice or part of a dress in which the breasts are confined.

महरमराज़, a confidant or confidential person.

महरा, *m.* a pālkee-bearer. [of song among cowherds.

महराई, *f.* the occupation of pālkee-bearer: a kind

महरि, **महरी** } *f.* a female, woman, wife.

महरू, a contraction of **माहरू**, *q.v.*

महरूम, prohibited, excluded; deprived of the support of life, plundered, unfortunate, wretched, disappointed.

महरूसा, *m.* a garrisoned or fortified place, well-governed or protected territory (as that which is subject to established power).

महर्लोक, *m. pr. n.* one of the divisions of the universe (a region said to be one crore of Yojans above the polar star, and to be the celestial paradise of those saints who survive a destruction of the world).

महर्षि, *m.* a preëminent class of saint-sages (said to be primeval, and to be the procreators of mankind): *lit.* a great saint.

महर्षी, *more prop.* **महर्षि**, *q.v.*

महल (corruption) = **महल्ल**, *q.v.*

महल्ल, *m.* (*pl.* āt) a place, building, house, abode, residence, mansion, castle, palace, seraglio; a district, quarter, station; time, occasion, opportunity.

महल्लक, *m.* a eunuch or attendant belonging to a seraglio. [mansion, the seraglio.

महल्लसरा, *f.* the inner or female apartments of a

महल्ला, *m.* a district, quarter, division of a town: a review of troops. [servant, a eunuch.

महल्ली, appertaining to the seraglio; *hence*, a

महवा = **महुआ**, *q.v.*

महवार, *m.* monthly salary; a deed settling the payment of revenue by monthly instalments.

महवारा, *m.*, **महवारी**, *f.* } = **महवार**, *q.v.*

महसूल, *m.* excise, tax, custom, duty, postage, public revenue, produce. — *lenā*, to collect taxes.

महा, 1, (used only in comp.) = **महत**, in the sense of great, illustrious; very, extremely: 2, *f.* (*m.* **मह**) a cow.

महाउत (*corruption*) = **महावत**, *q.v.*

महाकन्द, *m.* a certain very large esculent root, a sort of yam, garlic.

महाकर्म्म, *m.* a great work: *adj.* accomplishing great works, doing mighty deeds: an epithet of Shiv.

महाकाय, of great body, of high stature, large, bulky, stout, tall, gigantic.

महाकाल, *m.* an epithet of Shiv (as identified with Time) in his character of the Destroyer, in which he is represented of a black colour and of an aspect more or less terrific. In this chief, Shiv may be regarded as a personification of time that destroys all things.

महाकाली, *f.* (see **महाकाल**) an epithet of Durgā (wife of Shiv) in her more terrific form.

महाकुल, *m.* (*f.* ā) a noble: *lit.* eminent by birth, of good extraction, of great family, high-born.

महाकुलीन, *m.* (*f.* ā) = **महाकुल**, *q.v.*

महाकूप, *m.* a large or deep well.

महाकूल, *more prop.* **महाकुल**, *q.v.* [elephantiasis).

महाकोढ़, *m.* a certain species of leprosy (perhaps

महाखण्ड, *m.* an epithet of Bhāratvarsh.

महाखाल, *m.* a rush of the sea upon a contiguous flat region.

महागद, 1, *m.* a kind of medicinal compound ; a great sickness, severe illness, fever : 2, *m.* (*f.* ā) armed with a great club. [*jaṭā.*

महाजट, *m.* an epithet of Shiv: *lit.* having a great

महाजटा, *f.* a great *jaṭā* (*esp.* the *jaṭā* of Shiv).

महाजड़, utterly irrational, intensely stupid or insensible.

महाजन, *m.* (*f.* ī) a preëminent or distinguished person, a good or trustworthy person : a merchant, money-dealer, banker.

महाजनी, *f.* the business of a *mahājan*, commerce, trade ; interest, commission.

महाजान = **महाज्ञान**, *q.v.*

महाजाल, *m.* a large fishing-net, a seine.

महाजाला (dialectic) = **महाजाल**, *q.v.*

महाजोखिम, *f.* great peril, a great enterprise, a great achievement.

महाज्ञान, *m.* (*f.* ā) possessed of great knowledge or learning very wise. [or pālkee for great personages.

महाडोल, *m.* a large and splendid sort of sedan

महाड़ी = **म्हाड़ी**, *q.v.*

महातत्त्व, *m.* (the great principle, *i.e.*) the intellect (or second of the Sānkhya *tattvas*).

महातत्त्वा, *f. pr. n.* one of Durgā's attendants.

महातम, *m.* greatness, grandeur, rank, dignity ; the benefit accruing from any good work.

महातमप्रभा, *f. pr. n.* the nethermost division of

महातम्य, *m.* (*f.* ā) = **महात्मा**, *q.v.* [hell (*Narak*).

महातल, *m. pr. n.* the fifth in descent of the seven regions (*pātāl*) under the earth. It is said to be inhabited by various classes of evil beings, such as Nāgs, Asurs, Daityas, etc.

महातिक्त, *m.* the large *nimb*-tree (*Melia sempervirens*): *lit. m.* (*f.* ā) very bitter or sharp.

महातीक्ष्ण, *m.* (*f.* ā) an acute person: *lit.* very sharp (as a weapon, perception, etc.), very pungent.

महातेजा, *m. f.* very bright, very energetic, very

महात्म; see (1) **महात्मा** (2) **माहात्म्य**. [vigorous.

महात्मा, *m. f.* high-souled, lofty-minded, magnanimous, noble, high-bred, high-principled, generous, liberal.

महात्म्य (contraction) = **माहात्म्य**, *q.v.*

महात्व; see **महत्त्व** and **महातत्त्व**.

महादन्त, *m.* an elephant's tusk ; an elephant with large tusks. [a great giver.

महादाता, *m.* (*f.* trī) a very beneficent person,

महादान, *m.* (a great gift) an epithet of certain valuable gifts or the giving of different kinds of valuable presents to the priests. Sixteen such gifts are particularly enumerated.

महादीन, *m.* (*f.* ā) very meek, very poor. [bad.

महादुष्ट, *m.* (*f.* ā) exceedingly vile, exceptionally

महादुष्टत्व, *m.* (*f.* tā) great vileness.

महादेव, *m.* the epithet by which Shiv is most commonly known.

महादेवी, *f.* an epithet of Pārvatī (wife of Shiv).

महाधातु, *m.* gold: *lit.* the great or prime element.

महान, *m.* (*f.* **महती**) = **महन्त**, *q.v.*

महानगर, *m.* a great city : *pr. n.* a certain city.

महानन्द, *m.* the highest bliss, *i.e.* eternal emancipation, final beatitude. [day of the month Māgh.

महानन्दा, *f.* a certain Hindoo festival on the ninth

महानन्दि, *m. pr. n.* a certain ancient Hindoo king, son of Nandivardhan.

महानन्दी, *m.* (*f.* inī) one who has attained final beatitude : *lit.* relating to *Mahānand*.

महानरक, *m. pr. n.* one of the divisions of the infernal regions. [of the *shuklpaksh* of Aswin.

महानवमी, *f.* a Hindoo festival on the ninth day

महानिद्रा, *f.* an epithet of death or dying ; *lit.* the

महा निन्दा, *f.* rank blasphemy. [great sleep.

महानिम्ब, *m.* a large kind of *nimb*-tree (*Melia sempervirens*).

महानिशा, *f.* the dead of night, midnight.

महानील, *m.* the sapphire : *pr.n.* one of the Nāgas.

महानुभाव, (*f.* ā) a gentleman ; *lit.* preëminent, just, virtuous, magnanimous, liberal.

महापंक, *m.* deep mire, a great quagmire.

महापक्षी, *m.* (*f.* iṇī) an owl.

महापण्डित, very learned : hence, *m.* (*f.* ā) a great scholar, great philosopher, great teacher.

महापथ, *m.* a principal road or street, main entrance, chief route, highway ; the great way, *i.e.* the way of all flesh, the final exit, death.

महापद्म, *m.* 1, *pr.n.* (1) of one of the nine treasures (*nidhi*) of Kuver (2) of one of Kuver's attendants (3) of one of the Nāgas : 2, one hundred thousand billions.

महापाखण्ड (*colloquial*) = **महापाषण्ड**, *q.v.*

महापात = **महापातक**, *q.v.*

महापातक, *m.* falling with great force ; *hence*, great crime, a heinous offence, a crime of the highest degree. Five of these are taken cognizance of in the Hindoo system ; *viz.* (1) the killing a Brāhmaṇ (2) stealing gold from a priest (3) drinking spirits (4) adultery with the wife of a spiritual teacher, and (5) associating with persons who have committed these offences.

महापातकी, *m.* (*f.* inī) one who has been guilty of a crime of the highest degree, a great offender, an atrocious sinner.

महापाप, *m.* (see **महापातक**) guilt of the most heinous kind, great sin, atrocious crime.

महापापी, *m.* (*f.* inī) = **महापातकी**, *q.v.*

महापाषण्ड, 1, *m.* great heresy or hypocrisy : 2, a great heretic, great hypocrite, great blasphemer.

महापासक, *m.* a religious mendicant.

महापुरुष, *m.* (*f.* ī) a great personage, magnate, dignitary, chief, noble, saint ; a person invested with official authority.

महापुष्पा, *f.* a certain flower (*Clitoria ternatea*).

महाप्रभु, *m.* a great master, great personage, monarch, saint ; an epithet of Shiv, Vishṇu, and other deities.

महाप्रलय, *m. pr. n.* (1) of a general dissolution

of the world occurring (according to the Hindoos) after every period of 4320000000 years of mortals (2) of a total destruction of the universe which is to take place after a period commensurate with the life of Brahmā, *viz.* a hundred years, each day and each night of which is equal to the above-mentioned period (4320000000 years). At the expiration of this period, the seven states (*lok*), with the saints, gods, and Brahmā himself, are totally annihilated.

महाप्रसाद, *m.* the food which is offered to a deity (esp. to Jagannāth) and afterwards distributed.

महाप्राण, *m.* (in Gram.) an aspirated letter, aspirated pronunciation, spiritus asper.

महाब; for words beginning thus, but not given below, see under the more proper form **महाव**.

महाबल, *m.* (*f.* ā) a very powerful person; air, wind; lead: *lit.* very strong or powerful.

महाबला, *f.* (*m.* **महाबल**,) a very powerful female; a sort of Sida with yellow flowers.

महाबली, *m.* (*f.* inī) = **महाबल**, *q. v.*

महाब्राह्मण, *m.* a Brāhm ṇ who persides at funeral ceremonies (*shrāddh*) and is first fed after the mourning for a dead person.

महाभाग, *m.* (*f.* ā) fortunate, auspicious, prosperous, happy, virtuous in a high degree, exalted, eminent, holy.

महाभागत्व, *m.* (*f.* tā) great luck, auspiciousness, prosperity, felicity, exalted station or merit, possession of the eight cardinal virtues.

महाभागी, *m.* (*f.* inī) = **महाभाग**, *q. v.*

महाभाष्य, *m. pr. n.* the great commentary of Patañjali on the grammatical aphorisms of Paṇini.

महाभाग्य, 1, *m.* = **महाभागत्व**; 2, *m.* (*f.* ā) = **महाभाग**.

महाभारत, *m. pr. n.* (1) of the great war of the descendants of Bharat (2) of the great epic poem of the Hindoos. This poem is ascribed to Vyās, and contains an account of the dissensions and wars of the Kurus and Pāndus, two great collateral branches of the house of Bhārat, so called from Bharat its founder.

महाभीत, *m.* (*f.* ā) a great coward: *lit.* very timid, cowardly, pusillanimous.

महाभीता, *f.* (*m.* **महाभीत**) a timid female; a sensitive-plant (*Mimosa pudica*).

महाभ्रम, *m.* great error, heterodoxy.

महामणि, *m. f.* the greater gems, the more precious stones or metals (as diamonds, gold, etc.).

महामरी = **महामारी**, *q. v.* [ness.

महामहिमन्, *m.* excessive greatness, true great-

महामहिमा, 1, *m.* excessive greatness, true greatness: 2, *m. f.* very great, exceeding great, truly great, high and mighty.

महामांस, *m.* human flesh. One who takes money on giving his daughter in marriage, is said to sell (*mahāmāns*) human flesh.

महामाया, *f.* worldly illusion or unreality; the personification of the illusory nature of worldly objects; an epithet of Durgā. [great mortality.

महामारि, *f.* a great slaughter, great pestilence,

महामारी, *f.* a great pestilence or mortality, great plague, the cholera; (the great destroying goddess, *i. e.*) Durgā.

महामारु, 1, *m.* a great battle or slaughter; a great pestilence: 2, *m.* or *f.* a great fighter, hard hitter.

महामाष, *m.* a kind of bean (*Dolichos catsang*).

महामूर्ख, *m.* a great fool.

महामूर्खत्व, *m.* (*f.* tā) exceeding folly.

महामूल्य, *m.* the ruby: *lit. m.* (*f.* ā) high-priced, costly, precious.

महामेद, *m.* the coral-tree (*Erythrina Indica*); a certain drug classed among the principal drugs, and described as a tonic and stimulant.

महामोह (Rām.) = **अज्ञान**, *q. v.*

महायज्ञ, *m.* an essential sacrifice or ceremony, a sacrament of the Hindoo religion. Five acts of this description are enumerated, and they are severally considered as due to (1) the Veds (2) to the gods (3) to man (4) to the manes (5) to all created beings. These acts are (1) the study of scripture (2) the offering sacrifice to the gods (3) the hospital treatment of guests (4) libations of water, etc. to the manes of deceased ancestors (5) the casting food on the ground or into water, as an offering to created beings generally.

महायन्त्र, *m.* any great mechanical work, as a lock, dike, etc. [glorious.

महायशा, *m. f.* illustrious, celebrated, renowned,

महायाजक, *m.* a high priest, chief priest.

महायुग, *m.* the aggregate of the four ages (*Yug*), *i. e.* a period of 4320000000 years.

महारत, *f.* subtlety, acuteness, genius, excellence, skill, expertness, proficiency.

महारथ, 1, *m.* a large vehicle, great chariot: 2, *m.* (*f.* ī) one who has a large chariot, *i. e.* a hero.

महाराज, *m.* a great king, sovereign, emperor. The term is commonly used in respectful address = Your Majesty, Your Excellency, Your Honor, Sir.

महाराजा, *m.* (*f.* **महारानी**) an emperor, monarch, sovereign. [emperor.

महाराजाधिराज, *m.* a lord paramount, king of kings,

महाराज्य, *m.* sovereignty, dominion.

महारानी, (see **रानी**) . (*m.* **महाराजा**) an empress.

महाराति, 1, see (1) **महारात्रि** (2) **महाराष्ट्री**: 2, *m.* a great foe.

महारात्र, *m.* the dead of night, midnight, late at night, the time after midnight, close of night.

महारात्रि, *f.* midnight, the dead of night, time after midnight; the great night of the complete destruction of the world; the eighth day or night in the light half of the month Āshwin.

महारानी (*corruption*) = **महारानी**, *q. v.* [of Vālmiki.

महारामायण, *m. pr. n.* one of the many Rāmāyaṇs

महाराष्टी, *more prop.* **महाराष्ट्री**, *q. v.*

महाराष्ट्र, *m. pr. n.* the Marhaṭṭā country: a species of metre in Sanskrit prosody.

महाराष्ट्रा, *m.* (pl.: see **आ**, 22) the Marhaṭṭā people.

महाराष्ट्री, 1, *f.* the language of the Marhaṭṭās: 2, *m.* a Marhaṭṭā Brāhman.

महाराही, *m.* (*f.* ni, inī, nī) a great traveller.

महालची, *more prop.* **महालचो**, *q. v.*

महालय, *m.* an epithet of the Supreme Being; *lit.* the great refuge, an asylum, sanctuary.

महालोह, *m.* the loadstone, magnet.

महावठ, *m.* rain which falls in the month Māgh.

महावत, *m.* an elephant-keeper, elephant-driver, commonly pronounced "mahaut."

महावती / **महावत्नी** } *f.* an elephant-driver's wife.

महावथ, *more com.* **महावत**, *q. v.*

महावन, *m.* a great wood, dense forest.

महावर, *m.* lac (the red animal dye so called, extracted from the lac insect).

महावस, *m.* the Gangetic porpoise.

महावाक्य, *m.* the mystic syllable *Om.* [ditation.

महाविचार, *m.* deep consideration, profound me-

महाविनाश, *m.* great destruction, total ruin.

महाविरक्त, *m.* (*f.* ā) very destitute, utterly forlorn.

महाविष, *m.* a certain small highly-venomous snake (supposed to be two-headed).

महाविषुव, *m.* the *sankrānti,* or moment of the vernal equinox. [fernal regions.

महावीचि, *m. pr. n.* one of the divisions of the in-

महावीर, *m.* a hero; a lion; a white horse; sacrificial fire; a sacrificial vessel: *pr. n.* (1) of Vishṇu (2) of Gāruḍā (3) of Agni (4) of the thunderbolt of Indra (5) of the last and most celebrated Jain teacher of the present age (supposed to have flourished in the province of Bihār in the 6th century before the Christian era). [person: *lit.* very strong.

महावीर्य्य, *m.* (*f.* ā) a Brāhmaṇ; a very strong

महाशंख, *m.* a very large number (a thousand billions, a thousand millions); one of Kuver's treasures; the forehead.

महाशय, munificent, liberal, magnanimous. The term is used in respectful address = Your Honor, Sir.

महाष्टमी, *f.* the eighth day of Asin *shuklpaksh.*

महासंग्राम, *m.* a great battle. [virtuous, just.

महासत्त्व, *m.* (*f.* ā) a virtuous person: *lit.* good,

महासान्तपन, *m.* a severe kind of penance (the subsisting for six successive days respectively on the following six substances (1) cow's urine (2) cow's dung (3) milk (4) curds (5) ghee (6) water in which *kush*-grass has been boiled; and fasting on the seventh day). Some authorities assign (instead of one day) a period of three days to each, considering the first as the common *sāntpan*; while others omit the two last periods,—making it last fifteen days. [outrage.

महासाहस, *m.* excessive violence, brutal assault,

महासुख, *m.* copulation, coïtion.

महासुन्दर, *m* (*f.* ī) very beautiful, very handsome.

महासुन्दरी, *f.* a lovely female, a beauty. [cate.

महासूक्ष्म, *m.* (*f.* ā) minute, subtile, very fine, deli-

महाहास, *m.* a boisterous laugh, horse-laugh.

महि, 1, in poet. = **में**, *q. v.*: 2, *f.* (*prop.* **मही**) the earth.

महिखरी, *f.* (in Pros.) a species of metre.

महिदेव, *m.* (*f.* ī) an epithet of any Brāhmaṇ: *lit.*

महिधर, *m.* any mountain. [a deity on earth.

महिनवारी, *more prop.* **महीनवारी**, *q. v.*

महिप / **महिपति** / **महिपाल** / **महिपालक** } = **महीप**, *q. v.*

महिभार, *m.* the burden of the world as borne by the great serpent Anant; also the burden of human suffering said to have been borne by Vishṇu.

महिमा, *m.* (*f.* ?) greatness, magnitude, grandeur, majesty, exaltation. [treatment.

महिमानी, *f.* kind offices, hospitality, respectful

महिमासंयुक्त, *m.* (*f.* ā) great, magnificent, exalted, majestic.

महिराक, a dialectic form = **महिला**, *q. v.*

महिला, *f.* a female, a woman; a certain plant (commonly called *priyangu*).

महिष, 1, *m.* (*f.* ī) a buffalo; the emblem and vehicle of Yam: 2, *m. pr. n.* a certain *asur* (Vice personified) who was destroyed by Durgā.

महिषाक्ष, *m.* a certain plant (supposed to be the

महिषासुर = **महिष**, 2, *q. v.* [bdellium-tree),

महिषी, *f.* (*m.* **महिष**) a female buffalo; the wife of a king who has been consecrated with him, the queen-consort.

महिषेश = (1) **महिषासुर** (2) **यमराज**, *qq. v.*

महिषेस / **महिषेसा** } (*corruption*) = **महिषेश**, *q. v.*

महिष्मती, *m.* an epithet of Yam.

मही, *f.* (*m.* **मह**) the earth; landed property; (in Geom.) the basis of a plane figure; a species of metre in Sanskrit prosody; *pr. n.* a certain river which rises in the province of Mālwā, and after pursuing a westerly course of about 280 miles, falls into the upper part of the gulf of Cambay: buttermilk.

महींनवा, *more prop.* **महीनवा**, *q. v.*

महीत, *more prop.* **मुहीत**, *q. v.*

महीतल, *m.* the surface of the earth.

महीदेव = **महिदेव**, *q. v.*

महीधर, *m.* any mountain.

महीन, 1, *more prop.* **मिहीन**, *q. v.*: 2, *m.* (an earth-ruler, *i. e.*) a king, prince.

महीनवा, appertaining to a month.

महीनवारी, *f.* monthly salary, wages, stipend.

महीना, *m.* a month; monthly pay; *hence,* wages.
— *charhnā,* to be in arrears.

महीनादार, *m.* a monthly servant.

महीन्द्र, *more prop.* **महेन्द्र**, *q. v.*

महीप, *m.* an epithet of any king, sovereign, or prince; *lit.* nourisher or protector of the earth.

महीपत (contraction) = **महीपति**, *q. v.*

महीपति, *m.* (*f.* patnī) / **महीपाल**, *m.* (*f.* ā) / **महीपालक**, *m.* (*f.* ikā) } = **महीप**, *q. v.*

महीमय, *m.* (*f.* ī) abounding in earth, consisting of

महीरुह, *m.* a tree, a plant. [earth, earthen, earthy.

महीलता, *f.* an earthworm.

महीला, *more prop.* **महिला**, *q.v.*

महीशा = **महीश** = **महेश**, *q.v.*

महीसुर = **महिदेव**, *q.v.*

महुआ } **महुया** } = **महूआ**, *q.v.*

महुरत } **महुर्त** } *more prop.* **मुहूर्त्त**, *q.v.*

महूआ, *m.* a certain tree (*Bassia latifolia*) bearing sweet flowers from which a spirituous liquor is distilled, and whose nuts afford an oil which is used instead of butter.

महूरत } **महूर्त्त** } (*corruptions*) = **मुहूर्त्त**, *q.v.*

महेताब, *more prop.* **महताब**, *q.v.*

महेन्द्र, *m. pr. n.* (1) of Indra, the ruler of the celestial regions (2) of one of the seven principal chains of mountains in Bhāratvarsh, apparently the northern part of the Ghāṭs.

महेर, *m.* a kind of dish (consisting of rice or other grain, boiled in sour milk).

महेरी, *f.* = **महेर**, *q.v.*

महेरू = **महरू** = **माहरू**, *q.v.*

महेलत; see **मुहलत**.

महेला, *f.* 1, *more prop.* **महिला**, *q.v.*: 2, a kind of food given to horses (consisting of boiled kidney-beans); a mash.

महेश, *m.* (the great lord, *i. e.*) Shiv.

महेशदत्त, *m.* a proper name = given by Shiv.

महेश्वर = **महेश**, *q.v.*

महेश्वरी, *f.* an epithet of Pārvatī (wife of Shiv).

महेस (*corruption*) = **महेश**, *q.v.*

महेसुर in Braj = **महेश्वर**, *q.v.*

महैश्वर्य्य, *m.* great power or dominion, supreme lordship or sovereignty.

महोक्ष, *m.* a large bull, an ox, a great ox, a full-grown bull: *met.* a blockhead.

महोखा, *m.* a certain bird (*Cuculus castaneus* Buch.).

महोच्छो; see (1) **महोक्ष** (2) **महोखा**.

महोख (*colloquial*) = **महोक्ष**, *q.v.*

महोका, *m.* a funeral feast among fakeers.

महोत्सव, *m.* any great festival.

महोत्साह, 1, *m.* (*f.* ā) a very energetic person, a king possessing all the powers of monarchy: *lit.* adj. possessing great energy, making strenuous and unremitted exertion; persevering, diligent: 2, *m.* great effort, exertion, perseverence, diligence.

महोदय, *m.* final emancipation of the soul from matter and from existence, greatness, eminence, elevation, prosperity: a great man, lord, master: an epithet of the ancient city and district of Kanauj.

महोदार, powerful, mighty.

महोद्यम, 1, *m.* (*f.* ā) making great effort, zealous, persevering, eager: 2, *m.* great effort, energy, exertion.

महोर्म्मि, *f.* a large or tempestuous wave.

महोष, *m.* a kind of bird.

महोसः } **महोसा** } *m.* a freckle, spot.

महौत, a very com. corruption of **महावत**, *q.v.*

महौदार्य्य, *m.* great bountifulness or liberality.

महौषध, *m.* a great or sovereign remedy, a panacea; garlic (*Allium sativum*); another plant (*Betula*); long pepper.

महौषधि, *f.* a kind of grass (*dūb*); a kind of sensitive-plant (*Mimosa pudica*).

महौषधी, *f.* dry ginger; a kind of potherb (*Hingsta repens*).

मह्यौ, *m.* buttermilk.

मा, *f.* mother; an epithet of Lakshmī. The term is applied in respectful address to aged females generally.

माइ, *f.* (= **माई**) a mother.

माइया, (a voc. sing. of **माई**) O mother!

माइल, 1, *more prop.* **मैल**, *q.v.*: 2, (Engl.) mile: 3, inclined towards, taking delight in, affectionate; having a propensity, inclination, or partiality; addicted, apt.

माई, *f.* mother; a woman's breast.

माई, *f.* an aunt (the wife of a maternal uncle).

माईक्रस्कोप, *m.* (Engl.) microscope.

माईल; see **माइल**.

माउ } **माए** } *f.* a mother.

माएका, *m.* the maternal mansion (applied only to that of a woman).

मां, 1, *a corruption of* **मा**, *q.v.*: 2, (one of the many forms from **मध्य**) in: 3, (Rām.) = **मुझे**, *q.v.*

मांग, *f.* a line on the top of the head where the hair is parted; a betrothed damsel; a prow; division; an ornament of pearls or of gold worn by women on the top of the head along the line where the hair is parted. — *denā*, to borrow for another, to ask for and give. — *nikālnā*, to divide the hair in a straight line on the top of the head, to part the hair. — *lenā*, to borrow.

मांगचिकनी, *f.* a certain bird.

मांगटीका, *f.* (see **मांग**) an ornament worn along the line on the top of the head.

मांगदेना; see *s.v.* **मांग**.

मांगना, *t.* to ask for, demand, solicit, crave, desire, pray, beg, seek, require, want, betroth, will. *Māng tāng k.* to ask for.

मांगनी, *f.* asking or betrothing in marriage.

मांगलिक, *m.* (*f.* ā) auspicious, propitious, prosperous.

मांगलेना; see *s.v.* **मांग**.

मांगल्य, *m.* auspiciousness, prosperousness, prosperity; festivity; a festival.

मांगबौ in Braj = **मांगना**. See **ना**, 3.

मांगी, *f.* anything borrowed, a loan; betrothed (said of females).

मांगोग, a corruption of **मांगोगे** (**मांगना**).

मांज, *m.* pus, matter, serum.

मांजना, *t.* to scour, scrub, clean, polish, furbish. *Mānjmānjke le,āo*, scrub it well and bring it.

मांजा, *m.* (*f.* ī) cleansed, scoured, furbished, polished.

मांजिष्ठ, 1, *m.* (*f.* ā *or* ī) of a red colour, red: 2, *m.* the colour red.

मांजेमूंजे, a play on the word **मांजा**, *q.v.*

मांझ, 1, *m.* the middle; a certain musical mode (*rāgiṇī*); a kind of verse. 2, in the middle; in.

मांझल, *f.* state, dignity,

मांझधार, *f.* mid-stream.

मांझा, *m.* a kind of paste made of pounded glass and applied to the string of a kite to cut the strings of other kites: a feast given by a bridegroom previous to the wedding: the trunk of a tree.

मांझी, *m.* (*lit.* the midman) a master of a sailing-vessel; a steersman, helmsman; a boatman, sailor.

मांटी in Mārwāṛī = Master.

मांड, मांढ, मांद, मांध; for words beginning with either of these elements, see under the corresponding forms **मायड, मायढ, मान्द, मान्ध**.

मांथ / **मांथा** } *more prop.* **माथा**, *q.v.*

मांबाप, *m.* mother and father, parents.

मांशुक, *more prop.* **माशूक**, *q.v.*

मांस, *m.* flesh, butcher's-meat.

मांसखाद, *more prop.* **मांसाद**, *q.v.* [nourishing flesh.

मांसपोषक, *m.* (*f.* ikā) a cattle-breeder, etc,: lit. *adj.*

मांसभक्ष, *m.* (*f.* ā) = **मांसाद**, *q.v.* [flesh, flesh-eating.

मांसाद, any carnivorous creature: *lit.* feeding on

मांसाशी, *m.* (*f.* inī) / **मांसाहारी**, *m.* (*f.* iṇī) } = **मांसाद**, *q.v.*

मांसी, *f.* Indian spikenard (*Valeriana jatamansi*).

मांह = **में**, *q.v.* Very frequent in Braj, in poetry, and in the colloquial jargon of the villagers.

मांहि / **मांहिं** / **मांहीं** } emphatic forms of **मांह**, *q.v.*

मांहँ in Chand = **मांहि** = **मांह** (?) *q.v.*

माकन, *more prop.* (1) **मकान** (2) **माखन**, *qq.v.*

माकन्द, *m.* the mango. [town.

माकन्दी, *f.* emblic myrobalan: *pr. n.* a certain

माकूल, reasonable, probable, just, pertinent, proper.

माक्षिक, *m.* honey: pyrites of various kinds.

माक्षिकज, *m.* bee's-wax (*lit.* produced from honey).

माक्षी, *f.* (**मक्षिका**) a fly.

माख; see **मोख**.

माखड़ा, *m.* (*f.* ī) stupid, foolish, ignorant (?).

माखन, *m.* (prop. **मक्खन**) butter.

माखनचोर / **माखनप्रभु** / **माखनलाल** } *m.* epithets of Krishṇ.

माखी, *f.* (**मक्षिका**) a fly.

माखू, *m.* a weaver's shuttle.

माग = (1) **माघ** (2) **मार्ग** (3) **मांग**, *qq.v.*

मागध, *lit.* appertaining to the province of Magadh; *hence*, an inhabitant of Magadh, the inhabitants of Magadh: a bard or minstrel whose duty it is to recite the praises of sovereigns (their genealogy, and the deeds of their ancestors) in their presence and to attend an army on the march to animate the soldiers by martial songs. These minstrels form a particular caste said to have sprung from a Vaishya father by a Kshatriya mother; though in the mythology they are said to have been created at once by the will of Shiv. Under the name of *Bhāṭ* they are still numerous in some parts of India, especially in Guzerāt, where they are a privileged tribe.

मागधा, *m.* (pl.: see **आ**, 22) the inhabitants or the people of the province of Magadh.

मागधी, *f.* long pepper (*Piper longum*); a kind of jasmine (*Jasminum auriculatum*); a sort of cardamoms grown in Guzerāt; refined sugar; a certain dialect of the Sanskrit language (being one of the principal forms of Prākrit, and nearly the same as that used in the sacred books of the Bauddhs and Jains).

मागना, *more prop.* **मांगना**, *q.v.*

माघ, *m. pr. n.* (1) of the tenth Hindoo month (Jan.-Feb.) the full moon of which is near *Maghā* (2) of a certain Hindoo poet (author of the *Sisu-pāla badha* or *Maghākāvya*).

माघात, land broken up in Māgh for next year's crop. — *kī phasl*, the crops sown during Māgh or immediately after it.

माघी, *f.* a kind of potherb (*Hingsta repens*).

माचा, *m.* a large bedstead or platform; a frame or stage on which a watchman sits to drive away birds, etc. from corn-fields.

माचातोड़, a lazy person who never stirs from his bed; a kind of soldier among the Rājpūts, very indolent and much addicted to opium, but active and brave when roused.

माची, *f.* 1, (*provincial*) = **मक्षिका**, *q v.*: 2, (dim. of **माचा**) a small bedstead: 3, a harrow.

माचीन, *m. pr. n.* China or Chinese Tartary.

माछ, *m.* (*f.* ī) a fish.

माछर, *more com.* **मच्छर**, *q.v.*

माछरी, *more com.* **मछरी**, *q.v.* [male fish.

माछी, *f.* 1, (from **मक्षिका**) a fly: 2, (*m.* **माछ**) a fe-

माजरा, *m.* state, condition, circumstances: an event, occurrence, adventure, incident.

माजा, the foam of the water of the early rains.

माजाई, *f.* (*m.* **माजाया**) a uterine sister.

माजाया, *m.* (*f.* **माजाई**) a uterine brother; *lit.* born of one and the same mother.

माजिस्टेट, *m.* (Engl.) magistrate.

माजूज, *more prop.* **मजूज़**, *q.v.*

माजूफल, *m.* gall-nut, oak-apple.

माझ (*Rām.*) = **मांझ**, *q.v.* [mid-stream.

माझधार, *f.* the middle of the stream or current,

माझे / **माझें** } = **मझिले**, *q.v.*

माट, *m.* a boiler, a vat, a pan for the manufacture of indigo, a large vessel or jar. [to envy.

माटी, *f.* earth, mould, soil, clay, dust.—*phaknā*,

माट्ठा = (1) **मठा** (2) **मट्ठा**, *qq.v.*

माठ, see (1) **माट** (2) **मठ** (3) **मठा** (4) **मट्ठा**.

माठा = (1) **मठा** (2) **मट्ठा**, *qq.v.*

माठू, *m.* (a term of reproach) a buffoon.

माड़ना, *t.* to thresh corn; to flatten.

माड़नी, *f.* paste.

माड़वाड़, *m. pr. n.* (Sk. **मरु**) a certain province [to the west of Jainagar.

माड़िया, thin, lean.

माढा, *more prop.* **माण्ढा**, *q.v.*

माणव, *m.* a child; a man (in the contemptuous sense), a mannikin: a necklace of sixteen strings.

माणवक, *m.* a child; a boy under sixteen years of age, a mannikin: a childish or ignorant man.

माणिक } **माणिक्य** } *m.* a ruby, a precious stone.

माण्ड, *m.* rice-water, rice-gruel, starch, paste.

माण्डना, *t.* to rub; to tread or trample down; to knead: to make, occasion, excite, stir, commit, perpetrate: to starch.

माण्डव्य, *m. pr. n.* a certain Hindoo sage (*rishi*).

माण्डा, *m.* a film, a speck on the eye: a kind of bread.

माण्डी, *f.* starch made of rice-flour: the knee.

माण्ढा, *m.* a temporary building, an open shed or hall (adorned with flowers and erected on festive occasions, such as weddings, etc.).

मात, 1, *a contraction* (1) of **माता** (2) of **मात्रा** (3) of **मात्र**, *qq.v.*: 2, *f.* (in Chess) checkmate. — *k.* to give checkmate; to overcome in any affair, to win. — *kī bhāji*, *f.* the edible amaranth (*Amaranthus oleraceus*).

मातंग, *m.* (*f.* ī) an outcaste, a barbarian; an elephant; the sacred figtree (*Ficus religiosa*): *pr. n.* the 24th astronomical *yog*, or division of the moon's path.

मातंगी, *f.* an epithet of Pārvatī.

मातना, 1, see **मतना**: 2, *n.* to be intoxicated.

मातपिता (*contraction*) = **मातापिता**, *q.v.*

मातपितु = **मातापिता**, *q.v.*

मातम, *m.* grief, mourning (*esp.* public mourning, as that which is held for a prince, or at the Muharram).

मातर्द्धि, *f.* the wealth or prosperity of a mother.

मातल, intoxicated, drunk.

मातलि, *m. pr. n.* the charioteer of Indra.

मातह in Chand = **माता** = mother.

मातहि, 1, (*Rām.*) = **माता**, 2, *q.v.*: 2, an old acc. of **मात** = **माता** = mother.

माता, 1, *f.* (see **मातृ**) mother; the small-pox: 2, [*m.* (*f.* ī) intoxicated.

मातापिता, *m.* mother and father, parents.

मातापित्री (*corruption*) = **मातापितृ**, *q.v.*

मातापितृ, *more com.* **मातापिता**, *q.v.* [parent.

मातामह (**माता** + **मह**) *m.* (*f.* ī) a maternal grand-

मातामहः, *more prop.* **मातामह**, *q.v.*

मातामही, *f.* a maternal grandmother.

मातारी, *more com.* **महतारी**, *q.v.* [drunken female.

माती, 1, *more com.* **माटी**, *q.v.*: 2, *f.* (*m.* **माता**) a

मातु (provincial) = **माता**, *q.v.*

मातुघर, *m.* maternal relations, mother's family.

मातुपिता, *more prop.* **मातापिता**, *q.v.*

मातुल, *m.* (*f.* ā, ānī, ī) a maternal uncle: thorn-apple (*Datura metel* and *fastuosa*).

मातुलपुत्रक, *m.* (*f.* ā *or* ikā) the child of a maternal uncle: fruit of the thorn-apple.

मातुला = **मातुलानी**, *q.v.*

मातुलानी, *f.* (*m.* **मातुल**) an aunt (wife of a maternal uncle): hemp (*Cannabis sativa*).

मातुली = **मातुलानी**, *q.v.*

मातृ, *m.* a mother; a divine mother, a personified energy of a deity or of his wife (they are variously enumerated: according to some authorities they are seven, according to others eight, and according to others sixteen in number); the wife of a Brāhmaṇ; a cow; the earth; space, ether.

मातृका, *m.* a mother; a certain class of goddesses (see *mātṛi*); a nurse; the alphabet.

मातृगण, *m.* (see **मातृ**) the Divine Mothers (worshipped in a peculiar manner in the western parts of India).

मातृघात, *m.* the killing a mother, matricide.

मातृघातक, *m.* (*f.* ī) }
मातृघाती, *m.* (*f.* inī) } = **मातृघ्न**, *q.v.*
मातृघातुक, *m.* (*f.* ī) }

मातृघ्न, *m.* (*f.* ī) the murderer of his own mother, a matricide.

मातृदत्त, *m.* that which is given by a mother to [her daughter at her marriage.

मातृद्धि, *more prop.* **मातर्द्धि**, *q.v.*

मातृप्रतिष्ठा, *f.* the honour or reputation of a mo- [ther.

मातृबन्धु, *m. f.* a relation by the mother's side, [maternal relation.

मातृबान्धव = **मातृबन्धु**, *q.v.*

मातृहन } **मातृघ्न** } *m.* (*f.* **मातृघ्नी**) = **मातृघ्न**, *q.v.*

माते, *m.* (pl. of **माता**) drunken men. See **मातना**.

मात्र, *m.* measure, quantity; a little, trifle, atom, element, a moment, a short vowel; totality, the whole. It is often subjoined to substantives as a Taddhita suffix to restrict their meaning; so situated, it = mere, merely, only, nothing but, solely; *e.g.* **मनुष्यमात्र**, only a man, a mere man.

मात्रक, (only in comp.; like **मात्र**) that much, only, mere, solely: *lit.* of a certain measure or size.

मात्रा, *f.* an element; quantity (esp. in metre); a little; a dose; an ingredient; an instant; (in Pros.) the length of time requisite for the pronunciation of a short syllable; (in Gram.) (1) the horizontal stroke of a letter (2) a vowel-symbol.

मातानन्द, *f.* the joy of a mother (*esp.* at the birth [of a son).

मात्रिक, 1, at the end of compounds = **मात्र**, *q.v.*: 2, *m.* (*f.* ā) of the nature of matter, material: containing a short vowel.

मात्रिका, *f.* (= **मात्रा**) a prosodial instant, a simple [sound.

मात्सर, *m.* (*f.* ā) an envious person: *adj.* impatient of another's prosperity, envious.

मात्सर्य, *m.* envy, selfishness, malice.

माथ, 1, = **माथा**, *q.v.*: 2, *m.* churning: a road.

माथा, *m.* the top or head of anything; the ridge of a thatch; the forehead: a prow; pinnacle, summit. — *thanaknā* (*lit.* ringing or throbbing of the forehead) implies a presentiment of the conclusion of an affair from certain marks observed at its commencement: it is generally understood to indicate that the termination will be an unfortunate one. — *ragarnā*, (*lit.* to rub the forehead, *i. e.* on the ground at the feet of the person supplicated) to implore in deepest humility (as of God, of a saint, or of a great personage). *Māthepar charhnā*, to tyrannize, oppress.

माथी लेना, *t.* to make even (*esp.* a thatch).

माथुर, *m.* an inhabitant or a native of Mathurā: *pr. n.* (1) of a certain caste of Kāyaths (2) of a certain sect of Brāhmaṇs.

माद, *m.* intoxication; infatuation; pride; ecstasy, rapture, joy. [cinating, maddening.

मादक, *m.* (*f.* ikā) intoxicating; infatuating; fas-

मादकत्व, *m.* (*f.* tā) inebriating quality; the state of intoxication, drunkenness.

मादगी, *f.* female nature, feminality.

मादरजाज (corruption) = **मादरज़ाद**, *q.v.*

मादरज़ाद, as born of the mother, innate, congenital.

मादा, *adj.* female: *subst.* a female.

मादियान, *f.* a mare, a she-ass.

मादी } *f.* a female.
मादीन }

माद्री, *f.* a sample, specimen, model, pattern, example: *pr. n.* a certain *saut* of Kuntī.

माधव, (*lit.* made of honey; belonging to spring; *hence*) *m.* sweetness: an epithet (1) of Vishṇu or Krishṇ (2) of the month Vaisākh (3) of Spring (4) of a celebrated Hindoo scholar, son of Māyaṇ.

माधवी, *f.* sugar; spirituous liquor; a bawd: a certain large creeping-plant (*Gaertnera racemosa*); an epithet of Durgā.

माधवीलता, *f.* (see **माधवी**) a certain large creeping-plant (*Gaertnera racemosa*).

माधुरी, *f.* 1, = **माधुर्य्य**, *q.v*: 2, Arabian jasmine.

माधुर्य्यमूर्त्ति, *m.* an epithet of Krishṇ.

माधुर्य्य, *m.* (*f.* ī) sweetness, suavity, gracefulness, agreeableness, pleasantness.

माधो (colloquial) = **माधव**, *q.v.*

माधोलता (*corruption*) = **माधवीलता**, *q.v.*

माधा in Braj = **माधव**, *q.v.*

माध्य, *m.* (*f.* ā) } middle, central, mid.
माध्यम, *m.* (*f.* ī) }

माध्वक = **माध्वीक**, *q.v.*

माध्वी, *f.* 1, = **माध्वीक**, *q.v.*: 2, a certain fish.

माध्वीक, *m.* spirituous liquor distilled from the blossoms of the *Bassia latifolia*; spirit distilled from grapes, wine.

मान, 1, *a contraction of* **मानो**, *q.v.*: 2, *m.* (*f.* matī); a Taddhita suffix which serves to form adjectives implying possession, from substantives: 3, *m.* self-confidence, pride, arrogance, haughtiness; indignation, anger, sulkiness, caprice: honour, dignity, character, respect, rank, value, reputation: measuring, measure, weight; a particular measure (the fourth part of a *khārī*); the computation of the duration of a year: taking: blandishment: an agent: a blockhead; a barbarian. — *lenā*, to allow, admit, accept, own.

मानक, *m.* a certain plant (*Arum Indicum*) the root of which is sometimes eaten.

मानगुमान, *m.* state, dignity, honour.

मानगौन, *m.* respect.

मानत, *f.* a voluntary obligation, vow, promise, resolution, purpose: resemblance, likeness.

मानता = **मानत**, *q.v.* See also **मानना** and **मानिता**.

मानधाता, *more prop.* **मान्धाता**, *q.v.*

मानना, *t.* to respect, regard, mind, attend to, observe, obey, heed, esteem, honour, venerate, acknowledge, confess, submit, admit, receive, take, accept, allow, agree, assent, accede to, consent, grant, yield, trust, assume, own, permit; to be set on. *Burā* —, to take amiss, take as an affront, take offence at. *Bhalā* —, to take in good part. *Burā yā bhalā* —, to take ill or well. [gard, venerable.

माननीय, *m.* (*f.* ā) deserving of honour or of re-

मानपान, *m.* respecting, honouring.

मानन्द, *more prop.* **मानिन्द**, *q.v.*

मानमहत, *m.* dignity, state, honour, respect.

मानयुक्त, *m.* (*f.* ā) connected with or possessing honour or reputation. [respectful.

मानरहित, *m.* (*f.* ā) unhonoured, despised; dis-

मानव, *m.* (*f.* ī) a human being; a man; a child, boy; mankind; a multitude of men: *lit.* appertaining to (or descended from) Manu.

मानवक, *more prop.* **माणवक**, *q.v.* [angry.

मानवत, *m.* (*f.* vatī) proud, high-spirited, haughty,

मानवती, *f.* (*m.* °वन्त, etc.) a proud female.

मानवन्त, *m.* (*f.* vatī) = **मानवत**, *q.v.*

मानवर्ज्जित, *m.* (*f.* ā) destitute of pride, lowly,

मानवर्ज्जिता, *f.* lowliness, humility. [humble.

मानवान, *m.* (*f.* vatī) = **मानवन्त**, *q.v.*

मानवी, *f.* (*m.* **मानव**) a female descendant of Manu; *hence*, a female, a woman.

मानष in Chand = **मानुष**, *q.v.*

मानस, 1, = **मानस्सरोवर**, *q.v.*: 2, *m.* the mind (the seat of reason and of feeling); thought, wish, volition: *lit. m.* (*f.* ī) appertaining to the mind, mental.

मानसत्व, *m.* (*f.* tā) thoughtfulness.

मानसनवान, *more prop.* **मानसन्मान**, *q.v.*

मानसन्मान, *m.* welcome.

मानसमूल, *m.* an epithet of the river Saryū.

मानसरवर } (*corruption*) = **मानस्सरोवर**, *q.v.*
मानसरोवर }

मानसिक, mental, ideal, imaginary, rational: *lit.* appertaining to the mind.

मानसी, *f.* 1, *more prop.* **मांसी**, *q.v.*: 2, *pr. n.* a certain goddess of the Jains.

मानसुर (*corruption*) = **मानस्सरोवर**, *q.v.*

मानस्सरोवर, *m. pr. n.* a certain lake in the Himālaya mountains. It is a sacred place of Hindoo pilgrimage on mount Kailās, the native place of wild geese or swans. Constant allusions are made to this lake in Hindoo poetry, and the Hańs or Rājhańs is described as migrating to its shores every year at the breeding-season.

मानहानि, *f.* loss of honour or of respectability.

मानहीन, *m.* (*f.* ā) void of haughtiness or pride; destitute of honour or respectability.

मानहु / **मानहूँ** } in Braj = **मानो**, 1, *q.v.* See also **मानना**.

मानापमान, *m.* esteem and disesteem. [a horse.

मानिक (*corruption*) = **माणिक्य**, *q. v.* *Lidkā* —, *m.*

मानिकजोड़, *m.* a certain bird (*Ardea leucocephala*).

मानिता, *f.* (*m.* °त्व) arrogance, pride, haughtiness, dignity.

मानिनी, *f.* (*m.* **मानी**) a proud or sulky female (*esp.* one who is indignant towards her lover).

मानिन्द, *postp.* (*f.* or *m.*) like, resembling.

मानिहै (pl. °हैं) in Braj = **मानेंगे** (**मानना**).

मानी, *m.* (*f.* inī) mindful, fancying, weening; proud, arrogant, haughty, indignant, sulky.

मानींद, *more prop.* **मानिन्द**, *q.v.*

मानु in Braj = **मानो**, *q.v.* See also **मानना**.

मानुख / **मानुज** } = **मानुष**, *q. v.*

मानुष, *m.* (*f.* ī) a human being, person, individual, man: *lit.* appertaining to human-kind.

मानुषतन = **मनुष्यतन**, *q.v.*

मानुषी, *f.* (*m.* **मानुष**) a woman, a female.

मानुष्य, *m.* the condition or the quality of a human being, humanity; manhood, manliness: *lit.* appertaining to human-kind.

मानुस, 1, a corruption of **मानुष**, *q.v.*: 2, *m. f.* a companion, associate, friend.

मानो, 1, (2nd pers. pl. condit. of **मानना**) you would suppose, one might suppose, it seems as if, so to speak, it is the same as if, as it were, suppose, grant; as, like, resembling (generally preceded by *ki* expressed or understood: it is conjectured by some, that the form **मानों** = **मानूं** = I suppose: 2, *m.* a cat.

मानों = (1) **मानूं** (2) **मानूंगा** (3) **मानो**.

मानो / **मानों** } *in Braj* = **मानों**, *q.v.*

मान्सा, *f.* = **मानस**, *q.v.*

मान्द, 1, *f.* a dull colour: 2, a dunghill: the den of a wild beast, a lair: 3, faded.

मान्दगी, *f.* weariness, fatigue.

मान्दना, *n.* to be fatigued, be languid; to be ill.

मान्दा, *m.* (*f.* ī) tired, fatigued, weary, languid, indisposed, ailing.

मान्द्य, *m.* inferiority, badness, vileness; indisposition, sickness, languishing, torpor, slowness, indolence, stupidity.

मान्धाता, *m. pr. n.* a certain ancient Hindoo king.

मान्ना = **मानना**, *q. v.*

मान्य, *m.* (*f.* ā) to be respected, estimable, venerable.

मान्यत्व, *m.* (*f.* tā) venerableness, estimableness, credibility, respectability, honour.

मान्यमान, *m.* (*f.* matī) an estimable person: *lit.* honoured, regarded, esteemed, venerated.

मान्या, *f.* (*m.* **मान्य**) an estimable female.

मान्स, *more prop.* **मांस**, *q.v.*

माप, *m.* measurement, measure, size, dimensions.

मापक, *m.* (*f.* ikā) a measurer: lit. *adj.* determining by measure or quantity.

मापतूल, *m.* a system of measures and weights.

मापन, *m.* measuring; a balance.

मापना, *t.* to measure.

मापा, *m.* (*f.* ī) measured.—*shorbā aur ginī dālīyāṅ* is applied to express scarcity of provisions; also, penurious economy.

मापी (Rām.) = **मतवाली**, *q. v.*

माफ = **मुआफ़**, *q. v.*

माफल (*contraction*) = **मालूफल**, *q. v.*

माफिक, more prop. **मुवाफ़िक़**, *q. v.*

माब, a place of return, receptacle, repository.

माबाप, *m.* mother and father, parents.

माम, *f.* mother. The term is used in respectful address to any elderly female.

मामक, 1, (from Sk. **मम**) *m.* (*f.* ikā *or* ī) a niggard, selfish person, miser: a mother's brother: *lit.* mine: *hence*, selfish: 2, *f.* (a dim. form of **मा** or of **माम**) dear little mother, mother dear.

मामकी = **मामिका**, *q. v.*

मामला, *m.* affair, business, negotiation, transaction, procedure, concern, suit at law.

मामा, (not infl.) 1, = **माम**, *q. v.*: 2, *m.* an uncle [(mother's brother).

मामाई, *f.* midwifery.

मामिका, *f.* (*m.* **मामक**) a niggardly or selfish female: an aunt (maternal uncle's wife).

मामिनाफ़ = **मामनाफ़** = a midwife.

मामी, *f.* an aunt (maternal uncle's wife). — *pīnā* to shew partiality. [firm constant.

मामुन, rendered secure, preserved, exempted;

मामू, *m.* an uncle (mother's brother): a snake (the term so applied is euphemistic, and is used at night, when it is deemed unlucky to call a serpent by its proper name).

मामूं, 1, *more prop.* **मामू**, *q.v.*: 2, see **मामुन**.

मामूल, hoped for: *m.* hope.

माय, *more prop.* (1) **माई** (2) **माया**, *qq.v.*

मायका, *more prop.* **माइका**, *q.v.*

मायस, *adj.* walking proudly, waving from side to side: *subst.* a calumniator, whisperer.

माया, 1, *f.* illusion, delusion, fraud, deceit, hypocrisy, unreality; magical power; a deception depending on the power of the deity whereby mankind believe in the existence of external objects which are, in fact, nothing but idea; the external world (considered as a mere illusion, without reality, and personified in mythology as a female, the wife of Brahmā, and the immediate operative cause of creation); the wife of a juggler; a woman; prosperity, opulence, riches: wickedness: compassion, pity, sympathy, mercy, kindness, affection, feeling: 2, *m.* wealth, stock, money;

root, origin, principle; stock-in-trade, capital, store; measure, quantity, value.

मायातीत, *m.* (*f.* ā) = **मायारहित**, *q.v.* [causing illusion.

मायाद, *m.* (*f.* ī) an epithet of the alligator; *lit.*

मायापटु, *m. f.* a deceiver, etc.: *lit.* expert in deceiving, delusive, deceptive. [or of Rām.

मायापति, *m.* (see **प्रजा**) an epithet of the Deity

मायापात्र, *m.* (*f.* ī) a wealthy person; *lit.* a vessel of wealth; *hence,* opulent, wealthy, rich.

मायाभूमि, *f.* a place of deception, locality where wickedness abounds. [gical, wonderful.

मायामय, *m.* (*f.* ī) illusory, unreal, deceptive, ma-

मायामोह, *m.* (**माया + मोह**) illusion and ignorance.

मायायी, *m.* (*f.* inī) = **मायावी**, *q.v.*

मायारहित, *m.* (*f.* ā) without compassion, merciless, unfeeling, unloving.

मायारूप / **मायारूपी** } illusory, unreal, deceptive.

मायावत, *m.* (*f.* vatī) a deceiver; an epithet of Kaṅs: *lit.* illusory, unreal, deceitful.

मायावती, *f.* (*m.* °**वन्त**, etc.) a female deceiver; an epithet of the wife of Kām.

मायावन्त / **मायावान** } *m.* (*f.* vatī) = **मायावत**, *q.v.*

मायाविद्या, *f.* the science of illusion, magic.

मायावी, *m.* (*f.* inī) a deceiver; a juggler, conjuror, magician; a cat: *lit.* illusory, unreal, deceitful, magical, using tricks.

मायिक, *m.* (*f.* ā *or* ī) a juggler: *lit.* illusory, deceptive, fascinating; affectionate, benevolent.

मायी, *m.* (*f.* inī) a deceiver, cheat, juggler; an epithet of Brahmā, Vishṇu, and Agni: *lit.* illusory, deceptive, magical.

माये, the form of the infl. sing. of **माया**, 2, *q.v.*

मार, 1, *m.* (*f.* ī) *lit.* that which strikes or kills, striking, killing; a killer: *hence,* (1) *m.* an epithet of love, and of Kāmdev (its deity); plague, pestilence, epidemy; killing, dying, death; a serpent, snake; obstruction (2) *f.* a blow; beating; battle: 2, a black loam, a stiff clay or loamy soil with some sand or vegetable mould. — *khānā,* to be beaten, get a drubbing. — *girānā,* to knock down. — *ḍālnā,* to smite, kill, slay outright. — *denā,* to smite, beat; to dismiss a suit, quash a complaint. — *parnā,* to get a beating. — *marnā,* to commit suicide; to fall in battle after having killed some of the enemy. — *lānā,* to take by robbery, to rob. — *lenā,* to smite, overcome, conquer. — *saknā,* to be able to beat. — *haṭānā,* to overcome, beat and drive back. — *hārnā,* to beat severely.

मारक, *m.* (*f.* ikā) a slayer, destroyer, executioner; a hawk; plague, pestilence, epidemic: *lit. adj.* putting to death.

मारकण्डेय, *more prop.* **मार्कण्डेय**, *q.v.* [emerald.

मारकत, *m.* (*f.* ī) emerald-like, of the colour of an

मारकुटाई, *f.* a beating and bruising.

मारकुटिया, *m.* a turbulent quarrelsome person.

मारग (*colloquial*) = **मार्ग**, *q.v.*

मारगन, 1, *more prop.* **मार्गण**, *q.v.*: 2, a pl. of **मार्ग**.

मारगीर, *m.* a snake-catcher.

मारगीरी, *f.* snake-catching.

मारण, *m.* killing, slaughter. [derer.

मारणहारा, *m.* (*f.* ī) a slayer, slaughterman, mur-

मारतोल, *m.* a hammer: a turnscrew.

मारधार, *f.* thumping and beating severely.

मारना, *t.* to smite, strike, hit, beat, bang, to mortify, slay, kill, to punish, to drive, shoot, cast, toss, throw, to mar, spoil, blight, blast, ruin, destroy, to conquer, take, to crack, break, to take, to set, to smother, to stamp, to sting, to stop, to calm, quench, to run. *Apne monko* —, to practice self-denial.

मारपीट, *f.* a drubbing, beating and bruising, assault and battery.

मारपेच, *f.* serpentine twisting and winding, circumvolution. — *ki rāh, f.* a winding or crooked path.

मारयौ in Braj = **मारे**, *q.v.*

मारव, 1, = **मालव**, *q.v.*: 2, = **मैं मारूंगा**. See **व**, 4.

मारवा, *m.* a certain musical mode (*rāg*).

मारहि, 1, (pl. °**हिं**) = **मारता है**: 2, acc. or emphatic form of **मार**, *q.v.*

मारा, 1, *m.* a striking or beating: 2, *m.* (*f.* ī) a victim: *lit.* beaten, smitten, slain, overturned, foundered (as a boat, etc.). — *jānā,* to be overcome, be slain, be overturned, be sunk (as a boat), be cut off (as a detachment, etc.). — *parnā,* to be destroyed, be ruined, be killed. *Mārā mārā phirnā,* to wander.— *Mārā kāṭī k.,* to blot paper (in writing), to spoil a letter or document.

मारात्मक, *m.* (*f.* ikā) a cruel person, etc.: *lit.* of a cruel disposition, murderous, fatal, deadly.

मारामारि, *f.* a mutual beating or striking, scuffle, bickering, broil, fray, battle; preposteræ veneris usus reciprocus.

मारामारी = **मारामारि**, *q.v.*

मारि, *f.* killing; plague, epidemic.

मारिका, *f.* (*m.* **मारक**) a murderess, etc. [killed.

मारित, *m.* (*f.* ā) put to death, slaughtered, slain,

मारिष, *m.* a venerable person (in dramatic language), the manager of a theatre; a certain potherb (*Amaranthus oleraceus*).

मारिषा, *f. pr. n.* the mother of Daksh.

मारिहै (*pl.* **मारिहैं**) in Braj = **मारेगा**.

मारिहौ in Braj = **मारोगे**.

मारिहौं in Braj = **मारूंगा**.

मारी, *f.* plague, pestilence, epidemic, murrain, mortality: toil, labour. [certain Rakshas.

मारीच, *m. pr. n.* (1) of a certain Muni (2) of a

मारुत, *lit.* appertaining to the Maruts; *hence, m.* vital air, wind; a Marut; burnt offering on the occasion of corruption. [sen.

मारुति, *m.* an epithet (1) of Hanumān (2) of Bhīm-

मारू, *m.* a certain musical mode (*rāg*); a kind of warlike musical instrument, kettledrum; a certain deadly weapon composed of two antelope-horns pointed with steel; *lit.* adj. smiting, striking, warlike, destructive, deadly, fatal: (in comp.) = striker, hard hitter, killer.

मारूजन; a plural form of **मारू**, *q.v.*

मारूबाजा, *m.* an instrument of music played in battle (*esp.* the kettle-drum).

मारे, (past part. of **मारना** used as a subst. *m.* infl.: it takes genit. *m.* infl., and may be put either before its word or after it ; *e.g.* *Ḍarke māre* or *Māre ḍarke* by reason of, on account of, in consequence of, because of, for fear of, through, for the sake of, from, by, for.

मारेउ (an old form) = **मारा** (**मारना**).

मारें (an old form) = **मैं मारूं** or **मारूंगा**.

मार्कण्डेय, *m.pr. n.* a certain ancient Hindoo sage (the supposed author of the Mārkaṇḍey Purāṇ).

मार्ग, *m.* search, enquiry, trace; a road, path, way; the anus; a saw-kerf; doctrine, creed, belief.

मार्गगोरी, *f.* journeying, marching, proceeding.

मार्गण, *m.* enquiry, search, research; begging; a beggar; a solicitor; an arrow. [showing the way.

मार्गदर्शक, *m.* (*f.* ikā) a conductor, guide: lit. *adj.*

मार्गदर्शी, *m.* (*f.* iṇī) = **मार्गदर्शक**, *q.v.*

मार्गपाल, *m.* (*f.* ī) a guardian of the road, custos viarum, patrol, watchman.

मार्गलूट, *f.* highway robbery.

मार्गशिर = **मार्गशीर्ष**, *q.v.* [Dec.).

मार्गशीर्ष, *m.* the Hindoo month Agrahāyan (Nov.-

मार्गशीर्षी, *f.* the fifteenth day of the first half of the month Mārgashīrsh. [way.

मार्गाधीश, *m.* (*f.* ā) the lord or sovereign of the

मार्गी (*m. f.* inī) one who goes the road (literally or spiritually), *hence*, a traveller, follower, pilgrim.

मार्ग्ग, *more prop.* **मार्ग**, *q.v.*

मार्जन, *m.* a cleaning, rubbing, scouring, wiping; a cleaning the person by rubbing it with oil or fragrant unguents; a sprinkling with water for purification before the commencement of religious ceremonies; the clearing off a debt; pardon.

मार्जनी, *f.* 1, = **मार्जन**, *q.v.*: 2, a rubber, brush, broom, towel. [the pole-cat.

मार्जार, *m.* (*f.* ī) the common cat, the wild cat;

मार्तण्ड, *m.* the sun: a hog.

मार्तोल, *m.* a hammer: a turnscrew.

माल, 1, *f.* (*contraction*) = **माला**, *q.v.*: 2, *m.* a boxer, wrestler, prize-fighter, champion, hero: a field: a napkin, rubber, towel: property, goods, merchandise; wealth, capital; the public revenue of a State: 3, *m. pr. n.* (1) of a certain country (2) of a certain tribe: an epithet of Vishṇu.

मालकंगनी, *f.* staff-tree (*Celastrus*).

मालका, *f.* a garland.

मालकोश, *m.* a certain musical mode (*rāg*).

मालख़ाना, *m.* a store, store-house, treasury.

मालगाड़ी, *f.* a luggage-van, luggage-train.

मालगुज़ार, *m.* one who pays tribute, a landholder; tenant, subject.

मालगुज़ारी, *f.* the paying rent or revenue; land-revenue; rent of land. [of a debt.

मालज़ामिन, *m.* (in Law) security for the discharge

मालती, *f.* a bud, blossom; a young woman; moonlight: night; a river: the name of several plants and flowers (1) *Jasminum grandiflorum* (2) *Bignonia suaveolens* (3) *Echytes caryophillata*, Roxb. (4) *Gaertnera racemosa*, Roxb. or *Banisteria Bengalensis*, Linn.

मालतीलता, *f.* = **मालती** (4), *q.v.*

मालधनी, *m.* (*f.* inī) a possessor of much property (especially in land).

मालपुआ, *m.* a kind of sweetmeat, pancake.

मालम, *more prop.* **मालूम**, *q.v.* [of Mālwa.

मालव, *m.pr.n.* the province of Mālwa; the people

मालवश्री, *f.* a certain musical mode (*rāgiṇī*).

मालवा, *more prop.* **मालव**, *q.v.*

मालवान, *m. pr. n.* a certain demon (*daitya*).

मालवार, opulent, wealthy, rich.

मालवो, in Mārwāṛī = to play.

मालशिरी }
मालश्री } (corruptions) = **मालवश्री**, *q.v.*

माला, *f.* a line; a necklace, garland, wreath, chaplet of flowers, a chain, a string of breads, a Hindoo rosary: a field: a cocoanut-shell: a book.

मालाकार, *m* (*f.* ī) a maker of flower-chaplets or garlands, a florist, a gardener, flower-seller.

मालाफल, *m.* the seed of the *Eleocarpus* (of which common rosaries are made).

मालामाल, brimful, replete, abundant.

मालावान, *m.* (*f.* vatī) possessing a wreath or garland, garlanded, wreathed, crowned.

मालिक, 1, *m.* (*f.* ā) a flower-gatherer, chaplet-weaver, florist; a painter; a sort of bird: 2, *m.* proprietor, owner, possessor, lord, master. Very commonly applied to the Supreme Being as Lord of all.

मालिका, *f.* a garland of flowers; a necklace: a multitude: a daughter: a palace: a spirituous liquor: double jasmine.

मालिकाना, *m.* a monthly or annual allowance paid to a zamīndār by an occupant of his lands.

मालिन (*contraction*) = **मालिनी**, *q.v.*

मालिनी, *f.* (*m.* **माली**) the wife of a *mālī*; a female flower-dealer; a certain plant (*Hedysarum alhagi*): a certain shrub (*Echitis caryophyllata*); a certain musical mode (*rāgiṇī*); a species of metre in Sanskrit prosody: an epithet (1) of Pārvatī (2) of the Ganges of heaven.

माली, *m.* (*f.* inī) = **मालाकार**, *q.v.*

मालुक; see **मलुक**.

मालून, more prop. **मलऊन**, *q.v.*

मालूफ़, *m.* (*f.* ā) familiar, accustomed to live in friendship with, habituated, ordinary: fed, fattened.

मालूम, known, distinguished, notorious, evident, apparent, obvious. — *k.* to know, find out, perceive.

मालूल, indisposed, distempered, diseased, sick.

माल्य, *m.* a flower, a chaplet of flowers, wreath, garland for the forehead.

माल्यवत, *m. pr. n.* a certain mountainous range (eastward of mount Meru) described as one of the smaller ranges of India proper.

माल्यवती, *f. pr. n.* a certain river.

माल्यवन्त }
माल्यवान } = **माल्यवत**, *q.v.*

मावली, *f.* (*dialectic* = **मां**) mother.

मावस (*colloquial*) = **अमावस्या**, *q.v.* See **अ**, 18.

मावा, *f.* substance ; starch ; the yolk of an egg; leaven; milk inspissated by boiling: a dwelling, abode, habitation, mansion.

माशूक, *m.* (*f.* ā) a beloved object, a lover.

माशूका, *f.* a sweetheart, mistress.

माशूम, defended, preserved; innocent, simple: [*hence*, an infant.

माशोबी, *m. f.* a kind of bird.

माष, 1, = **मावा**, *q. v.*: 2, anger.

माषः } = **माषा**, *q. v.*
माषक }

माषपर्णी, *f.* a certain leguminous shrub (*Glycine debilis*).

माषा, *m.* a kind of black vetch or kidney-bean (*Phaseolus max* or *radiatus*); a certain cutaneous disease ; a fool ; a jeweller's or goldsmith's weight (variously reckoned at 5, 8, or 10 seeds (*ratti*) of the *Abrus precatorius* : the weight in common use is about 17 grs. Troy).

माषो (Rām.) = (1) **मक्खी** (2) **शहद**, *qq. v.*

माषीण, *m.* (**माष**) a field producing black kidney-beans.

माष्य = **माषीण**, *q. v.*

मास, 1, *a corruption of* (1) **माष** (2) **मांस** (3) **मच्छली** *qq. v.* : 2, *m.* the moon, a month, the twelfth part of the Hindoo year. It is usually the lunar month, consisting of thirty *tithi* ; but it may also be a solar month, being equal to the sun's passage through a sign of the zodiac. There is also a *sāwan* month, consisting of thirty risings and settings of the sun ; a *nakshatra* month, regulated by the lunar asterisms; also, a fifth description of month called *Vārhaspatya*, depending on the motions of the planet Jupiter ; while the lunar month also being of two kinds (as reckoned from the new or from the full moon) makes, in all, six different modes of monthly calculation.

मासकबार, the end of a month, the last day of a month ; a monthly abstract (of cases decided in court).

मासन, *m.* the medicinal seed *Serratula anthelmintica*.

मासला, *m.* a pattern, model.

मासव्विर, *more prop.* **मुसव्विर**, *q. v.*

मासवृद्धि, *f.* an intercalary month : monthly interest.

मासा (*corruption*) = (1) **माषा** (2) **मांस** (3) **मास**, 2.

मासान्त, *m. f.* ? the last day of the solar or lunar month, the day of new moon.

मासिक, *lit.* appertaining to a month, monthly, payable in a month, hired by the month, lasting for a month, falling at the end of a month, occurring monthly; *hence, m.* (*f.* ī) a monthly servant; monthly hire, stipend, wages; a certain obsequial offering (*shrāddh*) performed on the day of the new moon.

मासिकविभागकर्त्ता, *m.* (*f.* trī) a paymaster (*esp.* of monthly servants).

मासिका } *f.* monthly hire, stipend, wages.
मासिकी }

मासी, *f.* an aunt (mother's sister).

मासीन, *m.* (*f.* ā) any creature a month old : *lit.* of a month ; a month old ; monthly.

मासु (emphat.) = **मास** or **मांस**, *qq. v.* : see **उ**, 9.

मासुर ; see **मसूर** and **महसूल**.

मासुल } (colloquial) = **महसूल**, *q. v.*
मासूल }

माह, 1, = **माहीं**, *q. v.* : 2, *m.* the moon ; a month ; [*met.* a beloved person.

माहताब = **महताब**, *q. v.*

माहरू, (moon-faced, *i. e.*) beautiful, charming, elegant.

माहवारी, *f.* the revenue that is collected in a [month, monthly pay, wages.

माहा, 1, *f.* a cow : 2, see **माह**.

माहां ; see **माहा**.

माहाकुल, *m.* (*f.* ā) = **महाकुल**, *q. v.*

माहाजनिक, appertaining to great persons (fit for them, suitable to them).

माहात्मिक, majestic, glorious, of great honour or sanctity, magnanimous.

माहात्म्य, *m.* majesty, glory, greatness, celebrity, praise, might ; the peculiar efficacy or virtue of a deity or of a shrine; a literary work giving an account of the merits of any holy object or place.

माहाराजिक, appertaining to kings (fit for them, suitable to them), imperial, royal.

माहि } = **माहीं**, *q. v.*
माहिं }

माहिमा, *more prop.* **महिमा**, *q. v.*

माहियाना, *m.* monthly salary.

माहिर, acute, ingenious, sagacious, skilful, clever, [proficient.

माहिरी, *f.* cleverness, expertness, skill.

माहिष्मती, *f. pr. n.* a certain city founded by Mahishmat or by Muchukund.

माहिष्य, *m. pr. n.* one of the mixed tribes (sprung from a Kshatriya father by a Vaishya mother).

माही, 1, = **माहीं**, *q. v.* : 2, *f.* a fish ; *pr. n.* the fish on which the earth is supposed to rest.

माहीं = **में**, *q. v.* Very frequent in poetry, in Braj, and in the colloquial jargon of the villagers.

माहीयत, *f.* essence, quality, intrinsic worth, state, [condition, circumstances.

माहुर, *m.* poison, venom.

माहू, *m.* = **कनखलाई**, *q. v.*

मिंह ; see **मेंह** and **मेह**.

मिंहदी (*colloquial*) = **मेन्धी**, *q. v.*

मिंगनी, *f.* goat's-dung, sheep's-dung.

मिचकारना, *t.* to rinse.

मिचना, *t.* to shut, close.

मिचराना, *t.* to eat without appetite. *Michar michar k.* to eat without appetite.

मिचोलना, *t.* to shut or cover the eyes.

मिच्चरमिचर, *more prop.* **मिचरमिचर**. See **मिचराना**.

मिछा in old Hindee = **मिथ्या**, *q. v.*

मिज़ाज, *m.* temperament, constitution, habit of body, state of health, complexion, disposition, temper.

मिटका ; see **मटका**.

मिटना, *n.* to be effaced, be obliterated: *a. int.* to [cease to exist, to expire.

मिटाना, *t.* efface, erase, obliterate, blot out, abrogate, bring to nought, abolish.

मिटिया, *f.* a kind of earthen vessel.

मिट्ठी = **मट्ठी**, *q. v.*

मिट्ठा, 1, *more com.* **मीठा**, *q. v.*: 2, *m.* a kiss.

मिट्ठी, *f.* a kiss.—*lakṛī*, *f.* (**मिट्ठा**, 1) liquorice-root.
मिठ (*corruption*) = **मिष्ट**, *q. v.*
मिठरी, *f.* a kind of sweetmeat.
मिठाई, *f.* sweets, sweetmeats; sweetness.
मिठाईवाला, (*f.* ī) a maker or a vendor of sweetmeats, a confectioner.
मिठांस, *m.* (*f.* ?) sweetness.
मिठाला, a productive moisture inherent in a soil.
मिठास, *m.* (*f.* ?) sweetness. [frugal.
मित, measured; restricted, moderate, regular,
मितवाच, of measured speech, prudent in the use
मिताई (*corruption*) = **मित्रताई**, *q. v.* [of speech.
मिताक्षरा, *f. pr. n.* the designation of various celebrated commentaries of the Hindoos.
मिताशन, 1, *m.* abstemiousness, moderation in eating: 2, an abstemious person: *lit.* moderate in eating.
मिताशी, *m.* (*f.* inī), } = **मिताशन**, 2, *q. v.*
मिताहारी, *m.* (*f.* iṇī) }
मिति, 1, *f.* measuring, measurement, measure, weight, value: evidence, proof; 2, *m.* interest; date. *Kachchā* —, interest charged on money, dated from the day before the transaction. *Pakkā* —, interest allowed on money, dated from the day following receipt.
मिती, *f.* (see **मिति**, 2) date; interest.
मित्र, *m.* (*f.* ā) a friend, ally; the sun.
मित्रता, *f.* }
मित्रताई, *f.* } = **मित्राई**, *q. v.*
मित्रत्व, *m.* }
मित्रद्रुह, *m.* an injurer of his friend, a false or treacherous friend.
मित्रद्रोही, *m.* (*f.* inī) = **मित्रद्रुह**, *q.v.*
मित्रभाव, *m.* a state of friendship, friendliness, friendly disposition.
मित्रभेद, *m.* a breach of friendship.
मित्रलाभ, *m.* the acquisition of a friend, the forming friendship: *pr. n.* the first book of the *Hitopadesh.*
मित्रविन्दा, *f.* an epithet of an Ishṭi: *pr. n.* a wife of Krishṇ.
मित्रविन्द, *m. pr. n.* (1) of a son of the 12th Manu (2) of a son of Krishṇ; an epithet of Agni.
मित्रसेन, *m. pr. n.* (1) of a son of the 12th Manu (2) of a grandson of Krishṇ (3) of a certain Buddhist (4) of a certain king of the Draviḍ country.
मित्रा, *f.* (*m.* **मित्र**) a female friend.
मित्राई, *f.* friendship, alliance, intimacy, friendliness, friendly intercourse.
मित्रावरुण, *m. pr. n.* the father of Agasti.
मिथः = **मिथस**, *q. v.*
मिथस, in conjunction, in private union, in coition, privately, together, mutually, reciprocally.
मिथिला, *f. pr. n.* a certain city and district lying to the North-east of Bengal.
मिथिलानगर, *m.* (*f.* ī) } *pr. n.* the city of Mithilā.
मिथिलापुर, *m.* (*f.* ī) }
मिथिलेश, *m.* (the lord of Mithilā, *i.e.*) rājā Janak.
मिथिलेस; see **मिथिलेश** and **मिथिलेसि**.
मिथिलेसि, *f. pr. n.* the wife of king Janak.
मिथुन, *m.* copulation junction, union; a couple, pair, brace; male and female, man and woman: *pr. n.* the sign Gemini.
मिथुनी; see (1) **मिथुन** (2) **मैथुनी**.
मिथुनीभाव, *m.* amorous inclination. [swearing.
मिथ्यकिरिया, *f.* (**मिथ्या** + **किरिया**) a false oath, false
मिथ्यता, *f.* utter untruth, sheer falseness.
मिथ्या, 1, *m.* an untruth, falsehood; denial: 2, false, lying, untrue, feigned, counterfeit, delusory, wrong; 3, falsely, untruly, wrongly, feignedly, uselessly, in vain. [having falsely.
मिथ्याचार, *m.* (*f.* ā) a deceiver, etc.: *lit.* adj. be-
मिथ्यात्व, *m.* utter untruth, sheer falsehood.
मिथ्यात्वोक्ति, *f.* utter untruthfulness of speech, sheer falsehood. [infidelity, atheism.
मिथ्यादृष्टि, *f.* denial of future existence, heresy,
मिथ्यापूजक, *adj.* worshipping what is false, worshipping in vain: hence, *m.* (*f.* ikā) an idolater.
मिथ्याप्रतिज्ञ, guilty of breach of engagement, treacherous: hence, *m.* (*f.* ā) a promise-breaker. [mistake.
मिथ्यामति, *f.* ignorance, error; an erroneous opinion,
मिथ्यार्थ, with a view to deception, for the sake of falsehood. [falsehood, denying a charge.
मिथ्यावादी, *m.* (*f.* inī) a liar: *lit.* adj. speaking
मिथ्याशपथकर्त्ता, *m.* (*f.* trī) a perjuror.
मिन्ती (*colloquial*) = **विनति**, *q. v.*
मिन्न, *m.* (*f.* ā) unctuous, moist.
मिन्नत, *f.* an obligation, favour; humble and earnest supplication, entreaty.
मियाँ, (a term of address or of calling, expressive of respect and of kindly feeling) Sir! master! It is used especially to elderly persons and to eunuchs.
मियाँजी, *m.* the respected master (applied esp. to a school-master). [the waist, loins.
मियान, 1, *more prop.* **मियाँ**, *q. v.*: 2, *f.* a scabbard;
मिर, *more prop.* **मीर**, *q.v.*
मिरा, *m.* (*f.* ī) a contraction of **मेरा**, *q. v.*
मिरना, *more prop.* **मरना**, *q.v.*
मिरिच (*colloquial*) = **मरिच**, *q.v.* [patrol).
मिरोना, *a. int.* to perambulate, keep watch (as a
मिरोड़; for words beginning thus, see under the
मिर्ग (corruption) = **मृग**, *q. v.* [form **मरोड़**.
मिर्गि } *f.* epilepsy, falling-fits.
मिर्गी }
मिर्गीहा, (*f.* ī) an epileptic; *lit.* afflicted with epilep-
मिर्च = **मरिच**, *q. v.* [sy, epileptic.
मिर्चा, *m.* 1, (*dialectic*) = **मरिच**, *q. v.*: 2, Chili pepper
मिर्चाई = **मिर्चा**, 2, *q. v.* [(*Capsicum frutescens*).
मिर्चानी } (*dialectic*) = **मरिच**, *q. v.*
मिर्चा }

मिर्ज़ापुर, *m. pr. n.* (1) of a certain district of northern India (2) of the capital of that district.

मिर्त (corruption) = **मत्यु**, *q. v.*

मिर्था (*colloquial*) = **मिथ्या**, *q. v.* [मर्दंग.

मिर्दंग; for words beginning thus, see under the form

मिर्धा, *m.* an officer employed by Government in villages, an overseer, exciseman.

मिल; see (1) **मिलना** (2) **मोल**.

मिलई, (pl. °ईं) an old form = **मलेगा**.

मिलजुल, together. See **मिलेजुले**.

मिलन, *n.* the coming into contact or union with a thing. contact, coälescence, mixing with, union, agreement; encountering. meeting. [convivial.

मिलनसार, civil, affable, social, friendly, intimate,

मिलनसारी, *f.* civility, affableness, sociability, friendliness, concord, agreement.

मिलना, *n.* to be mixed, be confounded, to be attained, be met with, be got, to be connected, be united: *t.* to meet, assemble, to join, blend, coälesce, agree, accord, fit, suit, correspond, tally, harmonize with, become connected with, associate: *a. int.* to occur, to come (into one's possession).—*julnā* or *jhulnā*, to meet cordially, to have unrestricted intercourse. — *hilnā*, to be together, to act together, to coälesce, join.

मिलवट, shrivelling. (?) [mixed, cause to mix.

मिलवाना, *t.* (causat. of **मिलाना**) to cause to be

मिलहि, *m. f.* (pl. **मिलहिं**) in Braj = **मिलेगा**.

मिला, *m.* (*f.* ī) obtained, attained, mixed, united.

मिलाउव in Braj = (1) **मिलाव**, *q. v.* (2) **मिलाऊंगा**.

मिलाजुला, sociable, friendly, harmonious. *Milejule rahnā*, to live together in great harmony.

मिलान, *m.* the bringing things into contact, causing a mixture, making parties agree, adjustment of differences, producing harmony in music, reconcilement, union, unison, society.

मिलाना, *t.* (of **मिलना**) to cause to meet, to introduce, join, unite, attach, mix, blend, connect, adjust, accord, fit, apply, close, cement, assimilate, compare, reconcile, meet, visit, find. get.

मिलानी, *f.* comparison, adjustment.

मिलाप, *m.* agreement, reconciliation, accommodation, mixing, combination, coälescence, concord, union, understanding, adjustment, pacification, meeting, interview, visit, social converse, society.

मिलापी, *m.* (*f.* inī) a social person, etc.: *lit.* civil, affable, sociable, friendly, intimate, convivial.

मिलाव, *m.* mixing, mixture, accord, unison, assimilation; adjustment, arbitration; mixture, alloy, adulteration, corruption.

मिलावट, *f.* = **मिलाव**, *q. v.*

मिलावनीं in Braj = **मिलाना**, *q. v.*

मिलावा = **मिलाव**, *q. v.*

मिलाहिज़ा, *more prop.* **मुलाहज़ा**, *q. v.*

मिलि; see **मिलना** and **मिलो**.

मिलित, *m.* (*f.* ā) united, connected, combined, mixed; met with, encountered, found, obtained.

मलिवो = **मिलब** = **मिलेगा**. See **ब**, 4.

मलिहै, *m. f.* (pl. **मिलिहैं**) in Braj = **मिलेगा**.

मिलिहि, *m. f.* (pl. **मिलिहिं**) in Braj = **मिलेगा**.

मिली, *f.* (*m.* **मिला**) obtained, etc.

मिलेजुले, the inflected form of **मिलाजुला**, *q.v.*

मिलौनी, *f.* mixture, adulteration, alloy.

मिल्क, *m.* possession, property, right.

मिशर; see (1) **मिश्र** (2) **मिस्र**.

मिशन, *m.* (Engl.) a missionary society.

मिशि, *f.* the name of several plants:—(1) *Anethum panmorium*, a sort of fennel (2) *Valeriana jatamansi*, Indian spikenard (3) *Anethum sowa*, another sort of fennel (4) *Ligusticum ajwaen* a sort of lovage (5) *Pimpinella anisum*, common anise.

मिशी = (1) **मिशि** (2) **मीशी**, *qq. v.*

मिश्र, *lit. m.* (*f.* ā) mixed, mingled, blended, united; *hence, m.* a mixing, mixture; an elephant of the fourth of the four classes into which elephants are arranged; a Hindoo physician. The term is used as a title (= a respectable person, Sir), and as such is applied (1) to Brāhmaṇs who were brought to India from Shākdwip by Krishṇ, in order to cure the leprosy of his son Shāmb (2) to some Brāhmaṇs from Mithilā.

मिश्रक, *adj.* mixing, adulterating; mingled, miscellaneous: mixed, adulterated: hence (1) *m.* salt produced from salt soil (2) *m.* (*f.* ā) a mixer, compounder; an adulterator: a kind of song or singing: *pr. n.* (1) of a certain *tīrth*, i. e. Naimish (2) of a certain garden of paradise.

मिश्रण, *m.* a uniting, mixing: (in Math.) addition.

मिश्राह्न, *f.* = **मिशिणी**, *q. v.*

मिश्रिक = **मिश्रक**, *q v.*

मिश्रित, *m.* (*f.* ā) mixed, mingled, blended, united, joined, added; respectable, respected.

मिश्री, *more prop.* **मिस्री**, *q. v.*

मिष, 1, *m.* emulation; envy; fraud, trick, deception, stratagem, sham, pretence, excuse, apology: 2, *adv.* (with gen. *m.* infl.) under the pretence of.

मिषि / **मिषी** } = **मिशि**, *q. v.*

मिष्ट, *m.* (*f.* ā) sprinkled; sweet, pleasant, agreeable, sugary; hence, *m.* a sweetmeat.

मिष्टाचार, *m.* pleasing behaviour.

मिष्टान्न, *m.* sweetmeats; frumenty; a mixture of sugar and acids eaten with rice, etc.; sauce, gravy, seasoning.

मिस, *more prop.* **मिष**, *q. v.*

मिसकीनी, *f.* poverty, indigence. [and sand.

मिसन, *m.* a soil consisting of a mixture of clay

मिसना, *n.* to be pulverized, be ground.

मिसबाबा, *f.* (Engl. hybrid) an unmarried girl or lady (of European parentage).

मिसर, *more prop.* (1) **मिश्र** (2) **मिस्र**, *qq. v.*

मिसरा, *m.* a leaf of a folding door: (in Pros.) a single line, hemistich.

मिसरी, *more prop.* **मिस्री**, *q. v*

मिसि = **मिशि**, *q. v.*

मिसिर, *more prop.* **मिस्र**, *q. v.*

मिसिराह्न, *f.* = **मिशिणी**, *q. v.* [vetches.

मिसी, 1, = (1) **मिशि** (2) **मिस्सी**, *qq. v.*: 2, made of

मिसीदार, *m.* a box (generally made of some precious metal, as gold) for holding *missī*.

मिसौन, *m.* a vetch, pulse.

मिसोना, *f.* linseed (*Linum utilatissimum*).

मिसु(Rām.) = **मिष**, *q.v.* [level for treading out corn.

मिस्ता,, *m.* a desert without herbage: a place made

मिस्र, 1, *more prop.* **मिश्र**, *q. v.*: 2, *m.* any large city: [3, *m. pr. n.* Egypt; Cairo.

मिस्रिक = **मिश्रक**, *q.v.*

मिस्री, appertaining to Egypt or to Cairo: hence, (1) *m.* (*f.* iṇī) an Egyptian (2) *f.* sugar-candy.

मिस्सी, *f.* a kind of powder (made of vitriol, etc.) with which the teeth are tinged of a black colour.

मिहतर, *m.* (*f.* ānī) a sweeper, scavenger, nightmare: *lit.* greater: *hence*, a principal person, chief, prince.

मिहतरानी, *f.* (*m.* **मिहतर**) any female of the *mihtar* caste, a female sweeper; a female inn-keeper.

मिहदार, *m.* (see **बज़ीदार**) an agricultural servant who receives his remuneration in money.

मिहदी (*colloquial*) = **मेन्धी**, *q.v.*

मिहनत, *f.* labour, toil, exertion, pains, difficulty, trouble, calamity, affliction, trial, temptation, sorrow, perplexity.

मिहनती, *m.* (*f.* inī) a labourer, workman, etc.: *lit.* laborious, painstaking; unfortunate; difficult.

मिहना, *m.* sarcasm. — *ḍheknā*, to poke fun, to be sarcastic, to sneer. [in-law.

मिहमान, *m.* a stranger; a guest, a lodger; a son-

मिहमानदार, *m.* an entertainer, host; an officer whose business it is to receive and entertain ambassadors.

मिहमानी, 1, *f.* entertainment, hospitality: 2, appertaining to a guest.

मिहर, 1, *m.*; *more prop.* **मिहिर**, *q. v.*: 2, *f.* love, affection, kindness, friendliness.

मिहरबान, a friend: *lit.* kind, affectionate, friendly, indulgent, gracious.

मिहरबानी, *f.* kindness, friendliness, favour. — *k.* to exercise kindness, to confer a favour.

मिहरवा, *f.* a female, a woman. [a woman.

मिहरा, *m.* a man who appears in the costume of

मिहराई, *f.* the occupation of a pālkee-bearer: a kind of song among cowherds.

मिहराऊ
मिहरिया } *f.* (= **मिहरवा**) a female, a woman.
मिहरी

मिहाना, *a. int.* to become damp.

मिहानी, *f.* a churning-vessel, churn.

मिहिन्दी (colloquial) = **मेन्धी**, *q.v.* [a certain sage.

मिहिर, *m.* the sun; the moon; a cloud; air, wind:

मिहीन, fine, thin, subtle, not coarse.

मिहोघा, (in the hill dialect) a certain fungus filled (when ripe) with dry powder (*vulg.* puff-ball).

मींगी, *f.* marrow, pith, essence.

मींजना, *t.* to rub, to scour.

मींह, *more prop.* **मेंह**, *q.v.*

मीका, *m. pr. n.* of the prophet Micah and of the Book that bears his name.

मीच, *f.* death, extinction.

मीचना
मीछना } *t.* to close the eyes, wink.

मींजना, *t.* rub with the hands.

मीजू, *m.* (= **मसूर**) a lentil.

मीठा, *m.* (*f.* ī) sweet, pleasant, agreeable, gentle, slow; hence, *m.* a kiss; a certain fruit; an impotent man; a very active vegetable poison.

मीठाई, *f.* sweets, sweetmeats; sweetness.

मीठाईवाला, *m.* (*f.* ī) a maker or a vendor of sweetmeats, a confectioner.

मीठास, *f.* sweets, sweetmeats; sweetness.

मींठिया, *f.* a kiss.

मीठी, *f.* (*m.* **मीठा**) an agreeable female: a kiss.

मीठीकद्दू, *f.* red pumpkin or squash gourd (*Cucurbita melopepo*, Willd.).

मीठीलकड़ी, *f.* liquorice-root.

मीणा, *f.* a certain caste of Hindoos who are professedly thieves. [lover, sweetheart, namesake.

मीत, 1, = **मीता**, 2, *q.v.*: 2, (from **मित्र**) a friend,

मीतन, *f.* (*m.* **मीत**, 2) a female friend, sweetheart, female namesake. [er, porringer, cup.

मीता, 1, *m.* (*f.* ī *or* n) = **मीत**, 2, *q.v.*: 2, *m.* a pitch-

मींती, *f.* (*m.* **मीता**, 1) = **मीतन**, *q.v.*

मीन, *f. m.* (?) a fish: *pr. n.* (1) of the sign Pisces (2) of the first incarnation of Vishṇu (see *Avatār*).

मीनरंग, *m.* (*f.* ā) a kingfisher.

मीना, 1, = **मीणा**, *q.v.*: 2, *m.* a goblet, glass, decanter; a blue colour: enamel; the azure vault, heaven, paradise; the blue stone, blue vitriol, caustic.

मीनाघाती, *m.* (*f.* inī) a fisherman; a crane: *lit.* adj. [fish-killing.

मीनाण्ड, *m.* fish-spawn, roe, milt.

मीनाबाजार, *m.* a fancy bāzār, a bāzār where miscellaneous goods are sold.

मीमांसक, *m.* a follower of the Mīmāṅsā philosophy.

मीमांसा, *f. pr. n.* one of the systems of Hindoo philosophy. The Mīmāṅsā consists of two parts which form two of the six schools of philosophy (*darshan*), and it has for its object the interpretation of the Veds: the first part (called *Mīmāṅsā*, *Pūrvamīmāṅsā*, or *Karmamīmāṅsā*) originated with Jaimini, and illustrates the *Karmkānd* of the Veds, *i. e.* the practical part, or the ritual, of religion and devotion, including also moral and legal obligations: the second part (called *Mīmāṅsā*, *Uttarmīmāṅsā*, or *Brahmamīmāṅsā*) is ascribed to Vyās and is the same as the *Vedānt*, being founded on the *gyānkānd* (or theological portion) of the Veds: it has for its object the investigation of theological proof deducible from the Veds, and treats of the spiritual worship of the Supreme Soul of the universe.

मीमियाना, *a. int.* to bleat (said of kids).

मीर, *m.* the sea, ocean; a certain part of a mountain; a limit, boundary; a drink, beverage: a chief, leader; a title by which saiyids are addressed.

मील, (Engl.) a mile.

मीलन, *m.* twinkling, blinking, winking.

मीला (*Rām.*) = **मिल करके**.

मीवा, *f.* the worm of the intestines, ascarides, etc.

मोशी, *f.* chamois-leather.

मोसना, *t.* (of **मिसना**) to pulverize, grind, tweak, twitch, rumple, crumple. [trained, well-disciplined.

मुअद्दब, respectful, civil, polite, courteous, well-

मुआ, *m.* (*f.* **मुई**) *more com.* **मूआ**, *q. v.*

मुआजिज़ा, *more prop.* **मुजिज़ा**, *q.v.*

मुआतबत, *f.* reprehension, censure.

मुआफ़, dispensed with, exempted, forgiven, absolved. — *k.* to excuse, remit, absolve, forgive.

मुआफ़िक़, more prop. **मुवाफ़िक़**, *q.v.*

मुआफ़ी, *f.* immunity, exemption, absolution, pardon: (in Revenue) lands the rents of which, previously payable to Government, are remitted in perpetuity to the holder.

मुंगा, *m.* (*f.* ī) naked, bare.

मुंज, *m.* a species of grass (*Saccharum munja*) from the fibres of which a string is prepared of which the triple thread worn as a girdle by Brāhmaṇs should be formed; the Brāhmanical girdle: an arrow.

मुंजल, *m.* the fruit of the palmyra-tree.

मुंजा, more prop. **मुंज**, *q.v.*

मुंझ (dialectic) = **मुझ**, *q.v.*

मुंशी (corruption) = **मुनशी**, *q.v.*

मुंह, *m.* the fore part of anything, the mouth, face, countenance, presence, aspect; an orifice: respect, complaisance; power, ability, qualification, pretension, fitness. — *apnā sā leke phir jānā*, to return disappointed from any enterprize, to fail of success. *Apnā sā — lenā* is used to denote failure of success. — *ānā*, to be salivated. — *utar jānā*, to have the face sunk or withered by weakness and emaciation. — *k.* to confront, compare, put face to face; to give abuse; to burst or open (as an abscess); to make the first attempt at seizing game (said of young hunting-animals); to turn one's face towards, to direct the steps toward any particular object or place. — *kā niwālā*, anything easily obtained. — *kā phuhar*, abusive. — *kālā*, *m.* disgrace. — *ke bhal* (sc. *par*) face foremost, face downwards, pronus, prostrate. — *kālā k.* to incur disgrace; to punish, disgrace. — *ki loī utarnā* or *jānā*, to lose the sense of shame. — *ke kawwe uṛ jānā*, to look blank on any occasion. — *kholnā*, to abuse. — *chharhnā*, to become intimate with, attach oneself to; to face, confront. — *chalānā*, to bite or be inclined to bite (said of horses). — *chiṛānā*, to make mouths. — *chhipānā*, to hide one's face. — *ṭeṛhā k.* to make wry faces. — *thathānā*, to slap one's face, box one's ears. — *ḍālnā*, to beg, entreat. — *taknā*, to be astonished or afflicted. — *toṛnā*, to harass. — *to dekho*, look at his face! (applied to a person who pretends to something beyond his power or ability). — *thathānā*, to make mouths or faces, to fashion the face. — *dikhānā*, to shew one's face, to appear with confidence or satisfaction. — *dekhke bāt k.* to say what one supposes will be agreeable to the vanity of the hearers, to flatter. — *dekhnā*, to look up to, have a regard for one; to be astonished, to be helpless. — *dekh rahnā*, to stare at with surprize. — *dekhkeki prīti*, *f.* apparent friendship or affection, mere shew of friendship. — *par garm honā*, to behave disrespectfully in the presence of a superior. — *par lānā*, to relate, tell. — *par hawāī uṛnā* or *phirnā* or *chhuṭnā*, *lit.* to have a squib or rocket discharged against one's face; *i. e* to change colour. — *pasārnā*, to gape (with surprize, etc.). — *pānā*, to get into one's good graces; to presume on the favour of another. — *pīṭh k.* to speak in anger or in bitterness. — *phirnā* or *phir lenā*, to turn away the face from, to be displeased with, be disgusted at, to shun. — *phernā*, to abstain from. — *phailānā*, to presume, to desire much, to gape. — *band k.* to hold one's tongue. — *banānā*, to make mouths or faces, to fashion the face. — *bānā*, to open the mouth, gape. — *bārnā*, to refrain. — *bigarnā*, to have the taste blunted or depraved; to be displeased. — *bigārnā*, to make faces, to frown. — *mārnā*, to stop anyone's mouth, to silence him: to bite; to feed. — *meṅ pānī ānā* (the watering of the mouth) to desire with great eagerness. — *moṛnā*, to turn away, abstain, desist. — *rakhnā*, to keep on good terms with. — *lagnā*, to have the mouth burned by any pungent substance: to become intimate, be familiarized, become a favorite. — *lagānā*, to familiarize, to be intimate with inferiors, to countenance, to favour. — *laṭkanā*, to pull a long face, to be down in the mouth. — *leke rakh jānā*, to be silent from shame. — *sukaṛnā*, to change colour. — *se phūl jhaṛnā*, to abuse, reproach.

मुंहअखरी, verbal, by word of mouth.

मुंहअन्धेरा, *m.* twilight, evening, dusk: *adj.* dark, [obscure.

मुंहचंग, *m.* a jew's harp.

मुंहचोर, shamefaced, bashful, timid, sheepish.

मुंहचोरी, *f.* shamefacedness, bashfulness, timidness, sheepishness. [ceals his face.

मुंहछिपाऊ, *m.?* blind-man's buff: one who con-

मुंहज़बानी, vivā voce, verbal (as evidence or a

मुंहज़ोर, headstrong, obstinate. [message).

मुंहतोपा, *m.* a bribe, sop.

मुंहदिखाई, *f.* a present given by the friends of the family and by the women of the neighbourhood, on their first visit to a bride. [or of a tobacco-pipe.

मुंहनाल, *m. f.?* the mouth-piece of a hukkā-tube.

मुंहपकना = **मुंहअन्धेरा**, *q.v.*

मुंहपट्टा, *m.* a horse's head-stall.

मुंहबन्द, *m.* a muzzle.

मुंहबोला, *m.* (*f.* ī) in name or appellation, nominal. — *bhāī*, *m.* an intimate male friend; *lit.* one who is, as it were, a brother. *Muṅhbōlī bahin*, *f.* an intimate female friend.

मुंहभरी, *f.* a bribe, sop.

मुंहमांगा, *m.* (*f.* ī) solicited, demanded, asked for, requested by word of mouth. [thrush, aphthæ.

मुंहां, *m.* soreness in the mouth, salivation,

मुंहामुंह = **मुंहांमुंह**, *q. v.*

मुंहांमुंह, tête-à-tête, face to face, brimful, topful. — *jhuṭhālnā*, to give a man the lie to his face.

मुहांमुही, *f.* alteration, wrangling, squabbling.

मुककुन्द, *m. pr. n.* a son of Māndātā.

मुकतो in Braj = **मुक्ता**, *q.v.*

मुक़द्दमा, *m.* the first part, preämble, preface; business, subject, affair, matter, (in Law) a cause.

मुकर in Māṛwāṛī = **मुक़र्रर**, *q.v.*

मुकरना, *t.* to deny; to refuse. [infallible.

मुक़र्रर, certain, sure, established, unquestionable,

मुकरी, *f.* a kind of short poem of frequent use in the Braj dialect. It consists of four lines each composed of four trochees: in the first three the speaker (a female) appears to talk of her lover; but on the question being put by a friend, she applies the whole to some other subject: hence, the name from *mukarnā*, to deny.

मुकाबला, *m.* comparison, collation, confronting, presence. — *k.* to compare, confront, be hostile to.

मुकाम, *more prop.* **मक़ाम**, *q. v.*

मुकावा, *m.* a dressing-box, dressing-case.

मुकुट, *m.* a crest, diadem, tiara, crown.

मुकुटसाजा, *m.* (*f.* ī) adorned with a crest or crown.

मुकुता (Rām.) = **मुक्ता**, *q. v.*

मुकुताहल (Rām.) = **मुक्ताहल**, *q. v.*

मुकुन्द, *m.* gum olibanum; quicksilver; a precious gem: *pr. n.* (1) of one of Kuver's treasures (2) of various learned men (3) of a certain mountain (4) an epithet of Vishnu.

मुकुर, *m.* a looking-glass, mirror; the stick of a potter's wheel: a bud: Arabian jasmine; a certain tree (*Mimusops elengi*).

मुकुल, *m.* an opening bud, blossom: the body; the soul.

मुकुलित, half-closed (said of a bud, or of the eye), blinking, winking: blossoming.

मुक्का, *m.* a thump, blow, buffet. — *mārnā*, to administer a blow with the fist.

मुक्कियो, a colloquial form of **मुक्का**, *q. v.*

मुक्की, *f.* = **मुक्का**, *q. v.*

मुक्कूं / **मुक्कौ** } dialectic forms of **मुक्का**, *q. v.*

मुक्खी (dialectic) = **मुक्की**, *q. v.*

मुक्त, 1, *a contraction of* (1) **मुक्ता** (2) **मुक्ति**, *qq. v.*: 2, *m.* (*f.* ā) a liberated person; the spirit released from mundane existence and reïntegrated with its divine original: *lit.* loosed, liberated, let go, released, absolved, liberated from corporeal existence, finally happy.

मुक्तन in Braj, pl. of **मुक्ता**, *q. v.* See **न**, 6 (1).

मुक्तफल (*contraction*) = **मुक्ताफल**, *q. v.*

मुक्ता, 1, *f. m.?* a pearl: 2, much, many.

मुक्ताफल, *m.* a pearl: camphor: custard-apple.

मुक्तावलि / **मुक्तावली** } *f.* a pearl necklace.

मुक्तास्फोट, *m.* (*f.* ā) a pearl-oyster.

मुक्ताहार, *m.* a string of pearls, a pearl necklace.

मुक्ताहल, *m.* a pearl.

मुक्ति, *f.* leaving off; deliverance, release, liberation, absolution, acquittal; (esp.) the liberation of the soul from matter and body, and its exemption from further transmigration, absorption of the emancipated spirit into its Great Source, identification with with God, final beatitude.

मुक्तिखोजक, *m.* (*f.* ikā) a seeker of liberty.

मुक्तिदाता, *m.* (*f.* trī) an emancipator; (the term is used by Hindoos as an epithet of the Supreme, and by Christians also, as an epithet of Christ:) lit. *adj.* freedom-giving.

मुक्तिदायक, *m.* (*f.* ikā) / **मुक्तिदायी**, *m.* (*f.* inī) } = **मुक्तिदाता**, *q. v.*

मुक्तिसाधन, *m.* the accomplishing emancipation.

मुक्तिहेतु, for the sake of deliverance or salvation.

मुक्खो, a dialectic form of **मुक्का**, *q. v.*

मुख, 1, (*corruption*) = **मुख्य**, *q. v.*: 2, *m.* (= **मुंह**) the mouth, face, countenance; a bird's beak; an entrance, aperture, front; commencement.

मुखआभा, *f.* splendour of countenance.

मुखचन्द, *m.* a moon-like face, lovely face.

मुखड़ा, *m.* the mouth, face.

मुखपड, powerful, able, strong.

मुखपड़ाणी, *f.* powerfulness, strength.

मुख़्तार, chosen, selected; absolute, independent; invested with power and authority: *hence*, a free agent; an agent who acts with full power for another.

मुखन, a Braj pl. of **मुख**, *q. v.* See **न**, 6.

मुखनि, a Braj pl. of **मुख**, *q. v.* See **नि**.

मुखमंजन, *m.* cleaning the face, any substance for cleaning the face.

मुखपूरण, *m.* a mouthful.

मुखभिड़ / **मुखभेड़** } opposite, fronting, facing.

मुखर, *m.* (*f.* ā *or* ī) a leader; an abusive person; a conch shell: *lit.* speaking harshly or scurrilously, foul-mouthed, abusive; rallying; resounding, noisy.

मुखरज, *m.* an expenditure, anything given out.

मुखवचन, *m.* word of mouth, report, rumour, tradition.

मुखवैवर्ण्य, *m.* colourlessness of face, change of countenance.

मुखागर (Rām.) = **जबानी**, *q. v.*

मुखाग्नि, *m.* fire put into the mouth of a corpse at the time of lighting the funeral pile; a sacrificial fire; a forest conflagration; a kind of goblin with a face of fire.

मुखारविन्द, *m.* an epithet of the face or countenance of any deity: *lit.* the lotus-faced.

मुखिआ / **मुखिया** } (*colloquial*) = **मुख्य**, *q. v.*

मुखिरी, *f.* a bud.

मुख्य, *m.* (*f.* ā) appertaining to the face, or the mouth; *hence*, primary, initial, original, anterior, main, leading, principal, preëminent, noble, chief.

मुख्यत्व, *m.* (*f.* tā) the being chief or best, preëminence, distinction, chiefship.

मुगदर (by inversion) = **मुद्गर**, *q. v.*

मुगना, *a. int.* to become musty (said of grain).

मुग़ल, *m.* a native of Tartary or Tūrān, a Mughal. In India the term is erroneously applied to Persians, and in the Dakkhan, to Musalmans in general.

मुगलाणी, *f.* (in Māṛwāṛī) a Mughal female.

मुग्ध, *m.* (*f.* ā) a fool, idiot, etc.: *lit.* stupid, ignorant, simple, foolish, silly, idiotic; in love; lovely, beautiful.

मुग्धत्व, *m.* (*f.* tā) stupidity, ignorance, simpleness, foolishness; loveliness.

मुग्धबोध, *m. pr. n.* a certain popular work on Sanskrit Grammar, by Vopadev.

मुग्धा, *f.* (*m.* **मुग्ध**) an idiotic female; a lovely female.

मुचंग, *more prop.* **मुंहचंग**, *q. v.*

मुचकुन्द, *more prop.* **मुचुकुन्द**, *q. v.*

मुचलका, *m.* a bond, note of hand, agreement, a

binding over (to keep the peace), (in Law) a recognisance.

मुचुकुन्द, *m. pr. n.* (1) of a certain ancient Hindoo king or Muni (2) of a son of Māndātā (3) of a son of Yadu (4) of the father of Chandra-bhāg (5) of a certain poet of Kāshmīr (6) of a certain demon.

मुचुकुन्दप्रसादक, *m.* an epithet of Krishṇ (*i. e.* the one by whom it was vouchsafed that Kālyavan was destroyed by Muchukund).

मुच्चा, *m.* a large lump of flesh or of meat.

मुछनों in Chand = to be let loose, be set free.

मुछरक, the down on the lips.

मुछेव = **मुछयो** = **मुछा**, set free, loosened. (Chand.)

मुज; see (1) **मज** (2) **मुंज** (3) **मुझ**. [conqueror.

मुज़फ़्फ़र, victorious, superior, fortunate: *hence*, a

मुजरा, *m.* allowance, premium, deduction: obeisance, respects; a visit; audience.— *k.* to make obeisance, pay respects, wait on, visit. [of visitors.

मुजरेगाह, *f.* a place of audience for the reception

मुज़ायक़ा, *m.* poverty, necessity, distress; moment, consequence, significance; *e. g. Kuchh — nahīn*, it is of no consequence.

मुजायेका, *more prop.* **मुज़ायक़ा**, *q. v.*

मुजिज़ा, *m.* (*pl.* āt) miracle. The term is applied only to those miracles which are performed by prophets of the first order: those performed by inferior personages are called *Karāmāt*.

मुजिब, *adj.* listening to, granting, consenting, [taking well.

मुजे (*dialectic*) = **मुझे**, *q. v.*

मुझ (*an inflect. base of* **मैं**) = me.

मुझका, 1, *m.* (*f.* ī) *more com.* **मेरा**, *q. v.*: 2, see **मुझे**.

मुझला, *m.* (*f.* ī) *more prop.* **मझला**, *q. v.*

मुझसा, *m.* (*f.* ī) like me. See **सा**.

मुझी, *more prop.* **मुझही** (**मुझ** + **ही**).

मुझे (*a dat. or acc. of* **मैं**) = to me; me.

मुझै / **मुझैं** } in Braj = **मुझे**, *q. v.*

मुटाई, *f.* / **मुटापा**, *m.* } *more prop.* **मोटाई**, *q. v.*

मुटिया (*corruption*) = **मोटिया**, *q. v.*

मुट्ठा, *m.* the handle of a plough: a bundle.

मुट्ठी, *f.* a grasp of the hand, the fist, hand, clutch, grip; a handful; the wrist; a fetlock.

मुठ, *m. f.*? the fist, clutch, grasp; a blow with with the fist; a handle, haft, helve.

मुठभरे (Rām.) = **सन्मुख, निकट**, *qq. v.*

मुठभेरी (Rām.) = **निकटसे**.

मुठमर्द, *m.* a ruffian, a robber.

मुठिका, *f.* the fist.

मुठिया, *m.* a handful.

मुठी = **मुट्ठी**, *q. v.*

मुठोलिया, *m.* one who practises onanism.

मुठोली, *f.* (from **मुष्टि**) onanism.

मुड़कना = **मुरकना**, *q. v.*

मुड़कूमड़ी, inverted, topsy-turvy.

मुड़ना, *n.* to be turned back, be bent, be twisted, be turned (as the edge of a weapon): *a. int.* to turn, bend, twine.

मुड़वाना = **मुंड़वाना** = **मुण्डवाना**, *q. v.*

मुड़ेर, *f.* (= **मुण्डेर**) the coping of a wall.

मुढ़, *m.* the head; a chief, head-man.

मुढ़ता (corruption) = **मूढ़ता**, *q. v.*

मुढ़ियाना, *n.* to be twisted, be writhed.

मुण्ड, *m.* (*f.* ā) shaved, bald, having no hair on the head; uncovered; low, mean: blunt, obtuse, dull: *hence, m.* the head, skull; the forehead; a bald-pate; a barber: a headman; the trunk of a lopped tree: *pr. n.* (1) of Rāhu (2) of a certain Daitya.

मुण्डक, *m.* (*f.* ikā) a shaver, barber. [stomach.

मुण्डकारी मारना, to lie round with the knees to the

मुण्डन, *m.* shaving, shearing, cutting; the shaving a child (a certain religious ceremony among Hindoos).

मुण्डना, *n.* to be shaved.

मुण्डपना, *m.* bluntness, dulness.

मुण्डमाल, *m.* = **मूण्डमाल**, *q. v.*

मुण्डमाला, *f.* a necklace of human skulls.

मुण्डला, *m.* (*f.* ī) shaved. [cause to be shaved.

मुण्डवाना, *t.* (causat. of **मुण्डाना**) to cause to shave,

मुण्डा, 1, *f.* (*m.* **मुण्ड**) a bald-headed female: 2, *m.* the head; the head of a paper kite; the shoulder; a kind of uncovered pālkee (qy., *f.*?): 2, *f.* Bengal madder (*Rubia manjeth*).

मुण्डाना, *t.* (of **मुण्डना**) to cause to be shaved, *i.e.*

मुण्डासबन्द, *m.* (Dakkanī) a man. [to shave.

मुण्डासा, *m.* a kind of small turban. [wife.

मुण्डिका, *f.* (*m.* **मुण्डक**) a female barber, a barber's

मुण्डित, *m.* (*f.* ā) one who is shaven: *lit.* shaven, shorn, bald; lopped.

मुण्डितशिरा, *m. f.* shaven-headed, bald-pated.

मुण्डिया, *m.* the head.

मुण्डी, 1, *m.* (*f.* inī) a barber: 2, *f.* a certain medicinal plant (*Sphuranthus Indicus*): head, extremity, end. — *tornā*, to turn away the face.

मुण्डीरी, *f.* a certain creeping-plant which bears a red and yellow flower.

मुण्डू, *lit. m. f.* a shaved one, a bald-pate; *hence*, a monk, fakeer, sunnyāsī, gosāīn.

मुण्डेर / **मुण्डेरो** } *f.* the coping of a wall.

मुण्ठ, shameless, unblushing, impudent.

मुत, a corruption of **मुत्र**, *q. v.*

मुतना, 1, *more prop.* **मूतना**, *q. v.*: 2, *m.* (*f.* ī) one who discharges much urine, a piss-a-bed.

मुतनाही, finished, determined, terminated, arrived at the utmost extreme.

मुतफिक, *more prop.* **मुत्तफ़िक़**, *q. v.*

मुतरिब, *m.* a musician, singer, minstrel.

मुतलक, absolute, universal, principal, supreme: *adv.* wholly, entirely, altogether: (with a negative) not at all, not in the least, never.

मुतवज्जिह, turning, facing, travelling towards, attending to, favouring.

मुतसद्दी, 1, *m.* an accountant, writer, clerk: 2, *adj.* turning away the face, opposing; intent on, attempting, daring.

मुताजिब, full of admiration, wondering, astonished, amazed.

मुताना, *t.* (causat. of **मूतना**) to cause to discharge urine.

मुतानेवाला, *m.* (in Med.) a diuretic.

मुताबिक़, conformable, equal, corresponding, suitable, agreeable to.

मुतारा, *m.* } a block.
मुतारी, *f.* }

मुतास, *f.* desire or inclination to emit urine.

मुतासा, *m.* (*f.* ī) desirous of emitting urine.

मुति; see **मति** and **मिति**.

मुतिहर, *m.* straw, etc. mixed with horse's urine.

मुतिहरी, *f.* a hole in which the dirt of a stable (particularly urine) is collected.

मुत्तफ़िक़, united, agreeing, harmonious, consenting, unanimous: *hence*, an associate, accomplice.

मुत्तसिल, near, about, contiguous, adjoining.

मुद, *f.* pleasure, joy, delight; intoxication; a wife.

मुदगर } (*colloquial*) = **मुद्गर**, *q.v.*
मुदगल }

मुदत, ; see (1) **मदत** (2) **मुदित** (3) **मुद्दत**.

मुदद; see **मदद**.

मुदरी, *f.* (colloquial) = **मुद्रा**, *q.v.*

मुदा, *f.* pleasure, joy, delight, happiness.

मुदालक, *m. pr. n.* a certain ancient Hindoo sage.

मुदित, *m.* (*f.* ā) rejoiced, pleased, delighted, happy.

मुदिर, *m.* a cloud: a lover.

मुदुल, capital, stock, store.

मुदौअज }
मुदौअल } a closing up, covering up.
मुदौला }

मुद्ग, *m.* a sort of millet (*Phaseolus mungo*): a cover.

मुद्गर, *m.* a carpenter's hammer, a weapon formed like a carpenter's hammer, a mallet, a mace; a staff armed with iron and enlarged at the lower extremity (used for breaking clods of earth, etc.); a sort of flower (supposed to be the wild variety of *Jasminum zambac*); a club used for exercising with in the manner of dumb-bells: *pr. n.* the tenth astronomical *yog* or division of the moon's path.

मुद्दआ, *m.* desire, wish, meaning, suit, view, object, scope, intention.

मुद्दई, *m.* (*f.* **ईया**) a plaintiff, suitor, claimant, complainant, prosecutor, opponent, adversary.

मुद्दत, *f.* a space of time, a long time, antiquity.

मुद्दया, *more prop.* **मुद्दआ**, *q.v.*

मुद्दाह, *m.* encomiasts.

मुद्रा, *f.* a seal, signet; a seal-ring; the impression of a seal, a stamp, print; coin, cash; a medal, etc.; a ring worn by Yogees in their ears; a finger-ring, a collar; a mode of intwining the fingers in religious worship.

मुद्रांकित, stamped, sealed. — *k.* to stamp, seal.

मुद्राचिन्ह, *m.* the impression of a stamp or seal.

मुद्रिका, *f.* = **मुद्रा**, *q.v.*

मुद्रित, sealed, stamped, struck, marked, impressed, printed, imprinted, closed, unblown (said of flowers).

मुधा, to no purpose, uselessly, in vain.

मुन (contraction) = **मुनि**, *q.v.*

मुनकिर, *m.* a denier, opponent: lit. *adj.* denying, rejecting, opposing.

मुनक़्क़श, painted; embroidered.

मुनक़्क़ा, *m.* a species of dried grapes, raisins, currants.

मुनज्जिम, *m.* an astrologer, astronomer, almanac-maker.

मुनमुन (a mode of calling a cat) = puss! puss!

मुनशी, *m.* a writer, clerk, secretary, (esp.) a teacher of the Arabic and Persian languages.

मुनसिफ़, *m.* an administrator of justice, an arbitrator, a judge: *lit.* just, equitable.

मुनादी, 1, more prop. **मनादी**, *q.v.*: 2, *m.* (*f.* inī) a proclaimer, crier, herald, preacher.

मुनाफ़िक़, *m.* a hypocrite, atheist, enemy.

मुनासिब, proper, convenient, expedient, fit, pertinent congruous.

मुनि, *m.* a holy sage endowed with divine inspiration (either as the result of a divine nature within, or as the product of rigid abstraction and mortification); a pious and learned person, an ascetic, hermit, devotee. The term is applied as a title to the Ṛishis and Brahmādiks, and to a great number of persons (as Vyās, Pāṇini, etc.) distinguished for their writings and considered as inspired. Seven in particular are reckoned; and hence, in the ingenious system of reckoning by symbols adopted by Hindoos in their poetry, this word is a symbol for 7.

मुनिधर्म्म, *m.* the duties that appertain to the status of a *Muni*.

मुनिनाथ, *m.* an epithet of respectful address to superiors.

मुनिन, *m.* (an old pl. of **मुनि**) sages, the sages.

मुनिनायक; see **मुनिनाथ**, **मुनीवर**, and **मुनीश्वर**.

मुनिन्द } (*Rām.*) = **मुनीन्द्र**, *q.v.*
मुनिन्दा }

मुनिपट, *m.* the dress of the *munis*, i. e. the bark of the Bhojpatra.

मुनिया, *f.* the female of the little birds (*Fringilla amandava*) called *amadavat* or *lāl*.

मुनिराज, *m.* = **मुनीश्वर**, *q.v.*; also an epithet of Vashishṭh.

मुनिराजू } poet. forms of **मुनिराज**, *q.v.*
मुनिराया }

मुनिवर, *m.* an epithet of Shukrāchārya: *lit.* the best of ascetics or holy sages, an excellent *Muni*, an eminent saint.

मुनिवर्य्य, *m.* an eminent ascetic or saint.

मुनिश्रेष्ठ = **मुनिवर**, *q.v.*

मुनिश्वर, *more prop.* **मुनीश्वर**, *q.v.*

मुनिसन, 1, an abl. sing. of **मुनि**, *q.v.*: 2, a Braj pl. of **मुनीश**.

मुनिस्थान, *m.* any abode or place of retirement of holy sages or ascetics, a hermitage.

मुनिह, *more prop.* **मुनिः** = **मुनि**, *q.v.*

मुनी, 1, (*corruption*) = मुनि, *q.v.*: 2, *f.* a female saint.

मुनीन्द्र, *m.* chief of sages or ascetics; an epithet (1) of any Bauddh sage or teacher (2) Sâkyamuni (3) of Shiv (4) of Bharat (5) of a certain Dânav (6) of any great or eminent sage or ascetic.

मुनीश, *m.* any eminent ascetic or saint.

मुनीश्वर, *m.* any great sage or ascetic: an epithet (1) of Vishṇu (2) of Buddh: *pr. n.* a certain commentator on the Siddhânt-Shiromaṇi.

मुनीस, *more prop.* मुनीश, *q.v.* [of मुनीश.

मुनीसन, 1, an abl. sing. of मुनि, *q.v.*: 2, a Braj pl.

मुनीसा, a poet. form of मुनीश, *q. v.*

मुन्तज़िर, *adj.* expecting with impatience, tarrying for, looking out for: *hence*, an expectant.

मुन्य, *more prop.* मन्य, *q.v.*

मुन्दना, *n.* to be shut; be closed, be contracted: *t.* to close. [in anything, contents.

मुन्दरिजा, *m.* that which is included or contained

मुन्दरी = मुदरी (*colloquial*) = मुद्रा, *q. v.*

मुन्दिकुकुर, *more prop.* मन्दिकुकुर, *q. v.*

मुन्द, a hole, chasm, aperture, rent, fissure.

मुन्द्रा, *m.* } (*colloquial*) = मुद्रा, *q. v.*
मुन्द्री, *f.* }

मुफ़स्सिर, *m.* (pl. मुफ़स्सिरीन) an interpreter, commentator, explainer. [pense.

मुबादला, *m.* exchange, barter, retaliation, recom-

मुबार, *m.* a pudding, sausage.

मुबारक, happy, fortunate, blessed, august, sacred, holy, welcome, well, auspicious.

मुबाशरत, *f.* the undertaking or commencing an affair: having carnal knowledge of a woman.

मुबाहसा, *m.* a dispute, contest, debate, investigation, argumentation.

मुमकिन, *m.* (*pl.* ât) anything possible, a possibility: [*lit.* possible.

मुमाखी, *f.* (मधुमक्षिका) a honey-bee.

मुमानी, *f.* an aunt (mother's brother's wife).

मुमुक्षु, desirous of liberation from mundane existence; *hence*, a sage abstracted from human passions.

मुमूर्षु, *m. f.* a dying person: *lit.* about to die, at the point of death.

मुयस्सर, attainable, procurable; facilitated; easy, favourable, practicable, possible.

मुया, *m.* (*f.* मुयी or मुई) *more com.* मूआ, *q. v.*

मुर, 1, see मुरं: 2, *m. pr. n.* a certain Daitya slain by Krishṇ: 3, *m.* the head.

मुरई (*colloquial*) = मूली, *q. v.* See also मुरना.

मुरकना, *a. int.* to twist, writhe, cramp.

मुरकाना, *a. int.* (*t.* ?) to twist, writhe.

मुरकी, *f.* a kind of ornament worn in the ear; the *tragus* of the ear: dirt, filth.

मुरग़ *m.* a fowl, bird, cock (*esp.* a house-fowl).

मुरग़ा, *m.* a male fowl, a cock.

मुरग़ी, *f.* a female fowl, a hen.

मुरग़ीवाला, *m.* (*f.* ī) a fowl-dealer, poulterer.

मुरचंग (*corruption*) = मुंहचंग, *q. v.*

मुरछा, *more prop.* मूर्छा, *q. v.*

मुरझन, *m.* fading, drooping, pining, fainting.

मुरझाना, *a. int.* to wither, fade, droop, pine; to become dispirited or dejected.

मुरण्ड, *m. pr. n.* (1) of a country (called also *Lampak* or *Lamgan*) to the North-west of Hindūstān (2) of the people of that country.

मुरण्डा, 1 in Mārwāṛī = मुंड, *q.v.*: 2,—क°, *t.* to tie, to captivate.—*kar ḍālnā*, to captivate, entrance, enchant.

मुरद, *m.* (lit. *adj.* Mur-cutting) an epithet of the discus of Krishṇ. It was with his discus that he slew the demon.

मुरदा, *m.* a corpse: *lit.* dead.

मुरधर, *m. pr. n.* one of the names of Mārwāṛ.

मुरना, *t.* to acquire a taste.

मुरम, a kind of gravelly soil. [eaten raw).

मुरमुरा, *m.* a kind of food (rice pressed flat and

मुरला, 1, *m.* (*f.* ī) toothless: 2, *m.* a peacock.

मुरली, *f.* a flute, pipe, fife, whistle.

मुरलीधर, *m.* an epithet of Krishṇ: *lit.* the flute-holder, the fifer.

मुरलीमनोहर, *m.* an epithet of Krishṇ (as the one who delighted Rādhā and the cowherdesses with his performances on the flute). [prophet, apostle.

मुरसल, *m.* (*f.* īn) a messenger, divine messenger,

मुरसिदाबाद, *more prop.* मुर्शिदाबाद, *q. v.*

मुरहा, 1, *m.* = मुरही, *q. v.*: 2, *m.* an orphan: a peacock: 3, *m.* (*f.* ī) twisted.

मुरही, *f.* twist, contortion, convolution, writhe.

मुरा, *m.* a species of very small fish.

मुराई, *m.* (*f.* inī) 1, = मुराऊ, *q.v.*: 2, a seeming saint, hypocrite, dissembler.

मुराऊ, *m. f.* one whose business it is to cultivate vegetables and sell them. [sign, purpose.

मुराद, *f.* desire, wish, inclination, intention, de-

मुरार } poet. contractions of मुरारि, *q.v.*
मुरारा }

मुरारि, *m.* (the enemy of Mur, *i. e.*) Krishṇ.

मुरारिपु, *m.* (the enemy of Mur, *i. e.*) Krishṇ.

मुरारी = मुरारि, *q. v.*

मुरिल, (in Pros.) a species of metre.

मुरेला } *m.* (*f.* ī) a peachick, a peacock.
मुरैला }

मुर्ग़, *m.* (*f.* ī) *more com.* मुरग़, *q.v.*

मुर्ग़ाबी, *f.* a waterfowl, wild duck, teal: a certain plant (*Sanseviera zeylanica*).

मुर्चा; see (1) मूर्च्छा (2) मोरचा.

मुर्च्छा } *more prop.* मूर्च्छा, *q. v.*
मुर्छा }

मुर्छित, *m.* (*f.* ā) *more prop.* मूर्च्छित, *q. v.*

मुर्द; see मुरद and मुर्दा.

मुर्दा, *m.* a corpse: *lit.* dead.

मुर्द्धन्य, *more prop.* मूर्द्धन्य, *q. v.*

मुर्र, *m.* bitterness, myrrh.

मुर्रा, *m.* a squib.

मुर्शिदाबाद, *m. pr.n.* (1) of a certain district in Bengal (2) of the capital of that district.

मुलक, *more prop.* **मुल्क**, *q.v.*

मुलट्ठी (contraction) = **मुलहट्ठी**, *q.v.*

मुलतान, *m. pr.n.* a province in the Punjāb.

मुलतानी, 1, *m.* (*f.* inī) a Multānian: *lit.* appertaining to Multān : 2, *f.* a certain musical mode (*rāgiṇi*). — *maṭṭi*, *f.* Armenian bole.

मुलन; see (1) **मल** (2) **मलन** (3) **मूलन**.

मुलम्मा, 1, covered with gold or silver, plated, bright: 2, *m.* gilt, gilding.

मुलहट्ठी, *f.* liquorice.

मुलाई, *f.* appraisement, valuation.

मुलाक़ात, *f.* a falling in with, encountering, meeting, interview, visit, conversation. — *k.* (with abl. of object) to encounter, meet, have an interview with.

मुलाना, *t.* to appraise ; to sell.

मुलाघात in Māṛwāṛī = **मुलाक़ात**, *q.v.*

मुलाहज़ा, *m.* looking at, contemplation, consideration, notice, view, regard : kindness, an obliging disposition.

मुलुक ; see (1) **मलुक** (2) **मुल्क** (3) **मुलूक**.

मुलूक, *m.* (pl. of **मालिक**) kings.

मुल्क, *m.* kingdom, realm, land, country, region, district, province : sovereignty, reign.

मुल्कगीरी }
मुल्कदारी } = **मुल्कसितानी**, *q.v.*
मुल्करानी }

मुल्कसितानी, *f.* territorial conquest, sovereignty, dominion, ruling, empire, government.

मुल्की, appertaining to the empire or country, or to land and revenue affairs, civil, political.

मुवाफ़िक़, conformably to, proportionate to, consonant, congruous, suitable, favorable, propitious.

मुवार, *more prop.* **मुबार**, *q.v.*

मशकिल = **मश्किल**, *q.v.*

मुशगुल, *more prop.* **मशगूल**, *q.v.*

मुशताक, full of desire, desirous, wishful, longing (*esp.* to see a person).

मुशरिक, *m.* an infidel, idolater, polytheist.

मुशल = **मुसल**, *q.v.*

मुशली = (1) **मुषली** (2) **मुसली** (3) **मूसली**, *q.v.*

मुशाबिह, 1, *m.* resemblance, picture, similitude ; probability : 2, like, resembling, analogous.

मुश्क, *m.* musk.

मुश्किल, difficult, hard, painful, troublesome, intricate, bothersome, patience-trying.

मुश्कें चढ़ाना or **बान्धना**, *t.* to tie the hands behind the back, to pinion.

मुश्त, *m.* a fist; a blow with the fist ; a handful.

मुष, 1, *f.* stealing, robbing : 2, *m.* = **मुख**, 2, *q.v.*

मुषक, *more prop.* **मूषक**, *q.v.*

मुषल = **मुसल**, *q.v.*

मुषली, *f.* a small house-lizard : a certain plant (*Curculigo orchioides*).

मुषित, *m.* (*f.* ā) stolen, robbed, plundered, deprived of ; free from.

मुष्क, *m.* a testicle, the scrotum, a heap, multitude ; a thief ; a certain plant.

मुष्ट, *m.* theft, robbery, plunder.

मुष्टमार, *m.* a robber, pilferer, thief. — *kar baiṭhnā*, to sit with the knees held up (by the arms clasped around them) towards the face.

मुष्टामुष्टि }
मुष्टामुष्टी } = **मुष्टीमुष्टि**, *q.v.*

मुष्टि, *m. f.* the closed hand, the fist ; a handful ; the handle of a sword.

मुष्टिक, 1, *m.* a certain position of the hands : *pr. n.* a certain demon slain by Kṛishṇ : 2, *m.* (*f.* ā) a goldsmith.

मुष्टी, *f.* 1, *more prop.* **मुष्टि**, *q. v.* : 2, filching, pilfering, stealing, robbing.

मुष्टीपात, *m.* a boxing, pummelling.

मुष्टीबन्ध, *m.* a clenching the fist.

मुष्टीमुष्टि, *m.* fisticuffs, thumping and pulling, boxing : *adv.* fist to fist.

मुष्यमाण, *m.* (*f.* ā) *adj.* being robbed, being plundered.

मुस, land along the high banks of rivers.

मुसकन, *more com.* **मुसकान**, *q. v.*

मुसकराना = **मुसकुराना**, *q. v.*

मुसकान, *f.* a smile, grin, smirk, simper.

मुसकाना, *a. int.* to smile, smirk, grin, simper.

मुसकाहट = **मुसकुराहट**, *q. v.*

मुसकियाना, *more com.* **मुसकाना**, *q. v.*

मुसकिराना ; see (1) **मुसकान** (2) **मुसकाना**.

मुसकीन ; see (1) **मुसकान** (2) **मिसकीन**.

मुसकुटी }
मुसकुराई } = **मुसकुराहट**, *q. v.*
मुसकुराट }

मुसकुराना, *a. int.* to smile, grin, smirk, simper.

मुसकुराहट, *f.* a grinning, smiling, sniggering, smirking ; a smirk, simper, snigger, smile, grin. — *mārnā*, to grin, smirk, smile, simper, snigger.

मुसब्बर, *f.* aloes (the drug merely).

मुसब्बिर ; see (1) **मुसौविर** (2) **मुसब्बर**.

मुसर, *more com* **मुसल**, *q. v.*

मुसल, 1, *m.* a long, heavy, wooden pestle used in clearing rice from the husk ; a club, mace : 2, *m. pr.n.* the twenty-second astronomical *yog* or division of the moon's path.

मुसलधार, torrents of rain : an epithet of Baladev. — *barasnā*, to rain very heavily.

मुसलमान, *m.* (*f.* ī) a believer in and follower of the Muhammadan faith, a Musalmān.

मुसलमानी, 1, *f.* (*m.* **मुसलमान**) a female Musalmān : 2, *f.* the Muhammadan religion : *vulg.* circumcision : 3, appertaining to a Musalmān or to the Muhammadan religion.

मुसलमाची = **मुसलमानी**, 1, *q.v.*

मुसलिन, *m.* an epithet of Balarām or Baladev.

मुसलिम, *m.* = **मुसलमान**, *q. v.*

मुसली, 1, *m.* = **मुसलिन**, *q. v.* : 2, *f.* = **मुषली**, *q. v.* : 3, = **मूसली**, *q. v.*

मुसहर, *m.* (*f.* ī) a wild-man, man of the woods.

मुसायद, an effort, attempt; an assault, attack.

मुसान, (in Mārwāṛī) a heap of dust.

मुसाना, *t.* (causat. of **मोसना**) to cause to steal.

मुसान्या, *m.* one who dwells in a *musān*, i.e. a yogee.

मुसाफ़िर, *m.* a traveller, sojourner, passenger, stranger.

मुसाहबत, *f.* companionship, society, familiar intercourse, communion.

मुसाहिब, a companion, favorite, aide-de-camp.

मुसीबत, *f.* misfortune, disaster, affliction, adversity. evil, misery, ill.

मुसुकाई, *f.* = **मुसकान** or **मुसकुराहट**, *qq. v.*

मुसुकान = **मुसकान**, *q. v.*

मुसुकाना, *more com.* **मुसकाना**, *q. v.*

मुसौविर, *adj.* forming, figuring: *hence*, a painter, sculptor.

मुस्क; see (1) **मुश्क** (2) **मुष्क**.

मुस्कान = **मुसकान**, *q. v.*

मुस्तक, *m.* a certain fragrant grass (*Cyperus rotundus*): a sort of poison.

मुस्तरी, *m.* a lion.

मुस्से (*colloquial*) = **मुझसे**.

मुह, 1, for words beginning thus, but not given below, see under the form **मुंह**; 2, in old Hindee = **मुझ**, *q. v.*

मुहंकना, *t.* to smell.

मुहचंग = **मुंहचंग**, *q. v.*

मुहताज, necessitous, indigent, in want, needy, dependent, mendicant.

मुहताजी, *f.* indigence, poverty.

मुहकिल, *more prop.* **मुश्किल**, *q. v.*

मुहब्बत, *more prop.* **महब्बत**, *q. v.*

मुहमांगा, *m.* (*f.* ī) *more prop.* **मुंहमांगा**, *q. v.*

मुहम्मद, *m. pr. n.* Muhammad.

मुहम्मदी, appertaining to Muhammad or to his teachings, Muhammadan: hence, *m.* (*f.* in *or* inī) a Muhammadan.

मुहर, 1, (*dialectic*) = **मोर**, *q. v.*: 2, = **मुहुर**, *q. v.*

मुहरा, *m.* vanguard, van.

मुहरी, *f.* the cuff of the sleeve of a jacket, the extremity of the leg of a pair of trowsers, the bore of a gun, etc.: a drain, gutter, aqueduct, kennel, conduit.

मुहर्रम, sacred; forbidden: hence, *m. pr. n.* the first month of the Muhammadans. During this month fighting is forbidden: the month is held sacred on account of the death of Husain, son of 'Alī who was slain by Yazid near Kūfa.

मुहल्ला, *more prop.* **महल्ला**, *q. v.*

मुहाना, *m.* the mouth of a river, channel or bed of a river, conflux of two rivers, estuary, inlet, outlet.

मुहाल, formidable, dreadful: impossible, absurd.

मुहावरा, *m.* usage (in language), idiom, current speech, phraseology, dialogue, conversation, conference.

मुहासा, *m.* pimple on the face (in youths).

मुहि = **मोहि** = **मुझे**, *q. v.*

मुहिम्म, *f.* a momentous business, important affair, urgent matter, affair of consequence, exigence, exploit.

मुहीं; see (1) **महीं** (2) **मुहि**.

मुहुर, *f.* a seal, seal-ring, signet, stamp, a cautery, the impression of a seal: maidenhood, virginity: a certain gold coin in Indian currency [valued, according to some, at Rs. 15 (1*l.* 10*s.*), according to others, at Rs 16 (1*l.* 12*s.*), and according to others, at Rs. 18 (1*l.* 16*s.*)].—*k.* to seal.

मुहुर्त (*corruption*) = **मुहूर्त्त**, *q. v.*

मुहुर्मुहु, again and again, repeatedly.

मुहुर्मुहुः / **मुहुर्मुहुर** } **मुहुर्मुहु**, *q. v.*

मुहूर्त्त, *m.* a certain division of time (= 12 *kshaṇ* or 2 *ghaṛī*, or the thirtieth part of a day and night or an hour of 48 minutes); any short space of time indefinitely, a moment; (in Astrol.) a lucky moment; an astrologer, an astronomer.

मुहूर्त्ता, 1, *m.* (pl.: see **आ**, 22) the Muhūrttas or Hours personified as the children of Muhūrttā : 2, *f. pr. n.* a daughter of Daksh (wife of Dharm or Manu, and mother of the Muhūrttas).

मूअना (*dialectic*) = **मरना**, *q. v.*

मूआ, *m.* (*f.* **मूई**) dead, lifeless; dull; impotent (used as a term of vulgar abuse).

मूआप, *more prop.* **मुआफ़**, *q. v.*

मूआबादल, *m.* sponge.

मूआशो, a washer of dead bodies.

मूई, *f.* (*m.* **मूआ**) dead, etc.

मूं (*dialectic*) = **मुंह**, *q. v.*

मूंकी, *f.* a blow with the fist, buffet.

मूंग, *f.* a kind of pulse (*Phaseolus mungo*) commonly called 'black gram'.

मूंगची = **मूंगरी**, *q. v.*

मूंगफली, *f.* the ground-nut or pig-nut (*Arachis hypogœa*) of the West Indies.

मूंगरी, *f.* a certain dish made with *mūng*.

मूंगा, *m.* coral, red coral.

मूंगिया, *m.* the colour of red coral.

मूंगेर, headstrong, obstinate, stubborn.

मूंच / **मूंछ** } *more prop.* **मूछ**, *q. v.*

मूंज / **मूंजा** } (*colloquialisms*) = **मुंज**, *q. v.*

मूंजी, *more prop.* **मौंजी**, *q. v.*

मूंड, **मूंठ**, **मूंद**; for words beginning with either of these elements, see under the corresponding forms **मूण्ड**, **मूण्ठ**, **मून्द**.

मूंड़; for words beginning thus, see under the form **मूण्ड**.

मूंथ, *more com.* **मूथ**, *q. v.*

मूंसल, *more prop.* **मुसल**, *q. v.*

मूंसला = **मूसला**, *q. v.*

मूंह; for words beginning thus, see under the form **मुंह**.

मूक, 1, speechless, mute, dumb: 2, *m.* a poor man, pauper: a fish: a daitya.

मूकर, carrying a heavy burden, loaded, weighed down, oppressed; *hence*, pregnant; fruitful; depressed.

मूका, *m.* the fist; a thump, blow: a spy-hole.

मूकां, *more com.* **मूका**, *q. v.*

मूकी, *f.* a blow with the fist, a thump.
मूकीं, a Braj infl. pl. of मूका, *q.v.*
मूखतार, *more prop.* मुख़तार, *q.v.*
मूखा, *m.* the ridge of a thatch, the topping or coping of a wall.
मूखी, 1, *f.* = मूकी, *q.v.*: 2, *m.* a kind of pigeon.
मूगरा = मोगरा, *q.v.*
मूगरी, *f.* a mallet for beating clothes with.
मूचकाना, *t.* to sprain. [tweezers.
मूचना, 1, *t.* to shut, close: to pinch: 2, *m.* pincers,
मूछ, *f.* the hair of the upper lip, the moustache. — *marorā roṭī torā*, one who is proud of eating the bread of idleness.
मूछकड़े = मूछाकड़े, *q.v.*
मूछाकड़ा, *m.* a stiff and bushy moustache.
मूछाकड़े, *m.* (pl. of मूछाकड़ा) stiff and bushy
मूछें, *f.* (pl. of मूछ) moustachios. [moustachios.
मूछैल, *adj.* having a large moustache.
मूज; see (1) मुंज (2) मुझ.
मूजिब, *m.* cause, motive, reason, account.
मूजिबन, a Braj pl. (1) of मूजिब (2) of मूजिबा, *qq.v.*
मूजिबा, *m.* a thing of importance (whether good or bad); the rewards or punishments of eternity; (in Logic) an affirmative proposition.
मूझ, a corruption of मुझ, *q.v.*
मूठ, *f.* handle, hilt; fist, hand; handful: a certain game. *Mūṭhki* —, handful after handful, repeated handfuls, numerous handfuls.
मूठरा, *m.* a kind of printing (consisting of spots)
मूठा, *m.* a handle, hilt. [on cloth, leather, etc.
मूठिया, *m.* a handful.
मूठी, *f.* (मुष्टि) the fist.
मूड, मूड़ } *m.* (from मुण्ड) the head.
मूढ़, *m.* (*f.* ā) an idiot, fool, simpleton, sluggard: *lit.* perplexed, confused, stupid, blinded by passion or by ignorance, infatuated, brutish, ignorant, foolish.
मूढ़त्व, *m.* (*f.* tā) stupidity, ignorance, infatuation,
मूढ़मन, *m. f.* = मूढ़ात्मा, *q.v.* [foolishness, folly.
मूढ़ात्मा, *m. f.* stupid person, fool: *lit.* having the disposition of a fool, stupid in mind.
मूण्ड, *m.* (prop. मुण्ड) the head. — *pānā*, to get around a person, get the right side of him, get his ears, to wheedle, coax.
मूण्डछूरा, *m.* a kind of pillar.
मूण्डना, *t.* to shave: to instruct, make a disciple of, convert: to wheedle out of a thing. *Ulṭe usturese* —, to cheat anyone.
मूण्डला, *m.* (*f.* ī) shaved, shorn, cropped.
मूण्डी, *f.* (from मुण्ड) the head.
मूण्ढा, *more prop.* मोढ़ा and मोण्ढा, *qq.v.*
मूत (*colloquial*) = मूत्र, *q.v.*
मूतना, *t.* to discharge urine.
मूतलक़, *more prop.* मुतलक़, *q.v.*

मूत्र, *m.* urine. — *aṭaknā*, to labour under a total suppression of urine, to have strangury.
मूत्रकछ (*colloquial*) = मूत्रकृच्छ्र, *q.v.*
मूत्रकृच्छ्र, *m.* strangury; urinary affection in general (as gravel, etc.). [complaint).
मूत्रदोष, *m.* gonorrhæa (considered as a urinary
मूत्रपथ, *m.*, मूत्रप्रणाली, *f.* } = मूत्रमार्ग, *q.v.*
मूत्रमार्ग, *m.* the urethra or urinary passage (*Meatus urinarius*). [sediment).
मूत्रशुक्र, *m.* milky urine (depositing a thick white
मूत्रस्थान, *m.* the private parts.
मूत्राघात, *m.* suppression of urine. [sage of urine.
मूत्रातीत, *m.* difficulty in passing urine, slow pas-
मूद; see मुद and मोद.
मूदत; see मुदत.
मूदना, *more com.* मून्दना, *q.v.*
मूदव्वत, *more prop.* मुदव्वत, *q.v.*
मूनना, to forget; to be silent; to forsake. (?)
मूना, *a. int.* to expire, die.
मूनासिब, *more prop.* मुनासिब, *q.v.*
मूनु, little, of small quantity. [volve; to imprison.
मून्दना, *t.* (of मुन्दना) to shut, cover, close; to in-
मून्दरी, *f.* (from मुद्रा) a finger-ring.
मून्दा, *m.* (*f.* ī) closed, covered; involved; im-
मूबारक, *more prop.* मुबारक, *q.v.* [prisoned.
मूया, *m.* (*f.* मूयो or मूई) *more com.* मूआ, *q.v.*
मूरख; for words beginning thus, see under the
मूरचा, *more com.* मोर्चा, *q.v.* [form मूर्ख.
मूरत (*colloquial*) = मूर्त्ति, *q.v.*
मूरतपूजत; see मूर्त्तिपूजक.
मूराति (*corruption*) = मूर्त्ति, *q.v.*
मूरतिवंत, *more prop.* मूर्त्तिवन्त = मूर्त्तिमान, *q.v.*
मूरतें, *f.* (pl. of मूरत) images, etc.
मूरष in Braj = मूर्ख, *q.v.*
मूरि; see मूल and मूली.
मूरुख (colloq. and poet.) = मूर्ख, *q.v.*
मूर्ख, *m.* (*f.* ā) a fool, blockhead: *lit.* foolish, unwise, inconsiderate, ignorant, stupid, idiotic.
मूर्खगाण्ठ, *m.* stubbornness, the insisting of an ignorant fool on what he says.
मूर्खता, *f.* stupidity, dulness, ignorance, folly, idiotcy, foolishness, barbarousness.
मूर्खताई, *f.*, मूर्खत्व, *m.*, मूर्खपन, *m.*, मूर्खपना, *m.*, मूर्खपा, *m.* } = मूर्खता, *q.v.*
मूर्खलोग, *m.* fools, idiots, clowns, ignoramuses.
मूर्च्छित; see (1) मूर्च्छा (2) मूर्च्छिता
मूर्च्छन, 1, = मूर्च्छित, *q.v.*; 2, *m.* modulation; fainting, swooning, syncope.

मूर्च्छा, *f.* loss of consciousness, state of insensibility, fainting, swoon, stupefaction. — *ānā* or *khānā*, to faint, swoon.

मूर्च्छित, *m.* (*f.* ā) bereft of sensation, in a fainting-fit, swooned, faint.

मूर्छा = **मूर्च्छा**, *q.v.*

मूर्छागत } **मूर्छापन्न** } *m.* (*f.* ā) = **मूर्च्छित**, *q.v.*

मूर्छारोग, *m.* a fainting-fit, swoon.

मूर्छित, *m.* (*f.* ā) = **मूर्च्छित**, *q.v.*

मूर्त्ति, *f.* matter, substance; figure, shape, form, any definite image or shape (esp. the human frame; hence, the term signifies, among Vairāgees, an individual, a person), body, incarnation, image, likeness, resemblance, picture, statue, an idol.

मूर्त्तिपूजक, *m.* (*f.* ikā) an image-worshipper.

मूर्त्तिपूजा, *f.* image worship, idolatry.

मूर्त्तिमन्त, *m.* (*f.* matī) = **मूर्त्तिमान**, *q.v.*

मूर्त्तिमान, *m*, (*f.* matī) an incarnation, etc.: *lit.* endowed with a corporeal frame, having shape or form, embodied, incarnate, personified; accomplished, clever.

मूर्द्धन्य, appertaining to the head; hence, *m.* (in Gram.) the cerebral letters (*viz.* ऋ, ॠ, ट, ठ, ड, ढ, ण, र, ष). They are also called linguals, in consequence of the essential and peculiar part which the tongue plays in the enunciation of them.

मूर्द्धा } **मूर्धन** } *m.* the head, skull.

मूल, 1, *m.* (*f.* ?) root, origin, source, cause, commencement, foundation, generation, race, capital, principal, stock-in-trade; a text (as distinguished from the comment on it): *pr. n.* the 19th *Nakshatra* (containing eleven stars, which appear to be the same as those in the tail of Scorpio): 2, radical, original, proper, real: 3, really.

मूलक, 1, a corruption of **मुल्क**, *q.v.*: 2. *m.* a certain esculent root; a sort of yam; the radish (*Raphanus sativus*): a sort of poison.

मूलकर्त्ता, *m.* (*f.* tri) the author of an original work: *hence*, an epithet of the Great Creator.

मूलज्ञानाशय, *m.* the essence or drift of wisdom.

मूलतत्त्व, *m.* the essential root or origin.

मूलत्व, *m.* the having its root (or foundation or source) in anything, the being occasioned by (or due to or arising from) anything.

मूलन, a Braj pl. of **मूल**, *q.v.* See **न**, 6.

मूलपाठ, *m.* the basis or text of a discourse.

मूलम, the painful excrescences about the anus or extremity of the gut arising from the blind piles.

मूलमी, mad, insane. (?)

मूलवान, *m.* (*f.* vatī) *adj.* possessing roots, possessing edible roots; (perhaps) practising magic with roots.

मूलविद्या, *f.* elementary or fundamental instruction.

मूलसमानता, *f.* equality with (or resemblance to) the root or origin.

मूलसम्बन्ध, *m.* connexion with the root or origin.

मूलस्वर, *m.* (in Gram.) a primary or simple vowel.

मूला, 1, an angle, corner (!): 2, (see **मूल**) the 19th *Nakshatra*.

मूलिया, 1, born when the moon is in the sign Scorpio (*mūl*) which is considered unlucky: 2, (in Mārwārī) stupid.

मूली, *f.* an edible root, a radish.

मूलुक, *more prop.* **मुलुक**, *q.v.*

मूलू, a kind of horn trumpet used by faqeers: small bells used as music.

मूल्य, *m.* price, wages, hire.

मूल्लू; see (1) **मूलू** (2) **मल्लू**.

मूष, *m.* (*f.* ā *or* ī) a rat, a mouse.

मूषक, *m.* (*f.* ikā) a rat, a mouse, a thief: a certain tree (*Mimosa shirisha*): *pr. n.* a certain country.

मूषगीर, *m.* a mouse-taker, sparrow-hawk.

मूषण, *m.* pilfering, stealing.

मूषदान, *m.* a mousetrap, rat-trap.

मूषा, *f.* (*m.* **मूष**) = **मूषिका**, *q.v.*

मूषिक, *m.* (*f.* ā) = **मूषक**, *q.v.*

मूषिका, *f.* (*m.* **मूषक**, etc.) a female rat, female mouse; a female thief: a crucible.

मूषिकांचन, *m.* an epithet of Ganesh.

मूषित, *m.* (*f.* ā) stolen.

मूषिदस्ती, *m.* an epithet of the mole.

मूषी, *f.* (*m.* **मूष**) = **मूषिका**, *q.v.*

मूस, 1, *more prop.* **मूष**, *q.v.*: 2, *f.* a crucible.

मूसकराना, *more com.* **मुसकराना**, *q. v.*

मूसना, *t.* to pilfer, steal, filch, defraud, snatch or seize by force.

मूसरा, (**मूज**) *m.* (*f.* ī) a rat, mouse.

मूसरी, *f.* 1, (*m.* **मूसरा**) a female rat or mouse: 2, (dim. of **मूसरा**) a small rat, a mouse.

मूसल (*corruption*) = **मुसल**, *q.v.*

मूसलधार } **मूसलधारा** } (*corruptions*) = **मुसलधार**, *q.v.*

मूसला, *m.* a tap-root; the fusiform receptacle of a many-seeded fruit (as of the *Artocarpus*, *Annona*, etc.). — *dhār barasnā*, to rain very heavily.

मूसा, 1, = **मूषा**, *q.v.*: 2, *m.* (*f.* ī) a mouse, a rat: 3, *m. pr. n.* the patriarch and lawgiver Moses.

मूसाई, *f.* the following the religion and laws of Moses, Judaism.

मूसाना, *more prop.* **मुसाना**, *q.v.*

मूसाहेब, *more prop.* **मुसाहिब**, *q.v.*

मूस्कराना, *more com.* **मुसकराना**, *q.v.*

मूहाना = **मुहाना**, *q.v.*

मूहित, *m.* (*f.* ā) *more prop.* **मोहित**, *q.v.*

मूहुर्त्त (*corruption*) = **मुहूर्त्त**, *q.v.*

मृकण्डु, *m. pr. n.* (1) of a certain ancient Hindoo sage, father of Mārkandey (2) Mārkandey himself.

मृग, *m.* (*f.* ī) a deer, antelope; a kind of elephant; an animal generally: *pr. n.* the fifth *Nakshatra* (containing three stars, one of which is Orionis (λ), and figured by an antelope's head, whence its name).

मृगचिड़ा, *m.* (*f.* ī) a certain small bird.

मृगछाला, *m.* the skin of the antelope worn (and used as a bed) by Hindoo ascetics.

मृगछौना, *m.* (*f.* ī) the young of the deer.

मृगजल, *m.* = **मृगतृष**, *q. v.*

मृगतृष, *f.* vapour floating over sands or deserts and appearing at a distance like water, mirage.

मृगतृषा
मृगतृष्णा
मृगतृष्णिका } *f.* = **मृगतृष**, *q. v.*

मृगनयन, *m.* (*f.* ā) an epithet of anyone who has very beautiful eyes ; *lit.* deer-eyed, fawn-eyed.

मृगनयना
मृगनयनी } = **मृगनेत्री**, *q. v.*

मृगनाभि, *f. m.* musk ; a bag of musk.

मृगनाभिजा, *f.*
मृगनाभी, *m. f.* } musk.

मृगनी, *f.* (*m.* **मृग**) a female antelope or deer, a doe.

मृगनेत्री, *f.* an epithet of any female with beautiful eyes ; *lit.* a fawn-eyed female.

मृगनैनी = **मृगनयनी** = **मृगनेत्री**, *q. v.*

मृगपति = **मृगराज**, *q. v.*

मृगभोजनी, *f.* bitter apple (*Colocynth*).

मृगमद, *m.* musk.

मृगया, *f.* the chase, hunting.

मृगराज, *m.* the king of the animals, *i. e.* the lion.

मृगलोचन, *m.* (*f.* ā) an epithet of any one who has very beautiful eyes ; *lit.* deer-eyed.

मृगलोचना
मृगलोचनी } = **मृगनेत्री**, *q. v.*

मृगशिरः, *m. pr. n.* (see **आग्रहायणी**) the fifth *Nakshatra* (containing three stars, one of which is Orionis (λ). and figured by an antelope's head, whence its name).

मृगशिरस
मृगशिरा
मृगशीर्ष } = **मृगशिरः**, *q. v.*

मृगसाला, *f.* a deer-park.

मृगा, *m.* (*f.* ī) *more prop.* **मृग**, *q. v.* [the leopard.

मृगादन, *m.* (*f.* ī) an epithet of the hyæna and of

मृगादनी, *f.* colocynth (*Cucumis coloquintida*).

मृगाधीश = **मृगपति**, *q. v.*

मृगी, *f.* 1, *a corruption of* **मिर्गी**, *q. v.*: 2, (*m.* **मृग**) a female antelope or deer, a doe ; a species of metre in Sanskrit prosody.

मृगु, a poet. form of **मृग**, *q. v.* [in Sanskrit prosody.

मृगेन्द्र, *m.* 1, = **मृगराज**, *q. v.*: 2, a species of metre

मृणाल, *m.* the fibrous stalk of a lotus.

मृणालिनी, *f.* a place where lotuses grow.

मृणाली, 1, *m.* a lotus: 2, *m. f.* a small fibre of a lotus : 3, *f.* an assemblage of lotuses.

मृत, 1, *m.* (*f.* ā) dead, defunct, extinct ; calcined (said of metals): 2, *m.* death ; solicited alms.

मृतक, *m.* a dead body, corpse ; the dead.

मृतकर्पट, *m.* the habiliments of the dead, a shroud.

मृतकल्प, *m.* (*f.* ā) a dying person etc.: *lit.* seemingly dead, nearly dead, dying ; insensible, fainted.

मृतजनकर्म्माध्यक्ष, *m.* (*f.* ī) an executioner.

मृतप्राय, *m.* (*f.* ā) = **मृतकल्प**, *q. v.*

मृतमण्डल, *m.* an epithet of this world ; *lit.* the temple of the dead or of death.

मृतलोक, 1, = **मर्त्यलोक**, *q. v.* : 2, (*corruption*) = **मृत्युलोक**, *q. v.*

मृतवत, *m.* (*f.* ī) death-like. [**लोक**, *q. v.*

मृतस्नात, *m.* (*f.* ā) bathed after mourning : dead immediately after ablution. [lution.

मृतस्नान, *m* bathing after mourning, funeral ab-

मृता, *f.* (*m.* **मृत**) a deceased female.

मृताल, *m.* a certain kind of fragrant earth (called

मृतालक = **मृताल**, *q. v.* [also Surat-earth).

मृति, *f.* death, decease, dying.

मृतिका, *more prop.* **मृत्तिका**, *q. v.* [ly, mortal.

मृतिमय, possessed of or abounding in death, dead-

मृतु (corruption) = **मृत्यु**, *q. v.*

मृत्किरा, *f.* an earth-worm.

मृत्ताल
मृत्तालक } = **मृताल**, *q. v.*

मृत्तिका, *f.* earth, mould, soil, clay, fresh earth,

मृत्यका ; see (1) **मृत्तिका** (2) **मृत्यु**. [a fragrant earth.

मृत्यजनक, death-producing, deadly, mortal.

मृत्यवती, *f. pr. n.* a wife of Dharm.

मृत्यु, 1, *m. f.* dying, death : 2, *m. pr. n.* the seventeenth astronomical *yog* or division of the moon's path: 3, *m.* an epithet of Yam.

मृत्युंजय, *m.* an epithet of Shiv ; *lit.* conqueror of death. In Christian literature the epithet is applied to Christ. [the world of the dead.

मृत्युलोक, *m.* the abode of Yam, the world of death,

मृदंग, *m.* a kind of drum broader in the middle than at the ends, a long drum, a small drum, tabor, double drum ; a sound ; bamboo ; (in Geom.) a figure shaped like a drum. [borer, drummer.

मृदंगिया, a person who beats the *mridang*, a ta-

मृदंगी, *m.* (*f.* inī) = **मृदंगिया**, *q. v.*

मृदु, *m.* (*f.* **मृदवी**) soft, mild, gentle, slow, tame, quiet, affable, kind ; blunt (not sharp).

मृदुभाव, *m.* gentleness of disposition.

मृदुत्व, *m.* (*f.* tā) softness, gentleness, mildness.

मृदुल, 1, soft, mild, gentle : 2, *m.* water.

मृदुवाणी, 1, *f.* a sweet, mild, or soft, voice : 2, *m.* (*f.* inī) sweet-voiced, soft-voiced, mild in speech.

मृदुसम्भाषण, *m.* gentle conversation, pleasing intercourse. [ally tame or soft.

मृदुस्वभाव, of a mild or gentle disposition, natur-

मृनाल (*corruption*) = **मृणाल**, *q. v.*

मृषा, falsely ; uselessly, in vain.

मृषावाद, *m.* false speech, false accusation.

मृषावादी, *m.* (*f.* inī) a liar, trifler: *lit.* adj. speaking falsely or uselessly.

में, 1, *a corruption of* **मैं**, 2, *q. v.*: 2, (from Sk. **मध्ये**)

the termination of the locative case in Hindee = in, among, between, into, at, on, concerning.

मेंकना, *a. int.* to bleat (as sheep and goats).

मेंगनी, *f.* orbicular excrement (as that of goats, sheep, camels, rats, etc.).

मेंड, मेंढ; for words beginning thus, see under the corresponding forms **मेंड़, मेंढ़**.

मेंसे (a double termination of frequent occurrence, and made up of **में** + **से**) = from within, out of.

मेंह, *m.* rain.—*chhūṭna*, to rain heavily.—*barasnā*, *a. int.* to rain.—*barsānā*, *t.* to rain, shower down.

मेंहदी (*colloquial*) = **मेंन्धी**, *q. v.*

मेंहमानदारी, *more prop.* **मिहमान्दारी**, *q. v.*

मेकडम्बर, a canopy over the *hauda* of an elephant.

मेकलकन्यका }
मेकलकन्या } = **मेखलकन्यका**, *q.v.*
मेकलसुता }

मेख (*corruption*) = (1) **मेख़** (2) **मेष**, *qq. v.*

मेख़, *f.* a tent-pin, peg, nail, pin, hook, tenter.

मेखचू, *m.* a frog.

मेखलकन्यका, *f.* an epithet of the Narmadā river.

मेखला, *f.* the girdle or zone of a female, a triple zone or string worn around the loins by the first three classes, the sacrificial string of a Brāhmaṇ when made of deer-skin; a sword-belt, sword-knot: the edge or slope of a mountain: the sea: a sort of figure made on the four sides of a sacrificial pit: *pr. n.* the Narmadā river. The *mekhlā* of a Brāhmaṇ should be of the fibres of the *munj* or of *kush*-grass; that of the Kshatriya, of *murwā* or bowstring; and that of the Vaishya, of a thread of the *sun*.

मेखली, 1, *f.* sackcloth: 2, *m.* (*f.* inī) one who wears a girdle or zone (*mekhlā*).

मेग़, *m.* a cloud, mist, fog.

मेगम, the white leprosy.

मेगिज़ीन, *m.* (Engl.) a magazine.

मेघ, *m.* a cloud; a demon; a certain fragrant grass (*Cyperus rotundus*); a certain musical mode (*rāg*) appropriated to the rainy season and last watch of the night before the first dawn of day (said to have proceeded either from the head of Brahmā or from the sky).

मेघकाल, *m.* the rainy season, the rains.

मेघगर्ज्जन, *m.* thunder.

मेघघटा, *f.* a mass of clouds.

मेघज्योतिस, *m.* a flash of lightning.

मेघडम्बर }
मेघडम्बुर } = **मेघाडम्बर**, *q. v.*

मेघतिमिर, *m.* cloudiness; cloudy or rainy weather.

मेघदीप, *m.* lightning.

मेघद्वार, *m.* the sky, the heavens, ether.

मेघधनुष, *m.* the rainbow.

मेघनाद, *m.* the rumbling of clouds, thunder; the pulas-tree (*Butea frondosa*); a sort of amaranth (*Amaranthus polygamus*): *pr. n.* (1) of Varuṇ (2) of a son of his (3) of a younger brother of Rāvaṇ.

मेघनादानुलासी, *m.* (*f.* inī) a peacock.

मेघपति, *m.* an epithet of Indra; *lit.* lord of the clouds, the thunderer. [of the four horses of Krishṇ.

मेघपुष्प, *m.* water; river-water; hail: *pr. n.* one

मेघबनर; see **मेघबरन** and **मेघबानर**.

मेघबरन (*colloquial*) = **मेघवर्ण**, *q. v.*

मेघबानर, *m.* an epithet of the clouds.

मेघमाला, *f.* a gathering or succession of clouds.

मेघराग, *m.* one of the six modes in Hindoo music.

मेघराज }
मेघराजा } = **मेघपति**, *q. v.*

मेघरूपी, cloud-like, *i. e.* either (1) resounding; or (2) black and threatening.

मेघवर्ण, 1, *m.* the colour of the clouds: 2, *m.* (*f.* ā) cloud-coloured, dark like the clouds: 3. *m. pr. n.* (1) of a certain man (2) of a certain crow in the *Hitopadesh*.

मेघागम = **मेघकाल**, *q. v.*

मेघाच्छन्न, *m.* (*f.* ā) shaded by clouds, covered with clouds, clouded, beclouded.

मेघाडम्बर, *m.* a mass of clouds; thunder; the shadow of clouds: the umbrella of Indra.

मेघारम्भ, *m.* a gathering of clouds.

मेघारूढ़, *m.* (*f.* ā) seated on the clouds.

मेच; see **मेंच** and **मीच**.

मेचक, black, dark blue; hence, *m.* the colour black or dark blue, a cloud, smoke, darkness, the eye of a peacock's tail, sulphuret of antimony.

मेचकताई, *f.* blackness, darkness.

मेज़, *f.* a table. — *bichhānā*, to lay the cloth.

मेजिस्त्रेट, *m.* (Engl.) a magistrate.

मेझुका, *m.* (*f.* ī) a ram.

मेट; see **मेटना** and **मेटा**.

मेटना, *t.* (of **मिटना**) to efface, erase, blot out, annihilate, annul, cancel, expiate, atone for: to thwart.

मेटनिहार, *m.* (*f.* nī, ī, in) an eraser, expiator.

मेटा }
मेटिया } *f.* a small earthen water-jar.
मेटी }

मेटुला, *f.* a certain tree (*Spondias mangifera*).

मेठा, *m.* (*f.* ī) a corruption (1) of **मेटा** (2) of **मेढ़ा**, *qq. v.*

मेडक }
मेडुक } *m.* (*f.* ī) a frog.

मेड, 1, (*corruption*) = **मेड़**, *q. v.*: 2, gleanings of corn left on the field.

मेढ़क, *m.* (*f.* in, ī, nī) a ram.

मेढ़शृंगी, *f.* a certain milky plant (*Asclepias geminata*) the fruit of which is crooked, and is therefore compared to a ram's horn.

मेढ़ा, *m.* (*f.* ī) a ram.

मेढ़्र, *m.* a ram; the penis.

मेंड़, *f.* a bank, border, edge, hedge, fence, dam, dyke, mole, mound. —*parnā*, to rise (said of waves).

मेंडक, 1, *m.* (*f.* ī) a frog; 2, *m.* the rump of a horse.

मेंडककोड़ा, *m.* the frog-abscess.

मेंडकी, *f.* a female frog. — *ko zukām honā* (*lit.*

a frog having caught cold) expresses pride or consequential airs assumed by worthless or unsuitable persons.

मेंढकफल (*dialectic*) = मैंफल, *q. v.* [parapet of a well.

मेंढा, 1, *m.* (*f.* ī) a kind of goat: 2, *f.* the brim or

मेंड़ियाना, *t.* to skirt, enclose with a bank or fence.

मेंढी, 1, (colloquial) = मेन्धी, *q. v.*: 2, *f.* (*m.* मेंढा) a she-goat of a certain kind.

मेंढु; see मेंढ and मेंढुक.

मेंढुक, *m.* (*f.* in, ī, nī) a frog.

मेंढुकवि / मेंढुका } see मेंढुक.

मेंढल, *m.* a certain fruit (*Guilandina bondueella*, Linn.); a kind of fire-work which bursts with an explosion. [tide called the bore.

मेंढा, 1, *m.* (*f.* ī) a ram: 2, *m.* the swell of the

मेथि = मेधि, *q. v.*

मेथिका, *f.* = मेथी, *q. v.*

मेथी, *f.* the plant fenugreek (*Trigonella fœnum græcum*). [cessive corpulency.

मेद, *m.* marrow, fat, adeps, lymph, serum; ex-

मेदनी, a contraction of मेदिनी, *q. v.*

मेदस्वी, *m.* (*f.* inī) fat, stout, robust, strong.

मेदा, *f.* a certain root used as a drug. It is said to resemble ginger, and is brought from the Morung district. It is one of the eight principal medicaments, and is said to be of cooling and emollient properties, and of particular virtue in fever and consumption.

मेदान, *more prop.* मैदान, *q. v.*

मेदिनी, *f.* the earth; landed property, land, country: a body of pilgrims going to visit the tomb of a saint.

मेदोधरा, *f.* a membrane (the omentum) in the abdomen containing the fat. [lency.

मेदोवृद्धि, *f.* enlargement of the scrotum, corpu-

मेध, *m.* sacrifice, offering, oblation.

मेधा, *f.* understanding, apprehension, conception, sense, prudence.

मेधातिथि, *m. pr. n.* (1) of a certain Kāṇv, author of some of the hymns of the Reg-Ved (2) of the father of Kaṇv (3) of a son of Manu Swayambhuva (4) of one of the seven sages under Sāvarṇ (5) of a son of Priyavrat (6) of a certain lawyer or commentator on the Mānav Dharm-Shāstra (7) of a certain river.

मेधावी, *m.* (*f.* inī) intelligent, possessing a ready and just apprehension, wise, clever, learned, docile.

मेधि, *m.* the part of a threshingfloor around which cattle turn as they tread out the corn; the post fixed in the centre of a threshingfloor around which cattle turn in treading out the corn.

मेधिर, *m.* (*f.* ā) / मेधी, *m.* (*f.* inī) } = मेधावी, *q. v.*

मेनका, *f. pr. n.* a certain courtesan of Indra's heaven.

मेना = मेनका, *q. v.*

मेन्धी, *f.* a certain plant (*Lawsonia inermis*), from the leaves of which a reddish dye is prepared with which natives stain the palms of the hands, the tips of the fingers, the finger-nails, and the soles of the feet.

मेम, *f.* Ma'am, Madam. The term is applied by the natives to married European ladies. By some of the more ill-informed, the term Mem-Sāhib is applied to Her Majesty, Queen Victoria, whom they regard as the wife of the Lāṭ-Sāhib or Governor-General.

मेमना, *more prop.* मेम्ना, *q. v.*

मेमसाहिब / मेमसाहिबः } = मेम, *q. v.*

मेम्ना, *m.* a kid.

मेरखाने, a corruption of मिहरखानी, *q. v.*

मेरा, (gen. of मैं) *m.* (*f.* ī) my, mine,

मेरु, *m. pr. n.* (1) of the highland of Tartary north of the Himālaya (2) of a certain fabulous mountain situated in the centre of the seven continents (*dwip*) of Hindoo mythological geography. It is compared to the cup or seed-vessel of the lotus, the leaves of which are represented by the different dweeps. Its height is 84000 *yajans* (or near 672000 English miles) 16000 of which are below the surface of the earth. The shape of this mountain is variously described as square, conical, columnar, spherical, and spiral; and its four faces are of various colours, *viz.* white towards the east, black to the west, yellow to the south, and red to the north. The Ganges falls from heaven on its summit, and flows thence to the surrounding world in four streams, *viz.* the *Sitā* which flows eastward, the *Chakshu* (Oxus) which flows westward, the *Bhadrsomā* which runs northwards into Tartary, and the *Gangā* (Ganges) which flows southward into Hindūstān. On the summit of *Meru*, Brahmā resides, attended and worshipped by the Rishis, Gandharvas, etc.; while the regents of the points of the compass occupy the corresponding faces of the mountain, the whole of which consists of gold and gems (3) the north pole (in Astron.).

मेरुक, *m.* fragrant resin, incense.

मेरुदेवी, *f. pr. n.* a daughter of Meru, wife of Nābhi and mother of Rishab, who was an incarnation of Vishṇu.

मेरु, 1, *in Braj* = मेरा, *q. v.*: 2 *m.* (मरु) an axis.

मेरो (*colloquial and poet.*) = मेरा, *q. v.*

मेरौ, *in Braj* = मेरा, *q. v.*

मेरोई, an emphatic Braj form = मेरा भी.

मेल, *m.* an assemblage, meeting, fair, court of justice, counterpart: connexion, relation, agreement, compact, combination, intimacy, concord, mixture, mixing, association, union, reconciliation.

मेलक, *m.* an assembling, associating.

मेलकरवैया, *m.* one who brings about reconciliation, a promoter of concord, a peace-maker.

मेलन, *m.* meeting, coming together, union, junction, assembling, associating with; an encounter; mixing with, mixture; adding to. [to penetrate.

मेलना, *t*, to thrust in, stuff in, force in, cram in,

मेलमिलाप, *m.* friendly intercourse, reconcilement.

मेलवो, (1) in Māṛwāṛī = to send: 2, in Braj = मेलना, [*q. v.*

मेलनौ in Braj = मेलना, *q. v.*

मेला, *m. f.* a fair, a large concourse of people collected at stated periods for religious or commercial purposes, a mixed assemblage of fakeers.

मेलाठेला, *m.* a large concourse of people, a crowd, throng; a crowding and pushing.

मेलान, the feeding of cattle at night.

मेली, *m.* (*f.* inī) partaking, sociable, friendly.

मेव, *m. pr. n.* a certain tribe inhabiting the mountainous province of Mewāt, much addicted to robbing.

मेवड़ा = मेव, *q. v.*

मेवा, *m.* (pll. मेवजात, मेवहा, मेवे) fruit ; a certain plant (*Aanona squamosa*). [of India.

मेवात, *m. pr. n.* a certain mountainous district

मेवाती, *m.* (*f.* inī) = मेव, *q. v.*: *lit.* appertaining to Mewāt or to its people.

मेवादार, fruit-bearing, fruitful. [of drug.

मेष, *m.* (*f.* ī) a sheep, ram ; the sign Aries : a kind

मेषचक्षु, a blockhead: *lit.* sheep-eyed: *met.* sheepish. [ing or protecting sheep or flocks.

मेषपाल, *m.* (*f.* ī) a shepherd: *lit.* adj. nourish-

मेषपालक, *m.* (*f.* ikā)
मेषपाली, *m.* (*f.* inī) } = मेषपाल, *q. v.*

मेषशावक, *m.* (*f.* ikā) a lamb.

मेषाण्ड, *m.* an epithet of Indra.

मेषाण्डकोष, *m.* (see गोतम) an epithet of Indra.

मेषी, *f.* (*m.* मेष) a ewe.

मेस : see (1) मिस (2) मेज़ (3) मेष.

मेसी, *f.* goatskin or sheepskin leather uncoloured.

मेह, 1. *a corruption* of मेंह, *q. v.*: 2, = मेघ, *q. v*: 3, *m.* discharging urine ; urine ; urinary disease (*esp.* inflammation of the urethra, gonorrhœa, etc.).

मेहतर (*colloquial*) = मिहतर, *q. v.*

मेहतरानी (*colloquial*) = मिहतरानी, *q. v.*

मेहठी = मेन्धी, *q. v.*

मेहनत, *more prop.* मिहनत, *q. v.*

मेहना, *m.* a taunt. — *mārnā*, to taunt.

मेहन्ना, *m.* (*f.* मेहन्निन or मेहन्नी) a taunter.

मेहमान, *more prop.* मिहमान, *q. v.*

मेहमांदारी, *more prop.* मिहमान्दारी, *q. v.*

मेहर ; see मिहर and मिहराब.

मेहरबानी, *more prop.* मिहरबानी, *q. v.* [ment. (?)

मेहरा, 1, *more prop.* मिहरा, *q. v.*: 2, a female apart-

मेहराब, *more com.* मिहराब, *q. v.*

मेहूं (corruption) = मेंह, *q. v.*

मै, 1, in Braj = में, *q. v.*: 2, in Chand = मैं, *q. v.* : 3, *f.* wine ; spirituous liquor.

मैआ, (1) *more com.* मैया, *q. v.*: 2, in Braj = मा, *q. v.*

मैआते in Braj = माते (abl. of मा).

मैं, 1, (*corruption*) = में, 2, *q. v.* : 2, = मैया, *q. v.*; 3, (the personal pronoun 1st person singular) I. *Main hūn*, I am, it is I, I am he.

मैंआ, *more com.* मैया, *q. v.*

मैंढ़ा, *m.* (*f.* ī) a ram.

मैंनका, in Braj = मेनका, *q. v.*

मैंना, a corruption of मैना, *q. v.*

मैंनाक, *more prop.* मैनाक, *q. v.*

मैंने, *more com.* मैने, *q. v.*

मैंफल, *m.* a certain fruit (*Vangueria spinosa*, Roxb.) used in medicine, the emetic nut.

मैंभा = (1) मैभा (2) मैं भया.

मैका, *m.* maternal relations, kindred, family connexions.

मैख़ाना, *m.* a spirit-shop, tavern. [nexions.

मैख़ोर
मैख़्वारा
मैगुसार } = मैनोश, *q. v.*

मैडा, a kind of scaffold erected in a corn-field where a person is stationed to watch the crops.

मैड़ा = मैडा, *q. v.* [ings.

मैयठ, corn left on a field in small quantity, glean-

मैयठल = मेयठल, *q. v.*

मैतो, *more prop.* मैं तो.

मैत्र, 1, appertaining to a friend or to friendship, amicable, friendly : 2, *m.* friendship : any Brāhman who has arrived at the highest state of human perfection ; the son of an outcaste Vaishya ; a friend to all creatures: the anus; the discharging of excrement : *pr. n.* (1) of the seventeenth *Nakshatra* (2) of the twelfth astronomical *yog* or division of the moon's path.

मैत्री, *f.* friendship : *pr. n.* the 17th *Nakshatra.*

मैत्रेय, *m.* (*f.* ī) the offspring of a Vaideha by an Ayogava female : *lit.* appertaining to a friend.

मैत्रेयक, *m.* (*f.* ikā) the offspring of a Vaideha by an Ayogava female : a crier or chanter of the hours (an office occupied seemingly by men of this *Maitreyak* caste).

मैथिल, *m.* (*f.* ī) a native of Mithilā: *lit.* appertaining to Mithilā. [tive of Mithilā.

मैथिली, *f.* an epithet of Sītā : *prop.* a female na-

मैथुन, *m.* sexual intercourse, holy union, marriage ; union, association, matrimony.

मैथुनी, *m.* (*f.* inī) one who has experienced sexual intercourse. [embraces.

मैथुन्य, contracted for the purpose of amorous

मैदान, *m.* an open field, plain, field of battle, parade-ground. — *k.* to fight a duel.

मैदानी, *m.* a person who precedes a general or a wazīr and proclaims his titles ; a kind of *hukkā* used by faqeers ; flour made into dough for the preparation of sweetmeats.

मैन, 1, *m.* an epithet of Kāmdev : 2, a common short grass which grows on rich and inundated land, and chokes the crops.

मैनका in Braj = मेनका, *q. v.*

मैनफल = मैंफल, *q. v.*

मैनसिल, *m.* red orpiment, red arsenic; realgar (*Arsenicum rubrum*), the Sandaraca of Pliny.

मैना, 1, (*corruption*) = (1) मयना (2) मैन, *qq. v.* : 2, *f. pr. n.* the mother of Pārvatī. [certain demon.

मैनाक, *m. pr. n.* (1) of a certain mountain (2) of a

मैने, (the Agentive case of मैं) by me.

मैनोश, *m.* a wine-bibber, drunkard, sot.

मैभा, *f.* (मातृभा) a step-mother.

मैम in Mārwāṛī = मेम, *q. v.*

मैम्भा ; see (1) मैंभा (2) मैभा.

मैया = (1) मा (2) माइया, *qq. v.*

मैयारे ; see (1) मझारे (2) मया रे.

मैल, 1, in Mārwāṛī = महल्ल, *q. v.* : 2, *f.* dirt, filth,

pollutionscum, rust : 3, *m.* (Engl.) a mile. — *kāṭnā*, to refine, purify. — *chhāṇtnā*, to fine, strain, clarify, purify. — *baiṭhnā*, to gather a crust.

मैलकुचैल
मैलकुचैला } *more prop.* **मैलाकुचैला**, *q. v.*

मैलख़ोरा, *m.* an under-vestment (as under-petticoat, etc.); an apron; a saddlecloth.

मैला, 1, *m.* = **मैल**, *q. v.* : 2, *m.* (*f.* ī) dirty, foul, defiled, nasty. — *k.* to tarnish, foul, pollute. — *ho jānā*, *a. int.* to tarnish, become turbid or dirty.

मैलाकुचीला, *m.* (*f.* **मैलीकुचीली**) = **मैलाकुचैला**, *q. v.*

मैलाकुचैला, *m.* (*f.* **मैलीकुचैली**) dirty and ill-clad, filthy and rugged, polluted, foul. [nastiness.

मैलापन, *m.* filthiness of condition, pollutedness,

मैलेवेष, *m.* foul clothing.

मैंहका, (**महिष**) *m.* (*f.* ī) a buffalo.

मो in Braj = (1) **मुझ** (2) **मैं**, 2, *qq. v.*

मोआ, a certain plant and its flower.

मोई (Rām.) = **मोही**, *q. v.*

मों (dialectic) = (1) **मुंह** (2) **मैं**, *qq. v.*

मोंको (in Braj, dat. and acc.) = **मुझे**, *q. v.*

मोंखतार, *more prop.* **मुख़तार**, *q. v.*

मोंगरी (colloquial) = **मोगरी**, *q. v.*

मोंटी ; see **मोटी**, *q. v.*

मोंढा, *m.* 1, more prop. **मोढ़ा**, *q. v* : 2, the shoulder; a hump : shoots of the sugarcane.

मोंतें, an old form = **मुझसे**, *q. v.*

मोंसें, *more com.* **मोसें**, *q. v.*

मोंह (corruption) = (1) **मुंह** (2) **मोह**, *qq. v.*

मोंहरी, *f.* a kennel, drain.

मोंहि (in Braj, dat. and acc.) = **मुझे**, *q. v.*

मोकर; see (1) **मुयक्कर** (2) **मूक़र** (3) **मेरा**.

मोकलो, in Mārwārī = much.

मोकरर, *more prop.* **मुक़र्रर**, *q. v.* [panded, extended.

मोकला, *m.* a plant, vegetable : *lit.* opened, ex-

मोकलारूप, *m.* a young shoot, sprout.

मोका
मोकां } see (1) **मुझको** (2) **मूका** (3) **मौका**.

मोकान, *more prop.* **मकान**, *q. v.*

मोकाबिल, *more prop.* **मुक़ाबिल**, *q. v.*

मोकाबिला, *more prop.* **मुक़ाबिला**, *q. v.*

मोक़ाम, *more prop.* **मक़ाम**, *q. v.*

मोको
मोकों
मोकौ
मोकौं } Braj forms of **मुझको**, *q. v.*

मोक्ष, *m.* an untying ; liberation (esp. the liberation of the soul from the body, and its exemption from further transmigration ; *hence*) final beatitude ; death ; acquittance of an obligation.

मोक्षक, *m.* (*f.* ikā) one who sets at liberty, an emancipator, deliverer, saviour.

मोक्षज्ञान, *m.* knowledge of the beatitude attained through the entire emancipation of the soul from matter.

मोक्षज्ञानी, *m.* (*f.* inī) one who is acquainted with the beatitude of emancipation.

मोक्षण, *m.* a letting go, liberating, emancipating, exempting from further transmigration.

मोक्षदाता, *m.* (*f.* trī) an emancipator, deliverer, saviour : lit. *adj.* imparting emancipation.

मोक्षदायक, *m.* (*f.* ikā)
मोक्षदायी, *m.* (*f.* inī) } = **मोक्षदाता**, *q. v.*

मोक्षधर्म्म, *m.* law or rule of emancipation.

मोक्षपद, *m.* the way of emancipation or salvation ; the status of emancipation or salvation.

मोक्षिका, *f.* (*m.* **मोक्षक**) a female deliverer.

मोक्षित, *m.* (*f.* ā) let go, liberated, emancipated, [at large.

मोख = **मोखा**, *q. v.*

मोखतार, *more prop.* **मुख़तार**, *q. v.*

मोखतसर, *more prop.* **मुख़तसर**, *q. v.*

मोखा, *m.* a small hole in a wall for admitting light and air, an air-hole, aperture.

मोगरा, *m.* a mallet, pounder, rammer, ramrod ; the dog-head nail of the cock of a flint lock : a certain flower (*Jasminum zambac*, var. γ, Roxb. ; or *Mogorium*, Lamarck) commonly called Tuscan jasmine, or double Moogrie, or great double Arabian jasmine.

मोगरी, *f.* a mallet for beating clothes, etc. with.

मोघ, 1, *m.* a fence, hedge: 2, vain, useless, fruitless.

मोघज्ञान, *m.* (*f.* ā) one who cultivates vain knowledge or any but religious wisdom.

मोघा, *f.* trumpet-flower (*Bignonia swaveolens*).

मोघाश, *m.* (*f.* ā) one who indulges vain hopes.

मोच, *m.* a strain, sprain, twist: whiskers, moustachios : the nib or point of anything : a certain tree (*Hyperanthera morunga*) : the plantain.

मोचक, 1, *m.* (*f.* ikā) a liberator ; a devotee : 2, *m.* the silk-cotton tree (*Bombax heptaphyllum*) ; the plantain (*Musa sapientum*) ; a certain tree (*Hyperanthera morunga*).

मोचन, 1, *f.* = **मोचिन**, *q. v.* : 2, *m.* setting free, liberating, deliverance, discharge, dismissal, forgiveness, acquittal, release : robbery, theft.

मोचना, 1, *m.* pincers, tweezers: 2, *t.* to let go, set free, put off, shed, extinguish.

मोचनी ; see (1) **मोचिन** (2) **मोचना**.

मोचरस, *m.* the gum of the silk-cotton tree.

मोचा, 1, *m.* a large lump of flesh : crops beaten down by wind and rain : 2, *f.* the silk-cotton tree (*Bombax heptaphyllum*) ; the plantain-tree (*Musa sapientum*).

मोचाट, *m.* a certain pungent seed (*Nigella Indica*).

मोचिन, *f.* (*m.* **मोची**) the wife of any worker in leather, a shoemaker's wife. [prickly nightshade.

मोचिनी, *f.* 1, *more com.* **मोचिन**, *q. v.* : 2, a kind of

मोचिची, *more com.* **मोचिन**, *q. v.*

मोची, *m.* (*f.* in, inī, innī, nī,) a leather-worker, a saddler, harness-maker, a shoemaker, cobbler.

मोछ, *more prop.* (1) **मूछ** (2) **मोक्ष**, *qq. v.*

मोज; see (1) **मूज** (2) **मोज़ा** (3) **मौज**.

मोज़फर, *more prop.* **मुज़फ्फर**, *q.v.*

मोज़ा, *m.* a stocking, sock; a boot.

मोट, 1, = **मोठ**, *q.v.*: 2, (*contraction*) = **मोटा**, *q.v.*

मोटकी, *f.* a fat female; one of the female personifications (*rāginī*) of the musical modes; a mattock, pickaxe.

मोटक्क, *more prop.* (1) **मुक्क** (2) **मोख**, *qq.v.*

मोटरा, *m.* a bundle, package, load.

मोटरी, *f.* (dim. of **मोटरा**) a small bundle, a parcel, a knapsack.

मोटला, *m.* (*f.* ī) *more com.* **मोटा**, *q.v.*

मोटा, *m.* (*f.* ī) fat, plump, corpulent, thick, coarse, great, large, gross, big, bulky.

मोटाई, *f.* corpulency, fatness, thickness, grossness, bigness, bulkiness.

मोटापन / **मोटापना** / **मोटापा** } *m.* = **मोटाई**, *q.v.*

मोटिया, *m.* a bearer of burdens, a carrier, porter, labourer.

मोटी, *f.* (*m.* **मोटा**) a fat female, etc.

मोठ, *f.* a bundle, package, load, bale: amount, total: a leathern bucket for raising water: vetches, lentils.

मोठिया, 1, = **मोटिया**, *q.v.*: 2, a dim. of **मोठ**, *q.v.*

मोड़, 1, = **मोड़का**, *q.v.*: 2, *m.* a turn, twist sprain, convolution, writhe; a fistula. — *khānā*, to be defeated, be routed. — *denā*, to put to flight, defeat.

मोड़का, *m.* young shoots of a tree or of a plant.

मोड़ना, *t.* to twist, turn, bend, screw: *a. int.* to turn away.

मोड्डा; see (1) **मोड़ना** (2) **मुण्डना**.

मोड़े in Mārwāṛī = late.

मोढ़ा, *m.* 1, = **मोयला**, *q.v.*: 2, a low stool, footstool.

मोयट; see **मोट**.

मोयटा, *m.* (*f.* ī) *more com.* **मोटा**, *q.v.*

मोयटी; see **मोटी**.

मोयला, *m.* 1, = **मोढ़ा**, *q.v.*: 2, the shoulder, a hump, a lump: shoots of the sugarcane.

मोतअक्ज़िव, *more prop.* **मुताक्ज़िब**, *q.v.*

मोतन; see (1) **मोतिन** (2) **मेरा तन**.

मोतवज्जह / **मोतवज्जः** } *more prop.* **मुतवज्जिह**, *q.v.*

मोतरा = **मोथरा**, *q.v.*

मोतसील, *more prop.* **मुत्तसिल**, *q.v.*

मोताबिक, *more prop.* **मुताबिक**, *q.v.*

मोति, *more com.* **मोती**, *q.v.*

मोतिन, a Braj pl. of **मोती**, *q.v.*

मोतियराम, *m.* a common name of males.

मोतिया, *m.* a certain flower (*Jasminum zambac*, var. β, Roxb.): a pearl.

मोतियाबिन्द, *m.* a kind of blindness (*Gutta serena*).

मोती, *m.* a pearl. — *kī sī āb utarnā*, to be disgraced. — *kūṭkar bharnā*, to be very bright (the eye). — *pironā*, to string pearls: *met.* to speak eloquently; to weep (the tear-drops being compared to pearls).

मोतीचूर, *m.* a certain description of eye among pigeons; a kind of sweetmeat.

मोतीराम, *m. pr. n.* a son of Kānad.

मोतें in Braj = **मुझसे**.

मोत्रा, *more prop.* (1) **मोथरा** (2) **मुत्र**, *q.v.*

मोथरा, *m.* a certain disease in horses, splint, spavin.

मोथा, *m.* a kind of grass (*Cyperus rotundus*) the root of which is used in medicine.

मोथी, *f.* a kind of sweet yellow leguminous seed.

मोद, *m.* joy, gladness, delight, happiness, pleasure.

मोदक, 1, *m.* (*f.* ikā) one who causes delight; a confectioner: *lit.* gladdening, exhilarating, delighting, pleasing: 2, *m.* a kind of sweetmeat; sweetmeats.

मोदित, *m.* (*f.* ā) pleased, delighted, joyous, gratified.

मोदिन, 1, *f.* = **मोदिनी**, *q.v.*: 2, *m.* (*f.* ī) = **मोदी**, *q.v.*

मोदी, *m.* (*f.* inī) a merchant, grain-merchant, shopkeeper, purveyor, steward.

मोदीख़ाना, *m.* a grain-merchant's shop; a grocer's shop; a pantry.

मोधू, *m. f.* guileless, artless, innocent, simple, silly, foolish.

मोनक्कश; see **मुनक्कश** and **मिनकश**.

मोनासिब, *more prop.* **मुनासिब**, *q.v.*

मोनी, *f.* a point, end.

मोपर in Braj = **मुझपर**. See **मो**.

मोपास in Braj = **मेरे पास**. See **मो**.

मोपै / **मोपैं** } in Braj = (1) **मुझपर** (2) **मेरे पास**. See **मो**.

मोफस्सल / **मोफस्सिल** } *more prop.* **मुफ़स्सल**, *q.v.*

मोम, *m.* wax, bee's-wax. — *kī nāk*, a person of fickle disposition.

मोमजामा, *m.* / **मोमजाम**, *f.* } wax-cloth.

मोमदिल, tender-hearted.

मोमबत्ती, *f.* a wax candle.

मोमरौग़न, *m.* a mixture of wax and oil.

मोमिया, *m.* a mummy.

मोमियाई, 1, mummy-like, appertaining to a mummy: 2, *f.* a certain medicine.

मोमी, *m.* (*f.* inī) of the colour of wax; waxen; (as applied to chintz, it means) prepared after stamping by covering the flowers with wax to prevent their being spoiled by other colours afterwards applied.

मोयस्सर, *more prop.* **मुयस्सर**, *q.v.*

मोर, 1, (*contraction*) = **मोरा**, *q.v.*: 2, (*corruption*) = **मोड़**, 2, *q.v.*: 3, *m.* (*f.* nī, in, ī) a peacock: 4, *m.* an ant.

मोरचंग, *more prop.* **मुंहचंग**, *q.v.*

मोरचा; see (1) **मोर्चा** (2) **मूर्छा**.

मोरछल, *m.* a fan (made of peacock's feathers) for driving away flies; a brush.

मोरतूटा / **मोरतुत्ता** } *m.* sulphate of copper.

मोरन, *m.* (a Braj. pl. of मोर) peacocks, ants, etc.

मोरनी, *f.* (*m.* मोर, 3) a peahen. [See म, 6.

मोरपंख, *m.* a peacock's feather, a peacock's wing.

मोरपंखी, *f.* a kind of pleasure-boat, a barge.

मोरपख } मोरपच्छ } = मोरपंख, *q.v.*

मोरम in Māṛwāṛī = मुहर्रम, *q.v.*

मोरमुकुट, *m.* a peacock's crest; a crown or crest like that of the peacock.

मोरवा (poetical) = मोर, 3, *q.v.*

मोरस; see मूरिस.

मोरस्तुति (Rām.) = मेरी ओरसे.

मोरा, 1, *m.* (*f.* ī) = मेरा, *q.v.*: 2, = मोर, 3, *q.v.*

मोरि, a contracted form of मोरा, 1, or of मोरी, 2, [*qq.v.*

मोरिन, *more com.* मोरनी, *q.v.*

मोरी, 1, *more com.* मोरनी, *q.v.*: 2, *f.* (*m.* मोरा) my, mine: 3, *f.* a subterraneous passage for water, a drain, kennel, pipe, aqueduct, conduit.

मोरे in Braj (infl. of मोरा) = मेरे. See मेरा.

मोरेहु in Braj = मेरे भी.

मोरो } मोरौ } in Braj = मेरा, *q.v.*

मोर्चा, *m.* a small ant, emmet: rust: a battery, entrenchment: a poor weak fellow.

मोल, *m.* purchase: price, cost.—*ṭhahrānā*, to fix a price, appraise, value, estimate.—*baṛhānā*, to enhance the price.—*lenā*, to purchase.—*toṛnā*, to beat down the price.

मोलक, *m.* *pr. n.* a certain ancient Hindoo sage.

मोलतोल, *m.* the fixing a price; purchasing; trading, traffic.

मोलवान, *m.* *pr. n.* a certain demon.

मोलाहेजा, *more prop.* मुलाहज़ा, *q.v.*

मोलिया in Māṛwāṛī = stupid.

मोवाफिक, *more prop.* मुवाफ़िक़, *q.v.*

मोवासरत, *more prop.* मुआशरत, *q.v.*

मोष, 1, *more prop.* मूष, *q.v.*: 2, *m.* robbing, robbery, stealing, pilfering, swindling, theft.

मोषक, *m.* (*f.* ikā) a thief, robber, swindler.

मोषण, *m.*, } मोषा, *f.* } = मोष, 2, *q.v.*

मोसना, *t.* to pilfer, steal, filch, defraud, snatch or seize by force.

मोसम (*poet.*) = मेरे समान. See मेा.

मोसखिर, *more prop.* मुसख़्ख़िर, *q.v.*

मोसाफिर } मोसाफीर } *more prop.* मुसाफ़िर, *q.v.*

मोसाहेब, *more prop.* मुसाहिब, *q.v.*

मोसो } मोसों } मोसौ } मोसौं } in Braj = (1) मुझसा (2) मुझसे.

मोह, *m.* (*f.* ?) loss of consciousness, fainting, bewilderment, distraction, stupefaction, error, mistake, ignorance, weakness of intellect, foolishness, infatuation; fascination, allurement, affection, love, kindness, sympathy, compassion, pity. The term is specially applied to that spiritual ignorance and infatuation by which men are led to believe in the reality of worldly objects and to addict themselves to mundane and sensual enjoyment.—*jānā*, to become enamoured.—*men ānā*, to faint (as at the sudden appearance of a friend or mistress).—*lenā*, to attach, allure, captivate, charm, fascinate, entrance, enamour.

मोहक, *m.* (*f.* ikā) causing ignorance, folly, or error, stupefying, infatuating, fascinating.

मोहतम, *m.* the darkness occasioned by मोह, *q.v.*

मोहन, 1, *m.* (*f.* ī) a fascinator: *lit.* depriving of consciousness or understanding, stupefying, fascinating; winning, charming, captivating: 2, *m.* the overpowering reason and reflection by worldly or sensual pleasure, temptation, seduction, copulation: *pr. n.* one of the arrows of Kāmdev.

मोहनप्यारा, *m.* an epithet of Krishṇ.

मोहनभोग, *m.* a kind of sweetmeat, the being subject to an infatuation.

मोहनमाला, *f.* a string of golden beads and corals, an ornament.

मोहना, 1, *m.* (*f.* ī) = मोहन, 1, *q.v.*: 2, *t.* to allure, charm, fascinate, enchant, delude.

मोहनी, *f.* 1, (*m.* मोहन) an enchantress, courtesan: 2, incantation, charm, magic: 3, *pr. n.* (1) of a certain female demon (2) of a certain Apsaras.

मोहनीमूर्ति, *m.* an epithet of Krishṇ.

मोहब्बत, *more prop.* महब्बत, *q.v.*

मोहमय, *m.* (*f.* ī) abounding in (or under the influence of) *moh*; false, delusive.

मोहर (*corruption*) = मुहर, *q.v.*

मोहरा, *more prop.* मुहरा, *q.v.*

मोहा, 1, *more prop.* मोह, *q.v.*: 2, = महुआ, *q.v.*

मोहाना = मुहाना, *q.v.*

मोहापहारी, *m.* (*f.* inī) the destroyer of ignorance (an epithet of Shiv and of Wisdom).

मोहाफेज, *more prop.* मुहाफ़िज़, *q.v.*

मोहाल, *more prop.* मुहाल, *q.v.*

मोहि in Braj = (1) मुझे (2) मुझको (3) मोहित (4) मोही, *qq.v.*

मोहिका, *f.* (*m.* मोहक) an enchantress, etc.

मोहित, *m.* (*f.* ā) senseless, unconscious, faint; charmed, fascinated, enamoured, beguiled, deceived.

मोहिनी, *f.* (*m.* मोही) a fascinating female, charmer, courtesan: an epithet of Durgā; a kind of jasmine (called also *Tripurā-mālī*).

मोहिलियो a Braj form = मोह लिया. See *q.v.* मोह.

मोहिसन in Braj = मुझसेही. See मेा.

मोही, *m.* (*f.* inī) illusive, fascinating, bewildering, beguiling, charming.

मोहीं in Braj = (1) मुझे (2) मोही (3) मोहूकौं, *qq.v.*

मोहु in Braj = (1) मुझ ही (2) मोहूकौं, *q.v.*

मोहूकौं in Braj = (1) मुझको भी (2) मुझकोही, me too, me myself, me even, me forsooth.

मौ, *m.* (from मधु) honey.

मौं; see (1) मैं (2) मों (3) मौ (4) मौन.

मौंज, (see मुंज) *m.* (*f.* ī) made of *munj*.

मौंजी, *f.* (see मुंज) the girdle of a Brāhmaṇ (it is made of three strings of *munj*-grass.

मौंजीबन्धन, *m.* investiture with the distinguishing Brāhmaṇical cord.

मौंडा / **मौंड़ा** } *m.* (*f.* ī) shaven.

मौंसी, *more com.* **मौसी**, *q.v.*

मौका, fit, proper, suitable: *m.* a place where anything happens; a contingency.

मौकूफ, postponed, relinquished, deferred to, dependent on, devolved upon. —*k.* to cease, leave off, to abolish.

मौख्य, *m.* preëminence, chiefship.

मौग्ध, *m.* simplicity, artlessness, silliness, ignorance.

मौज, *f.* a wave; caprice, whim. — *mārnā*, to fluctuate, waver, to be capricious, to enjoy oneself without restraint. — *rakhnā*, to be whimsical, to be proud.

मौजफ्फर, *more prop.* **मुज़फ्फर**, *q.v.*

मौजूद, found, present, existing, existent, standing before, ready, at hand, in vogue.

मौड़, *m.* a kind of high-crowned hat or chaplet worn by Hindoo bridegrooms at the time of their marriage.

मौड़ा; see (1) **मौड़** (2) **मौण्डा**.

मौड़ी, *f.* (= **मौड़**) the head-dress of the bride.

मौढ्य, *more prop.* **मौग्ध**, *q.v.*

मौढ्य, *m.* ignorance, silliness, folly (*esp.* in relation to spiritual things).

मौण्डा, *m.* (*f.* ī) shaven.

मौण्ड्य, *m.* shaving the head; baldness.

मौत, *f.* death. — *lagnā*, to court death.

मौन, *m.* silence, taciturnity, speechless (assumed by Hindoo devotees as a vow). — *gahnā*, to be silent.

मौनता, *f.* = **मौन**, *q.v.*

मौनव्रत, 1, *m.* a vow of silence: 2, *m.* (*f.* ā) *adj.* observing a vow of silence, holding one's tongue.

मौना, *m.* a large jar: a basket.

मौनी, 1, *f.* (dim. of **मौना**) a small round basket, a work-basket: 2, *m.* (*f.* inī) a taciturn person; a class of Hindoo ascetics who make a vow to observe perpetual silence; hence, *generally*, one who has overcome his passions and retired from the world, an ascetic, hermit, religious sage.

मौमाखी, *f.* (**मधुमक्षिका**) a honey-bee.

मौर, 1, (*corruption*) = **मौड़**, *q.v.*: 2, *m.* the blossom of a tree (especially of the mango).

मौराना, *a. int.* to blossom, flourish (said especially of the mango-tree).

मौरु (*poet.*) = **मौड़**, *q.v.*

मौर्ख्य, *m.* stupidity, folly, fatuity.

मौल, proceeding from a root, of pure blood, descended from those who were resident in a place when it was built, original, ancient, radical, of long standing.

मौलना, *a. int.* to bloom, bud, blossom (said of the mango-tree): *t.* to intoxicate (said of bhang).

मौलरा; see **मौड़**.

मौलरी; see **मौड़ी**.

मौलसरी, *f.* a certain tree (*Mimusops elengi*) the flowers of which are highly fragrant.

मौलसिरी, *more com.* **मौलसरी**, *q.v.*

मौलि, *m. f.* a lock of hair on the crown of the head, hair ornamented and braided around the head; a crown, diadem, tiara; the head.

मौलिक, of inferior rank or caste among Kayasths.

मौली, *f.* 1, = **मौलि**, *q.v.*: 2, the earth.

मौवत; see (1) **मौत** (2) **नौबत**.

मौसम, *m.* season, time.

मौसरी; see (1) **मौलसरी** (2) **मूसरी**.

मौसिम, *m.* season, time.

मौसा, *m.* an uncle (mother's sister's husband).

मौसी, *f.* an aunt (mother's sister).

मौसेरा, *m.* (*f.* ī) belonging to or related to a mother's sister's husband.

मौसेरा भाई, *m.* a cousin (son of a mother's sister).

मौसेरी बहिन, *f.* a cousin (daughter of a mother's sister).

मौह; see (1) **मौह** (2) **महूआ**.

मौहा, *more com.* **महूआ**, *q. v.*

मौहि in Braj = **मुझको**.

मौहोव in Chand = **महोबा**, *q.v.*

म्यूं, (*onomatopoetic*) the cry of a cat, 'mew'. —*k.* to mew, to cry as a cat.

म्लान, *m.* (*f.* ā) withered, faded; languid, faint, melancholy; foul, dirty.

म्लानि, *f.* decay, fading, languor, weariness, faintness, sadness, melancholy, foulness, filth.

म्लेच्छ, *m.* a barbarian, foreigner, person of an outcaste race; an unclean person, a sinner. This epithet is applied by Hindoos to those who make no distinction between clean and unclean food, who are not subject to the recognized Hindoo institutions, or who speak any other language than Sanskrit or some language immediately derived from it. The tribes enumerated under this head by Manu (but who, he says, are properly speaking, degraded Kshatriyas) appear to be chiefly the inhabitants of the countries bordering immediately on India.

म्लेच्छजाति, *m. f.* (= **म्लेच्छ**) a person of an outcaste race, a barbarian.

म्लेच्छदेश, *m.* the countries bordering in India, or any country that may be inhabited by people whose language, institutions, and faith, differ from those of the Hindoos, any country where the black antelope is not found.

म्लेच्छभोजन, *m.* wheat; half-ripe barley. [dialect.

म्लेच्छवाक, *m.* (*f.* ī) one who speaks a barbarous

म्लेच्छित, *m.* foreign or barbarous language, ungrammatical speech; *adj.* spoken inaccurately or barbarously.

म्लेक, for words beginning thus, see under the form **म्लेच्छ**.

म्वाफिक, *more prop.* **मुवाफ़िक़**, *q. v.*

म्हाड़ी, *f.* an upper story, upper room; a house; a stately dwelling, mansion, palace, edifice.

म्हारा, *m.* (*f.* i) a dialectic form of **मेरा**, *q.v.*

म्हूर (*dialectic*) = **मोर**, *q.v.*

म्हूरी, *f.* a water-channel, drain, pipe.

म्हेन्दा, *m.* / **म्हेन्दी**, *f.* } (colloquial) = **मेन्धी**, *q. v.*

म्हैंस, a dialectic form of **भैंस**, *q. v.*

म्हेल in Māṛwāṛī = **महल्ल**, *q. v.*

य

य (y) is the twenty-sixth consonant in the Hindee alphabet, and has the following characteristics and functions:—1, It belongs to the class of palatals, and is the first of the semivowels or *antuhsth* letters; see अन्तःस्थ. 2, At the beginning of words and syllables its true pronunciation is that of the English letter *y* in 'young'; in other situations also (especially when it is part of a compound letter) this is its sound; *e. g.* सूर्य्य. When, however, it does not stand at the head of a word or syllable, its pronunciation (in Hindee, though not in Sanskrit) resembles that of the English letter *i*; thus जाय is pronounced as if it were spelt जाइ or जाई; and, indeed, it often is so spelt. This arises from the fact that in Hindee the inherent vowel (see अ, 2,3) is not, as a rule, pronounced at the end of words. 3, It is of very great importance to observe that this letter, in whatsoever situation it may be found (excepting when it ends a word, as in जाय, जय, etc.) is continually interchanged with ज; *e. g.* जुग = युग; सूरज = सूर्य्य (see ज, 2). In compiling the present work it has been thought advisable (even at the risk of the imputation of pedantry) to give the meanings of a word under its true form only, whenever that form has been ascertainable. There is scarcely one word beginning with this letter which is not continually pronounced and written as if it began with ज. 4, This letter is very frequently interchanged with ऐ; *e. g.* नैन = नयन; and occasionally with च; *e. g.* लोयन, properly लोचन; and with र; *e. g.* बिरोग, properly वियोग; and with श; *e. g.* संसा, properly संशय; समा, properly समय. 5, In the Rāmāyan, and in the poets generally, this letter is found in place of the proper sign of the second person plural of the imperative; *e. g.* दारय = दारो; धारिय = धारिये. 6, This letter is inserted euphonically in the formation of the masculine of the past participle passive of the historical tenses of those verbs whose base ends in a vowel; *e. g.* पाया, किया; in the feminine form of such words the proper spelling is resumed; *e. g.* पाई, किई. It may be important to guard against the remark of Shakespear (see *s. v.* आस; 4th edn. 1861) and of Forbes (see *s. v.* आस; 2nd edn. 1866) that पियास = पी + आशा; since, if this were an accurate account of the construction of पियास, this word (and others similar in appearance) might seem to point to another class of instances of a euphonic function of य. पियास is a Prākrit form of the Sanskrit word पिपास, which is formed in accordance with the rules for the formation of Desiderative words (see the Sanskrit Grammars). The point to guard against is, that पियास does not (as those learned gentlemen have affirmed it does) contain the word आशा. 7, As a Taddhita suffix it is employed to form patronymics; *e. g.* गार्ग्य, a male descendant of गर्ग. 8, As a Taddhita suffix it also forms a number of adjectives from substantives (*e. g.* नासिक्य, from नासिका; द्वैप्य, from द्वीप), the radical vowel of the word to which it is thus subjoined sometimes remaining unaltered (in which case the fem. is formed by the addition of ā), and sometimes undergoing a *vriddhi* change (in which case the fem. is formed by adding ī). 9, As a Taddhita suffix it also serves to form abstract substantives masculine equivalent to those ending in त्व; *e. g.* तरुणय = तरुणत्व; मौढ्य = मूढ़त्व. 10, When it follows a vowel it is liable to be interchanged with ए. This phenomenon takes place most frequently in the dependant mode of verbs whose base ends in a long vowel, and assumes a variety of forms; *e. g.* होए is most frequently written होय, होये, होवे. It is also continually found added to the first form of the conjunct participle of verbs of that description; *e. g.* जाय, more properly जा, *i. e.* जाके. These phenomena occur chiefly in colloquial speech, and seem to be occasioned by nature's *horror vacui.* 11, This is one of the terminations by which in Sanskrit the future participle of the passive is formed: it is important to notice this as this Sanskrit form is very largely represented in Hindee. The form is expressed in English by the phrase 'to be' and by the termination 'able'; *e. g.* ग्राह्य, to be accepted, *i. e.* acceptable: the *fem.* is formed by adding *ā*. 12, In some parts of the country this letter (when it occurs at the beginning of words) is frequently interchanged with ए: the most noteworthy instance of this is the word एक, which is continually pronounced and written after the Persian manner, यक. It is liable also to be interchanged with अ; *e. g.* यकेला. It is also occasionally corrupted into ए or ऐ; *e. g.* बिखे, बिखै, properly विषय. 13, In works on Prosody this letter is used for the metrical foot Bacchic or Bacchius (⏑ — —) consisting of a short syllable followed by two long ones. 14, In the older Hindee and in poetry, this letter is frequently joined to the final consonant in the past participial forms of certain verbs; *e. g.* बोल्यौ = बोला. 15, Not only do words which properly contain this letter frequently reject it for ज, but the reverse is also true, *viz.* that words which properly contain ज exchange it for य; *e. g.* राय, properly राजा. 16. This letter also stands occasionally for an original ज्ञ, and even for झ; *e. g.* सयाना = सज्ञान; and मयारे = मझारे. 17. In very corrupt Hindee this letter is occasionally found where we might properly expect यह.

यं (Rām.) = जिसको. See य, 17.

यंग, *more prop.* जंग, *q.v.*

यंत्र; for words beginning thus, see under the [form यन्त्र.

यद; see (1) जद (2) यहो.

यक (*colloquial*) = एक, *q. v.* See य, 12.

यकंग, alone, lonely, solitary.

यकता, *m.* (*f.* ī) single; simple; unique: hence, *m.* a garment without a lining.

यकतारा, *m.* a kind of guitar with one string.

यकत्रा (*colloquial*) = एकत्रा, *q.v.*

यकेला in Braj = अकेला, *q. v.*

यकलौता, *m.* (*f.* ī) (*colloquial*) = एकलौठा, *q. v.*

यकस (*dialectic*) = एक, *q.v.*

यकसां, *more com.* एकसां, *q.v.*

यकार, *m.* the letter **य**, or any or symbol that may represent it.

यक़ीन, 1, *m.* certainty, truth: 2, true, certain. — *k.* to ascertain.—*rakhnā* or *lānā*, to feel certain, to believe.—*honā*, to be certain.

यकेला, *m.* (*f.* ī) (*colloquial*) = **अकेला**, *q. v.*

यको = **एक भो**. See **यक**; **य**, 11; **ओ**, 5.

यकोत्रा (*colloquial*) = **एकत्रा**, *q. v.*

यक्तालोस (*colloquial*) = **एकतालोस**, *q. v.*

यक्ष, 1, *m.* (*f.* ī) a kind of demigod attendant especially on Kuver and employed in the care of his gardens and treasures: 2, *m.* an epithet (1) of Kuver (2) of the palace of Indra.

यक्षकुवेर, *m.* (see **यक्ष**) an epithet of Kuver.

यक्षणी }
यक्षनी } *more prop.* **यक्षिणी**, *q. v.*

यक्षपति, *m.* (see **यक्ष**) an epithet of Kuver.

यक्षिणी = **यक्षी**, *q. v.*

यक्षी, 1, *f. pr. n.* [see **यक्ष**, 2 (1)] the wife of Kuver: 2, *f.* any female *yaksh* or fairy.

यक्ष्म }
यक्ष्मन } *m.* pulmonary consumption.
यक्ष्मा }

यक्ष्मी, *m.* (*f.* iṇī) one who is afflicted with pulmonary consumption: *lit.* phthisical.

यगण, *m.* (in Pros.) a Bacchius: see **य**, 12.

यच्छ, **यछ**; for words beginning thus, see under the form **यक्ष**.

यजमान, *m.* (*f.* ī) a person who institutes the performance of a sacrifice, employs priests for the purpose, and pays the expenses of it: a customer: a person to whose custom Brāhmaṇs, barbers, and some others, have a legal claim. The hereditary Brāhman, barber, etc. of a village must be paid his fees whether one choose to employ him or another person.

यजमानी, *f.* the wife of a *yajmān*: the stipend paid by a *yajmān*: the status and the occupation of a *yajmān*.

यज़ीद, *m. pr. n.* a certain arch-heretic among Muhammadans (the prince by whose order the Imām Husain was put to death at Karbalā); *hence*, wicked, cruel, execrable, accused.

यजु }
यजुः } = **यजुस**, *q. v.*
यजुर }

यजुर्वेद (**यजुस** + **वेद**) = **यजुस**, 2, *q. v.*

यजुस, 1, *m.* a short prayer or invocation not restricted to metre: 2, *m. pr. n.* the second of the four Veds. It is divided into two portions, the white and the black: both portions of it are very full on the subject of religious rites, and the prayers peculiar to it are chiefly in measured and poetical prose.

यज्ञ, *m.* oblation, sacrifice; a religious offering; a ceremony in which oblations are offered.

यज्ञकरावन = **यजमान**, *q. v.*

यज्ञकर्म्म, *m.* any sacrificial act or ceremony.

यज्ञकेतु, *m. pr. n.* a certain Rākshas.

यज्ञडुम्बुर, *m.* a species of figtree (*Ficus glomerata*).

यज्ञपशु, *m.* any animal offered in sacrifice; a horse.

यज्ञपात्र, *m.* a sacrificial vessel.

यज्ञपुरुष, *m.* an epithet of Vishṇu.

यज्ञप्रलय, *m.* the destruction of a **यज्ञ**, *q. v.*

यज्ञभूमि, *f.* a locality prepared for a sacrifice, a place where sacrifice is offered.

यज्ञवेदि }
यज्ञवेदी } *f.* a sacrificial altar.

यज्ञशाला, *f.* a house or hall for the celebration of sacrifice, a temple, shrine.

यज्ञसिद्धि, *f.* the performance or accomplishment of a sacrifice: the obtaining the objects of sacrifice.

यज्ञसूत्र, *m.* the sacrificial thread originally worn (by the Brāhmaṇ, the Kshatriya, and the Vaishya) as distinctive of their castes, but now confined to the Brāhmanical order.

यज्ञस्थान, *m.* = **यज्ञभूमि**, *q. v.*

यज्ञावतार, *m. pr. n.* the boar-*avatār*. See **अवतार**.

यज्ञिय, appertaining to sacrifice, sacrificial, proper (or suitable) to be offered in sacrifice.

यज्ञियदेश, *m.* (see **म्लेच्छदेश**) an epithet of Hindūstān or the land of the Hindoos. Properly, that country in which the ritual and institutions of the Hindoo religion are performed, or the country in which the black antelope is found.

यज्ञोपवीत = **यज्ञसूत्र**, *q. v.* the sacrificial thread.

यज्ञोपवीती, *m.* (*f.* inī) a person who is invested with the sacrificial thread.

यतन; for words beginning thus, see under the form **यत्न**.

यतव्रत, *m.* (*f.* ā) one who is firm to an engagement or vow.

यति, 1, *m.* (*f.* **यती**) = **यती**, 2, *q. v.*: 2, *f.* cessation, pause, stopping, restraint, check; (in Pros.) pause.

यतिनी, *f.* (*m.* **यती**) a widow.

यती, 1, *f.* (*m.* **यति**) a widow: 2, *m.* (*f.* inī) a person whose passions are completely subdued; a religious mendicant, sage, ascetic devotee. The term is specially applied to mendicants of the Jain sect.

यतीम, *m.* a fatherless child, orphan; a ward, a pupil: a valuable jewel.

यतेन्द्रिय (*corruption*) = **जितेन्द्रिय**, *q. v.*

यत्न, *m.* effort, endeavour, exertion, striving, energy, perseverance, zeal, labour, diligence, care.

यत्नवत, *m.* (*f.* vatī) strenuous, making effort or exertion, persevering, laborious, energetic, diligent, careful.

यत्नवती, *f.* (*m.* **यत्नवान**, etc.) an energetic female.

यत्नवन्त }
यत्नवान } *m.* (*f.* vatī) = **यत्नवत**, *q. v.*

यत्नी, *m.* (*f.* inī) = **यत्नवत**, *q. v.*

यत्नीय, requiring to be made a matter of exertion or diligence, to be persevered in.

यत्र, in whatever place, wheresoever, where, wherein.

यथा, in which manner, like, as, according to, thus, so.

यथाउचित, *more prop.* **यथोचित**, *q. v.*

यथाकथंचित, in any manner, anywise, anyhow, in some way or other.

यथाकर्त्तव्य, according as is right or proper to be done.

यथाकल्प, according to design.

यथाकाम, according to pleasure, at pleasure, agreeably to one's wishes, optionally.

यथाकामी, according to inclination, self-willed, independent: hence, *m.* (*f.* inī) a wayward person.

यथाकाल, in due time, according to the time, opportunely.

यथाक्रम, in regular order, in due succession, orderly, successively, methodically.

यथाजोग (*colloquial*) = **यथायोग्य**, *q. v.*

यथातथा, in every way, by all means.

यथाथित = **यथास्थित**, *q. v.*

यथाभिमत, according to one's wish or purpose.

यथामुखीन, like, resembling, shewing similarly, reflecting an appearance.

यथायथा, in what proportion, in any manner, howsoever, anyhow.

यथायोग्य, according as is befitting, in a proper manner, suitably, appropriately.

यथार्थ, 1, according to the sense, accurate, genuine, suitable, proper, right: 2, truly, properly, suitably, exactly.

यथार्थत्व, *m.* (*f.* tā) genuineness, fitness, accurateness, propriety, suitableness.

यथावकाश, according to leisure, according to opportunity, as occasion offers.

यथावत, exactly as it was, truly, according to law or usage, in due manner or order, duly.

यथावसर = **यथावकाश**, *q. v.*.

यथावस्थित, *m.* (*f.* ā) reinstated.

यथाविध (contraction) = **यथाविधि**, *q. v.*

यथाविधि, conformably to the precept, according to the rule.

यथाशक्ति, to the extent of one's power or capability, according to one's capacity, as much as possible.

यथाशास्त्र, conformably to the codes of law or to the precepts of science, according to scripture.

यथासम्भव, according to circumstances, suitable.

यथास्थित, as it took place, circumstantially.

यथेच्छ, in harmony with one's desire, according to one's wishes, as one lists.

यथेच्छम / **यथेच्छा** / **यथेच्छुक** } = **यथेच्छ**, *q v.*

यथेष्ट, conformably to one's desire or wish; sufficient, enough.

यथोक्त, conformably to what has been already stated, as above-mentioned, as aforesaid.

यथोचित, according to fitness or propriety, as is right or befitting, suitable, appropriate, proportionate.

यदपि, *more prop.* **यद्यपि**, *q. v.*

यदभविष्य, *m.* (*f.* ā) one who believes in the power of fate, a fatalist: *pr. n.* a certain fish (in the *Hitopadesh*).

यदवधि, (**यदा** + **अवधि**) at the time when the allotted period shall be completed.

यदा, what time, when, at the time when, while, whilst.

यदातदा, somehow or other.

यदि, in case that, if, though, since.

यदु, *m. pr. n.* (1) of a celebrated ancient king, the eldest son of Yayāti and ancestor of Krishṇ (2) of the country (on the west of the Yamunā about Mathura and Vrindāvan) over which he ruled (3) of his descendants.

यदुकुल, *m.* (see **यदु**) the race of Yadu.

यदुगति, *f.* the manners or doings of the Yadus.

यदुनाथ, *m.* (see **यदु**) lord of the Yadus, *i.e.* Kṛishṇ.

यदुपति / **यदुराज** / **यदुराम** / **यदुराय** } = **यदुनाथ**, *q.v.*

यदुवंश, *m.* (see **यदु**) the race of Yadu.

यदुवंशी, appertaining to the race of Yadu; hence, *m.* (*f.* inī) a descendant of Yadu.

यदुबंस (*corruption*) = **यदुवंश**, *q. v.*

यद्दे, (a dialectic contraction of **यह देखो**) = see here! lo! here it is!

यद्यपि, though, although, though even, even if, notwithstanding that.

यन, in Braj a common inflexional termination of the base of the plural of substantives and adjectives; *e. g.* **स्त्रीयनकों** = **स्त्रियोंका**.

यनहीं = **या नहीं** = **अथवा नहीं**.

यना; see (1) **ज़ना** (2) **ज़िना** (3) **यनहीं**.

यनाम; see **यह नाम**.

यने, *more com.* **याने**, *q. v.*

यन्त्र, *m.* an engine or machine of any kind, instrument, apparatus, implement, a dial, an observatory, a musical instrument, an astrolabe, a diagram (of a mystical, astrological, or magical nature), an amulet; a thong; a sort of vessel; juggling.

यन्त्रक, *m.* a checking, controlling, binding: pain, anguish.

यन्त्रणा, *f.* restraint, control; anguish, pain, torture, affliction, torment.

यन्त्रमन्त्र, *m.* enchanting by figures and incantations, juggling, conjuring.

यन्त्रराज, *m.* the astrolabe.

यन्त्रालय, *m.* an engine-house, a printing-office, any establishment where machines are made, sold, or worked.

यन्त्रिका, *f.* any instrument or means for binding, a chain, fetters.

यन्त्रित, *m.* (*f.* ā) restrained, curbed, checked, bound.

यन्त्री, 1, *f.* an instrument for drawing wire: 2, *m.* (*f.* inī) a juggler, conjurer, wizard, a player on any instrument of music, etc: *lit.* having to do with instruments, mechanical, ingenious, crafty, designing.

यन्दरोज, *more prop.* **चन्दरोज़**, *q. v.*

यभी; see (1) **यहभी** (2) **अबही**.

यम, 1, *m.* (*f.* ī) of a pair, a twin, fellow (*hence*, in the ingenious system of reckoning by symbols adopted by Hindoos in their poetry, this word is a symbol for 2): 2, *m.* restraining, taming, subduing; penance; moral duty; a festival: 3, *m. pr. n.* the Pluto of the Hindoo mythology, regent of the infernal world, and judge of departed spirits; *hence*, 4, death; time.

यमक, 1, *m.* (*f.* ikā) = **यमल**, *q. v.*: 2, *m.* (in Rhet.) a species of alliteration (the repeating a word in different significations).

यमकरधार, *m.* the army of Yam.

यमकाल, *m.* an epithet of the time of death; also, of Yam.

यमज, *m.* (*f.* ā) one of a pair or brace, a twin-fellow.

यमदग्नि, *m.* the fire of hell.

यमदिया, *m.* a lamp or illumination sacred to Yam lighted on the 13th of the *Krishṇpaksh* of Karttik, *i.e.* three days before the Dewālee.

यमदुतिया ; see **यमद्वितीया** and **यमदूत**.

यमदूत, *m. pr. n.* the angel or messenger of death (an infernal spirit employed to bring the souls of the dead to the judgment-seat of Yam and to conduct them thence to their final destination).

यमद्वितीया, *f.* the second day in the light half of the mouth Kārttik. On this day brothers and sisters dress up and exchange gifts and compliments, in allusion to the attachment of Yam and his sister Yamunā.

यमन, 1, (*corruption*) = **यवन**, *q. v.* : 2, *m.* a certain musical mode (*rāg*).

यमनी, appertaining to Yaman : *m.* a cornelian.

यमपुर, *m.* = **यमपुरी**, *q. v.* [the city or abode of Yam.

यमपुरी, *f.* an epithet of the infernal regions ; *lit.*

यमराज = **यम**, 3, *q. v.*

यमल, *m.* a pair, brace, couple.

यमला, *f.* a kind of hiccough : *pr. n.* (1) of a certain Tantra deity (2) of a certain river.

यमलार्जुन, *m. pr. n.* two Arjun-trees which obstructed the path of Krishṇ when a child and were uprooted by him.

यमली, *f.* a sort of dress (body and petticoat).

यमलोक, *m.* Yam's world, the region of Yam.

यमानी ; see (1) **यमनी** (2) **यमी** (3) **यवानी** (4) **युमानी**.

यमालय, *m.* the residence of Yam.

यमिका, *f.* (*m.* **यमक**, 1,) a twin-sister.

यमी, *f.* (*m.* **यम**) a twin-sister : *pr. n.* (1) of the wife of Yam (2) of the Yamunā river.

यमुन, *more prop.* (1) **यमुना** (2) **जमुन**, 2, *qq. v.*

यमुना, *f. pr. n.* the river Jumna (Yamunā) which rises on the southern side of the Himālaya range at a short distance north-west of the source of the Ganges; and which, after a course of about 860 miles, falls into the Ganges at Pryāg (Allahabad). In mythology, this river is considered daughter of Sūrya and twin-sister of Yam.

यमुनातीर, *m.* the banks of the Yamunā.

यमुनोत्री, *f. pr. n.* the source of the Yamunā, the place where it issues from the mountains.

यमुहाई, *more prop.* **जमुहाई**, *q. v.*

ययाति, *m. pr. n.* (see **यदु**) a certain king (the fifth monarch of the lunar dynasty).

ययुर्वेद (corruption) = **यजुर्वेद**, *q. v.*

यरमियाह, *m. pr. n.* the prophet Jeremiah and the Book that bears his name.

यरु, *m.* manure, compost, dung.

यरुसलम, *f. pr. n.* the city of Jerusalem.

यर्दन, *f. pr. n.* the river Jordan.

यलाफैला, unconfined, extended, spread out, at ease.

यव, *m.* barley (*Hordeum hexastichum*); a corn of barley ; the measure of a barley corn (considered as equal to six mustard-seeds or the third part of an inch) ; a natural line across the joint of the thumb supposed to indicate good fortune : velocity. *Yav-yav hisāb lenā*, to take a strict and minute account.

यवक्षार, *m.* nitrate of potash (saltpetre, nitre).

यवखार (*corruption*) = **यवक्षार**, *q. v.*

यवन, *m.* (*f.* ī) 1, a swift horse : *lit.* swift : 2, *pr. n.* (1) of a certain country, most probably Bactria if not Ionia or Greece : by later Hindoo writers it is most commonly applied to Arabia, or in general to those countries inhabited by Musalmāns (2) of the inhabitants of that country, originally the Greeks, but subseqnently applied to both Muhammadan and European invaders of India, and to foreigners and barbarians generally.

यवनाचार्य, *m. pr. n.* a certain writer on Astronomy frequently alluded to by ancient Hindoo writers (perhaps Ptolemy or Greek astronomers collectively).

यवनाल, *m.* a certain grass (*Andropogon* or *Holcus bicolor*) which is very generally cultivated and the grain of which is very extensively eaten.

यवनिका, *f.* a curtain ; tent-curtains.

यवनी, *f.* (*m.* **यवन**) a female *Yavan*.

यवफल, *m.* a certain medicinal plant (*Wrightea antidysenterica*) : a bamboo.

यवमध्य, *m.* a certain species of penance (the diminishing the food daily during the dark fortnight, fasting on the new moon, and gradually augmenting the food till the full moon).

यवांकुर, *m.* a sprout or blade of barley.

यवानी, *f.* a certain plant (*Liqusticum ajwaen*).

यवास, *m.* a certain plant (*Hedysarum alhagi*) and its flower.

यश, *m.* glory, splendour, lustre, fame, celebrity, renown, praise, eulogium, reputation, name, character, luck.

यशअपयश, *m.* good and bad reputation, fame and ill-fame, praise and dispraise.

यशः = **यशस्**, *q. v.*

यशकर *m.* (*f.* ī) (*contraction*) = **यशस्कर**, *q. v.*

यशकाम, *m.* (*f.* ā) (*contraction*) = **यशस्काम**, *q. v.*

यशदाई, *m.* (*f.* inī) a panegyrist, eulogist, encomiast.

यशपत (*contraction*) = **यशपति**, *q. v.*

यशपति, famous, excellent, reputable, renowned: hence, *m.* (*f.* patnī) a celebrity.

यशवती, *f. pr. n.* a daughter of Vishwakarmā by Varhishmatī.

यशवन्त, *m.* (*f.* vati) = **यशस्वी**, *q. v.*

यशवी, *m.* (*f.* inī) = (1) **यशस्वी** (2) **योश्वी**, *qq. v.*

यशस (Sk. form) = **यश**, *q. v.*

यशस्क, 1, *m.* (*f.* ī) = **यशस्कर**, *q. v.* : 2, *m.* = **यश**, *q. v.* : 3, *m.* (*f.* ī) whose repute is but small.

यशस्कर, *m* (*f.* ī) *adj.* rendering famous or glorious, conferring distinction or celebrity.

यशस्काम, desirous of fame or glory: hence, *m.* (*f.* ā) an ambitious person.

यशस्की, *f.* ; see **यशस्क**.

यशस्वत / **यशस्वन्त** / **यशस्वान** } *m.* (*f.* vatī) = **यशस्वी**, *q. v.*

यशस्वी, glorious, famous, reputable, celebrated, renowned: hence, *m.* (*f.* inī) a celebrity, etc.

यशाया, *m. pr. n.* the prophet Isaiah, and the Book that bears his name.

यशी, *m.* (*f.* inī) = **यशस्वी**, *q. v.*

यशुति, a contraction of **यशुमति**, *q. v.*

यशुद्ध; see (1) **अशुद्ध** (2) **यह अशुद्ध**.

यशुमती = **यशोदा**, *q. v.*

यशोद (*contraction*) = **यशोदा**, *q. v.*

यशोदमति = **यशोदा**, *q. v.*

यशोदा, *f. pr. n.* (see **देवकी**) the wife of Nand and foster-mother of Krishṇ.

यशोमति, 1, = **यशोदा**, *q. v.* : 2, *f.* the third lunar night.

यष्टि, 1, *m. f.* a staff, stick, perch, stem, support, palisade, a staff armed with iron, etc. used as a weapon, a club, mace; a thread to be strung with pearls, a string, a necklace; any creeping-plant; liquorice, a certain shrub (*Siponanthus Indica*): 2, *m.* a flagstaff; the arm and fore-arm.

यष्टिक, *m.* (*f.* ā) the lapwing, [ice; a pond.

यष्टिका, *f.* a staff, club, mace; a necklace; liquor-

यष्टिमधु, *m.* (*f.* ā) liquorice, or the root of the *Abrus precatorius* which is used instead of it.

यष्टी, *f.* = **यष्टि**, 1, *q. v.* [see under the form **यश**.

यस; for words beginning thus, but not given below,

यसमन, a corruption of **यह समन**, *qq. v.*

यसअियाह, *m. pr. n.* the prophet Isaiah and the Book that bears his name. [affluence, plenty.

यसार, *m.* the left: an unlucky person: opulence,

यसू, *more prop.* **योशु**, *q. v.*

यस्सी; see (1) **यशस्वी** (2) **योज्यी**.

यह, (correl. of **वह**) the pronoun nearer demonstrative (gen. **इसका**) *m. f.* this, this person: (sometimes *plural*) these; but see **ये**: (sometimes *adverbial*) to this extent that; but see **यहालों**.

यहं (contraction) = **यहां**, *q. v.*

यहंलगि (colloquial) = **यहांलग**, *q. v.*

यहग्रीव, *m.* an epithet of Vishṇu.

यहां, 1, in this place, here; hereabout; hither: 2, *postp.* (takes gen. *m.* infl.) at the abode of, in the neighbourhood of, near, with, apud, chez, bei. *Yahāṅkā yahin*, in this very place, exactly, here.

यहांकहीं, here somewhere, here or hereabouts, somewhere here. [place.

यहांका, (gen. of **यहां**) *m.* (*f.* ī) appertaining to this

यहांतक / **यहांतलक** / **यहांलग** } = **यहालों**, *q. v.*

यहालों, thus far, to this degree, to such an extent that, so much so that, to this pitch, hitherto.

यहांसे, (abl. of **यहां**) from here, hence.

यहि (contraction) = **यही**, *q. v.*

यही, (see **ही**) nearer demonstrative pronoun emphatic: *m. f.* this very (person or thing), this same, this very same, this even.

यहीं, 1, a form of **यही**, *q. v.* : 2, (emphatic of **यहां**: see **हीं**) in this very place, exactly in this spot.

यहींसे, (abl. of **यहीं**) from this very place, on this very account hence.

यहु (Rām.) = **यह समय**.

यहूद = **यहूदी**, *q. v.*

यहूदा, *m pr. n.* Judah, Judas, Jude.

यहूदाह, *m. pr. n.* the land of Judea.

यहूदिनी, *f.* (*m.* **यहूदी**) a Jewess.

यहूदी, *m.* (*f.* inī) a Hebrew, Jew: *lit.* appertaining to the Hebrews, Israelitish, Jewish, Judean.

यहूदीय, appertaining to Judea or to the Jews: hence, *m.* (*f.* ā) = **यहूदी**, *q v.*

यहूदीया, *m. pr. n.* the land of Judea.

यहूवाह, *m. pr. n.* Jehovah.

यहै, an old form of **यही**, *q. v.*

या, 1, in Braj, the base of the oblique cases of the sing. of **यह**: 2, (*colloquial*) = **यह**, *q. v.* : 3, or, either, whether: 4, a Kridanta suffix forming certain substantives, *fem.* from verbal roots; *e. g.* **विद्या** (Rt. **विद्**): 5, a Taddhita suffix forming collective substantives, *e. g.* **रथ्या**: 6. It also forms many nominals by being added to substantives; *e. g.* **बटोहिया**.

यां, 1, (contraction) = **यहां**, *q. v.* : 2, *more prop.* **यह**, *q. v.*

यांते in Braj = (1) **यहांसे** (2) **इससे**.

याका, *m.* (*f.* ī) in Braj = **इसका**. See **या**, 2.

याकि, (1) *more prop.* **याकी** (2) = **अथवा**; see **या**, 3.

याकु in the Rīva dialect = **एक**, *q. v.*

याकूत, *m.* a precious stone, ruby, garnet.

याकूती, 1, appertaining to a ruby, ruby-coloured: 2, a kind of ornamental hand-writing: a kind of medicine.

याकूब, *m. pr. n.* Jacob, James.

याके in Braj = **इसके**. See **या**, 2.

याको; see (1) **याकि** (2) **याकी** (3) **याकीं**

याकी, *m.* (*f.* ī) in Braj = **इसका**. See **या**, 2.

याकीं in Braj = **इसे** (dat. and acc.). See **या**, 2.

याग (colloquial) = **यज्ञ**, *q. v.* See **आ**, 3.

याचक, *adj.* asking, soliciting: hence, *m.* (*f.* ikā) a petitioner, suitor, candidate, beggar, mendicant.

याचना, 1, *f.* asking, soliciting, begging: 2, *t.* (with gen.) to want, need, require, implore, solicit, ask, beg.

याचिका, *f.* (*m.* **याचक**) a female petitioner.

याचित, *m.* (*f.* ā) asked, solicited, prayed for, begged, acquired by begging: *hence*, any borrowed thing, (in Law) a particular form of deposit whereby the holder is allowed the use of the article deposited.

याचितक, *m.* = **याचित**, *q. v.* [begging.

याचितता, *f.* a collection of things acquired by

याजक, *m.* (*f.* ikā) an officiating or sacrificing priest: a player on cymbals or on the tabor: a royal elephant, a furious elephant: *lit.* adj. performing sacrifice.

याजकत्व, *m.* (*f.* tā) the status or the functions of a priest, priestship, priesthood.

याजकीय, appertaining to a priest or to the priestly office, priestly, sacredotal.

याजन, *m.* the conducting a sacrifice, the causing or assisting others to perform sacrifice, sacrificing.

याजिका, *f.* (*m.* **याजक**) a priestess, etc.

याजूजमाजूज, *m. pr. n.* Gog and Magog.

याज, *more prop.* यज्ञ, *q.v.* See आ, 3.

याज्ञवल्क्य, *m. pr. n.* a celebrated ancient Hindoo saint-sage and legislator.

याज्ञिक, *m.* (*f.* ā *or* ī) the institutor of a sacrifice, a sacrificer, officiating priest: *lit.* sacrificial.

याज्ञिय, *m.* (*f.* ā) fit for sacrifice.

याज्य, 1, *m.* (*f.* ā) fit to be offered in sacrifice, to be effected by sacrifice: 2, *m.* property or presents obtained by officiating at sacrifices: a place for sacrifice: 3, *m.* (*f.* ā) one for whom (and at whose expense) a sacrifice is offered; one who performs sacrifice for others.

याणा, in the hill dialect = snow, ice.—*ṭuṭṇo* describes the fall of an avalanche.

यातना, *f.* acute pain, torment, anguish, agony, punishment, requital, the pains of hell.

यातायात, *m.* a coming and going, intercourse, transmigration. [imp, goblin, *rākshas.*

यातु, *m. f.* (*lit.* a goer, traveller; *hence*) time; an

यातुधान, *m.* (*f.* ī) a goblin, demon, *rākshas.*

याते / यातें } in Braj = यातें = यहांसे, *q.v.* See या, 2.

याता = अथवा, *q.v.* See या, 3, and ता.

यात्रा, *f.* a going, travelling, proceeding, marching, going on pilgrimage, procession of idols, departure, march, journey, the passing away time; a theatrical representation; practice, conduct, usage; intercourse; an expedient, means of support, maintenance; a moment (generally a fortunate moment); the title of the book of Exodus. [pilgrimage.

यात्राकरण, *m.* the setting forth on a journey or

यात्रिक, *m.* (*f.* ā *or* ī) a wayfarer, traveller, pilgrim: *lit.* appertaining to a march or to an enterprize, marching, travelling, performing pilgrimage.

यात्रिन = (1) यात्री (2) यात्रिणी, *qq. v.*

यात्रिणी, *f.* (*m.* यात्री) a female traveller or pilgrim.

यात्री, *m.* (*f.* iṇī) = यात्रिक, *q.v.*

यात्रु / यात्रू } *m. f.* a traveller, pilgrim.

याथार्थ; see यथार्थ and याथार्थ्य. [real, genuine.

याथार्थिक, *m.* (*f.* ā *or* ī) just, right, righteous, true,

याथार्थिकता, *f.* / याथार्थिकत्व *m.* } = याथार्थ्य, *q.v.*

याथार्थ्य, *m.* justice, righteousness, truth, rectitude, genuineness.

याद, *f.* remembrance, memory, recollection.—*dilānā*, to remind.—*k.* or *rakhnā*, (with *gen.* or *acc.*) to bear in mind.—*honā*, (with dat. of the agent) to remember, recollect.

यादव, (patronym. of यदु) *m.* (*f.* ī) a descendant of Yadu; an epithet of Krishṇ; a stock of cattle.

यादवंशी, *more prop.* यदुवंशी, *q.v.*

यादवकुल, *m.* (see यदु) the race of Yadu.

यादवन, a Braj pl. of यादव, *q.v.* See न, 6.

यादवपति, *m.* (see यदु) an epithet of Krishṇ; *lit.* lord of Yadu.

यादवलोग, *m.* (see यदु) the race of Yadu.

यादववंशी, *more com.* यदुवंशी, *q.v.*

यादो (colloquial) = यादव, *q.v.*

यादोवंशी, *more prop.* यादववंशी = यदुवंशी, *q. v.*

यान, *m.* a going, moving, proceeding, marching; any means of locomotion (as a carriage, litter, pālkee, horse, elephant, etc.). [wit; or; for, because,

याने, that is, that is to say, namely, videlicet, to

यापन, *m.* a spending or passing away the time, the staying at a place; ejection, rejection.

यापर in Braj = इसपर. See या, 2.

याफ्त, *f* perquisite, earnings, gains, income, profit; fees, bribes, and douceurs extorted by official persons. A native official commonly speaks of a situation as being worth so much in *darmāhā* (*i. e.* regular salary), and so much in *yāft.*

याबिधि = याविधि, *q.v.*

याबू, *m.* a pony, galloway, nag.

याम, 1, *m.* a going, marching: forbearance; cessation, termination: a watch of three hours: 2, *m.* (*f.* i) appertaining to *Yam*: 3, *m.* season, time, weather.

यामत in Braj = यह मत. See या, 2.

यामनी, *more prop.* यावनी, *q.v.*

यामनीभाषा, *more prop.* यावनीभाषा, *q.v.*

यामह / यामहं } in Braj = इसमें. See (1) या, 2 (2) मह and महं.

यामाता, *m.* a son-in-law (daughter's husband); a husband, lord, master: the sunflower (*Helianthus annuus*).

यामातृ / यामातृक } *m.* = यामाता, *q.v.*

यामि, *f.* a sister; a daughter-in-law; a virtuous woman: night.

यामिक, *m.* (*f.* ā *or* ī) one who announces the watches (*yām*): *lit.* appertaining to the watches.

यामिका, *f.* night.

यामिनी, 1, (corruption) = यावनी, *q.v.*: 2, *f.* night.

यामी, *f.* 1, see याम, 2: 2, = यामि, *q.v.*

यामुन, *m.* antimony, (or rather) the sulphuret of antimony used as a collyrium.

यामें in Braj = इसमें. See या, 2.

यायो in Braj = आया (आमा) = उपजाया.

यार, (Sk. जार) *m.* (*f.* nī) a friend, lover, gallant, paramour; a companion, ally, assistant.

यारा, *m.* power, strength; boldness: a broad bracelet: the wrist: a wound: a shrewd man: friendship: necessity: toll, tax, revenue.

यारी, *f.* friendship, love; assistance, companionship; (generally) intriguing.

याला = वाला? See कौड़ियाला.

यावक, *m.* half-ripe barley, awnless barley, forced rice; barley-gruel: lac.

यावज्जीव = यावज्जीवन, *q.v.*

यावज्जीवन, as long as life shall last, to the end of life, through life, for life.

यावत, as much as, as many as, as far as, as long as; unto, till, until; in order that.

यावत्पर्य्यन्त, as long as, till, until.

यावन, *m.* (*f.* ī) appertaining to the Yavans or to their country; *hence*, Musalmān, foreign. Ionian. Greek, barbarian. [female Yavan.

यावनी, *f.* (*m.* **यावन**) the dialect of Yavans, a

यावनीभाषा, *f.* the dialect of Yavans.

यावरी, *f.* assistance, aid, help.

याविधि, in this way, after this manner.

याहे, a corruption (1) of **यहांसे** (2) of **इससे**. See **या**.

याहें in Braj = (1) **यहांसे** (2) **इससे**. See **या**.

याहां, *more prop.* **यहां**, *q.v.* [(dat. and acc.).

याहि (oblique form of **इस** or of **या**, 2) in Braj = **इसे**

याहीं in Braj = (1) **याहि** (2) **यहीं**, *qq.v.*

याहींविधि, an emphatic form of **याविधि**, *q.v.*

यिरमियाह, *more prop.* **यरमियाह**, *q.v.*

यिरुशलीम, *f. pr. n.* the city of Jerusalem.

यिशैयाह, *more prop.* **यशयियाह**, *q.v.*

यिह, *more com.* **यह**, *q.v.*

यिही, *more com.* **यही**, *q.v.*

यिहूद; for words beginning thus, see under the [form **यहूद**.

यीशु, *m. pr. n.* Jesus.

यीशवी, appertaining to Jesus or to His religion or to His followers, Christian: *hence*, 1, *m* (*f.* inī) a follower of Christ, a Christian: 2, *f.* the Christian era, anno domini. It is placed *after* the date (not *before* it, as in English); thus, १८७४ यी॰ = A. D 1874.

युक्त, *m.* (*f.* ā) joined, united, combined, identified with. adapted to, fit, proper, right, just; (used as a suffix in comp. =) endowed with, possessed of, attached to.

युक्तकरण, *m.* addition, identifying.

युक्तत्व, *m.* (*f.* tā) fitness, suitableness.

युक्तमान, *m.* (*f.* mati); see (1) **युक्त** (2) **युक्तिमान**.

युक्तरसा, *f.* a certain plant (*Mimosa octandra*).

युक्ति, *f.* junction, connexion, union, adjustment; fitness, propriety: contrivance, device, project; dexterity, skill, policy; reasoning, demonstration, inference; (in Gram.) the supplying an ellipsis.

युक्तिमान, *m.* (*f.* mati) joined, united, tied; possessing fitness, fertile in expedients, full of contrivances or plans, ingenious, clever, inventive, able competent; furnished with arguments, based on arguments, proved.

युग, *m.* a yoke; a pair, brace, couple; a term used in the game of *chausar* (the opposite of a blot, two or more men standing on the same square); a measure of four cubits; an age, period. epoch, cycle, an astronomical cycle, a lustre of five years, (in Myth.) a great period of the world. The Hindoos reckon four of these great cycles since the creation of the present world, *viz.* 1, *Krityug* or *Satyayug* which lasted 1728000 solar years: 2, *Tretāyug* which lasted 1296000 years: 3, *Dwāparyug* which lasted 864000 years: 4, *Kaliyug* (the present cycle) whose duration is to be 432000 years (of which nearly 5000 have already elapsed). In all these periods mankind are supposed to undergo a progressive deterioration; thus these four ages bear a noteworthy resemblance to the Golden, Silver, Brasen, and Iron ages of the classics. In the ingenious system of reckoning by symbols adopted by Hindoos in their poetry, this word is hence a symbol for 4. — *phūṭnā* or *phornā*, to cause a difference between friends; to fall out.

युगजोड़, *adv.* with the hands clasped (as in earnest entreaty). [once. suddenly.

युगपत, *adv.* at one time, together, conjointly, at

युगयुग, from age to age, constantly, perpetually, [eternally.

युगल, *m.* a pair, brace, couple.

युगविधि, *f.* the quality or manner of a **युग**, *q.v.*

युगव्यवस्था, *f.* the laws or economy of a **युग**, *q.v.*

युगानुयुग, from one age to another, during successive ages, to the ages of ages, for ever and ever, for ever and for evermore, to all eternity, eternally.

युगान्त, *m.* the end of an age; a destruction of the [universe.

युगान्तबन्धु, *m. f.* a fast friend.

युगान्तर, *m.* another epoch: *adv.* from age to age, in the midst of an epoch.

युग्म, *m.* a pair, brace, couple.

युत, *m.* (*f.* ā) a suffix in comp. = with, united or connected with, joined to, in contact with, endowed with, possessed of.

युथ, *more prop.* **यूथ**, *q.v.* [conflict, contest.

युद्ध, *m. f.* the use of arms, war, battle, combat,

युद्धमान, *m.* (*f.* matī) = **युध्मान**, *q.v.*

युध, 1, *f* = **युद्ध**, *q.v.*: 2, *m.* = **योधी**, *q.v.*

युधिष्ठिर, *m. pr. n.* the eldest of the five Pāṇḍav princes, and leader of the great war (related in the *Mahābhārat*) between them and the Kurus in the beginning of Kaliyug. [a warrior.

युध्मान, *adj.* fighting, warring: hence, *m.* (*f.* matī)

युनी, *f.* (*m.* **युवन**) = **युवती**, *q.v.*

युयुधान, *m. pr. n.* a certain ancient Hindoo king.

युवता, *f.* youthfulness, youth.

युवति, *f.* (*m.* **युवन**) = **युवती**, *q.v.*

युवतिन (colloquial) = **युवती**, *q.v.*

युवती, *f.* (*m.* **युवन** and **युवा**) a young woman (from 16 to 30 years of age).

युवत्व, *m.* youthfulness, youth.

युवन, *m.* (*f.* **युवती**, etc.) = **युवा**, *q.v.*

युवनाश्व, *m. pr. n.* of various persons, but especially of an ancient king, father of Māndhātā.

युवराज, *m.* a young prince associated to the throne, an heir-apparent, a king's son.

युवराज्य, *m.* the status of heir-apparent and associate in the throne, heir-apparency.

युवा, 1, (uninfl.) *m.* (*f.* **युवती**, etc.) one who has attained the age of puberty, a young man, a man from 16 to 17 years of age: *lit.* young, vigorous, strong: 2, *m.* a yoke (of a carriage or of a plough).

युवापन, *m.* the state or condition of puberty, youth (regarded as a state and condition, or as a time of life), youthfulness, adolescence.

युवावस्था, *f.* = **युवापन**, *q.v.*

युह, *more prop.* **यूह**, *q.v.* See **ह**. [bears his name.

यूएल, *m. pr. n.* the prophet Joel and the Book that

यूं, 1, = **यावत**, *q.v.*: 2, thus, in this manner, just like this. *Yūṅ na yūṅ*, one way or other, somehow or other.

यूंही (emphat. of यूं : see ही) = यूंहीं, *q.v.*

यूंहीं, (see हीं) in this very manner, exactly thus, accidentally, by chance, causelessly, cursorily, easily.

यूक, *m.* } a louse.
यूका, *f.* }

यूथ, *m.* a multitude of birds or beasts, a herd, flock, drove, band, company.

यूथप, *m.* a large elephant, the leader of a wild herd, the lord or chief among the herd (as the leader in a flock of geese, or the 'bell-wether' among sheep); the keeper or protector of a troop, the lord or captain of a band.

यूथनाथ } = यूथप, *q.v.*
यूथपति }

यूथपयूथ, *m.* a troop of leaders.

यूथा, *more prop.* यूथ, *q.v.*

यूथी, *f.* a species of jasmine (*Jasminum auriculatum*).

यूनः, *m. pr. n.* the prophet Jonah and the Book which bears his name.

यूनान, *m. pr. n.* Ionia, Ancient Greece. So calle l till subdued by the Romans; since then the term *Rūm* has been applied to the Eastern Roman Empire at large.

यूनानियान, *m.* (pl. of यूनानी) the Ionians, the Greeks.

यूनानी, appertaining to Yūnān, Greek: hence (1) *m.* (*f.* ini) an Ionian, Grecian (2) *f.* the Greek language.

यूनानीय, *m.* (*f.* ā) = यूनानी, *q. v.*

यूप, *m.* a sacrificial post to which the victim to be immolated is bound; a column erected as a trophy in honour of a victory.

यूया, *more prop.* जूआ, *q. v.*

यूरप, (Engl.) *m. pr. n.* Europe.

यूरपखण्ड, *m. pr. n.* the continent of Europe.

यूष, *m.* the water in which pulse of any kind has been boiled, pease-soup, pease-porridge, broth.

यूसुफ़, *m. pr. n.* the patriarch Joseph.

यूह, *more prop.* यूथ, *q.v.* See ह.

ये, (gen. इनका) *m. f.* (pl. of यह) these. See या, 2.

येई, (emphat. of ये : see ई, 4) = येही, *q. v.*

यें; see (1) ये (2) यहाँ.

येक, *more prop.* एक, *q. v.*

येलम, *more com.* नीलाम, *q. v.*

येवा = यावा, *q. v.*

येह in Braj = यह, *q. v.*

येही, (emphat. of ये : see ही) these very, these same, these very same, these even.

येहु (*emphat.*) = ये ही or ये भी.

यै (*provincial*) = ये, *q. v.*

यो, 1, (*dialectic*) = यह, *q. v.* : 2, = यूं, *q. v.*

योयल, *more prop.* यूयल, *q. v.*

यों, *more com.* यूं, *q. v.*

योंतों, in various ways, somehow or other.

योंही, see यूंहीं.

योंहीं, *more com.* यूंहीं, *q. v.*

योग, *m.* union, junction, joining, contact, mixture, combination, association, meeting, fitting, conflux, a lucky conjuncture, propriety, fitness, fortunate moment, occasion, opportunity; penance, devotion; a putting to (horses), connexion, the putting on armour; armour; a spy, a violator of truth or confidence; (in Arithm.) addition; (in Philos.) union with the Universal Soul by means of abstract contemplation; the concentration of the mental powers on one object only and that object the Universal Soul: *pr. n.* (1) of the system of philosophy taught by Patanjali (2) of the 27th part of a circle measured on the plane of the Ecliptic (3) of certain division of the moon's path corresponding to the twenty-eight Nakshatras: (as a suffix in comp. =) possible, capable, fit, able, worthy; *e. g. Varyog*, fit for a bridegroom, *i. e.* marriageable.

योगक्षेम, *m.* property, possessions (*esp.* such as is assigned for deeds of charity); sacrificial and conservatory acts; goods not liable to distribution among co-heirs; the custody or transport of goods; a charge for securing goods.

योगता (corruption) = योग्यता, *q. v.*

योगनाविक, *m.* a certain fish (*Silurus ascita*).

योगनिद्रा, *f.* a kind of sleep (supposed to be peculiar to devotees) which admits of the full exercise of the faculties of the mind, absorption in profound meditation; light sleep, wakefulness.

योगपट्ट, *m.* a cloth drawn by an ascetic around his lower extremities when he squats to perform religious abstraction.

योगपति, *m.* an epithet of Vishṇu.

योगबल, *m.* the power or strength derived from continued abstract meditation.

योगभाष्य, *m. pr. n.* a certain philosophical treatise of the Hindoos by Patanjali.

योगमाया, *f.* a certain illusionary power which yogees are supposed to possess, *viz.* the being able to assume at will any number of forms of their own body.

योगरूढ़, used in a particular sense or meaning.

योगरूढ़ि, *f.* (in Gram.) a compound word used in a sense different from the meanings of its component members, an epithet.

योगवह, *m.* (*f.* ā) *adj.* bringing about, causing, promoting, furthering.

योगवही; see (1) योगवाही (2) योगवह.

योगवाही, 1, *m.* a medium for mixing medicines, menstruum: 2, *f.* alkali: quicksilver.

योगसेवा, *f.* practising religious abstraction.

योगाभ्यास, *m.* the manner of life and practice of Hindoo ascetics (yogī).

योगारूढ़, *m.* (*f.* ā) a person engaged in profound and abstract meditation.

योगासन, *m.* (among Yogees) a certain posture. proper for profound and abstract meditation.

योगिन, 1, *m.* = योगी, *q.v.*: 2, *f.* more prop. योगिनी.

योगिनिद्रा, *f.* (योगनिद्रा) light sleep, wakefulness.

योगिनी, (see रिझाल) *f.* (*m.* योगी) a female fiend or sprite supposed to be attendant on Durgā and to be created by her: (in Astrol.) spirits governing periods of good and ill luck.

योगी, *m.* (*f.* inī) one who performs the kind of religious exercise called *yog*, an ascetic, hermit, devotee: a person who has acquired supernatural power, a conjuror, magician: a certain caste of Hindoos (they are commonly weavers, and their peculiarity is that they do not burn their dead but bury them, their widows sometimes being buried alive with the corpses of their husbands).

योगीश्वर, *more prop.* योगेश्वर, *q.v.*

योगेश्वर, *m.* a chief among ascetics or contemplative saints; an adorer, devotee; a teacher of sacred science; a magician; an object of devout contemplation, a deity: an epithet (1) of Shiv (2) of Yājnawalkya.

योग्य, 1, *m.* a vehicle: a cake: a certain drug (*Riddhi*): sandal: 2, *m.* (*f.* ā) fit, proper, suitable, befitting, becoming; accomplished, clever, skilful, powerful, able.

योग्यता, *f.* (*m.* °त्व) appropriateness, fitness, suitableness, propriety, consistency, expediency, lawfulness, merit, capability.

योजन, *m.* joining, union; an epithet of the Supreme Being; a certain measure of distance equal, according to some calculations, to 4 kos or 9 miles; according to others, 5 miles or 4½ miles.

योजना, *f.* an adding together, uniting, joining, meeting, a combination of circumstances.

योतिष (corruption) = ज्योतिष, *q.v.*

योतिषी (corruption) = ज्योतिषी, *q.v.*

योद्धा, *m.* (uninfl.) a warrior, combatant, soldier.

योद्धापन = योधापन, *q.v.*

योधान, *m.* fighting, warring, battle.

योधा = योद्धा, *q.v.*

योधापन, *m.* heroism, bravery, prowess; soldiering.

योधी, *m.* (*f.* inī) a warrior, combatant, soldier; *lit.* adj. warring, fighting.

योनि, *m. f.* the place from which a thing originates, source, origin, spring, fountain, mine, the vulva, *pudendum mulieris*, the womb.

योनिनासा, *f.* the upper part of the vulva, the union of the labiæ.

योनिलिंग, *m.* the clitoris.

योनी, *f.* more com. योनि, *q.v.*

योन्यर्शा, *f.* a certain affection of the vulva (menorrhagia or prolapsus uteri).

योम, *m.* (pl. अय्याम) a day. (Though this is an Arabic word it occurs occasionally in Hindee works.)

योषणा / **योषा** / **योषित** / **योषिता** } *f.* a woman, wife, *femme.*

योसिसों॑स (*Rām.*) = जो हो—सो हो.

योहन, *m. pr. n.* the evangelist John and the Book that bears his name.

यो in Braj sometimes = (1) य; *e. g.* घामको मारयो = घामके मारे, on account of the heat (2) या; *e.g.* कियो = किया (3) आ; *e. g.* कह्यो = कहा.

यौं in Braj = यूं, *q.v.*

यौगिक, (see योग) appertaining to the religious practice called *yog*; usual, proper, suitable; (in Gram.) derivative in form and meaning (as a word that retains its own proper etymological signification).

यौतक, *m.* property given to a bride at her marriage, a dower, a nuptial present.

यौतिक, *more prop.* (1) यौतक (2) ज्योतिष, *qq.v.*

यौतिष (*corruption*) = ज्योतिष, *q.v.*

यौतुक = यौतक, *q.v.*

यौन, 1, *m.* a contracting an affinity: 2, *m.* (*f.* ī) a uterine relative, etc.: *lit.* appertaining to the place of origin or to the womb, connected by female alliance, connubial, uterine.

यौनी, *f.* (*m.* यौन) a female relative.

यौवन, *m.* puberty, adolescence, the age of marriageableness, youth, prime, manhood; an assemblage of young women; *met.* the breast.

यौवनदर्प, *m.* pride of youth, rashness, conceit.

यौवनदशा, *f.* youthfulness, adolescence, the period or the condition of youth.

यौवनमान, *m.* (*f.* matī) = यौवनस्थ, *q.v.*

यौवनवती, *f.* (*m.* यौवनवान, etc.) a young marriageable female.

यौवनवन्त / **यौवनवान** } *m.* (*f.* vatī) = यौवनस्थ, *q.v.*

यौवनस्थ, *m.* (*f.* ā) a marriageable person, a youth: *lit.* arrived at the age of puberty, youthful.

यौवना = यौवनवती, *q.v.*

य्याद, a corruption of याद, *q.v.*

य्हां (colloquial and dialectic) = यहां, *q.v.*

य्हूं (colloquial and dialectic) = यूं, *q.v.*

र

र (r) is the twenty-seventh consonant in the Hindee alphabet, and has the following characteristics and functions:—1, It belongs to the class of cerebrals, and is the second of the semivowels or *antahsth* letters: see अन्तःस्थ. 2, It is uniformly pronounced like the *r* in the English word 'rough' (the 'r' being fully and distinctly rung) 3, When the secondary symbol of उ or of ऊ occurs after this letter their forms are unique; thus रु (rŭ) and रू (rū). 4, In conformity either to dialectic laws or colloquial and corrupt usage, this letter is continually interchanged (1) with ऋ; *e. g.* रिषि, properly ऋषि (2) with ड़; *e.g.* बाड़ी, properly बारी; again, खरक, properly खड़क; again बिराल, properly बिडाल (3) with ल; *e. g.* गारी, properly गाली (4) with य; *e. g.* बिरोग, properly बियोग. 5, When this letter is followed by a consonant without the intervention of the inherent vowel-sound, it undergoes a peculiar change of form and is then written over another letter; *e. g.* धर्म. If, when it is so written, the letter under it be an unaspirated consonant, or either of the letters घ, भ, म, this letter is generally doubled: great latitude is, however, exercised by writers as to the application of this principle; thus, properly धर्म्म, though many write धर्म. A good rule for the application of this secondary form seems to be that it is to be used when र is pronounced as if *virām* were written under it, *i. e.* when no vowel-sound intervenes between र and the letter that follows it: thus, the form दरशन would be pronounced in three syllables ('darashan'); while the form दर्शन (the true spelling of this word) would be pronounced in two syllables ('darshan') as if written दर्‌शन. As writers have done pretty much as they have liked in this matter, the student should, in all cases of words containing either र or ृ, but which may not be found in the Dictionary, look under the other form: thus, if he do not find the form दरशन he should look for the form दर्शन It is important to note this, lest the student infer that the word he has met with is not given in the Dictionary. 6, This letter occurs in Hindee (1) as a *Kridanta* suffix, by means of which adjectives are formed from verbal roots; *e. g.* हिंस्र, from the root हिंस्, hurting (2) as a *Taddhita* suffix, forming adjectives from substantives; *e. g.* अश्मर, from the root अश्मन्, a stone (3) as an *Uṇādi* suffix, forming a number of adjectives and substantives from verbal roots; *e. g.* शक्र, from the root शक्, to be able. 7, In works on Prosody this letter denotes the metrical foot (—⏑—) called *Amphimacer* or *Cretic*, consisting of two long syllables separated by a short one. 8, When this letter follows a consonant not attended by the inherent vowel-sound, it is represented by a short transverse stroke at the foot of the letter; thus क् + र = क्र; द् + र = द्र; ष + ट + र = ष्ट्र. This kind of nexus (as, indeed, all the other kinds) is continually liable in Hindee to dissolution: it is also (especially in the older Hindee) frequently used by attraction in the place of the other secondary form of र; thus, धरम, more properly धर्म्म; again, सग or सरग, more properly स्वर्ग.

रअद, *m.* thunder, fulmination.

रइयत, *more prop.* **रयैयत**, *q.v.*

रई. *f.* a churning staff: bran.

रईस, *m.* a prince, chief, head, commander, captain, pilot, principal, president: a citizen.

रउरा, *m.* (*f.* ī) = **रावरा**, *q.v.*

रऊनत, *f.* haughtiness, pride.

रयैयत, *m.* a subject, a tenant; a peasant; *vulg.* ryot.

रंक, *m.* (*f.* in, inī, ī, nī) a very poor man, a beggar; a miser: *lit.* niggardly, avaricious; indigent, poor; wretched; slow.

रंकु. *m.* a sort of deer (the spotted *Axis*).

रंखा, *more prop.* **रंक**, *q.v.*

रंग, *m.* colour, hue; colouring-matter, paint, dye: (in the Drama) a stage: dancing, acting, singing, amusement, merriment, pleasure: a suit (at cards): a field of battle: tin. —*uṛ jānā*, to change colour, turn pale with fear. —*utarnā*, to become pale; to be grieved. —*k.* to enjoy; to lead a life of pleasure. —*charhnā*, to be elated with liquor. —*dekhnā*, to look at or examine the state, condition, result, conclusion, or consequence of a thing. —*bigāṛnā*, to change the condition of anything. —*mārnā*, to win (in gaming: the expression is taken from the game of *chaupar*). —*ratnā*, to be affected or imbued with love, to become attached to anyone. —*lagānā*, to lay on colouring-matter, to paint, dye, colour; to excite a quarrel.

रंगड़ in Mārwāṛī = Rājpūt.

रंगढंग, *m.* a brilliant or pleasing sight.

रंगत, *f.* colour, dye, tint.

रंगना, *t.* to colour, stain, dye.

रंगनेवाला, *m.* (*f.* ī) a colourer, dyer, painter.

रंगबरंग, 1, *m.* various colours, various kinds: 2, *adj.* of various colours or kinds, various.

रंगभंग, *m.* lasciviousness, hilarity: spoiling of sport.

रंगभूति, *f.* the day of full moon in the month Ashwin (the night of which is devoted to Lakshmī, and spent in playing ancient chess, dancing, etc.).

रंगभूमि, *f.* = **रंगशाला**, *q. v.*

रंगमहल्ल, *m.* an apartment appropriated for festive or voluptuous enjoyment. [society of a lover.

रंगरलियां, *f.* merriment, pleasure, mirth, pleasant

रंगरस, *m.* merriment, sport, delight, pleasure,

रंगरूप, *m.* colour, form, appearance. [melody.

रंगरेज़, *m.* a dyer, painter.

रंगरेज़ी, *f.* dyeing, tinging, painting.

रंगवती, *f.pr.n.* a certain woman (wife of Rantidev)

रंगवय्या, *m.* a dyer, painter. [who killed her husband.

रंगवाई, *f.* the price paid for colouring (particu-

रंगवैया, *m.* a dyer, painter. [larly for dyeing).

रंगशाला, *f.* a dancing-saloon, place of amusement, ball-room, theatre, stage, palæstra.

रंगाई. *f.* 1, = **रंगवाई**, *q. v.*: 2, a certain space of time during which a cloth is dyed. [a person blush.

रंगाना, *t.* to colour, tinge, paint, dye; to make

रंगारंग, many-coloured, of a variety of kinds, va-

रंगारा, *m.* a colourer, dyer. [rious.

रंगावट, *f.* the business of colouring; colouring,

रंगिमा = **रंग**, *q. v.*: see **रूपा**. [colour.

रंगी, 1, *m.* (*f.* inī) a dyer; a passionate person; an actor: lit. *adj.* (1) colouring, dyeing, painting (2) passionate, impassioned, having a passion or propensity (3) acting or exhibiting on a stage: 2, *f.* chintz (the colour of which will not stand washing); a kind of cloth peculiar to Khairābād.

रंगीत, a kind of vulture with a white body and yellow neck (commonly called 'Pharaoh's chicken').

रंगीन, coloured, painted, showy, fine, gaudy, figurative, various: passionate, impassioned.

रंगीनी, *f.* the state of being coloured, gaudiness, figurativeness, variableness.

रंगीला, *m.* a man of pleasure, a rake: *lit.* coloured, gaudy, fine, showy, airy, buxom.

रंगीलाचंगीला, *m.* (*f.* **रंगीलीचंगीली**), a play on the word **रंगीला**, *q. v.*

रंगून, *m. pr. n.* the city of Rangoon.

रंच, a little, somewhat.

रंचित; see **रंजित** and **रचित**.

रंज, *m.* grief, affliction, trouble, anxiety, anguish of mind, offence, disgust: a forest, desert, wilderness

रंजक, 1, *m.* (*f.* ikā) a painter, dyer, colourer: an inciter of affection, a stimulous, biliary humour on which vision depends: lit *adj.* (1) exciting, affecting, gladdening (2) colouring: 2, *f.* priming-powder; the touch-hole of a gun: 3, *m.* red sandal.—*uṛānā*, to burn priming: to flash in the pan.—*uṛnā*, to flash in the pan (priming).—*pilānā*, to prime.

रंजकदान, *m.* a priming-pan, fire-pan.

रंजन, 1, *m.* the act of painting, dyeing, or colouring; the affecting the heart, exciting passion, pleasing, gladdening, delighting; conciliating, befriending: red sandal-wood: 2, *m.* (*f.* ī) *adj.* colouring, dyeing; exciting passion or love; gratifying, exhilarating, delighting, rejoicing.

रंजनि (*Rām.*) = **रंजनी**, *q. v.*

रंजनी, *f.* the female personification of a particular mode in Hindoo music: any female who excites passion or who imparts gratification; indigo.

रंजित, *m.* (*f.* ā) moved, affected.

रंजिनी, *more prop.* **रंजनी**, *q. v.*

रंजीदा, afflicted, vexed, tormented.

रंजूर, sick, afflicted, infirm.

रंत, रंद, रंध, रंभ; for words beginning with either of these forms, see under the corresponding forms **रन्त, रन्द, रंन्ध, रम्भ**, respectively.

रंस, *f.* (Sk. **रश्मि**) a sunbeam, ray.

रंहट, *more prop.* **रहट**, *q. v.*

रकअ़त, *f.* the bowing the body in prayer, genuflexion; gesticulations performed when reading the Ḳur,ān.

रकखना = **रखना**, *q. v.* [form **रक्त**.

रकत; for words beginning thus, see under the

रक़म, *f.* writing; handwriting, character: arithmetic: manner, method, sort, kind: a royal edict.

रक़बा, *m.* a neck: a slave: an enclosure, esplanade,

रकाब, *more prop.* **रिकाब**, *q. v.* [environs.

रकार, *m.* (see **रेफ**) the letter **र**, or any symbol that may represent it.

रक़ीक़, subtile, thin, fine, minute.

रक़ीब, *m.* a rival, an enemy: one who watches,

रक़्स, an answer: the North. [a guardian.

रक्खना = **रखना**, *q.v.*

रक्त, *m.* (*f.* ā) coloured, tinged; red; attached to: hence, *m.* the colour red; blood. [affected is red.

रक्तकोढ़, *m.* a kind of leprosy in which the part

रक्तगुल्म, *m.* a certain disease (a hard lump in the abdomen of a female after conception); a clot of blood. [*pus santolinus*).

रक्तचन्दन, *m.* saffron: red sandal-wood (*Pterocar-*

रक्तचूर्ण, *m.* red lead. [affected by passion.

रक्तता, *f.* redness; the nature of blood; the being

रक्तधातु, *m.* red chalk, red orpiment; copper.

रक्तप, *m.* (*f.* ā) any rakshas or demon: lit. *adj.* blood-drinking.

रक्तपा, *f.* (*m.* **रक्तप**) a female demon; a leech.

रक्तपात, *m.* spilling of blood, bleeding, blood-

रक्तपायिनी, *f.* a leech. [shedding.

रक्तपायी, *m.* (*f.* inī) a bug: lit. *adj.* blood-drinking.

रक्तपित्त, *m.* a certain painful and itchy eruption (supposed to arise from excess of blood and bile); a certain plant used for the cure of this disease: plethora, spontaneous hœmorrhages from the mouth, nose, rectum, and cuticle (accompanied with fever and headache, vomiting, purging, etc.).

रक्तपित्ती, *f.* }
रक्तपीठ, *m.* } = **रक्तपित्त**, *q. v.*

रक्तमय, *m.* (*f.* ī) consisting of blood, abounding in blood, full of blood, bloody, blood-stained.

रक्तलोचन, *m.* (*f.* ā) red-eyed.

रक्तवर्ण, *m.* (*f.* ā) red-coloured.

रक्तविकार, *m.* deterioration of the blood.

रक्तहीन, *m.* (*f.* ā) bloodless; cold-blooded.

रक्ताम्बर, *m.* (*f.* ā) any one dressed in red; a vagrant devotee wearing red garments: *lit.* whose clothing is red. [*purea*).

रक्तालु, *m.* a species of red yam (*Dioscorea pur-*

रक्ष, 1, *m.* (*f.* ā) = **रक्षक**, *q. v.*: 2, *m.* preserving, guarding, protecting; protection: lac.

रक्षक, *m.* (*f.* ikā) a guardian, protector, preserver, saviour, keeper, guard: lit *adj.* guarding, preserving, keeping, protecting. [ing, keeping, taking care of.

रक्षण, *m.* the act of preserving, protecting, guard-

रक्षन, 1, *m.* (*f.* ā) = **रक्षक**, *q. v.*: 2, *more prop.* **रक्षण**.

रक्षना; see (1) **रक्षण** (2) **रखना**.

रक्षपाल, *m.* (*f.* ī) = **रक्षक**, *q. v.*

रक्षस, *more com.* **राक्षस**, *q. v.*

रक्षा, *f.* protection, guardianship, care, preservation, defence, patronage, safety; shadowing: ashes: lac: a sort of bracelet, an amulet.

रक्षिका, *f.* (*m.* **रक्षक**) a protectress.

रक्षित, *m.* (*f.* ā) guarded, protected, kept, preserved, saved, defended, safe, detained.

रक्षिता }
रक्षितृ } *m.* (*f.* trī) = **रक्षक**, *q. v.*

रक्षोगण, *m.* a class or company of demons.

रक्षोगणभोजन, *m. pr. n.* a certain hell where human beings are eaten by demons (the *Rakshogaṇ*).

रक्ष्य, *m.* protection, preservation.

रक्ष्यमाण, *m.* (*f.* matī) one who is protected: *lit.* protected, preserved, guarded.

रख, (particip. of **रखना**) putting, placing, keeping. —*chhornā*, to put, place; to have keep, have in charge. —*denā*, to put down, place, put by, keep.—*lenā*, to take charge of, to take into service, to engage.

रखक, *m.* (*f.* ikā) *more prop.* **रक्षक**, *q. v.*

रखछोड़ना; see *s. v.* **रख**.

रखदेना; see *s. v.* **रख**.

रखन (*colloquial*) = **रक्षण**, *q. v.*

रखनहार, *m.* (*f.* ī) = **रखवाला**, *q. v.*

रखना, *t.* to keep, put, place, deposit, lay, set, station, to have, hold, harbour, entertain, to possess, own, to stop, to preserve, save, to reserve, to apply, ascribe, impute, to deem.

रखलेना; see *s. v.* **रख**.

रखवाई, *f.* the price paid for keeping, etc.

रखवाना, *t.* to cause a thing to be kept, to cause to keep. *Rakhwā lenā*, to take in charge.

रखवार }
रखवारा } *m.* (*f.* ī) = **रखवाला**, *q. v.*

रखवारी, 1, *f.* of **रखवारा**, *q. v.*: 2, = **रखवाली**, *q. v.*

रखवाल, *m.* (*f.* ī) = **रखवाला**, *q. v.*

रखवाला, *m.* (*f.* i) a keeper, guardian, protector, pastor, shepherd, goatherd, guard, watchman.

रखवाली, *f.* 1, (*m.* **रखवाला**) a protectress, shepherdess: 2, keeping, guarding, protection, guardianship, care; cattle-grazing: tribute or fees paid to a chief for protecting property: black-mail.

रखशान, resplendent, shining.

रखसत (*corruption*) = **रुख़सत**, *q.v.*

रखाई; see (1) **रखवाई** (2) **रखाना**.

रखाना, *t.* to cause to keep, to give in charge, to put, place.

रखिया, *f.* protection, keeping.

रखी, 1, *m.* (*f.* inī) = **रक्षक**, *q.v.*: 2, *f.* a kind of tribute or black-mail paid to a Sikh chief in return for protection: 3, *f.* (?) grass which has been reserved for cattle, cut down and dried, hay.

रखेल, *f.* an assault, attack.

रखेलना, *t.* to assault, attack.

रखेला, an assault, attack.

रखैया, *m.* = **रखवाला**, *q.v.*

रग, *f.* a vein, a fibre, a sinew, tendon, a nerve.

रगड़, *f.* attrition, friction, rubbing: the quick beating of a drum.

रगड़ना, *t.* to rub, grate, abrade, to excoriate, to scour, to fret.

रगड़ा, *m.* rubbing, scouring, polishing: quarrelling: a kind of collyrium.

रगड़ाझगड़ा, *m.* debate, disputation, discussion, altercation, quarrel.

रगण, (see **र**, 7) *m.* (in Pros.) a Cretic.

रगत, *m.* (prop. **रक्त**) blood.

रगना, *t.* to be attached to, to be in love with.

रग़म, *m.* looking down, shame, reproach, contempt, abhorrence, repugnance. [common form **रगड़**.

रगर; for words beginning thus, see under the more

रगरग, from vein to vein, in every vein.

रगवत, vein-like, having veins or fibres.

रगिनी in Chand = **राज्ञी**, *q.v.*

रगेद, *f.* pursuit, chase, hunt.

रगेदना, *t.* to pursue, chase, hunt.

रघु, *m. pr. n.* (1) of an ancient king of Oude, great-grandfather of Rāmchandra (2) of his offspring.

रघुकुल, *m.* the race or offspring of Raghu.

रघुकुलमणि, *m.* (the gem of the race of Raghu, *i.e.*) Rām.

रघुनन्दन, *m.* an epithet of Rām; *lit.* descended from Raghu.

रघुनाथ, *m.* an epithet of Dasharath and of Rām; [*lit.* lord of the race of Raghu.

रघुनायक
रघुपति
रघुराई
रघुराज
रघुराजा } = **रघुनाथ**, *q.v.*

रघुवंश, *m. pr. n.* (1) of the offspring of king Raghu; hence, also (2) of a poem by Kālidās (which treats of the ancestors of Rām).

रघुवंशमणि, *m.* (the gem of the race of Raghu, *i.e.*) Rām.

रघुवंशी, *m.* (*f.* inī) a descendant of Raghu: *lit.* appertaining to the race of Raghu.

रघुवर, *m.* an epithet of Rām; *lit.* the best (or the eldest or the chief) of the race of Raghu.

रघुवीर, *m.* an epithet of Rām; *lit.* the hero of the race of Raghu.

रघूत्तम, *more prop.* **रघूत्तम**, *q.v.*

रचक, *m.* (*f.* ikā) a maker, fabricator, contriver, composer, inventor: lit. *adj.* fabricating.

रचना, 1, *n.* to be made, be created, be fabricated, be prepared; to be set to work, be employed, be about (a business): *u.int.* to stain, colour; to love, like to penetrate; (in Music) to keep time; to predestinate: *t.* to make, form, fabricate, compose, contrive, make arrangements, perform: 2, *f.* making, forming, fabricating, composing, creating, inventing; workmanship, work, a created thing.

रचवा, *m.* the act of making or forming.

रचाना, *t.* (of **रचना**) to set to work, set a-going; to make, do; to make merry; to celebrate; to stain the hands, feet, etc. with *mendhī*.

रचावट, *f.* staining with **हिना**, *q.v.*

रचित, *m.* (*f.* ā) fabricated, manufactured, made, done, composed, compiled, written by.

रचेसि = **तूने रचा** (**रचना**). See **एसि**.

रच्छ, रछ; for words beginning with either of these elements, see under the form **रक्ष**.

रच्छन (*colloquial*) = **रक्षण**, *q.v.*

रच्छना = **रक्षण** = **रखना**, *q. v.*

रज, *m.* (see **गुण**) dust; pollen; the menstrual excretion; sexual passion, the second of the three inherent natural qualities of living beings (*gun*). It predominates in air, and is active, urgent, and variable: it produces sensual desire, worldly coveting, pride and falsehood and is the cause of vice and of pain.—*jānā*, to be satisfied.

रजक, *m.* (*f.* ī) a washerman: cloth.

रजकनी (*Rām.*) = **रजकी**, *q.v.*

रजकी, *f.* (*m.* **रजक**) a washerman's wife, a washerwoman: a woman on the third day of her courses.

रजगद्दी = **राजगद्दी**, *q.v.*: see **ग्र**, 15.

रजजाना; see *s.v.* **रज**.

रजत, *m.* the colour white; silver; gold; ivory; a necklace; blood; an asterism; mount Kailās: *lit.* white.

रजधानी (*contraction*) = **राजधानी**, *q.v.*

रजधामा, *more prop.* **राजधाम**, *q.v.*

रजनी, *f.* night: turmeric; the indigo-plant: lac.

रजनीकर, *m.* (the night-maker, *i. e.*) the moon.

रजनीगन्ध, *m.* the tuberose (*Polyanthes tuberosa*).

रजनीचर, *m.* (*f.* ī) a ghost, goblin, *rākshas*, thief, watchman: lit. *adj.* night-walking.

रजनीपति, *m.* (the lord of night, *i. e.*) the moon.

रजनीमुख, *m.* nightfall, evening.

रजनीश, *m.* (the lord of night, *i. e.*) the moon.

रजनीशाखा, *f.* a certain plant (*Nyctanthes arbor tristis*) which blossoms at night and whose flower diffuses a powerful odour after sunset.

रजपुत, रजपूत } m. (f. nī) a contraction of = राजपूत, q.v.

रजब, m. the seventh month of the Muhammadan year.

रजम, m. detestation, repulse, dejection; stoning to death; (in Muhammadan law) the punishment for adultery.

रजमण्डित, m. (f. ā) covered with dust.

रजवाड़ा, m. a country under the control of a *rājā*, a kingdom.

रजवीर्य्य, m. menstrual excretion and semen virile.

रजस = रज, q.v.

रजस्वला, f. a female during menstruation; a marriageable female.

रजा, f. hope; prayer, intercession.

रज़ा, f. consent, acquiescence, leave.

रजाइ, f. a royal decree, edict, mandate, order, command.

रजाई = (1) रज़ाई (2) रजाइ, qq. v.

रज़ाई, f. a quilt; a comforter, headgear.

रज़ामन्द, *adj.* acquiescing, consenting, permitting, willing, good, pleasure, well-pleasing.

रज़ामन्दी, f. acquiescence, consent, permission.

रजाय; see (1) रजाइ (2) रज़ाई (3) राज्य.

रजायसु, m. a royal decree, edict, mandate, order, command.

रजित, affected, excited, moved, attracted.

रजु (corruption) = रज्जु, q. v.

रजुल, m. (pl. रिजाल) a man. (The word is Arabic, but is occasionally found in Hindee literature.)

रजोगुण, m. (see रज) the quality of passion.

रजोगुणी, m. (f. inī) appertaining to *Rajojuṇ*.

रजोबन्ध, m. suppression of menstruation.

रज्जु, m. f. a rope, cord, string, thread, tie; a lock of braided hair.

रज्जू (corruption) = रज्जु, q. v.

रट, f. iteration, repetition.

रटघट, f. labour and toil.

रटना, t. to iterate, repeat, call out; to order or demand repeatedly; to labour.

रण, m. noise, sound; war, combat, battle; a mosquito; anxiety: a forest, desert, wilderness.

रणकामी, (f. inī) a warlike person: *lit.* wishing to fight, desirous of war.

रणगढ़ा, *m.* lines of intrenchment.

रणछोड़, m. an epithet of Krishṇ.

रणधीर, m. (f. ā) firm or composed in battle.

रणपुरा, m. = रणवास, q. v. See भा, 22.

रणभूमि, f. the region or locality of war, a battlefield.

रणरणक, regret, care, anxiety.

रणवन, m. (अरण्य + वन) a wilderness.

रणवास, m. (either रण्डा or राणी + वास) a rājā's female-apartments, the seraglio, the female-apartments in the house of any rich man, a harem.

रणसिंगा, रणसिंधा } *more prop.* रणसिंहा, q. v

रणसिंहा, f. a battle-conch, war-trumpet.

रणस्तम्भ, m. a pillar in commemoration of a battle, a monument of war, trophy.

रणस्थल, रणांगण } m. = रणभूमि, q. v.

रणि, night.

रणोत्साह, m. prowess, bravery in battle.

रण्ड, 1, m. (f. ā) one who neglects his religious duties; one who dies without male issue: *lit.* barren: the castor-oil plant (*Ricinus vulgaris* or *Palma Christi*).

रण्डक, m. a barren tree.

रण्डसाला, m. widow's weeds or dress.

रण्डा, f. (m. रण्ड) a widow (term of abuse): a certain plant (*Salvinia cucullata*): a species of metre in Sanskrit prosody.

रण्डापन, रण्डापना, रण्डापरो, रण्डापा } m. widowhood.

रण्डिया, f. (रण्डा) a widow; a woman.

रण्डी, f. a woman, a wench.—*ghar*, a brothel.

रण्डीबाज़, m. a whoremonger.

रण्डीबाज़ी, f. whoremongery.

रण्डुआ, m. a widower.

रत, 1, in comp. = रात, q.v.: 2, m. (f. ā) beloved; intent on, engaged by, occupied, delighted with, satisfied, inclined: 3, m. coïtion, copulation: a private part.

रतकेल, m. copulation, coïtion.

रतजगा, m. a vigil, watching all night on religious occasions (a female ceremony).

रतघट, f. toil and trouble.

रतन; for words beginning thus, but not given below, see under the form रत्न.

रतनार, m. (रक्त) red colour.

रतनारे (*Rām.*) = रतनार, q. v.

रतनिधि, m. a wagtail.

रतनियां, m. a kind of rice.

रतवाही, f. a night-attack: a concubine who comes at night.

रताना, a. *int.* to rut: n. to be lewd.

रतायनी, f. a lewd female, harlot.

रतार्थी, m. (f. inī) any libidinous person: *lit.* desirous of copulation, lascivious.

रतालु (contraction) = रक्तालु, q. v.

रतावा, m. an attack, assault, (more particularly) a sudden inroad on an enemy's country.

रति, f. (see कामदेव) pleasure, enjoyment, joy; the sexual passion; sexual intercourse, enjoyment of love; a private part: *pr. n.* the Venus of the Hindoos, and wife of Kāmdev; (in Pros.) a species of metre.

रतिकेलि, रतिक्रिया } f. sexual intercourse.

रतिदान, m. sexual intercourse, the enjoyment of carnal love.

रतिनाथ = रतिपति, q. v.

रतिपति, m. an epithet of Kāmdev; *lit.* the husband or lord of Rati.

रतिभामा, *f.* the name of one of the characters in the *Singhāsan-Batīsī*.

रतिमत्वरा, *f.* a certain plant (*Trigonella corniculata*) considered, perhaps, as aphrodisiac.

रती, 1, *more prop.* **रत्ती**, *q.v.*: 2. *f. pr. n.* (= **रति**) the Venus of the Hindoo mythology.

रतीवत }
रतीवन्त } = **रतीवान**, *q. v.*

रतीवान, *m.* (*f.* matī) a prosperous person : *lit.* fortunate, prosperous, flourishing.

रतू, *f.* 1, *pr. n.* (see **गंगा**) the Ganges of heaven: 2, a woman who speaks the truth.

रतूबत, *f.* humidity, moisture, freshness.

रतौन्धा, *m.* night-blindness, nyctalopia.

रतौन्धिया, blind at night.

रत्त, affected by love, enamoured, charmed.

रत्ती, *f.* fortune: the seed of the *Abrus precatorius* used as a weight; a weight equal to eight barleycorns. — *chamaknā*, to begin to prosper; to flourish.

रत्न, *m.* a jewel, gem, pearl, precious stone, treasure; the pupil of the eye (in comp.) anything particularly precious or excellent in its kind, the jewel of the species; *e. g. Strīratn*, a pearl of a woman.

रत्नकन्दल, *m.* coral.

रत्नखानि, *f.* a mine for precious stones, jewel-mine.

रत्नजटित }
रत्नजड़ा }
रत्नजड़ाव } set with jewels, begemmed.
रत्नजड़ित }

रत्नजोत, *f.* a certain plant, a certain medicine said to be good for the eyes.

रत्नमंज, *f.* the name of one of the characters in [the *Singhāsan-Batīsī*.

रत्नमंजरी, *f.* a certain flower: *pr. n.* (1) of one of the thirty-two images supporting the throne of king Vikram (2) of a certain Vidyādharī (3) of a certain woman in the Hitopadesh.

रत्नमय, *m.* (*f.* ī) abounding in gems, made of [gems, gemmed.

रत्नमाला, *f.* a necklace of precious stones: a certain book on astronomy: a certain flower.

रत्नवत, *m.* (*f.* vatī) = **रत्नमय**, *q. v.*

रत्नवृक्ष, *m.* the coral-tree.

रत्नसिंहासन, *m.* a throne adorned with precious [stones.

रत्नसेन, *m. pr. n.* a certain ancient Hindoo king.

रत्नाकर, *m.* a mine of jewels; an epithet of the [ocean.

रत्नावली, *f.* a necklace of gems.

रत्ब, moist, green, fresh, tender.

रथ, *m.* a car, a war-chariot, any vehicle, a carriage, coach, chariot.

रथकार, *m.* (*f.* ī) a car-maker, coach-builder.

रथन, a Braj pl. of **रथ**. See **न**, 6.

रथन्तर, *m.* the name of various Sāmans; a form of Agni (regarded as a son of Tapas).

रथबान, *more prop.* **रथवान**, *q. v.*

रथयात्रा, *f.* a festival at which the chariots go in procession. The term is more especially applied to the procession of the car of Jagannāth on the second day of the *Shuklpaksh* of Āshāṛh.

रथयुत, *m.* (*f.* ā) = **रथी**, *q. v.*

रथवान, *m.* (*f.* vatī) a charioteer, coachman, carriage-driver.

रथवानी, *f.* coachmanship, the office of carriage-driving.

रथस्व, a contraction of **रथाश्व**, *q. v.*

रथहीन, *m.* (*f.* ā) *adj.* not possessing a chariot, deprived of a chariot.

रथांग, *m.* any limb of a carriage; a wheel: the [ruddy goose (*Anas casarca*).

रथाश्व, *m.* a chariot and horse: a carriage-horse, chariot-horse.

रथी, *m.* (*f.* inī) the owner of (or rider in) a carriage, a charioteer, warrior who fights from a car.

रथ्या, *f.* a multitude of cars: a high street: a place where several roads meet.

रद, *m.* a splitting, rending, tearing; a split, rent; [a tooth, a tusk.

रदच्छद, *m.* the lip: *lit.* tooth-cover.

रदन, 1, = **रद**, *q. v.*: 2, a Braj pl. of **रद**. See **न**, 6.

रदपट, *m.* the lip: *lit.* tooth-cover.

रद्दा, *m.* a row, layer, line.

रदीफ़, 1, *m.* a man riding behind another on the same horse: 2, *f.* the rhyming-word of a poem.

रद्द, *m.* rejection, repulsion, resistance, refutation; *met.* vomiting. — *k.* to reject, repel, to oppose, refute; to vomit.

रद्दजवाब, *m.* a replication, rejoinder.

रद्दबदल, *f.* altercation, discussion, dispute.

रद्दा, *m.* a layer of a wall, a day's work.

रद्दी, *m.* rejected things, refuse, (*esp.*) waste-paper: *lit.* rejected.

रन, 1, = **रण**, *q. v.*: 2, *m.* a forest, desert, wilderness,

रनबन (*corruption*) = **रणवन**, *q. v.*

रनवास }
रनिवास } *more prop.* **रणवास**, *q. v.*
रनिवासा }

रन्ति, *m. pr. n.* the lexicographer Rantidev.

रन्तिदेव, *m.* 1, *pr. n.* (1) of a certain king (2) an epithet of Vishṇu (3) of a certain lexicographer: 2, a dog.

रन्दा, *m.* a hole, a loop-hole, an air-hole, an embrasure: a plane (carpenter's).

रन्धना, *n.* to be boiled (said of food).

रन्ध्र, *m.* a hole, fissure, cavity, cavern; a fault, defect, flaw, weak point. In the ingenious system of reckoning by symbols adopted by Hindoos in their poetry, this word is a symbol for 9 (in allusion to the nine apertures of the human body).

रपट, *f.* hard labour, fatigue: slipperiness: chase,

रपटना, *a. int.* to slip, slide.

रपरपाना, *a. int.* to gallop hard.

रपेट, *f.* chase, running, pursuing, hunting.

रपेटना, to chase, run down, hunt, worry.

रफतरफत (*contraction*) = **रफ़्तारफ़्ता**, *q. v.*

रफ़्तार, *f.* going, motion, procedure, gait, pace, [walk,

रफ़्तारफ़्ता, *adj.* (infl. **रफ़्तेरफ़्ते**) going, in the act of going: *adv.* by degrees, step by step, gradually, in process of time.

रफ़ू, *m.* mending (a garment), cementing (broken friendship), pacifying; tranquillity, peace.

रफ़ाक़त, *f.* society, companionship, friendship, fellowship, intercourse. [(especially on a journey).

रफ़ीक़, *m.* a friend, ally, associate, companion

रफ़ूतेरफ़ूते, a corruption of **रफ़्तेरफ़्ते**, *q.v.*

रबड़, *f.* fatigue, trudging, fruitless labour.

रबड़ना, *a. int.* to fatigue oneself, to run about fruitlessly.

रबड़ा, *m.* (*f.* ī) fatigue, worn, weary. [fatigue.

रबड़ाना, *t.* to cause to run about fruitlessly, to

रबड़ी, *f.* 1, (*m.* **रबड़ा**) a weary female: 2, thick milk; a kind of porridge made of Indian corn.

रबाब, *m.* a kind of violin, a rebeck.

रबि (colloquial) = **रवि**, *q.v.*

रबी, 1, a colloquial form of **रवि**, *q.v.*: 2, *f.* the spring; spring-grass; the spring-harvest, grain sown in October and November and cut in the spring months (Mar.-Ap.), such as peas, wheat, etc. (Vulg. *rubbee.*)

रबीब, *m.* (*f.* **ई**) a step-child, a child by a former husband. [hammadans) an epithet of God.

रब्ब, *m.* lord, protector, preserver; (among Mu-

रब्बानी, godly, divine.

रब्बो, (Arabic) = my lord! See **रब्ब**.

रम, *m.* flight, elopement. — *rahnā*, to turn, roam, range. [spirit.

रमक़, *m.* the last breath, the departing soul or

रमचेरा, (contr. of **रामचेरा**) *m.* (*f.* ī) a slave, a servant (frequently given as a name to slaves).

रमज़ान, *m.* the ninth month among Muhammadans. This period is their Lent, during which they are interdicted from eating, drinking, and conjugal duty between the morning dawn and the appearance of the stars in the evening. On the 27th of this month the Kurān began to descended from heaven, and every prayer offered up on that night will be complied with. Also, prayers offered up on the 19th, 21st, and 23rd of this month are peculiarly efficacious.

रमझोल, *f.* a kind of ornament for the foot.

रमण, 1, *m.* (*f.* ā *or* ī) a husband, lover; an epithet of Kāmdev: lit. *adj.* affording delight: 2, *m.* sporting, playing, amorous dalliance, coition.

रमणक, *m. pr. n.* (1) of a certain Varsh and of its king (2) of a certain Dweep.

रमणा, *f.* (*m.* **रमण**) = **रमणी**, *q.v.*

रमणी, *f.* (*m.* **रमण**) an agreeable female, a mistress, a wife; *mons veneris*; a species of metre in Sanskrit prosody.

रमणीक, agreeable, pleasing, pleasant.

रमणीय, *m.* (*f.* **ई**) beautiful, pleasing, delightsome, enjoyable, exhilarating, charming.

रमणीयता, *f.* (*m.* °**य**) delightsomeness, agreeableness, pleasantness, charm.

रमथ, *m.* pleasure, sport, dalliance.

रमत, pleasing; sporting.

रमता, *m.* (*f.* trī) a traveller, wanderer.

रमति, *m.* love: paradise: a crow: time.

रमदूफ़ट्टू, *m.* the populace, the vulgar, the tag-rag-and-bobtail, "Dick, Tom, and Harry."

रमन (corruption) = **रमण**, *q.v.*

रमनः = **रमना**, 3, *q.v.*

रमना, 1, *t.* to reap enjoyment, have sexual intercourse: 2, *a. int.* to turn; to roam, range, wander; to go: 3, *m.* a place to roam in, a park, a chase (for game).

रमल, *m.* geomancy, foretelling by figures, divination: sand. [tress; an epithet of Lakshmee.

रमा, *f.* (*m.* **रम**) a beloved female, a wife, a mis-

रमाइबेको in Braj = **रमानेको** (**रमाना**).

रमाना, *t.* to entice, beguile: to take possession of.

रमानिवास, *m.* (the one who dwelt with Lakshmee, *i. e.*) Vishṇu.

रमापति, *m.* (the lord of Lakshmee, *i. e.*) Vishṇu.

रमियान; see **रमज़ान**.

रमैं; see **रमना**.

रम्फ़्तरम्फ़्त = **रफ़्तारफ़्ता**, *q.v.*

रम्भ, *m.* 1, *pr.n.* a certain monkey: 2, a bamboo.

रम्भस, *m. pr. n.* a certain ancient Hindoo king.

रम्भा, *f.* the plantain-tree (*Musa paradisiaca*) and its fruit; a courtesan, harlot; delight: a sounding, roaring; the lowing of cattle: *pr. n.* (1) of a certain nymph (*apsaras*) in the court of Indra (2) of Gaurī.

रम्माज़, *m*, a propounder of enigmas, etc., one who speaks mysteriously.

रम्माल, *m.* a soothsayer, fortune-teller, prophet, conjuror. [lightful, beautiful.

रम्य, *m.* (*f.* ā) pleasing, agreeable, pleasant, de-

रम्यक, *m. pr. n.* one of the minor divisions of the world (*dwip*) lying to the north of Ilāvrit.

रय, *m.* speed, velocity; the current of a river.

रयन (*dialectic*) = **रैन**, *q.v*

रयना, *more prop.* **रहना**, *q.v.* [wine: afternoon.

रया; 1, see (1) **रय** (2) **रयना** (3) **राय** (3) **राया**: 2, *m.*

रये; see **रया**.

रलना, *n.* to be ground down, be mixed.

रलाना, *t.* to pound together, to mix.

रव, *m.* sound, noise, voice, cry.

रवणक, *m.* a filter made of cane or bamboo.

रवत, *m.* (*f.* vantī) *adj.* crying out, raising a cry,

रवथ, *m.* the Indian cuckoo. [bellowing.

रवन (*Rām.*) = **रमण**, *q.v.*

रवनक; see (1) **रमणक** (2) **रवणक** (3) **रौनक़**.

रवना, *a. int.* to give forth sound, make a noise.

रवनी (*Rām.*) = **रमणी**, *q.v.*

रवन्ना, *m.* a servant who attends at the gates of the female apartments to purchase articles that are required: a pass, passport, permit.

रवय्या; (1) **रवैया** (2) **कइँया** (3) **रोवाई**.

रवबो in Māṛwāṛī = **रहना**, *q.v.*

रवा, 1, *m.* a grain or particle (of sand, dust, gunpowder, etc.), gold or silver filings: 2, lawful, right, proper, accurate, worthy.

रवां, 1, *more prop.* (1) **रवा** (2) **रवाम**, *qq.v.* : 2, in Bhojpuri = **रावरा**, *q.v.*

रवांस, *m.* a kind of bean (*Dolichos sinensis*).

रवाज, *m.* usage, custom, fashion; currency; vent, sale: *adj*, customary, current; vendible.

रवान, 1, going, moving, flowing, running, fluent, current: 2, *m.* life, soul; text; reading.

रवानः, *m.* a pass, passport: a marching: *adj.* departed, despatched, proceeding.

रवाना = (1) **रवानः** (2) **रोआना**, *qq.v.*

रवाब, 1, *more prop.* **रबाब**, *q.v.*: 2, = **रोआऊं** or **रोआऊंगा**. See **ब**.

रवानगी, *f.* a running, flowing, flux; passing, going, travelling, departure.

रवांसिन = **रवांस**, *q.v.*

रवारवो, **रवारो**, **रवारोई**, *f.* going, travelling.

रवि, *m.* the sun.

रविउये (*Rām.*) = **रविका उदय**, sunrise.

रविकर, 1, *m. pr. n.* a certain Hindoo commentator: 2, an old genitive of **रवि** (see **कर**, 3).

रविकान्त, *m.* a sort of crystal, sunstone.

रवितनया = **रविनन्दिनी**, *q.v.*

रविदास, *more com.* **रैदास**, *q.v.*

रविनन्दिनी, *f.* an epithet of the Yamunā river; *lit.* daughter of the sun.

रविमण्डल, *m.* the sun's disc.

रविमणि, *m. f.* the sunstone.

रविमार्ग, *m.* the sun's path.

रविवार, *m.* Sunday.

रविश, *f.* custom, fashion, institution, rule, law: a way, passage, walk, avenue.

रवैया, *m.* custom, fashion, institution, law, rule, mode of procedure.

रशक; see (1) **रश्क** (2) **रसिक**.

रशती, *f.* the bonus paid by a cultivator in consideration of being allowed to reclaim waste lands.

रशना = **रसना**, *q.v.*

रशीद, sagacious, intelligent, wise; hence, *m.* a guide, conductor.

रश्क, *m.* malice, spite, envy, jealousy, emulation.

रश्मि, *m.* a rein: a ray of light: an eyelash.

रस, *m.* taste, flavour; the primary substance of a thing, essence, pith, marrow; any fluid, water, juice, humour, semen virile, quicksilver; exudation; poison; any affection of the mind, passion, relish, enjoyment, taste, sentiment, emotion (*esp.* as an object of poetry or composition); any fluid of the body, the serum, etc.; gum, myrrh. This term has certain technical applications:—1, It is used to indicate the passions which a literary composition describes or is calculated to excite: *by some*, these are reckoned to be nine in number; *viz.* (1) *Sringār-ras*, *i. e.* love, or the intercourse and mutual feeling of lovers (2) *Hāsya-ras* the ludicrous style (3) *Karunā-ras*, the pathetic (4) *Vir-ras*, the heroic or epic, describing deeds of courage and martial prowess (5) *Raudra-ras*, describing or exciting indignation or rage (6) *Bhayānak-ras*, the terrible, describing the fear and terrible apprehension of the writer (7) *Vibhatsa-ras*, expressing aversion (8) *Shānt-ras*, expressing confidence and security (9) *Adbhūt-ras*, the marvellous, expressing astonishment: *by others*, a tenth is added; viz. *Vātsalya*, paternal tenderness: 2, It is used to express the physical tastes, which are said to be six: *viz.* (1) sweet (2) sour (3) salt (4) bitter (5) acrid (6) astringent: *hence*, 3, In the ingenious system of reckoning by symbols adopted by Hindoos in their poetry, this word is a symbol for 6.

रसकपूर, *more prop.* **रसकर्पूर**, *q.v.*

रसकर्पूर, *m.* corrosive white sublimate, or a muriate of mercury similar to it but perhaps milder.

रसखान, *m.* an epithet of Krishṇ: *lit.* an abode or treasury of *ras*.

रसज्ञ, *m.* (*f.* ā) discriminating (or acquainted with) tastes, sentiments, etc.; *hence* (1) a poet, or writer who understands the different sentiments (*ras*) to be described or appealed to (2) an alchymist, or one who has obtained a command over the magical properties, of mercury (3) a physician, or medical preparer and administerer of mercurial and chemical compounds.

रसज्ञता, *f.* knowledge of flavours (*ras*); poetical or rhetorical taste or skill; alchymy.

रसज्ञा, *f.* (see **रसज्ञ**) the tongue.

रसता, 1, = **रस्ता**, *q.v.*: 2, thread.

रसद, *f.* store of grain laid in for an army, etc.: grain, provision, supplies.

रसधातु, *m.* quicksilver, mercury.

रसन, a Braj pl. of **रस**. See **न**, 6.

रसना, *f.* the tongue: a woman's girdle.

रसनिवृत्ति, *f.* loss of taste, flavour, etc.

रसपुष्प, *m.* a muriate of mercury (formed by subliming in close vessels a mixture of sulphur, mercury, and common salt).

रसभस्मन, *m.* the oxide of mercury, calx.

रसम, *f.* custom, law; model, plan: a certain game among children.

रसमसा, *m.* (*f.* ī) wet with perfumed essences or with perspiration.

रसमसाना, *n.* to be wet with perfumed essences or with perspiration.

रसमसीला, *m.* (*f.* ī) wet with perspiration or with perfumed essences. (Little used.)

रसरस (*Rām.*) = **धीरेधीरे**, *q.v.*

रसरा, *m.* a rope, cable.

रसराज, *m.* quicksilver, mercury.

रसरास, *more com.* **रासरस**, *q.v.*

रसरी, *f.* (dim. of **रसरा**) cord, string.

रसल, *m.* sending news.

रसवत = **रसोत**, *q.v.*

रसवती, *f.* (*m.* **रसवान**) an agreeable female: a cook-room, kitchen.

रसवाई, *more prop.* **रुसवाई**, *q.v.*

रसवाद, *m.* (*f.* ā) a mischief-maker: lit. *adj.* quarrel-exciting.

रसवान, *m.* (*f.* vatī) juicy, succulent; well-flavoured, savoury; agreeable; tasteful (said of literary composition).

रससा, *more prop.* **रस्सा**, *q.v.*

रससिन्दूर, *m.* a sort of artificial cinnabar (made with zinc, mercury, blue vitriol, and nitre fused together) used as an escharotic.

रसा, *f.* the earth; the tongue; a grape; a rope, halter, line: the name of several plants; *pr.n.* a certain river of the lower regions.

रसाइन; see (1) **रसायन** (2) **रसायिनी**.

रसाई, *f.* access, entrance, arrival: wisdom, penetration, quickness of apprehension, skill, cleverness.

रसांजन, *m.* a certain kind of collyrium (prepared either with the calx of brass or with the *Amomum anthorrhiza.*

रसातल, *m. pr. n.* (1) of the lowest of the seven divisions of the infernal regions (2) of the seven hells underneath the earth. [It is the abode of various monstrous and demonical beings (*Nāg, Asur, Daitya*, etc.); but should not be confounded with the Hindoo Tartarus (*Narak*) or hell proper,—the abode of guilty mortals after death.]

रसातललोक = **रसातल**, *q.v.*

रसाद, *m.* (*f.*ā) = **रस खानेवाला**.

रसाना, *t.* to solder.

रसायन, *m.* alchymy, chemistry; the employment of mercury in medicine; a medicine composed of mercury and other metals; a certain medicine (*Elixir vitæ*) preventing old age and prolonging life; poison: buttermilk: slowness, mildness: an epithet of Garuda: an alchymist. [mistry.

रसायनविद्या, *f.* the science of alchymy or of che-

रसायनी, 1, *m.* (*f.* inī) an alchymist, a chemist: 2, *f.* a vessel conveying nutrition.

रसाल, *m.* the sugarcane; the mango-tree (*Mangifera Indica*): *lit.* savoury, juicy.

रसालय, *m.* the seat or abode of the Rasas; the seat or abode of enjoyments. [nerve, tendon, etc.).

रसालसा, *f.* any tubular vessel of the body (as a

रसाला, 1, a corruption (1) of **रसालय** (2) of **रिसाला**, *qq.v.*: 2, *f.* curd mixed with sugar and spices.

रसावल, *m.* a kind of dish (rice and the juice of sugarcane boiled together).

रसिक, *m.* (*f.* ā) a libertine; a horse; an elephant: *lit.* savoury, flavoured; tasteful (said of composition); inclined, impassioned; sentimental; witty.

रसिकता, *f.* } **रसिकत्व**, *m.* } = **रसिकाई**, *q.v.*

रसिका, *f.* a woman's girdle; the tongue; curds mixed with sugar and spice; molasses.

रसिकाई, *f.* cunningness, shrewdness, amorousness, pleasure, humour, joviality.

रसिया, *m.* one who pursues enjoyment, an epicure, a voluptuary. [mence ripening, to ooze.

रसियाना, *n.* to be moist or juicy: *a. int.* to com-

रसी, *m.* (*f.* inī) impassioned; humourous, witty.

रसीद, *f.* acknowledgment of arrival or of receiving, a receipt.

रसीला, *m.* (*f.* ī) juicy, luscious; rakish, volup-

रसुन, *m.* garlic (*Allium sativum*). [tuous.

रसूत = **रसौत**, *q.v.*

रसूल, *m.* (*pl.* ān) a messenger, an apostle, (among Muhammadans) an epithet of Muhammad.

रसूली, *f.* apostleship, mission.

रसे, softly, gently.

रसेन्द्र, *m.* quicksilver; the philosopher's stone.

रसोइया, *m.* a dresser of food, a cook.

रसोई, *f.* victuals; a cook-room, kitchen.

रसोँई = **रसोई**, *q.v.*

रसोईदार, *m.* a dresser of food, a cook.

रसोन्त, *more com.* **रसौत**, *q.v.*

रसोय्या, *more prop.* **रसोइया**, *q.v.*

रसौत, *f*, a kind of collyrium (extracted from the root of the *Amomum anthorrhizum*, Roxb.).

रस्ता (contraction) = **रास्ता**, *q.v.*

रस्म, *f.* custom, law; model, plan.

रस्य, 1, juicy, savoury: 2, *m.* blood.

रस्सा, *m.* a rope, cable.

रस्सी, *f.* (dim. of **रस्सा**) string, cord, rope, reins.

रह, (base of **रहना**) staying.—*jānā*, to wait, stay, delay, desist, give up.

रहंट, *more prop.* **रहट**, *q. v.* [cart.

रहकला, *m.* a small cannon, a swivel, a field-piece; a

रहगीर, *m.* a traveller, wayfarer.

रहचोला, *m.* flattery, agreeable conversation.

रहज़न, *m.* a highwayman, robber.

रहज़नी, *f.* highway-robbery.

रहजाना; see *s.v.* **रह**. [for drawing water with.

रहट, *m.* the wheel (fixed at the top of a well)

रहटा, *m.* a spinning-wheel.

रहडू, *m.* a cart, a waggon.

रहण, *f.* manner, method, way.

रहपट, *more prop.* **रहट**, *q.v.*

रहत, *m.* a staying, remaining.

रहते, (sc. **में**; from **रहना**) during the existence of, in the presence of, in the face of the fact that, notwithstanding, in spite of: *lit.* in the remaining.

रहतेजाते, before and behind, in the presence or

रहन, *more prop.* **रहण**, *q.v.* [absence of.

रहनहार, *m.* (*f.* ī) a dweller, inhabitant: lit. *adj.* abiding, remaining, tarrying.

रहना, *a. int.* to stay, stop, remain, last, stand, continue, lie, exist, be; to inhabit, reside, dwell, live; to escape.

रहनुमा, *m.* one who shews the road, a guide, conductor, pilot, escort.

रहनेहारा } **रहनेवाला** } *m.* (*f.* ī) = **रहनहार**, *q.v.*

रहब = **रहूँगा**. See, **ब**, 4.

रहबर, *m.* a conductor, guide. [derness.

रहम, *m.* mercy, pity, kindness, compassion, ten-

रहमत, *f.* = **रहम**, *q. v.*

रहमदिल, tender-hearted, pitiful, merciful, kind.

रहमान, merciful, forgiving (an epithet of God).

रहमार, *m.* (*f.* ī) a highway-robber.

रहल = **रहा**. See **ल**, 3.

रहला, *m.* a kind of pulse (*Cicer arietinum*) commonly called *chanā* or chick-pea. [not purchased).
रहवा, (from **रहना**) *m.* (*f.* ī) a kind of slave (one
रहवाई, *f.* (see **रहना**) house-rent.
रहवार, *m.* an ambling horse, a sound roadster.
रहवास, *m.* a residence: a resident. [cupant.
रहवैया, *m.* a dweller, resident, inhabitant, oc-
रहस, 1, *m.* secrecy, privacy, solitariness; a secret, a mystic or religious truth; a privity; a place of privacy, hidingplace, solitude; copulation: merriment, waggery: trampling under foot, treading: 2, secretly; privily, in private, solitarily.
रहसना, *a. int.* to rejoice, be pleased.
रहसि; see **रहना** and **रहसना**.
रहस्य, *m.* a secret, mystery, recondite thing: *lit. m.* (*f.* ā) secret, private, mysterious, clandestine.
रहाइश } **रहाइस** } *f.* = **रहाव**, *q.v.*
रहाई, *f.* escape, liberation, relief, acquittal, discharge, freedom, release.
रहालत, *more prop.* **रिहालत**, *q.v.*
रहाव, *m.* (from **रहना**) stay, halt, remaining, an abode, residence, continuance.
रहित, *m.* (*f.* ā) relinquished, abandoned, left, forsaken; divested of, destitute of, devoid of, without, exempt from.—*k.* to divest of, deprive of. Much used as the latter element in compound adjectives.
रहिन (*Rām.*) = **रहन**, *q.v.*
रहिय, a poet. form = **रहो** and **रहिये** (**रहना**).
रहिहै, (pl. **रहिहैं**) in Braj = **रहेगा**. [tender.
रहीम, merciful, compassionate, pitiful, kind,
रहूगण, *m. pr. n.* (1) of a certain ancient Hindoo king (2) of the author of certain hymns of the Rig-Ved.
रहूगणाः, (see **आ**, 22) *m. pr. n.* a certain family belonging to the race of Angiras.
रहेउ in Braj = (1) **रहा** (2) **रहो** (**रहना**).
रहेना, *more prop.* **रहना**, *q.v.*
रहेव in Braj = (1) **रहा** (2) **रहो** (**रहना**).
रहेसि (*poet.*) = **रहता है**.
रा; 1, in Māṛwāṛī this is the regular termination of the masculine form of the genitive (= **को**): 2, in ordinary Hindee, this is the termination of the masculine singular and plural of the genitive of the first and second personal pronouns.
राआ, a Prākrit form of **राजा**, *q.v.*
राइ, in Chand = **राजा**, *q.v.*
राइज, customary, current, usual, common, fashionable; vendible. [chaff of wheat, bran.
राइया, *m.* a species of mustard with large seeds:
राई, 1, *more com.* **राय**, *q.v.*: 2, *f.* a kind of mustard (*Sinapis racemosa* or *S. chinensis*) with small seeds; mustard: 3; *f.* wisdom, opinion, thought, counsel.
राईकाई, broken to atoms.
राईया = **राइया**, *q.v.*
राउ (*Rām.*) = **राजा**, *q.v.*
राउत (*Rām.*) = (1) **महतो** (2) **सरदार** (3) **राजदूत**, *qq. v.*
राउर = (1) **रावरा** (2) **राजमन्दिर**, *qq. v.*
राउरा, *m.* (*f.* ī) = **रावरा**, *q.v.*
राउल = **राजकुल**, *q.v.*
राऊ (*Rām.*) = **राजा**, *q.v.*
राए, *more com.* **राय**, *q.v.*
राएगान, gratuitous; acquired without labour; useless: *adv.* gratis; in vain, uselessly.
राएता, *m.* pumpkins, etc. pickled in sour milk.
राएबांस, *m.* a kind of spear.
राएबेल, *f.* a certain flower (*Jasminum zambac*).
राएरायान, *more com.* **रायरायान**, *q.v.*
राओरा } **राओरी** } = **रावरा**, *q.v.*
रांग, *f.* (**रंग**) pewter, tin.
रांगभरा, (**रंग**) *m.* (*f.* ī) a toyman.
रांगा, *m.* (**रंग**) pewter, tin.
रांचना = (1) **रचना** (2) **राचना**, *qq. v.*
रांझन, *m.* an estimable person, a sweetheart: Leander, the lover of Hero (called in Hindee, *Hīr*).
रांझना } **रांझा** } *m.* = **रांझन**, *q.v.*
रांड, **रांद**, **रांध**, **रांप**, **रांभ**; for words beginning with either of these elements, see under the corresponding forms **राण्ड**, **रान्द**, **रान्ध**, **राम्प**, **राम्भ**, respectively.
रांडू = **राण्ड**, *q. v.*
राकस (corruption) = **राक्षस**, *q. v.*
राका, *f.* full moon; the day of full moon: a girl in whom menstruation has commenced: itch: a cup made of palmyra-leaf: *pr. n.* a certain river.
राकापति, *m.* (the lord of Rākā, *i.e.*) full moon.
राकानिशा, *f.* the night of full moon.
राकिब, *m.* a rider: a rival, an observer.
राक़िम, *m.* one who writes, a writer.
राकेश, *m.* the full moon: an epithet of Shiv.
राकेस, *more prop.* **राकेश**, *q. v.*
राकेसकर, *m.* moonbeams, moonlight.
राक्षस, *m.* (*f.* ī) appertaining to a demon, infested by demons, demoniacal, fiendish, infernal: *hence*, an evil spirit, demon, satyr, imp, ogre, vampire, goblin, fiend, the Devil; a certain form of marriage (the violent seizure and rape of a girl); one of the astronomical *yogs* or divisions of the moon's path. In the Hindoo mythology the Rākshas plays an important part, and is divisible into three classes:—1, One sort of Rākshas is of a demi-celestial nature and is ranked with the attendants on Kuver: 2, Another kind corresponds to the goblin, imp, or ogre; and is believed to haunt cemeteries, animate dead bodies, disturb sacrifices, and to ensnare and devour human beings: 3, The third kind approaches more to the idea of a Titan, and is a powerful and relentless enemy of the gods in a superhuman or incarnate form (such as *Rāvaṇ*).
राक्षसव्याह, *m.* a certain form of marriage (the violent seizure and rape of a girl, after the repulse or the destruction of her relatives).
राक्षसी, *f.* (*m.* **राक्षस**), a female demon: a large

tusk: a sort of perfume.—*belā*, *f.* the period between sunset and dark, twilight (*prop.* the time when evil spirits are abroad).

राख, *f.* (from **रखना**) ashes (*esp.* of cowdung).

राखना, *more com.* **रखना**, *q. v.*

राखनीं Braj = **रखना**, *q. v.*

राखस (*colloquial*) = **राक्षस**, *q. v.*

राखसगट्टा, a species of air-plant (*Bryonia epigœa*) called also, 'devil's-root'.

राखसपत्ता, *m.* the aloe-plant.

राखात, lands set apart for grazing.

राखी, *f.* an amulet (being a string which Hindoos tie around their arms on the occasion of a certain festival held at the full moon of *Shrāvan* in honour of Krishṇ).

राखेउ in Braj = **राखा** (**रखना**).

राख्यो in Braj = **रखा** (**रखना**).

राग, *m.* colour, hue, tint, dye: mental affection (as passion, desire, love, joy, sorrow, wrath, envy, greediness, etc.): music, harmony, melody, air, song, tune: a mode in music. The modes in music are personified, and are reckoned to be six, *viz.* (1) Bhairav (2) Mālav (3) Sārang (4) Hindol (5) Vasant (6) Dīpak or Megh: hence, in the ingenious system of reckoning by symbols adopted by Hindoos in their poetry, this word is a symbol for 6.—*chānā*, to be in concert.

रागचूखा, *m.* a certain tree (*Mimosa catechu*) which yields an astringent resin, and whose wood is used in dyeing.

रागद्वेष, *m.* love and hatred, affection and enmity.

रागन, a Braj pl. of **राग**, *q.v.* See **न**, 6.

रागना, *a. int.* to begin to sing.

रागनी, *more prop.* **रागिणी**, *q. v.*

रागमाला, *f. pr. n.* (see **राग**) a certain treatise on music. It is nothing more than a collection of pictures exhibiting the traditional history of the primary and subordinate modes, and the subjects appropriated to each.

रागरंग, *m.* music.

रागसागर, *m.* a song composed of many musical modes (*rāg*).

रागिणी, *f.* (*m.* **रागी**) a shrewd and intriguing female: a modification of a musical mode personified as the wife of a *Rāg*. These Rāgiṇis are thirty in number.

रागिनी, 1, (corruption) = **रागिणी**, *q. v.*: 2, in old Hindee = **रागी**, *q. v.*

रागिब, wishing; desirous, curious.

रागी, coloured; agitated by affections, impassioned, passionate, loving: hence, *m.* (*f.* iṇī) a lover, a libertine, a singer; a painter.

राघव, *m.* (*f* ī) a descendant of Raghu; an epithet of Rām, the ocean: an intruding guest: a certain fish (*Silurus pelorius?*).

राचना, *m.* to be affected or imbued with love, to be strongly attached.

राचा, *m.* (*f.* ī) imbued with love.

राच्छस, *m.* (*f.* in *or* ī) = **राक्षस**, *q.v.*

राछ, *m.* apparatus.

राछस, *m.* (*f.* in *or* ī) = **राक्षस**, *q.v.*

राछसनी (*colloquial*) = **राक्षसी**, *q.v.*

राज, 1, a very com. contraction of **राज्य**, *q.v.*: the word is also used inadvertently for **राजा**; and is very frequent in composition (1) as a prefix; in which event it is equivalent to the Sanskrit genitive of the word **राजा**; *e.g.* **राजदर्शन**, *i.e.* **राजाका दर्शन** (2) as a suffix; in which event it is equivalent to the nominative form **राजा**; *e.g.* **धर्मराज**, *i. e.* **धर्मका राजा**; 2, *m.* a mason, bricklayer, house-builder.

राजः, *more prop.* **राजा**, *q. v.*

राजकन्या, *f.* a king's daughter, princess.

राजकर, *m.* tax paid to royalty, king's taxes, royal tribute, revenue.

राजकशेरु, *m.* a certain fragrant grass (*Cyperus*).

राजकाज = **राजकार्य्य**, *q. v.*

राजकार, *more com.* **राजकर**, *q. v.*

राजकार्य्य, *m.* royal duties, state affairs, the functions of Government.

राजकीय, kingly, royal, princely.

राजकुंअर } **राजकुंवर** } *m.* (*f.* ī) = **राजकुमार**, *q. v.*

राजकुमार, *m* (*f.* ī) a king's son, a prince.

राजकुमारी, *f.* a king's daughter, a princess.

राजकुम्वर, *m.* (*f.* ī) = **राजकुमार**, *q.v.*

राजकुल, 1, *m.* a royal race: a king's court; a court of justice: 2, *m.* (*f.* ā) a prince, king's child.

राजकुवर, *m.* (*f.* ī) = **राजकुमार**, *q. v.*

राजगद्दी } **राजगादी** } = **राज्यगद्दी**, *q. v.*

राजगी, *f.* = **राजत्व**, *q. v.*

राजगीरा, the plant *Amaranthus polygamus.*

राजगीरी, *f.* masterly work, workmanship.

राजगुरु, *m.* the spiritual preceptor of a royal personage.

राजगृह, *m.* a royal dwelling, palace.

राजग्रीव, *m.* a sort of flat fresh-water fish.

राजघ } **राजघ्न** } *m.* (*f.* **राजघ्नी**) = **राजहन**, *q.v.*

राजचक्र, *m.* 1, = **सुदर्शनचक्र**, *q.v.*: 2, fear or perplexity occasioned by a monarch.

राजचिन्ह, *m.* the insignia of royalty.

राजजुध्या = **राजयुध्वा**, *q. v.*

राजटीका, *f.* the mark placed on the forehead of a royal personage on the occasion of coronation; a mark put on the forehead of a royal personage by his vassals.

राजत (*Rām.*) = **राजता** (pres. part. of **राजना**).

राजतरंगिणी, *f. pr. n.* a certain historical poem.

राजता, *f.* = **राजत्व**, *q. v.*

राजति (*Rām.*) = **राजती** (**राजना**).

राजतिलक, *m.* = **राजटीका**, *q. v.*

राजतेजस, *m.* royal splendour or dignity, majesty.

राजत्व, *m.* kingship, sovereignty, royalty; kingly authority, supremacy, government, reign.

राजदण्ड, *m.* the royal sceptre; punishment ordered by the sovereign; fine payable to royalty.

राजदण्डापहरण, *m.* confiscation (*lit.* the seizure of property in execution of a royal of a legal decree).

राजदत्त, *m.* (*f.* ā) given or allowed by the king or by Government. [or by Government.

राजदत्तभूमि, *f.* an allowance of land by the king

राजदर्शन, *m.* an audience of a royal personage, a royal levee. [spouse.

राजदार, *f.* a king's wife, queen-consort, royal

राजदुलारी, *f.* a king's darling. See **दुलारा**.

राजदूत, *m.* (*f.* i, in, nī, ī) a royal ambassador.

राजदेव, *m. pr. n.* a certain Hindoo lexicographer.

राजदेवी, *f. pr. n.* a certain ancient Hindoo prin-

राजद्रोह, *m.* high treason: tyranny. [cess.

राजद्रोही, *m. f.* inī) a person guilty of treason against the sovereign, a rebel, traitor.

राजद्वार, *m.* a palace-gate, a royal entrance.

राजधन, *m.* royal revenue or right to property.

राजधर, *m.* (*f.* ā) a prime minister.

राजधर्म्म, *m.* the duties of a sovereign; the functions or obligations of Government, the duty of the military tribe.

राजधान = **राजधानी**, *q.v.*

राजधानी, *f.* the residence of a sovereign, a palace; a royal city, metropolis, capital.

राजधाम, *m.* = **राजधानी**, *q.v.*

राजधुरा, *f.* kingly responsibility, royal functions, the burden of governing.

राजन, 1, *more com.* **राजा**, *q.v.*: 2, a Braj pl. of **राजा**:

राजनय (*Rām.*) = **राजनीति**, *q.v.* [see **न**, 6 (1).

राजना, *n.* to be adorned: *a. int.* to shine.

राजनीति, *f.* princely duties, regal polity, the science of government, the kingly art.

राजनील, *m.* the emerald.

राजपट्ट, *m.* a royal fillet, tiara; a royal cushion, throne; a kind of gem (said to be an inferior kind of diamond) brought from a country (*Virāṭ-desh*) in the north-west of India).

राजपत (*contraction*) = **राजपति**, *q.v.*

राजपति, *m.* prince (a Hindoo title).

राजपत्नी, *f.* a queen.

राजपथ, *m.* the king's highway (*i.e.* a path open to all the king's subjects), a public road, main road, a road forty cubits broad, and passable for horses and elephants.

राजपद, *m.* kingly status or office.

राजपदधारी, *m.* (*f.* inī) one who accedes to the position and office of sovereign.

राजपाट, *m.* a royal throne. See **राजपट्ट**.

राजपुत }
राजपुत्र } *more com.* **राजपूत**, *q.v.*

राजपुर, *m.* }
राजपुरी, *f.* } = **राजधानी**, *q.v.*

राजपूत, (prop. **राजपुत्र**) *m.* (*f.* nī) *lit.* a descendant or son of a king: the term is applied especially (1) to Hindoos of the second caste (*Kshatriya*) or military tribe (2) to a certain class of Hindoos who claim descent from the ancient Kshatriyas. [of Ajmeer.

राजपूताना, *m. pr. n.* another name for the province

राजपूती, *f.* prowess in war, courage.

राजप्रताप, *m.* royal power and splendour, kingly dignity, majesty.

राजफोड़ा, *m.* a kind of large boil or carbuncle which generally rises at the back of the neck and most commonly proves fatal.

राजबंश }
राजबंस } (*colloquial*) = **राजवंश**, *q.v.*

राजबहा, *m.* the main channel, the principal or common branch of a canal. [royal kitchen.

राजभण्डार, *m.* a royal storehouse or treasury; a

राजभवन }
राजभुवन } = **राजमन्दिर**, *q.v.*

राजभोग, *m.* food placed before idols at noon.

राजमन्त्री, *m.* (*f.* iṇī) a king's minister, counsellor of state, privy counsellor.

राजमन्दिर, *m.* a royal residence, a palace.

राजमन्दिल, *more prop.* **राजमन्दिर**, *q.v.*

राजमराल, *m.* (*f.* ī) any very beautiful swan.

राजमार्ग = **राजपथ**, *q.v.* [a monarch.

राजमुकुट, *m.* a royal crown, any diadem worn by

राजर्षि, *m.* a particular class of sages; a prince who has adopted a life of devotion.

राजयुध्वा, *m. f.* one who makes war against his sovereign, a rebel, mutineer, traitor.

राजयोग्य, *m.* (*f.* ā) suitable or proper for a royal personage, kingly, princely, royal.

राजराज = **राजाधिराज**, *q.v.*

राजराणी, *f.* a queen-consort, royal spouse. [tion).

राजरोग, *m.* any mortal disease (such as consump-

राजलक्षण, *m.* the insignia of royalty; any mark by which royalty may be indicated.

राजलेख, *m.* a royal letter or order.

राजवंश, *m.* a family of kings, a royal race, a dynasty.

राजवंशी, *m.* (*f.* inī) }
राजवंशीय, *m.* (*f.* ā) } = **राजवंश्य**, *q.v.*

राजवंश्य, appertaining to a royal family or dynasty, of royal parentage or ancestry: *hence, m.* (*f.* ā) the offspring of royalty: a tribe of Rājpūts.

राजवत, like a king, kingly, royal, princely.

राजवर, *m.* an excellent king, a chief king.

राजवाड़ा, *m.* the country of rājās, royal domains.

राजवीजी, *m.* (*f.* inī) a royal personage: *lit.* of royal, seed sprung from a royal race.

राजवीर, *m.* an epithet of any man of superior bravery; *lit.* a prince of heroes.

राजवैद्य, *m.* a king's physician. [edict, decree.

राजव्यवस्था, *f.* a royal institute or order, mandate,

राजशासन, *m.* a royal edict, a decree, mandate.

राजशाही, *f.* royal status, kingship, royalty.

राजस, *m.* (*f.* ī) appertaining to the quality of passion, endowed with passion.

राजसत्ता, *f.* royal dignity, majesty.

राजसभा, *m.* an assemblage of princes, an assembly in which the sovereign is present, a king's court, a king's privy council, a royal assembly, parliament.

राजसर्प, *m.* (the king-serpent, *i. e.*) the boa.

राजसिंहासन, *m.* a royal throne.

राजसी, *f.* (*m.* राजस) an epithet of Durgā.

राजसू = राजसूय, *q. v.*

राजसूय, *m.* a sacrifice performed only by a universal monarch attended by his tributary princes.

राजसेवक, *m.* (*f.* ikā) an attendant on a royal personage, a courtier. [sonage.

राजसेवा, *f.* service or attendance on a royal per-

राजस्थान, *m. pr. n.* another name for the province of Rājpūtānā.

राजस्व, *m.* royal revenue, tribute, tax.

राजहंस, *m.* (*f.* ī) a white goose with red legs and bill; the flamingo.

राजहन, राजहा } *m.* (*f.* राजघ्नी) a regicide.

राजहांस, *more prop.* राजहंस, *q.v.* [*us niloticus*).

राजहासक, *m.* a certain large kind of fish (*Cyprin-*

राजहिं = (1) राजाको (2) राजते हैं (राजना).

राजा, (uninfl.) *m.* (*f.* राज्ञी, *vulg.* रानी) a king, sovereign, monarch, prince, lord, master, governor.

राजाई, *f.* = राजत्व, *q.v.*

राजाऊ, *m. f.* kingly, royal, princely.

राजाज्ञा, *f.* a royal decree, an edict, mandate.

राजाधिकारी, *m.* (*f.* iṇī) one who holds sway, a governor, king.

राजाधिराज, *m.* a king of kings, a supreme ruler of princes, a paramount sovereign, an emperor.

राजापन, *m.* kingship, royalty.

राजामार्ग = राजपथ, *q. v.*

राजावर्त्त, *m.* (= राजपट्ट) a kind of diamond.

राजावलि = राजावली, *q.v.*

राजावली, *f.* a line of kings, royal pedigree or genealogy, a royal House, dynasty.

राजि, *f.* a rank, row, line, stripe, continuous or unbroken line, the line parting the hair.

राजिक, 1, = राजिका, *q.v.*: 2, *m.* (*f.* ā) a lord, chief, noble person: *pr. n.* a certain *muni.*

राजिका, *f.* a row, continuous line, a streak: a field: black mustard (*Sinapis racemosa*).

राजिव, a contraction of राजीव, *q.v.*

राज़ी, satisfied, contented, agreed, willing, pleas-

राजी = (1) राजि (2) राज़ी, *qq. v.* [ed, complacent.

राज़ीनामा, *m.* an acknowledgement of a cause being finally settled, given by the plaintiff. The defendant gives a *ṣāfi-nāma*, a general release, discharge from an obligation.

राजीव, *m.* 1, = राजहासक, *q.v.*: 2, the lotus (*Nelumbium speciosum*): the Indian crane: a kind of deer: an elephant.

राजीवनयन, राजीवनेत्र, राजीवलोचन } *m.* (*f.* ā *or* ī) lotus-eyed.

राजे, 1, (*Rām.*) = राज्ञी, *q.v.*: 2, a mistaken nominative plural and inflected singular of राजा.

राजेन्द्र, *m.* a powerful king, an emperor.

राजेश्वर, *m.* a sovereign, prince, governor.

राज्ञी, *f.* (*m.* राजा) a queen; a princess.

राज्य, *m.* a government, kingdom, empire, principality: the administration or exercise of empire, dominion, sovereignty, sway, empire, reign, administration; royalty, dynasty.

राज्यकाज = राजकार्य्य, *q. v.*

राज्यकुंवर, *m.* (*f.* ī) = राजकुमार, *q. v.* [throne.

राज्यगद्दी, *f.* the royal cushion or seat, a king's

राज्यच्युत, *m.* (*f.* ā) a deposed sovereign: *lit.* deprived of regal dignity, dethroned, deposed.

राज्यच्युति, *f.* loss of sovereignty, deposal, dethronement, subversion of regal dignity.

राज्यधर्म्म = राजधर्म्म, *q. v.*

राज्यपराक्रम, *m.* sovereign dominion, regal power.

राज्यपाट, *m.* a royal throne.

राज्यभंग, राज्यभ्रंश } *m.* = राज्यच्युति, *q. v.*

राज्यभ्रष्ट, *m.* (*f.* ā) = राज्यच्युत, *q. v.*

राज्यरक्षा, *f.* the protection or defence of a kingdom.

राज्यसुख, *m.* the enjoyment of possessing royalty or a kingdom, the happiness of governing.

राज्याधिकार, *m.* the right or title to the sovereignty of a kingdom.

राज्याधिकारी, *m.* (*f.* iṇī) a governor, king.

राठोड़, strong, firm, fixed, fast.

राठोर, *m.* a certain tribe of Rājpūts.

राड़, *f.*, राड़ा, *m.* } = रार, *q. v.*

राढ़ी, 1, = रारी, *q.v.*: 2, the sharp point of an arrow or of a pen. [to the west of the Ganges.

राढ़, *m. pr. n.* that portion of Bengal which lies

राढ़ा, *f. pr. n.* = राढ़, *q. v.*

राढ़ी, *m.* a Brāhmaṇ from Rāṛh; one of the four divisions of Brāhmaṇs: *lit.* appertaining to the coun-

राण; see (1) रान (2) रांड (3) राणा. [try of Rāṛh.

राणा, *m.* (among Hindoos) a title of a prince or rājā: a certain tribe of Rājpūts.

राणियां, *f.* (pl. of राणी) queens, princesses.

राणी, *f.* (from राज्ञी) a queen, a princess.

रांड, *f.* a widow; a woman.—*kā sāṇḍ* (*lit.* a widow's stallion, *i. e.*) a gallant, a cavaliere serviente; *hence*, a base, contemptible fellow, a spoilt child.

रांडा, *m.* (*f.* ī) barren. The term is particularly applied to unproductive trees (such as the male palm, etc.), also to the mango-fish without roes.

रांडापा, *m.* widowhood.

रात, *f.* (*contraction*) = रात्रि, night. *Ādhī*—, *f.* midnight. *Rāt thorī aur sāng bahut* is applied to express a hurry of business with but little time to perform it in (like the English saying. 'The devil to pay. and no pitch hot'): also great expense with a small income. *Rātoṅ* —, in the middle of the night. —*bkar*, all night. — *ko*. at night, by night —*din*, night and day, continually. *Baṛī* —, late at night, in the dead of night.

रातना, *t.* to dye, stain : *n.* to be strongly attached, be deeply in love (*lit.* stained, *i. e.* with the dye of love).

राता, 1, (*poet.*) = **रात**, *q.v.*: 2, (*poet.*) = **रत**, *q.v.*: 3, *m.* (*f.* ī) stained, dyed. coloured ; red.

राति (*contraction*) = **रात्रि**, *q. v.*

रातिदिन, night and day, continually.

रातिब, *m.* daily allowance of food (esp. to dogs and elephants) ; allowance, portion, provision.

रातिबा, *m.* salary, stipend, pay.

राती, 1, = **रात्रि**, *q. v.*: 2, appertaining to night.

रातीन्धा, *m.* night-blindness, nyctalopia.

रात्र, *m.* used in comp. for **रात्रि**, *q. v.*

रात्रि, *f.* night.

रात्रिचर, *m.* (*f.* ī) an evil spirit, fiend, goblin, ghost; a burglar; a patrol, watchman, guard : lit. *adj* moving at night, night-walking.

रात्री, *f.* night.

रात्रीकाल, *m.*
रात्रीवेला, *f.*
रात्रीसमय, *m.* } night-time.

राद
राध } *f.* pus, matter.

राधा, *f. pr. n.* (1) of the favorite mistress of Krishṇ during his residence among the cowherds (2) of the sixteenth *Nakshatra* (3) of the wife of the charioteer of Dhritarāshṭra by whom Karṇ was fostered.

राधाकुण्ड, *m. pr. n.* a certain sacred place of pilgrimage in Mathurā.

राधाकृष्ण, a kind of ejaculatory invocation much used by the devotees of Krishṇ and Rādhā.

राधानगरी, *f.* a kind of silk cloth made at Rādhānagar.

राधाप्यारी, *f.* an epithet of Rādhā as the beloved of [Krishṇ.

राधिक, *m. pr. n.* a certain king, son of Jaysen.

राधिका, *f. pr. n.* = **राधा** (1), *q. v.* (A diminutive form of that word expressive of endearment.)

रान, *f. m.* the thigh. — *chhoṛnā*, to expel. — *tale dabānā*, to have completely in one's power, to subdue. *Rānse rān bāndhnā*, to guard or watch diligently.

रानन, *f. m.* (a Braj pl. of **रान**) the thighs.

राना (*corruption*) = **राणा**, *q. v.*

रानियां = **राणियां**, *q. v.*

रानी (*corruption*) = **राणी**, *q. v.*

रान्दना, *t.* to expel, drive out, drive off, drive away.

रान्दनी, *f.* parsley.

रान्दपड़ोस, *m.* neighbourhood.

रान्दा, a carpenter's plane.

रान्धना, *t.* to cook, dress food.

रान्धनेवा, *m.* a cook, a baker.

रापी, *f.* a shoemaker's knife, currier's knife.

राब, *f.* syrup, molasses, treacle.

राबड़ी, *f.* a kind of food like pap.

राबन (*corruption*) = **रावण**, *q. v.*

राबना, *a. int.* to toil, labour.

राबिता, *m.* whatever serves to bind one thing to another, bond, connexion, conjunction, a catchword.

राम, *m.* (*f.* ā) beautiful, pleasing. This term is is applied as an appellation to three of the incarnations of Vishṇu ; *viz.* (1) to Parashurām (2) to Rāmchandra (3) to Balrām, *qq. v.* : hence, in the ingenious system of reckoning by symbols adopted by Hindoos in their poetry, this word is a symbol for 3.

रामकथा, *f.* the story of the exploits of Rām.

रामकरी
रामकली } = **रामकेली**, *q. v.*

रामकहानी, *f. pr. n.* the *Rāmāyaṇ* or story of Rām ; *hence*, any long story.

रामकान्त, *m.* a kind of sugarcane : *pr. n.* a certain [Scholiast.

रामकीर्त्ति, *f.* the renown of Rām-Chandra.

रामकेली, *f.* a certain musical mode (*rāgiṇī*).

रामगिरि, *m. pr. n.* (1) of a mountain called also *Kompte* or *Chitrkūṭ* in Bundelkhaṇḍ (2) of a mountain near Nāgpur, called also *Rāmṭek*.

रामगुरु, *m.* (Rām's guru, *i. e.*) Vashishṭ.

रामचन्द्र, *m. pr. n.* (see **अवतार**; **राम**) the second and chief of the three renowned Rāms and hero of the *Rāmāyaṇ*. He was the son of Dasharath by Kaushalyā and reigned as king of Ayodhyā (Oude) about B. C. 1600. He was the 7th *avatār* of Vishṇu, and conqueror of Ceylon (*Lankā*). In him the Deity is believed to have descended for the purpose of destroying Rāvaṇ, who, having (on account of his devotion) received a promise from Brahmā that he should not suffer death by any of the usual means, had become the tyrant and pest of mankind. The Devatās came in the shape of monkeys, as Rāvaṇ had received no promise of safety from them; hence, the monkey-god (Hanumān) was Rām's general. Rām's younger brother Bharat was son of Kaikeyī, who was the cause of his going to the desert to perform devotions on the banks of the Pampā-nadī, who insisted that her son should reign during the fourteen years that Rām was to employ in devotion. It was while performing his devotion (or during his stay in the forests) in company with Lakshmaṇ (his brother by Sumitrā) that Rāvāṇ appeared as a beggar while Rām was absent hunting, and enticed away Sītā, which was the immediate occasion of the war detailed in the Rāmāyaṇ. Sītā was daughter of Rājā Janak, who had promised to give her to any man who should break a certain bow; this was done by Rāmchandra. When in the forest, he drew a circle around Sītā, and forbade her to go beyond it. and left Lakshmaṇ to take care of her; but Lakshmaṇ, hearing some noise which alarmed him for his brother, left her to seek him. Then it was that Rāvaṇ appeared and enticed her out of the circle (*gaṇḍī*), and carried her off in his flying chariot : in the air he was opposed by the bird *Jaṭāyu*, whose wings he cut and so escaped.

रामचरण, *m.* the blessed feet of Rām-Chandra.

रमचरित, *m.* the exploits of Rām.

रामचेरा, *m.* (*f.* ī) a man's name, particularly that of a slave : *lit.* a slave of Rām.

रामजनी, *f.* (**रामा + जनी**) a Hindoo dancing-girl; a prostitute.

रामजस = रामयश, *q.v.*

रामटेक; see **रामगिरि**. [tic doctrines.

रामतापनी, *f.* a certain Hindoo work on the Vedan-

रामतारक, *m.* a certain *mantra* (*viz.* **रांरामायनमः**) by repeating which emancipation is obtained.

रामतुरई, *f.* a certain vegetable (*Hibiscus esculentus*) called ochra. [*mum gratissimum*).

रामतुलसी, *f.* a certain large species of basil (*Ocy-*

रामदुहाई, *f.* an asseveration on oath by Rām or by the Deity = "By God!"

रामधनुष, *m.* the rainbow.

रामधाई, *more prop.* **रामदुहाई**, *q.v.*

रामधामदा, *f.* an epithet of the Saryū river: *prop.* the donatrix of the abode of Rām (*i.e.* those who bathe in that river obtain emancipation).

रामपद, *m.* the feet of Rām; the religion of Rām; the salvation imparted by Rām; the status of Rām.

रामप्रताप, *m.* the splendour or glory of Rām.

रामबटाई, *f.* a division of a crop between landlord and tenant.

रामभक्त, *m.* (*f.* ā) a worshipper of Rām.

रामभति, *f.* a calling out for redress, a complaint.

राममून, *m.* a kind of goat.

रामयश, *m.* the renown of Rām-Chandra.

रामराम, a form of salutation (also, of invocation) very common among Hindoos.—*k.* or *kahnā*, to make the sound of invocation, to call 'Ram! Rām!'

रामलीला, *f.* one of the festivals of the Hindoos in which the deeds of Rām are celebrated.

रामसर, *m.* a kind of wood; a sort of reed.

रामसिंगा, *m.* a particular kind of wind instrument or horn of a deep bass sound.

रामा, *f.* (*m.* **राम**) a beautiful female.

रामानन्द, *m.* a certain disciple of Rāmānuj and founder of a subdivision of the Vaishnav sect.

रामानन्दी, *m.* a kind of Hindoo ascetics (followers of Rāmānand); believers in Rām.

रामानुज, *m. pr. n.* a celebrated Hindoo reformer, author of several Vedanta treatises. He belonged to the sect of the Vaishnavs, was regarded as an incarnation of Shesh, and flourished in the 12th century in southern India, where he combated the Shaivas.

रामानुजमत, *m.* the sect of Rāmānuj.

रामायण, *m. pr. n.* (1) of a great epic poem of the Hindoos written in Sanskrit by Vālmīki in which are detailed the adventures of Rāmchandra (2) of several other poems on the same subject by other authors.

रामायुध, *m.* a bow (the weapon).

रामावत, *m.* the system or tenets of that sect of Hindoo ascetics who are followers of Rāmānuj.

रामावतार, *m. pr. n.* (see **रामचन्द्र**) the seventh incarnation of Vishṇu.

रामी, *m.* an archer, shooter, thrower, hurler: a jester, scoffer: *pr. n.* the sign Sagittarius.

राम्पी, *f.* an iron leather-scraper.

रांभना, *a. int.* to bellow, to cry out. [wealth-

राय, *m.* (a title among Hindoos) prince, chief:

रायगान, *more prop.* **राएगान**, *q.v.*

रायज, *more prop.* **राइज**, *q.v.* [standard.

रायत, 1, *more prop.* **रय्यत**, *q.v.*: 2, *f.* a banner,

रायता = राइता, *q.v.*

रायबांस, *m.* a kind of spear.

रायबेल = राइबेल, *q.v.*

रायमनिया, *m.* a kind of rice (in the husk).

रायमनी(1) = **रायमनिया**, *q.v.*: 2, *more prop.* **रायमुनी**.

रायमुनी, *m.* a certain bird (*lāl*; the male of the *Fringilla amandava*).

रायरायान, *m.* (a title among Hindoos; *lit.* the chief of princes) the *dīwān* of the *Khālisa* or chief treasurer.

राया, 1, *more prop.* **राइया**, *q.v.*: 2, see **राजा** and **राय**.

रार, *f.* wrangling, contention, quarrel, fray, strife. —*machānā*, to occasion a fray, create a disturbance.

रारि = रार, *q.v.*

रारी, 1, *m.* (*f.* iṇī) a wrangler, etc.: *lit.* contentious, quarrelsome: 2, *f.* a coarse kind of grass.

राल, *m.* (*f.*?) the resinous exudation of the *Shorea robusta*; resin, rosin, pitch; saliva.

राला, *m.* a kind of millet.

राव, *m.* prince (a title among Hindoos).

रावकबक, *m.* the headman of a village.

रावचाव, *f.* gaiety, amusement, merriment, mirth; dalliance; affection, endearment.

रावटी, *f.* a kind of tent.

रावण, *m. pr. n.* (see **रामचन्द्र**) the king of the class of demons called *Rākshas*. He was the son of Vishravā by Kaikasī, and reigned as sovereign of Laṅkā (Ceylon). He stole away Sītā, and was at last destroyed by Rām-Chandra.

रावणि, *m. pr. n.* the eldest son of Rāvaṇ.

रावत, *m.* a hero: a sweeper (of a particular caste).

रावर, *more com.* **रावरा**, *q.v.*

रावरा, *m.* (*f.* ī) yours, of you. (Used chiefly in Braj.)

रावरो }
रावरी } in Braj = **रावरा**, *q.v.*

रावल, *m.* a soldier, chieftain, chief.

रावी, *m.* the author of a fable, romance, fiction, etc., a historian, relater, narrator.

राश, *m.* a heap of winnowed corn: a feather.

राशि, *m.* a heap, quantity, congeries, number; a part and its division, (in Math.) numerator and denominator; (in Astron.) any sign of the Zodiac.

राशिकरण, *m.* a heaping, piling, gathering into a heap.

राशिकृत, *m.* (*f.* ā) heaped, piled, collected together

राशिचक्र, *m. pr. n.* the Zodiac. [into a heap.

राशिद, pious, faithful, orthodox, following the

राशिभाग, *m.* (in Math.) a fraction. [right path.

राशिभोग, *m.* the passage of any planet through a sign of the Zodiac.

राशी, *m.* one who gives bribes.

राष ; see (1) **राख** (2) **राश** (3) **रास**.

राषना = **राखना** = **रखना**, *q.v.*

राषा, *m.* (*f.* ī) = **रखा** (**राषना**).

राष्ट्र, *m.* an inhabited country, a realm, kingdom, empire, region : a public calamity (as a famine, plague, etc.). [*num jacquini*).

राष्ट्रिका, *f.* a prickly sort of night-shade (*Sola-*

रास, 1, a corruption of **राशि**, *q.v.* : 2, *m.* sound, confused noise ; speech ; a chain ; amorous pastime; a certain Hindoo festival including songs and dances celebrated in the month Kārttik (*esp.* the circular dance in commemoration of the dances performed by Krishṇ and the cowherdesses) : 3, *f.* reins (of a bridle) : usury : adoption : corn separated from the chaff. —*ānā*, to be agreeable. —*biṭhānā* or *lenā*, to adopt a son.

रासचक (corruption) = **राशिचक्र**, *q.v.*

रासता, *more prop.* **रास्ता**, *q.v.*

रासधारी, 1, *m.* a dancing-boy (who imitates the *rās* of Krishṇ): 2, *m.* (*f.* inī) a composer of dances.

रासनिशीन, *m.* an adopted son.

रासभ, *m.*(*f.* ī) an ass. [of Krishṇ.

रासमण्डल, *m.* the circular dance or dancing-ground

रासयात्रा, *f.* a certain festival of the Hindoos held on the full moon of Kārttik in honour of Krishṇ and his dances with the cowherdesses *gopī*).

रासर 1, *m.* the dance known as *rāsyātra*; pastime, sport, festive mirth : a company, assembly, party : love, desire, sentiment : alchemy.

रासलीला, *f.* the amorous pastimes of Krishṇ (*esp.* on a certain night) with the cowherdesses of Mathurā.

रासविलास, *m.* = **रासलीला**, *q.v.*

रासि (*corruption*) = **राशि**, *q.v.* [sincere.

रासिख़, firm, durable, constant, rooted ; learned;

रासी, (said of horses) of middling breed, indifferent, so-so.

रासू, *m.* the mungoose (*Viverra mungo*).

रासो, an old form of **रास**, *q.v.*

रास्त, right, true, good, just, sincere; right (not left), straight, even, level : *adv.* actually, certainly. —*ānā*, to gain one's temper, be set to rights.

रास्तबाज़, *m.* (*lit.* one who plays or acts fairly; *hence*); faithful, to be depended on. —*ṭhahrānā*, to justify, to constitute (or reckon to be) just.

रास्ता, *m.* a road, way, path, street.

रास्ना, *f.* a sort of perfume: the name of two plants; *viz.* (1) *Mimosa octandra* (2) *Ophioxylon serpentaria*.

राह, *f.* a road, path, way; *met.* manner, method. —*taknā* or *dekhnā*, to look out for, wait for, expect.— *lūṭnā*, to rob anyone on the highway.

राहज़न, *m.* a highway-robber.

राहत, *f.* quiet, repose, rest, ease, tranquillity,

राहता; see (1) **राहना** (2) **रहना**. [pleasure.

राहदारी, *f.* collection of duties on roads (an authorized branch of revenue arising from duties collected from travellers by the officers of Government (*rāhdār*) stationed on the high roads for the protection of passengers. In Dakkhanī the term signifies (1) a guide (2) a warrant, passport, permit.

राहना, *t.* to roughen a millstone by digging little pits on its surface with a small pickaxe.

राहनुमा } *m.* a guide, conductor, leader.
राहबर }

राहब, a poet. fut. = **राहूंगा** (**राहना**) : 2, see **राहिब**.

राहम, see **रहम** and **राहिम**.

राहरविश, *f.* manners, habits, customs. [clear.

राहरुन्दन, barring the way, keeping the gangway

राहित्य, *m.* freedom from anything. [a mortgager.

राहिन, *m.* one who borrows on a pledge or pawn,

राहिब, *m.* a christian priest, monk ; a lion.

राहिम, compassionate, merciful.

राही, *m.* (*f.* inī) a traveller, wayfarer.

राहु, *m.* (in Astron.) the dragon's head or ascending node; (in Myth.) *pr. n.* a certain Daitya, the son of Sinhikā, who occasions eclipses by devouring the sun or the moon.

राहुग्रास } *m.* an eclipse. See **राहु**.
राहुग्राह }

राहू (*corruption*) = **राहु**, *q.v.*

रि ; it is quite common in Hindee to represent the forms **ऋ** and **ॠ** by this form **रि** ; for all words, therefore, beginning thus, but not given below, see under these latter forms.

रिआयती, *m.* a favoured person, a protégé, a tenant to whom abatement of rent is made.

रिआया, (pl. of **रईयत**) subjects, tenants.

रिंद, *more prop.* **रिन्द**, *q.v.*

रिक (*corruption*) = **ऋग**, *q.v.* See **रि**.

रिकाब, *f.* a stirrup : equipage, train : a dish, plate.

रिक्कत, *f.* thinness, minuteness, subtleness ; pity, sympathy, tenderness, affection ; weeping.

रिक्त, *m.* a vacuum, vacuity ; a wood, forest : *lit.* emptied, destitute of, cleared, empty, void.

रिक्तता, *f.* vacuity, void, space.

रिक्तहस्त, *m.* (*f.* ā) empty-handed.

रिखि (*corruption*) = **ऋषि**, *q.v.* See **रि**.

रिचक, *more prop.* **ऋचीक**, *q.v.*

रिचा (*corruption*) = **ऋच**, *q.v.* See **ऋ**, 4.

रिच्छेस, *more prop.* **ऋक्षेश**, *i.e.* **जाम्बवत**, *q.v.*

रिज़क़, *m.* food ; wealth ; pension, allowance, subsistence, support, daily bread.

रिजाल, *m.* (pl. of **रजुल**) men. —*ul-ghaib*, *m. pr. n.* an invisible being (called by the Hindoos *yogini*) which moves in a circular orbit around the world : on the 1st, 9th, 16th, and 24th days of a lunar month his station is in the east ; on the 3rd, 11th, 18th, and 25th, in the south-east ; on the 4th, 12th, 19th, and 27th, in the south-west ; on the 6th, 14th, 21st, and 29th, in the west ; on the 7th, 15th, and 27th, in the north-west; on the 2nd, 10th, 17th, and 25th, in the north ; and on the 8th, 23rd, and 30th, in the north-east. His influence on each day is especially exerted during nine gharees, or three hours and thirty-six minutes, at the close of that lunar day (*tith*), and in that interval it is unfortunate to begin a journey towards the station of this being or in such a direction as to place him on the right hand.

रिज़ाला, the worst (after the best has been picked out); mean, vile, base.

रिझवाड़ }
रिझवार } = रिझवैया, q v.

रिझवैया, having the quality of being pleased, easily gratified. [plex.

रिझाना, t. to please: met. to plague, teaze, per-

रिण = ऋण, q.v. See रि.

रित, more prop. (1) ऋतु (2) रीति, qq.v.

रिताना, t. (रिक्त) to cause to empty.

रिति, more prop. रीति, q.v.

रितु = ऋतु, q.v. See रि.

रितुराज = ऋतुराजा, q.v.

रिद्धि = ऋद्धि, q.v. See रि.

रिन = ऋण, q.v. See रि.

रिनि; see ऋण and ऋणी.

रिनी = ऋणी, q.v.

रिन्द, m. a rake, libertine, debauchee, profligate, blackguard, reprobate, vagabond, drunkard.

रिपु, m. an enemy.

रिपुता, f. hostility, enmity.

रिपुसूदन, m. the destroyer of enemies: pr. n. the the youngest of the three brothers of Rām-chandra.

रिफाकत, more prop. रफ़ाक़त, q.v.

रिया, m. hypocrisy, dissimulation, subterfuge, evasion, affectation.

रियाज़त, f. abstinence, austerity.

रियाज़ी, m. abstract science, mathematics.

रियासत, f. government, dominion, command.

रिवायत, f. history, narrative, tale, fiction, story,

रिशवत = रिश्वत, q.v. [fable.

रिश्ता, m. a thread, line, string; a series; relationship, connexion, kin.

रिश्वत, f. a bribe.—khānā, to accept a bribe (lit. to swallow a bribe).—denā, to give a bribe. — lenā, to take a bribe.

रिष, रिषि, रिषं; for words beginning with either of these elements, see under the form ऋषि. See रि.

रिष्ट, 1, (corruption) = हृष्ट, q.v.: 2, m. happiness; good luck: misfortune, loss, destruction: the soap-berry plant (Sapindus detergens). [gens.

रिष्टक, m. the soap-berry plant (Sapindus deter-

रिष्टपुष्ट (corruption) = हृष्टपुष्ट, q. v. See रि.

रिख and रिखि in Chand = ऋषि, q. v. See रि.

रिस, f. anger, passion, vexation.

रिसता; see (1) रिश्ता (2) रिसाना.

रिसना, a. int. to drop slowly: n. to be vexed, be angry. [vexed.

रिसहा, m. (f. ī) wrathful, passionate, angry,

रिसाना, 1, = रोसना, q.v.: 2, m. (f. ī) = रिसहा, q.v.

रिसानी, f. 1, anger: 2, (m. रिसाना) angry, etc.

रिसालत, f. mission, apostleship, the state (or the circumstance) of having received mission.

रिसाला, m. mission, sending a letter, etc.; a treatise, small tract, essay, a book: a troop of horse.

रिसिआना }
रिसियाना } = रिसाना, q.v.

रिह्न, m. pledging, giving in pawn; a pledge, pawn, sum lent on mortgage, anything given in security for a loan, (in Law) the detention of a thing on account of a claim which may be answered by means of that thing, as in the case of debt.

रिहलत, f. marching, departure (particularly to the other world), decease, death.

रिहाई, f. liberation, deliverance, escape, release, acquittal, discharge, freedom, salvation.

री, 1, (see रे) a vocative particle (= Holloa! Bravo! Sirrah! O!) used exclusively in adressing females, and expressive of admiration, contempt, disrespect, or woe: 2, frequent in poetry as a rhyme-syllable, or, to fill out the line: 3, (in Māṛwāṛī) = the feminine genitive termination की, q. v.: 4, in ordinary Hindee this is the termination of the feminine form of the pronouns, मेरा, तेरा, and हमारा, तुम्हारा.

रींगना = रेंगना, q.v.

रींछ = रीछ, q.v.

रींधना, t. to cook, dress victuals.

रीख in Gaṛhwālī = रीछ, q.v.

रीछ, (from ऋक्ष) m. (f. in or nī) a bear.

रीछपति, m. (lord of the bears, i. e.) Jāmbavant.

रीछनी }
रीछिन } f. (m. रीछ) a she-bear.

रीछेस, m. (the lord of the bears, i. e.) Jāmbavant.

रीझ, f. choice, approbation, love, desire, wish; pleasing, satisfying.—pachānā, to conceal one's gratification.

रीझना, n. to be pleased, be gratified, be delighted.

रीझपचाऊ, m. f. a person who conceals his inclin-

रीझलना (corruption) = रीझना, q. v. [ation.

रीठा, f. a certain fruit (Sapindus emarginatus or saponaria) commonly called soap-wort or soap-nut.

रीठिया }
रीठी } f. a small रीठा, q.v.

रीढ़, f. }
रीढ़क, m. } the backbone.

रीढ़ी, f. a young mango.

रीत (contraction) = रीति, q.v. See ॠ, 1.

रीतना (Rām.) = (1) खोतना (2) खाली होना.

रीता, m. (f. ī) empty, void, deprived of. — k. to hollow, scoop out.

रीति, f. a going; established observance or usage, custom, way, practice, rite, mode, method, regulation, rule, ceremony; natural property: oozing, distilling: brass, white brass: rust of iron; calx of brass.

रीतिज्ञ (= कानूनगो) m. (f. ā) one who is acquainted with established rules or observances.

रीतो (corruption) = रीति, q.v.

रोते, inflected form of **रोता**, *q.v.* See **रोतना**.

रोन्धना, *t.* to cook, dres; victuals.

रोर, *m.* noise, clamour, outcry.

रोंगियाना, *a. int.* to cry (as a child); to murmur: to importune, beg earnestly.

रोश, *f.* the beard. — *banānā*, to shave. [lation.

रोस, *f.* 1, *more com.* **रिस**, *q.v.*: 2, equality; emu-

रोह, *f.* wind, odour, exhalation.

रु (contraction) = **अरु**, *q.v.* (see **अ**, 18).

रुअब, *m* terrifying, fear, trembling with fear,

रुआई, *more com.* **रोआई**, *q.v.* [terror, awe.

रुआना (a causal form of **रोना**) = **रोलाना**, *q.v.*

रुई, 1, *more prop.* **रूई**, *q.v.*: 2, the white ant (*Termes bellicosus*): a certain fish (*Cyprinus rohita*).

रुंकना, *more prop.* **रुकना**, *q.v.*

रुंड, **रुंद**, **रुंध**; for words beginning with either of these elements, see under the corresponding forms **रुण्ड**, **रुन्द**, **रुन्ध**, respectively.

रुक, 1, *m.* stoppage, hindrance: 2, a Kridanta suffix by means of which a few adjectives are formed from verbal roots; *e. g.* **भीरुक**, from the root **भी**.

रुकन, *f.* a stopping, hindering, preventing.

रुकना, *a. int.* to stop, rest: *n.* to be hindered, be prohibited, be enclosed. [stopped.

रुकवाना, *t.* (causat. of **रुकना**) to cause to be

रुकवैया, *m.* a hinderer, preventer, prohibitor.

रुकात, *m.* bits, pieces; notes, letters, cards; a collection of epistles. [er, stop.

रुकाना, *t.* to cause to enclose; to surround, hind-

रुकाव, *m.* hindrance, prevention, stoppage, delay, detention, backwardness, prohibition, obstacle.

रुकावट, *f.* = **रुकाव**, *q.v.*

रुकू; see **रुक** and **रुकना**.

रुकूब, *m.* the act of riding (on a horse, carriage, etc.): the perpetration of a crime: expecting, waiting, watching, contemplating the stars. [a foot of a verse.

रुक्न, *m.* a pillar, prop, aid, support: a grandee;

रुक्म, 1, clear, bright: 2, *m.* gold; iron: 3, *m. pr. n.* a certain prince (the son of Bhīshmak and brother-in-law of Krishṇ, slain by Balrām).

रुक्मअग्रज, *m. pr. n.* the eldest son of Bhīshmak.

रुक्मकेश, *m. pr. n.* the second son of Bhīshmak.

रुक्मवती, *f.* a species of metre in Sanskrit prosody: *pr. n.* a granddaughter of Rukmin.

रुक्मिणी, *f. pr. n.* (1) of a certain princess (sister of Rukm) who was carried off and married by Krishṇ (2) an epithet of the goddess Lakshmee.

रुक्मिन } = **रुक्म**, *q.v.*
रुक्मी }

रुक्ष, rough, rugged, difficult, uneven, harsh, austere, morose, unkind, unfriendly, cruel.

रुख़, *m.* the cheek; face: point, side, quarter, direction: (in Chess) the castle. — *k.* to attend to, to pursue (a prey); to make for (a place). — *denā*, to familiariz:. — *phernā* or *badalnā*, to be inattentive; to be angry, be displeased; to turn away from: to reject. — *rakhnā*, to continue friendship, maintain friendly intercourse.

रुख़सत, *f.* leave, licence, congé, dismission, discharge, permission, indulgence.

रुख़सार, *m.* the cheek, face, complexion, mien, air.

रुखा, *m.* (*f.* ī) *more prop.* **रूखा**, *q.v.*

रुखाई = **रूखाई**, *q.v.* [acrimonious.

रुखाना, *m.* (*f.* ī) dry, uninteresting, indifferent,

रुखावट = **रुखाई**, *q.v.*

रुग्न, broken; bent, curved, crooked; injured; diseased, sick, infirm. [firmity, sickness.

रुग्नता, *f.* (*m.* °**त्व**) curvedness, crookedness; in-

रुच, *f.* light, lustre, splendour, beauty; lightning: desire, wish, craving, avidity, desire of (or pleasure from) eating. [cite desire.

रुचना, *n.* to be agreeable, be gratifying: *t.* to ex-

रुचाभानु, *f. pr. n.* the wife of Hiraṇyāksh.

रुचि, *f.* light, a ray of light; splendour, lustre: desire, wish, pleasure, passion, hunger, appetite, liking, taste, sentiment; intent application: *pr. n.* a certain *rishi*. — *k.* to have a taste for.

रुचिभोजन, *m.* tempting food, food that is to one's appetite or taste. [dial, restorative.

रुचिर, beautiful, pleasing, agreeable, sweet, cor-

रुज्ज (*Rām.*) = **रोग**, *q.v.*

रुजू, *m.* return, turning towards, appearing; reference. — *k.* to appeal (or have recourse) to a higher authority. — *lānā*, to turn towards, to side with, to submit, yield.

रुणा, *f. pr. n.* a certain river flowing into the

रुण्ड, *m.* a headless body, trunk. [Saraswatī.

रुण्डमुण्ड, *m.* the trunk and head (considered as severed from each other).

रुत in Māṛwāṛī = **ऋतु**, *q.v.*

रुतबा, *m.* rank, dignity, degree, stair, step.

रुदन (*contraction*) = **रोदन**, *q.v.*

रुद्ध, *m.* (*f.* ā) obstructed, stopped, impeded, hindered, opposed, besieged, surrounded, held, secured.

रुद्र, *m.* an epithet (1) of Shiv as the god of tempests (2) of the eleven inferior manifestations of Shiv (personified roaring of the wind); *hence*, in the ingenious system of reckoning by symbols adopted by Hindoos in their poetry, this word is a symbol for 11.

रुद्राक्ष, *m.* a certain tree (*Eleocarpus ganitrus*) from the dark-coloured seeds of which a kind of rosary is made.

रुद्राणी, *f.* (see **रुद्र**, 1) an epithet of Durgā.

रुद्राधिर, *m.* pain or solicitude occasioned by Ru-

रुद्री, *f.* a sort of lute. [dra.

रुधि in Chand = **रुधिर**, *q.v.*

रुधिर, *m.* blood.

रुनी, *f.* the guava.

रुन्दना, *n.* to be trodden on, be trampled.

रुन्दवाना, *t.* to cause to be trampled down.

रुन्धजाना, an intensive form of **रुन्धना**, *q.v.*

रुन्धना, *n.* to be confined, be restrained, be surrounded, be afflicted (in mind).

रुपए, *m.* (pl. of **रुपया**) rupees ; money.
रुपना, *n.* (of **रोपना**) to be at bay : *a. int.* to stop.
रुपया, *more prop.* **रुपिया**, *q.v.*
रुपहरा, *more prop.* **रूपहरा**, *q.v.*
रुपिया / **रुपोया** / **रुपैया** } *more prop.* **रुपिया**, *q.v.*
रुपे, 1, = **रुपिया**, *q.v.*: 2 a corrupt inflection of [**रुपा**, *q.v.*
रुपैयेपैसे, *m.* rupees and pice, *i.e.* money.
रुरु, *m.* a kind of deer : 2 *pr. n.* a certain demon (*daitya*) who was slain by Shiv.
रुलना, *n.* to be rolled or planed, be smoothened, to be pulverized.
रुलाना, 1, (a causal form of **रोना**) = **रोलाना**, *q. v.*: 2, *t.* (causat. of **रोलना** to cause to roll, cause to plane, cause to smoothe.
रुल्ल, land that requires to be left fallow for a year or two in order to recover its vigour.
रुवा ; see **रुई**.
रुषित, *m.* (*f.* ā) = **रुष्ट**, *q.v.*
रुष्ट, *m.* (*f.* ā) displeased, angry, enraged.
रुसना = **रोसना**, *q.v.*
रुसवा = **रुस्वा**, *q. v.*
रुसवाई, *f.* = **रुस्वा**, 2, *q.v.*
रुसाना = **रोसना**, *q.v.*
रुसूम, *f.* (pl. of **रसम**) customs, duties, taxes ; a fee ; postage of letters.
रुस्त, growth, increase : *adj.* courageous, hearty, [spirited, bold, firm.
रुस्तम, *m. pr. n.* a celebrated warrior (one of the twelve champions of Persia) ; *hence*, any hero.
रुस्वा, 1, infamous, ignominious, dishonoured, disgraced : 2, *m.* opprobrium, disgrace, infamy, disrepute, dishonour, ignominy.
रुह, *m.* (*f.* ā) used as the latter element in compound words in the sense of growing, produced from ; mounted, ascended ; *e.g.* **शिरोरुह**, *lit.* growing on the head ; *hence*, the hair.
रू, *m.* face ; surface : cause, reason, sake.
रूई, *f.* cotton.
रूईदार, quilted with cotton, stuffed with cotton.
रूईवस्त्र, *m.* cotton stuff.
रूईहा, *m.* (*f.* ī) a seller of cotton.
रूं, *f.* (*dialectic*) = **रोम**, *q.v.*
रूंगटा, *m.* the short hairs of the body. *Rūngṭe khare hona*, to be on end (said of the hair, from cold, astonishment, fear, etc.).
रूंघट, *f.* dirt, filth.
रूंथना ; see (1) **रुन्दना** (2) **रुन्धना** (3) **रुन्थना**.
रूंधना = **रुन्धना**, *q. v.*
रूक / **रूकन** } *f.* = **घुलवा**, *q.v.*
रूख, 1, = (1) **रुक्ष** (2) **रुख** (3) **रूखा**, *qq. v.*: 2, *m.* a tree.
रूखचढ़ा, *m.* (*f.* ī) an epithet of the monkey ; *lit. adj.* tree-climbing, tree-mounting.

रूखड़, *m.* a sort of Hindoo ascetic.
रूखड़ा, *m.* (dim. of **रूख**) a small tree.
रूखन, *m.* = **घुलवा**, *q.v.*
रूखा, *m.* (*f.* ī) dry, stale (as bread), rough, harsh, unkind, unfriendly ; pure, simple, plain, unseasoned.
रूखाई, *f.* plainness, dryness (of bread), roughness, unseasonedness, staleness, unkind looks, indifference, [unfriendliness.
रूखानी, *f.* a carpenter's chisel.
रूखासूखा, *m.* (*f.* **रूखीसूखी**) plain, blunt, unseasoned, harsh (said of words).
रूखी, *f.* 1, (*m.* **रूखा**) dry, etc. : 2, a squirrel.
रूक्ष, 1, *adj.* stern : 2, *m.* a violator.
रूज, *m.* a kind of insect very troublesome to birds.
रूजू, *more prop.* **रुजू**, *q. v.*
रूझा, *m.* (*f.* ī) any animal (*esp.* a bird) much teazed by the insect called *rūj*.
रूठना, (from **रुष्ट**) to have a misunderstanding with a friend, to be angry, be displeased, be cool, to have a quarrel.
रूठनी, 1, *f.* a species of sensitive-plant (*Mimosa* [*natans*) : 2, quarrelsome.
रूठा, *m.* (*f.* ī) displeased, cool, angry.
रूठारूठी, *f.* misunderstanding between friends, mutual coolness.
रूढ़, grown, arisen ; budded, blown, born, produced ; mounted, ascended ; ascertained ; hard, stiff, rough, grim, cross, rude, harsh, uncourteous, traditional, conventional (applied especially to words which, though familiar, are of obscure or unknown origin).
रूढ़वचन / **रूढ़वाक्य** } = **रूढ़शब्द**, *q.v.*
रूढ़शब्द, *m.* harsh language ; (in Gram.) a word of obscure or unknown origin though of familiar use and application.
रूढ़ि, *f.* growth, origin, birth, rise, notoriety ; (in Gram.) the traditional or conventional meaning of words as distinguished from their etymological signification.
रूपड़, *more prop.* **रुपड़**, *q. v.*
रूत, 1, *m.* any cry or noise (*esp.* that of birds) : 2, *f. pr. n.* the Book of Ruth.
रूदाद, *f.* (*m.* ?) an account of circumstances, narrative, statement ; occurrence, accident, incident.
रून्थना ; see (1) **रुन्धना** (2) **रुन्धना** (3) **रुन्दना**.
रून्धना, *t.* to surround, enclose (as with a hedge); to watch : *n.* to be restrained ; to be astonished or confounded.
रूप, 1, *m.* natural state or condition; form, shape, figure, appearance, semblance, image, kind, beauty, colour, picture, face, countenance, aspect, features, mode, manner, method : a dramatic poem, a play : silver: (in Arithm.) discrete quantity; the arithmetical unit; integer number : (in Algeb.) the known or absolute number : 2, *m.* (*f.* ā) this word is often found as the last member of compound adjectives (*bahuvrīhi*). in the sense of like, resembling, consisting of ; *e. g.* **मनुष्यरूप**, of the shape of a human being. In the ingenious system of reckoning by symbols adopted by Hindoos in their poetry, this word is a symbol for 1 (one).

रूपकरण, *m.* (in Gram.) declension.

रूपजस्त, *m.* pewter.

रूपज्ञान, *m.* acquaintance with any form.

रूपधारण, *m.* the assuming a form or guise.

रूपधारी, *m.* (*f.* iṇī) a disguised person, etc. : lit. *adj.* assuming a form, in disguise, disguised.

रूपनिधान, an epithet of any very beautiful person ; *lit.* a receptacle or abode of beauty.

रूपभानु, resembling the sun, sunlike.

रूपमान, *m.* (*f.* matī) = **रूपवान**, *q.v.*

रूपय:, *more com.* **रुपिया**, *q.v.*

रूपरस, *m.* killed or calcined silver.

रूपरेख } **रूपरेखा** } *f.* the countenance, features, visage.

रूपवती, *f.* (*m.* **रूपवान**, etc.) a handsome or well-formed female, a comely woman.

रूपवन्त, *m.* (*f.* vatī) = **रूपवान**, *q.v.*

रूपवान, *m* (*f.* vatī) possessing shape or form, well-shaped, comely, elegant, handsome, beautiful.

रूपसागर, an epithet of any very beautiful person; *lit.* an ocean of beauty.

रूपहना } **रूपहरा** } *m.* (*f.* ī) = **रूपहला**, *q.v.*

रूपहला, *m.* (*f.* ī) made of silver, silvery, silvered.

रूपा, 1, *m.* (from **रूप्य**) silver: 2, *f.* (*m.* **रूप**, 2) like, resembling.

रूपान्तर, *m.* change of appearance or form, transformation.—*k.* to transform.

रुपिय: = **रुपिया**, *q. v.*

रुपिया, *m.* (infl. **रुपिये**) a rupee (the well-known silver coin so called); *hence*, money, wealth. The Calcutta sicca rupee is worth about two shillings, and the silver of it is better than English standard silver by 2¾*d.* the ounce. By the regulations of Government passed in May 1793, the rupee should weigh 179⅝ grs. Troy.

रुपियावाला, *m.* (*f.* ī) a wealthy person.

रूपी, *m.* (*f.* iṇī) : this word is often found as the last member of compound adjectives, in the sense of possessed of shape or form, beautiful, handsome, having the shape or figure of; *e.g.* **मनुष्यरूपी**, of human form.

रुपैय: } **रुपै** } **रुपैय:** } *more com.* **रुपिया**, *q. v.*

रुपैयापैसा, *m.* rupees and pice, *i.e.* money.

रूपोश, concealed.—*honā*, to be concealed, to hide, one's face, to abscond.

रूप्य, *m.* silver, wrought silver ; wrought gold.

रूबकार, (*lit.* face to business ; *hence*) ready for business, intent on, in hand, on foot.

रूबकारी, *f.* proceedings (of a cause).

रूबराह, setting out ; fit for business, adjusted, prepared ; returned from an erroneous course, reformed.

रूबरू, *m.* presence: *adv.* in the presence of, in the sight of, face to face with, before, in front of.

रूम, *m. pr. n.* the eastern Roman empire ; the present Turkish empire, Greece, Romelia, Asia Minor.

रूमटी, *f.* subterfuge, trick ; wrangling.

रूमनिवासी, *m.* (*f.* inī) a dweller in *Rūm.*

रूमाल, *m.* a handkerchief, pocket-handkerchief, towel, napkin.

रूमी, *m.* (*f.* iṇī) a native of *Rūm*, a Grecian, a Turk : *lit.* appertaining to *Rūm.* — *mastakī*, *f.* the drug called gum mastic.

रूर ; see (1) **रूखा** (2) **रूढ़** (3) **रूरा.**

रूरा, *m.* (*f.* ī) beautiful, good.

रूवत, *f.* beauty, freshness, symmetry, gracefulness, splendour ; friendly attention, regard, kindness.

रूश ; see (1) **अटरूष** (2) **रोष.**

रूशिनास, conspicuous, celebrated, honourable, respectable : *hence*, a person whose face one knows, an acquaintance : (*pl.* ān) chiefs of a kingdom or city : stars.

रूष, 1, *more prop.* **रूख**, *q.v.* : 2, see **रोष.**

रूस; see (1) **अटरूष** (2) **रोष.**

रूसना = **रोसना**, *q.v.*

रूसफ़ेद, fair-faced, of a bright countenance; hence, *met.* unblameable, honest, respectable, select.

रूसबाई, *more prop.* **रुसवाई**, *q. v.*

रूसवा, *more prop.* **रुस्वा**, *q.v.*

रूसियाह, *m.* a criminal, sinner, guilty party : *lit.* black in the face ; hence, *met.* disgraced, criminal, unfortunate.

रूसियाही, *f.* disgrace, criminality, dishonour.

रूसी, *f.* (**रूक्षीय**) scurf.

रूस्याह, *more prop.* **रूसियाह**, *q.v.*

रूह, 1, *f.* soul, spirit : 2, *m.* the Holy Spirit.

रूहअफ़ज़ा, increasing the spirits, life-prolonging.

रूहउलक़ुदूस, *Arabic* (Rūh-ul-ḳudus) *m. pr. n.* (1) of the Holy Spirit (2) of the angel Gabriel.

रूहानी, appertaining to soul or spirit, spiritual.

रूहू ; see **रूह** and **रोहू.**

रे, 1, (see **री**) a vocative particle (= Holloa ! Bravo ! Sirrah ! O !) used exclusively in addressing *males*, and expressive of admiration, contempt, disrespect, or woe: 2, It is frequently found in poetry as a rhyme-syllable, or, to fill out the line.

रेंक, *f.* the braying of the ass.

रेंकना, *a. int.* to bray (said of the ass).

रेंगना, *a. int.* to creep, plod, crawl, go on all fours.

रेंगनी, *f.* a certain medicinal plant (*Solanum jacquini*, Willd.).

रेंगाई, *f.* creeping, crawling.

रेंगाना, *t.* to cause to creep, cause to crawl.

रेंट, *m.* = (1) **रहट** (2) **रेंटा**, *q.v.*

रेंटा, *m.* snivel, mucus, snot.

रेंड or **रेंड़**, *m.* } **रेंडी** or **रेंड़ी**, *f.* } = **रेवड़ी**, *q. v.*

रेंडु, a corruption of **रेणु**, *q. v.*

रेंकू, *m.* a vehicle, carriage, bullock-cart.

रेंटी, *f.* a small melon.

रेख, *f.* ; a contraction of **रेखा**, *q.v.*

रेखउठान, marked with lines.

रेख़ता, 1, scattered: 2, *m.* mortar, plaster: a Hindūstānī ode: the Hindustānī language (being a mixed one) is called *rekhtā*.

रेखरू (**रेखा + रू**) shape and form.

रेखा, *f.* (for **लेखा**) a line, row, series; a streak, stripe; a mark; writing, fate, destiny; a little; fraud; fulness, satisfaction: a saw-kerf; a furrow; (in Astron.) the meridian of Lankā.

रेखान, land that is beyond the reach of river-water.

रेग, *f.* sand.

रेगड़ / **रेगर** } = **लेगड़**, *q.v.*

रेगाना, *more prop.* **रेंगाना**, *q.v.*

रेगारी / **रेघारी** } *f.* (from **रेखा**) a furrow.

रेज़गी, *f.* a scrap, bit, piece; small change, small coin (as four-*ānā* pieces, etc.).

रेण (*contraction*) = **रेणु**, *q.v.*

रेणु, *m. f.* dust, sand, powder, pollen; an atom.

रेणुका, *f.* a certain perfume and medicine of a bitter and slightly pungent taste and greyish colour (it is procured in grains about the size of those of pepper): a species of pulse (*Ervum*): *pr. n.* the wife of Jamadagni and mother of Parashurām.

रेयट, *m.* = (1) **रहट** (2) **रेयटा**, *q.v.*

रेयटा, *m.* snivel, mucus, snot.

रेयड, *m.* (from **एरयड**) = **रेयडी**, *q.v.*

रेंयडी, *f.* (from **एरयडी**) the castor-oil plant (*Palma Christi* or *Ricinus vulgaris*. — *kā tel*, *m.* castor-oil.

रेयडु (*corruption*) = **रेणु**, *q.v.*

रेत, 1, a contraction of **रेतः**, *q.v.*: 2, a corruption of **रेयट**, 2 (= **रेयटा**), *q.v.*: 3, *f.* sand; filings.

रेतः / **रेतन** } = **रेतस**, *q.v.*

रेतना, *t.* to file, rasp, polish, thrum.

रेतनी, *f.* a file.

रेतल, 1, *f.* sand; sandy ground: 2, sandy, abounding in sand.

रेतला, abounding in sand, sandy.

रेतस, *m.* seminal fluid, sperm, sperma genitale (*viri aut mulieris*): quicksilver.

रेता, *m.* (see **रेत**, 3) sand; filings.

रेताई, *f.* the price paid for filing or for polishing.

रेतियाना, *t.* to file, polish.

रेती, *f.* sandy ground on the shore of a river: a file.

रेतीला, abounding in sand, sandy.

रेतूआ, *m.* (*f.* **रेतूई**) a filer, polisher.

रेन, 1, *more com.* **रैन**, *q.v.*: 2, *more prop.* **रेणु**, *q.v.*

रेनु (*corruption*) = **रेणु**, *q.v.*

रेन्दी, *f.* a small melon.

रेफ, *m.* (see **रकार** and **र**, 5) the letter **र** with the inherent vowel; the mark which represents this letter when it is placed over a following consonant.

रेब; see (1) **रेव** (2) **अवरेब**.

रेल, *m.* (Engl.) the railway.

रेलगाड़ी, *f.* a railway-carriage, the railway-train.

रेलढेल = **रेलपेल**, *q.v.*

रेलना, *t.* to shove, push, rush.

रेलपेल, *f.* abundance, plenty; a bustle, crowd, promiscuous crowd.

रेला, *m.* a rushing, rush, push, shove, assault: a flood: a line or string of animals.

रेव, deceit, stratagem, fraud: a ford: *m. pr. n.* a son of Ānart, and father of Raivat.

रेवड़ी, *f.* a kind of sweetmeat. — *ke phermen paṛnā*, to be involved in difficulties. The allusion is to a certain game constructed on the principle of geometrical progression, in which a person bets that he will eat one of these sweet cakes so many times doubled and is confounded at finding the quantity amount to something far beyond his expectation. The phrase also applies to a similar game founded on arithmetical progression, such as the well-known feat of gathering up a hundred stones, etc., placed at a distance of a yard asunder, in the space of an hour.

रेवत, *m. pr. n.* (see **रेवती**, 1) a certain ancient king, father-in-law of Balarām.

रेवती, *f. pr. n.* (1) of the daughter of Rewat and wife of Balarām (2) one of the female energies (*mātṛi*) of the gods (3) the 27th *Nakshatra* consisting of Piscium (ζ) and thirty-one other stars, and figured by a tabor.

रेवतीरमण, *m.* (the husband of Revatī, *i.e.*) Balarām.

रेवा, *f. pr. n.* (1) of the Narmada (Nerbudda) river (2) of the wife of Kāmdev.

रेश, *m.* a wound, sore; pus, matter.

रेशम, *m.* silk.

रेशमी, silken, woven with silk, made of silk.

रेशा, *m.* a fibre, filament, nerve, the string fibre of the mango.

रेसम, *more prop.* **रेशम**, *q.v.*

रेसमान, *f.* string, cord, thread, rope.

रेसमी, *more prop.* **रेशमी**, *q.v.*

रेसू (*Rām.*) = **ईर्षा**, *q.v.*

रेह, *f.* fossil alkali (used for washing and making soap).

रेहड़, barren (said of soil).

रेहडू, *m.* a sled, a sledge.

रेहना, *t.* to streak, to make lines, to delineate.

रेहर, barren (said of soil).

रेहला, *m.* a vetch.

रेहाई, *more prop.* **रहाई**, *q.v.*

रेही, *f.* fossil alkali.

रेहूपेहू, *f.* abundance.

रेंकना, *a. int.* to bray (said of the ass).

रेंगना = **रेंगना**, *q.v.*

रैंन, *more com.* **रैन**, *q.v.*

रैदास, *m. pr. n.* Ravidās (a certain fakeer, and leader of a sect of Hindoos).

रैन, *f.* (from **रजनी**) night (from the end of twilight till daybreak)

रैनदिन, day and night, continually.

रैना } **रैनि** } *more com.* **रैन**, *q.v.*

रैनु, a corruption (1) of **रैन** (2) of **रेणु**, *qq.v.*

रैयत, *more prop.* **रऐयत**, *q.v.*

रैवत, *m. pr. n.* (1) of the fifth Manu of the present cycle (2) of a certain Daitya (3) an epithet of Shiv (4) of a certain mountain (the eastern part of the Vindhya range).

रो in Māṛwāṛī = the well-known genit. termin. **का**. It also occurs in some Braj forms; *e.g.* **तोरो** = **तेरा**.

रोआई, *f.* (see **आई**, 3) lamentation, wailing.

रोआं, *m.* (from **रोम**) the small hair of the body, bristle, pile, nap, down; wool; moss.

रोआना (a causal form of **रोना**) = **रोलाना**, *q.v.*

रोआस, *f.* inclination to weep.

रोआसा, *m.* (*f.* ī) inclined to weep, vexed, afflicted, displeased.

रोई, *f.* (*m.* **रोयां**) past part. of the verb **रोना**, *q.v.*

रोईदगी, *f.* vegetation, growth of a plant.

रोएं, *f.* (pl. of **रोआं**) the small fine hairs of the body, bristles, down. — *badalnā*, to change his coat, to become sleek and fat (said of the horse).

रोंआ, 1, *m.* (*f.* **रोंई**) *more prop.* **रोया**, *q.v.*: 2, (pl. **रोंए**) *more com.* **रोआं**, *q.v.*

रोंआं (pl. **रोंएं**) = **रोआं**, *q.v.*

रोंआर, possessing down (or bristles, etc.) on the body, downy, woolly, bristly, mossy.

रोंए (pl. of **रोंआ**) } **रोंएं** (pl. of **रोंआं**) } = **रोएं**, *q.v.*

रोंगटी } **रोंघटा** } (by inversion) = **रोयटगी**, *q.v.*

रोंट, **रोंड**, **रोंध**, **रोंप**; for words beginning with either of these elements, see under the corresponding forms **रोपट**, **रोपड**, **रोन्ध**, **रोम्प**, respectively.

रोंजी, *more prop.* **रोजी**, *q.v.*

रोंवा (pl. **रोंवे**) } **रोंवां** (pl. **रोंवें**) } *more prop.* **रोआं**, *q.v.*

रोंशन, *more prop.* **रोशन**, *q.v.*

रोक, 1, *m.* ready money, cash; prompt payment in cash: 2, *f.* prevention, prohibition, stop, restraint, let, hindrance, check, barrier. — *rakhnā*, to keep, a check upon.

रोकटोक, *f.* let-and-hindrance, opposition, resistance, obstruction, challenge.

रोकड़, *f.* ready money, cash; prompt payment in cash: a cash-book.

रोकड़बही, *f.* a cash-book.

रोकड़िया, *m.* a cash-keeper, treasurer, banker.

रोकड़ी, *m.* (*f.* nī, inī, in) = **रोकड़िया**, *q.v.*

रोकड़े, *m.* ready money, cash; prompt payment in cash.

रोकन, *f.* an obstacle, obstruction, hindrance.

रोकना, *t.* to hem in, enclose, surround, stop, block, fend, to detain, restrain, hinder, coerce, prevent, to prohibit, interdict, forbid, interrupt.

रोकू, *m. f.* a hinderer, preventer.

रोख, *more com.* (1) **रूख** (2) **रोष**, *qq.v.*

रोखसत, *more prop.* **रुख़सत**, *q.v.*

रोखा, *m.* (*f.* ī); see (1) **रूखा** (2) **रोचना**.

रोग, *m.* disease, sickness: a species of costus (*Costus speciosus*).

रोगग्रस्त, *m.* (*f.* ā) an invalid: *lit.* taken ill, seized by a sickness, diseased.

रोगग्रस्तता, *f.* diseasedness, badness of health.

रोगनिवृत्यर्थ, (Sk.) for the purpose of removing disea e.

रोगभू, *f.* an epithet of the body; *lit.* the region (or seat) of disease.

रोगराज, *m.* an epithet of consumption; *lit.* the chief of diseases.

रोगलक्षण, *m.* a symptom of disease.

रोगशान्तक, *m.* (*f.* ikā) an epithet of any physician; *lit.* an alleviator of disease.

रोगशान्ति, *f.* the alleviation or cure of disease.

रोगहर, *m.* (*f.* ī) = **रोगहारी**, *q.v.*

रोगहारी, *m.* (*f.* iṇī) an epithet of any physician or of medicine; lit. *adj.* taking away (or removing) disease, medicinal, curative.

रोगिणी, *f.* (*m.* **रोगी**) a female invalid.

रोगियल } **रोगिया** } = **रोगी**, *q.v.*

रोगी, *m.* (*f.* iṇī) an invalid: *lit.* affected with sickness, diseased, invalided, ailing, sick, ill, unwell.

रोगील } **रोगीला** } *m.* (*f.* ī *or* in) = **रोगी**, *q.v.*

रोगीसोगी (alliteration) = **रोगी** + **सोगी**, *qq.v.*

रोगोत्पादक, *m.* a cause of disease: lit. *adj.* producing or occasioning disease.

रोचक, *m.* any medicine which strengthens the tone of the stomach and restores lost appetite, stomachic, a carminative.

रोचन, 1, *m.* (*f.* ā) irradiating, splendid, pleasing, sharpening to the appetite: 2, *m.* any stomachic; the name of several plants; the æther; turmeric.

रोचना, *f.* 1, a certain yellow pigment supposed to be the concrete bile of the cow or to be found in the head of that animal (it is used as a medicine, a dye, and a perfume): 2, an excellent female.

रोचनी, *f.* 1, = **रोचना**, 1, *q.v.*: 2, red arsenic.

रोज, 1, *more prop.* (1) **रोज़** (2) **रोझ**, *q.v.*: 2, *m.* lamentation, wailing, weeping.

रोज़, *m.* a day. *Roz-roz*, every day, always, constantly.

रोज़गार, *m.* service, livelihood, earning. — *k.* to serve, to earn a livelihood.

रोजड़ा, *m.* lamentation, wailing, weeping.

रोज़नामचा, *m.* a daily account-book.

रोज़मर्रा, 1, *m.* daily conversation, common discourse: 2, daily, always, constantly.

रोज़ा, *m.* a religious fast; Lent. — *rakhnā*, to keep or observe a fast. — *kholnā*, to break or terminate a fast, to eat during a fast at the ceremonially appointed time. — *toṛnā*, to violate a fast (*i.e.* to eat at a time other than that religiously enjoined).

रोज़ी, *f.* daily food or portion; daily work, employment; monthly wages; goods, chattels.

रोज़ीना, *m.* daily pay, daily food.

रोझ, *m.* the painted (or white-footed) antelope (*Antelope picta*).

रोट, *m.* thick bread: *met.* sweetmeats offered to the monkey-god (*Hanumān*).

रोटा, *m.* = रोट, *q. v.*

रोटी, *f.* bread; a loaf; any wheaten cake toasted on an iron plate or gridiron (without yeast). The term is applied to any bread whether leavened or unleavened; while the bread eaten by Europeans, and made with yeast, is, strictly speaking, called *Khamīrī roṭī.*

रोड़ा, *m.* a stone, a fragment of stone or brick, a brickbat: a certain Hindoo tribe of the military (*Kshatrī*) caste. *Bāṭkā* —, a stumblingblock (in one's path).

रोवो, in Māṛwāṛī = रोना, 2, *q. v.*

रोपट, *f.* subterfuge, trick, cheating.

रोपटगी, *f.* quarrelling, wrangling; subterfuge, deception, trick, trickery, cheating.

रोपटना, *t.* to deny, contradict, dispute.

रोपटिया, deceptive, treacherous, quarrelsome.

रोपटी, *f.* subterfuge, trick, cheating.

रोपड़ी, *f.* deceit, fraud, villainy.

रोद, *m.* a river, stream: the string of a musical instrument.

रोदन, *m.* weeping; lamentation, wailing; a tear, tears.

रोदा, *m.* a gut, intestine, catgut, sinew (used as a bowstring): the branch of a creeper.

रोदिति (*Rām.*) = रोता है. (The term is Sanskrit.)

रोध, *m.* an obstruction; a bank, shore.

रोधन, 1, *m.* an impediment, obstruction, obstacle, hindrance; the act of impeding: a beseiging: *pr. n.* the planet Mercury: 2, *m.* (*f.* ā) a hinderer: lit. *adj.* impeding, obstructing, hindering.

रोनक, *more prop.* रौनक़, *q. v.*

रोना, 1 = रवा, *q. v.*: 2, *a. int.* to weep, cry, lament; *n.* to be melancholy, be displeased: 3, *m.* weeping, wailing, lamentation, grief: 3, *m.* (*f.* ī) a weeper: *lit.* addicted to weeping. — *denā*, to weep, cry: to be filled with indignation, to be displeased.

रोनी, *f.* (*m.* रोना, 3,) a female addicted to weeping. — *sūrat*, 1, *f.* a melancholy or rueful countenance: 2, any person of a joyless countenance: *lit.* of a tearful face.

रोनीं, in Braj = रोना, 2, *q. v.*

रोन्धना, *more com.* रौन्दना, *q. v.*

रोप, *m.* the stalk of grass or corn when growing.

रोपक, *m.* (*f.* ikā) a planter, sower: lit. *adj.* planting, sowing, raising.

रोपण, *m.* the act of planting, sowing, or raising: cicatrizing.

रोपना, *t.* to sow, plant, transplant: to defend, block, obstruct.

रोपर, transplanted rice: a rate in a lease for crops of rice raised by transplanting.

रोपा, *m.* transplanted rice.

रोपित, *m.* (*f.* ā) planted, sown, raised.

रोपै, 1, in Braj = रोपे (रोपना): 2, *more com.* रुपया.

रोब, an old form = मैं रोऊंगा (रोना).

रोबाइयां, *more prop.* रोवाइयां, *q. v.*

रोबाह, *f.* a fox.

रोम, *m.* the small hair of the body, pile, nap, down, bristle, wool, moss: water: *pr. n.* Rome.

रोमकूप, **रोमछिद्र**, **रोमछेद** } *m.* a pore of the skin.

रोमदेश, *m. pr. n.* the country of Rome, Italy.

रोमपाट, *m.* woollen cloth.

रोमपाद, *m pr. n.* a certain ancient Hindoo king.

रोमवत, **रोमवन्त**, **रोमवान** } *m.* (*f.* vatī) = रोमश, *q. v.*

रोमविकार = रोमांच, *q. v.*

रोमश, *m.* (*f.* ā) any hairy or woolly creature; a hog, a ram: *lit.* hairy, downy, woolly.

रोमहर्ष, 1, *m.* = रोमांच, *q. v.*: 2, *m.* (*f.* ā) terrible: *lit.* causing the hair to stand erect.

रोमहर्षण, 1, = रोमहर्ष, 1 and 2: 2, *m. pr. n.* a certain Hindoo sage, promulgator of the Mahābhārat.

रोमांच, *m.* horripilation (considered as occasioned by rapture or exquisite delight).

रोमांचित, *m.* (*f.* ā) affected with horripilation through the sense of exquisite pleasure, enraptured, delighted.

रोमावली, *f.* the line of hair extending across the middle of the navel.

रोमीय, appertaining to Rome or to the Romans.

रोम्पना, *t.* to plant, to transplant.

रोया, *m.* (*f.* रोई) past part. of the verb रोना, *q. v.*

रोयां, (pl. रोयें) *more com.* रोआं, *q. v.*

रोर, *f.* (from रव) noise, clamour, outcry; fame, rumour, notoriety.

रोरा, *m.* (*f.* ī) profligate, blackguard.

रोरी, *f.* a kind of clay with which the *tilak* is occasionally made.

रोरोकर, (*lit.* with repeated weeping; hence) *adv.* in tears, with difficulty, with labour and pain.

रोल, *f.* a catalogue, roll.

रोलना, *t.* to roll, plane, polish, smoothe: to select, pick, winnow, sift.

रोलाना, *t.* (a causat. of रोना) to cause to weep, make one cry, to displease, affect, vex.

रोलाश, (in Māṛwāṛī) rocky jungle.

रोली, *f.* a certain mixture (of rice, turmeric, and alum, with acid) used by Hindoos to make the sectarial mark (*tilak*) on the forehead.

रोवना, *more com.* रोना, *q. v.*

रोवनी; see (1) रोनी (2) रोहिणी.

रोवनों, a plural form of रोवनी, *q. v.*

रोवनीं in Braj = रोना, *q. v.*

रोवां, (pl. रोवें) *more prop.* रोआं, *q. v.*

रोवा, 1 *more prop.* रवा, *q. v.*: 2, *m.* (*f.* ī) *more prop.* रोआ, *q. v.*

रोवाई, 1, (pl. रोवाइयां) *more com.* रोआई, *q. v.*: 2, *f.* = रोवाया, *q. v.*

रोवाना, 1, *more com.* रोआना, *q. v.*: 2, *more prop.* रवाना, *q. v.*

रोवाया, *m.* (*f.* रोवाई) past part. of रोवाना.

रौशन, bright, splendid, illuminated, lighted up, alight, manifest. conspicuous. — *k.* to illumine, to light (*e.g.* a candle or lamp).—*ho jānā*, to become, illuminated.

रौशनाई, *f.* light, brightness: ink.

रौशनी, *f.* light, brightne s, splendour, glare.

रोष, *m.* anger, wrath, passion, rage. — *k.* to be angry, be displeased, be enraged.

रोषण, 1, *m.* (*f.* ā) wrathful, passionate, angry: 2. *m.* a touchstone: quicksilver.

रोषना, *more com.* **रोसना**, *q.v.*

रोषवाहन, *m.* (*f.* ā) carrying or displaying wrath, wrathful. excitable, ira cible, choleric, angry.

रोषित, *m.* (*f.* ā) }
रोषी, *m.* (*f.* iṇī) } = **रुष्ट**, *q. v.*

रोसना, *n.* (from **रोष**) to be vexed, be displeased, be angry, be provoked, to have a misunderstanding with a friend.

रोसल, *m.* }
रोसली, *f.* } light soil of a good quality.

रोस्ताई, *m.* a village: a villager, peasant.

रोहण, *m. pr. n.* the mountain in Ceylon commonly known as "Adam's peak."

रोहट, *f.* weeping, crying; tears.

रोहण, *m.* a growing, rising, ascending, mounting: semen virile: a species of large forest-tree (*Swietenia febrifuga*): *pr. n.* (1) of the mountain in Ceylon commonly known as "Adam's peak" (2) of a certain ancient Hindoo king.

रोहणी (*contraction*) = **रोहिणी**, *q. v.*

रोहिण, *m.* the Indian figtree; a certain fragrant grass: a part of the forenoon.

रोहिणि = **रोहिणी**, 1 (1), *q.v.*

रोहिणी, 1, *f. pr. n.* (1) of the fourth *Nakshatra*, figured by a wheeled carriage, and comprising Aldebaran and four other stars in Taurus (2) of the mother of Balarām: 2, *f.* a cow; a woman stained with red pigments: a girl at the commencement of menstruation; inflammatory affection of the throat; Bengal madder; yellow myrobalan; lightning.

रोहित, *m.* a kind of fish (*Cyprinus rohita* or *C. denticulatus*, Buch.) commonly called the 'rohee': a kind of deer: Indra's bow unbent and invisible to mortals: *lit.* (1) red (2) *m.* the red colour.

रोहिताश्व, *m.* an epithet of Agni: *lit.* whose horses are red.

रोहिनि, *more prop.* **रोहिणि**, *q.v.*

रोहिष = **रोहिष**, *q.v.*

रोहू, *m. f.* = **रोहित**, *q.v.*

रौंद, **रौंध**; for words beginning thus, see under the form **रौन्द**.

रौग़न, *m.* grease, oil, boiled butter; varnish, lacker.

रौज, *more com.* **रोज**, *q.v.*

रौज़ा, *m.* a garden; a mausoleum, a shrine or tomb of a reputed saint.

रौता, *m.* pumpkins, etc. pickled in sour milk.

रौताई, *f.* chiefship.

रौद (*contraction*) = **रौद्र**, 2, *q.v.*

रौदना = **रौन्दना**, *q. v.*

रौद्र, 1, *m.* (*f.* ī) irascible, wrathful, violent, terrific, formidable: 2, *m.* heat, warmth, sunshine, wrath, rage.

रौद्रता, *f.* fierceness, horribleness, formidableness.

रौद्री, *f.* an epithet of Pārvatī; *lit.* a formidable female.

रौधना = **रौन्दना**, *q.v.*

रौनक़, *f.* beauty, elegance, splendour, ornament, gaiety; order, symmetry.

रौना, *m.* the bringing home a wife to consummate a marriage.

रौनौं in Braj = **रौना**, 2, *q.v.*

रौन्दन, *m.* a trampling, treading under-foot.

रौन्दना, *t.* to trample on, tread down, ride over.

रौन्धना = **रौन्दना**, *q v*

रौपै in Braj = (1) **रोपे** (**रोपना**) (2) **रुपिया**, *q. v.*

रौम }
रौमक } = **रौमलवण**, *q. v.*

रौमलवण, *m.* a kind of salt procured from a salt lake near the town of Sambhar in the district of Jainagar.

रौर, 1, = **रोर**, *q.v.*: 2, a contraction of **रावर**, *q.v.*

रौरव, 1, *m.* (*f.* ī) a savage, etc.: *lit.* proceeding from the deer called *ruru*; *hence*, formidable, horrible, terrific, frightful; dishonest: 2, *m. pr. n.* one of the divisions of the infernal regions.

रौला, *m.* noise, tumult, sedition, alarm.

रौलाधौला, a play on the word **रौला**, *q. v.*

रौशन, **रौसन**; for words beginning thus, see under the form **रोशन**.

रौहिण, 1, *m.* (*f.* ī) born under the asterism *Rohiṇī*: 2, *m.* the sandal-tree, sandal-wood: the Indian figtree: 3. *m.* an epithet of Agni: 4, *m. pr. n.* (1) of a certain demon vanquished by India (2) of the 9th Muhūrt of the day.

रौहिणी; see (1) **रोहिणी** (2) **रौहिण**.

रौहिणेय, 1, *m.* an epithet (1) of Balarām (2) of the planet Mercury: 2, *m.* an emerald.

रौहिष, *m.* 1, = **रोहित**, *q.v.*: 2, a kind of creeper: 3, *m.* (*f.* ī) a sort of deer said to resemble an ass.

ल

ल (1) is the twenty-eighth consonant in the Hindee alphabet, and has the following characteristics and functions: — 1, It belongs to the class of dentals and is the third of the semivowels or *antahsth* letters: see **अन्तःस्थ**. 2, Its sound is, as nearly as possible, that of the English letter '*l.*' 3, In the brogue of the rustics this letter is continually added to the past participial form of verbs; *e.g.* **लिखाल**; properly **लिखा**. Most frequently, however, when so used, it displaces the vowel at the end; *e. g.* **रहल**, **कहल**; properly **रहा**, **कहा**. 4, This letter is continually interchanged (1) with **ड़**; *e.g.* **दालिम**; properly **दाड़िम**: again **बिलाल**, properly **बिड़ाल** (2) with **न**; *e.g.* **लील**; properly **नील** (3) with **र**; *e.g.* **दीवाल**; properly **दीवार**: (4) with **औ**; *e. g.* **तीन सल**, properly **तीन सौ**. In one instance it changes places with **स**, *viz.* in the word **निकसना** and **निकासना** = **निकलना** and

निकासना. Lastly, It sometimes changes places with another letter in the same word; e.g. नखलेा; properly लखनेा. 5, In works on Prosody, this letter is used as an abbreviation for the word लघु. 6, This letter is frequently found as a Taddhita suffix [m. (f. ā)] by means of which adjectives are formed from substantives; e.g. मुख्य, पांशुल, शिराल, स्वादल.

लअ्नत, f. an imprecation, curse, anathema, execration.—k. to curse: (with par) to invoke a curse upon.

लअ्ल, m. a ruby; any bright gem: met. the lips

लइवेा in Braj = लाओ (लाना). [of a mistress.

लई, 1, more prop. लय, 3, q.v.: 2, much, many, extremely, more, very, excessively.

लउआ, a gourd. [bundance, much.

लंक, 1, f. the loins, the reins: 2, m. a heap, a-

लंका, f. pr. n. (1) of the capital of Rāvaṇ in Ceylon (2) of the island of Ceylon (3) of the place whence Hindoo astronomers calculate longitude (which is different in situation from Ceylon). According to the Hindoos, Laṅkā is much further from the continent than Ceylon is, and is much more considerable in size than that island, being equal to one twelfth of the equatorial circumference of the earth. It is one of the places lying under the first meridian, and is placed in the Eastern Ocean south of Ceylon, from which island Laṅkā is said to be just visible.

लंकाकाण्ड, m. pr. n. (see सातोंकाण्ड) the sixth section of the Rāmāyaṇ.

लंकापति } = लंकेश्वर, q.v.
लंकाभुआर }

लंकायिका, f. a certain gramineous plant (Trigonella corniculata).

लंकास्थायी, f. a certain plant (Euphorbia tirucalli).

लंकिनी, f. pr. n. (1) of the epithet of Laṅkā (2) of a certain caste of goddesses.

लंकेस, more prop. लंकेश = लंकेश्वर, q.v.

लंकेश्वर, m. an epithet of any king of Lankā, but

लंकेापिका = लंकायिका, q.v. [especially of Rāvaṇ.

लंग, 1, = लंगड़ा, q.v.: 2, m. limping, lameness: union: a gallant, lover: a certain plant (Eugenia caryophyllata).

लंगड़, 1, more prop. लंगर, q.v.: 2, (contraction) =

लंगड़ना (dialectic) = लंगड़ाना, q.v. [लंगड़ा, q.v.

लंगड़ा, lame, limping: hence, m. (f. ī) a cripple.

लंगड़ाई, f. lameness, limping.

लंगड़ाना, a. int. to limp, walk lame.

लंगड़ाहट, f. lameness, limping.

लंगर, m. the raphe of the perineum: an anchor; a stay or rope for supporting a tent; an almshouse. — uṭhānā, to weigh anchor. — ḍālnā or k. to cast anchor. — par honā, to be at anchor.

लंगरख़र्च, m. provisions or funds for the support of the poor and destitute, charitable funds.

लंगरख़ाना, m. an asylum for the poor and destitute, a poor-house, almshouse.

लंगरवारी, f. a place of anchorage, harbour, haven.

लंगराई, f. worthlessness.

लंगराना, more prop. लंगड़ाना, q.v.

लंगरी, f. a large shallow metal pan generally used to knead bread in or for serving up rice.

लंगू, 1, = लगूं = लग, q.v.: 2, see लंग.

लंगूचा, m. a sausage.

लंगूर, m. a baboon, monkey.

लंगोट, m. a narrow slip of cloth passed between the thighs and tucked into a waistband before and behind to conceal the privities.

लंगोटबन्द, m. a bandage to which the langoṭ is fastened: a person devoted to celibacy.

लंगोटा, m. = लंगोट, q.v.

लंगोटिया, f. (dim. of लंगोटा) a small langoṭ.—yār, an old friend, a friend from childhood, a very intimate friend, a crony.

लंगोटी, f. = लंगोट, q.v.

लंघन, m. a jumping over, passing over, stepping beyond a limit, exceeding, transgressing, going beyond the limits of propriety; a going by leaps or jumps, leaping, springing; coition: abstinence, fasting.

लंघना, t. to jump over, leap over: a. int. to pass, pass over: n. to be jumped over, be passed over.

लंघनी, f. abstinence, fasting, fast. [gressed.

लंघित, m. (f. ā) overstepped, passed beyond, trans-

लंड, लंद, लंप, लंब; for words beginning with either of these elements, see under the corresponding forms लण्ड, लन्द, लम्प, लम्ब, respectively.

लंड़, m. membrum virile. [cleanse, purify.

लक, m. a hundred thousands, a lac.—k. to

लकच, more prop. लकुच, q.v.

लकड़, m. wood, timber; a cudgel, beam, bar.

लकड़कोट, m. a stockade.

लकड़फोड़, m. the woodpecker.

लकड़बाज़, m. a cudgel-player, fencer.

लकड़बाज़ी, f. cudgel-play, fencing.

लकड़हारा, m. (f. ī) = लकड़ीहारा, q.v.

लकड़ा, 1, m. (f. ī) a hyæna: 2, m. a large piece of wood, a balk of timber, a beam, log, block; timber.

लकड़ी, f. (dim. of लकड़ा) a stick, staff; wood, timber, fire-wood: met. stiff.

लकड़ीहारा, m. (f. ī) a wood-cutter, woodman, wood-vendor, timber-merchant.

लकती, f. the total rent of a property or of an estate.

लकपति = लखपति, q.v.

लकर; for words beginning thus, see under the

लक़लक़, m. the stork. [form लकड़.

लकलक क°, a. int. to shine, glitter, twinkle.

लकलकाना, a. int. to gasp or pant (with heat or thirst): to shine, glitter, twinkle.

लकलोट = लखलुट, q.v.

लक़वा, m. a spasmodic distortion of the face.

लकसान, more prop. नुक़सान, q.v.

लक़ात, lean, thin, infirm. [represent it.

लकार, m. the letter ल, or any character that may

लकीर, *f.* a line, streak, lineament. [*puslakucha*).

लकुच, *m.* a species of the bread-fruit tree (*Artocar-*

लकुट, *m.* a stick, staff, club, bludgeon.

लकुटिया, *f.* (dim. of लकुट) a small bludgeon (*esp.* the one held by Krishṇ).

लक्का, *m.* a piece, lump : a kind of pigeon.

लक्खाबेस्वा, *f.* a certain cunning courtesan (mentioned in the *Gulistān Bakāwali*).

लत्तक, *m.* old cloth, a rag, rags : lac (the animal dye). [cessively.

लत्तालगत, one after another, in succession, suc-

लत्तुफली, *f.* the *sami*-tree (*Mimosa suma*).

लत्ती, *f.* the total rent of a property or of an estate.

लक्ष, *m.* a mark, butt, aim : disguise, fraud : one hundred thousands, a lac.

लक्षण, *m.* a characteristic mark, a sign, symptom, token, indication ; feature, spot; destiny; a definition, a predicate, an appellation, name : the Indian crane.

लक्षणा, *f.* metonymy, the metaphorical sense as distinguished from the literal : the female of the Indian crane ; a goose.

लक्षावधि, (लक्ष + अवधि, *i.e.*) up to a hundred

लच्छि (*Rām.*) = लक्ष्मी, *q.v.* [thousands.

लक्षित, *m.* (*f.* ā) seen, observed ; marked.

लछिमी, *more prop.* लक्ष्मी, *q.v.*

लक्ष्मण, 1, *m. pr n.* the son of Dasharath by Sumitrā, the younger half-brother and faithful companion of Rāmchandra : 2, *m.* (*f.* ā) the Indian crane 3, *m.* a mark, spot : a name : 3, *m.* (*f.* ā) prosperous, fortunate.

लक्ष्मणा, *f.* (*m.* लक्ष्मण, 2) the female of the Indian crane : *pr. n.* a wife of Krishṇ and mother of Shāmb.

लक्ष्मी, *f.* prosperty, wealth, success, fortune, luck; beauty, splendour ; royal power, dominion, superhuman power ; a pearl : *pr. n.* one of the principal female deities of the Hindoos, being the daughter of the ocean and wife of Vishṇu, and goddess of abundance, prosperity, and wealth : she is also called Padmā, Kamalā, and Shrī ; and is suppos'd to be the Ceres of the ancients : an epithet of Sitā the wife Rām.

लक्ष्मीच्छाया, *f.* (*lit.* the shadow of Lakshmī, *i.e.* her protection or favour, *i. e.*) good fortune, prosperousness.

लक्ष्मीपति, *m.* an epithet (1) of Vishṇu or (2) of a person of fortune : *lit.* lord of Lakshmee, or of wealth.

लक्ष्मीवान, *m.* (*f.* vatī) prosperous, fortunate, thriving, wealthy ; beautiful.

लक्ष्य, 1, to be seen or noted, observable, perceivable : 2, *m.* fraud, disguise ; a mark, sign, butt ; a hundred thousands, a lac.

लखन (*colloquial*) = लक्षण, *q.v.*

लखनऊ, *more com.* लखनौ, *q.v.*

लखना, *t.* to see, look at, behold, perceive : to understand : *a. int.* to appear, seem.

लखनौ, *m. pr. n.* the capital of Oude.

लखनौती, *f. pr. n.* a certain ancient city in the north of Bengal (now in ruins).

लखपति, *m.* (*f.* patnī) a wealthy person : *lit.* a master, master of a lac, a millionaire : *hence*, rich, prosperous.

लखपती = लखपति, *q.v.* [thirst (said of birds).

लखलखाना, *a. int.* to gasp or pant with heat or

लखलुट, *m.* a squanderer, spendthrift : *lit.* the squanderer of a lac : *hence*, extravagant, wasteful.

लखा, *m.* (pl.: see आ, 22) lacs, hundreds of thous-

लखाओ, *more com.* लखाव, *q.v.* [ands.

लखाऊ, *m. f.* significant, perceptible.

लखाना, *t.* to cause to see.

लखाव, *m.* } the act of seeing or perceiving.
लखावट, *f.* }

लखावनौ in Braj = लखाना, *q.v.*

लखासी, *f.* the act of seeing or perceiving.

लखि ; see (1) लखना (2) लच्छि.

लखिया, *m.* (noun of agency from लखना) one who sees or beholds, a spectator, on-looker, beholder, seër.

लखीर ; see (1) लकीर (2) लखिया (3) लखेरा.

लखेरा, (from लाखा) *m.* (*f.* i) a varnisher.

लखे ; see लखना.

लखोटा ; see लखौटा and लखावट.

लखौटा, *m.* (*f.* ī) besmeared with lac. — *k.* to smear with lac, to glaze.

लग, to, up to, asfar as, close to, near, till, until, whilst, during. — *chalnā*, to follow closely, to court friendship. — *rahnā*, to continue without interruption, to continue fixed.

लग़ज़िश, *f.* a slip, stumble, an error.

लगड़, *m.* a species of hawk or falcon.

लगड़ना, *t.* to rub. *Lagaṛkar mārnā*, to administer a violent beating.

लगड़ाना, *t.* to cause to rub. [instantly.

लगत, at that very instant, at the very time of,

लगता, *m.* assessment or stipulated rent of land.

लगतासार, without intermission, continual, successive. [the other.

लगतालगत, repeatedly, in succession, one after

लगती, *f.* = लगता, *q.v.*

लगन, 1, a corruption of लग्न, *q.v.* : 2, a dialectic form of लग, *q.v.* : 3, *m.* the coming in contact, the being attached to : a kind of large flat hollow copper utensil in the form of a basin.

लगनकुन्डली, *f.* a circle for a horoscope.

लगना, *n.* to be applied, be fixed, be attached, be close to, to be employed, be imputed, be connected with, to be : *a. int.* to apply, begin, adjoin, fetch home, reach the mark, touch, attain to, reach, suit, join, close, belong, become, happen, befall, seem, taste, to regard.

लगभग, (takes gen. *m.* infl.) close, near, about, almost, by, nearly, thereabouts.

लगलग, *m.* (prop. लक़लक़) the stork.

लगवाना, *t.* to cause to be put, etc. ; to cause to put, place, apply, plant, etc. ; to apply, fix, etc.

लगा, *m.* (*f.* ī) stuck, attached, connected with, occupied in, busied with. — *mārnā*, to calumniate. — *rakhnā*, to be occupied with, be busy in. — *lenā*, to attach to oneself, conciliate, win.

लगाई, *f.* the rent or revenue charged on a field or estate.

लगातार, *m.* close together; incessant, consecutive, repeated, successive.

लगान, *m.* a stopping or making fast (said of boats, etc.): a haltingplace for boats. — *k.* to make fast a boat.

लगाना, *t.* to put, place, set, apply, affix, attach, join, impose, lay, add, fix, plant, fasten, to impute, ascribe, to spread, to inflect, to shut, close, to connect, to plaster, to put to work, employ, engage, use, to report anything in the way of scandal or malice, to reserve — *bujhānā*, to excite quarrels. *Lahre* —, to feed with mere hopes.

लगाम, *f.* a bridle; a bit; bit and reins together.

लगालग, without intermission, uninterruptedly, incessantly, in close contact.

लगाव, *m.* application, connexion, contact, adherence, adhesion; intercourse, access, relation; series, symmetry.

लगावट, *f.* connexion, attachment, union, application.

लगावना (*colloquial*) = लगाना, *q. v.*

लगि, 1, *more prop.* लग, *q.v.*: 2, an old form = लिये, *q.v.* 3, लगके (लगना): see ड, 7.

लगित, *m.* (*f.* ā) connected with, attached to.

लगुड़ = लगुर, *q. v.*

लगुर, *m.* a staff, stick, club; an iron club, or a club bound with iron.

लगुरहस्त, *m.* (*f.* ā) a person armed with a *lagur*: lit. *adj.* having a *lagur* in the hand.

लगूआ, *m.* (*f.* लगूई) a lover, paramour.

लगूं (*dialectic*) = लग, *q. v.*

लगूंहा, *m.* (*f.* ī) pleasing, beautiful, delightful, alluring: thickly set, continuous, close together.

लगूंहां, *m.* (*f.* लगूंहीं) } = लगूंहा, *q.v.*
लगूहा, *m.* (*f.* लगूही) }

लगून, *more prop.* लगूं, *q.v.*

लगे, with, about one. See लगा.

लगेहात, together with, just after, immediately upon.

लगौंहा, *m.* (*f.* लगौंही) } = लगूंहा, *q. v.*
लगौंहां, *m.* (*f.* लगौंहीं) }

लग्गा, *m.* attachment, affection; interest or influence with a person; an applying or comparing one thing with another: a pole for propelling a boat. — *na khōnā*, to be incompatible or inconsistent with, to bear no comparison with.

लग्गी, *f.* a pole, staff, gibstaff, rod.

लग्न, 1, attached to, joined, in contact, adhering to, connected with; intent on, occupied in, concerned with: 2, *m.* (*f.* ā) a bard, panegyrist: 3, *m* (*f.* ?) affection, attachment, friendship, love: espousal, the appointing the day of marriage: (in Astron.) the rising of a sign of the Zodiac above the horizon; the sun's entrance into a sign of the Zodiac; the oblique ascension, on the divisions of the equator which rise in succession with each sign in an oblique sphere (also defined as the arc of the equator which passes the meridian in the same time with each sign of the ecliptic); in popular acceptation, it is the moment of the sun's entrance into a zodiacal sign; *hence*, a moment.

लग्ना, *f.* (*m.* लग्न, 2) a female bard, poetess.

लग्यो } old forms of लगा, *q. v.*
लग्यौ }
लगयौ }

लघु, *m.* (*f.* लघ्वी) light, easy, swift, small, short, trivial, insignificant, mean, low, narrow; young; feeble; vain, frivolous; (in Gram.) short (as a vowel or syllable); (in Arithm.) a smaller quantity, the lesser root in an equation.

लघुगर्ग, *m.* a kind of fish (*Pimelodus* ?).

लघुचेता, *m. f.* of a low or trivial type of mind, frivolous, light-minded.

लघुचेता = लघुचेता, *q, v.*

लघुता, *f.* lightness, levity, smallness, insignificance, meanness, diminution, humiliation, wantonness, disregard, disrespect.

लघुतापस, *m.* an epithet of Lakshmaṇ.

लघुत्व, *m.* = लघुता, *q. v.*

लघुदीट, short-sighted.

लघुदुन्दुभी, *m.* a small kettledrum.

लघुपतक; see लघुपतनक.

लघुपतनक, *m.* (*f.* ikā) *adj.* quick-flying, light-falling: *pr. n.* a certain crow in the Hitopadesh.

लघुबेले, shortly, in a short time.

लघुमांस, *m.* the francoline partridge.

लघुमित्र, *m.* (*f.* ā) a friend or ally of little power or value.

लघुमूल, *m.* (in Algebra) the lesser root of an equation, the least root with reference to the additive quantities.

लघुराशि, (in Algebra) consisting of fewer terms (as a side in an equation).

लघुशंका, *f.* urine. — *k.* to emit urine.

लघू, *more prop.* लघु, *p. v.*

लघूकरण, *m.* reducing in weight or consequence, thinking little of, contemning.

लघूदीठ, *more prop.* लघुदीठ, *q. v.*

लघूबेले, *more prop.* लघुबेले, *q. v.*

लघूर्मि, *f.* a light or small wave.

लघ्याहार, *m.* (*f.* ī) temperate in food or in eating.

लघ्वी, *f.* (*m.* लघु) a delicate, beautiful, or insignificant female: a light carriage: urine.

लङ्क, लङ्ग, लङ्घ; for words beginning with either of these elements, see under the corresponding forms, लंक, लंग, लंघ, respectively.

लचक, *f.* bending, elasticity, spring.

लचकता, *m.* (*f.* ī) elastic, springy.

लचकना, *a. int.* to spring, bend.

लचका, 1, *m.* jolt: a kind of boat, a barge: 2, *m.* (*f.* ī) bent.

लचकाना, *t.* to bolt, to strain.

लचना, *a. int.* to bend, low, become bent.

लचर, *m.* a foolish fellow, simpleton, ninny, noodle.

लचलच, the sound made by a dog when lapping or drinking.

लचलचाना, *n.* to be clammy or glutinous: to be elastic: *t.* to lick up.

लचाना, *t.* to bend, bow, cock.

लचार (*contraction*) = लाचार, *q. v.*

लचीला, *m.* (*f.* ī) elastic, flexible.

लच्चा, *m.* a kind of necklace or neck-ornament worn by females.

लच्छ = **लक्ष**, *q. v.*

लच्छन = **लक्षण**, *q. v.*

लच्छना, *m.* a species of grain (*Cynosurus coracanus*) called by Europeans "Natchenny."

लच्छा, *m.* a bundle of thread, a ball or skein of thread, etc.: a kind of necklace (of gold beads and brass beads) fitting tight around the neck.

लछ (*Rām.*) = (1) **लक्ष** (2) **लक्षण** (3) **लक्ष्म**, *qq. v.*

लछना; see **लक्षणा** and **लच्छना**.

लछमन = **लक्ष्मण**, *q. v.*

लछि (*Rām.*) = **लक्ष्मी**, *q. v.*

लछिमन = **लक्ष्मण**, *q. v.*

लछी, *f.* blood and water mixing.

लजकारिका, *f.* the sensitive-plant (*Mimosa pudica* or *natans*).

लजत, *more prop.* **लज़्ज़त**, *q. v.*

लजलजा, *m.* (*f.* ī) clammy, glutinous, viscous.

लजलजाना, *a. int.* to soften: *t.* to soften.

लजलाज, *m. pr. n.* (according to the Arabs) the inventor of chess: *hence*, an instructor in any game of hazard.

लजवन्ती, *more prop.* **लज्जावती**, *q. v.*

लजवाना, *t.* to cause to blush, cause to be ashamed, to put to shame, to shame.

लजाना, *n.* to be ashamed, be abashed: *a. int.* to blush.

लजालू, *more prop.* **लज्जालु**, *q. v.*

लजावन्ती, *more prop.* **लज्जावती**, *q. v.*

लज़िज, adhesive, tenacious, clammy, viscous.

लजियाना = **लजाना**, *q. v.*

लजीला, *m.* (*f.* ī) shamefaced, bashful.

लज्जत, *m.* (*f.* ā) ashamed, blushing, bashful.

लज़्ज़त, *f.* pleasure, enjoyment, delight, flavour, deliciousness, taste, savour, sweetness.

लज्जमान (*contraction*) = **लज्जामान**, *q. v.*

लज्जा, *f.* shame, bashfulness, modesty.

लज्जाकर }
लज्जाकार } *m.* (*f.* ī) = **लज्जाकारी**, *q. v.*

लज्जाकारी, *m.* (*f.* iṇī) *adj.* causing or occasioning shame, shameful.

लज्जान्वित, *m.* (*f.* ā) = **लज्जावत**, *q. v.*

लज्जाबान (*corruption*) = **लज्जावान**, *q. v.*

लज्जाबोधक शब्द, *m.* (in Gram.) any word expressive of shame or disgust; *e. g.* **छी**, **धिक्क**, **फिश**.

लज्जामन्त, *m.* (*f.* matī) }
लज्जामान, *m.* (*f.* matī) }
लज्जायुक्त, *m.* (*f.* ā) } = **लज्जावत**, *q. v.*

लज्जारहित, *m.* (*f.* ā) destitute of shame, bereft of modesty, shameless, immodest, impudent, bold.

लज्जालु, *m.* the sensitive-plant (*Mimosa natans* or *pudica*): *lit.* bashful, ashamed.

लज्जालू, *more prop.* **लज्जालु**, *q. v.*

लज्जावत, *m.* (*f.* vatī) bashful, shamefaced, modest, ashamed, abashed, blushing.

लज्जावती, *f.* (*m.* **लज्जावत**, etc.) a bashful female; the sensitive-plant (*Mimosa natans* or *pudica*).

लज्जावन्त }
लज्जावान } *m.* (*f.* vatī) = **लज्जावत**, *q. v.*

लज्जाशील, *m.* (*f.* ā) of a modest disposition, bashful, ashamed, modest.

लज्जाशून्य }
लज्जाहीन } *m.* (*f.* ā) = **लज्जारहित**, *q. v.*

लज्जित, *m.* (*f.* ā) ashamed, blushing, bashful.

लज्ज्या }
लज्या } (*corruptions*) = **लज्जा**, *q. v.*

लट, 1. *m.* one who speaks ignorantly or foolishly, a blockhead, fool: fault, defect: 2. *f.* tangled hair or silk thread, a clotted lock of hair: a tadpole. —*jānā*, to become entangled.

लटक, 1, *f.* hanging, dangling; a kind of affected motion in blandishment and coquetry: resemblance: 2 *m.* a bad man.

लटकचाल, *f.* affected gait, coquetry in walking.

लटकत = **लटकता** (**लटकना**). See **त**, 5.

लटकन, *m.* a hanging or being suspended; anything suspended or hanging; *hence*, ear-drops, pendants, ringlets, a certain handsome green bird (*Psittacus minor*?) which often remains hanging by the claws, a stand for waterpots, the drops of a crystal lustre, the clapper of a bell; a certain fruit (*Bixa orellana*?) with which clothes are dyed yellow.

लटकना, *a. int.* to hang, dangle, swing: *n.* to be suspended.

लटकवाना, *t.* to cause to be hung, cause to be suspended.

लटका, 1, *m.* incantation; a conjuring-rod, a philtre, a quack-medicine or nostrum: 2, *m.* (*f.* ī) hanging, suspended, swinging, dangling.

लटकाना, *t.* to cause to dangle, to hang, suspend, dangle, swing.

लटकाया, *m.* (*f.* **लटकाई**) suspended, dangling.

लटकाव, *m.* hanging, suspension.

लटत = **लटता** (**लटना**, 2): see **त**, 5.

लटन, an early-sown crop, a crop sown during the cold season.

लटना, 1, diminution: 2, to acquire a taste.

लटपट, *adj.* staggering, tripping, stammering; folded, entangled.

लटपटा, *m.* (*f.* ī) innocent, playful, frisky, wanton, humourous: irregularly folded (said of a turban).

लटपटाना, *a. int.* to stagger, trip; to stammer.

लटपटिया, frisky, wanton, humourous, double-dealing, not straight-forward, mischief-making.

लटपटी, *f.* a stumbling, staggering, swaggering.

लटवाटी; see **खटवाटी** and **अटवाटी**.

लटा, *m.* (*f.* ī) reduced (by sickness), emaciated, lean.

लटाई, *f.* a kind of roller on which the string of a kite is wound.

लटापटा, *m.* baggage, furniture, effects.

लटी, *f.* (in Mārwāṛī) tax, impost.

लटूड़ी }
लटूरिया } *f.* = लटूरी, *q. v.* [ringlets.

लटूरियाँ, *f.* (pl. of लटूरी) tangled short hairs; locks,

लटूरी, *f.* a small curl or lock of hair, a ringlet;

लटाड़ा = लटोरा, *q. v.* [tangled short hair.

लटोरा, *m.* (*f.* ī) the shrike or butcher-bird (*Lanius*).

लटोरी, *f.* a kind of head-dress.

लट्टा, *m.* a measuring rod or pole. Twenty square laṭṭās make one *bighā*. [fall in love.

लट्टू, *m.* a child's top. — *honā*, to be enamoured,

लट्टर, remiss, slack, lazy.

लट्ठा, *m.* a beam.

लट्ठी (*contraction*) = लाठी, *q. v.*

लठ, *m.* a stick, club, cudgel.

लठपठ, soaked through, drenched.

लठबाज़, *m.* a cudgel-player, fencer.

लठबाज़ी, *f.* cudgelling, fencing.

लठालठम, *m.* }
लठालठी, *f.* } a mutual cudgelling.

लठियाना, *t.* to belabour, cudgel, cane.

लठी, 1, (*contraction*) = लाठी, *q. v.*: 2, *f.* (in Māṛwāṛī) a piece of cloth forty yards long.

लठैवाला, *m.* (*f.* ī) a man armed with a bludgeon. Many such men are employed by zamīndārs, indigo-planters, and others, with a view to their settling all disputes respecting lands and boundaries.

लड़, *f.* a string (of pearls, etc.); a thread, row, a strand of rope or cord: a party. — *meṅ rahnā*, to be in one's party. — *marnā*, to engage in mortal strife.

लड़कपन (*contraction*) = लड़कापन, *q. v.*

लड़कबुद्धि, *f.* a child's understanding, the wisdom of childhood, childishness.

लड़का, *m.* a boy; a child, infant, babe.

लड़काई, *f.* the condition of being a child, the state of childhood, boyhood, childhood.

लड़काकूल, *m. pr. n.* a certain mountain tribe in

लड़कापन, *m.* = लड़काई, *q. v.* [Chattisghar.

लड़काबाला = लड़कावाला. *q. v.*

लड़कालड़की, *more prop.* लड़केलड़कियाँ, *q. v.*

लड़कावाला, *m.* (pl. लड़केवाले) a child.

लड़किनी (*corruption*) = लड़की, *q. v.*

लड़की, *f.* (*m.* लड़का) a girl, female child.

लड़के, *m.* (pl. of लड़का) boys; children. — *laṛkiyāṅ*, boys and girls, children, bairns, brats. [folk.

लड़केवाले, *m.* (pl. of लड़कावाला,) children, young

लड़कोड़ा, }
लड़कोरा } *m.* (*f.* ī) a parent.

लड़खड़ाना, *a. int.* to stagger, trip; to stutter, stam-

लड़खराना = लड़खड़ाना, *q. v.* [mer.

लड़ड़ु, = लड्डू, *q. v.*

लड़त, *f.* battle, war, strife, contest.

लड़ना, 1, *m.* fighting, battling, contending, warring: 2. *t.* to contend, quarrel, fight, make war.

लड़नेमरनेवाला, *m.* (*f.* ī) a great fighter, one who engages in mortal combat.

लड़न्त, 1, *f.* = लड़ना, 1, *q. v.*: 2, contentious, quar-

लड़बड़, stammering; reeling. [relsome.

लड़बड़ाना, *a. int.* to stutter, stammer; to stagger,

लड़बावला, *m.* (*f.* ī) mad, foolish. [reel.

लड़याना, *more com.* लड़ियाना, *q. v.*

लड़ला, a corruption of नहला, *q. v.*

लड़वैया, *m.* a fighter, warrior, quarrelsome, combative person: *adj.* fond of fighting, fighty, warlike.

लड़ा, *adj.* (used in comp.) of a string or thread; *e.g. Eklaṛā*, of one string: *Dolaṛā*, of two strings.

लड़ाई, *f.* quarrel, strife, fighting, battle, war, fight, conflict. — *k.* to war, fight, give battle.

लड़ाईभड़ाई }
लड़ाईभिड़ाई } jingles on the word लड़ाई, *q. v.*

लड़ांका = लड़ाक, *q. v.*

लड़ाक, a fighter, brawler, wrangler:-*adj.* quarrelsome, contentious, warlike, pugnacious, fighty.

लड़ाका = लड़ाक, *q. v.*

लड़ाख (*dialectic*) = लड़ाक, *q. v.*

लड़ाना, *t.* to cause to fight, to fight, bait: to play.

लड़ालड़ी, *f.* mutual quarrelling, wrangling.

लड़िकन, *m.* (a Braj pl. of लड़का) boys, children.

लड़ियाना, *t.* to thread, string.

लड़ी, *f.* a string (of pearls, etc.).

लडुआ }
लड्डू } *more com.* लड्डू, *q. v.*

लड्डुक, *m.* a kind of sweetmeat (a ball of flour fried with oil or ghee and mixed with sugar and spices).

लड्डू, *m.* a kind of sweetmeat. It is made chiefly of sugar, with the addition of cream, and of cocoanut-kernel rasped, the whole being formed into the shape of large boluses or balls. *Manke — khānā*, to build castles in the air. *Ṭhag ke — khā baiṭhnā*, to be distracted, foolish, or intoxicated (said of one who talks or acts absurdly in opposition to his usual good sense;—the allusion being to the notorious sharpers called *thags* who join a party of travellers, and having got into their confidence entertain them with sweetmeats impregnated with some intoxicating drug (such as *datura*) that they may murder and rob them with impunity while under its stupefying influence).

लढ़ा, *m.* a cart.

लढ़िया, *f.* (dim. of लढ़ा) a small cart, a sled, sledge.

लढ़ियाना, *more prop.* (1) लड़ियाना (2) लुढ़ियाना, *qq. v.*

लढ़ी = लढ़िया, *q. v.*

लण्ड, *m.* membrum virile.

लण्डन, *m. pr. n.* the city of London.

लण्डूआ, possessed of the membrum virile.

लण्डूरा, *m.* (*f.* ī) tailless, docked, bobtail: *met.* without friends, forlorn.

लत, *f.* the hanging branch of a creeper (*latā*): bad habits, whim, whimsey: (contract. of *lāt*) a kick (used in comp.). — *khānā*, to undergo a beating or kicking.

— *mardan k.* to trample or tread on. — *mardanmen̐ parnā*, to be trampled under-foot, be disgraced.
लतकुन्दन, *m.* ignominious treatment.
लतकोब, *adj.* cudgelling, beating.
लतख़ोरा, *m.* (*f.* ī) a slave : a threshold : *lit.* kicked, beaten : *hence*, mean, contemptible.
लतघत, *f.* nature, disposition, manners.
लतज़दा, of bad habits, vicious.
लतपत ; see लटपट and लतरपतर.
लतफल, *m.* the consequences of bad habits.
लतमा, *m.* a slap, blow, box, cuff.
लतर, *f.* an old shoe.
लतरपतर, soaked through, drenched.
लतरी, *f.* an old shoe : a kind of vetch.
लता, *f.* any winding or creeping-plant, a vine, a creeper, the musk-creeper (said to grow in the Dakkhan, and to be used medicinally), the plant commonly called *priyaṅgu*, a certain gramineous plant (*Trigonella corniculata*), heart-pea (*Cardiospermum halicacabum*) ; a branch : thread.
लताकाम, *f. pr. n.* ; more prop. कामलता, *q.v.*
लताड़, *f.* calamity, misfortune ; labour.
लताड़ना, *t.* to cause to toil, to exhaust by labour, to work, jade, bring down, fatigue ; to irritate, affront, insult.
लताद्रुम, *m.* a kind of timber-yielding tree (*Shorea robusta*).
लतिका, *f.* a twining-plant, creeper.
लतिया, *m. f.* of bad habits.
लतियाना, *t.* (from लात) to kick ; to beat.
लतीफ़, elegant, agreeable, courteous, kind, benevolent ; minute, subtile, fine ; exquisite, delicious : facetious, witty.
लतीफ़ा, *m.* elegance, rarity, a pleasantry, jest, joke, raillery.
लतेड़ना ; see लताड़ना and लथेड़ना.
लत्ता, *m.* a scrap of cloth, a rag, tatter.
लत्ती, *f.* the string of a child's top : a cloth tied to the end of a pole to direct the flight of pigeons ; a kick when swimming. — *k.* to run away.
लथड़, rigid, stiff.
लथड़ना, *n.* to be draggled : *a. int.* to draggle.
लथड़पथड़, besmeared with mud or any kind of filth, so as to walk with difficulty.
लथर, rigid, stiff.
लथेड़ना, *t.* (of लथड़ना) to draggle, to besmear with filth.
लदना, *n.* to be laden, be loaded. — *lenā*, to load oneself ; to mount (a horse, etc.).
लदफन्दा, *m.* loading and packing.
लदवाना, *t.* (causat. of लादना) to cause to load.
लदाना, *t.* (causat. of लादना) to cause to be loaded, *i. e.* to load, lade, freight.
लदाव, *m.* an arched roof or terrace : a load.
लद्दू, *more prop.* लड्डू, *q.v.*
लद्धिय in Chand = लिया, *q.v.*
लनतरानियां, *f.* (pl. of लनतरानी) conceited airs.
लनतरानी, *f.* boasting, gasconading, conceitedness.
लन्दन, *more prop.* लण्डन, *q.v.*
लप, *f.* the space formed in the palm of the hand when closed so as to hold water ; a handful.
लपक, *f.* a snatch, bounce, spring (as of a tiger), flash (as of lightning, etc.).
लपकना, *a. int.* to flash (as lightning), to rush forth, make a rush, spring, bounce, pounce : *t.* to make an attack upon, to snatch, to seize suddenly.
लपका, *m.* a snatch ; nimbleness : a bad habit or custom.
लपकाना, *t.* to put forth the hand for the purpose of taking something, to snatch, seize.
लपकी, *f.* a stitch.
लपची, *f.* the skate-fish.
लपझप, nimble, dapper, quick.
लपट, *f.* odour : warmth, glow.
लपटना, *a. int.* to adhere, cling, stick : (*n.* to be stuck, be in a state of adhesion ?).
लपटसपट, *f.* fawning, wriggling, writhing.
लपटा, *m.* 1, = लपटी, *q.v.* : 2, a kind of molasses : connexion, relation : a certain grass (*Panicum verticillatum*).
लपटाना, *a. int.* to adhere, cling, stick : (*t.* to cause to be stuck, *i. e.* to stick ?).
लपटी, *f.* any glutinous liquid food, pap.
लपतिया, *m. f.* a liar.
लपलप, 1, *m.* lapping (as dogs) : 2, nimble, dapper, quick. — *khānā*, to eat quickly.
लपसी, *f.* a glutinous kind of food, pap, spoon-meat, pottage.
लपाटिया, *m. f.* a tattler, liar.
लपाटी, *f.* tattling, lying.
लपानक, slender, spare, thin.
लपेट, *f. m.* a fold, ply, coil, plait, twist, envelope, bandage, fillet. — *k.* to fold up.
लपेटझपेट, *f.* evasion, subterfuge.
लपेटन, *f.* a roller on which cloth is wound in the loom ; a button.
लपेटना, *t.* to fold, furl, roll up, enclose, pack, wrap up, coil : to spread, smear.
लपेटवां, *m.* (*f.* wīn) twisted ; ornamented with gold or silver thread wound around.
लपेटसपेट, *f.* evasion, subterfuge.
लपेटा, *m.* (*f.* ī) folded, furled, wrapped up.
लपेटें, *f.* (pl. of लपेट) folds, coils, plaits.
लपोड़िया, *m.* a flatterer.
लप्पा, *m.* gold or silver cloth, brocade.
लफ़्ज़, *m. f.* (see फ) a word, expression, saying, phrase.
लब, *m. f.* a lip, brim, edge, rim, shore, coast, bank, margin (of a lake, etc.).
लबड़ख़न्दा, *m.* (*f.* ī) a mischievous child.
लबड़घटाई, *f.* the giving the breast to a child when it contains no milk.
लबड़ना, *a. int.* to act or speak absurdly, improperly, or foolishly.
लबड़सबड़ / लबड़सबर, *m.* tittle-tattle, nonsensical talk.
लबड़ा, *m.* (*f.* ī) a liar, tattler : *adj.* left-handed.

लबड़ी, false and talkative (applied to females).

लबदार, mud, thick mud formed by water flooding a stiff soil.

लबध, *more prop.* **लब्ध**, *q.v.* [collected from the tree.

लबनी, *f.* the pot in which palm-juice (*tāṛī*) is

लबरगट्टा / **लबरघट्टा** } *m.* (*f.* ī) fastidious, fretful, touchy.

लबरचटाई = **लबड़चटाई**, *q.v.*

लबरसबर, *m.* tittle-tattle, nonsensical talk.

लबरा, *m.* (*f.* ī) *more com.* **लबड़ा**, *q. v.*

लबलब, *m.* sand, gravel, grit. [glutinous.

लबलबा, 1, *m.* the pancreas: 2, *m.* (*f.* ī) clammy,

लबलेास, 1, *f.* flattery: 2, shameless, naked.

लबवादा; see **लुबादा**.

लबवार; see **लबार**.

लबाड़, *f.* spoil, plunder, plundering.

लबाड़ना, *t.* to plunder, spoil.

लबाड़ी, *m.* (*f.* in *or* inī) a plunderer, ravager.

लबादा, *more prop.* **लुबादा**, *q.v.*

लबान, *more prop.* **लुबान**, *q.v.*

लबार, *m.* a babbler, talker, liar. [into sugar.

लबी, *f.* the juice of the sugarcane when boiling

लबेदा, *m.* a club, cudgel.

लबेरा, *m.* a certain fruit (*Cordia myxa*).

लबेल, possessed of a lip or margin.

लब्ध, *m.* (*f.* ā) obtained, taken, acquired, received. got, attained. [one's right mind, recovered.

लब्धचेता, *m. f.* restored to one's senses, come to

लब्धदास, *m.* (*f.* ī) a slave received as a gift or transfer. [of a promise or vow.

लब्धपणास, one who has obtained the pulfilment

लब्धपुत्र, *m.* (*f.* ī) an adopted child. [faithless.

लब्धा, *f.* a woman whose husband or lover is

लब्धि, *f.* the getting or obtaining a thing, acquisition, gain; (in Arithm.) the quotient.

लभ्य, *m.* gain, profit, interest on money: lit. *m.* (*f.* ā) attainable, obtainable, procurable; proper, fitting.

लमकना, *m.* (**लम्बकर्ण**) a hare, rabbit.

लमकाना, 1, = **लमकना**, *q. v.*: 2, *t.* to stretch out the hand to take anything.

लमकड़, *f.* a long kind of musket.

लमकड़ा, *m.* (*f.* ī) tall, long.

लमटंगा, *m.* (*f.* ī) longlegged, spindle-shanks.

लमतरांग, long, tall. [fishing.

लमडोड़, a fishing-line, strings or cords used in

लमबर, *m.* (Engl.) number.

लमहर, a tree that has sprung up of itself in a cultivated field, and which the cultivator may legally [cut down.

लमहा, *m.* a hare, rabbit.

लम्पट, *m.* a lecher, libertine, gallant, whoremonger: *lit.* covetous, greedy, false, lying, reprobate, dissolute, lascivious, lecherous.

लम्पटता, *f.* (*m.* °त्व) greediness, dissoluteness, lasciviousness, lewdness, lecherousness, libertinism.

लम्ब, *m.* a perpendicular: a bribe: moving a man at a sort of backgammon.

लम्बकर्ण, *m.* (*f.* ā *or* ī) a goat; an elephant, a hare, rabbit; a Rākshas: *lit.* long-eared.

लम्बनकरण, *more prop.* **लम्बकरण**, *q.v.*

लम्बर, 1, *f.* a fox: 2, *m.* (Engl.) number.

लम्बा, 1, *f.* a bitter gourd: an epithet (1) of Lakshmī (2) of Durgā: 2. *m.* (*f.* ī) long tall —*k.* to lengthen, extend; to beat, drub. *Lambe muṅhse* (or *lambe muṅh karke*) *khānā*, to eat eagerly, eat with a zest, eat with a sharp appetite.

लम्बाई, *f.* length, tallness, height.

लम्बाईचौड़ाई, *f.* length and breadth, size; *met.* pomp, glory, pride.

लम्बाओं; see **लम्बाई** and **लम्बाना**. [grain, salt, etc.

लम्बाड़ा, *m.* a certain wandering tribe who deal in

लम्बान, *m.* length, tallness, height.

लम्बाना, *t.* to lengthen.

लम्बिका, *f.* the uvula or soft palate.

लम्बित, *m.* (*f.* ā) hanging down, pendulous, suspended, depending, pendant.

लम्बियां, *f.* (pl. of **लम्बी**, 2) bounding paces.—*k.* to prance (said of horses).

लम्बी, *f.* 1, (*m.* **लम्बा**) tall, long: 2, a kind of bounding pace in horses.—*k.* to make a horse capriole or throw out his fore-legs.— *sāṅs bharnā*, to fetch a long sigh, *i. e.* to lament, regret, repent.

लम्बुक, *m. pr. n.* the fifteen astronomical *yog* or division of the moon's path.

लम्बुका, *m. pr. n.* a certain *Apsarā*.

लम्बुको; see **लम्बुक** and **लम्बुका**.

लम्बुवा, *f.* a necklace of seven strings.

लम्बे, *m. f.* long, tall. [bellied.

लम्बोदर *m.* an epithet of Ganesh; *lit.* the long-

लम्भा, 1, *m.* a hare, rabbit: 2, *f.* a kind of chain enclosure or fence. [an eye, a moment, minute.

लम्हा, *m.* a hare, rabbit: a glance or twinkling of

लय, 1, a colloquial form of **ला**, **लाया**, or **लाके**; from the vb. **लाना**: 2, = **लई**, *q.v.*: 3, in Braj and in poetry (1) **लिया** (2) **लिये**, *qq.v.*: 4, *f.* equal time (in music and dancing), voice, sound, tone, melody, modulation, symphony, singing in tune: ardent affection or desire, absorption or immersion: destruction.

लयऊ (*Rām.*) = **लाया**, *q. v.*

लयकारी, *m.* (*f.* iṇī) destructive, etc. See **लय**, 4.

लयनो; see (1) **लगाना** (2) **लाना** (3) **लेना**.

लयल, 1, a dialectic form of **लाया**, *q.v.*: 2, *more*

लयलीन, *m.* (*f.* ā) = **लौलीन**, *q.v.* [*prop.* **लम्पल**, *q.v.*

लयारी, *more prop.* **ल्यारी**, *q.v.*

लये / **लयै** / **लयो** } see **लाये** and **लिये**.

लर, *f.* a kind of rod for the measurement of land. Four hundred square lars make one *bīghā*.

लरज़ना, *a. int.* to shake, quiver, tremble.

लरन, 1, a Braj pl. of **लर**, *q.v.*: 2, see **लड़ना**.

लरिकन, *more prop.* **लड़िकन**, *q.v.*

लरिका, *m.* (*f.* ī) *more prop.* **लड़का**, *q.v.*

लरिकाई, *more prop.* **लड़काई**, *q. v.*

लरिकिनी, a corrupt form of **लड़की**, *q.v.*

लरिवेको (*Rām.*) = **लड़नेको**. See **ना**, 3.

लर्का, *m.* a skein. [quake; fear, terror.

लर्ज़ा, *m.* a shivering, shaking, tremor, an earth-

ललक, *f.* a sudden gush of any liquid: *met.* whim,

ललकना, *t.* to attack, fall upon. [fancy, caprice.

ललकाना, *t.* (causat. of **ललकना**) to cause to attack, i. e. to set on to fight, egg on, to excite a quarrel.

ललकार, *f.* a calling, bawling, challenge.

ललकारना, *a. int.* to bawl, call out insultingly, to set up the war-whoop: *t.* to call out to, bawl after, halloo after, challenge.

ललगदहा, *m.* (*f.* ī) an epithet of the monkey; *lit.* the one with a red anus.

ललचत, *m.* (*f.* ā) desired, coveted.

ललचाना, *n.* to be tantalized: *a. int.* to long covet: *t.* to excite desire, tantalize, to covet.

ललदम्बु / **ललदम्बू** } *m.* a certain flower (*Nerium odorum*).

ललन, *m.* pleasure, sport, pastime; a lolling the tongue: a certain tree (*Shorea robusta*): a boy.

ललना, *f.* a woman, a woman of pleasure, a wanton woman, a playful woman: a species of metre in Sanskrit prosody.

ललसाना, to experience desire, be desirous for.

लला, 1, *m.* a boy: 2, *m.* (*f.* ī) impotent.

ललाट, *m.* the forehead: hence, *met.* fate, destiny, fortune (believed by Hindoos to be written on the forehead).

ललाटरेखा, *f.* a certain line on the forehead supposed to indicate long life; a coloured sectarial mark worn by Hindoos on the forehead.

ललाटिका, *f.* an ornament worn on the forehead; a mark made with sandal on the forehead.

ललाड़ = **ललाट**, *q.v.*

ललाम, *m.* a mark; a flag; an ornament; a mane; a tail; a line; a mark worn on the forehead. [forehead.

ललामक, *m.* a chaplet of flowers falling over the

ललामन, *m.* = **ललाम**, *q.v.*: 2, a Braj pl. of **ललाम**.

ललामा; see (1) **ललाम** (2) **नीलाम**.

ललामी, *f.* an ear-ornament.

ललित, *m.* (*f.* ā) enjoyed, played, sported; wished for; pleasing, beautiful, lovely.

ललिता, *f.* (*m.* **ललित**) a woman; a wanton: a certain musical mode (*rāgini*). [coax, wheedle.

ललियाना, *a. int.* to redden: *t.* to beg earnestly,

लली, *f.* 1, (*m.* **लला**) a girl: 2, impotent. [tery.

लल्लोपत्तो, *m.* wheedling, coaxing, adulation, flat-

लव, *m.* cutting, plucking, reaping: smallness: a drop: hair; wool: a kind of quail: loss, destruction: a nutmeg, cloves: (in Arithm.) the numerator of a fraction: a certain small division of time (the 60th part of the twinkling of an eye); a larger division of time (36 twinklings of the eye); a portion, bit; a moment: *pr. n.* one of Rām's sons.

लवंग, *m.* the clove-tree (*Eugenia caryophyllata*, Willd.; or *Caryophyllus aromaticus*, Gært.; or *Muristica caryophyllata*) and its fruit, cloves.

लवक, *m.* (*f.* ikā) a reaper: lit. *adj.* cutting, reaping.

लवड़; see **लवर**.

लवण, 1, *m.* salt, saltness, the sea of salt water, rock or fossil salt, sea salt: *pr. n.* a certain Rākshas: 2, *m.* (*f.* ā) salt, saline: charming, beautiful.

लवणखानि, *m.* a salt-mine; an epithet of the district of Sāmbhar in Ajmīr celebrated for its fossil salt.

लवणसमुद्र / **लवणसिन्धु** } *m.* the briny ocean.

लवणा, *f.* 1, (*m.* **लवण**, 2) saline: beautiful: 2, light, beauty: 3, *pr. n.* a certain river in Tirhut.

लवणाकर, *m.* a salt-mine.

लवणाम्बु, *m.* salt water, the sea.

लवणोत्तम, *m.* (lit. the best salt; *hence*) rock or river-salt; nitre. [reaping, harvesting.

लवन, 1, (*corruption*) = **लवण**, *q.v.*: 2, *m.* cutting,

लवनसिन्धु (*corruption*) = **लवणसिन्धु**, *q.v.*

लवना, 1, (*corruption*) = **लवणा**, *q.v.*: 2, *t.* to reap, to harvest.

लवनी, *f.* wages paid in kind to reapers at harvest-time: a coarse kind of custard-apple (*Annona squamosa* or *reticulata*).

लवर, *m.* flame. See **लौर**.

लवलीन, *m.* (*f.* ā) = **लौलीन**, *q.v.*

लवलेस, *m.* a very small particle, an atom.

लवा, *m.* a kind of quail (*Perdix chinensis*).

लवाई, *f.* tenderness, affection, fondness.

लवाक, *m.* a reapinghook, sickle.

लवाज़िम, *m.* (pl. of **लाज़िम**) necessaries, requisites, essentials, appurtenances, baggage.

लवाज़िमा / **लवाज़िमात** / **लवाजिमें** } (pll. of **लाज़िम**) = **लवाज़िम**, *q. v.*

लवाणक, *m.* a sickle, reapinghook.

लवार, *m.* a talker, babbler, liar.

लवास, *more prop.* **लिबास**, *q. v.*

लविन्द, free, independent; having no fixed residence; unlearned, ignorant, foolish: poor; scarce of provisions; uxorious: hence, *m.* a soldier, a volunteer, an adventurer, a rake.

लवे; see (1) **लवा** (2) **लवना** (3) **लेना**.

लवैया, *m.* a harvestman, reaper.

लशकर, *more prop.* **लश्कर**, *q. v.* [much ado.

लशटमपशटम, topsy-turvy: with difficulty, with

लशमामाटी, *f.* adhesive clay land.

लशुन, *m.* garlic (*Allium sativum*): a freckle.

लश्कर, *m.* an army. In India this term has gradually come to signify a native sailor (vulgarly called

a 'lascar'; or *per metathesin*, a 'rascal': it is also applied to soldiers, inferior artillerymen, camp-followers, tent-pitchers, and coolies.

लश्मामाटी, *f.* adhesive clay land.

लषन (*Rām.*) = (1) **लक्षण** (2) **लक्ष्मण** (3) **लखना**, *qq.v.*

लषना (*Rām.*) = (1) **लक्षणा** (2) **लखना**, *qq.v.*

लषहि, (pl. **लषहिं**) / **लषही**, (pl. **लषहीं**) } poet. forms = **लखते हैं** (**लखना**).

लषाऊ (*Rām.*) = (1) **चिन्ह** (2) **जानना**, *qq.v.*

लस, *m.* tenacity, viscosity, glutinousness, clamminess.

लसकना, *a. int.* to become viscous, become moist or stiff (as a field.

लसकर, *more prop.* **लश्कर**, *q.v.*

लसत, *m.* (*f.* antī) shining, glittering, flashing, glancing; befitting: sporting, playing.

लसदार, viscous, clammy, glutinous, adhesive.

लसदारी, *f.* = **लस**, *q.v.*

लसद्भाल, *adj.* having a brilliant countenance, moon-faced.

लसन, *more prop.* **लशुन**, *q.v.*

लसना, *a. int.* to become, befit: to shine.

लसन्त, *m.* (*f.* ī) = **लसत**, *q.v.*

लसलसा, *m.* (*f.* ī) viscous, clammy, glutinous, adhesive, ropy.

लसलसाहट, *f.* viscosity, clamminess, adhesiveness,

लसलसाना, *n.* to be clammy or glutinous: *a. int.* to agglutinate.

लसित, *m.* (*f.* ā) seen, evident, obvious.

लसियाना, *n.* to be viscous, be clammy.

लसुन, *more com.* **लशुन**, *q.v.*

लसोड़ा, *m.* a certain glutinous fruit (*Cordyamyxa*). *Baṛā*—, the plant *Cordia latifolia*, Roxb.

लस्कर, *more prop.* **लश्कर**, *q.v.*

लस्मामाटी, *f.* adhesive clay land.

लस्सानिकत, *f.* eloquence.

लस्सानी, *f.* eloquence; elocution.

लस्सी, *f.* milk and water.

लहई, *m. f.* (pl. **लहईं**) *poet.* = **लहता है** (**लहना**).

लहऊं (*poet.*) = **लूं** and **लूंगा**, *q.v.*

लहंगा, *m.* a petticoat, a kind of skirt which is tied around the loins and extends to the feet or ground.

लहंजा, *m.* misfortune, calamity.

लहक, *f.* flash, glare, glitter.

लहकना, *a. int.* to glitter, flash, glance, shine, rise up into a flame; to wave (as herbage before the wind) to warble, quaver.

लहकाना, *t.* to cause to warble or quaver, cause to shine or glitter, to blow up a fire.

लहकारना, *t.* to fondle, to pat and encourage a horse, etc,

लहकावट, *f.* a glittering, flashing.

लहकोला / **लहकेला** } *m.* (*f.* ā) glittering, flashing.

लहकौवर, *m.* rice-milk eaten by the bride and bridegroom.

लहजा, *m.* the tongue, voice, sound, tone, accent, cadence, speech, talk.

लहना, 1, *a. int.* to answer, avail, boot, signify, accrue: 2, *t.* to find, get, experience: 3, *m.* outstanding debt; fate, destiny.

लहबर, *m.* a kind of parroquet.

लहबेरा, *m.* a certain plant.

लहम, *m.* flesh, meat: solder.

लहमा (by inversion) = **लम्हा**, *q.v.*

लहर, *f.* (contr. of **लहरि**) a wave, a large wave or surf: undulation; emotion, excitement; a waving pattern in embroidery; whim, fancy: visionariness; the effect of the poison of a snake.

लहरना, *a. int.* to play as waves, to undulate, fluctuate.

लहरनी (*dialectic*) = **नहरणी**, *q.v.*

लहरबहर, *f.* prosperity.

लहरा, *m.* a quaver, shake, trill (in Music): evasion.—*lagānā*, to evade, to shirk an engagement; to feed with mere hopes.

लहराना, *t.* to undulate, fluctuate, wave; to tantalize: to play loosely, to put off, evade.

लहरि, *f.* a large wave or surf. See **लहर**.

लहरिया, waved (a mode of dyeing or painting).

लहरी, 1, *f.* a large wave or surf: 2, *m.* (*f.* iṇī) fluctuating, inconstant, capricious, whimsical.

लहर्रा, *m.* the grain called **बाजरा**, *q.v.*

लहलहा, *m.* (*f.* ī) flourishing, blooming.

लहलहाना, *a. int.* to flourish, bloom.

लहलही, *f.* stiff or thick mud.

लहलोट, *adj.* borrowing and never paying.

लहवार, *m.* (*f.* nī) *more prop.* **लोहार**, *q.v.*

लहसन, *more prop.* **लशुन**, *q.v.*

लहसनिया, *m.* a certain precious stone (cat's-eye?): *adj.* savouring of garlic, garlicky.

लहसुन, *more prop.* **लशुन**, *q.v.*

लहसोड़ा = **लसोड़ा**, *q.v.*

लहहि, (pl. **लहहिं**) / **लहही**, (pl. **लहहीं**) } old forms = **लेता है**.

लहाना, *more com.* **लहना**, 2, *q.v.*

लहू, *m.* blood.

लहूआ, *m.* a certain plant.

लहूलुहान, bloodstained, gory, covered with blood.

लहेऊ (*poet.*) = **लिया**, *q.v.*

लहै, an old form = **लहे** (**लहना**).

लहोवा, *m.* iron.

लहोवाटी, *f.* a poker.

लछमी, a corruption of **लक्ष्मी**, *q.v.*

ला, 1, = **लाके** (**लाना**): 2, (*contraction*) = **लाहा**.

लाइक़, suitable, fit, proper, adapted, worthy, able, capable, competent, qualified.

लाइये, respectful imperat. 2nd pers. of vb. **लाना**.

लाइलाहा, *m* (*f.* ī) one who possesses *chanā*.

लाइहि, (pl. °**हिं**) / **लाइही**, (pl. °**हीं**) / **लाइहै**, (pl. °**हैं**) } old forms = **लावेगा** (**लाना**).

लाई, 1, (*Rām.*) = **लिये**, *q.v.* : 2, *f.* (*m.* **लाया**) brought, fetched, produced : 3, *f.* a kind of sweetmeat (parched rice mixed with sugar).

लाउं, *more prop.* **लाऊं**, *q.v.*

लाउव (*Rām.*) = (1) **मैं लाऊं** (2) **मैं लाऊंगा**.

लाउक, *more prop.* **लायक़**, *q.v.*

लाऊ, *m. f.* one who brings, a bringer.

लाऊं, (from vb. **लाना**) I may bring.

लाएक, *more prop.* **लायक़**, *q.v.*

लाओ, 1, *more prop.* **लाव**, *q.v.* : 2, the imperat. 2nd pers. pl. of the verb **लाना**. [chaff.

लांक, *f.* quantity, measure : the loins ; birdlime :

लांगल, *m.* a plough : the penis : the main beam of a house : the palm-tree.

लांगलिक, *m.* one of the thirty-four species of the fixed (or mineral and vegetable) poisons.

लांगली, *f.* the designation of several plants (1) *Gloriosa superba* (2) *Commelina salicifolia* (3) *Jussiena repens* (4) *Nama zeylanica.*

लांगुल = **लांगूल**, *q.v.* [penis.

लांगूल, *m.* a tail, a hairy tail (as a horse's) ; the

लांघजाना, intensive of **लांघना**, *q.v.*

लांघना, *t.* to jump over, overleap.

लांच, a bribe, suborning-fee.

लांचख़ोर, *m.* one who takes a bribe.

लांछन, *m.* a spot, mark, sign ; a name, appellation : reproach, calumny.

लांछित, *m.* (*f.* **आ**) marked : reproached, blamed.

लांड़, *m.* membrum virile. *Jumerātkā* --- is a phrase applied to anything used up and unfit for service.

लांडगा, *m.* (*f.* ī) a wolf.

लांडा, *m.* (*f.* ī) tailless, docked, bobtail.

लांप, *f.* a bound, leap, spring.

लाक, *m.* a kneading-trough : a tortoise.

लाकड़ू in the hill dialect = **लकड़ी**.

लाक्षा, *f.* the red animal dye called 'lac'; the insect which produces lac (it is analogous to the cochineal insect ; and, like it, forms, when dried and prepared, a dye of a red colour ; its nest is formed of a resinous substance which is used as sealing-wax and is called "shell-lac" (*vulg.* shellac).

लाक्षागिर, *m. pr. n.* (prop. **लाक्षागृह**) a certain ancient palace near Benares.

लाक्षातरु = **लाक्षावृक्ष**, *q.v.*

लाक्षाप्रसादन, *m.* a certain tree (the red *Lodh*) from the bark of which an astringent infusion is prepared which is used to fix colour in dyeing.

लाक्षावृक्ष, *m.* the palās-tree (*Butea frondosa*).

लाख, *m.* gum lac, a kind of wax formed by the *Coccus lacca*; sealing-wax : one hundred thousands, a lac. — *ki butti*, a stick of sealing-wax. — *lagānā*, to shut up or conceal.

लाखन, *m.* [pl. of **लाख** : see **न**, 6 (1)] lacs.

लाखना, *t.* to apply lac.

लाखवां, *m.* (*f.* wīṅ) the hundred-thousandth.

लाखी, *f.* a red colour procured from lac.

लाखों, *m.* (pl. of **लाख** : see **ओं**, 4) lacs, hundreds of thousands, lacs and lacs, many lacs.

लाग, *f.* striking, hitting, fixing ; a stroke : grudge, enmity, rancour, spite : affection, love : expenditure, price, cost : a secret : approach. — *lagnā*, to fall in love.

लागऊं, *more prop.* **लगाऊं** (**लगाना**).

लागणीं in Mārwāṛī = **लगना**, *q.v.*

लागत, *f.* expense, cost, price.

लागना, *more com.* **लगना**, *q.v.*

लाग़र, lean, spare, meagre, thin.

लागि, 1, = **लागके** (**लागना**): 2, (poet.) = **लिये**, *q.v.*

लागिहि, (pl. °**हिं**) an old form = **लगता है** (**लगना**).

लागी, *f.* 1, (poet.) = **लिये**, *q.v.*: 2, past part. of **लागना**, *q.v.* : 3, a mark, butt : affection, love, attachment.

लागु ; see **लाग** and **लागू**. [desirous.

लागू, 1, (*Rām.*) = **लाग**, *q.v.* : 2, *m. f.* adhering to;

लागूट, *f.* attachment, affection, love.

लागे, frequent (*esp.* in poetry) for **लिये**, *q.v.*

लाघव, *m.* lightness, swiftness, readiness, dexterity; smallness, minuteness, insignificance, meanness ; (in Pros.) shortness (of a vowel); levity, frivolity; diminution ; contempt, undervaluing ; delicacy ; health.

लाङ्ग : see under the form **लांग**. [lorn, poor.

लाचार, without remedy, helpless; distitute, for-

लाचारी, *f.* the state of being without remedy, helplessness, destituteness, forlornness. The term is often used in the same sense as our expression 'Hobson's choice.'

लाची, a contraction of **इलाची**, *qv*.

लाज, 1, *f.* bashfulness, shame, modesty : 2, *m.* grain (wetted or sprinkled).

लाजन, a Braj pl. of **लाज**, *q.v.*

लाजना, to feel ashamed or abashed.

लाजरम, necessarily, undoubtedly, indispensably.

लाजवन्त, *more prop.* **लज्जावन्त**, *q.v.*

लाजवन्ती, *more prop.* **लज्जावती**, *q.v.*

लाजवाब, incapable of answering, disconcerted, silenced, speechless, confuted.

लाजवाला, *m.* (*f* ī) imperishable.

लाजा (*Rām.* = (1) **लज्जा** (2) **लावा**, *qq.v.*

लाज़िम, necessary, urgent, suitable, proper, important, inseparable. [ability, inseparableness.

लाज़िमी, *f.* necessity, urgency, importance, suit-

लाभा, *m.* glutinousness, viscosity, tenacity.

लाट, 1, *m.* cloth : entanglement, disorder, confusion : the Hindee form of the English title 'lord' : 2, *f.* an obelisk, pillar, minaret, steeple : a club, staff : 3, old or worn, dirty, soiled, spoiled, shabby (as cloth, ornaments, etc.).

लाटपादरी, *m.* the Lord Bishop.

लाटसाहिब, *m.* the Lord-Sahib, *i.e.* the Viceroy and Governor-General, the Lord Bishop, the Chief Justice.

लाटा, *m.* a kind of food eaten by the poor (consisting of *mahū,ā* pounded with grain).

लाटी, *more prop.* **लाठी**, *q.v.*

लाठ, *f.* an obelisk, pillar, steeple, minaret; a club, staff; the vertical part of an oil-mill; the upright beam which moves in a sugar-mill.

लाठा, *m.* a large club or stick.

लाठियाल } *m.* (*f.* ī *or* in) = **लठैवाला**, *q.v.*
लाठिवाल }

लाठी, *f.* a staff, pole, stick, club, crutch, mace, bludgeon, cudgel.

लाठीपाठी, *f.* a mutual cudgelling, a stick-fight.

लाड़, *m.* lovingness, blandishments, coaxing, caressing, endearment, sport, play, playfulness (of a child); saliva, spittle, slaver.—*laṛānā*, to fondle a child.

लाड, *more com.* **लाड़**, *q.v.*

लाड़कपूर, *m. pr.n.* two celebrated merry minstrels (*Lāṛ* and *Kapūr*) who lived at the court of Akbar.

लाड़प्यार, *m.* great fondness, love and dalliance.

लाड़ला, *m.* (*f.* ī) darling, dear, beloved.

लाडला }
लाड़िला } *m.* (*f.* ī) *more com.* **लाड़ला**, *q.v.*
लाड़ोला }

लाडु, 1, *more prop.* **लड्डू**, *q.v.*: 2, poet. = **लाड़**, *q.v.*

लाण्ड़ = **लांड़**, *q.v.*

लाण्डगा, *m.* (*f.* ī) a wolf.

लाण्डा, *m.* (*f.* ī) tailless, docked, bobtail.

लात, *f.* a kick.—*denā* or *mārnā*, to kick.

लातीनी, *f.* the Latin, language: *adj.* Latin.

लाद, *f.* a load: bowel.

लादना, *t.* (causat. of **लदना**) to cause to be loaded, *i. e.* to load, lade, freight.

लदफान्द, *f.* loading and packing.

लादवेा, in Māṛwārī = to meet. [full.

लादवी, *f.* a deed of release, an acquittance in

लादिया, *m.* one who loads, a loader. [man's).

लादी, *f.* (dim. of **लाद**) a small load (*esp.* a washer-

लादू, *m. f.* a burden-bearer, beast of burden (as an ass): *lit.* fit to carry a load.—*k.* to mount a horse or colt for the first time.

लानत, *more prop.* **लश्नत**, *q.v.*

लाना, (contr. of **ले** + **आना**) to bring, fetch; to adduce, introduce; to produce, breed, spread, propagate, make; to apply; to induce, persuade. This verb, though transitive in sense, is in its government active intransitive, *i. e.* its agent does not take *ne.*

लानाबन्दी, *f.* assessment of land according to the number of ploughs employed on it.

लाफना, *a. int.* to jump, leap. [ulant.

लाबाली, fearing nothing, insolent, licentious, pet-

लाबुद, necessarily, infallibly, assuredly, doubtless: *adj.* unavoidable.

लाभ, *m.* getting, obtaining, acquisition, acquirement, gain, profit, advantage, welfare, emolument, produce, interest.—*k.* to gain, acquire; to attain.

लाभकर, *m.* (*f.* ī) affording advantage, procuring gain or profit, profitable, advantageous, lucrative.

लाभका, (gen. of **लाभ**) *m.* (*f.* ī) advantageous, beneficial, profitable, of use.

लाभकारी, *m.* (*f.* iṇī) }
लाभजनक. *m.* (*f.* ikā) } = **लाभकर**, *q.v.*
लाभदाई, *m.* (*f.* inī) }
लाभदायक, *m.* (*f.* ikā) }

लाभमय. *m.* (*f.* ī) abounding in advantage or profit, profitable, advantageous, lucrative.

लाभाय, *more prop.* **लुभाय** (**लुभाना**).

लाभालाभ, *m.* (**लाभ** + **अलाभ**) advantage and disadvantage, gain and detriment, profit and loss.

लाम, *m.* a ringlet, curl.

लामड़ी, *more prop.* **लोमड़ी**, *q.v.*

लामिसा, *m.* feeling, touching, the sense of feeling.

लाय, 1, = **लाके** (**लाना**): 2, *more com.* **लिये**, *q.v.*

लायक, 1, *more prop.* **लाइक़**, *q.v.*: 2, *adj.* (in comp.) *m.* (*f.* ikā) bringing, getting, procuring.

लायना, 1, *more prop.* **लेना**, *q.v.*: 2, *m.* a kind of grain.

लायानी, unmeaning, insignificant, absurd; abusive; obscene.

लाया, *m.* (*f.* **लाई**) brought, fetched, produced.

लाये, 1, *m.* pl. of **लाया**, *q.v.*: 2, *more prop.* **लिये**.

लार, 1, *m.* (*f.* ?) spittle, saliva, slaver: 2, *adv.* in company with: (in Māṛwāṛī) after.

लारकोलार in Māṛwāṛī = immediately behind.

लारैब, unquestionable, doubtless.

लाल, 1, darling, dear, precious: inflamed: dumb: 2, *m.* an infant boy, a son: saliva, spittle: a ruby: a certain bird (the male of the *Fringilla amandava*).

लालक, *m.* (*f.* ikā) a seducer: lit. *adj.* seducing,

लालकद्दू, *m.* a kind of pumpkin. [seductive.

लालकार, *more prop.* **ललकार**, *q.v.*

लालच, *m.* (*f.* ?) strong desire, covetousness, greediness, longing, want, selfishness, avarice, occasion, view.

लालची, *m.* (*f.* inī) a greedy person: *lit.* greedy, covetous, interested, selfish, avaricious, miserly, niggardly. [ling a ruby.

लालड़ी, *f.* a kind of ruby; a false stone resemb-

लालन, 1, *adj.* wheedling, coaxing, caressing, over-indulging, spoiling: 2, *m.* a wheedling, coaxing, caressing, over-indulging, spoiling: 3, *f.* a mistress, sweetheart.

लालनपालन, *m.* caressing and cherishing.

लालबुझक्कड़, *m.* an intelligent person, one who comprehends quickly, or who readily divines what has happened (or is to happen) from certain symptoms. The term is, however, usually applied ironically (as an epithet) to a wiseacre, an ignorant foolish person who pretends to more sense and knowledge than his neighbours.

लालमिर्च, *f.* red pepper, cayenne, capsicum.

लालरी, *more com.* **लालड़ी**, *q.v.*

लालसमुद्र, *m. pr. n.* the Red Sea.

लालसा, *f.* ardent desire, a wishing for any absent person or object, longing, coveting, the longing of pregnant females, regret, sorrow, missing, asking, soliciting, dalliance. [*gangeticus*, Willd.).

लालसाग, *m.* a certain vegetable (*Amaranthus*

लालसित, *m.* (*f.* ā) very desirous or wishful.

लाला, 1, *f.* saliva, spittle, slaver: 2, *m.* (uninfl.) master, Sir, grandee, schoolmaster; a writer, clerk, copyist; a slave; a head servant, major domo; a prating fellow, babbler; talkativeness, frivolous talk: a kind of grain like sesamum; a tulip; a certain herb brought from the neighbourhood of Mecca (the smell of which keeps off the piles). This term is the designation of a certain tribe of Kāyaths who are schoolmasters, and is also applied (as a title) to certain Hindoo castes (*i. e.* the Vaishya, etc.).

लालाजी, (a mode of address used towards a respectable man not of high rank) master, Sir.

लालाटिक, *m.* (*f.* ī) an attentive servant: an idler: *lit.* appertaining to the forehead; appertaining to fate or to destiny.

लालाभक्ष, *m. pr. n.* (lit. feeding upon saliva) a certain hell appropriated to those who eat their food without offering some to the gods, to the manes, or to guests.

लालामेह, *m.* the passing unctuous urine.

लालिका, *f.* (*m.* **लालक**,) a female seducer, a wanton.

लालित, *m.* (*f.* ā) loved, desired, treated tenderly, cherished, coaxed, wheedled, seduced.

लालित्य, *m.* loveliness, pleasantness, beauty, gracefulness, sweetness, gentleness, gaiety.

लालित्यता, *f.* (*redundant*) = **लालित्य**, *q. v.*

लालिन, (1) *m.* (*f.* ī) = **लाली**, 1 (2) *f.* = **लालिनी**, *qq. v.*

लालिनी, *f.* (*m.* **लाली**) = **लालिका**, *q. v.*

लाली, 1, *m.* (*f.* inī) = **लालक**, *q. v.*: 2, *f.* redness, ruddiness, blood-colour.

लालेपड़ना, *n.* to be extremely desirous and unable to fully express one's wishes.

लालोपत्ती, *more com.* **लल्लोपत्तो**, *q. v.*

लाव, 1, *m.* a rope for raising water from a well, the cable of a boat: flattery: 2, *m.* (*f.* ā) a sort of quail (*Perdix chinensis*): 3, *adj.* cutting down.

लावक, *m.* a kind of quail (*Perdix chinensis*).

लावचरस, irrigation by water raised from wells in the leathern bag or bucket called *charas*.

लावणिक, 1, *m.* (*f.* ī) a salt-merchant: 2, *m.* a vessel holding salt: 3, *lit.* appertaining to salt, impregnated with salt, salted: *met.* savoury, beautiful, lovely.

लावणिकी, *f.* (*m.* **लावणिक**) a female salt-merchant, a salt-merchant's wife; a lovely female.

लावण्य, *m.* saltness: *met.* agreeableness, loveliness, beauty, charm, elegance, grace. [female's name.

लावण्यवती, *f.* (*m.* **लावण्यवान**) a lovely female: a

लावत, an old form = **लाता है**. See **त**, 5.

लावत्यवती, a corruption of **लावण्यवती**, *q. v.*

लावना (*colloquial*) = **लाना**, *q. v.*

लावन्य (*corruption*) = **लावण्य**, *q. v.*

लावलश्कर, *m.* an army. [covetousness, avarice.

लावलाव, *m.* (lit. "bring bring"; *hence*) greediness,

लावसाव, *m.* advantage, profit.

लावहि (pl. °हिं) } (poet.) = **लावेगा** (**लावना**).
लावही (pl. °हीं) }

लावा, 1, *f.* (*m.* **लाव**, 2,) a sort of quail; 2, *m.* parched grain: a joke; the game of tipcat: 3, *m.* (*f.* ī) *more com.* **लाया**, *q. v.*

लावालुत्र; see **लावालुत्रा**.

लावालुत्रा, *m.* (*f.* ī) a tale-bearer.

लावू, *f.* a pumpkin (*Cucurbita lagenaria*).

लाश, *f.* a dead body, corpse, carcass.

लाशा, 1, *f.* = **लाश**, *q. v.*: 2, *m.* = **लासा**, *q. v.*

लास, *m.* dancing; wantonness, dalliance: pea-water; pulse that has been lightly boiled. [a peacock.

लासक, *m.* (*f.* ā *or* ikā) an actor, dancer, mime;

लासन; see **लसन** and **श्रासन**.

लासना; see **लसना** and **लसलसाना**.

लासा, *m.* anything clammy or glutinous; *hence*, the milk of plants, birdlime, size, glue, starch.

लासानी; see **लसियाना** and **लस्सानी**.

लासिका, *f.* (*m.* **लासक**) a dancing-girl.

लास्य, 1, *m.* dancing; lascivious acting, dalliance, wantonness; union of dance and music; the dance of the Indian dancing-girls: 2, *m.* (*f.* ā) a dancer, actor, mime.

लाह, 1, *more prop.* **लाभ**, *q. v.* (see **ह**): 2, *m.* a kind of cloth resembling gauze: lac.

लाहल्ल, not to be untied, not to be solved, difficult, abstruse, indissoluble.

लाहा, *m.* (from **लाभ**) advantage, profit, gain.

लाहिक, *m.* an appendage, a dependent: *lit* touching, reaching, overtaking, adhering, adjoining, pertaining.

लाही, *f.* a certain plant: a sort of fine cloth.

लाहू (*Rām.*) = **लाभ**, *q. v.*

लाहेार = **लाहौर**, *q. v.* [salt procured in Lahore.

लाहेारी = **लाहौरी**, *q. v.* — *namak*, *m.* rock or fossil

लिश्रा, *m.* (*f.* **लिई**) *more com.* **लिया**, *q. v.*

लाहौर, *m. pr. n.* (1) of the province of Lahore in north western India (2) of its capital.

लाहौरी, *m.* (*f.* iṇī) a native or a resident of Lahore: *lit* appertaining to Lahore.

लिई, (pl. **लिईं**) the fem. form of **लिया**, *q. v.*

लिए, 1, a pl. of **लिया**, *q. v.*: 2, = **लिये**, *q. v.*

लिंग; see under the form **लिङ्ग**.

लिकुच = **लकुच**, *q. v.*

लिक्षा, *f.* a young louse, a nit.

लिखत, 1, *f.* (*m.* ?) anything written, a writing, inscription, missive, letter, scripture: 2, *adj.* writing.

लिखतं, *m.* a writing, document, deed.

लिखतम, *more com.* **लिखतं**, *q. v.*

लिखन, *m.* the act of writing, any written document, a letter, missive, writing, scripture; fate, destiny.

लिखना, *t.* to write; to delineate, paint.

लिखनी, *f.* an instrument for writing with, a reed, a pen, a style. [copyist, quill-driver.

लिखनीदास, *m.* (*f.* ī) a writer, amanuensis, clerk,

लिखनेहारा, *m.* (*f.* ī) a writer, scribe, author.

लिखन्त, *m.* fate, destiny, predestination.

लिखलेना, *t.* to write out, to copy.

लिखवाना, *t.* to cause to write; to cause to be delineated or written out; to cause (one's picture) to be drawn.

लिखा, 1, *m.* (*f.* ī) written: 2, *m.* writing; fate, destiny, predestination (*i. e.* what is written on the forehead).

लिखाई, *f.* the art or business of writing or penmanship; the labour of writing; wages paid for writing.

लिखात; see (1) **लिखावट** (2) **लिखाना**.

लिखाना, *t.* to cause to write, teach to write; to get

लिखापढ़ी, *f.* reading and writing. [a thing written.

लिखाव, *m.* the act of writing; a writing, inscrip-

लिखावट, *f.* = **लिखाव**, *q.v.* [tion.

लिखित, *m.* (*f.* ā) written, drawn, sketched, painted, delineated, specified; hence, *m.* a written book or paper, a writing, document, manuscript, scripture.

लिखोर; see **लखोर**.

लिङ्ग, *m.* a sign, token, spot, discriminative mark, symptom of disease; membrum virile, a priapus; the phallus (or Shiv under that emblem); a religious mark; the order of the religious student; (in Gram.) gender; (in Logic) the reason or middle term, premisses, an inference; (in the Sānkhya Philos.) nature (as the active power in creation); the primary body or subtle frame in which the soul is invested.

लिङ्गन, *m.* an embracing, caressing.

लिङ्गनाश, *m.* the destruction or the loss of the penis.

लिङ्गवचन, *m.* (in Gram.) that word in any sentence with which the other words have to agree in gender.

लिङ्गायत, *m.* the private parts: *adj.* possessing the organs of generation

लिङ्गार्च्चण, *m.* *ling*-worship (*i. e.* the worship of Shiv under the emblem of the phallus).

लिङ्गिवेष, *m* the dress or the insignia of a Hindoo student of theology (*i. e.* the skin, staff, bowl, etc.); the dress or the appearance of a follower of Shiv.

लिङ्गी, distinguished by a characteristic mark or sign; hence *m.* (*f.* inī) a certain sect of gymnosophists, a worshipper of Shiv under the phallic emblem, one who is intitled to wear religious marks, a Hindoo student of theology, a hypocrite, an elephant.

लिङ्गीचेय, *m.* the emission of urine (?).

लिङ्गैत, *adj.* possessed of the organs of generation.

लिचिक, *m.* a sprain, bruise.

लिचि }
लिची } *more prop.* **लीची**, *q.v.*
लिचू }

लिभड़ी, *f.* after-birth, placenta.

लिट, a kind of bead. [put to rest.

लिटवाना, *t.* to cause to be laid down, cause to be

लिटाना, *t.* (causat. of **लेटना**) to cause to lie down or repose, to lay, place.

लिटारना = **लिटाना**, *q.v.* [paste baked on coals.

लिट्टी, *f.* a certain kind of balls (or thick cakes) of

लिड़ना, *a. int.* to wallow, welter, draggle, grovel.

लियड़ना, *n.* to be draggled.

लिथाड़ना, *t.* to draggle.

लिन, *more prop* **लीन**, *q.v.* [form **लपट**.

लिपट; for words beginning thus, see under the

लिपटाव, *m.* adhesion.

लिपड़ी, *f.* an old ragged turban. [washed over.

लिपना, *n.* to be plastered over, be smeared over, be

लिपवाना, *t.* (causal of **लीपना**) to cause to plaster, etc.; to cause to be smeared, etc.

लिपाई, *f.* the act of smearing or plastering.

लिपाना, *t.* (causat. of **लेपना** or **लीपना**) to cause to smear or plaster.

लिपि, *f.* anointing, smearing, painting, writing; hand-writing; a written document, manuscript, book, etc.; an alphabet.

लिपिकर }
लिपिकार } *m.* (*f.* ī) a writer, scribe; a plasterer.

लिपित, *m.* (*f.* ā) written, besmeared, plastered.

लिपी, *f.* = **लिपि**, *q.v.*

लिप्त, 1, *m.* (*f.* ā) smeared, anointed, plastered, spread; tainted, defiled, contaminated; closely united, connected, embraced: 2, *m.* (in Astron.) the 60th part of a degree. [sure, envelope.

लिफ़ाफ़ा, *m.* an outer case, wrapper, cover, enclo-

लिबलिबा, *m.* the pancreas.

लिबास, *m.* apparel, garments, clothes, dress, attire, habit: a veil: forgery.

लिब्बई, *m. pr. n.* the apostle Lebbæus.

लिब्बा, *m.* a slap, blow, buffet. [trace: fault.

लिम, *f.* unjust censure, calumny: indication,

लिम्पट = **लम्पट**, *q.v.*

लिय; see **लिया** and **लिये**.

लिया, (past part. of **लेना**) *m.* (*f.* **लिई**: pl. **लिये** or **लिए**) brought. [fitness, knack.

लियाक़त, *f.* worth, merit, skill, abilities, dignity,

लिये, (infl. past part. *m.* of **लेना**) by occasion of, by reason of, on account of, with a view to, for the purpose of, for the sake of, in the interests of, for.

लिरवा = **लिरुआ**, *q.v.*

लिरावो in Māṛwāṛī = **लिवाना**, *q.v.*

लिरुआ, *m.* rice-straw (*esp.* such as is fit for fodder).

लिलयाना; see **रीरियाना** and **ललाना**.

लिलहिं (*Rām.*) = (1) **लीलासे** (2) **बिना श्रम**.

लिलाट }
लिलाड़ } = **ललाट**, *q.v.*

लिलाना, *a. int.* to long, wish, desire eagerly.

लिलार, *more com.* **लिलाड़**, *q.v.*

लिवलावो in Māṛwāṛī = to consider attentively.

लिवा, 1, in Braj = **लिया**, *q.v.*: 2, *m.* a standard,

लिवाकत, *more prop.* **लियाक़त**, *q.v.* [banner.

लिवाना, *t.* (causat. of **लेना**) to cause to take.

लिवालाना, *t.* to procure, bring.

लिवास, *more prop.* **लिबास**, *q.v.*

लिवैया, *m.* one who takes, a taker

लिखनौं in Chand = **लिखना**, *q.v.*

लिसा, *more prop.* **निसा**, *q.v.*

लिसान, *f.* the tongue; language, dialect.

लिसोड़ा = **लसोड़ा**, *q.v.*

लिहा, *more com.* **लिया**, *q.v.*

लिहाई, *f.* a kind of paste or glue (made from tamarind-stones pounded and boiled to a jelly) used by bookbinders.

लिहाज़, *m.* a look, glance, view; an observing attentively; sense; respect. — *k.* to observe, notice; to regard, mind, have respect for.

लिहाड़ा, *m.* (*f.* ī) vile, base, contemptible, mean.

लिहाफ़, *m.* a coverlet, quilt, counterpane; a quilted upper garment; *met.* a wife.

लिहैयहौ, *f.* the act of throwing up water for irrigation from a pond or river with a kind of basket worked by two persons.

लीश्रा, *m.* land that is annually flooded.

लीए, *more prop.* **लिए**, *q.v.*

लीक, *f.* marks of a carriage-wheel, rut, track, trace, path; strain, disgrace, ignominy.

लींका (*Rām.*) = (1) **लीक** (2) **मर्यादा** (3) **रेखा**)4) **गिन्ती**.

लीख, *f.* the egg of a louse, a nit.

लीखना, a corruption of **लिखना**, *q.v.*

लीच = **नीच**? *q.v.* — *jānā*, to succumb, subside, [submit.

लीचड़, stingy, niggardly.

लीची, *f.* the leechee-fruit (*Scytalia litchi*) first introduced from China. (*Vulg.* lichi.)

लीजे
लांजे } in Braj = **लीजिये** (**लेना**).

लीजो in Braj = **लीजियो** (**लेना**).

लीझी, *f.* dregs, sediment.

लीतरा, *m.* an old shoe or slipper. [phants, or asses.

लीद, *f.* the globular dung of horses, mules, ele-

लीन, 1, an old form = **लिया**, *q.v.*: 2, *m.* (*f.* ā) melted, dissolved, wiped away, removed, effaced, extinguished, perished: intimately united with, absorbed into, immersed, occupied in thought or contemplation; adhered to, embraced.

लीनछीन, captured, seized, enslaved.

लीनत, *f.* softness.

लीना, *m.* (*f.* ī) an old form = **लिया**, *q.v.*

लीनें, an old form = **लिया**, *q.v.*

लीन्हा, *m.* *f.* ī) an old form = **लिया**; see **न्हा**.

लीन्हे, *m.* (*f.* °**न्हीं**) pl. of **लीन्हा**, *q.v.*

लीन्हेसि, an old form = **लिया**, *q.v.*

लीन्हो
लीन्हौ } = **लीन्हा**, *q.v.*

लीपड़ी, *f.* a rag; a small turban.

लीपना, *t.* to plaster, besmear, whitewash.

लीबड़, *m.* rheum (of the eyes).

लीम, *m.* concord, peace.

लीमू, *m.* the lime-tree (*Citrus medica*) and its fruit, a lime, a lemon.

लीमून (*dialectic*) = **लीमू**, *q.v.*

लीया, a corruption of **लिया**, *q.v.*

लींयो, in Chand = **लिया**, *q.v.*

लीर, *f.* a strip or slip of cloth.

लील [*colloquialism*: see **ल**, 4 (2)] = **नील**, *q.v.*

लीलकण्ठ (*colloquialism*) = **नीलकण्ठ**, *q.v.*

लीलगाई, *f.* (*colloquialism*) = **नीलगाव**, *q.v.*

लीलना, *t.* to swallow, gulp. [or wanton sport.

लीला, *f.* play, sport, pastime, diversion; amorous

लीलावती, *f.* a wanton or sportful woman: *pr.n.* a certain well-known treatise (written in Sanskrit by Bhāshkar) on arithmetic, algebra, and mensuration.

लीलापीला, *m.* (*f* **लीलीपीली**) = **नीलापीला**, *q.v.*

लीवो, a corruption of **लेवो** (**लेना**).

लीस, in the hill dialect = pitch.

लु; a Taddhita suffix by means of which some adjectives are formed from substantives: *e.g.* **दयालु**, from **दया**.

लुआब, *m.* thirsting, thirst: saliva, spittle.

लुं, *more prop.* **लूं** = **लेऊं**, *q.v.*

लुंच
लुंजः
लुंजा } = **लुञ्जा**, *q.v.*

लुक, 1, *m.* a cutting off, elision, rejection: a falling star, meteor: varnish: 2, a Kridanta suffix by means of which a few adjectives are formed from verbal roots; *e.g.* **भीलुक** (from rt. **भी**).

लुकनत, *f.* stuttering, stammering, lisp.

लुकना, to be concealed, lie hid.

लुकन्दा, *m.* a rake, profligate, blackguard.

लुकमा, *m.* a morsel, mouthful, sop, bit.

लुका, *m.* (*f.* ī) concealed, hidden.

लुकांजन, *m* a certain ointment by the application of which to a person's eyes he is said to become invisible.

लुकाना, *t.* to hide, conceal.

लुकावना (*colloquial*) = **लुकाना**, *q.v.*

लुक्क, *m.* a kind of dye.

लुग़ज़, *m.* any ambiguous phrase, an enigma, riddle.

लुगटी, *f.* (= **लूकटी**) a poker.

लुग़त, *f.* tongue, speech, dialect, language; a glossary, dictionary; a word.

लुगाइ
लुगाई } = **लोगाई**, *q.v.*

लुच, mere, pure, stark, naked.

लुचई, *f.* a kind of cake.

लुचपन, *m.*
लुचपना, *m.*
लुचपनी, *f.* } = **लुच्चापनी**, *q.v.*

लुचबहादुर, *m.* a vagabond.

लुचरा, *m.* (*f.* ī) a spider.

लुच्चपन, *m.*
लुच्चपना, *m.* } = लुच्चामी, *q.v.*
लुच्चपनी, *f.*

लुच्चा, *m.* (*f.* ī) a vagabond; libertine, rake, profligate; a bankrupt: *adj.* low, mean, paltry, base; wanton, lascivious, lecherous.

लुच्चापन, *m.*
लुच्चोपना, *m.* } = लुच्चामी, *q.v.*
लुच्चापनी, *f.*

लुच्चामी, *f.* libertinism, profligacy, rakishness, wantonness, lasciviousness, lechery.

लुच्चावन; see लुच्चापन.

लुजलुजा = लजलजा, *q.v.* [ency, necessity.

लुज़ूम, *m.* what is behoving or requisite, expedi-

लुञ्जमुञ्ज, utterly lame.

लुञ्जा, *m.* (*f.* ī) lame of a hand or hands, having lost the use of hands or feet, without hands or feet, crippled, lame.

लुटना, *n.* to be plundered, be sacked.

लुटवाना, *t.* to cause to be sacked or given up to plunder, cause to be squandered.

लुटवैया, *m.* a squanderer, prodigal, spendthrift; plunderer, free-booter, robber: *lit.* thievish, squandering.

लुटस = लुट्टस, *q.v.*

लुटाना, *t.* 1, (causat. of लूटना) to cause to plunder or to be plundered, to spend or expend, to squander: 2, (causat. of लोटना) to cause to wallow or roll about.

लुटारा, *m.* (*f.* ī) = लुटवैया, *q.v.*

लुटिया, *f.* (dim. of लोटा) a small pot.

लुटेरा
लुटेरू } = लुटवैया, *q.v.*

लुट्टस, *f.* (*m.* ?) plundering, devastation, ruin.

लुट्टू, *m.* a child's top.

लुठना; see (1) लुटना (2) लोटना.

लुड़कना, *more prop.* लुढ़कना, *q.v.*

लुड़का, *m.* a kind of ear-ornament worn by Hindoos.

लुड़खना *a. int.* to roll, slip, slide, fall (or roll) off.

लुड़खुड़ी, *f.* rolling: flattery, coaxing, wheedling, fawning.

लुड़ना, *a. int.* to wallow, welter, draggle, grovel.

लुड़बुड़ा, *m.* (*f.* ī) rash, inconsiderate; acquainted with everybody, meddlesome, intrusive.

लुढ़कना, *a. int.* to roll, be tossed about, be upset,

लुढ़जाना, *a. int.* to die. [be spilt.

लुढ़ना = लुढ़कना, *q.v.*

लुढ़ाना, *t.* to cause to roll, cause to roll over, to

लुढ़िया, *f.* = लोढ़ा, *q.v.* [upset, spill.

लुढ़ियाना, *t.* to double-hem a garment.

लुढुकना; see लुढ़कना.

लुणटक, *m.* a sort of potherb (*Chironia centauroides*).

लुण्डा, 1, *m.* (*f.* ī) tailless, tailcropt, docked: 2,

लुण्डियाना, *a. int.* to roll. [*m.* a mass, lump.

लुथड़ना, for लुढ़ना, *q.v.*

लुतड़ा, *m.* (*f.* ī) *more com.* लुतरा, *q.v.*

लुतपुता, *m.* (*f.* ī) savoury, delicious.

लुत्फ़, *m.* courtesy, kindness, favour, benignity, graciousness, gentleness; pleasantry, wit.

लुतरा, *m.* (*f.* ī) a sycophant, tell-tale, babbler, tattler, backbiter, one who cannot restrain his tongue, a blab, a silly person: *adj.* driven off, expelled, rejected.

लुतरापन, *m.* the state or condition of a sycophant or

लुतरी, *f.* (*m.* लुतरा) a female blab, etc. [backbiter.

लुत्रा, *m.* (*f.* ī) *more com.* लुतरा, *q.v.*

लुपकी, *f.* fear, alarm, terror.

लुपरी, *f.* pap.

लुपलुप, *m.* lapping (as of dogs drinking).

लुप्त, cut off, elided, dropped, removed, obsolete, disused, extinct, disappeared, lost, gone.

लुप्तता, *f.* disappearance, non-existence.

लुबदी, *f.* a poultice, cataplasm.

लुबलुब, kind, benevolent to inferiors.

लुबादा, *m.* a wrapper, cloak, great coat, outer garment, pelisse.

लुबान, *m.* a kind of gum, frankincense, olibanum, benzoin, resin (of the *Boswellia serrata*, Roxb.).

लुबुध (*Rām.*) = लुब्ध, *q.v.*

लुब्ध, *m.* (*f.* ā) a hunter, a miser, covetous or greedy person, a lecher, rake, libertine, whoremonger: *lit.* desirous, covetous, greedy, avaricious, cupidinous.

लुब्धक, *m.* (*f.* ikā) = लुब्ध, *q.v.*

लुभाना, *t.* to excite desire, tantalize, allure, entice.

लुहपण्डा, *m.* an iron pot.

लुहरा, *m.* (*f.* ī) a junior, a younger; a cadet.

लुहांगी, *f.* a staff armed with iron.

लुहान, covered or smeared with blood, blood-

लुहानः = लुहान, *q.v.* [stained, bloody.

लुहार, *m.* (*f.* in) a worker in iron, a blacksmith.

लुहारिन, *f.* (*m.* लुहार) a blacksmith's wife.

लुहू, *m.* (from लोहू) blood.

लू (*contraction*) = लूक, *q.v.*

लूआट
लूआत } = लूकट, *q.v.*

लूई, *f.* a round lump of dough prepared for making into bread or cakes; a poultice.

लूं, a shortened form of लेऊं, *q.v.*

लूंगा, a shortened form of लेऊंगा, *q.v.*

लूक = (1) तारा (2) लुक्क (3) लूघ (4) लूख, *qq.v.*

लूकट, 1, half-burnt (said of wood): 2, *m.* a brand.

लूकटी, *f.* a wooden poker or stake burnt at one end; firebrand: a fox.

लूकना, *n.* to be scorched by the sun or hot wind; to have a *coup de soleil*: *t.* to see, behold.

लूकवाई, *f.* conflagration.

लूका, *m.* pieces of burning matter thrown out from a conflagration, burning grass.—*lagānā*, to inflame or excite quarrels, etc.

लूख, *f* a flame. — *chalānā*, (to enflame with love, (i. e.) to charm, fascinate.

लूगा, clothes.

लूट, *f*. depredation, plunder, spoil, pillage, booty.

लूटकोट, लूटखूट } *f*. = लूटपाट, *q. v.*

लूटना, *t*. to plunder, pillage, spoil; to squander.

लूटपाट, *f*. plunder and sacking, plundering and ravaging, pillaging.

लूटबाज़, *m*. a plunderer; a murderer.

लूटाई, *f*. booty, pillage, plunder, spoil.

लूटालाटी, लूटालूट, लूटालूटी } *f*. = लूटपाट, *q. v.*

लूटिया, *m*. a mounted robber, plunderer, pillager.

लूटी, *m*. (*f*. inī) = लूटिया, *q. v.*

लूटोवाला, *m*. (*f*. ī) one who lives by robbery.

लूण, 1, *m*. salt: 2, *adj*. salt, saline, brackish.

लूणया, *m*. (*f*. ī) salt, saline, brackish.

लूणी, *f*. the salt that effloresces from walls, etc.: butter.

लूतखरन, 1, *m*. the colour of a spider: 2, spider-coloured.

लूता, *f*. a spider: local inflammation produced by the urine of a spider: an ant.

लूथ, *f*. a dead body, carcase, corpse.

लूनि, *f*. a cutting, reaping: rice.

लून, 1, *m*. salt: 2, *adj*. salt, saline: 3, *m*. (*f*. ā) cut, clipped; cut off, served; wounded.

लूना; see लून and लोना.

लूनिया, 1, salt, saline, brackish: 2, *m*. purslain (*Portulaca oleracea*): a salt-maker: a certain tribe of native traders (*baniyā*): a pioneer.

लूनी = लूणी, *q. v.*

लूम, *m*. a tail; a hairy tail (as a horses's, monkey's, etc.)

लूरी, 1, (*corruption*) = नूरी, *q. v.*: 2, *f*. leprosy.

लूला, 1, *m*. (*f*. ī) lame of the hands, maimed: 2, *m*. a roll of paper.

लूलू, *m*. a pearl: a goblin to frighten children: *pr. n*. a certain people in Persia (called also Kārāji).

लूलुआ, *m*. a paw.

लूह, *f*. the hot wind of the months of Vaisākh and Jeth, a hot wind, simoom.

ले, 1, (conjunctive participle of लेना) having taken: 2, (2nd pers. sing. imperat. of that verb) take: 3, till, up to: 4, from: 5, come! well! 6, (2nd and 3rd pers. sing. of the aor. of vb. *lenā*) mayest take, may take: 7, in the Kumāonī dialect of Hindee this form is the case-sign of the Agent and of the Ablative. — *jānā*, to take away, carry off, run away with, carry, convey, export, submit, refer, win. — *parnā*, to lie with (*coïre*): to involve another in one's disgrace. — *pālnā*, to adopt, rear, bring up, father (a child). — *bhāgnā*, to run away with. — *marnā*, to calumniate. — *rakhnā*, to provide, keep ready, procure, reserve. — *rahnā*, to pilfer, to cheat. — *lenā*, to take, receive, accept of, take by force, extort, bereave.

लेअइहौं (see इहौं) in Braj = मैं लेआऊंगा.

लेआना (= लाना) to bring. *Le,ā-denā*, to bring and give, to fetch and present.

लेइ in Braj = लिई, लिया, ले, or लेई, *qq. v.*

लेइहै (pl. लेइहैं) in Braj = लेगा (लेना).

लेइहौं in Braj = मैं लेऊंगा (लेना).

लेई, *f*. paste, starch.

लेउगे in Braj = लेओगे or लोगे (लेना).

लेऊं, the 1st pers. sing. aor. of the verb लेना.

लेऊंगा, *m*. (*f*. ī) the 1st pers. sing. fut. of verb लेना.

लें (pl. of ले, 6) = लेवें, *q. v.*

लेंडी = लेंपड़ी, *q. v.*

लेंठा = लेंपठा, *q. v.*

लेंव, in Braj = लेऊं (लेना).

लेंहिगे, a corruption of लेंगे (लेना).

लेकर (a conjunct. part. of लेना, used idiomatically with the abl. before it, and forming, with it, an adverbial phrase; *e. g. Yahānse lekar wahāntak*, from here to there; *hence* =) from; with.

लेकिन, but, still, but still, on the other hand, yet, moreover, notwithstanding.

लेके = लेकर, *q. v.*

लेक्षण; see लेखन and लक्षण.

लेख, *m*. a letter, epistle, writing.

लेखई (*Rām.*) = लखती है (लखना).

लेखक, *m*. (*f*. ikā) a writer, clerk, copyist, amanuensis, scribe, author, accountant.

लेखकी, *f*. the business of a writer.

लेखति (*Rām.*) = लेखती है (लेखना).

लेखन, *m*. scarifying; writing, copying; scripture; the bark of the *bhoj*-tree (which is used for writing on in Nepāl and Upper India).

लेखना, *t*. to dig, delve, engrave, scoop.

लेखनी, *f*. any instrument for writing with, a reed, pen, style.

लेखय = लेख्य, *q. v.*

लेखा, *f*. a line, stripe, stroke, flash, mark, delineation, painting; a row; handwriting: account, reckoning, calculation, estimation. — *k*. to compute. — *lenā*, to take an account.

लेखाबही, *f*. an account-book, a day-book; book-keeping.

लेखे; the inflected form of लेखा, *q. v.*

लेखेवाला, *m*. (*f*. ī) an accountant.

लेख्य, *m*. a letter, epistle, writing, manuscript.

लेख्यपत्र, *m*. a written paper, a writing, letter, document.

लेख्यस्थान, *m*. an office: a country-house.

लेगड़, *m*. a sort of earth or mud, black alluvial soil, cotton-ground.

लेजइये (*poet.*) = ले जाइये.

लेजाना; see *s. v.* ले.

लेट, *m*. plaster, mortar, chunam.

लेटना, *a. int*. to lie down, recline, repose, rest.

लेड़वो in Mārwārī = impotent. A term of reproach applied by Rājputs to Banias.

लेणु; see रेणु.

लेंपड़ो, 1, *f*. goat's-dung: 2, a cur, a country dog: 3, impotent.

लेपड़ा, *m.* smut, mildew: a flock of goats or sheep; [a pack of dogs.

लेत, *m.* plaster, paste, batter.

लेताड़ना, *t.* to fatigue, weary.

लेन, *m.* the act of taking, receiving.

लेनदेन, *m.* taking and giving, borrowing and lending, buying and selling, trading, trade, traffic, barter, business — *k.* to carry on business. — *kā lekhā*, account-current.

लेना, *t.* to take, accept, get, hold, receive, to pick, to win, to assume, to buy.

लेनादेना, *m.* = लेनदेन, *q.v.*

लेप, *m.* smearing, plastering; a plaster, unguent, ointment, liniment; mortar, plaster, chunam; a stain, spot: food: the wipings of the hand which has offered funeral oblations to three ancestors (these wipings being considered as an oblation to ancestors in the fourth, fifth, and sixth degrees).

लेपक, *m.* (*f.* ikā) a bricklayer; a plasterer: lit. *adj.* smearing, plastering.

लेपड़ना; see *s.v.* ले. [tering; mortar, plaster.

लेपन, *m.* the act of anointing or smearing or plas-

लेपना, *t.* to plaster, smear over, besmear.

लेपालक, *m.* (*f.* ikā) an adopted child, foster-child: *adj.* adopted, fostered (as a child).

लेपालकपन, *m.* the state or condition of adoption.

लेपालना; see *s.v.* ले.

लेपालेप, *m.* complete plastering.

लेपी, *m.* (*f.* inī) = लेपक, *q.v.*

लेप्य, *m.* smearing, plastering, spreading.

लेफाफा, *more prop.* लिफ़ाफ़ा, *q.v.*

लेभागना }
लेमरना } see *s.v.* ले.

लेमू = लीमू, *q.v.*

लेरखना }
लेरहना } see *s.v.* ले.

लेरां in Māṛwāṛī = after.

लेरु }
लरू } *m.* a calf.

लेरुआ, *m.* (*f.* लेरुई) a calf.

लेला, *m.* a lamb.

लेलियाना, *a. int.* to bleat.

लेलूट, *adj.* borrowing and never paying.

लेलेना; see *s.v.* ले.

लेव, *more prop.* लेओ (लेना): 2, *m.* plaster falling [from a wall.

लेवहु (*poet*) = लेओ (लेना).

लेवा, *m.* a taker: plaster, the ashes or earth spread on the outside of a new cooking-vessel: an udder.

लेवादेई }
लेवादेवी } *f.* = लेनदेन, *q.v.*

लेवार, *m.* mud for plastering a wall.

लेवास, *m.* plaster.

लेवे, (pl. लेवें) 2nd and 3rd pers. sing. aor. of vb. लेना.

लेवेत्रे, *f.* (?) = लेनदेन, *q.v.*

लेवै (pl. लेवैं) in Braj = लेवे, *q.v.*

लेवैया, one who takes, a taker.

लेश, 1, *m.* smallness; a small portion, minute particle, a little; a mark, sign, trace, effect: 2, small, little.

लेस (*corruption*) = लेश, *q.v.* [to foment a quarrel.

लेसना, *t.* to plaster, smear, spread, daub: to kindle;

लेसालेस, *m.* plastering. [a licker, sipper.

लेह, 1, in Braj = लेओ, *q.v.*: 2, *m* licking, tasting;

लेहन, *m.* tasting with the tongue, licking.

लेहना, *m.* pasture, provender.

लेहरा, *m.* (*f.* ī) impure, filthy, dirty.

लेहाज, *more prop.* लिहाज़, *q.v.*

लेहिन, *m.* borax.

लेहि (pl. लेहिं) }
लेही (pl. लेहीं) } = लेता है (लेना).

लेहु }
लेहू } Braj forms of लेओ, *q.v.*

लेह्य, fit or proper to be licked; hence, *m.* food that is licked; nectar, ambrosia.

लै in Braj = ले, *q.v.*

लैग्रइहों (see इहों) in Braj = मैं लेआऊंगा.

लैग्रावनों in Braj = लेआना, *q.v.*

लैजैहों in Braj = मैं लेजाऊंगा. [row.

लैन, 1, *more prop.* लेन, *q.v.*: 2, *m.* (Engl.) a line,

लैना, *more com.* लेना, *q.v.*

लैर in Māṛwāṛī = after.

लैल, *f.* night.

लैली, appertaining to night, nocturnal: a beloved woman, mistress: one who works at night: *pr. n* the celebrated mistress of Majnūn.

लैलेनों in Braj = लेलेना. See. *s.v.* ले.

लैव्यव्यवस्था, *f. pr. n.* the Book of Leviticus.

लैस, *m.* a kind of vinegar: a practising-arrow: a spring: *adj.* ready, brought

लैहै (pl. लैहैं) in Braj = लेगा (लेना).

लैहों in Braj = लेऊंगा (लेना).

लो, look! see! lo! there now! take that! *lit.* (imperat.) take, hold.

लोई, 1, (*Rām.*) = लोग, *q.v.*: 2, *f.* flannel; a blanket: splendour of the countenance: honour.

लों, 1, *more prop.* लूह, *q.v.*; 2, = लग, *q.v.*

लोंग, *f.* = लवंग, *q.v.*

लोंड़ा, *m.* (*f.* ī); see (1) लौंडा (2) लोहरा (3) लोंदा.

लोंडा, *m.* (*f.* ī) *more prop.* लौंडा, *q.v.*

लोंठा, *m.* a lump of clay, a clod.

लोक, *m.* seeing, sight: the world, the universe; mankind, people, folk; a world, a division of the universe. In general, three divisions of the universe are enumerated; *viz.* (1) Swarglok (2) Pātāl (3) Mrityabhavan; or Heaven, Hill, and Earth. Another classification enumerates (1) *Bhūrlok* (2) *Swarglok* (3) *Bhūvarlok*; or Earth, Heaven, and intermediate space. A third classification enumerates seven divisions exclusive of the infernal regions; *viz.* (1) *Bhūrlok*, the Earth

(2) *Bhūvarlok*, the space between the earth and the sun, the region of the Munis, Siddhis, etc. (3) *Swarglok*, the heaven of Indra, between the sun and the polar star (4) *Maharlok*, the usual abode of Bhrigu and other saints: during the conflagration of these lower worlds the saints ascend to the next, *viz* (5) *Janlok*, which is described as the abode of Brahmā's sons: above this is the sixth world, *viz.* (6) *Tapolok*, where the deities called Vairāgis reside (7) *Satyalok* or *Brahmlok*, the abode of Brahma; translation to which world exempts from further birth. Of these seven worlds the first three are destroyed at the end of each *Kalp* or day of Brahm, the last three at the end of his life or of one hundred of his years; while the fourth, though equally permanent, is uninhabitable from heat at the time the first three are burning. Another enumeration calls these seven worlds (1) earth (2) sky (3) heaven (4) middle region (5) place of births (6) mansion of the blest, and (7) the abode of truth; placing the sons of Brahma in the sixth division, and stating the fifth (or *Janlok*) to be the state in which animals destroyed in the general conflagration are born again.

लोकक, *more com.* लौकिक, *q.v.*

लोककृत, an epithet of Brahmā: *lit.* the creator of the universe or of the worlds (*lok*).

लोकड़ी, *f.* (= लुकटी) a wooden poker.

लोकजित, *m.* a conqueror of the world (an epithet of a Buddh or deified Bauddh teacher).

लोकजीत = लोकजित, *q.v.*

लोकत्रय, *m.* (see लोक) the three worlds, *viz.* heaven, earth, and hell; *i. e.* the whole universe.

लोकन, 1, a Braj pl. of लोक: see न, 6 (1): 2, = लोकत्रय, *q.v.*: 3, *m.* a looking, viewing, beholding.

लोकना, *t.* to catch.

लोकनाथ, *m.* (the lord of the universe, *i.e.*) Shiv.

लोकनिन्दा, *f.* calumny, slander.

लोकनीय, worthy or suitable to be looked at or seen, visible, to be to be seen.

लोकप
लोकपति } *more com.* लोकपाल, *q.v.*

लोकपाल, *m.* a sovereign, king. The term is specially applied to a certain class of deities (Indra, Yam, Varun, Kuver) who are believed to protect the various regions of the universe.

लोकपालक, *m.* (*f.* ikā) = लोकपाल, *q.v.*

लोकप्रसिद्ध, generally acknowledged, universally admitted or understood; notorious, well-known.

लोकबुद्धि, *m. f.* one who knows the ways of the world: *lit.* worldly-wise.

लोकरंजन, *m.* popularity, gaining public confidence.

लोकरा, *m.* torn clothes, tatters.

लोकराक्षस, *m.* the spirit of a wicked man converted into a demon.

लोकरीति, *f.*
लोकलाज, *f.*
लोकव्यवहार, *m.*
लोकाचार, *m.* } = लोकाचारी, *q.v.*

लोकाचारी, *f.* the custom of a people, the honour or credit of a people, the way of the world.

लोकान्तर, *m.* the other world, another world; decease, death.

लोकापवाद, *m.* calumny, slander.

लोकालोक, *m.* a mountainous belt surrounding the outermost of the seven seas and bounding the world.

लोकिक; for words beginning thus, see under the [from लौकिक.

लोखड़ी, *f.* a fox.

लोखर, *m.* tools, old iron pots, pans, hardware.

लोग, *m.* mankind, people, folk. The word is often used for the purpose of pluralizing; *e. g. Purushlog*, men, males: *Strilog*, women-folk, females.

लोगन; see न 6 (1) and (2).

लोगाई, *f.* woman; a female; womenfolk.

लोगू in Braj = लोग, *q.v.*: see ऊ, 7.

लोचक, *m.* a lump of flesh, ball of meat: stibium, lampblack.

लोचन, *m.* the eye: seeing: filings, powder.

लोचनकर्कट
लोचनमस्तक } *m.* a flower (*Celosia cristata*).

लोचना, *m.* = लोचा, *q.v.*: 2, *more prop.* नोचना, *q.v.*

लोचनामय, *m.* diseased affection of the eye, ophthalmia.

लोचा, *m.* a lump of flesh, ball of meat.

लोचुन, *m.* filings, powder.

लोट, 1, *m.* = लोटा, *q.v.*: 2, *f.* a wallowing, rolling: 3, prize, plunder, pillage: a wave, billow: 4, (Engl.) a banknote.

लोटन, *m.* a rolling, tumbling, wallowing; a tumbler-pigeon: a braid of hair; a bush.

लोटना, *a.int.* to wallow, roll about, flounce, sprawl.

लोटनापोटना, *a. int.* (intensive of लोटना) to roll or turn over and over, to wallow.

लोटपुटिया, *m.* watercresses.

लोटपोट, *adj.* tumbling and tossing, rolling about, restless, wallowing. — *k.* to roll about, trumble and toss, wallow. — *honā*, to be in love. — *rahnā*, to continue restless or tossing about.

लोटा, *m.* an earthen cooking-pot, pipkin; a small metal pot (generally of brass or tinned iron).

लोटाना, *t.* to cause to flounder, cause to wallow.

लोटासज्जी, *f.* a kind of earth containing fossil alkali.

लोठड़ा = लोथड़ा, *q. v.*

लोढ़ना, *t.* to hem (a garment).

लोढ़ा, *m.* a stone pestle with which materials are triturated on a stone.

लोढ़ी, *f.* a hem of a garment.

लोण, 1, *m.* salt: 2, *adj.* salt, saline.

लोणद्रोही, *m.* (*f.* inī) *adj.* having an aversion to salt.

लोणा, 1, *m.* (*f.* ī) salt, saline, brackish, salted, seasoned: beautiful: barren or salt (said of land): 2, *m.* salt that effloresces from walls, etc.: purslain (*Portacula oleracea*).

लोणापन, *m.* saltness, brackishness; palatableness: beauty.

लोथ, *f.* a dead body, carcase, corpse.

लोथड़ा, *m.*
लोथड़ी, *f.*
लोथरा, *m.*
लोथरी, *f.* } a lump of flesh, ball of meat.

लोथा, *f.* a bag, sack, stupe.
लोथी, *f.* a staff, club (knotted).
लोदा, *m.* (*more com.* **लोन्दा**) a lump of clay, a clod.
लोदी, *m.* a certain agricultural tribe among the Paṭhāns ; *hence*, a husbandman.
लोध, a contraction of **लोध्र**, *q. v.*
लोधा / **लोधिया** / **लोधी** } = **लोदी**, *q.v.*
लोध्र, *m.* a certain tree (*Symplocos racemosa*) the bark of which is used in dyeing: a kind of medicine.
लोन, *m.* salt. — ***mirch lagānā***, to speak hyperbolically or in lofty diffuse language.
लोनवाई, *m.* (*f.* inī) a seller of salt.
लोना, 1, = **लोणा**, *q.v.*: 2, *m.* a certain fruit (*Annona reticulata*).
लोनाई, *f.* / **लोनायन**, *m.* } = **लोणापन**, *q.v.*
लोनार, *m.* salt lands ; a place where salt is produced, a salt-pit.
लोन्दा, *m.* a lump of clay, a clod.
लोप, *m.* cutting off, rejection, erasure, disappearance, destruction, omission, annulling, cancelling; (in Gram.) elision.
लोपड़ी, *f.* a lump of anything moist, a poultice composed of flour, turmeric, and oil or clarified butter.
लोपवो in Māṛwāṛī = to transgress.
लोबान, *more prop.* **लुबान**, *q.v.*
लोबिया, *m.* a kind of bean (*Dolichos sinensis*).
लोभ, *m.* intense or greedy desire, covetousness, greediness, cupidity, avarice.
लोभक, appertaining to **लोभ**; *hence*, greedy, avaricious.
लोभना, *n.* to be enamoured.
लोभमोहित, *m.* (*f.* ā) beguiled or overcome by greediness.
लोभविरह, *m.* freedom from greediness.
लोभविरही, *m.* (*f.* iṇī) free from greediness.
लोभाना, *more com.* **लुभाना**, *q. v.*
लोभाग्नि, *f.* the fire or lust of greed.
लोभावनौं in Braj **लुभाना**, *q.v.*
लोभी, *m.* (*f.* inī) a greedy person, etc.: *lit.* desirous, eager, covetous, avaricious, cupidinous.
लोम, *m.* hair, down, wool; a hairy tail (as that of the horse, monkey, etc.): (in Geom.) the base of a triangle : a piquet, outpost, sentry.
लोमकर्ण, *m.* (*f.* ī) the hare.
लोमकूप, *m.* a pore of the skin.
लोमड़ी, *f.* a fox.
लोमविष, *m.* any animal (as the tiger, etc.) whose hair is supposed to be poisonous.
लोमश, *m.* (*f.* ā) a ram : *lit.* hairy, mixed with hair, covered with hair, made of hair ; woollen.
लोमशपर्णिनी, *f.* a certain plant (*Glycine debilis*).
लोमशमार्जार, *m.* (*f.* ī) the pole-cat.
लोमशा, *f.* a fox: a female divine being (an attendant on Durgā): green vitriol : Indian spikenard (*Valeriana Jatamansi*); cowach (*Carpopogon pruriens*); another plant (*Leca hirta*) ; orris root.
लोमस, 1, *more prop.* **लोमश**, *q.v.*: 2, *m. pr.n.* a certain *rishi*.
लोमसार, *m.* the emerald.
लोमहर्षणा, *m.* horripilation.
लोयन, *m.* (from **लोचन**) the eye. See **च**, 4.
लोयनि (*Rām.*) = **लोयन**, *q.v.*
लोर, *m.* an earring, pendant; a tear.
लोल, 1, shaking, tremulous, trembling, agitated, waving, unsteady : 2, *m.* the fluid in which the eyes sometimes appear to be overwhelmed, tears ; undulation ; glimmer.
लोलक, *m.* a pendant, earring, nose-jewel.
लोलकी, *f.* the lobe of the ear.
लोलना, *t.* to cause to vibrate, to move, shake, wag.
लोला, 1, *f.* the tongue: an epithet of Lakshmī ; one of the female modes in music (*Rāgiṇī*) : 2, *m.* a suppository, a kind of solid clyster.
लोलार्क, *m.* a certain form of the sun.
लोलिका, *f.* a sort of dock or sorrel (*Rumex vescicarius*).
लोलुप, very desirous or covetous, insatiable, longing, greedy, very cupidinous.
लोलुपता / **लोलुपताई** } *f.* insatiableness, greed.
लोवा, a fox.
लोष्ट, *m.* a clod, lump of earth : rust of iron ; iron filings.
लोष्टमय, made of clods.
लोष्टु, *m.* a clod, lump of earth.
लोह, *m.* iron (whether crude or wrought), steel : a weapon : blood : aloe-wood or agallochum.
लोहकण्टक, *m.* a thorny shrub.
लोहकान्त, *m.* the loadstone.
लोहकार, *m.* (*f.* ī) an iron-smith, black-smith, locksmith, cutler.
लोहकिट्ट, *m.* rust of iron, iron filings.
लोहचुन / **लोहचून** / **लोहचूर** } (*contractions*) = **लोहचूर्ण**, *q. v.*
लोहचूर्ण, *m.* iron filings.
लोहज, *m.* bell-metal; rust of iron, iron filings.
लोहजित, *m.* an epithet of diamond ; *lit.* conquering (*i.e.* in hardness) iron.
लोहघड़ा, *m.* an iron pot.
लोहद्रावी, *m.* an epithet of borax, *lit.* the iron-fuser.
लोहबन्दा, loaded with iron, iron-bound : hence, *m.* an iron club or life-preserver.
लोहमय, made of iron, abounding in iron.
लोहमारक, *m.* a certain plant (*Achyranthes triandra*).
लोहरा, *m.* (*f.* ī) younger, junior ; a cadet.
लोहलाठ, *m.* an iron mace or club.
लोहशलाका, *f.* any missile (as a dart, etc.) made of iron.
लोहसार, *f.* an iron-mine.
लोहा, *m.* iron. — *bajānā*, to fight with swords.
लोहान, bloodstained, bloody.

लोहानी, *m.* a certain tribe among the Paṭhāns or Afghāns.

लोहाभिसार, *m.* a certain ceremony (the lustration of arms performed on the 9th of the light half of the month Ashwin: formerly a ceremony observed by princes before opening campaign, but now usually confined to the domestic decoration and worship of the soldier's weapons).

लोहामहल्ल, *m.* an iron-department; revenue derived from iron-mines.

लोहार, *m.* an iron-worker, blacksmith.

लोहारख़ाना, *m.* a blacksmith's shop, smithy, forge.

लोहारन } लोहारिन } *f.* a blacksmith's wife.

लोहित, 1, *adj.* red: 2, *m.* red (the colour): blood.

लोहितक, *m.* a ruby, calx of brass; an epithet of the planet Mars; *lit.* red. [*lit.* red-faced.

लोहितानन, *m.* (*f.* ī) an epithet of the ichneumon:

लोहिया, made of iron. [just before sunrise.

लोही, *f.* a lump, a mouthful; a kind of silk; dawn

लोहू *m.* blood. — *ḍālnā*, to spit blood. — *phaṭnā*, to have leprosy. — *bahānā*, to spill, to shed blood — *bāiṭhnā*, to pass blood at stool. [gory.

लोहूलहां, covered with blood, bloodstained, bloody,

लौ, 1, in Braj = लग, *q. v.*: 2, *f.* flame of a candle, any pointed flame: remembrance: love. — *lagnī*, *f.* the constantly and eagerly craving for a thing, the frequent and long-continued repetition of a saying (particularly the calling of a lover on his mistress or of a dying person on God). — *lagānī*. *f.* an intense and importunate praying or untiring meditation on God.

लौं in Braj = (1) लग (2) लूह (3) लौ, 2, *qq. v.*

लौंग, *f.* = लवंग, *q. v.* [meal.

लौंगचड़ा, *m.* a kind of dish prepared from pease-

लौंड़, *m.* membrum virile.

लौंडा, for words beginning thus, see under the corresponding form लौंडा.

लौंड़िया, *more prop.* लौंडिया, *q. v.*

लौंड़ी, *more com.* लौंडी, *q. v.* [lighten, flash.

लौकना, *t.* to see, behold: *a. int.* to shine, glitter,

लौका, *m.* lightning, flash, glitter, coruscation: a kind of pumpkin (*Cucurbita lagenaria*).

लौकायतिक, *m.* an atheist, materialist, Bauddh.

लौकिक, *m.* (*f.* ī) prevailing amongst (or familiar to) mankind, generally received, vulgar, appertaining to this world as distinguished from the next, mundane, worldly, human, customary; ceremonial; ceremonious.

लौकिकज्ञान, *m.* the knowledge or wisdom that pertains to the present world, worldly wisdom.

लौकिकज्ञानी, *m*, (*f.* ini) a worldy-wise person: *lit.* appertaining to worldly wisdom, possessing worldly wisdom.

लौकिकता, *f.* (*m.* °त्व) the being customary, worldly currency or custom, worldliness, popularity.

लौकिकधर्म्म, *m.* the prevailing order of things in religion, fashionable religion.

लौकी, *f.* a kind of pumpkin.

लौज़, *m.* an almond; a kind of sweetmeat.

लौट, *m.* a turning over, inverting; a returning.

लौटना, *a. int.* to turn over, to turn back, return, retreat. [turn, give back, reject.

लौटाना, *t.* to turn over, to invert, turn back, re-

लौठा, *m.* a young man. (Cf. Engl. 'lout'.)

लौठियन, a Braj pl. of लौठी, *q. v.*

लौठी in Braj = लाठी, *q. v.* [brum virile.

लौड़ा, *m.* (*f.* ī) *more prop.* लौंडा, *q. v.*: 2 *m.* mem-

लौड़िया, *more prop.* लौंडिया, *q. v.*

लौण्या, *m.* a certain medicine. [catamite.

लौंडा, *m.* (*f.* ī) a boy, lad, brat, a slave-boy; a

लौंडाबाज़, *m.* a sodomite. Also spelt लौंडेबाज़.

लौंडाबाज़ी, *f.* sodomy. Also spelt लौंडेबाज़ी.

लौंडिया = लौंडी, *q. v.* [girl, bondmaid.

लौंडी, *f.* (*m.* लौंडा) a girl, a servant-girl, slave-

लौन, *m.* colour, hue; external form; species, genus. [*t.* to reap, to harvest.

लौना, 1, *m.* balancing, making scales equal: 2,

लौनी, *f.* wages paid in kind to reapers in harvest-

लौन्द, *m.* an intercalary month. [time.

लौम, *m.* blaming, reprehending, accusing, reprov-

लौर = लवर, *q. v.* [ing, reproaching.

लौलगनी } लौलगानी } see *s. v.* लौ.

लौलास, a token, favour.

लौलीन, *m.* (*f.* ā) absorbed in, intent on, bent on, concentrated on, enamoured, rapt, eager.

लौलेश, *m.* an atom. [unsteadiness, fickleness.

लौल्य, *m.* greediness, desire, passion, agitation,

लौस, *m.* taste; tasting.

लौह, 1, made of iron: 2, *m.* iron.

लौहरा, *m.* (*f.* ī) younger, junior; a cadet.

लौहलाय, *more prop.* लौहलाठ, *q. v.*

लौहार, *m.* a trance.

ल्याई, *f.* (*m.* ल्याया) *more prop.* लेआई (लेआना).

ल्याऊं, *more prop.* लेआऊं (लेआनो).

ल्याना in Braj = लाना or लेआना, *qq. v.*

ल्यादेना = लेआ देना, *q. v.*

ल्याय, in Braj = लेआके (लेआना).

ल्याया, *m.* (*f.* ल्याई) *more prop.* लेआया (लेआना).

ल्यायहीं, in Braj = लेआऊंगा (लेआना).

ल्यायोहै, in Braj = लेआया है (लेआना).

ल्यारी, *m.* (*f.* iṇī) a wolf.

ल्याव, in Braj = लेआओ (लेआना).

ल्होवार, *m.* (*f.* nī) a worker in iron, ironsmith, black-

ल्हो, *m.* blood. [smith, locksmith, cutler.

ल्होपीव, *m.* a blood-drinker.

ल्होलुआन, *more com.* लोहूलहां, *q. v.*

ल्होवा, *m.* iron. — *chābnā*, (lit. to chew iron; *hence*) to act bravely or boldly.

व

व (v *or* w) is the twenty-ninth consonant in the Hindee alphabet, and has the following characteristics and functions:—1, It belongs to the class of labials, is sometimes called 'dento-labial,' and is the fourth of the semi-vowels or *antahsth* letters: see **अन्तःस्थ.** 2, The pronunciation of this letter is sometimes the same as that of the English letter *v*, and sometimes of *w*: it is not easy, however, to lay down rules that shall embrace all instances. When it occurs as the latter element in a compound letter, it is pronounced like *w*, unless the first element be **र**; *e. g.* **स्वर** *swar*: it is also pronounced like *w*, or better still, perhaps, like *o*, when it follows a vowel; *e. g.* **शिव,** 'Shiw' or 'Shio.' At the beginning of words it is generally pronounced like *v*, though sometimes like *w*; e. g. **विशेष,** properly *vishesh*, but sometimes also *wishesh.* 3, Some substantives [*m.* (*f.* ā)] are formed by the addition of this letter as a suffix; *e. g.* **अश्व.** 4, This letter is also found as a Taddhita suffix by means of which some adjectives and epithets [*m.* (*f.* ā)] are derived from substantives; *e. g.* **केशव,** from **केश.** 5, This letter is constantly interchanged (1) with **ब** (see **ब,** 1); for all words therefore beginning with this letter, but not found in the following pages, see under the form **ब** (2) with **न** [see **न,** 6 (3)], especially in the infinitive form of verbs in poetry and in Braj; *e. g.* **करवो = करना: देखवेके = देखनेके** (3) with **ओ**; *e. g.* **बवना,** properly **बोना** (4) with **औ**; *e. g.* **अनऔसर,** properly **अनवसर** (5) with **म**; *e. g.* **रवन,** more properly **रमण** (6) with **उ** and **ऊ**; *e. g.* **तरव,** properly **तरु,** etc. (7) with **य** or **अ**; *e. g.* **पुतलिवां,** more commonly **पुतलियां** or **पुतलिआं**; **किवा,** more commonly **किया** or **किआ** (8) with **ह**; *e. g.* **जोव** constantly found in poetry for **जोह.** 6, This letter is frequently put, interchangeably with **य,** (see **य,** 10, and **ह,** 4), for **ए** as a kind of euphonic fulcrum on which to rest the vowel; *e. g.* **हावे** or **होये** for **होए.** 7, It is also inserted like **अ,** and interchangeably with it, (see **अ,** 12), to create an additional syllable or to avoid a hiatus: *e. g.* **सोवत = सोअत = सोता है.** 8, It is frequently inserted redundantly before the signs of mode and tense in the case of those verbs whose base ends with **आ**; *e. g.* **नचावना, कहावता, जावेगा,** properly **नचाना, कहाता, जाएगा.** 9, This letter, inserted between the base of a verb and the sign of the causal form, gives what has been called the 'doubly causal' form; *e. g.* **लगना,** to be struck: **लगाना,** to cause a thing to stick: **लगवाना,** to cause that a thing be stuck on by someone else. This, however is a feature in Hindee that is beset with difficulty, for it is by no means always easy to perceive the exact function of the letter when it occurs in this position, and it may even be supposed that it is in some instances redundant.

वंक, *m.* crookedness; a bending, curvature; the bend (elbow or reach) of a river or winding stream.

वंकता, *f.* = **वंक,** *q. v.*

वंका, *f.* the pommel of a saddle.

वंकाई, *f.* = **वंक,** *q. v.*

वंग, *m.* cotton: lead: tin; the calx of tin taken internally as an aphrodisiac: the egg-plant (*Solanum melongena*): *pr. n.* (1) of the province of Bengal, or its eastern parts (2) of its inhabitants.

वंचक, *m.* (*f.* ikā) a deceiver, knave, cheat, rogue, vile man, a jackal, a tame ichneumon: *lit.* deceitful, crafty, fraudulent.

वंचन, *m.* (or *f.* ā) deceit, cheating, deception, [knavery, fraud.

वंचित, *m.* (*f.* a) deceived, defrauded, tricked, imposed upon.

वंचुक, *m.* (*f.* ā *or* ī) = **वंचक,** *q v.*

वंजर; see **बनजर.**

वंजरा, *f. pr. n.* a certain river.

वंभ; see (1) **बभु** (2) **ब्राह्मण.**

वंश, *m.* race, lineage, family, pedigree, stock, offspring, descendant; a multitude, assemblage: the backbone, spine: a bamboo, a staff; a tube, pipe, flute.

वंशक, *m.* a certain small fish (*Cynoglosus lingua*).

वंशचरित्र, *m.* a genealogical table or list, the history of a dynasty or race.

वंशपरम्परा, *f.* lineage, family, descent.

वंशभोज्य, *m.* hereditary estate.

वंशरोचना, *f.* the manna or sugar of the bamboo (an earthy concretion of a milk-white colour formed in the hollow of the bamboo: it has been found on analysis to contain siliceous earth).

वंशलोचन, *m.* } = **वंशरोचना,** *q. v.*
वंशलोचना, *f.* }

वंशवृद्धि, *f.* the prosperity of a family.

वंशसमाचार, *m.* family history, family affairs; family usage. [genealogy

वंशावली, *f.* (or °लि) a genealogical list, pedigree,

वंशिक, 1, appertaining to a family, or to a bamboo, etc. (see *vaṅs*): 2, *m.* aloe-wood (*Amyris agallocha*).

वंशिका, *f.* aloe-wood (*Amyris agallocha*).

वंशी, 1, *f.* a pipe, flute, fife: bamboo manna: a fish-hook: a kind of wheat with blackish ears: 2, (in comp.) *m.* (*f.* inī) appertaining to the race or lineage of.

वंशीधर, *adj.* holding or carrying a flute: hence, *m.* (*f.* ā) fluteplayer, piper; an epithet of Krishṇ.

वंशीधारी, *m.* (*f.* iṇī) = **वंशीधर,** *q. v.*

वंशीवट, *m. pr. n.* the figtree under which Krishṇ was wont to play the flute.

वंस, *more prop.* **वंश,** *q. v.*

वक, *m.* a certain aquatic bird that feeds on fishes, the crane (*Ardea nivea* or *A. torra* or *A. putea*): a certain tree (*Sesbana grandiflora* or *Œschynomene sesban*): a kind of apparatus for subliming metals an epithet of Kuver; *pr. n.* a certain demon.

वकचाल, *f.* a walking slowly (like a *vak*).

वकत (*corruption*) = **वक्त,** *q. v.*

वकध्यान, *m.* the seeming contemplativeness of the *vak*: hence, — *lagānā*, to act with dissimulation.

वकध्यानी, contemplative like the *vak*; hence, *m.* (*f.* inī) a treacherous person.

वकपान्ती, *f.* a row or line of cranes.

वकपुष्प, *m.* a certain tree (*Æschynomene sesban* or *Æschynomene grandiflora*).

वकराज, *m.* the king of the cranes (named Rājdharman: he was son of Kashyap).

वकराजा, *more prop.* **वकराज**, *q.v.*

वकार, *m.* the letter **व**, or any symbol that may [represent it.

वकासुर, *m. pr. n.* (see **वक**) a certain crane-shaped demon slain by Krishṇ.

वकील, *m.* an agent, ambassador, representative, (in Law an attorney, counsellor.

वकुल, *m.* a certain plant (*Mimusops elengi*).

वकुली, *f.* a sort of drug.

वक़्त, *m.* time, season, opportunity, circumstance: [*met.* adversity.

वक्तव्य, 1, fit or proper to be said or spoken; hence, *m.* speaking, speech; a rule; a subject treated of; the meaning of a passage: 2, *m.* (*f.* ā) vile, low, base, bad, reprehensible; dependent, subject.

वक्ता, (uninfl.) *m.* (*f.* trī) a speaker, talker, teacher, etc.: lit. *adj.* speaking, talking, loquacious, eloquent; wise.

वक्तृ, *m.* (*f.* trī) = **वक्ता**, *q. v.*

वक्त्र, *m.* the mouth, the face, the organ of speech; a verse; a sort of garment: (in Math.) the first term in a progression: (in Pros.) a species of metre.

वक्र, cooked, curved, tortuous, bowed, bent; indirect, evasive, ambiguous; fraudulent, dishonest, malignant, cruel: hence, *m.* the winding course of a river: an epithet (1) of Saturn (2) of Mars (3) of Rudra.

वक्रगति, *f.* a tortuous motion, crooked gait; *met.* [foppishness, airs.

वक्रगामी, *m.* (*f.* inī) a fraudulent person, etc.; lit. *adj.* going tortuously or in zigzag, tortuous; fraudulent, dishonest, evasvie.

वक्रता, *f.* (*m.* °**त्व**) tortuousness, crookedness; fraudulence, dishonesty, craft, cunning: evasive or indirect speech.

वक्रपुष्प, *m.* a certain tree (*Sesbana grandiflora*).

वक्री, *m.* (*f.* iṇī) crooked, tortuous, bent; fraudulent, dishonest.

वक्रीभाव, *m.* curvature; fraudulent disposition.

वक्रोक्ति, *f.* an evasive utterance, equivoque, double entendre, hint, pun, insinuation; sarcasm.

वक्ष:, *m.* the breast, the bosom.

वक्ष:स्थल, *m.* the breast (*esp.* the female breast).

वक्षस, *m.* the breast, the bosom.

वक्षस्थल }
वक्षोज } *m.* the female breast.
वक्षोरुह }

वखालना (*dialectic*) = **उखालना**, *q.v.* See **व**, 5 (6).

वगवर; see **वागवर**.

वग़ैरः, and the rest, and so forth, etcetera.

वगैरा }
वगैरे } = **वग़ैरा**, *q.v.*

वङ्क; see under the form **वंक**, *q.v.*

वच, 1, (*contraction*) = **वचन**, *q.v.*: 2, *m.* orris-root (*Acorus calamus* or *Zingiber zedoaria*): a parrot.

वचन, *m.* speaking; a speech, word, dictum, discourse, talk, expression, saying, statement, remark, adage, quotation, sentence, aphorism, rule; a promise, agreement. — *chhornā*, to break one's promise, go from one's word. — *ḍālnā*, to ask, inquire, question. — *toṛnā*, to break one's word. — *denā*, to give one's word, to promise, agree, consent. —*nibhānā* or *pālnā*, to abide by one's promise.—*pūrā k.* to be faithful to one's word.— *bandh k.* or *bandh kar lenā*, to bind by promise. — *bandh* (or *band*) *honā*, to give one's word, to promise, to be agreed upon. — *mānnā*, to obey. — *mārnā*, to conclude an agreement. — *lenā*, to receive a promise. — *hārnā*, to promise, agree, pledge one's word, to affirm. *Priya—kahnā*, to speak in affectionate terms. As used in the terminology of Grammar the meaning of this word is noteworthy; *e. g.* **एकवचन**, the singular number.

वचनकर, *m.* (*f.* ī) the author or enunciator of a precept: *adj.* obedient.

वचनक्रम, *m.* order of words or speech, discourse.

वचनक्रमभंग, *m.* an ellipsis.

वचनग्राही, *m.* (*f.* iṇī) an obedient person: *lit.* attentive to orders, compliant, conformable, submissive, humble.

वचनदत्त, *m.* (*f.* ā) betrothed, espoused.

वचनबन्ध, *m.* (in Gram.) composition.

वचनमात्र, *m* mere words, empty talk, assertion unsupported by facts.

वचवच, *m.* twaddle, babble, nonsense.

वचवचाना, *a. int.* to talk nonsense, to twaddle, [babble.

वचांसि, *m.* (*Rām.*: Sk. pl. of **वच**:) words.

वचवची, *m.* (*f.* inī) a twaddler, babbler: lit. *adj.* twaddling, talking nonsensically, babbling.

वचा, *f.* orris-root (*Acorus calamus*).

वज़्अ, *f.* situation, state, condition, mode, manner, procedure, conduct, position.

वजड़ी, *f.* intestines, entrails, bowels. [tripe, paunch.

वजड़ीवटी, *f.* the contents of the abdomen, the

वज़ीर, *m.* a minister of state, cabinet-minister: (in Chess) the queen; (at Cards) the knave.

वज्र, *m.* (*f.* ā *or* ī) hard, adamantine, impenetrable; hence, *m.* a thunderbolt, a diamond, the thunderbolt of Indra; a form of array; emblic myrobalan; a child or pupil; sour gruel; harsh language; the blossom of the sesamum; one of the lunar mansions.

वज्रांग, *m.* an epithet of Hanumān.

वज्रांगी, *f.* a kind of mark (*tilak*) made on a Hindoo's forehead with red lead.

वज्रकण्टक, *m.* an epithet of Hanumān (the monkey-god): *lit.* adamantine-armoured.

वज्रत्व, *m.* (*f.* tā) hardness; severity.

वज्रपात, *m.* a stroke of lightning, the fall of a thunderbolt.

वज्रकीट, *m.* (*lit.* lightning-insect) a species of the armadillo called by naturalists *Pangolin* or *Manis* and sometimes 'the scaly ant-eater.'

वज्रधर, *m.* (the holder of the thunderbolt, *i. e.*) Indra.

वज्रधारण, *m.* (the holder of the thunderbolt, *i. e.*) [Indra.

वज्रनाभ, *m. pr. n.* (1) of one of Skand's attendants

(2) of a certain Danav (3) of a certain king (4) of the discus of Krishṇ. [Indra.

वज्रपाणि, *m.* (the holder of the thunderbolt, *i. e.*)

वज्रपुष्प, *m.* the blossom of the sesamum.

वज्रबध, *m.* death by lightning.

वज्रबाध, *m.* (in Arithm.) cross-multiplication.

वज्रभांग, *m.* tobacco. This appears to have been the first name given to the weed which was introduced into India, as is supposed, in the time of Jehanghir. [Indra.

वज्रभृत, *m.* (the bearer of the thunderbolt, *i.e.*)

वज्रमय, *m.* (*f.* ī) adamantine, hard: *met.* hardhearted.

वज्रबाण, *m.* a thunderbolt.

वज्रवल्ली, *f.* a species of sunflower.

वज्रा, *f.* a species of Euphorbia; another plant (*Menispermum cordifolia*).

वज्राघात, *m.* the blow of a thunderbolt; *met.* a sudden shock, an astounding calamity.

वज्राभ, *m.* a precious opal; *lit.* like a diamond.

वज्राभ्यास, *m* (in Arithm.) cross-multiplication.

वज्री, 1, *f.* a species of Euphorbia: 2, *m.* an epithet of Indra; lit. *m.* (*f* iṇī) armed with a thunderbolt.

वञ्च; see under the form **वंच**.

वट, 1, *m.* a string, rope, tie: the large Indian figtree (*Ficus Indica*): a circle: equality in shape or dimension: a small shell, a single cowrie: a division, share, partition: pulse ground and fried with oil or butter: 2, this element forms the termination of many substantives *fem.* in Hindee; *e. g.* **बनावट**, etc.

वटपार, *more com.* **बटपाड़**, *q. v.*

वटवट, *m.* twaddle, babble, nonsense.

वटवटाना = **वचवचाना**, *q. v.*

वटवटी, *m.* (*f.* inī) = **वचवची**, *q. v.*

वटिका, *f.* a kind of dish made of pulse: a pill.

वटी, *f.* a string, rope; a bead.

वटु, *m.* 1, a lad, stripling, youth, young man; a Brahmachāri or young Brahmaṇ who is studying for the priesthood: 2, a certain flower (*Bignonia Indica*).

वटुक = **वटु**, 1, *q. v.*

वडवा = **बड़वा**, *q. v.*

वडा, *f.* pulse ground and fried with oil or butter; a ball or cake; a gingerbread-nut.

वड़िश, *m.* (also *f.* ā *or* ī) a fish-hook. [sickle.

वण्ट, *m.* a part, share, portion: the handle of a

वण्टक, 1, *m.* a part, portion, share: 2, *m.* (*f.* ikā) a distributor: *adj.* distributing, dividing, sharing out.

वण्टन, *m.* dividing, distributing, apportioning, sharing, dealing out.

वण्ड, *m.* (*f.* ā) a person whose hands have been cut off; a tailless animal; a circumcised man or one who has no prepuce: *lit.* maimed, crippled, defective; tailless, docked; emasculated, impotent.

वण्डा, *f.* an unchaste female. [home, abode.

वतन, *m.* native country, birthplace, residence,

वतना, *m.* (*f.* ī) *more com.* **उतना**, *q. v.*

वत, 1, an indeclinable termination denoting similitude (=as, like, similar to) by which adverbs implying similarity or comparison are derived from substantives; *e. g.* **पशुवत**, like a brute beast: 2, *m.* (*f.* vatī) a Taddhita suffix by means of which attributives of possession are derived from substantives: (in Sanskrit this is the termination for the neuter form of such words:) 3 this element forms the termination of many substantives *fem.* in Hindee, *e. g.* **कहावत** etc.: 4, sometimes in old Hindee = **वात**, *q. v.*

वती, *f.*: see **वत**, 2, and **वान**.

वत्स, 1, *m.* (*f.* ā) a calf; the young of any animal: child (as a term of endearment): 2, *m.* a year; the breast, chest: 3, *m. pr. n.* (1) of a certain *rishi* (2) of a certain people (3) of their country.

वत्सक, *m.* a calf; a child: a certain medicinal plant (*Wrightea antidysenterica*).

वत्सतर, *m.* (*f.* ī) a steer. [a bull.

वत्सतरी, *f.* a she-calf, a heifer given away with

वत्सदन्त, *m.* (calf-toothed) a kind of arrow having a point like the tooth of a calf.

वत्सनाभ, *m.* a certain poisonous tree (*Aconitum ferox*) brought from Nepāl; an active poison (the root of that tree) called 'Meethā zahar'.

वत्सर, *m.* a year: a young bullock.

वत्सरीय, *m.* (*f.* ā) yearly, annual.

वत्सरीयगमन, *m.* (in Astron.) the sun's annual course through all the signs of the zodiac.

वत्सरूप = **वत्सासुर**, *q. v.*

वत्सल, 1, *m.* (*f.* ā) affectionate kind, loving, tender, fond, indulgent: 2, *m.* fondness, affection.

वत्सलता, *f.* affection, tenderness, kindness, fondness, love. [cow anxious for her calf.

वत्सला, *f.* (*m.* **वत्सल**) an affectionate female; a

वत्सासुर, *m. pr. n.* a certain calf-shaped Asur slain

वथुआ, *m.* (in Pros.) a species of metre. [by Krishṇ.

वदन, *m.* the mouth, the face; a beginning; (in Math.) the initial term in a progression; (in Geom.) the summit of a figure, the part opposite its base.

वदर, *m.* nonsensical talk, babble, prate, jabber.

वदरना, *a. int.* to babble, jabber, prate, talk non-

वदरात, *f.* = **वदर**, *q. v.* [sense.

वदान्य, *m.* (*f.* ā) a liberal person, etc.: *lit.* munificent, liberal, generous: speaking kindly; eloquent.

वदामि, Sk. (*Rām.*) = **मैं बोलता हूं**.

वदाल, *m.* the sheat-fish (*Silurus boalis*).

वधक, *m.* (*f.* ikā) = **बधक**, *q. v.*

वधहीन, *m.* (*f.* ā) free from slaughter, uninjured by slaughter, preserved or rescued from murder.

वधिका, *f.* (*m.* **वधक**) = **बधिका**, *q. v.*

वधु = **वधू**, *q. v.*

वधुका }
वधुटी } = **वधूटी**, *q v.*

वधू *f.* a woman, a female relation, a wife, the wife of a relation (esp. of a son), a daughter-in-law, a wife recently married. This word is frequently suffixed to the name of a male person to designate his wife; *e. g.* **इन्द्रवधु**, the wife of Indra. [wife).

वधूटी, *f.* a young woman; a daughter-in-law (son's

स्त्रैश्वर्य्य, *m.* the wealth or dominion of females.

वन, *m.* (= **बन**) a wood, forest, grove, jungle: water, a fountain, a cascade; a dwellingplace, residence, house, abode.

वनकचु, *m.* a species of arum (*A. colocasia*).

वनचर, *m.* (*f.* ī) an epithet of any creature or wild animal that inhabits the jungle: hence, a monkey, forester, woodman, savage, etc.: *lit.* going (*i. e.* living or moving) in the forest, sylvan, savage.

वनचारक, *m.* (*f.* ikā) } = **वनचर**, *q. v.*
वनचारी, *m.* (*f.* iṇī) }

वनपशु, *m. f.* any animal of the forest, a wild beast.

वनप्रस्थ, *m.* (*f.* ā) a hermit, anchoret: lit. *adj.* retiring into a forest, withdrawing from society into the wilderness, leading the life of an anchoret.

वनप्रस्थायी, *m.* (*f.* inī) = **वनप्रस्थ**, *q. v.* [honey.

वनमधु, *m.* honey produced in the jungle, wild

वनयात्रा, *f.* the pilgrimage through the eighty-four forests of the Braj-country.

वनराज, *m.* an epithet of the lion; *lit.* king of the forest. [**सं**, 2, *q. v.*

वनवास, 1, *m.* (*f.* ā) = **वनवासी**, 1, *q. v.*: 2, *m.* = **वनवा-**

वनवासी, 1, *m.* (*f.* inī) one who dwells in the forest, a hermit, anchoret, a forester: *lit.* dwelling in a forest: 2, *f.* the state of one who dwells in the forest, the life of a hermit; dwelling in the forest.

वनविड़ाल, *m.* a species of wild cat (*Felis caracal*).

वनविहार, *m.* a wandering or sporting in the woods or forests.

वनस्थायी, *m.* (*f.* inī) = **वनवासी**, 1, *q. v.* [van.

वनस्थित, situated in a forest, wild, savage, syl-

वनस्पति, *m.* lit. a lord of the forest; *hence* (1) a tree (2) a tree (a certain species of the fig, jack, etc.) that bears fruit, but no apparent blossoms (3) an ascetic, hermit, anchoret.

वनान्त, *m.* the skirts of a forest. [another wood.

वनान्तर, *m.* the middle or interior of a wood;

वनाश्रय, *m.* dwelling in a forest. [a mistress.

वनिता, *f* a woman; a beloved woman, a wife,

वनेचर, *m.* (*f.* ā *or* ī) = **वनचर**, *q. v.*

वनेला, *m.* (*f.* ī) appertaining to the forest, wild,

वन्त, *m.* (*f.* vatī) = **वान**, 2, *q. v.* [sylvan, savage.

वन्दन, *m.* homage, salutation, adoration, respect, worship, praise, flattery; *esp.* obeisance to a Brāhman or other superior by touching the feet, etc.: the mouth, the face.

वन्दना, *f.* (= **वन्दन**) praise; praising (*esp.* the gods or great personages); prayer.

वन्दनी, *f.* (= **वन्दन**) reverence, adoration, worship; asking, begging: a drug for restoring the dead to life.

वन्दनीय, *m.* (*f.* ā) deserving to be adored or eulogized, praiseworthy, worshipful, adorable, laudable, commendable, estimable, acquiring or deserving salutation.

वन्दा, *f.* any parasitical plant, but especially mistletoe (*Epidendrum tassellatum*). [adored.

वन्दित, *m.* (*f.* ā) praised, celebrated, extolled,

वन्दी, 1, *m.* (*f.* inī) a panegyrist, flatterer, praiser, bard, herald, a servant whose office it is to proclaim the titles of a great man as he passes along; or a poet who sings the praises of a prince in his presence, or who accompanies an army to chant martial songs: 2, *f.* a captive, prisoner (male or female), a man or beast confined.

वन्द्य, *m.* (*f.* ā) = **वन्दनीय**, *q. v.*

वन्धी, *m.* (*f.* inī) *more prop.* **बन्धी**, *q v.*

वन्य, *m.* (*f.* ā) sylvan, rural, wild, savage, produced in the forest.

वन्यपशु, *m.* any animal of the forest, a wild beast.

वन्या, *f.* a multitude of groves or forests; a quantity of water, a flood, inundation, deluge: a certain plant (*Physalis flexuosa*).

वन्हि (by inversion) = **वह्नि**, *q. v.*

वपन, *m.* sowing seed; semen virile: shaving.

वपनी, *f.* a barber's shop.

वपुः, *m.* the corporeal frame, the body.

वपुष } = **वपुः**, *q. v.*
वपुस }

वप्ता, *m.* (*f.* trī) a sower, planter, husbandman; a progenitor, father; a poet.

वफ़ा, *f.* performing a promise, observation of faith, fulfilment, sincerity, fidelity, sufficiency.

वमन, *m.* the act of vomiting; vomit; anything occasioning vomiting, an emetic. — *k.* to spue, vomit.

वमनशील, *m.* (*f.* ā) inclined to vomit, sickish.

वमनी, *f.* a leech.

वमी, 1, *f.* sickness of stomach, vomiting; an emetic; vomit: 2, *m.* (*f.* inī) a person who is sick at stomach; *adj.* inclined to vomit, sick.

वमि, *m.* sickness of the stomach, vomiting; an emetic: fire: a rogue.

वय, *m.* (*f.* ī) a weaver. [a weaver.

वयत, 1, *more prop.* **बैत**, *q. v.*: 2, *m.* (*f.* vayantī)

वयन, 1, *m.* the act of weaving: 2, *more prop.* **बयन**, *q. v.*: 3, black grapes: excelling: interval, separation, distance: absence: union, connexion.

वयर; see **बयार** and **बैर**. [prime of life.

वयस, *m.* age, time of life; especially youth;

वयस्क, appertaining to age, of such or such an age, aged.

वयस्य, *m* (*f.* ā) a cotemporary, one of the same age, a friend, companion, associate: *lit.* appertaining to age, aged.

वयस्या, *f.* a woman's female friend.

वयार, *f.* wind, air.

वर, 1, *m.* (*f.* ā) better, best; excellent, precious, beautiful; eldest: 2, *m.* a selecting; a soliciting; a wish; a boon, blessing, favour, privilege, *esp.* the gift of a Brāhman or of a deity; one who solicits a girl for his wife; a bridegroom, husband; a catamite; a sparrow: saffron.—*rahnā*, to be victorious, have the advantage, to prevail, gain, win.

वरट, *m.* a wasp, hornet.

वरटा } *f.* a wasp, hornet: a goose.
वरटी }

वरण, 1, *more com.* **बरं**, *q.v.*: 2, *m.* choosing, selecting; choice: surrounding, screening, covering; nourishing; a promise of marriage: an enclosure, rampart, mound: a certain tree (*Capparis trifoliata*): a camel: a causeway, a bridge: 3, *f. pr. n.* a certain rivulet.

वरणसी = **वाराणसी**, *q.v.*

वरणना, *more prop.* **वर्णना**, *q.v.*

वरणा, *f. pr. n.* a certain rivulet near Benares.

वरण्डा, *m.* a portico, verandah: a kind of thrush: a dagger, knife: the wick of a lamp.

वरण्डालु, *m.* castor-oil tree (*Ricinus communis*).

वरद, *m.* (*f.* ā) conferring a boon or boons, granting a request or prayer, favorable, propitious.

वरदा, *f.* (*m.* **वरद**) a girl, virgin, maid: *pr. n.* a certain river.

वरदान, *m.* the granting a boon, benefaction, vouchsafement, bestowal: *pr. n.* a certain place of Hindoo pilgrimage.

वरदेखौनी, *f.* the negotiating a marriage.

वरन; see (1) **बरं** (2) **वरण** (3) **वर्ण**.

वरनना, *more prop.* **वर्णना**, *q.v.*

वरनों; see **बरना**.

वरनि, *m.* (an old pl. of **वर**) heroes. See **नि**, 2.

वरनहि, (pl. °**हिं**) } old forms = **वर्णता है** (**वर्णना**).
वरनहो, (pl. °**हीं**) }

वरपाश, the act of rubbing together the fingers of both hands.

वरपाशना, to rub together the fingers of both hands.

वरप्रदान, *m.* the granting a boon.

वररहना; see *s.v.* **वर**.

वररुचि, *m. pr. n.* a certain poet, grammarian, lexicographer, and writer on medicine. He is sometimes indentified with Katyāyan, the reputed author of the Vāttikas or supplementary rules of Pāṇini: he is placed, by some among the nine gems of the court of Vikramāditya, and by others, among the ornaments of the court of Bhoj: he was the author of the Prākṛit Grammar called Prākrit-Prakāsh and is said to be the first Grammarian who reduced the various Prākrit dialects to system. The term is also used as an epithet of Shiv.

वरल, *m.* a wasp, hornet.

वरला, 1. *f.* a wasp, hornet: a goose: 2, on this side (of a river, etc.).

वरष, *more prop.* **वर्ष**, *q.v.*

वरा, 1, *f.* a sort of perfume; the three myrobalans; a certain plant (*Cissampelos hexandra*): 2, situated on this side (of a river, etc); near, close by: 3, *f.* an excellent female (see *Var*).

वरां, the Sk. acc. case of **वरा**, 3, *q.v.*

वराक, 1, *m.* war, battle: *pr.n.* Shiv: 2, *m.* (*f.* ī) a sinner, etc.: *lit.* poor, unhappy, low, vile, impure.

वराटक, *m.* the small shell called a cowrie and used as a coin: a rope: the seed-vessel of the lotus.

वराणसी, a contraction of **वाराणसी**, *q.v.*

वराति; see **बरात** and **बराती**.

वरासन, *m.* a beautiful or glorious throne.

वराह, *m.* a hog, boar; a certain form of marching an army; a sort of measure; *pr.n.* (1) of the third incarnation (see *Avatār*) of Vishṇu in which he assumed the form of a boar (2) of one of the eighteen lesser divisions (*dwip*) of the world (3) of a certain sacred place.

वरिष्ठ, *m.* (*f.* ā) largest, greatest; best, most preferable, dearest, most beloved.

वरी, *f.* a certain plant (*Asparagus racemosus*): *pr.n.* Chhāyā the wife of the sun.

वरीयान, *m. pr. n.* the eighteenth of the astronomical periods or divisions of the ecliptic (called *yog*).

वरुण, *m. pr. n.* the deity of the waters and regent of the west (the Neptune of the Hindoos).

वरूथ, *m.* a wooden fender around a carriage to prevent collision; armour: skin, leather: a house.

वरूथिनी, *f.* an army: *pr.n.* a certain Apsaras.

वरे, 1, in Ayodhyā = **लिये**, *q.v.*: 2, (see **वरा**, 2) on this side, near. —*ānā*, to draw near, approach. —*girnā*, to fall short.

वरेखा, *m.* the negotiating a marriage.

वरेपरे, *adv.* far and near.

वरोरु, *m.* a beautiful thigh: *adj.* having beautiful thighs.

वर्ग, *m.* a multitude of similar things (whether animate or inanimate), a series, row, class, tribe, troop; a chapter, section, book; (in Gram.) any class of letters pronounced by the same part of the mouth, (as gutturals, dentals, etc); *e.g.* **कवर्ग**, the guttural class of consonants; (in Math.) a square number.

वर्गकर्म्म, *m.* (in Math.) any operation relating to square numbers.

वर्गघन, *m.* (in Math.) a square of a cube.

वर्गघनघात, *m.* (in Math.) the fifth power.

वर्गपद, *m.* (in Math.) the root of a square.

वर्गप्रकृति, *f.* (in Algeb.) an affected square.

वर्गमूल, *m.* (in Math.) a square root.

वर्गवर्ग, *m.* (in Math.) the square of a square, a biquadratic number.

वर्गवर्गवर्ग, *m.* (in Math.) the square of a squared square.

वर्गीकृत, *m.* (in Math.) squared, raised to a square.

वर्ज्जन, *m.* abandoning, dereliction, leaving, desertion, avoiding, shunning, quitting; exception, exclusion, omission.

वर्ज्जनीय, anything that ought to be shunned or relinquished, irregular, improper, censurable, wicked.

वर्ज्जित, *m.* (*f.* ā) abandoned, relinquished, excluded, omitted, excepted, avoided, shunned, free from, destitute of, forbidden, interdicted, unlawful.

वर्ण, *m.* colour, hue, tint; a class, tribe, order, caste (the Hindoos are divided into four principal varṇs, *viz.* (1) Brāhman (2) Kshatriya (3) Vaishya (4) Shūdra; fame, celebrity, praise, description; beauty; quality, property: theatrical dress; sort, kind; form, figure; the colour or fineness of gold as ascertained by its streak on the touchstone; fresh earth carried into hollows by means of water: (in Gram.) a letter of the alphabet; a syllable; (in Math.) a coëfficient. — *k.* to hire a priest for the performance of sacrifice or of any religious ceremony.

वर्णक्रम, *m.* order of colours or of castes; alphabetical arrangement, the alphabet.

वर्णगत, (in Math.) algebraic.

वर्णदुय, *more prop.* **वर्णद्वय**, *q.v.*

वर्णद्वय, two syllables, two colours, two castes or races.

वर्णधर्म, *m.* the particular duties that are religiously incumbent on the several castes of Hindoos.

वर्णन, *m.* colouring painting; describing, pointing out qualities or excellencies. expatiating. explaining; recital, explanation, praise, panegyric. — *k.* to describe, explain. extol. praise.

वर्णनाश्रमी ; see **वर्णाश्रमी**.

वर्णना, 1, *f.* = **वर्णन**, *q.v.* : 2, *t.* to explain, narrate, relate, tell, describe, praise, extol.

वर्णमाला, *f.* (uninfl.) an alphabet.

वर्णरेखा, *f.* a certain white aluminous fossil (often confounded with chalk, of which it is a species).

वर्णलिपि, *f.* a dissertation or treatise on an al-

वर्णविचार, *m.* = **वर्णलिपि**, *q.v.* [phabet

वर्णविपर्यय, *m.* (in Gram.) the substitution of one letter for another. [number of syllables.

वर्णवृत्त, *m.* (in Gram.) metre regulated by the

वर्णव्यवस्था, *f.* the institution of caste, caste-system; the rules of caste.

वर्णश्रेष्ठ, *m.* (*f.* ā) any Brāhmaṇ : *lit.* of the best caste, of good tribe or kind.

वर्णसंकर, *m.* mixture or confusion of castes or tribes by intermarriage: a person or tribe of mixed origin, or from parents of different castes.

वर्णहीन, casteless: hence, *m.* (*f.* ā) an outcaste.

वर्णाश्रम, *m.* the class and state of a person.

वर्णाश्रमा, *m.* (pl.: see **आ**, 22) the four Hindoo castes (*viz.* Brāhmaṇ. Kshatriya. Vaishya, and Shūdra) and the four states of Hindoo society (*viz.* Student, Householder, Mendicant, and Anchoret).

वर्णाश्रमी, *m.* (*f.* inī) posse sed of caste and order.

वर्णित, *m.* (*f.* ā) described, related, explained, praised.

वर्त्तक, 1, *m.* a hors.'s hoof: a sort of mixed metal commonly called *bidri* : 2, *m.* (*f.* ā *or* ikā) a species of quail (*Perdix olivacea*): *lit.* who is, or exists, or abides.

वर्त्तन, *m.* livelihood, subsistance, occupation, wages.

वर्त्तमान, existing, present, being, actu lly taking place: dwelling, abiding in; (in Gram.) present (said of tense).

वर्त्तमानकाल, *m.* (in Gram.) the present tense.

वर्त्तमानकालिक, (in Gram.) appertaining to present time or to the present tense.

वर्त्ता, *m.* a wooden pencil for writing on a board.

वर्त्ति, *f.* perfume for the person, a collyrium; a paint-brush; a ruled line; the wick of a lamp; a lamp, a candle, a match; the ends of a cloth; a bougie.

वर्त्तिका, *f.* the wick of a candle: a species of quail (*Perdix olivacea*).

वर्त्ती, 1, *f.* = **वर्त्ति**, *q.v.* : 2, (in comp.) *m.* (*f.* inī) existing, being, continuing, abiding, resting; *e g.* **मध्यवर्त्ती**, situated in the midst, etc.

वर्द्धन, 1, *adj.* growing, thriving, increasing; causing to increase or thrive: 2, *m.* growth, increase; growing, increasing, thriving.

वर्द्धनी, *f.* a small water-jar: a brush.

वर्द्धमान, *m.* (*f.* matī) increasing, growing, thriving, prosperous: *pr. n.* a certain mountain, district, and city (now called Burdwān).

वर्द्धा, *m.* a bull, a bullock. [panded.

वर्द्धित, *m.* (*f.* ā) grown, augmented, thriven, ex-

वर्मा, *more com.* **बर्मा**, *q.v.*

वर्य, *more prop.* **वर्य्य**, *q.v.* [chief: *pr n.* Kāmdev.

वर्य्य, *m.* (*f.* ā) fit to be chosen, estimable, worthy,

वर्य्या, *f.* (*m.* **वर्य्य**) a young maiden, a marriageable girl, a girl choosing her own husband.

वर्ला, on this side (of a river, etc.). See **वरला**.

वर्वट, *m.* = **वर्व्वटी**, *q.v*

वर्वर, *m.* a barbarian, ignorant person, outcaste; country inhabited by barbarians: woolly or curly hair: a sort of basil (*Ocymum pilosum*, Roxb): a mode of dancing: vermillion: the clash of weapons.

वर्व्वटी, *f.* a sort of kidney-bean (*Dolichos catjang*).

वर्ष, *m.* rain; a cloud; raining; the rainy season: a year: a division of the known world: India (*Jambudwip*). There are nine divisions reckoned, *viz* (1) Kuru (2) Hiraṇmay (3) Romāṇak (4) Ilāvrat (5) Hari (6) Ketumāl (7) Bhadrāswa (8) Kinnar (9) Bhārat.

वर्षण, *m.* the falling of rain, raining; rain.

वर्षत्, *adj.* raining, showering, sprinkling.

वर्षदिन, *m.* the period of a year.—*tak*, for the period of a year, for a whole year.

वर्षना, *a. int.* to rain.

वर्षपर्व्वत, *m. pr. n.* a certain mountainous range supposed to separate the various divisions (*varsh*) of the known world from each other. Six ranges are enumerated from south to north, *viz.* (1) Himavān (2) Hemkūt (3) Nishadh (4) Nil (5 Swet (6) Sringi or Sringvān: mount Meru constitutes a seventh. Other names are sometimes given to these ranges.

वर्षवां, *m.* (*f.* wīṅ) yearly, annual, anniversary.

वर्षशत, *m.* a century (*lit.* a hundred years).

वर्षसहस्र *m.* a period of a thousand years.

वर्षा, 1, *m.* (pl. of **वर्ष** : see **आ**, 22) the rains, the rainy season: 2, *m. f.* (!) rain, a shower. It is the third of the six seasons (see **ऋतु**) of the Hindoos, and is variously limited: according to some it embraces the months Shrāvaṇ and Bhādra: and according to others Bhādra and Āshwin; according to others, again, it extends from the 15th of Ashāṛh to the 15th of Bhādra: the actual duration of the monsoon is, however, longer, being reckoned from Ashāṛh to Kārttik, *i. e.* from the middle of June to the beginning of October.

वर्षाऊ, partic. act. *m. f.* raining.

वर्षाऋतु }
वर्षाकाल } *m.* (see **वर्षा**) the rainy season.

वर्षाती, *more com.* **बर्साती**, *q.v.* [rain down.

वर्षाना, *t.* to cause to rain, to shower down, to

वर्षायुत. *m.* a period of ten thousand years.

वर्षाविन्दु, *m.* a rain-drop.

वर्षावसान, *m.* the season of autumn.

वर्षाशन, *m.* subsistence for a year, annual salary.

वर्षिक }
वर्ष्यक } yearly, annual.

वर्हिणी, *f.* (*m.* **वर्ही**) a peahen.

वर्हिन, 1, *m.* (*f.* iṇī) = **वर्ही**, *q.v.*: 2, *f.* = **वर्हिणी**, *q. v.*

वर्हिष = **वर्हिस**, *q.v.*

वर्हिषत / **वर्हिषद** } = **बर्हिषद**, *q. v.*

वर्हिष्पन्द = **वर्हिषद**, *q.v.*

वर्हिष्मती, *f. pr. n.* (1) of a wife of Priyavrat and daughter of Vishwakarmā (2) of a city in Brahmāvart.

वर्हिस, *m.* a layer; a seat of sacred grass; sacred or sacrificial grass (*Poa cynosuroides*: sacrifice: fire, light, lustre, splendour; a species of perfume.

वर्ही, *m.* (*f.* iṇī) a peacock.

वलके, a corruption of **बल्कि**, *q.v.*

वलती / **वलथी** } *f.* the eaves of a house.

वलध; see **बलद** and **बलधारी**.

वलहना, *more prop.* **उलहना**, *q. v.*

वला, near, hither, on this side.

वलाक, *m.* (*f.* ā) a crane.

वलाका, *f.* a female crane: a small kind of crane: a line or row of cranes; a flight of cranes: a crane (in general): a mistress.

वलाकी, *m.* (*f.* inī) one who possesses cranes; a proper name: lit. *adj.* having cranes.

वलागत (*corruption*) = **बलाग़त**, *q. v.*

वलाहक, 1, = **बलाक**, *q.v.*: 2, *m.* a cloud, thunder-cloud: a mountain: *pr. n.* (1) of one of the seven clouds at the destruction of the world (2) of a certain *daitya* (3) of a brother of Jayadrath (4) of one of the Nāgas (5) of one of the four horses of Vishṇu.

वलि, *more com.* **बलि**, *q.v.*

वली, *m.* a prince, lord, master; a friend, a friend or favorite of God, a holy man, saint: a guardian: a servant, slave.

वल्कल, *m.* the bark of a tree; a cloth or garment made of bark.

वल्गा, *f.* a bridle, rein; the bit of a bridle.

वल्मिक / **वल्मिकि** / **वल्मीक** } *m.* an anthill, a mole-hill.

वल्लभ, *m.* a lover, husband, favorite, friend: a superintendent, overseer, master; a chief herdsman: a horse with good marks: lit. *m* (*f.* ā) beloved, dear, desired, amiable: supreme, superintending.

वल्लभा, *f.* (*m.* **वल्लभ**) a beloved female, a mistress.

वल्लाह, *exclam.* = by God! (A profane oath used by Muhammadans.)

ववस्वत; see **विवस्वत** and **वैवस्वत**.

वबुवाहन, *more prop.* **बभ्रुवाहन**, *q.v.*

वश, 1, *m.* (*f.* ā) willing; overpowered, subdued, tamed, humbled; subdued by charms and incantations, enthralled, fascinated, enchanted, charmed: 2, *m.* wish, desire; authority, power, will, mastership, supremacy, control, command, advantage, opportunity; the state of being completely overpowered or tamed, subjection: 3, *postp.* (takes gen. *m.* infl.: sc, *men*) in subjection to, under the control of. — *ānā* to come into one's power, to be obtained. — *k.* to bring into subjection, overpower.

वशकारी, *m.* (*f.* iṇī) one who overpowers another; lit. *adj.* overpowering, subduing, humbling.

वशक्रिया, *f.* the subjecting or overpowering any-one (esp. by incantations or by drugs); subduing, enchanting, charming.

वशा, *f.* (*m.* **वश**, 1) a woman, wife, daughter, husband's sister, a female elephant, a cow, a barren cow, a barren woman.

वशिता, *f.* (*m.* °**त्व**) fascinating, bewitching, subduing, overpowering, subjection, dominion; holding in subjection.

वशिष्ठ, *m. pr. n.* a certain celebrated Hindoo saint-sage (*rishi*) the spiritual preceptor (*guru*) of Rām-Chandra. He is also a Brahmādhika and Prajāpati, and is identified with one of the seven stars of Ursa Major.

वशिनी, *f.* a parasitical plant; a certain tree [(*Mimosa sama*, Roxb.).

वशी, *m.* (*f.* inī) one who has his passions under control; an ascetic, sage: *lit.* under control, subdued.

वशीकरण, *m.* = **वशक्रिया**, *q. v.*

वशीकृत, *m.* (*f.* ā) brought into subjection, overpowered, subdued, tamed; obedient; enthralled, fascinated.

वशीभूत, *m.* (*f.* ā) = **वशीकृत**, *q. v.*

वशीर, *m.* a certain pungent fruit (*Pothos officinalis*) resembling pepper.

वशीष्ठ (*corruption*) = **वशिष्ठ**, *q. v.*

वश्य, *m.* (*f.* ā) a subject, dependent, slave, etc.: *lit.* governable, subdued, obedient, under control, tame, tractable, humble.

वश्यता, *f.* disposition to (or fitness for) subjection; humility, subjection.

वश्या, *f.* (*m.* **वश्य**) an obedient wife; a female dependent or slave.

वश्यात्मा, *m.* or *f.* a humble or tractable person: *lit.* of a subdued or tractable spirit.

वस, 1, *more prop.* **वश**, *q v.*: 2, *f.* offspring, progeny, children.

वसति, *f.* a peopled or inhabited place, a house, abode, residence, dwelling, hamlet; a village; population: night.

वसतिस्थान, *m.* a place of abode.

वसतिरक्षक, *m.* (*f.* ikī) a village-watchman.

वसती = **वसति**, *q. v.*

वसन, *m.* a habitation, house, abode, residence: a covering; cloth; clothes, wearing-apparel, dress, habit, attire, a suit of clothes. *Asan* —, *m.* food and clothing

वसन्त, *m.* (see **ऋतु**) the vernal season, spring, the first of the six seasons of the Hindoos (from the 15th of Phālgun to the 15th of Vaisākh, or from the middle of March to the middle of May); the deified personification of spring: diarrhœa, dysentery, small-pox: a certain musical mode (*rāg*) of the Hindoos. *Ānkhoṅmeṅ — phūlnā*, to dazzle. — *kī khabar*, *f.* knowledge (or care) about futurity. — *phūlnā*, to put forth the blossoms of mustard-plants.

वसन्तकुसुम, *m.* a certain tree (*Cordia myxa* and *latifolia*).

वसन्तपंचमी, *f.* a certain festival of the Hindoos. It is held on the 5th of Māgh, which was formerly observed as the beginning of spring.

वसन्ती, 1, of a yellow colour, orange-coloured (this was Krishṇ's favorite colour): appertaining to spring: 2, *f.* a certain scale in Hindoo music.

वसन्तोत्सव, *m.* the celebration (among Hindoos) of the return of spring (formerly held on the full moon of Chaitra, but now on the full moon of Phālgun, being identified with the *Dolyātrā* or *Holi*.

वसवास, *m.* temptation, distraction, doubt, suspense, hesitation, perplexity, superstition, scrupulousness. [udation.

वसा, *f.* marrow, fat, suet, adeps, brain, oily ex-

वसारा, *m.* the verandah or porch of a house, a shed, thatch, awning.

वसिष्ट (*corruption*) = **वशिष्ठ**, *q.v.*

वसीठ, *m.* an agent, ambassador.

वसीठी, 1, = **वसीठ**, *q.v.*: 2, *f.* the business of a *vasit*, agency, ambassadorship.

वसीत = **वसीठ**, *q.v.*

वसीला, *m.* affinity, propinquity; cause, instrument, agency, means of effecting anything, instrumentality; conjuncture; support, prop; patronage. As a postposition (*wasile* or *wasilese*) it is most appropriately used when the instrument is an animate (and especially a human) one.

वसु, *m.* a kind of fish: the tie of a yoke: a gem, jewel: water: fossil salt: gold: a yellow kind of kidney-bean: a ray of light; the sun: a rein: wealth, substance, matter, thing: an epithet (1) of Shiv (2) of Kuver (3) of Agni (4) of a certain class of demigods of whom eight are enumerated, *viz.* (1) Dhav (2) Dhruv (3) Som (4) Vishṇu (5) Anil (6) Anal (7) Prabhūsh (8) Prabhāv: hence, in the ingenious system of reckoning by symbols adopted by Hindoos in their poetry, this word is a symbol for 8.

वसुक, *m.* Sāmbhar salt (a fossil salt brought from Sāmbhar in Ajmere): a certain tree (*Sesbana grandiflora*); a certain plant (*Æschynomena grandiflora*; a certain shrub (*Asclepias gigantea*).

वसुदा (*corruption*) = **वसुधा**, *q.v.*

वसुदेव, *m. pr. n.* the real father of Kṛishṇ. (His foster-father was Nand.)

वसुदेवता, *f. pr. n.* the twenty-fourth *Nakshatra.*

वसुदेवनन्दन, *m.* (the son of Vasudev, *i.e.*) Krishṇ.

वसुदेवभू, *m.* (sprung from Vasudev, *i. e.*) Kṛishṇ.

वसुधा, *f.* the earth, the world, the globe.

वसुमती, *f.* (*m.* **वसुमान**) a wealthy female: an epithet of the earth. [wealthy.

वसुमान, *m.* (*f.* matī) possessing, wealth, rich,

वसूक, *more com.* **वसुक**, *q.v.*

वसूरा, *f.* an unchaste woman, prostitute, harlot.

वसोवास, *more com.* **वसोबास**, *q.v.*

वस्ता, *m.* (*f.* trī) one who clothes, a clother.

वस्ती, *more prop.* **वसती**, *q.v.*

वस्तु, *f. m.* natural disposition or quality, essence, substance, object, thing, material, ingredient, stuff, baggage, goods, chattels.

वस्तुतः, owing to the nature of a thing, as a natural consequence, consequently, of course; in fine; in fact, in reality, in very deed, really, actually, verily, essentially; substantially.

वस्तुतस = **वस्तुतः**, *q.v.*

वस्तुता, *f.* (*m.* °**त्व**) substantiality.

वस्तुभाव, *m.* (*f.* ?) chattels, things, baggage.

वस्तुमात्र, *m.* outline of a subject, the substance or skeleton of a discourse, an epitome.

वस्तुहानि, *f.* loss of property. [clothes, garments.

वस्त्र, *m.* cloth, raiment, linen, apparel, dress,

वस्त्तृ, *m.* (*f.* trī) one who clothes, a clother.

वस्त्रभेदी, *m.* (*f.* inī) a tailor.

वस्त्रहीन, *m.* (*f.* ā) destitute of clothing.

वस्त्रांचल, *m.* the hem of a garment.

वस्त्रागार } **वस्त्रालय** } *m.* a wardrobe, a clother's shop.

वस्त्री, *f.* (*m.* **वस्त्ता**) a female clother.

वस्न, *m.* price; wages; wealth; a thing, substance; cloth, clothes; abiding, dwelling; skin; death.

वस्फ़, *m.* encomium, description of qualities, praise, merit, worth, virtue.

वह, (the remoter demonstrative pronoun) *m.* and *f.*(gen. **उसका**) that, that person, that thing; he, she, it; the. It sometimes = **वे**, *q.v.*

वहई, *f.* side, quarter, way.

वहऊ, in Braj = **वुह भी**. See **ऊ**, 7.

वहत, *m.* an ox: a traveller.

वहति, *m.* an ox: a friend: air, wind.

वहती, *f.* a river.

वहतु, *m.* an ox.

वहन, *m.* a bearing; a flowing; a raft, a boat.

वहनि = **वह्नि**, *q.v.*

वहन्त, *m.* wind, air.

वहर = (1) **बहर** (2) **उधर**, *qq.v.*

वहला, *m.* an attack, onset, assault.

वहां, there, yonder, thither. *Wahānkā wohān*, in that very place, in that very spot. This word is sometimes (though not very often) used with the second sense of the word **यहां**, *q. v.*

वहांका, (gen. of **वहां**) *m.* (*f.* ī) appertaining to that place, belonging there, made or produced there.

वहांसे, (abl. of **वहां**) thence.

वहांहीं, (an emphat. form of **वहां**) that very place.

वहिः } **वहिर** } = **वहिस**, *q. v.*

वहिर्देश, *m.* a place abroad, a foreign land, a remote country; the outskirts of a town.

वहिर्भूत, *m.* (*f.* ā) external; excluded, expelled; expired (as time); inattentive; irrelevant.

वहिश } **वहिष** } = **वहिस**, *q.v.*

वहिस, outwards, out, outside, on the outside, without, apart from. The final **स** is liable to be exchanged for :, र्, श्, or स्, by the rules of Sandhi, according to the nature of the initial letter of the word to which it is prefixed.

वही, (an emphat. form of **वह**; see **ई**, 4) the same, that same, that very one.

वहीं, (an emphat. advl. form of **वहां**) that very (time, place, etc.), immediately, thereupon, at once, forthwith, on that very spot, exactly there, so, even so, just so, in that very manner.

वहीभर = **उतनाही**, *q.v.*

वहुमित्र, *more prop.* **बहुमित्र**, *q.v.*

वहोत, *more prop.* **बहुत**, *q.v.*

वहोरि, *more com.* **बहोरि**, *q.v.*

वह्नि, *m.* fire: an epithet of the god of fire (*Agni*): digestion, appetite; the marking-nut plant; leadwort (*Plumbago zeylanica*). In the ingenious system of reckoning by symbols (see **अग्नित्रेता**) adopted by Hindoos in their poetry, this word is a symbol for 3.

वा, 1, in Braj = **वह**, *q.v.*: 2, in Braj, one of the bases (see **ता**, 1) of the singular of **वह** or **वुह**: 3, or (*i.e.* indifferently or optionally, this or that; *e.g.* *Vā — vō*, either-or, whether-or): 4, often (*esp.* in poetry) = **या** of the past part.; *e.g.* **गावा** = **गाया**: 5, this is one of the modifications of **वाला**, *q.v.*

वाई in Braj = **वही**, *q.v.*

वां, 1, (*colloquial*) = **वहां**, *q.v.*: 2, like the *th* of English ordinals, this element [*m.* (*f.* **वीं**)] added to the cardinal numbers (after **चौथा**, fourth), yields (1) the nom. sing. of ordinals; *e.g.* **बारहवां**, *m.* (*f.* °**वीं**) twelfth; and (2) distributives by repetition; *e.g.* **दशवां दशवां**, by tens, ten to each, every tenth.

वांका, *more prop.* (1) **वहांका** (2) **वाका**, *qq.v.*

वांगमय, 1, *m.* (*f.* ī) consisting of words, appertaining to speech; eloquent: 2, *m.* eloquence.

वांमय, 1, *m.* (*f.* ī) appertaining to speech; endowed with speech; consisting of words; eloquent; loquacious: 2, *m.* eloquence, rhetoric. [speech).

वांमयी, *f.* an epithet of Saraswatī (the goddess of

वांमुख, *m.* an exordium, introduction. [boo.

वांशी, 1, = **बांसी**, *q.v.*: 2, *f.* the manna of the bam-

वांह; see (1) **बांह** (2) **वहां**.

वांहीं, *more prop.* **वहांहीं**, *q.v.*

वाक, 1, *m.* word, speech, language, dialect: 2, *m.* a flight of cranes: 2, *m.* (*f.* i) appertaining to cranes.

वाक; see (1) **वाक** (2) **वाका** (3) **वाकि**.

वाकचपल, *m.* (*f.* ā) an inconsistent or frivolous talker: *lit.* inconsistent in speech, frivolous.

वाकचापल्य, *m.* inconsistency or frivolousness in speech; chatter, gossip, idle or improper talk.

वाकछल, *m.* equivocation, prevarication.

वाकपटु, *m.* (*f.* ṭu *or* ṭvī) an eloquent person: *lit.* clever in speech, eloquent.

वाकपटुता, *f.* cleverness in speech, eloquence.

वाकपारुष्य, *m.* slander, calumny, libel.

वाका, *m.* (*f.* ī) = **वाकौ**, *q.v.*

वाकि, 1, see **वाकी** and **बाकी**: 3, *adj.* falling; befalling, happening, appearing, intervening.

वाकिफ़, experienced, intelligent, knowing, acquainted with, learned, sensible.

वाकी, *f.* (*m.* **वाका**) his, her, hers, its.

वाके, *m.* inflected form of **वाका**.

वाको; see (1) **वाकौ** (2) **वाकौं**. [her, hers, its.

वाकौ, [in Braj, the gen. *m.* (*f.* **वाकी**) of **वह**] his,

वाकौं, (in Braj, the dat. and acc. of **वह**) to him, to her, to it, to that: him, her, it, that.

वाक्य, *m.* (in Gram.) a sentence, speech, word, rule, aphorism, expression, assertion.

वाक्यखण्डन, *m.* refutation, criticism (especially unfavourable criticism).

वाक्यविलारी, *f.* a kind of song.

वाक्यविन्यास, *m.* (in Gram.) the formation of sentences, syntax. [sentence, speech, etc.

वाक्यार्थ, *m.* the meaning or purport of a word,

वाग, in compos. = **वाक**, *q.v.*

वाग्जाल, *m.* an ensnaring utterance, a prevarication, equivocation: circumlocution; multiloquence; a collection of sentences.

वागदान, *more prop.* **वाग्दान**, *q.v.*

वागवर, *m.* (*f.* ā *or* ī) well-spoken.

वागवाद, *m.* war of words, altercation.

वागीश, *m.* (*f.* ā) an eloquent person: *lit.* a master of language, eloquent: hence, *m.* an epithet of Vṛihaspati, preceptor of the gods. [joy-inspiring.

वागुर, 1, see **वागुरा** (2) **बागर**: 2, *m.* (*f.* ā *or* ī) *adj.*

वागुरा, *f.* a net or snare for catching deer and other wild animals. [nets, a hunter.

वागुरिक, *m.* a man who catches deer, etc. in

वागे, *m.* (*more prop.* **बागे**) clothing, vestments.

वाग्दण्ड, *m.* reprimand, rebuke.

वाग्दत्त, *m.* (*f.* ā) promised, betrothed.

वाग्दत्ता, *f.* a betrothed virgin. [betrothment.

वाग्दान, *m.* the promising a damsel in marriage,

वाग्दुष्ट, *m.* (*f.* ā) defamatory, abusive: speaking badly or ungrammatically: vituperated.

वाग्देवी, *f.* an epithet of Saraswatī: *lit.* the goddess of speech or eloquence. [abuse.

वाग्दोष, *m.* evil-speaking, defamation, calumny,

वाग्मी, *m.* (*f.* inī) an eloquent person, etc.: *lit.* skilled in language, eloquent, talkative, loquacious.

वाग्विदग्ध, *m.* (*f.* ā) a bland or fascinating person: *lit.* skilled in speech, bland.

वाघरी, *m.* (*f.* iṇī) a certain caste of people who ensnare and catch wild beasts.

वाघा, (in Pros.) a species of metre.

वाङ्मय = **वांमय**, *q.v.*

वाच, *f.* speaking, speech, a word, phrase, adage, proverb; voice: an epithet of Saraswatī.

वाचक, 1, *adj.* speaking; expressed by sounds, (in Gram.) signifying, implying, expressive of: 2, *m.* a word, a significant sound: 3, *m.* (*f.* ikā) a speaker, a messenger: 4, *m.* (in Gram.) an explanatory particle.

वाचन, *m.* a preparatory rite in which the Brāhmaṇs invoke the blessing of the gods, etc.

वाचनिक, verbal, textual; enjoined, prescribed; mentioned, expressed.

वाचा, *f.* (= **वाच**) speech; affirmation, agreement, promise, pledge, vow, oath.

वाचाट } = **वाचालु**, *q. v.*
वाचाल }

वाचालत्व, *m.* (*f.* tā) loquaciousness, garrulity.

वाचालु, *m.* or *f.* talkative, garrulous, loquacious, chattering, gabbling, talking much and idly or blameably.

वाचिक, done by speech, verbal, conveyed by words, expressive of, signifying: hence, *m* news, intelligence, tidings.

वाचिकपत्र, *m.* a news-letter, gazette, newspaper, despatch.

वाचिका, *f.* (*m.* **वाचक**) a female speaker or messenger.

वाची, *m.* (*f.* inī) = **वाचक**, *q. v.*

वाच्य, *m.* blame, reproach, abuse; (in Gram.) a sentence, a predicate: *lit.* fit or proper to be spoken, suitable to be predicated, expressible; blameable, contemptible, vile, bad.

वाछिड़ा, most probably from **वाच्छलिओ**, the Prākṛit form of the Sanskṛit **वात्सल्यक**, dimin. of **वात्सल्य**. The term seems to occur only in the plural **वाछिड़े**.

वाछिड़े, *m.* praising, applauding: (pl.) blandishments, endearments, cajoleries; *exclam.* bravo! well done! aha!

वाजपेय, *m.* a certain kind of sacrifice.

वाजपेयी, *m.* one who performs the sacrifice called *Vājpey*.

वाजबी (*corruption*) = **वाजिबी**, *q. v.*

वाजिपृष्ट, *m.* globe amaranth.

वाजिब, necessary, requisite, expedient, convenient, proper, just, right, reasonable, worthy.

वाजिबी, 1, = **वाजिब**, *q. v.*: 2, *f.* necessity, expediency, propriety, justness, fitness: salary.

वाजी, 1, swift; hence, *m.* (*f.* inī) a horse, a bird, an arrow: 2, *m.* a certain plant (*Justicia adhenatoda*).

वाजीकर, *adj.* aphrodisiac.

वाजीकरण, *m.* the excitement of amorous desires by means of aphrodisiacs.

वाजीमेध, *m.* = **अश्वमेध**, *q. v.*

वाञ्छन, *m.* wishing, desiring.

वाञ्छा, *f.* wish, desire.

वाञ्छित, *m.* (*f.* ā) wished for, longed for, desired.

वाञ्छिनी, *f.* a libidinous female, a wanton.

वाञ्छी, *m.* (*f.* inī) wishful, wishing, desirous.

वाट, *m.* (*f.* ?) a road, path, way, highway, a journey. *Kisikā—johnā*, to be looking out for someone.—*nihārnā*, to expect.

वाटपाड, *m. f.* a wayfarer, traveller.

वाटिका, *f.* the site of a building; a villa; a small garden.

वाटी, *f.* the site of a building; a house, dwelling, habitation, home; a garden-house; a garden, orchard, plantation; an enclosure; a mud wall; the groin; a road: a rod, mace.

वाड़, (in comp.) a termination denoting place, enclosure, dwellingplace; *e. g. Satwāṛ*, the enclosure where a Hindoo widow is burned.

वाड़ा, *m.* a ward or quarter of a town where people of the same caste or trade dwell.

वाड़ी, 1, *most com.* **बाड़ी**, *q. v.*: 2, *f.* (= **वाड़**) in comp. a termination denoting place, enclosure, dwellingplace; *e. g. Phūlwāṛi*, a flower-garden.

वाण, *m.* an arrow, dart: a fire: the udder of a cow: a pipe; the feathered part of an arrow: a sky-rocket, grenade, a kind of rocket used in battle: *pr. n.* a certain *asur*, son of Rājā Bali. In allusion to the five arrows of Kāmdev, this word, in the ingenious system of reckoning by symbols adopted by Hindoos in their poetry, is a symbol for 5.

वाणपुर, *m. pr. n.* the capital of Vāṇ rājā.

वाणमारा, *m.* (*f.* ī) slain by a missile.

वाणशय्या, *f.* the bed or couch of arrows (a peculiar method of transfixing each other with arrows practised by the gods in their mutual strifes).

वाणावती, *f. pr. n.* the wife of Vāṇāsur.

वाणासुर, *m. pr. n.* a certain demon, son of Bali. He was an enemy of Vishṇu and a favorite of Shiv.

वाणि, *f.* weaving; a weaver's loom.

वाणिज्य, *most com.* **बाणिज्य**, *q. v.*

वाणिनी, *f.* an intriguing woman; an intoxicated woman; a dancing-girl, actress: (in Pros.) a species of metre.

वाणी, 1, *f.* weaving; a weaver's loom: voice, sound, speech, language: a literary production; an epithet of the goddess of speech (Saraswatī): 2, *m.* (*f.* inī) in comp. a termination of epithets = (1) having an arrow, or arrows, armed with arrows (2) speaking, voiced; *e. g. Mriduvāṇi*, sweet-voiced.

वात, *m.* air, wind, breeze; wind as one of the humours of the body: rheumatism, gout; inflammation of the joints, hypochondria.

वातक, *m.* a certain plant (*Marsilea quadrifolia*).

वातकी, *m.* (*f.* inī) a hypochondriac, etc.: *lit.* rheumatic, gouty, hypochondriac.

वातज्वर, *m.* fever arising from flatulency or vitiated wind.

वातपित्त, *m.* rheumatism attended with fever.

वातफुल्ल, *m.* (*f.* ā) puffed up with wind, inflated.

वातमांहि; see **मांहि**.

वातरक्त, *m.* acute gout or rheumatism.

वातरोग, *m.* rheumatism, gout.

वातरोगी, *m.* (*f.* inī) a person afflicted with gout or rheumatism: *lit.* rheumatic, gouty.

वातवृद्धि, *f.* swelled testicle.

वातवैरी, *m.* the castor-oil tree.

वातव्याधि, *f.* any morbid affection arising from disorder of the wind.

वातशूल, *m.* cholic with flatulence.

वातस्यायन, *more prop.* **वात्स्यायन**, *q. v.*

वातापि, *m. pr. n.* a certain *asur* (son of Prahlād) who was devoured by Agastya.

वातारि, *m.* the castor-oil tree; the plant *Asparagus racemosus*.

वातिन, perennial, perpetual, fixed: living or running (water).

वाती, *more prop.* **बाती**, *q. v.*

वातीय, appertaining to wind, windy.

वातुल, 1, gouty, rheumatic: mad, insane, foolish: 2, *m.* a whirlwind, hurricane, gale.

वाते / **वातें** / **वातैं** = उससे. See वा, 2, and ते, 3.

वात्सल्य, *m.* tenderness, affection, fondness, attachment, love.

वात्स्यायन, *m. pr. n.* a certain Muni.

वाद, *m.* speaking, sound; a word, sentence, discourse, report; assertion, affirmation; controversy, disputation, discussion, discourse, dispute, contradiction; demonstrated conclusion, result; accusation, plaint; an exposition of holy texts; an interlocution for discovering truth.

वादः, *m.* origin, source, essence, matter of anything.

वादक, *m.* (*f.* ikā) a speaker; a musician: lit. *adj.* speaking, saying, telling.

वादना, *a. int.* to speak, to discourse; to play on an instrument; to strike (said of a clock).

वादप्रतिवाद, *m.* a formal disputation, assertion, and counter assertion, statement and contradiction, controversy, verşy, dispute.

वादयुद्ध, *m.* a war of words, logomachy, controversy, dispute.

वादविवाद, *m.* discussion, disputation, debate, argumentation, litigation.

वादसाधन, *m.* maintaining a controversy; argument.

वादानुवाद, *m.* attack and rejoinder, plaint and reply. a controversy, disputation, dispute, altercation.

वादान्य, *m.* (*f.* ā) liberal munificent, generous.

वादिप्रतिवादित्व, *m.* (*f.* tā) the condition of plaintiff and defendant.

वादी, *adj.* speaking, saying, telling, discoursing, declaring; hence, *m.* (*f.* inī) a speaker, disputant, arguer, mischief-maker; (in Hindoo Theol.) an expounder of the laws and sacred writings, a sage; (in Law) a plaintiff, accuser, complainant, suitor, prosecutor, enemy; (in Music) the key-note.

वाद्य, *m.* any musical instrument.

वाद्यकर, *m.* (*f.* ī) a player on a musical instrument.

वाद्यभाण्ड, *m.* a multitude of musical instruments.

वान, 1, *more prop.* **वाण**, *q.v.*: 2, a Taddhita suffix *m.* (*f.* vati) by means of which attributives of possession are derived from substantives; *e.g. Dhanwān*, wealthy: 3, *m.* a moving; a flood, heavy sea, the high tide or swell (commonly called the 'bore') in some of the rivers of India: a mat of straw: a perfume: living: a hole in the wall of a house: a number of woods.

वानप्रस्थ, *m.* (see **आश्रम**) the third grade in the life of a Brāhman, Kshatriya or Vaishya; a hermit, anchoret: the designation of two plants (1) *Bassia latifolia* (2) *Butea frondosa.*

वानर, *m.* (*f.* ī) a monkey, ape.

वानरी, *f.* cowach (*Carpopogon pruriens*): a female monkey.

वानीय, 1, in Chand = **वाणी**, *q.v.*: 2, see **वानेय**.

वाने in Braj = **उसने**. See **वा**, 2.

वानें, *f.* (a pl. of **वाण**, 2) qualities, manners.

वानेय, 1, *m.* (*f.* ī) appertaining to wood or to water: 2, *m.* the fragrant grass *Cyperus rotundus.*

वापल, *m.* a kind of holy basil (*Ocymum sanctum*) distinguished as the black species of *tulsi.*

वापि, *f.* = **वापी**, *q.v.*

वापिका, *f.* = **बाओली**, *q.v.*

वापी, *f.* a large oblong reservoir of water, a pond, lake, tank, pool.

वाम, 1, left (not right); inverted, reverse, adverse, contrary, unfavorable, opposite; crooked; bad, wicked, base, vile; short: beautiful: 2, *m.* an animal a snake: an udder: an epithet (1) of Shiv (2) of Kāmdev

वामअंग, *m.* the left side.

वामता, *f.* (*m.*°त्व) perverseness, contrariety, wickedness, disfavour.

वामदार, *f.* an epithet of any beautiful female.

वामदेव, *m.* an epithet of Shiv.

वामन, *m.* (*f.* ī) a dwarf: *lit.* of low stature, dwarfish, short; low, base, vile. The term is specially applied (1) to the fifth incarnation of Vishṇu (see *Avatār*) in which he is believed to have appeared as a dwarf to prevent Bali from obtaining dominion of the three worlds (2) to the elephant that supports the south quarter.

वामनपुराण, *m.pr.n.* (see **अवतार** and **पुराण**) one of the Hindoo Purāns (containing an account of the fifth incarnation of Vishṇu).

वामना, *f. pr. n.* a certain **अप्सरस**, *q.v.*

वामनी, *f.* (*m.* **वामन**) a female dwarf.

वामभाग, *m.* 1, the left side; the reverse side: 2, good fortune or share.

वाममार्ग = **वामाचार**, *q.v.*

वाममार्गी, *m.* (*f.* inī) = **वामाचारी**, *q.v.*

वामह in Braj = **उसमें**. See **वा**, 2, and **मह**, 2.

वामांहिं / **वामांहीं** in Braj = **उसमें**. See **वा**, 2.

वामा, *f.* a female, woman; an epithet (1) of Saraswatī (2) of Lakshmī (3) of Gaurī.

वामाचार, *m.* the left-hand ritual (the use of flesh, spirits etc. forming part of the Vāmāchār ceremonies); the doctrine of the *Tantras* (according to one system); unsound doctrine, hetrodoxy.

वामाचारी, *m.* (*f.* iṇī) a heterodox person: *lit. adj.* following the left-hand portion of the Tantras, heterodox.

वामी, *f.* a mare; a she-ass; and young female elephant; the female of a jackal.

वाय, 1, (*contraction*) = **वायु**, *q.v.*: 2, *m.* weaving.

वायक, 1, *m.* a multitude: 2, *adj.* weaving: hence, *m.* (*f.* ikā) a weaver.

वायगोला = **बाओगोला**, *q. v.*

वायन, *m.* sweetmeats or cakes. They are used (1) as a light refreshment allowed to be taken during a religious fast (2) as part of an offering to a deity (3) on particular occasions, as marriages, etc. (4) as presents to friends and acquaintances.

वायव, appertaining to wind, windy.

वायवी, *f.* the region of the wind, *i.e.* the north-west.

वायव्य, appertaining to the wind, coming from (or belonging to) Vāyu the god of wind, sacred to Vāyu; north-western.

वायु, *m.* air, wind; the air of the body; morbid affection of the windy humour; *pr. n.* the deified personification of wind, and guardian deity of the north-west quarter. In the ingenious system of reckoning by symbols adopted by Hindoos in their poetry, this word is a symbol for 49.

वायस, 1, *m.* (*f.* ī) a crow: 2, *m.* two plants: 3, *adj.* long-lived.

वायुकोण, *m.* the north-west quarter.

वायुगण्ड, *m.* flatulence, indigestion.

वायुगुल्म, *m.* a whirlpool, a whirlwind.

वायुग्रस्त, *m.* (*f.* ā) affected by wind, flatulent, epileptic, hypochondriac, insane.

वायुजल, *m.* (wind and water, *i.e.*) climate.

वायुनिवृत्ति, *f.* a calm, lull; the cure of windy disorder.

वायुभक्षण, *m.* fasting; *lit.* feeding on air.

वायुशूल, *m.* the wind-colic.

वायुसम, *m.* (*f.* ā) swift; unsubstantial: *lit.* like the wind.

वार, 1, *m.* (*f.* ī) = **वाला**, 1, *q.v.*: 2, *m.* a flock, multitude, troop; a heap, quantity; a day of the week: a moment, time, turn, vicissitude, occasion, opportunity: a vessel for holding spirituous liquor: a door, gate: the hither side of a river: a blow, assault, gash, wound: water; an epithet of Shiv: 3, *f.* time, leisure, delay, waiting, patience. — *mārnā*, to administer a blow.

वारक, 1, *adj.* opposing, preventing, hindering, checking, thwarting; hence, *m.* (*f.* ikā) an opponent: 2, *m.* a horse; a horse's paces: the seat of pain: a sort of fragrant grass.

वारण, *m.* a warding off, resistance, opposition, prohibition, defence, guarding, protecting; armour, mail; an elephant.

वारन, *m.* sacrifices, oblations, offerings.

वारना, *t.* to surround, encircle, go around: to offer (in sacrifice, etc.): to devote oneself.

वारपार, 1, on this side and on that, on both sides, through and through, right through, across: 2, bounds.

वारा, 1, (*m. f.* ī) in Braj = **वाला** and **बारा**, *qq.v.*: 2, *m.* cheapness, thrift; benefit: gain, lucre: 3, *m.* (*f.* ī) cheap: 4, *m.* (*f.* ī) a victim (in sacrifice).

वाराणसक, *m.* (*f.* ikā) born in the Ganges.

वाराणसी, *f. pr. n.* Benares, the most sacred of the cities of the Hindoos. Several rival theories are put forward as to the origin and meaning of this word; among others the following: — *viz.* (1) **वर** (excellent) + **अनस** (water) + the feminine termination ी, *i.e.* the daughter (*i.e.* the city) of the excellent water: (2) **वरणा + असी**, the names of two rivulets in Benares.

वाराणसेय, *m.* (*f.* ī) born at or produced in Benares.

वारापार = **वारपार**, *q.v.*

वाराफेरी, *f.* the circumambulation of a thing sacrificed.

वाराह, 1, relating to a boar, boarish: 2, *m.* (*f.* ī) a boar.

वाराहक्षेत्र, *m. pr. n.* a certain place of Hindoo pilgrimage on the river Goomtee about 32 miles south of Ayodhyānāth, celebrated as the birthplace of Vishṇu under the form of the boar (see *Avatār*).

वाराही, *f.* a sow: the earth: one of the divine mothers (*mātṛi*): a measure: a certain esculent root (*Dioscorea*).

वारि, 1, *m.* water; fluidity: 2, *f.* a place where elephants are tied up: a captive: an epithet of Saraswati. In the ingenious system of reckoning by symbols adopted by Hindoos in their poetry, this word is a symbol for 4.

वारिक; see **वारि** (2) **वारिज** (3) **बारीक**.

वारिकण्टक, *m.* the designation of two plants (1) *Pistia stratioites* (2) *Trapa bispinosa*.

वारिकपूर, *m.* a certain fish (*Cluponodon Ilisha*) commonly called the ilis or hilsa.

वारिचर, *m.* (*f.* ī) a fish or any aquatic animal: *lit.* moving (or existing) in water, aquatic.

वारिज, *m.* a conch-shell; any bivalve shell; the lotus; salt: *lit. m.* (*f.* ā) water-born, *i.e.* produced in (or by) water.

वारिजनयन, *m.* (*f.* ā *or* ī) lotus-eyed.

वारित, *m.* (*f.* ā) hindered, prevented, impeded, kept off, obstructed.

वारिद, *m.* a cloud: *lit.* productive of water, water-yielding.

वारिदनाद, *m.* rumbling of the clouds, thunder.

वारिधर, *m.* a cloud.

वारिधि, *m.* an epithet of the ocean; *lit.* the treasury or reservoir of water.

वारिनिधि = **वारिधि**, *q.v.*

वारिपर्णी / **वारिपूर्णी** } = **वारिमूली**, *q.v.*

वारिप्रवाह, *m.* a flow of water, current, waterfall, cascade, cataract.

वारिमूली, *f.* a certain aquatic plant (*Pistia stratioites*).

वारिरथ, *m.* a raft, float.

वारिवदन, *m.* the fruit *Flacourtia cataphracta*.

वारिविहंग, *m.* (*f.* ā *or* ī) any aquatic bird.

वारिस, *m.* an heir, master, lord, owner.

वारी, *f.* 1, in Braj = **वाली** or **बारी**, *qq.v.* (see **वारा**, 1): 2, (*m.* **वारा**) cheap: 3, (*m.* **वारा**) a female victim (in sacrifice): 4, water: a waterpot; a milking-vessel: a hole for catching elephants: a rope for fastening elephants.

वारीचार, *more prop.* **वारिचर**, *q.v.*

वारीफेरी, *f.* a kind of religious or superstitious ceremony. —*k.* to be devoted to one; to be transported with joy.

वारुणी, *f.* any spirituous liquor (*esp.* a particular kind prepared from hogweed ground with the juice of the date or palm, and then distilled): *pr. n.* (1) of the region over which Varuṇ presides, *i.e.* the west (2) of a certain Upanishad in the Yajur-ved (3) of the twenty-fifth Nakshatra (4) of a certain Hindoo festival on the thirteenth day of the second half of the month Chaitra.

वारूत; see **बरूत** and **बारूत**.

वारे, see (1) **वार** (2) **वारना** (3) **वारा** (4) **बारे**.

वारौ, see **वारना** and **वारा**.

वार्त्ता, *f.* a report, rumour, tidings, news, account, information, intelligence, word, conversation: abiding: livelihood, business, profession, trade, agriculture.—*k.* to hold conversation with. *Khuli*—, plain speaking.

वार्त्ताकि / **वार्त्ताकी** } *f.* = **वार्त्ताकु**, *q.v.*

वार्त्ताकु, *m.* the egg plant (*Solanum melongena*).

वार्त्तालाभ } m. = कथावार्त्ता, q.v.
वार्त्तालाप }

वार्त्तिक, *m.* a man of the third caste, *i.e.* a husbandman, handicraftsman, tradesman; an informer, intelligencer, envoy; a commentary, gloss, *esp.* a supplementary explanation: *lit.* appertaining to news; commentary, explanatory.

वार्द्धक, *m.* a multitude of old men; old age; the infirmity of old age.

वार्द्धक्य, *m.* old age; the infirmity of old age.

वार्द्धवय, *m.* old age, senility, agedness.

वार्ष = वार्षिक, *q.v.*

वार्षिक, appertaining to a year, annual, yearly: appertaining to the rainy season.

वार्हत, *m.* the fruit of the *Solanum jacquini*.

वार्हस्पत्य, *m.* rules of conduct, ethics, morals: *lit.* derived from Vrihaspati (he being supposed to be the author of this science).

वाल, 1, *m.* (*f.* in *or* ī) = वाला, *q.v.*: 2, *m.* revenge: 3, high, eminent, superior.

वालकाएद, *more com.* वालकाएड, *q.v.*

वाला, *m.* (*f.* ī): this particle (with its modifications आर, आला, वा, वार, and वाल) corresponds in sense and usage with हारा. It occurs only in composition, and denotes agent, doer, keeper, man, inhabitant, lord, master, owner, possessor. It is sometimes added (1) to the root of a verb; *e.g.* *Rakhwālā* (2) sometimes (perhaps corruptly) to a mutilated form of the infinitive mode; *e.g.* *Khānwālā* (3) sometimes (and most frequently) to the nominative case of the inflected form of the infinitive mode; *e.g.* *Likhnewālā* (4) and very commonly to the unaltered form of the nominative case of a substantive; *e.g.* *Gharwālā* (5) sometimes it is added to substantives to form adjectives; *Gunjāishwālā*. The following are examples of its senses: 1, Proprietorship; *e.g.* *Gharwālā*, the master of a house: 2, Agency; *e.g.* *Mārnewālā*, a striker: 3, Residence; *e.g.* *Dilliwālā*, an inhabitant of Delhi: (under this head its meaning is sometimes restricted; *e.g.* *Gayāwāl*, a priest of Gayā:) 4, Occupation; *e.g.* *Nāowālā*, a boatman: 5, Adjectival, implying description or state: *e.g.* *Gunjāishwālā*, capacious, roomy: 6, Sometimes it imports a future sense; *e.g.* *Honewālā*, that has yet to come to pass: 7, Sometimes it implies future possibility: *e.g.* *Honewālā*, it is yet possible.

वालि = बालि, *q.v.*

वाली, *f.* (*m.* वाल or वाला) an agent, etc. This form is sometimes attached to the root of a verb to signify (not the agent, but) the act; *e.g.* *Rakhwāli*, protection, etc.

वाल्मीक (contraction) = वाल्मीकि, *q.v.*

वाल्मीकि, *m. pr. n.* the author of the Rāmāyaṇ.

वाल्य, *m.* childhood, infancy, boyhood, youth.

वाल्यकाल, *m.* } = वाल्यावस्था, *q. v.*
वाल्यदशा, *f.* }

वाल्यावस्था, *f.* the age or condition of childhood or infancy.

वावदूक, *m.* a great talker, an eloquent person: *lit.* talking much, garrulous, loquacious, gabbling, prattling; eloquent.

वावदूकता, *f.* (*m.* ·त्व) loquaciousness.

वाशा, *f.* a certain plant (*Justicia ganderussa*).

वाशिक; see आशिक.

वाशित, *m.* (*f.* ā) perfumed, scented.

वाशिता, *f.* a woman; a female elephant.

वाशिष्ठ, appertaining to Vashishṭh, composed by Vashishṭh, explained by Vashishṭh.

वाशिष्ठी, *f.* an epithet of the Gūmtī river which rising in the Kumaon hills pursues a winding course through Oude towards the S.E., and, passing Lakhnau and Jaunpur, falls into the Ganges below Banāras.

वाशें; see (1) वाशा (2) वासें (3) बाशा.

वाष्कल, *m. pr. n.* a certain demon, son of *Ahlād*.

वाष्प, *m.* vapour, hot mist, steam: a tear: iron: mention: the smallest quantity, an atom, a trace.

वाष्पकल } *m.* a steam-engine.
वाष्पयन्त्र }

वाष्पिका } = हिंगुपत्री, *q. v.*
वाष्पी }

वास, *m.* dwelling, resting, residing; a dwelling-place, habitation, house, abode; situation, site: cloth, a garment; perfuming, perfume, scent.

वासदेव (contraction) = वासुदेव, *q.v.*

वासन, 1, in Brāj = उसे (see वा, 2, and सन): 2, *m.* abiding, abode: cloth, clothing, apparel, garments: any receptacle, a box, casket, envelope, water-jar: a particular posture in sitting: perfuming, steeping, infusing: knowledge.

वासना, *f.* trust, confidence; imagination, fancy, inclination, fanciful desire, longing, wish, propensity.

वासन्त, 1, *m.* (*f.* ī) appertaining to spring, vernal; diligent in the performance of religious ceremonies: 2, *m.* the Indian cuckoo; the south wind; any young animal; a catamite; a camel.

वासन्ती, *f.* a certain festival in honour of Kāmdev; a festival in honour of Durgā (celebrated in the month Chaitra); a certain beautiful shrub (*Gœrtnera racemosa*) and several other plants; a certain goddess.

वासर, *m.* a day: a kind of snake: the sleeping together of a couple on the first night after marriage.

वासव, 1, *m.* (*f.* ī) appertaining to Indra: 2, *m.* an epithet of Indra.

वासवी, *f. pr. n.* the mother of Vyās.

वासा; see वास and बासा.

वासित, 1, *m.* (*f.* ā) perfumed, scented; spiced, seasoned: clothed, dressed, accoutred; peopled, populous, flourishing (said of a country): 2 *m.* sound; the cry of birds: knowledge.

वासिता, *f.* a woman; a female elephant.

वासी, *m.* (*f.* inī): used in comp. in the sense of an inhabitant, dweller, etc.: lit. *adj.* inhabiting, abiding, staying, residing: clothed.

वासु, 1, in Braj = उसे (see वा, 2): 2, *m.* an epithet [of Vishṇu.

वासुकि, *m. pr. n.* a certain serpent, sovereign of the snakes. Fable says that he supports the universe, and that he was used as a string to whirl the mountain *Mandar* in churning the ocean for the *amrit*, etc.

वासुकी in Braj = (1) वासुकी (2) वासुकि, *qq. v.*

वासू, *f.* a young girl (esp. in theatrical language).

वासुदेव, *m.* an epithet of Krishṇ or Vishṇu (*prop.* the son of Vasudev).

वासे, 1, = **वासें**, *q. v.* : 3, ample, wide, capacious.

वासें } in Braj = **उससे**. See **वा**, 2.
वासैं }

वास्तः = **वास्ता**, *q v.*

वास्तव, being anything in the true sense of the word. connected with the true nature of a thing, essential, material ; real genuine. substantial, fixed, determ'ned, demonstrated, manifest, evident.

वास्तविक = **वास्तव**, *q. v.*

वास्तव्य, suitable to be resided at, fit to be dwelt in or used as a habitation, habitable.

वास्ता, *m.* account, sake, cause, reason, means, medium. [of a building.

वास्तु, *m.* a habitation, residence, abode ; the site

वास्तुक } *m.* a potherb (*Chenopodium album*, etc.).
वास्तूक }

वास्ते, on account of, through the agency or instrumentality of, by reason of, for, because of.

वास्य, *more prop.* **वाच्य**, *q. v.*

वास्य = **वास्तव्य**, *q. v.*

वाह, *exclam.* (expressive of admiration, and occasionally of grief or fear) well done ! bravo ! excellent well ! admirable! well well ! alas ! fie ! It is generally repeated ; thus, *Wāh wā* or *Wāh wāh* !

वाहक, *adj.* carrying, bearing : hence, *m.* (*f.* ikā) a carrier, porter, a waterman, rower, a horse, a horseman.

वाहन, *adj.* carrying, bearing : hence, *m.* any animal or other conveyance by which anyone rides, as a vehicle, carriage, boat, horse, elephant, etc.

वाहा ; see **बाहा**.

वाहां, *more prop.* **वहां**, *q. v.*

वाहि in Braj = **उसे** (see **वा**, 2; and **हि**). It is the form for the dat. and acc. sing. of the pers. pron. (**उस**) in the 3rd person. [(in Gram.) singular.

वाहिद, one, sole, individual, undivided, single,

वाहिनी, *f.* an army, a cohort, a battalion ; a river ; a body of forces consisting of 81 elephants, 81 cars, 243 horse, and 405 foot.

वाहिनीपति, *m.* a general : the ocean : *lit.* (1) the lord or chief of a *Vāhinī* : (2) the lord or chief of the rivers. [premisses, etc.).

वाहीं, 1, = **वाहि**, *q. v.* : 2, weak, ill-founded (as

वाहे ; see **बाहना**.

वाह्य, outer, external, outward, relating to abroad, foreign : hence, *m.* (*f.* ā) a foreigner ; one of a low caste.

वि, I, an inseparable prefix, the reverse of **सं** or **सम्** : it implies (1) disunion, disjunction division, separation, distinction, difference, dispersion (2) privation (3) wrongness (4) baseness (5) opposition (6) manifoldness (7) spreading, falling in different directions (8) intenseness, and may be translated by away, off, apart, asunder, distinct, much ; or by the Latin prefixes *a, di, dis, e, ex, in, un, sc.* Sometimes it has but little or even no apparent influence on the sense of the word to which it is prefixed. II, a Kriddanta suffix (*m.* [*f.* vi]) by means of which a few adjectives are derived from verbal roots; *e. g.* **जागृवि** (Rt. **जागृ**). III. *subst.* (1) *m.* the eye : heaven : the region of the wind (2) *m.* (*f.* vi or vī) a bird.

विअक्षरी, *f.* (in Pros.) a species of metre.

विंशति, Sk., 1, twenty : 2, *f.* a score.

विंशतितम, Sk., *m.* (*f.* ī) the twentieth.

विकट, 1, large, great ; formidable, terrible, horrible. hideous, frightful ; distorted ; changed in form or appearance : obscure ; obsolete : pleasing, beautiful : 2, *m.* danger, jeopardy, fright, awe ; a tumour.

विकण्टक, *m.* a certain herbaceous plant (*Hedysarum alhagi*).

विकम्प, *m.* (*f.* ā) = **विकम्पित**, *q. v.*

विकम्पित, *m.* (*f.* ā) tremulous, agitated, unsteady, trembling ; heaving, palpitating. [ugly.

विकराल, *m.* (*f.* ā) formidable, dreadful, terrific,

विकर्ण, *m. pr. n.* one of the Kuru princes on the side of Duryodhan in the war against the Pāṇḍavs.

विकर्णिक, *m. pr. n.* the district of Sāraswat in the north-west of Hindūstān.

विकर्म, *m.* cessation from labour: an unlawful act, misdeed. fraud : various business.

विकर्मक्रिया, *f.* an illegal or immoral act.

विकल, 1, *m.* (*f.* ā) out of order, confused, confounded, discomposed, disconcerted, agitated, uneasy, restless, troubled, anxious, distressed ; defective, imperfect, on the wane. impaired, decayed : 2, *m.* one sixtieth of a *kalā*, the sixtieth part (or a second) of a degree.

विकलत्व, *m.* (*f.* tā) irregularity, disorder, confusion, agitation, uneasiness, distress, anxiety.

विकला, *f.* (*m.* **विकल**) a sorrowful female ; a woman in whom menstruation has ceased.

विकली = **विकला**, *q. v.*

विकल्प, *m.* option, alternative, distinction, alternation, doubt, indecision, error, mistake, ignorance, uncertainty, ambiguity ; (in Gram.) the admitting of more than one form or rule ; (in Rhet.) antithesis.

विकश्वित = **विकसित**, *q. v.*

विकसना, *a. int.* to expand or blow (said of flowers) : to smile, manifest delight.

विकसित, *m.* (*f.* ā) expanded, opened, unfolded, budded, blown (as a flower); cheered, delighted.

विकस्वर, *m.* (*f.* ī) expanded, blown ; delighted.

विकार, *m.* change, the change or deviation of anything from its original or natural state or form, alteration, undoing, ruin ; change of mind ; deterioration of the constituent humours of the body, disorder, disease, sickness ; mental agitation : a wound : badness, sin. [evening, dusk.

विकाल, *m.* the latter part of afternoon, twilight,

विकालक = **विकाल**, *q. v.* [the period called *vikāl*.

विकालिका, *f.* a sort of clepsydra which defines the

विकाश, *m.* expansion, opening, budding, blowing (as of flowers or as of the heart when falling in love); display, manifestation ; a shining, blooming ; an open or splendid appearance ; enjoyment, happiness, pleasure : æther, heaven : loneliness, solitude, privacy.

विकाशक, *m.* (*f.* ikā) *adj.* causing to expand, spreading, displaying, opening, unfolding. [publicity.

विकाशता, *f.* manifestation, appearance, display,

विकाशन, *m.* the act of displaying, manifestation, expansion, the blowing of a flower. [displayed.

विकाशित, *m.* (*f.* ā) expanded, opened, spread out,

विकाशी, *m.* (*f.* inī) *adj.* expanding, opening, budding, blowing (said of flowers).

विकाष, विकास; for words beginning thus, see under the form **विकाश**.

विकृत, 1, *m.* (*f.* ā) altered: estranged; averse; diseased; imperfect: 2, *m.* estrangement, aversion, disgust.

विकृतमुख, *m.* (*f.* ī) } = **विकृतानन**, *q.v.*
विकृतवदन, *m.* (*f.* ā) }

विकृताकार, of an altered or deformed shape or

विकृताकृति = **विकृताकार**, *q.v.* [appearance.

विकृतानन, *m.* (*f.* ī) a person with an altered face or a distorted countenance.

विकृति, *f.* change (of any kind whether permanent or temporary, as of nature, form, mind, purpose, or health: *hence*) sickness, disease; apprehension, fear.

विकृती, *more prop.* **विकृति**, *q. v.*

विक्रम, 1, = **विक्रमादित्य**, *q.v.*: 2. *m.* a step; proceeding: overpowering strength, great power, prowess, heroic valour, heroism; an overpowering.

विक्रमपुर, *m.* an epithet of Ujjain (*lit.* the city of Vikramāditya).

विक्रमसिंह
विक्रमसेन } = **विक्रमादित्य**, *q. v.*
विक्रमार्क

विक्रमाजीत (*corruption*) = **विक्रमादित्य**, *q. v.*

विक्रमादित्य, *m. pr. n.* a celebrated prince, sovereign of Ujjain and reputed founder of an æra (still in use among the Hindoos) which commenced 56 years before the Christian æra. There are, however, several other princes of this name, and it is variously spelt. [*m.* (*f.* inī) a hero; a lion.

विक्रमी, strong, mighty, powerful, valiant: hence,

विक्रय, *m.* selling, vending, sale, demand.

विक्रयिक, *m.* (*f.* ā *or* ī) } = **विक्रेता**, *q.v.*
विक्रयी, *m.* (*f.* inī) }

विक्रान्त, overcoming, victorious; courageous; preëminent; mighty; valiant: hence (1) *m.* (*f.* ā) a hero a warrior; a lion (2) *m* valour: gait.

विक्रान्ति, *f.* great strength; valour, boldness, prowess: a horse's canter or gallop.

विक्रीत, *m.* (*f.* ā) sold, vended.

विक्रेता, *m.* (*f.* trī) a seller, vendor, salesman, dealer.

विक्षिप्त, *m.* (*f.* ā) thrown, cast, sent, scattered, dispersed; agitated, bewildered, perplexed, foolish.

विक्षेप, *m.* a casting, throwing, throwing away, dispatching; confusion, perplexity, fear (arising from ignorance or error); dispersion, dissipation; (in Astron.) celestial latitude.

विक्षेपण, *m.* scattering, throwing, dispatching, confusion (proceeding from ignorance or error).

विख्यात, *m.* (*f.* ā) named, called, nominated, spoken of, celebrated, famous, renowned, notorious, known, glorious, victorious.

विख्याति, *f.* celebrity, notoriety, renown, fame.

विख्यापन, *m.* explaining, expounding.

विगत, *m.* (*f.* ā) gone away, departed, disappeared; obscure dark, gloomy. [demeanour.

विगति, *f.* badness, degeneracy, deterioration, mis-

विगन्ध, *m.* (*f.* ?) stink, fœtor.

विगुण, *m.* (*f.* ā) void of all qualities, void of distinguishing qualities; worthless, bad; imperfect.

विगूढ़, *m.* (*f.* ā) concealed, hidden, scarcely perceivable: blamed.

विग्रह, *m.* opposition, encounter, quarrel, strife, battle, war; disfavour: extension, diffusion: shape, form; the body: a portion; (in Gram.) the proper form of a compound word. [fortune.

विघटन, *m.* breaking up, distinction, ruin, mis-

विघात, *m.* prohibition, opposition; an impediment, obstacle, hindrance: abandoning: destruction, murder: a blow.

विघाती, *m.* (*f.* inī) a murderer, etc.: lit. *adj.* obstructing, impeding, opposing; destroying, murdering.

विघ्न, *m.* an obstacle, trouble, impediment, hindrance, stop, prevention, interruption, detriment, calamity.

विघ्नकर, *m* (*f.* ī) an opposer, disturber, etc.: lit. *adj.* causing an interruption or disturbance, impeding, obstructing, hindering, opposing.

विघ्नकारक, *m.* (*f.* ikā) } = **विघ्नकर**, *q. v.*
विघ्नकारी, *m.* (*f.* iṇī) }

विघ्ननाशक, *m.* (*f.* ikā) a remover of obstacles or difficulties: lit. *adj.* destroying impediments.

विघ्ननाशन, 1, = **विघ्नराज**, *q.v.*: 2, *m.* the removal of obstacles: 3, *m.* (*f.* ī) a remover of obstacles.

विघ्नराज, *m.* an epithet of Gaṇesh; *lit.* the lord of difficulties,—Gaṇesh being invoked at the commencement of an undertaking as the remover of difficulties and interruptions.

विघ्नविनायक = **विघ्नराज**, *q. v.*

विघ्नसिद्धि, *f.* the removal of obstacles.

विघ्नहारक, *m.* (*f.* ikā) } = (1) **विघ्ननाशक** (2) **विघ्नराज**.
विघ्नहारी, *m.* (*f.* iṇī) }

विघ्नित, *m.* (*f.* ā) obstructed, hindered, impeded, stopped, prevented.

विघ्नेश = **विघ्नराज**, *q. v.* [stopped, prevented.

विचक्षण, *m.* (*f.* ā) all-seeing, discerning, knowing, circumspect, wise, sensible, clever, able, skilful, proficient.

विचल, 1, *m.* (*f.* ā) unsteady, unfixed, moveable, fickle, moving, going: 2, *m.* deviation, perverseness, irregularity, disobedience.

विचलन, *m.* a deviating, fickleness, unsteadiness, self-praise, conceit. [fringe; to break one's promise.

विचलना, *a. int.* to turn, bend; to slip; to in-

विचलित, *m.* (*f.* ā) deviated, moved irregularly, slipped, displaced; unsteady, unsettled, not fixed, fickle.

विचार, *m.* the exercise of judgment or reason, consideration, investigation, deliberation, reflection, discrimination, judgment, discussion, prudence, opinion, decision; contrivance, apprehension, thought, will; a trial. — *k.* (with gen. of the object) to exercise the judgment upon.

विचारक, *m.* (*f.* ikā) an investigator, discriminator, inspector, judge: lit. *adj.* investigating, discussing deliberating, judging.

विचारकर्त्ता, *m.* (*f.* trī) an investigator, discriminator, judge, administrator of justice.

विचारण, *m.* enquiry, deliberation, investigation, discrimination, judgment, hesitation, doubt.

विचारणा, 1, *f.* = **विचारण**, *q.v.*: 2, *f. pr. n.* an epithet of the Mīmānsā system of philosophy.

विचारत, *adj.* thinking, reflecting, judging.

विचारना, to consider, reflect, discriminate, think, judge, apprehend, conceive, comprehend, investigate, estimate, give judgment, decide.

विचारशील, *m.* (*f.* ā) a person of a considerate or judicious disposition. [liberately.

विचारसे, *adv.* (abl. of **विचार**) considerately, de-

विचारस्थल }
विचारस्थान } *m.* a court of justice, a tribunal.

विचारा, 1, *m.* (*f.* ī) *more prop.* **बेचारा**, *q.v.*: 2, see

विचाराध्यक्ष, *m.* (*f.* ī) a chief justice. [**विचारना**.

विचारि, an old conjunct. part. of **विचारना**, *q. v.*

विचारिका, *f.* (*m.* **विचारक**) a female investigator or judge. [decided.

विचारित, *m.*(*f.* ā) judged, discussed, determined,

विचारी, *m.* (*f.* iṇī) }
विचारु, *m.* and *f.* } = **विचारक**, *q. v.*

विचार्य्य, requiring to be discussed, fit and proper to be discussed, etc.

विचाल, intervening, intermediate.

विचिकित्सा, *f.* doubt, uncertainty, error, mistake.

विचित्र, variegated, spotted, many-coloured, gaudy, ornamented, beautiful, wonderful.

विचित्रवीर्य्य, *m. pr. n.* one of the sons of king Śantanu by his wife Satyavatī.

विच्छन्द }
विच्छन्दक }
विच्छर्दक } *m.* a palace; a temple.

विच्छेद, *m.* cutting, dividing, breaking, separation, disjunction, interruption, dispersion, distribution; an interval; chapter, section; dissension, breach (of friendship, etc.): prohibition, prevention.

विछेद (*corruption*) = **विच्छेद**, *q. v.*

विजन, without people or inhabitants, uninhabited, unfrequented, private, solitary, lonely.

विजय, *m.* (*f.* ?) an overpowering, conquest, triumph, victory: *pr. n.* (1) of a certain auspicious hour (2) an epithet of Arjun (3) one of the two gate-keepers of the Hindoo paradise.

विजयदशमी, *f.* the tenth day of the light half of the month Āshwin, the day of Dashaharā, etc.

विजयन्त, *m.* an epithet of Indra.

विजयमन्त }
विजयमान } *m.* (*f.* matī) = **विजयी**, *q. v.*

विजया, *f.* the name of several plants, particularly of hemp (*Cannabis sativa*) and of the tops of the hemp-plant used as a narcotic; an epithet of Durgā; a festival in honour of Durgā on the 10th day of the light fortnight of Āswini. [of sauces, etc.).

विजयिन, mixed with rice-water or gruel (said

विजयी, *m.* (*f.* inī) a conqueror: *lit.* victorious, conquering, triumphant. [caste.

विजाति, *f.* a different species, kind, tribe, or

विजातीय, *m.* (*f.* ā) a bastard, etc.: *lit.* of another kind or caste, differing from its order or species, dissimilar, uncommon, of a bad description, base-born, bastard. [conquered.

विजित, *m.* (*f.* ā) overcome, subdued, defeated,

विजिताश्व, *m. pr. n.* the eldest son of king Pṛithu.

विजितेन्द्रिय, *m.* (*f.* ā) a person of subdued passions: *lit.* whose organs are subdued.

विजिन }
विजिल }
विजिविल }
विज्जल } = **विजयिन**, *q.v.*

विज्ञ, *m.* (*f.* ā) a scholar, etc.: *lit.* knowing, conversant, wise, learned, clever, skilful, able, experienced, ready. [readiness, experience.

विज्ञता, *f.* skill, cleverness, wisdom, learning,

विज्ञति, 1, a contraction of **विज्ञप्ति**, *q.v.*: 2, a cor-

विज्ञत्व, *m.* = **विज्ञता**, *q. v.* [ruption of **विज्ञता**, *q. v.*

विज्ञप्ति, *f.* a report, announcement, information, representation, communication.

विज्ञात, *m.* (*f.* ā) known, understood, famous, notorious, celebrated. [enced person, a witness.

विज्ञाता, *m.* (*f.* tri) one who knows, an experi-

विज्ञान, *m.* knowledge, learning, science, wisdom, intelligence, *esp.* acquaintance with worldly affairs and law or the arts, etc.: distinction; music; employment, business.

विज्ञानता, *f.* (*m.* °त्व) learnedness, intelligence.

विज्ञानविहान, *m.* the removal or destruction of learning.

विज्ञापक, *m.* (*f.* ikā) an instructor, an informant: lit. *adj.* making known, giving information.

विज्ञापन, *m.* the making a thing known, teaching, informing, representing, instructing, an announcement, information.

विज्ञापना, *f.* an announcement, information.

विज्ञाय, *adj.* having known or perceived, having understood, having ascertained, having recognized.

विज्वर, *m.* (*f.* ā) exempt from fever or pain, free from anxiety or distress.

विटप, *m.* the branch of a tree with its new sprout, a branch, a twig, a new shoot; a bush; a thicket; a bunch, cluster, tuft; a tree: spreading, expansion: the septum of the scrotum: a keeper of catamites.

विटसारिका, *f.* a sort of thrush (usually, though inaccurately, called in Bengal the *mainā*).

विटौरा, *more com.* **बिटोरा**, *q. v.* [noyance.

विडम्ब, *m.* imitation; afflicting, distressing, an-

विडम्बन, *m.* imitation, copying; disguise; the supernatural assumption of a borrowed form; an afflicting, distressing; frustrating; vexation, mortification.

विडम्बना, *f.* deceiving, fraud, breach of faith: pain, distress, vexation, affliction. [abject, low, poor.

विडम्बित, *m.* (*f.* ā) afflicted, vexed, distressed,

विडाल } m. a cat : the eyeball.
विड़ाल }

विडालक, *m.* a cat: the application of orpiment to the external part of the eye : yellow orpiment.

विडूरज (*corruption*) = **विदूरज**, *q.v.*

वितण्डा, *f.* controversy, debate, perverse argumentation, criticism, refutation of the assertion of an opponent without establishing a position of one's own : a ladle: the name of two plants.

वितत, *m.* spread, expanded, extended, diffused.

वितता, *f.* (*m.* °त्व) largeness.

वितति, *f.* spreading; quantity; a cluster, clump.

वितथ, 1, at variance with the fact, untrue, false : 2, *m. pr. n.* a certain ancient Hindoo King.

वितद्रु, *pr. n.* (*f.* ?) a certain river said to be situated in the Panjāb.

वितना, *m.* (*f.* ī) in Braj = उतना, *q. v.*

वितरण, *m.* a crossing over, passing : quitting, abandoning : a gift, donation, distribution of charity.

वितर्क, *m.* deliberation, consideration, opinion, conjecture, doubt, discussion, reasoning ; a teacher in divine knowledge.

वितर्कण, *m.* reasoning, discussion, doubt.

वितर्द्धि, *f.* a quadrangular building or a sort of covered terrace in the centre of the courtyard of a temple or palace; a verandah, a balcony: a seat, bench.

वितर्द्धी = **वितर्द्धि**, *q. v.*

वितल, *m.pr.n.* one of the seven divisions of Pātāl, *viz.*— the second in descent below the earth.

वितललोक = **वितल**. See **लोक**.

वितस्ता, *f. pr. n.* a certain river.

वितस्ति, *m. f.* a long span measured by the extended thumb and little finger, and considered equal to twelve fingers.

वितान, 1, empty, pithless, stupid, dull, abandoned, wicked : 2. *m.* expansion, spreading ; an awning, canopy, cover, cushion ; the warp of cloth ; a quantity, heap ; sacrifice, offering ; the hole in which sacred fire is kept : (in Pros.) a species of metre.

विताना ; see **बिताना**.

वितृष्ण, *m.* (*f.* ā) 1, content, satisfied, free from desire : 2, disinclined, disliking, dissatisfied with.

वितृष्णता, *f.* satiety, satisfaction, contentment : disinclination, disgust, indifference.

वितृष्णा, *f* = (1) **वितृष्ण** (2) **वितृष्णता**, *qq. v.*

वित्त, *m.* wealth, property, money: substance, thing; means, ability, power.

वित्तवान, *m.* (*f.* vatī) possessing property, wealthy, rich.

वित्तहीन, *m.* (*f.* ā) destitute of property, indigent, poor.

वित्रारना, *t.* to rescue, save, deliver.

विद, 1, *more com.* **बिद**, *q.v.*: 2, *m.* (*f.* ā) a knower, wise man, sage.

विदग्ध, *m.* (*f.* ā) a shrewd or clever person, a scholar, paṇḍit ; an intriguer, libertine, lecher: *lit.* clever, shrewd, knowing, learned, able, skilful ; intriguing : burnt.

विदग्धता, *f.* (*m.* °त्व) sharpness, shrewdness, cleverness, sagacity, cunning, learnedness.

विदर, *m.* the Indian prickly pear (*Cactus Indicus*): lit. *adj.* tearing, rending.

विदरना, *a. int.* to split, go asunder, burst.

विदर्भ, *m.* any dry or desert soil: *pr. n.* (1) of a certain country (2) of its king.

विदा, *f.* 1, knowledge, understanding, wisdom: 2, permission to go away, dismissal with good wishes, dismission, leave-taking, farewell, adieu: commencement. — *k.* to bid farewell, to dismiss. — *dend*, to send away, dismiss, give one leave of absence. — *honā*, to take one's leave.

विदारण, *m.* tearing, rending, breaking, cleaving, splitting ; dividing, severing, afflicting ; killing ; war.

विदारना, *t.* to tear, rend, cleave, sever.

विदिक, *f.* an intermediate or subordinate point of the compass, as North-West, South-east, etc.

विदित, 1, known, understood; promised ; represented : informed : 2, *m.* information ; representation : 3, *m.* (*f.* ā) a learned person, scholar, sage.

विदिश, *f.* = **विदिक**, *q.v.*

विदिशा, *f.* 1, = **विदिक**, *q.v.* : 2, *pr.n.* (1) of a certain town (2) of a certain river.

विदीर्ण, *m.* (*f.* ā) rent asunder, torn, split, burst open, broken open, ripped up, expanded, opened.

विदुर, 1, *m.* (*f.* ā) a learned or clever person ; an intriguer : *lit.* clever, skilful, wise, intelligent, learned: *pr. n.* the younger brother or Dhṛitrāshṭra and Pāṇḍu.

विदुष, *m.* (*f.* ī) = **विदुर**, 1, *q. v.*

विदुषक, *m.* (*f.* ikā) *more prop.* **विदूषक**, *q.v.*

विदुषण ; see **विदूषण** and **विदूषक**.

विदुषन्ह, a Braj pl. of **विदुष**. See **न्ह**.

विदूर, 1, far off, afar, distant, remote : 2, *m. pr. n.* a certain mountain and city whence the lapis lazuli is brought.

विदूरज, *m.* lapis lazuli.

विदूरथ, *m.pr.n.* (1) of a certain king, son of Sarath (2) of a son of Bhajamān.

विदूषक, *m.* (*f.* ikā) a clown, buffoon, jester ; a detractor ; (in the Drama) the jocose companion of the principal person ; a catamite : *lit.* censorious, detracting ; witty, facetious.

विदूषण, *m.* the act of corrupting or defiling ; contamination ; corruption ; censuring, reviling, abuse, satire.

विदूषना, *t.* to calumniate, detract, abuse.

विदेश, *m.* any other country than one's own, a foreign country, abroad, a distant land.

विदेशग, *m.* (*f.* ā) = **विदेशगामी**, *q. v.*

विदेशगमन, *m.* travelling, going abroad.

विदेशगामी, (*f.* inī) one who goes abroad, a traveller : lit. *adj.* going to foreign countries.

विदेशज, *m.* (*f.* ā) a foreigner : *lit.* born in a foreign land, foreign, exotic.

विदेशी, *m.* (*f.* inī) a foreigner, traveller : *lit.* appertaining to another country or to a foreign land, foreign, exotic, strange.

विदेह, 1, *m.* (*f.* ā) without a body, incoporeal : 2, *m. pr. n.* the king of Videhā.

विदेहा, 1, *m.* (pl. ; see आ, 22) the people of Videh: 2. *f. pr. n* the district of ancient Mithilā or the modern Tirhut in the province of Bihār.

विद्यमान, *m.* (*f.* matī) known, heard of; being, existent, being present or in existence.

विद्यमानत्व, *m.* (*f.* tī) existence ; presence.

विद्या, *f.* knowledge, learning, science (whether sacred or profane, but esp. the former) : a magical pill or bolus by putting which into the mouth one has the power of ascending to heaven : a certain tree (*Premna spinosa*) : an epithet of Durgā. *Vidyā* is sometimes classed into fourteen divisions; thus (1, 2, 3, 4) the Veds, (5, 6, 7, 8, 9, 10) the six auxiliary sciences (*ang*) towards the right understanding of the Veds, as Grammar, Prosody, Astronomy, etc., (11) the Purāns, (12) the *Mīmānsā* or Theology, (13) *Nyāy*, or Logic, (14) *Dharm.* or law.

विद्याघर, *more com.* **विद्यालय,** *q.v.*

विद्यादाता } **विद्यादातृ** } *m.* (*f.* tri) an instructor, teacher.

विद्यादान, *m.* the impartation of knowledge or science, instruction, teaching.

विद्याधन, *m.* property acquired by means of science, instruction, or learning.

विद्याधर, *m.* (*f.* ī) a demigod of a certain class. (They are attendants in the celestial courts.)

विद्यान, a corruption of **विद्यावान,** *q.v.*

विद्यानुराग, *m.* the passion for learning.

विद्यानुरागी, *m.* (*f.* inī) a studious person: lit. *adj.* having a passion for learning.

विद्यापठन, *m.* the study of science, study.

विद्याप्राप्ति *f.* the acquirement of knowledge ; anything acquired by knowledge or learning.

विद्याभ्यास, *m.* the study of science ; study, diligent application to knowledge. [of learning.

विद्यायुत, *m.* (*f.* ā) connected with or possessed

विद्यारूप, *m.* (*f.* ā) the very embodiment of learning, exceedingly learned, abounding in learning.

विद्यारूपी, *m.* (*f.* iṇī) = **विद्यारूप,** *q.v.*

विद्यार्थी, *m.* (*f* inī) a seeker after knowledge, a student, pupil, scholar : *lit.* desirous of knowledge, studious. [lege, seminary.

विद्यालय, *m.* an abode of learning, a school, col-

विद्यालाभ, *m.* = **विद्याप्राप्ति,** *q.v.*

विद्यावान, possessed of knowledge or learning : hence, *m.* (*f.* vatī) a learned person, a scholar.

विद्यावानी, *more prop.* **विद्यावान,** *q.v.*

विद्याहीन, destitute of knowledge, unlearned, ignorant : hence, *m.* (*f.* ā) an unlearned or illiterate person.

विद्युत, *f.* lightning.

विद्युद्विशिष्ट, *m.* (*f.* ā) possessed of lightning.

विद्रुम, *m.* coral, a coral-tree, a tree bearing precious gems : a young sprout.

विद्वन, 1, Sk. voc. sing. of **विद्वान,** *q. v.* : 2, see **विधन.**

विद्वलता, *f.* the strength of learning, power of knowledge. [ligent, wise, clever, learned.

विद्वान, *m.* (*f.* vatī) a learned person : *lit.* intel-

विद्वेष, *m.* enmity, hatred, dislike, contempt.

विद्वेषी, *m.* (*f.* iṇī) an enemy : *lit.* inimical, hating, hostile, malicious.

विध, 1, *f.* a contraction (1) of **विधा** (2) of **विधि,** *qq. v.* : 2, frequent in Bahuvrīhi compounds ; *e.g.* **द्विविध.**

विधन, *m.* (*f.* ā) without wealth, indigent, poor.

विधनता, *f.* (*m.* °त्व) poverty, indigence.

विधना, 1, *f.* (*m.* **विधन**) an indigent female : 2, *m.* an epithet of Brahmā. [heterodoxy ; apostasy.

विधर्म्म, *m.* a religion different from one's own ;

विधवा, 1, *m.* = **विधात्रा,** *q. v.* : 2, *f.* a widow.

विधवां, *f.* (pl. of **विधवा**) widows.

विधवावेदन, *m.* the marrying a widow.

विधव्यवहार, a contraction of **विधिव्यवहार,** *q. v.*

विधा, *f.* a prescribed form, a rule: manner, kind, sort : an act, action : thriving, prosperity : hire, wages : food of horses, elephants, etc. : a piercing.

विधाता, *m.* (*f.* trī) a ruler ; a maker : fate : an epithet (1) of Brahmā or Divine Providence (2) of [Kāmdev.

विधातृ, *m.* (*f.* trī) = **विधाता,** *q. v.*

विधान, *m.* sending, ordering, arrangement, disposition, creation ; an ordinance, injunction, precept, direction, regulation, rule, law ; form, manner, mode : act, action, *esp.* the performance of an act prescribed by religion or by law ; worship ; ceremony ; means, expedient : wealth ; gaining : an act of hostility ; conflict of opposite feelings : an elephant's fodder.

विधायक, *m.* (*f.* ikā) one who entrusts or deposits, etc. : lit. *adj.* establishing a rule or law, placing, fixing, securing, directing, prescribing, enjoining.

विधायी, *m.* (*f.* inī) = **विधायक,** *q. v.*

विधि, *m.* an order, injunction, command, rule, precept, ceremony, form, formula, ordinance, an act or rite prescribed by religion, a sacred precept ; a text prescribing any particular act ; action ; a sacred work; fate : kind, sort, manner, mode : time : creation : behaviour, life : food for horses, elephants, etc. : an epithet (1) of Brahmā (2) of Vishṇu.

विधिक्रिया, *f.* (in Gram.) the imperative mood.

विधिज्ञ, *m.* (*f.* ā) a well-informed person, etc. : *lit.* acquainted with the laws or precepts, knowing how to proceed.

विधिदर्शी, *m.* (*f.* iṇī) a priest whose business at a sacrifice is to see that all is done according to the prescribed rules. [feet of Brahm.

विधिपद, *m.* an epithet of Brahmlok; the blessed

विधिवत, 1, *adv.* agreeably to law or to prescribed rule, regularly, duly : 2, *m.* (*f.* vatī) one who acts agreeably to the prescribed rule.

विधिवती, *f.* (*m.* **विधिवान,** etc.) a female who conforms to the prescribed rules.

विधिवन्त } **विधिवान** } *m.* (*f.* vatī) = **विधिवत,** 2, *q.v.*

विधिव्यवहार, *m.* the conduct or the practices of Brahmā.

विधिहरिहरमय, consisting of (or abounding in) Brahmā, Vishṇu, and Shiv, possessed of (or imbued with) the divine.

विधु, *m.* the moon : an expiatory obligation : camphor : an epithet (1) of Brahmā (2) of Vishṇu (3) of a Rākshas.

विधुंतुद, *m.* an epithet of Rāhu.

विधुपुष्प, *m.* the sun and moon.

विधुयत्व, *m.* (*f.* tā) fitness; practicability.

विधुर, 1, *m.* (*f.* ī) trembling, agitated, bewildered, distressed, adverse, separated from one's lover, abandoned: 2, *m.* agitation of mind, confusion, distress, danger, separation. [or handsome face.

विधुवदन, *m.* (*f.* ī) moon-faced, having a moonlike

विधूदय, *m.* the rising of the moon.

विधेय, *m.* (*f.* ī) what requires to be accomplished or arranged; enjoined, prescribed: compliant, tractable, manageable; (in Gram.) the predicate.

विधेयता, *f.* (*m.* °त्व) necessary or proper act or conduct, fitness for enactment as a rule, practicability; submission.

विध्यक्षेत्र, a corruption of **विन्ध्याक्षेत्र**, *q.v.*

विध्याचल, a corruption of **विन्ध्याचल**, *q.v.*

विध्वंस, *m.* aversion, disrespect, enmity, dislike; offence; overthrow, ruin, destruction, slaughter, annihilation, non-existence.

विध्वंसी, *m.* (*f.* inī) a destroyer, etc.: lit. *adj.* falling asunder, causing to fall, overthrowing, destroying, adverse, hostile. [1, *q. v.*

विन, 1, (contraction) = **विना**, *q.v.*: 2, in Braj = **उन**,

विनत, *m.* (*f.* ā) sunk down, drooping, inclined, bowed, bent, curved, crooked, stooping, cast down, prostrate, humble, modest.

विनता, *f.* 1, = **विनत**, *q.v.*: 2, a sort of basket: 3, *pr. n.* the wife of Kashyap and mother of Aruṇ and Garuḍ.

विनति, *f.* a bowing, bending, stooping; humility, modesty; submission, apology, solicitation, entreaty. — *k.* (with abl.) to entreat.

विनती, *more prop.* **विनति**, *q.v.*

विननि in Braj = **उनने**. See (1) **विन**, 2: (2) **नि**, 2 (5).

विनय, *m.* training, discipline, good behaviour, decorum, decency, reverence, obeisance, modesty, propriety of conduct, humility, mildness, courtesy, affability.

विनयग्राही, *m.* (*f.* iṇī)
विनयवान, *m.* (*f.* vatī) } = **विनयी**, *q.v.*
विनयवन्त, *m.* (*f.* vatī)

विनयी, *m.* (*f.* inī) a modest person, etc.: *lit.* suppliant, mild, tractable, courteous, respectful, affable, humble, obedient.

विनशन, *m.* a destroying, destruction: *pr. n.* a certain country forming the western frontier of *Madhyadesh*.

विनशना, *a. int.* to deteriorate, spoil, perish: *n.* to be brought to nothing, be destroyed.

विनशाना, *t.* to cause a thing to deteriorate or to spoil, to spoil, destroy, ruin. [perishing, decaying.

विनश्यत, *m.* (*f.* antī) *adj.* being lost or ruined,

विनश्यन्त, *m.* (*f.* ī) = **विनश्यत**, *q.v.* [ished, lost.

विनष्ट, *m.* (*f.* ā) spoiled, destroyed, ruined, per-

विनष्टि, *f.* disappearance, destruction, ruin.

विनसना (*colloquial*) = **विनशना**, *q. v.*

विनस्सया, in Chand = **विनाश**, *q.v.*

विना, without, except, besides, unless, not having. The usage of this word in Hindee, both as to government and position, seems very uncertain. In Sanskrit it governs regularly the Acc. and Instr. cases; in Hindee, however, it is found not only with these cases but also with the uninflected Nom. and with the Gen., as also with the inflected form of inflectible words without any case-sign. Thus much may be said, that when it is used with a word in the Abl. or Instr. case, it precedes that word; and that when its word is in the Nom. or the Gen. case, it generally follows it.

विनाथ, *m.* (*f.* ā) an unprotected person: *lit.* without a protector, unowned, deserted.

विनायक, *m.* (*f.* ikā) a spiritual preceptor; an epithet (1) of Gaṇesh (2) of Garuḍ (3) of a Bauddh.

विनायिका, *f.* (*m.* **विनायक**) a spiritual preceptress, the wife of a spiritual preceptor; *pr. n.* the wife of Garuḍ. [truction, loss, death.

विनाश, *m.* disappearance, annihilation, ruin, des-

विनाशक, *m.* (*f.* ikī) a destroyer, spoiler: *lit.* destructive, destroying, ruining.

विनाशन, 1, *m.* (*f.* ā) = **विनाशक**; 2, *m.* = **विनाश**, *qq. v.*

विनाशना, *t.* to spoil, ruin, destroy.

विनाशमान, *m.* (*f.* matī) perishable, destructible.

विनाशित, *m.* (*f.* ā) effaced, destroyed, ruined.

विनाशिन, *m.* (*f.* ī) *more com.* **विनाशी**, *q. v.*

विनाशी, *m.* (*f.* inī) a destroyer, etc.: *lit.* destructive, destroying; perishable, destructible; perishing, being destroyed; undergoing change or transformation.

विनाश्यमान *m.* (*f.* matī) = **विनाशमान**, *q. v.*

विनास्या in Chand = **विनाश**, *q.v.*

विनिन्दक, *m.* (*f.* ikā) a reprover, reviler, blasphemer: lit. *adj.* reproving, reviling, blaspheming.

विनिन्दित, *m.* (*f.* ā) blamed, reprehended, reviled, blasphemed.

विनिपात, *m.* a falling, falling down, fall (literally or metaphorically); ruin; unavoidable evil, calamity; pain, distress; death; disrespect. [or destruction.

विनिपातशंसी, portentous, announcing misfortune

विनिमय, *m.* barter, exchange, substitution, retaliation, requital; a pledge, deposit.

विनिश्चित, *m.* (*f.* ā) ascertained, determined, settled, decided, certain. [unconcerned.

विनिश्चिन्त, *m.* (*f.* ā) thoughtless, inconsiderate,

विनीत, *m.* (*f.* ā) humble, modest, complaint, tractable, meek, placid, gentle

विनीतात्मा, *m. f.* a well-behaved person, etc.: *lit.* of a humble or tractable disposition, well-behaved lowly. [obeisance, homage.

विनीति, *f.* training, good behaviour, reverence,

विनोद, *m.* a dismissing, removing; dismissal, abandonment: play, sport, pastime, entertainment, pleasure, gratification, happiness, interest: eagerness, vehemence.

विन्द, 1, a contraction of **विन्दु**, *q.v.*: 2, found as a suffix to certain epithets in the sense of acquiring, obtaining; *e. g.* **गोविन्द**.

विन्दु, *m.* a drop (of any liquid); a spot, speck,

dot, mark, point; the dot over a letter (in Devanāgari) to represent *anuswār* or the nasal sound; the bite or mark of a tooth; a mark of colouring-matter on an elephant's face or trunk; the part of the forehead between the eyebrows.

विन्दुक, *m.* a drop (of any liquid).

विन्दुसर, *m. pr. n.* a certain sacred lake which is also a place of Hindoo pilgrimage.

विन्दुसार, *m. pr. n.* a certain ancient Hindoo king (son of Chandra-gupt).

विन्दुसेन, *m. pr. n.* a certain ancient Hindoo king, [son of Kshatraujas.

विन्ध्य, 1, *m. pr. n.* the range of mountains which stretches across India and divides Hindūstān from the Dakkhan, and marks the southern boundary of the sacred land of the Hindoos: 2, *m.* (*f.* ā) a hunter.

विन्ध्यक्षेत्र, *m.* = **विन्ध्यावासिनी** (2), *q.v.*

विन्ध्या, *f.* 1, see **विन्ध्य**, 2: 2, small cardamoms: a certain plant (*Annona reticulata*).

विन्ध्याचक्र, *m.* a triangle: *pr. n.* a certain place of Hindoo pilgrimage in the Vindhya mountains.

विन्ध्याचल, *m. pr. n.* = **विन्ध्य**, 1, *q.v.*

विन्ध्याटवी, *f. pr. n.* the great Vindhya forest (which appears, at one time, to have spread from near Mathurā to the Narmadā).

विन्ध्यावली, *f. pr. n.* the wife of the asur Bali.

विन्ध्यावलीपुत्र = **विन्ध्यावलीसुत**, *q.v.*

विन्ध्यावलीसुत, *m.* (the son of Vindhyāvalī, *i.e.*) Vāṇ.

विन्ध्यावासिनी, *f. pr. n.* (1) of Durgā (2) of a certain village and temple (sacred to that goddess under the forms of Yogmāyā and Bhogmāyā) situated on the Ganges about three miles from Mirzapur; — it is a place of great resort among the Hindoos.

विन्याक, *m.* a certain tree (*Echites scholaris*).

विन्यास, *m.* a laying down, entrusting, collecting, depositing orderly arrangement, adjustment; an assemblage, collection, deposit, a place, site; a receptacle.

विन्नें / **विन्नैं** } in Braj = **उन्नें** = **उनको**. See **उन** and **तिन**.

विपक्ष, *m.* an enemy, adversary, opponent, a member of the opposite party, disputant: (in Gram.) an exception: (in Logic) a negative instance: *lit.* adverse, hostile, opposed, contrary.

विपक्षता, *f.* (*m.* °**त्व**) contrariety, opposition, contradiction, enmity, hostility.

विपक्षपात, 1, *m.* impartiality, indifference: 2, impartial, indifferent.

विपक्षी, *m.* (*f.* iṇī) = **विपक्ष**, *q.v.*

विपच्छी, *m.* (*f.* inī) *more prop.* **विपक्षी**, *q.v.*

विपत, *f.* adversity, calamity, misfortune, disaster, distress, failing, pain, death.

विपता / **विपति** } = **विपत**, *q.v.*

विपतिनिदान, *m.* a cause or occasion of trouble.

विपत्काल, *m.* a time of calamity or misfortune, a season of distress or adversity.

विपत्त / **विपत्ति** } = **विपत**, *q.v.*

विपत्तियुक्त, *m.* (*f.* ā) calamitous, unfortunate, unhappy.

विपत्तिरहित, *m.* (*f.* ā) exempt from misfortune, [prosperous, happy.

विपत्सागर, *m.* an ocean of trouble, heavy calamity.

विपथ, *m.* a by-path; a wrong road, bad way, wrong [course, evil conduct.

विपद = **विपत**, *q.v.*

विपदग्रस्त, *m.* (*f.* ā) = **विपद्ग्रस्त**, *q.v.*

विपदयुक्त, *m.* (*f.* ā) = **विपत्तियुक्त**, *q.v.*

विपदरहित, *m.* (*f.* ā) = **विपत्तिरहित**, *q.v.*

विपदा = **विपत**, *q.v.*

विपदुद्धार, *m.* deliverance from misfortune.

विपद्ग्रस्त, *m.* (*f.* ā) in difficulties, overtaken by calamity, involved in disaster or misfortune.

विपद्युक्त, *m.* (*f.* ā) = **विपत्तियुक्त**, *q.v.*

विपद्रहित, *m.* (*f.* ā) = **विपत्तिरहित**, *q.v.*

विपरीत, 1, *m.* (*f.* ā) contrary, reverse, opposite, repugnant, inverse: 2, *f.* mischief, ruin.

विपरीतता, *f.* (*m.* °**त्व**) contrariness, contrariety, reverse, the reverse or opposite state or condition.

विपर्यय, *m.* change, a morbid change; failure of conception: the reverse or opposite; opposition, contrariety, opposedness, perverseness of disposition, repugnance, hostility, error, mistake.

विपर्याय / **विपर्यास** } = **विपर्यय**, *q.v.*

विपल, *m.* a moment, instant, a simple breathing; (in Astron.) a second.

विपाक, *m.* cooking, dressing, ripening, maturing; maturity, ripeness; a change of state or form; unexpected or inprobable result: flavour, taste; digestion: distress, embarrassment.

विपाट / **विपाश** } *f. pr. n.* = **विपाशा**, *q.v.*

विपाशा, *f. pr. n.* a certain river in the Punjāb (called also the *Beyah*).

विपिन, *m.* a wood, forest, thicket, grove.

विपुल, 1, large, great; broad, extensive; deep, profound; rash: 2, *m.* (*f.* ā) a respectable person: 3, *m. pr. n.* (1) of mount Meru (2) of the Himālaya range.

विपुलता, *f.* (*m.* °**त्व**) magnitude, extent.

विपुला, *f.* 1, (*m.* **विपुल**) a respectable female: the earth: (in Pros.) a species of metre.

विप्ता = **विपत**, *q.v.*

विप्य in Chand = **विप्र**, *q.v.*

विप्र, *m.* a poet or singer of Vedic hymns; a Brāhmaṇ; [a priest.

विप्रचरण, *m.* the sacred feet of a Brāhmaṇ.

विप्रचित्ती, *f. pr. n.* (in Myth.) a certain demon.

विप्रतिपत्ति, *f.* mutual connexion with: conservancy: perplexity, various acquirements: difference, opposition of interests, conflict of evidence, objection, contrariety, contest, dispute.

विप्रन, a Braj pl. of **विप्र**. See **न**, 6 (1).

विप्रवध *m.* the murder of a Brāhmaṇ,

विप्रहि, an emphatic or acc. form of **विप्र**, *q.v.*

विफल, *m.* (*f.* ā) fruitless, barren, useless, vain, idle, unmeaning.

विफलता, *f.* (*m.* °**त्व**) fruitlessness, barrenness, unproductiveness, unprofitableness, uselessness.

विबुद्ध, *m.* (*f.* ā) wide awake, awakened, aroused;

expanded, blossomed; clever, experienced, skilful, knowing: without consciousness, unconscious.

विबुधवैद्य, *m.* an epithet of the physicians of the gods, *i. e.* the *Ashwin.*

विबुध, 1, *m.* (*f.* ā) a wise or a learned man, a teacher, pandit; a god, an immortal: an epithet of the moon: *pr. n.* the author of the *Janmpradip.*

विबुधवन, *m.* an epithet of the pleasure-ground of Indra and paradise of the gods.

विभंजन, 1, *m.* a breaking, destroying: 2, *m.*(*f.* ā) a breaker, destroyer: *lit.* destructive.

विभंजना, *f.* (*m.* **विभंजन**) a female destroyer.

विभंजनि } **विभंजनो** } (*Rām.*) = **विभंजन**, *q. v.*

विभक्त, *m.* (*f.* ā) divided, portioned out, partitioned, separated, parted, distinct; (in Law) one who has received his portion of the patrimony and has set up for himself.

विभक्ति, *f.* a portion, share, partition; (in Gram.) an affix of declension or inflection; declension; inflection; case-sign.

विभचारी, *m.*(*f.* iṇī) a corruption of = **व्यभिचारी**, *q. v.*

विभव, *m.* power, supreme or superhuman power; wealth, property, substance, thing; magnanimity, emancipation from existence.

विभाग, *m.* a dividing; division, distribution, partition; part share, portion, lot; (in Arithm.) a fraction; the numerator of a fraction.

विभाजक, *adj.* dividing, distributing, distinguishing, (in Gram.) disjunctive.

विभात, *m.* daybreak, dawn: lit. *m.* (*f.* ā) become manifest.

विभाना, *a. int.* to become manifest, shine forth.

विभास, *f.* light, lustre, splendour.

विभासा, *f.* shining brightly; light, lustre: an alternative, option, one of two ways; (in Gram.) the allowing a rule to be optional.

विभिन्न, *m.* (*f.* ā) pierced, wounded, cleft, broken; scattered, disunited, separated, dispersed; different, various, contradictory, disappointed, bewildered.

विभिन्नता, *f.* (*m.* °त्व) distinctness, separation, dividedness, contrariety.

विभिन्ना, 1, *f.* of **विभिन्न**: 2, *m.* pl. of **विभिन्न**. See **न्ना**, 22.

विभीषण, 1, *m.* (*f.* ā) fearful, terrific, alarming, frightful, horrible: 2, *m.* the property of exciting fear; terrifying; a means of terrifying: *pr. n.* one of the brothers of Rāvaṇ.

विभीषणा, *f.* the property of exciting fear; terrifying; a means of terrifying.

विभु, omnipresent, all-pervading; firm, solid; eternal: hence, *m.* an epithet (1) of the Supreme Being (2) of Brahmā (3) of Vishṇu (4) of Shiv (5) of the soul (6) of time (7) of æther (8) of space (9) of a master or lord.

विभुता, *f.* (*m.* °त्व) supremacy, sovereignty, authority, power, might.

विभुन्ह, a Braj pl. of **विभु**. See **न्ह**.

विभूति, *f.* individual or separated existence as contrasted with union with the divine essence: superhuman power (attributed to Shiv, and attainable by mortals through continued austerities); power, dominion, majesty, dignity, glory: ashes of cowdung.

विभूतिमान, *m.* (*f.* matī) a person possessed of superhuman power.

विभूषण, *m.* ornament, decoration.

विभूषित, *m.* (*f.* ā) ornamented, decorated, adorned.

विभेद, *m.* a dividing, breaking, violating, wounding; bewildering; separation, division, distinction, disagreement, schism, dissension, contradiction, enmity.

विभेदक, *m.* (*f.* ikā) a discriminator, etc.: lit. *adj.* separating, distinguishing, discriminative, contradicting.

विभो (*colloquial*) = **विभव**, *q. v.*

विभ्रम, *m.* a whirling, going round; motion; hurry, flurry, perturbation; an error, mistake, blunder; apprehension, doubt; erroneous use; amorous actions, amatory caprice; grace, beauty.

विभ्रान्ति, *f.* a whirling round; hurry, precipitation, alarm; error; confusion.

विमर्श, *m.* examination by reasoning, discussion, investigation, trial, hesitation, doubt, regret, dislike.

विमल, *m.* (*f.* ā) free from stains, white, clear, clean, spotless, stainless, uncontaminated, undefiled: immaculate, pure (whether literally or metaphorically).

विमलमणि, *m.* crystal.

विमलात्मक, *m.* (*f.* ikā) a pure-minded person, etc: *lit.* of an uncontaminated mind, unpolluted, stainless, pure.

विमलात्मा } **विमलार्थक** } = **विमलात्मक**, *q. v.*

विमाता } **विमात** } *f.* a step-mother (father's wife).

विमान, *m.* a chariot of the gods (self-directed and self-moving); any car or vehicle; a horse; a palace: a measure.

विमार्ग, *m.* 1, = **विपथ** *q.v.*: 2, a brush, broom.

विमुक्त, *m.* (*f.* ā) let loose, released, liberated, emancipated, dismissed.

विमुक्ति, *f.* separation, release, emancipation, liberation (*esp.* of the spirit from matter and separate existence).

विमुख, *m.* (*f.* ī) having the face averted, averse to, disinclined, opposed, hostile.

विमुखता, *f.* turning away the face, disinclination, opposition; departure.

विमुखी, *m.* (*f.* inī) = **विमुख**, *q. v.*

विमूढ़, *m.* (*f.* ā) an infatuated person, etc.: *lit.* bewildered, beguiled, infatuated, foolish, stupid.

विमूढ़ात्मा, *m. f.* = **विमूढ़**, *q. v.*

विमोच, *m.* an untying, letting loose, release, liberation, dismissing, abandoning, final emancipation; forgiveness.

विमोचण, *m.* } **विमोचणा**, *f.* } **विमोचन**, *m.* } = **विमोच**, *q. v.*

विमोचित, *m.* (*f.* ā) released, emancipated; forgiven, wiped away, pardoned.

विमोह, *m.* temptation, allurement, seduction.

विमोहन, *m.* the act of confounding the mind and exciting the passions, tempting, alluring, seducing.

विमोहनी, *m.* (*f.* inī) a fascinator: lit. *adj.* fascinating, tempting, alluring, seductive.

विमोहित, *m.* (*f.* ā) fascinated, bewitched, seduced, beguiled, tempted.

विम्ब, *m.* 1, the disc of the sun or moon: a reflected form; an image, shadow, picture; a bubble: 2, a certain cucurbitaceous plant (*Momordica monadelpha*) and its fruit.

विम्बक, *m.* the disc of the sun or moon: the fruit of the *Momordica monadelpha.* [ed out, pictured.

विम्बित, *m.* (*f.* ā) reflected (as an image), shadow-

विम्बा / **विम्बिका** / **विम्बी** } *f.* = **विम्ब**, 2, *q.v.*

विम्बोष्ठ, 1, *m.* a *vimb*-like lip, *i.e.* a lip red like the *vimb*-fruit: 2, *m.* (*f.* ā *or* ī) a person with beautifully red lips: *lit.* having lips beautifully red like the *vimb*-fruit.

विम्बौष्ठ, *m.* (*f.* ā or ī) = **विम्बोष्ठ**, *q.v.*

विम्लान, *m.* (*f.* ā) fresh, pure, clean, free from soil or decay; refreshed.

वियत, *m.* the sky, heaven, atmosphere.

वियद्गगा, *f. pr. n.* (1) of the celestial Ganges (2) [of the Milky Way.

वियाज, *more prop.* **व्याज**, *q.v.*

वियारी / **वियालू** } *more prop.* **बियारी**, etc., *qq. v.*

वियोग, *m.* separation, disunion, disjunction, absence (esp. of lovers); death.

वियोगक, *m.* (ikā) = **वियोगी**, *q.v.*

वियोगन, *m.* a disjoining, separating.

वियोगिनी, *f.* (*m.* **वियोगी**) a female separated from her husband or lover.

वियोगी, *m.* (*f.* inī) a lover suffering the pain of absence the ruddy goose: *lit.* separated, apart, absent, remote, distressed from separation.

वियोर; see **बेवरा**.

विरंग, *adv.* in a variety of ways, in different ways.

विरंच / **विरंचि** } *m.* a Brāhmaṇ: an epithet of Brahmā.

विरक्त, *m.* (*f.* ā) an ascetic, etc.: *lit.* (1) disinclined, dégagé, indifferent to, free from passion or from attachment to worldly objects, averse (2) attached to, pleased with, fond of, impassioned.

विरक्तभाव, 1, *m.* disinclination, averseness: 2, disinclined to, averse, disliking.

विरक्ति, *f.* non-attachment, absence of affection, disinclination, disgust, aversion.

विरचन, *m.* a making, composing, embellishing.

विरचना, 1, *f.* = **विरचन**, *q.v.*: 2, *t.* to make, compose, fabricate, form, embellish.

विरचित, *m.* (*f.* ā) made, prepared, effected, written, composed, compiled.

विरज, *m.* (*f.* ā) one who is free from passion.

विरजा, *f.* a species of grass (*dūb*): *pr. n.* a certain river.

विरण, *m.* a certain fragrant grass (*Andropogon aromaticum* or *muricatum* or *schœnanthum*) used by the Hindoos in religious ceremonies.

विरत, *m.* (*f.* ā) desisted, stopped, ceased, rested.

विरति, *f.* stop, cessation, desisting, term, end, rest.

विरथ, *m.* (*f.* ā) having no car or chariot, chariotless.

विरद, *m.* fame, reputation, panegyric: the dress of heroes, military uniform or accoutrements, the habiliments of war.

विरल, *m.* (*f.* ā) fine, delicate, thin (but with interstices); few; little: loose, relaxed; apart, wide, separated by an interval; rare; remote, distant; occurring at distant or repeated intervals of time; scarce, uncommon, rare, wonderful.

विरला, *f. pr. n.* the mother of Vidur.

विरस, *m.* (*f.* ā) insipid, tasteless; ill-flavoured, nauseous; painful.

विरह, *m.* separation, parting, absence (*esp.* of lovers); abandonment, relinquishment, desertion, loneliness; cessation; a song complaining of a lover's absence.

विरहा, *m.* = (1) **विरह** (2) **विरहा**, *qq.v.*

विरहवन्त / **विरहवान** } *m.* (*f.* vatī) = **विरही**, *q. v.*

विरहाग्नि, *f.* the fire of separation (*i. e.* the disconsolateness of lovers during absence).

विरहिणी, *f.* (*m.* **विरही**) a female lover suffering the pangs of absence from the object of her affection: wages, hire.

विरहित, *m.* (*f.* ā) separated, left alone, deserted, forsaken; void of, exempt or free from.

विरहिन, 1, *m.* (*f.* ī) = **विरही**: 2, *f.* = **विरहिणी**, *qq.v.*

विरहिया, *m.* or *f.* suffering the pangs of absent love, amorous, sensual.

विरही, *m.* (*f.* inī) one who is suffering the pangs of absence from the object of affection: *lit.* separated from, sundered, lonely, deserted.

विराग, *m.* absence of desire or passion, disregard of sensual enjoyment, indifference, disaffection, aversion.

विरागी, *m.* (*f.* inī) a stoical person, ascetic: *lit.* void of passion or desire; entertaining aversion or dislike.

विराज्, *m.* splendour, beauty, display: the first progeny of Brahmā: a man of the military or regal class: (in Philos.) the consciousness which perceives collections or aggregates: (in Pros.) a species of metre.

विराजत = **विराजमान**, *q.v.*

विराजना, *a. int.* to appear, be conspicuous or splendid, to enjoy overself, live in health, ease, independence, and content.

विराजमान, *m.* (*f.* matī) shining, brilliant, splendid, appearing splendid, handsome. [displayed.

विराजित, *m.* (*f.* ā) made splendid, illuminated,

विराट, *m.* 1, the embodied spirit; beauty, splendour: *pr. n.* (1) of a certain sovereign (2) of Berar in central India; 3, enormous, gigantic.

विराटज, *m.* an inferior sort of diamond found in Virāṭ. [Rākshas.

विराध, *m.* prevention, opposition, vexation; a

विराम, 1, uneasy, unquiet, agitated: 2, *m.* cessation, desisting, stop, rest, repose, pause, end; (in Gram.) a certain mark put under a consonant to indicate that it is not to be pronounced with the inherent vowel-sound; *e. g.* **विराज्**, pronounced (not in three syllables, *virāja* but) *virāj*: see Art. **ब्**, 2,3.

विराल (*corruption*) = **बिड़ाल**, *q. v.* See **र**, 4 (2).

विरंच, *m.* an epithet of Brahmā.

विरिंचि, *m.* an epithet (1) of Brahmā (2) of Vishṇu

विरुज (*Rām.*) = निरोगी, *q.v.* [(3) of Shiv.

विरुदैत (*Rām.*) = बानावाले बीर.

विरुद्ध, *m.* (*f.* ā) contrary to, opposed to, opposite, against, averse, incongruous, hostile, inconsistent with : opposed, hindered, thwarted by, excluded.

विरुद्धता, *f.* (*m.* °त्व) opposition, contrariety, incongruity, enmity, aversion, hostility.

विरूप, 1, *m.* (*f.* ā) deformed, misshapen, disfigured, ugly, monstrous, unnatural, hideous, frightful : 2, *m.* difference of nature; deformity; ugly shape, a monstrosity : 3, *m.* opposition, dislike. — *honā*, to be disgraced.

विरूपक, *m.* (*f.* ikā) = **विरूप**, 1, *q.v.*

विरूपा, *f.* (*m.* **विरूप**) a female monstrosity ; *pr. n.* the wife of Yam.

विरूपी, *m.* (*f.* iṇī) = **विरूप**, 1, *q.v.*

विरेक }
विरेचन } *m.* purging, diarrhœa : a purgative.

विरोध, *m.* hindrance, impediment, restraint, check, opposition, contradiction; enmity, hostility, animosity; contention, contrariety, litigation, dispute, war, calamity.

विरोधचारी, *m.* (*f.* iṇī) *more prop.* **विरोधाचारी**, *q.v.*

विरोधयुत, *m.* (*f.* ā) obstructive, adverse.

विरोधाचारी, *m.* (*f.* iṇī) = **विरोधी**, 2, *q.v.*

विरोधी, 1, *f.* a fixed rule, an institute : 2, *m.* (*f.* iṇī) an antagonist, etc. : *lit.* opposing, counteracting, disputatious, litigious, obstructive, adverse, hostile, inimical, contentious, quarrelsome, contradictory, inconsistent, adverse, exclusive, beseiging, blockading.

विल, *m.* a hole, chasm, fissure, vacuity, cavern, cave, burrow, valley : *pr. n.* one of Indra's horses.

विलक्ष, *m.* (*f.* ā) astonished, surprized, ashamed, abashed, embarrassed.

विलक्षण, 1, *m.* a seeing : a state or condition for which no cause can be assigned : 2, other, different : good.

विलग = **बिलग**, *q.v.* [est, impudent.

विलज्ज, *m.* (*f.* ā) unabashed, shameless, immod-

विलम्ब, *m.* a falling, hanging down, depending; slowness, tardiness, delay. [crastination.

विलम्बन, *m.* a depending, delaying, delay, pro-

विलम्बना, *a. int.* to stay, tarry, delay, stop.

विलम्बाना, *t.* to detain, stop, delay.

विलम्बित, *m.* (*f.* ā) delayed, procrastinated.

विलम्भ, *m.* 1, *more prop.* **विलम्ब**, *q.v.* : 2, liberality; a donation, gift. [destruction of the world.

विलय, *m.* liquefaction ; death ; destruction ; the

विलयन, *m.* a liquefying, attenuating, corroding, removing, destroying : an attenuant, an escharotic.

विलसन, *m.* sporting, dallying; play, sport, mirth; flashing.

विलसना, *n.* to be pleased, be satisfied, be delighted.

विलाप, *m.* lamentation, complaint, the language of grief and distress.

विलापक, *m.* (*f.* ikā) = **विलापी**, *q.v.*

विलापना, *a. int.* to bewail, lament, complain, grieve, mourn, weep. [complaining, lamenting.

विलापी, *m.* (*f.* inī) a bewailer : lit. *adj.* bewailing,

विलायत, *f.* an inhabited country, a dominion, district; a foreign country : possession, the being master of anything. By the natives of India this term is used to denote any country excepting their own, but more especially Arabia, Persia, and Great Britain.

विलायती, *m.* (*f.* inī) a foreigner, European : *lit.* appertaining to *Wilāyat.*

विलाल (*corruption*) = **बिडाल**, *q.v.* See **ल**, 4 (1).

विलास, *m* amorous playfulness, dalliance, wantonness, coquetry, merriness, sport, play, pastime, pleasure, delight, gladness, enjoyment, charm, beauty.

विलासना, *a. int.* to enjoy oneself, take one's pleasure. [pleasure, coquette, harlot.

विलासिनी, *f.* (*m.* **विलासी**) a woman ; a woman of

विलासी, *m.* (*f.* inī) a sensualist, rake, coquet : a snake : fire : an epithet (1) of Shiv (2) of Vishṇu (3) of Krishṇ (4) of Kāmdev (5) of the moon : *lit.* wanton, amorous, dallying, sportive, addicted to pleasure, voluptuous.

विलोकन, *m.* the act of seeing, regarding, looking, view, sight, spying, inspection.

विलोकना, *t.* to see, look at, behold, view.

विलोकनीय, *m.* (*f.* ā) fit to be seen or looked at, beautiful, agreeable.

विलोकित, *m.* (*f.* ā) looked at, beheld, viewed, seen.

विलोचन, *m.* the eye.

विलोचनपात, *m.* a glance of the eye, a look.

विलोटक, *m.* a certain fish (*Cupea cultrata*).

विलोडन, *m.* an agitating, whirling round, stirring, rolling, churning.

विलोड़ना, *t.* to agitate, shake, whirl round, churn.

विलोभ, *m.* allurement, attraction, temptation, seduction, delusion.

विलोभन, *m.* a beguiling, alluring, tempting, attracting, seducing, perplexing : praise.

विलोम, contrary to the grain, against the natural or usual order, reverse, opposite, contrary, backward.

विलोमक्रिया, *f.* (in Math.) an inverse operation, the rule of inversion. [verse.

विलोमत्रैराशिक, *m.* (in Math.) the rule of three in-

विलोमविधि, *m.* = **विलोमक्रिया**, *q.v.*

विलोलन = **विलोडन**, *q.v.* See **ल**, 4 (1).

विलोवना, *t.* to agitate, shake, whirl round, churn.

विल्ल, *more prop.* **विल**, *q.v.*

विल्लव (*corruption*) = **विल्व**, *q.v.*

विल्लौ ; see **विल्व**, *q.v.*

विल्व, *m.* the wood-apple tree (*Ægle marmelos*) and its fruit (commonly called *bēl*). [Balarām.

विल्वल, *m. pr. n.* a certain monkey-demon slain by

विवक्षा, *f.* desire to speak : wish, desire : a question : a clear indication.

विवक्षित, *m.* (*f.* ā) desired to be spoken or said ; wished, desired ; meant, intended, signified.

विवक्षिता, *f.* wish, purpose, intention.

विवर, *m.* separation; a hole, cavern, cave, vacuity, fissure, breach, interval, space; a vulnerable part, a wound; fault, defect. In the ingenious system of reckoning by symbols adopted by Hindoos in their poetry, this word (probably in allusion to the nine apertures of the body, and like other words of similar import) is a symbol for 9.

विवरण, *m.* an uncovering, describing, detailing, a statement, description, account, history, explanation, specification, interpretation, gloss, comment.

विवर्जन, *m.* an abandoning, leaving, shunning.

विवर्जित, *m.* (*f.* ā) left, abandoned, avoided, shunned.

विवर्ण, *m.* (*f.* ā) a person of low caste, one of degrading occupation, an outcaste: *lit.* colourless, pale; bad-coloured, changing colour; of an inferior caste, low-bred, low.

विवर्द्ध, *m.* increase, augmentation, amplification.

विवर्द्धन, 1, *adj.* growing, furthering, increasing: 2, *m.* increase, augmentation, amplification.

विवश, *m.* (*f.* ā) an uncontrolled person, etc.; *lit.* (1) deprived of will, subjected, subject, helpless, disabled, destitute (2) uncontrolled, unsubdued, unrestrained, independent; having the soul free from worldly cares and fears, sedate at the time of death, desirous of death.

विवस्त्र, *m.* (*f.* ā) destitute of clothes, uncl d, naked.

विवस्वत = **विवस्वान**, *q. v.*

विवस्वती, *f. pr. n.* the city of the sun.

विवस्वन्त = **विवस्वान**, *q. v.*

विवस्वान, *m.* the sun; Aruṇ (the charioteer of the sun): a god: *Vaivaswat* (the seventh or present Manu)

विवाक, *m.* one who decides causes, a judge.

विवाकी, *f.* the completion of a case, judgment, decision.

विवाद, *m.* contest, strife, quarrel, contention, dispute, argument, litigation, controversy: *pr. n.* the Book of Deuteronomy.

विवादक, *m.* (*f.* ikā) = **विवादी**, *q. v.*

विवादी, *m.* (*f.* inī) a party in a lawsuit, a disputant, controversialist: *lit.* contentious, disputatious, quarrelsome, litigious.

विवास, *m.* banishment, exile.

विवासन, *m.* a banishing, banishment, exile.

विवाह, *m.* marriage; a wedding, nuptial form.

विवाहना, *t.* to marry, wed.

विवाहा, *m.* (*f.* ī) = **विवाहित**, *q. v.*

विवाहि, *more prop.* (1) *m.* **विवाह** (2) *f.* **विवाही**, 2 (3) **विवाहकरके** (**विवाहना**).

विवाहित, *m.* (*f.* ā) a married person: *lit.* married.

विवाही, 1, *m.* (*f.* inī) = **विवाहित**, *q. v.*: 2, *f.* (*m.* **विवाहा**) a married female.

विवाहीय, *m.* (*f.* ā) a marriageable person: *lit.* fit to be married, requiring to be married, marriageable.

विविक्त, *m.* (*f.* ā) separated, scattered, disunited; solitary, single, alone; discriminated, cleansed, pure.

विविध, of different kinds, of many sorts, various, manifold, multiform.

विवेक, *m.* discrimination, judgment, discernment; investigation, discussion; true knowledge; aversion to the world.

विवेकता, *f.* the faulty or property of judgment, discrimination.

विवेकी, *m.* (*f.* inī) a philosopher, sage, judge: *lit.* discriminative, judicious, prudent, sensible.

विवेचक, *m.* (*f.* ikā) = **विवेकी**, *q. v.*

विवेचन, *m.* the making distinctions, discriminating truth from falsehood; discrimination, judgment, an investigation, trial; decision.

विवेचना, *f.* = **विवेचन**, *q. v.*

विशंक, *m.* (*f.* ā) fearless, undaunted, safe.

विशद, 1, white, clean, clear, pure, spotless; beautiful; apparent, evident, manifest.

विशदवाणी, *f.* clear speech, a clear beautiful voice.

विशस्त्र, *m.* (*f.* ā) disarmed, unarmed.

विशाकार, *m.* a certain plant (*Euphorbia*).

विशाखा, *f. pr. n.* the sixteenth *Naksha'ra* (figured by a festoon, and containing four stars, or, according to some, two.)

विशारद, learned, wise, skilful, conversant with; celebrated, famous, eminent; confident, bold, presuming, daring.

विशाल, *m.* (*f.* ā) great, large, broad, widely spread, extensive; illustrious, eminent.

विशालता, *f.* (*m.* °त्व) extension, breadth, expansion, bulk, magnitude, eminence, distinction.

विशिख, *m.* an arrow: an iron crow.

विशिखा, *f.* a sort of needle, a minute arrow, a pin: a spade: a highway.

विशिष्ट, *m.* (*f.* ā) having distinctive and exclusive properties, endowed with, possessed of, invested with, having; superior, preëminent, best, respectable.

विशिष्टत्व, *m.* (*f.* tā) excellence, superiority, distinction.

विशुष्क, completely dried up, very dry, withered, thirsty.

विशूचिका, *f.* cholera.

विशेष, 1, *m.* difference, distinction, peculiarity, special property, speciality, characteristic mark, a mark on the forehead; superiority, excellence; sort, kind, manner; (in Law) a special rule or distinction; (in Med.) a change for the better: 2, especial, peculiar, special, distinctive, particular; abundant; excellent: 3, especially, particularly.—*karke*, more especially.

विशेषक, *m.* (*f.* ikā) distinguishing, discriminative, characteristic, attributive.

विशेषण, discriminative, distinctive, attributive: hence, *m.* a distinguishing, distinction, an attribute, an epithet, a peculiar mark; (in Gram.) the qualifying word, *i.e.* the adjective.

विशेषता, *f.* peculiarity, speciality; abundance.

विशेषभावना, *f.* a particular or special thought; (in Math.) a certain operation in extracting roots.

विशेषवान, *m.* (*f.* vatī) possessed of some distinguishing property, peculiar, excellent, superior, better.

विशेषित, *m.* (*f.* ā) distinguished, separated; excellent.

विशेषी, *m.* (*f.* iṇī) = **विशेषक**, *q. v.*

विशेष्य, 1, what is determinable, what is to be distinguished, what requires to be described or defined; principal, primary, chief: 2, *m.* (in Gram.) a substantive: the subject of a predicate; the words or clauses that are qualified by others.

विशेष्यनिघ्न, (in Gram.) dependent on, governed by.

विशोक, free from grief or sorrow, happy.

विश्रवस / **विश्रवा** } *m. pr. n.* a certain Hindoo sage.

विश्रान्त, *m.* (*f.* ā) rested, reposed, composed, calm.

विश्रान्ति, *f.* cessation from occupation, rest, repose, ease, composure, tranquillity, cessation, pause, stop. — *lenā*, to take rest, to repose, to pass the night (used esp. by wandering fakeers).

विश्रान्तिक, *m.* (*f.* ā) appertaining to rest, imparting rest.

विश्राम, *m.* = **विश्रान्ति**, *q v.*

विश्रामघाट, *f.pr.n.* a certain wharf near Mathurā where Krishṇ on one occasion rested.

विश्रामवार, *m.* the Sabbath day.

विश्लेष, *m.* separation, disunion, disjunction, chasm.

विश्व, 1, all, every, whole, entire, universal: 2, *m.* the universe, the world: dry ginger: 3, *m. pr. n* a deity of a particular class in which ten are enumerated, *viz.* Vasu, Satya, Kratu, Daksh, Kāl, Kām, Dhriti, Kuru, Purūrav, and Madrav: they are worshipped particularly at the funeral obsequies in honour of deceased progenitors, and receive oblations of clarified butter at the daily domestic *shrāddh*: 3, in the ingenious system of reckoning by symbols adopted by Hindoos in their poetry, this word is a symbol for 13.

विश्वकर्म्मा, *m.* the sun: a saint; *pr. n.* a son of Brahmā and architect and artist of the gods.

विश्वका, *f.* a species of gull (*Larus ridibundus*).

विश्वकृत, *m.* an epithet (1) of Vishwakarmmā (2) of the Supreme Creator; *lit.* the maker of all.

विश्वजन, *m.* the human race, mankind, all men.

विश्वजनीन / **विश्वजनीय** } = **विश्वजन्य**, *q.v.*

विश्वजन्य, *m.* (*f.* ā) good for all men, universally salutary.

विश्वजित, 1, *m.* (*f.* ā) all-subduing: 2, *m.* a certain sacrifice: *pr. n.* the noose of Varuṇ.

विश्वदेव, *m.* any god of the class called **विश्व**, *q.v.*

विश्वदेवा, *f.* a plant (*Hedysarum lagopodioides*).

विश्वधारिणी, *f.* an epithet of the Earth.

विश्वधारी, *m.* an epithet of the Deity: lit. *m.* (*f.* iṇi) all-sustaining.

विश्वनाथ, *m.* an epithet of Shiv; *lit.* lord of the universe.

विश्वम्भर, *m.* an epithet (1) of Vishṇu (2) of Indra (3) of the Supreme Being; *lit.* all-sustaining.

विश्वम्भरा, *f.* an epithet of the Earth.

विश्वराज, *m.* a universal sovereign.

विश्वरूप, *m.* an epithet of Vishṇu; *lit.* whose form is the universe; existing in all forms, universal, omnipresent.

विश्वरोचन, *m.* a certain esculent root (*Arum colocasia*).

विश्ववास, 1, *m.* dwelling in or occupying the universe: 2, *adj.* whose dwellingplace is the universe, universally situated, all-pervading: *hence,* an epithet of Vishṇu.

विश्वव्यापक, permeating all things, universally diffused, all pervading, omnipresent.

विश्वव्यापी = **विश्वव्यापक**, *q.v.*

विश्वव्याप्ति, *f.* universal diffusion or permeation, omnipresence.

विश्वसन, *m.* trusting, confiding in.

विश्वसर्ज, *more com.* **विश्वसृज** *q.v.*

विश्वसारक, *m.* the prickly pear (*Costus Indicus*).

विश्वसुखद, *m.* (*f.* ā) *adj.* imparting happiness to the universe (an epithet of Rām as the source of universal happiness).

विश्वसृक / **विश्वसृज** } **विश्वसृष्टा**, *q.v.*

विश्वसृष्टा, *m.* an epithet (1) of Brahmā (2) of the Supreme Being; *lit.* the creator of the universe.

विश्वस्त, *m.* (*f.* ā) trusted, confided in, relied upon; deserving confidence, trusty, faithful, bold fearless, full of confidence.

विश्वस्तता, *f.* (*m.* °**त्व**) trustworthiness, faithfulness, boldness, fearlessness.

विश्वस्ता, *f.* (*m.* **विश्वस्त**) a widow.

विश्वा, *f.* 1, = **अतिविषा**, *q.v.*: 2, *pr.n.* a daughter of Daksh and wife of Dharm.

विश्वात्म, *m.* an epithet (1) of Vishṇu (2) of the Supreme Being; *lit.* the soul of the universe, the universal spirit.

विश्वान्तर, *m. pr. n.* a son of Sushadman.

विश्वामित्र, *m. pr. n.* a certain Hindoo sage (*muni*) originally a monarch and of the military order, who by long and painful austerities, became a Brahmarshi, in which character he appears in the Rāmāyaṇ as the early preceptor and counsellor of Rām.

विश्वास, *m.* confidence, trust, faith. —*k.* or *dharnā* or *lānā*, to place confidence in, believe in, trust.

विश्वासक, *m.* (*f.* ikā) = **विश्वासी**, *q. v.*

विश्वासकृत, *m.* (*f.* ā) a confidant: lit. *adj.* producing confidence, inspiring trust or faith.

विश्वासघात, *m.* breach of faith, violation of trust, treachery, perfidy, betrayal.

विश्वासघातक, *m.* (*f.* ikā) = **विश्वासघाती**, *q.v.*

विश्वासघाति, *f.* = **विश्वासघात**, *q. v.*

विश्वासघातिका / **विश्वासघातिनी** } *f.* a traitress, etc.

विश्वासघाती, *m.* (*f.* inī) a perfidious person, traitor: *lit.* violating confidence, treacherous, perfidious.

विश्वासपात्र, *m.* (*f.* ī) a confidential agent, a trustworthy person, a faithful one: *lit.* a vessel of confidence

विश्वासभंग, *m.* = **विश्वासघात** *q.v.*

विश्वासयोग – **विश्वासयोग्य**, *q.v.*

विश्वासयोग्य, *m.* (*f.* ā) worthy of belief of confidence, credible, trustworthy.

विश्वासार्ह, *m.* (*f.* ā) = **विश्वासयोग्य**, *q.v.* See **अर्ह**.

विश्वासिका / **विश्वासिनी** } *f.*: see (1) **विश्वासक** (2) **विश्वासी**.

विश्वासी, *m.* (*f.* inī) a believer, truster; a confidant: *lit.* possessing faith, trustful, confiding, believing, faithful, honest, trusty.

विश्वास्य, *m.* (*f.* ā) = **विश्वासयोग्य**, *q.v.*

विश्वेदेव; see (1) **विश्वेदेवा** (2) **विश्वदेव**.

विश्वेदेवा, *m.* (pl.: see **श्रा**, 22) the Vishwadevas.

विश्वेश्वर, *m.pr.n.* an epithet of Shiv ; *lit.* lord of the universe. He is especially worshipped under this appellation at Benares where a temple is appropriated to him under his title of universal lord.

विष, 1, *m.* poison, venom (*met.* the word is sometimes applied to bitter things in general) : water : the film or fibres attached to the stalk of the water-lily: 2, *f.* excrement.

विषकन्या; see **विश्वकर्मा**.

विषकपः; see **विषखपरा** and **विषखोपरा**.

विषकीट, *m.* (*f.* ī) a certain insect that lives in (and subsists on) poison.

विषखपरा, *m.* a certain medicinal plant (*Trianthema petandra*).

विषखोपरा, *m.* a species of lizard (*Lacerta iguana*). about a yard long and said to be venomous.

विषग्रस्त, *m.* (*f.* ā) having taken poison, under the influence of any poison.

विषघाती, *m.* an antidote ; a certain tree (*Mimosa sirisa*) : lit. *m.* (*f.* inī) destroying or counteracting poison, antidotal.

विषघ्नि, *m.* a species of snake.

विषद, 1, *adj.* poison-giving ; water-shedding : 2, *m.* a cloud : green vitriol. [venomous. poisonous.

विषधर, *m.* (*f.* ā) a snake : *lit.* retaining poison,

विषनाशक, *m.* (*f.* ikā)
विषनाशन, *m.* (*f.* ā)
विषनाशी, *m.* (*f.* inī) } = **विषघाती**, *q.v.*

विषबटी, *more prop.* **विषवटी**, *q.v.*

विषभक्षण, *m.* taking poison.

विषभुजंग, *m.* (*f.* ī) any venomous snake.

विषम, 1, *m.* (*f.* ā) unequal, different, inconstant, (in numbers) odd, uneven, rough, difficult of access, hard to be comprehended, fearful, frightful, awful, bad, afflictive, disagreeable, dishonest, wicked, partial: hence, 2, *m.* unevenness, inequality, an inaccessible place, a precipice, thicket, pit, difficulty, misfortune, pain. [remittent fever.

विषमज्वर, *m.* high or violent fever ; irregularly

विषमता, *f.* (*m.* °त्व) = **विषम**, 2, *q.v.*

विषमत्रिभुज, *m.* (in Geom.) a scalene triangle.

विषमन्त्र, *m.* a snake-charmer, snake-catcher ; a charm for curing snake-bites.

विषमय, *m.* (*f.* ī) abounding in venom, poisonous.

विषमबान, *m.* a barbed arrow.

विषमवृत्त, *m.* (in Pros.) a species of metre in which the four feet are dissimilar. [ness.

विषमसाहस, *m.* temerity, rashness, daring, bold-

विषमान, *m.* a certain plant (*Arum cucullatum* or *Arum cordifolium*).

विषमिश्रित, *m.* (*f.* ā) mixed with poison.

विषय, 1, *m.* anything perceivable by the senses (as colour, form, flavour, odour, sound), an object (as of affection, desire, etc.), a worldly object or pursuit (as an affair, matter, thing, business, transaction): 2, (sc. *meṅ*) in the matter of, in relation to, in regard to, concerning, about. In the ingenious system of reckoning by symbols adopted by Hindoos in their poetry, this word (in allusion to the five classes of objects cognizable by the senses, and like other words of similar import) is a symbol for 5.

विषयक, *m.* (*f.* ā) relating to an object, (at the end of compounds) having for an object or subject, relating to, having reference to, on the subject of, treating of, concerning. [sual objects.

विषयभोग, *m.* the enjoyment of material or sen-

विषयासक्त, *m.* (*f.* ā) attached to objects of sense, devoted to the world, worldly.

विषयी, *m.* (*f.* iṇī) a person engaged in worldly pursuits, a man of business or of the world, a sensualist, epicurean, voluptuary, materialist, an epithet (1) of any king (2) of Kāmdev : *lit.* appertaining to sensual objects, carnal, sensual, worldly.

विषवटि, *m.*
विषवटी, *f.* } a ball or pill of poison.

विषवत, *m.* (*f.* ī) like poison ; possessing poison, poisonous.

विषविद्या, *f.* the science of the administration of antidotes, the cure of poison by drugs or by charms.

विषवैद्य, *m.* a dealer in antidotes, one who professes to cure snakebites.

विषसा, *m.* (*f.* ī) like poison.

विषसूचक, *m.* the Greek partridge (*Perdix rufa*).

विषहर, *m.* (*f.* ī) antidotal : an antidote.

विषहरा (or °री), *f. pr. n.* the sister of Vāsuki and wife of Jaratkāru and goddess of the serpent-race.

विषहा, *m.* (*f.* ī) venomous (said of reptiles).

विषहृदय, *m.* (*f.* ā) a person who cherishes hatred or hostility : *lit* poison-hearted, malignant, malicious.

विषाण, *m.* 1, the horn of any animal, the tusk of an elephant or of a boar : 2, a certain plant (*Costus speciosus*).

विषाणी, 1, *f.* = **विषाण**, 1, *q. v.* : 2, *m.* (*f.* inī) any horned animal, a bull, an elephant : *lit.* horned.

विषाद, *m.* lassitude, dejection, want of energy, fear, weakness, distress, affliction, sorrow, disappointment, despair.

विषादी, *m* (*f.* inī) dejected, disconsolate, sorrowful ; causing dejection, distressing.

विषाना ; see **बिसाना**.

विषापह, 1, *m.* (*f.* ā) antidotal : 2, *m.* an antidote.

विषापहा, *f.* a kind of birth-wort (*Aristolochia Indica*).

विषालु, venomous, poisonous.

विषाशा, *m.* (*f.* ī) desirous of poison.

विषास्य, *m.* (*f.* ā) an epithet of the snake ; *lit.* poison-mouthed. [*anacurdium*).

विषास्या, *f.* the marking-nut plant (*Semicarpus*

विषिधर, venomous, poisonous.

विषिष्ट (*corruption*) = **विशिष्ट**, *q. v.*

विषी, *m.* (*f.* iṇī) venomous, poisonous.

विषुप
विषुव } *m. pr. n.* the equinox.

विषुवकाल, *m.* the time of the equinox.

विषुवच्छाया, *f.* the shadow of the gnomon at noon when the sun is on the equinox.

विषुवत, *m. pr. n.* the equinox.

विषुवतरेखा, *f. pr. n.* the equinoctial line.

विषुवदिन, *m.* the day of the equinox.

विषैला, *m.* (*f.* ī) venomous, poisonous.

विषै, *more prop.* **विषय**, *q. v.*

विषौषधी, *f.* any antidote to poison.

विष्टम्भ, *m.* an obstacle, a stopping; paralysis, loss of motion; obstruction of urine or of fœces, ischury, constipation.

विष्टर, *m.* a handful of sacred grass (*Poa cynosuroides*); a seat made of a sheet of such grass for the Brāhmaṇ who officiates at a sacrifice; a tree; a layer, couch, seat, bed.

विष्टा, *f.* ordure, fœces, excrement.

विष्टि, *f.* working, labour, occupation; unpaid labour; act, action: a sending; a consigning to hell-torments after death: *pr. n.* the seventh of the variable astronomical periods called Karaṇ.

विष्टो } **विष्ठो** } (*corruptions*) = **विष्टि**, *q. v.*

विष्ठा, *f.* ordure, fœces, excrement.

विष्णु, *m. pr. n.* one of the persons of the Hindoo triad, or the Deity in his character of Preserver. The various incarnations (*avatār*) are considered as manifestations of this deity, while in Krishṇ he is believed to have been really and wholly incarnate. Vishṇu is the husband of Lakshmī, and is usually represented as a mild and benevolent deity. The name is also applied (1) to Agni (2) to one of the Vasus (3) to a certain ancient lawgiver.

विष्णुक्रान्ता, *f.* a flower (*Clitorea ternatea*).

विष्णुज्वर, *m.* ague.

विष्णुदार, *f.* (the wife of Vishṇu, *i.e.*) Mahā-Lakshmī.

विष्णुपद, *m.* the atmosphere, sky, heaven; the sea of milk; a lotus.

विष्णुपदी, *f. pr. n.* (1) of one of the twelve periods (*saṅkrānti*) at which the sun enters a sign of the zodiac esp. the first sign after the equinox (2) the sun's entrance into Taurus, Leo, Scorpio, or Aquarius (3) an epithet of the Ganges

विष्णुपुराण, *m. pr. n.* (see **पुराण**) one of the eighteen Purāṇs of Hindoos. [in the name of Vishṇu.

विष्णुप्रीत, 1, = **विष्णूत्तर**, *q. v.*: 2, *m.* a certain song

विष्णुप्रीतदार, *m.* a class of Brāhmaṇs to whom have been assigned grants of land in the name of Vishṇu.

विष्णुप्रीति, *f.* = **विष्णूत्तर**, *q. v.*

विष्णुभक्त, *m.* (*f.* ā) a worshipper of Vishṇu.

विष्णुभगवान, *m.* an epithet of Vishṇu.

विष्णुमय, *m.* (*f.* ī) emanated from Vishṇu, abounding in or permeated by Vishṇu.

विष्णुवल्लभा, *f.* a certain fragrant plant (*Echites caryophyllata*); a certain small fragrant shrub (*Ocymum sanctum*).

विष्णुवी, *more prop.* **वैष्णव**, *q v.*

विष्णुशर्मा, *m. pr. n.* (1) of a certain leader of the sect of the Bhattas (2) of the author of the *Panchtantra* (3) of a certain scribe.

विष्णूत्तर, *m.* a grant of rent-free lands to Brāhmaṇs in honour of Vishṇu or to maintain his worship.

विस, 1, in Braj = **उस**, *q. v.*: 2, *m.* the film or fibres of the stalk of the water lily.

विसद, *more prop.* **विशद**, *q. v.*

विसराना, *more com.* **बिसराना**, *q. v.*

विसर्ग, *m.* dereliction, abandoning, separation, dismission, departure; evacuation; final emancipation; a donation; light, lustre; (in Gram.) the sign: *q. v.*

विसर्गसन्धि, *f.* (in Gram.) the union of *visarg* with a vowel and a consonant (according to special rules) for the formation of a compound letter.

विसर्ज्जन, *m.* a relinquishing, sending away, dismissing; an offering, a donation; the throwing the image of a deity into holy-water as the concluding rite of a festival.

विसा; for words beginning thus, see under the form **विशा**.

विसे in Braj = **उसे**, *q. v.* See **विस**.

विसेश, **विसेष**; for words beginning with either of these elements, see under the form **विशेष**.

विस्तर, *m.* spreading, extension, prolixity; detail; abundance; a large company, assemblage, multitude; a bed, a seat.

विस्तार, *m.* spreading, extension, diffusion, vastness, expanse, length, breadth, amplitude, copiousness, abundance; (in Math.) the diameter of a circle; the branch of a tree with its new shoots; a shrub.

विस्तारक, *m.* (*f.* ikā) = **विस्तारी**, *q. v.*

विस्तारना, *t.* to extend, spread out, diffuse.

विस्तारपूर्व्वक, in detail, at length, fully.

विस्तारित, *m.* (*f.* ā) = **विस्तीर्ण**, *q. v.*

विस्तारी, *m.* (*f.* inī) *adj.* spreading, expanding, enlarging, amplifying, dwelling upon at length, explaining in detail.

विस्तीर्ण, *m.* (*f.* ā) spread, extended, expanded, diffused; large, great, vast.

विस्तृत, *m.* (*f.* ā) = **विस्तीर्ण**, *q. v.*

विस्तृतता, *f.* (*m.* °त्व) diffusedness, amplitude, largeness, extensiveness.

विस्तृति, *f.* spreading, expansion, breadth, width, extent; (in Math.) the diameter of a circle.

विस्व; for words beginning thus, see under the form **विश्व**.

विस्पष्ट, *m.* (*f.* ā) apparent, evident, manifest, open, clear, plain, intelligible.

विस्फोट, *m.* a boil, a pustule; small-pox.

विस्फोटक, *m.* } **विस्फोटा**, *f.* } **विस्फोड़ा**, *f.* } = **विस्फोट**, *q. v.*

विस्मय, *m.* surprize, amazement, wonder, disconcertedness, perplexity, uncertainty, doubt, dismay, pride.

विस्मयान्वित } **विस्मयापन्न** } *m.* (*f.* ā) = **विस्मयी**, *q. v.*

विस्मयी, *m.* (*f.* inī) amazed, taken by surprize, astonished, disconcerted, afraid, dismayed.

विस्मरण, *m.* forgetting, obliviousness.

विस्मित, *m.* (*f.* ā) = **विस्मयी**, *q. v.*

विस्मृत, *m.* (*f.* ā) forgotten.

विस्मृति, *f.* obliviousness, forgetting.

विस्र, विस्व; for words beginning thus, but not given below, see under the forms **विश्र, विश्व,** respectively.

विस्र, *m.* a smell like that of raw meat.

विस्रा, *f.* the substance called *hapushā*, which smells like raw meat.

विस्वर, inharmonious, discordant.

विस्वा; for words beginning thus, but not given below, see under the form **विश्वा.**

विस्वाद, 1. *m.* tastelessness, insipidity: 2, tasteless, insipid.

विहंग / **विहंगम** } *m.* (*f.* ā) = **विहग**, *q.v.*

विहंगमा, *f.* a pole for carrying burdens.

विहंगराज, *m.* the king of birds } *i. e.* Garuḍ.
विहंगवर, *m.* the best of birds }

विहंगिका, *f.* a pole for carrying burdens.

विहग, *m.* (*f.* ā) a bird, a cloud, an arrow, the sun, the moon, a planet: lit. *adj.* going or moving in the sky or air.

विहरण, *m.* a taking off, taking away: a going about for pleasure or exercise, a roaming, walk, airing, pastime, pleasure.

विहरना, *a.int.* to rejoice, enjoy pleasure: *t.* to take pleasure in, enjoy; to rejoice, delight.

विहवल, *more prop.* **विह्वल**, *q. v.*

विहसना, *a. int.* to smile, to laugh.

विहाग, *m.* (in Pros.) a species of metre.

विहाना, *more prop.* **बिहाना**, *q. v.*

विहाय, *more prop.* **बिहाय**, *q. v*

विहायस, *m.* the open air, sky, atmosphere, heavens; a bird.

विहार, *m.* wandering, roaming about, walk for pleasure; play, sport, pastime, recreation, amusement, diversion: a temple; a palace: the shoulder: a sort of bird: a Bauddh or Jain convent: *pr. n.* a certain province in northern India. —*k.* to roam about, enjoy oneself.

विहारस्थल, *m.* any place of amusement or pleasure.

विहारी, 1, *m.* (*f.* iṇī) *adj.* roaming about for pleasure; sportive; beautiful: 2, *m. pr. n.* a certain Hindoo poet: 3 *m.* an epithet of Krishṇ.

विहित, *m.* (*f.* ā) arranged, established, instituted, prescribed, proper, fit.

विहीन, *m* (*f.* ā) abandoned, relinquished, deserted, destitute of, deprived of.

विह्वल, (*f.* ā) agitated, overcome with fear (or grief or passion), alarmed, beside oneself, infatuated, delirious; fused; languishing; desponding.

विह्वलता, *f.* (*m.* °**त्व**) agitation, consternation, perturbation, anxiety.

वी, 1, a Kridanta suffix *fem.*; see **वि**, II: 2, *f.* [*m.* **वि** III, (2)] a female bird: 3, *f.* a going: 4, an adjectival suffix (*m.* [*f.* **विनी**]) of frequent occurrence in Hindee; *e. g.* **तेजस्वी**, etc.

वीं; the distinctive termination of the fem. form of ordinals (see **वां**, 2) from **पांचवां** upwards. The same form is used in all the cases; *e g.* **पांचवीं स्त्री**, the fifth woman: **दशवीं पुस्तकमें**, in the tenth book.

वीचि, 1, *m. f.* a wave: a ray of light: leisure; pleasure: 2, small, little.

वीची, *f.* = **वीचि**, *q. v.*

वीज, *m.* seed, grain, germ, spermum genitale (viri aut mulieris): primary cause, source, origin: algebra, analysis. — *bonā*, to sow.

वीजकोश, *m.* a pericarpium, seed-vessel.

वीजकोशी, *f.* a legume, pod.

वीजखाद, advance of seed and food to agriculturists.

वीजगणित, *m.* Algebra; *pr. n.* a certain ancient Hindoo work on Algebra; *lit.* elemental arithmetic.

वीजन, *m.* a being fanned; a fan; a sort of pheasant; the ruddy goose: a thing.

वीजनमार, *m.* failure of germination.

वीजाक्षर, *m.* the first syllable of a magical formula, the syllable at the commencement of a *mantra* or form of prayer.

वीजी, *m.* (*f.* inī) a sower; a parent, father, progenitor: lit. *adj.* having seed, sowing seed.

वीटिका, *f.* the betel-plant (*Piper betel*); the preparation (commonly called *pān*) of the areca-nut with spices and chunam and folded in the leaf of the betel-plant.

वीण, *f.* a contraction of **वीणा**, *q. v.*

वीणा, the Indian lute. It is a fretted instrument of the guitar kind usually having seven wires or strings and a large gourd at each end of the finger-board. The extent of the instrument is two octaves. It is supposed to be the invention of Nārad the son of Brahmā, and has many varieties which are enumerated according to the number of strings, etc.

वीणाकरण, *m. pr. n.* one of the Gandharvs.

वीथि, *f.* a row, line; a road; a terrace in front of a house; a stall, shop; a kind of drama: 2, a certain division of the planetary sphere (comprising three asterisms).

वीथी, *f.* = **वीथि**, 1, *q. v.*

वीधेय; see **विधेय.**

वीना, 1, = **बीना**, *q. v.*: 2, *m.* a bundle of thread, a skein.

वीय, an old form of **वीर्य्य**, *q. v.*

वीर, heroic, brave, valiant; strong, powerful, mighty; eminent, excellent: hence, (1) *m.* (*f.* ā) a brave person, hero, champion, soldier: a mime, actor (2) *m.* heroic sentiment: fire; sacrificial fire.

वीरता, *f.* (*m.* °**त्व**) heroism, valour, prowess, bravery, boldness, manliness.

वीरपुर, *m.* this word is a common proper name of Hindoo cities.

वीरभद्र, *m.* (*f.* ā) a renowned or distinguished warrior or hero: a sacrificial horse.

वीररस, *m.* heroic principle or sentiment.

वीरसिंह, *m. pr. n.* (1) of a certain king of Gūrjar (2) of the author of the *Durgābhaktitaranginī*.

वीरसेन, *m. pr. n.* the father of Nal (*lit.* having an army of heroes).

वीरसेव, *f.* hero-worship.

वीरा, *f.* (*m.* **वीर**) a heroine; a matron, a wife and mother: the plantain-tree: the name of several plants.

वीर्य्य, *m.* strength, power, vigour, fortitude, heroism, dignity, splendour; semen virile; seed.

वीर्य्यवान, *m.* (*f.* vati) stout, strong, robust, firm, heroic, energetic, illustrious, victorious.

वीर्य्यदान, *m.* the bestowal of semen. The allusion is to a certain ceremony among Hindoos, *viz.* when a husband of either of the three subordinate castes is either dead or in a distant part of the country, and the wife has not as yet borne a male child, the *purohit* of that household performs the office.

वीर्य्यविरहित, *m.* (*f.* ā) destitute of power or vigour.

वीर्य्यविशिष्ट, *m.* (*f.* ā) possessed of power or vigour.

वीर्य्यहानि, *f.* loss of vigour or courage, impotence.

वीर्य्यहीन, *m.* (*f.* ā) destitute of power or vigour, spiritless, cowardly; seedless.

वीवाह, in Chand = **ब्याह** = **बियाह**, *q. v.*

वुहीं, *more prop.* **वहीं**, *q. v.*

वुतना, *m.* (*f.* ī) in Braj = **उतना**, *q. v.*

वुह; for words beginning thus, see under the more [common form **वह**.

वूं = **वों**, *q. v.*

वूंहीं, *more prop.* (1) **वहीं** (2) **वोंहीं**, *qq. v.*

वृक, *m.* (*f.* ī) a wolf, a hyæna, a jackal, a crow: *pr. n.* (1) of a certain Asur (2) of a son of a Prithu (3) of a son of Vijay (4) of a son of Krishṇ.

वृकासुरवध, *m.* the killing of the *asur* Vṛik (name of the 96th chapter of the Krīḍā-khaṇḍ of the Gaṇesh Purāṇ).

वृक्ष, *m.* a tree (in general).

वृक्षक, *m.* a tree (in general): a certain tree (*Wrightea antidysenterica*).

वृक्षकेतु, *more prop.* **वृषकेतु**, *q. v.*

वृक्षचर, *m.* (*f.* ā *or* ī) a monkey.

वृक्षछाया, *f.* the shade of a tree or wood sylvan [shades.

वृक्षधूप, *m.* turpentine.

वृक्षनाथ, *m.* the Indian figtree.

वृक्षभिद, *f.* an axe.

वृक्षमय, *m.* (*f.* ī) abounding in trees.

वृक्षरोपण, *m.* tree-planting.

वृक्षादिक, (trees, etc.; *i.e.*) all things in the vegetable and animal kingdoms.

वृक्षादिविद्या, *f.* the science of botany.

वृख; for words beginning thus, see under the form [**वृष**.

वृज, a provincial form of **व्रज**, *q. v.*

वृजि, *f.* a provincial form of **व्रज**, *q. v.*

वृति, *f* selection, choice, appointment: a request: an enclosure, hedge; an enclosed piece of ground.

वृत्त, 1, existed, been, past, gone, finished, dead: chosen, appointed: covered: 2, *m* conduct, behaviour, practice, livelihood, profession: verse, metre: a circle.

वृत्तखण्ड, *m.* a segment of a circle.

वृतमान, *more prop.* **वर्त्तमान**, *q. v.*

वृत्तसूचक, *m.* (*f.* ikā) an explainer of **वृत्त**, *q. v.*

वृत्तान्त, *m.* an occurrence, event, fact; tidings, report, rumour, intelligence; a tale, story, narrative; topic, subject: opportunity: sort, kind: difference.

वृत्तान्तपत्र, *m.* any document containing a statement of events, a newspaper, a report.

वृत्तासुर, a corruption of **वृत्रासुर**, *q. v.*

वृत्ति, *f.* state, condition, existence; means of acquiring a subsistence, livelihood, possession; a pension: the circumference of a circle.

वृत्रासुर, *m. pr. n.* a certain demon slain by Indra.

वृथा, to no purpose, in vain, uselessly, fruitlessly, foolishly, wrongly, inaccurately.

वृथादान, *m.* an improper gift (*i. e.* one that may be annulled), an unprofitable donation, money lost in gaming or given to harlots.

वृथावाद, *m.* idle or fruitless talk.

वृद्ध, old, aged, ancient; wise, learned: hence *m.* (*f.* ā) an old person, one past the age of seventy; a sage; a respectable person.

वृद्धता, *f.* (*m.* °**त्व**) old age, senility, ancientness.

वृद्धसा, *m.* (*f.* ī) oldish, elderly. See **सा**.

वृद्धसेवा, *f.* reverence for old age.

वृद्धस्रवा, *adj.* having great glory: endowed with much food: an epithet of Indra.

वृद्धा, *f.* (*m.* **वृद्ध**) an old woman.

वृद्धापन, *m.* the condition of old age, agedness.

वृद्धावस्था, *f.* the condition or the period of old age agedness.

वृद्धि, *f.* augmentation (in bulk, in importance, in power, in wealth, etc.); an ascending, rise, increase; prosperity, success, usury; profit; a heap, quantity, multitude; a cutting off; (in Law) forfeiture; (in Astron.) the eleventh astronomical *yog*, or (2) the principal star of the eleventh lunar asterism (3) the increase of the digits of the sun or moon; (in Gram.) a peculiar protraction to which vowels are subject under certain conditions; (in Med.) enlargement of the scrotum.

वृद्धिवान, *m.* (*f.* vatī) augmented, increasing, [prosperous, wealthy, rich.

वृद्धिमन्त }
वृद्धिमान } *m.* (*f.* matī) = **वृद्धिवान**, *q. v.*

वृद्धिश्राद्ध, *m.* an offering or sacrifice made to departed ancestors on an occasion of prosperity (as at the birth of a son, etc.).

वृन्द, *m.* a heap, quantity, assemblage, multitude.

वृन्दस्रवा, a corruption of **वृद्धस्रवा**, *q. v.*

वृन्दा, *f.* 1, holy basil (*Ocymum sanctum*): 2, *pr. n.* a certain forest in which Krishṇ was educated.

वृन्दादेवी, *f. pr. n.* a certain goddess.

वृन्दावन, *m. pr. n.* = **वृन्दा**, 2, *q. v.*

वृन्दावनधाम, *m.* an epithet of the forest Vṛindā.

वृन्दावनवासी, *m.* (*f.* inī) an inhabitant of Vrindāvan.

वृन्दावनविहारी, *m.* an epithet of Krishṇ.

वृन्दाविपिन, *m. pr. n.* = **वृन्दा**, 2, *q. v.*

वृश्चिक, *m.* a scorpion, a caterpillar; a crab; a centipede; a kind of beetle; *pr. n.* (in Astron.) the sign Scorpio.

वृष, *m.* a bull, a rat; a peacock's tail; *pr. n.* (in Astron.) the sign Taurus.

वृषकेतु, *m.* an epithet (1) of the sign Taurus (2) of Mahādev.

वृषध्वज, *m.* an epithet of Shiv; *lit.* whose banner or emblem is a bull.

वृषपर्वा, *m. pr. n.* a certain demon-king (father of Sharmishṭhā).

वृषभ, *m.* a bull: the orifice of the ear: an elephant's ear: *in comp.*, *m.* (*f.* ī) principal, chief, excellent, best.

वृषभान = **वृषभानु**, *q. v.*

वृषभानु, *m. pr. n.* the son of Sūrbhānu and father of Rādhā.

वृषभानुकन्या } *f.* epithets of Rādhā.
वृषभानुसुता }

वृषभी, *f.* (see **वृषभ**) a widow.

वृषम, *more prop.* (1) **विषम** (2) **वृषभ**, *qq. v.*

वृषल, *m.* (*f.* ī) a person of low origin, one who by the neglect of his religious duties has lost his caste, a Shūdra, a sinner: a horse : garlic.

वृषली, *f.* (*m.* **वृषल**) a Shūdra female ; a woman during menstruation: a barren woman.

वृषा, 1, *m.* an epithet of Indra : *lit.* he who rains : 2, *f.* a certain plant (*Salvinia cucullata*).

वृषाकपायी, *f.* an epithet (1) of Lakshmī (2) of Gauri (3) of Swahā, wife of Agni (4) of Sachi, wife of Indra. [(2) of Shiv (3) of Agni.

वृषाकपि, *m.* an epithet (1) of Vishṇu or Krishṇ

वृषासुर, *m.* a certain demon (*asur*).

वृषोत्सर्ग, *m.* the setting a bull at liberty on the occasion of a sacrifice or obsequial oblation.

वृष्टि, *f.* rain ; a shower.

वृष्टिकाल, *m.* the rainy-season.

वृष्णि, *m.* an epithet (1) of Krishṇ (2) of Indra (3) of Angi : *pr. n.* a certain descendant of Yadu and ancestor of Krishṇ.

वृष्णिवंशी, *m.* (*f.* inī) a certain tribe or family, descendants of Vrishṇi and relations of Krishṇ : a certain class of Kshatriyas and Vaishyas.

वृहज्जन, *m.* (*f.* ā) a great or illustrious personage, [a celebrity.

वृहत, *m.* (*f.* ī) large, great ; much.

वृहतक्षत्र, *m. pr. n.* a certain king.

वृहतचैत्र, *m.* 1, *pr. n.* a certain ancient Hindoo king : 2, an epithet of Prayāg (*Tirthrāj*).

वृहती, *f.* a wrapper ; a mantle ; a reservoir, a large lute ; the name of two plants. [a miracle.

वृहत्कर्म्म, *m.* a weighty business, a great work,

वृहद्गृह, *m. pr. n.* a certain country lying behind the Vindhya mountains near the province of Mālwa.

वृहद्भानु, *m.* an epithet of Agni : *pr. n.* (1) of a son of Sattrāyan and a manifestation of Vishṇu (2) of a son of Krishṇ (3) of a certain king.

वृहद्बल, *m. pr. n.* (1) of a certain king of Koshal (2) of another king, son of Devbhāg.

वृहद्रथ, *m. pr. n.* a certain ancient Hindoo king.

वृहद्धर्मा, *m. pr. n.* a certain ancient Hindoo king.

वृहद्धल, *m.* (**वृहत + हल**) a large plough.

वृहन } *m.* (*f.* **वृहती**) = **वृहत**, *q. v.*
वृहन्त }

वृहन्नारदीय, *m. pr. n.* (see **पुराण**) one of the eighteen Purāṇs (*prop.* the large Nāradiya).

वृहस्पति, *m. pr. n.* (1) of a certain deity originally the lord of prayer (2) of the regent of the planet Jupiter : astronomically, he is identified with the planet, and in mythology, he is the preceptor of the gods (3) of a certain ancient sage and lawgiver (4) of Thursday.

वृहस्पतिचक्र, *m.* the cycle of sixty years.

वृहस्पतिवार, *m.* Thursday.

वृहस्पतिस्मृति, *f.* the law-book of Vrihaspati (said to be classed among the Tāmas-works).

वे, 1, *m. f.* (nom. pl. of **वह** or **वुह**) they: 2, like **वें** 2, this element sometimes terminates adverbial ordinals ; *e. g.* **आठवे**, in the eighth place, eighthly; 3, this element is often found as the distinctive termination of the 2nd and 3rd persons sing. of the aor. of verbs whose base ends in a long vowel ; *e. g.* **पावे, देवे, होवे**, etc. : 3, the inflection of the Braj termination **वेा** ; *e. g* **राखिवेको** in Braj = **राखनेको**.

वेऊ in Braj = **वे भो**. See **ऊ**, 7.

वें, 1, the distinctive termination of ordinals masculine (see **वां**, 2) in all cases excepting the nom. sing. from **पांचवां** upwards; *e. g.* **पांचवें पुरुषको**, to (as far as) the fifth man: 2, like **वे**, this element sometimes terminates adverbial ordinals ; *e. g.* **दसवें**, in the tenth place, tenthly : 3, this element is often found as the distinctive termination of all persons of the plural of verbs whose root ends in a long vowel ; *e. g.* **लावें, लेवें, बोवें**.

वेकट, *m.* a sort of fish (perhaps the common [*Bhektī*).

वेख (*colloquial*) = **वेष**, *q. v.*

वेग, 1, *m.* speed, despatch, velocity, celerity, haste, rapidity ; the current of water; impetus; impulse; evacuation; semen virile: 2, quickly, with haste, soon.

वेगवत, 1, *m.* (*f.* vatī) swift, rapid, fleet, impetuous, quick : 2, quickly, rapidly, speedily.

वेगवती, *f.* (in Pros.) a species of metre.

वेगवन्त } *m.* (*f.* vatī) = **वेगवत**, *q. v.*
वेगवान }

वेगाना, *more prop.* **बेगाना**, *q. v.*

वेगि, *adv.* quickly, with haste, soon, speedily.

वेगिता, *f.* rapidity, quickness, speed.

वेगिनी, *f.* (*m.* **वेगी**) a river.

वेगी, 1, *m.* (*f.* ini) a courier, an express ; a hawk: *lit.* speedy, rapid, fleet, swift, quick: 2, rapidly, quickly, speedily. [idol at Prayāg.

वेणिमाधव, *m. pr. n.* the large square-shaped stone

वेणी, *f.* 1, *pr. n.* = **त्रिवेणी**, *q. v.*: 2, unornamented hair (braided in a single braid and falling down the back like a tail, as worn by widows and by women whose husbands are absent): an assemblage of waters, the conflux of rivers.

वेणीलाल, *m.* an epithet of Krishṇ.

वेणु, *m.* a bamboo, a reed ; a flute, pipe, fife : *pr. n.* a [son of king Ang.

वेणुवाद्य, *m.* a player on a flute.

वेतन, *m.* hire, wages, pittance, reward: profession, livelihood: silver.

वेतना, *m.* (*f.* ī) in Braj = **उतना**, *q. v.*

वेतनादान, *m.* non-payment of wages.

वेतस, *m.* the ratan (*Calamus rotang*) ; the citron.

वेता, *m.* (*f.* ī) an old form = **उतना**, *q. v.*

वेताल, *m.* a goblin (esp. one that is supposed to haunt cemeteries and animate corpses); a dead body so occupied.

वेतौर, 1, see **बेठौर**: 2, (in Pros.) a species of metre.

वेत्ता, *m.* (*f.* tri) a sage, wise man, one who understands the nature of the soul and of God: *lit.* acquainted with, understanding, knowing.

वेत्र, *m.* the ratan (*Calamus rotang*) a reed, cane, staff, the staff of a doorkeeper. [keeper.

वेत्रधर, *m.* (*f.* ā) a staff-bearer, mace-bearer, door-

वेत्रवती, *f. pr. n.* a certain river which rising in the province of Mālwa falls into the Yamunā near Kalpi after a north-easterly course of about 340 miles.

वेद, *m.* knowledge, science, learning. The term is applied specially to the sacred scriptures of the Hindoos. The original Ved is believed to have been revealed by Brahmā, and to have been preserved by tradition until it was arranged in its present order by a certain sage, who thence obtained the surname of Vyās or Vedavyās, *i. e.* compiler of the Veds. He distributed the sacred writings into four parts, *viz.* (1) the Rig-Ved (2) the Yajush (*or* Yajur)-Ved (3) the Sām-Ved (4) the Atharva-Ved. The ancient history (*Itihās*) and the Purāṇs or mythological works are sometimes considered as a fifth Ved.

वेदक्रिया, *f.* the religious ceremonies enjoined in the Vedic writings. [struction or testimony).

वेदगिरा, *f.* the voice of the Veds (*i.e.* divine in-

वेदज्ञ, *m.* (*f.* ā) a person who knows the Veds, a learned person (esp. a Brāhmaṇ): *lit.* skilled in the knowledge of the Veds. [Veds.

वेदतत्त्व, *m.* the true doctrine (or essence) of the

वेदन, *m.* perception, knowledge, knowledge conveyed by the senses; pain, smart, ache, agony, torment, affliction, sickness, distress.

वेदनर्म, *m.* jest contained in the Veds, jest concerning the Veds, desecration or abuse of religious

वेदना, *f.* = **वेदन**, *q. v.* [things.

वेदपाठ, *m.* the study or recital of the Veds.

वेदपुण्य, *m.* the sanctity of the Veds.

वेदमग (*Rām.*) = **वेदमार्ग**, *q. v.*

वेदमाता, *f.* an epithet of the Gāyatrī personified as the source of the Veds, a sort of mystical prayer.

वेदमार्ग, *m.* the religion of the Veds.

वेदलभ्य, *m.* (*f.* ā) obtainable through the Veds.

वेदविद्वान, *m.* (*f.* vatī) a person who is learned in the Veds: lit. *adj.* knowing the Veds.

वेदव्यास, *m. pr. n.* (see **वेद** and **व्यास**) a certain ancient Hindoo sage the supposed compiler and arranger of the Veds. [tural, orthodox.

वेदसंमत, *m.* (*f.* ā) conformable to the Veds, scrip-

वेदांग, *m. pr. n.* the general term applied to the six auxiliary or subordinate branches of the Veds, *viz.* (1) *Shikshā*, or the rules of pronunciation and recital (2) *Kalp*, or the details of religious ceremonies (3) *Vyākaran*, or grammar (4) *Chhand*, or prosody (5) *Nirukti*, or the explanation of difficult, obscure, or obsolete words that occur in the Veds (6) *Jyotish*, or astronomy.

वेदानुक्रमणिका, *f.* an epitome of a Ved, a table of the

वेदानुक्रमणी = **वेदानुक्रमणिका**, *q. v.* [contents of a Ved.

वेदान्त, *m. pr. n.* (1) of the complete Ved (2) of a certain system of philosophy and theology based particularly on the Upanishads (3) of works concerning this philosophy and in support of it.

वेदान्तखण्डन, *m.* the opposition or refutation of the Vedāntic system of philosophy.

वेदान्तग
वेदान्तज्ञ } *m.* (*f.* ā) = **वेदान्ती**, *q. v.*

वेदान्ती, *m.* (*f.* inī) a follower of the Vedānt philosophy. [tion of the sacred syllable Ōm.

वेदाभ्यास, *m.* the study of the Veds; the repeti-

वेदार्थ, *m.* the meaning or sense of the Veds.

वेदासंमत, *m.* (*f.* ā) contrary to the Veds, unscriptural, unorthodox.

वेदि, *f.* a place or ground prepared for sacrifice, a purified place, an altar; a quadrangular spot in the courtyard of a temple or palace, usually furnished with a raised floor or seat and covered with a roof supported by pillars; a stool, bench, seat: a seal-ring: an epithet of Saraswatī.

वेदिका, *f.* ground prepared for sacrificial ceremonies; a rude altar; a quadrangular open shed in the middle of a courtyard, erected for various purposes and furnished with a seat.

वेदी, 1, *f.* = **वेदि**, *q. v.*: 2, *m.* (*f.* inī) a Brāhmaṇ, a learned Brāhmaṇ a scholar, teacher: *lit.* acquainted with, knowing. [or said in the Veds, scriptural.

वेदोक्त, *m.* (*f.* ā) sanctioned by holy writ, taught

वेध, *m.* a piercing or breaking through, perforation, excavation, depth, hole, bore, crack.

वेधक, *m.* (*f.* ikā) a perforator, piercer: *lit.* piercing, perforating, sharp.

वेधन, *m.* piercing, perforation; depth.

वेधना, *t.* to perforate, pierce, bore.

वेधनी, *f.* an instrument for piercing (an elephant's ear, gems, shells, etc.); a gimlet, auger, etc.

वेधि, an old form = **वेधके** (**वेधना**). See **कृ**, 7.

वेधित, *m.* (*f.* ā) pierced, perforated, bored.

वेधिया, *m.f.* a perforator, piercer, lover of gems, etc.

वेधी, *m.* (*f.* inī) = **वेधक**, *q. v.*

वेन, 1, (*corruption*) = **वेणु**, *q. v.*: 2, *m. pr. n.* Brahmā.

वेर, *m.* the body: saffron: the egg-plant.

वेरि
वेरी } *more prop.* **बेरि**, *q. v.*

वेला, *f.* time, season, while; tide, current, flow: sea-shore; boundary, limit; leisure, interval. —*kuvelā*, in season and out of season.

वेलार, *m.* (in Pros.) a species of metre.

वेवसाय = **व्यवसाय**, *q. v.*

वेश, *m.* entrance, access; an abode, house; a house of prostitutes: dress, apparel, habit, guise, disguise;

वेशदान, *m.* the sun-flower. [decoration, ornament.

वेशधारी, *m.* (*f.* iṇī) a hypocrite, a false devotee: *lit.* assuming a guise. [ornament for the nose.

वेशर, 1, *more prop.* **बेसर**, *q. v.*: 2, *m.* a nostril; an

वेश्या, 1, *f.* a harlot, courtesan: a certain plant (*Cissampelos hexandra*): (in Pros.) a species of metre: 2, *m.* a habitation of harlots.

वेश्यागमन, *m.* whoring, debauchery. [prostitutes.

वेश्यागामी, *m.* (*f.* inī) a whoremonger: lit. *adj.* visiting

वेश्याघर, *m.* a habitation of harlots, a resort of women of ill-fame, a brothel, house of assignation.

वेष, *m.* dress, guise, ornament, decoration.

वेषधारी, *m.* (*f.* iṇī) = **वेशधारी**, *q.v.*

वेषप्रताप, *m.* the splendour of clothing or of disguise.

वेष्टन, *m.* a surrounding; anything that encompasses, a girdle, envelope, enclosure, fence, wall.

वेष्टित, *m.* (*f.* ā) surrounded, encompassed, enclosed, wrapped up, enveloped.

वेसर, *m.* a mule.

वेसवा, *more prop.* **वेश्या**, *q.v.*

वेहळ, *more prop.* **बेहळ**, *q.v.*

वै; see (1) **बय** (2) **बाई** (3) **बे** (4) **वे** (5) **व्यय**.

वैंचना, *more prop.* **वैंकना**, *q.v.*

वैंकना, *t.* (Sk. **विछेद**) to skin.

वैकल्य, *m.* lameness; imbecility; deficiency, defect, want, insufficiency; non-existence; agitation, consternation, perplexity, confusion, surprize, astonishment, wonder.

वैकान्त, *m.* a kind of gem said to resemble the diamond.

वैकारिक, *m. pr. n.* a certain class of deities: *lit.* modified.

वैकाल = **विकाल**, *q.v.*

वैकालिक, appertaining to (or occurring in) the afternoon.

वैकुण्ठ, *m. pr. n.* (1) of Vishṇu (2) of the paradise of Vishṇu, described as either in the northern ocean or on the peak of mount Meru (3) of Indra.

वैकुण्ठनाथ, *m.* an epithet of Vishṇu.

वैकुण्ठवासी, *m.* (*f.* inī) a celestial being, an inhabitant of paradise: lit. *adj.* inhabiting paradise.

वैकुण्ठा, *m. pr. n.* (see **भा**, 22) a certain class of gods.

वैकुल्य, *more prop.* **वैकल्य**, *q.v.*

वैखानस, *m.* (*f.* ī) a hermit, anchoret.

वैखानसी, *f.* a vessel used for frying meat to be offered in sacrifice.

वैजयन्त, *m. pr. n.* (1) of the palace of Indra (2) of the banner or emblem of Indra: a flag or banner in general.

वैजयन्ती, *f.* 1, a flag, ensign, banner (*esp.* that of Indra): a kind of garland: the name of two trees: 2, *pr. n.* the necklace of Vishṇu composed of five gems produced from the five elements of nature, *viz.* (1) the sapphire, from the earth (2) the pearl, from water (3) the ruby, from fire (4) the topaz, from air (5) the diamond, from space or æther.

वैजयन्तीमाला = **वैजयन्ती**, 2, *q.v.*

वैण, *m.* a worker in bamboo-work, a bamboo-cutter.

वैणव, 1, made of bamboo: 2, *m.* a bamboo staff: *pr. n.* a certain sacred place of pilgrimage: 3, *m.* (*f.* ī) a worker in bamboo or wicker-work.

वैणविक, *m.* (*f.* ā *or* ī) a player on the *vīnā*, a lutist, fluteplayer.

वैणिक = **वैणविक**, *q.v.*

वैतरणी (or °**णि**), *f. pr. n.* (1) of the river of hell (2) of the mother of the Rākshasas.

वैताग, *m.* disgust, weariness. —*lenā*, to be tired or disgusted with any person or thing.

वैतागी, *m.* (*f.* inī) weary, disgusted.

वैताल, *more prop.* **वेताल**, *q.v.*

वैतालिक, *m.* a bard whose duty it is to awaken a chief or prince at dawn with music and song; a singer: one who has an evil spirit (*vetāl*) for a familiar, the worshipper of a *vetāl*; a magician, conjuror.

वैदिक, *m.* (*f.* ī) a Brāhmaṇ well versed in the Veds: *lit.* appertaining to the Veds, authorized by scripture, scriptural.

वैदिकी, *f.* a certain division of the Sanskrit grammar containing explanations of portions of the Veds.

वैदूर्य, *m.* a gem of a dark blue colour, the lapis lazuli.

वैदेशिक, *m.* (*f.* ā *or* ī) } = **विदेशी**, *q.v.*
वैदेशी, *m.* (*f.* inī) }

वैदेह, 1, *m.* (*f.* ī) the offspring of a Vaishya by a Brāhmaṇ woman; a trader by caste or by profession: 2, *m. pr. n.* (1) of the king of Videhā father of Sītā (2) of one of the mixed classes among Hindoos.

वैदेहक } *m.* (*f.* ā *or* ī) = **वैदेह**, 1, *q.v.*
वैदेहिक }

वैदेही, *f.* (*m.* **वैदेह**) the wife of a trader, a female of the Vaideh caste: an epithet of Sītā (as daughter of Vaideh).

वैद्य, *m.* a follower of the Veds; a physician; the offspring of a Brāhman by a Vaishya woman: *lit.* (1) appertaining to the Veds, conversant with the Veds (2) appertaining to medicine, medicinal, medical.

वैद्यक, *m.* (*f.* ikā) a physician: *lit.* appertaining to medicine, medical.

वैद्यन, a Braj pl. of **वैद्य**. See **न**, 6 (1).

वैद्यनाथ, *m.* an epithet (1) of Dhanvantari, chief physician in the court of Indra (2) of Shiv (3) of a certain poet (4) of a certain country.

वैध, *m.* (*f.* ī) enjoined by rule, conformable to rule, prescribed, appointed; giving rules or directions, preceptive, ritual; legal.

वैधृत, *m.* a certain position of the sun and moon when they are on the same side of either solstice and of equal declination but of opposite directions. (This is considered a malignant aspect.)

वैधृति, *f. pr. n.* the *yog*-star of the 27th *Nakshatra*.

वैनतेय, *m.* an epithet of Garuḍa.

वैपारिन (*colloquial*) = **व्यापारिणी**, a merchant's wife.

वैपरीत्य, *m.* contrariety, opposition; reverse, counterpart.

वैबस्वत, *more prop.* **वैवस्वत**, *q.v.*

वैभव, *m.* power, wealth, grandeur, preëminence, greatness.

वैमात्र, *m.* (*f.* ī) a step-mother's child, *i. e.* a child of the same father but by a different mother, a half-brother (or sister).

वैमात्रेय, *m.* (*f.* ī) = **वैमात्र**, *q.v.*

वैमानिक, *m.* (*f.* ā *or* ī) a god: *lit.* appertaining to (or borne in) chariots of the gods.

वैमानी, *m.* (*f.* inī) *more com.* **वैमानिक**, *q.v.*

वैया, *more prop.* **बया**, *q.v.*

वैयाकरण, *m.* a grammarian: *lit.* appertaining to grammar, grammatical.

वैर, *m.* heroism, valour, prowess: enmity, hostility, animosity, revenge, malice, spite. —*k.* (with abl.) to hate, etc. —*lenā*, to take revenge.

वैरभाव, 1, *m.* = **वैर**, *q.v.*: 2, *m. f.* = **वैरी**, 1, 2, *qq.v.*

वैरयुक्त, *m.* (*f.* ā) inimical, hostile, malicious, revengeful.

वैराग = **वैराग्य**, *q.v.*

वैरागिणी, *f.* (*m.* **वैरागी**) a female ascetic.

वैरागी, *m.* (*f.* iṇī) one who has subdued his worldly desires and passions, one who abandons the pursuits of this world, an ascetic, devotee, stoic, recluse: *lit.* separated from passion or worldly attachments. At present the term is applied to a certain class of Hindoo fakeers who roam the country and practice certain austerities.

वैराग्य, *m.* freedom from passion or from worldly attachments, subjection of the appetites, disaffection, stoicism, sorrow, despondency.

वैराग्यवान, *m.* (*f.* vatī) = **वैरागी**, *q.v.*

वैरान, 1, desolated, depopulated, laid waste, ruined: 2, a village under the headman of another village.

वैरानखेड़ा, the deserted site of a village.

वैरानी, *f.* desolation, depopulation, destruction; a desert country.

वैरिणी, *f.* (*m.* **वैरी**) a heroine; a female foe.

वैरिता, *f.* (*m.* °त्व) enmity, malice, hatred.

वैरी, *m.* (*f.* iṇī) a hero: an enemy, foe: *lit.* (1) heroic (2) inimical, hostile, malicious, revengeful.

वैरूप्य, *m.* (and *f.* °ता) difference of form, deformity; (in Gram.) change of form.

वैरोचन, *m. pr. n* (1) of the son of the Sun (2) of the son of Agni (3) of Bali, son of Virochan.

वैलक्षण, *m.* indifference, contrariety.

वैलक्षण्य, *m.* disparity, difference, contrariety.

वैलक्ष्य, *m.* absence of any characteristic; the contrary course to that which is usual or natural, contrariety, reverse.

वैला, near, hither, on this side.

वैलोचन, *more prop.* **वैरोचन**, *q.v.*

वैवर्त्त, *m.* revolution, change or modification of existence.

वैवस्वत, *m. pr. n.* (1) of Yam (2) of the seventh (or present) Manu (3) of one of the Rudras (4) of the planet Saturn.

वैवाहिक, appertaining to marriage, nuptial, matrimonial: hence (1) *m.* a wedding (2) *m.* (*f.* ā *or* ī) the parent of a daughter's husband or of a son's wife.

वैशम्पायन, *m. pr. n.* a certain sage (*muni*) the promulgator of the Yajur-Ved.

वैशाख, *m. pr. n.* the first solar month of the Hindoos (April-May) in which the moon is full near Vishākh (four stars in Libra and Scorpio).

वैशाखी, 1, *f.* the day of full moon in the month Vaishākh (the day on which the sun enters Aries); a large kind of myrobalan or citron-fruit: 2, appertaining to (or growing in) the month Vaishākh.

वैशेषिक, characteristic: appertaining to the Vaisheshik system: hence (1) *m.* a certain school of philosophy among the Hindoos, being an offshoot of the Nyāya school (2) *m.* (*f.* ā *or* ī) a follower of the Vaisheshik system.

वैश्य, *m.* (*f.* ā) a person of the third Hindoo caste, whose chief duties are agriculture and trade: *hence*, a trader, an agriculturist.

वैश्यक्रिया, *f.* the proper occupation etc. of a Vaishya, *i. e.* commerce, trade, agriculture.

वैश्यनी = **वैश्या**, *q. v.*

वैश्या, *f.* (*m.* **वैश्य**) a female of the Vaishya caste.

वैश्यानी (*corruption*) = **वैश्यनी**, *q. v.*

वैश्रवण, *m. pr. n* (1) of a son of Vishwasan (2) of a certain division of the infernal regions.

वैषम्भ; see (1) **वैष्णव** (2) **वैषम्य**.

वैषम्य, *m.* unevenness, inequality; solitariness, singleness; difficulty; injustice; distress, misery; harshness, rigour.

वैषयिक, appertaining to objects of sense, sensual, carnal: hence, *m.* (*f.* ī) a worldly person, sensualist.

वैष्णव, *m.* (*f.* ī) a follower or worshipper of Vishṇu: *lit.* appertaining to Vishṇu.

वैष्णवी, *f.* 1, *pr. n.* (1) of one of the Matris, the personified energy of Vishṇu (2) of Durgā: 2, a certain flower (*Clitora ternenta*); sacred basil (*Ocymum sanctum*).

वैष्णवोत्तर, *m.* lands granted rent-free to the worshippers of Vishṇu (*esp.* to those of the mendicant orders).

वैस (*colloquial*) = (1) **वयस** (2) **वैश्य**, *qq. v.*

वैसहो = **वैसाही**, *q. v.*

वैसा, 1, *m.* (*f.* ī) such as that, that-like: 2, in that manner, so, like that. *Waisekā waisā*, such as before.

वैसाख; for words beginning thus, see under the form **वैशाख**.

वैसाही, (emphat.) in the same manner, in that very same way, even like that, exactly so.

वैसी, *f.* (*m.* **वैसा**) that-like, etc.

वैसीही, the feminine form of **वैसाही**, *q. v.*

वैसे, 1, pl. of **वैसा**, *q. v.*: 2, *adv.* = **वैसा**, 2, *q. v.*

वैसें, free of cost, gratis, freely, gratuitously.

वैसेशिक, **वैसेषिक**, **वैसेसिक** } *more prop.* **वैशेषिक**, *q. v.*

वैसेही, the inflected form of the masc. of **वैसाही** *q. v.*

वैस्य; for words beginning thus, see under the form **वैश्य**.

वो, 1, in Braj = (1) **वह** (2) **वे**, 1 (3) **ओ**, 5, *qq. v.*: 2, = **वौ**, *q. v.*

वों, 1, so, that manner, like that: *Woṅkā woṅhi*, exactly the same as before or originally: 2, sometimes put corruptly for **ऊं**; *e. g.* **जलावोंगा** = **जलाऊंगा**.

वोंही, (emphat.) in that very manner; in that very instant.

वोंहीं = **वोंही**, *q. v.*

वोट, *m.* (*f.* ā) a slave.

वोड़ा = **वोढ़**, *q. v.*

वोढ़, *m.* (*f.* ī) a species of fish: the boa-constrictor.

वोढ़ी, *f.* the fourth part of a *paṇ*.

वोढ़ना, *more com.* **ओढ़ना**, *q. v.*

वोढ़वेको, a Braj form = **ओढ़नेको** (**ओढना**), See **वे**, 3.

वोढ़ा, *m.* one who carries or draws, a bearer, porter, carrier: a charioteer: a bull: a leader, guide: a bridegroom.

वोढ़ = **वोढ़ा**, *q. v.*

वोतना, *m.* (*f.* ī) *more com.* **उतना**, *q. v.*

वोद, wet, moist, damp.

वोदाल, *m.* sheat-fish (*Silurus boalis*).

वोपदेव, *m. pr. n.* a certain ancient Hindoo grammarian.

वोर in Braj = **ओर**, *q. v.*

वेाल, *m.* gum, myrrh.

वेाश्राश्रोन, the wi mowing of grain.

वेाह = **वुह** = **वह**, *q.v.*

वेाहित, *more prop.* **वेाहित्य**, *q.v.*

वेाहित्य, *m.* a sailing-vessel, ship, boat.

वेाही, 1, = **वेांही**, *q.v.* : 2, *more prop.* **वही**, *q.v.*

वेाहीं = **वेांहीं**, *q.v.*

वेा (infl. **वे** ; *e.g.* **राखिवेकेा** = **राखनेकेा**) in Braj = **ना** of the infinitive ; *e. g.* **मांगवेा** or **मांगवेां** = **मांगना**. See (1) **श्रेा**, 7 (2) **श्रेां**, 5 (3) **श्रेा**, 5 (4) **श्रेां** (5) **ना**, 3.

वेां. 1, in Braj = **वेां**, *q.v.* : 2, = **वेा**, *q.v.*

वेागिरह in Braj = **वग़ैरः**, *q.v.*

व्यंग, 1, *m.* (*f.* ā) a cripple ; a frog ; a 2, *m.* a freckle, spot ; a joke, sarcasm ; *lit.* deformed, mutilated, distorted, ill-arranged lame, bodiless.

व्यंगुल, *m.* the 60th part of a digit (*angul*).

व्यंजक, *m.* a sign, mark, symbol ; feeling, external indication of feeling : *lit.* making clear or plain.

व्यंजन, *m.* the distinguishing anything ; a mark, token, sign ; the beard ; the privities (of either sex). the marks of puberty ; sauce, condiment ; sarcasm ; insignia, paraphernalia ; (in Gram.) a consonant.

व्यंजनचक, *m.* (in Gram.) a table or paradigm of the consonant.

व्यंजनसन्धि, *f.* (in Gram.) the union of a vowel or consonant with a consonant (according to special rules) for the formation of a compound letter.

व्यंजना, *f.* the correct indication of any sentiment ; the third power of a word, suggestion ; irony, sarcasm, a joke.

व्यंजनान्त, (in Gram.) ending with a consonant.

व्यक्त, *m.* (*f.* ā) individuated, specific, individual ; apparent, manifest, evident : wise, learned.

व्यक्ति, *f.* distinctness, individuality : appearance, manifestation : an individual, a person : (in Gram.) inflexion, case.

व्यक्तिवाचक, *m.* (in Gram.) a proper name : *lit.* signifying or expressive of a person.

व्यग्र, *m.* (*f.* ā) bewildered, perplexed, distracted, agitated, occupied in, eager, zealous.

व्यग्रता, *f* (*m.* °**त्व**) zealousness, eagerness, perplexedness, agitation, alarm.

व्यजन, *m.* a fan, a ventilator.

व्यञ्जन; see **व्यंजन** and **व्यजन**, *q.v.*

व्यतिक्रम, *m.* inverted or retragrade order, reverse, contrariety, misfortune, opposition, deviation, transgression, fault, sin.

व्यतिरिक्त, *m.* (*f.* ā) different from, distinct, separate.

व्यतिरेक, *m.* separateness, distinctness, dissimilitude, negative inference, interception, exception, exclusion.

व्यतीत, *m.* (*f.* ā) passed, gone, elapsed, spent (as times) ; departed, dead ; excepted, omitted. — *k.* (with acc.) to spend or pass away time. [the dead.

व्यतीतन, (a Braj pl. of **व्यतीत** ; see **न**, 6) past events ;

व्यतीपात, *m.* disrespect ; a portent indicating calamity ; great calamity ; the day of new moon (when it falls on a Sunday and the moon is in certain mansions) ; *pr. n.* the 17th astronomical *Yog*.

व्यत्यय, *m.* inverted or retrograde order, contrariety, reverse, discrepancy, variety, interchange.

व्यथा, *f.* pain, agony, distress, alarm, fear.

व्यथाकर, painful, agonizing, excruciating.

व्यथारहित, free from pain, painless.

व्यभिचार, *m.* a going astray, following improper courses, trespass, crime, sin, vice, unchastity, adultery (*esp.* in a wife).

व्यभिचारी, *m.* (*f.* iṇī) an unchaste person, adulterer, etc. : lit. *adj.* going astray. deviating, trespassing, wanton, unchaste. adulterous.

व्यभिचारीपन, *m.* (= **व्यभिचार**) unchastity. etc.

व्यय, *m.* disapppearance, loss, destruction, expenditure, disbursement, expense, consumption, use, squandering : *pr. n.* the 20th year of the Hindoo cycle.

व्ययकारी, *adj.* squandering, extravagant, expensive : hence, *m.* (*f.* iṇi) a spendthrift.

व्ययभूत }
व्ययीकृत } *m.* (*f.* ā) expended, squandered, wasted.
व्ययीभूत }

व्यर्थ, ineffectual, meaningless, unmeaning, useless, vain, unprofitable, inefficient.

व्यर्थता, *f.* (*m.* °**त्व**) uselessness, unprofitableness, unmeaningness, nonsense, inefficiency, vanity, inoffensiveness.

व्यलीक, disagreeable, offensive, improper, painful, strange, unnatural ; hence, *m.* any displeasing or improper act, falsehood, cheating, fault, transgression ; pain, torture, grief, ; a catamite.

व्यव, (*i.e.* **वि + अव**) a particle used in comp. denoting separation, division, etc.

व्यवकलन, *m.* (in Arithm.) subtraction.

व्यवच्छेद, *m.* dividing, separating, discrimination, distinction. contrast, restriction.

व्यवधा; see **व्यवधा**. [disappearance, concealment.

व्यवधा, *f.* a covering, screen ; a being covered,

व्यवधान, *m.* an intervening, interposition, partition, space. [ing, concealing, hiding.

व्यवधायक, *adj.* intervening, separating, screen-

व्यवरा, *more prop.* **ब्योरा**, *q. v.*

व्यवरेवार, detailed. See **ब्योरेवार**.

व्यवसाय, *m.* perseverance, intentness. eagerness, exertion, effort, energy ; counsel, plan, device, trick ; business, occupation, profession.

व्यवसायी, *m.* (*f.* inī) a man of business : *lit.* persevering, energetic, active, engaged in a business.

व्यवस्था, *f.* a separating, placing remote or apart ; an adjustment ; contract, engagement ; a statute, a written declaration of the law, a decision. The term is applied in practice to the written extracts from the codes of law, stated as the opinions of the Hindoo law officers attached to the courts of justice.

व्यवस्थाज्ञाता, *m.* (*f.* trī) one who knows laws.

व्यवस्थादायक, *m.* (*f.* ikā) }
व्यवस्थादायी, *m.* (*f.* inī) } a law-giver.

व्यवस्थाधीन, *m.* (*f.* ā) subject to law.

व्यवस्थाधीनता, *f.* subjection to law.

व्यवस्थानुगमन, *m.* the observance of established laws, or customs, loyalty.

व्यवस्थानुगामी, *m.* (*f.* inī) an observer of established laws or customs, a loyal person: lit. *adj.* going according to law or established usage.

व्यवस्थापक, *m.* (*f.* ikā) an adjuster, legislator, judge, one who gives a legal opinion: lit. *adj.* deciding, adjusting, legislating.

व्यवस्थापत्र, *m.* an extract from a code of law, a document stating the opinion of a law officer on a controverted point.

व्यवस्थित, established, settled, arranged, adjusted, decreed, resolved upon.

व्यवहार, *m.* a doing, performing, action, occupation, affair, business, profession, practice, custom, usage, transaction, dealings, traffic, conduct, behaviour, lawsuit, litigation, the practice of the courts or civil and criminal law, judicial procedure, administrative justice (as the examination of evidence, etc.).

व्यवहारक, *m.* (*f.* ikā) = = **व्यवहारिक**, *q.v.*

व्यवहारगामन, *m.* conformity to custom.

व्यवहारगामी, *m.* (*f.* inī) one who conforms to current custom.

व्यवहारपद, *m.* a title of jurisprudence, a topic of litigation.

व्यवहारमार्ग, **व्यवहारविषय**, **व्यवहारस्थान** } = **व्यवहारपद**, *q.v.*

व्यवहारसम्बन्धी, *m.* (*f.* inī) appertaining to **व्यवहार**.

व्यवहारिक, *m.* (*f.* ā) a trader, etc.: *lit.* calculated for practical use, practical; practicable; customary; engaged in an avocation; appertaining to usage, to business, or to legal processes, litigant.

व्यवहारिका, *f.* a female trader, a trader's wife: usage: a brush.

व्यवहारित, *m.* (*f.* ā) rendered customary, brought into usage, established as a usage or custom: accustomed.

व्यवहारी, *m*, (*f.* iṇī) = **व्यवहारिक**, *q.v.*

व्यवहार्य्य, to be observed or practised (as a duty or an avocation). customary, current; subject to legal process, actionable; negociable; fit for use.

व्यवहित, *m.* (*f.* ā) placed near, intervening, concealed, interposed, separated, covered, connected with.

व्यवहृत, *m.* (*f.* ā) customarily done, followed in practice, used.

व्यश्न; for words beginning thus, see under the form **व्यसन**.

व्यसन, *m.* calamity, misfortune, affliction, destruction, loss; fruitless effort: incompetence, inability: fate: fault, vice, crime, sin: intent application or attachment to an object, diligence: individuality.

व्यसनासक्त, *m.* (*f.* ā) afflicted by misfortune or calamity, distressed, miserable, wretched, unfortunate.

व्यसनी, *m.* (*f.* inī) 1, = **व्यसनासक्त**, *q.v.*: 2, a wicked person, etc.: *lit.* wicked, vicious, ruled by passions, criminal; intent on, industrious, occupied.

व्यस्त, *m.* (*f.* ā) confounded, bewildered, annoyed, distressed; pervaded, penetrated, spread.

व्यस्तता, *f.* (*m.* °**त्व**) agitation, bewilderment, perplexity; several inherence.

व्यस्य, having thrown asunder, having thrown or tossed about, having dispersed or scattered; having arranged in order.

व्यहाल, *more prop.* **बेहाल**, *q.v.*

व्याकरण, *m.* the science of Grammar: *lit.* an explaining, expounding. It is accounted one of the six auxiliary branches (*vedāng*) of learning.

व्याकरणी, *m.* (*f.* inī) a grammarian.

व्याकुल, *m.* (*f.* ā) confused, bewildered, dimmed, perplexed, overcome with fear, agitated, uneasy, restless.

व्याकुलता, *f.* (*m.* °**त्व**) perturbation, confusion, perplexity, trouble, uneasiness.

व्याकुलमना, *m. f.* = **व्याकुलित**, *q.v.*

व्याकुलित, *m.* (*f.* ā) agitated, bewildered, flurried, perplexed, distressed, agitated.

व्याख्या, *f.* an exposition, explanation, gloss, comment, scholia.

व्याख्यान, *m.* commenting, expounding, explaining.

व्याघात, *m.* obstacle, impediment, percussion, striking, wounding, destroying; *pr. n.* the 13th astronomical *yog*.

व्याघाती, *adj.* striking against, opposing, thwarting, hindering: hence, *m.* (*f.* inī) a resister, striker, etc.

व्याघ्र, *m.* (*f.* ī) a tiger.

व्याघ्रनखी, *f.* a tiger's claw; a scratch of the claws or nails; a sort of perfume; a certain plant (*Galedupa arborea*).

व्याज, *m.* deceit, fraud, cunning, disguise; pretext, pretence; wickedness; appearance; means; overplus, deduction, discount, interest, usury.

व्याजख़ोर, *m.* one who takes interest, a usurer.

व्याजी, 1, *m.* (*f.* inī) one who takes interest, a usurer: 2, *f.* money that bears interest, or which is lent or borrowed at interest.

व्याजू, *m.* the principal or capital put out at interest.

व्याध, *m.* (*f.* ā *or* ī) a hunter, sportsman, fowler; a low or wicked man.

व्याधा, *f.* (*m.* **व्याध**) a female hunter, etc.

व्याधि, *f.* disease, sickness, ailment, pain, anguish, leprosy.

व्याधिकारक, *m.* (*f.* ikā) occasioning disease or pain.

व्याधित, *m.* (*f.* ā) diseased, afflicted, sick, ill.

व्याधिरहित, *m.* (*f.* ā) free from disease, in good health.

व्याधी, 1, *f.* (*m.* **व्याध**) a huntress, etc.: 2, diseased, afflicted, sick, ill: hence, *m.* (*f.* inī) an invalid.

व्यान, *m.* one of the five vital airs (that which is diffused throughout the body).

व्याप (*contraction*) = **व्यापार**, *q.v.*

व्यापक, diffusive, pervading, extensive, spreading widely, comprehensive; forward, impudent: hence, *m.* (*f.* ikā) an impudent person, etc.

व्यापकता, *f.* (*m.* °**त्व**) diffusion, pervadence, prevalence; influence; forwardness, impudence.

व्यापना, *t.* and *a. int.* to spread throughout, pervade, penetrate, occupy. effect, act, operate, work, affect.

व्यापार, *m.* occupation, business, trade, commerce, merchandise, traffic, profession, labour, work, affair, exercise, practice, exertion, activity.

व्यापारी, *m.* (*f.* iṇī) a man of business, tradesman, merchant: *lit.* occupied, transacting business, performing, busy.

व्यापिक = **व्यापक**, *q.v.*

व्यापिका, *f.* (*m.* **व्यापक**) an impudent female, termagnant.

व्यापी, *m.* (*f.* inī) = **व्यापक**, *q.v.*

व्याप्त, *m.*(*f.*ā) pervaded, penetrated, occupied, filled, full: obtained, gotten; placed: famous, celebrated.

व्याप्ति, *f.* diffusion, permeation, inherence, universal permeation (as an attribute of the Diety), omnipresence, (in Logic) the relation of the subject to the predicate in a universal proposition.

व्याप्तिमान, *m.* (*f.* matī) pervaded by, attended by; diffusive, pervading, permeating, omnipresent.

व्याप्य, permeable, pervadible; amenable, liable; anything that is invariably accompanied by something else; hence, *m.* (in Gram.) the subject to an attribute; (in Logic) the sign or middle term in an inference: a certain drug (*Costus speciosus*).

व्यायाम, *m.* 1, = **व्याम**, *q.v.*: 2, fatigue, exertion, exercise, labour, athletic exercise, gymnastics; fighting; manliness: difficulty; occupation, business.

व्यारे, in Garhwāl = yesterday.

व्याप्यत्व, *m.* (*f.* tā) the capacity of being pervaded or essentially affected, pervadibleness, permeableness.

व्याम, *m.* a fathom (or the space between the tips of the fingers of the hands when the arms are extended).

व्यामोह, *m.* error, mistake; foolishness; embarrassment, trouble, affliction.

व्याल, wicked, villainous, bad, cruel: hence, *m.* (*f.* ī) a beast of prey, vicious elephant, a snake, a rogue, a king.

व्यालग्राही, *m.* (*f.* iṇī) a serpent-catcher.

व्यालारि, *m.* an epithet of Garuṛ.

व्याली, *f.* (*m.* **व्याल**) a female snake, etc.

व्यावना, a corruption of **व्यापना**, *q.v.*

व्यावहारिक, *m.* (*f.* ā *or* ī) a counseller, minister, etc.: *lit.* active; customary; judicial; intended for use: practicable.

व्यावहारी, *m.* (*f.* iṇī) a counsellor, minister, etc.: *lit.* usual, customary; juridical, judicial, legal.

व्यास, *m.* extension; diffusion; distinction, detail: disposition of parts; (in Geom.) the diameter of a circle; *pr. n.* a celebrated ancient Hindoo sage (the reputed arranger or compiler of the Veds and Purāns, author of the Mahābhārat, and founder of the Vedānt school of philosophy.

व्यासगद्दी, *f.* any cushion or seat on which an instructor sits when imparting instruction.

व्यासदेव = **वेदव्यास**, *q.v.*

व्यासा, *f. pr. n.* a certain river.

व्याह; for words beginning thus, see under the form **बियाह**.

व्याहुती; see (1) **व्याहृति** (2) **विवाहिता**.

व्याहृति, *f.* voice, an articulate sound, speech, a word. The term is applied especially to the mystical words *Om, Bhur, Bhuvah, Svar*, pronounced by Brāhmans at the beginning of daily prayer.

व्युत्क्रम, *m.* inverted order, irregular arrangement, confusion.

व्युत्पत्ति, *f.* conservancy with literature or science; learning; descent, origin, derivation, etymology.

व्युत्पन्न, generated, descended from, derived from; versed in science, proficient, learned; (in Gram). derived.

व्यूह, *m.* military array, arrangement of troops; a flock, multitude, army, squadron: logic, reasoning: making: the body.

व्योपार = **व्यापार** or **ब्योपार**, *qq.v.*

व्योम, *m.* the sky, atmosphere, heaven; air, ether: water: a temple sacred to the sun: talc, mica.

व्योमकेश } *m.* epithets of Shiv.
व्योमकेशी }

व्योमन = **व्योम**, *q.v.*

व्योमनगंगा, *f. pr. n.* (see **गंगा**) the celestial Ganges.

व्योममण्डल, *m.* a flag, banner: *lit.* sky-circle.

व्योमा, *m. pr. n.* a certain ancient Hindoo king.

व्योमासुर, *m.pr. n.* a certain demon slain by Kṛishṇ.

व्योर; see **ब्योरा**.

व्योरा = **ब्योरा**, *q.v.*

व्योरेवार, detailed. See **ब्योरेवार**.

व्योपारी = **व्यापारी** or **ब्योपारी**, *qq.v.*

व्योरो in Braj = **ब्योरा**, *q.v.*

व्योवसाव = **व्यवसाय**, *q.v.*

व्रज, *m.* a multitude, flock, herd; a cowpen: a road: *pr.n.* the district about Agra and Mathurā. It is about 168 miles in circumference, and contains the several villages of Mathurā, Gokul and Vrindāvan. It was the birthplace of Krishṇ and is the Arcadia of India.

व्रजकिशोर, *m.* (the youth of Braj, *i.e.*) Kṛishṇ.

व्रजगोप, *m.* (*f.* ī) any cowherd of Braj.

व्रजचन्द, *m.* (the moon of Braj, *i.e.*) Kṛishṇ.

व्रजजन, *m.* the people of Braj.

व्रजतिय, *f.* = **व्रजनारी**, *q.v.*

व्रजनाथ, *m.* (the lord of Braj, *i.e.*) Kṛishṇ.

व्रजनारी, *f.* any female inhabitant of the Braj-country. The term is specially applied to Krishṇ's cowherdesses. [as votaries of Kṛishṇ.

व्रजभक्त, *m.* (*f.* ā) the people of Braj considered

व्रजभाषा, *f.* the dialectic form of Hindee that is spoken chiefly in the Braj district, the pastoral language of the Hindee-speaking people.

व्रजभूमि, *f. pr. n.* the Braj district.

व्रजमण्डल, *m. pr. n.* the Braj district.

व्रजमोहन, *m.* (the fascinator of Braj, *i.e.*) Kṛishṇ.

व्रजराज, *m.* (the lord of Braj, *i.e.*) Kṛishṇ.

व्रजलोग, *m.* the people of Braj.

व्रजवन, *m.* the forest or district of Braj.

व्रजवर, *m.* (the best man in Braj, *i.e.*) Kṛishṇ.

व्रजवाम, *f.* = **व्रजनारी**, *q.v.*

व्रजवाल, *m.* (*f.* ā) an inhabitant of Braj.

व्रजवाला, 1, *f.* = **व्रजनारी**, *q.v.*: 2, *m* (*f.* i) = **व्रजवाल**.

व्रजवासी, *m.* (*f.* inī) an inhabitant of the Braj-country.

व्रजविलास, *m.* the sports and exploits of Kṛishṇ in the Braj country: *pr. n.* a certain poetical work detailing those exploits.

व्रजहि, an old form = **व्रजको**, acc. of **व्रज**.

व्रण, *m.* a fracture, wound, ulcer, tumour, boil, sore.

व्रत, *m.* any self-chosen voluntary act of devotion undertaken as a work of religious merit (as penance, austerity, privation, fasting, continence, exposure to heat and cold, etc.), a religious vow, a fast. The word **उपवास** is often confounded with this word **व्रत**. The former of these words, however, is, properly speaking, applied to a compulsory abstention from food, as when one fasts through inability to obtain food or through sickness: the latter word has a strictly religious signification.

व्रतति, *f.* a spreading; expansion, extent; a creeper.

व्रतती = **व्रतति**, *q.v.*

व्रतमान, a corruption of **वर्तमान**, *q.v.*

व्रतस्थ, *m.* (*f.* ā) a person engaged in religious austerities.

व्रती, *m.* (*f.* inī) an ascetic, devotee; one who fasts; an employer of priests; a religious student: *lit.* engaged in religious ceremonies voluntarily undertaken, or in the observance of religious obligations or vows, pious.

व्राजबास, a corruption of **व्रजवास**, *q.v.*

व्रात, *m.* the company and attendants at a marriage feast; an assemblage, multitude: the son of an outcaste: bodily labour, day-labour.

व्रात्य, *m.* (*f.* ā) a person of either of the first three Hindoo castes (whether Brāhman, Kshatriya, or Vaishya) in whose youth the customary observances have been omitted, and who has not received his investiture with the sacred thread, one who has fallen from caste, an outcaste.

व्रात्या, *f.* (see **व्रात्य**) the wife or daughter of an outcaste.

व्रित्ति (*corruption*) = **वृत्ति**, *q.v.*

व्रीड, *m.* / **व्रीडा**, *f.* } bashfulness, modesty, shame.

व्रीड़ित, *m.* (*f.* ā) bashful, ashamed, modest.

व्रीहि, *m.* rice (of various kinds).

व्हां (*corruption*) = **वहां**, *q.v.*

श

श (sh) is the thirtieth consonant in the Hindee or Devanāgarī alphabet, and has the following characteristics and functions:—1, It belongs to the palatal class, and is the first of the three sibilants, which, including **ह**, form the class called *ūshma* or *ūshmānah*; it is hence called the palatal sibilant. 2, In pronunciation it has the sound of *sh* in the English word 'shun,' or of *s* in the English 'sure,' or of *ch* in the French 'cheval': it never has the *z* sound of *s* in the English word 'wise,' nor the *zh* sound of *s* in 'pleasure.' By many persons this letter is slightly aspirated, so that the word **शरीर** is pronounced by them as if it were spelt *shharīr*. It is of some importance to observe that though the natives of Bengal seldom make any perceptible difference in the pronunciation of the three sibilants, yet that among the Hindee-speaking people the sounds of these letters are distinctly marked even among the masses, excepting by persons of singular carelessness or of some vocal inability to produce the respective sounds. 3, This letter is constantly interchanged inaccurately with **ष** and **स**, and occasionally even with **ग** and **ह**; *e.g.* **दिग** = **दिक** = **दिश**; **केहर** = **केशर**. 4, When compounded with another letter it assumes (according to the option of the writer) the form **श्**, *e.g.* **श्व**, **श्च**, **श्र**, **श्ल**. When so compounded it is pronounced by many with a sharp sibilant sound; thus **परिश्रम** is often (though with questionable accuracy) pronounced *parisram* rather than *parishram*. 5. This letter occasionally occurs as a Taddhita suffix [*m.* (*f.* ā)] by means of which adjectives are formed from substantives; *e.g.* **लोमश**, from **लोम**. 6, In foreign words in this Dictionary it stands for ش; *e.g.* **निशान** = نشان.

शई, *more prop.* **शै**, *q.v.*

शं, happily, fortunately, auspiciously.

शंक; for words beginning thus, but not given below, see under the more proper form **शंख**.

शंकु, *more prop.* **शंकु**, *q.v.*

शंकर, *m.* (1) *pr. n.* a celebrated writer on the Vedānt philosophy (2) an epithet of Mahādev.

शंकरभाष्य, *m. pr. n.* a certain Sanskrit work.

शंकरवाणी, *f.* the voice or utterance of Mahādev, a divine oracle.

शंकरस्वामी, *m.* an epithet (1) of Shaṅkarāchārya (2) of Mahādev.

शंकरा, *f.* a certain musical mode (*rāginī*).

शंकराचारी, *m.* (*f.* inī) a follower of Shaṅkarāchārya.

शंकराचार्य्य, *m. pr. n.* a certain celebrated Hindoo ascetic who eradicated the Jain sect.

शंकराभरण, *m.* a certain musical mode.

शंकरी, *f.* an epithet of Pārvatī (wife of Shiv).

शंका, *f.* doubt, uncertainty; error; fear, apprehension, terror: presumption; hope.

शंकामय, *m.* (*f.* ī) apprehensive, fearful, doubting.

शंकाहीन, *m.* (*f.* ā) free from apprehension, fearless, undoubting.

शंकित, *m.* (*f.* ā) frightened, apprehensive, alarmed; uncertain, doubtful.

शंकु, *m.* the trunk of a lopped tree: a pin, style, stake, pale: a weapon, dart, javelin: fear: the gnomon of a dial: ten billions: sin: a demon: poison: a goose: an ant-hill: a certain tree (*Shorea robusta*) the skate-fish (*Raia sankur*): an epithet (1) of Shiv (2) of Kāmdev.

शंकेचुड़; see **शंखचूड़**.

शंकोच, *m.* a skate-fish (*Raia sankur*).

शंक्रान्ति (*colloquial*) = **संक्रान्ति**, *q.v.*

शंख, *m.* the conch-shell used by the Hindoos as a vessel for offering libations, and also for blowing as a horn; a shell: a military drum: the temple-bone: an elephant's cheek: a kind of perfume: a large number, ten or a hundred billions: *pr. n.* one of Kuver's treasures.

शंखचूड़, *m. pr. n.* a certain demon slain by Krishṇ.

शंखध्वनि, *f.* the sound of the *shaṅkh*.

शंखासुर, *m. pr. n.* a certain demon slain by Vishṇu.

शंखिनी, *f.* (see **पद्मिनी**) the third of the four classes or descriptions of females described in the erotic writings of the Hindoos. The Shaṅkhinī is said to be tall, long-haired, neither stout nor thin, and of irascible disposition and strong passions,—the worst description of woman, a very demon in look and in nature.

शंगर्फ़, *m.* cinnabar, vermilion.

शंब, **शंभ**; for words beginning thus, see under the corresponding forms **शम्ब**, **शम्भ**.

शक, *m.* a sovereign or prince who gives his name, to an era (esp. applied to Shālivāhan and to the era which takes his name, commencing 76 or 78 years after the Christian era): a certain caste (the followers or the descendants of Shālivāhan); an era.

शकट, *m.* a cart, a cartload: an implement for preparing grain: a form of marching an army: *pr. n.* (1) of the fourth mansion of the Hindoo zodiac (2) of a certain demon (*daitya*) slain by Krishn.

शकटासुर, *m. pr. n.* = शकट (2), *q.v.*

शकटिका, *f* a small cart, a toy-cart.

शकटी, *f.* a cart. [be perturbed.

शकना, 1, *more prop.* सकना, *q.v.*: 2, to doubt, fear,

शकर, *f.* sugar.

शकरकन्द, *m.* sweet potatoe (*Convolvulus battatas*).

शकरभता, *m.* a kind of sweetmeat (made of rice, butter, and sugar).

शकल, 1, *more prop.* शक्ल, *q.v.*: 2, *m.* a part, portion, piece; a potsherd: skin; bark; scales (of a fish): a kind of black pigment.

शकस (*corruption*) = शख्स, *q.v.*

शकार, *m.* the letter श, or any character that may represent it: the silly brother-in-law of a king.

शकित, capable of being accomplished.

शकी; see (1) शकना (2) शक्की.

शकील } **शकीला** } *m.* (*f.* ī) well-shaped, handsome.

शकुन, *m.* any auspicious (and sometimes, but not frequently, inauspicious) object, mark, or omen; an augury: any bird, but especially the vulture or eagle.

शकुनि, *m.* any bird: the Indian Kite (*Falco cheela*): *pr. n.* (1) of the Ashwin (2) of one of the astronomical periods called Karan.

शकुनी, 1, *f.* (*m.* शकुनि) a hen-sparrow: 2, *m.* (*f.* ini) one who understands omens.

शकुन्त, *m.* a bird; the blue jay; the Indian vulture.

शकुन्तक, *m.* (*f.* ikā) = शकुन्त, *q.v.*

शकुन्तला, *f. pr. n.* a certain famous drama written [in Sanskrit by Kālidās.

शकुन्ति, *m.* = शकुन्त, *q.v.*

शकुल, *m.* a fish.

शकुलगण्ड, *m.* a certain fish (the gilt-head).

शकुलार्भक, *m.* a species of the gilt-head (*Sparus emarginatus*).

शकेब, *f.* endurance, patience.

शक्क, *m.f.* doubt, suspense, hesitation, uncertainty.

शक्करलब, sugar-lipped (*esp.* a mistress).

शक्की, perplexing, doubtful. —— *mizāj*, undetermined, wavering, hesitating.

शक्कुलक़मर, *m.* the rending of the moon asunder. (A miracle attributed to Muhammad by certain sects.)

शक्त, *m.* (*f.* ā) powerful strong, able, capable; hard, compact, tight, fast: attentive, intent. diligent, clever: civil, polite, pleasing. [hardness.

शक्तता, *f.* strength, power, ability, capability,

शक्ति, *f.* might, main, power, strength, ascendancy, ability, prowess; the energy or active power of a deity personified as his wife, as Gaurī of Shiv, Lakshmi of Vishnu, etc.: the female organ as the counterpart of the phallic personification of Shiv, and worshipped (either literally or symbolically) by a certain sect of Hindoos, who are thence termed Shāktas.

शक्तिमत } **शक्तिमन्त** } *m.* (*f.* matī) = शक्तिमान, *q.v.*

शक्तिमान, *m.* (*f.* matī) strong, mighty, powerful, [able.

शक्तिबोधक, (in Gram.) potential.

शक्तिहीन, *m.* (*f.* ā) impotent, powerless.

शक्य, capable of being accomplished, possible, practicable; requiring to be effected: *m.* (in Gram.) the meaning of a word.

शक्यता, *f.* practicability, possibility.

शक्र, *m.* an epithet of Indra: the name of two trees (1) *Pentaptera arjuna* (2) *Nerium antidysentericum*.

शक्रगोप, *m.* the insect called the lady-bird (*Coccinella*).

शक्रधनुष, *m.* Indra's bow, the rainbow.

शक्रभूभवा, *f.* coloeynth (*Cucumis coloquintida*).

शक्राशन, *m.* a certain medicinal plant (*Wrightea antidysenterica*). [blance, mode.

शक्ल *f.* shape, form, effigy, appearance, semblance,

शख़, hard ground; the top of a hill, the peak of [a mountain.

शखश, a corruption of शख़्स, *q.v.*

शख़्स, *m.* a person, body, individual.

शखि, *more prop.* सखि, *q. v.*

शगल = शुग़ल, *q.v.*

शग़ाल, *m.* a jackal. —— *khor*, a jackal-eater (term applied to a certain gang of free-booters on the Oude frontier).

शगुन, *more prop.* (1) शुगुन (2) सगुण, *qq.v.*

शगुफता } **शगोफ़तन** } corruptions of शिगुफ़ता, *q.v.*

शचि, *f. pr. n.* a certain goddess (wife of Indra).

शचिपति, *m.* (the lord of Shachi, *i. e.*) Indra.

शची, *f.* 1, = शचि, *q.v.* . 2, strength,

शचु, *more prop.* सचु, *q.v.*

शजर, *m.* a tree, plant.

शज्या, *more prop.* शय्या, *q.v.*

शठ, wicked, crafty, deceitful, cunning, dishonest, perfidious: hence, *m.* a cheat, knave, rogue: an idler; a blockhead, fool; false lover; a mediator.

शठंगार, *m.* decoration.

शठता, *f.* (*m.* °त्व) deceitfulness, knavery, craftiness; perfidiousness, depravity, wickedness.

शठमना, *m.* or *f.* a person of an evil mind.

शण, *m.* hemp (*Cannabis sativa*); a certain plant (*Crotolaria juncea*) and its flax or fibre. It is commonly called Bengal *san*, and from it a kind of hemp is prepared.

शणसूत्र, *m.* the fibre or flax of the above-named plant (*Crotolaria juncea*) or string or net made from it; twine, cordage, packthread.

शणीर, *m. pr. n.* (1) of a certain rock or small island in the midst of the river Sone (2) of a certain island inclosed by the branches of the Saryū where it falls into the Ganges.

शगड, *m.* a bull at liberty ; a eunuch ; an impotent man ; a clown ; a collection of lotus-flowers.

शत, *m.* a hundred.

शतक, *m.* a hundred ; a hundred collectively.

शतगुण, a hundred times over, a hundredfold.

शतद्रु, *f. pr. n.* the river Sutlej in the Panjāb. It rises in the Himālayas (in the vicinity, it is supposed, of the *Rāvan hrad* or lake), and flowing in a south-westerly direction, unites, in the Panjāb, with the Beya and Vipasa (when it forms the Hypasis of the Greeks) and falls into the Indus below Mooltan.

शतधन्वा, *m.pr.n.* a certain person slain by Krishṇ [for having killed Satrājit.

शतपति, *m.* (*f.* patni) the lord or chief of a hundred men, a centurion, military officer.

शतपदी / **शतपाद** } *f.* a centipede, jaulus.

शतभिषा, *f.pr.n.* the 25th Nakshatra (containing one hundred stars, the chief of which is [λ] Aquarü).

शतम, *m.* reproach, contumely, contempt, outrage, injury, villainy, abuse not amounting to slander.

शतमूल, *m.* / **शतमूली**, *f.* } the plant *Asparagus racemosus.*

शतरंज, *more prop.* **शत्रंज**, *q.v.*

शतरूपा, *more prop.* **सतरूपा**, *q. v.*

शतलक्ष, *m.* ten millions ; *lit.* a hundred lacs.

शतलज, *m.pr.n.* the river Satlaj or Sutlej.

शतवर्ष, *m.* a century ; *lit.* a hundred years.

शतवेधी, *m.* a species of dock or sorrel (*Oxalis monadelpha* or *Rumex vesicarius*).

शतसहस्र, *m.* a lac ; *lit.* a hundred thousands.

शत्ता, *m.* (*f.* ī) ingenious, clever, cunning.

शत्रंज, *f.* chess ; a chess-board.

शत्रंजबाज़, *m.* (*f.* nī) a chessplayer.

शत्रंजबाज़ी, *f.* chessplaying.

शत्रंजी, 1, *m.* (*f.* inī) a person who excels at chess: 2, *f.* a kind of spotted carpet (esp. one on which games are played).

शत्रवन ; see (1) **शत्रुन** (2) **शत्रुवन** (3) **शत्रुहन**.

शत्री = **क्षत्री** = **खत्री**, *q.v.*

शत्रु, *m. f.* an enemy, adversary, foe.

शत्रुघ्न, *m. pr. n.* one of the brothers of Rām : lit. *m.* (*f.* ā *or* ī) a foe-slayer, a hosticide.

शत्रुता, *f.* (*m.* °त्व) enmity, animosity, hostility.

शत्रुताई (see ई, 14) = **शत्रुता**, *q.v.*

शत्रुन, a Braj pl. of **शत्रु**. See **न**, 6 (1).

शत्रुभाव, 1, *m.* a hostile disposition, enmity : 2, *adj.* of a hostile or quarrelsome disposition.

शत्रुवन, *m. pr. n.* a certain ancient Hindoo king, son of Dhrishtketu and Shrutikīrti.

शत्रुहन, *m.* (*f.* °नी *or* °घ्नी) = **शत्रुघ्न**, *q. v.* [strong.

शदीद, difficult ; afflicting ; violent, intrepid,

शद्ध, a corruption of **शुद्ध**, *q. v.*

शन ; see (1) **शण** (2) **शनि** (3) **सन**.

शनक, *more prop.* **सनक**, *q. v.*

शनि, *m. pr. n.* (1) of the planet Saturn (2) of its regent or mythological personification.

शनिग्रह, *m. pr. n.* the planet Saturn.

शनिप्रिय, *m.* the emerald or sapphire.

शनिवार, *m.* Saturday.

शनिश्चर, *m.* the planet Saturn, Saturday.

शनिसन्ध्या / **शनिसांझ** } *f.* Saturday evening.

शनीचर, *more com.* **सनीचर**, *q. v.*

शनीर, *more prop.* **शमीर**, *q.v.*

शनै, hesitatingly, slowly, tardily, stealthily, gradually, successively.

शनैशनै, slowly, stealthily, tardily, little by little, step by step, gradually, successively.

शनैश्चर, *m. pr. n.* the planet Saturn.

शपथ, *m.* a solemn asseveration, oath, imprecation, curse, asseveration by oath or ordeal ; abuse, malediction, cursing.

शपन = **शपथ**, *q. v.*

शपर ; see (1) **शप्पर** (2) **शफर**.

शप्त, 1, *m.* (*f.* ā) anthematized, accursed: 2, *m.* a certain grass (*Saccharum cylindricum*).

शप्पर, *m.* a bat ; *lit.* night-flier.

शप्पा, *m.* a butt or mark for archers.

शफ़क़, *f.* evening, twilight; the horizon; condolence, sympathy, kindness ; fear.

शफ़क़त, *f.* clemency, compassion, mercy, kindness, affection, sympathy, condolence.

शफ़्फ़ाफ़ी, *f.* clearness, transparency.

शफर, *m.* = **शफरी**, *q. v.*

शफरी, *f.* a certain small glistening fish (*Cyprinus sophore*, Ham.: or *Cyprinus chrysoparius*, Buch.). It is a sort of carp, and is also called *punthi*, and mango fish.

शफ़ाअत, *f.* deprecation, intercession, intreaty, recommendation.

शफ़ाख़ाना, *m.* a hospital, lazaretto.

शफ़ीक़, merciful, compassionate, affectionate.

शब, 1, *f.* night : 2, *more prop.* (1) **शव** (2) **सब**, *qq. v.*

शबका, *m.* a net, lattice, reticulated veil.

शबद = **शब्द**, *q. v.* [gauze : 2, *f.* night-moisture, dew.

शबनम, 1, *m.* kind of cloth, a very fine muslin or

शबय ; see **सबय**, *q. v.*

शबा, *m.* a nocturnal attack.

शबानगाह, *f.* evening (the entrance of night) ; a place or fold for lodging cattle at night.

शबाब, *m.* youth, prime of life.

शबारोज़, *m.* night and day, twenty-four hours.

शबाहत, *f.* resemblance, similarity.

शबीह, alike, resembling : hence, *f.* resemblance, likeness ; a picture.

शबोरोज़, night and day, continually.

शब्द, *m.* (*f.* ?) sound, noise, voice ; grammar : a word ; (in Gram.) a declinable word (as a noun, pronoun, etc.) without its termination : verbal communication : (among Nānakpanthis) a song.

शब्दकार, sonorous, sounding.

शब्दकोष, *m.* a dictionary.

शब्दचोर, *m.* (*f.* in) a plagiarist.

शब्दब्रह्म, *m.* Holy Writ, a Ved.

शब्दभेदी, *m.* an epithet of Arjun ; a certain fabled arrow or dart. [a radical word.

शब्दयोनि, *f.* the source or origin of a word, a root,

शब्दवेधी, *m.* (*f.* inī) one who has the skill of shooting an arrow, etc. on an unseen person on hearing a sound made by him.

शब्दशास्त्र, *m.* the science of grammatical inflection, rules of grammar, etymology, grammar, philology.

शब्दसाधन, *m.* (in Gram.) etymology.

शब्दाकर, *m.* = शब्दयोनि, *q.v.*

शब्दोत्पत्ति, *f.* the origin or the production of words.

शम, *m.* 1, rest, tranquillity, quiet, calmness, undisturbedness, quiet of mind, disregard of the objects of sense, the absence of passion, indifference, stoicism; abstract meditation on the Supreme Being ; emancipation from human existence, final happiness : 2, convalescence, cure : the hand : imprecation, abuse.

शमः, *more prop.* **शम्मा**, *q.v.*

शमत, potherbs and spices put into victuals whilst dressing: a mixture of black and white hairs.

शमता, *f.* } **शम**, 1, *q.v.*
शमथ, *m.* }

शमन, *m.* 1, = **शम**, *q.v.*: 2, the immolation of animals for sacrifice: hurt, injury : malediction, abuse: an antelope: *pr. n.* Yam (regent of the dead).

शमशेर, *f.* a sword, scimitar.

शम्स, *m.* the sun.

शमा, *more prop.* (1) **शम्मा** (2) **समा**, *qq.v.*

शमातत, *f.* rejoicing at the calamities or misfortunes of another.

शमादान, *m.* a perfume-box.

शमाल, *m.* the north ; the north wind; the left hand.

शमि, *f.* a pod, legume.

शमित, *m.* (*f.* ā) pacified, appeased, calm, tranquil, quiet, sedate ; pacific, tranquilized.

शमी, 1, *m.* (*f.* ini) = **शमित**, *q.v.*: 2, *f.* a pod, legume : a large stick ; a certain shrub (*Serratula anthelmintica*): a certain tree (*Acacia suma*, Roxb.).

शमीपत्री, *f.* a species of the sensitive-plant (*Mimosa pudica*).

शमीर, *m.* a certain small variety of the *Acacia suma.*

शमे; see (1) **शम्मा** (2) **समय**.

शमें, *more prop.* **समें** = **समय**, *q. v.*

शमेसे, *more prop.* **समयसे** (**समय**).

शम्बा, *m.* Saturday.

शम्बाली, *f.* the chaste tree (*Vitex negundo*).

शम्बु
शम्बुक } = **शम्बूक**, 1, *q.v.*
शम्बुक्क

शम्बूक, *m.* 1, a bivalve shell, a conch-shell ; a snail: 2, the edge of the frontal protuberance of an elephant: *pr. n.* a certain demon (*daitya*).

शम्बूका, *f.* = **शम्बूक**, *q.v.*

शम्भु, *m.* an epithet (1) of Brahmā (2) of Shiv (3) of any sage man (4) of a semi-divine being (*siddh*).

शम्भुमनु, *more prop.* **स्वयंभूमनु**, *q.v.*

शम्भूसुत, *m.* (*f.* ā) a child of Shambhu.

शम्मा, *m.* an atom, particle; a little: odour, perfume : habit, custom.

शयतान, *more prop.* **शैतान**, *q.v.*

शयन, *m.* a reposing, sleeping; sleep; a bed, couch: copulation.

शयनस्थान, *m.* a sleeping place, bed-chamber.

शयनेच्छुक, desirous of sleep or of copulation.

शयालु, 1, *m. f.* sluggish, slothful, sleepy: 2, *m.* a snake, a boa-constrictor : a dog.

शय्या, *f.* a bed, couch, sofa.

शर, *m.* a sort of reed (*Saccharum sara*); a reed, tube ; an arrow : (in Math.) the versed sine of an arc : the cream of slightly curdled milk: the swell of the tide : water.

शरई, *f.* tight drawers, trowsers.

शरकिस्तान, *m.* the East ; Asia (*lit.* the country of the unbelievers).

शरग, a Prākrit form of **स्वर्ग**, *q. v.*

शरच्चन्द्र, *m.* the autumnal moon.

शरट, *m.* a lizard, a chameleon: safflower.

शरण, 1, *m.* (*f.* ?) a place of shelter or refuge, an asylum, retreat, habitation, house ; preservation, security, safety. protection. defence, help : 2, *m.* (*f.* ā) a protector, etc : lit. *adj.* protecting, preserving. — *ānā* (sc. *meṅ*) or *lenā*, to take refuge in, have recourse to.

शरणद, *adj.* shelter-affording : hence, *m.* (*f.* ā) a shelterer, protector.

शरणा, *f.* (*m.* **शरण** 2) a protectress.

शरणागत, *m.* (*f.* ā) one who comes for protection or refuge, a refugee, appellant : lit. *adj.* having come for refuge.

शरणागतवत्सल, *m.* an epithet of the Supreme: *lit.* compassionate or merciful to those who come for sanctuary.

शरणागति, *m.* a taking refuge, flying for protection.

शरणागती, 1, *more prop.* **शरणागति**, *q.v.*: 2, *m.* (*f.* inī) *more prop.* **शरणागत**, *q. v.*

शरणापन्न, *m.* (*f.* ā) = **शरणागत**, *q.v.*

शरणार्थी, *m.* (*f.* inī) one who sues for protection: lit. *adj.* sueing for refuge, dependent on others for protection, wretched, unfortunate.

शरणि
शरणी } *f.* a row, line; a road, path, way.

शरण्य, 1, *m.* = **शरण**, 1, *q.v.*: 2, *m.* (*f.* ā) a protector, etc. : a refuge, etc.: lit. (1) fit to be resorted to for protection (2) needing to be protected, helpless, poor, miserable.

शरत, *f.* the sultry season, autumn, the two months succeeding the rains. According to the Vaidiks, it comprizes the months Bhādra and Ashwin ; and according to the Paurāṇiks, it comprizes Ashwin and Kārttik, thus fluctuating from August to November.

शरतकाल, *m.* = **शरत**, *q.v.*

शरतकालीन, autumnal (*lit.* appertaining to *sharat-kāl*).

शरद
शरदा } *f.* = **शरत**, *q. v.*

शरदी, *more com.* **सरदी**, *q.v.*

शरफ़, *m.* nobility, excellence, eminence, rank.

शरबत, *more prop.* **शर्बत**, *q.v.*

शरबन, *more prop.* **शरवन**, *q.v.*

शरभ, *m.* a certain fabulous animal (with eight legs and stronger than a lion) supposed to inhabit the snowy mountains : a young elephant : a grasshopper : a locust.

शरम, *f.* bashfulness, modesty, shame.

शरमन्दगी, *f.* shame, bashfulness, modesty.

शरमन्दा, *m.* (*f.* ī) blushing, abashed, ashamed, bashful, modest.

शरमल्ल, *m.* a certain small bird (*Turdus gosalica*) considered as a variety of the Salic or Maina.

शरमा ; see (1) **शर्म** (2) **शर्म्मा**.

शरमाना = **शर्माना**, *q v.* [ed, abashed.

शरमाया, *m.* (*f.* **शरमाई**) smitten with shame, asham-

शरमिन्दा, *m.* (*f.* ī) = **शरमन्दा**, *q.v.*

शरयु, 1, *m.* = **सरयु**, *q. v* : 2, *f* = **सरयू**, *q. v.*

शरयू. *more prop.* **सरयू**, *q.v.*

शरकिसतान (corruption) = **शरकिस्तान**, *q.v.* [सरल.

शरल; for words beginning thus, see under the form

शरवन, *m.* a thicket of reeds: *pr. n.* a certain forest in the Himālayas near mount Kailās.

शरह, *m.* desire, appetite, avidity, gluttony.

शरा, *m.* an eruption of pimples on the skin : desire, appetite, avidity, gluttony.

शराकत, *f.* participation, partnership.

शराटा, *m.* sound, noise, voice.

शराटि, *f.* a certain bird (*Tardus ginginianus*) commonly called the Āli or Sarāli.

शराडि, **शराति** = **शराटि**, *q.v.*

शराप; for words beginning thus, see under the

शराफ़त, *f.* nobility, eminence. [form **शाप**.

शराब, *f.* spirituous liquor, wine.

शराबी, appertaining to spiritous liquor, winebibbing, intoxicated: hence, *m.* (*f.* in *or* inī) a drunkard.

शराबोर, soused, dripping wet.

शरारत, *f.* vice, wickedness, depravity, villainy.

शरारि, **शरालि**, **शराली** = **शराटि**, *q.v.*

शराव, *m.* a lid, cover ; a shallow cup or dish, a tray, vessel, platter : a measure equal to two *kuḍavs*.

शरासन, *m.* arrow-shooting ; a bow.

शरिअत, **शरियत** more prop. **शरीअत**, *q. v.*

शरिर, *more prop.* **शरीर**, *q.v.* [mad in the Kur,ān.

शरीअत, *f.* law, justice, equity; the laws of Muham-

शरीक, *m.* a partner, associate, comrade, ally, accomplice, friend, participator.

शरीफ़, noble, excellent, eminent, illustrious. A title given to the rulers of Mecca.

शरीफ़ा, *m.* the custard-apple (*Annona squamosa*).

शरीर, 1, *m.* the body: life: 2, wicked, vicious.

शरीरक = (1) **शारीरक** (2) **शारीरिक**, *qq.v.*

शरीरबन्धक, *m.* (*f.* ī) a hostage.

शरीरसंस्कार, *m.* purification of the body by various ceremonies on the occasion of conception, birth, initiation, death, etc. [*i. e.* death.

शरीरान्त, *m.* the end or destruction of the body,

शरीरी, 1, *m.* the soul whilst it occupies the body : 2 *m.* (*f.* iṇī) an animal, a sentient being, an embodied spirit, a man : 3, appertaining to the body, corporeal, embodied, invested with a body, bodily.

शर्क़, *m.* the East; rising (as of the sun).

शर्करा, *f.* (*m.* ?) gravel, stone ; a potsherd ; the gravel (disease) ; a part ; a soil abounding in stony fragments ; clayed or candied sugar.

शर्करावन्त, **शर्करावान** *m.* (*f.* vatī) = **शर्करिल**, *q. v.*

शर्करिल, *m.* (*f.* ā) full of stony particles, gritty, gravelly. [a mark, sign, signal.

शर्त, *f.* agreement, condition, stipulation, wager :

शर्तव्रर्त, *f.* advantage, profit, success. — *karnā* or *denā*, to lavish. [medicine.

शर्बत, *m.* a beverage, drink, sherbet, dose of

शर्म, 1, *more prop.* **शर्म्म**, *q.v.* : 2, *f.* shame, bashfulness, modesty. [to blush.

शर्माना, to be abashed, be ashamed, to feel shame,

शर्म्म, *m.* blessing, happiness, delight, pleasure.

शर्म्मा, 1, *m.* = **शर्म्म**, *q.v.* : 2, *m.* an appellation commonly appended to the names of Brāhmaṇs : 3, *m.* (*f.* ī) glad, happy, prosperous.

शर्व्वरी, *f.* night: a woman : turmeric.

शल, *m.* porcupine's quill: a dart: a kind of field : an epithet of Brahmā. [sperma viri : vulva.

शलख़, *m.* a round, discharge, volley, broadside:

शलग़म, *m.* a turnip.

शलबोन, *f.* vice (in a horse).

शलभ, *m.* a grasshopper, a locust.

शलल, *m.*, **शलली**, *f.* a porcupine's quill.

शलवार, *m.* trowsers.

शलाक़, *f.* flogging, flagellation : coitus.

शलाका, *f.* a dart, arrow, javelin ; a rule, a ruler ; a probe ; a small stake, the bar of a cage, a rib of an umbrella, a fibrous stick used as a brush or pencil, a thin slip of bamboo serving (when tipped with sulphur) for a match ; a rod, peg, pin, pencil, ruler, brimstone match : a porcupine : a piece of ivory used in particular games, a domino : a bone : a certain bird (*Turdus gosalica*).

शलोत: = **शलोता**, *q. v.*

शलोता, *m.* a canvas sack, etc. in which baggage is fastened previously to being loaded on cattle.

शलूका, *m.* a child's bib.

शल्य, *m.* a dart, arrow, javelin ; a peg, pin ; a porcupine; a certain thorny shrub (*Vangueria spinosa*); a bamboo rod or stake; an iron crow ; any extraneous substance that has lodged in the body (as an arrow or a thorn); difficulty, embarrassment; a boundary; poison; sin; abuse; *pr. n.* (1) of the king of Madra, paternal uncle of the Pāṇḍav princes (2) of a son of Viprachitti.

शल्यशास्त्र, *m.* that branch of surgery which treats of extraneous substances lodged in the body.

शल्योद्धार, *m.* the extracting foreign substances (as arrows or thorns) from the body: the ceremony of cleansing the site of a new house from bones or other unclean substances.

शल्लक, *m.* a certain plant (*Bignonia Indica*): bark, rind.

शल्लकी, *f.* a porcupine: the gum-olibanum tree (*Boswellia thurifera*).

शल्लकीद्रव, *m.* incense, olibanum.

शल्व, *m. pr. n.* a certain country.

शव, *m.* a dead body, corpse: water.

शवर, 1, *m.* an epithet of Shiv: 2, water: 3, *m.* (*f.* ī) a member of a certain tribe of barbarians who inhabit the mountainous districts of India and wear peacock's feathers as decorations.

शवसाधन, *m.* a certain mystical and superstitious ceremony performed by means of a dead body.

शवाद; see **सवाद**.

शवाले; see (1) **सिवालय** (2) **सुवाल**.

शव्वाल, *m.* the 10th month of the Muhammadan year.

शश, *m.* a hare, a rabbit; the spots on the moon supposed to resemble the figure of a hare: gum-myrrh: a certain tree (*Symplocus racemosa*): an uxorious man.

शशक, *m.* a hare, a rabbit.

शशधर / **शशभृत** } *m.* epithets of the moon.

शशमुख, *m.* (*f.* ī) / **शशवदन**, *m.* (*f.* ā *or* ī) } = **शशिमुख**, *q.v.*

शशबिन्दु, *m.* (*lit.* hare-spotted) an epithet (1) of the moon (2) of Vishṇu or Krishṇ: *pr. n.* a certain king (son of Chitrarath).

शशस्थली, *f.* an epithet of the Doāb (the country lying between the Ganges and Jumna rivers).

शशा, *more com.* **शश**, *q.v.*

शशांक, *m.* an epithet of the moon.

शशि (*Rām.*) = **शशिन** (2) **रेवती**, *qq.v.*

शशिकर, *m.* a moonbeam.

शशिकिरण, *m.* a moonbeam.

शशिन, *m.* an epithet of the moon.

शशिपोषक, *m.* the nourisher of the moon (an epithet of Shuklpaksh).

शशिभूषण, *m.* (the moon-decorated, *i.e.*) Shiv.

शशिमुख, *m.* (*f.* ī) moon-faced, having a beautiful countenance.

शशिरस, *m.* ambrosia, nectar.

शशिललाट, *m.* (the moon-headed, *i.e.*) Shiv.

शशिलिलाट, *more prop.* **शशिललाट**, *q.v.*

शशिलेखा, *f.* a digit of the moon.

शशिशोषक, *m.* the destroyer of the moon (an epithet of Krishṇpaksh).

शशिसमाज, *m.* the moon's orbit.

शशी, *m.* an epithet of the moon.

शशुर, *more prop.* **श्वशुर**, *q.v.*

शश्मान (by inversion) = **श्मशान** *q.v.*

शसि, *more prop.* **शशि**, *q.v.*

शस्त्र, *m.* a weapon (*esp.* a hand-weapon), arms; a sword, scimitar: iron, steel: a hymn.—*bāndhnā*, to gird on weapons of war, take up arms.

शस्त्रकार, *m.* (*f.* ī) an armourer.

शस्त्रगृह, *m.* a repository of arms, armoury.

शस्त्रधारी, *adj.* seizing (holding, or possessing) weapons, armed: hence, *m.* (*f.* iṇī) an armed person, a warrior.

शस्त्रबन्ध, *m.* (*f.* ā) armed, accoutred, equipped.

शस्त्राभ्यास, *m.* military exercise.

शस्त्रविद्या, *f.* the science of arms.

शस्त्रशाला, *f.* = **शस्त्रगृह**, *q.v.*

शस्प, *m.* young grass: loss of intellect.

शस्मान (*corruption*) = **श्मशान**, *q.v.*

शस्य, *m.* a good quality, an excellence, a merit; grain, corn, fruit, kernel, harvest, grass.

शस्यभक्षक, *m.* (*f.* ikā) any graminivorous animal: lit. *adj.* grain-eating.

शस्याढ्यत्व, *m* (*f.* tā) wealth of merit; wealth of grain.

शह, *m.* a king: (at Chess) check.

शहचाल, *f.* a term used at chess when only the king can move.

शहज़ादा, *m.* a king's son, prince.

शहज़ादी, *f.* a king's daughter, princess.

शहज़ोर, stout, gallant, strong, brave, heroic.

शहतीर, *m.* a beam.

शहतूत, *m.* a mulberry.

शहद, *m.* honey. — *makkhī*, *f.* a bee.

शहन; see (1) **शहना** (2) **सहन**.

शहना, *m.* a representative, lieutenant, viceroy; a peon or servant of a taxgatherer.

शहनाई, *m.* a clarion, hautboy, flute.

शहबत, a corruption of **शहवत**, *q.v.*

शहबास; see (1) **शाबाश** (2) **सहवास**.

शहर, *m.* a city: a lunar month.

शहरपनाह, *m.* a wall or entrenchments around a town.

शहरयार, *m.* a prince, king.

शहवत, *m.* concupiscence, lust, appetite, desire.

शहसान, *more prop.* **सहसान**, *q.v.*

शहादत, *f.* evidence, testimony, martyrdom.

शहाना, *m.* (*f.* ī) appertaining to royalty, princely, kingly, royal.

शहीद, killed; martyred. — *honā*, to be killed, be martyred: *met.* to fall desperately in love.

शहीर, 1, celebrated, famous, notorious, well-known: 2, a sort of tree.

शहुवा; see **शहवत**.

शहेर / **शहैर** } see (1) **शहर** (2) **शहीर**.

शा, 1, *more prop.* **शाह**, *q.v.*: 2, *f.* an epithet of Durgā.

शाइर, *m.* (Pers.: *pl.* ān) a poet.

शांकड़ि; (1) शंकरी (2) सांकरी.

शांत; for all words beginning thus, see under the corresponding form **शान्त**.

शाक, *m.* any vegetable, a potherb, greens: any leaf, flower, fruit, stalk, root, etc. used as a vegetable; the teak-tree (*Tectona grandis*): power: one of the seven divisions of the world (*dwīp*), esp. the 6th surrounded by white or milky sea: an era, a period usually dating from the reign of some celebrated prince. The term is most generally applied to the era of Shālivāhan.

शाकनी, *more prop.* **शाकिनी**, *q.v.*

शाकपुणि / **शाकपूणि** } = **शाकपूर्णि**, *q.v.*

शाकपूर्णि, *m. pr. n.* a certain ancient interpreter of the Ved.

शाकम्भरी, *f. pr. n.* a certain city (supposed to be the modern Sāmbhar in the province of Ajmere)

शाकम्भरीय, *m.* a kind of salt brought from a lake in the vicinity of Sāmbhar.

शाकल, *f.* a certain mixture (of sesamum-seeds, fruits, ghee, barley, coarse sugar, etc.) used by Hindoos in oblations to the gods: *pr. n.* a certain school of the Rig-Ved.

शाकला, 1, = **शाकल**, *q.v.*: 2, *m.* (see **शा**, 22) a certain tribe inhabiting Bhāratvarsh; the followers of the Shākal school.

शाकल्य, *more prop.* **साकल्य**, *q.v.*

शाकिनी, *f.* a certain inferior class of female divinity (attendant chiefly on Shiv and Durgā).

शाकी, *m.* (*f.* inī) complainer, backbiter.

शाकेश्वर, *m.* (see **शाक**) an epithet of any prince (as Yudhisthir, Vikramāditya, Shālivāhan, etc.) who has established an era, or after whom an era is named.

शाक्त, *m.* (see **शक्ति**) a worshipper of Devī or the female principle.

शाक्य, *m.* an epithet of Buddh (the founder of the Bauddh faith).

शाक्यमुनि / **शाक्यसिंह** } = **शाक्य**, *q.v.*

शाख, *f.* a branch, bow, stalk; a horn.

शाखा, *f.* a branch, bow; an arm; a part; a division; a sect; any part of an animal devoid of sensibility (as a horn); a subdivision of the Veds according to the different schools and redactions of the holy writings.

शाखामृग, *m.* (*f.* ī) a monkey; a squirrel.

शाखी, 1, *m.* a tree; a Ved: 2, *m.* (*f.* inī) one who practices the injunctions of any particular branch of the Veds: *lit.* having branches, branched.

शाखोच्चार, *m.* the relating a genealogy, stating a pedigree.

शागिर्द, *m.* a pupil, disciple, apprentice, servant.

शागिर्दपेशा, *m.* a servant, menial; retinue.

शाचाल; see **शतचाल**.

शाट, *m.* a petticoat; a garment.

शाटक, *m.* a petticoat, a woman's garment.

शाटी, *f.* a petticoat; a gown; cloth.

शाठ्य, *m.* deceit, perfidy, craft, villainy, vice, wickedness, hatred.

शाण, *m.* a touchstone, whetstone, grindstone: coarse cloth, canvas.

शाणी, *f.* a ragged garment: a new, unseamed, single breadth of cloth given to the religious student at his investiture: a whetstone, grindstone, touchstone.

शातिर, wanton; clever; sly: hence, *m.* an expert player; a chess-player; a messenger.

शाद, pleased, delighted, cheerful, exulting.

शादकामी, *f.* happiness, gladness, delight, content.

शादी, *f.* delight, pleasure, rejoicing, festivity; marriage, wedding, a marriage-feast.

शान, 1, *f.* an affair, business: state, condition, degree, dignity, pomp: constitution, nature, disposition: 2, *m.* a honey-comb.

शाना, *m.* a comb, crest; the shoulder.

शानी, 1, *more prop.* **सानी**, *q.v.*: 2, of age, arrived at the age of puberty.

शान्त, 1, *f.* (*contraction*) = **शान्ति**, *q.v.*: 2, *m.* (*f.* ā) one whose passions are subdued, an ascetic: *lit.* allayed, pacified, appeased, hushed, calm, tranquil, meek, humble, content.

शान्तज्वर, *m.* fever.

शान्तता, *f.* (*m.* °त्व) quietness, meekness, calmness.

शान्तशील, *m.* (*f.* ā) a person of subdued passions or of tranquil disposition.

शान्तात्मा, *m. f.* a person of a composed or resigned disposition: *lit.* of a calm and tranquil mind, composed.

शान्ति, *f.* absence of passion, and indifference to objects of pleasure or pain, comfort, tranquillity, quiet, rest, repose; stoicism; remission, alleviation.

शान्तित, *m* (*f.* ā) consoled, comforted.

शान्तिदाई, *adj.* imparting rest or repose, alleviating, peace-importing: hence, *m.* (*f.* inī) a tranquilizer, comforter.

शान्तिदाता *m.* (*f.* trī) / **शान्तिदायक**, *m.* (*f.* ika) } = **शान्तिदाई**, *q.v.*

शान्तिपर्व, *m.pr.n.* one of the main divisions of the Mahābhārat.

शान्तिमय, peaceful, tranquil, calm.

शाप, *m.* an affirmation by oath or ordeal, asseveration, oath, imprecation, curse, abuse, malediction. — *denā*, to curse, imprecate, invoke curses.

शापग्रस्त, *m.* (*f.* ā) one who lies under a curse: *lit.* seized by a curse, having incurred a curse, accursed.

शापना, *t.* to curse, imprecate, invoke curses upon.

शापित, *m.* (*f.* ā) sworn, cursed, imprecated; accursed.

शापोद्धार, *m.* deliverance from a curse or its effects.

शाफ़ी, *m.* (*f.* inī) a healer: *lit.* sanative, salutary, healing.

शाबान, *m.* (Portug.) soap.

शाबाश, bravo! well done! excellent!

शाबाशी, *f.* applause, praise, plaudit.

शाबासि, a corruption of **शाबाशी**, *q.v.*

शाम, 1, *m.* conciliation, appeasing: 2, *m. pr. n.* (1) of Krishṇ (2) of Syria (3) of Damascus: 3, *f.* evening.

शामत, *f.* bad fortune, adversity.

शामदेश, *m. pr. n.* Syria.

शामदेशी, *adj.* Syrian : hence, *m.* (*f.* inī) a Syrian.

शामा, *m.* mouldiness : two species of grass or grain (1) *Panicum colonum* (2) *Panicum frumentaceum*: a certain small kind of song-bird (*Turdus macrourus*)

शामियाना, *m.* an awning, canopy.

शामिल, 1, united, confederated, gathered together with, numbered among, identified with: 2, *adv.* together : 3, *postp.* with, along with.

शामिलात, common concerns, partnership.

शामी, *f.* the iron head or ring of a wooden pestle. — *lagānā*, to shoe with iron.

शाम्ब, *m. pr. n.* a son of Krishṇ by Jambavatī.

शामुक } = **शाम्बूक**, *q. v.*
शामूक }

शाम्बरी, *f.* jugglery, sorcery, illusion (as practised by the *daitya* Shāmbar): a sorceress.

शाम्बुक = **शाम्बूक**, *q.v.*

शाम्बूक, *m.* a bivalve shell; a conch-shell; a kind of snail (*Helix ampullacea*) from the shell of which lime is made.

शायक, *m.* an arrow, dart; a sword.

शायजादा, *m.* (*f.* i) a corruption of **शाहज़ादा**, *q. v.*

शायद, may be, perhaps, perchance, possibly, probably. [suspicion.

शायबा, *m.* mixture, pollution, stain; doubt,

शायान, legal, worthy, suitable, agreeable.

शार, 1, variegated in colour : yellow : 2, *m.* hurting : a mixture of blue and yellow, a green : variegating : air, wind : a piece or man (at Chess, etc.).

शारंग, variegated, spotted : hence, *m.* (*f.* ī) a deer; an elephant a peacock; a large bee; the *chātak* (*Cuculus melanoleucus*).

शारंगी, *f.* 1, (*m.* **शारंग**) a female deer, etc. : a sort of fiddle : *pr. n.* the wife of Mandapāl.

शारघर, *m.* a cattle-shed.

शारद, appertaining to autumn, autumnal: hence *m.* grain or rice which ripens in the autumn; a sort of kidney-bean; autumnal sickness; autumnal sunshine; a year. [Saraswatī (2) of Durgā.

शारदा, *f.* a sort of guitar : an epithet (1) of

शारदी, *f.* the day of full moon in Kārttik : two plants (1) *Echites scholaris* (2) *Jussieua repens.*

शारस, *more prop.* **सारस**, *q. v.*

शारि, 1, *m.* a piece or man (at Chess, etc.) : an elephant's housings : fraud : 2, *m. f.* certain bird (*Gracula religiosa*).

शारिक, *m.* the sun.

शारिका = **सारिका**, *q. v.* [*Gracula religiosa*).

शारी, *f.* an arrow : *kush*-grass : a certain bird

शारीर, *m.* the soul whilst incorporate; excrement : *lit.* appertaining to the animal body, incorporate, corporeal, bodily.

शारीरक, incorporate, corporeal, material.—*mīmānsā*, a certain celebrated work on the Vedānt system in the form of aphorisms, by Bādarāyaṇ.

शारीरिक, appertaining to the body, bodily, corporeal, carnal, material.

शारीरी; see (1) **शरीरी** (2) **शारीरिक**.

शार्दूल, *m.* a tiger; a *rākshas*; a certain bird. As the latter element in compound epithets it conveys the idea of eminence or distinction : *e. g.* **नरशार्दूल**, a tiger of a man, *i. e.* an eminent man.

शार्दूलललित, *m.* (in Pros.) a species of metre.

शार्दूलविक्रीड़ित, *m.* (in Pros.) a species of metre.

शार्वर, 1, *m.* (*f.* ī) nocturnal, mischievous, pernicious : 2, *m.* darkness.

शार्वरी, *f.* night.

शाल, 1, *m.* a certain tree (*Shorea robusta*): ajackal: 2, *m. pr. n.* Shālivāhan : 3, *m.* (*f.* ā) a certain fish (*Ophiocephalus wrahl*, Ham.) : 4, *f.* a shawl.

शालग्राम, *m.* a kind of flinty stone found in the Gandhak river, containing one or more ammonites, conceived by the Hindoos to represent Vishṇu. It is hence worshipped by the Vaishṇavs. [*gangeticum*).

शालपर्णी, *f.* a certain plant or shrub (*Hedysarum*

शालबाफ़, *m.* a shawl-weaver.

शालबाब, *m.* shawl-cloths. [of India.

शालभंजिका, *f.* a doll; a kind of play in the east

शालभंजी, *f.* = **शालभंजिका**, *q. v.*

शाला, 1, *more prop.* **शुश्राला**, *q. v.*: 2, *f.* a large branch of a tree : a hall, room, house, stable, place. [cage.

शालार, *m.* a ladder : as elephant's claw : a bird-

शालि, *m.* 1, the civet or polecat : 2, rice [*esp.* two varieties (1) a white rice growing in deep water (2) a red sort requiring only a moist soil].

शालिक, 1, appertaining to the *Shorea robusta* or to a hall : 2. *m.* a weaver : a village of artificers: a tax.

शालिकपर्व, *m. pr. n.* one of the main divisions of the Mahābhārat.

शालिग्राम = **शालग्राम**, *q.v.*

शालिवाहन, *m. pr. n.* (see **शाकेश्वर**) a certain ancient sovereign of India, institutor of the era now called *Shāk*. He was the enemy of Vikramāditya, and held his capital at Pratisthān in the Dakkhan.

शालिहोत्र, 1, *m.* (*f.* ī) a horse: 2, *m. pr. n.* a certain writer on veterinary medicine.

शालिहोत्री, *m.* (*f.* iṇī) a horse.

शाली, 1, *m.* (*f.* inī) a weaver of shawls and similar articles : 2, = **शालि**, *q. v* : 3, *adj.* made of shawl: 4, *m.* (*f.* inī) appertaining to a house, domestic: 5, used in forming compound epithets [*m.* (*f.* inī)] in the sense of endowed with, possessed of, having, shining or resplendent with; inclined to, disposed to.

शाल्मलि, *f.* 1, *pr. n.* (see **द्वीप**) one of the seven greater divisions (*dwīp*) of the known world : 2, the silk-cotton tree (*Bombax heptaphyllum*).

शाल्मली, *f.* 1. = **शाल्मलि**, *q.v.*: 2, *pr. n.* a certain river in the infernal regions.

शाल्व, *m. pr. n.* (1) of the inhabitants of Shalv (2) of their king, who was slain by Krishṇ.

शावक, *m.* the young of any animal, a child.

शावर्णि, *more prop.* **सावर्णि**, *q. v.*

शावान, *m.* (Portug.) soap.

शाशक, *m.* (*f.* ikā) *more prop.* = **शासक**, *q. v.*

शाशन (*corruption*) = **शासन**, *q. v.*

शाश्वत, *m.* (*f.* ī) all ; eternal, perpetual ; immortal : hence, *m.* an epithet (1) of Shiv (2) of the sun (3) of Vyās (4) of heaven.

शाश्वती, *f.* an epithet of the earth.

शासक, *m.* (*f.* ikā) a governor ; a chastizer.

शासन, *m.* governing, ruling, command ; chastizement ; authority, control ; an order, command, precept, edict ; a written contract, a patent, a grant, a deed ; a royal grant of land or privileges a shāstra or scripture : governing the passions : instruction.

शासनपत्र, *m.* any substance (as a sheet of paper, a stone, or a plate of copper) on which an edict, etc. is inscribed. [ish, admonish.

शासना, 1, *f.* = **शासन**, *q.v.* : 2, *t.* to chastize, pun-

शासनीय, *m.* (*f.* ā) deserving correction or punishment ; suitable or proper to be governed.

शासिता / **शासितृ** } *m.* (*f.* trī) = **शास्ता**, *q.v.*

शास्तर (*corruption*) = **शास्त्र**, *q.v.*

शास्ता, *m.* (*f.* trī) a ruler, governor, commander, preceptor, teacher.

शास्ति, *f.* a command, order, edict ; governing, ruling ; correction, punishment inflicted by royal command.

शास्त्र, *m.* an order, command, precept, rule, law ; a code of laws ; a book, collection, treatise ; a science ; literature ; law : learning ; science, scripture, institutes of religion ; a work of a religious or scientific character ; certain sacred books of the Hindoos. Used singly the term implies works of literature or science in general ; it is therefore usual to connect it with some other word in order to limit its application ; thus *Vedānt-Shāstra*, the Hindoo treatises on philosophical theology ; *Kām-Shāstra* the erotic compositions of the Hindoos. In the singular number it is also used comprehensively to signify the body of all that has been written on the subject; thus, *Dharm-Shastra*, the institutes or codes of law ; *Kāvya Shāstra*, poetical works ; *Alaṅkār-Shāstra*, works on rhetoric, etc. See **षटशास्त्र**.

शास्त्रग, 1, a contraction of **शास्त्रज्ञ**, *q.v.*: 2, *m.* (*f.* ā) one who conducts himself according to law or religion.

शास्त्रजन्य, *m.* an epithet of religion (*lit.* born of the Shāstras).

शास्त्रजन्या, *f.* an epithet of religious deeds (*lit.* born of the Shāstras).

शास्त्रज्ञ, *m.* (*f.* ā) a learned person; a theologian; a theorist: *lit.* acquainted with the Shāstras: skilled in knowledge (*esp.* of law and religion): acquainted with science or with books, knowing by means of books

शास्त्रतः, according to law, in harmony with the precepts of science or the teachings of religion.

शास्त्रनि, a Braj pl. of **शास्त्र**. See **नि**, 2 (1).

शास्त्रविरुद्ध, contrary to law or to religion, illegal, forbidden.

शास्त्रवेत्ता / **शास्त्रवेत्तृ** } *m.* (*f.* trī) = **शास्त्रज्ञ**, *q.v.*

शास्त्राध्ययन, *m.* study (*esp.* of sacred science).

शास्त्रानुसार, conformably to the ordinances or precepts of law or of religion.

शास्त्रार्थ, *m.* the object or substance of a book, the purport of a passage of law or religion; argument, debate, dispute discussion, discourse.

शास्त्रिक = **शास्त्रीय**, *q.v.*

शास्त्री, *m.* (*f.* iṇī) a teacher of sacred science, one who is skilled in sacred science, a pandit.

शास्त्रीय, appertaining to (authorized by or conformable to) sacred institutes, legal, scriptural.

शास्त्रोक्त, said in a book, declared by law, sanctioned by a work of sacred authority.

शास्य, fit (or requiring) to be regulated or ordained; deserving punishment, punishable, corrigible.

शाह, *m.* a king ; (at Chess) the king. A title assumed by fakeers. [a prince,

शाहज़ादा, *m.* (*f.* ī) the offspring of a monarch,

शाहज़ादी, *f.* (*m.* **शाहज़ादा**) a princess.

शाहन्शाह, *m.* a king of kings, an emperor. A title adopted by the ancient kings of Persia.

शाहाज़ादा, *m.* (*f.* ī) a corruption of **शाहज़ादा**, *q.v.*

शाहाना, *m* (*f.* ī) appertaining to a king, princely, regal, royal: a kind of dress worn by a bridegroom.

शाहिद, *m.* a witness : (in Pers.) a beloved object, sweetheart, female friend.

शाहीन, *m.* a royal white falcon.

शिंशपा, *f.* the name of two trees (1) of the *ashoka*-tree (2) of the *Dalbergia sisu*.

शिंशिपा = **शिंशपा**, *q.v.* [fold, ply, curl, furrow.

शिकन, *f.* a shrinking, shrivelling, constringing; a

शिकम, *m.* the stomach.

शिकरा, *m.* a falcon, hawk (*Falco*).

शिकस्त, 1, broken, uneven, unpaired, odd : 2, *f.* deficiency, loss, defeat, breaking.

शिकायत, *f.* lamentation, complaint, accusation.

शिकार, *m.* hunting, the chase ; prey, game, plunder : a catch (of fishes); perquisites. — *khelnā*, to engage in the chase.

शिकारगाह, *f.* a place for hunting in.

शिकारबन्द, *m.* cords, etc. for tying game in, or to be tied to a horse's saddle.

शिकारबाज़, *m.* a sportsman, hunter.

शिकारी, *m.* (*f.* iṇī) one who hunts or 'takes' live animals (birds, beasts, or fishes) especially one who 'takes' them as a sport, a sportsman, hunter, fowler, angler or fisherman: *lit.* appertaining to hunting, etc.

शिकिल, *more prop.* **सैक़ल**, *q.v.*

शिक्षक, *m.* (*f.* ikā) a learner; a teacher; a preacher.

शिक्षा, *f.* instruction, teaching, sermon, doctrine, learning, knowledge ; a lesson ; study, the acquisition of knowledge, education; modesty : one of the six auxiliary branches (see **वेदांग**) of sacred study.

शिक्षाग्राहक, *m.* (*f.* ikā) one who receives instruction, a learner, pupil.

शिक्षानवीस, *m.* an apprentice.

शिक्षाशक्ति, *f.* skill, dexterity.

शिक्षित, *m.* (*f.* ā) taught, instructed, disciplined, exercised, docile, studied, learned, conversant, skilful, clever.

शिख, *more com.* **सिख**, 2, *q.v.*

शिखण्ड, *m.* a peacock's tail; the lock of hair left by Hindoos on the crown or side of the head.

शिखण्डक = **शिखण्ड**, *q.v.* [the crown of the head.

शिखण्डका, *f.* the lock of hair left by Hindoos on

शिखण्डिक, *m.* a cock-bird.

शिखण्डिनी, *f. pr. n.* the daughter of Drupad who was metamorphozed into a man.

शिखण्डी, 1, *m.* (*f.* inī) a peacock; a cock-bird: 2, *m.* a peacock's tail; an arrow: 3, *m. pr. n.* (1) of a certain *rishi* (2) of the son of Drupad who had formerly been a girl: 4, *lit.* crested.

शिखना = **सिखना**, *q. v.*

शिखर, *m.* point, end, summit, top, peak, pinnacle, the armpit: horripilation: a gem of a bright red colour: the bud of the Arabian jasmine.

शिखरिणी, *f.* a line of hair extending across the navel: an excellent woman: a dish of curds and sugar with spices: Arabian jasmine.

शिखरी, 1, *m.* a mountain; a tree; a stronghold, hill fort: 2, *m.* (*f.* iṇī) the lapwing: 3, *lit.* crested, peaked, pointed.

शिखा, *f.* a point, end, summit, top, peak, pinnacle, crest, tuft of feathers, a flame, a ray of light, a branch, a look of hair on the crown of the head, topknot.

शिखाण्डक = **शिखण्ड**, *q. v.*

शिखाना, *more prop.* **सिखाना**, *q v.*

शिखायत, *more prop.* **शिकायत**, *q.v.*

शिखाया, *more prop.* **सिखाया**, *q.v.* [pointed; burnt.

शिखावल, *m.* (*f.* ā *or* ī) a peacock: *lit.* crested,

शिखी, crested, pointed, having a lock of hair on the top of the head: hence, *m.* (*f.* inī) a peacock; a cock-bird; a religious mendicant; a mountain; an arrow; fire; a bull; a horse; a lamp; *pr. n.* Ketu, the personified descending node.

शिगाफ़, *m.* a split, rent, fissure, crack, crevice.

शिगुफ़ता, expanded, blown (as a flower). — *honā*, to be blown (said of flowers; to be delighted.

शिच्छा (*corruption*) = **शिक्षा**, *q. v.*

शितद्रु = **शतद्रु**, *q. v.*

शितलना; see **शीतला**.

शिता, *m.* the cold season, winter.

शिताब, *m.* quickness, haste. [or birch.

शिति, 1, black; dark blue: white: 2, *m.* the bhūrj

शितिकण्ठ, *m.* an epithet of Shiv; *lit.* blue-throat.

शितिरत्न, *m.* the sapphire.

शितिसारक, *m.* a sort of ebony (*Diospyros glutinosa*).

शिथिल, loosened, loose, slack, lax, flabby, flaccid, relaxed, dissolved; languid, feeble, inert, dilatory, not energetic; ineffectual; abandoned.

शिथिलता, *f.* (*m.* °**त्व**) looseness, relaxedness, state of dissolution, relaxation, slackness, want of energy, dilatoriness, indolence.

शिथिलबल, *m.* (*f.* ā) weakened, relaxed.

शिद; see **शीत** and **सिद्ध**.

शिद्दत, *f.* violence, force, vehemence, fervour: adversity, affliction; difficulty.

शिनाख़्त, *f.* knowledge, understanding.

शिनासाई, *f.* acquaintance, knowledge.

शिनि, *m. pr. n.* a certain class of Kshatriyas.

शिप्पा, a shell, cowrie. — *laṛānā*, to keep on good terms with. [a mother.

शिफा, *f.* a fibrous root: a small whip: a river:

शिफ़ा, *f.* recovery, convalescence; medicine, remedy, cure. [form **शिश्र**.

शिम; for words beginning thus, see under the

शिमोन, *m. pr. n.* Simon Peter. [pepper-plant.

शिर, *m.* the head; the top, summit: the root of the

शिरः = **शिरस**, *q. v.* [skull as his emblem.

शिरःकपाली, *m.* a devotee who carries a human

शिरःकम्प / **शिरःकम्पन** } *m.* vertigo.

शिरःपीड़ा, *f.* / **शिरःशूल**, *m.* } headache.

शिरकाटा, *m.* (*f.* ī) decapitated, headless.

शिरताज, *m.* a crown, diadem, crest.

शिरस, 1, *more com.* **शिर**, *q. v.*: 2, *m. pr. n.* a certain ancient Hindoo sage (*rishi*).

शिरा, 1, *f.* any tubular vessel of the body (as a gut, nerve, tendon, or vein): 2, *m.* traffic, purchase, sale.

शिराल, 1, *m.* (*f.* ā) veiny, shewing the veins or tendons, skinny, tendinous: 2, *m.* a certain acid fruit (*Averrhoa carambola*).

शिरिश्तेदार, *more prop.* **सरिश्तदार**, *q. v.*

शिरीष, *m.* a certain tree (*Acacia sirisa* or *Mimosa sirisa*) and its flower.

शिरोपांव, the head and feet. — *denā*, to place any one's foot on another's head or neck (a form of salutation intended to betoken submissiveness).

शिरोभूषण, *m.* an ornament for the head.

शिरोमणि, *m. f.* a gem or jewel worn in a crest or upon the head.

शिरोमणी, *f.* / **शिरोरत्न**, *m.* } = **शिरोमणि**, *q. v.*

शिरोरोग, *m.* / **शिरोर्त्ति**, *f.* } = **शिरोवेदना**, *q. v.*

शिरोवेदना, *f.* headache, any pain in the head, disease of the head.

शिर्क, *m.* company, society, partnership: paganism, infidelity (*i. e.* ascribing plurality to the Deity).

शिर्कत, *f.* going partners, partnership, society.

शिल, 1, *f.* (contraction) = **शिला**, *q. v.*: 2, *m.* glean-

शिलड़ी (*dialectic*) = **सिरी**, *q. v.* [ing ears of corn.

शिला, *f.* a stone, rock; a flat stone on which condiments are ground; a hailstone; arsenic; a threshhold, a door-frame; a stone or beam placed across a post or pillar; any transverse beam.

शिलाजतु / **शिलाजत** } *m.* storax, bitumen, red chalk.

शिलाधातु, *m.* a white fossil substance, an aluminous earth of a white colour, chalk; red chalk.

शिलापुष्प, *m.* storax or benzoin.

शिलामय, *m.* (*f.* ī) stony, abounding in stone, consisting of stone, made of stone.

शिलारस, *m.* incense: benjamin or olibanum; storax, bitumen, red chalk.

शिलावल्का, *f.* a certain medicinal substance (most commonly called *Silābāk*) said to be of cooling and lithonthriptic properties: a sort of lichen or moss (esp. a kind used in medicine).

शिलि, *f.* the lower timber of a door.

शिली, *f.* a dart, arrow, spike: an earthworm: a threshold; a stone or beam placed across a post or pillar, any transverse beam.

शिलीमुख, 1, *m.* (*f.* ā *or* ī) a bee; a fool; a monkey: 2, *m.* an arrow; war.

शिल्प, *m.* any art, any mechanical or handicraft trade; proficiency in any art or profession: a kind of spoon used in sacrificing to pour the butter on the fire.

शिल्पकर्म, *m.* manual labour, handicraft.

शिल्पकार, *m.* (*f.* ī) an artisan, mechanic.

शिल्पविद्या, *f.* the science of mechanics or architecture, mechanical or manual skill, art.

शिल्पिनी, *f.* 1, (*m.* शिल्पी) a female artisan, the wife of an artisan: 2, a kind of grass (commonly called *Lahānsipi*) described as sweet and cooling, and bearing seeds of tonic and restorative properties.

शिल्पशाला, *f.* a manufactory, workshop.

शिल्पशास्त्र, *m.* a treatise on architecture or any work of mechanical art.

शिल्पी, appertaining to a mechanical profession or art, mechanical: hence, *m.* (*f.* inī) an artificer, workman, artisan.

शिल्पता, *more prop.* शीतता, *q.v.*

शिव, 1, *m.* (*f.* ā) prosperous, auspicious, happy: 2, *m.* bliss, happiness, wellbeing; final emancipation; an auspicious planetary conjunction; water: a pillar to which cattle are tied: a sort of perfume: sea or fossil salt; 3, *m.* *pr. n.* (1) of the third person in the Hindoo triad, the Deity in the character of producer and destroyer, or Time personified (2) of one of the astronomical periods called *yog* (3) of the phallic emblem of Shiv (4) of the Veds.

शिवगण, *m.* the attendants of Shiv.

शिवचरण, *m.* the blessed feet of Shiv. The term is very common as a proper name.

शिवदीन, bestowed by Shiv = Theodore. Commonly used as a proper name of males among Hindoos.

शिवधातु, *m.* milkstone, opal, chalcedony.

शिवधाम, *m.* an epithet (1) of Kailās (2) of Benares.

शिवनारायण, *m.* an epithet (1) of Shiv (2) of another god: *pr. n.* a certain author.

शिवनारायणी, *m.* (*f.* inī) a follower of Shivnārāyan.

शिवपुर, *m.* = शिवपुरी, *q.v.*

शिवपुरी, *f.* an epithet of the city of Benares (which is especially sacred to Shiv).

शिवप्रिय, *m.* (*f.* ā) dear to (or esteemed by) Shiv: hence, *m.* the tree *Sesbana grandiflora*; the thorn-apple; crystal; the seeds of the *rudrāksh*.

शिवप्रिया, *f.* an epithet of Durgā. See शिवा.

शिवरात्रि, *f.* a certain festival held in honour of Shiv or of the birth of phallus (*ling*) on the 14th of the dark fortnight of the month Māgh (Jan.-Feb.).

शिवलिंग, *m.* the phallus or emblem of Shiv.

शिववाणी, *f.* the voice or the words of Shiv.

शिवशंकर, *m.* an epithet of Mahādev.

शिवशैल, *m.* an epithet of mount Kailās.

शिवसमाज, *m.* any assemblage of the worshippers of Shiv, but especially on mount Kailās).

शिवा, *f.* the goddess Durgā, wife of Shiv: the female jackal: a certain tree (*Mimosa suma*); yellow myrobalan (*Terminalia chebula*).

शिवाना, *more prop.* सिवाना, *q.v.*

शिवानी, *f.* the goddess Durgā, wife of Shiv.

शिवाल, *m.* any temple dedicated to Shiv: a cemetery: red basil (*Ocymum sanctum*).

शिवालय } **शिवाला** } = शिवाल, *q.v.*

शिवि, *m.* a beast of prey: *pr. n.* a certain king.

शिविका, *f.* a palanquin, litter; a tent, marquee: *pr. n.* a certain female.

शिश; see (1) शिशु (2) शीश (3) सीस.

शिशिर, cool, cold, chilly, frigid, freezing: hence *m.* coolness, cold, frost: the cold season.

शिशिरकाल, *m.* winter, the cold season (comprising two months, from about the middle of January to that of March).

शिशु, *m.* the young of any animal, an infant, calf, pup, etc.; a child under 8 years of age; a boy; a pupil.

शिशुक, *m.* a child: a porpoise; a certain fish (*Delphinus gangeticus*) resembling a porpoise. See सूढक.

शिशुता, *f.* (*m.* °त्व) infancy, early childhood, boyhood, pupilage.

शिशुनाग, *m.* a kind of demon (*rākshas*).

शिशुपन, *m.* the condition (or the period) of infancy or a childhood, pupilage.

शिशुपाल, *m.* *pr. n.* a certain ancient Hindoo king opposed to Krishn and slain by him.

शिशुमार, *m.* the Gangetic porpoise (*Delphinus gangeticus*); the heavenly porpoise or collection of the stars and planets; the north-west: *pr. n.* Vishnu or Krishn.

शिशुविन्द, *more prop.* शशबिन्दु, *q.v.*

शिश्न, *m.* membrum virile, penis.

शिष्ट, *m.* (*f.* ā) trained, disciplined, polished, good, polite, genteel, urbane, well-behaved, docile, obedient, ordered, commanded.

शिष्टता, *f.* (*m.* °त्व) good behaviour, gentleness, politeness, civility, urbanity, docility.

शिष्टसभा, *f.* an assembly of chief officers, a council of state.

शिष्टसमाचार, *m.* history or tradition of eminent persons.

शिष्टाचार, 1, *m.* the approved conduct of the wise and good, proper behaviour, good manners, gentlemanliness, urbanity, politeness: 2, *m.* (*f.* ā) a well-behaved person: *lit.* following the conduct of the wise and good, urbane, polite, gentlemanly, well-behaved.

शिष्टाचारी, *m.* (*f.* iṇī) = शिष्टाचार, 2, *q.v.*

शिष्टि, *f.* an order, precept, command.

शिष्य, *m.* (*f.* ā) a learner, pupil, disciple.

शिष्यता, *f.* the state or condition of a pupil, pupilage, discipleship.

शिष्या, *f.* (*m.* शिष्य) a female pupil or disciple.

शिसु, *more prop.* (1) शश (2) शिशु, *qq.v.*

शीश्र, *m.* a member of a certain sect of the Muhammadans, followers of 'Alī, son-in-law of Muhammad, a Shiyaite.

शीश्रई, appertaining to the sect of 'Alī, a Shīyaite.

शींग, *more prop..* सींग, *q.v.*

शीक, a kind of grass of which brooms are made.

शीकर, *m.* a drop of water, a drop of rain, thin rain, rain driven by wind, spray : a sort of pine or its resin.

शीकरान, hemlock.

शीघ्र,, 1, speedy, quick, rapid; violent: 2, quickly, speedily, rapidly. swiftly ; soon : 3, *m.* (in Astron.) parallax. — *k.* to make haste.

शीघ्रकेन्द्र, *m.* (in Astron.) the commutation.

शीघ्रगामी, *m.* (*f.* inī) any swift or fleet creature: *lit.* swift-going, fleet, rapid.

शीघ्रता, *f.* quickness, haste, speed, rapidity, fleetness, alertness, agility. — *k.* to accelerate.

शीघ्रतासे, *adv.* (abl.) quickly, hastily, speedily.

शीघ्रत्व, *m.* the quality or faculty of speed.

शीत, cold, chilly, frigid ; apathetic, stupid, idle : hence, *m.* cold, coldness, numbness, frigidity; dew; wet, wetness; water ; cold weather, winter, the cold season (including the six months of the rainy, dewy, and winter seasons).

शीतउष्ण, *more prop.* शीतोष्ण, *q.v.*

शीतऋतु / शीतकाल } *m.* the cold season, winter.

शीतजनक, *adj.* producing the sensation of cold, cooling, chilly, refrigerating.

शीतज्वर, *m.* chill fever, ague.

शीतता, *f.* (*m.* °त्व) coldness, cold.

शीतरस, *m.* the flux, dysentery.

शीतराज, *m.* (the lord of cold, *i.e.*) the moon.

शीतल, 1, *m.* (*f.* ā) cool, cold, chilly, frigid, stupefied, benumbed : 2, *m.* coldness, cold ; a pearl ; the moon ; a sort of camphor ; turpentine ; sulphate of iron ; a certain plant (*Marsilea quadrifolia*).

शीतलता, *f.* (*m.* °त्व) coldness, coolness, frigidity.

शीतलताई = शीतलता, *q v.*

शीतला, *f.* the name of several plants : small-pox; *pr. n.* the goddess who presides over small-pox.

शीतहर, *adj.* removing cold.

शीतांग, *m.* the being chilled ; numbness ; palsy.

शीतांशु, *m.* camphor; the moon.

शीतार्त्त, chilled, cold, shivering, suffering (or shrinking, from) cold.

शीताश्मन / शीताश्मा } *m.* the moonstone, crystal.

शीतोष्ण, *m.* a mixture of cold and heat, lukewarmness, the change of seasons, unsettledness of the weather. [unsettled (as weather).

शीतोष्णमान, *m.* (*f.* mati) cold and hot, lukewarm,

शीन, a kind of large tray.

शीफालिका, *more prop.* शेफालिका, *q. v.*

शीर, *m.* milk.

शीरध्वज, *more prop.* सीरध्वज, *q.v.*

शीरबिरंज, *m.* a certain kind of grain.

शीरमाल, *f.* bread made with milk.

शीरवा, *m.* broth, soup.

शीरस; (1) शिरस (2) सिरसा.

शीराज़ा, *m.* the stitching of the back of a book ; sewing button-holes.

शीरीनी, *f.* sweetness ; sweetmeats : eloquence.

शीर्ण, *m.* (*f.* ā) hurt, injured, broken, withered, decayed. thin, small, slender, emaciated, lean.

शीर्णता, *f.* (*m.*°त्व) withered or decayed condition, emaciation, slenderness, leanness.

शीर्वि, hurtful, distructive.

शीर्विका ; see शिविका.

शीर्ष, *m.* the head.

शीर्षछेद, *m.* beheading, decapitation.

शील, 1, *m.* nature, quality, character, natural disposition, inclination, moral practice, good conduct, propriety, amiableness, virtue, beauty : 2, *m.* (*f.* ā) well disposed, well-behaved. *Āṅkhoṁmeṅ—rahnā* or *honā*, to be polite, be generous. This word frequently occurs as the latter element of *bahavrīhi* compound adjectives in the sense of 'in the habit of', 'having a disposition for'; *e. g* स्नानशील, in the habit of performing religious ablution : भयशील, of a timid disposition.

शीलता, *f.* (*m.* °त्व) disposition, inclination ; quality; conversancy, practice.

शीलम, birdlime, cement.

शीलनिधान, *m.* epithet of any very excellent person (*lit.* a treasury of virtue).

शीलवत, of a good or amiable disposition, well-behaved : hence, *m.* (*f.* vatī) a well-disposed person.

शीलवती, (*m.* शीलवत, etc.) an amiable female.

शीलवन्त / शीलवान } *m.* (*f.* vatī) = शीलवत, *q. v.*

शीवन, 1, *more prop.* शेवन, *q. v.*: 2, *m.* (*f.* varī) the boa-constrictor.

शीवरी, *f.* an iguana.

शीविका, *more prop.* शिविका, *q. v.*

शीश, *m.* lead ; blacklead.

शीशम, *f.* Indian rosewood (*Dalbergia sisu*, Roxb.).

शीशमहल्ल, *m.* a glazed palace or house, an apartment fitted up with mirrors.

शीशा, *m.* glass ; a glass; a bottle.

शीशी, *f.* a small glass, small bottle, phial.

शीस, *more prop.* (1) शीश (2) सीस, *qq.v.*

शीसा, *more prop.* शीशा, *q. v.*

शुंभला, *m.* a flame, blaze, light, flash.

शुंघाना, *more prop.* सुंघाना, *q. v.*

शुक, *m.* a parrot : cloth, the hem of cloth, a turban; a sort of perfume : the name of several plants.

शुककीट, *m.* a caterpillar.

शुकदेव, *m.pr.n.* the son of Vyāsdev. He is famed for his sanctity, and was the narrator of the Bhāgavat and other Purāns composed by his father.

शुकन्तला (*corruption*) = शकुन्तला, *q.v.*

शुकर (*colloquial*) = शुक्र, 4, *q.v.*

शुकरान, hemlock.

शुकराना, *m.* gratitude, the giving thanks, a thank-offering; a fee paid by a plaintiff or a defendant on the case being decided in his favour (but not if he *lose* the case).

शुका, *m.* (*f.* ī) a parrot.

शुकूर, a corruption (1) of शुक (2) of शूकर (3) of सुकर, *qq.v.*

शुक्ति, *f.* a pearl-oyster (*Ostrea ephippium*) a cockle, a muscle; a conch; a small shell; a portion of the skull used as a cup; a curl or feather on a horse's neck or breast; a disease of the cornea; a sort of perfume; a weight of two *karshas*.

शुक्तिमान, *m.pr.n.* one of the seven principal mountanous ranges of India.

शुक्र, 1, pure, white, resplendent: 2, *m.* sperm, semen virile: male and female strength: a morbid affection of the iris: 3, *m.* an epithet (1) of Agni (2) of the planet Venus or its regent regarded as the son of Bhrigu and preceptor of the daityas (3) of the month Jyeshth (May-June): 4, *m.* thanks, gratitude.

शुक्रगुज़ार, thankful, grateful.

शुक्रगुज़ारी, *f.* thankfulness, gratitude, thanksgiving

शुक्रगुरु; see शुक्र, 3 (2).

शुक्रवार, *m.* Friday.

शुक्रसम्भव, *n.* the origin or the mixing of sperm.

शुक्राचार्य्य, *m.pr.n.* the regent of the planet Venus, and preceptor of the Daityas.

शुक्ल, 1, *m.* (*f.* ā) white, bright, pure, clean: 2, *m.* white (the colour), whiteness; the light half of the month (from new to full moon); silver; fresh butter; a disease of the cornea: *pr. n.* one of the astronomical periods called *yog*.

शुक्लकण्टक, *m.* a kind of gallinule or water-hen.

शुक्लता, *f.* (*m.*°त्व) whiteness, brightness.

शुक्लपक्ष, *m.* (see कृष्णपक्ष) the light half of the month (*i. e.* the fortnight of the moon's increase).

शुक्लपक्षी, *m.* (*f.* iṇī) = शुक्लपक्षीय, *q.v.*

शुक्लपक्षीय, appertaining to the light half of the month.

शुक्लाचौथ, *f.* the fourth day of the light half of any month.

शुक्लीकर्म्म, *m.* soap: lit. *adj.* whitening.

शुग़्ल, *m.* speech, language; a thing, business, affair.

शुग़ल, *m.* occupation, employment, labour, study.

शुगभ (by inversion) = शुभग, *q.v.*

शुगा, *m.* (*f.* ī) a parrot.

शुगुन / शुगून } *m.* an augury, omen.

शुचि, 1, white, resplendant, clear, pure, clean, cleansed, purified; exempt from passion, free from fault, upright, honest, innocent, virtuous, pious: 2, *m.* white (the colour); purity, virtue, correctness, goodness, holiness; purification by ablution; judicial acquittal, a tried and faithful minister; oblation to fire at the first feeding of an infant; the month Jyeshth (May-June); the month Āshādh (June-July): an epithet (1) of Shiv (2) of the planet Venus (3) of the sun (4) of the moon (5) of fire (6) of a Brāhman.

शुचिता, *f.* (*m.*°त्व) whiteness, resplendance, clearness, cleanness, purity, virtue, holiness.

शुचिमणि, *m. f.* crystal.

शुजा; see (1) सुजना (2) सूजना (3) सूजा.

शुजाअत, *f.* bravery, valour, prowess.

शुझना, *more prop.* सूझना, *q.v.*

शुण्ठ, a contraction of शुण्ठि, *q.v.*

शुण्ठि / शुण्ठी } *f.* dry ginger.

शुण्ड, *m.* the exudation from an elephant's temples; an elephant's trunk.

शुण्डा, *f.* an elephant's trunk: spirituous liquor: a tavern; a harlot: the stalk of the lotus.

शुतुर, *m.* a camel.

शुदी, *more com.* सुदी, *q.v.*

शुद्ध, *m.* (*f.* ā) pure, clean, white, perfect, faultless, unadulterated, uncorrupt, purified, cleansed, genuine, honest, correct, accurate, innocent, authorized, alone, only, mere, simple.

शुद्धतत्त्व, *m.* the very essence; genuineness.

शुद्धता, *f.* (*m.*°त्व) purity, cleanness, freedom from soil or from defect, accuracy, innocence, faultlessness.

शुद्धपत्र = शुद्धिपत्र, *q.v.*

शुद्धमति, *m.f.* of pure and sincere purpose, guileless, unsophisticated, innocent, honest; intelligent.

शुद्धसत्त्व, right, correct righteous, pure: hence, *m.* (*f.* ā) a virtuous person.

शुद्धस्वभाव, 1, *m.* a virtuous nature or disposition: 2, *adj.* of a virtuous nature or disposition.

शुद्धाशुद्धपत्र = शुद्धिपत्र, *q.v.*

शुद्धि, *f.* a cleaning, cleansing, purification, purity, correctness, rectitude, sanctity, truth, certainty, acquittal.

शुद्धिकर, cleansing, purifying, correcting, amending: hence, *m.* (*f.* ī) a correcter, cleanser, etc.

शुद्धिकारक, *m.* (*f.* ikā) / शुद्धिकारी, *m.* (*f.* iṇī) } = शुद्धिकर, *q.v.*

शुद्धिपत्र, *m.* a list of errata in a book.

शुनःशेप = शुनःशेफ, *q. v.*

शुनःशेफ, *m. pr. n.* a certain ancient Hindoo king, nephew of Vishwāmitra.

शुनक, *m.* a dog, a young dog.

शुनना, *more prop.* सुनना, *q. v.*

शुनी, *f.* (*m.* श्वन) a bitch.

शुन्य (*corruption*) = शून्य, *q.v.*

शुबहा; see (1) शुभा (2) सुभग.

शुभ, 1, *m.* (*f.* ā) shining, splendid, beautiful, handsome; good, virtuous; happy, well, right, fortunate, auspicious; eminent, clever, learned: 2, *m.* good fortune, hail, happiness, prosperity, welfare, auspiciousness: 3, *m. pr. n.* one of the astrological *yogs*.

शुभंकर, 1, conferring happiness or good fortune, auspicious, propitious, prosperous, lucky: 2, *m.* (*f.* ī) an accountant, arithmetician.

शुभकर = शुभंकर, *q. v.*

शुभकर्म्म, *m.* an auspicious action, a pious act, reputable occupation.

शुभकारक, *m.* (*f.* ikā) } = शुभंकर, *q. v.*
शुभकारी, *m.* (*f.* iṇī) }

शुभकाल, *m.* a good season or time, virtuous epoch, favorable opportunity.

शुभग, fortunate, propitious, auspicious.

शुभगुणसदन,, *m.* an epithet of Gaṇesh and of other deities (*lit.* the mansion of excellent quaties).

शुभगुण, *m.* excellent quality, virtue.

शुभग्रह, *m.* an auspicious planet, lucky star.

शुभचाल, *f.* good behaviour, virtuous conduct.

शुभचिन्तक, *m.* (*f.* ā, ikā *or* ī) a well-wisher, friend; one whose thoughts are excellent. [(*f.* ā) a benefactor.

शुभद, granting happiness, auspicious; hence, *m.*

शुभदत्त, 1, *m.* an excellent or auspicious gift: 2, *m.* (*f.* ā) the recipient of an auspicious gift.

शुभदन्ती, *f. pr. n.* the female elephant of the north-west quarter.

शुभदा, *f.* (*m.* शुभद) a benefactress.

शुभदाई, *m.* (*f.* inī) }
शुभदानी, *m. f.* inī) } = शुभद, *q.v.*
शुभदायक, *m.* (*f.* ikā) }

शुभदायनी, *more prop.* शुभदायिनी(शुभदाई) = शुभदा.

शुभद्रा, *more prop.* सुभद्रा, *q.v.*

शुभध्वनि, *m.* a glorious or a pleasing sound.

शुभफल, *m.* happy result or consequence, auspicious result.

शुभमुहूर्त्त, *m.* an auspicious moment.

शुभलग्न, *m.* an auspicious moment.

शुभशील, *m.* (*f.* ā) a good-natured person: *lit.* of a good disposition, good-natured.

शुभसाअत, *f.* an auspicious moment, lucky time.

शुभा, *m.* doubt, uncertainty, suspicion.

शुभांग, *m.* (*f.* ī) a handsome person: *lit.* elegant, handsome.

शुभाचार, *m.* (*f.* ī) a virtuous person: *lit.* well-behaved, virtuous.

शुभाशुभ, 1, *m.* (*f.* ā) good or wicked; auspicious and inauspicious, lucky and unlucky: 2, *m.* good and evil fortune, weal and woe.

शुभिता, *m.* prosperity, prosperousness, welfare, security; time, leisure, opportunity, convenience, accommodation.

शुभ्र, 1, white, shining, bright: 2, *m.* white (the colour); silver; sandal; talc.

शुभ्रकृत, *m.* the 36th year of the Indian cycle.

शुभ्रदन्ती = शुभदन्ती, *q. v.*

शुभ्रा, *f.* crystal; the manna of the bamboo: an epithet of the Ganges.

शुमार, 1, *m.* counting, computing, calculating: a multitude: 2, numerable, calculable.

शुम्भ, *m. pr. n.* a certain demon (brother of Nishumbh) slain by Durgā.

शुम्भपुर, *m. pr n.* a certain city and district (perhaps the modern Sambhalpur in the Gondwānā district).

शुरकी; see (1) सुरख़ी (2) सिरकी.

शुरज, *more prop.* सूर्य्य, *q. v.*

शुरत, *more prop.* सुरत, *q v.*

शुरना, *more prop.* सुरना, *q. v.*

शुरू, *m.* commencement, beginning.

शुलगाना, *more prop.* सुलगाना, *q. v.*

शुलमान, a corruption of सुलेमान, *q. v.*

शुलो, *more prop.* (1) शूलो (2) सूलो, *qq. v.*

शुलेमान, *more prop.* सुलेमान, *q. v.*

शुश, *m.* the lungs: the noise made by a person setting on a dog. — *k.* to set on, encourage, or stimulate a dog by crying "*shush.*"

शुशकारना = शुश क° *q. v.*

शुशकारी, *f.* the impelling or setting on a dog.

शुष्क, dried up, dry, withered, shrivelled.

शुष्कता, *f.* (*m.*° त्व) dryness, shrivelledness.

शुस, *more prop.* शुभ्र, *q. v.* See भ्र, 2.

शुहदा, *m.* a rake, debauchee, blackguard, vagabond, scoundrel, prodigal.

शुहदापन, *m.* rakishness, dissoluteness, debauchery.

शुहदाशिकस्ता, ruined and wretched.

शुहबत, *more prop.* सुहबत, *q.v.*

शुहरा, *m.* divulging, publishing; rumour, report; fame, renown, reputation.

शूअर, *m.* (*f.* ī) a hog.

शूक, *m.* the awn of barley; the bristle of insects; the spiculæ of plants: compassion.

शूककीट, *m.* a hairy caterpillar.

शूकर, *m.* (*f.* ī) a hog, a wild boar; the hog-deer.

शूकरखेत = शूकरक्षेत्र = वाराहक्षेत्र, *q.v.*

शूकरमुख, *m. pr. n.* a certain division of the infernal regions (filled with boiling oil).

शूकरान, hemlock.

शूकरी, *f.* (*m.* शूकर) a sow.

शूकापुट्ट, *m.* a kind of gem (perhaps amber).

शूक्ष्म, *more prop* सूक्ष्म, *q. v.*

शूद्र, (see वर्ण) *m.* (*f.* ā, āṇī, ī) a man of the fourth caste of the Hindoos.

शूद्रक, *m. pr. n.* (1) of the first Andhra king, also written Sindhuk, Shishuk, and Shūrak (2) of a certain ancient Hindoo king, author of the drama called Mṛichhakaṭika.

शूद्रता, *f.* (*m.* °त्व) the nature or condition of a person of the fourth caste, Shūdraship.

शूद्रनी } = शूद्राणी, *q. v.*
शूद्रा }

शूद्राणी, *f.* (*m.* शूद्र) the wife of a Shūdra, a female of the Shūdra caste.

शूद्री = शूद्राणी, *q. v.*

शून, *m.* 1, *more prop.* शून्य, *q. v.*: 2, a slaughter-house: the soft palate.

शूनना, *more prop.* सुनना, *q.v.*

शूना } *more prop.* शून्य, *q.v.* See also शून्या.
शूनी }

शून्य, *m.* (*f.* ā) empty, void, vacant, deserted, desert, ruined, destitute of, unsuspecting, unmeaning, indifferent: hence, *m.* vacuity, a vacuum, heaven, sky, ether, a dot, (in Arithm.) a cypher, naught.

शून्यता, *f.* (*m.* °त्व) **vacuity, emptiness, vanity,** unreality, the illusory nature of all existence.
शून्यवादी, *m.* (*f.* ini) an atheist, a Bauddh.
शून्या, *f.* (see **शून्य**) a hollow reed.
शूम, 1, black: unfortunate, unhappy; disgraceful, vile: 2, *m.* a miser, niggard. [avaricious, churlish.
शूमड़ा, *m.* (*f.* ī) ugly, miserly, stingy, niggardly,
शूमड़ी, *f.* a kind of fried food: a female miser.
शूर, *m.* a hero, champion; a lion; a boar; the sun.
शूरंग, *more prop.* **सुरंग**, *q.v.*
शूरक; see **शूद्रक**.
शूरज, a corruption of **सूर्य्य**, *q.v.*
शूरण, *m.* a certain plant (*Bignonia Indica*); a certain esculent root (*Arum campanulatum*).
शूरत, *more prop* **सुरत**, *q v.* [ess.
शूरता, *f.* courage, bravery, valour, heroism, prow-
शूरताई, *f.* = **शूरता**, *q.v.*
शूरताधारी, *m.* (*f.* iṇī) a hero: *lit.* heroic.
शूरत्व, *m.* = **शूरता**, *q.v.*
शूरमनुष्य, *m.* (*f.* ā) a heroic person, champion.
शूरमा, *more prop.* (1) **सुरमा** (2) **सूरमा**, *q.v.* [brave.
शूरवीर, *m.* (*f.* ā) a hero, champion: *adj.* heroic,
शूरसेन, *m. pr. n.* the country about Mathurā.
शूरसेनकाः, *m.* (pl.: see **आ**, 22) the people of Shūrsen.
शूरसेनज, *m.* (*f.* **आ**) a native of Shūrsen.
शूरसेनप, *m.* an epithet of **कार्त्तिकेय**, *q.v.*
शूक, *more prop.* **शुक**, *q.v.*
शूर्प = **शूर्प्प**, *q.v.*
शूर्पणखा, *more prop.* **सूर्पनखा**, *q.v.*
शूर्प्प, *m.* a winnowing-basket: a measure of two *dronas* or *ādhakas*. [children.
शूर्प्पी, *f.* a small winnowing-basket; a toy for
शूल, *m.* a spear, dart, weapon, pike, trident, stake, iron pin or spit; a banner; death; sharp pain (*esp.* in the belly as colic, or in the joints from rheumatism or gout): *pr. n.* a certain astronomical *yog* (that of the ninth lunar mansion).
शूलतानी, *more prop.* **सुलतानी**, *q.v.*
शूलनिर्मूलन, *m.* (the destroyer of pain, *i. e.*) Shiv.
शूलपाणि, trident-handed: hence, *m.* an epithet of Shiv: *pr. n.* a certain Hindoo author. [regions.
शूलपोत, *m. pr. n.* a certain division of the infernal
शूलशत्रु, *m.* the castor-oil plant (*Ricinus communis*).
शूलहत, *f.* assafœtida. [a harlot: a brick-kiln.
शूला, *f.* a spit; a stake for impaling criminals:
शूली, 1, *m.* (*f.* ini) one who suffers sharp pain; a stake-bearer, a spearman; an epithet of Mahādev: *lit.* (1) armed with a spear or dart (2) afflicted with colic or with rheumatism: 2, *f.* a gibbet; crucifixion. — *rakhnā*, to gibbet, crucify.
शूहरा, *m.* report, rumour, fame, reputation.
शृंखल, *m.* a chain, fetter, belt, a chain worn around a man's body.
शृंग, *m.* a horn; the peak of mountain; a precipice, height, cliff; dignity, sovereignty: a sign, mark: a lotus: an artficial fountain.
शृंगवेर, *m.* ginger: *pr. n.* a certain town.
शृंगा; see **शृंग**. [(*Trapa bispinosa*).
शृंगाट, *m.* a four-cross road: a certain plant
शृंगाटक = **शृंगाट**, *q.v.*
शृंगार, *m.* copulation, coition, love (as an object of poetical description): fragrant powder for the dress or the person; cloves; a mark; read lead; marks made with red lead on an elephant's head or trunk by way of ornament.
शृंगारी, 1, *m.* (*f.* iṇī) an amorous person, etc.: *lit.* appertaining to the passion of love, amorous, enamoured, lascivious; gaily dressed; stained with red lead: 2, *m.* dress, decoration, ornament.
शृंगि, 1, *m.* gold for ornaments: 2, *f.* a species of sheat-fish (*Silurus singio*).
शृंगिकनक, *m.* gold for ornaments.
शृंगिणी, *f.* a cow.
शृंगिया, *m.* a kind of musical instrument.
शृंगी, 1, having horns, summits, or peaks, horned, crested, peaked: hence, *m.* a mountain, an elephant, a tree: 2, *m. pr. n.* a certain Hindoo saint (*rishi*) son of Gautam.
शृंगीकनक, *m.* gold for ornaments.
शृगाल, *m.* a jackal; a rogue; a coward; a demon; an epithet of Krishn.
शृगाली, *f.* a female jackal; a fox.
शेखर, *m.* a crest, diadem, garland of flowers worn on the crown of the head; a mountain-peak.
शेख़ी, *f.* boasting, bragging, domineering.
शेप
शेपस } *m.* the penis.
शेफ
शेफ़ता, distracted, mad, enamoured.
शेफस, *m.* the penis.
शेफालिका, *f.* the flower *Nyctanthes arbor-tristis.*
शेब, *m.* a descent, declivity.
शेबरी = **सेवरी**, *q.v.*
शेबा, *more prop.* (1) **शेवा** (2) **सेवा**, *qq.v.*
शेर, *m.* a tiger, a lion.
शेरनी, *f.* a lioness, tigress.
शेरबबर, *m.* a full-grown, strong, and very fierce lion (as distinguished from an ordinary one and as distinguished from a mere whelp).
शेराइन, cold.
शेव, *m.* a snake: happiness: the penis.
शेवड़ा, *m.* any fakeer of the Jain sect.
शेवधि = **सेवधि**, *q.v.*
शेवन, *m.* grief, lamentation, mourning.
शेवनारायणी, *more prop.* **शिवनारायणी**, *q.v.*
शेवा, 1, *f.* the penis: 2, *m.* business, trade, profession: manner, habit, custom: amorous looks.
शेवाल, *m.* a certain aquatic plant (*Vallisneria octandra*).
शेष, 1, *m. pr. n.* = **शेषनाग**, *q. v.*: 2, *adj.* remain-

ing, other, all the other: 3 *m.* residue, remainder, leavings, arrears, the rest, the balance: killing, destroying; finishing; end: an epithet of Baldev. — *rahnā*, to remain, be over and above.

शेषकारक, *m.* (in Gram.) an oblique case.

शेषकाल, *m.* the last time, the last term, the latter end, the time of death.

शेषजाति, *f.* (in Arithm.) assimilation of residue, reduction of fractions of residues, or successive fractional remainders.

शेषनाग, *m. pr. n.* the king of the serpent-race, and of Pātāl as the abode of the snakes. He is represented as a large thousand-headed snake, at once the couch and the canopy of Vishṇu and upholder of the world, which rests on one of his heads. He is sometimes called *Anant* (the endless or infinite), and, as such, is regarded as an emblem of eternity.

शेषपथ, *m.* a journey's end.

शेषभुक, *adj.* eating remnants of food.

शेषरात्रि, *f.* the last watch of the night.

शेषशाई, *m.* (he who sleeps on *Sheshnāg*, *i.e.*) Vishṇu.

शेषा, *f.* flowers, etc. that have been offered to an idol and are then distributed amongst the worshippers and attendants.

शेषावस्था, *f.* the last state or condition of life.

शै, *f.* (pl. **अशिया**) a thing, affair, object.

शैक्य, placed between the ropes of a porter's yoke.

शैक्ष, *m.* a young Brāhmaṇ who has begun to read the Veds.

शैक्ष्य, *m.* learning, skill.

शैख, *m.* the offspring of an outcaste Brāhmaṇ.

शैख़, *m.* a venerable old man, a chief, a prelate. A title taken by the descendants of Muhammad and given to those who become proselytes to his religion.

शैतान, *m. pr. n.* Satan, the Devil: *met.* a very bad or diabolical person. — *ki ānt, lit.* the Devil's entrails; hence (1) anything long and winding (as a long and winding lane); (2) intricate.

शैतानत, *f.* devil's-tricks, devilry, wickedness such as originates in (or is worthy of) the Devil.

शैतानी, 1, *f.* = **शैतानत**, *q.v.*: 2, Satanic, devilish, diabolical, appertaining to Satan.

शैत्य, *m.* cold, coldness, frigidity.

शैथिल्य, *m.* looseness, laxity, flaccidity, weakness, dilatoriness, inattention, cowardice, smallness, relaxation of rule or of connexion.

शैदा, *m.* (*f.* ī) mad, insane, distraught, in love.

शैन, 1, a Prākṛit form of **शयन**, *q.v.*: 2, disgrace, dishonour, shame.

शैन्य, *more prop.* **सैन्य**, *q.v.*

शैय्या, *more prop.* **शय्या**, *q.v.*

शैर, *more prop.* (1) **सैर** (2) **शहर**, *qq.v.*

शैल, stony, rocky, mountainous: hence, (1) *m.* (*f.* ā or i) a mountaineer (2) *m.* a mountain, a rock; a dike; bitumen; storax; a sort of collyrium.

शैलकुमारी = **शैलजा**, *q.v.*

शैलपत्त, *m.* the mountain-dwelling (an epithet of the Himālaya mountains).

शैलज, *m.* (*f.* ā) produced in or on mountains or rocks, mountain-born.

शैलजा, *f.* (see **गिरिजा**) an epithet of Pārvatī.

शैलराज, *m.* (the lord or chief of mountains, *i.e.*) the Himālaya range.

शैलसुता = **शैलजा**, *q.v.*

शैला } *f*; see **शैल**.
शैली }

शैव, appertaining to Shiv: hence, *m.* a worshipper of Shiv, a Shivite: the plant *Vallisneria octandra.*

शैवल } = **शैवाल**, *q.v.*
शैवाल }

शो, a corruption (1) of **शव** (2) of **शौ** (3) of **सो** (= he, etc.) 3, *qq.v.*

शोक, *m.* grief, sorrow, mourning, regret, woe, affliction, lamentation, anguish.

शोकजनक, grief-producing, afflictive.

शोकडर, *m.* sorrow and fear.

शोकत, *more prop.* **शौकत**, *q.v.*

शोकपर, *m.* (*f.* ā) a person filled with grief: *lit.* whose principal occupation is grief.

शोकभंग, 1, *m.* a dissipating or removing sorrow: 2, *m.* (*f.* ā or i) a dissipator or remover of sorrow.

शोकमय, *m.* (*f.* ī) abounding in sorrow or woe.

शोकवत }
शोकवन्त } *m.* (*f.* vatī) = **शोकी**, *q.v.*
शोकवान }

शोकाकुल, *m.* (*f.* ā) overwhelmed with distress or sorrow, grieved.

शोकार्त्त, *m.* (*f.* ā) a very sorrowful person: *lit.* pained or afflicted with sorrow or grief, grieved, sorrowful.

शोकित, *m.* (*f.* ā) = **शोकी**, *q.v.*

शोकी, *m.* (*f.* inī) a mourner, etc.: *lit.* sorrowful, mourning, sad, grieved, distressed, afflicted.

शोकोक्ति, *f.* the language of grief, mourning, lamentation. — *sambandhanīya gīt*, a dirge.

शोख़ी, *f.* mischief, humour, playfulness, cheerfulness, sauciness, wantonness, coquetry, insolence.

शोग, a Prākrit form of **शोक**, *q.v.*

शोघात, a present.

शोच, *more prop.* (1) **शोचन**, 1, *q.v.* (2) **सोच**, *q.v.*

शोचडर, *m.* sorrow and fear.

शोचन, 1, *m.* (*f.* ā) sorrowful, sorrowing, regretful, sad: 2, *m.* sorrow, sadness, mourning, regret, distress, grief.

शोचना, *f.* (1) = **शोचन**, 1, *q.v.*: (2) = **शोचन**, 2, *q.v.*

शोचित, *m.* (*f.* ā) sorrowful, afflicted, grieved.

शोचिष्केश, *m.* an epithet (1) of the sun (2) of fire (3) of the god of fire (Agni): *lit.* whose rays are like hair.

शोण, 1, of a crimson colour; red in the face (from passion): 2, *m.* crimson (the colour); fire; a sort of red sugarcane; blood; red lead; a certain plant (*Bignonia Indica*): 3, *m. pr. n.* the river Sone, which, rising in the table land of Amarkaṇṭak and running first northerly and then easterly for 500 miles, falls into the Ganges above Patna.

शोणभद्र, *m.* } *pr. n.* = **शोण**, 3, *q.v.*
शोणभद्रा, *f.* }

शोणरत्न, *m.* (the crimson gem, *i. e.*) the ruby.

शोणित, *m.* (*f.* ā) red, crimson, purple: hence, *m.* blood; saffron.

शोणितपुर, *m.* an epithet of **बाणपुर**, *q.v.*

शोणितोपल, *m.* = **शोणरत्न**, *q.v.* [rising.

शोथ, *m.* swelling from disease, intumescence,

शोथघ्न, *adj.* removing swellings, discutient.

शोथघ्नी, *f.* hogweed (*Boerhavia diffusa*). [tion.

शोध, *f.* discharge of debt, liquidation, retalia-

शोधक, 1, *m.* (*f.* ikā) a purifier, a corrector: lit. *adj.* purifying, cleansing, paying off a debt, retaliating: 2, *m.* (in Arithm.) the subtrahend; (in Algebra) the quantity to be subtracted from a number in order to its being capable of yielding an exact square root.

शोधन, 1, *m.* (*f.* ā or ī) = **शोधक**, 1, *q.v.*: 2, *m.* removing what may be prejudicial, cleansing, purifying, expiation, punishment, correcting, freeing from faults or errors, liquidation, retaliation, payment, acquittance; green vitriol; ordure: (in Arithm.) subtraction.

शोधना, *more com.* **सोधना**, *q.v.*

शोधनी, *f.* a besom, a broom.

शोभन, 1, (*f.* ā) splendid, beautiful, handsome, pleasing; propitious, auspicious; virtuous, good; richly adorned: 2, *m.* a shining; comeliness, handsomeness, pleasantness; burnt-offering for auspicious results; a planet; a lotus; *pr. n.* the 5th of the astronomical divisions of the ecliptic.

शोभना, *a. int.* or *t.* to befit, beseem, become.

शोभमान, *m.* (*f.* matī) = **शोभी**, *q.v.*

शोभा, *f.* splendour, lustre, light, radiance; loveliness, comeliness, beauty; ornament, decoration, dress: (in Pros.) a species of metre.

शोभांजन, *m.* a tree (*Hyperanthera moringa*) called also *sajinā* and *sahajnā*. [trious.

शोभान्वित, *m.* (*f.* ā) beautiful, ornamented, illus-

शोभायमान, *m.* (*f.* matī) = **शोभी**, *q.v.*

शोभाविष्ट, *m* (*f.* ā) beautiful, lovely, ornamented.

शोभित, *m.* (*f.* ā) beautified, ornamented, adorned, made splendid. [tiful, conspicuous, adorning.

शोभी, *m.* (*f.* inī) shining, radiant, splendid, beau-

शोमारी, 1, *m.* (*f.* iṇī) indolent, lazy: 2, *f.* laziness, indolence.

शोमिरोन, *m. pr. n.* the province of Samaria.

शोमिरोनी, appertaining to the province of Samaria, Samaritan: hence, *m.* (*f.* iṇī) a Samaritan.

शोर, *m.* an outcry, noise, cry.

शोरबा, *m.* broth, soup. [saltpetre.

शोरा, *m.* marshy ground, barren ground: nitre,

शोरिश, *f.* tumult, insurrection, confusion.

शोला, *m.* Indian cork (*Æschynomene paludosa*) the wood of which, being very light and spongy, is used by fishermen for floating their nets. A variety of toys, such as artificial birds and flowers, are also made of it, garlands of these flowers being used in marriage ceremonies; and, when charred, it answers the purpose of tinder.

शोष, *m.* drying up, exsiccation, dryness; intumescence, swelling, pulmonary consumption. [cious.

शोषक, *m.* (*f.* ikā) absorbent; avaricious, rapa-

शोषण, *m.* a drying up, absorbing, sucking, suction, exhaustion: *pr. n.* one of the arrows of Kāmdev.

शौ, *m.* a husband; a bridegroom.

शौक़, *m.* desire, special leaning, fondness, eagerness, zest, relish, inclination, love; curiosity; cheerfulness, gaiety. [pomp.

शौकत, *f.* state, dignity, magnificence, majesty,

शौच, *m.* cleanness, freedom from defilement; honesty; purification by ablution; purification from any personal defilement; evacuation; ablution.

शौचापर, *m.* (*f.* ā) a cleanly or virtuous person: *lit.* intent on purity.

शौण्डिक, *m.* (*f.* ī) a vinter, distiller, vendor of spirituous liquors, tavern-keeper. [slaughterhouse.

शौन, 1, = **शौनिक**, 1, *q.v.*: 2, *m.* meat kept at a

शौनक, *m. pr. n.* a certain *Rishi*.

शौनिक, 1, *m.* (*f.* ī) a vendor of flesh, a butcher, poulterer; 2, *m.* hunting, the chase.

शौनिकप्रधान, *m.* a chief butcher, etc. See **शौनिक**.

शौभाग्य (*corruption*) = **सौभाग्य**, *q.v.*

शौर्य्य, *m.* valour, heroism, bravery, prowess.

शौहर, *m.* a husband.

श्मशान, *m.* any place where corpses are burned or buried, a crematory, a cemetery, buryingplace, sepulchre.

श्मशानक, appertaining to a buryingplace.

श्मशानवासी, *m.* (*f.* inī) a ghost, goblin, sprite: lit. *adj.* dwelling in buryingplaces: an epithet of Shiv.

श्यतान (*corruption*) = **शैतान**, *q.v.*

श्यमन्तक, *more prop.* **स्यमन्तक**, *q.v.*

श्यापर्ण, *m.* (*f.* ā) = **श्यापर्णीय**, *q.v.*

श्यापर्णा, *m.* (pl.; see **श्रा**, 22) a certain tribe or family. [family or race.

श्यापर्णीय, *m.* (*f.* ā) appertaining to the Shyaparṇ

श्याम, *m.* (*f.* ā) green; dark blue; black; shady; brown: hence, *m.* green, etc. (the colours); a cloud; the thorn-apple; sea salt; pepper; a species of grain (*Panicum frumentaceum*): an epithet of (1) the Indian cuckoo (2) of the sacred imperishable tree at Allahabad (called also *akshayvriksh*).

श्यामकर्ण, *m.* (*f.* ā or ī) any black-eared creature.

श्यामकर्णघोड़ा, *m.* a black-eared horse, *i. e.* a horse suitable for the horse sacrifice (*Ashwamedh*).

श्यामकार्त्तिक, a corruption of **स्वामिकार्त्तिक**, *q.v.*

श्यामघटा, *f.* a collection of black clouds.

श्यामता, *f.* (*m.* °**त्व**) darkness of colour, blackness, dark blue. [as jet.

श्यामभास, *m.* (*f.* ā) of a glassy black hue, black

श्यामरंग, green, dark blue, black, shady, brown. Used as a subst. *m.*, or as an adj. *m.* (*f.* ā).

श्यामल, of a black or dark blue colour, blackish: hence (1) *m.* black (the colour): pepper; the religious figtree (2) *m.* (*f.* ā) a large bee.

श्यामला, *f.* an epithet of Pārvatī.

श्यामवर्ण = **श्यामरंग**, *q.v.*

श्यामसुन्दर, *m.* an epithet of Kṛishṇ.

श्यामा, *f.* night; shade, shadow: a cow: a married female before she has borne children; several plants: a certain small singing-bird (*Turdus macrourus*) with black plumage, commonly called *shāmā*: a form of Durgā much worshipped by the Tāntrikas.

श्यामाक, *m.* a certain gramineous plant (*Panicum frumentaceum* or *P. colonum*) the grain of which (also called *sāṅwāṅ*) is much eaten by Hindoos.

श्यामारहस्य, *m. pr. n.* a certain Tāntrik work.

श्यार, *more prop.* **स्यार**, *q.v.*

श्यालक, *m.* a brother-in-law (wife's brother).

श्यालकी, *f.* a sister-in-law (wife's sister). [falcon.

श्येन, 1, *m.* white (the colour): 2, *m.* (*f.* ī) a hawk,

श्येनिका, *f.* (in Pros) a species of metre.

श्येनी, *f.* (*m.* **श्येन**) a white hawk or falcon.

श्रद्धधान, *adj.* giving credit to, having faith or reverence, believing, trusting, venerating, respecting.

श्रद्धा, *f.* faith, confidence, belief, reliance, credit; respect, reverence; purity; wish, desire, hope.

श्रद्धाकृत, done in faith.

श्रद्धान्वित, *m.* (*f.* ā) having faith, trustful.

श्रद्धामय, *m.* (*f.* ī) abounding in faith, believing.

श्रद्धायुक्त, *m.* (*f.* ā) having faith, believing, trustful.

श्रद्धारहित, *m.* (*f.* ā) destitute of faith, unbelieving.

श्रद्धालु, 1, *m.* (*f.* ī) having faith, believing, faithful: desirous. wishful; 2, *f.* a pregnant woman longing for anything.

श्रद्धावान, *m.* (*f.* vatī) having faith, believing.

श्रद्धाहीन, *m.* (*f.* ā) faithless, unbelieving.

श्रद्धेय, *m.* (*f.* ī) deserving trust, trustworthy.

श्रप } **श्रप्प** } in Chand = **श्राप** = **शाप**, *q.v.*

श्रब्ब in Chand = **सर्व**, *q. v.* [toil, fatigue, weariness.

श्रम, *m.* painstaking, exertion, industry, labour,

श्रमण, following a low business, base: hence, *m.* (*f.* ā *or* ī) a religious mendicant, a *yati*, a Bauddh friar, an ascetic.

श्रमणा, *f.* (*m.* **श्रमण**) a female mendicant; a female of low caste or business; a handsome woman.

श्रमणी = **श्रमणा**, *q.v.*

श्रमबिन्दु, *m.* perspiration, sweat. [riness.

श्रमहारी, *m.* (*f.* iṇī) *adj.* subduing or removing wea-

श्रमार्त्त, *m.* (*f.* ā) fatigued, wearied, exhausted.

श्रमी, *m.* (*f.* iṇī) a laborious person, etc.: *lit.* undergoing or incurring weariness, diligent, laborious; wearying. [ing; learning, study.

श्रवण, *m.* 1, *pr. n.* = **श्रवणा**, *q. v.*: 2, the ear; hear-

श्रवणन, *m.* (a Braj pl. of **श्रवण**) the ears.

श्रवणपूर, *m.* any ear-ornament.

श्रवणमार्ग } **श्रवणरन्ध्र** } *m.* the ear-hole.

श्रवणा, *f. pr. n.* the 23rd *Nakshatra* (represented by three footsteps and containing the three principal stars in Aquila). [voice, pleasing sound.

श्रवणामृत, *m.* (the ambrosia of the ear, *i. e.*) a sweet

श्रवणेन्द्रिय, *m.* the organ of hearing, the ear.

श्रवनन = **श्रवणन**, *q. v.*

श्रवननि, in Braj (1) a pl. of **श्रवण**; see **नि**, 2 (2): (2) an agentive form of **श्रवण**; see **नि**, 2 (5).

श्रविष्ठा, *f. pr. n.* the 24th *Nakshatra* (called also *Dhanishthā*, and corresponding to the Dolphin).

श्राद्ध, 1, believing, faithful: 2, *m.* a certain funeral ceremony observed by Hindoos at various fixed periods and for different purposes, consisting of offerings with water and fire to the gods and manes, and of food and gifts to the relatives present and to the assisting of Brāhmaṇs. It is especially performed for a parent recently deceased, or for three paternal ancestors, or for all ancestors collectively, and is believed essential to the ascent of departed spirits to a world appropriated to the manes and to their residence there. The term is also applied to the gifts presented on the occasion of the observance of the ceremony.

श्राद्धदेव, *m.* any god who presides over funeral rites: an epithet (1) of Yam (2) of Vishwa-dev (3) of Manu-Vaivaswat.

श्राद्धदेवमनु, *m.* an epithet of Manu-Vaivaswat.

श्रान्त, *m.* (*f.* ā) fatigued, weary: tranquil, calm.

श्रान्ति, *f.* weariness, fatigue, exhaustion.

श्राप = **शाप**, *q. v.*

श्रावक, *m.* a certain class of the Bauddh votaries; a lay votary of the Bauddh religion; a pupil of a Jain.

श्रावण, *m.* the fourth Hindoo month Shrāvaṇ (July-Aug.) beginning when the sun enters Cancer. Its full moon is near *Shrāvaṇ* or Aquilæ. — *hare na bhādoṅ sūkhe* (flourishing in summer and not failing in autumn) is applied to express continuance in the same state or condition. [2, *m.* the month Shrāvaṇ.

श्रावणिक, 1, *m.* (*f.* ī) appertaining to Shrāvaṇ:

श्रावणी, *f.* the day of full moon in the month Shrāvaṇ; one of the Hindoo domestic sacrifices.

श्रावणिक, *more prop.* **श्रावणिक**, *q. v.*

श्री, *f.* fortune, success, prosperity, thriving; wealth, property; beauty, light, lustre, splendour, glory; decoration; intellect: cloves: *pr. n.* (1) of the goddess Lakshmī, wife of Vishṇu, and deity of plenty and prosperity (2) of Saraswatī (3) the three objects of life collectively, *viz.* love, duty, and wealth. This term is usually prefixed, as an indication of respect, to names of deities and other revered persons, and also to literary productions, implying, 'holy' 'illustrious,' 'famous', *e. g.* **श्रीगणेश**, the illustrious or honoured Gaṇesh: **श्रीभागवत**, the famous or sacred Bhāgavat.

श्रीखण्ड, *m.* sandal-wood. [globe on earth.

श्रीचक्र, *m.* a magical diagram; the circle of the

श्रीनगर, *m. pr. n.* (the city of fortune) the name of several Indian cities.

श्रीनिवास, *m.* (the occupant of Lakshmī, *i.e.*) Vishṇu.

श्रीपति, *m.* (the husband of Lakshmī, *i. e.*) Vishṇu.

श्रीफल, *m.* the wood-apple tree (*Ægle marmelos*) and its fruit.

श्रीमत, *m.* (*f.* matī) a famous person, etc: *lit.* fortunate, prosperous, thriving, wealthy, famous, illustrious, pleasing, beautiful: an epithet (1) of Shiv (2) of Vishnu (3) of Kuver.

श्रीमती, *f.* (*m.* **श्रीमत**, etc.) an illustrious or beautiful female; *pr. n.* the mother of Mādhavācharya; an epithet of Rādhā. The term is also applied as a title to women.

श्रीमद, *m.* the intoxication produced by prosperity.

श्रीमन्त } **श्रीमान** } *m.* (*f.* matī) = **श्रीमत**, *q.v.*

श्रीमुख, *m.* the word **श्री** written on the back of a letter: the seventh year of the Indian cycle

श्रीयुक्त, *m.* (*f.* ā) attended or endowed with prosperity, auspicious, fortunate, illustrious, prosperous, wealthy, Your Honour.

श्रीयुत, *m.* (*f.* ā) = **श्रीयुक्त**. *q. v.*

श्रीरंग, *m.* an epithet of Vishṇu.

श्रीरस, *m.* turpentine.

श्रीराग, *m.* the third of the personified musical modes (see *rāg*). It is appropriated to the afternoon in winter, and proceeds from the womb of the earth.

श्रीवत्स, *m.* a certain mark or sign usually said to be a curl of hair on the breast of Vishṇu or Krishṇ and used as his mark or symbol; an epithet of Vishṇu: *pr. n.* one of the lunar asterisms (*Nakshatra*): a hole in a wall for felonious purposes.

श्रीहस्तिनी, *f.* sunflower (*Heliotropium Indicum*).

श्रुत, heard, heard of, reported, rumoured, said; understood, hence, *m.* sacred science or learning, holy writ.

श्रुतदेव, *m. pr. n.* a certain ancient Brāhmaṇ.

श्रुतदेवा, *f. pr. n.* a daughter of Sūr and wife of Vriddha-sharman.

श्रुतदेवी, *f.* (the goddess of learning, *i. e.*) Saraswatī.

श्रुतश्रवा, *f. pr. n.* the wife of Damghosh.

श्रुति, *f.* the sense of hearing; the being heard of or specially mentioned: the ear; report: (in Theol.) the revealed law, holy writ, the Veds: (in Geom.) the diagonal of a tetragon; the hypotenuse of a triangle: (in Music) a division of the octave, a quarter tone or interval, of which twenty-two are enumerated.

श्रुतिकीर्ति, *f. pr. n.* (1) of a wife of Dhrishtiketu, (2) of a certain Hindoo book.

श्रुतिवेचक, *m.* (*f.* ikā) an epithet of any Brāhmaṇ (*lit.* one who traffics in the Veds).

श्रुतिसार, *m.* the essence or substance of the Veds.

श्रेणि, *m. f.* = **श्रेणी**, *q. v.*

श्रेणी, *f.* a line, row, range; a row of trees, an avenue; a troop; a company of artisans following the same business; a corporation: a baling-vessel, bucket.

श्रेढ़ी, *f* a chain, a series. [auspiciousness, propriety.

श्रेय:, *m.* final beatitute, happiness; good fortune,

श्रेयस = **श्रेय:**, *q. v.*

श्रेष्ठ, *superl.* best, excellent, of higher rank, chief, oldest, senior: hence, *m.* (1) a king (2) a Brāhmaṇ (3) cow's milk (4) Kuver.

श्रेष्ठतर, *m.* (*f.* ā) more excellent; older.

श्रेष्ठता, *f.* (*m.*°**त्व**) superiority, excellence.

श्रोत, 1, *more prop.* **स्रोत**, *q. v.*: 2, *m.* the ear.

श्रोतव्य, fit to be heard, proper to be listened to, audible. [*pr. n.* a certain *yaksh.*

श्रोता, (uninfl.) *m.* (*f.* trī) a hearer, listener, pupil:

श्लाघा, *f.* panegyric, praise, eulogium, applause, flattery; boasting; service; wish, desire.

श्लाघ्य, *m.* (*f.* ā) entitled to praise or to veneration, praiseworthy, respectable, venerable.

श्लीपद, *m.* morbid enlargement of the legs, elephantiasis.

श्लेष्मा, *m.* one of the three principal humours of the human body, *viz.* phlegm, rheum, mucus; serum.

श्लेष, *m.* union, junction, association; a clinging to, an embrace; a paronomasia, double entendre, pun, sarcasm.

श्लोक, *m.* fame; a saying; a verse, a stanza (*esp.* the epic stanza, properly called **वक्त्र**, consisting of two verses, each of sixteen syllables).

श्वन्, *m.* (*f.* **शुनी**) a dog.

श्वपच, *m.* (*f.* ā) a dog-feeder, person of low caste, *chāṇḍāl.*

श्वपाक, *m.* (*f.* ī) a person of a low or outcaste tribe; the offspring of a Kshattṛi by an Ugrā woman.

श्वफल्क, *m. pr. n.* a son of Pṛishni (or, as some say, of Vṛishṇi). He was husband of Gāndinī, by whom he had a son called Akrūr.

श्वशुर, *m.* a father-in-law (a wife's or a husband's father).

श्वश्रू, *f.* a mother-in-law.

श्वसुर, *more prop.* **श्वशुर**, *q. v.*

श्वान, *m.* (*f.* ī) a dog, a hound.

श्वाना, *more prop.* **श्वानी**, *q. v.*

श्वानी, *f.* (*m.* **श्वान**) a bitch.

श्वास, *m.* breathing, respiration; a breath; sighing, a sigh; air, wind; life. — *khainchnā* or *lenā*, to take breath, draw breath, breathe.

श्वासा, *more prop.* **श्वास**, *q. v.*

श्वित्र, *m.* whiteness of the skin, white leprosy, vitiligo.

श्वित्री, *m.* (*f.* iṇī) a leper: *lit.* affected with vitiligo or with leprosy, leprous.

श्वेत, white: hence, (1) *m.* (*f.* ā *or* nī) a person clothed in white: (2) *m.* white (the colour); a conch; a small white shell used as a coin; a white cloud; cumin-seed; silver: *pr. n.* (1) of one of the minor divisions (*dwip*) of the world; in fable, the white Island (called also *Chandra-dwip*) identified geographically by Wilford with Britain (2) of the planet Venus, or its regent *Shukra* (3) of the 6th range of the mountains which are fabled to divide the known continent, *viz.* the white mountains separating the Varshas of Hiraumay and Romanak.

श्वेतचींवटी, *f.* the white ant.

श्वेतता, *f.* whiteness.

श्वेतद्वीप, *m. pr. n.* = **श्वेत**, 2 (1), *q. v.*

श्वेतधातु, *m.* milkstone, opal, chalcedony, chalk.

श्वेतनी, *f.* (*m.* **श्वेत**) white.

श्वेतवर्ण, *m.* (*f.* ā) white-coloured.

श्वेतसर्प, 1, *m.* (*f.* ī) a white snake: 2, *m.* a certain tree (*Tapia cratæva*).

श्वेतहस्ती, *m.* (*f.* inī) a white elephant.

श्वेता, *f.* (*m.* **श्वेत**) a female in a white dress; a small white shell used as a coin; crystal; candied sugar; the name of several plants.

श्वेतार्क, *m.* the gigantic swallow-wort (*Asclepias gigantea*) bearing white flowers.

श्वेती, *f.* white (the colour): *pr. n.* a certain river.

श्वेत्र / **श्वेत्र्य** } *m.* the white leprosy.

श्वेष्ट, *m.* (*f.* ā) *more prop.* **स्वेष्ट**, *q. v.*

ष

ष (sh *or* sḥ) is the thirty-first consonant in the Hindee or Devanāgarī alphabet, and has the following characteristics and functions :— 1, It belongs to the cerebral class, and is the second of the three sibilants ; it is hence called the cerebral sibilant. (See **श**, 1.) 2, It is generally represented in the Roman character by *sh*, but with a view to distinguishing between it and its predecessor (**श**), two dots (as indicated above) are sometimes placed under the *h*. 3, In pronunciation it has the sound of the English *sh* ; but its sound differs from that of **श** in being slightly rougher and more aspirated, as many persons pronounce the *ss* in 'session' or the *ti* in 'unction'. (See **श**, 2.) The difference, however, between the pronunciation of **श** and of **ष** is hardly sufficiently noticeable to be detected by a beginner, unless he has an acute ear and is on the alert in the matter. It should be added that by the larger portion of the Hindee-speaking people this letter is pronounced exactly like the aspirated letter **ख**. 4, This letter is frequently called "peṭkaṭā *sha*," seemingly in allusion to its form. 5, It is occasionally interchanged with **क**; *e. g.* **ज्योतिक**, more properly **ज्योतिष** ; and is constantly liable to be interchanged with **स**, **छ**, **ख**, **श**, and **स** ; *e. g.* **सन्तोख**, properly **सन्तोष**: again **वैषानस**, more properly **वैखानस**, etc. We have also noteworthy instances of interchange in the words **षटांक**, **षामपडलें**, and **षट**, 6, In the formation of the word **मानुष** from **मनु**, this letter appears as a Taddhita suffix. 7, As a cerebral, this letter requires **न** to be exchanged for **ण** in words in which it precedes the *n*-sound : See **ण**, 3, and notes on **ण**. 8, It should be observed that it is not always easy or even possible to ascertain whether **श** or **ष** should be used; *e.g.* **कोश** = **कोष**. 9, In Sandhi this letter undergoes important changes which will be found carefully specified at length in any good Hindee or Sanskrit Grammar.

षकार, *m.* the letter **ष**, or any character that may represent it.

षग in Chand = **खड्ग**, *q. v*,

षट, (prop. **षष**) six.

षटऋतु, *m.* (see **ऋतु**) the six seasons of the Hindoos.

षट्कर्म्म, *m.* 1, (pl.: see **श्रा**, 22) the six acts proper for a Brāhman, *viz.* (1) adoration (2) sacred study (3) alms-giving (4) offering sacrifice (5) teaching the Veds or scriptures (6) accepting suitable gifts: the six acts allowable to a Brāhman for subsistence, *viz.* (1) gleaning (2) accepting gifts (3) asking alms (4) agriculture (5) trade (6) tending cattle, or (according to some) lending money at interest: the six acts taught in the Tantras, *viz.* (1) killing (2) infatuating (3) enthralling (4) expelling (5) exciting animosity (6) the stopping or privation of any faculty: 2, any Brāhman who performs the six prescribed duties: 3, an adept in the Tantras.

षटकोण, *m.* any six-angled figure, a hexagon: *pr. n.* the thunderbolt of Indra : *lit.* hexangular.

षटकोना, *m.* (*f.* ī) = **षटकोण**, *q. v.*

षटचरण, *m.* an epithet of the bee : *lit.* six-footed.

षटदर्शण = **षटशास्त्र**, *q. v.*

षटपद, *m.* (*f.* ī) a large black bee.

षटपदिका, *f.* (in Pros.) a species of metre,

षटमुख, *m.* an epithet of Kārttikeya, the son of Shiv and god of war : *lit.* the six-faced.

षटरस, *m.* (see **रस**) the six tastes.

षटवदन = **षटमुख**, *q. v.*

षटशास्त्र, *m. pr. n.* the six philosophical sciences or schools of the Hindoos, *viz* (1) the *Nyāy*, Logic, taught by the sage Gotam : (2) the *Vaisheshik*, taught by Kanād or Kaṇād : it agrees with the *Nyāy* in some points but differs in others : (3) the *Mimānsā*, taught by Jaimani : it consists of rules for the right interpretation and construing of the Veds : (4) the *Vedānt*, taught by Vyāsdev : it consists of the science of Theology : (5) the *Sānkhya*, taught by Kapil : the followers of this sect disbelieve in a creator, and hold that the universe has existed from all eternity : (6) the *Patanjal*, introduced by Sheshnāg : it agrees in every point with the Sānkhya, excepting that it holds that God is the Creator.

षटांक, *most com.* **छटांक**, *q. v.*

षट.नन = **षटमुख**, *q. v.*

षट्खांग, *more prop.* **खट्वांग**, *q. v.*

षड्, in compos, = **षट**, six.

षडंग, *m.* six parts of the body taken collectively, *viz.* the arms, the legs, the head, and the waist : the six auxiliary or supplementary branches (*ang*) of sacred science, *viz.* (1) Grammar (2) Prosody (3) Pronunciation (4) Astronomy (5) the meanings of unusual terms (6) the ritual of the Hindoo religion : a certain set of six particular articles of offering at the first oblation of rice, etc. to the manes of deceased ancestors.

षड्गुण, 1, sixfold, six times; 2, *m.* an assemblage of six qualities or properties.

षड्दर्शण = **षटशास्त्र**, *q. v.*

षडमात्र, *m.* (*f.* ī) containing six *mātras*.

षडानन = **षटमुख**, *q. v.*

षड्डा, *m.* (*f.* ī) *more prop.* **खड्डा**, *q.v.*

षड्विंशति, *f.* (Sk.) twenty-six.

षड्विंशतितम, (Sk.) *m.* (*f.* ī) the twenty-sixth.

षड्विध, of six kinds or descriptions, in six ways.

षणादर्शण = **षटशास्त्र**, *q. v*,

[sixfold, six-times.

षणा, an old form = **खण्ड**, *q v.*

षण्ड, *m.* a bull at liberty : a eunuch : a quantity of lotuses : a multitude ; a wood, thicket.

षण्ढ, *m.* a eunuch,

षर्भर in Chand = **खब्बर**, *q. v*,

षरान, *m.* the foot.

षर्दर्शन = **षटशास्त्र**, *q. v.*

षष, six.

षष्ट, sixtieth.

षष्टि, *f.* sixty.

षष्टी, *more prop.* (1) **षष्टि** (2) **षष्ठी**, *qq. v.*

षष्ठ, *m.* (*f.* ā *or* ī) sixth,

[epithet of Durgā.

षष्ठा, *f.* the sixth day of a lunar fortnight ; an

षष्ठी = **षष्ठा**, *q. v.*

षामपडलें in Chand = **श्यामपडल**, *q. v.*

षासक, *more prop.* **शासक**, *q. v.*

षेत in Chand = **खेत**, *q. v*,

षोडश, 1, *m.* (*f.* ī) sixteenth: 2, sixteen: 3, *m.* a set of sixteen particular articles of offering.

ष्याति, *f. pr. n.* the wife of Bhṛigu.

ष्याल in Mārwārī = **ख्याल**, *q.v.*

स

स (s) is the thirty-second consonant in the Hindee or Devanāgarī alphabet, and has the following characteristics and functions:—1, It belongs to the dental class, and is the last of the three sibilants; which, including **ह**, form the class called by grammarians *ūshmā*, or *ūshmānah*: it is hence called the dental sibilant. 2, In pronunciation it has the common sound of *s* as in the English word 'son': it never has the *z*-sound of that letter in the English word 'nose', nor the *sh*-sound of *s* in 'measure'. By many persons this letter is slightly aspirated, so that the word **सकल** is sometimes pronounced as if it were spelt *shakal* or even *shhakal*. It may be of some importance to observe that though the natives of Bengal seldom make any perceptible difference in their pronunciation of the three sibilants, yet among the Hindee-speaking people the sounds of these letters are distinctly marked even among the masses, excepting by persons of singular carelessness or of some vocal inability to produce the respective sounds. 3, As a Taddhita suffix, it is used to form a few adjectives from substantives; *e.g.* **तृणास**, grassy; from **तृण**, grass. 4, This letter sometimes = the English personal pronoun 'he', 'that': in such case it is one of the Sanskrit forms of the nominative of the personal pronoun **तद्** he. 5, As, apparently, an abridged form of **सह** with, it is frequently found (1) as the first member in Bahuvṛīhi compounds; *e.g.* **सकमल**, with lotus-flowers: **सजीव**, alive (2) as = the same, like, equal; *e.g.* **सधर्म्मा**, *adj.* of the same caste, etc.: **सगोत्र**, of one ancestry or family. 6, This letter is sometimes found as an abbreviation (1) of **सु**; *e.g.* **सपुत** = **सुपुत्र**, a filial son (2) of **स्व**; *e.g.* **सगुण** = **स्वगुण**. 7, It is constantly interchanged with **श**, and not unfrequently with **ष**; while sometimes it interchanges with **क्ष** (**क्षिर्का** = **सिर्का**), and once with **ल** (**निकलना**, etc. = **निकसना**, etc.): it is also liable to be interchanged with **ह**. 8, In foreign words current in Hindee, this letter stands for (1) ث (2) ص, and (3) س. 9, In many words it is quite common to drop this letter; *e.g.* **हमें** (= **सहमें**); **नेह** (= **स्नेह**); **थान** (= **स्थान**); **थिति** (= **स्थिति**). 10, In Prosody, this letter represents the metrical foot (⏑⏑—) called anapæst, consisting of two short syllables followed by one long one.

सअद, *m.* felicity, prosperity, propitiousness.

सआदत, *f.* happiness, felicity, good fortune.

सइद; see (1) **सैयिद** (2) **शायद**.

सइल in Chand = **शैल**, *q.v.*

सई, 1, a corruption of **सहोत**, *q.v.*: 2, *f.* a wire chain: industry: *pr. n.* a certain river.

सईद; see (1) **सैयिद** (2) **शायद**.

सईस = **साईस**, *q.v.*

सउ in old Hindee = **सौ**, *q.v.*

सउबत, *more prop.* **सुहबत**, *q.v.*

सं [an inseparable prefix the reverse of **वि**, implying (like the Grk. σύν, and Lat. *con.* etc.) connexion, fulness, perfection, participation, or unity] = with, together with, much, very, wholly, beautifully, etc. Sometimes, however, it does not perceptibly affect the sense of a word.

सः (Sk. nom. sing. of the 3rd pers. pron. **तद्**) = **वह**.

संक (*corruption*) = (1) **शंका** (2) **शंख**, *qq.v.*

संकची, *f.* a skate.

संकट, narrow, contracted, crowded, impervious, impassable: hence, *m.* a strait, difficulty, trouble, vexation, anguish, pain, agony, pang, distress, misfortune, danger.

संकटचौथ, *f. m.* a certain Hindoo holiday in the month Māgh, sacred to Gaṇesh as the festival of his birth.

संकड़ई, *f.* a crowding; contracting.

संकड़ना, *n.* to be contracted, be narrowed.

संकड़ा, *m.* (*f.* ī) contracted, narrow, cramped.

संकड़ाना, *t.* to cause to be narrowed or contracted, to cramp.

संकर, 1, *more prop.* **शंकर**, *q.v.*: 2, *m.* a mixing, blending, confounding; the union of a man with a woman of a higher caste, culpable mixture; a mixed or degraded caste: dust, sweepings: the crackling of a flame. The term is specially applied to a mixed caste or race proceeding from the promiscuous intercourse of the four tribes in the first instance, and again, from their commerce with the descendants of such a connexion, or the indiscriminate cohabitation of those descendants among themselves. Most Hindoos of the present age are of one of the many branches of this race, the highest of which is impure, and is inferior to the Shūdra. According to the Rāmāyan, under the term *saṅkar* two kinds of men are included (1) *Yonisaṅkar*, mixed or degraded by birth (2) *Āchārsaṅkar*, degraded by conduct.

संकर्षण, *m.* an attracting, drawing; ploughing: *pr. n.* (1) of Baldev, brother of Krishṇ (2) of one of the eleven *Rudras*.

संकल, *m.* a collection, quantity; (in Arithm.) addition: a chain.

संकलताला, *m.* lock and chain (as of a door).

संकलन, *m.* a mixing, uniting, arranging; junction, collision, contact; collection, blending, intermixture; heaping; (in Arithm.) summation, addition.

संकलित, heaped together, piled up, added, joined, mixed, arranged: hence, *m.* (1) Arithmetic (2) addition.

संकल्प, *m.* volition, will, wish, desire, mind, thought, resolve, mental determination; a declaration of purpose, a solemn vow, expectation of advantage from a holy work.

संकल्पना, *a. int.* to vow: *t.* to give alms (by making a religious vow).

संकल्पा, *f. pr. n.* a daughter of Daksh and wife of Dharm.

संकल्पित, conceived, imagined, thought, contrived, intended, determined.

संका (*corruption*) = **शंका**, *q.v.*

संकार, 1, *m.* dust, sweepings; the crackling of flame: 2, *f.* a sign, nod, hint, wink, beckoning.

संकारना, *a. int.* to beckon, nod, make a signal, wink, hint: to inveigle.

संकाश, similar, resembling, like.

संकीर्ण, *m.* (*f.* ā) mixed, impure, confused: contracted, small: spread, diffused: crowded, confused.

संकीर्त्तन, *m.* (or *f.* ā) celebrating, praising, extolling: glorification, honour, glory.

संकुचित, *m.* (*f.* ā) shrivelled up, unopened, unblown; backward, diffident, abashed.

संकुल, *m.* (*f.* ā) filled so as to be impervious, crowded, full, thronged: mixed, confused, perplexed.

संकेत, *m.* a sign, hint, allusion, gesture, gesticulation: appointment, engagement, agreement, convention: conditions or circumstances under which a thing is effected.

संकेतस्थान, *m.* an appointed place, place of assignation.

संकेतित, adapted, accommodated, non-natural; [indicated.

संकोच, *m.* contraction, diminution, shutting, closing, shrivelling up; family honour; shame, backwardness, reserve, diffidence, fear: the skate-fish (*Raia sancara*): saffron.

संकोचन, *m.* a shrinking; an astringing; a causing to shrink or close.

संकोचित, shrivelled, shrunken, bashful, diffident, [reserved.

संकोची, *m.* (*f.* inī) a bashful person, etc.: *lit.* bashful, reserved, diffident; shrivelling up.

संक्रम, *m.* difficult progress, making way through almost impervious passes; the means of effecting such a passage, a causeway, bridge; a going, moving, travelling, traversing; concurrence; the passage of a planet through the zodiac.

संक्रांत / **संक्रात** } = (1) **संक्रान्त** (2) **संक्रान्ति**, *qq.v.*

संक्रान्त, passed, gone, transferred, proceeded from one station to the next, entered (into a new sign of the zodiac).

संक्रान्ति, *f.* union; procession, passage (*esp.* the passage of the sun or any planetary body from one sign of the zodiac into another).

संक्रान्ती, 1, (*corruption*) = **संक्रान्ति**, *q.v.*: 2, appertaining to the *Saṅkrānti*.

संक्षय, *m.* complete consumption, destruction, loss, ruin, the destruction of the world.

संक्षिप्त, *m.* (*f.* ā) compressed, condensed, abridged.

संक्षिप्ति, *f.* a throwing together, an abridgment; a sending; an ambuscade.

संक्षेप, 1, *m.* a throwing together, condensing, an abridgment, summary, abstract, epitome, abbreviation; conciseness; brevity, compression: 2, condensed, abridged, brief.

संक्षेपक, *m.* (*f.* ikā) an abridger, etc.: lit. *adj.* reducing to a small compass, abridging, abbreviating.

संक्षेपण, *m.* = **संक्षेप**, 1, *q.v.*

संक्षेपवक्ता, *m.* (*f.* trī) a laconic speaker.

संक्षोभ, *m.* a shaking, trembling, agitation, disturbance, upsetting; pride. [less.

संख, 1, a corruption of **शंख**, *q.v.*: 2, simple, art-

संखचूड़, *more prop.* **शंखचूड़**, *q.v.*

संखाहुली, *f.* a certain medicinal plant (*Andropogon aciculatum?*).

संखिनी (*corruption*) = **शंखिनी**, *q.v.*

संखिया, *m.* a kind of poison, arsenic.

संखी, *more prop.* **सखी**, *q.v.*

संख्यता, *f.* number, numeration, counting.

संख्या, *f.* number in general; a numeral; a sum, muster; (in Gram.) number; a calculation, account; intellect; reflection, deliberation, reasoning; manner.

संख्यावाचक, (in Gram.) expressive of number.

संख्येय, proper to be numbered or calculated, numerable, calculable.

संग, 1, *m.* joining, uniting, meeting, confluence of rivers, concurrence, encountering, touch, association, union, friendship, love, intercourse, attachment, fondness, propensity, desire, cupidity, copulation: a stone; a weight: 2, with, together with, in the company of, along with. —*k.* to have dealings with, companionate with.

संगकूर्पो, *f.* a certain plant (*Volkemeria inermis*) used in medicine. [ally.

संगजाति, *m.* (*f.* inī) an associate, companion, friend,

संगत, 1, *f.* a contraction of **संगति**, *q.v.*: 2, met, encountered, associated, united, collected, mixed: appropriate, apposite.

संगतराश, *m.* a stone-cutter, sculptor.

संगति, *f.* meeting, joining, union, association, congressus, intercourse, coïtion; a collection, congregation, company, society, companionship, acquaintance, friendship; appropriateness; opportunity; chance; a frequenting; questioning for further information; a place where the Sikhs celebrate their religious ceremonies. [rade.

संगती, *m.* (*f.* inī) an associate, companion, com-

संगतौल, equal in weight.

संगदाना, *m.* the gizzard.

संगदिल, hard-hearted. [close friendship.

संगपग, 1, very great intimacy: 2, on terms of very

संगपुश्त, *m.* a tortoise, turtle.

संगम, *m.* meeting, encounter, confluence, junction, union, association, copulation, mixture, touch; company: appropriateness; (in Astron.) planetary conjunction.

संगमरमर, *m.* marble.

संगमूसा, a certain black close-grained stone.

संगर, *m.* agreement, assent, promise; a bargain; transaction of sale: misfortune, calamity: war, battle; poison: lines, entrenchment: knowledge, the fruit of the *Shami*-tree.

संगलद्वीप, *more prop.* **सिंहलद्वीप**, *q.v.*

संगवाला, *m.* (*f.* ī), 1, an associate, companion, fellow: 2, made of stone, stony.

संगसंग = **साथसाथ**, *q.v.*

संगसी, *f.* pincers, forceps, tongs.

संगा (*Rām.*) = **संग**, *q.v.*

संगाती, *m.* (*f.* inī) *more prop.* **संघाती**, *q.v.*

संगिश्रा (*dialectic*) = **संग**, *q.v.*

संगिश्रासिया, a millstone.

संगिखारा, flint.

संगजराहत, a species of steatites.

संगबसरी, *f.* (the white stone, *i.e.*) zinc.

संगी, *m.* (*f.* inī) a companion, comrade, accomplice, confederate, ally, etc.: *lit.* uniting with, connected with, attached to, fond of, studious, desirous, lustful, libidinous.

संगीत, *m.* song in chorus, a public entertainment consisting of song, music, and dancing; the art of music and dancing.

संगीतदर्पण, *m.* a book on music.

संगीतनाच, *m.* a kind of dance.

संगीदास, *m.* (*f.* ī) a fellow-servant. [bayonet.

संगीन, 1, stony; weighty; solid; thick: 2, *f.* a

संगुण, *more prop.* **सगुण**, *q.v.*

संगे, *more com.* **संग**, 2, *q.v.*

संगेसंग (emphat. of **संगसंग**) = **साथोसाथ**, *q.v.*

संगोपन, *m.* concealment, hiding.

संगोरना, *t.* to lay up (as treasure).

संग्रह, *m.* a taking, seizing; mentioning; a clenching, grasping; collection, compilation, abridgment, catalogue; effort; restraining, governing; assent, promise; protecting; propitiating, attaching; elevation, loftiness.

संग्रहकरनेहारा, *m.* (*f.* ī) = **संग्रहकर्त्ता**, *q.v.*

संग्रहकर्त्ता, *m.* (*f.* trī) a seizer, collector, compiler.

संग्रहण, *m.* a collecting, compiling; enchasing; sexual intercourse, adultery; taking, accepting; hope.

संग्रहणी, *f.* an irregular state of the bowels, costiveness alternately with diarrhœa, dysentery, diarrhœa, cramp (as in cholera).

संग्रही, *m.* (*f.* iṇī) a compiler, collector.

संग्रहीत, accepted; compiled, collected.

संग्राम, *m.* scuffle, tussle, fighting, battle, war.

संग्रामजित, *m. pr. n.* one of the sons of Kṛishṇ.

संग्रामभूमि, *f.* a region or locality of war, a battle-field. [multitude, flock.

संघ, *m.* a collection, heap, quantity, number,

संघट, a contraction of **संघट्ट**, *q.v.*

संघटन, *m.* }
संघटना, *f.* } = **संघट्ट**, 1, *q.v.*

संघट्ट, 1, *m.* rubbing together, friction, clashing together, collision, shock; embracing, meeting, encounter, intertwining of wrestlers, close contact, concurrence, conflux, union: 2, *m.* (*f.* ikā) a pimp.

संघट्टन, *m.* = **संघट्ट**, 1, *q.v.*

संघट्टिका, *f.* (*m.* **संघट्ट**, 2) a procuress, bawd.

संघर, an intrenchment.

संघर्ष, *m.* trituration, grinding, rubbing, friction; collision: rivalry, emulation, envy: a going gently, gliding.

संघर्षण = **संघर्ष**, *q.v.* [ing, rivalling.

संघर्षी, *m.* (*f.* iṇī) an emulator, rival: lit. *adj.* emulat-

संघाट्टिका, *f.* (*m.* **संघट्ट**) a procuress, bawd.

संघात, *m.* an assemblage, collection, heap, cluster, multitude; society, companionship: striking, killing: phlegm: *pr. n.* a certain division of Tartarus.

संघाती, *m.* (*f.* inī) an associate, companion, friend, ally. [form **संहार**, *q.v.*

संघार; for words beginning thus, see under the

संघिया, *m. f.* an associate, companion.

संचकार, *m.* noise, sound of footsteps.

संचना, *t.* to collect, gather, accumulate, hoard.

संचनहार, *m.* (*f.* in, ī, nī) a hoarder, gatherer.

संचय, *m.* a collection, heaping up, accumulation, quantity, heap, hoard, crowd, multitude, number, saving, store, purse, stock, capital. — *k.* (with gen.) to keep in store, hoard up, save.

संचयी, *m.* (*f.* inī) one who accumulates or hoards: lit. *adj.* gathering, collecting accumulating, saving, hoarding.

संचरना, *a. int.* to go, proceed, be in motion.

संचल, *m.* noise, sound of footsteps.

संचार, *m.* difficult progress, difficulty, distress; going, motion, course; setting in motion, inciting, leading; a gem supposed to be in the head of a serpent; entrance, penetration, commencement; the entrance of the sun or any planet into a new sign; a gate, opening, access; contagion.

संचारिका, *f.* a female messenger, go-between, bawd, procuress: a pair: smell. [accumulated, saved.

संचित, *m.* (*f.* ā) collected, gathered, heaped up,

संचिता, *f.* a certain plant (*Salvinia cucullata*).

संक्षेप; for words beginning thus, see under the

संजना, *more prop.* **सहजना**, *q.v.* [form **संक्षेप**.

संजम, a Prākṛit form of **संयम**, *q.v.*

संजय, *m. pr. n.* (1) of the charioteer of king Dhṛitrāshtra (2) of a son of Supārshwa (3) of a son of Pratikshatra (4) of a son of Ranañjay.

संजात, *m.* (*f.* ā) begotten, produced, brought forth.

संजाफ़, *f.* border (tacked to the outer part of a garment), flouncing.

संजाब, *m.* ermine, the grey squirrel.

संजीवक, 1, *m.* (*f.* ikā) *adj.* living together; animating: 2, *m. pr. n.* a certain bull in the Hitopadesh.

संजीवन, *m.* an animating, bringing to life; reanimating, life-restoring: a cluster of four houses: *pr. n.* one of the divisions of the infernal regions.

संजीवनी, *f.* 1, a contraction of **संजीविनी**, *q.v.*: 2, a kind of elixir. — *vidyā*, f. the art of vivifying.

संजीविनी, *f.* (*m.* **संजीवी**) a female revivifyer, anything that reänimates.

संजीवी, *m.* (*f.* inī) a restorer to life, reänimator: lit. *adj.* restoring to life, reänimating.

संजुग, a Prākṛit form of **संयुग**, *q.v.*

संजूषा; see **मंजूषा**.

संजोउ (*Rām.*) = **सामग्री**, *q.v.*

संजोग, a Prākṛit form of **संयोग**, *q.v.*

संजोय; see **संयोग्य**.

संजोवना, *t.* to make ready, prepare.

संज्ञ, *m.* (*f.* ā) knock-kneed.

संज्ञक, *m.* (*f.* ā) having a name, named, called.

संज्ञा, *f.* consciousness, mind, intellect, thought, knowledge: gesture, gesticulation, sign: (in Gram.) a noun subtantive, name, appellation, designation; a metaphor; an idiomatical phrase.

संज्ञावन्त, *m.* (*f.* vatī, = **संज्ञावान**, *q. v.*

संज्ञावाचक, (in Gram.) appertaining to a name or appellation, substantival. [ty: having a name.

संज्ञावान, *m.* (*f.* vatī) recovered after insensibili-

संज्ञित, named, called, termed, designated.

संज्ञु, *m. f.* knock-kneed.

संज्वर, *m.* fever, heat, burning, scorching; a burn.

संझना, horse-radish.

संड, संत, संद, संध, संप, संब, संभ; for words beginning with either of these elements but not given below, see under the corresponding forms **सण्ड, सन्त, सन्द, सन्ध, सम्प, सम्ब, सम्भ**, respectively.

संड़सी, *f.* tongs, pincers, forceps.

संतनु, 1, possessing a body, embodied: 2, *m. pr. n.* a certain ancient Hindoo king.

संनिधि, *f.* = **सन्निधान**, *q. v.*

संन्यसन, *m.* abandonment or renunciation of all worldly affections and possessions: entrusting to.

संन्यास, *m.* abandonment of all worldly possessions and affections and fixing the mind only on the Supreme Spirit, abandonment, resignation, deposit, trust; a stake (at play); sudden death; Indian spikenard.

संन्यासी, *m.* (*f.* inī) one who has abandoned all worldly possessions and affections, a Brāhman of the fourth order, the religious mendicant, an ascetic, devotee.

संमत, 1, agreed, of one mind, consentient; assented or agreed to, concurred in, acknowledged; conformable or agreeable to: 2, *m.* opinion, sentiment.

संमतसे, consentiently, unanimously.

संमति, *f.* similarity of opinion or of purpose, unanimity, agreement, approbation; regard, respect; wish, desire; real knowledge; consultation, advice.

संमय, *more prop.* **समय**, *q. v.*

संमान, *m.* respect, esteem, regard, honour, reverence, veneration, homage: measure. — *k.* to honour, treat respectfully.

संमानी, *m.* (*f.* inī) a polite or reverential person: *lit.* reverential, respectful, civil, polite.

संमान्य, *m.* (*f.* ā) respectable, venerable, honorable, estimable.

संमुख, fronting, facing, confronting, in front of, before, opposite to, in the presence of.

संमुखीन = **संमुख**, *q. v.*

संम्यक = **सम्यक**, *q. v.*

संयत, *m. f.* war, battle, conflict, strife.

संयम, *m.* a restraining; restraint, continence, forbearance, sobriety, abstinence from certain food on particular days; the avoiding the infliction of pain on others, compassionateness.

संयमनी, *f. pr. n.* the capital of Yam.

संयमी, *m.* (*f.* inī) one who controls his passions, a continent person, sage, ascetic, saint: *lit.* abstemious, continent, temperate, sober.

संयुक्त, united, joined, connected, blended, mixed; (in comp.) endowed with, possessed of.

संयुक्तक्रिया, *f.* (in Gram.) a compound verb.

संयुक्तव्यंजन, *m.* (in Gram.) a compound consonant.

संयुक्तसंज्ञा, *f.* (in Gram.) a compound subsantive.

संयुक्ति, *f.* = **संयोग**, *q. v.* [coming united.

संयुग्य, *m.* (*f.* ā) *adj.* having joined together, be-

संयुग, *m.* a union, mixing: scuffle, battle, strife, war.

संयुत; see (1) **संयत** (2) **संयुक्त** (3) **संयुक्ति**.

संयोग, *m.* connexion, junction, cohesion, contact, adherence, union, association, conjunction, agreement, compounding; a coincidence, event, occurrence, accident, chance opportunity, hap, luck; a kind of alliance in which both parties unite only for one object, but attack with united power; (in the Sānkhya Philos.) simple conjunction as distinguished from constant aggregation.

संयोगन, *m.* a joining, connecting, uniting.

संयोगसे, by chance, by coincidence, accidentally.

संयोगी, *m.* (*f.* inī) an ascetic who does not observe his vow of continence, but has a family: lit. *adj.* connecting, joining, uniting, adjoining.

संयोग्य; see (1) **संयुग्य** (2) **संयोग** (3) **संयोज्य**.

संयोजक, *m.* (in Gram.) any word denoting connexion, a conjunction: *lit.* conjunctive; containing.

संयोज्य, *m.* (*f.* ā) *adj.* having joined together or united; having enjoined or directed.

संरक्षण, *m.* a protecting, guarding, saving.

संरक्षणार्थ, with the view of protecting or of saving.

संरक्षित, *m.* (*f.* ā) protected, guarded, saved.

संरम्भ, *m.* a beginning: anger, rage, wrath: pride, arrogance: agitation.

संरम्भी, angry; proud; agitated: hence, *m.* (*f.* inī) an arrogant or a wrathful person.

संराधन, *m.* propitiation: perfect meditation.

संराव, *m.* sound, noise, clamour, tumult.

संरोध, *m.* a hindering, stopping; an impediment, check, curb, fetter. [mixed, adherent; appropriate.

संलग्न, *m.* (*f.* ā) united with, joined, associated,

संलय, *m.* sleep.

संलाप, *m.* conversation.

संवत, *m.* a year; an era; a year of the era of Vikramāditya. The term is generally used by Hindoos in giving chronological dates. — *bāndhnā*, to establish an era, to distinguish oneself by illustrious actions.

संवत्सर, *m.* a year.

संवत्सरी, *f.* any annual ceremony.

संवर, *m.* self-command, restraint of the organs.

संवरना, *n.* to be dressed, be decorated, be prepared: *a. int.* to suit; to prosper; to improve.

संवराना = **संवारना**, *q. v.*

संवल, *more prop.* **सम्बल**, *q. v.*

संवाद, *m.* conversation; intelligence, information, news, report; communication of intelligence; assent, agreement, conformity, correspondence, sameness.

संवारना, *t.* to prepare, dress, decorate, adorn, deck, arrange, adjust, methodize, improve, ameliorate, mend.

संबुक (*Rām.*) = **शम्बूक**, *q. v.*

संशय, *m.* doubt, uncertainty, suspicion, dread, apprehension, fear, anxiety. [apprehension.

संशयछेत्ता, *m.* (*f.* trī) one who removes doubt or

संशयात्मा, *m. f.* a doubter, sceptic: *lit.* doubtful, uncertain, dubious, hesitating, apprehensive, sceptical, mistrustful, diffident.

संशयान / **संशयापन्न** / **संशयालु** } = **संशयात्मा**, *q. v.*

संशयावस्था, *f.* a state or condition of uncertainty or of apprehension.

संशयिता, *m.* (*f.* trī) / **संशयित्**, *m.* (*f.* trī) / **संशयी**, *m.* (*f.* inī) } = **संशयात्मा**, *q.v.*

संश्रय, *m.* a refuge, dwellingplace, asylum, protection, alliance. [mixture.

संश्रव, *m.* hearing; agreement, promise, assent;

संसगर, fertile, productive, fruitful.

संसना; see (1) **सनसनाना** (2) **सांसना**.

संसनाना, *a. int.* to jingle, ring; to faint; to simmer.

संसनाहट, *f.* an imitative sound; a ringing, jingling; a hissing, simmering; a fainting.

संसय (*corruption*) = **संशय**, *q. v.*

संसर्ग, *m.* union, junction, contiguousness, proximity, contact, approximation; acquaintance, familiarity, consorting with, intercourse, association, sensual attachment, coïtion.

संसर्गी, *m.* (*f.* iṇī) an associate, acquaintance, companion; *lit.* in contact with, connected, united, keeping company, acquainted, familiar.

संसा, *m.* = **संशय**, *q. v.*

संसाना; see (1) **सांसना** (2) **संसनाना**.

संसार, *m.* transmigration; mundane existence; the habitation of mortals, the world; domestic life, mundane concerns.

संसाररूपी, mundane, worldly, secular.

संसारा, *more prop.* **संसार**, *q.v.*

संसारिक (*contraction*) = **सांसारिक**, *q. v.*

संसारी, *m.* (*f.* iṇī) an animal or sentient being, a man: *lit.* secular, mundane, worldly, temporal, mixing up with mundane affairs. [tion; the world.

संसृति, *f.* course; a current, stream; transmigra-

संसे (*colloquial*) = **संशय**, *q. v.*

संसौ in Braj = **संशय**, *q. v.*

संस्कार, *m.* a completing, accomplishing, finishing, perfecting, perfection; embellishment, decoration, ornament; a purificatory rite; initiation, consecration; the marriage ceremony; institution; education; purification, ceremony; investiture with the sacred thread; obsequies; purity; conception; apprehension; impression, form, mould; the power of memory; the self-productive quality; a faculty, habit, instinct, passion; an idea, notion.

संस्कृत, finished, perfected, accomplished, wrought, artificially produced; decorated, ornamented; cleansed, purified; excellent, best; initiated, consecrated: hence, *m.* language formed according to perfect grammatical rules; *pr. n.* the sacred and classical language of the Hindoos.

संस्कृतानुयायी, *m.* (*f.* inī) in accordance with (or having relation to) the Sanskrit language, after the manner of the Sanskrit language, Sanskritized.

संस्थान, *m.* a heap, quantity, crowd; the aggregation of the primitive atoms; position, form, figure, shape; fabrication, construction; a neighbourhood, common place of abode, vicinity; a place where four roads meet; a place, station; a mark, spot, sign; death.

संस्पर्श, *m.* contact, touch, mixture, union; a being touched, being affected; a laying hold of; perception, sense: *adj.* contiguous; contagious.

संहत, united, aggregated, heaped up, collected, assembled; compact, closely joined, strongly knit: struck, wounded, killed.

संहतता, *f.* (*m.* °त्व) close approximation, contact, combination, union, agreement, compactness.

संहति, *f.* combination, union, junction; agreement; compactness: a collection, assemblage, heap, multitude; bulk.

संहात, *m. pr. n.* one of the divisions of hell.

संहार, 1, *m.* collection; comprehensive description; abridgement, abbreviation; restraining; practice, skill; murdering, killing, slaughter, carnage; destruction, ruin: *pr. n.* (1) of one of the divisions of the infernal regions (2) of the destruction of the world at the end of a *kalp*: 2, killed.

संहारक, *m.* (*f.* ikā) a destroyer, etc.: *lit.* destructive, ruinous: abridging, abbreviating.

संहारण, *m.* killing, murdering: *pr. n.* a certain demon slain by Krishṇ.

संहारना, *t.* to make away with, kill, destroy.

संहारिका, *f.* (*m.* **संहारक**) / **संहारिणी**, *f.* (*m.* **संहारी**) } a female destroyer.

संहारित, *m.* (*f.* ā) killed, slain, murdered.

संहारी, *m.* (*f.* iṇī) = **संहारक**, *q. v.*

संहिता, *f.* a collection, compilation; the complete collection of hymns and invocations belonging to one Ved, an arrangement of the texts of the Veds into short sentences; a compendium: (in Gram.) the coalescence of the final and the initial letter of consecutive words.

संहिदानी, *f.* a mark, sign, token. [ing.

संहूति, *f.* tumultuous exclamation, clamour, shout-

सक, 1, *more prop.* (1) **शक** (2) **शक्क**, *qq.v.*: 2, *f.* (?) strength, power, ability, capacity, authority.

सकट, 1, (*colloquial*) = (1) **शकट** (2) **संकट**, *qq. v.*: 2, *m.* a certain small tree (*Trophis aspera*): 3, bad, vile.

सकण्टक, 1, thorny, prickly; troublesome, perilous: 2, *m.* a certain aquatic plant (*Vallisneria*).

सकत (*colloquial*) = (1) **शक्त** (2) **शक्ति**, *qq. v.*

सकता, *m.* a trance; apoplexy; a pause, vacancy.

सकना, *n.* to be able. [ened, strait.

सकरा, *m.* (*f.* ī) not roomy, small, narrow, strait-

सकराई, *f.* want of room, smallness, straitened-

सकरात, *f.* agony; fainting. [ness, narrowness.

सकराना, *t.* to deprive of necessary room, to straiten: to cause anyone to accept (as a bill, etc.).

सकरान्त, *more prop.* (1) **सकरात** (2) **संक्रान्त**, *qq.v.*

सकरुण, *m.* (*f.* ā) commiserating, compassionate.

सकर्मक, (in Gram.) transitive, active.

सकल, all, the whole, entire, every. —— *urbāsī*, an epithet of Vishṇu (*lit.* dwelling in all hearts).

सका, might, power, main. [feel tired.
सकाना, *n.* to be grieved or sorrowful; to be weary,
सकाम, *m.* (*f.* ā) one who has attained his desire, etc.: *lit.* content, satisfied, happy: lascivious, sensual, in love: occupied: done with a desire of future reward or fruition.
सकार, 1, *more prop.* **सकाल**, *q.v.*: 2, *m.* the letter **स**, or any character that may represent it. [a cause.
सकारण, *adj.* having some cause, originating from
सकारना, *t.* to accept (as a bill, etc.); to approve of (or agree to) an arrangement.
सकारी, *more prop.* **सकाली**, *q. v.*
सकारे, in the early morning, at dawn.
सकाल, 1, *m.* early dawn, the morning: 2, betimes, early in the morning, at dawn: to-morrow.
सक़ालत, *f.* weight, heaviness.
सकालना = **सकारना**, *q. v.*
सकाली, *f.* early dawn, the morning. [purse.
सकिलना, *t.* to gather, collect, accumulate, convene,
सकिलि, old part. = **सकिलके** (**सकिलना**).
सक़ील, heavy; indigestible; lazy; phlegmatic.
सकुंतला (*corruption*) = **शकुन्तला**, *q. v.*
सकुच, *f.* shrinking, awe, fear, shame.
सकुचना, *n.* to be afraid, be apprehensive, be in awe, be abashed.
सकुचाई, *f.* apprehensiveness, bashfulness.
सकुचाना, 1, = **सकुचना**, *q. v.*: 2, *t.* to intimidate, overawe, abash.
सकुचानी, ; see (1) **सकुचाना** (2) **सकुचाया** (3) **सकुचाई**.
सकुचाया, *m.* (*f.* **सकुचाई**) apprehensive, intimidated, awe-stricken, abashed.
सकुन, *more prop.* **शकुन**, *q. v.*
सकुनि, *more prop.* **शकुनि**, *q. v.*
सकुनिअन्ह, 1, a Braj pl. of **शकुनि** (see **अन्ह**): 2, a Braj inflective base of the pl. of **शकुनी**, 2, *q. v.*
सकुनी, *more prop.* (1) **शकुनी** (2) **शकुनि**, *qq. v.*
सकुल, *m.* (*f.* ā) 1, = **सगोत्र**, *q. v.*: 2, a family person: lit. *adj.* having a family.
सकुल्य, *m.* (*f.* ā) = **सगोत्र**, *q. v.*
सकृत, once; always, ever: with, together with.
सकेत, 1, narrow, strait: 2, *f.* distress, want, straits, straitened circumstances, difficulty, fix.
सकेतना, *t.* to tighten, narrow, straiten.
सकेता, 1, *m.* = **सकेत**, 2, *q. v.*: *m.* (*f.* ī) straitened, tightened, narrow, strait.
सकेतो, *more com.* **सकेत**, 2, *q. v.*
सकेलना, *a. int.* to shrink, shrivel, gather up (as the limbs of a tortoise).
सकेला, *m.* a kind of iron.
सकेलि, old part. = **सकेलके** (**सकेलना**). See **इ**, 7.
सके; see **सकना**.
सकोच, *m.* regard, respect, esteem. See **संकोच**.
सकोचु; see **सकोच** and **संकोच**.
सकोड़ना, *a. int.* to shrink, shrivel, draw up, gather up, contract, tighten: *t.* to draw up, contract, tighten.
सकोप, *m.* (*f.* ā) enraged, angry, displeased.
सकोरा, *m.* a small earthen vessel.
सकोरी, *f.* a saucer.
सकोध = **सक्रोध**, *q. v.* See **स**.
सक्कर, *more prop.* **शुक्कर**, *q. v.*
सक्करी, *f.* (in Pros.) a species of metre.
सक्ति, 1, (*colloquial*) = **शक्ति**, *q. v.*: 2, *f.* contact; junction: attachment, addiction to.
सक्तिन, a Braj pl. of **सक्ती**, 2. See **न**, 6 (1).
सक्ती, 1, (*colloquial*) = **शक्ति**, *q. v.*: 2, *f.* a female, a woman: spear, javelin, dart.
सक्तुक, *m.* a species of poison.
सक्तुफला, *f.* the *sami*-tree (*Mimosa suma*).
सक्थि, *m.* the thigh; a bone; the frame of a cart.
सक्यो in Braj = **सका** (**सकना**).
सक्र (*colloquial*) = **शक्र**, *q. v.*
सक्रान्त = (1) **संक्रान्त** (2) **संक्रान्ति**, *q. v.*
सक्रान्ति, *more prop.* **संक्रान्ति**, *q. v.*
सक्रोध, *m.* (*f.* ā) angry, wrathful, enraged.
सख, 1, *m.* (*f.* ī) a friend, a dear friend: 2, *m.* a certain tree (*Mimosa catechu*).
सख़्त, hard, obdurate, stiff, rigid; difficult; strong; stingy; austere, severe, cruel, violent, troublesome, painful: *adv.* very, exceedingly, violently.
सख़्तता; see **सख़्त**.
सख़्ती, *f.* hardness; obstinacy; stinginess; indigence, distress.—*ko pinā*, to endure, bear patiently.
सखन, a Braj pl. of **सख**, 1. See **न**, 6 (1).
सखर, *m. pr. n.* a certain Rākshas (*lit.* possessed of
सखरस, *m.* butter. [a donkey or mule).
सख़रा, *m.* a rock: *pr. n.* a certain demon.
सखश, a corruption of **शख़्स**, *q. v.*
सखसावन, *m.* a palkee, easy chair, couch. [friend.
सखा, (not infl.) *m.* (*f.* ī) an associate, companion,
सखालोग, *m.* companions, associates, chums.
सख़ावत, *f.* generosity, liberality.
सखावृन्द, *m.* (a pl. of **सखा**) a host of companions.
सखि, 1, *m.* (*f.* **सखी**) = **सखा**, *q. v.*: 2, *more prop.* [**सखी**, *q. v.*
सखिअन, a Braj pl. of **सखी**, *q. v.*
सखित्व, *m.* (*f.* tā) friendship, intimacy.
सखिन, a Braj pl. of **सखी**, *q. v.*
सखियन, a Braj pl. of **सखी**, *q. v.*
सखिया, *more com.* **सखी**, *q. v.*
सखियां, *f.* (pl. of **सखी**) handmaids, cronies.
सखी, *f.* (*m.* **सखि**) a female friend or companion, a woman's female friend, a confidante, a handmaid.
सखीजन, *f.* a female friend or confidante.
सखुन, *m.* speech, language; a thing, business, affair.
सख्य, *m.* friendship, intimacy; equality.
सख्युक्त, *m.* (*f.* ā) the aforesaid friend, the friend referred to.

सग, *m.* a dog.

सगउती, *more com.* **सगोती**, *q.v.*

सगख़ाना, *m.* a dog's house, kennel. *Sagkhānemen sonā*, to kennel.

सगट, alike, similar, the same.

सगड़, *m.* a cart.

सगड़ी, *f.* (dim. of **सगड़**) a small cart.

सगण, *m.* (in Pros.) an anapæst. See **स**, 10.

सगतराश (*corruption*) = **संगतराश**, *q. v.*

सगन्ध, smelling, fragrant, odoriferous.

सगपहता, *m.* greens dressed with pulse.

सगभत्ता, *m.* a hash of vegetables.

सगमत्व, (*f.* tā) accessibility.

सगर, 1, poisonous : 2, *m. pr. n.* a certain ancient sovereign of Oude (*Ayodhyā*) whose great-grandson brought the Ganges from heaven to earth.

सगरा, *m.* (*f.* ī) all, the whole, every.

सगरी ; see (1) **सगरा** (2) **सगड़ी**.

सगरे, *m.* (pl. of **सगरा**) all.

सगर्भ, 1, pregnant : 2, *m.* (*f.* ā) a brother (or sister) of whole blood, *i. e.* by the same father and mother.

सगर्भ्य, *m.* (*f.* ā) = **सगर्भ**, 2, *q. v.*

सगर्व्व, proud, haughty, elated.

सगल ; see (1) **शक्ल** (2) **युगल** (3) **सकल**.

सगलगी, *f.* fawning, servility, flattery.

सगला, a dialectic form of **सकल**, *q. v.*

सगलानि (*colloquial*) = **सग्लानि**, *q. v.*

सगा, 1, *m.* (*f.* ī) born of the same parents, related, full, own : hence, 2, *m.* kin : 3, *m.* (*f.* ī) a relative, a kin. — *bhāī*, own brother.

सगाई, *f.* relationship by the same parents, consanguinity, family relation, kin ; betrothing for marriage; the second marriage of a woman of low tribe. — *k.* to contract a marriage; to affiance, betroth.

सगावत, *f.* = **सगाई**, *q. v.*

सगासोदा, kith and kin, relations.

सगी, *f.* (*m.* **सगा**) a female relative. — *bahin*, own sister.

सगुण, *m.* (*f.* ā) endowed with qualities or properties, possessing good qualities.

सगुणरूप, *m.* (*f.* ā) *adj.* possessed of a form that has qualities.

सगुणी, *m.* (*f.* inī) = **सगुण**, *q.v.*

सगुन = (1) **सगुण** (2) **शकुन**, *qq. v.*

सगोती, *f.* animal food, meat, flesh.

सगोत्र, 1, *m.* (*f.* ā *or* ī) one of the same family name and of common origin, a kinsman, distant kinsman, remote relation : *lit.* of one and the same family, of kin, related : 2, *m.* a family, race.

सगोत्ती, *f.* animal food, meat, flesh.

सग्गड़, *m.* a cart.

सग्गड़ी, *f.* (dim. of **सग्गड़**) a small cart.

सग्गा, *m.* (*f.* ī) *more com.* **सगा**, *q.v.*

सग्लानि, languidly, weakly : irreverently, reproachfully, slanderously, censoriously.

सघन, *m.* (*f.* ā) impervious, impassable, dense, crowded, thick (as fruit, clouds, hair, a forest, etc.).

सङ्क, **सङ्ग**, **सङ्ख**, **सङ्ग**, **सङ्घ**; for words beginning with either of these elements, see under the corresponding forms **संक**, **संच**, **संख**, **संग**, **संघ**, respectively.

सच = **सच्च**, *q. v.*

सचमुच, *adj.* or *adv.* true, truly, in truth, indeed, verily, indeed and in truth, really, in fact, verily verily.

सचराचर, all (whether animate or inanimate).

सचल, connected with moving things, having the ability to move, moving, locomotive.

सचसच, (emphatic redupl. of **सच**), verily verily.

सचा, *m.* (*f.* ī) = **सच्चा**, *q. v.*

सचाई, *f.* = **सच्चाई**, *q. v.*

सचान, *m.* a falcon, hawk (*Falco*).

सचापन, *m.*, **सचावट**, *f.*, **सचाहट**, *f.* } = **सच्चाई**, *q. v.*

सचि, 1, *f. more prop.* **शचि**, *q. v.* : 2, *m.* connexion, intimacy, friendship.

सचिच, *more com* **सचमुच**, *q.v.*

सचिदानन्द, *more prop.* **सच्चिदानन्द**, *q. v.*

सचिन्त, *m.* (*f.* ā) thoughtful, attentive, considerate.

सचिव, *m.* a friend, associate, companion : the minister or counsellor of a king.

सची, *f.* 1, *more prop.* **शची**, *q.v.* : 2, (*m.* **सचा**) = **सच्ची**, *q.v.*

सचोच, *more com.* **सचमुच**, *q. v.*

सचीरची, a play on the word **सची** (= **शचि**).

सचु, *m.* joy, pleasure, happiness.

सचेत, *m.* (*f.* ā) = **सचेतन**, *q.v.* — *honā*, to mind. — *rahnā*, to have a care, be on one's guard, be circumspect.

सचेतन, *m.* (*f.* ā) a rational creature, etc.: *lit.* recovering one's senses, animate, rational, sensible, feeling, intelligent, thinking, conscious, considerate, cautious, circumspect, watchful, on one's guard, attentive, alert, aware.

सचेता, 1, *m. f.* = **सचेतन**, *q. v.* : 2, *f.* (*m.* **सचेत**) a rational female.

सचेष्ट, 1, *m.* the mango (*Mangofera Indica*): 2, *m.* (*f.* ā) a zealous or active person : *lit.* making effort or exertion, energetic, active, zealous.

सचौटी, *f.* the habit of speaking the truth, sincerity, rectitude, good faith, honesty, fidelity, heartiness, impartiality.

सच्च, 1, = **सच्चा**, *q. v.* : 2, *m.* = **सच्चाई**, *q. v.* : 3, *adv.* indeed ; in earnest, actually, truly, verily.

सच्चा, *m.* (*f.* ī) true, genuine, real, honest, heartfelt, hearty, just, sincere, faithful, sure : *hence*, a truth-teller, etc.

सच्चाई, *f.* truth, sincerity, truthfulness, veracity, honesty, probity, authenticity, reality, fidelity, heartiness, impartiality.

सच्चिदानन्द, *m.* [**सत** (= **सन्त** ; from **अस**, to be) + **चित** + **आनन्द**] an epithet of the Supreme Spirit or of Brahm : *lit.* He who is the source of existence, intelligence, and happiness.

सच्ची, *f.* (*m.* **सच्चा**) a real or genuine person or thing (of the feminine gender).

सच्छन्द, *more prop.* **स्वच्छन्द**, *q. v.*

सज, *m. f.* ? shape, appearance, mien, manner ;

preparation ; ornament. — *sajānā*, to put into a state of preparation, to set out, adorn. [cautious, careful.

सजग, watchful, wideawake, vigilant, circumspect,

सजत = **सजता** (**सजना**).

सजदार, well-shaped, handsome.

सजधज, *f.* preparation and appearance.

सजन, *m.* (*f.* ā *or* ī) = **सज्जन**, *q.v.*

सजना, 1, *more prop.* **सज्जन**, *q.v.*: 2, *f* = **सज्जनी**, *q.v.*: 3, *n.* to be made ready or prepared : *a. int.* to fit, befit, become, beseem : to mend, improve : *t.* to adjust, rectify, dress, accoutre, ornament, adorn.

सजनी, *more prop.* **सज्जनी**, *q.v.*

सजल, containing water, filled with or abounding in water, wet, watery, moist.

सजला, *m.* the third brother of four or more.

सजव (*Rām.*) = **मैं सजूंगा** (**सजना**).

सजवाना, *t.* (causat. of **सजना**, *n.*) to cause a thing to be prepared, to get prepared, have rectified.

सजस, a Prākṛit form of **सुयश**, *q.v.*

सजसजाना; see *s.v.* **सज**.

सज़ा, *f.* one's deserts, retribution, correction, punishment.—*k.* or *denā*, to give one his deserts, to adjudge guilty and deserving of punishment, to condemn, to punishment, to award punishment, to punish, castigate. [making belts or scabbards.

सजाई, *f.* 1, = **सजावट**, *q.v.*: 2, the price paid for

सजात (*contraction*) = **सजाति**, *q.v.*

सजाति, *m. f.* a compeer, fellow-clansman, etc.: *lit.* of the same sort, species, kind, class, or tribe.

सजाती, *m.* (*f.* inī) } *more com.* **सजाति**, *q.v.*
सजातीय, *m.* (*f.* ā) }

सजाना, 1, *t.* (causat. of **सजना**, *t.*) to cause a person to prepare a thing : to methodize : to mend: 2, *m.* (*f.* ī) wise.

सजाव, *m.* = **सजावट**, *q.v.* [contrivance.

सजावट, *f.* preparation, ornament, arrangement,

सज़ावल, *m.* a tax-gatherer, land-steward, officer employed at a monthly salary to collect the revenues of a district the zamindār of which has fallen in arrear.

सज़ावार, liable to, worthy, excellent, able, applic-

सजिव (*Rām.*) = **सजीव**, *q.v.* [able, meritorious.

सजीया, *m.* nature, temper, disposition.

सजीला, *m.* (*f.* ī) well-shaped, graceful, handsome.

सजीव, *m.* (*f.* ā) any animate creature : *lit.* possessing (or endowed with) life, living, alive.

सजीवन = **संजीवन**, *q.v.*

सजीवनि; see (1) **संजीवनी** (2) in Braj, a pl. (or an agent. case) of **सजीव**. See **नि**, 2 (2) and 2 (5).

सजेरे, a corruption of **सवेरे**, *q.v.*

सँजोवन; see (1) **सजीवन** (2) **सयौवन**. [ing.

सजौटी, *f.* an adorning or "fixing" oneself, dress-

सज्ज, *m.* (*f.* ā) an armed person, etc.: *lit.* armed, fortified, accoutred; prepared, got ready ; covered, clothed, ornamented.

सज्जन, 1, *m.* (*f.* ā *or* ī) a respectable or virtuous person, a sweetheart, lover, etc.: *lit.* of good family, well-born, well bred, reputable, virtuous, good, benevolent, respectable: 2, *m.* fastening, arming, dressing, preparing ; 3, *m.* a guard, sentry, piquet : a ferry.

सज्जना, *f.* 1, = **सज्जनी**, *q.v.*: 2, = **सज्जन**, 2, *q.v.*: 3, ornamenting or caparisoning an elephant.

सज्जनी, *f.* (*m.* **सज्जन**) a respectable or a virtuous female, a mistress, sweetheart.

सज्जा, *f.* 1, (*m.* **सज्ज**) an armed female, etc.; 2, armour, mail; harness : equipage, apparatus, furniture, decoration, dress.

सज्जाति, *more com.* **सजाति**, *q.v.*

सज्जादा, *m.* a carpet or mat on which Muhammadans kneel at prayer ; an altar ; a mosque.

सज्जी, a contraction of **सर्जिका**, *q.v.*

सज्जीखून, *m.* } = **सर्जिका**, *q.v.*
सज्जीमती, *f.* }

सज्या; see (1) **संज्ञा** (2) **सज्जोया** (3) **सय्या**.

सज्वाना = **सजवाना**, *q.v.*

सज्ञात, 1, *more prop.* **स्वज्ञाति**, *q.v.*: 2, *m.* (*f.* ā) known, apprehended, perceived.

सज्ञान, *m.* (*f.* ā) = **सज्ञानी**, *q.v.*

सज्ञानता, *f.* intelligence, sagacity, wisdom.

सज्ञाना, *f.* (*m.* **सज्ञान**) a sagacious female.

सज्ञानी, *m.* (*f.* inī) an intelligent person, etc.: *lit.* possessed of knowledge, knowing, intelligent, wise, sagacious.

सझना, *more prop.* **सुझना**, *q.v.* [form **सँच**.

सञ्च, for all words beginning thus, see under the

सट, *m.* the clotted and matted hair of an ascetic. —*denā*, to cast, to knock out, to throw away, to deem a thing of no value, to deem worthless.

सटक, *f.* an elastic rod thick at one end and thin at the other.

सटकना, *a. int.* to run away, flee, sheer off, make oneself scarce, decamp, disappear, hide.

सटका, manageable.

सटकाई, *f.* the vanishing of a tapering body at its extreme point, taperingness, disappearance : lowering and raising. [baulk.

सटकाना, *t.* to cause to disappear, to disappoint,

सटकाला, a lock of hair.

सटदेना, *t.*: see *s.v.* **सट**, *q.v.*

सटना, *a. int.* to join, unite, knit (as bones), adhere, stick, inhere, permeate, to lay (said of arms).

सटपटाना, *n.* to be surprized, be confounded.

सटल } *f.* = **ज़टल**, *q.v.*
सटली }

सटा, *f.* an ascetic's clotted hair ; a braid of hair; a crest ; a mane ; bristles (of a boar).

सटाना, *t.* to cause to adhere, to join on, unite, paste, stick, graft, engraft. [ing, uniting.

सटासट, *f.* sticking or sticking together, adher-

सटिया, *f.* a stick.

सटी, *f.* zedoary (*Curcuma zerumbet* or *C. amhuldi* or *C. amada*). [commentary annexed.

सटीक, accompanied by a commentary, having a

सटोसटी, stuck together, glued, joined, crowded.
सट्टा, *m.* a hank: a market.
सट्टाबट्टा, *m.* an amour, combination, league, cabal, plot, intrigue, collusion.
सट्टी, *f.* a horse-market.
सठ, *more prop.* शठ, *q. v.*
सठियाना, *n.* to be turned of sixty years, to be decrepit, be in one's dotage; to be superannuated.
सठोड़ा, *m.* a kind of sweetmeat. It consists of meal, sugar, spices, etc., and is more particularly given to lying-in women, and distributed (as candle is) to gossips.
सड़क, *f.* the high-road, highway, main road, a road, path: *exclam.* away! be off! hence! make yourself scarce!
सड़कना, *more com.* सटकना, *q.v.*
सड़कं फांसी / सड़कवासी } *f.* a running knot, noose, loop, knittle.
सड़को, *exclam.* away! be off! hence! make yourself scarce!
सड़न, *f.* rottenness, putrefaction, rot; (in Surgery) a gangrene.
सड़ना, *a. int.* to decay, rot; to ferment.
सड़नेहार, *adj.* decaying, rotting, fermenting.
सड़सठ = सतसठ, *q. v.*
सड़सिन्ध; see सर्नस.
सड़ा, *m* (*f.* ī) putrid, rotten, decayed, musty, tainted, stinking.
सड़ांद (*contraction*) = सड़ाहिन्द, *q.v.*
सड़ाना, *t.* to cause to rot; to cause to ferment; to stink.
सड़ाहट, *f.* rottenness, mustiness.
सड़ाहिन्द, *f.* a disagreeable smell, the smell of putrid meat, fumette.
सड़ियल, *m.* (*f.* ā) rotten, putrid, stinking.
सथ, *more prop.* शथ, *q.v.*
सथसूत्र, *more prop.* शथसूत्र, *q.v.*
सथाई, *f.* (in the hill dialect =) the inflated buffalo-hide which the natives use as a boat.
सणि in the Garhwālī and Kumāonī dialects of Hindee = को, the case-sign of the dat. and accusative.
सपठ (= शठ) depraved, roguish; miserly.
सपठना, *a. int.* to league, combine.
सपड़, *more prop.* शपड़, *q.v.*
सपड़सन, *m. pr. n.* a certain division of the infernal regions.
सपड़सी, *f.* tongs, pincers, forceps.
सपड़ा, 1, *m.* hardened excrement, scybala: 2, *m.* (*f.* ī) strong, fat, stout: 3, *m. pr. n.* a son of Shukrāchārya.
सपड़ास, *m.* a water-closet opening into the street, a necessary, sewer, sink.
सपड़ासा, *m.* large pincers.
सपड़ासी, 1, *f.* (dim. of सपड़ासा) small pincers, forceps, tongs: 2, *m.* a corruption of संन्यासी, *q.v.*
सत, 1, *more prop.* शत, *q.v.*: 2, (*contraction*) = सत्य, *q.v.*: 3, true, right, actual: 4, actually, truly: 5, being, existing, existent: 6, *m.* (*f.* ī) good, virtuous, excellent, best, venerable, respectable: 7, *m.* power, strength, excellence: the principle of goodness: the true God, the ever-present and all-pervading Spirit: touch: sap, juice: 8, everlasting: 9, in compos. a contraction of सप्त and of सात, seven: 10, in Mārwārī = षट, *q. v.*
सतं in Chand = सातवां, *q.v.*
सतकर्म्म, *more com.* सत्कर्म्म, *q.v.*
सतकामो; see (1) सत्कर्म्म (2) सत्कर्म्मी.
सतकारी, *more com.* सत्कारी, *q.v.*
सतकोटि, a hundred crores (*i. e.* a thousand millions).
सतकृत, *m.* (*f.* ā) treated with respect or kindness, revered, adored, welcomed, saluted, worshipped.
सतकोना, *m.* (*f.* ī) heptagonal: *hence*, a heptagon.
सतखना = सतखन, *q.v.*
सतखन, of seven divisions or storeys (said of a building).
सतगुरु, *m.* a chief or excellent गुरु, *q.v.*
सतत, 1, *more prop.* सत्य, *q. v.*: 2, continual, perpetual, eternal.
सतधन्वा, *more prop.* शतधन्वा, *q.v.*
सतनजा, a hodge-podge, medley.
सतपंच (*Rām.*) = सात पांच.
सतबादी, *m.* (*f.* inī) colloquial = सत्यवादी, *q.v.*
सतबाहु, *m. pr. n.* a certain demon.
सतभामा, *more prop.* सत्यभामा, *q. v.*
सतभाव = सद्भाव, *q. v.*
सतभिषा, *more prop.* शतभिषा, *q. v.*
सतमत, *m.* the true or right way in morals or in religion.
सतमासा, *m.* a certain feast given in the seventh month of pregnancy.
सतमी, *f.* the seventh lunar day.
सतयुग (*colloquial*) = सत्ययुग, *q. v.*
सतर; see (1) शत्रु (2) सत्तर (3) सत्र (4) सत्रह.
सतरह = सत्रह, *q. v.*
सतराना, *n.* to be displeased, be vexed, be angry.
सतरूपा, *f. pr. n.* the wife of Swayambhu-Manu.
सतलड़ा, *m.* (*f.* ī) sevenfold, of seven strings or rows (as a chain of pearls, etc.).
सतलड़ी, *f.* a necklace of seven strings.
सतलोक, *more prop.* सत्यलोक, *q. v.*
सतवन्ता, *m.* (*f.* ī) good, virtuous, chaste, honest, adhering to truth; renowned.
सतवरता, *more com.* सत्वरता, *q.v.*
सतवांसा / सतवासा } = सत्वांसा, *q. v.*
सतसई, *f. pr. n.* = सतसैया, *q. v.*
सतसंग, *more com.* सत्संग, *q. v.*
सतसंगति, *more com.* सत्संगति, *q. v.*
सतसठ, sixty-seven (६७): see भों, वां, वीं, वे, वें.
सतसैया, *f. pr. n.* (lit. 700) a certain poetical work written in the Braj dialect by Bihārī lāl, an inhabitant of Goāliyār, containing 700 dohās of exquisite beauty and finish. 'Braj-bhākhā barnī kabin bahū bidh buddhi bilās, sabkau bhūkhan Satsaiyā karī Bihārī Dās,' the poets, each according to his capacity, have displayed the beauties of the Braj dialect, but Bihārī Dās composed the Satsaiyā, which is the jewel of the whole.
सतहत्तर, seventy-seven (७७): see भों, वां, वीं, वे, वें.

सता, *f.* a cotemporary wife, rival wife.

सताइस }
सताईस } *more prop.* **सत्ताईस**, *q.v.*

सताऊ, *m. f.* a vexer, teazer, tormentor.

सतां, a pl. of **सता**, *q.v.*

सतानन्द, *m. pr. n.* king Janak's family-priest.

सतानवे, *more prop.* **सत्तान्वे**, *q.v.*

सताना, *t.* to teaze, annoy, vex, fret, irk, trouble, afflict. grieve, interrupt, harass, ail, harm, inflict injury upon. [formed by Hindoo widows)

सतारोहण, *m.* the ascent of the funeral pile (per-

सतावन, *more prop.* **सत्तावन**, *q.v.*

सतावना (*colloquial*) = **सताना**, *q.v.*

सतासी, *more prop.* **सत्तासी**, *q.v.*

सति, 1, in *Rām.* = **सोधा**, *q.v.*: 2, *f.* end, destruction: [a gift, giving.

सतिकपट = **सतीकपट**, *q.v.*

सतिभाए (*Rām.*) = **सद्भाव**, *q.v.*

सतिभामा, *more prop.* **सत्यभामा**, *q.v.*

सतिहि, (pl. °**हिं**) an old acc. of **सती**, *q.v.*

सती, *f.* 1, (*m.* **सत**, 6) virtuous, constant, chaste: *hence*, 2. a chaste wife, *esp.* a widow who burns herself with her husband's corpse: 3, the ceremony of a widow burning herself on her husband's funeral pile: 4, an epithet of Pārvatī.

सतीकपट, *f. m.*? the dissimulation of Pārvatī when she went to Rām-Chandra pretending that she was Sītā.

सतीत्व, *m.* (*f.* tā) virtuousness in a wife, female chastity, purity and fidelity as evinced by the widow ascending the pile with her husband's corpse.

सतीर्थ, *m.* (*f* ā) = **सतीर्थ्य**, *q.v.*

सतीर्थ्य, *m.* (*f.* ā) a fellow-student, a pupil of the same spiritual preceptor: *adj.* possessing sacred bathing-places.

सतोल, *m.* 1, = **सतोला**, 2, *q.v*: 2, air, wind: bamboo.

सतोला, 1, *m.* (*f.* ī) powerful, strong: 2, *f.* peas, pulse in general, or of a particular kind.

सतीवाड़, *f.* a burning-ground, place where a widow (*sati*) has been burnt; a tomb, grave.

सतीवार = **सतीवाड़**, *q.v.*

सतुन, *more prop.* **सतून**, *q.v.*

सतुया }
सतुवा } = **सतूआ**, *q.v.*

सतूआ, 1, *m.* = **सत्तू**, *q.v.*: 2, pulverable, free from threads or fibres (applied to a kind of ginger).—*baitrā*, green ginger. — *sankrānti*, the entering of the sun into Aries, on which day the meal of parched grain (*satū,ā*) is distributed to Brāhmaṇs.

सतूकः, *m.* base coin (Gladwin).

सतून, *m.* a pillar, column, prop.

सतेसा = **सथिया**, *q.v.*

सतोंचा, (in Surveying) seven and a half.

सतोगुण, *more prop.* **सत्त्वगुण**, *q.v.*

सतोड़ा, 1, *m.* (*f.* ī) annihilated: 2, *m.* non-existence.

सत्कर्म्म, *m.* a good act, in virtuous action; virtuous demeanour, piety, virtue; worship; hospitality; funeral obsequies.

सत्कर्म्मी, *m.* (*f.* iṇī) a kind or virtuous person, etc.: *lit* one who practices *satkarmm.*

सत्कार, *m.* a kind or benevolent action, doing good; reverence, respect; attention; hospitable treatment or reception; a pious action: the act of regarding, rewarding or distinguishing; worship; obsequies; a meal; a festival ; care.

सत्कारी, *m.* (*f.* iṇī) a kind or virtuous person, etc.; one who burns the dead: *lit.* one who practices *satkār.*

सत्कार्य्य, *m.* incumbent acts of kindness or benevolence, religious duties, pious obligations.

सत्क्रिया, *f.* a good or virtuous action, doing good, virtue. charity; salutation, welcome, courtesy, respectful treatment, hospitable reception; funeral or obsequial ceremonies; any purificatory ceremony.

सत्त in Chand = **सात**, *q.v.*

सत्तति in Prākrit = **सत्तर**, *q.v.*

सत्तम, *m.* (*f.* ā) best, excellent; very venerable or respectable; most virtuous.

सत्तमो in Prākrit = **सातवां**, *q.v.*

सत्तर, seventy (७०): see **ओं, वां, वीं, वे, वें.**

सत्तरस in Prākrit = **सत्रह**, *q.v.*

सत्तरह = **सत्रह**, *q.v.*

सत्तराबहत्तरा, old, doting, decrepit: *lit.* 70 to 72 (which in India is reckoned a very advanced age).

सत्तरि in Prākrit = **सत्तर**, *q.v.*

सत्तवां, *m.* (*f.* °**वीं**) = **सत्तरवां**, *q.v.*

सत्ता, 1, *m.* power, strength: (at Cards) seven; 2, *f.* existence, being; reality: goodness, excellence.

सत्ताईस, twenty-seven (२७): see **ओं, वां, वीं, वे, वें.**

सत्तानवे }
सत्तान्व } *more prop.* **सत्तान्वे**, *q.v.*

सत्तान्वे, ninety-seven (९७) }
सत्तावन, fifty-seven (५७) } see **ओं, वां, वीं, वे, वें.**
सत्तासी, eighty-seven (८७) }

सत्तिया. *m.* power, strength.

सत्तुर, *m.* (prop. **शत्रु**) an enemy, foe.

सत्तू, *m.* parched grain reduced to meal and made into a paste. [veneri addictus.

सत्तूखोरा, *m.* pæderastes, pædicator, præposteræ

सत्त. a Prākrit form of **सात**, *q.v.*

सत्त्व, *m.* being, existence, entity, life; natural property, nature, character; essence; thing, substance; the quality of virtue or goodness (one of the three properties [*guṇ*] of man and nature); certainty; breath; mind; strength, power, vigour; courage; self-possession; wealth: an animal, being; a demon, goblin; a monster; a beast: (in Gram.) a substantive.

सत्त्वगुण, *m.* (see **गुण**) the quality of excellence or goodness.

सत्त्वता, *f.* purity, goodness.

सत्त्वरजतम, *m.* (see **गुण**) the three *guṇs.*

सत्पथ, *m.* a good road or way; good course of life, correct or virtuous conduct; sound or orthodox doctrine.

सत्पात्र, *m.* (*f.* ī) a worthy or virtuous person.

सत्पुत्र, *m.* (*f.* ī) a virtuous or filial child.

सत्पुरुष, *m.* a worthy or spirited man.

सत्फल, *m.* the pomegranate.

सत्मत, *m.* the true or right way in morals or in religion.

सत्य, 1, *m.* (*f.* ā) true, real, sincere, honest, truthful; accurate: 2. *m.* truth: a solemn asseveration. an oath: a demonstrated conclusion: *pr. n.* (1) of the golden age (*yug*) of the Hindoo mythology (2) of the uppermost of the seven worlds (*lok*).

सत्यक, 1, true, veracious: 2, *m.* the ratification of a bargain.

सत्यकरण, *m.* demonstration, proof.

सत्यकाम, *m.* (*f.* ā) a lover of truth, one whose deeds are good. A proper name among Hindoos.

सत्यकेतु, *m. pr. n.* a certain ancient Hindoo king.

सत्यजित, *m. pr. n.* a certain ancient Hindoo prince, son of Vṛihadrath.

सत्यता, *f.* (*m.* °**त्व**) truth, trueness, veracity, integrity, virtue.

सत्यत्वासत्यत्व, *m.* truth and untruth.

सत्यदेव, *m.* (*f.* ā) *adj.* shining through truth.

सत्यदेवी, *f. pr. n.* the wife of king Vṛihaddharm.

सत्यधर्म्मा, *m. f.* practising the duty of truth; ruling by fixed ordinances.

सत्यधाम, *m.* an epithet of the Supreme Being (*lit.* the dwellingplace of truth).

सत्यब; for words beginning thus, see under the form **सत्यव**°.

सत्यभामा, *f. pr. n.* the daughter of Satrājit and one of the eight wives of Krishṇ.

सत्यम, (a particle of interrogation and of asseveration) indeed, verily.

सत्यमत, *m.* the true or right way in morals or religion.

सत्यमन्त्र, *m.* (*f.* ā) having or repeating true prayers; praying effectually.

सत्ययुग, *m. pr. n.* the first of the four ages (*yug*) of the Hindoos. It is their Golden Age, or period of general virtue and purity, and comprizes a period of 1728000 years.

सत्ययुगी, appertaining to Satyayug: hence, *m.* (*f.* inī one who lived in that era.

सत्यरूपा, *more prop.* **सतरूपा**, *q.v.*

सत्यलोक, *m. pr. n.* the uppermost of the seven worlds (*lok*), the abode of Brahm and the heaven of truth (called also *Brahmlok*), to which human beings, once translated, are exempted from further birth.

सत्यवंत, *m.* (*f.* vatī) = **सत्यवान**, *q.v.*

सत्यवक्ता, *m.* (*f.* trī) = **सत्यवादी**, *q.v.*

सत्यवचन, *m.* truth-speaking, a true statement.

सत्यवत, *m.* (*f.* vatī) = **सत्यवान**, *q.v.*

सत्यवती, *f.* (*m.* **सत्यवन्त**, etc.) a veracious female. A frequent proper name of females.

सत्यवन्त, *m.* (*f.* vatī) = **सत्यवान**, *q.v.*

सत्यवरन, *more prop.* **सत्यवर्ण**, *q.v.*

सत्यवर्णा, 1, *m.* the Brāhmaṇical caste: 2, *m.* (*f.* ā) an epithet of any Brāhmaṇ.

सत्यवाद, 1, = **सत्यवादी**, *q.v.*: 2, *m.* truthfulness, veraciousness.

सत्यवादी, *m.* (*f.* inī) one who speaks the truth: *lit.* true to (his) words, veracious, truth-speaking.

सत्यवान, *m.* (*f.* vatī) a veracious person: *lit.* veracious, true, practising or speaking the truth.

सत्यव्रत, 1, *m.* (*f.* ā) veracious, honest: 2, *m. pr. n.* (1) of the 25th king of the solar dynasty (2) of Manu-Vaivasvat (3) of the author of a Dharm-Shāstra.

सत्यसंकल्प, *m.* a faithful agreement or promise: 2, *m.* (*f.* ā) one who is faithful to his engagements.

सत्यसाक्षी, *m.* (*f.* iṇī) a veracious or unexceptionable witness.

सत्यसेन, *m. pr. n.* one of the incarnations of Vishṇu.

सत्या, *f.* 1, veracity, sincerity: 2, *pr. n.* (1) of Sītā (2) of Satyavatī, mother of Vyās: 3, *m.* power, strength.

सत्यात्मा, *m. f.* a virtuous and upright person: lit. *adj.* of a true or upright disposition or spirit.

सत्यानाश, *m.* (a term of imprecation, signifying) depravation, destruction, total destruction.—*k.* (*kiskā*) to work another's mischief or destruction. —*jānā* or *honā* (1) with *kisikā* = to be the depravation or ruin of anyone or anything (2) to be depraved or ruined.

सत्यानाशी, 1, *m.* (*f.* inī) a depraved or ruined person: *lit.* damaged, depraved, bad, destroyed: 2, *m.* a certain thorny plant (it is a kind of thistle, the juice of which is of a yellow colour and is very acrid: it is used as a caustic).

सत्यानृत, *m.* commerce, trade, traffic: *lit.* truth and falsehood (of which trade is supposed to be a mixed practice).

सत्यापन, *m.* / **सत्यापना**, *f.* } the ratification of a bargain.

सत्यार्थी, *m.* (*f.* inī) one who is in search of truth.

सत्र, *m.* a sacrifice: munificence, liberality: covering, concealing, veiling, suppressing; a hidingplace; the privities; fraud, cheating: a house: wealth: a tank: a forest.

सत्रंग, a mandrake.

सत्रह, seventeen (१७): see **ओं**, **वां**, **वीं**, **वे**, **वें**.

सत्राजित, *m. pr. n.* a son of Nighn and father of Satyabhāmā.

सत्रु; for words beginning thus, see under the form **शत्रु**.

सत्व; for words beginning thus, but not given below, see under the more proper form **सत्त्व**.

सत्वर, 1, *m.* (*f.* ā) swift, quick, expeditious: 2, swiftly, quickly, expeditiously.

सत्वरता, *f.* (*m.* °**त्व**) swiftness, speed, quickness.

सत्वांसा, 1, *m.* (*f.* ī) a child born in the seventh month: 2, *m.* an entertainment given to a woman by her parents in the seventh month of her pregnancy.

सत्वू; see (1) **सत्तू** (2) **सत्त्व**.

सत्संग, 1, *m.* = **सत्संगति**, *q.v.*: 2, good, pious.

सत्संगत (*contraction*) = **सत्संगति**, *q.v.*

सत्संगति, *f.* intercourse or association with the good, good companionship, pious association.

सत्संगतिमहिमा, *f.* = **सत्संगप्रभाव**, *q.v.*

सत्संगप्रभाव, *m.* the excellence acquired by association with the good.

सत्संसर्ग, *m.* the society of good or virtuous persons.

सत्स्वभाव, *m.* a good disposition, goodness of nature.

सथन, *more prop.* **सुथन**, *q.v.*

सथरा, *m.* a mattress.

सथराव, *m.* (in War) a heap of slain.

सथवारा, *more com.* **सठोड़ा**, *q.v.*

सथिया, *m.* a surgeon: a mark in the form of a cross the four arms of which are bent at right angles. It is prefixed (in vermilion) by Hindoos to their account-books at the commencement of a new year; and is also formed on the ground with flour at marriages and other ceremonies.

सद, 1, sometimes in comp. = **सत**, *q.v.*: 2, *m.* any edible vegetable product (as fruit, etc.): 3, *f.* an ode or poem: 4, fresh, flourishing: 5, one hundred.

सदक़ा, *m.* alms, propitiatory offerings, voluntary or supererogatory alms.

सद्गत (*contraction*) = **सदगति**, *q.v.*

सदगति, *f.* a good state or condition, good estate; good behaviour; happiness, blessedness.

सदगुण, *more com.* **सद्गुण**, *q.v.*

सदग्रन्थ, *m.* a good or holy book.

सदज्ञानी, *m.* (*f.* inī) one who possesses good knowledge, one who is wise in the best sense.

सदन, *m.* a house, residence, mansion, palace: decaying, perishing; exhaustion.

सदना, *a. int.* to leak (as a ship, etc.).

सदफ़, *f.* a shell, pearl; mother-of-pearl.

सदबर्ग, a marigold.

सदमा, *m.* a blow, collision, adversity, adventure, stroke of fortune.

सदय, *m.* (*f.* ā) a compassionate person: *lit.* compassionate, commiserating, merciful, kind, favorable.

सदया, *m.* 1, = **सदिया**, *q.v.*: 2, *f.* (*m.* **सदय**) a compassionate female: 3, a kind of religious mendicant: 4, mercifully.

सदर, 1, chief, supreme: 2, *f.* exaltation, preëminence; Government, the seat of Government: the breast: the right side of cloth (or that which is worn outward).

सदरंज; for words beginning thus, see under the form **शत्रंज**.

सदस, *m.* a seat, abode; a meeting, assembly.

सदसत, being and not being, real and unreal, true and untrue, good and evil.

सदस्य, *m.* (*f.* ā) any person present at an assembly, a by-stander, spectator, member: one who assists at a sacrifice, a spectator of a ceremonial observance.

सदा, 1, always, at all times, ever, perpetually, constantly, continually. — *sarvadā*, at all times, constantly, for ever and ever: 2, *f.* sound, tone, echo, voice.

सदाई, 1, an emphat. form of **सदा**, *q.v*: 2, *f.* perpetuity.

सदां, *more com.* **सदा**, *q. v.*

सदाक़त, *f.* sincerity; friendship.

सदाकाल, at all times, constantly, always, for ever.

सदागति, *m.* final happiness, emancipation from existence: an epithet (1) of the Supreme Spirit (2) of the sun (3) of air or wind.

सदाचार, *m.* the immemorial observances of virtuous persons, customs sanctioned by immemorial usage, approved usage, good or virtuous conduct.

सदाचारी, of virtuous conduct, well-behaved: hence, *m.* (*f.* iṇī) a virtuous person.

सदातन, *m.* an epithet of Vishṇu: *lit.* eternal.

सदात्मा, *m. f.* good, virtuous, pious.

सदानन्द, *m.* (*f.* ā) always joyful, constantly happy.

सदानर्त्त, *m.* (*f.* ā) a wagtail.

सदापुष्पी, *f.* the white variety of the gigantic swallow-wort.

सदाफल, *m.* 1, a certain fabled fruit the eating of which confers long life: 2, *adj.* constantly in fruit; an epithet of several trees; *e.g.* (1) a kind of lemon (2) the glomerous figtree (3) the jack-fruit tree (4) the *bel*-tree (*Ægle marmelos*).

सदाबर्त्त / **सदाबत** / **सदावर्त्त** } corruptions of **सदाव्रत**, *q. v.*

सदाय; see (1) **सदय** (2) **सुदाय**.

सदाव्रत, *m.* alms or food distributed daily to the poor, to travellers, etc.

सदाशिव, *m.* an epithet of Mahādev: *lit.* always happy or prosperous.

सदास, *m.* (*f.* ā) *adj.* always honouring or giving.

सदासर्वदा; see *s.v.* **सदा**.

सदासुहागन, *f.* a certain bird (*Frogon dilectus*, Buch.); a certain flower (*Hibiscus phœniceus*. the white variety); a kind of mendicant dressed like a woman.

सदास्थिर, *m.* (*f.* ā) always firm, of eternal duration, abiding, permanent.

सदाही, an emphatic form of **सदा**, *q. v.*

सदिया, *f.* the female of the little bird called *amadavat*.

सदुत्तर, *m.* a proper or good reply.

सदुपदेश, *m.* salutary instruction, wholesome counsel.

सदूक़ी, *m.* a Sadducee.

सदृश, *m.* (*f.* ī) like, similar, resembling; conformable; right, proper, fit, suitable, worthy. The term is also used as a postposition, and when so used it takes the inflected form of the genitive masculine.

सदृशता, *f.* (*m.* °**त्व**) similarity, likeness.

सदेश, 1, (*colloquial*) = **स्वदेश**, *q. v.*: 2, of the same country or place: near, proximate, before, fronting.

सदेशी, *m.* (*f.* inī) = (1) **स्वदेशी** (2) **सदेश**, 2, *qq.v.*

सदेह, 1, possessed of a body, corporeal: 2, *adv.* bodily, with a body, in the body, in an embodied form.

सदेही, *m.* (*f.* inī) = **सदेह**, 1, *q.v.*

सदेव (*Rām.*) = **सदाही**, *q. v.* (Sk. **सदा** + **एव**.)

सदेसी in Braj = **सदेशी**, *q.v.*

सदोम, *m. pr. n.* the ancient city of Sodom.

सदोष, defective, faulty, sinful, guilty.

सदोषी, *m.* (*f.* iṇī) = **सदोष**, *q.v.*

सद्गति, *f.* felicity or fortune, good estate; salvation; good conduct.

सद्गुण, 1, *m.* a virtue, good trait, excellency: 2, *m.* (*f.* ā) good, pure, virtuous, excellent, eminent.

सद्द, 1, in Chand = **शब्द**, *q.v.*: 2, *f.* an obstruction of any kind, an obstacle, impediment, barrier, ditch, rampart, wall.

सद्भाव, *m.* reality, actual existence, the being alive or in existence: a pure or holy disposition or nature, the property of goodness, kindly feeling, good temper, amiability, courtesy.

सद्य, to-day; instantly, immediately, at that very time, forthwith, at once, just now.

सद्यंज; for words beginning thus, see under the form **शत्रंज**.

सधन, *m.* (*f.* ā) *adj.* possessed of property, opulent, wealthy, rich. [ciplined.

सधना, *n.* (see **साधना**) to be fully instructed or dis-

सधनी, *m.* (*f.* inī) = **सधन**, *q.v.*

सधर्म्म, *m.* (*f.* ā *or* ī) = **सधर्म्मी**, *q.v.*

सधर्म्मा, 1, *m.f.* = **सधर्म्मी**, *q.v.*: 2, *f.* of **सधर्म्म**, *q.v.*: 3, similar, like, analogous.

सधर्म्मिणी, *f.* a wife wedded according to the legal form or ritual of the Veds.

सधर्म्मी, *m.* (*f.* iṇī) a caste-fellow, etc.: *lit.* observing the same customs or laws, of the same caste, performing like duties, of the same properties, equal in respect of duty. [a happy wife.

सधवा, *f.* a married woman whose husband is alive;

सधवाना; see (1) **सधाना** (2) **सुधवाना**.

सधाऊ, 1, improveable: 2, *m.* or *f.* a maker.

सधाना, *t.* to train animals: to perform; to manage

सधारन, a corruption of **साधारण**, *q.v.* [a house.

सधाव, *m.* improvement.

सधि, 1, *more prop.* **सुधि**, *q.v.*: 2, *m.* an epithet of Agni.

सन, 1, in Braj = **से**; *e.g.* **वासन** = **वासे** = **उससे**: 2, In some provincial dialects this form is equivalent to **सा**; *e. g.* **कइसन** = **कैसा**: 3, a corruption of **शण**, *q.v.*: 4, *f.* a year. Though in this last sense the word is perhaps of Shemitic origin, it is nevertheless in regular use in Hindee, especially in dating; *e. g.* **सन १८७५ ईसवी** = the year of Christ (*lit.* the Christian year, anno domini) 1875. It is, however, most probably a degenerate form of **संवत**. [of Brahmā.

सनंदन, *more prop.* **सनन्दन**, *q.v.*

सनक, *m. pr. n.* (see **सनकादि**) one of the four sons

सनकादि, the four sons of Brahmā, *viz.* Sanak, Sanandan, Sanātan, and Sanatkumār.

सनकारना, *more com.* **संकारना**, *q.v.*

सनगरी sanagarī, *m.* (*f.* iṇī) a fellow-citizen.

सनत, 1, always, ever, continually: 2, *f.* the repetition of the same course of the sun, with its concomitant changes; a year.

सनत्कुमार, *m. pr. n.* (see **सनकादि**) one of the four sons of Brahmā, and eldest of the progenitors of mankind.

सनद, *f.* signature; the seal of a magistrate; a lease; a patent, grant, or charter from a man in authority; a deed, grant, order, license: a prop, support: relation, connexion.

सनना, *n.* to be impregnated: to be soiled, be stained, be smeared, be defiled: to be kneaded, be mixed up (said of flour, dough, earth, etc.). [of Brahmā.

सनन्दन, *m. pr. n.* (see **सनकादि**) one of the four sons

सनपात, *more prop.* (1) **सन्निपात** (2) **सनापत**, *qq.v.*

सनम, *m.* an idol; a lover, sweetheart: a certain

सनमान = **संमान**, *q.v.* [game among children.

सनमाना, *t.* to treat respectfully, to honour.

सनमानी, *m.* (*f.* inī) = **संमानी**, *q.v.*

सनसनाना = **संसनाना**, *q.v.*

सनसनाहट = **संसनाहट**, *q.v.*

सनसि; see **सनना**.

सनसूत्र, *more prop.* **शणसूत्र**, *q.v.*

सनह, a corruption of **स्नेह**, *q.v.*

सनहला, *m.* (*f.* ī) *more prop.* **सुनहला**, *q.v.*

सना, 1, always, ever, perpetually, continually: 2, *m.* senna (*Cassia senna* or *Senna Italica*).

सनाटा = **सन्नाटा**, *q.v.*

सनातन, *m.* an epithet (1) of Brahmā (2) of Vishṇu (3) of Shiv: *p. n.* one of the four sons of Brahmā: lit. *m.* (*f.* ī) eternal, perpetual, continual; fixed, firm, permanent; primeval.

सनाथ, *m.* (*f.* ā) having (or accompanied by) a master, protector, or husband.

सनाथा, *f.* a woman whose husband is still alive.

सनान, in Chand = **स्नान**, *q.v.*

सनापत, *f.* massacre.

सनाय, *f.* the senna-plant. See **सना**.

सनाह, 1, *more prop.* **सनाथ**, *q.v.*: 2, *m.* armour, mail.

सनि, 1, *m.* worship, service: a giving, donation: 2, *m. f.* a respectful solicitation, request.

सनिया, *m.* a kind of *tasar*-cloth.

सनी, *f.* a request, respectful solicitation: a quarter or point of the compass. [Saturday.

सनीचर, *m. pr. n.* (1) of the planet Saturn (2) of

सनीचरा, 1, *m.* (*f.* ī) an unlucky person: 2, *m. pr. n.* a certain mountain near Goāliyār.

सनीन, *f.* (prop. **संगीन**) a bayonet.

सनेह (*Rām*) = **स्नेह**, *q. v.*

सनेहनि, in Braj = 1, a pl. of **स्नेह**, *q.v.*; see **नि**, 2 (2): 2, the agent. case of **स्नेह**; see **नि**, 2 (5).

सनेहा, a poet. form of **स्नेह**, *q.v.*

सनेही, *m.* (*f.* inī) *more prop.* **स्नेही**, *q.v.*

सनेहू, *more prop.* **स्नेह भी**. See **ऊ**, 7.

सनै, *more prop.* (1) **शनै** (2) **सुनै**, *qq. v.*

सनोमान = **संमान**, *q. v.*

सन्त, *m.* (*f.* satī) a pious or venerable person, a saint: lit. *adj.* being, existing, being (in the true sense of the word) *i.e.* right, virtuous, pious, steady, venerable, excellent. [ual, perpetual, lasting, eternal.

सन्तत, 1, a contraction of **सन्तति**, *q.v.*: 2, contin-

सन्तति, *f.* a continuous line, continuity; extent, width, expansion; multitude; race, lineage, offspring, posterity, progeny, a son or a daughter.

सन्तन, *m.* [a Braj pl. of **सन्त**; see **न**, 6 (1)] the good, the righteous. [giver of joy to the pious).

सन्तनसुखद, *m.* an epithet of Vishṇu, etc.: *lit.* the

सन्तना, *f.* palliation, consolation, the act of appeasing. — *k.* to appease, still, quiet, lull, comfort.

सन्तनु, *more prop.* **संतनु**, *q.v.*

सन्तप्त, *m.* (*f.* ā) heated, burned; afflicted, distressed, vexed, wretched, pained.

सन्तवस्था, *f.* the state or condition of a saint, saintliness, venerableness.

सन्तसभा, *f.* = **सन्तसमाज**, *q. v.* [pious.

सन्तसमागम, *m.* the intercourse or union of the

सन्तसमाज, *m.* the assembly of the good. The term is applied chiefly to the Hindoo ascetics regarded as to their corporate capacity.

सन्ता, *m.* (*f.* ī) depraved, wicked; miserly.

सन्तान, *m.* (*f.* ī) spreading, extension; lineage, race, descent, family, offspring, progeny, children, a son or a daughter: *pr. n.* one of the trees of heaven.

सन्ताना, *more prop.* **सताना**, *q. v.*

सन्तानिक, appertaining to offspring: hence, *m.* (*f.* ā) one who possesses offspring, a parent.

सन्तानिका, *f.* froth; cream: a cobweb: the blade of a knife or sword.

सन्ताप, *m.* heat, fire, burning heat; pain, penance, affliction, distress, sorrow, misery; passion; repentance.

सन्तापित, *m.* (*f.* ā) = **सन्तापी**, *q. v.*

सन्तापी, *m.* (*f.* inī) an afflicted person, etc.: *lit.* heated, inflamed; pained, distressed, sad, sorrowful, afflicted, impassioned, penitent.

सन्ती, 1, *f.* (*m.* **सन्ता**) a depraved or miserly female: 2, *m.* (*f.* inī) a succedaneum, substitute: 3, *postp.* (takes fem. genit.) = **सन्ते**, 2, *q. v.*

सन्तुष्ट, *m.* (*f.* ā) content, satisfied, delighted, pleased, gratified, consoled, comforted, at rest, patient, resigned.

सन्तुष्टता / **सन्तुष्टि** } *f.* = **सन्तोष**, *q. v.*

सन्ते, 1, = **समयमें** *q.v.*: 2, *postp.* (takes gen. masc. infl.) instead of, in substitution for.

सन्तोख (*colloquial*) = **सन्तोष**, *q. v.*

सन्तोष, *m.* contentedness, settledness of the desires, satisfaction, gratification, pleasure, happiness, joy, delight; satiety; patience: the thumb and forefinger.

सन्तोषी, *m.* (*f.* inī) = **सन्तुष्ट**, *q. v.*

सन्था, *m.* a lesson, reading.

सन्दरोदन, *more prop.* **सुन्दरोदन**, *q. v.*

सन्दर्शन, *m.* seeing each other, meeting; a seeing, looking, shewing, presenting; sight, vision; appearance; consideration.

सन्दल, *m.* sandal-wood.

सन्दलसिल, *f.* a grinder (for spices).

सन्दलानी, *m.* (*f.* inī) a dealer in sandal-wood.

सन्दलासा, *m.* a flat stone on which sandal-wood is ground.

सन्दली, 1, appertaining to sandal-wood: 2, *m.* a species of eunuch: 3, *f.* a kind of chair: 4, *pr. n.* a certain city of Kashmīr.

सन्दलोटा = **सन्दलासा**, *q. v.*

सन्दसी; see **सन्दा** and **सण्डसी**.

सन्दा, *m.* an anvil: fetid excrement: a broad stone.

सन्दान, *m.* a rope, cord (*esp.* for tying cattle): an elephant's temples, or the part whence the ichorous fluid issues.

सन्दानिनी, *f.* a cowhouse.

सन्दिग्ध, *m.* (*f.* ā) indistinct, uncertain, doubtful, dubious, doubted, questioned, suspected; desponding.

सन्दिग्धभूत, *m.* (in Gram.) the doubtful past tense: *e. g. Tumne dekhā hogā*, it may be that you saw, perhaps (or probably) you saw.

सन्दिग्धवर्त्तमान, *m.* (in Gram.) the doubtful present tense: *e. g. Wuh sunti hogi*, perhaps she hears, it may be that she hears.

सन्दीपन, 1, *more prop.* **सान्दीपनि**, *q.v.*: 2, *m.* a lighting, enflaming, igniting: *pr. n.* one of the arrows of Kāmdev.

सन्दूक, *m. f.* a box, trunk, chest, coffer, casket.

सन्दूकचा, *m.* / **सन्दूकची**, *f.* } a small box, a casket.

सन्दूख, *more prop.* **सन्दूक**, *q. v.*

सन्दूचा, a contraction of **सन्दूकचा**, *q. v.*

सन्दूषण, *m.* a vice which causes infamy.

सन्देश, *m.* news, tidings, intelligence, information, report; message; commission; command.

सन्देशी, *m.* (*f.* inī) one who brings news, a messenger.

सन्देशु = (1) **सन्देश** (1) **सन्देशी**, *qq. v.*

सन्देस; for words beginning thus, see under the form **सन्देश**.

सन्देसो in Braj = **सन्देश**, *q. v.*

सन्देह, *m.* doubt, hesitation, uncertainty, apprehension, mistrust, suspicion, anxiety, danger.

सन्देही, doubtful, apprehensive, suspicious, mistrustful, scrupulous: hence, *m.* (*f.* inī) a mistrustful person, a doubter.

सन्देहू = (1) **सन्देह** (2) **सन्देही**, *qq. v.*

सन्दोरी, *f.* a narrow passage, alley, lane.

सन्दोह, *m.* an assemblage, multitude, concourse.

सन्धव, *m.* (prop. **सैन्धव**) rock-salt.

सन्धान, *m.* uniting, joining, fixing, tying, binding; union, association, junction, mixing, alliance; company; peace: supporting; receiving; contracting the skin, etc. by astringents: distillation: a relish, something eaten to excite thirst; pickles; sour rice-gruel; spirituous liquor: an aim, a guess, a discovery; search, inquiry, spying, prying into secrets; information about a lost thing or person; a secret. — *pānā*, to trace, discover.

सन्धाना, *m.* pickle, acid preparation of *bel* and other fruits.

सन्धानी, *f.* 1, = **सन्धाना**, *q.v.*: 2, distillation: a foundry.

सन्धाने, *m.* (pl. of **सन्धाना**) pickles.

सन्धि, *m.* union, junction, connexion, combination, alliance, peace, pacification, making a treaty, a treaty: a joint, articulation; a fold; an interval, pause, rest, stop; a hole, breach, chasm (*esp.* in a wall for felonious purposes); breaking, dividing, division; the vulva; a certain period at the expiration of each (*yug*) or age; (in Gram.) the euphonic combination or coälescence of the final letter of a word with the initial letter of a following word.

सन्धिकर्त्ता, *m.* (*f.* trī) one who brings about union or pacification, a reconciler.

सन्धिप्रकरण, *m.* (in Gram.) a treatise on Sandhi.

सन्ध्या, *f.* the mean between two things; twilight (either morning or evening); a period of time forenoon, mid-day, afternoon, or evening; holy rites of morning, noon, and evening; evening prayer; the period between the expiration of one age (*yug*) and the commencement of another; joining, union; promise, agreement; boundary: a certain flower: reflection, meditation: *pr. n.* a certain river.

सन्ध्याकाल / सन्ध्यासमय } m. eventide, twilight, dusk.

सन्नति, f. reverence, reverential salutation, obeisance; humility: sound.

सन्नद्ध, m. (f. ā) tied together, fastened; arranged, arrayed; ready; bordering; armed, accoutred; cruel, murderous.

सन्ना = सनना, q.v.

सन्नाटा, 1, = सुन्नाटा, q.v.: 2, m. (f. ī) entirely desolate (as an empty city, etc.).

सन्नाना, a. int. to hiss (as a snake, etc.).

सन्नासी, more prop. संन्यासी, q.v.

सन्निकर्ष, m. connexion, relation, approximation, attraction, proximity, vicinity.

सन्निध, m. = सन्निधान, q.v.

सन्निधान, m. proximity, nearness, vicinity: perceptibility, appearance, presence; a placing, depositing; a receptacle; a receiving, taking charge of.

सन्निधि, f. = सन्निधान, q.v.

सन्निपात, m. contact, collision; assemblage, multitude; union, junction, mixture, miscellaneous collection; alighting, descending; arrival; intent; a morbid state of the three humours (a disease in which the body is seized with universal chilliness: it is explained by the Hindoo physicians to be a disease in which the three humours [bile, phlegm, and atrabilis] are corrupted).

सन्निविष्ट, m. (f. ā) entered, near, close by, neighbouring; seated, encamped; assembled, collected; intent.

सन्निवेष्टन, m. (f. ā or ī) adj. entering; sitting; collected, folded. [jacent, close.

सन्निहित, near, proximate, at hand, present, ad-

सन्मख, more prop. संमुख, q.v.

सन्मपात; see (1) सन्निपात (2) सम्पात.

सन्मान = संमान, q.v.

सन्मानी, m. (f. inī) = संमानी, q.v.

सन्मित्र, m. (f. ā) a sincere friend.

सन्मुख = संमुख, q.v.

सन्यपात, more prop. सन्निपात, q.v.

सन्यवेष्टन, more prop. सन्निवेष्टन, q.v.

सन्यास / सन्न्यास } more prop. संन्यास, q.v.

सपक्ष, winged: having a side or party, belonging to the same party: hence, m. a partisan: a similar instance, i. e. one in which the major term is found: any winged creature.

सपच्छ (colloquial) = सपक्ष, q.v.

सपड़ना, n. to be caught, be involved.

सपड़ाना, t. to catch, arrest, involve.

सपथ, more prop. शपथ, q.v. [ment.

सपदि, instantly, immediately, quickly, in a mo-

सपन, सपना; for words beginning with either of these elements, see under the form स्वप्न.

सपनेहु in Braj = स्वप्न भो. See हु, 1.

सपन्नग, m. (f. ā) with the snake-shaped demons.

सपरब (Rām.) = सपर्व, q.v.

सपर्दा, m. a musician attendant on singing-women.

सपर्दाई, f. the corps of musicians who attend a

सपर्व, possessing knots, knotted. [dancing-girl.

सपल्लव, together with (or possessed of) sprouts, shoots, or twigs (as a pot, etc. in times of rejoicing).

सपहिरा, m. (f. in or ī) a snake-catcher.

सपाटा, m. a leap, spring, bound.

सपात, pure, clean, smooth, level.

सपाद, augmented by one fourth, with one fourth

सपुत = सपुत्र, q.v. [added to it, a quarter more.

सपुतह an old form = सपुत्र, q.v. [with child.

सपुत्र, 1, = सुपुत्र, q.v.: 2, m. (f. ā) possessing a son,

सपूत = सपुत्र, q.v. [filialness.

सपूताई, f. tractableness or dutifulness in a son,

सपूरन, 1, (dialectic) = सम्पूर्ण, q.v.: 2, m. the full

सपेड़ा, m. (f. in or ī) a snake-catcher. [moon.

सपेद (colloquial) = सफ़ेद, q.v.

सपेरा, m. (f. in or ī) a snake-catcher.

सपेला, m. (f. ī) a young snake just hatched.

सपोला, m. (f. ī) / सपोलिया, m. f. } = सपेला, q.v.

सप्त, seven. The word is Sk. and seldom occurs

सप्तऋषि, more prop. सप्तर्षि, q.v. [in Hindee.

सप्तति, f. (Sk.) seventy.

सप्तदश, (Sk.) 1, seventeen: 2, m. (f. ī) the seventeenth. [ing seven padas.

सप्तपद, m. (f. ā or ī) having seven steps, contain-

सप्तपदी, f. the seven steps at marriage.

सप्तपदीन, m. the state of seven steps, i. e. intimacy; the advance of seven steps taken by a bride to meet the bridegroom.

सप्तम, (Sk.) m. (f. ī) the seventh.

सप्तमा, more prop. सप्तम, q.v. [fortnight.

सप्तमी, f. the seventh day (tithi) of the lunar

सप्तर्षि, (see ऋषि) m. pr. n. (1) of the seven great saint-sages of the Hindoos (2) of the constellation Ursa Major, the seven stars of which represent the seven sages.

सप्तविंशति, f. (Sk.) twenty-seven.

सप्तविंशतितम, (Sk.) m. (f. ī) the twenty-seventh.

सप्तवारश, seven times. [after any other day.

सप्ताह, m. seven days, a week, the eighth day

सप्ताहपारायण, m. the ceremony of reading the Bhāgavat Purāṇ through in seven days. This is one of the many ways by which Hindoos believe that they may secure emancipation from the necessity for further transmigration immediately at the close of the present life.

सप्ताहयज्ञ = सप्ताहपारायण, q.v.

सप्ताहा, more prop. सप्ताह, q.v.

सप्तृख / सप्तृष } more prop. सप्तर्षि, q.v.

सप्न; for words beginning thus, see under the form [स्वप्न.

सप्रमाण, accompanied with proof or evidence, **सप्रीति**, *adj.* possessing affection. [authentic.

सफ, a contraction of **साफ़**, *q.v.*

सफक, *more prop.* **शफ़क़**, *q.v.*

सफ़्स, *f.* drinking a great deal without quenching thirst. [Book that bears his name.

सफनियाह, *m. pr. n.* the prophet Zephaniah and the

सफर = (1) **सफ़र** (2) **शफर**, *qq.v.*

सफ़र, *m.* a journey, voyage, travel.

सफरना, *a. int.* to go on a journey or voyage, to travel.

सफरी = **शफरी**, *q.v.*

सफल, *m.* (*f.* ā) productive, fruitful, profitable, advantageous, remunerative, efficient, successful, fulfilled, blessed.

सफलता, *f.* fruitfulness, profitableness, remunerativeness, efficiency, successfulness, fulfilment.

सफह; see (1) **सफ़ा** (2) **साफ़**.

सफहः, *more prop.* **सफ़हा**, *q.v.*

सफ़हा, *m.* a page, chapter; surface, face.

सफ़ा, 1, = **साफ़**, *q.v.*: 2, *f.* purity, cleanness: pleasure, content.

सफ़ाई, *f.* cleanness, purity; innocence; ingenuousness: levelness. — *batānā*, to reject a petition without ceremony, to refuse flatly.

सफारिस = **सिपारिश**, *q.v.* [fall.

सफ़ाल, *m.* meanness of rank, depression, descent,

सफ़ी, 1, pure, just, righteous: 2, *pr. n.* a certain Persian dynasty that reigned from 1503 to 1736, founded by Shāh Ishmāil Safi, and was overturned by Nādir Shāh. [book, common-place book.

सफ़ीना, *m.* a sailing-vessel, ship, boat: a blank

सफ़ीर, *f.* a sound, whistling, hissing noise, blowing, singing (as of a bird): a sapphire.

सफ़ेद, white. — *tulsī*, white basil.

सफ़ेदा = **सुफ़ेदा**, *q.v.*

सफ़ेदी, *f.* whiteness; white leprosy; whitewash; the lime used with betel. *Andeki* —, white of an egg.

सब, all, the whole, one and all, total, every, all and every. — *kuchh*, everything, all things, all. — *koi*, everyone, all. *Sab misriki hain dāliyān* is used to denote equality or similitude of form, state, etc.; *lit.* all are pieces of sugar, *i. e.* as like as two peas *Sab milākar*, in the lump. *Sabhi sab*, an intensive or emphatic form of *sab*. In the oblique cases it sometimes takes the plural form of inflection; e. g. *Sabhonkā*. It has also a sort of collective form that is very frequently used; e. g. *Sabkā sab*, m. (f. *sabki sab*) the whole, altogether, the whole of it together, completely: Pl. m. *Sabke sab*, the whole of them, the whole of them together, completely.

सबक़, *m.* a lesson, lecture, reading.

सबकसब (*corruption*) = **सबका सब**. See *s.v.* **सब**.

सबका, 1, *more prop.* **शबका**: 2, *m.* (*f.* ī): see **सब**.

सबकेसब, infl. form of **सबका सब**; see *s.v.* **सब**.

सबखव्वा, *m.* (*f.* ī) one who eats all kinds of food without exception: *lit.* omnivorous.

सबगबला, mash.

सबज़ा, *m.* verdure; incipient beard; bloom; the sweet basil (*Ocymum basilicum*); a green stone worn in the ear as an ornament; the jay-bird.

सबज़ी, *f.* greenness; culinary vegetables, greens; a kind of intoxicating potion made of *bhang*.

सबज्ञान, 1, *m.* all-knowledge, the knowledge of all: 2, *m.* (*f.* ā) all knowing, omniscient.

सबड़ा, *m.* (*f.* ī) a liar.

सबत = **सवत** = **सौत**, *q.v.*

सबतिश्रा = **सवतिया** = **सौतिया**, *q.v.*

सबते in Braj = **सबसे** (**सब**).

सबद (colloquial) = **शब्द**, *q.v.*

सबदरा, *m.* the bowsprit of a vessel.

सबन, 1, *more prop.* **सवन**, *q.v.*: 2, in Braj = **सबों** (**सब**).

सबन्ह, 1, a Braj. pl. of **सब**, *q.v.*: 2, (a Braj form of the infl. pl. of **सब**) = **सबों**. See *s. v.* **सब**.

सबब, *m.* cause, reason, motive; relation, affinity; instrument: *postp.* (takes gen. *m.* infl.) on account of, by reason of.

सबय; see (1) **सबहि** (2) **सबया** (3) **सब्य**.

सबर, *f.* endurance, patience. — *k.* to exercise patience, to wait.

सबर्स, *m.* a hare, a rabbit. [tience, to wait.

सबल, *m.* (*f.* ā) powerful, forcible, energetic.

सबलाई, *f.* powerfulness, strength, force, energy.

सबसन, an old form = **सबसे**. See **सन**.

सबसबाना, *a. int.* to creep (as a snake).

सबह, *more prop.* **सुबह**, *q.v.*

सबहि (*Rām.*) = **सबको** (**सब**): see **हि**, 2.

सबहिन, a Braj form = **सभों**, *q.v.*

सबा, *f.* a gentle breeze; an easterly breeze; a morning breeze.

सबां, to-morrow. [ing breeze.

सबाब (*colloquial*) = **सवाब**. *q.v.*

सबाह, *f.* the early dawn, morning: a certain bird.

सबाहत, *f.* gracefulness, beauty. [form **सवि**.

सबि; for words beginning thus, see under the

सबील, *f.* a road, way, path: mode, manner: water distributed to thirsty travellers during the first ten days of the Muharram. — *k.* to obtain money by borrowing or by begging.

सबीह, of a fine complexion, beautiful.

सबू, *m.* a cup, glass, ewer, jar, pitcher.

सबूत, *m.* firmness, stability, permanency; proof, proving, demonstration, confirmation by evidence.

सबूर, patient, enduring, mild.

सबूरा, *m.* instrumentum in membri virilis forma e corio concinnatum, quo mulieres libidinosæ utuntur.

सबे; see **सबय**. [more common form **सवेर**.

सबेर; for words beginning thus, see under the

सबै; see (1) **सबय** (2) **सवैश्रा** (3) **सवैं** (4) **सब**.

सबोतर, (from **सर्वत्र**) everywhere.

सब्द; for words beginning thus, see under the more proper form **शब्द**.

सब्बह in Chand = **सब**, *q.v.* [proper form **शब्द**.

सब्बाग़, *m.* a dyer.

सभ, an occasional Braj form of **सब**, *q.v.*

सभन, a Braj form = **सभों**, *q.v.*

सभय, *m.* (*f.* ā) apprehensive, timid, fearful.

सभहि, an old acc. of **सभा** and of **सब**, *qq.v.*

सभा, *f.* an assembly, meeting, company, council, levee: a much-frequented place, a judicial court, a hall of audience; a sitting of the king in council; a place, a house.

सभाध्यक्ष, *m.* (*f.* ī) the president or leader of an assembly.

सभानायक, *m.* (*f.* ikā) = **सभापति**, *q.v.*

सभापति, *m.* (*f.* patī) the president or chairman of an assembly; a gaming house keeper.

सभाय; see **सभय**.

सभाव, 1, *more prop.* **सुभाव**, *q.v.*: 2, (dialectic) = **सभा**.

सभावाला, *m.* (*f.* ī) a member of an assembly.

सभासद, *m.* one of a company; an assistant at an assembly or meeting; (in Law) an assessor.

सभासुभ (*colloquial*) = **शुभाशुभ**, *q.v.*

सभिक, *m.* the keeper of a gaming-house; the president of an assembly or feast.

सभें; see **सबहि**.

सभीत, *m.* (*f.* ā) timid, apprehensive, afraid.

सभीता, *f.* a timid female; an epithet of the goddess Kālī.

सभे; see (1) **सबहि** (2) **सभय**.

सभै in Braj = (1) **सबहि** (2) **सभय**, *qq.v.*

सभैं, a Braj form of **सभे**, *q.v.*

सभों, the inflective base of the oblique cases of the pl. of **सब**, *q.v.*

सभ्य, appertaining to an assembly; social, polite; confidential, trustworthy, faithful: hence, *m.* (*f.* ā) an assistant at any assembly, (in Law) an assessor: a person of respectable parentage: a gaming-house keeper.

सभ्यता, *f.* (*m.* **त्व°**) refinement in manners, good breeding, politeness.

सभ्राता, with a brother, with brethren.

सम, 1, in compos. = **सं**, *q.v.*: 2, in old Hindee = **से**, *q.v.*: 3, a corruption of **ग्राम**, *q.v.*: 4, *m.*(*f.* ā) even, level, smooth, plain; similar, like, equal, same; all, whole, entire, full, complete: 5, *m.* a level plain; (in Music) tone; (in Math.) a mean proportional segment in solving certain problems in a trapezium.

समइ / **समई** } old forms = **समय**, *q.v.*

समंजस = **समञ्जस**, *q.v.*

समंझौती = **समझावा**, *q.v.*

समंद; see (1) **समन्द** (2) **समुद्र** (3) **सम्बन्ध**.

समकन्या, *f.* a girl fit to be married.

समकालिक / **समकालिन** } *m.* (*f.* ā) = **समकालीन**, *q.v.*

समकालीन, *m.* (*f.* ā) appertaining to the same time or period, contemporary, contemporaneous.

समकिमि, alike, similar, equal, akin.

समकुराना (by inversion) = **मुसकुराना**, *q.v.*

समग्र, entire, complete, full, whole, all.

समग्रह; see (1) **समग्र** (2) **संग्रह** (3) **सामग्री**.

समच्छायक, *m.* (*f.* ikā) *more prop.* **समुच्छायक**, *q.v.*

समजातीय, *m.* (*f.* ā) of the same caste or class, of the same origin or kind, homogeneous.

समझ, *f.* comprehension, understanding, discernment, conception, thought, opinion, judgment, mind, knowledge.

समझना, *t.* to understand, comprehend, know, perceive; to come to an understanding with: *a. int.* to think, conceive, apprehend, perceive, know, suppose, infer, consider, deem, fancy.

समझबूझके, *adv.* in the exercise of the faculty of intelligence and of understanding, knowingly.

समझबूझना (reduplic.) = **समझना**, *q.v.*

समझवार, *m.* (*f.* ī) prudent, discerning, wise, intelligent, considerate.

समझाइश, *f.* a giving to understand or to know; a tampering with, subornation, instructing in false evidence.

समझातो (*corruption*) = **समझौती**, *q.v.*

समझाना, *t.* to cause to comprehend, to inform, intimate, give to understand, explain, describe, account for, to undeceive, warn, admonish, instruct, to satisfy, to apologize.

समझानाबुझाना (a freq. redupl.) = **समझाना**, *q.v.*

समझावा, *f.* the act of explaining, convincing, or imparting confidence.

समझौती = **समझावा**, *q.v.*

समञ्जस, 1, *m.* (*f.* ā) proper, right, fit, correct, accurate, true, virtuous, good, experienced: 2, *m.* truth, accuracy; fitness, propriety; agreement, consistency, correct evidence.

समत, 1, *more prop.* **संमत**, *q.v.*: 2, *f.* a way, path, side, quarter, part, direction.

समता, *f.* (*m.* **°त्व**) equality, sameness, identity, similarity, likeness, resemblance, similitude, parity, comparison, parallelism; evenness, equanimity, right, decision, perfectness, state of a common (*i.e.* not preëminent) person.

समताई, *f.* = **समता**, *q.v.*

समतूल, alike, similar, equal, akin.

समदरसी (*Rām.*) = **समदर्शी**, *q.v.*

समदर्शी, *m.* (*f.* inī) an impartial person: lit. *adj.* seeing all equally (and therefore, by supposition, equitably), viewing both sides.

समदाना, to worship, adore, venerate.

समदुःख, *adj.* sharing another's pain or grief, sympathizing: hence, *m.* (*f.* ā) a sympathizer.

समदुःखी, *m.* (*f.* inī) = **समदुःख**, *q.v.*

समदूर, *m.* the sea; a large river.

समदेशीय, *m.*(*f.* ā) belonging to the same country or locality.

समधन, *more prop.* **समधिन**, *q.v.*

समधमिलावा, *m.* the mutual embracing of two *samdhīs*.

समधरातल, level (*esp.* level with the ground).

समधर्मिय / **समधर्मीय** } *m.* (*f.* ā) = **सधर्मी**, *q.v.*

समधिन, *f.* a child's mother-in-law.

समधियाना, *m.* the family of a child's father-in-law.

समधी, *m.* a child's father-in law.

समन, 1, (*Rām.*) = **शमन**, *q.v.*: 2, *m.* lily of the valley, jasmine: price, value: 3, *m.* (Engl.) a summons.

समनक, *f. pr. n.* a certain fairy (*lit.* lily-face).

समन्द, *m.* a horse of noble breed, a steed, the bay colour in horses.

समन्दर (*colloquial*) = **समुद्र**, *q. v.*

समप्पनें, in Chand = **समर्पना**, *q. v.*

समभाव, 1, of like nature or property: 2, *m.* equality, similarity, equability, sameness, equilibrium, goodness.

समभिव्याहार, *m.* (in Rhet.) mentioning together; proximity of (or association with) a word whose meaning is well understood; bringing together, association, company.

समभूमि, *f.* level ground, even soil; a race-course.

समय, *m.* (*f.* ?) agreement, treaty, contract, bargain: time, season, the proper time for anything; opportunity, leisure; plenty, abundance; concord, harmony, unison, state, condition. — *bandhnā*, to be in concert.

समयक, appertaining to time, seasonable, periodical.

समयसमय, at times, from time to time, now and then, here and there, at intervals, occasionally, sometimes. — *par*, according to the times, on certain occasions, at certain seasons.

समया, 1, *more prop.* **समय**, *q.v.*: 2, within, in the midst, amidst; near: at a fixed time, in due time, seasonably.

समयात्री, *m.* (*f.* iṇi) a fellow-traveller.

समयानुगामी, *adj.* going according to the time, timeserving: hence *m.* (*f.* ini) a timeserver.

समर, *m.* conflict, battle, war: evening conversations: night, darkness: time: a vestibule: an adventure, mishap. — *k.* to make war, to fight.

समरण, 1, *more prop.* **स्मरण**, *q.v.*: 2, *m.* a coming together, approach; conflict, combat.

समरतरंग, *m.* a sharp conflict.

समरत्थ
समरथ } (*colloquialisms*) = **समर्थ**, *q.v.*

समरभूमि, *f.* a scene of war, battle-field.

समररस, *m.* heroic principle or sentiment, warlike spirit.

समरूत (*dialectic*) = **सामर्थ्य**, *q.v.*

समरून = **ग्रोमिरोन**, *q.v.*

समर्ज, (in Math.) parallel.

समर्थ, 1, a contraction of **सामर्थ्य**, *q. v.*: 2, *m.* (*f.* ā) able, capable, fit, proper, adequate; connected in sense: 3, *m.* the construction of words.

समर्थक, *m.* aloe-wood (*Amyris agallocha*).

समर्थता, *f.* (*m.* °त्व) strength, power, ability, capability, adequacy; prowess; maturity, puberty; the signification of terms.

समर्थी, *m.* (*f.* iṇi) a contraction of **सामर्थी**, *q. v.*

समर्पण, *m.* delivering, handing over, consigning, entrusting, committing, surrendering.

समर्पना, *t.* to deliver up to, hand over, consign, entrust, commit, surrender.

समर्पित, *m.* (*f.* ā) delivered up, made over, consigned, entrusted, surrendered.

समर्पे, entrusted to, delivered over to.

समर्य्याद, *m.* (*f.* ā) limited, bounded; proximate, contiguous, near; keeping within bounds, correct in conduct, respectful.

समल, 1 *m* (*f.* ā) dirty, muddy, filthy; *met.* sinful, polluted: 2 *m.* ordure.

समला, a crop which, after having been checked, has recovered.

समवृत, *m.* (in Pros.) species of metre in which all the four feet are equal.

समशान (*colloquial*) = **श्मशान**, *q. v.*

समसिया, *more prop.* **समस्या**, *q. v.*

समस्त, 1, thrown together, composed, compounded; abridged; entire, all, whole, complete: 2. *m.* a whole.

समस्या, *f.* the part of a stanza given to a person to complete it (as a trial of skill); the giving a person part of a stanza and requiring him to complete it.

समस्व, 1, *m.* equality in wealth: 2, *m.* (*f.* ā) *adj.* possessing equal wealth.

समस्वभावी, *m.* (*f.* ini) *adj.* possessing equal wealth.

समस्थान, *m.* the horizon.

समा, 1, (*colloquial*) = **समय**, *q. v.*: 2, *f.* a year: 3, *m.* the heavens, firmament, sky; a canopy; altitude.

समाई, 1, (*colloquial*) = **समय**, *q. v.*: 2, *f.* endurance, patience, firmness: power, capability, capacity. — *bōt*, hearsay.

समाउ, any vessel in which fire is kept.

समां (*colloquial*) = **समय**, *q. v.*

समाख्या, *f.* fame, notoriety, reputation, name.

समाख्यात, famed, notorious, celebrated, public.

समागत, 1, *m.* (*f.* ā) arrived, come, approached, met, encountered, assembled, united, joined: 2, *m.* arrival, assembly, meeting.

समागति, *f.* = **समागम**, *q. v.*

समागम, *m.* arrival, approach; meeting, encountering; union, joining, assembly, junction, association, acquaintance, intercourse; similar condition or progress.

समाचार, 1, *m.* (*f.* ā) equal or like in virtuous conduct; 2. *m.* proper practice or conduct, proceeding, conduct; going; way: information, notice, report, intelligence, news, tidings, message, advices, account of circumstances, health, etc.; an occurrence.

समाचारदायक, *m.* (*f.* ikā) a herald, intelligencer, courier, newsman.

समाचारपत्र, *m.* a newspaper.

समाचारलिखक, *m.* (*f.* ikā) a news-writer.

समाज, *m.* a multitude, number, assembly, meeting, a convivial meeting; society; equipage; the abode of a respectable community; an elephant.

समाजत, 1, *f* deformity; shamefulness; turpitude; adulteration; entreaty; humiliation: 2, deformed, filthy, base.

समाजी, *f.* (?) musicians that attend to dancers.

समादर, *m.* reverence, veneration, respect.

समाध, a contraction of **समाधि**, *q. v.*

समाधान, *m.* religious abstraction as practised by Hindoo ascetics (*i. e.* restraining the senses by confining the mind to contemplation on the true nature of spirit), meditation, contemplation; promising, declaring; adjustment, decision, determination; the act of satisfying, propitiating, pacification, comfort, consolation, solace.

समाधि, *m.* (*f*, ?) a putting together, composing or reconciling differences, the laying up a store of grain; an agreement, promise, engagement, vow, a religious vow or obligation; requital; silence: profound meditation, contemplation, devotion: a burial, tomb, grave; the joint of the neck; the attempting impossibilities: demonstrated conclusion. The term is particularly applied to the practice among Hindoo ascetics (*yogī*) of being buried alive; also to the tomb in which such a person is buried. It is also applied to that exercise of austerity among Hindoo ascetics whereby they are believed to acquire the power of suspending, during their own pleasure, the connexion between their body and soul.

समाधिस्थान, *m.* a buryingplace, cemetery.

समाधी, absorbed in contemplation, meditative: hence, *m.* (*f.* inī) a thoughtful person.

समाध्यक्ष, *m.* (*f.* ī) an overseer, superintendent.

समान, 1. *m.* (*f.* ā *or* ī) like, similar, equal, akin, alike, the same, one, uniform; adequate; good, virtuous, honoured: 2, *f.* (?) equality, level, rank: 3, *m.* one of the vital airs (*viz.* that one which is essential to digestion). *Tu merī samānkā nahīn*, thou art not my equal.—*k.* to proportion.

समानकालीन, appertaining to the same period.

समानचित्त, *m.* (*f.* ā) of an equitable or even disposition.

समानजन्मा, *m. f.* of equal age.

समानता, *f.* (*m.* °त्व) community of kind or quality, sameness, equality, likeness, resemblance, similarity.

समानवयस्क, *m.* (*f.* ā *or* ī) of equal age.

समाना, 1, *f.* (*m.* **समान**) a female friend or equal, etc.: 2, to be contained in, to go into: *e. g. Itnā pānī is bartanmen samāwegā*, this vessel will hold thus much of water.

समानान्तर, parallel.

समानी, *f.* 1, = **समाना**, 1, *q. v.*: 2, (in Pros.) a species of metre: 3, (in Gram.) neuter (as a verb).

समानु (*poet.*) = **समान**, *q. v.*

समापन, *m.* conclusion, completion, finishing: a section, chapter: profound meditation: acquisition: killing.

समापन्न } = **समाप्त**, *q. v.*
समापित }

समाप्त, *m.* (*f.* ā) completed, concluded, accomplished, finished, done, perfected: skilful.

समाप्ति, *f.* completion, finishing, accomplishment, end, conclusion, finis: putting an end to disputes, reconciling differences.

समाभिव्याहार, a corruption **समभिव्याहार**, *q. v.*

समार, crop-ploughing.

समारना, *t.* to relinquish: to prepare, decorate, adorn, ornament, beautify (?).

समारिया, *more prop.* **शामियान**, *q. v.*

समारी, *more prop.* **समाली**, *q. v.*

समारोह, *m.* ascending, riding upon; agreeing; concourse, crowd; magnificence, grandeur, pomp.

समारोहण, *m.* an ascending, riding upon; an agreeing.

समारोही, *m.* (*f.* inī) magnificent, grand, pompous.

समालना (*colloquial*) = **सम्भालना**, *q. v.*

समाली, *f.* a collection of flowers, a nosegay, etc.

समालू, *m.* a certain plant (*Vitex trifolia* or V. *negundo*) called also *me,orī*.

समाव, *m.* room, space.

समावी, celestial, heavenly.

समावेश, *m.* entrance; possession by evil spirits: affection, passion.

समास, *m.* aggregation, assemblage; contraction, abridgement; conciseness; (in Gram.) the composition of words, formation of compounds; a compound word.

समाहत, *f.* benevolence, liberality.

समित, *f.* battle, conflict, war: fuel: a kind of herb.

समिता, *f.* wheaten flour.

समिति, *f.* meeting, union; assembly, company; sameness, likeness, equality; war, conflict, battle.

समिध, *f.* material for kindling a fire, fuel, wood, grass.

समिर, *m.* air, wind.

समी, 1, *more prop.* **शमी**, *q. v.*: 2, *m.* a namesake.

समीक, *m.* war, battle, conflict: a pike, dart.

समीकरण, *m.* equalizing, assimilation, digestion; (in Arithm.) equation, the reducing fractions to a common denominator.

समीका, *more prop.* (1) **समीक** (2) **समीक्षा**, *qq. v.*

समीकार, *m.* } = **समीकरण**, *q. v.*
समीक्रिया, *f.* }

समीक्ष, *m. pr. n.* the Sānkhya system of philosophy.

समीक्षा, *f.* investigation, search, inspection, looking, sight; understanding, intellect; essential nature.

समीच, *m.* the ocean.

समीची, *f.* a doe.

समीचीन, 1, correct, accurate, right, proper, fit, true: 2, *m.* truth, reality.

समीत, *more prop.* **समित**, *q. v.*

समीती, *more prop.* **समिति**, *q. v.*

समीप, 1, proximate, neighbouring, contiguous, near, at hand: 2, *postp* (takes gen. *m.* infl.) near to, close by: 3, *m.* vicinity, proximity, neighbourhood.

समीपता, *f.* proximity, contiguousness.

समीपी, *f.* contiguity, proximity, vicinity: 2, *m.* (*f.* in *or* inī) a neighbour.

समीर, *m.* air, wind.

समीहा, *f.* (?) modesty, reserve: effort, exertion.

समुंद (*colloquial*) = **समुद्र**, *q. v.*

समुचा, *m.* (*f.* ī) entire, whole; complete, full.

समुचित, fit, right, appropriate, suitable, proper.

समुच्चय, *m.* assemblage, collection, accumulation, aggregate; (in Gram.) conjunction of words and sentences.

समुच्चयबोधक, *m.* (in Gram.) any word denoting connexion, a conjunction: lit. *adj.* importing conjunction, conjunctive.

समुच्चायक, *m.* (*f.* ikā) accumulative, collective, conjunctive.

समुझना, *more prop.* **समझना**, *q. v.*

समुझाना, *more prop.* **समझाना**, *q. v.*

समुझावल in Braj = (1) **समझाया** (2) **समझावा**, *qq. v.*

समुझि, 1, *more com.* **समझ**, *q. v.*: 2, see **समुझना**.

समुझेऊँ, an old form = **मैंने समझा**.

समुत्पत्ति, *f.* origin, production, formation, birth; occurrence, existence.

समुत्पन्न, *m.* (*f.* ā) born, produced.

समुत्सव, *m.* festivity.

समुदय, *m.* ascent, rise, rising (as of the sun) : a day : effort : revenue : a multitude, quantity, number, heap ; totality, a whole : war, battle : the rear or reserve of an army : *adj.* together, collected.

समुदाई, *more prop.* समुदाय, *q.v.*

समुदाय = समुदय, *q.v.*

समुद्र, 1, *m.* the sea, ocean : 2, *m.* (*f.* ā) sealed.

समुद्रकफ = समुद्रफेन, *q.v.*

समुद्रगामी, sea-going, sea-faring : hence, *m.* (*f.* inī) a sailor, sea-farer, mariner.

समुद्रतट } *m.* the sea-coast, the shore.
समुद्रतीर }

समुद्रदत्त, *m.* (*f.* ā) given or yielded by the sea (an epithet of anything obtained from the sea).

समुद्रफेन, *m.* the dorsal scale or bone of the cuttle-fish (*Sepia officinalis*) : *lit.* ocean-froth.

समुद्रलवण, *m.* sea-salt.

समुद्रवह्नि, *m.* submarine fire.

समुद्रसोख, *m.* a certain medicine (*Convolvulus argentius*).

समुद्रा, *more prop.* समुद्र, 1, *q.v.*

समुद्रान्त, *m.* the sea-shore : *adv.* as far as the sea.

समुद्रान्ता, *f.* the cotton-plant ; a certain gramineous plant (*Trigonella corniculata*) ; a certain shrub (*Hedysarum alhagi*).

समुद्रारु, *m.* a shark ; a large fabulous fish (perhaps the whale, hyperbolically described) : Rām's bridge.

समुद्रिक, *m.* (*f.* ī) a contraction of सामुद्रिक, *q.v.*

समुद्रिय, *m.* (*f.* ā) } *more com.* समुद्रीय, *q.v.*
समुद्री, *m.* (*f.* iṇī) }

समुद्रीय, *m.* (*f.* ā) marine, oceanic, maritime.

समुन्द ; see (1) समन्द (2) समुद्र (3) समुन्दन.

समुन्दन, *m.* moisture, wetness.

समुन्दर (*colloquial*) = समुद्र, *q.v.*

समुन्दरफल, *m.* a certain medicine.

समुन्दरफेन (*colloquial*) = समुद्रफेन, *q.v.*

समुन्दरसार ; see समुद्रफेन.

समुन्दरसोख } (*colloquial*) = समुद्रसोख, *q.v.*
समुन्दरसोग }

समुन्द्र (*colloquial*) = समुद्र, *q.v.*

समुहाना, *n.* to be in the presence of, be before, be fronting or facing, be present.

समुहानी (*Rām.*) = (1) समुहाई (2) समुहाना, *qq.v.*

समुहाया, *m.* (*f.* समुहाई) in the presence of, before, fronting, facing.

समू, *more prop.* (1) समय (2) समूह, *qq.v.*

समूएल, *m. pr. n.* the prophet Samuel or the Books that bear his name.

समूचा, *m.* (*f.* ī) *more prop.* समुचा, *q.v.*

समूढ़, *m.* (*f.* ā) brought together, collected, accumulated, assembled, associated, accompanying, enveloped ; produced quickly ; crooked, bent ; tamed, tranquillized ; purified, cleansed.

समूम, *f.* a hot pestilential wind (commonly called the Simoom).

समूर, *m.* a weasel, marten, sable ; sable-skin, fur.

समूल, roots and all, by the roots, completely, utterly.

समूह, *m.* assemblage, multitude, number, heap, quantity, aggregate, troop.

समूहक, appertaining to an assemblage or to a whole.

समूहन, *m.* collection, plenty.

समूहनी, *f.* a broom, besom.

समृत्ति (*Rām.*) = स्मृति, *q.v.*

समृद्धि, *f.* increase, thriving, prosperity, success, greatness, power, supremacy, wealth.

समै } *more prop.* समय, *q.v.*
समैं }

समेट, *f.* contraction ; an astringent, a medicine used by females ad constringendam vulvam.

समेटना, *t.* to cause to shrink or shrivel, to constringe, compress, contract, brace, to collect together, fold up, amass, hoard.

समेत, 1, *adj.* assembled, collected, associated with : 2, *adv.* together with, along with, with.

समेते, 1, *more prop.* समेत, 2 : 2, in Braj = समयसे.

समै }
समैं }
समैया } *more prop.* समय, *q.v.*
समो }
समों }

समैक ; see (1) समयक (2) सम्यक.

समोना, *t.* to cool warm water by mixing it with cold water, to make lukewarm.

सम्पत, 1, (*contraction*) = सम्पत्ति, *q.v.* : 2, = सम्पद, *q.v.*

सम्पतनौं in Chand = to arrive.

सम्पत्ति, *f.* prosperity, increase of wealth, opulence, success, wealth ; happiness ; power : a certain medicinal root.

सम्पत्तिवान, prosperous, wealthy : hence, *m.* (*f.* vatī) a wealthy person.

सम्पद, *f.* increase, success, prosperity, blessing, wealth ; advancement in good qualities, accomplishment, excellence, distinction, perfection : power : adornment : fate : a necklace of pearls : a treasure.

सम्पदा, *more prop.* सम्पद, *q.v.*

सम्पदारी, *m.* (*f.* iṇī) a devotee of prosperity and success.

सम्पन्न, *m.* (*f.* ā) prosperous, thriving, successful, fortunate, happy : accomplished, completed, effected ; obtained : *in comp.* = possessed of, endowed with.

सम्पन्नता, *f.* prosperousness, success ; completion.

सम्पर्क, *m.* mingling, mixture ; contact, junction, union, copulation ; relationship, connexion.

सम्परना, to become captive.

सम्पात, *m.* 1, concurrence, meeting, falling, descending, butting, lighting, flashing, going, moving : 2, *pr. n.* a certain fabulous bird (eldest son of Garuṛ, and elder brother of Jaṭāya).

सम्पाति, *m. pr. n.* = सम्पात, 2, *q.v.*

सम्पादक, *m.* (*f.* ikā) a causer, an agent, an officer, an editor : lit. *adj.* causing, producing, accomplishing, effecting.

सम्पादन, *m.* a gaining, acquiring, attaining, effecting, accomplishing, making ; cleansing.

सम्पादित, accomplished, effected, brought about, attained, obtained, gained, gotten.

सम्पारना, *t.* to complete a work already begun.

सम्पारा, *m.* (*f.* ī) *more com.* **सम्पेरा**, *q. v.*

सम्पुट, *m.* a cavity; the closely shutting any cavity; a box with its lid shut; a casket; a certain flower (commonly called *kuruvak*).

सम्पूर्ण, *m.* (*f.* ā) completed, finished; full; whole, entire, perfect: hence, *m.* (in Music) a tune in which all the notes of the gamut are employed. [tion.

सम्पूर्णता, *f.* (*m.*°**त्व**) fulness, completeness, perfec-

सम्पूर्णम (Sk.) = **सम्पूर्ण**, *q. v.* [er, snake-keeper.

सम्पेरा, *m.* (*f.* ī *or* in) a snake-catcher, snake-charm-

सम्पेला, *m.* (*f.* ī) a young snake just hatched.

सम्पोला, *m.* (*f.* ī) }
सम्पोलिया, *m.* or *f.* } = **सम्पेला**, *q. v.*

सम्प्रति, at this present time, now.

सम्प्रदान, *m.* a giving, bestowing; a gift, donation; the person to whom a thing is given; (in Gram.) the Dative case.

सम्प्रदाय, *m.* traditional doctrine regarded as of divine authority; a peculiar doctrine and exclusive worship of one divinity: a sect, band, company.

सम्प्रसाधन, *m.* an effecting, accomplishing, performing well or completely.

सम्प्रस्थान, *m.* a setting out on a journey.

सम्प्राप्त, *m.* (*f.* ā) attained, obtained, gotten.

सम्प्राप्ति, *f.* getting, obtaining, acquiring.

सम्प्रीत, *m.* (*f.* ā) well-pleased, delighted. [light.

सम्प्रीति, *f.* attachment, friendliness, affection, de-

सम्बंध = **सम्बन्ध**, *q. v.*

सम्बत, *more prop.* **संवत**, *q. v.*

सम्बन्ध, *m.* connexion, affinity, relation, union, relationship (by birth or by marriage), the having reference or relation to anything: (in Pros.) rhyme, metre; (in Gram.) the genitive or possessive case.

सम्बन्धता, *f.* connectedness, relatedness, unitedness.

सम्बन्धवाचक, (in Gram.) relative.

सम्बन्धवान, (in Gram.) genitival, possessive.

सम्बन्धसूचक, (in Gram.) construed with the genitive case, governing (or pointing out) the genitive case.

सम्बन्धी, connected with, belonging to, inhe.ent, relating to, related: hence, *m.* (*f.* inī) a relation by marriage, relative, kinsman; a son or daughter's father-in-law.

सम्बर, *m.* a mountain: a sort of deer: a fish: war: water: a religious observance: *pr. n.* a certain demon.

सम्बल, *m.* provender or stock for travelling expen-

सम्बाद, *more prop.* **संवाद**, *q.v.* [ses: water.

सम्बुक, *more prop.* **शम्बूक**, *q.v.* [Vocative case.

सम्बुद्धि, *f.* a calling, calling to; (in Gram.) the

सम्बुल, maidenhair.

सम्बु, much.

सम्बोधन, *m.* a call, calling, calling to, addressing; (in Gram.) the Vocative case: the act of consoling, comfort, soothing, encouragement.

सम्भ, *more prop.* **शम्भु**, *q. v.*

सम्भलना, *n.* to be supported or sustained, be propped, be erected; to be firm; *a. int.* to recover oneself from a fall, to stand, to stop.

सम्भलाना (by inversion) = **सम्भालना**, *q. v.*

सम्भव, *m.* mixing, union; appropriateness, adaptation, capacity; possibility, probability, compatibility, consistency, agreement; acquaintance: destruction, loss: origin, birth, production, rearing: cause, motive: *adj.* possible, probable, likely, suitable, proper, fit, right. [partaker, shareholder.

सम्भागी, *m.* (*f.* inī) a sharer, partner, participator,

सम्भारना, *more com.* **सम्भालना**, *q. v.*

सम्भालना, *t.* to support, sustain, hold up, prop; to maintain; to assist, help; to moderate; to shield, protect, stop, retain, restrain, check, repress.

सम्भावन, *m.* = **सम्भावना**, *q. v.*

सम्भावना, *f.* adequacy, competency, suitableness, ability, fitness, probability, possibility; considering, reflecting, thought, doubt; review; worship, honour; love: (in Gram.) the potential mode.

सम्भावनीय = **सम्भाव्य**, *q. v.*

सम्भावित, possible, probable, conjectured.

सम्भावितपुत्रा, *f.* a woman who is believed likely to become the mother of male issue.

सम्भाव्य, suitable, fit, possible, probable.

सम्भाव्यभविष्यत, (in Gram.) the doubtful or dependent future tense: *e. g. Main jātā hoūn*, I may perhaps go, it may be that I shall go.

सम्भाषण, *m.* conversation, intercourse; sexual intercourse; watch-cry, watch-word.

सम्भु, *m.* a parent, progenitor. [ed, born.

सम्भूत, *m.* (*f.* ā) sprung from, produced, originat-

सम्भूति, *f.* combination; birth, origin, production.

सम्भूमनु, *more prop.* **स्वयंभूमनु**, *q. v.*

सम्भृति, *f.* support, nourishment; preparation, provision; fulness, plenitude.

सम्भोग, *m.* enjoyment, pleasure, delight; sensual enjoyment; copulation: use, occupation: a catamite.

सम्भोगी, *m* (*f.* inī) a sensualist, etc.: lit. *adj.* enjoying; possessing: sensual; cohabiting.

सम्भोजन, 1, *m.* (*f.* ī) convivial: 2, *m.* a meal taken together, a convivial party.

सम्भ्रम, *m.* a turning round, revolving; confusion (arising from fear, joy, haste, etc.), alarm; error; ignorance: reverence, awe, honour, esteem, respect.

सम्भर्ई, *f.* the pipe of a drill-plough (generally made of a hollow bamboo).

सम्मत; for words beginning thus, see under the

सम्मन्ध, *more prop.* **सम्बन्ध**, *q. v.* [form **संमत**, *q. v.*

सम्मय, *more prop.* **समय**, *q. v.*

सम्मान, **सम्मुख**; for words beginning thus, see under the forms **संमान**, **संमुख**, respectively.

सम्मित, measured, meted: of equal measure or extent, like, similar, same. [ed.

सम्मुग्ध, fascinated, bewildered, stupefied, astound-

सम्मोद, *m.* pleasure, delight.

सम्मोह, *m.* fascination, beguilement, stupefaction, fainting, illusion. folly, ignorance.

सम्मोहित, *m.* (*f.* ā) overcome with delight, enraptured, fascinated. beguiled.

सम्यक, along with, together; all, wholly, entirely, thoroughly; in the right manner. properly. fitly, well.

सम्यकबोध, *m.* wisdom or intelligence that is good or befitting. omniscience.

सम्युक्ति, a corruption of **संयुक्ति**, *q. v.*

सम्सार, 1, a corruption of **संसार**, *q.v.*: 2, *m.* a household. family, tribe.—*k.* to live, domesticate oneself, provide for self and family.

सम्हारना, *more com.* **सम्भालना**, *q. v.*

सम्हाल; see (1) **संहार** (2) **सम्भाल**.

सम्हालना (*colloquial*) = **सम्भालना**, *q.v.*

सय, *more prop.* (1) **सई** (2) **से**, *qq. v.*

सयन (*Rām.*) = (1) **शयन** (2) **सैन** (3) **सेवन**, *qq. v.*

सयल in Chand = **शैल**, *q. v.*

सयान, *m.* shrewdness, cunning, artfulness, sagacity, cleverness, maturity.

सयानप, *m.* the condition of being mature, cunning, or clever; knowledge.

सयानपन } **सयानपना** } = **सयानप**, *q. v.*

सयाना, *m.* (*f.* ī) a knowing person, conjuror, etc.: *lit.* shrewd, cunning, artful, sagacious, knowing, prudent, clever, sly: grown up, mature, of age, marriageable. *Thoremen sayāne jānte hain* (= 'verbum sap.') a word to the wise is enough.

सयौवन, one who is experiencing the time or the condition of youth.

सय्या, *f.* a bed, couch, sofa.

सर, 1, *m.* (*f.* ī) *more prop.* **शर**, *q.v.*: 2, *m.* a pond, tank, pool, lake: a going, motion: the coagulum of curds or milk, cream: salt, saltness: a waterfall; water: the head, top, pinnacle; origin, beginning; point, intention, end, aim, will, desire, love: 3, *in comp.* [*m.* (*f.* ā or ī)] *adj.* going, moving.—*k.* to perform, complete.

सरंग, a contraction of **सरङ्ग**, *q.v.*

सरंजाम = **सरनजाम**, *q. v.*

सरंदद्वीप, *more pr p.* **सरान्द्वीप**, *q. v.*

सरक, *m.* a continuous line of road: spirituous liquor; spirit-drinking; distribution of spirits: a drinking-vessel: going: a lake: heaven: a noose; a snare.

सरकटा, *m.* (*f.* ī) decapitated, headless.

सरकड़ा, *m.* a kind of reed (*Saccharum procerum*, Roxb.) of which mats are made.

सरकण्डा = **सरकड़ा**, *q. v.*

सरकना, *n.* to be moved: *a. int.* to move, stir, budge, remove, get out of the way, get along.

सरकफांसी, *f.* a noose.

सरकवाना, *t.* to cause to be removed.

सरकशी, *f.* disobedience, rebellion, revolt, mutiny,

सरकाना, *t.* to move out of the way, put on one side, remove.

सरकार, 1, *f.* the king's court, the Government: a business firm: estate, property: 2, *m.* a superintendent. The term is also applied as a title of respect to a person whether he be present or absent = Your Highness, His Highness, Your Honor, etc.

सरकारकम्पनी, *f.* the British-Indian Government.

सरकारी, 1, appertaining to an estate, establishment, firm, or Government: 2, *f.* superintendence.

सरख़त, *m.* an agreement to hire service; a certificate of service performed; a bill of sale.

सरखप = **सर्षप**, *q. v.*

सरख़ुद, independent, one's own master.

सरग, a Prākṛit form of **स्वर्ग**, *q.v.*

सरगरदानी, *f.* distress, confusion, amazement, stupefaction.

सरगर्म, intent on, attentive; inflamed with love.

सरगुज़श्त, *f.* an event, accident, transaction, account of circumstances.

सरगुण (*contraction*) = **सर्वगुण**, *q. v.*

सरघा, *f.* a bee.

सरचापधर, *m.* (*f.* ā or ī) the holder of the bow and arrow; *hence*, an archer.

सरचापधारी, *m.* (*f.* inī) = **सरचापधर**, *q. v.*

सरज, *m.* fresh butter: a saddle.

सरजक = **सृजक**, *q. v.*

सरजदेव, a corruption of **सूर्य्यदेव**, *q. v.*

सरज़मीन, *f.* the earth; region, country; confines.

सरजाति, *m. pr. n.* a certain ancient Hindoo king.

सरजु } **सरजू** } *more prop.* **सरयू**, *q.v.*

सरज़ोरी, *f.* disobedience, rebellion, mutiny.

सरट, *m.* air, wind; a cloud; a lizard, chameleon, guana.

सरटा, a lizard, chameleon, guana.

सरटि, *m.* wind: a cloud.

सरण (*colloquial*) = **शरण**, *q. v.*

सरणा, *f.* a certain plant (*Pœderia fetida*).

सरणागत (*colloquial*) = **शरणागत**, *q. v.*

सरणि, *f.* a path, road; a straight or continuous line: a certain disease of the throat.

सरणी, *f.* = (1) **सरणा** (2) **सरणि**, *qq. v.*

सरण्ड, *m.* a bird: a rogue; a kind of ornament.

सरण्यु, *m.* air, wind; water; a cloud.

सरत (*colloquial*) = **शरत**, *q. v.*

सरतबरत = **शर्तबर्त**, *q. v.*

सरतान, *m.* a crab; the sign Cancer; a cancer; a certain disease incident to the feet of cattle.

सरताब, refractory, disobedient.

सरद, 1, = **शरद**, *q. v.*: 2, cold, damp, cool.

सरदकाल, *m.* the cold season, winter.

सरदचन्द्र, *m.* the autumnal moon.

सरदा, *m.* a kind of musk-melon, a water-melon.

सरदार, *m.* a head man, chief, leader, master.

सरदी, *f.* a cold; coldness, dampness; the cold, cold weather, the cold season.

सरन; for words beginning thus, but not given below, see under the form **शरण**.

सरनजाम, *m.* apparatus, utensils, materials, furniture, goods and chattels, ingredients; necessaries; conclusion, end, accomplishment.—*k.* to conclude, finish, to prepare, to manage.

सरना, 1, corruption of **शरण**, *q.v.*: 2, *n.* to be performed, be carried on; to be ended: *a.int.* to issue.

सरनाई (*Rām.*) = **सिरनाई**, *q.v.*

सरनामा, *m.* title, address, superscription.

सरन्हि, an old pl. of **सर**. See **न्हि**.

सरप (*colloquial*) = **सर्प**, *q.v.*

सरपट, *f.* galloping: *adv.* glibly: *adj.* level.—*dauṛnā* or *phenknā*, to set off in a gallop.—*dauṛānā*, to put one's horse to a gallop.

सरपत, *m.* a kind of reed (*Saccharum procerum*, Roxb.) of which mats are made.

सरपता = **सरपत**, *q.v.*

सरपर्दा, *m.* a certain musical mode supposed to have been published by Amir Khusraw of Delhi.

सरपि (*Rām.*) = **सर्पिस**, *q.v.*

सरपेंच, 1, *m.* head-dress, head-gear, a diadem; a turban; an ornament (of gold, silver, or jewels) worn in front of a turban.

सरपोश, *m.* a lid, cover.

सरफत; see **सरपत**.

सरफ़राज़, exalted, eminent, distinguished.

सरफ़राज़ी, *f.* eminence, exaltation, promotion, distinction.

सरफोड़ी, *f.* labour in vain.

सरब, an old form = **सर्व**, *q. v.*

सरबर (*colloquial*) = **सरोवर**, *q. v.*

सरबराह, *f.* supply, travelling-expenses.—*kār*, a commissary of supplies.

सरबस (*colloquial*) = **सर्वस्व**, *q. v.*

सरबसर, all, the whole, entirely.

सरबसु (*colloquial*) = **सर्वस्व**, *q. v.*

सरबस्ती, *m.* (*f.* inī) omnipresent.

सरबाज़ी, *f.* intrepidity, recklessness of life.

सरबासोधी, *f.* massacre.

सरम, 1, in Chand = **श्रम**, *q. v.*: 2, the ridge-pole of a house.

सरमग़ज़न, *m.* trouble, perplexity, vexation, fatigue, labour.

सरमजाम, *more prop.* **सरनजाम**, *q. v.*

सरमण्डल, *m.* a kind of musical instrument.

सरमा, 1, the cold season, winter: 2, *f. pr. n.* (1) of the bitch of the gods (2) of the daughter of Daksh (3) of the wife of Rāvaṇ's brother.

सरमाया, *m.* stock-in-trade, capital.

सरमिंदा, *more prop.* **शर्मिन्दा**, *q. v.*

सरमिष्टा, *f. pr. n.* (prop. **शर्मिष्ठा**) one of the wives of Yayāti (she was daughter of Vṛishparvan and mother of Puru).

सरमुख (*corruption*) = **संमुख**, *q. v.*

सरयाति, *more prop.* (1) **शर्याति** (2) **सरजाति**, *qq. v.*

सरयु, 1, *f.* = **सरयू**, *q. v.*: 2, *m.* air, wind.

सरयू, *f. pr. n.* a certain sacred river in Oude. It is in this river that Rām-Chandra is said to have drowned himself.

सरल, 1, (*Rām.*) = **सड़ा**, *q. v.*: 2, *m.* (*f.* ā) straight, perpendicular, tall, upright, honest, artless, sincere, simple, ingenuous, candid: 3, *m.* a certain beautiful bird (*Pavo bicalcarata*); a sort of pine (*Pinus longifolia*).

सरलता, *f.* (*m.* °**त्व**) uprightness, rectitude, sincerity, ingenuousness, simplicity, candour, honesty.

सरलचित्त, *m.* (*f.* ā) of an artless or straightforward disposition.

सरलमन = **सरलचित्त**, *q. v.*

सरला, *f.* (*m.* **सरल**) an ingenuous female, etc.: a variety of the *teori*-plant.

सरलान्तःकरण, 1, *m.* an upright mind, an honest heart: 2, *m.* (*f.* ī) a person of an honest mind or of an upright heart: 3, *m.* a chief, principal, leader.

सरवर, 1, a contraction of **सरोवर**, *q. v.*: 2, equal:

सरवरि (*Rām.*); see (1) **शर्वरी** (2) **बराबरी**.

सरवरी (*Rām.*) = **शर्वरी**, *q. v.*

सरवस / **सरवसु** } (*colloquial*) = **सर्वस्व**, *q. v.*

सरवा = **सर्वा**, *q. v.*

सरवां (Sk.), all, every.

सरवान, *more prop.* **सारबान**, *q. v.*

सरवैया, *m.* a mender.

सरशारी, *f.* fulness, redundance, intoxication.

सरश्वती, *more prop.* **सरस्वती**, *q. v.*

सरस, 1, *m.* a large pond, a large sheet of water in which the lotus grows, a tank, pool, lake: 2, best, excellent, prime; beautiful, charming, agreeable: more, abundant, plenty; new: impassioned: 3, beyond measure, much; overmuch, over, more.

सरसई (*Rām.*) = **सरस्वती**, *q. v.*

सरसठ, *more com.* **सतसठ**, *q. v.*

सरसत in Mārwāṛī = **सरस्वती**, *q. v.*

सरसब्ज़ी, *f.* verdure, greenness; prosperity, happiness.

सरसर, *f.* the noise made by a snake when creeping.

सरसराट (*contraction*) = **सरसराहट**, *q. v.*

सरसराना, *a.int.* to creep along as a snake, to make the noise a snake does when creeping.

सरसराहट, *f.* a creeping sensation, titillation; the noise made by a snake when creeping.

सरसरी, easy, feasible, facile, careless.

सरसा = **सरस**, *q. v.*

सरसार, high.

सरसाई, *f.* increase, abundance, excess; excellence, majority, plurality.

सरसि; see **सिरस**.

सरसिज, *m.* a lotus, water-lily.

सरसी, *f.* a large pond, tank, pool, lake; a piece of water in which the lotus grows: (in Pros.) a species of metre.

सरसीरुह, *m.* a lotus, water-lily.

सरसुती, *more prop.* **सरस्वती**, *q. v.*

सरसो = **सरसों**, *q. v.*

सरसों, *f.* a certain species of mustard-seed or plant (*Sinapis dichotoma*, Roxb.)

सरस्वत, *m.* (*f.* vatī) = **सरस्वन्त**, *q. v.*

सरस्वन्त, 1, *m.* (*f.* vatī) juicy, sapid; elegant; sentimental: 2, *m.* the ocean; a male river; a buffalo.

सरस्वती, *f.* 1, (*m.* **सरस्वन्त**) an excellent female: speech, eloquence: a river: a cow: 2, *pr. n.* (1) of the daughter of Brahmā, the goddess of speech and eloquence, patroness of music and the arts, and inventress of the Sanskrit language and of the Devanāgarī character (2) of the river commonly called Sarsootee. It rises in the mountains that bound the north-east part of the province of Delhi, whence it flows in a south-westerly direction and is lost in the sands of the great desert in the country of the Bhatti. According to the Hindoos, however, the river only *disappears* in this place, and, continuing its course underground, joins the Ganges and Yamunā at the junction at Allahabad.

सरहंग, *m.* a general, commander, captain, chief, myrmidon, overseer; a foot soldier; the mate of a ship (*vulg.* serāng).

सरहज, *f.* the wife of one's wife's brother.

सरहद्द, *f.* boundary, limit, confines, frontier, extremity, a boundary-mark, landmark.

सरहरी; see **सनफराई** and **सुरहुरी**.

सरा, 1, *m.* an earthen cover of a pot: 2, *f.* a caravansery, inn, halting place, temporary home for travellers; a house, a mansion: a waterfall.

सराई, *f.* 1, *more prop.* **सराय**, *q.v.*: 2, (dim. of **सरा**, 1) a small cover.

सराए, *f.* = **सरा**, 2, *q. v.*

सरांजाम = **सरनजाम**, *q. v.*

सराचा, *m.* a tent surrounded with an enclosure; an inner apartment.

सरात, *more prop.* (1) **श्राद्ध** (2) **सिरात**, *qq.v.*

सराधा, *more prop.* **श्राद्ध**, *q. v.*

सरान्दीप, *m. pr. n.* the island of Ceylon.

सराप = **शाप**, *q. v.*

सरापना = **शापना**, *q. v.*

सरापर्दा, *m.* a royal tent, a pavilion.

सरापा, 1, *m.* the whole body, the figure: 2, from head to foot, from end to end, head and ears, totally.

सराफ; for words beginning thus, see under the more proper form **सर्राफ़**.

सराब = (1) **शराब** (2) **सराव** (3) **सराह**, *qq. v.*

सराय, *more prop.* **सराए**, *q. v.*

सरालि = **शराटि**, *q. v.*

सराव (*colloquial*) = **सराव**, *q. v.*

सरावक (*colloquial*) = **श्रावक**, *q. v.*

सरावगी, *f.* a certain sect of Hindoos founded by Jayandev.

सरावन, 1, *more prop.* **श्रावण**, *q.v.*: 2, *m.* a harrow.

सरासन (*colloquial*) = **शरासन**, *q. v.*

सरासर, all, the whole, entirely, head and ears, in toto.

सरासरी, *f.* a kind of ornament that goes all around the head; summary.—*k.* or *banānā*, to perform anything in a hurry.

सरासुर, *m.* an epithet of Vāṇāsur.

सराह, *f.* praise, commendation, eulogy.

सराहत = **सराहता है**. See **त**, 5.

सराहन, *m.* the act of praising, praise, eulogy, panegyric, commendation.

सराहना, 1, *f.* = **सराहन**, *q. v.*: 2, *t.* to praise, eulogize, applaud, celebrate, commend, approve.

सराहहि, (pl. °हिं) } old forms = **सराहता है** (**सराहना**).
सराहही, (pl. °हीं) }

सराहि; (1) **सराह** (2) **सराहत** (3) **सराहना**.

सराहिय (*Rām.*) = **सराहो** (**सराहना**).

सराहिये, (poet.) it is necessary or right to praise.

सराहिहहि, (pl. °हिं) } old forms = **सराहेगा** (**सराहना**).
सराहिहही, (pl. °हीं) }

सराहो; see (1) **सराह** (2) **सराहत** (3) **सराहना**.

सरि, *m. f.* (?) a waterfall; a river.

सरिगम, *m.* the gamut; sol-faïng, sol-mization.

सरित, *f.* a river; thread; a clue.

सरितवर = **सरिद्वर**, *q. v.*

सरिता, in old Hindee = **सरित**, *q. v.*

सरितीर, *m.* the bank or margin of a river.

सरिद्वर, *m.* (the best or chief of rivers, *i.e.*) the Ganges.

सरिफ, *more prop.* **शरीफ़**, *q. v.*

सरिर, *more prop* (1) **सरीर** (2) **शरीर**, *qq. v.*

सरिरास, alike, the same.

सरिश, 1, (*Rām.*) = **सदृश**, *q.v.*: 2, *more prop.* **सरेश**, *q.v.*

सरिश्त, *f.* nature, temperament, constitution, disposition, intellect, complexion.

सरिस, 1, (*Rām.*) = **सदृश**, *q.v.*: 2, *more prop.* **सरेश**, *q.v.*

सरिस्त, *more prop.* **सरिश्त**, *q. v.*

सरी, *f.* the shaft of an arrow; a reed of which arrows are made: a waterfall: chiefship.

सरींदाप (by inversion) = **सरान्दीप**, *q. v.*

सरीका, *m.* (*f.* ī) *more com.* **सरीखा**, *q. v.*

सरीखा, *m.* a pattern: hence, *m.* (*f.* ī) like, resembling, as, that, so, such; e. g. *Ham sarikhi abalā*, such weak women as we are: *Tum sarikhe murkhoṅko pakarneke liye*, for the purpose of seizing such fools as you, i.e. "the likes of" you: *Us sarikheko mat māno*, don't heed "the likes of" him, i. e. such a fellow as that. It is sometimes used merely as an expletive or emphatic particle, and is sometimes scarcely translatable.

सरीफा, *more prop.* **शरीफ़ा**, *q. v.*

सरीर, 1, *more prop.* **शरीर**, *q.v.*: 2, *m.* a throne; a cot or bedstead: a grating, scratching (as of a pen, or of a door on rusty hinges).

सरीसो in Māṛwāṛī = chief.

सरुचि = **सुरुचि**, *q. v.*

सरुज, *m.* (*f.* ā) diseased, sickly, ill.

सरुष, *m.* (*f.* ā) wrathful, angry, furious.

सरु in Māṛwāṛī = **लिये**, *q. v.*

सरूप, 1, *more prop.* (1) **सुरूप** (2) **स्वरूप**, *qq. v.*: 2, *m.* (*f.* ā) possessing form or appearance, shapen, formed: like, resembling.—*k.* or *banānā* or *lānā*, to personate.

सरूपता, *f.* resemblance, likeness.

सरूपी, *m.* (*f.* inī) = (1) **सरूप**, 2, *q. v.*: (2) **स्वरूपी**, *q. v.*

सरे; this term is used in a sense equivalent to that of *a* or *per* in such English expressions as 'Two rupees a sér'; *e. g.* '*Sare gaz kai rūpaiye*,' How many rupees a (or per) yard?

सरेका, *m.* (*f.* ī) *more com.* **सरीखा**, *q. v.*

सरेखा, 1, *m.* (*f.* ī) *more prop.* **सरीखा**, *q.v.*: 2, *f. pr.n.* the ninth *Nakshatra* (consisting of five stars near the southern claw of Cancer): 3, *m.* (*f.* ī) cunning, sly.

सरेजमीन, *more com.* **सरज़मीन**, *q. v.*

सरेजव } **सरेजो** } *m.* shelter, protection, patronage.

सरेन (*Rām.*: Sk. instr. sing.) = **शरसे**, with an arrow.

सरेव, *m.* patronage, shelter, asylum.

सरेश, *m.* glue; starch.

सरेसाल, the beginning of the year.

सरैत, *f.* a mistress, concubine, paramour.

सरैतिन = **सरैत**, *q. v.*

सरोकार, *m.* business, intercourse.

सरोग, *m.* (*f.* ā) sick, diseased.

सरोज, *m.* the lotus: *lit.* water-born.

सरोजिनी, *f.* a female Brahman; a lotus; a multitude of lotuses; a pond abounding in lotuses.

सरोजी, *m.* (*f.* inī) an epithet of any Brāhman.

सरोतरसिह, *m.* a miser.

सरोता, *m.* a kind of scissors for cutting betel-nut; a nut-cracker.

सरोत्रा = **सरोता**, *q. v.*

सरोद, *m.* a song, modulation, melody, music.

सरोपा, 1, all, the whole: 2, *m.* a vest with which princes honour their subjects; investiture.

सरोबर, *more prop.* **सरोवर**, *q.v.*

सरोरुह, *m.* the lotus, water-lily.

सरोला, *m.* a kind of sweetmeat.

सरोवर, *m.* a large lake or pond, any piece of water deep enough for the lotus to grow in.

सरोष, *m.* (*f.* ā) angry, wrathful.

सरोसमान, *m.* apparatus, goods and chattels.

सरोही, *f.* a kind of scimitar.

सरौं (*Rām.*) = **डपड**, *q. v.*

सरौंज, *f.* a kind of seed.

सरौता = **सरोता**, *q.v.*

सर्कार = **सरकार**, *q. v.*

सर्ग, 1, *more prop.* **स्वर्ग**, *q.v.*: 2, *m.* letting go, relinquishment; creation, nature, the universe; nature, natural property: ascertainment, certainty; tendency; agreement, assent: a chapter, section; a book.

सर्गपताली, *m.* (*f.* inī) a squint-eyed person; an ox, etc. having one horn pointing upwards and the other downwards.

सर्गलोक (*colloquial*) = **स्वर्गलोक**, *q. v.*

सर्गुण (*colloquial*) = **सर्वगुण**, *q. v.*

सर्जि, *f.* = **सर्जिका**, *q. v.*

सर्जिका, *f.* natron, alkali, the impure carbonate of soda used in India instead of soap.

सर्जिकाक्षार, *m.* = **सर्जिका**, *q. v.*

सर्तबर्त = **शर्तबर्त**, *q. v.*

सर्तोल, *m.* an equal, compeer, consort.

सर्द, 1, = **शरद**, *q. v.*: 2, cold, damp, cool.

सर्दार, *m.* a head man, chief, leader.

सर्प, 1, *m.* a sliding serpentine motion: 2, *m.* (*f.* ī) a snake, serpent.

सर्पगन्धा, *f.* a certain plant (*Ophioxylon?*).

सर्पघ्न, *m.* (*f.* ī) = **सर्पहन**, *q.v.*

सर्पछत्र, *m.* a mushroom, toadstool.

सर्पज्ञ; see **सर्वज्ञ**.

सर्पनगरी, *f.* a dwellingplace of reptiles; (in Myth.) the name of several places on earth and in hell.

सर्पफणज, *m.* the snake-stone or carbuncle (a gem or pearl said to be found in the head of the snake, and resembling in form the berry of the *Abrus precatorius*, and possessing alexipharmic properties).

सर्पमणि, *m. f.* = **सर्पफणज**, *q. v.*

सर्पराज, *m.* an epithet of Vāsuki, king of the serpent-race.

सर्पहन, *m.* (*f.* ī) an epithet of the ichneumon or mongoose: *lit.* the snake-killer.

सर्पि; see (1) **सर्पिस** (2) **सर्पी**.

सर्पिस, *m.* clarified butter, ghee.

सर्पिस्तान, pap.

सर्पी, *f.* (*m.* **सर्प**) a female snake.

सर्पेच } **सर्पेश** } = **सरपेंच**, *q. v.*

सर्फराज, *more prop.* **सरफ़राज़**, *q. v.*

सर्ब, (prop. **सर्व**) all, the whole, complete.

सर्बपतन (*colloquial*) = **सर्वपतन**, *q. v.*

सर्बजान, *m.* omniscience.

सर्बभक्षी, *m.* (*f.* inī) *more prop.* **सर्वभक्षी**, *q.v.*

सर्बस, a corruption of **सर्वस्व**, *q. v.*

सर्बस } **सर्बसु** } (*colloquial*) = **सर्वस्व**, *q.v.*

सर्म; see (1) **शर्म** (2) **श्रम** (3) **सरम**.

सर्याति, *more prop.* **शर्याति**, *q. v.*

सर्राज, *m.* a saddler; a groom.

सर्राफ़, *m.* a banker, money-changer, money-jobber, officer (vulgarly called a *shroff*) employed to ascertain the value of different currencies.

सर्राफ़ा, *m.* a bank, exchange, place where bankers transact their business.

सर्राफ़ी, *f.* banking, money-changing.

सर्रिश्तादार, *m* the chief native revenue-officer in a district; a supervisor of revenue matters.

सर्रिश्ता, *m.* office, employment: connexion, affinity: a rope, thread, cord: desire.

सर्लो, *m.* (*f.* i) high.

सर्व, 1, all, the whole, entire, complete, universal, every, each: 2, an epithet (1) of Vishṇu (2) of Shiv.

सर्वकारी, *m.* an epithet of the Creator: *lit.* the maker or doer of all things.

सर्वकाल, *m.* all seasons, all times.

सर्वकालीन, appertaining to all seasons or times.

सर्वग, *m.* an epithet (1) of Brahmā (2) of Shiv (3) of soul or spirit (4) of water: *lit.* going everywhere, all-pervading, omnipresent.

सर्वगत, universally diffused, all-pervading, omnipresent.

सर्वगन्ध, *m.* a class of four aromatics, *viz.* cloves, *kakkol*, gum benjamin, and agallochum.

सर्वगुण, 1, *m.* all qualities: 2, *m.* (*f.* ā) *adj.* possessing all qualities (an epithet of the Supreme).

सर्वग्रहण } **सर्वग्रास** } *m.* a total eclipse.

सर्वग्रासी, all-devouring, omnivorous, rapacious: hence, *m.* (*f.* ini) a greedy person. [world.

सर्वजगत, *m.* (*f.* ī) the entire universe, the whole

सर्वजित, 1, *m.* (*f.* ā) all-subduing, irresistible, all-surpassing, excellent, incomparable: 2, *m.* the 21st year of the Hindoo cycle.

सर्वज्ञ, *m.* an epithet (1) of Shiv (2) of a Jain sage (3) of a certain Bauddh (4) of a certain *daitya*: *lit.* all-knowing, all-wise, omniscient.

सर्वज्ञत्व, *m.* (*f.* tā) omniscience.

सर्वज्ञानी, omniscient, all-wise.

सर्वतेजस, *m.* all-splendour, all-power, omnipotence.

सर्वतेजोमय, *m.* (*f.* ī) consisting of or containing every kind of splendour or omnipotence.

सर्वतोभद्र, good on all sides, everywhere auspicious: hence, *m.* (1) a temple or place of a square form with an entrance opposed to each point of the compass (2) a certain form of military army (3) a peculiar mystical square diagram (4) the *neem*-tree (5) a kind of charade (6) a kind of verse so contrived as to express the same meaning whether read forwards or backwards.

सर्वतोभाव, *m.* entireness, completeness, universality. [ways.

सर्वत्र, everywhere, in all places: at all times, al-

सर्वथा, in all ways, by all means; at every time; assuredly, certainly, for certain; exceedingly, entirely, completely, in every respect, in every manner, mostly.

सर्वदमन, 1, *m.* (*f.* ī) all-subduing, irresistible: 2, *m.* an epithet of Bharat, son of Shakuntalā.

सर्वदर्शक = **सर्वदर्शी**, *q.v.*

सर्वदर्शित्व, *m.* (*f.* tā) omniscience.

सर्वदर्शी, *m.* an epithet of the Supreme: *lit.* all-

सर्वदा, at all times, always. [seeing, omniscient.

सर्वदुःखक्षय, *m.* the end or destruction of all pain, *i. e.* final emancipation from separate existence.

सर्वधन, *m.* the total amount of one's wealth or property; (in Arithm.) the sum-total of a progression.

सर्वधारी, 1, *m.* an epithet of the Supreme; *lit.* all-sustaining: 2, *f.* the 22nd year of the Hindoo cycle.

सर्वनाम, *m.* (in Gram.) a pronoun or pronominal adjective. [thorough and irreversible destruction.

सर्वनाश, *m.* the destruction of all, complete ruin,

सर्वपूर्णता, *f.* entire completion or fulness, complete preparation or provision.

सर्वप्रकार, of all kinds, in all ways. [chief of all.

सर्वप्रधान, *m.* an epithet of the Most High: *lit.*

सर्वप्रिय, *m.* (*f.* ā) a much-loved or a much-loving person: *lit.* generally beloved: loving to all, generally friendly.

सर्वभक्ष, *m.* (*f.* ā) an omnivorous creature, a goat: *lit.* eating all sorts of things, all-devouring, omnivorous.

सर्वभक्षी, *m.* (*f.* ini) = **सर्वभक्ष**, *q.v.*

सर्वभाव, *m.* the entire disposition, all one's thoughts and purposes. [ed things.

सर्वभूत, *m.* all the elements, all essences or creat-

सर्वभूतमय, containing all living beings or existences, comprising all elementary matter. An epithet of the supreme all-pervading spirit.

सर्वभूतव्यापक, *m.* an epithet of the Supreme Being considered as pervading all existences.

सर्वम्, (Sk.) all, every.

सर्वमय, *m.* an epithet of the Supreme: *lit.* consisting of the whole or of everything, universal, general, comprehensive.

सर्वरात्र, *m.* the whole night.

सर्वलोक, *m.* all worlds, the entire universe.

सर्ववित, *m.* an epithet of the Supreme: *lit.* all-knowing, all-wise, omniscient.

सर्ववेदी = **सर्ववित**, *q.v.*

सर्वव्यापक, all-pervading, universal (in the Pantheistic sense). Applied to the Supreme Being.

सर्वव्यापकता, *f.* } **सर्वव्यापकत्व**, *m.* } = **सर्वव्यापित्व**, *q.v.*

सर्वव्यापित्व, *m.* all-pervadingness, universality; the embracing all the particular circumstances of a case.

सर्वव्यापी = **सर्वव्यापक**, *q.v.*

सर्वस (*colloquial*) = **सर्वस्व**, *q.v.* [sally.

सर्वसंगत, *m.* (*f.* ā) united with all, met with univer-

सर्वसंगा, a medley.

सर्वसंघा, *adj.* all-uniting: *f. pr. n.* a certain river.

सर्वसंचयी, miserly, niggardly: hence, *m.* (*f.* ini) a miser, niggard.

सर्वसिद्धि, *f.* accomplishment of every object, universal success: *m.* the *vilva*-tree.

सर्वसमता, *f.* sameness or identity with all things, equal regard for all, equanimity.

सर्वसर्वनाशक, *m.* (*f.* ikā) mutually, destructive.

सर्वसह, 1, *m.* (*f.* ā) bearing the whole, bearing all things with firmness and patience, all-enduring, very patient: 2, *m.* bdellium.

सर्वसामर्थ्यता, *f.* omnipotence.

सर्वसामर्थी, omnipotent, almighty.

सर्वसु (*colloquial*) = **सर्वस्व**, *q.v.*

सर्वस्य (Sk. gen. of **सर्व**) of all.

सर्वस्व, *m.* whole property or possessions, the whole essence of anything (its substance), one's all.

सर्वस्वदण्ड, 1, fined to the extent of one's all: 2, *m.* confiscation of an entire property.

सर्वस्वहरण, *m.* sequestration of a whole property.

सर्वस्वामी, *m.* an epithet (1) of a universal monarch or master (2) of the Supreme: *lit.* owner or master of all.

सर्वहार, *m.* confiscation of a whole property.

सर्वा, (Sk.) all, every.

सर्वा, *m.* a cup: a brother-in-law (wife's brother): excelling. — *k.* to break the ice. [of sacred science.

सर्वांग, *m.* the whole body; all the auxiliary branches

सर्वांगी, *m.* (*f.* iṇī) possessing all the limbs or parts, entire, complete, perfect. [beings collectively.

सर्वात्मा, *m.* the Supreme or All-pervading spirit; all

सर्वाधिकार, *m.* general superintendence or control.

सर्वाधिकारी, *m.* (*f.* iṇī) a head or general superin-

सर्वानिह. a corruption of **सवानिह**, *q.v.* [tendent.

सर्वार्थम, for (or on account of) all.

सर्वाश्रय, *m.* (*f.* ā) a universal protector: lit. *adj.* affording shelter or asylum to all.

सर्वेश. *m.* an epithet (1) of any supreme or universal monarch (2) of the Supreme : *lit.* lord of all.

सर्वैया, *m.* a mender.

सर्वोत्तम, *m.* an epithet of the Supreme Being: *lit.* *m.* (*f.* ā) best of all, the most excellent.

सर्वौषधिगण, *m.* a certain class of medicinal drugs, *viz.* (1) Mūra (2) Valeriana (3) Jatamansi (4) Orris root (5) Benzoin (6) Zedoary (7) Kūrk or Costus speciosus (8) Red sanders (9) Cyperus.

सर्वौषधिरस, *m.* the juice or infusion of a number of plants as used at a royal inauguration.

सर्षप, *m.* a kind of poison ; a species of mustard (*Sinapis dichotoma*); a weight equal to a mustard-seed.

सर्सों = **सरसों**, *q.v.*

सर्हना, *m.* the scale of a fish.

सल, 1, a colloquialism for **सेा**, *q.v.*: 2, *m.* the large green grasshopper, the mantis or leaf-insect : water: 3, *m. pr. n.* a certain demon slain by Krishṇ.

सलकंत, *f.* the root of the *Nymphæa lotus*.

सलग, intimacy, friendship, familiarity.

सलगम, *more prop.* **शलग़म**, *q.v.*

सलगी, familiar, friendly, sociable, attached, tame, domesticated, gentle, obedient. [modest, ashamed.

सलज्ज, *m.* (*f.* ā) affected with shame, bashful,

सलतनत, *f.* kingly sway, sovereignty, reign, dominion, royal power, the appurtenances of monarchship, empire, kingdom.

सलना, 1, *a. int.* to pierce, prick, perforate, penetrate, enter : 2, *m.* a rivulet.

सलनो, a contraction of **सलूनो**, *q. v.*

सलन्हार, *m.* (*f.* ī) penetrable.

सलब, *m.* (in Logic) a negative argument: plunder.

सलभ (*colloquial*) = **शलभ**, *q.v.*

सलम, *m.* peace, safety ; saluting, submitting, cultivating peace, friendship: *adj* free from fault or flaw.

सलवा, manna. [rankling, piercing.

सलसलाट, *f.* 1, (*contraction*) = **सलसलाहट**, *q.v.* : 2, a

सलसलाना, *a. int.* to creep along as a snake does, to make the noise a snake does when creeping : *t.* to beat : to pierce (as a thorn); to rankle ; to offend ; to doubt.

सलसलाहट, *f.* a creeping sensation, titillation ; the noise made by a snake when creeping.

सला, *f.* annunciation, proclamation, information, invitation, voice.

सलाई, *f.* a needle, probe, piece of wire for tinging the eyelids with collyrium (also used to deprive persons of sight by drawing it, while hot, close over the eyes of the sufferer) : a lead pencil.

सलाकना, *t.* to rule lines.

सलाका (*colloquial*) = **शलाका**, *q. v.*

सलात, *f.* prayer, benediction : the first chapter of the Kur,ān. [majesty, dignity, awe.

सलाबत, *f.* hardness, severity, firmness, valour,

सलाम, *m.* safety, peace ; salutation. — *k.* to salute : to refrain, desist, give up, bid adieu. — *lenā*, (to accept one's *sa'ām*, *i. e.*) to return a salutation.

सलामत, *f.* safety, tranquillity, health, recovery, salvation.

सलामोपयाम, *m.* salutations and kind messages.

सलाह, *f.* peace, concord ; treaty ; integrity, rec-

सलिता, *f.* a river, a stream. [titude: counsel, advice.

सलिल, *m.* water ; liquid (in general).

सलोक, whatever falls from a tree, leaves or branches ; withered thorns : honey : a roadside.

सलीक़ा, *m.* nature, genius, good disposition, knack, dexterity, address, knowledge. [crucify.

सलीब, *m. f.* 1 a cross, crucifix. —*par khaiṅchnā*, to

सलीमी, *f.* a kind of cloth.

सलोल, *m.* (*f.* ā) playful, sportive, wanton.

सलीस, not abstruse, easy, plain, simple.

सलू = **सल्लू**, *q. v.*

सलूक, *more prop.* **सुलूक**, *q. v.*

सलून = **सलोना**, *q. v.*

सलूनो, *f.* the full moon in *Shrāvaṇ* (at which time the ornament called *rākhī* is tied around the wrist).

सलूप, *m.* a little, very little.

सलोक, 1, (*corruption*) = **श्लोक**, *q. v.*: 2, *m.* good or respectable people, gentlefolk. [world as.

सलोकता, *f.* the condition of dwelling in the same

सलोन, 1, salted (said of food): 2, *m. pr. n.* a certain district.

सलोना, *m.* (*f.* ī) salt, salted, seasoned ; tasteful ; beautiful interesting; dark-complexioned, nutbrown, expressive (said of the countenance): *met.* piquant, intelligent (as opposed to insipid or dull).

सलोनी, *f.* (*m.* **सलोना**) seasoned ; tasteful ; beautiful (as applied to a mistress).

सलोल, *m.* (*f.* ā) playful, sportive, wanton.

सलौना, *m.* (*f* ī) = **सलोना**, *q. v.*

सल्य, *more prop.* **शल्य**, *q. v.* [*fera*).

सल्लकी, *f.* the gum-olibanum tree (*Boswellia thuri-*

सल्लम, *m.* a kind of coarse cloth.

सल्लाह, 1, *more prop.* **सलाह**, *q.v.*: 2, one who voids much excrement. [shoes are stitched, a latchet.

सल्लू, *m.* a thong, narrow slips of leather with which

सल्ला, foolish (said of women).

सव, 1, *more prop.* **सब**, *q.v.*: 2, (*provincial*) = **सेा**, *q.v.*:

सवगात, *more prop.* **सौग़ात**, *q.v.* [3, (*Rām.*) = **शव**, *q.v.*

सवत ; for words beginning thus, see under the more common form **सौत**.

सवत्स, *m.* (*f.* ā) together with a calf, having a calf, having offspring or descendants.

सवन, *m.* bringing forth offspring: extracting and drinking *som*-juice: a sacrifice: the moon: ablution (purificatory or expiatory). [porary, friend.

सवया, *adj.* cotemporary: hence, *m. f.* a cotem-

सवर, *m.* (*f.* ई) *more prop.* **शबर**, *q. v.*

सवरा; see **सवर** and **सूरा**.

सवरालवेा, in Mārwāṛī = **समालना**, *q.v.*

सवर्ण, *m.* (*f.* ā) appertaining to the same colour, class, tribe, kind, or caste, homogeneous, resembling, like.

सवर्णा, *f.* an epithet of Chhāyā, wife of the sun.

सववां, *m.* (*f.* °वीं) *more prop.* **सैावां**, *q. v.*

सवहन; see **सबहिन** and **सेाहन**.

सवहिन, an old form of **सभेां**, *q. v.*

सवा, 1, *more prop.* **सिवा**, *q. v.*: 2, with a quarter, augmented by one fourth, with one fourth added to it, a quarter more; *e. g.* (1) *Savā tīn*, three and a quarter (2) *Savā tīn sau*, three hundred and twenty-five.

सवाई, 1, = **सवा**, 2, *q. v.*: 2, *m.* a title of the *rājā* of Jaipur: 3, *f.* the venereal disease.

सवां, *m.* (*f.* °वीं) *more prop.* **सैावां**, *q. v.*

सवांग = **स्वांग**, *q. v.*

सवांगी, *m.* (*f.* inī) = **स्वांगी**, *q. v.*

सवांर, *more prop.* **सवार**, *q. v.*

सवांरना, *more com.* **संवारना**, *q. v.*

सवांरी, *more prop.* **सवारी**, *q. v.*

सवाखना, *t.* to test, try, prove.

सवाणी in Mārwāṛī = a giver of a good omen.

सवाद, 1, (*colloquial*) = **स्वाद**, *q. v.*: 2, *m.* blackening, soot, smoke; environs: reading: ability.

सवादिक, *more prop.* **स्वादिक**, *q. v.*

सवाना, *more com.* **सुलाना**, *q. v.* [rences, accidents.

सवानिह, *m.* (pl. of **सानिहा**) incidents, events, occur-

सवाब, *m.* rectitude, virtuous action, happy issue, success; premium; the reward of virtue; punishment.

सवाया, *more prop.* **सवैया**, *q. v.*

सवार, 1, mounted (on a horse, carriage, ship, or anything else): *met.* tipsy: 2, *m.* a rider, horseman, cavalier, trooper; cavalry.

सवारकार, *m.* (*f.* in, ī, nī) a horsebreaker, horseman.

सवारना, *more com.* **संवारना**, *q. v.*

सवारी, *f.* riding, horsemanship: equipage, suite.

सवाल, *more prop.* **सुवाल**, *q. v.*

सवाल्ले; see **सुवाल** and **शिवालय**.

सवास, *more prop.* **श्वास**, *q. v.*

सविकार, changed, transformed, transfigured.

सविता, *m.* the sun. This is the name by which the deity is invoked in the Gāyatrī.

सविलास, *m.* (*f.* ā *or* ī) amorous, wanton, sportive.

सविवेक, *adj.* possessing discrimination.

सविस्मय, *m.* (*f.* ā) astonished, surprized, doubtful.

सवीं, *f.* (*m.* **सवां**) *more prop.* **सैावीं**, *q. v.*

सवेाल = **वेाआधार सहित**.

सवेर, *adj.* early, in good time, soon.

सवेरा, *m.* the early morning, dawn.

सवेरे, *adv.* in the morning, at dawn, early, soon.

सवै an old form = **सबहि**, *q. v.*

सवैया, (Sk. **सपाद**), 1, *more com.* **सवा**, 2, *q. v.*: 2, *m.* (in Pros.) a species of metre.

सवैं, *f.* vermicelli, macaroni.

सवैया = **सवैया**, *q. v.*

सव्य, reverse, contrary, backward; left, to the left; south, southern: hence, *m.* the left hand; the south.

सशंक, *m.* (*f.* ā) timid, fearful, doubtful, suspicious: dangerous, alarming, terrifying, formidable.

सशंकना, to be possessed of fear, to be very fearful.

सशाला, *m.* (*f.* ī *or* in) a fellow-student.

ससुरा = **ससुर** = **श्वसुर**, *q. v.*

सशोक, *adj.* sorrowful, sad: *adv.* sorrowfully, sadly.

सस, 1, (*colloquial*) = **शश**, *q. v.*: 2, *m.* the moon;

ससंकेउ (*Rām.*) = **सशंका** (**सशंकना**). See **सउ**. [the sky.

ससंशय, *m.* (*f.* ā) doubtful, uncertain.

ससक (*colloquial*) = **शशक**, *q. v.*

ससयटी, *f.* (Engl.) a Society.

ससयर, *more prop.* **ससियर**, *q. v.*

ससरना, *a. int.* to move.

ससलोह (*Rām.*) = **सहसलोह**, *q. v.*

ससा, *m.* a hare. [form **शशि**.

ससि; for words beginning thus, see under the

ससि (*Rām.*) = (1) **शशिम** (2) **रेवती**, *qq. v.*

ससियर, *m.* the moon.

ससी, *f.* an epithet of the moon.

ससुगन्ध, *m.* (*f.* ā) *adj.* possessing a fragrant smell.

ससुर (*contraction*) = **श्वसुर**, *q. v.*

ससुरार / **ससुरारि** } *more prop.* **सुसरार**, *q. v.*

सस्ता, *m.* (*f.* ī) easily procured, cheap.

सस्ताई / **सस्तागी** } *f.* cheapness.

सस्ताना, *a. int.* to stop, rest, lie down: to have

सस्य (*colloquial*) = **शस्य**, *q. v.* [patience.

सह, 1, with, together, in company with: 2, *m.* strength, power, ability, endurance, forbearance, toleration: the Hindoo month Mārgahīrah (Nov.—Dec.): 3, frequently found (1) as an inseparable preposition = with, united, common; like; complete (2) as a postposition [*m.* (*f.* ā)] = bearing, enduring, suffering, sustaining; patient; able.

सहकर्मी, *m.* (*f.* iṇī) = **सहकारी**, *q. v.*

सहकार, 1, *m.* = **सहकारिता**, *q. v.*: 2, *m.* (*f.* ī) = **सहकारी**, *q. v.*: 3, *m.* a fragrant sort of mango.

सहकारिता, *f.* coöperation, assistance, aid.

सहकारी, *m.* (*f.* iṇī) a helper, assistant, associate; a fellow-worker, fellow-servant: lit. *adj.* coöperating, assisting, aiding.

सहगमन, *m.* a going with, accompanying; the voluntary burning of a widow on the funeral pile with her deceased husband.

सहगामिनी, *f.* a female associate; a woman who burns herself with the body of her deceased husband.

सहगामी, *m.* (*f.* inī) an attendant, companion, follower: lit. *adj.* going with, accompanying, following.

सहचर, *m.* (*f.* ī) = सहगामी, *q.v.*

सहचरी, *f.* a female associate or attendant, a woman's female friend, a confidante; a wife.

सहचार, 1, *m.* (*f.* ī) = सहगामी, *q.v.*: 2, *m.* (in Logic) the accompaniment of the middle term by the major.

सहचारी, *m.* (*f.* iṇī) = सहगामी, *q.v.*

सहज, 1, *m.* the natural state or disposition: 2, *m.* (*f.* ā) a brother (or sister) of whole blood: *lit.* born or produced with or together, cognate, innate, inherent, naturally belonging to: *hence*, 3, natural, not difficult, easy, facile, unaffected: *adv.* easily.

सहजना, *m.* a certain tree (*Guilandina morunga*, Linn.; or *Hyperanthera morunga*, Roxb.) the root of which is used as a substitute for horse-radish.

सहजन्य, *m. pr. n.* a certain यक्ष, *q.v.* [court of Indra.

सहजन्या, *f. pr. n.* a certain dancer (*Apsaras*) in the

सहजस्वभावसों, with natural ease.

सहजा, *f.* (*m.* सहज) a sister of whole blood.

सहजाई, *m.* (*f.* inī) a fellow-traveller, companion, associate.

सहत, 1 = सहता (see स, 5): 2, = शहद, *q.v.*

सहता, 1, *f.* = सहत्व, *q.v.*: 2, pres. part. of सहना. *Sahte sahte*, patiently. [tion, companionship.

सहत्व, *m.* sufferance, endurance: union, associa-

सहद, *more prop.* शहद, *q.v.* [princes.

सहदेव, *m. pr. n.* the youngest of the five Pāṇḍav

सहन, 1, *m.* (*f.* ā) patient, enduring, suffering, bearing: 2, *m.* enduring, bearing, suffering, patience.

सहनकार, *more com.* सहन्हार, *q.v.*

सहनशील, *m.* (*f.* ā) patiently disposed, enduring.

सहनशीलता, *f.* patience of disposition, forbearance.

सहनशीला, *f.* a female of a patient disposition.

सहना, 1, *f.* (*m.* सहन) a patient female: 2, *t.* (or *a.int.*) to bear, sustain, support, endure, suffer, have patience, 'pocket.'

सहनाई, *more prop.* शहनाई, *q.v.*

सहनी; see सहना and शहना.

सहन्हार, *m.* (*f.* ī) sufferable, bearable, supportable, tolerable; obnoxious to.

सहबान, *m. pr. n.* a certain Arabian orator whose eloquence is said to have been unrivalled.

सहबत; see शहवत and सुहबत.

सहभागी, *adj.* sharing; hence, *m.* (*f.* inī) a partaker, participator, sharer, shareholder, partner. [ness.

सहम, *m.* fear, terror, dread: gravity, venerable-

सहमना, to fear, dread, revere.

सहमरण, *m.* concremation, the voluntary burning of a widow on the funeral pile with her deceased husband.

सहमा, *m.* (*f.* ī) terrified, awestricken.

सहमाना, *t.* to overawe, strike terror into.

सहमि = सहमके (सहमना). See क, 7.

सहर, 1, = शहर, *q.v.*: 2, *m.* dawn of day: watching,

सहरगाह, *f.* the morning, the dawn. [wakefulness.

सहराना, 1, *more prop.* सहलाना, *q.v.*: 2, *a.int.* to thrill; to have the hair standing on end.

सहरावन, *more prop.* सहलावन, *q.v.*

सहरी, a Prākrit form of शफरी, *q.v.*

सहरोसा (*Rām.*) = सक्रोध, *q.v.* Cf. सह and रोष.

सहल, easy, not difficult, simple, soft.

सहलना, *t.* to stroke, rub gently, tickle: to tease,

सहलावन, *f.* = सहलाहट, *q.v.* [harass, tire.

सहलाहट, *f.* gentle rubbing, stroking, titillation.

सहवत, 1, *more prop.* शहवत, *q.v.*: 2, see सुहवत.

सहवसति, *f.* / **सहवास**, *m.* } a residing together.

सहवासी, *m.* (*f.* inī) one who resides with another, a fellow-resident, fellow-lodger.

सहवैया, *m. f.* an endurer, sufferer.

सहस, 1, (*colloquial*) = सहस्र, *q.v.*: 2, *m.* the Hindoo month *Agrahāyan* (Nov. — Dec.); the winter season strength, power; victory: light.

सहसबाहु (*corruption*) = सहस्रबाहु, *q.v.*

सहसा, without consideration or pause, precipitately, suddenly, quickly, hastily, rashly, at once.

सहसाक्षी, *m.* (*f.* iṇī) *adj.* possessing a witness.

सहसाखी (*Rām.*) = (1) सहसाक्षी (2) सहस्राक्ष.

सहसान, patient, enduring, suffering.

सहस्य, 1, a corruption of सहस, *q.v.*: 2, *m. pr. n.* the Hindoo month *Paush* (Dec. — Jan.).

सहस्यानन (*corruption*) = सहस्रानन, *q.v.*

सहस्र, *m.* a thousand (१०००): see ओं, वां, वीं, वे, वें.

सहस्रदन्त, *m.* a kind of sheat-fish (*Silurus pelorius*).

सहस्रदृग, *m.* (*f.* ā) / **सहस्रनयन**, *m.* (*f.* ā) / **सहस्रनेत्र**, *m.* (*f.* ī) } = सहस्राक्ष, *q.v.*

सहस्रपति, *m.* (*f.* patni) any high military officer: *lit.* the chief or governor of a thousand.

सहस्रबाहु / **सहस्रभुज** } *m.* epithets of अर्जुन, *q.v.*

सहस्रयुग, *m.* a period of a thousand ages. [Nāg.

सहस्रवदन, *m.* (the thousand-mouthed, *i.e.*) Shesh-

सहस्रसहस्र, *m.* thousands, thousands upon thousands, a thousand thousands, a billion.

सहस्रसीस, *m.* (the thousand-headed, *i.e.*) Sheshnāg.

सहस्राक्ष, *m.* an epithet of the god Indra: *lit.* thousand-eyed; hence *m.* (*f.* ī) vigilant, all-seeing, all-inspecting, Argus-eyed.

सहस्राक्षि = सहस्राक्ष, *q.v.* [nāg.

सहस्रानन, *m.* (the thousand-mouthed, *i.e.*) Shesh-

सहस्रार्जुन, *m.* an epithet of अर्जुन, *q.v.*

सहस्री, 1, *m.* a body of a thousand men; a fine amounting to a thousand: 2, *m.* (*f.* iṇī) the commander or prefect of a thousand: 3, *adj.* having a thousand; consisting of thousands.

सहस्रों, (see **ओं**, 4) thousands, many thousands, thousands upon thousands, by thousands.

सहा, *f.* the earth: the name of several plants.

सहाइफ़, *m.* (pl. **सहीफ़ा**) books, leaves, page , letters.

सहाई, *m.* more prop. (1) **सहाय** (2) **साहाय्य**, *qq.v.*

सहाऊ, 1, *m. f.* = **सहाय**, 1, *q.v.*: 2, *m. f.* sufferable, endurable, bearable: obnoxious to.

सहाओ, *m.* endurance, bearing, sufferance, patience.

सहाना, 1, *m.* a certain musical mode: *t.* to cause to sustain or support, to cause to endure or have patience.

सहाय, 1, *m. f.* a contraction of **साहाय्य**, *q.v.*: 2, *m* an assistant, aider, succourer, patron, supporter, helper, companion, adherent, ally: (in Geog.) a tributary: 3, the ruddy goose (*Anas casarca*): a sort of drug and perfume: 4, a multitude of companions and helpers.

सहायक, *m.* (*f.* ikā) = **सहाय**, 2, *q.v.*: *lit.* helpful, auxiliary, accompanied by; (in Geog.) tributary.

सहायकपत्र, *m.* a letter of recommendation, letter of introduction.

सहायता, *f.* (*m.* °**त्व**) companionship, association, friendship, aid, help, assistance.—*k.* to help.—*chāhnā*, to crave assistance.

सहायफ, *more prop.* **सहाइफ़**, *q.v.*

सहायवत / **सहायवन्त** } *m.* (*f.* vatī) = **सहायवान्**, *q.v.*

सहायवान्, *m.* (*f.* vatī) one who is befriended, etc.: *lit.* accompanied, befriended, assisted.

सहाया (*Rām.*) = **सहाय**, *q.v.*

सहायिका, *f.* (*m.* **सहायक**) a female helper.

सहायी, *m.* (*f.* inī) = **सहाय**, 2, *q.v.*

सहार, patience, endurance.

सहारना; see (1) **संहारना** (2) **सुहारना**.

सहारा, *m.* association, assistance, aid, help; dependence, hope: concord; gentleness.—*k.* to aid, to abet.

सहार्थ, having the same meaning, synonymous.

सहाव = **सहाओ**, *q.v.*

सहावट, *f.* passability, passableness.—*se.* passively.

सहित, accompanied or attended by, associated or connected with, possessed of; with, together with, along with.

सहियारना, *t.* to arrange.

सहिराना = (1) **सहराना**, 2 (2) **सहलाना**, *qq.v.*

सहिष्णु, *m. f.* of a disposition to bear, able to endure, patient, enduring, resigned.

सहिष्णुता, *f.* (*m.* °**त्व**) ability to support or bear, patience, forbearance, endurance, resignation.

सही, (a particle of accord or of emphasis =) it is true or correct; very good! very well! certainly! undoubtedly!

सहीफ़ा, *m.* a book, leave, page, letter.

सहीह, accurate, just, pure, perfect, entire, sound, certain.—*k.* to correct, rectify, to sign (as, a document).

सहुत, a corruption of **शब्द**, *q.v.*

सहूलत, *f.* ease, facility, smoothness, plainness.

सहेजना, *t.* to try, investigate, adjust: to provide.

सहेट, *f.* a mead, meadow.

सहेतु, having a cause or occasion, caused, occasioned.

सहेली, *f.* a woman's female companion, a lady who is the confidante of another, a maid-servant, handmaid, damsel; a concubine; female companions in a seraglio, handmaids, concubines.

सहो, *f. m.* ? error, mistake, oversight, fault, inadvertency, neglect, negligence, omission.

सहोटी, *more com.* **सहौटी**, *q. v.*

सहोढ़, *m.* the son of a female pregnant at the time of her marriage; a thief caught with stolen property upon him.

सहोत्रा, *f. pr. n.* the wife of Sahdev.

सहोदर, of the same womb, descended from the same mother: hence, *m.* (*f.* ī) a brother (or sister) of whole blood.—*bhāī*, a full brother.

सहोल, *m.* a plummet.

सहौटी, *f.* a kind of door-frame, a lintel.

सह्य, 1, fit to be borne or suffered, endurable, tolerable: 2, able to bear, strong, powerful, 3, *m.* health, convalescence: assistance: 4, *m. pr. n.* a certain range of mountains.

सा, a very common and most important adjunct in Hindee, is most probably the Prākrit form of **सदृश** or **सादृश्य** or **सम** (**समान**): by some, however, it is believed to be merely a contraction of the word **ऐसा** in one of the idiomatic usages of this word. It denotes, 1, similitude, likeness, resemblance; *e. g.* **हाथीसा मुंह**, an elephant-like face: **हाथी ऐसा मुंह**, a face like the elephant's: **लिखासा**, as if written: **बादलसा**, like a cloud, cloud-like: 2, When suffixed to adjectives, it is sometimes *intensive*; *e. g.* **थोड़ासा**, a very little; **बहुतसा**, very much: and sometimes *modificatory*, like the English 'ish', or '-like', or 'as if', or 'so to speak'; *e.g.* **कालासा**, blackish, black-like: similarly the English 'faintish', 'faint-like', 'as if in a swoon': 3, When suffixed to pronouns, it is sometimes added to the base, sometimes to the unaltered nominative, and sometimes to the genitive; *e.g.* **तुझसा** or **तूसा** or **तेरासा**, like thee, such as thee or thou: 4, It is to be observed that popular usage (with however much of questionable accuracy or logic) has decided in favour of treating the **आ** in in this particle as if it were an unquestioned adjectival termination; hence, it has become the fashion to inflect it (m. *sā*; f. *sī*; pl. m. *se*) as an adjective. Like many other inaccuracies or anomalies in language, it is probably past recovery now.

साअत, *f.* a moment, minute, hour; a time-piece, watch, clock.

साइका, *m.* (?) lightning, a thunderbolt.

साइत, *more prop.* (1) **साअत** (2) **साइद**, *qq. v.*

साइद, *f.* the arm from the wrist to the elbow, the fore-arm.

साइर, *m.* a whole: a remainder: a going, walking, wandering: tax, duty levied on personal property as distinguished from that levied on land.

साइल, *m.* an asker, interrogator, questioner; a petitioner, beggar, mendicant.

साइस, *more prop.* **साईस**, *q. v.*

साई, 1, *more com.* **सांई**, *q.v.*: 2, *f.* earnest-money:
साईं = सांईं, *q.v.* [3, *m.* (*f.* inī) industrious.
साईस, *m.* a horse-keeper, groom.
साईसी, *f.* the business of a groom.
साउज, *m.* (*f.* ā) a deer, antelope.
साऊ, *m. f.* 1, tractable: 2, a relation.
साऊंगी = सांगी, *q.v.*
साऊल, *m.* a plummet. (?)
साएद; see (1) **सैयिद** (2) **शायद**. [form **सांव**.
साओं; for words beginning thus, see under the
सां, *more com.* **सा**, *q.v.*
सांइ, *more com.* **सांई**, *q.v.*
सांइद्रोही (*Rām.*) = **स्वामीद्रोही**, *q.v.*
सांई, *m.* (fr. **स्वामी**) lord, master, Your Worship: an imitative sound (as of wind): *met.* an epithet (1) of the Supreme Being (2) of any religious mendicant or ascetic.
सांईं = सांई, *q.v.* [the *Jalevī*).
सांक, *f.* fear: asthma: a lump of sweetmeat (*esp.*
सांकर, 1, *f.* a chain: a kind of ornament worn by females: a strait; a narrow lane: *met.* difficulty, straits: 2 narrow (as cloth), strait, close, strict, tight.
सांकरी, *f.* = **सांकर**, *q.v.*
सांकल, *f.* a chain.
सांखला, in Gaṛhwāl = a honeycomb.
सांखू, *m.* a kind of wood (*Shorea robusta*): a bridge.
सांखा, *m.* a bridge.
सांख्य, 1, appertaining to number, numeral: deliberating, reasoning; rational, discriminative: 2, *m.* (in Logic) reasoning, argument: 3, *m. pr. n.* (among Hindoos) a certain system of philosophy ascribed originally to Kapil-Muni.
सांख्ययोग, *m. pr. n.* the 2nd chapter of the Bhagavadgitā. Properly, the term means the application of the Sāṅkhya doctrine to the knowledge of spirit; and the book is perhaps so named, because it sets forth the Sāṅkhya and Yog doctrines in regard to the soul.
सांख्यशास्त्र, *m.* the Sāṅkhya system of philosophy, or a treatise referring to it. [bhikshu.
सांख्यसार, *m.* a certain Sanskrit work by Vijnān-
सांग, 1, a corruption of **स्वांग**, *q.v.*: 2, *f.* a spear or javelin all of iron, a lance: 3, complete in all its parts, having all the members, finished; possessed of the auxiliary branches (*aṅg*) of sacred science.
सांगर, *m.* a cutter of grindstones. [propped.
सांगी, *f.* a support on which the pole of a cart is
सांगीत, *more prop.* **संगीत**, *q.v.*
सांगुस } **सांगूस** } *f.* the skate-fish (*Raia sankur*).
सांगा, in Gaṛhwāl = a suspension-bridge.
सांगोपांग, entire, complete: possessed of the *angas* or *upāngas*, or the principal and auxiliary branches of sacred science.
सांघर, *m.* a wife's son by a former husband.
सांच, true, proper, correct, accurate, exact, authentic, real: *adv.* only, indeed and in truth, really.
सांचरनोन, *m.* Glauber's or Epsom salts.
सांचा, 1, *m.* (*f.* ī) = **सांच**, *q.v.*: 2, *m.* a mould, a matrice, a form, an outline, a cone.
सांचेहु, an old emphatic form of **सांच**, *q.v.*
सांचो } **सांचौ** } in Braj = **सांचा**, *q.v.*
सांखी, *m.* (*f.* inī) *more prop.* **साखी**, *q.v.*
सांज, *more prop.* (1) **सांझ** (2) **साज**, *qq.v.*
सांजन; see **साजन**.
सांजना; see **साजना**.
सांझ, *f.* evening.—*samay*, the evening, eventide.
सांझा, *m.* images of cowdung made by children during the dark half of the month *āsin* to represent idols.
सांझी, *f.* = **सांझा**, *q.v.*
सांट, सांठ, सांड, सांत, सांथ, सांद, सांध, सांप, सांब, सांभ; for words beginning with either of these elements, see under the forms **साण्ट, साण्ठ, साण्ड, सान्त, सान्थ, सान्द, सान्ध, साम्प, साम्ब, साम्भ**, respectively.
सांइ; for words beginning thus, see under the form
सांया, a Prākrit form of **छाया**, *q.v.* [**सायड**.
सांय; see **छाया** and **श्रान्ति**.
सायंत; see (1) **सावन्त** (2) **सांगोपांग**.
सांयचीत, without anxiety, tranquil.
सांवरा, *m.* (*f.* ī) *more prop.* **सांवला**, *q.v.*
सांवरो } **सांवरों** } **सांवरौ** } in Braj = **सांवला**, *q.v.*
सांवल (*contraction*) = **सांवला**, *q.v.*
सांवला, *m.* (*f.* ī) of a dark or sallow complexion, of a nut-brown colour, of handsome countenance.
सांवलासलोना, *m.* (*f.* **सांवलीसलोनी**) pleasing.
सांवलीसूरत, *m.* (the one with a sallow or handsome complexion, *i.e.*) Krishṇ. [(*esp.* that of Krishṇ).
सांवलीसूरति, *f.* a sallow or handsome countenance
सांवा, *m.* a certain kind of very small grain (*Pani-*
सांवां = सांवा, *q.v.* [*cum frumentaceum*, Roxb.).
सांस, *f.* breath, breathing, respiration; a sigh.—*ulti lenā*, to gasp in agony.—*bharnā*, to sigh, to regret.—*ruknā*, to be smothered or throttled.—*rūknā* or *roknā*, to suffocate, stifle.—*lenā*, to breathe, take breath, draw breath. *Lambi*—*bharnā*, to sigh deeply.
सांसत, *m.* punishment; pain.
सांसना, *t.* to snub; to threaten; to distress.
सांसा, *m.* imagination, reflection, fancy, apprehension, fear. [worldly.
सांसारिक, appertaining to this present world; lay,
सांसारिकोपाय, 1, *m.* worldly contrivance, temporizing: 2, a time-server, temporizer: lit. *adj.* having recourse to secular measures.
साक, 1, *more prop.* **शाक**, *q.v.*: 2, *f.* the leg; the trunk of a tree, the stalk of a herb.
साकबनिक, *m.* a vendor of herbs, green-grocer.
साकला, *more prop.* **शाकला**, *q.v.*

साकल्य, *m.* totality, entireness, completeness, wholeness; the whole, all.

साका, *m.* (**शाक**) an era.— *k.* to establish an era; *met.* to distinguish oneself by heroic actions.

साकार, possession of form or shape.

साकित, silent, quiet, at rest.

साकी; see (1) **साखी** (2) **शाकी** (3) **शाखी**.

साकेअन्ध = **शाकेश्वर**, *q.v.*

साक्रमेयट, *m.* a corruption of the English word 'sacrament' introduced into the Hindee literature by some of the propagators of Christianity.

साक्ष, 1, a contraction of **साक्ष्य**, *q. v.*: 2, *m.* (*f.* ī) possessed of eyes: 3, *m.* (*f.* ā) possessed of the seeds of which rosaries are made; having a rosary.

साक्षर, *m.* orthography: adj. *m.* (*f.* ā) containing syllables or letters.

साक्षरी, *m.* (*f.* iṇī) orthographical.

साक्षा; see **साक्ष**.

साक्षात, 1, eye to eye, in the presence of, within sight of, before, face to face, openly, evidently, manifestly, visibly: as, like, like as: 2, evident, conspicuous, open: 3, *m.* an interview, meeting.

साक्षी, 1, *f.* = **साक्ष्य**, *q.v.*: 2, *m.* (*f.* iṇī) an eye-witness, (in Law) a witness, an evidence: lit. *adj.* bearing testimony, giving evidence, attesting, testifying. *Ishwarko* — *k.* to call God to witness.— *denā*, to give witness. —*k.* to bear witness.

साक्ष्य, *m.* testimony, evidence.

साख, *f.* credit, trust, reputation: season, time.

साखा (*colloquial*) = (1) **शाखा** (2) **साक्ष्य** (3) **साख**, *qq.v.*

साखामृग (*colloquial*) = **शाखामृग**, *q. v.*

साखी, a corruption (1) of **शाखी** (2) of **साक्षी**, *qq.v.*

साखोच्चार (*colloquial*) = **शाखोच्चार**, *q.v.*

साख्यात (*colloquial*) = **साक्षात**, *q. v.*

साग, *m.* a potherb, culinary vegetables, edible herbs, greens: (in Mārwāṛī =) a player, actor.

सागपात, *m.* 1, = **साग**, *q.v*: 2, petty dues paid in kind to village officials.—*honā*, to become soft.

सागमड़ी, *f.* cultivated ground, rice-fields, lands in full crop.

सागर, *m.* an ocean: a kind of deer: *pr.n.* a certain district and city in central India.

साग़र, *m.* a bowl, cup, goblet.

सागवान = **सागून**, *q. v.*

सागवाला, *m.* (*f.* ī) a dealer in herbs, herb-seller, herbalist, vegetarian.

सागू, *m.* sago (from the pith of the *Sagus rumphii*); a tree of the palm species. A flour is made from this tree, which when made into bread and fresh from the oven, eats like hot rolls: when hard it requires to be soaked in water before it is used. Three of these trees yield sufficient to maintain a man for a year; and an acre, properly planted, will afford subsistence for one hundred men during that time.

सागूदाना, *m.* sago.

सागून, *f.* the teak-tree (*Tectona grandis*) or its timber.

सागौती, *f.* meat, flesh, butcher's-meat.

सागोन = **सागून**, *q.v.*

साच, true, proper, correct, accurate, exact, authentic, real.

साचा, *more prop.* (1) **सांचा** (2) **साचा**, *qq. v.*

साझ; for words beginning thus, see under the form **साझ्**.

साज, *m.* preparation; harness, fittings, accoutrements: the teak-tree (*Tectona grandis*), the plane-tree.

साजन, 1, *m.* (*f.* ā or ī) *colloquial* = **सज्जन**, 1, *q.v.*: 2, *m.* a preparing, decorating, adorning.

साजना, *t.* to prepare, decorate, dress, bedeck; to regulate: *a. int.* to suit, fit, become.

साज़बाज़, *m.* ornament, apparatus, accoutrement: *adj.* trim, dressy.

साजा; see (1) **सजा** (2) **साज** (3) **साजना**.

साजिद, *m.* one who is prostrate in adoration, a worshipper, adorer.

साज़िश, *f.* combination, confederacy, conspiracy, cabal, collusion.

साज्जन, *m.* (*f.* ā or ī) *more prop.* **सज्जन**, *q.v.*

साझा, *m.* association, relation, connexion, partnership: *adj.* joint.

साझी, *m.* (*f.* iṇī) an associate, partner, partaker.

साझे, *adv.* (sc. **से**) jointly.

साट, 1, *more prop.* (1) **शाट** (2) **साठ**, *q. v.*: 2, *f.* junction.

साटक, *m.* (in Pros.) a species of metre.

साटन, 1, a Braj pl. of **साट**, *q.v.*: 2, a kind of cement or paste.

साटना, 1, *more com.* **सटाना**, *q.v.*: 2, see **सापटना**.

साटबाट, *f.* combining, leaguing, confederating, intrigue.

साटा; see (1) **साट** (2) **सट्टा** (3) **सटना** (4) **साटना**.

साठ, sixty (६०). See **ओं**, **वां**, **वों**, **वे**, **वें**.

साँठ; see (1) **साठ** (2) **साँठा**.

साठी, *m.* a kind of rice produced in the rains (so called because it ripens in sixty days from the time of sowing).

साठ्य (*colloquial*) = **शाठ्य**, *q. v.*

साड़ी, *f.* a kind of dress worn by Hindoo females. It consists of one long piece of cloth worn round the body and passing over the head.

साड़े, *more com.* **साढ़े**, *q. v.*

साढ़ी, *m.* the spring harvest, or grain cut in the spring.

साढ़ू, *m.* a wife's sister's husband.

साढ़े, *lit.* with one half more. This word is never used alone, but is prefixed to numerals, and denotes that a half of a unity is to be added to the numeral to which it is prefixed; *e.g. Sāṛhe chār* = four and a half. When prefixed to an aggregate number, a half of that aggregate has to be added; *e.g. Sāṛhe sau* = 150: *Sāṛhe pānch sahasra* = 7500.

साढ़ेसाती, *f.* a period of seven and a half years (*esp.* that occupied by Saturn in his revolution).

साणा, *more com.* **शाणा**, *q. v.*

सापट, *f.* joining, sticking; confederacy, collusion; a flail, stick for threshing corn with.

सापटना, *t.* (of **सटना**) to join thread, to splice, piece, unite, join, stick together; to apply.

सापटा, *m.* a stick or whip with which elephants are beaten at the time of fighting; a spur.

सापटी, *f.* a dimin. of **सापटा**, *q.v.*

सापठ, 1, = **सापट**, *q. v.*: 2, invention,

सापठना = **सापटना**, *q. v.*

साथठगाथठ = साठबाट, *q. v.*

साथठाना, *t.* to invent.

साथड, *m.* a bull; a stallion; *met.* an independent, extravagant fellow. *Rāṇḍkā* —, (*lit.* a widow's stallion or bull, *i. e.*) a kept man.

साथड़ = साथड, *q. v.*

साथड़नी, *f.* a female camel, a dromedary.

साथड़नीसवार, *m.* one who rides a camel.

साथड़ा, *m.* a certain animal (it resembles a lizard, and its oil is said to have restorative properties).

सात, seven (७): see सों, वां, वीं, वे, वें. *Sāt pānch k.*, to be in doubt, be unable to decide what to do.

सातभाई, *m.* a kind of thrush: *lit.* seven-brothers. It is so called from these birds being gregarious, and frequently seven of them are found together.

सातमें in Braj = सातवां, *q. v.*

सातवां, (see सात) *m.* (*f.* wīṅ) seventh.

सातसमुन्दर, *m.* a certain game (in play).

साताइस, *more prop.* सत्ताईस, *q. v.*

सातारोहवा, *m.* a dog that associates with six wolves.

सातिसार, *m.* (*f.* ā) a person afflicted with dysentery: [*lit.* dysenteric.

साती, *more prop.* साथी, *q. v.*

सातीलक, *m.* pulse in general, or of a particular kind.

सातु, see (1) सातों (2) सत्तु (3) सत्त्व.

सातूर, *m.* a large knife, a butcher's chopping-knife.

सातो, *more prop.* सातों, *q. v.*

सातों, the seven, all the seven, the seven of them. —*munh sarāhnā*, to praise or extol very much.

सातोंकाण्ड, *m.* the seven sections into which the *Rāmāyaṇ* is divided, *viz.* (1) Bālkāṇḍ (2) Ayodhyākāṇḍ (3) Āraṇyakāṇḍ (4) Kiskindākāṇḍ (5) Sundarkāṇḍ (6) Lankākāṇḍ (7) Uttarkāṇḍ.

सातोंद्वीप, *m.* (see द्वीप) the seven divisions of the world as recognized in the Hindoo system.

सात्यकि, *m. pr. n.* a certain warrior (son of Satyak) in the Pāṇḍu army who acted as the charioteer of Krishṇ.

सात्व, a corruption of सत्त्व, *q. v.*

सात्वकी, a corruption of सात्त्विकी, *q. v.*

सात्विक, *more prop.* सात्त्विक, *q. v.*

सात्विकी, *more prop.* सात्त्विकी, *q. v.*

सात्त्विक, endowed with सत्त्व (see गुण) *i.e.* with the best of the qualities, endowed with goodness, appertaining to that quality; hence (1) good, honest, true, sincere, disposed to truth and goodness, virtuous, excellent, pious, gentle, amiable: hence (2) *m.* (*f.* ī) a Brāhmaṇ; an excellent or amiable person.

साथ, 1, with, together, together with, along with, attended by: 2, *m.* a troop, society, company.—*iske*, along with this, *i.e.* besides, moreover.—*uske*, along with that, *i.e.* although, notwithstanding.—*denā*, to join, to associate with.—*lenā* or *ho lenā*, to partake, share.—*hone is bātke*, notwithstanding this.

साथरी, *f.* a kind of seat (*viz.* a small carpet or mat) on which Hindoos sit to worship.

साथवाला, *m.* (*f.* ī) = साथी, *q. v.*

साथसाथ, (an emphatic, a frequentative, or a distributive of साथ, 1) with, together, in one company, along with, together with, in society with.

साथा, a poetical form of साथ, *q. v.*

साथिन = साथिनी, *q. v.*

साथिनी, *f.* (*m.* साथी) a female attendant, associate, [or accomplice.

साथी, *m.* (*f.* inī) an associate, comrade, ally, companion, accomplice, attendant, partaker: lit. *adj.* being with, associated: *adv.* more.—*k.* to make a companion of one.

साथोंसाथ / साथेंसाथ } emphatic forms of साथसाथ, *q. v.*

साद, 1, *more prop.* साध, *q. v.*: 2, old form = शब्द, *q. v.*

सादःकार, *m.* a kind of goldsmith, a plain worker in gold or silver who makes articles which are subsequently ornamented by other hands.

सादर, 1, *m.* (*f.* ā) having or paying respect, respectful: impassioned: 2, with respect, respectfully.

सादरा, *m.* a kind of song.

सादरी, *m.* (*f.* iṇī) having or paying respect, respect- [ful.

सादा, 1. *more prop* सदा, *q. v.*: 2, *m.* (*f.* ī) plain, white, unadorned, simple, artless, open, sincere.

सादिक़, true, just, sincere. — *ānā*, to come true, be verified in (*par*) a person; *e. g.* prophecy.

सादी, 1, *more prop.* शादी, *q. v.*: 2, *f.* (*m.* सादा) plain, etc.—*silāī*, plain sewing, plainwork.

सादृश्य, *m. f.* (?) likeness, resemblance, similarity.

साध, 1, a contraction of साधु, *q. v.*: 2, *f.* wish, desire, inclination, effort. prayer, the longing of pregnant females: performance, fulfilment.

साधक, *m.* (*f.* ikā) an accomplisher, practiser; a devotee, etc.: lit. *adj.* accomplishing, completing, perfecting; helping; magical; adept; holy.

साधन, *m.* an accomplishing, effecting; a means of accomplishing; cause, instrument; wealth; practice.

साधना, 1, *f.* the act of familiarizing by habitude; practice, accomplishment; solicitation, entreaty; contrivance; devotion, adoration, worship: 2, *t.* to familiarize gradually to any habit, to habituate. accustom, teach, to use, practise, learn, to regulate, order, arrange, correct, rectify, settle, fix, determine, point (a gun), to accomplish, to pacify, to improve, ameliorate, to modulate.

साधनीय, feasible, accomplishable.

साधन्हार, *m.* (*f.* ī) improveable.

साधमत, *m.* good behaviour, moral conduct.

साधा, *m.* (*f.* ī); past part. of साधना, 2, *q. v.*

साधारण, belonging to many, common, general, joint; equal, like, similar; commonplace, well-known; ordinary, usual, middling, so-so, trite; public.

साधारणधर्म्म, *m.* duty or law binding on all the different castes in common, common or universal duty.

साधारणरूप, 1, *m.* plain features: 2, *m.* (*f.* ā) a person of plain features: *lit.* plain-featured, ordinary.

साधारणरूपी, *m.* (*f.* iṇī) = साधारणरूप, *q. v.*

साधि, an old conjunct. part. of साधना. See क, 7.

साधित, habituated, accomplished, settled: amerced, fined, awarded.

साधी, *f.* (*m.* साधा); past past. of साधना, 2, *q. v.*

साधु, perfect; fit, proper, right; good, excellent, pure, virtuous, righteous, holy, pious, honest: hence, (1) *m.* an honest man; a religious person, holy one, saint; a kind of Hindoo mendicant; a merchant, usurer (2) *f.* a virtuous woman.

साधुता, *f.* (*m.* °त्व) goodness, honesty, correctness, righteousness, piety, virtue.

साधुन, an old form = साधुश्रों (साधु).

साधुनि, in Braj (1) a pl. of साधु; see नि, 2 (2): (2) an agentive form of साधु; see नि, 2 (5).

साधुपुष्प, *m.* a certain flower (*Hibiscus mutabilis*).

साधुमहिमा, *f.* the majesty or excellence of Hindoo ascetics.

साधुवृक्ष, *m.* the *kadamb*-tree (*Nauclea cadamba*).

साधुशील, *m.* (*f.* ī) of a wise or virtuous disposition, righteous, virtuous.

साधुसमाज, *m.* any large gathering of Hindoo ascetics.

साधुसेवी, *m.* (*f.* inī) any person who administers to the wants or requirements of a Hindoo ascetic.

साधू (*corruption*) = साधु, *q. v.*

साध्य, 1, accomplishable, attainable, practicable, easy: 2. *m.* a thing that has to be accomplished or to be established by proof: accomplishment, perfection: 3. *m. pr. n.* (1) of a certain class of inferior deities whose number is variously given as twelve and seventeen (2) of the 22nd of the astronomical periods called *yog*.

साध्यगण, *i. e.* साध्य, 3 (1), *q. v.* See गण.

साध्यसम, possessed of the power of effecting a thing, equal to, adequate to, sufficient.

साध्यसम, *adj.* that may be accomplished by application or energy.

साध्या, 1, *m.* (pl.: see आ, 22) = साध्यगण, *q. v.*; 2, *f. pr. n.* the mother of that class of deities. She was a daughter of Daksh and one of the wives of Dharm.

साध्वी, *f.* a chaste female, virtuous wife.

सान, 1, *more prop.* शान, *q. v.*: 2, *m.* likeness, similitude; a sign: a muster of an army. — *bujhānā*, to cause one to understand by hints.

सानना, *t.* 1, (causat. of सनना) to knead, mash, mix up (as flour, dough, earth, etc): to impregnate, stain, soil, smear, defile: 2, to whet

साननासिक (*contraction*) = सानुनासिक, *q. v.*

सानने, *more prop.* साम्हने, *q. v.*

सानबुझाना; see *s. v.* सान.

सानहा; see शाना and सानिहा.

साना, 1, *more com.* शाना, *q v.*: 2, (from सानना) *m.* (*f.* ī) mixed, impregnated, etc.

सानि, an old conjunct. part. of सानना. See इ, 7.

सानिहा, *m.* an occurrence, incident, accident.

सानिहाल, *more prop.* सवानिह, *q. v.*

सानी, *f.* chaff or straw mixed with grain (*esp.* that from which the oil has been expressed) as food for cattle, mash.

सानु, *m.* end, point; the top of a mountain; level ground on the top or edge of a mountain, table-land; a forest: a sprout: a gale of wind: a road: a sage.

सानुकूल, attended by favorable circumstances.

सानुज (*Rām.*: स + अनुज) in company with one's younger brother.

सानुनासिक, (in Gram.) pronounced with the assistance of the nose, nasal The term is applied to any letter that has *Anuswār* or *Chandravindu* over it, also to the fifth letter of each of the first five classes of consonants.

सान्त, 1, (*colloquial*) = शान्त, *q. v.*: 2, the season of spring: a certain month.

सान्तरस, *more prop.* शान्तरस, *q. v.*

सान्ति (*colloquial*) = शान्ति, *q. v.*

सान्ता, *m.* the sugarcane.

सान्ती, 1, = सान्त, 2, *q. v.*: 2, *f.* stead: 3, *postp.* (takes gen. *fem.*) instead of, in substitution for.

सान्ते, *postp.* (takes gen. *masc.* infl.) instead of, in substitution for.

सान्त्वन, *m.* conciliation, reconcilement; appeasing; mildness; speaking kindly and in a conciliatory manner: friendly salutation and inquiry.

सान्थरी = साथरी, *q. v.*

सान्थरो, in Mārwāṛī = a bed of grass. See साथरी.

सान्दीपन; see (1) सन्दीपन (2) सान्दीपनि.

सान्दीपनि, *m. pr. n.* a certain sage, tutor of Krishn and Balarām.

सान्धना (*Rām.*) = साधना, 2, *q. v.*

साना = सानना, *q. v.*

सान्निध्य, *m.* proximity, vicinity, presence, attendance.

साप (*corruption*) = (1) शाप (2) साम्य, *qq. v.*

सापत, *m.* (*f.* ā) = शापित, *q. v.*

सापन, 1, a Braj pl. of साप, *q. v.*: 2, *m.* a kind of disorder in which the hair gradually falls off.

सापना = शापना, *q. v.*

सापराध, *m.* (*f.* ā) faulty, offending, criminal, guilty.

सापा, 1, mourning: 2, see (1) साप (2) सापना (3) सफ़ा.

सापित, *m.* (*f.* ā) = शापित, *q. v.*

सापिन, *more prop.* सर्पिणी, *q. v.*

सापेक्ष, having respect to, dependent on, proper, expedient.

सापेक्ष्यता, *f.* dependence on; expediency.

साफ़, clean, clear, distinct, manifest, plain, level, pure, candid, innocent. — *kahnā*, to speak distinctly or plainly.

साफल्य, *m.* productiveness, fruitfulness, effectiveness, efficiency, advantage, success.

साफ़ी, *f.* clearness, pureness; candour, sincerity; a filter or straining-cloth; a dish-clout.

साफ़ीख़त }
साफ़ीनामा } *m.*; see *s. v.* राज़ीनामा.

साब, in Mārwāṛī = साहिब, *q. v.*

साबधान (*colloquial*) = सावधान, *q. v.*

साबन = साबुन, *q. v.*

साबर, *m.* an elk (or more properly, a large species of stag); a leather of elk's or any kind of deer's hide for bedding; a small anvil.

साबरमन्त्र, *m.* a kind of spell composed in colloquial language.

साबल, *m.* an iron crow or lever.

साबस्त }
साबस्तो } *more prop.* सहवसति, *q. v.*

साबा in Mārwāṛī = the day of marriage.

साबासी, *more prop.* (1) शाबाशी (2) सहवासी. *qq.v.*

साबिक़, *adj.* former, preceding: *adv.* formerly, in the past, of yore.

साबित, fixed, established, firm, stable, durable, confirmed, proved, constant. — *k.* to render durable, to establish, confirm, prove (whether by evidence, by witness, by argument, or by demonstration).

साबुन, *m.* soap. — *kā phen*, lather, soapsuds.

साबुनगर, *m.* (*f.* nī) a soap-manufacturer.

साबुनगरी, *f.* the manufacture of soap, soap-making.

साबूत, whole, entire.

साबून = साबुन, *q.v.*

साम, 1, a contraction of श्याम, *q.v.*: 2, *f.* a ferrule: evening: 3, *m.* a hymn, a prayer that is to be chanted: hence, *pr. n.* (see वेद) the third Ved (the prayers of which are composed in metre, and are always sung or chanted).

सामक, appertaining to the Sām-Ved; hence, *m.* (*f.* ikā) one who sings the Sām-Ved.

सामग्री, *f.* entireness, wholeness, the whole; perfection; stock, implements, apparatus, tools, utensils, goods, chattels, baggage, things, furniture, effects, materials, necessaries, articles, scenery, train, retinue.

सामचार (by inversion) = समाचार, *q.v.*

सामग, *m.* (*f.* ā) one who believes in or observes the Sām-Ved. The term is more particularly used as an epithet of Garuṛ. [the Sām-Ved.

सामन, *m.* calming, conciliation, mildness; song:

सामना, *more prop.* साम्हना, *q. v.*

सामने, *more prop.* साम्हने, *q. v.*

सामयिक, appertaining to time or to some appointed or understood time, seasonable, opportune, timely, punctual; according to agreement, conventional, customary.

सामर, a contraction of साम्भर, *q. v.*

सामरी; see सामिरी and शाम्बरी.

सामर्थ, a contraction of सामर्थ्य, *q. v.*

सामर्थवान, *m.* (*f.* vatī) = सामर्थ्यवान, *q. v.*

सामर्थी, *m.* (*f.* iṇī) = सामर्थ्यवान, *q. v.*

सामर्थ्य, *m.* (*f.* ?) fitness, adequacy; the being entitled; profit; strength, power, fortitude, ability, capacity: (in Gram.) the mutual relation of words, the sense of words.

सामर्थ्यता, *f.* strongness, adequateness, ableness.

सामर्थ्यवती, *f.* a powerful or adequate female.

सामर्थ्यवन्त, *m.* (*f.* vatī) = सामर्थ्यवान, *q. v.*

सामर्थ्यवान, *m.* (*f.* vatī) powerful, mighty, adequate, fit, capable, able.

सामवेद, *m. pr. n.* (see साम) the third Ved.

सामवेदी, *m.* (*f.* inī) any Brāhmaṇ who studies the [Sām-Ved.

सामहो = साम्हने, *q. v.*

सामा, 1, *f.* = सामग्री, *q. v.*: 2, *m.* = सांवा, *q. v.*: 3, *f.* = श्यामा, *q. v.*: 4, in Mārwāṛī = साम्हने, *q. v.*: 5, *f.* eatables of various sorts, provisions.

सामाजिक, *m.* (*f.* ā *or* ī) an assistant or spectator at an assembly; *lit.* appertaining to an assembly, social.

सामाजिकता, *f.* (*m.* °त्व) the belonging to an assembly or society.

सामान, *m.* furniture, apparatus, instruments, tools: materials; necessaries; measure, quantity: understanding, reason, intellect: custom, habit, mode; order; proportion: opulence; power; probity: a land-mark.

सामानाधिकरण्य, *m.* common office; the being in the same predicament; the relating to the same object.

सामान्य, 1, *m.* (*f.* ā) common, equal, general, generic, universal; commonplace, low, plebeian: 2, *m.* totality, common affairs, common property; equanimity; the being common to many; a generic character; kind, species, genus; identity.

सामान्यभविष्यत, *m.* (in Gram.) the simple future.

सामान्यभूत, *m.* (in Gram.) the common or regular past tense, the aorist.

सामान्यलक्षण, *m.* a generic or specific character; a definition or description comprising many individuals.

सामान्यवर्त्तमान, *m.* (in Gram.) the present indicative.

सामान्यविश्वासी, *m.* (*f.* inī) one who believes what others also believe, one who believes anything on trust.

सामान्या, *f.* (*m.* सामान्य) a common female, a harlot.

सामिरी, appertaining to Samaria, Samaritan: hence (1) *f.* the Samaritan language (2) *m.* (*f.* iṇī) a native of Samaria (3) *m. pr. n.* a certain magician who is said to have been a contemporary of Moses and to have made by magic a speaking calf.

सामी, 1, (*contraction*) = (1) साम्हीं (2) स्वामी, *qq.v.*: 2, *f.* a ferrule: arable land: 3, exalted, sublime.

सामीप्य, 1, *m.* nearness, proximity, vicinity: 2, *m.* (*f.* ā) [a neighbour.

सामुझि (*Rām.*) = समझ, *q. v.*

सामुद्र, appertaining to the sea, marine, sea-born: hence, *m.* a mariner, voyager; cuttle-fish bone; sea-salt; a mark or stain on the body.

सामुद्रक, *m.* (*f.* ī) = सामुद्रिक, *q. v.*

सामुद्रकविद्या, *f.* the art of interpreting the marks on the body, palmistry, chiromancy, the art of physiognomy, fortune-telling.

सामुद्रकी, 1, *f.* of सामुद्रक, *q. v.*: 2, = सामुद्रिकी, *q. v.*

सामुद्रिक, 1, *m.* = सामुद्रकविद्या, *q. v.*: 2, *m.* (*f.* ā *or* ī) one who interprets marks on the body, a palmister, fortune teller, physiognomist.

सामुद्रिकविद्या = सामुद्रकविद्या, *q. v.*

सामुद्रिकी, 1, *f.*: 2, *m.* (*f.* inī) = सामुद्रिक, *q. v.*

सामुने, a corruption of साम्हने, *q. v.*

सामुहे (*Rām.*) = साम्हने, *q. v.*

साम्हा, *more prop.* साम्हना, *q. v.*

साम्हे, *more prop.* साम्हने, *q. v.*

साम्प, *m.* (*f.* n *or* in) a snake, a serpent. — *kī ṭopī*, a mushroom, toadstool. [a kind of defect in horses.

साम्पन, 1, *f.* a female snake, female serpent: 2,

साम्पा, a passing-bell.

साम्पिन = साम्पन, 1, *q. v.* [ly.

साम्प्रत°, now, at this time: seasonably, fitly, proper-

साम्ब, 1, *more prop.* शाम्ब, *q. v.*: 2, *m.* an epithet of

साम्बर, *m.* an elk. [Shiv: *lit.* attended by Ambā.

साम्भर, *m.* 1, *pr. n.* a certain town near Ajmeer, in the vicinity of which there is a lake from which salt is extracted: 2. the salt procured at Sāmbhar.

साम्हना, *m.* an encountering, confronting, opposing, facing, fronting; opposition; the front.— *k.* (with gen. of object) to face, confront, encounter, oppose.

साम्हने, *postp.* (takes gen. *m.* infl.) in front of, fronting, opposite, facing, before, over against, in comparison with —*rakhnā*, to offer.

साम्हों = **साम्हने** *q. v.*

साय, *m.* end, close; evening: an arrow.

सायंकाल, *m.* eventide, evening.

सायक, *m.* an arrow, dart; a sword.

सायण, *m. pr. n.* a certain learned Brāhmaṇ. He is thought to have flourished about A.D. 1370, and is celebrated as a well-known commentator on the Rig-Ved, the Shatpatha-Brāhmaṇa, the Tāṇḍya Brāhmaṇa, and other works. He was associated in many of his writings with his elder brother Mādhav, also called Vidyāraṇya, who became Prime Minister to two kings, Bukka rāya and Harihara after having aided them to found a new capital called Vijayā-nagar, in the native kingdom of Karnāṭ about A.D. 1344.

सायणाचार्य्य = **सायण**, *q. v.*

सायत, *more prop.* **साअत**, *q. v.*

सायद, *more prop.* (1) **शायद** (2) **सैयिद**, *qq. v.*

सायन, *m.* the longitude of a planet reckoned from the vernal equinoctial point.

सायब, in Māṛwāṛī = **साहिब**, *q. v.*

सायबान, *m.* a canopy, umbrella, parasol, the fly of a tent.

साया, *m.* shadow, shade; shelter, protection; an apparition, spectre; a petticoat.

सायुज्य, *m.* union, identification, intimate union (*esp.* the ultimate reäbsorption of the soul into the Divine Essence); similarity, likeness.

सायेत, *more prop.* **साअत**, *q. v.*

सार, 1, essential; excellent, best: hard, irrefragable; proved: 2, *m.* pith or sap of trees; the essence or the vital part of anything, cream, marrow, quintessence: strength, vigour, valour, heroism, prowess: value, worth; wealth: fresh butter: air, wind: sickness, disease; dysentery: pus: manure: a piece (at *chaupar*, chess, backgammon, etc.): iron: water: propriety, fitness: climax: a cow-house.

सारंग, 1, *m* (*f.* ī) many-coloured, variegated, spotted, gaudy: hence, 2, *m.* the chātak (*Cuculus melanoleucus*), the Indian cuckoo, a kind of crane, a snake, serpent, a peacock, a deer, a large bee, the third of the personified musical modes (*rāg*), a woman, a lion, an elephant, a cloud, a tree, a parasol, the lotus, hair, a garment, a flower, a conch-shell, a jewel, a gold, a bow, manure, sandal, camphor: 3, *m. pr. n.* a certain country: 4, *m.* an epithet (1) of Shiv (2) of Kāmdev.

सारंगधर, *m.* (the possessor of *sāraṅg, i.e.*) Vishṇu.

सारंगपाणी = **सारंगधर**, *q. v.*

सारंगिया, *m. f.* a fiddler.

सारंगी, *f.* a musical instrument like a fiddle.

सारक, 1, cathartic, laxative: 2, a kind of bird.

सारगधर, *more prop.* **सारंगधर**, *q. v.*

सारग्रहण, *m.* the extracting the essence or the best part of a thing.

सारग्राही, *m.* (*f.* iṇī) *adj.* extracting the essence or the best part of a thing.

सारता, *f.* essence, substance, strength, highest degree.

सारथि }
सारथी } *m.* (*f.* inī) a charioteer.

सारद; for words beginning thus, see under the form **शारद**.

सारना, *t.* to make, effect, accomplish, complete, perform, perfect; to mend, improve, ameliorate; to ornament, adorn; to polish; to manure; to manage a house: to marshal: to mind, observe.

सारनाथ, *m.* (the lord of essences, *i.e.*) the Almighty.

सारनी, *m.* (*f.* in *or* inī) = **सारन्हार**, *q. v.*

सारन्हार, *m.* (*f.* in *or* ī) a mender, a perfecter, completer.

सारबान, *m.* a camel-driver.

सारभाटा, low-water (as opposed to *high-water*).

सारमेय, *m.* (*f.* ī) a dog.

सारमेयादन, 1, *m.* the eating of dog's flesh: 2, *adj.* dog-eating: 3, *m. pr. n.* (in Myth.) one of the hells.

सारलोह, *m.* steel.

सारवत, *m.* (*f.* vatī) having pith or substance, strong, substantial, pithy, fertile.

सारवर्जित, *m.* (*f.* ā) destitute of pith or substance, pithless, sapless, unsubstantial.

सारसा, in Māṛwāṛī = a ranting spear.

सारस, appertaining to a lake: hence, 1, *m.* (*f.* ī) the Indian crane (*Ardea sibirica*); a bird in general: 2, *m.* a lotus: the moon.

सारसी, *f.* (*m.* **सारस**) the female of the Indian crane.

सारस्वत, 1, appertaining to the goddess Saraswatī or to the river which bears her name: 2, *m.* (*f.* ī) eloquent: 3, *m.* a staff of the *vilva*-tree: 4, *m. pr. n.* (1) of the people of the Saraswat country in the north-west of the province of Delhi (2) of their country.

सारा, 1, *m.* (*f.* ī) restored, recovered, repaired, completed: all, whole, entire: 2, *m.* a brother-in-law (wife's brother): *kush*-grass: 3, a funeral pile.

सारांश, *m.* the best part of a thing, the substance, essence; an epitome, summary; a table of contents.

सारांशरूप, consisting of the essence or best or essential part of a thing.

सारार्थ, *m.* an abridgment, epitome.

सारात्सार, 1, most essential: 2, *m.* quintessence.

सारालि = **सरिखा** = **सरीखा**, *q. v.* See **शरालि**.

सारिका, *f.* a certain bird (*Turdus salica*); the *mainā*-bird (*Gracula religiosa*).

सारिख (*Rām.*) = **सारिखा** = **सरीखा**, *q. v.*

सारिखना, *t.* to liken: *a. int.* to resemble.

सारिखा, *m.* (*f.* ī) *more prop.* **सरीखा**, *q. v.*

सारिन्दा, *m.* a violin, fiddle, lute.

सारी, 1, *f.* a corruption of **साड़ी**, *q. v.*: 2, *f.* cream: a man or piece (at chess, backgammon, etc.): the *mainā*-bird (*Turdus salica*): 3, *m.* (*f.* iṇī) in comp. = (1) going, proceeding (2) having the essence or substance of.

सारू, 1, in Māṛwāṛī = **लिये**, *q. v.*: 2, *more prop.* **साहू**, *q. v.*: 3, *f.* a species of blackbird or starling: 4 *m. f.* in comp. = performer, accomplisher.

सारे in Māṛwāṛī = in the power of.

सार्थर, a kind of hut in the jungles used by cowherds.

सार्थक, fit for the purpose, effectual, useful, profitable, advantageous, substantial; having a meaning or purpose.

सार्पी, *f. pr. n.* the ninth *Nakshatra.*

सार्वकालिक, *m.* (*f.* ī) appertaining to all times or seasons, everlasting, perennial.

सार्वधातुक, *m.* (in Gram.) a certain class of terminations in the inflection of the Sanskrit verb.

सार्वभौम, appertaining to (or comprising) the whole earth: hence, *m.* (*f.* ī) an epithet (1) of an emperor or universal monarch (2) of the elephant of Kuver as regent of the north quarter.

सार्वलौकिक, prevailing throughout the universe, universally known.

सार्ववर्णिक, appertaining to every kind, sort, or tribe. [Veds.

सार्ववेद, *m.* a Brāhman conversant with all the

साल, 1, *m.* a wall surrounding a building, a wall in general; a common kind of timber-tree (*Shorea robusta*), the plane-tree; a kind of fish (*Ophiocephalus wrahl*): a thorn: affliction, trouble, pain: a perforation, orifice, mortise, a hole made by driving a pin into the ground, etc.: a jackal: the gilthead fish (*Sparus spilotus*); a year; 2, *f.* a house, a place, a school-house.

सालक, afflictive, troublous, painful.

सालगम, *more prop.* शलगम, *q. v.*

सालग्राम, *more prop.* शालग्राम, *q. v.*

सालन, *m.* meat, fowl, fish, or vegetables dressed with condiments in various ways and eaten with bread or rice; the dish commonly called 'curry'. The curry eaten by Hindoos consists of vegetable only. (See *Kārī*, 5.)

सालना, 1, *m.* = सालन, *q.v.*: 2, *t.* to penetrate, perforate, bore, pierce, prick, drill; *a. int.* to ache, smart, pain.

सालपर्णी / **सालपर्णि** } = शालपर्णी, *q. v.*

सालपुष्प, *m.* a certain shrub (*Hibiscus mutabilis*).

सालम, good and fertile land.

सालमलि, *more prop.* शाल्मलि, *q. v,*

सालरस, *m.* the resinous juice of the *sāl*-tree.

सालवाहन (*corruption*) = शालिवाहन, *q. v.*

सालहतरी, *more prop.* सालिहोत्री, *q. v.*

सालसा, *m.* sarsaparilla; a certain medicinal plant (*Ichnocarpus frutescens*).

सालहोत्री, *more prop.* सालिहोत्री = सालोतरी, *q. v.*

साला, 1, *more prop.* शाला, *q. v.*: 2, *m.* a brother-in-law (wife's brother). The term is also used in a grossly abusive sense. [marshal, general.

सालार, *m.* a chief, head, leader, prince, captain,

सालि, *more prop.* शालि, *q. v.*

सालिक, 1, *more prop* सारिका, *q. v.*: 2, *m.* a traveller: *met.* a devotee; a class of Muhammadans who observe the law and lead a domestic life.

सालिग्राम, *more prop.* शालिग्राम, *q. v,*

सालिम, safe, free, perfect.

सालियाना, appertaining to a year, annual: hence, *m.* a yearly salary; an annuity.

सालिवाहन (*colloquial*) = शालिवाहन, *q. v,*

सालिस, the third: hence, *m.* (*f.* ā) an arbitrator, mediator, umpire.

सालिसी, *f.* umpireship, arbitration, mediation.

सालिहोत्री = सालोतरी, *q. v.*

साली, *f.* 1, a sister-in-law (wife's sister, *esp.* her younger sister): land taken by the year: *lit.* appertaining to a year, annual.

सालू, *m.* a kind of red cloth (dyed with *Morinda*); a sort of fine cloth (usually of a red or violet colour).

सालूसी, *f.* hypocrisy, trick, fraud, subterfuge.

सालोतर = सालोतरी, *q. v.*

सालोतरी, (from शालिहोत्री) 1, *m.* (inī) a farrier, a horse-doctor: 2, *f.* veterinary practice, farriery.

साल्मलि, *more prop.* शाल्मलि, *q. v.*

साल्व, 1, *more prop.* शाल्व, *q. v*: 2, *m. pr. n.* a certain [demon.

सावक, *more prop.* शावक, *q. v.*

सावकरन (*Rām.*) = श्यामकर्ण, *q. v.*

सावकाश, 1, *m.* leisure, opportunity: 2, *m.* (*f.* ā) with leisure, leisurely. [animals for the chase).

सावज, 1, wild, savage: 2, *m.* sport; game (*i.e.* wild

सावधान, careful, cautious, attentive, circumspect, prudent.—*rahnā* or *honā* (with abl.) to be cautious of; *e.g. Kuttese—ho*, beware of the dog.

सावधानत्व, *m.* (*f.* tā) = सावधानी, *q. v.*

सावधानी, *f.* carefulness, caution, circumspection, attention, prudence.

सावन, *m.* 1, (*colloquial*) = श्रावण, *q. v.*: 2, an employer of priests for a sacrifice; the ceremonies by which sacrifice is terminated: a month of thirty solar days; a day reckoned from sunrise to sunrise (of which 1577917828 are counted in a cycle [*yug*] of 4320000 years): 3, an epithet Varuṇ.

सावना, *more com.* सेवना, *q. v.*

सावन्त, *m.* (*f.* vatī) a leader, general, champion, hero: *lit.* brave, heroic.

सावन्ती, *f.* bravery, valour, heroism.

सावयव, possessed of limbs or members.

सावर, 1, *more com.* साबर, *q. v.*: 2, *m.* fault, offence; sin, wickedness, crime; the Lodhra-tree: a plumbline (!).

सावरो, in Braj = सांवला, *q. v.*

सावर्णि, *m. pr. n.* the eighth Manu.

सावर्ण्य, *m.* identity of caste.

सावस्त / **सावस्ती** } *more prop.* श्रावस्ति, *q. v.*

सावित; see सावित्र and साबित.

सावित्र, 1, descended from the sun; appertaining to the dynasty descended from the sun: 2, *m.* an epithet (1) of the sun (2) of Shiv (3) of a certain Vasu (4) of Karṇ, the child of the sun (5) of one of the Nakshatras.

सावित्री, *f.* a beam of light, a cluster of rays: the sacrificial thread; the ceremony of investiture with the sacred thread; *pr. n.* (1) of the wife of Satyavān (2) of Umā (3) of the most holy verse of the Rig-Ved.

साष्टांग (स + अष्ट + अंग) *m.* the ceremony of touching the ground (in prostration in worship) with eight parts of the body, *viz.* the forehead, the breast, the shoulders, the hands, and the feet.

सास, 1, a corruption of सांस, *q.v.*: 2, a contraction of सासु, *q. v.*: 3, *m.* a bug, a flea, a louse.

सासत } *more prop.* शास्ति, *q.v.*
सासति }

सासन; for words beginning thus, see under the [form शासन.

सासु, *f.* (श्वश्रू) a mother-in-law.

सास्ति (*colloquial*) = शास्ति, *q.v.*

सास्ना, *f.* the dewlap of an ox.

सास्वतं (*Rām.*) = शाश्वत, *q.v.*

साह, *m.* (*f.* n or nī) a merchant, shop-keeper; a title of respect given to merchants, bankers, etc.: an innocent, an honest person: *adj.* penurious.

साहज़ादा, *m.* (*f.* ī) *more prop.* शाहज़ादा, *q.v.*

साहत, *f.* the inner part of a building, a court, quadrangle: shore, coast: tract of country.

साहन, *f.* the wife of a *sāh*; a female *sāh.*

साहनी; see साहन and सहनी.

साहब, *more prop.* साहिब, *q.v.*

साहम (Sk. स + अहम) = वह मैं हूं.

साहस, *m.* violence, oppression, cruelty, assault, outrage, rape: punishment, chastisement: hatred: boldness, daring, courage, spirit, valour, intrepidity, resoluteness: encouragement, reässurance: rashness: suicide.

साहसिक, *m.* (*f.* ī) = साहसी, *q.v.*

साहसी, *m.* (*f.* inī) violent, rapacious, cruel; bold, daring, rash, impetuous, resolute, determined, brave, undaunted, intrepid, courageous, forward, obtrusive, impudent, saucy.

साहाना, *m.* (*f.* ī) *more prop.* शाहाना, *q.v.*

साहाय, *more prop.* (1) सहाय (2) साहाय्य, *qq. v.*

साहाय्य, *m.* mutual help, alliance, confederation, assistance, succour, help, friendship, fellowship.

साहि, 1, Chand = शाह, *q.v.*: 2, in Mārwārī (= सांई) a Muhammadan fakeer. [association, society.

साहित्य, *m.* conjunction, connexion, combination,

साहिब, *m.* a lord, master, owner, proprietor; Sir: (in Mārwārī =) God. The collective plural form *Sāhib-log* signifies *par excellence* gentlemen, gentlefolks, gentry; and is applied in some parts of India to the Muhammadan race of the Saiyids, but more generally to Europeans or to persons of European extraction.

साहिबख़ाना, *m.* the master of the house, head of the family.

साहिबा, *f.* a lady, mistress, proprietress, dame, gentlewoman; Madam. The expression (as also the term *Bibi-sāhib*) is most generally applied to a European lady or to a lady of European extraction.

साहिर, *m.* (*f.* ā) an enchanter, magician, wizard.

साहिल, *m.* a plumb-line: a porcupine.

साहिस, a corruption of साईस, *q. v.*

साही, *f.* a porcupine, hedgehog: nightmare.

साहु, *m.* (*f.* ni) = साह, *q.v.*

साहुनि, *f.* (*m.* साहु) = साहन, *q.v.*

साहू, *m.* (*f.* ni) = साह. *q.v.*

साहूकार, *m.* (*f.* i) a wealthy person, great man, great merchant, banker, broker, shopkeeper, tradesman.

साहूकारी, *f.* the condition or duties of a wealthy person, trade, traffic, commerce, exchange of money.

साहूनि, *f.* (*m.* साहू) = साहन, *q. v.*

साहूल, *m.* a plummet.

साहेब, *m.* (*f.* ā) *more prop.* साहिब, *q. v.*

साहो; see सहो and साहु.

ंस, a termination = एस. 2, *q. v*

सिअनि; see (1) सिकनि (2) सोंचनी.

सिआरा, *m.* (*f.* ī) *more prop.* सियार, *q. v.*

सिंकोरना = सकोड़ना, *q.v.*

सिंग, *more prop.* (1) सिंह (2) सींग, *qq. v.*

सिंगड़ा, *m.* a powder horn.

सिंगड़ी, *f.* a small powder-horn (for priming).

सिंगरौर } (*Rām.*) = शृंगवेर, *q.v.*
सिंगरौर }

सिंगलदीप, *more prop.* सिंहलद्वीप, *q.v.*

सिंगसिंगोटी, *f.* a general term for horned beasts.

सिंगा, *m.* a musical horn, trumpet; a powder-horn.

सिंगार, *m.* dress, ornament, decoration, embellishment.—*k.* to wear, be clad with; to adjust.

सिंगारना, *t.* to dress, decorate, adorn, embellish.

सिंगाररस, *m.* the sentiment (*ras*) of love, considered as one of the nine sentiments. [*arbor-tristis*).

सिंगारहार, *m.* the weeping nyctanthes (*Nyctanthes*

सिंगारा (*Ram.*) = सिंगार, *q.v.*

सिंगारिया, *m.* one whose business it is to dress an

सिंगारू (*Rām.*) = (1) सिंगार (2) सिंगारिया, *q.v.* [idol.

सिंगिया, *m.* a kind of poison.

सिंगौटी, *f.* a polishing-tool made of horn: an ornament of metal on the horns of a bullock: a last.

सिंघ, *m.* (*f.* nī) a frequent form of सिंह, *q.v.*

सिंघल (*Rām.*) = सिंहल, *q.v.*

सिंघाड़ा, *m.* a certain plant (*Trapa natans*): a handkerchief folded diagonally: water-chesnut or water-caltrops: the root of the esculent water-lily.

सिंचाना, *t.* to cause to irrigate. (?)

सिंचासिंचाई, *more com.* सींचासींचाई, *q.v.*

सिंय, सिंद, सिंध; for words beginning with either of these elements, see under the corresponding forms सिन्य, सिन्द, सिन्ध, respectively.

सिंसुपा (*Rām.*) = सिसुपा, *q.v.*

सिंह, 1, *m.* (*f.* ī) a lion: 2, *m. pr. n.* the zodiacal sign Leo: 3, in comp. = preëminent, distinguished: 4, the term is much used among Hindoos as a title. *Sarotar* —, a miser. [*musops elengi*).

सिंहकेशर, *m.* a lion's mane: a certain plant (*Mi-*

सिंहगति } *f.* a lion's gait.
सिंहठवनि }

सिंहद्वार, *m.* a gate, entrance, portal, grand entrance, the royal gate or chief entrance to a palace (that on which is placed the effigy of a lion).

सिंहध्वनि, *m.* a lion's roar; war-cry.

सिंहनाद, *m.* war-cry, war-whoop: the roar or yelp of a lion: (in Pros.) a species of metre.

सिंहनादक, *m.* = **सिंहनाद**, *q. v.*

सिंहनादका, *f.* a certain plant (*Hedysarum a'hagi*).

सिंहनी, *f.* (*m.* **सिंह**) a lioness.

सिंहपर्णी, *f.* the plant *Justicia adhenatoda.*

सिंहपुच्छी, *f.* the plant *Hedysarum lagopodioides.*

सिंहपौर } **सिंहपौल** } = **सिंहद्वार**, *q. v.*

सिंहल, *m.* tin; brass: cassia-bark: *pr. n.* Ceylon.

सिंहलद्वीप, *m. pr. n.* the island of Ceylon.

सिंहलाद, *m. pr. n.* one of the four sons of Hiranyakashyap by his wife Kiyadhū.

सिंहासन, *m.* a throne. [fiction.

सिंहासनबत्तीसी, *f. pr. n.* a certain Hindee work of

सिंहिका, *f. pr. n.* the daughter of *Hiranyakashyap* and mother of Rāhu.

सिंहिनी (*colloquial*) = **सिंहनी**, *q. v.*

सिंही, *f.* (*m.* **सिंह**) a lioness: the egg-plant (*Solanum melongena*). [shard, potsherd.

सिकटा, *m.* a fragment of an earthen vessel, a

सिकता, *f.* a kind of disease (the stone).

सिकना, *n.* (see **सेंकना**) to be roasted, be parched.

सिकनि, *f.* the mucus of the nose. [Great.

सिकन्दर, *m. pr. n.* Alexander, *esp.* Alexander the

सिकरा, *m.* a falcon, hawk (*Falco*).

सिकरी, *f* the staple of a lock.

सिकल, *f.* (prop. **शृंखल**) a chain.

सिकली, *f.* the staple of a lock.

सिकलीगढ़ = **सैक़लगर** *q. v.*

सिका; see (1) **सिकना** (2) **शिखा** (3) **सिखा** (4) **सिक्का**.

सिकार; for words beginning thus, see under the

सिकिल, *more prop.* **सैक़ल**, *q. v.* [form **शिकार**.

सिकुड़ना = **सुकड़ना**, *q. v.*

सिकुड़ा, *m.* (*f.* ī) = **सुकड़ा**, *q. v.*

सिकोड़ना } **सिकोरना** } = **सकोड़ना**, *q. v.*

सिक्का, 1, *m.* a die for coining; the stamp or impression on money; stamped coin; a rupee; a certain weight =7 dwt. 11·5511 grs.: 2, sterling, current (as coin).

सिक्थ, *m.* boiled rice; a lump of boiled rice: beeswax: indigo.

सिख, 1, *more prop.* **शिखा**, *q. v.*: *m.* 2, (from **शिष्य**) a disciple, pupil, scholar, apprentice: 3, *m.* (*f.* ni) a people (followers of Nânak) who reside in the Panjāb, a Sikh.

सिखण्ड; for words beginning thus, see under the more proper form **शिखण्ड**.

सिखनहारा, *m.* (*f.* ī) *more prop.* **सीखनेहारा**, *q. v.*

सिखना, a corruption of **सीखना**, *q. v.*

सिखनावद, *m.* tuition, instruction.

सिखनी, *f.* (*m.* **सिख**) a female Sikh, the wife of a Sikh.

सिखनौतू, *m.* a new learner, novice.

सिखर, *m.* 1, *more prop.* **शिखर**, *q. v.*: 2, three or more strings tied together to form a support for hanging anything on; netting; the cords of a bahangi in which the baskets rest.

सिखरन, 1, a Braj pl. of **सिखर**, *q. v.*: 2, *m.* a kind of dish made of coagulated milk and sugar.

सिखलाना = **सिखाना**, *q. v.*

सिखवैं in Braj = (1) **सिखाऊं** (2) **सीखूं**.

सिखा (*Rām.*) = (1) **शिखा** (2) **शिखा** (3) **शिष्य**, *qq. v.*

सिखाई, *f.* teaching, instruction.

सिखाना, *t.* (of **सीखना**) to instruct, teach, inculcate; *met.* to admonish, chastise.

सिखानेवाला } **सिखानेहारा** } *m.* (*f.* ī) an instructor, admonisher.

सिखापन, *m.* teaching, etc.—*k.* to be true, admonish.

सिखाया, *m.* teaching, instruction. [ish.

सिखावट, *f.* teaching, instruction, admonition.

सिखावना (*colloquial*) = **सिखाना**, *q. v.*

सिखावनिहार, in Braj = **सिखानेहारा**, *q. v.*

सिखिनी, *f.* (prop. **शिखिनी**) a pea-hen.

सिखी, appertaining to the Sikhs or to their religion.

सिगरा, *m.* (*f.* ī) all, the whole, every.

सिगरे in Braj = **सिगरा**, *q. v.*

सिगलीगर = **सैक़लगर**, *q. v.* [hatred, calumny.

सिगाल, thought, suspicion; word, speech; enmity,

सिङ्; for words beginning thus, see under the

सिचना, *more com.* **सींचना**, *q. v.* [form **सिंग**.

सिचाना, *t.* to irrigate: (to cause to irrigate ?).

सिच्छक (*colloquial*) = **शिक्षक**, *q. v.*

सिच्छा (*colloquial*) = **शिक्षा**, *q. v.*

सिजदा, *m.* the touching the ground with the forehead in prostration as an act of adoration to God.

सिजिल, 1, = **सिजिल्ल**, *q. v.*: 2, *m.* the recording angel.

सिजिल्ल, 1, *m.* a register, the decree or the seal of a judge, the written attestation of a notary: 2, right, proper, good, well-arranged.

सिज्जिल; see (1) **सिजिल** (2) **सिजिल्ल**.

सिझाना, *t.* to tan, boil, seethe, melt.

सिटकारी, tapering, fusiform.

सिट्टा, *f.* Indian corn.

सिट्टी, *f.* whistling.

सिट्ठी, *f.* dross, lees.

सिठनी, *f.* (*m.* **सेठ**) = **सेठन**, *q. v.*

सिठाई, *f.* tastelessness, insipidity.

सिठानी, *f.* (*m.* **सेठ**) = **सेठन**, *q. v.*

सिड़, *f.* madness, insanity.

सिड़न, *f.* mad (said of females).

सिड़पन, *m.* insanity, madness, lunacy.

सिड़बिलिल्ला, *m.* (*f.* ī) mad, insane.

सिड़ा, *m.* (*f.* ī) mad, insane, lunatic.

सिड़ी, 1, *more prop.* **सीढ़ी**, *q. v.*: 2, *f.* (*m.* **सिड़ा**) a

सिढ़ी, *more prop.* **सीढ़ी**, *q. v.* [mad female.

सित, 1, *adj.* white: 2, *m.* white (the colour): 3,

m. pr. n. the planet Venus: 4, *m.* the light half of the month: an arrow: silver: sandal. [cold.

सितंग, *m.* palsy, numbness, the being chilled with

सितंगी, chilled with cold, numbed, palsied, paralytic: hence, *m.* (*f.* inī) a paralytic, etc.

सितकाल = शीतकाल, *q. v.*

सितचिह्न, *m.* a certain fish (*Lacerta scincus*).

सितम, *m.* tyranny, violence, oppression, injury.

सितमकश, subjected to tyranny, injured, oppressed.

सितरी, *f.* perspiration, sweat.

सिता, *f.* candied sugar; moonlight; a beautiful female; spirituous liquor; the name of several plants.

सिताइश, *f.* thanksgiving, praise.

सितांक, *m.* a certain fish (*Lacerta scincus*).

सितांग (*colloquial*) = शीतांग, *q. v.*

सिताबि, (*prop.* शिताबी) *f.* quickness: *adv.* quickly.

सितार, *m.* a kind of guitar with three strings.

सितारा, *m.* 1, = सितार, *q.v.*: 2, *m.* a star; a kind of firework. [*more com.* से, *q. v.*

सिती, 1, *more prop.* (1) सिती (2) शीति, *qq.v.*: 2,

सितीलक = सातीलक, *q. v.*

सितून, *m.* a pillar, column, prop.

सितेज़खोर, quarrelsome, contentious.

सितेज़ा, *m.* controversy, altercation, contention, quarrelling, conflict, battle.

सितोपल, *m.* chalk (or a mineral substance of similar appearance, considered as a variety of it); crystal.

सिताह, *f.* affliction, uneasiness, distress, indigence.

सितरी, *f.* perspiration, sweat.

सिथल (*colloquial*) = शीतल, *q. v.*

सिथिल (*colloquial*) = शिथिल, *q. v.*

सिद, 1, *more prop.* सिद्ध, *q.v.*: 2, *f. pr.n.* (in Māṛwāṛī) the wife of Gaṇesh.

सिद्ध, 1, *m.* (*f.* ā) accomplished, effected, brought about, settled, completed, finished, perfected; successful: ready, prepared; cooked; accomplished (in ability, in sanctity, or in holiness); emancipated; endowed with supernatural powers; judged, decided; celebrated, famous; shining, splendid; eternal: initiated; discharged (said of debt); (in Law) valid: (in Logic) demonstrated, proved: 2, *m.* a divine personage of undefined attributes or character; a saint, sage, seer; an adept; a magician; one who by the performance of certain mystical and magical rites has acquired superhuman powers; one who has subjected his will to the eight *siddhis*; an ascetic who by mystic and austere practices has effected all or any of five purposes, *viz.* (1) the influence of the gods (2) their form (3) their society (4) residence in the divine *loks* (5) identification with a deity: an inspired or prophetic writer (as Vyās and others), one to whom the past, present, and future are supposed to be known: 3, *m. pr. n.* (1) of a certain class of demigods who inhabit the middle air, or Indra's heaven (2) of the 21st of the astronomical period called *yog*.

सिद्धकारी, *m.* (*f.* iṇī) an observer of the laws.

सिद्धता, *f.* completion, accomplishment, success.

सिद्धधातु }
सिद्धपारा } *m.* mercury, quicksilver.

सिद्धपुरुष, *m.* a man who by abstraction and austerities has attained that degree of divine perfection which enables him to accomplish anything he desires.

सिद्धरस, 1, mineral, metallic: 2, *m.* mercury.

सिद्धलोक = सिद्धपुरुष, *q. v.*

सिद्धसाधन, *m.* the performance of magical rites: the materials employed in alchymical processes.

सिद्धाना, *t.* to exercise or accomplish सिद्धि, *q.v.*

सिद्धान्त, *m.* demonstrated conclusion, established truth, reliable doctrine, the result attained by a process of demonstration, an end accomplished, conclusion, decision, result, consequence; any system of science (*esp.* of astronomy, geometry, etc.).

सिद्धान्तकोटि = सिद्धान्तपक्ष, *q. v.*

सिद्धान्तपक्ष, *m.* a logical conclusion, an argument by which one opinion is refuted and another undoubtedly established.

सिद्धान्ती, *m.* (*f.* inī) a follower of the Mīmāṅsā philosophy; a logician, demonstrator: *lit.* appertaining to a logical demonstration.

सिद्धार्थ, 1, *m.* (*f.* ī) *adj.* having attained one's aim, successful: 2, *m.* white mustard.

सिद्धि, *f.* accomplishment, fulfilment, completion, success, prosperity; accuracy, correctness; an indisputable conclusion or position; knowledge, understanding, intellect; acquittance, discharge (of debt); concealment: the fruit of the adoration of the gods or of ascetic severities; the acquisition of supernatural powers by the completion af magical, mystical, or alchymical rites and processes; a magical shoe which is supposed to convey its wearer wherever he lists; a certain medicinal plant; (in Law) validity; the decision of a court of justice; (in Math.) the solution of a problem; *pr. n.* of a certain *yog* [either (1) the sixteenth of the astronomical periods so termed, or (2) the nineteenth of the twenty-eight astrological periods so termed].

सिद्धिप्रद, *m.* (*f.* ā) a giver of सिद्धि, *q. v.*

सिद्धिफोला, *f.*? (in Gram.) the junction of a consonant with a vowel.

सिद्धिवाला, *m.* (*f.* ī) one who possesses सिद्धि, *q.v.*

सिद्धोन्मुख, fit for business. (?)

सिध, *more com.* सिद्ध, *q. v. Sidh kar lānā*, to obey.

सिधाना; see (1) सिद्धाना (2) सिधारना.

सिधारना, *a. int.* to depart, set out, set off, take one's farewell, take leave, go.

सिधारो, *interj.* on! off! [plicity.

सिधावट, *f.* straightforwardness, candour, sim-

सिधि, *more prop.* सिद्धि, *q. v.* [occ sion intoxication.

सिधी, *f.* a species of hemp the leaves of which

सिधोड़, *f.* the longing of pregnant females.

सिन, *more prop.* (1) सिन (2) सीन, *qq. v.*

सिनक, *m.* blowing the nose; mucus of the nose.

सिनकना, *a. int.* to blow the nose.

सिनीवाली, *f.* the day of new moon, or the day preceding that of the new moon.

सिनेह (*corruption*) = स्नेह, *q. v.*

सिन्धु, a corruption of सिन्धु, *q. v.*

सिन्दुर (*corruption*) = सिन्दूर, *q. v.*

सिन्दूर, *m.* minium, red lead, vermilion.

सिन्दूरी, *f.* the name of three plants, *viz.* (1) the plant called *rockani* (2) *Grislea tomentosa* (3) *Lythrum fruticosum.*

सिन्ध (*contraction*) = सिन्धु, *q. v.* See उ, 3.

सिन्धु, *m.* the ocean : the juice that exudes from an elephant's temples; an elephant : *pr. n.* (1) of the river Indus (2) of the country along the Indus, commonly called Scinde or Sindh (3) of the inhabitants of that country (4) of a certain musical mode (*rāgiṇī*). In the ingenious system of reckoning by symbols adopted by Hindoos in their poetry, this word is a symbol for 4.

सिन्धुक ; see (1) सुतक (2) सन्दूक.

सिन्धुज, 1, *m.* (*f.* ā) river-produced, sea-produced, marine: produced in the country along the Indus: 2, *m.* rock-salt.

सिन्धुपुष्प, *m.* a conch.

सिन्धमथ, सिन्धुमथन, सिन्धुमन्थ } *m.* the churning of the ocean.

सिन्धुर, *m.* (*f.* ā) an elephant.

सिन्धुलवण, *m.* rock-salt.

सिन्धू, *more prop.* सिन्धु, *q. v.*

सिन, *m.* an age; period of life: a tooth: the nib of a pen.

सिपकली, *more prop.* छिपकली, *q. v.* See स,

सिपर, *f.* a shield, target.

सिपरदारी, *f.* shielding, protecting.

सिपविष्ट, *more prop.* शिपिविष्ट, *q. v.*

सिपहर, *m.* the sphere, world, celestial globe ; fortune ; time : afternoon.

सिपारस, *more prop.* सिपारिश, *q. v.*

सिपारा = सीपारा, *q. v.*

सिपारिश, *f.* recommendation, intercession, introduction, presentation, entrée.

सिपास, *f.* thanksgiving, praise.

सिपाह, *f.* (used in the pl.) soldiers, an army.— *phir jānā*, to revolt (said of an army).

सिपाही, *m.* a military man, soldier (*vulg.* sepoy).

सिपिविष्ट, *more prop.* शिपिविष्ट, *q. v.*

सिप्र, *m.* perspiration, sweat : the moon.

सिप्रा, *f.* a woman's zone; a female buffalo: *pr. n.* a certain river near Oujain or Ujjayan.

सिफ्लक, *m.* a small lizard (commonly found in houses, and subsisting on flies and insects).

सिफत, *f.* praise; quality, attribute; description, manner.

सिफारिश = सिपारिश, *q. v.*

सिब in Chand = शिव, *q. v.*

सिबत, *m.* progeny, family, tribe.

सिबाब, an abusing, reviling.

सिबार ; see (1) सवार (2) सिवार.

सिभ in Chand = शिव, *q. v.*

सिमट, *f.* the act of condensing, collecting, or constringing; tone, elasticity. — *jānā*, to shrivel, shrink.

सिमटना, *a. int.* to become concentrated or contracted or condensed, to shrivel, shrink.

सिमटा, *m.* (*f.* ī) collected, gathered, shrivelled.

सिमत, *f.* a mark (*esp.* one made by burning).

सिमसिमाहट, *f.* moisture, moistness.

सिमिटना = सिमटना, *q. v.*

सिम्बल = सेमल, *q. v.*

सिय, a Prākṛit form of सीता, *q. v.*

सियन (*Rām.*) = सीना, *q. v.*

सियपिय (*Rām.*) = सीताका प्रिय, *i.e.* Rām-Chandra.

सियराम = सीताराम, *q. v.*

सियरना, *a. int.* to become joined, to unite.

सिया, 1, a Prākrit form of सीता, *q v.* : 2, *m.* (*f.* सिई) sewn, stitched.

सियाक़, *m.* arithmetic or enumeration by the Arabic alphabet ; accounts.

सियादत, *f.* dominion, rule, sovereignty, reigning, governing.

सियान ; for words beginning thus, see under the form सयान.

सियानत, *f.* defence, guarding, keeping, preserving, support.

सियार, सियाल } *m.* (*f.* ī) a jackal.

सियालकाँटा, *m.* an epithet of the prickly poppy (*Argemone Mexicana*) ; *lit.* jackal's thorn.

सियासत, *f.* government, administration of justice ; chastisement, pain, pang, agony.

सियाह, black.—*k.* to take an account of.

सियाहगोश, *m.* a certain animal (*Felis caracal*, Gmel.; *Persian lynx*, Penn.) of the panther kind with which they hunt deer.

सियाहा, *m.* an account-book, written account, list, inventry.

सियाहरू, blackfaced : *hence*, disgraced, unlucky.

सियाही, *f.* blackness (moral as well as physical); ink; blacking.

सियोन, *m. pr. n.* the Mount Sion.

सिर, *m.* the head, top, summit.—*uṭhātehī pā·nāl ho-jānā*, to be crushed in the commencement of one's undertaking.—*uṭhānā*, to rise up against one, rise in rebellion.—*k.* to make a commencement.—*kāṛhnā*, to become conspicuous, to become impudent.—*ke zor*, with all one's might.—*ke bhal*, headlong head-foremost.—*ko kadam k.* to go quickly but with respect.—*khujānā*, to court punishment.—*chaṛhnā*, to become impudent.—*chaṛhke marnā*, to lay the guilt of one's blood at another's door.—*chaṛhānā*, to exalt ; to assume, to be arrogant ; to shew respect.—*dolānā*, to nod (from sleepiness).—*dulānā* or *dhunnā*, to shake the head from affliction.—*ṭālnā*, to have the menses. —*toṛnā*, to subdue.—*dharnā*, to be obedient.—*nānā*, to bow the head (*esp.* in obeisance or in worship).—*niwānā*, to be humble, to be obedient.—*papolnā bhejā khānā*, to shew kindness externally and harbour enmity in the breast.—*par*, on the head of, on the neck of.—*par khāk ḍālnā*, to throw ashes on the head, to lament.—*par chaṛhānā*, to spoil (a child, etc); to raise an inferior above oneself ; to show respect.—*parasti k.*, to protect, aid.—*pīṭnā*, to lament.—*phirānā*, to labour in vain.—*phaṭnā*, to have the menses. —*phernā*, to revolt from a state of obedience.—*mailā honā*, to have the menses.—*mārnā*, to be at great pains, to search diligently, to cudgel one's brains.—*muṇḍānā*, to quit one's connexions and adopt a life of mendicity.—*se kafan bāndhnā*, to engage in a desperate undertaking (giving up all regard for one's own safety)—*se sirwā* (or *sirwāhe*), the turban is for the head, or turbans are like the head, *i e.* without a chief the people fall into ruin and confusion.—*de-de mārnā*, to be desperate.—*hilānā*, to nod (from sleepiness).

सिरकटा, *m.* (*f.* ī) beheaded, decapitated.

सिरका, *m.* vinegar.

सिरकी, *f.* a kind of reed of which mats are made, reed-grass (the upper joint of *Saccharum procerum*, Roxb); a sort of mat to keep off rain.

सिरखप, resolute, adventurous (said of soldiers).

सिरखपी, *f.* resoluteness, adventurousness, enterprize, perseverance.

सिरगिरी, *f.* the comb of a cock, crest of a bird.

सिरचढ़ा, *m.* (*f.* ī) high-headed, haughty, proud.

सिरचोट, *f.* aversion, disgust.

सिरजन; for words beginning thus, see under the form **सजन**.

सिरजनहार, **सिरजनहारा**, **सिरजन्हार** } *m.* (*f.* ī) = **सजनहार**, *q.v.*

सिरजा, *m.* (*f.* ī) *more prop.* **सजा**, *q.v.*

सिरजाना, *more prop.* (1) **सजाना** (2) **सिराजना**, *qq.v.*

सिरठौवर, **सिरठौवल** } *m.* salutation (with displeasure).

सिरडूब, perfectly wet, soaking, dripping.

सिरदवाल, *f.* reins of a bridle, headstall.

सिरन, *m.* (a Braj pl. of **सिर**) heads. See **न**, 6.

सिरना, *more com.* **सईना**, *q.v.*

सिरनाई, *f.* bowing the head, obeisance.

सिरनाय; see **सिर नाना** under the word **सिर**.

सिरन्ह, *m.* (a Braj pl. of **सिर**) heads. See **न्ह**.

सिरपर; see *s.v.* **सिर**.

सिरपिड़ात, *f.* headache.

सिरपै, *more com.* **सिरपर**, *q.v.* See **पै**.

सिरफटौवर, *m.* wrangling: affectation of civility with internal hatred.

सिरफोड़ी, *f.* headache.

सिरमनि, *more com.* **शिरोमणि**, *q.v.*

सिरमाथा, *m.* assent, nodding assent.

सिरविन्दु, *m.* the sign *Anuswār* or *Chandravindu*.

सिरवंहिया, *m.* an overseer.

सिरस; see (1) **सिरसा** (2) **शिरस**.

सिरसा = **शिरीष**, *q.v.*

सिरसख्याक, head of cattle, a herd (?).

सिरसींग, rebellious, mutinous.

सिरहना, *more prop.* **सईना**, *q.v.*

सिरहाना, *m.* the place where the head rests when a person is asleep or dead, the head of a bed or of a tomb, a pillow, bolster.

सिरा, 1, the head, top, tip, end, extremity: 2, *f.* any tubular vessel of the body (as a nerve, vein, or artery); a bucket, a baling vessel.

सिराज, *m.* a luminary; a candle; a lamp; the sun.

सिराजना, *t.* to create, produce, form.

सिराजाल, *m.* enlargement of the vessels of the eye.

सिराजुद्दौला, *m. pr. n.* (*lit.* the luminary of the State) the viceroy of Bengal who in 1756 took Calcutta and caused the death of 131 Englishmen by confining them in a close dungeon famed as 'The Black Hole of Calcutta'.

सिराजुलकुत्रब *m.* the fairy's lamp; a certain plant that shines at night like the glowworm.

सिरात, *adj.* cold, becoming cold.

सिराना, *a. int.* to cool: 2, *t.* to cool, make cold: to float, set afloat; to set off, despatch.

सिरानी, (*Rām.*) a fem. form of **सिराना**, *q.v.*

सिरावन, *m.* a harrow.

सिरावनों in Braj = **सिराना**, *q.v.*

सिराहि, (pl. °हिं), **सिराहीं**, (pl. °हीं) } old forms = **सिराता है** (**सिराना**).

सिरि; see (1) **सिढ़ी** (2) **श्री** (3) **सिरी**.

सिरिजना (*Rām.*) = **सजना**, *q.v.*

सिरिस = **शिरीष**, *q.v.*

सिरिस्त; see (1) **सरिश्त** (2) **सरिश्त** (3) **सृष्टि**.

सिरी, 1, *more prop.* **सिर्री**, *q.v.*: 2, *f.* the head (*esp.* when severed from the trunk): improvement.

सिरीखा, *m.* (*f.* ī) = **सरीखा**, *q.v.*

सिरीष, *more prop.* **शिरीष**, *q.v.*

सिरोत्पात, *m.* redness and inflammation of the eyes.

सिरोमनि (*colloquial*) = **शिरोमणि**, *q.v.*

सिर्का, *m.* vinegar.

सिर्फ़, unmixed, pure, alone, only, mere, merely.

सिर्र, *m.* (pl. **असरार**) a secret, a mystery.

सिर्री, *m.* (*f.* iṇī) mad, insane, lunatic.

सिल, *f.* (*contraction*) = **सिला**, 1, *q.v.*

सिलः, *more prop.* **शिला**, *q.v.*

सिलक, 1, *more prop.* **तिलक**, *q.v.*: 2, *m.* a thread, string; order, series, train; a road, path.

सिलगना = **सुलगना**, *q.v.*

सिलगाना = **सुलगाना**, *q.v.*

सिलन, (a Braj pl. of **सिल**; see **न**, 6) stones, rocks.

सिलपची = **चिलमची**, *q.v.*

सिलपट, smooth, even, level.

सिलबट्टा, *m.* two stones with which spices, paint, etc. are ground.

सिलवट, 1, = **सिलौट**, *q.v.*: 2. *f.* a fold, ply.

सिलवाना, *t.* to cause to sew or stitch, to cause to be sewn or stitched.

सिलसिला, *m.* a chain, series, concatenation; succession, pedigree, genealogy; a catalogue.

सिलसिलाहट, *f.* concatenation: moisture, moistness.

सिलहदार, *m.* an armour-bearer, esquire, armed attendant.

सिला, 1, *f.* = **शिला**, *q.v.*: 2, *m.* (*f.* ī) = **सीला**, *q.v.*: 3, *m.* ? the gleanings of a cornfield.

सिलाई, *f.* the act or the business of sewing, needle-work, sewing; a seam; the price paid for sewing: a match tipped with sulphur.

सिलाईदार, striped (as cloth) with narrow stripes.

सिलाजित (*colloquial*) = **शिलाजित**, *q. v.*

सिलाना, *t.* (causat. of **सीना**) to cause to sew or stitch: to moisten: *a. int.* to melt: 2, *m.* (*f.* ई) moist.

सिलाबाक; see **शिलावल्का.**

सिलारस (*colloquial*) = **शिलारस**, *q.v.* [armour.

सिलाह, *f.* implements of war, arms, weapons,

सिली, *f.* a whetstone, a hone: a small kiln: the grain and chaff on the threshingfloor before winnowing: the trunk of a tree: a plank: a teal, a large species of teal commonly called 'whistling teal' (from the sharp cry of this bird).

सिलीमुख (*colloquial*) = **शिलीमुख**, *q. v.*

सिलेदार in Mārwārī = **सिलहदार**, *q. v.*

सिलोट, *f.* a small grindingstone, a muller, stone for grinding spices.

सिल्प (*colloquial*) = **शिल्प**, *q. v.*

सिल्ली, *f.* a whetstone, grindstone, hone: a plank.

सिव; for words beginning thus, but not given below, see under the more proper form **शिव.**

सिवईं, *more prop.* **सवैं**, *q.v.*

सिवरबो in Mārwārī = **सुमरना**, *q.v.*

सिवहि (*Rām.*) = **शिवको** (**शिव**).

सिवा, 1, (*colloquial*) = **शिवा**, *q. v.*: 2, = **सिवाय**, *q.v.*

सिवाना, *m.* a verge, limit, boundry, landmark, march. [more, without.

सिवाय, except, besides, beyond, over and above,

सिवार, *m.* a kind of green vegetation (*Vallisneria spiralis* or *V. octandra*) which grows at the bottom of pools or other water; vegetable mould, moss.

सिवाला (*colloquial*) = **शिवाला**, *q. v.*

सिवासन (*Rām.*) = **शिवासे** (**शिव**). See **सन.**

सिवि; for words beginning thus, see under the

सिवैया; see (1) **सवैया** (2) **सुवैया.** [form **शिवि.**

सिष्ट; for words beginning thus, but not given below, see under the more proper form **शिष्ट.**

सिष्ट in Mārwārī = **सृष्टि**, *q. v.*

सिष्ट; see (1) **स्रष्ट** (2) **श्रेष्ठ.**

सिष्य; for words beginning thus, see under the

सिस; see (1) **शिशु** (2) **शिष्य** (3) **सीस.** [form **शिष्य.**

सिसकना, *a. int.* to sob.

सिसकी, *f.* sobbing; a sob. *Siskiyāṅ bharnā,* to sob.

सिसि (*Rām.*) = **शशि**, *q. v.*

सिसियाईन्द, *f.* a disagreeable smell.

सिसिर (*Rām.*) = **शिशिर**, *q. v.* [form **शिशु.**

सिसु; for words beginning thus, see under the

सिसुपा, *f.* the sisoo-tree; the custard-apple tree.

सिस्न (*Rām.*) = **शिश्न**, *q. v.*

सिहत; see (1) **सहत** (2) **सहित.**

सिहर, *m.* enchantment, magic.

सिहरना, *a. int.* to shiver, shake with cold: *t.* to scrape.

सिहरा, *m.* a chaplet, garland, wreath (worn on the head by the bride and bridegroom at a marriage ceremony).

सिहराऊ, *m. f.* tiresome, tedious.

सिहराना = **सहराना**, 1, 2, *q.v.*

सिहाई, *more prop.* **सियाही**, *q.v.*

सिहात = **सिहाता है** (**सिहाना**). See **त**, 5.

सिहाना (*Rām.*) = **सुहाना**, *q.v.*

सिहाहि, (pl. °हिं) } = **सिहाता** (**सिहाना**).
सिहाही, (pl. °हीं) }

सिहिरना, *a. int.* to liquefy.

सिहुड़ारी, *f.* a hedge of euphorbium.

सी; 1, the feminine inflection of **सा**, *q.v.*: 2, *more* [*prop.* **सोई**, *q.v.*

सीअन, *more prop.* **सीवन**, *q.v.*

सीआ, 1, *m.* (*f.* **सीई**) *more com.* **सोया**, *q.v.*: 2, *more*

सीई, *f.* (pl. **सीईं**); see **सोया**, 1. [*prop.* **सीवन**, *q.v.*

सीं, *more prop.* **सोईं**, *q.v.*

सींक, *f.* the culm of the grass (*Andropogon muricatum*) of which brooms are made.

सींकर, *m.* the flower of the *sīṅk.*

सींका, *m.* a groove. *Sīṅke banānā,* to groove.

सींकिया, *m. f.* striped.

सींकुर, *m.* beard.

सींग, *m.* a horn. *Sīṅg—honā,* to put out horns.

सींगड़ा, *m.* a powder-horn.

सींगवाला, *m.* (*f.* ī) horned.

सींगा, *m.* a musical horn, trumpet; a powder-horn.

सींगिया, *m.* a kind of poison.

सींगी, *f.* a small musical horn: a certain fish, *viz.* the hornbeak (*Silurus pungentissimus*, Buch.): a cup for cupping. — *lagānā*, to cup.

सींघ, *m.* a horn: a fin (?). [cattle.

सींघाटीमहसूल, *m.* a tax or poll raised on horned

सींच, *f.* irrigation, watering fields.

सींचना, *t.* to water, irrigate.

सींचाई, *f.* the price paid of irrigation.

सींचासींचाई, *f.* artificial irrigation of land.

सींचो, *f.* the season for irrigation.

सींन, *more prop.* **सीन**, *q. v.*

सींना, *more prop.* **सीना**, *q.v.*

सींव (*Rām.*) = **सीमा**, *q.v.*

सींवन, *more prop.* **सीवन**, *q.v.*

सींवा (*Rām.*) = **सीमा**, *q.v.*

सींह, *m.* hedgehog.

सीकर, 1, (*colloquial*) = **शीकर**, *q.v.*: 2, *f.* a chain.

सीकरी, *f.* a wire-chain.

सीख, *f.* instruction, lesson, learning, study, admonition. — *lenā*, to acquire knowledge, to learn.

सीखन, *f.* (a Braj pl. of **सीख**) lessons; admonitions.

सीखना, *t.* to acquire knowledge, to learn, master.

सीखनेवारा, *m.* (*f.* ī) a learner, student.

सीग़ा, *m.* a mould (for casting metal): trade, profession: a form of words used at marriage ceremonies, etc.

सीगारः, *m.* thick cloth.

सींचना, *t.* to water, irrigate; to lave; to empty.

सीज, *m.* the milky hedge-plant (*Euphorbia neriifolia* or *Euphorbia antiquorum*).

सीजना, *a. int.* to exude, filtrate, sweat: to seethe, boil, dissolve or become soft by boiling: *n.* to be received (said of money); to be liquidated (said of debt).

सीटी, *f.* whistling.—*bajānā*, to whistle.—*bandhnā*, or *gum honā* or *bhūlnā*, to be confounded or distracted, to become senseless.

सीटीबाज़, *m.* a whistler. [chewed; indigo-refuse.

सीठ, *f.* dregs of betel or of anything that has been

सीठन, *f.* (a Braj pl. of सीठ) dregs, refuse.

सीठना, *m.* abusive or lascivious songs sung by fe-

सीठनी, *f.* = सीठना, *q.v.* [males at weddings.

सीठा, *m* (*f.* ī) insipid, tasteless, pithless, vapid, faded, languid, weak, sickly, pale.

सीठी, *f.* = (1) सीठ (2) सीठा, *qq.v.*

सीडरवो, in Māṛwāṛī = सड़ना, *q.v.*

सीड़ा, *m.* a channel through which fields are watered: an overflowing field.

सीढ़ी, *f.* a ladder, stair, step: degree.

सीत; for words beginning thus, but not given below, see under the more proper form शीत.

सीतंग, *more com.* सितंग, *q.v.*

सीतबाई, *f.* the palsy.

सीतल; for all words beginning thus, but not given below, see under the more proper form शीतल.

सीतलचीनी, *f.* allspice (*Myrtus pimenta*).

सीतलपाटी, *f.* a kind of fine cool mat (for sleeping on). [pox.

सीतलामुंह, *m.* (*f.* ī) having a face pitted with small-

सीता, *f.* the track of a ploughshare, a furrow: husbandry: spirituous liquor: *pr. n.* (1) of the daughter of king Janak, wife of Rāmchandra (2) of the wife of Indra presiding over fruits (3) of Lakshmī (4) of Umā (5) of one of the fabulous branches of the Ganges.

सीतांग (*colloquial*) = शीतांग, *q. v.*

सीतानाथ / सीतापति } *m.* (the lord of Sītā, *i. e.*) Rām.

सीताफल, *m.* custard-apple (*Annona squamosa*).

सीताबिर्च = सीतारवन, *q.v.*

सीतार; see (1) सितार (2) सीताहार.

सीतारमण, *m.* (the enamoured of Sītā, *i.e.*) Rām.

सीतारवन (*Rām.*) = सीतारमण, *q.v.*

सीताराम, a kind of ejaculatory invocation much used by the devotees of Rām and Sītā.

सीतार्त, *more prop.* शीतार्त, *q.v.*

सीतावृक्ष, *m.* an epithet of the oak-tree.

सीतासुपारी, *f.* an epithet of the acorn.

सीताहार, *m.* a certain cryptogamous plant (*Lycopodium phlegmaria*): a kind of musical instrument.

सीती, *f.* the plant *Magnolia.*

सीते (*Rām.*: Sk. voc. sing. fem.) = O Sītā!

सीथ, *m.* boiled rice, a grain of boiled rice, rice sowins,

सीदना, to suffer affliction, be afflicted. [gruel.

सीदहि (pl. हिं) = सीदता है (सीदना).

सीदी, a negro.

सीदोन, *m. pr. n.* the ancient city of Sidon.

सीध (*contraction*) = सीधा, *q. v.* *Nākkī sīdh chale jāo*, follow your nose.

सीधा, 1, *m.* (*f.* ī) straight, direct, accurate, right; close (as a translation); erect; simple, artless, candid, plain, pointblank, fair, upright; opposite, facing: 2, *m.* undressed victuals, provisions, forage.—*k.* to straighten, smoothe, plane, rectify.

सीधाई, *f.* straightness, directness, simplicity, candour, uprightness, rectitude, straightforwardness, harmlessness.

सीधापन, *m.* = सीधाई, *q.v.*

सीधारना, *more com.* सिधारना, *q. v.*

सीधी, *f.* = (1) सीधा (2) सीधाई, *qq. v.*

सीन, *f.* a metal dish or salver.

सीनई, *pr. n.* the Mount Sinai.

सीना, 1, *t.* to stitch, sew: 2, *m.* the breast, bosom: 3, *pr.n.* the Mount Sinai: 4, (in the hill dialect) a cliff.

सीनापिरोना, *m.* needlework, sewing, stitching.

सीप, *f.* a shell (*esp.* bivalve): the first mangoes that fall from the tree.

सीपल, a fragment of earthenware.

सीपलक, the small house-lizard.

सीपारा, *m. pr. n.* one of the sections of the Kur,ān. It contains thirty *sipāras* [*kīṛā*, a muscle, shell fish.

सीपी, *f.* any bivalve shell; mother-of-pearl.—*kā*

सीफ़, bank, margin, shore, coast.

सीफल, a Prākṛit form of श्रीफल, *q.v.* [form शिव.

सीब; for words beginning thus, see under the

सीम, 1, a contraction of सीमा, *q. v.*: 2, *m.* silver.

सीमन, 1, *m.* more com. सीमा, *q.v.*: 2, a Braj pl. of सीमा, *q. v.*

सीमन्त, *m.* the separating the hair on each side so as to leave a distinct line on the top of the head; the head.

सीमन्तिनी, *f.* a female, a woman. See सीमन्त.

सीमर, a Prākṛit form of सेमल, *q.v.*

सीमा, 1, *f.* a limit, restriction, boundary, confines, border, skirt, landmark: observance of due bounds in morals: a field: the nape of the neck: the scrotum: 2, *m.* the forehead, face, countenance, aspect.

सीमाब, *m.* mercury, quicksilver. [daries.

सीमाबन्ध, *m.* the laying down or making of boun-

सीमावर्ती, *m.* (*f.* inī) one who dwells within certain boundaries, a well-regulated or orthodox person.

सीमावृक्ष, *m.* a tree serving as a boundary-mark.

सीमासन्धि, *m.* the meeting of two boundaries.

सीमिया, *m.* metallurgy, alchemy: magic, necromancy, enchantment: poetry; rhetoric.

सीय, a Prākrit form of सीता, *q.v.*

सीया, 1, = (1) सीता (2) सीवन, *qq.v.*: 2, *m.* (*f* सीई)

सीयाह, *more prop.* सियाह, *q.v.* [sewn, stitched.

सीर, 1, *more prop.* सिर, *q.v.*: 2, a contraction of सीरा, 1, *q.v.*: 3. *m.* a plough: the sun: 4, *m. f* husbandry, agriculture; 5, *m.* lands in a village cultivated by the hereditary proprietors; *hence*, firstrate land; 6, *m.* garlic: 7, *f.* damp.

सीरक, *f.* coolness, rawness, dampness.

सीरत, *f.* disposition, temperament, nature, qualities, manners, conduct.

सीरध्वज, *m.* an epithet of rājā Janak.

सीरा, 1, *m.* (*f.* ī) cool, raw, damp: 2, *m.* a kind of sweetmeat made of meal and sugar.

सीरी, *m.* (*f.* iṇī) a partner: a plough-holder (an epithet of Balarām). [dampness, moistness, moisture.

सील, 1, (*colloquial*) = शील, *q.v.*: 2, *f.* cold, wetness,

सीलन, *f.* coolness, rawness, moisture, dampness.

सीलना, *a. int.* to moisten. [form शीलव.

सीलव; for words beginning thus, see under the

सीला, *m.* (*f.* ī) damp, moist, wet, marshy, cool.

सीलाई, *more com.* सिलाई, *q.v.*

सीवं (*Rām.*) = सीमा, *q.v.* [binding of a book.

सीवन, *m.* sewing, darning, stitching; a seam; the

सीवनी, *f.* the frenum of the prepuce.

सीवली, *f.* a certain caste whose occupation it is to draw juice from the date-tree.

सीवां (*Rām.*) = सीमा, *q.v.*

सीष, in Chand = सीस, *q.v.*

सीषनौं, in old Hindee = सीखना, *q.v.*

सीस, *m.* the head: a freckle, a flame, a spike: lead. --*charhānā*, to place upon the head; to exalt the head, to assume, be arrogant; to exalt; to shew respect.

सीसक, *m.* lead.

सीसफूल, *m.* a head-ornament worn by females.

सीसमहल, *more prop.* शीशमहल्ल, *q.v.*

सीसा, 1, *more prop.* (1) शीशा (2) सीस, *qq.v.*: 2, *m.* lead; blacklead.

सीसेका, *m.* (*f.* ī) made of lead, leaden.

सीसो, *m.* a certain tree (*Dalbergia sisoo*, Roxb.) and its wood (much used in manufactures).

सीसों = सीसो, *q.v.*

सींह, *m.* a hedgehog, porcupine.

सु, 1, An inseparable prefix, the reverse of दुर or कु corresponding to the Greek εὖ. It signifies good, well, beautifully, easily, much, exceedingly; and conveys, therefore, the idea of goodness, excellence, intensity, worship, reverence, honour. As this particle is prefixable almost *ad lib.* to substantives, many words commencing with it will be found in Hindee literature which it has been deemed superfluous to insert in a Dictionary: 2, In Braj this particle is frequently found as equivalent to से, the sign of the ablative case: it is also occasionally equivalent to का or के of the genitive: while sometimes it is equivalent to सो 2, the remoter demonstrative pronoun.

सुअंजन (*Rām.*) = अच्छा अंजन } See सु, 1.
सुअंजली (*Rām*) = अच्छी अंजली }

सुअंर, *m.* (*f.* ī) *more com.* सूअर, *q. v.*

सुअन, *m.* a son.

सुअर, *m.* (*f.* ī) *more com.* सूअर, *q. v.*

सुआ, *m.* (*f.* सुई) a parrot. [seller of food.

सुआर, (Sk. सूपकार) *m.* (*f.* in) a cook, a dresser and

सुआरा, *m.* (*f.* in *or* ī) = सुआर, *q.v.*

सुआस, *more com.* सुवास, *q.v.*

सुआसिनिन्ह, a poet. pl. of सुवासिनी, *q.v.* [parrot.

सुई, 1, *more prop.* सूई, *q.v.*: 2, *f.* (*m.* सुआ) a female

सुंगना } *more prop.* सूंघना, *q v.*
सुंघना }

सुंघाई, *f.* smell, odour, perfume, fragrance.

सुंघाना, *t.* (causat. of सूंघना) to cause to smell, to

सुंघावट, *f.* odour, perfume, fragrance. [nuzzle.

सुंद, सुंध, सुंभ; for words beginning with either of these elements, see under the corresponding forms सुन्द, सुन्ध, सुम्भ, respectively.

सुंसान, *more com.* सुन्सान, *q. v.*

सुक = (1) शुक (2) शुकदेव (3) शुक्र (4) शुक्ल (5) शूक (6) सुख.

सुकंठ, *m.* (*f.* ā *or* ī) = सुग्रीव, *q. v.*

सुकचाना (by inversion) = सकुचाना, *q. v.*

सुकटा, *m.* (*f.* ī) lean, thin, meagre, emaciated, dry.

सुकटी, *f.* dried fish.

सुकड़ना, *a. int.* to shrink, shrivel, gather up, collect, contract, dwindle, draw in, constrain.

सुकड़ा, *m.* (*f.* i) shrivelled, contracted, tight, drawn in, narrow, circumscribed.

सुकड़ाव, *m.* a shrivelling, contraction.

सुकण्ठ, (*f.* ā *or* ī) = सुग्रीव, *q.v.*

सुकदेव, *more prop.* शुकदेव, *q.v.*

सुकना (*colloquial*) = सूखना, *q.v.*

सुकन्या, *f.* a good daughter: *pr. n.* a certain princess (daughter of king Saryāti).

सुकर, 1, (*colloquial*) = शुक्र, *q. v.* 2, *m.* doing good, well-doing, beneficence: 3, *m.* (*f.* ī) *adj.* doing good, beneficent, benevolent: easy, practicable, attainable.

सुकरा, 1, *f.* a tractable cow: 2, the month of May.

सुकरी, *f.* (*m.* सुकर) a beneficent or a tractable female.

सुकर्कश (*Rām.*) = अति कठोर.

सुकर्म्म, *m* = सुक्रिया, *q.v.* [deities.

सुकर्म्मा, *m.pr.n.* (pl.; see आ, 22) a certain class of

सुकर्म्मी, *m.* (*f.* iṇī) = सुकर, 3, *q.v.* [form शुक्ल.

सुकल; for words beginning thus, see under the

सुकवार = (1) शुक्रवार (2) सुकुमार, *qq. v.*

सुकवि, *m.* an excellent poet, a first-class poet.

सुका, *m.* (*f.* ī) *more prop.* शुका, *q.v.*

सुकाल; *m.* goodness of seasons, good times, plenty, cheapness, abundance. [manes of the Shūdras).

सुकाली, *m.* (*f.* iṇī) a certain class of demigods (the

सुकि; see (1) सुकना (2) सुका (3) सूकी.

सुकीर्ति, *f.* good report, good character; celebration; an epithet of a certain hymn.

सुकुचना = सकुचना, *q.v.*

सुकुचाना = सकुचाना, *q.v.*

सुकुमार, *m.* (*f.* ā *or* ī) beautifully young or youthful, very soft, smooth, tender, delicate, young, youthful, elegant.

सुकुमारता, *f.* softness, smoothness, tenderness, delicateness, youthfulness, elegance.

सुकुल, 1, *m.* a good or virtuous family: 2, *m.* (*f.* ā) of good family, well born: 3, *m.* a certain caste of Brāhmaṇs.

सुकूत, *f.* silence, quietness, peace.

सुकून, *m.* quiet, tranquillity, peace, rest, ease.

सुकूनत, *f.* tranquillity; a dwelling, residence.

सुकृत, 1, *m.* = सुकृति, *q. v.*: 2, *m.* (*f.* ā) well done, easily accomplished; virtuous, pious; fortunate, auspicious; assisted, befriended.

सुकृति, *f.* a good action; virtue, moral merit; kindness, bounty, friendliness, auspiciousness.

सुकृती, *m.* (*f.* inī) a well-doer, etc.: *lit.* virtuous, pious, beneficent, benevolent, benign, good, auspicious.

सुकृपा, *f.* pitifulness, tenderness, compassion.

सुकृपानिधान, *m.* an epithet of God: *lit.* the blessed mansion of compassion.

सुकेड़ना; see (1) सकेतना (2) सकेलना (3) सकोड़ना.

सुकेतु, *m. pr. n.* (1) of a certain demigod (2) of a son of Nandivardhan (3) of a son of Sunith.

सुकेतुसुता, *f.* an epithet of Sītā and certain other [goddesses.

सुक्कर, *m.* sugar.

सुक्का, *m.* (*f.* ī) *more prop.* (1) सूखा (2) शुक्का, *qq.v.*

सुक्कानगीर, *m.* a helmsman.

सुक्कानी, *m.* (*f.* in *or* inī) a helmsman.

सुक्को; see सुक्का.

सुक्त, *more prop.* सूक्त, *q.v.*

सुक्तकर्त्ता, *m.* (*f.* trī) *more prop.* सूक्तकर्त्ता, *q. v.*

सुक्र (*colloquial*) = शुक्र, *q. v.*

सुक्रिया, *f.* a good work, good action, meritorious deed, moral or religious observance, merit.

सुक्ल, *more prop.* शुक्ल, *q.v.*

सुक्लीकर्म, *m.* soap: lit. *adj.* whitening.

सुख, 1, happy, joyful, agreeable, sweet, delightful; virtuous, pious; easy: 2, *m.* happiness, joy, pleasure, tranquillity, ease, contentment, easy circumstances, rest, relief, easiness: water: an epithet of paradise. — *mānnā*, to regard as a matter for happiness, to entertain joy, be glad.

सुखअयन = सुखधाम, *q.v.*

सुखकन्द = शकरकन्द (?), *q.v.*

सुखकर, imparting happiness, generous, delightsome: hence, *m.* (*f.* ī) a generous or benevolent person.

सुखकारक, *m.* (*f.* ikā)
सुखकारी, *m.* (*f.* inī) } = सुखकर, *q. v.*

सुखचैन, *m.* (सुख + चैन) ease, tranquillity, rest, leisure.

सुखतला, *m.* a piece of leather placed on the sole within a shoe to protect the foot from friction.

सुखद, ease-affording, pleasure-giving, salubrious, pleasant, comforting: hence, (1) *m.* (*f.* ā) one who confers happiness, a comforter (2) an epithet of the seat of Vishṇu (3) an epithet of the Supreme Being.

सुखदर्शन, *m.* a certain shrub (*Crinum Asiaticum* and *Crinum zeylanicum*) the juice of which is given for the ear-ache.

सुखदा, *f.* (*m.* सुखद) a female who affords happiness, a courtesan of the paradise of Indra.

सुखदाई, *m.* (*f.* inī)
सुखदाता, *m.* (*f.* trī) } = सुखद, *q. v.*
सुखदातृ, *m.* (*f.* trī)

सुखदान, 1, *m.* (*f.* ā) = सुखद, *q.v.*: 2, *m.* the act of imparting ease, comfort, or contentment, beneficence.

सुखदानी, *m.* (*f.* inī)
सुखदायक, *m.* (*f.* ikā) } = सुखद, *q.v.*
सुखदायी, *m.* (*f.* inī)

सुखदास, *m.* a certain kind of rice (very superior [and delicious).

सुखदेव, *more prop.* शुकदेव, *q.v.*

सुखदेन, 1, *adj.* imparting happiness, pleasure-yielding: 2, *m.* prosperity and poverty, happiness and unhappiness.

सुखधाम, *m.* a blissful place, an abode of happiness, paradise.

सुखन, *m.* (Braj pl. of सुख) joys, comforts, pleasures.

सुखना, *more prop.* सूखना, *q.v.*

सुखनिधान, *m.* an epithet of the Supreme Being: *lit.* [the mansion of bliss.

सुखनींद, *f.* good sleep, refreshing slumber.

सुखपाल, *m.* a pālkī, easy chair, couch.

सुखपूर्वक, with ease, without difficulty, easily.

सुखप्रद, *m.* (*f.* ā) = सुखद, *q.v.*

सुखप्राप्ति, *f.* the possession or enjoyment of happiness.

सुखबास (*colloquial*) = सुखवास, *q.v.*

सुखबिलास = सुखविलास, *q.v.*

सुखभाग, *m.* good fortune, happiness, bliss.

सुखभागी, fortunate, happy, delighted: hence, *m.* (*f.* inī) a fortunate person, etc.

सुखभोग, *m.* the enjoyment of pleasure.

सुखभोगी, enjoying pleasure or happiness, luxurious: hence, *m.* (*f.* inī) a luxurious person.

सुखमय, *m.* (*f.* ī) consisting of or abounding in happiness, blissful, joyous.

सुखमा, 1, (*Rām.*) = सुखमय (?): 2, *f. pr. n.* one of Krishṇ's female companions.

सुखराशि, *m.* an accumulation of happiness (epithet of the Deity).

सुखरास, *m.* melodious sound, pleasant speech.

सुखरासी, *more prop.* सुखराशि, *q.v.*

सुखलव, *m.* a minute portion of happiness, a trace [of happiness.

सुखलाना = सुखाना, *q.v.*

सुखलेश, *m.* insignificant pleasure, a small portion [of happiness.

सुखवास = सुखधाम, *q. v.*

सुखविलास, *m.* enjoyment, pleasure, gaiety, fastness.

सुखविलासी, *m.* (*f.* inī) one who devotes himself to enjoyment, a pleasure-seeker.

सुखशान्ति, *f.* the pleasure arising from *Sāntras.*

सुखशील, *m.* (*f.* ā) of a happy or pleasant disposition.

सुखसन्दोह, *m.* an accumulation of happiness (epithet of the Deity).

सुखसवान, *m.* a pālkī, easy chair, couch.

सुखसागर, *m.* an epithet of the Bhāgavat Purāṇ, also of any popular deity such as Rām-chandra.

सुखसाध्य, easy of accomplishment or of attainment.

सुखसावन, *m.* a pālkī, easy chair, couch.

सुखसील, *m.* (*f.* ā) *more prop.* **सुखशील**, *q.v.*

सुखस्थान, *m.* an epithet of paradise or heaven: *lit.* the place of happiness.

सुखस्वभाव = **सुखिस्वभाव**, *q.v.*

सुखाना, *t.* (causat. of **सूखना**) to cause to dry up, cause to pine away or be emaciated, cause to evaporate, to dry, dry up, evaporate, to kill, wither, to parch, to emaciate.

सुखारना, *t.* to contribute to one's happiness.

सुखार्थ, for the sake of happiness, ease, etc.

सुखार्थी, *m.* (*f.* inī) a seeker after happiness: lit. wishful for happiness or contentment.

सुखालय = **सुखधाम**, *q.v.*

सुखाला, 1, = **सुखधाम**, *q.v.*: 2, *m.* (*f.* ī) easy, not difficult, facile.

सुखासन, *m.* a pālkī, easy chair, couch.

सुखास्वाद, 1, well-flavoured, agreeable, delightful: 2, *m.* pleasantness, flavour, enjoyment.

सुखावि, (pl. °वें)
सुखावी, (pl °वीं) } = **सुखाता है (सुखाना)**.

सुखिस्वभाव, 1, *m.* a happy or contented disposition: 2, *adj.* of a happy or contented disposition.

सुखित
सुखिया } = **सुखी**, *q. v.*

सुखी, *m.* (*f.* inī) at ease, happy, glad, content, comfortable, tranquil, pleasant, possessing happiness or pleasure.

सुखीभाव = **सुखिस्वभाव**, *q. v.*

सुखेच्छा, *f.* desire for happiness.

सुखेन (*Rām.*: Sk. instr. sing.) = with joy, *i.e.* joyfully.

सुखोदय, *m.* the occurrence or the realization of happiness or pleasure.

सुखोपयोगी, *m.* (*f.* inī) *adj.* contributing to or producing happiness or pleasure.

सुख्यात, *m.* (*f.* ā) well spoken-of, of good repute, celebrated, famous.

सुख्याति, *f.* good repute, celebrity, fame.

सुग, 1. *m.* (*f.* ā) going well; graceful; well rid of: plain, intelligible; easy of access: 2, *m.* ordure.

सुगंद = **सुगन्ध**, *q.v.*

सुगत, *m.* a Buddh; a Bauddh deified preceptor.

सुगति, *f.* a good gait; a good or happy state or condition.

सुगन, *m.* an augury, omen.

सुगन्द. *more com.* **सुगन्ध**, *q.v.*

सुगन्ध, 1, *m.* = **सुगन्धि**, *q.v.*: 2, *m.* (*f.* ā) sweet-scented, fragrant, odoriferous, spicy, aromatic.

सुगन्धपात्र, *m.* any vessel containing sweet odours; a scent-bottle.

सुगन्धराए, a kind of flower.

सुगन्धवाला, *m.* (*f.* ī) impregnated with perfume.

सुगन्धाविष्ट, *m.* (*f.* ā) *adj.* possessing sweet odour.

सुगन्धि, 1, *m. f.* = **सुगन्ध**, 2, *q.v.*: 2, *f.* a good or pleasing smell, sweet odour, fragrance, aroma, spiciness, perfume, odour, scent, perfumery.

सुगन्धित, *m.* (*f.* ā) sweet-smelling, fragrant, perfumed.

सुगन्धिता, *f.* agreeableness of smell such as is produced by the trituration of perfumes, fragrance.

सुगन्धें, *f.* (a pl. of **सुगन्ध**) scents, perfumery.

सुगम, *m.* (*f.* ā) easy to travel over, easy to get at, easy, accessible, attainable, plain, practicable, intelligible, going well.

सुगमता, *f.* accessibleness, attainableness, ease, plainness, practicability, intelligibleness; easy flow, euphony.

सुगमित, *m.* (*f.* ā) come-at-able, accessible, easily attainable.

सुगम्य, 1, *m.* (*f.* ā) = **सुगम**, *q.v.*: 2, *m.* = **सुगमता**, *q. v.*

सुगवा, *m.* (*f.* ī) a parrot.

सुगाना, *t.* to apply to, fix on, appropriate.

सुगीति, *f.* (in Pros.) a species of metre.

सुगुन, *m.* an augury, omen; luck.

सुगुनिया, lucky.

सुगुप्त, 1, *m.* (*f.* ā) well hidden, well kept secret; secret: 2, very secretly, very privately.

सुगुप्ति, *f.* closeness, secrecy.

सुग्गा, *m.* (*f.* ī *or* iyā) a parrot.

सुघई, *f.* a certain musical mode (*rāginī*) sung in the afternoon.

सुग्रीव, handsome-necked: hence (1) *m.* (*f.* ā) a goose; a hero (2) *m.* a sort of weapon (3) *m.* *pr. n.* (1) of one of Krishn's horses (2) of a certain monkey, the ally of Rām (3) of Indra (4) of Shiv (5) of a certain mountain (6) of a certain serpent of the lower regions.

सुघटित, *m.* (*f.* ā) well-joined, well-contrived, well-managed, well arranged.

सुघड़, elegant, beautiful, accomplished, virtuous; neat; handy.

सुघड़ई, *f.* elegancy, accomplishment, beauty, virtuousness.

सुघड़ाई = **सुघड़ई**, *q. v.*

सुघड़ी, *f.* a lucky hour, auspicious moment, suitable time.

सुघर, *more prop.* **सुघड़**, *q. v.*

सुघरी, *more prop.* **सुघड़ी**, *q. v.*

सुघती, *f. pr. n.* a wife of rājā Sagar.

सुच, 1, pure, clear, clean, white, undefiled, unpolluted: 2, *m.* the month of June.

सुचक, *m.* (*f.* ikā) cautious, reflective.

सुचकना, *n.* to be astonished, be startled.

सुचकार, *m.* lustration.

सुचकारी, *m.* (*f.* iṇī) lustral.

सुचाई, *f.* straightforwardness, sincerity, simplicity.

सुचारु, *m.* (*f.* rvī) very agreeable.

सुचाल, *m.* graceful gait; good behaviour, propriety of character and deportment: *adj.* walking gracefully; behaving with propriety.

सुचि (*colloquial*) = **शुचि**, *q. v.*

सुचिंतित, *more prop.* **सुचिन्तित**, *q. v.*

सुचित, *m.* (*f.* ā) unoccupied, disengaged, at one's ease, easy, at leisure, thoughtless; attentive, careful: occupied.

सुचिता, *more prop.* **शुचिता**, *q.v.* [ness, carefulness.

सुचिताई, *f.* ease, freedom from care: attentive-

सुचित्ताई, *m.*(*f.* ā) worthy of attention or care.

सुचितो in Braj = **सुचित**, *q.v.*

सुचिन्ता, *f.* due consideration or reflection.

सुचिन्तित, well-considered, duly considered, much reflected on.

सुचेत, 1, = **सचेत**, *q.v.*: 2, contented, happy.

सुचेती, *f.* discreetness, caution.

सुजन, *m.* (*f.* a) goodnatured, benevolent, kind; virtuous, respectable.

सुजनता, *f.*(*m.*°त्व) benevolence, kindness, urbanity, goodness, virtuousness, respectability.

सुजनसमाज, *m.* the assembly of the good. The term is applied chiefly to the Hindoo ascetics regarded in their corporate capacity.

सुजना, 1, *more prop.* **सूझना**, *q.v*: 2, *f.* (*m.* **सुजन**) a benevolent or a respectable female.

सुजराल, *more com.* **सुसराल**, *q.v.*

सुजस (*colloquial*) = **सुयश**, *q.v.* [or caste.

सुजाति, *m. f.* of good race, lineage, tribe, species,

सुजान = (1) **सुजन** (2) **सुज्ञान**, 2, *qq. v.*

सुजाना, 1, (*poet.*) = **सुज्ञान**, *q.v.*: 2, *t.* (causat. of **सूजना**)

सुजि = **सूजि**, *q.v.* [to cause to swell.

सुजोग (*colloquial*) = **सुयोग**, *q.v.*

सुज्ञान, 1, *m.* wisdom, intelligence, sagacity: 2, *m.* (*f.* ā) well-informed, intelligent, knowing, wise.

सुझना, *more prop.* **सूझना**, *q.v.* [to shew.

सुझाना, *t.* (causat. of **सूझना**) to cause to understand,

सुटकुन, *f.* a rod. [to gulp down.

सुटुकना, *t.* to swallow by gulps and with a noise,

सुटुकि, an old conjunt. part. of **सुटुकना**. See **क**, 7.

सुठाम, *m. f.* a good place, pleasant spot, abode of

सुठि, much, very, exceedingly. [bliss, paradise.

सुड़की, *f.* the act of suddenly slackening the string

सुड़्की = **सुड़की**, *q.v.* [of a paper kite.

सुड़प, *f.* sipping or sucking up (as broth); the noise made in sipping or sucking up.

सुड़पना, *t.* to sip, suck, lick.

सुढुकना = **सुटुकना**, *q.v.* [pretty, handsome, neat.

सुडोल, well-formed, well-shapen, elegant, graceful,

सुडोलता, *f.* goodness of shape, elegance, handsomeness, gracefulness, prettiness. [someness.

सुडोलदेही, *f.* gracefulness of bodily shape, hand-

सुढव
सुढाल } = **सुडोल**, *q.v.*

सुण्ड, *m.* an elephant's proboscis.

सुण्डका, *m.* the hump of a camel, bullock, etc.

सुत, *m.* a male child, a son: a prince: lit. *m.* (*f.* ā) generated, produced, born.

सुतघात, *f.* the murder of a son.

सुतघातक, *m.* (*f.* ikā)
सुतघाती, *m.* (*f.* inī) } one who slays his son.

सुतन, *m.* [a Braj pl. of **सुत**; see **न**, 6 (1)] offspring, progeny, descendants, children, sons.

सुतना, *a. int.* to sleep.

सुतन्त्र, *more prop.* **स्वतन्त्र**, *q.v.*

सुतन्ह = **सुतन**, *q.v.* See **न्ह**.

सुतपाल, *m.* (*f.* ī) a nourisher of children: *pr. n.* a certain class of deities. [regions.

सुतल, *m. pr. n.* one of the divisions of the infernal

सुतललोक = **सुतल**, *q.v.*

सुतली, *more com.* **सूतली**, *q.v.* [thet of Brahmlok.

सुतलोक, 1, *more prop.* **सुतललोक**, *q.v.*: 2, *m.* an epi-

सुतवत, 1, *adj.* having offspring: 2, *m.* (*f.* vati) the parent of a son: a drinker of *som*-juice.

सुतवती, *f.* (*m.* **सुतवत**, etc.) a mother (*esp.* of a son).

सुतवन्त
सुतवान } *m.* (*f.* vatī) = **सुतवत**, *q.v.*

सुता, *f.* (*m.* **सुत**) a female child, a daughter.

सुतान, *m.* a good time. [2, *m.* opportunity, time.

सुतार, 1, *m.* (*f.* in *or* ī) a carpenter, wheelwright:

सुतारी, *f.* an awl, a bodkin: a carpenter's wife.

सुतार्थी, *m.* (*f.* inī) desirous of having a son.

सुतिनी, *f.* (*m.* **सुती**) a mother.

सुतिय, *f.* a good woman, good wife.

सुतियमणि, *f.* an epithet of Pārvatī and of Sītā; *lit.* the pearl of excellent women.

सुती, *adj.* having offspring: hence, *m.*(*f.* inī) a parent.

सुतीक्ष्ण, *m.* (*f.* ā) very sharp, very subtle; very pungent; acutely painful.

सुतीछन, *more prop.* **सुतीक्ष्ण**, *q.v.*

सुतीछा, *m.* (*f.* ī) *more com.* **सुतीक्ष्ण**, *q.v.*

सुतीयमनि, *more prop.* **सुतियमणि**, *q.v.*

सुतुही, *f.* a pearl-oyster, oyster-shell.

सुतून, *m.* a piller, column, prop.

सुतोतरि; see (1) **सुतोतला** (2) **स्वाद्**.

सुतोतला, *m.* (*f.* ī) one who has a pleasant lisp, one who e lispings or attempts to speak are productive of pleasurable sensations.

सुत्या, *f.* parturition.

सुत्रा, *more com.* **सुथरा**, *q.v.*

सुत्रामा, *m.* an epithet of Indra.

सुत्वन, *m.* a student who has performed his ablutions subsequent (or preparatory) to a sacrifice; an offerer or a drinker of *som*-juice.

सुत्वा, *m.* = **सुत्वन**, *q.v.*

सुथन, *more com.* **सूथन**, *q.v.*

सुथना; see (1) **सुतना** (2) **सूतना** (3) **सूथना**.

सुथनी, *more com.* **सूथनी**, *q.v.*

सुथरा, *m.* (*f.* ī) neat, elegant, adorned, beautiful, handsome, excellent, well.

सुथराई, *f.* neatness, elegance, beauty, goodness.

सुथरासाह, *m. pr. n.* a certain religious mendicant.

सुथरासाही, *m.* (*f.* inī) a follower of Suthrāsāh.

सुदक्षिण, 1, *m.*(*f.* ā) a good present: 2, *m.* (*f.* ā) very sincere or upright; very liberal in sacrificial gifts: 3, *m. pr. n.* a son of Puṇḍarik and king of Vidarbh.

सुदन्ती, *f. pr. n.* the female elephant of the north-west quarter.

सुदसुद, quite, perfectly, exactly.

सुदर्शन, 1, *m.* (*f.* ā) good-looking, pleasing, handsome: 2, *m* (*f.* ā) a vulture: 3, *m.* an epithet (1) of the discus of Krishṇ or Vishṇu (2) of mount Meru (3) of the rose-apple (*Eugenia jambu*).

सुदर्शनचक्र, *m.* (see **चक्र**) the discus of Krishṇ.

सुदामन, *m.* = **सुदामा**, 1, *q.v.*

सुदामा, 1, *m.* (not infl.) a cloud; a mountain; the sea: *pr. n.* (1) of Indra's elephant Airāvat (2) of a certain cowherd (3) of a certain poor Brāhman who came to Dwārkā to ask Krishṇ's aid, and was raised to wealth by him (4) of a certain mountain (5) of a certain river: 2, *f. pr. n.* a certain river in Northern India.

सुदामापुरी, *f.pr.n.* a certain sacred place of Hindoo pilgrimage.

सुदास, 1, *m. pr. n.* a certain ancient Hindoo king at whose court both Vasishṭ and Vishwamitra appear to have acted as family-priests: 2, *m.* (*f.* ī) a good slave or servant.

सुदि = **सुदी**, *q.v.*

सुदिन, 1, *more prop.* **शिवदीन**, *q.v.*: 2, *m.* a fine or auspicious day; good or prosperous times.

सुदी, *f.* the light half of the lunar month, *i. e.* from the new to full moon.

सुदीचौथ, *f.* the fourth day of the light half of the month.

सुदुराचार, *m.* (*f.* ā) a profligate: *lit.* very wicked, abandoned, profligate.

सुदुर्लभ, difficult of attainment, inaccessible.

सुदुष्कर, very difficult.

सुदृढ़, very hard, very firm, solid.

सुदेश, *m.* a beautiful country: a limb.

सुदेशे, 1, (*Rām.*: Sk. loc. sing. of **सुदेश**) = **अच्छे देशमें**; [2, = **अच्छी वस्तु देनेवाला** (?).

सुदेसु (*Rām.*) = **सुदेश**, *q.v.*

सुदेसे; see **सुदेशे**.

सुद्धां, with, together with: only, merely.

सुद्युम्न, *m. pr. n.* (in Myth.) a certain king who became alternately (month by month) a male and a female.

सुध = (1) **शुद्ध** (2) **सुधि**, *qq.v.*—*lenā*, to remember; to take care of or for; to look after, inquire into; to accommodate.

सुधंग, well-formed, handsome, graceful, polite.

सुधकना, *a. int.* to burn, kindle, ignite.

सुधकाना, *t.* to kindle, light, enflame.

सुधड़न, well-behaved.

सुधड़ना = **सुधरना**, *q. v.*

सुधबुध, *f.* correct knowledge; sense; sensation, perception; care.

सुधमुचा, *m.* (*f.* ī) well-shaped, handsome.

सुधरना, to be correct, be mended, be rectified, be set right; to be or seem right or good; to avail, answer, succeed; to improve, mend.

सुधरहि (pl. °**हिं**) = **सुधरता है** (**सुधरना**).

सुधराई, *f.* improvement, amendment, rectification, management.

सुधराव, *m.* = **सुधराई**, *q.v.*

सुधर्म्मा, *m.* the council or assembly of the gods.

सुधलेना; see *s.v.* **सुध**.

सुधवाना, *t.* to cause to be reminded.

सुधा, *f.* plaster, mortar; a brick; the nectar of flowers, the nectar of the gods, ambrosia; juice; water: lightning: 2, *m.* (*f.* ī) peaceable.

सुधाई, *f.* straightforwardness, sincerity, simplicity.

सुधां, with, together with: only, merely.

सुधांशु } **सुधांसु** } = **सुधाकर**, *q.v.*

सुधाकर, *m.* an epithet of the moon regarded as the repository of the nectar (*sudhā*) of the gods: moonlight.

सुधाना, *t.* to cause to remember, to put in mind, remind.

सुधारना, *t.* (causat. of **सुधरना**) to adorn, adjust, arrange, rectify, mind, improve, to palliate, to polish, to marshal, methodize.

सुधारनेवाला, *m.* (*f.* ī) an adorner, adjuster, good manager, adjuster, ameliorator, methodizer, framer, maker.

सुधारस, *m.* nectar, ambrosia.

सुधारा, *m.* (*f.* ī) polished.

सुधारी, *m.* (*f.* iṇī) } **सुधारू**, *m.* or *f.* } = **सुधारनेवाला**, *q.v.*

सुधि, *f.* remembrance, memory; sensation, consciousness; notice; care; intelligence.

सुधी, *m.* (*f.* inī) a learned or intelligent person, a pandit: *lit.* learned.

सुधीर, *m.* (*f.* ā) learned; considerate; firm.

सुन, 1, (Sk. **शून्य**) empty, void: insensible, without sensation, numb, palsied; indolent (said of tumours); too patient, passive: 2, *m.* (in Arithm.) a cypher, naught: (in Gram.) the sign of abbreviation (viz. °); a dot. —*k.* to numb.—*pānā*, to overhear, get to hear.—*lenā*, to hearken, overhear, pay attention.—*honā*, to be numb.

सुनःसेफ (*colloquial*) = **शुनःशेफ**, *q. v.*

सुनकरनेवाला, *m.* a narcotic medicine.

सुनकातर, *m.* a species of snake.

सुनखत, *more prop.* **सुनक्षत्र**, *q.v.*

सुनक्षत्र, *m.* a fortunate star or constellation: *pr. n.* a certain ancient Hindoo king.

सुनक्षत्रा, *f.* the second night of the civil month.

सुनना, *t.* (or *a. int.*) to listen, hearken, hear, attend to, mind, observe, keep. *Sun pānā* or *lenā*, to overhear, to get to hear.

सुनन्द, 1, *m.* (*f.* ā) delighting, affording pleasure: 2, *m. pr. n.* the club of Baldev.

सुनन्दा, *f.* a woman; an epithet of Umā.

सुनन्हार, *m.* (*f.* in, ī, nī) a hearer, listener, auditor.

सुनबहरी, *f.* a certain disease (*Elephantiasis*).

सुनमुख, *more prop.* **सम्मुख**, *q.v.*

सुनय, 1, see (1) **सुनाय** (2) **सुनै**: 2, *m.* good conduct; policy.

सुनयन, *m.* (*f.*ā) an epithet of the deer: *lit.* beautiful-eyed. [(2) of any female.
सुनयना, *f.* an epithet (1) of the wife of king Janak
सुनरे (an invocation to listen); see **सुन** and **रे**.
सुनमेना; see *s. v.* **सुन**.
सुनवय्या = **सुनवैया**, *q. v.*
सुनवैया, *m. f.* a listener, hearer, auditor.
सुनसर, *m.* a kind of ornament.
सुनसान, *more prop.* **सुन्सान**, *q. v.*
सुनसार, *m.* a kind of ornament.
सुनसुनी, *f.* a mole (the animal).
सुनहरा } **सुनहला** } *m.* (*f.* ī) golden; gilded.
सुनहि, (pl. °**हिं**) } **सुनही**, (pl. °**हीं**) } poet. forms = **सुनता है** (**सुनना**).
सुना, 1, *m.* gold: a cypher: 2, *m.* (*f.*ī) heard.
सुनाई, 1, *f.* (*m.* **सुनाया**) proclaimed: 2, *f.* hearing. — *denā*, to come within hearing, to be heard.
सुनाड़ी = **सुनारी**, 3, *q. v.*
सुनाना, *t.* (causat. of **सुनना**) to cause to hear, to inform, tell, advise, bid, warn.
सुनानेवाला, *m.* (*f.*ī) an informant, herald, preacher.
सुनापट, *f.* stillness, dreariness. [ern India.
सुनाभ, *m.* a mountain; part of the ranges of south-
सुनाम, *m.* a good name; good reputation.
सुनामन, *m.* (*f.* ī) well-named; of good repute.
सुनामी, *m.* (*f.* inī) = **सुनामन**, *q. v.*
सुनाय; see (1) **सुनाई** (2) **सुनाया** (3) **सुनाना**.
सुनायउ in Braj = **सुनाया**, *q. v.*
सुनाया, *m.* (*f.* **सुनाई**) made known, heralded, pro-
सुनायो in Braj = **सुनाया**, *q. v.* [claimed, announced.
सुनार, *m.* a worker in gold, a goldsmith. [goldsmith.
सुनारनी, *f.* (*m.* **सुनार**) a goldsmith's wife, a female
सुनारिणी, *f.* (*m.* **सुनारी**, 3) a clever female.
सुनारिन = **सुनारनी**, *q. v.*
सुनारी, 1, *f.* = **सुनारनी**, *q. v.*: 2, *f.* the business or the pay of a goldsmith: a good or handsome female: 3, *m.* (*f.* inī) a clever person, etc: *lit.* clever, alert, skilful, handy; neat.
सुनावट, *f.* hearing. [foreign country.
सुनावनी, *f.* tidings of the death of some one in a
सुनावनों in Braj = **सुनाना**, *q. v.*
सुनाशीर } **सुनासीर** } *m.* an epithet of Indra.
सुनि = **सुनके** (**सुनना**): see **स**, 7.
सुनिया, a contraction of **सुनैया**, *q. v.*
सुनिद्रा, *f.* sound sleep, healthy slumber.
सुनिहहि, (pl. °**हिं**) } **सुनिहही**, (pl. °**हीं**) } poet. forms = **सुनेगा** (**सुनना**).
सुनी, *f.* (*m.* **सुना**,) heard. [haved; politic.
सुनीत, 1, *m.* = **सुनीति**, *q. v.*: 2, *m.* (*f.* ā) well-be-
सुनीता, *f.* (*m.* **सुनीत**) a well-behaved female.
सुनीति, *f.* propriety of behaviour, good manners, good conduct; policy; *pr. n.* a wife of Uttānapād.
सुनीलक, *m.* the blue shrike: the emerald or sap-
सुनीथा, *f. pr. n.* the mother of king Veṇu. [phire.
सुनीसुनाई, *adj.* hearsay, rumoured.
सुनु, 1, = **सूनु**, *q. v*, 2, in Braj = **सुनो** (**सुनना**).
सुनै (*Rām.*) = **सुनता है** or **सुने**. See **से**, 3.
सुनौं (*poet.*) = (1) **मैं सुनूं** (2) **मैं सुनूंगा**.
सुन्न, 1, insensibility, stupidity, a swoon: 2, insensible, faint, lifeless: 3, *m. pr. n.* a certain man.
सुन्दर, *m.* (*f.* ī) handsome, beautiful, elegant, charming, comely, seemly, virtuous, good, neat, pure.
सुन्दरकाण्ड, *m. pr. n.* (see **सातकाण्ड**) the fifth section of the Rāmāyan.
सुन्दरचाल, 1, *adj.* moving gracefully or with a pleasing gait: 2, *m.* a graceful gait.
सुन्दरता, *f.* } **सुन्दरताई**, *f.* } **सुन्दरत्व**, *m.* } = **सुन्दराई**, *q. v.*
सुन्दरश्याम, *more com.* **श्यामसुन्दर**, *q. v.*
सुन्दराई, *f.* beauty, handsomeness, elegance, comeliness, goodness, virtuousness.
सुन्दरी, *f.* 1, = **सुन्दराई**, *q. v.*: 2, (*m.* **सुन्दर**) a beautiful female: 3, (in Pros.) a species of metre: a certain small timber-tree (*Heritiera minor*): turmeric.
सुन्दरौदन, *m.* good rice. [earthy smell.
सुन्धावट, *m.* smell, perfume, odour, scent; an
सुन्न (*colloquial*) = **शून्य**, *q. v.*
सुन्नत, *f.* circumcision: the traditions of Muhammad; rite, ordinance; ordination, confirmation. — *k.* to circumcise.
सुन्नसान = **सुन्सान**, *q. v.*
सुन्ना, 1, = **सुनना**, *q. v.*: 2, *m.* hearing, listening, attending: (in Arithm.) a cypher, naught; (in Gram.) the sign of abbreviation (viz. °); a dot: gold.
सुन्नाटा, *m.* the roaring of waves, the rumbling noise made by wind and rain at a distance, bluster, noise, sound.
सुन्नी, 1, *m.* an orthodox Muhammadan who reveres equally the four successors of Muhammad: 2, *f.* hearing, listening to.
सुन्या in old Hindee = **सुना**, heard.
सुन्सान, destitute of people, desolate and silent, deserted, lonely, still, dreary, dismal, void.
सुपक्ष, 1, = **सुपक्षी**, *q. v.*: 2, *m.* the fortunate half of the month, *i. e.* from the new to the full moon.
सुपक्षी, *m.* (*f.* iṇī) the party which has justice on its side, an advocate of the just cause.
सुपच = **स्वपच** = **श्वपच**, *q. v.*
सुपच्छ = **सुपक्ष**, *q. v.*
सुपच्छी, *m.* (*f.* inī) = **सुपक्षी**, *q. v.*
सुपत्र, *m.* the leaf of the *Laurus cassia*.
सुपथ, *m.* (the antithesis of **कुपथ**) a good road; good conduct; orthodoxy.
सुपथी, *m.* (*f.* inī) well-behaved; orthodox.

सुपन, an old form = **स्वप्न**, *q. v.*

सुपनखा, *more prop.* **शूर्पणखा**, *q.v.*

सुपना, *more prop.* **स्वप्न**, *q. v.*

सुपन्थ = **सुपथ**, *q. v.*

सुपाई, in Mārwāṛī = **सिपाही**, *q. v.*

सुपात्र, 1, *m.* (*f.* ī) a worthy person, an able, clever, or respectable person: 2, *adj.* worthy, fit, creditable: 3, *m.* an earthen vessel.

सुपारा, *m.* glans penis.

सुपारी, *f.* = (1) **सुपारा** (2) **सुपियारी**, *qq.v.*

सुपावीना, *m.* (*f.* ī) *more prop.* **सूपाबेना**, *q.v.*

सुपास, *m.* security, preservation, safety, happiness.

सुपासी, *m.* (*f.* inī) safe, secure, preserved, happy.

सुपियड, handsome, elegant, beautiful; personable; muscular, brawny. [its fruit.

सुपियारी, *f.* the betel-nut tree (*Areca catechu*) and

सुपुत्र, *m.* an excellent or dutiful son, a tractable

सुपुनीत, (a poet. redundancy) = **पुनीत**, *q. v.* [son,

सुपुर्द, *f.* charge, care, keeping, trust; handing over to, entrusting. — *k.* to consign, entrust,

सुपुर्दनामा, *m.* a deed of delivery.

सुपूत = **सुपुत्र**, *q. v.*

सुपेती (*Rām.*) = **सफ़ेदी**, *q. v.* [senseless, numbed.

सुप्त, 1, *m.* = **सुप्ति**, *q.v.*; 2, *m.* (*f.* ā) asleep, sleeping;

सुप्ति, *f.* sleeping, sleep, deep sleep; drowsiness; numbness, insensibility.

सुप्तोत्थित, *m.* (*f.* ā) aroused (or risen) from sleep.

सुप्रकाश, manifest, apparent, public.

सुप्रतिष्ठा, *f.* consecration, erection (as of a temple or idol): (in Pros.) a species of metre. [able.

सुप्रसन्न, *m.* (*f.* ā) well-pleased, favouring, favour-

सुफरा, *m.* a table-cloth, a napkin; the anus.

सुफल, *m.* (*f.* ā) bearing good fruit, attended with good results, fruitful for good, profitable, advantageous, useful, beneficial, efficacious. [Yuyudhān.

सुफलक, 1, *m.* (*f.* ikā) = **सुफल**, *q.v.*: 2, *m. pr. n.* a son of

सुफलता, *f.* advantageousness, usefulness, profit-

सुफेन, *m.* cuttle-fishbone: yeast, barm. [ableness.

सुफ़ेद, *adj.* (= **सफ़ेद**) white.

सुफ़ेदा, *m.* whiteness; white of egg; dawn of day; white lead; hair-powder.

सुबक्ता, *m.* (*f.* trī) = **सुवक्ता**, *q. v.*

सुबद्ध; see **सुभद्द**.

सुबन्ध, well-secured, having a good binding, well-

सुबर्च, *more prop.* **सुवर्च**, *q. v.* [fastened.

सुबरण / **सुबरन** / **सुबर्ण** / **सुबर्न** } *more prop.* **सुवर्ण**, *q. v.*

सुबह, *f.* morning, dawn.—*kā tārā*, the morning

सुबहा; see (1) **शुभा** (2) **सुब्ह** (3) **सुबहा**. [star.

सुबहान, *m.* praising, glorifying: an epithet of the Deity.

सुबहोशाम, morning and evening.

सुबा; see **सुबहा**.

सुबानी, *more prop.* **सुवाणी**, *q. v.*

सुबारि, *more prop.* **सुवारि**, *q. v.*

सुबास, *more prop.* **सुवास**, *q. v.*

सुबासनायुक्त, *m.* (*f.* ā) *more prop.* **सुवासनायुक्त**, *q. v.*

सुबाहु = **सुभुज**, *q. v.*

सुबिप्र, *m.* (*f.* ā) *more prop.* **सुविप्र**, *q. v.*

सुबिरति, *more prop.* **सुविरति**, *q. v.*

सुबिस्ता, *m. f.* security, preservation, safety.

सुबिहिता; see (1) **सुबिस्ता** (2) **सुविहित** (3) **सुभिता**.

सुबुद्धि, 1, *m. f.* intelligent, wise, clever, cunning, shrewd; 2, *f.* a good understanding, good sense, a correct notion.

सुबूत = **सबूत**, *q. v.*

सुबेदार = **सूबादार**, *q. v.*

सुबेष (*colloquial*) = **सुवेष**, *q. v.*

सुबोधनी, *f. pr. n.* (1) of a commentry on the Krishnkarnāmrit (2) of a commentary on the Bhagavad-Gītā (3) of a commentary on the Shrutbodh by Manohar-Sharman.

सुबोधिनी, *f. pr.n.* (1) of a commentary on Vijñāneshwar's Mitākshara by Visheshwar (2) of a commentary on the Bhagavad-Gītā by Shrī-dhar Swāmin (3) of a short treatise on ritual by Shiv-Rām.

सुभ, 1, (*colloquial*) = **शुभ**, *q.v.*: 2, *more prop.* **सुबह**, *q.v.*

सुभग, 1, *m.* (*f.* ā) auspicious, fortunate, happy; beautiful, charming, lovely, agreeable, pleasant, good; neat, pure; beloved, amiable: 2, *m.* fortune: the *Ashoka*-tree; the *Champaca*-tree.

सुभगता, *f.* auspiciousness, fortunateness; agreeableness, loveliness, amiableness.

सुभगा, *f.* (*m.* **सुभग**) a woman beloved by her husband, a favorite wife, a respectable and auspicious mother.

सुभगुन (*colloquial*) = **शुभगुण**, *q. v.*

सुभट, *more prop.* **सुभट्ट**, *q. v.* [rior, champion, hero.

सुभट्ट, *m.* a very learned man: a distinguished war-

सुभदत्त, *m.* (*f.* ā) *more prop.* **शुभदत्त**, *q. v.*

सुभद्र, 1, *m.* (*f.* ā) propitious, auspicious, fortunate 2, *m.* an epithet of Vishṇu. [a certain river.

सुभद्रा, *f. pr.n.* (1) of the sister of Jagannāth (2) of

सुभलच्छण, *more prop.* **शुभलक्षण**, *q. v.*

सुभलगन, *more prop.* **शुभलग्न**, *q. v.*

सुभा, *more prop.* **शुभा**, *q. v.*

सुभाउ / **सुभाऊ** / **सुभाओ** } *more prop.* (1) **सुभाव** (2) **स्वभाव**, *qq. v.*

सुभाग, *more com.* **सौभाग्य**, *q. v.*

सुभागी, *m.* (*f.* inī) = **सौभागी**, *q. v.*

सुभाग्य, *more com.* **सौभाग्य**, *q. v.*

सुभान; see **सुभाना** and **सुबहान**.

सुभाना, *t.* to afford pleasure to.

सुभाय, a poet. form of the conjunct. part. of **सुभाना**.

सुभाया, 1, = सुभाव, *q. v.*: 2, *m.* (*f.* सुभाई) past part. of सुभाना, *q. v.*

सुभाव, 1, *more prop.* स्वभाव, *q. v.*: 2, *m.* a good disposition: 3, of a good disposition, well-disposed.

सुभाषा, *f.* good language, pleasant speech.

सुभाषित, 1, *m.* (*f.* ā) well-spoken, well-said, spoken elegantly: eloquent: 2, *m.* eloquence, elegant speech.

सुभाषी, *m.* (*f.* iṇī) a fair speaker, elegant or eloquent speaker.

सुभास, *m. pr. n.* a certain ancient Hindoo king.

सुभासा, *more prop.* (1) सुभास (2) सुभाषा, *qq. v.*

सुभासुभ (*colloquial*) = शुभाशुभ, *q. v.*

सुभिता }
सुभीता } (*colloquial*) = शुभिता, *q. v.*

सुभुज, *m.* an epithet of Rāvaṇ: *lit.* having powerful arms, very strong.

सुभ्र (*Rām.*): see (1) सुभ्रु (2) शुभ्र.

सुभ्राता, *m.* a good brother.

सुभ्रु, *adj.* having beautiful eyebrows: hence, *f.* a woman.

सुम, *m.* a flower: a hoof, a hoofed foot.

सुमंगल, *m.* (*f.* ā) very fortunate or auspicious, bringing good fortune; abounding in sacrifices.

सुमंगला, *f. pr. n.* (1) of a certain river in the district of Kāmākhyā (2) of one of the mothers of the twenty-four Arhats.

सुमंत्र = सुमन्त्र, *q. v.*

सुमड़ा, *more prop.* शूमड़ा, *q. v.*

सुमत, friendly, well-disposed, kindly disposed: *m. pr. n.* a certain ancient Hindoo king.

सुमतचन्द, an epithet of any person who is remarkable for friendliness.

सुमति, 1, *f.* friendliness, kindness, benevolence; good conscience, good understanding; favour of the gods, blessing, gift, desire, wish: 2, *m. f.* of a good understanding or conscience, very wise; benevolent.

सुमती, *f. pr. n.* (1) of the wife of Sagar, and mother of 60,000 sons (2) of the wife of Vishṇu-yashas, and mother of Kalkī.

सुमदुम, very corpulent.

सुमन, 1, of good disposition; fair, handsome, beautiful: satisfied: 2, *m.* a god: a learned man, a student of the Veds: wheat; a flower; the thorn-apple.

सुमनचाप }
सुमनधनुष } *m.* epithets of the bow of Kāmdev.

सुमनवृष्टि, *f.* a shower of flowers.

सुमनसी, *f.* the great flowered jasmine.

सुमनोहर, very charming, very delightful, agreeable, pleasing, beautiful.

सुमन्त्र, 1, = सुमन्त्रण, *q. v.*: 2, well-deliberated, well-advised.

सुमन्त्रण, *m.* }
सुमन्त्रणा, *f.* } good advice, wise counsel.

सुमर, 1, = शुमर, *q. v.*: 2, *adj.* dying easily.

सुमरण }
सुमरन } = स्मरण, *q. v.*

सुमरना, *t.* to remember, keep in memory; to mention; to invoke.

सुमर्य्याद, *m.* (*f.* ā) good, upright, pious.

सुमसुम, *f.* the noise of moist wood when burning, a simmering.

सुमानस, *m.* an epithet of lake *Mānas.*

सुमार = (1) शुमार (2) सुमर, 2, *qq. v.*

सुमाली, 1, *m.* (*f.* inī) well-garlanded, possessed of a good garland: 2, *m. pr. n.* a certain daitya.

सुमित्र, *m.* (*f.* ā) a friend, a good friend.

सुमित्रा, *f. pr. n.* one of the wives of Dasharath, and mother of Lakshmaṇ.

सुमिर, *m.* remembrance, recollection.

सुमिरत, remembered, made mention of.

सुमिरन = स्मरण, *q. v.*

सुमिरना, *t.* to remember, keep in memory; to mention, tell, celebrate in song, relate.

सुमिरनी, *f.* a rosary; a memento.

सुमिरहि, (pl. °हिं) }
सुमिरही, (pl. °हीं) } poet. forms = सुमिरता है.

सुमिरि, an old conjunct, part. of सुमिरना, *q. v.*

सुमिरिय, an old Imperat. of सुमिरना, *q. v.*

सुमिरेसि (*Rām.*) = सुमिरा (सुमिरना). See एसि.

सुमिरै, (pl. °रैं) an old form = सुमिरे (सुमिरना).

सुमुख, 1, *m.* (*f.* ā *or* ī) handsome-faced, pleasing, propitious: 2, *m.* (*f.* ā) a teacher: 3, *m.* a beautiful mouth: the scratch of a finger-nail.

सुमुखा, *f* (*m.* सुमुख) a handsome-faced female.

सुमुखि; see सुमुखी.

सुमुखित, *m.* (*f.* ā) well-adorned.

सुमुखी, *f.* 1, = सुमुखा, *q. v.*: 2, (in Pros.) a species of metre.

सुमृति (*Rām.*) = स्मृति, *q. v.*

सुमेर, a leader.

सुमेरु, an epithet of mount मेरु, *q. v.*

सुमेरुगिर = मेरु, 2, *q. v.*

सुमेल, suitable; of pleasing manners, affable.

सुम्न, *m.* a hymn.

सुम्नयु, a chanter of hymns.

सुम्बा, *m.* a sponge-staff; a ramrod.

सुम्बात *f.* a hoof.

सुम्बुलखार, *m.* arsenic, orpiment.

सुम्भ, *m.* a hole made in a wall.

सुयज्ञ, *m. pr. n.* a certain Yaksh.

सुयज्ञ, *m.* a good oblation, excellent sacrifice: *pr. n.* a certain ancient Hindoo king.

सुयश, 1, *m.* good repute, renown: 2, of good repute, renowned.

सुयशी, *m.* (*f.* inī) of good repute, renowned.

सुयोग, *m.* a favorable juncture, good opportunity, auspicious occasion.

सुर, 1, (*colloquial*) = स्वर, *q. v.*: 2, *m.* the sun; a god, deity: the stars of the northern hemisphere. In the ingenious system of reckoning by symbols adopted by Hindoos in their poetry, this word is a symbol for 33.

सुरंग, 1, *m.* bright colour, orange, red colour; red sanders; vermilion: 2, red-coloured, light bay or chesnut (horses): 2, m. (f. ?) a mine; a hole cut in a wall for burglarious purposes; a gallery; a subterraneous passage; an adit.

सुरंगधातु, *m.* red chalk.

सुरंगा, *f* a hole cut in a wall for burglarious purposes: a kind of fragrant grass: crystal.

सुरंगी, *m.* (*f.* inī) 1, bright-coloured, red-coloured: 2, a miner, housebreaker, burglar.

सुरकुल, *m.* the race or family of the gods.

सुरखंड, *more prop.* **सुर्खंड** *q.v.* [proportion of leaves.

सुरखा, *m.* a tall plant running up without a due

सुरख़ी, *f.* redness, a red tincture, blood, brickdust.

सुरग, in Chand = **स्वर्ग**, *q. v.*

सुरगण, *m.* a class or company of divinities; a host of gods; an epithet of Shiv.

सुरगुरु, *m.* (instructor of the gods, *i. e.*) Vrihaspatī.

सुरज, 1, = **सूर्य्य**, *q. v.*: 2, *m.* (*f.* ā) born of a deity.

सुरजन, 1, a Prākṛit form of **सज्जन**, *q. v.*: 2, *m.* (a pl. of **सुर**; see **जन**) the gods. [of the gods.

सुरज्येष्ठ, *m.* an epithet of Brahmā: *lit.* the eldest

सुरत, 1, *more prop.* **सूरत**, *q. v.*: 2, *m.* (*f.* ā) much pleased, highly delighted; compassionate, tender: 2, *f.* recollection, memory; consideration, reflection, attention; caution; accuracy: copulation.—*k.* to recollect, bear in mind.

सुरतरु, *m.* an epithet of **कल्पवृक्ष**, *q. v.*

सुरता, 1, *f.* = **सुरत**, 1, *q. v.*: 2, *m.* = **स्मर्त्ता**, *q. v.*

सुरति, *more prop.* (1) **स्मृति** (2) **सूरति**, *qq. v.*

सुरतीला, *m.* (*f.* ī) considerate, prudent.

सुरत्राता, *m.* an epithet of Vishṇu; *lit.* the preserver

सुरत्रिय, *f.* the wives of the gods. [of the gods.

सुरधूप, *m.* resin, turpentine.

सुरधेनु, *more com.* **कामधेनु**, *q. v.*

सुरन, 1, (a Braj pl. of **सुर**), gods: 2, *more prop.* **स्वर्ण**, *q. v.*

सुरनर, *m.* gods and men, mortals and immortals.

सुरना, *m.* a kind of pipe, a clarion.

सुरनाई, *m.* (*f.* in *or* inī) a clarion-player, piper.

सुरनाथ, *m.* (chief of the gods, *i. e.*) Indra.

सुरनारी, *f.* the wives of the gods.

सुरन्ह / **सुरन्हि** } old oblique pll. of **सुर**. See **न्ह** and **न्हि**.

सुरपति, *m.* (chief of the gods, *i. e.*) Indra.

सुरपुर, *m. pr. n.* the abode of the immortal gods.

सुरबर्चा, *more prop.* **सुरवर्चा**, *q. v.*

सुरब्राता (*Rām.*) = **सुरव्रात**, *q. v.*

सुरभि, 1, *f.* = **सुरभी**, *q. v.*: 2, *m.* fragrance, perfume; the spring; resin; a nutmeg; a certain plant (*Michelia champaca*); the month Chaitra (March—April): *lit.* fragrant, sweet-smelling; pleasing; handsome; good; friendly; wise; celebrated.

सुरभी, *f.* the earth; a fabulous cow (the cow of plenty); a cow: spirituous liquor: the name of several plants.

सुरभूप, *m.* (the lord of the gods, *i. e.*) Indra.

सुरमनि (*Rām.*) = **सूर्य्यमणि**, *q. v.*

सुरमा, *m.* a collyrium, antimony.

सुरयानी, appertaining to Syria, Syrian, Syriac: hence (1) *m.* (*f.* ini) a native of Syria (2) *f.* the Syrian language.

सुरराजा, *m.* the king or chief of the gods (an epithet of Indra and of Vishṇu).

सुरराय in Braj = **सुरराजा**, *q. v.*

सुररुख, *adv.* in the direction of the gods.

सुररुख, *m.* either (or the whole) of the five trees of Indra's paradise. [of the gods.

सुरलोक, *m. pr. n.* the heaven of Indra, and abode

सुरवा, *m.* a ladle in the form of a hand with which clarified butter (*ghi*) is thrown into the fire for a burnt-offering.

सुरवर्चा, *f. pr. n.* a certain female *rākshas.*

सुरवानी, *f.* the voice of the gods, celestial sounds.

सुरवीथी, *f.* an epithet of the ecliptic: *lit.* the road of the gods. [host or army of the gods.

सुरव्रात, *m.* a class or company of divinities, a

सुरस, 1, *m.* (*f.* ā) well-flavoured, savoury, sweet, juicy, sapid; elegant: 2, *m.* the name of several plants.

सुरसती in Mārwāṛī = **सरस्वती**, *q. v.*

सुरसमाज, *m.* = **सुरसमुदाई**, *q. v.*

सुरसमुदाई, *f.* the gods of the Hindoo pantheon regarded in their collective and corporate capacity.

सुरसर, *m.* an epithet of **मानसरोवर**, *q v.* [Ganges.

सुरसरि, *f.* (see **गंगा**) the celestial Ganges; the earthly

सुरसरित / **सुरसरिता** } = **सुरसरि**, *q. v.*

सुरसरिधार, *f.* the stream or flow of the Ganges.

सुरसा, *f.* the name of several plants; an epithet of Durgā; (in Pros.) a species of metre.

सुरसाईं / **सुरसांई** } = **सुरस्वामी**, *q. v.*

सुरसाल, *m.* the churningstaff of the gods.

सुरसुराना = **सरसराना**, *q. v.*

सुरसुराहट = **सरसराहट**, *q. v.*

सुरसुरी, *f.* 1, = **सरसराहट**, *q. v.*: 2, a kind of insect bred in grain: a kind of fireworks. [form **शूरसेन**.

सुरसेन; for words beginning thus, see under the

सुरस्वामी, *m.* (lord or chief of the deities, *i.e.*) Indra.

सुरहित beloved of the gods: hence, *m.* an epithet (1) of sacrifice (2) of Kṛishṇ. [uncultivated land.

सुरही, *f.* a kind of grass that grows on neglected or

सुरा, *f.* spirituous or inebriating liquor: a drinking-vessel: a snake.

सुराई, *f.* courage, bravery, valour, heroism, prowess.

सुराख़ना, *t.* to perforate, pierce, penetrate, bore.

सुराग़, *m.* search, inquiry, spying; a sign, mark, trace.—*lenā*, to search, seek, inquire for, spy.

सुरातन, *m.* bravery, valour, heroism, prowess.

सुराति (*Rām.*) = **सुरात्रि**, *q. v.*

सुरात्रि, *f.* a fine or auspicious night.

सुराती (*Rām.*) = **सुरात्रि**, *q. v.*

सुरानीक, *adv.* in the direction of (or as far as to) the gods.

सुराब, *m.* a vapour which at a distance resembles [the sea, mirage, glare.

सुरिया, *m. pr. n.* the province of Syria.

सुरियानी = **सुरयानी**, *q.v.*

सुरी, *f.* = **सुरा**, *q.v.*

सुरीत (*contraction*) = **सुरीति**, *q. v.*

सुरीति, *f.* good behaviour, good practice.

सुरीन, the hip.

सुरुकना = **सुड़ुकना**, *q. v.*

सुरुचि, *f.* 1, (*Rām.*) = **अच्छी रुचि**: 2, *pr. n.* a wife of [Uttānapād.

सुरुब, *m.* lead.

सुरुवा, *more prop.* (1) **सुरवा** (2) **शोरबा**, *qq.v.*

सुरू, *more prop.* **शुरू**, *q.v.*

सुरूप, 1, *m.* a handsome or elegant form: 2, *m.* (*f.* ā) handsome, symmetrical, well-formed, beautiful.

सुरूपता, *f.* handsomeness, elegance, beauty.

सुरूपवत, *m.* (*f.* vatī) well-shaped, symmetrical, handsome, beautiful.

सुरूपवती, *f.* (*m.* **सुरूपवान** etc.) a beautiful female.

सुरूपवन्त / **सुरूपवान** } *m.* (*f.* vatī) = **सुरूपवत**, *q.v.*

सुरूपी, *m.* (*f.* iṇī) = **सुरूप**, 2, *q.v.*

सुरेश, *m.* (the lord or chief of the gods, *i. e.*) Indra.

सुरेश्वर, *m.* (the lord or chief of the gods, *i.e.*) Indra.

सुरेसा (*Rām.*) = **सुरेश**, *q.v.*

सुरैत, *f.* a paramour, mistress, concubine.

सुरैतिन = **सुरैत**, *q. v.*

सुर्ख़, red: hence, *m.* a red tincture, red ink.

सुर्ख़रू, red in the face; honourable, unabashed, nullâ culpâ pallescens (not pale from the consciousness of any guilt): acquitted; pleased, contented.

सुर्ख़ी, *f.* redness, a red tincture, blood, brickdust.

सुर्ब, *m.* lead.

सुर्मा, *m.* collyrium, antimony.

सुर्रा, *m.* the sword-fish: a purse filled with gold [or silver.

सुलक्खण = **सुलक्षण**, *q.v.*

सुलक्षण, 1, *m.* a good or distinct mark, an auspicious mark; beauty, excellence: a determining: 2, *m.* (*f.* ā) clearly distinguished by marks; of good omen, auspicious, fortunate; beautiful; clever, expert.

सुलक्षणा, *f.* (*m.* **सुलक्षण**) a beautiful female, etc.: a proper name of females.

सुलगना, *a. int.* to light, ignite, become kindled or enflamed; to burn without smoke or flame.

सुलगाट, *m.* place where Hindoos burn their dead.

सुलगाना; *t.* to light, kindle, enflame.

सुलच्छन = **सुलक्षण**, *q.v.*

सुलच्छनि; see (1) **सुलक्षण** (2) **सुलक्षणा**.

सुलझना, *n.* to be unravelled, be disentangled.

सुलझाना, *t.* to unravel, disentangle.

सुलझाव, *m.* disentanglement, solution.

सुलतान, *m.* a prince, king, monarch, emperor, gov-[ernor.

सुलतानी, 1, appertaining to a monarch, regal, royal, princely: 2, *f.* the office or status of a monarch, sultanship.

सुलभ, *m.* (*f.* ā) easy of acquisition, easily obtainable, easy to be perceived or effected, easy, feasible.

सुलभता, *f.* easiness of acquisition, feasibleness.

सुलभावकाश, *m.* (*f.* ā) easily gaining room or admis-[sion.

सुलभ्य = **सुलभ**, *q. v.*

सुलवाना, *t.* to cause to be put to sleep, to cause to [put to sleep.

सुलसली, *f.* continued rains.

सुला देना, an intensive form of **सुलाना**, *q.v.*

सुलाना, *t.* (a causat. of **सोना**) to cause to sleep, to put to sleep, to lull: *met.* to murder, kill.

सुलाभ = **सुलभ**, *q. v.*

सुलूक, *m.* road, way; manner, mode, conduct; usage, treatment; intercourse.—*k.* to treat with, negotiate with, have dealings with, proceed with.

सुलैमान, *m. pr. n.* king Solomon.

सुलोक, *m.* the abode of the good, the good state, [heaven.

सुलैमानी, 1, *m.* an onyx: 2, *f.* the state or dignity of king Solomon: 3, appertaining to Solomon.

सुवक्ता, *m.* (*f.* trī) an eloquent or elegant speaker: lit. *adj.* speaking elegantly or well.

सुवचन, *m.* elegant speech, eloquence.

सुवन, *m.* a son.

सुवरन (*colloquial*) = **सुवर्ण**, *q. v.*

सुवर्च, *m. pr. n.* a certain demon (*rākshas*).

सुवर्ण, 1, *m.* (*f.* ā) of a good colour, tribe, or caste, bright, brilliant: golden: 2, *m.* a good colour; good rank or class in society: a kind of red chalk or ochre; a species of sandal-wood: gold, pure gold; a gold coin, gold mohur, a weight of gold equal to sixteen *mashās*: a certain tree (*Cassia fistula*); a sort of sacrifice.

सुवर्णगणित, *m.* computation of gold, *i. e.* of its weight and fineness; (in Arithm.) allegation medial.

सुवर्णमय, *m.* (*f.* ī) golden, consisting of (or abounding in) gold.

सुवर्णा, *f.* the name of several plants.

सुवर्नो (*colloquial*) = (1) **सुवर्ण** (2) **सुवर्णा**, *qq. v.*

सुवस्तु, *f.* any good or excellent thing.

सुवहा, *f.* the Indian lute; the name of several [plants.

सुवांग, *more prop.* **स्वांग**, *q. v.*

सुवांगी, *m.* (*f.* inī) *more com.* **स्वांगी**, *q. v.*

सुवाणी, *f.* a sweet voice, pleasant sound or speech.

सुवाना, *t.* (a causat. of **सोना**) to cause to sleep, to [put to sleep.

सुवानी, *more prop.* **सुवाणी**, *q. v.*

सुवारि, excellent or beautiful water.

सुवाल, *m.* an interrogation, question; a proposition; a petition, request.—*k.* to interrogate, ask, solicit, beg.

सुवास, *m.* a pleasant or reputable residence: an agreeable perfume, sweet smell, fragrance, scent: *adj.* odorous, sweet scented.

सुवासनायुक्त, *m.* (*f.* ā) possessed of a pleasant smell, sweet-smelling, odorous, fragrant.

सुवासिनी, *f.* a married female residing in her father's house; a perfumed female. [fumed.

सुवासी, *m.* (*f.* inī) *adj.* dwelling comfortably: per-

सुविक्रम, *m.* valour, bravery, prowess.

सुविचार, *m.* due consideration, deliberation.

सुविज्ञ, *m.* (*f.* ā) very knowing or skilful.

सुविध, of a good kind: *adv.* in a good or easy way, easily, well.

सुविप्र, *m.* (*f.* ā) a good or excellent Brāhmaṇ.

सुविरति, *f.* a good or fortunate rest or termination.

सुविश्वस्त, *m.* (*f.* ā) very trustful, confiding, very trusty, dependable, confidential.

सुविहित, *m.* (*f.* ā) well-placed, well-deposited; well-provided; well-arranged: well performed, well done.

सुवेल, 1, *m.* the sea-shore: a good time, fitting, season: 2, *m.* (*f.* ā) bowed or stopping greatly; very humble, very quiet: 3, *m. pr. n.* a certain mountain.

सुवेलशैल, *m. pr. n.* a certain mountain. See **सुवेल**.

सुवेष, 1, *m.* a good or ornamental dress or guise: 2, *m.* (*f.* ā) well-dressed, ornamented, decorated.

सुवेषी, *m.* (*f.* iṇī) = **सुवेष**, 2, *q.v.*

सुवैया, *m. f.* one who sleeps, a sleeper.

सुवोधिनी, *more prop.* **सुबोधिनी**, *q.v.*

सुव्यवहार, *m.* good behaviour; good usage. [or.

सुशिक्षक, *m.* (*f.* ikā) a good learner; a good instruct-

सुशिच्छक = **सुशिक्षक**, *q.v.*

सुशीतल, *m.* (*f.* ā) very cool, very cold, frigid, freez-

सुशीतलता *f.* great coldness, frigidity. [ing.

सुशील, *m.* (*f.* ā) well-disposed, of a good disposition, good-natured, kind, benevolent.

सुशीलता, *f.* goodness of disposition, amiability, good-naturedness, kindness.

सुशीला, *f.* (*m.* **सुशील**) a well-disposed or benevolent female: *pr. n.* (1) of one of Krishṇ's eight wives (2) of the wife of Sudāmā (3) of a daughter of Huriswāmī (4) of Yam's wife.

सुशीली, *m.* (*f.* inī) = **सुशील**, *q.v.* [compassion.

सुशोक, *m.* tender or auspicious grief, sympathy,

सुशोभ, well-adorned, beautified, handsome, comely.

सुशोभन, 1, *m.* (*f.* ā) handsome, well-looking, comely: 2, *m.* handsomeness, comeliness.

सुशोभित, *m.* (*f.* ā) well-adorned, beautified.

सुश्राव्य, pleasing or agreeable to the hearing; distinctly audible.

सुषुप्त, *m.* (*f.* ā) sound asleep, fast asleep.

सुषुप्ति, *f.* deep sleep, dead sleep, profound repose, entire insensibility, unconsciousness.

सुषेण, *m.* an epithet of Vishṇu: a certain plant (*Carissa carondas*).

सुसंग, *m.* good association, good company.

सुसंगति, *f.* the association or companionship of the good. [ted, well connected.

सुसंगत, *m.* (*f.* ā) well united, auspiciously associa-

सुसंगी, *m.* (*f.* inī) a suitable companion or associate (whether for good or for evil).

सुसंगू; see (1) **सुसंग** (2) **सुसंगी**.

सुसकारना, *more prop.* **सुस्कारना**, *q.v.*

सुसताना, *more prop.* **सुस्ताना**, *q.v.*

सुसन्देश, *m.* good news, glad tidings.

सुसमय, *m.* a period of prosperity, good times, a season of plenty, a good season. [excellent judgment.

सुसमझ, *f.* a good intellect or understanding, an

सुसमाचार, *m.* an epithet of the Gospel: *lit.* good

सुसयटी, *f.* (Engl.) a Society. [news.

सुसर } very common forms of **श्वशुर**, *q.v.*
सुसरा }

सुसरार, a colloquial form of **सुसराल**, *q.v.*

सुसराल, *f.* (Sk. **श्वशुरालय**) a father-in-law's house or family. The term is sometimes applied ironically to a gaol, just as in English the pawnbroker's shop is sometimes called "the mansion of mine uncle:" Again, *Wah -- ko gayā*, he has gone nobody knows where, he has made himself scarce, he has bolted.

सुसाखी, *m.* (*f.* iṇī) a good or favourable witness.

सुसामुझि (*Rām.*) = **सुसमझ**, *q.v.*

सुसार, *m.* cook, a dresser and seller of food: a kind of jewel or crystal: property, competence; convenience, accommodation.

सुसाहसी, *m.* (*f.* inī) brave, courageous, valiant.

सुसाहिब, *m.* a good or excellent master or lord.

सुसीतल (*colloquial*) = **सुशीतल**, *q.v.*

सुसीतलताई, *f.* = **सुशीतलता**, *q.v.* [form **सुशील**.

सुसील; for words beginning thus, see under the

सुसुम, lukewarm, tepid.

सुसेवक, *m.* (*f.* ikā) a good or faithful servant or attendant. [**सुसेवक**).

सुसेवकनि (*Rām.*) = **सुसेवकानि** (the Sk. nom. pl. of

सुसेवित, *m.* (*f.* ā) well served, much attended to.

सुसैश्रटी }
सुसैटी } = **सुसयटी**, *q.v.*
सुसैयटी }

सुस्कारना, *a. int.* to sibilate, to hiss (said of snakes).

सुस्त, relaxed, languid, feeble, slow, indolent, lazy, idle, negligent. — *k.* to relax.

सुस्तर, a string for making images dance.

सुस्ता; see (1) **सुस्त** (2) **सुस्ताना** (3) **सस्ता**.

सुस्ताना, *a. int.* to stop, rest, lie down.

सुस्ती, *f.* relaxedness, dilatoriness, laziness, negligence, remissness, slothfulness.

सुस्थ, *m.* (*f.* ā) well, healthy; well off, in a good condition, in easy circumstances, happy.

सुस्थता, *f.* (*m.* °त्व) healthiness, good condition, ease, comfort, happiness.

सुस्थित, *m.* (*f.* ā) living well, being well, safe.

सुस्थिर, *m.* (*f.* ā) firm, steady, stable, resolute, calm, cool. [ness.

सुस्थिरत्व, *m.* (*f.* tā) steadiness, resoluteness, calm-

सुस्पष्ट, very distinct, very clear, easy intelligible.

सुस्वभाव, 1, *m.* a good disposition, goodness of nature: 2, *adj.* of a good disposition, good-natured.

सुस्वभावना, *m.* (*f.* ī) of a good disposition, good-natured.

सुस्वाद, *m.* a pleasant taste, delicious flavour.

सुस्वादित, *m.* (*f.* ā) rendered pleasing to the taste, well-flavoured. [delicious.

सुस्वादु, very pleasant to the taste, very sweet,

सुहबत, *f.* companionship, society; discourse; a meeting, assemblage; a fair; coïtion.

सुहरना, *a. int.* to trail, draggle, drag.

सुहला, *m.* a kind of song.

सुहाई, *f.* (*m.* **सुहाया**) = **सुहानी**, *q.v.*

सुहाऊ = **सुहावा**, *q.v.*

सुहाग, *m.* auspiciousness, good fortune; the affection of a husband, an act of endearment, a caress; the happy state of being a wife as contrasted with widowhood; ornaments worn by married women while their husbands are alive.

सुहागन, *f.* a woman whose husband is alive; a woman beloved of her husband; a favorite wife.

सुहागपिटारा, *m.* a casket of jewels presented by a bridegroom to his bride.

सुहागपुड़ा, *m.* = **सुहागपिटारा**, *q.v.*

सुहागलहर, *f.* a cool refreshing breeze.

सुहागा, *m.* borax.

सुहागिन; see (1) **सुहागन** (2) **सुहागिनी**. [er's house.

सुहागिनी, *f.* a married female residing in her fath-

सुहागी, 1, *more com.* **सुहागिनी**, *q.v.*: 2, *m.* (*f.* inī) a

सुहात; see **सुहाता** and **सुहाना**, 2. [fortunate person.

सुहाता, *m.* (*f.* ī) agreeable, pleasant, charming.

सुहान; see **सुहाना** and **सूहान**.

सुहाना, 1, *m.* (*f.* ī) agreeable, pleasant, charming: 2, *a. int.* to please, be agreeable, be liked, be approved of; to become, befit, to shine: *t.* to ornament, adorn.

सुहामनी in Chand = **सुहाना**, *q.v.*

सुहाय, a contraction of **सुहाया**, *q.v.*

सुहायमान, *m.* (*f.* mati) } = **सुहाना**, 1, *q.v.*
सुहाया, *m.* (*f.* **सुहाई**) }

सुहारना, *t.* to trail, draggle, drag.

सुहाल, *m.* bread or cakes fried in butter.

सुहाली, *f.* = **सुहाल**, *q.v.* [ornament.

सुहावन, agreeable, pleasant, charming. —*k.* to

सुहावना, 1, adj. *m.* (*f.* ī): 2, *a. int.* = **सुहाना**, *q.v.*

सुहावनी, *f.* an agreeable or charming female.

सुहावा, 1, *m.* (*f.* ī) agreeable, pleasing: 2, *m.* decoration, garniture, ornament; splendidness, handsomeness.

सुहावी, *f.* agreeableness, pleasantness.

सुहाहि, (pl °हिं) } = **सुहाता** (**सुहाना**).
सुहाही, (pl. °हीं) }

सुहृद, *m.* (*f.* ā) = **सुहृदय**, *q.v.*

सुहृदभेद, *m.* the separation of friends, dissension among friends.

सुहृदय, *m.* (*f.* ā) a kind-hearted person: *lit.* good-hearted, friendly, kind.

सुहृदयभेद = **सुहृदभेद**, *q.v.* [birth of a son).

सुहैया, *f.* a birth-song (sung by the females at the

सुहैला, *m.* a kind of descriptive or eulogistic song.

सू, 1, *more prop.* **सु**, good, etc. *q.v.*: 2, *f.* a side, part, quarter, direction: 3, in the direction of, towards: 4, in Braj = **से**, *q.v.* [stye.— *kī charbī*, lard.

सूअर, *m.* (*f.* ī) a hog, a wild boar.—*kī bhār*, a hog-

सूअरख़ाना, *m.* a pork-establishment, any place where swine are slain or sold, a pig's-house, hogstye.

सूआ, *m.* a parrot, a parroquet: any large needle, a needle with which gunny-bags are sewed, a packing-needle; a prick, prickle; an awn of corn.

सूआपाटी } *f.* a certain game among children.
सूआपाती }

सूआस, *m.* a kind of rice.

सूइया, pointed (said of needles).

सूइस, *m.* a porpoise.

सूई, *f.* a needle; the hand of a watch; the needle of a compass; a prick, prickle.—*kā kām*, needlework. —*ke nākese khudāiko nikālnā* is applied to express the performance of seeming impossibilities.—*bhar*, a needleful.

सूईगल, (*lit.* the needle-melter) a certain very acid kind of lemon in which needles are said to dissolve.

सूईभर; see *s.v.* **सूई**.

सूं, 1, in Braj and in Mārwarī = **से**, 1, *q.v.*: 2, *more prop.* **सोंह**, *q.v.*

सूंगरा, *m.* (*f.* ī) a buffalo-calf.

सूंगा, *m.* the clitoris.

सूंघ, *f.* smell; a smelling, inhaling.

सूंघन, *f.* anything to smell to, snuff; smelling.

सूंघना, *t.* to scent, smell, nose, sniff, snuff, inhale. *Sūnghtā* [*m.* (*f.* ī)] *phirnā*, to prowl about.

सूंघनी, *f.* snuff, scent. —*lenā*, to nuzzle.

सूंघा, 1, *m.* (*f.* ī) staunch (said of dogs); a setter of jewels: 2, *m.* a person employed in Marhatta armies who is said to be able to detect hidden treasure or grain by the smell of the earth.

सूंट, **सूंड**, **सूंत**, **सूंथ**; for all words beginning with either of these elements, see under the corresponding forms **सुघट**, **सुघड़**, **सुन्त**, **सुन्थ** respectively.

सूंड़, *f.* an elephant's trunk. [liquors.

सूंड़ी, *m.* (*f.* inī) a distiller and vendor of spirituous

सूंड़ीमुआमलसी, *f.* a tax on vendors of spirituous

सूंस, *m.* porpoise. [liquors.

सूक (*colloquial*) = **शूक**, *q.v.*

सूकटा, *m.* (*f.* ī) lean, emaciated, weak.

सूकड़ा, *more prop.* **सुकड़ा**, *q.v.*

सूकना, *more prop.* **सूखना**, *q.v.*

सूकर (*colloquial*) = (1) **शूकर** (2) **शूक**, *qq.v.*

सूकरमुख, *more prop.* **शूकरमुख**, *q.v.*

सूकरखेत = **शूकरखेत** = **वाराहक्षेत्र**, *q.v.*

सूकरी, 1, (*colloquial*) = **शूकरी**, *q.v.*: 2, *f.* a species of moss (*Lycopodium imbricatum*).

सूकचा, *m.* a kind of vetch.

सूका, 1, *m.* (*f.* ī) *more prop.* **सूखा**, *q.v.*: 2, *m.* a four-anna piece (a silver coin equal to a quarter of a rupee).

सूकाश, *m.* leisure opportunity.

सूकी, *m.* 1, *more prop.* **सूखी**, *q.v.*: 2, = **सूका**, *q.v.*

सूक्त, *m.* an invocation, prayer in metre, a hymn; a sentence. [invocations.

सूक्तकर्त्ता, *m.* (*f.* trī) an epithet of any maker of

सूक्ती, *f.* a snail.

सूक्ष (*colloquial*) = **सूक्ष्म**, *q.v.*

सूक्ष्म, *m.* (*f.* ā) thin, fine, attenuated, minute, subtle, small, atom-like, atomic; delicate; tender; slender; shrill; ingenious; accurate, correct, exact: hence, *m.* an atom: the clearing-nut plant (*Strychnos potatorum*); fine thread; subtlety, craft, fraud; an epithet of the Supreme Soul.

सूक्ष्मता, *f.*, (*m.* °**त्व**) thinness, fineness, minuteness, subtlety, acuteness, shrillness.

सूक्ष्मदर्शक, *m.* (*f.* ikā) = **सूक्ष्मदर्शी**, 1, *q.v.*

सूक्ष्मदर्शी, *m.* (*f.* iṇī) an acute or sharpsighted person: *lit.* of acute discernment, sharpsighted, quick, intelligent.

सूक्ष्मबुद्धि, 1, *f.* mental acumen; an acute intellect: 2, *m.* *f.* sharp, shrewd, acute, intelligent, ingenious, penetrating, witty.

सूक्ष्मबोध, *m.* = **सूक्ष्मबुद्धि**, 1, *q.v.*

सूक्ष्मशरीर, *m.* (in the Vedantic Philos.) the atom-like body, *i. e.* the subtle person or immediate frame in which the human soul is enveloped within the grosser body.

सूक्ष्मा, *f.* 1, (*m.* **सूक्ष्म**) subtle, etc.: 2, a kind of jasmine; small cardamoms; a sort of perfume.

सूखकड़ी, *f.* consumption, atrophy.

सूखद, *more prop.* **सुखद**, *q.v.*

सूखना, *a. int.* to dry, dry up, evaporate, wither, pine away, languish, fall away, become emaciated, shrivel, dwindle, parch. [more proper form **सूक्ष्म**.

सूखम; for words beginning thus, see under the

सूखा, *m.* (*f.* ī) dry, dried, withered, sapless, juiceless: hence, *m.* dry land, terra firma, dry tobacco eaten with betel-leaf; consumption, atrophy: the croup in children.

सूखाधान, *m.* rice burnt up by the sun's rays.

सूखेसूखे, *adj.* by land (as opposed to *Pānī-pānī*,

सूगंध, *more prop.* **सुगन्ध**, *q.v.* [by water).

सूगन्धसना, *m.* (*f.* ī) impregnated with perfume.

सूगरासियान, officious.

सूगा, *m.* (*f.* ī) a parrot, parroquet.

सूघड़, *more com.* **सुघड़**, *q.v.*

सूच, *m.* the shoot of *kush*-grass.

सूचक, 1, *adj.* indicating, pointing out, indicative, making known, betraying: hence, *m.* (*f.* ikā) a spy, informer; an instructor, teacher; a detractor; the manager or chief actor of a company; a crow; an imp; a dog; a cat: 2, *m.* a needle.

सूचत; see (1) **सुचित** (2) **सोचता है**.

सूचा, *f.* a piercing: gesticulation: light.

सूचि, *f.* = **सूची**, *q. v.*

सूचित, *m.* (*f.* ā) *more prop.* **सुचित**, *q. v.*

सूची, *f.* a piercing; a needle; indication of a feeling by signs; a mode of dancing; a mode of array (a sharp file or column); a cone; a triangle formed by the flanks of a trapezium produced until they meet; the table of contents of a book.

सूचीपत्र, *m.* a table of contents, a book; an index.

सूचेत, *more prop.* **सुचेत**, *q. v.* [form **सूक्ष्म**.

सूछम; for words beginning thus, see under the

सूच्चारण, *m.* agreeable enunciation, euphony.

सूज } *f.* a swelling, rising.
सूजन }

सूजना, 1, *more prop.* **सूझना**, *q. v.*: 2, *a. int.* to swell, rise.

सूजा, *m*, a borer, gimlet, augur, awl, a large needle.

सूजि, *f.* = **सूजी**, *q. v.*

सूजी, 1, *f.* a needle: meal, coarse-ground flour, the entire inside of corn after the external part or bran has been rubbed off by the action of the millstone: 2, *m.* (*f.* in *or* inī) one who sews, a stitcher, tailor.

सूझ, *f.* sight, perception, vision, seeing.

सूझना, *a. int.* (construed with the dat.) to appear, become visible, be seen, be able to be seen; to seem, look. *Mujhe kyūṅkar andheremeṅ sūjhe* (*lit.* how can it be seen to me in the dark, *i. e.*) how can I see in the dark? *Mujhe sūjhtā* (or *sūjh ātā* or *sūjh partā*) *hai*, it seems to me, me thinks. [visible.

सूझा, 1, *more prop.* **सूझ**, *q. v.*: 2, *m.* (*f.* ī) apparent,

सूझेबूझे, a jingle made up of the combined past tenses of the verbs **सूझना** and **बूझना**.

सूड़, *f.* retaliation, revenge.

सूडौल, *more prop.* **सुडौल**, *q.v.*

सूढार, *adj.* level.

सूढाल, *more prop.* **सुढाल**, *q.v.*

सूणट, *f.* silence.—*bharnā* or *mārnā*, to maintain or observe silence, be silent.—*māre jānā*, to depart in silence.

सूणड, *f.* an elephant's trunk.

सूणडका, *m.* a saddle-cloth, a pillow under a saddle, a pad; the hump on the back of a camel, bullock, etc.

सूणडा, *m.* a small insect in corn, a weevil.

सूणडी, *m.* (*f.* inī) a distiller and vendor of spirit-

सूणढ, *more com.* **सूणड**, *q.v.* [uous liquors.

सूत, *m.* a charioteer; a bard; a rehearser of ancient legends; a carpenter; the sun; quicksilver; one of the mixed tribes among Hindoos (*viz.* the offspring of a Kshatriya by a Brāhmaṇ female): direct way, range: thread, yarn; a silver thread; wire: (in Botany) a stamen, tendril. *Tāgā bhar*—, a needleful of thread.

सूतक, *m.* birth; impurity from child-birth or from

सूतका = **सूतिका**, *q. v.* [miscarriage: quicksilver.

सूतधार, *m.* (*f.* in, ī, nī) a rope-dancer. [sleep.

सूतना, 1, *more prop.* **सुस्ताना**, *q.v.*: 2, *a. int.* to repose,

सूतपुत्र, *m.* (*f.* ī) the offspring of a **सूत**, *q. v.*

सूतपौराणिक, *m.* (*f.* ī) any rehearser of ancient legends.

सूतखूण्टो, *f.* a kind of needle-work.

सूतर; for words beginning thus, see under the

सूतन्न, *more prop.* सुतन्न, *q. v.* [more proper form सूत्र.

सूतन्ना, *m.* the reins of a carriage: the little skin that rises backwards near the nails at the end of the fingers.

सूतली, *f.* string, lace, twine, packthread.

सूता, *f.* thread: a lying-in female.

सूतार, *more prop.* सुतार, *q. v.*

सूति, *f.* birth, production; offspring; source: sewing, stitching. [delivered.

सूतिका, *f.* a lying-in woman, a female recently

सूतिकागृह, *m.* a house or a room appropriated to lying-in females. [female in childbirth.

सूती, 1, made of cotton-thread, threaden: 2, *f.* a

सूतीमास, *m.* the last month of pregnancy.

सूत्र, *m.* thread, fibre, string: a rule, axiom, aphorism, short precept (in morals or in science): origin: (in Law) an opinion or decree.

सूत्रकर्ता, *m.* (*f.* trī) = सूत्रकार, *q. v.*

सूत्रकार, *m.* (*f.* ī) an author of any work containing rules or precepts.

सूत्रधर, *m.* (*f.* ā) = सूत्रधार, *q. v.*

सूत्रधार, *m.* (*f.* ī) the manager or chief actor in a company of theatricals; one who causes wooden dolls to dance: a carpenter; the author of a set of rules: an epithet (1) of Indra (2) of the Supreme God.

सूत्रधारक, *m.* (*f.* ikā) } = सूत्रधार, *q. v.*
सूत्रधारी, *m.* (*f* iṇī) }

सूथन, *f.* drawers (*esp.* those worn by males), trow-

सूथना, *more com.* सूथन, *q. v.* [sers.

सूथनी, *f.* drawers (*esp.* those worn by females): a certain edible bulbous root (*Dioscorea fasciculata*, Roxb.).

सूथरा, *m.* (*f.* ī) *more prop.* सुथरा, *q. v.*

सूद, *m.* profit, gain, interest, usury.

सूदी, *f.* money borrowed at interest. [form शूद.

सूद; for words beginning thus, see under the

सूधा, 1, *more prop.* सुधा, *q. v.*: 2, *m.* (*f.* ī) straight, true, proper, simple, artless, sincere.

सूधाई, *f.* trueness, propriety, artlessness, simplicity, sincerity.

सूधे, sincerely, artlessly, with simplicity.

सूधो, 1, in Braj = सूधा, *q v.*: 2, *more prop.* सोधो, *q. v.*

सून = शून्य, *q. v.*

सूनबहरी, *more com.* सुनबहरी, *q. v.*

सूनसान, *more prop.* सुन्सान, *q. v.*

सूना, 1, *m.* (*f.* ī) = शून्य, *q. v.*: 2, a point, mark: 3, *m.* (*f.* ī) a dog. —*kuturnā*, to pup.

सूनाड़ी, *more com.* सुनाड़ी, *q. v.*

सूनु, 1, *m.* a son: a younger brother: the sun: 2, *f.*

सूनू, *f.* (*m.* सूनु) a daughter. [a daughter.

सूनो, a Braj form of शून्य, *q. v.*

सून्तना, 1, = सून्थना, *q. v.*: 2, *t.* to rub. [draw a sword.

सून्थना, *t.* to strip leaves off from vegetables: to

सून्य (*colloquial*) = शून्य, *q. v.*

सूप, *m.* broth, soup; sauce, condiment; a cook; a vessel; an arrow: a kind of winnowing-basket.

सूपकारक, *m.* (*f.* ikā) } a cook.
सूपकारी, *m.* (*f.* iṇī) }

सूपली, *f.* a kind of winnowing-basket.

सूपशास्त्र, *m.* the art of cooking.

सूपसाख, *more prop.* सूपशास्त्र, *q. v.*

सूपान, a ladder. [*batassia*, Buch.).

सूपाखेना, *m.* (*f.* ī) the swallow-bird (*Hirundo apus*

सूपारा, *m.* glans penis.

सूपारी, *more prop.* सुपारी, *q. v.*

सूपियड, *more prop.* सुपियड, *q. v.*

सूपियारी, *more prop.* सुपियारी, *q. v.*

सूफल, *more prop.* सुफल, *q. v.*

सूबर, impure, alloyed (said of silver).

सूबरण } *more prop.* सुवर्ण, *q. v.*
सूबरन }

सूब्रस, *m.* a pleasant or reputable residence.

सूबा, *m.* a province; one of the large divisions of the Moghal empire (such as Bengal, Bihār, etc.): a governor.

सूबादार, *m.* a chief, viceroy, lieutenant or governor of a province; an Indian military officer whose rank corresponds to that of captain.

सूबास, *more prop.* सुवास, *q. v.*

सूबिभता, *more prop.* शुभिता, *q. v.*

सूबे, *m.* (pl. of सूबा) provinces: governors.

सूबेदार = सूबादार, *q v.*

सूबेर, *more prop.* सुबेर, *q. v.*

सूभग, a corruption of सुभग, *q. v.*

सूभाव, *more prop.* (1) सुभाव (2) स्वभाव, *qq. v.*

सूम, *m.* milk; water: the sky: a miser, niggard: *adj.*

सूमड़ा, *more prop.* सूमड़ा, *q. v.* [penurious.

सूमता, *f.* niggardliness, stinginess, meanness.

सूमनात, *more prop.* सोमनाथ, *q. v.*

सूमपना, *m.* niggardliness, avarice.

सूर, *m.* 1, = सूरदास, *q. v.*: 2, the sun: a wise man; a teacher: a hero: a rampart: tenesmus: (in Māṛwāṛī); a boar.

सूरः = सरा, *q. v.*

सूरखक, a corruption of सुर्खक, *q. v.*

सूरज, *m.* (Sk. सूर्य्य) the sun. For words beginning thus,

सूरजगहन = सूर्य्यग्रहण, *q. v.* [see under the form सूर्य्य.

सूरजमुखी } = सूर्य्यमुखी, *q. v.*
सूरजमूखी }

सूरड़ा, *m.* (in Māṛwāṛī, pl. of सूरा,) boars, swine.

सूरण, *more prop.* शूरण, *q. v.*

सूरत, 1, *m.* any chapter or section of the Kurān (it contains 114 surats): 2, *f.* form, face, countenance, appearance, portrait; manner, condition, state: 3, *m.* (*f.* ī) playful; calm, tranquil; compassionate, tender: 4 *m.* love; sexual intercourse.

सूरतहाल, *m.* a likeness, representation.

सूरता, 1, *more prop.* **शूरता**, *q.v.*: 2, *f.* a tractable cow.

सूरताई, *more prop.* **शूरताई**, *q. v.*

सूरताधारी, *more prop.* **शूरताधारी**, *q.v.*

सूरति, *more prop.* **सुरत**, 2, *q. v.*

सूरतिहाल, *f.* a statement, form or state of condition or case, a written declaration.

सूरदास, *m. pr. n.* a certain blind Hindee poet and singer: *hence*, among Hindoos the term is applied as an epithet to any blind man.

सूरवीर, *more prop.* **शूरवीर**, *q. v.*

सूरमलार, *more prop.* **सूरमल्लार**, *q. v.*

सूरमल्लार, *m.* a certain musical mode (*rāgiṇī*).

सूरमा, *m.* (*f.* ī)
सूरमां, *m.* (*f.* īn) } = **सूरमार**, *q. v.*

सूरमापन, *m.* boldness, bravery, heroism.

सूरमार, bold, brave, valiant, heroic.

सूरसती, *more prop.* **सरस्वती**, *q.v.*

सूरसूत, *m.* an epithet of dawn (*Aruṇa*) personified as the charioteer of the sun.

सूरसुती, *more prop.* **सरस्वती**, *q.v.*

सूरसेन (*colloquial*) = **शूरसेन**, *q. v.*

सूरस, *more prop.* **सुरस**, *q. v.*

सूरा, *m.* a hero: a tale, story, fable; a chapter or section of the Kurān (in which there are 114 sūras); a millepede.

सूराख़, *m.* a hole, passage, orifice, puncture.

सूरातन, *m.* bravery, valour, prowess.

सूरि, *m.* the sun: a wise or learned man; a teacher.

सूरी, wise: hence, *m* (*f.* iṇī) a learned person, wise person, teacher.

सूरुप; see (1) **सुरूप** (2) **स्वरूप**.

सूरे:; see (1) **सूर** (2) **सूरा** (3) **सूर्य्य**.

सूर्ख़, *more prop.* **सुर्ख़**, *q. v.*

सूर्त, *more prop.* **सूरत**, *q. v.*

सूर्प, *m.* a winnowing-basket.

सूर्पनखा = **शूर्पणखा**, *q. v.*

सूर्मा, *m.* a collyrium, antimony.

सूर्य्य, *m.* the sun: gigantic swallow-wort: *pr. n.* the son of Bali. In the ingenious system of reckoning by symbols adopted by Hindoos in their poetry, this word (in allusion to the passage of the sun through the signs of the zodiac) is a numeral for 12.

सूर्य्यकान्त, *m.* a certain gem (crystal, jasper?).

सूर्य्यक्रान्ति, *f.* (in Astron.) the course of the sun.

सूर्य्यग्रहण, *m.* an eclipse of the sun.

सूर्य्यचमक, *f.* (*m.*?) the splendour or glare of the sun.

सूर्य्यतनय, *m.* an epithet (1) of Karṇ (2) of Sugrīv.

सूर्य्यतनया, *f.* an epithet of the river Yamunā.

सूर्य्यदेव, *m.* one of the epithets of the sun personified as a deity.

सूर्य्यदेवता, *m.* an epithet of the sun regarded as a deity.

सूर्य्यनारायण, *m.* the sun personified (*esp.* as Vishṇu).

सूर्य्यभगवान, *m.* the sun personified (*esp.* as Vishṇu).

सूर्य्यमणि, *m.* the sun-stone (a certain fabulous gem supposed to yield its possessor whatever he may desire): a certain tree (*Hibiscus phœniceus*).

सूर्य्यमण्डल, *m.* the sun's orb or disc.

सूर्य्यमुखी, *f.* the sun-flower (*Helianthus annuus*): a kind of fan or parasol.

सूर्य्यवंश, *m.* the solar race or dynasty.

सूर्य्यवंशी, *m.* a certain tribe of Kshatriyas who claim to have descended from the sun: *lit.* appertaining to the solar race: hence, *m.* (*f.* inī) a descendant of the sun, a person of the solar race.

सूर्य्यसंक्रान्ति, *f.* (in Astron.) the sun's entrance into a new sign.

सूर्य्यसिद्धान्त, *m. pr. n.* a certain celebrated Sanskrit work on astronomy (by Varāha Mihir).

सूर्य्या, *f.* a bitter gourd: a new bride: *pr. n.* the wife of the sun.

सूर्य्यास्त, *m.* sunset.

सूर्य्योदय, *m.* sunrise.

सूल, 1, *more prop.* **शूल**, *q. v.*: 2, *m.* a thorn: compassion, tenderness: situation, condition.

सूली, 1, *more prop.* **शूली**, *q. v.*: 2, *f.* an impaling-stake.—*charhānā* or *denā*, to impale.

सूवा, *more prop.* **सुआ**, *q. v.*

सूस, *m.* a porpoise (*Delphinus*): liquorice.

सूसः, *m.* gasping, panting.

सूसंदेस, *more prop.* **सुसन्देश**, *q. v.*

सूसमार, *m.* a porpoise (*Delphinus*).

सूसी, *f.* a kind of cloth.

सूसूम, lukewarm, tepid.

सूहा, 1, *m.* (*f.* ī) red, crimson: 2, *m.* a certain musical mode (*rāg*).

सूहाकुसुम्भा, red as the dye of safflower.

सूहान, *m.* a file (the instrument so called).

सृंकाल; see (1) **शृंखल** (2) **शृंगार** (3) **शृगाल**.

सृंग; for words beginning thus, see under the form **शृंग**.

सृंगार; see (1) **शृंगार** (2) **शृगाल**.

सृकाल
सृगाल } (*colloquial*) = **शृगाल**, *q. v.*

सृजक, *m.* (*f.* ikā) a maker, former, creator, producer.

सृजन, *m.* a forming, creating, producing.

सृजनहार, *m.* (*f.* ī) a maker, producer, former, creator: *hence*, an epithet of the Creator.

सृजना, *t.* to create, produce, form, make.

सृजनेश्वर, *m.* (the Creator-God, *i.e.*) the Almighty.

सृजा, *m.* (*f.* ī) created, produced, formed, made.

सृजाना, *t.* to cause to produce or make.

सृष्ट, *m.* (*f.* ā) created, produced, made: abandoned, deserted: connected: adorned: *adj.* much, many.

सृष्ट्याद्यार्थ (Sk.) = **सृष्टि आदि का अर्थ**.

सृष्टि, *f.* creation, production, invention; the creation; nature; natural state, property, or disposition: a liberal gift.

सृष्टिकर्त्ता, (*f.* trī) a creator, maker, inventor.

सृष्टिचक्र, *m.* (*lit.* the wheel of creation) the entire system of created things.

से, 1, the distinctive termination of the ablative or

instrumental case = from.of out of: by the instrumentality of.by, in consequence of,on account of,according to,by reason of,after, since. through. with,at, to, than, concerning, in reference to, upon, among : 2, in Braj =(1) सा (2) सो, 2 (3) as a sign of the instrumental case it sometimes yields adverbial expressions; *e. g.* सहजसे, easily; *lit.* with ease (4) sometimes: 3, the inflected form masculine of the terminational particle सा.

सेइ, in the Pūrbī dialect of Hindee = से, 1, *q. v.*

सेइय (*Rām.*) = तू सेवता है (सेवना).

सेइये (pl.°यें) = सेवेगा (सेवना).

सेइहि, (pl.°हिं) } **सेइहै**, (pl°हैं) } old forms = सेवेगा (सेवना).

सेउ in Braj = सेवो (सेवना) = सेवा करो.

सेओंती } **सेओती** } *more com.* सेवती, *q. v.*

सेओना, *more com.* सेवना, *q. v.*

सेऊं, the 1st pers. sing. condit. of सेवना, *q.v.*

सें, *more prop.* (1) से, 1, (2) सेन, *qq. v.*

सेंओंती, *more com.* सेवती, *q. v.*

सेंक, *m.* toasting, fomentation.—*k.* to toast, warm.

सेंकड़ा, *more com.* सैकड़ा, *q. v.*

सेंकना, *t.* to toast, parch, heat, warm before (or with) anything hot; to foment; to incubate.

सेंकसांक, a play on the word सेंक, *q.v.*

सेंगरी, *f.* a pod, siliqua (*esp.* of the radish).

सेंठ, सेंड, सेंत, सेंद, सेंध, सेंब, सेंभ; for words beginning with either of these elements see under the corresponding forms सेण्ठ,सेण्ड,सेन्त,सेन्द,सेन्ध, सेम्ब, सेम्भ, respectively.

सेंली, *more prop.* सेली, *q.v.*

सेंवियां, *m.* macaroni, vermicelli.

सेंहुआ } **सेंहूआ** } *m.* a tetter.

सेकची, *f.* a skate (for sliding on).

सेकना, *more com.* सेंकना, *q. v.*

सेखरन, *m.* a kind of food.

सेचन, *m.* sprinkling, aspersion, irrigation, watering, baling, dripping: a bucket.

सेचनी, *f.* a baling-vessel, a bucket. [for a horse.

सेज, *f.* a bed, couch; bedding; a layer of straw

सेजचतुर, *m.*(*f.* ā)one who is a skilful judge of the goodness or comfort of a bed.

सेजदा, *more prop.* सिजदा, *q.v.*

सेजबन्द, *m.* a cord for fastening bedding to a bedstead, the lacing of a bed.

सेजसोहाग, the nuptial bed.

सेज्या, a common form of शय्या, *q v.*

सेट, *f.* the hair about the groin, or that of the armpits, and in the nostrils.

सेटु, *m.* the water-melon; a kind of cucumber.

सेठ, *m.* a money-broker. banker, millionaire, capitalist, wholesale merchant. The term is applied to bankers, etc. as a title of respect.

सेठन, *f.* the wife of a *seṭh*: a whisk, a kind of [brush.

सेण्ट } **सेण्ठ** } *more prop.* (1) सेंट (2) सेंठ, *qq. v.*

सेण्ठा, *m.* a kind of reed-grass (*Saccharum sara*, Roxb.) of which morhās are made.

सेण्ठी, *f.* = सेण्ठा, *q.v.*

सेण्ड, *m.* the milk-plant or spurge (*Euphorbia*), of which there are many species.

सेत, 1, a Prākrit form of श्वेत, *q.v.*: 2, a contraction of सेतु, *q.v.*

सेतकवा, *m.* a rook.

सेतद्वीप in Prākrit = श्वेतद्वीप, *q.v.*

सेतना, *t.* to take care of, keep carefully, husband.

सेतबन्ध, *more prop.* सेतुबन्ध, *q.v.*

सेतमेंत = सेन्त, *q. v.*

सेती in Kanauji Hindee = से, 1, *q.v.*

सेतु, *m.* a mound, bank, dam, dike; a high causeway in fields; a landmark; a pass, defile; a bridge.

सेतुबन्ध, *m. pr. n.* the ridge of rocks extending from the south extremity of the Coromandel coast towards the island of Ceylon. It is fabled to have been formed by Hanumān at the bidding of Rām, as a bridge for the passage of Rām's forces when marching against Rāvaṇ, and is hence also called Setubandhrāmeshwar.

सेतुबन्धरामेश्वर; see सेतुबन्ध.

सेदना, *t.* to foment, stupe.

सेन, 1, a Prākrit form of श्येन, *q.v.*: 2, *f.* a contraction of सेना, *q. v.*: 3, in the Avadhī dialect of Hindee, this is one of the signs of the ablative case = से, 1, *q.v*: 4, *m. pr. n.* a certain *rākshas*.

सेनग्रगामी, *m.* a vanguard. [Indra's paradise.

सेनजिता, *f. pr. n.* a certain courtesan (*apsarā*) of

सेनप = सेन.पति, *q.v.*

सेना, 1, a contraction of सेवना, *q.v.*: 2, *f.* (not infl.) an army: 3, *f. pr. n.* the wife of Kārttikeya, god of war: 4, *m.* an officer who collects the revenue in a village: the commander of an army.

सेनादल, *m.* military troops.

सेनादार, *m.* a military chief, officer.

सेनानी, appertaining to an army, military: hence, (1) *m.* (*f.* ini) the commander of an army, a general, military chief (2) *m.* an epithet of Kārttikeya.

सेनापति, *m.* = सेनानी, *q.v.* The term is applied as a title of Prime Ministers, and is particularly a title of the *rājā* of Berar.

सेनावाला, *m.*(*f.* ī) a person belonging to an army.

सेनास्थल = सेनास्थान, *q. v.*

सेनास्थान, *m.* any place where an army is collected.

सेनी; in the Avadhī dialect of Hindee, this is one of the signs of the ablative case = से, *q.v.*

सेन्त, gratis, free of charge, for nothing, gratuitously, of no expense.

सेन्तना, *t.* to put to rights, adjust.

सेन्तमेत } **सेन्तमेन्त** } = सेन्त, *q. v.*

सेन्द, *f.* the vegetable *Cucumis Madraspatanus.*

सेन्दकचरिया, *m.* = **सेन्द**, *q.v.*

सेन्दना, *t.* to draw water ; to irrigate.

सेन्दूक, *more prop.* **सन्दूक**, *q.v.*

सेन्दूर, *m.* minium, red lead, vermilion.

सेन्दूरिया, *f.* a species of mango.

सेन्ध, *m.* a hole made in a wall by thieves or besiegers, house-breaking, burglary.– *denā* or *mārnā*, to make a hole in a wall for a burglarious purpose, to sap.

सेन्धचोर, *m.* a burglar, house-breaker.

सेन्धचोरी, *f.* house-breaking, burglary.

सेन्धना, *t.* to mine, dig, excavate.

सेन्धमार, *m.* (*f.* in, ī, nī) a house-breaker, burglar.

सेन्धमारी, *f.* house-breaking, burglary.

सेन्धव = (1) **सेन्धा** (2) **सैन्धव**, *qq.v.*

सेन्धा, *m.* rock-salt.

सेन्धिया, *m.* a burglar, house-breaker : poison : a certain Marhatta tribe (probably so named as originating on the banks of the river Sindh).

सेन्धी, 1, *f.* the juice of the wild date-tree (*Phœnix sylvestris*, Roxb.) used for intoxication, toddy, palm-wine: 2, *m.* (*f.* inī) a miner, house-breaker, burglar.

सेम, *f.* (*m.* ī) the flat bean (*Dolichos lablab*) : leprosy producing discoloration of the skin.

सेमल, *m.* the silk-cotton tree (*Bombax heptaphyllum*) and the coarse kind of cotton it yields. *Sīkā* –, a bubble.

सेम्बल } = **सेमल**, *q.v.*
सेम्भल }

सेय in Māṛwāṛī = sewn.

सेयाना, *m.* (*f.* ī) *more prop.* **सयाना**, *q.v.*

सेयाय, *more prop.* **सिवाय**, *q.v.*

सेयेउं (*Rām.*) = **सेवा किया** (**सेना**, 1).

सेर. 1, *more prop.* **शेर**, *q.v.* : 2, full, satiated, sated, replete, tired: 3. *m.* a certain Indian weight or measure. In Calcutta, the factory *ser* = 1 *lb.* 13 *oz.* 13·86 *drs.* Avoirdupois; and the bāzār *ser* = 2 *lb.* 0 *oz.* 13·853 *drs.*

सेरभर; see **सेर** 3, and **भर**, 7.

सेरांग, *more prop.* **सरहंग**, *q.v.*

सेराना, *t.* to set afloat ; to despatch: to cool.

सेरी, *f.* satiety, fulness, repletion: glut, plenitude: the *ser*-weight.

सेरुआ, *m.* the head and foot parts of a bed-frame.

सेल, *m.* a spear: a species of carp.

सेलह in Chand = **शैल**, *q.v.*

सेला, *m.* a kind of sheet constituting a part of dress (worn especially in the Dakkhan and given as a present) : muslin, lawn (fine linen) : a kind of rice: a spear : a royal tiger.

सेलिया, *m.* tabby, puss.

सेली, *f.* a necklace of threads worn by mendicants; a belt, sash ; a rope: a blow with the edge of the open hand, a slap, cuff.

सेले (*i. e.* **से**, 1, + **ले**, 4) is used in the colloquial speech of the Do,āb for **से** of the ablative case.— the particle **ले** emphasizing the idea of 'source,' 'beginning,' 'place from whence,' *e.g.* **पहाड़सेले नदीतक**, 'quite from the mountain to the river.'

सेल्हो; see (1) **सेलको** (2) **सेलो**.

सेव, 1, *f.* a contraction of **सेवा**, *q.v.*: 2, *m.* a kind of sweetmeat : an apple.

सेवई, *f.* vermicelli, macaroni.

सेवक, servile, dependent : hence, *m.* (*f.* ikā) a servant, worshipper, votary, loyal person, subject, dependent.

सेवकाई, *f.* = **सेवा**, 2, *q.v.*

सेवकिन } *more prop.* **सेविका**, *q.v.*
सेवकी }

सेवट, *f.* end, extremity, summit.

सेवड़ा, *m.* any fakeer of the Jain sect : a certain plant (*Trophis aspera*).

सेवत (*Rām.*) = **सेवत**. (**सेवना**).

सेवती, *f.* the dog-rose (*Rosa grandulifera*, Roxb.).

सेवन, *m.* the act of serving, service.

सेवधि, *m.* a divine treasure owned by Kuver, the god of wealth: a treasure.

सेवना, *t.* to attend on, serve, worship: to brood, rear, sit, incubate, hatch, to litter. *Aṇḍ*ā –, to brood, mope.

सेवनीय, requiring or deserving service or attendance, worshipful: hence, *m.* (*f.* ā) a master, etc.

सेवरा, *m.* 1, *more prop.* **सेवड़ा**, *q.v.* : 2, half-baked earthenware.

सेवरी, 1, see **सेवारी**: 2. *f.* a certain female worshipper of Rām-Chandra.

सेवा, 1, *more prop.* **सिवा** = **सिवाय**, *q.v.*: 2, *f.* service, servitude, situation, office, province, post, attendance on, homage, worship, piety, addiction to, practice. — *k.* (with *fem.* gen.) to serve, attend on, worship.

सेवाए } = **सिवाय**, *q.v.*
सेवाय }

सेवार, *more com.* **सिवार**, *q.v.*

सेवारी, *f.* sugar that has been purified with *siwār.*

सेवास्थान, *m.* a place of worship, temple.

सेवि = **सेवके** (**सेवना**) : see **इ**, 7.

सेविका, *f.* (*m.* **सेवक**) a female servant (or disciple, or votary, or worshipper).

सेवी, *m.* (*f.* inī) *more com.* **सेवक** *q.v.*

सेवीं, *f.* vermicelli, macaroni.

सेवे (pl. **सेवैं**) in Braj = **सेवे** (**सेवना**).

सेवैई, *f.* vermicelli, macaroni.

सेवैं (*poet.*) = **मैं सेवूं** (**सेवना**).

सेव्य, *m.* (*f.* ā) deserving or requiring to be served, or obeyed, honourable, worshipful, respectable, estimable.

सेव्या, 1, *more prop.* **शैव्या**, *q.v.* : 2, see **सेव्य**.

सेश, **सेष**, **सेस**; for words beginning with either of these elements, see under the more proper form **शेष**.

सेसर, *m.* the gripe of a bow : a certain game at cards.

सेह, *m.* a hedgehog, porcupine.

सेहथना, *t.* to whisk.

सेहना ; see (1) **सहना** (2) **सेवना**.

सैहरा, *more com.* (1) **सिहरा** (2) **सहना**, *qq.v.*

सैही, *f.* a porcupine, hedgehog.

सैहुण्ड, *m.* a species of Euphorbia, or, indeed, a general name for plants of that kind.

सै, 1, one hundred : 2, *f.* success, prosperity.

सैओं, many hundreds. See **ओं**, 4.

सैं, 1, *more prop.* **साईं**, *q.v.*: 2, in comp. = **सात**, *q. v.*

सैंकड़ा, *more com.* **सैकड़ा**, *q.v.*

सैंगर, *m.* the bean of the *Mimosa suma.*

सैंत, सैंद ; for words beginning with either of these elements, see under the forms **सैन्त, सैन्द**, respectively.

सैकड़ा, *m.* a hundred: *adv.* per cent., a hundred per cent. [hundreds. See **ओं**, 4.

सैकड़ों, hundreds, hundreds upon hundreds, many

सैक़ल, *m.* scouring, polishing, cleaning, furbishing; any instrument for polishing with.

सैक़लगर, *m.* a burnisher, furbisher, polisher, scourer, cutler, armourer, man who cleans and brightens rusty metal instruments.

सैक़लीगर = **सैक़लगर**, *q.v.*

सैतना, *t.* to take care of, keep carefully, husband.

सैथावार, *m.* an agricultural tribe near Benares.

सैद, 1, *more prop.* (1) **शायद** (2) **सैयिद**, *qq. v.* : 2. *f.* game, prey ; hunting, the chase.

सैदा, *m.pr.n.* the ancient city of Sidon. [Sidonian.

सैदानी, appertaining to Sidon : hence, *m.* (*f.* inī) a

सैन, 1, a form (1) of **शयन** (2) of **सेना**, *qq. v.* : 2, *f.* a sign, signal, token, hint, wink, nod. — *k.* to beckon.

सैना, *more prop.* **सेना**, *q. v.*

सैनासैनी, *f.* a mutual beckoning or giving hints, etc., a mutual winking or nodding, a mutual signalling.

सैनिक, appertaining to an army : hence, *m.* a soldier, sentinel, guard, picket; a body of forces in array.

सैनी, *f.* a ladder.

सैन्तना, *t.* to set in order, put to rights, adjust, rectify ; to keep, tend ; to provide, supply. *Saint k.* to lay in. *Saint rakhnā*, to preserve.

सैन्तालीस, forty-seven (४७). See **ओं, वां, वीं, वे, वें.**

सैन्ताव, *m.* arrangement.

सैन्ती, *f.* a dart, javelin.

सैन्तीस, thirty-seven (३७). See **ओं, वां, वीं, वे, वें.**

सैन्दिया ; see (1) **सैन्धिया** (2) **सैन दिया.**

सैन्धव, appertaining to the sea or to Sindh, marine, Sindhian : hence, *m.* a horse; rock-salt; the people of the country along the Indus.

सैन्य, *m.* a soldier ; a guard : an army.

सैन्यवेष्टन, *m.* the surrounding of an army.

सैन्या, 1, *more prop.* **सैन्य**, *q. v.*: 2, a pl. of **सैन्य** (see **आ**, 22).

सैफ़, *m.* a sword.

सैयाद, *m.* a hunter, fowler, fisherman.

सैयादी, *f.* hunting, fowling, sport.

सैयिद, *m.* a lord, prince. The term is assumed as a title by those who profess to be the descendants of Muhammad through his son in law and successor 'Alī and his daughter Fātima.

सैयिदानी, 1, *f.* a female Saiyid: 2, *m.* (Arab. dual) Hasan and Husain, the sons of 'Alī by Fātima.

सैयें, many hundreds. See **सै** and **ओं**, 4.

सैर, 1, in Māṛwāṛī = **शहर**, *q.v.*: 2, *f.* perambulation, taking the air, a ramble : perusal ; amusement ; moving about. — *k* to travel, ramble : to take the air ; to peruse ; to view or contemplate a beautiful landscape scene from an eminence.

सैराना, *a. int.* to increase, augment. [**शैल.**

सैल; for words beginning thus, see under the form

सैल, *f.* flowing; a current, torrent, flood; walking, going about for airing or for amusement.

सैलाब, *m.* a flood, torrent, deluge, inundation.

सैव ; see (1) **शैव** (2) **सेव.**

सैवां, *m.* (*f.* **सैवीं**) *adj.* the hundredth. See **सै.**

सैस (*colloquial*) = **साईस**, *q. v.*

सैहरन, *f.* sufferance.

सैहरनी, *m.* (*f.* in *or* inī) a sufferer.

सैहारना, *t.* to put.

सो, 1, in Braj = (1) **से** (2) **सा**, *qq.v.*: 2, an occasional corruption of **सौ**, *q. v.*: 3, that, that one, that person or thing, he, she, it : 3, hence, therefore, so, so that, consequently, accordingly.

सोअर, *m.* a lying-in chamber. [anise.

सोआ, *m.* fennel (*Anethum sowa*, Roxb.), also called

सोआना, *more com.* **सुलाना**, *q. v.*

सोआवनो in Braj = **सोआना** = **सुलाना**, *q.v.*

सोइ, *more prop.* **सोई**, *q. v.* [2, *f.* an augury, omen.

सोई (see **ई**, 4) that very one, he himself, that same

सोउ
सोऊ } in Braj = **सोई**, *q. v.*

सोऊं, 1, in Braj = **सोई**, *q.v.*: 2, aor. 1st sing. of **सोना.**

सोए, 1, infl. of **सोआ** : 2, aor. sing. of **सोना** (2nd

सोएन, prolific (said of females). [and 3rd pers.).

सों, 1, in Braj = (1) **सा** (2) **से**, *qq. v.*: 2, *more prop.* **सौंह**, *q. v.* : 3, in Braj, sometimes = **ही** emphatic ; *e. g.* **काचसों काच** = **काचही काच**, *i. e.* mere glass and nothing else (that is, they are not diamonds as they are intended to seem).

सोंग ; see (1) **सूंगा** (2) **स्वांग** (3) **सूंघ.**

सोंगड़ा ; see **सूंगरा.**

सोंगी, *m.* (*f.* inī) ; see (1) **शौक़ी** (2) **स्वांगी.**

सोंट, सोंठ, सोंद, सोंध, सोंप ; for words beginning with either of these elements, see under the corresponding forms **सोंट, सोंठ, सोन्द, सोन्ध, सोम्प**, respectively.

सोंणभद्र, *more prop.* **शोणभद्र**, *q. v.*

सोंह, *f.* an oath, asseveration.—*khilānā* or *denā*, to administer an oath, adjure, swear.—*ḍālnā*, to conjure.

सोंहो
सोंहीं } = **सोहीं**, *q. v.*

सोंहें, *f.* (pl. of **सोंह**) asseverations, oaths.

सोक, 1, *more prop.* **शोक**, *q. v.* : 2, *m.* the holes in a bedstead through which the strings for bracing it pass.

सोख़तगी, *f.* burning; combustion; vexation; heart-burning. [a cook-boy, scullion.

सोख़ता, *m.* a slow match, tinder, brand, torch:

सोखना, *t.* (of सूखना) to soak up, dry up, absorb.

सोग = शोक, *q. v.*

सोगंध, *more prop.* सौगन्ध, *q. v.*

सोगवारी, *f.* grief.

सोगी, *m.* (*f.* inī) = शोकी, *q. v.*

सोच, *m.* consideration, reflection, thought, meditation, reverie, imagination, idea, attention, regard, notice; prudence; seriousness; regret, penitence.

सोचना, *t.* or *a. int.* to consider, meditate, reflect, mark, note, observe, mind, regard, notice, think, conceive, imagine, advert, to contrive.

सोचनीय, requiring (or deserving or capable of) [consideration.

सोचवन्त, *m.* (*f.* vatī) pensive.

सोचवन्ती, *f.* pensiveness.

सोचविचार, *m.* reflection and discrimination.

सोचसंकोच, merely a jingling combination of the corresponding words सोच and संकोच.

सोची, *m.* (*f.* inī) meditative, considerate, thoughtful, serious, observant, taking note, regardful.

सोज, *f.* a swelling, rising: *adj.* near, direct, close (as a translation). [of a gun.

सोज़न, *f.* a needle; a prick, prickle; the pricker

सोज़नी, *f.* a kind of small embroidered carpet; quilting, quilted linen: a kind of coverlet: a small throne; a seat of state.

सोज़ा, *m.* (*f.* ī) burning violently, giving excruciating pain: *hence*, a boil, whitlow.

सोज़िश, *f.* burning, vexation, pain, solicitude.

सोज़ी, a conflagration.

सोझ, *f.* straightness, directness.

सोझा, *m.* (*f.* ī) direct, straight.

सोटा; see सोंटा.

सोढना, *t.* to review.

सोंटा, *m* a mace, club, cudgel, pestle.

सोंटाना, a kind of sweetmeat.

सोंटाबरदार = सोंटेबर्दार, *q. v.*

सोंटेबर्दार, *m.* a person in the retinue of a great personage who is armed with a short curved club generally covered with silver, any mace-bearer.

सोंटेवाला, *m.* (*f.* ī) सोंटेबर्दार, *q.v.*

सोंठ, *f.* dry ginger: *met.* a miser, niggard.—*kī sī nās le rahnā*, to wait patiently, suffer, endure.—*kī nās na lenā*, to be very covetous.

सोंठी, penurious, niggardly, miserly. [hard.

सोंठूराय, *lit.* the chief of misers: *hence*, miserly,

सोंठौरा, *m.* ginger-bread.

सोत, *m. f.* a spring, fountain, jet d'eau; a stream, rivulet; an arm of the sea. [*m.* (*f.* ī) asleep, sleeping.

सोता, 1, *m.* = सोत, *q.v.*: 2, sleep; a sleeping: 3,

सोति, 1, *more prop.* सोती (2) in Chand = सोत, *qq.v.*

सोती, *f.* (dimin. of सोत) a rill.

सोथ (*colloquial*) = शोथ, *q. v.*

सोदना; see (1) सोधना (2) सोन्धना.

सोदर / सोदरा } *m.* (*f.* ī) = सहोदर, *q. v.*

सोदा, *more prop.* सौदा, *q.v.* [enquiry, search.

सोध, *f.* discharge of debt, liquidation: correction;

सोधना, *t.* to discharge a debt, pay back, liquidate; to collate: to refine metals: to inquire, search.

सोधेउ in Braj = सोधा (सोधना).

सोन = शोण, *q.v.*

सोनधोआ / सोनधोया } *m.* (*f.* सोनधोई) a washer of gold.

सोनभद्र, *more com.* शोणभद्र, *q. v.*

सोनमाखी, *f.* gold-stone, marcasite.

सोनहरा / सोनहला } *m.* (*f.* ī) made of gold, golden; gilded.

सोनहलापानी, *m.* gilt, gilding.

सोनहुला, *m.* (*f.* ī) made of gold, golden; gilded.

सोना, 1, *a. int.* to sleep: *met.* to die: 2, *m.* gold.

सोनामक्खी, *f.* gold-stone, marcasite.

सोनार, *more com.* सुनार, *q. v.*

सोनारिन, *more com.* सुनारिन, *q. v.*

सोनासा, *m.* (*f.* ī) like gold, of a golden colour.

सोनित, *m.* (*f.* ā) = शोणित, *q. v.* [etc. in the mint.

सोनिया, *m.* one who separates gold from ashes,

सोनोघन, *m.* a sign, signal, hint, symbol. [cloth.

सोन्धी, *f.* the wash in which washermen steep their

सोन्धना, *t.* to rub cloth in mud preparatory to washing; to mix; to smear.

सोन्धा, 1, *m.* a composition of fragrant substances used for washing the hair; perfume, pomatum, pomander, sweet scent, fragrant smell: 2, *m.* (*f.* ī) smelling like the perfume of a new earthen vessel when wetted, or from the parching of pulse; fragrant, savoury, nidorous.—*k.* to perfume, to season.

सोन्धाना, *t.* to perfume. [grance.

सोन्धाहट, *f.* a smell like that of new earth; fra-

सोन्धे, fragrant, smelling like new earth.

सोपान, *m.* stairs, steps, a ladder, staircase, scale;

सोपारी, *more prop.* सुपारी, *q.v.* [a way, road.

सोपि / सोपी } (*Rām.*: Sk. सः + अपि) = सोभी, *q.v.*

सोपो in Mārwārī = sleep; carelessness.

सोब्रन in Chand = सुवर्ण, *q. v.*

सोभ; for words beginning thus, but not given below, see under the form शोभ.

सोभाना, *t.* to ornament, decorate, adorn.

सोभामान, *m.* (*f.* matī) = शोभायमान, *q. v.*

सोभाव (*colloquial*) = स्वभाव, *q. v.* [even.

सोभी, (emphat.) he (she, or it) too, he (she, or it)

सोम, *m.* the moon: ambrosia, nectar: water: the moon-plant (*Sarcostema viminalis* or *Asclepias acida*)

and its acid juice prescribed to be drunk at sacrifices: air, wind: camphor: rice-gruel: the sky: an epithet (1) of Kuver (2) of Yam: *pr. n.* (1) of a certain mountainous range (2) of one the eight guardian deities (*lokpāl*) of the world (3) of Monday.

सोमतीर्थ, *m. pr. n.* a certain place of pilgrimage in the west of India.

सोमदत्त, *m. pr. n.* a certain king of Vaisālī.

सोमनात = सोमनाथ, *q. v.*

सोमनाथ, *m.* (the lord of Som, *i. e.* the divinity set up by Som, or the moon) an epithet of Mahādev. The term is applied as a proper name to many of the temples of Shiv in various parts of India, also to the idol contained in them; more particularly to a celebrated Hindoo shrine in Gujerat where there is a celebrated *Ling* or columnar emblem of Shiv. This temple was established in the town of Somnāthpattan, and was one of the twelve celebrated *ling*-temples which in various parts of India are held in special veneration. The temple built there was so famed for its enormous wealth that it attracted the attention of Mahmud of Ghazni, who, in A.D. 1024, under pretext of destroying its idols, carried off its treasures along with its renowned gates.

सोमनाथपत्तन, *m. pr. n.* a certain town on the western coast of India in the peninsula of Kattywar and province of Gujerāt. It was celebrated as the place of the famous temple of Somnāth.

सोमप, *m.* one who drinks the juice of the moon-plant; the performer of a sacrifice: a certain order of *pitris*; the manes of the Brāhmans.

सोमपत्र, *m.* the grass *Saccharum cylindricum.*

सोमपा, *m.* (and *f.* ?) = सोमप, *q. v.* [kept.

सोमपात्र, *m.* any vessel in which the *som*-juice is

सोमपान, *m.* the drinking the celebrated *som*-juice.

सोमपीती, *m.* (*f.* inī) a drinker of the *som*-juice.

सोमब; for words beginning thus, see under the form **सोमव**.

सोमयज्ञ, *m.* a sacrifice or oblation consisting of a libation of the celebrated *som* juice.

सोमरस, *m.* the juice of the moon-plant, *som*-juice.

सोमराज, *m.* a certain medicinal plant (*Serratula anthelmintica*; *i.e.* black cumin-seed).

सोमराजी, *m.* = सोमराज, *q.v.*

सोमवत, moon-like; lunar.

सोमवल्लरि / **सोमवल्लरी** } *f.* = सोमवल्लिका, *q. v.*

सोमवल्लिका, *f.* the moon-plant (*Asclepias acida*).

सोमवल्ली, *f.* the moon plant (*Asclepias acida*): another plant (*Menispermum glabrum*).

सोमवार, *m.* Monday.

सोम्पना, *t.* to commit to one's charge, deliver over, give, consign, refer, commend, entrust, repose, deposit, resign, give up, surrender. *Dāiko—*, to give out to nurse.

सोय = (1) सोई (2) सोय, 2, *qq. v.*

सोयन, *f.* a mare for breeding.

सोर, 1, *more prop.* शोर, *q. v.*: 2, *f.* root, ramification: 3, *m. pr. n.* the ancient city of Tyre.

सोरठी, *f. pr. n.* a certain village in Māṛwāṛ celebrated for its swords which are said to inflict incurable wounds.

सोरठ, *f.* a certain musical mode (*rāgiṇī*).

सोरठा, *m.* a certain Braj metre (the quatrain).

सोरनाली, *f.* a species of greens.

सोरह, 1, *more com.* सोलह, *q. v.*: 2, = शोरा, *q. v.*

सोरहों, *more com.* सोलहों, *q. v.*

सोरहोंशृंगार = षोड़शृंगार. See शृंगार.

सोरा, *more prop.* (1) शोरा (2) सुरा (3) सोलह, *qq. v.*

सोरियाना, *t.* to ramify.

सोलह, sixteen (१६): see वां, वीं, वे, वें.

सोलहों, (see ओं, 4) by sixteens, in groups of sixteen, sixteen times, the whole sixteen of them.

सोलाऊ, *m.* a sleeping-draught, opiate. [arms.

सोलाना, 1, *more com.* सुलाना, *q. v.*: 2, *t.* to ground

सोवत, 1, = सोता है (सोना): 2, the state of sleeping.

सोवना, *more prop.* सोना, *q. v.*

सोष, *more prop.* शोष, *q. v.*

सोसन, 1, in Braj = उससे *q. v.*: 2, *f.* a lily, the iris.

सोसना, *t.* to take patiently, bear, endure, suffer, [feel.

सोसाइटी, *more prop.* ससपटी, *q. v.*

सोसि; see सोसना. [oration, dress.

सोह, 1, *more com.* सोंह, *q. v.*: 2, *f.* ornament, dec-

सोहन, 1, *more prop.* सोहान, *q. v.*: 2, *m.* a lover, friend: *lit.* pleasing: 3, *m. f.* a kind of sweetmeat: 4, *f.* a whetstone.

सोहना, *a. int.* to befit, beseem, become: to shine, be splendid, be glorious: *t.* to weed.

सोहमस्मि (*Rām.*: Sk.) = वही मैं हूं, *i. e.* मैं ब्रह्म हूं.

सोहर, beautiful, pleasing, charming.

सोहला, a nuptial song.

सोहबत, *more prop.* सुहबत, *q.v.*

सोहा, 1, see सूहा: 2, *m.* (*f.* ī) splendid, etc.

सोहहि, (pl. °हिं) *Rām.* = सोहता है (सोहना).

सोहाग, *m.* affection, love, caress: a nuptial song.

सोहागन, 1, a Braj pl. of सोहाग (see न, 6): 2, = सुहागन.

सोहागपुरिया, *f.* a perfume, pomatum, pomander.

सोहागा, *m.* borax: a harrow.

सोहागिन; see (1) सोहागिनी (2) सुहागन.

सोहागिनी, *f.* a beloved female.

सोहान, *m.* a rasp (large rough file).

सोहाना, *m.* (*f.* ī) see सुहाना.

सोहाय; see (1) सहाय (2) सुहाया (सुहाना).

सोहावन / **सोहावना** } *m.* (*f.* ī) *more com.* सुहावन, *q. v.*

सोहीं = सोहीं, *q. v.*

सोहीं, 1, (emphat. form of सो; see हीं) that very one, he himself, he (she, or it) too: 2, *postp.* (takes gen masc. infl.) face to face, facing, fronting, opposite, in front of, before.

सौ, 1, one hundred: *Sau sirkā* [*m.* (*f.* ī)] *honā*, possessing a hundred heads; of which, if one or more be cut off, the others still remain: *hence*, excessively persevering or obstinate: 2, in Braj = (1) सा (2) से (3) सो, *qq. v.*

सौं, 1, *f.* in Braj = **सौंह**, *q. v.*: 2, in old Hindee = **से**, *q. v.*

सौंग, *more prop.* **स्वांग**, *q. v.*

सौंद, सौंध, सौंप; for words beginning thus, see under the forms **सौन्द, सौन्ध, सौम्प**, respectively.

सौंफ }
सौंफ़ } *f.* anise-seed (*Pimpinella anisum*).

सौंरा, *m.* anything black, as soot, etc.

सौंसार, *f.* family, wife and children, progeny, tribes; housewifery; the world.

सौंसारी, *f.* a housewife, dame.

सौंह (*Rām.*) = **सोंह**, *q. v.*

सौंहैं (*Rām.*) = **सोंहैं**, *q. v.*

सौक, *more prop.* **शौक**, *q. v.*

सौकन, *f.* a rival wife, contemporary wife (*saut*).

सौकनापा, *m.* rivalry between wives of the same husband. [hence, *m.* (*f.* ī) a swinish person.

सौकर, appertaining to swine, hoggish, swinish:

सौगद; see (1) **सौगन्द** (2) **सौगन्ध**.

सौगन्द, *f.* an asseveration, oath. — ***khānā*** or ***dharnā***, to make oath, asseverate, swear.

सौगन्दासौगन्दी, *f.* mutual asseveration upon oath.

सौगन्ध, 1, (*corruption*) = **सौगन्द**, *q. v.*: 2, *m.* sweet-scentedness, fragrance; a fragrant grass: *adj.* sweet-scented, fragrant.

सौगन्धसना, *m.* (*f.* ī) impregnated with perfume.

सौगन्ध्य, *m.* a sweet scent, odour, fragrance.

सौग़ात, *f.* a rarity, curiosity, present.

सौगाति, *more prop.* (1) **सौग़ात** (2) **सौग़ाती**, *qq. v.*

सौग़ाती, given as a present or memento, fit for a present, curious, rare.

सौगुण = **सौगुणा**, *q. v.*

सौगुणा, *m.* (*f.* ī) a hundred-fold.

सौगुना, *more prop.* **सौगुणा**, *q v.*

सौच, *more prop.* **शौच**, *q. v.*

सौजन्य, *m.* goodness, magnanimousness, generosity, benevolence, kindness, compassion, clemency, urbanity, friendliness.

सौज़ा, *m.* prey, game.

सौत, *f.* (**सपत्नी**) a secondary wife, rival wife, contemporary wife. (One wife is *saut* to another.) The term is also used for two mangoes that grow together; also in the sense of 'rival' in general.

सौतडाही, *m.* (*f.* inī) a malicious person, a rival.

सौतन, *f.* 1, = **सौत**, *q. v.*: 2, a Braj pl. of **सौत**.

सौति in Chand = **सौत**, *q. v.*

सौतिआ, *more com.* **सौतिया**, *q. v.*

सौतिन = **सौतन**, *q. v.*

सौतिया, appertaining to a **सौत**, *q. v.*

सौतियाझाल, *m.* = **सौतियाडाह**, *q. v.*

सौतियाडाह, *f.* the malice of a rival wife, *i. e.* malice of the most virulent kind; *hence*, any rivalry that partakes of malice.

सौतितादाह = **सौतियाडाह**, *q. v.*

सौती, 1, in Chand = **सौत**, *q. v.*: 2, *m.* (*f.* in *or* inī) a malicious person, rival.

सौतेला, *m.* (*f.* ī) appertaining to a *saut*, of one and the same father by different mothers, of one and the same mother by different fathers (like the English prefix 'half'): hence, *Sautelā bhāī*, a step-brother; *Sautelī bahin*, a step-sister; *Sautelī mā*, a step-mother.

सौदा, *m.* trade, traffic, marketing, purchase: enthusiasm, ambition; rage; atrabilis; phrenitis, melancholy, insanity, madness; concupiscence, love. — *k.* to traffic, to purchase. — *lenā*, to market.

सौदाई, *m.* (*f.* inī) melancholic, insane, mad.

सौदागर, *m.* a merchant, trader.

सौदागरी, *f.* trade, commerce, merchandise, business.

सौदापत्तर, *m.* (in Commerce) a note, bill.

सौध, *m.* a mansion, palace: silver: opal.

सौधाई in Braj = **सूधाई**, *q. v.*

सौनक, 1, *more prop.* **शौनक**, *q. v.*: 2, *m.* the month of July.

सौना, in Braj = **सोना**, *q. v.*

सौनिक = **शौनिक**, *q. v.*

सौनो in Braj = **सोना**, *q. v.*

सौन्दना, *t.* to knead, mash, mix, to rinse.

सौन्दर्य्य, *m.* elegance, beauty, comeliness, loveliness.

सौन्दर्य्यता, *f.* (not com.) = **सौन्दर्य्य**, *q. v.*

सौन्धा, *more com.* **सोन्धा**, *q. v.*

सौप्तिक, 1, somnolent: 2, *m.* nocturnal combat.

सौब, *m.* a side, tract, way.

सौबत, *more prop.* (1) **सुहबत** (2) **सौत**, *qq. v.*

सौबरनी, made of gold, golden.

सौभरि, *m. pr. n.* a certain ancient Hindoo sage who married the 50 daughters of Māndhātṛi and became the father of 150 sons.

सौभागी, *m.* (*f.* inī) auspicious, fortunate, well-to-do.

सौभागिनी = **सौभाग्यवती**, *q. v.*

सौभाग्य, *m.* good fortune, auspiciousness: *pr. n.* the fourth of the astronomical *yogs*.

सौभाग्यवत, *m.* (*f.* vatī) fortunate, auspicious.

सौभाग्यवती, *f.* a married female whose husband is alive (*esp.* if she also have offspring).

सौभाग्यवन्त }
सौभाग्यवान } *m.* (*f.* vatī) = **सौभाग्यवत**, *q. v.*

सौमिक, appertaining to the moon, lunar.

सौमिकी, *f.* a sacrifice performed on the day of full moon.

सौमित्र = **सौमित्रि**, *q. v.*

सौमित्रि, *m.* (sprung from Sumitrā, *i. e.*) Lakshmaṇ.

सौम्प, *f.* (?) charge, custody, protectorship, care.

सौम्पना = **सौम्पना**, *q. v.*

सौम्पे, entrusted to, delivered over to.

सौम्फ, *more prop.* **सौंफ**, *q. v.*

सौयज्ञ, *m.* the sacrifice of a hundred horses.

सौर, appertaining to the sun, solar, sacred to Sūrya, *i. e.* the sun; celestial: *hence* (1) *m.* a solar month, a solar day, the planet Saturn: a kind of fish (2) *m.* (*f.* ī) a worshipper of the sun.

सौरज (*Rām.*) = **शौर्य्य**, *q. v.*

सुस्वभाव, 1, *m.* a good disposition, goodness of nature: 2, *adj.* of a good disposition, good-natured.

सुस्वभावना, *m.* (*f.* ī) of a good disposition, good-natured.

सुस्वाद, *m.* a pleasant taste, delicious flavour.

सुस्वादित, *m.* (*f.* ā) rendered pleasing to the taste, well-flavoured. [delicious.

सुस्वादु, very pleasant to the taste, very sweet,

सुहबत, *f.* companionship, society; discourse; a meeting, assemblage; a fair; coïtion.

सुहरना, *a. int.* to trail, draggle, drag.

सुहला, *m.* a kind of song.

सुहाई, *f.* (*m.* सुहाया) = सुहानी, *q. v.*

सुहाऊ = सुहावा, *q. v.*

सुहाग, *m.* auspiciousness, good fortune; the affection of a husband, an act of endearment, a caress; the happy state of being a wife as contrasted with widowhood; ornaments worn by married women while their husbands are alive.

सुहागन, *f.* a woman whose husband is alive; a woman beloved of her husband; a favorite wife.

सुहागपिटारा, *m.* a casket of jewels presented by a bridegroom to his bride.

सुहागपुड़ा, *m.* = सुहागपिटारा, *q.v.*

सुहागलहर, *f.* a cool refreshing breeze.

सुहागा, *m.* borax.

सुहागिन; see (1) सुहागन (2) सुहागिनी. [er's house.

सुहागिनी,*f.* a married female residing in her fath-

सुहागी, 1, *more com.* सुहागिनी, *q.v.*: 2,*m.*(*f.* inī) a

सुहात; see सुहाता and सुहाना,2. [fortunate person.

सुहाता, *m.* (*f.* ī) agreeable, pleasant, charming.

सुहान; see सुहाना and सूहान.

सुहाना, 1, *m.* (*f.*ī) agreeable, pleasant, charming: 2, *a. int.* to please, be agreeable, be liked, be approved of; to become, befit, to shine: *t.* to ornament, adorn.

सुहावनी in Chand = सुहाना, *q.v.*

सुहाय, a contraction of सुहाया, *q.v.*

सुहायमान, *m.* (*f.* matī) } = सुहाना, 1, *q.v.*
सुहाया, *m.* (*f.* सुहाई) }

सुहारना, *t.* to trail, draggle, drag.

सुहाल, *m.* bread or cakes fried in butter.

सुहाली, *f.* = सुहाल, *q.v.* [ornament.

सुहावन, agreeable, pleasant, charming. — *k.* to

सुहावना, 1, adj. *m.* (*f.* ī): 2, *a. int.* = सुहाना, *q.v.*

सुहावनी, *f.* an agreeable or charming female.

सुहावा, 1, *m.* (*f.* ī) agreeable, pleasing: 2, *m.* decoration, garniture, ornament; splendidness, handsomeness.

सुहावो, *f.* agreeableness, pleasantness.

सुहाति, (pl °ति) } = सुहाता (सुहाना).
सुहाती, (pl. °तीं) }

सुहृद, *m.* (*f.* ā) = सुहृदय, *q.v.*

सुहृदभेद, *m.* the separation of friends, dissension among friends.

सुहृदय, *m.* (*f.* ā) a kind-hearted person: *lit.* good-hearted, friendly, kind.

सुहृदयभेद = सुहृदभेद, *q.v.* [birth of a son).

सुहेया, *f.* a birth-song (sung by the females at the

सुहेला, *m.* a kind of descriptive or eulogistic song.

सू, 1, *more prop.* सु, good, etc. *q.v.*: 2, *f.* a side, part, quarter, direction: 3, in the direction of, towards: 4, in Braj = से, *q. v.* [stye.— *kī charbī*, lard.

सूअर, *m.*(*f.* ī) a hog, a wild boar.—*kī bhār*, a hog-

सूअरख़ाना, *m.* a pork-establishment, any place where swine are slain or sold, a pig's-house, hogstye.

सूआ, *m.* a parrot, a parroquet: any large needle, a needle with which gunny-bags are sewed, a packing-needle; a prick, prickle; an awn of corn.

सूआपाटी } *f.* a certain game among children.
सूआपाती }

सूआस, *m.* a kind of rice.

सूइया, pointed (said of needles).

सूइस, *m.* a porpoise.

सूई, *f.* a needle; the hand of a watch; the needle of a compass; a prick, prickle.—*kā kām*, needlework. —*ke nākese khudāko nikālnā* is applied to express the performance of seeming impossibilities.—*bhar*, a needleful.

सूईगल, (*lit.* the needle-melter) a certain very acid kind of lemon in which needles are said to dissolve.

सूईभर; see *s.v.* सूई.

सूं, 1, in Braj and in Mārwaṛī = से, 1, *q.v.*: 2, *more* **सूंगरा**, *m.* (*f.* ī) a buffalo-calf. [*prop.* सोंस, *q.v.*

सूंगा, *m.* the clitoris.

सूंघ, *f.* smell; a smelling, inhaling.

सूंघन, *f.* anything to smell to, snuff; smelling.

सूंघना, *t.* to scent, smell, nose, sniff, snuff, inhale. *Sūnghtā* [*m.* (*f.* ī)] *phirnā*, to prowl about.

सूंघनी, *f.* snuff, scent. — *lenā*, to nuzzle.

सूंघा, 1, *m.* (*f.* ī) staunch (said of dogs); a setter of jewels: 2, *m.* a person employed in Marhatta armies who is said to be able to detect hidden treasure or grain by the smell of the earth.

सूंट, सूंड, सूंत, सूंघ; for all words beginning with either of these elements, see under the corresponding forms सुघट, सुघड़, सुन्त, सुन्ध respectively.

सूंड़, *f.* an elephant's trunk. [liquors.

सूंड़ी, *m.*(*f.*iṇī) a distiller and vendor of spirituous

सूंड़ीमुसख़्ख़सी, *f.* a tax on vendors of spirituous

सूंस, *m.* porpoise. [liquors.

सूक (*colloquial*) = शूक, *q.v.*

सूकटा, *m.* (*f.* ī) lean, emaciated, weak.

सूकड़ा, *more prop.* सुकड़ा, *q.v.*

सूकना, *more prop.* सूखना, *q.v.*

सूकर (*colloquial*) = (1) शूकर (2) शूक, *qq.v.*

सूकरमुख, *more prop.* शूकरमुख, *q. v.*

सूकरखेत = शूकरखेत = वाराहक्षेत्र, *q.v.*

सूकरी, 1, (*colloquial*) = शूकरी, *q.v.*: 2, *f.* a species of moss (*Lycopodium imbricatum*).

स्थापि = **स्थापके** (**स्थापना**, 2). See **स**, 7.

स्थापित, *m.* (*f.* ā) placed, founded, established, situated, fixed, erected, ordained, decreed, ascertained.

स्थापनी, *f.* the plant *Cissampelos hexandra.*

स्थामी, *f.* a certain *sūtra.*

स्थायी, *m.* (*f.* inī) standing, staying, continuing, enduring, fixed, steady, firm, unchangeable, residing.

स्थायीभाव, *m.* permanent or fixed condition.

स्थायुक, 1, stopping, staying, abiding, stationary, steady, firm: 2, *m.* the overseer of a village.

स्थाली, *f.* a small flat metal or earthen dish or boiler, a salver, platter, tray.

स्थावर, fixed, stable, immoveable, stationary, established, regular: hence, *m.* a mountain; real estate, unalienable property; an heirloom; a bowstring.

स्थित, standing, stayed, steady, firm, immoveable, established, decreed, determined, resolved, permanent.

स्थिति, *f.* the being fixed or stationary; a stay, staying; steadiness, continuance, permanence, consistency; stop, cessation, pause; decision, decree, maxim.

स्थिर, 1, fixed, immoveable, firm, steady, stable, permanent, durable, lasting, settled, steadfast, constant, faithful; tranquil, serene, collected, cool, mild, quiet, quiescent: 2, *m.* a deity; a mountain; final emancipation; a tree; a bull; Kārttikiya, god of war; the planet Saturn; one of the astronomical *yogs.* — *honā*, to be at rest, be firm.

स्थिरचित, *m.*(*f.* ā) firm of thought, resolved, determined, constant, steady, sedate.

स्थिरचेता, *m. f.* = **स्थिरचित**, *q. v.*

स्थिरता, *f.* (*m.*°**त्व**) steadiness, stability, permanence, perpetuity, firmness, steadfastness, rectitude, fortitude, serenity, rest.

स्थिरमति, *m. f.* steady, firm, deliberate.

स्थिरात्मा, *m. f.* stable, steady, firm, unmoved, resolute.

स्थूणा, *f.* the post or pillar of a house: an iron image; an anvil; a disease.

स्थूल, 1, *m.* (*f.* ā) great, large, bulky, fat, corpulent; jolly; dull, clumsy, stupid; gross, coarse: 2, *m.* the jack-tree; a heap; a tent.

स्थूलता, *f.* (*m.*°**त्व**) thickness, bulkiness, corpulency, coarseness, dulness, stupidity.

स्थूलबुद्धि, *m.* ... crass of intellect, thick-headed, fat-headed, stupid, senseless, dull, coarse-minded.

स्थैर्य, *m.* firmness, steadiness, stability, constancy, patience, fortitude, resoluteness.

स्थौल्य, *m.* thickness, fatness; largeness, bulkiness, size; dulness.

स्नान, *m.* bathing, ablution, purification, lustration.

स्नानकारक, *adj.* effecting ablution.

स्नाननहान, *m.* (**स्नान** + **नहान**) bathing and washing.

स्नानस्थान, *m.* a bathingplace.

स्नानीय, fit for bathing in, ablutionary, requiring to be bathed, to be used in bathing.

स्नेह, *m.* oil, unguent, grease; vicidity, unctuosity; affection, love, kindness, friendliness.

स्नेहवान, *m.* (*f.* vati) possessed of love, affectionate, loving.

स्नेहार्थ, with a view to (or on account of) love, for love's sake.

स्नेही, greasy, oily, unctuous; tender, affectionate, loving, kind: hence, *m.* (*f.* inī) a painter; a lover, friend, spouse.

स्पन्दन, *m.* motion, trembling, quivering, throbbing, shaking, vibration; the quickening of a child in the womb.

स्पर्द्धा, *f.* emulation, rivalry, jealousy, envy.

स्पर्द्धी, *m.* (*f.* inī) emulous, envious, rivaling, proud.

स्पर्श, *m.* touch, contract, feeling, touching; sexual intercourse; morbid heat: (in Gram.) the five classes (*varg*) of consonants embracing the letters from **क** to **म** inclusive.

स्पर्शनीय, *m.*(*f.* ā) *adj.* admitting of being touched, tangible, palpable, sensible, perceptible by the touch.

स्पर्शी, *m.* (*f.* inī) 1, = **स्पर्शनीय**, *q. v.*: 2, handling, touching.

स्पर्शेन्द्रिय, *m.* the function or sense of touch.

स्पष्ट, clear, evident, manifest, intelligible, easy, apparent, plain.

स्पष्टता *f.* (*m.* °**त्व**) clearness, plainness.

स्पष्टरूप, clearly, distinctly, manifestly.

स्पानी, appertaining to Spain, Spanish: hence (1) *f.* the Spanish language (2) *m.* (*f.* inī) a Spaniard.

स्पेन, *m. pr. n.* the country of Spain.

स्पृहा, *f.* desire, wish, longing.

स्पृही, *m.* (*f.* inī) wishful, desirous.

स्फट, *m.* a snake's expanded hood.

स्फटक, *m.* crystal, quartz.

स्फटा, *f.* a snake's expanded hood.

स्फटिक, *m.* crystal, quartz.

स्फटिकमय, *m.* (*f.* ī) made of crystal.

स्फटी, *f.* alum.

स्फाटिक, 1, crystalline: 2, *m.* crystal.

स्फुट, opened, blown, expanded; evident, manifest, apparent; known, understood.

स्फुरत (*Rām.*) = **स्फरित**, *q.v.*

स्फुरन्मौलि, *f. m.*? a brilliant head-dress, sparkling diadem.

स्फुरित, *m.* (*f.* ā) shaken, agitated, trembling, throbbing.

स्फूर्ति, *f.* a throbbing, palpitating, shaking.

स्फोट, *m.* a breaking through, bursting; a boil, tumour; (in the *Pūrva-Mimāṅsā*) the eternal sound.

स्फोटक, *m.* a tumour, boil.

स्फोटा, *f.* the hood of the snake.

स्मति; see (1) **संमति** (2) **स्मृति**.

स्मरण, 1, *m.* remembering, remembrance, recollecting; memory; regretting; mentioning: 2, *f.* a small rosary.

स्मरणकारक *m.*(*f.* ikā) calculated to bring to remembrance, provocative of recollection, commemorative.

स्मरणकारी, *m.* (*f.* inī) = **स्मरणकारक**, *q.v.*

स्मरणार्थक्रिया, *f.* commemoration.

स्मरणार्थिक, with a view to remembering, in remembrance or memory of.

स्मरणी, *f.* a small rosary.

स्मरणीय, fit or requiring to be remembered, memorable.

स्मरन, *m.* (*f.* ā) *adj.* remembering; considering.

स्मरामहे (*Rām.*) = **हम स्मरण करते हैं**.

स्मर्त्ता, *m.* (*f.* trī) one who remembers, etc.: *lit.* mindful, considerate, attentive, prudent, intelligent, accurate.

स्मशान, *more prop.* **श्मशान**, *q.v.*

स्मारक, *adj.* causing to remember, refreshing the memory, reminding: hence, *m.* a remembrancer.

स्मृति, *f.* remembrance, recollection, memory: the body of law as delivered originally by tradition; a law-book; law, tradition; a code of laws; didactic poems.

स्यन्दन, quick, fast: hence, *m.* a war-chariot, air, oozing, water, going swiftly: a certain tree (*Dalbergia ougeinensis*).

स्यमन्तक, *m.* the gem worn by Krishṇ. [kshetra.

स्यमन्तकक्षेत्र, *m. pr. n.* the former name of Kuru-

स्यान, **स्याम**; for words beginning thus, see under the forms **सयान**, **श्याम**, respectively.

स्यामचिड़ी, *f.* a certain bird.

स्यार, *m.* (*f.* in, ī, nī) a jackal.

स्यारक, *more prop.* **श्यालक**, *q.v.*

स्यारनी } **स्यारिन** } = **स्यारी**, *q. v.*

स्यारी, *f.* (*m.* **स्यार**) a female jackal.

स्याला, 1, *more prop.* **सियाल**, *q.v.*: 2, *m.* (*f.* ī) a brother-in-law (wife's brother).

स्यालापोका, *m.* a barnacle. [poor.

स्यावड़, small heaps of grain set apart for the

स्याही, *more prop.* **सियाही**, *q.v.*

स्यूपठा, *m.* tongs.

स्यून्यना; see (1) **स्यूपठा** (2) **सूथना** (3) **सून्यना**.

स्योना, *more com.* **सेवना**, *q. v.*

स्रंग, 1, in Chand = **शृङ्ग**, *q.v.*: 2, = **स्रज**, *qq.v.*

स्रक = **स्रज**, *q.v.*

स्रग, 1, = **स्रज**, *q.v.*: 2, an old form = **स्वर्ग**, *q.v.*

स्रज, *f.* a wreath of flowers, chaplet, garland.

स्रजत, **स्रद्धा**, **स्रम**, **स्रवन**, **स्राद**; for words beginning with either of these elements, see under the forms **सृजत**, **श्रद्धा**, **श्रम**, **श्रवण**, **श्राद्ध**, respectively.

स्रब्ब in Chand = **सर्व** = **सब**, *q. v.*

स्रवनमगु (*Rām.*) = **श्रवणमार्ग**, *q. v.*

स्रवनैं, 1, *more com.* **सुनना**, *q.v.*: 2, *a. int.* to drop, dribble, leak, ooze, stream, flow.

स्रावकी, *m.* a certain tribe of Hindoos.

स्राप = **श्राप**, *q.v.*

स्रापना = **श्रापना**, *q.v.*

स्रापित, *m.* (*f.* ā) = **श्रापित**, *q.v.*

स्रावन, *more prop.* **श्रावण**, *q.v.*

स्रिंग, **स्री**; for all words beginning thus, see under the forms **शृंग**, **श्री**, respectively.

स्रीवस्त, *m.* a certain tribe of Kāyasths.

स्रीहत, *m.* (*f.* ī) whose splendour has disappeared.

स्रुत; see under the form **श्रुत**.

स्रुव, *m.* a kind of sacrificial ladle with two excavations used for pouring ghee on the sacrificial fire.

स्रुवा, *f.* 1, = **स्रुव**, *q.v.*: 2, the name of two plants (1) *Sansviera zeylanica* (2) *Aletris hyacinthoides* and *Dracona nervosa*.

स्रेनी (*colloquial*) = **श्रेणी**, *q.v.* [form **श्रेष्ठ**.

स्रेष्ठ; for words beginning thus, see under the

स्रोत, *m.* a current, rapid stream, torrent, course of water, wave, river, spring: an organ of sense.

स्रोतस = **स्रोत**, *q.v.*

स्रोता, 1, *more prop.* **स्रोत**, *q v.*: 2, – **श्रोता**, *q.v.*

स्लेट, *m.* (Eng.) slate, a slate.

स्लेश } **स्लेष** } *more prop.* **श्लेष**, *q.v.*

स्लोक, *more prop.* **श्लोक**, *q.v.*

स्व, 1, *m.* (*f.* ā) own, one's own (Lat. *suus*): hence, 2, *m.* soul; a kinsman; property, wealth, belongings: (in Algebra) a positive or affirmative quantity. It may be of some importance to note that this word, in its first sense, is seldom used in Hindee excepting as the first member of compounds, and that its exact meaning is modified by the pronoun with which it is associated in the sentence; thus, it sometimes signifies 'my own', sometimes 'thy own', 'his (or her) own', 'our own', etc.

स्वइच्छा; for words beginning thus, see under the more proper form **स्वेच्छा**.

स्वकार्य्य, *m.* a person's own peculiar duty or occu-

स्वकर्म्म = **स्वकार्य्य**, *q.v.* [pation, one's own business.

स्वकीय, *m.* (*f.* ā) appertaining to one's self or to one's own family, own, proper, peculiar.

स्वकुटम्ब, *m.* one's own family.

स्वकुल, *m.* one's own race or tribe. [one's own self.

स्वकृत, *m.* (*f.* ā) self-performed, *i.e.* made or done by

स्वंगी, *m.* (*f.* ini) *more com.* **स्वांगी**, *q.v.*

स्वगति, *f.* one's own course or condition.

स्वच्छ, (**सु** + **अच्छ**) *m* (*f.* ā) clean, pure, clear, transparent, free from stain or soil, pellucid, polished; sound, healthy. [cy; healthiness, soundness.

स्वच्छता, (*f.* *m.* °**त्व**) cleanness, purity, transparen-

स्वच्छन्द, 1, following one's own will, unrestrained, independent, self-willed; spontaneous; uncultivated; free, contented, happy: 2, *m.* one's own will, independence; ease, security, peace.

स्वजन, *m.* (*f.* ā *or* ī) a kinsman, distant relative.

स्वजाति, *f.* own caste or tribe, own kind or species.

स्वज्ञाति, 1, *f.* kin, kindred: 2, *m.* *f.* a relation.

स्वतः, *adv.* of (or by) one's own self, of itself.

स्वतन्त्र, *m.* (*f.* ī) unrestrained, uncontrolled, independent, free, absolute, self-willed: of age, *i. e.* no longer subject to the authority of another.

स्वतन्त्रता, *f.* (*m.* °**त्व**) independence, uncontrolledness, absoluteness, freedom, self-will. [disposition.

स्वतन्त्रस्वभाव, *m.* (*f.* ā) of an unbridled or selfwilled

स्वतन्त्राधिराज, *m.* (*f.* °**राज्ञी**) one who is of a self-willed or despotic disposition.

स्वत्व, *m.* (*f.* tā) self-existence, personal identity, ownness, independence, proprietary right, ownership, proprietorship, possession. [one's home.

स्वदेश, *m.* one's native country, one's own place,

स्वदेशत्याग, *m.* forsaking or quitting one's native country, emigration, voluntary exile.

स्वदेशत्यागी, *m.* (*f.* inī) one who quits his own country, an emigrant, voluntary exile.

स्वदेशानुराग, 1, *m.* = **स्वदेशानुरागता**, *q.v.*: 2, *m.* (*f.* ā) = **स्वदेशानुरागी**, *q.v.* [patriotism.

स्वदेशानुरागता, *f.* passion for one's own country,

स्वदेशानुरागी, *m.* (*f.* iṇī) one who has a passion for his native country, a patriot.

स्वदेशी, appertaining to one's own (or to the same) country or locality: hence, *m.* (*f.* inī) a fellow-countryman.

स्वदेशीय, *m.* (*f.* ā) = **स्वदेशी**, *q.v.*

स्वदृष्टि, *f.* one's own eye, one's own sight, personal inspection. — *dekhnā*, to see wish one's own eyes.

स्वधर्म्म, *m.* the peculiar duty of any person, or those duties that appertain to any particular class of society.

स्वधर्म्मत्याग, *m.* dereliction of duty; apostasy.

स्वधर्म्मत्यागी, *m.* (*f.* inī) one who is guilty of dereliction of duty; an apostate.

स्वधर्म्मपक्षपाती, *m.* (*f.* inī) one who is prepossessed in favour of his own religion, a religious partisan, a bigot.

स्वधर्म्मार्थ, for the sake of one's own **धर्म्म**, *q.v.*

स्वधर्म्मार्थप्राण, *m.* one who is ready to give up his life for the sake of his *dharm*, one who has the martyr-spirit.

स्वधर्म्मी, appertaining to one's own duty or religion: hence, *m.* (*f.* iṇī) a dutiful person; a religious partisan.

स्वनगर, *m.* one's own town, one's native city.

स्वनाश, *m.* self-destruction, suicide.

स्वन्घ; see **सूँघ** and **स्वाँग**.

स्वपच, *more prop.* **श्वपच**, *q.v.*

स्वपत, *m.* (*f.* antī) asleep, sleeping, reposing.

स्वपाणि, *m.* one's own hand.

स्वप्त, *more prop.* (1) **स्वपत** (2) **सुप्त**, *qq.v.*

स्वप्न, *m.* sleep; dreaming, a dream: indolence.

स्वप्नदर्शी, *m.* (*f.* inī) a visionary: lit. *adj.* dreaming, [visionary.

स्वप्नदोष, *m.* nocturnal pollution.

स्वप्नध्यायी, *m.* (*f.* inī) an interpreter of dreams.

स्वप्नफल, *m.* the realization of things seen in dreams.

स्वप्नविचार, *m.* the interpretation of dreams.

स्वप्नविचारी, *m.* (*f.* iṇī) an interpreter of dreams.

स्वप्नवत्, like a dream, dreamy, unreal.

स्वप्ना, *more prop.* **स्वप्न**, *q.v.*

स्वप्नेहूँमें in Braj = **स्वप्नमें भी**.

स्वप्नोदय, seen or revealed in a dream.

स्वप्रकाश, *m.* (*f.* ā) shining by its own light, self-en-

स्वबस, *more prop.* **स्ववश**, *q.v.* [lightened, self-taught.

स्वबुद्धि, *f.* the conceiving a thing to be one's own property. [dom.

स्वबुध्यानुसार, in accordance with one's own wis-

स्वभाव, *m.* natural disposition, innate quality or property, natural state, nature, quality, essence; temperament; habit, fashion, custom, practice.

स्वभाववश, 1, *m.* subjection to natural disposition: 2, *m.* (*f.* ā) under the control of the natural dispositions.

स्वभाववाला, *m.* (*f.* ī) *adj.* possessed of **स्वभाव**, *q.v.*

स्वभाविक, appertaining to the innate quality or natural disposition.

स्वभू, *m.* 1, an epithet (1) of Brahm (2) of Vishṇu (3) of Shiv: *lit.* the self-existent: 2, time; love.

स्वभूमि, *f.* one's own land or estate, one's native place or country. [own religion.

स्वमत, *m.* one's own opinion or sentiments, one's

स्वयं, self; one's self; of or by one's self.

स्वयंबर, *more prop.* **स्वयंवर**, *q.v.* [Supreme Being.

स्वयंब्रह्म, *m.* (the self-existent, *i. e.*) Brahm or the

स्वयंभु
स्वयंभुव
स्वयंभू } = **स्वभू**, *q.v.*

स्वयंभूदय, *m.* the origin or creation of Brahm.

स्वयंभूमनु, *m. pr. n.* a certain king, the first of the six Manus and husband of Satrūpā. [princess.

स्वयंवर, *m.* the public choice of a husband by a

स्वयंवरा, *f.* a girl or princess who publicly selects her husband from a number of suitors assembled.

स्वयम; for words beginning thus, see under the more proper form **स्वयं**.

स्वर, *m.* sound, noise, voice; snoring; a note or key in music, a tune, music; (in Gram.) a vowel, pronunciation, an accent: the sun; splendour; heaven; paradise: (a mystical word signifying) the space between the sun and the polar star. *Gambhir* —, (in Music) the bass. In the ingenious system of reckoning by symbols adopted by Hindoos in their poetry, this word (in allusion to the notes in music) is a symbol for 7.

स्वरचक्र, *m.* (in Gram.) a table or paradigm of the vowels.

स्वरसन्धि, *f.* (in Gram.) the union of one or more simple vowels for the formation of a compound one, in accordance with special rules.

स्वरान्त, (in Gram.) ending with a vowel.

स्वरूप, 1, *m.* (*f.* ā) identified with, analogous, having the same nature or qualities as, similar, like; suitable; pleasing; learned, wise: hence, 2, *m.* own shape or kind, natural condition or state, natural and obvious purpose or inference, kind, sort, shape, identity, appearance; the reality as distinguished from the mere shadow, truth. [state, self-knowledge.

स्वरूपज्ञान, knowledge of one's own condition or

स्वरूपता, *f.* identity, sameness, likeness. [tion.

स्वरूपवान, *m.* (*f.* vatī) possessed of natural condi-

स्वरूपा, *f. pr. n.* (1) of a certain place (2) of a certain

स्वरूपान्तर, transformed. [demon.

स्वरूपी, *m.* (*f.* iṇī) = **स्वरूप**, 1, *q.v.*

स्वर्ग, *m.* the sky, heaven, the residence of the pious

dead or of deified mortals, the paradise of Indra. In the ingenious system of reckoning by symbols adopted by Hindoos in their poetry, this word (in allusion to the twenty-one heavens) is a symbol for 21.

स्वर्गंगा, *f. pr. n.* (see **गंगा**) the celestial Ganges.

स्वर्गगमन, *m.* the going to heaven.

स्वर्गति = **स्वर्गागति**, *q. v.*

स्वर्गधाम / **स्वर्गलोक** } = **स्वर्लोक**, *q. v.*

स्वर्गवासी, *m.* (*f.* inī) dwelling heaven, heavenly, [celestial.

स्वर्गविद्याधरी, *f.* a certain class of demigoddesses.

स्वर्गागत, *m.* (*f.* ā) gone to heaven.

स्वर्गागति, *f.* the going to heaven; future felicity; dying, death. [*lit.* the road of heaven.

स्वर्गाधिपति, *m.* an epithet of the Supreme Being:

स्वर्गारूढ़, *adj.* ascended to heaven.

स्वर्गारोहण, *m.* the ascending to heaven.

स्वर्गी, *m.* (*f.* inī) 1, = **स्वर्गीय**, *q. v.*: 2, a deity: 3, (in Law) dead.

स्वर्गीय, *m.* (*f.* ā) appertaining to heaven, paradisiacal, celestial, heavenly, divine.

स्वर्ग्य, *m.* (*f.* ā) 1 = **स्वर्गीय**, *q. v.*: 2, *adj.* procuring a [place in heaven.

स्वर्जिका = **सर्जिका**, *q. v.*

स्वर्जिकाक्षार = **सर्जिकाक्षार**, *q. v.*

स्वर्ण, *m.* (a contraction of **सुवर्ण**) gold.

स्वर्णक, golden, of gold.

स्वर्णकार, *m.* (*f.* ī) a worker in gold, a goldsmith.

स्वर्णकृत, *m.* (*f.* ā) 1, = **स्वर्णकार**, *q. v.*: 2, made of gold.

स्वर्णक्षीरी, *f.* a medicinal kind of moon-plant with a yellow juice (said to be brought from the Himālayas).

स्वर्णगैरिक, *m.* golden ochre.

स्वर्णचूड़, *m.* the blue jay.

स्वर्णदी, *f.* (see **गंगा**) the Ganges of heaven.

स्वर्णपुष्पी, *f.* a medicinal sort of moon-plant; the [*Cassia fistula.*

स्वर्णमय, *m.* (*f.* ī) golden.

स्वर्णमुद्रा, *f.* a golden coin, golden signet.

स्वर्नदी, *more prop.* **स्वर्णदी**, *q. v.*

स्वर्वेश्या, *f.* any nymph of Indra's paradise.

स्वर्भानु, *m.* Rāhu, the personified ascending node.

स्वर्मध्य, *m.* (in Astron.) the zenith.

स्वर्लोक, *m.* the celestial regions, the heavenly state, heaven, the abode of heaven, paradise.

स्वर्वैद्य, *m.* an epithet of either of the two Ashwins: *lit.* a physician of heaven.

स्वल्प, *m.* (*f.* ā) very small, very little, very few.

स्ववर्ण, *m.* one's own colour, tribe, or caste.

स्ववश, self-controlled, ruled by one's own free-will, independent, headstrong: hence, *m.* (*f.* ā) a free agent, etc.

स्ववासिनी, *f.* a female (whether married or unmarried) residing in her father's house.

स्ववृत्ति, 1, *f.* own or peculiar occupation or duty: 2, adj. *m. f.* subsisting by one's own exertion.

स्वशास्त्र, *m.* one's own Shāstra.

स्वसुर, *more prop.* **श्वशुर**, *q. v.*

स्वसेव्य, *m.* (*f.* ā) deserving of adoration by virtue of something in oneself.

स्वस्तता, *more prop.* **स्वस्थता**, *q. v.*

स्वस्ति, 1, *f.* welfare; blessing: 2, a particle of benediction = hail! health to you! prosperity! 3, a particle of sanction = so be it! Amen!

स्वस्तिक, *m.* a kind of temple with a portico in front; any auspicious object; the meeting of four roads; a palace with a portico on three sides; a mystical mark; a cross; the crossing the arms; a kind of posture; a kind of cake; a libertine; garlic.

स्वस्तिमन्त / **स्वस्तिमान** } *m.* (*f.* matī) happy, auspicious.

स्वस्तिवाचन, *m.* a certain rite (preparatory to any important observance, in which the Brāhmans strew boiled rice on the ground and invoke the blessing of the gods on the ceremonies about to commence).

स्वस्त्ययन, auspicious, producing happiness: hence, *m.* a means of attaining prosperity, the repetition of sacred texts or the performance of rites for divine propitiation or the averting of evil; benediction.

स्वस्थ, *m.* (*f.* ā) self-reliant, resolute, firm, confident; content; self-sufficient, independent; healthy, well, safe.

स्वस्थता *f.* health, well-being, soundness in health.

स्वस्थदाई, *m.* (*f.* inī) salutary, comforting, nourishing, tending to promote recovery from sickness.

स्वस्थान, *m.* home, residence, one's own place.

स्वस्वामित्यक्त, *m.* (*f.* ā) *adj.* forsaking one's own protector or husband.

स्वांग, *m.* mimicry, acting, imitation, disguise, sham, mockery; a scene, a part in a play, a character, impersonation. —*k.* to act foolishly. —*lānā*, to imitate, mimic.

स्वांगी, *m.* (*f.* inī) a mimic, actor, satirist, mocker.

स्वांस / **स्वांसा** } (*colloquial*) = **श्वास**, *q. v.*

स्वाक्षर, *m.* one's own handwriting, attestation, signature, imprimature.

स्वागत, *m.* welcome, salutation.

स्वागता, *f.* (in Pros.) a species of metre.

स्वात, a contraction of **स्वाति**, *q. v.*

स्वाति, *f.* 1, *pr. n.* (1) of one of the wives of the sun (2) of the star Arcturus, the 15th *Nakshatra* consisting of but one star: 2, an auspicious constellation: a sword.

स्वातिसुत, *m.* an epithet of a pearl: *lit.* the offspring of Arcturus (from a popular belief that in October, when the sun's longitude corresponds to that of Arcturus, the drops of rain that fall into shells are converted into pearls).

स्वाती, *f.* = **स्वाति**, *q. v.*

स्वाद, *m.* a tasting, eating, drinking; taste, flavour, relish sweetness; pleasure —*chikhnā*, (with gen.) to taste.

स्वादक / **स्वादन** } = **स्वादिक**, *q. v.*

स्वादिक, appertaining to flavour, etc., of high flavour, delicious, relishing, palatable.

स्वादित, tasted, touched: flavoured, seasoned, palatable. [ing, drinking.

स्वादी, *m.* (*f.* inī) a taster, drinker: lit. *adj.* tast-

स्वादु, grateful to the palate, sweet, dainty, delicate, agreeable, pleasing: hence (1) *m.* sweetness; a relish, taste; molasses; a certain medicinal root (2) *f.* a grape.

स्वाधिकार, *m.* one's own or peculiar authority, office, or station.

स्वाधिकारी, *m.* (*f.* iṇi) one who is his own master: *lit* under the authority of himself.

स्वाधिपत्य, *m.* supreme sway, sovereignty.

स्वाधीन, *m.* (*f.* ā) being one's own master, independent, uncontrolled, absolute, despotic; (in Gram.) *m.* a neuter verb

स्वाधीनता, *f.* (*m.* °त्व) = स्वाधीनी, *q.v.*

स्वाधीनी, *f.* independence, uncontrolledness, liberty.

स्वान, 1, *more prop.* श्वान, *q.v.*: 2, *m.* sound, noise.

स्वाभाव, *more prop.* स्वभाव, *q.v.*

स्वाभाविक, being by one's own nature, innate, natural, inherent, peculiar, essential.—*bhikshuk*, a beggar born.

स्वामकार्त्तिक, *m.* an epithet of Kārttikeya.

स्वामिन्, *more com.* हे स्वामी.

स्वामित्व, *m.* (*f.* tā) proprietorship, ownership, mastership, sovereignty.

स्वामिधर्म, *m.* the duties specially incumbent on a sovereign.

स्वामिनी, *f.* (*m.* स्वामी) a proprietress, mistress, protectress, patroness.

स्वामिभक्त, *m.* (*f.* ā) attached to one's own protector or husband.

स्वामी, *adj.* having proprietary rights: hence, *m.* (*f* inī) an owner, proprietor, lord, master, sovereign, prince, monarch; a lover, husband; a spiritual preceptor; a certain class of mendicants; an epithet (1) of the Supreme Being (2) of Vishṇu (3) of Shiv (4) of Kārttikeya (5) of Garuḍa.

स्वामिद्रोह, *m.* the injuring one's master or sovereign, treachery, perfidy.

स्वामिद्रोही, *m.* (*f.* inī) a perfidious person, traitor.

स्वायंभव, *m. pr. n.* (see मनु) the first Manu.

स्वायंभूमनु = स्वायंभव, *q.v.*

स्वारथ (*colloquial*) = स्वार्थ, *q.v.*

स्वारथहि in Braj = स्वार्थको, *q.v.*

स्वाराज्य, *m.* the state of Brahm, final felicity; heaven.

स्वारोचिष, *m. pr. n.* (see मनु) the second Manu.

स्वार्थ, *adj.* having one's own object, having a literal meaning; pleonastic; self-interested: hence, *m.* one's own desire or advantage, one's own object or cause, one's own interest; selfishness, the having an eye to one's own interests, the same meaning, pleonasm; mundane affairs; desire, wish, pleasure, object, end, aim, purpose, drift.

स्वार्थक, 1, *more prop.* स्वार्थिक, *q.v.*: 2, appertaining to one's own purpose or meaning.

स्वार्थिक, done with one's own property, having one's own object, answering its design, expressing its own or literal meaning, succeeding in one's purpose, effective, successful, profitable, advantageous, useful.

स्वार्थी, *m.* (*f.* iṇī) self-gratifying, selfish.

स्वार्थ्य, *m.* (in Gram.) the indicative mode.

स्वार्पितवस्तुक, *adj.* keeping anything in one's own possession.

स्वास = श्वास, *q.v.*

स्वासा, *m.* (*f.* ी) = श्वास, *q.v.*

स्वास्थ्य, *m.* health, happiness, satisfaction, content, pleasure, ease, relief; self-reliance, firmness, prowess; wealth.

स्वाहा, 1, an exclamation used on making an offering to a deity: 2 *f.* a personification of the preceding as the wife of Agni, who presides over burnt offerings.

स्वीकरण, *m.* assenting; promising; marriage.

स्वीकार, *m.* assent, consent, agreement, promise, avowal. — *k* to agree to, confess, own, approve of, acquiesce in, bear patiently.

स्वीकारक, *m.* (*f.* ikī) = स्वीकारी, *q.v.*

स्वीकारी, *adj.* acknowledging, confessing, assenting, accepting: hence, *m.* (*f.* iṇī) promiser, avower.

स्वीकृत, assented to, acknowledged, confessed, approved, avowed, promised, accepted, appropriated.

स्वेच्छा, *f.* one's own will or pleasure, the following one's own inclination, wilfulness, waywardness.

स्वेच्छाचर, *m.* (*f.* ī or ā)
स्वेच्छाचार, *m.* (*f.* ā) } = स्वेच्छाचारी, *q.v.*

स्वेच्छाचारी, *adj.* following one's own inclination, acting without restraint: hence, *m.* (*f.* iṇi) a self-willed person.

स्वेत (*colloquial*) = श्वेत, *q.v.*

स्वेता in Braj = श्वेत or श्वेता, *qq.v.*

स्वेद, *m.* perspiration, hot moisture, vapour; warmth, heat; hot work, labour.

स्वेदज, *m.* (*f.* ā) an epithet of worms and insects: *lit.* engendered by heat and moisture.

स्वेष्ट, *m.* (*f.* ā) self-desired, wished-for.

स्वेदज, *more prop.* स्वेदज, *q.v.*

स्वैरण (*colloquial*) = स्वैरिन, *q.v.*

स्वैरत्व, *m.* (*f.* tā) = स्वैरिता, *q.v.*

स्वैरिणी, *f.* (*m.* स्वैरी) a wanton female, an unchaste wife, an adulteress.

स्वैरिता, *f.* wilfulness, independence, freedom.

स्वैरिन, *more com.* स्वैरी, *q.v.*

स्वैरी, *m.* (*f.* iṇī) an independent or wanton person, an adulterer: *lit.* self-willed, wanton, uncontrolled.

स्वोपार्जित, self-earned, self-acquired.

स्वोरस, *m.* the sediment of oil, etc. ground with a stone and muller.

ह

ह (h) is the thirty-third consonant in the Hindee or Devanāgari alphabet, and has invariably the aspirated sound of the English letter *h*, as in the word 'hard.' It belongs to the class of gutturals, is the aspirate of the Devanāgari alphabet, and is the last letter of the class called by grammarians *ūshmā* or *ūshmāṇah*: it is hence called the guttural sibilant. By inaccurate writers and speakers this letter is constantly corrupted into *ai* (see ऐ, 7); *e.g.* ठैरना, properly ठहरना; again, गैना, properly गहना. Great care should be taken not to confound the 'inaudible *h*' (see आ, 19) with this aspirate. Lastly, this letter is occasionally displaced by घ; *e.g.* सिंघनी; again,

रघुगया, properly रहुगया ; it is also occasionally interchanged with ख ; e.g. केहरी, properly केखरी; and even with ख and भ; thus, बिलम्हना, properly बिलम्बना ; and सम्हालना, properly सम्भालना. Very frequently, also, and especially in poetry, it is interchanged with थ; thus, नाह, properly नाथ; and with प ; thus, कोह, properly कोप, and with व ; e.g जीह, properly जीव. One instance occurs in the *Rāmāyaṇ* in which this letter in used euphonically as a kind of fulcrum for the plural termination ; thus भौंहें = भौंहें, eyebrows.

हई, *f.* (*m.* हया) smitten, killed.

हउआ ; see (1) हवा (2) हव्वा (3) हूआ (4) हौवा.

हउदा, *more prop.* हौदा, *q.v.*

हए. *m.* (pl. of हया) smitten, killed.

हंकराना, हंकाटना } *more prop.* हंकारना, *q.v.*

हंकाटा, *m.* a shout, noise, cry, call.

हंकाना = (1) हंकारना (2) हांकना, *qq.v.*

हंकार, *m.* a cry, outcry, calling, bawling, an alarm: a driving, driving away.

हंकारना, *t.* or *a. int.* to call, bawl, halloo: to brave: *t.* to drive, drive away, expel : to hoist (as sails, etc.).

हंकारा, *more prop.* हंकार, *q.v.*

हंकारी, *m.* (*f.* iṇi) = अहंकारी, *q.v.* See अ, 18.

हंकालना (*colloquial*) = हंकारना, *q.v.*

हंगामा, *m.* an assembly, crowd ; an uproar, tumult, seditious riot; assault.—*k.* or *uṭhānā* or *machānā*, to raise a disturbance, to riot.

हंजरा, *m.* the throat, gullet, windpipe.

हंजार, *m.* a straight road ; a true method ; a mason's rule; a plumb-line, a level.

हंड, हंड़ ; for words beginning thus, see under the [form हण्ड.

हंता, *more prop.* हन्ता, *q.v.*

हंथिनी (*corruption*) = हाथिनी, *q.v.*

हंपना, *more com.* हांपना, *q.v.*

हंपनी, *f.* shortness of breath, panting, gasping.

हंपाना, *t.* (causat. of हांपना) to cause to pant or gasp, to put out of breath.

हंफना, *more com.* हांफना, *q.v.*

हंफेल, *m.* (*f.* ā) short-winded.

हंस, 1, *m.* (*f.* ī) a goose, gander, swan, drake, duck : 2, *m.* one of the vital breaths : 3, *m.* an epithet (1) of Brahm (2) of Vishṇu (3) of Shiv (4) of Kāmdev (5) of the soul (6) of the sun (7) of a devotee (8) of a liberal prince (9) of a sort of horse : 4, *m.* laughter,—*denā*, to give a smile, to laugh.

हंसक, 1, *m.* (*f.* ikā) a flamingo ; a gander: 2, *m.* a kind of ornament for the feet (made to resemble a duck's foot). [goose, graceful gait, goose-step.

हंसगमन, *m.* the moving gracefully like a swan or

हंसगमनी, हंसगवनी } = हंसगामिनी, *q. v.*

हंसगामिनी, *f.* a female with a graceful gait ; lit. *adj.* walking like a swan, *i. e.* gracefully.

हंसनियां, nom. pl. of हंसनी (हंसना).

हंसना, 1, *t.* or *a. int.* to laugh, smile, ridicule, deride, joke, make fun, (with acc.) to laugh at : 2, *m.* (*f.* i) (1) a laugher, ridiculer, jester (2) risible.

हंसनूआ, *m.* (*f.* हंसनूई) a laughingstock.

हंसपुर, *m. pr. n.* a certain city.

हंसमुख, *m.* (*f.* i) merry-faced, laughing, blithesome, cheerful, jocular, facetious, merry, jovial, jolly.

हंसराज, 1, = परेशावशान, *q.v.* : 2, a kind of rice.

हंसरूपी, goose-like. The term is used to describe an exceedingly graceful gait.

हंसली, *f.* the collar-bone, clavicle ; a collar (of gold, silver, etc.) worn as a neck-ornament.

हंसलोना, *m.* (*f.* I) humorous, jocular, waggish.

हंसहि, (pl. °हिं), हंसहो, (pl. °हीं) } poet. forms of हंसता है (हंसना).

हंसा, *m.* laughter, laughing, laugh.

हंसाई, *f.* laughter, ridicule, derision.

हंसाऊ, ridiculous, laughable.

हंसाना, *t.* to cause to laugh, to please, to tickle.

हंसाय, 1, *more prop.* हंसाई, *q.v.* : 2, see हंसाना.

हंसि, *m.* laughter. — *denā*, to laugh.

हंसिका, *f.* (*m.* हंसक) a goose ; a female flamingo.

हंसिबे (the inflected form of the old infinitive in बा or इबा) = हंसने (हंसना).

हंसिया, *m.* a reapinghook, sickle.

हंसिहहि, (pl. °हिं), हंसिहहो, (pl. °हीं) } poet. forms = हंसेगा (हंसना).

हंसिहहु (*Rām.*) = हंसोगे (हंसना).

हंसी, *f.* 1, (*m.* हंस) a female goose or swan : 2, laughter, ridicule, mockery, mirth, sport, fun, laugh : (in Pros.) a species of metre. — *k.* (with gen. fem.) to laugh at..

हंसै (pl. हंसैं) a poet form = हंसेगा (हंसना).

हंसीखुशी, *f.* merriment, hilarity.

हंसुआ, हंसूआ } *m.* a sickle, reapinghook, pruning-hook.

हंसे, *f.* laughter, mirth, fun, ridicule.

हंसोड़, facetious, humorous, jocular, cheerful, merry, waggish : hence, *m.* (*f.* in) a laugher, a wag.

हंसोड़ना, to exercise facetiousness or merriment.

हंसोड़पन, हंसोड़पना } *m.* jocularity, facetiousness.

हंस्यो, a Braj form of हंसा (हंसना).

हंहो in Māṛwāṛī = of belonging to.

हक, *more prop.* हक़्क़, *q.v.*

हक़दार, *m.* an owner, proprietor.

हकताला, *more prop.* हक़्क़तआला, *q.v.*

हकबकाना, *n.* to be confused or irresolute when anything is to be done, to be aghast.

हकम, *m.* an umpire, arbitrator, mediator.

हकमें, *more prop.* हक्कमें, *q.v.*

हकरावा, *m.* a calling, summoning. [ing.
हकला, *m.* (*f.* ī) *adj.* stuttering, stammering, lisp-
हकलाना, *a.int.* to stammer, stutter, falter. [ing.
हकलाहा, *m.* (*f.* ī) *adj.* stuttering, stammering, lisp-
हकाइक़, *f.* (pl. of **हक़ीक़त**) explanations; truths.
हकाम; see (1) **अहकाम** (2) **हुक्काम**.
हकार, *m.* the letter **ह**, or any character that may express the sound of it. [(as when treading out corn).
हकारना, *t.* to drive oxen or other cattle in a circle
हकालना = **हकारना**, *q.v.*
हक़ीक़त, *f.* account, narration, relation, explanation; reality, truth, sincerity. [tain, accurate, just; own.
हक़ीक़ी, true, veritable, unmistakeable, real, cer-
हकीम, *m.* a sage, philosopher; a physician, doctor.
हकीमी, *f.* the practice of medicine, doctoring.
हक़ीर, contemptible, vile; lean, thin.
हक़्क़, right, correct, true, just: hence, *m.* the truth rectitude, justice, equity; righteous due; the Deity.
हक़्क़तआला, *m.* an epithet of the Most High God.
हक़्क़ुभेंट, *f.* presents of ceremony made by inferiors or suppliants to officers in authority.
हक़्क़ुमें, *postp.* (takes gen. *m.* infl.) with respect to, concerning, about. [a lapidary.
हक्काक, *m.* a cutter and polisher of precious stones,
हक्काबक्का, *m.* (*f.* **हक्कीबक्की**) confused when anything is to be done, aghast.
हगवड़ा, *m.* (*f.* ī) defiled with excrement.
हगना, *a.int.* to go to stool, evacuate, mute, dung (said of birds).
हगनेटी, *f.* any place (as a field, etc.) to which people resort to evacuate: the anus, rectum.
हगनैटी = **हगनेटी**, *q.v.* [excrement.
हगभरना, *a.int.* to go to stool: *n.* to be defiled with
हगवान, *m.* flux, purging, diarrhœa. [ate, to purge.
हगाना, *t.* to cause to go to stool, cause to evacu-
हगास, *f.* inclination to evacuate, tenesmus.
हगासीबत्तख़, a restless fidgetting person.
हचका, *m.* a shock, jog, jolt (as of a carriage, etc.).
हचकोला = **हचका**, *q.v.*
हचरमचर, *m.* a dispute, cavil, excuse.
हच्चिदानन्द, *more prop.* **सच्चिदानन्द**, *q.v.*
हज, *more prop.* **हज्ज**, *q.v.*
हजब, *m.* interposing, secluding, fencing round.
हज़म, *m.* digestion.—*k.* to digest: *met.* to embezzle.
हजर, *m.* a stone: hindrance, prohibition: (in Law) annulment: disjunction.
हज़रत, *f.* presence, dignity, majesty. The term is addressed, as a title, to the great = Majesty, Excellency, Eminence, Grace, Holiness.
हजानत, *f.* the bringing up children in the Muhammadan faith. [the entire head).
हजामत, *f.* cupping, scarifying, shaving (*esp.* of
हज़ार, *m.* a thousand: a kind of bird.

हज़ारहां (see **हां**, 2) } in Urdoo = **सहस्रों**, *q.v.*
हज़ारों (see **ओं**, 4) }
हज़ारीबाग़, *m.* an orchard (or garden) of a thousand trees. The name of a certain city in Bihār (usually termed Hāzribāg or Hauzreebaugh).
हजू = **हजो**, *q. v.*
हजूर, *more pvop.* **हुज़ूर**, *q.v.* [lampoon.
हजो, *f.* satire, a lampoon, pasquinade.—*k.* to
हजोड़ा, *m.* (*f.* ī) a satirist.
हज्ज, *m.* the act of moving round or going to a place; pilgrimage to Mecca.
हज्जाम, *m.* a cupper, scarificer, shaver.
हज्जी; see **हज्ज** and **हाजी**.
हट, 1, a corruption of **हठ**, *q. v.*: 2, this particle (added to substantives, adjectives, or the roots of verbs) forms many abstract substantives feminine.
हटकना, *n.* to be repulsed, be driven back: *a. int.* to move, retreat, boggle, stop. *Haṭak rahanā*, to refrain. *Man*—, to have a misgiving. [prevent.
हटकाना, *t.* to cause to retreat, to hinder, stop,
हटकाहटकी, *f.* a driving back, a struggling.
हटताल, *f.* (**हाट** + **ताला**) the shutting up all the shops in a market (on account of oppression, etc.).
हटना, *a.int.* to fall back, get out of the way, retire, move, shrink, recoil, budge, retreat, return, recede, be driven back, be defeated; *hence*, to go back, fall away from virtue, backslide, apostatize. *Haṭ jānā*, to get out of the way, remove, retire. *Haṭ haṭke*, *adv.* again and again, repeatedly, often, oftentimes: obstinately.
हटवा, *m.* (*f.* in or ī) a person employed in a market or fair to measure rice, grain, etc., a market-man.
हटवाई, *f.* the office, the functions, or the wages [of a *haṭwā*.
हटाऊ, *m.* or *f.* marketable.
हटाकटा, *m.* (*f.* **हटीकटी**) stout and active, vigorous, robust.
हटाना, *t.* to cause to recede, to drive back, repel, move, remove, take out of the way, put back, put aside, back, worst, foil. *Haṭā denā*, to repel, repulse.
हटाव, *m.* a falling back, retreating, flinching, repulse, repulsion, removal, dismission.
हटिया, *m.* a market, fair.
हटीला } *m.* (*f.* ī) *more prop.* **हठीला**, *q.v.*
हटेला }
हट्ट, *m.* a market, moveable market, fair.
हट्टा, *m.* a large wooden shovel or ladle for watering fields from aqueducts.
हट्टाकट्टा = **हटाकटा**, *q.v.* [a sheepfold, pen, pound.
हट्टी, a petty market or fair: a flock, herd, drove:
हट्टर, *m.* hurry, impatience.
हठ, 1, *m.* violence, oppression, repine: a certain plant (*Pistia stratiotes*); 2, *f.* perverseness, refractoriness, obstinacy, unpersuadeableness, disobedience, crossness: teasing: pet, displeasure: allegation.—*k.* or *ki ṭekpar honā*, to resist or disobey through obstinacy, to be perverse, be peevish.
हठधर्मी, *m.* (*f.* iṇī) perverse, obstinate.

हठना, *n.* to be peevish, be perverse, be pettish : to importune, dun. *Haṭh-haṭh ke*, obstinately.

ह ठस, under the influence of a refractory disposition.

हठयाहा, *m.* (*f.* in *or* ī) = **हटवा**, *q. v.*

हठसील, of a refractory disposition.

हठात, by force; by chance; by surprize, unawares, suddenly, immediately, forthwith, instantly.

हठी, 1, *m.* (*f.* inī) peevish, obstinate, perverse, pettish : 2, *f.* a certain plant (*Pistia stratiotes*).

हठीला, *m.* (*f.* ī) teasing, tiresome ; pettish, perverse, obstinate, peevish, humoursome.

हठीले, *m.* a certain class of reputed saints (one of whom is buried at Barech).

हठुआ, *m.* (*f.* **हठुई**) = **हटवा**, *q. v.*

हड, *m.* a bone.—*phūṭnā*, to make progress, advance, promote.

हड़, 1, *m.* the stocks, bilboes : a bone : 2, *f.* a kind of nut (*Myrobalan*) ; a kind of ornament resembling that nut.

हड़ंगा, ruination, destruction, ruin.

हड़ंबा, *more prop.* **हिड़म्बा**, *q.v.*

हड़कत, *m.* a certain plant (*Acanthus ilicifolius*).

हड़काना, *t.* to estrange.

हड़खंगखारी, *m.* (*f.* iṇī) scraggy.

हड़गिला, *m.* (*f.* ī) = **हड़गीला**, *q. v.*

हड़गीला, *m.* (*f.* ī) ossivorous : *hence*, the gigantic crane (*Ardea argala*).

हड़जोड़ = **हड़जोड़ा**, *q.v.*

हड़जोड़ा, *m.* a certain medicinal plant (*Cissus quadrangularis*).

हड़ड़ा = **हर्रा**, *q. v.*

हड़डि, *more prop.* **हड्डी**, *q. v.*

हड़फूटन, *m.* pains in the bones, rheumatics, lassitude.

हड़बड़ाना, *a. int.* to be in a hurry, be precipitate, be confused : *t.* perplex, confuse.

हड़बड़िया, easily agitated, irritable, hasty, precipitate.

हड़बड़ी, *f.* hurry, haste, precipitation, rashness, hastiness, prematureness, disorder, confusion, confusedness, alarm, uproar, hurly-burly, pother, hubbub, riot, mutiny.— *k.* to hurry.—*uṭhānā*, to pother, create a hubbub.

हड़बैर, *m.* rancour.

हड़माला, *f.* the science of osteology.

हड़म्बा, *more prop.* **हिड़म्बा**, *q. v.*

हड़वाड़, *m.* a place where bones are laid, an ossuary, charnel-house.

हड़वार = **हड़वाड़**, *q.v.*

हड़हड़ाना, *a. int.* to shudder, shiver ; to rumble, rustle, rattle, crash : to hurry.

हड़हड़ाहट, *f.* a crash, crack, sound.

हड़हड़ी, *f.* the twang of a bow; hurry.

हड़ा, 1, *m.* a sky-rocket: 2, a kind of nut (*Myrobalan*.

हड़ावर ; see (1) **हड़वार** (2) **हरावल**.

हड़ाहड़ी, *f.* the twang of a bow.

हड्डा, *m.* a wasp: a bone; an osselet or ossicle, spavin. *Haḍḍe mothre nikālnā*, to break out in spavins and œdematous swellings : *met.* to adopt an evil course of conduct. *Gurgik ī—*, the kneepan.

हड्डा, *more prop.* **हर्रा**, *q. v.*

हड्डिया, *f.* an osselet or ossicle.

हड्डियाना, *a. int.* to ossify.

हड्डियाहट, *f.* ossification.

हड्डी, *f.* a bone: the hard part in the centre of a carrot or other similar root.

हड्डीला, *m.* (*f.* ī) full of bones, bony.

हड्डीसा, *m.* (*f.* ī) bonelike, osseous. *Haḍḍīsī ho jānā*, to ossify.

हण्डा, *m.* an earthen pot or boiler, a caldron : a species of grass.—*phornā*, to break the pot, *i.e.* to disclose a secret, let the cat out of the bag.

हण्डाना, *t.* to banish, expel, drive out of a city, disgrace by public banishment or by public exposure on an ass's back: to move around.

हण्डाभाड़ा, *m.* contract for the transportation of goods (including the payment of duties).

हण्डिका / **हण्डिया** } *f.* = **हण्डी**, *q. v.*

हण्डी, *f.* (dim. of **हण्डा**) a small earthen boiler or pot for boiling meat, etc.

हण्डोला = **हिण्डोला**, *q.v.*

हत, 1, *m.* (in Arithm.) multiplication : 2, begone! fie ; 3, this particle (added to substantives, adjectives, and the roots of verbs) forms many abstract substantives feminine : 4, this particle is sometimes interchanged inaccurately with **हथ** ; for all words, therefore, beginning with it, but not given below, see under those beginning with this latter form.

हतत्तक, a blow with the open hand, a slap.

हतन, *m.* the act of slaying.

हतना, *t.* to slaughter, slay, kill.

हता, *m.* (*f.* ī) slain, killed, murdered.

हते, *more com.* **हुते**, *q. v.*

हतेरीबतेरी, *f.* a prostitute.

हतोटी, *f.* an anvil; a hammer.

हतोड़ा, *m.* an anvil ; a sledge-hammer.

हतोड़ी, *f.* an anvil ; a hammer.

हत्तर (in compos.) = **सत्तर** ; *e.g.* **बहत्तर**.

हत्ता ; see (1) **हट्टा** (2) **हता**.

हत्थ in Chand = **हाथ**, *q. v.*

हत्य, *m.* / **हत्या**, *f.* } killing, slaughter, murder.

हत्याई, *f.* murder, slaughter, violence.

हत्यारा, murderous, bloodthirsty, bloody, inhuman : hence, *m.* (*f.* ī) a murderer, assassin, villain, wretch.

हत्यौ in Braj = (1) **हता** (2) **हता हुआ** (**हतना**).

हथ, 1, a contraction of **हाथ**, used as the former member of compound words : 2, *m.* a man in despondency.

हथकटी, *f.* a kind of stroke with the sword intended to take off or to disable the adversary's hand.

हथकड़ा, *m.* 1, = **हथकड़ी**, *q.v.* : 2, anything to hold fast by, a holdfast, handle, ring, hook, the handle of a shield.—*rakhnā*, to lead by the nose, lead one nolens volens.

हथकड़ी, *f.* handcuffs, manacles ; *met.* a leading-string —*denā* or *lagānā*, to handcuff, manacle.

हथलपका, *m.* custom, habit, knack, readiness: handicraft, profession. [handcuff, manacle.

हथखोड़, *m.* handcuffs, manacles.—*lagānā*, to

हथगाड़ी, *f.* a hand-barrow, wheel-barrow.

हथचक्की, *f.* a small handmill, a quern.

हथचल; see **हाथचलना**.

हथचपूआ, *m.* a snack, share.

हथचिठा, a note of hand, a receipt.

हथकूट, *m.* a beater, one who beats: a missile.

हथझोला, *m.* a hand-barrow.

हथटोकरी, *f.* a hand-basket, a hamper.

हथनाल, *f.* a small cannon carried on elephants, etc.

हथनी, *f.* (**हस्तिनी**) a she-elephant.

हथफूल, *m.* a kind of firework.

हथफेर, *m.* palmistry, legerdemain, sleight of hand (*esp.* in money-changers, who substitute bad money for good and insist on returning it to the customer): borrowing.—*denā*, to borrow.

हथफेरी, *f.* = **हथफेर**, *q.v.*

हथबन्धा, *m.* (*f.* ī) handcuffed, manacled.

हथबली, *f.* strength (of hand); force; dishonesty.

हथबेड़ी, *f.* handcuffs, manacles.—*lagānā*, to handcuff, manacle.

हथमार, *m.* or *f.* a pilferer.

हथयार, *more prop.* **हथियार**, *q.v.*

हथरस, *m.* toying, amorous dalliance: onanism; the itch.

हथरी, *f.* a handle; a winch of a spinning-wheel.

हथल, *m.* a metallic handle (of drawers, etc.).

हथलप, a light-fingered person, filcher.

हथलेवा, *m.* a kind of ceremony in Hindoo marriage. The hands of the couple are joined palm to palm with some flour put between them, when they are tied with a red thread.

हथवासहु, an emphat. form of **हथवासा**, *q.v.*

हथवासा, *m.* a handle (of drawers, etc.), that part of the beam of scales that remains in the hand.

हथा, *m.* a handle; the handle of a wheel, mill, etc; a ladle; a scoop; a baker's peel; a shovel; a sleeve.—*mārnā*, to pilfer.

हथाई, *f.* a meeting, assembly.

हथापेंची, *f.* a scuffle.

हथाबांहे, *f.* a set-to at fisticuffs.

हथामोरी, *f.* a romping, romp.

हथाहथी, *f.* a scuffle: *adv.* hand in hand.

हथिनी, *f.* (**हस्तिनी**) a she-elephant.

हथिया, *m.* the breaking up of the rains: *pr. n.* Corvus or the 13th Nakshatra.—*kī rāh*, the Milky-way.

हथियाना, *t.* to lay hands on, seize, occupy; to purloin, pilfer, to pocket.

हथियार, *m.f.*? a tool, apparatus, implements, arms, an offensive weapon; *met.* membrum virile.—*bāndhnā*, to arm, equip.

हथियारबन्द / **हथियारबन्ध** } armed, accoutred, equipped.

हथी, *f.* a rubber, hair-glove, brush for rubbing down horses with.

हथोना, *m.* (*f.* ī) handy.

हथोनी, *f.* the handle of a plough.

हथेबाज़, *m.* (*f.* nī) a peculator, pilferer.

हथेमार, a filcher.

हथेला, *m.* (*f.* ī) a pilferer, thief, robber.

हथेली, *f.* the palm of the hand, or an impression of it; a handful.

हथोड़ा, *m.* a hammer, large hammer, sledge-hammer.

हथोड़ी, *f.* (dim.) a small hammer.

हथोटिया, handy, skilful, dexterous.

हथोटी, 1, *f.* dexterity, skill, art; operation; handicraft, handiwork: 2, *m.* (*f.* inī) a person who does some work, a 'hand', a master-hand: 3, mechanical.

हथौड़ा, *m.* a hammer, large hammer, sledge-hammer.

हथौड़ियाना, *t.* to beat with a hammer, to hammer.

हथौड़ी, *f.* (dim.) a small hammer.

हथ्थ in Chand = **हाथ**, *q.v.*

हथ्याई, *f.* violence, slaughter, murder.

हद, *more prop* **हद्द**, *q.v.*

हदयारु, *m.* a kind of thumb-ring.

हदस, *m.* anything existing for the first time, a novelty, event, contingency: an accidental cause of impurity (according to Muhammadan traditions) whereby it becomes unlawful to commence or finish a prayer without previously undergoing ablution.

हदिया, *m.* the price of a copy of the Kur,ān.—*k.* to sell the Kur,ān, to sell scripture.

हदियाना, *a. int.* to hesitate, shrink, scruple, be apprehensive.

हदियाहट, *f.* hesitation, scrupulousness, apprehensiveness, coyness, shyness, sheepishness.

हदियाहा, *m.* (*f.* ī) hesitant, scrupulous, apprehensive, timid, coy, bashful, shy, sheepish.

हदी, *f.* cattle carried to Mecca to be sacrificed: a bride: a captive: *adj.* given as an offering.

हदीस, *m.* a history, a tradition (*esp.* the traditional sayings of Muhammad, which now bear the force of Laws).—*k.* to forswear, abjure, renounce.

हद्द, 1, *f.* a boundary, limit; precinct, pale; degree, pitch; an impediment; a definition; a starting-post; punishment agreeably to the laws of Muhammad, which fix the exact number of lashes, etc. to be awarded for certain crimes: 2, *m.* breaking, demolishing, ruining.

हद्दबन्दी, *f.* limitation, restriction.

हन, (in Comp.) *m.* (*f.* **हनी** or **घ्नी**) *adj.* killing: *hence*, a slaughterer, murderer.

हनत, *m.* (*f.* ā) striken, injured, slain.

हनन, *m.* a striking, injuring, hurting, destroying, killing: (in Arithm.) multiplication.

हननशील, *m.* (*f.* ā) cruel, murderous.

हनना, *t.* to smite, strike, murder, kill.

हनमत (*dialectic*) = **हनुमत** = **हनुमान**, *q. v.*

हनस, *more prop.* **हलस**, *q.v.* See **ल**, 4 (2).

हनान, a colloquial form of **स्नान**, *q.v.*

हनि, an old conjunct. part. of **हनना**, *q.v.*

हनु, 1, *m. f.* the jaw: 2, *f.* a weapon: sickness: death: a sort of vegetable perfume.
हनुफाल, *m.* (in Pros.) a species of metre.
हनुमत / **हनुमन्त** } *m.* (*f.* matī) = **हनुमान**, *q. v.*
हनुमान large-jawed: hence, *m.* (*f.* matī) a monkey, baboon: a miser; *pr. n.* the monkey-god or chief who acted as leader, ally, and spy to Rāmchandra in his march against Rāvaṇ at the invasion of Lankā.
हनू, 1, *f.* the jaw: 2, *m. pr. n.* Hanūmān.
हनूमान, *m.* (*f.* matī) = **हनुमान**, *q. v.*
हनूमानी, appertaining to Hanūmān.
हनें (*Rām.*) pl. of **हना** (**हनना**).
हन्तव्य, *m.* (*f.* ā) fit to be killed, deserving death.
हन्ता, *m* (*f.* trī) a striker, injurer, murderer, slayer, a thief, robber, assassin: *lit.* killing, mortal, murderous.
हन्तु, *m.* death: a bull.
हन्तृ, *m.* (*f.* trī) = **हन्ता**, *q. v.*
हना, 1, = **हनना**, *q. v.*: 2, *m.* the pommel of a saddle.
हन्विनी, *more prop.* **हथिनी**, *q. v.*
हन्दा, *m.* (*f.* **हन्दी**); this is one of the case-signs of of the genitive in Mārwāṛī Hindee.
हप, *m.* the act of suddenly snapping with the mouth and then swallowing.
हपकना, *a. int.* to wonder, marvel.
हपझप, quick. — *khānā*, to eat quickly and voraciously. [munch.
हपराना, *a. int.* to munch. *Haparāke khānā*, to
हपुषा, *f.* a certain substance forming an article of trade and having the smell of raw meat or fish. It is said to be of two kinds, is commonly called *Habush*, and is said to be of a long form and black colour.
हफ़तपहलू, septilateral: hence, *m.* a heptagon.
हफ़्ता, *m.* a week, seven days.
हफदफाना, *a. int.* to gasp, pant.
हबक्कूक, *m. pr. n.* the prophet Habbakuk and the Book that bears his name.
हबड़ा, *m.* (*f.* ī) ill-shapen, clumsy.
हबल, *m.* a rope; a tendon; a compact.
हबश, *m.* the people or race of Abyssinia.
हबशत = **हबशा**, *q. v.*
हबशन, *f.* (*m.* **हबश**) = **हबशिनी**, *q. v.*
हबशानी = **हबशिनी**, *q. v.* [southern Arabia.
हबशा, *m.* Ethiopia, people of Ethiopia, people of
हबशिन = **हबशिनी**, *q. v.*
हबशिनी, *f.* (*m.* **हबशी**) an Abyssinian female, Ethiopian woman, female Caffre, negress, female slave.
हबशी, appertaining to Abyssinia or its people: hence, *m.* (*f.* ini) an Abyssinian, Ethiopian, African, Caffre; a moor, negro, slave. [teething)
हबाड़बा, *m.* convulsions (in children, *esp.* when
हबि, *more prop.* **हवि**, *q. v.*
हबेली, *more prop.* **हवेली**, *q. v.*
हब्बा, *m.* one berry, one grain, one seed; a pill; a particle, a part; a measure = two barleycorns.
हब्बाडब्बा, *m.* the whooping-cough, chincough.
हब्बिय / **हब्बो** } in Chand = **हाव**, *q. v.*
हम, (pl. of **मैं**) pers. pron. of the 1st pers. pl. = we.
हमकार, *m.* egotism.
हमकारना, to egotize.
हमजम, a friend, intimate.
हमते in Braj = **हमसे**. See **ते**, 3.
हमदा, *m.* apoplexy. [sia, north-west of Ispahan.
हमदान, *m. pr. n.* a certain town and district of Per-
हमन (*dialectic*) = (1) **हम** (2) **हमारा** (3) **हमें**, *qq. v.*
हमना / **हमनां** } (*dialectic*) = **हमें**, *q. v.*
हमनी in Bhojpurī = **हम**, *q. v.*
हमनींका, in Bhojpurī = **हमारा**, *q. v.*
हमनीके, in Bhojpurī = **हमें**, *q. v.*
हमनींसे in Bhojpurī = **हमसे**, *q. v.*
हमने (the agentive or instrumental case of **हम**) = by us, *i. e.* through the agency or instrumentality of us.
हमर (*contraction*) = **हमारा**, *q. v.*
हमरा, *m.* (*f.* ī) a contraction of **हमारा**, *q. v.*
हमराके in Bhojpurī = **हमें**, *q. v.*
हमरासें / **हमरासों** } in Bhojpurī = **हमसे**.
हमराही, 1, *f.* companionship in travelling: 2, *m.* (*f.* iṇī) a travelling-companion, fellow-traveller.
हमरी (*contraction*) = **हमारी**, *q. v.*
हमरो / **हमरौ** } in Braj = **हमारा**, *q. v.*
हमल, *m.* a load, burden; fruit; the fruit of the womb, pregnancy: *pr. n.* the sign Aries. — *k.* to load, impute, accuse, ascribe.—*honā*, to be enceinte.
हमला, *m.* an attack, onset, assault, storming: *fig.* [concubitus.
हमसन (*Rām.*) = **हमसे**, *q. v.*
हमसाया, *m.* a neighbour; neighbourhood.
हमसे, by (with, or from) us. See **हम**.
हमसों / **हमसौं** } in Braj = **हमसे**, *q. v.*
हमहिं = (1) **हम भी** (2) **हमें**. See **हिं**.
हमहूं = **हम भी**. See **हूं**, 3.
हमातम, *m.* contest, competition, rivalry, equality, matching, equalling, evenness.
हमातमी, *f.* = **हमातम**, *q. v.*
हमादानी, *f.* the knowing everything, omniscience.
हमाम, *m.* a mortar for pounding in: a pigeon.
हमार (*contraction*) = **हमारा**, *q. v.*
हमारा, (gen. of **हम**) *m.* (*f.* ī) of us, our, ours.
हमारो (*colloquial*) = **हमारा**, *q. v.*
हमारोई in Braj = **हमाराही**. See **ई**, 4.
हमारौ in Braj = **हमारा**, *q. v.*
हमाल, like, equal, alike, resembling: coëval, co-

temporary: hence, *m.* (*f.* ā) an equal, comrade, companion, associate

हमियानी, *f.* a purse.

हमीं, we ourselves, we even, even we.

हमीद, *m.* (*f.* ā) praised, laudable, glorious.

हमीन, this very, even this, even so; only, solely, neither more nor less.

हमें, (dat. and acc. of **हम**) to us, us. — *kyā, jāne do*, (*lit.* what is it to us? let it go: *hence*) never mind, no matter.

हमेव, *m.* egotism, vanity, arrogance, pride.

हमेशा, always, perpetually, continually, ever.

हमैं / **हमैं** } in Braj = **हमें**, *q.v.*

हम्पल्ला, *m.* (*f.* ī) equidistant.

हम्बे, yes.

हम्माम, *m.* a warm bath, a bagnio.

हम्माल, *m.* (*f.* ā) a porter, carrier, pālkī-bearer.

हम्यानी, *f.* a purse.

हय, 1, *more prop.* **है**, *q.v.*: 2, *m.* (*f.* ī) a horse; the yak: 3, *m.* a man of a particular tribe: an epithet of Indra.

हयगन्धा, *f.* a certain plant (*Physalis flexuosa*).

हयगय, *m.* (in Chand) horses and elephants.

हयगृह, *m.* a horse-repository, a stable.

हयग्रीव, *m pr. n.* a certain demon-prince who (during Brahmā's sleep at the end of a *kalp*) stole the Veds. In order to recover them, Vishnu assumed the form of a fish (*Matsya-avatār*) and slew this demon.

हयप्रधान, *m.* (*f.* ā) a chief horse; a chief horseman, master of horse.

हयवर, *m.* (*f.* ā *or* ī) a war-horse, charger.

हयशाला, *f.* a horse-repository, a stable.

हया, 1, *more prop.* (1) **हय** (2) **हिया**, *qq.v.*: 2, *m.* (*f.* **हई**) smitten, killed, murdered: 3, *f.* shame, modesty.

हयात, *f.* life.

हयाशना, *f.* the gum-olibanum tree. [yak: a mare.

हयी, 1, *more prop.* **हई**, *q.v.*: 2, *f.* (*m.* **हय**) the female

हयोबंस / **हयोवंस** } *more prop.* **हयोवंश**, *q.v.*

हयोवंश, *m.* a certain tribe of Rājpūts in the province of Benares.

हर, 1, a colloquial form of **हल**, *q.v.*: 2, *adj.* taking, seizing, depriving of, carrying: 3, *m.* a rogue, wag: an ass: (in Arithm.) division. a divisor. the denominator of a fraction: 4, *m.* an epithet (1) of Mahādev (2) of Agni: 5, every, each, all and every.—*kahīṅ*, everywhere, wherever. — *din* or *roz*, every day, day by day, daily.

हरएक, each, every, each and every, every one.

हरक, 1, *m.* (*f.* ikī) a taker, seizer; a rogue; a person of reflection: 2, *m.* an epithet of Mahādev: (in Arithm.) division, a divisor.

हरकट, cutting rice while it is green and unripe.

हरकत, *f.* motion, gesture, action, procedure, conduct: prevention, hindrance. [scorched.

हरकाना, 1, *a. int.* to stop: to remove: 2, *n.* to be

हरका, *m.* a crying, whining.

हरकाना, *t.* to stop, prevent, forbid: to scorch.

हरकारा, *m.* a running footman, courier, messenger, emissary, scout, spy; a factotum.

हरकिया, *m. f.* snappish, peevish. [form **हर्ष**.

हरख; for words beginning thus, see under the

हरगिज़, ever, at any time, on any account.

हरगिरि, *m.* an epithet of mount *Kailās*.

हरगीला, *more com.* **हड़गीला**, *q.v.* [every quality.

हरगुणी, *m.* (*f.* inī) skilful, clever: *lit.* possessing

हरगुनी / **हरगूनी** } *more prop.* **हरगुणी**, *q.v.*

हरगौरि, Mahādev and his consort Pārvatī.

हरघसोट, all the cultivated land of a village.

हरचन्द, whensoever, howsoever, as often as, although. [Divine Being.

हरचरण, *m.* an epithet of the blessed feet of the

हरजाई, *m.* (*f.* inī) = **हरजायी**, *q.v.*

हरजाना, an intensive form of **हरना**, 3, *q.v.*

हरजायी, *m.* (*f.* inī) one who goes gadding about, a stroller, vagabond, vagrant. The term (even in its masculine form) is very generally applied to a female street-walker (like the English expression 'common prostitute').

हरट (*by inversion*) = **रहट**, *q.v.* [Brāhmaṇs.

हरटकुन, *m.* one of the sub-divisions of the Gaur

हरण, 1, *more prop.* **हरिण**, *q.v.*: 2, *m.* taking, seizing, carrying off, rape, removing, stealing, withholding, annulling, disregarding, accepting; the hand, the arm; subtraction, abstraction; (in Arithm.) division, dividing; *semen virile*: gold: boiling water. — *k.* to divide; to seize, plunder.

हरणदुःख, *m.* (*f.* ā) *adj.* taking away or dissipating pain, trouble, or grief.

हरणा, *more prop.* (1) **हरण** (2) **हरना**, *qq.v.*

हरणी, *more prop.* **हरिणी**, *q.v.*

हरता, 1, *m* (*f.* trī) = **हर्ता**, *q.v.*: 2, *m.* (*f.* ī) taken away, kidnapped, spoiled, captivated, charmed.

हरताल, *more prop.* **हरिताल**, *p.v.*

हरति (*Rām.*) = **हरती** (**हरता**, 2).

हरद, *f.* turmeric (*Cucurma longa*). [(in corn).

हरदा, 1, *more prop.* **हृदय**, *q.v.*: 2, *m.* mildew, smut

हरदावल, a kind of defect in horses.

हरदिन, *more prop.* **हर दिन**. See *s. v.* **हर**.

हरदी, *more prop.* (1) **हलदी** (2) **हृदय**, *qq.v.*

हरदुवास, *m.* a certain class of Rājpūts.

हरदेहा, a certain tribe of Hindoos. [**हरिद्वार**.

हरद्वार, *m. pr. n.* the town of Hardwār: but see *s.v.*

हरन (*colloquial*) = (1) **हरण** (2) **हरिण**, *q.v.*

हरनबाड़ी, *f.* a house of correction, a penitentiary; *lit.* a fold or enclosure for antelopes.

हरना, 1, a Prākṛit form of **हरिण**, *q.v.*: 2, *m.* the pommel of a saddle: 3, *t.* to size hold of, take by force, take away, kidnap, steal, plunder, spoil, destroy; to captivate, charm, bewitch.

हरनाम, *m.* an epithet of the Almighty.

हरनाहरनी, *pr. n.* the constellation Gemini.

हरनी 1, (*colloquial*) = **हरिणी**, *q.v.*: 2, a fem. form of the verb **हरना**, *q.v.*

हरनौटा, *m.* a fawn.

हरन्हार, *m.* (*f.* in, ī, nī) a filcher.

हरपूजी, *f.* the worship of the plough (a ceremony held on the day on which ploughing closes, when the plough is washed and decorated with garlands: to use or to lend it after this day is deemed unlucky).

हरफ़ = **हर्फ़**, *q.v.*

हरफरौरी, *f.* a certain sour kind of fruit (*Averrhoa acida*, Linn.; *Cicca disticha*, Gmel.; *Phyllanthus longifolius*, Jacq.; *Phyllanthus cheramela*, Roxb.) commonly called the 'Indian gooseberry.'

हरफारेवड़ी = **हरफरौरी**, *q.v.*

हरबरा, *m.* chick-pea (*Cicer arietinum*).

हरबोंग, *m.* anarchy, confusion, uproar: *pr. n.* a certain very foolish *rājā* or king-noodle, said to have flourished at one time at Jhoonsie (also called *Harbhongpūr*) near Allahabad: he is proverbial for his stupidity and misrule: whence the phrase *Harbong kā rāj* is applied to signify civil disorder and mal-administration in general.

हरभरा, *m.* / **हरभरी**, *f.* = **हरबरा**, *q.v.*

हरभूम / **हरभंग** / **हरभोग** = **हरबोंग**, *q.v.*

हरम, sacred, forbidden: hence, (1) *m. pr. n.* the sacred inclosure of the temple of Mecca (2) *f.* a concubine, wife, daughter; female apartments, harem, seraglio.

हरमुष्टा, *m.* (*f.* ī) stout, robust, active.

हरमुष्टी, *f.* robustness; thick-headedness.

हरया; see **हरिया**.

हरयाला, *m.* (*f.* ī) = **हरियाला**, *q.v.*

हरयाली = **हरियाली**, *q.v.*

हररोज़, *more prop.* **हर रोज़**. See *s.v.* **हर**.

हरला = **हर्रा**, *q.v.*

हरलोक, *m.* an epithet of this present world (as distinguished from the world to come), but more especially of mount Kailās in the Himālayas which is believed to be the abode of Mahādev.

हरलोकपरलोक, *m.* this world and the world to come.

हरवल, advances without interest (made to ploughmen).

हरवा, *m.* (*f.* ī) a kind of bird (the green pigeon?).

हरवाणि, *f.* the voice of God, an oracle.

हरवाना, *m.* a hospital: pain, torture, the rack.

हरवाहा, *m.* (*f.* in *or* ī) an agricultural bondsman, a ploughman.

हरवैया, *m.* a loser.

हरष (*colloquial*) = **हर्ष**, *q.v.*

हरषत (*Rām.*) = (1) **हर्षता है** (2) **हर्षित**, *qq.v.*

हरषानी, *f.* (*Rām.*) = **हर्षना**, *q.v.*

हरषाहि, (pl. °**हिं**) / **हरषाही**, (pl. °**हीं**) poet. forms = **हर्षाता है** (**हर्षाना**).

हरषि = **हर्षके** (**हर्षना**). See **क**, 7.

हरषित, *m.* (*f.* ā) = **हर्षित**, *q.v.*

हरस, 1, a Prākrit form of **हर्ष**, *q.v.*: 2, = **हरिस**, *q.v.*

हरसज्जा, 1, *m.* reciprocal aid in ploughing a field: 2, *m.* (*f.* ī) a sharer in a plough.

हरसाल, *adv.* every year, year by year.

हरसिंगार, *m.* the weeping nyctanthes (*Nyctanthes arbor tristis*) and its flower.

हरसोत, *f.* the first furrow ploughed, the first ploughing of the season, affording assistance in ploughing, the bringing home the plough.

हरसोतिया = **हरसोत**, *q.v.*

हरहटगी, unsettled, discontented, unsatisfied.

हरहा, *m.* stray oxen; unbroken and vicious cattle; plough-bullocks.

हरहाई, *f.* unsettledness, discontentedness, unsatisfiedness.

हरहिय (*Rām.*) = **हरका हृदय**, *qq.v.* See **हिय**.

हरा, *m.* (*f.* ī) 1, = **हरता**, 2, *q.v.*: 2, green, verdant, fresh; gladsome.

हराई, 1, *more prop.* **हलाई**, *q.v.*: 2, *f.* greenness, verdure, freshness; gladsomeness.

हरांस, female nature, feminality.

हरातर, any place where ploughs are working for a day.

हराती, appertaining to a plough.

हराना, *t.* (causat. of **हारना**) to cause to be defeated, to put *hors de combat*, to overcome, prevail, defeat, win, overthrow, conquer, beat, foil, worst, outface, outwit, weary, tire.

हरापन, *m.* greenness, freshness, verdure.

हराभरा, *m.* (*f.* **हरीभरी**) overgrown.

हराम, unlawful, wrong, forbidden, sacred. — *kā māl*, good-for-nothing. — *khānā*, to subsist on the wages of iniquity. — *rakhnā*, to prohibit, to deem a thing sacred or forbidden.

हरामकार, *m.* (*f.* in *or* nī) a fornicator.

हरामकारी, *f.* forbidden acts (*esp.* adultery or fornication).

हरामख़ोर, *m.* one who subsists on the wages of iniquity.

हरामज़ादा, unlawfully begotten; *hence*, a bastard. Generally used as a term of abuse, like our 'rogue,' 'scoundrel,' etc.

हरामज़ादी, *f* a wicked woman, a strumpet, a jade.

हरामज़ादगी, *f.* roguery, rascality. — *k.* to abuse, to ill-treat.

हरामी, *m.* (*f.* inī) a rogue, robber, assassin.

हराया, *m.* (*f.* **हराई**) defeated, foiled, etc.

हरारत, *f.* heat; a burning fever; warmth, zeal.

हराव, *m.* defeat (at games, etc.).

हरावल, *m.* the advanced guard of an army, the vanguard.

हरासा, *m.* (*f.* **हरीसी**) greenish. See **सा**.

हरास, sorrow, affliction, grief.

हरि, green; tawny; yellow: hence, *m.* green; tawny; yellow (the colours); the sun, the moon, a ray of light, fire, wind, a horse, a lion, a parrot, the Indian cuckoo, a peacock, a goose, an ape, a frog, a snake; (in Pros.) a species of metre; one of the divisions (*varsh*) into which the continent is divided: an epithet (1) of Vishṇu or Krishṇ 2) of Shiv (3) of Brahmā (4) of Indra (5) of Yam.

हरिअर, the close of the sowing-season.

हरिअवतार, *m.* either of the incarnations of the Hindo › Mythology.

हरिआली, *more com.* हरियाली, *q.v.*

हरिइच्छा, *more prop.* हरोच्छा, *q v.*

हरिकथा, *f.* the story of the incarnation of Vishṇu.

हरिकीर्त्ति, *f.* = हरियश, *q.v.*

हरिगुण, *m.* the qualities of Vishṇu or of the Divine Being, divine excellences, divine attributes.

हरिचन्द, *m. pr. n.* a certain king.

हरिचन्दन, *m.* a yellow and fragrant sort of sandal-wood: saffron: moonlight: the farina of the lotus: the person of a beloved one: *pr.n.* a tree of paradise.

हरिचरण, *m.* the blessed feet of the Divine Being.

हरिचरित = हरिचरित्र, *q.v.*

हरिचर्चा, *f.* conversation or investigation of or concerning Vishṇu, religious conversation.

हरिचरित्र, *m.* the exploits or behaviour (1) of Krishṇ as the incarnation of Vishṇu (2) of *any* avatar.

हरिजन = हरिभक्त, *q.v.*

हरिजस, *more prop.* हरियश, *q.v.*

हरिजाना, *more prop.* (1) हरजाना (2) हरियान (3) हरियाना, *qq.v.*

हरिजू, (see जू, 1) a respectful form of address (in poetry and in Braj) for Mahādev.

हरिण, yellowish-white: hence, *m.* (*f.* ī) a deer, antelope, hart, stag, buck; a goose; an epithet (1) of Shiv (2) of Vishṇu.

हरिणनयनी
हरिणलोचनी } *f.* a fawn-eyed damsel.
हरिणाक्षी

हरिणी, *f.* (*m.* हरिण) a hind, doe: one of the four kinds of women (the same as *Chatriṇi*); a beautiful woman: yellow jasmine.

हरित, *m.* (*f.* tā *or* iṇī) of a green colour, verdant, fresh.

हरिताल, *m.* orpiment, yellow arsenic, ratsbane.

हरितालक, *m.* yellow orpiment: the green pigeon: theatrical decoration of the person.

हरितालिका, *f.* a sort of grass: an epithet (1) of the fourth lunar day of the month Bhādra (2) of a festival on that day.

हरिताली, *f.* bent grass: a line in the sky: a sort of creeper.

हरिताश्मन, *m.* blue vitriol: a turquoise: an emerald.

हरिदास, *m.* (*f.* ī) a devotee of Vishṇu.

हरिदेव, *m. pr. n.* the asterism Shrāvaṇ.

हरिदौर, a kind of oblong mound raised in villages and studded with flags to avert epidemics.

हरिद्रा, *f.* turmeric (*Curcuma longa*).

हरिद्वार, *m. pr.n.* the town of Haridwār (the gate of Hari) where the Ganges issues from the Himālayas and enters the plains of Hindūstān. It is (among Hindoos) one of the chief places of pilgrimage, and is vulgarly called Hurdwār. The Sannyāsis argue that it is the gate of *Shiv*, and should be spelt Hardwār; while the Vaishṇavs hold that it is the place in which ablution at the proper season leads to Vishṇu or to Vaikuṇṭ, and that it should be spelt Haridwār.

हरिन, *m.* (*f.* ī) *more prop.* हरिण, *q.v.*

हरिना, 1, *m.* (*f.* ī) = हरिण, *q.v.*: 2, see हरना.

हरिनाथ, *m.* an epithet of Vishṇu or Krishṇ: the name of several Sanskrit authors.

हरिनियां, *more prop.* हरिणियां, pl. of हरिणी.

हरिन्मणि, *m.* an emerald.

हरिपैड़ी, *f.* any landingplace dedicated to Vishṇu.

हरिप्रिया, *f.* an epithet (1) of Lakshmī (see प्रिया) (2) of the earth (3) of the *tulsi*-plant (4) of the twelfth day of the lunar fortnight.

हरिपुर, *m.* an epithet of the paradise of the Hindoos.

हरिबोल, *m.* the famous cry of 'Hari-bol.' The raising this cry is usually an indication that death is about to be inflicted on some human being, and the word is an exhortation to the person to call out the name of Vishṇu with the view of settling his last account (like our expression 'Make your peace with God').

हरिभक्त, *m.* (*f.* ā) worshipper of Vishṇu; a pious person.

हरिभक्तन, a Braj pl. of हरिभक्त. See न, 6.

हरिभक्ति, *f.*
हरिभजन, *m.* } the worship of Vishṇu.

हरिमन्दल, *more prop.* हरिमन्दिर, *q..v.*

हरिमन्दिर, *m.* a temple of Vishṇu.

हरियर, the close of the sowing-season: *adj.* green, verdant.

हरियल, *m.* a green pigeon (*Columba hurriyala*).

हरियश, *m.* the fame of the exploits of any incarnation of Vishṇu, the reputation or renown of Vishṇu.

हरिया, 1, verdant, green: 2, *m. f.* a ploughman: 3, *m. f.* a worshipper, devotee.

हरियांव, a certain division of a crop by which the zamīndār receives seven parts and the cultivator retains nine.

हरियान, *m.* (the vehicle of Vishṇu, *i. e.*) Garuḍ.

हरियाना, *t.* to stop, prevent: *a. int.* to become green.

हरियाल = (1) हरियल (2) हरियाला, *qq.v.*

हरियाला, *m.* (*f.* ī) 1, green, verdant, grassy, irriguous: 2, a small green bird (*Merops viridis*) commonly called the "fly-catcher."

हरियाली, *f.* greenness, verdure, freshness; grass: *dūb*-grass.

हरियावल, *f.* verdure, freshness.

हरिला; see (1) हरियल (2) हरियाला (3) हरोला.

हरिलीला, *f.* the exploits of any *avatār* of Vishṇu (but *esp.* those of Krishṇ).

हरिवंश, *m. pr.n.* (1) of the family of Krishṇ, (*i. e.* Vishṇu) (2) of a celebrated poem supplementary to the Mahābhārat, on the history and adventures of Krishṇ and his family. It is usually regarded as part of the greater epic, though really a comparatively modern addition to it.

हरी, 1, *f.* (*m.* हरा) green: 2, *f.* (*m.* हरा, 1) taken away, etc.: 3, *more prop.* हरि, *q. v.*: 4, *f.* contribution of assistance by cultivators in ploughing the field of zamindārs.

हरिवार्त्ता, *f.* discourse about Vishṇu; religious conversation.

हरिवासर, *m.* the eleventh day of the moon's increase or wane (sacred to *Hari*).

हरिश्च; see (1) हरिस (2) हरीश (3) हर्ष (4) हरिश्चन्द्र.

हरिश्चन्द्र, *m. pr.n.* a certain ancient Hindoo king.

हरिस, *f.* the tail or the beam of a plough.

हरिसन (an old abl. of हरि) = हरिसे (हरि).

हरिहरकथा, *f.* the stories of the exploits of the various incarnations of Vishṇu and of Shiv.

हरीच्छा, *f.* the will of the Supreme Being.

हरीतः = हरौता, *q.v.*

हरीतक, *m.* = हरीतकी, *q.v.*

हरीतकी, *f.* yellow myrobalan (*Terminalia chebula*) of which there are seven varieties.

हरौता, *m.* the first commencement of ploughing in the rainy season.

हरीम; see (1) हरिया (2) हरा.

हरीफ़, clever, cunning; factious, pleasant; hence, *m.* (*f.* ā) a rival, enemy; an associate, friend, partner at play.

हरीभरी, *f.* (*m.* हराभरा) an overgrown female.

हरीर, *m.* silk; silken cloth.

हरीरा, *more com.* हरीला, *q.v.*

हरीला, *m.* (*f.* ī) 1, verdant, green, fresh: 2, a coward, a runaway.

हरीवा, *m.* a kind of parroquet.

हरीस, covetous, greedy, gluttonous.

हरु, 1, (*Rāmāyaṇ*) = हलका, *q.v.*: 2, = भरु, *q.v.*

हरुअ (*Rām.*) = हरुआ, *q.v.*

हरुआ, *m.* (*f.* हरुई) *Rāmāyaṇ* = हलका, *q.v.*

हरुवाई (*Rām.*) = हलकाई, *q.v.*

हरुवो in Braj = हलका, *q.v.*

हरे (the Sk. voc. sing. of हरि, *q.v.*) = O Vishṇu.

हरेऊ, an old form = हरा (हरना).

हरेणु, 1, *m.* peas, pulse: 2, *f.* a certain drug and perfume (commonly called *reṇuka*): a reputable woman.

हरेरा, 1, *m.* (*f.* ī) verdant, green, fresh: 2, *m.* verdure; a vegetable.

हरेरी, *f.* the colour green.

हरेला, *m.* (*f.* ī) a loser.

हरो, (2nd pers. pl. imperat. of हरना) take away, remove.

हरोरी, *f.* money lent by a cultivator to a ploughman.

हरौटी, *f.* a cane, a staff.

हरौता, the beginning of the ploughing-season.

हरौरी, *f.* the occupation of ploughing; a place where ploughing is going on.—*par jāo*, go and put your hand to the plough.

हर्कारा = हरकारा, *q. v.*

हर्गिज़, ever at any time, on any account.

हर्ज, *m.* tumult, sedition, confusion, loss, detriment, harm, injury; interruption.

हर्जमर्ज, *m.* agitation, tumult, sedition, hubbub, hurly-burly, pother.—*uṭhānā*, to pother, create a hubbub.

हर्डा, *m.* a kind of astringent nut, myrobalan (*Terminalia chebula* or *T. citrina*).

हर्ड़ा = हर्डा, *q. v.*

हर्ताल, *more com.* हरिताल, *q. v.*

हर्ता, *m.* (*f.* trī) a taker away, stealer, plunderer, depredator, spoiler, thief.

हर्दी, *f.* turmeric (*Curcuma longa*).

हर्फ़, *m.* (in Urdoo Gram.) a letter (vowel or consonant); a particle; a word.

हर्ब, *f.* war, battle, contest.

हर्बा, *m.* warlike apparatus, arms.

हर्बाबी, *m.* a jack-of-all-trades.

हर्मिस, (Grk.) *m. pr. n.* (1) of the planet Mercury (2) of the god Mercurius.

हर्या, green, verdant, fresh.

हर्यश्व, *m.* an epithet of Indra.

हर्रा, 1, = हर्डा, *q. v.*: 2, *m.* a sound, voice, shout: 3, the neck or collar of a cane, pillar, etc.

हर्राफ़, ingenious, clever, facetious, pleasant, talkative, chatty.

हर्ष, 1, *m.* (*f.* ā) joyful, delighted, glad, happy: 2, *m.* joy, delight, pleasure, happiness, gladness, mirth, exultation; blowing, blooming.

हर्षकारक, exhilarating, gladdening, delightsome: hence, *m.* (*f.* ikā) a gladdener, delighter.

हर्षना, *a. int.* to be delighted, to rejoice, to bloom, blow (said of flowers).

हर्षमन्त / **हर्षमान** } *m.* (*f.* matī) = हर्षवत, *q. v.*

हर्षवत, *m.* (*f.* vatī) joyful, delighted, happy.

हर्षवन्त / **हर्षवान** } *m.* (*f.* vatī) = हर्षवत, *q. v.*

हर्षान = हर्षित, *q. v.*

हर्षाना, *t.* to cause to be delighted, to delight, rejoice.

हर्षि = हर्षके (हर्षना). See क, 7.

हर्षित, *m.* (*f.* ā) gladdened, exhilarated, rejoiced, pleased, happy, gladsome, cheerful, elate.

हर्षितगात, *f.* the body when so overjoyed that the hair stands on end.

हर्षोदय, *m.* the dawn of happiness, the appearance or occurrence of joy or bliss.

हर्स; see (1) हर्ष (2) हरिस (3) ह्रस्व.

हल, *m.* a plough: the afterbirth: (in Gram): a consonant not followed by vowel sound (*e.g.* क्). — *chalānā* or *jotnā*, to plough, till.

हलक, 1, = हचका, *q. v.*; 2, *adj.* like a plough.

हलकना, *a. int.* to move.

हलका, *m.* (*f.* ī) light (in weight, in character, or in colour), of no consequence, puerile, trifling, mean, pitiful, scurvy, despicable, debased, silly, soft, cheap; neap (said of tide); pale, faint; manageable.—*k.* to lighten, assuage, ease, exonerate; to debase, depreciate, abase, affront.—*jānā*, to disesteem, disdain, think lightly or meanly of, to scorn, despise.

हलकाई, *f.* lightness, littleness, poorness, insignificance, levity, silliness, vanity, despicableness.

हलकाना, *t.* to lighten; to abet.

हलकापन, *m.* = हलकाई, *q. v.*

हलकाबगोश, *m.* slave, servant (*i. e.* one who wears a ring in his ear as a badge of servitude).

हलकारा; see (1) हरकारा (2) हलकारा.

हलकी, *f.* (*m.* **हलका**) light, trifling, etc.—*jawār*, the neap-tide. [wave.

हलकोरना, *t.* to gather, collect: *a. int.* to billow, surge,

हलकोरा, *m.* a wave, billow, surge.

हलगे, 1, gently, softly: 2, *f.* a small kind of drum.

हलचल, *f.* freight, perturbation, hubbub, tumult, anarchy; motion, gait.

हलजोता, *m.* a ploughman, tiller.

हलड़ा = **हरां**, *q. v.*

हलतड्डी, *f.* a drill-plough.

हलता, *m.* (*f.* ī) navigable.

हलदरा, *m.* a disease of the *cerealia* by which the plant withers and assumes a yellow tinge.

हलदार, *m.* the owner of a plough: a village-officer.

हलदिया, 1, yellow: 2, *m.* a certain poisonous root: a certain class of merchants: the jaundice.

हलदी, *f.* turmeric (*Curcuma longa*): a kind of marriage ceremony in which the parties are anointed with turmeric.

हलद्दा, a Prākṛit form of **हरिद्रा**, *q. v.*

हलधर, *m.* an epithet of Balarām (Krishṇ's elder brother): lit. *m.* (*f.* ā) the plough-holder.

हलन, 1, *more prop.* **हिलन**, *q. v.*: 2, a Braj pl. of **हल**.

हलन्त, (in Gram.) ending with a consonant.

हलफना, *a. int.* to toss about, tumble about; to shudder with fever.

हलफ़नामा, *m.* an affidavit, declaration on oath.

हलफल, *f.* affability: hurry, perturbation.

हलबन्दी / **हल . रार** } = **हलसारी**, *q. v.*

हलबल, hurry, confusion, bustle, haste.

हलबलाना, *a. int.* to hurry, be confused: to impair.

हलबलाहट, *f.* the effect of hurry, confusion, hurry.

हलभल, *m.* help; officiousness.—*k.* to lend a hand.

हलभलिया, *m.* a helper: *adj.* officious.

हलभलो, *f.* politeness.

हलभृत, *m.* an epithet of Balrām: *lit.* having a plough.

हलमूसल, *m.* the plough and pestle (the implements of Sheshnāg).

हलरा, *m.* a wave, billow, surge.

हलराना, *t.* to amuse, play with, dandle.

हलरावत = **हलरावता है**. See **त**, 5.

हलरावना, *t.* to amuse, play with, dandle.

हलवर्ण, *m.* (in Gram.) a consonant.

हलवा, *m.* a kind of sweetmeat (made of flour, ghee, and sugar).—*nikālnā*, to beat severely.

हलवाई, *m.* (*f.* in *or* inī) a maker or a vendor of *halwā* or sweetmeats: *pr. n.* a certain caste or tribe in the lower Doāb.

हलवान, *m.* a kid, a lamb.

हलवाहा, *m.* (*f.* in *or* ī) a tiller, ploughman.

हलवाही, *f.* agriculture, ploughing, tillage.—*k.* to plough, till.

हलस, the beam of a plough.

हलसन्धी, *m.* the combination of vowelless consonants in the formation of compound letters or words.

हलसारी, *f.* assessment according to the number of ploughs; a kind of tenure; the quantity of land under cultivation by any party.

हलसो, *f.* a certain small tree (*Ægiceras majus*).

हलहना, in Chand = **हिलना** (?), *q.v.*

हलहल, *m.* a sort of mortal poison.

हलहला, *m.* poison, venom.

हलहलाट, *f.* shaking, trembling (through fever or fear).

हलहलाना, *a. int.* to tremble, quiver, shake (through fever or fear): *t.* to cause to tremble, to shake.

हलहलाशब्द, *m.* shout, tumult, noise.

हलहलिया, *m.* poison, venom.

हलहली, *f.* sickness, disease; an ague.

हलहाई, a corruption of **हलाई**, *q. v.*

हलहाक, a corruption of **हलाक**, *q. v.*

हलाहिन, *m.* a sort of mortal poison.

हला, 1, *f.* the earth: vinous liquor: water: 2, (in theatrical language) a vocative particle used in addressing a female friend. [plough, till.

हलाई, *f.* ploughing, tillage, agriculture.—*k.* to

हलाक, 1, fatigued, lost, killed, dead: 2, *m.* slaughter, death, ruin, perdition. [slaughter.

हलाकत, *f.* destruction, death: (in Law) man-

हलाकी, *f.* ruin, destruction, perdition; pang.

हलाकू, *m. f.* a destroyer, murderer, ruffian: *lit.* destructive, operose, deadly.

हलायता, the first ploughing of the season.

हलायुध, *m.* an epithet of Balarām: *lit.* whose weapon is a plough.

हलाल, legal, legitimate, right; (a female) laying aside mourning for the death of her husband at the expiration of 100 days during which time she is not allowed by law to marry.

हलालख़ोर, *m.* (*f.* ī) a person of the lowest caste (*e g.* a sweeper), so called because everything is lawful food to him.

हलावत, *f.* sweetness, deliciousness.

हलावा, *more prop.* **हिलाव**, *q. v.*

हलाहल, *m.* a sort of mortal poison.

हलिकारा, *more prop.* **हरकारा**, *q. v.*

हलिया, *m.* a herd (of oxen), a flock, drove (of cows).

हलियाक / **हलियाग** } wages of ploughmen.

हलियाना, *a. int.* to nauseate.

हली, appertaining to a plough: hence (1) *m.* (*f.* *ini*) a ploughman (2) *m.* an epithet of Balarām.

हलीम, 1, *more com.* **हालिम**, *q. v.*: 2, a kind of food dressed in the Muharram.

हलुक; see (1) **हलका** (2) **हलक**.

हलुकई, *more com.* **हलकाई**, *q. v.*

हलुका, *m.* (*f.* ī) *more com.* **हलका**, *q. v.*

हलुआ, battered (as a harlot).

हले, *exclam.* ho! hoa! holloa!

हलेलज / **हलेला** } *m.* a kind of nut (*Myrobalan*).

हनोरना, *t.* to collect, gather.

हलोरा, *m.* a wave, billow, surge.

हल्ल, *m.* solution, loosening, untying.

हल्ला, *m.* uproar, tumult; assault, onset; the yellow myrobalan.

हल्लाकल्ला, *m.* foolish talking, loquacity, clamour.

हल्लाज, *m.* a comber, carder of cotton.

हल्लू, slowly, easily, gently, by degrees.

हव, *m.* sacrifice, oblation; a call, invitation; an order, command; a challenge.

हवन, *m.* sacrifice, offering, oblation. [rificial fire.

हवनी, *f.* a hole in the ground for receiving the sac-

हवस, *m. f.*? desire, lust; inordinate desire; ambition; curiosity.—*pakānā*, to form an inordinate desire.

हवा, *f.* wind, air, atmosphere: sensuality, lust, desire, affection, love. —*k.* fan; to broach, divulge.—*khānā*, to take the air.—*jānnā*, to set at nought. —*batānā*, to reject one's petition, to disappoint. —*ho-jānā*, to vanish, to scud.

हवाना, *a. int.* to screech, scream.

हवाम, *m.* (pl. of **हामा**) reptiles, insects, serpents.

हवाल, in Māṛwāṛī = **अहवाल**, *q. v.* See **अ**, 18.

हवालदार, *m.* a man employed to protect grain before it is stored; an agent employed for the management of a village; a military officer of inferior rank (*vulg.* havildar).

हवाला, *m.* charge, custody, care. [custody.

हवालात, *f.* things given in charge, trust, deposits;

हवाली, *f.* environs, suburbs, outskirts.

हवाशी, *m.* (pl. of **हाशिया**) borders, margins: attend-

हवि, *m.* an offering to the gods. [ants, followers.

हविर्धान, *m pr. n.* (1) of a certain ancient Hindoo prince (2) of the author of certain hymns of the Rig-Ved.

हविर्धानी, *f. pr. n.* a certain cow which appeared at the churning of the ocean; an epithet of the goddess Kālī.

हविर्भाग, 1, *m.* a share of an oblation: 2, *m.* (*f.* ā) one who shares in a sacrifice (an epithet of the deities).

हविर्भुज, *m.* fire: *pr. n.* the manes of Kshatriyas.

हविष = **हविस**, *q. v.*

हविष्मत / **हविष्मान** } *m.* (*f.* matī) possessed of oblations.

हविष्मन्ता, *m. pr n.* (pl.: see **आ**, 22,) a certain class of Pitṛis (regarded as progenitors of Kshatriyas, and as descended from Aṅgiras).

हविष्य, *m.* clarified butter; rice mixed with ghee; an oblation; wild grains. [(*esp.* of clarified butter).

हविस, *m.* clarified butter; an oblation; sacrifice

हवेली, *f.* a house, habitation: lands in the vicinity of towns the revenues of which were devoted to the support of the military garrison.

हव्य, *m.* an offering to the gods.

हव्यवाह, *m.* an epithet (1) of fire (2) Agni, the god of fire: lit *adj.* bearing away the oblation.

हव्यवाहन = **हव्यवाह**, *q. v.*

हव्याश, *m.* an epithet (1) of fire (2) of Agni, the god of fire (3) of Shiv: lit. *adj.* devouring the oblation.

हव्याशन = **हव्याश**, *q. v.*

हव्वा, *f. pr. n.* Eve (the mother of mankind).

हव्विय / **हव्वौ** } in Chand = **हाथ**, *q. v.*

हशम, *m.* pomp, equipage, suite, retinue.

हशमत, *f.* state, dignity, grandeur, glory, majesty, equipage, retinue, train, parade.

हशर, *m.* a meeting, concourse, congregation; the general resurrection of the dead.

हशो, *m.* stuffing (a pillow, cushion, bed, etc.); the materials for stuffing: people of the meanest condition: small camels.

हस, *m.* 1, *more prop.* **हंस**, *q.v.*: 2, *m.* (in Gram.) a consonant: laughter, mirth, derision.

हसत, *m.* (*f.* ā) *adj.* smiling, laughing.

हसद, *f.* envy, malice; emulation, ambition.

हसन, *m*, 1, *pr. n.*: see **हसनहुसैन**: 2, the act of laughing or of smiling.

हसनहुसैन, *m. pr. n.* the two sons of 'Alī (by Fātima) son-in-law of Muhammad, who both suffered martyrdom.

हसना, *more com.* **हंसना**, *q. v.*

हसनी = **हसन्तिका**, *q. v.* [ingdish.

हसन्तिका, *f.* a portable fire-pan, a furnace, a chaf-

हसन्ती = **हसन्तिका**, *q. v.*

हसपिटल, *m.* (Engl.) a hospital.

हसब, *m.* pedigree, nobility; computation; measure, proportion; value; way, mode, manner; religion.

हसमुख, *more com.* **हंसमुख**, *q. v.*

हसरत, *f.* regret, grief; desire.

हसली, *more prop.* **हस्ली**, *q. v.* [tense of **हसना**.

हसा, 1, *more com.* **हंसा**, *q. v.*: 2, *m.* (*f.* ī) a past

हसाई, *more com.* **हंसाई**, *q. v.* [continence, chastity.

हसानत, *f.* stability, firmness, duration, steadiness;

हसाना, *more com.* **हंसाना**, *q. v.*

हसिया, *m.* a reapinghook, sickle.

हसिबे, *more com.* **हंसिबे**, *q. v.* [past tense of **हसना**.

हसी, *f.* 1, *more com.* **हंसी**, *q. v.*: 2, *f.* (*m.* **हसा**) a

हसीन, beautiful, elegant: fortified, strong.

हसूद, envious, spiteful, malignant.

हस्त, *m.* 1, = **हस्ता**, *q. v.*: 2, the hand; an elephant's trunk; bellows; a cubit (measured from the elbow, to the tip of the middle finger).

हस्तक्रिया, *f.* the deeds of the hand, handiwork.

हस्ता, *f. pr. n.* the 13th *Nakshatra* (Corvus) represented by a hand and containing five stars.

हस्ताचर / **हस्ताक्षर** } *m.* a signature; handwriting.

हस्ति, *m.* (*f.* nī) an elephant.

हस्तिदन्त, *m.* elephant's tooth, ivory.

हस्तिनानगर, *more com.* **हस्तिनापुर**, *q. v.*

हस्तिनापुर, *m. pr. n.* the ancient capital of Yudhishthir and his brethren, the remains of which still exist about 57 miles N. E. of the modern city of Delhi on the banks of the old channel of the Ganges.

हस्तिनी, *f.* (*m.* **हस्ती**) a she-elephant: the fourth description of females (see *Padmini*) in the amatory writings of the Hindoos (the worst of the four classes).

हस्तिनीपुर, *more com.* **हस्तिनापुर**, *q. v.*

हस्तिपाल, *m.* (*f.* ī) an elephant-keeper or driver.

हस्तिमद, *m.* the juice that exudes from an elephant's temples when in rut.

हस्ती, 1, *m.* (*f.* inī) an elephant: 2, *m. pr. n.* a certain ancient Hindoo king, founder of Hastināpur.

हस्तीय, appertaining to the elephant.

हस्त्य, appertaining to the hand, given with the hand, done with the hand, manual.

हस्र, stupid, ignorant: hence, *m.* (*f.* ā) a fool.

हस्ली, *f.* the collar-bone, clavicle: a collar (of gold, silver, etc.) worn as an ornament, a necklace.

हहरना, *a. int.* to lament, be put out, be embarrassed.

हा, an interjection expressive of (1) surprize or wonder (2) of weariness (3) of pain, sorrow, or grief (4) of reproach (5) of wrath (6) of joy or pleasure = ah! oh! alas! well! excellent! just so! very well! yes indeed.

हाइल, a rudder, helm, stern-oar.

हाऊ, a kind of bird.

हाए, *more com.* **हाय**, *q. v.*

हां, 1, a contraction of **यहां**, *q.v.*: 2, as a termination to Persian numerals it is equivalent to the Hindee termination **ओं** (see **ओं**, 4); *e. g.* **हज़ारहां** = **हज़ारों**: 3, yes, yea, ay, indeed, by the by, forsooth; indeed, verily.—*k.* to agree, yield, assent.

हांक, *f.* a cry, call, bawling, calling aloud to: driving: renown: rule, government.—*mārnā*, to bawl after, call to.

हांकना, *t.* to drive; to drive away; to push out or away: *t.* or *a. int.* to bawl to. *Jhak* —, to rave.

हांकपुकार, *f.* outcry, uproar, hue and cry.—*k.* to protest.—*kahnā*, to own.

हांकाहांक, *m.* a mutual pushing and driving, reёncounter.

हांकहांकी, *f.* = **हांकाहांक**, *q. v.*

हांकी, *f.* a sieve: a kind of vessel in which they make vermicelli.

हांकेपुकारे, plainly, with a loud, clear, distinct voice.

हांखिला, in Garhwāl = a honeycomb.

हांगर, *m.* a shark.

हांजी, *f.* (see **हां**, 3 and **जी**, 1) obsequiousness, superficial assent.

हांड; for words beginning thus, see under the form **हाण्ड**.

हांड़ी, *f.* an earthen pot, small cauldron.

हांनि, *more prop.* **हानि**, *q. v.*

हांपना = **हांफना**, *q. v.*

हांफना, *a. int.* to puff and blow, pant, gasp, be out of breath.

हांफवों, an old form = (1) **हांफूं** (2) **हांफूंगा** (3) **हांफेगा**.

हांस, 1, *m.* (*f.* ī) a duck, gander, goose, swan; 2, *m.* the neck; the collar-bone, halse or hause.

हांसी, *f.* laughter, laughing, joking, ridicule, derision.

हांहां, 1, *more prop.* **हाहा**, *q.v.*: 2, a very common reduplication of **हां**, 3, *q. v.*

हांहों, (emphat.) yes, yes indeed, yea truly.

हांहों = **हांहो**, *q. v.*

हांहू, 1, = **हांहों**, *q. v.*: 2, off and on: 3, prevarication, ambiguous talk.

हाकिम, *m.* a ruler, governor, commander, master.

हाकिमी, 1, appertaining to a ruler: 2, *f.* the status or the functions of a ruler, magistracy.

हाजत, *f.* necessity, poverty, want, need, wish, hope.

हाजिब, *m.* a door-keeper, porter; a chamberlain privy-counsellor, minister of state; a curtain, screen; the eyebrow: an attorney at law.

हाज़िर, present, ready, willing, content. *Main* — *hūn*, I am at your service.

हाज़िरज़ामिन, *m.* (in Law) security for personal appearance.

हाज़िरी, *f.* breakfast; dessert: levee, presence, audience, muster-roll: an offering made to a saint.

हाजी, *m.* a Muhammadan who has made the pilgrimage to Mecca: a satirical poet.

हाट, *f.* a market, a fair or moveable market, a mart, a shop.

हाटक, 1, golden: 2, *m.* gold.

हाटकघट, *m.* any golden pot or jar.

हाटकेश्वर, *m. pr. n.* a certain form of Shiv which is worshipped on the banks of the Godāvarī.

हाटू, *m. f.* a market-person, market-man.

हाठ = **हाट**, *q. v.*

हाड़, *m.* a bone. — *lenā*, to examine the correctness of a pair of scales or of weights and measures. *Ga'ekā* — *honā*, to persecute.

हाडजोड़ा, *m.* the plant *Cissus quadrangularis*.

हाड़ा, *m.* a certain tribe of Rājpoots.

हाण्ड; see (1) **हाण्डा** (2) **हाण्डना**.

हाण्डना, *a. int.* to ramble, wander, move.

हाण्डा, *f.* a large cooking-pot (whether of clay or of metal), a cauldron.

हाण्डी, *f.* (dim.) a pot, small cauldron, an earthen pot.

हाढ़, *more prop.* **हाड़**, *q. v.*

हात, *more com.* **हाथ**, *q. v.*

हातसूंका, *m.* means, capital, stock.

हाता, a contraction of **अहाता**, *q. v.*

हाती, *m.* (*f.* inī) *more prop.* **हाथी**, *q.v.*

हातेहात, *more prop.* **हाथोंहाथ**, *q.v.*

हाथ, *m.* the hand; a paw; an elephant's claw; (in Measure) a cubit: *met.* possession, reach, power. — *ānā* (sc. *men*) to come into one's possession or power, to be gained, be obtained; to receive, reach. — *uthānā*, to beat; to salute by raising the hand to the head; to desist, leave off, cease, refrain from, abandon, relinquish, resign: — *uthāo*, hands off! — *ot lenā*, to receive with both hands open and stretched out together. *Auronke kāmmen* — *ḍālnā*, to interfere in other people's affairs. — *kamarpar rakhnā*, to be very feeble. — *k.* to subdue, to have possession. — *kāṭnā*, to express regret, to grieve. — *kānoṅpar rakhnā*, to be astonished, to deny vehemently. — *khainchnā*, to refrain from, desist, abstain. — *chalānā*, to act on the offensive, to offer violence, to attack. — *chāṭnā*, to lick one's lips, to relish exceedingly. — *jornā*, to clasp the hands, to knock under, knuckle down, to entreat earnestly, supplicate. — *jhārnā*, to bestow. — *jhūṭā honā*, to have the hands defiled; to lose the power of the hands. — *ḍālnā*, to thrust or put the hand (in or on), to undertake; to meddle, interfere, intrude, encroach. — *denā*, to lend a hand; to concern one self in or about, to take (a thing) in hand, to undertake; to make a bargain by taking hold of the hands of the other party under a cloth (a practice chiefly observed in settling the price of jewels or of horses) to promise. — *dhonā*, to resign, relinquish; to lose all hope, to be disappointed, be hopeless. — *p karnā*, to seize one by the hand, to shake hands, to hand a person. — *pakre le jānā*, to hand a person. — *parnā* (sc. *meṅ*) to come into one's possession. — *patthar tale dabnā*, to be unable to act, be helpless. — *pasārnā*, to spread out the hands, to supplicate, intreat, beg. *Pīṭhpar — phernā*, to pacify, satisfy, assure. — *pheṅknā*, to fence. — *phernā*, to rub, stroke, caress, coax, to retouch. — *band honā*, to have no leisure, be much occupied; to be indigent. — *baṛhānā*, to endeavour to get anything; to get possession of the property of others. — *bāndhnā*, to join the hands in a supplicating posture. — *baiṭhnā*, to acquire perfection in any art by practice, to get a set. — *bharnā*, to have the hands wearied or fatigued. — *malnā*, to regret, repent, lament. — *mārnā*, to promise; to acquire; to pilfer, plunder; to wound with a sword. — *milānā*, to claim equality; to prepare to wrestle. *Muṅh*—(or *Hāth pāṅw*) *dhonā*, to go to the necessary. — *rangnā*, to pilfer. — *roknā*, to prevent. — *lagnā*, to come to hand, to be got, be obtained, be acquired. — *lagānā*, to put or thrust the hand (into), to meddle (in), to handle; to lend a hand; to be employed in in any business; to reprove; to punish, torment. — *sameṭnā*, to refrain from giving, etc. — *sikoṛnā*, to retrench. — *sūā jānā*, to be without choice, be helpless.

हाथचला, *m.* (*f.* ī) quick of hand, dexterous, expert, active, alert, nimble, smart, laborious, light-fingered.

हाथचालाक = **हाथचला**, *q.v.*

हाथचालाकी, *f.* nimbleness, dexterity, expertness, alertness, activity, laboriousness.

हाथचिट्ठी, *f.* an autograph letter.

हाथजोड़, *adv.* with the hands folded in the manner of entreaty.

हाथपर, *adv.* on the nail.

हाथपांव, hand and foot, hands and feet: *hence*, a right-hand man, factotum. — *dhonā*, to go to the necessary. — *phūl jānā*, to be distressed or confounded. — *phailānā*, to extend one's business or schemes. — *bāndhnā*, to bind (anyone) hand and foot. — *mārnā*, to sprawl; to be agitated: to struggle, strive, endeavour, strain, toil.

हाथपांवों = **हाथपांव**, *q.v.* See **पांवों**.

हाथफूल, *m.* a certain plant (*Pothos*).

हाथफेड़, *f.* lending, loan. — *denā*, to lend.

हाथमें, (*lit.* in the hand; *hence*) in the possession of, in the power of, at the mercy of, under the control of, liable to: *e. g.* *Hāthmeṅ rakhnā*, to possess, hold in subjection. *Ham sabke sab mautke — haiṅ*, we are all liable to death. *Yah sab uske — hai*, all this is under his authority. *Nakel — rakhnā* or *honā* to lead one nolens volens, to lead by the nose. *Uske swāmikī bāg uske — hai*, she leads her husband by the nose. — *lapāṭmeṅ dhar choṭnā*, to squander, lavish.

हाथा, *more com.* **हाथ**, *q v.*

हाथाजोड़ी, *f.* a plant (*Lycopodium imbricatum*).

हाथापाई, *f.* a mutual beating, fisticuffs, struggle, tussle. — *k.* to have a scuffle, play at fisticuffs.

हाथाकची, *f.* a sort of game.

हाथाबांही = **हाथापाई**, *q.v.*

हाथाहाथी, *f.* a handing about, passing from hand to hand.

हाथिवान, *more prop.* **हाथीवान**, *q.v.*

हाथी, 1, *m.* (*f.* inī) the elephant; (at Chess) the rook: 2, *m. pr. n.* the 13th *Nakshatra*. —*sundkā pānī*, a waterspout. — *kī rāh*, the Milky-way.

हाथीख़ाना, *m.* an elephant's house or stable.

हाथीचक, *m.* a kind of grass which grows about a foot high and is used as fodder: artichoke.

हाथीदान्त, *m.* elephant's tooth, ivory.

हाथीपांव, *m.* elephantiasis, Barbadoes leg.

हाथीवान, *m.* an elephant-driver: *pr. n.* the 13th *Nakshatra*.

हाथीहंगाम, remission of rent, etc. for losses arising from depredations by wild elephants.

हाथोहाथ, *m.* acting in accord. —*k.* to act in accord, to pull together.

हाथों लेना, *t.* to handle roughly.

हाथोंहाथ, out of hand, over hand, quickly, expertly, expeditiously: from hand to hand. — *uṭhānā*, to raise by manual power. — *le jānā*, to carry away quickly; to snatch away at once or suddenly.

हादसा, a corruption of **हादिस**, *q. v.*

हादिक़, cutting, sharp, sour, acute, penetrating, ingenious, skilful, intelligent, industrious, excelling.

हादिस, new, just appearing. — *honā*, to appear, emerge, happen.

हादिसा, *m.* a novelty, event, occurrence, misfortune, calamity.

हान, 1, a contraction of **हानि**, *q. v.* (see **ह**, 1): 2, *m.* relinquishing, abandonment: prowess.

हानि, *f.* abandonment, desertion, quittance, absence, privation, deficiency, diminution, harm, detriment, loss; want; neglecting; injury, destruction, slaughter, murder.

हानिकर, occasioning loss, injurious, harmful, noxious, hurtful, prejudicial, pernicious, baneful: hence, *m.* (*f.* ī) a marrer, marplot.

हानिकरि = (1) **हानिकर** (2) **हानि करके**.

हानिकारक, *m.* (*f.* ikā), **हानिकारी**, *m* (*f.* iṇī), **हानिजनक**, *m.* (*f.* ikā) = **हानिकर**, *q. v.*

हानिस, a false-swearer, purjurer.

हानी, *m.* (*f.* inī) = **हानिकर**, *q. v.*

हापना, *more prop.* **हांपना**, *q. v.*

हापर, *f.* a seed-bed or nursery for sugarcane.

हापुस, a munching, *Hāpus hāpus khānā*, to munch.

हाफ़िज़, *m.* a guardian, governor, preserver: having a good memory; one who has the whole Kur,ān by heart; the poetical name of a certain Persian poet.

हामा, a kind of reptile (?).

हामारा, *m.* (*f.* ī) *more prop.* **हमारा**, *q. v.*

हामिल, 1, *m.* a porter, carrier: 2, *f.* a pregnant female.

हामिला, *f.* pregnant, enceinte, fruitful.

हामी, *m.* (*f.* inī) a protector, defender, guardian.

हाय, 1, *excl.* (expressive of pain) alas! ah! 2, *f.* a sigh; sighing. —*mārnā*, to sigh; to lament.

हायन, *m.* a twelvemonth, a year: a flame: a sort of rice.

हायहाय, (redupl. of intensity) 1, alas, alas! 2, *f.* a sigh; sighing. —*mārnā*, to sigh; to lament.

हार, 1, *m.* a necklace, string of pearls, etc.; a wreath, chaplet; a garland: a flock of cattle: pasturage; a village-common, the cultivated space immediately round a village; a subdivision of an estate; a tract of land: (in Arithm.) a divisor, the denominator of a fraction: taking: a porter: war, battle: 2, *f.* discomfiture, forfeiture, defeat, loss: 3. this particle [*m.* (*f.* ī] is sometimes added to some relic of the infinitive mode to indicate (1) agency: it thus equals *hārā* (2) futurity: it thus equals *wālā*: 4, *part.* being overcome. — *mānnā* or — *mān lenā*, to give up a dispute, give up in despair, acknowledge oneself beaten. — *denā*, to gamble away, squander.

हारक, 1, *m.* (*f.* ikā) a seizer, plunderer, ravisher, thief, cheat, rogue, gambler: lit. *adj.* seizing, taking, carrying off: 2, *m.* (in Arithm.) a divisor: a certain tree (*Trophis aspera*).

हारजीत, *m.* risk; hazard, gambling. — *k.* to gamble.

हारर्यो, 1, (*contraction*) = **हरियारी**, *q.v.*: 2, see **हारी**, 2.

हारना, *n.* to be tired out, be overcome, be unsuccessful: *a. int.* to lose (in play or in battle, to lose ground: *t.* to lose: *Bachan* —, to promise.

हारमान, see *s. v.* **हार**.

हारल, *more prop.* **हारियल**, 2, *q. v.*

हारसिंगार, *more prop.* **हरसिंगार**, *q. v.*

हारहूर, *m.* vinous liquor.

हारहूरा, *f.* a grape.

हारा, 1, *more prop.* **हार**, 1, *q. v.*: 2, *m.* (*f.* ī) this particle (with its modifications **अर**, **आर**, **आरा**, **र**, and **हार**) corresponds in sense and in usage with **वाला**, *q. v.*

हाराई, *f.* losing (as opposed to *winning*), loss.

हारि, *f.* defeat (in war or in gaming), losing, failure: a caravan.

हारिका, *f.* (*m.* **हारक**) a female thief, etc.

हारियाँ, *f.* (in Pros.) a species of metre.

हारियल, 1, *adj.* of a green colour: 2, *m.* a green pigeon (*Columba hurriala*, Buch.). [3, *f.* a pearl.

हारी, 1, *f.* = **हारा**, 2, *q. v.*: 2, *m.* (*f.* iṇī) = **हारक**, *q. v.*:

हारीत, *m.* the green pigeon: a rogue: a Muni, author of a law-book: *pr. n.* a certain Hindoo king.

हारू, *m.*, *f.* a loser, defeated party.

हारोन, *m. pr. n.* Aaron the priest.

हार्द, 1, appertaining to the heart: hence, 2, *m.* affection, love, kindness; will.

हार्य, 1, proper to be taken, to be taken away; 2, *m.* a certain plant (*Beleric myrobalan*).

हाल, 1, quick: 2, *m.* a plough: 3, *m.* an epithet (1) of Balrām (2) of Shālivāhan: 4, *m.* state, condition; business, affair; ecstasy: (in Gram.) present time: (in Revenue) the actual state of the collections.

हालगरा, land that retains moisture.

हालड़, moving, motion, agitation, swinging.

हालत, *f.* condition, circumstance, posture of affairs.

हालडे, quickly, hastily, speedily.

हालना, *a. int.* to move, shake, vibrate, tremble. *Yah dawā mat khānā tapke hālnemeṅ*, don't take this medicine during the paroxysm of the fever.

हालहल }
हलाहल } *m.* a sort of strong poison.

हाला, 1, *m.* a circle around the moon: 2, *f.* vinous or spirituous liquor, wine.

हालांकि, whereas, though, yet, however, even, although, notwithstanding.

हालाडोला, *m.* shaking, agitation; an earthquake.

हालाहल, *m.* a sort of strong poison.

हालाहलधर, *m.* (*f.* ā) a small black venomous kind of snake.

हालाहली, *f.* spirituous liquor, wine.

हालि, *f.* a helm, rudder.

हालिम, *m.* garden-cresses (*Lepidum sativum*).

हाली, 1, *f.* a sister-in-law (wife's younger sister): 2, *m.* (*f.* inī) a man employed for the duties of ploughing, an agricultural labourer.

हाव, *m.* calling, a call: any act of amorous pastime (on the part of a female), any act tending to excite amorous sensations, coquetry, blandishment, airs, dalliance.

हावभाव, *m.* charm, attraction, welcome, coquetry, blandishment, airs, dalliance.

हावा; see (1) **हवा** (2) **हाव**.

हाशिया, *m.* a margin, hem, border; a marginal note: persons of inferior rank; attendants, retinue, troops; facings of a military uniform.

हास, *m.* laughing, laughter; derision; joy.

हासकर, *m.* (*f.* ī) laughable, causing laughter, merry, ridiculous.

हासरस = **हास्यरस**, *q. v.*

हासहर, occasioning laughter, ridiculous.

हासिका, *f.* laughter, mirth.

हासिद, envious: hence, *m.* (*f.* ā) an enemy.

हासिल, *m.* produce; acquiring; profit; tax, duty, custom, revenue; corn. —*k.* to get, acquire, gain; to produce, bring about; to collect; to learn. —*honā*, to be attained or got.

हासी, *m.* (*f.* inī) *adj.* laughing, smiling.

हास्तिन, 1, *m.* = **हस्तिनापुर**, *q. v.*: 2, *m.* (*f.* ī) elephantine, as big as an elephant, very large, huge.

हस्तिनपुर }
हस्तिनापुर } *more com.* **हस्तिनापुर**, *q. v.*

हास्य, 1, *m.* (*f.* ā) laughable, ridiculous: 2, *m.* laughter, laughing, mirth.

हास्यरस, *m.* (see **रस**) the sentiment of humour, sense of humour, the comic vein, facetiousness.

हाहा, 1, *m* flattery; importunity, earnest request, supplication: 2, *m. pr. n.* a certain Gandharv: 3, an interjection of surprize, grief, or pain = ah! alas! oh! —*khānā*, to flatter, wheedle; to entreat, beseech.

हाहाकर, *m.* (*f.* ī) *adj.* exclaiming 'alas!'

हाहाकार, *m.* consternation: the uproar of battle: the sound of grief, distress, pain, or pity; lamentation, complaint, wailing, a cry.

हाहाजिगीजिगी is an expression of approbation, also of earnest request.

हाहाहीही, *f.* laughing, jeering. — *k.* to laugh, jeer, giggle.

हि, 1, often found instead of the more common emphatic particle **ही**, *q. v.* : 2, an old or poetic termination (1) of the third pers. sing. pres. or fut. (irrespective of gender) = °**ता** or **एगा** (2) of the 2nd pers. pl. imperat. = **हु** (3) of the dat. or acc. case. = **को** (4) it is occasionally found in poetry as an abl. termin. = **से**.

हिं, 1, an old or poetic termin. of the 3rd pers. pl., pres. or fut. irrespective of gender : 2, an old accusative plural termin. : *e. g.* **तिन्हिं** = **तिनको** = **उनको** ; 3, in poetry and in old Hindee sometimes = **से** (abl.).

हिंगन, a kind of fire work.

हिंगलाज, a temple of Devī, a place of pilgrimage.

हिंगु, *m.* assafœtida (*Ferula assafœtida*).

हिंगुल, *m.* vermilion.

हिंगुली, *f.* the egg-plant (*Solanum melongena*).

हिंड ; for words beginning thus, see under the

हिंयां, a dialectic form of **यहां**, *q.v.* [form **हिण्ड**.

हिंस, *f.* (?) the neighing of a horse.

हिंसक, mischievous, injurious, noxious, malignant, ferocious, savage, murderous : hence, *m.* (*f.* ikā) an enemy, a beast of prey : a Brāhmaṇ skilled in the Atharva-Ved.

हिंसन, *m.* injuring, injury, hurting, slaying.

हिंसा, *f.* injuring, injury, hurt, mischief, spoiling : slaughter, killing slaying ; malice.

हिंसालु, *m. f.* mischievous, hurtful, injurious.

हिंस्र, hurtful, injurious, mischievous, destructive, terrible, formidable, fierce, savage, cruel, murderous : hence, (1) *m.* (*f.* ā) one who delights in mischief; a beast of prey (2) *m.* an epithet of Shiv.

हिंस्रक, *m.* (*f.* ikā) = **हिंस्र**, *q. v.*

हिंहिंनाहि, (pl. °**हिं**) } – **हिनहिनाता है**.
हिंहिंनाहीं, (pl. °**हीं**) }

हिकरी, *f.* cultivated reeds grown on low marshy

हिकवा, *f.* the hiccough. See **हिचकी**. [grounds.

हिके (*Rām.*) = **हृदयके** (**हृदय**).

हिकाइत, *more prop.* **हिकायत**, *q. v.*

हिकायत, *f.* a story, tale, romance, narration, history.—*k.* to relate. [vileness, baseness.

हिक़ारत, *f.* contempt, scorn, affront, disgrace,

हिक्का, *f.* the hiccough. See **हिचकी**.

हिकमत, *f.* wisdom, knowledge ; cleverness, skill; philosophy, mystery; principle.

हिचक, *f.* a hitch.

हिचकना, *a. int.* to draw back, shrink, boggle, waver, decline, hitch, loathe.

हिचकाना, *t.* (causat. of **हिचकना**) to jolt.

हिचकिचाना, *a. int.* to doubt, hesitate, be in suspense, falter. *Hichkichāke bolnā*, to hum and haw.

हिचकिचाहट = **हिचकिची**, *q. v.*

हिचकिची, *f.* hesitation, hesitancy.—*bāndhnā*, to gnash the teeth. [from crying. sobbing.

हिचकिन, *m.* (*f.* I) *adj.* having hiccough, choking

हिचकियाना, *a. int.* to hiccough.

हिचकी, *f.* the hiccough: sobbing, choking in crying. *Hichki* (or *Hichkiyāṅ*) *lenā*, to hiccough, to sob bitterly.

हिचना, to loathe. [Book that bears his name.

हिज़क़ियेल, *m. pr. n.* the prophet Ezekiel and the

हिजड़ा, *m.* a hermaphrodite, a eunuch.

हिजानत = **हज़ानत**, *q. v.* [curtain; night.

हिजाब, *m.* modesty, bashfulness, shame ; a veil,

हिडम्ब ; for words beginning thus, see under the

हिड़हिड़ाना, *more com.* **हड़हड़ाना**, *q. v.* [form **हिडिम्ब**.

हिडिम्ब, *m. pr. n.* a certain Rākshas slain by Bhīm.

हिडिम्बजित, *m.* (the conqueror of Hiḍimb, *i. e.*) Bhīm. [Bhīm.

हिडिम्बनिसूदन, *m.* (the destroyer of Hiḍimb, *i. e.*)

हिडिम्बबध = **हिडिम्बवध**, *q. v.*

हिडिम्बभिद, *m.* (the destroyer of Hiḍimb, *i. e.*) Bhīm.

हिडिम्बवध, *m.* the slaying of Hiḍimb (the name of an episode of the Mahābhārat).

हिडिम्बा, *f. pr. n.* (1) of the sister of Hiḍimb, who changed herself into a very beautiful woman and married Bhīm, by whom she had a son named Ghaṭotkach (2) of the wife of Hanumat.

हिडिम्बापति, *m.* (the lord of Hiḍimbā, *i.e.*) Bhīm.

हिडिम्बारमण, *m.* (the husband of Hiḍimbā, *i. e.*)

हिडोला, *more com.* **हिण्डोला**, *q. v.* [Bhīm.

हिण्डन, *m.* wandering, roaming : copulation : writ-

हिण्डना, *a. int.* to walk, travel, journey. [ing.

हिण्डी, *f.* an epithet of Durgā. [stomachic.

हिण्डीर, *m.* cuttle-fish bone : a pomegranate : a tonic,

हिण्डोरा, *more com.* **हिण्डोला**, *q. v.*

हिण्डोल = (1) **हिण्डोला** (2) **हिन्डोल**, *qq. v.*

हिण्डोला, *m.* a swing, a cradle ; a song describing the swing and sung during that exercise.

हित, 1, *m.* (*f.* ā) laid hold of, seized, taken : suitable, proper, beneficial, fit, worthy, right, good ; useful; friendly, kind, affectionate : 2, *m.* benefit, welfare, wellbeing ; a good, a benefit ; benevolence, friendship; affection, love.

हितकर, kind, favorable, friendly, benevolent, beneficent, beneficial, improving, salutary, profitable, advantageous : hence, *m.* (*f.* ī) a benefactor, friend.

हितकार, *m.* (*f.* ī) = **हितकर**, *q. v.*

हितकारक, *m.* (*f.* ikā) = **हितकर**, *q. v.*

हितकारी, 1, *m.* (*f* iṇī) = **हितकर**, *q. v.* : 2, *f.* (*m.* **हितकार**) a benefactress: 3, *f.* beneficence, friendship, love, affection.

हितदायक, *m.* (*f.* ikā) = **हितकर**, *q. v.*

हितमित, a jingle on the word **हित**, *q. v.*

हितवान, *m.* (*f.* vatī) benevolent, beneficent, friendly, favorable, useful.

हितसों (a Braj abl. of **हित**) = **हितसे** (**हित**).

हितार्थ, *m.* the seeking the welfare of others, benevolence.

हितार्थी, desirous of the welfare of others, benevolent : hence, *m.* (*f.* inī) a benevolent person, well-wisher.

हितु } हितू } m. f. a benefactor, friend.

हितैषी, benevolent, seeking another's welfare, well-wishing: hence, m. (f. iṇī) a well-wisher.

हितोपदेश, m. salutary instruction, wholesome counsel, friendly or proper advice: pr. n. a certain popular Sanskrit work.

हित्या, in Māṛwāṛī = हत्या, q.v.

हिन, m. (f. ā) more prop. हीन, q.v.

हिनहिनाट (contraction) = हिनहिनाहट, q.v.

हिनहिनाना, a. int. to neigh (said of the horse).

हिनहिनाहट, f. neighing; a neigh.

हिनोता, m. f. (?) supplication, entreaty, humility.

हिन्ताल, m. the marshy date-tree (Phœnix paludosa or Elate paludosa. [India.

हिन्द, 1, m. (f. nī more com. हिन्दू, q.v.: 2, m. pr. n.

हिन्दनी, f. (m. हिन्द) a female Hindoo.

हिन्दवान, m. a water-melon, a kind of pumpkin.

हिन्दवाना = हिन्दवान, q.v.

हिन्दविन (fem. of हिन्दवी) = हिन्दनी, q.v.

हिन्दवी = हिन्दूई, q.v.

हिन्दिनी (fem. of हिन्दी) = हिन्दनी, q.v.

हिन्दी, the most com. form of हिन्दूई, q.v.

हिन्दुवाना = हिन्दवान, q.v.

हिन्दुविन (fem. of हिन्दुवी) = हिन्दनी, q.v.

हिन्दुई (corruption) = हिन्दूई, q.v.

हिन्दुवी = हिन्दूई, q.v.

हिन्दुस्थान = हिन्दुस्तान, q v.

हिन्दू, m. a negro, a black Arabian, an Ethiopian, an Indian, Hindoo, Gentoo, a native of India who observes the precepts of the Hindoo scriptures: met. a mole or lock of a mistress.

हिन्दूइनी (fem. of हिन्दूई) = हिन्दनी, q.v.

हिन्दूई, appertaining to India, to the blacks, or to the Hindoos: hence, (1) Indian, Hindoo (2) m. (f. inī) an Indian, a Hindoo (3) f. the language or dialect of the Hindoos, the Hindee or Hindūī language (4) f. blackness (of the hair, etc.).

हिन्दूमत, m. the Hindoo religion, Hindooism, the followers of the Hindoo religion.

हिन्दूमतसूर्मा, m. (lit. the eyesalve of Hindooism; hence) an epithet (1) of the Hindoo religion (2) of any person regarded as recondite in that religion.

हिन्दूवान = हिन्दवान, q.v.

हिन्दूस्तान, m pr. n. India. The designation is applied particularly to the Upper Provinces.

हिन्दूस्तानी, appertaining to Hindūstān or to the Hindūstānī people: hence (1) m. (f. in or inī) a native of Hindūstān (2) f. the language of Hindūstān.

हिन्दोरना, t. to puddle.

हिन्दोल, m. a swing, a cradle: one of the personified musical modes (rāg) sung in the morning of spring.

हिन्दोलना, t. to muddle.

हिना, f. a certain tree (Lawsonia inermis) with which Indians stain their hands and feet.

हिफ़्ज़, f. memory; guardianship, custody.

हिफ़ाज़त, f. memory; custody, guardianship, protection. — k. or rakhnā, to keep in memory; to repeat from memory: to preserve, guard, depend.

हिम, 1, m. (f. ā) cold, frigid, frosty: 2, m. frost, snow: cold: the moon; the Himālaya mountains; the cold season.

हिमउपल (Rām.) = हिमोपल, q.v.

हिमकर, frigorific, cold, frosty, chilly: hence, m. (1) the moon (2) camphor.

हिमगिरि } हिमभूधर } = हिमालय, q.v.

हिमर्तु, m. the cold season, the winter.

हिमवंत } हिमवत } हिमवन्त } m. (f. vatī) = हिमालय, q.v.

हिमवान, m. (f. vatī) chilly, cold, frostly, frigorific, freezing, wintry, snowy: hence, m. an epithet of the Himālaya range.

हिमशैल = हिमालय, q.v. [mountains, i.e.) Pārvatī.

हिमशैलसुता, f. (the daughter of the Himālaya

हिमा, f. winter: small cardamoms: a certain fragrant grass (Cyperus): a sort of perfume.

हिमाउपल (Rām.) = हिमोपल, q.v.

हिमाक़त, f. stupidity, folly.

हिमाचल = हिमालय, q.v.

हिमाचलगेह, m. the house of the Himālayas (an epithet of those mountains).

हिमाद्रि, m. pr. n. the Himālaya mountains.

हिमाद्रिजा, f. (the daughter of the Himālayas, i.e.) Pārvatī. [patronage, countenance.

हिमायत, f. protection, defence, guardianship,

हिमायती, m. (f. inī) protector, deliverer.

हिमार, m. the male ass; a wild ass.

हिमालय, m. pr. n. the snowy range of mountains which bounds India on the North-east (the Imaus and Emodus of the ancients): lit. the abode of cold or snow.

हिमाला = हिमालय, q.v.

हिमावती, f. a species of moon-plant.

हिमेनी, f. a purse.

हिमोपल, m. hail.

हिम्मत, f. resolution, spirit, inclination, bravery, courage; liberality; purpose, design: auspices, favour.

हिम्मतवाला, m. (f. ī) courageous, spirited, brave.

हिय, more com. हिया, q.v. [or won.

हियहार, m. (f. ī) adj. whose heart is conquered

हिया, m. the heart, mind, soul, life; the breast.

हियां, grief for separation or absence.

हियाव, m. courage, spirit, heart, bravery, valour, boldness, energy, manliness. [made when calling cattle.

हियो, 1, a poetic form of हिया, q.v.: 2, the sound

हियौ in Braj = हिया, q.v.

हिर; see हीर.

हिरकना, to loathe: to meet: to scamper.

हिरकाना, *t.* to join : to move.

हिरकी, *f.* shift, contrivance, scheme.

हिरन, 1, *m.* (*f.* ī) *more com.* **हरिण**, *q. v.*: 2, *m.* gold: a cowrie : semen virile.

हिरणाक्षदैत्य, *more prop.* **हिरण्याक्षदैत्य**, *q. v.*

हिरणी, *f.* (*m.* **हिरण**) *more com.* **हरिणी**, *q. v.*

हिरण्य, *m.* any precious metal unwrought ; gold ; silver ; wealth ; a cowrie : imperishable matter : substance : *semen virile.*

हिरण्यक, *m. pr. n.* a certain demon (*daitya*).

हिरण्यकश्यप = **हिरण्यकशिपु**, *q. v.*

हिरण्यकशिपु, *m. pr. n.* a certain demon (brother of Hiranyāksh and son of Kashyap by Diti) slain by Vishṇu.

हिरण्यगर्भ, *m.* an epithet of Brahmā (in allusion to his fabled origin from the golden mundane egg).

हिरण्यबाहु = **हिरण्यवाह**, *q. v.*

हिरण्यरेता, *m.* an epithet (1) of Shiv (2) of fire (3) of the sun.

हिरण्यवाह, *m.* an epithet (1) of Shiv (2) of the river Sone.

हिरण्याक्ष, *m. pr. n.* a certain demon slain by Vishṇu.

हिरद, a Prākṛit form of **हृद**, *q. v.*

हिरदा, a Prākṛit form of **हृदय**, *q. v.*

हिरदावल, a Prākṛit form of **हृदावर्त्त**, *q. v.*

हिरन, a Prākṛit form of **हरिण**, *q. v.*

हिरनी, a Prākṛit form of **हरिणी**, *q. v.*

हिरनौटा, *m.* a fawn.

हिरन्य; for words beginning thus, see under the form **हिरण्य**

हिरस ; see (1) **हिर्स** (2) **हरिस** (3) **ह्रस्व**.

हिराना, *t.* to lose, to mislay.

हिरार, raw, fresh, rare.

हिरावल, *m.* the advanced guard of an army.

हिरासत, *f.* care, watching, guarding.

हिर्ज़, *m.* an amulet, charm : a place of refuge, fortification, asylum : custody, keeping.

हिर्द, a Prākṛit form of **हृद**, *q. v.*

हिर्द्रय = **हृदय**, *q. v.*

हिर्फ़त, *f.* trade, profession, art ; skill, cleverness.

हिर्स, *f.* desiring eagerly, greediness, avarice.

हिलक ; see (1) **हिलकना** (2) **होरक**.

हिलकना, *a. int.* to writhe, suffer contortions (from affliction or from pain). The term is chiefly applied to children.

हिलकोर, *f.* agitation, fluctuation ; a wave.

हिलकोरना, *t.* to collect, gather, accumulate : to agitate, shake, disturb, perplex : *a. int.* to fluctuate, waver, wave, billow.

हिलकोरा, *m.* a wave, billow, surge.

हिलगना, *n.* to be hung on ; to be entangled : to be constant : *t.* or *a. int.* to adhere, stick, hang.

हिलगाना, *t.* to suspend, hang.

हिलडोल, *m.* moving, swinging, motion, agitation.

हिलन, *m.* movement, motion, agitation.

हिलनडोलन, *m.* swinging to and fro, motion, agitation.

हिलना, *a. int.* to move, shake, vibrate, rock, tremble, ruffle, be agitated, be moved ; to be tamed ; to be familiarized.

हिलम, *m.* coolness, temperateness, mildness, affability, gravity.

हिलमिल, mixed, jumbled together ; intimate, hand-in-glove. —*jānā*, to be mixed, be jumbled together, to join ; to be intimate.

हिलमोचिका = **हिलमोची**, *q. v.*

हिलमोची, *f.* a certain potherb (*Hingtsha repens*).

हिलसा, the most com. form of **इलीश**, *q. v.*

हिला, 1, *m.* (*f.* ī) vibrating, swinging, wagging : domesticated, tame : 2, *m.* moist ground trodden soft by cattle, mud, slime, quagmire.

हिलाकुला, *m.* (*f.* **हिलाकुली**) a play on the word **हिलना**.

हिलाना, *t.* to cause to vibrate, to move, rock, shake, wag, agitate : to inure, to familiarize, to tame : to cause to swim. *Kaprā* —, to beat a parley.

हिलामिला, *m.* (*f.* **हिलामिली**) tame, familiarized, attached, amicable. —*rahnā*, to be on terms of familiarity.

हिलार = **हिलोर** (?), *q. v.*

हिलारना = **हिलाना** (?), *q. v.*

हिलाव, *m.* swinging, motion, moving, agitation.

हिलावहुलाव, a jingling redupl. of **हिलाव**, *q. v.*

हिली, *f.* (*m.* **हिला**) tame, domesticated.

हिलोर, *f.* agitation, shaking ; a wave, surge.

हिलोरना, *a. int.* to shake, wave, surge, billow.

हिलोरा, *m.* a wave, billow, surge.—*mārnā*, to rise (said of the sea). *Hilore lenā*, to heave (said of the sea), to surge.

हिलोरी, *f.* a shaking ; a wave.—*mārnā*, to heave, rise (said of the sea).

हिव्राव = **हिश्राव**, *q. v.*

हिश्त, *m.* a hiss : *exclam.* hist ! pish ! avaunt ! away ! be off ! out !

हिस, *more prop.* **हिस्स**, *q. v.*

हिसका, *m.* imitation, copying, rivalry, emulation, contention.—*k.* to imitate, copy, ape, vie with.

हिसकाहिसकी, *f.* mutual imitation.

हिसक़ियेल, *m. pr. n.* the prophet Ezekiel and the Book that bears his name.

हिसानत ; see **हसानत** and **हज़ानत**.

हिसाब, *m.* computation, calculation, account, arithmetic.

हिसार, *m.* an enclosure, fence, fortified place, castle ; besieging.

हिसिका
हिसिषा } (*Rām.*) = **हिसका**, *q. v.*

हिस्त, *more com.* **हिश्त**, *q. v.*

हिस्न, *m.* a castle, fortification : destruction, perdition : armour, arms : female chastity.

हिस्स, *m.* a sense, sentiment, imagination, feeling, sympathy.

हिस्सा, *m.* a portion, quota, share, division, part, lot.

हिहिनाहि, (pl. °**हिं**) = **हिनहिनाता है**. (**हिनहिनाना**).

ही, 1, a contraction of **हिया**, *q. v.*: 2, an emphatic suffix of frequent occurrence = very, exactly, even, indeed, truly, only, merely, solely, altogether, outright : 3, sometimes = **हि** in its 2nd function. *Usne larke* *ko mārhi dālā*, he killed the boy outright, he actually murdered the boy. *Wah merāhi thā*, it was my own, it was mine and only mine.

हीयो हियो, 1 and 2, *qq. v.*

हीं, 1, emphatic = **ही**, 2, *q. v.* : 2, as an emphatic particle it is often inserted between a base and the termination; *e.g.* **इन्हींका**, of these very persons : 3, in Braj (when the nom. is *fem.*) = **हैं**, *q.v.*: 4, frequent in poetry = **हि** in its 1st function.

हींकारना, *a. int.* to low (as cattle).

हींग, a Prākṛit form of **हिगु**, *q. v.*—*hagnā*, to void by stool involuntarily, to linger : *met.* to pine.

हींगलू, (in Mārwāṛī) a mahogany colour.

हींगू, *more prop.* **हिगु**, *q. v.*

हींच = **ऍंच** = **ऐंच**, *q. v.*

हींचना, *t.* to draw, attract, pull, haul.

हींसना, *a. int.* to neigh, scream, make a noise as a horse when kicking.

हींहां भरना, to make a concession.

हीक, *m.* sickness at stomach, qualm, disgust.

हीकायत, *more prop.* **हिकायत**, *q. v.*

हीजड़ा, *m.* a species of eunuch : *met.* unmanly, pusillanimous.

हीठा = **अहीठा**, *q. v.* See **अ**, 18.

हीडना (in Mārwāṛī) = **हेरना**, *q. v.*

हीड़ा, *m.* flesh ; bulk, body.

हीत, *m.* (*f.* ā) *more prop.* **हित**, *q. v.*

हीति ; see (1) **हित** (2) **हेति**.

हीतो ; see (1) **हेतो** (2) **हेति** (3) **हित**.

हीन, *m.* (*f.* ā) quitted, abandoned, left, deserted, bereft deprived, destitute, free from, void of; worn, wasted, lean, decayed, feeble ; defective, deficient; abated, less, lower, little; blameable ; worthless, vile, low, bad.

हीनजाति, *m. f.* outcaste, degraded, vile, base.

हीनता, *f.* (*m.* °**त्व**) privation, deficiency, abatement, alleviation.

हीनमति, *m. f.* bereft of one's senses.

हीनवर्णा, *m.* (*f.* ā) of an inferior order or rank, of a low caste, low, vile, outcaste.

हीना, *f.* (*m.* **हीन**) abandoned, etc.

हीनांग, minus a limb, maimed, crippled: hence, *m.* (*f.* i) a cripple.

हीनांगी, *f.* an ant ; a female cripple.

हीम, *m.* (prop. **हिम**) snow, etc.

हीर, 1, *m.* the elemental part, quintessence, pith; energy, vigour: a diamond : a necklace : the thunderbolt of Indra : 2, *m.* (*f.* ā) a lion : a snake: 3, *m.* an epithet (1) of Shiv (2) of the thunderbolt of Indra : 4, essential, pure : 5, *f. pr. n.* Hero, the celebrated mistress of Leander (*Rānjhā*).

हीरक, *m.* a diamond ; adamant.

हीरया, *m.* gold : a cowrie : *semen virile.*

हीरा, 1, *m.* a diamond ; adamant : 2, *f.* an ant: a cockroach : an epithet of Lakshmee.

हीराना, *m.* the manuring a field by penning cattle or sheep on it.

हीरामन, *m.* a kind of parrot or parroquet (*Psittacus Sinensis*).

हीरावल, *m.* a kind of chequered blanket worn by mendicants.

हीरावलि } **हीरावली** } *f.* a row or string of diamonds.

हील, *m.* mud, slime, ooze, quagmire.

हीलना, *more prop.* (1) **हिलना** (2) **हिलाना**, *qq. v.*

हीला, *m.* 1, = **हील**, *q. v.* : 2, stratagem, deceit, pretence, trick.

हीही, (an interj. of surprize, merriment, or laughter) ah ! ha ha ! he he !

हु, 1, in old Hindee (1) a common sign of the imperat. 2nd pers. pl ; *e.g.* **करहु** = **करो**: (2) = **ही** emphatic : (3) = **भी**, *q v.*: (4) = **भो**, 3 and 4 ; *e. g.* **दशहुं** = **दशों**.

हुअ, *m.* Chand = **हुआ**, *q. v.*

हुआ, *m.* (pl. **हुए** : *f.* **हुई**) *more prop.* **हुआ**, *q v.*

हुआं, a dialectic form of **वहां**, *q. v.*

हुश्रि, in Chand = **है**, *q. v.*

हुई, (pl. **हुईं**) *more prop.* **हुई**, *q. v.*

हुं, an old from = (1) **में** (2) **मैं हूं**.

हुंकार, *m.* the uttering a menacing sound; a shout, roaring, bellowing; the twang of a bow.—*denā*, to give forth a sound, to roar, bellow, shout.

हुंड ; for words beginning thus, see under the form **हुण्ड**.

हुंडार, *m.* a wolf.

हुंतो in Chand = (1) **से** = from: or (2) = **हुतो**, *q. v.*

हुंआर, *more prop.* **हुंडार**, *q. v.*

हुकम, *more prop.* **हुक्म**, *q. v.*

हुकहुक, a sobbing, crying.—*kar ronā*, to burst repeatedly into tears, to keep on (or go on) cry, to sob and cry.

हुकुम, *more prop.* **हुक्म**, *q. v.*

हुक़ूक़, *m.* (pl. of **हक़्क़**) rights, duties.

हुकूमत, *f.* dominion, sovereignty, government, jurisdiction, authority.

हुक्का, *m.* the pipe, etc. in which the Indians smoke tobacco ; a grenade or bomb ; a box for holding jewels or drugs.

हुक्काम, *m.* (pl. of **हाकिम**) governors, rulers, commanders, magistrates.

हुक्म, *m.* order, command, decree, permission, warrant.

हुक्मत ; see **हुकूमत** and **हिकमत**.

हुक्मनामा, *m.* a written order, edict, decree,

हुक्मरान, *adj.* ruling, exercising sovereignty.

हुखास, *more com.* **हुलास**, *q. v.*

हुज़्न, *m.* grief, sadness, affliction.

हुजरा, *m.* a cell, closet, chamber.

हुजियो, *more prop.* **हूजियो**, *q. v.*

हुज़ूर, *m.* presence, appearance, attendance ; court, Government ; the town at which the chief authority resides : a title of respect = Your Honor, Your Highness.

हुज्जत, *f.* argument, proof, reason ; disputation, altercation, controversy.

हुज़्ज़ार, *m.* (pl. of **हाज़िर**) those present, spectators, on-lookers, auditors, assistants.

हुड़ = हूड़ *q. v.*

हुड़कना, *a. int.* to pine.

हुड़का, *m.* 1, pining (*esp.* of children separated from their parents): 2, the bar of a door.

हुड़काई, *f.* = **हुड़का**, *q. v.*

हुड़दंगा. *m.* (*f.* ī) turbulent.

हुड़दंगी, *f.* turbulence: a turbulent female.

हुड़हुड़, *f.* the twang of a bow.

हुड़ाहुड़ी, *f.* haste, precipitation.

हुडुक, *more prop.* **हुडुक्क**, *q. v.*

हुडुक्क, *m.* a gallinule: a drunken man: an iron-bound staff: the bar of a door: a kind of small drum (of the shape of an hour glass): generally played on by [bearers).

हुड्डा *m.* unripe or uncooked grain.

हुणा, is (in the Kumāonī dialect of Hindee) one of the case-signs of the dat. and acc. = **को**. [blockhead.

हुण्ड, *m.* a tiger: a ram: a village hog: an imp: a

हुण्डवी, *f.* a bill of exchange, money-order.

हुण्डा, *m.* (*f.* ī) = **मुण्डा** (?) *q. v.*

हुण्डाभाड़ा, *m.* contract for transportation of goods (including the payment of duties); insurance on goods.

हुण्डाभाड़ावाला, *m.* (*f.* in *or* ī) an insurer.

हुण्डार, *m.* (*more com.* **हुंड़ार**) a wolf.

हुण्डावन, *m.* exchange, or the price paid to a person for granting a bill of exchange.

हुण्डियान
हुण्डियावन } = **हुण्डावन**, *q. v.*
हुण्डीआन

हुण्डी, *f.* a bill of exchange, money-order.

हुण्डीदर्शनी, *f.* a bill payable at sight.

हुण्डीमीय्यादी, *f.* a bill payable after a certain stipulated interval. [an insurer.

हुण्डीवाल, *m.* (*f.* in *or* ī) an exchange-merchant;

हुण्डीवाला, *m.* (*f.* ī) *more com.* **हुण्डीवाल**, *q. v.*

हुण्डेत, *m.* an insurer.

हुण्ड, mutual assistance in tillage.

हुत, 1, offered with fire, burnt in sacrifice: called, invited: 2, *m.* an oblation, burnt sacrifice.

हुति, 1, *more prop.* **हुती**, *q. v.*: 2, (*Rām.*) = **सन्ती**, *q. v.*: 3, *f.* offering oblations: calling, invocation; calling defiantly, challenging.

हुती, *f.* (*m.* **हुतो**) in Braj = she was.

हुते, plural of **हुतो**, *q. v.*

हुतो, *m.* (*f.* ī) an old Hindee form = **हुतौ**, *q. v.*

हुतौ, *m.* (*f.* ī) in Braj = **था** = was.

हुत्यो
हुत्यौ } = **हुतौ**, *q. v.*

हुदल, *m.* a quagmire, slough.

हुक्कातुक्की, *f.* a mutual threatening.

हुन, *more prop.* **हून**, *q. v.*

हुनना, *t.* to offer up sacrifice.

हुनर, *m.* cleverness, dexterity, skill, ingenuity, talent: experience: virtue; handicraft, art, science; qualification.

हुना, *m.* (*f.* ī) offered up, sacrificed.

हुनूद, *m.* (pl. of **हिन्द** or **हिन्दू**) Hindoos, Gentoos.

हुन्दुवी, *f.* a bill of exchange.

हुबल, *m. pr. n.* a certain idol at Mecca, worshipped before the time of Muhammad. [Caffres, negroes, slaves.

हुबशान, *m.* (pl. of **हबश**) Ethiopians, Abyssinians,

हुमुक़, *m.* foolishness, inadvertency, stupidity.

हुमकना, *a. int.* to stretch forward, leap forward: *t.* [to assault.

हुमगना, *more com.* **हुमकना**, *q. v.*

हुमर, *m.* bitumen, naphtha.

हुमसाना, *t.* to scare, raise.

हुमा, *m.* a bird of paradise: the sudden influx of the tide on rivers at new and full moon (commonly called "the bore"), a strong flood.

हुम्मा = **हुमा**, *q. v.*

हुया, *m* (pl. **हुये**; *f.* **हुई**) *more prop.* **हूआ**, *q. v.*

हुर, rout, dispersion (of an army). — *ho jānā*, to [send.

हुरगुयडा, *m.* a certain vegetable.

हुरना, *t.* to beat down (as paviers do), to obtund.

हुरला, *m.* (*f.* ī) *adj.* (see **हुर**) running away in terror.

हुरहुर, *m.* a certain medicinal plant (*Cleome viscosa* or *Gynandropsis pentaphylla* ?).

हुरहुराना, to purl.

हुरुक्नी, *f.* a dancing-girl, courtesan, harlot.

हुरूफ़, *m.* (pl. of **हर्फ़**) letters of the alphabet.

हुरा, *m.* dispersion (of an army, assembly, etc.): general jail-delivery: *exclam.* hurrah! —*k.* to rush.

हुर्सा, *m.* a stone on which sandal-wood is ground.

हुलकना, *t.* to rush upon, attack, charge: *a. int.* to peep. [*mārnā*, to peep.

हुलकबुलक, a play on the base of **हुलकना**, *q.v.* —

हुलकारना, *t.* to instigate, set on (as cocks, etc.) halloo on (as in setting on a dog at a bull).

हुलकी, 1, see **हुलकना**: 2, *f.* choler: an epithet of the goddess *Kālī*. [to rejoice.

हुलसना, *n.* to be rejoiced, be pleased, be delighted,

हुलसाना, *t.* to gladden, delight, rejoice, cheer.

हुलसि (*part.*) = **हुलसके** (**हुलसना**).

हुलसित, *m.* (*f.* ā) gladdened, rejoiced, delighted, cheerful, happy. [mother of Tulsee Dās.

हुलसी, 1, *m.* (*f.* inī) = **हुलसित**, *q.v.*: 2, *f. pr. n.* the

हुलहुल, *m.* 1, = **हुरहुर**, *q.v.*: 2, snow.

हुलहुली, *f.* inarticulate sounds of pleasure made by women. [*f.* snuff.

हुलास, 1, *m.* alacrity; joy, happiness, delight: 2,

हुलासी
हुलासू } = **हुलसित**, *q.v.*

हुलाहुली, *f.* an exclamation of pleasure.

हुलियाना, *t.* to gore, butt: to nauseate.

हुलूल, *m.* descent: sojourning: penetrating: transmigration. [of the goddess Kālī.

हुल्कार, 1, see (1) **हुल्कारना** (2) **हूलना**: 2, *f.* an epithet

हुल्कारना = **हुलकारना**, *q. v.*

हुल्लड़, *m.* uproar, tumult, commotion, riot, row, mutiny, disturbance, hurly-burly, alarm, bustle.

हुल्ला, *m.* a robe, garment.

हुवंत in Chand = **होता**, 1, *q. v.*

हुवा, *m.* (*f.* ī) *more prop.* **हुआ**, *q. v.*

हुश, *m.* understanding, care, attention, study: *interj.* used in driving away birds.

हुशकारना, *t.* to put to flight, scare away (birds).

हुशन / **हुश्न** } *more prop.* **हुस्न**, *q. v.*

हुस, *more prop.* **हुश**, *q. v.*

हुसन, *more prop.* **हुस्न**, *q. v.*

हुसियार, *more prop.* **होशियार**, *q. v.* [advantage.

हुसूल, *m.* acquisition, gaining, attaining, profit,

हुसैन, *m. pr. n.* (see **हसनहुसैन**) the younger of the two sons of 'Ali. [tity.

हुस्न, *m.* beauty, elegance, goodness: female chas-

हुहु, *m. pr. n.* (in Hindoo Myth.) one of the heavenly choristers (*gandharv*).

हू, 1, = **भी** (both expletive and emphatic), *q.v.*: 2, an interjection (1) of calling (2) of contempt (3) of pride (4) of weeping: 3, report.

हूआ, *m.* (*f.* **हूई**) past part. sing. of vb. **होना**, = was, became. Idiomatically, this word may also mean 'is'; *e. g. Pānī garm hūā*, the water is hot: it may also be used as equivalent to the English word 'ago'; *e. g. Ek baras hūā*, a year ago.

हूआं, *more prop.* **वहां**, *q.v.*

हूए, *more prop.* **हूई**. See **हूआ**.

हूए, *m.* (*f.* **हूईं**) past part. pl. of verb **होना**. This word may also be used as equivalent to the English word 'ago'; *e.g. Pāñch baras hūē*, five years ago. [to pine.

हूकना, *a. int.* to make a mistake, miss, err, slip:

हूं, 1, = **मैं हूं**, I am: 2, = **हां**, 3, *q.v.*: 3, in Braj and in poetry freq. = **भी** (both expletive and emphatic): 4, *more prop.* (1) **हून** (2) **हुंआ**, *qq. v.*: 5, (= **ओंम** ?) a magical and mystical monosyllable.

हूंत, in Chand = **से** = from. [and haw.

हूंहां, *m.* uproar, tumult, alarm, riot.—*k.* to hum

हूक, *f.* shooting-pain, twitch, stitch, ache, pain.

हूकना, *a. int.* to make a mistake, miss, err, slip: [to pine.

हूकहूक = **हुकहुक**, *q.v.*

हूकुम, a corruption of **हुक्म**, *q.v.*

हूके in Braj = **होके**, *q.v.* [grass.'

हूगला, *m.* a kind of reed commonly called, 'elephant

हूचना, *t.* to miss, err, mistake.

हूजिये / **हूजियेगा** / **हूजियो** } respectful imperatt. of vb. **होना**.

हूज़र / **हूज़ूर** } *more prop.* **हुज़ूर**, *q.v.*

हूड़, 1, *f.* wrangling: 2, ignorant, foolish: 3, a fool, simpleton.

हूड़पना, *m.* ignorance, stupidity, senselessness.

हूड़ाहूड़ो, *f.* striving, wrangling.

हूण, *m.* a certain barbarous tribe.

हूणदेश, *m. pr. n.* the country around the lake [Mānasarovar.

हूणटा = **होपटा**, *q.v.*

हूणडार, *m.* a wolf. [valued at 3½ to 3¾ rupees.

हून, *m. f.* ? a certain Madras coin (called also *pagoda*)

हून्हार, *more com.* **होन्हार**, *q.v.*

हूपाहप, secretly, silently.

हूया, *m.* (pl. **हूये** or **हूए**; fem. **हूयी** or **हूई**) = **हूआ**, *q.v.*

हूरव, *m.* a jackal.

हूर, *f.* a virgin of paradise, black-eyed nymph. The term is applied more particularly to the celestial brides promised in the Kurān to all good Muhammadans in the next world.

हूरिया, *m.* a certain small class of Rājpoots.

हूल, *f.* a thrust, push, stab, an attack, a pass (in fencing).—*denā* or *mārnā*, to thrust, push, goad, drive, impel, urge,—*chalānā*, to make a pass in fencing.

हूलकना, *a. int.* to peep.

हूलड़, *more prop.* **हुल्लड़**, *q.v.*

हूलना, *t.* to goad, thrust, push, drive (as an elephant); to rush upon, attack.

हूवा, *m.* (*f.* ī) *more com.* **हूआ**, *q.v.*

हूस, *more prop.* (1) **होश** (2) **हुश**, *qq.v.*

हूस्न, a corruption of **हुस्न**, *q.v.*

हूसीअ, *m. pr. n.* the prophet Hosea, and the Book [that bears his name.

हूह (*Rām.*) = **हू**, 2, *q. v.*

हूहा, *m.* report, rumour, fame: a storm: pomp. ostentation, parade, pageantry; hue and cry, hurrah. —*k.* to hoop. [intensity.

हूहू, 1, *more prop.* **हुहु**, *q.v.*: 2, = **हू**, 2 (repeated for

हृद, *m.* (= **हृदय**) the heart, the mind.

हृदय, *m.* the seat or faculty of feeling and reflection, the heart, the mind; the life, the soul: knowledge. This word is sometimes found as the latter part of epithets or compound adjectives, in which case its fem. ends in *ā*; *e. g.* **सुहृदय**, *etc.*

हृदयनिकेत, *m.* an epithet of Kāmdev.

हृदयवान, *m.* (*f.* vatī) = **हृदयालु**, *q. v.*

हृदयवेधक, heart-piercing, painful.

हृदयालु, *m. f.* good-hearted, kind,

हृदयिक, *m.* (*f.* ā *or* ī) / **हृदयी**, *m.* (*f.* inī) } = **हृदयालु**, *q. v.*

हृदयेश, *m.* (*lit.* lord of the heart, *i.e.*) a husband, a lover. [a sweetheart.

हृदयेशा, *f.* (*lit.* the mistress of heart, *i.e.*) a wife,

हृदा (*colloquial*) = **हृदय**, *q.v.* See **आ**, 23, and **य**, 4.

हृदावर्त्त, *m.* a lock of hair on a horse's neck or breast or immediately behind the fore-legs. It is regarded as a defect in a horse, and is reckoned unlucky for the rider.

हृदीय, appertaining to the heart.

हृदै (*Rām.*) = **हृदय**, *q. v.* [ṇu or Krishṇ.

हृषीकेश, *m.* (lord of the organs of sense, *i.e.*) Vish-

हृष्ट, *m.* (*f.* ā) having the hair of the body erect; pleased, delighted, glad; smiling; astonished; disappointed.

हृष्टपुष्ट, happy and well-fed, well-conditioned.

हे, 1, (pl. **हें**) *more prop.* **है**, *q.v.*: 2, a vocative particle, = O!; *e.g.* **हे लड़के**, O boy! 3, in Braj = were: 4, in Bhojpurī = **यह**, *q.v.*

हेंगा, *m.* a harrow.—*phernā*, to harrow.

हेंगाऊ, *m.* *f.* a harrower.

हेंगाना, *t.* to harrow.

हेच, nothing: worthless, good-for-nothing: any, anything. — *jānnā*, to contemn, to outbrave.

हेचपूच, nugatory, useless: *hence*, things of no account, trifles; a ninnyhammer, nincompoop.

हेट, bowed, bent, submissive: hence, *m.* an overturning, bending, stooping.

हेठ, 1, *adv.* or *postp.* (takes gen. *m.* infl.) down, below, under, 2, bent down, stooped, dropped down: 3, *m.* hindering, obstructing, hurting; injury.

हेठा, *m.* (*f.* ī) low, pusillanimous, cowardly, indolent. — *k.* to humble. [lence.

हेठापन, *m.* pusillanimity, cowardliness, indo-

हेडा, *m.* meat, flesh.

हेड़ी, *m.* (*f.* in or inī) a beast of prey.

हेत, *more prop.* (1) **हेति** 2, (2) **हेतु**, *qq.v.*

हेति, 1, (*Rām.*) = **हा इति** = **हां यह**: 2, *f.* a weapon, a missile, a sword: a flame: a ray of the sun.

हेती, *m. pr. n.* the first Rākshas king, father of Vidyut-kesh. He is represented as residing in the sun's chariot in the month of Chaitra or Madhu.

हेतु, *m.* origin, cause, motive, sake, reason, purpose, meaning, drift, intention, object: (in Logic) the second of the five component parts of a complete syllogism, the middle term.

हेतुहेतुमद्भूत, *m.* (in Gram.) the conditional mode.

हेत्वाभास, *m.* (in Logic) a fallacious reason or middle term, a fallacy: *lit.* the semblance of a reason.

हेत्वाभासाः, *m.* (Sk. pl.: see **आ**, 22) fallacies.

हेनबेना, *m.* (*f.* ī) despoiled, ruined, spoilt, miser-

हेनबेनाई, *f.* ruin, spoliation. [able.

हेन्दा, *m.* (*f.* ī) ill-bred, clownish, stupid.

हेन्दागी, *f.* } clownishness, stupidity.
हेन्दापन, *m.* }

हेम, *m.* gold: a dark-coloured horse.

हेमकर्त्ता, *m.* (*f.* trī) } a worker in gold, a goldsmith.
हेमकार, *m.* (*f.* ī) }

हेमकूट, *m. pr. n.* one of the ranges of mountains that divide the known continent into nine regions (*varsh*). It is the second to the south of the central division (*Ilāvrit*), and lies immediately north of the Himālayas, forming with them, the boundaries of the *Kinnar Varsham.*

हेमक्षीरी, *f.* a medicinal species of the moon-plant.

हेमचन्द्र, *m. pr. n.* (1) of a certain king of Vaishāli (2) of a certain philosopher (3) of a celebrated author and lexicographer.

हेमतरु, *m.* the thorn-apple.

हेमतार, *m.* blue vitriol.

हेमन्त, *m.* (*f.* ?) the fifth season of the year among Hindoos, *i.e.* the cold season or winter, embracing the months *Agrahāyan* and *Paush*, or about Nov. —Dec.

हेमर in Chand = **हयवर**, *q.v.*

हेमवर्ण, gold-coloured, yellow.

हेमांग, 1, golden: 2, *m.* (*f.* ī) a lion: 3, *m.* an epithet (1) of Brahmā (2) of the fabulous bird Garur.

हेमाचल, *m. pr. n.* mount Sumeru.

हेरना, to look after; to observe, see; to search for; to hunt, pursue, chase; to catch, stop.

हेरम्ब, *m.* a buffalo: a proud hero: Gaṇesh.

हेराना, 1, *more com.* **हिराना**, *q.v.*: 2, *t.* a causative

हेराफेरी, *f.* strolling about. [form of **हेरना**, *q.v.*

हेरि (*Rām.*) = **हेरके** (**हेरना**): see **क**, 7.

हेरी, a certain tribe of Muhammadan Rājpoots in Jaipur; a certain pargana of Murādābād.

हेरे, *interj.* = ho!

हेलना, *a. int.* to swim.

हेलमेल, 1, = **हिलमिल**, *q.v.*: 2, intimacy.

हेला, *f.* sport; wanton dalliance, lascivious endearment; delight; disrespect, disregard, neglect, contempt: facility: oscillation; a jolt: a low caste. — *mārnā*, to shove, launch, dash through water.

हेलि, *f.* embracing, wantonness, dalliance.

हेवन्त } = **हेमन्त**, *q.v.*
हेवान्त }

हेसबेस, *more prop.* **हैसबैस**, *q.v.*

है, 1, *more com.* **हाय**, *q.v.*: 2, (the 2nd and 3rd persons sing. [*m. f.*] pres. indic. act. of **होना**) = art, is: 3, in Chand = **हय**, *q.v.*: 4, in the Kumāoni dialect of Hindee, this is one of the case-signs of the Ablative = **से**, *q.v.*: 5, yes, indeed. [act. of **होना**) = are.

हैं (the 1st and 3rd persons pl. [*m. f.*] pres. indic.

हैंगा, 1, = (1) **हैंगे** (2) **हेगा**, *qq.v.*: 2, *m.* a harrow.

हैंगे, 1, *m.* (*f.* **हैंगी**) in Gaṅwārī = **हैं**, *q.v.*: 2, an old form

हैंवर in Chand = **हयवर**, *q.v.* [of **होयंगे**, *q.v.*

हैक, *m.* a horse.

हैकल, *f.* any great building, a palace, temple; figure, form, face, stature, appearance, person: a neck-ornament.

हैकोर्ट, *m.* (Engl.) the High Court (*i.e.* the Supreme Court of English Judicature in India).

हैगा, *m.* (*f.* **हैगी**; pl. **हैंगे**) provincial = **है**, *q.v.*

हैगै, *m.* (in Chand) horses and elephants.

हैज़ा, *m.* cholera morbus, flux and vomit, cholic.

हैजे, an emphatic form of **हैज़ा** (?), *q.v.*

हैदराबाद, *m. pr. n.* a certain province and city in the Dakkhan and in Guzerat.

हैफ़, *m.* iniquity, violence, oppression.

हैमर in Chand = **हयवर**, *q.v.*

हैरत, *f.* stupor, astonishment, perturbation.

हैरान, perplexed, astonished, confounded, disturbed, fatigued. — *k.* to pose, puzzle.

हैरानी, *f.* astonishment, perturbation, confusion or distraction of mind, disconcertedness, distress, pressure.

हैवान, *m.* an irrational creature, a brute (as distinguished from *insān*, a human being).

हैसबैस, *f.* perplexity, hesitation, pause, suspense; a perplexing affair, hobble, dilemma. — *meṅ honā*, to be in a dilemma, to hesitate.

हैसियत, *f.* ubiquity, universality; ability, capacity, merit: a conditional proposition.

हैहै, 1, *more com.* **हायहाय**: 2, in Braj = **होगा**, *qq. v.*

हो, 1, a vocative particle = ho! (most commonly put after its word): 2, (the 2nd pers. pl. of the pres. indic. act. of **होना**) you are: 3, (the shortest form of the conjunctive participle of that verb) being, having been: 4, (the second pers. sing. and pl. of the conditional or of the imperative of vb. **होना**) = be thou, be ye: 5, in Braj, sometimes found for **है**, *q.v.*: 6, in Bhojpurī = **वह**, *q.v.* *Ho ānā*, to have gone and then returned. — *chalā*, *m.* (*f.* ī) near done, etc. — *chuknā*, to be finished, be expired, to have happened, to have elapsed. — *jānā*, to settle, become, to happen, turn out, prove, to have happened. — *rahnā*, to become, to be. — *lenā*, to be completed. — *saknā*, to be possible. *Ho na ho*, right or wrong; it must be so, necessarily. *Ho to ho*, perhaps. *Ho so ho* or *Hona ho so ho*, happen what will. *Honī ho so ho*, neck or nothing.

होआ, *m.* (*f.* **होई**) *more prop.* **हूआ**, *q.v.*

होइ (pl. **होइं**) = (1) **होता** (2) **होय** (3) **होइहि**.

होइब (*poet.*) = **होगा**, *q.v.*

होइय, (pl. **होंइय**) an old form = **होगा**, *q.v.*

होइहहि, *m. f.* (pl. °**हिं**) in old Hindee = **होगा**, *q. v.*

होइहहु, an old poetic form = **होगे**, *q. v.*

होइहि, *m. f.* (pl. **होइहिं**) in Braj = **होगा**, *q. v.*

होइहै, *m. f.* (pl. **होइहैं**) in Braj = **होगा**, *q. v.*

होइहों, an old form = **होऊंगा**, *q. v.*

होई; this word is very common in the poetry of the language, and seems to be used (according to the caprice of the poet or the exigencies of his metre) as equivalent to (1) **होतो** (2) **होए** (3) **होगो**; while in Chand it is regularly used for the Sanskrit **भवति** = **है**.

होईहहु, *more com.* **होइहहु**, *q. v.*

होईहि, (pl. °**हि**) *more com.* **होइहि**, *q. v.*

होउ (*Rām.*) = (1) **हो** (2) **होउब**, *qq. v.*

होउब (*poet.*) = **होऊंगा**, *q. v.*

होउं (*Rām.*) = (1) **हों** (2) **होऊं** (3) **होऊंगा**, *qq. v.*

होऊं (the 1st pers. sing. [*m. f.*] of the conditional mode of the verb **होना**) = I may be.

होऊंगा, (the 1st pers. sing. of the future tense of the verb **होना**) *m.* (*f.* ī) I shall (or will) be.

होऊंगे, (the 1st pers. pl. of the future tense of the verb **होना**) *m.* (*f.* iṅ) we shall (or will) be.

होए, (the 2nd and 3rd persons sing. of the conditional mode of the verb **होना**) = thou mayest be; he (she, or it) may be.

होएं, (the 1st and 3rd pers. pl. of the conditional mode of the verb **होना**) = we may be; they may be.

होएगा, *m.* (*f.* ī) *more com.* **होगा**, *q.v.*

होएंगे, *m.* (*f.* iṅ) *more com.* **होगे**, *q.v.*

होओ, (the 2nd pers. pl. of the conditional or the imperative mode of the verb **होना**) = (1) you may be (2) do you be, be you.

होओगे, *m.* (*f.* ī) *more com.* **होगे**, *q.v.*

हों, 1, in Braj = **मैं हूं**, I am: 2, (pl. of **हो**) they (or we) may be: 3, in Chand = **मैं**, *q.v.*

हांकना, *a. int.* to puff and blow, pant, gasp.

होंगा, *m.* (*f.* ī) *more prop.* **होऊंगा**, *q.v.*

होंगे, (the 1st and 3rd pers. pl. of the future of the verb **होना**) *m.* (*f.* iṅ) we shall be; they will be.

होंट, *m.* the lip. *Hontāṅ chābnā*, to bite the lips; to be mortified, be penitent, be apprehensive.

होंटा, (in Surveying) three and a half.

होंठ, *m.* the lip. See **होंट**.

होंठी, *f.* the bit of a bridle.

होंम, *more prop*, **होम**, *q. v.*

होंय (pl. of **होय**) = **होएं**, *q. v.*

होंस, *more com.* **हौस**, *q. v.*

होके (a form of the conjunctive participle of the verb **होना**) = (1) having been (2) through, by, proceeding from.

होगया, *m.* (*f.* **होगई**) the past tense of **होजाना**, *q. v.*

होगा, (the 2nd and 3rd pers. sing. of the future tense of **होना**) *m.* (*f.* ī) will be: may be, perhaps.

होगे, (the 2nd pers. pl. of the future tense of **होना**). [*m.* (*f.* ī) you will be.

होचला, *m.* (*f.* ī); see *s.v.* **हो**.

होचुकना } see *s. v.* **हो**.
होजाना }

होठ, *m.* the lip. See **होंठ** and **होपठ**.

होड़, *f.* a wager, bet, bargain, agreement, stipulation, condition, promise. — *badnā*, to wager, bet. — *bāndhnā*, to make an agreement, to bargain, to bet. — *lagānā*, to make an agreement, to wager: to be positive, be obstinate, be perverse. — *hārnā*, to lose a wager, etc.

होड़ल, *m.* talc, mica.

होपट, *m.* the lip. See **होंट**.

होपटा, (in Surveying) three and a half.

होपठ, *m.* the lip; margin. — *bichkānā* or *laṭkānā*, to make a lip, to pout.

होपठी, *f.* the bit of a bridle.

होत, 1, a contraction of **होता**, 1, *q. v.*: 2, *f.* wealth, means, ability; 3, *exclam.* (attached at the end of words) Ho! Hoa! Holloa!

होतव, *m.* destiny, predestination, fate.

होतव्यता, *f.* destiny, fate; that which is foreordained to happen.

होता, 1, (the pres. part. of **होना**) *m.* (*f.* ī) being, becoming, taking place: 2, *m.* wealth, means, ability: 3, *m.* (*f.* tri) a sacrificing priest who is conversant with the hymns of the Rig-Ved and recites them during his sacrificial performances. — *rahegā*, (an expression used in reply to terms of abuse, implying 'what you said of me is applicable to yourself;' hence = tu quoque, you're another.

होताजाता, *m.* coming and going.

होति (*poet.*) = (1) **होती** (2) **होत**, *qq. v.*

होती, *f.* (*m.* **होता**) being, becoming.

होतृ, *m.* (*f.* tri) = **होता**, 3, *q.v.*

होते, in the being, in the presence of, during, whilst. *Makānse*—, near the house, or just outside it.

होतेहोते, gradually, progressively, bit by bit, step by step, little by little.

होत्यौं, an old form = **होता**, *q.v.*

होत्र, *m.* a burnt sacrifice; an oblation of clarified butter.

होत्री, *f.* (*m.* **होता**, 3) the wife of a sacrificing priest, a priestess.

होय, *interj.* of calling to some one at a distance = ho! hallo! hallo there!

होनहार, *more prop.* **होन्हार**, *q. v.*

होना, 1, *n.* to be, to exist: *a. int.* to come to be, get to be, become; to come, accrue, come to pass, answer, pass as, serve, do, stand: to occur, happen, prove; to have; to belong: to desist, stop, die: 2, *m.* being, becoming, existence, possibility: 3, *m.* (*f.* ī) possible. *Honā ho so ho*, happen what will. *Sāth hone is bātke*, notwithstanding this, in spite of this.

होनारी, *f.* likelihood, promise, hopefulness, feasibility.

होनिहार = **होन्हार**, *q. v.*

होनिहारा, *m.* (*f.* ī) = **होन्हार**, *q. v.*

होनी, a *fem.* form of **होना**, = existence, birth, origin. *Honī ho so ho*, neck or nothing.

होनेका, *m.* (*f.* ī) future; possible. (The genitive sing. of **होना**.) See **होनेहार**.

होनेजोग, worthy (or likely) to take place, possible.

होनेवाला } **होनेहार** } **होनेहारा** } *m.* (*f.* ī) = **होन्हार**, *q. v.*

होनौ } **होनौं** } in Braj = **होना**, *q. v.*

होन्हार, future, appertaining to the future; yet to be, yet to take place, what is to happen, likely; possible; feasible, promising, hopeful.

होन्हारी, *f.* hopefulness, promise, likelihood, feasibility.

होब; see **होव**.

होम, *m.* a burnt-offering, burnt sacrifice an oblation of clarified butter, the casting clarified butter, etc. into fire as an offering to the gods, accompanied with invocations and prayers according to the objects of sacrifice. —*karnewālā*, *m.* (*f.* i) one who performs the *hom*; a fire-worshipper. —*k.* to perform the *hom*.

होमना, *t.* to perform the mode of sacrifice called *hom*.

होमी, *m.* (*f.* inī) a priest who makes an oblation of clarified butter.

होय, 1, (pl. **होंय**), *q.v.*: 2, frequently found in poetry as a participle for **हो**, 3. *q. v.*

होये, 1, (pl. **होयें**) = **होए**, *q. v.*

होर; see **होड़** and **हूर**.

होरधान = **हविर्धान**, *q. v.*

होरधानी; see (1) **होराधनी** (2) **हविर्धानी**.

होरहना; see *s. v.* **हो**.

होरा, *f.* the rising of a zodiacal sign; part of the duration of a sign; an hour; a mark, line.

होराधनी, *f. pr. n.* the daughter of Agni and wife of Hordhān.

होराफल, *m.* the result or effect of the rising of an astronomical sign.

होरी, *more prop.* **होली**, *q. v.*

होला, *m.* the chickpea after having been parched in the pod: green vetches: a kind of large flat-bottomed boat: hail.

होलाका } **होलिका** } *more com.* **होली**, *q. v.*

होलिये; see **होलेना**.

होली, *f.* the great Hindoo festival of the red powder (the grand jubilee and saturnalia of the Hindoos) held at the approach of the vernal equinox: the song which they sing during that festival. —*khelnā*, to observe the holee festival, to carry on the proceedings which are usual on the occasion of that festival.

होलेना; see *s. v.* **हो**.

होव in Braj = (1) **हो** 2 (2) **होय** (3) **होश्रो** (4) **होऊंगा**, *qq. v.*

होवह (poet. = **हो**, 4) be thou, be ye.

होवहि, (pl. °**हिं**) an old form = **होएगा**, *q.v.*

होवहु (poet. = **हो**, 4) be thou, be ye.

होवे (pl. **होवें**) = **होए**, *q. v.*

होवेगा, *m.* (*f.* ī) = **होगा**, *q.v.*

होवेंगे, *m.* (*f.* īṅ) = **होंगे**, *q. v.*

होवै (pl. **होवैं**) in Braj = **होए**, *q. v.*

होश, *m.* understanding, sense, judgment; prudence; mind, soul. —*pakarnā*, to recollect. —*meṅ ānā*, to come to one's senses (after intoxication or a swoon).

होशकारना, *t.* to disappoint, baulk.

होशियार, intelligent, attentive, careful, clever, sensible, sagacious, shrewd, circumspect, quick-witted, wide-awake, devoid of verdure in the white of the eye.

होशियारी, *f.* sobriety, carefulness, cleverness, shrewdness, attentiveness.

होष } **होस** } *more prop.* **होश**, *q.v.*

होसकना; see *s. v.* **हो**.

होहि, (pl. **होहिं**) (*poet.*) = (1) **होएगा** (2) **होता है**.

होहु in old Hindee = **होश्रो**, *q. v.*

होहो, an interj. of calling = ho! hallo there!

हौ; see (1) **हो** (2) **होहो** (3) **हौं**.

हौश्राना, *a. int.* to screech, scream.

हौं, 1, in Braj = **मैं हूं**, I am: 2, in Braj sometimes found for **है**, *q. v.*: 3, a Braj termination = **ऊंगा**; *e. g.* **कहिहौं** = **कहुंगा**: 4, in old Hindee = **मैं**, *q. v.*

हौंकना, *a. int.* to puff and blow, pant, gasp.

हौंय in Braj = (1) **होय** (2) **होएं**, *qq. v.*

हौंस, *f.* desire, wish, want, ambition, lust. —*k.* to desire.

हौंसना, *n.* to be jealous, be envious.

हौंसा, *m.* envy, jealousy.

हौंसी, *m.* (*f.* inī) jealous, desirous, emulous, ambitious.

हौंहू = (1) मैं भी (2) मैं भी हूं.

हौहूं, 1, = **हौंहू**, *q.v.*: 2, = **मैं हूं**.

हौका, *m.* cupidity, covetousness, profitless desire, greediness, ambition.

हौखा = **हौका**, *q.v.*

हौज़, *m.* a reservoir, pond, tank, vat, basin of a fountain.

हौज़ा, *m.* a track, side, part, middle.

हौदा, *m.* a kind of litter (or an open seat) on the back of elephants or camels for travelling.

हौनो, *more prop.* **होना**, *q.v.*

हौनौं in Braj = **होना**, *q.v.*

हौन्हार in Braj = **होन्हार**, *q.v.*

हौर, a dialectic form of **और**, *q.v.*

हौरा, *m.* a disturbance, row, tumult.

हौल, *m.* terror: a year: strength: deceit.

हौलनाक, formidable, frightful, terrible.

हौली, *f.* a liquor-shop.

हौले, gently, quietly, slowly, gradually, little by little, easily, fairly.

हौवा, *m*, a bugbear, hobgoblin, ogre.

हौवाना, *a. int.* to scream, screech.

हौवे, (pl. **हौवें**)
हौवै, (pl. **हौवैं**) } in Braj = **होय**, *q. v.*

हौसिला, *m.* the stomach, maw, crop: *met.* capacity, desire, ambition, resolution, spirit.

ह्यां in Braj = **यहां**, *q.v.*

ह्याव, *more prop.* **हियाव**, *q.v.*

ह्रद, *m.* a large piece of water, a deep lake, a pond lake, a tank, cistern: a ray of light.

ह्रस्व, low in stature, short, dwarfish, small, narrow; humble: hence, *m.* a dwarf: (in Gram.) a short vowel.

ह्राद, *m.* noise, sound.

ह्रादिनी, *f.* lightning: the olibanum-tree: a river: the thunder-bolt of Indra.

ह्रादी, *m.* (*f.* inī) *adj.* making a noise, sounding.

ह्रास, *m.* sound, noise: decrease, diminution, paucity, desertion, falling away, forsaking.

ह्लाद, *m.* pleasure, joy, delight.

ह्लादिनी = **ह्रादिनी**, *q. v.*

ह्लादी, *m.* (*f.* inī) *adj.* delighting; happy, glad.

ह्वां in Braj = **वहां**, *q. v.*

ह्वांते in Braj = **वहांसे**, *q. v.*

ह्वांहीं in Braj = **वहांही**, in that very place, in that very same place.

ह्वै, 1, (pl. **ह्वैं**) = **होय**, *q. v.*: 2, (from verb **ह्वैबो**) = was, became: 2, (= **हो**, 3) the conjunctive participle of **ह्वैबो**, in Braj = having been, having taken place; *hence*, through, by means of, by.

ह्वैके in Braj = **होके**, *q. v.*

ह्वैबेको in Braj = **होनेको** (**होना**).

ह्वैबो in Braj = **होना**, to be, exist.

ह्वैहै, (pl. **ह्वैहैं**)
ह्वैहे, (pl. **ह्वैहें**) } (fut. of **ह्वैबो**) in Braj = **होगा**.

ह्वैहौ in Braj (2nd pers. pl. fut. of **ह्वैबो**) = **होगे**, *q. v.*

THE END.